P9-DGH-076

Do not let anyone look down on you because you are young,
but be an example for the believers in your speech,
your conduct, your love, faith, and purity.

1 Timothy 4:12

This Bible belongs to:

Given by:

Date:

Occasion:

God wants to be in a close, loving relationship with all people. The Bible's stories tell how he has broken though to men and women throughout human history. God's biggest breakthrough was when his son, Jesus Christ, became human and lived among us. Now God wants to break through to you—to let you know how much you are loved. Here is a simple prayer to say whenever you read God's word:

Heavenly Father, through these words help me understand the things you wish to teach me.

Dear Jesus, through these words let me feel the love you have for me as you feel your Father's love for you.

Holy Spirit, through these words inspire me to live as a follower of Jesus and bring your love to everyone I meet today.

Amen.

Break Through!

Pray It! Study It! Live It!®
resources offer a holistic approach to learning, living, and passing on the Catholic faith.

Imprimatur information for the text of the articles and the introductions:
Nihil Obstat: Rev. Robert S. Horihan, STL
Censor Librorum
October 28, 2005
Imprimatur: † Most Reverend Bernard J. Harrington, DD
Bishop of Winona
October 28, 2005
The nihil obstat and imprimatur are official declarations that a book or pamphlet is free of doctrinal or moral error. No implication is contained therein that those who have granted the nihil obstat or imprimatur agree with the contents, opinions, or statements expressed, nor do they assume any legal responsibility associated with publication.

Imprimatur information for the text of the Good News Translation, Catholic Edition:
Imprimatur: † Most Reverend William H. Keeler, DD
President, National Conference of Catholic Bishops
March 10, 1993

Writers:
Nora Bradbury-Haehl, Lisa-Marie Calderone-Stewart, Shirley Kelter, Marilyn Kielbasa, Larry Schatz, Victoria Shepp, Brian Singer-Towns

Publishing team:
Brian Singer-Towns, general editor; Virginia Halbur, co-editor; Lorraine Kilmartin, reviewer; Mary Koehler, permissions editor; prepress and manufacturing coordinated by the prepublication and production services departments of Saint Mary's Press.

Copyright information for the text of the Good News Translation:
Today's English Version, Second Edition © 1976, 1979, 1992 American Bible Society. Used by permission. All rights reserved.

The American Bible Society is glad to grant authors and publishers the right to use up to five hundred (500) verses from the Good News Translation (GNT) text in Church, religious, and other publications without the need to seek and receive written permission. However, the extent of quotation must not comprise a complete book of the Bible nor should it amount to more than 25 percent of the work. The proper copyright notice must appear on the title or copyright page.

When quotations from GNT are used in non-saleable media, such as church bulletins, orders of service, posters, transparencies, and similar media, a complete copyright notice is not required, but the initials (GNT) must appear at the end of each quotation.

Requests for quotations in excess of five hundred (500) verses in any publication must be directed to, and written approval received from, the American Bible Society, 1865 Broadway, New York, NY 10023.

Copyright information for all other text:
Copyright © 2006 by Saint Mary's Press, Christian Brothers Publications, 702 Terrace Heights, Winona, MN 55987-1318, www.smp.org. All rights reserved. No part of this book may be reproduced by any means without the written permission of the publisher.

Printed in Canada

4119

ISBN 978-0-88489-862-7, paper
ISBN 978-0-88489-884-9, hardcover

Library of Congress Cataloging-in-Publication Data

Bible. English. Good News Translation. 2006.
Breakthrough! : the Bible for young Catholics: Good News Translation. — Catholic ed.
p. cm.
ISBN 978-0-88489-884-9 (hardbound) —
ISBN 978-0-88489-862-7 (pbk.)
I. Saint Mary's Press. II. Title.
BS195.T63 2006
220.5'20824—dc22

2005025578

Break Through!

The **Bible** for Young Catholics

Good News Translation
Catholic Edition

Saint Mary's Press®

Contents

the Old Testament

the New Testament

The Gospels and the Acts of the Apostles

The Letters and Revelation

Study Helps

Bible People Interviews

Read This First!

Welcome to *Breakthrough! The Bible for Young Catholics.* Growing out of childhood and into your teens is an exciting time of life. It can also be hard sometimes. You will be making some important decisions about what kind of person you want to be. The good news is that you are not alone—God is with you!

Sometimes it is difficult to feel God's love. Sometimes it seems as if no one else you know cares about listening to God—so why should you? Some people are in difficult or even abusive situations that make them wonder if God really cares for them. Some people have never had the opportunity to really learn the truth about God. The good news is that no matter what we are feeling or what our situation is, God never stops trying to **break through** and let us know that he loves us. That is why the title of this special Bible for young people is *Breakthrough!*

God has provided us with many ways to experience his love and to understand how

Catholic Connections

Scripture and Tradition

God wants us to know him. So throughout history God has revealed himself to human beings. We call this "revelation." God's most complete revelation was through the person of his son, Jesus Christ. Through the power of the Holy Spirit, the Apostles handed on to others what they had learned from their experience of Jesus. They passed on everything that our loving God revealed to save us from sin and death. Through the power of the Holy Spirit, the bishops of the Church continue to pass on this revelation without error for all ages.

This revelation is handed on in a special way through the Bible--in both the Old and New Testaments. It is also handed on through something called Tradition, a word which actually means "handing on." Tradition includes some teachings and practices that may not be found explicitly in the Scriptures (another word for the Bible). In fact, some of God's revelation is known chiefly through Tradition rather than through the Bible. That is why the Bible alone is not enough to learn about all of God's revelation. Both the Bible and Tradition are needed to learn the fullness of God's revelation.

"Catholic Connections" articles explain how Catholic beliefs are part of God's revelation and are taught through the Bible. They discuss things like our belief in the sacraments, our devotion to Mary, and the special role of the Pope and bishops. If you read all the "Catholic Connections" articles, it will be like getting a mini-introduction to the main beliefs of the Catholic Church!

he wants us to live. Hopefully, you experience God's love through your family, your friends, and the people of your church. But another way to know God's love is through reading his word, which we call the Bible or the Scriptures. Through the words of the Bible, God speaks to all people. That is why we read from the Bible when we gather at church to pray. But God also wants us to read the Bible on our own, and the Catholic Church encourages every person to do so.

This Bible was specifically created to help young people read and understand the Bible. We started by using the Good News Translation, a version of the Bible that is easier for young people to read. Then we added articles to forty of the Bible's seventy-three books to help you understand what God is saying in those books. You will find four different types of articles in those books: Study It!, Pray It!, Live It!, and Catholic Connections. There are samples of those articles on these pages so you can see what they look like. But read on for explanations of some other great *Breakthrough!* features.

Helps for Starting to Read the Bible

Everyone needs help reading the Bible. It is not an easy book for beginners to pick up and understand. The events the books talk

Study it!

Background for Understanding

The Bible was written a long time ago. So it is not surprising that we might need some help understanding the full meaning of the stories and teachings. This is true for adults as well as youth!

The Study It! articles give you information to help you better understand the Bible story you are reading. Some of the Study It! articles focus on the symbols the author used in the stories. Some help you understand the history behind the story. Some help you understand the story by explaining how people lived back then. The main purpose of the Study It! articles is to help you understand what the original author of the story was trying to get across.

Pray it!

Talking with God

Think of reading the Bible as sort of like having a conversation with God. Whenever you read the Bible, start by asking God for help in understanding what you read. After you read a section, listen for what God is telling you in the story. Then you will want to respond to God. This is one way of praying—by talking to God and listening for God's voice in what you read.

The Pray It! articles will help you do that. They contain prayers or ideas for how you might pray. Sometimes they make connections with the way we pray together at church. You may want to keep a journal to write down your thoughts—and to make up your own prayers—as you read the Bible.

about go all the way back to the creation of the universe. To fully understand the Bible's stories, it is helpful to know how they fit in biblical history. But many of the books don't give dates for their stories, and the books are not always in chronological order. So to help you see how the books and people fit into the big picture of the Bible's history, the very next section is a Bible timeline, called "God Breaks Through: Salvation History Timeline." You will find it helpful to read it over before you start reading the Bible.

You will also want to look at the section following the timeline, titled "Introduction to the Bible." It contains answers to questions like, "Who wrote the Bible?" and "How do I know the Bible is true?" and "What is a good way to study the Bible?"

It is also good to have a plan for reading the Bible. An important spiritual practice for all Christians, including Catholics, is to read complete books of the Bible. But don't start by trying to read through the whole Bible from beginning to end! In fact, for young Christians we don't even suggest you try to read all seventy-three books. We have picked forty books for you to focus on. The section "*Breakthrough!* Reading Plan" gives you a chart for keeping track of your progress.

Bible People Interviews

In the Bible we read about how God **broke through** to certain people as part of his plan of salvation. (Think of "plan of salvation" as God's design for saving us from sin and death so we can have full and everlasting life.) You will meet some of those people through imaginative interviews contained in the color sections inserted throughout the Bible. The interviews will help you understand the role these people had in God's great plan. You will be surprised by the variety of people God called—nomads, warriors, teens, people who didn't speak well, working people, fathers and mothers. Let them inspire you to answer God's call in your life!

Study Helps

You will find some important study helps in the back of *Breakthrough!* There are lists to help you find important Bible stories, lists for locating Jesus' miracles and parables, and a list of all the "Catholic Connections" articles. "Bible Passages for Special Occasions" suggests Bible passages for you to read at important moments in your life.

But there is more! "Word List" is a mini-dictionary of some hard to understand Bible words. Also included is an index of all the topics covered in the *Breakthrough!* articles. Finally, nine maps show the location of important events in the Bible. The more you use these study helps, the more expert you will become in using and understanding the Bible.

Live it!

Following God in Everyday Life

Reading the Bible will change your life, especially if you are open to hearing God's call in the Bible. Even though the stories and teachings of the Bible were written long ago, they still apply today. God's word is eternal—which is a way of saying that it applies to everyone, all through history.

The Live It! articles will help you understand how these ancient stories apply to your life today. They show how the Bible is a guide to building good relationships—with your friends, your family, and other people in your school and community. Live It! articles also show how God wants us to serve others who are in need and bring justice and peace to the world.

God Breaks Through:

The Bible tells the story of how God breaks through to save human beings from sin and bring us to eternal life. History told from the perspective of God's breaking though is called salvation history. This timeline shows the major periods of salvation history as told in the Bible's stories. Each period briefly describes what God is doing during that time in history, lists some of the Bible books that tell the stories from that period, and lists some of the important people of that period. The Bible books listed are only the ones used in the *Breakthrough!* reading plan. The Bible people whose names are in bold have interviews in the color insert pages.

Primeval History

The Bible begins with imaginative stories about how God created everything that exists. These are sometimes called "primeval" stories, meaning they are stories of things that happened before recorded history. The stories of Adam and Eve, Cain and Abel, Noah and the flood, and the tower of Babylon teach us that God created every-thing and that human beings have a special place in creation. They teach us that sin destroys our relationships with God and each other. They teach us that sin spreads and that without God's help, sin leads to death and destruction.

BIBLE BOOK

Genesis, chapters 1–11

BIBLE PEOPLE

• **Adam & Eve** • Cain & Abel • **Noah**

CREATION — 2000 BC

Patriarchs

In this period of salvation history, God begins to form a special relationship with a chosen race of people. He makes a special promise, called a Covenant, with a man named Abraham and his wife, Sarah. God promises that their descendants will be numerous and that they will inherit a Promised Land. This is followed by the stories of Abraham and Sarah's son, Isaac; their grandsons, Jacob and Esau; and their great-grandchildren, Joseph and his brothers and sister. These stories show us that even though Abraham and Sarah's descendents had many problems, God was faithful to his Covenant with them. Jacob's sons become the patriarchs—that is, founding fathers—of the twelve tribes of Israel.

BIBLE BOOK

Genesis, chapters 12–50

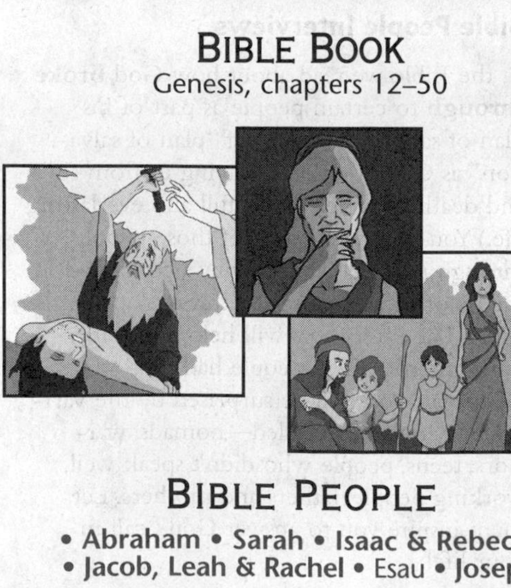

BIBLE PEOPLE

• **Abraham** • **Sarah** • **Isaac & Rebecca**
• **Jacob, Leah & Rachel** • Esau • **Joseph**

2000 BC — 1700 BC

Salvation History Timeline

Egypt and the Exodus

At the beginning of the Book of Exodus, we discover that the descendants of Jacob's children—now called Israelites—are in slavery in Egypt. God hears their cries and calls Moses to lead the people out of slavery. But Pharaoh, the Egyptian leader, has a hard heart. God has to send terrible plagues to make him let the Israelites go. The Israelites' escape from Egypt and journey to the Holy Land is called the Exodus.

On the way to the Promised Land, the Israelites stop at Mount Sinai. There God extends the Covenant he made with Abraham to all the Israelites. He gives Moses the Ten Commandments, which the people must obey as part of the Covenant. During the Exodus the people frequently complain and lose their faith in God. As a consequence they must wander in the desert for forty years, and only their children will be able to enter the Promised Land.

BIBLE BOOK

Exodus

BIBLE PEOPLE

• **Moses** • **Aaron & Miriam** • Pharaoh

1700 BC — 1250 BC

Settling the Promised Land

Moses dies before the Israelites enter the Promised Land. God calls a new leader, Joshua, to lead the people into the land. Much of the land is inhabited by other people. The Israelites must fight to gain control of the land. When they trust God, they are successful in their battles; when they do not trust God, they fail. Eventually they gain control of the land, and each of the twelve tribes is given their own section of the land.

New invaders, the Philistines, try to capture the land. At this time the Israelites have no king, because God is their ruler. But God calls special prophets and warriors, called judges, to help deliver justice and defend the land against the Philistine invasion.

BIBLE BOOKS

Joshua, Judges, Ruth

BIBLE PEOPLE

• **Joshua** • **Deborah** • **Gideon** • **Samson** • **Ruth**

1250 BC — 1050 BC

Timeline (continued)

Kingdoms of Judah & Israel

At the end of the period of the judges, the Israelites want their own king. God reluctantly answers their plea. He has Samuel—the last of the judges—anoint Saul as the first king of Israel. David follows Saul as the next king. David is a mighty warrior and unites all the twelve Tribes into one kingdom. David's son, Solomon, builds a Temple at Jerusalem, the capital city.

After Solomon's death there is disagreement between the tribes, and the kingdom splits in two. Israel is the name of the northern kingdom and Judah is the name of the southern kingdom. Many of the kings of Israel and Judah worshiped foreign gods and allowed injustice in the kingdom. So God called prophets to call the people to obey their Covenant with God. Prophets like Amos, Hosea, and Isaiah called the people to stop worshiping idols, to practice justice, and to care for people in need.

Bible Books

1 Samuel, 2 Samuel, 1 Kings, 2 Kings, Micah, Isaiah, Jeremiah

Bible People

- Samuel • King Solomon • Elijah and Elisha • King Saul • King David • King Hezekiah • King Josiah • Amos • Hosea • Isaiah • Jeremiah

1050 BC — 587 BC

Exile and Return

Despite the prophets' warnings, the people of Israel and Judah continued to turn away from God's Covenant with them. So God let their kingdoms be conquered. Israel was conquered by the Assyrians in 721 BC. Judah was conquered by the Babylonians in 587 BC. Many of the people were taken into captivity, so this time was called the Exile. Prophets like Ezekiel comforted the Israelites with the promise that God was still with them. Fifty years passed in exile. Then a new king allowed the people—now called Judeans or Jews—to return to rebuild Jerusalem and the Temple. The people saw God's hand at work.

Alexander the Great came along, and the Greeks ruled Israel. About 150 BC the Maccabees, a Jewish family, led a successful revolt against the Greeks to restore Jewish independence. During this troubled time, the people were hoping for a messiah, or savior, to make them great again.

Bible Books

Ezra, Nehemiah, Esther, Isaiah, 2 Maccabees, Ezekiel, Daniel, Jonah

Bible People

- Ezekiel • Ezra & Nehemiah • the Maccabees • Judith • Esther

587 BC — AD 1

Life of Jesus Christ

God never abandoned his Chosen People, even though so often they did not keep their part of the Covenant. When the time was right, God sent his only Son, Jesus Christ, into the world. When Jesus was born, the Romans ruled Israel. Some of the Jews were hoping for a mighty warrior and king like David, who would drive the Romans out. Instead, Jesus showed a different way. He preached love, justice, and forgiveness. He healed and worked miracles as signs of God's power.

Jesus' followers, called disciples, came to see that he was the Messiah, the Savior. Jesus showed that salvation comes through faith and a change of heart, not through violence and political power. When Jesus was killed by the Romans—with the approval of the Jewish leaders—his followers thought that all was lost. Instead, after three days God raised Jesus from the dead!

BIBLE BOOKS

Matthew, Mark, Luke, John

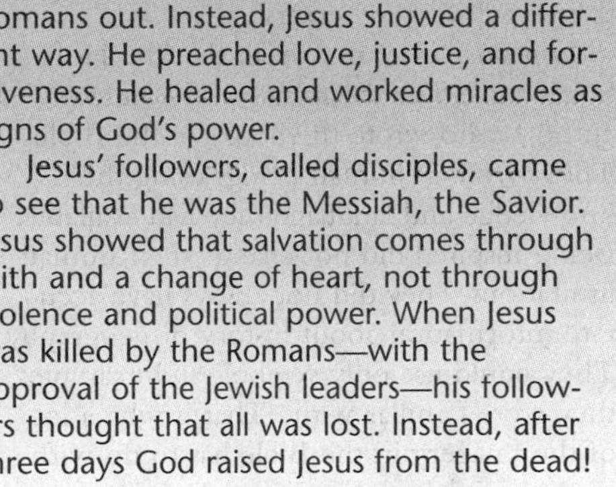

BIBLE PEOPLE

- **Mary of Nazareth** • **John the Baptist**
- Jesus of Nazareth, the Christ
- **Peter** • **Mary Magdalene**
- The Twelve Apostles
- Mary & Martha of Bethany

AD 1 — AD 33

Early Christian Church

After his Resurrection, Jesus instructed his closest followers, the Apostles, to go and spread the Good News of salvation to all people. After Jesus ascended to heaven, Peter and the other Apostles received the Holy Spirit. The Holy Spirit gave them the courage to tell others about Jesus Christ. They started by first preaching to other Jews. Sometimes they were persecuted by Jewish leaders who did not believe in Jesus.

One of those persecutors—whose name was Paul—had a vision of Jesus and became a Christian. God revealed to Paul that Christ came for all people. Paul began preaching to non-Jews, who were called Gentiles. Wherever he traveled he started new Christian communities. He was helped by many other believers, women and men. Soon Christianity spread throughout the whole Roman Empire—even to Rome.

BIBLE BOOKS

Acts of the Apostles, Romans, 1 Corinthians, Galatians, James, Philippians, 1 Timothy, Hebrews, 1 Peter, 1,2,3 John, Revelation

BIBLE PEOPLE

- **Peter** • **Paul** • **Barnabas** • **Timothy**
- **Priscilla & Aquila**

AD 33 — AD 100

Introduction to the Bible

What is the Bible?

The Bible is a holy book, which means that God speaks to us through it. It is the story of God's love relationship with the human race. Actually, the Bible is really not one book; it is a collection of books. There are seventy-three books in Catholic Bibles, forty-six books in the Old Testament and twenty-seven books in the New Testament.

Who wrote the Bible?

Many of the Bible's stories were first told by storytellers around campfires and in religious gatherings. Or they were messages given in public places by prophets and evangelists. Eventually these stories and messages were written down. Other people added to them, combined them, and rewrote them. Under the guidance of the Holy Spirit, some of the books in the Old Testament may have gone through hundreds of years of rewriting before they became the books we have today.

The Bible was written so long ago that we have no idea who most of these writers and editors were. What we do know is that the Holy Spirit was at work through the whole process, inspiring these authors to communicate God's truth.

What does *inspired* mean?

The Bible was written by people who were inspired by the Holy Spirit. This means that God is the ultimate author of the Bible. God made sure the Bible contains the things we need to know about God and how God saves us. By inspiring the human authors, God made sure they communicated these things without any errors.

Inspiration does not mean that the Holy Spirit took over the minds of the human authors who wrote the books of the Bible. They wrote as human beings using the knowledge and language they had available. Being inspired did not change their human limitations. They did not always have accurate information about history or geography. They could use only symbols and examples they were familiar with. (That is why a lot of the imagery in the Bible has to do with raising animals and farming.) Despite these limitations, under the Holy Spirit's guidance they were able to communicate the things we need to know about God and God's plan for humanity.

How do I know the Bible is true?

You can count on the Bible teachings to be true because the human authors were inspired by the Holy Spirit. God wants to communicate his truth and love to us. So everything the human authors wrote about God and how God saves us is true and without error. You can also count on the Bible's teachings to be true, because for two thousand years people have experienced God's truth and love through the stories of the Bible.

Sometimes understanding the truth in the Bible takes work. Sometimes we have to look at the teaching of the entire Bible to see the whole truth about a topic like suffering or God's justice. Sometimes we have to understand the world of the original authors in order to discover the truth God wants us to know. We also need the Church's guidance to understand some of the more difficult passages in the Bible. The articles in *Breakthrough!* will help you with these things. But most of the time, God's truth in the Bible is pretty clear for those who really want to find it.

How do I find things in the Bible?

The Bible has a system for helping you locate specific passages. Each book in the Bible is divided into chapters (except for some very short books). The chapter numbers are the larger ones on the page. Each chapter is divided into verses. A verse is usually about a sentence long. The verse numbers are the smaller numbers in each chapter and start with verse 1 in each new chapter.

A Bible citation is a code for finding a passage using this system. A citation has three parts: the Bible book name, a chapter number, and verse numbers. So John 3:16–17 means the Gospel of John, chapter three, verse sixteen through verse seventeen. Go ahead, try and find it. If you need help finding where the book is in the Bible, use the handy chart in the back of *Breakthrough!*

What is a good way to study the Bible?

It is not a good idea to start at the beginning of the Bible and try to read it all the way through to the end, like you would a novel. Start with a book you find interesting and read a chapter or two every day until you finish it. Then pick another book and read through it. *Breakthrough!* has a suggested reading plan for doing this. The chart on the next page will help you keep track of your progress.

It is a good idea to have a little ritual each time you read. This will help you be more focused on what God wants to say to you as you read the Bible. Here are some simple steps you might try:

1. Start with a short prayer asking for God's help in understanding what you read. There is a prayer in the front of *Breakthrough!* that you can use.
2. Read carefully through the chapter or passage. Don't rush. Try to hear every word and let its meaning sink in.
3. Think about what you just read. Try to imagine yourself in the story. How would you feel? What do you think God is saying to you through the words you read?
4. Read the Study It!, Pray It!, Live It!, or "Catholic Connections" article if there is one connected to the passage you read.
5. Finish by thinking about how the reading might apply to your life. Is God comforting you about a hard situation? Is God calling you to make a change or try something new? Talk with God about whatever you are thinking or feeling.

Breakthrough! Reading Plan

As a young person, you will want to get familiar with the people and stories in the Bible. A good way to do this is by reading complete books of the Bible. However, we do not recommend that you start at the beginning of the Bible and try to read it straight through. Because the Bible is a collection of many different kinds of books, it was not meant to be read like that. A better approach is to go back and forth between books in the Old and New Testaments. That way you can see the connections between both testaments.

The following chart lists the forty books that we have filled with extra articles. We chose these books because reading them will help you see the big picture of God's Revelation. You don't have to read the books in this order though; read them in whatever order you wish. We have listed all the chapters in each book so you can check them off as you read them. There are 943 chapters all together. To read them all in one year, you would have to read about two or three chapters a day; to read them over three years, you would have to read about one chapter a day. There is no need to rush, the important thing is to open yourself up to what God wishes to say to you.

MARK

❑ 1 ❑ 2 ❑ 3 ❑ 4 ❑ 5 ❑ 6 ❑ 7 ❑ 8 ❑ 9 ❑ 10 ❑ 11
❑ 12 ❑ 13 ❑ 14 ❑ 15 ❑ 16

GENESIS

❑ 1 ❑ 2 ❑ 3 ❑ 4 ❑ 5 ❑ 6 ❑ 7 ❑ 8 ❑ 9 ❑ 10 ❑ 11
❑ 12 ❑ 13 ❑ 14 ❑ 15 ❑ 16 ❑ 17 ❑ 18 ❑ 19 ❑ 20
❑ 21 ❑ 22 ❑ 23 ❑ 24 ❑ 25 ❑ 26 ❑ 27 ❑ 28 ❑ 29
❑ 30 ❑ 31 ❑ 32 ❑ 33 ❑ 34 ❑ 35 ❑ 36 ❑ 37 ❑ 38
❑ 39 ❑ 40 ❑ 41 ❑ 42 ❑ 43 ❑ 44 ❑ 45 ❑ 46 ❑ 47
❑ 48 ❑ 49 ❑ 50

EXODUS

❑ 1 ❑ 2 ❑ 3 ❑ 4 ❑ 5 ❑ 6 ❑ 7 ❑ 8 ❑ 9 ❑ 10 ❑ 11
❑ 12 ❑ 13 ❑ 14 ❑ 15 ❑ 16 ❑ 17 ❑ 18 ❑ 19 ❑ 20
❑ 21 ❑ 22 ❑ 23 ❑ 24 ❑ 25 ❑ 26 ❑ 27 ❑ 28 ❑ 29
❑ 30 ❑ 31 ❑ 32 ❑ 33 ❑ 34 ❑ 35 ❑ 36 ❑ 37 ❑ 38
❑ 39 ❑ 40

JOSHUA

❑ 1 ❑ 2 ❑ 3 ❑ 4 ❑ 5 ❑ 6 ❑ 7 ❑ 8 ❑ 9 ❑ 10 ❑ 11
❑ 12 ❑ 13 ❑ 14 ❑ 15 ❑ 16 ❑ 17 ❑ 18 ❑ 19 ❑ 20
❑ 21 ❑ 22 ❑ 23 ❑ 24

LUKE

❑ 1 ❑ 2 ❑ 3 ❑ 4 ❑ 5 ❑ 6 ❑ 7 ❑ 8 ❑ 9 ❑ 10 ❑ 11
❑ 12 ❑ 13 ❑ 14 ❑ 15 ❑ 16 ❑ 17 ❑ 18 ❑ 19 ❑ 20
❑ 21 ❑ 22 ❑ 23 ❑ 24

ACTS

❑ 1 ❑ 2 ❑ 3 ❑ 4 ❑ 5 ❑ 6 ❑ 7 ❑ 8 ❑ 9 ❑ 10 ❑ 11
❑ 12 ❑ 13 ❑ 14 ❑ 15 ❑ 16 ❑ 17 ❑ 18 ❑ 19 ❑ 20
❑ 21 ❑ 22 ❑ 23 ❑ 24 ❑ 25 ❑ 26 ❑ 27 ❑ 28

JUDGES

❑ 1 ❑ 2 ❑ 3 ❑ 4 ❑ 5 ❑ 6 ❑ 7 ❑ 8 ❑ 9 ❑ 10 ❑ 11
❑ 12 ❑ 13 ❑ 14 ❑ 15 ❑ 16 ❑ 17 ❑ 18 ❑ 19 ❑ 20
❑ 21

RUTH

❑ 1 ❑ 2 ❑ 3 ❑ 4

1 SAMUEL

❑ 1 ❑ 2 ❑ 3 ❑ 4 ❑ 5 ❑ 6 ❑ 7 ❑ 8 ❑ 9 ❑ 10 ❑ 11
❑ 12 ❑ 13 ❑ 14 ❑ 15 ❑ 16 ❑ 17 ❑ 18 ❑ 19 ❑ 20
❑ 21 ❑ 22 ❑ 23 ❑ 24 ❑ 25 ❑ 26 ❑ 27 ❑ 28 ❑ 29
❑ 30 ❑ 31

1 TIMOTHY

❑ 1 ❑ 2 ❑ 3 ❑ 4 ❑ 5 ❑ 6

2 TIMOTHY

❑ 1 ❑ 2 ❑ 3 ❑ 4

1 CORINTHIANS

❑ 1 ❑ 2 ❑ 3 ❑ 4 ❑ 5 ❑ 6 ❑ 7 ❑ 8 ❑ 9 ❑ 10 ❑ 11
❑ 12 ❑ 13 ❑ 14 ❑ 15 ❑ 16

2 SAMUEL

❑ 1 ❑ 2 ❑ 3 ❑ 4 ❑ 5 ❑ 6 ❑ 7 ❑ 8 ❑ 9 ❑ 10 ❑ 11
❑ 12 ❑ 13 ❑ 14 ❑ 15 ❑ 16 ❑ 17 ❑ 18 ❑ 19 ❑ 20
❑ 21 ❑ 22 ❑ 23 ❑ 24

1 KINGS

❑ 1 ❑ 2 ❑ 3 ❑ 4 ❑ 5 ❑ 6 ❑ 7 ❑ 8 ❑ 9 ❑ 10 ❑ 11
❑ 12 ❑ 13 ❑ 14 ❑ 15 ❑ 16 ❑ 17 ❑ 18 ❑ 19 ❑ 20
❑ 21 ❑ 22

2 KINGS

❑ 1 ❑ 2 ❑ 3 ❑ 4 ❑ 5 ❑ 6 ❑ 7 ❑ 8 ❑ 9 ❑ 10 ❑ 11
❑ 12 ❑ 13 ❑ 14 ❑ 15 ❑ 16 ❑ 17 ❑ 18 ❑ 19 ❑ 20
❑ 21 ❑ 22 ❑ 23 ❑ 24 ❑ 25

ISAIAH
❑ 1 ❑ 2 ❑ 3 ❑ 4 ❑ 5 ❑ 6 ❑ 7 ❑ 8 ❑ 9 ❑ 10 ❑ 11
❑ 12 ❑ 13 ❑ 14 ❑ 15 ❑ 16 ❑ 17 ❑ 18 ❑ 19 ❑ 20
❑ 21 ❑ 22 ❑ 23 ❑ 24 ❑ 25 ❑ 26 ❑ 27 ❑ 28 ❑ 29
❑ 30 ❑ 31 ❑ 32 ❑ 33 ❑ 34 ❑ 35 ❑ 36 ❑ 37 ❑ 38
❑ 39 ❑ 40 ❑ 41 ❑ 42 ❑ 43 ❑ 44 ❑ 45 ❑ 46 ❑ 47
❑ 48 ❑ 49 ❑ 50 ❑ 51 ❑ 52 ❑ 53 ❑ 54 ❑ 55 ❑ 56
❑ 57 ❑ 58 ❑ 59 ❑ 60 ❑ 61 ❑ 62 ❑ 63 ❑ 64 ❑ 65
❑ 66

MATTHEW
❑ 1 ❑ 2 ❑ 3 ❑ 4 ❑ 5 ❑ 6 ❑ 7 ❑ 8 ❑ 9 ❑ 10 ❑ 11
❑ 12 ❑ 13 ❑ 14 ❑ 15 ❑ 16 ❑ 17 ❑ 18 ❑ 19 ❑ 20
❑ 21 ❑ 22 ❑ 23 ❑ 24 ❑ 25 ❑ 26 ❑ 27 ❑ 28

PSALMS
❑ 1 ❑ 2 ❑ 3 ❑ 4 ❑ 5 ❑ 6 ❑ 7 ❑ 8 ❑ 9 ❑ 10 ❑ 11
❑ 12 ❑ 13 ❑ 14 ❑ 15 ❑ 16 ❑ 17 ❑ 18 ❑ 19 ❑ 20
❑ 21 ❑ 22 ❑ 23 ❑ 24 ❑ 25 ❑ 26 ❑ 27 ❑ 28 ❑ 29
❑ 30 ❑ 31 ❑ 32 ❑ 33 ❑ 34 ❑ 35 ❑ 36 ❑ 37 ❑ 38
❑ 39 ❑ 40 ❑ 41 ❑ 42 ❑ 43 ❑ 44 ❑ 45 ❑ 46 ❑ 47
❑ 48 ❑ 49 ❑ 50 ❑ 51 ❑ 52 ❑ 53 ❑ 54 ❑ 55 ❑ 56
❑ 57 ❑ 58 ❑ 59 ❑ 60 ❑ 61 ❑ 62 ❑ 63 ❑ 64 ❑ 65
❑ 66 ❑ 67 ❑ 68 ❑ 69 ❑ 70 ❑ 71 ❑ 72 ❑ 73 ❑ 74
❑ 75 ❑ 76 ❑ 77 ❑ 78 ❑ 79 ❑ 80 ❑ 81 ❑ 82 ❑ 83
❑ 84 ❑ 85 ❑ 86 ❑ 87 ❑ 88 ❑ 89 ❑ 90 ❑ 91 ❑ 92
❑ 93 ❑ 94 ❑ 95 ❑ 96 ❑ 97 ❑ 98 ❑ 99 ❑ 100 ❑ 101
❑ 102 ❑ 103 ❑ 104 ❑ 105 ❑ 106 ❑ 107 ❑ 108
❑ 109 ❑ 110 ❑ 111 ❑ 112 ❑ 113 ❑ 114 ❑ 115
❑ 116 ❑ 117 ❑ 118 ❑ 119 ❑ 120 ❑ 121 ❑ 122
❑ 123 ❑ 124 ❑ 125 ❑ 126 ❑ 127 ❑ 128 ❑ 129
❑ 130 ❑ 131 ❑ 132 ❑ 133 ❑ 134 ❑ 135 ❑ 136
❑ 137 ❑ 138 ❑ 139 ❑ 140 ❑ 141 ❑ 142 ❑ 143
❑ 144 ❑ 145 ❑ 146 ❑ 147 ❑ 148 ❑ 149 ❑ 150

PHILIPPIANS
❑ 1 ❑ 2 ❑ 3 ❑ 4

AMOS
❑ 1 ❑ 2 ❑ 3 ❑ 4 ❑ 5 ❑ 6 ❑ 7 ❑ 8 ❑ 9

MICAH
❑ 1 ❑ 2 ❑ 3 ❑ 4 ❑ 5 ❑ 6 ❑ 7

JEREMIAH
❑ 1 ❑ 2 ❑ 3 ❑ 4 ❑ 5 ❑ 6 ❑ 7 ❑ 8 ❑ 9 ❑ 10 ❑ 11
❑ 12 ❑ 13 ❑ 14 ❑ 15 ❑ 16 ❑ 17 ❑ 18 ❑ 19 ❑ 20
❑ 21 ❑ 22 ❑ 23 ❑ 24 ❑ 25 ❑ 26 ❑ 27 ❑ 28 ❑ 29
❑ 30 ❑ 31 ❑ 32 ❑ 33 ❑ 34 ❑ 35 ❑ 36 ❑ 37 ❑ 38
❑ 39 ❑ 40 ❑ 41 ❑ 42 ❑ 43 ❑ 44 ❑ 45 ❑ 46 ❑ 47
❑ 48 ❑ 49 ❑ 50 ❑ 51 ❑ 52

JAMES
❑ 1 ❑ 2 ❑ 3 ❑ 4 ❑ 5

GALATIANS
❑ 1 ❑ 2 ❑ 3 ❑ 4 ❑ 5 ❑ 6

ESTHER
❑ A ❑ 1 ❑ 2 ❑ 3 ❑ B ❑ 4 ❑ C ❑ D ❑ 5 ❑ 6 ❑ 7
❑ 8 ❑ E ❑ 9 ❑ 10 ❑ F

DANIEL
❑ 1 ❑ 2 ❑ 3 ❑ 4 ❑ 5 ❑ 6 ❑ 7 ❑ 8 ❑ 9 ❑ 10 ❑ 11
❑ 12 ❑ 13 ❑ 14

JOB
❑ 1 ❑ 2 ❑ 3 ❑ 4 ❑ 5 ❑ 6 ❑ 7 ❑ 8 ❑ 9 ❑ 10 ❑ 11
❑ 12 ❑ 13 ❑ 14 ❑ 15 ❑ 16 ❑ 17 ❑ 18 ❑ 19 ❑ 20
❑ 21 ❑ 22 ❑ 23 ❑ 24 ❑ 25 ❑ 26 ❑ 27 ❑ 28 ❑ 29
❑ 30 ❑ 31 ❑ 32 ❑ 33 ❑ 34 ❑ 35 ❑ 36 ❑ 37 ❑ 38
❑ 39 ❑ 40 ❑ 41 ❑ 42

1 PETER
❑ 1 ❑ 2 ❑ 3 ❑ 4 ❑ 5

EZEKIEL
❑ 1 ❑ 2 ❑ 3 ❑ 4 ❑ 5 ❑ 6 ❑ 7 ❑ 8 ❑ 9 ❑ 10 ❑ 11
❑ 12 ❑ 13 ❑ 14 ❑ 15 ❑ 16 ❑ 17 ❑ 18 ❑ 19 ❑ 20
❑ 21 ❑ 22 ❑ 23 ❑ 24 ❑ 25 ❑ 26 ❑ 27 ❑ 28 ❑ 29
❑ 30 ❑ 31 ❑ 32 ❑ 33 ❑ 34 ❑ 35 ❑ 36 ❑ 37 ❑ 38
❑ 39 ❑ 40 ❑ 41 ❑ 42 ❑ 43 ❑ 44 ❑ 45 ❑ 46 ❑ 47
❑ 48

JONAH
❑ 1 ❑ 2 ❑ 3 ❑ 4

EZRA
❑ 1 ❑ 2 ❑ 3 ❑ 4 ❑ 5 ❑ 6 ❑ 7 ❑ 8 ❑ 9 ❑ 10

NEHEMIAH
❑ 1 ❑ 2 ❑ 3 ❑ 4 ❑ 5 ❑ 6 ❑ 7 ❑ 8 ❑ 9 ❑ 10 ❑ 11
❑ 12 ❑ 13

HEBREWS
❑ 1 ❑ 2 ❑ 3 ❑ 4 ❑ 5 ❑ 6 ❑ 7 ❑ 8 ❑ 9 ❑ 10 ❑ 11
❑ 12 ❑ 13

ROMANS
❑ 1 ❑ 2 ❑ 3 ❑ 4 ❑ 5 ❑ 6 ❑ 7 ❑ 8 ❑ 9 ❑ 10 ❑ 11
❑ 12 ❑ 13 ❑ 14 ❑ 15 ❑ 16

PROVERBS
❑ 1 ❑ 2 ❑ 3 ❑ 4 ❑ 5 ❑ 6 ❑ 7 ❑ 8 ❑ 9 ❑ 10 ❑ 11
❑ 12 ❑ 13 ❑ 14 ❑ 15 ❑ 16 ❑ 17 ❑ 18 ❑ 19 ❑ 20
❑ 21 ❑ 22 ❑ 23 ❑ 24 ❑ 25 ❑ 26 ❑ 27 ❑ 28 ❑ 29
❑ 30 ❑ 31

SONG OF SONGS
❑ 1 ❑ 2 ❑ 3 ❑ 4 ❑ 5 ❑ 6 ❑ 7 ❑ 8

2 MACCABEES
❑ 1 ❑ 2 ❑ 3 ❑ 4 ❑ 5 ❑ 6 ❑ 7 ❑ 8 ❑ 9 ❑ 10 ❑ 11
❑ 12 ❑ 13 ❑ 14 ❑ 15

JOHN
❑ 1 ❑ 2 ❑ 3 ❑ 4 ❑ 5 ❑ 6 ❑ 7 ❑ 8 ❑ 9 ❑ 10 ❑ 11
❑ 12 ❑ 13 ❑ 14 ❑ 15 ❑ 16 ❑ 17 ❑ 18 ❑ 19 ❑ 20
❑ 21

1 JOHN
❑ 1 ❑ 2 ❑ 3 ❑ 4 ❑ 5

REVELATION
❑ 1 ❑ 2 ❑ 3 ❑ 4 ❑ 5 ❑ 6 ❑ 7 ❑ 8 ❑ 9 ❑ 10 ❑ 11
❑ 12 ❑ 13 ❑ 14 ❑ 15 ❑ 16 ❑ 17 ❑ 18 ❑ 19 ❑ 20
❑ 21 ❑ 22

Foreword to the Catholic Edition of the Good News Translation

In the *Dogmatic Constitution on Divine Revelation* (*Dei Verbum*), promulgated in 1965, the Second Vatican Council urged that "easy access to Sacred Scripture should be provided for all the Christian faithful," and encouraged the preparation of new translations of the Scriptures "since the word of God should be accessible at all times" (*Dei Verbum* 22). Just one year later, the American Bible Society published *Good News for Modern Man: The New Testament in the Today's English Version*, and it immediately became an international best-seller. This success encouraged the American Bible Society to undertake the translation of the Old Testament and to publish the first edition of the *Good News Bible* in 1976. Even as the Old Testament was being translated from Hebrew, discussions between the ABS and Roman Catholic officials began concerning the possibility of translating the Old Testament books that Roman Catholic Bibles always include but which are not based on Hebrew texts. These books are sometimes called "deuterocanonical" to suggest that they were added to the list (canon) of books that Catholics consider to be sacred Scripture and a worthy basis for doctrine at a somewhat later date than those books that were translated from Hebrew. The deuterocanonical books exist in Greek and Latin sources and have always been included in English Bibles translated from the Latin Vulgate.

Consequently, the American Bible Society published the *Good News Bible with Deuterocanonicals/Apocrypha* in 1979. This "interconfessional" text included all the deuterocanonical books plus a number of additional books not usually found in Catholic Bibles, but which other Christian traditions revere and employ in worship. This was the first edition of the *Good News Bible* to receive an *Imprimatur* (which means "let it be printed") from a Roman Catholic bishop, the Archbishop John Francis Whealon, the late archbishop of Hartford, Connecticut. While the *Imprimatur* does not constitute an endorsement, it assures the reader that the book does not contain anything contrary to the Catholic faith. When the *Good News Translation* was revised in 1992, it too received the *Imprimatur,* this time from the National Conference of Catholic Bishops under the signature of the then-Archbishop (now Cardinal) William H. Keeler, Archbishop of Baltimore.

The Catholic edition of the *Good News Bible* you hold in your hands contains the 1992 revised text in the order and format most preferred by Roman Catholics. It contains only those books considered sacred Scripture by Catholics and presents them in the sequence that follows the one used in all Catholic Bibles in the Latin Vulgate tradition. If you are unfamiliar with the *Good News Translation*, or if you are looking for a translation that will help you better understand the Good News of Jesus Christ for you and the world today, I encourage you to read on.

Jean-Pierre Ruiz, STD
St. John's University, New York
Epiphany 2003

OLD TESTAMENT

The Bible is divided into two major sections, the Old Testament and the New Testament. The Old Testament in Catholic Bibles contains forty-six books. The Bibles that most Protestants use has thirty-nine books in the Old Testament. They do not include the books of Tobit, Judith, 1 and 2 Maccabees, Wisdom, Sirach, Baruch, and some parts of Esther and Daniel. That is the main difference between Catholic and Protestant Bibles.

The Old Testament books include many different kinds of writings. You will find history, poetry, legends, laws, wise sayings, short stories, and the words of prophets. The Old Testament books are primarily about God's special relationship with his Chosen People. At different times these people are called Hebrews, Israelites, Judeans, and Jews. During their history God breaks through and calls the Chosen People to recognize him as their one and only God. God promises to bless them in a special way, and he asks the Chosen People to be faithful in following his commands.

This holy promise between God and the Chosen People is called a covenant. *Testament* is another word for *covenant,* so the Old Testament is the story of the Covenant between God and his special people—the Jews. Because of this, most of the books of the Old Testament are also the sacred Scriptures of the Jewish people. Since the books were written in Hebrew, they are sometimes called the Hebrew Scriptures. So the Old Testament isn't "old" because it is out of date. It is "old" because it is the story of how God first made his Covenant with his Chosen People.

The Old Testament in Christian Bibles is divided into four different sections. The table of contents shows the books that are in each section. Here is some information on each section:

The Pentateuch or Torah. These five books are the heart of the Old Testament. They contain the stories of Creation and stories about how sin entered the world. They tell how God broke through to first make his Covenant with Noah and Abraham. The Book of Exodus

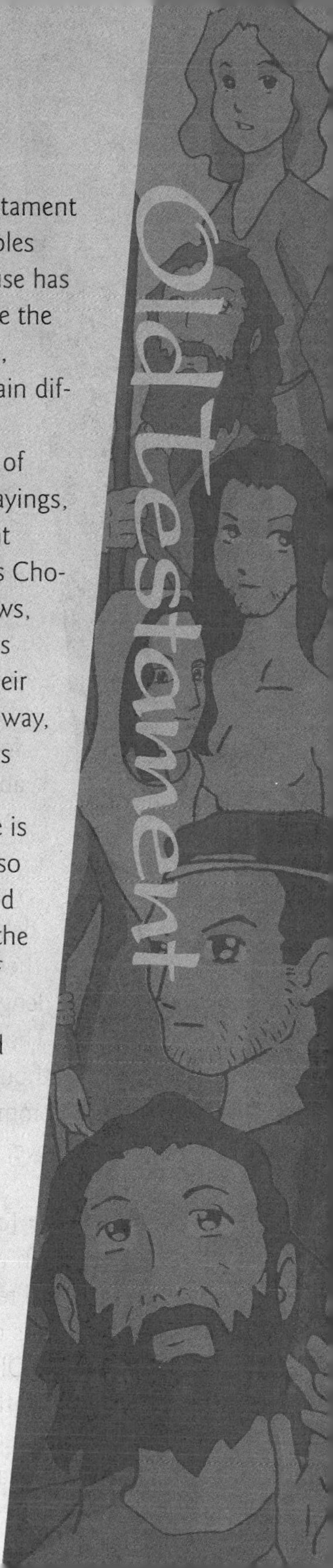

tells how God led his people out of slavery through the leadership of Moses. At Mount Sinai, God extended the Covenant to all his Chosen People and gave them the Ten Commandments.

The Historical Books. These sixteen books are mostly religious history and some short novels. They tell how the Chosen People settled in the Promised Land. Eventually they became a kingdom led by kings like Saul, David, and Solomon. But the rulers and the people often worshiped false gods and ignored the poor. So God sent prophets like Elijah and Elisha to call the people to be faithful to the Covenant. The historical books have imaginative stories about heroes like Ruth, Tobit, Judith, and Esther.

The Wisdom Books. These seven books contain the collected wisdom of the Chosen People. They contain the songs they used in worship and prayer. They contain advice for living a good and holy life. The Song of Songs has poetry about the goodness of sexuality. The Book of Job is a debate about why good people suffer bad things.

The Books of the Prophets. These eighteen books contain the messages of important prophets. The prophets delivered God's message to the Chosen People. They warned the Chosen People against worshiping false gods. They challenged the Chosen People to act fairly and to care for the poor. The prophets also offered comfort and hope when the people thought God had abandoned them. And some of the prophets promised a future savior, the Messiah, who would bring God's love, justice, and peace to the world.

To fully understand God's plan for the human race, we need both the Old and the New Testaments. In the Old Testament, God reveals the love he has for us. The stories teach us how sin keeps us from being in a completely loving relationship with God. The Old Testament shows how, through various people, God broke through to put his Chosen People on the right path. The stories prepare us to understand how Jesus Christ fulfills God's promise to save us from sin and death.

THE BOOK OF Genesis

Jake's mom keeps photo albums and scrapbooks. Chantal's dad videotapes the major moments in her life—and the not-so-major ones. Frederick's grandparents tell stories about what life was like when they were young. Human beings need to keep track of their memories. They also need to understand where they came from and where they are going.

The Book of Genesis does these things for the family of God. It starts out with stories about how God created the world, how evil came to be, and what God did about it. Then it tells the history of God's people—people who are holy (sometimes), good (except when they're bad), and faithful to God (eventually). Most of all, the Book of Genesis is the beginning of a love story between God and us.

Chap. 22

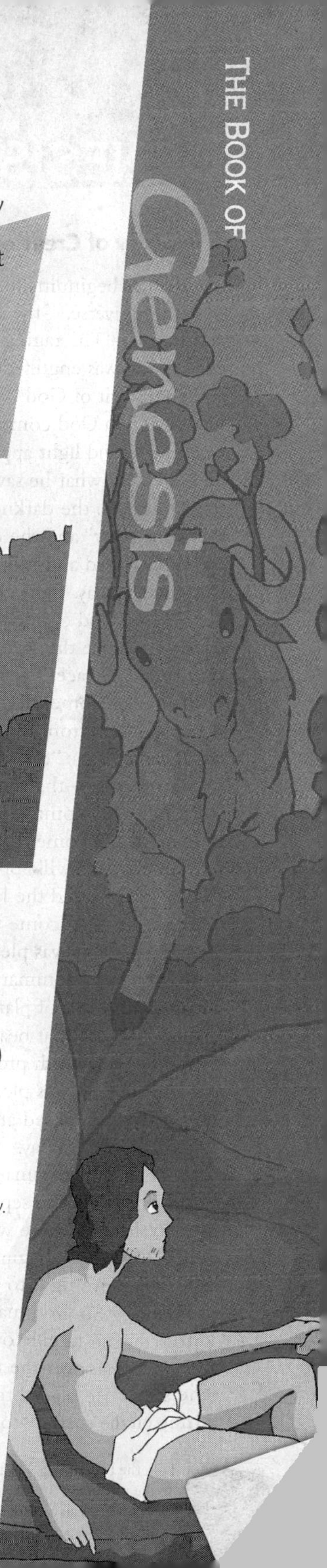

Headlines

- God Creates Stars, Seas, and Slimy Things (chapters 1–2)
- First Sin Leads to First Punishment (3:1–24)
- Flood Warning! Noah Evacuates (chapters 7–8)
- God Calls, Abram Listens (12:1–9)
- Treachery and Trickery: Twin Steals Inheritance (27:1–45)
- Jacob Tricked, Marries Wrong Sister! (29:15–30)
- Pharaoh Appoints Israelite Governor (41:37–57)

FACTOIDS

Who wrote this book? A tradition says Moses wrote Genesis, but that is unlikely. It was probably written by one or more authors who collected stories that were passed from generation to generation by word of mouth.

Why was it written? Genesis was written to explain how God created the world, how sin became part of life, and how the Israelites came to be God's Chosen People.

How does it fit into the Bible? Genesis is the first book of the Bible. It is part of the Pentateuch, the five books of the Bible that Jews call the Torah.

How is it organized? The first eleven chapters tell the story of Creation, the Fall, and God's Covenant with Noah. The rest of the book starts the history of God's Chosen People, beginning with Abraham and Sarah.

Important themes

- Everything God created is good and holy.
- Sin and evil are real.
- God promises to care for those who are faithful.

GENESIS

The Story of Creation

1 In the beginning, when God created
the universe,[a] 2the earth was formless
and desolate. The raging ocean that covered
everything was engulfed in total darkness,
and the Spirit of God[b] was moving over the
water. 3Then God commanded, "Let there
be light"—and light appeared. 4God was
pleased with what he saw. Then he separated
the light from the darkness, 5and he named
the light "Day" and the darkness "Night."
Evening passed and morning came—that
was the first day.

6-7Then God commanded, "Let there be a
dome to divide the water and to keep it in
two separate places"—and it was done. So
God made a dome, and it separated the
water under it from the water above it. 8He
named the dome "Sky." Evening passed and
morning came—that was the second day.

9Then God commanded, "Let the water
below the sky come together in one place,
so that the land will appear"—and it was
done. 10He named the land "Earth," and the
water which had come together he named
"Sea." And God was pleased with what he
saw. 11Then he commanded, "Let the earth
produce all kinds of plants, those that bear
grain and those that bear fruit"—and it was
done. 12So the earth produced all kinds of
plants, and God was pleased with what he
saw. 13Evening passed and morning came—
that was the third day.

14Then God commanded, "Let lights
appear in the sky to separate day from night
and to show the time when days, years, and
religious festivals[c] begin; 15they will shine in
the sky to give light to the earth"—and it
was done. 16So God made the two larger
lights, the sun to rule over the day and the
moon to rule over the night; he also made
the stars. 17He placed the lights in the sky to
shine on the earth, 18to rule over the day
and the night, and to separate light from
darkness. And God was pleased with what he
saw. 19Evening passed and morning came—
that was the fourth day.

20Then God commanded, "Let the water
be filled with many kinds of living beings,

Live it!

And God Was Pleased

The Bible says that every time God created something, God was pleased. God never made a mistake in creation, never started over, never even said "oops!" Poison ivy, stinkbugs, gray skies, mosquitoes, seaweed, vultures, and aardvarks were all worthy of God's pride.

God was especially proud of the human beings he made on the sixth day (Genesis 1:31). No human being who lives on this planet was a mistake. You are here because God wanted YOU at this time in this place for a special reason. The same goes for the person at school whom you really don't like and the person halfway across the world who lives in an "enemy" country.

The next time you're down on yourself or you see someone you don't really like, close your eyes and imagine God saying, "I am *very* pleased! I do great work!"

— Genesis 1:1—2:4

[a] **1:1** In the beginning . . . the universe; *or* In the beginning God created the universe; *or* When God began to create the universe. [b] **1:2** the Spirit of God; *or* the power of God; *or* a wind from God; *or* an awesome wind. [c] **1:14** religious festivals; *or* seasons.

1:3 2 Macc 7:28; 2 Cor 4:6 **1:6–8** 2 Pet 3:5

So God made them all, and was pleased with what he saw. (1:25)

and let the air be filled with birds." 21So God
created the great sea monsters, all kinds of
creatures that live in the water, and all kinds
of birds. And God was pleased with what he
saw. 22He blessed them all and told the crea-
tures that live in the water to reproduce and
to fill the sea, and he told the birds to
increase in number. 23Evening passed and
morning came—that was the fifth day.
24Then God commanded, "Let the earth
produce all kinds of animal life: domestic
and wild, large and small"—and it was done.
25So God made them all, and he was pleased
with what he saw.
26Then God said, "And now we will make
human beings; they will be like us and
resemble us. They will have power over the
fish, the birds, and all animals, domestic and
wild,[d] large and small." 27So God created
human beings, making them to be like him-
self. He created them male and female,
28blessed them, and said, "Have many chil-
dren, so that your descendants will live all
over the earth and bring it under their con-
trol. I am putting you in charge of the fish,
the birds, and all the wild animals. 29I have
provided all kinds of grain and all kinds of
fruit for you to eat; 30but for all the wild
animals and for all the birds I have provided
grass and leafy plants for food"—and it was
done. 31God looked at everything he had
made, and he was very pleased. Evening
passed and morning came—that was the
sixth day.

2 And so the whole universe was com-
pleted. 2By the seventh day God fin-
ished what he had been doing and stopped
working. 3He blessed the seventh day and set
it apart as a special day, because by that day
he had completed his creation[e] and stopped
working. 4And that is how the universe was
created.

So God created human beings . . . and he was very pleased. (1:27–31)

[d] **1:26** *One ancient translation* animals, domestic and wild; *Hebrew* domestic animals and all the earth. [e] **2:3** by that day he had completed his creation; *or* on that day he completed his creation.

1:26 Wis 2:23; Sir 17:3, 4; 1 Cor 11:7 **1:27, 28** Gen 5:1, 2 **1:27** Mt 19:4; Mk 10:6 **2:2, 3** Ex 20:11 **2:2** Heb 4:4, 10

Count the number of times the phrase "God was pleased" appears in Genesis, chapter 1.

The Garden of Eden

When the LORD[f] God made the universense,
5 there were no plants on the earth and no
seeds had sprouted, because he had not sent
any rain, and there was no one to cultivate
the land; 6 but water would come up from
beneath the surface and water the ground.
7 Then the LORD God took some soil
from the ground[g] and formed a man[g] out of
it; he breathed life-giving breath into his
nostrils and the man began to live.
8 Then the LORD God planted a garden in
Eden, in the East, and there he put the man
he had formed. 9 He made all kinds of beauti-
ful trees grow there and produce good fruit.
In the middle of the garden stood the tree
that gives life and the tree that gives knowl-
edge of what is good and what is bad.[h]
10 A stream flowed in Eden and watered
the garden; beyond Eden it divided into four
rivers. 11 The first river is the Pishon; it flows
around the country of Havilah. (12 Pure gold
is found there and also rare perfume and
precious stones.) 13 The second river is the
Gihon; it flows around the country of Cush.[i]
14 The third river is the Tigris, which flows
east of Assyria, and the fourth river is the
Euphrates.
15 Then the LORD God placed the man in
the Garden of Eden to cultivate it and guard
it. 16 He told him, "You may eat the fruit of
any tree in the garden, 17 except the tree that
gives knowledge of what is good and what is
bad.[j] You must not eat the fruit of that tree;
if you do, you will die the same day."
18 Then the LORD God said, "It is not
good for the man to live alone. I will make a
suitable companion to help him." 19 So he
took some soil from the ground and formed
all the animals and all the birds. Then he
brought them to the man to see what he
would name them; and that is how they all

Study it!

Uncovering the Truth

The first two chapters of Genesis tell two different stories of Creation. Some people believe that everything happened just as the Bible says it did. But Bible scholars tell us that neither of these stories gives us the scientific or historical *facts* about Creation. For example, God did not really create the world in six twenty-four-hour days. Neither God nor Adam named anything. And God did not take a rib from Adam to create Eve.

The stories in Genesis are symbolic stories. They may not contain scientific facts, but they tell us some important truths about God:

- **God always was, even before the universe was created.**
- **God created everything.**
- **God loves all of Creation.**
- **God created humans in the image of God.**
- **God created us to be happy and live in perfect harmony with him, each other, and all creation.**

There are many ways to communicate religious truth, and the Bible uses most of them. Believing the religious truth that the Bible teaches is the thing that really matters.

— Genesis 2:5–25

[f] **2:4** THE LORD: *Where the Hebrew text has Yahweh, traditionally transliterated as Jehovah, this translation employs LORD with capital letters, following a usage which is widespread in English versions.* [g] **2:7** GROUND . . . MAN: *The Hebrew words for "man" and "ground" have similar sounds.* [h] **2:9** knowledge of what is good and what is bad; *or* knowledge of everything. [i] **2:13** CUSH: *usually means Ethiopia, but here may refer to a place in Mesopotamia.* [j] **2:17** knowledge of what is good and what is bad; *or* knowledge of everything.

2:7 Wis 15:8, 11; 1 Cor 15:45 **2:9** Rev 2:7; 22:2, 14

***Genesis* means "source" or "beginning." It means that this book is about the beginning of things: the world, human beings, sin, the Covenant with God.**

got their names. 20 So the man named all the birds and all the animals; but not one of them was a suitable companion to help him.

21 Then the LORD God made the man fall into a deep sleep, and while he was sleeping, he took out one of the man's ribs and closed up the flesh. 22 He formed a woman out of the rib and brought her to him. 23 Then the man said,

"At last, here is one of my own kind—
Bone taken from my bone, and flesh from
my flesh.
'Woman' is her name because she was
taken out of man."[k]

24 That is why a man leaves his father and mother and is united with his wife, and they become one.

25 The man and the woman were both naked, but they were not embarrassed.

Human Disobedience

3 Now the snake was the most cunning animal that the LORD God had made. The snake asked the woman, "Did God really tell you not to eat fruit from any tree in the garden?"

2 "We may eat the fruit of any tree in the garden," the woman answered, 3 "except the tree in the middle of it. God told us not to eat the fruit of that tree or even touch it; if we do, we will die."

4 The snake replied, "That's not true; you will not die. 5 God said that because he knows that when you eat it, you will be like God[l] and know what is good and what is bad."[m]

6 The woman saw how beautiful the tree was and how good its fruit would be to eat, and she thought how wonderful it would be to become wise. So she took some of the fruit and ate it. Then she gave some to her husband, and he also ate it. 7 As soon as they had eaten it, they were given understanding and realized that they were naked; so they sewed fig leaves together and covered themselves.

How wonderful it would be to become wise! (3:6)

8 That evening they heard the LORD God walking in the garden, and they hid from him among the trees. 9 But the LORD God called out to the man, "Where are you?"

10 He answered, "I heard you in the garden; I was afraid and hid from you, because I was naked."

11 "Who told you that you were naked?" God asked. "Did you eat the fruit that I told you not to eat?"

12 The man answered, "The woman you put here with me gave me the fruit, and I ate it."

13 The LORD God asked the woman, "Why did you do this?"

She replied, "The snake tricked me into eating it."

God Pronounces Judgment

14 Then the LORD God said to the snake, "You will be punished for this; you alone of all the animals must bear this curse: From now on you will crawl on your belly, and you will have to eat dust as long as you live. 15 I will make you and the woman hate each other; her offspring and yours will always be enemies. Her offspring will crush your head, and you will bite her offspring's[n] heel."

16 And he said to the woman, "I will increase your trouble in pregnancy and your pain in giving birth. In spite of this, you will still have desire for your husband, yet you will be subject to him."

17 And he said to the man, "You listened to your wife and ate the fruit which I told you not to eat. Because of what you have done, the ground will be under a curse. You will have to work hard all your life to make it produce enough food for you. 18 It will produce weeds and thorns, and you will have to eat wild plants. 19 You will have to work

[k] **2:23** WOMAN . . . MAN: *The Hebrew words for "woman" and "man" have rather similar sounds.* [l] **3:5** God; *or* the gods. [m] **3:5** know what is good and what is bad; *or* know everything. [n] **3:15** her offspring's; *or* their.

2:24 Mt 19:5; Mk 10:7, 8; 1 Cor 6:16; Eph 5:31 **3:1** Wis 2:24; Rev 12:9; 20:2 **3:13** 2 Cor 11:3; 1 Tim 2:14 **3:15** Rev 12:17 **3:17, 18** Heb 6:8

Catholic Connections

Original Sin

In Genesis, chapter 3, a serpent told Adam and Eve that they could be just like God if they ate fruit from a certain tree. The trouble was that God told them not to. They knew it was wrong, but they ate it anyway. As a consequence God told them to leave the garden and promised that they would now have a hard life. Their problems were passed to all future generations—including ours.

Just like the Creation stories, the story about the serpent is a symbolic story that teaches a great truth: human beings turned away from God. The Church calls this turning away from God original sin. Just as you got your brown eyes from your mom or your gift for music from your grandfather, you were born with original sin because of the sin of the first human beings—Adam and Eve.

Because of original sin, human beings are more likely to disobey God; there is evil in the world; our relationships are sometimes difficult. But through our Baptism, original sin is forgiven and we are born to a new life as sons and daughters of God.

— Genesis 3:1–24

hard and sweat to make the soil produce
anything, until you go back to the soil from
which you were formed. You were made
from soil, and you will become soil again."
20 Adam[o] named his wife Eve,[p] because
she was the mother of all human beings.
21 And the LORD God made clothes out of
animal skins for Adam and his wife, and he
clothed them.

Adam and Eve Are Sent Out of the Garden

22 Then the LORD God said, "Now these
human beings have become like one of us
and have knowledge of what is good and
what is bad.[q] They must not be allowed to
take fruit from the tree that gives life, eat it,
and live forever." 23 So the LORD God sent
them out of the Garden of Eden and made
them cultivate the soil from which they had
been formed. 24 Then at the east side of the
garden he put living creatures[r] and a flaming
sword which turned in all directions. This
was to keep anyone from coming near the
tree that gives life.

Cain and Abel

4 Then Adam had intercourse with his
wife, and she became pregnant. She
bore a son and said, "By the LORD's help I
have gotten a son." So she named him Cain.[s]
2 Later she gave birth to another son, Abel.
Abel became a shepherd, but Cain was a
farmer. 3 After some time Cain brought some
of his harvest and gave it as an offering to
the LORD. 4 Then Abel brought the first
lamb born to one of his sheep, killed it, and
gave the best parts of it as an offering. The
LORD was pleased with Abel and his offer-
ing, 5 but he rejected Cain and his offering.
Cain became furious, and he scowled in
anger. 6 Then the LORD said to Cain, "Why

[o] **3:20** ADAM: *This name in Hebrew means "all human beings."* [p] **3:20** EVE: *This name sounds similar to the Hebrew word for "living," which is rendered in this context as "human beings."* [q] **3:22** knowledge of what is good and what is bad; *or* knowledge of everything. [r] **3:24** LIVING CREATURES: *See Word List.* [s] **4:1** CAIN: *This name sounds like the Hebrew for "gotten."*

3:22 Rev 22:14 **4:4** Heb 11:4

Pray it!

Am I Like Cain?

Am I like Cain, God?
I know I sometimes don't do my best. I do just enough to barely get by. Then when someone tells me it's not good enough, I get angry.
Am I like Cain, God?
Sometimes I hurt those who do well at the things I'd like to be good at. I hurt them with my words, my attitudes, and my actions.
Am I like Cain, God?
When I'm punished for something I did wrong, I complain about the unfairness of it all. I don't take responsibility for what I did.
Am I like Cain, God?
If I am, I'm sorry. Please help me let go of the anger and jealousy that's in my heart. Replace it with kindness, fairness, and the ability to see myself as you see me.
Amen.

—Genesis 4:1–16

are you angry? Why that scowl on your face?
7If you had done the right thing, you would
be smiling;[t] but because you have done evil,
sin is crouching at your door. It wants to
rule you, but you must overcome it."
8Then Cain said to his brother Abel, "Let's
go out in the fields."[u] When they were out
in the fields, Cain turned on his brother and
killed him.
9The LORD asked Cain, "Where is your
brother Abel?"

He answered, "I don't know. Am I supposed to take care of my brother?"

10Then the LORD said, "Why have you
done this terrible thing? Your brother's blood
is crying out to me from the ground, like a
voice calling for revenge. 11You are placed
under a curse and can no longer farm the
soil. It has soaked up your brother's blood as
if it had opened its mouth to receive it when

"Why that scowl on your face?" (4:6)

[t] **4:7** you would be smiling; *or* I would have accepted your offering. [u] **4:8** *Some ancient translations* Let's go out in the fields; *Hebrew does not have these words.*
4:8 Wis 10:3; Mt 23:35; Lk 11:51; 1 Jn 3:12 **4:10** Heb 12:24

The Fall is the name given to the events that led to Adam and Eve's being thrown out of the Garden of Eden.

Catholic Connections

Respecting Life

Cain tried to hide it at first. When God asked about Abel, he said, "I don't know. Am I supposed to take care of my brother?" (Genesis 4:9) But God knew the truth: Cain killed his brother.

In many parts of the world (including the United States), if someone kills another person, he or she can be put to death for the crime. But God spared Cain from that fate. He even put a mark on Cain to warn others not to kill him. The rest of his life was miserable, but he lived.

The Catholic Church teaches that all of life is sacred—even the life of a person who takes someone else's life. For that reason the death penalty must not be used if there are other ways to keep the murderer from hurting someone else. God calls us to have respect for all life.

— Genesis 4:8–16

you killed him. 12 If you try to grow crops,
the soil will not produce anything; you will
be a homeless wanderer on the earth."
13 And Cain said to the LORD, "This pun-
ishment is too hard for me to bear. 14 You are
driving me off the land and away from your
presence. I will be a homeless wanderer on
the earth, and anyone who finds me will kill
me."
15 But the LORD answered, "No. If anyone
kills you, seven lives will be taken in
revenge." So the LORD put a mark on Cain
to warn anyone who met him not to kill
him. 16 And Cain went away from the
LORD's presence and lived in a land called
"Wandering," which is east of Eden.

The Descendants of Cain

17 Cain and his wife had a son and named
him Enoch. Then Cain built a city and
named it after his son. 18 Enoch had a son
named Irad, who was the father of Mehu-
jael, and Mehujael had a son named
Methushael, who was the father of Lamech.
19 Lamech had two wives, Adah and Zillah.
20 Adah gave birth to Jabal, who was the
ancestor of those who raise livestock and live
in tents. 21 His brother was Jubal, the ancestor
of all musicians who play the harp and the
flute. 22 Zillah gave birth to Tubal Cain, who
made all kinds of tools out of bronze and
iron.[v] The sister of Tubal Cain was Naamah.
23 Lamech said to his wives,
"Adah and Zillah, listen to me:
I have killed a young man because he
struck me.
24 If seven lives are taken to pay for killing
Cain,
Seventy-seven will be taken if anyone kills
me."

Seth and Enosh

25 Adam and his wife had another son. She
said, "God has given me a son to replace
Abel, whom Cain killed." So she named him
Seth.[w] 26 Seth had a son whom he named

[v] **4:22** who made all kinds of tools out of bronze and iron; *one ancient translation* who was the ancestor of all metalworkers. [w] **4:25** SETH: *This name sounds like the Hebrew for "has given."*

Cain committed the sin of murder, but his story also contains other sins, such as jealous behavior and lying. Can you find more?

Enosh. It was then that people began using
the LORD's holy name in worship.

The Descendants of Adam
(1 Chronicles 1:1–4)

5 This is the list of the descendants of
Adam. (When God created human
beings, he made them like himself. 2He cre-
ated them male and female, blessed them,
and named them "Human Beings.") 3When
Adam was 130 years old, he had a son who
was like him, and he named him Seth. 4After
that, Adam lived another 800 years. He had
other children 5and died at the age of 930.
6When Seth was 105, he had a son,
Enosh, 7and then lived another 807 years.
He had other children 8and died at the age
of 912.
9When Enosh was 90, he had a son,
Kenan, 10and then lived another 815 years.
He had other children 11and died at the age
of 905.
12When Kenan was 70, he had a son,
Mahalalel, 13and then lived another 840
years. He had other children 14and died at
the age of 910.
15When Mahalalel was 65, he had a son,
Jared, 16and then lived another 830 years. He
had other children 17and died at the age of
895.
18When Jared was 162, he had a son,
Enoch, 19and then lived another 800 years.
He had other children 20and died at the age
of 962.
21When Enoch was 65, he had a son,
Methuselah. 22After that, Enoch lived in fel-
lowship with God for 300 years and had
other children. 23He lived to be 365 years
old. 24He spent his life in fellowship with
God, and then he disappeared, because God
took him away.
25When Methuselah was 187, he had a
son, Lamech, 26and then lived another 782
years. He had other children 27and died at
the age of 969.
28When Lamech was 182, he had a son
29and said, "From the very ground on which
the LORD put a curse, this child will bring us
relief from all our hard work"; so he named
him Noah.[x] 30Lamech lived another 595
years. He had other children 31and died at
the age of 777.
32After Noah was 500 years old, he had
three sons, Shem, Ham, and Japheth.

Human Wickedness

6 When people had spread all over the
world, and daughters were being born,
2some of the heavenly beings[y] saw that these
young women were beautiful, so they took
the ones they liked. 3Then the LORD said, "I
will not allow people to live forever; they are
mortal. From now on they will live no

Live it!

God's Bright Spot

God was fed up with human beings. Even though they were created in God's image, they insisted on disobeying God—*big* time! So God decided to destroy everyone and start from scratch. "I will wipe out these people I have created, and also the animals and the birds, because I am sorry that I made any of them" (Genesis 6:7).

But there was one bright spot: Noah and his family. They were good people who always made God number one in their life. They were the only ones in the world who lived as God wanted them to live. Because of them, God decided that the world was worth saving after all.

Does God always come first in your life? Are you God's bright spot?

— Genesis 6:1–12

[x] **5:29** NOAH: *This name sounds like the Hebrew for "relief."* [y] **6:2** heavenly beings; *or* sons of the gods; *or* sons of God.

5:1, 2 Gen 1:27, 28 **5:2** Mt 19:4; Mk 10:6 **5:24** Sir 44:16; 49:14; Heb 11:5; Jude 14 **6:1–4** Job 1:6; 2:1

longer than 120 years." 4In those days, and
even later, there were giants on the earth
who were descendants of human women
and the heavenly beings. They were the great
heroes and famous men of long ago.
5When the LORD saw how wicked every-
one on earth was and how evil their
thoughts were all the time, 6he was sorry
that he had ever made them and put them
on the earth. He was so filled with regret
7that he said, "I will wipe out these people I
have created, and also the animals and the
birds, because I am sorry that I made any of
them." 8But the LORD was pleased with
Noah.

Noah

9-10This is the story of Noah. He had
three sons, Shem, Ham, and Japheth. Noah
had no faults and was the only good man of
his time. He lived in fellowship with God,
11but everyone else was evil in God's sight,
and violence had spread everywhere. 12God
looked at the world and saw that it was evil,
for the people were all living evil lives.
13God said to Noah, "I have decided to
put an end to all people. I will destroy them
completely, because the world is full of their
violent deeds. 14Build a boat for yourself out
of good timber; make rooms in it and cover
it with tar inside and out. 15Make it 450 feet
long, 75 feet wide, and 45 feet high. 16Make
a roof[z] for the boat and leave a space of 18
inches between the roof[z] and the sides.
Build it with three decks and put a door in
the side. 17I am going to send a flood on the
earth to destroy every living being. Every-
thing on the earth will die, 18but I will
make a covenant with you. Go into the boat
with your wife, your sons, and their wives.
19-20Take into the boat with you a male and
a female of every kind of animal and of
every kind of bird, in order to keep them
alive. 21Take along all kinds of food for you
and for them." 22Noah did everything that
God commanded.

The Flood

7 The LORD said to Noah, "Go into the
boat with your whole family; I have
found that you are the only one in all the
world who does what is right. 2Take with
you seven pairs of each kind of ritually clean
animal, but only one pair of each kind of
unclean animal. 3Take also seven pairs of
each kind of bird. Do this so that every kind
of animal and bird will be kept alive to
reproduce again on the earth. 4Seven days
from now I am going to send rain that will
fall for forty days and nights, in order to
destroy all the living beings that I have
made." 5And Noah did everything that the
LORD commanded.
6Noah was six hundred years old when
the flood came on the earth. 7He and his
wife, and his sons and their wives, went into
the boat to escape the flood. 8A male and a
female of every kind of animal and bird,
whether ritually clean or unclean, 9went into
the boat with Noah, as God had command-
ed. 10Seven days later the flood came.

*Every kind of animal and bird . . .
went into the boat. (7:8, 9)*

11When Noah was six hundred years old,
on the seventeenth day of the second month
all the outlets of the vast body of water
beneath the earth burst open, all the flood-
gates of the sky were opened, 12and rain fell
on the earth for forty days and nights. 13On
that same day Noah and his wife went into
the boat with their three sons, Shem, Ham,
and Japheth, and their wives. 14With them
went every kind of animal, domestic and
wild, large and small, and every kind of bird.
15A male and a female of each kind of living

[z] **6:16** roof; *or* window.

6:4 Num 13:33; Sir 16:7; Bar 3:26 **6:5–8** Mt 24:37; Lk 17:26; 1 Pet 3:20 **6:9** Sir 44:17, 18; 2 Pet 2:5
6:22 Heb 11:7 **7:7** Mt 24:38, 39; Lk 17:27 **7:11** 2 Pet 3:6

being went into the boat with Noah, 16 as
God had commanded. Then the LORD shut
the door behind Noah.
17 The flood continued for forty days, and
the water became deep enough for the boat
to float. 18 The water became deeper, and the
boat drifted on the surface. 19 It became so
deep that it covered the highest mountains;
20 it went on rising until it was about twen-
ty-five feet above the tops of the mountains.
21 Every living being on the earth died—
every bird, every animal, and every person.
22 Everything on earth that breathed died.
23 The LORD destroyed all living beings on
the earth—human beings, animals, and birds.
The only ones left were Noah and those
who were with him in the boat. 24 The water
did not start going down for a hundred and
fifty days.

Everything on earth that breathed died. (7:22)

The End of the Flood

8 God had not forgotten Noah and all the
animals with him in the boat; he caused
a wind to blow, and the water started going
down. 2 The outlets of the water beneath the
earth and the floodgates of the sky were
closed. The rain stopped, 3 and the water
gradually went down for 150 days. 4 On the
seventeenth day of the seventh month the
boat came to rest on a mountain in the
Ararat range. 5 The water kept going down,
and on the first day of the tenth month the
tops of the mountains appeared.
6 After forty days Noah opened a window
7 and sent out a raven. It did not come back,
but kept flying around until the water was
completely gone. 8 Meanwhile, Noah sent
out a dove to see if the water had gone
down, 9 but since the water still covered all
the land, the dove did not find a place to
light. It flew back to the boat, and Noah
reached out and took it in. 10 He waited
another seven days and sent out the dove
again. 11 It returned to him in the evening
with a fresh olive leaf in its beak. So Noah
knew that the water had gone down. 12 Then
he waited another seven days and sent out
the dove once more; this time it did not
come back.

The water had gone down. (8:11)

13 When Noah was 601 years old, on the
first day of the first month, the water was
gone. Noah removed the covering of the
boat, looked around, and saw that the
ground was getting dry. 14 By the twenty-
seventh day of the second month the earth
was completely dry.
15 God said to Noah, 16 "Go out of the
boat with your wife, your sons, and their
wives. 17 Take all the birds and animals out
with you, so that they may reproduce and
spread over all the earth." 18 So Noah went
out of the boat with his wife, his sons, and
their wives. 19 All the animals and birds went
out of the boat in groups of their own kind.

Noah Offers a Sacrifice

20 Noah built an altar to the LORD; he took
one of each kind of ritually clean animal and
bird, and burned them whole as a sacrifice
on the altar. 21 The odor of the sacrifice
pleased the LORD, and he said to himself,

The name *Noah* means "to comfort" or "to give rest" in Hebrew.

Live it!

Got Gratitude?

When Noah and his family left the boat, the first thing Noah did was build an altar and offer prayers of thanksgiving to God. He was grateful to God for saving them and giving them a chance to start all over again. After receiving Noah's act of gratitude God decided never to destroy the world again.

If you never say thank you to the people in your life, they might feel like you take them for granted or don't appreciate them. Gratitude is also an important part of your relationship with God. Have you thanked God lately? For what are you grateful?

— Genesis 8:20–22

"Never again will I put the earth under a
curse because of what people do; I know that
from the time they are young their thoughts
are evil. Never again will I destroy all living
beings, as I have done this time. 22As long as
the world exists, there will be a time for
planting and a time for harvest. There will
always be cold and heat, summer and winter,
day and night."

God's Covenant with Noah

9 God blessed Noah and his sons and
said, "Have many children, so that your
descendants will live all over the earth. 2All
the animals, birds, and fish will live in fear of
you. They are all placed under your power.
3Now you can eat them, as well as green
plants; I give them all to you for food. 4The
one thing you must not eat is meat with
blood still in it; I forbid this because the life
is in the blood. 5If anyone takes human life,
he will be punished. I will punish with death
any animal that takes a human life. 6Human
beings were made like God, so whoever
murders one of them will be killed by some-
one else.
7"You must have many children, so that
your descendants will live all over the earth."
8God said to Noah and his sons, 9"I am
now making my covenant with you and with
your descendants, 10and with all living
beings—all birds and all animals—everything
that came out of the boat with you. 11With
these words I make my covenant with you: I
promise that never again will all living beings
be destroyed by a flood; never again will a
flood destroy the earth. 12As a sign of this
everlasting covenant which I am making with
you and with all living beings, 13I am putting
my bow in the clouds. It will be the sign of
my covenant with the world. 14Whenever I

The sign of my covenant with the world (9:13)

cover the sky with clouds and the rainbow
appears, 15I will remember my promise to
you and to all the animals that a flood will
never again destroy all living beings. 16When
the rainbow appears in the clouds, I will see it
and remember the everlasting covenant
between me and all living beings on earth.

9:1 Gen 1:28 **9:4** Lev 7:26, 27; 17:10–14; 19:26; Deut 12:16, 23; 15:23 **9:6** Ex 20:13; Gen 1:26 **9:7** Gen 1:28

Compare Genesis 1:29 and 9:2–3. What did God add to the human diet?

Pray it!

A Promising Sign

"I am putting my bow in the clouds. It will be the sign of my covenant with the world" (Genesis 9:13). After it was all over, God sent a rainbow as a sign to Noah, his family, and all living beings that God would never leave them and would never use a flood to destroy the world again. The rainbow was a symbol of God's *covenant,* a solemn promise made to Noah and to everyone who lived after him—including *you.*

Draw a rainbow, cut out a picture of one, or find a piece of rainbow ribbon. Put it someplace where you will see it often; for example, you could hang it near your bed or in your locker. Every time you look at it, close your eyes and take a deep breath. Think of God's promise. Fill yourself with the peace that comes with knowing that God is all around you and will never leave you.

— Genesis 9:8–17

17 That is the sign of the promise which I am
making to all living beings."

Noah and His Sons

18 The sons of Noah who went out of the
boat were Shem, Ham, and Japheth. (Ham
was the father of Canaan.) 19 These three
sons of Noah were the ancestors of all the
people on earth.

20 Noah, who was a farmer, was the first
man to plant a vineyard. 21 After he drank
some of the wine, he became drunk, took off
his clothes, and lay naked in his tent. 22 When
Ham, the father of Canaan, saw that his
father was naked, he went out and told his
two brothers. 23 Then Shem and Japheth took
a robe and held it behind them on their
shoulders. They walked backward into the
tent and covered their father, keeping their
faces turned away so as not to see him naked.
24 When Noah sobered up and learned what
his youngest son had done to him, 25 he said,

"A curse on Canaan!
He will be a slave to his brothers.
26 Give praise to the LORD, the God of
Shem!
Canaan will be the slave of Shem.
27 May God cause Japheth[a] to increase!
May his descendants live with the people
of Shem!
Canaan will be the slave of Japheth."

28 After the flood Noah lived 350 years
29 and died at the age of 950.

The Descendants of Noah's Sons
(1 Chronicles 1:5–23)

10 These are the descendants of Noah's
sons, Shem, Ham, and Japheth. These
three had sons after the flood.

2 The sons of Japheth—Gomer, Magog,
Madai, Javan, Tubal, Meshech, and Tiras—
were the ancestors of the peoples who bear
their names. 3 The descendants of Gomer
were the people of Ashkenaz, Riphath, and
Togarmah. 4 The descendants of Javan were
the people of Elishah, Spain, Cyprus, and
Rhodes; 5 they were the ancestors of the
people who live along the coast and on the
islands. These are the descendants of Japheth,
living in their different tribes and countries,
each group speaking its own language.

6 The sons of Ham—Cush, Egypt, Libya,
and Canaan—were the ancestors of the peo-
ples who bear their names. 7 The descendants
of Cush were the people of Seba, Havilah,
Sabtah, Raamah, and Sabteca. The descendants

[a] **9:27** JAPHETH: *This name sounds like the Hebrew for "increase."*

of Raamah were the people of Sheba and
Dedan. [8]Cush had a son named Nimrod, who
became the world's first great conqueror. [9]By
the LORD's help he was a great hunter, and
that is why people say, "May the LORD make
you as great a hunter as Nimrod!" [10]At first
his kingdom included Babylon, Erech, and
Accad, all three of them in Babylonia. [11]From
that land he went to Assyria and built the
cities of Nineveh, Rehoboth Ir, Calah, [12]and
Resen, which is between Nineveh and the
great city of Calah.

[13]The descendants of Egypt were the
people of Lydia, Anam, Lehab, Naphtuh,
[14]Pathrus, Casluh, and of Crete, from whom
the Philistines are descended.[b]

[15]Canaan's sons—Sidon, the oldest, and
Heth—were the ancestors of the peoples
who bear their names. [16]Canaan was also
the ancestor of the Jebusites, the Amorites,
the Girgashites, [17]the Hivites, the Arkites,
the Sinites, [18]the Arvadites, the Zemarites,
and the Hamathites. The different tribes
of the Canaanites spread out, [19]until the
Canaanite borders reached from Sidon
southward to Gerar near Gaza, and eastward
to Sodom, Gomorrah, Admah, and Zeboiim
near Lasha. [20]These are the descendants of
Ham, living in their different tribes and
countries, each group speaking its own lan-
guage.

[21]Shem, the older brother of Japheth, was
the ancestor of all the Hebrews. [22]Shem's
sons—Elam, Asshur, Arpachshad, Lud, and
Aram—were the ancestors of the peoples
who bear their names. [23]The descendants of
Aram were the people of Uz, Hul, Gether,
and Meshek. [24]Arpachshad was the father of
Shelah, who was the father of Eber. [25]Eber
had two sons: one was named Peleg,[c]
because during his time the people of the
world were divided; and the other was
named Joktan. [26]The descendants of Joktan
were the people of Almodad, Sheleph, Ha-
zarmaveth, Jerah, [27]Hadoram, Uzal, Diklah,
[28]Obal, Abimael, Sheba, [29]Ophir, Havilah,
and Jobab. All of them were descended from
Joktan. [30]The land in which they lived
extended from Mesha to Sephar in the east-
ern hill country. [31]These are the descendants
of Shem, living in their different tribes and
countries, each group speaking its own lan-
guage.

[32]All these peoples are the descendants of
Noah, nation by nation, according to their
different lines of descent. After the flood all
the nations of the earth were descended
from the sons of Noah.

The Tower of Babylon

11 At first, the people of the whole
world had only one language and
used the same words. [2]As they wandered
about in the East, they came to a plain in
Babylonia and settled there. [3]They said to
one another, "Come on! Let's make bricks
and bake them hard." So they had bricks to
build with and tar to hold them together.
[4]They said, "Now let's build a city with a
tower that reaches the sky, so that we can
make a name for ourselves and not be scat-
tered all over the earth."

[5]Then the LORD came down to see the
city and the tower which they had built,
[6]and he said, "Now then, these are all one
people and they speak one language; this is
just the beginning of what they are going
to do. Soon they will be able to do any-
thing they want! [7]Let us go down and mix
up their language so that they will not
understand each other." [8]So the LORD scat-
tered them all over the earth, and they
stopped building the city. [9]The city was
called Babylon,[d] because there the LORD
mixed up the language of all the people,
and from there he scattered them all over
the earth.

The Descendants of Shem

(1 Chronicles 1:24–27)

[10]These are the descendants of Shem. Two
years after the flood, when Shem was 100
years old, he had a son, Arpachshad. [11]After
that, he lived another 500 years and had
other children.

[12]When Arpachshad was 35 years old, he

[b] **10:14** *Probable text* and of Crete . . . descended; *Hebrew* from whom the Philistines are descended, and Crete.
[c] **10:25** PELEG: *This name sounds like the Hebrew for "divide."* [d] **11:9** BABYLON: *This name sounds like the Hebrew for "mixed up."*

Study it!

Watch Your Language!

As the Bible story goes, people used to speak the same language—until the people of Babylon tried to build a tower to the sky, that is. They wanted to show off their greatness; they wanted to be like God. God wanted to put a stop to their work, so God "mixed up the language of all the people, and from there he scattered them all over the earth" (Genesis 11:9).

The writers of Genesis were trying to explain the fact that people around the world spoke different languages, so they used a story about a tower. Like the other stories in the first eleven chapters of Genesis, it may not contain many historical facts, but it is true. Language can be used in ways that are hurtful or helpful. It can be used to build up relationships or to tear them down. It can be a source of prejudice, or it can be a source of pride.

God gave human beings the gift of language for a reason: to build a world that pleases and honors God.

— Genesis 11:1–9

had a son, Shelah; 13 after that, he lived
another 403 years and had other children.
14 When Shelah was 30 years old, he had a
son, Eber; 15 after that, he lived another 403
years and had other children.
16 When Eber was 34 years old, he had a
son, Peleg; 17 after that, he lived another 430
years and had other children.
18 When Peleg was 30 years old, he had a
son, Reu; 19 after that, he lived another 209
years and had other children.
20 When Reu was 32 years old, he had a
son, Serug; 21 after that, he lived another 207
years and had other children.
22 When Serug was 30 years old, he had a
son, Nahor; 23 after that, he lived another 200
years and had other children.
24 When Nahor was 29 years old, he had a
son, Terah; 25 after that, he lived another 119
years and had other children.
26 After Terah was 70 years old, he became
the father of Abram, Nahor, and Haran.

The Descendants of Terah

27 These are the descendants of Terah, who
was the father of Abram, Nahor, and Haran.
Haran was the father of Lot, 28 and Haran
died in his hometown of Ur in Babylonia,
while his father was still living. 29 Abram
married Sarai, and Nahor married Milcah,
the daughter of Haran, who was also the
father of Iscah. 30 Sarai was not able to have
children.
31 Terah took his son Abram, his grandson
Lot, who was the son of Haran, and his
daughter-in-law Sarai, Abram's wife, and
with them he left the city of Ur in Babylo-
nia to go to the land of Canaan. They went
as far as Haran and settled there. 32 Terah
died there at the age of 205.

God's Call to Abram

12 The LORD said to Abram, "Leave
your country, your relatives, and
your father's home, and go to a land that I
am going to show you. 2 I will give you
many descendants, and they will become a
great nation. I will bless you and make your
name famous, so that you will be a blessing.
3 I will bless those who bless you,
But I will curse those who curse you.

12:1 Wis 10:5; Acts 7:2, 3; Heb 11:8 **12:3** Gal 3:8

For the next month or so, try to learn at least one new word or phrase a day in another language.

Study it!

From Story to History

In the first part of the Book of Genesis (chapters 1–11), God speaks to us through stories about symbolic people in a time before recorded history. Though these chapters do not contain many historical facts, they are full of truth about God. The genealogy, or family tree, in Genesis 11:10–32 makes a transition to the second part of Book of Genesis.

Starting with the story of Abram and Sarai (who are later renamed Abraham and Sarah) in chapter 12, Genesis becomes more like a history book. The names of people and places are real. The events described in the second part of the book are not unusual; they are events that happen to real people. The characters struggle with some of the same things that we struggle with.

Both parts of Genesis are important. They are the foundation of all that we believe about God and God's relationship with us since the beginning of time.

— Genesis 11:10–32

And through you I will bless all the
nations."[e]
4 When Abram was seventy-five years old,
he started out from Haran, as the LORD had
told him to do; and Lot went with him.
5 Abram took his wife Sarai, his nephew Lot,
and all the wealth and all the slaves they had
acquired in Haran, and they started out for
the land of Canaan.
When they arrived in Canaan, 6 Abram
traveled through the land until he came to
the sacred tree of Moreh, the holy place at
Shechem. (At that time the Canaanites were
still living in the land.) 7 The LORD appeared
to Abram and said to him, "This is the coun-
try that I am going to give to your descen-
dants." Then Abram built an altar there to
the LORD, who had appeared to him. 8 After
that, he moved on south to the hill country
east of the city of Bethel and set up his camp
between Bethel on the west and Ai on the
east. There also he built an altar and wor-
shiped the LORD. 9 Then he moved on from
place to place, going toward the southern
part of Canaan.

Abram in Egypt

10 But there was a famine in Canaan, and
it was so bad that Abram went farther
south to Egypt, to live there for a while.
11 When he was about to cross the border
into Egypt, he said to his wife Sarai, "You
are a beautiful woman. 12 When the Egyp-
tians see you, they will assume that you are
my wife, and so they will kill me and let
you live. 13 Tell them that you are my sister;
then because of you they will let me live
and treat me well." 14 When he crossed the
border into Egypt, the Egyptians did see
that his wife was beautiful. 15 Some of the
court officials saw her and told the king
how beautiful she was; so she was taken to
his palace. 16 Because of her the king treat-
ed Abram well and gave him flocks of
sheep and goats, cattle, donkeys, slaves, and
camels.
17 But because the king had taken Sarai,
the LORD sent terrible diseases on him and
on the people of his palace. 18 Then the king
sent for Abram and asked him, "What have
you done to me? Why didn't you tell me
that she was your wife? 19 Why did you say

[e] **12:3** And through . . . nations; *or* All the nations will ask me to bless them as I have blessed you.
12:7 Acts 7:5; Gal 3:16 **12:13** Gen 20:2; 26:7

Chapters 12–50 of the Book of Genesis are mainly about Abraham, his son Isaac, Abraham's grandson Jacob, and Abraham's great-grandson Joseph.

Live it!

An Act of Faith

What would you do if someone told you to leave your home, your family, and your friends and move to a new country? This person says that if you do as asked, you will be famous. Would you trust him or her? Would you do it?

That's exactly what happened to Abram. He and his wife Sarai were living a comfortable life in Haran. God told them to pick up everything and move—not just to the next town, but to a new country. And they listened.

Why did Abram do it? Because he had faith. Through his faith, he came to know that God had great plans for him. He knew that his faith was a gift; he worked hard to understand what God wanted of him and took the steps to make it happen. It wasn't always easy, but every time Abram acted out of faith, his relationship with God got deeper.

God also gave you the gift of faith. Though God may not be telling you to leave home, he is inviting you to live out your faith every day. Are you listening carefully? What do you think God is asking of you?

— Genesis 12:1–9

that she was your sister, and let me take her
as my wife? Here is your wife; take her and
get out!" 20The king gave orders to his men,
so they took Abram and put him out of the
country, together with his wife and every-
thing he owned.

Abram and Lot Separate

13 Abram went north out of Egypt to
the southern part of Canaan with
his wife and everything he owned, and Lot
went with him. 2Abram was a very rich
man, with sheep, goats, and cattle, as well as
silver and gold. 3Then he left there and
moved from place to place, going toward
Bethel. He reached the place between Bethel
and Ai where he had camped before 4and
had built an altar. There he worshiped the
LORD.

5Lot also had sheep, goats, and cattle, as
well as his own family and servants. 6And so
there was not enough pasture land for the
two of them to stay together, because they
had too many animals. 7So quarrels broke
out between the men who took care of
Abram's animals and those who took care of
Lot's animals. (At that time the Canaanites
and the Perizzites were still living in the
land.)

8Then Abram said to Lot, "We are rela-
tives, and your men and my men shouldn't
be quarreling. 9So let's separate. Choose any
part of the land you want. You go one way,
and I'll go the other."

10Lot looked around and saw that the
whole Jordan Valley, all the way to Zoar, had
plenty of water, like the Garden of the
LORD[f] or like the land of Egypt. (This was
before the LORD had destroyed the cities of
Sodom and Gomorrah.) 11So Lot chose the
whole Jordan Valley for himself and moved
away toward the east. That is how the two
men parted. 12Abram stayed in the land of
Canaan, and Lot settled among the cities in
the valley and camped near Sodom, 13whose
people were wicked and sinned against the
LORD.

Abram Moves to Hebron

14After Lot had left, the LORD said to
Abram, "From where you are, look carefully
in all directions. 15I am going to give you
and your descendants all the land that you
see, and it will be yours forever. 16I am going
to give you so many descendants that no one

f **13:10** GARDEN OF THE LORD: *a reference to the Garden of Eden.*

13:10 Gen 2:10 **13:15** Acts 7:5

will be able to count them all; it would be as
easy to count all the specks of dust on earth!
17 Now, go and look over the whole land,
because I am going to give it all to you."
18 So Abram moved his camp and settled near
the sacred trees of Mamre at Hebron, and
there he built an altar to the LORD.

Abram Rescues Lot

14 Four kings, Amraphel of Babylonia,
Arioch of Ellasar, Chedorlaomer of
Elam, and Tidal of Goiim, 2 went to war
against five other kings: Bera of Sodom, Bir-
sha of Gomorrah, Shinab of Admah, Sheme-
ber of Zeboiim, and the king of Bela (or
Zoar). 3 These five kings had formed an
alliance and joined forces in Siddim Valley,
which is now the Dead Sea. 4 They had
been under the control of Chedorlaomer
for twelve years, but in the thirteenth year
they rebelled against him. 5 In the fourteenth
year Chedorlaomer and his allies came with
their armies and defeated the Rephaim in
Ashteroth Karnaim, the Zuzim in Ham, the
Emim in the plain of Kiriathaim, 6 and the
Horites in the mountains of Edom, pursu-
ing them as far as Elparan on the edge of
the desert. 7 Then they turned around and
came back to Kadesh (then known as
Enmishpat). They conquered all the land of
the Amalekites and defeated the Amorites
who lived in Hazazon Tamar.
8 Then the kings of Sodom, Gomorrah,
Admah, Zeboiim, and Bela drew up their
armies for battle in Siddim Valley and fought
9 against the kings of Elam, Goiim, Babylonia,
and Ellasar, five kings against four. 10 The valley
was full of tar pits, and when the kings of
Sodom and Gomorrah tried to run away from
the battle, they fell into the pits; but the other
three kings escaped to the mountains. 11 The
four kings took everything in Sodom and
Gomorrah, including the food, and went away.
12 Lot, Abram's nephew, was living in Sodom,
so they took him and all his possessions.
13 But a man escaped and reported all this
to Abram, the Hebrew, who was living near
the sacred trees belonging to Mamre the
Amorite. Mamre and his brothers Eshcol and
Aner were Abram's allies. 14 When Abram
heard that his nephew had been captured, he
called together all the fighting men in his
camp, 318 in all, and pursued the four kings
all the way to Dan. 15 There he divided his
men into groups, attacked the enemy by
night, and defeated them. He chased them as
far as Hobah, north of Damascus, 16 and got
back all the loot that had been taken. He
also brought back his nephew Lot and his
possessions, together with the women and
the other prisoners.

Catholic Connections

Priest of the Most High God

When Abram won a battle, Melchizedek—a king and a "priest of the Most High God" (Genesis 14:18)—blessed him. But it was an unusual blessing. Melchizedek offered Abram bread and wine, just as Jesus did at the Last Supper. It was different for Jesus, though. When he blessed the bread and shared it with his Apostles, it was no longer bread and wine. It was his body and blood.

Melchizedek is a priest of the Covenant between God and Abram. Jesus Christ is the High Priest of the New Covenant that God made with the whole human race—the Most High Priest of the Most High God. Every priest ordained in the Catholic Church carries on the work of Melchizedek and above all of Jesus in serving God's people.

— Genesis 14:17–20

Pray it!

Fear and Faith

Dear God,

Abram trusted you all the time. He did what you asked him to do and went where you asked him to go. But even he was afraid. He worried a lot. He was so afraid that he had nightmares.

Sometimes I'm afraid, too, God. I'm afraid of what the future will bring. I'm afraid that I won't know what to do when I grow up. I'm afraid of what will happen to the people I love. I'm afraid of the tests I have in school and the tests I have in life.

I believe in you, God. I know that you are with me all the time—especially when I'm afraid. Please take care of me.

— Genesis 15:1–15

Melchizedek Blesses Abram

17 When Abram came back from his victory over Chedorlaomer and the other kings, the king of Sodom went out to meet him in Shaveh Valley (also called King's Valley).
18 And Melchizedek, who was king of Salem and also a priest of the Most High God, brought bread and wine to Abram,
19 blessed him, and said, "May the Most High God, who made heaven and earth, bless Abram!
20 May the Most High God, who gave you victory over your enemies, be praised!" And Abram gave Melchizedek a tenth of all the loot he had recovered.

21 The king of Sodom said to Abram, "Keep the loot, but give me back all my people."

22 Abram answered, "I solemnly swear before the LORD, the Most High God, Maker of heaven and earth,
23 that I will not keep anything of yours, not even a thread or a sandal strap. Then you can never say, 'I am the one who made Abram rich.'
24 I will take nothing for myself. I will accept only what my men have used. But let my allies, Aner, Eshcol, and Mamre, take their share."

God's Covenant with Abram

15 After this, Abram had a vision and heard the LORD say to him, "Do not be afraid, Abram. I will shield you from danger and give you a great reward."

2 But Abram answered, "Sovereign LORD, what good will your reward do me, since I have no children? My only heir is Eliezer of Damascus.[g]
3 You have given me no children, and one of my slaves will inherit my property."

4 Then he heard the LORD speaking to him again: "This slave Eliezer will not inherit your property; your own son will be your heir."
5 The LORD took him outside and said, "Look at the sky and try to count the stars; you will have as many descendants as that."

6 Abram put his trust in the LORD, and because of this the LORD was pleased with him and accepted him.

7 Then the LORD said to him, "I am the LORD, who led you out of Ur in Babylonia, to give you this land as your own."

8 But Abram asked, "Sovereign LORD, how can I know that it will be mine?"

9 He answered, "Bring me a cow, a goat,

[g] **15:2** My . . . Damascus; *Hebrew unclear; literally,* The heir of my house, he of Damascus, Eliezer.

14:18–20 Heb 7:1–10 **15:5** Rom 4:18; Heb 11:12 **15:6** 1 Macc 2:52; Rom 4:3; Gal 3:6; Jas 2:23

Check out Hebrews 7:1–10 for more about Melchizedek. You may also hear his name at Mass in the Eucharistic prayer.

and a ram, each of them three years old, and
a dove and a pigeon." 10Abram brought the
animals to God, cut them in half, and placed
the halves opposite each other in two rows;
but he did not cut up the birds. 11Vultures
came down on the bodies, but Abram drove
them off.

12When the sun was going down, Abram
fell into a deep sleep, and fear and terror
came over him. 13The LORD said to him,
"Your descendants will be strangers in a for-
eign land; they will be slaves there and will
be treated cruelly for four hundred years.
14But I will punish the nation that enslaves
them, and when they leave that foreign land,
they will take great wealth with them. 15You
yourself will live to a ripe old age, die in
peace, and be buried. 16It will be four gener-
ations before your descendants come back
here, because I will not drive out the Amo-
rites until they become so wicked that they
must be punished."

17When the sun had set and it was dark, a
smoking fire pot and a flaming torch sud-
denly appeared and passed between the
pieces of the animals. 18Then and there the
LORD made a covenant with Abram. He
said, "I promise to give your descendants all
this land from the border of Egypt to the
Euphrates River, 19including the lands of the
Kenites, the Kenizzites, the Kadmonites,
20the Hittites, the Perizzites, the Rephaim,
21the Amorites, the Canaanites, the Gir-
gashites, and the Jebusites."

Hagar and Ishmael

16 Abram's wife Sarai had not borne
him any children. But she had an
Egyptian slave woman named Hagar, 2and
so she said to Abram, "The LORD has kept
me from having children. Why don't you
sleep with my slave? Perhaps she can have a
child for me." Abram agreed with what Sarai
said. 3So she gave Hagar to him to be his
concubine. (This happened after Abram had
lived in Canaan for ten years.) 4Abram had
intercourse with Hagar, and she became
pregnant. When she found out that she was
pregnant, she became proud and despised
Sarai.

5Then Sarai said to Abram, "It's your fault
that Hagar despises me.[h] I myself gave her to
you, and ever since she found out that she
was pregnant, she has despised me. May the
LORD judge which of us is right, you or
me!"

6Abram answered, "Very well, she is your
slave and under your control; do whatever
you want with her." Then Sarai treated
Hagar so cruelly that she ran away.

7The angel of the LORD met Hagar at a
spring in the desert on the road to Shur
8and said, "Hagar, slave of Sarai, where have
you come from and where are you going?"

She answered, "I am running away from
my mistress."

9He said, "Go back to her and be her
slave." 10Then he said, "I will give you so
many descendants that no one will be able
to count them. 11You are going to have a
son, and you will name him Ishmael,[i]
because the LORD has heard your cry of dis-
tress. 12But your son will live like a wild
donkey; he will be against everyone, and
everyone will be against him. He will live
apart from all his relatives."

13Hagar asked herself, "Have I really seen
God and lived to tell about it?"[j] So she
called the LORD, who had spoken to her, "A
God Who Sees." 14That is why people call
the well between Kadesh and Bered "The
Well of the Living One Who Sees Me."

15Hagar bore Abram a son, and he named
him Ishmael. 16Abram was eighty-six years
old at the time.

[h] **16:5** It's your fault...me; *or* May you suffer for this wrong done against me. [i] **16:11** ISHMAEL: *This name in Hebrew means "God hears."* [j] **16:13** *Probable text* lived to tell about it?; *Hebrew unclear.*

15:12 Job 4:13, 14 **15:13** Ex 1:1–14; Acts 7:6 **15:14** Ex 12:40, 41; Acts 7:7 **15:18** Acts 7:5 **16:15** Gal 4:22

What is the meaning of your name? Why did your parents choose it for you?

Circumcision, the Sign of the Covenant

17 When Abram was ninety-nine years
old, the LORD appeared to him and
said, "I am the Almighty God. Obey me and
always do what is right. 2I will make my
covenant with you and give you many
descendants." 3Abram bowed down with his
face touching the ground, and God said, 4"I
make this covenant with you: I promise that
you will be the ancestor of many nations.
5Your name will no longer be Abram, but
Abraham,[k] because I am making you the
ancestor of many nations. 6I will give you
many descendants, and some of them will be
kings. You will have so many descendants
that they will become nations.
7"I will keep my promise to you and to
your descendants in future generations as an
everlasting covenant. I will be your God and
the God of your descendants. 8I will give to
you and to your descendants this land in
which you are now a foreigner. The whole
land of Canaan will belong to your descen-
dants forever, and I will be their God."
9God said to Abraham, "You also must
agree to keep the covenant with me, both
you and your descendants in future genera-
tions. 10You and your descendants must all
agree to circumcise every male among you.
11-12From now on you must circumcise every
baby boy when he is eight days old, includ-
ing slaves born in your homes and slaves
bought from foreigners. This will show that
there is a covenant between you and me.
13Each one must be circumcised, and this
will be a physical sign to show that my
covenant with you is everlasting. 14Any male
who has not been circumcised will no longer
be considered one of my people, because he
has not kept the covenant with me."
15God said to Abraham, "You must no
longer call your wife Sarai; from now on her
name is Sarah.[l] 16I will bless her, and I will
give you a son by her. I will bless her, and
she will become the mother of nations, and
there will be kings among her descendants."
17Abraham bowed down with his face
touching the ground, but he began to laugh
when he thought, "Can a man have a child
when he is a hundred years old? Can Sarah
have a child at ninety?" 18He asked God,
"Why not let Ishmael be my heir?"
19But God said, "No. Your wife Sarah will

Study it!

What's in a Name?

Abram was faithful to God, and God was faithful to Abram. As a sign of that faithfulness, God made a covenant with him—a solemn promise to bless Abram with many descendants. Abram did not understand how this could happen—he had only one son at the time, Ishmael, whose mother was a slave. Abram's real wife, Sarai, was old—too old to have children. But Abram trusted God, just like he always did.

As a sign of the covenant between them, God changed Abram's name from Abram (which means "father") to Abraham (which means "father of many"). His wife's name was changed from Sarai to Sarah (meaning "princess"). As a physical sign of the covenant, God told Abram to be circumcised and to have his son and all the males in his house circumcised.

It happened just as God said it would. Sarah had a son named Isaac (meaning "God laughs"). Ishmael (meaning "God hears") also took his place among Abraham's descendants.

— Genesis 17:1–22

[k] **17:5** ABRAHAM: *This name sounds like the Hebrew for "ancestor of many nations."* [l] **17:15** SARAH: *This name in Hebrew means "princess."*

17:5 Rom 4:17 **17:7** Lk 1:55 **17:8** Acts 7:5 **17:10** Acts 7:8; Rom 4:11

bear you a son and you will name him
Isaac.[m] I will keep my covenant with him
and with his descendants forever. It is an
everlasting covenant. 20I have heard your
request about Ishmael, so I will bless him and
give him many children and many descen-
dants. He will be the father of twelve princes,
and I will make a great nation of his descen-
dants. 21But I will keep my covenant with
your son Isaac, who will be born to Sarah
about this time next year." 22When God fin-
ished speaking to Abraham, he left him.
23On that same day Abraham obeyed God
and circumcised his son Ishmael and all the
other males in his household, including the
slaves born in his home and those he had
bought. 24Abraham was ninety-nine years
old when he was circumcised, 25and his son
Ishmael was thirteen. 26They were both cir-
cumcised on the same day, 27together with
all of Abraham's slaves.

A Son Is Promised to Abraham

18 The LORD appeared to Abraham at
the sacred trees of Mamre. As Abra-
ham was sitting at the entrance of his tent
during the hottest part of the day, 2he
looked up and saw three men standing there.
As soon as he saw them, he ran out to meet
them. Bowing down with his face touching
the ground, 3he said, "Sirs, please do not pass
by my home without stopping; I am here to
serve you. 4Let me bring some water for you
to wash your feet; you can rest here beneath
this tree. 5I will also bring a bit of food; it
will give you strength to continue your jour-
ney. You have honored me by coming to my
home, so let me serve you."
They replied, "Thank you; we accept."
6Abraham hurried into the tent and said
to Sarah, "Quick, take a sack of your best
flour, and bake some bread." 7Then he ran to
the herd and picked out a calf that was ten-
der and fat, and gave it to a servant, who
hurried to get it ready. 8He took some
cream, some milk, and the meat, and set the
food before the men. There under the tree
he served them himself, and they ate.

Live it!

Surprises from God

One day Abraham and Sarah had visitors—one of whom was actually God. God promised Abraham that Sarah would have a baby. When Sarah heard the visitors' comments, she laughed. She couldn't *possibly* have a baby at this point in her life. She was too old. But Sarah didn't understand that it was God talking. And God can do surprising things.

Did God ever surprise you? Did something wonderful but unexpected ever happen to you? It might be something small, like a phone call from a friend or a piece of music that brings back good memories. Maybe it's something bigger, like a new job for a parent who is unemployed or finding out that you really like being a teacher's aide for younger kids. Those are gifts from God.

God is full of surprises. All you have to do is keep your eyes, your ears, and your heart open.

— Genesis 18:1–15

9Then they asked him, "Where is your
wife Sarah?"
"She is there in the tent," he answered.
10One of them said, "Nine months from
now[n] I will come back, and your wife Sarah
will have a son."
Sarah was behind him, at the door of the
tent, listening. 11Abraham and Sarah were
very old, and Sarah had stopped having her
monthly periods. 12So Sarah laughed to her-
self and said, "Now that I am old and worn
out, can I still enjoy sex? And besides, my
husband is old too."
13Then the LORD asked Abraham, "Why

[m] **17:19** ISAAC: *This name in Hebrew means "he laughs."* [n] **18:10** Nine months from now; *or* This time next year.

18:2a Heb 13:2 **18:10** Rom 9:9 **18:12** 1 Pet 3:6

did Sarah laugh and say, 'Can I really have a
child when I am so old?' 14 Is anything too hard
for the LORD? As I said, nine months from
now I will return, and Sarah will have a son."
15 Because Sarah was afraid, she denied it.
"I didn't laugh," she said.
"Yes, you did," he replied. "You laughed."

Abraham Pleads for Sodom

16 Then the men left and went to a place
where they could look down at Sodom, and
Abraham went with them to send them on
their way. 17 And the LORD said to himself, "I
will not hide from Abraham what I am
going to do. 18 His descendants will become
a great and mighty nation, and through him
I will bless all the nations.[o] 19 I have chosen
him in order that he may command his sons
and his descendants to obey me and to do
what is right and just. If they do, I will do
everything for him that I have promised."
20 Then the LORD said to Abraham,
"There are terrible accusations against
Sodom and Gomorrah, and their sin is very
great. 21 I must go down to find out whether
or not the accusations which I have heard
are true."
22 Then the two men left and went on
toward Sodom, but the LORD remained with
Abraham. 23 Abraham approached the LORD
and asked, "Are you really going to destroy
the innocent with the guilty? 24 If there are
fifty innocent people in the city, will you
destroy the whole city? Won't you spare it in
order to save the fifty? 25 Surely you won't
kill the innocent with the guilty. That's
impossible! You can't do that. If you did, the
innocent would be punished along with the
guilty. That is impossible. The judge of all
the earth has to act justly."
26 The LORD answered, "If I find fifty
innocent people in Sodom, I will spare the
whole city for their sake."
27 Abraham spoke again: "Please forgive
my boldness in continuing to speak to you,
Lord. I am only a man and have no right to
say anything. 28 But perhaps there will be
only forty-five innocent people instead of
fifty. Will you destroy the whole city because
there are five too few?"
The LORD answered, "I will not destroy
the city if I find forty-five innocent people."
29 Abraham spoke again: "Perhaps there
will be only forty."
He replied, "I will not destroy it if there
are forty."
30 Abraham said, "Please don't be angry,
Lord, but I must speak again. What if there
are only thirty?"
He said, "I will not do it if I find thirty."
31 Abraham said, "Please forgive my bold-
ness in continuing to speak to you, Lord.
Suppose that only twenty are found?"
He said, "I will not destroy the city if I
find twenty."
32 Abraham said, "Please don't be angry,
Lord, and I will speak only once more. What
if only ten are found?"
He said, "I will not destroy it if there are
ten." 33 After he had finished speaking with
Abraham, the LORD went away, and Abra-
ham returned home.

The Sinfulness of Sodom

19 When the two angels came to
Sodom that evening, Lot was sitting
at the city gate. As soon as he saw them, he
got up and went to meet them. He bowed
down before them 2 and said, "Sirs, I am here
to serve you. Please come to my house. You
can wash your feet and spend the night. In
the morning you can get up early and go on
your way."
But they answered, "No, we will spend
the night here in the city square."
3 He kept on urging them, and finally they
went with him to his house. Lot ordered his
servants to bake some bread and prepare a
fine meal for the guests. When it was ready,
they ate it.

[o] **18:18** through . . . nations; *or* all the nations will ask me to bless them as I have blessed him.
18:14 Lk 1:37

In Genesis 18:16–33 Abraham takes the daring step of questioning God. Are you willing to share with God everything you are thinking and feeling?

[4]Before the guests went to bed, the men of Sodom surrounded the house. All the men of the city, both young and old, were there. [5]They called out to Lot and asked, "Where are the men who came to stay with you tonight? Bring them out to us!" The men of Sodom wanted to have sex with them.

[6]Lot went outside and closed the door behind him. [7]He said to them, "Friends, I beg you, don't do such a wicked thing! [8]Look, I have two daughters who are still virgins. Let me bring them out to you, and you can do whatever you want with them. But don't do anything to these men; they are guests in my house, and I must protect them."

[9]But they said, "Get out of our way, you foreigner! Who are you to tell us what to do? Out of our way, or we will treat you worse than them." They pushed Lot back and moved up to break down the door. [10]But the two men inside reached out, pulled Lot back into the house, and shut the door. [11]Then they struck all the men outside with blindness, so that they couldn't find the door.

Lot Leaves Sodom

[12]The two men said to Lot, "If you have anyone else here—sons, daughters, sons-in-law, or any other relatives living in the city—get them out of here, [13]because we are going to destroy this place. The LORD has heard the terrible accusations against these people and has sent us to destroy Sodom."

[14]Then Lot went to the men that his daughters were going to marry, and said, "Hurry up and get out of here; the LORD is going to destroy this place." But they thought he was joking.

[15]At dawn the angels tried to make Lot hurry. "Quick!" they said. "Take your wife and your two daughters and get out, so that you will not lose your lives when the city is destroyed." [16]Lot hesitated. The LORD, however, had pity on him; so the men took him, his wife, and his two daughters by the hand and led them out of the city. [17]Then one of the angels said, "Run for your lives! Don't look back and don't stop in the valley. Run to the hills, so that you won't be killed."

Live it!

Don't Look Back

Evil surrounded Lot and his family. They lived in Sodom, a town where people did awful things. Finally, God had enough. He decided to destroy Sodom and Gomorrah, a neighboring town. But Lot and his family were good people. God wanted to spare them, so he told them to "Run for your lives! Don't look back . . . (Genesis 19:17)."

As you grow up you, too, will come face to face with evil. You may face pressure to drink or do drugs. Friends may try to convince you that seeing pornography doesn't hurt anyone. You may get caught up in a group that sees acts of violence or destruction as fun. These activities may not seem dangerous at first, but if you get deeper into them they will eventually lead to death and destruction.

When you are faced with a situation you know is wrong, do the right thing and take God's advice: "Run for your lives! Don't look back."

— Genesis 19:1–29

19:5–8 Judg 19:22–24 **19:11** 2 Kings 6:18 **19:16** 2 Pet 2:7

What is the connection between the story of Lot and his family (Genesis, chapter 19) and the story of Noah (Genesis, chapter 7)?

18But Lot answered, "No, please don't make us do that, sir. 19You have done me a great favor and saved my life. But the hills are too far away; the disaster will overtake me, and I will die before I get there. 20Do you see that little town? It is near enough. Let me go over there—you can see it is just a small place—and I will be safe."

21He answered, "All right, I agree. I won't destroy that town. 22Hurry! Run! I can't do anything until you get there."

Because Lot called it small, the town was named Zoar.[p]

The Destruction of Sodom and Gomorrah

23The sun was rising when Lot reached Zoar. 24Suddenly the LORD rained burning sulfur on the cities of Sodom and Gomorrah 25and destroyed them and the whole valley, along with all the people there and everything that grew on the land. 26But Lot's wife looked back and was turned into a pillar of salt.

Lot's wife looked back. (19:26)

27Early the next morning Abraham hurried to the place where he had stood in the presence of the LORD. 28He looked down at Sodom and Gomorrah and the whole valley and saw smoke rising from the land, like smoke from a huge furnace. 29But when God destroyed the cities of the valley where Lot was living, he kept Abraham in mind and allowed Lot to escape to safety.

The Origin of the Moabites and Ammonites

30Because Lot was afraid to stay in Zoar, he and his two daughters moved up into the hills and lived in a cave. 31The older daughter said to her sister, "Our father is getting old, and there are no men in the whole world[q] to marry us so that we can have children. 32Come on, let's get our father drunk, so that we can sleep with him and have children by him." 33That night they gave him wine to drink, and the older daughter had intercourse with him. But he was so drunk that he didn't know it.

34The next day the older daughter said to her sister, "I slept with him last night; now let's get him drunk again tonight, and you sleep with him. Then each of us will have a child by our father." 35So that night they got him drunk, and the younger daughter had intercourse with him. Again he was so drunk that he didn't know it. 36In this way both of Lot's daughters became pregnant by their own father. 37The older daughter had a son, whom she named Moab.[r] He was the ancestor of the present-day Moabites. 38The younger daughter also had a son, whom she named Benammi.[s] He was the ancestor of the present-day Ammonites.

Abraham and Abimelech

20 Abraham moved from Mamre to the southern part of Canaan and lived between Kadesh and Shur. Later, while he was living in Gerar, 2he said that his wife Sarah was his sister. So King Abimelech of Gerar had Sarah brought to him. 3One night God appeared to him in a dream and said, "You are going to die, because you have taken this woman; she is already married."

4But Abimelech had not come near her, and he said, "Lord, I am innocent! Would

[p] **19:22** ZOAR: *This name sounds like the Hebrew for "small."* [q] **19:31** the whole world; *or* this land.
[r] **19:37** MOAB: *This name sounds like the Hebrew for "from my father."* [s] **19:38** BENAMMI: *This name in Hebrew means "son of my relative" and sounds like the Hebrew for "Ammonite."*

19:24, 25 Mt 10:15; 11:23, 24; Lk 10:12; 17:29; 2 Pet 2:6; Jude 7 **19:26** Wis 10:7; Lk 17:32 **20:2** Gen 12:13; 26:7

you destroy me and my people? [5]Abraham
himself said that she was his sister, and she
said the same thing. I did this with a clear
conscience, and I have done no wrong."
[6]God replied in the dream, "Yes, I know
that you did it with a clear conscience; so I
kept you from sinning against me and did
not let you touch her. [7]But now, give the
woman back to her husband. He is a
prophet, and he will pray for you, so that
you will not die. But if you do not give her
back, I warn you that you are going to die,
you and all your people."
[8]Early the next morning Abimelech called
all his officials and told them what had hap-
pened, and they were terrified. [9]Then Abim-
elech called Abraham and asked, "What have
you done to us? What wrong have I done to
you to make you bring this disaster on me
and my kingdom? No one should ever do
what you have done to me. [10]Why did you
do it?"
[11]Abraham answered, "I thought that
there would be no one here who has rever-
ence for God and that they would kill me to
get my wife. [12]She really is my sister. She is
the daughter of my father, but not of my
mother, and I married her. [13]So when God
sent me from my father's house into foreign
lands, I said to her, 'You can show how loyal
you are to me by telling everyone that I am
your brother.' "
[14]Then Abimelech gave Sarah back to
Abraham, and at the same time he gave him
sheep, cattle, and slaves. [15]He said to Abra-
ham, "Here is my whole land; live anywhere
you like." [16]He said to Sarah, "I am giving
your brother a thousand pieces of silver as
proof to all who are with you that you are
innocent; everyone will know that you have
done no wrong."
[17-18]Because of what had happened to
Sarah, Abraham's wife, the LORD had made it
impossible for any woman in Abimelech's
palace to have children. So Abraham prayed
for Abimelech, and God healed him. He also
healed his wife and his slave women, so that
they could have children.

The Birth of Isaac

21 The LORD blessed Sarah, as he had
promised, [2]and she became pregnant
and bore a son to Abraham when he was
old. The boy was born at the time God had
said he would be born. [3]Abraham named
him Isaac, [4]and when Isaac was eight days
old, Abraham circumcised him, as God had
commanded. [5]Abraham was a hundred years
old when Isaac was born. [6]Sarah said, "God
has brought me joy and laughter.[t] Everyone
who hears about it will laugh with me."
[7]Then she added, "Who would have said to
Abraham that Sarah would nurse children?
Yet I have borne him a son in his old age."
[8]The child grew, and on the day that he
was weaned, Abraham gave a great feast.

Hagar and Ishmael Are Sent Away

[9]One day Ishmael, whom Hagar the
Egyptian had borne to Abraham, was playing
with[u] Sarah's son Isaac.[v] [10]Sarah saw them
and said to Abraham, "Send this slave and
her son away. The son of this woman must
not get any part of your wealth, which my
son Isaac should inherit." [11]This troubled
Abraham very much, because Ishmael also
was his son. [12]But God said to Abraham,
"Don't be worried about the boy and your
slave Hagar. Do whatever Sarah tells you,
because it is through Isaac that you will have
the descendants I have promised. [13]I will also
give many children to the son of the slave
woman, so that they will become a nation.
He too is your son."
[14]Early the next morning Abraham gave
Hagar some food and a leather bag full of
water. He put the child on her back and sent
her away. She left and wandered about in the
wilderness of Beersheba. [15]When the water
was all gone, she left the child under a bush
[16]and sat down about a hundred yards away.
She said to herself, "I can't bear to see my
child die." While she was sitting there, she[w]
began to cry.
[17]God heard the boy crying, and from

[t] **21:6** LAUGHTER: *The name Isaac in Hebrew means "he laughs" (see also 17:17–19).* [u] **21:9** playing with; *or* making fun of. [v] **21:9** *Some ancient translations* with Sarah's son Isaac; *Hebrew does not have these words.* [w] **21:16** she; *one ancient translation* the child.

21:2 Heb 11:11 **21:4** Gen 17:12; Acts 7:8 **21:10** Gal 4:29, 30 **21:12** Rom 9:7; Heb 11:18

Live it!

Jealousy

Tina was beautiful, smart, and athletic. Her closets were bursting with the latest fashions. If Tina wanted something, she got it. Rene had the things she needed, but seldom got anything just because she wanted it. Both girls were on the softball team.

Everyone liked Rene. She was a great softball player and captain of the team. Just like Sarah was jealous of Hagar, Tina was jealous of Rene's success and happiness. Tina tried hard to get everyone on the team to turn on Rene. Some people did. Most did not.

It was a good year for Rene. She loved softball and loved being captain of the team. For Tina it wasn't a great season. Her jealousy got the best of her. She hurt a lot of people. Finally, she quit the team.

Jealousy is a feeling that keeps on growing like mold on a peach. It destroys the goodness of a person and hurts everyone around him or her. Are you jealous of someone? How does your jealousy affect your relationship with that person? Ask God to help you to let go of your jealousy.

— Genesis 21:9–21

heaven the angel of God spoke to Hagar,
"What are you troubled about, Hagar? Don't
be afraid. God has heard the boy crying.
18 Get up, go and pick him up, and comfort
him. I will make a great nation out of his
descendants." 19 Then God opened her eyes,
and she saw a well. She went and filled the
leather bag with water and gave some to the
boy. 20 God was with the boy as he grew up;
he lived in the wilderness of Paran and
became a skillful hunter. 21 His mother got
an Egyptian wife for him.

The Agreement between Abraham and Abimelech

22 At that time Abimelech went with
Phicol, the commander of his army, and said
to Abraham, "God is with you in everything
you do. 23 So make a vow here in the pres-
ence of God that you will not deceive me,
my children, or my descendants. I have been
loyal to you, so promise that you will also be
loyal to me and to this country in which
you are living."
24 Abraham said, "I promise."
25 Abraham complained to Abimelech
about a well which the servants of Abim-
elech had seized. 26 Abimelech said, "I don't
know who did this. You didn't tell me about
it, and this is the first I have heard of it."
27 Then Abraham gave some sheep and cattle
to Abimelech, and the two of them made an
agreement. 28 Abraham separated seven lambs
from his flock, 29 and Abimelech asked him,
"Why did you do that?"
30 Abraham answered, "Accept these seven
lambs. By doing this, you admit that I am
the one who dug this well." 31 And so the
place was called Beersheba,[x] because it was
there that the two of them made a vow.
32 After they had made this agreement at
Beersheba, Abimelech and Phicol went back
to Philistia. 33 Then Abraham planted a
tamarisk tree in Beersheba and worshiped
the LORD, the Everlasting God. 34 Abraham
lived in Philistia for a long time.

[x] **21:31** BEERSHEBA: *This name in Hebrew means "Well of the Vow" or "Well of Seven" (see also 26:33).*
21:22 Gen 26:26

The story of Hagar and Ishmael in Genesis, chapter 21, shows that God takes care of poor and powerless people.

Catholic Connections

The Ultimate Sacrifice

God asked Abraham to do the unthinkable: kill his son Isaac. Abraham must have been horrified! After all, God promised him that he would have many descendants. But Abraham trusted God, so he loaded his donkey with wood and took Isaac up the mountain. Just as Abraham raised the knife, an angel stopped him. This story teaches us two things. First, that Abraham had complete faith in God. Second, that human sacrifice is against God's will.

In the New Testament, God again asks the unthinkable: he asks Jesus to be willing to sacrifice his life. Like Abraham, Jesus totally trusts his Father and obeys. Those who wish to kill Jesus do not listen to God as Abraham did. Jesus suffers a horrible death. But that is not the end, for God raised Jesus from the dead, thus sealing once and for all the New Covenant through which all people can have eternal life.

Because Abraham trusted God, his descendants would become God's special people. Because Jesus trusted God, all people can become part of God's family.

— Genesis 22:1–19

God Commands Abraham to Offer Isaac

22 Some time later God tested Abra-
ham; he called to him, "Abraham!"
And Abraham answered, "Yes, here I am!"
2"Take your son," God said, "your only
son, Isaac, whom you love so much, and go
to the land of Moriah. There on a mountain
that I will show you, offer him as a sacrifice
to me."
3Early the next morning Abraham cut
some wood for the sacrifice, loaded his don-
key, and took Isaac and two servants with
him. They started out for the place that God
had told him about. 4On the third day Abra-
ham saw the place in the distance. 5Then he
said to the servants, "Stay here with the don-
key. The boy and I will go over there and
worship, and then we will come back to
you."
6Abraham made Isaac carry the wood for
the sacrifice, and he himself carried a knife
and live coals for starting the fire. As they
walked along together, 7Isaac spoke up,
"Father!"
He answered, "Yes, my son?"
Isaac asked, "I see that you have the coals
and the wood, but where is the lamb for the
sacrifice?"
8Abraham answered, "God himself will
provide one." And the two of them walked
on together.
9When they came to the place which
God had told him about, Abraham built an
altar and arranged the wood on it. He tied
up his son and placed him on the altar, on
top of the wood. 10Then he picked up the
knife to kill him. 11But the angel of the
LORD called to him from heaven, "Abraham,
Abraham!"

22:1–13 Wis 10:5; Sir 44:20; Heb 11:17–19 **22:2** 2 Chr 3:1 **22:9** Jas 2:21

"All the nations will ask me to bless them as I have blessed your descendants—all because you obeyed my command" *(Genesis 22:18)*.

He answered, "Yes, here I am."
12 "Don't hurt the boy or do anything to him," he said. "Now I know that you honor and obey God, because you have not kept back your only son from him."

"Now I know that you honor and obey God." (22:12)

13 Abraham looked around and saw a ram caught in a bush by its horns. He went and got it and offered it as a burnt offering
instead of his son. 14 Abraham named that place "The LORD Provides."[y] And even today people say, "On the LORD's mountain he provides."[z]
15 The angel of the LORD called to Abraham from heaven a second time, 16 "I make a vow by my own name—the LORD is speaking—that I will richly bless you. Because you did this and did not keep back your only son from me,
17 I promise that I will give you as many descendants as there are stars in the sky or grains of sand along the seashore. Your descendants will conquer their enemies.
18 All the nations will ask me to bless them as I have blessed your descendants—all because you obeyed my command."
19 Abraham went back to his servants, and they went together to Beersheba, where Abraham settled.

The Descendants of Nahor

20 Some time later Abraham learned that Milcah had borne eight children to his brother Nahor:
21 Uz the first-born, Buz his brother, Kemuel the father of Aram,
22 Chesed, Hazo, Pildash, Jidlaph, and Bethuel,
23 Rebecca's father. Milcah bore these eight sons to Nahor, Abraham's brother.
24 Reumah, Nahor's concubine, bore Tebah, Gaham, Tahash, and Maacah.

Sarah Dies and Abraham Buys a Burial Ground

23 Sarah lived to be 127 years old.
2 She died in Hebron in the land of Canaan, and Abraham mourned her death.
3 He left the place where his wife's body was lying, went to the Hittites, and said,
4 "I am a foreigner living here among you; sell me some land, so that I can bury my wife."
5 They answered,
6 "Listen to us, sir. We look upon you as a mighty leader; bury your wife in the best grave that we have. Any of us would be glad to give you a grave, so that you can bury her."
7 Then Abraham bowed before them
8 and said, "If you are willing to let me bury my wife here, please ask Ephron son of Zohar
9 to sell me Machpelah Cave, which is near the edge of his field. Ask him to sell it to me for its full price, here in your presence, so that I can own it as a burial ground."
10 Ephron himself was sitting with the other Hittites at the meeting place at the city gate; he answered in the hearing of everyone there,
11 "Listen, sir; I will give you the whole field and the cave that is in it. Here in the presence of my own people, I will give it to you, so that you can bury your wife."
12 But Abraham bowed before the Hittites
13 and said to Ephron, so that everyone could hear, "May I ask you, please, to listen. I will buy the whole field. Accept my payment, and I will bury my wife there."
14 Ephron answered,
15 "Sir, land worth only four hundred pieces of silver—what is that between us? Bury your wife in it."

[y] **22:14** Provides; *or* Sees. [z] **22:14** provides; *or* is seen.
22:16, 17 Heb 6:13, 14 **22:17** Heb 11:12 **22:18** Acts 3:25 **23:4** Heb 11:9, 13; Acts 7:16

16 Abraham agreed and weighed out the
amount that Ephron had mentioned in the
hearing of the people—four hundred pieces
of silver, according to the standard weights
used by the merchants.
17 That is how the property which had
belonged to Ephron at Machpelah east of
Mamre, became Abraham's. It included the
field, the cave which was in it, and all the
trees in the field up to the edge of the prop-
erty. 18 It was recognized as Abraham's prop-
erty by all the Hittites who were there at the
meeting.
19 Then Abraham buried his wife Sarah in
that cave in the land of Canaan. 20 So the
field which had belonged to the Hittites, and
the cave in it, became the property of Abra-
ham for a burial ground.

A Wife for Isaac

24 Abraham was now very old, and the
LORD had blessed him in everything
he did. 2 He said to his oldest servant, who
was in charge of all that he had, "Place your
hand between my thighs[a] and make a vow. 3 I
want you to make a vow in the name of the
LORD, the God of heaven and earth, that
you will not choose a wife for my son from
the people here in Canaan. 4 You must go
back to the country where I was born and
get a wife for my son Isaac from among my
relatives."
5 But the servant asked, "What if the
young woman will not leave home to come
with me to this land? Shall I send your son
back to the land you came from?"
6 Abraham answered, "Make sure that you
don't send my son back there! 7 The LORD,
the God of heaven, brought me from the
home of my father and from the land of my
relatives, and he solemnly promised me that
he would give this land to my descendants.
He will send his angel before you, so that
you can get a wife there for my son. 8 If the
young woman is not willing to come with
you, you will be free from this promise. But
you must not under any circumstances take
my son back there." 9 So the servant put his
hand between the thighs of Abraham, his
master, and made a vow to do what Abra-
ham had asked.
10 The servant, who was in charge of
Abraham's property, took ten of his master's
camels and went to the city where Nahor
had lived in northern Mesopotamia. 11 When
he arrived, he made the camels kneel down
at the well outside the city. It was late after-
noon, the time when women came out to
get water. 12 He prayed, "LORD, God of my
master Abraham, give me success today and
keep your promise to my master. 13 Here I
am at the well where the young women of
the city will be coming to get water. 14 I will
say to one of them, 'Please, lower your jar
and let me have a drink.' If she says, 'Drink,
and I will also bring water for your camels,'
may she be the one that you have chosen for
your servant Isaac. If this happens, I will
know that you have kept your promise to
my master."
15 Before he had finished praying, Rebecca
arrived with a water jar on her shoulder. She
was the daughter of Bethuel, who was the
son of Abraham's brother Nahor and his wife
Milcah. 16 She was a very beautiful young
woman and still a virgin. She went down to
the well, filled her jar, and came back. 17 The
servant ran to meet her and said, "Please give
me a drink of water from your jar."
18 She said, "Drink, sir," and quickly low-
ered her jar from her shoulder and held it
while he drank. 19 When he had finished, she
said, "I will also bring water for your camels

Rebecca arrived. (24:15)

[a] **24:2** PLACE . . . THIGHS: *This was the way in which a vow was made absolutely unchangeable.*

and let them have all they want." 20She
quickly emptied her jar into the animals'
drinking trough and ran to the well to get
more water, until she had watered all his
camels. 21The man kept watching her in
silence, to see if the LORD had given him
success.

22When she had finished, the man took
an expensive gold ring and put it in her nose
and put two large gold bracelets on her
arms. 23He said, "Please tell me who your
father is. Is there room in his house for my
men and me to spend the night?"

24"My father is Bethuel son of Nahor and
Milcah," she answered. 25"There is plenty of
straw and fodder at our house, and there is a
place for you to stay."

26Then the man knelt down and wor-
shiped the LORD. 27He said, "Praise the
LORD, the God of my master Abraham, who
has faithfully kept his promise to my master.
The LORD has led me straight to my master's
relatives."

28The young woman ran to her mother's
house and told the whole story. 29Now
Rebecca had a brother named Laban, and he
ran outside to go to the well where Abra-
ham's servant was. 30Laban had seen the nose
ring and the bracelets on his sister's arms and
had heard her say what the man had told
her. He went to Abraham's servant, who was
standing by his camels at the well, 31and said,
"Come home with me. You are a man
whom the LORD has blessed. Why are you
standing out here? I have a room ready for
you in my house, and there is a place for
your camels."

32So the man went into the house, and
Laban unloaded the camels and gave them
straw and fodder. Then he brought water for
Abraham's servant and his men to wash their
feet. 33When food was brought, the man
said, "I will not eat until I have said what I
have to say."

Laban said, "Go on and speak."

34"I am the servant of Abraham," he
began. 35"The LORD has greatly blessed my
master and made him a rich man. He has
given him flocks of sheep and goats, cattle,
silver, gold, male and female slaves, camels,
and donkeys. 36Sarah, my master's wife, bore
him a son when she was old, and my master
has given everything he owns to him. 37My
master made me promise with a vow to obey
his command. He said, 'Do not choose a wife
for my son from the young women in the
land of Canaan. 38Instead, go to my father's
people, to my relatives, and choose a wife for
him.' 39And I asked my master, 'What if she
will not come with me?' 40He answered,
'The LORD, whom I have always obeyed, will
send his angel with you and give you success.
You will get for my son a wife from my own
people, from my father's family. 41There is
only one way for you to be free from your
vow: if you go to my relatives and they refuse
you, then you will be free.'

42"When I came to the well today, I
prayed, 'LORD, God of my master Abraham,
please give me success in what I am doing.
43Here I am at the well. When a young
woman comes out to get water, I will ask
her to give me a drink of water from her jar.
44If she agrees and also offers to bring water
for my camels, may she be the one that you
have chosen as the wife for my master's son.'
45Before I had finished my silent prayer,
Rebecca came with a water jar on her
shoulder and went down to the well to get
water. I said to her, 'Please give me a drink.'
46She quickly lowered her jar from her
shoulder and said, 'Drink, and I will also
water your camels.' So I drank, and she
watered the camels. 47I asked her, 'Who is
your father?' And she answered, 'My father is
Bethuel son of Nahor and Milcah.' Then I
put the ring in her nose and the bracelets on
her arms. 48I knelt down and worshiped the
LORD. I praised the LORD, the God of my
master Abraham, who had led me straight to
my master's relative, where I found his
daughter for my master's son. 49Now, if you
intend to fulfill your responsibility toward
my master and treat him fairly, please tell me;
if not, say so, and I will decide what to do."

50Laban and Bethuel answered, "Since this

After Sarah died Abraham married again and had more children. He died at a very old age. God's promises were fulfilled.

matter comes from the LORD, it is not for us
to make a decision. 51 Here is Rebecca; take
her and go. Let her become the wife of your
master's son, as the LORD himself has said."
52 When the servant of Abraham heard this,
he bowed down and worshiped the LORD.
53 Then he brought out clothing and silver
and gold jewelry, and gave them to Rebecca.
He also gave expensive gifts to her brother
and to her mother.

54 Then Abraham's servant and the men
with him ate and drank, and spent the night
there. When they got up in the morning, he
said, "Let me go back to my master."

55 But Rebecca's brother and her mother
said, "Let her stay with us a week or ten
days, and then she may go."

56 But he said, "Don't make us stay. The
LORD has made my journey a success; let me
go back to my master."

57 They answered, "Let's call her and find
out what she has to say." 58 So they called
Rebecca and asked, "Do you want to go
with this man?"

"Yes," she answered.

59 So they let Rebecca and her old family
servant go with Abraham's servant and his
men. 60 And they gave Rebecca their blessing
in these words:

"May you, sister, become the mother of
millions!
May your descendants conquer the cities
of their enemies!"

61 Then Rebecca and her young women got
ready and mounted the camels to go with
Abraham's servant, and they all started out.

62 Isaac had come into the wilderness of[b]
"The Well of the Living One Who Sees Me"
and was staying in the southern part of
Canaan. 63 He went out in the early evening
to take a walk in the fields and saw camels
coming. 64 When Rebecca saw Isaac, she got
down from her camel 65 and asked Abraham's
servant, "Who is that man walking toward us
in the field?"

"He is my master," the servant answered.
So she took her scarf and covered her face.

Live it!

A Match Made in Heaven

Isaac and Rebecca were meant for each other. God guided Abraham's servant and Rebecca's family to bring these two young people together so that they could be married. They raised a family and had a long life. "Isaac loved Rebecca . . ." (Genesis 24:67). And we presume that Rebecca loved Isaac, too.

What do you think you will be doing twenty years from now? Will you be married? Will you have children? Would you consider being a priest or a brother or a sister? Will you stay single? These lifestyles are known as *vocations,* and each one is a unique way to live the life God intends for you.

As you grow up, choosing a vocation will be one of your main responsibilities. Just as God brought Isaac and Rebecca together, God will guide you in lots of different ways. Keep your eyes, ears, and heart open to all possibilities. If you do, twenty years from now you and your life will be a match made in heaven!

— Genesis 24:57–67

66 The servant told Isaac everything he had
done. 67 Then Isaac brought Rebecca into
the tent that his mother Sarah had lived in,
and she became his wife. Isaac loved Rebec-
ca, and so he was comforted for the loss of
his mother.

[b] **24:62** *Some ancient translations* into the wilderness of; *Hebrew* from coming.

Rebecca had a gift for hospitality. She welcomed strangers and took care of them *(Genesis 24:15–20)*. **Who do you know who has the gift of hospitality?**

Pray it!

Thanks for Siblings

Jacob and Esau were brothers, twin sons of Isaac and Rebecca. They were very different from each other. Sometimes they got along, sometimes they didn't. Their conflicts continued throughout their life.

How do you get along with your brothers and sisters, your siblings? Do you help one another or hurt one another? Have you ever said thank you to God for them? Here's a prayer to help you do that.

Dear God,
I don't often say thanks for my siblings.
Usually, I complain to you about them.
We argue, we fight, and we get in one another's way.
We also laugh a lot and have fun together.
Deep down, I love them, and I know they love me.
My life would be a lot more boring without them.
So thank you, God, for sisters and brothers.
Please keep them safe and happy. Amen.

— Genesis 25:19–34

Other Descendants of Abraham
(1 Chronicles 1:32, 33)

25 Abraham married another woman,
whose name was Keturah. 2She bore
him Zimran, Jokshan, Medan, Midian, Ish-
bak, and Shuah. 3Jokshan was the father of
Sheba and Dedan, and the descendants of
Dedan were the Asshurim, the Letushim, and
the Leummim. 4The sons of Midian were
Ephah, Epher, Hanoch, Abida, and Eldaah.
All these were Keturah's descendants.
5Abraham left everything he owned to
Isaac; 6but while he was still alive, he gave
presents to the sons his other wives had
borne him. Then he sent these sons to the
land of the East, away from his son Isaac.

The Death and Burial of Abraham

7-8Abraham died at the ripe old age of
175. 9His sons Isaac and Ishmael buried him
in Machpelah Cave, in the field east of
Mamre that had belonged to Ephron son of
Zohar the Hittite. 10It was the field that
Abraham had bought from the Hittites; both
Abraham and his wife Sarah were buried
there. 11After the death of Abraham, God
blessed his son Isaac, who lived near "The
Well of the Living One Who Sees Me."

The Descendants of Ishmael
(1 Chronicles 1:28–31)

12Ishmael, whom Hagar, the Egyptian
slave of Sarah, bore to Abraham, 13had the
following sons, listed in the order of their
birth: Nebaioth, Kedar, Adbeel, Mibsam,
14Mishma, Dumah, Massa, 15Hadad, Tema,
Jetur, Naphish, and Kedemah. 16They were
the ancestors of twelve tribes, and their
names were given to their villages and
camping places. 17Ishmael was 137 years old
when he died. 18The descendants of Ishmael
lived in the territory between Havilah and
Shur, to the east of Egypt on the way to
Assyria. They lived apart from the other
descendants of Abraham.

25:10 Gen 23:3–16

The Birth of Esau and Jacob

19 This is the story of Abraham's son Isaac.
20 Isaac was forty years old when he married
Rebecca, the daughter of Bethuel (an
Aramean from Mesopotamia) and sister of
Laban. 21 Because Rebecca had no children,
Isaac prayed to the LORD for her. The LORD
answered his prayer, and Rebecca became
pregnant. 22 She was going to have twins, and
before they were born, they struggled against
each other in her womb. She said, "Why
should something like this happen to me?"
So she went to ask the LORD for an answer.
23 The LORD said to her,

"Two nations are within you;
You will give birth to two rival peoples.
One will be stronger than the other;
The older will serve the younger."

24 The time came for her to give birth,
and she had twin sons. 25 The first one was
reddish, and his skin was like a hairy robe, so
he was named Esau.[c] 26 The second one was
born holding on tightly to the heel of Esau,
so he was named Jacob.[d] Isaac was sixty years
old when they were born.

Esau Sells His Rights as the First-Born Son

27 The boys grew up, and Esau became a
skilled hunter, a man who loved the out-
doors, but Jacob was a quiet man who stayed
at home. 28 Isaac preferred Esau, because he
enjoyed eating the animals Esau killed, but
Rebecca preferred Jacob.
29 One day while Jacob was cooking some
bean soup, Esau came in from hunting. He
was hungry 30 and said to Jacob, "I'm starv-
ing; give me some of that red stuff." (That is
why he was named Edom.[e])
31 Jacob answered, "I will give it to you if
you give me your rights as the first-born
son."
32 Esau said, "All right! I am about to die;
what good will my rights do me?"
33 Jacob answered, "First make a vow that
you will give me your rights."
Esau made the vow and gave his rights to
Jacob. 34 Then Jacob gave him some bread
and some of the soup. He ate and drank and
then got up and left. That was all Esau cared
about his rights as the first-born son.

Then Jacob gave him . . . some of the soup. (25:34)

Isaac Lives at Gerar

26 There was another famine in the
land besides the earlier one during
the time of Abraham. Isaac went to Abim-
elech, king of the Philistines, at Gerar. 2 The
LORD had appeared to Isaac and had said,
"Do not go to Egypt; stay in this land, where
I tell you to stay. 3 Live here, and I will be
with you and bless you. I am going to give
all this territory to you and to your descen-
dants. I will keep the promise I made to
your father Abraham. 4 I will give you as
many descendants as there are stars in the
sky, and I will give them all this territory. All
the nations will ask me to bless them as I
have blessed your descendants. 5 I will bless
you, because Abraham obeyed me and kept
all my laws and commands."
6 So Isaac lived at Gerar. 7 When the men
there asked about his wife, he said that she
was his sister. He would not admit that she
was his wife, because he was afraid that the
men there would kill him to get Rebecca,
who was very beautiful. 8 When Isaac had

[c] **25:25** ESAU: *This name is taken to refer to Seir, the territory later inhabited by Esau's descendants; Seir sounds like the Hebrew for "hairy."* [d] **25:25** JACOB: *This name sounds like the Hebrew for "heel."* [e] **25:30** EDOM: *This name sounds like the Hebrew for "red."*

25:23 Rom 9:12 **25:33** Heb 12:16 **26:3, 4** Gen 22:16–18 **26:7** Gen 12:13; 20:2

been there for some time, King Abimelech looked down from his window and saw Isaac and Rebecca making love. 9 Abimelech sent for Isaac and said, "So she is your wife! Why did you say she was your sister?"

He answered, "I thought I would be killed if I said she was my wife."

10 "What have you done to us?" Abimelech said. "One of my men might easily have slept with your wife, and you would have been responsible for our guilt." 11 Abimelech warned all the people: "Anyone who mistreats this man or his wife will be put to death."

12 Isaac sowed crops in that land, and that year he harvested a hundred times as much as he had sown, because the LORD blessed him. 13 He continued to prosper and became a very rich man. 14 Because he had many herds of sheep and cattle and many servants, the Philistines were jealous of him. 15 So they filled in all the wells which the servants of his father Abraham had dug while Abraham was alive.

16 Then Abimelech said to Isaac, "Leave our country. You have become more powerful than we are." 17 So Isaac left and set up his camp in Gerar Valley, where he stayed for some time. 18 He dug once again the wells which had been dug during the time of Abraham and which the Philistines had stopped up after Abraham's death. Isaac gave the wells the same names that his father had given them.

19 Isaac's servants dug a well in the valley and found water. 20 The shepherds of Gerar quarreled with Isaac's shepherds and said, "This water belongs to us." So Isaac named the well "Quarrel."

21 Isaac's servants dug another well, and there was a quarrel about that one also, so he named it "Enmity." 22 He moved away from there and dug another well. There was no dispute about this one, so he named it "Freedom." He said, "Now the LORD has given us freedom to live in the land, and we will be prosperous here."

23 Isaac left and went to Beersheba. 24 That night the LORD appeared to him and said, "I am the God of your father Abraham. Do not be afraid; I am with you. I will bless you and give you many descendants because of my promise to my servant Abraham." 25 Isaac built an altar there and worshiped the LORD. Then he set up his camp there, and his servants dug another well.

The Agreement between Isaac and Abimelech

26 Abimelech came from Gerar with Ahuzzath his adviser and Phicol the commander of his army to see Isaac. 27 So Isaac asked, "Why have you now come to see me, when you were so unfriendly to me before and made me leave your country?"

28 They answered, "Now we know that the LORD is with you, and we think that there should be a solemn agreement between us. We want you to promise 29 that you will not harm us, just as we did not harm you. We were kind to you and let you go peacefully. Now it is clear that the LORD has blessed you." 30 Isaac prepared a feast for them, and they ate and drank. 31 Early next morning each man made his promise and sealed it with a vow. Isaac said good-bye to them, and they parted as friends.

32 On that day Isaac's servants came and told him about the well which they had dug. They said, "We have found water." 33 He named the well "Vow." That is how the city of Beersheba[f] got its name.

Esau's Foreign Wives

34 When Esau was forty years old, he married two Hittites, Judith the daughter of Beeri, and Basemath the daughter of Elon. 35 They made life miserable for Isaac and Rebecca.

[f] **26:33** BEERSHEBA: *This name in Hebrew means "Well of the Vow" or "Well of Seven" (see also 21:31).*

26:26 Gen 21:22

How were Jacob and Esau different? Read Genesis 25:19–34 to find out. How are you different from your siblings?

Isaac Blesses Jacob

27 Isaac was now old and had become
blind. He sent for his older son Esau
and said to him, "Son!"
"Yes," he answered.
2 Isaac said, "You see that I am old and
may die soon. 3 Take your bow and arrows,
go out into the country, and kill an animal
for me. 4 Cook me some of that tasty food
that I like, and bring it to me. After I have
eaten it, I will give you my final blessing
before I die."
5 While Isaac was talking to Esau, Rebecca
was listening. So when Esau went out to
hunt, 6 she said to Jacob, "I have just heard
your father say to Esau, 7 'Bring me an ani-
mal and cook it for me. After I have eaten it,
I will give you my blessing in the presence
of the LORD before I die.' 8 Now, son,"
Rebecca continued, "listen to me and do
what I say. 9 Go to the flock and pick out
two fat young goats, so that I can cook them
and make some of that food your father likes
so much. 10 You can take it to him to eat, and
he will give you his blessing before he dies."
11 But Jacob said to his mother, "You
know that Esau is a hairy man, but I have
smooth skin. 12 Perhaps my father will touch
me and find out that I am deceiving him; in
this way, I will bring a curse on myself
instead of a blessing."
13 His mother answered, "Let any curse
against you fall on me, my son; just do as I
say, and go and get the goats for me." 14 So
he went to get them and brought them to
her, and she cooked the kind of food that his
father liked. 15 Then she took Esau's best
clothes, which she kept in the house, and put
them on Jacob. 16 She put the skins of the
goats on his arms and on the hairless part of
his neck. 17 She handed him the tasty food,
along with the bread she had baked.
18 Then Jacob went to his father and said,
"Father!"
"Yes," he answered. "Which of my sons
are you?"
19 Jacob answered, "I am your older son
Esau; I have done as you told me. Please sit
up and eat some of the meat that I have
brought you, so that you can give me your
blessing."

Study it!

Esau's Dilemma

My brother Jacob did it to me again. First he tricked me into giving him my rights as the oldest son (Genesis 25:27–34). Then he tricked my father into giving him his blessing—the blessing of a dying father for his firstborn son (Genesis 27:1–29). My mother was behind it all, I know. She always liked Jacob best. My father is upset. He only had one blessing to give, and Jacob stole it from me.

Mom said God wanted it this way. God had plans for Jacob. But what about me? What about my life and my plans? With our father's blessing, Jacob will have a good life. The rest of my life will probably be miserable—all because Jacob is a thief and a liar. My father says what's done is done, and we all have to move on with our life. I'm not so sure I can let it go. Jacob ruined my life, and I'd like to kill him for it.

What would you do? Do you think what my mother and brother did to me and my father was fair? Okay, maybe I have some responsibility—I did make a stupid decision because of my hunger. But does doing wrong in the name of God make it right? Can God make good come out of deceit and trickery?

— Genesis 27:1–29

The oldest son was entitled to a position of honor in the family and to a double share of the father's inheritance.

[20]Isaac said, "How did you find it so
quickly, son?"
Jacob answered, "The LORD your God
helped me find it."
[21]Isaac said to Jacob, "Please come closer
so that I can touch you. Are you really
Esau?" [22]Jacob moved closer to his father,
who felt him and said, "Your voice sounds
like Jacob's voice, but your arms feel like
Esau's arms." [23]He did not recognize Jacob,
because his arms were hairy like Esau's. He
was about to give him his blessing, [24]but
asked again, "Are you really Esau?"
"I am," he answered.
[25]Isaac said, "Bring me some of the meat.
After I eat it, I will give you my blessing."
Jacob brought it to him, and he also brought
him some wine to drink. [26]Then his father
said to him, "Come closer and kiss me, son."
[27]As he came up to kiss him, Isaac smelled
his clothes—so he gave him his blessing. He
said, "The pleasant smell of my son is like
the smell of a field which the LORD has
blessed. [28]May God give you dew from
heaven and make your fields fertile! May he
give you plenty of grain and wine! [29]May
nations be your servants, and may peoples
bow down before you. May you rule over all
your relatives, and may your mother's
descendants bow down before you. May
those who curse you be cursed, and may
those who bless you be blessed."

He gave him his blessing. (27:27)

Esau Begs for Isaac's Blessing

[30]Isaac finished giving his blessing, and as
soon as Jacob left, his brother Esau came in
from hunting. [31]He also cooked some tasty
food and took it to his father. He said,
"Please, father, sit up and eat some of the
meat that I have brought you, so that you
can give me your blessing."
[32]"Who are you?" Isaac asked.
"Your older son Esau," he answered.
[33]Isaac began to tremble and shake all
over, and he asked, "Who was it, then, who
killed an animal and brought it to me? I ate
it just before you came. I gave him my final
blessing, and so it is his forever."
[34]When Esau heard this, he cried out
loudly and bitterly and said, "Give me your
blessing also, father!"
[35]Isaac answered, "Your brother came and
deceived me. He has taken away your bless-
ing."
[36]Esau said, "This is the second time that
he has cheated me. No wonder his name is
Jacob.[g] He took my rights as the first-born
son, and now he has taken away my blessing.
Haven't you saved a blessing for me?"
[37]Isaac answered, "I have already made
him master over you, and I have made all his
relatives his slaves. I have given him grain
and wine. Now there is nothing that I can
do for you, son!"
[38]Esau continued to plead with his father:
"Do you have only one blessing, father?
Bless me too, father!" He began to cry.
[39]Then Isaac said to him,

"No dew from heaven for you,
No fertile fields for you.
[40]You will live by your sword,
But be your brother's slave.
Yet when you rebel,[h]
You will break away from his control."

[41]Esau hated Jacob, because his father had
given Jacob the blessing. He thought, "The
time to mourn my father's death is near;
then I will kill Jacob."
[42]But when Rebecca heard about Esau's
plan, she sent for Jacob and said, "Listen, your
brother Esau is planning to get even with

[g] **27:36** JACOB: *This name sounds like the Hebrew for "cheat."* [h] **27:40** rebel; *or* grow restless.

27:27–29 Heb 11:20 **27:29** Gen 12:3 **27:36** Gen 25:29–34 **27:38** Heb 12:17 **27:39, 40** Heb 11:20
27:40 Gen 36:8; 2 Kings 8:20 **27:42** Wis 10:10

you and kill you. 43Now, son, do what I say. Go at once to my brother Laban in Haran, 44and stay with him for a while, until your brother's anger cools down 45and he forgets what you have done to him. Then I will send someone to bring you back. Why should I lose both of my sons on the same day?"

Isaac Sends Jacob to Laban

46Rebecca said to Isaac, "I am sick and tired of Esau's foreign wives. If Jacob also marries one of these Hittites, I might as well die."

28 Isaac called Jacob, greeted him, and told him, "Don't marry a Canaanite.
2Go instead to Mesopotamia, to the home of your grandfather Bethuel, and marry one of the young women there, one of your uncle Laban's daughters. 3May Almighty God bless your marriage and give you many children, so that you will become the father of many nations! 4May he bless you and your descendants as he blessed Abraham, and may you take possession of this land, in which you have lived and which God gave to Abraham!" 5Isaac sent Jacob away to Mesopotamia, to Laban, who was the son of Bethuel the Aramean and the brother of Rebecca, the mother of Jacob and Esau.

Esau Takes Another Wife

6Esau learned that Isaac had blessed Jacob and sent him away to Mesopotamia to find a wife. He also learned that when Isaac blessed him, he commanded him not to marry a Canaanite woman. 7He found out that Jacob had obeyed his father and mother and had gone to Mesopotamia. 8Esau then understood that his father Isaac did not approve of Canaanite women. 9So he went to Ishmael son of Abraham and married his daughter Mahalath, who was the sister of Nebaioth.

Jacob's Dream at Bethel

10Jacob left Beersheba and started toward Haran. 11At sunset he came to a holy place[i] and camped there. He lay down to sleep, resting his head on a stone. 12He dreamed that he saw a stairway reaching from earth to heaven, with angels going up and coming down on it. 13And there was the LORD standing beside him.[j] "I am the LORD, the God of Abraham and Isaac," he said. "I will give to you and to your descendants this land on which you are lying. 14They will be as numerous as the specks of dust on the earth. They will extend their territory in all directions, and through you and your descendants I will bless all the nations.[k] 15Remember, I will be with you and protect you wherever you go, and I will bring you

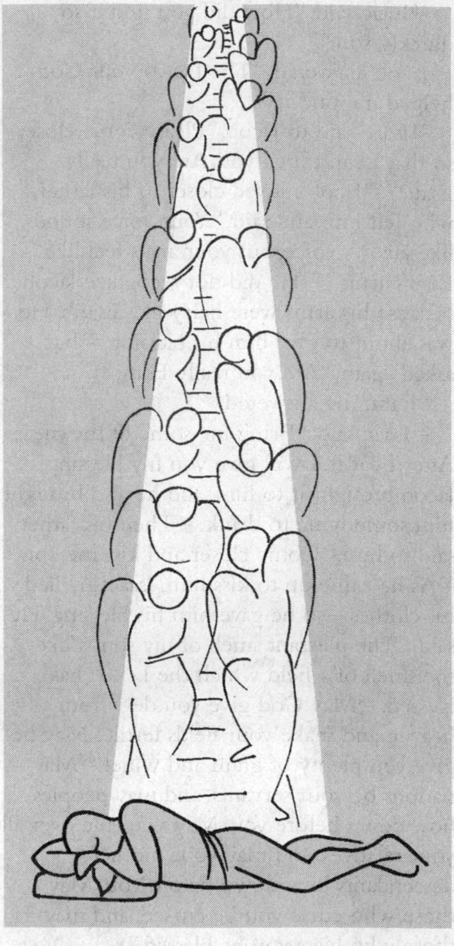

A stairway reaching from earth to heaven (28:12)

[i] **28:11** a holy place; *or* a place. [j] **28:13** beside him; *or* on it. [k] **28:14** through you . . . nations; *or* all the nations will ask me to bless them as I have blessed you and your descendants.

28:4 Gen 17:4–8 **28:10** Wis 10:10 **28:12** Jn 1:51 **28:13** Gen 13:14, 15 **28:14** Gen 12:3; 22:18

back to this land. I will not leave you until I
have done all that I have promised you."
16Jacob woke up and said, "The LORD is
here! He is in this place, and I didn't know
it!" 17He was afraid and said, "What a terrify-
ing place this is! It must be the house of God;
it must be the gate that opens into heaven."
18Jacob got up early next morning, took
the stone that was under his head, and set it
up as a memorial. Then he poured olive oil
on it to dedicate it to God. 19He named the
place Bethel.[l] (The town there was once
known as Luz.) 20Then Jacob made a vow to
the LORD: "If you will be with me and pro-
tect me on the journey I am making and
give me food and clothing, 21and if I return
safely to my father's home, then you will be
my God. 22This memorial stone which I
have set up will be the place where you are
worshiped, and I will give you a tenth of
everything you give me."

Jacob Arrives at Laban's Home

29 Jacob continued on his way and
went toward the land of the East.
2Suddenly he came upon a well out in the
fields with three flocks of sheep lying around
it. The flocks were watered from this well,
which had a large stone over the opening.
3Whenever all the flocks came together
there, the shepherds would roll the stone
back and water them. Then they would put
the stone back in place.
4Jacob asked the shepherds, "My friends,
where are you from?"
"From Haran," they answered.
5He asked, "Do you know Laban, grand-
son of Nahor?"
"Yes, we do," they answered.
6"Is he well?" he asked.
"He is well," they answered. "Look, here
comes his daughter Rachel with his flock."
7Jacob said, "Since it is still broad daylight
and not yet time to bring the flocks in, why
don't you water them and take them back to
pasture?"
8They answered, "We can't do that until
all the flocks are here and the stone has been
rolled back; then we will water the flocks."
9While Jacob was still talking with them,
Rachel arrived with the flock. 10When Jacob
saw Rachel with his uncle Laban's flock, he
went to the well, rolled the stone back, and
watered the sheep. 11Then he kissed her and
began to cry for joy. 12He told her, "I am
your father's relative, the son of Rebecca."
She ran to tell her father; 13and when he
heard the news about his nephew Jacob, he
ran to meet him, hugged him and kissed
him, and brought him into the house. When
Jacob told Laban everything that had hap-
pened, 14Laban said, "Yes, indeed, you are my
own flesh and blood." Jacob stayed there a
whole month.

Jacob Serves Laban for Rachel and Leah

15Laban said to Jacob, "You shouldn't
work for me for nothing just because you
are my relative. How much pay do you
want?" 16Laban had two daughters; the older
was named Leah, and the younger Rachel.
17Leah had lovely[m] eyes, but Rachel was
shapely and beautiful.
18Jacob was in love with Rachel, so he
said, "I will work seven years for you, if you
will let me marry Rachel."
19Laban answered, "I would rather give
her to you than to anyone else; stay here
with me." 20Jacob worked seven years so that
he could have Rachel, and the time seemed
like only a few days to him, because he loved
her.
21Then Jacob said to Laban, "The time is
up; let me marry your daughter." 22So Laban
gave a wedding feast and invited everyone.
23But that night, instead of Rachel, he took
Leah to Jacob, and Jacob had intercourse
with her. (24Laban gave his slave woman Zil-
pah to his daughter Leah as her maid.) 25Not
until the next morning did Jacob discover
that it was Leah. He went to Laban and said,

[l] **28:19** BETHEL: *This name in Hebrew means "house of God."* [m] **29:17** lovely; *or* weak.

Jacob asked three things from God. Read Genesis 28:20–22 to find out what they are. What do you need from God?

"Why did you do this to me? I worked to get Rachel. Why have you tricked me?"

26Laban answered, "It is not the custom here to give the younger daughter in marriage before the older. 27Wait until the week's marriage celebrations are over, and I will give you Rachel, if you will work for me another seven years."

28Jacob agreed, and when the week of marriage celebrations was over, Laban gave him his daughter Rachel as his wife. (29Laban gave his slave woman Bilhah to his daughter Rachel as her maid.) 30Jacob had intercourse with Rachel also, and he loved her more than Leah. Then he worked for Laban another seven years.

The Children Born to Jacob

31When the LORD saw that Leah was loved less than Rachel, he made it possible for her to have children, but Rachel remained childless. 32Leah became pregnant and gave birth to a son. She said, "The LORD has seen my trouble, and now my husband will love me"; so she named him Reuben.[n] 33She became pregnant again and gave birth to another son. She said, "The LORD has given me this son also, because he heard that I was not loved"; so she named him Simeon.[o] 34Once again she became pregnant and gave birth to another son. She said, "Now my husband will be bound more tightly to me, because I have borne him three sons"; so she named him Levi.[p] 35Then she became pregnant again and gave birth to another son. She said, "This time I will praise the LORD"; so she named him Judah.[q] Then she stopped having children.

30 But Rachel had not borne Jacob any children, and so she became jealous of her sister and said to Jacob, "Give me children, or I will die."

2Jacob became angry with Rachel and said, "I can't take the place of God. He is the one who keeps you from having children."

3She said, "Here is my slave Bilhah; sleep with her, so that she can have a child for me. In this way I can become a mother through her." 4So she gave Bilhah to her husband, and he had intercourse with her. 5Bilhah became pregnant and bore Jacob a son. 6Rachel said, "God has judged in my favor. He has heard my prayer and has given me a son"; so she named him Dan.[r] 7Bilhah became pregnant again and bore Jacob a second son. 8Rachel said, "I have fought a hard fight with my sister, but I have won"; so she named him Naphtali.[s]

9When Leah realized that she had stopped having children, she gave her slave Zilpah to Jacob as his wife. 10Then Zilpah bore Jacob a son. 11Leah said, "I have been lucky"; so she named him Gad.[t] 12Zilpah bore Jacob another son, 13and Leah said, "How happy I am! Now women will call me happy"; so she named him Asher.[u]

14During the wheat harvest Reuben went into the fields and found mandrakes,[v] which he brought to his mother Leah. Rachel said to Leah, "Please give me some of your son's mandrakes."

15Leah answered, "Isn't it enough that you have taken away my husband? Now you are even trying to take away my son's mandrakes."

Rachel said, "If you will give me your son's mandrakes, you can sleep with Jacob tonight."

16When Jacob came in from the fields in the evening, Leah went out to meet him and said, "You are going to sleep with me tonight, because I have paid for you with my son's mandrakes." So he had intercourse with her that night.

17God answered Leah's prayer, and she

[n] **29:32** REUBEN: *This name sounds like the Hebrew for "see, a son" and "has seen my trouble."* [o] **29:32** SIMEON: *This name sounds like the Hebrew for "hear."* [p] **29:32** LEVI: *This name sounds like the Hebrew for "bound."* [q] **29:32** JUDAH: *This name sounds like the Hebrew for "praise."* [r] **30:6** DAN: *This name sounds like the Hebrew for "judge in favor."* [s] **30:8** NAPHTALI: *This name sounds like the Hebrew for "fight."* [t] **30:11** GAD: *This name in Hebrew means "luck."* [u] **30:13** ASHER: *This name in Hebrew means "happy."* [v] **30:14** MANDRAKES: *Plants which were believed to produce fertility and were used as love charms.*

Rachel had a difficult time getting pregnant. Who was another woman in Genesis with the same difficulty? (Hint: It was Jacob's grandmother.)

Live it!

An Imperfect Believer

Jacob was not the most honest guy in the world. Most of what he had he got from tricking or cheating other people:

- **He took advantage of Esau's hunger to get Esau's rights as a firstborn son (Genesis 25:27–34).**
- **He tricked Isaac into giving him the blessing that was rightfully Esau's (27:1–29).**
- **He cleverly arranged to receive Laban's strongest sheep as payment for his service to his father-in-law. After twenty years of working for Laban, Jacob was a rich man (30:25–43).**

Jacob's trickery had consequences. His brother, Esau, hated him and wanted to kill him. His father-in-law tricked him into working for him for fourteen years. Yet with all his shortcomings, Jacob loved God deeply, and God had big plans for him. The twelve tribes that made up the great nation of Israel were descendants of Jacob's sons. Jacob's story teaches us something important: God can work through everyone—not just those who appear to be saintly or perfect. As long as you keep working on your relationship with God, God will work through you. You don't need to be perfect, just willing to trust God and do your best!

— Genesis 30:25–43

became pregnant and bore Jacob a fifth son.
18 Leah said, "God has given me my reward,
because I gave my slave to my husband"; so
she named her son Issachar.[w] 19 Leah became
pregnant again and bore Jacob a sixth son.
20 She said, "God has given me a fine gift.
Now my husband will accept me, because I
have borne him six sons"; so she named him
Zebulun.[x] 21 Later she bore a daughter,
whom she named Dinah.

22 Then God remembered Rachel; he
answered her prayer and made it possible for
her to have children. 23 She became pregnant
and gave birth to a son. She said, "God has
taken away my disgrace by giving me a son.
24 May the LORD give me another son"; so
she named him Joseph.[y]

Jacob's Bargain with Laban

25 After the birth of Joseph, Jacob said to
Laban, "Let me go, so that I can return
home. 26 Give me my wives and children that
I have earned by working for you, and I will
leave. You know how well I have served
you."

27 Laban said to him, "Let me say this: I
have learned by divination that the LORD
has blessed me because of you. 28 Name your
wages, and I will pay them."

29 Jacob answered, "You know how I have
worked for you and how your flocks have
prospered under my care. 30 The little you
had before I came has grown enormously,
and the LORD has blessed you wherever I
went.[z] Now it is time for me to look out for
my own interests."

31 "What shall I pay you?" Laban asked.

Jacob answered, "I don't want any wages. I
will continue to take care of your flocks if
you agree to this suggestion: 32 Let me go
through all your flocks today and take every
black lamb[a] and every spotted or speckled
young goat. That is all the wages I want. 33 In
the future you can easily find out if I have
been honest. When you come to check up
on my wages, if I have any goat that isn't

[w] **30:18** ISSACHAR: *This name sounds like the Hebrew for "a man is hired" and "there is reward."* [x] **30:20** ZEBULUN: *This name sounds like the Hebrew for "accept" and "gift."* [y] **30:24** JOSEPH: *This name sounds like the Hebrew for "may he give another" and "he has taken away."* [z] **30:30** wherever I went; *or* because of me. [a] **30:32** *One ancient translation* every black lamb; *Hebrew* every spotted and speckled lamb, and every black lamb.

speckled or spotted or any sheep that isn't black, you will know that it has been stolen."

34 Laban answered, "Agreed. We will do as you suggest." 35 But that day Laban removed the male goats that had stripes or spots and all the females that were speckled and spotted or which had white on them; he also removed all the black sheep. He put his sons in charge of them, 36 and then went away from Jacob with this flock as far as he could travel in three days. Jacob took care of the rest of Laban's flocks.

37 Jacob got green branches of poplar, almond, and plane trees and stripped off some of the bark so that the branches had white stripes on them. 38 He placed these branches in front of the flocks at their drinking troughs. He put them there, because the animals mated when they came to drink. 39 So when the goats bred in front of the branches, they produced young that were streaked, speckled, and spotted.

40 Jacob kept the sheep separate from the goats and made them face in the direction of the streaked and black animals of Laban's flock. In this way he built up his own flock and kept it apart from Laban's.

41 When the healthy animals were mating, Jacob put the branches in front of them at the drinking troughs, so that they would breed among the branches. 42 But he did not put the branches in front of the weak animals. Soon Laban had all the weak animals, and Jacob all the healthy ones. 43 In this way Jacob became very wealthy. He had many flocks, slaves, camels, and donkeys.

Jacob Flees from Laban

31 Jacob heard that Laban's sons were saying, "Jacob has taken everything that belonged to our father. He got all his wealth from what our father owned." 2 He also saw that Laban was no longer as friendly as he had been earlier. 3 Then the LORD said to him, "Go back to the land of your fathers and to your relatives. I will be with you."

4 So Jacob sent word to Rachel and Leah to meet him in the field where his flocks were. 5 He said to them, "I have noticed that your father is not as friendly toward me as he used to be; but my father's God has been with me. 6 You both know that I have worked for your father with all my strength. 7 Yet he has cheated me and changed my wages ten times. But God did not let him harm me. 8 Whenever Laban said, 'The speckled goats shall be your wages,' all the flocks produced speckled young. When he said, 'The striped goats shall be your wages,' all the flocks produced striped young. 9 God has taken flocks away from your father and given them to me.

10 "During the breeding season I had a dream, and I saw that the male goats that were mating were striped, spotted, and speckled. 11 The angel of God spoke to me in the dream and said, 'Jacob!' 'Yes,' I answered. 12 'Look,' he continued, 'all the male goats that are mating are striped, spotted, and speckled. I am making this happen because I have seen all that Laban is doing to you. 13 I am the God who appeared to you at Bethel, where you dedicated a stone as a memorial by pouring olive oil on it and where you made a vow to me. Now get ready and go back to the land where you were born.' "

14 Rachel and Leah answered Jacob, "There is nothing left for us to inherit from our father. 15 He treats us like foreigners. He sold us, and now he has spent all the money he was paid for us. 16 All this wealth which God has taken from our father belongs to us and to our children. Do whatever God has told you."

17-18 So Jacob got ready to go back to his father in the land of Canaan. He put his children and his wives on the camels, and drove all his flocks ahead of him, with everything that he had gotten in Mesopotamia. 19 Laban had gone to shear his sheep, and during his absence Rachel stole the household gods that belonged to her father. 20 Jacob deceived Laban by not letting him know that he was leaving. 21 He took everything he owned and left in a hurry. He crossed the Euphrates River and started for the hill country of Gilead.

31:13 Gen 28:18–22

Jacob drove all his flocks ahead of him. (31:18)

Laban Pursues Jacob

22 Three days later Laban was told that Jacob had fled. 23 He took his men with him and pursued Jacob for seven days until he caught up with him in the hill country of Gilead. 24 In a dream that night God came to Laban and said to him, "Be careful not to threaten Jacob in any way." 25 Jacob had set up his camp on a mountain, and Laban set up his camp with his relatives in the hill country of Gilead.

26 Laban said to Jacob, "Why did you deceive me and carry off my daughters like women captured in war? 27 Why did you deceive me and slip away without telling me? If you had told me, I would have sent you on your way with rejoicing and singing to the music of tambourines and harps. 28 You did not even let me kiss my grandchildren and my daughters good-bye. That was a foolish thing to do! 29 I have the power to do you harm, but last night the God of your father warned me not to threaten you in any way. 30 I know that you left because you were so anxious to get back home, but why did you steal my household gods?"

31 Jacob answered, "I was afraid, because I thought that you might take your daughters away from me. 32 But if you find that anyone here has your gods, he will be put to death. Here, with our men as witnesses, look for anything that belongs to you and take what is yours." Jacob did not know that Rachel had stolen Laban's gods.

33 Laban went and searched Jacob's tent; then he went into Leah's tent, and the tent of the two slave women, but he did not find his gods. Then he went into Rachel's tent. 34 Rachel had taken the household gods and put them in a camel's saddlebag and was sitting on them. Laban searched through the whole tent, but did not find them. 35 Rachel said to her father, "Do not be angry with me, sir, but I am not able to stand up in your presence; I am having my monthly period." Laban searched but did not find his household gods.

36 Then Jacob lost his temper. "What crime have I committed?" he asked angrily. "What law have I broken that gives you the right to hunt me down? 37 Now that you have searched through all my belongings, what household article have you found that belongs to you? Put it out here where your men and mine can see it, and let them decide which one of us is right. 38 I have been with you now for twenty years; your sheep and your goats have not failed to

Jacob's name fit his life perfectly. It means "he deceives."

reproduce, and I have not eaten any rams from your flocks. 39 Whenever a sheep was killed by wild animals, I always bore the loss myself. I didn't take it to you to show that it was not my fault. You demanded that I make good anything that was stolen during the day or during the night. 40 Many times I suffered from the heat during the day and from the cold at night. I was not able to sleep. 41 It was like that for the whole twenty years I was with you. For fourteen years I worked to win your two daughters—and six years for your flocks. And even then, you changed my wages ten times. 42 If the God of my fathers, the God of Abraham and Isaac, had not been with me, you would have already sent me away empty-handed. But God has seen my trouble and the work I have done, and last night he gave his judgment."

The Agreement between Jacob and Laban

43 Laban answered Jacob, "These young women are my daughters; their children belong to me, and these flocks are mine. In fact, everything you see here belongs to me. But since I can do nothing to keep my daughters and their children, 44 I am ready to make an agreement with you. Let us make a pile of stones to remind us of our agreement."

45 So Jacob got a stone and set it up as a memorial. 46 He told his men to gather some rocks and pile them up. Then they ate a meal beside the pile of rocks. 47 Laban named it Jegar Sahadutha,[b] while Jacob named it Galeed.[c] 48 Laban said to Jacob, "This pile of rocks will be a reminder for both of us." That is why that place was named Galeed. 49 Laban also said, "May the LORD keep an eye on us while we are separated from each other." So the place was also named Mizpah.[d] 50 Laban went on, "If you mistreat my daughters or if you marry other women, even though I don't know about it, remember that God is watching us. 51 Here are the rocks that I have piled up between us, and here is the memorial stone. 52 Both this pile and this memorial stone are reminders. I will never go beyond this pile to attack you, and you must never go beyond it or beyond this memorial stone to attack me. 53 The God of Abraham and the God of Nahor[e] will judge between us." Then, in the name of the God whom his father Isaac worshiped, Jacob solemnly vowed to keep this promise. 54 He killed an animal, which he offered as a sacrifice on the mountain, and he invited his men to the meal. After they had eaten, they spent the night on the mountain. 55 Early the next morning Laban kissed his grandchildren and his daughters good-bye, and left to go back home.

Jacob Prepares to Meet Esau

32 As Jacob went on his way, some angels met him. 2 When he saw them, he said, "This is God's camp"; so he named the place Mahanaim.[f]

3 Jacob sent messengers ahead of him to his brother Esau in the country of Edom. 4 He instructed them to say: "I, Jacob, your obedient servant, report to my master Esau that I have been staying with Laban and that I have delayed my return until now. 5 I own cattle, donkeys, sheep, goats, and slaves. I am sending you word, sir, in the hope of gaining your favor."

6 When the messengers came back to Jacob, they said, "We went to your brother Esau, and he is already on his way to meet you. He has four hundred men with him." 7 Jacob was frightened and worried. He divided into two groups the people who were with him, and also his sheep, goats, cattle, and camels. 8 He thought, "If Esau comes and attacks the first group, the other may be able to escape."

[b] **31:47** JEGAR SAHADUTHA: *This name in Aramaic means "a pile to remind us."* [c] **31:47** GALEED: *This name in Hebrew means "a pile to remind us."* [d] **31:49** MIZPAH: *This name sounds like the Hebrew for "place from which to watch."* [e] **31:53** ABRAHAM . . . NAHOR: *Abraham was Jacob's grandfather and Nahor was Laban's grandfather.*
[f] **32:2** MAHANAIM: *This name in Hebrew means "two camps."*

Have you ever felt like God wanted you to do something you didn't want to do? If so, you've wrestled with God.

9Then Jacob prayed, "God of my grand-
father Abraham and God of my father Isaac,
hear me! You told me, LORD, to go back to
my land and to my relatives, and you would
make everything go well for me. 10I am not
worth all the kindness and faithfulness that
you have shown me, your servant. I crossed
the Jordan with nothing but a walking stick,
and now I have come back with these two
groups. 11Save me, I pray, from my brother
Esau. I am afraid—afraid that he is coming
to attack us and destroy us all, even the
women and children. 12Remember that you
promised to make everything go well for me
and to give me more descendants than any-
one could count, as many as the grains of
sand along the seashore."

13-15After spending the night there, Jacob
chose from his livestock as a present for his
brother Esau: 200 female goats and 20 males,
200 female sheep and 20 males, 30 milk
camels with their young, 40 cows and 10
bulls, 20 female donkeys and 10 males. 16He
divided them into herds and put one of his
servants in charge of each herd. He said to
them, "Go ahead of me, and leave a space
between each herd and the one behind it."
17He ordered the first servant, "When my
brother Esau meets you and asks, 'Who is
your master? Where are you going? Who
owns these animals in front of you?' 18you
must answer, 'They belong to your servant
Jacob. He sends them as a present to his mas-
ter Esau. Jacob himself is right behind us.' "
19He gave the same order to the second, the
third, and to all the others who were in
charge of the herds: "This is what you must
say to Esau when you meet him. 20You must
say, 'Yes, your servant Jacob is right behind
us.' " Jacob was thinking, "I will win him over
with the gifts, and when I meet him, perhaps
he will forgive me." 21He sent the gifts on
ahead of him and spent that night in camp.

Jacob Wrestles at Peniel

22That same night Jacob got up, took his
two wives, his two concubines, and his
eleven children, and crossed the Jabbok
River. 23After he had sent them across, he
also sent across all that he owned, 24but he
stayed behind, alone.

Then a man came and wrestled with him
until just before daybreak. 25When the man
saw that he was not winning the struggle, he
hit Jacob on the hip, and it was thrown out

Study it!

Jacob's Wrestling Match

Did you ever have your favorite television show interrupted by an important announcement? That's what happens in the story about Jacob and Esau. They are just about to meet after twenty years when the writer stops the action and switches to another story: Jacob's wrestling match.

Jacob must have planned to get a good night's sleep before the meeting with Esau, which he was dreading. He sent everyone ahead while he stayed behind. That night a man came to him and started wrestling with him. They wrestled all night long. The man would not tell Jacob his name, but Jacob knew it was God. When they finished God blessed him and changed his name: Jacob's new name was Israel, which means "he struggles with God."

Jacob's life changed that day. He knew he was destined for great things. He worked hard to be the person God wanted him to be. He knew he had to make things right with Esau. After all, he had God's promise that he would be the founder and the father of the great nation of Israel.

— Genesis 32:22–32

32:12 Gen 22:17 **32:23** Wis 10:12 **32:24–26** Hos 12:3, 4

A man came and wrestled with him. (32:24)

of joint. 26The man said, "Let me go; day-
light is coming."
"I won't, unless you bless me," Jacob
answered.
27"What is your name?" the man asked.
"Jacob," he answered.
28The man said, "Your name will no
longer be Jacob. You have struggled with
God and with men, and you have won; so
your name will be Israel."[g]
29Jacob said, "Now tell me your name."
But he answered, "Why do you want to
know my name?" Then he blessed Jacob.
30Jacob said, "I have seen God face to
face, and I am still alive"; so he named the
place Peniel.[h] 31The sun rose as Jacob was
leaving Peniel, and he was limping because
of his hip. 32Even today the descendants of
Israel do not eat the muscle which is on the
hip joint, because it was on this muscle that
Jacob was hit.

Jacob Meets Esau

33 Jacob saw Esau coming with his four
hundred men, so he divided the
children among Leah, Rachel, and the two
concubines. 2He put the concubines and
their children first, then Leah and her chil-
dren, and finally Rachel and Joseph at the
rear. 3Jacob went ahead of them and bowed
down to the ground seven times as he

Esau . . . threw his arms around him. (33:4)

approached his brother. 4But Esau ran to
meet him, threw his arms around him, and
kissed him. They were both crying. 5When
Esau looked around and saw the women and
the children, he asked, "Who are these peo-
ple with you?"
"These, sir, are the children whom God
has been good enough to give me," Jacob
answered. 6Then the concubines came up
with their children and bowed down; 7then
Leah and her children came, and last of all
Joseph and Rachel came and bowed down.
8Esau asked, "What about that other
group I met? What did that mean?"
Jacob answered, "It was to gain your
favor."
9But Esau said, "I have enough, my broth-
er; keep what you have."
10Jacob said, "No, please, if I have gained
your favor, accept my gift. To see your face is

"If I have gained your favor" (33:10)

[g] **32:28** ISRAEL: *This name sounds like the Hebrew for "he struggles with God" or "God struggles."* [h] **32:30** PENIEL: *This name sounds like the Hebrew for "the face of God."*

32:28 Gen 35:10 **32:29** Judg 13:17, 18

Pray it!

A Moment of Great Power

The story of Jacob and Esau ends with a powerful moment: a moment of reconciliation. Jacob begs for Esau's forgiveness, and Esau forgives him. Esau did not hold a grudge against his brother. Jacob must have felt tremendous relief after so many years of worrying. In fact, meeting for the first time was such an intense experience that both brothers cried as they hugged each other. Their relationship was healed.

Are you more like Jacob who needed forgiveness? Or are you more like Esau who needed to forgive? Is there a relationship in your life that needs healing? Pray for the courage to let go of your grudges. Pray for the virtue of humility. Ask God to make your heart ready for a moment of great power.

— Genesis 33:1–11

for me like seeing the face of God, now that
you have been so friendly to me. 11 Please
accept this gift which I have brought for
you; God has been kind to me and given me
everything I need." Jacob kept on urging
him until he accepted.
12 Esau said, "Let's get ready and leave. I
will go ahead of you."
13 Jacob answered, "You know that the
children are weak, and I must think of the
sheep and livestock with their young. If they
are driven hard for even one day, the whole
herd will die. 14 Please go on ahead of me,
and I will follow slowly, going as fast as I can
with the livestock and the children until I
catch up with you in Edom."
15 Esau said, "Then let me leave some of
my men with you."
But Jacob answered, "There is no need for
that for I only want to gain your favor."[i]
16 So that day Esau started on his way back
to Edom. 17 But Jacob went to Sukkoth,
where he built a house for himself and shel-
ters for his livestock. That is why the place
was named Sukkoth.[j]
18 On his return from Mesopotamia Jacob
arrived safely at the city of Shechem in the
land of Canaan and set up his camp in a field
near the city. 19 He bought that part of the
field from the descendants of Hamor father
of Shechem for a hundred pieces of silver.
20 He put up an altar there and named it for
El, the God of Israel.

The Rape of Dinah

34 One day Dinah, the daughter of
Jacob and Leah, went to visit some
of the Canaanite women. 2 When Shechem
son of Hamor the Hivite, who was chief of
that region, saw her, he took her and raped
her. 3 But he found the young woman so
attractive that he fell in love with her and
tried to win her affection.[k] 4 He told his
father, "I want you to get Dinah for me as
my wife."
5 Jacob learned that his daughter had been
disgraced, but because his sons were out in
the fields with his livestock, he did nothing
until they came back. 6 Shechem's father

[i] **33:15** for I only want to gain your favor; *or* if it's all right with you. [j] **33:17** SUKKOTH: *This name in Hebrew means "shelters."* [k] **34:3** tried to win her affection; *or* comforted her.
33:19 Josh 24:32; Jn 4:5

Jacob was *really* nervous about meeting Esau. Read 32:13–21 and 33:1–17. How would you have handled it?

Hamor went out to talk with Jacob, 7just as
Jacob's sons were coming in from the fields.
When they heard about it, they were
shocked and furious that Shechem had done
such a thing and had insulted the people of
Israel by raping Jacob's daughter. 8Hamor said
to him, "My son Shechem has fallen in love
with your daughter; please let him marry her.
9Let us make an agreement that there will be
intermarriage between our people and yours.
10Then you may stay here in our country
with us; you may live anywhere you wish,
trade freely, and own property."

11Then Shechem said to Dinah's father
and brothers, "Do me this favor, and I will
give you whatever you want. 12Tell me what
presents you want, and set the payment for
the bride as high as you wish; I will give you
whatever you ask, if you will only let me
marry her."

13Because Shechem had disgraced their
sister Dinah, Jacob's sons answered Shechem
and his father Hamor in a deceitful way.
14They said to him, "We cannot let our sister
marry a man who is not circumcised; that
would be a disgrace for us. 15We can agree
only on the condition that you become like
us by circumcising all your males. 16Then we
will agree to intermarriage. We will settle
among you and become one people with
you. 17But if you will not accept our terms
and be circumcised, we will take her and
leave."

18These terms seemed fair to Hamor and
his son Shechem, 19and the young man lost
no time in doing what was suggested,
because he was in love with Jacob's daugh-
ter. He was the most important member of
his family.

20Hamor and his son Shechem went to
the meeting place at the city gate and spoke
to the people of the town: 21"These men are
friendly; let them live in the land with us
and travel freely. The land is large enough for
them also. Let us marry their daughters and
give them ours in marriage. 22But these men
will agree to live among us and be one peo-
ple with us only on the condition that we
circumcise all our males, as they are circum-
cised. 23Won't all their livestock and every-
thing else they own be ours? So let us agree
that they can live among us." 24All the citi-
zens of the city agreed with what Hamor
and Shechem proposed, and all the males
were circumcised.

25Three days later, when the men were
still sore from their circumcision, two of
Jacob's sons, Simeon and Levi, the brothers
of Dinah, took their swords, went into the
city without arousing suspicion, and killed all
the men, 26including Hamor and his son
Shechem. Then they took Dinah from
Shechem's house and left. 27After the slaugh-
ter Jacob's other sons looted the town to
take revenge for their sister's disgrace. 28They
took the flocks, the cattle, the donkeys, and
everything else in the city and in the fields.
29They took everything of value, captured all
the women and children, and carried off
everything in the houses.

30Jacob said to Simeon and Levi, "You
have gotten me into trouble; now the
Canaanites, the Perizzites, and everybody
else in the land will hate me. I do not have
many men; if they all band together against
me and attack me, our whole family will be
destroyed."

31But they answered, "We cannot let our
sister be treated like a common whore."

God Blesses Jacob at Bethel

35 God said to Jacob, "Go to Bethel at
once, and live there. Build an altar
there to me, the God who appeared to you
when you were running away from your
brother Esau."

2So Jacob said to his family and to all who
were with him, "Get rid of the foreign gods
that you have; purify yourselves and put on
clean clothes. 3We are going to leave here
and go to Bethel, where I will build an altar
to the God who helped me in the time of
my trouble and who has been with me

35:1 Gen 28:11–17

In Genesis, chapter 49, Jacob blesses his sons. But he will curse Simeon and Levi because of the violent actions they took in revenge of their sister's rape.

Study it!

A Crime Then and Now

The story of Dinah in Genesis, chapter 34, is shocking. Dinah was raped. Even though life was different then, rape was still considered a crime. But we don't hear how Dinah felt about it, just how her brothers felt. Back then people were more concerned about bringing dishonor to the family rather than the hurt caused to a living, breathing human being.

The man who raped Dinah, Shechem, wants to marry her. So Shechem's father and Dinah's father, Jacob, arrange the marriage of Shechem and Dinah. Dinah was never even asked how she felt about this! In biblical times, girls and women were the property of men—like land, animals, and tools. They could not own anything. They had little say in whom they married. They were expected to have many children—especially male children. They had no rights.

Today we see men and women as persons with equal rights. And our definition of sexual abuse includes not only rape but also unwanted sexual touching and unwanted sexual language and suggestions. You have probably heard about sexual abuse at school. If you or someone you know is being abused, tell an adult whom you trust. The adult should help bring an end to the abuse; if not, tell another adult. Rape and sexual abuse were horrible crimes in biblical times. They are still horrible crimes today.

— Genesis, chapter 34

everywhere I have gone." 4So they gave
Jacob all the foreign gods that they had and
also the earrings that they were wearing. He
buried them beneath the oak tree near
Shechem.
5When Jacob and his sons started to leave,
great fear fell on the people of the nearby
towns, and they did not pursue them. 6Jacob
came with all his people to Luz, which is
now known as Bethel, in the land of
Canaan. 7He built an altar there and named
the place for the God of Bethel, because
God had revealed himself to him there when
he was running away from his brother.
8Rebecca's nurse Deborah died and was
buried beneath the oak south of Bethel. So
it was named "Oak of Weeping."
9When Jacob returned from
Mesopotamia, God appeared to him again
and blessed him. 10God said to him, "Your
name is Jacob, but from now on it will be
Israel." So God named him Israel. 11And
God said to him, "I am Almighty God. Have
many children. Nations will be descended
from you, and you will be the ancestor of
kings. 12I will give you the land which I
gave to Abraham and to Isaac, and I will also
give it to your descendants after you."
13Then God left him. 14There, where God
had spoken to him, Jacob set up a memorial
stone and consecrated it by pouring wine
and olive oil on it. 15He named the place
Bethel.

The Death of Rachel

16Jacob and his family left Bethel, and
when they were still some distance from
Ephrath, the time came for Rachel to have
her baby, and she was having difficult labor.
17When her labor pains were at their worst,
the midwife said to her, "Don't be afraid,
Rachel; it's another boy." 18But she was
dying, and as she breathed her last, she
named her son Benoni,[l] but his father
named him Benjamin.[m]
19When Rachel died, she was buried

[l] **35:18** BENONI: *This name in Hebrew means "son of my sorrow."* [m] **35:18** BENJAMIN: *This name in Hebrew means "son who will be fortunate."*

35:10 Gen 32:28 **35:11, 12** Gen 17:4–8
35:14, 15 Gen 28:18, 19

beside the road to Ephrath, now known as
Bethlehem. 20Jacob set up a memorial stone
there, and it still marks Rachel's grave to this
day. 21Jacob moved on and set up his camp
on the other side of the tower of Eder.

The Sons of Jacob
(1 Chronicles 2:1, 2)

22While Jacob was living in that land,
Reuben had sexual intercourse with Bilhah,
one of his father's concubines; Jacob heard
about it and was furious.[n]

Jacob had twelve sons. 23The sons of Leah
were Reuben (Jacob's oldest son), Simeon,
Levi, Judah, Issachar, and Zebulun. 24The
sons of Rachel were Joseph and Benjamin.
25The sons of Rachel's slave Bilhah were
Dan and Naphtali. 26The sons of Leah's slave
Zilpah were Gad and Asher. These sons were
born in Mesopotamia.

The Death of Isaac

27Jacob went to his father Isaac at Mamre,
near Hebron, where Abraham and Isaac had
lived. 28Isaac lived to be a hundred and
eighty years old 29and died at a ripe old age;
and his sons Esau and Jacob buried him.

The Descendants of Esau
(1 Chronicles 1:34–37)

36 These are the descendants of Esau,
also called Edom. 2Esau married
Canaanite women: Adah, the daughter of
Elon the Hittite; Oholibamah, the daughter
of Anah son[o] of Zibeon the Hivite; 3and
Basemath, the daughter of Ishmael and sister
of Nebaioth. 4Adah bore Eliphaz; Basemath
bore Reuel; 5and Oholibamah bore Jeush,
Jalam, and Korah. All these sons were born
to Esau in the land of Canaan.

6Then Esau took his wives, his sons, his
daughters, and all the people of his house,
along with all his livestock and all the pos-
sessions he had gotten in the land of
Canaan, and went away from his brother
Jacob to another land. 7He left because the
land where he and Jacob were living was
not able to support them; they had too
much livestock and could no longer stay
together. 8So Esau lived in the hill country
of Edom.

9These are the descendants of Esau, the
ancestor of the Edomites. 10-13Esau's wife
Adah bore him one son, Eliphaz, and Eliphaz
had five sons: Teman, Omar, Zepho, Gatam,
and Kenaz. And by another wife, Timna, he
had one more son, Amalek.

Esau's wife Basemath bore him one son,
Reuel, and Reuel had four sons: Nahath,
Zerah, Shammah, and Mizzah.

14Esau's wife Oholibamah, the daughter of
Anah son[o] of Zibeon, bore him three sons:
Jeush, Jalam, and Korah.

15These are the tribes descended from
Esau. Esau's first son Eliphaz was the ances-
tor of the following tribes: Teman, Omar,
Zepho, Kenaz, 16Korah, Gatam, and Amalek.
These were all descendants of Esau's wife
Adah.

17Esau's son Reuel was the ancestor of the
following tribes: Nahath, Zerah, Shammah,
and Mizzah. These were all descendants of
Esau's wife Basemath.

18The following tribes were descended
from Esau by his wife Oholibamah, the
daughter of Anah: Jeush, Jalam, and Korah.
19All these tribes were descended from
Esau.

The Descendants of Seir
(1 Chronicles 1:38–42)

20-21The original inhabitants of the land
of Edom were divided into tribes which
traced their ancestry to the following
descendants of Seir, a Horite: Lotan, Shobal,
Zibeon, Anah, Dishon, Ezer, and Dishan.

22Lotan was the ancestor of the clans of
Hori and Heman. (Lotan had a sister named
Timna.)

23Shobal was the ancestor of the clans of
Alvan, Manahath, Ebal, Shepho, and Onam.

24Zibeon had two sons, Aiah and Anah.
(This is the Anah who found the hot springs
in the wilderness when he was taking care of

[n] **35:22** *One ancient translation* and was furious; *Hebrew does not have these words.* [o] **36:2,14** *Some ancient translations* son; *Hebrew* daughter; *or* granddaughter.

35:22 Gen 49:4 **35:27** Gen 13:18 **36:2** Gen 26:34 **36:3** Gen 28:9

his father's donkeys.) 25-26 Anah was the father
of Dishon, who was the ancestor of the clans
of Hemdan, Eshban, Ithran, and Cheran. Anah
also had a daughter named Oholibamah.

27 Ezer was the ancestor of the clans of
Bilhan, Zaavan, and Akan.

28 Dishan was the ancestor of the clans of
Uz and Aran.

29-30 These are the Horite tribes in the
land of Edom: Lotan, Shobal, Zibeon, Anah,
Dishon, Ezer, and Dishan.

The Kings of Edom
(1 Chronicles 1:43–54)

31-39 Before there were any kings in Israel,
the following kings ruled the land of Edom
in succession:

Bela son of Beor from Dinhabah
Jobab son of Zerah from Bozrah
Husham from the region of Teman
Hadad son of Bedad from Avith (he defeated the Midianites in a battle in the country of Moab)
Samlah from Masrekah
Shaul from Rehoboth-on-the-River
Baal Hanan son of Achbor
Hadad from Pau (his wife was Mehetabel, the daughter of Matred and granddaughter of Mezahab)

40-43 Esau was the ancestor of the following Edomite tribes: Timna, Alvah, Jetheth, Oholibamah, Elah, Pinon, Kenaz, Teman, Mibzar, Magdiel, and Iram. The area where each of these tribes lived was known by the name of the tribe.

Joseph and His Brothers

37 Jacob continued to live in the land
of Canaan, where his father had
lived, 2 and this is the story of Jacob's family.
Joseph, a young man of seventeen, took care of the sheep and goats with his brothers, the sons of Bilhah and Zilpah, his father's concubines. He brought bad reports to his father about what his brothers were doing.

Live it!

Favored Sibling

Richard and William were goofing around in the living room. The lamp fell and smashed into many pieces. William told his dad that it was Richard's fault. His dad believed him. Richard was older and stronger, he said. He should have known better.

Maya was the baby in the family. Even though she was eleven, she acted like a baby—when it suited her. She got everything she wanted. LeBron had to save his own money to buy a CD player. Maya got one for her birthday.

Do you ever feel like your parents favor your brother or sister over you? It may be true sometimes, as in the case with Joseph and his brothers (Genesis 37:3), but most parents love their children equally. They try to be fair, and that means occasionally giving someone special treatment. The next time you feel like your parents are unjust, try to remember a time when you were on the receiving end of their favoritism. If you can't remember, ask your siblings. They are sure to come up with a time when it seemed that your mom or dad liked you best.

— Genesis, chapter 37

3 Jacob loved Joseph more than all his
other sons, because he had been born to him
when he was old. He made a long robe with
full sleeves[p] for him. 4 When his brothers saw
that their father loved Joseph more than he

[p] **37:3** robe with full sleeves; *or* decorated robe.

Starting with Genesis, chapter 37, through the end of the book, Joseph takes over as the main character.

loved them, they hated their brother so
much that they would not speak to him in a
friendly manner.
5 One time Joseph had a dream, and when
he told his brothers about it, they hated him
even more. 6 He said, "Listen to the dream I
had. 7 We were all in the field tying up
sheaves of wheat, when my sheaf got up and
stood up straight. Yours formed a circle
around mine and bowed down to it."
8 "Do you think you are going to be a
king and rule over us?" his brothers asked.
So they hated him even more because of his
dreams and because of what he said about
them.
9 Then Joseph had another dream and told
his brothers, "I had another dream, in which
I saw the sun, the moon, and eleven stars
bowing down to me."
10 He also told the dream to his father, and
his father scolded him: "What kind of a
dream is that? Do you think that your moth-
er, your brothers, and I are going to come
and bow down to you?" 11 Joseph's brothers
were jealous of him, but his father kept
thinking about the whole matter.

Joseph Is Sold and Taken to Egypt

12 One day when Joseph's brothers had
gone to Shechem to take care of their
father's flock, 13 Jacob said to Joseph, "I want
you to go to Shechem, where your brothers
are taking care of the flock."
Joseph answered, "I am ready."
14 His father told him, "Go and see if your
brothers are safe and if the flock is all right;
then come back and tell me." So his father
sent him on his way from Hebron Valley.
Joseph arrived at Shechem 15 and was
wandering around in the country when a
man saw him and asked him, "What are you
looking for?"
16 "I am looking for my brothers, who are
taking care of their flock," he answered.
"Can you tell me where they are?"
17 The man said, "They have already left.
I heard them say that they were going to
Dothan." So Joseph went after his brothers
and found them at Dothan.
18 They saw him in the distance, and
before he reached them, they plotted against
him and decided to kill him. 19 They said to
one another, "Here comes that dreamer.
20 Come on now, let's kill him and throw his
body into one of the dry wells. We can say
that a wild animal killed him. Then we will
see what becomes of his dreams."
21 Reuben heard them and tried to save
Joseph. "Let's not kill him," he said. 22 "Just
throw him into this well in the wilderness,
but don't hurt him." He said this, planning
to save him from them and send him back to
his father. 23 When Joseph came up to his
brothers, they ripped off his long robe with
full sleeves.[p] 24 Then they took him and
threw him into the well, which was dry.
25 While they were eating, they suddenly
saw a group of Ishmaelites traveling from
Gilead to Egypt. Their camels were loaded
with spices and resins. 26 Judah said to his
brothers, "What will we gain by killing our
brother and covering up the murder? 27 Let's
sell him to these Ishmaelites. Then we won't
have to hurt him; after all, he is our brother,
our own flesh and blood." His brothers
agreed, 28 and when some Midianite traders
came by, the brothers[q] pulled Joseph out of
the well and sold him for twenty pieces of
silver to the Ishmaelites, who took him to
Egypt.
29 When Reuben came back to the well
and found that Joseph was not there, he tore
his clothes in sorrow. 30 He returned to his
brothers and said, "The boy is not there!
What am I going to do?"
31 Then they killed a goat and dipped
Joseph's robe in its blood. 32 They took the
robe to their father and said, "We found this.
Does it belong to your son?"
33 He recognized it and said, "Yes, it is his!
Some wild animal has killed him. My son

[p] **37:23** robe with full sleeves; *or* decorated robe. [q] **37:28** the brothers; *Hebrew* they.

37:11 Acts 7:9 **37:28** Wis 10:13; Acts 7:9

The story of Joseph was made into a popular musical called *Joseph and the Amazing Technicolor Dreamcoat.*

The Ishmaelites . . . took him to Egypt. (37:28)

Joseph has been torn to pieces!" 34Jacob tore his clothes in sorrow and put on sackcloth. He mourned for his son a long time. 35All his sons and daughters came to comfort him, but he refused to be comforted and said, "I will go down to the world of the dead still mourning for my son." So he continued to mourn for his son Joseph.

36Meanwhile, in Egypt the Midianites had sold Joseph to Potiphar, one of the king's officers, who was the captain of the palace guard.

Judah and Tamar

38 About that time Judah left his brothers and went to stay with a man named Hirah, who was from the town of Adullam. 2There Judah met a young Canaanite woman whose father was named Shua. He married her, 3and she bore him a son, whom he named Er. 4She became pregnant again and bore another son and named him Onan. 5Again she had a son and named him Shelah. Judah was at Achzib when the boy was born.

6For his first son Er, Judah got a wife whose name was Tamar. 7Er's conduct was evil, and it displeased the LORD, so the LORD killed him. 8Then Judah said to Er's brother Onan, "Go and sleep with your brother's widow. Fulfill your obligation to her as her husband's brother, so that your brother may have descendants." 9But Onan knew that the children would not belong to him, so when he had intercourse with his brother's widow, he let the semen spill on the ground, so that there would be no children for his brother. 10What he did displeased the LORD, and the LORD killed him also. 11Then Judah said to his daughter-in-law Tamar, "Return to your father's house and remain a widow until my son Shelah grows up." He said this because he was afraid that Shelah would be killed, as his brothers had been. So Tamar went back home.

12After some time Judah's wife died. When he had finished the time of mourning, he and his friend Hirah of Adullam went to Timnah, where his sheep were being sheared. 13Someone told Tamar that her father-in-law was going to Timnah to shear his sheep. 14So she changed from the widow's clothes she had been wearing, covered her face with a veil, and sat down at the entrance to Enaim, a town on the road to Timnah. As she well knew, Judah's youngest son Shelah was now grown up, and yet she had not been given to him in marriage.

15When Judah saw her, he thought that she was a prostitute, because she had her face covered. 16He went over to her at the side of the road and said, "All right, how much do you charge?" (He did not know that she was his daughter-in-law.)

She said, "What will you give me?"

17He answered, "I will send you a young goat from my flock."

She said, "All right, if you will give me something to keep as a pledge until you send the goat."

18"What shall I give you as a pledge?" he asked.

She answered, "Your seal with its cord and the walking stick you are carrying." He gave them to her. Then they had intercourse, and she became pregnant. 19Tamar went home, took off her veil, and put her widow's clothes back on.

20Judah sent his friend Hirah to take the goat and get back from the woman the articles he had pledged, but Hirah could not find her. 21He asked some men at Enaim, "Where is the prostitute who was here by the road?"

"There has never been a prostitute here," they answered.

22He returned to Judah and said, "I couldn't find her. The men of the place said that there had never been a prostitute there."

23Judah said, "Let her keep the things. We
don't want people to laugh at us. I did try to
pay her, but you couldn't find her."
24About three months later someone told
Judah, "Your daughter-in-law Tamar has
been acting like a whore, and now she is
pregnant."
Judah ordered, "Take her out and burn
her to death."
25As she was being taken out, she sent
word to her father-in-law: "I am pregnant by
the man who owns these things. Look at
them and see whose they are—this seal with
its cord and this walking stick."
26Judah recognized them and said, "She is
in the right. I have failed in my obligation to
her—I should have given her to my son
Shelah in marriage." And Judah never had
intercourse with her again.
27When the time came for her to give
birth, it was discovered that she was going to
have twins. 28While she was in labor, one of
them put out an arm; the midwife caught it,
tied a red thread around it, and said, "This
one was born first." 29But he pulled his arm
back, and his brother was born first. Then
the midwife said, "So this is how you break
your way out!" So he was named Perez.[r]
30Then his brother was born with the red
thread on his arm, and he was named
Zerah.[s]

Joseph and Potiphar's Wife

39 Now the Ishmaelites had taken
Joseph to Egypt and sold him to
Potiphar, one of the king's officers, who was
the captain of the palace guard. 2The LORD
was with Joseph and made him successful.
He lived in the house of his Egyptian mas-
ter, 3who saw that the LORD was with
Joseph and had made him successful in
everything he did. 4Potiphar was pleased
with him and made him his personal ser-
vant; so he put him in charge of his house
and everything he owned. 5From then on,
because of Joseph the LORD blessed the
household of the Egyptian and everything
that he had in his house and in his fields.
6Potiphar turned over everything he had to
the care of Joseph and did not concern him-
self with anything except the food he ate.
Joseph was well-built and good-looking,
7and after a while his master's wife began to
desire Joseph and asked him to go to bed
with her. 8He refused and said to her, "Look,
my master does not have to concern himself
with anything in the house, because I am
here. He has put me in charge of everything
he has. 9I have as much authority in this
house as he has, and he has not kept back
anything from me except you. How then
could I do such an immoral thing and sin
against God?" 10Although she asked Joseph
day after day, he would not go to bed with
her.
11But one day when Joseph went into the
house to do his work, none of the house ser-
vants was there. 12She caught him by his
robe and said, "Come to bed with me." But
he escaped and ran outside, leaving his robe
in her hand. 13When she saw that he had left
his robe and had run out of the house, 14she
called to her house servants and said, "Look
at this! This Hebrew that my husband
brought to the house is insulting us. He
came into my room and tried to rape me,
but I screamed as loud as I could. 15When
he heard me scream, he ran outside, leaving
his robe beside me."
16She kept his robe with her until Joseph's
master came home. 17Then she told him the
same story: "That Hebrew slave that you
brought here came into my room and insult-
ed me. 18But when I screamed, he ran out-
side, leaving his robe beside me."
19Joseph's master was furious 20and had
Joseph arrested and put in the prison where
the king's prisoners were kept, and there he
stayed. 21But the LORD was with Joseph and
blessed him, so that the jailer was pleased
with him. 22He put Joseph in charge of all
the other prisoners and made him responsi-
ble for everything that was done in the
prison. 23The jailer did not have to look
after anything for which Joseph was respon-
sible, because the LORD was with Joseph
and made him succeed in everything he did.

[r] **38:29** PEREZ: *This name in Hebrew means "breaking out" for the red brightness of dawn.*

[s] **38:29** ZERAH: *This name sounds like a Hebrew word*

39:2 Acts 7:9 **39:21** Acts 7:9

Live it!

Joseph's Tough Times

Joseph was in a tough spot. He was a slave in Egypt, having been sold by his brothers. But he made the best of it. He kept at it and worked hard. His master was pleased, so he made him his personal servant. Later, when Joseph was falsely accused of a crime and thrown into jail, the jailer recognized that Joseph had a special gift for understanding dreams. Eventually, he became governor of Egypt with power over many people—including his brothers.

Joseph could not have done it without God. He knew that God was everywhere, and he called on God for help. "The LORD was with Joseph and made him successful" (Genesis 39:2).

Do you ever feel like nothing is right? Does it seem like you'll never get ahead sometimes? Are you stressed and worried? Do what Joseph did:

- **Persevere. That means keep on doing what you have to do.**
- **Do your very best.**
- **Ask God for help.**

Someday you will look back at your tough times and say, "The Lord was with me and made me successful."

— Genesis 39:1–6

Joseph Interprets the Prisoners' Dreams

40 Some time later the king of Egypt's wine steward and his chief baker offended the king. 2He was angry with these two officials 3and put them in prison in the house of the captain of the guard, in the same place where Joseph was being kept. 4They spent a long time in prison, and the captain assigned Joseph as their servant.

5One night there in prison the wine steward and the chief baker each had a dream, and the dreams had different meanings. 6When Joseph came to them in the morning, he saw that they were upset. 7He asked them, "Why do you look so worried today?"

8They answered, "Each of us had a dream, and there is no one here to explain what the dreams mean."

"It is God who gives the ability to interpret dreams," Joseph said. "Tell me your dreams."

9So the wine steward said, "In my dream there was a grapevine in front of me 10with three branches on it. As soon as the leaves came out, the blossoms appeared, and the grapes ripened. 11I was holding the king's cup; so I took the grapes and squeezed them into the cup and gave it to him."

12Joseph said, "This is what it means: the three branches are three days. 13In three days the king will release you, pardon you, and restore you to your position. You will give him his cup as you did before when you were his wine steward. 14But please remember me when everything is going well for you, and please be kind enough to mention me to the king and help me get out of this prison. 15After all, I was kidnapped from the land of the Hebrews, and even here in Egypt I didn't do anything to deserve being put in prison."

16When the chief baker saw that the interpretation of the wine steward's dream was favorable, he said to Joseph, "I had a dream too; I was carrying three breadbaskets on my head. 17In the top basket there were all kinds of baked goods for the king, and the birds were eating them."

18Joseph answered, "This is what it means: the three baskets are three days. 19In three days the king will release you—and have your

God gave Joseph the gift of interpreting dreams. What special gifts did God give you?

Study it!

Catching Dreams

Long ago, a spiritual leader of the Lakota people, a Native American nation, had a vision of a spider named Iktomi who spoke in a sacred language. Iktomi took a willow hoop with beads, feathers, and horsehair on it. He began to spin a web as he spoke to the leader about the cycle of life and good and bad dreams. He said that the good dreams will lead a person in the right direction. Bad dreams will lead a person astray.

Iktomi gave the leader the hoop, which was a perfect circle with a hole in the center of the web. He told the leader that if he believed in the Great Spirit, the web would catch his good dreams, and he would lead his people well. The bad ones would pass through the hole in the center and disappear with the morning sun.

Even today, Lakota people—as well as many other people—hang dream catchers in their homes to sift their dreams and visions. They believe that dreams are messages from the Great Spirit, whom we call God. Their belief reflects the Bible stories of people like Joseph who had the gift of interpreting dreams as messages from God.

— Genesis 41:1–36

head cut off! Then he will hang your body on
a pole, and the birds will eat your flesh."
20On his birthday three days later the king
gave a banquet for all his officials; he released
his wine steward and his chief baker and
brought them before his officials. 21He
restored the wine steward to his former
position, 22but he executed the chief baker.
It all happened just as Joseph had said. 23But
the wine steward never gave Joseph another
thought—he forgot all about him.

Joseph Interprets the King's Dreams

41 After two years had passed, the king
of Egypt dreamed that he was standing
by the Nile River, 2when seven cows, fat
and sleek, came up out of the river and
began to feed on the grass. 3Then seven
other cows came up; they were thin and
bony. They came and stood by the other
cows on the riverbank, 4and the thin cows
ate up the fat cows. Then the king woke up.
5He fell asleep again and had another dream.
Seven heads of grain, full and ripe, were
growing on one stalk. 6Then seven other
heads of grain sprouted, thin and scorched
by the desert wind, 7and the thin heads of
grain swallowed the full ones. The king
woke up and realized that he had been
dreaming. 8In the morning he was worried,
so he sent for all the magicians and wise
men of Egypt. He told them his dreams, but
no one could explain them to him.
9Then the wine steward said to the king,
"I must confess today that I have done
wrong. 10You were angry with the chief
baker and me, and you put us in prison in
the house of the captain of the guard. 11One
night each of us had a dream, and the
dreams had different meanings. 12A young
Hebrew was there with us, a slave of the
captain of the guard. We told him our
dreams, and he interpreted them for us.
13Things turned out just as he said: you
restored me to my position, but you executed the baker."
14The king sent for Joseph, and he was
immediately brought from the prison. After
he had shaved and changed his clothes, he

41:8 Dan 2:2

Because God helped Joseph interpret Pharoah's dream, Joseph, a lowly shepherd, became the second-most-powerful ruler in Egypt. God is an awesome God!

HIGHLIGHTS IN JOSEPH'S LIFE (37—46)

(Numbers refer to chapter and verse in Genesis)

came into the king's presence. [15]The king
said to him, "I have had a dream, and no one
can explain it. I have been told that you can
interpret dreams."

[16]Joseph answered, "I cannot, Your
Majesty, but God will give a favorable inter-
pretation."

[17]The king said, "I dreamed that I was
standing on the bank of the Nile, [18]when
seven cows, fat and sleek, came up out of the
river and began feeding on the grass. [19]Then
seven other cows came up which were thin
and bony. They were the poorest cows I have
ever seen anywhere in Egypt. [20]The thin
cows ate up the fat ones, [21]but no one
would have known it, because they looked
just as bad as before. Then I woke up. [22]I also
dreamed that I saw seven heads of grain

which were full and ripe, growing on one
stalk. 23 Then seven heads of grain sprouted,
thin and scorched by the desert wind, 24 and
the thin heads of grain swallowed the full
ones. I told the dreams to the magicians, but
none of them could explain them to me."

25 Joseph said to the king, "The two
dreams mean the same thing; God has told
you what he is going to do. 26 The seven fat
cows are seven years, and the seven full heads
of grain are also seven years; they have the
same meaning. 27 The seven thin cows which
came up later and the seven thin heads of
grain scorched by the desert wind are seven
years of famine. 28 It is just as I told you—
God has shown you what he is going to do.
29 There will be seven years of great plenty in
all the land of Egypt. 30 After that, there will
be seven years of famine, and all the good
years will be forgotten, because the famine
will ruin the country. 31 The time of plenty
will be entirely forgotten, because the
famine which follows will be so terrible.
32 The repetition of your dream means that
the matter is fixed by God and that he will
make it happen in the near future.

33 "Now you should choose some man
with wisdom and insight and put him in
charge of the country. 34 You must also
appoint other officials and take a fifth of the
crops during the seven years of plenty.
35 Order them to collect all the food during
the good years that are coming, and give
them authority to store up grain in the cities
and guard it. 36 The food will be a reserve
supply for the country during the seven years
of famine which are going to come on
Egypt. In this way the people will not starve."

Joseph Is Made Governor over Egypt

37 The king and his officials approved this
plan, 38 and he said to them, "We will never
find a better man than Joseph, a man who
has God's spirit in him." 39 The king said to
Joseph, "God has shown you all this, so it is
obvious that you have greater wisdom and
insight than anyone else. 40 I will put you in
charge of my country, and all my people will
obey your orders. Your authority will be sec-
ond only to mine. 41 I now appoint you gov-
ernor over all Egypt." 42 The king removed
from his finger the ring engraved with the
royal seal and put it on Joseph's finger. He
put a fine linen robe on him, and placed a
gold chain around his neck. 43 He gave him
the second royal chariot to ride in, and his
guard of honor went ahead of him and cried
out, "Make way! Make way!" And so Joseph
was appointed governor over all Egypt.
44 The king said to him, "I am the king—and
no one in all Egypt shall so much as lift a
hand or a foot without your permission."
45-46 He gave Joseph the Egyptian name
Zaphenath Paneah, and he gave him a wife,
Asenath, the daughter of Potiphera, a priest
in the city of Heliopolis.

Joseph was thirty years old when he began
to serve the king of Egypt. He left the king's
court and traveled all over the land. 47 During
the seven years of plenty the land produced
abundant crops, 48 all of which Joseph collected
and stored in the cities. In each city he stored
the food from the fields around it. 49 There was
so much grain that Joseph stopped measuring
it—it was like the sand of the sea.

50 Before the years of famine came, Joseph
had two sons by Asenath. 51 He said, "God
has made me forget all my sufferings and all
my father's family"; so he named his first son
Manasseh.[t] 52 He also said, "God has given
me children in the land of my trouble"; so
he named his second son Ephraim.[u]

53 The seven years of plenty that the land
of Egypt had enjoyed came to an end, 54 and
the seven years of famine began, just as
Joseph had said. There was famine in every
other country, but there was food through-
out Egypt. 55 When the Egyptians began to
be hungry, they cried out to the king for
food. So he ordered them to go to Joseph
and do what he told them. 56 The famine
grew worse and spread over the whole
country, so Joseph opened all the storehouses
and sold grain to the Egyptians. 57 People
came to Egypt from all over the world to
buy grain from Joseph, because the famine
was severe everywhere.

[t] **41:51** MANASSEH: *This name sounds like the Hebrew for "cause to forget."* [u] **41:51** EPHRAIM: *This name sounds like the Hebrew for "give children."*

41:40 Acts 7:10 **41:42** Dan 5:29 **41:54** Acts 7:11

Joseph's Brothers Go to Egypt to Buy Grain

42 When Jacob learned that there was
grain in Egypt, he said to his sons,
"Why don't you do something? 2I hear that
there is grain in Egypt; go there and buy
some to keep us from starving to death." 3So
Joseph's ten half brothers went to buy grain
in Egypt, 4but Jacob did not send Joseph's full
brother Benjamin with them, because he was
afraid that something might happen to him.

5The sons of Jacob came with others to
buy grain, because there was famine in the
land of Canaan. 6Joseph, as governor of the
land of Egypt, was selling grain to people
from all over the world. So Joseph's brothers
came and bowed down before him with
their faces to the ground. 7When Joseph saw
his brothers, he recognized them, but he
acted as if he did not know them. He asked
them harshly, "Where do you come from?"

"We have come from Canaan to buy
food," they answered.

8Although Joseph recognized his brothers,
they did not recognize him. 9He remem-
bered the dreams he had dreamed about
them and said, "You are spies; you have come
to find out where our country is weak."

10"No, sir," they answered. "We have come
as your slaves, to buy food. 11We are all broth-
ers. We are not spies, sir, we are honest men."

12Joseph said to them, "No! You have
come to find out where our country is
weak."

13They said, "We were twelve brothers in
all, sir, sons of the same man in the land of
Canaan. One brother is dead, and the
youngest is now with our father."

14"It is just as I said," Joseph answered.
"You are spies. 15This is how you will be
tested: I swear by the name of the king that
you will never leave unless your youngest
brother comes here. 16One of you must go
and get him. The rest of you will be kept
under guard until the truth of what you say
can be tested. Otherwise, as sure as the king
lives, you are spies." 17With that, he put them
in prison for three days.

18On the third day Joseph said to them, "I
am a God-fearing man, and I will spare your
lives on one condition. 19To prove that you

Live it!

The Great River of Blessings

People were starving. There just was not enough food to feed everyone. A drought made growing crops difficult. Many people outside of Egypt went there to see if they could buy grain. Thanks to Joseph the Egyptians had storehouses of grain. He shared it with both Egyptians and non-Egyptians.

The Egyptians had the Nile River to thank for their good fortune. The Nile is the longest river in the world, and the land along the river is rich and fertile. So even when a drought hit the land, the river provided water for the crops.

God's creation provides plenty of food for the people of the world. Unfortunately, those countries that are blessed with riches often do not share with struggling countries. Even in our own country, every day people go hungry while others eat too much, waste food, or throw it away.

What can you do to make a difference in the world's hunger problem? What can you do to help with hunger in your own city or community?

— Genesis 42:1–11

42:2 Acts 7:12 **42:9** Gen 37:5–10

Remember Joseph's dream in Genesis 37:5–11? It comes true in Egypt *(see Genesis 42:6)*. **But this time, Joseph doesn't brag about it.**

are honest, one of you will stay in the prison where you have been kept; the rest of you may go and take back to your starving families the grain that you have bought. [20]Then you must bring your youngest brother to me. This will prove that you have been telling the truth, and I will not put you to death."

They agreed to this [21]and said to one another, "Yes, now we are suffering the consequences of what we did to our brother; we saw the great trouble he was in when he begged for help, but we would not listen. That is why we are in this trouble now."

[22]Reuben said, "I told you not to harm the boy, but you wouldn't listen. And now we are being paid back for his death." [23]Joseph understood what they said, but they did not know it, because they had been speaking to him through an interpreter. [24]Joseph left them and began to cry. When he was able to speak again, he came back, picked out Simeon, and had him tied up in front of them.

Joseph's Brothers Return to Canaan

[25]Joseph gave orders to fill his brothers' packs with grain, to put each man's money back in his sack, and to give them food for the trip. This was done. [26]The brothers loaded their donkeys with the grain they had bought, and then they left. [27]At the place where they spent the night, one of them opened his sack to feed his donkey and found his money at the top of the sack. [28]"My money has been returned to me," he called to his brothers. "Here it is in my sack!" Their hearts sank, and in fear they asked one another, "What has God done to us?"

[29]When they came to their father Jacob in Canaan, they told him all that had happened to them: [30]"The governor of Egypt spoke harshly to us and accused us of spying against his country. [31]'We are not spies,' we answered, 'we are honest men. [32]We were twelve brothers in all, sons of the same father. One brother is dead, and the youngest is still in Canaan with our father.' [33]The man answered, 'This is how I will find out if you are honest men: One of you will stay with me; the rest will take grain for your starving families and leave. [34]Bring your youngest brother to me. Then I will know that you are not spies, but honest men; I will give your brother back to you, and you can stay here and trade.' "

[35]Then when they emptied out their sacks, every one of them found his bag of money; and when they saw the money, they and their father Jacob were afraid. [36]Their father said to them, "Do you want to make me lose all my children? Joseph is gone; Simeon is gone; and now you want to take away Benjamin. I am the one who suffers!"

[37]Reuben said to his father, "If I do not bring Benjamin back to you, you can kill my two sons. Put him in my care, and I will bring him back."

[38]But Jacob said, "My son cannot go with you; his brother is dead, and he is the only one left. Something might happen to him on the way. I am an old man, and the sorrow you would cause me would kill me."

Joseph's Brothers Return to Egypt with Benjamin

43 The famine in Canaan got worse, [2]and when the family of Jacob had eaten all the grain which had been brought from Egypt, Jacob said to his sons, "Go back and buy a little food for us."

[3]Judah said to him, "The man sternly warned us that we would not be admitted to his presence unless we had our brother with us. [4]If you are willing to send our brother with us, we will go and buy food for you. [5]If you are not willing, we will not go, because the man told us we would not be admitted to his presence unless our brother was with us."

[6]Jacob said, "Why did you cause me so much trouble by telling the man that you had another brother?"

42:22 Gen 37:21, 22

Genesis 43:34 says Benjamin was served five times as much food as the others. It was just a way of saying "much more."

7 They answered, "The man kept asking about us and our family, 'Is your father still living? Do you have another brother?' We had to answer his questions. How could we know that he would tell us to bring our brother with us?"

8 Judah said to his father, "Send the boy with me, and we will leave at once. Then none of us will starve to death. 9 I will pledge my own life, and you can hold me responsible for him. If I do not bring him back to you safe and sound, I will always bear the blame. 10 If we had not waited so long, we could have been there and back twice by now."

11 Their father said to them, "If that is how it has to be, then take the best products of the land in your packs as a present for the governor: a little resin, a little honey, spices, pistachio nuts, and almonds. 12 Take with you also twice as much money, because you must take back the money that was returned in the top of your sacks. Maybe it was a mistake. 13 Take your brother and return at once. 14 May Almighty God cause the man to have pity on you, so that he will give Benjamin and your other brother back to you. As for me, if I must lose my children, I must lose them."

15 So the brothers took the gifts and twice as much money, and set out for Egypt with Benjamin. There they presented themselves to Joseph. 16 When Joseph saw Benjamin with them, he said to the servant in charge of his house, "Take these men to my house. They are going to eat with me at noon, so kill an animal and prepare it." 17 The servant did as he was commanded and took the brothers to Joseph's house.

18 As they were being brought to the house, they were afraid and thought, "We are being brought here because of the money that was returned in our sacks the first time. They will suddenly attack us, take our donkeys, and make us his slaves." 19 So at the door of the house, they said to the servant in charge, 20 "If you please, sir, we came here once before to buy food. 21 When we set up camp on the way home, we opened our sacks, and each man found his money in the top of his sack—every bit of it. We have brought it back to you. 22 We have also brought some more money with us to buy more food. We do not know who put our money back in our sacks."

23 The servant said, "Don't worry. Don't be afraid. Your God, the God of your father, must have put the money in your sacks for you. I received your payment." Then he brought Simeon to them.

24 The servant took the brothers into the house. He gave them water so that they could wash their feet, and he fed their donkeys. 25 They got their gifts ready to present to Joseph when he arrived at noon, because they had been told that they were to eat with him. 26 When Joseph got home, they took the gifts into the house to him and bowed down to the ground before him. 27 He asked about their health and then said, "You told me about your old father—how is he? Is he still alive and well?"

28 They answered, "Your humble servant, our father, is still alive and well." And they knelt and bowed down before him.

29 When Joseph saw his brother Benjamin, he said, "So this is your youngest brother, the one you told me about. God bless you, my son." 30 Then Joseph left suddenly, because his heart was full of tender feelings for his brother. He was about to break down, so he went to his room and cried. 31 After he had washed his face, he came out, and controlling himself, he ordered the meal to be served. 32 Joseph was served at one table and his brothers at another. The Egyptians who were eating there were served separately, because they considered it beneath their dignity to eat with Hebrews. 33 The brothers had been seated at the table, facing Joseph, in the order of their age from the oldest to the youngest. When they saw how they had been seated, they looked at one another in amazement. 34 Food was served to them from Joseph's table, and Benjamin was served five times as much as the rest of them. So they ate and drank with Joseph until they were drunk.

The Missing Cup

44 Joseph commanded the servant in charge of his house, "Fill the men's sacks with as much food as they can carry, and put each man's money in the top of his

Study it!

Another Name for the Israelites

You may have noticed that the word *Hebrew* is used several times in Genesis to refer to Abraham, Jacob, and Jacob's sons. It is a name that foreigners used to refer to Abraham and his descendants. They were called Hebrews before they were called Israelites. It described the Chosen People as an ethnic group, just as we would use terms like Hmong or Hispanic to describe a person's ethnicity.

Hebrew is also the name of the language of the Jewish people and is still used in Jewish worship around the world.

—Genesis 43:32

sack. 2Put my silver cup in the top of the
youngest brother's sack, together with the
money for his grain." He did as he was told.
3Early in the morning the brothers were sent
on their way with their donkeys. 4When
they had gone only a short distance from the
city, Joseph said to the servant in charge of
his house, "Hurry after those men. When
you catch up with them, ask them, 'Why
have you paid back evil for good? 5Why did
you steal my master's silver cup?[v] It is the
one he drinks from, the one he uses for div-
ination. You have committed a serious
crime!' "

6When the servant caught up with them,
he repeated these words. 7They answered
him, "What do you mean, sir, by talking like
this? We swear that we have done no such
thing. 8You know that we brought back to
you from the land of Canaan the money we
found in the top of our sacks. Why then
should we steal silver or gold from your
master's house? 9Sir, if any one of us is found
to have it, he will be put to death, and the
rest of us will become your slaves."

10He said, "I agree; but only the one who
has taken the cup will become my slave, and
the rest of you can go free." 11So they quick-
ly lowered their sacks to the ground, and
each man opened his sack. 12Joseph's servant
searched carefully, beginning with the oldest
and ending with the youngest, and the cup
was found in Benjamin's sack. 13The broth-
ers tore their clothes in sorrow, loaded their
donkeys, and returned to the city.

14When Judah and his brothers came to
Joseph's house, he was still there. They
bowed down before him, 15and Joseph said,
"What have you done? Didn't you know
that a man in my position could find you
out by practicing divination?"

16"What can we say to you, sir?" Judah
answered. "How can we argue? How can we
clear ourselves? God has uncovered our
guilt. All of us are now your slaves and not
just the one with whom the cup was found."

17Joseph said, "Oh, no! I would never do
that! Only the one who had the cup will be
my slave. The rest of you may go back safe
and sound to your father."

Judah Pleads for Benjamin

18Judah went up to Joseph and said,
"Please, sir, allow me to speak with you
freely. Don't be angry with me; you are like
the king himself. 19Sir, you asked us, 'Do you
have a father or another brother?' 20We
answered, 'We have a father who is old and a
younger brother, born to him in his old age.
The boy's brother is dead, and he is the only
one of his mother's children still alive; his
father loves him very much.' 21Sir, you told
us to bring him here, so that you could see
him, 22and we answered that the boy could
not leave his father; if he did, his father
would die. 23Then you said, 'You will not be
admitted to my presence again unless your
youngest brother comes with you.'

24"When we went back to our father, we
told him what you had said. 25Then he told
us to return and buy a little food. 26We

[v] **44:5** *One ancient translation* Why did you steal my master's silver cup?; *Hebrew does not have these words.*

answered, 'We cannot go; we will not be
admitted to the man's presence unless our
youngest brother is with us. We can go only
if our youngest brother goes also.' 27 Our
father said to us, 'You know that my wife
Rachel bore me only two sons. 28 One of
them has already left me. He must have been
torn to pieces by wild animals, because I
have not seen him since he left. 29 If you take
this one from me now and something hap-
pens to him, the sorrow you would cause me
would kill me, as old as I am.'

30-31 "And now, sir," Judah continued, "if I
go back to my father without the boy, as
soon as he sees that the boy is not with me,
he will die. His life is wrapped up with the
life of the boy, and he is so old that the sor-
row we would cause him would kill him.
32 What is more, I pledged my life to my
father for the boy. I told him that if I did not
bring the boy back to him, I would bear the
blame all my life. 33 And now, sir, I will stay
here as your slave in place of the boy; let
him go back with his brothers. 34 How can I
go back to my father if the boy is not with
me? I cannot bear to see this disaster come
upon my father."

Joseph Tells His Brothers Who He Is

45 Joseph was no longer able to control
his feelings in front of his servants, so
he ordered them all to leave the room. No
one else was with him when Joseph told his
brothers who he was. 2 He cried with such
loud sobs that the Egyptians heard it, and the
news was taken to the king's palace. 3 Joseph
said to his brothers, "I am Joseph. Is my
father still alive?" But when his brothers
heard this, they were so terrified that they
could not answer. 4 Then Joseph said to
them, "Please come closer." They did, and he
said, "I am your brother Joseph, whom you
sold into Egypt. 5 Now do not be upset or
blame yourselves because you sold me here.
It was really God who sent me ahead of you
to save people's lives. 6 This is only the sec-
ond year of famine in the land; there will be
five more years in which there will be nei-
ther plowing nor reaping. 7 God sent me
ahead of you to rescue you in this amazing
way and to make sure that you and your
descendants survive. 8 So it was not really you
who sent me here, but God. He has made
me the king's highest official. I am in charge
of his whole country; I am the ruler of all
Egypt.

9 "Now hurry back to my father and tell
him that this is what his son Joseph says:
'God has made me ruler of all Egypt; come
to me without delay. 10 You can live in the
region of Goshen, where you can be near
me—you, your children, your grandchildren,
your sheep, your goats, your cattle, and
everything else that you have. 11 If you are in
Goshen, I can take care of you. There will
still be five years of famine; and I do not
want you, your family, and your livestock to
starve.' "

12 Joseph continued, "Now all of you, and
you too, Benjamin, can see that I am really
Joseph. 13 Tell my father how powerful I am
here in Egypt and tell him about everything
that you have seen. Then hurry and bring
him here."

14 He threw his arms around his brother
Benjamin and began to cry; Benjamin also
cried as he hugged him. 15 Then, still weep-
ing, he embraced each of his brothers and
kissed them. After that, his brothers began to
talk with him.

16 When the news reached the palace that
Joseph's brothers had come, the king and his
officials were pleased. 17 He said to Joseph,
"Tell your brothers to load their animals and
to return to the land of Canaan. 18 Let them
get their father and their families and come
back here. I will give them the best land in
Egypt, and they will have more than enough
to live on. 19 Tell them also to take wagons
with them from Egypt for their wives and
small children and to bring their father with
them. 20 They are not to worry about leaving

45:1 Acts 7:13 **45:9–11** Acts 7:14

The news that Joseph was alive brought Jacob great joy. What news would bring you great joy?

Pray it!

The Way to Peace

Joseph had every reason to get even with his brothers, and he had the power to do it. But instead Joseph used his power to reunite his family. He made his father, Jacob, a very happy man in his old age. Joseph knew that revenge does not bring peace. Only forgiveness does.

The next time you want to get even with someone, think about Joseph and his brothers. Then say this famous prayer for peace, which is attributed to Saint Francis of Assisi:

Lord, make me an instrument of your peace:
where there is hatred, let me sow love;
where there is injury, pardon;
where there is doubt, faith;
where there is despair, hope;
where there is darkness, light;
and where there is sadness, joy.
O Divine Master,
grant that I may not so much seek
to be consoled as to console,
to be understood as to understand,
to be loved as to love.
For it is in giving that we receive,
it is in pardoning that we are pardoned,
and it is in dying that we are born to eternal life.

— Genesis, chapter 45

their possessions behind; the best in the whole land of Egypt will be theirs."

21Jacob's sons did as they were told. Joseph gave them wagons, as the king had ordered,
and food for the trip. 22He also gave each of
them a change of clothes, but he gave Benjamin three hundred pieces of silver and five
changes of clothes. 23He sent his father ten
donkeys loaded with the best Egyptian goods and ten donkeys loaded with grain, bread, and other food for the trip. 24He sent
his brothers off and as they left, he said to them, "Don't quarrel on the way."

25They left Egypt and went back home to
their father Jacob in Canaan. 26"Joseph is still
alive!" they told him. "He is the ruler of all Egypt!" Jacob was stunned and could not believe them.

27But when they told him all that Joseph had said to them, and when he saw the wagons which Joseph had sent to take him to
Egypt, he recovered from the shock. 28"My
son Joseph is still alive!" he said. "This is all I could ask for! I must go and see him before I die."

Jacob and His Family Go to Egypt

46 Jacob packed up all he had and went to Beersheba, where he offered sac-
rifices to the God of his father Isaac. 2God

Journeys to buy grain from Egypt in times of famine were so common that they are illustrated in Egyptian art.

spoke to him in a vision at night and called, “Jacob, Jacob!”

“Yes, here I am,” he answered.

3“I am God, the God of your father,” he said. “Do not be afraid to go to Egypt; I will make your descendants a great nation there. 4I will go with you to Egypt, and I will bring your descendants back to this land. Joseph will be with you when you die.”

5Jacob set out from Beersheba. His sons put him, their small children, and their wives in the wagons which the king of Egypt had sent. 6They took their livestock and the possessions they had acquired in Canaan and went to Egypt. Jacob took all his descendants with him: 7his sons, his grandsons, his daughters, and his granddaughters.

8The members of Jacob’s family who went to Egypt with him were his oldest son Reuben 9and Reuben’s sons: Hanoch, Pallu, Hezron, and Carmi. 10Simeon and his sons: Jemuel, Jamin, Ohad, Jachin, Zohar, and Shaul, the son of a Canaanite woman. 11Levi and his sons: Gershon, Kohath, and Merari. 12Judah and his sons: Shelah, Perez, and Zerah. (Judah’s other sons, Er and Onan, had died in Canaan.) Perez’ sons were Hezron and Hamul. 13Issachar and his sons: Tola, Puah, Jashub, and Shimron. 14Zebulun and his sons: Sered, Elon, and Jahleel. 15These are the sons that Leah had borne to Jacob in Mesopotamia, besides his daughter Dinah. In all, his descendants by Leah numbered thirty-three.

16Gad and his sons: Zephon, Haggi, Shuni, Ezbon, Eri, Arod, and Areli. 17Asher and his sons: Imnah, Ishvah, Ishvi, Beriah, and their sister Serah. Beriah’s sons were Heber and Malchiel. 18These sixteen are the descendants of Jacob by Zilpah, the slave woman whom Laban gave to his daughter Leah.

19Jacob’s wife Rachel bore him two sons: Joseph and Benjamin. 20In Egypt Joseph had two sons, Manasseh and Ephraim, by Asenath, the daughter of Potiphera, a priest in Heliopolis. 21Benjamin’s sons were Bela, Becher, Ashbel, Gera, Naaman, Ehi, Rosh, Muppim, Huppim, and Ard. 22These fourteen are the descendants of Jacob by Rachel.

23Dan and his son Hushim. 24Naphtali and his sons: Jahzeel, Guni, Jezer, and Shillem. 25These seven are the descendants of Jacob by Bilhah, the slave woman whom Laban gave to his daughter Rachel.

26The total number of the direct descendants of Jacob who went to Egypt was sixty-six, not including his sons’ wives. 27Two sons were born to Joseph in Egypt, bringing to seventy the total number of Jacob’s family who went there.

Jacob and His Family in Egypt

28Jacob sent Judah ahead to ask Joseph to meet them in Goshen. When they arrived, 29Joseph got in his chariot and went to Goshen to meet his father. When they met, Joseph threw his arms around his father’s neck and cried for a long time. 30Jacob said to Joseph, “I am ready to die, now that I have seen you and know that you are still alive.”

31Then Joseph said to his brothers and the rest of his father’s family, “I must go and tell the king that my brothers and all my father’s family, who were living in Canaan, have come to me. 32I will tell him that you are shepherds and take care of livestock and that you have brought your flocks and herds and everything else that belongs to you. 33When the king calls for you and asks what your occupation is, 34be sure to tell him that you have taken care of livestock all your lives, just as your ancestors did. In this way he will let you live in the region of Goshen.” Joseph said this because Egyptians will have nothing to do with shepherds.

47 So Joseph took five of his brothers and went to the king. He told him, “My father and my brothers have come from Canaan with their flocks, their herds, and all that they own. They are now in the region of Goshen.” 2He then presented his brothers to the king. 3The king asked them, “What is your occupation?”

“We are shepherds, sir, just as our ancestors were,” they answered. 4“We have come to live in this country, because in the land of Canaan the famine is so severe that there is no pasture for our flocks. Please give us

46:6 Acts 7:15 **46:20** Gen 41:50–52 **46:27** Acts 7:14

permission to live in the region of Goshen." [5]The king said to Joseph, "Now that your father and your brothers have arrived, [6]the land of Egypt is theirs. Let them settle in the region of Goshen, the best part of the land. And if there are any capable men among them, put them in charge of my own livestock."

[7]Then Joseph brought his father Jacob and presented him to the king. Jacob gave the king his blessing, [8]and the king asked him, "How old are you?"

[9]Jacob answered, "My life of wandering has lasted a hundred and thirty years. Those years have been few and difficult, unlike the long years of my ancestors in their wanderings." [10]Jacob gave the king a farewell blessing and left. [11]Then Joseph settled his father and his brothers in Egypt, giving them property in the best of the land near the city of Rameses, as the king had commanded. [12]Joseph provided food for his father, his brothers, and all the rest of his father's family, including the very youngest.

The Famine

[13]The famine was so severe that there was no food anywhere, and the people of Egypt and Canaan became weak with hunger. [14]As they bought grain, Joseph collected all the money and took it to the palace. [15]When all the money in Egypt and Canaan was spent, the Egyptians came to Joseph and said, "Give us food! Don't let us die. Do something! Our money is all gone."

[16]Joseph answered, "Bring your livestock; I will give you food in exchange for it if your money is all gone." [17]So they brought their livestock to Joseph, and he gave them food in exchange for their horses, sheep, goats, cattle, and donkeys. That year he supplied them with food in exchange for all their livestock.

[18]The following year they came to him and said, "We will not hide the fact from you, sir, that our money is all gone and our livestock belongs to you. There is nothing left to give you except our bodies and our lands. [19]Don't let us die. Do something! Don't let our fields be deserted. Buy us and our land in exchange for food. We will be the king's slaves, and he will own our land. Give us grain to keep us alive and seed so that we can plant our fields."

[20]Joseph bought all the land in Egypt for the king. Every Egyptian was forced to sell his land, because the famine was so severe; and all the land became the king's property. [21]Joseph made slaves of the people from one end of Egypt to the other. [22]The only land he did not buy was the land that belonged to the priests. They did not have to sell their lands, because the king gave them an allowance to live on. [23]Joseph said to the people, "You see, I have now bought you and your lands for the king. Here is seed for you to sow in your fields. [24]At the time of harvest you must give one-fifth to the king. You can use the rest for seed and for food for yourselves and your families."

[25]They answered, "You have saved our lives; you have been good to us, sir, and we will be the king's slaves." [26]So Joseph made it a law for the land of Egypt that one-fifth of the harvest should belong to the king. This law still remains in force today. Only the lands of the priests did not become the king's property.

Jacob's Last Request

[27]The Israelites lived in Egypt in the region of Goshen, where they became rich and had many children. [28]Jacob lived in Egypt seventeen years, until he was a hundred and forty-seven years old. [29]When the time drew near for him to die, he called for his son Joseph and said to him, "Place your hand between my thighs[w] and make a solemn vow that you will not bury me in Egypt. [30]I want to be buried where my fathers are; carry me out of Egypt and bury me where they are buried."

Joseph answered, "I will do as you say."

[31]Jacob said, "Make a vow that you will." Joseph made the vow, and Jacob gave thanks there on his bed.

[w] **47:29** PLACE . . . THIGHS: *See 24:2.*

47:29, 30 Gen 49:29–32; 50:6

Jacob Blesses Ephraim and Manasseh

48 Some time later Joseph was told that his father was ill. So he took his two sons, Manasseh and Ephraim, and went to see Jacob. 2When Jacob was told that his son Joseph had come to see him, he gathered his strength and sat up in bed. 3Jacob said to Joseph, "Almighty God appeared to me at Luz in the land of Canaan and blessed me. 4He said to me, 'I will give you many children, so that your descendants will become many nations; I will give this land to your descendants as their possession forever.' "

5Jacob continued, "Joseph, your two sons, who were born to you in Egypt before I came here, belong to me; Ephraim and Manasseh are just as much my sons as Reuben and Simeon. 6If you have any more sons, they will not be considered mine; the inheritance they get will come through Ephraim and Manasseh. 7I am doing this because of your mother Rachel. To my great sorrow she died in the land of Canaan, not far from Ephrath, as I was returning from Mesopotamia. I buried her there beside the road to Ephrath." (Ephrath is now known as Bethlehem.)

8When Jacob saw Joseph's sons, he asked, "Who are these boys?"

9Joseph answered, "These are my sons, whom God has given me here in Egypt."

Jacob said, "Bring them to me so that I may bless them." 10Jacob's eyesight was failing because of his age, and he could not see very well. Joseph brought the boys to him, and he hugged them and kissed them. 11Jacob said to Joseph, "I never expected to see you again, and now God has even let me see your children." 12Then Joseph took them from Jacob's lap and bowed down before him with his face to the ground.

13Joseph put Ephraim at Jacob's left and Manasseh at his right. 14But Jacob crossed his hands, and put his right hand on the head of Ephraim, even though he was the younger, and his left hand on the head of Manasseh, who was the older. 15Then he blessed Joseph:[x]

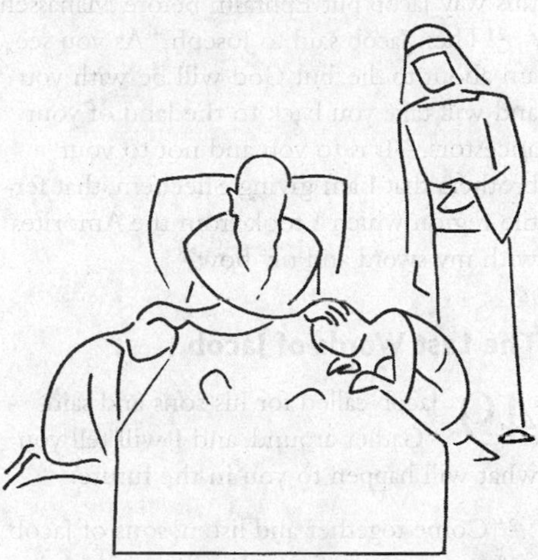

"May God . . . bless these boys!" (48:15)

"May God, whom my fathers Abraham
and Isaac served, bless these boys!
May God, who has led me to this very
day, bless them!
16May the angel, who has rescued me from
all harm, bless them!
May my name and the name of my
fathers Abraham and Isaac live on
through these boys!
May they have many children, many
descendants!"

17Joseph was upset when he saw that his father had put his right hand on Ephraim's head; so he took his father's hand to move it from Ephraim's head to the head of Manasseh. 18He said to his father, "Not that way, father. This is the older boy; put your right hand on his head."

19His father refused, saying, "I know, son, I know. Manasseh's descendants will also become a great people. But his younger brother will be greater than he, and his descendants will become great nations."

20So he blessed them that day, saying, "The

[x] **48:15** JOSEPH: *In blessing Ephraim and Manasseh, Jacob was in fact blessing Joseph.*

48:3, 4 Gen 28:13, 14 **48:7** Gen 35:16–19 **48:20** Heb 11:21

Jacob adopted Joseph's sons as his own. Read about it in Genesis 48:5–7.

Israelites will use your names when they pronounce blessings. They will say, 'May God make you like Ephraim and Manasseh.' " In this way Jacob put Ephraim before Manasseh.
21 Then Jacob said to Joseph, "As you see, I am about to die, but God will be with you and will take you back to the land of your ancestors.
22 It is to you and not to your brothers that I am giving Shechem, that fertile region which I took from the Amorites with my sword and my bow."

The Last Words of Jacob

49 Jacob called for his sons and said, "Gather around, and I will tell you what will happen to you in the future:

2 "Come together and listen, sons of Jacob.
Listen to your father Israel.

3 "Reuben, my first-born, you are my strength
And the first child of my manhood,
The proudest and strongest of all my sons.
4 You are like a raging flood,
But you will not be the most important,
For you slept with my concubine
And dishonored your father's bed.

5 "Simeon and Levi are brothers.
They use their weapons to commit violence.
6 I will not join in their secret talks,
Nor will I take part in their meetings,
For they killed people in anger
And they crippled bulls for sport.
7 A curse be on their anger, because it is so fierce,
And on their fury, because it is so cruel.
I will scatter them throughout the land of Israel.
I will disperse them among its people.

8 "Judah, your brothers will praise you.
You hold your enemies by the neck.
Your brothers will bow down before you.
9 Judah is like a lion,
Killing his victim and returning to his den,
Stretching out and lying down.
No one dares disturb him.
10 Judah will hold the royal scepter,
And his descendants will always rule.
Nations will bring him tribute[y]
And bow in obedience before him.
11 He ties his young donkey to a grapevine,
To the very best of the vines.
He washes his clothes in blood-red wine.
12 His eyes are bloodshot from drinking wine,
His teeth white from drinking milk.[z]

13 "Zebulun will live beside the sea.
His shore will be a haven for ships.
His territory will reach as far as Sidon.

14 "Issachar is no better than a donkey
That lies stretched out between its saddlebags.
15 But he sees that the resting place is good
And that the land is delightful.
So he bends his back to carry the load
And is forced to work as a slave.

16 "Dan will be a ruler for his people.
They will be like the other tribes of Israel.
17 Dan will be a snake at the side of the road,
A poisonous snake beside the path,
That strikes at the horse's heel,
So that the rider is thrown off backward.

18 "I wait for your deliverance, LORD.

19 "Gad will be attacked by a band of robbers,
But he will turn and pursue them.

20 "Asher's land will produce rich food.
He will provide food fit for a king.

21 "Naphtali is a deer that runs free,
Who bears lovely fawns.[a]

22 "Joseph is like a wild donkey by a spring,

[y] **49:10** *Probable text* Nations . . . tribute; *Hebrew unclear.* [z] **49:12** His eyes . . . milk; *or* His eyes are darker than wine, his teeth are whiter than milk. [a] **49:21** Naphtali . . . fawns *or* Naphtali is a spreading tree that puts out lovely branches.

49:9 Num 24:9; Rev 5:5

Jacob's sons are the patriarchs, or fathers, of families that will become the twelve tribes of Israel.

Study it!

The Tribe of Judah

In his final words, Jacob blesses or curses each of his sons. Some of the blessings also include predictions of what will happen to each of the twelve tribes that descend from his sons. For example, Jacob predicted that people will bring Judah tribute and bow down before him. It was his way of saying that the tribe of Judah would become the strongest of the twelve tribes of Israel. He also predicted that Judah "will hold the royal scepter" (Genesis 49:10). This was another way of saying that a descendant of Judah would be king. Sure enough, King David was a descendant of Judah. You can read about him in the Second Book of Samuel.

Jesus was a descendant of David. He is often referred to as the Son of David. Jesus is the one who Jacob predicts "will always rule" (49:10). Jesus is the fulfillment of God's Covenant, or promise, with Abraham and Jacob.

— Genesis 49:8–12

A wild colt on a hillside.[b]
23 His enemies attack him fiercely
And pursue him with their bows and
arrows.
24 But his bow remains steady,
And his arms are made strong[c]
By the power of the Mighty God of Jacob,
By the Shepherd, the Protector of Israel.
25 It is your father's God who helps you,
The Almighty God who blesses you
With blessings of rain from above
And of deep waters from beneath the
ground,
Blessings of many cattle and children,
26 Blessings of grain and flowers,[d]
Blessings of ancient mountains,[e]
Delightful things from everlasting hills.
May these blessings rest on the head of
Joseph,
On the brow of the one set apart from his
brothers.

27 "Benjamin is like a vicious wolf.
Morning and evening he kills and
devours."

28 These are the twelve tribes of Israel, and
this is what their father said as he spoke a
suitable word of farewell to each son.

The Death and Burial of Jacob

29 Then Jacob commanded his sons, "Now
that I am going to join my people in death,
bury me with my fathers in the cave that is
in the field of Ephron the Hittite, 30 at
Machpelah east of Mamre in the land of
Canaan. Abraham bought this cave and field
from Ephron for a burial ground. 31 That is
where they buried Abraham and his wife
Sarah; that is where they buried Isaac and his
wife Rebecca; and that is where I buried
Leah. 32 The field and the cave in it were
bought from the Hittites. Bury me there."
33 When Jacob had finished giving instruc-
tions to his sons, he lay back down and died.

50 Joseph threw himself on his father,
crying and kissing his face. 2 Then
Joseph gave orders to embalm his father's
body. 3 It took forty days, the normal time
for embalming. The Egyptians mourned for
him seventy days.

4 When the time of mourning was over,
Joseph said to the king's officials, "Please take
this message to the king: 5 'When my father
was about to die, he made me promise him
that I would bury him in the tomb which

[b] **49:22** Joseph . . . hillside; *or* Joseph is like a tree by a spring, a fruitful tree that spreads over a wall.
[c] **49:24** But . . . strong; *or* But their bows were broken and splintered, the muscles of their arms torn apart.
[d] **49:26** *Probable text* grain and flowers; *Hebrew* your fathers are mightier than. [e] **49:26** *One ancient translation* ancient mountains; *Hebrew* my ancestors to.

49:30 Gen 23:3–20 **49:31** **a** Gen 25:9, 10; **b** Gen 35:29 **49:33** Acts 7:15 **50:5** Gen 47:29–31

he had prepared in the land of Canaan. So
please let me go and bury my father, and
then I will come back.' "
6 The king answered, "Go and bury your
father, as you promised you would."
7 So Joseph went to bury his father. All
the king's officials, the senior men of his
court, and all the leading men of Egypt
went with Joseph. 8 His family, his brothers,
and the rest of his father's family all went
with him. Only their small children and
their sheep, goats, and cattle stayed in the
region of Goshen. 9 Men in chariots and
men on horseback also went with him; it
was a huge group.
10 When they came to the threshing place
at Atad east of the Jordan, they mourned
loudly for a long time, and Joseph performed
mourning ceremonies for seven days.
11 When the citizens of Canaan saw those
people mourning at Atad, they said, "What a
solemn ceremony of mourning the Egyp-
tians are holding!" That is why the place was
named Abel Mizraim.[f]
12 So Jacob's sons did as he had com-
manded them; 13 they carried his body to
Canaan and buried it in the cave at Mach-
pelah east of Mamre in the field which
Abraham had bought from Ephron the Hit-
tite for a burial ground. 14 After Joseph had
buried his father, he returned to Egypt with
his brothers and all who had gone with him
for the funeral.

Joseph Reassures His Brothers

15 After the death of their father, Joseph's
brothers said, "What if Joseph still hates us
and plans to pay us back for all the harm we
did to him?" 16 So they sent a message to
Joseph: "Before our father died, 17 he told us
to ask you, 'Please forgive the crime your
brothers committed when they wronged
you.' Now please forgive us the wrong that
we, the servants of your father's God, have
done." Joseph cried when he received this
message.
18 Then his brothers themselves came and
bowed down before him. "Here we are
before you as your slaves," they said.
19 But Joseph said to them, "Don't be
afraid; I can't put myself in the place of God.
20 You plotted evil against me, but God
turned it into good, in order to preserve the
lives of many people who are alive today
because of what happened. 21 You have noth-
ing to fear. I will take care of you and your
children." So he reassured them with kind
words that touched their hearts.

Study it!

To Be Continued

The Book of Genesis ends on a positive note. Jacob and his family are reunited. He blesses his sons and their children and tells them what they can expect in the future. Then he dies a happy man at a very old age. Joseph's brothers were afraid that Joseph would get even with them after the death of Jacob, but Joseph told them not to be afraid.

Joseph and his brothers and their families continued to live in Egypt, far away from home and far from the land that God promised to Abraham and his descendants. The next book of the Bible, Exodus, is a continuation of the story, long after the death of Joseph and his brothers.

Life will get very difficult for the descendants of Abraham, Isaac, and Jacob. But as always, God will be with them. The main message of Genesis is that God will not abandon his Creation, his promises, or his people.

— Genesis; chapter 50

f **50:11** ABEL MIZRAIM: *This name sounds like the Hebrew for "mourning of the Egyptians."*
50:13 Acts 7:16

The Death of Joseph

22Joseph continued to live in Egypt with
his father's family; he was a hundred and ten
years old when he died. 23He lived to see
Ephraim's children and grandchildren. He
also lived to receive the children of Machir
son of Manasseh into the family. 24He said to
his brothers, "I am about to die, but God
will certainly take care of you and lead you
out of this land to the land he solemnly
promised to Abraham, Isaac, and Jacob."
25Then Joseph asked his people to make a
vow. "Promise me," he said, "that when God
leads you to that land, you will take my body
with you." 26So Joseph died in Egypt at the
age of a hundred and ten. They embalmed
his body and put it in a coffin.

50:25 Ex 13:19; Josh 24:32; Heb 11:22

Your Next Step

Congratulations on finishing the Book of Genesis! Use this space to write your thoughts and questions about this book. If you are following the suggested reading plan, go on to the Book of Exodus to find out how God delivered the people from slavery in Egypt.

THE BOOK OF Exodus

A bold escape! A reluctant hero! Spectacular effects! Plagues of insects! Outbursts of rage! Passion and tenderness! Sounds like a blockbuster film, doesn't it? Hollywood film producers thought so too. In fact, only the story of Jesus has probably been the subject of more Bible-based movies than the Book of Exodus.

Aside from some great movie moments, Exodus is the story of how the Israelites came to be God's people. It is a story of slavery and freedom from slavery, promises and broken promises, anger and compassion, disappointment and hope. Led by Moses and his siblings, the Israelites came to know that God loves them, watches over them, and is *always* faithful.

Headlines

- Midwives Trick Pharaoh, Boy Lives (1:15—2:10)
- God's Voice Heard in Burning Bush! (3:1—4:17)
- Forecast: Hail with a Chance of Locusts (7:14—10:29)
- Angel of Death Passes Over (12:21–42)
- Red Sea Parts for Israelites (14:1–31)
- God Lays Down the Laws (20:1–17)
- Doubting Israelites Worship Gold Calf (32:1–24)

FACTOIDS

Who wrote this book? Exodus was written by an unknown author, possibly a group. The author collected stories that had been passed down for hundreds of years and put them together to make this book.

How does it fit into the Bible? It is the second book of the Bible. It is also the second book of the Pentateuch, that is, the Jewish Torah.

Who are the main characters? Moses, the Israelites, and Yahweh (God)

How is it organized? It has two main sections. The first section is about the freeing of the Israelites from slavery and their journey out of Egypt. The second section begins in chapter 19, when the Israelites reach Mount Sinai.

Important themes

- God frees people from slavery.
- God is always with the Chosen People, taking care of them.
- The Covenant between God and his people is rooted in love.

EXODUS

The Israelites Are Treated Cruelly in Egypt

1 The sons of Jacob who went to Egypt with him, each with his family, were 2Reuben, Simeon, Levi, Judah, 3Issachar, Zebulun, Benjamin, 4Dan, Naphtali, Gad, and Asher. 5The total number of these people directly descended from Jacob was seventy.[a] His son Joseph was already in Egypt. 6In the course of time Joseph, his brothers, and all the rest of that generation died, 7but their descendants, the Israelites, had many children and became so numerous and strong that Egypt was filled with them.

8Then, a new king, who knew nothing about Joseph, came to power in Egypt. 9He said to his people, "These Israelites are so numerous and strong that they are a threat to us. 10In case of war they might join our enemies in order to fight against us, and might escape from[b] the country. We must find some way to keep them from becoming even more numerous." 11So the Egyptians put slave drivers over them to crush their spirits with hard labor. The Israelites built the cities of Pithom and Rameses to serve as supply centers for the king. 12But the more the Egyptians oppressed the Israelites, the more they increased in number and the farther they spread through the land. The Egyptians came to fear the Israelites 13-14and made their lives miserable by forcing them into cruel slavery. They made them work on their building projects and in their fields, and they had no pity on them.

15Then the king of Egypt spoke to Shiphrah and Puah, the two midwives who helped the Hebrew women. 16"When you help the Hebrew women give birth," he said to them, "kill the baby if it is a boy; but if it is a girl, let it live." 17But the midwives were God-fearing and so did not obey the king; instead, they let the boys live. 18So the king sent for the midwives and asked them, "Why

Live it!

Doing the Right Thing

At the end of the Book of Genesis, life was good for the Israelites. But a few hundred years passed, and life was terrible. They were slaves and were treated cruelly by the Egyptians.

The family of Jacob's descendants—which was big to begin with—grew even bigger. His descendants numbered in the thousands. The Egyptians were afraid that the Israelites would gain power and take over. As a way of controlling the population, Pharaoh told the midwives—women skilled in helping with births—to kill all baby boys born to Hebrew women. Two midwives—Puah and Shiphrah—decided that it was the wrong thing to do. They knew they would be in trouble if Pharaoh found out, so they made up a story about why they did not kill the babies. Because of their decision to do the right thing, a baby boy named Moses grew up to free the Israelites from slavery and lead them out of Egypt.

Doing the right thing is not always easy, but it is always the best choice for those who want to be right with God.

— Exodus 1:15–22

[a] **1:5** *One ancient translation* seventy-five *(see Acts 7:14).* [b] **1:10** escape from; *or* take control of.

1:1–4 Gen 46:8–27 **1:7** Acts 7:17 **1:8** Acts 7:18 **1:10** Acts 7:19

are you doing this? Why are you letting the boys live?"

19 They answered, "The Hebrew women are not like Egyptian women; they give birth easily, and their babies are born before either of us gets there." 20-21 Because the midwives were God-fearing, God was good to them and gave them families of their own. And the Israelites continued to increase and become strong. 22 Finally the king issued a command to all his people: "Take every newborn Hebrew boy and throw him into the Nile, but let all the girls live."

The Birth of Moses

2 During this time a man from the tribe of Levi married a woman of his own tribe, 2 and she bore him a son. When she saw what a fine baby he was, she hid him for three months. 3 But when she could not hide him any longer, she took a basket made of reeds and covered it with tar to make it watertight. She put the baby in it and then placed it in the tall grass at the edge of the river. 4 The baby's sister stood some distance away to see what would happen to him.

5 The king's daughter came down to the river to bathe, while her servants walked along the bank. Suddenly she noticed the basket in the tall grass and sent a slave woman to get it. 6 The princess opened it and saw a baby boy. He was crying, and she felt sorry for him. "This is one of the Hebrew babies," she said.

The king's daughter . . . noticed the basket. (2:5)

7 Then his sister asked her, "Shall I go and call a Hebrew woman to nurse the baby for you?"

8 "Please do," she answered. So the girl went and brought the baby's own mother. 9 The princess told the woman, "Take this baby and nurse him for me, and I will pay you." So she took the baby and nursed him. 10 Later, when the child was old enough, she took him to the king's daughter, who adopted him as her own son. She said to herself, "I pulled him out of the water, and so I name him Moses."[c]

Moses Escapes to Midian

11 When Moses had grown up, he went out to visit his people, the Hebrews, and he saw how they were forced to do hard labor. He even saw an Egyptian kill a Hebrew, one of Moses' own people. 12 Moses looked all around, and when he saw that no one was watching, he killed the Egyptian and hid his body in the sand. 13 The next day he went back and saw two Hebrew men fighting. He said to the one who was in the wrong, "Why are you beating up a fellow Hebrew?"

14 The man answered, "Who made you our ruler and judge? Are you going to kill me just as you killed that Egyptian?" Then Moses was afraid and said to himself, "People have found out what I have done." 15-16 When the king heard about what had happened, he tried to have Moses killed, but Moses fled and went to live in the land of Midian.

One day, when Moses was sitting by a well, seven daughters of Jethro, the priest of Midian, came to draw water and fill the troughs for their father's sheep and goats. 17 But some shepherds drove Jethro's daughters away. Then Moses went to their rescue

[c] **2:10** MOSES: *This name sounds like the Hebrew for "pull out."*

1:22 Acts 7:19 **2:2** Acts 7:20; Heb 11:23 **2:10** Acts 7:21 **2:11–14** Acts 7:23–28 **2:11** Heb 11:24 **2:15** Acts 7:29; Heb 11:27

The king wanted all Jewish boys killed because they could be future leaders. Only men were expected to be leaders at that time.

are you doing this? Why are you letting the boys live?"

19 They answered, "The Hebrew women are not like Egyptian women; they give birth easily, and their babies are born before either of us gets there." 20-21 Because the midwives were God-fearing, God was good to them and gave them families of their own. And the Israelites continued to increase and become strong. 22 Finally the king issued a command to all his people: "Take every newborn Hebrew boy and throw him into the Nile, but let all the girls live."

The Birth of Moses

2 During this time a man from the tribe of Levi married a woman of his own tribe, 2 and she bore him a son. When she saw what a fine baby he was, she hid him for three months. 3 But when she could not hide him any longer, she took a basket made of reeds and covered it with tar to make it watertight. She put the baby in it and then placed it in the tall grass at the edge of the river. 4 The baby's sister stood some distance away to see what would happen to him.

5 The king's daughter came down to the river to bathe, while her servants walked along the bank. Suddenly she noticed the basket in the tall grass and sent a slave

The king's daughter . . . noticed the basket. (2:5)

woman to get it. 6 The princess opened it and saw a baby boy. He was crying, and she felt sorry for him. "This is one of the Hebrew babies," she said.

7 Then his sister asked her, "Shall I go and call a Hebrew woman to nurse the baby for you?"

8 "Please do," she answered. So the girl went and brought the baby's own mother. 9 The princess told the woman, "Take this baby and nurse him for me, and I will pay you." So she took the baby and nursed him. 10 Later, when the child was old enough, she took him to the king's daughter, who adopted him as her own son. She said to herself, "I pulled him out of the water, and so I name him Moses."[c]

Moses Escapes to Midian

11 When Moses had grown up, he went out to visit his people, the Hebrews, and he saw how they were forced to do hard labor. He even saw an Egyptian kill a Hebrew, one of Moses' own people. 12 Moses looked all around, and when he saw that no one was watching, he killed the Egyptian and hid his body in the sand. 13 The next day he went back and saw two Hebrew men fighting. He said to the one who was in the wrong, "Why are you beating up a fellow Hebrew?"

14 The man answered, "Who made you our ruler and judge? Are you going to kill me just as you killed that Egyptian?" Then Moses was afraid and said to himself, "People have found out what I have done." 15-16 When the king heard about what had happened, he tried to have Moses killed, but Moses fled and went to live in the land of Midian.

One day, when Moses was sitting by a well, seven daughters of Jethro, the priest of Midian, came to draw water and fill the troughs for their father's sheep and goats. 17 But some shepherds drove Jethro's daughters away. Then Moses went to their rescue

[c] **2:10** MOSES: *This name sounds like the Hebrew for "pull out."*

1:22 Acts 7:19 **2:2** Acts 7:20; Heb 11:23 **2:10** Acts 7:21 **2:11–14** Acts 7:23–28 **2:11** Heb 11:24 **2:15** Acts 7:29; Heb 11:27

The king wanted all Jewish boys killed because they could be future leaders. Only men were expected to be leaders at that time.

EXODUS

The Israelites Are Treated Cruelly in Egypt

1 The sons of Jacob who went to Egypt
with him, each with his family, were
2Reuben, Simeon, Levi, Judah, 3Issachar,
Zebulun, Benjamin, 4Dan, Naphtali, Gad,
and Asher. 5The total number of these peo-
ple directly descended from Jacob was seven-
ty.[a] His son Joseph was already in Egypt. 6In
the course of time Joseph, his brothers, and
all the rest of that generation died, 7but their
descendants, the Israelites, had many children
and became so numerous and strong that
Egypt was filled with them.
8Then, a new king, who knew nothing
about Joseph, came to power in Egypt. 9He
said to his people, "These Israelites are so
numerous and strong that they are a threat to
us. 10In case of war they might join our ene-
mies in order to fight against us, and might
escape from[b] the country. We must find some
way to keep them from becoming even
more numerous." 11So the Egyptians put
slave drivers over them to crush their spirits
with hard labor. The Israelites built the cities
of Pithom and Rameses to serve as supply
centers for the king. 12But the more the
Egyptians oppressed the Israelites, the more
they increased in number and the farther
they spread through the land. The Egyptians
came to fear the Israelites 13-14and made
their lives miserable by forcing them into
cruel slavery. They made them work on their
building projects and in their fields, and they
had no pity on them.
15Then the king of Egypt spoke to
Shiphrah and Puah, the two midwives who
helped the Hebrew women. 16"When you
help the Hebrew women give birth," he said
to them, "kill the baby if it is a boy; but if it
is a girl, let it live." 17But the midwives were
God-fearing and so did not obey the king;
instead, they let the boys live. 18So the king
sent for the midwives and asked them, "Why

Live it!

Doing the Right Thing

At the end of the Book of Genesis, life was good for the Israelites. But a few hundred years passed, and life was terrible. They were slaves and were treated cruelly by the Egyptians.

The family of Jacob's descendants—which was big to begin with—grew even bigger. His descendants numbered in the thousands. The Egyptians were afraid that the Israelites would gain power and take over. As a way of controlling the population, Pharaoh told the midwives—women skilled in helping with births—to kill all baby boys born to Hebrew women. Two midwives—Puah and Shiphrah—decided that it was the wrong thing to do. They knew they would be in trouble if Pharaoh found out, so they made up a story about why they did not kill the babies. Because of their decision to do the right thing, a baby boy named Moses grew up to free the Israelites from slavery and lead them out of Egypt.

Doing the right thing is not always easy, but it is always the best choice for those who want to be right with God.

— Exodus 1:15–22

[a] **1:5** *One ancient translation* seventy-five *(see Acts 7:14).* [b] **1:10** escape from; *or* take control of.

1:1–4 Gen 46:8–27 **1:7** Acts 7:17 **1:8** Acts 7:18 **1:10** Acts 7:19

Live it!

Standing Up for Right

Moses had a good life as the adopted son of Pharaoh's daughter. While his fellow Hebrews were working as slaves, Moses had the best of everything. Still, it bothered him when he saw people hurting others.

- **When he saw an Egyptian slave master beating a Hebrew slave, he was so angry that he killed the Egyptian (Exodus 2:11–12).**
- **He stepped in and tried to stop two Hebrews from fighting (2:13).**
- **He defended seven sisters against some shepherds and helped them get water (2:16–17).**

Moses should not have killed the slave master, and he ran away to save his life. God knew that his heart was in the right place, though, and used Moses to lead the people out of Egypt.

When you see someone being hurt by the actions or words of others, how do you react? Do you always stand up for what is right? How is God using you to right the wrongs of the world?

— Exodus 2:11–17

and watered their animals for them. 18When
they returned to their father, he asked, "Why
have you come back so early today?"
19"An Egyptian rescued us from the shep-
herds," they answered, "and he even drew
water for us and watered our animals."
20"Where is he?" he asked his daughters.
"Why did you leave the man out there? Go
and invite him to eat with us."

21So Moses decided to live there, and
Jethro gave him his daughter Zipporah in
marriage, 22who bore him a son. Moses said
to himself, "I am a foreigner in this land, and
so I name him Gershom."[d]
23Years later the king of Egypt died, but
the Israelites were still groaning under their
slavery and cried out for help. Their cry
went up to God, 24who heard their groaning
and remembered his covenant with Abra-
ham, Isaac, and Jacob. 25He saw the slavery of
the Israelites and was concerned for them.[e]

God Calls Moses

3 One day while Moses was taking care
of the sheep and goats of his father-in-
law Jethro, the priest of Midian, he led the
flock across the desert and came to Sinai, the
holy mountain. 2There the angel of the
LORD appeared to him as a flame coming
from the middle of a bush. Moses saw that
the bush was on fire but that it was not
burning up. 3"This is strange," he thought.
"Why isn't the bush burning up? I will go
closer and see."
4When the LORD saw that Moses was
coming closer, he called to him from the
middle of the bush and said, "Moses! Moses!"
He answered, "Yes, here I am."
5God said, "Do not come any closer. Take
off your sandals, because you are standing on
holy ground. 6I am the God of your ances-
tors, the God of Abraham, Isaac, and Jacob."
So Moses covered his face, because he was
afraid to look at God.
7Then the LORD said, "I have seen how
cruelly my people are being treated in
Egypt; I have heard them cry out to be res-
cued from their slave drivers. I know all
about their sufferings, 8and so I have come
down to rescue them from the Egyptians
and to bring them out of Egypt to a spa-
cious land, one which is rich and fertile and
in which the Canaanites, the Hittites, the
Amorites, the Perizzites, the Hivites, and the
Jebusites now live. 9I have indeed heard the
cry of my people, and I see how the Egyp-
tians are oppressing them. 10Now I am

[d] **2:22** GERSHOM: *This name sounds like the Hebrew for "foreigner."* [e] **2:25** was concerned for them; *one ancient translation* revealed himself to them.

2:24 Gen 15:13, 14 **3:2–10** Acts 7:30–34

Pray it!

A God of Many Names

When Moses asks for God's name, God tells him it is "I am who I am." Jews consider this name of God to be too sacred to say or even to write. To make sure no one reading the Hebrew Bible accidentally pronounced the name of God, Jewish scholars used the vowel symbols for the word "Lord" when writing the consonants for God's name (YHWH). Readers encountered this unusual spelling in the text would then either say "Lord" or "the Name." In a similar way, many English Bibles signal the specialness of God's name by representing it as "LORD".

God is a God of many names. We call God healer, creator, and comforter. We say God is a God of hope, a wonder worker, and our eternal friend. We talk about God the Father and sometimes also God as Mother.

What names for God do you hear in the words and music during Mass? Which names are most meaningful to you? Make a list of your favorite names for God. Each day, say one name over and over and think about what it means.

— Exodus 3:14

sending you to the king of Egypt so that you
can lead my people out of his country."
11 But Moses said to God, "I am nobody.
How can I go to the king and bring the
Israelites out of Egypt?"
12 God answered, "I will be with you, and
when you bring the people out of Egypt,
you will worship me on this mountain. That
will be the proof that I have sent you."
13 But Moses replied, "When I go to the
Israelites and say to them, 'The God of your
ancestors sent me to you,' they will ask me,
'What is his name?' So what can I tell them?"
14 God said, "I am who I am. You must tell
them: 'The one who is called I AM[f] has sent
me to you.' 15 Tell the Israelites that I, the
LORD, the God of their ancestors, the God
of Abraham, Isaac, and Jacob, have sent you
to them. This is my name forever; this is
what all future generations are to call me.
16 Go and gather the leaders of Israel togeth-
er and tell them that I, the LORD, the God
of their ancestors, the God of Abraham,
Isaac, and Jacob, appeared to you. Tell them
that I have come to them and have seen
what the Egyptians are doing to them. 17 I
have decided that I will bring them out of
Egypt, where they are being treated cruelly,
and will take them to a rich and fertile
land—the land of the Canaanites, the Hit-
tites, the Amorites, the Perizzites, the
Hivites, and the Jebusites.
18 "My people will listen to what you say
to them. Then you must go with the leaders

"I am who I am. . . . This is my name forever." (3:14-15)

[f] **3:14** I am who I am . . . I AM; *or* I will be who I will be . . . I WILL BE. *"I am" sounds like the Hebrew name Yahweh traditionally transliterated as Jehovah. This name is represented in this translation by "the LORD" in capital letters, following a usage which is widespread in English versions.*

3:13 Ex 6:2, 3 **3:14** Rev 1:4, 8

of Israel to the king of Egypt and say to him,
'The LORD, the God of the Hebrews, has
revealed himself to us. Now allow us to travel
three days into the desert to offer sacrifices to
the LORD, our God.' 19I know that the king
of Egypt will not let you go unless he is
forced to do so. 20But I will use my power
and will punish Egypt by doing terrifying
things there. After that he will let you go.
21"I will make the Egyptians respect you
so that when my people leave, they will not
go empty-handed. 22Every Israelite woman
will go to her Egyptian neighbors and to
any Egyptian woman living in her house and
will ask for clothing and for gold and silver
jewelry. The Israelites will put these things
on their sons and daughters and carry away
the wealth of the Egyptians."

God Gives Moses Miraculous Power

4 Then Moses answered the LORD, "But
suppose the Israelites do not believe me
and will not listen to what I say. What shall I
do if they say that you did not appear to me?"
2So the LORD asked him, "What are you
holding?"
"A walking stick," he answered.
3The LORD said, "Throw it on the
ground." When Moses threw it down, it
turned into a snake, and he ran away from it.
4Then the LORD said to Moses, "Reach
down and pick it up by the tail." So Moses
reached down and caught it, and it became a
walking stick again. 5The LORD said, "Do
this to prove to the Israelites that the LORD,
the God of their ancestors, the God of Abra-
ham, Isaac, and Jacob, has appeared to you."
6The LORD spoke to Moses again, "Put
your hand inside your robe." Moses obeyed;
and when he took his hand out, it was dis-
eased, covered with white spots, like snow.
7Then the LORD said, "Put your hand inside
your robe again." He did so, and when he
took it out this time, it was healthy, just like
the rest of his body. 8The LORD said, "If they
will not believe you or be convinced by the

3:21, 22 Ex 12:35, 36 **3:21** Wis 10:17

Live It! Exod

Moses' ...

Are you self-conscious about your height or your weight? Do you have a funny scar or wild hair? Do you believe that you're not very smart? Are you afraid of being made fun of? So was Moses.

Moses kept trying to tell God that he was the wrong guy for the job of leading the Israelites out of Egypt. He kept coming up with excuses. In Exodus, chapter 4, we find out that Moses had a speech problem and he was self-conscious about it. "I am a poor speaker, slow and hesitant" (Exodus 4:10). God did not back down though. God knew that Moses could do the job and promised to help him. Aaron would be his assistant, God said. Aaron would do the speaking. Moses would do the leading.

God created Moses—and you—for a purpose. God loves you just the way you are and plans to use every bit of who you are to build a better world. You are a perfect creation in God's eyes—flaws and all.

— Exodus 4:1–17

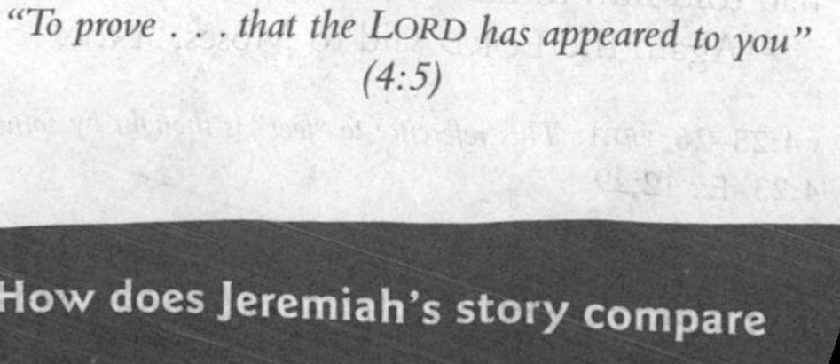

"To prove . . . that the LORD has appeared to you" (4:5)

Read chapter 1 in the Book of Jeremiah. How does Jeremiah's story compare with Moses' story in Exodus, chapter 3?

…one will convince
…these two miracles they
…lieve you, and if they refuse to
…at you say, take some water from
…and pour it on the ground. The
…will turn into blood."
10But Moses said, "No, LORD, don't send
me. I have never been a good speaker, and
I haven't become one since you began to
speak to me. I am a poor speaker, slow and
hesitant."
11The LORD said to him, "Who gives man
his mouth? Who makes him deaf or dumb?
Who gives him sight or makes him blind? It
is I, the LORD. 12Now, go! I will help you to
speak, and I will tell you what to say."
13But Moses answered, "No, Lord, please
send someone else."
14At this the LORD became angry with
Moses and said, "What about your brother
Aaron, the Levite? I know that he can speak
well. In fact, he is now coming to meet you
and will be glad to see you. 15You can speak
to him and tell him what to say. I will help
both of you to speak, and I will tell you both
what to do. 16He will be your spokesman
and speak to the people for you. Then you
will be like God, telling him what to say.
17Take this walking stick with you; for with
it you will perform miracles."

Moses Returns to Egypt

18Then Moses went back to Jethro, his
father-in-law, and said to him, "Please let me
go back to my relatives in Egypt to see if
they are still alive." Jethro agreed and told
him good-bye.
19While Moses was still in Midian, the
LORD said to him, "Go back to Egypt, for all
those who wanted to kill you are dead." 20So
Moses took his wife and his sons, put them
on a donkey, and set out with them for
Egypt, carrying the walking stick that God
had told him to take.
21Again the LORD said to Moses, "Now
that you are going back to Egypt, be sure to
perform before the king all the miracles
which I have given you the power to do.
But I will make the king stubborn, and he
will not let the people go. 22Then you must
tell him that I, the LORD, say, 'Israel is my
first-born son. 23I told you to let my son go,
so that he might worship me, but you
refused. Now I am going to kill your first-
born son.' "
24At a camping place on the way to
Egypt, the LORD met Moses and tried to kill
him. 25-26Then Zipporah, his wife, took a
sharp stone, cut off the foreskin of her son,
and touched Moses' feet[g] with it. Because of
the rite of circumcision she said to Moses,
"You are a husband of blood to me." And so
the LORD spared Moses' life.
27Meanwhile the LORD had said to Aaron,
"Go into the desert to meet Moses." So he
went to meet him at the holy mountain; and
when he met him, he kissed him. 28Then
Moses told Aaron everything that the LORD
had said when he told him to return to
Egypt; he also told him about the miracles
which the LORD had ordered him to per-
form. 29So Moses and Aaron went to Egypt
and gathered all the Israelite leaders together.
30Aaron told them everything that the LORD
had said to Moses, and then Moses per-
formed all the miracles in front of the peo-
ple. 31They believed, and when they heard
that the LORD had come to them and had
seen how they were being treated cruelly,
they bowed down and worshiped.

Moses and Aaron before the King of Egypt

5 Then Moses and Aaron went to the
king of Egypt and said, "The LORD, the
God of Israel, says, 'Let my people go, so that
they can hold a festival in the desert to
honor me.' "
2"Who is the LORD?" the king demand-
ed. "Why should I listen to him and let Israel

g **4:25–26** FEET: *This reference to "feet" is thought by some to be a euphemism for the genitals.*
4:23 Ex 12:29

"Now, go! I will help you to speak, and I will tell you what to say"
(Exodus 4:12).

go? I do not know the LORD; and I will not
let Israel go."
3 Moses and Aaron replied, "The God of
the Hebrews has revealed himself to us. Allow
us to travel three days into the desert to offer
sacrifices to the LORD our God. If we don't
do so, he will kill us with disease or by war."
4 The king said to Moses and Aaron,
"What do you mean by making the people
neglect their work? Get those slaves back to
work! 5 You people have become more
numerous than the Egyptians. And now you
want to stop working!"
6 That same day the king commanded the
Egyptian slave drivers and the Israelite fore-
men: 7 "Stop giving the people straw for
making bricks. Make them go and find it for
themselves. 8 But still require them to make
the same number of bricks as before, not one
brick less. They don't have enough work to
do, and that is why they keep asking me to
let them go and offer sacrifices to their God!
9 Make them work harder and keep them
busy, so that they won't have time to listen
to a pack of lies."
10 The slave drivers and the Israelite fore-
men went out and said to the Israelites, "The
king has said that he will not supply you
with any more straw. 11 He says that you
must go and get it for yourselves wherever
you can find it, but you must still make the
same number of bricks." 12 So the people
went all over Egypt looking for straw. 13 The
slave drivers kept trying to force them to
make the same number of bricks every day
as they had made when they were given
straw. 14 The Egyptian slave drivers beat the
Israelite foremen, whom they had put in
charge of the work. They demanded, "Why
aren't you people making the same number
of bricks that you made before?"
15 Then the foremen went to the king and
complained, "Why do you do this to us, Your
Majesty? 16 We are given no straw, but we are
still ordered to make bricks! And now we are
being beaten. It is your people that are at
fault."
17 The king answered, "You are lazy and
don't want to work, and that is why you ask
me to let you go and offer sacrifices to the
LORD. 18 Now get back to work! You will
not be given any straw, but you must still
make the same number of bricks." 19 The
foremen realized that they were in trouble
when they were told that they had to make
the same number of bricks every day as they
had made before.
20 As they were leaving, they met Moses
and Aaron, who were waiting for them.
21 They said to Moses and Aaron, "The

Live it!

Now What?

Moses and Aaron did just as God wanted them to do. They returned to Egypt to tell the king to free the Israelites. Everything went according to the plan except for one thing: the king refused. In fact, he treated the Israelites even more cruelly than before. Moses and Aaron weren't sure what to do next.

Did you ever try to fix something that was wrong, only to have it turn out worse than before? For example, you might have decided to stop cheating, only to be accused by a teacher of copying someone's answers on a big test. Maybe you tried to patch up a relationship with someone, but had a huge fight instead.

When that happens to you, follow Moses' example and do two things:

- **Talk to God. Of course God knew what happened, but Moses made his feelings known anyway.**
- **Be patient. God had a plan to change Pharaoh's mind, but it would take time. Moses had to let God do his work.**

Bad things happen to everyone, but if you are right with God, everything will work out. Believe it!

— Exodus 5:1–22

LORD has seen what you have done and will
punish you for making the king and his offi-
cers hate us. You have given them an excuse
to kill us."

Moses Complains to the LORD

22 Then Moses turned to the LORD again
and said, "Lord, why do you mistreat your
people? Why did you send me here? 23 Ever
since I went to the king to speak for you, he
has treated them cruelly. And you have done
nothing to help them!"

6 Then the LORD said to Moses, "Now
you are going to see what I will do to
the king. I will force him to let my people
go. In fact, I will force him to drive them
out of his land."

God Calls Moses

2 God spoke to Moses and said, "I am the
LORD. 3 I appeared to Abraham, to Isaac, and
to Jacob as Almighty God, but I did not
make myself known to them by my holy
name, the LORD.[h] 4 I also made my covenant
with them, promising to give them the land
of Canaan, the land in which they had lived
as foreigners. 5 Now I have heard the groan-
ing of the Israelites, whom the Egyptians
have enslaved, and I have remembered my
covenant. 6 So tell the Israelites that I say to
them, 'I am the LORD; I will rescue you and
set you free from your slavery to the Egyp-
tians. I will raise my mighty arm to bring ter-
rible punishment upon them, and I will save
you. 7 I will make you my own people, and I
will be your God. You will know that I am
the LORD your God when I set you free
from slavery in Egypt. 8 I will bring you to
the land that I solemnly promised to give to
Abraham, Isaac, and Jacob; and I will give it
to you as your own possession. I am the
LORD.' " 9 Moses told this to the Israelites, but
they would not listen to him, because their
spirit had been broken by their cruel slavery.
10 Then the LORD said to Moses, 11 "Go
and tell the king of Egypt that he must let
the Israelites leave his land."
12 But Moses replied, "Even the Israelites

Live it!

Not Me, Lord!

Logan was fed up. "I can't do anything about stuff that happens in places I don't know anything about!" he said. He kept hearing about how young people could make a difference, how they could change the world. He was tired of hearing that it was all up to him. His parents wouldn't let him stay up past 9 o'clock on school nights. Like Moses, Logan was thinking, "How could I change the world?"

One day Logan saw a poster: "We must be the change we wish to see in the world." At first, he was confused, but when he thought about it, it started to make sense. He could make things better in *his* world. If he was kind to people, those people might start doing nice things for others. And on it would go.

Logan secretly started doing things for others every day. His kindness changed his attitude. It made people smile. It changed his world—one kind act at a time.

— Exodus 6:12–13

will not listen to me, so why should the
king? I am such a poor speaker."
13 The LORD commanded Moses and
Aaron: "Tell the Israelites and the king of
Egypt that I have ordered you to lead the
Israelites out of Egypt."

The Family Record of Moses and Aaron

14 Reuben, Jacob's first-born, had four
sons: Hanoch, Pallu, Hezron, and Carmi;
they were the ancestors of the clans that bear

[h] **6:3** THE LORD: *See 3:14.*
6:2, 3 Gen 17:1; 28:3; 35:11; Ex 3:13–15

their names. 15Simeon had six sons: Jemuel,
Jamin, Ohad, Jachin, Zohar, and Shaul, the
son of a Canaanite woman; they were the
ancestors of the clans that bear their names.
16Levi had three sons: Gershon, Kohath, and
Merari; they were the ancestors of the clans
that bear their names. Levi lived 137 years.
17Gershon had two sons: Libni and Shimei,
and they had many descendants. 18Kohath
had four sons: Amram, Izhar, Hebron, and
Uzziel. Kohath lived 133 years. 19Merari had
two sons: Mahli and Mushi. These are the
clans of Levi with their descendants.

20Amram married his father's sister
Jochebed, who bore him Aaron and Moses.
Amram lived 137 years. 21Izhar had three
sons: Korah, Nepheg, and Zichri. 22Uzziel
also had three sons: Mishael, Elzaphan, and
Sithri.

23Aaron married Elisheba, the daughter of
Amminadab and sister of Nahshon; she bore
him Nadab, Abihu, Eleazar, and Ithamar.
24Korah had three sons: Assir, Elkanah, and
Abiasaph; they were the ancestors of the
divisions of the clan of Korah. 25Eleazar,
Aaron's son, married one of Putiel's daugh-
ters, who bore him Phinehas. These were the
heads of the families and the clans of the
tribe of Levi.

26Aaron and Moses were the ones to
whom the LORD said, "Lead the tribes of
Israel out of Egypt." 27They were the men
who told the king of Egypt to free the
Israelites.

The LORD's Command to Moses and Aaron

28When the LORD spoke to Moses in the
land of Egypt, 29he said, "I am the LORD. Tell
the king of Egypt everything I tell you."

30But Moses answered, "You know that
I am such a poor speaker; why should the
king listen to me?"

7 The LORD said, "I am going to make
you like God to the king, and your
brother Aaron will speak to him as your
prophet. 2Tell Aaron everything I command
you, and he will tell the king to let the
Israelites leave his country. 3-4But I will
make the king stubborn, and he will not lis-
ten to you, no matter how many terrifying
things I do in Egypt. Then I will bring
severe punishment on Egypt and lead the
tribes of my people out of the land. 5The
Egyptians will then know that I am the
LORD, when I raise my hand against them
and bring the Israelites out of their country."
6Moses and Aaron did what the LORD com-
manded. 7At the time when they spoke to
the king, Moses was eighty years old, and
Aaron was eighty-three.

Aaron's Walking Stick

8The LORD said to Moses and Aaron, 9"If
the king demands that you prove yourselves
by performing a miracle, tell Aaron to take
his walking stick and throw it down in front
of the king, and it will turn into a snake."
10So Moses and Aaron went to the king and
did as the LORD had commanded. Aaron
threw his walking stick down in front of the
king and his officers, and it turned into a
snake. 11Then the king called for his wise
men and magicians, and by their magic they
did the same thing. 12They threw down
their walking sticks, and the sticks turned
into snakes. But Aaron's stick swallowed
theirs. 13The king, however, remained stub-
born and, just as the LORD had said, the king
would not listen to Moses and Aaron.

Disasters Strike Egypt

Blood

14Then the LORD said to Moses, "The
king is very stubborn and refuses to let the
people go. 15So go and meet him in the
morning when he goes down to the Nile.
Take with you the walking stick that was
turned into a snake, and wait for him on the
riverbank. 16Then say to the king, 'The
LORD, the God of the Hebrews, sent me to

6:16–19 Num 3:17–20; 26:57, 58; 1 Chr 6:16–19 **7:3** Acts 7:36 **7:14–24** Wis 11:6–8

Moses tried *again* to get out of leading the Israelites. Read Exodus 6:10–13 and Exodus 6:28—7:7 to see what he said and how God replied.

tell you to let his people go, so that they can
worship him in the desert. But until now
you have not listened. 17 Now, Your Majesty,
the LORD says that you will find out who he
is by what he is going to do. Look, I am
going to strike the surface of the river with
this stick, and the water will be turned into
blood. 18 The fish will die, and the river will
stink so much that the Egyptians will not be
able to drink from it.' "

19 The LORD said to Moses, "Tell Aaron to
take his stick and hold it out over all the
rivers, canals, and pools in Egypt. The water
will become blood, and all over the land
there will be blood, even in the wooden tubs
and stone jars."

20 Then Moses and Aaron did as the LORD
commanded. In the presence of the king and
his officers, Aaron raised his stick and struck
the surface of the river, and all the water in
it was turned into blood. 21 The fish in the
river died, and it smelled so bad that the
Egyptians could not drink from it. There was
blood everywhere in Egypt. 22 Then the
king's magicians did the same thing by
means of their magic, and the king was as
stubborn as ever. Just as the LORD had said,
the king refused to listen to Moses and
Aaron. 23 Instead, he turned and went back
to his palace without paying any attention
even to this. 24 All the Egyptians dug along
the bank of the river for drinking water,
because they were not able to drink water
from the river.

25 Seven days passed after the LORD struck
the river.

Frogs

8 Then the LORD said to Moses, "Go to
the king and tell him that the LORD
says, 'Let my people go, so that they can
worship me. 2 If you refuse, I will punish
your country by covering it with frogs. 3 The
Nile will be so full of frogs that they will
leave it and go into your palace, your bed-
room, your bed, the houses of your officials
and your people, and even into your ovens
and baking pans. 4 They will jump up on
you, your people, and all your officials.' "

5 The LORD said to Moses, "Tell Aaron to
hold out his walking stick over the rivers,
the canals, and the pools, and make frogs
come up and cover the land of Egypt." 6 So
Aaron held it out over all the water, and the
frogs came out and covered the land. 7 But
the magicians used magic, and they also
made frogs come up on the land.

8 The king called for Moses and Aaron and
said, "Pray to the LORD to take away these

Study it!

Ten Terrible Troubles

The king would not listen to God's message through Moses and Aaron, so God did ten terrible things to Egypt to change the king's mind. Each one was worse than the others. Because of these ten plagues, God said, "The Egyptians will then know that I am the LORD" (Exodus 7:5).

Biblical scholars think that most of the plagues were like natural disasters that occasionally happened in Egypt anyway. What made them different in this story is that each plague started and stopped when Moses commanded it to.

Highlight or make a list of the ten plagues that God sent to the Egyptians. Which was the one that finally changed the king's mind and heart?

— Exodus 7:14–18

7:17 Rev 16:4

How old were Moses and Aaron when they started the journey out of Egypt? Check the first few verses of Exodus, chapter 7.

Pray it!

On Being Stubborn

The king of Egypt was stubborn, God. He refused to listen to you. His heart was hard. He was too proud to pay attention to your messengers.
I'm afraid that I'm like the king sometimes, God.
I laugh at people who are hurting.
I don't treat people fairly.
I ignore people who talk about you.
I refuse to change my ways.
Soften my heart, God, so that it is a more welcoming place for you. When I feel like being stubborn, fill my mind with thoughts of your love. When I act proudly, help me remember that you are a God of justice. When I refuse to listen to those who share your words, speak to me of the comfort that your Word brings. Amen.

— Exodus 8:5–19

frogs, and I will let your people go, so that
they can offer sacrifices to the LORD."
9Moses replied, "I will be glad to pray for
you. Just set the time when I am to pray for
you, your officers, and your people. Then
you will be rid of the frogs, and there will be
none left except in the Nile."
10The king answered, "Pray for me
tomorrow."
Moses said, "I will do as you ask, and then
you will know that there is no other god
like the LORD, our God. 11You, your offi-
cials, and your people will be rid of the
frogs, and there will be none left except in

They will jump up on you. (8:4)

the Nile." 12Then Moses and Aaron left the
king, and Moses prayed to the LORD to take
away the frogs which he had brought on the
king. 13The LORD did as Moses asked, and
the frogs in the houses, the courtyards, and
the fields died. 14The Egyptians piled them
up in great heaps, until the land stank with
them. 15When the king saw that the frogs
were dead, he became stubborn again and,
just as the LORD had said, the king would
not listen to Moses and Aaron.

Gnats

16The LORD said to Moses, "Tell Aaron to
strike the ground with his stick, and all over
the land of Egypt the dust will change into
gnats." 17So Aaron struck the ground with
his stick, and all the dust in Egypt was
turned into gnats, which covered the people
and the animals. 18The magicians tried to
use their magic to make gnats appear, but
they failed. There were gnats everywhere,
19and the magicians said to the king, "God
has done this!" But the king was stubborn
and, just as the LORD had said, the king
would not listen to Moses and Aaron.

8:19 Lk 11:20

Flies

20The LORD said to Moses, "Early tomor-
row morning go and meet the king as he
goes to the river, and tell him that the LORD
says, 'Let my people go, so that they can
worship me. 21I warn you that if you refuse,
I will punish you by sending flies on you,
your officials, and your people. The houses of
the Egyptians will be full of flies, and the
ground will be covered with them. 22But I
will spare the region of Goshen, where my
people live, so that there will be no flies
there. I will do this so that you will know
that I, the LORD, am at work in this land. 23I
will make a distinction[i] between my people
and your people. This miracle will take place
tomorrow.' " 24The LORD sent great swarms
of flies into the king's palace and the houses
of his officials. The whole land of Egypt was
brought to ruin by the flies.

25Then the king called for Moses and
Aaron and said, "Go and offer sacrifices to
your God here in this country."

26"It would not be right to do that,"
Moses answered, "because the Egyptians
would be offended by our sacrificing the
animals that we offer to the LORD our God.
If we use these animals and offend the Egyp-
tians by sacrificing them where they can see
us, they will stone us to death. 27We must
travel three days into the desert to offer sac-
rifices to the LORD our God, just as he com-
manded us."

28The king said, "I will let you go to sac-
rifice to the LORD, your God, in the desert,
if you do not go very far. Pray for me."

29Moses answered, "As soon as I leave, I
will pray to the LORD that tomorrow the
flies will leave you, your officials, and your
people. But you must not deceive us again
and prevent the people from going to sacri-
fice to the LORD."

30Moses left the king and prayed to the
LORD, 31and the LORD did as Moses asked.
The flies left the king, his officials, and his
people; not one fly remained. 32But even this
time the king became stubborn, and again
he would not let the people go.

Death of the Animals

9 The LORD said to Moses, "Go to the
king and tell him that the LORD, the
God of the Hebrews, says, 'Let my people
go, so that they may worship me. 2If you
again refuse to let them go, 3I will punish
you by sending a terrible disease on all your
animals—your horses, donkeys, camels, cat-
tle, sheep, and goats. 4I will make a distinc-
tion between the animals of the Israelites
and those of the Egyptians, and no animal
that belongs to the Israelites will die. 5I, the
LORD, have set tomorrow as the time when
I will do this.' "

6The next day the LORD did as he had
said, and all the animals of the Egyptians
died, but not one of the animals of the
Israelites died. 7The king asked what had
happened and was told that none of the ani-
mals of the Israelites had died. But he was
stubborn and would not let the people go.

Boils

8Then the LORD said to Moses and
Aaron, "Take a few handfuls of ashes from a
furnace; Moses is to throw them into the air
in front of the king. 9They will spread out
like fine dust over all the land of Egypt, and
everywhere they will produce boils that
become open sores on the people and the
animals." 10So they got some ashes and stood
before the king; Moses threw them into the
air, and they produced boils that became
open sores on the people and the animals.
11The magicians were not able to appear
before Moses, because they were covered
with boils, like all the other Egyptians. 12But
the LORD made the king stubborn and, just
as the LORD had said, the king would not
listen to Moses and Aaron.

Hail

13The LORD then said to Moses, "Early
tomorrow morning meet with the king and
tell him that the LORD, the God of the
Hebrews, says, 'Let my people go, so that they
may worship me. 14This time I will punish
not only your officials and your people, but I

[i] **8:23** *Some ancient translations* a distinction; *Hebrew* redemption.
9:10 Rev 16:2

Promise Breakers and Promise Keepers?

It was a huge hailstorm—the worst the king had ever seen. Finally he had enough. He called Moses and Aaron and told them to take the Israelites away. In return, Moses promised to stop the storm. As soon as he got outside the city, he raised his hands to God, and the rain, thunder, and hail stopped. But when things were back to normal, the king refused to let the people go. Just because life got better, he broke the promise he had made to Moses and Aaron—and to God.

Many people turn to God when life gets hard. They promise that if God will help them, they will pray more, help poor people, and resist temptation. But when life gets back to normal, they forget about their promises—and about God. But God promised to be with us always, no matter what happens.

Have you made any promises to God lately? How about to other people? Are you a promise breaker, like Pharaoh? Or are you a promise keeper, like God?

— Exodus 9:13–35

will punish you as well, so that you may
know that there is no one like me in all the
world. 15If I had raised my hand to strike you
and your people with disease, you would
have been completely destroyed. 16But to
show you my power I have let you live so
that my fame might spread over the whole
world. 17Yet you are still arrogant and refuse
to let my people go. 18This time tomorrow I
will cause a heavy hailstorm, such as Egypt
has never known in all its history. 19Now
give orders for your livestock and everything
else you have in the open to be put under
shelter. Hail will fall on the people and ani-
mals left outside unprotected, and they will
all die.' " 20Some of the king's officials were
afraid because of what the LORD had said,
and they brought their slaves and animals
indoors for shelter. 21Others, however, paid
no attention to the LORD's warning and left
their slaves and animals out in the open.

22Then the LORD said to Moses, "Raise
your hand toward the sky, and hail will fall
over the whole land of Egypt—on the peo-
ple, the animals, and all the plants in the
fields." 23So Moses raised his stick toward the
sky, and the LORD sent thunder and hail, and
lightning struck the ground. The LORD sent
24a heavy hailstorm, with lightning flashing
back and forth. It was the worst storm that
Egypt had ever known in all its history. 25All
over Egypt the hail struck down everything
in the open, including all the people and all
the animals. It beat down all the plants in the
fields and broke all the trees. 26The region of
Goshen, where the Israelites lived, was the
only place where there was no hail.

27The king sent for Moses and Aaron and
said, "This time I have sinned; the LORD is
in the right, and my people and I are in the
wrong. 28Pray to the LORD! We have had
enough of this thunder and hail! I promise
to let you go; you don't have to stay here
any longer."

29Moses said to him, "As soon as I go out
of the city, I will lift up my hands in prayer
to the LORD. The thunder will stop, and
there will be no more hail, so that you may
know that the earth belongs to the LORD.
30But I know that you and your officials do
not yet fear the LORD God."

31The flax and the barley were ruined,
because the barley was ripe, and the flax was

9:16 Rom 9:17 **9:24** Rev 8:7; 16:21

The king refused to give in, even though he was only hurting himself. Have you ever been that stubborn?

budding. 32But none of the wheat was
ruined, because it ripens later.
33Moses left the king, went out of the city,
and lifted up his hands in prayer to the
LORD. The thunder, the hail, and the rain all
stopped. 34When the king saw what had
happened, he sinned again. He and his offi-
cials remained as stubborn as ever 35and, just
as the LORD had foretold through Moses, the
king would not let the Israelites go.

Locusts

10 Then the LORD said to Moses, "Go
and see the king. I have made him
and his officials stubborn, in order that I may
perform these miracles among them 2and in
order that you may be able to tell your chil-
dren and grandchildren how I made fools of
the Egyptians when I performed the miracles.
All of you will know that I am the LORD."
3So Moses and Aaron went to the king
and said to him, "The LORD, the God of the
Hebrews, says, 'How much longer will you
refuse to submit to me? Let my people go, so
that they may worship me. 4If you keep on
refusing, then I will bring locusts into your
country tomorrow. 5There will be so many
that they will completely cover the ground.
They will eat everything that the hail did
not destroy, even the trees that are left. 6They
will fill your palaces and the houses of all
your officials and all your people. They will
be worse than anything your ancestors ever
saw.' "Then Moses turned and left.
7The king's officials said to him, "How
long is this man going to give us trouble?
Let the Israelite men go, so that they can
worship the LORD their God. Don't you
realize that Egypt is ruined?"
8So Moses and Aaron were brought back
to the king, and he said to them, "You may
go and worship the LORD your God. But
exactly who will go?"
9Moses answered, "We will all go, includ-
ing our children and our old people. We will
take our sons and daughters, our sheep and
goats, and our cattle, because we must hold a
festival to honor the LORD."
10The king said, "I swear by the LORD
that I will never let you take your women
and children! It is clear that you are plotting
to revolt. 11No! Only the men may go and
worship the LORD if that is what you want."
With that, Moses and Aaron were driven out
of the king's presence.
12Then the LORD said to Moses, "Raise
your hand over the land of Egypt to bring
the locusts. They will come and eat every-
thing that grows, everything that has sur-
vived the hail." 13So Moses raised his stick,
and the LORD caused a wind from the east
to blow on the land all that day and all that
night. By morning it had brought the
locusts. 14They came in swarms and settled
over the whole country. It was the largest
swarm of locusts that had ever been seen or
that ever would be seen again. 15They cov-
ered the ground until it was black with
them; they ate everything that the hail had
left, including all the fruit on the trees. Not a
green thing was left on any tree or plant in
all the land of Egypt.
16Then the king hurriedly called Moses
and Aaron and said, "I have sinned against
the LORD your God and against you. 17Now
forgive my sin this one time and pray to the
LORD your God to take away this fatal pun-
ishment from me." 18Moses left the king and
prayed to the LORD. 19And the LORD
changed the east wind into a very strong
west wind, which picked up the locusts and
blew them into the Gulf of Suez.[j] Not one
locust was left in all of Egypt. 20But the
LORD made the king stubborn, and he did
not let the Israelites go.

Darkness

21The LORD then said to Moses, "Raise
your hand toward the sky, and a darkness
thick enough to be felt will cover the land

[j] **10:19** GULF OF SUEZ: *See Red Sea in 13:18.*
10:14, 15 Rev 9:2, 3 **10:21–23** Wis 17:1–21

"I have sinned against the LORD your God and against you" *(Exodus 10:16)*. **The king said it, but he didn't mean it.**

Live it!

Breaking Families Apart

The king of Egypt was getting tired of Moses and Aaron pestering him to let the Israelites go to worship their God. Finally, he told Moses to take just the men. But Moses wanted everyone to go. He wanted to keep families together. The king refused.

Today, no evil leader is probably forcing your family members to separate from one another. But we face other challenges that make it hard for us to build strong relationships. Work schedules and responsibilities, extreme busyness, poor attitudes, and different priorities are some of the reasons families cannot find time to do things together.

Do you think your family spends enough time together? If not, what are some of the reasons? What can you do to build stronger relationships with the people you live with? Say a prayer asking God to bless all the people you consider to be "family."

— Exodus 10:7–11

of Egypt." 22Moses raised his hand toward
the sky, and there was total darkness
throughout Egypt for three days. 23The
Egyptians could not see each other, and no
one left his house during that time. But the
Israelites had light where they were living.
24The king called Moses and said, "You
may go and worship the LORD; even your
women and children may go with you. But
your sheep, goats, and cattle must stay here."
25Moses answered, "Then you would have
to provide us with animals for sacrifices and
burnt offerings to offer to the LORD our
God. 26No, we will take our animals with us;
not one will be left behind. We ourselves
must select the animals with which to worship the LORD our God. And until we get
there, we will not know what animals to sacrifice to him."
27The LORD made the king stubborn, and
he would not let them go. 28He said to Moses,
"Get out of my sight! Don't let me ever see
you again! On the day I do, you will die!"
29"You are right," Moses answered. "You
will never see me again."

Moses Announces the Death of the First-Born

11 Then the LORD said to Moses, "I
will send only one more punishment
on the king of Egypt and his people. After
that he will let you leave. In fact, he will
drive all of you out of here. 2Now speak to
the people of Israel and tell all of them to ask
their neighbors for gold and silver jewelry."
3The LORD made the Egyptians respect the
Israelites. Indeed, the officials and all the people considered Moses to be a very great man.
4Moses then said to the king, "The LORD
says, 'At about midnight I will go through
Egypt, 5and every first-born son in Egypt
will die, from the king's son, who is heir to
the throne, to the son of the slave woman
who grinds grain. The first-born of all the
cattle will die also. 6There will be loud crying all over Egypt, such as there has never
been before or ever will be again. 7But not
even a dog will bark at the Israelites or their
animals. Then you will know that I, the
LORD, make a distinction between the
Egyptians and the Israelites.' " 8Moses concluded by saying, "All your officials will
come to me and bow down before me, and
they will beg me to take all my people and
go away. After that, I will leave." Then in
great anger Moses left the king.
9The LORD said to Moses, "The king will
continue to refuse to listen to you, in order
that I may do more of my miracles in
Egypt." 10Moses and Aaron performed all
these miracles before the king, but the LORD
made him stubborn, and he would not let
the Israelites leave his country.

10:22 Ps 105:28; Rev 16:10

The Passover

12 The LORD spoke to Moses and Aaron in Egypt: 2"This month is to be the first month of the year for you. 3Give these instructions to the whole community of Israel: On the tenth day of this month each man must choose either a lamb or a young goat for his household. 4If his family is too small to eat a whole animal, he and his next-door neighbor may share an animal, in proportion to the number of people and the amount that each person can eat. 5You may choose either a sheep or a goat, but it must be a one-year-old male without any defects. 6Then, on the evening of the fourteenth day of the month, the whole community of Israel will kill the animals. 7The people are to take some of the blood and put it on the doorposts and above the doors of the houses in which the animals are to be eaten. 8That night the meat is to be roasted, and eaten with bitter herbs and with bread made without yeast. 9Do not eat any of it raw or boiled, but eat it roasted whole, including the head, the legs, and the internal organs. 10You must not leave any of it until morning; if any is left over, it must be burned. 11You are to eat it quickly, for you are to be dressed for travel, with your sandals on your feet and your walking stick in your hand. It is the Passover Festival to honor me, the LORD.

12"On that night I will go through the land of Egypt, killing every first-born male, both human and animal, and punishing all the gods of Egypt. I am the LORD. 13The blood on the doorposts will be a sign to mark the houses in which you live. When I see the blood, I will pass over you and will not harm you when I punish the Egyptians. 14You must celebrate this day as a religious festival to remind you of what I, the LORD, have done. Celebrate it for all time to come."

The Festival of Unleavened Bread

15The LORD said, "For seven days you must not eat any bread made with yeast—eat only unleavened bread. On the first day you are to get rid of all the yeast in your houses, for if anyone during those seven days eats bread made with yeast, he shall no longer be considered one of my people. 16On the first day and again on the seventh day you are to meet for worship. No work is to be done on those days, but you may prepare food. 17Keep this festival, because it was on this day that I brought your tribes out of Egypt. For all time to come you must celebrate this day as a festival. 18From the evening of the fourteenth day of the first month to the evening of the twenty-first day, you must not eat any bread made with yeast. 19-20For seven days no yeast must be found in your houses, for if anyone, native-born or foreign, eats bread made with yeast, he shall no longer be considered one of my people."

The First Passover

21Moses called for all the leaders of Israel and said to them, "Each of you is to choose a lamb or a young goat and kill it, so that your families can celebrate Passover. 22Take a sprig of hyssop, dip it in the bowl containing[k] the animal's blood, and wipe the blood on the doorposts and the beam above the door of your house. Not one of you is to leave the house until morning. 23When the LORD goes through Egypt to kill the Egyptians, he will see the blood on the beams and the doorposts and will not let the Angel of Death enter your houses and kill you. 24You and your children must obey these rules forever. 25When you enter the land that the LORD has promised to give you, you must perform this ritual. 26When your children ask you, 'What does this ritual mean?' 27you will answer, 'It is the sacrifice of Passover to honor the LORD, because he passed over the houses of the Israelites in Egypt. He killed the Egyptians, but spared us.' "

The Israelites knelt down and worshiped. 28Then they went and did what the LORD had commanded Moses and Aaron.

[k] **12:22** dip it in the bowl containing; *or* put it on the threshold covered with.

12:1–13 Lev 23:5; Num 9:1–5; 28:16; Deut 16:1, 2 **12:14–20** Ex 23:15; 34:18; Lev 23:6–8; Num 28:17–25; Deut 16:3–8 **12:23** Heb 11:28

Catholic Connections

Saved by the Blood of the Lamb

Every spring Jewish families celebrate Passover to remember the story described in Exodus, chapter 12. God gave the Israelites specific instructions for preparing the last meal they would eat as slaves of the Egyptians. God also told them to sacrifice a lamb and spread its blood on their doorposts. Their families would then be saved from the Angel of Death that God would send to kill the Egyptian first-born males.

Jesus and his disciples were probably sharing a Passover meal (also known as a Paschal feast or a seder meal) on the night before he died. Through this meal, which we know as the Last Supper, Jesus helped his followers understand his own death. The sacrifice of his body and blood would save the world. Just as the blood of the lamb freed the Israelites from the slavery of the Egyptians, Jesus freed the world from the slavery of sin. That is why the New Testament calls Jesus the Lamb of God.

We commemorate the life, death, and Resurrection of Jesus—the Paschal sacrifice—every time we celebrate the Eucharist.

— Exodus 12:21–28

The Death of the First-Born

29 At midnight the LORD killed all the
first-born sons in Egypt, from the king's son,
who was heir to the throne, to the son of
the prisoner in the dungeon; all the first-
born of the animals were also killed. 30 That
night, the king, his officials, and all the other
Egyptians were awakened. There was loud
crying throughout Egypt, because there was
not one home in which there was not a
dead son. 31 That same night the king sent
for Moses and Aaron and said, "Get out, you
and your Israelites! Leave my country; go
and worship the LORD, as you asked. 32 Take
your sheep, goats, and cattle, and leave. Also
pray for a blessing on me."
33 The Egyptians urged the people to
hurry and leave the country; they said, "We
will all be dead if you don't leave." 34 So the
people filled their baking pans with unleav-
ened dough, wrapped them in clothing, and
carried them on their shoulders. 35 The
Israelites had done as Moses had said, and had
asked the Egyptians for gold and silver jewel-
ry and for clothes. 36 The LORD made the
Egyptians respect the people and give them
what they asked for. In this way the Israelites
carried away the wealth of the Egyptians.

The Israelites Leave Egypt

37 The Israelites set out on foot from Rame-
ses for Sukkoth. There were about 600,000
men, not counting women and children. 38 A

The people filled their baking pans with unleavened dough. (12:34)

12:29 Ex 4:22–32 **12:35, 36** Ex 3:21, 22

The event described in Exodus, chapter 12, is called Passover because God's destroyer "passed over" the homes of the Israelites.

large number of other people and many sheep, goats, and cattle also went with them. 39 They baked unleavened bread from the dough that they had brought out of Egypt, for they had been driven out of Egypt so suddenly that they did not have time to get their food ready or to prepare leavened dough.

40 The Israelites had lived in Egypt for 430 years. 41 On the day the 430 years ended, all the tribes of the LORD's people left Egypt. 42 It was a night when the LORD kept watch to bring them out of Egypt; this same night is dedicated to the LORD for all time to come as a night when the Israelites must keep watch.

Regulations about Passover

43 The LORD said to Moses and Aaron, "These are the Passover regulations: No foreigner shall eat the Passover meal, 44 but any slave that you have bought may eat it if you circumcise him first. 45 No temporary resident or hired worker may eat it. 46 The whole meal must be eaten in the house in which it was prepared; it must not be taken outside. And do not break any of the animal's bones. 47 The whole community of Israel must celebrate this festival, 48 but no uncircumcised man may eat it. If a foreigner has settled among you and wants to celebrate Passover to honor the LORD, you must first circumcise all the males of his household. He is then to be treated like a native-born Israelite and may join in the festival. 49 The same regulations apply to native-born Israelites and to foreigners who settle among you." 50 All the Israelites obeyed and did what the LORD had commanded Moses and Aaron. 51 On that day the LORD brought the Israelite tribes out of Egypt.

Dedication of the First-Born

13 The LORD said to Moses, 2 "Dedicate all the first-born males to me, for every first-born male Israelite and every first-born male animal belongs to me."

The Festival of Unleavened Bread

3 Moses said to the people, "Remember this day—the day on which you left Egypt, the place where you were slaves. This is the day the LORD brought you out by his great power. No leavened bread is to be eaten. 4 You are leaving Egypt on this day in the first month, the month of Abib. 5 The LORD solemnly promised your ancestors to give you the land of the Canaanites, the Hittites, the Amorites, the Hivites, and the Jebusites. When he brings you into that rich and fertile land, you must celebrate this festival in the first month of every year. 6 For seven days you must eat unleavened bread and on the seventh day there is to be a festival to honor the LORD. 7 For seven days you must not eat any bread made with yeast; there must be no yeast or leavened bread anywhere in your land. 8 When the festival begins, explain to your sons that you do all this because of what the LORD did for you when you left Egypt. 9 This observance will be a reminder, like something tied on your hand or on your forehead; it will remind you to continue to recite and study the Law of the LORD, because the LORD brought you out of Egypt by his great power. 10 Celebrate this festival at the appointed time each year.

The First-Born

11 "The LORD will bring you into the land of the Canaanites, which he solemnly promised to you and your ancestors. When he gives it to you, 12 you must offer every first-born male to the LORD. Every first-born male of your animals belongs to the LORD, 13 but you must buy back from him every first-born male donkey by offering a lamb in its place. If you do not want to buy back the donkey, break its neck. You must buy back every first-born male child of yours. 14 In the future, when your son asks what this observance means, you will answer him, 'By using

12:40 Gen 15:13; Gal 3:17 **12:46** Num 9:12; Jn 19:36 **13:2** Num 3:13; Lk 2:23 **13:12** Ex 34:19, 20; Lk 2:23

Why didn't the Israelites take the shortest way out of Egypt? The answer is somewhere in the last part of Exodus, chapter 13.

Pray it!

God, Be My Pillar

God of light and God of darkness, the Israelites knew you were with them as they made their way out of Egypt. They saw you as a pillar of cloud in front of them during the day and a pillar of fire lighting their way at night.

I wish I could see you sometimes. It would make life a lot easier. At least I would know that I'm heading in the right direction. I know that you're always with me, too, but sometimes I don't **feel** ***it.***

I think that you put "pillars" in my life to guide me, just as you guided the Israelites. After all, I have parents, teachers, relatives, and friends who look out for me. They teach me, give me directions, and light my way when I'm lost or confused. They are gifts from you your way of being my very own pillar of cloud and fire. Thank you, God, for them. Amen.

— Exodus 13:20–22

great power the LORD brought us out of
Egypt, the place where we were slaves.
15 When the king of Egypt was stubborn and
refused to let us go, the LORD killed every
first-born male in the land of Egypt, both
human and animal. That is why we sacrifice
every first-born male animal to the LORD,
but buy back our first-born sons. 16 This
observance will be a reminder, like something tied on our hands or on our foreheads;
it will remind us that the LORD brought us
out of Egypt by his great power.' "

The Pillar of Cloud and the Pillar of Fire

17 When the king of Egypt let the people
go, God did not take them by the road that
goes up the coast to Philistia, although it was
the shortest way. God thought, "I do not
want the people to change their minds and
return to Egypt when they see that they are
going to have to fight." 18 Instead, he led
them in a roundabout way through the
desert toward the Red Sea.[l] The Israelites
were armed for battle.
19 Moses took the body of Joseph with
him, as Joseph had made the Israelites
solemnly promise to do. Joseph had said,
"When God rescues you, you must carry my
body with you from this place."
20 The Israelites left Sukkoth and camped
at Etham on the edge of the desert. 21 During the day the LORD went in front of them
in a pillar of cloud to show them the way,
and during the night he went in front of
them in a pillar of fire to give them light, so
that they could travel night and day. 22 The
pillar of cloud was always in front of the
people during the day, and the pillar of fire
at night.

Crossing the Red Sea

14 Then the LORD said to Moses,
2 "Tell the Israelites to turn back and
camp in front of Pi Hahiroth, between
Migdol and the Red Sea, near Baal Zephon.
3 The king will think that the Israelites are
wandering around in the country and are
closed in by the desert. 4 I will make him
stubborn, and he will pursue you, and my
victory over the king and his army will
bring me honor. Then the Egyptians will

[l] **13:18** RED SEA: *(in Hebrew literally "Sea of Reeds") evidently referred to (1) a series of lakes and marshes between the head of the Gulf of Suez and the Mediterranean, the region generally regarded as the site of the events described in Exodus 13, and was also used to designate (2) the Gulf of Suez, and (3) the Gulf of Aqaba.*

13:19 Gen 50:25; Josh 24:32 **13:22** Wis 10:17, 18; 18:3

The LORD went in front of them. (13:21)

know that I am the LORD." The Israelites did
as they were told.
5 When the king of Egypt was told that
the people had escaped, he and his officials
changed their minds and said, "What have
we done? We have let the Israelites escape,
and we have lost them as our slaves!" 6 The
king got his war chariot and his army ready.
7 He set out with all his chariots, including
the six hundred finest, commanded by their
officers. 8 The LORD made the king stub-
born, and he pursued the Israelites, who
were leaving triumphantly.[m] 9 The Egyptian
army, with all the horses, chariots, and driv-
ers, pursued them and caught up with them
where they were camped by the Red Sea
near Pi Hahiroth and Baal Zephon.
10 When the Israelites saw the king and his
army marching against them, they were ter-
rified and cried out to the LORD for help.
11 They said to Moses, "Weren't there any
graves in Egypt? Did you have to bring us
out here in the desert to die? Look what
you have done by bringing us out of Egypt!
12 Didn't we tell you before we left that this
would happen? We told you to leave us
alone and let us go on being slaves of the
Egyptians. It would be better to be slaves
there than to die here in the desert."

Live it!

Remember Who's in Charge

The Israelites were on their way out of Egypt when Pharaoh changed his mind again. He decided he didn't want them to leave after all, so he went with his army to bring them back. When the Israelites saw this, they were terrified. Moses reminded them that they should trust in God who cares for them: "The LORD will fight for you, and all you have to do is keep still" (Exodus 14:14).

Sometimes we forget that we are not in charge of our life—God is. When things get rough, we worry, we get stressed, and we feel alone. Moses' advice to the Israelites is good advice for us, too: "The LORD will fight for you, and all you have to do is keep still."

Make a poster of that verse and put it in your locker. Copy it into your notebook. Memorize it. And most of all, write it on your heart.

— Exodus 14:10–14

13 Moses answered, "Don't be afraid! Stand
your ground, and you will see what the
LORD will do to save you today; you will
never see these Egyptians again. 14 The LORD
will fight for you, and all you have to do is
keep still."
15 The LORD said to Moses, "Why are you
crying out for help? Tell the people to move
forward. 16 Lift up your walking stick and
hold it out over the sea. The water will
divide, and the Israelites will be able to walk
through the sea on dry ground. 17 I will make
the Egyptians so stubborn that they will go
in after them, and I will gain honor by my
victory over the king, his army, his chariots,

[m] **14:8** triumphantly; *or* under the protection of the LORD.

and his drivers. 18When I defeat them, the
Egyptians will know that I am the LORD."
19The angel of God, who had been in
front of the army of Israel, moved and went
to the rear. The pillar of cloud also moved
until it was 20between the Egyptians and the
Israelites. The cloud made it dark for the
Egyptians, but gave light to the people of
Israel,[n] and so the armies could not come
near each other all night.
21Moses held out his hand over the sea,
and the LORD drove the sea back with a
strong east wind. It blew all night and turned
the sea into dry land. The water was divided,
22and the Israelites went through the sea on
dry ground, with walls of water on both
sides. 23The Egyptians pursued them and
went after them into the sea with all their
horses, chariots, and drivers. 24Just before
dawn the LORD looked down from the pillar
of fire and cloud at the Egyptian army and
threw them into a panic. 25He made the
wheels of their chariots get stuck, so that
they moved with great difficulty. The Egyp-
tians said, "The LORD is fighting for the
Israelites against us. Let's get out of here!"

The Egyptians will know that I am the LORD. *(14:18)*

26The LORD said to Moses, "Hold out
your hand over the sea, and the water will
come back over the Egyptians and their
chariots and drivers." 27So Moses held out
his hand over the sea, and at daybreak the
water returned to its normal level. The
Egyptians tried to escape from the water, but
the LORD threw them into the sea. 28The
water returned and covered the chariots, the
drivers, and all the Egyptian army that had
followed the Israelites into the sea; not one
of them was left. 29But the Israelites walked
through the sea on dry ground, with walls of
water on both sides.
30On that day the LORD saved the people
of Israel from the Egyptians, and the
Israelites saw them lying dead on the
seashore. 31When the Israelites saw the great
power with which the LORD had defeated
the Egyptians, they stood in awe of the
LORD; and they had faith in the LORD and
in his servant Moses.

The Song of Moses

15 Then Moses and the Israelites sang this song to the LORD:

"I will sing to the LORD, because he has
won a glorious victory;
he has thrown the horses and their
riders into the sea.
2The LORD is my strong defender;
he is the one who has saved me.
He is my God, and I will praise him,
my father's God, and I will sing about
his greatness.
3The LORD is a warrior;
the LORD is his name.
4"He threw Egypt's army and its chariots
into the sea;
the best of its officers were drowned in
the Red Sea.
5The deep sea covered them;
they sank to the bottom like a stone.

[n] **14:20** *Probable text* The cloud . . . Israel; *Hebrew unclear.*
14:22 1 Cor 10:1, 2; Heb 11:29 **15:1** Rev 15:3 **15:2** Ps 118:14; Isa 12:2

Why couldn't Pharaoh's army see the Israelites crossing the Red Sea? Read Exodus 14:19–20 to find out.

Pray it!

We Did It, God!

After the Israelites make it across the Red Sea, they stopped to thank God and sing a song of praise. After all, they could not have done it without God's help.

What has God done for you lately? How has God gotten you through your own "Red Sea"?

- **Has God gotten you through a hard time? Maybe God gave you the right words to say to someone you needed to apologize to after a huge fight.**
- **Has God blessed you with a special gift? Maybe God sent a new friend or a great tutor that has given you a better handle on math.**
- **Has God taken care of someone in your family? Maybe God led your mom to a better job or gave a relative the strength to get through an illness.**

Read through Moses' prayer of praise and thanksgiving, then write your own. In it, tell the story of God's goodness in your life. Praise God with all the enthusiasm you can muster in your heart.

— Exodus, chapter 15

6 "Your right hand, LORD, is awesome in
power;
it breaks the enemy in pieces.
7 In majestic triumph you overthrow your
foes;
your anger blazes out and burns them
up like straw.
8 You blew on the sea and the water piled
up high;
it stood up straight like a wall;
the deepest part of the sea became
solid.
9 The enemy said, 'I will pursue them and
catch them;
I will divide their wealth and take all I
want;
I will draw my sword and take all they
have.'
10 But one breath from you, LORD, and the
Egyptians were drowned;
they sank like lead in the terrible water.
11 "LORD, who among the gods is like you?
Who is like you, wonderful in holiness?
Who can work miracles and mighty
acts like yours?
12 You stretched out your right hand,
and the earth swallowed our enemies.
13 Faithful to your promise, you led the
people you had rescued;
by your strength you guided them to
your sacred land.
14 The nations have heard, and they tremble
with fear;
the Philistines are seized with terror.
15 The leaders of Edom are terrified;
Moab's mighty men are trembling;
the people of Canaan lose their
courage.
16 Terror and dread fall upon them.
They see your strength, O LORD,
and stand helpless with fear
until your people have marched past—
the people you set free from slavery.
17 You bring them in and plant them on
your mountain,
the place that you, LORD, have chosen
for your home,
the Temple that you yourself have built.
18 You, LORD, will be king forever and
ever."

Moses' sister led the women in singing praises to God and dancing. What was her name? You'll find it in Exodus, chapter 15.

The Song of Miriam

[19]The Israelites walked through the sea on
dry ground. But when the Egyptian chariots
with their horses and drivers went into the
sea, the LORD brought the water back, and it
covered them.
[20]The prophet Miriam, Aaron's sister, took
her tambourine, and all the women followed
her, playing tambourines and dancing.
[21]Miriam sang for them:

"Sing to the LORD, because he has won a
glorious victory;
he has thrown the horses and their
riders into the sea."

Bitter Water

[22]Then Moses led the people of Israel
away from the Red Sea into the desert of
Shur. For three days they walked through the
desert, but found no water. [23]Then they
came to a place called Marah, but the water
there was so bitter that they could not drink
it. That is why it was named Marah.[o] [24]The
people complained to Moses and asked,
"What are we going to drink?" [25]Moses
prayed earnestly to the LORD, and the LORD
showed him a piece of wood, which he
threw into the water; and the water became
fit to drink.

There the LORD gave them laws to live
by, and there he also tested them. [26]He said,
"If you will obey me completely by doing
what I consider right and by keeping my
commands, I will not punish you with any
of the diseases that I brought on the Egyp-
tians. I am the LORD, the one who heals
you."
[27]Next they came to Elim, where there
were twelve springs and seventy palm trees;
there they camped by the water.

The Manna and the Quails

16 The whole Israelite community set
out from Elim, and on the fifteenth
day of the second month after they had left
Egypt, they came to the desert of Sin, which
is between Elim and Sinai. [2]There in the
desert they all complained to Moses and
Aaron [3]and said to them, "We wish that the
LORD had killed us in Egypt. There we
could at least sit down and eat meat and as
much other food as we wanted. But you
have brought us out into this desert to starve
us all to death."
[4]The LORD said to Moses, "Now I am
going to cause food to rain down from the
sky for all of you. The people must go out
every day and gather enough for that day. In
this way I can test them to find out if they
will follow my instructions. [5]On the sixth
day they are to bring in twice as much as
usual and prepare it."
[6]So Moses and Aaron said to all the
Israelites, "This evening you will know that
it was the LORD who brought you out of
Egypt. [7]In the morning you will see the daz-
zling light of the LORD's presence. He has
heard your complaints against him—yes,
against him, because we are only carrying
out his instructions." [8]Then Moses said, "It is
the LORD who will give you meat to eat in
the evening and as much bread as you want
in the morning, because he has heard how
much you have complained against him.
When you complain against us, you are real-
ly complaining against the LORD."
[9]Moses said to Aaron, "Tell the whole
community to come and stand before the
LORD, because he has heard their com-
plaints." [10]As Aaron spoke to the whole
community, they turned toward the desert,
and suddenly the dazzling light of the LORD
appeared in a cloud. [11]The LORD said to
Moses, [12]"I have heard the complaints of the
Israelites. Tell them that at twilight they will
have meat to eat, and in the morning they
will have all the bread they want. Then they
will know that I, the LORD, am their God."
[13]In the evening a large flock of quails
flew in, enough to cover the camp, and in
the morning there was dew all around the
camp. [14]When the dew evaporated, there
was something thin and flaky on the surface
of the desert. It was as delicate as frost.
[15]When the Israelites saw it, they didn't

[o] **15:23** MARAH: *This name in Hebrew means "bitter."*

15:25 Sir 38:5 **16:4** Wis 16:20–29; Jn 6:31 **16:15** 1 Cor 10:3

The food that the LORD *has given you to eat (16:15)*

know what it was and asked each other, "What is it?"

Moses said to them, "This is the food that the LORD has given you to eat. 16 The LORD has commanded that each of you is to gather as much of it as he needs, two quarts for each member of his household."

17 The Israelites did this, some gathering more, others less. 18 When they measured it, those who gathered much did not have too much, and those who gathered less did not have too little. Each had gathered just what he needed. 19 Moses said to them, "No one is to keep any of it for tomorrow." 20 But some of them did not listen to Moses and saved part of it. The next morning it was full of worms and smelled rotten, and Moses was angry with them. 21 Every morning each one gathered as much as he needed; and when the sun grew hot, what was left on the ground melted.

22 On the sixth day they gathered twice as much food, four quarts for each person. All the leaders of the community came and told Moses about it, 23 and he said to them, "The LORD has commanded that tomorrow is a holy day of rest, dedicated to him. Bake today what you want to bake and boil what you want to boil. Whatever is left should be put aside and kept for tomorrow." 24 As Moses had commanded, they kept what was left until the next day; it did not spoil or get worms in it. 25 Moses said, "Eat this today, because today is the Sabbath, a day of rest

Study it!

Come and Get It!

The Israelites hadn't had much to eat since they left Egypt. They were hungry, so they complained to Moses. Moses did his usual thing—talked to God about it. God sent manna, a kind of sweet, flaky breadlike substance. It was the first time the Israelites had seen this. In fact, manna means "what is it?" in Hebrew. God also sent small birds called quails so the travelers would have some meat.

Small quantities of manna and quails still appear in that part of the world today. The miracle was that God sent enough to feed everyone for a long time. Manna in the morning. Quails at night. Quite a feast!

When we celebrate Eucharist, the priest consecrates bread and wine, and it becomes the body and blood of Jesus. This is God's way of giving us food for our spiritual journey, just like he did for the Israelites.

— Exodus, chapter 16

dedicated to the LORD, and you will not find any food outside the camp. 26 You must gather food for six days, but on the seventh day, the day of rest, there will be none."

27 On the seventh day some of the people went out to gather food, but they did not find any. 28 Then the LORD said to Moses, "How much longer will you people refuse to obey my commands? 29 Remember that I, the LORD, have given you a day of rest, and that is why on the sixth day I will always give you enough food for two days. Everyone is to stay where he is on the seventh day

16:18 2 Cor 8:15 **16:23** Ex 20:8–11

and not leave his home." 30So the people did
no work on the seventh day.
31The people of Israel called the food
manna.[p] It was like a small white seed, and
tasted like thin cakes made with honey.
32Moses said, "The LORD has commanded us
to save some manna, to be kept for our
descendants, so that they can see the food
which he gave us to eat in the desert when
he brought us out of Egypt." 33Moses said to
Aaron, "Take a jar, put two quarts of manna
in it, and place it in the LORD's presence to be
kept for our descendants." 34As the LORD had
commanded Moses, Aaron put it in front of
the Covenant Box, so that it could be kept.
35The Israelites ate manna for the next forty
years, until they reached the land of Canaan,
where they settled. (36The standard dry mea-
sure then in use equaled twenty quarts.)

Water from the Rock
(Numbers 20:1–13)

17 The whole Israelite community left
the desert of Sin, moving from one
place to another at the command of the
LORD. They camped at Rephidim, but there
was no water there to drink. 2They com-
plained to Moses and said, "Give us water to
drink."
Moses answered, "Why are you complain-
ing? Why are you putting the LORD to the
test?"
3But the people were very thirsty and
continued to complain to Moses. They said,
"Why did you bring us out of Egypt? To kill
us and our children and our livestock with
thirst?"
4Moses prayed earnestly to the LORD and
said, "What can I do with these people?
They are almost ready to stone me."
5The LORD said to Moses, "Take some of
the leaders of Israel with you, and go on
ahead of the people. Take along the stick
with which you struck the Nile. 6I will stand
before you on a rock at Mount Sinai. Strike
the rock, and water will come out of it for
the people to drink." Moses did so in the
presence of the leaders of Israel.

Live it!

No More Whining!

Moses was trying his best to lead the Israelites out of Egypt. But life was hard, and the Israelites complained a lot. They were hungry. They were thirsty. They were lost. Let's face it: These Israelites were whiners.

Parents, teachers, and others in authority do their best to lead the way God wants them to, but some people do not appreciate their efforts. They whine because they are only concerned about themselves. When the Israelites complained, Moses went to God and said, "What can I do with these people?" (Exodus 17:4). Could your parents, teachers, and friends be asking God the same question about you?

The next time you feel like complaining, check your attitude and ask yourself two questions:

- **Is complaining going to make things better or worse for everyone?**
- **What can I do *myself* to make the situation better?**

Then say a prayer for the people in your life who do their best to listen to God and guide you in the right direction.

— Exodus 17:1–7

p **16:31** MANNA: *This word sounds like the Hebrew for "what is it?" (see verse 15).*
16:31 Num 11:7, 8 **16:33** Heb 9:4 **16:35** Josh 5:12 **17:1–7** Num 20:2–13

Compare the story in Exodus, chapter 16, with the story in Matthew 14:13–21. How are they similar?

7 The place was named Massah and Meribah,[q] because the Israelites complained and put the LORD to the test when they asked, "Is the LORD with us or not?"

War with the Amalekites

8 The Amalekites came and attacked the Israelites at Rephidim. 9 Moses said to Joshua, "Pick out some men to go and fight the Amalekites tomorrow. I will stand on top of the hill holding the stick that God told me to carry." 10 Joshua did as Moses commanded him and went out to fight the Amalekites, while Moses, Aaron, and Hur went up to the top of the hill. 11 As long as Moses held up his arms, the Israelites won, but when he put his arms down, the Amalekites started winning. 12 When Moses' arms grew tired, Aaron and Hur brought a stone for him to sit on, while they stood beside him and held up his arms, holding them steady until the sun went down. 13 In this way Joshua totally defeated the Amalekites.

They held his arms steady until the sun went down. (17:12)

14 Then the LORD said to Moses, "Write an account of this victory, so that it will be remembered. Tell Joshua that I will completely destroy the Amalekites." 15 Moses built an altar and named it "The LORD is my Banner." 16 He said, "Hold high the banner of the LORD![r] The LORD will continue to fight against the Amalekites forever!"

Jethro Visits Moses

18 Moses' father-in-law Jethro, the priest of Midian, heard about everything that God had done for Moses and the people of Israel when he led them out of Egypt. 2 So he came to Moses, bringing with him Moses' wife Zipporah, who had been left behind, 3 and Gershom and Eliezer, her two sons. (Moses had said, "I have been a foreigner in a strange land"; so he had named one son Gershom.[s] 4 He had also said, "The God of my father helped me and saved me from being killed by the king of Egypt"; so he had named the other son Eliezer.[t]) 5 Jethro came with Moses' wife and her two sons into the desert where Moses was camped at the holy mountain. 6 He had sent word to Moses that they were coming, 7 so Moses went out to meet him, bowed before him, and kissed him. They asked about each other's health and then went into Moses' tent. 8 Moses told Jethro everything that the LORD had done to the king and the people of Egypt in order to rescue the Israelites. He also told him about the hardships the people had faced on the way and how the LORD had saved them. 9 When Jethro heard all this, he was happy 10 and said, "Praise the LORD, who saved you from the king and the people of Egypt! Praise the LORD, who saved his people from slavery! 11 Now I know that the LORD is greater than all the gods, because he did this when the Egyptians treated the Israelites with such contempt." 12 Then Jethro brought an offering to be burned whole and other sacrifices to be offered to God; and Aaron and all the leaders of Israel went with him to eat the sacred meal as an act of worship.

[q] **17:7** MASSAH . . . MERIBAH: *These names in Hebrew mean "testing" and "complaining."* [r] **17:16** *Probable text* Hold . . . LORD; *Hebrew unclear.* [s] **18:3** GERSHOM: *This name sounds like the Hebrew for "foreigner."* [t] **18:4** ELIEZER: *This name sounds like the Hebrew for "God helps me."*

17:14 Deut 25:17–19; 1 Sam 15:2–9 **18:2, 3** Ex 2:21, 22 **18:3** Acts 7:29

How many examples of the Israelites' complaining can you find in Exodus, chapters 15–20?

Pray it!

A Friend in Need

Jethro must have known that Moses needed someone to talk to. When he heard about everything that had happened, he went to find his son-in-law. Moses was glad to see him. He told him about what God had done for them and how hard the journey had been. Jethro was thrilled at everything Moses had accomplished and praised God. He also gave Moses some good advice to help ease Moses' burden. Maybe he helped Moses see all his struggles in a new light.

Does someone in your life seem to know when you need a friend? This person is probably a good listener and helps you see things in a way you never thought about before. Say the following prayer for the Jethro in your life:

Thank you, God, for my friend (name of person).
She (or he) . . .
Knows when I need someone to listen.
Lets me talk about my worries and struggles.
Shows me the good side when I can only see the bad.
Laughs with me, not at me.
Gives me good advice.
Lets me talk about you.
Thank you, God, for (name). Please let me be a friend like that for someone else.

— Exodus 18:1–27

The Appointment of Judges
(Deuteronomy 1:9–18)

13 The next day Moses was settling dis-
putes among the people, and he was kept
busy from morning till night. 14 When Jethro
saw everything that Moses had to do, he
asked, "What is all this that you are doing for
the people? Why are you doing this all
alone, with people standing here from
morning till night to consult you?"

15 Moses answered, "I must do this because
the people come to me to learn God's will.
16 When two people have a dispute, they
come to me, and I decide which one of them
is right, and I tell them God's commands and
laws."

17 Then Jethro said, "You are not doing this
right. 18 You will wear yourself out and these
people as well. This is too much for you to
do alone. 19 Now let me give you some good
advice, and God will be with you. It is right
for you to represent the people before God
and bring their disputes to him. 20 You should
teach them God's commands and explain to
them how they should live and what they
should do. 21 But in addition, you should
choose some capable men and appoint them
as leaders of the people: leaders of thousands,
hundreds, fifties, and tens. They must be
God-fearing men who can be trusted and
who cannot be bribed. 22 Let them serve as
judges for the people on a permanent basis.
They can bring all the difficult cases to you,
but they themselves can decide all the smaller
disputes. That will make it easier for you, as
they share your burden. 23 If you do this, as
God commands, you will not wear yourself
out, and all these people can go home with
their disputes settled."

24 Moses took Jethro's advice 25 and chose
capable men from among all the Israelites.
He appointed them as leaders of thousands,
hundreds, fifties, and tens. 26 They served as
judges for the people on a permanent basis,
bringing the difficult cases to Moses but
deciding the smaller disputes themselves.

27 Then Moses said good-bye to Jethro,
and Jethro went back home.

The Israelites at Mount Sinai

19 1-2 The people of Israel left
Rephidim, and on the first day of the
third month after they had left Egypt they
came to the desert of Sinai. There they set up
camp at the foot of Mount Sinai, 3 and Moses
went up the mountain to meet with God.
The LORD called to him from the moun-
tain and told him to say to the Israelites,
Jacob's descendants: 4 "You saw what I, the
LORD, did to the Egyptians and how I car-
ried you as an eagle carries her young on
her wings, and brought you here to me.
5 Now, if you will obey me and keep my
covenant, you will be my own people. The
whole earth is mine, but you will be my
chosen people, 6 a people dedicated to me
alone, and you will serve me as priests." 7 So
Moses went down and called the leaders of
the people together and told them every-
thing that the LORD had commanded him.
8 Then all the people answered together, "We
will do everything that the LORD has said,"
and Moses reported this to the LORD.
9 The LORD said to Moses, "I will come to
you in a thick cloud, so that the people will
hear me speaking with you and will believe
you from now on."
Moses told the LORD what the people had
answered, 10 and the LORD said to him, "Go to
the people and tell them to spend today and
tomorrow purifying themselves for worship.
They must wash their clothes 11 and be ready
the day after tomorrow. On that day I will
come down on Mount Sinai, where all the
people can see me. 12 Mark a boundary
around the mountain that the people must
not cross, and tell them not to go up the
mountain or even get near it. If any of you set
foot on it, you are to be put to death; 13 you
must either be stoned or shot with arrows,
without anyone touching you. This applies to
both people and animals; they must be put to
death. But when the trumpet is blown, then
the people are to go up to the mountain."
14 Then Moses came down the mountain
and told the people to get ready for worship.
So they washed their clothes, 15 and Moses
told them, "Be ready by the day after tomor-
row and don't have sexual intercourse in the
meantime."
16 On the morning of the third day there
was thunder and lightning, a thick cloud
appeared on the mountain, and a very loud
trumpet blast was heard. All the people in
the camp trembled with fear. 17 Moses led
them out of the camp to meet God, and
they stood at the foot of the mountain. 18 All
of Mount Sinai was covered with smoke,
because the LORD had come down on it in
fire. The smoke went up like the smoke of a
furnace, and the whole mountain[u] trembled
violently. 19 The sound of the trumpet
became louder and louder. Moses spoke, and
God answered him with thunder. 20 The
LORD came down on the top of Mount
Sinai and called Moses to the top of the
mountain. Moses went up 21 and the LORD
said to him, "Go down and warn the people
not to cross the boundary to come and look
at me; if they do, many of them will die.
22 Even the priests who come near me must
purify themselves, or I will punish them."

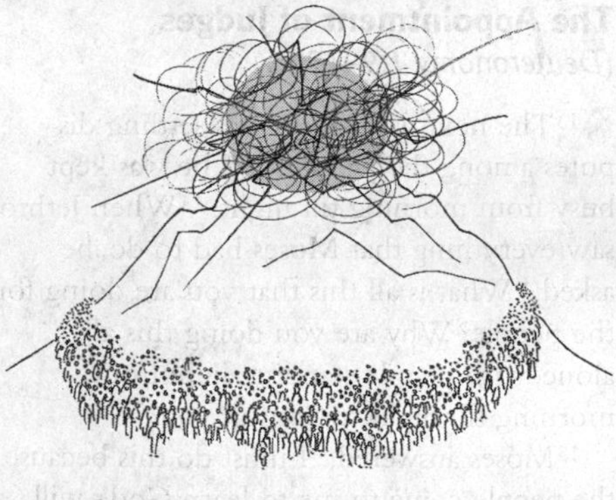

God answered him with thunder. (19:19)

23 Moses said to the LORD, "The people
cannot come up, because you commanded
us to consider the mountain sacred and to
mark a boundary around it."
24 The LORD replied, "Go down and bring
Aaron back with you. But the priests and the

[u] **19:18** the whole mountain; *one ancient translation and some Hebrew manuscripts* all the people.

19:5, 6 1 Pet 2:9 **19:5** Deut 4:20; 7:6; 14:2; 26:18; Titus 2:14 **19:6** Rev 1:6; 5:10 **19:12, 13** Heb 12:18–20 **19:16** Rev 4:5 **19:16–18** Deut 4:11, 12

Pray it!

Sensing God's Power

It's no wonder the Israelites were petrified. Wouldn't you be? Mount Sinai was in flames and shaking violently. There was thunder, lightning, and trumpets. Let's just say it was a powerful day—one that the Israelites would not forget.

We usually think of God's power as flashy and showy, like a disaster film at the theater. But God's power can be quiet, too. Every one of your senses experiences God's power. All you have to do is pay attention.

Try these "power prayers":

- **Look at a baby, a tree, or a fish and see God's power.**
- **Listen to a gentle rain, people laughing, or your heartbeat to hear God's power.**
- **Touch a furry animal, a leaf, or your own skin to feel God's power.**
- **Breathe in the scent of fire, a flower, or fresh-baked bread to smell God's power.**
- **Enjoy an orange, a slice of pizza, or a bowl of soup to taste God's power.**

When you are aware of God's power all around you, repeat the words of the Israelites: "We will do everything that the LORD has said" (Exodus 19:8).

— Exodus 19:16–25

people must not cross the boundary to come
up to me, or I will punish them." 25 Moses
then went down to the people and told
them what the LORD had said.

The Ten Commandments
(Deuteronomy 5:1–21)

20 God spoke, and these were his
words: 2 "I am the LORD your God
who brought you out of Egypt, where you
were slaves.
3 "Worship no god but me.
4 "Do not make for yourselves images of
anything in heaven or on earth or in the
water under the earth. 5 Do not bow down
to any idol or worship it, because I am the
LORD your God and I tolerate no rivals. I
bring punishment on those who hate me
and on their descendants down to the third
and fourth generation. 6 But I show my love
to thousands of generations[v] of those who
love me and obey my laws.
7 "Do not use my name for evil purposes,
for I, the LORD your God, will punish any-
one who misuses my name.
8 "Observe the Sabbath and keep it holy.
9 You have six days in which to do your
work, 10 but the seventh day is a day of rest
dedicated to me. On that day no one is to
work—neither you, your children, your
slaves, your animals, nor the foreigners who
live in your country. 11 In six days I, the
LORD, made the earth, the sky, the seas, and
everything in them, but on the seventh day I

[v] **20:6** thousands of generations; *or* thousands.

20:4, 5 Ex 34:17; Lev 19:4; 26:1; Deut 4:15–18; 27:15 **20:5, 6** Ex 34:6, 7; Num 14:18; Deut 7:9, 10 **20:7** Lev 19:12 **20:8** Ex 16:23–30; 31:12–14 **20:9, 10** Ex 23:12; 31:15; 34:21; 35:2; Lev 23:3 **20:11** Gen 2:1–3; Ex 31:17

God makes a covenant with the Israelites in Exodus 19:3–8. With whom did God make other covenants? Hint: Check out Genesis.

The Ten Commandments

Catholic Connections

The Ten Commandments are one of the most famous parts of the Bible. They are a summary of the entire Law God gave to Moses on Mount Sinai. For Christians and Jews, these Commandments play a key role in how we make decisions, how we treat each other, and how we go about being right with God.

As Catholics, we believe that the Ten Commandments and the teachings of Jesus (especially the Beatitudes in Matthew 5:3–11) are the core of what God reveals about morality. (Morality is knowing what is good and evil, right and wrong.) The *Catechism of the Catholic Church*—which is the official summary of Church teachings—uses the Ten Commandments as the outline for Christian morality.

Can you name all Ten Commandments? If not, try to memorize them. More important, try to live by them at all times.

— Exodus 20:1–17

rested. That is why I, the LORD, blessed the Sabbath and made it holy.

12 "Respect your father and your mother, so that you may live a long time in the land that I am giving you.

13 "Do not commit murder.

14 "Do not commit adultery.

15 "Do not steal.

16 "Do not accuse anyone falsely.

17 "Do not desire another man's house; do not desire his wife, his slaves, his cattle, his donkeys, or anything else that he owns."

The People's Fear
(Deuteronomy 5:22–33)

18 When the people heard the thunder and the trumpet blast and saw the lightning and the smoking mountain, they trembled with
fear and stood a long way off. 19 They said to
Moses, "If you speak to us, we will listen; but we are afraid that if God speaks to us, we will die."

20 Moses replied, "Don't be afraid; God has only come to test you and make you keep on obeying him, so that you will not sin."
21 But the people continued to stand a long way off, and only Moses went near the dark cloud where God was.

Laws about Altars

22 The LORD commanded Moses to tell the Israelites: "You have seen how I, the LORD, have spoken to you from heaven.
23 Do not make for yourselves gods of silver or gold to be worshiped in addition to me.
24 Make an altar of earth for me, and on it sacrifice your sheep and your cattle as offerings to be completely burned and as fellowship offerings. In every place that I set aside for you to worship me, I will come to you

20:12 a Deut 27:16; Mt 15:4; 19:19; Mk 7:10; 10:19; Lk 18:20; Eph 6:2; b Eph 6:3 **20:13** Gen 9:6; Lev 24:17; Mt 5:21; 19:18; Mk 10:19; Lk 18:20; Rom 13:9; Jas 2:11 **20:14** Lev 20:10; Mt 5:27; 19:18; Mk 10:19; Lk 18:20; Rom 13:9; Jas 2:11 **20:15** Lev 19:11; Mt 19:18; Mk 10:19; Lk 18:20; Rom 13:9 **20:16** Ex 23:1; Mt 19:18; Mk 10:19; Lk 18:20 **20:17** Rom 7:7; 13:9 **20:18, 19** Heb 12:18, 19

Jesus summed up the Ten Commandments in two statements. Read Mark 12:28–31 to find out what they are.

and bless you. 25If you make an altar of stone for me, do not build it out of cut stones, because when you use a chisel on stones, you make them unfit for my use. 26Do not build an altar for me with steps leading up to it; if you do, you will expose yourselves as you go up the steps.

The Treatment of Slaves

(Deuteronomy 15:12–18)

21 "Give the Israelites the following laws: 2If you buy a Hebrew slave, he shall serve you for six years. In the seventh year he is to be set free without having to pay anything. 3If he was unmarried when he became your slave, he is not to take a wife with him when he leaves; but if he was married when he became your slave, he may take his wife with him. 4If his master gave him a wife and she bore him sons or daughters, the woman and her children belong to the master, and the man is to leave by himself. 5But if the slave declares that he loves his master, his wife, and his children and does not want to be set free, 6then his master shall take him to the place of worship. There he is to make him stand against the door or the doorpost and put a hole through his ear. Then he will be his slave for life.

7"If a man sells his daughter as a slave, she is not to be set free, as male slaves are. 8If she is sold to someone who intends to make her his wife, but he doesn't like her, then she is to be sold back to her father; her master cannot sell her to foreigners, because he has treated her unfairly. 9If a man buys a female slave to give to his son, he is to treat her like a daughter. 10If a man takes a second wife, he must continue to give his first wife the same amount of food and clothing and the same rights that she had before. 11If he does not fulfill these duties to her, he must set her free and not receive any payment.

Laws about Violent Acts

12"Whoever hits someone and kills him is to be put to death. 13But if it was an accident and he did not mean to kill him, he can escape to a place which I will choose for you, and there he will be safe. 14But when someone gets angry and deliberately kills someone else, he is to be put to death, even if he has run to my altar for safety.

15"Whoever hits his father or his mother is to be put to death.

16"Whoever kidnaps someone, either to sell him or to keep him as a slave, is to be put to death.

17"Whoever curses his father or his mother is to be put to death.

18-19"If there is a fight and someone hits someone else with a stone or with his fist, but does not kill him, he is not to be punished. If the one who was hit has to stay in bed, but later is able to get up and walk outside with the help of a cane, the one who hit him is to pay for his lost time and take care of him until he gets well.

20"If a slave owner takes a stick and beats his slave, whether male or female, and the slave dies on the spot, the owner is to be punished. 21But if the slave does not die for a day or two, the master is not to be punished. The loss of his property is punishment enough.

22"If some men are fighting and hurt a pregnant woman so that she loses her child, but she is not injured in any other way, the one who hurt her is to be fined whatever amount the woman's husband demands, subject to the approval of the judges. 23But if the woman herself is injured, the punishment shall be life for life, 24eye for eye, tooth for tooth, hand for hand, foot for foot, 25burn for burn, wound for wound, bruise for bruise.

26"If someone hits his male or female slave in the eye and puts it out, he is to free the slave as payment for the eye. 27If he knocks out a tooth, he is to free the slave as payment for the tooth.

The Responsibility of Owners

28"If a bull gores someone to death, it is to be stoned, and its flesh shall not be eaten; but its owner is not to be punished. 29But if

20:25 Deut 27:5–7; Josh 8:31 **21:2–6** Lev 25:39–46 **21:12** Lev 24:17 **21:13** Num 35:10–34; Deut 19:1–13; Josh 20:1–9 **21:16** Deut 24:7 **21:17** Lev 20:9; Mt 15:4; Mk 7:10 **21:24** Lev 24:19, 20; Deut 19:21; Mt 5:38

Live it!

Getting Even

Riley just wanted to punch something, he was so mad. Zach made fun of him in gym class, and all the other guys laughed. That wasn't the worst of it though. It carried over to the cafeteria. It was the longest lunch period of his life. Now he was trying to figure out a way to get back at Zach. He wanted revenge.

Many people use Exodus 21:23–25 to justify getting even with someone. Even some laws are based on it, like the death penalty for a person who commits murder. But Jesus had a different idea. He said, "If anyone slaps you on the right cheek, let him slap your left cheek too" (Matthew 5:39).

An eye for an eye only leaves two people who can't see very well. A wound for a wound only leaves two people who are hurting. Instead of getting back at Zach, Riley should use his energy to do something kind for someone else who might be hurting.

Is there someone you want to get even with? What can you do instead that will make you feel better and help someone else? What would Jesus do?

— Exodus 21:23–25

the bull had been in the habit of attacking people and its owner had been warned, but did not keep it penned up—then if it gores someone to death, it is to be stoned, and its owner is to be put to death also. 30 However, if the owner is allowed to pay a fine to save his life, he must pay the full amount required. 31 If the bull kills a boy or a girl, the same rule applies. 32 If the bull kills a male or female slave, its owner shall pay the owner of the slave thirty pieces of silver, and the bull shall be stoned to death.

33 "If someone takes the cover off a pit or if he digs one and does not cover it, and a bull or a donkey falls into it, 34 he must pay for the animal. He is to pay the money to the owner and may keep the dead animal. 35 If someone's bull kills someone else's bull, the two of them shall sell the live bull and divide the money; they shall also divide up the meat from the dead animal. 36 But if it was known that the bull had been in the habit of attacking and its owner did not keep it penned up, he must make good the loss by giving the other man a live bull, but he may keep the dead animal.

Laws about Repayment

22 "If someone steals a cow or a sheep and kills it or sells it, he must pay five cows for one cow and four sheep for one sheep. 2-4 He must pay for what he stole. If he owns nothing, he shall be sold as a slave to pay for what he has stolen. If the stolen animal, whether a cow, a donkey, or a sheep, is found alive in his possession, he shall pay two for one.

"If a thief is caught breaking into a house at night and is killed, the one who killed him is not guilty of murder. But if it happens during the day, he is guilty of murder.

5 "If someone lets his animals graze in a field or a vineyard and they stray away and eat up the crops[w] growing in someone else's field, he must make good the loss with the crops from his own fields or vineyards.

They . . . eat up the crops growing in someone else's field. (22:5)

[w] **22:5** If . . . crops; *or* If someone burns off a field or a vineyard, and lets the fire get out of control and burn up the crops.

6 "If someone starts a fire in his own field
and it spreads through the weeds to someone
else's field and burns up grain that is grow-
ing or that has been cut and stacked, the one
who started the fire is to pay for the damage.
7 "If anyone agrees to keep someone else's
money or other valuables for him and they
are stolen from his house, the thief, if found,
shall repay double. 8 But if the thief is not
found, the one who was keeping the valu-
ables is to be brought to the place of wor-
ship and there he must take an oath that he
has not stolen the other one's property.
9 "In every case of a dispute about proper-
ty, whether it involves cattle, donkeys, sheep,
clothing, or any other lost object, the two
people claiming the property shall be taken
to the place of worship. The one whom God
declares to be guilty shall pay double to the
other one.
10 "If anyone agrees to keep someone else's
donkey, cow, sheep, or other animal for him,
and the animal dies or is injured or is carried
off in a raid, and if there was no witness,
11 the man must go to the place of worship
and take an oath that he has not stolen the
other man's animal. If the animal was not
stolen, the owner shall accept the loss, and
the other man need not repay him; 12 but
if the animal was stolen, the man must repay
the owner. 13 If it was killed by wild animals,
the man is to bring the remains as evidence;
he need not pay for what has been killed by
wild animals.
14 "If anyone borrows an animal from
someone else and it is injured or dies when
its owner is not present, he must pay for it.
15 But if that happens when the owner is
present, he need not repay. If it is a rented
animal, the loss is covered by the rental
price.

Moral and Religious Laws

16 "If a man seduces a virgin who is not
engaged, he must pay the bride price for her
and marry her. 17 But if her father refuses to
let him marry her, he must pay the father a
sum of money equal to the bride price for a
virgin.
18 "Put to death any woman who practices
magic.
19 "Put to death anyone who has sexual
relations with an animal.

Live it!

Rules and More Rules

"This place has too many rules!" Erika cried. "I'm afraid to say anything, do anything, or be different anymore. I might break a rule." Too many rules can be frustrating, but without them life would be a mess. Think of what the school day would be like without rules. What would it be like to ride in a car if there were no traffic laws? What would life be like at home without rules?

Many laws are listed in the Book of Exodus, after the Ten Commandments. These new laws helped the Israelites to build a fair society rather than one that was based on greed and violence. Some of the laws still hold true for us. Others no longer apply because of changes in culture, and the teaching of Jesus.

Rules are made for good reasons, and it is best to try to follow them. If you think a rule is unfair, talk to the people who made it. Try to understand why they felt the rule was necessary. Maybe you can work together to change it in a way that is fair to everyone.

— Exodus 22:1–8

22:16, 17 Deut 22:28, 29 **22:18** Deut 18:10, 11 **22:19** Lev 18:23; 20:15, 16; Deut 27:21

Which laws in Exodus, chapters 21–23, seem fair to you? Find some that no longer make sense in our culture or because of the teaching of Jesus.

20“Condemn to death anyone who offers sacrifices to any god except to me, the LORD.

21“Do not mistreat or oppress a foreigner; remember that you were foreigners in Egypt. 22Do not mistreat any widow or orphan. 23If you do, I, the LORD, will answer them when they cry out to me for help, 24and I will become angry and kill you in war. Your wives will become widows, and your children will be fatherless.

25“If you lend money to any of my people who are poor, do not act like a moneylender and require him to pay interest. 26If you take someone's cloak as a pledge that he will pay you, you must give it back to him before the sun sets, 27because it is the only covering he has to keep him warm. What else can he sleep in? When he cries out to me for help, I will answer him because I am merciful.

28“Do not speak evil of God,[x] and do not curse a leader of your people.

29“Give me the offerings from your grain, your wine, and your olive oil when they are due.

“Give me your first-born sons. 30Give me the first-born of your cattle and your sheep. Let the first-born male stay with its mother for seven days, and on the eighth day offer it to me.

31“You are my people, so you must not eat the meat of any animal that has been killed by wild animals; instead, give it to the dogs.

Justice and Fairness

23 “Do not spread false rumors, and do not help a guilty person by giving false testimony. 2Do not follow the majority when they do wrong or when they give testimony that perverts justice. 3Do not show partiality to a poor person at his trial.

4“If you happen to see your enemy's cow or donkey running loose, take it back to him. 5If his donkey has fallen under its load, help him get the donkey to its feet again; don't just walk off.

6“Do not deny justice to a poor person when he appears in court. 7Do not make false accusations, and do not put an innocent person to death, for I will condemn anyone who does such an evil thing. 8Do not accept a bribe, for a bribe makes people blind to what is right and ruins the cause of those who are innocent.

9“Do not mistreat a foreigner; you know how it feels to be a foreigner, because you were foreigners in Egypt.

The Seventh Year and the Seventh Day

10“For six years plant your land and gather in what it produces. 11But in the seventh year let it rest, and do not harvest anything that grows on it. The poor may eat what grows there, and the wild animals can have what is left. Do the same with your vineyards and your olive trees.

12“Work six days a week, but do no work on the seventh day, so that your slaves and the foreigners who work for you and even your animals can rest.

13“Listen to everything that I, the LORD, have said to you. Do not pray to other gods; do not even mention their names.

The Three Great Festivals

(Exodus 34:18–26; Deuteronomy 16:1–17)

14“Celebrate three festivals a year to honor me. 15In the month of Abib, the month in which you left Egypt, celebrate the Festival of Unleavened Bread in the way that I commanded you. Do not eat any bread made with yeast during the seven days of

[x] **22:28** God; *or* the judges.

22:20 Deut 17:2–7 **22:21, 22** Ex 23:9; Lev 19:33, 34; Deut 24:17, 18; 27:19 **22:25** Lev 25:35–38; Deut 15:7–11; 23:19, 20 **22:26, 27** Deut 24:10–13 **22:28** Acts 23:5 **22:31** Lev 17:15 **23:1** Ex 20:16; Lev 19:11, 12; Deut 5:20 **23:3** Lev 19:15 **23:4, 5** Deut 22:1–4 **23:6–8** Lev 19:15; Deut 16:19 **23:9** Ex 22:21; Lev 19:33, 34; Deut 24:17, 18; 27:19 **23:10, 11** Lev 25:1–7 **23:12** Ex 20:9–11; 31:15; 34:21; 35:2; Lev 23:3; Deut 5:13, 14 **23:15** Ex 12:14–20; Lev 23:6–8; Num 28:17–25

Which verse in Exodus 23:1–9 deals with peer pressure? What does it say about following the crowd?

Live it!

Everyday Justice

If a teacher asked you and your friends to come up with guidelines for being a person who is well liked and respected, your list would probably include some of the following rules:

- **Don't spread rumors.**
- **Don't cover for someone who has done something wrong.**
- **Don't give in to peer pressure, especially when peers lie or cheat.**
- **If you find something that belongs to someone else, return it to that person.**
- **Be fair to everyone, even those who are different or don't seem to fit in.**

The words may be different, but these rules come straight from the Bible (Exodus 23:1–9). They were written hundreds of years ago, but they make as much sense today as they did then. If you want to be well liked and respected as you grow up, you will want to live by these rules.

The Bible is not just a book for and about people who lived many centuries ago. It is a book that was written for and about you, too. Read it often and use it as a guide to becoming the person God wants you to be.

— Exodus 23:1–9

this festival. Never come to worship me
without bringing an offering.
16 "Celebrate the Harvest Festival when
you begin to harvest your crops.
"Celebrate the Festival of Shelters in the
autumn, when you gather the fruit from
your vineyards and orchards. 17 Every year at
these three festivals all your men must come
to worship me, the Lord your God.
18 "Do not offer bread made with yeast
when you sacrifice an animal to me. The fat
of animals sacrificed to me during these fes-
tivals is not to be left until the following
morning.
19 "Each year bring to the house of the
LORD your God the first grain that you har-
vest.
"Do not cook a young sheep or goat in
its mother's milk.

Promises and Instructions

20 "I will send an angel ahead of you to
protect you as you travel and to bring you to
the place which I have prepared. 21 Pay atten-
tion to him and obey him. Do not rebel
against him, for I have sent him, and he will
not pardon such rebellion. 22 But if you obey
him and do everything I command, I will
fight against all your enemies. 23 My angel will
go ahead of you and take you into the land of
the Amorites, the Hittites, the Perizzites, the
Canaanites, the Hivites, and the Jebusites, and
I will destroy them. 24 Do not bow down to
their gods or worship them, and do not adopt
their religious practices. Destroy their gods
and break down their sacred stone pillars. 25 If
you worship me, the LORD your God, I will
bless you with food and water and take away
all your sicknesses. 26 In your land no woman
will have a miscarriage or be without chil-
dren. I will give you long lives.
27 "I will make the people who oppose
you afraid of me; I will bring confusion
among the people against whom you fight,
and I will make all your enemies turn and
run from you. 28 I will throw your enemies
into panic;[y] I will drive out the Hivites, the
Canaanites, and the Hittites as you advance.
29 I will not drive them out within a year's
time; if I did, the land would become
deserted, and the wild animals would be too
many for you. 30 Instead, I will drive them
out little by little, until there are enough of
you to take possession of the land. 31 I will
make the borders of your land extend from

[y] **23:28** I will . . . panic; *or* I will send hornets among your enemies.

23:16 a Lev 23:15–21; Num 28:26–31; **b** Lev 23:39–43 **23:19** Deut 26:2; Ex 34:26; Deut 14:21

the Gulf of Aqaba to the Mediterranean Sea and from the desert to the Euphrates River. I will give you power over the inhabitants of the land, and you will drive them out as you advance. [32]Do not make any agreement with them or with their gods. [33]Do not let those people live in your country; if you do, they will make you sin against me. If you worship their gods, it will be a fatal trap for you."

The Covenant Is Sealed

24 The LORD said to Moses, "Come up the mountain to me, you and Aaron, Nadab, Abihu, and seventy of the leaders of Israel; and while you are still some distance away, bow down in worship. [2]You alone, and none of the others, are to come near me. The people are not even to come up the mountain."

[3]Moses went and told the people all the LORD's commands and all the ordinances, and all the people answered together, "We will do everything that the LORD has said." [4]Moses wrote down all the LORD's commands. Early the next morning he built an altar at the foot of the mountain and set up twelve stones, one for each of the twelve tribes of Israel. [5]Then he sent young men, and they burned sacrifices to the LORD and sacrificed some cattle as fellowship offerings. [6]Moses took half of the blood of the animals and put it in bowls; and the other half he threw against the altar. [7]Then he took the book of the covenant, in which the LORD's commands were written, and read it aloud to the people. They said, "We will obey the LORD and do everything that he has commanded."

[8]Then Moses took the blood in the bowls and threw it on the people. He said, "This is the blood that seals the covenant which the LORD made with you when he gave all these commands."

[9]Moses, Aaron, Nadab, Abihu, and seventy of the leaders of Israel went up the mountain [10]and they saw the God of Israel. Beneath his feet was what looked like a pavement of sapphire, as blue as the sky.

Study it!

The Covenant of Covenants

God made important covenants before this one. In the Bible a covenant is a set of promises made between God and a person or a group. The Book of Genesis tells about covenants God made with Noah, Abraham, and Jacob. But the Sinai Covenant is the Covenant of Covenants. At Sinai God made clear what his covenant with Abraham would now mean for all of Abraham's descendants. When Moses read the Law—the Ten Commandments—from the book of the Covenant, the Israelites replied, "We will obey the LORD and do everything that he has commanded" (Exodus 24:7). To seal the deal, Moses went up Mount Sinai, where God gave him stone tablets on which the Law was written. The Sinai Covenant and the Law that was part of that Covenant continue to guide Jewish and Christian believers today.

God's Covenant with the Israelites meant that they were now and forever the People of God. Nothing would ever change that, even though the Israelites would make some huge mistakes. As sons and daughters of Abraham through our faith, we are also the People of God—now and forever.

— Exodus 24:1–18

[11]God did not harm these leading men of Israel; they saw God, and then they ate and drank together.

24:8 a Mt 26:28; Mk 14:24; Lk 22:20; 1 Cor 11:25; Heb 10:29; **b** Heb 9:19, 20

Moses on Mount Sinai

12 The LORD said to Moses, "Come up the
mountain to me, and while you are here, I
will give you two stone tablets which con-
tain all the laws that I have written for the
instruction of the people." 13 Moses and his
helper Joshua got ready, and Moses began[z]
to go up the holy mountain. 14 Moses said to
the leaders, "Wait here in the camp for us
until we come back. Aaron and Hur are here
with you; and so whoever has a dispute to
settle can go to them."

15 Moses went up Mount Sinai, and a
cloud covered it. 16-17 The dazzling light of
the LORD's presence came down on the
mountain. To the Israelites the light looked
like a fire burning on top of the mountain.
The cloud covered the mountain for six
days, and on the seventh day the LORD
called to Moses from the cloud. 18 Moses
went on up the mountain into the cloud.
There he stayed for forty days and nights.

Offerings for the Sacred Tent
(Exodus 35:4–9)

25 The LORD said to Moses, 2 "Tell the
Israelites to make an offering to me.
Receive whatever offerings anyone wishes to
give. 3 These offerings are to be: gold, silver,
and bronze; 4 fine linen; blue, purple, and red
wool; cloth made of goats' hair; 5 rams' skin
dyed red; fine leather; acacia wood; 6 oil for
the lamps; spices for the anointing oil and
for the sweet-smelling incense; 7 carnelians
and other jewels to be set in the ephod[a] of
the High Priest and in his breastpiece. 8 The
people must make a sacred Tent for me, so
that I may live among them. 9 Make it and all
its furnishings according to the plan that I
will show you.

The Covenant Box
(Exodus 37:1–9)

10 "Make a Box out of acacia wood, 45
inches long, 27 inches wide, and 27 inches
high. 11 Cover it with pure gold inside and
out and put a gold border all around it.
12 Make four carrying rings of gold for it and
attach them to its four legs, with two rings
on each side. 13 Make carrying poles of acacia
wood and cover them with gold 14 and put
them through the rings on each side of the
Box. 15 The poles are to be left in the rings
and must not be taken out. 16 Then put in
the Box the two stone tablets that I will give
you, on which the commandments are writ-
ten.

17 "Make a lid of pure gold, 45 inches long
and 27 inches wide. 18 Make two winged
creatures[b] of hammered gold, 19 one for each
end of the lid. Make them so that they form
one piece with the lid. 20 The winged crea-
tures are to face each other across the lid,
and their outspread wings are to cover it.
21 Put the two stone tablets inside the Box
and put the lid on top of it. 22 I will meet
you there, and from above the lid between
the two winged creatures I will give you all
my laws for the people of Israel.

The Table for the Bread Offered to God
(Exodus 37:10–16)

23 "Make a table out of acacia wood, 36
inches long, 18 inches wide, and 27 inches
high. 24 Cover it with pure gold and put a
gold border around it. 25 Make a rim 3 inch-
es wide around it and a gold border around
the rim. 26 Make four carrying rings of gold
for it and put them at the four corners,
where the legs are. 27 The rings to hold the
poles for carrying the table are to be placed
near the rim. 28 Make the poles of acacia
wood and cover them with gold. 29 Make

[z] **24:13** Moses began; *one ancient translation* they began. [a] **25:7** EPHOD: *In most contexts the term ephod refers to a type of shoulder garment, in certain respects resembling a vest. It was made of costly and colorful cloth and to it was attached a kind of pouch containing the Urim and Thummim, two objects used in determining God's will.* [b] **25:18** WINGED CREATURES: *See Word List.*

24:18 Deut 9:9 **25:17** Heb 9:5

The stone tablets were to be kept in the Covenant Box described in Exodus 25:10–22. The Covenant Box is also called the Ark of the Covenant in other Bibles.

plates, cups, jars, and bowls to be used for
the wine offerings. All of these are to be
made of pure gold. 30The table is to be
placed in front of the Covenant Box, and on
the table there is always to be the sacred
bread offered to me.

The Lampstand
(Exodus 37:17–24)

31"Make a lampstand of pure gold. Make
its base and its shaft of hammered gold; its
decorative flowers, including buds and petals,
are to form one piece with it. 32Six branches
shall extend from its sides, three from each
side. 33Each of the six branches is to have
three decorative flowers shaped like almond
blossoms with buds and petals. 34The shaft of
the lampstand is to have four decorative
flowers shaped like almond blossoms with
buds and petals. 35There is to be one bud
below each of the three pairs of branches.
36The buds, the branches, and the lampstand
are to be a single piece of pure hammered
gold. 37Make seven lamps for the lampstand
and set them up so that they shine toward
the front. 38Make its tongs and trays of pure
gold. 39Use seventy-five pounds of pure gold
to make the lampstand and all this equip-
ment. 40Take care to make them according to
the plan that I showed you on the mountain.

The Tent of the LORD's Presence[c]
(Exodus 36:8–38)

26 "Make the interior of the sacred
Tent, the Tent of my presence, out of
ten pieces of fine linen woven with blue,
purple, and red wool. Embroider them with
figures of winged creatures. 2Make each
piece the same size, 14 yards long and 2
yards wide. 3Sew five of them together in
one set, and do the same with the other five.
4Make loops of blue cloth on the edge of
the outside piece in each set. 5Put fifty loops
on the first piece of the first set and fifty
loops matching them on the last piece of the
second set. 6Make fifty gold hooks with
which to join the two sets into one piece.

7"Make a cover for the Tent out of eleven
pieces of cloth made of goats' hair. 8Make
them all the same size, 15 yards long and 2
yards wide. 9Sew five of them together in
one set, and the other six in another set. Fold
the sixth piece double over the front of the
Tent. 10Put fifty loops on the edge of the last
piece of one set, and fifty loops on the edge
of the other set. 11Make fifty bronze hooks
and put them in the loops to join the two
sets so as to form one cover. 12Hang the
extra half piece over the back of the Tent.
13The extra half yard on each side of the
length is to hang over the sides of the Tent
to cover it.

14"Make two more coverings, one of
rams' skin dyed red and the other of fine
leather, to serve as the outer cover.

15"Make upright frames for the Tent out
of acacia wood. 16Each frame is to be 15 feet
long and 27 inches wide, 17with two match-
ing projections, so that the frames can be
joined together. All the frames are to have
these projections. 18Make twenty frames for
the south side 19and forty silver bases to go
under them, two bases under each frame to
hold its two projections. 20Make twenty
frames for the north side of the Tent 21and
forty silver bases, two under each frame.
22For the back of the Tent on the west, make
six frames, 23and two frames for the corners.
24These corner frames are to be joined at
the bottom and connected all the way to the
top. The two frames that form the two cor-
ners are to be made in this way. 25So there
will be eight frames with their sixteen silver
bases, two under each frame.

26"Make fifteen crossbars of acacia wood,
five for the frames on one side of the Tent,
27five for the frames on the other side, and
five for the frames on the west end, at the
back. 28The middle crossbar, set halfway up
the frames, is to extend from one end of the

[c] **26:1** TENT OF THE LORD'S PRESENCE: *See Word List.*
25:30 Lev 24:5–8 **25:40** Acts 7:44; Heb 8:5

The Tent of the LORD's presence is also called a tabernacle in other Bible translations.

Live it!

Portable God

Martina was going away with her friend's family for a few days. Her mom went shopping and bought several travel-sized items for Martina to take along—shampoo, toothpaste, and other things she needed for the trip. They were small and a lot easier to pack than the stuff she had at home.

Exodus, chapters 25–31, contain instructions for building a travel-sized worship space. As the Israelites continued their journey from Sinai, God wanted them to know that he was always with them, always blessing them. They needed a place to worship God and listen to him. The Tent of the LORD's presence and its furnishings weren't exactly small and light, but they could be packed up and carried from place to place.

God is always with us, but sometimes we need to be reminded of his presence. Some people wear a cross or medal. Others pray when they hear church bells. Others post pictures and poems that remind them of God in places where they will see them every day.

As you travel on your journey through life, what reminds you that God is with you?

— Exodus, chapter 26

Tent to the other. 29 Cover the frames with
gold and fit them with gold rings to hold
the crossbars, which are also to be covered
with gold. 30 Set up the Tent according to the
plan that I showed you on the mountain.
31 "Make a curtain of fine linen woven
with blue, purple, and red wool. Embroider
it with figures of winged creatures. 32 Hang it
on four posts of acacia wood covered with
gold, fitted with hooks, and set in four silver
bases. 33 Place the curtain under the row
of hooks in the roof of the Tent, and put
behind the curtain the Covenant Box containing the two stone tablets. The curtain
will separate the Holy Place from the Most
Holy Place. 34 Put the lid on the Covenant
Box. 35 Outside the Most Holy Place put the
table against the north side of the Tent and
the lampstand against the south side.
36 "For the entrance of the Tent make a
curtain of fine linen woven with blue, purple, and red wool and decorated with
embroidery. 37 For this curtain make five
posts of acacia wood covered with gold and
fitted with gold hooks; make five bronze
bases for these posts.

The Altar
(Exodus 38:1–7)

27 "Make an altar out of acacia wood. It
is to be square, 7½ feet long and 7½
feet wide, and it is to be 4½ feet high. 2 Make
projections at the top of the four corners.
They are to form one piece with the altar,
and the whole is to be covered with bronze.
3 Make pans for the greasy ashes, and make
shovels, bowls, hooks, and fire pans. All this
equipment is to be made of bronze. 4 Make a
bronze grating and put four bronze carrying
rings on its corners. 5 Put the grating under
the rim of the altar, so that it reaches halfway
up the altar. 6 Make carrying poles of acacia
wood, cover them with bronze, 7 and put
them in the rings on each side of the altar
when it is carried. 8 Make the altar out of
boards and leave it hollow, according to the
plan that I showed you on the mountain.

The Enclosure for the Tent of the LORD's Presence
(Exodus 38:9–20)

9 "For the Tent of my presence make an
enclosure out of fine linen curtains. On the
south side the curtains are to be 50 yards

26:33 Heb 6:19; 9:3–5

Pray it!

A Traveler's Prayer

Saint Patrick was a missionary who brought Christ to the people of Ireland. Because of his efforts to spread the Gospel, Patrick is known as the Apostle of Ireland and its patron saint.

Inside the Tent of the LORD's presence, in front of the Covenant Box, a lamp was to be kept burning all night as a sign of God's presence. Like that lamp, this prayer of Saint Patrick will remind you that God is always with you and around you on the journey of life.

Christ, be with me, Christ before me, Christ behind me.
Christ in me, Christ beneath me, Christ above me,
Christ on my right, Christ on my left.
Christ where I lie, Christ where I sit, Christ where I arise.
Christ in the heart of every one who thinks of me,
Christ in the mouth of every one who speaks of me.
Christ in every eye that sees me.
Christ in every ear that hears me.

— Exodus 27:20–21

long, 10supported by twenty bronze posts in
twenty bronze bases, with hooks and rods
made of silver. 11Do the same on the north
side of the enclosure. 12On the west side
there are to be curtains 25 yards long, with
ten posts and ten bases. 13On the east side,
where the entrance is, the enclosure is also
to be 25 yards wide. 14-15On each side of
the entrance there are to be 7½ yards of
curtains, with three posts and three bases.
16For the entrance itself there is to be a
curtain 10 yards long made of fine linen
woven with blue, purple, and red wool, and
decorated with embroidery. It is to be sup-
ported by four posts in four bases. 17All the
posts around the enclosure are to be con-
nected with silver rods, and their hooks are
to be made of silver and their bases of
bronze. 18The enclosure is to be 50 yards
long, 25 yards wide, and 2½ yards high. The
curtains are to be made of fine linen and
the bases of bronze. 19All the equipment
that is used in the Tent and all the pegs for
the Tent and for the enclosure are to be
made of bronze.

Taking Care of the Lamp
(Leviticus 24:1–4)

20"Command the people of Israel to
bring you the best olive oil for the lamp, so
that it can be lit each evening. 21Aaron and
his sons are to set up the lamp in the Tent of
my presence outside the curtain which is in
front of the Covenant Box. There in my
presence it is to burn from evening until
morning. This command is to be kept for-
ever by the Israelites and their descendants.

Garments for the Priests
(Exodus 39:1–7)

28 "Summon your brother Aaron and
his sons, Nadab, Abihu, Eleazar, and
Ithamar. Separate them from the people of
Israel, so that they may serve me as priests.
2Make priestly garments for your brother
Aaron, to provide him with dignity and
beauty. 3Call all the skilled workers to whom
I have given ability, and tell them to make
Aaron's clothes, so that he may be dedicated
as a priest in my service. 4Tell them to make
a breastpiece, an ephod, a robe, an embroi-

Vestments

Catholic Connections

In Exodus, chapter 28, God gave Moses directions for the clothing—called *vestments*—that the priests of the temple were to wear to honor God. It was to be brightly colored and made of the finest materials.

Catholic priests and deacons also wear vestments when they celebrate the sacraments. The next time you are at Mass, see if you can identify the following vestments:

- **Alb: a long, white tunic. It may be tied around the waist with a rope, known as a *cincture*.**
- **Stole: a long, narrow strip of fabric. Priests wear a stole over both shoulders. Deacons wear a stole over one shoulder.**
- **Chasuble: the outer garment worn by a priest. The color of the chasuble is determined by the liturgical season or type of Mass being celebrated.**

— Exodus, chapter 28

dered shirt, a turban, and a sash. They are to
make these priestly garments for your broth-
er Aaron and his sons, so that they can serve
me as priests. [5]The skilled workers are to use
blue, purple, and red wool, gold thread, and
fine linen.

[6]"They are to make the ephod of blue,
purple, and red wool, gold thread, and fine
linen, decorated with embroidery. [7]Two
shoulder straps, by which it can be fastened,
are to be attached to the sides. [8]A finely
woven belt made of the same materials is to
be attached to the ephod so as to form one
piece with it. [9]Take two carnelian stones and
engrave on them the names of the twelve
sons of Jacob, [10]in the order of their birth,
with six on one stone and six on the other.
[11]Have a skillful jeweler engrave on the two
stones the names of the sons of Jacob, and
mount the stones in gold settings. [12]Put
them on the shoulder straps of the ephod to
represent the twelve tribes of Israel. In this
way Aaron will carry their names on his
shoulders, so that I, the LORD, will always
remember my people. [13]Make two gold set-
tings [14]and two chains of pure gold twisted
like cords, and attach them to the settings.

The Breastpiece
(Exodus 39:8–21)

[15]"Make a breastpiece for the High Priest
to use in determining God's will. It is to be
made of the same materials as the ephod and
with similar embroidery. [16]It is to be square
and folded double, 9 inches long and 9 inch-
es wide. [17]Mount four rows of precious
stones on it; in the first row mount a ruby, a
topaz, and a garnet; [18]in the second row, an
emerald, a sapphire, and a diamond; [19]in the
third row, a turquoise, an agate, and an
amethyst; [20]and in the fourth row, a beryl,
a carnelian, and a jasper. These are to be
mounted in gold settings. [21]Each of these
twelve stones is to have engraved on it the
name of one of the sons of Jacob, to repre-
sent the tribes of Israel. [22]For the breastpiece
make chains of pure gold, twisted like cords.

Breastpiece: A linen pocket that was attached to another garment and worn like an apron. It held special items.

[23]Make two gold rings and attach them to the upper corners of the breastpiece, [24]and fasten the two gold cords to the two rings. [25]Fasten the other two ends of the cords to the two settings, and in this way attach them in front to the shoulder straps of the ephod. [26]Then make two rings of gold and attach them to the lower corners of the breastpiece on the inside edge next to the ephod. [27]Make two more gold rings and attach them to the lower part of the front of the two shoulder straps of the ephod, near the seam and above the finely woven belt. [28]Tie the rings of the breastpiece to the rings of the ephod with a blue cord, so that the breastpiece rests above the belt and does not come loose.

29"When Aaron enters the Holy Place, he will wear this breastpiece engraved with the names of the tribes of Israel, so that I, the LORD, will always remember my people. [30]Put the Urim and Thummim[d] in the breastpiece, so that Aaron will carry them when he comes into my holy presence. At such times he must always wear this breastpiece, so that he can determine my will for the people of Israel.

The Other Priestly Garments
(Exodus 39:22–31)

31"The robe that goes under the ephod is to be made entirely of blue wool. [32]It is to have a hole for the head, and this hole is to be reinforced with a woven binding to keep it from tearing. [33-34]All around its lower hem put pomegranates of blue, purple, and red wool, alternating with gold bells. [35]Aaron is to wear this robe when he serves as priest. When he comes into my presence in the Holy Place or when he leaves it, the sound of the bells will be heard, and he will not be killed.

36"Make an ornament of pure gold and engrave on it 'Dedicated to the LORD.' [37]Tie it to the front of the turban with a blue cord. [38]Aaron is to wear it on his forehead, so that I, the LORD, will accept all the offerings that the Israelites dedicate to me, even if the people commit some error in offering them.

39"Weave Aaron's shirt of fine linen and make a turban of fine linen and also a sash decorated with embroidery.

40"Make shirts, sashes, and caps for Aaron's sons, to provide them with dignity and beauty. [41]Put these clothes on your brother Aaron and his sons. Then ordain them and dedicate them by anointing them with olive oil, so that they may serve me as priests. [42]Make linen shorts for them, reaching from the waist to the thighs, so that they will not expose themselves. [43]Aaron and his sons must always wear them when they go into the Tent of my presence or approach the altar to serve as priests in the Holy Place, so that they will not be killed for exposing themselves. This is a permanent rule for Aaron and his descendants.

Instructions for Ordaining Aaron and His Sons as Priests
(Leviticus 8:1–36)

29 "This is what you are to do to Aaron and his sons to dedicate them as priests in my service. Take one young bull and two rams without any defects. [2]Use the best wheat flour, but no yeast, and make some bread with olive oil, some without it, and some in the form of thin cakes brushed with oil. [3]Put them in a basket and offer them to me when you sacrifice the bull and the two rams.

4"Bring Aaron and his sons to the entrance of the Tent of my presence, and have them take a ritual bath. [5]Then dress Aaron in the priestly garments—the shirt, the robe that goes under the ephod, the ephod, the breastpiece, and the belt. [6]Put the turban on him and tie on it the sacred sign of dedication engraved 'Dedicated to the

[d] **28:30** URIM AND THUMMIM: *Two objects used by the priest to determine God's will; it is not known precisely how they were used.*

28:30 Num 27:21; Deut 33:8; Ezra 2:63; Neh 7:65 **28:33, 34** Sir 45:9

Ordination is the religious ritual in which someone becomes a priest by being given priestly powers and responsibilities.

LORD.' 7Then take the anointing oil, pour it
on his head, and anoint him.

8"Bring his sons and put shirts on them;
9put sashes around their waists and tie caps
on their heads. That is how you are to ordain
Aaron and his sons. They and their descen-
dants are to serve me as priests forever.

10"Bring the bull to the front of the Tent
of my presence and tell Aaron and his sons
to put their hands on its head. 11Kill the bull
there in my holy presence at the entrance of
the Tent. 12Take some of the bull's blood and
with your finger put it on the projections of
the altar. Then pour out the rest of the blood
at the base of the altar. 13Next, take all the
fat which covers the internal organs, the best
part of the liver, and the two kidneys with
the fat on them, and burn them on the altar
as an offering to me. 14But burn the bull's
flesh, its skin, and its intestines outside the
camp. This is an offering to take away the
sins of the priests.

15"Take one of the rams and tell Aaron
and his sons to put their hands on its head.
16Kill it, and take its blood and throw it
against all four sides of the altar. 17Cut the
ram in pieces; wash its internal organs and its
hind legs, and put them on top of the head
and the other pieces. 18Burn the whole ram
on the altar as a food offering. The odor of
this offering pleases me.

19"Take the other ram—the ram used for
dedication—and tell Aaron and his sons to
put their hands on its head. 20Kill it, and take
some of its blood and put it on the lobes of
the right ears of Aaron and his sons, on the
thumbs of their right hands and on the big
toes of their right feet. Throw the rest of the
blood against all four sides of the altar.
21Take some of the blood that is on the altar
and some of the anointing oil, and sprinkle
it on Aaron and his clothes and on his sons
and their clothes. He, his sons, and their
clothes will then be dedicated to me.

22"Cut away the ram's fat, the fat tail, the
fat covering the internal organs, the best part
of the liver, the two kidneys with the fat on
them, and the right thigh. 23From the basket
of bread which has been offered to me, take
one loaf of each kind: one loaf made with
olive oil and one made without it and one
thin cake. 24Put all this food in the hands of
Aaron and his sons and have them dedicate
it to me as a special gift. 25Then take it from
them and burn it on the altar, on top of the
burnt offering, as a food offering to me. The
odor of this offering pleases me.

26"Take the breast of this ram and dedi-
cate it to me as a special gift. This part of the
animal will be yours.

27"When a priest is ordained, the breast
and the thigh of the ram being used for the
ordination are to be dedicated to me as a
special gift and set aside for the priests. 28It is
my unchanging decision that when my peo-
ple make their fellowship offerings, the
breast and the thigh of the animal belong to
the priests. This is the people's gift to me, the
LORD.

29"Aaron's priestly garments are to be
handed on to his sons after his death, for
them to wear when they are ordained. 30The
son of Aaron who succeeds him as priest and
who goes into the Tent of my presence to
serve in the Holy Place is to wear these gar-
ments for seven days.

31"Take the meat of the ram used for the
ordination of Aaron and his sons and boil it
in a holy place. 32At the entrance of the Tent
of my presence they are to eat it along with
the bread left in the basket. 33They shall eat
what was used in the ritual of forgiveness at
their ordination. Only priests may eat this
food, because it is sacred. 34If some of the
meat or some of the bread is not eaten by
morning, it is to be burned; it is not to be
eaten, for it is sacred.

35"Perform the rites of ordination for
Aaron and his sons for seven days exactly as I
have commanded you. 36Each day you must
offer a bull as a sacrifice, so that sin may be
forgiven. This will purify the altar. Then
anoint it with olive oil to make it holy. 37Do
this every day for seven days. Then the altar
will be completely holy, and anyone or any-
thing that touches it will be harmed by the
power of its holiness.[e]

[e] **29:37** BE HARMED BY THE POWER OF ITS HOLINESS: *It was believed that ordinary people or things would be harmed by touching something holy.*

29:18 Eph 5:2; Phil 4:18

The Daily Offerings
(Numbers 28:1–8)

38“Every day for all time to come, sacri-
fice on the altar two one-year-old lambs.
39Sacrifice one of the lambs in the morning
and the other in the evening. 40With the
first lamb offer two pounds of fine wheat
flour mixed with one quart of pure olive
oil. Pour out one quart of wine as an offer-
ing. 41Sacrifice the second lamb in the
evening, and offer with it the same amounts
of flour, olive oil, and wine as in the morn-
ing. This is a food offering to me, the LORD,
and its odor pleases me. 42For all time to
come, this burnt offering is to be offered in
my presence at the entrance of the Tent of
my presence. That is where I will meet my
people and speak to you. 43There I will
meet the people of Israel, and the dazzling
light of my presence will make the place
holy. 44I will make the Tent and the altar
holy, and I will set Aaron and his sons apart
to serve me as priests. 45I will live among
the people of Israel, and I will be their God.
46They will know that I am the LORD their
God who brought them out of Egypt so
that I could live among them. I am the
LORD their God.

The Altar for Burning Incense
(Exodus 37:25–28)

30 “Make an altar out of acacia wood,
for burning incense. 2It is to be
square, 18 inches long and 18 inches wide,
and it is to be 36 inches high. Its projec-
tions at the four corners are to form one
piece with it. 3Cover its top, all four sides,
and its projections with pure gold, and put
a gold border around it. 4Make two gold
carrying rings for it and attach them below
the border on two sides to hold the poles
with which it is to be carried. 5Make these
poles of acacia wood and cover them with
gold. 6Put this altar outside the curtain
which hangs in front of the Covenant Box.
That is the place where I will meet you.
7Every morning when Aaron comes to take
care of the lamps, he is to burn sweet-
smelling incense on it. 8He must do the
same when he lights the lamps in the
evening. This offering of incense is to con-
tinue without interruption for all time to
come. 9Do not offer on this altar any for-
bidden incense, any animal offering, or any
grain offering, and do not pour out any
wine offering on it. 10Once a year Aaron is
to perform the ritual for purifying the altar
by putting on its four projections the blood
of the animal sacrificed for sin. This is to be
done every year for all time to come. This
altar is to be completely holy, dedicated to
me, the LORD.”

The Tax for the Tent of the LORD’s Presence

11The LORD said to Moses, 12“When you
take a census of the people of Israel, each
man is to pay me a price for his life, so that
no disaster will come on him while the cen-
sus is being taken. 13Everyone included in
the census must pay the required amount of
money, weighed according to the official
standard. Everyone must pay this as an offer-
ing to me. 14Everyone being counted in the
census, that is, every man twenty years old or
older, is to pay me this amount. 15The rich
man is not to pay more, nor the poor man
less, when they pay this amount for their
lives. 16Collect this money from the people
of Israel and spend it for the upkeep of the
Tent of my presence. This tax will be the
payment for their lives, and I will remember
to protect them.”

The Bronze Basin

17The LORD said to Moses, 18“Make a
bronze basin with a bronze base. Place it
between the Tent and the altar, and put
water in it. 19Aaron and his sons are to use
the water to wash their hands and feet
20before they go into the Tent or approach
the altar to offer the food offering. Then
they will not be killed. 21They must wash
their hands and feet, so that they will not
die. This is a rule which they and their
descendants are to observe forever.”

30:13 Ex 38:25, 26; Mt 17:24 **30:18** Ex 38:8

The Anointing Oil

22The LORD said to Moses, 23"Take the
finest spices—12 pounds of liquid myrrh,
6 pounds of sweet-smelling cinnamon, 6
pounds of sweet-smelling cane, 24and 12
pounds of cassia (all weighed according to the
official standard). Add one gallon of olive oil,
25and make a sacred anointing oil, mixed like
perfume. 26Use it to anoint the Tent of my
presence, the Covenant Box, 27the table and
all its equipment, the lampstand and its equip-
ment, the altar for burning incense, 28the altar
for burning offerings, together with all its
equipment, and the washbasin with its base.
29Dedicate these things in this way, and they
will be completely holy, and anyone or any-
thing that touches them will be harmed by
the power of its holiness.[f] 30Then anoint
Aaron and his sons, and ordain them as priests
in my service. 31Say to the people of Israel,
'This holy anointing oil is to be used in my
service for all time to come. 32It must not be
poured on ordinary men, and you must not
use the same formula to make any mixture
like it. It is holy, and you must treat it as holy.
33Whoever makes any like it or uses any of it
on anyone who is not a priest will no longer
be considered one of my people.' "

The Incense

34The LORD said to Moses, "Take an
equal part of each of the following sweet
spices—stacte, onycha, galbanum, and pure
frankincense. 35Use them to make incense,
mixed like perfume. Add salt to keep it pure
and holy. 36Beat part of it into a fine pow-
der, take it into the Tent of my presence, and
sprinkle it in front of the Covenant Box.
Treat this incense as completely holy. 37Do
not use the same formula to make any
incense like it for yourselves. Treat it as a
holy thing dedicated to me. 38If anyone
makes any like it for use as perfume, he will
no longer be considered one of my people."

Live it!

God-Given Gifts

Bezalel could do just about anything. He was skilled at working with wood, precious metals, and cloth. He was famous for his wonderful designs. Where did he get such talent? From God. "I have filled him with my power. I have given him understanding, skill, and ability for every kind of artistic work" (Exodus 31:3).

God gave you a special gift, too, and is counting on you to use it to honor him. You may have a gift of working with your hands or for working with people. Maybe you are good at decorating or writing. Perhaps you are a good leader or a good follower. We use our gifts from God in ways that honor him.

- **What special gift or gifts has God given you?**
- **What do you think God is asking you to do with your gift right now?**
- **How will you honor God with your gift?**

— Exodus 31:1–11

Craftsmen for the Tent of the LORD's Presence

(Exodus 35:30—36:1)

31 The LORD said to Moses, 2"I have
chosen Bezalel, the son of Uri and
grandson of Hur, from the tribe of Judah,
3and I have filled him with my power.[g] I have
given him understanding, skill, and ability for

[f] **30:29** HARMED BY THE POWER OF ITS HOLINESS: *See 29:37.* [g] **31:3** power; *or* spirit.
30:22–38 Ex 37:29

The Jewish Sabbath (like Sunday in the Christian Church) is supposed to be a day of rest. Why? Check out Exodus, chapter 31.

every kind of artistic work— 4for planning
skillful designs and working them in gold, sil-
ver, and bronze; 5for cutting jewels to be set;
for carving wood; and for every other kind of
artistic work. 6I have also selected Oholiab
son of Ahisamach, from the tribe of Dan, to
work with him. I have also given great ability
to all the other skilled workers, so that they
can make everything I have commanded to
be made: 7the Tent of my presence, the
Covenant Box and its lid, all the furnishings
of the Tent, 8the table and its equipment, the
lampstand of pure gold and all its equipment,
the altar for burning incense, 9the altar for
burnt offerings and all its equipment, the
washbasin and its base, 10the magnificent
priestly garments for Aaron and his sons to
use when they serve as priests, 11the anointing
oil, and the sweet-smelling incense for the
Holy Place. In making all these things, they
are to do exactly as I have commanded you."

Sabbath, the Day of Rest

12The LORD commanded Moses 13to tell
the people of Israel, "Keep the Sabbath, my
day of rest, because it is a sign between you
and me for all time to come, to show that I,
the LORD, have made you my own people.
14You must keep the day of rest, because it is
sacred. Whoever does not keep it, but works
on that day, is to be put to death. 15You have
six days in which to do your work, but the
seventh day is a solemn day of rest dedicated
to me. Whoever does any work on that day is
to be put to death. 16The people of Israel are
to keep this day as a sign of the covenant. 17It
is a permanent sign between the people of
Israel and me, because I, the LORD, made
heaven and earth in six days, and on the sev-
enth day I stopped working and rested."

18When God had finished speaking to
Moses on Mount Sinai, he gave him the two
stone tablets on which God himself had
written the commandments.

The Gold Bull-Calf

(Deuteronomy 9:6–29)

32 When the people saw that Moses
had not come down from the
mountain but was staying there a long time,
they gathered around Aaron and said to him,
"We do not know what has happened to
this man Moses, who led us out of Egypt; so
make us a god[h] to lead us."

2Aaron said to them, "Take off the gold
earrings which your wives, your sons, and
your daughters are wearing, and bring them
to me." 3So all the people took off their gold
earrings and brought them to Aaron. 4He
took the earrings, melted them, poured the
gold into a mold, and made a gold bull-calf.

The people said, "Israel, this is our god,
who led us out of Egypt!"

5Then Aaron built an altar in front of the
gold bull-calf and announced, "Tomorrow
there will be a festival to honor the LORD."
6Early the next morning they brought some
animals to burn as sacrifices and others to
eat as fellowship offerings. The people sat
down to a feast, which turned into an orgy
of drinking and sex.

7The LORD said to Moses, "Hurry and go
back down, because your people, whom you
led out of Egypt, have sinned and rejected
me. 8They have already left the way that I
commanded them to follow; they have made
a bull-calf out of melted gold and have wor-
shiped it and offered sacrifices to it. They are
saying that this is their god, who led them
out of Egypt. 9I know how stubborn these
people are. 10Now, don't try to stop me. I am
angry with them, and I am going to destroy
them. Then I will make you and your
descendants into a great nation."

11But Moses pleaded with the LORD his
God and said, " LORD, why should you be so
angry with your people, whom you rescued
from Egypt with great might and power?
12Why should the Egyptians be able to say

[h] **32:1** a god; *or* some gods.

31:15 Ex 20:8–11; 23:12; 34:21; 35:2; Lev 23:3; Deut 5:12–14 **31:17** Ex 20:11 **32:1** Acts 7:40
32:4 1 Kings 12:28; Acts 7:41 **32:6** 1 Cor 10:7 **32:11–14** Num 14:13–19

**How did God punish the Israelites? You'll find the answer near the end of
Exodus, chapter 32.**

that you led your people out of Egypt, plan-
ning to kill them in the mountains and
destroy them completely? Stop being angry;
change your mind and do not bring this di-
saster on your people. [13]Remember your
servants Abraham, Isaac, and Jacob. Remem-
ber the solemn promise you made to them
to give them as many descendants as there
are stars in the sky and to give their descen-
dants all that land you promised would be
their possession forever." [14]So the LORD
changed his mind and did not bring on his
people the disaster he had threatened.
[15]Moses went back down the mountain,
carrying the two stone tablets with the com-
mandments written on both sides. [16]God
himself had made the tablets and had
engraved the commandments on them.
[17]Joshua heard the people shouting and
said to Moses, "I hear the sound of battle in
the camp."
[18]Moses said, "That doesn't sound like a
shout of victory or a cry of defeat; it's the
sound of singing."
[19]When Moses came close enough to the
camp to see the bull-calf and to see the peo-
ple dancing, he became furious. There at the
foot of the mountain, he threw down the
tablets he was carrying and broke them. [20]He
took the bull-calf which they had made,
melted it, ground it into fine powder, and
mixed it with water. Then he made the peo-
ple of Israel drink it. [21]He said to Aaron,
"What did these people do to you, that you
have made them commit such a terrible sin?"
[22]Aaron answered, "Don't be angry with
me; you know how determined these people
are to do evil. [23]They said to me, 'We don't
know what has happened to this man
Moses, who brought us out of Egypt; so
make us a god to lead us.' [24]I asked them to
bring me their gold ornaments, and those
who had any took them off and gave them
to me. I threw the ornaments into the fire
and out came this bull-calf!"
[25]Moses saw that Aaron had let the people
get out of control and make fools of them-
selves in front of their enemies. [26]So he
stood at the gate of the camp and shouted,
"Everyone who is on the LORD's side come
over here!" So all the Levites gathered

32:13 Gen 22:16, 17; Gen 17:8

Live it!

Sinful but Forgiven

How could the Israelites do something like this! Forty days earlier they promised God that they would obey his commandments. Then, while Moses was on Mount Sinai, they asked Aaron to make a bull-calf out of gold so that they could worship it. They broke the very first commandment, "Do not bow down to any idol or worship it" (Exodus 20:5).

Moses was so angry that he threw the stone tablets, and they cracked into pieces. God wanted to destroy the Israelites, but Moses knew that God loved them. Even though the people sinned, Moses asked God to forgive them. God did just that—over and over again.

We shouldn't be too hard on the Israelites. Most of us do something to betray God on a pretty regular basis. But as soon as we say we're sorry and promise to do better, God forgives us. And he keeps on forgiving us, simply because we are God's people, God is our God, and God loves us. No sin is big enough to change that.

It is important to be aware of your sins—even though you might not have angry people breaking stone tablets nearby. When you are aware of a sin, say a prayer asking God's forgiveness and try to go to the sacrament of Penance and Reconciliation, especially if it is a serious sin. Then let yourself feel God's love surround you.

— Exodus, chapter 32

around him, 27 and he said to them, "The
LORD God of Israel commands every one of
you to put on your sword and go through
the camp from this gate to the other and kill
your brothers, your friends, and your neigh-
bors." 28 The Levites obeyed, and killed about
three thousand men that day. 29 Moses said to
the Levites, "Today you have consecrated
yourselves[i] as priests in the service of the
LORD by killing your sons and brothers, so
the LORD has given you his blessing."
30 The next day Moses said to the people,
"You have committed a terrible sin. But
now I will again go up the mountain to the
LORD; perhaps I can obtain forgiveness for
your sin." 31 Moses then returned to the
LORD and said, "These people have commit-
ted a terrible sin. They have made a god out
of gold and worshiped it. 32 Please forgive
their sin; but if you won't, then remove my
name from the book in which you have
written the names of your people."
33 The LORD answered, "It is those who
have sinned against me whose names I will
remove from my book. 34 Now go, lead the
people to the place I told you about.
Remember that my angel will guide you,
but the time is coming when I will punish
these people for their sin."
35 So the LORD sent a disease on the peo-
ple, because they had caused Aaron to make
the gold bull-calf.

The LORD Orders Israel to Leave Mount Sinai

33 The LORD said to Moses, "Leave this
place, you and the people you
brought out of Egypt, and go to the land
that I promised to give to Abraham, Isaac,
and Jacob and to their descendants. 2 I will
send an angel to guide you, and I will drive
out the Canaanites, the Amorites, the Hit-
tites, the Perizzites, the Hivites, and the
Jebusites. 3 You are going to a rich and fertile
land. But I will not go with you myself,
because you are a stubborn people, and I
might destroy you on the way."
4 When the people heard this, they began
to mourn and did not wear jewelry any more.
5 For the LORD had commanded Moses to tell
them, "You are a stubborn people. If I were to
go with you even for a moment, I would
completely destroy you. Now take off your
jewelry, and I will decide what to do with
you." 6 So after they left Mount Sinai, the
people of Israel no longer wore jewelry.

The Tent of the LORD's Presence

7 Whenever the people of Israel set up camp,
Moses would take the sacred Tent and put it up
some distance outside the camp. It was called
the Tent of the LORD's presence, and anyone
who wanted to consult the LORD would go
out to it. 8 Whenever Moses went out there,
the people would stand at the door of their
tents and watch Moses until he entered it.
9 After Moses had gone in, the pillar of cloud
would come down and stay at the door of the
Tent, and the LORD would speak to Moses
from the cloud. 10 As soon as the people saw
the pillar of cloud at the door of the Tent, they
would bow down. 11 The LORD would speak
with Moses face to face, just as someone speaks
with a friend. Then Moses would return to the
camp. But the young man who was his helper,
Joshua son of Nun, stayed in the Tent.

The LORD Promises to Be with His People

12 Moses said to the LORD, "It is true that
you have told me to lead these people to
that land, but you did not tell me whom you
would send with me. You have said that you
know me well and are pleased with me.
13 Now if you are, tell me your plans, so that
I may serve you and continue to please you.

They would bow down. (33:10)

[i] **32:29** *Some ancient translations* Today you have consecrated yourselves; *Hebrew* Consecrate yourselves today; *or* You have been consecrated today.

32:32 Ps 69:28; Rev 3:5 **33:1** **a** Gen 12:7; **b** Gen 26:3; **c** Gen 28:13

Pray it!

How Will I Know, God?

Moses had a lot of questions for God. He wanted to be sure he was headed in the right direction and that God was pleased with him. In Exodus 33:12–23, Moses and God have a conversation that shows the love they have for each other. Moses' prayer might have sounded something like this:

God, I try to do what I think you want me to do, but am I doing it right?
How will I know?
Are you pleased with me, God? When you look at me, do you feel proud?
How will I know?
I want to believe that you're on the journey with me—even when I mess things up, but how will I know?
I wish I could see you, God. Maybe I do—but I just don't know it's you.
How will I know?
I'd like some answers soon, God. But I have to trust that you will show me what I need to know even if it isn't everything that I would want to know.

— Exodus 33:12–23

Remember also that you have chosen this nation to be your own."
14The LORD said, "I will go with you, and I will give you victory."
15Moses replied, "If you do not go with us, don't make us leave this place. 16How will anyone know that you are pleased with your people and with me if you do not go with us? Your presence with us will distinguish us from any other people on earth."
17The LORD said to Moses, "I will do just as you have asked, because I know you very well and I am pleased with you."
18Then Moses requested, "Please, let me see the dazzling light of your presence."
19The LORD answered, "I will make all my splendor pass before you and in your presence I will pronounce my sacred name. I am the LORD, and I show compassion and pity on those I choose. 20I will not let you see my face, because no one can see me and stay alive, 21but here is a place beside me where you can stand on a rock. 22When the dazzling light of my presence passes by, I will put you in an opening in the rock and cover you with my hand until I have passed by. 23Then I will take my hand away, and you will see my back but not my face."

The Second Set of Stone Tablets
(Deuteronomy 10:1–5)

34 The LORD said to Moses, "Cut two stone tablets like the first ones, and I will write on them the words that were on the first tablets, which you broke. 2Get ready tomorrow morning, and come up Mount Sinai to meet me there at the top. 3No one is to come up with you; no one is to be seen on any part of the mountain; and no sheep or cattle are to graze at the foot of the mountain." 4So Moses cut two more stone tablets, and early the next morning he carried them up Mount Sinai, just as the LORD had commanded.
5The LORD came down in a cloud, stood

33:19 Rom 9:15

Why did God think about sending an angel to go with the Israelites instead of going himself? Read Exodus 33:1–6.

Party Time!

Catholic Connections

The Harvest Festival mentioned in Exodus 34:22 was a celebration of the wheat harvest. It was also known as Pentecost. Some Bibles also call it the Feast of Weeks. The Israelites received the Covenant Law from God on Mount Sinai during harvest time, so the feast of Pentecost came to be a celebration of the Covenant between God and his Chosen People.

When Jesus' followers were celebrating Pentecost after Jesus ascended into heaven, an important event happened. The Holy Spirit came to be with them, just as Jesus promised before he died. Check out Acts, chapter 2, to read all about it. In the New Testament, Pentecost marks the time when Jesus' followers began going out to preach and baptize new believers. So Pentecost is sometimes called the birthday of the Church. Catholics celebrate the feast of Pentecost fifty days after Easter.

— Exodus 34:22

with him there, and pronounced his holy
name, the LORD.[j] 6The LORD then passed in
front of him and called out, "I, the LORD, am a
God who is full of compassion and pity, who
is not easily angered and who shows great love
and faithfulness. 7I keep my promise for thou-
sands of generations[k] and forgive evil and sin;
but I will not fail to punish children and
grandchildren to the third and fourth genera-
tion for the sins of their parents."
8Moses quickly bowed down to the
ground and worshiped. 9He said, "Lord, if
you really are pleased with me, I ask you to
go with us. These people are stubborn, but
forgive our evil and our sin, and accept us as
your own people."

The Covenant Is Renewed

(Exodus 23:14–19; Deuteronomy 7:1–5; 16:1–17)

10The LORD said to Moses, "I now make
a covenant with the people of Israel. In their
presence I will do great things such as have
never been done anywhere on earth among
any of the nations. All the people will see
what great things I, the LORD, can do,
because I am going to do an awesome thing
for you. 11Obey the laws that I am giving
you today. I will drive out the Amorites, the
Canaanites, the Hittites, the Perizzites, the
Hivites, and the Jebusites, as you advance.
12Do not make any treaties with the people
of the country into which you are going,
because this could be a fatal trap for you.
13Instead, tear down their altars, destroy their
sacred pillars, and cut down their symbols of
the goddess Asherah.
14"Do not worship any other god, because
I, the LORD, tolerate no rivals. 15Do not
make any treaties with the people of the
country, because when they worship their
pagan gods and sacrifice to them, they will
invite you to join them, and you will be
tempted to eat the food they offer to their
gods. 16Your sons might marry those foreign
women, who would lead them to be unfaith-
ful to me and to worship their pagan gods.

[j] **34:5** THE LORD: *See 3:14, and Word List.* [k] **34:7** thousands of generations; *or* thousands.

34:6, 7 Ex 20:5, 6; Num 14:18; Deut 5:9, 10; 7:9, 10 **34:13** Deut 16:21

"I, the LORD, am a God who is full of compassion and pity, who is not easily angered and who shows great love and faithfulness" *(Exodus 34:6)*.

Pray it!

A Moment with God

Moses' face was beaming! He had just come down from Mount Sinai, where he spent some time talking to God. His time on Mount Sinai was just what he needed to continue living the life God wanted him to live.

You can be with God whenever you want to. You do not need to do anything special—except be mindful that God is with you. To help you find that place of mindfulness, you might say a short prayer over and over, like "Be with me, God" or "God, you are my God, and I am yours." When you are focused, you can talk to God, read a prayer, say one that you know, or just be quiet and feel God's love for you.

Don't be too concerned about *how* you pray. It's more important *that* you pray. God is waiting for you to climb Mount Sinai in your heart.

— Exodus 34:29–35

17"Do not make gods of metal and wor-
ship them.
18"Keep the Festival of Unleavened Bread.
As I have commanded you, eat unleavened
bread for seven days in the month of Abib,
because it was in that month that you left
Egypt.
19"Every first-born son and first-born
male domestic animal belongs to me, 20but
you are to buy back every first-born donkey
by offering a lamb in its place. If you do not
buy it back, break its neck. Buy back every
first-born son.
"No one is to appear before me without
an offering.
21"You have six days in which to do your
work, but do not work on the seventh day,
not even during plowing time or harvest.
22"Keep the Harvest Festival when you
begin to harvest the first crop of your wheat,
and keep the Festival of Shelters in the
autumn when you gather your fruit.
23"Three times a year all of your men
must come to worship me, the LORD, the
God of Israel. 24After I have driven out the
nations before you and extended your terri-
tory, no one will try to conquer your coun-
try during the three festivals.
25"Do not offer bread made with yeast
when you sacrifice an animal to me. Do not
keep until the following morning any part of
the animal killed at the Passover Festival.
26"Each year bring to the house of the
LORD the first grain that you harvest.
"Do not cook a young sheep or goat in
its mother's milk."
27The LORD said to Moses, "Write these
words down, because it is on the basis of
these words that I am making a covenant
with you and with Israel." 28Moses stayed
there with the LORD forty days and nights,
eating and drinking nothing. He wrote on
the tablets the words of the covenant—the
Ten Commandments.

Moses Goes Down from Mount Sinai

29When Moses went down from Mount
Sinai carrying the Ten Commandments, his
face was shining because he had been speak-
ing with the LORD; but he did not know it.
30Aaron and all the people looked at Moses
and saw that his face was shining, and they
were afraid to go near him. 31But Moses
called them, and Aaron and all the leaders of
the community went to him, and Moses

34:17 Ex 20:4; Lev 19:4; Deut 5:8; 27:15 **34:18** Ex 12:14–20; Lev 23:6–8; Num 28:16–25 **34:19** Ex 13:2 **34:20** Ex 13:13 **34:21** Ex 20:9, 10; 23:12; 31:15; 35:2; Lev 23:3; Deut 5:13, 14 **34:22** **a** Lev 23:15–21; Num 28:26–31; **b** Lev 23:39–43 **34:25** Ex 12:10 **34:26** **a** Deut 26:2; **b** Deut 14:21 **34:29–35** 2 Cor 3:7–16 spoke with them. [32]After that, all the people of Israel gathered around him, and Moses gave them all the laws that the LORD had given him on Mount Sinai. [33]When Moses had finished speaking with them, he covered his face with a veil. [34]Whenever Moses went into the Tent of the LORD's presence to speak to the LORD, he would take the veil off. When he came out, he would tell the people of Israel everything that he had been commanded to say, [35]and they would see that his face was shining. Then he would put the veil back on until the next time he went to speak with the LORD.

Regulations for the Sabbath

35 Moses called together the whole community of the people of Israel and said to them, "This is what the LORD has commanded you to do: [2]You have six days in which to do your work, but the seventh day is to be sacred, a solemn day of rest dedicated to me, the LORD. Anyone who does any work on that day is to be put to death. [3]Do not even light a fire in your homes on the Sabbath."

Offerings for the Sacred Tent
(Exodus 25:1–9)

[4]Moses said to all the people of Israel, "This is what the LORD has commanded: [5]Make an offering to the LORD. Everyone who wishes to do so is to bring an offering of gold, silver, or bronze; [6]fine linen; blue, purple, and red wool; cloth made of goats' hair; [7]rams' skin dyed red; fine leather; acacia wood; [8]oil for the lamps; spices for the anointing oil and for the sweet-smelling incense; [9]carnelians and other jewels to be set in the High Priest's ephod and in his breastpiece.

Articles for the Tent of the LORD's Presence
(Exodus 39:32–43)

[10]"All the skilled workers among you are to come and make everything that the LORD commanded: [11]the Tent, its covering and its outer covering, its hooks and its frames, its crossbars, its posts, and its bases; [12]the Covenant Box, its poles, its lid, and the curtain to screen it off; [13]the table, its poles, and all its equipment; the bread offered to God; [14]the lampstand for the light and its equipment; the lamps with their oil; [15]the altar for burning incense and its poles; the anointing oil; the sweet-smelling incense; the curtain for the entrance of the Tent; [16]the altar on which to burn offerings, with its bronze grating attached, its poles, and all its equipment; the washbasin and its base; [17]the curtains for the enclosure, its posts and bases; the curtain for the entrance of the enclosure; [18]the Tent pegs and ropes for the Tent and the enclosure; [19]and the magnificent garments the priests are to wear when they serve in the Holy Place—the sacred clothes for Aaron the priest and for his sons."

The People Bring Their Offerings

[20]All the people of Israel left, [21]and everyone who wished to do so brought an offering to the LORD for making the Tent of the LORD's presence. They brought everything needed for use in worship and for making the priestly garments. [22]All who wanted to, both men and women, brought decorative pins, earrings, rings, necklaces, and all kinds of gold jewelry and dedicated them to the LORD. [23]Everyone who had fine linen; blue, purple, or red wool; cloth of goats' hair; rams' skin dyed red; or fine leather, brought it. [24]All who were able to contribute silver or bronze brought their offering for the LORD, and all who had acacia wood which could be used for any of the work brought it. [25]All the skilled women brought fine linen thread and thread of blue, purple, and red wool, which they had made. [26]They also made thread of goats' hair. [27]The leaders brought carnelians and other jewels to be set in the ephod and the breastpiece [28]and spices and oil for the lamps, for the anointing oil, and for the sweet-smelling incense. [29]All the people of Israel who wanted to brought their offering to the LORD for the work which he had commanded Moses to do.

35:2 Ex 20:8–11; 23:12; 31:15; 34:21; Lev 23:3; Deut 5:12–14

Workers to Make the Tent of the LORD's Presence
(Exodus 31:1–11)

30 Moses said to the Israelites, "The LORD
has chosen Bezalel, the son of Uri and grand-
son of Hur from the tribe of Judah. 31 God has
filled him with his power[l] and given him
skill, ability, and understanding for every kind
of artistic work, 32 for planning skillful designs
and working them in gold, silver, and bronze;
33 for cutting jewels to be set; for carving
wood; and for every other kind of artistic
work. 34 The LORD has given to him and to
Oholiab son of Ahisamach, from the tribe of
Dan, the ability to teach their crafts to others.
35 He has given them skill in all kinds of work
done by engravers, designers, and weavers of
fine linen; blue, purple, and red wool; and
other cloth. They are able to do all kinds of
work and are skillful designers.

36 "Bezalel, Oholiab, and all the other
workers to whom the LORD has
given skill and understanding, who know
how to make everything needed to build the
sacred Tent, are to make everything just as
the LORD has commanded."

The People Bring Many Gifts

2 Moses called Bezalel, Oholiab, and all the
other skilled men to whom the LORD had
given ability and who were willing to help,
and Moses told them to start working.
3 They received from him all the offerings
which the Israelites had brought for con-
structing the sacred Tent. But the people of
Israel continued to bring Moses their offer-
ings every morning. 4 Then the skilled men
who were doing the work went 5 and told
Moses, "The people are bringing more than
is needed for the work which the LORD
commanded to be done."

6 So Moses sent a command throughout
the camp that no one was to make any fur-
ther contribution for the sacred Tent; so the
people did not bring any more. 7 What had
already been brought was more than enough
to finish all the work.

l **35:31** power; *or* spirit.

Live it!

Every Little Something Counts

When work finally started on the portable worship space, everyone wanted to contribute something. People brought jewels, colorful cloths, animal skins, oil, and whatever else they could think of to create a proper place to worship God together. In the end, the craftsmen had "more than enough to finish all the work" (Exodus 36:7).

How do you contribute to the life of your parish community? Do you help with parish programs and events? Do you contribute money to support the work of the Church and help those who are needy? Do you use the gifts God gave you to make your parish a better place? Do you share your ideas with parish leaders? You may be young, but you have a lot to give. Being young is no excuse for not doing your part.

Everyone can do something, and every little something counts. What *can* you do? What *will* you do?

— Exodus 36:2–7

Making the Tent of the LORD's Presence
(Exodus 26:1–37)

8 The most skilled men among those
doing the work made the Tent of the LORD's

The future Temple in Jerusalem, built by King Solomon, would follow the design of the Tent of the LORD's Presence.

presence. They made it out of ten pieces of fine linen woven with blue, purple, and red wool and embroidered with figures of winged creatures. [9]Each piece was the same size, 14 yards long and 2 yards wide. [10]They sewed five of them together in one set and did the same with the other five. [11]They made loops of blue cloth on the edge of the outside piece in each set. [12]They put fifty loops on the first piece of the first set and fifty loops matching them on the last piece of the second set. [13]They made fifty gold hooks, with which to join the two sets into one piece.

[14]Then they made a cover for the Tent out of eleven pieces of cloth made of goats' hair. [15]They made them all the same size, 15 yards long and 2 yards wide. [16]They sewed five of them together in one set and the other six in another set. [17]They put fifty loops on the edge of the last piece of one set and fifty loops on the edge of the other set. [18]They made fifty bronze hooks to join the two sets, so as to form one cover. [19]They made two more coverings, one of rams' skin dyed red and the other of fine leather, to serve as an outer cover.

[20]They made upright frames of acacia wood for the Tent. [21]Each frame was 15 feet tall and 27 inches wide, [22]with two matching projections, so that the frames could be joined together. All the frames had these projections. [23]They made twenty frames for the south side [24]and forty silver bases to go under them, two bases under each frame to hold its two projections. [25]They made twenty frames for the north side of the Tent [26]and forty silver bases, two under each frame. [27]For the back of the Tent, on the west, they made six frames [28]and two frames for the corners. [29]These corner frames were joined at the bottom and connected all the way to the top. The two frames that formed the two corners were made in this way. [30]So there were eight frames and sixteen silver bases, two under each frame.

[31]They made fifteen crossbars of acacia wood, five for the frames on one side of the Tent, [32]five for the frames on the other side, and five for the frames on the west end, at the back. [33]The middle crossbar, set halfway up the frames, extended from one end of the Tent to the other. [34]They covered the frames with gold and fitted them with gold rings to hold the crossbars, which were also covered with gold.

[35]They made a curtain of fine linen, woven with blue, purple, and red wool and embroidered it with figures of winged creatures. [36]They made four posts of acacia wood to hold the curtain, covered them with gold, and fitted them with gold hooks. Then they made four silver bases to hold the posts. [37]For the entrance of the Tent they made a curtain of fine linen woven with blue, purple, and red wool and decorated with embroidery. [38]For this curtain they made five posts fitted with hooks, covered their tops and their rods with gold, and made five bronze bases for the posts.

Making the Covenant Box

(Exodus 25:10–22)

37 Bezalel made the Covenant Box out of acacia wood, 45 inches long, 27 inches wide, and 27 inches high. [2]He covered it with pure gold inside and out and put a gold border all around it. [3]He made four carrying rings of gold for it and attached them to its four feet, with two rings on each side. [4]He made carrying poles of acacia wood, covered them with gold, [5]and put them through the rings on each side of the Box. [6]He made a lid of pure gold, 45 inches long and 27 inches wide. [7]He made two winged creatures of hammered gold, [8]one for each end of the lid. He made them so that they formed one piece with the lid. [9]The winged creatures faced each other across the lid, and their outspread wings covered it.

Can you think of a movie about finding the Covenant Box (the Ark of the Covenant)? If not, ask a relative or a teacher.

Making the Table for the Bread Offered to God
(Exodus 25:23–30)

[10]He made the table out of acacia wood, 36 inches long, 18 inches wide, and 27 inches high. [11]He covered it with pure gold and put a gold border around it. [12]He made a rim 3 inches wide around it and put a gold border around the rim. [13]He made four carrying rings of gold for it and put them at the four corners, where the legs were. [14]The rings to hold the poles for carrying the table were placed near the rim. [15]He made the poles of acacia wood and covered them with gold. [16]He made the dishes of pure gold for the table: the plates, the cups, the jars, and the bowls to be used for the wine offering.

Making the Lampstand
(Exodus 25:31–40)

[17]He made the lampstand of pure gold. He made its base and its shaft of hammered gold; its decorative flowers, including buds and petals, formed one piece with it. [18]Six branches extended from its sides, three from each side. [19]Each of the six branches had three decorative flowers shaped like almond blossoms with buds and petals. [20]The shaft of the lampstand had four decorative flowers shaped like almond blossoms with buds and petals. [21]There was one bud below each of the three pairs of branches. [22]The buds, the branches, and the lampstand were a single piece of pure hammered gold. [23]He made seven lamps for the lampstand, and he made its tongs and trays of pure gold. [24]He used seventy-five pounds of pure gold to make the lampstand and all its equipment.

Making the Altar for Burning Incense
(Exodus 30:1–5)

[25]He made an altar out of acacia wood, for burning incense. It was square, 18 inches long and 18 inches wide, and it was 36 inches high. Its projections at the four corners formed one piece with it. [26]He covered its top, all four sides, and its projections with pure gold and put a gold border around it. [27]He made two gold carrying rings for it and attached them below the border on the two sides, to hold the poles with which it was to be carried. [28]He made the poles of acacia wood and covered them with gold.

Making the Anointing Oil and the Incense
(Exodus 30:22–38)

[29]He also made the sacred anointing oil and the pure sweet-smelling incense, mixed like perfume.

Making the Altar for Burning Offerings
(Exodus 27:1–8)

38 For burning offerings, he made an altar out of acacia wood. It was square, 7½ feet long and 7½ feet wide, and it was 4½ feet high. [2]He made the projections at the top of the four corners, so that they formed one piece with the altar. He covered it all with bronze. [3]He also made all the equipment for the altar: the pans, the shovels, the bowls, the hooks, and the fire pans. All this equipment was made of bronze. [4]He made a bronze grating and put it under the rim of the altar, so that it reached halfway up the altar. [5]He made four carrying rings and put them on the four corners. [6]He made carrying poles of acacia wood, covered them with bronze, [7]and put them in the rings on each side of the altar. The altar was made of boards and was hollow.

Making the Bronze Basin
(Exodus 30:18)

[8]He made the bronze basin and its bronze base out of the mirrors belonging to the women who served at the entrance of the Tent of the LORD's presence.

The Enclosure for the Tent of the LORD's Presence
(Exodus 27:9–19)

[9]For the Tent of the LORD's presence he made the enclosure out of fine linen curtains.

37:29 Ex 30:22–38 **38:8** Ex 30:18

On the south side the curtains were 50 yards
long, [10]supported by twenty bronze posts in
twenty bronze bases, with hooks and rods
made of silver. [11]The enclosure was the same
on the north side. [12]On the west side there
were curtains 25 yards long, with ten posts and
ten bases and with hooks and rods made of
silver. [13]On the east side, where the entrance
was, the enclosure was also 25 yards wide.
[14-15]On each side of the entrance there were
7½ yards of curtains, with three posts and
three bases. [16]All the curtains around the
enclosure were made of fine linen. [17]The bases
for the posts were made of bronze, and the
hooks, the rods, and the covering of the tops
of the posts were made of silver. All the posts
around the enclosure were connected with sil-
ver rods. [18]The curtain for the entrance of the
enclosure was made of fine linen woven with
blue, purple, and red wool and decorated with
embroidery. It was 10 yards long and 2½ yards
high, like the curtains of the enclosure. [19]It
was supported by four posts in four bronze
bases. Their hooks, the covering of their tops,
and their rods were made of silver. [20]All the
pegs for the Tent and for the surrounding
enclosure were made of bronze.

Metals Used in the Tent of the LORD's Presence

[21]Here is a list of the amounts of the met-
als used in the Tent of the LORD's presence,
where the two stone tablets were kept on
which the Ten Commandments were writ-
ten. The list was ordered by Moses and made
by the Levites who worked under the direc-
tion of Ithamar son of Aaron the priest.
[22]Bezalel, the son of Uri and grandson of
Hur from the tribe of Judah, made everything
that the LORD had commanded. [23]His helper,
Oholiab son of Ahisamach, from the tribe of
Dan, was an engraver, a designer, and a weaver
of fine linen and of blue, purple, and red wool.
[24]All the gold that had been dedicated to
the LORD for the sacred Tent weighed 2,195
pounds, weighed according to the official
standard. [25]The silver from the census of the
community weighed 7,550 pounds, weighed
according to the official standard. [26]This
amount equaled the total paid by all persons
enrolled in the census, each one paying the
required amount, weighed according to the
official standard. There were 603,550 men
twenty years old or older enrolled in the
census. [27]Of the silver, 7,500 pounds were
used to make the hundred bases for the
sacred Tent and for the curtain, 75 pounds
for each base. [28]With the remaining 50
pounds of silver Bezalel made the rods, the
hooks for the posts, and the covering for
their tops. [29]The bronze which was dedicat-
ed to the LORD amounted to 5,310 pounds.
[30]With it he made the bases for the entrance
of the Tent of the LORD's presence, the
bronze altar with its bronze grating, all the
equipment for the altar, [31]the bases for the
surrounding enclosure and for the entrance
of the enclosure, and all the pegs for the Tent
and the surrounding enclosure.

Making the Garments for the Priests
(Exodus 28:1–14)

39 With the blue, purple, and red wool
they made the magnificent garments
which the priests were to wear when they
served in the Holy Place. They made the
priestly garments for Aaron, as the LORD had
commanded Moses.
[2]They made the ephod of fine linen; blue,
purple, and red wool; and gold thread. [3]They
hammered out sheets of gold and cut them
into thin strips to be worked into the fine
linen and into the blue, purple, and red wool.
[4]They made two shoulder straps for the
ephod and attached them to its sides, so that
it could be fastened. [5]The finely woven belt,
made of the same materials, was attached to
the ephod so as to form one piece with it, as
the LORD had commanded Moses. [6]They
prepared the carnelians and mounted them
in gold settings; they were skillfully engraved
with the names of the twelve sons of Jacob.
[7]They put them on the shoulder straps of the
ephod to represent the twelve tribes of Israel,
just as the LORD had commanded Moses.

38:25, 26 Ex 30:11–16 **38:26** Mt 17:24

Making the Breastpiece
(Exodus 28:15–30)

8 They made the breastpiece of the same materials as the ephod and with similar embroidery. 9 It was square and folded double, 9 inches long and 9 inches wide. 10 They mounted four rows of precious stones on it: in the first row they mounted a ruby, a topaz, and a garnet; 11 in the second row, an emerald, a sapphire, and a diamond; 12 in the third row, a turquoise, an agate, and an amethyst; 13 and in the fourth row, a beryl, a carnelian, and a jasper. These were mounted in gold settings. 14 Each of the twelve stones had engraved on it the name of one of the sons of Jacob, in order to represent the twelve tribes of Israel. 15 For the breastpiece they made chains of pure gold, twisted like cords. 16 They made two gold settings and two gold rings and attached the two rings to the upper corners of the breastpiece. 17 They fastened the two gold cords to the two rings 18 and fastened the other two ends of the cords to the two settings and in this way attached them in front to the shoulder straps of the ephod. 19 They made two rings of gold and attached them to the lower corners of the breastpiece, on the inside edge next to the ephod. 20 They made two more gold rings and attached them to the lower part of the front of the two shoulder straps of the ephod, near the seam and above the finely woven belt. 21 Just as the LORD had commanded Moses, they tied the rings of the breastpiece to the rings of the ephod with a blue cord, so that the breastpiece rested above the belt and did not come loose.

Making the Other Priestly Garments
(Exodus 28:31–43)

22 The robe that goes under the ephod was made entirely of blue wool. 23 The hole for the head was reinforced with a woven binding to keep it from tearing. 24-26 All around its lower hem they put pomegranates of fine linen and of blue, purple, and red wool, alternating with bells of pure gold, just as the LORD had commanded Moses.

27 They made the shirts for Aaron and his sons, 28 and the turban, the caps, the linen shorts, 29 and the sash of fine linen and of blue, purple, and red wool, decorated with embroidery, as the LORD had commanded Moses. 30 They made the ornament, the sacred sign of dedication, out of pure gold, and they engraved on it "Dedicated to the LORD." 31 They tied it to the front of the turban with a blue cord, just as the LORD had commanded Moses.

The Completion of the Work
(Exodus 35:10–19)

32 All the work on the Tent of the LORD's presence was finally completed. The Israelites made everything just as the LORD had commanded Moses. 33 They brought to Moses the Tent and all its equipment, its hooks, its frames, its crossbars, its posts, and its bases; 34 the covering of rams' skin dyed red; the covering of fine leather; the curtain; 35 the Covenant Box containing the stone tablets, its poles, and its lid; 36 the table and all its equipment, and the bread offered to God; 37 the lampstand of pure gold, its lamps, all its equipment, and the oil for the lamps; 38 the gold altar; the anointing oil; the sweet-smelling incense; the curtain for the entrance of the Tent; 39 the bronze altar with its bronze grating, its poles, and all its equipment; the washbasin and its base; 40 the curtains for the enclosure and its posts and bases; the curtain for the entrance of the enclosure and its ropes; the Tent pegs; all the equipment to be used in the Tent; 41 and the magnificent garments the priests were to wear in the Holy Place—the sacred clothes for Aaron the priest and for his sons. 42 The Israelites had done all the work just as the LORD had commanded Moses. 43 Moses examined everything and saw that they had made it all just as the LORD had commanded. So Moses blessed them.

How many stones were in the breastpiece? Why that number? What was engraved on each? Check out Exodus, chapter 39.

Live it!

Way to Go!

When the Israelites finished their work, Moses looked it over, and because they had done what God asked, he blessed them. They had every reason to be proud of themselves, just like these three people who are about your age:

- **Mitchell's scout leader told his mom that he could always count on Mitch to get things done. Mitch and his mom were very proud.**
- **Desiree was proud of her family. They all worked together, supported one another, and cared for one another.**
- **Amanda was proud of her ability to play the clarinet. She was thrilled when the music director at church asked her to be part of the music group for the first Communion liturgy.**

What are you proud of? Is it a special talent? a personality trait? something you work hard at? something you are part of? You can have pride in anything you do or are that is pleasing to God. When you are proud of yourself for the right reasons, God blesses you.

— Exodus 39:32–43

Setting Up and Dedicating the Tent of the LORD's Presence

40 The LORD said to Moses, 2“On the
first day of the first month set up the
Tent of the LORD's presence. 3Place in it the
Covenant Box containing the Ten Com-
mandments and put the curtain in front of
it. 4Bring in the table and place the equip-
ment on it. Also bring in the lampstand and
set up the lamps on it. 5Put the gold altar for
burning incense in front of the Covenant
Box and hang the curtain at the entrance of
the Tent. 6Put in front of the Tent the altar
for burning offerings. 7Put the washbasin
between the Tent and the altar and fill it
with water. 8Put up the surrounding enclo-
sure and hang the curtain at its entrance.
9“Then dedicate the Tent and all its equip-
ment by anointing it with the sacred oil, and
it will be holy. 10Next, dedicate the altar and
all its equipment by anointing it, and it will
be completely holy. 11Also dedicate the
washbasin and its base in the same way.
12“Bring Aaron and his sons to the
entrance of the Tent, and have them take a
ritual bath. 13Dress Aaron in the priestly gar-
ments, anoint him, and in this way conse-
crate him, so that he can serve me as priest.
14Bring his sons and put the shirts on them.
15Then anoint them, just as you anointed
their father, so that they can serve me as
priests. This anointing will make them priests
for all time to come.”
16Moses did everything just as the LORD
had commanded. 17So on the first day of the
first month of the second year after they left
Egypt, the Tent of the LORD's presence was set
up. 18Moses put down its bases, set up its
frames, attached its crossbars, and put up its
posts. 19He spread out the covering over the
Tent and put the outer covering over it, just as
the LORD had commanded. 20Then he took
the two stone tablets and put them in the
Covenant Box. He put the poles in the rings
of the Box and put the lid on it. 21Then he
put the Box in the Tent and hung up the cur-
tain. In this way he screened off the Covenant
Box, just as the LORD had commanded.
22He put the table in the Tent, on the north
side outside the curtain, 23and placed on it the
bread offered to the LORD, just as the LORD
had commanded. 24He put the lampstand in
the Tent, on the south side, opposite the table,
25and there in the LORD's presence he lit the
lamps, just as the LORD had commanded.
26He put the gold altar in the Tent, in front of

How many times does the phrase “LORD had commanded” appear in chapter 40? Why does it appear so many times?

the curtain, 27 and burned the sweet-smelling
incense, just as the LORD had commanded.
28 He hung the curtain at the entrance of the
Tent, 29 and there in front of the curtain he
placed the altar for burning offerings. On it he
sacrificed the burnt offering and the grain
offering, just as the LORD had commanded.
30 He put the washbasin between the Tent and
the altar and filled it with water. 31 Moses,
Aaron, and his sons washed their hands and
their feet there 32 whenever they went into the
Tent or to the altar, just as the LORD had
commanded. 33 Moses set up the enclosure
around the Tent and the altar and hung the
curtain at the entrance of the enclosure. So he
finished all the work.

The Cloud over the Tent of the LORD's Presence

(Numbers 9:15–23)

34 Then the cloud covered the Tent and
the dazzling light of the LORD's presence
filled it. 35 Because of this, Moses could not
go into the Tent. 36 The Israelites moved
their camp to another place only when the
cloud lifted from the Tent. 37 As long as the
cloud stayed there, they did not move their
camp. 38 During all their wanderings they
could see the cloud of the LORD's presence
over the Tent during the day and a fire burning above it during the night.

40:34 1 Kings 8:10, 11; Isa 6:4; Ezek 43:4, 5; Rev 15:8

Study it!

To Be Continued

At the end of the Book of Exodus, the Israelites leave Mount Sinai. They would not reach Canaan—the land that God promised to Abraham—for many years. The story of the journey to the Promised Land is continued in the Book of Numbers, then in Deuteronomy, and finally in the Book of Joshua.

During their years of wandering through the desert, the Israelites experienced many encounters with God and made many mistakes. They celebrated together and they fought. People died and babies were born. In other words, in their journey to the Promised Land, life happened.

The same is true for us. Each day, we move toward our own promised land: heaven. Like the Israelites, we walk with other people who are headed in the same direction, guided by God.

— Exodus, chapter 40

Your Next Step

Congratulations on finishing the Book of Exodus! Use this space to write your thoughts and questions about this book. If you are following the suggested reading plan, move ahead to the Book of Joshua, which tells how the Israelites moved into the Promised Land.

The Book of Leviticus

"Leviticus Rules!" That's what you might say if you really liked rules. Leviticus is a law book for God's people. The book is named for a group of priests from the tribe of Levi. God's Chosen People were expected to live by these laws. The laws in Leviticus helped the Chosen People put God first and live lives of holiness and justice. In the same way, Christians are called to live lives of holiness and justice—even when it doesn't seem to be very popular.

Most of these laws are no longer followed by Christians. The Holy Spirit led the early Christians to understand that many of these laws were no longer necessary for Christians. But we can appreciate the intent of these laws, to live lives that are holy and pleasing to God!

Chap. 8

Headlines

- Moses's Brother Is Ordained a Priest (8:1–36)
- Be Careful What You Eat (chapter 11)
- Scapegoat Takes Rap for Sinners! (16:20–22)
- God's People Told to Love Neighbors (19:1–18)
- Fifty Year Celebration: Time to Party! (25:8–17)
- Blessings Promised for Obeying Laws! (26:1–13)

FACTOIDS

Who wrote this book? This collection of laws and regulations, which were handed down orally, was probably compiled by several priestly writers and editors over a long period of time.

When was it written? The laws were established in the desert wilderness, after the Israelites escaped from Egypt. However, the writing and editing was probably done hundreds of years later.

Why was it written? Leviticus was written to bring about holiness and to unify the Israelite people.

What literary style is used? This book is written in the "priestly style," which is formal and portrays God as distant. Rules are rules, and it is the job of God's People to follow them.

Important themes

- Actions have consequences. If we follow the laws, we will be holy.
- Don't let the negative influence of others persuade you to sin.
- The blessings that God gives us are meant to be shared.

Sacrifices Burned Whole

1 The LORD called to Moses from the Tent of the LORD's presence and gave him the following rules [2]for the Israelites to observe when they offer their sacrifices.

When you offer an animal sacrifice, it may be one of your cattle or one of your sheep or goats. [3]If you are offering one of your cattle as a burnt offering, you must bring a bull without any defects. You must present it at the entrance of the Tent of the LORD's presence so that the LORD will accept you. [4]You shall put your hand on its head, and it will be accepted as a sacrifice to take away your sins. [5]You shall kill the bull there, and the Aaronite priests shall present the blood to the LORD and then throw it against all four sides of the altar located at the entrance of the Tent. [6]Then you shall skin the animal and cut it up, [7]and the priests shall arrange firewood on the altar and light it. [8]They shall put on the fire the pieces of the animal, including the head and the fat. [9]You must wash the internal organs and the hind legs, and the officiating priest will burn the whole sacrifice on the altar. The odor of this food offering is pleasing to the LORD.

[10]If you are offering one of your sheep or goats, it must be a male without any defects. [11]You shall kill it on the north side of the altar, and the priests shall throw its blood on all four sides of the altar. [12]After you cut it up, the officiating priest shall put on the fire all the parts, including the head and the fat. [13]You must wash the internal organs and the hind legs, and the priest will present the sacrifice to the LORD and burn all of it on the altar. The odor of this food offering is pleasing to the LORD.

[14]If you are offering a bird as a burnt offering, it must be a dove or a pigeon. [15]The priest shall present it at the altar, wring its neck, and burn its head on the altar. Its blood shall be drained out against the side of the altar. [16]He shall remove the crop and its contents and throw them away on the east side of the altar where the ashes are put. [17]He shall take hold of its wings and tear its body open, without tearing the wings off, and then burn it whole on the altar. The odor of this food offering is pleasing to the LORD.

Grain Offerings

2 When any of you present an offering of grain to the LORD, you must first grind it into flour. You must put olive oil and incense on it [2]and bring it to the Aaronite priests. The officiating priest shall take a handful of the flour and oil and all of the incense and burn it on the altar as a token that it has all been offered to the LORD. The odor of this food offering is pleasing to the LORD. [3]The rest of the grain offering belongs to the priests; it is very holy, since it is taken from the food offered to the LORD.

[4]If the offering is bread baked in an oven, it must be made without yeast. It may be thick loaves made of flour mixed with olive oil or thin cakes brushed with olive oil.

[5]If the offering is bread cooked on a griddle, it is to be made of flour mixed with olive oil but without yeast. [6]Crumble it up and pour the oil on it when you present it as an offering.

[7]If the offering is bread cooked in a pan, it is to be made of flour and olive oil. [8]Bring it as an offering to the LORD and present it to the priest, who will take it to the altar. [9]The priest will take part of it as a token that it has all been offered to the LORD, and he will burn it on the altar. The odor of this food offering is pleasing to the LORD. [10]The rest of the offering belongs to the priests; it is very holy, since it is taken from the food offered to the LORD.

[11]None of the grain offerings which you present to the LORD may be made with yeast; you must never use yeast or honey in food offered to the LORD. [12]An offering of the first grain that you harvest each year shall be brought to the LORD, but it is not to be burned on the altar. [13]Put salt on every grain offering, because salt represents the covenant

between you and God. (You must put salt on
all your offerings.) 14When you bring to the
LORD an offering of the first grain harvest-
ed, offer roasted grain or ground meal.
15Add olive oil and put incense on it. 16The
priest will burn that part of the meal and oil
that is to serve as a token, and also all the
incense, as a food offering to the LORD.

Fellowship Offerings

3 When any of you offer one of your cat-
tle as a fellowship offering, it is to be a
bull or a cow without any defects. 2You shall
put your hand on the head of the animal and
kill it at the entrance of the Tent of the
LORD's presence. The Aaronite priests shall
throw the blood against all four sides of the
altar 3and present the following parts of the
animal as a food offering to the LORD: all the
fat on the internal organs, 4the kidneys and
the fat on them, and the best part of the liver.
5The priests shall burn all this on the altar
along with the burnt offerings. The odor of
this food offering is pleasing to the LORD.

6If a sheep or goat is used as a fellowship
offering, it may be male or female, but it
must be without any defects. 7If you offer a
sheep, 8you shall put your hand on its head
and kill it in front of the Tent. The priests
shall throw its blood against all four sides of
the altar 9and present the following parts of
the animal as a food offering to the LORD:
the fat, the entire fat tail cut off near the
backbone, all the fat covering the internal
organs, 10the kidneys and the fat on them,
and the best part of the liver. 11The officiat-
ing priest shall burn all this on the altar as a
food offering to the LORD.

12If you offer a goat, 13you shall put your
hand on its head and kill it in front of the
Tent. The priests shall throw its blood against
all four sides of the altar 14and present the
following parts as a food offering to the
LORD: all the fat on the internal organs,
15the kidneys and the fat on them, and the
best part of the liver. 16The priest shall burn
all this on the altar as a food offering pleas-
ing to the LORD. All the fat belongs to the
LORD. 17No Israelite may eat any fat or any
blood; this is a rule to be kept forever by all
Israelites wherever they live.

Offerings for Unintentional Sins

4 The LORD commanded Moses 2to tell
the people of Israel that anyone who
sinned and broke any of the LORD's com-
mands without intending to, would have to
observe the following rules.

3If it is the High Priest who sins and so
brings guilt on the people, he shall present a
young bull without any defects and sacrifice
it to the LORD for his sin. 4He shall bring
the bull to the entrance of the Tent, put his
hand on its head, and kill it there in the
LORD's presence. 5Then the High Priest shall
take some of the bull's blood and carry it
into the Tent. 6He shall dip his finger in the
blood and sprinkle it in front of the sacred
curtain seven times. 7Then he shall put some
of the blood on the projections at the cor-
ners of the incense altar in the Tent. He shall
pour out the rest of the blood at the base of
the altar used for burning sacrifices, which is
at the entrance of the Tent. 8From this bull
he shall take all the fat, the fat on the inter-
nal organs, 9the kidneys and the fat on them,
and the best part of the liver. 10The priest
shall take this fat and burn it on the altar
used for the burnt offerings, just as he does
with the fat from the animal killed for the
fellowship offering. 11But he shall take its
skin, all its flesh, its head, its legs, and its
internal organs, including the intestines,
12carry it all outside the camp to the ritually
clean place where the ashes are poured out,
and there he shall burn it on a wood fire.

13If it is the whole community of Israel

He shall bring the bull. (4:4)

that sins and becomes guilty of breaking one of the LORD's commands without intending to, [14]then as soon as the sin becomes known, the community shall bring a young bull as a sin offering. They shall bring it to the Tent of the LORD's presence; [15]the leaders of the community shall put their hands on its head, and it shall be killed there. [16]The High Priest shall take some of the bull's blood into the Tent, [17]dip his finger in it, and sprinkle it in front of the curtain seven times. [18]He shall put some of the blood on the projections at the corners of the incense altar inside the Tent and pour out the rest of it at the base of the altar used for burning sacrifices, which is at the entrance of the Tent. [19]Then he shall take all its fat and burn it on the altar. [20]He shall do the same thing with this bull as he does with the bull for the sin offering, and in this way he shall make the sacrifice for the people's sin, and they will be forgiven. [21]Then he shall take the bull outside the camp and burn it, just as he burns the bull offered for his own sin. This is an offering to take away the sin of the community.

[22]If it is a ruler who sins and becomes guilty of breaking one of the LORD's commands without intending to, [23]then as soon as the sin is called to his attention, he shall bring as his offering a male goat without any defects. [24]He shall put his hand on its head and kill it on the north side of the altar, where the animals for the burnt offerings are killed. This is an offering to take away sin. [25]The priest shall dip his finger in the blood of the animal, put it on the projections at the corners of the altar, and pour out the rest of it at the base of the altar. [26]Then he shall burn all of its fat on the altar, just as he burns the fat of the animals killed for the fellowship offerings. In this way the priest shall offer the sacrifice for the sin of the ruler, and he will be forgiven.

[27]If any of you people sin and become guilty of breaking one of the LORD's commands without intending to, [28]then as soon as the sin is called to your attention, you shall bring as your offering a female goat without any defects. [29]You shall put your hand on its head and kill it on the north side of the altar, where the animals for the burnt offerings are killed. [30]The priest shall dip his finger in the blood of the animal, put it on the projections at the corners of the altar, and pour out the rest of it at the base of the altar. [31]Then he shall remove all its fat, just as the fat is removed from the animals killed for the fellowship offerings, and he shall burn it on the altar as an odor pleasing to the LORD. In this way the priest shall offer the sacrifice for the man's sin, and he will be forgiven.

[32]If you bring a sheep as a sin offering, it must be a female without any defects. [33]You shall put your hand on its head and kill it on the north side of the altar, where the animals for the burnt offerings are killed. [34]The priest shall dip his finger in the blood of the animal, put it on the projections at the corners of the altar, and pour out the rest of it at the base of the altar. [35]Then he shall remove all its fat, just as the fat is removed from the sheep killed for the fellowship offerings, and he shall burn it on the altar along with the food offerings given to the LORD. In this way the priest shall offer the sacrifice for your sin, and you will be forgiven.

Cases Requiring Sin Offerings

5 Sin offerings are required in the following cases.

If you are officially summoned to give evidence in court and do not give information about something you have seen or heard, you must suffer the consequences.

[2]If you unintentionally touch anything ritually unclean, such as a dead animal, you are unclean and guilty as soon as you realize what you have done.

[3]If you unintentionally touch anything of human origin that is unclean, whatever it may be, you are guilty as soon as you realize what you have done.

[4]If you make a careless vow, no matter what it is about, you are guilty as soon as you realize what you have done.

[5]When you are guilty, you must confess the sin, [6]and as the penalty for your sin you must bring to the LORD a female sheep or

4:27–31 Num 15:27, 28

goat as an offering. The priest shall offer the sacrifice for your sin.

7 If you cannot afford a sheep or a goat, you shall bring to the LORD as the payment for your sin two doves or two pigeons, one for a sin offering and the other for a burnt offering. 8 You shall bring them to the priest, who will first offer the bird for the sin offering. He will break its neck without pulling off its head 9 and sprinkle some of its blood against the side of the altar. The rest of the blood will be drained out at the base of the altar. This is an offering to take away sin. 10 Then he shall offer the second bird as a burnt offering, according to the regulations. In this way the priest shall offer the sacrifice for your sin, and you will be forgiven.

11 If you cannot afford two doves or two pigeons, you shall bring two pounds of flour as a sin offering. You shall not put any olive oil or any incense on it, because it is a sin offering, not a grain offering. 12 You shall bring it to the priest, who will take a handful of it as a token that it has all been offered to the LORD, and he will burn it on the altar as a food offering. It is an offering to take away sin. 13 In this way the priest shall offer the sacrifice for your sin, and you will be forgiven. The rest of the flour belongs to the priest, just as in the case of a grain offering.

Repayment Offerings

14 The LORD gave the following regulations to Moses. 15 If any of you sin unintentionally by failing to hand over the payments that are sacred to the LORD, you shall bring as your repayment offering to the LORD a male sheep or goat without any defects. Its value is to be determined according to the official standard. 16 You must make the payments you have failed to hand over and must pay an additional 20 percent. You shall give it to the priest, and the priest shall offer the animal as a sacrifice for your sin, and you will be forgiven.

17 If any of you sin unintentionally by breaking any of the LORD's commands, you are guilty and must pay the penalty. 18 You must bring to the priest as a repayment offering a male sheep or goat without any defects. Its value is to be determined according to the official standard. The priest shall offer the sacrifice for the sin which you committed unintentionally, and you will be forgiven. 19 It is a repayment offering for the sin you committed against the LORD.

6 The LORD gave the following regulations to Moses. 2 An offering is to be made if any of you sin against the LORD by refusing to return what another Israelite has left as a deposit or by stealing something from him or by cheating him 3 or by lying about something that has been lost and swearing that you did not find it. 4-5 When you sin in any of these ways, you must repay whatever you got by dishonest means. On the day you are found guilty, you must repay the owner in full, plus an additional 20 percent. 6 You shall bring to the priest as your repayment offering to the LORD a male sheep or goat without any defects. Its value is to be determined according to the official standard. 7 The priest shall offer the sacrifice for your sin, and you will be forgiven.

Sacrifices Burned Whole

8 The LORD commanded Moses 9 to give Aaron and his sons the following regulations for burnt offerings. A burnt offering is to be left on the altar all night long, and the fire is to be kept burning. 10 Then the priest, wearing his linen robe and linen shorts, shall remove the greasy ashes left on the altar and put them at the side of the altar. 11 Then he shall change his clothes and take the ashes outside the camp to a ritually clean place. 12 The fire on the altar must be kept burning and never allowed to go out. Every morning the priest shall put firewood on it, arrange the burnt offering on it, and burn the fat of the fellowship offering. 13 The fire must always be kept burning on the altar and never allowed to go out.

Grain Offerings

14 The following are the regulations for grain offerings. An Aaronite priest shall present the grain offering to the LORD in front

6:1–7 Num 5:5–8

of the altar. 15Then he shall take a handful of the flour and oil, and the incense on it, and burn it on the altar as a token that all of it has been offered to the LORD. The odor of this offering is pleasing to the LORD. 16-17The priests shall eat the rest of it. It shall be made into bread baked without yeast and eaten in a holy place, the courtyard of the Tent of the LORD's presence. The LORD has given it to the priests as their part of the food offerings. It is very holy, like the sin offerings and the repayment offerings. 18For all time to come any of the male descendants of Aaron may eat it as their continuing share of the food offered to the LORD. Anyone else who touches a food offering will be harmed by the power of its holiness.

19The LORD gave Moses the following regulations 20for the ordination of an Aaronite priest. On the day he is ordained, he shall present as an offering to the LORD two pounds of flour (the same amount as the daily grain offering), half in the morning and half in the evening. 21It is to be mixed with oil and cooked on a griddle and then crumbled and presented as a grain offering, an odor pleasing to the LORD. 22For all time to come this offering is to be made by every descendant of Aaron who is serving as High Priest. It shall be completely burned as a sacrifice to the LORD. 23No part of a grain offering that a priest makes may be eaten; all of it must be burned.

Sin Offerings

24The LORD commanded Moses 25to give Aaron and his sons the following regulations for sin offerings. The animal for a sin offering shall be killed on the north side of the altar, where the animals for the burnt offerings are killed. This is a very holy offering. 26The priest who sacrifices the animal shall eat it in a holy place, the courtyard of the Tent of the LORD's presence. 27Anyone or anything that touches the flesh of the animal will be harmed by the power of its holiness. If any article of clothing is spattered with the animal's blood, it must be washed in a holy place. 28Any clay pot in which the meat is boiled must be broken, and if a metal pot is used, it must be scrubbed and rinsed with water. 29Any male of the priestly families may eat this offering; it is very holy. 30But if any of the blood is brought into the Tent and used in the ritual to take away sin, the animal must not be eaten; it must be burned.

Repayment Offerings

7 The following are the regulations for repayment offerings, which are very holy. 2The animal for this offering is to be killed on the north side of the altar, where the animals for the burnt offerings are killed, and its blood is to be thrown against all four sides of the altar. 3All of its fat shall be removed and offered on the altar: the fat tail, the fat covering the internal organs, 4the kidneys and the fat on them, and the best part of the liver. 5The priest shall burn all the fat on the altar as a food offering to the LORD. It is a repayment offering. 6Any male of the priestly families may eat it, but it must be eaten in a holy place, because it is very holy.

7There is one regulation that applies to both the sin offering and the repayment offering: the meat belongs to the priest who offers the sacrifice. 8The skin of an animal offered as a burnt offering belongs to the priest who offers the sacrifice. 9Every grain offering that has been baked in an oven or prepared in a pan or on a griddle belongs to the priest who has offered it to God. 10But all uncooked grain offerings, whether mixed with oil or dry, belong to all the Aaronite priests and must be shared equally among them.

Fellowship Offerings

11The following are the regulations for the fellowship offerings presented to the LORD. 12If you make this offering as a thanksgiving offering to God, you shall present, together with the animal to be sacrificed, an offering of bread made without yeast: either thick loaves made of flour mixed with olive oil or thin cakes brushed with olive oil or cakes made of flour mixed with olive oil. 13In addition, you shall offer loaves of bread baked with yeast. 14You shall present one part of each kind of bread as a special contribution to the LORD; it belongs to the priest who takes the blood of the animal and throws it against the altar. 15 The flesh of the animal must be eaten on the day it is sacrificed; none of it may be left until the next morning.

16 If you bring a fellowship offering as fulfillment of a vow or as your own freewill offering, not all of it has to be eaten on the day it is offered, but any that is left over may be eaten on the following day. 17 Any meat that still remains on the third day must be burned. 18 If any of it is eaten on the third day, God will not accept your offering. The offering will not be counted to your credit but will be considered unclean, and whoever eats it will suffer the consequences. 19 If the meat comes into contact with anything ritually unclean, it must not be eaten, but must be burned.

Any of you that are ritually clean may eat the meat, 20 but if any of you who are not clean eat it, you shall no longer be considered one of God's people. 21 Also, if you eat the meat of this offering after you have touched anything ritually unclean, whether from a person or an animal, you shall no longer be considered one of God's people.

22 The LORD gave Moses the following regulations 23 for the people of Israel. No fat of cattle, sheep, or goats shall be eaten. 24 The fat of an animal that has died a natural death or has been killed by a wild animal must not be eaten, but it may be used for any other purpose. 25 Anyone who eats the fat of an animal that may be offered as a food offering to the LORD will no longer be considered one of God's people. 26 No matter where the Israelites live, they must never use the blood of birds or animals for food. 27 Anyone who breaks this law will no longer be considered one of God's people.

28 The LORD gave Moses the following regulations 29 for the people of Israel. When any of you offer a fellowship offering you must bring part of it as a special gift to the LORD, 30 bringing it with your own hands as a food offering. You shall bring the fat of the animal with its breast and present it as a special gift to the LORD. 31 The priest shall burn the fat on the altar, but the breast shall belong to the priests. 32 The right hind leg of the animal shall be given as a special contribution 33 to the priest who offers the blood and the fat of the fellowship offering. 34 The breast of the animal is a special gift, and the right hind leg is a special contribution that the LORD has taken from the people of Israel and given to the priests. This is what the people of Israel must give to the priests for all time to come. 35 This is the part of the food offered to the LORD that was given to Aaron and his sons on the day they were ordained as priests. 36 On that day the LORD commanded the people of Israel to give them this part of the offering. It is a regulation that the people of Israel must obey for all time to come.

37 These, then, are the regulations for the burnt offerings, the grain offerings, the sin offerings, the repayment offerings, the ordination offerings, and the fellowship offerings. 38 There on Mount Sinai in the desert, the LORD gave these commands to Moses on the day he told the people of Israel to make their offerings.

The Ordination of Aaron and His Sons
(Exodus 29:1–37)

8 The LORD said to Moses, 2 "Take Aaron and his sons to the entrance of the Tent of my presence and bring the priestly garments, the anointing oil, the young bull for the sin offering, the two rams, and the basket of unleavened bread. 3 Then call the whole community together there."

4 Moses did as the LORD had commanded, and when the community had assembled, 5 he said to them, "What I am now about to do is what the LORD has commanded."

6 Moses brought Aaron and his sons forward and had them take a ritual bath. 7 He put the shirt and the robe on Aaron and the sash around his waist. He put the ephod[a] on him and fastened it by putting its finely woven belt around his waist. 8 He put the breastpiece on him and put the Urim and Thummim[b] in it. 9 He placed the turban on his head, and on the front of it he put the

[a] **8:7** EPHOD: *See Word List.* [b] **8:8** URIM AND THUMMIM: *Two objects used by the priest to determine God's will; it is not known precisely how they were used.*

7:26, 27 Gen 9:4; Lev 17:10–14; 19:26; Deut 12:16, 23; 15:23

gold ornament, the sacred sign of dedication,
just as the LORD had commanded him.
10 Then Moses took the anointing oil and
put it on the Tent of the LORD's presence
and everything that was in it, and in this way
he dedicated it all to the LORD. 11 He took
some of the oil and sprinkled it seven times
on the altar and its equipment and on the
basin and its base, in order to dedicate them
to the LORD. 12 He ordained Aaron by pour-
ing some of the anointing oil on his head.
13 Next, Moses brought the sons of Aaron
forward and put shirts on them, put sashes
around their waists, and tied caps on their
heads, just as the LORD had commanded.
14 Then Moses brought the young bull for
the sin offering, and Aaron and his sons put
their hands on its head. 15 Moses killed it and
took some of the blood, and with his finger
put it on the projections at the corners of
the altar, in order to dedicate it. He then
poured out the rest of the blood at the base
of the altar. In this way he dedicated it and
purified it. 16 Moses took all the fat on the
internal organs, the best part of the liver, and
the kidneys with the fat on them, and
burned it all on the altar. 17 He took the rest
of the bull, including its skin, flesh, and
intestines, and burned it outside the camp,
just as the LORD had commanded.
18 Next, Moses brought the ram for the
burnt offering, and Aaron and his sons put
their hands on its head. 19 Moses killed it and
threw the blood on all four sides of the altar.
20-21 He cut the ram in pieces, washed the
internal organs and the hind legs with water,
and burned the head, the fat, and all the rest
of the ram on the altar, just as the LORD had
commanded. This burnt offering was a food
offering, and its odor was pleasing to the
LORD.
22 Then Moses brought the second ram,
which was for the ordination of priests, and
Aaron and his sons put their hands on its
head. 23 Moses killed it and took some of the
blood and put it on the lobe of Aaron's right
ear, on the thumb of his right hand, and on
the big toe of his right foot. 24 Then he
brought Aaron's sons forward and put some
of the blood on the lobes of their right ears,
on the thumbs of their right hands, and on
the big toes of their right feet. Moses then
threw the rest of the blood on all four sides
of the altar. 25 He took the fat, the fat tail, all
the fat covering the internal organs, the best
part of the liver, the kidneys with the fat on
them, and the right hind leg. 26 Then he took
one loaf of bread from the basket of unleav-
ened bread dedicated to the LORD, one loaf
made with oil, and one thin cake, and he put
them on top of the fat and the right hind
leg. 27 He put all of this food in the hands of
Aaron and his sons, and they presented it as a
special gift to the LORD. 28 Then Moses took
the food from them and burned it on the
altar, on top of the burnt offering, as an ordi-
nation offering. This was a food offering, and
its odor was pleasing to the LORD. 29 Then
Moses took the breast and presented it as a
special gift to the LORD. It was Moses' part of
the ordination ram. Moses did everything just
as the LORD had commanded.[c]
30 Moses took some of the anointing oil
and some of the blood that was on the altar
and sprinkled them on Aaron and his sons
and on their clothes. In this way he conse-
crated them and their clothes to the LORD.
31 Moses said to Aaron and his sons, "Take
the meat to the entrance of the Tent of the
LORD's presence, boil it, and eat it there with
the bread that is in the basket of ordination
offerings, just as the LORD commanded.[c]
32 Burn up any meat or bread that is left
over. 33 You shall not leave the entrance of
the Tent for seven days, until your ordination
rites are completed. 34 The LORD command-
ed us to do what we have done today, in
order to take away your sin. 35 You must stay
at the entrance of the Tent day and night for

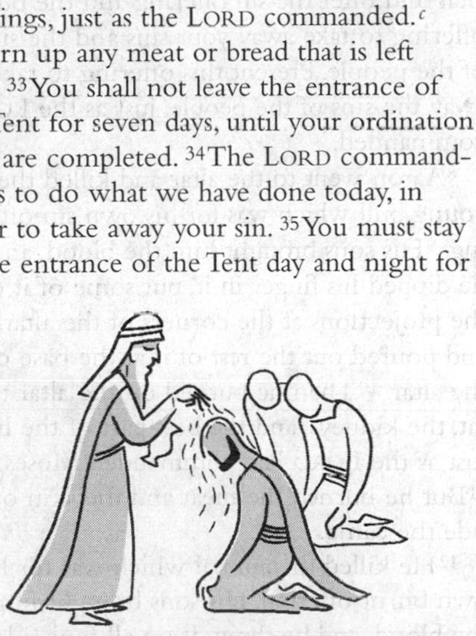

In this way he consecrated them. (8:30)

[c] **8:31** as the LORD commanded; *or* as I commanded.

seven days, doing what the LORD has com-
manded. If you don't, you will die. This is
what the LORD has commanded me." 36So
Aaron and his sons did everything that the
LORD had commanded through Moses.

Aaron Offers Sacrifices

9 The day after the ordination rites were
completed, Moses called Aaron and his
sons and the leaders of Israel. 2He said to
Aaron, "Take a young bull and a ram with-
out any defects and offer them to the LORD,
the bull for a sin offering and the ram for a
burnt offering. 3Then tell the people of
Israel to take a male goat for a sin offering, a
one-year-old calf, and a one-year-old lamb
without any defects for a burnt offering,
4and a bull and a ram for a fellowship offer-
ing. They are to sacrifice them to the LORD
with the grain offering mixed with oil. They
must do this because the LORD will appear
to them today."

5They brought to the front of the Tent
everything that Moses had commanded, and
the whole community assembled there to
worship the LORD. 6Moses said, "The LORD
has commanded you to do all this, so that
the dazzling light of his presence can appear
to you." 7Then he said to Aaron, "Go to the
altar and offer the sin offering and the burnt
offering to take away your sins and the sins
of the people. Present this offering to take
away the sins of the people, just as the LORD
commanded."

8Aaron went to the altar and killed the
young bull which was for his own sin offer-
ing. 9His sons brought him the blood, and
he dipped his finger in it, put some of it on
the projections at the corners of the altar,
and poured out the rest of it at the base of
the altar. 10Then he burned on the altar the
fat, the kidneys, and the best part of the liver,
just as the LORD had commanded Moses.
11But he burned the meat and the skin out-
side the camp.

12He killed the animal which was for his
own burnt offering. His sons brought him
the blood, and he threw it on all four sides
of the altar. 13They handed him the head
and the other pieces of the animal, and he
burned them on the altar. 14Then he washed
the internal organs and the hind legs and
burned them on the altar on top of the rest
of the burnt offering.

15After that, he presented the people's
offerings. He took the goat that was to be
offered for the people's sins, killed it, and of-
fered it, as he had done with his own sin
offering. 16He also brought the animal for
the burnt offering and offered it according
to the regulations. 17He presented the grain
offering and took a handful of flour and
burned it on the altar. (This was in addition
to the daily burnt offering.) 18He killed the
bull and the ram as a fellowship offering for
the people. His sons brought him the blood,
and he threw it on all four sides of the altar.
19Aaron put the fat parts of the bull and the
ram 20on top of the breasts of the animals
and carried it all to the altar. He burned the
fat on the altar 21and presented the breasts
and the right hind legs as the special gift to
the LORD for the priests, as Moses had com-
manded.

22When Aaron had finished all the sacri-
fices, he raised his hands over the people and
blessed them, and then stepped down.
23Moses and Aaron went into the Tent of the
LORD's presence, and when they came out,
they blessed the people, and the dazzling
light of the LORD's presence appeared to all
the people. 24Suddenly the LORD sent a fire,
and it consumed the burnt offering and the
fat parts on the altar. When the people saw
it, they all shouted and bowed down with
their faces to the ground.

The Sin of Nadab and Abihu

10 Aaron's sons, Nadab and Abihu, each
took his fire pan, put live coals in it,
added incense, and presented it to the LORD.
But this fire was not holy, because the LORD
had not commanded them to present it.
2Suddenly the LORD sent fire, and it burned
them to death there in the presence of the
LORD. 3Then Moses said to Aaron, "This is
what the LORD was speaking about when he
said, 'All who serve me must respect my

9:7 Heb 7:27 **9:18** Lev 3:1–11 **9:22** Num 6:22–26

holiness; I will reveal my glory to my peo-
ple.' "[d] But Aaron remained silent.
4 Moses called Mishael and Elzaphan, the
sons of Uzziel, Aaron's uncle, and said to
them, "Come here and carry your cousins'
bodies away from the sacred Tent and put
them outside the camp." 5 So they came and
took hold of the clothing on the corpses and
carried them outside the camp, just as Moses
had commanded.
6 Then Moses said to Aaron and to his
sons Eleazar and Ithamar, "Do not leave
your hair uncombed or tear your clothes to
show that you are in mourning. If you do,
you will die, and the LORD will be angry
with the whole community. But all other
Israelites are allowed to mourn this death
caused by the fire which the LORD sent.
7 Do not leave the entrance of the Tent or
you will die, because you have been conse-
crated by the anointing oil of the LORD." So
they did as Moses said.

Rules for Priests

8 The LORD said to Aaron, 9 "You and your
sons are not to enter the Tent of my pres-
ence after drinking wine or beer; if you do,
you will die. This is a law to be kept by all
your descendants. 10 You must distinguish
between what belongs to God and what is
for general use, between what is ritually
clean and what is unclean. 11 You must teach
the people of Israel all the laws which I have
given to you through Moses."
12 Moses said to Aaron and his two
remaining sons, Eleazar and Ithamar, "Take
the grain offering that is left over from the
food offered to the LORD, make unleavened
bread with it and eat it beside the altar,
because this offering is very holy. 13 Eat it in
a holy place; it is the part that belongs to
you and your sons from the food offered to
the LORD. That is what the LORD com-
manded me. 14 But you and your families
may eat the breast and the hind leg that are
presented as the special gift and the special
contribution to the LORD for the priests. You
may eat them in any ritually clean place.
These offerings have been given to you and
your children as the part that belongs to you
from the fellowship offerings of the people
of Israel. 15 They shall bring the hind leg and
the breast at the time the fat is presented as
a food offering to the LORD. These parts
belong to you and your children forever, just
as the LORD commanded."
16 Moses asked about the goat for the sin
offering and learned that it had already been
burned. This made him angry at Eleazar and
Ithamar, and he demanded, 17 "Why didn't
you eat the sin offering in a sacred place? It
is very holy, and the LORD has given it to
you in order to take away the sin of the
community. 18 Since its blood was not
brought into the sacred Tent, you should
have eaten the sacrifice there, as I com-
manded."
19 Aaron answered, "If I had eaten the sin
offering today, would the LORD have
approved? The people presented their sin
offering to the LORD today, and they
brought their burnt offering, but still these
terrible things have happened to me."
20 When Moses heard this, he was satisfied.

Animals That May Be Eaten

(Deuteronomy 14:3–21)

11 The LORD gave Moses and Aaron
the following regulations 2 for the
people of Israel. You may eat any land animal
3 that has divided hoofs and that also chews
the cud, 4-6 but you must not eat camels, rock
badgers, or rabbits. These must be considered
unclean; they chew the cud, but do not have
divided hoofs. 7 Do not eat pigs. They must
be considered unclean; they have divided
hoofs, but do not chew the cud. 8 Do not eat
these animals or even touch their dead bod-
ies; they are unclean.
9 You may eat any kind of fish that has fins
and scales, 10 but anything living in the water
that does not have fins and scales must not
be eaten. 11 Such creatures must be consid-
ered unclean. You must not eat them or even
touch their dead bodies. 12 You must not eat
anything that lives in the water and does not
have fins and scales.
13-19 You must not eat any of the following

[d] **10:3** I will reveal my glory to my people; *or* my people must honor me.
10:12, 13 Lev 6:14–18 **10:14, 15** Lev 7:30–34 **10:17** Lev 6:24–26

The unclean animals (11)

birds: eagles, owls, hawks, falcons; buzzards, vultures, crows; ostriches; seagulls, storks, herons, pelicans, cormorants;[e] hoopoes; or bats.

[20]All winged insects are unclean, [21]except those that hop. [22]You may eat locusts, crickets, or grasshoppers. [23]But all other small things that have wings and also crawl must be considered unclean.

[24-28]If you touch the dead bodies of the following animals, you will be unclean until evening: all animals with hoofs, unless their hoofs are divided and they chew the cud, and all four-footed animals with paws. If you carry their dead bodies, you must wash your clothes, but you will still be unclean until evening.

[29-30]Moles, rats, mice, and lizards must be considered unclean. [31]Whoever touches them or their dead bodies will be unclean until evening. [32]And if their dead bodies fall on anything, it will be unclean. This applies to any article of wood, cloth, leather, or sacking, no matter what it is used for. It shall be dipped in water, but it will remain unclean until evening. [33]And if their bodies fall into a clay pot, everything that is in it shall be unclean, and you must break the pot. [34]Any food which could normally be eaten, but on which water from such a pot has been poured, will be unclean, and anything drinkable in such a pot is unclean. [35]Anything on which the dead bodies fall is unclean; a clay stove or oven shall be broken, [36]but a spring or a cistern remains clean, although anything else that touches their dead bodies is unclean. [37]If one of them falls on seed that is going to be planted, the seed remains clean. [38]But if the seed is soaking in water and one of them falls on it, the seed is unclean.

[39]If any animal that may be eaten dies, anyone who touches it will be unclean until evening. [40]And if any of you eat any part of the animal, you must wash your clothes, but you will still be unclean until evening; any of you who carry the dead body must wash your clothes, but you will still be unclean until evening.

[41]You must not eat any of the small animals that move on the ground, [42]whether they crawl, or walk on four legs, or have many legs. [43]Do not make yourselves unclean by eating any of these. [44]I am the LORD your God, and you must keep yourselves holy, because I am holy. [45]I am the LORD who brought you out of Egypt so that I could be your God. You must be holy, because I am holy.

[46]This, then, is the law about animals and birds, about everything that lives in the water, and everything that moves on the

[e] **11:13–19** *The identification of some of the birds in verses 13–19 is uncertain.*
11:44 Lev 19:2; 1 Pet 1:16

ground. [47]You must be careful to distinguish between what is ritually clean and unclean, between animals that may be eaten and those that may not.

The Purification of Women after Childbirth

12 The LORD gave Moses the following regulations [2]for the people of Israel. For seven days after a woman gives birth to a son, she is ritually unclean, as she is during her monthly period. [3]On the eighth day, the child shall be circumcised. [4]Then it will be thirty-three more days until she is ritually clean from her loss of blood; she must not touch anything that is holy or enter the sacred Tent until the time of her purification is completed.

[5]For fourteen days after a woman gives birth to a daughter, she is ritually unclean, as she is during her monthly period. Then it will be sixty-six more days until she is ritually clean from her loss of blood.

[6]When the time of her purification is completed, whether for a son or daughter, she shall bring to the priest at the entrance of the Tent of the LORD's presence a one-year-old lamb for a burnt offering and a pigeon or a dove for a sin offering. [7]The priest shall present her offering to the LORD and perform the ritual to take away her impurity, and she will be ritually clean. This, then, is what a woman must do after giving birth.

[8]If the woman cannot afford a lamb, she shall bring two doves or two pigeons, one for a burnt offering and the other for a sin offering, and the priest shall perform the ritual to take away her impurity, and she will be ritually clean.

Laws concerning Skin Diseases

13 The LORD gave Moses and Aaron these regulations. [2]If any of you have a sore on your skin or a boil or an inflammation which could develop into a dreaded skin disease, you shall be brought to the Aaronite priest. [3]The priest shall examine the sore, and if the hairs in it have turned white and the sore appears to be deeper than the surrounding skin, it is a dreaded skin disease, and the priest shall pronounce you unclean. [4]But if the sore is white and does not appear to be deeper than the skin around it and the hairs have not turned white, the priest shall isolate you for seven days. [5]The priest shall examine you again on the seventh day, and if in his opinion the sore looks the same and has not spread, he shall isolate you for another seven days. [6]The priest shall examine you again on the seventh day, and if the sore has faded and has not spread, he shall pronounce you ritually clean; it is only a sore. You shall wash your clothes and be ritually clean. [7]But if the sore spreads after the priest has examined you and pronounced you clean, you must appear before the priest again. [8]The priest will examine you again, and if it has spread, he shall pronounce you unclean; it is a dreaded skin disease.

[9]If any of you have a dreaded skin disease, you shall be brought to the priest, [10]who will examine you. If there is a white sore on your skin which turns the hairs white and is full of pus, [11]it is a chronic skin disease. The priest shall pronounce you unclean; there is no need to isolate you, because you are obviously unclean. [12]If the skin disease spreads and covers you from head to foot, [13]the priest shall examine you again. If he finds that it actually has covered the whole body, he shall pronounce you ritually clean. If your whole skin has turned white, you are ritually clean. [14]But from the moment an open sore appears, you are unclean. [15]The priest shall examine you again, and if he sees an open sore, he shall pronounce you unclean. An open sore means a dreaded skin disease, and you are unclean. [16]But when the sore heals and becomes white again, you shall go to the priest, [17]who will examine you again. If the sore has turned white, you are ritually clean, and the priest shall pronounce you clean.

[18]If any of you have a boil that has healed [19]and if afterward a white swelling or a reddish-white spot appears where the boil was, you shall go to the priest. [20]The priest shall

12:3 Gen 17:12; Lk 2:21 **12:8** Lk 2:24

examine you, and if the spot seems to be
deeper than the surrounding skin and the
hairs in it have turned white, he shall pro-
nounce you unclean. It is a dreaded skin dis-
ease that has started in the boil. [21]But if the
priest examines it and finds that the hairs in
it have not turned white and that it is not
deeper than the surrounding skin, but is light
in color, the priest shall isolate you for seven
days. [22]If the spot spreads, the priest shall pro-
nounce you unclean; you are diseased. [23]But
if it remains unchanged and does not spread,
it is only the scar left from the boil, and the
priest shall pronounce you ritually clean.

The priest shall examine you. (13:20)

[24]In case any of you have been burned, if
the raw flesh becomes white or reddish-
white, [25]the priest shall examine you. If the
hairs in the spot have turned white and it
appears deeper than the surrounding skin, it
is a dreaded skin disease that has started in
the burn, and the priest shall pronounce you
unclean. [26]But if the hairs in it have not
turned white and it is not deeper than the
surrounding skin, but is light in color, the
priest shall isolate you for seven days. [27]The
priest shall examine you again on the sev-
enth day, and if it is spreading, it is a dreaded
skin disease, and the priest shall pronounce
you unclean. [28]But if the spot remains
unchanged and does not spread and is light
in color, it is not a dreaded skin disease. The
priest shall pronounce you ritually clean,
because it is only a scar from the burn.

[29]When any of you, male or female, have
a sore on your head or chin, [30]the priest
shall examine it. If it seems to be deeper
than the surrounding skin and the hairs in it
are yellowish and thin, it is a dreaded skin
disease, and he shall pronounce you unclean.
[31]If, when the priest examines you, the sore
does not appear to be deeper than the sur-
rounding skin, but there are still no healthy
hairs in it, he shall isolate you for seven days.
[32]The priest shall examine the sore again on
the seventh day, and if it has not spread and
there are no yellowish hairs in it and it does
not seem to be deeper than the surrounding
skin, [33]you shall shave the head except the
area around the sore. The priest shall then
isolate you for another seven days. [34]On the
seventh day the priest shall again examine
the sore, and if it has not spread and does not
seem to be deeper than the surrounding
skin, he shall pronounce you ritually clean.
You shall wash your clothes, and you will be
clean. [35]But if the sore spreads after you have
been pronounced clean, [36]the priest shall
examine you again. If the sore has spread, he
need not look for yellowish hairs; you are
obviously unclean. [37]But if in the priest's
opinion the sore has not spread and healthy
hairs are growing in it, the sore has healed,
and the priest shall pronounce you ritually
clean.

[38]When any of you, male or female, have
white spots on the skin, [39]the priest shall
examine you. If the spots are dull white, it is
only a blemish that has broken out on the
skin; you are ritually clean.

[40-41]If you lose your hair at the back or
the front of your head, this does not make
you unclean. [42]But if a reddish-white sore
appears on the bald spot, it is a dreaded skin
disease. [43]The priest shall examine you, and
if there is a reddish-white sore, [44]the priest
shall pronounce you unclean, because of the
dreaded skin disease on your head.

[45]If you have a dreaded skin disease, you
must wear torn clothes, leave your hair
uncombed, cover the lower part of your
face, and call out, "Unclean, unclean!" [46]You
remain unclean as long as you have the dis-
ease, and you must live outside the camp,
away from others.

Laws concerning Mildew

47When there is mildew[f] on clothing,
whether wool or linen, 48or on any piece of
linen or wool cloth or on leather or any-
thing made of leather, 49if it is greenish or
reddish, it is a spreading mildew and must be
shown to the priest. 50The priest shall exam-
ine it and put the object away for seven days.
51He shall examine it again on the seventh
day, and if the mildew has spread, the object
is unclean. 52The priest shall burn it, because
it is a spreading mildew which must be
destroyed by fire.

53But if, when he examines it, the priest
finds that the mildew has not spread on the
object, 54he shall order that it be washed and
put away for another seven days. 55Then he
shall examine it, and if the mildew has not
changed color, even though it has not
spread, it is still unclean; you must burn the
object, whether the rot is on the front or the
back. 56But if, when the priest examines it
again, the mildew has faded, he shall tear it
out of the clothing or leather. 57Then, if the
mildew reappears, it is spreading again, and
the owner shall burn the object. 58If he
washes the object and the spot disappears, he
shall wash it again, and it will be ritually
clean.

59This, then, is the law about mildew on
clothing, whether it is wool or linen, or on
linen or wool cloth or on anything made of
leather; this is how the decision is made as to
whether it is ritually clean or unclean.

Purification after Having Skin Diseases

14 The LORD gave Moses 2the follow-
ing regulations about the ritual
purification of those of you cured of a
dreaded skin disease. On the day you are to
be pronounced clean, you shall be brought
to the priest, 3and the priest shall take you
outside the camp and examine you. If the
disease is healed, 4the priest shall order that
two ritually clean birds be brought, along
with a piece of cedar wood, a red cord, and a
sprig of hyssop. 5Then the priest shall order
that one of the birds be killed over a clay
bowl containing fresh spring water. 6He shall
take the other bird and dip it, together with
the cedar wood, the red cord, and the hys-
sop, in the blood of the bird that was killed.
7He shall sprinkle the blood seven times on
the one of you who is to be purified from
your skin disease, and then he shall pro-
nounce you clean. He shall let the live bird
fly away over the open fields. 8You shall
wash your clothes, shave off all your hair, and
take a bath; you will then be ritually clean.
You may enter the camp, but you must live
outside your tent for seven days. 9On the
seventh day you shall again shave your head,
your beard, your eyebrows, and all the rest of
the hair on your body; you shall wash your
clothes and take a bath, and then you will be
ritually clean.

10On the eighth day you shall bring two
male lambs and one female lamb a year old
that are without any defects, five pounds of
flour mixed with olive oil, and half a pint of
olive oil. 11The priest shall take you and
these offerings to the entrance of the Tent of
the LORD's presence. 12Then the priest shall
take one of the male lambs and together
with the half pint of oil he shall offer it as a
repayment offering. He shall present them as
a special gift to the LORD for the priest.
13He shall kill the lamb in the holy place
where the animals for the sin offerings and
the burnt offerings are killed. He must do
this because the repayment offering, like the
sin offering, belongs to the priest and is very
holy. 14The priest shall take some of the
blood of the lamb and put it on the lobe of
the right ear, on the thumb of the right
hand, and on the big toe of the right foot of
the one of you to be declared ritually clean.
15The priest shall take some of the olive oil
and pour it in the palm of his own left hand,
16dip a finger of his right hand in it, and
sprinkle some of it seven times there in the
LORD's presence. 17He shall take some of the
oil that is in the palm of his hand and some
of the blood of the lamb and put them on
the lobe of the right ear, on the thumb of
the right hand, and on the big toe of the
right foot of the one of you to be declared

[f] **13:47** MILDEW: *The Hebrew word for "dreaded skin disease" and "mildew" is the same.*
14:2 Mt 8:4; Mk 1:44; Lk 5:14; 17:14

ritually clean. 18He shall put the rest of the oil that is in the palm of his hand on your head. In this way he shall perform the ritual of purification.

19Then the priest shall offer the sin offering and perform the ritual of purification. After that, he shall kill the animal for the burnt offering 20and offer it with the grain offering on the altar. In this way the priest shall perform the ritual of purification, and you will be ritually clean.

21If you are poor and cannot afford any more, you shall bring for your purification only one male lamb as your repayment offering, a special gift to the LORD for the priest. You shall bring only two pounds of flour mixed with olive oil for a grain offering and half a pint of olive oil. 22You shall also bring two doves or two pigeons, one for the sin offering and one for the burnt offering. 23On the eighth day of your purification you shall bring them to the priest at the entrance of the Tent. 24The priest shall take the lamb and the olive oil and present them as a special gift to the LORD for the priest. 25He shall kill the lamb and take some of the blood and put it on the lobe of your right ear, on the thumb of your right hand, and on the big toe of your right foot. 26The priest shall pour some of the oil into the palm of his own left hand 27and with a finger of his right hand sprinkle some of it seven times there in the LORD's presence. 28He shall put some of the oil on the same places he put the blood: on the lobe of your right ear, on the thumb of your right hand, and on the big toe of your right foot. 29The rest of the oil that is in his palm he shall put on your head and in this way perform the ritual of purification. 30Then he shall offer one of the doves or pigeons 31as the sin offering and the other as the burnt offering with the grain offering. In this way the priest shall perform the ritual of purification. 32This is the law for those who have a dreaded skin disease but who cannot afford the normal offerings required for his purification.

Mildew in Houses

33The LORD gave Moses and Aaron
34-35the following regulations about houses affected by spreading mildew. (These were to apply after the people of Israel entered the land of Canaan, which the LORD was going to give them as their possession.) If any of you find that the LORD has sent mildew on your house, then you must go and tell the priest about it. 36The priest shall order everything to be moved out of the house before he goes to examine the mildew; otherwise everything in the house will be declared unclean. Then he shall go to the house 37and examine the mildew. If there are greenish or reddish spots that appear to be eating into the wall, 38he shall leave the house and lock it up for seven days. 39On the seventh day he shall return and examine it again. If the mildew has spread, 40he shall order that the stones on which the mildew is found be removed and thrown into some unclean place outside the city. 41After that he must have all the interior walls scraped and the plaster dumped in an unclean place outside the city. 42Then other stones are to be used to replace the stones that were removed, and new plaster will be used to cover the walls.

The stones shall be removed. (14:40)

43If the mildew breaks out again in the house after the stones have been removed and the house has been scraped and plastered, 44the priest shall go and look. If it has spread, the house is unclean. 45It must be torn down, and its stones, its wood, and all its plaster must be carried out of the city to an unclean place. 46Any who enter the house while it is locked up will be unclean until evening. 47Any who lie down or eat in the house must wash their clothes.

48 If, when the priest comes to look, the mildew has not reappeared after the house has been replastered, he shall pronounce the house ritually clean, because the mildew has been completely removed. 49 To purify the house, he shall take two birds, some cedar wood, a red cord, and a sprig of hyssop. 50 He shall kill one of the birds over a clay bowl containing fresh spring water. 51 Then he shall take the cedar wood, the hyssop, the red cord, and the live bird and shall dip them in the blood of the bird that was killed and in the fresh water. And he shall sprinkle the house seven times. 52 In this way he shall purify the house with the bird's blood, the fresh water, the live bird, the cedar wood, the hyssop, and the red cord. 53 Then he shall let the live bird fly away outside the city over the open fields. In this way he shall perform the ritual of purification for the house, and it will be ritually clean.

54 These are the laws about dreaded skin diseases; 55-56 sores, boils, or inflammations; and about mildew in clothes or houses. 57 These laws determine when something is unclean and when it is clean.

Unclean Bodily Discharges

15 The LORD gave Moses and Aaron the following regulations 2 for the people of Israel. When any man has a discharge from his penis, the discharge is unclean, 3 whether the penis runs with it or is stopped up by it. 4 Any bed on which he sits or lies is unclean. 5 Anyone who touches his bed 6 or sits on anything the man has sat on must wash his clothes and take a bath, and he remains unclean until evening. 7 Anyone who touches the man with the discharge must wash his clothes and take a bath, and he remains unclean until evening. 8 If the man with the discharge spits on anyone who is ritually clean, that person must wash his clothes and take a bath, and he remains unclean until evening. 9 Any saddle or seat on which the man with the discharge sits is unclean. 10 Anyone who touches anything on which the man sat is unclean until evening. Anyone who carries anything on which the man sat must wash his clothes and take a bath, and he remains unclean until evening. 11 If a man who has a discharge touches one of you without first having washed his hands, you must wash your clothes and take a bath, and you remain unclean until evening. 12 Any clay pot that the man touches must be broken, and any wooden bowl that he touches must be washed.

13 After the man is cured of his discharge, he must wait seven days and then wash his clothes and take a bath in fresh spring water, and he will be ritually clean. 14 On the eighth day he shall take two doves or two pigeons to the entrance of the Tent of the LORD's presence and give them to the priest. 15 The priest shall offer one of them as a sin offering and the other as a burnt offering. In this way he will perform the ritual of purification for the man.

16 When a man has an emission of semen, he must bathe his whole body, and he remains unclean until evening. 17 Anything made of cloth or leather on which the semen falls must be washed, and it remains unclean until evening. 18 After sexual intercourse both the man and the woman must take a bath, and they remain unclean until evening.

19 When a woman has her monthly period, she remains unclean for seven days. Anyone who touches her is unclean until evening. 20 Anything on which she sits or lies during her monthly period is unclean. 21-23 Any who touch her bed or anything on which she has sat must wash their clothes and take a bath, and they remain unclean until evening. 24 If a man has sexual intercourse with her during her period, he is contaminated by her impurity and remains unclean for seven days, and any bed on which he lies is unclean.

25 If a woman has a flow of blood for several days outside her monthly period or if her flow continues beyond her regular period, she remains unclean as long as the flow continues, just as she is during her monthly period. 26 Any bed on which she lies and anything on which she sits during this time is unclean. 27 Any who touch them are unclean and must wash their clothes and take a bath; they remain unclean until evening. 28 After her flow stops, she must wait seven days, and then she will be ritually clean. 29 On the eighth day she shall take two

doves or two pigeons to the priest at the entrance of the Tent of the LORD's presence. 30 The priest shall offer one of them as a sin offering and the other as a burnt offering, and in this way he will perform the ritual of purification for her.

31 The LORD told Moses to warn the people of Israel about their uncleanness, so that they would not defile the Tent of his presence, which was in the middle of the camp. If they did, they would be killed.

32 These are the regulations about a man who has a discharge or an emission of semen, 33 a woman during her monthly period, or a man who has sexual intercourse with a woman who is ritually unclean.

The Day of Atonement

16 The LORD spoke to Moses after the death of the two sons of Aaron who were killed when they offered unholy fire to the LORD. 2 He said, "Tell your brother Aaron that only at the proper time is he to go behind the curtain into the Most Holy Place, because that is where I appear in a cloud above the lid on the Covenant Box. If he disobeys, he will be killed. 3 He may enter the Most Holy Place only after he has brought a young bull for a sin offering and a ram for a burnt offering."

4 Then the LORD gave the following instructions. Before Aaron goes into the Most Holy Place, he must take a bath and put on the priestly garments: the linen robe and shorts, the belt, and the turban.

5 The community of Israel shall give Aaron two male goats for a sin offering and a ram for a burnt offering. 6 He shall offer a bull as a sacrifice to take away his own sins and those of his family. 7 Then he shall take the two goats to the entrance of the Tent of the LORD's presence. 8 There he shall draw lots, using two stones, one marked "for the LORD" and the other "for Azazel."[g] 9 Aaron shall sacrifice the goat chosen by lot for the LORD and offer it as a sin offering. 10 The goat chosen for Azazel shall be presented alive to the LORD and sent off into the desert to Azazel, in order to take away the sins of the people.

11 When Aaron sacrifices the bull as the sin offering for himself and his family, 12 he shall take a fire pan full of burning coals from the altar and two handfuls of fine incense and bring them into the Most Holy Place. 13 There in the LORD's presence he shall put the incense on the fire, and the smoke of the incense will hide the lid of the Covenant Box so that he will not see it and die. 14 He shall take some of the bull's blood and with his finger sprinkle it on the front of the lid and then sprinkle some of it seven times in front of the Covenant Box.

15 After that, he shall kill the goat for the sin offering for the people, bring its blood into the Most Holy Place, and sprinkle it on the lid and then in front of the Covenant Box, as he did with the bull's blood. 16 In this way he will perform the ritual to purify the Most Holy Place from the uncleanness of the people of Israel and from all their sins. He must do this to the Tent, because it stands in the middle of the camp, which is ritually unclean. 17 From the time Aaron enters the Most Holy Place to perform the ritual of purification until he comes out, there must be no one in the Tent. When he has performed the ritual for himself, his family, and the whole community, 18 he must then go out to the altar for burnt offerings and purify it. He must take some of the bull's blood and some of the goat's blood and put it all over the projections at the corners of the altar. 19 With his finger he must sprinkle some of the blood on the altar seven times. In this way he is to purify it from the sins of the people of Israel and make it holy.

The Scapegoat

20 When Aaron has finished performing the ritual to purify the Most Holy Place, the rest of the Tent of the LORD's presence, and the altar, he shall present to the LORD the live goat chosen for Azazel.[g] 21 He shall put both of his hands on the goat's head and confess over it all the evils, sins, and rebellions of the people of Israel, and so transfer them to the

[g] **16:8,20** AZAZEL: *The meaning of this Hebrew word is unknown; it may be the name of a desert demon.*

16:2 Heb 6:19 **16:3** Heb 9:7 **16:15** Heb 9:12 **16:21, 22** Tob 8:3

goat's head. Then the goat is to be driven off into the desert by someone appointed to do it. 22 The goat will carry all their sins away with him into some uninhabited land.

The goat will carry all their sins away. (16:22)

23 Then Aaron shall go into the Tent, take off the priestly garments that he had put on before entering the Most Holy Place, and leave them there. 24 He must take a bath in a holy place and put on his own clothes. After that, he shall go out and offer the burnt offering to remove his own sins and those of the people. 25 He shall burn on the altar the fat of the animal for the sin offering. 26 The man who drove the goat into the desert to Azazel must wash his clothes and take a bath before he comes back into camp. 27 The bull and the goat used for the sin offering, whose blood was brought into the Most Holy Place to take away sin, shall be carried outside the camp and burned. Skin, meat, and intestines shall all be burned. 28 The one who burns them must wash his clothes and take a bath before he returns to camp.

Observing the Day of Atonement

29 The following regulations are to be observed for all time to come. On the tenth day of the seventh month the Israelites and the foreigners living among them must fast and must not do any work. 30 On that day the ritual is to be performed to purify them from all their sins, so that they will be ritually clean. 31 That day is to be a very holy day, one on which they fast and do no work at all. These regulations are to be observed for all time to come. 32 The High Priest, properly ordained and consecrated to succeed his father, is to perform the ritual of purification. He shall put on the priestly garments 33 and perform the ritual to purify the Most Holy Place, the rest of the Tent of the LORD's presence, the altar, the priests, and all the people of the community. 34 These regulations are to be observed for all time to come. This ritual must be performed once a year to purify the people of Israel from all their sins.

So Moses[h] did as the LORD had commanded.

The Sacredness of Blood

17 The LORD commanded Moses 2 to give Aaron and his sons and all the people of Israel the following regulations. 3-4 Any Israelites who kill a cow or a sheep or a goat as an offering to the LORD anywhere except at the entrance of the Tent of the LORD's presence have broken the Law. They have shed blood and shall no longer be considered God's people. 5 The meaning of this command is that the people of Israel shall now bring to the LORD the animals which they used to kill in the open country. They shall now bring them to the priest at the entrance of the Tent and kill them as fellowship offerings. 6 The priest shall throw the blood against the sides of the altar at the entrance of the Tent and burn the fat to produce an odor that is pleasing to the LORD. 7 The people of Israel must no longer be unfaithful to the LORD by killing their animals in the fields as sacrifices to the goat demons. The people of Israel must keep this regulation for all time to come.

8 Any Israelites or any foreigners living in the community who offer a burnt offering or any other sacrifice 9 as an offering to the LORD anywhere except at the entrance of the Tent shall no longer be considered God's people.

10 If any Israelites or any foreigners living

[h] **16:34** Moses; *or* Aaron.

16:23 Ezek 44:19 **16:27** Heb 13:11 **16:29–34** Lev 23:26–32; Num 29:7–11 **17:10** Gen 9:4; Lev 7:26, 27; 19:26; Deut 12:16, 23; 15:23

in the community eat meat with blood still
in it, the LORD will turn against them and
no longer consider them his people. 11 The
life of every living thing is in the blood, and
that is why the LORD has commanded that
all blood be poured out on the altar to take
away the people's sins. Blood, which is life,
takes away sins. 12 That is why the LORD has
told the people of Israel that neither they
nor any foreigner living among them shall
eat any meat with blood still in it.

13 If any Israelites or any foreigners living
in the community catch an animal or a bird
which is ritually clean, they must pour its
blood out on the ground and cover it with
dirt. 14 The life of every living thing is in the
blood, and that is why the LORD has told the
people of Israel that they shall not eat any
meat with blood still in it and that anyone
who does so will no longer be considered
one of his people.

15 Any people, Israelites or foreigners, who
eat meat from an animal that has died a natural death or has been killed by wild animals
must wash their clothes, take a bath, and wait
until evening before they are ritually clean.
16 If they do not, they must suffer the consequences.

Forbidden Sexual Practices

18 The LORD told Moses 2 to say to the
people of Israel, "I am the LORD
your God. 3 Do not follow the practices of
the people of Egypt, where you once lived,
or of the people in the land of Canaan,
where I am now taking you. 4 Obey my laws
and do what I command. I am the LORD
your God. 5 Follow the practices and the laws
that I give you; you will save your life by
doing so. I am the LORD."

6 The LORD gave the following regulations.
Do not have sexual intercourse with any of
your relatives. 7 Do not disgrace your father
by having intercourse with your mother. You
must not disgrace your own mother. 8 Do not
disgrace your father by having intercourse
with any of his other wives. 9 Do not have
intercourse with your sister or your half sister, whether or not she was brought up in
the same house with you. 10 Do not have
intercourse with your granddaughter; that
would be a disgrace to you. 11 Do not have
intercourse with a stepsister; she, too, is your
sister. 12-13 Do not have intercourse with an
aunt, whether she is your father's sister or
your mother's sister. 14 Do not have intercourse with your uncle's wife; she, too, is
your aunt. 15 Do not have intercourse with
your daughter-in-law 16 or with your brother's wife. 17 Do not have intercourse with the
daughter or granddaughter of a woman with
whom you have had intercourse; they may be
related to you, and that would be incest.
18 Do not take your wife's sister as one of
your wives, as long as your wife is living.

19 Do not have intercourse with a woman
during her monthly period, because she is ritually unclean. 20 Do not have intercourse with
another man's wife; that would make you ritually unclean. 21 Do not hand over any of your
children to be used in the worship of the god
Molech, because that would bring disgrace on
the name of God, the LORD. 22 No man is to
have sexual relations with another man; God
hates that. 23 No man or woman is to have
sexual relations with an animal; that perversion makes you ritually unclean.

24 Do not make yourselves unclean by any
of these acts, for that is how the pagans made
themselves unclean, those pagans who lived
in the land before you and whom the LORD
is driving out so that you can go in. 25 Their
actions made the land unclean, and so the
LORD is punishing the land and making it
reject the people who lived there. 26-27 They
did all these disgusting things and made the
land unclean, but you must not do them. All
of you, whether Israelites or foreigners living
with you, must keep the LORD's laws and
commands, 28 and then the land will not
reject you, as it rejected the pagans who lived
there before you. 29 You know that whoever
does any of these disgusting things will no
longer be considered one of God's people.

30 And the LORD said, "Obey the com-

17:11 Heb 9:22 **18:5** Neh 9:29; Ezek 18:9; 20:11–13; Lk 10:28; Rom 10:5; Gal 3:12 **18:8** Lev 20:11; Deut 22:30; 27:20 **18:9** Lev 20:17; Deut 27:22 **18:12–14** Lev 20:19, 20 **18:15** Lev 20:12 **18:16** Lev 20:21 **18:17** Lev 20:14; Deut 27:23 **18:19** Lev 20:18 **18:20** Lev 20:10 **18:21** Lev 20:1–5 **18:22** Lev 20:13 **18:23** Ex 22:19; Lev 20:15, 16; Deut 27:21

mands I give and do not follow the practices of the people who lived in the land before you, and do not make yourselves unclean by doing any of these things. I am the LORD your God."

Laws of Holiness and Justice

19 The LORD told Moses 2to say to the
community of Israel, "Be holy,
because I, the LORD your God, am holy.
3Each of you must respect your mother and
your father, and must keep the Sabbath, as I
have commanded. I am the LORD your God.
4"Do not abandon me and worship idols;
do not make gods of metal and worship
them. I am the LORD your God.
5"When you kill an animal for a fellow-
ship offering, keep the regulations that I have
given you, and I will accept the offering.
6The meat must be eaten on the day the
animal is killed or on the next day. Any meat
left on the third day must be burned,
7because it is ritually unclean, and if anyone
eats it, I will not accept the offering. 8Any
who eat it will be guilty of treating as ordi-
nary what is dedicated to me, and they will
no longer be considered my people.
9"When you harvest your fields, do not
cut the grain at the edges of the fields, and
do not go back to cut the heads of grain that
were left. 10Do not go back through your
vineyard to gather the grapes that were
missed or to pick up the grapes that have
fallen; leave them for poor people and for-
eigners. I am the LORD your God.
11"Do not steal or cheat or lie. 12Do not
make a promise in my name if you do not
intend to keep it; that brings disgrace on my
name. I am the LORD your God.
13"Do not rob or take advantage of any-
one. Do not hold back the wages of someone
you have hired, not even for one night. 14Do
not curse the deaf or put something in front
of the blind so as to make them stumble over
it. Obey me; I am the LORD your God.
15"Be honest and just when you make
decisions in legal cases; do not show

Live it!

You Can Be Holy!

Chapters 17–26 of Leviticus are called the holiness code, or holiness laws. In these chapters God says, "Be holy, because I, the LORD your God, am holy" (19:2), and, "Obey my laws, because I am the LORD and I make you holy" (20:8). The message is clear: God wants us to be holy as he is holy. To be holy is to be like God, and holiness is basically imitating God.

All of these laws in the holiness code were ways of living God's values. The laws had to do with avoiding sinful behavior, how to avoid sickness and disease, how to worship God properly, and how to live fairly with other people. Some of these laws don't apply to us today because Christians have a different understanding today of how to live out these same values. But the values are still there for us to live out in every part of our lives.

The call to holiness takes a new twist in the New Testament. Because Jesus is God we are now called to imitate Jesus. Imitating Jesus means being peacemakers, being forgiving even to those who hate us, caring for everyone, especially people with special needs, and accepting suffering with grace. Try this. Make a list of all the things you can do to be like Jesus. Then ask Jesus to help you do them!

— Leviticus 19:1–3

19:2 Lev 11:44, 45; 1 Pet 1:16 **19:3 a** Ex 20:12; Deut 5:16; **b** Ex 20:8; Deut 5:12 **19:4 a** Lev 26:1; **b** Ex 20:23; 34:17; Deut 17:25 **19:9, 10** Lev 27:15; Deut 24:19–22 **19:11 a** Ex 20:15; Deut 5:19; **b** Ex 20:16; Deut 5:20 **19:12** Ex 20:7; Deut 5:11; Mt 5:33 **19:13** Deut 24:14, 15 **19:14** Deut 27:18 **19:15** Ex 23:6–8; Deut 16:19

favoritism to the poor or fear the rich. 16 Do
not spread lies about anyone, and when
someone is on trial for his life, speak out if
your testimony can help him. I am the LORD.
17 "Do not bear a grudge against others,
but settle your differences with them, so that
you will not commit a sin because of them.[i]
18 Do not take revenge on others or continue
to hate them, but love your neighbors as you
love yourself. I am the LORD.

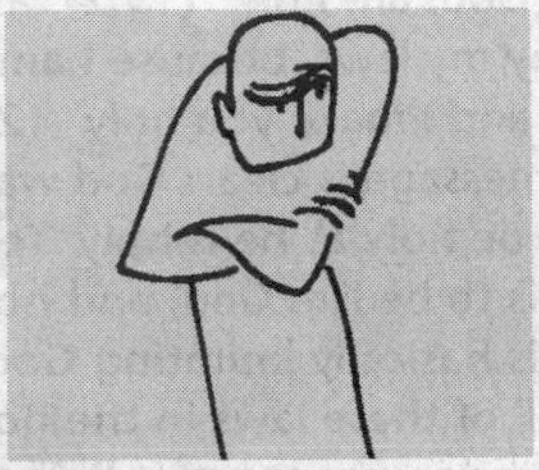

"Do not bear a grudge." (19:17)

19 "Obey my commands. Do not cross-
breed domestic animals. Do not plant two
kinds of seed in the same field. Do not wear
clothes made of two kinds of material.
20 "If a slave woman is the recognized con-
cubine of a man and she has not been paid
for and freed, then if another man has sexual
relations with her, they will be punished, but
not[j] put to death, since she is a slave. 21 The
man shall bring a ram to the entrance of the
Tent of my presence as his repayment offer-
ing, 22 and with it the priest shall perform the
ritual of purification to remove the man's sin,
and God will forgive him.
23 "When you come into the land of
Canaan and plant any kind of fruit tree, con-
sider the fruit ritually unclean for the first
three years. During that time you must not
eat it. 24 In the fourth year all the fruit shall
be dedicated as an offering to show your
gratitude to me,[k] the LORD. 25 But in the
fifth year you may eat the fruit. If you do all
this, your trees will bear more fruit. I am the
LORD your God.

Show respect for old people. (19:32)

26 "Do not eat any meat with blood still in
it. Do not practice any kind of magic. 27 Do
not cut the hair on the sides of your head or
trim your beard 28 or tattoo yourselves or cut
gashes in your body to mourn for the dead. I
am the LORD.
29 "Do not disgrace your daughters by
making them temple prostitutes;[l] if you do,
you will turn to other gods and the land will
be full of immorality. 30 Keep the Sabbath,
and honor the place where I am worshiped.
I am the LORD.
31 "Do not go for advice to people who
consult the spirits of the dead. If you do, you
will be ritually unclean. I am the LORD your
God.
32 "Show respect for old people and honor
them. Reverently obey me; I am the LORD.
33 "Do not mistreat foreigners who are liv-
ing in your land. 34 Treat them as you would
an Israelite, and love them as you love your-
selves. Remember that you were once for-
eigners in the land of Egypt. I am the LORD
your God.
35 "Do not cheat anyone by using false
measures of length, weight, or quantity.
36 Use honest scales, honest weights, and
honest measures. I am the LORD your God,

[i] **19:17** so . . . them; *or* so that you do not commit this sin against them. [j] **19:20** they . . . not; *or* an investigation will be made but they will not be. [k] **19:24** to show your gratitude to me; *or* in praise of me.
[l] **19:29** TEMPLE PROSTITUTES: *These women were found in Canaanite temples, where fertility gods were worshiped. It was believed that intercourse with these prostitutes assured fertile fields and herds.*

19:17 Mt 18:15 **19:18** Mt 5:43; 19:19; 22:39; Mk 12:31; Lk 10:27; Rom 13:9; Gal 5:14; Jas 2:8 **19:19** Deut 22:9–11 **19:26 a** Gen 9:4; Lev 7:26, 27; 17:10–14; Deut 12:16, 23; 15:23; **b** Deut 18:10 **19:27, 28** Lev 21:5; Deut 14:1 **19:29** Deut 23:17 **19:30** Lev 26:2 **19:31** Deut 18:11; 1 Sam 28:3; 2 Kings 23:4; Isa 8:19 **19:33, 34** Ex 22:21; Deut 24:17, 18; 27:19 **19:35, 36** Deut 25:13–16; Prov 20:10; Ezek 45:10

Love them as you love yourselves. (19:34)

and I brought you out of Egypt. [37]Obey all
my laws and commands. I am the LORD."

Penalties for Disobedience

20 The LORD told Moses [2]to say to the
people of Israel, "Any of you or any
foreigner living among you who gives any
children to be used in the worship of the
god Molech shall be stoned to death by the
whole community. [3]If any of you give one
of your children to Molech and make my
sacred Tent unclean and disgrace my holy
name, I will turn against you and will no
longer consider you my people. [4]But if the
community ignores what you have done and
does not put you to death, [5]I myself will
turn against you and your whole family and
against all who join you in being unfaithful
to me and worshiping Molech. I will no
longer consider any of you my people.

[6]"If any of you go for advice to people
who consult the spirits of the dead, I will
turn against you and will no longer consider
you one of my people. [7]Keep yourselves
holy, because I am the LORD your God.
[8]Obey my laws, because I am the LORD and
I make you holy."

[9]The LORD gave the following regula-
tions. Any of you that curse your father or
mother shall be put to death; you are
responsible for your own death.

[10]If a man commits adultery with the wife
of an Israelite, both he and the woman shall
be put to death. [11]A man who has inter-
course with one of his father's wives dis-
graces his father, and both he and the
woman shall be put to death. They are
responsible for their own death. [12]If a man
has intercourse with his daughter-in-law,
they shall both be put to death. They have
committed incest and are responsible for
their own death. [13]If a man has sexual rela-
tions with another man, they have done a
disgusting thing, and both shall be put to
death. They are responsible for their own
death. [14]If a man marries a woman and her
mother, all three shall be burned to death
because of the disgraceful thing they have
done; such a thing must not be permitted
among you. [15]If a man has sexual relations
with an animal, he and the animal shall be
put to death. [16]If a woman tries to have
sexual relations with an animal, she and
the animal shall be put to death. They are
responsible for their own death.

[17]If a man marries his sister or half sister,
they shall be publicly disgraced and driven
out of the community. He has had inter-
course with his sister and must suffer the
consequences. [18]If a man has intercourse
with a woman during her monthly period,
both of them are to be driven out of the
community, because they have broken the
regulations about ritual uncleanness.

[19]If a man has intercourse with his aunt,
both of them must suffer the consequences
for incest. [20]If a man has intercourse with his
uncle's wife, he disgraces his uncle, and he
and the woman will pay the penalty; neither
one will have children. [21]If a man takes his
brother's wife, they will die childless. He has
done a ritually unclean thing and has dis-
graced his brother.

[22]The LORD said, "Keep all my laws and
commands, so that you will not be rejected
by the land of Canaan, into which I am
bringing you. [23]Do not adopt the customs of
the people who live there; I am driving out
those pagans so that you can enter the land.
They have disgusted me with all their evil
practices. [24]But I have promised you this
rich and fertile land as your possession, and I
will give it to you. I am the LORD your

20:9 Ex 21:17; Mt 15:4; Mk 7:10 **20:10** Ex 20:14; Lev 18:20; Deut 5:18 **20:11** Lev 18:8; Deut 22:30; 27:20 **20:12** Lev 18:15 **20:13** Lev 18:22 **20:14** Lev 18:17; Deut 27:23 **20:15, 16** Ex 22:19; Lev 18:23; Deut 27:21 **20:17** Lev 18:9; Deut 27:22 **20:18** Lev 18:19 **20:19, 20** Lev 18:12–14 **20:21** Lev 18:16

God, and I have set you apart from the other
nations. 25So then, you must make a clear
distinction between animals and birds that
are ritually clean and those that are not. Do
not eat unclean animals or birds. I have
declared them unclean, and eating them
would make you unclean. 26You shall be
holy and belong only to me, because I am
the LORD and I am holy. I have set you apart
from the other nations so that you would
belong to me alone.

27"Any man or woman who consults the
spirits of the dead shall be stoned to death;
any of you that do this are responsible for
your own death."

The Holiness of the Priests

21 The LORD commanded Moses to
tell the Aaronite priests, "No priest is
to make himself ritually unclean by taking
part in the funeral ceremonies when a rela-
tive dies, 2unless it is his mother, father, son,
daughter, brother, 3or unmarried sister living
in his house. 4He shall not make himself
unclean at the death of those related to him
by marriage.[m]

5"No priest shall shave any part of his
head or trim his beard or cut gashes on his
body to show that he is in mourning. 6He
must be holy and must not disgrace my
name. He offers food offerings to me, and he
must be holy. 7A priest shall not marry a
woman who has been a prostitute or a
woman who is not a virgin or who is
divorced; he is holy. 8The people must con-
sider the priest holy, because he presents the
food offerings to me. I am the LORD; I am
holy and I make my people holy. 9If a priest's
daughter becomes a prostitute, she disgraces
her father; she shall be burned to death.

10"The High Priest has had the anointing
oil poured on his head and has been conse-
crated to wear the priestly garments, so he
must not leave his hair uncombed or tear his
clothes to show that he is in mourning.
11-12He has been dedicated to me and is not
to make himself ritually unclean nor is he to
defile my sacred Tent by leaving it and enter-
ing a house where there is a dead person,
even if it is his own father or mother. 13He
shall marry a virgin, 14not a widow or a
divorced woman or a woman who has been
a prostitute. He shall marry only a virgin
from his own clan. 15Otherwise, his children,
who ought to be holy, will be ritually
unclean. I am the LORD and I have set him
apart as the High Priest."

16The LORD commanded Moses 17to tell
Aaron, "None of your descendants who has
any physical defects may present the food
offering to me. This applies for all time to
come. 18No man with any physical defects
may make the offering: no one who is blind,
lame, disfigured, or deformed; 19no one with
a crippled hand or foot; 20no one who is a
hunchback or a dwarf; no one with any eye
or skin disease; and no eunuch. 21No descen-
dant of Aaron the priest who has any physical
defects may present the food offering to me.
22Such a man may eat the food offered to
me, both the holy food offering and the very
holy food offering, 23but because he has a
physical defect, he shall not come near the
sacred curtain or approach the altar. He must
not profane these holy things, because I am
the LORD and I make them holy."

24This, then, is what Moses said to Aaron,
the sons of Aaron, and to all the people of
Israel.

The Holiness of the Offerings

22 The LORD commanded Moses 2to
tell Aaron and his sons, "You must
not bring disgrace on my holy name, so treat
with respect the sacred offerings that the
people of Israel dedicate to me. I am the
LORD. 3If any of your descendants, while he
is ritually unclean, comes near the sacred
offerings which the people of Israel have
dedicated to me, he can never again serve at
the altar. This applies for all time to come. I
am the LORD.

4"None of the descendants of Aaron who
has a dreaded skin disease or a discharge may
eat any of the sacred offerings until he is
ritually clean. Any priest is unclean if he
touches anything which is unclean through
contact with a corpse or if he has an emis-

[m] **21:4** *Verse 4 in Hebrew is unclear.*

21:5 Lev 19:27, 28; Deut 14:1

sion of semen 5or if he has touched an unclean animal or person. 6Any priest who becomes unclean remains unclean until evening, and even then he may not eat any of the sacred offerings until he has taken a bath. 7After the sun sets he is clean, and then he may eat the sacred offerings, which are his food. 8He shall not eat the meat of any animal that has died a natural death or has been killed by wild animals; it will make him unclean. I am the LORD.

9"All priests shall observe the regulations that I have given. Otherwise, they will become guilty and die, because they have disobeyed the sacred regulations. I am the LORD and I make them holy.

10"Only a member of a priestly family may eat any of the sacred offerings; no one else may eat them—not even someone staying with a priest or hired by him. 11But a priest's slaves, bought with his own money or born in his home, may eat the food the priest receives. 12A priest's daughter who marries someone who is not a priest may not eat any of the sacred offerings. 13But a widowed or divorced daughter who has no children and who has returned to live in her father's house as a dependent may eat the food her father receives as a priest. Only a member of a priestly family may eat any of it.

14"If any people who are not members of a priestly family eat any of the sacred offerings without intending to, they must repay the priest its full value plus an additional 20 percent. 15The priests shall not profane the sacred offerings 16by letting any unauthorized people eat them; this would bring guilt and punishment on such people. I am the LORD and I make the offerings holy."

17The LORD commanded Moses 18to give Aaron and his sons and all the people of Israel the following regulations. When any Israelite or any foreigner living in Israel presents a burnt offering, whether as fulfillment of a vow or as a freewill offering, the animal must not have any defects. 19To be accepted, it must be a male without any defects. 20If you offer any animal that has any defects, the LORD will not accept it. 21When anyone presents a fellowship offering to the LORD, whether as fulfillment of a vow or as a freewill offering, the animal must be without any defects if it is to be accepted. 22Do not offer to the LORD any animal that is blind or crippled or mutilated, or that has a running sore or a skin eruption or scabs. Do not offer any such animals on the altar as a food offering. 23As a freewill offering you may offer an animal that is stunted or not perfectly formed, but it is not acceptable in fulfillment of a vow. 24Do not offer to the LORD any animal whose testicles have been crushed, cut, bruised, or torn off. This is not permitted in your land.

25Do not offer as a food offering any animal obtained from a foreigner. Such animals are considered defective and are not acceptable.

26-27When a calf or a lamb or a kid is born, it must not be taken from its mother for seven days, but after that it is acceptable as a food offering. 28Do not sacrifice a cow and its calf or a sheep and its lamb or a goat and its kid on the same day. 29When you offer a sacrifice of thanksgiving to the LORD, follow the rules so that you will be accepted; 30eat it the same day and leave none of it until the next morning.

31The LORD said, "Obey my commands; I am the LORD. 32Do not bring disgrace on my holy name; all the people of Israel must acknowledge me to be holy. I am the LORD and I make you holy; 33and I brought you out of Egypt to become your God. I am the LORD."

The Religious Festivals

23 The LORD gave Moses 2the following regulations for the religious festivals, when the people of Israel are to gather for worship. 3You have six days in which to do your work, but remember that the seventh day, the Sabbath, is a day of rest. On that day do not work, but gather for worship. The Sabbath belongs to the LORD, no matter where you live. 4Proclaim the following festivals at the appointed times.

22:20 Deut 17:1 **23:3** Ex 20:8–10; 23:12; 31:15; 34:21; 35:2; Deut 5:12–14

Passover and Unleavened Bread
(Numbers 28:16–25)

[5]The Passover, celebrated to honor the
LORD, begins at sunset on the fourteenth
day of the first month. [6]On the fifteenth day
the Festival of Unleavened Bread begins, and
for seven days you must not eat any bread
made with yeast. [7]On the first of these days
you shall gather for worship and do none of
your daily work. [8]Offer your food offerings
to the LORD for seven days. On the seventh
day you shall again gather for worship, but
you shall do none of your daily work.

[9-10]When you come into the land that the
LORD is giving you and you harvest your
grain, take the first sheaf to the priest. [11]He
shall present it as a special offering to the
LORD, so that you may be accepted. The
priest shall present it the day after the Sab-
bath. [12]On the day you present the offering
of grain, also sacrifice as a burnt offering a
one-year-old male lamb that has no defects.
[13]With it you shall present four pounds of
flour mixed with olive oil as a food offering.
The odor of this offering is pleasing to the
LORD. You shall also present with it an offer-
ing of one quart of wine. [14]Do not eat any
of the new grain, whether raw, roasted, or
baked into bread, until you have brought this
offering to God. This regulation is to be
observed by all your descendants for all time
to come.

The Harvest Festival
(Numbers 28:26–31)

[15]Count seven full weeks from the day
after the Sabbath on which you bring your
sheaf of grain to present to the LORD. [16]On
the fiftieth day, the day after the seventh Sab-
bath, present to the LORD another new
offering of grain. [17]Each family is to bring
two loaves of bread and present them to the
LORD as a special gift. Each loaf shall be
made of four pounds of flour baked with
yeast and shall be presented to the LORD as
an offering of the first grain to be harvested.
[18]And with the bread the community is to
present seven one-year-old lambs, one bull,
and two rams, none of which may have any
defects. They shall be offered as a burnt
offering to the LORD, along with a grain
offering and a wine offering. The odor of
this offering is pleasing to the LORD. [19]Also
offer one male goat as a sin offering and two
one-year-old male lambs as a fellowship
offering. [20]The priest shall present the bread
with the two lambs as a special gift to the
LORD for the priests. These offerings are
holy. [21]On that day do none of your daily
work, but gather for worship. Your descen-
dants are to observe this regulation for all
time to come, no matter where they live.

[22]When you harvest your fields, do not
cut the grain at the edges of the fields, and
do not go back to cut the heads of grain that
were left; leave them for poor people and
foreigners. The LORD is your God.

Leave them for poor people. (23:22)

The New Year Festival
(Numbers 29:1–6)

[23-24]On the first day of the seventh month
observe a special day of rest, and come
together for worship when the trumpets
sound. [25]Present a food offering to the
LORD and do none of your daily work.

The Day of Atonement
(Numbers 29:7–11)

[26-27]The tenth day of the seventh month
is the day when the annual ritual is to be
performed to take away the sins of the peo-
ple. On that day do not eat anything at all;
come together for worship, and present a
food offering to the LORD. [28]Do no work
on that day, because it is the day for per-
forming the ritual to take away sin. [29]Any

23:5 Ex 12:1–13; Deut 16:1, 2 **23:6–8** Ex 12:14–20; 23:15; 34:18; Deut 16:3–8 **23:15–21** Ex 23:16; 34:22; Deut 16:9–12 **23:22** Lev 19:9, 10; Deut 24:19–22 **23:26–32** Lev 16:29–34 who eat anything on that day will no longer be considered God's people. 30 And if any do any work on that day, the LORD himself will put them to death. 31 This regulation applies to all your descendants, no matter where they live. 32 From sunset on the ninth day of the month to sunset on the tenth observe this day as a special day of rest, during which nothing may be eaten.

The Festival of Shelters
(Numbers 29:12–40)

33-34 The Festival of Shelters begins on the fifteenth day of the seventh month and continues for seven days. 35 On the first of these days come together for worship and do none of your daily work. 36 Each day for seven days you shall present a food offering. On the eighth day come together again for worship and present a food offering. It is a day for worship, and you shall do no work.

(37 These are the religious festivals on which you honor the LORD by gathering together for worship and presenting food offerings, burnt offerings, grain offerings, sacrifices, and wine offerings, as required day by day. 38 These festivals are in addition to the regular Sabbaths, and these offerings are in addition to your regular gifts, your offerings as fulfillment of vows, and your freewill offerings that you give to the LORD.)

39 When you have harvested your fields, celebrate this festival for seven days, beginning on the fifteenth day of the seventh month. The first day shall be a special day of rest. 40 On that day take some of the best fruit from your trees, take palm branches and limbs from leafy trees, and begin a religious festival to honor the LORD your God. 41 Celebrate it for seven days. This regulation is to be kept by your descendants for all time to come. 42 All the people of Israel shall live in shelters for seven days, 43 so that your descendants may know that the LORD made the people of Israel live in simple shelters when he led them out of Egypt. He is the LORD your God.

44 So in this way Moses gave the people of Israel the regulations for observing the religious festivals to honor the LORD.

Taking Care of the Lamps
(Exodus 27:20, 21)

24 The LORD told Moses 2 to give the following orders to the people of Israel: Bring pure olive oil of the finest quality for the lamps in the Tent, so that a light might be kept burning regularly. 3 Each evening Aaron shall light them and keep them burning until morning, there in the LORD's presence outside the curtain in front of the Covenant Box, which is in the Most Holy Place. This regulation is to be observed for all time to come. 4 Aaron shall take care of the lamps on the lampstand of pure gold and must see that they burn regularly in the LORD's presence.

The Bread Offered to God

5 Take twenty-four pounds of flour and bake twelve loaves of bread. 6 Put the loaves in two rows, six in each row, on the table covered with pure gold, which is in the LORD's presence. 7 Put some pure incense on each row, as a token food offering to the LORD to take the place of the bread. 8 Every Sabbath, for all time to come, the bread must be placed in the presence of the LORD. This is Israel's duty forever. 9 The bread belongs to Aaron and his descendants, and they shall eat it in a holy place, because this is a very holy part of the food offered to the LORD for the priests.

An Example of Just and Fair Punishment

10-11 There was a man whose father was an Egyptian and whose mother was an Israelite named Shelomith, the daughter of Dibri from the tribe of Dan. There in the camp this man quarreled with an Israelite. During the quarrel he cursed the LORD, so they took him to Moses, 12 put him under guard, and waited for the LORD to tell them what to do with him.

13 The LORD said to Moses, 14 "Take that man out of the camp. Everyone who heard him curse shall put his hands on the man's head to testify that he is guilty, and then the

23:33–36 Deut 16:13–15 **24:5, 6** Ex 25:30 **24:9** Mt 12:4; Mk 2:26; Lk 6:4

whole community shall stone him to death.
[15]Then tell the people of Israel that anyone
who curses God must suffer the conse-
quences [16]and be put to death. Any Israelite
or any foreigner living in Israel who curses
the LORD shall be stoned to death by the
whole community.

[17]"Any who commit murder shall be put
to death, [18]and any who kill an animal
belonging to someone else must replace it.
The principle is a life for a life.

[19]"If any of you injure another person,
whatever you have done shall be done to
you. [20]If you break a bone, one of your bones
shall be broken; if you put out an eye, one of
your eyes shall be put out; if you knock out a
tooth, one of your teeth shall be knocked
out. Whatever injury you cause another per-
son shall be done to you in return. [21]Whoev-
er kills an animal shall replace it, but whoever
kills a human being shall be put to death.
[22]This law applies to all of you, to Israelites
and to foreigners living among you, because I
am the LORD your God."

[23]When Moses had said this to the people
of Israel, they took the man outside the
camp and stoned him to death. In this way
the people of Israel did what the LORD had
commanded Moses.

The Seventh Year

(Deuteronomy 15:1–11)

25 The LORD spoke to Moses on
Mount Sinai and commanded him
[2]to give the following regulations to the
people of Israel. When you enter the land
that the LORD is giving you, you shall honor
the LORD by not cultivating the land every
seventh year. [3]You shall plant your fields,
prune your vineyards, and gather your crops
for six years. [4]But the seventh year is to be a
year of complete rest for the land, a year
dedicated to the LORD. Do not plant your
fields or prune your vineyards. [5]Do not even
harvest the grain that grows by itself without
being planted, and do not gather the grapes
from your unpruned vines; it is a year of
complete rest for the land. [6]Although the
land has not been cultivated during that
year, it will provide food for you, your slaves,
your hired men, the foreigners living with
you, [7]your domestic animals, and the wild
animals in your fields. Everything that it pro-
duces may be eaten.

The Year of Restoration

[8]Count seven times seven years, a total of
forty-nine years. [9]Then, on the tenth day of
the seventh month, the Day of Atonement,
send someone to blow a trumpet throughout
the whole land. [10]In this way you shall set
the fiftieth year apart and proclaim freedom
to all the inhabitants of the land. During this
year all property that has been sold shall be
restored to the original owner or the descen-
dants, and any who have been sold as slaves
shall return to their families. [11]You shall not
plant your fields or harvest the grain that
grows by itself or gather the grapes in your
unpruned vineyards. [12]The whole year shall
be sacred for you; you shall eat only what the
fields produce of themselves.

[13]In this year all property that has been
sold shall be restored to its original owner.
[14]So when you sell land to an Israelite or
buy land, do not deal unfairly. [15]The price is
to be set according to the number of years
the land can produce crops before the next
Year of Restoration. [16]If there are many
years, the price shall be higher, but if there
are only a few years, the price shall be lower,
because what is being sold is the number of
crops the land can produce. [17]Do not cheat
an Israelite, but obey the LORD your God.

The Problem of the Seventh Year

[18]Obey all the LORD's laws and com-
mands, so that you may live in safety in the
land. [19]The land will produce its crops, and
you will have all you want to eat and will
live in safety.

[20]But someone may ask what there will
be to eat during the seventh year, when no
fields are planted and no crops gathered.
[21]The LORD will bless the land in the sixth
year so that it will produce enough food for
two years. [22]When you plant your fields in

24:17 Ex 21:12 **24:20** Ex 21:23–25; Deut 19:21; Mt 5:38 **24:22** Num 15:16 **25:1–7** Ex 23:10, 11.

the eighth year, you will still be eating what you harvested during the sixth year, and you will have enough to eat until the crops you plant that year are harvested.

Restoration of Property

23 Your land must not be sold on a permanent basis, because you do not own it; it belongs to God, and you are like foreigners who are allowed to make use of it.

24 When land is sold, the right of the original owner to buy it back must be recognized. 25 If any of you Israelites become poor and are forced to sell your land, your closest relative is to buy it back. 26 If you have no relative to buy it back, you may later become prosperous and have enough to buy it back yourself. 27 In that case you must pay to the one who bought it a sum that will make up for the years remaining until the next Year of Restoration, when you would in any event recover your land. 28 But if you do not have enough money to buy the land back, it remains under the control of the one who bought it until the next Year of Restoration. In that year it will be returned to its original owner.

29 If you sell a house in a walled city, you have the right to buy it back during the first full year from the date of sale. 30 But if you do not buy it back within the year, you lose the right of repurchase, and the house becomes the permanent property of the purchasers and their descendants; it will not be returned in the Year of Restoration. 31 But houses in unwalled villages are to be treated like fields; the original owner has the right to buy them back, and they are to be returned in the Year of Restoration. 32 However, Levites have the right to buy back at any time their property in the cities assigned to them. 33 If a house in one of these cities is sold by a Levite and is not bought back, it must be returned in the Year of Restoration,[n] because the houses which the Levites own in their cities are their permanent property among the people of Israel. 34 But the pasture land around the Levite cities shall never be sold; it is their property forever.

Loans to the Poor

35 If any Israelites living near you become poor and cannot support themselves, you must provide for them as you would for a hired worker, so that they can continue to live near you. 36 Do not charge Israelites any interest, but obey God and let them live near you. 37 Do not make them pay interest on the money you lend them, and do not make a profit on the food you sell them. 38 This is the command of the LORD your God, who brought you out of Egypt in order to give you the land of Canaan and to be your God.

You must provide for them. (25:35)

Release of Slaves

39 If any Israelites living near you become so poor that they sell themselves to you as a slave, you shall not make them do the work of a slave. 40 They shall stay with you as hired workers and serve you until the next Year of Restoration. 41 At that time they and their children shall leave you and return to their family and to the property of their ancestors. 42 The people of Israel are the LORD's slaves, and he brought them out of Egypt; they must not be sold into slavery. 43 Do not treat them harshly, but obey your God. 44 If you need slaves, you may buy them from the nations around you. 45 You may also buy the children of the foreigners who are living among you. Such children born in your land may become your property, 46 and you may leave them as an inheritance to your children,

[n] **25:33** *Probable text* If a house . . . Restoration; *Hebrew unclear.*

25:35 Deut 15:7, 8 **25:37** Ex 22:25; Deut 23:19, 20 **25:39–46** Ex 21:2-6; Deut 15:12–18

whom they must serve as long as they live.
But you must not treat any Israelites harshly.

47 Suppose a foreigner living with you
becomes rich, while some Israelites become
poor and sell themselves as slaves to that for-
eigner or to a member of that foreigner's
family. 48 After they are sold, they still have
the right to be bought back. A brother 49 or
an uncle or a cousin or another close relative
may buy them back; or if they themselves
earn enough, they may buy their own free-
dom. 50 They must consult the one who
bought them, and they must count the years
from the time they sold themselves until the
next Year of Restoration and must set the
price for their release on the basis of the
wages paid hired workers. 51-52 They must
refund a part of the purchase price according
to the number of years left, 53 as if they had
been hired on an annual basis. Their master
must not treat them harshly. 54 If they are not
set free in any of these ways, they and their
children must be set free in the next Year of
Restoration. 55 Israelites cannot be perma-
nent slaves, because the people of Israel are
the LORD's slaves. He brought them out of
Egypt; he is the LORD their God.

Blessings for Obedience
(Deuteronomy 7:12–24; 28:1–14)

26 The LORD said, "Do not make idols
or set up statues, stone pillars, or
carved stones to worship. I am the LORD
your God. 2 Keep the religious festivals and
honor the place where I am worshiped. I am
the LORD.

3 "If you live according to my laws and
obey my commands, 4 I will send you rain at
the right time, so that the land will produce
crops and the trees will bear fruit. 5 Your
crops will be so plentiful that you will still
be harvesting grain when it is time to pick
grapes, and you will still be picking grapes
when it is time to plant grain. You will have
all that you want to eat, and you can live in
safety in your land.

6 "I will give you peace in your land, and
you can sleep without being afraid of any-
one. I will get rid of the dangerous animals
in the land, and there will be no more war
there. 7 You will be victorious over your ene-
mies; 8 five of you will be able to defeat a
hundred, and a hundred will be able to
defeat ten thousand. 9 I will bless you and
give you many children; I will keep my part
of the covenant that I made with you.
10 Your harvests will be so plentiful that they
will last for a year, and even then you will
have to throw away what is left of the old
harvest to make room for the new. 11 I will
live among you in my sacred Tent, and I will
never turn away from you. 12 I will be with
you; I will be your God, and you will be my
people. 13 I, the LORD your God, brought
you out of Egypt so that you would no
longer be slaves. I broke the power that held
you down and I let you walk with your head
held high."

Punishment for Disobedience
(Deuteronomy 28:15–68)

14 The LORD said, "If you will not obey
my commands, you will be punished. 15 If
you refuse to obey my laws and commands
and break the covenant I have made with
you, 16 I will punish you. I will bring disaster
on you—incurable diseases and fevers that
will make you blind and cause your life to
waste away. You will plant your crops, but it
will do you no good, because your enemies
will conquer you and eat what you have
grown. 17 I will turn against you, so that you
will be defeated, and those who hate you will
rule over you; you will be so terrified that
you will run when no one is chasing you.

18 "If even after all of this you still do not
obey me, I will increase your punishment
seven times. 19 I will break your stubborn
pride; there will be no rain, and your land
will be dry and as hard as iron. 20 All your
hard work will do you no good, because
your land will not produce crops and the
trees will not bear fruit.

21 "If you still continue to resist me and
refuse to obey me, I will again increase your
punishment seven times. 22 I will send dan-
gerous animals among you, and they will kill
your children, destroy your livestock, and

26:1 Lev 19:4 **26:3–5** Deut 11:13–15; 28:1–14 **26:12** 2 Cor 6:16 **26:14–33** Deut 28:15–68 leave so few of you that your roads will be deserted.

[23]"If after all of this punishment you still do not listen to me, but continue to defy me, [24]then I will turn on you and punish you seven times harder than before. [25]I will bring war on you to punish you for breaking our covenant, and if you gather in your cities for safety, I will send incurable diseases among you, and you will be forced to surrender to your enemies. [26]I will cut off your food supply, so that ten women will need only one oven to bake all the bread they have. They will ration it out, and when you have eaten it all, you will still be hungry.

[27]"If after all of this you still continue to defy me and refuse to obey me, [28]then in my anger I will turn on you and again make your punishment seven times worse than before. [29]Your hunger will be so great that you will eat your own children. [30]I will destroy your places of worship on the hills, tear down your incense altars, and throw your dead bodies on your fallen idols. In utter disgust [31]I will turn your cities into ruins, destroy your places of worship, and refuse to accept your sacrifices. [32]I will destroy your land so completely that the enemies who occupy it will be shocked at the destruction. [33]I will bring war on you and scatter you in foreign lands. Your land will be deserted, and your cities left in ruins. [34-35]Then the land will enjoy the years of complete rest that you would not give it; it will lie abandoned and get its rest while you are in exile in the land of your enemies.

[36]"I will make those of you who are in exile so terrified that the sound of a leaf blowing in the wind will make you run. You will run as if you were being pursued in battle, and you will fall when there is no enemy near you. [37]You will stumble over one another when no one is chasing you, and you will be unable to fight against any enemy. [38]You will die in exile, swallowed up by the land of your enemies. [39]The few of you who survive in the land of your enemies will waste away because of your own sin and the sin of your ancestors.

[40]"But your descendants will confess their sins and the sins of their ancestors, who resisted me and rebelled against me, [41]and caused me to turn against them and send them into exile in the land of their enemies. At last, when your descendants are humbled and they have paid the penalty for their sin and rebellion, [42]I will remember my covenant with Jacob and with Isaac and with Abraham, and I will renew my promise to give my people the land. [43]First, however, the land must be rid of its people, so that it can enjoy its complete rest, and they must pay the full penalty for having rejected my laws and my commands. [44]But even then, when they are still in the land of their enemies, I will not completely abandon them or destroy them. That would put an end to my covenant with them, and I am the LORD their God. [45]I will renew the covenant that I made with their ancestors when I showed all the nations my power by bringing my people out of Egypt, in order that I, the LORD, might be their God."

[46]All these are the laws and commands that the LORD gave to Moses on Mount Sinai for the people of Israel.

Laws concerning Gifts to the LORD

27 The LORD gave Moses [2]the following regulations for the people of Israel. When any of you have been given to the LORD in fulfillment of a special vow, you may be set free by the payment of the following sums of money, [3-7]according to the official standard:

- adult male, twenty to sixty years old: 50 pieces of silver
- adult female: 30 pieces of silver
- young male, five to twenty years old: 20 pieces of silver
- young female: 10 pieces of silver
- infant male under five: 5 pieces of silver
- infant female: 3 pieces of silver
- male above sixty years of age: 15 pieces of silver
- female above sixty: 10 pieces of silver

[8]If any of you make a vow and are too poor to pay the standard price, you shall bring the person to the priest, and the priest

26:42 **a** Gen 28:13, 14; **b** Gen 26:3, 4; **c** Gen 17:7, 8

will set a lower price, according to your abil-
ity to pay.

9 If your vow concerns an animal that is
acceptable as an offering to the LORD, then
every gift made to the LORD is sacred, 10 and
you may not substitute another animal for it.
If you do, both animals belong to the LORD.
11 But if your vow concerns a ritually
unclean animal, which is not acceptable as an
offering to the LORD, you shall take the ani-
mal to the priest. 12 The priest shall set a
price for it, according to its good or bad
qualities, and the price will be final. 13 If you
wish to buy it back, you must pay the price
plus an additional 20 percent.

14 When any of you dedicate your house
to the LORD, the priest shall set the price
according to its good or bad points, and the
price will be final. 15 If you wish to buy your
house back, you must pay the price plus an
additional 20 percent.

16 If any of you dedicate part of your land
to the LORD, the price shall be set according
to the amount of seed it takes to sow it, at
the rate of ten pieces of silver per bushel of
barley. 17 If you dedicate the land immediate-
ly after a Year of Restoration, the full price
applies. 18 If you dedicate it any time later,
the priest shall estimate the cash value
according to the number of years left until
the next Year of Restoration, and set a
reduced price. 19 If you wish to buy your
field back, you must pay the price plus an
additional 20 percent. 20 If you sell the field
to someone else without first buying it back
from the LORD, you lose the right to buy it
back. 21 At the next Year of Restoration the
field will become the LORD's permanent
property; it shall belong to the priests.

22 If you dedicate to the LORD a field that
you have bought, 23 the priest shall estimate
its value according to the number of years
until the next Year of Restoration, and you
must pay the price that very day; the money
belongs to the LORD. 24 At the Year of
Restoration the field shall be returned to the
original owner or to the descendants.

25 All prices shall be set according to the
official standard.

26 The first-born of an animal already
belongs to the LORD, so no one may dedi-
cate it to him as a freewill offering. A calf, a
lamb, or a kid belongs to the LORD, 27 but
the first-born of an unclean animal may be
bought back at the standard price plus an
additional 20 percent. If it is not bought
back, it may be sold to someone else at the
standard price.

28 None of you may sell or buy back
what you have unconditionally dedicated[o]
to the LORD, whether it is a human being,
an animal, or land. It belongs permanently
to the LORD. 29 Not even human beings
who have been unconditionally dedicated
may be bought back; they must be put to
death.

30 One tenth of all the produce of the
land, whether grain or fruit, belongs to the
LORD. 31 If you wish to buy any of it back,
you must pay the standard price plus an
additional 20 percent. 32 One of every ten
domestic animals belongs to the LORD.
When the animals are counted, every tenth
one belongs to the LORD. 33 You may not
arrange the animals so that the poor animals
are chosen, and you may not make any sub-
stitutions. If you do substitute one animal for
another, then both animals will belong to
the LORD and may not be bought back.

34 These are the commands that the LORD
gave Moses on Mount Sinai for the people
of Israel.

[o] **27:28** UNCONDITIONALLY DEDICATED: *Anything dedicated in this way belonged completely to the LORD and could not be used; it had to be destroyed.*

27:28 Num 18:14 **27:30–33** Num 18:21; Deut 14:22–29

THE BOOK OF Numbers

Are we there yet? I'm hungry! He's bugging me! Why do you get the front seat? Traveling together can have its joys, and its struggles. The Book of Numbers tells the story of the Israelites' journey from Sinai to Moab as they prepare to enter the Promised Land.

As with most trips, the Israelites' journey began by making sure everyone was counted and knew the rules for the journey. The trip had its memorable moments—a fiery cloud, spies, and even a talking donkey. And then there were those who complained about everything. Their rebellion stood in contrast to God's faithfulness, patience, and love. As time passed, a new generation emerged that was more faithful and obedient to God. They were the ones to finally settle the Promised Land.

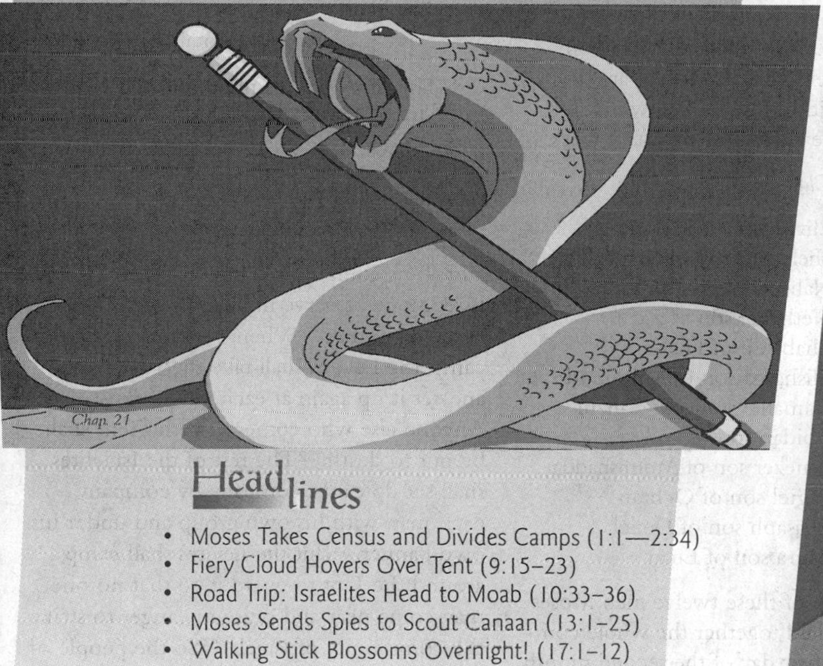

Headlines

- Moses Takes Census and Divides Camps (1:1—2:34)
- Fiery Cloud Hovers Over Tent (9:15–23)
- Road Trip: Israelites Head to Moab (10:33–36)
- Moses Sends Spies to Scout Canaan (13:1–25)
- Walking Stick Blossoms Overnight! (17:1–12)
- Donkey Talks, Owner Confesses! (22:22–33)
- Joshua Chosen as Moses' Successor (27:15–23)

FACTOIDS

Who wrote this book? Priestly scribes most likely wrote this book hundreds of years after the events took place.

When was it written? The final version of the book was probably composed sometime during the Babylonian exile (587–538 BC).

Why was it written? This book records the story of the Israelites where Exodus leaves off. It makes clear for God's people the importance of being holy, faithful, and grateful for God's blessings.

How does it fit into the Bible? It is the fourth book in the Pentateuch (the first five books of the Bible) and tells the early experiences of God's people.

Important themes

- Faithfulness and gratefulness to God is rewarded.
- Don't lose faith in God when things get hard.
- God is always patient, present, and caring despite the faults and failings of his people.

NUMBERS

The First Census of Israel

1 On the first day of the second month in the second year after the people of Israel left Egypt, the LORD spoke to Moses there in the Tent of his presence in the Sinai Desert. He said, 2"You and Aaron are to take a census of the people of Israel by clans and families. List the names of all the men 3twenty years old or older who are fit for military service. 4Ask one clan chief from each tribe to help you." 5-16These are the men, leaders within their tribes, who were chosen from the community for this work:

Tribe	*Clan chief*
Reuben	Elizur son of Shedeur
Simeon	Shelumiel son of Zurishaddai
Judah	Nahshon son of Amminadab
Issachar	Nethanel son of Zuar
Zebulun	Eliab son of Helon
Ephraim	Elishama son of Ammihud
Manasseh	Gamaliel son of Pedahzur
Benjamin	Abidan son of Gideoni
Dan	Ahiezer son of Ammishaddai
Asher	Pagiel son of Ochran
Gad	Eliasaph son of Deuel
Naphtali	Ahira son of Enan

17With the help of these twelve men Moses and Aaron 18called together the whole community on the first day of the second month and registered all the people by clans and families. The names of all the men twenty years old or older were recorded and counted, 19as the LORD had commanded. In the Sinai Desert, Moses registered the people. 20-46The men twenty years old or older who were fit for military service were registered by name according to clan and family, beginning with the tribe of Reuben, Jacob's oldest son. The totals were as follows:

Tribe	*Number*
Reuben	46,500
Simeon	59,300
Gad	45,650
Judah	74,600
Issachar	54,400
Zebulun	57,400
Ephraim	40,500
Manasseh	32,200
Benjamin	35,400
Dan	62,700
Asher	41,500
Naphtali	53,400
Total:	603,550

47The Levites were not registered with the other tribes, 48because the LORD had said to Moses, 49"When you take a census of the men fit for military service, do not include the tribe of Levi. 50Instead, put the Levites in charge of the Tent of my presence and all its equipment. They shall carry it and its equipment, serve in it, and set up their camp around it. 51Whenever you move your camp, the Levites shall take the Tent down and set it up again at each new campsite. Anyone else who comes near the Tent shall be put to death. 52The rest of the Israelites shall set up camp, company by company, each man with his own group and under his own banner. 53But the Levites shall camp around the Tent to guard it, so that no one may come near and cause my anger to strike the community of Israel." 54So the people of Israel did everything that the LORD had commanded Moses.

The Arrangement of the Tribes in Camp

2 The LORD gave Moses and Aaron the following instructions. 2When the Israelites set up camp, each man will camp under the banner of his division and the flag of his own clan. The camp is to be set up all around the Tent.

3-9On the east side, those under the banner of the division of Judah shall camp in their groups, under their leaders, as follows:

1:1–46 Num 26:1–51

Tribe	Leader	Number
Judah	Nahshon son of Amminadab	74,600
Issachar	Nethanel son of Zuar	54,400
Zebulun	Eliab son of Helon	57,400
	Total:	186,400

The division of Judah shall march first.

10-16On the south, those under the banner of the division of Reuben shall camp in their groups, under their leaders, as follows:

Tribe	Leader	Number
Reuben	Elizur son of Shedeur	46,500
Simeon	Shelumiel son of Zurishaddai	59,300
Gad	Eliasaph son of Deuel	45,650
	Total:	151,450

The division of Reuben shall march second.

17Then, between the first two divisions and the last two the Levites are to march carrying the Tent. Each division shall march in the same order as they camp, each in position under its banner.

18-24On the west, those under the banner of the division of Ephraim shall camp in their groups, under their leaders, as follows:

Tribe	Leader	Number
Ephraim	Elishama son of Ammihud	40,500
Manasseh	Gamaliel son of Pedahzur	32,200
Benjamin	Abidan son of Gideoni	35,400
	Total:	108,100

The division of Ephraim shall march third.

25-31On the north, those under the banner of the division of Dan shall camp in their groups, under their leaders, as follows:

Tribe	Leader	Number
Dan	Ahiezer son of Ammishaddai	62,700
Asher	Pagiel son of Ochran	41,500
Naphtali	Ahira son of Enan	53,400
	Total:	157,600

The division of Dan shall march last.

32The total number of the people of Israel enrolled in the divisions, group by group, was 603,550. 33As the LORD had commanded Moses, the Levites were not registered with the rest of the Israelites.

34So the people of Israel did everything the LORD had commanded Moses. They camped, each under his own banner, and they marched, each with his own clan.

Aaron's Sons

3 This is the family of Aaron and Moses at the time the LORD spoke to Moses on Mount Sinai. 2Aaron had four sons: Nadab, the oldest, Abihu, Eleazar, and Ithamar. 3They were anointed and ordained as priests, 4but Nadab and Abihu were killed when they offered unholy fire to the LORD in the Sinai Desert. They had no children, so Eleazar and Ithamar served as priests during Aaron's lifetime.

The Levites Are Appointed to Serve the Priests

5The LORD said to Moses, 6"Bring forward the tribe of Levi and appoint them as servants of Aaron the priest. 7They shall do the work required for the Tent of my presence and perform duties for the priests and for the whole community. 8They shall take charge of all the equipment of the Tent and perform the duties for the rest of the Israelites. 9The only responsibility the Levites have is to serve Aaron and his sons. 10You shall appoint Aaron and his sons to carry out the duties of the priesthood; anyone else who tries to do so shall be put to death."

11The LORD said to Moses, 12-13"The Levites are now to be mine. When I killed all the first-born of the Egyptians, I consecrated as my own the oldest son of each Israelite family and the first-born of every animal. Now, instead of having the first-born sons of

3:2 Num 26:60 **3:4** Lev 10:1, 2; Num 26:61 **3:13** Ex 13:2

Israel as my own, I have the Levites; they
will belong to me. I am the LORD."

The Census of the Levites

14 In the Sinai Desert the LORD com-
manded Moses 15 to register the Levites by
clans and families, enrolling every male a
month old or older, 16 and Moses did so.
17-20 Levi had three sons: Gershon, Kohath,
and Merari, who were the ancestors of the
clans that bear their names. Gershon had two
sons: Libni and Shimei; Kohath had four
sons: Amram, Izhar, Hebron, and Uzziel; and
Merari had two sons: Mahli and Mushi.
They were the ancestors of the families that
bear their names.

21 The clan of Gershon was composed of
the families of Libni and Shimei. 22 The total
number of males one month old or older
that were enrolled was 7,500. 23 This clan
was to camp on the west behind the Tent,
24 with Eliasaph son of Lael as chief of the
clan. 25 They were responsible for the Tent, its
inner cover, its outer cover, the curtain for
the entrance, 26 the curtains for the court
which is around the Tent and the altar, and
the curtain for the entrance of the court.
They were responsible for all the service
connected with these items.

27 The clan of Kohath was composed of
the families of Amram, Izhar, Hebron, and
Uzziel. 28 The total number of males one
month old or older that were enrolled was
8,600. 29 This clan was to camp on the south
side of the Tent, 30 with Elizaphan son of
Uzziel as chief of the clan. 31 They were
responsible for the Covenant Box, the table,
the lampstand, the altars, the utensils the
priests use in the Holy Place, and the curtain
at the entrance to the Most Holy Place.
They were responsible for all the service
connected with these items.

32 The chief of the Levites was Eleazar son
of Aaron the priest. He was in charge of
those who carried out the duties in the
Holy Place.

33 The clan of Merari was composed of
the families of Mahli and Mushi. 34 The total
number of males one month old or older
that were enrolled was 6,200. 35 This clan
was to camp on the north side of the Tent,
with Zuriel son of Abihail as chief of the
clan. 36 They were assigned responsibility for
the frames for the Tent, its bars, posts, bases,
and all its fittings. They were responsible for
all the service connected with these items.
37 They were also responsible for the posts,
bases, pegs, and ropes for the outer court.

38 Moses and Aaron and his sons were to
camp in front of the Tent on the east. They
were responsible for carrying out the servic-
es performed in the Holy Place for the peo-
ple of Israel. Anyone else who tried to do so
was to be put to death. 39 The total number
of all the Levite males one month old or
older that Moses enrolled by clans at the
command of the LORD, was 22,000.

The Levites Take the Place of the First-Born Sons

40-41 The LORD said to Moses, "All of
Israel's first-born sons belong to me. So reg-
ister by name every first-born male Israelite,
one month old or older. But in place of
them I claim all the Levites as mine! I am
the LORD! I also claim the livestock of the
Levites in place of all the first-born of the
livestock." 42 Moses obeyed, and registered all
the first-born males 43 one month old or
older; the total was 22,273.

44 The LORD said to Moses, 45 "Now dedi-
cate the Levites as mine in place of all the
first-born Israelite sons, and dedicate the
livestock of the Levites in place of the first-
born of the Israelites' livestock. 46 Since the
first-born Israelite sons outnumber the
Levites by 273, you must buy back the extra
sons. 47 For each one pay five pieces of silver,
according to the official standard, 48 and give
this money to Aaron and his sons." 49 Moses
obeyed and took 50 the 1,365 pieces of silver
51 and gave them to Aaron and his sons.

The Duties of the Levite Clan of Kohath

4 The LORD told Moses 2 to take a census
of the Levite clan of Kohath by subclans
and families, 3 and to register all the men
between the ages of thirty and fifty who
were qualified to work in the Tent of the

LORD's presence. [4]Their service involves the
most holy things.

[5]The LORD gave Moses the following
instructions. When it is time to break camp,
Aaron and his sons shall enter the Tent, take
down the curtain in front of the Covenant
Box, and cover the Box with it. [6]They shall
put a fine leather cover over it, spread a cloth
of solid blue on top, and then insert the car-
rying poles.

[7]They shall spread a blue cloth over the
table for the bread offered to the LORD and
put on it the dishes, the incense bowls, the
offering bowls, and the jars for the wine
offering. There shall always be bread on the
table. [8]They shall spread a red cloth over all
of this, put a fine leather cover over it, and
then insert the carrying poles.

[9]They shall take a blue cloth and cover
the lampstand, with its lamps, tongs, trays,
and all the olive oil containers. [10]They shall
wrap it and all its equipment in a fine leather
cover and place it on a carrying frame.

[11]Next they shall spread a blue cloth over
the gold altar, put a fine leather cover over it,
and then insert the carrying poles. [12]They
shall take all the utensils used in the Holy
Place, wrap them in a blue cloth, put a fine
leather cover over them, and place them on
a carrying frame. [13]They shall remove the
greasy ashes from the altar and spread a pur-
ple cloth over it. [14]They shall put on it all
the equipment used in the service at the
altar: fire pans, hooks, shovels, and basins.
Then they shall put a fine leather cover over
it and insert the carrying poles. [15]When it is
time to break camp, the clan of Kohath shall
come to carry the sacred objects only after
Aaron and his sons have finished covering
them and all their equipment. The Kohath
clan must not touch the sacred objects, or
they will die.

These are the responsibilities of the
Kohath clan whenever the Tent is moved.

[16]Eleazar son of Aaron the priest shall be
responsible for the whole Tent and for the
oil for the lamps, the incense, the grain
offerings, the anointing oil, and everything
else in the Tent that has been consecrated to
the LORD.

[17]The LORD said to Moses and Aaron,
[18]"Do not let the clan of Kohath [19]be killed
by coming near these most sacred objects. To
prevent this from happening, Aaron and his
sons shall go in and assign each man his task
and tell him what to carry. [20]But if the
Kohathites enter the Tent and see the priests
preparing the sacred objects for moving,[a]
they will die."

The Duties of the Levite Clan of Gershon

[21]The LORD told Moses [22]to take a census
of the Levite clan of Gershon by subclans
and families, [23]and to register all the men
between the ages of thirty and fifty who
were qualified to work in the Tent of the
LORD's presence. [24]They shall be responsible
for carrying the following objects: [25]the Tent,
its inner cover, its outer cover, the fine leather
cover on top of it, the curtain for the
entrance, [26]the curtains and ropes for the
court that is around the Tent and the altar,

[a] **4:20** see . . . moving; *or* see the sacred objects even for a moment.

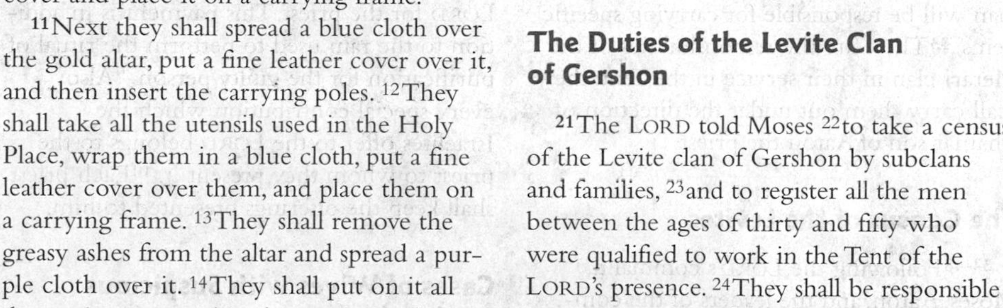

Qualified to work in the Tent (4:23)

the curtains for the entrance of the court, and all the fittings used in setting up these objects. They shall perform all the tasks required for these things. 27Moses and Aaron shall see to it that the Gershonites perform all the duties and carry everything that Aaron and his sons assign to them. 28These are the responsibilities of the Gershon clan in the Tent; they shall carry them out under the direction of Ithamar son of Aaron the priest.

The Duties of the Levite Clan of Merari

29The LORD told Moses to take a census of the Levite clan of Merari by subclans and families, 30and to register all the men between the ages of thirty and fifty who were qualified to work in the Tent of the LORD's presence. 31They shall be responsible for carrying the frames, bars, posts, and bases of the Tent, 32and the posts, bases, pegs, and ropes of the court around the Tent, with all the fittings used in setting them up. Each man will be responsible for carrying specific items. 33These are the responsibilities of the Merari clan in their service in the Tent; they shall carry them out under the direction of Ithamar son of Aaron the priest.

The Census of the Levites

34-48Following the LORD's command, Moses, Aaron, and the leaders of the community took a census of the three Levite clans, Kohath, Gershon, and Merari. They did this by subclans and families and registered all the men between the ages of thirty and fifty who were qualified to work in the Tent of the LORD's presence, as follows:

Clan	*Number*
Kohath	2,750
Gershon	2,630
Merari	3,200
Total:	8,580

49Each man was registered as the LORD had commanded Moses; and at the command of the LORD given through Moses, each man was assigned responsibility for his task of serving or carrying.

Unclean People

5 The LORD said to Moses, 2"Command the people of Israel to expel from the camp everyone with a dreaded skin disease or a bodily discharge and everyone who is unclean by contact with a corpse. 3Send all these ritually unclean people out, so that they will not defile the camp, where I live among my people." 4The Israelites obeyed and expelled them all from the camp.

Repayment for Wrongs Done

5The LORD gave Moses 6the following instructions for the people of Israel. When any of you are unfaithful to the LORD and commit a wrong against someone, 7you must confess your sin and make full repayment, plus an additional 20 percent, to the person you have wronged. 8But if that person has died and has no near relative to whom payment can be made, it shall be given to the LORD for the priest. This payment is in addition to the ram used to perform the ritual of purification for the guilty person. 9Also every special contribution which the Israelites offer to the LORD belongs to the priest to whom they present it. 10Each priest shall keep the offerings presented to him.

Cases of Wives with Suspicious Husbands

11The LORD commanded Moses 12-14to give the Israelites the following instructions. It may happen that a man becomes suspicious that his wife is unfaithful to him and has defiled herself by having intercourse with another man. But the husband may not be certain, for his wife may have kept it secret—there was no witness, and she was not caught in the act. Or it may happen that a husband becomes suspicious of his wife, even though she has not been unfaithful. 15In either case the man shall take his wife to the priest. He shall also take the required offering of two pounds of barley flour, but he shall not pour any olive oil on it or put any incense on it, because it is an offering

5:5–8 Lev 6:1–7

from a suspicious husband, made to bring
the truth to light.
[16]The priest shall bring the woman for-
ward and have her stand in front of the altar.
[17]He shall pour some holy water into a clay
bowl and take some of the earth that is on
the floor of the Tent of the LORD's presence
and put it in the water to make it bitter.
[18]Then he shall loosen the woman's hair and
put the offering of flour in her hands. In his
hands the priest shall hold the bowl contain-
ing the bitter water that brings a curse.
[19]Then the priest shall make the woman
agree to this oath spoken by the priest: "If
you have not committed adultery, you will
not be harmed by the curse that this water
brings. [20]But if you have committed adul-
tery, [21]may the LORD make your name a
curse among your people. May he cause
your genital organs to shrink and your stom-
ach to swell up. [22]May this water enter your
stomach and cause it to swell up and your
genital organs to shrink."
The woman shall respond, "I agree; may
the LORD do so."
[23]Then the priest shall write this curse
down and wash the writing off into the
bowl of bitter water. [24]Before he makes the
woman drink the water, which may then
cause her bitter pain, [25]the priest shall take
the offering of flour out of the woman's
hands, hold it out in dedication to the
LORD, and present it on the altar. [26]Then he
shall take a handful of it as a token offering
and burn it on the altar. Finally, he shall
make the woman drink the water. [27]If she
has committed adultery, the water will cause
bitter pain; her stomach will swell up and
her genital organs will shrink. Her name will
become a curse among her people. [28]But if
she is innocent, she will not be harmed and
will be able to bear children.
[29-30]This is the law in cases where a man
is jealous and becomes suspicious that his
wife has committed adultery. The woman
shall be made to stand in front of the altar,
and the priest shall perform this ritual. [31]The
husband shall be free of guilt, but the
woman, if guilty, must suffer the conse-
quences.

Rules for Nazirites

6 The LORD commanded Moses [2]to give
the following instructions to the people
of Israel. Any of you, male or female, who
make a special vow to become a nazirite and
dedicate yourself to the LORD [3]shall abstain
from wine and beer. You shall not drink any
kind of drink made from grapes or eat any
grapes or raisins. [4]As long as you are a
nazirite, you shall not eat anything that
comes from a grapevine, not even the seeds
or skins of grapes.
[5]As long as you are under the nazirite
vow, you must not cut your hair or shave.
You are bound by the vow for the full time
that you are dedicated to the LORD, and you
shall let your hair grow. [6-7]Your hair is the
sign of your dedication to God, and so you
must not defile yourself by going near a
corpse, not even that of your father, mother,
brother, or sister. [8]As long as you are a
nazirite, you are consecrated to the LORD.
[9]If your consecrated hair is defiled
because you are right beside someone who
suddenly dies, you must wait seven days and
then shave your head; and so you become
ritually clean. [10]On the eighth day you shall
bring two doves or two pigeons to the priest
at the entrance of the Tent of the LORD's
presence. [11]The priest shall offer one as a sin
offering and the other as a burnt offering, to
perform the ritual of purification for you
because of your contact with a corpse. On
the same day you shall reconsecrate your hair
[12]and rededicate to the LORD your time as a
nazirite. The previous period of time doesn't
count, because your consecrated hair was
defiled. As a repayment offering you shall
bring a one-year-old lamb.
[13]When you complete your nazirite vow,
you shall perform this ritual. You shall go to
the entrance of the Tent [14]and present to the
LORD three animals without any defects: a
one-year-old male lamb for a burnt offering,
a one-year-old ewe lamb for a sin offering,
and a ram for a fellowship offering. [15]You
shall also offer a basket of bread made with-
out yeast: thick loaves made of flour mixed
with olive oil and thin cakes brushed with

6:3 Lk 1:15 **6:13–21** Acts 21:23, 24

olive oil, and in addition the required offer-
ings of grain and wine.
16 The priest shall present all these to the
LORD and offer the sin offering and the
burnt offering. 17 He shall sacrifice the ram
to the LORD as a fellowship offering, and
offer it with the basket of bread; he shall also
present the offerings of grain and wine. 18 At
the entrance of the Tent you nazirites shall
shave off your hair and put it on the fire on
which the fellowship offering is being
burned.
19 Then, when the shoulder of the ram is
boiled, the priest shall take it and put it,
together with one thick loaf of bread and
one thin cake from the basket, into the
hands of the nazirite. 20 Next, the priest shall
present them as a special gift to the LORD;
they are a sacred offering for the priest, in
addition to the breast and the leg of the ram
which by law belong to the priest. After that,
the nazirite may drink wine.
21 These are the regulations for you
nazirites; but if you promise an offering
beyond what your vow requires you to give,
you must fulfill exactly the promise you
made.

The Priestly Blessing

22 The LORD commanded Moses 23 to tell
Aaron and his sons to use the following
words in blessing the people of Israel:
24 May the LORD bless you and take care of
you;
25 May the LORD be kind and gracious to
you;
26 May the LORD look on you with favor
and give you peace.
27 And the LORD said, "If they pronounce
my name as a blessing upon the people of
Israel, I will bless them."

The Offerings of the Leaders

7 On the day Moses finished setting up
the Tent of the LORD's presence, he
anointed and dedicated the Tent and all its
equipment, and the altar and all its equip-
ment. 2 Then the clan chiefs who were lead-
ers in the tribes of Israel, the same men who
were in charge of the census, 3 brought their
offerings to the LORD: six wagons and
twelve oxen, a wagon for every two leaders
and an ox for each leader. After they had
presented them, 4 the LORD said to Moses,
5 "Accept these gifts for use in the work to
be done for the Tent; give them to the
Levites according to the work they have to
do." 6 So Moses gave the wagons and the
oxen to the Levites. 7 He gave two wagons
and four oxen to the Gershonites, 8 and four
wagons and eight oxen to the Merarites. All
their work was to be done under the direc-
tion of Ithamar son of Aaron. 9 But Moses
gave no wagons or oxen to the Kohathites,
because the sacred objects they took care of
had to be carried on their shoulders.
10 The leaders also brought offerings to
celebrate the dedication of the altar. When
they were ready to present their gifts at the
altar, 11 the LORD said to Moses, "Tell them
that each day for a period of twelve days one
of the leaders is to present his gifts for the
dedication of the altar."
12-83 They presented their offerings in the
following order:

Day	*Tribe*	*Leader*
1st	Judah	Nahshon son of Amminadab
2nd	Issachar	Nethanel son of Zuar
3rd	Zebulun	Eliab son of Helon
4th	Reuben	Elizur son of Shedeur
5th	Simeon	Shelumiel son of Zurishaddai
6th	Gad	Eliasaph son of Deuel
7th	Ephraim	Elishama son of Ammihud
8th	Manasseh	Gamaliel son of Pedahzur
9th	Benjamin	Abidan son of Gideoni
10th	Dan	Ahiezer son of Ammishaddai
11th	Asher	Pagiel son of Ochran
12th	Naphtali	Ahira son of Enan

The offerings each one brought were
identical: one silver bowl weighing 50
ounces and one silver basin weighing 30
ounces, by the official standard, both of them
full of flour mixed with oil for the grain
offering; one gold dish weighing 4 ounces,
full of incense; one young bull, one ram, and

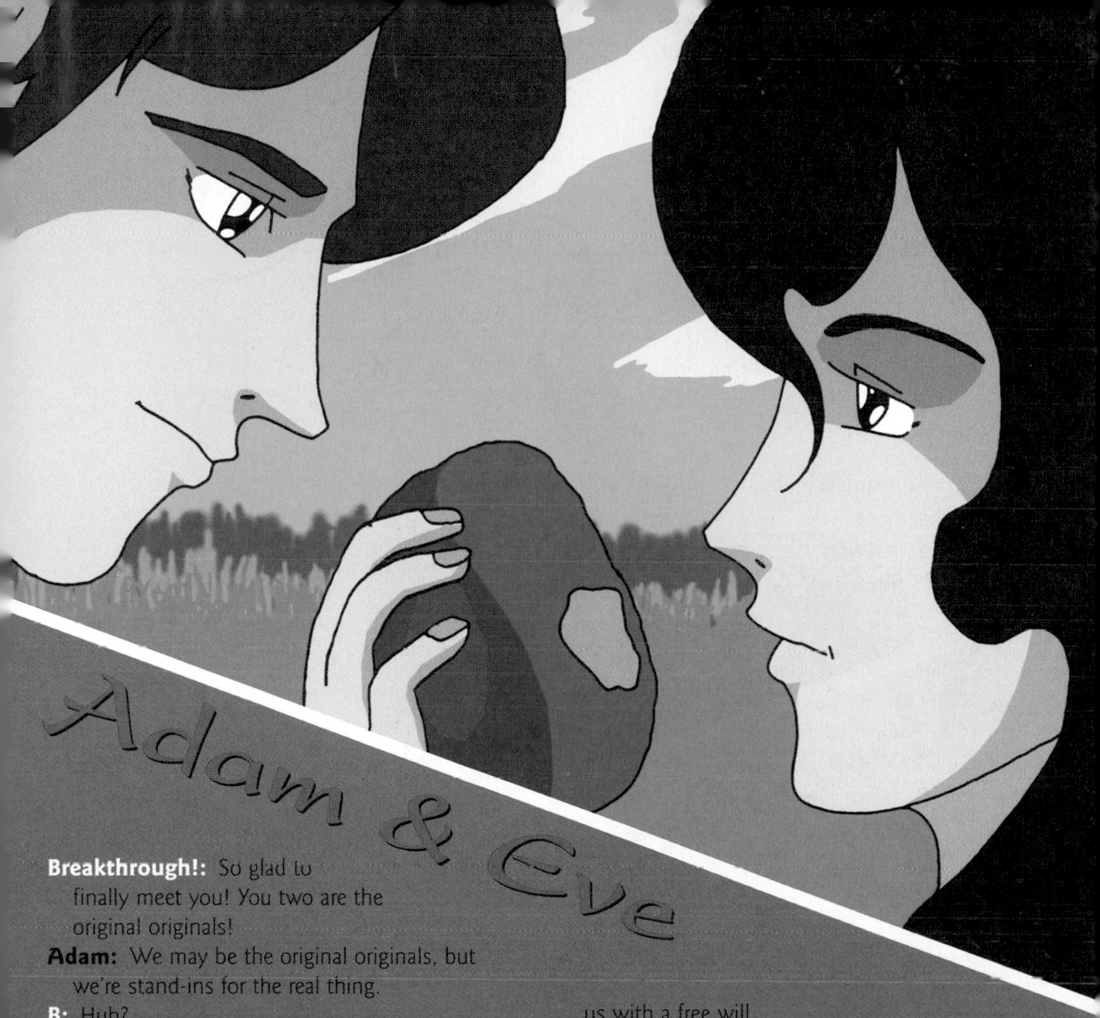

Adam & Eve

Breakthrough!: So glad to finally meet you! You two are the original originals!

Adam: We may be the original originals, but we're stand-ins for the real thing.

B: Huh?

Eve: What Adam is trying to say is that we're characters in a story that isn't really history.

B: But you've got real names! And you're in the Bible!

Adam: Actually, my name simply means "human being."

Eve: And my name means "living."

B: You mean, you never existed?

Adam: I wouldn't say that. God created human beings and there was a first set of human parents, right? But the first human beings lived long before recorded history. So in the opening stories of the Bible, we are the symbols for the first man and woman.

B: Then what about the part about the Garden of Eden?

Eve: The garden is another symbolic part of the story. It explains the way things should be between God and human beings. God created us with a free will and meant us to live in perfect harmony with him, each other, and all creation. But we chose to give in to temptation and disobeyed God.

Adam: Our sin has been passed on to everyone who lived after us—except Jesus and his mother, Mary.

Eve: Have you ever heard of original sin? That's what Adam is talking about. It means that every person is born somewhat separated from God and has a tendency to choose sin.

B: Does that mean we're all bad?

Adam: Absolutely not. Everything God created is good and holy. Sometimes we make bad choices, but God's love is much greater than our weaknesses.

Eve: Right. Even though we sometimes turn away from God, God never turns away from us. And that's the truth!

Abraham

Breakthrough!: Abraham. That wasn't always your name, was it?

Abraham: No, it was Abram at first. God changed it as a sign of the Covenant he made with me. My wife's name was changed to Sarah.

B: Covenant?

Abraham: That's a special agreement between God and me. I promised to do what God asked. God promised to give me many descendants and a land to call our own. That took some faith because Sarah and I were both pretty old, but I didn't ask too many questions—God being God and all.

B: Speaking of being old, you were not a young man when God asked you to pack up and leave your family. What was that all about?

Abraham: Like I said, I didn't ask too many questions. God promised to bless me and make me famous. Did you expect me to say no?

B: Wasn't it hard though?

Abraham: Sure it was. We had a comfortable life in Haran. It was not an easy trip. It was downright terrifying sometimes.

B: What are some of the amazing things God did during your lifetime?

Abraham: Well, of course, there was the wonderful day Isaac was born. The destruction of Sodom and Gomorrah showed me how God treats those who do not live a good life. Then there was the day God told me to sacrifice Isaac. It was the worst day of my life. I had to make a choice: my son or my God. I didn't know it at the time, but God was testing me. You can read about my and Sarah's adventures in the Book of Genesis.

B: What's the most important thing you learned from God?

Abraham: Listen, and have faith. God may surprise you. Look what happened to me. I became the father of the Jewish, Christian, and Moslem peoples.

Sarah

Breakthrough!: Should we call you Sarah or Sarai?

Sarah: Sarah, please. Sarai was my name before God made the Covenant with my husband, Abraham.

B: What was life like for you and Abraham?

Sarah: Abraham was a good man. We lived a comfortable life in Haran. The other women and I were good friends. Then one day God told Abraham to pick up everything and leave. I had nothing to say about it. Women did not have much say back then. So we went—Abraham, his nephew Lot, all our belongings, our servants, and me.

B: How was the trip?

Sarah: Long. We ended up in Egypt because of a famine. The Pharaoh took me to live with him, but he let me go when God gave him a terrible disease.

B: Any children?

Sarah: That's a sore spot—and the high point of my life. Abraham and I wanted a son in the worst way, but God never gave us any children. Then one day I overheard some visitors telling Abraham that I would have a son. I laughed to myself; I was much too old to have children. We found out later that these visitors were from God.

B: Then what happened?

Sarah: Nine months later I had a bouncing baby boy. We named him Isaac.

B: Isaac is an unusual name. What does it mean?

Sarah: It means, "He laughs."

B: What lessons did you try to pass on to Isaac?

Sarah: Nothing is impossible with God. Put your trust in the God who is always with you. And keep on laughing.

Isaac

Breakthrough!: Isaac, how would you describe yourself?

Isaac: I'm a peaceful guy. I may get upset, but I'm not one to get even. I trust that God will take care of things. I guess I learned that from my dad, Abraham.

B: Tell me about your wife.

Isaac: Oh, how I loved Rebecca! I didn't exactly choose her. Like all weddings at that time, our families arranged for us to marry. God had a hand in it, I'm sure.

B: Did you have children?

Isaac: We had twin boys, Esau and Jacob. Esau was my favorite, partly because he always brought me meat from his hunting trips. Jacob was quiet but feisty—just like his mother. Rebecca liked him better.

B: Didn't Esau give away his special rights as your first-born son?

Isaac: Yes, he gave away his birthright. For what? Food! I swear, that guy would eat anything that didn't eat him first!

B: Tell us about "the switch."

Isaac: I couldn't believe I was tricked like that! I was supposed to give Esau a special blessing, but Rebecca decided that Jacob should have it. She put an animal skin on Jacob's arm. I was blind, so I had to go by what I felt. I knew Esau was a lot hairier than his brother, so when I touched Jacob's hairy arm, I thought he was Esau. So I blessed the wrong son—or was it the right one?

B: How did Esau react?

Isaac: He was upset, and so was I. He begged me for a blessing, but I only had one special blessing to give. Esau wanted to get even with Jacob, but we sent Jacob away for his own protection.

B: What did you try to teach your sons about God?

Isaac: Trust in God. God has a way of making things work out.

Jacob

Breakthrough!: You had a major role in the history of the Chosen People, didn't you?

Jacob: I'd like to think so.

B: How do you explain the dishonest start to your career?

Jacob: You must be talking about the birthright and blessing that I tricked my brother, Esau, out of. I'm not proud of it, but let's just say that God intended things to be different. Don't forget that I was on the receiving end of one of those switches, too.

B: Do you mean your father-in-law, Laban?

Jacob: Yes. When I met Rachel, I fell in love with her immediately. I told her father that I would work for him for seven years if he would let me marry her. He agreed, but when the time came, he secretly gave me his older daughter, Leah, instead. So I hung around and worked another seven years so I could marry Rachel, too.

B: Did you father any children?

Jacob: Twelve sons and one daughter. The twelve tribes of Israel are named for my sons and two grandsons. That must have been what God meant when he promised my grandfather, Abraham, that he would have many descendants.

B: Did you have a favorite?

Jacob: Yes; Joseph and Benjamin, the sons of Rachel. That caused a few problems.

B: Tell us more.

Jacob: My older sons were jealous, especially of Joseph. They sold Joseph as a slave and told me he was dead. I was heartbroken. But our amazing God made it all come out okay in the end.

B: Do you have a message for our readers?

Jacob: Never lose hope. God came through for us and made me the father of the Twelve Tribes of Israel!

Leah & Rachel

Breakthrough!: You two are sisters, right?

Leah: Yes. We are the daughters of Laban. I am the oldest.

B: You were both married to Jacob. How did that happen?

Rachel: Jacob was in love with me. He promised to work for my father for seven years if he would let us get married. My father agreed, but at the last minute, he tricked Jacob into marrying Leah.

Leah: My face was covered with a veil, so Jacob couldn't see me. I didn't know what was going on. I just did as my father told me. Besides, it was our custom that the oldest daughter married first. If Rachel married before me, people would have thought there was something terribly wrong with me.

B: How did Jacob react?

Rachel: He was angry, but I think he understood why my father tricked him. We got married a week later, but he had to work for my father for another seven years. I knew that he must have loved me very much to do that.

Leah: It was very obvious that Jacob loved Rachel more than me. She was prettier. Sometimes it hurt.

B: So you both had children?

Leah: I gave Jacob many children—six sons and a daughter. That pleased him.

Rachel: I was jealous of Leah. It seemed like I would never have children. Finally, I had Joseph. Such a joy! A few years later, I got pregnant again. It was a difficult birth. I died after Benjamin was born.

B: What do you think your greatest contribution to God's plan is?

Leah: Rachel and I, along with Sarah and Rebecca, were the founding mothers of Israel.

Rachel: That's right. The men could not have done it without our faith and wisdom!

Joseph

Breakthrough!: Nice coat!

Joseph: Thanks. It was a gift from my father.

B: Colorful! Is that how you would describe your life?

Joseph: Yes. I was the son of Jacob and Rachel. I didn't know my mother well. She died when my brother, Benjamin, was born. My father talked about her all the time. He really loved her.

B: You had eleven brothers and a sister. Was there any sibling rivalry?

Joseph: Big time. My brothers were so jealous of me that they sold me. I ended up as a slave in Egypt.

B: It must have been a hard life.

Joseph: It was, but God was with me. I did well, and became the slave of an important official. But then I was accused of something I didn't do and got thrown into prison. Luckily, God gave me the gift of understanding dreams. That's how I got out of prison.

B: Whose dreams did you interpret?

Joseph: First it was the baker and the wine steward. Eventually Pharaoh called me in to interpret his dreams. He was so pleased that he made me governor of Egypt.

B: Did you ever see your family again?

Joseph: Yes. Because of a drought in Canaan, there was no food. My brothers came to Egypt to buy grain. They didn't recognize me, but I knew who they were. I made them sweat a little before I gave them food. It was payback time, if you know what I mean. You can read the story in Genesis chapters 42–47. Eventually the entire family came to Egypt.

B: Any advice for our readers?

Joseph: Three things: Do your best wherever you are, take care of the needy, and don't try to get even.

Moses

Breakthrough!: So, Moses, it's great to finally meet you! You have many fans. Many people even call you a hero!

Moses: Well, I don't know about that. Early in my life, I didn't even know who I was.

B: Really?

Moses: Yes, I was actually born a slave, but my mother and sister saved my life. The pharaoh's daughter adopted me, and I lived like an Egyptian prince. When I finally realized how badly my blood relatives were treated, I kind of flew off the handle. But God has always come through for me.

B: Could you tell us a little about a time God came through for you?

Moses: Well, the most amazing time was when I led my people to freedom. Pharaoh and his whole army were after us! We were pretty scared, but God told me to stretch my staff out over the water, and we crossed over on dry land. But the water closed over Pharaoh's army and drowned them, and we were able to escape.

B: Why do you think God chose you to lead the people out of Egypt?

Moses: You know, that's something I never could figure out. I'm not a good public speaker. I'm not very brave. I killed a man, a soldier who was beating a slave, and had to run away and hide. I was really afraid. I certainly didn't want to go back to Egypt. I pleaded with God to send someone else. I guess God must have seen something in me that I couldn't.

B: What advice would you like to give our readers?

Moses: I have to say that the Ten Commandments God gave me on Mount Sinai are the best advice I could give anyone.

a one-year-old lamb, for the burnt offering; one goat for the sin offering; and two bulls, five rams, five goats, and five one-year-old lambs, for the fellowship offering.

84-88 The totals of the offerings brought by the twelve leaders for the dedication of the altar were as follows:

- twelve silver bowls and twelve silver basins weighing a total of 60 pounds
- twelve gold dishes weighing a total of 48 ounces, filled with incense
- twelve bulls, twelve rams, and twelve one-year-old lambs, plus the grain offerings that go with them, for the burnt offerings
- twelve goats for the sin offerings
- twenty-four bulls, sixty rams, sixty goats, sixty one-year-old lambs, for the fellowship offerings

89 When Moses went into the Tent to talk with the LORD, he heard the LORD speaking to him from above the lid on the Covenant Box, between the two winged creatures.[b]

Placing the Lamps

8 The LORD said to Moses, 2 "Tell Aaron that when he puts the seven lamps on the lampstand, he should place them so that the light shines toward the front." 3 Aaron obeyed and placed the lamps facing the front of the lampstand. 4 From top to bottom the lampstand was made of hammered gold, according to the pattern that the LORD had shown Moses.

The Purification and Dedication of the Levites

5 The LORD said to Moses, 6 "Separate the Levites from the rest of the people of Israel and purify them 7 in the following way: sprinkle them with the water of purification and have them shave their whole bodies and have them wash their clothes. Then they will be ritually clean. 8 Then they are to take a young bull and the required grain offering of flour mixed with olive oil; and you are to take another bull for the sin offering. 9 Then assemble the whole community of Israel and have the Levites stand in front of the Tent of my presence. 10 The people of Israel are to place their hands on the heads of the Levites, 11 and then Aaron shall dedicate the Levites to me as a special gift from the Israelites, so that they may do my work. 12 The Levites shall then put their hands on the heads of the two bulls; one is to be offered as a sin offering and the other as a burnt offering, in order to perform the ritual of purification for the Levites.

13 "Dedicate the Levites as a special gift to me, and put Aaron and his sons in charge of them. 14 Separate the Levites in this way from the rest of the Israelites, so that they will belong to me. 15 After you have purified and dedicated the Levites, they will be qualified to work in the Tent. 16 I have claimed them in the place of all the first-born sons of the Israelites, and they belong to me alone. 17 When I killed all the first-born in Egypt, I consecrated as my own the oldest son of each Israelite family and the first-born of every animal. 18 I am now taking the Levites instead of all the first-born of the Israelites, 19 and I assign the Levites to Aaron and his sons, as a gift from the Israelites, to work in the Tent for the people of Israel and to protect the Israelites from the disaster that would strike them if they came too near the Holy Place."

20 So Moses, Aaron, and all the people of Israel dedicated the Levites, as the LORD commanded Moses. 21 The Levites purified themselves and washed their clothes, and Aaron dedicated them as a special gift to the LORD. He also performed the ritual of purification for them. 22 The people did everything the LORD had commanded Moses concerning the Levites. And so the Levites were qualified to work in the Tent under Aaron and his sons.

23 The LORD said to Moses, 24 "From the age of twenty-five each Levite shall perform his duties in the Tent of my presence, 25 and at the age of fifty he shall retire. 26 After that, he may help his fellow Levites in performing their duties in the Tent, but he must not perform any service by himself. This is how you are to regulate the duties of the Levites."

[b] **7:89** WINGED CREATURES: *See Word List.*

8:1–4 Ex 25:31–40; 37:17–24 **8:17** Ex 13:2

The Second Passover

9 The LORD spoke to Moses in the Sinai Desert in the first month of the second year after the people of Israel had left Egypt. He said, 2-3“On the fourteenth day of this month, beginning at sunset, the people of Israel are to observe the Passover according to all the rules and regulations for it.” 4So Moses told the people to observe the Passover, 5and on the evening of the fourteenth day of the first month they did so in the Sinai Desert. The people did everything just as the LORD had commanded Moses.

6But there were some people who were ritually unclean because they had touched a corpse, and they were not able to keep the Passover on that day. They went to Moses and Aaron 7and said, “We are unclean because we have touched a corpse, but why should we be excluded from presenting the LORD’s offering with the rest of the Israelites?”

8Moses answered, “Wait until I receive instructions from the LORD.”

9The LORD told Moses 10to say to the people of Israel, “When any of you or your descendants are unclean from touching a corpse or are far away on a journey, but still want to keep the Passover, 11you are permitted to observe it one month later instead, on the evening of the fourteenth day of the second month. Celebrate it with unleavened bread and bitter herbs. 12Do not leave any of the food until the following morning and do not break any of the animal’s bones. Observe the Passover according to all the regulations. 13But if any of you are ritually clean and not away on a journey and do not observe the Passover, you shall no longer be considered my people, because you did not present the offering to me at the appointed time. You must suffer the consequences of your sin.

14“If foreigners living among you want to keep the Passover, they must observe it according to all the rules and regulations. The same law applies to everyone, whether native or foreigner.”

The Fiery Cloud
(Exodus 40:34–38)

15-16On the day the Tent of the LORD’s presence was set up, a cloud came and covered it. At night the cloud looked like fire. 17Whenever the cloud lifted, the people of Israel broke camp, and they set up camp again in the place where the cloud came down. 18The people broke camp at the command of the LORD, and at his command they set up camp. As long as the cloud stayed over the Tent, they stayed in the same camp. 19When the cloud stayed over the Tent for a long time, they obeyed the LORD and did not move on. 20Sometimes the cloud remained over the Tent for only a few days; in any case, they remained in camp or moved, according to the command of the LORD. 21Sometimes the cloud remained only from evening until morning, and they moved on as soon as the cloud lifted. Whenever the cloud lifted, they moved on. 22Whether it was two days, a month, a year, or longer, as long as the cloud remained over the Tent, they did not move on; but when it lifted, they moved. 23They set up camp and broke camp in obedience to the commands which the LORD gave through Moses.

The Silver Trumpets

10 The LORD said to Moses, 2“Make two trumpets of hammered silver to use for calling the people together and for breaking camp. 3When long blasts are sounded on both trumpets, the whole community is to gather around you at the entrance to the Tent of my presence. 4But when only one trumpet is sounded, then only the leaders of the clans are to gather around you. 5When short blasts are sounded, the tribes camped on the east will move out. 6When short blasts are sounded a second time, the tribes on the south will move out. So short blasts are to be sounded to break camp, 7but in order to call the community together, long blasts are to be sounded. 8The trumpets are to be blown by Aaron’s sons, the priests.

“The following rule is to be observed for

9:1–5 Ex 12:1–13 **9:12** Ex 12:46; Jn 19:36

all time to come. 9When you are a... r in
your land, defending yourselves agai... n
enemy who has attacked you, sound t... sig-
nal for battle on these trumpets. I, the L...
your God, will help you and save you fro...
your enemies. 10Also on joyful occasions—
at your New Moon Festivals and your other
religious festivals—you are to blow the
trumpets when you present your burnt
offerings and your fellowship offerings. Then
I will help you. I am the LORD your God."

The Israelites Break Camp

11On the twentieth day of the second
month in the second year after the people
left Egypt, the cloud over the Tent of the
LORD's presence lifted, 12and the Israelites
started on their journey out of the Sinai
Desert. The cloud came to rest in the
wilderness of Paran.

13They began to march at the command
of the LORD through Moses, 14and each
time they moved, they were in the same
order. Those under the banner of the divi-
sion led by the tribe of Judah started out
first, company by company, with Nahshon
son of Amminadab in command. 15Nethanel
son of Zuar was in command of the tribe of
Issachar, 16and Eliab son of Helon was in
command of the tribe of Zebulun.

17Then the Tent would be taken down,
and the clans of Gershon and Merari, who
carried it, would start out.

When only one trumpet is sounded (10:4)

18Next, those under th...
division led by the tribe of R...
start out, company by company, w...
son of Shedeur in command. 19Shelumi...
son of Zurishaddai was in command of the
tribe of Simeon, 20and Eliasaph son of Deuel
was in command of the tribe of Gad.

21Then the Levite clan of Kohath would
start out, carrying the sacred objects. By the
time they arrived at the next camp, the Tent
had been set up again.

22Next, those under the banner of the
division led by the tribe of Ephraim would
start out, company by company, with
Elishama son of Ammihud in command.
23Gamaliel son of Pedahzur was in com-
mand of the tribe of Manasseh, 24and Abidan
son of Gideoni was in command of the tribe
of Benjamin.

25Finally, those under the banner of the
division led by the tribe of Dan, serving as
the rear guard of all the divisions, would start
out, company by company, with Ahiezer son
of Ammishaddai in command. 26Pagiel son
of Ochran was in command of the tribe of
Asher, 27and Ahira son of Enan was in com-
mand of the tribe of Naphtali. 28This, then,
was the order of march, company by compa-
ny, whenever the Israelites broke camp and
set out.

29Moses said to his brother-in-law Hobab
son of Jethro the Midianite, "We are about
to start out for the place which the LORD
said he would give us. He has promised to
make Israel prosperous, so come with us, and
we will share our prosperity with you."

30Hobab answered, "No, I am going back
to my native land."

31"Please don't leave us," Moses said. "You
know where we can camp in the wilderness,
and you can be our guide. 32If you come
with us, we will share with you all the bless-
ings that the LORD gives us."

The People Set Out

33When the people left Sinai, the holy
mountain, they traveled three days. The
LORD's Covenant Box always went ahead of
them to find a place for them to camp. 34As
they moved on from each camp, the cloud of
the LORD was over them by day.

…henever the Covenant Box started
… Moses would say, "Arise, LORD; scatter
…our enemies and put to flight those who
hate you!" 36 And whenever it stopped, he
would say, "Return, LORD, to the thousands
of families of Israel."[c]

The Place Named Taberah

11 The people began to complain to
the LORD about their troubles.
When the LORD heard them, he became
angry and sent fire on the people. It burned
among them and destroyed one end of the
camp. 2 The people cried out to Moses for
help; he prayed to the LORD, and the fire
died down. 3 So the place was named Tabe-
rah,[d] because there the fire of the LORD
burned among them.

Moses Chooses Seventy Leaders

4 There were foreigners traveling with the
Israelites. They had a strong craving for meat,
and even the Israelites themselves began to
complain: "If only we could have some
meat! 5 In Egypt we used to eat all the fish
we wanted, and it cost us nothing. Remem-
ber the cucumbers, the watermelons, the
leeks, the onions, and the garlic we had?
6 But now our strength is gone. There is
nothing at all to eat—nothing but this
manna day after day!"

(7 Manna was like small seeds, whitish yel-
low in color. 8-9 It fell on the camp at night
along with the dew. The next morning the
people would go around and gather it, grind
it or pound it into flour, and then boil it and
make it into flat cakes. It tasted like bread
baked with olive oil.)

10 Moses heard all the people complaining
as they stood around in groups at the
entrances of their tents. He was distressed
because the LORD had become angry with
them, 11 and he said to the LORD, "Why have
you treated me so badly? Why are you dis-
pleased with me? Why have you given me
the responsibility for all these people? 12 I
didn't create them or bring them to birth!

Live it!

Quit Your Griping

Throughout the Book of Numbers, there were many times when the Israelites complained to Moses. They complained about a lot of things, including a lack of food and water and Moses' leadership. When they got to the Promised Land, they complained because strong people were already living there. They complained so much that Moses asked God to kill him so he wouldn't have to listen to their complaints anymore!

The Israelites complained so much because they were discouraged and afraid. What the author of Numbers wants us to know is that when things get hard, we need to trust in God even more. Our grumbling, griping, and complaining may sound like we don't appreciate what God does for us. It might be a symptom that we don't trust that God is there for us.

Think about how you act at home. Do you grumble and gripe about what your parents feed you? Do you complain about your chores or your sisters and brothers? Does your griping make you sound ungrateful? If so, you may want to try to replace griping with either silence or praise. What if you praise the brussels sprouts at your table because God did create them? What if you praise your siblings for keeping you from being bored? The next time you're ready to complain, grumble, or gripe, remember these stories.

— Numbers 11:1–15

[c] **10:36** Return . . . Israel; *or* Return, LORD, you who are like an army of millions for Israel. [d] **11:3** TABERAH: *This name sounds like the Hebrew for "burning."*

10:35 Ps 68:1 **11:7, 8** Ex 16:31 **11:9** Ex 16:13–15

Why should you ask me to act like a nurse
and carry them in my arms like babies all
the way to the land you promised to their
ancestors? 13 Where could I get enough meat
for all these people? They keep whining and
asking for meat. 14 I can't be responsible for
all these people by myself; it's too much for
me! 15 If you are going to treat me like this,
have pity on me and kill me, so that I won't
have to endure your cruelty any longer."

"I can't be responsible for all these people!" (11:14)

16 The LORD said to Moses, "Assemble
seventy respected men who are recognized
as leaders of the people, bring them to me
at the Tent of my presence, and tell them to
stand there beside you. 17 I will come down
and speak with you there, and I will take
some of the spirit I have given you and give
it to them. Then they can help you bear the
responsibility for these people, and you will
not have to bear it alone. 18 Now tell the
people, 'Purify yourselves for tomorrow; you
will have meat to eat. The LORD has heard
you whining and saying that you wished
you had some meat and that you were bet-
ter off in Egypt. Now the LORD will give
you meat, and you will have to eat it. 19 You
will have to eat it not just for one or two
days, or five, or ten, or even twenty days,
20 but for a whole month, until it comes out
of your ears, until you are sick of it. This
will happen because you have rejected the
LORD who is here among you and have
complained to him that you should never
have left Egypt.'"
21 Moses said to the LORD, "Here I am
leading 600,000 people, and you say that you
will give them enough meat for a month?
22 Could enough cattle and sheep be killed
to satisfy them? Are all the fish in the sea
enough for them?"
23 "Is there a limit to my power?" the
LORD answered. "You will soon see whether
what I have said will happen or not!"
24 So Moses went out and told the people
what the LORD had said. He assembled sev-
enty of the leaders and placed them around
the Tent. 25 Then the LORD came down in
the cloud and spoke to him. He took some
of the spirit he had given to Moses and gave
it to the seventy leaders. When the spirit
came on them, they began to shout like
prophets, but not for long.
26 Two of the seventy leaders, Eldad and
Medad, had stayed in the camp and had not
gone out to the Tent. There in the camp the
spirit came on them, and they too began to
shout like prophets. 27 A young man ran out
to tell Moses what Eldad and Medad were
doing.
28 Then Joshua son of Nun, who had been
Moses' helper since he was a young man,
spoke up and said to Moses, "Stop them,
sir!"
29 Moses answered, "Are you concerned
about my interests? I wish that the LORD
would give his spirit to all his people and
make all of them shout like prophets!"
30 Then Moses and the seventy leaders of
Israel went back to camp.

The LORD Sends Quails

31 Suddenly the LORD sent a wind that
brought quails from the sea, flying three feet
above the ground. They settled on the camp
and all around it for miles and miles in every
direction.[e] 32 So all that day, all night, and all
the next day, the people worked catching
quails; no one gathered less than fifty
bushels. They spread them out to dry all
around the camp. 33 While there was still
plenty of meat for them to eat, the LORD
became angry with the people and caused
an epidemic to break out among them.
34 That place was named Kibroth Hattaavah
(which means "Graves of Craving"), because
there they buried the people who had
craved meat.

[e] **11:31** sea, flying . . . direction; *or* sea. They settled in the camp and all around it for miles and miles in every direction, until they were piled up three feet deep on the ground.

Catching quails (11:32)

35From there the people moved to Hazeroth, where they made camp.

Miriam Is Punished

12 Moses had married a Cushite[f]
woman, and Miriam and Aaron crit-
icized him for it. 2They said, "Has the LORD
spoken only through[g] Moses? Hasn't he also
spoken through[g] us?" The LORD heard what
they said. (3Moses was a humble man, more
humble than anyone else on earth.)
4Suddenly the LORD said to Moses,
Aaron, and Miriam, "I want the three of
you to come out to the Tent of my pres-
ence." They went, 5and the LORD came
down in a pillar of cloud, stood at the
entrance of the Tent, and called out,
"Aaron! Miriam!" The two of them stepped
forward, 6and the LORD said, "Now hear
what I have to say! When there are prophets
among you,[h] I reveal myself to them in
visions and speak to them in dreams. 7It is
different when I speak with my servant
Moses; I have put him in charge of all my
people Israel.[i] 8So I speak to him face to
face, clearly and not in riddles; he has even
seen my form! How dare you speak against
my servant Moses?"
9The LORD was angry with them; and so
as he departed 10and the cloud left the Tent,
Miriam's skin was suddenly covered with a
dreaded disease and turned as white as snow.
When Aaron looked at her and saw that she
was covered with the disease, 11he said to
Moses, "Please, sir, do not make us suffer this
punishment for our foolish sin. 12Don't let
her become like something born dead with
half its flesh eaten away."
13So Moses cried out to the LORD, "O
God, heal her!"

"O God, heal her!" (12:13)

14The LORD answered, "If her father had
spit in her face, she would have to bear her
disgrace for seven days. So let her be shut
out of the camp for a week, and after that
she can be brought back in." 15Miriam was
shut out of the camp for seven days, and
the people did not move on until she was
brought back in. 16Then they left Hazeroth
and set up camp in the wilderness of Paran.

[f] **12:1** Cushite *(compare Heb 3:7); or* Midianite; *or* Ethiopian. [g] **12:2** through; *or* to. [h] **12:6** *Some ancient translations* When . . . you; *Hebrew unclear.* [i] **12:7** I have put . . . Israel; *or* he can be trusted with all my affairs.

12:3 Sir 45:4 **12:7** Heb 3:2 **12:14** Num 5:2, 3

The Spies
(Deuteronomy 1:19–33)

13 The LORD said to Moses, 2 “Choose one of the leaders from each of the twelve tribes and send them as spies to explore the land of Canaan, which I am giving to the Israelites.” 3-15 Moses obeyed and from the wilderness of Paran he sent out leaders, as follows:

Tribe	*Leader*
Reuben	Shammua son of Zaccur
Simeon	Shaphat son of Hori
Judah	Caleb son of Jephunneh
Issachar	Igal son of Joseph
Ephraim	Hoshea son of Nun
Benjamin	Palti son of Raphu
Zebulun	Gaddiel son of Sodi
Manasseh	Gaddi son of Susi
Dan	Ammiel son of Gemalli
Asher	Sethur son of Michael
Naphtali	Nahbi son of Vophsi
Gad	Geuel son of Machi

16 These are the spies Moses sent to explore the land. He changed the name of Hoshea son of Nun to Joshua.

17 When Moses sent them out, he said to them, “Go north from here into the southern part of the land of Canaan and then on into the hill country. 18 Find out what kind of country it is, how many people live there, and how strong they are. 19 Find out whether the land is good or bad and whether the people live in open towns or in fortified cities. 20 Find out whether the soil is fertile and whether the land is wooded. And be sure to bring back some of the fruit that grows there.” (It was the season when grapes were beginning to ripen.)

21 So the men went north and explored the land from the wilderness of Zin in the south all the way to Rehob, near Hamath Pass in the north. 22 They went first into the southern part of the land and came to Hebron, where the clans of Ahiman, Sheshai, and Talmai, the descendants of a race of giants called the Anakim, lived. (Hebron was founded seven years before Zoan in Egypt.) 23 They came to Eshcol Valley, and there they cut off a branch which had one bunch of grapes on it so heavy that it took two men to carry it on a pole between them. They also brought back some pomegranates and figs. (24 That place was named Eshcol[j] Valley because of the bunch of grapes the Israelites cut off there.)

It took two men to carry it. (13:23)

25 After exploring the land for forty days, the spies returned 26 to Moses, Aaron, and the whole community of Israel at Kadesh in the wilderness of Paran. They reported what they had seen and showed them the fruit they had brought. 27 They told Moses, “We explored the land and found it to be rich and fertile; and here is some of its fruit. 28 But the people who live there are powerful, and their cities are very large and well fortified. Even worse, we saw the descendants of the giants there. 29 Amalekites live in the southern part of the land; Hittites, Jebusites, and Amorites live in the hill country; and Canaanites live by the Mediterranean Sea and along the Jordan River.”

30 Caleb silenced the people who were complaining against[k] Moses, and said, “We should attack now and take the land; we are strong enough to conquer it.”

31 But the men who had gone with Caleb said, “No, we are not strong enough to attack them; the people there are more powerful than we are.” 32 So they spread a false report among the Israelites about the land they had explored. They said, “That land doesn't even produce enough to feed the people who live there. Everyone we saw was very tall, 33 and we even saw giants there, the

[j] **13:24** ESHCOL: *This name in Hebrew means “bunch of grapes.”* [k] **13:30** complaining against; *or* gathered around.
13:33 Gen 6:4

descendants of Anak. We felt as small as grasshoppers, and that is how we must have looked to them."

The People Complain

14 All night long the people cried out in distress. 2They complained against Moses and Aaron, and said, "It would have been better to die in Egypt or even here in the wilderness! 3Why is the LORD taking us into that land? We will be killed in battle, and our wives and children will be captured. Wouldn't it be better to go back to Egypt?" 4So they said to one another, "Let's choose a leader and go back to Egypt!"

5Then Moses and Aaron bowed to the ground in front of all the people. 6And Joshua son of Nun and Caleb son of Jephunneh, two of the spies, tore their clothes in sorrow 7and said to the people, "The land we explored is an excellent land. 8If the LORD is pleased with us, he will take us there and give us that rich and fertile land. 9Do not rebel against the LORD and don't be afraid of the people who live there. We will conquer them easily. The LORD is with us and has defeated the gods who protected them; so don't be afraid." 10The whole community was threatening to stone them to death, but suddenly the people saw the dazzling light of the LORD's presence appear over the Tent.

Moses Prays for the People

11The LORD said to Moses, "How much longer will these people reject me? How much longer will they refuse to trust in me, even though I have performed so many miracles among them? 12I will send an epidemic and destroy them, but I will make you the father of a nation that is larger and more powerful than they are!"

13But Moses said to the LORD, "You brought these people out of Egypt by your power. When the Egyptians hear what you have done to your people, 14they will tell it to the people who live in this land. These people have already heard that you, LORD, are with us, that you appear in plain sight when your cloud stops over us, and that you go before us in a pillar of cloud by day and a pillar of fire by night. 15Now if you kill all your people, the nations who have heard of your fame will say 16that you killed your people in the wilderness because you were not able to bring them into the land you promised to give them. 17So now, LORD, I pray, show us your power and do what you promised when you said, 18'I, the LORD, am not easily angered, and I show great love and faithfulness and forgive sin and rebellion. Yet I will not fail to punish children and grandchildren to the third and fourth generation for the sins of their parents.' 19And now, LORD, according to the greatness of your unchanging love, forgive, I pray, the sin of these people, just as you have forgiven them ever since they left Egypt."

20The LORD answered, "I will forgive them, as you have asked. 21But I promise that as surely as I live and as surely as my presence fills the earth, 22none of these people will live to enter that land. They have seen the dazzling light of my presence and the miracles that I performed in Egypt and in the wilderness, but they have tried my patience over and over again and have refused to obey me. 23They will never enter the land which I promised to their ancestors. None of those who have rejected me will ever enter it. 24But because my servant Caleb has a different attitude and has remained loyal to me, I will bring him into the land which he explored, and his descendants will possess the land 25in whose valleys the Amalekites and the Canaanites now live. Turn back tomorrow and go into the wilderness in the direction of the Gulf of Aqaba."

The LORD Punishes the People for Complaining

26The LORD said to Moses and Aaron, 27"How much longer are these wicked people going to complain against me? I have heard enough of these complaints! 28Now give them this answer: 'I swear that as surely as I live, I will do to you just what you have

14:9 Heb 3:16 **14:13–19** Ex 32:11–14 **14:18** Ex 20:5, 6; 34:6, 7; Deut 5:9, 10; 7:9, 10 **14:21–23** Heb 3:18 **14:24** Josh 14:9–12

asked. I, the LORD, have spoken. 29You will
die and your corpses will be scattered across
this wilderness. Because you have com-
plained against me, none of you over twenty
years of age will enter that land. 30I promised
to let you live there, but not one of you will,
except Caleb and Joshua. 31You said that
your children would be captured, but I will
bring them into the land that you rejected,
and it will be their home. 32You will die
here in this wilderness. 33Your children will
wander in the wilderness for forty years, suf-
fering for your unfaithfulness, until the last
one of you dies. 34You will suffer the conse-
quences of your sin for forty years, one year
for each of the forty days you spent explor-
ing the land. You will know what it means to
have me against you! 35I swear that I will do
this to you wicked people who have gath-
ered together against me. Here in the
wilderness every one of you will die. I, the
LORD, have spoken.' "

36-37 The men Moses had sent to explore
the land brought back a false report which
caused the people to complain against the
LORD. And so the LORD struck them with a
disease, and they died. 38Of the twelve spies
only Joshua and Caleb survived.

The First Attempt to Invade the Land
(Deuteronomy 1:41–46)

39When Moses told the Israelites what the
LORD had said, they mourned bitterly.
40Early the next morning they started out to
invade the hill country, saying, "Now we are
ready to go to the place which the LORD
told us about. We admit that we have
sinned."

41But Moses said, "Then why are you dis-
obeying the LORD now? You will not suc-
ceed! 42Don't go. The LORD is not with you,
and your enemies will defeat you. 43When
you face the Amalekites and the Canaanites,
you will die in battle; the LORD will not be
with you, because you have refused to follow
him."

44Yet they still dared to go up into the hill
country, even though neither the LORD's
Covenant Box nor Moses left the camp.
45Then the Amalekites and the Canaanites
who lived there attacked and defeated them,
and pursued them as far as Hormah.[l]

Laws about Sacrifice

15 The LORD gave Moses 2the follow-
ing regulations for the people of
Israel to observe in the land that he was
going to give them. 3A bull, a ram, a sheep,
or a goat may be presented to the LORD as a
burnt offering or as a sacrifice in fulfillment
of a vow or as a freewill offering or as an
offering at your regular religious festivals; the
odor of these food offerings is pleasing to
the LORD. 4-5Whoever presents a sheep or a
goat as a burnt offering to the LORD is to
bring with each animal 2 pounds of flour
mixed with 2 pints of olive oil as a grain
offering, together with 2 pints of wine.
6When a ram is offered, 4 pounds of flour
mixed with 3 pints of olive oil are to be pre-
sented as a grain offering, 7together with 3
pints of wine. The odor of these sacrifices is
pleasing to the LORD. 8When a bull is
offered to the LORD as a burnt offering or as
a sacrifice in fulfillment of a vow or as a fel-
lowship offering, 9a grain offering of 6
pounds of flour mixed with 4 pints of olive
oil is to be presented, 10together with 4 pints
of wine. The odor of this sacrifice is pleasing
to the LORD.

11That is what shall be offered with each
bull, ram, sheep, or goat. 12When more than
one animal is offered, the accompanying
offering is to be increased proportionately.
13All native Israelites are to do this when
they present a food offering, an odor pleas-
ing to the LORD. 14And if at any time for-
eigners living among you, whether on a
temporary or a permanent basis, make a
food offering, an odor that pleases the
LORD, they are to observe the same regula-
tions. 15For all time to come, the same[m] rules
are binding on you and on the foreigners
who live among you. You and they are alike
in the LORD's sight; 16the same laws and reg-
ulations apply to you and to them.

[l] **14:45** HORMAH: *This name in Hebrew means "destruction."* [m] **15:15** *Some ancient translations* the same; *Hebrew* the congregation the same.

14:29 Heb 3:17 **14:33** Acts 7:36 **15:16** Lev 24:22

[17]The LORD gave Moses [18]the following regulations for the people of Israel to observe in the land that he was going to give them. [19]When any food produced there is eaten, some of it is to be set aside as a special contribution to the LORD. [20]When you bake bread, the first loaf of the first bread made from the new grain is to be presented as a special contribution to the LORD. This is to be presented in the same way as the special contribution you make from the grain you thresh. [21]For all time to come, this special gift is to be given to the LORD from the bread you bake.

[22]But suppose someone unintentionally fails to keep some of these regulations which the LORD has given Moses. [23]And suppose that in the future the community fails to do everything that the LORD commanded through Moses. [24]If the mistake was made because of the ignorance of the community, they are to offer a bull as a burnt offering, an odor that pleases the LORD, with the proper grain offering and wine offering. In addition, they are to offer a male goat as a sin offering. [25]The priest shall perform the ritual of purification for the community, and they will be forgiven, because the mistake was unintentional and they brought their sin offering as a food offering to the LORD. [26]The whole community of Israel and the foreigners living among them will be forgiven, because everyone was involved in the mistake.

[27]If any of you sin unintentionally, you are to offer a one-year-old female goat as a sin offering. [28]At the altar the priest shall perform the ritual of purification to purify you from your sin, and you will be forgiven. [29]The same regulation applies to all who unintentionally commit a sin, whether they are native Israelites or resident foreigners.

[30]But any who sin deliberately, whether they are natives or foreigners, are guilty of treating the LORD with contempt, and they shall be put to death, [31]because they have rejected what the LORD said and have deliberately broken one of his commands. They are responsible for their own death.

The Man Who Broke the Sabbath

[32]Once, while the Israelites were still in the wilderness, a man was found gathering firewood on the Sabbath. [33]He was taken to Moses, Aaron, and the whole community, [34]and was put under guard, because it was not clear what should be done with him. [35]Then the LORD said to Moses, "The man must be put to death; the whole community is to stone him to death outside the camp." [36]So the whole community took him outside the camp and stoned him to death, as the LORD had commanded.

Rules about Tassels

[37]The LORD commanded Moses [38]to say to the people of Israel: "Make tassels on the corners of your garments and put a blue cord on each tassel. You are to do this for all time to come. [39]The tassels will serve as reminders, and each time you see them you will remember all my commands and obey them; then you will not turn away from me and follow your own wishes and desires. [40]The tassels will remind you to keep all my commands, and you will belong completely to me. [41]I am the LORD your God; I brought you out of Egypt to be your God. I am the LORD."

The Rebellion of Korah, Dathan, and Abiram

16 [1-2]Korah son of Izhar, from the Levite clan of Kohath, rebelled against the leadership of Moses. He was joined by three members of the tribe of Reuben—Dathan and Abiram, the sons of Eliab, and On son of Peleth—and by 250 other Israelites, well-known leaders chosen by the community. [3]They assembled before Moses and Aaron and said to them, "You have gone too far! All the members of the community belong to the LORD, and the LORD is with all of us. Why, then, Moses, do you set yourself above the LORD's community?"

[4]When Moses heard this, he threw himself on the ground and prayed. [5]Then he said to Korah and his followers, "Tomorrow morning the LORD will show us who belongs to

15:27, 28 Lev 4:27–31 **15:38** Deut 22:12 **16:1–35** Sir 45:18–20 **16:1** Jude 11

him; he will let the one who belongs to him, that is, the one he has chosen, approach him at the altar. [6-7]Tomorrow morning you and your followers take fire pans, put live coals and incense on them, and take them to the altar. Then we will see which of us the LORD has chosen. You Levites are the ones who have gone too far!"

[8]Moses continued to speak to Korah. "Listen, you Levites! [9]Do you consider it a small matter that the God of Israel has set you apart from the rest of the community, so that you can approach him, perform your service in the LORD's Tent, and minister to the community and serve them? [10]He has let you and all the other Levites have this honor—and now you are trying to get the priesthood too! [11]When you complain against Aaron, it is really against the LORD that you and your followers are rebelling."

[12]Then Moses sent for Dathan and Abiram, but they said, "We will not come! [13]Isn't it enough that you have brought us out of the fertile land of Egypt to kill us here in the wilderness? Do you also have to lord it over us? [14]You certainly have not brought us into a fertile land or given us fields and vineyards as our possession, and now you are trying to deceive us. We will not come!"

[15]Moses became angry and said to the LORD, "Do not accept any offerings these men bring. I have not wronged any of them; I have not even taken one of their donkeys."

[16]Moses said to Korah, "Tomorrow you and your 250 followers must come to the Tent of the LORD's presence; Aaron will also be there. [17]Each of you will take his fire pan, put incense on it, and then present it at the altar." [18]So they each took their fire pans, put live coals and incense on them, and stood at the entrance of the Tent with Moses and Aaron. [19]Then Korah gathered the whole community, and they stood facing Moses and Aaron at the entrance of the Tent. Suddenly the dazzling light of the LORD's presence appeared to the whole community, [20]and the LORD said to Moses and Aaron, [21]"Move back from these people, and I will destroy them immediately."

[22]But Moses and Aaron bowed down with their faces to the ground and said, "O God, you are the source of all life. When one of us sins, do you become angry with the whole community?"

[23]The LORD said to Moses, [24]"Tell the people to move away from the tents of Korah, Dathan, and Abiram."

[25]Then Moses, accompanied by the leaders of Israel, went to Dathan and Abiram. [26]He said to the people, "Get away from the tents of these wicked men and don't touch anything that belongs to them. Otherwise, you will be wiped out with them for all their sins." [27]So they moved away from the tents of Korah, Dathan, and Abiram.

Dathan and Abiram had come out and were standing at the entrance of their tents, with their wives and children. [28]Moses said to the people, "This is how you will know that the LORD has sent me to do all these things and that it is not by my own choice that I have done them. [29]If these men die a natural death without some punishment from God, then the LORD did not send me. [30]But if the LORD does something unheard of, and the earth opens up and swallows them with all they own, so that they go down alive to the world of the dead, you will know that these men have rejected the LORD."

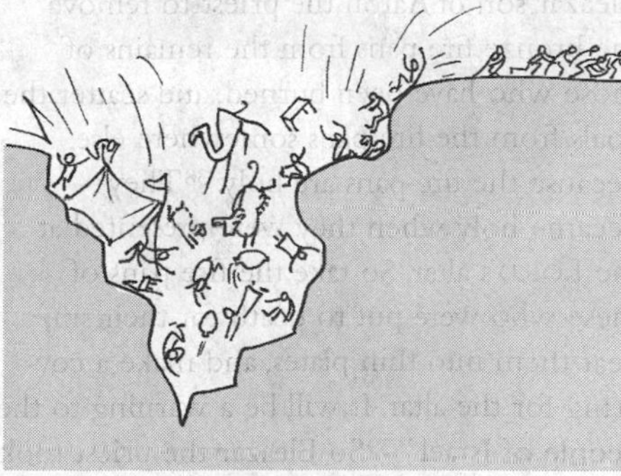

The earth opens up and swallows them. (16:30)

[31]As soon as he had finished speaking, the ground under Dathan and Abiram split open [32]and swallowed them and their families, together with all of Korah's followers and their possessions. [33]So they went down alive to the world of the dead, with their possessions. The earth closed over them, and they vanished. [34]All the people of Israel who were

Between the living and the dead (16:48)

there fled when they heard their cry. They shouted, "Run! The earth might swallow us too!"

35 Then the LORD sent a fire that blazed out and burned up the 250 men who had presented the incense.

The Fire Pans

36 Then the LORD said to Moses, 37 "Tell Eleazar son of Aaron the priest to remove the bronze fire pans from the remains of those who have been burned, and scatter the coals from the fire pans somewhere else, because the fire pans are holy. 38 They became holy when they were presented at the LORD's altar. So take the fire pans of these who were put to death for their sin, beat them into thin plates, and make a covering for the altar. It will be a warning to the people of Israel." 39 So Eleazar the priest took the fire pans and had them beaten into thin plates to make a covering for the altar. 40 This was a warning to the Israelites that no one who was not a descendant of Aaron should come to the altar to burn incense for the LORD. Otherwise he would be destroyed like Korah and his men. All this was done as the LORD had commanded Eleazar through Moses.

Aaron Saves the People

41 The next day the whole community complained against Moses and Aaron and said, "You have killed some of the LORD's people." 42 After they had all gathered to protest to Moses and Aaron, they turned toward the Tent and saw that the cloud was covering it and that the dazzling light of the LORD's presence had appeared. 43 Moses and Aaron went and stood in front of the Tent, 44 and the LORD said to Moses, 45 "Move back from these people, and I will destroy them on the spot!"

The two of them bowed down with their faces to the ground, 46 and Moses said to Aaron, "Take your fire pan, put live coals from the altar in it, and put some incense on the coals. Then hurry with it to the people and perform the ritual of purification for them. Hurry! The LORD's anger has already broken out and an epidemic has already begun." 47 Aaron obeyed, took his fire pan and ran into the middle of the assembled people. When he saw that the plague had already begun, he put the incense on the coals and performed the ritual of purification for the people. 48 This stopped the plague, and he was left standing between the living and the dead. 49 The number of people who died was 14,700, not counting those who died in Korah's rebellion. 50 When the

16:44–48 Wis 18:20–25

plague had stopped, Aaron returned to Moses at the entrance of the Tent.

Aaron's Walking Stick

17 The LORD said to Moses, [2]"Tell the people of Israel to give you twelve walking sticks, one from the leader of each tribe. Write each man's name on his stick [3]and then write Aaron's name on the stick representing Levi. There will be one stick for each tribal leader. [4]Take them to the Tent of my presence and put them in front of the Covenant Box, where I meet you. [5]Then the stick of the man I have chosen will sprout. In this way I will put a stop to the constant complaining of these Israelites against you."

[6]So Moses spoke to the Israelites, and each of their leaders gave him a stick, one for each tribe, twelve in all, and Aaron's stick was put with them. [7]Moses then put all the sticks in the Tent in front of the LORD's Covenant Box.

[8]The next day, when Moses went into the Tent, he saw that Aaron's stick, representing the tribe of Levi, had sprouted. It had budded, blossomed, and produced ripe almonds! [9]Moses took all the sticks and showed them to the Israelites. They saw what had happened, and each leader took his own stick back. [10]The LORD said to Moses, "Put Aaron's stick back in front of the Covenant Box. It is to be kept as a warning to the rebel Israelites

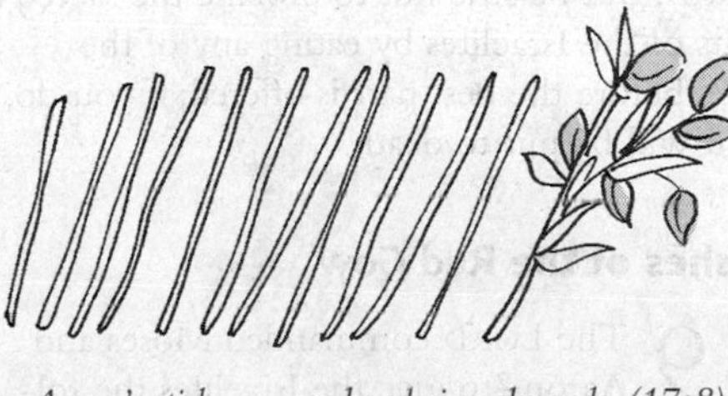

Aaron's stick . . . produced ripe almonds. (17:8)

that they will die unless their complaining stops." [11]Moses did as the LORD commanded.

[12]The people of Israel said to Moses, "Then that's the end of us! [13]If anyone who even comes near the Tent must die, then we are all as good as dead!"

Duties of Priests and Levites

18 The LORD said to Aaron, "You, your sons, and the Levites must suffer the consequences of any guilt connected with serving in the Tent of my presence; but only you and your sons will suffer the consequences of service in the priesthood. [2]Bring in your relatives, the tribe of Levi, to work with you and help you while you and your sons are serving at the Tent. [3]They are to fulfill their duties to you and their responsibilities for the Tent, but they must not have any contact with sacred objects in the Holy Place or with the altar. If they do, both they and you will be put to death. [4]They are to work with you and fulfill their responsibilities for all the service in the Tent, but no unqualified person may work with you. [5]You and your sons alone must fulfill the responsibilities for the Holy Place and the altar, so that my anger will not again break out against the people of Israel. [6]I am the one who has chosen your relatives the Levites from among the Israelites as a gift to you. They are dedicated to me, so that they can carry out their duties in the Tent. [7]But you and your sons alone shall fulfill all the responsibilities of the priesthood that concern the altar and what is in the Most Holy Place. These things are your responsibility, because I have given you the gift of the priesthood. Any unqualified person who comes near the sacred objects shall be put to death."

The Share of the Priests

[8]The LORD said to Aaron, "Remember that I am giving you all the special contributions made to me that are not burned as sacrifices. I am giving them to you and to your descendants as the part assigned to you forever. [9]Of the most sacred offerings not burned on the altar, the following belong to you: the grain offerings, the sin offerings, and the repayment offerings. Everything that is presented to me as a sacred offering belongs to you and your sons. [10]You must eat these things in a holy place, and only males may eat them; consider them holy.

17:8–10 Heb 9:4

11“In addition, any other special contribu-
tions that the Israelites present to me shall be
yours. I am giving them to you, your sons,
and your daughters for all time to come.
Every member of your family who is ritually
clean may eat them.
12“I am giving you all the best of the first
produce which the Israelites give me each
year: olive oil, wine, and grain. 13It all
belongs to you. Every member of your fami-
ly who is ritually clean may eat it.
14“Everything in Israel that has been
unconditionally dedicated to me belongs to
you.
15“Every first-born child or animal that
the Israelites present to me belongs to you.
But you must accept payment to buy back
every first-born child, and must also accept
payment for every first-born animal that is
ritually unclean. 16Children shall be bought
back at the age of one month for the fixed
price of five pieces of silver, according to the
official standard. 17But the first-born of
cows, sheep, and goats are not to be bought
back; they belong completely to me and are
to be sacrificed. Throw their blood against
the altar and burn their fat as a food offer-
ing, an odor pleasing to me. 18The meat
from them belongs to you, like the breast
and the right hind leg of the special offering.
19“I am giving to you, to your sons, and
to your daughters, for all time to come, all
the special contributions which the Israelites
present to me. This is an unbreakable
covenant that I have made with you and
your descendants.”
20The LORD said to Aaron, “You will not
receive any property that can be inherited,
and no part of the land of Israel will be
assigned to you. I, the LORD, am all you
need.”

The Share of the Levites

21The LORD said, “I have given to the
Levites every tithe that the people of Israel
present to me. This is in payment for their
service in taking care of the Tent of my pres-
ence. 22The other Israelites must no longer
approach the Tent and in this way bring on
themselves the penalty of death. 23From now
on only the Levites will take care of the Tent
and bear the full responsibility for it. This is
a permanent rule that applies also to your
descendants. The Levites shall have no perma-
nent property in Israel, 24because I have given
to them as their possession the tithe which
the Israelites present to me as a special contri-
bution. That is why I told them that they
would have no permanent property in Israel.”

The Levites’ Tithe

25The LORD commanded Moses 26to say
to the Levites: “When you receive from the
Israelites the tithe that the LORD gives you
as your possession, you must present a tenth
of it as a special contribution to the LORD.
27This special contribution will be consid-
ered as the equivalent of the offering which
the farmer makes of new grain and new
wine. 28In this way you also will present the
special contribution that belongs to the
LORD from all the tithes which you receive
from the Israelites. You are to give this spe-
cial contribution for the LORD to Aaron the
priest. 29Give it from the best that you
receive. 30When you have presented the best
part, you may keep the rest, just as the
farmer keeps what is left after he makes his
offering. 31You and your families may eat the
rest anywhere, because it is your wages for
your service in the Tent. 32You will not
become guilty when you eat it, as long as
you have presented the best of it to the
LORD. But be sure not to profane the sacred
gifts of the Israelites by eating any of the
gifts before the best part is offered; if you do,
you will be put to death.”

Ashes of the Red Cow

19 The LORD commanded Moses and
Aaron 2to give the Israelites the fol-
lowing regulations. Bring to Moses and
Aaron a red cow which has no defects and
which has never been worked, 3and they
will give it to Eleazar the priest. It is to be
taken outside the camp and killed in his
presence.[n] 4Then Eleazar is to take some of

[n] **19:3** It . . . presence; *or* He is to take it outside to the east of the camp and kill it.

18:14 Lev 27:28 **18:21** Lev 27:30–33; Deut 14:22–29

its blood and with his finger sprinkle it seven times in the direction of the Tent. [5]The whole animal, including skin, meat, blood, and intestines, is to be burned in the presence of the priest. [6]Then he is to take some cedar wood, a sprig of hyssop, and a red cord and throw them into the fire. [7]After that, he is to wash his clothes and pour water over himself, and then he may enter the camp; but he remains ritually unclean until evening. [8]The one who burned the cow must also wash his clothes and pour water over himself, but he also remains unclean until evening. [9]Then someone who is ritually clean is to collect the ashes of the cow and put them in a ritually clean place outside the camp, where they are to be kept for the Israelite community to use in preparing the water for removing ritual uncleanness. This ritual is performed to remove sin. [10]The one who collected the ashes must wash his clothes, but he remains unclean until evening. This regulation is valid for all time to come, both for the Israelites and for the foreigners living among them.

Contact with a Corpse

[11]Those who touch a corpse are ritually unclean for seven days. [12]They must purify themselves with the water for purification on the third day and on the seventh day, and then they will be clean. But if they do not purify themselves on both the third and the seventh day, they will not be clean. [13]Those who touch a corpse and do not purify themselves remain unclean, because the water for purification has not been thrown over them. They defile the LORD's Tent, and they will no longer be considered God's people.

[14]In the case of a person who dies in a tent, anyone who is in the tent at the time of death or who enters it becomes ritually unclean for seven days. [15]Every jar and pot in the tent that has no lid[o] on it also becomes unclean. [16]If any touch a person who has been killed or has died a natural death outdoors or if any touch a human bone or a grave, they become unclean for seven days.

[17]To remove the uncleanness, some ashes from the red cow which was burned to remove sin shall be taken and put in a pot, and fresh water added. [18]In the first case, someone who is ritually clean is to take a sprig of hyssop, dip it in the water, and sprinkle the tent, everything in it, and the people who were there. In the second case, someone who is ritually clean is to sprinkle the water on those who had touched the human bone or the dead body or the grave. [19]On the third day and on the seventh the person who is ritually clean is to sprinkle the water on the unclean persons. On the seventh day he is to purify those, who, after washing their clothes and pouring water over themselves, become ritually clean at sunset.

[20]Those who have become ritually unclean and do not purify themselves remain unclean, because the water for purification has not been thrown over them. They defile the LORD's Tent and will no longer be considered God's people. [21]You are to observe this rule for all time to come. The person who sprinkles the water for purification must also wash his clothes; anyone who touches the water remains ritually unclean until evening. [22]Whatever an unclean person touches is unclean, and anyone else who touches it remains unclean until evening.

Events at Kadesh
(Exodus 17:1–7)

20 In the first month the whole community of Israel came to the wilderness of Zin and camped at Kadesh. There Miriam died and was buried.

[2]There was no water where they camped, so the people gathered around Moses and Aaron [3]and complained: "It would have been better if we had died in front of the LORD's Tent along with the other Israelites. [4]Why have you brought us out into this wilderness? Just so that we can die here with our animals? [5]Why did you bring us out of Egypt into this miserable place where nothing will grow? There's no grain, no figs, no grapes, no

[o] **19:15** no lid; *or* no lid fastened.

19:9 Heb 9:13 **20:2–13** Ex 17:1–7

pomegranates. There is not even any water to drink!" 6 Moses and Aaron moved away from the people and stood at the entrance of the Tent. They bowed down with their faces to the ground, and the dazzling light of the LORD's presence appeared to them.

7 The LORD said to Moses, 8 "Take the stick that is in front of the Covenant Box, and then you and Aaron assemble the whole community. There in front of them all speak to that rock over there, and water will gush out of it. In this way you will bring water out of the rock for the people, for them and their animals to drink." 9 Moses went and got the stick, as the LORD had commanded.

10 He and Aaron assembled the whole community in front of the rock, and Moses said, "Listen, you rebels! Do we have to get water out of this rock for you?" 11 Then Moses raised the stick and struck the rock twice with it, and a great stream of water gushed out, and all the people and animals drank.

12 But the LORD reprimanded Moses and Aaron. He said, "Because you did not have enough faith to acknowledge my holy power before the people of Israel, you will not lead them into the land that I promised to give them."

A great stream of water gushed out. (20:11)

13 This happened at Meribah,[p] where the people of Israel complained against the LORD and where he showed them that he is holy.

The King of Edom Refuses to Let Israel Pass

14 Moses sent messengers from Kadesh to the king of Edom. They said, "This message is from your kinsmen, the tribes of Israel. You know the hardships we have suffered, 15 how our ancestors went to Egypt, where we lived many years. The Egyptians mistreated our ancestors and us, 16 and we cried to the LORD for help. He heard our cry and sent an angel, who led us out of Egypt. Now we are at Kadesh, a town at the border of your territory. 17 Please permit us to pass through your land. We and our cattle will not leave the road or go into your fields or vineyards, and we will not drink from your wells. We will stay on the main road[q] until we are out of your territory."

18 But the Edomites answered, "We refuse to let you pass through our country! If you try, we will march out and attack you."

19 The people of Israel said, "We will stay on the main road, and if we or our animals drink any of your water, we will pay for it—all we want is to pass through."

20 The Edomites repeated, "We refuse!" and they marched out with a powerful army to attack the people of Israel. 21 Because the Edomites would not let the Israelites pass through their territory, the Israelites turned and went another way.

The Death of Aaron

22 The whole community of Israel left Kadesh and arrived at Mount Hor, 23 on the border of Edom. There the LORD said to Moses and Aaron, 24 "Aaron is not going to enter the land which I promised to give to Israel; he is going to die, because the two of you rebelled against my command at Meribah. 25 Take Aaron and his son Eleazar up Mount Hor, 26 and there remove Aaron's priestly robes and put them on Eleazar. Aaron is going to die there." 27 Moses did

[p] **20:13** MERIBAH: *This name in Hebrew means "complaining."* [q] **20:17** main road; *or* King's Highway.

20:11 Wis 11:4

what the LORD had commanded. They went up Mount Hor in the sight of the whole community, [28]and Moses removed Aaron's priestly robes and put them on Eleazar. There on the top of the mountain Aaron died, and Moses and Eleazar came back down. [29]The whole community learned that Aaron had died, and they all mourned for him for thirty days.

Victory over the Canaanites

21 When the Canaanite king of Arad in the southern part of Canaan heard that the Israelites were coming by way of Atharim, he attacked them and captured some of them. [2]Then the Israelites made a vow to the LORD: "If you will let us conquer these people, we will unconditionally dedicate[r] them and their cities to you and will destroy them." [3]The LORD heard them and helped them conquer the Canaanites. So the Israelites completely destroyed them and their cities, and named the place Hormah.[s]

The Snake Made of Bronze

[4]The Israelites left Mount Hor by the road that leads to the Gulf of Aqaba, in order to go around the territory of Edom. But on the way the people lost their patience [5]and spoke against God and Moses. They complained, "Why did you bring us out of Egypt to die in this desert, where there is no food or water? We can't stand any more of this miserable food!" [6]Then the LORD sent poisonous snakes among the people, and many Israelites were bitten and died. [7]The people came to Moses and said, "We sinned when we spoke against the LORD and against you. Now pray to the LORD to take these snakes away." So Moses prayed for the people. [8]Then the LORD told Moses to make a metal snake and put it on a pole, so that anyone who was bitten could look at it and be healed. [9]So Moses made a bronze snake and put it on a pole. Anyone who had been bitten would look at the bronze snake and be healed.

From Mount Hor to the Valley of the Moabites

[10]The Israelites moved on and camped at Oboth. [11]After leaving that place, they camped at the ruins of Abarim in the wilderness east of Moabite territory. [12]Then they camped in Zered Valley. [13]From there they moved again and camped on the north side of the Arnon River, in the wilderness which extends into Amorite territory. (The Arnon was the border between the Moabites and the Amorites.) [14]That is why The Book of the LORD's Battles speaks of ". . . the town of Waheb in the area of Suphah, and the valleys; the Arnon River, [15]and the slope of the valleys that extend to the town of Ar and toward the border of Moab."

[16]From there they went on to a place called Wells, where the LORD said to Moses, "Bring the people together, and I will give them water." [17]At that time the people of Israel sang this song:

"Wells, produce your water;
And we will greet it with a song—
[18]The well dug by princes
And by leaders of the people,
Dug with a royal scepter
And with their walking sticks."

They moved from the wilderness to Mattanah, [19]and from there they went on to Nahaliel, and from Nahaliel to Bamoth, [20]and from Bamoth to the valley in the

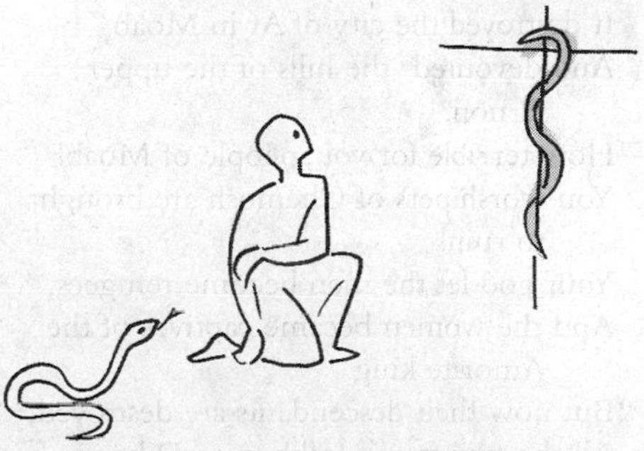

Anyone who was bitten could look at it and be healed. (21:8)

[r] **21:2** UNCONDITIONALLY DEDICATE: *Anything dedicated in this way belonged completely to the LORD and could not be used; it had to be destroyed.* [s] **21:3** HORMAH: *This name in Hebrew means "destruction."*

20:28 Ex 29:29; Num 33:38, Deut 10:6 **21:1** Num 33:40 **21:4** Deut 2:1 **21:5, 6** 1 Cor 10:9 **21:9** 2 Kings 18:4; Jn 3:14

territory of the Moabites, below the top of
Mount Pisgah, looking out over the desert.

Victory over King Sihon and King Og
(Deuteronomy 2:26—3:11)

21 Then the people of Israel sent messen-
gers to the Amorite king Sihon to say:
22 "Let us pass through your land. We and
our cattle will not leave the road and go into
your fields or vineyards, and we will not
drink water from your wells; we will stay on
the main road[t] until we are out of your ter-
ritory." 23 But Sihon would not permit the
people of Israel to pass through his territory.
He gathered his army and went out to Jahaz
in the wilderness and attacked the Israelites.
24 But the Israelites killed many of the enemy
in battle and occupied their land from the
Arnon River north to the Jabbok, that is, to
the Ammonites, because the Ammonite bor-
der was strongly defended.[u] 25 So the people
of Israel captured all the Amorite cities,
including Heshbon and all the surrounding
towns, and settled in them. 26 Heshbon was
the capital city of the Amorite king Sihon,
who had fought against the former king of
Moab and had captured all his land as far as
the Arnon River. 27 That is why the poets
sing,

"Come to Heshbon, to King Sihon's city!
We want to see it rebuilt and restored.
28 Once from this city of Heshbon
Sihon's army went forth like a fire;
It destroyed the city of Ar in Moab
And devoured[v] the hills of the upper
Arnon.
29 How terrible for you, people of Moab!
You worshipers of Chemosh are brought
to ruin!
Your god let the men become refugees,
And the women became captives of the
Amorite king.
30 But now their descendants are destroyed,
All the way from Heshbon to Dibon,
From Nashim to Nophah, near
Medeba."[w]

31 So the people of Israel settled in the ter-
ritory of the Amorites, 32 and Moses sent
men to find the best way to attack the city
of Jazer. The Israelites captured it and its sur-
rounding towns and drove out the Amorites
living there.
33 Then the Israelites turned and took the
road to Bashan, and King Og of Bashan
marched out with his army to attack them at
Edrei. 34 The LORD said to Moses, "Do not be
afraid of him. I will give you victory over
him, all his people, and his land. Do to him
what you did to Sihon, the Amorite king
who ruled at Heshbon." 35 So the Israelites
killed Og, his sons, and all his people, leaving
no survivors, and then they occupied his land.

The King of Moab Sends for Balaam

22 The Israelites moved on and set up
camp in the plains of Moab east of
the Jordan and opposite Jericho.
2 When the king of Moab, Balak son of
Zippor, heard what the Israelites had done to
the Amorites and how many Israelites there
were, 3 he and all his people became terri-
fied. 4 The Moabites said to the leaders of the
Midianites, "This horde will soon destroy
everything around us, like a bull eating the
grass in a pasture." So King Balak 5 sent mes-
sengers to summon Balaam son of Beor,
who was at Pethor near the Euphrates River
in the land of Amaw. They brought him this
message from Balak: "I want you to know
that a whole nation has come from Egypt; its
people are spreading out everywhere and
threatening to take over our land. 6 They
outnumber us, so please come and put a
curse on them for me. Then perhaps we will
be able to defeat them and drive them out
of the land. I know that when you pro-
nounce a blessing, people are blessed, and
when you pronounce a curse, they are
placed under a curse."
7 So the Moabite and Midianite leaders
took with them the payment for the curse,
went to Balaam, and gave him Balak's mes-
sage. 8 Balaam said to them, "Spend the night

[t] **21:22** main road; *or* King's Highway. [u] **21:24** because . . . strongly defended; *some ancient translations* as far as Jazer on the Ammonite border. [v] **21:28** *One ancient translation* devoured; *Hebrew* the lords of. [w] **21:30** *Verse 30 in Hebrew is unclear.*

21:28, 29 Jer 48:45, 46 **22:5** Num 31:8; 2 Pet 2:15, 16; Jude 11

here, and tomorrow I will report to you
whatever the LORD tells me." So the
Moabite leaders stayed with Balaam.
9 God came to Balaam and asked, "Who
are these people that are staying with you?"
10 He answered, "King Balak of Moab has
sent them to tell me 11 that a people who
came from Egypt has spread out over the
whole land. He wants me to curse them for
him, so that he can fight them and drive
them out."
12 God said to Balaam, "Do not go with
them, and do not put a curse on the people
of Israel, because they have my blessing."
13 The next morning Balaam went to
Balak's messengers and said, "Go back home;

HIGHLIGHTS FROM THE STORY OF BALAAM
(Numbers refer to chapter and verse in Numbers)

the LORD has refused to let me go with
you." 14So they returned to Balak and told
him that Balaam had refused to come with
them.

15Then Balak sent a larger number of
leaders, who were more important than the
first. 16They went to Balaam and gave him
this message from Balak: "Please don't let
anything prevent you from coming to me!
17I will reward you richly and do anything
you say. Please come and curse these people
for me."

18But Balaam answered, "Even if Balak
gave me all the silver and gold in his palace,
I could not disobey the command of the
LORD my God in even the smallest matter.
19But please spend the night, as the others
did, so that I may learn whether or not the
LORD has something else to tell me."

20That night God came to Balaam and
said, "If these men have come to ask you to
go with them, get ready and go, but do only
what I tell you." 21So the next morning Ba-
laam saddled his donkey and went with the
Moabite leaders.

Balaam and His Donkey

22God was angry that Balaam was going,
and as Balaam was riding along on his don-
key, accompanied by his two servants, the
angel of the LORD stood in the road to bar
his way. 23When the donkey saw the angel
standing there holding a sword, it left the
road and turned into the fields. Balaam beat
the donkey and brought it back onto the
road. 24Then the angel stood where the
road narrowed between two vineyards and
had a stone wall on each side. 25When the
donkey saw the angel, it moved over against
the wall and crushed Balaam's foot against
it. Again Balaam beat the donkey. 26Once
more the angel moved ahead; he stood in a
narrow place where there was no room at
all to pass on either side. 27This time, when
the donkey saw the angel, it lay down. Ba-
laam lost his temper and began to beat the
donkey with his stick. 28Then the LORD
gave the donkey the power of speech, and it
said to Balaam, "What have I done to you?
Why have you beaten me these three
times?"

29Balaam answered, "Because you have
made a fool of me! If I had a sword, I would
kill you."

30The donkey replied, "Am I not the same
donkey on which you have ridden all your
life? Have I ever treated you like this
before?"

"No," he answered.

31Then the LORD let Balaam see the angel
standing there with his sword; and Balaam
threw himself face downward on the
ground. 32The angel demanded, "Why have
you beaten your donkey three times like
this? I have come to bar your way, because
you should not be making this journey.[x]
33But your donkey saw me and turned aside
three times. If it hadn't, I would have killed
you and spared the donkey."

34Balaam replied, "I have sinned. I did not
know that you were standing in the road to
oppose me; but now if you think it is wrong
for me to go on, I will return home."

35But the angel said, "Go on with these
men, but say only what I tell you to say." So
Balaam went on with them.

Balak Welcomes Balaam

36When Balak heard that Balaam was
coming, he went to meet him at Ar, a city
on the Arnon River at the border of Moab.
37Balak said to him, "Why didn't you come
when I sent for you the first time? Did you
think I wasn't able to reward you enough?"

38Balaam answered, "I came, didn't I? But
now, what power do I have? I can say only
what God tells me to say." 39So Balaam went
with Balak to the town of Huzoth, 40where
Balak slaughtered cattle and sheep and gave
some of the meat to Balaam and the leaders
who were with him.

Balaam's First Prophecy

41The next morning Balak took Balaam
up to Bamoth Baal, from where Balaam
could see a part of the people of Israel.

[x] **22:32** *Probable text* you should . . . journey; *Hebrew unclear.*

23 1 He said to Balak, "Build seven altars
here for me, and bring me seven
bulls and seven rams."
2 Balak did as he was told, and he and Ba-
laam offered a bull and a ram on each altar.
3 Then Balaam said to Balak, "Stand here by
your burnt offering, while I go to see
whether or not the LORD will meet me. I
will tell you whatever he reveals to me." So
he went alone to the top of a hill, 4 and God
met him. Balaam said to him, "I have built
the seven altars and offered a bull and a ram
on each."
5 The LORD told Balaam what to say and
sent him back to Balak to give him his mes-
sage. 6 So he went back and found Balak still
standing by his burnt offering with all the
leaders of Moab.
7 Balaam uttered this prophecy:

"Balak king of Moab has brought me
From Syria, from the eastern mountains.
'Come speak for me,' he said.
'Put a curse on the people of Israel.'
8 How can I curse what God has not cursed,
Or speak of doom when the LORD has
not?
9 From the high rocks I can see them;
I can watch them from the hills.
They are a nation that lives alone;
They know they are blessed more than
other nations.
10 The descendants of Israel are like the
dust—
There are too many of them to be
counted.
Let me end my days like one of God's
people;
Let me die in peace like the righteous."

11 Then Balak said to Balaam, "What have
you done to me? I brought you here to
curse my enemies, but all you have done is
bless them."
12 He answered, "I can say only what the
LORD tells me to say."

Balaam's Second Prophecy

13 Then Balak said to Balaam, "Come with
me to another place from which you can see
only some of the Israelites. Curse them for
me from there." 14 He took him to the field
of Zophim on the top of Mount Pisgah.
There also he built seven altars and offered a
bull and a ram on each of them.
15 Balaam said to Balak, "Stand here by
your burnt offering, and I will meet God
over there."
16 The LORD met Balaam, told him what
to say, and sent him back to Balak to give
him his message. 17 So he went back and
found Balak still standing by his burnt offer-
ing, with the leaders of Moab. Balak asked
what the LORD had said, 18 and Balaam
uttered this prophecy:

"Come, Balak son of Zippor,
And listen to what I have to say.
19 God is not like people, who lie;
He is not a human who changes his
mind.
Whatever he promises, he does;
He speaks, and it is done.
20 I have been instructed to bless,
And when God blesses, I cannot call it
back.
21 I foresee that Israel's future
Will bring her no misfortune or trouble.
The LORD their God is with them;
They proclaim that he is their king.
22 God has brought them out of Egypt;
He fights for them like a wild ox.
23 There is no magic charm, no witchcraft,
That can be used against the nation of
Israel.[y]
Now people will say about Israel,
'Look what God has done!'
24 The nation of Israel is like a mighty lion:
It doesn't rest until it has torn and
devoured,
Until it has drunk the blood of those it
has killed."

25 Then Balak said to Balaam, "You refuse
to curse the people of Israel, but at least
don't bless them!"
26 Balaam answered, "Didn't I tell you that
I had to do everything that the LORD told
me?"

y 23:23 There . . . Israel; *or* No magic charms are used in Israel, no witchcraft is practiced there.

Balaam's Third Prophecy

[27]Balak said, "Come with me, and I will take you to another place. Perhaps God will be willing to let you curse them for me from there." [28]So he took Balaam to the top of Mount Peor overlooking the desert. [29]Balaam said to him, "Build seven altars for me here and bring me seven bulls and seven rams." [30]Balak did as he was told, and offered a bull and a ram on each altar.

24 By now Balaam knew that the LORD wanted him to bless the people of Israel, so he did not go to look for omens, as he had done before. He turned toward the desert [2]and saw the people of Israel camped tribe by tribe. The spirit of God took control of him, [3]and he uttered this prophecy:

"The message of Balaam son of Beor,
The words of the man who can see clearly,[z]
[4]Who can hear what God is saying.
With staring eyes I see in a trance
A vision from Almighty God.
[5]The tents of Israel are beautiful,
[6]Like long rows of palms
Or gardens beside a river,
Like aloes planted by the LORD
Or cedars beside the water.
[7]They will have abundant rainfall
And plant their seed in well-watered fields.[a]
Their king shall be greater than Agag,
And his rule shall be extended far and wide.
[8]God brought them out of Egypt;
He fights for them like a wild ox.
They devour their enemies,
Crush their bones, smash their arrows.
[9]The nation is like a mighty lion;
When it is sleeping, no one dares wake it.
Whoever blesses Israel will be blessed,
And whoever curses Israel will be cursed."

[10]Balak clenched his fists in anger and said to Balaam, "I called you to curse my enemies, but three times now you have blessed them instead. [11]Now get on home! I promised to reward you, but the LORD has kept you from getting the reward."

[12]Balaam answered, "I told the messengers you sent to me that [13]even if you gave me all the silver and gold in your palace, I could not disobey the command of the LORD by doing anything of myself. I will say only what the LORD tells me to say."

Balaam's Final Prophecies

[14]Balaam said to Balak, "Now I am going back to my own people, but before I go, I am warning you what the people of Israel will do to your people in the future." [15]Then he uttered this prophecy:

"The message of Balaam son of Beor,
The words of the man who can see clearly,[b]
[16]Who can hear what God is saying
And receive the knowledge that comes from the Most High.
With staring eyes I see in a trance
A vision from Almighty God.
[17]I look into the future,
And I see the nation of Israel.
A king, like a bright star, will arise in that nation.
Like a comet he will come from Israel.
He will strike the leaders of Moab
And beat down all the people of Seth.[c]
[18]He will conquer his enemies in Edom
And make their land his property,
While Israel continues victorious.
[19]The nation of Israel will trample them down
And wipe out the last survivors."

[20]Then in his vision Balaam saw the Amalekites and uttered this prophecy:

"Amalek was the most powerful nation of all,
But at the end it will perish forever."

[21]In his vision he saw the Kenites, and uttered this prophecy:

"The place where you live is secure,
Safe as a nest set high on a cliff,

[z] **24:3** who can see clearly; *or* whose eyes are closed. [a] **24:7** *One ancient translation* They . . . fields; *Hebrew unclear.* [b] **24:15** who can see clearly; *or* whose eyes are closed. [c] **24:17** the people of Seth; *or* who are proud and violent.

24:9 a Gen 49:9; **b** Gen 12:3

22But you Kenites will be destroyed
When Assyria takes you captive."[d]
23Balaam uttered this prophecy:
"Who are these people gathering in the
north?[e]
24Invaders will sail from Cyprus;
They will conquer Assyria and Eber,
But they, in turn, will perish forever."
25Then Balaam got ready and went back
home, and Balak went on his way.

The People of Israel at Peor

25 When the Israelites were camped at
Acacia Valley, the men began to have
sexual intercourse with the Moabite women
who were there. 2These women invited
them to sacrificial feasts, where the god of
Moab was worshiped. The Israelites ate the
food and worshiped the god 3Baal of Peor.
So the LORD was angry with them 4and said
to Moses, "Take all the leaders of Israel and,
in obedience to me, execute them in broad
daylight,[f] and then I will no longer be angry
with the people." 5Moses said to the officials,
"Each of you is to kill every man in your
tribe who has become a worshiper of Baal
of Peor."
6One of the Israelites took a Midianite
woman into his tent in the sight of Moses
and the whole community, while they were
mourning at the entrance of the Tent of the
LORD's presence. 7When Phinehas, the son
of Eleazar and grandson of Aaron the priest,
saw this, he got up and left the assembly. He
took a spear, 8followed the man and the
woman into the tent, and drove the spear
through both of them. In this way the epi-
demic that was destroying Israel was stopped,
9but it had already killed twenty-four thou-
sand people.
10The LORD said to Moses, 11"Because of
what Phinehas has done, I am no longer
angry with the people of Israel. He refused
to tolerate the worship of any god but me,
and that is why I did not destroy them in my
anger. 12So tell him that I am making a
covenant with him that is valid for all time
to come. 13He and his descendants are per-
manently established as priests, because he
did not tolerate any rivals to me and brought
about forgiveness for the people's sin."
14The name of the Israelite who was
killed with the Midianite woman was Zimri
son of Salu, the head of a family in the tribe
of Simeon. 15The woman's name was Cozbi.
Zur, her father, was chief of a group of Mid-
ianite clans.
16The LORD commanded Moses,
17"Attack the Midianites and destroy them,
18because of the evil they did to you when
they deceived you at Peor, and because of
Cozbi, who was killed at the time of the
epidemic at Peor."

The Second Census

26 After the epidemic the LORD said to
Moses and Eleazar son of Aaron,
2"Take a census by families of the whole
community of Israel, of all men twenty years
old or older who are fit for military service."
3-4Moses and Eleazar obeyed and called
together all the men of that age group. They
assembled in the plains of Moab across the
Jordan River from Jericho.
These were the Israelites who came out of
Egypt:
5The tribe of Reuben (Reuben was the
oldest son of Jacob): the clans of Hanoch,
Pallu, 6Hezron, and Carmi. 7These clans
numbered 43,730 men. 8The descendants of
Pallu were Eliab 9and his sons Nemuel,
Dathan, and Abiram. (These are the Dathan
and Abiram who were chosen by the com-
munity. They defied Moses and Aaron and
joined the followers of Korah when they
rebelled against the LORD. 10The ground
opened and swallowed them, and they died
with Korah and his followers when fire
destroyed 250 men; they became a warning
to the people. 11But the sons of Korah were
not killed.)
12The tribe of Simeon: the clans of
Nemuel, Jamin, Jachin, 13Zerah, and Shaul.
14These clans numbered 22,200 men.
15The tribe of Gad: the clans of Zephon,

[d] **24:22** *Verse 22 in Hebrew is unclear.* [e] **24:23** *Probable text* Who . . . north; *Hebrew unclear.* [f] **25:4** in broad daylight; *or* publicly.
26:1–51 Num 1:1–46

Haggi, Shuni, 16 Ozni, Eri, 17 Arod, and Areli.
18 These clans numbered 40,500 men.
19-21 The tribe of Judah: the clans of She-
lah, Perez, Zerah, Hezron, and Hamul. (Two
of Judah's sons, Er and Onan, had died in the
land of Canaan.) 22 These clans numbered
76,500 men.
23 The tribe of Issachar: the clans of Tola,
Puah, 24 Jashub, and Shimron. 25 These clans
numbered 64,300 men.
26 The tribe of Zebulun: the clans of
Sered, Elon, and Jahleel. 27 These clans num-
bered 60,500 men.
28 The tribes of Joseph, who was the father
of two sons, Manasseh and Ephraim.
29 The tribe of Manasseh. Machir son of
Manasseh was the father of Gilead, and the
following clans traced their ancestry to Gilead:
30 the clans of Iezer, Helek, 31 Asriel, Shechem,
32 Shemida, and Hepher. 33 Zelophehad son of
Hepher had no sons, but only daughters; their
names were Mahlah, Noah, Hoglah, Milcah,
and Tirzah. 34 These clans numbered 52,700
men.
35 The tribe of Ephraim: the clans of
Shuthelah, Becher, and Tahan. 36 The clan of
Eran traced its descent from Shuthelah.
37 These clans numbered 32,500 men.
These are the clans descended from
Joseph.
38 The tribe of Benjamin: the clans of
Bela, Ashbel, Ahiram, 39 Shephupham, and
Hupham. 40 The clans of Ard and Naaman
traced their descent from Bela. 41 These clans
numbered 45,600 men.
42 The tribe of Dan: the clan of Shuham,
43 which numbered 64,400 men.
44 The tribe of Asher: the clans of Imnah,
Ishvi, and Beriah. 45 The clans of Heber and
Malchiel traced their descent from Beriah.
46 Asher had a daughter named Serah.
47 These clans numbered 53,400 men.
48 The tribe of Naphtali: the clans of
Jahzeel, Guni, 49 Jezer, and Shillem. 50 These
clans numbered 45,400 men.
51 The total number of the Israelite men
was 601,730.
52 The LORD said to Moses, 53 "Divide the
land among the tribes, according to their
size. 54-56 Divide the land by drawing lots,
and give a large share to a large tribe and a
small one to a small tribe."
57 The tribe of Levi consisted of the clans
of Gershon, Kohath, and Merari. 58 Their
descendants included the subclans of Libni,
Hebron, Mahli, Mushi, and Korah. Kohath
was the father of Amram, 59 who was mar-
ried to Levi's daughter Jochebed, who was
born in Egypt. She bore Amram two sons,
Aaron and Moses, and a daughter, Miriam.
60 Aaron had four sons, Nadab, Abihu,
Eleazar, and Ithamar. 61 Nadab and Abihu
died when they offered unholy fire to the
LORD. 62 The male Levites who were one
month old or older numbered 23,000. They
were listed separately from the rest of the
Israelites, because they were not given any
property in Israel.
63 All these clans were listed by Moses and
Eleazar when they took a census of the
Israelites in the plains of Moab across the
Jordan River from Jericho. 64 There was not
even one man left among those whom
Moses and Aaron had listed in the first cen-
sus in the Sinai Desert. 65 The LORD had said
that all of them would die in the wilderness,
and except for Caleb son of Jephunneh and
Joshua son of Nun they all did.

The Daughters of Zelophehad

27 Mahlah, Noah, Hoglah, Milcah, and
Tirzah were the daughters of
Zelophehad son of Hepher, son of Gilead,
son of Machir, son of Manasseh, son of
Joseph. 2 They went and stood before Moses,
Eleazar the priest, the leaders, and the whole
community at the entrance of the Tent of
the LORD's presence and said, 3 "Our father
died in the wilderness without leaving any
sons. He was not among the followers of
Korah, who rebelled against the LORD; he
died because of his own sin. 4 Just because he
had no sons, why should our father's name
disappear from Israel? Give us property
among our father's relatives."
5 Moses presented their case to the LORD,
6 and the LORD said to him, 7 "What the
daughters of Zelophehad request is right;
give them property among their father's rela-

26:52–56 Num 34:13; Jas 14:1, 2 **26:60** Num 3:2 **26:61** Lev 10:1, 2; Num 3:4 **26:65** Num 14:26–35
27:7 Num 36:2

Take Joshua . . . a capable man. (27:18)

tives. Let his inheritance pass on to them.
8Tell the people of Israel that whenever a
man dies without leaving a son, his daughter
is to inherit his property. 9If he has no
daughter, his brothers are to inherit it. 10If he
has no brothers, his father's brothers are to
inherit it. 11If he has no brothers or uncles,
then his nearest relative is to inherit it and
hold it as his own property. The people of Israel are to observe this as a legal requirement, just as I, the LORD, have commanded you."

Joshua Is Chosen as Successor to Moses

(Deuteronomy 31:1–8)

12The LORD said to Moses, "Go up the
Abarim Mountains and look out over the
land that I am giving to the Israelites. 13After
you have seen it, you will die, as your brother Aaron did, 14because both of you rebelled
against my command in the wilderness of Zin. When the whole community complained against me at Meribah, you refused to acknowledge my holy power before them." (Meribah is the spring at Kadesh in the wilderness of Zin.)

15Moses prayed, 16"LORD God, source of
all life, appoint, I pray, a man who can lead
the people 17and can command them in battle, so that your community will not be like sheep without a shepherd."

18The LORD said to Moses, "Take Joshua
son of Nun, a capable man, and place your
hands on his head. 19Have him stand in front
of Eleazar the priest and the whole community, and there before them all proclaim him
as your successor. 20Give him some of your
own authority, so that the whole community
of Israel will obey him. 21He will depend on
Eleazar the priest, who will learn my will by
using the Urim and Thummim.[g] In this way
Eleazar will direct Joshua and the whole
community of Israel in all their affairs."
22Moses did as the LORD had commanded
him. He had Joshua stand before Eleazar the
priest and the whole community. 23As the
LORD had commanded, Moses put his hands on Joshua's head and proclaimed him as his successor.

[g] **27:21** URIM AND THUMMIM: *Two objects used by the priest to determine God's will; it is not known precisely how they were used.*

27:12–14 Deut 3:23–27; 32:48–52 **27:17** 1 Kings 22:17; Ezek 34:5; Mt 9:36; Mk 6:34 **27:18** Ex 24:13
27:21 Ex 28:30; 1 Sam 14:41; 28:6 **27:23** Deut 31:23

The Regular Offerings
(Exodus 29:38–46)

28 The LORD commanded Moses [2]to instruct the Israelites to present to God at the appointed times the required food offerings that are pleasing to him.

[3]These are the food offerings that are to be presented to the LORD: for the daily burnt offering, two one-year-old male lambs without any defects. [4]Offer the first lamb in the morning, and the second in the evening, [5]each with a grain offering of 2 pounds of flour, mixed with 2 pints of the best olive oil. [6]This is the daily offering that is completely burned, which was first offered at Mount Sinai as a food offering, an odor pleasing to the LORD. [7]As the wine offering with the first lamb, pour out at the altar 2 pints of wine. [8]In the evening offer the second lamb in the same way as the morning offering, together with its wine offering. It also is a food offering, an odor pleasing to the LORD.

The Sabbath Offering

[9]On the Sabbath day offer two one-year-old male lambs without any defects, 4 pounds of flour mixed with olive oil as a grain offering, and the wine offering. [10]This burnt offering is to be offered every Sabbath in addition to the daily offering with its wine offering.

The Offering on the First Day of the Month

[11]Present a burnt offering to the LORD at the beginning of each month: two young bulls, one ram, seven one-year-old male lambs, all without any defects. [12]As a grain offering, offer flour mixed with olive oil: with each bull, 6 pounds of flour; with the ram, 4 pounds; [13]and with each lamb, 2 pounds. These burnt offerings are food offerings, an odor pleasing to the LORD. [14]The proper wine offering is 4 pints of wine with each bull, 3 pints with the ram, and 2 pints with each lamb. This is the regulation for the burnt offering for the first day of each month throughout the year. [15]And in addition to the daily burnt offering with its wine offering, offer one male goat as a sin offering.

The Offerings at the Festival of Unleavened Bread
(Leviticus 23:5–14)

[16]The Passover Festival in honor of the LORD is to be held on the fourteenth day of the first month. [17]On the fifteenth day a religious festival begins which lasts seven days, during which only bread prepared without yeast is to be eaten. [18]On the first day of the festival you are to gather for worship, and no work is to be done. [19]Offer a burnt offering as a food offering to the LORD: two young bulls, one ram, and seven one-year-old male lambs, all without any defects. [20]Offer the proper grain offering of flour mixed with olive oil: 6 pounds with each bull, 4 pounds with the ram, [21]and 2 pounds with each lamb. [22]Also offer one male goat as a sin offering, and in this way perform the ritual of purification for the people. [23]Offer these in addition to the regular morning burnt offering. [24]In the same way, for seven days offer to the LORD a food offering, an odor pleasing to him. Offer this in addition to the daily burnt offering and wine offering. [25]Meet for worship on the seventh day and do no work.

The Offerings at the Harvest Festival
(Leviticus 23:15–22)

[26]On the first day of the Harvest Festival, when you present the offering of new grain to the LORD, you are to gather for worship, and no work is to be done. [27]Offer a burnt offering as an odor pleasing to the LORD: two young bulls, one ram, and seven one-year-old male lambs, all without any defects. [28]Offer the proper grain offering of flour mixed with olive oil: 6 pounds with each bull, 4 pounds with the ram, [29]and 2 pounds with each lamb. [30]Also offer one male goat as a sin offering, and in this way perform the ritual of purification for the people.

28:16 Ex 12:1–13; Deut 16:1, 2 **28:17–25** Ex 12:14–20; 23:15; 34:18; Deut 16:3–8 **28:26–31** Ex 23:16; 34:22; Deut 16:9–12

31 Offer these and the wine offering in addition to the daily burnt offering and grain offering.

The Offerings at the New Year Festival

(Leviticus 23:23–25)

29 On the first day of the seventh month you are to gather for worship, and no work is to be done. On that day trumpets are to be blown. 2 Present a burnt offering to the LORD, an odor pleasing to him: one young bull, one ram, and seven one-year-old male lambs, all without any defects. 3 Offer the proper grain offering of flour mixed with olive oil: 6 pounds of flour with the bull, 4 pounds with the ram, 4 and 2 pounds with each lamb. 5 Also offer one male goat as a sin offering, and in this way perform the ritual of purification for the people. 6 Offer these in addition to the regular burnt offering for the first day of the month with its grain offering, and the daily burnt offering with its grain offering and wine offering. These food offerings are an odor pleasing to the LORD.

The Offerings at the Day of Atonement

(Leviticus 23:26–32)

7 Gather for worship on the tenth day of the seventh month; eat no food and do no work. 8 Offer a burnt offering to the LORD, an odor pleasing to him: one young bull, one ram, and seven one-year-old male lambs, all without any defects. 9 Offer the proper grain offering of flour mixed with olive oil: 6 pounds of flour with the bull, 4 pounds with the ram, 10 and 2 pounds with each lamb. 11 Also offer one male goat as a sin offering, in addition to the goat offered in the ritual of purification for the people, and the daily burnt offering with its grain offering and wine offering.

The Offerings at the Festival of Shelters

(Leviticus 23:33–44)

12 Gather for worship on the fifteenth day of the seventh month. Celebrate this festival in honor of the LORD for seven days and do no work. 13 On this first day offer a food offering to the LORD, an odor pleasing to him: thirteen young bulls, two rams, and fourteen one-year-old male lambs, all without any defects. 14 Offer the proper grain offering of flour mixed with olive oil: 6 pounds of flour with each bull, 4 pounds with each ram, 15 and 2 pounds with each lamb, with the required wine offerings. 16 Also offer one male goat as a sin offering. Offer these in addition to the daily burnt offering with its grain offering and wine offering.

17 On the second day offer twelve young bulls, two rams, and fourteen one-year-old male lambs, all without any defects. 18-19 Offer with them all the other offerings required for the first day.

20 On the third day offer eleven young bulls, two rams, and fourteen one-year-old male lambs, all without any defects. 21-22 Offer with them all the other offerings required for the first day.

23 On the fourth day offer ten young bulls, two rams, and fourteen one-year-old male lambs, all without any defects. 24-25 Offer with them all the other offerings required for the first day.

26 On the fifth day offer nine young bulls, two rams, and fourteen one-year-old male lambs, all without any defects. 27-28 Offer with them all the other offerings required for the first day.

29 On the sixth day offer eight young bulls, two rams, and fourteen one-year-old male lambs, all without any defects. 30-31 Offer with them all the other offerings required for the first day.

32 On the seventh day offer seven young bulls, two rams, and fourteen one-year-old male lambs, all without any defects. 33-34 Offer with them all the other offerings required for the first day.

35 On the eighth day gather for worship

29:7–11 Lev 16:29–34 **29:12–38** Lev 23:34; Deut 16:13–15

and do no work. 36 Offer a burnt offering as
a food offering to the LORD, an odor pleas-
ing to him: one young bull, one ram, and
seven one-year-old male lambs, all without
any defects. 37-38 Offer with them all the
other offerings required for the first day.
39 These are the regulations concerning
the burnt offerings, grain offerings, wine
offerings, and fellowship offerings that you
are to make to the LORD at your appointed
festivals. These are in addition to the offer-
ings you give in fulfillment of a vow or as
freewill offerings.
40 So Moses told the people of Israel every-
thing that the LORD had commanded him.

Rules about Vows

30 Moses gave the following instruc-
tions to the leaders of the tribes of
Israel. 2 When a man makes a vow to give
something to the LORD or takes an oath to
abstain from something, he must not break
his promise, but must do everything that he
said he would.
3 When a young woman still living in her
father's house makes a vow to give some-
thing to the LORD or promises to abstain
from something, 4 she must do everything
that she vowed or promised unless her father
raises an objection when he hears about it.
5 But if her father forbids her to fulfill the
vow when he hears about it, she is not
required to keep it. The LORD will forgive
her, because her father refused to let her
keep it.
6 If an unmarried woman makes a vow,
whether deliberately or carelessly, or promis-
es to abstain from something, and then mar-
ries, 7 she must do everything that she vowed
or promised unless her husband raises an
objection when he hears about it. 8 But if her
husband forbids her to fulfill the vow when
he hears about it, she is not required to keep
it. The LORD will forgive her.
9 A widow or a divorced woman must
keep every vow she makes and every prom-
ise to abstain from something.
10 If a married woman makes a vow or
promises to abstain from something, 11 she
must do everything that she vowed or prom-
ised unless her husband raises an objection
when he hears about it. 12 But if her husband
forbids her to fulfill the vow when he hears
about it, she is not required to keep it. The
LORD will forgive her, because her husband
prevented her from keeping her vow. 13 Her
husband has the right to affirm or to annul
any vow or promise that she has made. 14 But
if, by the day after he hears of the vow, he
has raised no objection, she must do every-
thing that she has vowed or promised. He
has affirmed the vow by not objecting on
the day he heard of it. 15 But if he later
annuls the vow, he must suffer the conse-
quences for the failure to fulfill the vow.
16 These are the rules that the LORD gave
Moses concerning vows made by an unmar-
ried woman living in her father's house or
by a married woman.

The Holy War against Midian

31 The LORD said to Moses, 2 "Punish
the Midianites for what they did to
the people of Israel. After you have done
that, you will die."
3 So Moses said to the people, "Get ready
for war, so that you can attack Midian and
punish them for what they did to the LORD.
4 From each tribe of Israel send a thousand
men to war."
5 So a thousand men were chosen from
each tribe, a total of twelve thousand men
ready for battle. 6 Moses sent them to war
under the command of Phinehas son of
Eleazar the priest, who took charge of the
sacred objects and the trumpets for giving
signals. 7 They attacked Midian, as the LORD
had commanded Moses, and killed all the
men, 8 including the five kings of Midian:
Evi, Rekem, Zur, Hur, and Reba. They also
killed Balaam son of Beor.
9 The people of Israel captured the Midi-
anite women and children, took their cattle
and their flocks, plundered all their wealth,
10 and burned all their cities and camps.
11 They took all the loot that they had cap-
tured, including the prisoners and the ani-
mals, 12 and brought them to Moses and

30:2 Deut 23:21–23; Mt 5:33

Eleazar and to the community of the people of Israel, who were at the camp on the plains of Moab across the Jordan from Jericho.

The Army Returns

13 Moses, Eleazar, and all the other leaders of the community went out of the camp to meet the army. 14 Moses became angry with the officers, the commanders of battalions and companies, who had returned from the war. 15 He asked them, "Why have you kept all the women alive? 16 Remember that it was the women who followed Balaam's instructions and at Peor led the people to be unfaithful to the LORD. That was what brought the epidemic on the LORD's people. 17 So now kill every boy and kill every woman who has had sexual intercourse, 18 but keep alive for yourselves all the girls and all the women who are virgins. 19 Now all of you who have killed anyone or have touched a corpse must stay outside the camp for seven days. On the third day and on the seventh day purify yourselves and the women you have captured. 20 You must also purify every piece of clothing and everything made of leather, goats' hair, or wood."

21 Eleazar the priest said to the men who had returned from battle, "These are the regulations that the LORD has given to Moses. 22-23 Everything that will not burn, such as gold, silver, bronze, iron, tin, or lead, is to be purified by passing it through fire. Everything else is to be purified by the water for purification. 24 On the seventh day you must wash your clothes; then you will be ritually clean and will be permitted to enter the camp."

Division of the Loot

25 The LORD said to Moses, 26 "You and Eleazar, together with the other leaders of the community, are to count everything that has been captured, including the prisoners and the animals. 27 Divide what was taken into two equal parts, one part for the soldiers and the other part for the rest of the community. 28 From the part that belongs to the soldiers, withhold as a tax for the LORD one out of every five hundred prisoners and the same proportion of the cattle, donkeys, sheep, and goats. 29 Give them to Eleazar the priest as a special contribution to the LORD. 30 From the part given to the rest of the people, take one out of every fifty prisoners and the same proportion of the cattle, donkeys, sheep, and goats. Give them to the Levites who are in charge of the LORD's Tent." 31 Moses and Eleazar did what the LORD commanded.

32-35 The following is a list of what was captured by the soldiers, in addition to what they kept for themselves: 675,000 sheep and goats, 72,000 cattle, 61,000 donkeys, and 32,000 virgins. 36-40 The half share of the soldiers was 337,500 sheep and goats, of which 675 were the tax for the LORD; 36,000 cattle for the soldiers, of which 72 were the tax for the LORD; 30,500 donkeys for the soldiers, of which 61 were the tax for the LORD; and 16,000 virgins for the soldiers, of which 32 were the tax for the LORD. 41 So Moses gave Eleazar the tax as a special contribution to the LORD, as the LORD had commanded.

42-46 The share of the community was the same as that for the soldiers: 337,500 sheep and goats, 36,000 cattle, 30,500 donkeys, and 16,000 virgins. 47 From this share Moses took one out of every fifty prisoners and animals, and as the LORD had commanded, gave them to the Levites who were in charge of the LORD's Tent.

48 Then the officers who had commanded the army went to Moses 49 and reported, "Sir, we have counted the soldiers under our command and not one of them is missing. 50 So we are bringing the gold ornaments, armlets, bracelets, rings, earrings, and necklaces that each of us has taken. We offer them to the LORD as a payment for our lives, so that he will protect us." 51 Moses and Eleazar received the gold, all of which was in the form of ornaments. 52 The total contribution of the officers weighed over four hundred pounds. 53 Those who were not officers kept the loot they had taken. 54 So Moses and Eleazar took the gold to the Tent, so that the LORD would protect the people of Israel.

31:16 Num 25:1–9

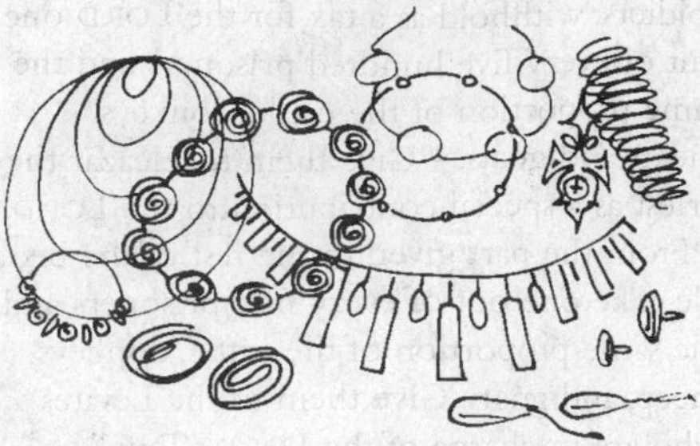

The gold ornaments. (31:50)

The Tribes East of the Jordan
(Deuteronomy 3:12–22)

32 The tribes of Reuben and Gad had
a lot of livestock. When they saw
how suitable the land of Jazer and Gilead
was for cattle, 2they went to Moses, Eleazar,
and the other leaders of the community and
said, 3-4"This region which the LORD has
helped the Israelites occupy—the towns of
Ataroth, Dibon, Jazer, Nimrah, Heshbon,
Elealeh, Sibmah, Nebo, and Beon—is good
land for livestock, and we have so much live-
stock. 5Please give us this land as our proper-
ty, and do not make us cross the Jordan
River and settle there."

6Moses replied, "Do you want to stay here
while the other Israelites go to war? 7How
dare you try to discourage the people of
Israel from crossing the Jordan into the land
which the LORD has given them? 8That is
what your fathers did when I sent them
from Kadesh Barnea to explore the land.
9They went as far as Eshcol Valley and saw
the land, but when they returned, they dis-
couraged the people from entering the land
which the LORD had given them. 10The
LORD became angry that day and made a
promise: 11'I swear that because they did not
remain loyal to me, none of the men twenty
years old or older who came out of Egypt
will enter the land that I promised to Abra-
ham, Isaac, and Jacob.' 12This included every-
one, except Caleb son of Jephunneh the
Kenizzite and Joshua son of Nun; they
remained loyal to the LORD. 13The LORD
became angry with the people and made
them wander in the wilderness forty years
until that whole generation that had dis-
pleased him was dead. 14And now you have
taken your ancestors' place, a new generation
of sinful people ready to bring down the
fierce anger of the LORD on Israel again. 15If
you people of Reuben and Gad refuse to
follow him now, he will once again abandon
all these people in the wilderness, and you
will be responsible for their destruction."

16They approached Moses and said, "First,
allow us to build stone enclosures here for
our sheep and fortified towns for our
dependents. 17Then we will be ready to go
with the other Israelites into battle and lead
the attack until we have settled them in the
land that will be theirs. In the meantime, our
dependents can live here in the fortified
towns, safe from the people of this land. 18We
will not return to our homes until all the
other Israelites have taken possession of the
land assigned to them. 19We will not take
possession of any property among them on
the other side of the Jordan, because we have
received our share here east of the Jordan."

20Moses answered, "If you really mean
what you say, then here in the presence of
the LORD get ready to go into battle. 21All
your fighting men are to cross the Jordan and
under the command of the LORD they are to
attack our enemies until the LORD defeats
them 22and takes possession of the land. After
that, you may return, because you will have
fulfilled your obligation to the LORD and to
the other Israelites. Then the LORD will
acknowledge that this land east of the Jordan
is yours. 23But if you do not keep your
promise, I warn you that you will be sinning
against the LORD. Make no mistake about it;
you will be punished for your sin. 24So build
your towns and the enclosures for your
sheep, but do what you have promised!"

25The men of Gad and Reuben said, "Sir,
we will do as you command. 26Our wives
and children and our cattle and sheep will
remain here in the towns of Gilead. 27But all
of us are ready to go into battle under the
LORD's command. We will cross the Jordan
and fight, just as you have said."

28So Moses gave these commands to
Eleazar, Joshua, and the other leaders of
Israel: 29"If the men of Gad and Reuben

32:8, 9 Num 13:17–33 **32:10–13** Num 14:26–35 **32:28–32** Josh 1:12–15 cross the Jordan ready for battle at the LORD's command and if with their help you are able to conquer the land, then give them the land of Gilead as their property. 30 But if they do not cross the Jordan and go into battle with you, they are to receive their share of the property in the land of Canaan, as you do."

31 The men of Gad and Reuben answered, "Sir, we will do as the LORD has commanded. 32 Under his command we will cross into the land of Canaan and go into battle, so that we can retain our property here east of the Jordan."

33 So Moses assigned to the tribes of Gad and Reuben and to half the tribe of Manasseh all the territory of King Sihon of the Amorites and King Og of Bashan, including the towns and the country around them. 34 The tribe of Gad rebuilt the fortified towns of Dibon, Ataroth, Aroer, 35 Atroth Shophan, Jazer, Jogbehah, 36 Beth Nimrah, and Beth Haran. 37 The tribe of Reuben rebuilt Heshbon, Elealeh, Kiriathaim, 38 Nebo, Baal Meon (this name was changed), and Sibmah. They gave new names to the towns they rebuilt.

39 The clan of Machir son of Manasseh invaded the land of Gilead, occupied it, and drove out the Amorites who were there. 40 So Moses gave Gilead to the clan of Machir, and they lived there. 41 Jair, of the tribe of Manasseh, attacked and captured some villages and named them "Villages of Jair." 42 Nobah attacked and captured Kenath and its villages, and he renamed it Nobah, after himself.

The Journey from Egypt to Moab

33 The following account gives the names of the places where the Israelites set up camp after they left Egypt in their tribes under the leadership of Moses and Aaron. 2 At the command of the LORD, Moses wrote down the name of the place each time they set up camp.

3 The people of Israel left Egypt on the fifteenth day of the first month of the year, the day after the first Passover. Under the LORD's protection they left the city of Rameses in full view of the Egyptians, 4 who were burying the first-born sons that the LORD had killed. By doing this, the LORD showed that he was more powerful than the gods of Egypt.

5 The people of Israel left Rameses and set up camp at Sukkoth. 6 Their next camp was at Etham on the edge of the desert. 7 From there they turned back to Pi Hahiroth, east of Baal Zephon, and camped near Migdol. 8 They left Pi Hahiroth and passed through the Red Sea[h] into the desert of Shur; after a three days' march they camped at Marah. 9 From there they went to Elim, where they camped, because there were twelve springs of water and seventy palm trees there.

10 They left Elim and camped near the Gulf of Suez. 11 Their next camp was in the desert of Sin. 12 Then they camped at Dophkah, 13 and after that at Alush. 14 Next was Rephidim, where there was no water for them to drink.

15-37 From Rephidim to Mount Hor they set up camp at the following places: the Sinai Desert, Kibroth Hattaavah (or "Graves of Craving"), Hazeroth, Rithmah, Rimmon Perez, Libnah, Rissah, Kehelathah, Mount Shepher, Haradah, Makheloth, Tahath, Terah, Mithkah, Hashmonah, Moseroth, Bene Jaakan, Hor Haggidgad, Jotbathah, Abronah, Eziongeber, the wilderness of Zin (that is, Kadesh), and Mount Hor, at the edge of the land of Edom.

38-39 At the command of the LORD, Aaron the priest climbed Mount Hor. At the age of 123 he died there on the first day of the fifth month of the fortieth year after the Israelites had left Egypt.

40 The king of Arad in southern Canaan heard that the Israelites were coming.

41-49 From Mount Hor to the plains of Moab the Israelites set up camp at the following places: Zalmonah, Punon, Oboth, the ruins of Abarim in the territory of Moab, Dibon Gad, Almon Diblathaim, the Abarim Mountains near Mount Nebo, and in the plains of Moab across the Jordan River from Jericho, between Beth Jeshimoth and Acacia Valley.

[h] **33:8** RED SEA: *See Word List.*

33:38 Num 20:22–28; Deut 10:6; 32:50 **33:40** Num 21:1

Instructions before Crossing the Jordan

50 There in the plains of Moab across the Jordan from Jericho the LORD gave Moses 51 the following instructions for Israel: "When you cross the Jordan into the land of Canaan, 52 you must drive out all the inhabitants of the land. Destroy all their stone and metal idols and all their places of worship. 53 Occupy the land and settle in it, because I am giving it to you. 54 Divide the land among the various tribes and clans by drawing lots, giving a large piece of property to a large clan and a small one to a small clan. 55 But if you do not drive out the inhabitants of the land, those that are left will be as troublesome as splinters in your eyes and thorns in your sides, and they will fight against you. 56 If you do not drive them out, I will destroy you, as I planned to destroy them."

The Boundaries of the Land

34 The LORD gave Moses 2 the following instructions for the people of Israel: "When you enter Canaan, the land which I am giving you, the borders of your territory will be as follows. 3 The southern border will extend from the wilderness of Zin along the border of Edom. It will begin on the east at the southern end of the Dead Sea. 4 Then it will turn southward toward Akrabbim Pass and continue on through Zin as far south as Kadesh Barnea. Then it will turn northwest to Hazar Addar and on to Azmon, 5 where it will turn toward the valley at the border of Egypt and end at the Mediterranean.

6 "The western border will be the Mediterranean Sea.

7 "The northern border will follow a line from the Mediterranean to Mount Hor 8 and from there to Hamath Pass. It will continue to Zedad 9 and to Ziphron, and will end at Hazar Enan.

10 "The eastern border will follow a line from Hazar Enan to Shepham. 11 It will then go south to Harbel, east of Ain, and on to the hills on the eastern shore of Lake Galilee, 12 then south along the Jordan River to the Dead Sea.

"These will be the four borders of your land."

13 So Moses said to the Israelites, "This is the land that you will receive by drawing lots, the land that the LORD has assigned to the nine and one-half tribes. 14 The tribes of Reuben and Gad and the eastern half of Manasseh have received their property, divided according to their families, 15 on the eastern side of the Jordan, opposite Jericho."

The Leaders Responsible for Dividing the Land

16 The LORD said to Moses, 17 "Eleazar the priest and Joshua son of Nun will divide the land for the people. 18 Take also one leader from each tribe to help them divide it."
19-28 These are the men the LORD chose:

Tribe	*Leader*
Judah	Caleb son of Jephunneh
Simeon	Shelumiel son of Ammihud
Benjamin	Elidad son of Chislon
Dan	Bukki son of Jogli
Manasseh	Hanniel son of Ephod
Ephraim	Kemuel son of Shiphtan
Zebulun	Elizaphan son of Parnach
Issachar	Paltiel son of Azzan
Asher	Ahihud son of Shelomi
Naphtali	Pedahel son of Ammihud

29 These are the men that the LORD assigned to divide the property for the people of Israel in the land of Canaan.

The Cities Assigned to the Levites

35 In the plains of Moab across the Jordan from Jericho the LORD said to Moses, 2 "Tell the Israelites that from the property they receive they must give the Levites some cities to live in and pasture land around the cities. 3 These cities will belong to the Levites, and they will live there. The pasture land will be for their cattle and all their other animals. 4 The pasture land is to extend outward from the city walls five hundred yards in each direction, 5 so that

33:54 Num 26:54–56 **34:13** Num 26:52–56 **34:13–15** Josh 14:1–5 **35:1–8** Josh 21:1–42

there is a square area measuring one thousand yards on each side, with the city in the middle. 6 You are to give the Levites six cities of refuge to which any of you can escape if you kill someone accidentally. In addition, give them forty-two other cities 7 with their pasture land, making a total of forty-eight. 8 The number of Levite cities in each tribe is to be determined according to the size of its territory."

The Cities of Refuge

(Deuteronomy 19:1–13; Joshua 20:1–9)

9 The LORD told Moses 10 to say to the people of Israel: "When you cross the Jordan River and enter the land of Canaan, 11 you are to choose cities of refuge to which any of you can escape if you kill someone accidentally. 12 There you will be safe from the dead person's relative who seeks revenge. No one accused of manslaughter is to be put to death without a public trial. 13 Choose six cities, 14 three east of the Jordan and three in the land of Canaan. 15 These will serve as cities of refuge for Israelites and for foreigners who are temporary or permanent residents. Anyone who kills someone accidentally can escape to one of them.

16-18 "If, however, any of you use a weapon of iron or stone or wood to kill someone, you are guilty of murder and are to be put to death. 19 The dead person's nearest relative has the responsibility for putting the murderer to death. When he finds you, he is to kill you.

20 "If you hate someone and kill him by pushing him down or by throwing something at him 21 or by striking him with your fist, you are guilty of murder and are to be put to death. The dead person's nearest relative has the responsibility for putting the murderer to death. When he finds you, he is to kill you.

22 "But suppose you accidentally kill someone you do not hate, whether by pushing him down or by throwing something at him. 23 Or suppose that, without looking, you throw a stone that kills someone whom you did not intend to hurt and who was not your enemy. 24 In such cases the community shall judge in your favor and not in favor of the dead person's relative who is seeking revenge. 25 You are guilty only of manslaughter, and the community is to rescue you from the dead person's relative, and they are to return you to the city of refuge to which you had escaped. You must live there until the death of the man who is then High Priest. 26 If you leave the city of refuge to which you have escaped 27 and if the dead person's relative finds you and kills you, this act of revenge is not murder. 28 Any of you guilty of manslaughter must remain in the city of refuge until the death of the High Priest, but after that you may return home. 29 These rules apply to you and your descendants wherever you may live.

30 "Those accused of murder may be found guilty and put to death only on the evidence of two or more witnesses; the evidence of one witness is not sufficient to support an accusation of murder. 31 Murderers must be put to death. They cannot escape this penalty by the payment of money. 32 If they have fled to a city of refuge, do not allow them to make a payment in order to return home before the death of the High Priest. 33 If you did this, you would defile the land where you are living. Murder defiles the land, and except by the death of the murderer there is no way to perform the ritual of purification for the land where someone has been murdered. 34 Do not defile the land where you are living, because I am the LORD and I live among the people of Israel."

The Inheritance of Married Women

36 The heads of the families in the clan of Gilead, the son of Machir and grandson of Manasseh son of Joseph, went to Moses and the other leaders. 2 They said, "The LORD commanded you to distribute the land to the people of Israel by drawing lots. He also commanded you to give the property of our relative Zelophehad to his daughters. 3 But remember, if they marry men of another tribe, their property will then belong to that tribe, and the total

35:9–28 Deut 19:2–4; Jas 20:1–9 **35:30** Deut 17:6; 19:15 **36:2** Num 27:7

allotted to us will be reduced. [4]In the Year of
Restoration, when all property that has been
sold is restored to its original owners, the
property of Zelophehad's daughters will be
permanently added to the tribe into which
they marry and will be lost to our tribe."

[5]So Moses gave the people of Israel the
following command from the LORD. He
said, "What the tribe of Manasseh says is
right, [6]and so the LORD says that the
daughters of Zelophehad are free to marry
anyone they wish but only within their
own tribe. [7]The property of every Israelite
will remain attached to his tribe. [8]Every
woman who inherits property in an
Israelite tribe must marry a man belonging
to that tribe. In this way all Israelites will
inherit the property of their ancestors, [9]and
the property will not pass from one tribe to
another. Each tribe will continue to possess
its own property."

10-11 So Mahlah, Tirzah, Hoglah, Milcah,
and Noah, the daughters of Zelophehad, did
as the LORD had commanded Moses, and
they married their cousins. [12]They married
within the clans of the tribe of Manasseh
son of Joseph, and their property remained
in their father's tribe.

13These are the rules and regulations that
the LORD gave the Israelites through Moses
in the plains of Moab across the Jordan
River from Jericho.

THE BOOK OF Deuteronomy

Has your family ever had to move to a brand new city where you didn't know anyone? If you have, you know that you can feel both scared and excited at the same time. So picture a whole nation of people about to enter a foreign country, and not sure what kind of welcome they are going to receive. This was the situation of the Israelites after their years of wandering in the desert. They were feeling both excited and afraid and needed a morale boost. Deuteronomy is made up of Moses' last words of encouragement to the Israelites before he dies and turns over the leadership to Joshua.

Before Moses gives his final blessing, he tells the people that they have to choose—life or death, blessings or curses, faithfulness to God or disobedience. Moses encourages them to choose life by loving and holding fast to God so that they and their children may live and prosper in the land that God promised.

Chap. 34

Headlines

- Obedience Has Its Rewards (4:1–14)
- Remember This One Thing (6:4–9)
- Don't Make God Angry Again! (chapter 9)
- Seven Is the Magic Number (15:1–11)
- Remember to Celebrate! (16:1–17)
- Be Sexually Pure (22:13–30)
- Moses' Final Farewell (32:45–52)

FACTOIDS

Who wrote this book? It was written by elders or scribes who summarized the first Law given to the Israelites in the desert to meet the Israelites' changing needs. *Deuteronomy* means a "second Law."

When was it written? During the Babylonian exile, while the Israelites were figuring out how to preserve their laws and beliefs.

Why was it written? Deuteronomy was written to encourage the people to have hope and to trust in their Covenant relationship with God.

What is the Jesus connection? Jesus quotes Deuteronomy 6:4–9 when asked about the greatest commandment. See Matthew 22:37–39.

Important themes

- God promises to bless those who are faithful.
- God's people are called to protect the weak, feed and clothe poor people, bring justice for widows and orphans, and welcome the stranger.

DEUTERONOMY

Introduction

1 In this book are the words that Moses spoke to the people of Israel when they were in the wilderness east of the Jordan River. They were in the Jordan Valley near Suph, between the town of Paran on one side and the towns of Tophel, Laban, Hazeroth, and Dizahab on the other. (2 It takes eleven days to travel from Mount Sinai to Kadesh Barnea by way of the hill country of Edom.) 3 On the first day of the eleventh month of the fortieth year after they had left Egypt, Moses told the people everything the LORD had commanded him to tell them. 4 This was after the LORD[a] had defeated King Sihon of the Amorites, who ruled in the town of Heshbon, and King Og of Bashan, who ruled in the towns of Ashtaroth and Edrei. 5 It was while the people were east of the Jordan in the territory of Moab that Moses began to explain God's laws and teachings.

He said, 6 "When we were at Mount Sinai, the LORD our God said to us, 'You have stayed long enough at this mountain. 7 Break camp and move on. Go to the hill country of the Amorites and to all the surrounding regions—to the Jordan Valley, to the hill country and the lowlands, to the southern region, and to the Mediterranean coast. Go to the land of Canaan and on beyond the Lebanon Mountains as far as the great Euphrates River. 8 All of this is the land which I, the LORD, promised to give to your ancestors, Abraham, Isaac, and Jacob, and to their descendants. Go and occupy it.' "

Moses Appoints Judges
(Exodus 18:13–27)

9 Moses said to the people, "While we were still at Mount Sinai, I told you, 'The responsibility for leading you is too much for me. I can't do it alone. 10 The LORD your God has made you as numerous as the stars in the sky. 11 May the LORD, the God of your ancestors, make you increase a thousand times more and make you prosperous, as he promised! 12 But how can I alone bear the heavy responsibility for settling your disputes? 13 Choose some wise, understanding, and experienced men from each tribe, and I will put them in charge of you.' 14 And you agreed that this was a good thing to do. 15 So I took the wise and experienced leaders you chose from your tribes, and I placed them in charge of you. Some were responsible for a thousand people, some for a hundred, some for fifty, and some for ten. I also appointed other officials throughout the tribes.

16 "At that time I instructed them, 'Listen to the disputes that come up among your people. Judge every dispute fairly, whether it concerns only your own people or involves foreigners who live among you. 17 Show no partiality in your decisions; judge everyone on the same basis, no matter who they are. Do not be afraid of anyone, for the decisions you make come from God. If any case is too difficult for you, bring it to me, and I will decide it.' 18 At the same time I gave you instructions for everything else you were to do.

The Spies Are Sent Out from Kadesh Barnea
(Numbers 13:1–33)

19 "We did what the LORD our God commanded us. We left Mount Sinai and went through that vast and fearful desert on the way to the hill country of the Amorites. When we reached Kadesh Barnea, 20-21 I told you, 'You have now come to the hill country of the Amorites, which the LORD our God, the God of our ancestors, is giving us. Look, there it is. Go and occupy it as he commanded. Do not hesitate or be afraid.'

22 "But you came to me and said, 'Let's send men ahead of us to spy out the land, so

[a] **1:4** the LORD; *or* Moses.

1:4 Num 21:21–35

that they can tell us the best route to take
and what kind of cities are there.’
23“That seemed like a good thing to do,
so I selected twelve men, one from each
tribe. 24They went into the hill country as
far as Eshcol Valley and explored it. 25They
brought us back some fruit they found there,
and reported that the land which the LORD
our God was giving us was very fertile.
26“But you rebelled against the command
of the LORD your God, and you would not
enter the land. 27You grumbled to one
another: ‘The LORD hates us. He brought us
out of Egypt just to hand us over to these
Amorites, so that they could kill us. 28Why
should we go there? We are afraid. The men
we sent tell us that the people there are
stronger and taller than we are, and that they
live in cities with walls that reach the sky.
They saw giants there!’
29“But I told you, ‘Don’t be afraid of
those people. 30The LORD your God will
lead you, and he will fight for you, just as
you saw him do in Egypt 31and in the
desert. You saw how he brought you safely
all the way to this place, just as a father
would carry his son.’ 32But in spite of what
I said, you still would not trust the LORD,
33even though he always went ahead of you
to find a place for you to camp. To show you
the way, he went in front of you in a pillar of
fire by night and in a pillar of cloud by day.

The LORD Punishes Israel
(Numbers 14:20–45)

34“The LORD heard your complaints and
became angry, and so he solemnly declared,
35‘Not one of you from this evil generation
will enter the fertile land that I promised to
give your ancestors. 36Only Caleb son of
Jephunneh will enter it. He has remained
faithful to me, and I will give him and his
descendants the land that he has explored.’
37Because of you the LORD also became
angry with me and said, ‘Not even you,
Moses, will enter the land. 38But strengthen
the determination of your helper, Joshua son
of Nun. He will lead Israel to occupy the
land.’
39“Then the LORD said to all of us, ‘Your
children, who are still too young to know
right from wrong, will enter the land—the
children you said would be seized by your
enemies. I will give the land to them, and
they will occupy it. 40But as for you people,
turn around and go back into the desert on
the road to the Gulf of Aqaba.’
41“You replied, ‘Moses, we have sinned
against the LORD. But now we will attack,
just as the LORD our God commanded us.’
Then each one of you got ready to fight,
thinking it would be easy to invade the hill
country.
42“But the LORD said to me, ‘Warn them
not to attack, for I will not be with them,
and their enemies will defeat them.’ 43I told
you what the LORD had said, but you paid
no attention. You rebelled against him, and in
your pride you marched into the hill coun-
try. 44Then the Amorites who lived in those
hills came out against you like a swarm of
bees. They chased you as far as Hormah and
defeated you there in the hill country of
Edom. 45So you cried out to the LORD for
help, but he would not listen to you or pay
any attention to you.

The Years in the Desert

46“So then, after we had stayed at Kadesh
2 for a long time, 1we finally turned and
went into the desert, on the road to the
Gulf of Aqaba, as the LORD had command-
ed, and we spent a long time wandering
about in the hill country of Edom.
2“Then the LORD told me 3that we had
spent enough time wandering about in those
hills and that we should go north. 4He told
me to give you the following instructions
‘You are about to go through the hill coun-
try of Edom, the territory of your distant rel-
atives, the descendants of Esau. They will be
afraid of you, 5but you must not start a war
with them, because I am not going to give
you so much as a square foot of their land. I
have given Edom to Esau’s descendants. 6You
may buy food and water from them.’
7“Remember how the LORD your God
has blessed you in everything that you have

1:26 Deut 9:23; Heb 3:16 **1:31** Acts 13:18 **1:32** Heb 3:19 **1:34, 35** Heb 3:18 **2:1** Num 21:4
2:4 Gen 36:8

done. He has taken care of you as you wan-
dered through this vast desert. He has been
with you these forty years, and you have had
everything you needed.

8“So we moved on and left the road that
goes from the towns of Elath and Eziongeber
to the Dead Sea, and we turned northeast
toward Moab. 9The LORD said to me, ‘Don’t
trouble the people of Moab, the descendants
of Lot, or start a war against them. I have
given them the city of Ar, and I am not
going to give you any of their land.’ ”

(10A mighty race of giants called the
Emim used to live in Ar. They were as tall as
the Anakim, another race of giants. 11Like
the Anakim they were also known as
Rephaim; but the Moabites called them
Emim. 12The Horites used to live in Edom,
but the descendants of Esau chased them
out, destroyed their nation, and settled there
themselves, just as the Israelites later chased
their enemies out of the land that the LORD
gave them.)

13“Then we crossed the Zered River as
the LORD told us to do. 14This was thirty-
eight years after we had left Kadesh Barnea.
All the fighting men of that generation had
died, as the LORD had said they would.
15The LORD kept on opposing them until
he had destroyed them all.

16“After they had all died, 17the LORD said
to us, 18‘Today you are to pass through the
territory of Moab by way of Ar. 19You will
then be near the land of the Ammonites, the
descendants of Lot. Don’t trouble them or
start a war against them, because I am not
going to give you any of the land that I have
given them.’ ”

(20This territory is also known as the land
of the Rephaim, the name of the people
who used to live there; the Ammonites
called them Zamzummim. 21They were as
tall as the Anakim. There were many of
them, and they were a mighty race. But the
LORD destroyed them, so that the
Ammonites took over their land and settled
there. 22The LORD had done the same thing
for the Edomites, the descendants of Esau,
who live in the hill country of Edom. He
destroyed the Horites, so that the Edomites
took over their land and settled there, where
they still live. 23The land along the Mediter-
ranean coast had been settled by people from
the island of Crete. They had destroyed the
Avvim, the original inhabitants, and had
taken over all their land as far south as the
city of Gaza.)

24“After we had passed through Moab, the
LORD told us, ‘Now, start out and cross the
Arnon River. I am placing in your power
Sihon, the Amorite king of Heshbon, along
with his land. Attack him, and begin occupy-
ing his land. 25From today on I will make
people everywhere afraid of you. Everyone
will tremble with fear at the mention of
your name.’

Israel Defeats King Sihon
(Numbers 21:21–30)

26“Then I sent messengers from the desert
of Kedemoth to King Sihon of Heshbon
with the following offer of peace: 27‘Let us
pass through your country. We will go
straight through and not leave the road.
28We will pay for the food we eat and the
water we drink. All we want to do is to pass
through your country, 29until we cross the
Jordan River into the land that the LORD
our God is giving us. The descendants of
Esau, who live in Edom, and the Moabites,
who live in Ar, allowed us to pass through
their territory.’

30“But King Sihon would not let us pass
through his country. The LORD your God
had made him stubborn and rebellious, so
that we could defeat him and take his terri-
tory, which we still occupy.

31“Then the LORD said to me, ‘Look, I
have made King Sihon and his land helpless
before you; take his land and occupy it.’
32Sihon came out with all his men to fight
us near the town of Jahaz, 33but the LORD
our God put him in our power, and we
killed him, his sons, and all his men. 34At the
same time we captured and destroyed every
town, and put everyone to death, men,
women, and children. We left no survivors.
35We took the livestock and plundered the
towns. 36The LORD our God let us capture

2:9 Gen 19:37 **2:14** Num 14:28–35 **2:19** Gen 19:38

all the towns from Aroer, on the edge of the
Arnon Valley, and the city in the middle of
that valley, all the way to Gilead. No town
had walls too strong for us. 37 But we did not
go near the territory of the Ammonites or to
the banks of the Jabbok River or to the
towns of the hill country or to any other
place where the LORD our God had com-
manded us not to go.

Israel Conquers King Og
(Numbers 21:31–35)

3 "Next, we moved north toward the
region of Bashan, and King Og came
out with all his men to fight us near the
town of Edrei. 2 But the LORD said to me,
'Don't be afraid of him. I am going to give
him, his men, and all his territory to you. Do
the same thing to him that you did to Sihon
the Amorite king who ruled in Heshbon.'

3 "So the LORD also placed King Og and
his people in our power, and we slaughtered
them all. 4 At the same time we captured all
his towns—there was not one that we did
not take. In all we captured sixty towns—the
whole region of Argob, where King Og of
Bashan ruled. 5 All these towns were fortified
with high walls, gates, and bars to lock the
gates, and there were also many villages
without walls. 6 We destroyed all the towns
and put to death all the men, women, and
children, just as we did in the towns that
belonged to King Sihon of Heshbon. 7 We
took the livestock and plundered the towns.

8 "At that time we took from those two
Amorite kings the land east of the Jordan
River, from the Arnon River to Mount Her-
mon. (9 Mount Hermon is called Sirion by
the Sidonians, and Senir by the Amorites.)
10 We took all the territory of King Og of
Bashan: the cities on the plateau, the regions
of Gilead and of Bashan, as far east as the
towns of Salecah and Edrei."

(11 King Og was the last of the Rephaim.
His coffin,[b] made of stone,[c] was six feet wide
and almost fourteen feet long, according to
standard measurements. It can still be seen in
the Ammonite city of Rabbah.)

The Tribes That Settled East of the Jordan
(Numbers 32:1–42)

12 "When we took possession of the land,
I assigned to the tribes of Reuben and Gad
the territory north of the town of Aroer
near the Arnon River and part of the hill
country of Gilead, along with its towns. 13 To
half the tribe of Manasseh I assigned the rest
of Gilead and also all of Bashan, where Og
had ruled, that is, the entire Argob region."

(Bashan was known as the land of the
Rephaim. 14 Jair, from the tribe of Manasseh,
took the entire region of Argob, that is,
Bashan, as far as the border of Geshur and
Maacah. He named the villages after himself,
and they are still known as the villages of Jair.)

15 "I assigned Gilead to the clan of Machir
of the tribe of Manasseh. 16 And to the tribes
of Reuben and Gad I assigned the territory
from Gilead to the Arnon River. The middle
of the river was their southern boundary, and
their northern boundary was the Jabbok
River, part of which formed the Ammonite
border. 17 On the west their territory extend-
ed to the Jordan River, from Lake Galilee in
the north down to the Dead Sea in the south
and to the foot of Mount Pisgah on the east.

18 "At the same time, I gave them the fol-
lowing instructions: 'The LORD our God has
given you this land east of the Jordan to occu-
py. Now arm your fighting men and send
them across the Jordan ahead of the other
tribes of Israel, to help them occupy their
land. 19 Only your wives, children, and live-
stock—I know you have a lot of livestock—
will remain behind in the towns that I have
assigned to you. 20 Help the other Israelites
until they occupy the land that the LORD is
giving them west of the Jordan and until the
LORD lets them live there in peace, as he has
already done here for you. After that, you may
return to this land that I have assigned to you.'

21 "Then I instructed Joshua: 'You have
seen all that the LORD your God did to
those two kings, Sihon and Og; and he will
do the same thing to everyone else whose
land you invade. 22 Don't be afraid of them,
for the LORD your God will fight for you.'

[b] **3:11** coffin; *or* bed. [c] **3:11** stone; *or* iron.
3:18–20 Josh 1:12–15

Moses Is Not Permitted to Enter Canaan

23 “At that time I earnestly prayed, 24 ‘Sov-
ereign LORD, I know that you have shown
me only the beginning of the great and won-
derful things you are going to do. There is no
god in heaven or on earth who can do the
mighty things that you have done! 25 Let me
cross the Jordan River, LORD, and see the
fertile land on the other side, the beautiful
hill country and the Lebanon Mountains.’

26 “But because of you people the LORD
was angry with me and would not listen.
Instead, he said, ‘That’s enough! Don’t men-
tion this again! 27 Go to the peak of Mount
Pisgah and look to the north and to the
south, to the east and to the west. Look care-
fully at what you see, because you will never
go across the Jordan. 28 Give Joshua his
instructions. Strengthen his determination,
because he will lead the people across to
occupy the land that you see.’

29 “So we remained in the valley opposite
the town of Bethpeor.”

Moses Urges Israel to Be Obedient

4 Then Moses said to the people, “Obey
all the laws that I am teaching you, and
you will live and occupy the land which
the LORD, the God of your ancestors, is
giving you. 2 Do not add anything to what I
command you, and do not take anything
away. Obey the commands of the LORD
your God that I have given you. 3 You your-
selves saw what the LORD did at Mount
Peor. He destroyed everyone who wor-
shiped Baal there, 4 but those of you who
were faithful to the LORD your God are
still alive today.

5 “I have taught you all the laws, as the
LORD my God told me to do. Obey them in
the land that you are about to invade and
occupy. 6 Obey them faithfully, and this will
show the people of other nations how wise
you are. When they hear of all these laws,
they will say, ‘What wisdom and understand-
ing this great nation has!’

7 “No other nation, no matter how great,
has a god who is so near when they need
him as the LORD our God is to us. He
answers us whenever we call for help. 8 No
other nation, no matter how great, has laws
so just as those that I have taught you today.
9 Be on your guard! Make certain that you
do not forget, as long as you live, what you
have seen with your own eyes. Tell your
children and your grandchildren 10 about the
day you stood in the presence of the LORD
your God at Mount Sinai, when he said to
me, ‘Assemble the people. I want them to
hear what I have to say, so that they will
learn to obey me as long as they live and so
that they will teach their children to do the
same.’

11 “Tell your children how you went and
stood at the foot of the mountain which was
covered with thick clouds of dark smoke and
fire blazing up to the sky. 12 Tell them how
the LORD spoke to you from the fire, how
you heard him speaking but did not see him
in any form at all. 13 He told you what you
must do to keep the covenant he made with
you—you must obey the Ten Command-
ments, which he wrote on two stone tablets.
14 The LORD told me to teach you all the
laws that you are to obey in the land that
you are about to invade and occupy.

Warning against Idolatry

15 “When the LORD spoke to you from
the fire on Mount Sinai, you did not see any
form. For your own good, then, make cer-
tain 16 that you do not sin by making for
yourselves an idol in any form at all—
whether man or woman, 17 animal or bird,
18 reptile or fish. 19 Do not be tempted to
worship and serve what you see in the sky—
the sun, the moon, and the stars. The LORD
your God has given these to all other peo-
ples for them to worship. 20 But you are the
people he rescued from Egypt, that blazing
furnace. He brought you out to make you
his own people, as you are today. 21 Because
of you the LORD your God was angry with
me and solemnly declared that I would not

3:23–27 Num 27:12–14; Deut 32:48–52 **4:2** Rev 22:18, 19 **4:3** Num 25:1–9 **4:11, 12** Ex 19:16–18; Heb 12:18, 19 **4:13** Ex 31:18; 34:28; Deut 9:10 **4:14** Ex 21:1 **4:16** Ex 20:4; Lev 26:1; Deut 5:8; 27:15 **4:17, 18a** Rom 1:23 **4:20** Ex 19:5; Deut 7:6; 14:2; 26:18; Titus 2:14; 1 Pet 2:9 **4:21** Num 20:12

cross the Jordan River to enter the fertile land which he is giving you. [22]I will die in this land and never cross the river, but you are about to go across and occupy that fertile land. [23]Be certain that you do not forget the covenant that the LORD your God made with you. Obey his command not to make yourselves any kind of idol, [24]because the LORD your God is like a flaming fire; he tolerates no rivals.

[25]"Even when you have been in the land a long time and have children and grandchildren, do not sin by making for yourselves an idol in any form at all. This is evil in the LORD's sight, and it will make him angry. [26]I call heaven and earth as witnesses against you today that, if you disobey me, you will soon disappear from the land. You will not live very long in the land across the Jordan that you are about to occupy. You will be completely destroyed. [27]The LORD will scatter you among other nations, where only a few of you will survive. [28]There you will serve gods made by human hands, gods of wood and stone, gods that cannot see or hear, eat or smell. [29]There you will look for the LORD your God, and if you search for him with all your heart, you will find him. [30]When you are in trouble and all those things happen to you, then you will finally turn to the LORD and obey him. [31]He is a merciful God. He will not abandon you or destroy you, and he will not forget the covenant that he himself made with your ancestors.

[32]"Search the past, the time before you were born, all the way back to the time when God created human beings on the earth. Search the entire earth. Has anything as great as this ever happened before? Has anyone ever heard of anything like this? [33]Have any people ever lived after hearing a god speak to them from a fire, as you have? [34]Has any god ever dared to go and take a people from another nation and make them his own, as the LORD your God did for you in Egypt? Before your very eyes he used his great power and strength; he brought plagues and war, worked miracles and wonders, and caused terrifying things to happen. [35]The LORD has shown you this, to prove to you that he alone is God and that there is no other. [36]He let you hear his voice from heaven so that he could instruct you; and here on earth he let you see his holy fire, and he spoke to you from it. [37]Because he loved your ancestors, he chose you, and by his great power he himself brought you out of Egypt. [38]As you advanced, he drove out nations greater and more powerful than you, so that he might bring you in and give you their land, the land which still belongs to you. [39]So remember today and never forget: the LORD is God in heaven and on earth. There is no other god. [40]Obey all his laws that I have given you today, and all will go well with you and your descendants. You will continue to live in the land that the LORD your God is giving you to be yours forever."

The Cities of Refuge East of the Jordan

[41]Then Moses set aside three cities east of the Jordan River [42]to which a man could escape and be safe if he had accidentally killed someone who had not been his enemy. He could escape to one of these cities and not be put to death. [43]For the tribe of Reuben there was the city of Bezer, on the desert plateau; for the tribe of Gad there was Ramoth, in the territory of Gilead; and for the tribe of Manasseh there was Golan, in the territory of Bashan.

Introduction to the Giving of God's Law

[44]Moses gave God's laws and teachings to the people of Israel. [45-46]It was after they had come out of Egypt and were in the valley east of the Jordan River, opposite the town of Bethpeor, that he gave them these laws. This was in the territory that had belonged to King Sihon of the Amorites, who had ruled in the town of Heshbon. Moses and the people of Israel defeated him when they came out of Egypt. [47]They occupied his land and the land of King Og of Bashan, the other Amorite king who lived east of the

4:24 Heb 12:29 **4:27, 28** Deut 28:36 **4:29** Jer 29:13 **4:35** Mk 12:32 **4:41–43** Josh 20:8, 9

Jordan. 48This land extended from the town
of Aroer, on the edge of the Arnon River, all
the way north to Mount Sirion,[d] that is,
Mount Hermon. 49It also included all the
region east of the Jordan River as far south
as the Dead Sea and east to the foot of
Mount Pisgah.

The Ten Commandments
(Exodus 20:1–17)

5 Moses called together all the people of
Israel and said to them, "People of Israel,
listen to all the laws that I am giving you
today. Learn them and be sure that you obey
them. 2At Mount Sinai the LORD our God
made a covenant, 3not only with our fathers,
but with all of us who are living today. 4There
on the mountain the LORD spoke to you face
to face from the fire. 5I stood between you
and the LORD at that time to tell you what he
said, because you were afraid of the fire and
would not go up the mountain.

"The LORD said, 6'I am the LORD your
God, who rescued you from Egypt, where
you were slaves.

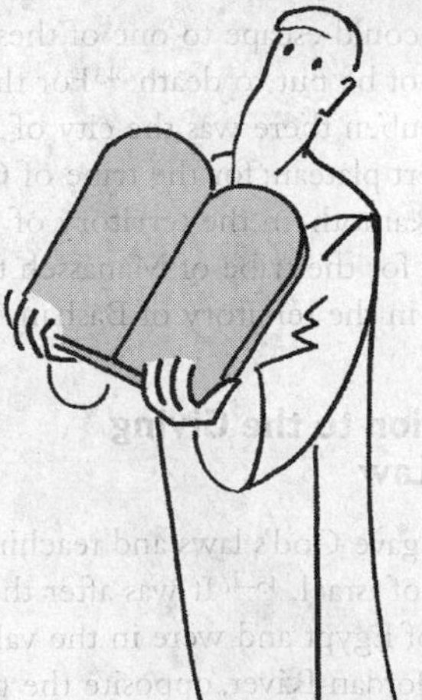

The LORD our God made a covenant. (5:2)

7" 'Worship no god but me.

8" 'Do not make for yourselves images of
anything in heaven or on earth or in the
water under the earth. 9Do not bow down
to any idol or worship it, for I am the LORD
your God and I tolerate no rivals. I bring
punishment on those who hate me and on
their descendants down to the third and
fourth generation. 10But I show my love to
thousands of generations[e] of those who love
me and obey my laws.

11" 'Do not use my name for evil purpos-
es, for I, the LORD your God, will punish
anyone who misuses my name.

12" 'Observe the Sabbath and keep it holy,
as I, the LORD your God, have commanded
you. 13You have six days in which to do
your work, 14but the seventh day is a day of
rest dedicated to me. On that day no one is
to work—neither you, your children, your
slaves, your animals, nor the foreigners who
live in your country. Your slaves must rest just
as you do. 15Remember that you were slaves
in Egypt, and that I, the LORD your God,
rescued you by my great power and strength.
That is why I command you to observe the
Sabbath.

16" 'Respect your father and your mother,
as I, the LORD your God, command you, so
that all may go well with you and so that
you may live a long time in the land that I
am giving you.

17" 'Do not commit murder.

18" 'Do not commit adultery.

19" 'Do not steal.

20" 'Do not accuse anyone falsely.

21" 'Do not desire another man's wife; do
not desire his house, his land, his slaves, his cat-
tle, his donkeys, or anything else that he owns.'

22"These are the commandments the
LORD gave to all of you when you were
gathered at the mountain. When he spoke
with a mighty voice from the fire and from
the thick clouds, he gave these command-
ments and no others. Then he wrote them
on two stone tablets and gave them to me.

[d] **4:48** *One ancient translation* Sirion; *Hebrew* Sion. [e] **5:10** thousands of generations; *or* thousands.

5:8, 9 Lev 26:1; Deut 4:15–18; 27:15 **5:9, 10** Ex 34:6, 7; Num 14:18; Deut 7:9, 10 **5:11** Lev 19:12 **5:12** Ex 16:23–30; 31:12–14 **5:13, 14** Ex 23:12; 31:15; 34:21; 35:2; Lev 23:3 **5:16** **a** Deut 27:16; Sir 3:1–16; Mt 15:4; 19:19; Mk 7:10; 10:19; Lk 18:20; Eph 6:2; **b** Eph 6:3 **5:17** Gen 9:6; Lev 24:17; Mt 5:21; 19:18; Mk 10:19; Lk 18:20; Rom 13:9; Jas 2:11 **5:18** Lev 20:10; Mt 5:27; 19:18; Mk 10:19; Lk 18:20; Rom 13:9; Jas 2:11 **5:19** Lev 19:11; Mt 19:18; Mk 10:19; Lk 18:20; Rom 13:9 **5:20** Ex 23:1; Mt 19:18; Mk 10:19; Lk 18:20 **5:21** Rom 7:7; 13:9 **5:22–27** Heb 12:18, 19

The People's Fear
(Exodus 20:18–21)

23 “When the whole mountain was on fire
and you heard the voice from the darkness,
your leaders and the chiefs of your tribes
came to me 24 and said, ‘The LORD our God
showed us his greatness and his glory when
we heard him speak from the fire! Today we
have seen that it is possible for people to
continue to live, even though God has spo-
ken to them. 25 But why should we risk
death again? That terrible fire will destroy us.
We are sure to die if we hear the LORD our
God speak again. 26 Has any human being
ever lived after hearing the living God speak
from a fire? 27 Go back, Moses, and listen to
everything that the LORD our God says.
Then return and tell us what he said to you.
We will listen and obey.’

28 “When the LORD heard this, he said to
me, ‘I have heard what these people said, and
they are right. 29 If only they would always
feel this way! If only they would always
honor me and obey all my commands, so
that everything would go well with them
and their descendants forever. 30 Go and tell
them to return to their tents. 31 But you,
Moses, stay here with me, and I will give
you all my laws and commands. Teach them
to the people, so that they will obey them in
the land that I am giving them.’

32 “People of Israel, be sure that you do
everything that the LORD your God has
commanded you. Do not disobey any of his
laws. 33 Obey them all, so that everything will
go well with you and so that you will con-
tinue to live in the land that you are going
to occupy.

The Great Commandment

6 “These are all the laws that the LORD
your God commanded me to teach
you. Obey them in the land that you are
about to enter and occupy. 2 As long as you
live, you and your descendants are to honor
the LORD your God and obey all his laws
that I am giving you, so that you may live in
that land a long time. 3 Listen to them, peo-
ple of Israel, and obey them! Then all will
go well with you, and you will become a
mighty nation and live in that rich and fer-
tile land, just as the LORD, the God of our
ancestors, has promised.

4 “Israel, remember this! The LORD—and
the LORD alone—is our God.[f] 5 Love the
LORD your God with all your heart, with all
your soul, and with all your strength. 6 Never
forget these commands that I am giving you
today. 7 Teach them to your children. Repeat
them when you are at home and when you
are away, when you are resting and when
you are working. 8 Tie them on your arms
and wear them on your foreheads as a
reminder. 9 Write them on the doorposts of
your houses and on your gates.

Write them on the doorposts. (6:9)

Warning against Disobedience

10 “Just as the LORD your God promised
your ancestors, Abraham, Isaac, and Jacob, he
will give you a land with large and prosper-
ous cities which you did not build. 11 The
houses will be full of good things which you
did not put in them, and there will be wells
that you did not dig, and vineyards and olive
orchards that you did not plant. When the
LORD brings you into this land and you
have all you want to eat, 12 make certain that
you do not forget the LORD who rescued

[f] **6:4** The LORD . . . is our God; *or* The LORD, our God, is the only God; *or* The LORD our God is one.
6:4 Mk 12:29 **6:5** Mt 22:37; Mk 12:30; Lk 10:27 **6:6–9** Deut 11:18–20 **6:10** **a** Gen 12:7; **b** Gen 26:3; **c** Gen 28:13

Study it!

How Shall You Love God?

Deuteronomy 6:4–9 is part of a prayer called the Shema. Chapter 6, verse 4 may even be the most famous verse of the Old Testament, "Israel, remember this! The LORD—and the LORD alone—is our God." The next verse also tells you how to love God: "Love the LORD your God with all your heart, with all your soul, and with all your strength." Being surrounded by people who do not believe in their God was a temptation for the Israelites. They could and often did start following the false gods of other nations. The Shema was a constant reminder to be faithful to God—heart, soul, and strength.

The passage goes on to say don't just believe this, but talk about it with your family, wear the words on your clothing, and display the words on your doorposts (6:7–9)! Even today, this happens. When they pray, Orthodox Jews wear phylacteries, which are tiny leather pouches that hold small scrolls. The scrolls have the words of Deuteronomy 6:4–9 written on them. Their homes also have a mezuzah, a small container holding such a scroll, on their doorpost.

In the Gospel of Matthew (22:34–39) Jesus was asked what the greatest commandment was. He quoted this passage from Deuteronomy as his answer.

— Deuteronomy 6:4–9

you from Egypt, where you were slaves.
13 Honor the LORD your God, worship only
him, and make your promises in his name
alone. 14 Do not worship other gods, any of
the gods of the peoples around you. 15 If you
do worship other gods, the LORD's anger
will come against you like fire and will
destroy you completely, because the LORD
your God, who is present with you, tolerates
no rivals.

16 "Do not put the LORD your God to the
test, as you did at Massah. 17 Be sure that you
obey all the laws that he has given you. 18 Do
what the LORD says is right and good, and
all will go well with you. You will be able to
take possession of the fertile land that the
LORD promised your ancestors, 19 and you
will drive out your enemies, as he promised.

20 "In times to come your children will ask
you, 'Why did the LORD our God command
us to obey all these laws?' 21 Then tell them,
'We were slaves of the king of Egypt, and the
LORD rescued us by his great power. 22 With
our own eyes we saw him work miracles and
do terrifying things to the Egyptians and to
their king and to all his officials. 23 He freed
us from Egypt to bring us here and give us
this land, as he had promised our ancestors he
would. 24 Then the LORD our God commanded
us to obey all these laws and to
honor him. If we do, he will always watch
over our nation and keep it prosperous. 25 If
we faithfully obey everything that God has
commanded us, he will be pleased with us.'[g]

The LORD's Own People
(Exodus 34:11–16)

7 "The LORD your God will bring you
into the land that you are going to
occupy, and he will drive many nations out
of it. As you advance, he will drive out seven
nations larger and more powerful than you:
the Hittites, the Girgashites, the Amorites,
the Canaanites, the Perizzites, the Hivites,
and the Jebusites. 2 When the LORD your
God places these people in your power and
you defeat them, you must put them all to
death. Do not make an alliance with them

[g] **6:25** If we faithfully . . . with us; *or* The right thing for us to do is to obey faithfully everything that God has commanded us.

6:13 Mt 4:10; Lk 4:8 **6:16** **a** Mt 4:7; Lk 4:12; **b** Ex 17:1–7 **7:1** Acts 13:19

or show them any mercy. [3]Do not marry any of them, and do not let your children marry any of them, [4]because then they would lead your children away from the LORD to worship other gods. If that happens, the LORD will be angry with you and destroy you at once. [5]So then, tear down their altars, break their sacred stone pillars in pieces, cut down their symbols of the goddess Asherah, and burn their idols. [6]Do this because you belong to the LORD your God. From all the peoples on earth he chose you to be his own special people.

[7]"The LORD did not love you and choose you because you outnumbered other peoples; you were the smallest nation on earth. [8]But the LORD loved you and wanted to keep the promise that he made to your ancestors. That is why he saved you by his great might and set you free from slavery to the king of Egypt. [9]Remember that the LORD your God is the only God and that he is faithful. He will keep his covenant and show his constant love to a thousand generations of those who love him and obey his commands, [10]but he will not hesitate to punish those who hate him. [11]Now then, obey what you have been taught; obey all the laws that I have given you today.

The Blessings of Obedience
(Deuteronomy 28:1–14)

[12]"If you listen to these commands and obey them faithfully, then the LORD your God will continue to keep his covenant with you and will show you his constant love, as he promised your ancestors. [13]He will love you and bless you, so that you will increase in number and have many children; he will bless your fields, so that you will have grain, wine, and olive oil; and he will bless you by giving you many cattle and sheep. He will give you all these blessings in the land that he promised your ancestors he would give to you. [14]No people in the world will be as richly blessed as you. None of you nor any of your livestock will be sterile. [15]The LORD will protect you from all sickness, and he will not bring on you any of the dreadful diseases that you experienced in Egypt, but he will bring them on all your enemies. [16]Destroy every nation that the LORD your God places in your power, and do not show them any mercy. Do not worship their gods, for that would be fatal.

[17]"Do not tell yourselves that these peoples outnumber you and that you cannot drive them out. [18]Do not be afraid of them; remember what the LORD your God did to the king of Egypt and to all his people. [19]Remember the terrible plagues that you saw with your own eyes, the miracles and wonders, and the great power and strength by which the LORD your God set you free. In the same way that he destroyed the Egyptians, he will destroy all these people that you now fear. [20]He will even cause panic[h] among them and will destroy those who escape and go into hiding. [21]So do not be afraid of these people. The LORD your God is with you; he is a great God and one to be feared. [22]Little by little he will drive out these nations as you advance. You will not be able to destroy them all at once, for, if you did, the number of wild animals would increase and be a threat to you. [23]The LORD will put your enemies in your power and make them panic until they are destroyed. [24]He will put their kings in your power. You will kill them, and they will be forgotten. No one will be able to stop you; you will destroy everyone. [25]Burn their idols. Do not desire the silver or gold that is on them, and do not take it for yourselves. If you do, that will be fatal, because the LORD hates idolatry. [26]Do not bring any of these idols into your homes, or the same curse will be on you that is on them. You must hate and despise these idols, because they are under the LORD's curse.

A Good Land to Be Possessed

8 "Obey faithfully all the laws that I have given you today, so that you may live, increase in number, and occupy the land that the LORD promised to your ancestors.

[h] **7:20** cause panic; *or* send hornets, *or* send plagues.

7:5 Deut 12:3 **7:6** Ex 19:5; Deut 4:20; 14:2; 26:18; Titus 2:14; 1 Pet 2:9 **7:9, 10** Ex 20:5, 6; 34:6, 7; Num 14:18; Deut 5:9, 10 **7:12–16** Deut 11:13–17

[2]Remember how the LORD your God led you on this long journey through the desert these past forty years, sending hardships to test you, so that he might know what you intended to do and whether you would obey his commands. [3]He made you go hungry, and then he gave you manna to eat, food that you and your ancestors had never eaten before. He did this to teach you that you must not depend on bread alone to sustain you, but on everything that the LORD says. [4]During these forty years your clothes have not worn out, nor have your feet swollen up. [5]Remember that the LORD your God corrects and punishes you just as parents discipline their children. [6]So then, do as the LORD has commanded you: live according to his laws and obey him. [7]The LORD your God is bringing you into a fertile land—a land that has rivers and springs, and underground streams gushing out into the valleys and hills; [8]a land that produces wheat and barley, grapes, figs, pomegranates, olives, and honey. [9]There you will never go hungry or ever be in need. Its rocks have iron in them, and from its hills you can mine copper. [10]You will have all you want to eat, and you will give thanks to the LORD your God for the fertile land that he has given you.

Warnings against Forgetting the LORD

[11]"Make certain that you do not forget the LORD your God; do not fail to obey any of his laws that I am giving you today. [12]When you have all you want to eat and have built good houses to live in [13]and when your cattle and sheep, your silver and gold, and all your other possessions have increased, [14]be sure that you do not become proud and forget the LORD your God who rescued you from Egypt, where you were slaves. [15]He led you through that vast and terrifying desert where there were poisonous snakes and scorpions. In that dry and waterless land he made water flow out of solid rock for you. [16]In the desert he gave you manna to eat, food that your ancestors had never eaten. He sent hardships on you to test you, so that in the end he could bless you with good things. [17]So then, you must never think that you have made yourselves wealthy by your own power and strength. [18]Remember that it is the LORD your God who gives you the power to become rich. He does this because he is still faithful today to the covenant that he made with your ancestors. [19]Never forget the LORD your God or turn to other gods to worship and serve them. If you do, then I warn you today that you will certainly be destroyed. [20]If you do not obey the LORD, then you will be destroyed just like those nations that he is going to destroy as you advance.

The People's Disobedience

9 "Listen, people of Israel! Today you are about to cross the Jordan River and occupy the land belonging to nations greater and more powerful than you. Their cities are large, with walls that reach the sky. [2]The people themselves are tall and strong; they are giants, and you have heard it said that no one can stand against them. [3]But now you will see for yourselves that the LORD your God will go ahead of you like a raging fire. He will defeat them as you advance, so that you will drive them out and destroy them quickly, as he promised.

[4]"After the LORD your God has driven them out for you, do not say to yourselves that he brought you in to possess this land because you deserved it. No, the LORD is going to drive these people out for you because they are wicked. [5]It is not because you are good and do what is right that the LORD is letting you take their land. He will drive them out because they are wicked and because he intends to keep the promise that he made to your ancestors, Abraham, Isaac, and Jacob. [6]You can be sure that the LORD is not giving you this fertile land because you deserve it. No, you are a stubborn people.

[7]"Never forget how you made the LORD your God angry in the desert. From the day that you left Egypt until the day you arrived here, you have rebelled against him. [8]Even at Mount Sinai you made the LORD angry—angry enough to destroy you. [9]I went up the

8:3 Mt 4:4; Lk 4:4 **8:5** Wis 11:9, 10 **8:11–16** Hos 13:5, 6 **9:9** Ex 24:18

mountain to receive the stone tablets on
which was written the covenant that the
LORD had made with you. I stayed there
forty days and nights and did not eat or
drink anything. 10Then the LORD gave me
the two stone tablets on which he had writ-
ten with his own hand what he had said to
you from the fire on the day that you were
gathered there at the mountain. 11Yes, after
those forty days and nights the LORD gave
me the two stone tablets on which he had
written the covenant.

12"Then the LORD said to me, 'Go down
the mountain at once, because your people,
whom you led out of Egypt, have become
corrupt and have done evil. They have
already turned away from what I command-
ed them to do, and they have made an idol
for themselves.'

13"The LORD also said to me, 'I know
how stubborn these people are. 14Don't try
to stop me. I intend to destroy them so that
no one will remember them any longer.
Then I will make you the father of a nation
larger and more powerful than they are.'

15"So I turned and went down the moun-
tain, carrying the two stone tablets on which
the covenant was written. Flames of fire were
coming from the mountain. 16I saw that you
had already disobeyed the command that the
LORD your God had given you, and that you
had sinned against him by making yourselves
a metal idol in the form of a bull-calf. 17So
there in front of you I threw the stone tablets
down and broke them to pieces. 18Then
once again I lay face downward in the
LORD's presence for forty days and nights and
did not eat or drink anything. I did this
because you had sinned against the LORD
and had made him angry. 19I was afraid of
the LORD's fierce anger, because he was furi-
ous enough to destroy you; but once again
the LORD listened to me. 20The LORD was
also angry enough with Aaron to kill him, so
I prayed for Aaron at the same time. 21I took
that sinful thing that you had made—that
metal bull-calf—and threw it into the fire.
Then I broke it in pieces, ground it to dust,
and threw the dust into the stream that
flowed down the mountain.

22"You also made the LORD your God
angry when you were at Taberah, Massah,
and Kibroth Hattaavah. 23And when he sent
you from Kadesh Barnea with orders to go
and take possession of the land that he was
giving you, you rebelled against him; you did
not trust him or obey him. 24Ever since I
have known you, you have rebelled against
the LORD.

25"So I lay face downward in the LORD's

9:19 Heb 12:21 **9:22 a** Num 11:3; **b** Ex 17:7; **c** Num 11:34 **9:23 a** Num 13:17; **b** Deut 1:21; **c** Num 13:31; Deut 1:26; Heb 3:16

I threw the stone tablets down and broke them to pieces. (9:17)

presence those forty days and nights, because
I knew that he was determined to destroy
you. 26And I prayed, 'Sovereign LORD, don't
destroy your own people, the people you
rescued and brought out of Egypt by your
great strength and power. 27Remember your
servants, Abraham, Isaac, and Jacob, and do
not pay any attention to the stubbornness,
wickedness, and sin of this people. 28Other-
wise, the Egyptians will say that you were
unable to take your people into the land that
you had promised them. They will say that
you took your people out into the desert to
kill them, because you hated them. 29After
all, these are the people whom you chose to
be your own and whom you brought out of
Egypt by your great power and might.'

Moses Receives the Commandments Again

(Exodus 34:1–10)

10 "Then the LORD said to me, 'Cut
two stone tablets like the first ones
and make a wooden Box to put them in.
Come up to me on the mountain, 2and I
will write on those tablets what I wrote on
the tablets that you broke, and then you are
to put them in the Box.'
3"So I made a Box of acacia wood and
cut two stone tablets like the first ones and
took them up the mountain. 4Then the
LORD wrote on those tablets the same words
that he had written the first time, the Ten
Commandments that he gave you when he
spoke from the fire on the day you were
gathered at the mountain. The LORD gave
me the tablets, 5and I turned and went down
the mountain. Then, just as the LORD had
commanded, I put them in the Box that I
had made—and they have been there ever
since."
(6The Israelites set out from the wells that
belonged to the people of Jaakan, and went
to Moserah. There Aaron died and was
buried, and his son Eleazar succeeded him as
priest. 7From there they went to Gudgodah
and then on to Jotbathah, a well-watered
place. 8At that time the LORD appointed the
men of the tribe of Levi to be in charge of
the Covenant Box, to serve him as priests,
and to pronounce blessings in his name. And
these are still their duties. 9That is why the
tribe of Levi received no land as the other
tribes did; what they received was the privi-
lege of being the LORD's priests, as the LORD
your God promised.)
10"I stayed on the mountain forty days
and nights, as I did the first time. The LORD
listened to me once more and agreed not to
destroy you. 11Then he told me to go and
lead you, so that you could take possession
of the land that he had promised to give to
your ancestors.

What God Demands

12"Now, people of Israel, listen to what
the LORD your God demands of you: Wor-
ship the LORD and do all that he commands.
Love him, serve him with all your heart,
13and obey all his laws. I am giving them to
you today for your benefit. 14To the LORD
belong even the highest heavens; the earth is
his also, and everything on it. 15But the
LORD's love for your ancestors was so strong
that he chose you instead of any other peo-
ple, and you are still his chosen people. 16So
then, from now on be obedient to the LORD
and stop being stubborn. 17The LORD your
God is supreme over all gods and over all
powers. He is great and mighty, and he is to
be obeyed. He does not show partiality, and
he does not accept bribes. 18He makes sure
that orphans and widows are treated fairly;
he loves the foreigners who live with our
people, and gives them food and clothes.
19So then, show love for those foreigners,
because you were once foreigners in Egypt.
20Have reverence for the LORD your God
and worship only him. Be faithful to him
and make your promises in his name alone.
21Praise him—he is your God, and you have
seen with your own eyes the great and
astounding things that he has done for you.
22When your ancestors went to Egypt, there
were only seventy of them. But now the
LORD your God has made you as numerous
as the stars in the sky.

10:6 Num 20:28; 33:38 **10:8** Num 3:5–8 **10:10** Ex 34:28 **10:17** 1 Tim 6:15; Rev 17:14; 19:16; Acts 10:34; Rom 2:11; Gal 2:6; Eph 6:9 **10:18** Sir 35:12–15 **10:22** **a** Gen 46:27; **b** Gen 15:5; 22:17

The Lord's Greatness

11 "Love the Lord your God and always obey all his laws. 2 Remember today what you have learned about the Lord through your experiences with him. It was you, not your children, who had these experiences. You saw the Lord's greatness, his power, his might, 3 and his miracles. You saw what he did to the king of Egypt and to his entire country. 4 You saw how the Lord completely wiped out the Egyptian army, along with their horses and chariots, by drowning them in the Red Sea[i] when they were pursuing you. 5 You know what the Lord did for you in the desert before you arrived here. 6 You recall what he did to Dathan and Abiram, the sons of Eliab of the tribe of Reuben. In the sight of everyone the earth opened up and swallowed them, along with their families, their tents, and all their servants and animals. 7 Yes, you are the ones who have seen all these great things that the Lord has done.

The Blessings of the Promised Land

8 "Obey everything that I have commanded you today. Then you will be able to cross the river and occupy the land that you are about to enter. 9 And you will live a long time in the rich and fertile land that the Lord promised to give your ancestors and their descendants. 10 The land that you are about to occupy is not like the land of Egypt, where you lived before. There, when you planted grain, you had to work hard to irrigate the fields; 11 but the land that you are about to enter is a land of mountains and valleys, a land watered by rain. 12 The Lord your God takes care of this land and watches over it throughout the year.

13 "So then, obey the commands that I have given you today; love the Lord your God and serve him with all your heart. 14 If you do, he will send rain on your land when it is needed, in the autumn and in the spring, so that there will be grain, wine, and olive oil for you, 15 and grass for your livestock. You will have all the food you want. 16 Do not let yourselves be led away from the Lord to worship and serve other gods. 17 If you do, the Lord will become angry with you. He will hold back the rain, and your ground will become too dry for crops to grow. Then you will soon die there, even though it is a good land that he is giving you.

18 "Remember these commands and cherish them. Tie them on your arms and wear them on your foreheads as a reminder. 19 Teach them to your children. Talk about them when you are at home and when you are away, when you are resting and when you are working. 20 Write them on the doorposts of your houses and on your gates. 21 Then you and your children will live a long time in the land that the Lord your God promised to give to your ancestors. You will live there as long as there is a sky above the earth.

Teach them to your children. (11:19)

22 "Obey faithfully everything that I have commanded you: Love the Lord your God, do everything he commands, and be faithful to him. 23 Then he will drive out all those nations as you advance, and you will occupy

[i] **11:4:** RED SEA: *See Word List.*

11:3 Ex 7:8—12:13 **11:4** Ex 14:28 **11:6** Num 16:31, 32 **11:13–17** Lev 26:3–5; Deut 7:12–16; 28:1–14 **11:18–20** Deut 6:6–9

the land belonging to nations greater and
more powerful than you. [24]All the ground
that you march over will be yours. Your terri-
tory will extend from the desert in the south
to the Lebanon Mountains in the north, and
from the Euphrates River in the east to the
Mediterranean Sea in the west. [25]Wherever
you go in that land, the LORD your God will
make the people fear you, as he has prom-
ised, and no one will be able to stop you.

[26]"Today I am giving you the choice
between a blessing and a curse— [27]a bless-
ing, if you obey the commands of the LORD
your God that I am giving you today; [28]but
a curse, if you disobey these commands and
turn away to worship other gods that you
have never worshiped before. [29]When the
LORD brings you into the land that you are
going to occupy, you are to proclaim the
blessing from Mount Gerizim and the curse
from Mount Ebal. ([30]These two mountains
are west of the Jordan River in the territory
of the Canaanites who live in the Jordan Val-
ley. They are toward the west, not far from
the sacred trees of Moreh near the town of
Gilgal.) [31]You are about to cross the Jordan
River and occupy the land that the LORD
your God is giving you. When you take it
and settle there, [32]be sure to obey all the
laws that I am giving you today.

The One Place for Worship

12 "Here are the laws that you are to
obey as long as you live in the land
that the LORD, the God of your ancestors, is
giving you. Listen to them! [2]In the land that
you are taking, destroy all the places where
the people worship their gods on high
mountains, on hills, and under green trees.
[3]Tear down their altars and smash their
sacred stone pillars to pieces. Burn their
symbols of the goddess Asherah and chop
down their idols, so that they will never
again be worshiped at those places.

[4]"Do not worship the LORD your God in
the way that these people worship their gods.
[5]Out of the territory of all your tribes the
LORD will choose the one place where the
people are to come into his presence and
worship him. [6]There you are to offer your
sacrifices that are to be burned and your
other sacrifices, your tithes and your offer-
ings, the gifts that you promise to the LORD,
your freewill offerings, and the first-born of
your cattle and sheep. [7]There, in the presence
of the LORD your God, who has blessed you,
you and your families will eat and enjoy the
good things that you have worked for.

[8]"When that time comes, you must not
do as you have been doing. Until now you
have all been worshiping as you please,
[9]because you have not yet entered the land
that the LORD your God is giving you,
where you can live in peace. [10]When you
cross the Jordan River, the LORD will let you
occupy the land and live there. He will keep
you safe from all your enemies, and you will
live in peace. [11]The LORD will choose a sin-
gle place where he is to be worshiped, and
there you must bring to him everything that
I have commanded: your sacrifices that are
to be burned and your other sacrifices, your
tithes and your offerings, and those special
gifts that you have promised to the LORD.
[12]Be joyful there in his presence, together
with your children, your servants, and the
Levites who live in your towns; remember
that the Levites will have no land of their
own. [13]You are not to offer your sacrifices
wherever you choose; [14]you must offer them
only in the one place that the LORD will
choose in the territory of one of your tribes.
Only there are you to offer your sacrifices
that are to be burned and do all the other
things that I have commanded you.

Tear down their altars. (12:3)

11:24, 25 Josh 1:3–5 **11:29** Deut 27:11–14; Josh 8:33–35 **12:3** Deut 7:5

15 “But you are free to kill and eat your animals wherever you live. You may eat as many as the LORD gives you. All of you, whether ritually clean or unclean, may eat them, just as you would eat the meat of deer or antelope. 16 But you must not eat their blood; you must pour it out on the ground like water. 17 Nothing that you offer to the LORD is to be eaten in the places where you live: neither the tithes of your grain, your wine, or your olive oil, nor the first-born of your cattle and sheep, the gifts that you promise to the LORD, your freewill offerings, or any other offerings. 18 You and your children, together with your servants and the Levites who live in your towns, are to eat these offerings only in the presence of the LORD your God, in the one place of worship chosen by the LORD your God. And you are to be happy there over everything that you have done. 19 Be sure, also, not to neglect the Levites, as long as you live in your land.

20 “When the LORD your God enlarges your territory, as he has promised, you may eat meat whenever you want to. 21 If the one place of worship is too far away, then, whenever you wish, you may kill any of the cattle or sheep that the LORD has given you, and you may eat the meat at home, as I have told you. 22 Anyone, ritually clean or unclean, may eat that meat, just as he would eat the meat of deer or antelope. 23 Only do not eat meat with blood still in it, for the life is in the blood, and you must not eat the life with the meat. 24 Do not use the blood for food; instead, pour it out on the ground like water. 25 If you obey this command, the LORD will be pleased, and all will go well for you and your descendants. 26 Take to the one place of worship your offerings and the gifts that you have promised the LORD. 27 Offer there the sacrifices which are to be completely burned on the LORD’s altar. Also offer those sacrifices in which you eat the meat and pour the blood out on the altar. 28 Obey faithfully everything that I have commanded you, and all will go well for you and your descendants forever, because you will be doing what is right and what pleases the LORD your God.

Warning against Idolatry

29 “The LORD your God will destroy the nations as you invade their land, and you will occupy it and settle there. 30 After the LORD destroys those nations, make sure that you don’t follow their religious practices, because that would be fatal. Don’t try to find out how they worship their gods, so that you can worship in the same way. 31 Do not worship the LORD your God in the way they worship their gods, for in the worship of their gods they do all the disgusting things that the LORD hates. They even sacrifice their children in the fires on their altars.

32 “Do everything that I have commanded you; do not add anything to it or take anything from it.

13 “Prophets or interpreters of dreams may promise a miracle or a wonder, 2 in order to lead you to worship and serve gods that you have not worshiped before. Even if what they promise comes true, 3 do not pay any attention to them. The LORD your God is using them to test you, to see if you love the LORD with all your heart. 4 Follow the LORD and honor him; obey him and keep his commands; worship him and be faithful to him. 5 But put to death any interpreters of dreams or prophets that tell you to rebel against the LORD, who rescued you from Egypt, where you were slaves. Such people are evil and are trying to lead you away from the life that the LORD has commanded you to live. They must be put to death, in order to rid yourselves of this evil.

6 “Even your brother or your son or your daughter or the wife you love or your closest friend may secretly encourage you to worship other gods, gods that you and your ancestors have never worshiped. 7 Some of them may encourage you to worship the gods of the people who live near you or the gods of those who live far away. 8 But do not let any of them persuade you; do not even listen to them. Show them no mercy or pity, and do not protect them. 9 Kill them! Be the first to stone them, and then let everyone else stone them too. 10 Stone them to death! They tried to lead you away from the LORD your God, who

12:16 Gen 9:4; Lev 7:26, 27; 17:10–14; 19:26; Deut 15:23 **12:23, 24** Lev 17:10–14 **12:32** Deut 4:2; Rev 22:18, 19

Do not even listen to them. (13:8)

rescued you from Egypt, where you were
slaves. 11Then all the people of Israel will hear
what happened; they will be afraid, and no
one will ever again do such an evil thing.
12"When you are living in the towns that
the LORD your God gives you, you may hear
13that some worthless people of your nation
have misled the people of their town to
worship gods that you have never worshiped
before. 14If you hear such a rumor, investi-
gate it thoroughly; and if it is true that this
evil thing did happen, 15then kill all the peo-
ple in that town and all their livestock too.
Destroy that town completely. 16Bring
together all the possessions of the people
who live there and pile them up in the town
square. Then burn the town and everything
in it as an offering to the LORD your God. It
must be left in ruins forever and never again
be rebuilt. 17Do not keep for yourselves any-
thing that was condemned to destruction,
and then the LORD will turn from his fierce
anger and show you mercy. He will be mer-
ciful to you and make you a numerous peo-
ple, as he promised your ancestors, 18if you
obey all his commands that I have given you
today, and do what he requires.

A Forbidden Mourning Practice

14 "You are the people of the LORD
your God. So when you mourn for
the dead, don't gash yourselves or shave the
front of your head, as other people do. 2You
belong to the LORD your God; he has cho-
sen you to be his own people from among
all the peoples who live on earth.

Clean and Unclean Animals
(Leviticus 11:1–47)

3"Do not eat anything that the LORD has
declared unclean. 4You may eat these animals:
cattle, sheep, goats, 5deer, wild sheep, wild
goats, or antelopes— 6any animals that have
divided hoofs and that also chew the cud.
7But no animals may be eaten unless they
have divided hoofs and also chew the cud.
You may not eat camels, rabbits, or rock
badgers. They must be considered unclean;
they chew the cud but do not have divided
hoofs. 8Do not eat pigs. They must be consid-
ered unclean; they have divided hoofs but do
not chew the cud. Do not eat any of these
animals or even touch their dead bodies.
9"You may eat any kind of fish that has
fins and scales, 10but anything living in the
water that does not have fins and scales may
not be eaten; it must be considered unclean.
11"You may eat any clean bird. 12-18But
these are the kinds of birds you are not to
eat: eagles, owls, hawks, falcons; buzzards, vul-
tures, crows; ostriches; seagulls, storks, herons,
pelicans, cormorants;[j] hoopoes; and bats.
19"All winged insects are unclean; do not
eat them. 20You may eat any clean insect.
21"Do not eat any animal that dies a natu-
ral death. You may let the foreigners who
live among you eat it, or you may sell it to
other foreigners. But you belong to the
LORD your God; you are his people.
"Do not cook a young sheep or goat in
its mother's milk.

The Law of the Tithe

22"Set aside a tithe—a tenth of all that
your fields produce each year. 23Then go to
the one place where the LORD your God
has chosen to be worshiped; and there in his
presence eat the tithes of your grain, wine,
and olive oil, and the first-born of your cat-

[j] **14:12–18** *The identification of some of these birds is uncertain.*

14:1 Lev 19:28; 21:5 **14:2** Ex 19:5, 6; Deut 4:20; 7:6; 26:18; Titus 2:14; 1 Pet 2:9 **14:21** Ex 23:19; 34:26 **14:22–29** Lev 27:30–33; Num 18:21

tle and sheep. Do this so that you may learn
to honor the LORD your God always. 24 If
the place of worship is too far from your
home for you to carry there the tithe of the
produce that the LORD has blessed you with,
then do this: 25 Sell your produce and take
the money with you to the one place of
worship. 26 Spend it on whatever you want—
beef, lamb, wine, beer—and there, in the
presence of the LORD your God, you and
your families are to eat and enjoy yourselves.
27 "Do not neglect the Levites who live in
your towns; they have no property of their
own. 28 At the end of every third year bring
the tithe of all your crops and store it in
your towns. 29 This food is for the Levites,
since they own no property, and for the for-
eigners, orphans, and widows who live in
your towns. They are to come and get all
they need. Do this, and the LORD your God
will bless you in everything you do.

The Seventh Year
(Leviticus 25:1–7)

15 "At the end of every seventh year
you are to cancel the debts of those
who owe you money. 2 This is how it is to be
done. Each of you who has lent money to
any Israelite is to cancel the debt; you must
not try to collect the money; the LORD him-
self has declared the debt canceled. 3 You
may collect what a foreigner owes you, but
you must not collect what any of your own
people owe you.
4 "The LORD your God will bless you in
the land that he is giving you. Not one of
your people will be poor 5 if you obey him
and carefully observe everything that I com-
mand you today. 6 The LORD will bless you,
as he has promised. You will lend money to
many nations, but you will not have to bor-
row from any; you will have control over
many nations, but no nation will have con-
trol over you.
7 "If in any of the towns in the land that
the LORD your God is giving you there are
Israelites in need, then do not be selfish and
refuse to help them. 8 Instead, be generous
and lend them as much as they need. 9 Do
not refuse to lend them something, just
because the year when debts are canceled is
near. Do not let such an evil thought enter
your mind. If you refuse to make the loan,
they will cry out to the LORD against you,
and you will be held guilty. 10 Give to them
freely and unselfishly, and the LORD will
bless you in everything you do. 11 There will
always be some Israelites who are poor and
in need, and so I command you to be gener-
ous to them.

The Treatment of Slaves
(Exodus 21:1–11)

12 "If any Israelites, male or female, sell
themselves[k] to you as slaves, you are to
release them after they have served you for
six years. When the seventh year comes, you
must let them go free. 13 When you set them
free, do not send them away empty-handed.
14 Give to them generously from what the
LORD has blessed you with—sheep, grain,
and wine. 15 Remember that you were slaves
in Egypt and the LORD your God set you
free; that is why I am now giving you this
command.

Do not send them away empty-handed. (15:13)

16 "But your slave may not want to leave;
he may love you and your family and be con-
tent to stay. 17 Then take him to the door of
your house and there pierce his ear; he will

[k] **15:12** sell themselves; *or* are sold.

15:7, 8 Lev 25:35 **15:11** Mt 26:11; Mk 14:7; Jn 12:8 **15:12–18** Lev 25:39–46

then be your slave for life. Treat your female
slave in the same way. 18 Do not be resentful
when you set slaves free; after all, they have
served you for six years at half the cost of
hired servants.[l] Do this, and the LORD your
God will bless you in all that you do.

The First-Born Cattle and Sheep

19 "Set aside for the LORD your God all
the first-born males of your cattle and sheep;
don't use any of these cattle for work and
don't shear any of these sheep. 20 Each year
you and your family are to eat them in the
LORD's presence at the one place of worship.
21 But if there is anything wrong with the
animals, if they are crippled or blind or have
any other serious defect, you must not sacri-
fice them to the LORD your God. 22 You
may eat such animals at home. All of you,
whether ritually clean or unclean, may eat
them, just as you eat deer or antelope. 23 But
do not use their blood for food; instead, you
must pour it out on the ground like water.

The Passover
(Exodus 12:1–20)

16 "Honor the LORD your God by cel-
ebrating Passover in the month of
Abib; it was on a night in that month that he
rescued you from Egypt. 2 Go to the one
place of worship and slaughter there one of
your sheep or cattle for the Passover meal to
honor the LORD your God. 3 When you eat
this meal, do not eat bread prepared with
yeast. For seven days you are to eat bread
prepared without yeast, as you did when you
had to leave Egypt in such a hurry. Eat this
bread—it will be called the bread of suffer-
ing—so that as long as you live you will
remember the day you came out of Egypt,
that place of suffering. 4 For seven days no
one in your land is to have any yeast in the
house; and the meat of the animal killed on
the evening of the first day must be eaten
that same night.
5-6 "Slaughter the Passover animals at the
one place of worship—and nowhere else in
the land that the LORD your God will give
you. Do it at sunset, the time of day when
you left Egypt. 7 Boil the meat and eat it at
the one place of worship; and the next
morning return home. 8 For the next six days
you are to eat bread prepared without yeast,
and on the seventh day assemble to worship
the LORD your God, and do no work on
that day.

The Harvest Festival
(Exodus 34:22; Leviticus 23:15–21)

9 "Count seven weeks from the time that
you begin to harvest the grain, 10 and then
celebrate the Harvest Festival, to honor the
LORD your God, by bringing him a freewill
offering in proportion to the blessing he has
given you. 11 Be joyful in the LORD's pres-
ence, together with your children, your ser-
vants, and the Levites, foreigners, orphans,
and widows who live in your towns. Do this
at the one place of worship. 12 Be sure that
you obey these commands; do not forget
that you were slaves in Egypt.

The Festival of Shelters
(Leviticus 23:33–43)

13 "After you have threshed all your grain
and pressed all your grapes, celebrate the
Festival of Shelters for seven days. 14 Enjoy it
with your children, your servants, and the
Levites, foreigners, orphans, and widows
who live in your towns. 15 Honor the LORD
your God by celebrating this festival for
seven days at the one place of worship. Be
joyful, because the LORD has blessed your
harvest and your work.
16 "All the men of your nation are to
come to worship the LORD three times a
year at the one place of worship: at Passover,
Harvest Festival, and the Festival of Shelters.
Each man is to bring a gift 17 as he is able, in
proportion to the blessings that the LORD
your God has given him.

[l] **15:18** at half . . . servants; *or* and have worked twice as hard as hired servants.

15:19 Ex 13:12 **15:23** Gen 9:4; Lev 7:26, 27; 17:10–14; 19:26; Deut 12:16, 23 **16:1–8** Ex 12:1–20; Lev 23:5–8; Num 28:16–25 **16:9–12** Lev 23:15–21; Num 28:26–31 **16:13–15** Lev 23:33–36, 39–43; Num 29:12–38

Each man is to bring a gift. (16:16)

The Administration of Justice

[18]“Appoint judges and other officials in
every town that the LORD your God gives
you. These men are to judge the people
impartially. [19]They are not to be unjust or
show partiality in their judgments; and they
are not to accept bribes, for gifts blind the
eyes even of wise and honest men, and cause
them to give wrong decisions. [20]Always be
fair and just, so that you will occupy the land
that the LORD your God is giving you and
so that you will continue to live there.

[21]“When you make an altar for the LORD
your God, do not put beside it a wooden
symbol of the goddess Asherah. [22]And do
not set up any stone pillar for idol worship;
the LORD hates them.

17 “Do not sacrifice to the LORD your
God cattle or sheep that have any
defects; the LORD hates this.

[2]“Suppose you hear that in one of your
towns some men or women have sinned
against the LORD and broken his covenant
[3]by worshiping and serving other gods or
the sun or the moon or the stars, contrary
to the LORD's command. [4]If you hear such a
report, then investigate it thoroughly. If it is
true that this evil thing has happened in
Israel, [5]then take them outside the town and
stone them to death. [6]However, they may be
put to death only if two or more witnesses
testify against them; they are not to be put
to death if there is only one witness. [7]The
witnesses are to throw the first stones, and
then the rest of the people are to stone
them; in this way you will get rid of this
evil.

[8]“It may be that some cases will be too
difficult for the local judges to decide, such
as certain cases of property rights or of bodi-
ly injury or those cases that involve a dis-
tinction between murder and manslaughter.
When this happens, go to the one place of
worship chosen by the LORD your God,
[9]and present your case to the levitical priests
and to the judge who is in office at that
time, and let them decide the case. [10]They
will give their decision, and you are to do
exactly as they tell you. [11]Accept their ver-
dict and follow their instructions in every
detail. [12]Anyone who dares to disobey either
the judge or the priest on duty is to be put
to death; in this way you will remove this
evil from Israel. [13]Then everyone will hear
of it and be afraid, and no one else will dare
to act in such a way.

Instructions concerning a King

[14]“After you have taken possession of the
land that the LORD your God is going to
give you and have settled there, then you
will decide you need a king like all the
nations around you. [15]Be sure that the man
you choose to be king is the one whom the
LORD has chosen. He must be one of your
own people; do not make a foreigner your

16:19 Ex 23:6–8; Lev 19.15 **16:21** Ex 34:13 **16:22** Lev 26:1 **17:3** Ex 22:20 **17:6** Num 35:30; Deut 19:15; Mt 18:16; 2 Cor 13:1; 1 Tim 5:19; Heb 10:28 **17:7** 1 Cor 5:13 **17:14** 1 Sam 8:5

king. 16 The king is not to have a large num-
ber of horses for his army, and he is not to
send people to Egypt to buy horses,[m]
because the LORD has said that his people
are never to return there. 17 The king is not
to have many wives, because this would
make him turn away from the LORD; and he
is not to make himself rich with silver and
gold. 18 When he becomes king, he is to have
a copy of the book of God's laws and teach-
ings made from the original copy kept by
the levitical priests. 19 He is to keep this book
near him and read from it all his life, so that
he will learn to honor the LORD and to
obey faithfully everything that is command-
ed in it. 20 This will keep him from thinking
that he is better than other Israelites and
from disobeying the LORD's commands in
any way. Then he will reign for many years,
and his descendants will rule Israel for many
generations.

The Share of the Priests

18 "The priestly tribe of Levi is not to
receive any share of land in Israel;
instead, they are to live on the offerings and
other sacrifices given to the LORD. 2 They
are to own no land, as the other tribes do;
their share is the privilege of being the
LORD's priests, as the LORD has promised.

3 "Whenever cattle or sheep are sacrificed,
the priests are to be given the shoulder, the
jaw, and the stomach. 4 They are to receive
the first share of the grain, wine, olive oil,
and wool. 5 The LORD chose from all your
tribes the tribe of Levi to serve him as
priests forever.

6 "Any Levite who wants to may come
from any town in Israel to the one place of
worship 7 and may serve there as a priest of
the LORD his God, like the other Levites
who are serving there. 8 He is to receive the
same amount of food as the other priests,
and he may keep whatever his family sends
him.[n]

Warning against Pagan Practices

9 "When you come into the land that the
LORD your God is giving you, don't follow
the disgusting practices of the nations that
are there. 10 Don't sacrifice your children in
the fires on your altars; and don't let your
people practice divination or look for omens
or use spells 11 or charms, and don't let them
consult the spirits of the dead. 12 The LORD
your God hates people who do these dis-
gusting things, and that is why he is driving
those nations out of the land as you advance.
13 Be completely faithful to the LORD."

The Promise to Send a Prophet

14 Then Moses said, "In the land you are
about to occupy, people follow the advice of
those who practice divination and look for
omens, but the LORD your God does not
allow you to do this. 15 Instead, he will send
you a prophet like me from among your
own people, and you are to obey him.[o]

16 "On the day that you were gathered at
Mount Sinai, you begged not to hear the
LORD speak again or to see his fiery pres-
ence any more, because you were afraid you
would die. 17 So the LORD said to me, 'They
have made a wise request. 18 I will send them
a prophet like you from among their own
people; I will tell him what to say, and he[p]
will tell the people everything I command.
19 He will speak in my name, and I[q] will
punish anyone who refuses to obey him.
20 But if any prophet dares to speak a mes-
sage in my name when I did not command
him to do so, he must die for it, and so must
any prophet who speaks in the name of
other gods.'

21 "You may wonder how you can tell
when a prophet's message does not come
from the LORD. 22 If a prophet speaks in the
name of the LORD and what he says does
not come true, then it is not the LORD's
message. That prophet has spoken on his
own authority, and you are not to fear him.

[m] **17:16** to buy horses; *or* in exchange for horses. [n] **18:8** *Probable text* and he may keep . . . sends him; *Hebrew unclear.* [o] **18:15** a prophet . . . him; *or* prophets . . . them. [p] **18:18** a prophet . . . him . . . he; *or* prophets . . . them . . . they. [q] **18:19** He will speak . . . and I; *or* When a prophet speaks in my name, I.

17:16 1 Kings 10:28; 2 Chr 1:16; 9:28 **17:17 a** 1 Kings 11:1–8; **b** 1 Kings 10:14–22, 27; 2 Chr 1:15; 9:27 **18:2** Num 18:20 **18:10 a** Lev 19:26; **b** Ex 22:18 **18:11** Lev 19:31 **18:13** Mt 5:48 **18:15** Acts 3:22; 7:37 **18:19** Acts 3:23

The Cities of Refuge
(Numbers 35:9–34; Joshua 20:1–9)

19 "After the LORD your God has
destroyed the people whose land he
is giving you and after you have taken their
cities and houses and settled there, 2-3divide
the territory into three parts, each with a
city that can be easily reached. Then any of
you that kill will be able to escape to one of
them for protection. 4If you accidentally kill
someone who is not your enemy, you may
escape to any of these cities and be safe. 5For
example, if two of you go into the forest
together to cut wood and if, as one of you is
chopping down a tree, the ax head comes off
the handle and kills the other, you can run
to one of those three cities and be safe. 6If
there were only one city, the distance to it
might be too great, and the relative who is
responsible for taking revenge for the killing
might catch you and angrily kill an innocent
person. After all, it was by accident that you
killed someone who was not your enemy.
7This is why I order you to set aside three
cities.
8"When the LORD your God enlarges
your territory, as he told your ancestors he
would, and gives you all the land he has
promised, 9then you are to select three more
cities. (He will give you this land if you do
everything that I command you today and if
you love the LORD your God and live
according to his teachings.) 10Do this, so that
innocent people will not die and so that you
will not be guilty of putting them to death
in the land that the LORD is giving you.
11"But suppose you deliberately murder
your enemy in cold blood and then escape to
one of those cities for protection. 12In that
case, the leaders of your own town are to send
for you and hand you over to the relative
responsible for taking revenge for the murder,
so that you may be put to death. 13No mercy
will be shown to you. Israel must rid itself of
murderers, so that all will go well.

Ancient Property Lines

14"Do not move your neighbor's property
line, established long ago in the land that the
LORD your God is giving you.

Concerning Witnesses

15"One witness is not enough to convict
someone of a crime; at least two witnesses
are necessary to prove that someone is guilty.
16If any of you try to harm another by false
accusations, 17both of you are to go to the
one place of worship and be judged by the
priests and judges who are then in office.
18The judges will investigate the case thor-
oughly; and if you have made a false accusa-
tion, 19you are to receive the punishment the
accused would have received. In this way
your nation will get rid of this evil. 20Then
everyone else will hear what happened; they
will be afraid, and no one will ever again do
such an evil thing. 21In such cases show no

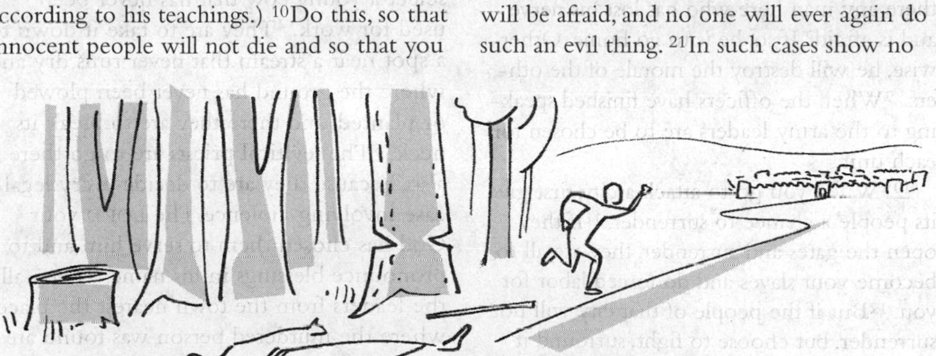

It was by accident that you killed someone. (19:6)

19:1–13 Josh 20:1–9 **19:14** Deut 27:17 **19:15** Num 35:30; Deut 17:6; Mt 18:16; Jn 8:17; 2 Cor 13:1; 1 Tim 5:19; Heb 10:28 **19:21** Ex 21:23–25; Lev 24:19, 20; Mt 5:38

mercy; the punishment is to be a life for a
life, an eye for an eye, a tooth for a tooth,
a hand for a hand, and a foot for a foot.

Concerning War

20 "When you go out to fight against
your enemies and you see chariots
and horses and an army that outnumbers
yours, do not be afraid of them. The LORD
your God, who rescued you from Egypt, will
be with you. 2Before you start fighting, a
priest is to come forward and say to the
army, 3'Men of Israel, listen! Today you are
going into battle. Do not be afraid of your
enemies or lose courage or panic. 4The
LORD your God is going with you, and he
will give you victory.'
5"Then the officers will address the men
and say, 'Is there any man here who has just
built a house, but has not yet dedicated it? If
so, he is to go home. Otherwise, if he is
killed in battle, someone else will dedicate
his house. 6Is there any man here who has
just planted a vineyard, but has not yet had
the chance to harvest its grapes? If so, he is
to go home. Otherwise, if he is killed in bat-
tle, someone else will enjoy the wine. 7Is
there anyone here who is engaged to be
married? If so, he is to go home. Otherwise,
if he is killed in battle, someone else will
marry the woman he is engaged to.'
8"The officers will also say to the men, 'Is
there any man here who has lost his nerve
and is afraid? If so, he is to go home. Other-
wise, he will destroy the morale of the oth-
ers.' 9When the officers have finished speak-
ing to the army, leaders are to be chosen for
each unit.
10"When you go to attack a city, first give
its people a chance to surrender. 11If they
open the gates and surrender, they are all to
become your slaves and do forced labor for
you. 12But if the people of that city will not
surrender, but choose to fight, surround it
with your army. 13Then, when the LORD
your God lets you capture the city, kill every
man in it. 14You may, however, take for
yourselves the women, the children, the live-
stock, and everything else in the city. You
may use everything that belongs to your
enemies. The LORD has given it to you.
15That is how you are to deal with those
cities that are far away from the land you
will settle in.
16"But when you capture cities in the
land that the LORD your God is giving you,
kill everyone. 17Completely destroy all the
people: the Hittites, the Amorites, the
Canaanites, the Perizzites, the Hivites, and
the Jebusites, as the LORD ordered you to do.
18Kill them, so that they will not make you
sin against the LORD by teaching you to do
all the disgusting things that they do in the
worship of their gods.
19"When you are trying to capture a city,
do not cut down its fruit trees, even though
the siege lasts a long time. Eat the fruit, but
do not destroy the trees; the trees are not
your enemies. 20You may cut down the
other trees and use them in the siege
mounds until the city is captured.

Concerning Unsolved Murders

21 "Suppose someone is found mur-
dered in a field in the land that the
LORD your God is going to give you, and
you do not know who killed him. 2Your
leaders and judges are to go out and mea-
sure the distance from the place where the
body was found to each of the nearby
towns. 3Then the leaders of the town near-
est to where the body was found are to
select a young cow that has never been
used for work. 4They are to take it down to
a spot near a stream that never runs dry and
where the ground has never been plowed
or planted, and there they are to break its
neck. 5The levitical priests are to go there
also, because they are to decide every legal
case involving violence. The LORD your
God has chosen them to serve him and to
pronounce blessings in his name. 6Then all
the leaders from the town nearest the place
where the murdered person was found are
to wash their hands over the cow 7and say,
'We did not murder this one, and we do
not know who did it. 8LORD, forgive your
people Israel, whom you rescued from
Egypt. Forgive us and do not hold us
responsible for the murder of an innocent
person.' 9And so, by doing what the LORD

requires, you will not be held responsible for the murder.

Concerning Women Prisoners of War

10“When the LORD your God gives you victory in battle and you take prisoners, 11you may see among them a beautiful woman that you like and want to marry. 12Take her to your home, where she will shave her head,[r] cut her fingernails, 13and change her clothes. She is to stay in your home and mourn for her parents for a month; after that, you may marry her. 14Later, if you no longer want her, you are to let her go free. Since you forced her to have intercourse with you, you cannot treat her as a slave and sell her.

Concerning the First Son's Inheritance

15“Suppose a man has two wives and they both bear him sons, but the first son is not the child of his favorite wife. 16When the man decides how he is going to divide his property among his children, he is not to show partiality to the son of his favorite wife by giving him the share that belongs to the first-born son. 17He is to give a double share of his possessions to his first son, even though he is not the son of his favorite wife. A man must acknowledge his first son and give him the share he is legally entitled to.

Concerning a Disobedient Son

18“Suppose someone has a son who is stubborn and rebellious, a son who will not obey his parents, even though they punish him. 19His parents are to take him before the leaders of the town where he lives and make him stand trial. 20They are to say to them, ‘Our son is stubborn and rebellious and refuses to obey us; he wastes money and is a drunkard.’ 21Then the men of the city are to stone him to death, and so you will get rid of this evil. Everyone in Israel will hear what has happened and be afraid.

Various Laws

22“If someone has been put to death for a crime and the body is hung on a post, 23it is not to remain there overnight. It must be buried the same day, because a dead body hanging on a post brings God's curse on the land. Bury the body, so that you will not defile the land that the LORD your God is giving you.

22 “If you see an Israelite's cow or sheep running loose, do not ignore it; take it back. 2But if its owner lives a long way off or if you don't know who owns it, then take it home with you. When its owner comes looking for it, give it to him. 3Do the same thing if you find a donkey, a piece of clothing, or anything else that an Israelite may have lost.

When its owner comes . . . give it to him. (22:2)

4“If an Israelite's donkey or cow has fallen down, don't ignore it; help him get the animal to its feet again.

If an Israelite's donkey . . . has fallen down (22:4)

[r] **21:12** shave her head; *or* trim her hair.

21:23 Gal 3:13 **22:1–4** Ex 23:4, 5

5 “Women are not to wear men’s clothing,
and men are not to wear women’s clothing;
the LORD your God hates people who do
such things.

6 “If you happen to find a bird’s nest in a
tree or on the ground with the mother bird
sitting either on the eggs or with her young,
you are not to take the mother bird. 7 You
may take the young birds, but you must let
the mother bird go, so that you will live a
long and prosperous life.

8 “When you build a new house, be sure
to put a railing around the edge of the roof.
Then you will not be responsible if someone
falls off and is killed.

9 “Do not plant any crop in the same field
with your grapevines; if you do, you are for-
bidden to use either the grapes or the pro-
duce of the other crop.

10 “Do not hitch an ox and a donkey
together for plowing.

11 “Do not wear cloth made by weaving
wool and linen together.

12 “Sew tassels on the four corners of your
clothes.

Laws concerning Sexual Purity

13 “Suppose a man marries a young
woman and later he decides he doesn’t want
her. 14 So he makes up false charges against
her, accusing her of not being a virgin when
they got married.

15 “If this happens, the young woman’s
parents are to take the blood-stained wed-
ding sheet that proves she was a virgin, and
they are to show it in court to the town
leaders. 16 Her father will say to them, ‘I gave
my daughter to this man in marriage, and
now he doesn’t want her. 17 He has made
false charges against her, saying that she was
not a virgin when he married her. But here
is the proof that my daughter was a virgin;
look at the bloodstains on the wedding
sheet!’ 18 Then the town leaders are to take
the husband and beat him. 19 They are also to
fine him a hundred pieces of silver and give
the money to the young woman’s father,
because the man has brought disgrace on an
Israelite woman. Moreover, she will continue
to be his wife, and he can never divorce her
as long as he lives.

20 “But if the charge is true and there is no
proof that she was a virgin, 21 then they are
to take her out to the entrance of her
father’s house, where the men of her city are
to stone her to death. She has done a shame-
ful thing among our people by having inter-
course before she was married, while she
was still living in her father’s house. In this
way you will get rid of this evil.

22 “If a man is caught having intercourse
with another man’s wife, both of them are to
be put to death. In this way you will get rid
of this evil.

23 “Suppose a man is caught in a town
having intercourse with a young woman
who is engaged to someone else. 24 You are
to take them outside the town and stone
them to death. She is to die because she did
not cry out for help, although she was in a
town, where she could have been heard. And
the man is to die because he had intercourse
with someone who was engaged. In this way
you will get rid of this evil.

25 “Suppose a man out in the countryside
rapes a young woman who is engaged to
someone else. Then only the man is to be
put to death; 26 nothing is to be done to the
woman, because she has not committed a
sin worthy of death. This case is the same as
when one man attacks another man and
murders him. 27 The man raped the engaged
woman in the countryside, and although she
cried for help, there was no one to help her.

28 “Suppose a man is caught raping a young
woman who is not engaged. 29 He is to pay
her father the bride price of fifty pieces of sil-
ver, and she is to become his wife, because he
forced her to have intercourse with him. He
can never divorce her as long as he lives.

30 “No man is to disgrace his father by hav-
ing intercourse with any of his father’s wives.

Exclusion from the LORD’s People

23 “No man who has been castrated or
whose penis has been cut off may be
included among the LORD’s people.

2 “No one born out of wedlock or any

22:9–11 Lev 19:19 **22:12** Num 15:37–41 **22:28, 29** Ex 22:16, 17 **22:30** Lev 18:8; 20:11; Deut 27:20

descendant of such a person, even in the tenth generation, may be included among the LORD's people.

3"No Ammonite or Moabite—or any of their descendants, even in the tenth generation—may be included among the LORD's people. 4They refused to provide you with food and water when you were on your way out of Egypt, and they hired Balaam son of Beor, from the city of Pethor in Mesopotamia, to curse you. 5But the LORD your God would not listen to Balaam; instead he turned the curse into a blessing, because he loved you. 6As long as you are a nation, never do anything to help these nations or to make them prosperous.

7"Do not despise the Edomites; they are your relatives. And do not despise the Egyptians; you once lived in their land. 8From the third generation onward their descendants may be included among the LORD's people.

Keeping the Military Camp Clean

9"When you are in camp in time of war, you are to avoid anything that would make you ritually unclean. 10If a man becomes unclean because he has had a wet dream during the night, he is to go outside the camp and stay there. 11Toward evening he is to wash himself, and at sunset he may come back into camp.

12"You are to have a place outside the camp where you can go when you need to relieve yourselves. 13Carry a stick as part of your equipment, so that when you have a bowel movement you can dig a hole and cover it up. 14Keep your camp ritually clean, because the LORD your God is with you in your camp to protect you and to give you victory over your enemies. Do not do anything indecent that would cause the LORD to turn his back on you.

Various Laws

15"If slaves run away from their owners and come to you for protection, do not send them back. 16They may live in any of your towns that they choose, and you are not to treat them harshly.

17"No Israelite, man or woman, is to become a temple prostitute. 18Also, no money earned in this way may be brought into the house of the LORD your God in fulfillment of a vow. The LORD hates temple prostitutes.

19"When you lend money or food or anything else to Israelites, do not charge them interest. 20You may charge interest on what you lend to foreigners, but not on what you lend to Israelites. Obey this rule, and the LORD your God will bless everything you do in the land that you are going to occupy.

21"When you make a vow to the LORD your God, do not put off doing what you promised; the LORD will hold you to your vow, and it is a sin not to keep it. 22It is no sin not to make a vow to the LORD, 23but if you make one voluntarily, be sure that you keep it.

24"When you walk along a path in someone else's vineyard, you may eat all the grapes you want, but you must not carry any away in a container. 25When you walk along a path in someone else's grainfield, you may eat all the

You may eat all the grapes you want. (23:24)

But you must not carry any away in a container. (23:24)

23:3–5 Neh 13:1, 2 **23:4** Num 22:1–6 **23:5** Num 23:7—24:9 **23:17** Lev 19:29 **23:19, 20** Ex 22:25; Lev 25:36, 37; Deut 15:7–11 **23:21** Num 30:1–16; Mt 5:33

grain you can pull off with your hands, but
you must not cut any grain with a sickle.

Divorce and Remarriage

24 "Suppose a man marries a woman
and later decides that he doesn't want
her, because he finds something about her
that he doesn't like.[s] So he writes out divorce
papers, gives them to her, and sends her away
from his home. 2Then suppose she marries
another man, 3and he also decides that he
doesn't want her, so he also writes out
divorce papers, gives them to her, and sends
her away from his home. Or suppose her sec-
ond husband dies. 4In either case, her first
husband is not to marry her again; he is to
consider her defiled. If he married her again,
it would be offensive to the LORD. You are
not to commit such a terrible sin in the land
that the LORD your God is giving you.

Various Laws

5"When a man is newly married, he is
not to be drafted into military service or any
other public duty; he is to be excused from
duty for one year, so that he can stay at
home and make his wife happy.[t]

6"When you lend someone something,
you are not to take as security his millstones
used for grinding his grain. This would take
away the family's means of preparing food to
stay alive.

7"If any of you kidnap Israelites and make
them your slaves or sell them into slavery,
you are to be put to death. In this way your
nation will get rid of this evil.

8"When you are suffering from a dreaded
skin disease, be sure to do exactly what the
levitical priests tell you; follow the instruc-
tions that I have given them. 9Remember
what the LORD your God did to Miriam as
you were coming from Egypt.

10"When you lend someone something,
do not go into his house to get the garment
he is going to give you as security; 11wait
outside and let him bring it to you himself.
12If he is poor, do not keep it overnight;
13return it to him each evening, so that he
can have it to sleep in. Then he will be
grateful, and the LORD your God will be
pleased with you.

14"Do not cheat poor and needy hired
servants, whether they are Israelites or for-
eigners living in one of your towns. 15Each
day before sunset pay them for that day's
work; they need the money and have count-
ed on getting it. If you do not pay them,
they will cry out against you to the LORD,
and you will be guilty of sin.

16"Parents are not to be put to death for
crimes committed by their children, and
children are not to be put to death for
crimes committed by their parents; people
are to be put to death only for a crime they
themselves have committed.

17"Do not deprive foreigners and orphans
of their rights; and do not take a widow's
garment as security for a loan. 18Remember
that you were slaves in Egypt and that the
LORD your God set you free; that is why I
have given you this command.

19"When you gather your crops and fail to
bring in some of the grain that you have cut,
do not go back for it; it is to be left for the
foreigners, orphans, and widows, so that the
LORD your God will bless you in everything
you do. 20When you have picked your olives
once, do not go back and get those that are
left; they are for the foreigners, orphans, and
widows. 21When you have gathered your
grapes once, do not go back over the vines a
second time; the grapes that are left are for
the foreigners, orphans, and widows. 22Never
forget that you were slaves in Egypt; that is
why I have given you this command.

25 "Suppose two Israelites go to court
to settle a dispute, and one is
declared innocent and the other guilty. 2If
the guilty one is sentenced to be beaten, the
judge is to make him lie face downward and
have him whipped. The number of lashes
will depend on the crime he has committed.

[s] **24:1** something . . . like; *or* that she is guilty of some shameful conduct. [t] **24:5** make his wife happy; *or* be happy with his wife.

24:1 Mt 5:31; 19:7; Mk 10:4 **24:7** Ex 21:16 **24:8** Lev 13:1—14:54 **24:9** Num 12:10 **24:10–13** Ex 22:26, 27 **24:14, 15** Lev 19:13 **24:16** 2 Kings 14:6; 2 Chr 25:4; Ezek 18:20 **24:17, 18** Ex 23:9; Lev 19:33, 34; Deut 27:19 **24:19–21** Lev 19:9, 10; 23:22

3He may be given as many as forty lashes,
but no more; more than that would humili-
ate him publicly.
4"Do not muzzle an ox when you are
using it to thresh grain.

Duty to a Dead Brother

5"If two brothers live on the same property
and one of them dies, leaving no son, then his
widow is not to be married to someone out-
side the family; it is the duty of the dead man's
brother to marry her. 6The first son that they
have will be considered the son of the dead
man, so that his family line will continue in
Israel. 7But if the dead man's brother does not
want to marry her, she is to go before the
town leaders and say, 'My husband's brother
will not do his duty; he refuses to give his
brother a descendant among the people of
Israel.' 8Then the town leaders are to summon
him and speak to him. If he still refuses to
marry her, 9his brother's widow is to go up to
him in the presence of the town leaders, take
off one of his sandals, spit in his face, and say,
'This is what happens to the man who refuses
to give his brother a descendant.' 10His family
will be known in Israel as 'the family of the
man who had his sandal pulled off.'

Other Laws

11"If two men are having a fight and the
wife of one tries to help her husband by
grabbing hold of the other man's genitals,
12show her no mercy; cut off her hand.
13-14"Do not cheat when you use weights
and measures. 15Use true and honest weights
and measures, so that you may live a long
time in the land that the LORD your God is
giving you. 16The LORD hates people who
cheat.

The Command to Kill the Amalekites

17"Remember what the Amalekites did to
you as you were coming from Egypt. 18They
had no fear of God, and so they attacked you
from the rear when you were tired and
exhausted, and killed all who were straggling
behind. 19So then, when the LORD your
God has given you the land and made you
safe from all your enemies who live around
you, be sure to kill all the Amalekites, so that
no one will remember them any longer. Do
not forget!

Harvest Offerings

26 "After you have occupied the land
that the LORD your God is giving
you and have settled there, 2each of you
must place in a basket the first part of each
crop that you harvest and you must take it
with you to the one place of worship. 3Go
to the priest in charge at that time and say to
him, 'I now acknowledge to the LORD my
God that I have entered the land that he
promised our ancestors to give us.'
4"The priest will take the basket from you
and place it before the altar of the LORD
your God. 5Then, in the LORD's presence
you will recite these words: 'My ancestor was
a wandering Aramean, who took his family
to Egypt to live. They were few in number
when they went there, but they became a
large and powerful nation. 6The Egyptians
treated us harshly and forced us to work as
slaves. 7Then we cried out for help to the
LORD, the God of our ancestors. He heard
us and saw our suffering, hardship, and mis-
ery. 8By his great power and strength he res-
cued us from Egypt. He worked miracles
and wonders, and caused terrifying things to
happen. 9He brought us here and gave us
this rich and fertile land. 10So now I bring to
the LORD the first part of the harvest that he
has given me.'
"Then set the basket down in the LORD's
presence and worship there. 11Be grateful for
the good things that the LORD your God
has given you and your family; and let the
Levites and the foreigners who live among
you join in the celebration.
12"Every third year give the tithe—a
tenth of your crops—to the Levites, the
foreigners, the orphans, and the widows, so

25:3 2 Cor 11:24 **25:4** 1 Cor 9:9; 1 Tim 5:18 **25:5, 6** Mt 22:24; Mk 12:19; Lk 20:28 **25:7–10** Ruth 4:7, 8 **25:13–16** Lev 19:35, 36 **25:17–19** Ex 17:8–14; 1 Sam 15:2–9 **26:2** Ex 23:19 **26:12** Deut 14:28, 29

that in every community they will have all
they need to eat. When you have done this,
[13]say to the LORD, 'None of the sacred tithe
is left in my house; I have given it to the
Levites, the foreigners, the orphans, and the
widows, as you commanded me to do. I
have not disobeyed or forgotten any of
your commands concerning the tithe. [14]I
have not eaten any of it when I was
mourning; I have not taken any of it out of
my house when I was ritually unclean; and
I have not given any of it as an offering for
the dead.[u] I have obeyed you, O LORD; I
have done everything you commanded
concerning the tithe. [15]Look down from
your holy place in heaven and bless your
people Israel; bless also the rich and fertile
land that you have given us, as you prom-
ised our ancestors.'

The LORD's Own People

[16]"Today the LORD your God commands
you to obey all his laws; so obey them faith-
fully with all your heart. [17]Today you have
acknowledged the LORD as your God; you
have promised to obey him, to keep all his
laws, and to do all that he commands.
[18]Today the LORD has accepted you as his
own people, as he promised you; and he
commands you to obey all his laws. [19]He
will make you greater than any other nation
that he has created, and you will bring praise
and honor to his name.[v] You will be his own
people, as he promised."

God's Laws Written on Stones

27 Then Moses, together with the lead-
ers of Israel, said to the people,
"Obey all the instructions that I am giving
you today. [2]On the day you cross the Jordan
River and enter the land that the LORD your
God is giving you, you are to set up some
large stones, cover them with plaster, [3]and
write on them all these laws and teachings.
When you have entered the rich and fertile
land that the LORD, the God of your ances-
tors, promised you, [4]and you are on the
other side of the Jordan, set up these stones
on Mount Ebal, as I am instructing you
today, and cover them with plaster. [5]Build an
altar there made of stones that have had no
iron tools used on them, [6]because any altar
you build for the LORD your God must be
made of uncut stones. There you are to offer
the sacrifices that are to be burned, [7]and
there you are to sacrifice and eat your fel-
lowship offerings and be grateful in the pres-
ence of the LORD your God. [8]On the stones
covered with plaster write clearly every
word of God's laws."

[9]Then Moses, together with the levitical
priests, said to all the people of Israel, "Give
me your attention, people of Israel, and listen
to me. Today you have become the people of
the LORD your God; [10]so obey him and
keep all his laws that I am giving you today."

"People of Israel . . . listen to me." (27:9)

The Curses on Disobedience

[11]Then Moses said to the people of Israel,
[12]"After you have crossed the Jordan, the
following tribes are to stand on Mount Ge-
rizim when the blessings are pronounced on
the people: Simeon, Levi, Judah, Issachar,
Joseph, and Benjamin. [13]And the following
tribes will stand on Mount Ebal when the
curses are pronounced: Reuben, Gad, Asher,
Zebulun, Dan, and Naphtali. [14]The Levites
will speak these words in a loud voice:

[15]" 'God's curse on anyone who makes an
idol of stone, wood, or metal and secretly
worships it; the LORD hates idolatry.'

"And all the people will answer, 'Amen!'

[16]" 'God's curse on anyone who dishonors
his father or mother.'

[u] **26:14** for the dead; *or* to the dead. [v] **26:19** bring praise . . . name; *or* receive praise and honor.
26:18 Ex 19:5; Deut 4:20; 7:6; 14:2; Titus 2:14; 1 Pet 2:9 **27:2–8** Josh 8:30–32 **27:5, 6** Ex 20:25 **27:12** Deut 11:29; Josh 8:33–35 **27:15** Ex 20:4; 34:17; Lev 19:4; 26:1; Deut 4:15–18; 5:8 **27:16** Ex 20:12; Deut 5:16

"And all the people will answer, 'Amen!'
17 " 'God's curse on anyone who moves a
neighbor's property line.'
"And all the people will answer, 'Amen!'
18 " 'God's curse on anyone who leads a
blind person in the wrong direction.'
"And all the people will answer, 'Amen!'
19 " 'God's curse on anyone who deprives
foreigners, orphans, and widows of their
rights.'
"And all the people will answer, 'Amen!'
20 " 'God's curse on anyone who disgraces
his father by having intercourse with any of
his father's wives.'
"And all the people will answer, 'Amen!'
21 " 'God's curse on anyone who has sexu-
al relations with an animal.'
"And all the people will answer, 'Amen!'
22 " 'God's curse on anyone who has inter-
course with his sister or half sister.'
"And all the people will answer, 'Amen!'
23 " 'God's curse on anyone who has inter-
course with his mother-in-law.'
"And all the people will answer, 'Amen!'
24 " 'God's curse on anyone who secretly
commits murder.'
"And all the people will answer, 'Amen!'
25 " 'God's curse on anyone who accepts
money to murder an innocent person.'
"And all the people will answer, 'Amen!'
26 " 'God's curse on anyone who does not
obey all of God's laws and teachings.'
"And all the people will answer, 'Amen!'

The Blessings of Obedience
(Leviticus 26:3–13; Deuteronomy 7:12–24)

28 "If you obey the LORD your God
and faithfully keep all his commands
that I am giving you today, he will make you
greater than any other nation on earth.
2 Obey the LORD your God and all these
blessings will be yours:
3 "The LORD will bless your towns and
your fields.
4 "The LORD will bless you with many
children, with abundant crops, and with
many cattle and sheep.
5 "The LORD will bless your grain crops
and the food you prepare from them.
6 "The LORD will bless everything you do.
7 "The LORD will defeat your enemies
when they attack you. They will attack from
one direction, but they will run from you in
all directions.
8 "The LORD your God will bless your
work and fill your barns with grain. He will
bless you in the land that he is giving you.
9 "If you obey the LORD your God and do
everything he commands, he will make you
his own people, as he has promised. 10 Then
all the peoples on earth will see that the
LORD has chosen you to be his own people,
and they will be afraid of you. 11 The LORD
will give you many children, many cattle,
and abundant crops in the land that he
promised your ancestors to give you. 12 He
will send rain in season from his rich store-
house in the sky and bless all your work, so
that you will lend to many nations, but you
will not have to borrow from any. 13 The
LORD your God will make you the leader
among the nations and not a follower; you
will always prosper and never fail if you obey
faithfully all his commands that I am giving
you today. 14 But you must never disobey
them in any way, or worship and serve other
gods.

The Consequences of Disobedience
(Leviticus 26:14–46)

15 "But if you disobey the LORD your God
and do not faithfully keep all his commands
and laws that I am giving you today, all these
evil things will happen to you:
16 "The LORD will curse your towns and
your fields.
17 "The LORD will curse your grain crops
and the food you prepare from them.
18 "The LORD will curse you by giving
you only a few children, poor crops, and few
cattle and sheep.
19 "The LORD will curse everything you
do.
20 "If you do evil and reject the LORD, he
will bring on you disaster, confusion, and

27:17 Deut 19:14 **27:18** Lev 19:14 **27:19** Ex 22:21; 23:9; Lev 19:33, 34; Deut 24:17, 18 **27:20** Lev 18:8; 20:11; Deut 22:30 **27:21** Ex 22:19; Lev 18:23; 20:15 **27:22** Lev 18:9; 20:17 **27:23** Lev 18:17; 20:14 **27:26** Gal 3:10 **28:1–14** Deut 11:13–17

But if you disobey the LORD *(28:15)*

trouble in everything you do, until you are
quickly and completely destroyed. 21He will
send disease after disease on you until there
is not one of you left in the land that you
are about to occupy. 22The LORD will strike
you with infectious diseases, with swelling
and fever; he will send drought and scorch-
ing winds to destroy your crops. These disas-
ters will be with you until you die. 23No
rain will fall, and your ground will become
as hard as iron. 24Instead of rain, the LORD
will send down duststorms and sandstorms
until you are destroyed.

25"The LORD will give your enemies vic-
tory over you. You will attack them from
one direction, but you will run from them in
all directions, and all the people on earth
will be terrified when they see what hap-
pens to you. 26When you die, birds and wild
animals will come and eat your bodies, and
there will be no one to scare them off.
27The LORD will send boils on you, as he
did on the Egyptians. He will make your
bodies break out with sores. You will be cov-
ered with scabs, and you will itch, but there
will be no cure. 28The LORD will make you
lose your mind; he will strike you with
blindness and confusion. 29You will grope
about in broad daylight like someone blind,
and you will not be able to find your way.
You will not prosper in anything you do. You
will be constantly oppressed and robbed, and
there will be no one to help you.

30"You will be engaged to a young
woman—but someone else will marry her.
You will build a house—but never live in it.
You will plant a vineyard—but never eat its
grapes. 31Your cattle will be butchered
before your very eyes, but you will not eat
any of the meat. Your donkeys will be
dragged away while you look on, and they
will not be given back to you. Your sheep
will be given to your enemies, and there will
be no one to help you. 32Your sons and
daughters will be given as slaves to foreigners
while you look on. Every day you will strain
your eyes, looking in vain for your children
to return. 33A foreign nation will take all the
crops that you have worked so hard to grow,
while you receive nothing but constant
oppression and harsh treatment. 34Your suf-
ferings will make you lose your mind. 35The
LORD will cover your legs with incurable,
painful sores; boils will cover you from head
to foot.

36"The LORD will take you and your king
away to a foreign land, where neither you
nor your ancestors ever lived before; there
you will serve gods made of wood and
stone. 37In the countries to which the LORD
will scatter you, the people will be shocked
at what has happened to you; they will make
fun of you and ridicule you.

38"You will plant plenty of seed, but reap
only a small harvest, because the locusts will
eat your crops. 39You will plant vineyards
and take care of them, but you will not gath-
er their grapes or drink wine from them,
because worms will eat the vines. 40Olive
trees will grow everywhere in your land, but
you will not have any olive oil, because the
olives will drop off. 41You will have sons and
daughters, but you will lose them, because
they will be taken away as prisoners of war.
42All your trees and crops will be devoured
by insects.

43"Foreigners who live in your land will
gain more and more power, while you grad-
ually lose yours. 44They will have money to

lend you, but you will have none to lend
them. In the end they will be your rulers.
45 "All these disasters will come on you,
and they will be with you until you are
destroyed, because you did not obey the
LORD your God and keep all the laws that
he gave you. 46 They will be the evidence of
God's judgment on you and your descen-
dants forever. 47 The LORD blessed you in
every way, but you would not serve him
with glad and joyful hearts. 48 So then, you
will serve the enemies that the LORD is
going to send against you. You will be hun-
gry, thirsty, and naked—in need of every-
thing. The LORD[w] will oppress you harshly
until you are destroyed. 49 The LORD will
bring against you a nation from the ends of
the earth, a nation whose language you do
not know. They will swoop down on you
like an eagle. 50 They will be ruthless and
show no mercy to anyone, young or old.
51 They will eat your livestock and your
crops, and you will starve to death. They will
not leave you any grain, wine, olive oil, cat-
tle, or sheep; and you will die. 52 They will
attack every town in the land that the LORD
your God is giving you, and the high, forti-
fied walls in which you trust will fall.
53 "When your enemies are besieging your
towns, you will become so desperate for
food that you will even eat the children that
the LORD your God has given you. 54-55 Even
the most refined man of noble birth will
become so desperate during the siege that he
will eat some of his own children because he
has no other food. He will not even give any
to his brother or to the wife he loves or to
any of his children who are left. 56-57 Even
the most refined woman of noble birth, so
rich that she has never had to walk any-
where, will behave in the same way. When
the enemy besieges her town, she will
become so desperate for food that she will
secretly eat her newborn child and the after-
birth as well. She will not share them with
the husband she loves or with any of her
children.
58 "If you do not obey faithfully all of
God's teachings that are written in this book
and if you do not honor the wonderful and
awesome name of the LORD your God, 59 he
will send on you and on your descendants
incurable diseases and horrible epidemics
that can never be stopped. 60 He will bring
on you once again all the dreadful diseases
you experienced in Egypt, and you will
never recover. 61 He will also send all kinds
of diseases and epidemics that are not men-
tioned in this book of God's laws and teach-
ings, and you will be destroyed. 62 Although
you become as numerous as the stars in the
sky, only a few of you will survive, because
you did not obey the LORD your God. 63 Just
as the LORD took delight in making you
prosper and in making you increase in num-
ber, so he will take delight in destroying you
and in bringing ruin on you. You will be
uprooted from the land that you are about to
occupy.
64 "The LORD will scatter you among all
the nations, from one end of the earth to the
other, and there you will serve gods made of
wood and stone, gods that neither you nor
your ancestors have ever worshiped before.
65 You will find no peace anywhere, no place
to call your own; the LORD will overwhelm
you with anxiety, hopelessness, and despair.
66 Your life will always be in danger. Day and
night you will be filled with terror, and you
will live in constant fear of death. 67 Your
hearts will pound with fear at everything
you see. Every morning you will wish for
evening; every evening you will wish for
morning. 68 The LORD will send you back to
Egypt in ships, even though he[x] said that you
would never have to go there again. There
you will try to sell yourselves to your enemies
as slaves, but no one will want to buy you."

The LORD's Covenant with Israel in the Land of Moab

29 These are the terms of the covenant
that the LORD commanded Moses
to make with the people of Israel in the land
of Moab; all this was in addition to the
covenant which the LORD had made with
them at Mount Sinai.

[w] **28:48** The LORD; *or* Your enemies. [x] **28:68** he; *or* I.
28:57 2 Kings 6:28, 29; Lam 4:10

2 Moses called together all the people of
Israel and said to them, "You saw for your-
selves what the LORD did to the king of
Egypt, to his officials, and to his entire coun-
try. 3 You saw the terrible plagues, the mira-
cles, and the great wonders that the LORD
performed. 4 But to this very day he has not
let you understand what you have experi-
enced. 5 For forty years the LORD led you
through the desert, and your clothes and
sandals never wore out. 6 You did not have
bread to eat or wine or beer to drink, but
the LORD provided for your needs in order
to teach you that he is your God. 7 And
when we came to this place, King Sihon of
Heshbon and King Og of Bashan came out
to fight against us. But we defeated them,
8 took their land, and divided it among the
tribes of Reuben and Gad, and half the tribe
of Manasseh. 9 Obey faithfully all the terms
of this covenant, so that you will be success-
ful in everything you do.

10 "Today you are standing in the presence
of the LORD your God, all of you—your
leaders and officials, your men, 11 women,
and children, and the foreigners who live
among you and cut wood and carry water
for you. 12 You are here today to enter into
this covenant that the LORD your God is
making with you and to accept its obliga-
tions, 13 so that the LORD may now confirm
you as his people and be your God, as he
promised you and your ancestors, Abraham,
Isaac, and Jacob. 14 You are not the only ones
with whom the LORD is making this
covenant with its obligations. 15 He is making
it with all of us who stand here in his pres-
ence today and also with our descendants
who are not yet born.

16 "You remember what life was like in
Egypt and what it was like to travel through
the territory of other nations. 17 You saw
their disgusting idols made of wood, stone,
silver, and gold. 18 Make sure that no man,
woman, family, or tribe standing here today
turns from the LORD our God to worship
the gods of other nations. This would be like
a root that grows to be a bitter and poison-
ous plant. 19 Make sure that there is no one
here today who hears these solemn demands
and yet convinces himself that all will be well
with him, even if he stubbornly goes his own
way. That would destroy all of you, good and
evil alike. 20 The LORD will not forgive such a
man. Instead, the LORD's burning anger will
flame up against him, and all the disasters
written in this book will fall on him until the
LORD has destroyed him completely. 21 The
LORD will make an example of him before
all the tribes of Israel and will bring disaster
on him in accordance with all the curses list-
ed in the covenant that is written in this
book of the LORD's teachings.

22 "In future generations your descendants
and foreigners from distant lands will see the
disasters and sufferings that the LORD has
brought on your land. 23 The fields will be a
barren waste, covered with sulfur and salt;
nothing will be planted, and not even weeds
will grow there. Your land will be like the
cities of Sodom and Gomorrah, of Admah
and Zeboiim, which the LORD destroyed
when he was furiously angry. 24 Then the
whole world will ask, 'Why did the LORD
do this to their land? What was the reason
for his fierce anger?' 25 And the answer will
be, 'It is because the LORD's people broke
the covenant they had made with him, the
God of their ancestors, when he brought
them out of Egypt. 26 They served other
gods that they had never worshiped before,
gods that the LORD had forbidden them to
worship. 27 And so the LORD became angry
with his people and brought on their land all
the disasters written in this book. 28 The
LORD became furiously angry, and in his
great anger he uprooted them from their
land and threw them into a foreign land, and
there they are today.'

29 "There are some things that the LORD
our God has kept secret; but he has revealed
his Law, and we and our descendants are to
obey it forever.

Conditions for Restoration and Blessing

30 "I have now given you a choice
between a blessing and a curse. When
all these things have happened to you, and

29:7 **a** Num 21:21–30; **b** Num 21:31–35 **29:8** Num 32:33 **29:18** Heb 12:15 **29:23** Gen 19:24, 25 you are living among the nations where the LORD your God has scattered you, you will remember the choice I gave you. [2]If you and your descendants will turn back to the LORD and with all your heart obey his commands that I am giving you today, [3]then the LORD your God will have mercy on you. He will bring you back from the nations where he has scattered you, and he will make you prosperous again. [4]Even if you are scattered to the farthest corners of the earth, the LORD your God will gather you together and bring you back, [5]so that you may again take possession of the land where your ancestors once lived. And he will make you more prosperous and more numerous than your ancestors ever were. [6]The LORD your God will give you and your descendants obedient hearts, so that you will love him with all your heart, and you will continue to live in that land. [7]He will turn all these curses against your enemies, who hated you and oppressed you, [8]and you will again obey him and keep all his commands that I am giving you today. [9]The LORD will make you prosperous in all that you do; you will have many children and a lot of livestock, and your fields will produce abundant crops. He will be as glad to make you prosperous as he was to make your ancestors prosperous, [10]but you will have to obey him and keep all his laws that are written in this book of his teachings. You will have to turn to him with all your heart.

11"The command that I am giving you today is not too difficult or beyond your reach. [12]It is not up in the sky. You do not have to ask, 'Who will go up and bring it down for us, so that we can hear it and obey it?' [13]Nor is it on the other side of the ocean. You do not have to ask, 'Who will go across the ocean and bring it to us, so that we may hear it and obey it?' [14]No, it is here with you. You know it and can quote it, so now obey it.

15"Today I am giving you a choice between good and evil, between life and death. [16]If you obey the commands of the LORD your God,[y] which I give you today, if you love him, obey him, and keep all his laws, then you will prosper and become a nation of many people. The LORD your God will bless you in the land that you are about to occupy. [17]But if you disobey and refuse to listen, and are led away to worship other gods, [18]you will be destroyed—I warn you here and now. You will not live long in that land across the Jordan that you are about to occupy. [19]I am now giving you the choice between life and death, between God's blessing and God's curse, and I call heaven and earth to witness the choice you make. Choose life. [20]Love the LORD your God, obey him and be faithful to him, and then you and your descendants will live long in the land that he promised to give your ancestors, Abraham, Isaac, and Jacob."

Choose life. (30:19)

Joshua Becomes Moses' Successor

31 Moses continued speaking to the people of Israel, [2]and said, "I am now a hundred and twenty years old and am

y **30:16** *One ancient translation* If you obey the commands of the LORD your God; *Hebrew does not have these words.*

30:12–14 Rom 10:6–8 **30:15** Sir 15:16, 17 **30:20** **a** Gen 12:7; **b** Gen 26:3; **c** Gen 28:13 **31:2** Num 20:12

no longer able to be your leader. And besides
this, the LORD has told me that I will not
cross the Jordan. 3The LORD your God him-
self will go before you and destroy the
nations living there, so that you can occupy
their land; and Joshua will be your leader, as
the LORD has said. 4The LORD will destroy
those people, just as he defeated Sihon and
Og, kings of the Amorites, and destroyed
their country. 5The LORD will give you vic-
tory over them, and you are to treat them
exactly as I have told you. 6Be determined
and confident. Do not be afraid of them.
Your God, the LORD himself, will be with
you. He will not fail you or abandon you."

7Then Moses called Joshua and said to
him in the presence of all the people of
Israel, "Be determined and confident; you
are the one who will lead these people to
occupy the land that the LORD promised to
their ancestors. 8The LORD himself will lead
you and be with you. He will not fail you or
abandon you, so do not lose courage or be
afraid."

The Law Is to Be Read Every Seven Years

9So Moses wrote down God's Law and
gave it to the levitical priests, who were in
charge of the LORD's Covenant Box, and
to the leaders of Israel. 10He commanded
them, "At the end of every seven years,
when the year that debts are canceled comes
around, read this aloud at the Festival of
Shelters. 11Read it to the people of Israel
when they come to worship the LORD your
God at the one place of worship. 12Call
together all the men, women, and children,
and the foreigners who live in your towns,
so that everyone may hear it and learn to
honor the LORD your God and to obey his
teachings faithfully. 13In this way your
descendants who have never heard the Law
of the LORD your God will hear it. And so
they will learn to obey him as long as they
live in the land that you are about to occupy
across the Jordan."

The LORD's Last Instructions to Moses

14Then the LORD said to Moses, "You do
not have much longer to live. Call Joshua
and bring him to the Tent, so that I may give
him his instructions." Moses and Joshua went
to the Tent, 15and the LORD appeared to
them there in a pillar of cloud that stood by
the door of the Tent.

16The LORD said to Moses, "You will
soon die, and after your death the people
will become unfaithful to me and break the
covenant that I made with them. They will
abandon me and worship the pagan gods of
the land they are about to enter. 17When
that happens, I will become angry with
them; I will abandon them, and they will be
destroyed. Many terrible disasters will come
upon them, and then they will realize that
these things are happening to them because
I, their God, am no longer with them. 18And
I will refuse to help them then, because they
have done evil and worshiped other gods.

19"Now, write down this song. Teach it to
the people of Israel, so that it will stand as
evidence against them. 20I will take them
into this rich and fertile land, as I promised
their ancestors. There they will have all the
food they want, and they will live comfort-
ably. But they will turn away and worship
other gods. They will reject me and break
my covenant, 21and many terrible disasters
will come on them. But this song will still
be sung, and it will stand as evidence against
them. Even now, before I take them into the
land that I promised to give them, I know
what they are thinking."

22That same day Moses wrote down the
song and taught it to the people of Israel.

23Then the LORD spoke to Joshua son of
Nun and told him, "Be confident and deter-
mined. You will lead the people of Israel into
the land that I promised them, and I will be
with you."

24Moses wrote God's Law in a book, taking
care not to leave out anything. 25When he
finished, he said to the levitical priests, who
were in charge of the LORD's Covenant Box,
26"Take this book of God's Law and place it
beside the Covenant Box of the LORD your

31:4 Num 21:21–35 **31:8** Josh 1:5; Heb 13:5 **31:10** **a** Deut 15:1, 2; **b** Deut 16:13–15 **31:23** Num 27:23; Josh 1:6

God, so that it will remain there as a witness against his people. [27]I know how stubborn and rebellious they are. They have rebelled against the LORD during my lifetime, and they will rebel even more after I am dead.
[28]Assemble all your tribal leaders and officials before me, so that I can tell them these things; I will call heaven and earth to be my witnesses against them. [29]I know that after my death the people will become wicked and reject what I have taught them. And in time to come they will meet with disaster, because they will have made the LORD angry by doing what he has forbidden."

The Song of Moses

[30]Then Moses recited the entire song while all the people of Israel listened.

32 "Earth and sky, hear my words,
listen closely to what I say.
[2]My teaching will fall like drops of rain
and form on the earth like dew.
My words will fall like showers on young plants,
like gentle rain on tender grass.
[3]I will praise the name of the LORD,
and his people will tell of his greatness.

[4]"The LORD is your mighty defender,
perfect and just in all his ways;
Your God is faithful and true;
he does what is right and fair.
[5]But you are unfaithful, unworthy to be his people,[z]
a sinful and deceitful nation.
[6]Is this the way you should treat the LORD,
you foolish, senseless people?
He is your father, your Creator,
he made you into a nation.

[7]"Think of the past, of the time long ago;
ask your parents to tell you what happened,
ask the old people to tell of the past.
[8]The Most High assigned nations their lands;
he determined where peoples should live.
He assigned to each nation a heavenly being,
[9] but Jacob's descendants he chose for himself.

[10]"He found them wandering through the desert,
a desolate, wind swept wilderness.
He protected them and cared for them,
as he would protect himself.
[11]Like an eagle teaching its young to fly,[a]
catching them safely on its spreading wings,
the LORD kept Israel from falling.
[12]The LORD alone led his people
without the help of a foreign god.

[13]"He let them rule the highlands,
and they ate what grew in the fields.
They found wild honey among the rocks;
their olive trees flourished in stony ground.
[14]Their cows and goats gave plenty of milk;
they had the best sheep, goats, and cattle,
the finest wheat, and the choicest wine.

[15]"The LORD's people grew rich, but rebellious;
they were fat and stuffed with food.
They abandoned God their Creator
and rejected their mighty savior.
[16]Their idolatry made the LORD jealous;
the evil they did made him angry.
[17]They sacrificed to gods that are not real,
new gods their ancestors had never known,
gods that Israel had never obeyed.
[18]They forgot their God, their mighty savior,
the one who had given them life.

[19]"When the LORD saw this, he was angry
and rejected his sons and daughters.
[20]'I will no longer help them,' he said;
'then I will see what happens to them,
those stubborn, unfaithful people.
[21]With their idols they have made me angry,
jealous with their so-called gods,
gods that are really not gods.

[z] **32:5** *Probable text* But you . . . people; *Hebrew unclear.* [a] **32:11** teaching its young to fly; *or* watching over its young.

32:8 Acts 17:26 **32:17** 1 Cor 10:20 **32:21** **a** 1 Cor 10:22; **b** Rom 10:19

So I will use a so-called nation to make
them angry;
I will make them jealous with a nation
of fools.
22 My anger will flame up like fire
and burn everything on earth.
It will reach to the world below[b]
and consume the roots of the
mountains.

23 " 'I will bring on them endless disasters
and use all my arrows against them.
24 They will die from hunger and fever;
they will die from terrible diseases.
I will send wild animals to attack them,
and poisonous snakes to bite them.
25 War will bring death in the streets;
terrors will strike in the homes.
Young men and young women will die;
neither babies nor old people will be
spared.
26 I would have destroyed them completely,
so that no one would remember them.
27 But I could not let their enemies boast
that they had defeated my people,
when it was I myself who had crushed
them.'

28 "Israel is a nation without sense;
they have no wisdom at all.
29 They fail to see why they were defeated;
they cannot understand what happened.
30 Why were a thousand defeated by one,
and ten thousand by only two?
The LORD, their God, had abandoned
them;
their mighty God had given them up.
31 Their enemies know that their own gods
are weak,
not mighty like Israel's God.
32 Their enemies, corrupt as Sodom and
Gomorrah,
are like vines that bear bitter and
poisonous grapes,
33 like wine made from the venom of
snakes.
34 "The LORD remembers what their
enemies have done;
he waits for the right time to punish
them.
35 The LORD will take revenge and punish
them;
the time will come when they will fall;
the day of their doom is near.
36 The LORD will rescue his people
when he sees that their strength is
gone.
He will have mercy on those who serve
him,
when he sees how helpless they are.
37 Then the LORD will ask his people,
'Where are those mighty gods you
trusted?
38 You fed them the fat of your sacrifices
and offered them wine to drink.
Let them come and help you now;
let them run to your rescue.

39 " 'I, and I alone, am God;
no other god is real.
I kill and I give life, I wound and I heal,
and no one can oppose what I do.
40 As surely as I am the living God,
I raise my hand and I vow
41 that I will sharpen my flashing sword
and see that justice is done.
I will take revenge on my enemies
and punish those who hate me.
42 My arrows will drip with their blood,
and my sword will kill all who oppose
me.
I will spare no one who fights against me;
even the wounded and prisoners will
die.'

43 "Nations, you must praise the LORD's
people—
he punishes all who kill them.
He takes revenge on his enemies
and forgives the sins of his people."

44 Moses and Joshua son of Nun recited this song, so that the people of Israel could hear it.

Moses' Final Instructions

45 When Moses had finished giving God's
teachings to the people, 46 he said, "Be sure to
obey all these commands that I have given
you today. Repeat them to your children, so
that they may faithfully obey all of God's

[b] **32:22** THE WORLD BELOW: *This refers to the world of the dead.*

32:35 Rom 12:19; Heb 10:30 **32:36a** Ps 135:14 **32:43** Rom 15:10; Rev 19:2

teachings. 47 These teachings are not empty
words; they are your very life. Obey them
and you will live long in that land across the
Jordan that you are about to occupy."
48 That same day the LORD said to Moses,
49 "Go to the Abarim Mountains in the land
of Moab opposite the city of Jericho; climb
Mount Nebo and look at the land of
Canaan that I am about to give the people
of Israel. 50 You will die on that mountain as
your brother Aaron died on Mount Hor,
51 because both of you were unfaithful to me
in the presence of the people of Israel. When
you were at the waters of Meribah, near the
town of Kadesh in the wilderness of Zin,
you dishonored me in the presence of the
people. 52 You will look at the land from a
distance, but you will not enter the land that
I am giving the people of Israel."

Moses Blesses the Tribes of Israel

33 These are the blessings that Moses, the man of God, pronounced on the people of Israel before he died.

2 The LORD came from Mount Sinai;
he rose like the sun over Edom
and shone on his people from Mount Paran.
Ten thousand angels were with him,
a flaming fire at his right hand.[c]
3 The LORD loves his people[d]
and protects those who belong to him.
So we bow at[e] his feet
and obey his commands.
4 We obey the Law that Moses gave us,
our nation's most treasured possession.
5 The LORD became king of his people Israel
when their tribes and leaders were gathered together.

6 Moses said about the tribe of Reuben:
"May Reuben never die out,
Although their people are few."

7 About the tribe of Judah he said:
"LORD, listen to their cry for help;
Unite them again with the other tribes.
Fight for them, LORD,
And help them against their enemies."[f]

8 About the tribe of Levi he said:
"You, LORD, reveal your will by the Urim and Thummim[g]
Through your faithful servants, the Levites;
You put them to the test at Massah
And proved them true at the waters of Meribah.
9 They showed greater loyalty to you
Than to parents, brothers, or children.
They obeyed your commands
And were faithful to your covenant.
10 They will teach your people to obey your Law;
They will offer sacrifices on your altar.
11 LORD, help their tribe to grow strong;
Be pleased with what they do.
Crush all their enemies;
Let them never rise again."

12 About the tribe of Benjamin he said:
"This is the tribe the LORD loves and protects;
He guards them all the day long,
And he dwells in their midst."[h]

13 About the tribe of Joseph he said:
"May the LORD bless their land with rain
And with water from under the earth.
14 May their land be blessed with sun-ripened fruit,
Rich with the best fruits of each season.
15 May their ancient hills be covered with choice fruit.
16 May their land be filled with all that is good,
Blessed by the goodness of the LORD,
Who spoke from the burning bush.
May these blessings come to the tribe of Joseph,
Because he was the leader among his brothers.
17 Joseph has the strength of a bull,
The horns of a wild ox.

[c] **33:2** *Probable text* Ten thousand . . . right hand; *Hebrew unclear.* [d] **33:3** *One ancient translation* his people; *Hebrew* the peoples. [e] **33:3** *Probable text* bow at; *Hebrew unclear.* [f] **33:7** *Probable text* Fight for . . . enemies; *Hebrew* The tribe of Judah will fight for itself, and the LORD will help it against its enemies. [g] **33:8** URIM AND THUMMIM: *Two objects used by the priest to determine God's will; it is not known precisely how they were used.* [h] **33:12** And he . . . midst; *or* They live under his protection.

32:48–52 Num 27:12–14; Deut 3:23–27 **33:8** **a** Ex 28:30; **b** Ex 17:7; **c** Ex 17:7; Num 20:13

His horns are Manasseh's thousands
And Ephraim's ten thousands.
With them he gores the nations
And pushes them to the ends of the
earth."

18 About the tribes of Zebulun and
Issachar he said:
"May Zebulun be prosperous in their
trade on the sea,
And may Issachar's wealth increase at
home.
19 They invite foreigners to their mountain
And offer the right sacrifices there.
They get their wealth from the sea
And from the sand along the shore."

20 About the tribe of Gad he said:
"Praise God, who made their territory
large.
Gad waits like a lion
To tear off an arm or a scalp.
21 They took the best of the land for
themselves;
A leader's share was assigned to them.
They obeyed the LORD's commands and
laws
When the leaders of Israel were gathered
together."[i]

22 About the tribe of Dan he said:
"Dan is a young lion;
He leaps out from Bashan."

23 About the tribe of Naphtali he said:
"Naphtali is richly blessed by the LORD's
good favor;
Their land reaches to the south from Lake
Galilee."

24 About the tribe of Asher he said:
"Asher is blessed more than the other
tribes.
May he be the favorite of his brothers,
And may his land be rich with olive trees.
25 May his towns be protected with iron
gates,
And may he always live secure."

26 People of Israel, no god is like your God,
riding in splendor across the sky,
riding through the clouds to come to
your aid.
27 God has always been your defense;
his eternal arms are your support.
He drove out your enemies as you
advanced,
and told you to destroy them all.
28 So Jacob's descendants live in peace,
secure in a land full of grain and wine,
where dew from the sky waters the
ground.
29 Israel, how happy you are!
There is no one like you,
a nation saved by the LORD.
The LORD himself is your shield and your
sword,
to defend you and give you victory.
Your enemies will come begging for
mercy,
and you will trample them down.

[i] **33:21** *One ancient translation* When the leaders . . . together; *Hebrew unclear.*

The LORD showed him the whole land. (34:1)

The Death of Moses

34 Moses went up from the plains of
Moab to Mount Nebo, to the top of
Mount Pisgah east of Jericho, and there the
LORD showed him the whole land: the terri-
tory of Gilead as far north as the town of
Dan; 2the entire territory of Naphtali; the
territories of Ephraim and Manasseh; the
territory of Judah as far west as the Mediter-
ranean Sea; 3the southern part of Judah; and
the plain that reaches from Zoar to Jericho,
the city of palm trees. 4Then the LORD said
to Moses, "This is the land that I promised
Abraham, Isaac, and Jacob I would give to
their descendants. I have let you see it, but I
will not let you go there."
5So Moses, the LORD's servant, died there
in the land of Moab, as the LORD had said
he would. 6The LORD buried him in a valley
in Moab, opposite the town of Bethpeor, but
to this day no one knows the exact place of
his burial. 7Moses was a hundred and twenty
years old when he died; he was as strong as
ever, and his eyesight was still good. 8The
people of Israel mourned for him for thirty
days in the plains of Moab.
9Joshua son of Nun was filled with wis-
dom, because Moses had appointed him to
be his successor. The people of Israel obeyed
Joshua and kept the commands that the
LORD had given them through Moses.
10There has never been a prophet in Israel
like Moses; the LORD spoke with him face
to face. 11No other prophet has ever done
miracles and wonders like those that the
LORD sent Moses to perform against the
king of Egypt, his officials, and the entire
country. 12No other prophet has been able
to do the great and terrifying things that
Moses did in the sight of all Israel.

34:4 **a** Gen 12:7; **b** Gen 26:3; **c** Gen 28:13 **34:10** Ex 33:11; Sir 45:1–5

The Book of Joshua

Action, adventure, spies, sieges, battles—the Book of Joshua is full of great stories. It is also part of a larger story, the story of the People of God. Moses led them out of slavery and through the wilderness. Now Joshua is their leader. They are about to enter the Promised Land. The people see their military victories as God's reward for their obedience. The Book of Joshua shows God's faithfulness in fulfilling his promise to his people.

Chap. 6

Headlines

- Rahab Rescues Spies on the Roof! (2:1–24)
- The Walls Come Tumbling Down (5:13—6:27)
- Disguise Fools Joshua (9:3–15)
- Women Request Right to Land! (17:3–6)
- Argument Erupts Over Monument (22:13–20)
- People Vow to Serve the Lord (24:14–18)

FACTOIDS

Who wrote this book? The author is not known. Some scholars think it was the same person or group who wrote Deuteronomy.

When was it written? The book probably went through several stages as various stories were collected and written down. The final version was probably written during the Babylonian Exile.

Why was it written? The Book of Joshua was written to reinforce the idea that obedience to God will be rewarded and disobedience will be punished.

What is the Jesus connection? The name Jesus is the Greek form of the Hebrew name Joshua.

Important themes

- God is always with his people, no matter where they are.
- God gives those who are faithful and obedient the Promised Land.
- Do not worship false gods but serve only the God of Israel.

JOSHUA

Live it!

Big Shoes to Fill

Moses had led the Israelites out of Egypt and through the wilderness. He had been with them as their leader for forty years! Now Joshua is chosen as the one to lead the people after Moses died. That must have been scary for Joshua. But God promises Joshua, "I will always be with you; I will never abandon you" (1:5). Read chapter 34 of Deuteronomy to see how Joshua's story is a continuation of the story of Moses and God's Chosen People, the Israelites.

It can be hard to follow others who were really good at something. Maybe you are on the basketball team the year after the previous team won the regional title. Maybe you're following an older brother or sister who got all A's in school. If you sometimes feel like you have big shoes to fill, remember Joshua and fear not! God will be with you and never abandon you. God doesn't ask you to be successful, just to be faithful to him.

— Joshua 1:1–9

God Commands Joshua to Conquer Canaan

1 After the death of the LORD's servant
Moses, the LORD spoke to Moses'
helper, Joshua son of Nun. 2He said, "My ser-
vant Moses is dead. Get ready now, you and
all the people of Israel, and cross the Jordan
River into the land that I am giving them.
3As I told Moses, I have given you and all my
people the entire land that you will be
marching over. 4Your borders will reach from
the desert in the south to the Lebanon
Mountains in the north; from the great
Euphrates River in the east, through the Hit-
tite country, to the Mediterranean Sea in the
west. 5Joshua, no one will be able to defeat
you as long as you live. I will be with you as
I was with Moses. I will always be with you; I
will never abandon you. 6Be determined and
confident, for you will be the leader of these
people as they occupy this land which I
promised their ancestors. 7Just be deter-
mined, be confident; and make sure that you
obey the whole Law that my servant Moses
gave you. Do not neglect any part of it and
you will succeed wherever you go. 8Be sure
that the book of the Law is always read in
your worship. Study it day and night, and
make sure that you obey everything written
in it. Then you will be prosperous and suc-
cessful. 9Remember that I have commanded
you to be determined and confident! Do not
be afraid or discouraged, for I, the LORD
your God, am with you wherever you go."

Joshua Gives Orders to the People

10Then Joshua ordered the leaders to 11go
through the camp and say to the people, "Get
some food ready, because in three days you are
going to cross the Jordan River to occupy the
land that the LORD your God is giving you."
12Joshua said to the tribes of Reuben and
Gad and to half the tribe of Manasseh,
13"Remember how the LORD's servant Moses
told you that the LORD your God would give
you this land on the east side of the Jordan as
your home. 14Your wives, your children, and
your livestock will stay here, but your soldiers,
armed for battle, will cross over ahead of the
other Israelites in order to help them 15until

1:3–5 Deut 11:24, 25 **1:5** Deut 31:6, 8; Heb 13:5 **1:6** Deut 31:6, 7, 23 **1:12–15** Num 32:28–32; Deut 3:18–20; Josh 22:1–6 they have occupied the land west of the Jordan that the LORD your God has given them. When he has given safety to all the tribes of Israel, then you may come back and settle here in your own land east of the Jordan, which Moses, the LORD's servant, gave to you."

16They answered Joshua, "We will do everything you have told us and will go anywhere you send us. 17We will obey you, just as we always obeyed Moses, and may the LORD your God be with you as he was with Moses! 18Whoever questions your authority or disobeys any of your orders will be put to death. Be determined and confident!"

Joshua Sends Spies into Jericho

2 Then Joshua sent two spies from the camp at Acacia with orders to go and secretly explore the land of Canaan, especially the city of Jericho. When they came to the city, they went to spend the night in the house of a prostitute named Rahab. 2The king of Jericho heard that some Israelites had come that night to spy out the country, 3so he sent word to Rahab: "The men in your house have come to spy out the whole country! Bring them out!"

4-6"Some men did come to my house," she answered, "but I don't know where they were from. They left at sundown before the city gate was closed. I didn't find out where they were going, but if you start after them quickly, you can catch them." (Now Rahab had taken the two spies up on the roof and hidden them under some stalks of flax that she had put there.) 7The king's men left the city, and then the gate was shut. They went looking for the Israelite spies as far as the place where the road crosses the Jordan.

8Before the spies settled down for the night, Rahab went up on the roof 9and said to them, "I know that the LORD has given you this land. Everyone in the country is terrified of you. 10We have heard how the LORD dried up the Red Sea in front of you when you were leaving Egypt. We have also heard how you killed Sihon and Og, the two Amorite kings east of the Jordan. 11We were afraid as soon as we heard about it; we have all lost our courage because of you. The LORD your God is God in heaven above and here on earth. 12Now swear by him that you will treat my family as kindly as I have treated you, and give me some sign that I can trust you. 13Promise me that you will save my father and mother, my brothers and sisters, and all their families! Don't let us be killed!"

14The men said to her, "May God take our lives if we don't do as we say![a] If you do not tell anyone what we have been doing, we promise you that when the LORD gives us this land, we will treat you well."

15Rahab lived in a house built into the city

Explore the land . . . especially the city of Jericho. (2:1)

[a] **2:14** May God . . . say; *or* We will protect you if you protect us.

2:1 Heb 11:31; Jas 2:25 **2:10** **a** Ex 14:21; **b** Num 21:21–35

Remember the parable of the good Samaritan *(Luke 10:30–37)***? What similarities are there between Rahab and the good Samaritan?**

Pray it!

The Lord Your God Is God

God is all around us, all the time, every minute of every day. And yet we fail to recognize God's power and presence. Rahab, the woman who hides the Israelite spies, tells them that she believes their God is the true God of heaven and earth. This story has a little irony in it. Rahab is a Canaanite. She is the enemy of the Israelites. But her belief in the power of their God is what saves the Israelite spies.

Take a few minutes to write down the evidence of God you have seen in your own life. What are the signs, big and small, that come your way and remind you of God's power and presence? Some people like to keep a journal of the times they notice God's action in their lives and look back on it from time to time. It can help us recognize God's power and presence the way Rahab did.

— Joshua 2:1–13

wall, so she let the men down from the window by a rope.
16"Go into the hill country," she said, "or the king's men will find you. Hide there for three days until they come back. After that, you can go on your way."
17The men said to her, "We will keep the promise that you have made us give.
18This is what you must do. When we invade your land, tie this red cord to the window you let us down from. Get your father and mother, your brothers, and all your father's family together in your house.
19If anyone goes out of the house, his death will be his own fault, and we will not be responsible; but if anyone in the house with you is harmed, then we will be responsible.
20However, if you tell anyone what we have been doing, then we will not have to keep our promise which you have made us give you."
21She agreed and sent them away. When they had gone, she tied the red cord to the window.
22The spies went into the hills and hid. The king's men looked for them all over the countryside for three days, but they did not find them, so they returned to Jericho.
23Then the two spies came down from the hills, crossed the river, and went back to Joshua. They told him everything that had happened,
24and then said, "We are sure that the LORD has given us the whole country. All the people there are terrified of us."

The People of Israel Cross the Jordan

3 The next morning Joshua and all the people of Israel got up early, left the camp at Acacia, and went to the Jordan, where they camped while waiting to cross it.
2Three days later the leaders went through the camp
3and told the people, "When you see the priests carrying the Covenant Box of the LORD your God, break camp and follow them.
4You have never been here before, so they will show you the way to go. But do not get near the Covenant Box; stay about half a mile behind it."
5Joshua told the people, "Purify yourselves, because tomorrow the LORD will perform miracles among you."
6Then he told the priests to take the Covenant Box and go with it ahead of the people. They did as he said.
7The LORD said to Joshua, "What I do today will make all the people of Israel begin to honor you as a great man, and they will realize that I am with you as I was with Moses.
8Tell the priests carrying the Covenant Box that when they reach the river, they must wade in and stand near the bank."
9Then Joshua said to the people, "Come here and listen to what the LORD your God has to say.
10As you advance, he will surely drive out the Canaanites, the Hittites, the Hivites, the Perizzites, the Girgashites, the

Study it!

Remember When . . .

Remember when Moses brought the people of Israel across the Red Sea (Exodus 14:21–31)? The story of Joshua leading the people across the Jordan is meant to remind people of Moses. A miracle happens. The waters are parted. All the people are able to cross over safely. Why might the author want people to compare Joshua to Moses?

— Joshua 3:14–17

Amorites, and the Jebusites. You will know
that the living God is among you 11when
the Covenant Box of the Lord of all the
earth crosses the Jordan ahead of you. 12Now
choose twelve men, one from each of the
tribes of Israel. 13When the priests who
carry the Covenant Box of the LORD of all
the earth put their feet in the water, the Jordan will stop flowing, and the water coming
downstream will pile up in one place."

14-15It was harvest time, and the river was
in flood.

When the people left the camp to cross
the Jordan, the priests went ahead of them,
carrying the Covenant Box. As soon as the
priests stepped into the river, 16the water
stopped flowing and piled up, far upstream at
Adam, the city beside Zarethan. The flow
downstream to the Dead Sea was completely
cut off, and the people were able to cross
over near Jericho. 17While the people
walked across on dry ground, the priests carrying the LORD's Covenant Box stood on
dry ground in the middle of the Jordan until
all the people had crossed over.

Memorial Stones Are Set Up

4 When the whole nation had crossed the
Jordan, the LORD said to Joshua,
2"Choose twelve men, one from each tribe,
3and command them to take twelve stones
out of the middle of the Jordan, from the
very place where the priests were standing.
Tell them to carry these stones with them
and to put them down where you camp
tonight."

4Then Joshua called the twelve men he
had chosen, 5and he told them, "Go into the
Jordan ahead of the Covenant Box of the
LORD your God. Each one of you take a
stone on your shoulder, one for each of the

The people hurried across the river. (4:10)

tribes of Israel. 6These stones will remind
the people of what the LORD has done. In
the future, when your children ask what
these stones mean to you, 7you will tell
them that the water of the Jordan stopped
flowing when the LORD's Covenant Box
crossed the river. These stones will always
remind the people of Israel of what hap-
pened here."

8The men followed Joshua's orders. As the
LORD had commanded Joshua, they took
twelve stones from the middle of the Jordan,
one for each of the tribes of Israel, carried
them to the camping place, and put them
down there. 9Joshua also set up twelve stones
in the middle of the Jordan, where the
priests carrying the Covenant Box had
stood. (Those stones are still there.) 10The
priests stood in the middle of the Jordan
until everything had been done that the
LORD ordered Joshua to tell the people to
do. This is what Moses had commanded.

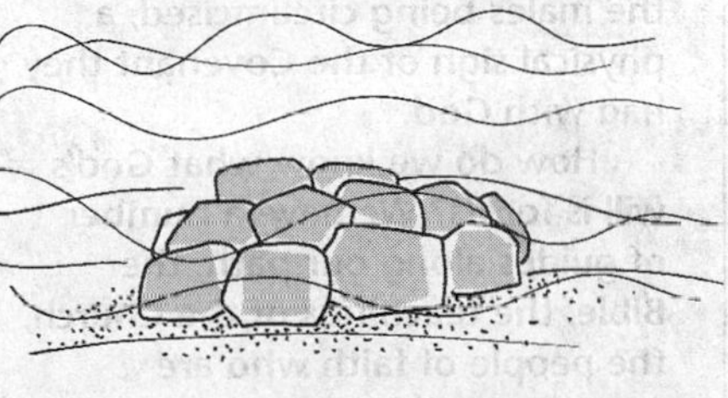

Twelve stones in the middle of the Jordan (4:9)

The people hurried across the river.
11When they were all on the other side, the
priests with the LORD's Covenant Box went
on ahead of the people. 12The men of the
tribes of Reuben and Gad and of half the
tribe of Manasseh, ready for battle, crossed
ahead of the rest of the people, as Moses had
told them to do. 13In the presence of the
LORD about forty thousand men ready for
war crossed over to the plain near Jericho.
14What the LORD did that day made the
people of Israel consider Joshua a great man.
They honored him all his life, just as they
had honored Moses.

15Then the LORD told Joshua 16to com-
mand the priests carrying the Covenant Box

Study it!

An Important Dozen

There are twelve tribes of Israel, descended from the twelve sons of Jacob (Genesis 35:23–26). After the Israelites had passed through the Jordan, the Lord had each tribe take a large stone from the riverbed. They carried the stones to dry land and made an altar in honor of God's power. It was a custom to make an altar to honor God as a memorial wherever a special event occurred.

Throughout the Old Testament, God guides the twelve tribes that make up the whole nation. Sometimes they fight among themselves, but often, especially in the Book of Joshua, they work together and try hard to be unified. Jesus chose twelve Apostles to be his closest followers. The number is meant to remind everyone that Jesus' mission is a continuation of the salvation begun in the Hebrew Scriptures.

— Joshua 4:19–24

to come up out of the Jordan. 17Joshua did
so, 18and when the priests reached the river-
bank, the river began flowing once more
and flooded its banks again.

19The people crossed the Jordan on the
tenth day of the first month and camped at
Gilgal, east of Jericho. 20There Joshua set up
the twelve stones taken from the Jordan.
21And he said to the people of Israel, "In the
future, when your children ask you what these
stones mean, 22you will tell them about the
time when Israel crossed the Jordan on dry

The Covenant Box is also called the Ark of the Covenant. It was a sign of God's presence and leadership.

ground. 23Tell them that the LORD your God
dried up the water of the Jordan for you until
you had crossed, just as he dried up the Red
Sea for us. 24Because of this everyone on earth
will know how great the LORD's power is, and
you will honor the LORD your God forever."

5 All the Amorite kings west of the Jor-
dan and all the Canaanite kings along
the Mediterranean Sea heard that the LORD
had dried up the Jordan until the people of
Israel had crossed it. They became afraid and
lost their courage because of the Israelites.

The Circumcision at Gilgal

2Then the LORD told Joshua, "Make some
knives out of flint and circumcise the
Israelites." 3So Joshua did as the LORD had
commanded, and he circumcised the
Israelites at a place called Circumcision Hill.
4-6When the people of Israel left Egypt, all
the males were already circumcised. Howev-
er, during the forty years the people spent
crossing the desert, none of the baby boys
had been circumcised. Also, by the end of
that time all the men who were of fighting
age when they left Egypt had died because
they had disobeyed the LORD. Just as he had
sworn, they were not allowed to see the rich
and fertile land that he had promised their
ancestors. 7The sons of these men had never
been circumcised, and it was this new gener-
ation that Joshua circumcised.
8After the circumcision was completed,
the whole nation stayed in the camp until
the wounds had healed. 9The LORD said to
Joshua, "Today I have removed from you the
disgrace of being slaves in Egypt." That is
why the place was named Gilgal,[b] the name
it still has.
10While the Israelites were camping at
Gilgal on the plain near Jericho, they
observed Passover on the evening of the
fourteenth day of the month. 11The next day
was the first time they ate food grown in
Canaan: roasted grain and bread made with-
out yeast. 12The manna stopped falling then,
and the Israelites no longer had any. From
that time on they ate food grown in Canaan.

Live it!

Following God's Will

The Israelites have done what God has asked them to do. God rewards them by bringing them into the Promised Land. But even though they had Moses and Aaron to lead them, they have not always followed God's will. They had to wander in the desert for forty years because they had been disobedient. All the adult men and women who had been adults when they left their life of slavery in Egypt had died during those years. Now a new generation would pick up where the older generation left off, and they would start with all the males being circumcised, a physical sign of the Covenant they had with God.

How do we know what God's will is for us? We have a number of guides along our path: the Bible, the teachings of the Church, the people of faith who are around us, and our own conscience. All these things help us understand what God wants for us. And the sacraments of the Church are a physical sign of God's power in our life and our promise to follow God's will. You have a responsibility for keeping the mission of Jesus alive in the world!

— Joshua 5:2–9

[b] **5:9** GILGAL: *This name sounds like the Hebrew for "removed."*
5:6 Num 14:28–35 **5:10** Ex 12:1–13 **5:12** Ex 16:35

"Everyone on earth will know how great the LORD's power is, and you will honor the LORD your God forever" *(Joshua 4:24)*.

Live it!

The Angel's Promise

In the Bible, angels have a number of different roles. They bring messages, they give advice, they guide, and they encourage. After the Israelites enter the Promised Land, an angel with a sword appears to Joshua as a sign that God will be with them in the battles to come. The angel is a reminder that God is with Joshua in the same way God was with Moses. The angel in this story even uses the same words as the angel who spoke to Moses (Exodus 3:5): "Take your sandals off; you are standing on holy ground" (Joshua 5:15).

What are some times when you feel a special need for God's reassurance? During those times look for little signs that God is with you. Joshua had to notice the angel and even go ask him why he was there. The signs of God's love and presence are often just little things: the smile of a stranger or a song on the radio with a special message for you. And don't be afraid to ask a parent, a friend, or another adult you trust for a little extra support. They are also God's messengers in your life.

– Joshua 5:13–15

Joshua and the Man with a Sword

13 While Joshua was near Jericho, he suddenly saw a man standing in front of him, holding a sword. Joshua went up to him and asked, "Are you one of our soldiers, or an enemy?"
14 "Neither," the man answered. "I am here as the commander of the LORD's army."

Joshua threw himself on the ground in worship and said, "I am your servant, sir. What do you want me to do?"

15 And the commander of the LORD's army told him, "Take your sandals off; you are standing on holy ground." And Joshua did as he was told.

The Fall of Jericho

6 The gates of Jericho were kept shut and guarded to keep the Israelites out. No
one could enter or leave the city. 2 The
LORD said to Joshua, "I am putting into your hands Jericho, with its king and all its brave
soldiers. 3 You and your soldiers are to march around the city once a day for six days.
4 Seven priests, each carrying a trumpet, are to go in front of the Covenant Box. On the seventh day you and your soldiers are to march around the city seven times while the
priests blow the trumpets. 5 Then they are to sound one long note. As soon as you hear it, all the people are to give a loud shout, and the city walls will collapse. Then the whole army will go straight into the city."
6 Joshua called the priests and told them, "Take the Covenant Box, and seven of you
go in front of it, carrying trumpets." 7 Then he ordered the people to start marching around the city, with an advance guard going on ahead of the LORD's Covenant Box.
8-9 So, just as Joshua had ordered, an advance guard started out ahead of the priests who were blowing trumpets; behind these came the priests who were carrying the Covenant Box, followed by a rear guard. All this time the trumpets were sounding.
10 But Joshua had ordered the people not to shout, not to say a word until he gave the
order. 11 So he had this group of men take the LORD's Covenant Box around the city one time. Then they came back to camp and spent the night there.
12-13 Joshua got up early the next morning, and for the second time the priests and soldiers marched around the city in the same order as the day before: first, the advance guard; next, the seven priests blowing the seven trumpets; then, the priests carrying the LORD's Covenant Box; and finally, the rear guard. All this time the trumpets were
sounding. 14 On this second day they again marched around the city one time and then returned to camp. They did this for six days.

Study it!

Whose Power Won?

The fall of Jericho is important because it is the first military victory of the Israelites. But when you read the story, notice the strange way they win. God has Joshua's army march around the city once a day for seven days. They are led by the priests who carry the Covenant Box. On the seventh day the priests blow their trumpets, and the army shouts, and the walls that protect the city collapse, leaving it defenseless! What does this mean?

In the Bible, numbers have symbolic meanings. Seven is a number that symbolizes completeness and God's power—remember the seven days of creation in the opening chapters of the Book of Genesis? The seven marches on seven days show that the victory belongs not to a leader or an army but to God.

— Joshua 6:1–20

15 On the seventh day they got up at day-
break and marched seven times around the
city in the same way—this was the only day
that they marched around it seven times.
16 The seventh time around, when the priests
were about to sound the trumpets, Joshua
ordered the people to shout, and he said,
"The LORD has given you the city! 17 The
city and everything in it must be totally
destroyed as an offering to the LORD. Only
the prostitute Rahab and her household will
be spared, because she hid our spies. 18 But
you are not to take anything that is to be
destroyed; if you do, you will bring trouble
and destruction on the Israelite camp.
19 Everything made of silver, gold, bronze,
or iron is set apart for the LORD. It is to be
put in the LORD's treasury."
20 So the priests blew the trumpets. As
soon as the people heard it, they gave a loud
shout, and the walls collapsed. Then all the
army went straight up the hill into the city
and captured it. 21 With their swords they
killed everyone in the city, men and women,
young and old. They also killed the cattle,
sheep, and donkeys.
22 Joshua then told the two men who had
served as spies, "Go into the prostitute's
house, and bring her and her family out, as
you promised her." 23 So they went and

6:20 Heb 11:30

They gave a loud shout, and the walls collapsed. (6:20)

Study it!

Can There Be Holy War?

In the Old Testament there are many stories of war victories that are portrayed as the fulfillment of God's wishes. Joshua and the Israelites saw the Canaanites as a threat to their beliefs and felt that it was God's will that they should kill them all. They even felt that wars against unbelievers were holy and commanded by God. When their army was victorious in battle, the Israelites understood it to mean that God was on their side.

For Christians this view of war is a problem. Because of Jesus' teachings, the terms *holy* and *war* seem to contradict each other. Jesus taught us to love our enemies and to do good to those who persecute us. We interpret the Old Testament in the light of Jesus' teachings. Because of this, the Church teaches that war is only to be used as a last resort under very specific circumstances. War is not holy and marks a failure by somebody to live by God's will. Every effort should be made to find nonviolent solutions before resorting to war.

— Joshua 6:21

brought Rahab out, along with her father
and mother, her brothers, and the rest of her
family. They took them all, family and slaves,
to safety near the Israelite camp. 24 Then they
set fire to the city and burned it to the
ground, along with everything in it, except
the things made of gold, silver, bronze, and
iron, which they took and put in the LORD's
treasury. 25 But Joshua spared the lives of the
prostitute Rahab and all her relatives,
because she had hidden the two spies that he
had sent to Jericho. (Her descendants have
lived in Israel to this day.)
26 At this time Joshua issued a solemn
warning: "Anyone who tries to rebuild the
city of Jericho will be under the LORD's
curse.

Whoever lays the foundation will lose his
oldest son;
Whoever builds the gates will lose his
youngest."

27 So the LORD was with Joshua, and his
fame spread through the whole country.

Achan's Sin

7 The LORD's command to Israel not to
take from Jericho anything that was to
be destroyed was not obeyed. A man named
Achan disobeyed that order, and so the
LORD was furious with the Israelites. (Achan
was the son of Carmi and grandson of
Zabdi, and belonged to the clan of Zerah, a
part of the tribe of Judah.)
2 Joshua sent some men from Jericho to
Ai, a city east of Bethel, near Bethaven, with
orders to go and explore the land. When
they had done so, 3 they reported back to
Joshua: "There is no need for everyone to
attack Ai. Send only about two or three
thousand men. Don't send the whole army
up there to fight; it is not a large city." 4 So
about three thousand Israelites made the
attack, but they were forced to retreat. 5 The
men of Ai chased them from the city gate as
far as some quarries and killed about thirty-
six of them on the way down the hill. Then
the Israelites lost their courage and were
afraid.
6 Joshua and the leaders of Israel tore their
clothes in grief, threw themselves to the
ground before the LORD's Covenant Box,
and lay there till evening, with dust on their

6:25 Heb 11:31 **6:26** 1 Kings 16:34

Rahab of Jericho was spared by the Israelites. She became the great-great-grandmother of King David and an ancestor of Jesus *(Matthew 1:2–6)*.

heads to show their sorrow. 7 And Joshua
said, "Sovereign LORD! Why did you bring
us across the Jordan at all? To turn us over to
the Amorites? To destroy us? Why didn't we
just stay on the other side of the Jordan?
8 What can I say, O Lord, now that Israel has
retreated from the enemy? 9 The Canaanites
and everyone else in the country will hear
about it. They will surround us and kill every
one of us! And then what will you do to
protect your honor?"

10 The LORD said to Joshua, "Get up! Why
are you lying on the ground like this?
11 Israel has sinned! They have broken the
agreement with me that I ordered them to
keep. They have taken some of the things
condemned to destruction. They stole them,
lied about it, and put them with their own
things. 12 This is why the Israelites cannot
stand against their enemies. They retreat
from them because they themselves have
now been condemned to destruction! I will
not stay with you any longer unless you
destroy the things you were ordered not to
take! 13 Get up! Purify the people and get
them ready to come before me. Tell them to
be ready tomorrow, because I, the LORD
God of Israel, have this to say: 'Israel, you
have in your possession some things that I
ordered you to destroy! You cannot stand
against your enemies until you get rid of
these things!' 14 So tell them that in the
morning they will be brought forward, tribe
by tribe. The tribe that I pick out will then
come forward, clan by clan. The clan that I
pick out will come forward, family by fami-
ly. The family that I pick out will come for-
ward, one by one. 15 The one who is then
picked out and found with the condemned
goods will be burned, along with his family
and everything he owns, for he has brought
terrible shame on Israel and has broken my
covenant."

16 Early the next morning Joshua brought
Israel forward, tribe by tribe, and the tribe of
Judah was picked out. 17 He brought the
tribe of Judah forward, clan by clan, and the
clan of Zerah was picked out. Then he
brought the clan of Zerah forward, family by
family, and the family of Zabdi was picked
out. 18 He then brought Zabdi's family for-

Live it!

Consequences

Actions have consequences. Have you ever gotten grounded by your parents for breaking the rules? Ever had a friend stop trusting you because of something you did or said? Usually the people who love us and care about us will forgive us when we make mistakes or even when we do something wrong on purpose. Sometimes, though, the consequences are bigger than we can handle or fix. We might spread a rumor that ruins a person's reputation. When someone drives drunk and kills another person in an accident, the consequences affect many people for years to come.

This is what happened to the Israelites with Achan. God commanded the people not to take anything from the city of Jericho. It seemed God wanted this first battle to not be about gaining wealth or possessions. But Achan took gold, silver, and clothing. His disobedience had consequences not only for him but also for all the Israelites. They lost the very next battle they fought.

The next time you're tempted to do something wrong, consider the consequences. How will this action hurt you and possibly other people?

— Joshua, chapter 7

The valley of trouble is called Achor, which means "misery" or "affliction" in the Hebrew language.

Pray it!

Courage

"Don't be afraid or discouraged. I will give you victory" (Joshua 8:1). Joshua and the people of Israel trusted their lives to God. Do you rely on God? Trusting in God can be a hard thing to do. We want to do it ourselves, our own way. God sometimes asks us to take chances and step beyond where we are comfortable.

God help me to rely on you.
Give me the courage to follow your will
as I reach out to others and as I learn new things.
Help me to have the confidence that you
will always be there to guide me and protect me.

— Joshua 8:1–2

ward, one by one, and Achan, the son of
Carmi and grandson of Zabdi, was picked
out. [19]Joshua said to him, "My son, tell the
truth here before the LORD, the God of
Israel, and confess. Tell me now what you
have done. Don't try to hide it from me."
[20]"It's true," Achan answered. "I have
sinned against the LORD, Israel's God, and
this is what I did. [21]Among the things we
seized I saw a beautiful Babylonian cloak,
about five pounds of silver, and a bar of gold
weighing over one pound. I wanted them so
much that I took them. You will find them
buried inside my tent, with the silver at the
bottom."
[22]So Joshua sent some men, who ran to
the tent and found that the condemned
things really were buried there, with the sil-
ver at the bottom. [23]They brought them out
of the tent, took them to Joshua and all the
Israelites, and laid them down in the pres-
ence of the LORD. [24]Joshua, along with all
the people of Israel, seized Achan, the silver,
the cloak, the bar of gold, together with
Achan's sons and daughters, his cattle, don-
keys, and sheep, his tent, and everything else
he owned; and they took them to Trouble
Valley. [25]And Joshua said, "Why have you
brought such trouble on us? The LORD will
now bring trouble on you!" All the people
then stoned Achan to death; they also stoned
and burned his family and possessions.
[26]They put a huge pile of stones over him,
which is there to this day. That is why that
place is still called Trouble Valley.
Then the LORD was no longer furious.

The Capture and Destruction of Ai

8 The LORD said to Joshua, "Take all the
soldiers with you and go on up to Ai.
Don't be afraid or discouraged. I will give
you victory over the king of Ai; his people,
city, and land will be yours. [2]You are to do
to Ai and its king what you did to Jericho
and its king, but this time you may keep
its goods and livestock for yourselves. Pre-
pare to attack the city by surprise from the
rear."
[3]So Joshua got ready to go to Ai with all
his soldiers. He picked out thirty thousand
of his best troops and sent them out at
night [4]with these orders: "Hide on the
other side of the city, but not too far away
from it; be ready to attack. [5]My men and I
will approach the city. When the men of Ai
come out against us, we will turn and run,
just as we did the first time. [6]They will pur-
sue us until we have led them away from
the city. They will think that we are run-
ning from them, as we did before. [7]Then
you will come out of hiding and capture
the city. The LORD your God will give it to
you. [8]After you have taken the city, set it on
fire, just as the LORD has commanded.

These are your orders." 9 So Joshua sent
them out, and they went to their hiding
place and waited there, west of Ai, between
Ai and Bethel. Joshua spent the night in
camp.

10 Early in the morning Joshua got up and
called the soldiers together. Then he and the
leaders of Israel led them to Ai. 11 The sol-
diers with him went toward the main
entrance to the city and set up camp on the
north side, with a valley between themselves
and Ai. 12 He took about five thousand men
and put them in hiding west of the city,
between Ai and Bethel. 13 The soldiers were
arranged for battle with the main camp
north of the city and the rest of the men to
the west. Joshua spent the night in the val-
ley. 14 When the king of Ai saw Joshua's
men, he acted quickly. He and all his men
went out toward the Jordan Valley to fight
the Israelites at the same place as before, not
knowing that he was about to be attacked
from the rear. 15 Joshua and his men pre-
tended that they were retreating, and ran
away toward the barren country. 16 All the
men in the city had been called together to
go after them, and as they pursued Joshua,
they kept getting farther away from the city.
17 Every man in Ai[c] went after the Israelites,
and the city was left wide open, with no
one to defend it.

18 Then the LORD said to Joshua, "Point
your spear at Ai; I am giving it to you."
Joshua did as he was told, 19 and as soon as he
lifted his hand, the men who had been hid-
ing got up quickly, ran into the city and cap-
tured it. They immediately set the city on
fire. 20 When the men of Ai looked back,
they saw the smoke rising to the sky. There
was no way for them to escape, because the
Israelites who had run toward the barren
country now turned around to attack them.
21 When Joshua and his men saw that the
others had taken the city and that it was on
fire, they turned around and began killing
the men of Ai. 22 The Israelites in the city
now came down to join the battle. So the
men of Ai found themselves completely sur-
rounded by Israelites, and they were all
killed. No one got away, and no one lived
through it 23 except the king of Ai. He was
captured and taken to Joshua.

24 The Israelites killed every one of the
enemy in the barren country where they
had chased them. Then they went back to Ai
and killed everyone there. 25-26 Joshua kept
his spear pointed at Ai and did not put it
down until every person there had been
killed. The whole population of Ai was killed
that day—twelve thousand men and women.
27 The Israelites kept for themselves the live-
stock and goods captured in the city, as the
LORD had told Joshua. 28 Joshua burned Ai
and left it in ruins. It is still like that today.
29 He hanged the king of Ai from a tree and
left his body there until evening. At sun-
down Joshua gave orders for the body to be
removed, and it was thrown down at the
entrance to the city gate. They covered it
with a huge pile of stones, which is still
there today.

The Law Is Read at Mount Ebal

30 Then Joshua built on Mount Ebal an
altar to the LORD, the God of Israel. 31 He
made it according to the instructions that
Moses, the LORD's servant, had given the
Israelites, as it says in the Law of Moses: "an
altar made of stones which have not been
cut with iron tools." On it they offered
burnt sacrifices to the LORD, and they also
presented their fellowship offerings.
32 There, with the Israelites looking on,
Joshua made on the stones[d] a copy of the
Law which Moses had written. 33 The
Israelites, with their leaders, officers, and
judges, as well as the foreigners among
them, stood on two sides of the LORD's
Covenant Box, facing the levitical priests
who carried it. Half of the people stood
with their backs to Mount Gerizim and the
other half with their backs to Mount Ebal.
The LORD's servant Moses had commanded
them to do this when the time came for
them to receive the blessing. 34 Joshua then
read aloud the whole Law, including the
blessings and the curses, just as they are

[c] **8:17** *One ancient translation* Ai; *Hebrew* Ai and Bethel. [d] **8:32** the stones; *or* stones.

8:30–32 Deut 27:2–8 **8:31** Ex 20:25 **8:33–35** Deut 11:29; 27:11–14

Catholic Connections

Altars

The Israelites built an altar at Mount Ebal to offer sacrifice in praise and thanksgiving to God. This altar was a renewal of their promise to be obedient to God. Altars were a way to offer thanksgiving and praise to God. The altar at Mount Ebal reminded them that even though they were in a new place, their identity was the same. They were still the People of God. Joshua emphasized this by reading aloud the whole Law to the people.

Every Catholic church has an altar. We also offer thanks and praise to God. It's where we celebrate who we are. At the alter we celebrate and renew Jesus' sacrifice and gather as one family around the table of the Lord. The altar helps us remember our identity as followers of Jesus, the family of God.

— Joshua 8:30–35

written in the book of the Law. 35 Every one
of the commandments of Moses was read
by Joshua to the whole gathering, which
included women and children, as well as
the foreigners living among them.

The Gibeonites Deceive Joshua

9 The victories of Israel became known
to all the kings west of the Jordan—in
the hills, in the foothills, and all along the
coastal plain of the Mediterranean Sea as far
north as Lebanon; these were the kings of
the Hittites, the Amorites, the Canaanites,
the Perizzites, the Hivites, and the Jebusites.
2 They all came together and joined forces to
fight against Joshua and the Israelites.
3 But the people of Gibeon, who were
Hivites, heard what Joshua had done to Jeri-
cho and Ai, 4 and they decided to deceive
him. They went and got some food and
loaded their donkeys with worn-out sacks
and patched-up wineskins. 5 They put on
ragged clothes and worn-out sandals that
had been mended. The bread they took
with them was dry and moldy. 6 Then they
went to the camp at Gilgal and said to
Joshua and the Israelites, "We have come
from a distant land. We want you to make a
treaty with us."
7 But the Israelites said, "Why should we
make a treaty with you? Maybe you live
nearby."
8 They said to Joshua, "We are at your
service."
Joshua asked them, "Who are you? Where
do you come from?"
9 Then they told him this story: "We have
come from a very distant land, sir, because
we have heard of the LORD your God. We
have heard about everything that he did in
Egypt 10 and what he did to the two Amorite
kings east of the Jordan: King Sihon of
Heshbon and King Og of Bashan, who lived
in Ashtaroth. 11 Our leaders and all the peo-
ple that live in our land told us to get some
food ready for a trip and to go and meet
you. We were told to put ourselves at your
service and ask you to make a treaty with us.
12 Look at our bread. When we left home
with it and started out to meet you, it was
still warm. But look! Now it is dry and

9:7 Ex 23:32; 34:12; Deut 7:2 **9:10** Num 21:21–35

Sometimes in the Bible it's the crafty or clever people who succeed. The people of Gibeon trick Joshua into an alliance, and so they survive.

moldy. 13When we filled these wineskins,
they were new, but look! They are torn. Our
clothes and sandals are worn out from the
long trip."

"But look! They are torn." (9:13)

14The Israelites accepted some food from
them, but did not consult the LORD about it.
15Joshua made a treaty of friendship with the
people of Gibeon and allowed them to live.
The leaders of the community of Israel gave
their solemn promise to keep the treaty.
16Three days after the treaty had been
made, the Israelites learned that these people
did indeed live nearby. 17So the people of
Israel started out and three days later arrived
at the cities where these people lived:
Gibeon, Chephirah, Beeroth, and Kiriath
Jearim. 18But the Israelites could not kill
them, because their leaders had made a
solemn promise to them in the name of the
LORD, Israel's God. All the people com-
plained to the leaders about this, 19but they
answered, "We have made our solemn prom-
ise to them in the name of the LORD God of
Israel. Now we cannot harm them. 20We
must let them live because of our promise; if
we don't, God will punish us. 21Let them
live, but they will have to cut wood and
carry water for us." This was what the lead-
ers suggested.
22Joshua ordered the people of Gibeon to
be brought to him, and he asked them,
"Why did you deceive us and tell us that
you were from far away, when you live right
here? 23Because you did this, God has con-
demned you. Your people will always be
slaves, cutting wood and carrying water for
the sanctuary of my God."
24They answered, "We did it, sir, because
we learned that it was really true that the
LORD your God had commanded his servant
Moses to give you the whole land and to kill
the people living in it as you advanced. We
did it because we were terrified of you; we
were in fear of our lives. 25Now we are in
your power; do with us what you think is
right." 26So this is what Joshua did: he pro-
tected them and did not allow the people of
Israel to kill them. 27But at the same time he
made them slaves, to cut wood and carry
water for the people of Israel and for the
LORD's altar. To this day they have continued
to do this work in the place where the
LORD has chosen to be worshiped.

The Amorites Are Defeated

10 Adonizedek, the king of Jerusalem,[e]
heard that Joshua had captured and
totally destroyed Ai and had killed its king,
just as he had done to Jericho and its king.
He also heard that the people of Gibeon had
made peace with the Israelites and were liv-
ing among them. 2The people of Jerusalem
were greatly alarmed at this because Gibeon
was as large as any of the cities that had a
king; it was larger than Ai, and its men were
good fighters. 3So Adonizedek sent the fol-
lowing message to King Hoham of Hebron,
King Piram of Jarmuth, King Japhia of
Lachish, and to King Debir of Eglon:
4"Come and help me attack Gibeon,
because its people have made peace with
Joshua and the Israelites." 5These five Amo-
rite kings, the kings of Jerusalem, Hebron,
Jarmuth, Lachish, and Eglon, joined forces,
surrounded Gibeon, and attacked it.
6The men of Gibeon sent word to Joshua
at the camp in Gilgal: "Do not abandon us,
sir! Come at once and help us! Save us! All

[e] **10:1** JERUSALEM: *At that time it was a Jebusite city.*

What other miracles of nature are recorded in the Scriptures? Can you find a flood, an earthquake, a storm at sea, and a drought?

Pray it!

Helpful Hail

Have you ever witnessed a powerful storm? It can be scary, but it can be beautiful. It can also remind us of the tremendous power of nature. As Joshua's army chased down its enemies, strange things were going on in the sky that helped their battle. In biblical times, natural phenomena like earthquakes, solar and lunar eclipses, volcanic eruptions, and powerful storms were often seen as signs of God's punishment or power. Because we understand how weather develops and what causes earthquakes, we can sometimes take the forces of nature for granted.

God of all creation,
you made everything
from the depths of the earth to the farthest star.
Wind and water, sun and sky,
you made everything.
Help me to remember
when I see a beautiful sunset or a powerful storm,
when nature amazes me,
that you made everything.

— Joshua 10:11–14

the Amorite kings in the hill country have joined forces and have attacked us!"
7So Joshua and his whole army, including the best troops, started out from Gilgal. 8The
LORD said to Joshua, "Do not be afraid of them. I have already given you the victory. Not one of them will be able to stand
against you." 9All night Joshua and his army marched from Gilgal to Gibeon, and they made a surprise attack on the Amorites.
10The LORD made the Amorites panic at the sight of Israel's army. The Israelites slaughtered them at Gibeon and pursued them down the mountain pass at Beth Horon, keeping up the attack as far south as Azekah
and Makkedah. 11While the Amorites were running down the pass from the Israelite army, the LORD made large hailstones fall down on them all the way to Azekah. More were killed by the hailstones than by the Israelites.
12On the day that the LORD gave the men of Israel victory over the Amorites, Joshua spoke to the LORD. In the presence of the Israelites he said,

"Sun, stand still over Gibeon;
Moon, stop over Aijalon Valley."

13The sun stood still and the moon did not move until the nation had conquered its enemies. This is written in the Book of Jashar. The sun stood still in the middle of the sky and did not go down for a whole
day. 14Never before, and never since, has there been a day like it, when the LORD obeyed a human being. The LORD fought on Israel's side!
15After this, Joshua and his army went back to the camp at Gilgal.

Joshua Captures the Five Amorite Kings

16The five Amorite kings, however, had escaped and were hiding in the cave at
Makkedah. 17Someone found them, and Joshua was told where they were hiding.
18He said, "Roll some big stones in front of the entrance to the cave. Place some guards

there, [19]but don't stay there yourselves. Keep
on after the enemy and attack them from the
rear; don't let them get to their cities! The
LORD your God has given you victory over
them." [20]Joshua and the men of Israel
slaughtered them, although some managed
to find safety inside their city walls and were
not killed. [21]Then all of Joshua's men came
back safe to him at the camp at Makkedah.

No one in the land dared even to speak
against the Israelites.

Bring those five kings out to me. (10:22)

[22]Then Joshua said, "Open the entrance to
the cave and bring those five kings out to
me." [23]So the cave was opened, and the kings
of Jerusalem, Hebron, Jarmuth, Lachish, and
Eglon were brought out [24]and taken to
Joshua. Joshua then called all the men of Israel
to him and ordered the officers who had
gone with him to come and put their feet on
the necks of the kings. They did so. [25]Then
Joshua said to his officers, "Don't be afraid or
discouraged. Be determined and confident
because this is what the LORD is going to do
to all your enemies." [26]Then Joshua killed the
kings and hanged them on five trees, where
their bodies stayed until evening. [27]At sun-
down Joshua gave orders, and their bodies
were taken down and thrown into the same
cave where they had hidden earlier. Large
stones were placed at the entrance to the
cave, and they are still there.

Joshua Captures More Amorite Territory

[28]Joshua attacked and captured Makkedah
and its king that day. He put everyone in the
city to death; no one was left alive. He did to
the king of Makkedah what he had done to
the king of Jericho.

[29]After this, Joshua and his army went on
from Makkedah to Libnah and attacked it.
[30]The LORD also gave the Israelites victory
over this city and its king. They spared no
one, but killed every person in it. They did
to the king what they had done to the king
of Jericho.

[31]After this, Joshua and his army went on
from Libnah to Lachish, surrounded it and
attacked it. [32]The LORD gave the Israelites
victory over Lachish on the second day of
the battle. Just as they had done at Libnah,
they spared no one, but killed every person
in the city. [33]King Horam of Gezer came to
the aid of Lachish, but Joshua defeated him
and his army and left none of them alive.

[34]Next, Joshua and his army went on
from Lachish to Eglon, surrounded it and
attacked it. [35]They captured it the same day
and put everyone there to death, just as they
had done at Lachish.

[36]After this, Joshua and his army went
from Eglon up into the hills to Hebron,
attacked it [37]and captured it. They killed the
king and everyone else in the city as well as
in the nearby towns. Joshua condemned the
city to total destruction, just as he had done
to Eglon. No one in it was left alive.

[38]Then Joshua and his army turned back
to Debir and attacked it. [39]He captured it,
with its king and all the nearby towns. They
put everyone there to death. Joshua did to
Debir and its king what he had done to
Hebron and to Libnah and its king.

[40]Joshua conquered the whole land. He
defeated the kings of the hill country, the
eastern slopes, and the western foothills, as
well as those of the dry country in the
south. He spared no one; everyone was put
to death. This was what the LORD God of
Israel had commanded. [41]Joshua's campaign
took him from Kadesh Barnea in the south
to Gaza near the coast, including all the area
of Goshen, and as far north as Gibeon.
[42]Joshua conquered all these kings and their
territory in one campaign because the
LORD, Israel's God, was fighting for Israel.

10:13 2 Sam 1:18; Sir 46:4–6

43 After this, Joshua and his army went back to the camp at Gilgal.

Joshua Defeats Jabin and His Allies

11 When the news of Israel's victories reached King Jabin of Hazor, he sent word to King Jobab of Madon, to the kings of Shimron and Achshaph, 2 and to the kings in the hill country in the north, in the Jordan Valley south of Lake Galilee, in the foothills, and on the coast near Dor. 3 He also sent word to the Canaanites on both sides of the Jordan, to the Amorites, the Hittites, the Perizzites, and the Jebusites in the hill country, as well as to the Hivites who lived at the foot of Mount Hermon in the land of Mizpah. 4 They came with all their soldiers—an army with as many men as there are grains of sand on the seashore. They also had many horses and chariots. 5 All of these kings joined forces and came together and set up camp at Merom Brook to fight against Israel.

6 The LORD said to Joshua, "Do not be afraid of them. By this time tomorrow I will have killed all of them for Israel. You are to cripple their horses and burn their chariots." 7 So Joshua and all his men attacked them by surprise at Merom Brook. 8 The LORD gave the Israelites victory over them; the Israelites attacked and pursued them as far north as Misrephoth Maim and Sidon, and as far east as the valley of Mizpah. The fight continued until none of the enemy was left alive. 9 Joshua did to them what the LORD had commanded: he crippled their horses and burned their chariots.

10 Joshua then turned back, captured Hazor and killed its king. (At that time Hazor was the most powerful of all those kingdoms.) 11 They put everyone there to death; no one was left alive, and the city was burned.

12 Joshua captured all these cities and their kings, putting everyone to death, just as Moses, the LORD's servant, had commanded. 13 However, the Israelites did not burn any of the cities built on mounds, except Hazor, which Joshua did burn. 14 The people of Israel took all the valuables and livestock from these cities and kept them for themselves. But they put every person to death; no one was left alive. 15 The LORD had given his commands to his servant Moses, Moses had given them to Joshua, and Joshua obeyed them. He did everything that the LORD had commanded Moses.

The Territory Taken by Joshua

16 Joshua captured all the land—the hill country and foothills, both north and south, all the area of Goshen and the dry country south of it, as well as the Jordan Valley. 17-18 The territory extended from Mount Halak in the south near Edom, as far as Baalgad in the north, in the valley of Lebanon south of Mount Hermon. Joshua was at war with the kings of this territory for a long time, but he captured them all and put them to death. 19 The only city that made peace with the people of Israel was Gibeon, where some of the Hivites lived. All the others were conquered in battle. 20 The LORD had made them determined to fight the Israelites, so that they would be condemned to total destruction and all be killed without mercy. This was what the LORD had commanded Moses.

21 At this time Joshua went and destroyed the race of giants called the Anakim who lived in the hill country—in Hebron, Debir, Anab, and in all the hill country of Judah and Israel. Joshua completely destroyed them and their cities. 22 None of the Anakim were left in the land of Israel; a few, however, were left in Gaza, Gath, and Ashdod.

23 Joshua captured the whole land, as the LORD had commanded Moses. Joshua gave it to the Israelites as their own and divided it into portions, one for each tribe.

So the people rested from war.

11:20 Deut 7:16

The city of Hazor *(Joshua 11:10)* **was the largest city of Joshua's time. With 40,000 inhabitants, it was almost ten times the size of Jerusalem.**

The Kings Defeated by Moses

12 The people of Israel had already
conquered and occupied the land
east of the Jordan, from the Arnon Valley up
the Jordan Valley and as far north as Mount
Hermon. They defeated two kings. 2One
was Sihon, the Amorite king who ruled at
Heshbon. His kingdom included half of
Gilead: from Aroer (on the edge of the
Arnon Valley) and from the city in[f] the mid-
dle of that valley, as far as the Jabbok River,
the border of Ammon; 3it included the Jor-
dan Valley from Lake Galilee south to Beth
Jeshimoth (east of the Dead Sea) and on
toward the foot of Mount Pisgah.
4They also defeated King Og of Bashan,
who was one of the last of the Rephaim; he
ruled at Ashtaroth and Edrei. 5His kingdom
included Mount Hermon, Salecah, and all of
Bashan as far as the boundaries of Geshur
and Maacah, as well as half of Gilead, as far
as the territory of King Sihon of Heshbon.
6These two kings were defeated by Moses
and the people of Israel. Moses, the LORD's
servant, gave their land to the tribes of
Reuben and Gad and to half the tribe of
Manasseh, to be their possession.

The Kings Defeated by Joshua

7Joshua and the people of Israel defeated
all the kings in the territory west of the Jor-
dan, from Baalgad in the valley of Lebanon
to Mount Halak in the south near Edom.
Joshua divided this land among the tribes
and gave it to them as a permanent posses-
sion. 8This portion included the hill country,
the western foothills, the Jordan Valley and its
foothills, the eastern slopes, and the dry
country in the south. This land had been the
home of the Hittites, the Amorites, the
Canaanites, the Perizzites, the Hivites, and
the Jebusites. 9The people of Israel defeated
the kings of the following cities: Jericho, Ai
(near Bethel), 10Jerusalem, Hebron, 11Jar-
muth, Lachish, 12Eglon, Gezer, 13Debir,
Geder, 14Hormah, Arad, 15Libnah, Adullam,
16Makkedah, Bethel, 17Tappuah, Hepher,
18Aphek, Lasharon, 19Madon, Hazor,
20Shimron Meron, Achshaph, 21Taanach,
Megiddo, 22Kedesh, Jokneam (in Carmel),
23Dor (on the coast), Goiim (in Galilee[g]),
24and Tirzah—thirty-one kings in all.

Study it!

Conquering Canaan

In a time when winning a battle was seen as a sign of God's blessing, Joshua was very blessed. Chapter 12 of Joshua lists all the kings defeated by Moses and Joshua. Even though Joshua was not a king himself, God had given him victory over kings. This list shows that the Israelites had won everything that God had promised them so far. The list includes all the different types of land in Palestine: hill country, the Jordan river valley, foothills, and plains. The Israelites were well on their way to gaining control over the Promised Land.

— Joshua, chapter 12

The Land Still to Be Taken

13 Joshua was now very old. The LORD
said to him, "You are very old, but
there is still much land to be taken: 2all the
territory of Philistia and Geshur, 3as well as
all the territory of the Avvim to the south.

[f] **12:2** *Probable text (see 13:16; Deut 2:36)* the city in; *Hebrew does not have these words.* [g] **12:23** *One ancient translation* Galilee; *Hebrew* Gilgal.

12:1–5 Num 21:21–35; Deut 2:26—3:11 **12:6** Num 32:33; Deut 3:12

The tribes mentioned in Joshua 12:6 will have a big argument over an altar with the rest of the tribes of Israel in Joshua, chapter 22.

(The land from the stream Shihor, at the Egyptian border, as far north as the border of Ekron was considered Canaanite; the kings of the Philistines lived at Gaza, Ashdod, Ashkelon, Gath, and Ekron.) [4]There is still all the Canaanite country, and Mearah (which belonged to the Sidonians), as far as Aphek, at the Amorite border; [5]the land of the Gebalites; all of Lebanon to the east, from Baalgad, which is south of Mount Hermon, to Hamath Pass. [6]This includes all the territory of the Sidonians, who live in the hill country between the Lebanon Mountains and Misrephoth Maim. I will drive all these peoples out as the people of Israel advance. You must divide the land among the Israelites, just as I have commanded you to do. [7]Now then, divide this land among the other nine tribes and half of the tribe of Manasseh, for them to possess as their own."

The Division of the Territory East of the Jordan

[8]The tribes of Reuben and Gad and the other half of the tribe of Manasseh had already received the land that Moses, the LORD's servant, had given them; it was on the east side of the Jordan River. [9]Their territory extended to Aroer (on the edge of the Arnon Valley) and the city in the middle of that valley and included all of the plateau from Medeba to Dibon. [10]It went as far as the border of Ammon and included all the cities that had been ruled by the Amorite king Sihon, who had ruled at Heshbon. [11]It included Gilead, the regions of Geshur and Maacah, all of Mount Hermon, and all of Bashan as far as Salecah. [12]It included the kingdom of Og, the last of the Rephaim, who had ruled at Ashtaroth and Edrei. Moses had defeated these people and driven them out. [13]However, the Israelites did not drive out the people of Geshur and Maacah; they still live in Israel.

[14]Moses had given no land to the tribe of Levi. As the LORD had told Moses, they were to receive as their possession a share of the sacrifices burned on the altar to the LORD God of Israel.

Live it!

Older and Wiser

Do you know an older person who has a strong faith in God? What do you think made their faith so strong? Often it's not because they've had an easy life but because they've learned that they needed to count on God. They've learned that when life got hard, they couldn't get by when they tried to do it on their own power.

When God commands Joshua to divide the land, Joshua is an old man. Joshua has followed God faithfully all his life. He has learned by experience that if you rely on God, God will always be there for you. During the rest of the book, Joshua doesn't fight any more battles. But he is still the wise leader the people come to for advice and inspiration.

What older person can you go to for advice and inspiration? Many young people have grandparents who fill that role. Ask that older person what he or she has learned about getting through life's hard times. Let that person's experiences inspire you.

— Joshua 13:1–7

The Territory Assigned to Reuben

[15]Moses had given a part of the land to the families of the tribe of Reuben as their possession. [16]Their territory extended to Aroer (on the edge of the Arnon Valley) and the city in the middle of that valley and included all the plateau around Medeba. [17]It included Heshbon and all the cities on the plateau: Dibon, Bamoth Baal, Beth Baalmeon, [18]Jahaz, Kedemoth, Mephaath, [19]Kiriathaim, Sibmah, Zereth Shahar on the hill in the valley,

13:6 Num 33:54 **13:8** Num 32:33; Deut 3:12 **13:14** Deut 18:1

Study it!

Dividing the Land

Chapter 13 of Joshua begins the second major part of this book. In this section the Promised Land is divided among the twelve tribes of Israel. Even though the major battles have been fought and most of the land has been won, there is still work to be done. In these chapters you will read about promises made and kept. Even though the division of the land all sounds pretty peaceful and orderly, the reality was probably a lot messier. Keep in mind that the guiding theme is that the promises God made to Moses and the Israelites at Mount Sinai are now being fulfilled.

— Joshua, chapter 13

20 Bethpeor, the slopes of Mount Pisgah, and
Beth Jeshimoth. 21 It included all the cities of
the plateau and the whole kingdom of the
Amorite king Sihon, who had ruled at Hesh-
bon. Moses defeated him, as well as the rulers
of Midian: Evi, Rekem, Zur, Hur, and Reba.
All of them had ruled the land for King
Sihon. 22 Among those whom the people of
Israel killed was the fortune teller Balaam son
of Beor. 23 The Jordan was the western border
of the tribe of Reuben. These were the cities
and towns given to the families of the tribe of
Reuben as their possession.

The Territory Assigned to Gad

24 Moses had also given a part of the land
to the families of the tribe of Gad as their
possession. 25 Their territory included Jazer
and all the cities of Gilead, half the land of
Ammon as far as Aroer, which is east of
Rabbah; 26 their land extended from Hesh-
bon to Ramath Mizpeh and Betonim, from
Mahanaim to the border of Lodebar. 27 In
the Jordan Valley it included Beth Haram,
Bethnimrah, Sukkoth, and Zaphon, the rest
of the kingdom of King Sihon of Heshbon.
Their western border was the Jordan River
as far north as Lake Galilee. 28 These were
the cities and towns given to the families of
the tribe of Gad as their possession.

The Territory Assigned to East Manasseh

29 Moses had given a part of the land to
the families of half the tribe of Manasseh as
their possession. 30 Their territory extended
to Mahanaim and included all of Bashan—
the whole kingdom of Og, the king of
Bashan, as well as all sixty of the villages of
Jair in Bashan. 31 It included half of Gilead, as
well as Ashtaroth and Edrei, the capital cities
of Og's kingdom in Bashan. All this was
given to half the families descended from
Machir son of Manasseh.

32 This is how Moses divided the land east
of Jericho and the Jordan when he was in
the plains of Moab. 33 But Moses did not
assign any land to the tribe of Levi. He told
them that their possession was to be a share
of the offerings to the LORD God of Israel.

The Division of the Territory West of the Jordan

14 What follows is an account of how
the land of Canaan west of the Jor-
dan was divided among the people of Israel.
Eleazar the priest, Joshua son of Nun, and
the leaders of the families of the Israelite
tribes divided it among the population. 2 As
the LORD had commanded Moses, the terri-
tories of the nine and one-half tribes west of
the Jordan were determined by drawing
lots.[h] 3-4 Moses had already assigned the land
east of the Jordan to the other two and one-
half tribes. (The descendants of Joseph were
divided into two tribes: Manasseh and
Ephraim.) However, Moses gave the Levites

[h] **14:2** DRAWING LOTS: *This was usually done by using specially marked stones to determine God's will.*

13:33 Num 18:20; Deut 18:2 **14:2** Num 26:52–56; 34:13 **14:3, 4** Num 32:33; 34:14, 15; Deut 3:12–17

no portion of the territory. Instead, they
received cities to live in, with fields for their
cattle and flocks. 5The people of Israel divid-
ed the land as the LORD had commanded
Moses.

Hebron Is Given to Caleb

6One day some people from the tribe of
Judah came to Joshua at Gilgal. One of
them, Caleb son of Jephunneh the Kenizzite,
said to him, "You know what the LORD said
in Kadesh Barnea about you and me to
Moses, the man of God. 7I was forty years
old when the LORD's servant Moses sent me
from Kadesh Barnea to spy out this land. I
brought an honest report back to him. 8The
men who went with me, however, made our
people afraid. But I faithfully obeyed the
LORD my God. 9Because I did, Moses prom-
ised me that my children and I would cer-
tainly receive as our possession the land
which I walked over. 10But now, look. It has
been forty-five years since the LORD said
that to Moses. That was when Israel was
going through the desert, and the LORD, as
he promised, has kept me alive ever since.
Look at me! I am eighty-five years old 11and
am just as strong today as I was when Moses
sent me out. I am still strong enough for war
or for anything else. 12Now then, give me
the hill country that the LORD promised me
on that day when my men and I reported.
We told you then that the race of giants
called the Anakim were there in large walled
cities. Maybe the LORD will be with me, and
I will drive them out, just as the LORD said."
13Joshua blessed Caleb son of Jephunneh
and gave him the city of Hebron as his pos-
session. 14Hebron still belongs to the descen-
dants of Caleb son of Jephunneh the
Kenizzite, because he faithfully obeyed the
LORD, the God of Israel. 15Before this,
Hebron was called the city of Arba. (Arba
had been the greatest of the Anakim.)
There was now peace in the land.

Live it!

Caleb's Reward

Caleb is given a special reward when the land is divided because of his faithfulness to God. We are also rewarded when we are faithful to God. Have you ever experienced any of the following rewards?

- **Feeling good about yourself because you've been kind to others.**
- **Becoming more happy and joyful because you made a decision based upon what God wants rather than on what other people think or do.**
- **Becoming less stressed because you know that God is with you.**

What other rewards have you received for trying to follow God's way?

— Joshua 14:6–15

The Territory Assigned to Judah

15 The families of the tribe of Judah
received a part of the land described
as follows:
The land reached south to the southern-
most point of the wilderness of Zin, at the
border of Edom. 2This southern border ran
from the south end of the Dead Sea, 3went
southward from the Akrabbim Pass and on
to Zin. It ran south of Kadesh Barnea, past
Hezron and up to Addar, turned toward
Karka, 4went on to Azmon, and followed the
stream on the border of Egypt to the
Mediterranean Sea, where the border ended.
That was the southern border of Judah.
5The eastern border was the Dead Sea, all

14:6 Num 14:30 **14:7** Num 13:1–30 **14:9** Num 14:24

What was special about the tribe of Levi, and why don't they receive land like the rest of the tribes? *(See Deuteronomy 18:1–8.)*

the way up to the inlet where the Jordan empties into it.

The northern border began there, 6 extended up to Beth Hoglah, and went north of the ridge overlooking the Jordan Valley. Then it went up to the Stone of Bohan (Bohan was a son of Reuben), 7 from Trouble Valley up to Debir, and then turned north toward Gilgal, which faces Adummim Pass on the south side of the valley. It then went on to the springs of Enshemesh, out to Enrogel, 8 and up through Hinnom Valley on the south side of the hill where the Jebusite city of Jerusalem was located. The border then proceeded up to the top of the hill on the west side of Hinnom Valley, at the northern end of Rephaim Valley. 9 From there it went to the Springs of Nephtoah and out to the cities near Mount Ephron. There it turned toward Baalah (or Kiriath Jearim), 10 where it circled west of Baalah toward the hill country of Edom, went on the north side of Mount Jearim (or Chesalon), down to Beth Shemesh, and on past Timnah. 11 The border then went out to the hill north of Ekron, turned toward Shikkeron, past Mount Baalah, and on to Jamnia. It ended at the Mediterranean Sea, 12 which formed the western border.

Within these borders lived the people of the families of Judah.

Caleb Conquers Hebron and Debir
(Judges 1:11–15)

13 As the LORD commanded Joshua, part of the territory of Judah was given to Caleb son of Jephunneh, from the tribe of Judah. He received Hebron, the city belonging to Arba, father of Anak. 14 Caleb drove the descendants of Anak out of the city—the clans of Sheshai, Ahiman, and Talmai. 15 From there he went to attack the people living in Debir. (This city used to be called Kiriath Sepher.) 16 Caleb said, "I will give my daughter Achsah in marriage to the man who succeeds in capturing Kiriath Sepher." 17 Othniel, the son of Caleb's brother Kenaz, captured the city, so Caleb gave him his daughter Achsah in marriage. 18 On the wedding day Othniel urged her[i] to ask her father for a field. She got down from her donkey, and Caleb asked her what she wanted. 19 She answered, "I want some water holes. The land you have given me is in the dry country." So Caleb gave her the upper and lower springs.

The Cities of Judah

20 This is the land that the families of the tribe of Judah received as their possession. 21 The cities farthest south that belonged to them, those that were near the border of Edom, were Kabzeel, Eder, Jagur, 22 Kinah, Dimonah, Adadah, 23 Kedesh, Hazor, Ithnan, 24 Ziph, Telem, Bealoth, 25 Hazor Hadattah, Kerioth Hezron (or Hazor), 26 Amam, Shema, Moladah, 27 Hazar Gaddah, Heshmon, Bethpelet, 28 Hazar Shual, Beersheba, Biziothiah, 29 Baalah, Iim, Ezem, 30 Eltolad, Chesil, Hormah, 31 Ziklag, Madmannah, Sansannah, 32 Lebaoth, Shilhim, Ain, and Rimmon: twenty-nine cities in all, along with the towns around them.

33 The cities in the foothills were Eshtaol, Zorah, Ashnah, 34 Zanoah, Engannim, Tappuah, Enam, 35 Jarmuth, Adullam, Socoh, Azekah, 36 Shaaraim, Adithaim, Gederah, and Gederothaim: fourteen cities, along with the towns around them.

37 There were also Zenan, Hadashah, Migdalgad, 38 Dilean, Mizpah, Joktheel, 39 Lachish, Bozkath, Eglon, 40 Cabbon, Lahmam, Chitlish, 41 Gederoth, Bethdagon, Naamah, and Makkedah: sixteen cities, along with the towns around them.

42 There were also Libnah, Ether, Ashan, 43 Iphtah, Ashnah, Nezib, 44 Keilah, Achzib, and Mareshah: nine cities, along with the towns around them.

45 There was Ekron with its towns and vil-

[i] **15:18** *Probable text (see Judg 1:14)* Othniel urged her; *Hebrew* she urged Othniel.
15:13, 14 Judg 1:20

Othniel *(Joshua 15:17)* **will become the first judge of Israel. More of his story appears in Judges 3:7–11.**

lages, 46 and all the cities and towns near Ash-
dod, from Ekron to the Mediterranean Sea.
47 There were Ashdod and Gaza, with
their towns and villages, reaching to the
stream on the border of Egypt and the coast
of the Mediterranean Sea.
48 In the hill country there were Shamir,
Jattir, Socoh, 49 Dannah, Kiriath Sepher (or
Debir), 50 Anab, Eshtemoa, Anim, 51 Goshen,
Holon, and Giloh: eleven cities, along with
the towns around them.
52 There were Arab, Dumah, Eshan,
53 Janim, Beth Tappuah, Aphekah, 54 Humtah,
Hebron, and Zior: nine cities, along with the
towns around them.
55 There were Maon, Carmel, Ziph, Juttah,
56 Jezreel, Jokdeam, Zanoah, 57 Kain, Gibeah,
and Timnah: ten cities, along with the towns
around them.
58 There were Halhul, Bethzur, Gedor,
59 Maarath, Bethanoth, and Eltekon: six cities,
along with the towns around them.
60 There were Kiriath Baal (or Kiriath
Jearim) and Rabbah: two cities, along with
the towns around them.
61 In the desert there were Beth Arabah,
Middin, Secacah, 62 Nibshan, Salt City, and
Engedi: six cities, along with the towns
around them.
63 But the people of Judah were not able
to drive out the Jebusites, who lived in
Jerusalem. The Jebusites still live there with
the people of Judah.

The Territory Assigned to Ephraim and West Manasseh

16 The southern boundary of the land
assigned to the descendants of
Joseph started from the Jordan near Jericho,
at a point east of the springs of Jericho, and
went into the desert. It went from Jericho
up into the hill country as far as Bethel.
2 From Bethel it went to Luz, passing on to
Ataroth Addar, where the Archites lived. 3 It
then went west to the area of the Japhletites,
as far as the area of Lower Beth Horon. It
went on from there to Gezer and ended at
the Mediterranean Sea.
4 The descendants of Joseph, the tribes of
Ephraim and West Manasseh, received this
land as their possession.

Ephraim

5 This was the territory of the Ephraimite
families: their border ran from Ataroth Addar
eastward to Upper Beth Horon, 6 and from
there to the Mediterranean Sea. Mich-
methath was on their north. East of there the
border bent toward Taanath Shiloh and went
past it on the east to Janoah. 7 Then it went
down from Janoah to Ataroth and Naarah,
reaching Jericho and ending at the Jordan.
8 The border went west from Tappuah to the
stream Kanah and ended at the Mediter-
ranean Sea. This was the land given to the
families of the tribe of Ephraim as their pos-
session, 9 along with some towns and villages
that were within the borders of Manasseh,
but given to the Ephraimites. 10 But they did
not drive out the Canaanites who lived in
Gezer, so the Canaanites have lived among
the Ephraimites to this day, but they have
been forced to work as slaves.

West Manasseh

17 A part of the land west of the Jordan
was assigned to some of the families
descended from Joseph's older son Manasseh.
Machir, the father of Gilead, was Manasseh's
oldest son and a military hero, so Gilead and
Bashan, east of the Jordan, were assigned to
him. 2 Land west of the Jordan was assigned
to the rest of the families of Manasseh:
Abiezer, Helek, Asriel, Shechem, Hepher,
and Shemida. These were male descendants
of Manasseh son of Joseph, and they were
heads of families. 3 Zelophehad, son of He-
pher, son of Gilead, son of Machir, son of
Manasseh, did not have any sons, but only
daughters. Their names were Mahlah, Noah,
Hoglah, Milcah, and Tirzah. 4 They went to
Eleazar the priest and to Joshua son of Nun
and to the leaders, and said, "The LORD
commanded Moses to give us, as well as our
male relatives, a part of the land to possess."
So, as the LORD had commanded, they were
given land along with their male relatives.

15:63 Judg 1:21; 2 Sam 5:6; 1 Chr 11:4 **16:10** Judg 1:29 **17:4** Num 27:1–7

5This is why Manasseh received ten shares in addition to Gilead and Bashan on the east side of the Jordan, 6since his female descendants as well as his male descendants were assigned land. The land of Gilead was assigned to the rest of the descendants of Manasseh.

7The territory of Manasseh reached from Asher to Michmethath, east of Shechem. The border then went south to include the people of Entappuah. 8The land around Tappuah belonged to Manasseh, but the town of Tappuah, on the border, belonged to the descendants of Ephraim. 9The border then went down to the stream Kanah. The cities south of the stream belonged to Ephraim, even though they were in the territory of Manasseh. The border of Manasseh proceeded along the north side of the stream and ended at the Mediterranean Sea. 10Ephraim was to the south, and Manasseh was to the north, with the Mediterranean Sea as their western border. Asher was to the northwest, and Issachar to the northeast. 11Within the territories of Issachar and Asher, Manasseh possessed Beth Shan and Ibleam, along with their surrounding towns, as well as Dor (the one on the coast),[j] Endor, Taanach, Megiddo, and their surrounding towns. 12The people of Manasseh, however, were not able to drive out the people living in those cities, so the Canaanites continued to live there. 13Even when the Israelites became stronger, they did not drive out all the Canaanites, but they did force them to work for them.

Ephraim and West Manasseh Request More Land

14The descendants of Joseph said to Joshua, "Why have you given us only one part of the land to possess as our own? There are very many of us because the LORD has blessed us."

15Joshua answered, "If there are so many of you and the hill country of Ephraim is too small for you, then go into the forests and clear ground for yourselves in the land of the Perizzites and the Rephaim."

Live it!

Women Have Rights, Too!

In Numbers, chapter 27, the daughters of Zelophehad have a serious talk with Moses. Keep in mind that at this time, women cannot inherit land. Their father is dead, and they don't have any brothers. They ask Moses for the right to inherit land so that their father will be remembered. These remarkable women are mentioned four times in the Scriptures: twice in Numbers, once in Joshua, and again in Chronicles. Joshua keeps the promise that Moses made to these women. Because they speak up and ask that their rights be protected, they are given land to preserve their family name.

Many people find the story of these outspoken women an important one today. It is a story that shows that women are entitled to human rights and human dignity. Are boys and girls treated the same in your school and community? Does either group get more attention or more privileges? Can you think of any ways that the dignity and rights of women still need protection today?

— Joshua 17:3–6

16They replied, "The hill country is not big enough for us, but the Canaanites in the plains have iron chariots, both those who live in Beth Shan and its surrounding towns and those who live in Jezreel Valley."

17Joshua said to the tribes of Ephraim and West Manasseh, "There are indeed many of

[j] **17:11** *Probable text* Dor (the one on the coast); *Hebrew unclear.*

17:12, 13 Judg 1:27, 28

you, and you are very powerful. You shall have more than one share. 18The hill country will be yours. Even though it is a forest, you will clear it and take possession of it from one end to the other. As for the Canaanites, you will drive them out, even though they do have iron chariots and are a strong people."

The Division of the Rest of the Land

18 After they had conquered the land, the entire community of Israel assembled at Shiloh and set up the Tent of the LORD's presence. 2There were still seven tribes of the people of Israel who had not yet been assigned their share of the land. 3So Joshua said to the people of Israel, "How long are you going to wait before you go in and take the land that the LORD, the God of your ancestors, has given you? 4Let me have three men from each tribe. I will send them out over the whole country to map out the territory that they would like to have as their possession. Then they are to come back to me. 5The land will be divided among them in seven parts; Judah will stay in its territory in the south, and Joseph in its territory in the north. 6Write down a description of these seven divisions and bring it to me. Then I will draw lots[k] to consult the LORD our God for you. 7The Levites, however, will not receive a share of the land with the rest of you, because their share is to serve as the LORD's priests. And of course, the tribes of Gad, Reuben, and East Manasseh have already received their land east of the Jordan, which Moses, the LORD's servant, gave to them."

8The men went on their way to map out the land after Joshua had given them these instructions: "Go all over the land and map it out, and come back to me. And then here in Shiloh I will consult the LORD for you by drawing lots." 9So the men went all over the land and set down in writing how they divided it into seven parts, making a list of the towns. Then they went back to Joshua in the camp at Shiloh. 10Joshua drew lots to consult the LORD for them, and assigned each of the remaining tribes of Israel a certain part of the land.

The Territory Assigned to Benjamin

11The territory belonging to the families of the tribe of Benjamin was the first to be assigned. Their land lay between the tribes of Judah and Joseph. 12On the north their border began at the Jordan and then went up

[k] **18:6** DRAW LOTS: *See 14:2.*

Go all over the land and map it out. (18:8)

Many of the names of people became the names of places as the tribes settled into the territories that were given to them.

the slope north of Jericho and westward through the hill country as far as the desert of Bethaven. [13]The border then went to the slope on the south side of Luz (also called Bethel), then down to Ataroth Addar, on the mountain south of Lower Beth Horon. [14]The border then went in another direction, turning south from the western side of this mountain and going to Kiriath Baal (or Kiriath Jearim), which belongs to the tribe of Judah. This was the western border. [15]The southern border started on the edge of Kiriath Jearim and went[l] to the Springs of Nephtoah. [16]It then went down to the foot of the mountain that overlooks Hinnom Valley, at the north end of Rephaim Valley. It then went south through Hinnom Valley, south of the Jebusite ridge, toward Enrogel. [17]It then turned north to Enshemesh and then on to Geliloth, opposite Adummim Pass. The border then went down to the Stone of Bohan (Bohan was a son of Reuben) [18]and passed north of the ridge overlooking the Jordan Valley. It then went down into the valley, [19]passing north of the ridge of Beth Hoglah, and ended at the northern inlet on the Dead Sea, where the Jordan River empties into it. This was the southern border. [20]The Jordan was the eastern border. These were the borders of the land which the families of the tribe of Benjamin received as their possession.

[21]The cities belonging to the families of the tribe of Benjamin were Jericho, Beth Hoglah, Emek Keziz, [22]Beth Arabah, Zemaraim, Bethel, [23]Avvim, Parah, Ophrah, [24]Chepharammoni, Ophni, and Geba: twelve cities, along with the towns around them. [25]There were also Gibeon, Ramah, Beeroth, [26]Mizpah, Chephirah, Mozah, [27]Rekem, Irpeel, Taralah, [28]Zela, Haeleph, Jebus (or Jerusalem), Gibeah, and Kiriath Jearim: fourteen cities, along with the towns around them. This is the land which the families of the tribe of Benjamin received as their possession.

The Territory Assigned to Simeon

19 The second assignment made was for the families of the tribe of Simeon. Its territory extended into the land assigned to the tribe of Judah. [2]It included Beersheba, Sheba, Moladah, [3]Hazar Shual, Balah, Ezem, [4]Eltolad, Bethul, Hormah, [5]Ziklag, Beth Marcaboth, Hazar Susah, [6]Beth Lebaoth, and Sharuhen: thirteen cities, along with the towns around them.

[7]There were also Ain, Rimmon, Ether, and Ashan: four cities, along with the towns around them. [8]This included all the towns around these cities as far as Baalath Beer (or Ramah), in the south. This was the land which the families of the tribe of Simeon received as their possession. [9]Since Judah's assignment was larger than was needed, part of its territory was given to the tribe of Simeon.

The Territory Assigned to Zebulun

[10]The third assignment made was for the families of the tribe of Zebulun. The land which they received reached as far as Sarid. [11]From there the border went west to Mareal, touching Dabbesheth and the stream east of Jokneam. [12]On the other side of Sarid it went east to the border of Chisloth Tabor, then to Daberath and up to Japhia. [13]It continued east from there to Gath Hepher and Ethkazin, turning in the direction of Neah on the way to Rimmon. [14]On the north the border turned toward Hannathon, ending at Iphtahel Valley. [15]It included Kattath, Nahalal, Shimron, Idalah, and Bethlehem: twelve cities, along with the towns around them. [16]These cities and their towns were in the land which the families of the tribe of Zebulun received as their possession.

The Territory Assigned to Issachar

[17]The fourth assignment made was for the families of the tribe of Issachar. [18]Its area

[l] **18:15** *Probable text* and went; *Hebrew* and went westward.

19:2–8 1 Chr 4:28–33

Shiloh *(Joshua 19:51)* **was an important place. The Tent of the Lord's presence, which is also called the Tent of meeting, is set up there. It was a holy place.**

included Jezreel, Chesulloth, Shunem,
19 Hapharaim, Shion, Anaharath, 20 Rabbith,
Kishion, Ebez, 21 Remeth, Engannim, Enhad-
dah, and Bethpazzez. 22 The border also
touched Tabor, Shahazumah, and Beth
Shemesh, ending at the Jordan. It included
sixteen cities along with the towns around
them. 23 These cities and their towns were in
the land which the families of the tribe of
Issachar received as their possession.

The Territory Assigned to Asher

24 The fifth assignment made was for the
families of the tribe of Asher. 25 Its area
included Helkath, Hali, Beten, Achshaph,
26 Allam Melech, Amad, and Mishal. On the
west it touched Carmel and Shihor Libnath.
27 As it turned east, the border went to
Bethdagon, touching Zebulun and Iphtahel
Valley on the way north to Bethemek and
Neiel. It continued north to Cabul, 28 Ebron,
Rehob, Hammon, and Kanah, as far as
Sidon. 29 The border then turned to Ramah,
reaching the fortified city of Tyre; then it
turned to Hosah and ended at the Mediter-
ranean Sea. It included Mahalab, Achzib,
30 Ummah, Aphek, and Rehob: twenty-two
cities, along with the towns around them.
31 These cities and their towns were in the
land which the families of the tribe of Asher
received as their possession.

The Territory Assigned to Naphtali

32 The sixth assignment made was for the
families of the tribe of Naphtali. 33 Its border
went from Heleph to the oak in Zaanannim,
on to Adaminekeb and to Jamnia, as far as
Lakkum, and ended at the Jordan. 34 There
the border turned west to Aznoth Tabor,
from there to Hukkok, touching Zebulun
on the south, Asher on the west, and the Jor-
dan[m] on the east. 35 The fortified cities were
Ziddim, Zer, Hammath, Rakkath, Chin-
nereth, 36 Adamah, Ramah, Hazor, 37 Kedesh,
Edrei, Enhazor, 38 Yiron, Migdalel, Horem,
Bethanath, and Beth Shemesh: nineteen
cities, along with the towns around them.
39 These cities and their towns were in the
land which the families of the tribe of
Naphtali received as their possession.

The Territory Assigned to Dan

40 The seventh assignment made was for
the families of the tribe of Dan. 41 Its area
included Zorah, Eshtaol, Irshemesh, 42 Shaal-
bim, Aijalon, Ithlah, 43 Elon, Timnah, Ekron,
44 Eltekeh, Gibbethon, Baalath, 45 Jehud,
Beneberak, Gathrimmon, 46 Mejarkon, and
Rakkon, as well as the territory around
Joppa. 47 When the people of Dan lost their
land, they went to Laish and attacked it.
They captured it, killed its people, and
claimed it for themselves. They settled there
and changed the name of the city from Laish
to Dan, naming it after their ancestor Dan.
48 These cities and their towns were in the
land which the families of the tribe of Dan
received as their possession.

The Final Assignment of the Land

49 When the people of Israel finished
dividing up the land, they gave Joshua son of
Nun a part of the land as his own. 50 As the
LORD had commanded, they gave him the
city he asked for: Timnath Serah, in the hill
country of Ephraim. He rebuilt the city and
settled there.

51 Eleazar the priest, Joshua son of Nun,
and the leaders of the families of the tribes
of Israel assigned these parts of the land by
drawing lots[n] to consult the LORD at Shiloh,
at the entrance of the Tent of the LORD's
presence. In this way they finished dividing
the land.

The Cities of Refuge

20 Then the LORD told Joshua 2 to say
to the people of Israel, "Choose the
cities of refuge that I had Moses tell you
about. 3 If any of you accidentally kills some-
one, you can go there and escape the one
who is looking for revenge. 4 You can run
away to one of these cities, go to the place
of judgment at the entrance to the city, and
explain to the leaders what happened. Then

[m] **19:34** *One ancient translation* the Jordan; *Hebrew* Judah at the Jordan. [n] **19:51** DRAWING LOTS: *See 14:2.*
19:47 Judg 18:27–29 **20:1–9** Num 35:9–34; Deut 4:41–43; 19:1–13

Pray it!

A Second Chance

If someone killed another person in ancient Israel, the dead person's family was expected to take revenge. They could, by law, kill the killer. That was the justice of the time, even if the death was accidental. This passage from Joshua establishes safe places for anyone in danger of being killed for the sake of revenge. The cities of refuge were places where someone could start a new life and be assured of protection. They were places where the hopeless could get a second chance.

Have you ever needed a second chance? Maybe you made a big mistake, or maybe you started hanging around the wrong people. Maybe you just forgot the kind of person you wanted to be and started doing things you knew you shouldn't do. Well, fortunately, God is a God of second chances. In the same way the cities of refuge were established to protect and give new life, Jesus gives us new life—forgiveness, safety, a second chance.

God of new life,
be my city of refuge
When I have done wrong,
I will come to you.
You will be my safe place in this world
until I can set things right again.

— Joshua, chapter 20

they will let you into the city and give you a
place to live in, so that you can stay there. 5If
the one looking for revenge follows you
there, the people of the city must not hand
you over to that one. They must protect you
because you killed the person accidentally
and not out of anger. 6You may stay in the
city until you have received a public trial
and until the death of the man who is then
the High Priest. Then you may go back
home to your own town, from which you
had run away."

7So, on the west side of the Jordan they
set aside Kedesh in Galilee, in the hill coun-
try of Naphtali; Shechem, in the hill country
of Ephraim; and Hebron, in the hill country
of Judah. 8East of the Jordan, on the desert
plateau east of Jericho, they chose Bezer in
the territory of Reuben; Ramoth in Gilead,
in the territory of Gad; and Golan in
Bashan, in the territory of Manasseh. 9These
were the cities of refuge chosen for all the
people of Israel and for any foreigner living among them. Any who killed a person accidentally could find protection there from the one looking for revenge; they could not be killed unless they had first received a public trial.

The Cities of the Levites

21 The leaders of the Levite families
went to Eleazar the priest, Joshua
son of Nun, and to the heads of the families
of all the tribes of Israel. 2There at Shiloh in
the land of Canaan they said to them, "The
LORD commanded through Moses that we
were to be given cities to live in, as well as
pasture land around them for our livestock."
3So in accordance with the LORD's com-
mand the people of Israel gave the Levites
certain cities and pasture lands out of their
own territories.

4The families of the Levite clan of Kohath

21:2 Num 35:1–8

were the first to be assigned cities. The fami-
lies who were descended from Aaron the
priest were assigned thirteen cities from the
territories of Judah, Simeon, and Benjamin.
5The rest of the clan of Kohath was assigned
ten cities from the territories of Ephraim,
Dan, and West Manasseh.

6The clan of Gershon was assigned thir-
teen cities from the territories of Issachar,
Asher, Naphtali, and East Manasseh.

7The families of the clan of Merari were
assigned twelve cities from the territories of
Reuben, Gad, and Zebulun.

8By drawing lots,[n] the people of Israel
assigned these cities and their pasture lands
to the Levites, as the LORD had commanded
through Moses.

9These are the names of the cities from
the territories of Judah and Simeon which
were given 10to the descendants of Aaron
who were of the clan of Kohath, which was
descended from Levi. Their assignment was
the first to be made. 11They were given the
city of Arba (Arba was Anak's father), now
called Hebron, in the hill country of Judah,
along with the pasture land surrounding it.
12However, the fields of the city, as well as its
towns, had already been given to Caleb son
of Jephunneh as his possession.

13In addition to Hebron (one of the cities
of refuge), the following cities were assigned
to the descendants of Aaron the priest: Lib-
nah, 14Jattir, Eshtemoa, 15Holon, Debir,
16Ain, Juttah, and Beth Shemesh, with their
pasture lands: nine cities from the tribes of
Judah and Simeon. 17From the territory of
Benjamin they were given four cities:
Gibeon, Geba, 18Anathoth, and Almon, with
their pasture lands. 19Thirteen cities in all,
with their pasture lands, were given to the
priests, the descendants of Aaron.

20The other families of the Levite clan of
Kohath were assigned some cities from the
territory of Ephraim. 21They were given
four cities: Shechem and its pasture lands in
the hill country of Ephraim (one of the
cities of refuge), Gezer, 22Kibzaim, and Beth
Horon, with their pasture lands. 23From the
territory of Dan they were given four cities:
Eltekeh, Gibbethon, 24Aijalon, and Gathrim-
mon, with their pasture lands. 25From the
territory of West Manasseh they were given
two cities: Taanach and Gathrimmon, with
their pasture lands. 26These families of the
clan of Kohath received ten cities in all, with
their pasture lands.

27Another group of Levites, the clan of
Gershon, received from the territory of East
Manasseh two cities: Golan in Bashan (one
of the cities of refuge) and Beeshterah, with
their pasture lands. 28From the territory of
Issachar they received four cities: Kishion,
Daberath, 29Jarmuth, and Engannim, with
their pasture lands. 30From the territory of
Asher they received four cities: Mishal,
Abdon, 31Helkath, and Rehob, with their
pasture lands. 32From the territory of
Naphtali they received three cities: Kedesh
in Galilee, with its pasture lands (one of the
cities of refuge), Hammoth Dor, and Kar-
tan, with their pasture lands. 33The various
families of the clan of Gershon received a
total of thirteen cities with their pasture
lands.

34The rest of the Levites, the clan of Me-
rari, received from the territory of Zebulun
four cities: Jokneam, Kartah, 35Dimnah, and
Nahalal, with their pasture lands. 36From the
territory of Reuben they received four
cities: Bezer, Jahaz, 37Kedemoth, and
Mephaath, with their pasture lands. 38From
the tribe of Gad they received four cities:
Ramoth in Gilead, with its pasture lands
(one of the cities of refuge), Mahanaim,
39Heshbon, and Jazer, with their pasture
lands. 40So the clan of Merari was assigned a
total of twelve cities.

41-42From the land that the people of
Israel possessed, a total of forty-eight cities,
with the pasture lands around them, was
given to the Levites.

[n] **21:8** DRAWING LOTS: *See 14:2.*

There are six cities of refuge: Kedesh, Shechem, Hebron, Bezer, Ramoth, and Golan. Can you find all six on Map 3 in the back of this Bible?

Israel Takes Possession of the Land

43 So the LORD gave to Israel all the land
that he had solemnly promised their ancestors
he would give them. When they had taken
possession of it, they settled down there. 44 The
LORD gave them peace throughout the land,
just as he had promised their ancestors. Not
one of all their enemies had been able to stand
against them, because the LORD gave the
Israelites the victory over all their enemies.
45 The LORD kept every one of the promises
that he had made to the people of Israel.

Joshua Sends the Eastern Tribes Home

22 Then Joshua called together the peo-
ple of the tribes of Reuben, Gad, and
East Manasseh. 2 He said to them, "You have
done everything that Moses the LORD's ser-
vant ordered you to do, and you have obeyed
all my commands. 3 All this time you have
never once deserted the other Israelites. You
have been careful to obey the commands of
the LORD your God. 4 Now, as he promised,
the LORD your God has given the other
Israelites peace. So go back home to the land
which you claimed for your own, the land
on the east side of the Jordan, that Moses, the
LORD's servant, gave you. 5 Make sure you
obey the law that Moses commanded you:
love the LORD your God, do his will, obey
his commandments, be faithful to him, and
serve him with all your heart and soul."
6-8 Joshua sent them home with his blessing
and with these words: "You are going back
home very rich, with a lot of livestock, silver,
gold, bronze, iron, and many clothes. Share
with your fellow tribesmen what you took
from your enemies." Then they left for home.

Moses had given land east of the Jordan to
one half of the tribe of Manasseh, but to the
other half Joshua had given land west of the
Jordan, along with the other tribes.

9 So the people of the tribes of Reuben,
Gad, and East Manasseh went back home.
They left the rest of the people of Israel at

22:2 Num 32:20–32; Josh 1:12–15

Live it!

Who Do They Think They Are?

"Look at the way he's dressed!" "She thinks she's so great." Sometimes we judge people without really understanding them. That's what happens in Joshua, chapter 22. The tribes that settled on the eastern side of the Jordan wanted to make sure that the rest of Israel knew that they also served God, so they built an altar that was big enough to be seen all the way across the river. They even named it Witness.

But the tribes on the western side of the Jordan saw the altar as a threat. They thought it meant the tribes on the eastern side were worshiping foreign gods. They talked about going to war against their fellow Israelites! Phinehas is sent to talk to the eastern tribes and quickly sees that the eastern tribes have been misjudged.

When we quickly judge somebody's actions, we might be in danger of misjudgment. We can end up angry or hateful, and the other person can feel attacked or left out. When you see something happening you don't understand, be sure to do what the Israelites did. Take time to find out what the other person really meant by what he or she did.

— Joshua, chapter 22

Chapter 22 begins the third major section of the Book of Joshua. This section describes what happens after all the tribes were settled in their given lands.

Shiloh in the land of Canaan and started out
for their own land, the land of Gilead, which
they had taken as the LORD had commanded
them through Moses.

The Altar by the Jordan

[10]When the tribes of Reuben, Gad, and
East Manasseh arrived at Geliloth, still on
the west side[o] of the Jordan, they built a
large, impressive altar there by the river.
[11]The rest of the people of Israel were told,
"Listen! The people of the tribes of Reuben,
Gad, and East Manasseh have built an altar at
Geliloth, on our side of the Jordan!" [12]When
the people of Israel heard this, the whole
community came together at Shiloh to go to
war against the eastern tribes.
[13]Then the people of Israel sent Phinehas,
the son of Eleazar the priest, to the people
of the tribes of Reuben, Gad, and East Ma-
nasseh in the land of Gilead. [14]Ten leading
men went with Phinehas, one from each of
the western tribes and each one the head of
a family among the clans. [15]They came to
the land of Gilead, to the people of Reuben,
Gad, and East Manasseh, [16]and speaking for
the whole community of the LORD, they
said to them, "Why have you done this evil
thing against the God of Israel? You have
rebelled against the LORD by building this
altar for yourselves! You are no longer fol-
lowing him! [17]Remember our sin at Peor,
when the LORD punished his own people
with an epidemic? We are still suffering
because of that. Wasn't that sin enough?
[18]Are you going to refuse to follow him
now? If you rebel against the LORD today, he
will be angry with everyone in Israel tomor-
row. [19]Now then, if your land is not fit to
worship in, come over into the LORD's land,
where his Tent is. Claim some land among
us. But don't rebel against the LORD or make
rebels out of us by building an altar in addi
tion to the altar of the LORD our God.
[20]Remember how Achan son of Zerah
refused to obey the command about the
things condemned to destruction; the whole
community of Israel was punished for that.
Achan was not the only one who died
because of his sin."
[21]The people of the tribes of Reuben,
Gad, and East Manasseh answered the heads
of the families of the western tribes: [22]"The
Mighty One is God! He is the LORD! The
Mighty One is God! He is the LORD! He
knows why we did this, and we want you to
know too! If we rebelled and did not keep
faith with the LORD, do not let us live any
longer! [23]If we disobeyed the LORD and built
our own altar to burn sacrifices on or to use
for grain offerings or fellowship offerings, let
the LORD himself punish us. [24]No! We did it
because we were afraid that in the future
your descendants would say to ours, 'What
do you have to do with the LORD, the God
of Israel? [25]He made the Jordan a boundary
between us and you people of Reuben and
Gad. You have nothing to do with the LORD.'
Then your descendants might make our
descendants stop worshiping the LORD. [26]So
we built an altar, not to burn sacrifices or
make offerings, [27]but instead, as a sign for our
people and yours, and for the generations
after us, that we do indeed worship the
LORD before his sacred Tent with our offer-
ings to be burned and with sacrifices and fel-
lowship offerings. This was to keep your
descendants from saying that ours have noth-
ing to do with the LORD. [28]It was our idea
that, if this should ever happen, our descen-
dants could say, 'Look! Our ancestors made
an altar just like the LORD's altar. It was not
for burning offerings or for sacrifice, but as a
sign for our people and yours.' [29]We would
certainly not rebel against the LORD or stop
following him now by building an altar to
burn offerings on or for grain offerings or
sacrifices. We would not build any other altar
than the altar of the LORD our God that
stands in front of the Tent of his presence."
[30]Phinehas the priest and the ten leading
men of the community who were with him,
the heads of families of the western tribes,
heard what the people of the tribes of
Reuben, Gad, and East Manasseh had to say,
and they were satisfied. [31]Phinehas, the son of
Eleazar the priest, said to them, "Now we

[o] **22:10** still on the west side; *or* on the east side.
22:16 Deut 12:13, 14 **22:17** Num 25:1–9 **22:20** Josh 7:1–26

know that the LORD is with us. You have not
rebelled against him, and so you have saved the
people of Israel from the LORD's punishment."
32 Then Phinehas and the leaders left the
people of Reuben and Gad in the land of
Gilead and went back to Canaan, to the
people of Israel, and reported to them. 33 The
Israelites were satisfied and praised God.
They no longer talked about going to war
to devastate the land where the people of
Reuben and Gad had settled.
34 The people of Reuben and Gad said,
"This altar is a witness to all of us that the
LORD is God." And so they named it "Wit-
ness."

Joshua's Farewell Address

23 Much later the LORD gave Israel
security from their enemies around
them. By that time Joshua was very old, 2 so
he called all Israel, the elders, leaders, judges,
and officers of the people, and said, "I am
very old now. 3 You have seen everything that
the LORD your God has done to all these
nations because of you. The LORD your God
has been fighting for you. 4 I have assigned as
the possession of your tribes the land of the
nations that are still left, as well as of all the
nations that I have already conquered, from
the Jordan River in the east to the Mediter-
ranean Sea in the west. 5 The LORD your
God will make them retreat from you, and he
will drive them away as you advance. You
shall have their land, as the LORD your God
has promised you. 6 So be careful to obey and
do everything that is written in the book of
the Law of Moses. Do not neglect any part
of it, 7 and then you will not associate with
these peoples left among you or speak the
names of their gods or use those names in
taking vows or worship those gods or bow
down to them. 8 Instead, be faithful to the
LORD, as you have been till now. 9 The LORD
has driven great and powerful nations out as
you advanced, and no one has ever been able
to stand against you. 10 Any one of you can
make a thousand men run away, because the
LORD your God is fighting for you, just as he
promised. 11 Be careful, then, to love the
LORD your God. 12 If you are disloyal and
join with the nations that are still left among
you and intermarry with them, 13 you may be
sure that the LORD your God will no longer
drive these nations out as you advance.
Rather, they will be as dangerous for you as a
trap or a pit and as painful as a whip on your
back or thorns in your eyes. And this will last
until none of you are left in this good land
which the LORD your God has given you.
14 "Now my time has come to die. Every
one of you knows in his heart and soul that
the LORD your God has given you all the
good things that he promised. Every promise
he made has been kept; not one has failed.
15 But just as he kept every promise that he
made to you, so he will carry out every
threat. 16 If you do not keep the covenant
which the LORD your God commanded you
to keep and if you serve and worship other
gods, then in his anger he will punish you,
and soon none of you will be left in this
good land that he has given you."

Joshua Speaks to the People at Shechem

24 Joshua gathered all the tribes of
Israel together at Shechem. He
called the elders, the leaders, the judges, and
the officers of Israel, and they came into the
presence of God. 2 Joshua said to all the peo-
ple, "This is what the LORD, the God of
Israel, has to say: 'Long ago your ancestors
lived on the other side of the Euphrates
River and worshiped other gods. One of
those ancestors was Terah, the father of Abra-
ham and Nahor. 3 Then I took Abraham,
your ancestor, from the land across the
Euphrates and led him through the whole
land of Canaan. I gave him many descen-
dants. I gave him Isaac, 4 and to Isaac I gave
Jacob and Esau. I gave Esau the hill country
of Edom as his possession, but your ancestor
Jacob and his children went down to Egypt.
5 Later I sent Moses and Aaron, and I
brought great trouble on Egypt. But I led
you out; 6 I brought your ancestors out of
Egypt, and the Egyptians pursued them with
chariots and cavalry. But when your ances-

23:10 a Deut 32:30; **b** Deut 3:22 **24:2** Gen 11:27 **24:3 a** Gen 12:1–9; **b** Gen 21:1–3 **24:4 a** Gen 25:24–26; **b** Gen 36:8; Deut 2:5; **c** Gen 46:1–7 **24:5** Ex 3:1—12:42

Pray it!

Remembering God's Goodness

Joshua recounts to the people all the things God has done for them. He reminds them of God's goodness and guidance to them throughout the years. Just like these ancient Israelites, every good thing we have comes from God. Take some time to remember all the times God has been good to you. Remember all your friendships, the love of your family, and the important lessons that you've learned.

As part of their prayer, some people like to keep a gratitude list or gratitude journal. At the end of every day, they write down all the good things that happened to them that day. No matter how bad the day was, they try to write down at least one good thing. It is surprising how something this simple can help you see God at work in your life! Is this something you might try?

— Joshua 24:1–15

tors got to the Red Sea 7they cried out to
me for help, and I put darkness between
them and the Egyptians. I made the sea
come rolling over the Egyptians and drown
them. You know what I did to Egypt.
" 'You lived in the desert a long time.
8Then I brought you to the land of the Amo-
rites, who lived on the east side of the Jordan.
They fought you, but I gave you victory over
them. You took their land, and I destroyed
them as you advanced. 9Then the king of
Moab, Balak son of Zippor, fought against
you. He sent word to Balaam son of Beor and
asked him to put a curse on you. 10But I
would not listen to Balaam, so he blessed you,
and in this way I rescued you from Balak.
11You crossed the Jordan and came to Jericho.
The men of Jericho fought you, as did the
Amorites, the Perizzites, the Canaanites, the
Hittites, the Girgashites, the Hivites, and the
Jebusites. But I gave you victory over them all.
12As you advanced, I threw them into panic in
order to drive out the two Amorite kings.
Your swords and bows had nothing to do with
it. 13I gave you a land that you had never
worked and cities that you had not built. Now
you are living there and eating grapes from
vines that you did not plant, and olives from
trees that you did not plant.'
14"Now then," Joshua continued, "honor
the LORD and serve him sincerely and faith-
fully. Get rid of the gods which your ances-
tors used to worship in Mesopotamia and in
Egypt, and serve only the LORD. 15If you are
not willing to serve him, decide today
whom you will serve, the gods your ances-
tors worshiped in Mesopotamia or the gods
of the Amorites, in whose land you are now
living. As for my family and me, we will
serve the LORD."
16The people replied, "We would never
leave the LORD to serve other gods! 17The
LORD our God brought our fathers and us
out of slavery in Egypt, and we saw the mir-
acles that he performed. He kept us safe
wherever we went among all the nations
through which we passed. 18As we advanced
into this land, the LORD drove out all the
Amorites who lived here. So we also will
serve the LORD; he is our God."

24:6, 7 Ex 14:1–31 **24:8** Num 21:21–35 **24:9, 10** Num 22:1—24:25 **24:11 a** Josh 3:14–17; **b** Josh 6:1–21 **24:12** Ex 23:28; Deut 7:20 **24:13** Deut 6:10, 11

"As for my family and me, we will serve the LORD" *(Joshua 24:15)*.

"As for my family and me, we will serve the LORD." (24:15)

[19]Joshua said to the people, "But you may
not be able to serve the LORD. He is a holy
God and will not forgive your sins. He will
tolerate no rivals, [20]and if you leave him to
serve foreign gods, he will turn against you
and punish you. He will destroy you, even
though he was good to you before."
[21]The people said to Joshua, "No! We will
serve the LORD."
[22]Joshua told them, "You are your own
witnesses to the fact that you have chosen to
serve the LORD."
"Yes," they said, "we are witnesses."
[23]"Then get rid of those foreign gods that
you have," he demanded, "and pledge your
loyalty to the LORD, the God of Israel."
[24]The people then said to Joshua, "We
will serve the LORD our God. We will obey
his commands."
[25]So Joshua made a covenant for[p] the
people that day, and there at Shechem he
gave them laws and rules to follow. [26]Joshua
wrote these commands in the book of the
Law of God. Then he took a large stone and
set it up under the oak tree in the LORD's
sanctuary. [27]He said to all the people, "This
stone will be our witness. It has heard all the
words that the LORD has spoken to us. So it
will be a witness against you, to keep you
from rebelling against your God." [28]Then
Joshua sent the people away, and everyone
returned to their own part of the land.

Joshua and Eleazar Die

[29]After that, the LORD's servant Joshua son
of Nun died at the age of a hundred and
ten. [30]They buried him on his own land at
Timnath Serah in the hill country of
Ephraim north of Mount Gaash.
[31]As long as Joshua lived, the people of
Israel served the LORD, and after his death
they continued to do so as long as those lead-
ers were alive who had seen for themselves
everything that the LORD had done for Israel.
[32]The body of Joseph, which the people of
Israel had brought from Egypt, was buried at
Shechem, in the piece of land that Jacob had
bought from the sons of Hamor, the father of
Shechem, for a hundred pieces of silver. This
land was inherited by Joseph's descendants.
[33]Eleazar son of Aaron died and was
buried at Gibeah, the town in the hill coun-
try of Ephraim which had been given to his
son Phinehas.

[p] **24:25** for; *or* with.
24:30 Josh 19:49, 50 **24:32** Gen 33:19; 50:24, 25; Ex 13:19; Jn 4:5; Acts 7:16

Your Next Step

Congratulations on finishing the Book of Joshua! Use this space to write your thoughts and questions about this book. If you are following the suggested reading plan, go ahead to the New Testament and the Gospel according to Luke. Look for ways the Gospel makes connections with the Old Testament people you have read about so far.

THE BOOK OF Judges

Have you ever met someone who just seems born to lead? Maybe that person is good at talking to people, or they are very athletic. After the strong leadership of Moses and Joshua and before the great kings, the leaders of the Israelites were called judges. They were not like the judges you see in a courtroom. Some were military leaders or local heroes. Others were simply respected members of the community. They were natural leaders.

The Book of Judges tells the story of Israel in an in-between time. Even though the Israelites had entered the Promised Land, they needed to remain faithful to their covenant with God. Yet even the judges failed to always be faithful to God. Still, no matter how many times the people of Israel turned away from God, God was always ready to rescue them.

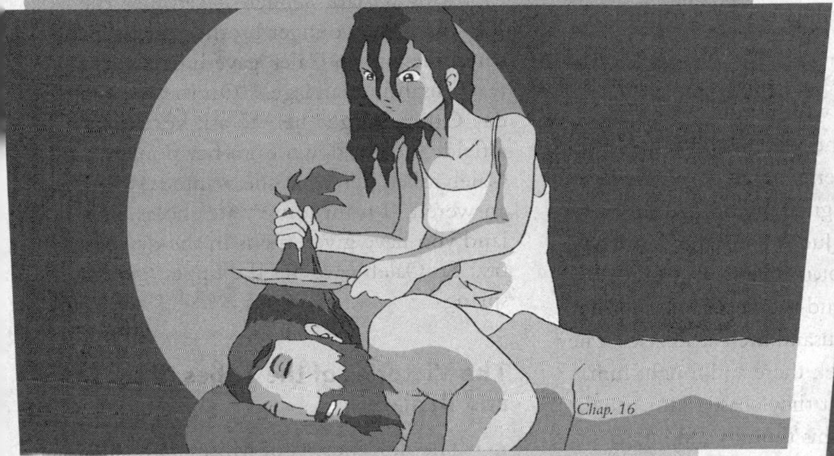

Chap. 16

Headlines

- Israelites Abandon God, Had a Baal! (2:11–15)
- Woman Murders Sleeping General (4:12–24)
- Deborah's Song: A New Top 40 Hit! (chapter 5)
- Gideon Looks for a Sign (6:36–40)
- Judge Makes Foolish Promise (11:29–39)
- Angel Announces Child's Birth (chapter 13)
- Bad Haircut Leads to Blindness (16:1–22)

FACTOIDS

Who wrote this book? The author is unknown, but someone during the Exile gathered these stories into this one collection. Some think it was the same person or group who wrote Deuteronomy.

When did these events take place? After the conquest of Canaan and before the time of the Israelite kings.

Why was it written? The Book of Judges was written to record the stories of the judges and show that whenever Israel turned away from God, it fell into ruin. Faithfulness to God was the key to the Israelites' survival.

Important themes
- When the people turn to God, God raises up heroes to lead them.
- Faithfulness leads to blessings, and unfaithfulness is punished.
- God is always merciful when the people repent.

JUDGES

The Tribes of Judah and Simeon Capture Adonibezek

1 After Joshua's death the people of Israel
asked the LORD, "Which of our tribes
should be the first to go and attack the
Canaanites?"
2 The LORD answered, "The tribe of Judah
will go first. I am giving them control of the
land."
3 The people of Judah said to the people
of Simeon, "Go with us into the territory
assigned to us, and we will fight the Canaan-
ites together. Then we will go with you into
the territory assigned to you." So the tribes
of Simeon 4 and Judah went into battle
together. The LORD gave them victory over
the Canaanites and the Perizzites, and they
defeated ten thousand men at Bezek. 5 They
found Adonibezek there and fought him.
6 He ran away, but they chased him, caught
him, and cut off his thumbs and big toes.
7 Adonibezek said, "Seventy kings with their
thumbs and big toes cut off have picked up
scraps under my table. God has now done to
me what I did to them." He was taken to
Jerusalem, where he died.

The Tribe of Judah Conquers Jerusalem and Hebron

8 The people of Judah attacked Jerusalem
and captured it. They killed its people and
set fire to the city. 9 After this they went on
to fight the Canaanites who lived in the hill
country, in the foothills, and in the dry
country to the south. 10 They marched
against the Canaanites living in the city of
Hebron, which used to be called Kiriath
Arba. There they defeated the clans of She-
shai, Ahiman, and Talmai.

Othniel Conquers the City of Debir
(Joshua 15:13–19)

11 From there the men of Judah marched
against the city of Debir, at that time called
Kiriath Sepher. 12 One of them, called
Caleb, said, "I will give my daughter Achsah
in marriage to the man who succeeds in
capturing Kiriath Sepher." 13 Othniel, the
son of Caleb's younger brother Kenaz, cap-
tured the city, so Caleb gave him his daugh-
ter Achsah in marriage. 14 On the wedding
day Othniel urged her[a] to ask her father for
a field. She got down from her donkey, and
Caleb asked her what she wanted. 15 She
answered, "I want some water holes. The
land you have given me is in the dry coun-
try." So Caleb gave her the upper and lower
springs.

The Victories of the Tribes of Judah and Benjamin

16 The descendants of Moses' father-in-
law, the Kenite, went on with the people of
Judah from Jericho, the city of palm trees,
into the barren country south of Arad in
Judah. There they settled among the
Amalekites.[b] 17 The people of Judah went
with the people of Simeon, and together
they defeated the Canaanites who lived in
the city of Zephath. They put a curse
on the city, destroyed it, and named it
Hormah.[c] 18-19 The LORD helped the peo-
ple of Judah, and they took possession of
the hill country. But they did not capture[d]
Gaza, Ashkelon, or Ekron, with their sur-
rounding territories. These people living
along the coast had iron chariots, and so the
people of Judah were not able to drive
them out. 20 As Moses had commanded,
Hebron was given to Caleb, who drove out
of the city the three clans descended from
Anak. 21 But the people of the tribe of Ben-

[a] **1:14** *Some ancient translations* Othniel urged her; *Hebrew* she urged Othniel. [b] **1:16** *Some ancient translations* Amalekites; *Hebrew* people. [c] **1:17** HORMAH: *This name in Hebrew means "destruction."* [d] **1:18-19** *One ancient translation* But they did not capture; *Hebrew* And they captured.

1:20 Josh 15:13, 14 **1:21** Josh 15:63; 2 Sam 5:6; 1 Chr 11:4

Live it!

Speak Up

Caleb's daughter Achsah knows that her people will need water. The land they are given is in the desert. She asks her father, and he gives her two springs, or watering holes. Do you suffer in silence when you need something? Be bold like Achsah and ask for what you need. You can ask God for help with any problem. But sometimes you need to ask a parent or a friend for help, too. People can't help you if they don't know what you need!

— Judges 1:12–15

jamin did not drive out the Jebusites living in Jerusalem, and the Jebusites have continued to live there with the people of Benjamin ever since.

The Tribes of Ephraim and Manasseh Conquer Bethel

22-23 The tribes of Ephraim and Manasseh went to attack the city of Bethel, at that time called Luz. The LORD helped them. They sent spies to the city, 24 who saw a man leaving and said to him, "Show us how to get into the city, and we won't hurt you." 25 So he showed them, and the people of Ephraim and Manasseh killed everyone in the city, except this man and his family. 26 He later went to the land of the Hittites, built a city there, and named it Luz, which is still its name.

People Who Were Not Driven Out by the Israelites

27 The tribe of Manasseh did not drive out the people living in the cities of Beth Shan, Taanach, Dor, Ibleam, Megiddo, and the nearby towns; the Canaanites continued to live there. 28 When the Israelites became stronger, they forced the Canaanites to work for them, but still they did not drive them all out.

29 The tribe of Ephraim did not drive out the Canaanites living in the city of Gezer, and so the Canaanites continued to live there with them.

30 The tribe of Zebulun did not drive out the people living in the cities of Kitron and Nahalal, and so the Canaanites continued to live there with them and were forced to work for them.

31 The tribe of Asher did not drive out the people living in the cities of Acco, Sidon, Ahlab, Achzib, Helbah, Aphek, and Rehob. 32 The people of Asher lived with the local Canaanites, since they had not been driven out.

33 The tribe of Naphtali did not drive out the people living in the cities of Beth Shemesh and Bethanath. The people of Naphtali lived with the local Canaanites, but forced them to work for them.

34 The Amorites forced the people of the tribe of Dan into the hill country and did not let them come down to the plain. 35 The Amorites continued to live at Aijalon, Shaalbim, and Mount Heres, but the tribes of Ephraim and Manasseh kept them under their rule and forced them to work for them.

36 North of Sela, the Edomite[e] border ran through Akrabbim Pass.

The Angel of the LORD at Bochim

2 The angel of the LORD went from Gilgal to Bochim and said to the Israelites, "I took you out of Egypt and brought you

[e] **1:36** *One ancient translation* Edomite; *Hebrew* Amorite.
1:27, 28 Josh 17:11–13 **1:29** Josh 16:10

The story continues . . . the Book of Judges picks up right where the Book of Joshua left off. The author even begins by reviewing the events of Joshua.

Pray it!

Turning Your Back on God

The Israelites turned their back on God by worshiping the Baals and Astartes, the gods and goddesses of other peoples. They had promised to have no other God but Yahweh. It is hard to imagine why they would do this after all that God had done for them.

We should be careful, though, before judging the Israelites too harshly. There is more than one way to turn your back on God. We can put other things before God. We're too busy to pray or go to church. We don't notice other people in need because we're too distracted by things we want. It's all too easy to do.

God, help me never to turn my back on you,
because you never turn your back on me.
Remind me when I forget you,
that I am yours and you are mine.
Help me commit to putting you first,
by praying,
by doing something for someone in need,
by being an active member of my church.

— Judges 2:10–13

to the land that I promised to your ancestors. I said, 'I will never break my covenant
with you. 2You must not make any covenant
with the people who live in this land. You must tear down their altars.' But you have not done what I told you. You have done
just the opposite! 3So I tell you now that I
will not drive these people out as you advance. They will be your enemies,[f] and you will be trapped by the worship of their
gods." 4When the angel had said this, all the
people of Israel began to cry, 5and that is
why the place is called Bochim.[g] There they offered sacrifices to the LORD.

The Death of Joshua

6Joshua sent the people of Israel on their
way, and each man went to take possession of his own share of the land. 7As long as Joshua
lived, the people of Israel served the LORD, and even after his death they continued to do so as long as the leaders were alive who had seen for themselves all the great things that
the LORD had done for Israel. 8The LORD's
servant Joshua son of Nun died at the age of
a hundred and ten. 9He was buried in his
own part of the land at Timnath Serah in the hill country of Ephraim north of Mount
Gaash. 10That whole generation also died,
and the next generation forgot the LORD and what he had done for Israel.

Israel Stops Worshiping the LORD

11Then the people of Israel sinned against
the LORD and began to serve the Baals.
12They stopped worshiping the LORD, the

[f] 2:3 *Some ancient translations* enemies; *Hebrew* sides. [g] 2:5 BOCHIM: *This name in Hebrew means "those who cry."*
2:2 Ex 34:12, 13; Deut 7:2–5 **2:9** Josh 19:49, 50

Baals were the gods of the Canaanites, and the Astartes their goddesses.

God of their ancestors, the God who had
brought them out of Egypt, and they began
to worship other gods, the gods of the peo-
ples around them. They bowed down to
them and made the LORD angry. 13They
stopped worshiping the LORD and served
the Baals and the Astartes. 14And so the
LORD became furious with Israel and let
raiders attack and rob them. He let the ene-
mies all around overpower them, and the
Israelites could no longer protect themselves.
15Every time they would go into battle, the
LORD was against them, just as he had said
he would be. They were in great distress.

16Then the LORD gave the Israelites lead-
ers who saved them from the raiders. 17But
the Israelites paid no attention to their lead-
ers. Israel was unfaithful to the LORD and
worshiped other gods. Their fathers had
obeyed the LORD's commands, but this new
generation soon stopped doing so. 18When-
ever the LORD gave Israel a leader, the LORD
would help that leader and would save the
people from their enemies as long as that
leader lived. The LORD would have mercy
on them because they groaned under their
suffering and oppression. 19But when the
leader died, the people would return to the
old ways and behave worse than the previous
generation. They would serve and worship
other gods, and stubbornly continue their
own evil ways. 20Then the LORD would
become furious with Israel and say, "This

Israel . . . worshiped other gods. (2:17)

nation has broken the covenant that I com-
manded their ancestors to keep. Because
they have not obeyed me, 21I will no longer
drive out any of the nations that were still in
the land when Joshua died. 22I will use them
to find out whether or not these Israelites
will follow my ways, as their ancestors did."
23So the LORD allowed these nations to
remain in the land; he did not give Joshua
victory over them, nor did he drive them
out soon after Joshua's death.

The Nations Remaining in the Land

3 So then, the LORD left some nations in
the land to test the Israelites who had
not been through the wars in Canaan. 2He
did this only in order to teach each genera-
tion of Israelites about war, especially those
who had never been in battle before. 3Those
left in the land were the five Philistine cities,
all the Canaanites, the Sidonians, and the
Hivites who lived in the Lebanon Moun-
tains from Mount Baal Hermon as far as
Hamath Pass. 4They were to be a test for
Israel, to find out whether or not the
Israelites would obey the commands that the
LORD had given their ancestors through
Moses. 5And so the people of Israel settled
down among the Canaanites, the Hittites,
the Amorites, the Perizzites, the Hivites, and
the Jebusites. 6They intermarried with them
and worshiped their gods.

Othniel

7The people of Israel forgot the LORD
their God; they sinned against him and wor-
shiped the idols of Baal and Asherah. 8So the
LORD became angry with Israel and let King
Cushan Rishathaim of Mesopotamia con-
quer them. They were subject to him for
eight years. 9Then the Israelites cried out to
the LORD, and he sent someone to free
them. This was Othniel, the son of Caleb's
younger brother Kenaz. 10The spirit of the
LORD came upon him, and he became
Israel's leader. Othniel went to war, and the
LORD gave him the victory over the king of
Mesopotamia. 11There was peace in the land
for forty years, and then Othniel died.

Ehud

12 The people of Israel sinned against the
LORD again. Because of this the LORD made
King Eglon of Moab stronger than Israel.
13 Eglon joined the Ammonites and the
Amalekites; they defeated Israel and captured
Jericho, the city of palm trees. 14 The Israelites
were subject to Eglon for eighteen years.

15 Then the Israelites cried out to the
LORD, and he sent someone to free them.
This was Ehud, a left-handed man, who was
the son of Gera, from the tribe of Benjamin.
The people of Israel sent Ehud to King
Eglon of Moab with gifts for him. 16 Ehud
had made himself a double-edged sword
about a foot and a half long. He had it fas-
tened on his right side under his clothes.
17 Then he took the gifts to Eglon, who was
a very fat man. 18 When Ehud had given him
the gifts, he told the men who had carried
them to go back home. 19 But Ehud himself
turned back at the carved stones near Gilgal,
went back to Eglon, and said, "Your Majesty,
I have a secret message for you."

So the king ordered his servants, "Leave us
alone!" And they all went out.

20 Then, as the king was sitting there alone
in his cool room on the roof, Ehud went
over to him and said, "I have a message from
God for you." The king stood up. 21 With his
left hand Ehud took the sword from his
right side and plunged it into the king's
belly. 22 The whole sword went in, handle
and all, and the fat covered it up. Ehud did
not pull it out of the king's belly, and it stuck
out behind, between his legs.[h] 23 Then Ehud
went outside, closed the doors behind him,
locked them, 24 and left. The servants came
and saw that the doors were locked, but they
only thought that the king was inside, reliev-
ing himself. 25 They waited as long as they
thought they should, but when he still did
not open the door, they took the key and
opened it. And there was their master, lying
dead on the floor.

26 Ehud got away while they were waiting.
He went past the carved stones and escaped
to Seirah. 27 When he arrived there in the hill
country of Ephraim, he blew a trumpet to
call the people of Israel to battle; then he led
them down from the hills. 28 He told them,
"Follow me! The LORD has given you victo-
ry over your enemies, the Moabites." So they
followed Ehud down and captured the place
where the Moabites were to cross the Jordan;
they did not allow anyone to cross. 29 That
day they killed about ten thousand of the
best Moabite soldiers; none of them escaped.
30 That day the Israelites defeated Moab, and
there was peace in the land for eighty years.

Shamgar

31 The next leader was Shamgar son of
Anath. He too rescued Israel, and did so by
killing six hundred Philistines with an
oxgoad.

Deborah and Barak

4 After Ehud died, the people of Israel
sinned against the LORD again. 2 So the
LORD let them be conquered by Jabin, a
Canaanite king who ruled in the city of
Hazor. The commander of his army was Sis-
era, who lived at Harosheth-of-the-Gentiles.
3 Jabin had nine hundred iron chariots, and
he ruled the people of Israel with cruelty
and violence for twenty years. Then the peo-
ple of Israel cried out to the LORD for help.

4 Now Deborah, the wife of Lappidoth,
was a prophet, and she was serving as a judge
for the Israelites at that time. 5 She would sit
under a certain palm tree between Ramah
and Bethel in the hill country of Ephraim,
and the people of Israel would go there for
her decisions. 6 One day she sent for Barak
son of Abinoam from the city of Kedesh in
Naphtali and said to him, "The LORD, the
God of Israel, has given you this command:
'Take ten thousand men from the tribes of
Naphtali and Zebulun and lead them to
Mount Tabor. 7 I will bring Sisera, the com-
mander of Jabin's army, to fight you at the
Kishon River. He will have his chariots and
soldiers, but I will give you victory over
him.' "

8 Then Barak replied, "I will go if you go
with me, but if you don't go with me, I
won't go either."

[h] **3:22** *Probable text* it stuck . . . legs; *Hebrew unclear.*

Study it!

A Brave and Wise Woman

Deborah is very unusual for her time. She is the fourth judge of Israel, and the only woman known to be a judge. She sits under her palm tree and gives wise advice to all the people who come to her. Then she receives a message from God and commands Barak to go to war. Barak refuses unless Deborah agrees to go with him. Barak must have felt the army would only follow him if they saw that Deborah was with him. Barak and the people who came to Deborah for judgment and advice must have trusted her a lot.

What woman do you know who is wise and courageous?

— Judges 4:1–8

9She answered, "All right, I will go with
you, but you won't get any credit for the victory, because the LORD will hand Sisera over
to a woman." So Deborah set off for Kedesh
with Barak. 10Barak called the tribes of Zebulun and Naphtali to Kedesh, and ten thousand
men followed him. Deborah went with him.

11In the meantime Heber the Kenite had
set up his tent close to Kedesh near the oak
tree at Zaanannim. He had moved away
from the other Kenites, the descendants of
Hobab, the brother-in-law of Moses.

12When Sisera learned that Barak had
gone up to Mount Tabor, 13he called out his
nine hundred iron chariots and all his men,
and sent them from Harosheth-of-the-Gentiles to the Kishon River.

14Then Deborah said to Barak, "Go! The
LORD is leading you! Today he has given you
victory over Sisera." So Barak went down
from Mount Tabor with his ten thousand
men. 15When Barak attacked with his army,
the LORD threw Sisera into confusion
together with all his chariots and men. Sisera
got down from his chariot and fled on foot.
16Barak pursued the chariots and the army
to Harosheth-of-the-Gentiles, and Sisera's
whole army was killed. Not a man was left.

The LORD threw . . . into confusion . . . all his chariots and men. (4:15)

17Sisera ran away to the tent of Jael, the
wife of Heber the Kenite, because King
Jabin of Hazor was at peace with Heber's
family. 18Jael went out to meet Sisera and
said to him, "Come in, sir; come into my
tent. Don't be afraid." So he went in, and she
hid him behind a curtain.[i] 19He said to her,
"Please give me a drink of water; I'm
thirsty." She opened a leather bag of milk,
gave him a drink, and hid him again. 20Then
he told her, "Stand at the door of the tent,
and if anyone comes and asks you if anyone
is here, say no."

21Sisera was so tired that he fell sound
asleep. Then Jael took a hammer and a tent
peg, quietly went up to him, and killed him
by driving the peg right through the side of
his head and into the ground. 22When Barak
came looking for Sisera, Jael went out to
meet him and said to him, "Come here! I'll
show you the man you're looking for." So he
went in with her, and there was Sisera on
the ground, dead, with the tent peg through
his head.

23That day God gave the Israelites victory

[i] **4:18** hid him behind a curtain; *or* covered him with a rug.

Jael is not an Israelite, but she is connected to them. Moses' wife was also a Kenite *(Judges 1:16)*, **the same group that Jael is from.**

Pray it!

Sing a Song

After their victory over the Canaanites, Deborah and Barak sing the song in Judges, chapter 5. The song recounts the victory over Sisera's army and the brave acts of those who helped. If you wrote a song that praised God for the good he has done in your life, what would you say? If you could choose a song that celebrates what God has done for you, what song would you choose?

Some people find that music helps them pray. They may listen to popular music on the radio or music by Christian singers or bands. If you want to pray with music, you might ask a youth leader at your church for some suggestions.

— Judges, chapter 5

over Jabin, the Canaanite king. 24 They pressed harder and harder against him until they destroyed him.

The Song of Deborah and Barak

5 On that day Deborah and Barak son of Abinoam sang this song:

2 Praise the LORD!
The Israelites were determined to fight;
the people gladly volunteered.
3 Listen, you kings!
Pay attention, you rulers!
I will sing and play music
to Israel's God, the LORD.
4 LORD, when you left the mountains of Seir,
when you came out of the region of Edom,
the earth shook, and rain fell from the sky.
Yes, water poured down from the clouds.
5 The mountains quaked before the LORD of Sinai,
before the LORD, the God of Israel.
6 In the days of Shamgar son of Anath,
in the days of Jael,
caravans no longer went through the land,
and travelers used the back roads.
7 The towns of Israel stood abandoned, Deborah;
they stood empty until you came,[j]
came like a mother for Israel.
8 Then there was war in the land
when the Israelites chose new gods.
Of the forty thousand men in Israel,
did anyone carry shield or spear?
9 My heart is with the commanders of Israel,
with the people who gladly volunteered.
Praise the LORD!
10 Tell of[k] it, you that ride on white donkeys,
sitting on saddles,
and you that must walk wherever you go.
11 Listen! The noisy crowds around the wells
are telling of the LORD's victories,
the victories of Israel's people!
Then the LORD's people marched down
from their cities.[l]

[j] **5:7** abandoned, Deborah . . . you came; *or* abandoned; they stood empty until I, Deborah, came.
[k] **5:10** Tell of; *or* Think about. [l] **5:11** from their cities; *or* to their gates.
5:5 Ex 19:18

"May your friends shine like the rising sun!" *(Judges 5:31)*.

12 Lead on, Deborah, lead on!
Lead on! Sing a song! Lead on!
Forward, Barak son of Abinoam,
lead your captives away!
13 Then the faithful ones came down to
their leaders;
the LORD's people came to him[m] ready
to fight.
14 They came[n] from Ephraim into the
valley,[o]
behind the tribe of Benjamin and its
people.
The commanders came down from
Machir,
the officers down from Zebulun.
15 The leaders of Issachar came with
Deborah;
yes, Issachar came and Barak too,
and they followed him into the valley.
But the tribe of Reuben was divided;
they could not decide to come.
16 Why did they stay behind with the sheep?
To listen to shepherds calling the
flocks?
Yes, the tribe of Reuben was divided;
they could not decide to come.
17 The tribe of Gad stayed east of the
Jordan,
and the tribe of Dan remained by the
ships.
The tribe of Asher stayed by the seacoast;
they remained along the shore.
18 But the people of Zebulun and Naphtali
risked their lives on the battlefield.

19 At Taanach, by the stream of Megiddo,
the kings came and fought;
the kings of Canaan fought,
but they took no silver away.
20 The stars fought from the sky;
as they moved across the sky,
they fought against Sisera.
21 A flood in the Kishon swept them
away—
the onrushing Kishon River.
I shall march, march on, with strength!
22 Then the horses came galloping on,
stamping the ground with their hoofs.

23 "Put a curse on Meroz," says the angel of
the LORD,
"a curse, a curse on those who live
there.
They did not come to help the LORD,
come as soldiers to fight for him."
24 The most fortunate of women is Jael,
the wife of Heber the Kenite—
the most fortunate of women who live
in tents.
25 Sisera asked for water, but she gave him
milk;
she brought him cream in a beautiful
bowl.
26 She took a tent peg in one hand,
a worker's hammer in the other;
she struck Sisera and crushed his skull;
she pierced him through the head.
27 He sank to his knees,
fell down and lay still at her feet.
At her feet he sank to his knees and fell;
he fell to the ground, dead.
28 Sisera's mother looked out of the
window;
she gazed[p] from behind the lattice.
"Why is his chariot so late in coming?"
she asked.
"Why are his horses so slow to
return?"
29 Her wisest friends answered her,
and she told herself over and over,
30 "They are only finding things to capture
and divide,
a woman or two for every soldier,
rich cloth for Sisera,
embroidered pieces for the neck of the
queen."[q]
31 So may all your enemies die like that,
O LORD,
but may your friends shine like the
rising sun!

And there was peace in the land for forty
years.

[m] **5:13** *One ancient translation* him; *Hebrew* me. [n] **5:14** *Probable text* They came; *Hebrew* Their root.
[o] **5:14** *One ancient translation* into the valley; *Hebrew* in Amalek. [p] **5:28** *Some ancient translations* gazed; *Hebrew* cried out. [q] **5:30** *Probable text* queen; *Hebrew* plunder.

Gideon

6 Once again the people of Israel sinned against the LORD, so he let the people of Midian rule them for seven years. 2The Midianites were stronger than Israel, and the people of Israel hid from them in caves and other safe places in the hills. 3Whenever the Israelites would plant their crops, the Midianites would come with the Amalekites and the desert tribes and attack them. 4They would camp on the land and destroy the crops as far south as the area around Gaza. They would take all the sheep, cattle, and donkeys, and leave nothing for the Israelites to live on. 5They would come with their livestock and tents, as thick as locusts. They and their camels were too many to count. They came and devastated the land, 6and Israel was helpless against them.

7Then the people of Israel cried out to the LORD for help against the Midianites, 8and he sent them a prophet who brought them this message from the LORD, the God of Israel: "I brought you out of slavery in Egypt. 9I rescued you from the Egyptians and from the people who fought you here in this land. I drove them out as you advanced, and I gave you their land. 10I told you that I am the LORD your God and that you should not worship the gods of the Amorites, whose land you are now living in. But you have not listened to me."

11Then the LORD's angel came to the village of Ophrah and sat under the oak tree that belonged to Joash, a man of the clan of Abiezer. His son Gideon was threshing some wheat secretly in a wine press, so that the Midianites would not see him. 12The LORD's angel appeared to him there and said, "The LORD is with you, brave and mighty man!"

13Gideon said to him, "If I may ask, sir, why has all this happened to us if the LORD is with us? What happened to all the wonderful things that our fathers told us the LORD used to do—how he brought them out of Egypt? The LORD has abandoned us and left us to the mercy of the Midianites."

14Then the LORD ordered him, "Go with all your great strength and rescue Israel from the Midianites. I myself am sending you."

15Gideon replied, "But Lord, how can I rescue Israel? My clan is the weakest in the tribe of Manasseh, and I am the least important member of my family."

16The LORD answered, "You can do it because I will help you. You will crush the Midianites as easily as if they were only one man."

17Gideon replied, "If you are pleased with me, give me some proof that you are really the LORD. 18Please do not leave until I bring you an offering of food."

He said, "I will stay until you come back."

19So Gideon went into his house and cooked a young goat and used a bushel of flour to make bread without any yeast. He put the meat in a basket and the broth in a pot, brought them to the LORD's angel under the oak tree, and gave them to him. 20The angel told him, "Put the meat and the bread on this rock, and pour the broth over them." Gideon did so. 21Then the LORD's angel reached out and touched the meat and the bread with the end of the stick he was holding. Fire came out of the rock and burned up the meat and the bread. Then the angel disappeared.

22Gideon then realized that it was the LORD's angel he had seen, and he said in terror, "Sovereign LORD! I have seen your angel face to face!"

23But the LORD told him, "Peace. Don't be afraid. You will not die." 24Gideon built an altar to the LORD there and named it "The LORD is Peace." (It is still standing at Ophrah, which belongs to the clan of Abiezer.)

"The LORD is with you, brave and mighty man!" *(6:12)*

Live it!

But Lord . . .

It's a familiar pattern in the Bible. God calls someone, and they have a long list of reasons why they can't respond. Gideon tells the Lord that he can't lead because he's too unimportant. God tells Gideon though, "You can do it because I will help you" (Judges 6:16).

Have you ever thought that you would like to make a difference in the world, but felt as though you were too young or too shy or not smart enough or not popular enough? God says, "You can do it because I will be there to help you!"

That's one of the great things about God. Things that may not have seemed possible before *are* possible. God calls all sorts of people (usually not the richest or the prettiest) to do good in the world. God's calling you too! Gideon said yes. What will your answer be?

— Judges 6:11–16

25 That night the LORD told Gideon,
"Take your father's bull and another bull
seven years old,[r] tear down your father's altar
to Baal, and cut down the symbol of the
goddess Asherah, which is beside it. 26 Build a
well-constructed altar to the LORD your
God on top of this mound. Then take the
second bull[s] and burn it whole as an offering, using for firewood the symbol of Asherah you have cut down." 27 So Gideon took
ten of his servants and did what the LORD
had told him. He was too afraid of his family
and the people in town to do it by day, so he
did it at night.
28 When the people in town got up early
the next morning, they found that the altar
to Baal and the symbol of Asherah had been
cut down, and that the second bull had been
burned on the altar that had been built
there. 29 They asked each other, "Who did
this?" They investigated and found out that
Gideon son of Joash had done it. 30 Then
they said to Joash, "Bring your son out here,
so that we can kill him! He tore down the
altar to Baal and cut down the symbol of
Asherah beside it."
31 But Joash said to all those who confronted him, "Are you arguing for Baal? Are
you defending him? Anyone who argues for
him will be killed before morning. If Baal is
a god, let him defend himself. It is his altar
that was torn down." 32 From then on
Gideon was known as Jerubbaal,[t] because
Joash said, "Let Baal defend himself; it is his
altar that was torn down."
33 Then all the Midianites, the Amalekites,
and the desert tribes assembled, crossed the
Jordan River, and camped in Jezreel Valley.
34 The spirit of the LORD took control of
Gideon, and he blew a trumpet to call the
men of the clan of Abiezer to follow him.
35 He sent messengers throughout the territory of both parts of Manasseh to call them
to follow him. He sent messengers to the
tribes of Asher, Zebulun, and Naphtali, and
they also came to join him.
36 Then Gideon said to God, "You say that
you have decided to use me to rescue Israel.
37 Well, I am putting some wool on the
ground where we thresh the wheat. If in the
morning there is dew only on the wool but
not on the ground, then I will know that
you are going to use me to rescue Israel."
38 That is exactly what happened. When
Gideon got up early the next morning, he
squeezed the wool and wrung enough dew

[r] **6:25** bull and another bull seven years old; *or* bull, the seven-year-old one. [s] **6:26** the second bull; *or* the bull.
[t] **6:32** JERUBBAAL: *This name in Hebrew means "Let Baal defend himself."*

The Midianites were descendents of Abraham! Midian was Abraham's son by Keturah *(Genesis 25:1–2)*.

Miracles

Gideon asks for a sign from God. He wants to be sure that this is what God really wants him to do. God's response to Gideon is to show him not just one but two miracles. In one miracle God caused fire to come from a rock and burn up bread and meat. In the second miracle God caused the morning dew to be only on some wool Gideon put out, while leaving no dew on the ground. The next day the morning dew was only on ground, and the wool was completely dry.

The Catholic Church teaches that miracles still happen today. Many miracles are healings of people who are sick or diseased. These healings happen without any medical explanation. We cannot force God to perform a miracle, especially as a test, like Gideon. But we can ask God for what we need and trust he will give us what is best for us.

— Judges 6:17–22,36–40

out of it to fill a bowl with water. 39 Then
Gideon said to God, "Don't be angry with
me; let me speak just once more. Please let
me make one more test with the wool. This
time let the wool be dry, and the ground be
wet." 40 That night God did that very thing.
The next morning the wool was dry, but the
ground was wet with dew.

Gideon Defeats the Midianites

7 One day Gideon and all his men got up
early and camped beside Harod Spring.
The Midianite camp was in the valley to the
north of them by Moreh Hill.
2 The LORD said to Gideon, "The men
you have are too many for me to give them
victory over the Midianites. They might
think that they had won by themselves, and
so give me no credit. 3 Announce to the
people, 'Anyone who is afraid should go
back home, and we will stay here at Mount
Gilead.' " So twenty-two thousand went
back, but ten thousand stayed.
4 Then the LORD said to Gideon, "You
still have too many men. Take them down to
the water, and I will separate them for you
there. If I tell you a man should go with
you, he will go. If I tell you a man should
not go with you, he will not go." 5 Gideon
took the men down to the water, and the
LORD told him, "Separate everyone who laps
up the water with his tongue like a dog,
from everyone who gets down on his knees
to drink." 6 There were three hundred men
who scooped up water in their hands and
lapped it; all the others got down on their
knees to drink. 7 The LORD said to Gideon,
"I will rescue you and give you victory over
the Midianites with the three hundred men
who lapped the water. Tell everyone else to

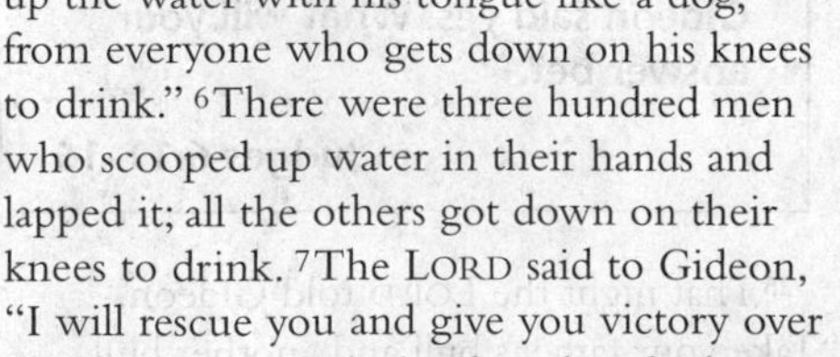

"Separate everyone who laps up the water." (7:5)

7:3 Deut 20:8

Gideon's strategy is surprise! Check out the strategy he used to defeat the Midianites with only a handful of soldiers!

go home." 8So Gideon sent all the Israelites
home, except the three hundred, who kept
all the supplies and trumpets. The Midianite
camp was below them in the valley.
9That night the LORD commanded
Gideon, "Get up and attack the camp; I am
giving you victory over it. 10But if you are
afraid to attack, go down to the camp with
your servant Purah. 11You will hear what
they are saying, and then you will have the
courage to attack." So Gideon and his
servant Purah went down to the edge of
the enemy camp. 12The Midianites, the
Amalekites, and the desert tribesmen were
spread out in the valley like a swarm of
locusts, and they had as many camels as there
are grains of sand on the seashore.
13When Gideon arrived, he heard a man
telling a friend about a dream. He was say-
ing, "I dreamed that a loaf of barley bread
rolled into our camp and hit a tent. The tent
collapsed and lay flat on the ground."
14His friend replied, "It's the sword of the
Israelite, Gideon son of Joash! It can't mean
anything else! God has given him victory
over Midian and our whole army!"
15When Gideon heard about the man's
dream and what it meant, he fell to his knees
and worshiped the LORD. Then he went back
to the Israelite camp and said, "Get up! The
LORD is giving you victory over the Midian-
ite army!" 16He divided his three hundred
men into three groups and gave each man a
trumpet and a jar with a torch inside it. 17He
told them, "When I get to the edge of the
camp, watch me, and do what I do. 18When
my group and I blow our trumpets, then you
blow yours all around the camp and shout,
'For the LORD and for Gideon!' "
19Gideon and his one hundred men came
to the edge of the camp a while before mid-
night, just after the guard had been changed.
Then they blew the trumpets and broke the
jars they were holding, 20and the other two
groups did the same. They all held the torch-
es in their left hands, the trumpets in their
right, and shouted, "A sword for the LORD
and for Gideon!" 21Every man stood in his
place around the camp, and the whole
enemy army ran away yelling. 22While
Gideon's men were blowing their trumpets,
the LORD made the enemy troops attack
each other with their swords. They ran
toward Zarethan as far as Beth Shittah, as far
as the town of Abel Meholah near Tabbath.
23Then men from the tribes of Naphtali,
Asher, and both parts of Manasseh were
called out, and they pursued the Midianites.
24Gideon sent messengers through all the
hill country of Ephraim to say, "Come down
and fight the Midianites. Hold the Jordan
River and the streams as far as Bethbarah, to
keep the Midianites from crossing them."
The men of Ephraim were called together,
and they held the Jordan River and the
streams as far as Bethbarah. 25They captured
the two Midianite chiefs, Oreb and Zeeb;
they killed Oreb at Oreb Rock, and Zeeb at
the Winepress of Zeeb. They continued to
pursue the Midianites and brought the heads
of Oreb and Zeeb to Gideon, who was now
east of the Jordan.

The Final Defeat of the Midianites

8 Then the people of Ephraim said to
Gideon, "Why didn't you call us when
you went to fight the Midianites? Why did
you treat us like this?" They complained bit-
terly about it.
2But he told them, "What I was able to
do is nothing compared with what you have
done. Even the little that you people of
Ephraim did is worth more than what my
whole clan has done. 3After all, through the
power of God you killed the two Midianite
chiefs, Oreb and Zeeb. What have I done to
compare with that?" When he said this, they
were no longer so angry.
4By this time Gideon and his three hun-
dred men had come to the Jordan River and
had crossed it. They were exhausted, but
were still pursuing the enemy. 5When they
arrived at Sukkoth, he said to the men of the
town, "Please give my men some loaves of
bread. They are exhausted, and I am chasing
Zebah and Zalmunna, the Midianite kings."
6But the leaders of Sukkoth said, "Why
should we give your army any food? You
haven't captured Zebah and Zalmunna yet."

8:3–5 Ps 83:11

While Gideon's men were blowing their trumpets, the LORD *made the enemy troops attack each other. (7:22)*

7So Gideon said, "All right! When the
LORD has handed Zebah and Zalmunna over
to me, I will beat you with thorns and briers
from the desert!" 8Gideon went on to
Penuel and made the same request of the
people there, but the men of Penuel gave the
same answer as the men of Sukkoth. 9So he
said to them, "I am going to come back safe
and sound, and when I do, I will tear this
tower down!"

10Zebah and Zalmunna were at Karkor
with their army. Of the whole army of
desert tribesmen, only about 15,000 were
left; 120,000 soldiers had been killed.
11Gideon went on the road along the edge
of the desert, east of Nobah and Jogbehah,
and attacked the army by surprise. 12The
two Midianite kings, Zebah and Zalmunna,
ran away, but he pursued them and captured
them, and caused their whole army to panic.

13When Gideon was returning from the
battle by way of Heres Pass, 14he captured a
young man from Sukkoth and questioned
him. The young man wrote down for
Gideon the names of the seventy-seven lead-
ing men of Sukkoth. 15Then Gideon went to
the men of Sukkoth and said, "Remember
when you refused to help me? You said that
you couldn't give any food to my exhausted
army because I hadn't captured Zebah and
Zalmunna yet. Well, here they are!" 16He
then took thorns and briers from the desert
and used them to punish the leaders of
Sukkoth. 17He also tore down the tower at
Penuel and killed the men of that city.

18Then Gideon asked Zebah and Zal-
munna, "What about the men you killed at
Tabor?"

They answered, "They looked like you—
every one of them like the son of a king."

19Gideon said, "They were my brothers,
my own mother's sons. I solemnly swear that
if you had not killed them, I would not kill
you." 20Then he said to Jether, his oldest son,
"Go ahead, kill them!" But the boy did not

draw his sword. He hesitated, because he was still only a boy.

21 Then Zebah and Zalmunna said to Gideon, "Come on, kill us yourself. It takes a man to do a man's job." So Gideon killed them and took the ornaments that were on the necks of their camels.

22 After that, the Israelites said to Gideon, "Be our ruler—you and your descendants after you. You have saved us from the Midianites."

23 Gideon answered, "I will not be your ruler, nor will my son. The LORD will be your ruler." 24 But he went on to say, "Let me ask one thing of you. Every one of you give me the earrings you took." (The Midianites, like other desert people, wore gold earrings.)

25 The people answered, "We'll be glad to give them to you." They spread out a cloth, and everyone put on it the earrings that he had taken. 26 The gold earrings that Gideon got weighed over forty pounds, and this did not include the ornaments, necklaces, and purple clothes that the kings of Midian wore, nor the collars that were around the necks of their camels. 27 Gideon made an idol from the gold and put it in his hometown, Ophrah. All the Israelites abandoned God and went there to worship the idol. It was a trap for Gideon and his family.

28 So Midian was defeated by the Israelites and was no longer a threat. The land was at peace for forty years, until Gideon died.

The Death of Gideon

29 Gideon went back to his own home and lived there. 30 He had seventy sons, because he had many wives. 31 He also had a concubine in Shechem; she bore him a son, and he named him Abimelech. 32 Gideon son of Joash died at a ripe old age and was buried in the tomb of his father Joash, at Ophrah, the town of the clan of Abiezer.

33 After Gideon's death the people of Israel were unfaithful to God again and worshiped the Baals. They made Baal-of-the-Covenant their god, 34 and no longer served the LORD their God, who had saved them from all their enemies around them. 35 They were not grateful to the family of Gideon for all the good that he had done for Israel.

Study it!

I Will Not Rule Over You

The Israelites had many powerful leaders through the years: Abraham, Moses, Joshua, and now the judges. But they had never had a king. They want to make Gideon a king, but he refuses the honor. He feels that the Israelites should only honor God as their king.

After the time of the judges, the Israelites will have their own kings. During this time you will see that Gideon's opinion about kings is justified. Many of the kings are not faithful to God and the Covenant God made with the Israelites.

— Judges 8:22–23

Abimelech

9 Gideon's son Abimelech went to the town of Shechem, where all his mother's relatives lived, and told them 2 to ask the men of Shechem, "Which would you prefer? To have all seventy of Gideon's sons govern you or to have just one man? Remember that Abimelech is your own flesh and blood." 3 His mother's relatives talked to the men of Shechem about this for him, and the men of Shechem decided to follow Abimelech because he was their relative. 4 They gave him seventy pieces of silver from the temple of Baal-of-the-Covenant, and with this money he hired a bunch of worthless

"I will not be your ruler, nor will my son. The LORD will be your ruler" *(Judges 8:23)*.

Pray it!

Prayer of a Humble Leader

Abimelech's father, Gideon, was a humble hero. Abimelech was not like his father at all. God chose Gideon. Abimelech chose himself. He decided that he wanted to lead, so he killed all seventy of his brothers except one. The surviving brother curses Abimelech and the people of Shechem who supported him. Even though Abimelech experiences some military successes, he dies without honor. His own people turn on him.

God make me a humble leader.
Help me to lead not because I want to
but when you call me to lead.
Help me to lead not for my personal glory
but to bring glory to you.
Help me not to think of what I want
but to put the needs of others before my own needs.

— Judges, chapter 9

scoundrels to join him. 5He went to his
father's house at Ophrah, and there on top of
a single stone he killed his seventy brothers,
Gideon's sons. But Jotham, Gideon's
youngest son, hid and was not killed. 6Then
all the men of Shechem and Bethmillo got
together and went to the sacred oak tree at
Shechem, where they made Abimelech king.
7When Jotham heard about this, he went
and stood on top of Mount Gerizim and
shouted out to them, "Listen to me, you
men of Shechem, and God may listen to
you! 8Once upon a time the trees went out
to choose a king for themselves. They said to
the olive tree, 'Be our king.' 9The olive tree
answered, 'In order to govern you, I would
have to stop producing my oil, which is used
to honor gods and human beings.' 10Then
the trees said to the fig tree, 'You come and
be our king.' 11But the fig tree answered, 'In
order to govern you, I would have to stop
producing my good sweet fruit.' 12So the
trees then said to the grapevine, 'You come
and be our king.' 13But the vine answered,
'In order to govern you, I would have to
stop producing my wine, that makes gods
and human beings happy.' 14So then all the
trees said to the thorn bush, 'You come and
be our king.' 15The thorn bush answered, 'If
you really want to make me your king, then
come and take shelter in my shade. If you
don't, fire will blaze out of my thorny
branches and burn up the cedars of
Lebanon.'
16"Now then," Jotham continued, "were
you really honest and sincere when you
made Abimelech king? Did you respect
Gideon's memory and treat his family prop-
erly, as his actions deserved? 17Remember
that my father fought for you. He risked his
life to save you from the Midianites. 18But
today you turned against my father's family.
You killed his sons—seventy men on a single
stone—and just because Abimelech, his son
by his servant woman, is your relative, you
have made him king of Shechem. 19Now
then, if what you did today to Gideon and
his family was sincere and honest, then be
happy with Abimelech and let him be happy
with you. 20But if not, may fire blaze out

Part of Abimelech's problem is that he is pretty stuck on himself. Who else in the Bible has a similar problem?

Study it!

Write a Masal

Abimelech's brother Jotham uses a story about trees to describe what Abimelech's leadership will be like and to predict Abimelech's doom. In ancient Israel this kind of story is called a *masal.* A *masal* uses a saying or story to make a comparison with a situation the listeners are familiar with. In Jotham's story, he says Abimelech is like the thorn bush that is good only for burning. Sooner or later those who follow him will be destroyed by him.

Think of some situation of wrongdoing or injustice in the world today. What kind of story could you tell to describe to people what will happen if they don't set things right? Write your own masal that tells about this problem.

— Judges 9:7–15

from Abimelech and burn up the men of
Shechem and Bethmillo. May fire blaze out
from the men of Shechem and Bethmillo
and burn Abimelech up." 21 Then because he
was afraid of his brother Abimelech, Jotham
ran away and went to live at Beer.
22 Abimelech ruled Israel for three years.
23 Then God made Abimelech and the men
of Shechem hostile to each other, and they
rebelled against Abimelech. 24 This happened
so that Abimelech and the men of Shechem,
who encouraged him to murder Gideon's
seventy sons, would pay for their crime.
25 The men of Shechem put men in ambush
against Abimelech on the mountaintops, and
they robbed everyone who passed their way.
Abimelech was told about this.
26 Then Gaal son of Ebed came to
Shechem with his brothers, and the men of
Shechem put their confidence in him.
27 They all went out into their vineyards and
picked the grapes, made wine from them,
and held a festival. They went into the tem-
ple of their god, where they ate and drank
and made fun of Abimelech. 28 Gaal said,
"What kind of men are we in Shechem?
Why are we serving Abimelech? Who is he,
anyway? The son of Gideon! And Zebul
takes orders from him, but why should we
serve him? Be loyal to your ancestor Hamor,
who founded your clan! 29 I wish I were
leading this people! I would get rid of
Abimelech! I would tell[u] him, 'Reinforce
your army, come on out and fight!'"
30 Zebul, the ruler of the city, became
angry when he heard what Gaal had said.
31 He sent messengers to Abimelech at
Arumah[v] to say, "Gaal son of Ebed and his
brothers have come to Shechem, and they
are not going to let you into the city. 32 Now
then, you and your men should move by
night and hide in the fields. 33 Get up tomor-
row morning at sunrise and make a sudden
attack on the city. Then when Gaal and his
men come out against you, hit them with all
you've got!"
34 So Abimelech and all his men made
their move at night and hid outside
Shechem in four groups. 35 When Abimelech
and his men saw Gaal come out and stand at
the city gate, they got up from their hiding
places. 36 Gaal saw them and said to Zebul,
"Look! There are men coming down from
the mountaintops!"
"Those are not men," Zebul answered.
"They are just shadows on the mountains."
37 Gaal said again, "Look! There are men
coming down the crest of the mountain and
one group is coming along the road from
the oak tree of the fortunetellers!"
38 Then Zebul said to him, "Where is all
your big talk now? You were the one who
asked why we should serve this man Abim-
elech. These are the men you were making
fun of. Go on out now and fight them."
39 Gaal led the men of Shechem out and
fought Abimelech. 40 Abimelech started after
Gaal, and Gaal ran. Many were wounded,
even at the city gate. 41 Abimelech lived in

[u] **9:29** *One ancient translation* I would tell; *Hebrew* He told. [v] **9:31** *Probable text* Arumah; *Hebrew unclear.*

Arumah, and Zebul drove Gaal and his
brothers out of Shechem, so that they could
no longer live there.
42The next day Abimelech found out that
the people of Shechem were planning to go
out into the fields, 43so he took his men,
divided them into three groups, and hid in
the fields, waiting. When he saw the people
coming out of the city, he came out of hid-
ing to kill them. 44While Abimelech and his
group hurried forward to guard the city
gate, the other two companies attacked the
people in the fields and killed them all.
45The fighting continued all day long. Abim-
elech captured the city, killed its people, tore
it down, and covered the ground with salt.
46When all the leading men in the fort at
Shechem heard about this, they sought safety
in the stronghold of the temple of Baal-of-
the-Covenant. 47Abimelech was told that
they had gathered there, 48so he went up to
Mount Zalmon with his men. There he took
an ax, cut a limb off a tree, and put it on his
shoulder. He told his men to hurry and do
the same thing. 49So everyone cut off a tree
limb; then they followed Abimelech and
piled the wood up against the stronghold.
They set it on fire, with the people inside,
and all the people of the fort died—about a
thousand men and women.
50Then Abimelech went to Thebez, sur-
rounded that city, and captured it. 51There
was a strong tower there, and every man and
woman in the city, including the leaders, ran
to it. They locked themselves in and went up
to the roof. 52When Abimelech came to
attack the tower, he went up to the door to
set the tower on fire. 53But a woman threw a
millstone down on his head and fractured his
skull. 54Then he quickly called the young
man who was carrying his weapons and told
him, "Draw your sword and kill me. I don't
want it said that a woman killed me." So the
young man ran him through, and he died.
55When the Israelites saw that Abimelech
was dead, they all went home.
56And so it was that God paid Abimelech
back for the crime that he committed
against his father in killing his seventy broth-
ers. 57God also made the men of Shechem
suffer for their wickedness, just as Jotham,
Gideon's son, said they would when he
cursed them.

Tola

10 After Abimelech's death Tola, the son
of Puah and grandson of Dodo,
came to free Israel. He was from the tribe of
Issachar and lived at Shamir in the hill coun-
try of Ephraim. 2He was Israel's leader for
twenty-three years. Then he died and was
buried at Shamir.

Jair

3After Tola came Jair from Gilead. He led
Israel for twenty-two years. 4He had thirty
sons who rode thirty donkeys. They had
thirty cities in the land of Gilead, which are
still called the villages of Jair. 5Jair died and
was buried at Kamon.

Jephthah

6Once again the Israelites sinned against
the LORD by worshiping the Baals and the
Astartes, as well as the gods of Syria, of
Sidon, of Moab, of Ammon, and of Philistia.
They abandoned the LORD and stopped
worshiping him. 7So the LORD became
angry with the Israelites, and let the
Philistines and the Ammonites conquer
them. 8For eighteen years they oppressed
and persecuted all the Israelites who lived in
Amorite country east of the Jordan River in
Gilead. 9The Ammonites even crossed the
Jordan to fight the tribes of Judah, Benjamin,
and Ephraim. Israel was in great distress.
10Then the Israelites cried out to the LORD
and said, "We have sinned against you, for we
left you, our God, and worshiped the Baals."
11The LORD gave them this answer: "The
Egyptians, the Amorites, the Ammonites, the
Philistines, 12the Sidonians, the Amalekites,
and the Maonites oppressed you in the past,
and you cried out to me. Did I not save you
from them? 13But you still left me and wor-
shiped other gods, so I am not going to res-
cue you again. 14Go and cry out to the gods

9:53 2 Sam 11:21

you have chosen. Let them rescue you when
you get in trouble."
15 But the people of Israel said to the
LORD, "We have sinned. Do whatever you
like, but please, save us today." 16 So they got
rid of their foreign gods and worshiped the
LORD; and he became troubled over Israel's
distress.
17 Then the Ammonite army prepared for
battle and camped in Gilead. The people of
Israel came together and camped at Mizpah
in Gilead. 18 There the people and the lead-
ers of the Israelite tribes asked one another,
"Who will lead the fight against the
Ammonites? Whoever does will be the
leader of everyone in Gilead."

11 Jephthah, a brave soldier from
Gilead, was the son of a prostitute.
His father Gilead 2 had other sons by his
wife, and when they grew up, they forced
Jephthah to leave home. They told him, "You
will not inherit anything from our father;
you are the son of another woman." 3 Jeph-
thah fled from his brothers and lived in the
land of Tob. There he attracted a group of
worthless men, and they went around with
him.
4 It was some time later that the
Ammonites went to war against Israel.
5 When this happened, the leaders of Gilead
went to bring Jephthah back from the land
of Tob. 6 They told him, "Come and lead us,
so that we can fight the Ammonites."
7 But Jephthah answered, "You hated me
so much that you forced me to leave my
father's house. Why come to me now that
you're in trouble?"
8 They said to Jephthah, "We are turning
to you now because we want you to go with
us and fight the Ammonites and lead all the
people of Gilead."
9 Jephthah said to them, "If you take me
back home to fight the Ammonites and the
LORD gives me victory, I will be your ruler."
10 They replied, "We agree. The LORD is
our witness." 11 So Jephthah went with the
leaders of Gilead, and the people made him
their ruler and leader. Jephthah stated his
terms at Mizpah in the presence of the LORD.
12 Then Jephthah sent messengers to the
king of Ammon to say, "What is your quarrel
with us? Why have you invaded our coun-
try?"
13 The king of Ammon answered Jeph-
thah's messengers, "When the Israelites came
out of Egypt, they took away my land from
the Arnon River to the Jabbok River and
the Jordan River. Now you must give it back
peacefully."
14 Jephthah sent messengers back to the
king of Ammon 15 with this answer: "It is

Live it!

An Unexpected Leader

Sometimes prejudice and jealousy can get in the way of someone using his or her gifts. Jephthah was driven away from his home by his half-brothers. His mother and father weren't married, and his brothers did not want to share their inheritance with him.

Have you ever been discriminated against because you dress or talk differently? Have you ever kept someone else from being a part of the group because they like to do different things than you? Fortunately for the Israelites, Jephthah helped them anyway, even though they had rejected him. He was a brave soldier and a good leader. God works through all kinds of people! We risk missing out on some really great people when we only stick with the ones who are just like us! Branch out and see what God has in store for you!

— Judges 11:1–11

"We have sinned. . . . Please, save us" *(Judges 10:15)*. **This pattern repeats again and again throughout the Scriptures. Try saying it yourself.**

not true that Israel took away the land of Moab or the land of Ammon. 16This is what happened: when the Israelites left Egypt, they went through the desert to the Gulf of Aqaba and came to Kadesh. 17Then they sent messengers to the king of Edom to ask permission to go through his land. But the king of Edom would not let them. They also asked the king of Moab, but neither would he let them go through his land. So the Israelites stayed at Kadesh. 18Then they went on through the desert, going around the land of Edom and the land of Moab until they came to the east side of Moab, on the other side of the Arnon River. They camped there, but they did not cross the Arnon because it was the boundary of Moab. 19Then the Israelites sent messengers to Sihon, the Amorite king of Heshbon, and asked him for permission to go through his country to their own land. 20But Sihon would not let Israel do it. He brought his whole army together, camped at Jahaz, and attacked Israel. 21But the LORD, the God of Israel, gave the Israelites victory over Sihon and his army. So the Israelites took possession of all the territory of the Amorites who lived in that country. 22They occupied all the Amorite territory from the Arnon in the south to the Jabbok in the north and from the desert on the east to the Jordan on the west. 23So it was the LORD, the God of Israel, who drove out the Amorites for his people, the Israelites. 24Are you going to try to take it back? You can keep whatever your god Chemosh has given you. But we are going to keep everything that the LORD, our God, has taken for us. 25Do you think you are any better than Balak son of Zippor, king of Moab? He never challenged Israel, did he? Did he ever go to war against us? 26For three hundred years Israel has occupied Heshbon and Aroer, and the towns around them, and all the cities on the banks of the Arnon River. Why haven't you taken them back in all this time? 27No, I have not done you any wrong. You are doing wrong by making war on me. The LORD is the judge. He will decide today between the Israelites and the Ammonites." 28But the king of Ammon paid no attention to this message from Jephthah.

29Then the spirit of the LORD came upon Jephthah. He went through Gilead and Manasseh and returned to Mizpah in Gilead and went on to Ammon. 30Jephthah promised the LORD: "If you will give me victory over the Ammonites, 31I will burn as an offering the first person that comes out of my house to meet me, when I come back from the victory. I will offer that person to you as a sacrifice."

32So Jephthah crossed the river to fight the Ammonites, and the LORD gave him victory. 33He struck at them from Aroer to the area around Minnith, twenty cities in all, and as far as Abel Keramim. There was a great slaughter, and the Ammonites were defeated by Israel.

Jephthah's Daughter

34When Jephthah went back home to Mizpah, there was his daughter coming out

Dancing and playing the tambourine (11:34)

11:17 Num 20:14–21 **11:18** Num 21:4 **11:19–22** Num 21:21–24 **11:25** Num 22:1–6

Jephthah makes a vow to sacrifice a human being even though the Abraham and Isaac story teaches that God doesn't want that.

Pray it!

Friends to Count On

Jephthah made a terrible promise, and his daughter is sacrificed. She will die without getting married or having children. Her friends go with her into the mountains to help her mourn. It couldn't have been easy being with her when they knew she was going to be killed. Have you ever known someone who knew they were dying? A lot of people pull away when someone is dying or even just very sick. They just don't want to have to deal with pain or struggle.

God of love, give me friends I can count on
when I have something difficult to face
or if I just need a shoulder to cry on.
Help me in turn to be a good friend
and offer comfort to the people who count on me.

— Judges 11:34–40

to meet him, dancing and playing the tambourine. She was his only child. 35When he saw her, he tore his clothes in sorrow and said, "Oh, my daughter! You are breaking my heart! Why must it be you that causes me pain? I have made a solemn promise to the LORD, and I cannot take it back!"

36She told him, "If you have made a promise to the LORD, do what you said you would do to me, since the LORD has given you revenge on your enemies, the Ammonites." 37But she asked her father, "Do this one thing for me. Leave me alone for two months, so that I can go with my friends to wander in the mountains and grieve that I must die a virgin." 38He told her to go and sent her away for two months. She and her friends went up into the mountains and grieved because she was going to die unmarried and childless. 39After two months she came back to her father. He did what he had promised the LORD, and she died still a virgin.

This was the origin of the custom in Israel 40that the Israelite women would go out for four days every year to grieve for the daughter of Jephthah of Gilead.

Jephthah and the Ephraimites

12 The men of Ephraim prepared for battle; they crossed the Jordan River to Zaphon and said to Jephthah, "Why did you cross the border to fight the Ammonites without calling us to go with you? We'll burn the house down over your head!"

2But Jephthah told them, "My people and I had a serious quarrel with the Ammonites. I did call you, but you would not rescue me from them. 3When I saw that you were not going to, I risked my life and crossed the border to fight them, and the LORD gave me victory over them. So why are you coming up to fight me now?" 4Then Jephthah brought all the men of Gilead together, fought the men of Ephraim and defeated them. (The Ephraimites had said, "You Gileadites in Ephraim and Manasseh, you are deserters from Ephraim!") 5In order to keep the Ephraimites from escaping, the Gileadites captured the places where the Jordan could be crossed. When any Ephraimite who was trying to escape would ask permission to cross, the men of Gilead would ask, "Are you an Ephraimite?" If he said, "No," 6they would tell him to say "Shibboleth." But he would say "Sibboleth," because he could not

11:35 Num 30:2

pronounce it correctly. Then they would
grab him and kill him there at one of the
Jordan River crossings. At that time forty-
two thousand of the Ephraimites were
killed.
7 Jephthah led Israel for six years. Then he
died and was buried in his hometown[w] in
Gilead.

Ibzan, Elon, and Abdon

8 After Jephthah, Ibzan from Bethlehem
led Israel. 9 He had thirty sons and thirty
daughters. He gave his daughters in marriage
outside the clan and brought thirty young
women from outside the clan for his sons to
marry. Ibzan led Israel for seven years, 10 then
he died and was buried at Bethlehem.
11 After Ibzan, Elon from Zebulun led
Israel for ten years. 12 Then he died and was
buried at Aijalon in the territory of Zebulun.
13 After Elon, Abdon son of Hillel from
Pirathon led Israel. 14 He had forty sons and
thirty grandsons, who rode on seventy don-
keys. Abdon led Israel for eight years, 15 then
he died and was buried at Pirathon in the
territory of Ephraim in the hill country of
the Amalekites.

The Birth of Samson

13 The Israelites sinned against the
LORD again, and he let the
Philistines rule them for forty years.
2 At that time there was a man named
Manoah from the town of Zorah. He was a
member of the tribe of Dan. His wife had
never been able to have children. 3 The
LORD's angel appeared to her and said, "You
have never been able to have children, but
you will soon be pregnant and have a son.
4 Be sure not to drink any wine or beer, or
eat any forbidden food; 5 and after your son
is born, you must never cut his hair, because
from the day of his birth he will be dedicat-
ed to God as a nazirite.[x] He will begin the
work of rescuing Israel from the Philistines."
6 Then the woman went and told her hus-
band, "A man of God has come to me, and
he looked as frightening as the angel[y] of
God. I didn't ask him where he came from,
and he didn't tell me his name. 7 But he did
tell me that I would become pregnant and
have a son. He told me not to drink any
wine or beer, or eat any forbidden food,
because the boy is to be dedicated to God as
a nazirite as long as he lives."
8 Then Manoah prayed to the LORD,
"Please, LORD, let the man of God that you
sent come back to us and tell us what we
must do with the boy when he is born."
9 God did what Manoah asked, and his
angel came back to the woman while she
was sitting in the field. Her husband Manoah
was not with her, 10 so she ran at once and

Study it!

A Sneak Preview

Pay attention when an angel visits! You can usually bet something big is about to happen. It's a sneak preview, a way to let the audience know that something important is coming soon. Manoah and his wife each see an angel who promises them they will have a son. They have not been able to have a child, so this is wonderful news. However, they must raise him as a nazirite—someone who is especially dedicated to God.

Can you think of other childless couples in the Bible who receive special visits from angels? One couple is in the Book of Genesis, and two others are in the beginning of the Gospel of Luke.

— Judges 13:2–24

[w] **12:7** *One ancient translation* his hometown; *Hebrew* the towns. [x] **13:5** NAZIRITE: *A person who showed devotion to God by taking vows not to drink wine or beer or allow any hair to be cut or touch corpses (see Num 6:1–8).*
[y] **13:6** the angel; *or* an angel.

13:5 Num 6:1–5

told him, "Look! The man who came to me the other day has appeared to me again."
11 Manoah got up and followed his wife. He went to the man and asked, "Are you the man who talked to my wife?"

"Yes," he answered.
12 Then Manoah said, "Now then, when your words come true, what must the boy do? What kind of a life must he lead?"
13 The LORD's angel answered, "Your wife must be sure to do everything that I have
told her. 14 She must not eat anything that comes from the grapevine; she must not drink any wine or beer, or eat any forbidden food. She must do everything that I have told her."
15-16 Not knowing that it was the LORD's angel, Manoah said to him, "Please do not go yet. Let us cook a young goat for you."

But the angel said, "If I do stay, I will not eat your food. But if you want to prepare it, burn it as an offering to the LORD."
17 Manoah replied, "Tell us your name, so that we can honor you when your words come true."
18 The angel asked, "Why do you want to know my name? It is a name of wonder."[z]
19 So Manoah took a young goat and some grain, and offered them on the rock altar to the LORD who works wonders.[a]
20-21 While the flames were going up from the altar, Manoah and his wife saw the LORD's angel go up toward heaven in the flames. Manoah realized then that the man had been the LORD's angel, and he and his wife threw themselves face downward on the ground. They never saw the angel again.
22 Manoah said to his wife, "We are sure to die, because we have seen God!"
23 But his wife answered, "If the LORD had wanted to kill us, he would not have accepted our offerings; he would not have shown us all this or told us such things at this time."
24 The woman gave birth to a son and named him Samson. The child grew and the LORD blessed him. 25 And the LORD's power

Manoah and his wife saw the LORD's angel. (13:21)

began to strengthen him while he was between Zorah and Eshtaol in the Camp of Dan.

Samson and the Woman from Timnah

14 One day Samson went down to Timnah, where he noticed a certain young Philistine woman. 2 He went back home and told his father and mother, "There is a Philistine woman down at Timnah who caught my attention. Get her for me; I want to marry her."
3 But his father and mother asked him, "Why do you have to go to those heathen Philistines to get a wife? Can't you find someone in our own clan, among all our people?"

But Samson told his father, "She is the one I want you to get for me. I like her."

[z] **13:18** name of wonder; *or* mysterious name. [a] **13:19** *Some ancient translations* who works wonders; *Hebrew* and working wonders while Manoah and his wife watched.

Samson eats wild honey and is known as something of a wild man. Can you think of a wild man from the Gospels that eats wild honey?

4His parents did not know that it was the
LORD who was leading Samson to do this,
for the LORD was looking for a chance to
fight the Philistines. At this time the
Philistines were ruling Israel.
5So Samson went down to Timnah with
his father and mother. As they were going
through the vineyards there, he heard a
young lion roaring. 6Suddenly the power of
the LORD made Samson strong, and he tore
the lion apart with his bare hands, as if it
were a young goat. But he did not tell his
parents what he had done.
7Then he went and talked to the young
woman, and he liked her. 8A few days later
Samson went back to marry her. On the way
he left the road to look at the lion he had
killed, and he was surprised to find a swarm
of bees and some honey inside the dead
body. 9He scraped the honey out into his
hands and ate it as he walked along. Then he
went to his father and mother and gave
them some. They ate it, but Samson did not
tell them that he had taken the honey from
the dead body of a lion.
10His father went to the woman's house,
and Samson gave a banquet there. This was a
custom among the young men. 11When the
Philistines saw him, they sent thirty young
men to stay with him. 12-13Samson said to
them, "Let me tell you a riddle. I'll bet each
one of you a piece of fine linen and a
change of fine clothes that you can't tell me
its meaning before the seven days of the
wedding feast are over."

"Tell us your riddle," they said. "Let's hear
it."
14He said,

"Out of the eater came something to eat;
Out of the strong came something sweet."

Three days later they had still not figured
out what the riddle meant.
15On the fourth[b] day they said to Sam-
son's wife, "Trick your husband into telling
us what the riddle means. If you don't, we'll
set fire to your father's house and burn you
with it.[c] You two invited us so that you
could rob us, didn't you?"
16So Samson's wife went to him in tears
and said, "You don't love me! You just hate

Live it!

Samson in Trouble

Samson, for all his feats of strength, seems to keep getting himself in trouble. If he would only think first, he might not get into trouble so much. His anger also gets him into trouble. First, he told a riddle at his wedding feast that he thought no one could guess. But the guests found out the answer from his new wife, which made Samson furious. Besides killing thirty Philistine men, he stormed away from his new wife. When her father then married her to the best man, Samson was even more furious. He tied burning torches to foxes' tails, and they set fire to the Philistine crops and orchards. In revenge the Philistines killed his wife and her family. It just kept getting worse and worse.

When you get upset, do you stop and think, or do you just react? In the end Samson forgets that God is where his real strength lies. Can you remember and keep cool when things around you heat up? Try remembering that God is your strength next time you get angry or upset!

— Judges 14:15—15:8

[b] **14:15** *Some ancient translations* fourth; *Hebrew* seventh.
[c] **14:15** set fire . . . you with it; *or* burn you and your family.

Three thousand men came to capture one man! Silly? Well, not if he can kill a thousand men with a jawbone of a donkey!

me! You told my friends a riddle and didn't
tell me what it means!"
He said, "Look, I haven't even told my
father and mother. Why should I tell you?"
17She cried about it for the whole seven
days of the feast. But on the seventh day he
told her what the riddle meant, for she
nagged him so about it. Then she told the
Philistines. 18So on the seventh day, before
Samson went into the bedroom,[d] the men of
the city said to him,

"What could be sweeter than honey?
What could be stronger than a lion?"

Samson replied,

"If you hadn't been plowing with my
cow,
You wouldn't know the answer now."

19Suddenly the power of the LORD made
him strong, and he went down to Ashkelon,
where he killed thirty men, stripped them,
and gave their fine clothes to the men who
had solved the riddle. After that, he went
back home, furious about what had hap-
pened, 20and his wife was given to the man
that had been his best man at the wedding.

15 Some time later Samson went to
visit his wife during the wheat har-
vest and took her a young goat. He told her
father, "I want to go to my wife's room."
But he wouldn't let him go in. 2He told
Samson, "I really thought that you hated her,
so I gave her to your friend. But her
younger sister is prettier, anyway. You can
have her, instead."
3Samson said, "This time I'm not going
to be responsible for what I do to the
Philistines!" 4So he went and caught three
hundred foxes. Two at a time, he tied their
tails together and put torches in the knots.
5Then he set fire to the torches and turned
the foxes loose in the Philistine wheat fields.
In this way he burned up not only the
wheat that had been harvested but also the
wheat that was still in the fields. The olive
orchards were also burned. 6When the
Philistines asked who had done this, they
learned that Samson had done it because his
father-in-law, a man from Timnah, had
given Samson's wife to a friend of Samson's.
So the Philistines went and burned the
woman to death and burned down her
father's house.[e]
7Samson told them, "So this is how you
act! I swear that I won't stop until I pay you
back!" 8He attacked them fiercely and killed
many of them. Then he went and stayed in
the cave in the cliff at Etam.

Samson Defeats the Philistines

9The Philistines came and camped in
Judah, and attacked the town of Lehi. 10The
men of Judah asked them, "Why are you
attacking us?"
They answered, "We came to take Samson
prisoner and to treat him as he treated us."
11So these three thousand men of Judah
went to the cave in the cliff at Etam and said
to Samson, "Don't you know that the
Philistines are our rulers? What have you
done to us?"
He answered, "I did to them just what
they did to me."
12They told him, "We have come here to
tie you up, so we can hand you over to
them."
Samson said, "Give me your word that
you won't kill me yourselves."
13"All right," they said, "we are only going
to tie you up and hand you over to them.
We won't kill you." So they tied him up
with two new ropes and brought him back
from the cliff.
14When he got to Lehi, the Philistines
came running toward him, shouting at him.

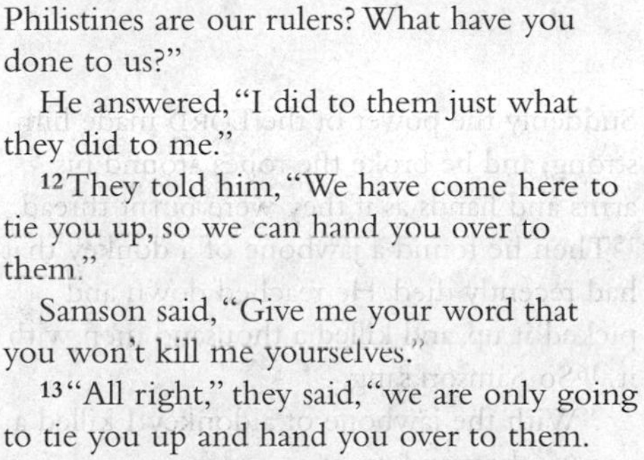

He tied their tails together and put torches in the knots. (15:4)

[d] **14:18** *Probable text* bedroom; *Hebrew* sun. [e] **15:6** burned the woman . . . house; *or* burned the woman and her family to death.

He broke the ropes around his arms. (15:14)

Suddenly the power of the LORD made him strong, and he broke the ropes around his arms and hands as if they were burnt thread.
15Then he found a jawbone of a donkey that had recently died. He reached down and picked it up, and killed a thousand men with
it. 16So Samson sang,

"With the jawbone of a donkey I killed a thousand men;
With the jawbone of a donkey I piled them up in piles."[f]

17After that, he threw the jawbone away. The place where this happened was named Ramath Lehi.[g]
18Then Samson became very thirsty, so he called to the LORD and said, "You gave me this great victory; am I now going to die of thirst and be captured by these heathen Philistines?"
19Then God opened a hollow place in the ground there at Lehi, and water came out of it. Samson drank it and began to feel much better. So the spring was named Hakkore;[h] it is still there at Lehi.
20Samson led Israel for twenty years while the Philistines ruled the land.

Samson at Gaza

16 One day Samson went to the Philistine city of Gaza, where he met a prostitute and went to bed with her.
2The people of Gaza found out that Samson was there, so they surrounded the place and waited for him all night long at the city gate. They were quiet all night, thinking to themselves, "We'll wait until daybreak, and then we'll kill him."
3But Samson stayed in bed only until midnight. Then he got up and took hold of the city gate and pulled it up—doors, posts, lock, and all. He put them on his shoulders and carried them far off to the top of the hill overlooking Hebron.

Samson and Delilah

4After this, Samson fell in love with a woman named Delilah, who lived in Sorek Valley.
5The five Philistine kings went to her and said, "Trick Samson into telling you why he is so strong and how we can overpower him, tie him up, and make him helpless. Each one of us will give you eleven hundred pieces of silver."
6So Delilah said to Samson, "Please tell me what makes you so strong. If someone wanted to tie you up and make you helpless, how could he do it?"
7Samson answered, "If they tie me up with seven new bowstrings that are not dried out, I'll be as weak as anybody else."
8So the Philistine kings brought Delilah seven new bowstrings that were not dried out, and she tied Samson up.
9She had some men waiting in another room, so she shouted, "Samson! The Philistines are coming!" But he snapped the bowstrings just as thread breaks when fire touches it. So they still did not know the secret of his strength.
10Delilah told Samson, "Look, you've been making a fool of me and not telling me the truth. Please tell me how someone could tie you up."
11He told her, "If they tie me with new ropes that have never been used, I'll be as weak as anybody else."
12So Delilah got some new ropes and tied

[f] **15:16** PILES: *This word sounds like the Hebrew for "donkey."* [g] **15:17** RAMATH LEHI: *This name in Hebrew means "Jawbone Hill."* [h] **15:19** HAKKORE: *This name in Hebrew means "caller."*

Live it!

Be Careful Whom You Trust

Lisa didn't like her middle name. It was old fashioned, and it embarrassed her. She never told anyone what it was, especially at school. Then one day Marci invited Lisa over after school. Lisa didn't know Marci very well, but Marci was popular. They did their homework and had a nice time. Then Marci wanted to play Truth or Dare. She asked Lisa what her middle name was. Lisa wasn't sure if Marci would keep her secret, but she wanted Marci to like her. Lisa told Marci her middle name and asked her not to tell anyone else. The next day at school Lisa walked into the classroom and someone had written her whole name in big letters on the board at the front of the classroom. Lisa had never been so embarrassed or felt such betrayal in her whole life.

Samson, like Lisa, shared his secret with someone who wasn't trustworthy. What was wrong with Samson? Why couldn't he see that Delilah was trying to trick him? Why did he trust her with his most important secret? What about Lisa? Why would she tell someone she hardly knew one of her biggest secrets? Read Sirach 6:5–17 and write down your own advice about being taken advantage of.

— Judges 16:4–22

him up. Then she shouted, "Samson! The
Philistines are coming!" The men were wait-
ing in another room. But he snapped the
ropes off his arms like thread.
13 Delilah said to Samson, "You're still mak-
ing a fool of me and not telling me the truth.
Tell me how someone could tie you up."
He told her, "If you weave my seven locks
of hair into a loom, and make it tight with a
peg, I'll be as weak as anybody else."
14 Delilah then lulled him to sleep, took
his seven locks of hair, and wove them into
the loom.[i] She made it tight with a peg and
shouted, "Samson! The Philistines are com-
ing!" But he woke up and pulled his hair
loose from the loom.
15 So she said to him, "How can you say
you love me, when you don't mean it?
You've made a fool of me three times, and
you still haven't told me what makes you so
strong." 16 She kept on asking him, day after
day. He got so sick and tired of her bother-
ing him about it 17 that he finally told her
the truth. "My hair has never been cut," he
said. "I have been dedicated to God as a
nazirite[j] from the time I was born. If my hair
were cut, I would lose my strength and be as
weak as anybody else."
18 When Delilah realized that he had told
her the truth, she sent a message to the
Philistine kings and said, "Come back one
more time. He has told me the truth." Then
they came and brought the money with
them. 19 Delilah lulled Samson to sleep in her
lap and then called a man, who cut off[k]
Samson's seven locks of hair. Then she began
to torment him, for he had lost his strength.
20 Then she shouted, "Samson! The
Philistines are coming!" He woke up and
thought, "I'll get loose and go free, as
always." He did not know that the LORD had
left him. 21 The Philistines captured him and
put his eyes out. They took him to Gaza,
chained him with bronze chains, and put
him to work grinding at the mill in the
prison. 22 But his hair started growing back.

[i] **16:14** *One ancient translation* and make it tight *(in verse 13)* . . . into the loom *(in verse 14)*; *Hebrew does not have these words.* [j] **16:17** NAZIRITE: *See 13:5.* [k] **16:19** *Probable text* who cut off; *Hebrew* and she cut off.

Samson gave in to Delilah because she kept bothering him. What should Samson have done instead?

Pray it!

Prayer in Despair

Samson had once been strong and in control of every situation. He lost his strength because he forgot that it came from the Lord. But even though he has nothing left, he turns to God and asks for help. The next time you are in despair, try Samson's prayer:

"Sovereign LORD, please remember me; please, God, give me my strength" **(Judges 16:28).**

— Judges 16:23–31

The Death of Samson

23 The Philistine kings met together to
celebrate and offer a great sacrifice to their
god Dagon. They sang, "Our god has given
us victory over our enemy Samson!"
24-25 They were enjoying themselves, and so
they said, "Call Samson, and let's make him
entertain us!"[l] When they brought Samson
out of the prison, they made him entertain
them[m] and made him stand between the
columns. When the people saw him, they
sang praise to their god: "Our god has given
us victory over our enemy, who devastated
our land and killed so many of us!"
26 Samson said to the boy who was leading him by
the hand, "Let me touch the columns that
hold up the building. I want to lean on
them."
27 The building was crowded with
men and women. All five Philistine kings
were there, and there were about three thousand men and women on the roof, watching
Samson entertain them.[n]
28 Then Samson prayed, "Sovereign LORD,
please remember me; please, God, give me
my strength just this one time more, so that
with this one blow I can get even with the
Philistines for putting out my two eyes."
29 So Samson took hold of the two middle
columns holding up the building. Putting
one hand on each column, he pushed against
them
30 and shouted, "Let me die with the
Philistines!" He pushed with all his might,
and the building fell down on the five kings
and everyone else. Samson killed more people at his death than he had killed during his
life.
31 His brothers and the rest of his family
came down to get his body. They took him
back and buried him between Zorah and
Eshtaol in the tomb of his father Manoah.
He had been Israel's leader for twenty years.

He pushed with all his might. (16:30)

[l] **16:24–25** make him entertain us; *or* make fun of him. [m] **16:24–25** made him entertain them; *or* made fun of him. [n] **16:27** entertain them; *or* and making fun of him.

In the Book of Judges, the people worship God at Shiloh in a tent. Do you know which king builds a Temple to worship God? What city is it built in?

Micah's Idols

17 There was once a man named
Micah, who lived in the hill country
of Ephraim. 2He told his mother, "When
someone stole those eleven hundred pieces
of silver from you, you put a curse on the
robber. I heard you do it. Look, I have the
money. I am the one who took it."

His mother said, "May the LORD bless
you, my son!" 3He gave the money back to
his mother, and she said, "To keep the curse
from falling on my son, I myself am solemn-
ly dedicating the silver to the LORD. It will
be used to make a wooden idol covered
with silver. So now I will give the pieces of
silver back to you." 4Then he gave them
back to his mother. She took two hundred
of the pieces of silver and gave them to a
metalworker, who made an idol, carving it
from wood and covering it with the silver. It
was placed in Micah's house.

5This man Micah had his own place of
worship. He made some idols and an
ephod,[o] and appointed one of his sons as his
priest. 6There was no king in Israel at that
time; everyone did whatever they wanted.

7At that same time there was a young
Levite who had been living in the town of
Bethlehem in Judah. 8He left Bethlehem to
find another place to live. While he was trav-
eling, he came to Micah's house in the hill
country of Ephraim. 9Micah asked him,
"Where do you come from?"

He answered, "I am a Levite from Bethle-
hem in Judah. I am looking for a place to
live."

10Micah said, "Stay with me. Be my advis-
er and priest, and I will give you ten pieces
of silver a year, some clothes, and your
food."[p] 11The young Levite agreed to stay
with Micah and became like a son to him.
12Micah appointed him as his priest, and he
lived in Micah's home. 13Micah said, "Now
that I have a Levite as my priest, I know that
the LORD will make things go well for me."

Study it!

What's Wrong with This Picture?

Read Judges, chapters 17–18, carefully. Does anything strike you as terribly wrong with the actions of the people in this story? Did you notice the following?

- **Micah steals from his mother (17:2).**
- **Micah has the stolen silver made into an idol. In addition he has several other idols (17:4–5).**
- **The spies steal from Micah. The priest doesn't stop the spies from stealing (18:18).**
- **When Micah and his neighbors try to stop the Danite army, they act like nothing is wrong (18:23).**
- **The Danites kill a whole town of peaceful people and burn it to the ground (18:27).**

These actions are against several of the Ten Commandments. Twice the author mentions, "There was no king in Israel at that time" (17:6; 18:1). The Book of Judges was written later, at a time when there was a king. It seems like the author may be suggesting that things are better with kings.

— Judges, chapters 17–18

Micah and the Tribe of Dan

18 There was no king in Israel at that
time. In those days the tribe of Dan
was looking for territory to claim and settle
in because they had not yet received any
land of their own among the tribes of Israel.
2So the people of Dan chose five qualified[q]
men out of all the families in the tribe and

[o] 17:5 EPHOD: *See Word List.* [p] 17:10 *Probable text* your food; *Hebrew* your food. So the Levite went.
[q] 18:2 qualified; *or* brave.
17:6 Judg 21:25

sent them from the towns of Zorah and Esh-
taol with instructions to explore the land
and spy on it. When they arrived in the hill
country of Ephraim, they stayed at Micah's
house. 3While they were there, they recog-
nized the accent of the young Levite, so they
went up to him and asked, "What are you
doing here? Who brought you here?"

4He answered, "I have an arrangement
with Micah, who pays me to serve as his
priest."

5They said to him, "Please ask God if we
are going to be successful on our trip."

6The priest answered, "You have nothing
to worry about. The LORD is taking care of
you on this trip."

7So the five men left and went to the
town of Laish. They saw how the people
there lived in security like the Sidonians.
They were a peaceful, quiet people, with no
argument with anyone; they had all they
needed.[r] They lived far away from the Sido-
nians and had no dealings with any other
people. 8When the five men returned to
Zorah and Eshtaol, the people asked them
what they had found out. 9"Come on," they
replied. "Let's attack Laish. We saw the land,
and it's very good. Don't stay here doing
nothing; hurry! Go on in and take it over!
10When you get there, you will find that the
people don't suspect a thing. It is a big coun-
try; it has everything a person could want,
and God has given it to you."

11So six hundred men from the tribe of
Dan left Zorah and Eshtaol, ready for battle.
12They went up and camped west of Kiriath
Jearim in Judah. That is why the place is still
called Camp of Dan. 13They went on from
there and came to Micah's house in the hill
country of Ephraim.

14Then the five men who had gone to spy
on the country around Laish said to their
companions, "Did you know that here in
one of these houses there is a wooden idol
covered with silver? There are also other
idols and an ephod. What do you think we
should do?" 15So they went into Micah's
house, where the young Levite lived, and
asked the Levite how he was getting along.
16Meanwhile the six hundred Danite sol-
diers, ready for battle, were standing at the
gate. 17The five spies went straight on into
the house and took the wooden idol covered
with silver, the other idols, and the ephod,
while the priest stayed at the gate with the
six hundred armed men.

18When the men went into Micah's house
and took the sacred objects, the priest asked
them, "What are you doing?"

19They told him, "Keep quiet. Don't say a
word. Come with us and be our priest and
adviser. Wouldn't you rather be a priest for a
whole Israelite tribe than for the family of
one man?" 20This made the priest very
happy, so he took the sacred objects and
went along with them.

21They turned around and started off,
with their children, their livestock, and their
belongings going ahead. 22They had traveled
a good distance from the house when Micah
called his neighbors out for battle. They
caught up with the Danites 23and shouted at
them. The Danites turned around and asked
Micah, "What's the matter? Why all this
mob?"

24Micah answered, "What do you mean,
'What's the matter?' You take my priest and
the gods that I made, and walk off! What
have I got left?"

25The Danites told him, "You had better
not say anything else unless you want these
men to get angry and attack you. You and
your whole family would die." 26Then the
Danites went on. Micah saw that they were
too strong for him, so he turned and went
back home.

27-28After the Danites had taken the priest
and the things that Micah had made, they
went and attacked Laish, that town of peace-
ful, quiet people which was in the same val-
ley as Bethrehob. They killed the inhabitants
and burned the town. There was no one to
save them, because Laish was a long way
from Sidon, and they had no dealings with
any other people. The Danites rebuilt the
town and settled down there. 29They
changed its name from Laish to Dan, after
their ancestor Dan, the son of Jacob. 30The
Danites set up the idol to be worshiped, and
Jonathan, the son of Gershom and grandson

[r] **18:7** *Probable text* They were . . . needed; *Hebrew unclear.*

of Moses, served as a priest for the Danites,
and his descendants served as their priests
until the people were taken away into exile.
31 Micah's idol remained there as long as the
Tent where God was worshiped remained at
Shiloh.

The Levite and His Concubine

19 In those days before Israel had a
king, there was a Levite living far
back in the hill country of Ephraim. He
took a young woman from Bethlehem in
Judah to be his concubine. 2 But she became
angry with him,[s] went back to her father's
house in Bethlehem, and stayed there four
months. 3 Then the man decided to go after
her and try to persuade her to return to
him. He took his servant and two donkeys
with him. The woman showed the Levite
into the house, and when her father saw
him, he gave him a hearty greeting. 4 The
father insisted that he stay, and so he stayed
for three days. The couple had their meals
and spent the nights there. 5 On the morning
of the fourth day they woke up early and
got ready to go. But the woman's father said
to the Levite, "Have something to eat first.
You'll feel better. You can go later."
6 So the two men sat down and ate and
drank together. Then the woman's father
told him, "Please spend the night and enjoy
yourself."
7 The Levite got up to go, but the father
urged him to stay, so he spent another night
there. 8 Early in the morning of the fifth day
he started to leave, but the woman's father
said, "Eat something, please. Wait until later
in the day." So the two men ate together.
9 When the man, his concubine, and the
servant once more started to leave, the father
said, "Look, it's almost evening now; you
might as well stay all night. It will be dark
soon; stay here and have a good time.
Tomorrow you can get up early for the trip
and go home."

[s] **19:2** *One ancient translation* became angry with him; *another translation* left him; *Hebrew* was faithful to him.

Live it!

No More Violence Against Women

In the last few chapters of the Book of Judges, things go terribly wrong. The story starts with a man—a Levite or a priest—who has reclaimed his concubine. Ironically he passes by a non-Israelite town to stay overnight in a city of Israelites. Only an old man shows them any hospitality. Then a gang shows up and wants to rape the visiting Levite. To save himself he hands over his concubine, and overnight the gang rapes and abuses her to death.

The story doesn't get any better. The Levite takes the dead woman and cuts her into twelve pieces, and sends them to all twelve tribes of Israel. Of course everyone Is shocked, and they agree to go to war against the tribe of Benjamin. The whole nation of Israel ends up in civil war.

In this disturbing story, women were treated as objects used by men. Not just the gang but even by the Levite who fails to defend his concubine. Unfortunately, this horrible behavior still happens today. Women are treated as objects for display in advertising and pornography. Men abuse women violently every day. Violence against women is wrong. Men and women (including young men and young women) need to stand up and speak out against this kind of violence.

— Judges, chapter 19

Do you know where to find help if someone you know has been physically or sexually abused?

10-11 But the man did not want to spend another night there, so he and his concubine started on their way, with their servant and two donkeys with pack saddles. It was late in the day when they came near Jebus (that is, Jerusalem), so the servant said to his master, "Why don't we stop and spend the night here in this Jebusite city?"

12-13 But his master said, "We're not going to stop in a city where the people are not Israelites. We'll pass on by and go a little farther and spend the night at Gibeah or Ramah." 14 So they passed by Jebus and continued on their way. It was sunset when they came to Gibeah in the territory of the tribe of Benjamin. 15 They turned off the road to go and spend the night there. They went into town and sat down in the city square, but no one offered to take them home for the night.

16 While they were there, an old man came by at the end of a day's work on the farm. He was originally from the hill country of Ephraim, but he was now living in Gibeah. (The other people there were from the tribe of Benjamin.) 17 The old man noticed the traveler in the city square and asked him, "Where do you come from? Where are you going?"

18 The Levite answered, "We have been in Bethlehem in Judah, and now we are on our way home[t] deep in the hill country of Ephraim. No one will put us up for the night, 19 even though we have fodder and straw for our donkeys, as well as bread and wine for my concubine and me and for my servant. We have everything we need."

20 The old man said, "You are welcome in my home! I'll take care of you; you don't have to spend the night in the square." 21 So he took them home with him and fed their donkeys. His guests washed their feet and had a meal.

22 They were enjoying themselves when all of a sudden some sexual perverts from the town surrounded the house and started beating on the door. They said to the old man, "Bring out that man that came home with you! We want to have sex with him!"

23 But the old man went outside and said to them, "No, my friends! Please! Don't do such an evil, immoral thing! This man is my guest. 24 Look! Here is his concubine and my own virgin daughter. I'll bring them out now, and you can have them. Do whatever you want to with them. But don't do such an awful thing to this man!" 25 But the men would not listen to him. So the Levite took his concubine and put her outside with them. They raped her and abused her all night long and didn't stop until morning.

26 At dawn the woman came and fell down at the door of the old man's house, where her husband was. She was still there when daylight came. 27 Her husband got up that morning, and when he opened the door to go on his way, he found his concubine lying in front of the house with her hands reaching for the door. 28 He said, "Get up. Let's go." But there was no answer. So he put her body across the donkey and started on his way home. 29 When he arrived, he went in the house and got a knife. He took his concubine's body, cut it into twelve pieces, and sent one piece to each of the twelve tribes of Israel. 30 Everyone who saw it said, "We have never heard of such a thing! Nothing like this has ever happened since the Israelites left Egypt! We have to do something about this! What will it be?"

Israel Prepares for War

20 All the people of Israel from Dan in the north to Beersheba in the south, as well as from the land of Gilead in the east, answered the call. They gathered in one body in the LORD's presence at Mizpah. 2 The leaders of all the tribes of Israel were present at this gathering of God's people,

[t] **19:18** *One ancient translation* home; *Hebrew* to the house of the LORD.
19:22–24 Gen 19:5–8 **19:29** 1 Sam 11:7

Concubine: A servant woman who, although not a wife, has sexual relations with her master. She was often treated like a second wife.

and there were 400,000 foot soldiers.
3 Meanwhile the people of Benjamin heard
that all the other Israelites had gathered at
Mizpah.
The Israelites asked, "Tell us, how was this
crime committed?" 4 The Levite whose con-
cubine had been murdered answered, "My
concubine and I went to Gibeah in the ter-
ritory of Benjamin to spend the night. 5 The
men of Gibeah came to get me and sur-
rounded the house at night. They intended
to kill me; instead they raped my concubine,
and she died. 6 I took her body, cut it in
pieces, and sent one piece to each of the
twelve tribes of Israel. These people have
committed an evil and immoral act among
us. 7 All of you here are Israelites. What are
we going to do about this?"
8 All the people stood up together and
said, "None of us, whether he lives in a tent
or in a house, will go home. 9 This is what
we will do: we will draw lots and choose
some men to attack Gibeah.[u] 10 One tenth of
the men in Israel will provide food for the
army, and the others will go and punish
Gibeah[v] for this immoral act that they have
committed in Israel." 11 So all the men in
Israel assembled with one purpose—to
attack the town.
12 The Israelite tribes sent messengers all
through the territory of the tribe of Ben-
jamin to say, "What is this crime that you
have committed? 13 Now hand over those
perverts in Gibeah, so that we can kill them
and remove this evil from Israel." But the
people of Benjamin paid no attention to the
other Israelites. 14 From all the cities of Ben-
jamin they came to Gibeah to fight the
other people of Israel. 15-16 They called out
twenty-six thousand soldiers from their cities
that day. Besides these, the citizens of Gibeah
gathered seven hundred specially chosen
men[w] who were left-handed. Every one of
them could sling a stone at a strand of hair
and never miss. 17 Not counting the tribe of
Benjamin, the Israelites gathered 400,000
trained soldiers.

The War against the Benjaminites

18 The Israelites went to the place of wor-
ship at Bethel, and there they asked God,
"Which tribe should attack the Benjaminites
first?"
The LORD answered, "The tribe of Judah."
19 So the Israelites started out the next
morning and camped near the city of
Gibeah. 20 They went to attack the army of
Benjamin, and placed the soldiers in position
facing the city. 21 The army of Benjamin
came out of the city, and before the day was
over they had killed twenty-two thousand
Israelite soldiers. 22-23 Then the Israelites went
to the place of worship and mourned in the
presence of the LORD until evening. They
asked him, "Should we go again into battle
against our brothers the Benjaminites?"
The LORD answered, "Yes."
So the Israelite army was encouraged,
and they placed their soldiers in position
again, where they had been the day before.
24 They marched against the army of Ben-
jamin a second time. 25 And for the second
time the Benjaminites came out of Gibeah,
and this time they killed eighteen thousand
trained Israelite soldiers. 26 Then all the
people of Israel went up to Bethel and
mourned. They sat there in the LORD's
presence and did not eat until evening.
They offered fellowship sacrifices and
burned some sacrifices whole—all in the
presence of the LORD. 27-28 God's Covenant
Box was there at Bethel in those days, and
Phinehas, the son of Eleazar and grandson
of Aaron, was in charge of it. The people
asked the LORD, "Should we go out to fight
our brothers the Benjaminites again, or
should we give up?"
The LORD answered, "Fight. Tomorrow I
will give you victory over them."
29 So the Israelites put some soldiers in
hiding around Gibeah. 30 Then for the third
straight day they marched against the army
of Benjamin and placed their soldiers in
battle position facing Gibeah, as they had
done before. 31 The Benjaminites came out
to fight and were led away from the city. As

[u] **20:9** *One ancient translation* to attack Gibeah; *Hebrew* to Gibeah. [v] **20:10** *One ancient translation* Gibeah; *Hebrew* Geba. [w] **20:15–16** *Some ancient translations* men; *Hebrew* men. In all this number there were seven hundred specially chosen men.

they had before, they began killing some
Israelites in the open country, on the road to
Bethel and on the road to Gibeah. They
killed about thirty Israelites. 32 The Ben-
jaminites said, "We've beaten them just as
before."

But the Israelites had planned to retreat
and lead them away from the city onto the
roads. 33 So when the main army of the
Israelites pulled back and regrouped at
Baaltamar, the men surrounding Gibeah
suddenly rushed out of their hiding places
in the rocky country around the city.[x]
34 Ten thousand men, specially chosen out
of all Israel, attacked Gibeah, and the
fighting was hard. The Benjaminites had
not realized that they were about to be
destroyed. 35 The LORD gave Israel victory
over the army of Benjamin. The Israelites
killed 25,100 of the enemy that day, 36 and
the Benjaminites realized they were
defeated.

How the Israelites Won

The main body of the Israelite army had
retreated from the Benjaminites because they
were relying on the men that they had put
in hiding around Gibeah. 37 These men ran
quickly toward Gibeah; they spread out in
the city and killed everyone there. 38 The
main Israelite army and the men in hiding
had arranged a signal. When they saw a big
cloud of smoke going up from the town,
39 the Israelites out on the battlefield were to
turn around. By this time the Benjaminites
had already killed the thirty Israelites. They
told themselves, "Yes, we've beaten them just
as before." 40 Then the signal appeared; a
cloud of smoke began to go up from the
town. The Benjaminites looked behind them
and were amazed to see the whole city
going up in flames. 41 Then the Israelites
turned around, and the Benjaminites were
thrown into panic because they realized that
they were about to be destroyed. 42 They
retreated from the Israelites and ran toward
the open country, but they could not escape.
They were caught between the main army
and the men who were now coming out of
the city,[y] and they were destroyed. 43 The
Israelites had the enemy trapped, and with-
out stopping they pursued them as far as a
point east of Gibeah, killing them as they
went.[z] 44 Eighteen thousand of the best Ben-
jaminite soldiers were killed. 45 The others
turned and ran toward the open country to
Rimmon Rock. Five thousand of them were
killed on the roads. The Israelites continued
to pursue the rest to Gidom, killing two
thousand. 46 In all, twenty-five thousand Ben-

Live it!

Civil War

The rape of the Levite's concubine has resulted in a horrible civil war. This is not the first time, and it won't be the last, that Israel has gone to war against itself. The Israelites realize just before it's too late that they must stop the fighting or the tribe of Benjamin will come to an end. Since the other tribes have killed all the Benjaminite women, the remaining men have no one left to marry. So they commit even more violence so the men of Benjamin will have wives. Yikes! This is a frightening story of violence and revenge gone out of control.

Have you ever been in an argument with a group of friends? Has it ever happened that people take sides with each side acting worse and worse to each other? The only way this can end is with everyone hating each other—or if someone says *stop* and reaches out a hand asking for forgiveness. Can you be that person?

— Judges, chapters 20–21

[x] **20:33** *One ancient translation* the city *(that is, Gibeah); Hebrew* Geba. [y] **20:42** *Probable text* city; *Hebrew* cities.
[z] **20:43** *Verse 43 in Hebrew is unclear.*

jaminites were killed that day—all of them
brave soldiers.
47 But six hundred men were able to
escape to the open country to Rimmon
Rock, and they stayed there four months.
48 The Israelites turned back against the rest
of the Benjaminites and killed them all—
men, women, and children, and animals as
well. They burned every town in the area.

Wives for the Tribe of Benjamin

21 When the Israelites had gathered at
Mizpah, they had made a solemn
promise to the LORD: "None of us will allow
a Benjaminite to marry a daughter of ours."
2 So now the people of Israel went to Bethel
and sat there in the presence of God until
evening. Loudly and bitterly they mourned:
3 "LORD God of Israel, why has this hap-
pened? Why is the tribe of Benjamin about
to disappear from Israel?"
4 Early the next morning the people got
up and built an altar there. They offered fel-
lowship sacrifices and burned some sacrifices
whole. 5 They asked, "Is there any group out
of all the tribes of Israel that did not go to
the gathering in the LORD's presence at
Mizpah?" (They had taken a solemn oath
that anyone who had not gone to Mizpah
would be put to death.) 6 The people of
Israel felt sorry for their brothers the Ben-
jaminites and said, "Today Israel has lost one
of its tribes. 7 What shall we do to provide
wives for the men of Benjamin who are left?
We have made a solemn promise to the
LORD that we will not give them any of our
daughters."
8 When they asked if there was some
group out of the tribes of Israel that had not
gone to the gathering at Mizpah, they found
out that no one from Jabesh in Gilead had
been there; 9 at the roll call of the army no
one from Jabesh had responded. 10 So the
assembly sent twelve thousand of their
bravest men with the orders, "Go and kill
everyone in Jabesh, including women and
children. 11 Kill all the males, and also every
woman who is not a virgin." 12 They found
four hundred young virgins among the peo-
ple in Jabesh, so they brought them to the
camp at Shiloh, which is in the land of
Canaan.
13 Then the whole assembly sent word to
the Benjaminites who were at Rimmon
Rock and offered to end the war. 14 The
Benjaminites came back, and the other
Israelites gave them the young women from
Jabesh whom they had not killed. But there
were not enough of them.
15 The people felt sorry for the Ben-
jaminites because the LORD had broken the
unity of the tribes of Israel. 16 So the leaders
of the gathering said, "There are no more
women in the tribe of Benjamin. What shall
we do to provide wives for the men who
are left? 17 Israel must not lose one of its
twelve tribes. We must find a way for the
tribe of Benjamin to survive, 18 but we can-
not allow them to marry our daughters,
because we have put a curse on anyone who
allows a Benjaminite to marry one of our
daughters."
19 Then they thought, "The yearly festival
of the LORD at Shiloh is coming soon."
(Shiloh is north of Bethel, south of
Lebonah, and east of the road between
Bethel and Shechem.) 20 They told the Ben-
jaminites, "Go and hide in the vineyards
21 and watch. When the young women of
Shiloh come out to dance during the festi-
val, you come out of the vineyards. Each of
you take a wife by force from among them
and take her back to the territory of Ben-
jamin with you. 22 If their fathers or brothers
come to you[a] and protest, you[b] can tell
them, 'Please let us keep them, because we
did not take them from you in battle to be
our wives. And since you did not give them
to us, you are not guilty of breaking your
promise.' "
23 The Benjaminites did this; each of them
chose a wife from the young women who

[a] **21:22** *One ancient translation* you; *Hebrew* us. [b] **21:22** *Probable text* you; *Hebrew* we.

The city of Gibeah had 700 left-handed warriors who were excellent with slings. Do you recall an earlier judge who was also left-handed?

were dancing at Shiloh and carried her away. Then they went back to their own territory, rebuilt their towns, and lived there. 24 At the same time the rest of the Israelites left, and every man went back to his own tribe and family and to his own property.

25 There was no king in Israel at that time. Everyone did whatever they pleased.

21:25 Judg 17:6

Your Next Step

Congratulations on finishing the Book of Judges! Use this space to write your thoughts and questions about this book. If you are following the suggested reading plan, go on to the Book of Ruth. This little short story about faithful love happens during the time of the judges.

THE BOOK OF Ruth

Ruth is a love story, but not the kind that we're used to hearing. It is the story of the love and devotion of a daughter-in-law for her mother-in-law. The story begins with Ruth as a poor widow. She has nothing but her faith in God and her love for Naomi, her widowed mother-in-law. Ruth refuses to leave Naomi. Ruth's faithfulness is rewarded with marriage to a wealthy man. Even more, the Bible tells us that Ruth will become the great-grandmother of the famous King David. So Ruth is also an ancestor of Jesus. You will enjoy this dramatic story of tragedy, hope for the future, and faith in God.

Chap. 3

Headlines

- Desperate Widow Sends Sons' Wives Away! (1:1–14)
- Faithful Daughter-in-law Refuses to Leave (1:16–22)
- Rich Relative Helps Ruth (2:1–16)
- Boaz Takes Off Sandal, Seals Deal! (4:1–12)
- Boy Destined for Fame! (4:13–22)

FACTOIDS

Who wrote this book? The author is not known.

When was it written? The story of Ruth is set during the time of the judges, but the book was written much later than that.

Why was it written? Ruth was written to remind people of the values of faithfulness, obedience, and love. Ruth is offered as the model of all these things even though she is a foreigner.

What is the Jesus connection? Ruth is the great-grandmother of King David. David was a shepherd as a young man. He was the ancestor of Jesus who would also be called shepherd and king.

Important themes

- Faithfulness and generosity will be rewarded.
- God works through ordinary people.
- God's love and favor extends to people of different faiths and cultures.

RUTH

Elimelech and His Family Move to Moab

1 1-2Long ago, in the days before Israel had
a king, there was a famine in the land. So
a man named Elimelech, who belonged to
the clan of Ephrath and who lived in Bethle-
hem in Judah, went with his wife Naomi and
their two sons Mahlon and Chilion to live for
a while in the country of Moab. While they
were living there, 3Elimelech died, and
Naomi was left alone with her two sons,
4who married Moabite women, Orpah and
Ruth. About ten years later 5Mahlon and
Chilion also died, and Naomi was left all
alone, without husband or sons.

Naomi and Ruth Return to Bethlehem

6Some time later Naomi heard that the
LORD had blessed his people by giving them
good crops; so she got ready to leave Moab
with her daughters-in-law. 7They started out
together to go back to Judah, but on the way
8she said to them, "Go back home and stay
with your mothers. May the LORD be as
good to you as you have been to me and to
those who have died. 9And may the LORD
make it possible for each of you to marry
again and have a home."

So Naomi kissed them good-bye. But
they started crying 10and said to her, "No!
We will go with you to your people."

11"You must go back, my daughters,"
Naomi answered. "Why do you want to
come with me? Do you think I could have
sons again for you to marry? 12Go back
home, for I am too old to get married again.
Even if I thought there was still hope, and so
got married tonight and had sons, 13would
you wait until they had grown up? Would
this keep you from marrying someone else?
No, my daughters, you know that's impossi-
ble. The LORD has turned against me, and I
feel very sorry for you."[a]

Live it!

When Bad Things Happen

The events in the Book of Ruth happened a long time ago, but the lessons it teaches can still help us today. Ruth was a widow. Her husband died at a young age before they had any children. In Ruth's time a widow faced poverty and even starvation unless she remarried. Her mother-in-law, Naomi, wants Ruth to go back to her birth family. But Ruth holds tight to her new faith in God and to Naomi, whom she loves and who probably taught Ruth about God. Ruth knows that staying with her new family and counting on God's help is better than each facing hard times alone.

When things get hard, prayer, family, and friendship are sometimes the only things that can get us through. Can you think of the last time you faced something really sad or difficult? How did you handle it? Whom did you rely on? The next time something bad happens, remember the people you can count on and remember to turn to God.

— Ruth, chapter 1

14Again they started crying. Then Orpah
kissed her mother-in-law good-bye and
went back home,[b] but Ruth held on to her.
15So Naomi said to her, "Ruth, your sister-
in-law has gone back to her people and to
her god.[c] Go back home with her."

[a] **1:13** sorry for you; *or* bitter about what has happened to you. [b] **1:14** *One ancient translation* and went back home; *Hebrew does not have these words.* [c] **1:15** god; *or* gods.

16But Ruth answered, "Don't ask me to
leave you! Let me go with you. Wherever you
go, I will go; wherever you live, I will live. Your
people will be my people, and your God will
be my God. 17Wherever you die, I will die, and
that is where I will be buried. May the LORD's
worst punishment come upon me if I let any-
thing but death[d] separate me from you!"

18When Naomi saw that Ruth was deter-
mined to go with her, she said nothing more.

19They went on until they came to Beth-
lehem. When they arrived, the whole town
became excited, and the women there
exclaimed, "Is this really Naomi?"

They went on until they came to Bethlehem. (1:19)

20"Don't call me Naomi," she answered;
"call me Marah,[e] because Almighty God has
made my life bitter. 21When I left here, I had
plenty, but the LORD has brought me back
without a thing. Why call me Naomi when
the LORD Almighty has condemned me and
sent me trouble?"

22This, then, was how Naomi came back
from Moab with Ruth, her Moabite daugh-
ter-in-law. When they arrived in Bethlehem,
the barley harvest was just beginning.

Ruth Works in the Field of Boaz

2 Naomi had a relative named Boaz, a
rich and influential man who belonged
to the family of her husband Elimelech.

2One day Ruth said to Naomi, "Let me go
to the fields to gather the grain that the har-
vest workers leave. I am sure to find some-
one who will let me work with him."

Naomi answered, "Go ahead, daughter."

3So Ruth went out to the fields and
walked behind the workers, picking up the
heads of grain which they left. It so happened
that she was in a field that belonged to Boaz.

Ruth went out . . . picking up the heads of grain. (2:3)

4Some time later Boaz himself arrived
from Bethlehem and greeted the workers.
"The LORD be with you!" he said.

"The LORD bless you!" they answered.

5Boaz asked the man in charge, "Who is
that young woman?"

6The man answered, "She is the foreigner
who came back from Moab with Naomi.
7She asked me to let her follow the workers
and gather grain. She has been working since
early morning and has just now stopped to
rest for a while under the shelter."

8Then Boaz said to Ruth, "Let me give
you some advice. Don't gather grain any-
where except in this field. Work with the
women here; 9watch them to see where they
are reaping and stay with them. I have

[d] **1:17** anything but death; *or* even death. [e] **1:20** NAOMI . . . MARAH: *In Hebrew Naomi means "pleasant" and Marah means "bitter."*

2:2 Lev 19:9, 10; Deut 24:19

"Wherever you go, I will go; wherever you live, I will live. Your people will be my people, and your God will be my God" *(Ruth 1:16)*.

Catholic Connections

Caring for Poor People

The Law of Moses had strict laws regarding how poor people were to be cared for. They recognized that orphans and widows relied on the kindness of other people. For example, Ruth gleaned in the fields of Boaz, which means she followed the harvesters and picked the grain they left behind. The Law of Moses required that this be allowed to provide for poor people and foreigners (Leviticus 19:9–10).

In a similar way, the Catholic Church teaches that we must love poor people and help provide for their needs. This is sometimes called the preferential love for the poor. There are a number of organizations that put this teaching into action on a national and global scale. The Catholic Campaign for Human Development helps people in the United States. Catholic Relief Services helps people in need all over the world. Both organizations are sponsored by the Catholic Church in the United States and have special opportunities for youth to help. Find their Web sites online and learn more about what you can do.

— Ruth 2:1–3

ordered my men not to molest you. And
whenever you are thirsty, go and drink from
the water jars that they have filled."
10Ruth bowed down with her face touch-
ing the ground, and said to Boaz, "Why
should you be so concerned about me? Why
should you be so kind to a foreigner?"
11Boaz answered, "I have heard about
everything that you have done for your
mother-in-law since your husband died. I
know how you left your father and mother
and your own country and how you came
to live among a people you had never
known before. 12May the LORD reward you
for what you have done. May you have a full
reward from the LORD God of Israel, to
whom you have come for protection!"
13Ruth answered, "You are very kind[f] to
me, sir. You have made me feel better by
speaking gently to me, even though I am not
the equal of one of your servants."
14At mealtime Boaz said to Ruth, "Come
and have a piece of bread, and dip it in the
sauce." So she sat with the workers, and Boaz
passed some roasted grain to her. She ate
until she was satisfied, and she still had some
food left over. 15-16After she had left to go
and gather grain, Boaz ordered the workers,
"Let her gather grain even where the bun-
dles are lying, and don't say anything to stop
her. Besides that, pull out some heads of
grain from the bundles and leave them for
her to pick up."
17So Ruth gathered grain in the field until
evening, and when she had beaten it out, she
found she had nearly twenty-five pounds.
18She took the grain back into town and
showed her mother-in-law how much she had
gathered. She also gave her the food left over
from the meal. 19Naomi asked her, "Where
did you gather all this grain today? Whose
field have you been working in? May God
bless the man who took an interest in you!"
So Ruth told Naomi that she had been

[f] **2:13** You are very kind; *or* Please be kind.

Ruth is also a love story. What signs do you see in chapter 2 that Boaz is falling in love with Ruth?

Live it!

A Good Reputation

What kind of reputation do you have? Do people know you as a kind person? a hard worker? a person with good morals?

Ruth's faithfulness to her mother-in-law is already the talk of the town when Boaz meets her. Often we hear about ugly rumors and negative gossip, but word can also spread when people do good things. Normally, someone like Boaz would be suspicious of Ruth because she is a foreigner. But Ruth's good reputation has made her path smoother. Because Ruth has been kind to Naomi, Boaz is generous to her.

A good reputation generally takes time to build. It comes from consistently being generous, positive, and faithful over time. A good reputation doesn't guarantee success, but it can be a valuable asset. Think about what you want your reputation to be and what you have to do to build it.

—Ruth 2:11–12

working in a field belonging to a man
named Boaz.
20 "May the LORD bless Boaz!" Naomi
exclaimed. "The LORD always keeps his prom-
ises to the living and the dead." And she went
on, "That man is a close relative of ours, one
of those responsible for taking care of us."
21 Then Ruth said, "Best of all, he told me
to keep gathering grain with his workers
until they finish the harvest."
22 Naomi said to Ruth, "Yes, daughter, it
will be better for you to work with the
women in Boaz' field. You might be molest-
ed if you went to someone else's field." 23 So
Ruth worked with them and gathered grain
until all the barley and wheat had been har-
vested. And she continued to live with her
mother-in-law.

Ruth Finds a Husband

3 Some time later Naomi said to Ruth, "I
must find a husband for you, so that you
will have a home of your own. 2 Remember
that this man Boaz, whose women you have
been working with, is our relative. Now lis-
ten. This evening he will be threshing the
barley. 3 So wash yourself, put on some per-
fume, and get dressed in your best clothes.
Then go where he is threshing, but don't let
him know you are there until he has finished
eating and drinking. 4 Be sure to notice
where he lies down, and after he falls asleep,
go and lift the covers and lie down at his
feet. He will tell you what to do."
5 Ruth answered, "I will do everything
you say."
6 So Ruth went to the threshing place and
did just what her mother-in-law had told
her. 7 When Boaz had finished eating and
drinking, he was in a good mood. He went
to the pile of barley and lay down to sleep.
Ruth slipped over quietly, lifted the covers
and lay down at his feet. 8 During the night
he woke up suddenly, turned over, and was
surprised to find a woman lying at his feet.
9 "Who are you?" he asked.
"It's Ruth, sir," she answered. "Because
you are a close relative, you are responsible
for taking care of me. So please marry me."
10 "The LORD bless you," he said. "You are
showing even greater family loyalty in what
you are doing now than in what you did for
your mother-in-law. You might have gone
looking for a young man, either rich or
poor, but you haven't. 11 Now don't worry,
Ruth. I will do everything you ask; as every-
one in town knows, you are a fine woman.
12 It is true that I am a close relative and am
responsible for you, but there is a man who
is a closer relative than I am. 13 Stay here the
rest of the night, and in the morning we will
find out whether or not he will take respon-
sibility for you. If so, well and good; if not,

2:20 Lev 25:25 **3:12** Ruth 2:20

Study it!

Marriage Then and Now

It probably seems strange that Boaz feels he has to clear it with another relative to marry Ruth. Marriage in Ruth's time was rarely about love. Usually it was an arrangement made by fathers of different families. If the father was dead or far away, then the next closest male relative could make arrangements. The male relative may even have married a widowed woman himself. Ruth's actions are surprising because she appeals on her own behalf to Boaz for his protection.

Boaz does indeed love Ruth and wants to marry her, but he has to clear it with the other male relative. So he makes the arrangements with the city elders and her closest male relative for the marriage. Christian marriage is different because we see marriage as a sacrament that requires the consent of both the man and the woman. This is another sign that our understanding of the rights of women has come quite a way since biblical times.

— Ruth 4:1–12

then I swear by the living LORD that I will take the responsibility. Now lie down and stay here till morning."

14 So she lay there at his feet, but she got up before it was light enough for her to be seen, because Boaz did not want anyone to know that she had been there. 15 Boaz said to her, "Take off your cloak and spread it out here." She did, and he poured out almost fifty pounds of barley and helped her lift it to her shoulder. Then she returned to town with it. 16 When she arrived home, her mother-in-law asked her, "How did you get along, daughter?"

Ruth told her everything that Boaz had done for her. 17 She added, "He told me I must not come back to you empty-handed, so he gave me all this barley."

18 Naomi said to her, "Now be patient, Ruth, until you see how this all turns out. Boaz will not rest today until he settles the matter."

Boaz Marries Ruth

4 Boaz went to the meeting place at the town gate and sat down there. Then Elimelech's nearest relative, the man whom Boaz had mentioned, came by, and Boaz called to him, "Come over here, my friend, and sit down." So he went over and sat down. 2 Then Boaz got ten of the leaders of the town and asked them to sit down there too. When they were seated, 3 he said to his relative, "Now that Naomi has come back from Moab, she wants to sell the field that belonged to our relative Elimelech, 4 and I think you ought to know about it. Now then, if you want it, buy it in the presence of these men sitting here. But if you don't want it, say so, because the right to buy it belongs first to you and then to me."

The man said, "I will buy it."

5 Boaz said, "Very well, if you buy the field from Naomi, then you are also buying Ruth,[g] the Moabite widow, so that the field will stay in the dead man's family."

6 The man answered, "In that case I will give up my right to buy the field, because it would mean that my own children would not inherit it. You buy it; I would rather not."

7 Now in those days, to settle a sale or an exchange of property, it was the custom for the seller to take off his sandal and give it to the buyer. In this way the Israelites showed that the matter was settled.

8 So when the man said to Boaz, "You buy it," he took off his sandal and gave it to Boaz.[h] 9 Then Boaz said to the leaders and all

[g] **4:5** *Some ancient translations* Naomi . . . Ruth; *Hebrew* Naomi and from Ruth. [h] **4:8** *One ancient translation* and gave it to Boaz; *Hebrew does not have these words.*

4:7, 8 Deut 25:9 **4:10** Deut 25:5, 6

It was the custom for the seller to take off his sandal.
(4:7)

the others there, "You are all witnesses today
that I have bought from Naomi everything
that belonged to Elimelech and to his sons
Chilion and Mahlon. 10In addition, Ruth the
Moabite, Mahlon's widow, becomes my wife.
This will keep the property in the dead man's
family, and his family line will continue
among his people and in his hometown. You
are witnesses to this today."
11The leaders and the others said, "Yes, we
are witnesses. May the LORD make your
wife become like Rachel and Leah, who
bore many children to Jacob. May you
become rich in the clan of Ephrath and
famous in Bethlehem. 12May the children
that the LORD will give you by this young
woman make your family like the family of
Perez, the son of Judah and Tamar."

Boaz and His Descendants

13So Boaz took Ruth home as his wife.
The LORD blessed her, and she became
pregnant and had a son. 14The women said
to Naomi, "Praise the LORD! He has given
you a grandson today to take care of you.
May the boy become famous in Israel!
15Your daughter-in-law loves you, and has
done more for you than seven sons. And
now she has given you a grandson, who will
bring new life to you and give you security
in your old age." 16Naomi took the child,
held him close,[i] and took care of him.
17The women of the neighborhood
named the boy Obed. They told everyone,
"A son has been born to Naomi!"
Obed became the father of Jesse, who was
the father of David.
18-22This is the family line from Perez to
David: Perez, Hezron, Ram, Amminadab,
Nahshon, Salmon, Boaz, Obed, Jesse, David.

[i] **4:16** held him close; *or* adopted him.
4:11 Gen 29:31 **4:12** Gen 38:27–30

Your Next Step

Congratulations on finishing the Book of Ruth! Use this space to write your thoughts and questions about this book. If you are following the suggested reading plan, go on to the First Book of Samuel. This book tells about Samuel, the last judge of Israel, and about Saul, the first king of Israel.

The First Book of Samuel

"Okay, okay—have it your way. But don't say I didn't warn you!"

Perhaps you have heard these words somewhere along the line. This is the message God gives the people through Samuel, the last of the judges. The people want a king. It seems as if that's all they care about. They want to be just like every other nation. So God agrees. That sets into motion a new era in Israel's history. The two books of Samuel, which were originally one long book, tell the stories of the time of change in leadership—from the judges, the military rulers of Israel, to the kings. This will pose a whole new set of challenges for the people. The Israelites and their kings will have to remember that the true king of Israel is God.

Chap. 17

Headlines

- Sleeping Boy Is Awakened by Voice (3:1–19)
- Saul Is Chosen as First King (10:17–27)
- Disobedient King Rejected by God (15:10–23)
- Shepherd Boy Is Anointed Next King (16:1–13)
- Giant Slain with a Slingshot (17:41–54)
- Loyal Prince Risks Life for David (20:9–17)
- Wise Wife Saves Foolish Husband (25:2–35)

FACTOIDS

Why was it written? This book was probably compiled using ancient court records and stories of heroes. It was written to tell the story of the beginning of the monarchy (kings) in Israel.

What time period does it cover? About 1040 to 1000 BC.

How does it fit into the Bible? First and Second Samuel are very important books because they tell the story of Israel's greatest king, David.

Jesus connection: Jesus is from the line of David and is often compared to David.

Important themes

- Faithfulness to God leads to success; disobedience leads to disaster.
- Israel's kings are chosen by God and are responsible for God's interests.
- The person God chooses is often not the person we might choose.

1 SAMUEL

Elkanah and His Family at Shiloh

1 There was a man named Elkanah, from
the tribe of Ephraim, who lived in the
town of Ramah in the hill country of
Ephraim. He was the son of Jeroham and
grandson of Elihu, and belonged to the family
of Tohu, a part of the clan of Zuph. [2]Elkanah
had two wives, Hannah and Peninnah. Penin-
nah had children, but Hannah did not. [3]Every
year Elkanah went from Ramah to worship
and offer sacrifices to the LORD Almighty at
Shiloh, where Hophni and Phinehas, the two
sons of Eli, were priests of the LORD. [4]Each
time Elkanah offered his sacrifice, he would
give one share of the meat to Peninnah and
one share to each of her children. [5]And even
though he loved Hannah very much he
would give her only one share, because[a] the
LORD had kept her from having children.
[6]Peninnah, her rival, would torment and
humiliate her, because the LORD had kept her
childless. [7]This went on year after year; when-
ever they went to the house of the LORD,
Peninnah would upset Hannah so much that
she would cry and refuse to eat anything.
[8]Her husband Elkanah would ask her, "Han-
nah, why are you crying? Why won't you eat?
Why are you always so sad? Don't I mean
more to you than ten sons?"

Hannah and Eli

[9-10]One time, after they had finished their
meal in the house of the LORD at Shiloh,
Hannah got up. She was deeply distressed,
and she cried bitterly as she prayed to the
LORD. Meanwhile, Eli the priest was sitting
in his place by the door. [11]Hannah made a
solemn promise: "LORD Almighty, look at
me, your servant! See my trouble and
remember me! Don't forget me! If you give
me a son, I promise that I will dedicate him
to you for his whole life and that he will
never have his hair cut."[b]
[12]Hannah continued to pray to the LORD
for a long time, and Eli watched her lips.
[13]She was praying silently; her lips were

[a] **1:5** And even . . . because; *or* To Hannah, however, he would give a special share, because he loved her very much, even though. [b] **1:11** NEVER HAVE HIS HAIR CUT: *A sign of dedication to the LORD (see Num 6:5).*

1:11 Num 6:5

Pray it!

I'm Praying, Really!

Hannah is praying silently to the Lord, but her lips are moving. She is begging the Lord to give her a son. Eli, the priest, is watching her and thinks that she must be drunk and tells her to sober up. Have you ever judged someone else's behavior only to find out you were wrong? Try this prayer when you are tempted to judge someone else without knowing what is really going on.

Lord, help me not to be too quick to judge others, especially during a prayer service or Mass. Even though it may look like they are sleeping or daydreaming, they may also be deep in prayer, as I should be at those times. Give me the deep faith of Hannah and let me focus on you during prayer, not the actions of those around me. Amen.

—1 Samuel 1:12–18

moving, but she made no sound. So Eli
thought that she was drunk, 14and he said to
her, "Stop making a drunken show of your-
self! Stop your drinking and sober up!"

"Stop making a drunken show of yourself!" (1:14)

15"No, I'm not drunk, sir," she answered.
"I haven't been drinking! I am desperate, and
I have been praying, pouring out my trou-
bles to the LORD. 16Don't think I am a
worthless woman. I have been praying like
this because I'm so miserable."
17"Go in peace," Eli said, "and may the
God of Israel give you what you have asked
him for."
18"May you always think kindly of me,"
she replied. Then she went away, ate some
food, and was no longer sad.

Samuel's Birth and Dedication

19The next morning Elkanah and his fam-
ily got up early, and after worshiping the
LORD, they went back home to Ramah.
Elkanah had intercourse with his wife Han-
nah, and the LORD answered her prayer. 20So
it was that she became pregnant and gave
birth to a son. She named him Samuel,[c] and
explained, "I asked the LORD for him."
21The time came again for Elkanah and
his family to go to Shiloh and offer to the
LORD the yearly sacrifice and the special sac-
rifice he had promised. 22But this time Han-
nah did not go. She told her husband, "As
soon as the child is weaned, I will take him
to the house of the LORD, where he will stay
all his life."
23Elkanah answered, "All right, do what-
ever you think best; stay at home until you
have weaned him. And may the LORD make
your[d] promise come true." So Hannah stayed
at home and nursed her child.
24After she had weaned him, she took him
to Shiloh, taking along a three-year-old
bull,[e] a bushel of flour, and a leather bag full
of wine. She took Samuel, young as he was,
to the house of the LORD at Shiloh. 25After
they had killed the bull, they took the child
to Eli. 26Hannah said to him, "Excuse me,
sir. Do you remember me? I am the woman
you saw standing here, praying to the LORD.
27I asked him for this child, and he gave me
what I asked for. 28So I am dedicating him
to the LORD. As long as he lives, he will
belong to the LORD."
Then they[f] worshiped the LORD there.

Hannah's Prayer

2 Hannah prayed:

"The LORD has filled my heart with joy;
how happy I am because of what he
has done!
I laugh at my enemies;
how joyful I am because God has
helped me!
2"No one is holy like the LORD;
there is none like him,
no protector like our God.

[c] **1:20** SAMUEL: *This name, which in Hebrew means "name of God," is here related to the Hebrew verb for "ask."*
[d] **1:23** *Some ancient translations* your; *Hebrew* his. [e] **1:24** *Some ancient translations* a three-year-old bull; *Hebrew* three bulls. [f] **1:28** *Some ancient translations* they; *Hebrew* he.
2:1–10 Lk 1:46–55

No haircut—ever! This was a sign in biblical times that a man was a Nazirite—someone specially dedicated to God.

3 Stop your loud boasting;
silence your proud words.
For the LORD is a God who knows,
and he judges all that people do.
4 The bows of strong soldiers are broken,
but the weak grow strong.
5 The people who once were well fed
now hire themselves out to get food,
but the hungry are hungry no more.
The childless wife has borne seven
children,
but the mother of many is left with
none.
6 The LORD kills and restores to life;
he sends people to the world of the
dead
and brings them back again.
7 He makes some people poor and others
rich;
he humbles some and makes others
great.
8 He lifts the poor from the dust
and raises the needy from their misery.
He makes them companions of princes
and puts them in places of honor.
The foundations of the earth belong to
the LORD;
on them he has built the world.

9 "He protects the lives of his faithful
people,
but the wicked disappear in darkness;
a man does not triumph by his own
strength.
10 The LORD's enemies will be destroyed;
he will thunder against them from
heaven.
The LORD will judge the whole world;
he will give power to his king,
he will make his chosen king
victorious."

11 Then Elkanah went back home to
Ramah, but the boy Samuel stayed in Shiloh
and served the LORD under the priest Eli.

The Sons of Eli

12 The sons of Eli were scoundrels. They
paid no attention to the LORD 13 or to the
regulations concerning what the priests
could demand from the people. Instead,
when someone was offering a sacrifice, the
priest's servant would come with a three-
pronged fork. While the meat was still cook-
ing, 14 he would stick the fork into the cook-
ing pot, and whatever the fork brought out
belonged to the priest. All the Israelites who
came to Shiloh to offer sacrifices were treat-
ed like this. 15 In addition, even before the fat
was taken off and burned, the priest's servant
would come and say to the one offering the
sacrifice, "Give me some meat for the priest
to roast; he won't accept boiled meat from
you, only raw meat."
16 If the person answered, "Let us do what
is right and burn the fat first; then take what
you want," the priest's servant would say,

Study it!

Two Women at Prayer

Read Hannah's prayer at the beginning of 1 Samuel, chapter 2. Hannah is filled with joy because God heard her prayer for a son. Now turn to the Gospel of Luke and read Luke 1:46–55. This is Mary's prayer when she visits her cousin Elizabeth. Notice all the similarities between the two prayers. Both women gave birth to sons who were destined for greatness.

Hannah and Elizabeth, although separated by one thousand years, also have a lot in common. Neither woman could have children, but finally both were given a son. Their sons, Samuel and John the Baptist, play key roles in preparing the way for great kings. Samuel anointed King David, and John baptized Jesus.

— 1 Samuel 2:1–10

2:6 Wis 16:13; Tob 13:2

"No! Give it to me now! If you don't, I will have to take it by force!"

[17]This sin of the sons of Eli was extremely serious in the LORD's sight, because they treated the offerings to the LORD with such disrespect.

Samuel at Shiloh

[18]In the meantime the boy Samuel continued to serve the LORD, wearing a sacred linen apron. [19]Each year his mother would make a little robe and take it to him when she accompanied her husband to offer the yearly sacrifice. [20]Then Eli would bless Elkanah and his wife, and say to Elkanah, "May the LORD give you other children by this woman to take the place of the one you dedicated to him."

Each year his mother would make a little robe. (2:19)

After that they would go back home.

[21]The LORD did bless Hannah, and she had three more sons and two daughters. The boy Samuel grew up in the service of the LORD.

Eli and His Sons

[22]Eli was now very old. He kept hearing about everything his sons were doing to the Israelites and that they were even sleeping with the women who worked at the entrance to the Tent of the LORD's presence. [23]So he said to them, "Why are you doing these things? Everybody tells me about the evil you are doing. [24]Stop it, my sons! This is an awful thing the people of the LORD are talking about! [25]If anyone sins against someone else, God can defend the one who is wrong; but who can defend someone who sins against the LORD?"

But they would not listen to their father, for the LORD had decided to kill them.

[26]The boy Samuel continued to grow and to gain favor both with the LORD and with people.

The Prophecy against Eli's Family

[27]A prophet came to Eli with this message from the LORD: "When your ancestor Aaron and his family were slaves of the king of Egypt, I revealed myself to Aaron. [28]From all the tribes of Israel I chose his family to be my priests, to serve at the altar, to burn the incense, and to wear the ephod[g] to consult me. And I gave them the right to keep a share of the sacrifices burned on the altar. [29]Why, then, do you look with greed[h] at the sacrifices and offerings which I require from my people? Why, Eli, do you honor your sons more than me by letting them fatten themselves on the best parts of all the sacrifices my people offer to me? [30]I, the LORD God of Israel, promised in the past that your family and your clan would serve me as priests for all time. But now I say that I won't have it any longer! Instead, I will honor those who honor me, and I will treat with contempt those who despise me. [31]Listen, the time is coming when I will kill all the young men in your family and your clan, so that no man in your family will live to be old. [32]You will be troubled and look with envy[i] on all the blessings I will give to the other people of Israel, but no one in your family will ever again live to old age. [33]Yet I will keep one of your descendants alive, and he will serve me as priest. But he[j] will become blind and lose all

[g] **2:28** EPHOD: *See Word List.* [h] **2:29** *One ancient translation* look with greed; *Hebrew unclear.* [i] **2:32** *Probable text* look with envy; *Hebrew unclear.* [j] **2:33** *One ancient translation* he; *Hebrew* you.

2:26 Sir 46:13; Lk 2:52 **2:28** **a** Ex 28:1–4; **b** Lev 7:35, 36

Pray it!

Speak, Lord

Read the wonderful story of God calling young Samuel (1 Samuel 3:1–14). At first Samuel thinks it is Eli calling him, and so he asks Eli what he wants. Then Eli catches on. He knows that God is calling Samuel, and suggests a great response to Samuel: "Speak, LORD, your servant is listening." This is a great way for us to hear God as well. Here are a few prayer ideas you can try using.

- **Read a Bible passage and then say, "Speak, Lord, your servant is listening."**
- **Tell God about a problem you are dealing with. Then say, "Speak, Lord, your servant is listening."**
- **Place yourself in a quiet space and say, "Speak, Lord, your servant is listening." To make it even more personal, add your own name after the phrase "your servant." Repeat the phrase a few times, and then sit quietly and listen.**

— 1 Samuel 3:1–10

hope, and all your other descendants will die
a violent death. 34 When your two sons
Hophni and Phinehas both die on the same
day, this will show you that everything I have
said will come true. 35 I will choose a priest
who will be faithful to me and do everything
I want him to. I will give him descendants,
who will always serve in the presence of my
chosen king. 36 Any of your descendants who
survive will have to go to that priest and ask
him for money and food, and beg to be
allowed to help the priests, in order to have
something to eat."

The LORD Appears to Samuel

3 In those days, when the boy Samuel was
serving the LORD under the direction of
Eli, there were very few messages from the
LORD, and visions from him were quite rare.
2 One night Eli, who was now almost blind,
was sleeping in his own room; 3 Samuel was
sleeping in the sanctuary, where the sacred
Covenant Box was. Before dawn, while the
lamp was still burning, 4 the LORD called
Samuel. He answered, "Yes, sir!" 5 and ran to
Eli and said, "You called me, and here I am."
But Eli answered, "I didn't call you; go
back to bed." So Samuel went back to bed.
6-7 The LORD called Samuel again. The
boy did not know that it was the LORD,
because the LORD had never spoken to him
before. So he got up, went to Eli, and said,
"You called me, and here I am."
But Eli answered, "My son, I didn't call
you; go back to bed."
8 The LORD called Samuel a third time; he
got up, went to Eli, and said, "You called me,
and here I am."
Then Eli realized that it was the LORD
who was calling the boy, 9 so he said to him,
"Go back to bed; and if he calls you again,
say, 'Speak, LORD, your servant is listening.' "
So Samuel went back to bed.
10 The LORD came and stood there, and
called as he had before, "Samuel! Samuel!"
Samuel answered, "Speak; your servant is
listening."
11 The LORD said to him, "Some day I am
going to do something to the people of Israel

2:34 1 Sam 4:11

Eli's ancestor is Aaron, the first high priest of the Israelites.
Who were Aaron's brother and sister (see Exodus, chapters 4 and 15)?

"Speak; your servant is listening." (3:10)

that is so terrible that everyone who hears
about it will be stunned. 12On that day I will
carry out all my threats against Eli's family,
from beginning to end. 13I have already told
him[k] that I am going to punish his family
forever because his sons have spoken evil
things against me. Eli knew they were doing
this, but he did not stop them. 14So I
solemnly declare to the family of Eli that no
sacrifice or offering will ever be able to
remove the consequences of this terrible sin."

15Samuel stayed in bed until morning;
then he got up and opened the doors of the
house of the LORD. He was afraid to tell Eli
about the vision. 16Eli called him, "Samuel,
my boy!"

"Yes, sir," answered Samuel.

17"What did the LORD tell you?" Eli
asked. "Don't keep anything from me. God
will punish you severely if you don't tell me
everything he said." 18So Samuel told him
everything; he did not keep anything back.
Eli said, "He is the LORD; he will do what-
ever seems best to him."

19As Samuel grew up, the LORD was with
him and made come true everything that
Samuel said. 20So all the people of Israel,
from one end of the country to the other,
knew that Samuel was indeed a prophet of
the LORD. 21The LORD continued to reveal
himself at Shiloh, where he had appeared to
Samuel and had spoken to him. And when
Samuel spoke, all Israel listened.

The Capture of the Covenant Box

4 At that time the Philistines gathered to
go to war against Israel, so[l] the Israelites
set out to fight them. The Israelites set up
their camp at Ebenezer and the Philistines at
Aphek. 2The Philistines attacked, and after
fierce fighting they defeated the Israelites and
killed about four thousand men on the bat-
tlefield. 3When the survivors came back to
camp, the leaders of Israel said, "Why did the
LORD let the Philistines defeat us today? Let's
go and bring the LORD's Covenant Box from
Shiloh, so that he[m] will go with us and save
us from our enemies." 4So they sent messen-
gers to Shiloh and got the Covenant Box of
the LORD Almighty, who is enthroned above
the winged creatures.[n] And Eli's two sons,
Hophni and Phinehas, came along with the
Covenant Box.

5When the Covenant Box arrived, the
Israelites gave such a loud shout of joy that
the earth shook. 6The Philistines heard the
shouting and said, "Listen to all that shouting
in the Hebrew camp! What does it mean?"
When they found out that the LORD's
Covenant Box had arrived in the Hebrew
camp, 7they were afraid, and said, "A god has
come into their camp! We're lost! Nothing
like this has ever happened to us before!
8Who can save us from those powerful gods?
They are the gods who slaughtered the
Egyptians in the desert! 9Be brave,
Philistines! Fight like men, or we will
become slaves to the Hebrews, just as they
were our slaves. So fight like men!"

10The Philistines fought hard and defeated
the Israelites, who went running to their
homes. There was a great slaughter: thirty
thousand Israelite soldiers were killed.
11God's Covenant Box was captured, and Eli's
sons, Hophni and Phinehas, were both killed.

[k] **3:13** *One ancient translation* I have already told him; *Hebrew* I will tell him. [l] **4:1** *One ancient translation* the Philistines . . . so; *Hebrew does not have these words.* [m] **4:3** he; *or* it. [n] **4:4** WINGED CREATURES: *See Word List.*
4:4 Ex 25:22

Thousands! Add up the number of Israelites the Philistines killed in I Samuel, chapter 4. Keep in mind that sometimes numbers are exaggerated in the Bible.

The Death of Eli

12A man from the tribe of Benjamin ran all the way from the battlefield to Shiloh and arrived there the same day. To show his grief, he had torn his clothes and put dirt on his head. 13Eli, who was very worried about the Covenant Box, was sitting in his seat beside the road, staring. The man spread the news throughout the town, and everyone cried out in fear. 14Eli heard the noise and asked, "What is all this noise about?" The man hurried to Eli to tell him the news. (15Eli was now ninety-eight years old and almost completely blind.) 16The man said, "I have escaped from the battle and have run all the way here today."

Eli asked him, "What happened, my son?"

17The messenger answered, "Israel ran away from the Philistines; it was a terrible defeat for us! Besides that, your sons Hophni and Phinehas were killed, and God's Covenant Box was captured!"

18When the man mentioned the Covenant Box, Eli fell backward from his seat beside the gate. He was so old and fat that the fall broke his neck, and he died. He had been a leader in Israel for forty years.

The Death of the Widow of Phinehas

19Eli's daughter-in-law, the wife of Phinehas, was pregnant, and it was almost time for her baby to be born. When she heard that God's Covenant Box had been captured and that her father-in-law and her husband were dead, she suddenly went into labor and gave birth. 20As she was dying, the women helping her said to her, "Be brave! You have a son!" But she paid no attention and did not answer. 21She named the boy Ichabod,[o] explaining, "God's glory has left Israel"—referring to the capture of the Covenant Box and the death of her father-in-law and her husband. 22"God's glory has left Israel," she said, "because God's Covenant Box has been captured."

The Covenant Box among the Philistines

5 After the Philistines captured the Covenant Box, they carried it from Ebenezer to their city of Ashdod, 2took it into the temple of their god Dagon, and set it up beside his statue. 3Early the next morning the people of Ashdod saw that the statue of Dagon had fallen face downward on the ground in front of the LORD's Covenant Box. So they lifted it up and put it back in its place. 4Early the following morning they saw that the statue had again fallen down in front of the Covenant Box. This time its head and both its arms were broken off and were lying in the doorway; only the body was left. (5That is why even today the priests of Dagon and all his worshipers in Ashdod step over that place and do not walk on it.)

6The LORD punished the people of Ashdod severely and terrified them. He punished them and the people in the surrounding territory by causing them to have tumors.[p] 7When they saw what was happening, they said, "The God of Israel is punishing us and our god Dagon. We can't let the Covenant Box stay here any longer." 8So they sent messengers and called together all five of the Philistine kings and asked them, "What shall we do with the Covenant Box of the God of Israel?"

"Take it over to Gath," they answered; so they took it to Gath, another Philistine city. 9But after it arrived there, the LORD punished that city too and caused a great panic. He punished them with tumors which developed in all the people of the city, young and old alike. 10So they sent the Covenant Box to Ekron, another Philistine city; but when it arrived there, the people cried out, "They have brought the Covenant Box of the God of Israel here, in order to kill us all!" 11So again they sent for all the Philistine kings and said, "Send the Covenant Box of Israel back to its own place, so that it won't kill us and our families." There was panic throughout the city because God was punishing them so severely. 12Even those who did not die developed tumors and the people cried out to their gods for help.

[o] **4:21** ICHABOD: *This name in Hebrew means "no glory."* [p] **5:6** TUMORS: *The association of tumors with an abundance of mice suggests that this was a case of bubonic plague (see 6:5).*

Live it!

Stealing Has Consequences

The Covenant Box—also know as the Ark of the Covenant—was the holiest object in all of Israel. That it had been stolen was so shocking that it caused old Eli to fall out of his chair and break his neck (1 Samuel 4:18). Note what happened to the Philistines after they had stolen the Covenant Box. Many people developed tumors, and some even died. Soon, they couldn't wait to get rid of it. So, what's the point of this story?

One point is that there are consequences for stealing. When we take something that is of value to someone else, we rarely get away with it. We may not get tumors like the Philistines, but we may get caught and have to face legal consequences or the loss of a friendship. Even if we don't get caught, we have taken what does not belong to us, and that is a violation of God's Law, a sin. If we don't seek forgiveness, our hearts begin to harden. We no longer care about the effects of our actions on others. We drift away from God.

Have you ever had to return something you stole and ask for forgiveness? That can serve as a powerful lesson and helps to make things right—with others and with God.

— 1 Samuel, chapter 5

The Return of the Covenant Box

6 After the LORD's Covenant Box had
been in Philistia for seven months, 2 the
people called the priests and the magicians
and asked, "What shall we do with the
Covenant Box of the LORD? If we send it
back where it belongs, what shall we send
with it?"

3 They answered, "If you return the
Covenant Box of the God of Israel, you
must, of course, send with it a gift to him to
pay for your sin. The Covenant Box must
not go back without a gift. In this way you
will be healed, and you will find out why he
has kept on punishing you."

4 "What gift shall we send him?" the people asked.

They answered, "Five gold models of
tumors and five gold mice, one of each for
each Philistine king. The same plague was
sent on all of you and on the five kings.
5 You must make these models of the tumors
and of the mice that are ravaging your country, and you must give honor to the God of
Israel. Perhaps he will stop punishing you,
your gods, and your land. 6 Why should you
be stubborn, as the king of Egypt and the
Egyptians were? Don't forget how God
made fools of them until they let the
Israelites leave Egypt. 7 So prepare a new
wagon and two cows that have never been
yoked; hitch them to the wagon and drive
their calves back to the barn. 8 Take the
LORD's Covenant Box, put it on the wagon,
and place in a box beside it the gold models
that you are sending to him as a gift to pay
for your sins. Start the wagon on its way and
let it go by itself. 9 Then watch it go; if it
goes toward the town of Beth Shemesh, this
means that it is the God of the Israelites who
has sent this terrible disaster on us. But if it
doesn't, then we will know that he did not
send the plague; it was only a matter of
chance."

10 They did what they were told: they
took two cows and hitched them to the
wagon, and shut the calves in the barn.
11 They put the Covenant Box in the wagon,
together with the box containing the gold
models of the mice and of the tumors. 12 The
cows started off on the road to Beth
Shemesh and headed straight toward it,
without turning off the road. They were
mooing as they went. The five Philistine
kings followed them as far as the border of
Beth Shemesh.

13 The people of Beth Shemesh were
reaping wheat in the valley, when suddenly

they looked up and saw the Covenant Box. They were overjoyed at the sight. [14]The wagon came to a field belonging to a man named Joshua, who lived in Beth Shemesh, and it stopped there near a large rock. The people chopped up the wooden wagon and killed the cows and burned them as a burnt sacrifice to the LORD. [15]The Levites lifted off the Covenant Box of the LORD and the box with the gold models in it, and placed them on the large rock. Then the people of Beth Shemesh offered burnt sacrifices and other sacrifices to the LORD. [16]The five Philistine kings watched them do this and then went back to Ekron that same day.

The wagon came to a field belonging to a man named Joshua. (6:14)

[17]The Philistines sent the five gold tumors to the LORD as a gift to pay for their sins, one each for the cities of Ashdod, Gaza, Ashkelon, Gath, and Ekron. [18]They also sent gold mice, one for each of the cities ruled by the five Philistine kings, both the fortified towns and the villages without walls. The large rock in the field of Joshua of Beth Shemesh, on which they placed the LORD's Covenant Box, is still there as a witness to what happened.

[19]The LORD killed seventy of the men of Beth Shemesh because they looked inside the Covenant Box. And the people mourned because the LORD had caused such a great slaughter among them.

The Covenant Box at Kiriath Jearim

[20]So the men of Beth Shemesh said, "Who can stand before the LORD, this holy God? Where can we send him to get him away from us?" [21]They sent messengers to the people of Kiriath Jearim to say, "The Philistines have returned the LORD's Covenant Box. Come down and get it."

7 So the people of Kiriath Jearim got the LORD's Covenant Box and took it to the house of a man named Abinadab, who lived on a hill. They consecrated his son Eleazar to be in charge of it.

Samuel Rules Israel

[2]The Covenant Box of the LORD stayed in Kiriath Jearim a long time, some twenty years. During this time all the Israelites cried to the LORD for help.

[3]Samuel said to the people of Israel, "If you are going to turn to the LORD with all your hearts, you must get rid of all the foreign gods and the images of the goddess Astarte. Dedicate yourselves completely to the LORD and worship only him, and he will rescue you from the power of the Philistines." [4]So the Israelites got rid of their idols of Baal and Astarte, and worshiped only the LORD.

[5]Then Samuel called for all the Israelites to meet at Mizpah, telling them, "I will pray to the LORD for you there." [6]So they all gathered at Mizpah. They drew some water and poured it out as an offering to the LORD and fasted that whole day. They said, "We have sinned against the LORD." (It was at Mizpah where Samuel settled disputes among the Israelites.)

[7]When the Philistines heard that the Israelites had gathered at Mizpah, the five Philistine kings started out with their men to attack them. The Israelites heard about it and

7:1 2 Sam 6:2–4; 1 Chr 13:5–7

Can you find the five main cities of the Philistines listed in I Samuel, chapter 6? Which city is still in the news today?

were afraid, 8and said to Samuel, "Keep pray-
ing to the LORD our God to save us from
the Philistines." 9Samuel killed a young lamb
and burned it whole as a sacrifice to the
LORD. Then he prayed to the LORD to help
Israel, and the LORD answered his prayer.
10While Samuel was offering the sacrifice,
the Philistines moved forward to attack; but
just then the LORD thundered from heaven
against them. They became completely con-
fused and fled in panic. 11The Israelites
marched out from Mizpah and pursued the
Philistines almost as far as Bethcar, killing
them along the way.
12Then Samuel took a stone, set it up
between Mizpah and Shen, and said, "The
LORD has helped us all the way"—and he
named it "Stone of Help." 13So the
Philistines were defeated, and the LORD pre-
vented them from invading Israel's territory
as long as Samuel lived. 14All the cities
which the Philistines had captured between
Ekron and Gath were returned to Israel, and
so Israel got back all its territory. And there
was peace also between the Israelites and the
Canaanites.
15Samuel ruled Israel as long as he lived.
16Every year he would go around to Bethel,
Gilgal, and Mizpah, and in these places he
would settle disputes. 17Then he would go
back to his home in Ramah, where also he
would serve as judge. In Ramah he built an
altar to the LORD.

The People Ask for a King

8 When Samuel grew old, he made his
sons judges in Israel. 2The older son was
named Joel and the younger one Abijah;
they were judges in Beersheba. 3But they did
not follow their father's example; they were
interested only in making money, so they
accepted bribes and did not decide cases
honestly.
4Then all the leaders of Israel met together,
went to Samuel in Ramah, 5and said to him,
"Look, you are getting old and your sons
don't follow your example. So then, appoint a
king to rule over us, so that we will have a
king, as other countries have." 6Samuel was
displeased with their request for a king; so he
prayed to the LORD, 7and the LORD said,
"Listen to everything the people say to you.

Live it!

Who's the King?

So, who is in charge around here?

That is a question that could have been asked by almost any of Israel's neighbors because the Israelites had no clear ruler. The question is one of authority. A lot of times, we don't really like to be told what to do. You probably feel this way a lot at home or in school. It almost seems as if adults have it in for you. Why can't they just leave you alone?

That's a good question. Here's an answer. We need to realize that in order for the world to work right, we need leaders. Good leaders challenge us to work together and inspire us to be the best people we can be. Ultimately, our leader is God. God is The Authority. The best leaders are those who carry out the will of God in all that they do.

Like all their neighbors, the Israelites wanted to have a king, a definite person in charge. Samuel is worried that they will forget who is really in charge. We may forget, too. If God is not number 1 in our lives, we need to look at what is.

— 1 Samuel, chapter 8

7:9 Sir 46:16–18 **8:5** Deut 17:14

Samuel tells the people that having a king will change their lives. Name at least five changes that Samuel lists.

You are not the one they have rejected; I am the one they have rejected as their king. 8Ever since I brought them out of Egypt, they have turned away from me and worshiped other gods; and now they are doing to you what they have always done to me. 9So then, listen to them, but give them strict warnings and explain how their kings will treat them."

10Samuel told the people who were asking him for a king everything that the LORD had said to him. 11"This is how your king will treat you," Samuel explained. "He will make soldiers of your sons; some of them will serve in his war chariots, others in his cavalry, and others will run before his chariots. 12He will make some of them officers in charge of a thousand men, and others in charge of fifty men. Your sons will have to plow his fields, harvest his crops, and make his weapons and the equipment for his chariots. 13Your daughters will have to make perfumes for him and work as his cooks and his bakers. 14He will take your best fields, vineyards, and olive groves, and give them to his officials. 15He will take a tenth of your grain and of your grapes for his court officers and other officials. 16He will take your servants and your best cattle[q] and donkeys, and make them work for him. 17He will take a tenth of your flocks. And you yourselves will become his slaves. 18When that time comes, you will complain bitterly because of your king, whom you yourselves chose, but the LORD will not listen to your complaints."

19The people paid no attention to Samuel, but said, "No! We want a king, 20so that we will be like other nations, with our own king to rule us and to lead us out to war and to fight our battles." 21Samuel listened to everything they said and then went and told it to the LORD. 22The LORD answered, "Do what they want and give them a king." Then Samuel told all the men of Israel to go back home.

Saul Meets Samuel

9 There was a wealthy and influential man named Kish, from the tribe of Benjamin; he was the son of Abiel and grandson of Zeror, and belonged to the family of Becorath, a part of the clan of Aphiah. 2He had a son named Saul, a handsome man in the prime of life. Saul was a foot taller than anyone else in Israel and more handsome as well.

3Some donkeys belonging to Kish had wandered off, so he said to Saul, "Take one of the servants with you and go and look for the donkeys." 4They went through the hill country of Ephraim and the region of Shalishah, but did not find them; so they went on through the region of Shaalim, but the donkeys were not there. Then they went through the territory of Benjamin, but still did not find them. 5When they came into the region of Zuph, Saul said to his servant, "Let's go back home, or my father might stop thinking about the donkeys and start worrying about us."

6The servant answered, "Wait! In this town there is a holy man who is highly respected because everything he says comes true. Let's go to him, and maybe he can tell us where we can find the donkeys."

7"If we go to him, what can we give him?" Saul asked. "There is no food left in our packs, and we don't have a thing to give him, do we?"

8The servant answered, "I have a small silver coin. I can give him that, and then he will tell us where we can find them."

9-11 Saul replied, "A good idea! Let's go." So they went to the town where the holy man lived. As they were going up the hill to the town, they met some young women who were coming out to draw water. They asked these women, "Is the seer in town?"

(At that time a prophet was called a seer, and so whenever someone wanted to ask God a question, he would say, "Let's go to the seer.")

12-13"Yes, he is," the young women answered. "In fact, he is just ahead of you. If you hurry, you will catch up with him. As soon as you go into town, you will find him. He arrived in town today because the people are going to offer a sacrifice on the altar on the hill. The people who are invited won't start eating until he gets there, because

q **8:16** *One ancient translation* cattle; *Hebrew* young men.

Live it!

Tall Saul

Saul, the first king, is described as the most handsome man in Israel. He was also a foot taller than anyone else in Israel. No doubt that in our society he would be on the cover of almost every magazine.

Next time you are at a magazine rack, look at all the covers that feature people. Do you see any without someone beautiful or handsome on them? It is very clear that looks and appearance matter a lot in our society. So, where does that leave us? Most of us can never hope to measure up to the standards set by Hollywood. Almost everyone wishes they were better looking or taller or thinner or . . . you fill in the blank!

To the biblical writers, it was important that the first king of Israel stand apart, so Saul is described as being tall and very handsome. However, as we will find out in the stories about Saul, there are other things that are much more important than looks. We cannot all be models or movie stars, but we can be people whom others admire in the things that really matter. And we can all be models of faith, if we work at it.

What one thing can you do today to deepen your relationship with God and strengthen your faith?

— 1 Samuel 9:2

he has to bless the sacrifice first. If you go
now, you will find him before he goes up
the hill to eat." 14So Saul and his servant
went on to the town, and as they were going
in, they saw Samuel coming out toward
them on his way to the place of worship.
15Now on the previous day the LORD had
told Samuel, 16"Tomorrow about this time I
will send you a man from the tribe of Benjamin; anoint him as ruler of my people
Israel, and he will rescue them from the
Philistines. I have seen the suffering of my
people and have heard their cries for help."
17When Samuel caught sight of Saul, the
LORD said to him, "This is the man I told
you about. He will rule my people." 18Then
Saul went over to Samuel, who was near the
gate, and asked, "Tell me, where does the
seer live?"
19Samuel answered, "I am the seer. Go on
ahead of me to the place of worship. Both of
you are to eat with me today. Tomorrow
morning I will answer all your questions and
send you on your way. 20As for the donkeys
that were lost three days ago, don't worry
about them; they have already been found.
But who is it that the people of Israel want
so much?[r] It is you—you and your father's
family."
21Saul answered, "I belong to the tribe of
Benjamin, the smallest tribe in Israel, and my

"I am the seer." (9:19)

[r] **9:20** who is it . . . much?; *or* who is to have the most desirable thing in Israel?

family is the least important one in the tribe.
Why, then, do you talk like this to me?"
22 Then Samuel led Saul and his servant
into the large room and gave them a place at
the head of the table where the guests, about
thirty in all, were seated. 23 Samuel said to the
cook, "Bring the piece of meat I gave you,
which I told you to set aside." 24 So the cook
brought the choice piece of the leg and
placed it before Saul. Samuel[s] said, "Look,
here is the piece that was kept for you. Eat
it. I saved it for you to eat at this time with
the people I invited."[t]

So Saul ate with Samuel that day. 25 When
they went down from the place of worship
to the town, they fixed up a bed for Saul[u] on
the roof,[v] 26 and he slept there.[w]

Samuel Anoints Saul as Ruler

At dawn Samuel called to Saul on the
roof, "Get up, and I will send you on your
way." Saul got up, and he and Samuel went
out to the street together. 27 When they
arrived at the edge of town, Samuel said to
Saul, "Tell the servant to go on ahead of us."
The servant left, and Samuel continued,
"Stay here a minute, and I will tell you what
God has said."

10 Then Samuel took a jar of olive oil
and poured it on Saul's head, kissed
him, and said, "The LORD anoints you as
ruler of his people Israel. You will rule his
people and protect them from all their ene-
mies. And this is the proof to you that the
LORD has chosen you[x] to be the ruler of his
people: 2 When you leave me today, you will
meet two men near Rachel's tomb at Zelzah
in the territory of Benjamin. They will tell
you that the donkeys you were looking for
have been found, so that your father isn't
worried any more about them but about
you, and he keeps asking, 'What shall I do
about my son?' 3 You will go on from there
until you come to the sacred tree at Tabor,
where you will meet three men on their way
to offer a sacrifice to God at Bethel. One of
them will be leading three young goats,
another one will be carrying three loaves of
bread, and the third one will have a leather
bag full of wine. 4 They will greet you and
offer you two of the loaves, which you are to
accept. 5 Then you will go to the Hill of God
in Gibeah, where there is a Philistine camp.
At the entrance to the town you will meet a
group of prophets coming down from the
altar on the hill, playing harps, drums, flutes,
and lyres. They will be dancing and shouting.
6 Suddenly the spirit of the LORD will take
control of you, and you will join in their reli-
gious dancing and shouting and will become
a different person. 7 When these things hap-
pen, do whatever God leads you to do. 8 You
will go ahead of me to Gilgal, where I will
meet you and offer burnt sacrifices and

"The LORD anoints you as ruler of his people." (10:1)

[s] **9:24** *Some ancient translations* Samuel; *Hebrew* He (that is, the cook). [t] **9:24** *Probable text* I saved it . . . invited; *Hebrew unclear.* [u] **9:25** *One ancient translation* they fixed up a bed for Saul; *Hebrew* he spoke with Saul. [v] **9:25** ON THE ROOF: *At that time houses had flat roofs, and it was common for people to sleep on them.* [w] **9:26** *Some ancient translations* and he slept there; *Hebrew* and they got up early. [x] **10:1** *Some ancient translations* as ruler of his people . . . the LORD has chosen you; *Hebrew does not have these words.*

Can you find three things that looked like accidents that led to Saul's meeting Samuel? What does this say about how God works?

Study it!

Being Anointed

It may seem rather odd that the kings of Israel are anointed rather than crowned, especially when we realize that to be anointed means having olive oil poured over your head. Yet this action is indeed a very important sign. When Samuel pours oil over Saul's head and blesses him, Samuel tells him that he has been chosen and anointed by God. Every king from then on will be anointed in the same way. Anointing with oil is an ancient symbol of holiness. The word *Messiah* in Hebrew and *Christ* in Greek translate as "the Anointed One."

In the Catholic Church, we continue that tradition in the sacraments of Baptism, Confirmation, and Anointing of the Sick. In each of these sacraments, oil is used in the blessing and is a sign that the power of the Holy Spirit is being poured out on the person.

— 1 Samuel 10:1

fellowship sacrifices. Wait there seven days
until I come and tell you what to do."
9 When Saul turned to leave Samuel, God
gave Saul a new nature. And everything
Samuel had told him happened that day.
10 When Saul and his servant arrived at
Gibeah, a group of prophets met him. Sud-
denly the spirit of God took control of him,
and he joined in their ecstatic dancing and
shouting. 11 People who had known him
before saw him doing this and asked one
another, "What has happened to the son of
Kish? Has Saul become a prophet?" 12 A man
who lived there asked, "How about these
other prophets—who do you think their
fathers are?" This is how the saying originat-
ed, "Has even Saul become a prophet?"
13 When Saul finished his ecstatic dancing
and shouting, he went to the altar on the
hill.
14 Saul's uncle saw him and the servant,
and he asked them, "Where have you been?"

"Looking for the donkeys," Saul answered. "When we couldn't find them, we went to see Samuel."

15 "And what did he tell you?" Saul's uncle
asked.

16 "He told us that the animals had been
found," Saul answered—but he did not tell
his uncle what Samuel had said about his
becoming king.

Saul Is Acclaimed as King

17 Samuel called the people together for a
religious gathering at Mizpah 18 and said to
them, "The LORD, the God of Israel, says, 'I
brought you out of Egypt and rescued you
from the Egyptians and all the other peoples
who were oppressing you. 19 I am your God,
the one who rescues you from all your trou-
bles and difficulties, but today you have
rejected me and have asked me to give you a
king. Very well, then, gather yourselves
before the LORD by tribes and by clans.' "
20 Then Samuel had each tribe come for-
ward, and the LORD picked the tribe of
Benjamin. 21 Then Samuel had the families
of the tribe of Benjamin come forward, and
the family of Matri was picked out. Then the
men of the family of Matri came forward,[y]
and Saul son of Kish was picked out. They
looked for him, but when they could not
find him, 22 they asked the LORD, "Is there
still someone else?"

[y] **10:21** *One ancient translation* Then the men of the family of Matri came forward; *Hebrew does not have these words.*

10:12 1 Sam 19:23, 24

Saul is acclaimed as king at Mizpah. Locate Mizpah on Map 3 in the back of this Bible. What other important city is it close to?

The LORD answered, "Saul is over there,
hiding behind the supplies."
23 So they ran and brought Saul out to the
people, and they could see that he was a foot
taller than anyone else. 24 Samuel said to the
people, "Here is the man the LORD has cho-
sen! There is no one else among us like
him."
All the people shouted, "Long live the
king!"
25 Samuel explained to the people the
rights and duties of a king, and then wrote
them in a book, which he deposited in a
holy place. Then he sent everyone home.
26 Saul also went back home to Gibeah.
Some powerful men,[z] whose hearts God
had touched, went with him. 27 But some
worthless people said, "How can this fellow
do us any good?" They despised Saul and did
not bring him any gifts.

Saul Defeats the Ammonites

11 About a month later King Nahash
of Ammon led his army against the
town of Jabesh in the territory of Gilead and
besieged it. The men of Jabesh said to
Nahash, "Make a treaty with us, and we will
accept you as our ruler."
2 Nahash answered, "I will make a treaty
with you on one condition: I will put out
everyone's right eye and so bring disgrace on
all Israel."
3 The leaders of Jabesh said, "Give us seven
days to send messengers throughout the land
of Israel. If no one will help us, then we will
surrender to you."
4 The messengers arrived at Gibeah, where
Saul lived, and when they told the news, the
people started crying in despair. 5 Saul was
just then coming in from the field with his
oxen, and he asked, "What's wrong? Why is
everyone crying?" They told him what the
messengers from Jabesh had reported.
6 When Saul heard this, the spirit of God
took control of him, and he became furious.
7 He took two oxen, cut them in pieces, and
had messengers carry the pieces throughout
the land of Israel with this warning: "Who-
ever does not follow Saul and Samuel into
battle will have this done to his oxen!"
The people of Israel were afraid of what
the LORD might do, and all of them, without
exception, came out together. 8 Saul gathered
them at Bezek: there were 300,000 from
Israel and 30,000 from Judah. 9 They said to
the messengers from Jabesh, "Tell your peo-
ple that before noon tomorrow they will be
rescued." When the people of Jabesh
received the message, they were overjoyed
10 and said to Nahash, "Tomorrow we will
surrender to you, and you can do with us
whatever you wish."
11 That night Saul divided his men into
three groups, and at dawn the next day they
rushed into the enemy camp and attacked
the Ammonites. By noon they had slaugh-
tered them. The survivors scattered, each
man running off by himself.
12 Then the people of Israel said to
Samuel, "Where are the people who said
that Saul should not be our king? Hand
them over to us, and we will kill them!"
13 But Saul said, "No one will be put to
death today, for this is the day the LORD res-
cued Israel." 14 And Samuel said to them,
"Let us all go to Gilgal and once more pro-
claim Saul as our king." 15 So they all went to
Gilgal, and there at the holy place they pro-
claimed Saul king. They offered fellowship
sacrifices, and Saul and all the people of
Israel celebrated the event.

Samuel Addresses the People

12 Then Samuel said to the people of
Israel, "I have done what you asked
me to do. I have given you a king to rule
you, 2 and now you have him to lead you. As
for me, I am old and gray, and my sons are
with you. I have been your leader from my
youth until now. 3 Here I am. If I have done
anything wrong, accuse me now in the pres-
ence of the LORD and the king he has cho-
sen. Have I taken anybody's cow or any-
body's donkey? Have I cheated or oppressed
anyone? Have I accepted a bribe from

[z] **10:26** *One ancient translation* Some powerful men; *Hebrew* The army.
12:3 Sir 46:19

anyone? If I have done any of these things, I
will pay back what I have taken."
4 The people answered, "No, you have not
cheated us or oppressed us; you have not
taken anything from anyone."
5 Samuel replied, "The LORD and the king
he has chosen are witnesses today that you
have found me to be completely innocent."
"Yes, the LORD is our witness," they
answered.
6 Samuel continued, "The LORD is the one
who chose Moses and Aaron and who
brought your ancestors out of Egypt. 7 Now
stand where you are, and I will accuse you
before the LORD by reminding you[a] of all
the mighty actions the LORD did to save you
and your ancestors. 8 When Jacob and his
family went to Egypt and the Egyptians
oppressed them,[b] your ancestors cried to the
LORD for help, and he sent Moses and
Aaron, who brought them out of Egypt and
settled them in this land. 9 But the people
forgot the LORD their God, and so he let the
Philistines and the king of Moab and Sisera,
commander of the army of the city of
Hazor, fight against your ancestors and con-
quer them. 10 Then they cried to the LORD
for help and said, 'We have sinned, because
we turned away from you, LORD, and wor-
shiped the idols of Baal and Astarte. Rescue
us from our enemies, and we will worship
you!' 11 And the LORD sent Gideon, Barak,[c]
Jephthah, and finally me. Each of us rescued
you from your enemies, and you lived in
safety. 12 But when you saw that King
Nahash of Ammon was about to attack you,
you rejected the LORD as your king and said
to me, 'We want a king to rule us.'
13 "Now here is the king you chose; you
asked for him, and now the LORD has given
him to you. 14 All will go well with you if
you honor the LORD your God, serve him,
listen to him, and obey his commands, and if
you and your king follow him. 15 But if you
do not listen to the LORD but disobey his
commands, he will be against you and your
king.[d] 16 So then, stand where you are, and

Live it!

A Simple Choice

Okay, the Israelites got what they wanted: a king. So now, Samuel lays out for them in simple terms what they need to do: honor, serve, listen, and obey God, and all will go well. If you don't listen to God and disobey, things will not go well.

Isn't this also our choice in life? It seems that when our faith is strong and we try our best to follow God's will, things have a way of working out. Even terrible things—like losing someone we love or dealing with addictions—will gradually get better when we keep trying to put God first. But when we follow another path and shut God out, it doesn't take long for our lives to get pretty messed up.

Think of the bad choices so many young people make: drugs, alcohol, gangs, violence. None of these will bring us closer to God and true happiness. Oh, it may seem so at the time, but it doesn't take long and soon we find ourselves very far from the person God wants us to be. We have not honored, served, listened, or obeyed God. However, it is never too late to turn to God and start over. The Israelites learned this lesson time and time again through their history. What about us?

—1 Samuel 12:13–15

[a] **12:7** *One ancient translation* by reminding you; *Hebrew does not have these words.* [b] **12:8** *One ancient translation* and the Egyptians oppressed them; *Hebrew does not have these words.* [c] **12:11** *Some ancient translations* Barak; *Hebrew* Bedan. [d] **12:15** *One ancient translation* your king; *Hebrew* your ancestors.

12:6 Ex 6:26 **12:8** Ex 2:23 **12:9** **a** Judg 4:2; **b** Judg 13:1; **c** Judg 3:12 **12:10** Judg 10:10–15
12:11 **a** Judg 7:1; **b** Judg 4:6; **c** Judg 11:29; **d** 1 Sam 3:20 **12:12** 1 Sam 8:19

you will see the great thing which the LORD
is going to do. 17 It's the dry season, isn't it?
But I will pray, and the LORD will send thun-
der and rain. When this happens, you will
realize that you committed a great sin against
the LORD when you asked him for a king."
18 So Samuel prayed, and on that same day
the LORD sent thunder and rain. Then all the
people became afraid of the LORD and of
Samuel, 19 and they said to Samuel, "Please,
sir, pray to the LORD your God for us, so
that we won't die. We now realize that,
besides all our other sins, we have sinned by
asking for a king."
20 "Don't be afraid," Samuel answered.
"Even though you have done such an evil
thing, do not turn away from the LORD, but
serve him with all your heart. 21 Don't go
after[e] false gods; they cannot help you or
save you, for they are not real. 22 The LORD
has made a solemn promise, and he will not
abandon you, for he has decided to make
you his own people. 23 As for me, the LORD
forbid that I should sin against him by no
longer praying for you. Instead, I will teach
you what is good and right for you to do.
24 Obey the LORD and serve him faithfully
with all your heart. Remember the great
things he has done for you. 25 But if you
continue to sin, you and your king will be
destroyed."

War against the Philistines

13 [f] 2 Saul picked three thousand men,
keeping two thousand of them with
him in Michmash and in the hill country of
Bethel and sending one thousand with his
son Jonathan to Gibeah, in the territory of
the tribe of Benjamin. The rest of the men
Saul sent home.
3 Jonathan killed the Philistine com-
mander[g] in Geba, and all the Philistines
heard about it. Then Saul sent messengers to
call the Hebrews to war by blowing a trum-
pet throughout the whole country. 4 All the
Israelites were told that Saul had killed the
Philistine commander and that the
Philistines hated them. So the people
answered the call to join Saul at Gilgal.
5 The Philistines assembled to fight the
Israelites; they had thirty thousand war char-
iots, six thousand cavalry troops, and as many
soldiers as there are grains of sand on the
seashore. They went to Michmash, east of
Bethaven, and camped there. 6 Then they
launched a strong attack against the
Israelites, putting them in a desperate situa-
tion. Some of the Israelites hid in caves and
holes or among the rocks or in pits and
wells; 7 others crossed the Jordan River into
the territories of Gad and Gilead.
Saul was still at Gilgal, and the people
with him were trembling with fear. 8 He
waited seven days for Samuel, as Samuel had
instructed him to do, but Samuel still had
not come to Gilgal. The people began to
desert Saul, 9 so he said to them, "Bring me
the burnt sacrifices and the fellowship sacri-
fices." He offered a burnt sacrifice, 10 and just
as he was finishing, Samuel arrived. Saul
went out to meet him and welcome him,
11 but Samuel said, "What have you done?"
Saul answered, "The people were deserting
me, and you had not come when you said
you would; besides that, the Philistines are
gathering at Michmash. 12 So I thought, 'The
Philistines are going to attack me here in Gil-
gal, and I have not tried to win the LORD's
favor.' So I felt I had to offer a sacrifice."
13 "That was a foolish thing to do," Samuel
answered. "You have not obeyed the com-
mand the LORD your God gave you. If you
had obeyed, he would have let you and your
descendants rule over Israel forever. 14 But
now your rule will not continue. Because

[e] **12:21** *Some ancient translations* after; *Hebrew* because after. [f] **13:1** *One ancient translation does not have verse 1; Hebrew has as verse 1* Saul was . . . years old when he became king, and he was king of Israel for two years. *The Hebrew text is defective at two points in this verse.* [g] **13:3** killed the Philistine commander; *or* defeated the Philistines camping.

13:8 1 Sam 10:8

"Obey the LORD and serve him faithfully with all your heart. Remember the great things he has done for you" *(1 Samuel 12:24)*.

you have disobeyed him, the LORD will find the kind of man he wants and make him ruler of his people."

[15]Samuel left Gilgal and went on his way. The rest of the people followed Saul as he went to join his soldiers. They went from Gilgal[h] to Gibeah in the territory of Benjamin. Saul inspected his troops, about six hundred men. [16]Saul, his son Jonathan, and their men camped in Geba in the territory of Benjamin; the Philistine camp was at Michmash. [17]The Philistine soldiers went out on raids from their camp in three groups: one group went toward Ophrah in the territory of Shual, [18]another went toward Beth Horon, and the other one went to the border overlooking Zeboim Valley and the wilderness.

[19]There were no blacksmiths in Israel because the Philistines were determined to keep the Hebrews from making swords and spears. ([20]The Israelites had to go to the Philistines to get their plows, hoes, axes, and sickles[i] sharpened; [21]the charge was one small coin for sharpening axes and for fixing goads,[j] and two coins for sharpening plows or hoes.) [22]And so on the day of battle none of the Israelite soldiers except Saul and his son Jonathan had swords or spears.

[23]The Philistines sent a group of soldiers to defend Michmash Pass.

Jonathan's Daring Deed

14 One day Jonathan said to the young man who carried his weapons, "Let's go across to the Philistine camp." But Jonathan did not tell his father Saul, [2]who was camping under a pomegranate tree in Migron, not far from Gibeah; he had about six hundred men with him. [3](The priest carrying the ephod was Ahijah, the son of Ichabod's brother Ahitub, who was the son of Phinehas and grandson of Eli, the priest of the LORD in Shiloh.) The men did not know that Jonathan had left.

[4]In Michmash Pass, which Jonathan had to go through to get over to the Philistine camp, there were two large jagged rocks, one on each side of the pass: one was called Bozez and the other Seneh. [5]One was on the north side of the pass, facing Michmash, and the other was on the south side, facing Geba.

[6]Jonathan said to the young man, "Let's cross over to the camp of those heathen Philistines. Maybe the LORD will help us; if he does, nothing can keep him from giving us the victory, no matter how few of us there are."

[7]The young man answered, "Whatever you want to do,[k] I'm with you."

[8]"All right," Jonathan said. "We will go across and let the Philistines see us. [9]If they tell us to wait for them to come to us, then we will stay where we are. [10]But if they tell us to go to them, then we will, because that will be the sign that the LORD has given us victory over them."

[11]So they let the Philistines see them, and the Philistines said, "Look! Some Hebrews are coming out of the holes they have been hiding in!" [12]Then they called out to Jonathan and the young man, "Come on up here! We have something to tell[l] you!"

Jonathan said to the young man, "Follow me. The LORD has given Israel victory over them." [13]Jonathan climbed up out of the pass on his hands and knees, and the young man followed him. Jonathan attacked the Philistines and knocked them down, and the young man killed them. [14]In that first slaughter Jonathan and the young man killed about twenty men in an area of about half an acre.[m] [15]All the Philistines in the countryside were terrified; the raiders and the sol-

[h] **13:15** *Some ancient translations* on his way . . . went from Gilgal; *Hebrew does not have these words.* [i] **13:20** *One ancient translation* sickles; *Hebrew* plows. [j] **13:21** *Probable text* the charge . . . fixing goads; *Hebrew unclear.*
[k] **14:7** *One ancient translation* you want to do; *Hebrew* you want to do. Turn. [l] **14:12** tell; *or* show.
[m] **14:14** *Probable text* in an area of about half an acre; *Hebrew unclear.*

13:14 Acts 13:22

Saul's son Jonathan *(I Samuel 13:2)* **will play a very important role in David's life. Stay tuned.**

diers in the camp trembled with fear; the earth shook, and there was great panic.

The Defeat of the Philistines

[16]Saul's men on watch at Gibeah in the territory of Benjamin saw the Philistines running in confusion. [17]So Saul said to his men, "Count the soldiers and find out who is missing." They did so and found that Jonathan and the young man who carried his weapons were missing. [18]"Bring the ephod[n] here," Saul said to Ahijah the priest. (On that day Ahijah was carrying it in front of the people of Israel.)[o] [19]As Saul was speaking to the priest, the confusion in the Philistine camp kept getting worse, so Saul said to him, "There's no time to consult the LORD!" [20]Then he and his men marched into battle against the Philistines, who were fighting each other in complete confusion. [21]Some Hebrews, who had been on the Philistine side and had gone with them to the camp, changed sides again[p] and joined Saul and Jonathan. [22]Others, who had been hiding in the hills of Ephraim, heard that the Philistines were running away, so they also joined in and attacked the Philistines, [23]fighting all the way beyond Bethaven. The LORD saved Israel that day.

Events after the Battle

[24]The Israelites were weak with hunger that day, because Saul, with a solemn oath, had given the order: "A curse be on anyone who eats any food today before I take revenge on my enemies." So nobody had eaten anything all day. [25]They all[q] came into a wooded area and found honey everywhere. [26]The woods were full of honey, but no one ate any of it because they were all afraid of Saul's curse. [27]But Jonathan had not heard his father threaten the people with a curse; so he reached out with the stick he was carrying, dipped it in a honeycomb, and ate some honey. At once he felt much better. [28]But one of the men told him, "We are all weak from hunger, but your father threatened us and said, 'A curse be on anyone who eats any food today.' "

[29]Jonathan answered, "What a terrible thing my father has done to our people! See how much better I feel because I ate some honey! [30]How much better it would have been today if our people had eaten the food they took when they defeated the enemy. Just think how many more Philistines they would have killed!"

[31]That day the Israelites defeated the Philistines, fighting all the way from Michmash to Aijalon. By this time the Israelites were very weak from hunger, [32]and so they rushed over to what they had captured from the enemy, took sheep and cattle, slaughtered them on the spot, and ate the meat with the blood still in it. [33]Saul was told, "Look, the people are sinning against the LORD by eating meat with the blood in it."

"You are traitors!" Saul cried out. "Roll a big stone over here[r] to me." [34]Then he gave another order: "Go among the people and tell them all to bring their cattle and sheep here. They are to slaughter them and eat them here; they must not sin against the LORD by eating meat with blood in it." So that night they all brought their cattle and slaughtered them there. [35]Saul built an altar to the LORD, the first one that he built.

[36]Saul said to his men, "Let's go down and attack the Philistines in the night, plunder them until dawn, and kill them all."

"Do whatever you think best," they answered.

But the priest said, "Let's consult God first."

[37]So Saul asked God, "Shall I attack the Philistines? Will you give us victory?" But God did not answer that day. [38]Then Saul said to the leaders of the people, "Come here and find out what sin was committed today. [39]I promise by the living LORD, who gives Israel victory, that the guilty one will be put to death, even if he is my son

[n] **14:18** *One ancient translation* ephod *(see 2:28); Hebrew* Covenant Box. [o] **14:18** *One ancient translation* On that day . . . Israel; *Hebrew* Because on that day God's Covenant Box and the people of Israel. [p] **14:21** *Some ancient translations* changed sides again; *Hebrew* around also. [q] **14:25** *Probable text* They all; *Hebrew* All the land. [r] **14:33** *One ancient translation* here; *Hebrew* today.

14:33 Gen 9:4; Lev 7:26, 27; 17:10–14; 19:26; Deut 12:16, 23; 15:23

Pray it!

"Do Whatever You Think Best"

"Do whatever you think best" is repeated twice by Saul's troops (1 Samuel 14:36,40). It shows that they have confidence in Saul's decisions and will do what he tells them.

This sentence also serves as a deep statement of faith in another person. To know that others are counting on you to do whatever you think best means that they have a lot of confidence in you. This responsibility can be almost scary when you are babysitting or watching over younger brothers or sisters. If there's any danger—a bad storm, someone gets sick, or there is an accident—people are counting on you to do whatever you think is best. If you are in a difficult situation and are unsure what to do, say a prayer to God for guidance. You'd be amazed at how God can calm your fears and show you a way. Even if it doesn't work out perfectly, you will remember that God is with you.

— 1 Samuel 14:36,40

Jonathan." But no one said anything. 40 Then
Saul said to them, "All of you stand over
there, and Jonathan and I will stand over
here."

"Do whatever you think best," they
answered.

41 Saul said to the LORD, the God of Israel,
"LORD, why have you not answered me
today? LORD, God of Israel, answer me by
the sacred stones. If the guilt is Jonathan's or
mine, answer by the Urim; but if it belongs
to your people Israel,[s] answer by the Thummim."[t] The answer indicated Jonathan and
Saul; and the people were cleared. 42 Then
Saul said, "Decide between my son Jonathan
and me." And Jonathan was indicated.
43 Then Saul asked Jonathan, "What have
you done?"

Jonathan answered, "I ate a little honey
with the stick I was holding. Here I am—I
am ready to die."

44 Saul said to him, "May God strike me
dead if you are not put to death!"

45 But the people said to Saul, "Will
Jonathan, who won this great victory for
Israel, be put to death? No! We promise by
the living LORD that he will not lose even a
hair from his head. What he did today was
done with God's help." So the people saved
Jonathan from being put to death.

46 After that, Saul stopped pursuing the
Philistines, and they went back to their own
territory.

Saul's Reign and Family

47 After Saul became king of Israel, he
fought all his enemies everywhere: the people of Moab, of Ammon, and of Edom, the
kings of Zobah, and the Philistines. Wherever he fought he was victorious.[u] 48 He
fought heroically and defeated even the people of Amalek. He saved the Israelites from
all attacks.

49 Saul's sons were Jonathan, Ishvi, and
Malchishua. His older daughter was named
Merab, and the younger one Michal. 50 His
wife was Ahinoam, the daughter of Ahimaaz;
his army commander was his cousin Abner,
the son of his uncle Ner. 51 Saul's father Kish
and Abner's father Ner were sons of Abiel.

52 As long as he lived, Saul had to fight

[s] **14:41** *Some ancient translations* answer me by the sacred stones . . . your people Israel; *Hebrew does not have these words.* [t] **14:41** URIM . . . THUMMIM: *Two stones used by the priest to determine God's will; it is not known precisely how they were used.* [u] **14:47** *One ancient translation* was victorious; *Hebrew* acted wickedly.

14:41 Num 27:21; 1 Sam 28:6

fiercely against the Philistines. So whenever he found a man who was strong or brave, he would enlist him in his army.

War against the Amalekites

15 Samuel said to Saul, "I am the one whom the LORD sent to anoint you king of his people Israel. Now listen to what the LORD Almighty says. 2He is going to punish the people of Amalek because their ancestors opposed the Israelites when they were coming from Egypt. 3Go and attack the Amalekites and completely destroy everything they have. Don't leave a thing; kill all the men, women, children, and babies; the cattle, sheep, camels, and donkeys."

4Saul called his forces together and inspected them at Telem: there were 200,000 soldiers from Israel and 10,000 from Judah. 5Then he and his men went to the city of Amalek and waited in ambush in a dry riverbed. 6He sent a warning to the Kenites, a people whose ancestors had been kind to the Israelites when they came from Egypt: "Go away and leave the Amalekites, so that I won't kill you along with them." So the Kenites left.

7Saul defeated the Amalekites, fighting all the way from Havilah to Shur, east of Egypt; 8he captured King Agag of Amalek alive and killed all the people. 9But Saul and his men spared Agag's life and did not kill the best sheep and cattle, the best calves and lambs,[v] or anything else that was good; they destroyed only what was useless or worthless.[w]

Saul Is Rejected as King

10The LORD said to Samuel, 11"I am sorry that I made Saul king; he has turned away from me and disobeyed my commands." Samuel was angry, and all night long he pleaded with the LORD. 12Early the following morning he went off to find Saul. He heard that Saul had gone to the town of Carmel, where he had built a monument to himself, and then had gone on to Gilgal. 13Samuel went up to Saul, who greeted him, saying, "The LORD bless you, Samuel! I have obeyed the LORD's command."

14Samuel asked, "Why, then, do I hear cattle mooing and sheep bleating?"

15Saul answered, "My men took them from the Amalekites. They kept the best sheep and cattle to offer as a sacrifice to the LORD your God, and the rest we have destroyed completely."[x]

16"Stop," Samuel ordered, "and I will tell you what the LORD said to me last night."

"Tell me," Saul said.

17Samuel answered, "Even though you consider yourself of no importance, you are the leader of the tribes of Israel. The LORD anointed you king of Israel, 18and he sent you out with orders to destroy those wicked people of Amalek. He told you to fight until you had killed them all. 19Why, then, did you not obey him? Why did you rush to grab the loot, and so do what displeases the LORD?"

20"I did obey the LORD," Saul replied. "I went out as he told me to, brought back King Agag, and killed all the Amalekites. 21But my men did not kill the best sheep and cattle that they captured; instead, they brought them here to Gilgal to offer as a sacrifice to the LORD your God."

22Samuel said, "Which does the LORD prefer: obedience or offerings and sacrifices? It is better to obey him than to sacrifice the best sheep to him. 23Rebellion against him is as bad as witchcraft, and arrogance is as sinful as idolatry. Because you rejected the LORD's command, he has rejected you as king."

24"Yes, I have sinned," Saul replied. "I disobeyed the LORD's command and your instructions. I was afraid of my men and did

[v] **15:9** *One ancient translation* the best calves and lambs; *Hebrew unclear.* [w] **15:9** *Some ancient translations* useless or worthless; *Hebrew unclear.* [x] **15:15** DESTROYED COMPLETELY: *These animals had been unconditionally dedicated to the LORD and had to be destroyed (see Lev 27:28).*

15:1 1 Sam 10:1 **15:2** Ex 17:8–14; Deut 25:17–19

Urim and Thummim were two stones or sticks used by Israelite priests to try to determine God's will. They were probably thrown like dice.

Live it!

Who Do You Think You Are?

Samuel tells the disobedient Saul that arrogance is as sinful as idolatry. Idolatry means worshiping false gods. What does arrogance mean, and why is it so bad?

To be arrogant is to think that you are better than other people and to act like it. We might also call such a person a snob. While it is not right for us to judge others, we can usually tell when we are in the presence of someone who is arrogant. They have a way of making us feel unimportant or of even ignoring us. It is almost as if they assume that somehow God has made them superior to others. We all know that some of us are richer than others and some of us are better looking or better athletes, but we also know that all of us are created in God's image. God does not approve when we act as if we're better than other people—because then we are not only arrogant toward other people, but we are also arrogant toward God!

Arrogance is often easy to spot in others, but not always easy to see in ourselves. Ask Jesus to help you see if any of your actions or behavior could be seen as arrogant by someone else.

— 1 Samuel 15:17–25

what they wanted. 25 But now I beg you, for-
give my sin and go back with me, so that I
can worship the LORD."
26 "I will not go back with you," Samuel
answered. "You rejected the LORD's command,
and he has rejected you as king of Israel."
27 Then Samuel turned to leave, but Saul
caught hold of his cloak, and it tore.
28 Samuel said to him, "The LORD has torn
the kingdom of Israel away from you today
and given it to someone who is a better man
than you. 29 Israel's majestic God does not lie
or change his mind. He is not a human
being—he does not change his mind."

"The LORD has torn the kingdom . . . away from you." (15:28)

30 "I have sinned," Saul replied. "But at
least show me respect in front of the leaders
of my people and all of Israel. Go back with
me so that I can worship the LORD your
God." 31 So Samuel went back with him, and
Saul worshiped the LORD.
32 "Bring King Agag here to me," Samuel
ordered. Agag came to him, trembling with
fear, thinking to himself, "What a bitter
thing it is to die!"[y] 33 Samuel said, "As your
sword has made many mothers childless, so
now your mother will become childless."
And he cut Agag to pieces in front of the
altar in Gilgal.
34 Then Samuel went to Ramah, and King
Saul went home to Gibeah. 35 As long as
Samuel lived, he never again saw the king;
but he grieved over him. The LORD was
sorry that he had made Saul king of Israel.

y **15:32** trembling with fear . . . die; *or* confidently, thinking to himself, "Surely the bitter danger of death is past!"
15:27, 28 1 Sam 28:17; 1 Kings 11:30, 31

Jesse is the son of Obed, and Obed is Ruth and Boaz's son. That makes Ruth—who was not an Israelite by birth—King David's great-grandmother.

David Is Anointed King

16 The LORD said to Samuel, "How
long will you go on grieving over
Saul? I have rejected him as king of Israel.
But now get some olive oil and go to Beth-
lehem, to a man named Jesse, because I have
chosen one of his sons to be king."
2"How can I do that?" Samuel asked. "If
Saul hears about it, he will kill me!"
The LORD answered, "Take a calf with
you and say that you are there to offer a sac-
rifice to the LORD. 3Invite Jesse to the sacri-
fice, and I will tell you what to do. You will
anoint as king the man I tell you to."
4Samuel did what the LORD told him to
do and went to Bethlehem, where the city
leaders came trembling to meet him and
asked, "Is this a peaceful visit, seer?"
5"Yes," he answered. "I have come to offer
a sacrifice to the LORD. Purify yourselves
and come with me." He also told Jesse and
his sons to purify themselves, and he invited
them to the sacrifice.
6When they arrived, Samuel saw Jesse's son
Eliab and said to himself, "This man standing
here in the LORD's presence is surely the one
he has chosen." 7But the LORD said to him,
"Pay no attention to how tall and handsome
he is. I have rejected him, because I do not
judge as people judge. They look at the out-
ward appearance, but I look at the heart."
8Then Jesse called his son Abinadab and
brought him to Samuel. But Samuel said,
"No, the LORD hasn't chosen him either."
9Jesse then brought Shammah. "No, the
LORD hasn't chosen him either," Samuel
said. 10In this way Jesse brought seven of his
sons to Samuel. And Samuel said to him,
"No, the LORD hasn't chosen any of these."
11Then he asked him, "Do you have any
more sons?"
Jesse answered, "There is still the youngest,
but he is out taking care of the sheep."
"Tell him to come here," Samuel said. "We
won't offer the sacrifice until he comes." 12So
Jesse sent for him. He was a handsome,
healthy young man, and his eyes sparkled.
The LORD said to Samuel, "This is the one—
anoint him!" 13Samuel took the olive oil and
anointed David in front of his brothers.
Immediately the spirit of the LORD took

Study it!

The Heart of the Matter

God gives Samuel a very important message when he visits Jesse. Samuel has to determine which one of Jesse's eight sons will become the next king. It would make perfect sense that Eliab, the oldest son, would become the king. In biblical times, that's the way it worked: the first-born son would inherit the most. Eliab was also tall and handsome. He seemed like the natural choice. But God tells Samuel: "Pay no attention to how tall and handsome he is. . . . I do not judge as people judge. They look at the outward appearance, but I look at the heart" (1 Samuel 16:7).

So much for being the best looking or the richest or the smartest or the best athlete. That matters little in God's eyes. God cuts right through all of what the world considers important and sees the heart of each person. It is there that the true greatness of a person lies. David is the youngest of his family. In fact, he is not even present when Samuel comes to visit. He is tending the sheep. But God saw in young David what no one else did—a person after his own heart. Sometimes on a team, the coach may choose a player who clearly isn't as gifted an athlete as someone else, but that coach knows that this young person will put his or her heart in it. That often counts for more than ability. Don't ever underestimate yourself. God knows what is in your heart. It doesn't matter what the world thinks.

— 1 Samuel 16:1–13

control of David and was with him from that
day on. Then Samuel returned to Ramah.

David in Saul's Court

14The LORD's spirit left Saul, and an evil
spirit sent by the LORD tormented him.
15His servants said to him, "We know that an
evil spirit sent by God is tormenting you.
16So give us the order, sir, and we will look
for a man who knows how to play the harp.
Then when the evil spirit comes on you, the
man can play his harp, and you will be all
right again."
17Saul ordered them, "Find me a man
who plays well and bring him to me."
18One of his attendants said, "Jesse of the
town of Bethlehem has a son who is a good
musician. He is also a brave and handsome
man, a good soldier, and an able speaker. The
LORD is with him."
19So Saul sent messengers to Jesse to say,
"Send me your son David, the one who takes
care of the sheep." 20Jesse sent David to Saul
with a young goat, a donkey loaded with
bread, and a leather bag full of wine. 21David
came to Saul and entered his service. Saul
liked him very much and chose him as the
man to carry his weapons. 22Then Saul sent a
message to Jesse: "I like David. Let him stay
here in my service." 23From then on, when-
ever the evil spirit sent by God came on
Saul, David would get his harp and play it.
The evil spirit would leave, and Saul would
feel better and be all right again.

David would get his harp and play it. (16:23)

Live it!

The Power of Music

David had many talents. One was that he could write songs and play the harp. In fact, whenever Saul was tormented by an evil spirit causing Saul to feel bad, David would play his harp. Saul's advisers knew what all of us know today: music can have a powerful effect on our moods. If we've had a bad day, often we turn to our favorite music to help us feel better. Or if we're feeling great, we often turn to music to celebrate as well. Everyone has their favorite songs, their favorite performers, and their favorite types of music. Music is a great gift, and there is an amazing variety of it.

Music should raise us to a higher level. Every major religion includes music in its worship, because music has power to lift us up. It is also true that there are songs and artists whose music often sends negative messages about life and relationships. Music that accepts violence, drug use, and immoral sex does not lift us up but can tear us down. Look at the lyrics (words) of the music you listen to most often. What messages are coming through? What choices can you make to limit your exposure to negative messages in music?

— 1 Samuel 16:14–23

Goliath Challenges the Israelites

17 The Philistines gathered for battle
in Socoh, a town in Judah; they
camped at a place called Ephes Dammim,
between Socoh and Azekah. 2Saul and the
Israelites assembled and camped in Elah Val-
ley, where they got ready to fight the
Philistines. 3The Philistines lined up on one
hill and the Israelites on another, with a val-
ley between them.
4A man named Goliath, from the city of
Gath, came out from the Philistine camp to

"I dare you to pick someone to fight me!" (17:10)

challenge the Israelites. He was over nine
feet[z] tall 5and wore bronze armor that
weighed about 125 pounds and a bronze
helmet. 6His legs were also protected by
bronze armor, and he carried a bronze
javelin slung over his shoulder. 7His spear
was as thick as the bar on a weaver's loom,
and its iron head weighed about fifteen
pounds. A soldier walked in front of him
carrying his shield. 8Goliath stood and
shouted at the Israelites, "What are you
doing there, lined up for battle? I am a
Philistine, you slaves of Saul! Choose one of
your men to fight me. 9If he wins and kills
me, we will be your slaves; but if I win and
kill him, you will be our slaves. 10Here and
now I challenge the Israelite army. I dare you
to pick someone to fight me!" 11When Saul
and his men heard this, they were terrified.

David in Saul's Camp

12David was the son of Jesse, who was an
Ephrathite from Bethlehem in Judah. Jesse
had eight sons, and at the time Saul was
king, he was already a very old man.[a] 13His
three oldest sons had gone with Saul to war.
The oldest was Eliab, the next was Abinadab,
and the third was Shammah. 14David was the
youngest son, and while the three oldest
brothers stayed with Saul, 15David would go
back to Bethlehem from time to time, to
take care of his father's sheep.

16Goliath challenged the Israelites every
morning and evening for forty days.

17One day Jesse said to David, "Take a
half-bushel of this roasted grain and these
ten loaves of bread, and hurry with them to
your brothers in the camp. 18And take these
ten cheeses to the commanding officer. Find
out how your brothers are getting along and
bring back something to show that you saw
them and that they are well. 19King Saul,
your brothers, and all the other Israelites are
in Elah Valley fighting the Philistines."

20David got up early the next morning,
left someone else in charge of the sheep,
took the food, and went as Jesse had told
him to. He arrived at the camp just as the
Israelites were going out to their battle line,
shouting the war cry. 21The Philistine and
the Israelite armies took positions for battle,
facing each other. 22David left the food with
the officer in charge of the supplies, ran to

[z] **17:4** *Hebrew* nine feet; *one ancient Hebrew manuscript and one ancient translation* seven feet.
[a] **17:12** *Some ancient translations* a very old man; *Hebrew unclear.*

Philistia is the land of the Philistines. Locate Goliath's homeland on Map 3 in the back of this Bible.

the battle line, went to his brothers, and
asked how they were getting along. 23 As he
was talking with them, Goliath came for-
ward and challenged the Israelites as he had
done before. And David heard him. 24 When
the Israelites saw Goliath, they ran away in
terror. 25 "Look at him!" they said to each
other. "Listen to his challenge! King Saul has
promised to give a big reward to the man
who kills him; the king will also give him
his daughter to marry and will not require
his father's family to pay taxes."[b]
26 David asked the men who were near
him, "What will the man get who kills this
Philistine and frees Israel from this disgrace?
After all, who is this heathen Philistine to
defy the army of the living God?" 27 They
told him what would be done for the man
who killed Goliath.
28 Eliab, David's oldest brother, heard David
talking to the men. He became angry with
David and said, "What are you doing here?
Who is taking care of those sheep of yours
out there in the wilderness? You smart aleck,
you! You just came to watch the fighting!"
29 "Now what have I done?" David asked.
"Can't I even ask a question?" 30 He turned
to another man and asked him the same
question, and every time he asked, he got
the same answer.
31 Some men heard what David had said,
and they told Saul, who sent for him.
32 David said to Saul, "Your Majesty, no one
should be afraid of this Philistine! I will go
and fight him."
33 "No," answered Saul. "How could you
fight him? You're just a boy, and he has been
a soldier all his life!"
34 "Your Majesty," David said, "I take care
of my father's sheep. Any time a lion or a
bear carries off a lamb, 35 I go after it, attack
it, and rescue the lamb. And if the lion or
bear turns on me, I grab it by the throat and
beat it to death. 36 I have killed lions and
bears, and I will do the same to this heathen
Philistine, who has defied the army of the
living God. 37 The LORD has saved me from

[b] **17:25** to pay taxes; *or* either to pay taxes or serve him.

Live it!

Taking a Big Risk

The story of David defeating Goliath is one of the best known in the Bible. Think about what a risk David was taking. With only a slingshot, he took on a giant warrior dressed in full armor. We can be sure that what drove David to take on Goliath was his deep faith and trust that God was with him.

Taking risks is an important part of life, but we always have to weigh those risks. At times, some of the risks we face may seem like Goliaths. Sometimes our fears make the risk seem even bigger than it is. Sometimes we decide that the risk is not worth it or will not be a healthy choice for us. We know that taking illegal drugs and having sex before marriage are very dangerous and harmful behaviors. These are bad risks to take! However, challenging ourselves to try a new activity and to reach out to a new person in friendship are risks worth taking. If our faith and trust in God guide us in our decision making, we will most likely take risks that will help us grow, no matter how challenging they seem.

The next time you are thinking of trying something that involves risk, picture David approaching giant Goliath armed with only his slingshot and his deep faith in God.

— 1 Samuel, chapter 17

When David fought Goliath he put his complete trust in God. A good reminder that we also need to put our trust in God every day.

lions and bears; he will save me from this Philistine."

"All right," Saul answered. "Go, and the LORD be with you." 38He gave his own armor to David for him to wear: a bronze helmet, which he put on David's head, and a coat of armor. 39David strapped Saul's sword over the armor and tried to walk, but he couldn't, because he wasn't used to wearing them. "I can't fight with all this," he said to Saul. "I'm not used to it." So he took it all off. 40He took his shepherd's stick and then picked up five smooth stones from the stream and put them in his bag. With his sling ready, he went out to meet Goliath.

He . . . picked up five smooth stones. (17:40)

David Defeats Goliath

41The Philistine started walking toward David, with his shield bearer walking in front of him. He kept coming closer, 42and when he got a good look at David, he was filled with scorn for him because he was just a nice, good-looking boy. 43He said to David, "What's that stick for? Do you think I'm a dog?" And he called down curses from his god on David. 44"Come on," he challenged David, "and I will give your body to the birds and animals to eat."

45David answered, "You are coming against me with sword, spear, and javelin, but I come against you in the name of the LORD Almighty, the God of the Israelite armies, which you have defied. 46This very day the LORD will put you in my power; I will defeat you and cut off your head. And I will give the bodies of the Philistine soldiers to the birds and animals to eat. Then the whole

"Do you think I'm a dog?" (17:43)

world will know that Israel has a God, 47and everyone here will see that the LORD does not need swords or spears to save his people. He is victorious in battle, and he will put all of you in our power."

48Goliath started walking toward David again, and David ran quickly toward the Philistine battle line to fight him. 49He reached into his bag and took out a stone, which he slung at Goliath. It hit him on the forehead and broke his skull, and Goliath fell face downward on the ground. 50And so, without a sword, David defeated and killed Goliath with a sling and a stone! 51He ran to him, stood over him, took Goliath's sword out of its sheath, and cut off his head and killed him.

When the Philistines saw that their hero was dead, they ran away. 52The men of Israel and Judah shouted and ran after them,

David defeated and killed Goliath. (17:50)

17:50 2 Sam 21:19 **17:51** 2 Sam 21:19

pursuing them all the way to Gath[c] and to the
gates of Ekron. The Philistines fell wounded
all along the road that leads to Shaaraim, as far
as Gath and Ekron. 53When the Israelites
came back from pursuing the Philistines, they
looted their camp. 54David got Goliath's head
and took it to Jerusalem, but he kept Goliath's
weapons in his own tent.

David Is Presented to Saul

55When Saul saw David going out to
fight Goliath, he asked Abner, the command-
er of his army, "Abner, whose son is he?"
"I have no idea, Your Majesty," Abner
answered.
56"Then go and find out," Saul ordered.
57So when David returned to camp after
killing Goliath, Abner took him to Saul.
David was still carrying Goliath's head. 58Saul
asked him, "Young man, whose son are you?"
"I am the son of your servant Jesse from
Bethlehem," David answered.
18 Saul and David finished their conver-
sation. After that, Saul's son Jonathan
was deeply attracted to David and came to
love him as much as he loved himself. 2Saul
kept David with him from that day on and
did not let him go back home. 3Jonathan
swore eternal friendship with David because
of his deep affection for him. 4He took off
the robe he was wearing and gave it to
David, together with his armor and also his
sword, bow, and belt. 5David was successful in
all the missions on which Saul sent him, and

Jonathan swore eternal friendship with David. (18:3)

Live it!

Friends for Life

Throughout the rest of First Samuel, it is clear that David and Jonathan have become very close friends. Jonathan even shares his clothes with David, probably like you might do with some of your friends. It is not easy to be a good and loyal friend. It takes a lot of work, and in Jonathan's case, he has to deal with the growing jealousy of his father, King Saul, toward David. Several times, Jonathan takes great risks to help David because of their deep friendship. There are things you trust your best friend with that you tell no one else. It is all about trust and staying loyal to each other through thick and thin. Most of us can count on one hand those individuals we call true friends.

Think about how good and loyal a friend you are. Think about how you can make friends and also deepen a friendship you already have. Ask God to help you. Pray for your friends every day. Pray that you will be a loyal friend.

— 1 Samuel 18:1–5

so Saul made him an officer in his army. This
pleased all of Saul's officers and men.

Saul Becomes Jealous of David

6As David was returning after killing
Goliath and as the soldiers were coming back
home, women from every town in Israel
came out to meet King Saul. They were
singing joyful songs, dancing, and playing
tambourines and lyres. 7In their celebration

[c] **17:52** *One ancient translation* Gath; *Hebrew* a valley.
18:7 1 Sam 21:11; 29:5

the women sang, "Saul has killed thousands, but David tens of thousands." 8 Saul did not like this, and he became very angry. He said, "For David they claim tens of thousands, but only thousands for me. They will be making him king next!" 9 And so he was jealous and suspicious of David from that day on.

10 The next day an evil spirit from God suddenly took control of Saul, and he raved in his house like a madman. David was playing the harp, as he did every day, and Saul was holding a spear. 11 "I'll pin him to the wall," Saul said to himself, and he threw the spear at him twice; but David dodged each time.

12 Saul was afraid of David because the

"I'll pin him to the wall." (18:11)

LORD was with David but had abandoned him. 13 So Saul sent him away and put him in command of a thousand men. David led his men in battle 14 and was successful in all he did, because the LORD was with him. 15 Saul noticed David's success and became even more afraid of him. 16 But everyone in Israel and Judah loved David because he was such a successful leader.

David Marries Saul's Daughter

17 Then Saul said to David, "Here is my older daughter Merab. I will give her to you as your wife on condition that you serve me as a brave and loyal soldier, and fight the LORD's battles." (Saul was thinking that in this way the Philistines would kill David, and he would not have to do it himself.)

18 David answered, "Who am I and what is my family that I should become the king's son-in-law?" 19 But when the time came for Merab to be given to David, she was given instead to a man named Adriel from Meholah.

20 Saul's daughter Michal, however, fell in love with David, and when Saul heard of this, he was pleased. 21 He said to himself, "I'll give Michal to David; I will use her to trap him, and he will be killed by the Philistines." So for the second time Saul said to David, "You will be my son-in-law." 22 He ordered his officials to speak privately with David and tell him, "The king is pleased with you and all his officials like you; now is a good time for you to marry his daughter."

23 So they told this to David, and he answered, "It's a great honor to become the king's son-in-law, too great for someone poor and insignificant like me."

24 The officials told Saul what David had said, 25 and Saul ordered them to tell David: "All the king wants from you as payment for the bride are the foreskins of a hundred dead Philistines, as revenge on his enemies." (This was how Saul planned to have David killed by the Philistines.) 26 Saul's officials reported to David what Saul had said, and David was delighted with the thought of becoming the king's son-in-law. Before the day set for the wedding, 27 David and his men went and killed two hundred Philistines. He took their foreskins to the king and counted them all out to him, so that he might become his son-in-law. So Saul had to give his daughter Michal in marriage to David.

28 Saul realized clearly that the LORD was with David and also that his daughter Michal loved him. 29 So he became even more afraid of David and was his enemy as long as he lived.

30 The Philistine armies would come and fight, but in every battle David was more successful than any of Saul's other officers. As a result David became very famous.

Saul's oldest daughter, Merab, was first promised in marriage to David, but David ended up marrying a different daughter. What was her name?

Pray it!

The Jealousy Monster

Jealousy can really eat away at our relationships and destroy friendships. Jealousy turns Saul into a crazed man who publicly tries to kill David! Eventually it destroys this once great man. When you feel jealousy for another, try this prayer:

Dear God, I need your help in dealing with my jealousy toward _______.
Help me to step back and not judge this person.
Help me to realize how quickly my feelings of jealousy can take over and can lead me to say and do things that go against your command to love one another.
I want to pray that you bless _______ and that I can accept whatever differences there are between us.
Help me to move on and not let jealousy get the best of me.
Amen.

— 1 Samuel, chapter 19

David Is Persecuted by Saul

19 Saul told his son Jonathan and all his
officials that he planned to kill[d] David.
But Jonathan was very fond of David, 2and so
he told him, "My father is trying to kill you.
Please be careful tomorrow morning; hide in
some secret place and stay there. 3I will go and
stand by my father in the field where you are
hiding, and I will speak to him about you. If I
find out anything, I will let you know."

4Jonathan praised David to Saul and said,
"Sir, don't do wrong to your servant David.
He has never done you any wrong; on the
contrary, everything he has done has been a
great help to you. 5He risked his life when
he killed Goliath, and the LORD won a great
victory for Israel. When you saw it, you were
glad. Why, then, do you now want to do
wrong to an innocent man and kill David
for no reason at all?"

6Saul was convinced by what Jonathan
said and made a vow in the LORD's name
that he would not kill David. 7So Jonathan
called David and told him everything; then
he took him to Saul, and David served the
king as he had before.

8War with the Philistines broke out again.
David attacked them and defeated them so
thoroughly that they fled.

9One day an evil spirit from the LORD
took control of Saul. He was sitting in his
house with his spear in his hand, and David
was there, playing his harp. 10Saul tried to
pin David to the wall with his spear, but
David dodged, and the spear stuck in the
wall. David ran away and escaped.

11That same night Saul sent some men to
watch David's house and kill him the next
morning. Michal, David's wife, warned him,
"If you don't get away tonight, tomorrow
you will be dead." 12She let him down from
a window, and he ran away and escaped.
13Then she took the household idol, laid it
on the bed, put a pillow made of goats' hair

[d] **19:1** that he planned to kill; *or* to kill.
19:11 Ps 59 Title

How does David's wife fool Saul's soldiers into thinking he is sick? It's a trick you sometimes see in movies.

at its head, and put a cover over it. 14When
Saul's men came to get David, Michal told
them that he was sick. 15But Saul sent them
back to see David for themselves. He
ordered them, "Carry him here in his bed,
and I will kill him." 16They went inside and
found the household idol in the bed and the
goats' hair pillow at its head. 17Saul asked
Michal, "Why have you tricked me like this
and let my enemy escape?"

She answered, "He said he would kill me
if I didn't help him escape."

18David escaped and went to Samuel in
Ramah and told him everything that Saul had
done to him. Then he and Samuel went to
Naioth and stayed there. 19Saul was told that
David was in Naioth in Ramah, 20so he sent
some men to arrest him. They saw[e] the group
of prophets dancing and shouting, with
Samuel as their leader. Then the spirit of God
took control of Saul's men, and they also
began to dance and shout. 21When Saul heard
of this, he sent more messengers, and they also
began to dance and shout. He sent messen-
gers the third time, and the same thing hap-
pened to them. 22Then he himself started out
to Ramah. When he came to the large well in
Secu, he asked where Samuel and David were
and was told that they were at Naioth. 23As
he was going there, the spirit of God took
control of him also, and he danced and shout-
ed all the way to Naioth. 24He took off his
clothes and danced and shouted in Samuel's
presence, and lay naked all that day and all
that night. (This is how the saying originated,
"Has even Saul become a prophet?")

Jonathan Helps David

20 Then David fled from Naioth in
Ramah and went to Jonathan. "What
have I done?" he asked. "What crime have I
committed? What wrong have I done to your
father to make him want to kill me?"

2Jonathan answered, "God forbid that you
should die! My father tells me everything he
does, important or not, and he would not
hide this from me. It just isn't so!"

3But David answered,[f] "Your father knows
very well how much you like me, and he has
decided not to let you know what he plans
to do, because you would be deeply hurt. I
swear to you by the living LORD that I am
only a step away from death!"

4Jonathan said, "I'll do anything you
want."

5"Tomorrow is the New Moon Festival,"
David replied, "and I am supposed to eat
with the king. But if it's all right with you, I
will go and hide in the fields until the
evening of the day after tomorrow. 6If your
father notices that I am not at the table, tell
him that I begged your permission to hurry
home to Bethlehem, since it's the time for
the annual sacrifice there for my whole
family. 7If he says, 'All right,' I will be safe;
but if he becomes angry, you will know that
he is determined to harm me. 8Please do
me this favor, and keep the sacred promise
you made to me. But if I'm guilty, kill me
yourself! Why take me to your father to be
killed?"

9"Don't even think such a thing!"
Jonathan answered. "If I knew for sure that
my father was determined to harm you,
wouldn't I tell you?"

10David then asked, "Who will let me
know if your father answers you angrily?"

11"Let's go out to the fields," Jonathan
answered. So they went, 12and Jonathan said
to David, "May the LORD God of Israel be
our witness![g] At this time tomorrow and on
the following day I will question my father.
If his attitude toward you is good, I will send
you word. 13If he intends to harm you, may
the LORD strike me dead if I don't let you
know about it and get you safely away. May
the LORD be with you as he was with my
father! 14And if I remain alive, please keep
your sacred promise and be loyal to me; but
if I die,[h] 15show the same kind of loyalty to
my family forever. And when the LORD has
completely destroyed all your enemies,
16may our promise to each other still be
unbroken. If it is broken, the LORD will
punish you."[i]

[e] **19:20** *Some ancient translations* They saw; *Hebrew* He saw. [f] **20:3** *One ancient translation* answered; *Hebrew* made a vow again. [g] **20:12** *One ancient translation* be our witness; *Hebrew does not have these words.* [h] **20:14** *Some ancient translations* if I die; *Hebrew* that I may not die. [i] **20:16** *Verses 15–16 in Hebrew are unclear.*

19:24 1 Sam 10:11, 12 **20:5** Num 28:11 **20:15** 2 Sam 9:1

17 Once again Jonathan made David promise to love him, for Jonathan loved David as much as he loved himself. 18 Then Jonathan said to him, "Since tomorrow is the New Moon Festival, your absence will be noticed if you aren't at the meal. 19 The day after tomorrow your absence will be noticed[j] even more; so go to the place where you hid yourself the other time, and hide behind the pile of stones there.[k] 20 I will then shoot three arrows at it, as though it were a target. 21 Then I will tell my servant to go and find them. And if I tell him, 'Look, the arrows are on this side of you; get them,' that means that you are safe and can come out. I swear by the living LORD that you will be in no danger. 22 But if I tell him, 'The arrows are on the other side of you,' then leave, because the LORD is sending you away. 23 As for the promise we have made to each other, the LORD will make sure that we will keep it forever."

24 So David hid in the fields. At the New Moon Festival, King Saul came to the meal 25 and sat in his usual place by the wall. Abner sat next to him, and Jonathan sat across the table from him.[l] David's place was empty, 26 but Saul said nothing that day, because he thought, "Something has happened to him, and he is not ritually pure." 27 On the following day, the day after the New Moon Festival, David's place was still empty, and Saul asked Jonathan, "Why didn't David come to the meal either yesterday or today?"

28 Jonathan answered, "He begged me to let him go to Bethlehem. 29 'Please let me go,' he said, 'because our family is celebrating the sacrificial feast in town, and my brother ordered me to be there. So then, if you are my friend, let me go and see my relatives.' That is why he isn't in his place at your table."

30 Saul became furious with Jonathan and said to him, "How rebellious and faithless your mother was! Now I know you are taking sides with David and are disgracing yourself and that mother of yours! 31 Don't you realize that as long as David is alive, you will never be king of this country? Now go and bring him here—he must die!"

32 "Why should he die?" Jonathan replied. "What has he done?"

33 At that, Saul threw his spear at Jonathan to kill him, and Jonathan realized that his father was really determined to kill David. 34 Jonathan got up from the table in a rage and ate nothing that day—the second day of the New Moon Festival. He was deeply distressed about David, because Saul had insulted him. 35 The following morning Jonathan went to the fields to meet David, as they had agreed. He took a young boy with him 36 and said to him, "Run and find the arrows I'm going to shoot." The boy ran, and Jonathan shot an arrow beyond him. 37 When the boy reached the place where the arrow had fallen, Jonathan shouted to him, "The arrow is farther on! 38 Don't just stand there! Hurry up!" The boy picked up the arrow and returned to his master, 39 not knowing what it all meant; only Jonathan and David knew. 40 Jonathan gave his weapons to the boy and told him to take them back to town.

41 After the boy had left, David got up from behind the pile of stones,[m] fell on his knees and bowed with his face to the ground three times. Both he and Jonathan were crying as they kissed each other; David's grief was even greater than Jonathan's.[n] 42 Then Jonathan said to David, "God be with you. The LORD will make sure that you and I, and your descendants and mine, will forever keep

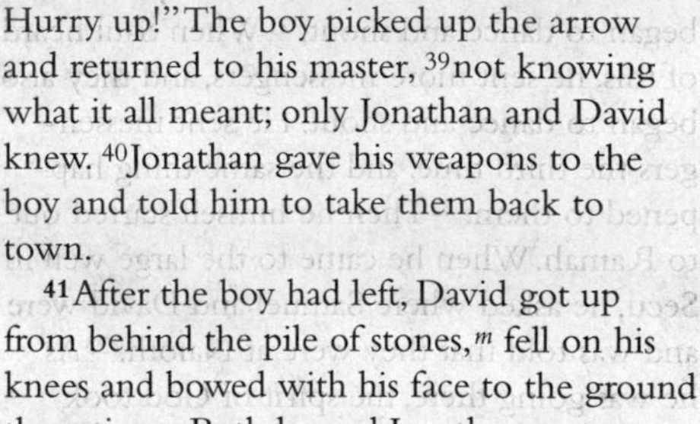

"God be with you!" (20:42)

[j] **20:19** *Some ancient translations* your absence will be noticed; *Hebrew* go down. [k] **20:19** *Probable text* the pile of stones there; *Hebrew* the Ezel Stone. [l] **20:25** *One ancient translation* sat across the table from him; *Hebrew* stood up. [m] **20:41** *Probable text* the pile of stones; *Hebrew* the south. [n] **20:41** *Probable text* David's grief was even greater than Jonathan's; *Hebrew unclear.*

the sacred promise we have made to each
other." Then David left, and Jonathan went
back to the town.

David Flees from Saul

21 David went to the priest Ahimelech
in Nob. Ahimelech came out trem-
bling to meet him and asked, "Why did you
come here all by yourself?"
2"I am here on the king's business," David
answered. "He told me not to let anyone
know what he sent me to do. As for my
men, I have told them to meet me at a cer-
tain place. 3Now, then, what supplies do you
have? Give me five loaves of bread or any-
thing else you have."
4The priest said, "I don't have any ordi-
nary bread, only sacred bread; you can have
it if your men haven't had sexual relations
recently."
5"Of course they haven't," answered
David. "My men always keep themselves rit-
ually pure even when we go out on an ordi-
nary mission; how much more this time
when we are on a special mission!"
6So the priest gave David the sacred
bread, because the only bread he had was the
loaves offered to God, which had been
removed from the sacred table and replaced
by fresh bread.
(7Saul's chief herdsman, Doeg, who was
from Edom, happened to be there that day,
because he had to fulfill a religious obliga-
tion.)
8David said to Ahimelech, "Do you have a
spear or a sword you can give me? The
king's orders made me leave in such a hurry
that I didn't have time to get my sword or
any other weapon."
9Ahimelech answered, "I have the sword
of Goliath the Philistine, whom you killed in
Elah Valley; it is behind the ephod, wrapped
in a cloth. If you want it, take it—it's the
only weapon here."
"Give it to me," David said. "There is not
a better sword anywhere!"

Study it!

Innocent Blood

Saul has clearly let his anger and jealousy overtake him. Because the priest Ahimelech has helped David feed his men, Saul decides to take revenge and orders eighty-five priests killed. Then he has everyone else in the city of Nob killed as well, including children and even babies. This slaughter of innocent blood is a terrible sin. Throughout history we have examples of innocent people being killed. Every continent and every century has its own horror stories about innocent people being put to death.

To some people in power, life is cheap. They have no regard for the sanctity of human life. They are like bullies on the playground who pick on people or beat them up simply to show that they are tougher, but they do it on a larger and much deadlier scale. Bullies—large and small—often come to a violent end themselves.

If you are being bullied, let a trusted adult know. If you are involved in being a bully, take a good, hard look at who you are bullying and why. Decide not to add to the violence in the world.

— 1 Samuel 21:1–6; 22:9–19

10So David left, fleeing from Saul, and
went to King Achish of Gath. 11The king's
officials said to Achish, "Isn't this David, the
king of his country? This is the man about

21:1–6 Mt 12:3, 4; Mk 2:25, 26; Lk 6:3 **21:6** Lev 24:5–9 **21:9** 1 Sam 17:51 **21:11** 1 Sam 18:7; 29:5

This story of the sacred bread in I Samuel, chapter 21, is used by Jesus to make a point about the Sabbath. Check it out in Matthew 12:1–4.

whom the women sang, as they danced, 'Saul
has killed thousands, but David has killed
tens of thousands.' "
12 Their words made a deep impression on
David, and he became very much afraid of
King Achish. 13 So whenever David was
around them, he pretended to be insane and
acted like a madman when they tried to
restrain him; he would scribble on the city[o]
gates and let spit drool down his beard. 14 So
Achish said to his officials, "Look! The man
is crazy! Why did you bring him to me?
15 Don't I have enough madmen already?
Why bring another one to bother me with
his crazy actions right here in my own
house?"

The Slaughter of the Priests

22 David fled from the city of Gath and
went to a cave near the town of
Adullam. When his brothers and the rest of
the family heard that he was there, they
joined him. 2 People who were oppressed or
in debt or dissatisfied went to him, about
four hundred men in all, and he became
their leader.
3 David went on from there to Mizpah in
Moab and said to the king of Moab, "Please
let my father and mother come and stay
with you until I find out what God is going
to do for me." 4 So David left his parents
with the king of Moab, and they stayed there
as long as David was hiding out in the cave.
5 Then the prophet Gad came to David
and said, "Don't stay here; go at once to the
land of Judah." So David left and went to the
forest of Hereth.
6 One day Saul was in Gibeah, sitting
under a tamarisk tree on a hill, with his spear
in his hand, and all his officers were standing
around him. He was told that David and his
men had been located, 7 and he said to his
officers, "Listen, men of Benjamin! Do you
think that David will give fields and vine-
yards to all of you, and make you officers in
his army? 8 Is that why you are plotting
against me? Not one of you told me that my
own son had made an alliance with David.
No one is concerned about me or tells me
that David, one of my own men, is right
now looking for a chance to kill me, and
that my son has encouraged him!"
9 Doeg was standing there with Saul's offi-
cers, and he said, "I saw David when he
went to Ahimelech son of Ahitub in Nob.
10 Ahimelech asked the LORD what David
should do, and then he gave David some
food and the sword of Goliath the Philis-
tine."
11 So King Saul sent for the priest Ahim-
elech and all his relatives, who were also
priests in Nob, and they came to him. 12 Saul
said to Ahimelech, "Listen, Ahimelech!"
"At your service, sir," he answered.
13 Saul asked him, "Why are you and
David plotting against me? Why did you
give him some food and a sword, and con-
sult God for him? Now he has turned
against me and is waiting for a chance to kill
me!"
14 Ahimelech answered, "David is the most
faithful officer you have! He is your own
son-in-law, captain of[p] your bodyguard, and
highly respected by everyone in the royal
court. 15 Yes, I consulted God for him, and it
wasn't the first time.[q] As for plotting against
you, Your Majesty must not accuse me or
anyone else in my family. I don't know any-
thing about this matter!"
16 The king said, "Ahimelech, you and all
your relatives must die." 17 Then he said to
the guards standing near him, "Kill the
LORD's priests! They conspired with David
and did not tell me that he had run away,
even though they knew it all along." But the
guards refused to lift a hand to kill the
LORD's priests. 18 So Saul said to Doeg, "You

[o] **21:13** city; *or* palace. [p] **22:14** *Some ancient translations* captain of; *Hebrew* he turned to. [q] **22:15** Yes, I consulted . . . time; *or* Now, have I done something wrong today by consulting God for him? Not at all!

21:12 Ps 56 Title **21:13** Ps 34 Title **22:1** Ps 57 Title; Ps 142 Title **22:9, 10** 1 Sam 21:7–9; Ps 52 Title

The wilderness near Ziph where David hid from Saul was most likely a very rocky and difficult area in which to travel, so no one lived there.

kill them!"—and Doeg killed them all. On
that day he killed eighty-five priests who
were qualified to carry the ephod. 19Saul
also had all the other inhabitants of Nob, the
city of priests, put to death: men and
women, children and babies, cattle, donkeys,
and sheep—they were all killed.

20But Abiathar, one of Ahimelech's sons,
escaped, and went and joined David. 21He
told him how Saul had slaughtered the
priests of the LORD. 22David said to him,
"When I saw Doeg there that day, I knew
that he would be sure to tell Saul. So I am
responsible[r] for the death of all your rela-
tives. 23Stay with me and don't be afraid.
Saul wants to kill both you and me, but you
will be safe with me."

David Saves the Town of Keilah

23 David heard that the Philistines were
attacking the town of Keilah and
were stealing the newly harvested grain. 2So
he asked the LORD, "Shall I go and attack
the Philistines?"

"Yes," the LORD answered. "Attack them
and save Keilah."

3But David's men said to him, "We have
enough to be afraid of here in Judah; it will
be much worse if we go to Keilah and attack
the Philistine forces!" 4So David consulted
the LORD again, and the LORD said to him,
"Go and attack Keilah, because I will give
you victory over the Philistines." 5So David
and his men went to Keilah and attacked the
Philistines; they killed many of them and
took their livestock. And so it was that David
saved the town.

6When Abiathar son of Ahimelech
escaped and joined David in Keilah, he took
the ephod with him.

7Saul was told that David had gone to
Keilah, and he said, "God has put him in my
power. David has trapped himself by going
into a walled town with fortified gates." 8So
Saul called his troops to war, to march against
Keilah and besiege David and his men.

9When David heard that Saul was plan-
ning to attack him, he said to the priest Abi-
athar, "Bring the ephod here." 10Then David
said, " LORD, God of Israel, I have heard that
Saul is planning to come to Keilah and
destroy it on account of me, your servant.
11Will the citizens of Keilah hand me over
to Saul? Will Saul really come, as I have
heard? LORD, God of Israel, I beg you to
answer me!"

The LORD answered, "Saul will come."

12"And will the citizens of Keilah hand
my men and me over to Saul?" David asked
again.

"They will," the LORD answered.

13So David and his men—about six hun-
dred in all—left Keilah at once and kept on
the move. When Saul heard that David had
escaped from Keilah, he gave up his plan.

David in the Hill Country

14David stayed in hiding in the hill coun-
try, in the wilderness near Ziph. Saul was
always trying to find him, but God did not
turn David over to him. 15David saw that
Saul was out to kill him.

David was at Horesh, in the wilderness
near Ziph. 16Jonathan went to him there and
encouraged him with assurances of God's
protection, 17saying to him, "Don't be afraid.
My father Saul won't be able to harm you.
He knows very well that you are the one
who will be the king of Israel and that I will
be next in rank to you." 18The two of them
made a sacred promise of friendship to each
other. David stayed at Horesh, and Jonathan
went home.

19Some people from Ziph went to Saul at
Gibeah and said, "David is hiding out in our
territory at Horesh on Mount Hachilah, in
the southern part of the Judean wilderness.
20We know, Your Majesty, how much you
want to capture him; so come to our territo-
ry, and we will make sure that you catch
him."

21Saul answered, "May the LORD bless you
for being so kind to me! 22Go and make
sure once more; find out for certain where
he is and who has seen him there. I hear that
he is very cunning. 23Find out exactly the

[r] **22:22** *Some ancient translations* I am responsible; *Hebrew* I have turned.
23:18 1 Sam 18:3 **23:19** Ps 54 Title

places where he hides, and be sure to bring back a report to me right away. Then I will go with you, and if he is still in the region, I will hunt him down, even if I have to search the whole land of Judah."

24So they left and returned to Ziph ahead of Saul. David and his men were in the wilderness of Maon, in a desolate valley in the southern part of the Judean wilderness. 25Saul and his men set out to look for David, but he heard about it and went to a rocky hill in the wilderness of Maon and stayed there. When Saul heard about this, he went after David. 26Saul and his men were on one side of the hill, separated from David and his men, who were on the other side. They were hurrying to get away from Saul and his men, who were closing in on them and were about to capture them. 27Just then a messenger arrived and said to Saul, "Come back at once! The Philistines are invading the country!" 28So Saul stopped pursuing David and went to fight the Philistines. That is why that place is called Separation Hill. 29David left and went to the region of Engedi, where he stayed in hiding.

David Spares Saul's Life

24 When Saul came back from fighting the Philistines, he was told that David was in the wilderness near Engedi. 2Saul took three thousand of the best soldiers in Israel and went looking for David and his men east of Wild Goat Rocks. 3He came to a cave close to some sheep pens by the road and went in to relieve himself. It happened to be the very cave in which David and his men were hiding far back in the cave. 4They said to him, "This is your chance! The LORD has told you that he would put your enemy in your power and you could do to him whatever you wanted to." David crept over and cut off a piece of Saul's robe without Saul's knowing it. 5But then David's conscience began to hurt, 6and he said to his men, "May the LORD keep me from doing any harm to my master, whom the LORD chose as king! I must not harm him in the least, because he is the king chosen by the LORD!" 7So David convinced his men that they should not attack Saul.

David . . . cut off a piece of Saul's robe. (24:4)

Saul got up, left the cave, and started away. 8Then David went out after him and called to him, "Your Majesty!" Saul turned around, and David bowed down to the ground in respect 9and said, "Why do you listen to people who say that I am trying to harm you? 10You can see for yourself that just now in the cave the LORD put you in my power. Some of my men told me to kill you, but I felt sorry for you and said that I would not harm you in the least, because you are the one whom the LORD chose to be king. 11Look, my father, look at the piece of your robe I am holding! I could have killed you, but instead I only cut this off. This should convince you that I have no thought of rebelling against you or of harming you. You are hunting me down to kill me, even though I have not done you any wrong. 12May the LORD judge which one of us is wrong! May he punish you for your action against me, for I will not harm you in the least. 13You know the old saying, 'Evil is done only by evil people.' And

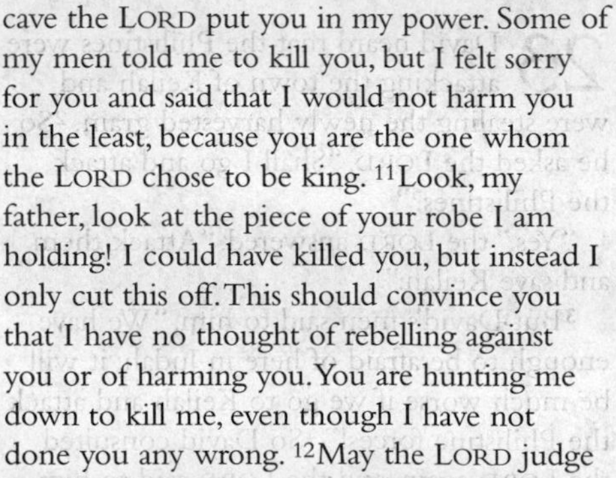

"I could have killed you!" (24:11)

24:3 Ps 57 Title; Ps 142 Title **24:6** 1 Sam 26:11

Pray it!

Respect

Try to imagine David's situation in 1 Samuel, chapter 24. He could very easily have killed Saul. He knew that Saul would kill him, if given the chance. So why did he spare Saul's life?

It's simple: respect. David knew that even though Saul had fallen out of favor with God, Saul was still God's chosen king, and he had great respect for both God and for his king. This says a lot about David's character.

Respect is a very important virtue and is a sign of maturity. We need to respect those in authority. We may not always agree with them, but we still respect their position. One way you can show your respect for people in authority is to pray for them. Here is a checklist of people you could pray for:

- **your parents or guardians**
- **your principal and teachers**
- **your mayor and city council or county board**
- **your state's governor and representatives**
- **state and federal judges**
- **the president and Congress**
- **leaders of all the nations of the world**

— 1 Samuel, chapter 24

so I will not harm you. 14Look at what the
king of Israel is trying to kill! Look at what
he is chasing! A dead dog, a flea! 15The LORD
will judge, and he will decide which one of
us is wrong. May he look into the matter,
defend me, and save me from you."
16When David had finished speaking, Saul
said, "Is that really you, David my son?" And
he started crying. 17Then he said to David,
"You are right, and I am wrong. You have
been so good to me, while I have done such
wrong to you! 18Today you have shown how
good you are to me, because you did not kill
me, even though the LORD put me in your
power. 19How often does someone catch an
enemy and then let him get away unharmed?
The LORD bless you for what you have done
to me today! 20Now I am sure that you will
be king of Israel and that the kingdom will
continue under your rule. 21But promise me
in the LORD's name that you will spare my
descendants, so that my name and my family's name will not be completely forgotten."
22David promised that he would.

Then Saul went back home, and David and his men went back to their hiding place.

The Death of Samuel

25 Samuel died, and all the Israelites came together and mourned for him. Then they buried him at his home in Ramah.

David and Abigail

After this, David went to the wilderness of
Paran. 2-3There was a man of the clan of
Caleb named Nabal, who was from the town
of Maon, and who owned land near the

24:14 1 Sam 26:20

"Then he (Saul) said to David, 'You are right and I am wrong. You have been so good to me, while I have done such wrong to you!' " *(1 Samuel 24:17)*.

town of Carmel. He was a very rich man,
the owner of three thousand sheep and one
thousand goats. His wife Abigail was beauti-
ful and intelligent, but he was a mean, bad-
tempered man.
Nabal was shearing his sheep in Carmel,
4 and David, who was in the wilderness,
heard about it, 5 so he sent ten young men
with orders to go to Carmel, find Nabal, and
give him his greetings. 6 He instructed them
to say to Nabal: "David sends you greetings,
my friend, with his best wishes for you, your
family, and all that is yours. 7 He heard that
you were shearing your sheep, and he wants
you to know that your shepherds have been
with us and we did not harm them. Nothing
that belonged to them was stolen all the
time they were at Carmel. 8 Just ask them,
and they will tell you. We have come on a
feast day, and David asks you to receive us
kindly. Please give what you can to us your
servants and to your dear friend David."
9 David's men delivered this message to
Nabal in David's name. Then they waited
there, 10 and Nabal finally answered, "David?
Who is he? I've never heard of him! The
country is full of runaway slaves nowadays!
11 I'm not going to take my bread and water,
and the animals I have butchered for my
sheepshearers, and give them to people who
come from I don't know where!"
12 David's men went back to him and told
him what Nabal had said. 13 "Buckle on your
swords!" he ordered, and they all did. David
also buckled on his sword and left with
about four hundred of his men, leaving two
hundred behind with the supplies.
14 One of Nabal's servants said to Nabal's
wife Abigail, "Have you heard? David sent
some messengers from the wilderness with
greetings for our master, but he insulted
them. 15 Yet they were very good to us; they
never bothered us, and all the time we were
with them in the fields, nothing that
belonged to us was stolen. 16 They protected
us day and night the whole time we were
with them looking after our flocks. 17 Please
think this over and decide what to do. This
could be disastrous for our master and all his
family. He is so mean that he won't listen to
anybody!"
18 Abigail quickly gathered two hundred
loaves of bread, two leather bags full of wine,
five roasted sheep, two bushels of roasted
grain, a hundred bunches of raisins, and two
hundred cakes of dried figs, and loaded them
on donkeys. 19 Then she said to the servants,
"You go on ahead and I will follow you."
But she said nothing to her husband.
20 She was riding her donkey around a
bend on a hillside when suddenly she met
David and his men coming toward her.
21 David had been thinking, "Why did I ever
protect that fellow's property out here in the
wilderness? Not a thing that belonged to
him was stolen, and this is how he pays me
back for the help I gave him! 22 May God
strike me[s] dead if I don't kill every last one
of those men before morning!"
23 When Abigail saw David, she quickly
dismounted and threw herself on the ground
24 at David's feet, and said to him, "Please, sir,
listen to me! Let me take the blame. 25 Please,
don't pay any attention to Nabal, that good-
for-nothing! He is exactly what his name
means—a fool![t] I wasn't there when your

When Abigail saw David . . . (25:23)

[s] **25:22** *One ancient translation* me; *Hebrew* my enemies. *Nabal.*

[t] **25:25** A FOOL: *This is the meaning of the Hebrew name*

Did you ever wonder what kind of food the ancient Israelites ate? Check the list in 1 Samuel 25:18.

servants arrived, sir. 26It is the LORD who has
kept you from taking revenge and killing
your enemies. And now I swear to you by
the living LORD that your enemies and all
who want to harm you will be punished like
Nabal. 27Please, sir, accept this present I have
brought you, and give it to your men.
28Please forgive me, sir, for any wrong I have
done. The LORD will make you king, and
your descendants also, because you are fight-
ing his battles; and you will not do anything
evil[u] as long as you live. 29If anyone should
attack you and try to kill you, the LORD
your God will keep you safe, as someone
guards a precious treasure. As for your ene-
mies, however, he will throw them away, as
someone hurls stones with a sling. 30And
when the LORD has done all the good things
he has promised you and has made you king
of Israel, 31then you will not have to feel
regret or remorse, sir, for having killed with-
out cause or for having taken your own
revenge. And when the LORD has blessed
you, sir, please do not forget me."
32David said to her, "Praise the LORD, the
God of Israel, who sent you today to meet
me! 33Thank God for your good sense and
for what you have done today in keeping me
from the crime of murder and from taking
my own revenge. 34The LORD has kept me
from harming you. But I swear by the living
God of Israel that if you had not hurried to
meet me, all of Nabal's men would have
been dead by morning!" 35Then David
accepted what she had brought him and said
to her, "Go back home and don't worry. I
will do what you want."
36Abigail went back to Nabal, who was at
home having a feast fit for a king. He was
drunk and in a good mood, so she did not
tell him anything until the next morning.
37Then, after he had sobered up, she told
him everything. He suffered a stroke and was
completely paralyzed. 38Some ten days later
the LORD struck Nabal and he died.
39When David heard that Nabal had died,
he said, "Praise the LORD! He has taken
revenge on Nabal for insulting me and has
kept me his servant from doing wrong. The
LORD has punished Nabal for his evil."
Then David sent a proposal of marriage
to Abigail. 40His servants went to her at
Carmel and said to her, "David sent us to
take you to him to be his wife."
41Abigail bowed down to the ground and
said, "I am his servant, ready to wash the feet
of his servants." 42She rose quickly and
mounted her donkey. Accompanied by her
five maids, she went with David's servants
and became his wife.
43David had married Ahinoam from
Jezreel, and now Abigail also became his
wife. 44Meanwhile, Saul had given his
daughter Michal, who had been David's
wife, to Palti son of Laish, who was from the
town of Gallim.

Study it!

David's Wives

The final verses of 1 Samuel, chapter 25, list a few of David's wives. The religious and civil laws in our country forbid polygamy, which means having more than one spouse. However, during the time of David, it was very common for men to have more than one wife. It was especially common for a ruler or military leader to have several wives. One of the reasons was to protect women. In biblical times, women had no rights and were generally considered property. An adult woman who wasn't married didn't "belong" to anyone and had no protector. We have a very different attitude toward women and marriage today.

— 1 Samuel 25:43–44

[u] **25:28** you will not do anything evil; *or* no evil will happen to you.
25:44 2 Sam 3:14–16

David Spares Saul's Life Again

26 Some men from Ziph came to Saul
at Gibeah and told him that David
was hiding on Mount Hachilah at the edge
of the Judean wilderness. 2 Saul went at once
with three thousand of the best soldiers in
Israel to the wilderness of Ziph to look for
David, 3 and camped by the road on Mount
Hachilah. David was still in the wilderness,
and when he learned that Saul had come to
look for him, 4 he sent spies and found out
that Saul was indeed there. 5 He went at once
and located the exact place where Saul and
Abner son of Ner, commander of Saul's
army, slept. Saul slept inside the camp, and
his men camped around him.

6 Then David asked Ahimelech the Hittite,
and Abishai the brother of Joab (their moth-
er was Zeruiah), "Which of you two will go
to Saul's camp with me?"

"I will," Abishai answered.

7 So that night David and Abishai entered
Saul's camp and found Saul sleeping in the
center of the camp with his spear stuck in
the ground near his head. Abner and the
troops were sleeping around him. 8 Abishai
said to David, "God has put your enemy in
your power tonight. Now let me plunge his
own spear through him and pin him to the
ground with just one blow—I won't have to
strike twice!"

9 But David said, "You must not harm
him! The LORD will certainly punish who-
ever harms his chosen king. 10 By the living
LORD," David continued, "I know that the
LORD himself will kill Saul, either when his
time comes to die a natural death or when
he dies in battle. 11 The LORD forbid that I
should try to harm the one whom the
LORD has made king! Let's take his spear
and his water jar, and go." 12 So David took
the spear and the water jar from right beside
Saul's head, and he and Abishai left. No one
saw it or knew what had happened or even
woke up—they were all sound asleep,
because the LORD had sent a heavy sleep on
them all.

13 Then David crossed over to the other
side of the valley to the top of the hill, a safe
distance away, 14 and shouted to Saul's troops
and to Abner, "Abner! Can you hear me?"

"Who is that shouting and waking up the
king?" Abner asked.

15 David answered, "Abner, aren't you the
greatest man in Israel? So why aren't you
protecting your master, the king? Just now
someone entered the camp to kill your mas-
ter. 16 You failed in your duty, Abner! I swear
by the living LORD that all of you deserve to
die, because you have not protected your
master, whom the LORD made king. Look!
Where is the king's spear? Where is the
water jar that was right by his head?"

17 Saul recognized David's voice and asked,
"David, is that you, my son?"

"Yes, Your Majesty," David answered.
18 And he added, "Why, sir, are you still pur-
suing me, your servant? What have I done?
What crime have I committed? 19 Your
Majesty, listen to what I have to say. If it is
the LORD who has turned you against me,
an offering to him will make him change his
mind; but if some people have done it, may
the LORD's curse fall on them. For they have
driven me out from the LORD's land to a
country where I can only worship foreign
gods. 20 Don't let me be killed on foreign
soil, away from the LORD. Why should the
king of Israel come to kill a flea like me?
Why should he hunt me down like a wild
bird?"

21 Saul answered, "I have done wrong.
Come back, David, my son! I will never
harm you again, because you have spared my
life tonight. I have been a fool! I have done a
terrible thing!"

22 David replied, "Here is your spear, Your
Majesty. Let one of your men come over and
get it. 23 The LORD rewards those who are
faithful and righteous. Today he put you in
my power, but I did not harm you, whom
the LORD made king. 24 Just as I have spared
your life today, may the LORD do the same
to me and free me from all troubles!"

25 Saul said to David, "God bless you, my
son! You will succeed in everything you do!"

So David went on his way, and Saul
returned home.

26:1 Ps 54 Title **26:11** 1 Sam 24:6

David among the Philistines

27 David said to himself, "One of these
days Saul will kill me. The best thing
for me to do is to escape to Philistia. Then
Saul will give up looking for me in Israel,
and I will be safe." 2So David and his six
hundred men went over at once to Achish
son of Maoch, king of Gath. 3David and his
men settled there in Gath with their fami-
lies. David had his two wives with him,
Ahinoam from Jezreel, and Abigail, Nabal's
widow, from Carmel. 4When Saul heard that
David had fled to Gath, he gave up trying to
find him.

5David said to Achish, "If you are my
friend, let me have a small town to live in.
There is no need, sir, for me to live with you
in the capital city." 6So Achish gave him the
town of Ziklag, and for this reason Ziklag
has belonged to the kings of Judah ever
since. 7David lived in Philistia for sixteen
months.

8During that time David and his men
would attack the people of Geshur, Girzi,
and Amalek, who had been living in the
region a very long time. He would raid their
land as far as Shur, all the way down to
Egypt, 9killing all the men and women and
taking the sheep, cattle, donkeys, camels, and
even the clothes. Then he would come back
to Achish, 10who would ask him, "Where
did you go on a raid this time?" and David
would tell him that he had gone to the
southern part of Judah or to the territory of
the clan of Jerahmeel or to the territory
where the Kenites lived. 11David would kill
everyone, men and women, so that no one
could go back to Gath and report what he
and his men had really done. This is what
David did the whole time he lived in Philis-
tia. 12But Achish trusted David and said to
himself, "He is hated so much by his own
people the Israelites that he will have to
serve me all his life."

28 Some time later the Philistines gath-
ered their troops to fight Israel, and
Achish said to David, "Of course you under-
stand that you and your men are to fight on
my side."

2"Of course," David answered. "I am your
servant, and you will see for yourself what I
can do."

Achish said, "Good! I will make you my
permanent bodyguard."

Saul Consults a Medium

3Now Samuel had died, and all the
Israelites had mourned for him and had
buried him in his hometown of Ramah. Saul
had forced all the fortunetellers and medi-
ums to leave Israel.

4The Philistine troops assembled and
camped near the town of Shunem; Saul
gathered the Israelites and camped at Mount
Gilboa. 5When Saul saw the Philistine army,
he was terrified, 6and so he asked the LORD
what to do. But the LORD did not answer
him at all, either by dreams or by the use of
Urim and Thummim or by prophets. 7Then
Saul ordered his officials, "Find me a woman
who is a medium, and I will go and consult
her."

"There is one in Endor," they answered.

8So Saul disguised himself; he put on dif-
ferent clothes, and after dark he went with
two of his men to see the woman. "Consult
the spirits for me and tell me what is going
to happen," he said to her. "Call up the spirit
of the man I name."

9The woman answered, "Surely you know
what King Saul has done, how he forced the
fortunetellers and mediums to leave Israel.[v]
Why, then, are you trying to trap me and get
me killed?"

10Then Saul made a sacred vow. "By the
living LORD I promise that you will not be
punished for doing this," he told her.

11"Whom shall I call up for you?" the
woman asked.

[v] **28:9** he forced . . . Israel; *or* he put to death the fortunetellers and mediums in Israel.

28:3 1 Sam 25:1 **28:3** Lev 20:27; Deut 18:10, 11 **28:6** Num 27:21 **28:11** Sir 46:20

Twice David has a chance to kill Saul; twice he takes something of Saul's to prove he was close to him. What are the two objects?

Study it!

Calling Up the Dead

In a rather frightening episode, Saul contacts a medium, that is, someone who calls people back from the dead. Saul, who is terrified of the Philistines, grows more and more desperate. He has the medium conjure up the spirit of the dead judge and prophet Samuel. This is a very serious violation of God's Law. The Israelites were supposed to trust in God, not in magic and the rituals used by people who worshiped false gods. In the end, Saul is given a message by Samuel's spirit that he and his sons would die in battle. This message hurt more than it helped because it terrified Saul.

We must avoid things like séances and Ouija boards, which supposedly allow communication with the spirits of dead people. People who get deeply involved in this get taken advantage of by con artists. They get fooled into thinking there are powers other than God. It is all a lack of trust in God's power. Our faith tells us that if we follow God's path of life, we have little to worry about when our own life ends.

— 1 Samuel 28:3–19

"Samuel," he answered.
12 When the woman saw Samuel, she
screamed and said to Saul, "Why have you
tricked me? You are King Saul!"
13 "Don't be afraid!" the king said to her.
"What do you see?"
"I see a spirit coming up from the earth,"
she answered.
14 "What does it look like?" he asked.
"It's an old man coming up," she
answered. "He is wearing a cloak."
Then Saul knew that it was Samuel, and
he bowed to the ground in respect.
15 Samuel said to Saul, "Why have you dis-
turbed me? Why did you make me come
back?"
Saul answered, "I am in great trouble! The
Philistines are at war with me, and God has
abandoned me. He doesn't answer me any
more, either by prophets or by dreams. And
so I have called you, for you to tell me what
I must do."
16 Samuel said, "Why do you call me when
the LORD has abandoned you and become
your enemy? 17 The LORD has done to you
what he told you through me: he has taken
the kingdom away from you and given it to
David instead. 18 You disobeyed the LORD's
command and did not completely destroy
the Amalekites and all they had. That is why
the LORD is doing this to you now. 19 He
will give you and Israel over to the
Philistines. Tomorrow you and your sons will
join me, and the LORD will also give the
army of Israel over to the Philistines."
20 At once Saul fell down and lay stretched
out on the ground, terrified by what Samuel
had said. He was weak, because he had not
eaten anything all day and all night. 21 The
woman went over to him and saw that he
was terrified, so she said to him, "Please, sir,
I risked my life by doing what you asked.
22 Now please do what I ask. Let me fix you
some food. You must eat so that you will be
strong enough to travel."
23 Saul refused and said he would not eat
anything. But his officers also urged him to
eat. He finally gave in, got up from the
ground, and sat on the bed. 24 The woman
quickly killed a calf which she had been fat-
tening. Then she took some flour, prepared it,

28:17 1 Sam 15:28 **28:18** 1 Sam 15:3–9

Why don't the Philistine commanders want David to fight with them against Saul?

and baked some bread without yeast. 25She set the food before Saul and his officers, and they ate it. And they left that same night.

David Is Rejected by the Philistines

29 The Philistines brought all their troops together at Aphek, while the Israelites camped at the spring in Jezreel Valley. 2The five Philistine kings marched out with their units of a hundred and of a thousand men; David and his men marched in the rear with King Achish. 3The Philistine commanders saw them and asked, "What are these Hebrews doing here?"

Achish answered, "This is David, an official of King Saul of Israel. He has been with me for quite some time now. He has done nothing I can find fault with since the day he came over to me."

4But the Philistine commanders were angry with Achish and said to him, "Send that fellow back to the town you gave him. Don't let him go into battle with us; he might turn against us during the fighting. What better way is there for him to win back his master's favor than by the death of our men? 5After all, this is David, the one about whom the women sang, as they danced, 'Saul has killed thousands, but David has killed tens of thousands.' "

6Achish called David and said to him, "I swear by the living God of Israel that you have been loyal to me; and I would be pleased to have you go with me and fight in this battle. I have not found any fault in you from the day you came over to me. But the other kings don't approve of you. 7So go back home in peace, and don't do anything that would displease them."

8David answered, "What have I done wrong, sir? If, as you say, you haven't found any fault in me since the day I started serving you, why shouldn't I go with you, my master and king, and fight your enemies?"

9"I agree," Achish replied. "I consider you as loyal as an angel of God. But the other kings have said that you can't go with us into battle. 10So then, David, tomorrow morning all of you who left Saul and came over to me will have to get up early and leave as soon as it's light."

11So David and his men started out early the following morning to go back to Philistia, and the Philistines went on to Jezreel.

The War against the Amalekites

30 Two days later David and his men arrived back at Ziklag. The Amalekites had raided southern Judah and attacked Ziklag. They had burned down the town 2and captured all the women; they had not killed anyone, but had taken everyone with them when they left. 3When David and his men arrived, they found that the town had been burned down and that their wives, sons, and daughters had been carried away. 4David and his men started crying and did not stop until they were completely exhausted. 5Even David's two wives, Ahinoam and Abigail, had been taken away.

6David was now in great trouble, because his men were all very bitter about losing their children, and they were threatening to stone him; but the LORD his God gave him courage. 7David said to the priest Abiathar son of Ahimelech, "Bring me the ephod," and Abiathar brought it to him. 8David asked the LORD, "Shall I go after those raiders? And will I catch them?"

He answered, "Go after them; you will catch them and rescue the captives."

9So David and his six hundred men started out, and when they arrived at Besor Brook, some of them stayed there. 10David continued on his way with four hundred men; the other two hundred men were too tired to cross the brook and so stayed behind. 11The men with David found a young Egyptian out in the country and brought him to David. They gave him some food and water, 12some dried figs, and two bunches of raisins. After he had eaten, his strength returned; he had not had anything to eat or drink for three full days. 13David asked him, "Who is your master, and where are you from?"

"I am an Egyptian, the slave of an Amalekite," he answered. "My master left me behind three days ago because I got sick.

29:5 1 Sam 18:7; 21:11 **30:5** 1 Sam 25:42, 43 **30:7** 1 Sam 22:20–23

14 We had raided the territory of the
Cherethites in the southern part of Judah
and the territory of the clan of Caleb, and
we burned down Ziklag."

15 "Will you lead me to those raiders?"
David asked him.

He answered, "I will if you promise me in
God's name that you will not kill me or
hand me over to my master." 16 And he led
David to them.

The raiders were scattered all over the
place, eating, drinking, and celebrating
because of the enormous amount of loot
they had captured from Philistia and Judah.
17 At dawn the next day David attacked them
and fought until evening. Except for four
hundred young men who mounted camels
and got away, none of them escaped. 18 David
rescued everyone and everything the
Amalekites had taken, including his two
wives; 19 nothing at all was missing. David
got back all his men's sons and daughters,
and all the loot the Amalekites had taken.
20 He also recovered all the flocks and herds;
his men drove all the livestock in front of
them[w] and said, "This belongs to David!"

21 Then David went back to the two hun-
dred men who had been too weak to go
with him and had stayed behind at Besor
Brook. They came forward to meet David
and his men, and David went up to them and
greeted them warmly. 22 But some mean and
worthless men who had gone with David
said, "They didn't go with us, and so we
won't give them any of the loot. They can
take their wives and children and go away."

23 But David answered, "My brothers, you
can't do this with what the LORD has given
us! He kept us safe and gave us victory over
the raiders. 24 No one can agree with what
you say! All must share alike: whoever stays
behind with the supplies gets the same share
as the one who goes into battle." 25 David
made this a rule, and it has been followed in
Israel ever since.

26 When David returned to Ziklag, he sent
part of the loot to his friends, the leaders of
Judah, with the message, "Here is a present
for you from the loot we took from the
LORD's enemies." 27 He sent it to the people
in Bethel, to the people in Ramah in the
southern part of Judah, and to the people in
the towns of Jattir, 28 Aroer, Siphmoth, Eshte-
moa, 29 and Racal; to the clan of Jerahmeel,
to the Kenites, 30 and to the people in the
towns of Hormah, Borashan, Athach, 31 and
Hebron. He sent it to all the places where he
and his men had roamed.

Live it!

Share and Share Alike

Sharing. David makes it a rule for his troops to follow. It is something we are taught and reminded of often as little children. Why is sharing so difficult? Probably because sharing goes against our culture which says to get as much as you can. God always calls us not to think of just ourselves. We have a duty to share what we have with others. If we make a practice of sharing when we are younger, as we grow older sharing becomes a habit. From something as simple as offering others a piece of gum to putting money into the collection basket each week, we are better people when we share what we have. Sharing reminds us that everything we have is really a gift from God.

- **Who has shared something with you recently?**
- **What have you shared with others?**

— 1 Samuel 30:17–25

The Death of Saul and His Sons
(I Chronicles 10:1–12)

31 The Philistines fought a battle against
the Israelites on Mount Gilboa.
Many Israelites were killed there, and the rest
of them, including King Saul and his sons,

[w] **30:20** *Probable text* his men . . . front of them; *Hebrew unclear.*

fled. [2]But the Philistines caught up with
them and killed three of Saul's sons, Jonathan,
Abinadab, and Malchishua. [3]The fighting was
heavy around Saul, and he himself was hit by
enemy arrows and badly wounded. [4]He said
to the young man carrying his weapons,
"Draw your sword and kill me, so that these
godless Philistines won't gloat over me and
kill me." But the young man was too terri-
fied to do it. So Saul took his own sword and
threw himself on it. [5]The young man saw
that Saul was dead, so he too threw himself
on his own sword and died with Saul. [6]And
that is how Saul, his three sons, and the
young man died; all of Saul's men died that
day. [7]When the Israelites on the other side of
Jezreel Valley and east of the Jordan River
heard that the Israelite army had fled and that
Saul and his sons had been killed, they aban-
doned their towns and fled. Then the
Philistines came and occupied the towns.

[8]The day after the battle the Philistines
went to plunder the corpses, and they found
the bodies of Saul and his three sons lying
on Mount Gilboa. [9]They cut off Saul's
head, stripped off his armor, and sent mes-
sengers with them throughout Philistia to
tell the good news to their idols and to their
people. [10]Then they put his weapons in the
temple of the goddess Astarte, and they
nailed his body to the wall of the city of
Beth Shan.

[11]When the people of Jabesh in Gilead
heard what the Philistines had done to Saul,
[12]the bravest men started out and marched
all night to Beth Shan. They took down the
bodies of Saul and his sons from the wall,
brought them back to Jabesh, and burned
them there. [13]Then they took the bones and
buried them under the tamarisk tree in
town, and fasted for seven days.

Study it!

A Tragic End

Saul's story is a very sad one. He and his sons meet a brutal and bloody end. What happened to this once-promising king of Israel? There are lots of answers, but the simplest is ego. Saul let his ego take over, and he forgot about God; he disobeyed, and he did not follow God's will. He spent his last days chasing after David, slaughtering priests, calling up Samuel's spirit, and finally committing suicide. His sons, including David's best friend Jonathan, are also dead.

Saul failed as king. He failed and met such a tragic end because he turned away from God. And he was too stubborn or too proud to change his ways and get off the path of destruction he was on. Let us remember that it is never too late to turn away from sin and return to God.

— 1 Samuel, chapter 31

Your Next Step

Congratulations on finishing the First Book of Samuel! Use this space to write your thoughts and questions about this book. If you are following the suggested reading plan, move ahead to the First Letter of Timothy in the New Testament. This letter is filled with advice to a Christian leader in the early Church about how to lead wisely.

The Second Book of Samuel

If you are thinking that there might be a sequel to First Samuel, you're right! First and Second Samuel were originally one book that was split into two separate books.

In the first book, Samuel, a prophet of the Lord, anoints the first two kings of Israel—Saul, who is later rejected by God because of his disobedience, and David, a shepherd boy well-known for defeating a giant with a slingshot.

In the second book, David reigns as king. Even though David is a good warrior and a successful king, he's not perfect. David commits some very serious sins and has to pay the consequences. He also has to deal with the violent death of two of his sons. David is a good example for us because he admitted his sins and remained faithful to God, no matter what.

Chap. 11

Headlines

- David Grieves for Dead Friend and King (1:1–12)
- David Named King of Israel and Judah (5:1–12)
- Sex Scandal in the Palace (chapter 11)
- Prophet Uncovers Crime, King Repents (chapter 12)
- King's Son Plans Rebellion! (15:1–12)
- King's Son Dies in Tree (18:4–18)
- David's Song Praises God's Victory (chapter 22)

FACTOIDS

Why was this book written? This book was written to tell the story of David's rise to power as the second king of Israel, his fall into sin, and his reliance on God.

What time period does it cover? About 1000 to 960 BC.

How does it fit into the Bible? This book continues the saga begun in First Samuel and covers the reign of Israel's greatest king, David.

Jesus connection: David is promised an eternal dynasty, from which Jesus will come one thousand years later (7:1–17).

Important themes

- When David sins, he admits it and asks God for forgiveness.
- Violence, jealousy, and power easily lead to a multitude of sins.
- God keeps the Covenant with his people through all of history.

2 SAMUEL

David Learns of Saul's Death

1 After Saul's death David came back
from his victory over the Amalekites
and stayed in Ziklag for two days. 2The next
day a young man arrived from Saul's camp.
To show his grief, he had torn his clothes
and put dirt on his head. He went to David
and bowed to the ground in respect. 3David
asked him, "Where have you come from?"
"I have escaped from the Israelite camp,"
he answered.
4"Tell me what happened," David said.
"Our army ran away from the battle," he
replied, "and many of our men were killed.
Saul and his son Jonathan were also killed."
5"How do you know that Saul and
Jonathan are dead?" David asked him.
6He answered, "I happened to be on
Mount Gilboa, and I saw that Saul was lean-
ing on his spear and that the chariots and
cavalry of the enemy were closing in on
him. 7Then he turned around, saw me, and
called to me. I answered, 'Yes, sir!' 8He asked
who I was, and I told him that I was an
Amalekite. 9Then he said, 'Come here and
kill me! I have been badly wounded, and I'm
about to die.' 10So I went up to him and
killed him, because I knew that he would
die anyway as soon as he fell. Then I took
the crown from his head and the bracelet
from his arm, and I have brought them to
you, sir."
11David tore his clothes in sorrow, and all
his men did the same. 12They grieved and
mourned and fasted until evening for Saul
and Jonathan and for Israel, the people of the
LORD, because so many had been killed in
battle.
13David asked the young man who had
brought him the news, "Where are you
from?"
He answered, "I'm an Amalekite, but I live
in your country."
14David asked him, "How is it that you

David tore his clothes in sorrow. (1:11)

dared kill the LORD's chosen king?" 15Then
David called one of his men and said, "Kill
him!" The man struck the Amalekite and
mortally wounded him, 16and David said to
the Amalekite, "You brought this on your-
self. You condemned yourself when you
confessed that you killed the one whom the
LORD chose to be king."

David's Lament for Saul and Jonathan

17David sang this lament for Saul and his
son Jonathan, 18and ordered it[a] to be taught
to the people of Judah. (It is recorded in *The
book of Jashar.*)

19"On the hills of Israel our leaders are dead!
The bravest of our soldiers have fallen!
20Do not announce it in Gath
or in the streets of Ashkelon.
Do not make the women of Philistia glad;
do not let the daughters of pagans
rejoice.

21"May no rain or dew fall on Gilboa's hills;
may its fields be always barren!

[a] **1:18** *One ancient translation* it; *Hebrew* the bow.
1:6–10 1 Sam 31:1–6; 1 Chr 10:1–6 **1:18** Josh 10:13

Live it!

Torn Apart

When David learned that both Saul and Jonathan were dead, he "tore his clothes in sorrow, and all his men did the same" (2 Samuel 1:11). This may strike us as a bit strange, and definitely a waste of clothing! But think for a moment about this action and what it might stand for. Many of us have experienced the loss of someone we are close to, either a family member or a close friend. Doesn't it often feel as if he or she were suddenly torn from our lives?

No matter how good someone is at sewing or patching, once a piece of clothing is ripped, it is never the same. So it is with us: when people we love die, they leave their mark on our lives, and we will never be the same. When we trust in God's goodness, the pain and grief we experience will be replaced by good memories over time. Think about someone in your life who died and how it felt when he or she was gone.

— 2 Samuel 1:1–12

For the shields of the brave lie there in disgrace;
the shield of Saul is no longer polished with oil.
22 Jonathan's bow was deadly,
the sword of Saul was merciless,
striking down the mighty, killing the enemy.

23 "Saul and Jonathan, so wonderful and dear;
together in life, together in death;
swifter than eagles, stronger than lions.

24 "Women of Israel, mourn for Saul!
He clothed you in rich scarlet dresses
and adorned you with jewels and gold.

25 "The brave soldiers have fallen,
they were killed in battle.
Jonathan lies dead in the hills.

26 "I grieve for you, my brother Jonathan;
how dear you were to me!
How wonderful was your love for me,
better even than the love of women.

27 "The brave soldiers have fallen,
their weapons abandoned and useless."

David Is Made King of Judah

2 After this, David asked the LORD, "Shall
I go and take control of one of the
towns of Judah?"
"Yes," the LORD answered.
"Which one?" David asked.
"Hebron," the LORD said. 2 So David went
to Hebron, taking with him his two wives:
Ahinoam, who was from Jezreel, and Abigail,
Nabal's widow, who was from Carmel. 3 He
also took his men and their families, and
they settled in the towns around Hebron.
4 Then the men of Judah came to Hebron
and anointed David as king of Judah.
When David heard that the people of
Jabesh in Gilead had buried Saul, 5 he sent
some men there with the message: "May the
LORD bless you for showing your loyalty to
your king by burying him. 6 And now may
the LORD be kind and faithful to you. I too
will treat you well because of what you have
done. 7 Be strong and brave! Saul your king is
dead, and the people of Judah have anointed
me as their king."

2:2 1 Sam 25:42, 43 **2:4** 1 Sam 31:11–13

Find out how long David ruled over Judah *(2 Samuel 2:11)*, **and locate Judah on Map 3 in the back of this Bible.**

Ishbosheth Is Made King of Israel

8The commander of Saul's army, Abner
son of Ner, had fled with Saul's son Ish-
bosheth across the Jordan to Mahanaim.
9There Abner made Ishbosheth king of the
territories of Gilead, Asher,[b] Jezreel, Ephraim,
and Benjamin, and indeed over all Israel.
10He was forty years old when he was made
king of Israel, and he ruled for two years.

But the tribe of Judah was loyal to David,
11and he ruled in Hebron over Judah for
seven and a half years.

War between Israel and Judah

12Abner and the officials of Ishbosheth
went from Mahanaim to the city of Gibeon.
13Joab, whose mother was Zeruiah, and
David's other officials met them at the pool,
where they all sat down, one group on one
side of the pool and the other group on the
opposite side. 14Abner said to Joab, "Let's
have some of the young men from each side
fight an armed contest."

"All right," Joab answered.

15So twelve men, representing Ishbosheth
and the tribe of Benjamin, fought twelve of
David's men. 16Each man caught his oppo-
nent by the head and plunged his sword into
his opponent's side, so that all twenty-four of
them fell down dead together. And so that
place in Gibeon is called "Field of Swords."

17Then a furious battle broke out, and
Abner and the Israelites were defeated by
David's men. 18The three sons of Zeruiah
were there: Joab, Abishai, and Asahel. Asahel,
who could run as fast as a wild deer, 19start-
ed chasing Abner, running straight for him.
20Abner looked back and said, "Is that you,
Asahel?"

"Yes," he answered.

21"Stop chasing me!" Abner said. "Run
after one of the soldiers and take what he
has." But Asahel kept on chasing him.
22Once more Abner said to him, "Stop chas-
ing me! Why force me to kill you? How
could I face your brother Joab?" 23But Asa-
hel would not quit; so Abner, with a back-
ward thrust[c] of his spear, struck him through
the stomach so that the spear came out at his
back. Asahel dropped to the ground dead,
and everyone who came to the place where
he was lying stopped and stood there.

24But Joab and Abishai started out after
Abner, and at sunset they came to the hill of
Ammah, which is to the east of Giah on the
road to the wilderness of Gibeon. 25The
men from the tribe of Benjamin gathered
around Abner again and took their stand on
the top of a hill. 26Abner called out to Joab,
"Do we have to go on fighting forever?
Can't you see that in the end there will be
nothing but bitterness? We are your relatives.
How long will it be before you order your
men to stop chasing us?"

27"I swear by the living God," Joab
answered, "that if you had not spoken, my
men would have kept on chasing you until
tomorrow morning." 28Then Joab blew the
trumpet as a signal for his men to stop pur-
suing the Israelites; and so the fighting
stopped.

29Abner and his men marched through
the Jordan Valley all that night; they crossed
the Jordan River, and after marching all the
next morning, they arrived back at
Mahanaim.

30When Joab gave up the chase, he gath-
ered all his men and found that nineteen of
them were missing, in addition to Asahel.
31David's men had killed 360 of Abner's men
from the tribe of Benjamin. 32Joab and his
men took Asahel's body and buried it in the
family tomb at Bethlehem. Then they
marched all night and at dawn arrived back
at Hebron.

3 The fighting between the forces sup-
porting Saul's family and those support-
ing David went on for a long time. As David
became stronger and stronger, his opponents
became weaker and weaker.

David's Sons

2The following six sons, in order of their
birth, were born to David at Hebron:
Amnon, whose mother was Ahinoam, from
Jezreel; 3Chileab, whose mother was Abigail,
Nabal's widow, from Carmel; Absalom, whose
mother was Maacah, the daughter of King

[b] **2:9** *One ancient translation* Asher; *Hebrew* Assyria. [c] **2:23** *Probable text* with a backward thrust; *Hebrew unclear.*

Talmai of Geshur; [4]Adonijah, whose mother
was Haggith; Shephatiah, whose mother was
Abital; [5]Ithream, whose mother was Eglah.
All of these sons were born in Hebron.

Abner Joins David

[6]As the fighting continued between
David's forces and the forces loyal to Saul's
family, Abner became more and more pow-
erful among Saul's followers.
[7]One day Ishbosheth son of Saul accused
Abner of sleeping with Saul's concubine Riz-
pah, the daughter of Aiah. [8]This made Abner
furious. "Do you think that I would betray
Saul? Do you really think I'm serving Judah?"
he exclaimed. "From the very first I have been
loyal to the cause of your father Saul, his
brothers, and his friends, and I have kept you
from being defeated by David; yet today you
find fault with me about a woman! [9-10]The
LORD promised David that he would take the
kingdom away from Saul and his descendants
and would make David king of both Israel
and Judah, from one end of the country to the
other. Now may God strike me dead if I don't
make this come true!" [11]Ishbosheth was so
afraid of Abner that he could not say a word.
[12]Abner sent messengers to David, who at
that time was at Hebron,[d] to say, "Who is
going to rule this land? Make an agreement
with me, and I will help you win all Israel
over to your side."
[13]"Good!" David answered. "I will make
an agreement with you on one condition:
you must bring Saul's daughter Michal to
me when you come to see me." [14]And
David also sent messengers to Ishbosheth to
say, "Give me back my wife Michal. I paid a
hundred Philistine foreskins in order to
marry her." [15]So Ishbosheth had her taken
from her husband Paltiel son of Laish.
[16]Paltiel followed her all the way to the
town of Bahurim, crying as he went. But
when Abner said, "Go back home," he did.
[17]Abner went to the leaders of Israel and
said to them, "For a long time you have
wanted David to be your king. [18]Now here
is your chance. Remember that the LORD
has said, 'I will use my servant David to res-
cue my people Israel from the Philistines and
from all their other enemies.' " [19]Abner
spoke also to the people of the tribe of Ben-
jamin and then went to Hebron to tell
David what the people of Benjamin and of
Israel had agreed to do.
[20]When Abner came to David at Hebron
with twenty men, David gave a feast for
them. [21]Abner told David, "I will go now
and win all Israel over to Your Majesty. They
will accept you as king, and then you will
get what you have wanted and will rule over
the whole land." David gave Abner a guaran-
tee of safety and sent him on his way.

Abner Is Murdered

[22]Later on Joab and David's other officials
returned from a raid, bringing a large
amount of loot with them. Abner, however,
was no longer there at Hebron with David,
because David had sent him away with a
guarantee of safety. [23]When Joab and his
men arrived, he was told that Abner had
come to King David and had been sent away
with a guarantee of safety. [24]So Joab went to
the king and said to him, "What have you
done? Abner came to you—why did you let
him go like that? [25]He came here to deceive
you and to find out everything you do and
everywhere you go. Surely you know that!"
[26]After leaving David, Joab sent messen-
gers to get Abner, and they brought him back
from Sirah Well; but David knew nothing
about it. [27]When Abner arrived in Hebron,
Joab took him aside at the gate, as though he
wanted to speak privately with him, and
there he stabbed him in the stomach. And so
Abner was murdered because he had killed
Joab's brother Asahel. [28]When David heard
the news, he said, "The LORD knows that my
subjects and I are completely innocent of the
murder of Abner. [29]May the punishment for
it fall on Joab and all his family! In every
generation may there be some man in his
family who has gonorrhea or a dreaded skin
disease or is fit only to do a woman's work or
is killed in battle or doesn't have enough to

[d] **3:12** *One ancient translation* at Hebron; *Hebrew* where he (Abner) was.

3:10 1 Sam 15:28 **3:14** 1 Sam 18:27

Live it!

Afflictions

David curses the descendants of Joab, asking that in every generation someone be afflicted with gonorrhea, a skin disease, weakness, death in battle, or hunger. It doesn't sound very nice but neither was Joab's sneaky killing of Abner. Jesus taught us that God doesn't punish children for their parents' sins, but it was a popular belief in Old Testament times.

You probably know that gonorrhea is a sexually transmitted disease (STD). It has been around a very long time. Keep in mind that it is transmitted almost only though sexual intercourse. Also keep in mind that if you and your future spouse follow the Church's teaching on sexuality, you should not need to worry unduly about gonorrhea or any other STD.

Make a pledge now to avoid intimate sexual activity until you get married. You might want to visit the True Love Waits Web site for more information.

— 2 Samuel 3:26–30

eat!" 30So Joab and his brother Abishai took
revenge on Abner for killing their brother
Asahel in the battle at Gibeon.

Abner Is Buried

31Then David ordered Joab and his men
to tear their clothes, wear sackcloth, and
mourn for Abner. And at the funeral King
David himself walked behind the coffin.
32Abner was buried at Hebron, and the king
wept aloud at the grave, and so did all the
people. 33David sang this lament for Abner:

"Why did Abner have to die like a fool?
34His hands were not tied,
And his feet were not bound;
He died like someone killed by
criminals!"

And the people wept for him again.
35All day long the people tried to get
David to eat something, but he made a
solemn promise, "May God strike me dead if
I eat anything before the day is over!" 36They
took note of this and were pleased. Indeed,
everything the king did pleased the people.
37All of David's people and all the people in
Israel understood that the king had no part
in the murder of Abner. 38The king said to
his officials, "Don't you realize that this day a
great leader in Israel has died? 39Even though
I am the king chosen by God, I feel weak
today. These sons of Zeruiah are too violent
for me. May the LORD punish these criminals
as they deserve!"

Ishbosheth Is Murdered

4 When Saul's son Ishbosheth heard that
Abner had been killed in Hebron, he
was afraid, and all the people of Israel were
alarmed. 2Ishbosheth had two officers who
were leaders of raiding parties, Baanah and
Rechab, sons of Rimmon, from Beeroth in
the tribe of Benjamin. (Beeroth is counted as
part of Benjamin. 3Its original inhabitants
had fled to Gittaim, where they have lived
ever since.)
4Another descendant of Saul was
Jonathan's son Mephibosheth, who was five
years old when Saul and Jonathan were
killed. When the news about their death
came from the city of Jezreel, his nurse
picked him up and fled; but she was in such
a hurry that she dropped him, and he
became crippled.

4:4 2 Sam 9:3

Mephibosheth is Jonathan's son. How did he become crippled?

5Rechab and Baanah set out for Ish-
bosheth's house and arrived there about
noon, while he was taking his midday rest.
6The woman at the door had become
drowsy while she was sifting wheat and had
fallen asleep, so Rechab and Baanah slipped
in.[e] 7Once inside, they went to Ishbosheth's
bedroom, where he was sound asleep, and
killed him. Then they cut off his head, took
it with them, and walked all night through
the Jordan Valley. 8They presented the head
to King David at Hebron and said to him,
"Here is the head of Ishbosheth, the son of
your enemy Saul, who tried to kill you.
Today the LORD has allowed Your Majesty to
take revenge on Saul and his descendants."

9David answered them, "I take a vow by
the living LORD, who has saved me from
all dangers! 10The messenger who came to
me at Ziklag and told me of Saul's death
thought he was bringing good news. I seized
him and had him put to death. That was the
reward I gave him for his good news! 11How
much worse it will be for evil men who
murder an innocent man asleep in his own
house! I will now take revenge on you for
murdering him and will wipe you off the
face of the earth!" 12David gave the order,
and his soldiers killed Rechab and Baanah
and cut off their hands and feet, which they
hung up near the pool in Hebron. They
took Ishbosheth's head and buried it in
Abner's tomb there at Hebron.

David Becomes King of Israel and Judah
(1 Chronicles 11:1–9; 14:1–7)

5 Then all the tribes of Israel went to
David at Hebron and said to him, "We
are your own flesh and blood. 2In the past,
even when Saul was still our king, you led
the people of Israel in battle, and the LORD
promised you that you would lead his people
and be their ruler." 3So all the leaders of
Israel came to King David at Hebron. He
made a sacred alliance with them, they
anointed him, and he became king of Israel.
4David was thirty years old when he became
king, and he ruled for forty years. 5He ruled
in Hebron over Judah for seven and a half
years, and in Jerusalem over all Israel and
Judah for thirty-three years.

6The time came when King David and
his men set out to attack Jerusalem. The
Jebusites, who lived there, thought that
David would not be able to conquer the
city, and so they said to him, "You will never
get in here; even the blind and the crippled
could keep you out." (7But David did cap-
ture their fortress of Zion, and it became
known as "David's City.")

8That day David said to his men, "Does
anybody here hate the Jebusites as much as I
do? Enough to kill them? Then go up
through the water tunnel and attack those
poor blind cripples." (That is why it is said,
"The blind and the crippled cannot enter
the LORD's house.")[f]

9After capturing the fortress, David lived
in it and named it "David's City." He built
the city around it, starting at the place where
land was filled in on the east side of the hill.
10He grew stronger all the time, because the
LORD God Almighty was with him.

11King Hiram of Tyre sent a trade mission
to David; he provided him with cedar logs
and with carpenters and stone masons to
build a palace. 12And so David realized that
the LORD had established him as king of
Israel and was making his kingdom prosper-
ous for the sake of his people.

13After moving from Hebron to
Jerusalem, David took more concubines and
wives, and had more sons and daughters.
14The following children were born to him
in Jerusalem: Shammua, Shobab, Nathan,
Solomon, 15Ibhar, Elishua, Nepheg, Japhia,
16Elishama, Eliada, and Eliphelet.

[e] **4:6** *Verse 6 follows one ancient translation; Hebrew* They went on into the house carrying wheat, and struck him in the belly. Then Rechab and his brother Baanah escaped. [f] **5:8** *Verse 8 in Hebrew is unclear.*

4:10 2 Sam 1:1–16 **5:4, 5** 1 Kings 2:11; 1 Chr 3:4; 29:27 **5:6** Josh 15:63; Judg 1:21

How old was David when he became king of Israel and Judah? How long was he king?

Study it!

Jerusalem, the Holy City

When David captured the city of Jerusalem from the Jebusites, it became known as David's City. When David captured it, it wasn't all that big or famous. But under David and Solomon's rule, it became the largest and most important city in Israel.

Jerusalem today continues to be a very important city. It has become a holy city for three of the world's major religions: Judaism, Christianity, and Islam. For Jews, Jerusalem contains a wall from the Great Temple built by King Herod and destroyed by the Romans in AD 70. For Christians, Jerusalem is the city where Jesus was crucified, buried, and raised from the dead. For Islam, Jerusalem is one of the three holy cities. It contains the Dome of the Rock, a mosque built over the site where all three faiths believe Abraham took his son to be sacrificed.

— 2 Samuel 5:6–9

Victory over the Philistines
(1 Chronicles 14:8–17)

17The Philistines were told that David had
been made king of Israel, so their army set out
to capture him. When David heard of it, he
went down to a fortified place. 18The Phi-
listines arrived at Rephaim Valley and occupied
it. 19David asked the LORD, "Shall I attack the
Philistines? Will you give me the victory?"

"Yes, attack!" the LORD answered. "I will
give you the victory!"

20So David went to Baal Perazim and
there he defeated the Philistines. He said,
"The LORD has broken through my enemies
like a flood." And so that place is called Baal
Perazim.[g] 21When the Philistines fled, they
left their idols behind, and David and his
men carried them away.

22Then the Philistines went back to
Rephaim Valley and occupied it again.
23Once more David consulted the LORD,
who answered, "Don't attack them from
here, but go around and get ready to attack
them from the other side, near the balsam
trees. 24When you hear the sound of march-
ing in the treetops, then attack because I will
be marching ahead of you to defeat the
Philistine army." 25David did what the LORD
had commanded, and was able to drive the
Philistines back from Geba all the way to
Gezer.

The Covenant Box Is Brought to Jerusalem
(1 Chronicles 13:1–14; 15:25 —16:6, 43)

6 Once more David called together the
best soldiers in Israel, a total of thirty
thousand men, 2and led them to Baalah[h] in
Judah, in order to bring from there God's
Covenant Box, bearing the name of the
LORD Almighty, whose throne is above the
winged creatures.[i] 3They took it from Abin-
adab's home on the hill and placed it on a
new cart. Uzzah and Ahio, sons of Abinadab,
were guiding the cart, 4with Ahio walking in
front. 5David and all the Israelites were danc-
ing and singing with all their might[j] to
honor the LORD. They were playing harps,
lyres, drums, rattles, and cymbals.

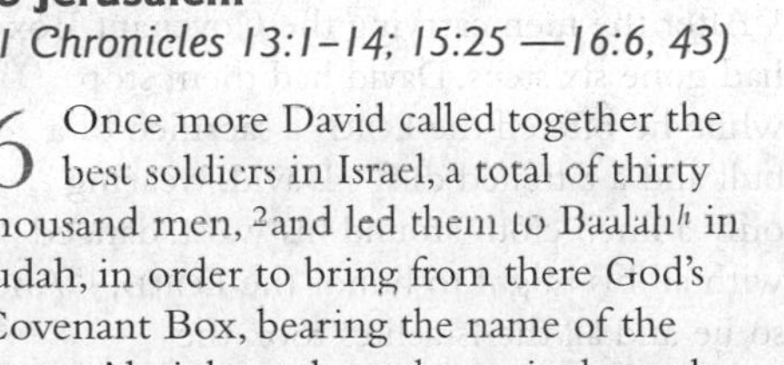

The Israelites were dancing and singing. (6:5)

[g] **5:20** BAAL PERAZIM: *This name in Hebrew means "Lord of the Breakthrough."* [h] **6:2** *Probable text (see 1 Chr 13:6)* to Baalah; *Hebrew* from Baaley, *or* from the leaders. [i] **6:2** WINGED CREATURES: *See Word List.* [j] **6:5** *One ancient translation (and see 1 Chr 13:8)* and singing with all their might; *Hebrew* with all the fir trees.

6:2 Ex 25:22 **6:3** 1 Sam 7:1, 2

6 As they came to the threshing place of
Nacon, the oxen stumbled, and Uzzah
reached out and took hold of the Covenant
Box. 7 At once the LORD God became angry
with Uzzah and killed him because of his
irreverence.[k] Uzzah died there beside the
Covenant Box, 8 and so that place has been
called Perez Uzzah[l] ever since. David was
furious because the LORD had punished
Uzzah in anger.

9 Then David was afraid of the LORD and
said, "How can I take the Covenant Box
with me now?" 10 So he decided not to take
it with him to Jerusalem; instead, he turned
off the road and took it to the house of
Obed Edom, a native of the city of Gath.
11 It stayed there three months, and the LORD
blessed Obed Edom and his family.

12 King David heard that because of the
Covenant Box the LORD had blessed Obed
Edom's family and all that he had; so he got
the Covenant Box from Obed's house to
take it to Jerusalem with a great celebration.
13 After the men carrying the Covenant Box
had gone six steps, David had them stop
while he offered the LORD a sacrifice of a
bull and a fattened calf. 14 David, wearing
only a linen cloth around his waist, danced
with all his might to honor the LORD. 15 And
so he and all the Israelites took the
Covenant Box up to Jerusalem with shouts
of joy and the sound of trumpets.

16 As the Box was being brought into the
city, Michal, Saul's daughter, looked out of the
window and saw King David dancing and
jumping around in the sacred dance, and she
was disgusted with him. 17 They brought the
Box and put it in its place in the Tent that
David had set up for it. Then he offered sacri-
fices and fellowship offerings to the LORD.
18 When he had finished offering the sacri-
fices, he blessed the people in the name of the
LORD Almighty 19 and distributed food to
them all. He gave each man and woman in
Israel a loaf of bread, a piece of roasted meat,[m]
and some raisins. Then everyone went home.

20 Afterward, when David went home to
greet his family, Michal came out to meet
him. "The king of Israel made a big name

Live it!

It's a Party!

Try to imagine the president of the United States leading a parade to the Capitol building in Washington, D.C., by dancing in his underclothes! When King David did something similar in the capital city of Jerusalem, he certainly got people's attention. He was leading the holiest object of the Jewish faith, the Covenant Box or Ark of the Covenant. It was going to its new home in the center of the city. To fully praise God, King David decided to throw a party, or festival, which he would lead. He also served everyone a meal.

One of David's wives, Michal, thought he was being a show-off, but he told her that this was the least he could do to honor God. What David did may not have seemed very kingly, but he did it out of a deep desire to show his love for God. And he wasn't the least bit embarrassed. Sometimes because religion isn't "cool," we get embarrassed when others find out that we pray or read the Bible or go to Church every Sunday.

Think of a time when you became embarrassed about your faith. What caused you to react in such a way, and how would you do it differently now? Next time you feel yourself becoming embarrassed about your faith, picture David dancing before the Lord.

— 2 Samuel 6:12–23

[k] **6:7** *Probable text* his irreverence; *Hebrew unclear.* [l] **6:8** PEREZ UZZAH: *This name in Hebrew means "Punishment of Uzzah."* [m] **6:19** a piece of roasted meat; *or* a cake of dates.

6:11 1 Chr 26:4, 5 **6:19, 20** 1 Chr 16:43

for himself today!" she said. "He exposed
himself like a fool in the sight of the servant
women of his officials!"
21 David answered, "I was dancing to honor
the LORD, who chose me instead of your
father and his family to make me the leader
of his people Israel. And I will go on dancing
to honor the LORD, 22 and will disgrace myself
even more. You[n] may think I am nothing, but
those women will think highly of me!"
23 Michal, Saul's daughter, never had any
children.

Nathan's Message to David
(1 Chronicles 17:1–15)

7 King David was settled in his palace,
and the LORD kept him safe from all his
enemies. 2 Then the king said to the prophet
Nathan, "Here I am living in a house built of
cedar, but God's Covenant Box is kept in a
tent!"
3 Nathan answered, "Do whatever you have
in mind, because the LORD is with you."
4 But that night the LORD said to Nathan,
5 "Go and tell my servant David that I say to
him, 'You are not the one to build a temple
for me to live in. 6 From the time I rescued
the people of Israel from Egypt until now, I
have never lived in a temple; I have traveled
around living in a tent. 7 In all my traveling
with the people of Israel I never asked any of
the leaders[o] that I appointed why they had
not built me a temple made of cedar.'
8 "So tell my servant David that I, the LORD
Almighty, say to him, 'I took you from looking
after sheep in the fields and made you the ruler
of my people Israel. 9 I have been with you
wherever you have gone, and I have defeated all
your enemies as you advanced. I will make you
as famous as the greatest leaders in the world.
10-11 I have chosen a place for my people Israel
and have settled them there, where they will live
without being oppressed any more. Ever since
they entered this land, they have been attacked
by violent people, but this will not happen
again. I promise to keep you safe from all your
enemies and to give you descendants. 12 When
you die and are buried with your ancestors, I
will make one of your sons king and will keep
his kingdom strong. 13 He will be the one to
build a temple for me, and I will make sure that
his dynasty continues forever. 14 I will be his
father, and he will be my son. When he does
wrong, I will punish him as a father punishes his
son. 15 But I will not withdraw my support from
him as I did from Saul, whom I removed so that
you could be king. 16 You will always have
descendants, and I will make your kingdom last
forever. Your dynasty will never end.'"
17 Nathan told David everything that God
had revealed to him.

David's Prayer of Thanksgiving
(1 Chronicles 17:16–27)

18 Then King David went into the Tent of
the LORD's presence, sat down and prayed,
"Sovereign LORD, I am not worthy of what
you have already done for me, nor is my
family. 19 Yet now you are doing even more,
Sovereign LORD; you have made promises
about my descendants in the years to come.
And you let a man see this,[p] Sovereign
LORD! 20 What more can I say to you! You
know me, your servant. 21 It was your will
and purpose to do this; you have done all
these great things in order to instruct me.
22 How great you are, Sovereign LORD!
There is none like you; we have always
known that you alone are God. 23 There is
no other nation on earth like Israel, whom
you rescued from slavery to make them your
own people. The great and wonderful things
you did for them[q] have spread your fame
throughout the world. You drove out[r] other

[n] **6:22** *One ancient translation* You; *Hebrew* I. [o] **7:7** *Probable text (see 1 Chr 17:6)* leaders; *Hebrew* tribes.
[p] **7:19** *Probable text* you let a man see this; *Hebrew* this is a law for human beings. [q] **7:23** *Probable text* them; *Hebrew* you *(plural)*. [r] **7:23** *One ancient translation (and see 1 Chr 17:21)* You drove out; *Hebrew* for your land.
7:12 Ps 89:3, 4; 132:11; Jn 7:42; Acts 2:30 **7:14** Ps 89:26, 27; 2 Cor 6:18; Heb 1:5 **7:16** Ps 89:36, 37
7:23 Deut 4:34

Notice the musical instruments used in David's time *(2 Samuel 6:5)*. **Which ones do we still use today?**

Study it!

An Eternal Kingdom

In 2 Samuel, chapter 7, Nathan gives David a very important message from God. David is promised by God that his kingdom will last forever, that David's dynasty will never end. A dynasty is the line of rulers or powerful people who are descendants of one person. What this promise, or covenant, seemed to mean was that a descendant of David would always sit on the throne of Israel.

But as we will see, there comes a time when David's descendants no longer sit on the throne. It's not that the covenant was wrong, it was just going to be fulfilled in an unexpected way. This covenant God makes with David is fulfilled in Jesus Christ. Jesus was a descendant of David. Jesus established God's kingdom on earth, a kingdom that has no end.

During Advent we hear the phrase "the root of Jesse." That refers to Jesus, who traces his ancestry back to David, the son of Jesse. David responds to this covenant with a beautiful prayer in 2 Samuel 7:18–29.

— 2 Samuel 7:12–29

nations and their gods as your people
advanced, the people whom you set free
from Egypt to be your own. 24You have
made Israel your own people forever, and
you, LORD, have become their God.

25"And now, LORD God, fulfill for all time
the promise you made about me and my
descendants, and do what you said you
would. 26Your fame will be great, and people
will forever say, 'The LORD Almighty is God
over Israel.' And you will preserve my
dynasty for all time. 27LORD Almighty, God
of Israel! I have the courage to pray this
prayer to you, because you have revealed all
this to me, your servant, and have told me
that you will make my descendants kings.

28"And now, Sovereign LORD, you are
God; you always keep your promises, and you
have made this wonderful promise to me. 29I
ask you to bless my descendants so that they
will continue to enjoy your favor. You, Sovereign LORD, have promised this, and your
blessing will rest on my descendants forever."

David's Military Victories
(1 Chronicles 18:1–17)

8 Some time later King David attacked
the Philistines again, defeated them, and
ended their control over the land.[s]

2Then he defeated the Moabites. He
made the prisoners lie down on the ground
and put two out of every three of them to
death. So the Moabites became his subjects
and paid taxes to him.

3Then he defeated the king of the Syrian
state of Zobah, Hadadezer son of Rehob, as
Hadadezer was on his way to restore his control over the territory by the upper Euphrates
River. 4David captured seventeen hundred of
his cavalry and twenty thousand of his foot
soldiers. He kept enough horses for a hundred chariots and crippled all the rest.

5When the Syrians of Damascus sent an
army to help King Hadadezer, David
attacked it and killed twenty-two thousand
men. 6Then he set up military camps in[t]
their territory, and they became his subjects
and paid taxes to him. The LORD made
David victorious everywhere. 7David captured the gold shields carried by Hadadezer's

[s] **8:1** *Probable text* over the land; *Hebrew unclear.* [t] **8:6** set up military camps in; *or* placed military commanders over.

Joram gives David presents made of what three metals? How are they connected to the Olympics today?

officials and took them to Jerusalem. 8He also took a great quantity of bronze from Betah and Berothai, cities ruled by Hadadezer.

9King Toi of Hamath heard that David had defeated all of Hadadezer's army. 10So he sent his son Joram to greet King David and congratulate him for his victory over Hadadezer, against whom Toi had fought many times. Joram took David presents made of gold, silver, and bronze. 11King David dedicated them for use in worship, along with the silver and gold he took from the nations he had conquered—12Edom, Moab, Ammon, Philistia, and Amalek—as well as part of the loot he had taken from Hadadezer.

13David became even more famous when he returned from killing eighteen thousand Edomites in Salt Valley. 14He set up military camps[u] throughout Edom, and the people there became his subjects. The LORD made David victorious everywhere.

15David ruled over all of Israel and made sure that his people were always treated fairly and justly. 16Joab, whose mother was Zeruiah, was the commander of the army; Jehoshaphat son of Ahilud was in charge of the records; 17Zadok son of Ahitub and Ahimelech son of Abiathar were priests; Seraiah was the court secretary; 18Benaiah son of Jehoiada was in charge of[v] David's bodyguards; and David's sons were priests.

David and Mephibosheth

9 One day David asked, "Is there anyone left of Saul's family? If there is, I would like to show him kindness for Jonathan's sake."

2There was a servant of Saul's family named Ziba, and he was told to go to David. "Are you Ziba?" the king asked.

"At your service, sir," he answered.

3The king asked him, "Is there anyone left of Saul's family to whom I can show loyalty and kindness, as I promised God I would?"

Ziba answered, "There is still one of Jonathan's sons. He is crippled."

4"Where is he?" the king asked.

"At the home of Machir son of Ammiel

He is crippled. (9:3)

in Lodebar," Ziba answered. 5So King David sent for him.

6When Mephibosheth, the son of Jonathan and grandson of Saul, arrived, he bowed down before David in respect. David said, "Mephibosheth," and he answered, "At your service, sir."

7"Don't be afraid," David replied. "I will be kind to you for the sake of your father Jonathan. I will give you back all the land that belonged to your grandfather Saul, and you will always be welcome at my table."

8Mephibosheth bowed again and said, "I am no better than a dead dog, sir! Why should you be so good to me?"

9Then the king called Ziba, Saul's servant, and said, "I am giving Mephibosheth, your master's grandson, everything that belonged

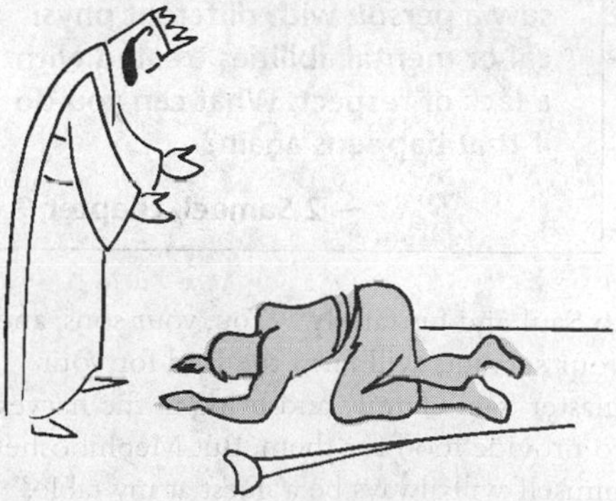

"Don't be afraid . . . I will be kind to you." (9:7)

[u] **8:14** set up military camps; *or* placed military commanders. [v] **8:18** *Some ancient translations* was in charge of; *Hebrew does not have these words.*

8:13 Ps 60 Title **9:1** 1 Sam 20:15–17 **9:3** 2 Sam 4:4

Live it!

Live Your Potential

In 2 Samuel, chapter 9, King David met the only surviving son of his best friend, Jonathan. He saw that Mephibosheth was injured in both legs. David treated him like his own son and made sure all the land taken from his family was returned. Just because Mephibosheth was injured was not a reason for him not to be treated fairly.

Today we have a variety of terms for people who have physical disabilities. The term often used to describe such persons is "differently abled." We want to emphasize the positive, that people can live full and satisfying lives even with a disability. Often in biblical times such persons were avoided because people believed that God was punishing them for their sins. Today, we know better. We understand that there are a variety of people, that everyone has different abilities, and that all people are to be treated with fairness and respect because they are created in the image of God.

Think about a time when you saw a person with different physical or mental abilities treated with a lack of respect. What can you do if that happens again?

— 2 Samuel, chapter 9

to Saul and his family. 10 You, your sons, and
your servants will farm the land for your
master Saul's family and bring in the harvest,
to provide food for them. But Mephibosheth
himself will always be a guest at my table."
(Ziba had fifteen sons and twenty servants.)
11 Ziba answered, "I will do everything
Your Majesty commands."
So Mephibosheth ate at the king's[w] table,
just like one of the king's sons. 12 Mephib-
osheth had a young son named Mica. All the
members of Ziba's family became servants of
Mephibosheth. 13 So Mephibosheth, who was
crippled in both feet, lived in Jerusalem, eat-
ing all his meals at the king's table.

David Defeats the Ammonites and the Syrians
(1 Chronicles 19:1–19)

10 Some time later King Nahash of
Ammon died, and his son Hanun
became king. 2 King David said, "I must
show loyal friendship to Hanun, as his father
Nahash did to me." So David sent messen-
gers to express his sympathy.
When they arrived in Ammon, 3 the
Ammonite leaders said to the king, "Do you
think that it is in your father's honor that
David has sent these men to express sympa-
thy to you? Of course not! He has sent them
here as spies to explore the city, so that he
can conquer us!"
4 Hanun seized David's messengers, shaved
off one side of their beards, cut off their
clothes at the hips, and sent them away.
5 They were too ashamed to return home.
When David heard about what had hap-
pened, he sent word for them to stay in Jeri-
cho and not return until their beards had
grown again.
6 The Ammonites realized that they had
made David their enemy, so they hired twen-
ty thousand Syrian soldiers from Bethrehob
and Zobah, twelve thousand men from Tob,
and the king of Maacah with a thousand
men. 7 David heard of it and sent Joab against
them with the whole army. 8 The Ammonites
marched out and took up their position at
the entrance to Rabbah, their capital city,
while the others, both the Syrians and the
men from Tob and Maacah, took up their
position in the open countryside.
9 Joab saw that the enemy troops would
attack him in front and from the rear, so he
chose the best of Israel's soldiers and put
them in position facing the Syrians. 10 He
placed the rest of his troops under the com-

[w] **9:11** *One ancient translation* the king's; *Hebrew* my.

Live it!

Cruelty

In 2 Samuel 10:3–4, we read about how Hanun, the king of Ammon, treats David's messengers. He cuts off one side of their beards and cuts off their clothes at the hips. They are too ashamed and embarrassed to return home until their beards have grown back. This is a grave insult to King David, who sent them to express his sympathy for Hanun's father, who had died.

Perhaps the actions done to David's men seem strange to us, but they were done to make fun of these men and to embarrass them and their king, David. It seems like a childish thing to do, until we think about the ways that we make fun of others, especially those we don't like. We can do it through actions that belittle others, or we can do it through words. Either way, the result is the same: we have tried to make ourselves better than someone else, while in reality we have only shown our immaturity.

Think about a time when you made fun of someone else or did something cruel to them. How do you feel about it now? How do you think it made them feel? Is it possible to make it up to them?

— 2 Samuel 10:4–5

mand of his brother Abishai, who put them
in position facing the Ammonites. [11]Joab said
to him, "If you see that the Syrians are
defeating me, come and help me, and if the
Ammonites are defeating you, I will go and
help you. [12]Be strong and courageous! Let's
fight hard for our people and for the cities of
our God. And may the LORD's will be done!"
[13]Joab and his men advanced to attack,
and the Syrians fled. [14]When the Ammonites
saw the Syrians running away, they fled from
Abishai and retreated into the city. Then Joab
turned back from fighting the Ammonites
and went back to Jerusalem.
[15]The Syrians realized that they had been
defeated by the Israelites, and so they called
all their troops together. [16]King Hadadezer
sent for the Syrians who were on the east
side of the Euphrates River, and they came
to Helam under the command of Shobach,
commander of the army of King Hadadezer
of Zobah. [17]When David heard of it, he
gathered the Israelite troops, crossed the Jordan
River, and marched to Helam, where
the Syrians took up their position facing
him. The fighting began, [18]and the Israelites
drove the Syrian army back. David and his
men killed seven hundred Syrian chariot
drivers and forty thousand cavalry, and they
wounded Shobach, the enemy commander,
who died on the battlefield. [19]When the
kings who were subject to Hadadezer realized
that they had been defeated by the
Israelites, they made peace with them and
became their subjects. And the Syrians were
afraid to help the Ammonites any more.

David and Bathsheba

11 The following spring, at the time of
the year when kings usually go to
war, David sent out Joab with his officers
and the Israelite army; they defeated the
Ammonites and besieged the city of Rabbah.
But David himself stayed in Jerusalem.
[2]One day, late in the afternoon, David got
up from his nap and went to the palace roof.
As he walked around up there, he saw a
woman taking a bath in her house. She was
very beautiful. [3]So he sent a messenger to

11:1 1 Chr 20:1

"Be strong and courageous! Let's fight hard for our people and for the cities of our God. And may the LORD's will be done!" *(2 Samuel 10:12).*

Pray it!

Facing the Truth

King David seemed to have it all. So much was going his way. But one day, he seemed to forget who he was and what God had called him to be. He saw a beautiful woman and decided he wanted her for himself. The only problem was that she happened to be married to a man named Uriah. Because the woman—named Bathsheba—became pregnant with David's child, he had her husband, Uriah, killed. Clearly, he abused his power. Nathan the prophet served as God's voice here. Through a clever story, he got David to admit his own sin. It was a powerful moment for both men. David could not undo what had been done, but he did repent and admitted that he had sinned. He didn't try to make excuses or have Nathan silenced.

David may have written Psalm 51 as a way of asking for forgiveness. You can read Psalm 51 as a prayer asking for forgiveness, too.

Be merciful to me, O God,
because of your constant love.
Because of your great mercy
wipe away my sins!
Wash away all my evil
***and make me clean from my sin!* (Psalm 51:1–2)**

— 2 Samuel, chapters 11–12

find out who she was, and learned that she
was Bathsheba, the daughter of Eliam and
the wife of Uriah the Hittite. 4David sent
messengers to get her; they brought her to
him and he made love to her. (She had just
finished her monthly ritual of purification.)
Then she went back home. 5Afterward she
discovered that she was pregnant and sent a
message to David to tell him.

6David then sent a message to Joab: "Send
me Uriah the Hittite." So Joab sent him to
David. 7When Uriah arrived, David asked
him if Joab and the troops were well, and
how the fighting was going. 8Then he said
to Uriah, "Go on home and rest a while."
Uriah left, and David had a present sent to
his home. 9But Uriah did not go home;
instead he slept at the palace gate with the
king's guards. 10When David heard that
Uriah had not gone home, he asked him,
"You have just returned after a long absence;
why didn't you go home?"

11Uriah answered, "The men of Israel and
Judah are away in battle, and the Covenant
Box is with them; my commander Joab and
his officers are camping out in the open.
How could I go home, eat and drink, and
sleep with my wife? By all that's sacred, I
swear that I could never do such a thing!"

12So David said, "Then stay here the rest
of the day, and tomorrow I'll send you
back." So Uriah stayed in Jerusalem that day
and the next. 13David invited him to supper
and got him drunk. But again that night
Uriah did not go home; instead he slept on
his blanket[x] in the palace guardroom.

[x] **11:13** blanket; *or* cot.

David wants Uriah to go home and sleep with his wife, Bathsheba. Why does David want this?

14 The next morning David wrote a letter
to Joab and sent it by Uriah. 15 He wrote: "Put
Uriah in the front line, where the fighting is
heaviest, then retreat and let him be killed."
16 So while Joab was besieging the city, he sent
Uriah to a place where he knew the enemy
was strong. 17 The enemy troops came out of
the city and fought Joab's forces; some of
David's officers were killed, and so was Uriah.

18 Then Joab sent a report to David telling
him about the battle, 19 and he instructed the
messenger, "After you have told the king all
about the battle, 20 he may get angry and ask
you, 'Why did you go so near the city to
fight them? Didn't you realize that they
would shoot arrows from the walls? 21 Don't
you remember how Abimelech son of
Gideon was killed? It was at Thebez, where a
woman threw a millstone down from the
wall and killed him. Why, then, did you go so
near the wall?' If the king asks you this, tell
him, 'Your officer Uriah was also killed.' "

22 So the messenger went to David and
told him what Joab had commanded him to
say. 23 He said, "Our enemies were stronger
than we were and came out of the city to
fight us in the open, but we drove them
back to the city gate. 24 Then they shot
arrows at us from the wall, and some of Your
Majesty's officers were killed; your officer
Uriah was also killed."

25 David said to the messenger, "Encourage
Joab and tell him not to be upset, since you
never can tell who will die in battle. Tell him
to launch a stronger attack on the city and
capture it."

26 When Bathsheba heard that her husband
had been killed, she mourned for him.
27 When the time of mourning was over,
David had her brought to the palace; she
became his wife and bore him a son. But the
LORD was not pleased with what David had
done.

Nathan's Message and David's Repentance

12 The LORD sent the prophet Nathan
to David. Nathan went to him and
said, "There were two men who lived in the
same town; one was rich and the other poor.
2 The rich man had many cattle and sheep,
3 while the poor man had only one lamb,
which he had bought. He took care of it,
and it grew up in his home with his chil-
dren. He would feed it some of his own
food, let it drink from his cup, and hold it in
his lap. The lamb was like a daughter to him.
4 One day a visitor arrived at the rich man's
home. The rich man didn't want to kill one
of his own animals to fix a meal for him;
instead, he took the poor man's lamb and
prepared a meal for his guest."

5 David became very angry at the rich
man and said, "I swear by the living LORD
that the man who did this ought to die! 6 For
having done such a cruel thing, he must pay
back four times as much as he took."

7 "You are that man," Nathan said to David.
"And this is what the LORD God of Israel
says: 'I made you king of Israel and rescued
you from Saul. 8 I gave you his kingdom and
his wives; I made you king over Israel and
Judah. If this had not been enough, I would
have given you twice as much. 9 Why, then,
have you disobeyed my commands? Why did

The rich man had many cattle and sheep. (12:2) • *The poor man had only one lamb. (12:3)*

11:21 Judg 9:53 **12:1** Ps 51 Title

He took the poor man's lamb. (12:4)

you do this evil thing? You had Uriah killed
in battle; you let the Ammonites kill him, and
then you took his wife! 10Now, in every gen-
eration some of your descendants will die a
violent death because you have disobeyed me
and have taken Uriah's wife. 11I swear to you
that I will cause someone from your own
family to bring trouble on you. You will see it
when I take your wives from you and give
them to another man; and he will have inter-
course with them in broad daylight. 12You
sinned in secret, but I will make this happen
in broad daylight for all Israel to see.' "

13"I have sinned against the LORD," David
said.

Nathan replied, "The LORD forgives you;
you will not die. 14But because you have
shown such contempt for the LORD in
doing this, your child will die." 15Then
Nathan went home.

David's Son Dies

The LORD caused the child that Uriah's
wife had borne to David to become very sick.
16David prayed to God that the child would
get well. He refused to eat anything, and every
night he went into his room and spent the
night lying on the floor. 17His court officials
went to him and tried to make him get up,
but he refused and would not eat anything
with them. 18A week later the child died, and
David's officials were afraid to tell him the
news. They said, "While the child was living,
David wouldn't answer us when we spoke to
him. How can we tell him that his child is
dead? He might do himself some harm!"

19When David noticed them whispering
to each other, he realized that the child had
died. So he asked them, "Is the child dead?"

"Yes, he is," they answered.

20David got up from the floor, took a
bath, combed his hair, and changed his
clothes. Then he went and worshiped in the
house of the LORD. When he returned to
the palace, he asked for food and ate it as
soon as it was served. 21"We don't under-
stand this," his officials said to him. "While
the child was alive, you wept for him and
would not eat; but as soon as he died, you
got up and ate!"

22"Yes," David answered, "I did fast and
weep while he was still alive. I thought that
the LORD might be merciful to me and not
let the child die. 23But now that he is dead,
why should I fast? Could I bring the child
back to life? I will some day go to where he
is, but he can never come back to me."

Solomon Is Born

24Then David comforted his wife Bathshe-
ba. He had intercourse with her, and she bore
a son, whom David named Solomon. The
LORD loved the boy 25and commanded the
prophet Nathan to name the boy Jedidiah,[y]
because the LORD loved him.

David Captures Rabbah
(1 Chronicles 20:1–3)

26Meanwhile Joab continued his cam-
paign against Rabbah, the capital city of
Ammon, and was about to capture it. 27He
sent messengers to David to report: "I have
attacked Rabbah and have captured its water

[y] **12:25** JEDIDIAH: *This name in Hebrew means "Beloved of the LORD."*
12:11, 12 2 Sam 16:22

supply. 28Now gather the rest of your forces, attack the city and take it yourself. I don't want to get the credit for capturing it." 29So David gathered his forces, went to Rabbah, attacked it, and conquered it. 30From the head of the idol of the Ammonite god Molech[z] David took a gold crown which weighed about seventy-five pounds and had a jewel in it. David took the jewel and put it in his own crown.[a] He also took a large amount of loot from the city 31and put its people to work with saws, iron hoes, and iron axes, and forced them to work at[b] making bricks. He did the same to the people of all the other towns of Ammon. Then he and his men returned to Jerusalem.

Amnon and Tamar

13 David's son Absalom had a beautiful unmarried sister named Tamar. Amnon, another of David's sons, fell in love with her. 2He was so much in love with her that he became sick, because it seemed impossible for him to have her; as a virgin, she was kept from meeting men. 3But he had a friend, a very shrewd man named Jonadab, the son of David's brother Shammah. 4Jonadab said to Amnon, "You are the king's son, yet day after day I see you looking sad. What's the matter?"

"I'm in love with Tamar, the sister of my half brother Absalom," he answered.

5Jonadab said to him, "Pretend that you are sick and go to bed. When your father comes to see you, say to him, 'Please ask my sister Tamar to come and feed me. I want her to fix the food here where I can see her, and then serve it to me herself.' " 6So Amnon pretended that he was sick and went to bed.

King David went to see him, and Amnon said to him, "Please let Tamar come and make a few cakes here where I can see her, and then serve them to me herself."

7So David sent word to Tamar in the palace: "Go to Amnon's house and fix him some food." 8She went there and found him in bed. She took some dough, prepared it, and made some cakes there where he could see her. Then she baked the cakes 9and

Live it!

Tell Someone!

In the beginning of 2 Samuel, chapter 13, we read about a horrible event: David's oldest son, Amnon, rapes his half sister, Tamar. It may surprise us to read that people in the Bible do such things, but it reminds us that biblical people are human beings like us. And often human beings do cruel things to one another. When bad things happen within families, it is especially difficult because family members are supposed to look out for one another. What Amnon did to Tamar is a sin and a crime. His actions also tore David's family apart.

Today we would counsel Tamar to tell someone about what happened and to make sure that she receives the care she needs. Amnon would be arrested for his crime to his sister.

If you or someone you know is ever the victim of sexual abuse, whether the perpetrator is a family member or someone else, make sure to let someone know about it. Tell a trusted adult outside the family—a teacher or a counselor perhaps. The abused person's welfare is more important than someone's reputation.

— 2 Samuel 13:1–21

[z] **12:30** idol of the Ammonite god Molech; *or* Ammonite king. [a] **12:30** jewel . . . crown; *or* crown and put it on his own head. [b] **12:31** *Probable text (see 1 Chr 20:3)* work at; *Hebrew* pass through.

Look back at Nathan's prophecy to David in 2 Samuel 12:10. How is it fulfilled in chapter 13?

emptied them out of the pan for him to eat,
but he wouldn't. He said, "Send everyone
away"—and they all left. 10 Then he said to
her, "Bring the cakes here to my bed and
serve them to me yourself." She took the
cakes and went over to him. 11 As she offered
them to him, he grabbed her and said,
"Come to bed with me!"

12 "No," she said. "Don't force me to do
such a degrading thing! That's awful! 13 How
could I ever hold up my head in public
again? And you—you would be completely
disgraced in Israel. Please, speak to the king,
and I'm sure that he will give me to you."
14 But he would not listen to her; and since
he was stronger than she was, he overpow-
ered her and raped her.

15 Then Amnon was filled with a deep
hatred for her; he hated her now even more
than he had loved her before. He said to her,
"Get out!"

16 "No," she answered. "To send me away
like this is a greater crime[c] than what you
just did!"

But Amnon would not listen to her; 17 he
called in his personal servant and said, "Get
this woman out of my sight! Throw her out
and lock the door!" 18 The servant put her
out and locked the door.

Tamar was wearing a long robe with full
sleeves,[d] the usual clothing for an unmarried
princess in those days.[e] 19 She sprinkled ashes
on her head, tore her robe, and with her face
buried in her hands went away crying.
20 When her brother Absalom saw her, he
asked, "Has Amnon molested you? Please,
sister, don't let it upset you so much. He is
your half brother, so don't tell anyone about
it." So Tamar lived in Absalom's house, sad
and lonely.

21 When King David heard what had hap-
pened, he was furious. 22 And Absalom hated
Amnon so much for having raped his sister
Tamar that he would no longer even speak
to him.

Absalom's Revenge

23 Two years later Absalom was having his
sheep sheared at Baal Hazor, near the town
of Ephraim, and he invited all the king's sons
to be there. 24 He went to King David and
said, "Your Majesty, I am having my sheep
sheared. Will you and your officials come
and take part in the festivities?"

25 "No, my son," the king answered. "It
would be too much trouble for you if we
all went." Absalom insisted, but the king
would not give in, and he asked Absalom to
leave.

26 But Absalom said, "Well, then, will you
at least let my brother Amnon come?"

"Why should he?" the king asked. 27 But
Absalom kept on insisting until David finally
let Amnon and all his other sons go with
Absalom.

Absalom prepared a banquet fit for a king[f]
28 and instructed his servants: "Notice when
Amnon has had too much to drink, and
then when I give the order, kill him. Don't
be afraid. I will take the responsibility
myself. Be brave and don't hesitate!" 29 So the
servants followed Absalom's instructions and
killed Amnon. All the rest of David's sons
mounted their mules and fled.

30 While they were on their way home,
David was told: "Absalom has killed all your
sons—not one of them is left!" 31 The king
stood up, tore his clothes in sorrow, and
threw himself to the ground. The servants
who were there with him tore their clothes
also. 32 But Jonadab, the son of David's broth-
er Shammah, said, "Your Majesty, they
haven't killed all your sons. Only Amnon is
dead. You could tell by looking at Absalom
that he had made up his mind to do this
from the time that Amnon raped his sister
Tamar. 33 So don't believe the news that all
your sons are dead; only Amnon was killed."

34 In the meantime Absalom had fled.

Just then the soldier on sentry duty saw a
large crowd coming down the hill on the

[c] **13:16** *Probable text* To send me . . . crime; *Hebrew unclear.* [d] **13:18** long robe with full sleeves; *or* decorated robe *(see Gen 37:3).* [e] **13:18** *Probable text* in those days; *Hebrew* garments. [f] **13:27** *Some ancient translations* Absalom prepared a banquet fit for a king; *Hebrew does not have these words.*

The sexual abuse and family violence in the story of Amnon, Tamar, and Absalom still happens today. Say a prayer for the victims of abuse.

"Those are your sons coming." (13:35)

road from Horonaim.[g] He went to the king
and reported what he had seen.[h] 35Jonadab
said to David, "Those are your sons coming,
just as I said they would." 36As soon as he
finished saying this, David's sons came in;
they started crying, and David and his offi-
cials also cried bitterly.
37-38Absalom fled and went to the king of
Geshur, Talmai son of Ammihud, and stayed
there three years. David mourned a long
time for his son Amnon; 39but when he got
over Amnon's death, he was filled with long-
ing for his son Absalom.

Joab Arranges for Absalom's Return

14 Joab knew that King David missed
Absalom very much, 2so he sent for
a clever woman who lived in Tekoa. When
she arrived, he said to her, "Pretend that you
are in mourning; put on your mourning
clothes, and don't comb your hair. Act like a
woman who has been in mourning for a
long time. 3Then go to the king and say to
him what I tell you to say." Then Joab told
her what to say.
4The woman went to the king, bowed
down to the ground in respect, and said,
"Help me, Your Majesty!"
5"What do you want?" he asked her.
"I am a poor widow, sir," she answered.

Live it!

Fathers and Sons

No matter how much parents and children love one another, there will come times when they won't get along. It happens in every family. Even the great King David had difficulties with his son Absalom, big ones. Absalom had killed his half brother, Amnon, because Amnon had raped Absalom's sister Tamar. Talk about your family troubles! Eventually David and Absalom were reconciled, but the struggles continued.

In some families, certain family members or relatives do not talk to one another. This may have gone on for years. As hard as it is sometimes, we have to be willing to do two things with our parents or guardians and siblings: show them the respect and love they deserve and always try to make things right. We shouldn't leave the house or go to our room at the end of the day angry with a family member. Try to reconcile. Take the first step if you need to. Family is just too important a part of our lives for us to stay mad at one another.

Is there someone in your family you need to be reconciled with? What's keeping you from doing it? Ask God for help.

— 2 Samuel, chapter 14

"My husband is dead. 6Sir, I had two sons,
and one day they got into a quarrel out in
the fields, where there was no one to sepa-
rate them, and one of them killed the other.
7And now, sir, all my relatives have turned

[g] **13:34** *Probable text* from Horonaim; *Hebrew* behind him. [h] **13:34** *One ancient translation* He went . . . had seen; *Hebrew does not have these words.*

13:37 2 Sam 3:3

against me and are demanding that I hand
my son over to them, so that they can kill
him for murdering his brother. If they do
this, I will be left without a son. They will
destroy my last hope and leave my husband
without a son to keep his name alive."
8"Go back home," the king answered,
"and I will take care of the matter."
9"Your Majesty," she said, "whatever you
do, my family and I will take the blame; you
and the royal family are innocent."
10The king replied, "If anyone threatens
you, bring him to me, and he will never
bother you again."
11She said, "Your Majesty, please pray to
the LORD your God, so that my relative who
is responsible for avenging the death of my
son will not commit a greater crime by
killing my other son."
"I promise by the living LORD," David
replied, "that your son will not be harmed in
the least."
12"Please, Your Majesty, let me say just one
more thing," the woman said.
"All right," he answered.
13She said to him, "Why have you done
such a wrong to God's people? You have not
allowed your own son to return from exile,
and so you have condemned yourself by
what you have just said. 14We will all die; we
are like water spilled on the ground, which
can't be gathered again. Even God does not
bring the dead back to life, but the king can
at least find a way to bring a man back from
exile.[i] 15Now, Your Majesty, the reason I have
come to speak to you is that the people
threatened me, and so I said to myself that I
would speak to you in the hope that you
would do what I ask. 16I thought you would
listen to me and save me from the one who
is trying to kill my son and me and so
remove us from the land God gave his peo-
ple. 17I said to myself that your promise, sir,
would make me safe, because the king is like
God's angel and can distinguish good from
evil.[j] May the LORD your God be with you!"
18The king answered, "I'm going to ask
you a question, and you must tell me the
whole truth."
"Ask me anything, Your Majesty," she
answered.
19"Did Joab put you up to this?" he asked
her.
She answered, "I swear by all that is
sacred, Your Majesty, that there is no way to
avoid answering your question.[k] It was
indeed your officer Joab who told me what
to do and what to say. 20But he did it in
order to straighten out this whole matter.
Your Majesty is as wise as the angel of God
and knows everything that happens."
21Later on the king said to Joab, "I have
decided to do what you want. Go and get
the young man Absalom and bring him back
here."
22Joab threw himself to the ground in
front of David in respect, and said, "God
bless you, Your Majesty! Now I know that
you are pleased with me, because you have
granted my request." 23Then he got up and
went to Geshur and brought Absalom back
to Jerusalem. 24The king, however, gave
orders that Absalom should not live in the
palace. "I don't want to see him," the king
said. So Absalom lived in his own house and
did not appear before the king.

Absalom Is Reconciled to David

25There was no one in Israel as famous for
his good looks as Absalom; he had no defect
from head to toe. 26His hair was very thick,
and he had to cut it once a year, when it
grew too long and heavy. It would weigh
about five pounds according to the royal
standard of weights. 27Absalom had three
sons and one daughter named Tamar, a very
beautiful woman.
28Absalom lived two years in Jerusalem
without seeing the king. 29Then he sent for
Joab, to ask him to go to the king for him;
but Joab would not come. Again Absalom
sent for him, and again Joab refused to
come. 30So Absalom said to his servants,
"Look, Joab's field is next to mine, and it has
barley growing in it. Go and set fire to it."
So they went and set the field on fire.
31Joab went to Absalom's house and

[i] **14:14** *Probable text* Even God . . . from exile; *Hebrew unclear.* [j] **14:17** can distinguish good from evil; *or* knows everything. [k] **14:19** there is . . . question; *or* you are absolutely right.

14:17 2 Sam 19:27

demanded, "Why did your servants set fire to
my field?"
32 Absalom answered, "Because you
wouldn't come when I sent for you. I wanted
you to go to the king and ask for me: 'Why
did I leave Geshur and come here? It would
have been better for me to have stayed
there.' " And Absalom went on, "I want you
to arrange for me to see the king, and if I'm
guilty, then let him put me to death."
33 So Joab went to King David and told
him what Absalom had said. The king sent
for Absalom, who went to him and bowed
down to the ground in front of him. The
king welcomed him with a kiss.

Absalom Plans Rebellion

15 After this, Absalom provided a chari-
ot and horses for himself, and an
escort of fifty men. 2 He would get up early
and go and stand by the road at the city gate.
Whenever someone came there with a dis-
pute that he wanted the king to settle, Absa-
lom would call him over and ask him where
he was from. And after the man had told
him what tribe he was from, 3 Absalom
would say, "Look, the law is on your side, but
there is no representative of the king to hear
your case." 4 And he would add, "How I wish
I were a judge! Then anyone who had a dis-
pute or a claim could come to me, and I
would give him justice." 5 When the man
would approach Absalom to bow down
before him, Absalom would reach out, take
hold of him, and kiss him. 6 Absalom did this
with every Israelite who came to the king
for judgment, and so he won their loyalty.
7 After four[l] years Absalom said to King
David, "Sir, let me go to Hebron and keep a
promise I made to the LORD. 8 While I was
living in Geshur in Syria, I promised the
LORD that if he would take me back to
Jerusalem, I would worship him in Hebron."[m]
9 "Go in peace," the king said. So Absalom
went to Hebron. 10 But he sent messengers

Absalom would . . . take hold of him . . . and kiss him. (15:5)

to all the tribes of Israel to say, "When you
hear the sound of trumpets, shout, 'Absalom
has become king at Hebron!' " 11 There were
two hundred men who at Absalom's invita-
tion had gone from Jerusalem with him;
they knew nothing of the plot and went in
all good faith. 12 And while he was offering
sacrifices, Absalom also sent to the town of
Gilo for Ahithophel, who was one of King
David's advisers. The plot against the king
gained strength, and Absalom's followers
grew in number.

David Flees from Jerusalem

13 A messenger reported to David, "The
Israelites are pledging their loyalty to Absa-
lom."
14 So David said to all his officials who were
with him in Jerusalem, "We must get away at
once if we want to escape from Absalom!
Hurry! Or else he will soon be here and
defeat us and kill everyone in the city!"
15 "Yes, Your Majesty," they answered. "We
are ready to do whatever you say." 16 So the
king left, accompanied by all his family and
officials, except for ten concubines, whom
he left behind to take care of the palace.
17 As the king and all his men were leaving
the city, they stopped at the last house. 18 All

[l] **15:7** *Some ancient translations* four; *Hebrew* forty. [m] **15:8** *One ancient translation* in Hebron; *Hebrew does not have these words.*

How did Absalom get Joab's attention when Joab was ignoring him?

So the king left, accompanied by all his family. (15:16)

his officials stood[n] next to him as the royal
bodyguards passed by in front of him. The
six hundred soldiers who had followed him
from Gath also passed by, 19and the king said
to Ittai, their leader, "Why are you going
with us? Go back and stay with the new
king. You are a foreigner, a refugee away
from your own country. 20You have lived
here only a short time, so why should I
make you wander around with me? I don't
even know where I'm going. Go back and
take all your people with you—and may the
LORD be kind and faithful to you."[o]

21But Ittai answered, "Your Majesty, I
swear to you in the LORD's name that I will
always go with you wherever you go, even if
it means death."

22"Fine!" David answered. "March on!" So
Ittai went on with all his men and their
dependents. 23The people cried loudly as
David's followers left. The king crossed Kidron
Brook, followed by his men, and together they
went out toward the wilderness.

24Zadok the priest was there, and with him
were the Levites, carrying the sacred Covenant
Box. They set it down[p] and didn't pick it up
again until all the people had left the city. The
priest Abiathar was there too.[q] 25Then the
king said to Zadok, "Take the Covenant Box
back to the city. If the LORD is pleased with
me, some day he will let me come back to see
it and the place where it stays. 26But if he isn't
pleased with me—well, then, let him do to me
what he wishes." 27And he went on to say to
Zadok, "Look,[r] take your son Ahimaaz and
Abiathar's son Jonathan and go back to the
city in peace. 28Meanwhile, I will wait at the
river crossings in the wilderness until I receive
news from you." 29So Zadok and Abiathar
took the Covenant Box back into Jerusalem
and stayed there.

30David went on up the Mount of Olives
crying; he was barefoot and had his head cov-
ered as a sign of grief. All who followed him
covered their heads and cried also. 31When
David was told[s] that Ahithophel had joined
Absalom's rebellion, he prayed, "Please, LORD,
turn Ahithophel's advice into nonsense!"

32When David reached the top of the hill,
where there was a place of worship, his trust-
ed friend Hushai the Archite met him with
his clothes torn and with dirt on his head.
33David said to him, "You will be of no help
to me if you come with me, 34but you can
help me by returning to the city and telling
Absalom that you will now serve him as
faithfully as you served his father. And do all
you can to oppose any advice that Ahith-
ophel gives. 35The priests Zadok and Abi-
athar will be there; tell them everything you

David went on up the Mount of Olives crying. (15:30)

[n] **15:18** *Probable text* stood; *Hebrew* passed. [o] **15:20** *One ancient translation* and may the LORD be kind and faithful to you; *Hebrew* kindness and faithfulness. [p] **15:24** *Probable text* set it down; *Hebrew* poured it out. [q] **15:24** *Probable text* was there too; *Hebrew* went up. [r] **15:27** *Some ancient translations* Look; *Hebrew* Are you the seer? [s] **15:31** *One ancient translation* was told; *Hebrew* told.

Did Mephibosheth really betray David as his servant Ziba says he did? Check out 2 Samuel 19:24–30 for Mephibosheth's side of the story.

hear in the king's palace. 36They have their
sons Ahimaaz and Jonathan with them, and
you can send them to me with all the infor-
mation you gather."
37So Hushai, David's friend, returned to
the city just as Absalom was arriving.

David and Ziba

16 When David had gone a little
beyond the top of the hill, he was
suddenly met by Ziba, the servant of
Mephibosheth, who had with him a couple
of donkeys loaded with two hundred loaves
of bread, a hundred bunches of raisins, a
hundred bunches of fresh fruit, and a leather
bag full of wine. 2King David asked him,
"What are you going to do with all that?"
Ziba answered, "The donkeys are for Your
Majesty's family to ride, the bread and the
fruit are for the men to eat, and the wine is
for them to drink when they get tired in the
wilderness."
3"Where is Mephibosheth, the grandson
of your master Saul?" the king asked him.
"He is staying in Jerusalem," Ziba
answered, "because he is convinced that the
Israelites will now restore to him the king-
dom of his grandfather Saul."
4The king said to Ziba, "Everything that
belonged to Mephibosheth is yours."
"I am your servant," Ziba replied. "May I
always please Your Majesty!"

David and Shimei

5When King David arrived at Bahurim,
one of Saul's relatives, Shimei son of Gera,
came out to meet him, cursing him as he
came. 6Shimei started throwing stones at
David and his officials, even though David was
surrounded by his men and his bodyguards.
7Shimei cursed him and said, "Get out! Get
out! Murderer! Criminal! 8You took Saul's
kingdom, and now the LORD is punishing you
for murdering so many of Saul's family. The
LORD has given the kingdom to your son
Absalom, and you are ruined, you murderer!"
9Abishai, whose mother was Zeruiah, said
to the king, "Your Majesty, why do you let
this dog curse you? Let me go over there
and cut off his head!"
10"This is none of your business," the king
said to Abishai and his brother Joab. "If he
curses me because the LORD told him to, who
has the right to ask why he does it?" 11And
David said to Abishai and to all his officials,
"My own son is trying to kill me; so why
should you be surprised at this Benjaminite?
The LORD told him to curse; so leave him
alone and let him do it. 12Perhaps the LORD
will notice my misery[t] and give me some
blessings to take the place of his curse." 13So
David and his men continued along the road.
Shimei kept up with them, walking on the
hillside; he was cursing and throwing stones
and dirt at them as he went. 14The king and
all his men were worn out when they reached
the Jordan,[u] and there they rested.

Shimei kept up with them, . . . cursing and throwing stones. (16:13)

Absalom in Jerusalem

15Absalom and all the Israelites with him
entered Jerusalem, and Ahithophel was with
them. 16When Hushai, David's trusted
friend, met Absalom, he shouted, "Long live
the king! Long live the king!"
17"What has happened to your loyalty to
your friend David?" Absalom asked him.
"Why didn't you go with him?"
18Hushai answered, "How could I? I am
for the one chosen by the LORD, by these
people, and by all the Israelites. I will stay
with you. 19After all, whom should I serve, if

[t] **16:12** *Some ancient translations* misery; *Hebrew* wickedness. [u] **16:14** *One ancient translation* the Jordan; *Hebrew does not have these words.*

16:1 2 Sam 9:9, 10 **16:3** 2 Sam 19:25–27

not my master's son? As I served your father,
so now I will serve you."

20 Then Absalom turned to Ahithophel
and said, "Now that we are here, what do
you advise us to do?"

21 Ahithophel answered, "Go and have
intercourse with your father's concubines
whom he left behind to take care of the
palace. Then everyone in Israel will know
that your father regards you as his enemy,
and your followers will be greatly encour-
aged." 22 So they set up a tent for Absalom
on the palace roof, and in the sight of every-
one Absalom went in and had intercourse
with his father's concubines.

23 Any advice that Ahithophel gave in
those days was accepted as though it were
the very word of God; both David and Absa-
lom followed it.

Hushai Misleads Absalom

17 Not long after that, Ahithophel said
to Absalom, "Let me choose twelve
thousand men, and tonight I will set out after
David. 2 I will attack him while he is tired and
discouraged. He will be frightened, and all his
men will run away. I will kill only the king
3 and then bring back all his men to you, like
a bride returning to her husband. You want to
kill only one man;[v] the rest of the people will
be safe." 4 This seemed like good advice to
Absalom and all the Israelite leaders.

5 Absalom said, "Now call Hushai, and let
us hear what he has to say." 6 When Hushai
arrived, Absalom said to him, "This is the
advice that Ahithophel has given us; shall we
follow it? If not, you tell us what to do."

7 Hushai answered, "The advice Ahithophel
gave you this time is no good. 8 You know that
your father David and his men are hard fight-
ers and that they are as fierce as a mother bear
robbed of her cubs. Your father is an experi-
enced soldier and does not stay with his men
at night. 9 Right now he is probably hiding in a
cave or some other place. As soon as David
attacks your men, whoever hears about it will
say that your men have been defeated. 10 Then
even the bravest men, as fearless as lions, will be
afraid because everyone in Israel knows that
your father is a great soldier and that his men
are hard fighters. 11 My advice is that you bring
all the Israelites together from one end of the
country to the other, as many as the grains of
sand on the seashore, and that you lead them
personally in battle. 12 We will find David
wherever he is, and attack him before he
knows what's happening. Neither he nor any
of his men will survive. 13 If he retreats into a
city, our people will all bring ropes and just
pull the city[w] into the valley below. Not a sin-
gle stone will be left there on top of the hill."

14 Absalom and all the Israelites said,
"Hushai's advice is better than Ahithophel's."
The LORD had decided that Ahithophel's
good advice would not be followed, so that
disaster would come on Absalom.

David Is Warned and Escapes

15 Then Hushai told the priests Zadok and
Abiathar what advice he had given to Absa-
lom and the Israelite leaders and what advice
Ahithophel had given. 16 Hushai added,
"Quick, now! Send a message to David not
to spend the night at the river crossings in
the wilderness, but to cross the Jordan at
once, so that he and his men won't all be
caught and killed."

17 Abiathar's son Jonathan and Zadok's son
Ahimaaz were waiting at the spring of Enro-
gel, on the outskirts of Jerusalem, because they
did not dare be seen entering the city. A ser-
vant woman would regularly go and tell them
what was happening, and then they would go
and tell King David. 18 But one day a boy hap-
pened to see them, and he told Absalom; so
they hurried off to hide in the house of a cer-
tain man in Bahurim. He had a well near his
house, and they got down in it. 19 The man's
wife took a covering, spread it over the open-
ing of the well and scattered grain over it, so
that no one would notice anything. 20 Absa-
lom's officials came to the house and asked the
woman, "Where are Ahimaaz and Jonathan?"

"They crossed the river," she answered.

The men looked for them but could not
find them, and so they returned to Jerusalem.

[v] **17:3** *One ancient translation* like a bride . . . only one man; *Hebrew* like the return of the whole, so is the man you seek. [w] **17:13** *Some ancient translations* the city; *Hebrew* him.

16:22 2 Sam 12:11, 12

21 After they left, Ahimaaz and Jonathan came
up out of the well and went and reported to
King David. They told him what Ahithophel
had planned against him and said, "Hurry up
and cross the river." 22 So David and his men
started crossing the Jordan, and by daybreak
they had all gone across.
23 When Ahithophel saw that his advice
had not been followed, he saddled his don-
key and went back to his hometown. After
putting his affairs in order, he hanged him-
self. He was buried in the family grave.
24 David had reached the town of
Mahanaim by the time Absalom and the
Israelites had crossed the Jordan. (25 Absalom
had put Amasa in command of the army in
the place of Joab. Amasa was the son of
Jether the Ishmaelite;[x] his mother was Abi-
gail, the daughter of Nahash and the sister of
Joab's mother Zeruiah.) 26 Absalom and his
men camped in the land of Gilead.
27 When David arrived at Mahanaim, he
was met by Shobi son of Nahash, from the
city of Rabbah in Ammon, and by Machir
son of Ammiel, from Lodebar, and by Barzil-
lai, from Rogelim in Gilead. 28-29 They
brought bowls, clay pots, and bedding, and
also food for David and his men: wheat, bar-
ley, meal, roasted grain, beans, peas,[y] honey,
cheese, cream, and some sheep. They knew
that David and his men would get hungry,
thirsty, and tired in the wilderness.

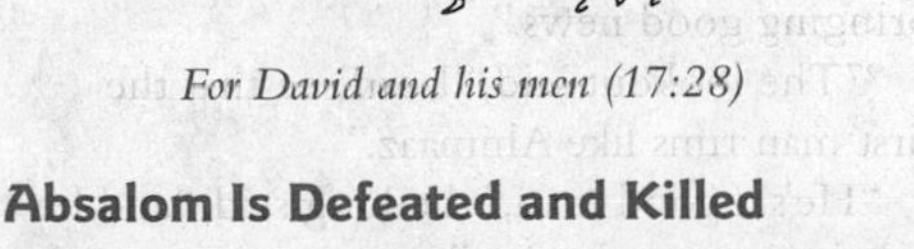

For David and his men (17:28)

Absalom Is Defeated and Killed

18 King David brought all his men
together, divided them into units of
a thousand and of a hundred, and placed
officers in command of them. 2 Then he sent
them out in three groups, with Joab and
Joab's brother Abishai and Ittai from Gath,
each in command of a group. And the king
said to his men, "I will go with you myself."
3 "You mustn't go with us," they answered.
"It won't make any difference to the enemy
if the rest of us turn and run, or even if half
of us are killed; but you are worth ten thou-
sand of us. It will be better if you stay here
in the city and send us help."
4 "I will do whatever you think best," the
king answered. Then he stood by the side of
the gate as his men marched out in units of a
thousand and of a hundred. 5 He gave orders
to Joab, Abishai, and Ittai: "For my sake don't
harm the young man Absalom." And all the
troops heard David give this command to his
officers.

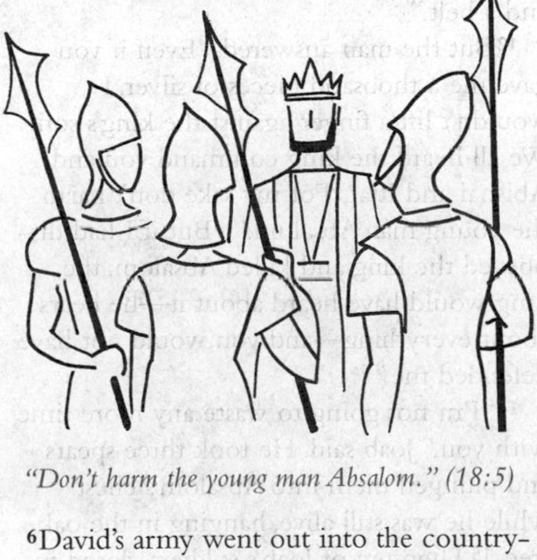

"Don't harm the young man Absalom." (18:5)

6 David's army went out into the country-
side and fought the Israelites in Ephraim For-
est. 7 The Israelites were defeated by David's
men; it was a terrible defeat, with twenty
thousand men killed that day. 8 The fighting
spread over the countryside, and more men
died in the forest than were killed in battle.
9 Suddenly Absalom met some of David's
men. Absalom was riding a mule, and as it
went under a large oak tree, Absalom's head

[x] **17:25** *One ancient translation (and see 1 Chr 2:17)* Ishmaelite; *Hebrew* Israelite. [y] **17:28-29** *Some ancient translations* peas; *Hebrew* peas and roasted grain.

Where did Abiathar and Zadok's sons hide, and why weren't they seen?

Absalom's head got caught in the branches. (18:9)

got caught in the branches. The mule ran on and Absalom was left hanging in midair. 10 One of David's men saw him and reported to Joab, "Sir, I saw Absalom hanging in an oak tree!"

11 Joab answered, "If you saw him, why didn't you kill him on the spot? I myself would have given you ten pieces of silver and a belt."

12 But the man answered, "Even if you gave me a thousand pieces of silver, I wouldn't lift a finger against the king's son. We all heard the king command you and Abishai and Ittai, 'For my sake don't harm the young man Absalom.' 13 But if I had disobeyed the king and killed Absalom, the king would have heard about it—he hears about everything—and you would not have defended me."

14 "I'm not going to waste any more time with you," Joab said. He took three spears and plunged them into Absalom's chest while he was still alive, hanging in the oak tree. 15 Then ten of Joab's soldiers closed in on Absalom and finished killing him.

16 Joab had the trumpet blown to stop the fighting, and his troops came back from pursuing the Israelites. 17 They took Absalom's body, threw it into a deep pit in the forest, and covered it with a huge pile of stones. All the Israelites fled to their own hometowns.

18 During his lifetime Absalom had built a monument for himself in King's Valley, because he had no son to keep his name alive. So he named it after himself, and to this day it is known as Absalom's Monument.

David Is Told of Absalom's Death

19 Then Ahimaaz son of Zadok said to Joab, "Let me run to the king with the good news that the LORD has saved him from his enemies."

20 "No," Joab said, "today you will not take any good news. Some other day you may do so, but not today, for the king's son is dead." 21 Then he said to his Ethiopian[z] slave, "Go and tell the king what you have seen." The slave bowed and ran off.

22 Ahimaaz insisted, "I don't care what happens; please let me take the news also."

"Why do you want to do it, my son?" Joab asked. "You will get no reward for it."

23 "Whatever happens," Ahimaaz said again, "I want to go."

"Then go," Joab said. So Ahimaaz ran off down the road through the Jordan Valley, and soon he passed the slave.

24 David was sitting in the space between the inner and outer gates of the city. The lookout went up to the top of the wall and stood on the roof of the gateway; he looked out and saw a man running alone. 25 He called down and told the king, and the king said, "If he is alone, he is bringing good news." The runner kept coming closer.

26 Then the lookout saw another man running alone, and he called down to the gatekeeper, "Look! There's another man running!"

The king answered, "This one also is bringing good news."

27 The lookout said, "I can see that the first man runs like Ahimaaz."

"He's a good man," the king said, "and he is bringing good news."

28 Ahimaaz called out a greeting to the king, threw himself down to the ground

[z] **18:21** *Hebrew* Cushite: *Cush is the ancient name of the extensive territory south of the First Cataract of the Nile River. This region was called Ethiopia in Graeco-Roman times, and included within its borders most of modern Sudan and some of present-day Ethiopia (Abyssinia).*

Check out 2 Samuel 14:25–26 to understand what caused Absalom to get caught in the tree.

Pray it!

If Only

David grieves over the death of his son Absalom, and says: "If only I had died in your place" (2 Samuel 18:33). We understand David's mourning for his dead son, but we have to be careful of getting too caught up in "if onlys." David becomes so trapped wishing things were different that he fails to be the strong leader his people need him to be. We can always find something about ourselves or our lives that we would like to change. Sometimes we can change things, but not always. We need to ask God for the ability to determine what we can and cannot change. Next time you find yourself saying, "If only . . . ," try this prayer.

Dear God, things haven't turned out like I hoped.
Sometimes I find myself wishing things had gone differently.
When I am tempted to say, "If only . . . ," open my eyes to all the blessings around me.
Let me make the most of what you have given me.
Help me to know when to work at changing things,
and when to accept things as they are and make the best of them.
I need your help God, please. Amen.

— 2 Samuel 18:33

before him, and said, "Praise the LORD your
God, who has given you victory over the
men who rebelled against Your Majesty!"
29 "Is the young man Absalom all right?"
the king asked.
Ahimaaz answered, "Sir, when your officer
Joab sent me, I saw a great commotion, but I
couldn't tell what it was."
30 "Stand over there," the king told him;
and he went over and stood there.
31 Then the Ethiopian[z] slave arrived and
said to the king, "I have good news for Your
Majesty! Today the LORD has given you vic-
tory over all who rebelled against you!"
32 "Is the young man Absalom all right?"
the king asked.
The slave answered, "I wish that what has
happened to him would happen to all your
enemies, sir, and to all who rebel against you."
33 The king was overcome with grief. He
went up to the room over the gateway and
wept. As he went, he cried, "O my son! My
son Absalom! Absalom, my son! If only I had
died in your place, my son! Absalom, my
son!"

Joab Reprimands David

19 Joab was told that King David was
weeping and mourning for Absalom.
2 And so the joy of victory was turned into
sadness for all of David's troops that day,
because they heard that the king was
mourning for his son. 3 They went back into
the city quietly, like soldiers who are
ashamed because they are running away
from battle. 4 The king covered his face and
cried loudly, "O my son! My son Absalom!
Absalom, my son!"
5 Joab went to the king's house and said to
him, "Today you have humiliated your
men—the men who saved your life and the
lives of your sons and daughters and of your
wives and concubines. 6 You oppose those
who love you and support those who hate
you! You have made it clear that your

[z] **18:31** *Hebrew* Cushite: *Cush is the ancient name of the extensive territory south of the First Cataract of the Nile River. This region was called Ethiopia in Graeco-Roman times, and included within its borders most of modern Sudan and some of present-day Ethiopia (Abyssinia).*

"O my son! My son Absalom!" (19:4)

officers and men mean nothing to you. I can see that you would be quite happy if Absalom were alive today and all of us were dead. 7Now go and reassure your men. I swear by the LORD's name that if you don't, not one of them will be with you by tomorrow morning. That would be the worst disaster you have suffered in all your life." 8Then the king got up, and went and sat near the city gate. His men heard that he was there, and they all gathered around him.

David Starts Back to Jerusalem

Meanwhile all the Israelites had fled to their own hometowns. 9All over the country they started quarreling among themselves. "King David saved us from our enemies," they said to one another. "He rescued us from the Philistines, but now he has fled from Absalom and left the country. 10We anointed Absalom as our king, but he has been killed in battle. So why doesn't somebody try to bring King David back?"

11The news of what the Israelites were saying reached King David.[a] So he sent the priests Zadok and Abiathar to ask the leaders of Judah, "Why should you be the last to help bring the king back to his palace? 12You are my relatives, my own flesh and blood; why should you be the last to bring me back?" 13David also told them to say to Amasa, "You are my relative. From now on I am putting you in charge of the army in place of Joab. May God strike me dead if I don't!" 14David's words won the complete loyalty of all the men of Judah, and they sent him word to return with all his officials.

15On his way back the king was met at the Jordan River by the men of Judah, who had come to Gilgal to escort him across the river. 16At the same time the Benjaminite Shimei son of Gera from Bahurim hurried to the Jordan to meet King David. 17He had with him a thousand men from the tribe of Benjamin. And Ziba, the servant of Saul's family, also came with his fifteen sons and twenty servants, and they arrived at the Jordan before the king. 18They crossed[b] the river to escort the royal party across and to do whatever the king wanted.

David Shows Kindness to Shimei

As the king was getting ready to cross, Shimei threw himself down in front of him 19and said, "Your Majesty, please forget the wrong I did that day you left Jerusalem. Don't hold it against me or think about it any more. 20I know, sir, that I have sinned, and this is why I am the first one from the northern tribes to come and meet Your Majesty today."

21Abishai son of Zeruiah spoke up: "Shimei should be put to death because he cursed the one whom the LORD chose as king."

22But David said to Abishai and his brother Joab, "Who asked your opinion? Are you going to give me trouble? I am the one who is king of Israel now, and no Israelite will be put to death today." 23And he said to Shimei, "I give you my word that you will not be put to death."

David Shows Kindness to Mephibosheth

24Then Mephibosheth, Saul's grandson, came down to meet the king. He had not washed his feet, trimmed his beard, or washed his clothes from the time the king left

[a] **19:11** *Some ancient translations* The news . . . David; *Hebrew* The news . . . David, to his palace, *and places this sentence at the end of the verse.* [b] **19:18** *Probable text* They crossed; *Hebrew* The crossing crossed.

19:16 2 Sam 16:5–13 **19:24** 2 Sam 9:1–13; 16:1–4

Live it!

Old Friends

Most young people don't like going into care facilities where lots of older adults live. They don't like being around old people. They often say, "It's too depressing." One of King David's supporters, Barzillai, is eighty years old. He tells David some of the things he struggles with, which are the same things old people deal with today.

Think about what a difference you can make in the lives of older adults when you go to visit them. It is rare that they see any young people. See if you can volunteer at a nearby residence for older adults. Often residents like to play cards or checkers or just to visit. They each have a lifetime of stories to tell. Look around their rooms and ask them about photos and objects that you see. All you need to bring with you is a smile and the willingness to be patient. You can really be a gift in an older person's life!

— 2 Samuel 19:31–39

Jerusalem until he returned victorious. 25 When
Mephibosheth arrived from[c] Jerusalem to meet
the king, the king said to him, "Mephibosheth,
you didn't go with me. Why not?"
26 He answered, "As you know, Your
Majesty, I am crippled. I told my servant to
saddle my donkey so that I could ride along
with you, but he betrayed me. 27 He lied about
me to Your Majesty, but you are like God's
angel, so do what seems right to you. 28 All of
my father's family deserved to be put to death
by Your Majesty, but you gave me the right to
eat at your table. I have no right to ask for any
more favors from Your Majesty."
29 The king answered, "You don't have to
say anything more. I have decided that you
and Ziba will share Saul's property."
30 "Let Ziba have it all," Mephibosheth
answered. "It's enough for me that Your
Majesty has come home safely."

David Shows Kindness to Barzillai

31 Barzillai, from Gilead, had also come
down from Rogelim to escort the king
across the Jordan. 32 Barzillai was a very old
man, eighty years old. He was very rich and
had supplied the king with food while he
was staying at Mahanaim. 33 The king said to
him, "Come with me to Jerusalem, and I
will take care of you."
34 But Barzillai answered, "I don't have
long to live; why should I go with Your
Majesty to Jerusalem? 35 I am already eighty
years old, and nothing gives me pleasure any
more. I can't taste what I eat and drink, and I
can't hear the voices of singers. I would only
be a burden to Your Majesty. 36 I don't
deserve such a great reward. So I will go just
a little way with you beyond the Jordan.
37 Then let me go back home and die near
my parents' grave. Here is my son Chimham,
who will serve you; take him with you, Your
Majesty, and do for him as you think best."
38 The king answered, "I will take him
with me and do for him whatever you want.
And I will do for you anything you ask."
39 Then David and all of his men crossed the
Jordan. He kissed Barzillai and gave him his
blessing, and Barzillai went back home.

Judah and Israel Argue over the King

40 When the king had crossed, escorted by
all the people of Judah and half the people

[c] **19:25** *One ancient translation* from; *Hebrew* at.
19:31 2 Sam 17:27–29

After his son Absalom's death, David could be angry and revengeful or kind and forgiving. Which does he choose?

of Israel, he went on to Gilgal, and
Chimham went with him. 41 Then all the
Israelites went to the king and said to him,
"Your Majesty, why did our brothers, the
men of Judah, think they had the right to
take you away and escort you, your family,
and your men across the Jordan?"
42 The men of Judah answered, "We did it
because the king is one of us. So why should
this make you angry? He hasn't paid for our
food nor has he given us anything."
43 The Israelites replied, "We have ten times
as many claims on King David as you have,
even if he is one of you. Why do you look
down on us? Don't forget that we were the
first to talk about bringing the king back!"

But the men of Judah were more violent in making their claims than the men of Israel.

Sheba's Rebellion

20 There happened to be in Gilgal a
worthless character named Sheba
son of Bikri, of the tribe of Benjamin. He
blew the trumpet and called out, "Down
with David! We won't follow him! Men of
Israel, let's go home!" 2 So the Israelites
deserted David and went with Sheba, but
the men of Judah remained loyal and followed David from the Jordan to Jerusalem.
3 When David arrived at his palace in
Jerusalem, he took the ten concubines he
had left to take care of the palace, and put
them under guard. He provided for their
needs, but did not have intercourse with
them. They were kept confined for the rest
of their lives, living like widows.
4 The king said to Amasa, "Call the men of
Judah together and be back here with them
by the day after tomorrow." 5 Amasa went to
call them, but he did not get back by the
time the king had told him to. 6 So the king
said to Abishai, "Sheba will give us more
trouble than Absalom. Take my men and go
after him, or else he may occupy some fortified towns and escape from us." 7 So Joab's
men, the royal bodyguards, and all the other
soldiers left Jerusalem with Abishai to go
after Sheba. 8 When they reached the large
rock at Gibeon, Amasa met them. Joab was
dressed for battle, with a sword in its sheath
fastened to his belt. As he came forward, the
sword fell out. 9 Joab said to Amasa, "How are
you, my friend?" and took hold of his beard
with his right hand in order to kiss him.
10 Amasa was not on guard against the sword
that Joab was holding in his other hand, and
Joab stabbed him in the belly, and his insides
spilled out on the ground. He died immediately, and Joab did not have to strike again.

Then Joab and his brother Abishai went
on after Sheba. 11 One of Joab's men stood
by Amasa's body and called out, "Everyone
who is for Joab and David follow Joab!"
12 Amasa's body, covered with blood, was
lying in the middle of the road. Joab's man
saw that everybody was stopping, so he
dragged the body from the road out into the
field and threw a blanket over it. 13 After the
body had been removed from the road,
everyone followed Joab in pursuit of Sheba.
14 Sheba passed through the territory of all
the tribes of Israel and came to the city of
Abel Beth Maacah, and all the members of
the clan of Bikri[d] assembled and followed
him into the city. 15 Joab's men heard that
Sheba was there, and so they went and
besieged the city. They built ramps of earth
against the outer wall and also began to dig
under the wall to make it fall down. 16 There
was a wise woman in the city who shouted
from the wall, "Listen! Listen! Tell Joab to
come here; I want to speak with him."
17 Joab went, and she asked, "Are you Joab?"

"Yes, I am," he answered.

"Listen to me, sir," she said.

"I'm listening," he answered.

18 She said, "Long ago they used to say, 'Go
and get your answer in the city of Abel'—and
that's just what they did. 19 Ours is a great city,
one of the most peaceful and loyal in Israel.

[d] **20:14** *Probable text* Bikri; *Hebrew* Beri.

20:1 1 Kings 12:16; 2 Chr 10:16 **20:3** 2 Sam 16:22

The cabinet of the president is made up of the officials who help the president run the country. Who is in David's cabinet, and what are their duties?

Why are you trying to destroy it? Do you want to ruin what belongs to the LORD?”

20“Never!” Joab answered. “I will never ruin or destroy your city! 21That is not our plan. A man named Sheba son of Bikri, who is from the hill country of Ephraim, started a rebellion against King David. Hand over this one man, and I will withdraw from the city.”

“We will throw his head over the wall to you,” she said. 22Then she went to the people of the city with her plan, and they cut off Sheba's head and threw it over the wall to Joab. He blew the trumpet as a signal for his men to leave the city, and they went back home. And Joab returned to Jerusalem to the king.

David's Officials

23Joab was in command of the army of Israel; Benaiah son of Jehoiada was in charge of David's bodyguards; 24Adoniram was in charge of the forced labor; Jehoshaphat son of Ahilud was in charge of the records; 25Sheva was the court secretary; Zadok and Abiathar were the priests, 26and Ira from the town of Jair was also one of David's priests.

Saul's Descendants Are Put to Death

21 During David's reign there was a severe famine which lasted for three full years. So David consulted the LORD about it, and the LORD said, “Saul and his family are guilty of murder; he put the people of Gibeon to death.” (2The people of Gibeon were not Israelites; they were a small group of Amorites whom the Israelites had promised to protect, but Saul had tried to destroy them because of his zeal for the people of Israel and Judah.) 3So David summoned the people of Gibeon and said to them, “What can I do for you? I want to make up for the wrong that was done to you, so that you will bless the LORD's people.”

4They answered, “Our quarrel with Saul and his family can't be settled with silver or gold, nor do we want to kill any Israelite.”

“What, then, do you think I should do for you?” David asked.

5They answered, “Saul wanted to destroy us and leave none of us alive anywhere in Israel. 6So hand over seven of his male descendants, and we will hang them before the LORD at Gibeah, the hometown of Saul, the LORD's chosen king.”

“I will hand them over,” the king answered.

7But because of the sacred promise that he and Jonathan had made to each other, David spared Jonathan's son Mephibosheth, the grandson of Saul. 8However, he took Armoni and Mephibosheth, the two sons that Rizpah the daughter of Aiah had borne to Saul; he also took the five sons of Saul's daughter Merab, whom she had borne to Adriel son of Barzillai, who was from Meholah. 9David handed them over to the people of Gibeon, who hanged them on the mountain before the LORD—and all seven of them died together. It was late in the spring, at the beginning of the barley harvest, when they were put to death.

10Then Saul's concubine Rizpah, the daughter of Aiah, used sackcloth to make a shelter for herself on the rock where the corpses were, and she stayed there from the beginning of harvest until the autumn rains came. During the day she would keep the birds away from the corpses, and at night she would protect them from wild animals.

11When David heard what Rizpah had done, 12he went and got the bones of Saul and of his son Jonathan from the people of Jabesh in Gilead. (They had stolen them from the public square in Beth Shan, where the Philistines had hanged the bodies on the day they killed Saul on Mount Gilboa.) 13David took the bones of Saul and Jonathan and also gathered up the bones of the seven men who had been hanged. 14Then they buried the bones of Saul and Jonathan in the grave of Saul's father Kish, in Zela in the territory of Benjamin, doing all that the king had commanded. And after that, God answered their prayers for the country.

Battles against Philistine Giants
(1 Chronicles 20:4–8)

15There was another war between the Philistines and Israel, and David and his me

21:2 Josh 9:3–15 **21:7** 1 Sam 20:15–17; 2 Sam 9:1–7 **21:8** 1 Sam 18:19 **21:12** 1 Sam 31:8–13

Catholic Connections

Respect for the Dead

Notice how David pays respect to the remains of Saul and Jonathan. Honoring the dead is a strong tradition in the Catholic Church. A special day has been set aside in the year to do that. It is November 2 and is often called All Souls' Day. Mexicans have a tradition called Day of the Dead, in which they celebrate with those who have died by having picnics at the graves of departed family members. The Church also has a tradition of honoring relics, which sometimes are bones or bone fragments of saints and holy people. Because these relics were once part of the living body of a saint, they too are considered holy.

All this comes from the belief that we are to honor and revere the memory and resting places of the dead. We know that the souls of those who die in God's friendship will one day be united with God and with all the saints in heaven after death. At the end of the world, their bodies will rise again to be united with their souls. So even though our dead loved ones are no longer physically here on earth, we can be connected to them spiritually. We call this spiritual family of living and dead believers the communion of saints. If we remain faithful to God, we too will be part of the communion of saints in this life and after our death.

— 2 Samuel 21:11–14

went and fought the Philistines. During one
of the battles David grew tired. 16 A giant
named Ishbibenob, who was carrying a
bronze spear that weighed about seven and a
half pounds and who was wearing a new
sword, thought he could kill David. 17 But
Abishai son of Zeruiah came to David's help,
attacked the giant, and killed him. Then
David's men made David promise that he
would never again go out with them to battle. "You are the hope of Israel, and we don't
want to lose you," they said.

18 After this there was a battle with the
Philistines at Gob, during which Sibbecai
from Hushah killed a giant named Saph.

19 There was another battle with the
Philistines at Gob, and Elhanan son of Jair[e]
from Bethlehem killed Goliath from Gath,
whose spear had a shaft as thick as the bar
on a weaver's loom.

20 Then there was another battle at Gath,
where there was a giant who loved to fight.
He had six fingers on each hand and six toes
on each foot. 21 He defied the Israelites, and
Jonathan, the son of David's brother
Shammah, killed him.

22 These four were descendants of the
giants of Gath, and they were killed by
David and his men.

David's Song of Victory
(Psalm 18)

22 When the LORD saved David from
Saul and his other enemies, David
sang this song to the LORD:

2 The LORD is my protector;
he is my strong fortress.
3 My God is my protection,
and with him I am safe.
He protects me like a shield;
he defends me and keeps me safe.
He is my savior;
he protects me and saves me from violence.
4 I call to the LORD,
and he saves me from my enemies.
Praise the LORD!

[e] **21:19** *Probable text (see 1 Chr 20:5)* Jair; *Hebrew* Jaareoregim.

21:17 1 Kings 11:36; Ps 132:17

5 The waves of death were all around
me;
the waves of destruction rolled over
me.
6 The danger of death was around me,
and the grave set its trap for me.
7 In my trouble I called to the LORD;
I called to my God for help.
In his temple he heard my voice;
he listened to my cry for help.

8 Then the earth trembled and shook;
the foundations of the sky rocked and
quivered
because God was angry!
9 Smoke poured out of his nostrils,
a consuming flame and burning coals
from his mouth.
10 He tore the sky open and came down,
with a dark cloud under his feet.
11 He flew swiftly on his winged creature;[f]
he traveled on the wings of the wind.

The LORD is my protector! (22:2)

12 He covered himself with darkness;
thick clouds, full of[g] water, surrounded
him;
13 burning coals flamed up from the
lightning before him.

14 Then the LORD thundered from the sky,
and the voice of Almighty God was
heard.
15 He shot his arrows and scattered his
enemies;
with flashes of lightning he sent them
running.
16 The floor of the ocean was laid bare,
and the foundations of the earth were
uncovered
when the LORD rebuked his enemies
and roared at them in anger.

17 The LORD reached down from above and
took hold of me;
he pulled me out of the deep waters.
18 He rescued me from my powerful enemies
and from all those who hate me—
they were too strong for me.
19 When I was in trouble, they attacked
me,
but the LORD protected me.
20 He helped me out of danger;
he saved me because he was pleased
with me.

21 The LORD rewards me because I do what
is right;
he blesses me because I am innocent.
22 I have obeyed the law of the LORD;
I have not turned away from my God.
23 I have observed all his laws;
I have not disobeyed his commands.
24 He knows that I am faultless,
that I have kept myself from doing
wrong.
25 And so he rewards me because I do what
is right,
because he knows that I am
innocent.

[f] **22:11** WINGED CREATURE: *See Word List.* [g] **22:12** *Some ancient translations (and see Ps 18:11)* full of; *Hebrew unclear.*

"You, LORD, are my light; / you dispel my darkness" *(2 Samuel 22:29)*.

26 O LORD, you are faithful to those who are faithful to you,
and completely good to those[h] who are perfect.
27 You are pure to those who are pure,
but hostile to those who are wicked.
28 You save those who are humble,
but you humble those who are proud.

29 You, LORD, are my light;
you dispel my darkness.
30 You give me strength to attack my enemies
and power to overcome their defenses.

31 This God—how perfect are his deeds,
how dependable his words!
He is like a shield
for all who seek his protection.
32 The LORD alone is God;
God alone is our defense.
33 This God is my strong refuge;
he makes[i] my pathway safe.
34 He makes me sure-footed as a deer;
he keeps me safe on the mountains.
35 He trains me for battle,
so that I can use the strongest bow.
36 O LORD, you protect me and save me;
your help has made me great.
37 You have kept me from being captured,
and I have never fallen.
38 I pursue my enemies and defeat them;
I do not stop until I destroy them.
39 I strike them down, and they cannot rise;
they lie defeated before me.
40 You give me strength for the battle
and victory over my enemies.
41 You make my enemies run from me;
I destroy those who hate me.
42 They look for help, but no one saves them;
they call to the LORD, but he does not answer.
43 I crush them, and they become like dust;
I trample on them like mud in the streets.

44 You saved me from my rebellious people
and maintained my rule over the nations;
people I did not know have now become my subjects.
45 Foreigners bow before me;
when they hear me, they obey.
46 They lose their courage
and come trembling[j] from their fortresses.

47 The LORD lives! Praise my defender!
Proclaim the greatness of the strong God who saves me!
48 He gives me victory over my enemies;
he subdues the nations under me
49 and saves me from my foes.
O LORD, you give me victory over my enemies
and protect me from violent men.
50 And so I praise you among the nations;
I sing praises to you.
51 God gives great victories to his king;
he shows constant love to the one he has chosen,
to David and his descendants forever.

David's Last Words

23 David son of Jesse was the man whom God made great, whom the God of Jacob chose to be king, and who was the composer of beautiful songs for Israel. These are David's last words:

2 The spirit of the LORD speaks through me;
his message is on my lips.
3 The God of Israel has spoken;
the protector of Israel said to me:
"The king who rules with justice,
who rules in obedience to God,

[h] **22:26** *Probable text (see Ps 18:25)* those; *Hebrew* the strong. [i] **22:33** *Probable text (see Ps 18:32)* he makes; *Hebrew unclear.* [j] **22:46** *Probable text (see Ps 18:45)* come trembling; *Hebrew* come ready to fight.
22:34 Hab 3:19 **22:50** Rom 15:9

Who were "The Three," and what did each of them do to become famous?

Live it!

The Man Whom God Made Great

David is described well in the first sentence of 2 Samuel, chapter 23. Think about how far David has come. When we first met him back in 1 Samuel, chapter 16, he was a lowly shepherd, the youngest of eight sons. And yet God knew what was in David's heart and could see what kind of man David would become. He certainly wasn't perfect, but through all his life David remained faithful to God.

There is so much potential in each one of us. We too have greatness within us. We only have to believe in ourselves and trust that God can and will call forth marvelous things from us. After all, we are created in God's image. Let God's grace flow through you. Ask God to help you become the person you were created to be. David composed beautiful songs for Israel. Let your life be a song of God's grace.

— 2 Samuel 23:1

4 is like the sun shining on a cloudless dawn,
the sun that makes the grass sparkle
after rain."
5 And that is how God will bless my
descendants,
because he has made an eternal
covenant with me,
an agreement that will not be broken,
a promise that will not be changed.
That is all I desire;
that will be my victory,
and God will surely bring it about.
6 But godless people are like thorns that are
thrown away;
no one can touch them barehanded.
7 You must use an iron tool or a spear;
they will be burned completely.[k]

David's Famous Soldiers
(1 Chronicles 11:10–41)

8 These are the names of David's famous
soldiers: the first was Josheb Basshebeth from
Tachemon, who was the leader of "The
Three";[l] he fought with his spear[m] against
eight hundred men and killed them all in
one battle.
9 The second of the famous three was
Eleazar son of Dodo, of the clan of Ahoh.
One day he and David challenged the
Philistines who had gathered for battle. The
Israelites fell back, 10 but he stood his ground
and fought the Philistines until his hand was
so cramped that he could not let go of his
sword. The LORD won a great victory that
day. After it was over, the Israelites returned
to where Eleazar was and stripped the armor
from the dead.
11 The third of the famous three was
Shammah son of Agee from Harar. The
Philistines had gathered at Lehi, where there
was a field of peas. The Israelites fled from
the Philistines, 12 but Shammah stood his
ground in the field, defended it, and killed
the Philistines. The LORD won a great victo-
ry that day.
13 Near the beginning of harvest time[n]
three of "The Thirty" went down to Adul-
lam Cave, where David was, while a band of
Philistines was camping in Rephaim Valley.
14 At that time David was on a fortified hill,
and a group of Philistines had occupied
Bethlehem. 15 David grew homesick and
said, "How I wish someone would bring me
a drink of water from the well by the gate at
Bethlehem!" 16 The three famous soldiers
forced their way through the Philistine
camp, drew some water from the well, and
brought it back to David. But he would not
drink it; instead he poured it out as an offer-
ing to the LORD 17 and said, "LORD, I could

[k] **23:7** *Verses 6-7 in Hebrew are unclear.* [l] **23:8** *One ancient translation* "The Three"; *Hebrew* the third.
[m] **23:8** *Probable text (see 1 Chr 11:11)* he fought with his spear; *Hebrew unclear.* [n] **23:13** *Probable text* Near the beginning of harvest time; *Hebrew unclear.*

never drink this! It would be like drinking
the blood of these men who risked their
lives!" So he refused to drink it.

Those were the brave deeds of the three
famous soldiers.

18 Joab's brother Abishai (their mother
was Zeruiah) was the leader of "The
Famous Thirty." He fought with his spear
against three hundred men and killed
them, and became famous among "The
Thirty."[o] 19 He was the most famous of
"The Thirty"[p] and became their leader, but
he was not as famous as "The Three."

20 Benaiah son of Jehoiada from Kabzeel
was another famous soldier; he did many
brave deeds, including killing two great
Moabite warriors. He once went down into
a pit on a snowy day and killed a lion. 21 He
also killed an Egyptian, a huge man who was
armed with a spear. Benaiah attacked him
with his club, snatched the spear from the
Egyptian's hand, and killed him with it.
22 Those were the brave deeds of Benaiah,
who was one of "The Thirty."[p] 23 He was
outstanding among them, but was not as
famous as "The Three." David put him in
charge of his bodyguard.

24-39 Other members of "The Thirty"
included:

Asahel, Joab's brother
Elhanan son of Dodo from Bethlehem
Shammah and Elika from Harod
Helez from Pelet
Ira son of Ikkesh from Tekoa
Abiezer from Anathoth
Mebunnai from Hushah
Zalmon from Ahoh
Maharai from Netophah
Heleb son of Baanah from Netophah
Ittai son of Ribai from Gibeah in Benjamin
Benaiah from Pirathon
Hiddai from the valleys near Gaash
Abialbon from Arabah
Azmaveth from Bahurim
Eliahba from Shaalbon
The sons of Jashen
Jonathan
Shammah from Harar
Ahiam son of Sharar from Harar
Eliphelet son of Ahasbai from Maacah
Eliam son of Ahithophel from Gilo
Hezro from Carmel
Paarai from Arab
Igal son of Nathan from Zobah
Bani from Gad
Zelek from Ammon
Naharai from Beeroth, Joab's armorbearer
Ira and Gareb from Jattir
Uriah the Hittite.

There were thirty-seven famous soldiers
in all.

David Takes a Census
(1 Chronicles 21:1–27)

24 On another occasion the LORD was
angry with Israel, and he made
David bring trouble on them. The LORD said
to him, "Go and count the people of Israel
and Judah." 2 So David gave orders to Joab,
the commander of his army: "Go with your
officers through all the tribes of Israel from
one end of the country to the other, and
count the people. I want to know how many
there are."

3 But Joab answered the king, "Your
Majesty, may the LORD your God make the
people of Israel a hundred times more
numerous than they are now, and may you
live to see him do it. But why does Your
Majesty want to do this?" 4 But the king
made Joab and his officers obey his order;
they left his presence and went out to count
the people of Israel.

5 They crossed the Jordan and camped
south of Aroer, the city in the middle of the
valley, in the territory of Gad.[q] From there
they went north to Jazer, 6 and on to Gilead
and to Kadesh, in Hittite territory.[r] Then
they went to Dan, and from Dan they went[s]
west to Sidon. 7 Then they went south to the
fortified city of Tyre, on to all the cities of
the Hivites and the Canaanites, and finally to
Beersheba, in the southern part of Judah. 8 So

[o] **23:18** *One ancient translation* "The Thirty"; *Hebrew* "The Three." [p] **23:19,22** *Probable text* "The Thirty"; *Hebrew* "The Three." [q] **24:5** *Probable text* Aroer . . . Gad; *Hebrew unclear.* [r] **24:6** *One ancient translation* Kadesh, in Hittite territory; *Hebrew* to the land of Tahtim, Hodshi. [s] **24:6** *Probable text* and from Dan they went; *Hebrew unclear.*

Pray it!

Guilty Conscience

What do we do when, like David, our conscience begins to hurt? Try this prayer.

O God, sometimes I can coast along in life, and everything seems to be going great. At other times, I know something is wrong. I don't feel right inside. Help me to pay attention to my conscience. If I am feeling guilty, help me to be honest with myself and with you. Help me to ask forgiveness if I've done something wrong. Help me to do the right thing, and when I fail, help me to learn from my failure and make up my mind to do better. You are with me through it all. Don't let me forget that! Amen.

— 2 Samuel 24:10

after nine months and twenty days they
returned to Jerusalem, having traveled
through the whole country. 9 They reported
to the king the total number of men capable
of military service: 800,000 in Israel and
500,000 in Judah.
10 But after David had taken the census, his
conscience began to hurt, and he said to the
LORD, "I have committed a terrible sin in
doing this! Please forgive me. I have acted
foolishly."
11-12 The LORD said to Gad, David's
prophet, "Go and tell David that I am giving
him three choices. I will do whichever he
chooses." The next morning, after David had
gotten up, 13 Gad went to him, told him
what the LORD had said, and asked, "Which
is it to be? Three[t] years of famine in your
land or three months of running away from
your enemies or three days of an epidemic
in your land? Now think it over, and tell me
what answer to take back to the LORD."
14 David answered, "I am in a desperate
situation! But I don't want to be punished
by people. Let the LORD himself be the one
to punish us, for he is merciful." 15 So the
LORD sent an epidemic on Israel, which
lasted from that morning until the time that
he had chosen. From one end of the coun-
try to the other seventy thousand Israelites
died. 16 When the LORD's angel was about
to destroy Jerusalem, the LORD changed his
mind about punishing the people and said
to the angel who was killing them, "Stop!
That's enough!" The angel was by the
threshing place of Araunah, a Jebusite.
17 David saw the angel who was killing the
people, and said to the LORD, "I am the
guilty one. I am the one who did wrong.
What have these poor people done? You
should punish me and my family."
18 That same day Gad went to David and
said to him, "Go up to Araunah's threshing
place and build an altar to the LORD."
19 David obeyed the LORD's command and
went as Gad had told him to. 20 Araunah
looked down and saw the king and his offi-
cials coming up to him. He threw himself
on the ground in front of David 21 and asked,
"Your Majesty, why are you here?"
David answered, "To buy your threshing
place and build an altar for the LORD, in
order to stop the epidemic."
22 "Take it, Your Majesty," Araunah said,
"and offer to the LORD whatever you wish.
Here are these oxen to burn as an offering
on the altar; here are their yokes and the
threshing boards to use as fuel." 23 Araunah

[t] **24:13** *Some ancient translations (and see 1 Chr 21:12)* Three; *Hebrew* Seven.

What is the total number of men capable of military service in David's kingdom? You will have to add those in Israel and those in Judah.

gave it all to the king[u] and said to him,
"May the LORD your God accept your
offering."
24But the king answered, "No, I will pay
you for it. I will not offer to the LORD my
God sacrifices that have cost me nothing."
And he bought the threshing place and the
oxen for fifty pieces of silver. 25Then he built
an altar to the LORD and offered burnt
offerings and fellowship offerings. The LORD
answered his prayer, and the epidemic in
Israel was stopped.

[u] **24:23** *Probable text* to the king; *Hebrew* to the king the king.

Your Next Step

Congratulations on finishing the Second Book of Samuel! Use this space to write your thoughts and questions about this book. If you are following the suggested reading plan, go ahead to the First Book of Kings. It continues with the story of King Solomon and the kings who followed him.

THE FIRST BOOK OF Kings

Just as the great pyramids record the golden years of Egypt, Israel's golden years are recorded in the First Book of Kings. The story of Israel's kings began in First and Second Samuel with Saul and David. The story continues in First Kings when David's son Solomon becomes the next king. He is a powerful and wise king who accumulates great wealth and builds Jerusalem into a great city.

Solomon is famous for building the Temple in Jerusalem. However, Solomon does not remain obedient to God, and his kingdom is eventually split in two—the kingdom of Judah in the south and the kingdom of Israel in the north. Prophets, who speak for God and are often critical of the kings, begin to play an important role in both First and Second Kings.

Headlines

- Young Solomon Prays for Wisdom (3:4–15)
- King Orders Baby Cut in Two! (3:16–28)
- Temple Construction Begins (6:1–14)
- Northern Tribes Revolt, Kingdom Splits (12:1–20)
- Prophet's Prayers Restore Child's Life (17:8–24)
- Elijah Proves Yahweh Supreme (18:16–40)
- Evil Deeds by King and Queen (chapter 21)

FACTOIDS

Who wrote this book? First and Second Kings were originally one book, but the author is unknown.

When was it written? It was probably written sometime after the fall of Jerusalem (587 BC). The author or authors used court records and other written histories as sources.

What time period does it cover? From 960 to 850 BC.

Why was it written? It was written to show that Israel's history was guided by God.

Important themes

- The success of the king's reign relies on his obedience to God.
- Disobeying God's Law and worshipping false gods result in the loss of the kingdom.
- God offers hope and continues to speak to his people through the prophets.

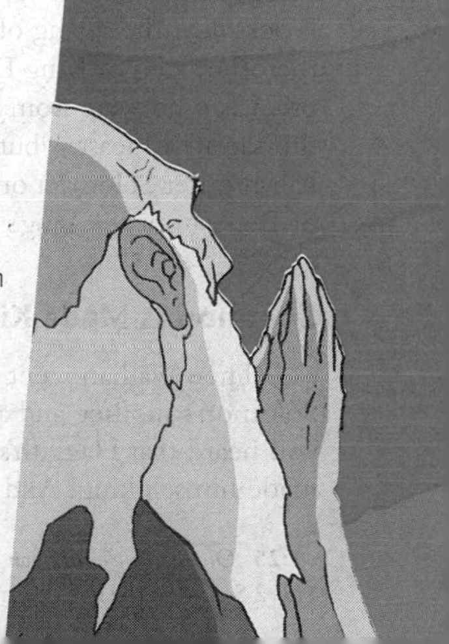

1 KINGS

King David in His Old Age

1 King David was now a very old man,
and although his servants covered him
with blankets, he could not keep warm. 2So
his officials said to him, "Your Majesty, let us
find a young woman to stay with you and
take care of you. She will lie close to you
and keep you warm." 3A search was made all
over Israel for a beautiful young woman, and
in Shunem they found such a woman named
Abishag, and brought her to the king. 4She
was very beautiful, and waited on the king
and took care of him, but he did not have
intercourse with her.

Adonijah Claims the Throne

5-6Now that Absalom was dead, Adonijah,
the son of David and Haggith, was the oldest
surviving son. He was a very handsome man.
David had never reprimanded him about
anything, and he was ambitious to be king.
He provided for himself chariots, horses, and
an escort of fifty men. 7He talked with Joab
(whose mother was Zeruiah) and with Abi-
athar the priest, and they agreed to support
his cause. 8But Zadok the priest, Benaiah son
of Jehoiada, Nathan the prophet, Shimei,
Rei, and David's bodyguards were not on
Adonijah's side.
9One day Adonijah offered a sacrifice of
sheep, bulls, and fattened calves at Snake
Rock, near the spring of Enrogel. He invited
the other sons of King David and the king's
officials who were from Judah to come to
this sacrificial feast, 10but he did not invite his
half brother Solomon or Nathan the prophet
or Benaiah or the king's bodyguards.

Solomon Is Made King

11Then Nathan went to Bathsheba,
Solomon's mother, and asked her, "Haven't
you heard that Haggith's son Adonijah has
made himself king? And King David doesn't
know anything about it! 12If you want to
save your life and the life of your son
Solomon, I would advise you to 13go at once
to King David and ask him, 'Your Majesty,
didn't you solemnly promise me that my son
Solomon would succeed you as king? How is
it, then, that Adonijah has become king?' "
14And Nathan added, "Then, while you are
still talking with King David, I will come in
and confirm your story."
15So Bathsheba went to see the king in his
bedroom. He was very old, and Abishag, the
young woman from Shunem, was taking care
of him. 16Bathsheba bowed low before the
king, and he asked, "What do you want?"
17She answered, "Your Majesty, you made
me a solemn promise in the name of the
LORD your God that my son Solomon
would be king after you. 18But Adonijah has
already become king, and you don't know
anything about it. 19He has offered a sacri-
fice of many bulls, sheep, and fattened calves,
and he invited your sons, and Abiathar the
priest, and Joab the commander of your
army to the feast, but he did not invite your
son Solomon. 20Your Majesty, all the people
of Israel are looking to you to tell them who
is to succeed you as king. 21If you don't, as
soon as you are dead, my son Solomon and
I will be treated as traitors."
22She was still speaking, when Nathan
arrived at the palace. 23The king was told
that the prophet was there, and Nathan went
in and bowed low before the king. 24Then
he said, "Your Majesty, have you announced
that Adonijah would succeed you as king?
25This very day he has gone and offered a
sacrifice of many bulls, sheep, and fattened
calves. He invited all your sons, Joab the
commander of your army,[a] and Abiathar the
priest, and right now they are feasting with
him and shouting, 'Long live King Adoni-
jah!' 26But he did not invite me, sir, or
Zadok the priest or Benaiah or Solomon.
27Did Your Majesty approve all this and not

[a] **1:25** *One ancient translation* Joab the commander of your army; *Hebrew* your army commanders.

1:5 2 Sam 3:4 **1:11** 2 Sam 12:24

even tell your officials who is to succeed you
as king?"
28 King David said, "Ask Bathsheba to
come back in"—and she came and stood
before him. 29 Then he said to her, "I prom-
ise you by the living LORD, who has rescued
me from all my troubles, 30 that today I will
keep the promise I made to you in the name
of the LORD, the God of Israel, that your son
Solomon would succeed me as king."
31 Bathsheba bowed low and said, "May
my lord the king live forever!"
32 Then King David sent for Zadok,
Nathan, and Benaiah. When they came in,
33 he said to them, "Take my court officials
with you; have my son Solomon ride my
own mule, and escort him down to Gihon
Spring, 34 where Zadok and Nathan are to
anoint him as king of Israel. Then blow the
trumpet and shout, 'Long live King
Solomon!' 35 Follow him back here when he
comes to sit on my throne. He will succeed
me as king, because he is the one I have
chosen to be the ruler of Israel and Judah."
36 "It shall be done," answered Benaiah,
"and may the LORD your God confirm it!
37 As the LORD has been with Your Majesty,
may he also be with Solomon and make his
reign even more prosperous than yours."
38 So Zadok, Nathan, Benaiah, and the
royal bodyguards put Solomon on King
David's mule and escorted him to Gihon
Spring. 39 Zadok took the container of olive
oil which he had brought from the Tent of
the LORD's presence, and anointed Solomon.
They blew the trumpet, and all the people
shouted, "Long live King Solomon!" 40 Then
they all followed him back, shouting for joy
and playing flutes, making enough noise to
shake the ground.
41 As Adonijah and all his guests were fin-
ishing the feast, they heard the noise. And
when Joab heard the trumpet, he asked,
"What's the meaning of all that noise in the
city?" 42 Before he finished speaking,
Jonathan, the son of the priest Abiathar,
arrived. "Come on in," Adonijah said.
"You're a good man—you must be bringing
good news."
43 "I'm afraid not," Jonathan answered.
"His Majesty King David has made
Solomon king. 44 He sent Zadok, Nathan,
Benaiah, and the royal bodyguards to escort
him. They had him ride on the king's mule,
45 and Zadok and Nathan anointed him as
king at Gihon Spring. Then they went into
the city, shouting for joy, and the people are
now in an uproar. That's the noise you just
heard. 46 Solomon is now the king. 47 What is
more, the court officials went in to pay their
respects to His Majesty King David and said,
'May your God make Solomon even more
famous than you, and may Solomon's reign
be even more prosperous than yours.' Then
King David bowed in worship on his bed
48 and prayed, 'Let us praise the LORD, the
God of Israel, who has today made one of
my descendants succeed me as king, and has
let me live to see it!' "
49 Then Adonijah's guests were afraid, and
they all got up and left, each going his own
way. 50 Adonijah, in great fear of Solomon,
went to the Tent of the LORD's presence and
took hold of the corners of the altar.[b] 51 King
Solomon was told that Adonijah was afraid
of him and that he was holding on to the
corners of the altar and had said, "First, I
want King Solomon to swear to me that he
will not have me put to death."
52 Solomon replied, "If he is loyal, not even
a hair on his head will be touched; but if he
is not, he will die." 53 King Solomon then
sent for Adonijah and had him brought
down from the altar. Adonijah went to the
king and bowed low before him, and the
king said to him, "You may go home."

David's Last Instructions to Solomon

2 When David was about to die, he called
his son Solomon and gave him his last
instructions: 2 "My time to die has come. Be

[b] **1:50** CORNERS OF THE ALTAR: *Small projections at the four corners of the altar that looked like horns. Anyone holding on to them was safe from being killed.*

Read about King David as a young hero in I Samuel, chapters 16–18. This shivering old man was once a handsome shepherd boy.

Live it!

Good Advice

Solomon has just become king. David's advice to his son Solomon is to follow the Law of Moses and to obey God in everything. Even though David made some pretty big mistakes, he always tried to obey God. When he was wrong, he admitted it and tried to set things right.

Think of someone you know who seems to have a good relationship with God—someone whose actions match his or her words, someone who puts his or her complete faith and trust in God. What advice do you think that person would give you about following God? Why not ask him or her?

— 1 Kings 2:1–4

confident and determined, 3and do what the
LORD your God orders you to do. Obey all
his laws and commands, as written in the
Law of Moses, so that wherever you go you
may prosper in everything you do. 4If you
obey him, the LORD will keep the promise
he made when he told me that my descen-
dants would rule Israel as long as they were
careful to obey his commands faithfully with
all their heart and soul.
5"There is something else. You remember
what Joab did to me by killing the two
commanders of Israel's armies, Abner son of
Ner and Amasa son of Jether. You remember
how he murdered them in time of peace as
revenge for deaths they had caused in time
of war. He killed innocent men,[c] and now I
bear the responsibility for what he did, and I
suffer[d] the consequences. 6You know what
to do; you must not let him die a natural
death.
7"But show kindness to the sons of
Barzillai from Gilead and take care of them,
because they were kind to me when I was
fleeing from your brother Absalom.
8"There is also Shimei son of Gera, from
the town of Bahurim in Benjamin. He
cursed me bitterly the day I went to Maha-
naim, but when he met me at the Jordan
River, I gave him my solemn promise in the
name of the LORD that I would not have
him killed. 9But you must not let him go
unpunished. You know what to do, and you
must see to it that he is put to death."

The Death of David

10David died and was buried in David's
City. 11He had been king of Israel for forty
years, ruling seven years in Hebron and thir-
ty-three years in Jerusalem. 12Solomon suc-
ceeded his father David as king, and his royal
power was firmly established.

The Death of Adonijah

13Then Adonijah, whose mother was
Haggith, went to Bathsheba, who was
Solomon's mother. "Is this a friendly visit?"
she asked.
"It is," he answered, 14and then he added,
"I have something to ask of you."
"What is it?" she asked.
15He answered, "You know that I should
have become king and that everyone in
Israel expected it. But it happened different-
ly, and my brother became king because it
was the LORD's will. 16And now I have one
request to make; please do not refuse me."
"What is it?" Bathsheba asked.

[c] **2:5** *Some ancient translations* innocent men; *Hebrew* men in battle. [d] **2:5** *Some ancient translations* I bear . . . and I suffer; *Hebrew* he bears . . . and he suffers.

2:5 a 2 Sam 3:27; **b** 2 Sam 20:10 **2:7** 2 Sam 17:27–29 **2:8** 2 Sam 16:5–13; 19:16–23 **2:11** 2 Sam 5:4, 5; 1 Chr 3:4 **2:12** 1 Chr 29:23

Solomon is anointed with oil when he becomes king. Catholics use oil for anointing in four of the seven sacraments. Can you name them?

17 He answered, "Please ask King Solomon—I know he won't refuse you—to let me have Abishag, the young woman from Shunem, as my wife."

18 "Very well," she answered. "I will speak to the king for you."

19 So Bathsheba went to the king to speak to him on behalf of Adonijah. The king stood up to greet his mother and bowed to her. Then he sat on his throne and had another one brought in on which she sat at his right. 20 She said, "I have a small favor to ask of you; please do not refuse me."

"What is it, mother?" he asked. "I will not refuse you."

21 She answered, "Let your brother Adonijah have Abishag as his wife."

22 "Why do you ask me to give Abishag to him?" the king asked. "You might as well ask me to give him the throne too. After all, he is my older brother, and Abiathar the priest and Joab are on his side!"[e] 23 Then Solomon made a solemn promise in the LORD's name, "May God strike me dead if I don't make Adonijah pay with his life for asking this! 24 The LORD has firmly established me on the throne of my father David; he has kept his promise and given the kingdom to me and my descendants. I swear by the living LORD that Adonijah will die this very day!"

25 So King Solomon gave orders to Benaiah, who went out and killed Adonijah.

Abiathar's Banishment and Joab's Death

26 Then King Solomon said to Abiathar the priest, "Go to your country home in Anathoth. You deserve to die, but I will not have you put to death now, for you were in charge of the LORD's Covenant Box while you were with my father David, and you shared in all his troubles." 27 Then Solomon dismissed Abiathar from serving as a priest of the LORD, and so made come true what the LORD had said in Shiloh about the priest Eli and his descendants.

28 Joab heard what had happened. (He had supported Adonijah, but not Absalom.) So he fled to the Tent of the LORD's presence and took hold of the corners of the altar.[f] 29 When the news reached King Solomon that Joab had fled to the Tent and was by the altar, Solomon sent a messenger to Joab to ask him why he had fled to the altar. Joab answered that he had fled to the LORD because he was afraid of Solomon. So King Solomon sent Benaiah[g] to kill Joab. 30 He went to the Tent of the LORD's presence and said to Joab, "The king orders you to come out."

"No," Joab answered. "I will die here."

Benaiah went back to the king and told him what Joab had said.

31 "Do what Joab says," Solomon answered. "Kill him and bury him. Then neither I nor any other of David's descendants will any longer be held responsible for what Joab did when he killed innocent men. 32 The LORD will punish Joab for those murders, which he committed[h] without my father David's knowledge. Joab killed two innocent men who were better men than he: Abner, commander of the army of Israel, and Amasa, commander of the army of Judah. 33 The punishment for their murders will fall on Joab and on his descendants forever. But the LORD will always give success to David's descendants who sit on his throne."

34 So Benaiah went to the Tent of the LORD's presence and killed Joab, and he was buried at his home in the open country. 35 The king made Benaiah commander of the army in Joab's place and put Zadok the priest in Abiathar's place.

The Death of Shimei

36 Then the king sent for Shimei and said to him, "Build a house for yourself here in Jerusalem. Live in it and don't leave the city. 37 If you ever leave and go beyond Kidron Brook, you will certainly die—and you yourself will be to blame."

38 "Very well, Your Majesty," Shimei answered. "I will do what you say." So he lived in Jerusalem a long time.

[e] **2:22** *Some ancient translations* and Abiathar the priest . . . on his side; *Hebrew unclear.* [f] **2:28** CORNERS OF THE ALTAR: *See 1:50.* [g] **2:29** *One ancient translation* Solomon sent a messenger . . . sent Benaiah; *Hebrew* Solomon sent Benaiah. [h] **2:32** will punish . . . committed; *or* will kill Joab, because he committed those murders.

2:17 1 Kings 1.3, 4 **2:26** **a** 2 Sam 15:24; **b** 1 Sam 22:20–23 **2:27** 1 Sam 2:27–36

39 Three years later, however, two of
Shimei's slaves ran away to the king of Gath,
Achish son of Maacah. When Shimei heard
that they were in Gath, 40 he saddled his
donkey and went to King Achish in Gath, to
find his slaves. He found them and brought
them back home. 41 When Solomon heard
what Shimei had done, 42 he sent for him
and said, "I made you promise in the LORD's
name not to leave Jerusalem. And I warned
you that if you ever did, you would certainly
die. Did you not agree to it and say that you
would obey me? 43 Why, then, have you bro-
ken your promise and disobeyed my com-
mand? 44 You know very well all the wrong
that you did to my father David. The LORD
will punish you for it. 45 But he will bless
me, and he will make David's kingdom
secure forever."

46 Then the king gave orders to Benaiah,
who went out and killed Shimei. Solomon
was now in complete control.

Solomon Prays for Wisdom
(2 Chronicles 1:3–12)

3 Solomon made an alliance with the
king of Egypt by marrying his daughter.
He brought her to live in David's City until
he had finished building his palace, the Tem-
ple, and the wall around Jerusalem. 2 A tem-
ple had not yet been built for the LORD, and
so the people were still offering sacrifices at
many different altars. 3 Solomon loved the
LORD and followed the instructions of his
father David, but he also slaughtered animals
and offered them as sacrifices on various
altars.

4 On one occasion he went to Gibeon to
offer sacrifices because that was where the
most famous altar was. He had offered hun-
dreds of burnt offerings there in the past.
5 That night the LORD appeared to him in a
dream and asked him, "What would you like
me to give you?"

6 Solomon answered, "You always showed
great love for my father David, your servant,
and he was good, loyal, and honest in his
relation with you. And you have continued
to show him your great and constant love by
giving him a son who today rules in his
place. 7 O LORD God, you have let me suc-
ceed my father as king, even though I am
very young and don't know how to rule.
8 Here I am among the people you have
chosen to be your own, a people who are so
many that they cannot be counted. 9 So give
me the wisdom I need to rule your people
with justice and to know the difference
between good and evil. Otherwise, how
would I ever be able to rule this great people
of yours?"

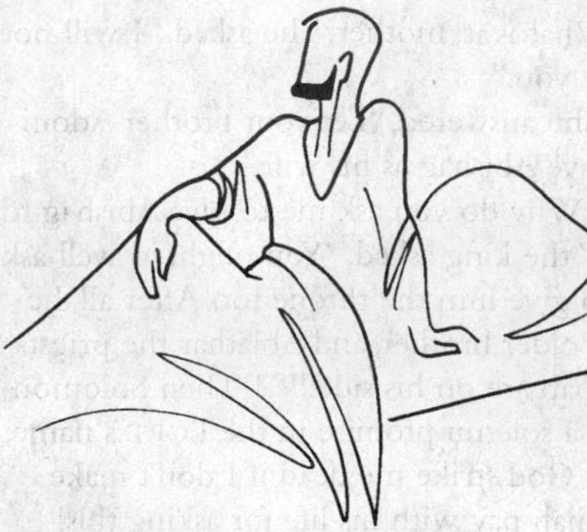

"Give me the wisdom I need." (3:9)

10 The Lord was pleased that Solomon had
asked for this, 11 and so he said to him,
"Because you have asked for the wisdom to
rule justly, instead of long life for yourself or
riches or the death of your enemies, 12 I will
do what you have asked. I will give you
more wisdom and understanding than any-
one has ever had before or will ever have
again. 13 I will also give you what you have
not asked for: all your life you will have
wealth and honor, more than that of any
other king. 14 And if you obey me and keep
my laws and commands, as your father
David did, I will give you a long life."

15 Solomon woke up and realized that
God had spoken to him in the dream. Then
he went to Jerusalem and stood in front of
the LORD's Covenant Box and offered burnt
offerings and fellowship offerings to the
LORD. After that he gave a feast for all his
officials.

3:4–9 Wis 9:1–18

Pray it!

Not a Perfect Person

Solomon has gained the throne and scarcely begun to rule. Already we see he is jealous and fearful of his half brother Adonijah. Solomon even has him killed. So why is it that long after Solomon's death, people will refer to Solomon's wisdom and his riches? Probably because even though Solomon is far from perfect, he struggles to follow God's laws.

Every person has strengths and weaknesses. Solomon realizes this. So he turns to God and asks for the gift of wisdom. You can do this, too. When you're feeling less than perfect, pray this prayer patterned after Solomon's prayer.

Loving God,
You have showed great love to your people.
You have given me many gifts
even though I am very young
and don't yet know everything I will need to know.
Here I am
among your people.
Give me the wisdom I need to follow you.
Help me to see what is right and what is wrong.
Help me to be a sign of your love in the world.

— 1 Kings 3:6–9

Solomon Judges a Difficult Case

16 One day two prostitutes came and pre-
sented themselves before King Solomon.
17 One of them said, "Your Majesty, this
woman and I live in the same house, and I
gave birth to a baby boy at home while she
was there. 18 Two days after my child was
born, she also gave birth to a baby boy. Only
the two of us were there in the house—no
one else was present. 19 Then one night she
accidentally rolled over on her baby and
smothered it. 20 She got up during the night,
took my son from my side while I was
asleep, and carried him to her bed; then she
put the dead child in my bed. 21 The next
morning, when I woke up and was going to
nurse my baby, I saw that it was dead. I
looked at it more closely and saw that it was
not my child."

22 But the other woman said, "No! The
living child is mine, and the dead one is
yours!"

The first woman answered back, "No! The dead child is yours, and the living one is mine!"

And so they argued before the king.

23 Then King Solomon said, "Each of you
claims that the living child is hers and that
the dead child belongs to the other one."
24 He sent for a sword, and when it was
brought, 25 he said, "Cut the living child in
two and give each woman half of it."

26 The real mother, her heart full of love
for her son, said to the king, "Please, Your
Majesty, don't kill the child! Give it to her!"

But the other woman said, "Don't give it to either of us; go on and cut it in two."

27 Then Solomon said, "Don't kill the

Solomon makes a wise political move by marrying the King of Egypt's daughter, but it may not be the best choice as far as God is concerned. Why?

"Don't kill the child!" (3:27)

child! Give it to the first woman—she is its real mother."

28 When the people of Israel heard of Solomon's decision, they were all filled with deep respect for him, because they knew then that God had given him the wisdom to settle disputes fairly.

Solomon's Officials

4 Solomon was king of all Israel, 2 and these were his high officials:

The priest: Azariah son of Zadok
3 The court secretaries: Elihoreph and Ahijah, sons of Shisha
In charge of the records: Jehoshaphat son of Ahilud
4 Commander of the army: Benaiah son of Jehoiada
Priests: Zadok and Abiathar
5 Chief of the district governors: Azariah son of Nathan
Royal Adviser: the priest Zabud son of Nathan
6 In charge of the palace servants: Ahishar
In charge of the forced labor: Adoniram son of Abda

7 Solomon appointed twelve men as district governors in Israel. They were to provide food from their districts for the king and his household, each man being responsible for one month out of the year. 8 The following are the names of these twelve officers and the districts they were in charge of:

Benhur: the hill country of Ephraim
9 Bendeker: the cities of Makaz, Shaalbim, Beth Shemesh, Elon, and Beth Hanan
10 Benhesed: the cities of Arubboth and Socoh and all the territory of Hepher
11 Benabinadab, who was married to Solomon's daughter Taphath: the whole region of Dor
12 Baana son of Ahilud: the cities of Taanach, Megiddo, and all the region near Beth Shan, near the town of Zarethan, south of the town of Jezreel, as far as the city of Abel Meholah and the city of Jokmeam
13 Bengeber: the city of Ramoth in Gilead, and the villages in Gilead belonging to the clan of Jair, a descendant of Manasseh, and the region of Argob in Bashan, sixty large towns in all, fortified with walls and with bronze bars on the gates
14 Ahinadab son of Iddo: the district of Mahanaim
15 Ahimaaz, who was married to Basemath, another of Solomon's daughters: the territory of Naphtali
16 Baana son of Hushai: the region of Asher and the town of Bealoth
17 Jehoshaphat son of Paruah: the territory of Issachar
18 Shimei son of Ela: the territory of Benjamin
19 Geber son of Uri: the region of Gilead, which had been ruled by King Sihon of the Amorites and King Og of Bashan

Besides these twelve, there was one governor over the whole land.

Solomon's Prosperous Reign

20 The people of Judah and Israel were as numerous as the grains of sand on the seashore; they ate and drank, and were happy.

Do you remember hearing the phrase "grains of sand on the seashore" before? Check out Genesis 22:17.

Study it!

Three Thousand Proverbs!

Solomon's fame spread. His rule was a time of peace and riches. Even though some of the numbers might be exaggerated to make a point, clearly there was something special about Solomon. He was not only wise about leadership and human nature, but he knew about science, the natural world, plants, and animals. He was a writer and a composer, making over three thousand proverbs and one thousand songs! No wonder people thought that he might have been the author of other Old Testament books, such as the Song of Songs, Ecclesiastes, Proverbs, and the Book of Wisdom.

—1 Kings 4:20–34

21 Solomon's kingdom included all the
nations from the Euphrates River to Philistia
and the Egyptian border. They paid him
taxes and were subject to him all his life.
22 The supplies Solomon needed each day
were 150 bushels of fine flour and 300
bushels of meal; 23 10 stall-fed cattle, 20 pas-
ture-fed cattle, and 100 sheep, besides deer,
gazelles, roebucks, and poultry.
24 Solomon ruled over all the land west of
the Euphrates River, from Tiphsah on the
Euphrates as far west as the city of Gaza. All
the kings west of the Euphrates were subject
to him, and he was at peace with all the
neighboring countries. 25 As long as he lived,
the people throughout Judah and Israel lived
in safety, each family with its own grapevines
and fig trees.
26 Solomon had forty thousand stalls for
his chariot horses and twelve thousand caval-
ry horses. 27 His twelve governors, each one
in the month assigned to him, supplied the
food King Solomon needed for himself and
for all who ate in the palace; they always
supplied everything needed. 28 Each governor
also supplied his share of barley and straw,
where it was needed,[i] for the chariot horses
and the work animals.
29 God gave Solomon unusual wisdom and
insight, and knowledge too great to be mea-
sured. 30 Solomon was wiser than the wise
men of the East or the wise men of Egypt.
31 He was the wisest of all men: wiser than
Ethan the Ezrahite, and Heman, Calcol, and
Darda, the sons of Mahol, and his fame
spread throughout all the neighboring coun-
tries. 32 He composed three thousand
proverbs and more than a thousand songs.
33 He spoke of trees and plants, from the
Lebanon cedars to the hyssop that grows on
walls; he talked about animals, birds, reptiles,
and fish. 34 Kings all over the world heard of
his wisdom and sent people to listen to him.

Solomon Prepares to Build the Temple
(2 Chronicles 2:1–18)

5 King Hiram of Tyre had always been a
friend of David's, and when he heard
that Solomon had succeeded his father
David as king, he sent ambassadors to him.
2 Solomon sent back this message to Hiram:
3 "You know that because of the constant
wars my father David had to fight against
the enemy countries all around him, he
could not build a temple for the worship of
the LORD his God until the LORD had given
him victory over all his enemies. 4 But now
the LORD my God has given me peace on
all my borders. I have no enemies, and there
is no danger of attack. 5 The LORD promised
my father David, 'Your son, whom I will
make king after you, will build a temple for
me.' And I have now decided to build that
temple for the worship of the LORD my
God. 6 So send your men to Lebanon to cut
down cedars for me. My men will work
with them, and I will pay your men whatev-
er you decide. As you well know, my men

[i] **4:28** where it was needed; *or* wherever King Solomon was.

4:21 Gen 15:18; 2 Chr 9:26 **4:26** 1 Kings 10:26; 2 Chr 1:14; 9:25 **4:31** Ps 89 Title **4:32** Prov 1:1; 10:1; 25:1; Song 1:1 **5:5** 2 Sam 7:12, 13; 1 Chr 17:11, 12 don't know how to cut down trees as well as yours do."

7 Hiram was extremely pleased when he received Solomon's message, and he said, "Praise the LORD today for giving David such a wise son to succeed him as king of that great nation!" 8 Then Hiram sent Solomon the following message: "I have received your message, and I am ready to do what you ask. I will provide the cedars and the pine trees. 9 My men will bring the logs down from Lebanon to the sea and will tie them together in rafts to float them down the coast to the place you choose. There my men will untie them, and your men will take charge of them. On your part, I would like you to supply the food for my men."

10 So Hiram supplied Solomon with all the cedar and pine logs that he wanted, 11 and Solomon provided Hiram with 100,000 bushels of wheat and 110,000 gallons[j] of pure olive oil every year to feed his men.

12 The LORD kept his promise and gave

Hiram supplied Solomon with . . . cedar and pine logs. (5:10)

Solomon wisdom. There was peace between Hiram and Solomon, and they made a treaty with each other.

13 King Solomon drafted 30,000 men as forced labor from all over Israel, 14 and put Adoniram in charge of them. He divided them into three groups of 10,000 men, and each group spent one month in Lebanon and two months back home. 15 Solomon also had 80,000 stone cutters in the hill country, with 70,000 men to carry the stones, 16 and he placed 3,300 foremen in charge of them to supervise their work. 17 At King Solomon's command they cut fine large stones for the foundation of the Temple. 18 Solomon's and Hiram's workers and men from the city of Byblos prepared the stones and the timber to build the Temple.

Solomon Builds the Temple

6 Four hundred and eighty years after the people of Israel left Egypt, during the fourth year of Solomon's reign over Israel, in the second month, the month of Ziv, Solomon began work on the Temple. 2 Inside it was 90 feet long, 30 feet wide, and 45 feet high. 3 The entrance room was 15 feet deep and 30 feet wide, as wide as the sanctuary itself. 4 The walls of the Temple had openings in them, narrower on the outside than on the inside. 5 Against the outside walls, on the sides and the back of the Temple, a three-storied annex was built, each story 7½ feet high. 6 Each room in the lowest story was 7½ feet wide, in the middle story 9 feet wide, and in the top story 10½ feet wide. The Temple wall on each floor was thinner than on the floor below, so that the rooms could rest on the wall without having their beams built into it.

7 The stones with which the Temple was built had been prepared at the quarry, so that there was no noise made by hammers, axes, or any other iron tools as the Temple was being built.

8 The entrance to the lowest[k] story of the annex was on the south side of the Temple, with stairs leading up to the second and third stories. 9 So King Solomon finished building the Temple. He put in a ceiling made of beams and boards of cedar. 10 The three-storied annex, each story[l] 7½ feet high, was built against the outside walls of the Temple, and was joined to them by cedar beams.

11 The LORD said to Solomon, 12 "If you

[j] **5:11** *Some ancient translations (and see 2 Chr 2:10)* 110,000 gallons; *Hebrew* 1,100 gallons. [k] **6:8** *Some ancient translations* lowest; *Hebrew* middle. [l] **6:10** *Probable text* three-storied annex, each story; *Hebrew* three-storied annex.

5:14 1 Kings 12:18

Catholic Connections

A Place to Worship

The Temple building is described here in great detail. Solomon spared no expense and built an impressive resting place for the Covenant Box, also called the Ark of the Covenant. Christians have done the same thing. In many of the great cities of the world are beautiful cathedrals and churches where people go to worship God. Some people make it a practice to visit famous churches when they visit a new city. They may try to attend Mass at well-known Catholic churches. If your family travels a lot, you might want to try this. It is inspiring to see the beautiful buildings and art created to honor God. Though the Temple and our churches today were built centuries apart, they were built for the same purpose: "for the worship of the LORD my God" (1 Kings 5:5).

— 1 Kings, chapters 5–6

obey all my laws and commands, I will do
for you what I promised your father David.
13 I will live among my people Israel in this
Temple that you are building, and I will
never abandon them."

14 So Solomon finished building the Temple.

The Interior Furnishings of the Temple

(2 Chronicles 3:8–14)

15 The inside walls were covered with
cedar panels from the floor to the ceiling,
and the floor was made of pine. 16 An inner
room, called the Most Holy Place, was built
in the rear of the Temple. It was 30 feet long
and was partitioned off by cedar boards
reaching from the floor to the ceiling.[m]
17 The room in front of the Most Holy Place
was 60 feet long. 18 The cedar panels were
decorated with carvings of gourds and flow-
ers; the whole interior was covered with
cedar, so that the stones of the walls could
not be seen.

19 In the rear of the Temple an inner room
was built, where the LORD's Covenant Box
was to be placed. 20 This inner room was 30
feet long, 30 feet wide, and 30 feet high, all
covered with pure gold. The altar was cov-
ered with cedar panels.[n] 21 The inside of the
Temple was covered with gold, and gold
chains were placed across the entrance of the
inner room, which was also covered with
gold. 22 The whole interior of the Temple
was covered with gold, as well as the altar in
the Most Holy Place.

23 Two winged creatures were made of
olive wood and placed in the Most Holy
Place, each one 15 feet tall. 24-26 Both were
of the same size and shape. Each had two
wings, each wing 7½ feet long, so that the
distance from one wing tip to the other was
15 feet. 27 They were placed side by side in
the Most Holy Place, so that two of their
outstretched wings touched each other in
the middle of the room, and the other two

[m] **6:16** *One ancient translation* ceiling; *Hebrew* walls. [n] **6:20** *Verse 20 in Hebrew is unclear.*

6:16 Ex 26:33, 34 **6:22** Ex 30:1–3 **6:23–28** Ex 25:18–20

The plants and animals carved and gilded in the Temple had symbolic meaning. They represented power, happiness, and blessing.

wings touched the walls. 28 The two winged
creatures were covered with gold.
29 The walls of the main room and of the
inner room were all decorated with carved
figures of winged creatures, palm trees, and
flowers. 30 Even the floor was covered with
gold.
31 A double door made of olive wood was
set in place at the entrance of the Most Holy
Place; the top of the doorway was a pointed
arch. 32 The doors were decorated with carved
figures of winged creatures, palm trees, and
flowers. The doors, the winged creatures, and
the palm trees were covered with gold. 33 For
the entrance to the main room a rectangular
doorframe of olive wood was made. 34 There
were two folding doors made of pine 35 and
decorated with carved figures of winged crea-
tures, palm trees, and flowers, which were
evenly covered with gold.
36 An inner court was built in front of the
Temple, enclosed with walls which had one
layer of cedar beams for every three layers of
stone.
37 The foundation of the Temple was laid
in the second month, the month of Ziv, in
the fourth year of Solomon's reign. 38 In the
eighth month, the month of Bul, in the
eleventh year of Solomon's reign, the Temple
was completely finished exactly as it had
been planned. It had taken Solomon seven
years to build it.

Solomon's Palace

7 Solomon also built a palace for himself,
and it took him thirteen years. 2-3 The
Hall of the Forest of Lebanon[o] was 150 feet
long, 75 feet wide, and 45 feet high. It had
three[p] rows of cedar pillars, 15 in each row,
with cedar beams resting on them. The ceil-
ing was of cedar, extending over storerooms,
which were supported by the pillars. 4 On
each of the two side walls there were three
rows of windows. 5 The doorways and the
windows[q] had rectangular frames, and the
three rows of windows in each wall faced
the opposite rows.
6 The Hall of Columns was 75 feet long
and 45 feet wide. It had a covered porch,
supported by columns.
7 The Throne Room, also called the Hall
of Judgment, where Solomon decided cases,
had cedar panels from the floor to the
rafters.[r]
8 Solomon's own quarters, in another
court behind the Hall of Judgment, were
made like the other buildings. He also built
the same kind of house for his wife, the
daughter of the king of Egypt.
9 All these buildings and the great court
were made of fine stones from the founda-
tions to the eaves. The stones were prepared
at the quarry and cut to measure, with their
inner and outer sides trimmed with saws.
10 The foundations were made of large stones
prepared at the quarry, some of them twelve
feet long and others fifteen feet long. 11 On
top of them were other stones, cut to mea-
sure, and cedar beams. 12 The palace court,
the inner court of the Temple, and the
entrance room of the Temple had walls with
one layer of cedar beams for every three lay-
ers of cut stones.

Huram's Task
(2 Chronicles 2:13,14)

13 King Solomon sent for a man named
Huram, a craftsman living in the city of Tyre,
who was skilled in bronze work. 14 His
father, who was no longer living, was from
Tyre, and had also been a skilled bronze
craftsman; his mother was from the tribe of
Naphtali. Huram was an intelligent and
experienced craftsman. He accepted King
Solomon's invitation to be in charge of all
the bronze work.

[o] **7:2–3** HALL OF THE FOREST OF LEBANON: *A large ceremonial hall in the palace, probably so called because it was paneled in cedar.* [p] **7:2–3** *One ancient translation* three; *Hebrew* four. [q] **7:5** *One ancient translation* windows; *Hebrew* doorposts. [r] **7:7** *Some ancient translations* rafters; *Hebrew* floor.
7:8 1 Kings 3:1

Huram was a busy guy! Read the list of everything he made for the Temple in I Kings 7:40–45.

The Two Bronze Columns
(2 Chronicles 3:15–17)

15 Huram cast two bronze columns, each
one 27 feet tall and 18 feet in circum-
ference,[s] and placed them at the entrance of
the Temple. 16 He also made two bronze cap-
itals, each one 7½ feet tall, to be placed on
top of the columns. 17 The top of each col-
umn was decorated with a design of inter-
woven chains[t] 18 and two rows of bronze
pomegranates.

19 The capitals were shaped like lilies, 6
feet tall, 20 and were placed on a rounded
section which was above the chain design.
There were 200 pomegranates in two rows
around each[u] capital.

21 Huram placed these two bronze
columns in front of the entrance of the Tem-
ple: the one on the south side was named
Jachin[v] and the one on the north was named
Boaz.[w] 22 The lily-shaped bronze capitals
were on top of the columns.

And so the work on the columns was
completed.

The Bronze Tank
(2 Chronicles 4:2–5)

23 Huram made a round tank of bronze,
7½ feet deep, 15 feet in diameter, and 45 feet
in circumference. 24 All around the outer
edge of the rim of the tank[x] were two rows
of bronze gourds, which had been cast all in
one piece with the rest of the tank. 25 The
tank rested on the backs of twelve bronze
bulls that faced outward, three facing in each
direction. 26 The sides of the tank were 3
inches thick. Its rim was like the rim of a
cup, curving outward like the petals of a lily.
The tank held about 10,000 gallons.

The Bronze Carts

27 Huram also made ten bronze carts; each
was 6 feet long, 6 feet wide, and 4½ feet
high. 28 They were made of square panels
which were set in frames, 29 with the figures
of lions, bulls, and winged creatures on the
panels; and on the frames, above and under-
neath the lions and bulls, there were spiral
figures in relief. 30 Each cart had four bronze
wheels with bronze axles. At the four cor-
ners were bronze supports for a basin; the
supports were decorated with spiral figures
in relief. 31 There was a circular frame on top
for the basin. It projected upward 18 inches
from the top of the cart and 7 inches down
into it. It had carvings around it. 32 The
wheels were 25 inches high; they were
under the panels, and the axles were of one
piece with the carts. 33 The wheels were like
chariot wheels; their axles, rims, spokes, and
hubs were all of bronze. 34 There were four
supports at the bottom corners of each cart,
which were of one piece with the cart.
35 There was a 9-inch band around the top
of each cart; its supports and the panels were
of one piece with the cart. 36 The supports
and panels were decorated with figures of
winged creatures, lions, and palm trees,
wherever there was space for them, with spi-
ral figures all around. 37 This, then, is how the
carts were made; they were all alike, having
the same size and shape.

38 Huram also made ten basins, one for
each cart. Each basin was 6 feet in diameter
and held 200 gallons. 39 He placed five of the
carts on the south side of the Temple, and
the other five on the north side; the tank he
placed at the southeast corner.

Summary List of Temple Furnishings
(2 Chronicles 4:11—5:1)

40-45 Huram also made pots, shovels, and
bowls. He completed all his work for King
Solomon for the LORD's Temple. This is
what he made:

The two columns
The two bowl-shaped capitals on top of
the columns

[s] **7:15** *Some ancient translations* each one . . . circumference; *Hebrew* the first column was 27 feet tall and the second column was 18 feet in circumference. [t] **7:17** *Verse 17 in Hebrew is unclear.* [u] **7:20** *One ancient translation* each; *Hebrew* the second. [v] **7:21** JACHIN: *This name sounds like the Hebrew for "he (God) establishes."* [w] **7:21** BOAZ: *This name sounds like the Hebrew for "by his (God's) strength."* [x] **7:24** *Probable text* All around . . . tank; *Hebrew unclear.*

7:38 Ex 30:17–21

The design of interwoven chains on each capital
The 400 bronze pomegranates, in two rows of 100 each around the design on each capital
The ten carts
The ten basins
The tank
The twelve bulls supporting the tank
The pots, shovels, and bowls

All this equipment for the Temple, which
Huram made for King Solomon, was of pol-
ished bronze. 46 The king had it all made in
the foundry between Sukkoth and Zarethan,
in the Jordan Valley. 47 Solomon did not have
these bronze objects weighed, because there
were too many of them, and so their weight
was never determined.

48 Solomon also had gold furnishings made
for the Temple: the altar, the table for the
bread offered to God, 49 the ten lampstands
that stood in front of the Most Holy Place,
five on the south side and five on the north;
the flowers, lamps, and tongs; 50 the cups,
lamp snuffers, bowls, dishes for incense, and
the pans used for carrying live coals; and the
hinges for the doors of the Most Holy Place
and of the outer doors of the Temple. All
these furnishings were made of gold.

51 When King Solomon finished all the
work on the Temple, he placed in the Tem-
ple storerooms all the things that his father
David had dedicated to the LORD—the sil-
ver, gold, and other articles.

The Covenant Box Is Brought to the Temple
(2 Chronicles 5:2— 6:2)

8 Then King Solomon summoned all the
leaders of the tribes and clans of Israel
to come to him in Jerusalem in order to take
the LORD's Covenant Box from Zion,
David's City, to the Temple. 2 They all assem-
bled during the Festival of Shelters in the
seventh month, in the month of Ethanim.
3 When all the leaders had gathered, the
priests lifted the Covenant Box 4 and carried
it to the Temple. The Levites and the priests
also moved the Tent of the LORD's presence
and all its equipment to the Temple. 5 King
Solomon and all the people of Israel assem-
bled in front of the Covenant Box and sacri-
ficed a large number of sheep and cattle—
too many to count. 6 Then the priests carried
the Covenant Box into the Temple and put
it in the Most Holy Place, beneath the
winged creatures. 7 Their outstretched wings
covered the box and the poles it was carried
by. 8 The ends of the poles could be seen by
anyone standing directly in front of the Most
Holy Place, but from nowhere else. (The
poles are still there today.) 9 There was noth-
ing inside the Covenant Box except the two
stone tablets which Moses had placed there
at Mount Sinai, when the LORD made a

Study it!

Old and New

After the Temple is built, the people come together to place the Covenant Box in the Most Holy Place. The Most Holy Place was a special room in the back of the Temple. Only the high priest could enter the Most Holy Place after the Covenant Box was placed there.

The Covenant Box contained the stone tablets with the laws that Moses brought down from Mount Sinai. It connected the Israelite people with their history. It was a coming together of their old way of life, when they were wandering tribes, with their new way of life, as a nation with a king. Even though they had changed their way of life, they were still the Chosen People, blessed by God and made holy by God's presence.

— 1 Kings 8:1–9

7:48 **a** Ex 30:1–3; **b** Ex 25:23–30 **7:49** Ex 25:31–40 1 Chr 15:25–29 **8:2** Lev 23:34 **8:9** Deut 10:5 **7:51** 2 Sam 8:11; 1 Chr 18:11 **8:1** 2 Sam 6:12–16;

covenant with the people of Israel as they
were coming from Egypt.
10 As the priests were leaving the Temple,
it was suddenly filled with a cloud 11 shining
with the dazzling light of the LORD's pres-
ence, and they could not go back in to per-
form their duties. 12 Then Solomon prayed:

"You, LORD, have placed the sun in the
sky,[y]
yet you have chosen to live in clouds
and darkness.
13 Now I have built a majestic temple for
you,
a place for you to live in forever."

Solomon's Address to the People
(2 Chronicles 6:3–11)

14 As the people stood there, King
Solomon turned to face them, and he asked
God's blessing on them. 15 He said, "Praise the
LORD God of Israel! He has kept the promise
he made to my father David, when he told
him, 16 'From the time I brought my people
out of Egypt, I have not chosen any city in
all the land of Israel in which a temple
should be built where I would be worshiped.
But I chose you, David, to rule my people.' "
17 And Solomon continued, "My father
David planned to build a temple for the
worship of the LORD God of Israel, 18 but
the LORD said to him, 'You were right in
wanting to build a temple for me, 19 but you
will never build it. It is your son, your own
son, who will build my temple.'
20 "And now the LORD has kept his prom-
ise. I have succeeded my father as king of
Israel, and I have built the Temple for the
worship of the LORD God of Israel. 21 I have
also provided a place in the Temple for the
Covenant Box containing the stone tablets
of the covenant which the LORD made with
our ancestors when he brought them out of
Egypt."

Solomon's Prayer
(2 Chronicles 6:12–42)

22 Then in the presence of the people
Solomon went and stood in front of the
altar, where he raised his arms 23 and prayed,
"LORD God of Israel, there is no god like
you in heaven above or on earth below! You
keep your covenant with your people and
show them your love when they live in
wholehearted obedience to you. 24 You have
kept the promise you made to my father
David; today every word has been fulfilled.
25 And now, LORD God of Israel, I pray that
you will also keep the other promise you
made to my father when you told him that
there would always be one of his descen-
dants ruling as king of Israel, provided they
obeyed you as carefully as he did. 26 So now,
O God of Israel, let everything come true
that you promised to my father David, your
servant.
27 "But can you, O God, really live on
earth? Not even all of heaven is large
enough to hold you, so how can this Temple
that I have built be large enough? 28 LORD
my God, I am your servant. Listen to my
prayer, and grant the requests I make to you
today. 29 Watch over this Temple day and
night, this place where you have chosen to
be worshiped. Hear me when I face this
Temple and pray. 30 Hear my prayers and the
prayers of your people when they face this
place and pray. In your home in heaven hear
us and forgive us.
31 "When a person is accused of wronging
another and is brought to your altar in this
Temple to take an oath that he is innocent,
32 O LORD, listen in heaven and judge your
servants. Punish the guilty one as he deserves,
and acquit the one who is innocent.
33 "When your people Israel are defeated
by their enemies because they have sinned
against you, and then when they turn to you
and come to this Temple, humbly praying to

[y] **8:12** *One ancient translation* You . . . sky; *Hebrew does not have these words.*

8:10, 11 Ex 40:34, 35 **8:12** Ps 18:11; 97:2 **8:16** 2 Sam 7:4–11; 1 Chr 17:3–10 **8:17, 18** 2 Sam 7:1–3; 1 Chr 17:1, 2 **8:19** 2 Sam 7:12, 13; 1 Chr 17:11, 12 **8:25** 1 Kings 2:4 **8:27** 2 Chr 2:6 **8:29** Deut 12:11

"LORD God of Israel, there is no god like you in heaven above or on earth below!" *(1 Kings 8:23)*.

Live it!

God in a Box?

Solomon recognizes that even though he has built a magnificent temple, God cannot be held inside a building. He wisely prays, "Not even all of heaven is large enough to hold you" (1 Kings 8:27). Sometimes we make the mistake of thinking that God is only in a building, our church. We think that somehow God is only with us when we go to church. The amazing thing we must remember is that God is present to us every minute of every day. All we have to do is open our eyes!

Jesse Manibusan, a popular Catholic singer and speaker, wrote a great song called "Open My Eyes." It makes a great prayer. Try using it throughout the day to remember God is with you.

Open my eyes, Lord, help me to see
your face.
Open my eyes, Lord, help me to see.
Open my ears, Lord, help me to hear
your voice.
Open my ears, Lord, help me to hear.

— 1 Kings 8:27

© 1988 Jesse Manibusan

you for forgiveness, 34listen to them in heav-
en. Forgive the sins of your people and bring
them back to the land which you gave to
their ancestors.
35"When you hold back the rain because
your people have sinned against you, and
then when they repent and face this Temple,
humbly praying to you, 36listen to them in
heaven. Forgive the sins of the king and of
the people of Israel, and teach them to do
what is right. Then, O LORD, send rain on
this land of yours, which you gave to your
people as a permanent possession.
37"When there is famine in the land or an
epidemic or the crops are destroyed by
scorching winds or swarms of locusts, or
when your people are attacked by their ene-
mies, or when there is disease or sickness
among them, 38listen to their prayers. If any
of your people Israel, out of heartfelt sorrow,
stretch out their hands in prayer toward this
Temple, 39hear their prayer. Listen to them
in your home in heaven, forgive them, and
help them. You alone know the thoughts of
the human heart. Deal with each person as
he deserves, 40so that your people may obey
you all the time they live in the land which
you gave to our ancestors.
41-42"When a foreigner who lives in a dis-
tant land hears of your fame and of the great
things you have done for your people and
comes to worship you and to pray at this
Temple, 43listen to his prayer. In heaven,
where you live, hear him and do what he
asks you to do, so that all the peoples of the
world may know you and obey you, as your
people Israel do. Then they will know that
this Temple I have built is the place where
you are to be worshiped.
44"When you command your people to
go into battle against their enemies and they
pray to you, wherever they are, facing this
city which you have chosen and this Temple
which I have built for you, 45listen to their
prayers. Hear them in heaven and give them
victory.
46"When your people sin against you—
and there is no one who does not sin—and
in your anger you let their enemies defeat
them and take them as prisoners to some
other land, even if that land is far away, 47lis-
ten to your people's prayers. If there in that
land they repent and pray to you, confessing
how sinful and wicked they have been, hear
their prayers, O LORD. 48If in that land they
truly and sincerely repent and pray to you as
they face toward this land which you gave to
our ancestors, this city which you have cho-

King Solomon had many important allies. King Hiram of Tyre was one of them. Can you name one of the favors that King Hiram did for Solomon?

sen, and this Temple which I have built for
you, 49then listen to their prayers. In your
home in heaven hear them and be merciful
to them. 50Forgive all their sins and their
rebellion against you, and make their ene-
mies treat them with kindness. 51They are
your own people, whom you brought out of
Egypt, that blazing furnace.

52"Sovereign LORD, may you always look
with favor on your people Israel and their
king, and hear their prayer whenever they
call to you for help. 53You chose them from
all the peoples to be your own people, as you
told them through your servant Moses when
you brought our ancestors out of Egypt."

The Final Prayer

54After Solomon had finished praying to
the LORD, he stood up in front of the altar,
where he had been kneeling with uplifted
hands. 55In a loud voice he asked God's bless-
ings on all the people assembled there. He
said, 56"Praise the LORD who has given his
people peace, as he promised he would. He
has kept all the generous promises he made
through his servant Moses. 57May the LORD
our God be with us as he was with our
ancestors; may he never leave us or abandon
us; 58may he make us obedient to him, so
that we will always live as he wants us to live,
keeping all the laws and commands he gave
our ancestors. 59May the LORD our God
remember at all times this prayer and these
petitions I have made to him. May he always
be merciful to the people of Israel and to
their king, according to their daily needs.
60And so all the nations of the world will
know that the LORD alone is God—there is
no other. 61May you, his people, always be
faithful to the LORD our God, obeying all his
laws and commands as you do today."

The Dedication of the Temple
(2 Chronicles 7:4–10)

62Then King Solomon and all the people
there offered sacrifices to the LORD. 63He
sacrificed 22,000 head of cattle and 120,000
sheep as fellowship offerings. And so the
king and all the people dedicated the Tem-
ple. 64That same day he also consecrated the
central part of the courtyard, the area in
front of the Temple, and then he offered
there the sacrifices burned whole, the grain
offerings, and the fat of the animals for the
fellowship offerings. He did this because the
bronze altar was too small for all these offer-
ings.

65There at the Temple, Solomon and all
the people of Israel celebrated the Festival of
Shelters for seven[z] days. There was a huge
crowd of people from as far away as Hamath
Pass in the north and the Egyptian border in
the south. 66On the eighth day Solomon
sent the people home. They all praised him
and went home happy because of all the
blessings that the LORD had given his servant
David and his people Israel.

God Appears to Solomon Again
(2 Chronicles 7:11–22)

9 After King Solomon had finished build-
ing the Temple and the palace and
everything else he wanted to build, 2the
LORD appeared to him again, as he had in
Gibeon. 3The LORD said to him, "I have
heard your prayer. I consecrate this Temple
which you have built as the place where I
shall be worshiped forever. I will watch over
it and protect it for all time. 4If you will
serve me in honesty and integrity, as your
father David did, and if you obey my laws
and do everything I have commanded you,
5I will keep the promise I made to your
father David when I told him that Israel
would always be ruled by his descendants.
6But if you or your descendants stop follow-
ing me, disobey the laws and commands I
have given you, and worship other gods,
7then I will remove my people Israel from
the land that I have given them. I will also
abandon this Temple which I have conse-
crated as the place where I am to be wor-
shiped. People everywhere will ridicule
Israel and treat her with contempt. 8This
Temple will become a pile of ruins,[a] and

[z] **8:65** *One ancient translation* seven; *Hebrew* fourteen. [a] **9:8** *Some ancient translations* a pile of ruins; *Hebrew* high.

8:56 Deut 12:10; Josh 21:44, 45 **9:2** 1 Kings 3:5; 2 Chr 1:7 **9:5** 1 Kings 2:4 **9:8** 2 Kings 25:9; 2 Chr 36:19

everyone who passes by will be shocked and
amazed. 'Why did the LORD do this to this
land and this Temple?' they will ask. 9People
will answer, 'It is because they abandoned
the LORD their God, who brought their
ancestors out of Egypt. They gave their alle-
giance to other gods and worshiped them.
That is why the LORD has brought this di-
saster on them.' "

Solomon's Agreement with Hiram
(2 Chronicles 8:1, 2)

10It took Solomon twenty years to build
the Temple and his palace. 11King Hiram of
Tyre had provided him with all the cedar
and pine and with all the gold he wanted
for this work. After it was finished, King
Solomon gave Hiram twenty towns in the
region of Galilee. 12Hiram went to see them,
and he did not like them. 13So he said to
Solomon, "So these, my brother, are the
towns you have given me!" For this reason
the area is still called Cabul.[b] 14Hiram had
sent Solomon almost five tons of gold.

Further Achievements of Solomon
(2 Chronicles 8:3–18)

15King Solomon used forced labor to
build the Temple and the palace, to fill in
land on the east side of the city, and to build
the city wall. He also used it to rebuild the
cities of Hazor, Megiddo, and Gezer. (16The
king of Egypt had attacked Gezer and cap-
tured it, killing its inhabitants and setting fire
to the city. Then he gave it as a wedding
present to his daughter when she married
Solomon, 17and Solomon rebuilt it.) Using
his forced labor, Solomon also rebuilt Lower
Beth Horon, 18Baalath, Tamar in the wilder-
ness of Judah, 19the cities where his supplies
were kept, the cities for his horses and chari-
ots, and everything else he wanted to build
in Jerusalem, in Lebanon, and elsewhere in
his kingdom. 20-21For his forced labor
Solomon used the descendants of the people
of Canaan whom the Israelites had not killed
when they took possession of their land.
These included Amorites, Hittites, Perizzites,
Hivites, and Jebusites, whose descendants
continue to be slaves down to the present
time. 22Solomon did not make slaves of
Israelites; they served as his soldiers, officers,
commanders, chariot captains, and cavalry.

23There were 550 officials in charge of
the forced labor working on Solomon's vari-
ous building projects.

24Solomon filled in the land on the east
side of the city, after his wife, the daughter of
the king of Egypt, had moved from David's
City to the palace Solomon built for her.

25Three times a year Solomon offered
burnt offerings and fellowship offerings on
the altar he had built to the LORD. He also
burned incense[c] to the LORD. And so he fin-
ished building the Temple.

26King Solomon also built a fleet of ships
at Eziongeber, which is near Elath on the
shore of the Gulf of Aqaba, in the land of
Edom. 27King Hiram sent some experienced
sailors from his fleet to serve with Solomon's
men. 28They sailed to the land of Ophir and
brought back to Solomon about sixteen tons
of gold.

The Visit of the Queen of Sheba
(2 Chronicles 9:1–12)

10 The queen of Sheba heard of
Solomon's fame,[d] and she traveled to
Jerusalem to test him with difficult ques-
tions. 2She brought with her a large group of
attendants, as well as camels loaded with
spices, jewels, and a large amount of gold.
When she and Solomon met, she asked him
all the questions that she could think of. 3He
answered them all; there was nothing too
difficult for him to explain. 4The queen of
Sheba heard Solomon's wisdom and saw the
palace he had built. 5She saw the food that
was served at his table, the living quarters for
his officials, the organization of his palace
staff and the uniforms they wore, the ser-
vants who waited on him at feasts, and the
sacrifices he offered in the Temple. It left her

[b] **9:13** CABUL: *This name sounds like "ke-bal," the Hebrew for "worthless."* [c] **9:25** *Hebrew has two additional words, the meaning of which is unclear.* [d] **10:1** *Probable text (see 2 Chr 9:1)* Solomon's fame; *Hebrew* Solomon's fame concerning the name of the LORD.

9:25 Ex 23:17; 34:23; Deut 16:16 **10:1–10** Mt 12:42; Lk 11:31

The queen of Sheba heard of Solomon's fame. (10:1)

breathless and amazed. [6]She said to King
Solomon, "What I heard in my own country
about you[e] and your wisdom is true! [7]But I
couldn't believe it until I had come and seen
it all for myself. But I didn't hear even half
of it; your wisdom and wealth are much
greater than what I was told. [8]How fortu-
nate are your wives![f] And how fortunate
your servants, who are always in your pres-
ence and are privileged to hear your wise
sayings! [9]Praise the LORD your God! He has
shown how pleased he is with you by mak-
ing you king of Israel. Because his love for
Israel is eternal, he has made you their king
so that you can maintain law and justice."
[10]She presented to King Solomon the
gifts she had brought: almost five tons of
gold and a very large amount of spices and
jewels. The amount of spices she gave him
was by far the greatest that he ever received
at any time.
([11]Hiram's fleet, which had brought
gold from Ophir, also brought from there a
large amount of juniper wood and jewels.
[12]Solomon used the wood to build railings
in the Temple and the palace, and also to
make harps and lyres for the musicians. It
was the finest juniper wood ever imported
into Israel; none like it has ever been seen
again.)
[13]King Solomon gave the queen of Sheba
everything she asked for, besides all the other
customary gifts that he had generously given
her. Then she and her attendants returned to
the land of Sheba.

King Solomon's Wealth
(2 Chronicles 9:13–29)

[14]Every year King Solomon received over
twenty-five tons of gold, [15]in addition to the
taxes[g] paid by merchants, the profits from
trade, and tribute paid by the Arabian kings
and the governors of the Israelite districts.
[16]Solomon made two hundred large
shields and had each one overlaid with
almost fifteen pounds of gold. [17]He also
made three hundred smaller shields, overlay-
ing each one of them with nearly four
pounds of gold. He had all these shields
placed in the Hall of the Forest of Lebanon.[h]
[18]He also had a large throne made. Part of
it was covered with ivory and the rest of it
was covered with the finest gold. [19-20]The

[e] **10:6** you; *or* your deeds. [f] **10:8** *Some ancient translations* wives; *Hebrew* men. [g] **10:15** *Some ancient translations* taxes; *Hebrew* men. [h] **10:17** HALL OF THE FOREST OF LEBANON: *See 7:2–3.*

If a ton is two thousand pounds, what was the weight in pounds of the queen of Sheba's gift of five tons of gold?

Study it!

A Royal Visit

The queen of Sheba is quite a character! Hearing of Solomon's fame she comes with lavish gifts and examines everything about Solomon's kingdom. She quizzes Solomon and finds that he is even wiser than she expected. She was known for being noble and wise. Her respect means a lot and helps make Solomon even more famous.

— 1 Kings 10:1–13

throne had six steps leading up to it, with
the figure of a lion at each end of every step,
a total of twelve lions. At the back of the
throne was the figure of a bull's head, and
beside each of the two armrests was the fig-
ure of a lion. No throne like this had ever
existed in any other kingdom.
21All of Solomon's drinking cups were
made of gold, and all the utensils in the Hall
of the Forest of Lebanon were of pure gold.
No silver was used, since it was not consid-
ered valuable in Solomon's day. 22He had a
fleet of ocean-going ships sailing with
Hiram's fleet. Every three years his fleet
would return, bringing gold, silver, ivory,
apes, and monkeys.
23King Solomon was richer and wiser
than any other king, 24and the whole world
wanted to come and listen to the wisdom
that God had given him. 25Everyone who
came brought him a gift—articles of silver
and gold, robes, weapons, spices, horses, and
mules. This continued year after year.
26Solomon built up a force of fourteen
hundred chariots and twelve thousand caval-
ry horses. Some of them he kept in
Jerusalem and the rest he stationed in vari-
ous other cities. 27During his reign silver was
as common in Jerusalem as stone, and cedar
was as plentiful as ordinary sycamore in the
foothills of Judah. 28The king's agents con-
trolled the export of horses from Musri[i] and
Cilicia,[j] 29and the export of chariots from
Egypt. They supplied the Hittite and Syrian
kings with horses and chariots, selling chari-
ots for 600 pieces of silver each and horses
for 150 each.

Solomon Turns Away from God

11 Solomon loved many foreign
women. Besides the daughter of the
king of Egypt he married Hittite women
and women from Moab, Ammon, Edom, and
Sidon. 2He married them even though the
LORD had commanded the Israelites not to
intermarry with these people, because they
would cause the Israelites to give their loyal-
ty to other gods. 3Solomon married seven
hundred princesses and also had three hun-
dred concubines. They made him turn away
from God, 4and by the time he was old they
had led him into the worship of foreign
gods. He was not faithful to the LORD his
God, as his father David had been. 5He wor-
shiped Astarte, the goddess of Sidon, and
Molech, the disgusting god of Ammon. 6He
sinned against the LORD and was not true to
him as his father David had been. 7On the
mountain east of Jerusalem he built a place
to worship Chemosh, the disgusting god of
Moab, and a place to worship Molech, the
disgusting god of Ammon. 8He also built
places of worship where all his foreign wives
could burn incense and offer sacrifices to
their own gods.
9-10Even though the LORD, the God of
Israel, had appeared to Solomon twice and
had commanded him not to worship foreign

[i] **10:28** *Probable text* Musri; *Hebrew* Egypt. [j] **10:28** MUSRI AND CILICIA: *Two ancient countries in what is now southeast Turkey which were centers of horse breeding in Solomon's time.*

10:26 1 Kings 4:26 **10:27** Deut 17:17 **10:28** Deut 17:16 **11:1** Deut 17:17 **11:2** Ex 34:16; Deut 7:3, 4

Can you find the names of a foreign goddess and two foreign gods that Solomon worshiped *(1 Kings 11:1–8)*.

gods, Solomon did not obey the LORD but
turned away from him. So the LORD was
angry with Solomon 11and said to him,
"Because you have deliberately broken your
covenant with me and disobeyed my com-
mands, I promise that I will take the king-
dom away from you and give it to one of
your officials. 12However, for the sake of
your father David I will not do this in your
lifetime, but during the reign of your son.
13And I will not take the whole kingdom
away from him; instead, I will leave him one
tribe for the sake of my servant David and
for the sake of Jerusalem, the city I have
made my own."

Solomon's Enemies

14So the LORD caused Hadad, of the royal
family of Edom, to turn against Solomon.
15-16Long before this, when David had con-
quered Edom, Joab the commander of his
army had gone there to bury the dead. He
and his men remained in Edom six months,
and during that time they killed every male
in Edom 17except Hadad and some of his
father's Edomite servants, who escaped to
Egypt. (At that time Hadad was just a child.)
18They left Midian and went to Paran, where
some other men joined them. Then they trav-
eled to Egypt and went to the king, who gave
Hadad some land and a house and provided
him with food. 19Hadad won the friendship
of the king, and the king gave his sister-in-
law, the sister of Queen Tahpenes, to Hadad in
marriage. 20She bore him a son, Genubath,
who was raised by the queen in the palace,
where he lived with the king's sons.

21When the news reached Hadad in
Egypt that David had died and that Joab the
commander of the army was dead, Hadad
said to the king, "Let me go back to my own
country."

22"Why?" the king asked. "Have I failed
to give you something? Is that why you
want to go back home?"

"Just let me go," Hadad answered the
king. And he went back to his country.[k]

Study it!

Too Many Gods . . . or Wives?

You knew it would happen. Throughout 1 Kings the author keeps reminding us that God's blessing will stay with Solomon *as long as* he is obedient to God. But he wasn't. According to this passage, he turned away from God and started worshiping foreign gods and goddesses. What happened to the man who prayed, "Make us obedient to him [God], so that we will always live as he wants us to live" (1 Kings 8:58)?

Maybe it had something to do with the fact that Solomon had seven hundred wives! That is surely an exaggeration, but the fact remains that he married many foreign princesses as a way of creating alliances with other people. These princesses wanted to worship the gods and goddesses of their people, and Solomon not only let them, he built altars and shrines for them. God warned the Israelites not to marry foreign people for this very reason, but Solomon ignored that warning.

Solomon broke the Covenant, and the nation began to crumble.

— 1 Kings 11:1–8

As king of Edom, Hadad was an evil, bit-
ter enemy of Israel.[l]

23God also caused Rezon son of Eliada to
turn against Solomon. Rezon had fled from
his master, King Hadadezer of Zobah, 24and
had become the leader of a gang of outlaws.
(This happened after David had defeated

[k] **11:22** *One ancient translation* And he went back to his country; *Hebrew does not have these words.*
[l] **11:22** *One ancient translation* As king . . . Israel; *in Hebrew this sentence, with some differences, comes at the end of verse 25.*

Hadadezer and had slaughtered his Syrian allies.) Rezon and his gang went and lived in Damascus, where his followers made him king of Syria. 25He was an enemy of Israel during the lifetime of Solomon.

God's Promise to Jeroboam

26Another man who turned against King Solomon was one of his officials, Jeroboam son of Nebat, from Zeredah in Ephraim. His mother was a widow named Zeruah. 27This is the story of the revolt.

Solomon was filling in the land on the east side of Jerusalem and repairing the city walls. 28Jeroboam was an able young man, and when Solomon noticed how hard he worked, he put him in charge of all the forced labor in the territory of the tribes of Manasseh and Ephraim. 29One day, as Jeroboam was traveling from Jerusalem, the prophet Ahijah from Shiloh met him alone on the road in the open country. 30Ahijah took off the new robe he was wearing, tore it into twelve pieces, 31and said to Jeroboam, "Take ten pieces for yourself, because the LORD, the God of Israel, says to you, 'I am going to take the kingdom away from Solomon, and I will give you ten tribes.

"Take ten pieces for yourself." (11:31)

32Solomon will keep one tribe for the sake of my servant David and for the sake of Jerusalem, the city I have chosen to be my own from the whole land of Israel. 33I am going to do this because Solomon has rejected me and has[m] worshiped foreign gods: Astarte, the goddess of Sidon; Chemosh, the god of Moab; and Molech, the god of Ammon. Solomon has[n] disobeyed me; he has done wrong and has not kept my laws and commands as his father David did. 34But I will not take the whole kingdom away from Solomon, and I will keep him in power as long as he lives. This I will do for the sake of my servant David, whom I chose and who obeyed my laws and commands. 35I will take the kingdom away from Solomon's son and will give you ten tribes, 36but I will let Solomon's son keep one tribe, so that I will always have a descendant of my servant David ruling in Jerusalem, the city I have chosen as the place where I am worshiped. 37Jeroboam, I will make you king of Israel, and you will rule over all the territory that you want. 38If you obey me completely, live by my laws, and win my approval by doing what I command, as my servant David did, I will always be with you. I will make you king of Israel and will make sure that your descendants rule after you, just as I have done for David. 39Because of Solomon's sin I will punish the descendants of David, but not for all time.' "

40And so Solomon tried to kill Jeroboam, but he escaped to King Shishak of Egypt and stayed there until Solomon's death.

The Death of Solomon
(2 Chronicles 9:29–31)

41Everything else that Solomon did, his career, and his wisdom, are all recorded in *The History of Solomon.* 42He was king in Jerusalem over all Israel for forty years. 43He died and was buried in David's City, and his son Rehoboam succeeded him as king.

The Northern Tribes Revolt
(2 Chronicles 10:1–19)

12 Rehoboam went to Shechem, where all the people of northern Israel had gathered to make him king. 2When Jeroboam son of Nebat, who had gone to Egypt to escape from King Solomon, heard this news, he returned from[o] Egypt. 3The

[m] **11:33** *Some ancient translations* Solomon has . . . and has; *Hebrew* they have . . . and have. [n] **11:33** *Some ancient translations* Solomon has; *Hebrew* They have. [o] **12:2** *Some ancient translations (and see 2 Chr 10:2)* returned from; *Hebrew* remained in.

people of the northern tribes sent for him,
and then they all went together to Reho-
boam and said to him, 4"Your father Solo-
mon treated us harshly and placed heavy
burdens on us. If you make these burdens
lighter and make life easier for us, we will be
your loyal subjects."
5"Come back in three days and I will give
you my answer," he replied. So they left.
6King Rehoboam consulted the older
men who had served as his father Solomon's
advisers. "What answer do you advise me to
give these people?" he asked.
7They replied, "If you want to serve this
people well, give a favorable answer to their
request, and they will always serve you loy-
ally."
8But he ignored the advice of the older
men and went instead to the young men
who had grown up with him and who were
now his advisers. 9"What do you advise me
to do?" he asked. "What shall I say to the
people who are asking me to make their
burdens lighter?"
10They replied, "This is what you should
tell them: 'My little finger is thicker than my
father's waist!' 11Tell them, 'My father placed
heavy burdens on you; I will make them
even heavier. He beat you with whips; I'll
flog you with bullwhips!' "
12Three days later Jeroboam and all the
people returned to King Rehoboam, as he
had instructed them. 13The king ignored the
advice of the older men and spoke harshly
to the people, 14as the younger men had
advised. He said, "My father placed heavy
burdens on you; I will make them even
heavier. He beat you with whips; I'll flog
you with bullwhips!" 15It was the will of the
LORD to bring about what he had spoken to
Jeroboam son of Nebat through the prophet
Ahijah from Shiloh. This is why the king did
not pay any attention to the people.
16When the people saw that the king
would not listen to them, they shouted,
"Down with David and his family! What
have they ever done for us? People of Israel,
let's go home! Let Rehoboam look out for
himself!"
So the people of Israel rebelled, 17leaving
Rehoboam as king only of the people who
lived in the territory of Judah.
18Then King Rehoboam sent Adoniram,
who was in charge of the forced labor, to
go to the Israelites, but they stoned him to
death. At this, Rehoboam hurriedly got in
his chariot and escaped to Jerusalem. 19Ever
since that time the people of the northern

12:16 2 Sam 20:1

Live it!

Not So Smart

Rehoboam gets two conflicting pieces of advice. He asks the experienced, older advisers on whom his father depended for their advice. He also asks the young, inexperienced men to tell him what to do. The young men are impatient and arrogant. They seem to want to stay in power and boss everybody around. Like his dad, Solomon, Rehoboam does not choose wisely in this case. He follows the advice of the younger men and tries to increase his own power instead of thinking what is best for the people.

Being older doesn't necessarily mean being wiser. But neither does being younger. When someone gives you advice, consider it carefully. A wise person doesn't think about his or her own needs first. A wise person thinks about what will be best for everyone. What impact will your choices have on others?

— 1 Kings 12:1

The split! Israel has one king through the reigns of Saul, David, and Solomon. Now after Solomon's death there will be two kingdoms.

kingdom of Israel have been in rebellion against the dynasty of David.

20 When the people of Israel heard that Jeroboam had returned from Egypt, they invited him to a meeting of the people and made him king of Israel. Only the tribe of Judah remained loyal to David's descendants.

Shemaiah's Prophecy

(2 Chronicles 11:1–4)

21 When Rehoboam arrived in Jerusalem, he called together 180,000 of the best soldiers from the tribes of Judah and Benjamin. He intended to go to war and restore his control over the northern tribes of Israel. 22 But God told the prophet Shemaiah 23 to give this message to Rehoboam and to all the people of the tribes of Judah and Benjamin: 24 "Do not attack your own relatives, the people of Israel. Go home, all of you. What has happened is my will." They all obeyed the LORD's command and went back home.

Jeroboam Turns Away from God

25 King Jeroboam of Israel fortified the town of Shechem in the hill country of Ephraim and lived there for a while. Then he left and fortified the town of Penuel. 26-27 He said to himself, "As things are now, if my people go to Jerusalem and offer sacrifices to the LORD in the Temple there, they will transfer their allegiance to King Rehoboam of Judah and will kill me."

28 After thinking it over, he made two bull-calves of gold and said to his people, "You have been going long enough to Jerusalem to worship. People of Israel, here are your gods who brought you out of Egypt!" 29 He placed one of the gold bull-calves in Bethel and the other in Dan. 30 And so the people sinned, going to worship in Bethel and in Dan.[p] 31 Jeroboam also built places of worship on hilltops, and he chose priests from families who were not of the tribe of Levi.

Worship at Bethel Is Condemned

32 Jeroboam also instituted a religious festival on the fifteenth day of the eighth month, like the festival in Judah. On the altar in Bethel he offered sacrifices to the gold bull-calves he had made, and he placed there in Bethel the priests serving at the places of worship he had built. 33 And on the fifteenth day of the eighth month, the day that he himself had set, he went to Bethel and offered a sacrifice on the altar in celebration of the festival he had instituted for the people of Israel.

13 At the LORD's command a prophet from Judah went to Bethel and arrived there as Jeroboam stood at the altar to offer the sacrifice. 2 Following the LORD's command, the prophet denounced the altar: "O altar, altar, this is what the LORD says: A child, whose name will be Josiah, will be born to the family of David. He will slaughter on you the priests serving at the pagan altars who offer sacrifices on you, and he will burn human bones on you." 3 And the prophet went on to say, "This altar will fall apart, and the ashes on it will be scattered. Then you will know that the LORD has spoken through me."

4 When King Jeroboam heard this, he pointed at him and ordered, "Seize that man!" At once the king's arm became paralyzed so that he couldn't pull it back. 5 The altar suddenly fell apart and the ashes spilled to the ground, as the prophet had predicted in the name of the LORD. 6 King Jeroboam said to the prophet, "Please pray for me to the LORD your God, and ask him to heal my arm!"

The prophet prayed to the LORD, and the king's arm was healed. 7 Then the king said to the prophet, "Come home with me and have something to eat. I will reward you for what you have done."

8 The prophet answered, "Even if you gave me half of your wealth, I would not go with you or eat or drink anything with you. 9 The

p **12:30** *One ancient translation* in Bethel and in Dan; *Hebrew* in Dan.

12:28 Ex 32:4 **12:32, 33** Lev 23:33, 34 **13:2** 2 Kings 23:15, 16

Bethel was the place where Jacob had a vision and built an altar to God *(Genesis 35:1–15).*

LORD has commanded me not to eat or
drink a thing, and not to return home the
same way I came." 10 So he did not go back
the same way he had come, but by another
road.

The Old Prophet of Bethel

11 At that time there was an old prophet
living in Bethel. His sons[q] came and told
him what the prophet from Judah had done
in Bethel that day and what he had said to
King Jeroboam. 12 "Which way did he go
when he left?" the old prophet asked them.
They showed him[r] the road 13 and he told
them to saddle his donkey for him. They did
so, and he rode off 14 down the road after the
prophet from Judah and found him sitting
under an oak tree. "Are you the prophet
from Judah?" he asked.

"I am," the man answered.

15 "Come home and have a meal with
me," he said.

16 But the prophet from Judah answered, "I
can't go home with you or accept your hos-
pitality. And I won't eat or drink anything
with you here, 17 because the LORD has com-
manded me not to eat or drink a thing, and
not to return home the same way I came."

18 Then the old prophet from Bethel said to
him, "I, too, am a prophet just like you, and at
the LORD's command an angel told me to
take you home with me and offer you my
hospitality." But the old prophet was lying.

19 So the prophet from Judah went home
with the old prophet and had a meal with
him. 20 As they were sitting at the table, the
word of the LORD came to the old prophet,
21 and he cried out to the prophet from Judah,
"The LORD says that you disobeyed him and
did not do what he commanded. 22 Instead,
you returned and ate a meal in a place he had
ordered you not to eat in. Because of this you
will be killed, and your body will not be
buried in your family grave."

23 After they had finished eating, the old
prophet saddled the donkey for the prophet
from Judah, 24 who rode off. On the way a
lion met him and killed him. His body lay
on the road, and the donkey and the lion
stood beside it. 25 Some men passed by and
saw the body on the road, with the lion
standing near by. They went on into Bethel
and reported what they had seen.

26 When the old prophet heard about it,
he said, "That is the prophet who disobeyed
the LORD's command! And so the LORD sent
the lion to attack and kill him, just as the
LORD said he would." 27 Then he said to his
sons, "Saddle my donkey for me." They did
so, 28 and he rode off and found the prophet's
body lying on the road, with the donkey and
the lion still standing by it. The lion had not
eaten the body or attacked the donkey.
29 The old prophet picked up the body, put it
on the donkey, and brought it back to Bethel
to mourn over it and bury it. 30 He buried it
in his own family grave, and he and his sons
mourned over it, saying, "Oh my brother, my
brother!" 31 After the burial the prophet said
to his sons, "When I die, bury me in this
grave and lay my body next to his. 32 The
words that he spoke at the LORD's command
against the altar in Bethel and against all the
places of worship in the towns of Samaria
will surely come true."

Jeroboam's Fatal Sin

33 King Jeroboam of Israel still did not
turn from his evil ways but continued to
choose priests from ordinary families to
serve at the altars he had built. He ordained
as priest anyone who wanted to be one.
34 This sin on his part brought about the ruin
and total destruction of his dynasty.

The Death of Jeroboam's Son

14 At that time King Jeroboam's son
Abijah got sick. 2 Jeroboam said to
his wife, "Disguise yourself so that no one
will recognize you, and go to Shiloh, where
the prophet Ahijah lives, the one who said
I would be king of Israel. 3 Take him ten
loaves of bread, some cakes, and a jar of
honey. Ask him what is going to happen to
our son, and he will tell you."

4 So she went to Ahijah's home in Shiloh.
Old age had made Ahijah blind. 5 The LORD

[q] **13:11** *Some ancient translations* sons; *Hebrew* son. [r] **13:12** *Some ancient translations* showed him; *Hebrew* saw.

had told him that Jeroboam's wife was com-
ing to ask him about her son, who was sick.
And the LORD told Ahijah what to say.
When Jeroboam's wife arrived, she pre-
tended to be someone else. 6But when Ahijah
heard her coming in the door, he said, "Come
in. I know you are Jeroboam's wife. Why are
you pretending to be someone else? I have
bad news for you. 7Go and tell Jeroboam that
this is what the LORD, the God of Israel, says
to him: 'I chose you from among the people
and made you the ruler of my people Israel.
8I took the kingdom away from David's
descendants and gave it to you. But you have
not been like my servant David, who was
completely loyal to me, obeyed my com-
mands, and did only what I approve of. 9You
have committed far greater sins than those
who ruled before you. You have rejected me
and have aroused my anger by making idols
and metal images to worship. 10Because of
this I will bring disaster on your dynasty and
will kill all your male descendants, young and
old alike. I will get rid of your family; they
will be swept away like dung. 11Any members
of your family who die in the city will be
eaten by dogs, and any who die in the open
country will be eaten by vultures. I, the
LORD, have spoken.' "
12And Ahijah went on to say to Jer-
oboam's wife, "Now go back home. As soon
as you enter the town, your son will die.
13All the people of Israel will mourn for him
and bury him. He will be the only member
of Jeroboam's family who will be properly
buried, because he is the only one with
whom the LORD, the God of Israel, is
pleased. 14The LORD is going to place a king
over Israel who will put an end to Jer-
oboam's dynasty.[s] 15The LORD will punish
Israel, and she will shake like a reed shaking
in a stream. He will uproot the people of
Israel from this good land which he gave to
their ancestors, and he will scatter them
beyond the Euphrates River, because they
have aroused his anger by making idols of
the goddess Asherah. 16The LORD will aban-
don Israel because Jeroboam sinned and led
the people of Israel into sin."
17Jeroboam's wife went back to Tirzah.
Just as she entered her home, the child died.
18The people of Israel mourned for him and
buried him, as the LORD had said through
his servant, the prophet Ahijah.

The Death of Jeroboam

19Everything else that King Jeroboam did,
the wars he fought and how he ruled, are all
recorded in *The History of the Kings of Israel.*
20Jeroboam ruled as king for twenty-two
years. He died and was buried, and his son
Nadab succeeded him as king.

King Rehoboam of Judah
(2 Chronicles 11:5—12:15)

21Solomon's son Rehoboam was forty-
one years old when he became king of
Judah, and he ruled seventeen years in
Jerusalem, the city which the LORD had
chosen from all the territory of Israel as the
place where he was to be worshiped.
Rehoboam's mother was Naamah from
Ammon.
22The people of Judah sinned against the
LORD and did more to arouse his anger
against them than all their ancestors had
done. 23They built places of worship for false
gods and put up stone pillars and symbols of
Asherah to worship on the hills and under
shady trees. 24Worst of all, there were men
and women who served as prostitutes at
those pagan places of worship. The people of
Judah practiced all the shameful things done

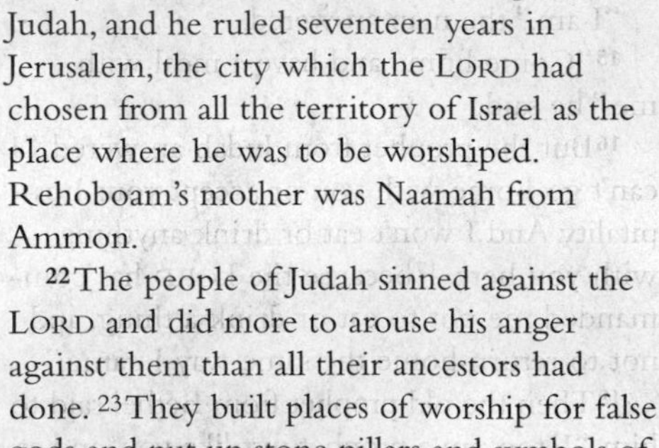

They built places of worship for false gods. (14:23)

[s] **14:14** *Hebrew has five additional words, the meaning of which is unclear.*
14:10 1 Kings 15:29 **14:23** 2 Kings 17:9, 10 **14:24** Deut 23:17

Live it!

Constantly Fighting

Unlike Solomon, whose reign was marked by peace, the new kings are at war with each other. Is there someone in your family whom you have a hard time getting along with? Constant fighting, whether it's between countries or family members, is destructive.

Did you ever get stuck in the middle of an argument between friends? When friends get angry with each other, it's easy to take sides and have things blow up into a huge disagreement. The next time conflict begins, ask yourself:

- **Is this an argument I should get involved in, or would it be better if I let the people involved work it out?**
- **What could I do or say to help people get along better?**

Remember to avoid gossiping. Encourage your friends to talk to each other. Don't let them use you to deliver hurtful messages. Even when somebody has said or done something hurtful, it is possible to be friends again. People need to be willing to talk to each other and say, "I'm sorry."

— 1 Kings 14:21–30

by the people whom the LORD had driven
out of the land as the Israelites advanced into
the country.
25 In the fifth year of Rehoboam's reign
King Shishak of Egypt attacked Jerusalem.
26 He took away all the treasures in the Temple
and in the palace, including the gold shields
Solomon had made. 27 To replace them, King
Rehoboam made bronze shields and entrusted
them to the officers responsible for guarding
the palace gates. 28 Every time the king went
to the Temple, the guards carried the shields
and then returned them to the guardroom.
29 Everything else that King Rehoboam
did is recorded in *The History of the Kings of
Judah*. 30 During all this time Rehoboam and
Jeroboam were constantly at war with each
other. 31 Rehoboam died and was buried in
the royal tombs in David's City and his son
Abijah succeeded him as king.

King Abijah of Judah
(2 Chronicles 13:1—14:1)

15 In the eighteenth year of the reign
of King Jeroboam of Israel, Abijah
became king of Judah, 2 and he ruled three
years in Jerusalem. His mother was Maacah,
the daughter of Absalom. 3 He committed
the same sins as his father and was not com-
pletely loyal to the LORD his God, as his
great-grandfather David had been. 4 But for
David's sake the LORD his God gave Abijah a
son to rule after him in Jerusalem and to
keep Jerusalem secure. 5 The LORD did this
because David had done what pleased him
and had never disobeyed any of his com-
mands, except in the case of Uriah the Hit-
tite. 6 The war which had begun between
Rehoboam and Jeroboam continued
throughout Abijah's lifetime. 7 And every-
thing else that Abijah did is recorded in *The
History of the Kings of Judah*.
8 Abijah died and was buried in David's
City, and his son Asa succeeded him as king.

King Asa of Judah
(2 Chronicles 14:1–5; 15:16—16:6; 11–14)

9 In the twentieth year of the reign of
King Jeroboam of Israel, Asa became king of

14:25 2 Chr 12:2–8 **14:26** 1 Kings 10:16, 17; 2 Chr 9:15, 16 **15:4** 1 Kings 11:36 **15:5** 2 Sam 11:1–27 **15:6** 2 Chr 13:3–21

Jeroboam was the first king of Israel, the kingdom in the north. Rehoboam was the first king of Judah, the kingdom in the south. It can be confusing!

Judah, [10]and he ruled forty-one years in Jerusalem. His grandmother was Maacah, the daughter of Absalom. [11]Asa did what pleased the LORD, as his ancestor David had done.
[12]He expelled from the country all the male and female prostitutes serving at the pagan places of worship, and he removed all the idols his predecessors had made. [13]He
removed his grandmother Maacah from her position as queen mother, because she had made an obscene idol of the fertility goddess Asherah. Asa cut down the idol and burned it in Kidron Valley. [14]Even though Asa did not destroy all the pagan places of worship, he remained faithful to the LORD all his life.
[15]He placed in the Temple all the objects his father had dedicated to God, as well as the gold and silver objects that he himself dedicated.

[16]King Asa of Judah and King Baasha of Israel were constantly at war with each other as long as they were in power. [17]Baasha
invaded Judah and started to fortify Ramah in order to cut off all traffic in and out of
Judah. [18]So King Asa took all the silver and gold that was left in the Temple and the palace, and sent it by some of his officials to Damascus, to King Benhadad of Syria, the son of Tabrimmon and grandson of Hezion, with this message: [19]"Let us be allies, as our fathers were. This silver and gold is a present for you. Now break your alliance with King Baasha of Israel, so that he will have to pull his troops out of my territory."

[20]King Benhadad agreed to Asa's proposal and sent his commanding officers and their armies to attack the cities of Israel. They captured Ijon, Dan, Abel Beth Maacah, the area near Lake Galilee, and the whole territory of Naphtali. [21]When King Baasha heard
what had happened, he stopped fortifying Ramah and went to Tirzah.

[22]Then King Asa sent out an order throughout all of Judah requiring everyone, without exception, to help carry away from Ramah the stones and timber that Baasha had been using to fortify it. With this material Asa fortified Mizpah and Geba, a city in the territory of Benjamin.

[23]Everything else that King Asa did, his brave deeds and the towns he fortified, are all recorded in *The History of the Kings of Judah*. But in his old age he was crippled by a foot disease. [24]Asa died and was buried in
the royal tombs in David's City, and his son Jehoshaphat succeeded him as king.

King Nadab of Israel

[25]In the second year of the reign of King Asa of Judah, King Jeroboam's son Nadab became king of Israel, and he ruled for two years. [26]Like his father before him, he sinned
against the LORD and led Israel into sin.

[27]Baasha son of Ahijah, of the tribe of Issachar, plotted against Nadab and killed him as Nadab and his army were besieging the city of Gibbethon in Philistia. [28]This hap-
pened during the third year of the reign of King Asa of Judah. And so Baasha succeeded Nadab as king of Israel. [29]At once he began
killing all the members of Jeroboam's family. In accordance with what the LORD had said through his servant, the prophet Ahijah from Shiloh, all of Jeroboam's family were killed; not one survived. [30]This happened because
Jeroboam aroused the anger of the LORD, the God of Israel, by the sins that he committed and that he caused Israel to commit.

[31]Everything else that Nadab did is recorded in *The History of the Kings of Israel.*
[32]King Asa of Judah and King Baasha of Israel were constantly at war with each other as long as they were in power.

King Baasha of Israel

[33]In the third year of the reign of King Asa of Judah, Baasha son of Ahijah became king of all Israel, and he ruled in Tirzah for twenty-four years. [34]Like King Jeroboam
before him, he sinned against the LORD and led Israel into sin.

15:12 2 Chr 15:8–15 **15:29** 1 Kings 14:10

Maacah was the daughter of Absalom. Who was Absalom?

16 The LORD spoke to the prophet Jehu son of Hanani and gave him this message for Baasha: 2“You were a nobody, but I made you the leader of my people Israel. And now you have sinned like Jeroboam and have led my people into sin. Their sins have aroused my anger, 3and so I will do away with you and your family, just as I did with Jeroboam. 4Any members of your family who die in the city will be eaten by dogs, and any who die in the open country will be eaten by vultures.”

5Everything else that Baasha did and all his brave deeds are recorded in *The History of the Kings of Israel.* 6Baasha died and was buried in Tirzah, and his son Elah succeeded him as king.

7That message from the LORD against Baasha and his family was given by the prophet Jehu because of the sins that Baasha committed against the LORD. He aroused the LORD's anger not only because of the evil he did, just as King Jeroboam had done before him, but also because he killed all of Jeroboam's family.

King Elah of Israel

8In the twenty-sixth year of the reign of King Asa of Judah, Elah son of Baasha became king of Israel, and he ruled in Tirzah for two years. 9Zimri, one of his officers who was in charge of half of the king's chariots, plotted against him. One day in Tirzah, Elah was getting drunk in the home of Arza, who was in charge of the palace. 10Zimri entered the house, assassinated Elah, and succeeded him as king. This happened in the twenty-seventh year of the reign of King Asa of Judah.

11As soon as Zimri became king he killed off all the members of Baasha's family. Every male relative and friend was put to death. 12And so, in accordance with what the LORD had said against Baasha through the prophet Jehu, Zimri killed all the family of Baasha. 13Because of their idolatry and because they led Israel into sin, Baasha and his son Elah had aroused the anger of the LORD, the God of Israel. 14Everything else that Elah did is recorded in *The History of the Kings of Israel.*

King Zimri of Israel

15In the twenty-seventh year of the reign of King Asa of Judah, Zimri ruled in Tirzah over Israel for seven days. The Israelite troops were besieging the city of Gibbethon in Philistia, 16and when they heard that Zimri had plotted against the king and assassinated him, then and there they all proclaimed their commander Omri king of Israel. 17Omri and his troops left Gibbethon and went and besieged Tirzah. 18When Zimri saw that the city had fallen, he went into the palace's inner fortress, set the palace on fire, and died in the flames. 19This happened because of his sins against the LORD. Like his predecessor Jeroboam, he displeased the LORD by his own sins and by leading Israel into sin. 20Everything else that Zimri did, including the account of his conspiracy, is recorded in *The History of the Kings of Israel.*

King Omri of Israel

21The people of Israel were divided: some of them wanted to make Tibni son of Ginath king, and the others were in favor of Omri. 22In the end, those in favor of Omri won out; Tibni died and Omri became king. 23So in the thirty-first year of the reign of King Asa of Judah, Omri became king of Israel, and he ruled for twelve years. The first six years he ruled in Tirzah, 24and then he bought the hill of Samaria for six thousand pieces of silver from a man named Shemer. Omri fortified the hill, built a town there, and named it Samaria, after Shemer, the former owner of the hill.

25Omri sinned against the LORD more than any of his predecessors. 26Like Jeroboam before him, he aroused the anger of the LORD, the God of Israel, by his sins and by leading the people into sin and idolatry. 27Everything else that Omri did and all his accomplishments are recorded in *The History of the Kings of Israel.* 28Omri died and was buried in Samaria, and his son Ahab succeeded him as king.

King Ahab of Israel

29In the thirty-eighth year of the reign of King Asa of Judah, Ahab son of Omri

became king of Israel, and he ruled in
Samaria for twenty-two years. 30 He sinned
against the LORD more than any of his pre-
decessors. 31 It was not enough for him to
sin like King Jeroboam; he went further and
married Jezebel, the daughter of King Eth-
baal of Sidon, and worshiped Baal. 32 He
built a temple to Baal in Samaria, made an
altar for him, and put it in the temple. 33 He
also put up an image of the goddess Asherah.
He did more to arouse the anger of the
LORD, the God of Israel, than all the kings of
Israel before him. 34 During his reign Hiel
from Bethel rebuilt Jericho. As the LORD had
foretold through Joshua son of Nun, Hiel
lost his oldest son Abiram when he laid the
foundation of Jericho, and his youngest son
Segub when he built the gates.

Elijah and the Drought

17 A prophet named Elijah, from Tishbe
in Gilead, said to King Ahab, "In the
name of the LORD, the living God of Israel,
whom I serve, I tell you that there will be
no dew or rain for the next two or three
years until I say so."
2 Then the LORD said to Elijah, 3 "Leave
this place and go east and hide yourself near
Cherith Brook, east of the Jordan. 4 The
brook will supply you with water to drink,
and I have commanded ravens to bring you
food there."

I have commanded ravens to bring you food. (17:4)

5 Elijah obeyed the LORD's command, and
went and stayed by Cherith Brook. 6 He
drank water from the brook, and ravens
brought him bread and meat every morning
and every evening. 7 After a while the brook
dried up because of the lack of rain.

Elijah and the Widow in Zarephath

8 Then the LORD said to Elijah, 9 "Now go
to the town of Zarephath, near Sidon, and
stay there. I have commanded a widow who
lives there to feed you." 10 So Elijah went to
Zarephath, and as he came to the town gate,
he saw a widow gathering firewood. "Please
bring me a drink of water," he said to her.
11 And as she was going to get it, he called
out, "And please bring me some bread, too."
12 She answered, "By the living LORD your
God I swear that I don't have any bread. All I
have is a handful of flour in a bowl and a bit
of olive oil in a jar. I came here to gather
some firewood to take back home and pre-
pare what little I have for my son and me.
That will be our last meal, and then we will
starve to death."
13 "Don't worry," Elijah said to her. "Go
on and prepare your meal. But first make a
small loaf from what you have and bring it
to me, and then prepare the rest for you
and your son. 14 For this is what the LORD,
the God of Israel, says: 'The bowl will not
run out of flour or the jar run out of oil
before the day that I, the LORD, send
rain.' "

"Go on and prepare your meal." (17:13)

15 The widow went and did as Elijah had
told her, and all of them had enough food
for many days. 16 As the LORD had promised
through Elijah, the bowl did not run out of
flour nor did the jar run out of oil.

16:34 Josh 6:26 **17:1** Jas 5:17 **17:9** Lk 4:25, 26

Study it!

Elijah

This passage marks a shift in 1 Kings. We'll still be hearing the stories of the kings, but now we also begin to find out about the prophets. First we meet Elijah, a very important prophet and miracle worker. Elijah predicts famine. He stays with a widow and her son. God saves all of them from starvation with a bowl of flour that is always full and a jar of oil that never runs dry. Later, when the son dies, Elijah brings him back to life. Do these miracles remind you of anything Jesus did?

Then God sends Elijah as a prophet to the evil King Ahab. To show that the foreign god Baal is powerless, he challenges the prophets of Baal to a contest. They will both set up altars with wood to burn an animal sacrifice. Then they will each pray to their god to light the fire. Of course nothing happens to the altar of Baal. Elijah douses his wood with jars of water for dramatic effect. When he prays, God sends down fire that burns everything, including the stones! Seems like that would get Ahab's attention, but unfortunately it doesn't.

— 1 Kings, chapters 17–18

17 Some time later the widow's son got
sick; he got worse and worse, and finally he
died. 18 She said to Elijah, "Man of God, why
did you do this to me? Did you come here
to remind God of my sins and so cause my
son's death?"

19 "Give the boy to me," Elijah said. He
took the boy from her arms, carried him
upstairs to the room where he was staying,
and laid him on the bed. 20 Then he prayed
aloud, "O LORD my God, why have you
done such a terrible thing to this widow?
She has been kind enough to take care of
me, and now you kill her son!" 21 Then Eli-
jah stretched himself out on the boy three
times and prayed, "O LORD my God, restore
this child to life!" 22 The LORD answered Eli-
jah's prayer; the child started breathing again
and revived.

23 Elijah took the boy back downstairs to
his mother and said to her, "Look, your son
is alive!"

24 She answered, "Now I know that you
are a man of God and that the LORD really
speaks through you!"

Elijah and the Prophets of Baal

18 After some time, in the third year of
the drought, the LORD said to Elijah,
"Go and present yourself to King Ahab, and
I will send rain." 2 So Elijah started out.

The famine in Samaria was at its worst,
3 so Ahab called in Obadiah, who was in
charge of the palace. (Obadiah was a devout
worshiper of the LORD, 4 and when Jezebel
was killing the LORD's prophets, Obadiah
took a hundred of them, hid them in caves
in two groups of fifty, and provided them
with food and water.) 5 Ahab said to Obadi-
ah, "Let us go and look[t] at every spring and
every stream bed in the land to see if we can
find enough grass to keep the horses and
mules alive. Maybe we won't have to kill any
of our animals." 6 They agreed on which part
of the land each one would explore, and set
off in different directions.

7 As Obadiah was on his way, he suddenly

[t] **18:5** *One ancient translation* Let us go and look; *Hebrew* You go and look.
17:21 2 Kings 4:34, 35

"Now I know that you are a man of God and that the LORD really speaks through you!" *(1 Kings 17:24)*.

met Elijah. He recognized him, bowed low before him, and asked, "Is it really you, sir?"

8 "Yes, I'm Elijah," he answered. "Go and tell your master the king that I am here."

9 Obadiah answered, "What have I done that you want to put me in danger of being killed by King Ahab? 10 By the living LORD, your God, I swear that the king has made a search for you in every country in the world. Whenever the ruler of a country reported that you were not in his country, Ahab would require that ruler to swear that you could not be found. 11 And now you want me to go and tell him that you are here? 12 What if the spirit of the LORD carries you off to some unknown place as soon as I leave? Then, when I tell Ahab that you are here and he can't find you, he will put me to death. Remember that I have been a devout worshiper of the LORD ever since I was a boy. 13 Haven't you heard that when Jezebel was killing the prophets of the LORD I hid a hundred of them in caves, in two groups of fifty, and supplied them with food and water? 14 So how can you order me to go and tell the king that you are here? He will kill me!"

15 Elijah answered, "By the living LORD Almighty, whom I serve, I promise that I will present myself to the king today."

16 So Obadiah went to King Ahab and told him, and Ahab set off to meet Elijah. 17 When Ahab saw him, he said, "So there you are—the worst troublemaker in Israel!"

18 "I'm not the troublemaker," Elijah answered. "You are—you and your father. You are disobeying the LORD's commands and worshiping the idols of Baal. 19 Now order all the people of Israel to meet me at Mount Carmel. Bring along the 450 prophets of Baal and the 400 prophets of the goddess Asherah who are supported by Queen Jezebel."

20 So Ahab summoned all the Israelites and the prophets of Baal to meet at Mount Carmel. 21 Elijah went up to the people and said, "How much longer will it take you to make up your minds? If the LORD is God, worship him; but if Baal is God, worship him!" But the people didn't say a word. 22 Then Elijah said, "I am the only prophet of the LORD still left, but there are 450 prophets of Baal. 23 Bring two bulls; let the prophets of Baal take one, kill it, cut it in pieces, and put it on the wood—but don't light the fire. I will do the same with the other bull. 24 Then let the prophets of Baal pray to their god, and I will pray to the LORD, and the one who answers by sending fire—he is God."

The people shouted their approval.

25 Then Elijah said to the prophets of Baal, "Since there are so many of you, you take a bull and prepare it first. Pray to your god, but don't set fire to the wood."

26 They took the bull that was brought to them, prepared it, and prayed to Baal until noon. They shouted, "Answer us, Baal!" and kept dancing around the altar they had built. But no answer came.

27 At noon Elijah started making fun of them: "Pray louder! He is a god! Maybe he is day-dreaming or relieving himself, or perhaps he's gone off on a trip! Or maybe he's sleeping, and you've got to wake him up!" 28 So the prophets prayed louder and cut themselves with knives and daggers, according to their ritual, until blood flowed. 29 They kept on ranting and raving until the middle of the afternoon; but no answer came, not a sound was heard.

30 Then Elijah said to the people, "Come closer to me," and they all gathered around him. He set about repairing the altar of the LORD which had been torn down. 31 He took twelve stones, one for each of the twelve tribes named for the sons of Jacob, the man to whom the LORD had given the name Israel. 32 With these stones he rebuilt the altar for the worship of the LORD. He dug a trench around it, large enough to hold about four gallons of water. 33 Then he placed the wood on the altar, cut the bull in pieces, and laid it on the wood. He said, "Fill four jars with water and pour it on the

18:31 Gen 32:28; 35:10

Elijah used twelve stones to make his altar. For another story about twelve stones that represent the twelve tribes, read Joshua, chapter 4.

offering and the wood." They did so, 34and
he said, "Do it again"—and they did. "Do it
once more," he said—and they did. 35The
water ran down around the altar and filled
the trench.

36At the hour of the afternoon sacrifice
the prophet Elijah approached the altar and
prayed, "O LORD, the God of Abraham,
Isaac, and Jacob, prove now that you are the
God of Israel and that I am your servant and
have done all this at your command.
37Answer me, LORD, answer me, so that this
people will know that you, the LORD, are
God and that you are bringing them back to
yourself."[u]

38The LORD sent fire down, and it burned
up the sacrifice, the wood, and the stones,
scorched the earth and dried up the water
in the trench. 39When the people saw this,
they threw themselves on the ground and
exclaimed, "The LORD is God; the LORD
alone is God!"

The LORD sent fire down. (18:38)

40Elijah ordered, "Seize the prophets of
Baal; don't let any of them get away!" The
people seized them all, and Elijah led them
down to Kishon Brook and killed them.

The End of the Drought

41Then Elijah said to King Ahab, "Now,
go and eat. I hear the roar of rain approach-
ing." 42While Ahab went to eat, Elijah
climbed to the top of Mount Carmel, where
he bowed down to the ground, with his
head between his knees. 43He said to his ser-
vant, "Go and look toward the sea."

The servant went and returned, saying, "I
didn't see a thing." Seven times in all Elijah
told him to go and look. 44The seventh time
he returned and said, "I saw a little cloud no
bigger than a man's hand, coming up from
the sea."

Elijah ordered his servant, "Go to King
Ahab and tell him to get in his chariot and
go back home before the rain stops him."

"I saw a little cloud." (18:44)

45In a little while the sky was covered
with dark clouds, the wind began to blow,
and a heavy rain began to fall. Ahab got in
his chariot and started back to Jezreel. 46The
power of the LORD came on Elijah; he fas-
tened his clothes tight around his waist and
ran ahead of Ahab all the way to Jezreel.

Elijah on Mount Sinai

19 King Ahab told his wife Jezebel
everything that Elijah had done and
how he had put all the prophets of Baal to
death. 2She sent a message to Elijah: "May
the gods strike me dead if by this time
tomorrow I don't do the same thing to you
that you did to the prophets." 3Elijah was
afraid and fled for his life; he took his servant
and went to Beersheba in Judah.

Leaving the servant there, 4Elijah walked a
whole day into the wilderness. He stopped
and sat down in the shade of a tree and
wished he would die. "It's too much, LORD,"

[u] **18:37** you are bringing them back to yourself; *or* you yourself made them turn away from you.

18:42–45 Jas 5:18 **19:4** Jon 4:3

Pray it!

A Whisper

Now we get to meet King Ahab's wife, Queen Jezebel. She is just as evil as Ahab, maybe even worse! She threatens to kill Elijah. Elijah goes into hiding in the wilderness in fear and despair. He is overwhelmed with the task before him and the situation he is in. He even prays that he will die. God has a different plan though. Elijah is fed by an angel, witnesses an earthquake, a great wind, and fire. But he doesn't see God in any of these dramatic events. Then in a soft whisper, God speaks to him.

Dear God,
I want to hear your voice.
I want it to be loud and dramatic, something I can't miss!
But that's not the way you usually speak to us.
Help me to be patient and listen for you
in the quiet of my heart.
Help me to make time and space
where I can hear the gentle whisper of your voice.

— 1 Kings, chapter 19

he prayed. "Take away my life; I might as
well be dead!"
5 He lay down under the tree and fell
asleep. Suddenly an angel touched him and
said, "Wake up and eat." 6 He looked around
and saw a loaf of bread and a jar of water
near his head. He ate and drank, and lay
down again. 7 The LORD's angel returned
and woke him up a second time, saying, "Get
up and eat, or the trip will be too much for
you." 8 Elijah got up, ate and drank, and the
food gave him enough strength to walk forty
days to Sinai, the holy mountain. 9 There he
went into a cave to spend the night.
Suddenly the LORD spoke to him, "Elijah,
what are you doing here?"
10 He answered, "LORD God Almighty, I
have always served you—you alone. But the
people of Israel have broken their covenant
with you, torn down your altars, and killed
all your prophets. I am the only one left—
and they are trying to kill me!"
11 "Go out and stand before me on top of
the mountain," the LORD said to him. Then
the LORD passed by and sent a furious wind
that split the hills and shattered the rocks—
but the LORD was not in the wind. The
wind stopped blowing, and then there was
an earthquake—but the LORD was not in
the earthquake. 12 After the earthquake there
was a fire—but the LORD was not in the fire.
And after the fire there was the soft whisper
of a voice.
13 When Elijah heard it, he covered his
face with his cloak and went out and stood
at the entrance of the cave. A voice said to
him, "Elijah, what are you doing here?"
14 He answered, " LORD God Almighty, I
have always served you—you alone. But the
people of Israel have broken their covenant
with you, torn down your altars, and killed
all your prophets. I am the only one left—
and they are trying to kill me."
15 The LORD said, "Return to the wilder-
ness near Damascus, then enter the city and
anoint Hazael as king of Syria; 16 anoint Jehu
son of Nimshi as king of Israel, and anoint
Elisha son of Shaphat from Abel Meholah
to succeed you as prophet. 17 Anyone who
escapes being put to death by Hazael will be

19:10, 14 Rom 11:3 **19:15** 2 Kings 8:7–13 **19:16** 2 Kings 9:1–6

killed by Jehu, and anyone who escapes Jehu
will be killed by Elisha. 18Yet I will leave
seven thousand people alive in Israel—all
those who are loyal to me and have not
bowed to Baal or kissed his idol."

The Call of Elisha

19Elijah left and found Elisha plowing
with a team of oxen; there were eleven
teams ahead of him, and he was plowing
with the last one. Elijah took off his cloak
and put it on Elisha. 20Elisha then left his
oxen, ran after Elijah, and said, "Let me kiss
my father and mother good-bye, and then I
will go with you."

Elijah answered, "All right, go back. I'm
not stopping you!"[v]

21Then Elisha went to his team of oxen,
killed them, and cooked the meat, using the
yoke as fuel for the fire. He gave the meat to
the people, and they ate it. Then he went
and followed Elijah as his helper.

War with Syria

20 King Benhadad of Syria gathered all
his troops, and supported by thirty-
two other rulers with their horses and chari-
ots, he marched up, laid siege to Samaria, and
launched attacks against it. 2He sent messen-
gers into the city to King Ahab of Israel to
say, "King Benhadad demands that 3you sur-
render to him your silver and gold, your
women and the strongest of your children."

4"Tell my lord, King Benhadad, that I
agree; he can have me and everything I
own," Ahab answered.

5Later the messengers came back to Ahab
with another demand from Benhadad: "I
sent you word that you were to hand over to
me your silver and gold, your women and
your children. 6Now, however, I will send
my officers to search your palace and the
homes of your officials, and to take every-
thing they[w] consider valuable. They will be
there about this time tomorrow."

7King Ahab called in all the leaders of the
country and said, "You see that this man
wants to ruin us. He sent me a message
demanding my wives and children, my silver
and gold, and I agreed."

Live it!

Elisha

Elisha was a wealthy farmer who gives up everything to take over for Elijah. Like the call of the Apostles in the Gospels, the call in this story is one that Elisha answers almost immediately. It is hard to imagine what we might do if a messenger from God came up to us in the middle of a school day and said, "Leave everything and come follow me. God has work for you to do." Okay, maybe there are some things we would be happy to give up, like homework and chores. But it would be hard to leave everything behind, such as your favorite things and the people you love and care about.

But God *does* ask us every day not to be attached to the things of this world. Every day we need to live as God wants and stay focused on God's will for us. God has called you through your Baptism to speak his truth to the people you meet, just like he called Elisha.

— 1 Kings 19:19–21

[v] **19:20** All right . . . you; *or* Go on, but come back, because what I have just done to you is important.
[w] **20:6** *Some ancient translations* they; *Hebrew* you.
19:18 Rom 11:4

When the kings of his Chosen People won't listen, God uses foreign kings like Hazael of Syria *(1 Kings 19:15-17)* **to get their attention.**

8The leaders and the people answered,
"Don't pay any attention to him; don't give
in."
9So Ahab replied to Benhadad's messen-
gers, "Tell my lord the king that I agreed to
his first demand, but I cannot agree to the
second."
The messengers left and then returned
with another message 10from Benhadad: "I
will bring enough men to destroy this city
of yours and carry off the rubble in their
hands. May the gods strike me dead if I
don't!"
11King Ahab answered, "Tell King Ben-
hadad that a real soldier does his bragging
after a battle, not before it."
12Benhadad received Ahab's answer as he
and his allies, the other rulers, were drinking
in their tents. He ordered his men to get
ready to attack the city, and so they moved
into position.
13Meanwhile, a prophet went to King
Ahab and said, "The LORD says, 'Don't be
afraid of that huge army! I will give you vic-
tory over it today, and you will know that I
am the LORD.' "
14"Who will lead the attack?" Ahab asked.
The prophet answered, "The LORD says
that the young soldiers under the command
of the district governors are to do it."
"Who will command the main force?" the
king asked.
"You," the prophet answered.
15So the king called out the young sol-
diers who were under the district com-
manders, 232 in all. Then he called out the
Israelite army, a total of seven thousand men.
16The attack began at noon, as Benhadad
and his thirty-two allies were getting drunk
in their tents. 17The young soldiers advanced
first. Scouts sent out by Benhadad reported
to him that a group of soldiers was coming
out of Samaria. 18He ordered, "Take them
alive, no matter whether they are coming to
fight or to ask for peace."
19The young soldiers led the attack, fol-
lowed by the Israelite army, 20and each one
killed the man he fought. The Syrians fled,
with the Israelites in hot pursuit, but Ben-
hadad escaped on horseback, accompanied
by some of the cavalry. 21King Ahab took to
the field, captured[x] the horses and chariots,
and inflicted a severe defeat on the Syrians.
22Then the prophet went to King Ahab
and said, "Go back and build up your forces
and make careful plans, because the king of
Syria will attack again next spring."

The Second Syrian Attack

23King Benhadad's officials said to him,
"The gods of Israel are mountain gods, and
that is why the Israelites defeated us. But we
will certainly defeat them if we fight them
in the plains. 24Now, remove the thirty-two
rulers from their commands and replace
them with field commanders. 25Then call up
an army as large as the one that deserted
you, with the same number of horses and
chariots. We will fight the Israelites in the
plains, and this time we will defeat them."
King Benhadad agreed and followed their
advice. 26The following spring he called up
his men and marched with them to the city
of Aphek to attack the Israelites. 27The
Israelites were called up and equipped; they
marched out and camped in two groups fac-
ing the Syrians. The Israelites looked like
two small flocks of goats compared to the
Syrians, who spread out over the country-
side.
28A prophet went to King Ahab and said,
"This is what the LORD says: 'Because the
Syrians say that I am a god of the hills and
not of the plains, I will give you victory over
their huge army, and you and your people
will know that I am the LORD.' "
29For seven days the Syrians and the
Israelites stayed in their camps, facing each
other. On the seventh day they started fight-
ing, and the Israelites killed a hundred thou-
sand Syrians. 30The survivors fled into the
city of Aphek, where the city walls fell on
twenty-seven thousand of them.

[x] **20:21** *One ancient translation* captured; *Hebrew* destroyed.

Find Syria on Map 3 in the back of this Bible. According to the map, what is another name for Syria?

Benhadad also escaped into the city and
took refuge in the back room of a house.
31 His officials went to him and said, "We
have heard that the Israelite kings are merci-
ful. Give us permission to go to the king of
Israel with sackcloth around our waists and
ropes around our necks, and maybe he will
spare your life." 32 So they wrapped sackcloth
around their waists and ropes around their
necks, went to Ahab and said, "Your servant
Benhadad pleads with you for his life."

Ahab answered, "Is he still alive? Good!
He's like a brother to me!"

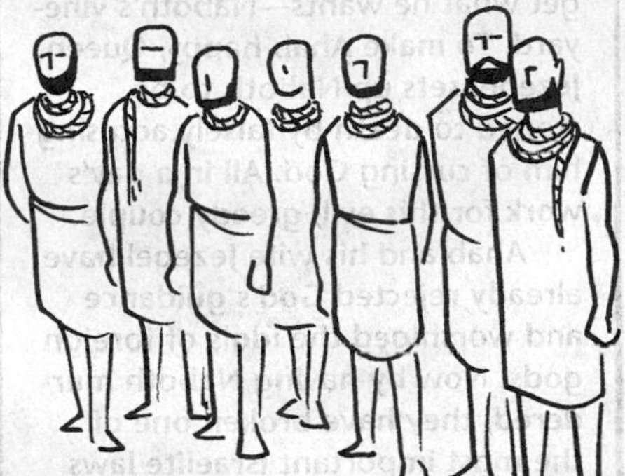

They wrapped . . . ropes around their necks. (20:32)

33 Benhadad's officials were watching for a
good sign, and when Ahab said "brother,"
they took it up at once, and said, "As you
say, Benhadad is your brother!"

"Bring him to me," Ahab ordered. When
Benhadad arrived, Ahab invited him to get
in the chariot with him. 34 Benhadad said to
him, "I will restore to you the towns my
father took from your father, and you may
set up a commercial center for yourself in
Damascus, just as my father did in Samaria."

Ahab replied, "On these terms, then, I will
set you free." He made a treaty with him and
let him go.

A Prophet Condemns Ahab

35 At the LORD's command a member of a
group of prophets ordered a fellow prophet
to hit him. But he refused, 36 so he said to
him, "Because you have disobeyed the
LORD's command, a lion will kill you as
soon as you leave me." And as soon as he
left, a lion came along and killed him.

37 Then this same prophet went to another
man and said, "Hit me!" This man did so; he
hit him a hard blow and hurt him. 38 The
prophet bandaged his face with a cloth, to
disguise himself, and went and stood by the
road, waiting for the king of Israel to pass.
39 As the king was passing by, the prophet
called out to him and said, "Your Majesty,
I was fighting in the battle when a soldier
brought a captured enemy to me and said,
'Guard this man; if he escapes, you will pay
for it with your life or else pay a fine of
three thousand pieces of silver.' 40 But I got
busy with other things, and the man
escaped."

The king answered, "You have pro-
nounced your own sentence, and you will
have to pay the penalty."

41 The prophet tore the cloth from his
face, and at once the king recognized him as
one of the prophets. 42 The prophet then said
to the king, "This is the word of the LORD:
'Because you allowed the man to escape
whom I had ordered to be killed, you will
pay for it with your life, and your army will
be destroyed for letting his army escape.' "

43 The king went back home to Samaria,
worried and depressed.

Naboth's Vineyard

21 Near King Ahab's palace in Jezreel
there was a vineyard owned by a
man named Naboth. 2 One day Ahab said to
Naboth, "Let me have your vineyard; it is
close to my palace, and I want to use the
land for a vegetable garden. I will give you a
better vineyard for it or, if you prefer, I will
pay you a fair price."

3 "I inherited this vineyard from my ances-
tors," Naboth replied. "The LORD forbid that
I should let you have it!"

4 Ahab went home, depressed and angry
over what Naboth had said to him. He lay
down on his bed, facing the wall, and would
not eat. 5 His wife Jezebel went to him and

20:36 1 Kings 13:24

asked, "Why are you so depressed? Why
won't you eat?"
6 He answered, "Because of what Naboth
said to me. I offered to buy his vineyard or, if
he preferred, to give him another one for it,
but he told me that I couldn't have it!"
7 "Well, are you the king or aren't you?"
Jezebel replied. "Get out of bed, cheer up,
and eat. I will get you Naboth's vineyard!"
8 Then she wrote some letters, signed
Ahab's name to them, sealed them with his
seal, and sent them to the officials and lead-
ing citizens of Jezreel.
9 The letters said: "Pro-
claim a day of fasting, call the people togeth-
er, and give Naboth the place of honor.
10 Get a couple of scoundrels to accuse him
to his face of cursing God and the king.
Then take him out of the city and stone him
to death."
11 The officials and leading citizens of
Jezreel did what Jezebel had commanded.
12 They proclaimed a day of fasting, called
the people together, and gave Naboth the
place of honor.
13 The two scoundrels pub-
licly accused him of cursing God and the
king, and so he was taken outside the city
and stoned to death.
14 The message was sent
to Jezebel: "Naboth has been put to death."
15 As soon as Jezebel received the message,
she said to Ahab, "Naboth is dead. Now go
and take possession of the vineyard which he
refused to sell to you."
16 At once Ahab went
to the vineyard to take possession of it.
17 Then the LORD said to Elijah, the
prophet from Tishbe,
18 "Go to King Ahab of
Samaria. You will find him in Naboth's vine-
yard, about to take possession of it.
19 Tell
him that I, the LORD, say to him, 'After mur-
dering the man, are you taking over his
property as well?' Tell him that this is what I
say: 'In the very place that the dogs licked up
Naboth's blood they will lick up your
blood!' "
20 When Ahab saw Elijah, he said, "Have
you caught up with me, my enemy?"
"Yes, I have," Elijah answered. "You have
devoted yourself completely to doing what is
wrong in the LORD's sight.
21 So the LORD
says to you, 'I will bring disaster on you. I
will do away with you and get rid of every
male in your family, young and old alike.
22 Your family will become like the family of
King Jeroboam son of Nebat and like the
family of King Baasha son of Ahijah, because
you have stirred up my anger by leading
Israel into sin.'
23 And concerning Jezebel, the
LORD says that dogs will eat her body in the
city of Jezreel.
24 Any of your relatives who
die in the city will be eaten by dogs, and any
who die in the open country will be eaten
by vultures."
(25 There was no one else who had devot-
ed himself so completely to doing wrong in
the LORD's sight as Ahab—all at the urging
of his wife Jezebel.
26 He committed the

Study it!

No Shame

Naboth is a holy man who is devoted to God and holds sacred the trust God has given him, the land of his ancestors. He is the opposite of the greedy, pouty King Ahab who sulks because he can't get what he wants—Naboth's vineyard. To make Ahab happy, Queen Jezebel sets up Naboth to be stoned to death by falsely accusing him of cursing God. All in a day's work for this evil, greedy couple.

Ahab and his wife Jezebel have already rejected God's guidance and worshiped the idols of foreign gods. Now by having Naboth murdered, they have broken one of the most important Israelite laws about land ownership. They have abused their power at the expense of a lowly person. This is the last straw for God. He sends Elijah to prophesy that they will die shamefully.

— 1 Kings, chapter 21

21:23 2 Kings 9:36

most shameful sins by worshiping idols, as the Amorites had done, whom the LORD had driven out of the land as the people of Israel advanced.)

27 When Elijah finished speaking, Ahab tore his clothes, took them off, and put on sackcloth. He refused food, slept in the sackcloth, and went about gloomy and depressed.

28 The LORD said to the prophet Elijah, 29 "Have you noticed how Ahab has humbled himself before me? Since he has done this, I will not bring disaster on him during his lifetime; it will be during his son's lifetime that I will bring disaster on Ahab's family."

The Prophet Micaiah Warns Ahab

(2 Chronicles 18:2–27)

22 There was peace between Israel and Syria for the next two years, 2 but in the third year King Jehoshaphat of Judah went to see King Ahab of Israel.

3 Ahab asked his officials, "Why is it that we have not done anything to get back Ramoth in Gilead from the king of Syria? It belongs to us!" 4 And Ahab asked Jehoshaphat, "Will you go with me to attack Ramoth?"

"I am ready when you are," Jehoshaphat answered, "and so are my soldiers and my cavalry. 5 But first let's consult the LORD."

6 So Ahab called in the prophets, about four hundred of them, and asked them, "Should I go and attack Ramoth, or not?"

"Attack it," they answered. "The Lord will give you victory."

7 But Jehoshaphat asked, "Isn't there another prophet through whom we can consult the LORD?"

8 Ahab answered, "There is one more, Micaiah son of Imlah. But I hate him because he never prophesies anything good for me; it's always something bad."

"You shouldn't say that!" Jehoshaphat replied.

9 Then Ahab called in a court official and told him to go and get Micaiah at once.

10 The two kings, dressed in their royal robes, were sitting on their thrones at the threshing place just outside the gate of Samaria, and all the prophets were prophesying in front of them. 11 One of them, Zedekiah son of Chenaanah, made iron horns and said to Ahab, "This is what the LORD says: 'With these you will fight the Syrians and totally defeat them.' " 12 All the other prophets said the same thing. "March against Ramoth and you will win," they said. "The LORD will give you victory."

13 Meanwhile, the official who had gone to get Micaiah said to him, "All the other prophets have prophesied success for the king, and you had better do the same."

14 But Micaiah answered, "By the living LORD I promise that I will say what he tells me to!"

15 When he appeared before King Ahab, the king asked him, "Micaiah, should King Jehoshaphat and I go and attack Ramoth, or not?"

"Attack!" Micaiah answered. "Of course you'll win. The LORD will give you victory."

16 But Ahab replied, "When you speak to me in the name of the LORD, tell the truth! How many times do I have to tell you that?"

17 Micaiah answered, "I can see the army of Israel scattered over the hills like sheep without a shepherd. And the LORD said, 'These men have no leader; let them go home in peace.' "

18 Ahab said to Jehoshaphat, "Didn't I tell you that he never prophesies anything good for me? It's always something bad!"

19 Micaiah went on: "Now listen to what the LORD says! I saw the LORD sitting on his throne in heaven, with all his angels standing beside him. 20 The LORD asked, 'Who will deceive Ahab so that he will go and be killed at Ramoth?' Some of the angels said one thing, and others said something else, 21 until

22:17 Num 27:17; Mt 9:36; Mk 6:34 **22:19** Job 1:6; Isa 6:1

"Ahab tore his clothes" *(1 Kings 21:27)*. **This is a sign that a person has realized she or he has done something terrible.**

a spirit stepped forward, approached the
LORD, and said, 'I will deceive him.'
22'How?' the LORD asked. The spirit replied,
'I will go and make all of Ahab's prophets
tell lies.' The LORD said, 'Go and deceive
him. You will succeed.' "
23And Micaiah concluded: "This is what
has happened. The LORD has made these
prophets of yours lie to you. But he himself
has decreed that you will meet with disas-
ter!"
24Then the prophet Zedekiah went up to
Micaiah, slapped his face, and asked, "Since
when did the LORD's spirit leave me and
speak to you?"
25"You will find out when you go into
some back room to hide," Micaiah replied.
26Then King Ahab ordered one of his
officers, "Arrest Micaiah and take him to
Amon, the governor of the city, and to
Prince Joash. 27Tell them to throw him in
prison and to put him on bread and water
until I return safely."
28"If you return safely," Micaiah
exclaimed, "then the LORD has not spoken
through me!" And he added, "Listen, every-
one, to what I have said!"

The Death of Ahab

(2 Chronicles 18:28–34)

29Then King Ahab of Israel and King
Jehoshaphat of Judah went to attack the city
of Ramoth in Gilead. 30Ahab said to
Jehoshaphat, "As we go into battle, I will dis-
guise myself, but you wear your royal gar-
ments." So the king of Israel went into battle
in disguise.
31The king of Syria had ordered his thir-
ty-two chariot commanders to attack no
one else except the king of Israel. 32So
when they saw King Jehoshaphat, they all
thought that he was the king of Israel, and
they turned to attack him. But when he
cried out, 33they realized that he was not
the king of Israel, and they stopped their
attack. 34By chance, however, a Syrian sol-
dier shot an arrow which struck King Ahab
between the joints of his armor. "I'm
wounded!" he cried out to his chariot driv-
er. "Turn around and pull out of the bat-
tle!"
35While the battle raged on, King Ahab
remained propped up in his chariot, facing
the Syrians. The blood from his wound ran
down and covered the bottom of the chari-
ot, and at evening he died. 36Near sunset the
order went out through the Israelite ranks:
"Each of you go back to your own country
and city!"
37So died King Ahab. His body was taken
to Samaria and buried. 38His chariot was
cleaned up at the pool of Samaria, where
dogs licked up his blood and prostitutes
washed themselves, as the LORD had said
would happen.
39Everything else that King Ahab did,
including an account of his palace decorated
with ivory and of all the cities he built, is
recorded in *The History of the Kings of Israel.*
40At his death his son Ahaziah succeeded
him as king.

King Jehoshaphat of Judah

(2 Chronicles 20:31—21:1)

41In the fourth year of the reign of King
Ahab of Israel, Jehoshaphat son of Asa
became king of Judah 42at the age of thirty-
five, and he ruled in Jerusalem for twenty-
five years. His mother was Azubah, the
daughter of Shilhi. 43Like his father Asa
before him, he did what was right in the
sight of the LORD; but the places of worship
were not destroyed, and the people contin-
ued to offer sacrifices and burn incense
there. 44Jehoshaphat made peace with the
king of Israel.
45Everything else that Jehoshaphat did, all
his bravery and his battles, are recorded in
The History of the Kings of Judah. 46He got
rid of all the male and female prostitutes
serving at the pagan altars who were still left
from the days of his father Asa.
47The land of Edom had no king; it was

Many kings had court prophets like Zedekiah. Rather than speaking for God, they often told the king what he wanted to hear.

ruled by a deputy appointed by the king of
Judah.
48 King Jehoshaphat had ocean-going
ships built to sail to the land of Ophir for
gold; but they were wrecked at Eziongeber
and never sailed. 49 Then King Ahaziah
of Israel offered to let his men sail with
Jehoshaphat's men, but Jehoshaphat refused
the offer.
50 Jehoshaphat died and was buried in the
royal tombs in David's City, and his son
Jehoram succeeded him as king.

King Ahaziah of Israel

51 In the seventeenth year of the reign of
King Jehoshaphat of Judah, Ahaziah son of
Ahab became king of Israel, and he ruled in
Samaria for two years. 52 He sinned against
the LORD, following the wicked example of
his father Ahab, his mother Jezebel, and King
Jeroboam, who had led Israel into sin. 53 He
worshiped and served Baal, and like his
father before him, he aroused the anger of
the LORD, the God of Israel.

Your Next Step

Congratulations on finishing the First Book of Kings! Use this space to write your thoughts and questions about this book. If you are following the suggested reading plan, go ahead to the Second Book of Kings. It continues with the story of the prophets Elijah and Elisha and the kings of Israel and Judah.

THE SECOND BOOK OF Kings

Have you ever watched a character in a movie and you just knew they were going to make a big mistake? The other characters warn them, but they just can't seem to stop themselves. The people of Israel are kind of like that in the Second Book of Kings. This book continues the story of the Israelites' history, but it doesn't end well. The two kingdoms—Judah in the south and Israel in the north—each have their own challenges even though their stories are still connected.

The prophet Elisha and other prophets continue the work begun by Elijah in calling the leaders and the people away from idolatry and injustice. In the end, the warning is ignored, and the people are led farther and farther away from their promise to serve only God. Eventually, all is lost.

Chap. 25

Headlines

- Elijah Rides Fiery Chariot to Heaven (2:1–18)
- Elisha Brings Boy Back to Life (4:8–37)
- Evil Queen Meets Her Fate (9:30–37)
- A Great Prophet Dies (13:14–21)
- Assyrians Conquer Samaria (Israel)! (17:5–23)
- Faithful King Rules Judah (18:1–8)
- Jerusalem and the Temple Destroyed (25:1–17)

FACTOIDS

How does this book fit into the Bible? This book concludes the story of Israel's kings. It is a major turning point in the history of the Israelites. The Temple and city of Jerusalem are destroyed, and the people are led away in exile.

Why was it written? It was written to show that Israel's history was guided by God.

Jesus connection: The story of Jesus feeding the crowds in all four Gospels recalls Elisha's feeding the prophets in 2 Kings 4:42–44.

Important themes

- God answers those who call on his name.
- God continually calls his people to repent and be faithful.
- Those who refuse to repent and turn to God will suffer the consequences and be expelled from God's presence.

2 KINGS

Elijah and King Ahaziah

1 After the death of King Ahab of Israel
the country of Moab rebelled against
Israel.
2 King Ahaziah of Israel fell off the balcony
on the roof of his palace in Samaria and was
seriously injured. So he sent some messen-
gers to consult Baalzebub, the god of the
Philistine city of Ekron, in order to find out
whether or not he would recover. 3 But an
angel of the LORD commanded Elijah, the
prophet from Tishbe, to go and meet the
messengers of King Ahaziah and ask them,
"Why are you going to consult Baalzebub,
the god of Ekron? Is it because you think
there is no god in Israel? 4 Tell the king that
the LORD says, 'You will not recover from
your injuries; you will die!' "
Elijah did as the LORD commanded, 5 and
the messengers returned to the king. "Why
have you come back?" he asked.
6 They answered, "We were met by a man
who told us to come back and tell you that
the LORD says to you, 'Why are you sending
messengers to consult Baalzebub, the god of
Ekron? Is it because you think there is no
god in Israel? You will not recover from your
injuries; you will die!' "
7 "What did the man look like?" the king
asked.
8 "He was wearing a cloak made of animal
skins, tied with[a] a leather belt," they
answered.
"It's Elijah!" the king exclaimed.
9 Then he sent an officer with fifty men to
get Elijah. The officer found him sitting on a
hill and said to him, "Man of God, the king
orders you to come down."
10 "If I am a man of God," Elijah answered,
"may fire come down from heaven and kill
you and your men!" At once fire came down
and killed the officer and his men.
11 The king sent another officer with fifty
men, who went up[b] and said to Elijah, "Man
of God, the king orders you to come down
at once!"
12 "If I am a man of God," Elijah answered,
"may fire come down from heaven and kill
you and your men!" At once the fire of God
came down and killed the officer and his
men.
13 Once more the king sent an officer with
fifty men. He went up the hill, fell on his
knees in front of Elijah, and pleaded, "Man
of God, be merciful to me and my men.
Spare our lives! 14 The two other officers and
their men were killed by fire from heaven;
but please be merciful to me!"
15 The angel of the LORD said to Elijah,
"Go down with him, and don't be afraid."
So Elijah went with the officer to the king
16 and said to him, "This is what the LORD
says: 'Because you sent messengers to consult
Baalzebub, the god of Ekron—as if there
were no god in Israel to consult—you will
not get well; you will die!' "
17 Ahaziah died, as the LORD had said
through Elijah. Ahaziah had no sons, so his
brother[c] Joram succeeded him as king in the
second year of the reign of Jehoram son of
Jehoshaphat, king of Judah.
18 Everything else that King Ahaziah did
is recorded in *The History of the Kings of
Israel*.

Elijah Is Taken Up to Heaven

2 The time came for the LORD to take
Elijah up to heaven in a whirlwind. Eli-
jah and Elisha set out from Gilgal, 2 and on
the way Elijah said to Elisha, "Now stay
here; the LORD has ordered me to go to
Bethel."
But Elisha answered, "I swear by my loyal-
ty to the living LORD and to you that I will
not leave you." So they went on to Bethel.
3 A group of prophets who lived there
went to Elisha and asked him, "Do you

[a] **1:8** was wearing . . . with; *or* was a hairy man and wore. [b] **1:11** *One ancient translation* went up; *Hebrew* answered. [c] **1:17** *Some ancient translations* his brother; *Hebrew does not have these words.*

1:8 Mt 3:4; Mk 1:6 **1:10, 12** Lk 9:54

Live it!

Saying Good-bye

Have you ever had to say good-bye to someone close to you? Maybe a friend moved, or someone you love passed away. Letting go of someone you care about is a very hard thing to do. Elisha doesn't want Elijah to leave him, but Elijah knows that it's his time to go. Something of Elijah remains with Elisha, though—Elijah's cloak. It is a symbol that Elisha now has Elijah's power.

Even when someone leaves us, we keep a part of him or her. It doesn't have to be a piece of clothing or even a picture. Our memories, the lessons we learned from the person, the love we have shared remains with us. When we entrust the person we love to God, we can stay connected. If you've lost someone, pray for him or her. If he or she has died or is just far away, ask God to look after him or her.

— 2 Kings 2:1–15

know that the LORD is going to take your
master away from you today?"
"Yes, I know," Elisha answered. "But let's
not talk about it."
4Then Elijah said to Elisha, "Now stay
here; the LORD has ordered me to go to
Jericho."
But Elisha answered, "I swear by my loyal-
ty to the living LORD and to you that I will
not leave you." So they went on to Jericho.
5A group of prophets who lived there
went to Elisha and asked him, "Do you
know that the LORD is going to take your
master away from you today?"
"Yes, I know," Elisha answered. "But let's
not talk about it."
6Then Elijah said to Elisha, "Now stay
here; the LORD has ordered me to go to the
Jordan River."
But Elisha answered, "I swear by my loyal-
ty to the living LORD and to you that I will
not leave you." So they went on, 7and fifty
of the prophets followed them to the Jordan.
Elijah and Elisha stopped by the river, and
the fifty prophets stood a short distance
away. 8Then Elijah took off his cloak, rolled
it up, and struck the water with it; the water
divided, and he and Elisha crossed to the
other side on dry ground. 9There, Elijah said
to Elisha, "Tell me what you want me to do
for you before I am taken away."
"Let me receive the share of your power
that will make me your successor,"[d] Elisha
answered.
10"That is a difficult request to grant," Eli-
jah replied. "But you will receive it if you see
me as I am being taken away from you; if
you don't see me, you won't receive it."
11They kept talking as they walked on;
then suddenly a chariot of fire pulled by
horses of fire came between them, and Elijah
was taken up to heaven by a whirlwind.
12Elisha saw it and cried out to Elijah, "My
father, my father! Mighty defender of Israel!
You are gone!" And he never saw Elijah
again.
In grief Elisha tore his cloak in two.
13Then he picked up Elijah's cloak that had
fallen from him, and went back and stood on
the bank of the Jordan. 14He struck the
water with Elijah's cloak and said, "Where is
the LORD, the God of Elijah?" Then he
struck the water again, and it divided, and he
walked over to the other side. 15The fifty
prophets from Jericho saw him and said,

[d] **2:9** THE SHARE . . . SUCCESSOR: *Elisha asked for the share that the first-born son inherited by law from his father (see Deut 21:17).*

2:9 Deut 21:17 **2:12** 2 Kings 13:14; Sir 48:9, 12

Can you find a story in 1 Kings in which God also sent down fire from heaven in response to Elijah's prayer?

"My father! . . . You are gone!" (2:12)

"The power of Elijah is on Elisha!" They
went to meet him, bowed down before him,
16and said, "There are fifty of us here, all
strong men. Let us go and look for your
master. Maybe the spirit of the LORD has
carried him away and left him on some
mountain or in some valley."
"No, you must not go," Elisha answered.
17But they insisted until he gave in and let
them go. The fifty of them went and looked
high and low for Elijah for three days, but
didn't find him. 18Then they returned to
Elisha, who had waited at Jericho, and he
said to them, "Didn't I tell you not to go?"

Miracles of Elisha

19Some men from Jericho went to Elisha
and said, "As you know, sir, this is a fine city,
but the water is bad and causes miscar-
riages."
20"Put some salt in a new bowl and bring
it to me," he ordered. They brought it to
him, 21and he went to the spring, threw the
salt in the water, and said, "This is what the
LORD says: 'I make this water pure, and it
will not cause any more deaths or miscar-
riages.' " 22And that water has been pure
ever since, just as Elisha said it would be.
23Elisha left Jericho to go to Bethel, and
on the way some boys came out of a town
and made fun of him. "Get out of here,
baldy!" they shouted.
24Elisha turned around, glared at them,
and cursed them in the name of the LORD.
Then two she-bears came out of the woods
and tore forty-two of the boys to pieces.
25Elisha went on to Mount Carmel and
later returned to Samaria.

War between Israel and Moab

3 In the eighteenth year of the reign of
King Jehoshaphat of Judah, Joram son of
Ahab became king of Israel, and he ruled in
Samaria for twelve years. 2He sinned against
the LORD, but he was not as bad as his father
or his mother Jezebel; he pulled down the
image his father had made for the worship
of Baal. 3Yet, like King Jeroboam son of
Nebat before him, he led Israel into sin and
would not stop.
4King Mesha of Moab raised sheep, and
every year he gave as tribute to the king of
Israel 100,000 lambs and the wool from
100,000 sheep. 5But when King Ahab of
Israel died, Mesha rebelled against Israel. 6At
once King Joram left Samaria and gathered
all his troops. 7He sent word to King
Jehoshaphat of Judah: "The king of Moab
has rebelled against me; will you join me in
war against him?"
"I will," King Jehoshaphat replied. "I am
at your disposal, and so are my men and my
horses. 8What route shall we take for the
attack?"
"We will go the long way through the
wilderness of Edom," Joram answered.
9So King Joram and the kings of Judah
and Edom set out. After marching seven
days, they ran out of water, and there was
none left for the men or the pack animals.
10"We're done for!" King Joram exclaimed.
"The LORD has put the three of us at the
mercy of the king of Moab!"
11King Jehoshaphat asked, "Is there a
prophet here through whom we can consult
the LORD?"
An officer of King Joram's forces
answered, "Elisha son of Shaphat is here. He
was Elijah's assistant."
12"He is a true prophet," King Jehosh-
aphat said. So the three kings went to
Elisha.
13"Why should I help you?" Elisha said to
the king of Israel. "Go and consult those
prophets that your father and mother con-
sulted."
"No!" Joram replied. "It is the LORD who
has put us three kings at the mercy of the
king of Moab."
14Elisha answered, "By the living LORD,

whom I serve, I swear that I would have nothing to do with you if I didn't respect your ally, King Jehoshaphat of Judah. 15 Now get me a musician."

As the musician played his harp, the power of the LORD came on Elisha, 16 and he said, "This is what the LORD says: 'Dig ditches all over this dry stream bed. 17 Even though you will not see any rain or wind, this stream bed will be filled with water, and you, your livestock, and your pack animals will have plenty to drink.' " 18 And Elisha continued, "But this is an easy thing for the LORD to do; he will also give you victory over the Moabites. 19 You will conquer all their beautiful fortified cities; you will cut down all their fruit trees, stop all their springs, and ruin all their fertile fields by covering them with stones."

"This is what the LORD says." (3:16)

20 The next morning, at the time of the regular morning sacrifice, water came flowing from the direction of Edom and covered the ground.

21 When the Moabites heard that the three kings had come to attack them, all the men who could bear arms, from the oldest to the youngest, were called out and stationed at the border. 22 When they got up the following morning, the sun was shining on the water, making it look as red as blood. 23 "It's blood!" they exclaimed. "The three enemy armies must have fought and killed each other! Let's go and loot their camp!"

24 But when they reached the camp, the Israelites attacked them and drove them back. The Israelites kept up the pursuit,[e] slaughtering the Moabites 25 and destroying their cities. As they passed by a fertile field, every Israelite would throw a stone on it until finally all the fields were covered; they also stopped up the springs and cut down the fruit trees. At last only the capital city of Kir Heres[f] was left, and the slingers surrounded it and attacked it.

26 When the king of Moab realized that he was losing the battle, he took seven hundred swordsmen with him and tried to force his way through the enemy lines and escape to the king of Syria,[g] but he failed. 27 So he took his oldest son, who was to succeed him as king, and offered him on the city wall as a sacrifice to the god of Moab. The Israelites were terrified[h] and so they drew back from the city and returned to their own country.

Elisha Helps a Poor Widow

4 The widow of a member of a group of prophets went to Elisha and said, "Sir, my husband has died! As you know, he was a God-fearing man, but now a man he owed money to has come to take away my two sons as slaves in payment for my husband's debt."

2 "What shall I do for you?" he asked. "Tell me, what do you have at home?"

"Nothing at all, except a small jar of olive oil," she answered.

3 "Go to your neighbors and borrow as many empty jars as you can," Elisha told her. 4 "Then you and your sons go into the house, close the door, and start pouring oil into the jars. Set each one aside as soon as it is full."

5 So the woman went into her house with her sons, closed the door, took the small jar of olive oil, and poured oil into the jars as her sons brought them to her. 6 When they had filled all the jars, she asked if there were any more. "That was the last one," one of her sons answered. And the olive oil stopped flowing. 7 She went back to Elisha, the prophet, who said to her, "Sell the olive oil and pay all your debts, and there will be enough money left over for you and your sons to live on."

[e] **3:24** *One ancient translation* kept up the pursuit; *Hebrew unclear.* [f] **3:25** *Probable text* only the capital city of Kir Heres; *Hebrew unclear.* [g] **3:26** *One ancient translation* Syria; *Hebrew* Edom. [h] **3:27** TERRIFIED: *either because of what Chemosh, the god of the Moabites, might do, or because of what the* LORD, *the God of the Israelites, might do.*

> **Study it!**
>
> ### Elisha the Rescuer
>
> **It may not sound like a very important miracle, making one small jar of olive oil enough to fill many bottles, but for this poor widow it made all the difference. Her husband had been a prophet. The family had lived simply. Now her sons were to be taken away as slaves to pay off the family's debt. This practice was one of the ways that poor people were robbed of their land.**
>
> **The woman was about to lose everything. Olive oil was very precious; it was even used as a kind of money. But more importantly it was one of the basic foods for both rich people and poor people. Elisha's miracle saved the woman's land and her sons. It was a sign of God's care for poor and powerless people.**
>
> **— 2 Kings 4:1–7**

Elisha and the Rich Woman from Shunem

8One day Elisha went to Shunem, where
a rich woman lived. She invited him to a
meal, and from then on every time he went
to Shunem he would have his meals at her
house. 9She said to her husband, "I am sure
that this man who comes here so often is a
holy man. 10Let's build a small room on the
roof, put a bed, a table, a chair, and a lamp in
it, and he can stay there whenever he visits
us."
11One day Elisha returned to Shunem and
went up to his room to rest. 12He told his
servant Gehazi to go and call the woman.
When she came, 13he said to Gehazi, "Ask
her what I can do for her in return for all
the trouble she has had in providing for our
needs. Maybe she would like me to go to
the king or the army commander and put in
a good word for her."
"I have all I need here among my own
people," she answered.
14Elisha asked Gehazi, "What can I do for
her then?"
He answered, "Well, she has no son, and
her husband is an old man."
15"Tell her to come here," Elisha ordered.
She came and stood in the doorway, 16and
Elisha said to her, "By this time next year
you will be holding a son in your arms."
"Oh!" she exclaimed. "Please, sir, don't lie
to me. You are a man of God!"
17But, as Elisha had said, at about that time
the following year she gave birth to a son.
18Some years later, at harvest time, the boy
went out one morning to join his father,
who was in the field with the harvest work-
ers. 19Suddenly he cried out to his father,
"My head hurts! My head hurts!"
"Carry the boy to his mother," the father
said to a servant. 20The servant carried the
boy back to his mother, who held him in
her lap until noon, at which time he died.

So the woman . . . poured oil into the jars. (4:5)

4:16 Gen 18:4

What horrible thing did the king of Moab do that terrified the Israelites and made them turn back?

21 She carried him up to Elisha's room, put
him on the bed and left, closing the door
behind her. 22 Then she called her husband
and said to him, "Send a servant here with a
donkey. I need to go to the prophet Elisha.
I'll be back as soon as I can."
23 "Why do you have to go today?" her
husband asked. "It's neither a Sabbath nor a
New Moon Festival."[i]
"Never mind," she answered. 24 Then she
had the donkey saddled, and ordered the ser-
vant, "Make the donkey go as fast as it can,
and don't slow down unless I tell you to."
25 So she set out and went to Mount
Carmel, where Elisha was.

"Make the donkey go as fast as it can." (4:24)

Elisha saw her coming while she was still
some distance away, and he said to his ser-
vant Gehazi, "Look, there comes the woman
from Shunem! 26 Hurry to her and find out
if everything is all right with her, her hus-
band, and her son."
She told Gehazi that everything was all
right, 27 but when she came to Elisha, she
bowed down before him and took hold of
his feet. Gehazi was about to push her away,
but Elisha said, "Leave her alone. Can't you
see she's deeply distressed? And the LORD
has not told me a thing about it."
28 The woman said to him, "Sir, did I ask
you for a son? Didn't I tell you not to get
my hopes up?"
29 Elisha turned to Gehazi and said,
"Hurry! Take my walking stick and go.
Don't stop to greet anyone you meet, and if
anyone greets you, don't take time to answer.
Go straight to the house and hold my stick
over the boy."
30 The woman said to Elisha, "I swear by
my loyalty to the living LORD and to you
that I will not leave you!" So the two of
them started back together. 31 Gehazi went
on ahead and held Elisha's stick over the
child, but there was no sound or any other
sign of life. So he went back to meet Elisha
and said, "The boy didn't wake up."
32 When Elisha arrived, he went alone into
the room and saw the boy lying dead on the
bed. 33 He closed the door and prayed to the
LORD. 34 Then he lay down on the boy, plac-
ing his mouth, eyes, and hands on the boy's
mouth, eyes, and hands. As he lay stretched
out over the boy, the boy's body started to
get warm. 35 Elisha got up, walked around
the room, and then went back and again
stretched himself over the boy. The boy
sneezed seven times and then opened his
eyes. 36 Elisha called Gehazi and told him to
call the boy's mother. When she came in, he
said to her, "Here's your son." 37 She fell at
Elisha's feet, with her face touching the
ground; then she took her son and left.

Two More Miracles

38 Once, when there was a famine
throughout the land, Elisha returned to
Gilgal. While he was teaching a group of
prophets, he told his servant to put a big pot
on the fire and make some stew for them.
39 One of them went out in the fields to get
some herbs. He found a wild vine and
picked as many gourds as he could carry. He
brought them back and sliced them up into
the stew, not knowing what they were.
40 The stew was poured out for the men to
eat, but as soon as they tasted it they
exclaimed to Elisha, "It's poisoned!"—and
wouldn't eat it. 41 Elisha asked for some meal,
threw it into the pot, and said, "Pour out

[i] **4:23** SABBATH . . . NEW MOON FESTIVAL: *Such holy days were thought to be the best time to consult a prophet.*
4:34, 35 1 Kings 17:21

The gourds in 2 Kings 4:39 were probably wild pumpkins. They were used as a medicine, but too much can be poisonous!

Pray it!

Seek Healing

Naaman, the commander of the mighty Syrian army, had a bad skin disease. He heard from a captured Israelite girl that he could be cured. Naaman went to his own king, who sent him to the king of Israel, who sent him to Elisha, who sent him to the Jordan River. And he was healed! One of the signs of the power and presence of God throughout the Bible is healing. We know that God wants to heal us. God wants to heal our bodies, but more importantly God wants to heal our hearts.

Healing God,
Naaman sought healing from the prophet Elisha.
He washed in the Jordan River, and his suffering ended.
I come to you now in need of healing.
Heal my heart in the broken places,
just as you healed Naaman.
Make me whole again.
Give me a fresh start.

— 2 Kings 5:1–14

some more stew for them." And then there
was nothing wrong with it.
42Another time, a man came from Baal
Shalishah, bringing Elisha twenty loaves of
bread made from the first barley harvested
that year, and some freshly-cut heads of
grain. Elisha told his servant to feed the
group of prophets with this, 43but he
answered, "Do you think this is enough for
a hundred men?"
Elisha replied, "Give it to them to eat,
because the LORD says that they will eat and
still have some left over." 44So the servant set
the food before them, and as the LORD had
said, they all ate, and there was still some left
over.

Naaman Is Cured

5 Naaman, the commander of the Syrian
army, was highly respected and esteemed
by the king of Syria, because through Naa-
man the LORD had given victory to the Syri-
an forces. He was a great soldier, but he suf-
fered from a dreaded skin disease. 2In one of
their raids against Israel, the Syrians had car-
ried off a little Israelite girl, who became a
servant of Naaman's wife. 3One day she said
to her mistress, "I wish that my master could
go to the prophet who lives in Samaria! He
would cure him of his disease." 4When Naa-
man heard of this, he went to the king and
told him what the girl had said. 5The king
said, "Go to the king of Israel and take this
letter to him."
So Naaman set out, taking thirty thousand
pieces of silver, six thousand pieces of gold,
and ten changes of fine clothes. 6The letter
that he took read: "This letter will introduce
my officer Naaman. I want you to cure him
of his disease."
7When the king of Israel read the letter,
he tore his clothes in dismay and exclaimed,
"How can the king of Syria expect me to
cure this man? Does he think that I am
God,[j] with the power of life and death? It's
plain that he is trying to start a quarrel with
me!"

j **5:7** God; *or* a god.
5:1–14 Lk 4:27

8 When the prophet Elisha heard what had
happened, he sent word to the king: "Why
are you so upset? Send the man to me, and
I'll show him that there is a prophet in
Israel!"
9 So Naaman went with his horses and
chariot and stopped at the entrance to
Elisha's house. 10 Elisha sent a servant out to
tell him to go and wash himself seven times
in the Jordan River, and he would be com-
pletely cured of his disease. 11 But Naaman
left in a rage, saying, "I thought that he
would at least come out to me, pray to the
LORD his God, wave his hand over the dis-
eased spot,[k] and cure me! 12 Besides, aren't
the rivers Abana and Pharpar, back in
Damascus, better than any river in Israel? I
could have washed in them and been cured!"
13 His servants went up to him and said,
"Sir, if the prophet had told you to do some-
thing difficult, you would have done it. Now
why can't you just wash yourself, as he said,
and be cured?" 14 So Naaman went down to
the Jordan, dipped himself in it seven times,
as Elisha had instructed, and he was com-
pletely cured. His flesh became firm and
healthy like that of a child. 15 He returned to
Elisha with all his men and said, "Now I
know that there is no god but the God of
Israel; so please, sir, accept a gift from me."

"If the prophet had told you to do something difficult, you would have done it." (5:13)

16 Elisha answered, "By the living LORD,
whom I serve, I swear that I will not accept
a gift."
Naaman insisted that he accept it, but he
would not. 17 So Naaman said, "If you won't
accept my gift, then let me have two mule-
loads of earth to take home with me,[l]
because from now on I will not offer sacri-
fices or burnt offerings to any god except
the LORD. 18 So I hope that the LORD will
forgive me when I accompany my king to
the temple of Rimmon, the god of Syria,
and worship him. Surely the LORD will for-
give me!"
19 "Go in peace," Elisha said. And Naaman
left.
He had gone only a short distance,
20 when Elisha's servant Gehazi said to him-
self, "My master has let Naaman get away
without paying a thing! He should have
accepted what that Syrian offered him. By
the living LORD I will run after him and
get something from him." 21 So he set off
after Naaman. When Naaman saw a man
running after him, he got down from his
chariot to meet him, and asked, "Is some-
thing wrong?"
22 "No," Gehazi answered. "But my master
sent me to tell you that just now two mem-
bers of the group of prophets in the hill
country of Ephraim arrived, and he would
like you to give them three thousand pieces
of silver and two changes of fine clothes."
23 "Please take six thousand pieces of sil-
ver," Naaman replied. He insisted on it, tied
up the silver in two bags, gave them and two
changes of fine clothes to two of his ser-
vants, and sent them on ahead of Gehazi.
24 When they reached the hill where Elisha
lived, Gehazi took the two bags and carried
them into the house. Then he sent Naaman's
servants back. 25 He went back into the
house, and Elisha asked him, "Where have
you been?"
"Oh, nowhere, sir," he answered.
26 But Elisha said, "Wasn't I there in spirit
when the man got out of his chariot to meet
you? This is no time to accept money and
clothes, olive groves and vineyards, sheep and
cattle, or servants! 27 And now Naaman's dis-
ease will come upon you, and you and your
descendants will have it forever!"
When Gehazi left, he had the disease—his
skin was as white as snow.

[k] **5:11** the diseased spot; *or* this place. [l] **5:17** EARTH TO TAKE HOME WITH ME: *It was then believed that a god could be worshiped only on his own land.*

The Recovery of the Ax Head

6 One day the group of prophets that
Elisha was in charge of complained to
him, "The place where we live is too small!
2 Give us permission to go to the Jordan and
cut down some trees, so that we can build a
place to live."
"All right," Elisha answered.
3 One of them urged him to go with
them; he agreed, 4 and they set out together.
When they arrived at the Jordan, they began
to work. 5 As one of them was cutting down
a tree, suddenly his iron ax head fell in the
water. "What shall I do, sir?" he exclaimed to
Elisha. "It was a borrowed ax!"
6 "Where did it fall?" Elisha asked.
The man showed him the place, and
Elisha cut off a stick, threw it in the water,
and made the ax head float. 7 "Take it out,"
he ordered, and the man reached down and
picked it up.

The Syrian Army Is Defeated

8 The king of Syria was at war with Israel.
He consulted his officers and chose a place
to set up his camp. 9 But Elisha sent word to
the king of Israel, warning him not to go
near that place, because the Syrians were
waiting in ambush there. 10 So the king of
Israel warned the people who lived in that
place, and they were on guard. This hap-
pened several times.
11 The Syrian king became greatly upset
over this; he called in his officers and asked
them, "Which one of you is on the side of
the king of Israel?"
12 One of them answered, "No one is, Your
Majesty. The prophet Elisha tells the king of
Israel what you say even in the privacy of
your own room."
13 "Find out where he is," the king
ordered, "and I will capture him."
When he was told that Elisha was in
Dothan, 14 he sent a large force there with
horses and chariots. They reached the town
at night and surrounded it. 15 Early the next
morning Elisha's servant got up, went out of
the house, and saw the Syrian troops with
their horses and chariots surrounding
the town. He went back to Elisha and
exclaimed, "We are doomed, sir! What shall
we do?"
16 "Don't be afraid," Elisha answered. "We
have more on our side than they have on
theirs." 17 Then he prayed, "O LORD, open
his eyes and let him see!" The LORD
answered his prayer, and Elisha's servant
looked up and saw the hillside covered with
horses and chariots of fire all around Elisha.
18 When the Syrians attacked, Elisha
prayed, "O LORD, strike these men blind!"
The LORD answered his prayer and struck
them blind. 19 Then Elisha went to them and
said, "You are on the wrong road; this is not
the town you are looking for. Follow me,
and I will lead you to the man you are after."
And he led them to Samaria.
20 As soon as they had entered the city,

Live it!

Mercy Not Revenge

It must have been so tempting for Elisha. The king would have been happy to kill these enemy soldiers who had come to kill Elisha. He would have been justified, right? But Elisha makes a different choice—feed them and send them home! Have you ever had a chance at revenge that you passed up? Did you ever face a situation where someone had been unkind to you, but you responded with kindness to him or her? It's a pretty good feeling. The story goes that after this, the King of Syria stopped raiding the land of Israel. Mercy can be a powerful force. Try it!

— 2 Kings 6:8–23

Check Map 3 in the back of this Bible to see how far Naaman traveled. He started in Syria and ended up at the Jordan River near Samaria.

Elisha prayed, "Open their eyes, LORD, and
let them see." The LORD answered his
prayer; he restored their sight, and they saw
that they were inside Samaria.
21 When the king of Israel saw the Syrians,
he asked Elisha, "Shall I kill them, sir? Shall I
kill them?"
22 "No," he answered. "Not even soldiers
you had captured in combat would you put
to death. Give them something to eat and
drink, and let them return to their king."
23 So the king of Israel provided a great feast
for them; and after they had eaten and
drunk, he sent them back to the king of
Syria. From then on the Syrians stopped
raiding the land of Israel.

The Siege of Samaria

24 Some time later King Benhadad of Syria
led his entire army against Israel and laid
siege to the city of Samaria. 25 As a result of
the siege the food shortage in the city was so
severe that a donkey's head cost eighty pieces
of silver, and half a pound of dove's dung[m]
cost five pieces of silver.
26 The king of Israel was walking by on
the city wall when a woman cried out,
"Help me, Your Majesty!"
27 He replied, "If the LORD won't help
you, what help can I provide? Do I have any
wheat or wine? 28 What's your trouble?"
She answered, "The other day this woman
here suggested that we eat my child, and
then eat her child the next day. 29 So we
cooked my son and ate him. The next day I
told her that we would eat her son, but she
had hidden him!"
30 Hearing this, the king tore his clothes in
dismay, and the people who were close to
the wall could see that he was wearing sack-
cloth under his clothes. 31 He exclaimed,
"May God strike me dead if Elisha is not
beheaded before the day is over!" 32 And he
sent a messenger to get Elisha.

Meanwhile Elisha was at home with some
elders who were visiting him. Before the
king's messenger arrived, Elisha said to the
elders, "That murderer is sending someone
to kill me! Now, when he gets here, shut the
door and don't let him come in. The king
himself will be right behind him." 33 He had
hardly finished saying this, when the king[n]
arrived and said, "It's the LORD who has
brought this trouble on us! Why should I
wait any longer for him to do something?"
7 Elisha answered, "Listen to what the
LORD says! By this time tomorrow you
will be able to buy in Samaria ten pounds of
the best wheat or twenty pounds of barley
for one piece of silver."
2 The personal attendant of the king said to
Elisha, "That can't happen—not even if the
LORD himself were to send grain[o] at once!"
"You will see it happen, but you won't get
to eat any of the food," Elisha replied.

The Syrian Army Leaves

3 Four men who were suffering from a
dreaded skin disease were outside the gates of
Samaria, and they said to each other, "Why
should we wait here until we die? 4 It's no use
going into the city, because we would starve
to death in there; but if we stay here, we'll die
also. So let's go to the Syrian camp; the worst
they can do is kill us, but maybe they will
spare our lives." 5 So, as it began to get dark,
they went to the Syrian camp, but when they
reached it, no one was there. 6 The Lord had
made the Syrians hear what sounded like the
advance of a large army with horses and char-
iots, and the Syrians thought that the king of
Israel had hired Hittite and Egyptian kings
and their armies to attack them. 7 So that
evening the Syrians had fled for their lives,
abandoning their tents, horses, and donkeys,
and leaving the camp just as it was.
8 When the four men reached the edge of
the camp, they went into a tent, ate and drank

[m] **6:25** DOVE'S DUNG: *This may be a popular term for a vegetable such as wild onions.* [n] **6:33** *Probable text* king; *Hebrew* messenger. [o] **7:2** grain; *or* rain.

6:29 Deut 28:57; Lam 4:10

A siege is when an army surrounds a city for days or weeks and does not let supplies in. A city's defenses are weakened so that the army can enter easily.

Study it!

The Last Shall Be First

The Syrians are winning. Their siege is starving out the people of the city of Samaria. Just when all seems to be lost, some lepers discover the Syrian army's camp has been suddenly deserted. In this dramatic story of despair turned to victory, the people at the bottom of society are the first ones to realize the good news. Lepers are outcasts. Because of their contagious skin disease, they have to live outside the city. People turn away from them. Now they are the heroes and get to deliver the good news that the Syrians are gone.

Throughout the Bible we see unlikely heroes, people no one would notice who end up playing key roles in God's plans. God seems to have a special place in his heart for the people who don't have it all together.

— 2 Kings 7:3–9

what was there, grabbed the silver, gold, and
clothing they found, and went off and hid
them; then they returned, entered another
tent, and did the same thing. 9 But then they
said to each other, "We shouldn't be doing
this! We have good news, and we shouldn't
keep it to ourselves. If we wait until morning
to tell it, we are sure to be punished. Let's go
right now and tell the king's officers!" 10 So
they left the Syrian camp, went back to
Samaria, and called out to the guards at the
gates: "We went to the Syrian camp and
didn't see or hear anybody; the horses and
donkeys have not been untied, and the tents
are just as the Syrians left them."

11 The guards announced the news, and it
was reported in the palace. 12 It was still
night, but the king got out of bed and said
to his officials, "I'll tell you what the Syrians
are planning! They know about the famine
here, so they have left their camp to go and
hide in the countryside. They think that we
will leave the city to find food, and then
they will take us alive and capture the city."

13 One of his officials said, "The people
here in the city are doomed anyway, like
those that have already died. So let's send
some men with five of the horses that are
left, so that we can find out what has hap-
pened."[p] 14 They chose some men, and the
king sent them in two chariots with instruc-
tions to go and find out what had happened
to the Syrian army. 15 The men went as far as
the Jordan, and all along the road they saw
the clothes and equipment that the Syrians
had abandoned as they fled. Then they
returned and reported to the king. 16 The
people of Samaria rushed out and looted the
Syrian camp. And as the LORD had said, ten
pounds of the best wheat or twenty pounds
of barley were sold for one piece of silver.

17 It so happened that the king of Israel
had put the city gate under the command of
the officer who was his personal attendant.
The officer was trampled to death there by
the people and died, as Elisha had predicted
when the king went to see him. 18 Elisha had
told the king that by that time the following
day ten pounds of the best wheat or twenty
pounds of barley would be sold in Samaria
for one piece of silver, 19 to which the officer
had answered, "That can't happen—not even
if the LORD himself were to send grain[q] at
once!" And Elisha had replied, "You will see
it happen, but you won't get to eat any of
the food." 20 And that is just what happened
to him—he died, trampled to death by the
people at the city gate.

The Woman from Shunem Returns

8 Now Elisha had told the woman who
lived in Shunem, whose son he had
brought back to life, that the LORD was

[p] **7:13** *Verse 13 in Hebrew is unclear.* [q] **7:19** grain; *or* rain.
8:1 2 Kings 4:8–37

sending a famine on the land, which would
last for seven years, and that she should leave
with her family and go and live somewhere
else. 2She had followed his instructions and
had gone with her family to live in Philistia
for the seven years.
3At the end of the seven years she
returned to Israel and went to the king to
ask that her house and her land be restored
to her. 4She found the king talking with
Gehazi, Elisha's servant; the king wanted to
know about Elisha's miracles. 5While Gehazi
was telling the king how Elisha had brought
a dead person back to life, the woman made
her appeal to the king. Gehazi said to him,
"Your Majesty, here is the woman and here
is her son whom Elisha brought back to
life!" 6In answer to the king's question, she
confirmed Gehazi's story, and so the king
called an official and told him to give back
to her everything that was hers, including
the value of all the crops that her fields had
produced during the seven years she had
been away.

Elisha and King Benhadad of Syria

7Elisha went to Damascus at a time when
King Benhadad of Syria was sick. When the
king was told that Elisha was there, 8he said
to Hazael, one of his officials, "Take a gift
to the prophet and ask him to consult the
LORD to find out whether or not I am
going to get well." 9So Hazael loaded forty
camels with all kinds of the finest products
of Damascus and went to Elisha. When
Hazael met him, he said, "Your servant
King Benhadad has sent me to ask you
whether or not he will recover from his
sickness."
10Elisha answered, "The LORD has
revealed to me that he will die; but go to
him and tell him that he will recover."
11Then Elisha stared at him with a horrified
look on his face until Hazael became ill at
ease. Suddenly Elisha burst into tears.
12"Why are you crying, sir?" Hazael asked.
"Because I know the horrible things you
will do against the people of Israel," Elisha
answered. "You will set their fortresses on
fire, slaughter their finest young men, batter
their children to death, and rip open their
pregnant women."
13"How could I ever be that powerful?"
Hazael asked. "I'm a nobody!"
"The LORD has shown me that you will
be king of Syria," Elisha replied.
14Hazael went back to Benhadad, who
asked him, "What did Elisha say?"
"He told me that you would certainly get
well," Hazael answered. 15But on the follow-
ing day Hazael took a blanket, soaked it in
water, and smothered the king.
And Hazael succeeded Benhadad as king
of Syria.

Live it!

Refugees

Do you know anyone who is a refugee? A refugee is someone who has been forced to leave his or her home and land because of war, famine, natural disaster, or persecution. Elisha showed a special concern for people in need—widows, sick people, poor people. He had warned this same woman that there would be a famine, and he comes to her aid once again so that she can regain her land.

There are thousands of refugees in the world today. As Christians we are called to actively help those in need. Find out about refugees in your area. Where are they from? What needs do they have? Why did they have to leave their homes? What can you do to help them?

— 2 Kings 8:1–6

8:13 1 Kings 19:15

King Jehoram of Judah
(2 Chronicles 21:1–20)

16 In the fifth year of the reign of Joram son of Ahab as king of Israel,[r] Jehoram son of Jehoshaphat became king of Judah 17 at the age of thirty-two, and he ruled in Jerusalem for eight years. 18 His wife was Ahab's daughter, and like the family of Ahab he followed the evil ways of the kings of Israel. He sinned against the LORD, 19 but the LORD was not willing to destroy Judah, because he had promised his servant David that his descendants would always continue to rule.

20 During Jehoram's reign Edom revolted against Judah and became an independent kingdom. 21 So Jehoram set out with all his chariots to Zair, where the Edomite army surrounded them. During the night he and his chariot commanders managed to break out and escape, and his soldiers scattered to their homes. 22 Edom has been independent of[s] Judah ever since. During this same period the city of Libnah also revolted.

23 Everything else that Jehoram did is recorded in *The History of the Kings of Judah*. 24 Jehoram died and was buried in the royal tombs in David's City, and his son Ahaziah succeeded him as king.

King Ahaziah of Judah
(2 Chronicles 22:1–6)

25 In the twelfth year of the reign of Joram son of Ahab as king of Israel, Ahaziah son of Jehoram became king of Judah 26 at the age of twenty-two, and he ruled in Jerusalem for one year. His mother was Athaliah, the daughter of King Ahab and granddaughter of King Omri of Israel. 27 Since Ahaziah was related to King Ahab by marriage, he sinned against the LORD, just as Ahab's family did.

28 King Ahaziah joined King Joram of Israel in a war against King Hazael of Syria. The armies clashed at Ramoth in Gilead, and Joram was wounded in battle. 29 He returned to the city of Jezreel to recover from his wounds, and Ahaziah went there to visit him.

Jehu Is Anointed King of Israel

9 Meanwhile the prophet Elisha called one of the young prophets and said to him, "Get ready and go to Ramoth in Gilead. Take this jar of olive oil with you, 2 and when you get there look for Jehu, the son of Jehoshaphat and grandson of Nimshi. Take him to a private room away from his companions, 3 pour this olive oil on his head, and say, 'The LORD proclaims that he anoints you king of Israel.' Then leave there as fast as you can."

4 So the young prophet went to Ramoth, 5 where he found the army officers in a conference. He said, "Sir, I have a message for you."

Jehu asked, "Which one of us are you speaking to?"

"To you, sir," he replied. 6 Then the two of them went indoors, and the young prophet poured the olive oil on Jehu's head and said to him, "The LORD, the God of Israel, proclaims: 'I anoint you king of my people Israel. 7 You are to kill your master the king, that son of Ahab, so that I may punish Jezebel for murdering my prophets and my other servants. 8 All of Ahab's family and descendants are to die; I will get rid of every male in his family, young and old alike. 9 I will treat his family as I did the families of King Jeroboam of Israel and of King Baasha of Israel. 10 Jezebel will not be buried; her body will be eaten by dogs in the territory of Jezreel.'" After saying this, the young prophet left the room and fled.

11 Jehu went back to his fellow officers, who asked him, "Is everything all right? What did that crazy fellow want with you?"

[r] **8:16** *Some ancient translations* Israel; *Hebrew* Israel, Jehoshaphat being king of Judah. [s] **8:22** independent of; *or* in revolt against.
8:19 1 Kings 11:36 **8:20** Gen 27:40 **9:6** 1 Kings 19:16 **9:10** 1 Kings 21:23

Edom *(2 Kings 8:20–22)* **was not one of the Twelve Tribes of Israel. The people of Edom were descendents of Esau, Jacob's twin brother.**

"You know what he wanted," Jehu answered.

12"No we don't!" they replied. "Tell us what he said!"

"He told me that the LORD proclaims: 'I anoint you king of Israel.' "

13At once Jehu's fellow officers spread their cloaks at the top of the steps for Jehu to stand on, blew trumpets, and shouted, "Jehu is king!"

King Joram of Israel Is Killed

14-15Then Jehu plotted against King Joram, who was in Jezreel, where he had gone to recover from the wounds which he had received in the battle at Ramoth against King Hazael of Syria. So Jehu said to his fellow officers, "If you are with me, make sure that no one slips out of Ramoth to go and warn the people in Jezreel."
16Then he got into his chariot and set off for Jezreel. Joram had still not recovered, and King Ahaziah of Judah was there, visiting him.

17A guard on duty in the watchtower at Jezreel saw Jehu and his men approaching. "I see some men riding up!" he called out.

Joram replied, "Send a rider to find out if they are friends or enemies."

18The messenger rode out to Jehu and said to him, "The king wants to know if you come as a friend."

"That's none of your business!" Jehu answered. "Fall in behind me."

The guard on the watchtower reported that the messenger had reached the group but was not returning.
19Another messenger was sent out, who asked Jehu the same question. Again Jehu answered, "That's none of your business! Fall in behind me."

20Once more the guard reported that the messenger had reached the group but was not returning. And he added, "The leader of the group is driving his chariot like a madman, just like Jehu!"

21"Get my chariot ready," King Joram ordered. It was done, and he and King Ahaziah rode out, each in his own chariot, to meet Jehu. They met him at the field which had belonged to Naboth.
22"Are you coming in peace?" Joram asked him.

"How can there be peace," Jehu answered, "when we still have all the witchcraft and idolatry that your mother Jezebel started?"

23"It's treason, Ahaziah!" Joram cried out, as he turned his chariot around and fled.
24Jehu drew his bow, and with all his strength shot an arrow that struck Joram in the back and pierced his heart. Joram fell dead in his chariot,
25and Jehu said to his aide Bidkar, "Get his body and throw it in the field that belonged to Naboth. Remember that when you and I were riding together behind King Joram's father Ahab, the LORD spoke these words against Ahab:
26'I saw the murder of Naboth and his sons yesterday. And I promise that I will punish you here in this same field.' So take Joram's body," Jehu ordered his aide, "and throw it in the field that belonged to Naboth, so as to fulfill the LORD's promise."

King Ahaziah of Judah Is Killed

27King Ahaziah saw what happened, so he fled in his chariot toward the town of Beth Haggan, pursued by Jehu. "Kill him too!" Jehu ordered his men, and they wounded him[t] as he drove his chariot on the road up to Gur, near the town of Ibleam. But he managed to keep on going until he reached the city of Megiddo, where he died.
28His officials took his body back to Jerusalem in a chariot and buried him in the royal tombs in David's City.

29Ahaziah had become king of Judah in the eleventh year that Joram son of Ahab was king of Israel.

[t] **9:27** *Some ancient translations* and they wounded him; *Hebrew does not have these words.*

9:26 1 Kings 21:19

Jezebel insults Jehu by calling him a Zimri. Read the story of Zimri in 1 Kings 16:8–12 to see what he did.

Queen Jezebel Is Killed

30 Jehu arrived in Jezreel. Jezebel, having
heard what had happened, put on eye shad-
ow, arranged her hair, and stood looking
down at the street from a window in the
palace. 31 As Jehu came through the gate, she
called out, "You Zimri![u] You assassin! Why
are you here?"
32 Jehu looked up and shouted, "Who is
on my side?" Two or three palace officials
looked down at him from a window, 33 and
Jehu said to them, "Throw her down!" They
threw her down, and her blood spattered on
the wall and on the horses. Jehu drove his
horses and chariot over her body, 34 entered
the palace, and had a meal. Only then did he
say, "Take that cursed woman and bury her;
after all, she is a king's daughter." 35 But the
men who went out to bury her found noth-
ing except her skull and the bones of her
hands and feet. 36 When they reported this to
Jehu, he said, "This is what the LORD said
would happen, when he spoke through his
servant Elijah: 'Dogs will eat Jezebel's body
in the territory of Jezreel. 37 Her remains will
be scattered there like dung, so that no one
will be able to identify them.' "

Study it!

A Bad End

Do you remember the evil Queen Jezebel from the end of 1 Kings? The story of her death is told with drama and graphic violence. The author wanted to make a point—those who did not obey God would be punished. After she falls to her death, she is consumed by dogs—just as Elijah had prophesied. This was a great dishonor for someone who expected to be buried in a royal tomb.

The death of Queen Jezebel, King Joram, and his son King Ahaziah of Judah mark the end of the Omri dynasty. King Omri and his descendants all got the "thumbs down" from the author. They had each sinned against the Lord by worshiping foreign gods and treating the people of their kingdoms with injustice. Their violent deaths are seen as punishment for leading Israel astray.

— 2 Kings 9:30–37

The Descendants of Ahab Are Killed

10 There were seventy descendants of
King Ahab living in the city of
Samaria. Jehu wrote a letter and sent copies
to the rulers of the city,[v] to the leading citi-
zens, and to the guardians of Ahab's descen-
dants. The letter read: 2 "You are in charge of
the king's descendants, and you have at your
disposal chariots, horses, weapons, and forti-
fied cities. So then, as soon as you receive
this letter, 3 you are to choose the best quali-
fied of the king's descendants, make him
king, and fight to defend him."
4 The rulers of Samaria were terrified.
"How can we oppose Jehu," they said,
"when neither King Joram nor King Ahazi-
ah could?" 5 So the officer in charge of the
palace and the official in charge of the city,
together with the leading citizens and the
guardians, sent this message to Jehu: "We are
your servants, and we are ready to do any-
thing you say. But we will not make anyone
king; do whatever you think best."
6 Jehu wrote them another letter: "If you
are with me and are ready to follow my
orders, bring the heads of King Ahab's
descendants to me at Jezreel by this time
tomorrow."
The seventy descendants of King Ahab
were under the care of the leading citizens
of Samaria, who were bringing them up.
7 When Jehu's letter was received, the leaders
of Samaria killed all seventy of Ahab's

[u] **9:31** ZIMRI: *An Israelite army officer who assassinated the king of Israel (see 1 Kings 16:8–12).* [v] **10:1** *Some ancient translations* the city; *Hebrew* Jezreel.

9:36 1 Kings 21:23

descendants, put their heads in baskets, and
sent them to Jehu at Jezreel.
8 When Jehu was told that the heads of
Ahab's descendants had been brought, he
ordered them to be piled up in two heaps at
the city gate and to be left there until the
following morning. 9 In the morning he
went out to the gate and said to the people
who were there, "I was the one who plotted
against King Joram and killed him; you are
not responsible for that. But who killed all
these? 10 This proves that everything that the
LORD said about the descendants of Ahab
will come true. The LORD has done what
he promised through his prophet Elijah."
11 Then Jehu put to death all the other rela-
tives of Ahab living in Jezreel, and all his
officers, close friends, and priests; not one of
them was left alive.

The Relatives of King Ahaziah Are Killed

12 Jehu left Jezreel to go to Samaria. On
the way, at a place called "Shepherds' Camp,"
13 he met some relatives of the late King
Ahaziah of Judah and asked them, "Who are
you?"
"Ahaziah's relatives," they answered. "We
are going to Jezreel to pay our respects to
the children of Queen Jezebel and to the
rest of the royal family." 14 Jehu ordered his
men, "Take them alive!" They seized them,
and he put them to death near a pit there.
There were forty-two people in all, and not
one of them was left alive.

All Remaining Relatives of Ahab Are Killed

15 Jehu started out again, and on his way
he was met by Jonadab son of Rechab. Jehu
greeted him and said, "You and I think alike.
Will you support me?"
"I will," Jonadab answered.
"Give me your hand, then," Jehu replied.
They clasped hands, and Jehu helped him up
into the chariot, 16 saying, "Come with me
and see for yourself how devoted I am to the
LORD." And they rode on together to
Samaria. 17 When they arrived there, Jehu
killed all of Ahab's relatives, not sparing even
one. This is what the LORD had told Elijah
would happen.

The Worshipers of Baal Are Killed

18 Jehu called the people of Samaria
together and said, "King Ahab served the
god Baal a little, but I will serve him much
more. 19 Call together all the prophets of
Baal, all his worshipers, and all his priests. No
one is excused; I am going to offer a great
sacrifice to Baal, and whoever is not present
will be put to death." (This was a trick on
the part of Jehu by which he meant to kill
all the worshipers of Baal.) 20 Then Jehu
ordered, "Proclaim a day of worship in
honor of Baal!" The proclamation was made,
21 and Jehu sent word throughout all the land
of Israel. All who worshiped Baal came; not
one of them failed to come. They all went
into the temple of Baal, filling it from one
end to the other. 22 Then Jehu ordered the
priest in charge of the sacred robes to bring
the robes out and give them to the wor-
shipers. 23 After that, Jehu himself went into
the temple with Jonadab son of Rechab and
said to the people there, "Make sure that
only worshipers of Baal are present and that
no worshiper of the LORD has come in."
24 Then he and Jonadab went in to offer sac-
rifices and burnt offerings to Baal. He had
stationed eighty men outside the temple and
had instructed them: "You are to kill all
these people; anyone who lets one of them
escape will pay for it with his life!"
25 As soon as Jehu had presented the offer-
ings, he said to the guards and officers, "Go
in and kill them all; don't let anyone escape!"
They went in with drawn swords, killed
them all, and dragged the bodies outside.
Then they went on into the inner sanctuary
of the temple, 26 brought out the sacred pillar
that was there, and burned it. 27 So they
destroyed the sacred pillar and the temple,
and turned the temple into a latrine—which
it still is today.
28 That was how Jehu wiped out the
worship of Baal in Israel. 29 But he imitated

10:11 Hos 1:4 **10:29** 1 Kings 12:28–30

the sin of King Jeroboam, who led Israel
into the sin of worshiping the gold bull-
calves he set up in Bethel and in Dan.
30The LORD said to Jehu, "You have done
to Ahab's descendants everything I wanted
you to do. So I promise you that your
descendants, down to the fourth genera-
tion, will be kings of Israel." 31But Jehu did
not obey with all his heart the Law of the
LORD, the God of Israel; instead, he fol-
lowed the example of Jeroboam, who led
Israel into sin.

The Death of Jehu

32At that time the LORD began to reduce
the size of Israel's territory. King Hazael of
Syria conquered all the Israelite territory
33east of the Jordan, as far south as the town
of Aroer on the Arnon River—this included
the territories of Gilead and Bashan, where
the tribes of Gad, Reuben, and East Manas-
seh lived.
34Everything else that Jehu did, including
his brave deeds, is recorded in *The History of
the Kings of Israel.* 35He died and was buried
in Samaria, and his son Jehoahaz succeeded
him as king. 36Jehu had ruled in Samaria as
king of Israel for twenty-eight years.

Queen Athaliah of Judah
(2 Chronicles 22:10—23:15)

11 As soon as King Ahaziah's mother
Athaliah learned of her son's murder,
she gave orders for all the members of the
royal family to be killed. 2Only Ahaziah's son
Joash escaped. He was about to be killed
with the others, but was rescued by his aunt
Jehosheba, who was King Jehoram's daughter
and Ahaziah's half sister. She took him and
his nurse into a bedroom in the Temple and
hid him from Athaliah, so that he was not
killed. 3For six years Jehosheba took care of
the boy and kept him hidden in the Temple,
while Athaliah ruled as queen.
4But in the seventh year Jehoiada the priest
sent for the officers in charge of the royal
bodyguard and of the palace guards, and told
them to come to the Temple, where he made
them agree under oath to what he planned to
do. He showed them King Ahaziah's son Joash
5and gave them the following orders: "When
you come on duty on the Sabbath, one third
of you are to guard the palace; 6another third

Live it!

Protectors and Defenders

The child Joash would never have survived if he had not been rescued by his aunt Jehosheba and then guarded by the priest Jehoiada. Most of us don't have to worry about assassination attempts, but we do face different kinds of troubles and need people around us who can protect us. Sometimes this protection comes when others help us make good choices. Young people are sometimes faced with things like cheating, lying, stealing, smoking, drinking, fighting, and other risky behaviors. If you make bad choices about these things, you could get hurt or even killed.

Who are the people in your life who have looked out for you? Who gives you guidance in making good choices to keep you from danger? Do you have friends who give you good advice? Is there an adult in your life you can really count on if you have a question or a problem? Think about who those protectors are in your life. Let them know how important they are to you.

— 2 Kings 11:1–12

Queen Athaliah tore her clothes when she saw that Joash had been crowned as king. This was an expression of sorrow or dismay.

are to stand guard at the Sur Gate, and the
other third are to stand guard at the gate
behind the other guards.[w] 7The two groups
that go off duty on the Sabbath are to stand
guard at the Temple to protect the king. 8You
are to guard King Joash with drawn swords
and stay with him wherever he goes. Anyone
who comes near you is to be killed."

9The officers obeyed Jehoiada's instructions and brought their men to him—those
going off duty on the Sabbath and those
going on duty. 10He gave the officers the
spears[x] and shields that had belonged to
King David and had been kept in the Temple, 11and he stationed the men with drawn
swords all around the front of the Temple, to
protect the king. 12Then Jehoiada led Joash
out, placed the crown on his head, and gave
him a copy of the laws governing kingship.
Then Joash was anointed and proclaimed
king. The people clapped their hands and
shouted, "Long live the king!"

13Queen Athaliah heard the noise being
made by the guards and the people, so she
hurried to the Temple, where the crowd had
gathered. 14There she saw the new king
standing by the column at the entrance of
the Temple, as was the custom. He was surrounded by the officers and the trumpeters,
and the people were all shouting joyfully and
blowing trumpets. Athaliah tore her clothes
in distress and shouted, "Treason! Treason!"

Athaliah tore her clothes in distress. (11:14)

15Jehoiada did not want Athaliah killed in
the Temple area, so he ordered the army officers: "Take her out between the rows of
guards, and kill anyone who tries to rescue
her." 16They seized her, took her to the
palace, and there at the Horse Gate they
killed her.

Jehoiada's Reforms
(2 Chronicles 23:16–21)

17The priest Jehoiada had King Joash and
the people make a covenant with the LORD
that they would be the LORD's people; he
also made a covenant between the king and
the people. 18Then the people went to the
temple of Baal and tore it down; they
smashed the altars and the idols, and killed
Mattan, the priest of Baal, in front of the
altars.

Jehoiada put guards on duty at the Temple, 19and then he, the officers, the royal
bodyguard, and the palace guards escorted
the king from the Temple to the palace, followed by all the people. Joash entered by the
Guard Gate and took his place on the
throne. 20All the people were filled with
happiness, and the city was quiet, now that
Athaliah had been killed in the palace.

21Joash became king of Judah at the age of
seven.

King Joash of Judah
(2 Chronicles 24:1–16)

12 In the seventh year of the reign of
King Jehu of Israel, Joash became
king of Judah, and he ruled in Jerusalem for
forty years. His mother was Zibiah from the
city of Beersheba. 2Throughout his life he
did what pleased the LORD, because Jehoiada
the priest instructed him. 3However, the
pagan places of worship were not destroyed,
and the people continued to offer sacrifices
and burn incense there.

[w] **11:6** *Hebrew has an additional word, the meaning of which is unclear.* [x] **11:10** *Some ancient translations (and see 2 Chr 23:9)* spears; *Hebrew* spear.
11:14 2 Kings 23:3

What did King Joash tell the priests they had to do?

4Joash called the priests and ordered them
to save up the money paid in connection
with the sacrifices in the Temple, both the
dues paid for the regular sacrifices and the
money given as freewill gifts. 5Each priest
was to be responsible for the money brought
by those he served, and the money was to be
used to repair the Temple, as needed.

6But by the twenty-third year of Joash's
reign the priests still had not made any
repairs in the Temple. 7So he called in
Jehoiada and the other priests and asked
them, "Why aren't you repairing the Temple?
From now on you are not to keep the
money you receive; you must hand it over,
so that the repairs can be made." 8The priests
agreed to this and also agreed not to make
the repairs in the Temple.

9Then Jehoiada took a box, made a hole
in the lid, and placed the box by the altar, on
the right side as one enters the Temple. The
priests on duty at the entrance put in the
box all the money given by the worshipers.
10Whenever there was a large amount of
money in the box, the royal secretary and
the High Priest would come, melt down the
silver, and weigh it.[y] 11After recording the
exact amount, they would hand the silver
over to the men in charge of the work in
the Temple, and these would pay the carpen-
ters, the builders, 12the masons, and the stone
cutters, buy the timber and the stones used
in the repairs, and pay all other necessary
expenses. 13None of the money, however,
was used to pay for making silver cups,
bowls, trumpets, or tools for tending the
lamps, or any other article of silver or of
gold. 14It was all used to pay the workers and
to buy the materials used in the repairs.
15The men in charge of the work were thor-
oughly honest, so there was no need to
require them to account for the funds. 16The
money given for the repayment offerings
and for the offerings for sin was not deposit-
ed in the box; it belonged to the priests.

17At that time King Hazael of Syria
attacked the city of Gath and conquered it;
then he decided to attack Jerusalem. 18King
Joash of Judah took all the offerings that his
predecessors Jehoshaphat, Jehoram, and
Ahaziah had dedicated to the LORD, added
to them his own offerings and all the gold
in the treasuries of the Temple and the
palace, and sent them all as a gift to King
Hazael, who then led his army away from
Jerusalem.

19Everything else that King Joash did is
recorded in *The History of the Kings of Judah*.

20-21King Joash's officials plotted against
him, and two of them, Jozacar son of
Shimeath and Jehozabad son of Shomer,
killed him at the house built on the land that
was filled in on the east side of Jerusalem, on
the road that goes down to Silla. Joash was
buried in the royal tombs in David's City,
and his son Amaziah succeeded him as king.

King Jehoahaz of Israel

13 In the twenty-third year of the reign
of Joash son of Ahaziah as king of
Judah, Jehoahaz son of Jehu became king of
Israel, and he ruled in Samaria for seventeen
years. 2Like King Jeroboam before him, he
sinned against the LORD and led Israel into
sin; he never gave up his evil ways. 3So the
LORD was angry with Israel, and he allowed
King Hazael of Syria and his son Benhadad
to defeat Israel time after time. 4Then Jeho-
ahaz prayed to the LORD, and the LORD,
seeing how harshly the king of Syria was
oppressing the Israelites, answered his prayer.
5The LORD sent Israel a leader, who freed
them from the Syrians, and so the Israelites
lived in peace, as before. 6But they still did
not give up the sins into which King Jer-
oboam had led Israel, but kept on[z] commit-
ting them; and the image of the goddess
Asherah remained in Samaria.

7Jehoahaz had no armed forces left except
fifty cavalry troops, ten chariots, and ten
thousand foot soldiers, because the king of
Syria had destroyed the rest, trampling them
down like dust.

8Everything else that Jehoahaz did and all
his brave deeds are recorded in *The History of
the Kings of Israel*. 9He died and was buried

[y] **12:10** melt down the silver, and weigh it; *or* count the money, and tie it up in bags. [z] **13:6** *Some ancient translations* kept on; *Hebrew* he kept on.

12:4 Ex 30:11–16 **12:15** 2 Kings 22:7 **12:16** Lev 7:7

Pray it!

The Same Old Sins

The Israelites kept committing the same sins. They couldn't seem to break their sinful habits. We can be like that sometimes. When we fall into bad or sinful habits, they can be very hard to break.

God of Love
I know you want me to stay close to you.
Whenever I sin it's like I'm
turning my back on you,
taking a step away from you,
refusing your gift of love.
Help me to avoid the things that lead me into sin.
Help me to seek you when I need forgiveness.
Help me to remember both your love and your mercy.

— 2 Kings 13:1–11

in Samaria, and his son Jehoash succeeded him as king.

King Jehoash of Israel

10 In the thirty-seventh year of the reign of King Joash of Judah, Jehoash son of Jehoahaz became king of Israel, and he ruled in Samaria for sixteen years.
11 He too sinned against the LORD and followed the evil example of King Jeroboam, who had led Israel into sin.
12 Everything else that Jehoash did, including his bravery in the war against King Amaziah of Judah, is recorded in *The History of the Kings of Israel*.
13 Jehoash died and was buried in the royal tombs in Samaria, and his son Jeroboam II succeeded him as king.

The Death of Elisha

14 The prophet Elisha was sick with a fatal disease, and as he lay dying, King Jehoash of Israel went to visit him. "My father, my father!" he exclaimed as he wept. "You have been the mighty defender of Israel!"
15 "Get a bow and some arrows," Elisha ordered him. Jehoash got them,
16 and Elisha told him to get ready to shoot. The king did so, and Elisha placed his hands on the king's hands.
17 Then, following the prophet's instructions, the king opened the window that faced toward Syria. "Shoot the arrow!" Elisha ordered. As soon as the king shot the arrow, the prophet exclaimed, "You are the LORD's arrow, with which he will win victory over Syria. You will fight the Syrians in Aphek until you defeat them."
18 Then Elisha told the king to take the other arrows and strike the ground with them. The king struck the ground three times, and then stopped.
19 This made Elisha angry, and he said to the king, "You should have struck five or six times, and then you would have won complete victory over the Syrians; but now you will defeat them only three times."
20 Elisha died and was buried.

Every year bands of Moabites used to invade the land of Israel.
21 One time during a funeral, one of those bands was seen, and the people threw the corpse into Elisha's tomb and ran off.[a] As soon as the body came

[a] **13:21** *One ancient translation* and ran off; *Hebrew* and he ran off.
13:14 2 Kings 2:12

into contact with Elisha's bones, the man came back to life and stood up.

War between Israel and Syria

[22]King Hazael of Syria oppressed the Israelites during all of Jehoahaz' reign, [23]but the LORD was kind and merciful to them. He would not let them be destroyed, but helped them because of his covenant with Abraham, Isaac, and Jacob. He has never forgotten his people.

[24]At the death of King Hazael of Syria his son Benhadad became king. [25]Then King Jehoash of Israel defeated Benhadad three times and recaptured the cities that had been taken by Benhadad during the reign of Jehoahaz, the father of Jehoash.

King Amaziah of Judah
(2 Chronicles 25:1–24)

14 In the second year of the reign of Jehoash son of Jehoahaz as king of Israel, Amaziah son of Joash became king of Judah [2]at the age of twenty-five, and he ruled in Jerusalem for twenty-nine years. His mother was Jehoaddin from Jerusalem. [3]He did what was pleasing to the LORD, but he was not like his ancestor King David; instead, he did what his father Joash had done. [4]He did not tear down the pagan places of worship, and the people continued to offer sacrifices and burn incense there.

[5]As soon as Amaziah was firmly in power, he executed the officials who had killed his father, the king. [6]However, he did not kill their children but followed what the LORD had commanded in the Law of Moses: "Parents are not to be put to death for crimes committed by their children, and children are not to be put to death for crimes committed by their parents; people are to be put to death only for a crime they themselves have committed."

[7]Amaziah killed ten thousand Edomite soldiers in Salt Valley; he captured the city of Sela in battle and called it Joktheel, the name it still has.

[8]Then Amaziah sent messengers to King Jehoash of Israel, challenging him to fight.[b] [9]But King Jehoash sent back the following reply: "Once a thorn bush on the Lebanon Mountains sent a message to a cedar: 'Give your daughter in marriage to my son.' A wild animal passed by and trampled the bush down. [10]Now Amaziah, you have defeated the Edomites, and you are filled with pride. Be satisfied with your fame and stay at home. Why stir up trouble that will only bring disaster on you and your people?"

[11]But Amaziah refused to listen, so King Jehoash marched out with his men and fought against him at Beth Shemesh in Judah. [12]Amaziah's army was defeated, and all his soldiers fled to their homes. [13]Jehoash took Amaziah prisoner, advanced on Jerusalem, and tore down the city wall from Ephraim Gate to the Corner Gate, a distance of two hundred yards. [14]He took all the silver and gold he could find, all the Temple equipment and all the palace treasures, and carried them back to Samaria. He also took hostages with him.

[15]Everything else that Jehoash did, including his bravery in the war against King Amaziah of Judah, is recorded in *The History of the Kings of Israel.* [16]Jehoash died and was buried in the royal tombs in Samaria, and his son Jeroboam II succeeded him as king.

The Death of King Amaziah of Judah
(2 Chronicles 25:25–28)

[17]King Amaziah of Judah lived fifteen years after the death of King Jehoash of Israel. [18]Everything else that Amaziah did is recorded in *The History of the Kings of Judah.*

[19]There was a plot in Jerusalem to assassinate Amaziah, so he fled to the city of Lachish, but his enemies followed him there

[b] **14:8** challenging him to fight; *or* inviting him to a conference.
14:6 Deut 24:16

Elisha was responsible for a miracle even after he was dead! What was it?

and killed him. 20 His body was carried back
to Jerusalem on a horse and was buried in
the royal tombs in David's City. 21 The peo-
ple of Judah then crowned his sixteen-year-
old son Uzziah as king. 22 Uzziah recon-
quered and rebuilt Elath after his father's
death.

King Jeroboam II of Israel

23 In the fifteenth year of the reign of
Amaziah son of Joash as king of Judah, Jer-
oboam son of Jehoash became king of Israel,
and he ruled in Samaria for forty-one years.
24 He sinned against the LORD, following the
wicked example of his predecessor King Jer-
oboam son of Nebat, who led Israel into sin.
25 He reconquered all the territory that had
belonged to Israel, from Hamath Pass in the
north to the Dead Sea in the south. This was
what the LORD, the God of Israel, had
promised through his servant the prophet
Jonah son of Amittai from Gath Hepher.
26 The LORD saw the terrible[c] suffering of
the Israelites; there was no one at all to help
them. 27 But it was not the LORD's purpose
to destroy Israel completely and forever, so
he rescued them through King Jeroboam II.
28 Everything else that Jeroboam II did, his
brave battles, and how he restored Damascus
and Hamath to Israel,[d] are all recorded in *The
History of the Kings of Israel.* 29 Jeroboam died
and was buried in the royal tombs, and his
son Zechariah succeeded him as king.

King Uzziah of Judah
(2 Chronicles 26:1–23)

15 In the twenty-seventh year of the
reign of King Jeroboam II of Israel,
Uzziah son of Amaziah became king of
Judah 2 at the age of sixteen, and he ruled in
Jerusalem for fifty-two years. His mother was
Jecoliah from Jerusalem. 3 Following the
example of his father, he did what was pleas-
ing to the LORD. 4 But the pagan places of
worship were not destroyed, and the people
continued to offer sacrifices and burn
incense there. 5 The LORD struck Uzziah
with a dreaded skin disease that stayed with
him the rest of his life. He lived in a separate
house, relieved of all duties, while his son
Jotham governed the country.
6 Everything else that Uzziah did is
recorded in *The History of the Kings of Judah.*
7 Uzziah died and was buried in the royal
burial ground in David's City, and his son
Jotham succeeded him as king.

King Zechariah of Israel

8 In the thirty-eighth year of the reign of
King Uzziah of Judah, Zechariah son of Jer-
oboam II became king of Israel, and he
ruled in Samaria for six months. 9 He, like his
predecessors, sinned against the LORD. He
followed the wicked example of King Jer-
oboam son of Nebat, who led Israel into sin.
10 Shallum son of Jabesh conspired against
King Zechariah, assassinated him at Ibleam,[e]
and succeeded him as king.
11 Everything else that Zechariah did is
recorded in *The History of the Kings of Israel.*
12 So the promise was fulfilled which the
LORD had made to King Jehu: "Your descen-
dants down to the fourth generation[f] will be
kings of Israel."

King Shallum of Israel

13 In the thirty-ninth year of the reign of
King Uzziah of Judah, Shallum son of Jabesh
became king of Israel, and he ruled in
Samaria for one month.
14 Menahem son of Gadi went from Tirzah
to Samaria, assassinated Shallum, and suc-
ceeded him as king. 15 Everything else that
Shallum did, including an account of his

[c] **14:26** *Some ancient translations* terrible; *Hebrew* rebellious. [d] **14:28** *One ancient translation* to Israel; *Hebrew* for Judah in Israel. [e] **15:10** *One ancient translation* at Ibleam; *Hebrew* before people. [f] **15:12** FOURTH GENERATION: *Zechariah was Jehu's great-great-grandson.*
14:25 Jon 1:1 **15:7** Isa 6:1 **15:12** 2 Kings 10:30

***The History of the Kings of Judah* and *The History of the Kings of Israel* are books that were lost long ago.**

Live it!

Plots and Schemes

Chapter 15 of 2 Kings mentions seven different kings, four of whom were assassinated! This was not a bright spot in the history of God's people. Their leaders were not good men, committed to following God.

You don't have to kill someone to plot against him or her. Once there was a group of teens who wanted to get revenge on another student. They wrote nasty notes about teachers and signed the notes with their victim's name. They left the notes in classrooms where they would be found. At first the group got away with it. Everyone thought that the student being picked on was guilty. But soon a teacher realized what was really happening. All the people in the group received detentions for their behavior.

Beware of things that are done in secret! Plots and schemes—except for planning surprise birthday parties—are big trouble for everyone involved.

— 2 Kings, chapter 15

conspiracy, is recorded in *The History of the Kings of Israel.*
16As Menahem was on his way from Tirzah, he completely destroyed the city of Tappuah,[g] its inhabitants, and the surrounding territory, because the city did not surrender to him. He even ripped open the bellies of all the pregnant women.

King Menahem of Israel

17In the thirty-ninth year of the reign of King Uzziah of Judah, Menahem son of Gadi became king of Israel, and he ruled in
Samaria for ten years.
18He sinned against the LORD, for until the day of his death he followed the wicked example of King Jeroboam son of Nebat, who led Israel into sin.
19Tiglath Pileser, the emperor of Assyria, invaded Israel, and Menahem gave him thirty-eight tons of silver to gain his support in strengthening Menahem's power over the
country.
20Menahem got the money from the rich men of Israel by forcing each one to contribute fifty pieces of silver. So Tiglath Pileser went back to his own country.
21Everything else that Menahem did is recorded in *The History of the Kings of Israel.*
22He died and was buried, and his son Pekahiah succeeded him as king.

King Pekahiah of Israel

23In the fiftieth year of the reign of King Uzziah of Judah, Pekahiah son of Menahem became king of Israel, and he ruled in
Samaria for two years.
24He sinned against the LORD, following the wicked example of King Jeroboam son of Nebat, who led Israel
into sin.
25An officer of Pekahiah's forces, Pekah son of Remaliah, plotted with fifty men from Gilead, assassinated Pekahiah in the palace's inner fortress[h] in Samaria, and succeeded him as king.
26Everything else that Pekahiah did is recorded in *The History of the Kings of Israel.*

King Pekah of Israel

27In the fifty-second year of the reign of King Uzziah of Judah, Pekah son of Remaliah became king of Israel, and he ruled in
Samaria for twenty years.
28He sinned against the LORD, following the wicked example of King Jeroboam son of Nebat, who led Israel into sin.
29It was while Pekah was king that Tiglath Pileser, the emperor of Assyria, captured the cities of Ijon, Abel Beth Maacah, Janoah, Kedesh, and Hazor, and the territories of Gilead, Galilee, and Naphtali, and took the people to Assyria as prisoners.

[g] **15:16** *One ancient translation* Tappuah; *Hebrew* Tiphsah.
[h] **15:25** *Hebrew has two additional words, the meaning of which is unclear.*

30 In the twentieth year of the reign of
Jotham son of Uzziah as king of Judah,
Hoshea son of Elah plotted against King
Pekah, assassinated him, and succeeded him
as king. 31 Everything else that Pekah did
is recorded in *The History of the Kings of
Israel*.

King Jotham of Judah
(2 Chronicles 27:1–9)

32 In the second year of the reign of Pekah
son of Remaliah as king of Israel, Jotham
son of Uzziah became king of Judah 33 at the
age of twenty-five, and he ruled in Jerusalem
for sixteen years. His mother was Jerusha, the
daughter of Zadok. 34 Following the example
of his father Uzziah, Jotham did what was
pleasing to the LORD. 35 But the pagan places
of worship were not destroyed, and the peo-
ple continued to offer sacrifices and burn
incense there. It was Jotham who built the
North Gate of the Temple.
36 Everything else that Jotham did is
recorded in *The History of the Kings of Judah*.
37 It was while he was king that the LORD
first sent King Rezin of Syria and King
Pekah of Israel to attack Judah. 38 Jotham
died and was buried in the royal tombs in
David's City, and his son Ahaz succeeded
him as king.

King Ahaz of Judah
(2 Chronicles 28:1–27)

16 In the seventeenth year of the reign
of Pekah son of Remaliah as king of
Israel, Ahaz son of Jotham became king of
Judah 2 at the age of twenty, and he ruled in
Jerusalem for sixteen years. He did not fol-
low the good example of his ancestor King
David; instead, he did what was not pleasing
to the LORD his God 3 and followed the
example of the kings of Israel. He even sac-
rificed his own son as a burnt offering to
idols, imitating the disgusting practice of the
people whom the LORD had driven out of
the land as the Israelites advanced. 4 At the
pagan places of worship, on the hills, and
under every shady tree, Ahaz offered sacri-
fices and burned incense.
5 King Rezin of Syria and King Pekah of
Israel attacked Jerusalem and besieged it, but
could not defeat Ahaz. (6 At the same time
the king of Edom[i] regained control of the
city of Elath and drove out the Judeans who
lived there. The Edomites settled in Elath
and still live there.) 7 Ahaz sent men to
Tiglath Pileser, the emperor of Assyria, with
this message: "I am your devoted servant.
Come and rescue me from the kings of Syria
and of Israel, who are attacking me." 8 Ahaz
took the silver and gold from the Temple
and the palace treasury, and sent it as a pres-
ent to the emperor. 9 Tiglath Pileser, in
answer to Ahaz' plea, marched out with his
army against Damascus, captured it, killed
King Rezin, and took the people to Kir as
prisoners.
10 When King Ahaz went to Damascus to
meet Emperor Tiglath Pileser, he saw the altar
there and sent back to Uriah the priest an
exact model of it, down to the smallest
details. 11 So Uriah built an altar just like it
and finished it before Ahaz returned. 12 On his
return from Damascus, Ahaz saw that the altar
was finished, 13 so he burned animal sacrifices
and grain offerings on it and poured a wine
offering and the blood of a fellowship offer-
ing on it. 14 The bronze altar dedicated to the
LORD was between the new altar and the
Temple, so Ahaz moved it to the north side of
his new altar. 15 Then he ordered Uriah: "Use
this large altar of mine for the morning burnt
offerings and the evening grain offerings, for
the burnt offerings and grain offerings of the
king and the people, and for the people's
wine offerings. Pour on it the blood of all the
animals that are sacrificed. But keep the
bronze altar for me to use for divination."
16 Uriah did as the king commanded.
17 King Ahaz took apart the bronze carts
used in the Temple and removed the basins
that were on them. He also took the bronze
tank from the backs of the twelve bronze
bulls and placed it on a stone foundation.
18 And in order to please the Assyrian emper-
or, Ahaz also removed from the Temple the

[i] **16:6** *Probable text* the king of Edom; *Hebrew* King Rezin of Syria.

16:3 Deut 12:31 **16:5** Isa 7:1 **16:14** Ex 27:1, 2; 2 Chr 4:1 **16:17** 1 Kings 7:23–39; 2 Chr 4:2–6

platform for the royal throne and closed up
the king's private entrance to the Temple.[j]
19 Everything else that King Ahaz did is
recorded in *The History of the Kings of Judah.*
20 Ahaz died and was buried in the royal
tombs in David's City, and his son Hezekiah
succeeded him as king.

King Hoshea of Israel

17 In the twelfth year of the reign of
King Ahaz of Judah, Hoshea son of
Elah became king of Israel, and he ruled in
Samaria for nine years. 2 He sinned against
the LORD, but not as much as the kings who
had ruled Israel before him. 3 Emperor Shal-
maneser of Assyria made war against him;
Hoshea surrendered to Shalmaneser and
paid him tribute every year. 4 But one year
Hoshea sent messengers to So, king of
Egypt,[k] asking for his help, and stopped pay-
ing the annual tribute to Assyria. When Shal-
maneser learned of this, he had Hoshea
arrested and put in prison.

The Fall of Samaria

5 Then Shalmaneser invaded Israel and
besieged Samaria. In the third year of the
siege, 6 which was the ninth year of the reign
of Hoshea, the Assyrian emperor[l] captured
Samaria, took the Israelites to Assyria as prison-
ers, and settled some of them in the city of
Halah, some near the Habor River in the dis-
trict of Gozan and some in the cities of Media.
7 Samaria fell because the Israelites sinned
against the LORD their God, who had res-
cued them from the king of Egypt and had
led them out of Egypt. They worshiped
other gods, 8 followed the customs of the
people whom the LORD had driven out as
his people advanced, and adopted customs
introduced by the kings of Israel.[m] 9 The
Israelites did[n] things that the LORD their

They worshiped other gods. (17:7)

God disapproved of. They built pagan places
of worship in all their towns, from the small-
est village to the largest city. 10 On all the
hills and under every shady tree they put up
stone pillars and images of the goddess
Asherah, 11 and they burned incense on all
the pagan altars, following the practice of the
people whom the LORD had driven out of
the land. They aroused the LORD's anger
with all their wicked deeds 12 and disobeyed
the LORD's command not to worship idols.
13 The LORD had sent his messengers and
prophets to warn Israel and Judah: "Abandon
your evil ways and obey my commands, which
are contained in the Law I gave to your ances-
tors and which I handed on to you through
my servants the prophets." 14 But they would
not obey; they were stubborn like their ances-
tors, who had not trusted in the LORD their
God. 15 They refused to obey his instructions,
they did not keep the covenant he had made
with their ancestors, and they disregarded his
warnings. They worshiped worthless idols and
became worthless themselves, and they fol-
lowed the customs of the surrounding nations,
disobeying the LORD's command not to imi-
tate them. 16 They broke all the laws of the
LORD their God and made two metal bull-
calves to worship; they also made an image of
the goddess Asherah, worshiped the stars, and
served the god Baal. 17 They sacrificed their
sons and daughters as burnt offerings to pagan
gods; they consulted mediums and fortune-
tellers, and they devoted themselves completely
to doing what is wrong in the LORD's sight,
and so aroused his anger. 18 The LORD was

[j] **16:18** *Verse 18 in Hebrew is unclear.* [k] **17:4** So, king of Egypt; *or* the king of Egypt at Sais. [l] **17:6** ASSYRIAN EMPEROR: *Probably Sargon II, the successor of Shalmaneser.* [m] **17:8** *Probable text* and adopted . . . Israel; *Hebrew unclear.* [n] **17:9** did; *or* said.

16:20 Isa 14:28 **17:10** 1 Kings 14:23 **17:16** 1 Kings 12:28 **17:17** Deut 18:10

Ahaz was a very bad king. Make a list of all the evil things he did from chapter 16. For a short chapter, it will be a pretty big list!

They disregarded his warnings. (17:15)

angry with the Israelites and banished them
from his sight, leaving only the kingdom of
Judah.
19 But even the people of Judah did not
obey the laws of the LORD their God; they
imitated the customs adopted by the people
of Israel. 20 The LORD rejected all the
Israelites, punishing them and handing them
over to cruel enemies until at last he had
banished them from his sight.
21 After the LORD had separated Israel
from Judah, the Israelites made Jeroboam son
of Nebat their king. Jeroboam caused them
to abandon the LORD and led them into ter-
rible sins. 22 They followed Jeroboam and
continued to practice all the sins he had
committed, 23 until at last the LORD banished
them from his sight, as he had warned
through his servants the prophets that he
would do. So the people of Israel were taken
into exile to Assyria, where they still live.

The Assyrians Settle in Israel

24 The emperor of Assyria took people
from the cities of Babylon, Cuth, Ivvah,
Hamath, and Sepharvaim, and settled them
in the cities of Samaria[o] in place of the
exiled Israelites. They took possession of
these cities and lived there. 25 When they first
settled there, they did not worship the
LORD, and so he sent lions, which killed
some of them. 26 The emperor of Assyria was
told that the people he had settled in the
cities of Samaria did not know the law of
the god of that land, and so the god had sent
lions, which were killing them. 27 So the
emperor commanded: "Send back one of the
priests we brought as prisoners; have him[p]
go back and live there, in order to teach the

Live it!

Monkey See Monkey Do

People have a funny habit of imitating one another's behavior. The Israelites who settled in Samaria began to imitate the practices of the people who had lived there before them. They worshiped other gods and even built idols to them. People imitate bad behavior for all kinds of reasons—to fit in, so people will be impressed with them, sometimes just out of curiosity.

Maybe you've had friends do this. They start hanging around with a new group of people. They dress differently than they used to, listen to different music, and do things they wouldn't have done before. Maybe you've even done this yourself. Part of it is just the process of finding out who you want to be. It can be a problem, though. If you're always looking for someone else to decide what's right and wrong for you, you can end up like the Israelites. You will be doing things that you know are really wrong. It's okay to want to fit in, but take a close look at your behavior. Does it match up with what you say you believe? Do your actions fit the person you are and want to become?

— 2 Kings 17:7–18

[o] **17:24** SAMARIA: *The name of the capital city was applied to the territory of the former kingdom of Israel.*
[p] **17:27** *Some ancient translations* him; *Hebrew* them.

In Jesus' time Samaria was seen as a place of polluted religion. Read these stories about Samaritans in the New Testament: John 4:1–26 and Luke 10:30–37.

people the law of the god of that land." 28 So
an Israelite priest who had been deported
from Samaria went and lived in Bethel,
where he taught the people how to worship
the LORD.
29 But the people who settled in Samaria
continued to make their own idols, and they
placed them in the shrines that the Israelites
had built. Each different group made idols in
the cities they were living in: 30 the people of
Babylon made idols of the god Succoth
Benoth; the people of Cuth, idols of Nergal;
the people of Hamath, idols of Ashima; 31 the
people of Ivvah, idols of Nibhaz and Tartak;
and the people of Sepharvaim sacrificed
their children as burnt offerings to their gods
Adrammelech and Anammelech. 32 These
people also worshiped the LORD and chose
from among their own number all sorts of
people to serve as priests at the pagan places
of worship and to offer sacrifices for them
there. 33 So they worshiped the LORD, but
they also worshiped their own gods accord-
ing to the customs of the countries from
which they had come.
34 They still carry on their old customs to
this day. They do not worship the LORD nor
do they obey the laws and commands which
he gave to the descendants of Jacob, whom
he named Israel. 35 The LORD had made a
covenant with them and had ordered them:
"Do not worship other gods; do not bow
down to them or serve them or offer sacri-
fices to them. 36 You shall obey me, the
LORD, who brought you out of Egypt with
great power and strength; you are to bow
down to me and offer sacrifices to me. 37 You
shall always obey the laws and commands
that I wrote for you. You shall not obey
other gods, 38 and you shall not forget the
covenant I made with you. 39 You shall obey
me, the LORD your God, and I will rescue
you from your enemies." 40 But those people
would not listen, and they continued to fol-
low their old customs.
41 So those people worshiped the LORD,
but they also worshiped their idols; and to
this day their descendants continue to do the
same.

Study it!

One of the Good Guys

As each king is named in 1 and 2 Kings, the author tells us either that "he sinned against the LORD" or "he did what was pleasing to the LORD." The kings who worshiped only God, resisted the pagan gods, treated people fairly, and destroyed their idols and altars are the good guys. King Hezekiah was one of the good guys. He is even compared with the great King David who was thought of as the most faithful, the most devoted to the Lord, of any king, ever.

This doesn't mean that King Hezekiah's life was without problems. The Assyrians tried to conquer the kingdom of Judah after taking over the northern kingdom of Israel. Because Hezekiah turned to God and relied on the advice of the prophet Isaiah, the Assyrians eventually turned away. But Hezekiah got a good scare.

— 2 Kings 18:1–8

King Hezekiah of Judah

(2 Chronicles 29:1, 2; 31:1)

18 In the third year of the reign of
Hoshea son of Elah as king of Israel,
Hezekiah son of Ahaz became king of Judah
2 at the age of twenty-five, and he ruled in
Jerusalem for twenty-nine years. His mother
was Abijah, the daughter of Zechariah. 3 Fol-
lowing the example of his ancestor King
David, he did what was pleasing to the
LORD. 4 He destroyed the pagan places of
worship, broke the stone pillars, and cut
down the images of the goddess Asherah. He

17:34 Gen 32:28; 35:10 **17:35** Ex 20:5; Deut 5:9 **17:36** Deut 6:13 **18:4** Num 21:9

also broke in pieces the bronze snake that Moses had made, which was called Nehushtan. Up to that time the people of Israel had burned incense in its honor. [5]Hezekiah trusted in the LORD, the God of Israel; Judah never had another king like him, either before or after his time. [6]He was faithful to the LORD and never disobeyed him, but carefully kept all the commands that the LORD had given Moses. [7]So the LORD was with him, and he was successful in everything he did. He rebelled against the emperor of Assyria and refused to submit to him. [8]He defeated the Philistines and raided their settlements, from the smallest village to the largest city, including Gaza and its surrounding territory.

[9]In the fourth year of Hezekiah's reign—which was the seventh year of King Hoshea's reign over Israel—Emperor Shalmaneser of Assyria invaded Israel and besieged Samaria. [10]In the third year of the siege Samaria fell; this was the sixth year of Hezekiah's reign and the ninth year of Hoshea's reign. [11]The Assyrian emperor[q] took the Israelites to Assyria as prisoners and settled some of them in the city of Halah, some near the Habor River in the district of Gozan, and some in the cities of Media.

[12]Samaria fell because the Israelites did not obey the LORD their God, but broke the covenant he had made with them and disobeyed all the laws given by Moses, the servant of the LORD. They would not listen and they would not obey.

The Assyrians Threaten Jerusalem

(2 Chronicles 32:1–19; Isaiah 36:1–22)

[13]In the fourteenth year of the reign of King Hezekiah, Sennacherib, the emperor of Assyria, attacked the fortified cities of Judah and conquered them. [14]Hezekiah sent a message to Sennacherib, who was in Lachish: "I have done wrong; please stop your attack, and I will pay whatever you demand." The emperor's answer was that Hezekiah should send him ten tons of silver and one ton of gold. [15]Hezekiah sent him all the silver in the Temple and in the palace treasury; [16]he also stripped the gold from the temple doors and the gold with which he himself had covered the doorposts, and he sent it all to Sennacherib. [17]The Assyrian emperor sent a large army from Lachish to attack Hezekiah at Jerusalem; it was commanded by his three highest officials. When they arrived at Jerusalem, they occupied the road where the cloth makers work by the ditch that brings water from the upper pool. [18]Then they sent for King Hezekiah, and three of his officials went out to meet them: Eliakim son of Hilkiah, who was in charge of the palace; Shebna, the court secretary; and Joah son of Asaph, who was in charge of the records. [19]One of the Assyrian officials told them that the emperor wanted to know what made King Hezekiah so confident. [20]He demanded, "Do you think that words can take the place of military skill and might? Who do you think will help you rebel against Assyria? [21]You are expecting Egypt to help you, but that would be like using a reed as a walking stick—it would break and jab your hand. That is what the king of Egypt is like when anyone relies on him."

[22]The Assyrian official went on, "Or will you tell me that you are relying on the LORD your God? It was the LORD's shrines and altars that Hezekiah destroyed, when he told the people of Judah and Jerusalem to worship only at the altar in Jerusalem. [23]I will make a bargain with you in the name of the emperor. I will give you two thousand horses if you can find that many men to ride them! [24]You are no match for even the lowest ranking Assyrian official, and yet you

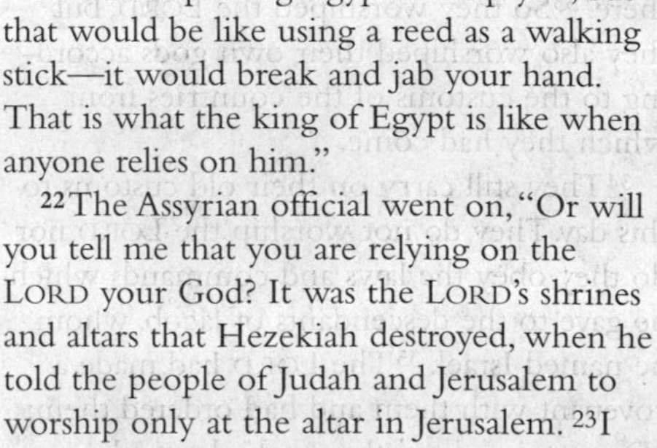

Sennacherib . . . attacked the fortified cities. (18:13)

[q] **18:11** ASSYRIAN EMPEROR: *See 17:6.*

expect the Egyptians to send you chariots and cavalry! 25 Do you think I have attacked your country and destroyed it without the LORD's help? The LORD himself told me to attack it and destroy it."

26 Then Eliakim, Shebna, and Joah told the official, "Speak Aramaic to us, sir. We understand it. Don't speak Hebrew; all the people on the wall are listening."

27 He replied, "Do you think you and the king are the only ones the emperor sent me to say all these things to? No, I am also talking to the people who are sitting on the wall, who will have to eat their excrement and drink their urine, just as you will."

28 Then the official stood up and shouted in Hebrew, "Listen to what the emperor of Assyria is telling you! 29 He warns you not to let Hezekiah deceive you. Hezekiah can't save you. 30 And don't let him persuade you to rely on the LORD. Don't think that the LORD will save you and that he will stop our Assyrian army from capturing your city. 31 Don't listen to Hezekiah. The emperor of Assyria commands you to come out of the city and surrender. You will all be allowed to eat grapes from your own vines and figs from your own trees, and to drink water from your own wells— 32 until the emperor resettles you in a country much like your own, where there are vineyards to give wine and there is grain for making bread; it is a land of olives, olive oil, and honey. If you do what he commands, you will not die, but live. Don't let Hezekiah fool you into thinking that the LORD will rescue you. 33 Did the gods of any other nations save their countries from the emperor of Assyria? 34 Where are they now, the gods of Hamath and Arpad? Where are the gods of Sepharvaim, Hena, and Ivvah? Did anyone save Samaria? 35 When did any of the gods of all these countries ever save their country from our emperor? Then what makes you think the LORD can save Jerusalem?"

36 The people kept quiet, just as King Hezekiah had told them to; they did not say a word. 37 Then Eliakim, Shebna, and Joah

The official stood up and shouted in Hebrew. (18:28)

tore their clothes in grief, and went and reported to the king what the Assyrian official had said.

The King Asks Isaiah's Advice
(Isaiah 37:1–7)

19 As soon as King Hezekiah heard their report, he tore his clothes in grief, put on sackcloth, and went to the Temple of the LORD. 2 He sent Eliakim, the official in charge of the palace, Shebna, the court secretary, and the senior priests to the prophet Isaiah son of Amoz. They also were wearing sackcloth. 3 This is the message which he told them to give Isaiah: "Today is a day of suffering; we are being punished and are in disgrace. We are like a woman who is ready to give birth, but is too weak to do it. 4 The Assyrian emperor has sent his chief official to insult the living God. May the LORD your God hear these insults and punish those who spoke them. So pray to God for those of our people who survive."

5 When Isaiah received King Hezekiah's message, 6 he sent back this answer: "The LORD tells you not to let the Assyrians frighten you with their claims that he cannot save you. 7 The LORD will cause the emperor to hear a rumor that will make him go back to his own country, and the LORD will have him killed there."

Remember how Israel split into two kingdoms? Second Kings 18:9–12 tells how the northern kingdom was taken over by the Assyrians in 721 BC.

Pray it!

Pour Out Your Heart

Have you ever felt hopeless? Like the world was closing in on you? King Hezekiah must have felt like that. The Assyrian Emperor sent a threatening letter meant to frighten Hezekiah and drive him to despair. Instead Hezekiah went to the Temple and poured out his heart to the Lord. Sometimes we need to do that, too.

Dear God,
I don't know what to do,
The situation seems hopeless.
I don't want to give up, but I don't see a way out.
I know we cannot solve this by ourselves.
We can only do it with your help.
Be with us, Lord.
Guide us, protect us, and give us courage.
I know we can only get through this with you.

— 2 Kings 19:14–19

The Assyrians Send Another Threat
(Isaiah 37:8–20)

8The Assyrian official learned that the
emperor had left Lachish and was fighting
against the nearby city of Libnah; so he went
there to consult him. 9Word reached the
Assyrians that the Egyptian army, led by
King Tirhakah of Ethiopia,[r] was coming to
attack them. When the emperor heard this,
he sent a letter to King Hezekiah of Judah
10to tell him, "The god you are trusting in
has told you that you will not fall into my
hands, but don't let that deceive you. 11You
have heard what an Assyrian emperor does
to any country he decides to destroy. Do you
think that you can escape? 12My ancestors
destroyed the cities of Gozan, Haran, and
Rezeph, and killed the people of Betheden
who lived in Telassar, and none of their gods
could save them. 13Where are the kings of
the cities of Hamath, Arpad, Sepharvaim,
Hena, and Ivvah?"
14King Hezekiah took the letter from the
messengers and read it. Then he went to the
Temple, placed the letter there in the pres-
ence of the LORD, 15and prayed, "O LORD,
the God of Israel, seated on your throne
above the winged creatures, you alone are
God, ruling all the kingdoms of the world.
You created the earth and the sky. 16Now,
LORD, look at what is happening to us. Lis-
ten to all the things that Sennacherib is say-
ing to insult you, the living God. 17We all
know, LORD, that the emperors of Assyria
have destroyed many nations, made their
lands desolate, 18and burned up their gods—
which were no gods at all, only images of
wood and stone made by human hands.
19Now, LORD our God, rescue us from the
Assyrians, so that all the nations of the world
will know that only you, O LORD, are God."

[r] **19:9** *Hebrew* Cush: *Cush is the ancient name of the extensive territory south of the First Cataract of the Nile River. This region was called Ethiopia in Graeco-Roman times, and included within its borders most of modern Sudan and some of present-day Ethiopia (Abyssinia).*
19:15 Ex 25:22

How does Hezekiah know that he will recover from his illness? What sign does he ask for?

Isaiah's Message to the King
(Isaiah 37:21–38)

20 Then Isaiah sent a message telling King
Hezekiah that in answer to the king's prayer
21 the LORD had said, "The city of Jerusalem
laughs at you, Sennacherib, and makes fun of
you. 22 Whom do you think you have been
insulting and ridiculing? You have been disre-
spectful to me, the holy God of Israel. 23 You
sent your messengers to boast to me that
with all your chariots you had conquered the
highest mountains of Lebanon. You boasted
that there you cut down the tallest cedars and
the finest cypress trees and that you reached
the deepest parts of the forests. 24 You boasted
that you dug wells and drank water in for-
eign lands and that the feet of your soldiers
tramped the Nile River dry.

25 "Have you never heard that I planned
all this long ago? And now I have carried it
out. I gave you the power to turn fortified
cities into piles of rubble. 26 The people who
lived there were powerless; they were fright-
ened and stunned. They were like grass in a
field or weeds growing on a roof when the
hot east wind blasts them.[s]

27 "But I know everything about you,
what you do and where you go. I know how
you rage against me. 28 I have received the
report of that rage and that pride of yours,
and now I will put a hook through your
nose and a bit in your mouth, and take you
back by the same road you came."

29 Then Isaiah said to King Hezekiah,
"Here is a sign of what will happen. This year
and next you will have only wild grain to eat,
but the following year you will be able to
plant your grain and harvest it, and plant vines
and eat grapes. 30 Those in Judah who survive
will flourish like plants that send roots deep
into the ground and produce fruit. 31 There
will be people in Jerusalem and on Mount
Zion who will survive, because the LORD is
determined to make this happen.

32 "And this is what the LORD has said
about the Assyrian emperor: 'He will not
enter this city or shoot a single arrow against
it. No soldiers with shields will come near
the city, and no siege mounds will be built
around it. 33 He will go back by the same
road he came, without entering this city. I,
the LORD, have spoken. 34 I will defend this
city and protect it, for the sake of my own
honor and because of the promise I made to
my servant David.' "

35 That night an angel of the LORD went
to the Assyrian camp and killed 185,000 sol-
diers. At dawn the next day there they lay, all
dead! 36 Then the Assyrian emperor Sen-
nacherib withdrew and returned to Nin-
eveh. 37 One day, when he was worshiping in
the temple of his god Nisroch, two of his
sons, Adrammelech and Sharezer, killed him
with their swords and then escaped to the
land of Ararat. Another of his sons, Esarhad-
don, succeeded him as emperor.

King Hezekiah's Illness and Recovery
(Isaiah 38:1–8, 21, 22; 2 Chronicles 32:24–26)

20 About this time King Hezekiah
became sick and almost died. The
prophet Isaiah son of Amoz went to see him
and said to him, "The LORD tells you that
you are to put everything in order, because
you will not recover. Get ready to die."

2 Hezekiah turned his face to the wall and
prayed: 3 "Remember, LORD, that I have
served you faithfully and loyally and that I
have always tried to do what you wanted me
to." And he began to cry bitterly.

4 Isaiah left the king, but before he had
passed through the central courtyard of the
palace the LORD told him 5 to go back to
Hezekiah, ruler of the LORD's people, and
say to him, "I, the LORD, the God of your
ancestor David, have heard your prayer and
seen your tears. I will heal you, and in three
days you will go to the Temple. 6 I will let
you live fifteen years longer. I will rescue
you and this city Jerusalem from the emper-
or of Assyria. I will defend this city, for the
sake of my own honor and because of the
promise I made to my servant David."

7 Then Isaiah told the king's attendants to
put on his boil a paste made of figs, and he
would get well.[t] 8 King Hezekiah asked,
"What is the sign to prove that the LORD

[s] **19:26** *Probable text* when the hot east wind blasts them; *Hebrew* blasted before they are grown. [t] **20:7** *One ancient translation (and see Isa 38:21)* figs, and he would get well; *Hebrew* figs. They did so, and he got well.

will heal me and that three days later I will
be able to go to the Temple?"
9 Isaiah replied, "The LORD will give you a
sign to prove that he will keep his promise.
Now, would you prefer to have the shadow
on the stairway go forward ten steps or go
back ten steps?"[u]
10 Hezekiah answered, "It's easy to have
the shadow go forward ten steps![v] Have it go
back ten steps."[v]
11 Isaiah prayed to the LORD, and the
LORD made the shadow go back ten steps[v]
on the stairway[w] set up by King Ahaz.

Messengers from Babylonia

(Isaiah 39:1–8)

12 About that same time the king of Bab-
ylonia, Merodach Baladan, the son of Bal-
adan, heard that King Hezekiah had been
sick, so he sent him a letter and a present.
13 Hezekiah welcomed the messengers and
showed them his wealth—his silver and
gold, his spices and perfumes, and all his mil-
itary equipment. There was nothing in his
storerooms or anywhere in his kingdom that
he did not show them. 14 Then the prophet
Isaiah went to King Hezekiah and asked,
"Where did these men come from and what
did they say to you?"

Hezekiah answered, "They came from a
very distant country, from Babylonia."
15 "What did they see in the palace?"

"They saw everything. There is nothing in
the storerooms that I didn't show them."
16 Isaiah then told the king, "The LORD
Almighty says that 17 a time is coming when
everything in your palace, everything that
your ancestors have stored up to this day, will
be carried off to Babylonia. Nothing will be
left. 18 Some of your own direct descendants
will be taken away and made eunuchs to
serve in the palace of the king of Babylonia."
19 King Hezekiah understood this to mean
that there would be peace and security dur-
ing his lifetime, so he replied, "The message
you have given me from the LORD is good."

The End of Hezekiah's Reign

(2 Chronicles 32:32, 33)

20 Everything else that King Hezekiah did,
his brave deeds, and an account of how he
built a reservoir and dug a tunnel to bring
water into the city, are all recorded in *The
History of the Kings of Judah.* 21 Hezekiah
died, and his son Manasseh succeeded him as
king.

King Manasseh of Judah

(2 Chronicles 33:1–20)

21 Manasseh was twelve years old when
he became king of Judah, and he
ruled in Jerusalem for fifty-five years. His
mother was Hephzibah. 2 Following the dis-
gusting practices of the nations whom the
LORD had driven out of the land as his peo-
ple advanced, Manasseh sinned against the
LORD. 3 He rebuilt the pagan places of wor-
ship that his father Hezekiah had destroyed;
he built altars for the worship of Baal and
made an image of the goddess Asherah, as
King Ahab of Israel had done. Manasseh also
worshiped the stars. 4 He built pagan altars in
the Temple, the place that the LORD had said
was where he should be worshiped. 5 In the
two courtyards of the Temple he built altars
for the worship of the stars. 6 He sacrificed
his son as a burnt offering. He practiced
divination and magic and consulted[x] for-
tunetellers and mediums. He sinned greatly
against the LORD and stirred up his anger.
7 He placed the symbol of the goddess
Asherah in the Temple, the place about
which the LORD had said to David and his
son Solomon: "Here in Jerusalem, in this
Temple, is the place that I have chosen out
of all the territory of the twelve tribes of
Israel as the place where I am to be wor-
shiped. 8 And if the people of Israel will obey
all my commands and keep the whole Law
that my servant Moses gave them, then I will
not allow them to be driven out of the land
that I gave to their ancestors." 9 But the peo-
ple of Judah did not obey the LORD, and

[u] **20:9** stairway . . . steps . . . steps . . . ; *or* sundial . . . degrees . . . degrees. [v] **20:10,11** steps; *or* degrees.
[w] **20:11** stairway; *or* sundial. *Archaeological evidence suggests that the stairway referred to in this passage was one specially constructed to tell time.* [x] **21:6** consulted; *or* brought back.

20:17 2 Kings 24:13; 2 Chr 36:10 **20:18** 2 Kings 24:14, 15; Dan 1:1–7 **21:2** Jer 15:4 **21:4** 2 Sam 7:13
21:7, 8 1 Kings 9:3–5; 2 Chr 7:12–18

Pray it!

In the Face of Evil

King Manasseh was powerful, violent, and brutal. He ruled longer than any other Israelite king. He followed the good King Hezekiah and led people astray. How could Hezekiah's son turn out so bad?

Where do we see this kind of behavior in the world today? Think of some of the places, people, or situations that are violent today: war, fighting, abuse, murder. What about the things that lead people astray? Greed, materialism, the media, peer pressure. How do you deal with these things in your own life? Do you try not to think about them? One thing we can do in the face of evil is to pray—for strength to resist it and for the power to change it. Read Psalm 71 for comfort and strength against evil.

— 2 Kings 21:1–10

Manasseh led them to commit even greater
sins than those committed by the nations
whom the LORD had driven out of the land
as his people advanced.
10 Through his servants the prophets the
LORD said, 11 "King Manasseh has done these
disgusting things, things far worse than what
the Canaanites did; and with his idols he has
led the people of Judah into sin. 12 So I, the
LORD God of Israel, will bring such a disas-
ter on Jerusalem and Judah that everyone
who hears about it will be stunned. 13 I will
punish Jerusalem as I did Samaria, as I did
King Ahab of Israel and his descendants. I
will wipe Jerusalem clean of its people, as
clean as a plate that has been wiped and
turned upside down. 14 I will abandon the
people who survive, and will hand them
over to their enemies, who will conquer
them and plunder their land. 15 I will do this
to my people because they have sinned
against me and have stirred up my anger
from the time their ancestors came out of
Egypt to this day."
16 Manasseh killed so many innocent peo-
ple that the streets of Jerusalem were flowing
with blood; he did this in addition to leading
the people of Judah into idolatry, causing
them to sin against the LORD.
17 Everything else that Manasseh did,
including the sins he committed, is recorded
in *The History of the Kings of Judah.* 18 Manas-
seh died and was buried in the palace garden,
the garden of Uzza, and his son Amon suc-
ceeded him as king.

King Amon of Judah
(2 Chronicles 33:21–25)

19 Amon was twenty-two years old when
he became king of Judah, and he ruled in
Jerusalem for two years. His mother was
Meshullemeth, the daughter of Haruz from
the town of Jotbah. 20 Like his father Manas-
seh, he sinned against the LORD; 21 he imitat-
ed his father's actions, and he worshiped the
idols that his father had worshiped. 22 He
rejected the LORD, the God of his ancestors,
and disobeyed the LORD's commands.
23 Amon's officials plotted against him and
assassinated him in the palace. 24 The people
of Judah killed Amon's assassins and made his
son Josiah king.
25 Everything else that Amon did is
recorded in *The History of the Kings of Judah.*

Compare King Manasseh with King Josiah in 2 Kings, chapters 22–23. What words would you use to describe each of them?

26 Amon was buried in the tomb in the gar-
den of Uzza, and his son Josiah succeeded
him as king.

King Josiah of Judah
(2 Chronicles 34:1, 2)

22 Josiah was eight years old when he
became king of Judah, and he ruled
in Jerusalem for thirty-one years. His mother
was Jedidah, the daughter of Adaiah from the
town of Bozkath. 2 Josiah did what was pleas-
ing to the LORD; he followed the example of
his ancestor King David, strictly obeying all
the laws of God.

The Book of the Law Is Discovered
(2 Chronicles 34:8–28)

3 In the eighteenth year of his reign, King
Josiah sent the court secretary Shaphan, the
son of Azaliah and grandson of Meshullam,
to the Temple with the order: 4 "Go to the
High Priest Hilkiah and get a report on the
amount of money that the priests on duty at
the entrance to the Temple have collected
from the people. 5 Tell him to give the
money to the men who are in charge of the
repairs in the Temple. They are to pay 6 the
carpenters, the builders, and the masons, and
buy the timber and the stones used in the
repairs. 7 The men in charge of the work are
thoroughly honest, so there is no need to
require them to account for the funds."
8 Shaphan delivered the king's order to
Hilkiah, and Hilkiah told him that he had
found the book of the Law in the Temple.
Hilkiah gave him the book, and Shaphan
read it. 9 Then he went back to the king and
reported: "Your servants have taken the
money that was in the Temple and have
handed it over to the men in charge of the
repairs." 10 And then he said, "I have here a
book that Hilkiah gave me." And he read it
aloud to the king.
11 When the king heard the book being
read, he tore his clothes in dismay, 12 and gave
the following order to Hilkiah the priest, to
Ahikam son of Shaphan, to Achbor son of
Micaiah, to Shaphan, the court secretary, and
to Asaiah, the king's attendant: 13 "Go and
consult the LORD for me and for all the
people of Judah about the teachings of this
book. The LORD is angry with us because
our ancestors have not done what this book
says must be done."
14 Hilkiah, Ahikam, Achbor, Shaphan, and
Asaiah went to consult a woman named
Huldah, a prophet who lived in the newer
part of Jerusalem. (Her husband Shallum, the

Live it!

An Amazing Woman

We know that King Josiah is going to be a good king because he "did what was pleasing to the LORD" (2 Kings 22:2). But after all those years of evil under King Manasseh, people didn't know how God wanted them to live anymore. Then someone found a book of the Law of Moses. After reading it and realizing how far astray they had gone from the Law, King Josiah was worried and afraid.

So King Josiah looked for guidance. He sent his aides out to find the prophet and holy woman Huldah. Huldah had words of challenge and words of comfort for the king. To whom do you go when you need guidance or advice, when you are worried or afraid? Who are the Huldahs in your life? Who are the people who can help you see right and wrong?

— 2 Kings, chapter 22

22:1 Jer 3:6 **22:7** 2 Kings 12:15

Before reading 2 Kings, had you ever heard of the prophet Huldah? How many other women can you name from the Bible?

son of Tikvah and grandson of Harhas, was in charge of the Temple robes.) They described to her what had happened, 15and she told them to go back to the king and give him 16the following message from the LORD: "I am going to punish Jerusalem and all its people, as written in the book that the king has read. 17They have rejected me and have offered sacrifices to other gods, and so have stirred up my anger by all they have done. My anger is aroused against Jerusalem, and it will not die down. 18As for the king himself, this is what I, the LORD God of Israel, say: You listened to what is written in the book, 19and you repented and humbled yourself before me, tearing your clothes and weeping, when you heard how I threatened to punish Jerusalem and its people. I will make it a terrifying sight, a place whose name people will use as a curse. But I have heard your prayer, 20and the punishment which I am going to bring on Jerusalem will not come until after your death. I will let you die in peace."

The men returned to King Josiah with this message.

Josiah Does Away with Pagan Worship
(2 Chronicles 34:3–7, 29–33)

23 King Josiah summoned all the leaders of Judah and Jerusalem, 2and together they went to the Temple, accompanied by the priests and the prophets and all the rest of the people, rich and poor alike. Before them all the king read aloud the whole book of the covenant which had been found in the Temple. 3He stood by the royal column and made a covenant with the LORD to obey him, to keep his laws and commands with all his heart and soul, and to put into practice the demands attached to the covenant, as written in the book. And all the people promised to keep the covenant.

4Then Josiah ordered the High Priest Hilkiah, his assistant priests, and the guards on duty at the entrance to the Temple to bring out of the Temple all the objects used in the worship of Baal, of the goddess Asherah, and of the stars. The king burned all

The king read aloud the whole book of the covenant. (23:2)

The king burned all these objects outside the city. (23:4)

these objects outside the city near Kidron Valley and then had the ashes taken to Bethel. 5He removed from office the priests that the kings of Judah had ordained to offer sacrifices[y] on the pagan altars in the cities of Judah and in places near Jerusalem—all the

[y] **23:5** *Some ancient translations* to offer sacrifices; *Hebrew* and he offered sacrifices.

23:4–6 2 Kings 21:3; 2 Chr 33:3

priests who offered sacrifices to Baal, to the
sun, the moon, the planets, and the stars. 6 He
removed from the Temple the symbol of the
goddess Asherah, took it out of the city to
Kidron Valley, burned it, pounded its ashes to
dust, and scattered it over the public burying
ground. 7 He destroyed the living quarters in
the Temple occupied by the temple prosti-
tutes.[z] (It was there that women wove robes
used in the worship of Asherah.) 8 He
brought to Jerusalem the priests who were
in the cities of Judah, and throughout the
whole country he desecrated the altars
where they had offered sacrifices. He also
tore down the altars dedicated to the goat
demons near the gate built by Joshua, the
city governor, which was to the left of the
main gate as one enters the city. 9 Those
priests were not allowed to serve in the Tem-
ple, but they could eat the unleavened bread
provided for their fellow priests.

10 King Josiah also desecrated Topheth, the
pagan place of worship in Hinnom Valley, so
that no one could sacrifice his son or daugh-
ter as a burnt offering to the god Molech.
11 He also removed the horses that the kings
of Judah had dedicated to the worship of the
sun, and he burned the chariots used in this
worship. (These were kept in the temple
courtyard, near the gate and not far from the
living quarters of Nathan Melech, a high
official.) 12 The altars which the kings of
Judah had built on the palace roof above
King Ahaz' quarters, King Josiah tore down,
along with the altars put up by King Manas-
seh in the two courtyards of the Temple; he
smashed the altars to bits[a] and threw them
into Kidron Valley. 13 Josiah desecrated the
altars that King Solomon had built east of
Jerusalem, south of the Mount of Olives,[b]
for the worship of disgusting idols—Astarte
the goddess of Sidon, Chemosh the god of
Moab, and Molech the god of Ammon.
14 King Josiah broke the stone pillars to
pieces, cut down the symbols of the goddess
Asherah, and the ground where they had
stood he covered with human bones.

15 Josiah also tore down the place of wor-
ship in Bethel, which had been built by
King Jeroboam son of Nebat, who led Israel
into sin. Josiah pulled down the altar, broke
its stones into pieces,[c] and pounded them to
dust; he also burned the image of Asherah.
16 Then Josiah looked around and saw some
tombs there on the hill; he had the bones
taken out of them and burned on the altar.
In this way he desecrated the altar, doing

Study it!

A Faith-Filled King

King Josiah gathered all the people together and had the book of the Law read to them. By doing this he imitated Moses and Joshua:

- **"Then [Moses] took the book of the covenant, in which the LORD's commands were written, and read it aloud to the people" (Exodus 24:7).**
- **"Joshua then read aloud the whole Law . . . Every one of the commandments of Moses was read by Joshua to the whole gathering" (Joshua 8:34–35).**

Josiah began a renewal. He tore down all the altars and places of worship that had been built to false gods. The people began to follow God again. They stopped worshiping idols and pagan gods. Josiah helped the people of Israel regain their sense of identity and their faith in God.

— 2 Kings 23:1–14

[z] **23:7** TEMPLE PROSTITUTES: *Men and women who practiced prostitution in the worship of fertility gods.*
[a] **23:12** *Probable text* smashed . . . to bits; *Hebrew unclear.* [b] **23:13** MOUNT OF OLIVES: *Hebrew here refers to it as "Mount of Destruction" or "Mount of Sin."* [c] **23:15** *One ancient translation* broke its stones into pieces; *Hebrew* burned the altar.

23:10 a Jer 7:31; 19:1–6; 32:35; **b** Lev 18:21 **23:12** 2 Kings 21:5; 2 Chr 33:5 **23:13** 1 Kings 11:7
23:15 1 Kings 12:33 **23:16** 1 Kings 13:2

what the prophet had predicted long before
during the festival as King Jeroboam was
standing by the altar. King Josiah looked
around and saw the tomb of the prophet[d]
who had made this prediction. 17“Whose
tomb is that?” he asked.

The people of Bethel answered, “It is the
tomb of the prophet who came from Judah
and predicted these things that you have
done to this altar.”

18“Leave it as it is,” Josiah ordered. “His
bones are not to be moved.”

So his bones were not moved, neither
were those of the prophet who had come
from Samaria.

19In every city of Israel King Josiah tore
down all the pagan places of worship which
had been built by the kings of Israel, who
thereby aroused the LORD’s anger. He did to
all those altars what he had done in Bethel.
20He killed all the pagan priests on the altars
where they served, and he burned human
bones on every altar. Then he returned to
Jerusalem.

Josiah Celebrates the Passover
(2 Chronicles 35:1–19)

21King Josiah ordered the people to cele-
brate the Passover in honor of the LORD
their God, as written in the book of the
Covenant. 22No Passover like this one had
ever been celebrated by any of the kings of
Israel or of Judah, since the time when
judges ruled the nation. 23Now at last, in the
eighteenth year of the reign of Josiah, the
Passover was celebrated in Jerusalem.

Other Changes Made by Josiah

24In order to enforce the laws written in
the book that the High Priest Hilkiah had
found in the Temple, King Josiah removed
from Jerusalem and the rest of Judah all the
mediums and fortunetellers, and all the
household gods, idols, and all other pagan
objects of worship. 25There had never been a
king like him before, who served the LORD
with all his heart, mind, and strength, obey-
ing all the Law of Moses; nor has there been
a king like him since.

There had never been a king like him before. (23:25)

26But the LORD’s fierce anger had been
aroused against Judah by what King Manas-
seh had done, and even now it did not die
down. 27The LORD said, “I will do to Judah
what I have done to Israel: I will banish the
people of Judah from my sight, and I will
reject Jerusalem, the city I chose, and the
Temple, the place I said was where I should
be worshiped.”

The End of Josiah’s Reign
(2 Chronicles 35:20—36:1)

28Everything else that King Josiah did is
recorded in *The History of the Kings of Judah.*
29While Josiah was king, King Neco of
Egypt led an army to the Euphrates River to
help the emperor of Assyria. King Josiah
tried to stop the Egyptian army at Megiddo
and was killed in battle. 30His officials placed
his body in a chariot and took it back to
Jerusalem, where he was buried in the royal
tombs.

The people of Judah chose Josiah’s son
Joahaz and anointed him king.

[d] **23:16** *One ancient translation* during the festival . . . the prophet; *Hebrew does not have these words.*
23:17 1 Kings 13:30–32

Josiah “served the LORD with all his heart, mind, and strength” *(2 Kings 23:25)*. **Read Deuteronomy 6:5 and Matthew 22:34–38. Notice anything similar?**

King Joahaz of Judah
(2 Chronicles 36:2–4)

31 Joahaz was twenty-three years old when
he became king of Judah, and he ruled in
Jerusalem for three months. His mother was
Hamutal, the daughter of Jeremiah from the
city of Libnah. 32 Following the example of
his ancestors, he sinned against the LORD.
33 His reign ended when King Neco of
Egypt took him prisoner in Riblah, in the
land of Hamath, and made Judah pay 7,500
pounds of silver and 75 pounds of gold as
tribute. 34 King Neco made Josiah's son Eli-
akim king of Judah as successor to Josiah,
and changed his name to Jehoiakim. Joahaz
was taken to Egypt by King Neco, and there
he died.

King Jehoiakim of Judah
(2 Chronicles 36:5–8)

35 King Jehoiakim collected a tax from the
people in proportion to their wealth, in
order to raise the amount needed to pay the
tribute demanded by the king of Egypt.
36 Jehoiakim was twenty-five years old
when he became king of Judah, and he ruled
in Jerusalem for eleven years. His mother
was Zebidah, the daughter of Pedaiah from
the town of Rumah. 37 Following the exam-
ple of his ancestors, Jehoiakim sinned against
the LORD.

24 While Jehoiakim was king, King
Nebuchadnezzar of Babylonia
invaded Judah, and for three years Jehoi-
akim was forced to submit to his rule; then
he rebelled. 2 The LORD sent armed bands
of Babylonians, Syrians, Moabites, and
Ammonites against Jehoiakim to destroy
Judah, as the LORD had said through his
servants the prophets that he would do.
3 This happened at the LORD's command, in
order to banish the people of Judah from
his sight because of all the sins that King
Manasseh had committed, 4 and especially
because of all the innocent people he had
killed. The LORD could not forgive Manas-
seh for that.
5 Everything that Jehoiakim did is record-
ed in *The History of the Kings of Judah*.
6 Jehoiakim died, and his son Jehoiachin suc-
ceeded him as king.
7 The king of Egypt and his army never
marched out of Egypt again, because the
king of Babylonia now controlled all the ter-
ritory that had belonged to Egypt, from the
Euphrates River to the northern border of
Egypt.

King Jehoiachin of Judah
(2 Chronicles 36:9, 10)

8 Jehoiachin was eighteen years old when
he became king of Judah, and he ruled in
Jerusalem for three months. His mother
was Nehushta, the daughter of Elnathan
from Jerusalem. 9 Following the example of
his father, Jehoiachin sinned against the
LORD.
10 It was during his reign that the Babylo-
nian army, commanded by King Nebuchad-
nezzar's officers, marched against Jerusalem
and besieged it. 11 During the siege Neb-
uchadnezzar himself came to Jerusalem, 12 and
King Jehoiachin, along with his mother, his
sons, his officers, and the palace officials, sur-
rendered to the Babylonians. In the eighth
year of Nebuchadnezzar's reign he took
Jehoiachin prisoner 13 and carried off to
Babylon all the treasures in the Temple and
the palace. As the LORD had foretold, Neb-
uchadnezzar broke up all the gold utensils
which King Solomon had made for use in
the Temple. 14 Nebuchadnezzar carried away
as prisoners the people of Jerusalem, all the
royal princes, and all the leading men, ten
thousand in all. He also deported all the
skilled workers, including the blacksmiths,
leaving only the poorest of the people
behind in Judah.
15 Nebuchadnezzar took Jehoiachin to

23:34 Jer 22:11, 12 **23:36** Jer 22:18, 19; 26:1–6; 35:1–19 **24:1** Jer 25:1–38; Dan 1:1, 2 **24:12** Jer 22:24–30; 24:1–10; 29:1, 2 **24:15** Ezek 17:12

Jehoiachin became king when he was 18 years old. Who was Jehoiachin's father?

Live it!

The Cost of Sin

King Manasseh had killed innocent people and had been unfaithful to God. The author viewed the destruction and loss of the southern Kingdom as the cost of the king's sin. Sin has a cost in our own lives. When we lie it destroys our relationships. When we cheat we lose our own sense of self-worth. What price have you paid for sin? What can you do to repair the damage you've done? In addition to receiving the sacrament of Reconciliation, here are a few things you could do:

- **If you've lost a friend or friends because of gossip or unkindness, apologize to the person or people you've hurt. See if you can do something good that would help repair the relationship.**
- **If you've disobeyed your parents, offer to help out around the house a little more than usual.**
- **If you've done something to hurt your own self-esteem, build it back up by working extra hard on a tough assignment or challenging yourself to give up a bad habit and start a good one.**

— 2 Kings 24:1–4

Babylon as a prisoner, together with
Jehoiachin's mother, his wives, his officials,
and the leading men of Judah. 16Nebuchad-
nezzar deported all the important men to
Babylonia, seven thousand in all, and one
thousand skilled workers, including the
blacksmiths, all of them able-bodied men fit
for military duty.
17Nebuchadnezzar made Jehoiachin's
uncle Mattaniah king of Judah and changed
his name to Zedekiah.

King Zedekiah of Judah
(2 Chronicles 36:11, 12; Jeremiah 52:1–3a)

18Zedekiah was twenty-one years old
when he became king of Judah, and he
ruled in Jerusalem for eleven years. His
mother was Hamutal, the daughter of Jere-
miah from the city of Libnah. 19King
Zedekiah sinned against the LORD, just as
King Jehoiakim had done. 20The LORD
became so angry with the people of
Jerusalem and Judah that he banished them
from his sight.

The Fall of Jerusalem
(2 Chronicles 36:13–21; Jeremiah 52:3b–11)

25 Zedekiah rebelled against King
Nebuchadnezzar of Babylonia, and
so Nebuchadnezzar came with all his army
and attacked Jerusalem on the tenth day of
the tenth month of the ninth year of Zed-
ekiah's reign. They set up camp outside the
city, built siege walls around it, 2and kept it
under siege until Zedekiah's eleventh year.
3On the ninth day of the fourth month[e] of
that same year, when the famine was so bad
that the people had nothing left to eat, 4the
city walls were broken through. Although
the Babylonians were surrounding the city,
all the soldiers escaped during the night.
They left by way of the royal garden, went
through the gateway connecting the two
walls, and fled in the direction of the Jor-
dan Valley. 5But the Babylonian army pur-
sued King Zedekiah, captured him in the
plains near Jericho, and all his soldiers
deserted him. 6Zedekiah was taken to King
Nebuchadnezzar, who was in the city of
Riblah, and there Nebuchadnezzar passed
sentence on him. 7While Zedekiah was
looking on, his sons were put to death;
then Nebuchadnezzar had Zedekiah's eyes
put out, placed him in chains, and took
him to Babylon.

[e] **25:3** *Probable text (see Jer 52:6)* the fourth month; *Hebrew* the month.

24:17 Jer 37:1; Ezek 17:13 **24:18** Jer 27:1–22; 28:1–17 **24:20** Ezek 17:15 **25:1** Jer 21:1–10; 34:1–5; Ezek 24:2 **25:4** Ezek 33:21 **25:7** Ezek 12:13

Pray it!

Utter Destruction

You don't know what you have until you lose it. Have you ever heard someone say that? Have you ever felt that way yourself? In this chapter we see the utter destruction of what the Israelites once had. King Zedekiah's sons are killed; the king is taken away, blinded, and put in chains. The Temple is looted and destroyed. All the important officials are taken away as prisoners, then beaten and put to death.

First the northern kingdom was taken over, and now the southern kingdom of Judah is no more. Can you imagine the despair the people must have felt? Maybe you can. Maybe you've experienced a loss that made you feel like your whole world was coming to an end.

O God,
I don't know what to do.
I feel like life will never be the same again.
There seems to be no reason to hope.
I want to hide and cry.
Hold me and comfort me.
Remind me that you're here with me.
Help me find something to be hopeful about.
Bring me back to life.

— 2 Kings 25:1–21

The Destruction of the Temple
(Jeremiah 52:12–33)

8On the seventh day of the fifth month of
the nineteenth year of King Nebuchadnezzar
of Babylonia, Nebuzaradan, adviser to the
king and commander of his army, entered
Jerusalem. 9He burned down the Temple, the
palace, and the houses of all the important
people in Jerusalem, 10and his soldiers tore
down the city walls. 11Then Nebuzaradan
took away to Babylonia the people who were
left in the city, the remaining skilled workers,[f]
and those who had deserted to the Babyloni-
ans. 12But he left in Judah some of the poor-
est people, who owned no property, and put
them to work in the vineyards and fields.
13The Babylonians broke in pieces the
bronze columns and the carts that were in the
Temple, together with the large bronze tank,
and they took all the bronze to Babylon.
14They also took away the shovels and the ash
containers used in cleaning the altar, the tools
used in tending the lamps, the bowls used for
catching the blood from the sacrifices, the
bowls used for burning incense, and all the
other bronze articles used in the Temple ser-
vice. 15They took away everything that was
made of gold or silver, including the small
bowls and the pans used for carrying live
coals. 16The bronze objects that King Sol-
omon had made for the Temple—the two
columns, the carts, and the large tank—were
too heavy to weigh. 17The two columns were
identical: each one was 27 feet high, with a
bronze capital on top, 4½ feet high. All around
each capital was a bronze grillwork decorated
with pomegranates made of bronze.

[f] **25:11** *Probable text (see Jer 52:15)* skilled workers; *Hebrew* crowd.

25:9 1 Kings 9:8 **25:13** **a** 1 Kings 7:15–26; 2 Chr 3:15–17; **b** 1 Kings 7:23–26; 2 Chr 4:2–5 **25:14** 1 Kings 7:45; 2 Chr 4:16

The people of Judah were carried away from their land into exile. (25:21)

The People of Judah Are Taken to Babylonia
(Jeremiah 52:24–27)

18 In addition, Nebuzaradan, the com-
manding officer, took away as prisoners
Seraiah the High Priest, Zephaniah the
priest next in rank, and the three other
important Temple officials. 19 From the city
he took the officer who had been in com-
mand of the troops, five of the king's person-
al advisers who were still in the city, the
commander's assistant, who was in charge of
military records, and sixty other important
men. 20 Nebuzaradan took them to the king
of Babylonia, who was in the city of Riblah
21 in the territory of Hamath. There the king
had them beaten and put to death.

So the people of Judah were carried away from their land into exile.

Gedaliah, Governor of Judah
(Jeremiah 40:7–9; 41:1–3)

22 King Nebuchadnezzar of Babylonia
made Gedaliah, the son of Ahikam and
grandson of Shaphan, governor of Judah, and
placed him in charge of all those who had
not been taken away to Babylonia. 23 When
the Judean officers and soldiers who had not
surrendered heard about this, they joined
Gedaliah at Mizpah. These officers were Ish-
mael son of Nethaniah, Johanan son of
Kareah, Seraiah son of Tanhumeth from the
town of Netophah, and Jezaniah from Maa-
cah. 24 Gedaliah said to them, "I give you my
word that there is no need for you to be
afraid of the Babylonian officials. Settle in
this land, serve the king of Babylonia, and all
will go well with you."

25 But in the seventh month of that year,
Ishmael, the son of Nethaniah and grandson
of Elishama, a member of the royal family,
went to Mizpah with ten men, attacked
Gedaliah, and killed him. He also killed the
Israelites and Babylonians who were there
with him. 26 Then all the Israelites, rich and
poor alike, together with the army officers,
left and went to Egypt, because they were
afraid of the Babylonians.

Jehoiachin Is Released from Prison
(Jeremiah 52:31–34)

27 In the year that Evilmerodach became
king of Babylonia, he showed kindness to
King Jehoiachin of Judah by releasing him
from prison. This happened on the twenty-
seventh day of the twelfth month of the

25:22–24 Jer 40:7–9 **25:25** Jer 41:1–3 **25:26** Jer 43:5–7

The destruction of Jerusalem leads to the Babylonian Exile, when all the leaders of Judah are taken to Babylon as slaves in 587 BC.

thirty-seventh year after Jehoiachin had been
taken away as prisoner. 28 Evilmerodach
treated him kindly and gave him a position
of greater honor than he gave the other
kings who were exiles with him in Babylo-
nia. 29 So Jehoiachin was permitted to change
from his prison clothes and to dine at the
king's table for the rest of his life. 30 Each day,
for as long as he lived, he was given a regular
allowance for his needs.

Your Next Step

Congratulations on finishing the Second Book of Kings! Use this space to write your thoughts and questions about this book. If you are following the suggested reading plan, move ahead to the Book of Isaiah. The prophet Isaiah and his followers have many things to say about the idolatry and injustice that happened during the time of the kings.

THE FIRST BOOK OF Chronicles

"Wow, that was an interesting Web site, wasn't it? The Mesopotamian people sure had lots of enemies, didn't they?" Doug's dad said. "Let's see what the next site listed on your homework sheet is like." When they opened the next Web site, the same time period was highlighted, but this site gave different information. It talked about how the kings of the Mesopotamian people came to power.

The First Book of Chronicles is similar. It covers the same period of history that the books of Samuel and Kings cover but from a different viewpoint. The writer (called the Chronicler) wants the reader to know the family tree of Israel's leaders. Most importantly, he wants to make sure the Israelites have hope for the future and continue their religious practices.

Chap. 15

Headlines

- Lists, Lists, and More Lists (chapters 1–9)
- Famous Soldiers Help David (11:10–25)
- Victory Declared! (14:8–17)
- Covenant Box Moved to Jerusalem (15:25–29)
- Giants Defeated in Battle (20:4–8)
- Levites Assigned Temple Duties (23:2–5)
- David Declares Temple to Be Built (28:1–8)

FACTOIDS

Who wrote this book? The author (or authors) of First and Second Chronicles was called the Chronicler. He was a scribe who wrote sometime after the people returned to Jerusalem after the Exile.

What time period does it cover? First Chronicles covers the events that took place from Creation until King David's death.

Why was it written? It was written to give hope for the future. It also emphasizes the importance of the priests and the Jerusalem Temple.

What is the literary style? The Chronicler used both stories and genealogies (family histories) to record the history of the Israelites.

Important themes

- Even though the Israelites have experienced many disasters, there is still hope for the future.
- The future of Israel can be secured if the people continue to worship God and keep their religious practices.

1 CHRONICLES

From Adam to Abraham

(Genesis 5:1–32; 10:1–32; 11:10–26)

1 Adam was the father of Seth, Seth was the father of Enosh, Enosh the father of Kenan, 2 Kenan the father of Mahalalel, Mahalalel the father of Jared. 3 Jared was the father of Enoch, who was the father of Methuselah; Methuselah was the father of Lamech, 4 who was the father of Noah. Noah had three sons: Shem, Ham, and Japheth.

5 The sons of Japheth—Gomer, Magog, Madai, Javan, Tubal, Meshech, and Tiras—were the ancestors of the peoples who bear their names. 6 The descendants of Gomer were the people of Ashkenaz, Riphath, and Togarmah. 7 The descendants of Javan were the people of Elishah, Spain, Cyprus, and Rhodes.

8 The sons of Ham—Cush, Egypt, Libya, and Canaan—were the ancestors of the peoples who bear their names. 9 The descendants of Cush were the people of Seba, Havilah, Sabtah, Raamah, and Sabteca. The descendants of Raamah were the people of Sheba and Dedan. (10 Cush had a son named Nimrod, who became the world's first great conqueror.) 11 The descendants of Egypt were the people of Lydia, Anam, Lehab, Naphtuh, 12 Pathrus, Casluh, and of Crete (from whom the Philistines were descended). 13 Canaan's sons—Sidon, the oldest, and Heth—were the ancestors of the peoples who bear their names. 14 Canaan was also the ancestor of the Jebusites, the Amorites, Girgashites, 15 Hivites, Arkites, Sinites, 16 Arvadites, Zemarites, and Hamathites.

17 Shem's sons—Elam, Asshur, Arpachshad, Lud, Aram, Uz, Hul, Gether, and Meshek—were the ancestors of the peoples who bear their names. 18 Arpachshad was the father of Shelah, who was the father of Eber. 19 Eber had two sons; one was named Peleg,[a] because during his time the people of the world were divided, and the other was named Joktan. 20 The descendants of Joktan were the people of Almodad, Sheleph, Hazarmaveth, Jerah, 21 Hadoram, Uzal, Diklah, 22 Ebal, Abimael, Sheba, 23 Ophir, Havilah, and Jobab.

24 The family line from Shem to Abram is as follows: Shem, Arpachshad, Shelah, 25 Eber, Peleg, Reu, 26 Serug, Nahor, Terah, 27 and Abram (also known as Abraham).

The Descendants of Ishmael

(Genesis 25:12–16)

28 Abraham had two sons, Isaac and Ishmael. 29 The sons of Ishmael became the heads of twelve tribes: Nebaioth (from the name of Ishmael's oldest son), Kedar, Adbeel, Mibsam, 30 Mishma, Dumah, Massa, Hadad, Tema, 31 Jetur, Naphish, and Kedemah.

32 Abraham had a concubine named Keturah, who bore him six sons: Zimran, Jokshan, Medan, Midian, Ishbak, and Shuah. Jokshan had two sons: Sheba and Dedan. 33 Midian had five sons: Ephah, Epher, Hanoch, Abida, and Eldaah.

The Descendants of Esau

(Genesis 36:1–19)

34 Abraham's son Isaac had two sons, Esau and Jacob. 35 Esau's sons were Eliphaz, Reuel, Jeush, Jalam, and Korah. 36 Eliphaz became the ancestor of the following tribes: Teman, Omar, Zephi, Gatam, Kenaz, Timna, and Amalek. 37 And Reuel became the ancestor of the tribes of Nahath, Zerah, Shammah, and Mizzah.

The Original Inhabitants of Edom

(Genesis 36:20–30)

38-42 The original inhabitants of Edom were descended from the following sons of Seir:

Lotan, who was the ancestor of the clans of Hori and Homam. (Lotan had a sister named Timna.)

[a] **1:19** PELEG: *This name sounds like the Hebrew for "divide."*

Shobal, who was the ancestor of the clans
of Alvan, Manahath, Ebal, Shephi, and
Onam.

Zibeon, who had two sons, Aiah and
Anah. Anah was the father of Dishon, and
Dishon was the ancestor of the clans of
Hamran, Eshban, Ithran, and Cheran.

Ezer, who was the ancestor of the clans of
Bilhan, Zaavan, and Jaakan.

Dishan, who was the ancestor of the clans
of Uz and Aran.

The Kings of Edom
(Genesis 36:31–43)

43-50 The following kings ruled the land of
Edom one after the other, in the time before
there were any kings in Israel:

Bela son of Beor from Dinhabah
Jobab son of Zerah from Bozrah
Husham from the region of Teman
Hadad son of Bedad from Avith (he
defeated the Midianites in a battle in
the country of Moab)
Samlah from Masrekah
Shaul from Rehoboth-on-the-River
Baal Hanan son of Achbor
Hadad from Pau (his wife was
Mehetabel, the daughter of Matred
and granddaughter of Mezahab)

51 The people of Edom were divided into
the following tribes: Timna, Alvah, Jetheth,
52 Oholibamah, Elah, Pinon, 53 Kenaz, Teman,
Mibzar, 54 Magdiel, and Iram.

The Descendants of Judah

2 Jacob had twelve sons: Reuben, Simeon,
Levi, Judah, Issachar, Zebulun, 2 Dan,
Joseph, Benjamin, Naphtali, Gad, and Asher.
3 Judah had five sons in all. By his wife
Bathshua, a Canaanite, he had three sons: Er,
Onan, and Shelah. His oldest son, Er, was so
evil that the LORD killed him. 4 By his
daughter-in-law Tamar, Judah had two more
sons, Perez and Zerah.
5 Perez had two sons, Hezron and Hamul.
6 His brother Zerah had five sons: Zimri,
Ethan, Heman, Calcol, and Darda. 7 Achan[b]
son of Carmi, one of Zerah's descendants,
brought disaster on the people of Israel by
keeping loot that had been devoted to God.
8 Ethan had one son, Azariah.

The Family Tree of King David

9 Hezron had three sons: Jerahmeel, Ram,
and Caleb.
10 The family line from Ram to Jesse is
as follows: Ram, Amminadab, Nahshon (a
prominent man of the tribe of Judah),
11 Salmon, Boaz, 12 Obed, and Jesse.
13 Jesse had seven sons. In order of age
they were: Eliab, Abinadab, Shammah,
14 Nethanel, Raddai, 15 Ozem, and David.
16 He also had two daughters, Zeruiah and
Abigail.
Jesse's daughter Zeruiah had three sons:
Abishai, Joab, and Asahel. 17 His other daugh-
ter Abigail married Jether, a descendant of
Ishmael, and they had a son named Amasa.

The Descendants of Hezron

18 Hezron's son Caleb married Azubah and
had a daughter named Jerioth. She had[c]
three sons: Jesher, Shobab, and Ardon. 19 After
the death of Azubah, Caleb married
Ephrath, and they had a son named Hur.
20 Hur's son was Uri, and his grandson was
Bezalel.
21 When Hezron was sixty years old, he
married Machir's daughter, the sister of
Gilead. They had a son named Segub, 22 and
Segub had a son named Jair. Jair ruled[d]
twenty-three cities in the territory of Gilead.
23 But the kingdoms of Geshur and Aram
conquered sixty towns there, including the
villages of Jair and Kenath, and the towns
nearby. All the people who lived there were
descendants of Machir, the father of Gilead.
24 After Hezron died, his son Caleb married
Ephrath, his father's widow.[e] They had a son
named Ashhur, who founded the town of
Tekoa.

[b] **2:7** ACHAN: *This is his name in Josh 7:1. The Hebrew text here calls him "Achar," which means "disaster."*
[c] **2:18** *Some ancient translations* had a daughter . . . She had; *Hebrew unclear.* [d] **2:22** ruled; *or* owned.
[e] **2:24** *Some ancient translations* his son . . . widow; *Hebrew unclear.*

2:7 Josh 7:1

The Descendants of Jerahmeel

25 Jerahmeel, the oldest son of Hezron, had five sons: Ram, the oldest, Bunah, Oren, Ozem, and Ahijah. 26-27 Ram had three sons: Maaz, Jamin, and Eker. Jerahmeel had another wife, a woman named Atarah, and they had a son, Onam. 28 Onam had two sons, Shammai and Jada, and Shammai also had two sons, Nadab and Abishur.

29 Abishur married a woman named Abihail, and they had two sons, Ahban and Molid. 30 Abishur's brother Nadab had two sons, Seled and Appaim, but Seled died without having any sons. 31 Appaim was the father of Ishi, Ishi was the father of Sheshan, and Sheshan the father of Ahlai.

32 Jada, the brother of Shammai, had two sons, Jether and Jonathan, but Jether died without having any sons. 33 Jonathan had two sons, Peleth and Zaza. All these were descendants of Jerahmeel.

34 Sheshan had no sons, only daughters. He had an Egyptian servant named Jarha, 35 to whom he gave one of his daughters in marriage. They had a son named Attai. 36 The family line from Attai to Elishama is as follows: Attai, Nathan, Zabad, 37 Ephlal, Obed, 38 Jehu, Azariah, 39 Helez, Eleasah, 40 Sismai, Shallum, 41 Jekamiah, and Elishama.

Other Descendants of Caleb

42 The oldest son of Caleb, Jerahmeel's brother, was named Mesha. Mesha was the father of Ziph, who was the father of Mareshah, who was the father of Hebron.[f] 43 Hebron had four sons: Korah, Tappuah, Rekem, and Shema. 44 Shema was the father of Raham and the grandfather of Jorkeam. Rekem, Shema's brother, was the father of Shammai, 45 who was the father of Maon, who was the father of Bethzur.

46 Caleb had a concubine named Ephah, and by her he had three more sons: Haran, Moza, and Gazez. Haran also had a son named Gazez.

(47 A man named Jahdai had six sons: Regem, Jotham, Geshan, Pelet, Ephah, and Shaaph.)

48 Caleb had another concubine, Maacah, who bore him two sons, Sheber and Tirhanah. 49 Later she had two more sons: Shaaph, who founded the town of Madmannah; and Shevah, who founded the towns of Machbenah and Gibea.

In addition, Caleb had a daughter named Achsah.

50 The following are also descendants of Caleb.

Hur was the oldest son of Caleb and his wife Ephrath. Hur's son Shobal founded Kiriath Jearim, 51 his second son Salma founded Bethlehem, and his third son Hareph founded Bethgader.

52 Shobal, the founder of Kiriath Jearim, was the ancestor of the people of Haroeh, of half the inhabitants of Menuhoth, 53 and of the following clans that lived in Kiriath Jearim: the Ithrites, Puthites, Shumathites, and Mishraites. (The people of the cities of Zorah and Eshtaol were members of these clans.)

54 Salma, the founder of Bethlehem, was the ancestor of the people of Netophath, of Atroth Beth Joab, and of the Zorites, who were one of the two clans in Manahath.

(55 The following clans of experts in writing and copying documents lived in the town of Jabez: the Tirathites, Shimeathites, and Sucathites. They were Kenites who had intermarried with the Rechabites.)

King David's Children

3 1-3 The following, in order of age, are David's sons who were born while he was in Hebron:

Amnon, whose mother was Ahinoam from Jezreel

Daniel, whose mother was Abigail from Carmel

Absalom, whose mother was Maacah, daughter of King Talmai of Geshur

Adonijah, whose mother was Haggith

Shephatiah, whose mother was Abital

Ithream, whose mother was Eglah

4 All six were born in Hebron during the seven and a half years that David ruled there.

f **2:42** *Probable text* father of Mareshah . . . Hebron; *Hebrew unclear.*

3:4 2 Sam 5:4, 5; 1 Kings 2:11; 1 Chr 29:27

In Jerusalem he ruled as king for thirty-
three years, 5 and many sons were born to
him there.

His wife Bathsheba, daughter of Ammiel,
bore him four sons: Shimea, Shobab, Nathan,
and Solomon.

6 He had nine other sons: Ibhar, Elishua,
Elpelet, 7 Nogah, Nepheg, Japhia, 8 Elishama,
Eliada, and Eliphelet. 9 In addition to all these
sons, David had sons by his concubines. He
also had a daughter, Tamar.

The Descendants of King Solomon

10 This is the line of King Solomon's
descendants from father to son: Solomon,
Rehoboam, Abijah, Asa, Jehoshaphat, 11 Jeho-
ram, Ahaziah, Joash, 12 Amaziah, Uzziah,
Jotham, 13 Ahaz, Hezekiah, Manasseh,
14 Amon, and Josiah. 15 Josiah had four sons:
Johanan, Jehoiakim, Zedekiah, and Joahaz.
16 Jehoiakim had two sons: Jehoiachin and
Zedekiah.

The Descendants of King Jehoiachin

17 These are the descendants of King
Jehoiachin, who was taken prisoner by the
Babylonians. Jehoiachin had seven sons:
Shealtiel, 18 Malchiram, Pedaiah, Shenazzar,
Jekamiah, Hoshama, and Nedabiah. 19 Peda-
iah had two sons, Zerubbabel and Shimei.
Zerubbabel was the father of two sons,
Meshullam and Hananiah, and one daughter,
Shelomith. 20 He had five other sons:
Hashubah, Ohel, Berechiah, Hasadiah, and
Jushab Hesed.

21 Hananiah had two sons, Pelatiah and
Jeshaiah. Jeshaiah was the father of Repha-
iah, who was the father of Arnan, the father
of Obadiah, the father of Shecaniah.[g]
22 Shecaniah had one son, Shemaiah, and five
grandsons: Hattush, Igal, Bariah, Neariah,
and Shaphat. 23 Neariah had three sons:
Elioenai, Hizkiah, and Azrikam. 24 Elioenai
had seven sons: Hodaviah, Eliashib, Pelaiah,
Akkub, Johanan, Delaiah, and Anani.

The Descendants of Judah

4 These are some of the descendants of
Judah: Perez, Hezron, Carmi, Hur, and
Shobal. 2 Shobal was the father of Reaiah,
who was the father of Jahath, the father of
Ahumai and Lahad, the ancestors of the peo-
ple who lived in Zorah.

3-4 Hur was the oldest son of his father
Caleb's wife Ephrath, and his descendants
founded the city of Bethlehem. Hur had
three sons: Etam, Penuel, and Ezer. Etam had
three sons:[h] Jezreel, Ishma, and Idbash, and
one daughter, Hazzelelponi. Penuel founded
the city of Gedor, and Ezer founded
Hushah.

5 Ashhur, who founded the town of Tekoa,
had two wives, Helah and Naarah. 6 He and
Naarah had four sons: Ahuzzam, Hepher,
Temeni, and Haahashtari. 7 Ashhur and Helah
had three sons: Zereth, Izhar, and Ethnan.

8 Koz was the father of Anub and Zobe-
bah, and the ancestor of the clans descended
from Aharhel son of Harum.

9 There was a man named Jabez, who was
the most respected member of his family. His
mother had given him the name Jabez,[i]
because his birth had been very painful.
10 But Jabez prayed to the God of Israel,
"Bless me, God, and give me much land. Be
with me and keep me from anything evil
that might cause me pain." And God gave
him what he prayed for.

Other Family Lists

11 Caleb, the brother of Shuhah, had a son,
Mehir. Mehir was the father of Eshton,
12 who had three sons: Bethrapha, Paseah, and
Tehinnah. Tehinnah was the founder of the
city of Nahash. The descendants of these
men lived in Recah.

13 Kenaz had two sons, Othniel and Sera-
iah. Othniel also had two sons, Hathath and
Meonothai.[j] 14 Meonothai was the father of
Ophrah.

Seraiah was the father of Joab, the founder
of Handcraft Valley, where all the people
were skilled workers.

[g] **3:21** *Verse 21 in Hebrew is unclear.* [h] **4:3–4** *Some ancient translations* sons; *Hebrew* fathers. [i] **4:9** JABEZ: *This name sounds like the Hebrew for "pain."* [j] **4:13** *Some ancient translations* Meonothai; *Hebrew does not have this name.*
3:5 2 Sam 11:3

15 Caleb son of Jephunneh had three sons:
Iru, Elah, and Naam. And Elah was the
father of Kenaz.
16 Jehallelel had four sons: Ziph, Ziphah,
Tiria, and Asarel.
17-18 Ezrah had four sons: Jether, Mered,
Epher, and Jalon. Mered married Bithiah, a
daughter of the king of Egypt, and they had
a daughter, Miriam, and two sons, Shammai
and Ishbah. Ishbah founded the town of
Eshtemoa. Mered also married a woman
from the tribe of Judah, and they had three
sons: Jered, who founded the town of
Gedor; Heber, founder of the town of Soco;
and Jekuthiel, founder of the town of
Zanoah.
19 Hodiah married the sister of Naham.
Their descendants founded the clan of
Garm, which lived in the town of Keilah,
and the clan of Maacath, which lived in the
town of Eshtemoa.[k]
20 Shimon had four sons: Amnon, Rinnah,
Benhanan, and Tilon.

Ishi had two sons: Zoheth and Benzoheth.

The Descendants of Shelah

21 Shelah was one of Judah's sons. His
descendants included Er, who founded the
town of Lecah; Laadah, founder of the town
of Mareshah; the clan of linen weavers, who
lived in the town of Beth Ashbea; 22 Jokim
and the people who lived in the town of
Cozeba; and Joash and Saraph, who married
Moabite women and then settled in Bethle-
hem.[l] (These traditions are very old.) 23 They
were potters in the service of the king and
lived in the towns of Netaim and Gederah.

Potters in the service of the king (4:23)

The Descendants of Simeon

24 Simeon had five sons: Nemuel, Jamin,
Jarib, Zerah, and Shaul. 25 Shaul's son was Shal-
lum, his grandson was Mibsam, and his great-
grandson was Mishma. 26 Then from Mishma
the line descended through Hammuel, Zaccur,
and Shimei. 27 Shimei had sixteen sons and six
daughters, but his relatives had fewer children,
and the tribe of Simeon did not grow as
much as the tribe of Judah did.
28 Down to the time of King David the
descendants of Simeon lived in the following
towns: Beersheba, Moladah, Hazarshual,
29 Bilhah, Ezem, Tolad, 30 Bethuel, Hormah,
Ziklag, 31 Beth Marcaboth, Hazarsusim,
Bethbiri, and Shaaraim. 32 They also lived in
five other places: Etam, Ain, Rimmon,
Tochen, and Ashan, 33 and the surrounding
villages, as far southwest as the town of
Baalath. These are the records which they
kept of their families and of the places where
they lived.
34-38 The following men were the heads of
their clans:

Meshobab, Jamlech, Joshah son of
Amaziah, Joel,
Jehu (the son of Joshibiah, the son of
Seraiah, the son of Asiel),
Elioenai, Jaakobah, Jeshohaiah, Asaiah,
Adiel, Jesimiel, Benaiah,
Ziza (the son of Shiphi, the son of Allon,
a descendant of Jedaiah, Shimri, and
Shemaiah).

Because their families continued to grow,
39 they spread out westward almost to Gerar[m]
and pastured their sheep on the eastern side
of the valley in which that city is located.

They . . . pastured their sheep. (4:39)

[k] **4:19** *Verse 19 in Hebrew is unclear.* [l] **4:22** *Probable text* settled in Bethlehem; *Hebrew unclear.* [m] **4:39** *Some ancient translations* Gerar; *Hebrew* Gedor.

4:28–33 Josh 19:2–8

40They found plenty of fertile pasture lands
there in a stretch of open country that was
quiet and peaceful. The people who had
lived there before were Hamites.
41In the time of King Hezekiah of Judah,
the men named above went to Gerar and
destroyed the tents and huts of the people
who lived there.[n] They drove the people out
and settled there permanently because there
was plenty of pasture for their sheep. 42Five
hundred other members of the tribe of
Simeon went east to Edom. They were led
by the sons of Ishi: Pelatiah, Neariah, Repha-
iah, and Uzziel. 43There they killed the sur-
viving Amalekites, and they have lived there
ever since.

The Descendants of Reuben

5 These are the descendants of Reuben,
the oldest of Jacob's sons. (Because he
had sex with one of his father's concubines,
he lost the rights belonging to the first-born
son, and those rights were given to Joseph.
2It was the tribe of Judah, however, that
became the strongest and provided a ruler
for all the tribes.) 3Reuben, the oldest of
Jacob's sons, had four sons: Hanoch, Pallu,
Hezron, and Carmi.
4-6These are the descendants of Joel from
generation to generation: Shemaiah, Gog,
Shimei, Micah, Reaiah, Baal, and Beerah.
The Assyrian emperor, Tiglath Pileser, cap-
tured Beerah, a leader of the tribe, and
deported him.
7The family records list the following clan
leaders in the tribe of Reuben: Jeiel, Zech-
ariah, 8and Bela, the son of Azaz and grand-
son of Shema, of the clan of Joel. This clan
lived in Aroer and in the territory from there
north to Nebo and Baal Meon. 9They had
large herds in the land of Gilead, and so they
occupied the land as far east as the desert
that stretches all the way to the Euphrates
River.
10In the time of King Saul the tribe of
Reuben attacked the Hagrites, killed them
in battle, and occupied their land in the east-
ern part of Gilead.

The Descendants of Gad

11The tribe of Gad lived to the north of
Reuben in the land of Bashan as far east as
Salecah. 12Joel was the founder of the leading
clan, and Shapham of the second most
important clan. Janai and Shaphat were
founders of other clans in Bashan. 13The
other members of the tribe belonged to the
following seven clans: Michael, Meshullam,
Sheba, Jorai, Jacan, Zia, and Eber. 14They
were descendants of Abihail son of Huri,
whose ancestors were traced back as follows:
Abihail, Huri, Jaroah, Gilead, Michael,
Jeshishai, Jahdo, Buz. 15Ahi, the son of Abdiel
and grandson of Guni, was head of these
clans. 16They lived in the territory of Bashan
and Gilead, in the towns there and all over
the pasture lands of Sharon. (17These records
were compiled in the days of King Jotham of
Judah and King Jeroboam II of Israel.)

The Armies of the Eastern Tribes

18In the tribes of Reuben, Gad, and East
Manasseh there were 44,760 soldiers, well-
trained in the use of shields, swords, and
bows. 19They went to war against the Hagrite
tribes of Jetur, Naphish, and Nodab. 20They
put their trust in God and prayed to him for
help, and God answered their prayers and
made them victorious over the Hagrites and
their allies. 21They captured from the enemy
50,000 camels, 250,000 sheep, and 2,000 don-
keys, and took 100,000 prisoners of war.
22They killed many of the enemy, because the
war was God's will. And they went on living
in that territory until the exile.[o]

The People of East Manasseh

23The people of East Manasseh settled in
the territory of Bashan as far north as Baal
Hermon, Senir, and Mount Hermon, and
their population increased greatly. 24The

[n] **4:41** the tents and huts . . . there; *or* the tents of the people who lived there, and the Meunites also.
[o] **5:22** THE EXILE: *About 733 B.C. the Assyrians conquered northern Israel and the Israelite territory east of the Jordan River and deported the people (see 2 Kings 15:29).*

5:1 Gen 35:22; 49:3, 4 **5:2** Gen 49:8–10 **5:6** 2 Kings 15:29

following were the heads of their clans: Epher, Ishi, Eliel, Azriel, Jeremiah, Hodaviah, and Jahdiel. They were all outstanding soldiers, well-known leaders of their clans.

The Eastern Tribes Are Deported

[25]But the people were unfaithful to the God of their ancestors and deserted him to worship the gods of the nations whom God had driven out of the land. [26]So God caused Emperor Pul of Assyria (also known as Tiglath Pileser) to invade their country. He deported the tribes of Reuben, Gad, and East Manasseh and settled them permanently in Halah, Habor, and Hara, and by the Gozan River.

The Family Line of the High Priests

6 Levi had three sons: Gershon, Kohath, and Merari. [2]Kohath had four sons: Amram, Izhar, Hebron, and Uzziel.

[3]Amram had two sons, Aaron and Moses, and one daughter, Miriam.

Aaron had four sons: Nadab, Abihu, Eleazar, and Ithamar.

[4]The descendants of Eleazar from generation to generation are as follows: Phinehas, Abishua, [5]Bukki, Uzzi, [6]Zerahiah, Meraioth, [7]Amariah, Ahitub, [8]Zadok, Ahimaaz, [9]Azariah, Johanan, [10]Azariah (the one who served in the Temple which King Solomon built in Jerusalem), [11]Amariah, Ahitub, [12]Zadok, Shallum, [13]Hilkiah, Azariah, [14]Seraiah, Jehozadak. [15]King Nebuchadnezzar deported Jehozadak along with the other people of Judah and Jerusalem whom the LORD sent into exile.

Other Descendants of Levi

[16]Levi had three sons: Gershon, Kohath, and Merari. [17]Each of them also had sons. Gershon was the father of Libni and Shimei; [18]Kohath was the father of Amram, Izhar, Hebron, and Uzziel; [19]and Merari was the father of Mahli and Mushi.

[20]These are the descendants of Gershon from generation to generation: Libni, Jahath, Zimmah, [21]Joah, Iddo, Zerah, Jeatherai.

[22]These are the descendants of Kohath from generation to generation: Amminadab, Korah, Assir, [23]Elkanah, Ebiasaph, Assir, [24]Tahath, Uriel, Uzziah, Shaul.

[25]Elkanah had two sons, Amasai and Ahimoth. [26]These are Ahimoth's descendants from generation to generation: Elkanah, Zophai, Nahath, [27]Eliab, Jeroham, Elkanah.

[28]Samuel had two sons: Joel,[p] the older, and Abijah, the younger.

[29]These are the descendants of Merari from generation to generation: Mahli, Libni, Shimei, Uzzah, [30]Shimea, Haggiah, Asaiah.

The Temple Musicians

[31]These are the men whom King David put in charge of the music at the place of worship in Jerusalem after the Covenant Box was moved there. [32]They took regular turns of duty at the Tent of the LORD's presence during the time before King Solomon built the Temple. [33]The family lines of those who held this office are as follows:

The clan of Kohath: Heman, the leader of the first choir, was the son of Joel. His family line went back to Jacob as follows: Heman, Joel, Samuel, [34]Elkanah, Jeroham, Eliel, Toah, [35]Zuph, Elkanah, Mahath, Amasai, [36]Elkanah, Joel, Azariah, Zephaniah, [37]Tahath, Assir, Ebiasaph, Korah, [38]Izhar, Kohath, Levi, Jacob.

[39]Asaph was leader of the second choir. His family line went back to Levi as follows: Asaph, Berechiah, Shimea, [40]Michael, Baaseiah, Malchijah, [41]Ethni, Zerah, Adaiah, [42]Ethan, Zimmah, Shimei, [43]Jahath, Gershon, Levi.

[44]Ethan of the clan of Merari was the leader of the third choir. His family line went back to Levi as follows: Ethan, Kishi, Abdi, Malluch, [45]Hashabiah, Amaziah, Hilkiah, [46]Amzi, Bani, Shemer, [47]Mahli, Mushi, Merari, Levi.

[48]The other Levites were assigned all the other duties at the place of worship.

p **6:28** *Some ancient translations (see also 1 Sam 8:2)* Joel; *Hebrew does not have this name.*

5:26 **a** 2 Kings 15:19; **b** 2 Kings 15:29; **c** 2 Kings 17:6 **6:16–19** Ex 6:16–19

The Descendants of Aaron

49 Aaron and his descendants presented the offerings of incense and offered the sacrifices that were burnt on the altar. They were responsible for all the worship in the Most Holy Place and for the sacrifices by which God forgives Israel's sins. They did all this in accordance with the instructions given by Moses, God's servant. 50 This is the line of Aaron's descendants: Eleazar, Phinehas, Abishua, 51 Bukki, Uzzi, Zerahiah, 52 Meraioth, Amariah, Ahitub, 53 Zadok, Ahimaaz.

Where the Levites Lived

54 This is the territory assigned to the descendants of Aaron of the clan of Kohath. They received the first share of the land assigned to the Levites. 55 This included Hebron in the territory of Judah and the pasture lands around it. 56 The fields and villages, however, that belonged to the city were assigned to Caleb son of Jephunneh. 57-59 The following towns were assigned to Aaron's descendants: Hebron, a city of refuge,[q] Jattir, and the towns of Libnah, Eshtemoa, Hilen, Debir, Ashan, and Beth Shemesh, with their pasture lands. 60 In the territory of Benjamin they were assigned the following towns with their pasture lands: Geba, Alemeth, and Anathoth. This made a total of thirteen towns for all their families to live in. 61 Ten towns in the territory of West Manasseh were assigned by lot to the rest of the clan of Kohath, family by family.

62 To the clan of Gershon, family by family, were assigned thirteen towns in the territories of Issachar, Asher, Naphtali, and East Manasseh in Bashan. 63 In the same way, twelve towns in the territories of Reuben, Gad, and Zebulun were assigned to the clan of Merari, family by family. 64 In this way the people of Israel assigned towns for the Levites to live in, together with the pasture lands around the towns. (65 The towns in the territories of Judah, Simeon, and Benjamin, mentioned above, were also assigned by drawing lots.)

66 Some of the families of the clan of Kohath were assigned towns and pasture lands in the territory of Ephraim: 67 Shechem, the city of refuge in the hills of Ephraim, Gezer, 68 Jokmeam, Beth Horon, 69 Aijalon, and Gath Rimmon. 70 In the territory of West Manasseh they were assigned the towns of Aner and Bileam with the surrounding pasture lands.

71 The families of the clan of Gershon were assigned the following towns, with the surrounding pasture lands:

In the territory of East Manasseh: Golan in Bashan, and Ashtaroth.

72 In the territory of Issachar: Kedesh, Daberath, 73 Ramoth, and Anem.

74 In the territory of Asher: Mashal, Abdon, 75 Hukok, and Rehob.

76 In the territory of Naphtali: Kedesh in Galilee, Hammon, and Kiriathaim.

77 The remaining families of the clan of Merari were assigned the following towns with the surrounding pasture lands:

In the territory of Zebulun: Rimmono and Tabor.

78 In the territory of Reuben, east of the Jordan River beyond Jericho: Bezer on the plateau, Jahzah, 79 Kedemoth, and Mephaath.

80 In the territory of Gad: Ramoth in Gilead, Mahanaim, 81 Heshbon, and Jazer.

The Descendants of Issachar

7 Issachar had four sons: Tola, Puah, Jashub, and Shimron.

2 Tola had six sons: Uzzi, Rephaiah, Jeriel, Jahmai, Ibsam, and Shemuel. They were heads of families of the clan of Tola and were famous soldiers. At the time of King David their descendants numbered 22,600.

3 Uzzi had one son, Izrahiah. Izrahiah and his four sons, Michael, Obadiah, Joel, and Isshiah, were all heads of families. 4 They had so many wives and children that their descendants were able to provide 36,000 men for military duty.

5 The official records of all the families of the tribe of Issachar listed 87,000 men eligible for military duty.

[q] **6:57–59** CITY OF REFUGE: *If anyone accidentally killed someone, he could escape to one of these cities and be safe from revenge (see Josh 20:1–9).*

The Descendants of Benjamin and Dan

6 Benjamin had three sons: Bela, Becher, and Jediael.

7 Bela had five sons: Ezbon, Uzzi, Uzziel, Jerimoth, and Iri. They were heads of families in the clan and were all famous soldiers. Their descendants included 22,034 men eligible for military duty.

8 Becher had nine sons: Zemirah, Joash, Eliezer, Elioenai, Omri, Jeremoth, Abijah, Anathoth, and Alemeth. 9 The official record of their descendants by families listed 20,200 men eligible for military duty.

10 Jediael had one son, Bilhan, and Bilhan had seven sons: Jeush, Benjamin, Ehud, Chenaanah, Zethan, Tarshish, and Ahishahar. 11 They were heads of families in the clan and were all famous soldiers. Their descendants included 17,200 men eligible for military duty. 12 Shuppim and Huppim also belonged to this tribe.

Dan had one son, Hushim.[r]

The Descendants of Naphtali

13 Naphtali had four sons: Jahziel, Guni, Jezer, and Shallum. (They were descendants of Bilhah.[s])

The Descendants of Manasseh

14 By his Aramean concubine, Manasseh had two sons, Asriel and Machir. Machir was the father of Gilead. 15 Machir found a wife for Huppim and one for Shuppim. His sister's name was Maacah. Machir's second son was Zelophehad, and he had only daughters.

16 Maacah, Machir's wife, gave birth to two sons, whom they named Peresh and Sheresh. Peresh had two sons, Ulam and Rakem, 17 and Ulam had a son named Bedan. These are all descendants of Gilead, the son of Machir and grandson of Manasseh.

18 Gilead's sister Hammolecheth had three sons: Ishod, Abiezer, and Mahlah. (19 Shemida had four sons: Ahian, Shechem, Likhi, and Aniam.)

The Descendants of Ephraim

20 These are the descendants of Ephraim from generation to generation: Shuthelah, Bered, Tahath, Eleadah, Tahath, 21 Zabad, Shuthelah. Ephraim had two other sons besides Shuthelah: Ezer and Elead, who were killed when they tried to steal the livestock belonging to the native inhabitants of Gath. 22 Their father Ephraim mourned for them for many days, and his relatives came to comfort him. 23 Then he had intercourse with his wife again, and she became pregnant and had a son. They named him Beriah,[t] because of the trouble that had come to their family.

24 Ephraim had a daughter named Sheerah. She built the towns of Upper and Lower Beth Horon, and Uzzen Sheerah.

25 Ephraim also had a son named Rephah, whose descendants were as follows: Resheph, Telah, Tahan, 26 Ladan, Ammihud, Elishama, 27 Nun, Joshua.

28 The territory which they took and settled included Bethel and the towns around it, as far east as Naaran and as far west as Gezer and the towns around it. It also included the cities of Shechem and Ayyah, and the towns around them.

29 The descendants of Manasseh controlled the cities of Beth Shan, Taanach, Megiddo, and Dor, and the towns around them.

All these are the places where the descendants of Joseph son of Jacob lived.

The Descendants of Asher

30 These are the descendants of Asher. He had four sons: Imnah, Ishvah, Ishvi, and Beriah; and one daughter, Serah.

31 Beriah had two sons, Heber and Malchiel. (Malchiel founded the city of Birzaith.)

32 Heber had three sons: Japhlet, Shomer, and Hotham; and one daughter, Shua.

33 Japhlet also had three sons: Pasach, Bimhal, and Ashvath.

34 His brother Shomer had three sons: Rohgah, Jehubbah, and Aram.

[r] **7:12** *Probable text* Shuppim . . . Hushim *(see Gen 46:23; Num 26:39, 42); Hebrew* And Shuppim and Huppim, sons of Ir; Hushim son of Aher. [s] **7:13** BILHAH: *A concubine of Jacob and the mother of his two sons Dan and Naphtali.* [t] **7:23** BERIAH: *This name sounds like the Hebrew for "in trouble."*

35 His brother Hotham[u] had four sons:
Zophah, Imna, Shelesh, and Amal.
36 The descendants of Zophah were Suah,
Harnepher, Shual, Beri, Imrah, 37 Bezer, Hod,
Shamma, Shilshah, Ithran, and Beera.
38 The descendants of Jether were Jephun-
neh, Pispa, and Ara, 39 and the descendants of
Ulla were Arah, Hanniel, and Rizia.
40 All of these were descendants of Asher.
They were heads of families, famous fighting
men, outstanding leaders. Asher's descendants
included 26,000 men eligible for military
duty.

The Descendants of Benjamin

8 Benjamin had five sons. In order of
age they were Bela, Ashbel, Aharah,
2 Nohah, and Rapha.
3 The descendants of Bela were Addar,
Gera, Abihud, 4 Abishua, Naaman, Ahoah,
5 Gera, Shephuphan, and Huram.
6-7 The descendants of Ehud were Naa-
man, Ahijah, and Gera. They were heads of
families that lived in Geba, but which were
forced out and went to live in Manahath.
Gera, the father of Uzza and Ahihud, led
them in this move.
8-9 Shaharaim divorced two wives, Hushim
and Baara. Later, when he lived in the coun-
try of Moab, he married Hodesh and had
seven sons: Jobab, Zibia, Mesha, Malcam,
10 Jeuz, Sachia, and Mirmah. His sons all
became heads of families.
11 He also had two sons by Hushim:
Abitub and Elpaal.
12 Elpaal had three sons: Eber, Misham, and
Shemed. It was Shemed who built the cities
of Ono and Lod and the surrounding villages.

The Benjaminites in Gath and Aijalon

13 Beriah and Shema were heads of fami-
lies that settled in the city of Aijalon and
drove out the people who lived in the city
of Gath. 14 Beriah's descendants included
Ahio, Shashak, Jeremoth, 15 Zebadiah, Arad,
Eder, 16 Michael, Ishpah, and Joha.

The Benjaminites in Jerusalem

17 Elpaal's descendants included Zebadiah,
Meshullam, Hizki, Heber, 18 Ishmerai, Izliah,
and Jobab.
19 Shimei's descendants included Jakim,
Zichri, Zabdi, 20 Elienai, Zillethai, Eliel,
21 Adaiah, Beraiah, and Shimrath.
22 Shashak's descendants included Ishpan,
Eber, Eliel, 23 Abdon, Zichri, Hanan, 24 Hana-
niah, Elam, Anthothijah, 25 Iphdeiah, and
Penuel.
26 Jeroham's descendants included Sham-
sherai, Shehariah, Athaliah, 27 Jaareshiah, Eli-
jah, and Zichri.
28 These were the ancestral heads of fami-
lies and their principal descendants who
lived in Jerusalem.

The Benjaminites in Gibeon and Jerusalem

29 Jeiel[v] founded the city of Gibeon and
settled there. His wife was named Maacah,
30 and his oldest son, Abdon. His other sons
were Zur, Kish, Baal, Ner,[w] Nadab, 31 Gedor,
Ahio, Zechariah, 32 and Mikloth, the father
of Shimeah. Their descendants lived in
Jerusalem near other families of their clan.

The Family of King Saul

33 Ner was the father of Kish, and Kish
was the father of King Saul. Saul had four
sons: Jonathan, Malchishua, Abinadab, and
Eshbaal.[x] 34 Jonathan was the father of
Meribbaal,[y] who was the father of Micah.
35 Micah had four sons: Pithon, Melech,
Tarea, and Ahaz. 36 Ahaz was the father of
Jehoaddah, who was the father of three sons:
Alemeth, Azmaveth, and Zimri. Zimri was
the father of Moza, 37 Moza the father of
Binea, Binea of Raphah, Raphah of Eleasah,
and Eleasah of Azel.
38 Azel had six sons: Azrikam, Bocheru,
Ishmael, Sheariah, Obadiah, and Hanan.
39 Azel's brother Eshek had three sons: Ulam,
Jeush, and Eliphelet.

[u] **7:35** *Probable text (see verse 32)* Hotham; *Hebrew* Helem. [v] **8:29** *Probable text (and see 9:35)* Jeiel; *Hebrew does not have this name.* [w] **8:30** *One ancient translation (and see 9:36)* Ner; *Hebrew does not have this name.* [x] **8:33** ESHBAAL: *Called Ishbosheth in 2 Sam 2:8 and elsewhere in 2 Samuel.* [y] **8:34** MERIBBAAL: *Called Mephibosheth in 2 Sam 4:4 and elsewhere in 2 Samuel.*

40 Ulam's sons were outstanding soldiers and archers. He had a hundred and fifty sons and grandsons in all. All those named above were members of the tribe of Benjamin.

The People Who Returned from Captivity

9 All the people of Israel were listed according to their families, and this information was recorded in *The History of the Kings of Israel.*

The people of Judah had been deported to Babylon as punishment for their sins.
2 The first to return to their property in the cities included Israelite citizens, priests, Levites, and Temple workers.
3 People from the tribes of Judah, Benjamin, Ephraim, and Manasseh went to live in Jerusalem.

4-6 There were 690 families of the tribe of Judah who lived in Jerusalem.

The descendants of Judah's son Perez had as their leader Uthai, the son of Ammihud and grandson of Omri. His other ancestors included Imri and Bani.

The descendants of Judah's son Shelah had as their leader Asaiah, who was the head of his family.

The descendants of Judah's son Zerah had Jeuel as their leader.

7-8 The following members of the tribe of Benjamin lived in Jerusalem:

Sallu son of Meshullam, who was the son of Hodaviah, the son of Hassenuah
Ibneiah son of Jeroham
Elah, the son of Uzzi and grandson of Michri
Meshullam son of Shephatiah, who was the son of Reuel, the son of Ibnijah

9 There were 956 families of this tribe living there. All the men named above were heads of families.

The Priests Who Lived in Jerusalem

10-12 The following priests lived in Jerusalem:

Jedaiah, Jehoiarib, and Jachin
Azariah son of Hilkiah (the chief official in the Temple), whose ancestors included Meshullam, Zadok, Meraioth, and Ahitub
Adaiah son of Jeroham, whose ancestors included Pashhur and Malchijah
Maasai son of Adiel, whose ancestors included Jahzerah, Meshullam, Meshillemith, and Immer

13 The priests who were heads of families totaled 1,760. They were experts in all the work carried on in the Temple.

The Levites Who Lived in Jerusalem

14-16 The following Levites lived in Jerusalem:

Shemaiah son of Hasshub, whose ancestors included Azrikam and Hashabiah, of the clan of Merari
Bakbakkar, Heresh, and Galal
Mattaniah son of Mica, whose ancestors included Zichri and Asaph
Obadiah son of Shemaiah, whose ancestors included Galal and Jeduthun
Berechiah, the son of Asa and grandson of Elkanah, who lived in the territory that belonged to the town of Netophah

The Temple Guards Who Lived in Jerusalem

17 The following Temple guards lived in Jerusalem: Shallum, Akkub, Talmon, and Ahiman. Shallum was their leader.
18 Down to that time members of their clans had been stationed at the eastern entrance to the King's Gate.[z] Formerly they had stood guard at the gates to the camps of the Levites.

19 Shallum, the son of Kore and grandson of Ebiasaph, together with his fellow members of the clan of Korah, was responsible for guarding the entrance to the Tent of the LORD's presence, just as their ancestors had been when they were in charge of the LORD's camp.
20 Phinehas son of Eleazar—may the LORD be with him!—had supervised them at one time.

[z] **9:18** KING'S GATE: *The east gate of the Temple, through which the king usually entered.*
9:2, 3 Ezra 2:70; 7:6-9; Neh 7:73

21 Zechariah son of Meshelemiah was also a guard at the entrance to the Tent of the LORD's presence.

22 In all, 212 men were chosen as guards for the entrances and gates. They were registered according to the villages where they lived. It was King David and the prophet Samuel who had put their ancestors in these responsible positions. 23 They and their descendants continued to guard the gates to the Temple. 24 There was a gate facing in each direction, north, south, east, and west, and each had a chief guard. 25 These guards were assisted by their relatives, who lived in the villages and who had to take turns at guard duty for seven days at a time. 26 The four chief guards were Levites and had the final responsibility. They were also responsible for the rooms in the Temple and for the supplies kept there. 27 They lived near the Temple, because it was their duty to guard it and to open the gates every morning.

The Other Levites

28 Other Levites were responsible for the utensils used in worship. They checked them out and checked them back in every time they were used. 29 Others were in charge of the other sacred equipment, and of the flour, wine, olive oil, incense, and spices. 30 But the responsibility for mixing the spices belonged to the priests.

31 A Levite named Mattithiah, oldest son of Shallum, of the clan of Korah, was responsible for preparing the baked offerings.[a] 32 Members of the clan of Kohath were responsible for preparing the sacred bread[b] for the Temple every Sabbath.

33 Some Levite families were responsible for the Temple music. The heads of these families lived in some of the Temple buildings and were free from other duties, because they were on call day and night.

34 The men named above were heads of Levite families, according to their ancestral lines. They were the leaders who lived in Jerusalem.

The Ancestors and Descendants of King Saul
(1 Chronicles 8:29–38)

35 Jeiel founded the city of Gibeon and settled there. His wife was named Maacah. 36 His oldest son was Abdon, and his other sons were Zur, Kish, Baal, Ner, Nadab, 37 Gedor, Ahio, Zechariah, and Mikloth, 38 the father of Shimeah. Their descendants lived in Jerusalem near other families of their clan.

39 Ner was the father of Kish, and Kish was the father of Saul. Saul had four sons: Jonathan, Malchishua, Abinadab, and Eshbaal.[c] 40 Jonathan was the father of Meribbaal,[d] who was the father of Micah. 41 Micah had four sons: Pithon, Melech, Tarea, and Ahaz.[e] 42 Ahaz was the father of Jarah, who was the father of three sons: Alemeth, Azmaveth, and Zimri. Zimri was the father of Moza, 43 Moza the father of Binea, Binea of Rephaiah, Rephaiah of Eleasah, and Eleasah of Azel.

44 Azel had six sons: Azrikam, Bocheru, Ishmael, Sheariah, Obadiah, and Hanan.

The Death of King Saul
(1 Samuel 31:1–13)

10 The Philistines fought a battle against the Israelites on Mount Gilboa. Many Israelites were killed there, and the rest of them, including King Saul and his sons, fled. 2 But the Philistines caught up with them and killed three of Saul's sons, Jonathan, Abinadab, and Malchishua. 3 The fighting was heavy around Saul, and he was hit by enemy arrows and badly wounded. 4 He said to the young man carrying his weapons, "Draw your sword and kill me, to keep these godless Philistines from gloating over me." But the young man was too terrified to do it. So Saul took his own sword and threw himself on it. 5 The young man

[a] **9:31** BAKED OFFERINGS: *Thin cakes of flour and olive oil which were baked and then presented as offerings to God (see Lev 2:4–6).* [b] **9:32** SACRED BREAD: *Twelve loaves of bread which were placed on a table in the Temple each Sabbath as an offering to God (see Lev 24:5–9).* [c] **9:39** ESHBAAL: *Called Ishbosheth in 2 Sam 2:8 and elsewhere in 2 Samuel.* [d] **9:40** MERIBBAAL: *Called Mephibosheth in 2 Sam 4:4 and elsewhere in 2 Samuel.* [e] **9:41** *Some ancient translations* Ahaz *(see 1 Chr 8:35); Hebrew does not have this name.*

saw that Saul was dead, so he too threw
himself on his sword and died. 6So Saul and
his three sons all died together, and none
of his descendants ever ruled. 7When the
Israelites who lived in Jezreel Valley heard
that the army had fled and that Saul and his
sons had died, they abandoned their towns
and ran off. Then the Philistines came and
occupied them.

8The day after the battle the Philistines
went to plunder the corpses, and they found
the bodies of Saul and his sons lying on
Mount Gilboa. 9They cut off Saul's head,
stripped off his armor, and sent messengers
with them throughout Philistia to tell the
good news to their idols and to their people.
10They put his weapons in one of their tem-
ples and hung his head in the temple of their
god Dagon. 11When the people of Jabesh in
Gilead heard what the Philistines had done
to Saul, 12the bravest men went and got the
bodies of Saul and his sons and took them to
Jabesh. They buried them there under an oak
and fasted for seven days.

13Saul died because he was unfaithful to
the LORD. He disobeyed the LORD's com-
mands; he tried to find guidance by consult-
ing the spirits of the dead 14instead of con-
sulting the LORD. So the LORD killed him
and gave control of the kingdom to David
son of Jesse.

David Becomes King of Israel and Judah
(2 Samuel 5:1–10)

11 All the people of Israel went to
David at Hebron and said to him,
"We are your own flesh and blood. 2In the
past, even when Saul was still our king, you
led the people of Israel in battle, and the
LORD your God promised you that you
would lead his people and be their ruler."
3So all the leaders of Israel came to King
David at Hebron. He made a sacred alliance
with them, they anointed him, and he
became king of Israel, just as the LORD had
promised through Samuel.

4King David and all the Israelites went and
attacked the city of Jerusalem. It was then
known as Jebus, and the Jebusites, the origi-
nal inhabitants of the land, were still living
there. 5The Jebusites told David he would
never get inside the city, but David captured
their fortress of Zion, and it became known
as "David's City." 6David said, "The first man
to kill a Jebusite will be commander of the
army!" Joab, whose mother was Zeruiah, led
the attack and became commander. 7Because
David went to live in the fortress, it came to
be called "David's City." 8He rebuilt the city,
starting at the place where land was filled in
on the east side of the hill, and Joab restored
the rest of the city. 9David grew stronger and
stronger, because the LORD Almighty was
with him.

David's Famous Soldiers
(2 Samuel 23:8–39)

10This is the list of David's famous sol-
diers. Together with the rest of the people of
Israel, they helped him become king, as the
LORD had promised, and they kept his king-
dom strong.

11First was Jashobeam of the clan of
Hachmon, the leader of "The Three."[f] He
fought with his spear against three hundred
men and killed them all in one battle.
12Next among the famous "Three" was
Eleazar son of Dodo, of the clan of Ahoh.
13He fought on David's side against the
Philistines at the battle of Pas Dammim. He
was in a barley field when the Israelites start-
ed to run away, 14so he and his men took a
stand in the middle of the field and fought
the Philistines. The LORD gave him a great
victory.

15One day three of the thirty leading sol-
diers went to a rock where David was stay-
ing near Adullam Cave, while a band of
Philistines was camping in Rephaim Valley.
16At that time David was on a fortified hill,
and a group of Philistines had occupied
Bethlehem. 17David got homesick and said,
"How I wish someone would bring me a
drink of water from the well by the gate in
Bethlehem!" 18The three famous soldiers
forced their way through the Philistine
camp, drew some water from the well, and

[f] **11:11** *One ancient translation (see also 2 Sam 23:8)* "The Three"; *Hebrew* "The Thirty."
10:13 **a** 1 Sam 13:8–14; 15:1–24; **b** Lev 19:31; 20:6; 1 Sam 28:7, 8 **11:4** Josh 15:63; Judg 1:21

The three famous soldiers (11:18)

brought it back to David. But he would not
drink it; instead he poured it out as an offer-
ing to the LORD 19 and said, "I could never
drink this! It would be like drinking the
blood of these men who risked their lives!"
So he refused to drink it. These were the
brave deeds of the three famous soldiers.
20 Joab's brother Abishai was the leader of
"The Famous Thirty."[g] He fought with his
spear against three hundred men and killed
them, and became famous among "The
Thirty."[h] 21 He was the most famous of "The
Thirty"[i] and became their leader, but he was
not as famous as "The Three."
22 Benaiah son of Jehoiada from Kabzeel
was a famous soldier; he did many brave
deeds, including killing two great Moabite
warriors. He once went down into a pit on a
snowy day and killed a lion. 23 He also killed
an Egyptian, a huge man seven and a half
feet tall, who was armed with a gigantic
spear. Benaiah attacked him with a club,
snatched the spear from the Egyptian's hand,
and killed him with it. 24 Those were the
brave deeds of Benaiah, who was one of
"The Thirty."[j] 25 He was outstanding among
"The Thirty," but not as famous as "The
Three." David put him in charge of his
bodyguard.
26-47 These are the other outstanding sol-
diers:

Asahel, Joab's brother
Elhanan son of Dodo from Bethlehem
Shammoth from Harod
Helez from Pelet
Ira son of Ikkesh from Tekoa
Abiezer from Anathoth
Sibbecai from Hushah
Ilai from Ahoh
Maharai from Netophah
Heled son of Baanah from Netophah
Ithai son of Ribai from Gibeah in Benjamin
Benaiah from Pirathon
Hurai from the valleys near Gaash
Abiel from Arbah
Azmaveth from Bahurum
Eliahba from Shaalbon
Hashem[k] from Gizon
Jonathan son of Shagee from Harar
Ahiam son of Sachar from Harar
Eliphal son of Ur
Hepher from Mecherah
Ahijah from Pelon
Hezro from Carmel
Naarai son of Ezbai
Joel brother of Nathan
Mibhar son of Hagri
Zelek from Ammon
Naharai, Joab's armorbearer, from Beeroth
Ira and Gareb from Jattir
Uriah the Hittite
Zabad son of Ahlai
Adina son of Shiza (a leading member of the tribe of Reuben, with his own group of thirty soldiers)
Hanan son of Maacah
Joshaphat from Mithan
Uzzia from Ashterah
Shamma and Jeiel, sons of Hotham, from Aroer
Jediael and Joha, sons of Shimri, from Tiz
Eliel from Mahavah
Jeribai and Joshaviah, sons of Elnaam
Ithmah from Moab
Eliel, Obed, and Jaasiel from Zobah[l]

David's Early Followers from the Tribe of Benjamin

12 David was living in Ziklag, where he
had gone to escape from King Saul.
There he was joined by many experienced,
reliable soldiers, 2 members of the tribe of
Benjamin, to which Saul belonged. They
could shoot arrows and sling stones either

[g] **11:20** *One ancient translation* Thirty; *Hebrew* Three. [h] **11:20** *One ancient translation (see also 2 Sam 23:18)* "The Thirty"; *Hebrew* "The Three." [i] **11:21** *Probable text (see 2 Sam 23:19)* most famous of "The Thirty"; *Hebrew unclear.* [j] **11:24** *Probable text* "The Thirty"; *Hebrew* "The Three." [k] **11:26–47** *Probable text* Hashem; *Hebrew* the sons of Hashem. [l] **11:26–47** *Probable text* from Zobah; *Hebrew unclear.*

right-handed or left-handed. 3-7They were under the command of Ahiezer and Joash, sons of Shemaah, from Gibeah.

These were the soldiers:

Jeziel and Pelet, sons of Azmaveth
Beracah and Jehu from Anathoth
Ishmaiah from Gibeon, a famous soldier and one of the leaders of "The Thirty"
Jeremiah, Jahaziel, Johannan, and Jozabad, from Gederah
Eluzai, Jerimoth, Bealiah, Shemariah, and Shephatiah, from Hariph
Elkanah, Isshiah, Azarel, Joezer, and Jashobeam, of the clan of Korah
Joelah and Zebadiah, sons of Jeroham, from Gedor

David's Followers from the Tribe of Gad

8These are the names of the famous, experienced soldiers from the tribe of Gad who joined David's troops when he was at the desert fort. They were experts with shields and spears, as fierce looking as lions and as quick as mountain deer. 9-13They were ranked in the following order: Ezer, Obadiah, Eliab, Mishmannah, Jeremiah, Attai, Eliel, Johanan, Elzabad, Jeremiah, and Machbannai.

14Some of these men from the tribe of Gad were senior officers in command of a thousand men, and others were junior officers in command of a hundred. 15In the first month of one year, the time when the Jordan River overflowed its banks, they crossed the river, scattering the people who lived in the valleys both east and west of the river.

Followers from Benjamin and Judah

16Once a group of men from the tribes of Benjamin and Judah went out to the fort where David was. 17David went to meet them and said, "If you are coming as friends to help me, you are welcome here. Join us! But if you intend to betray me to my enemies, even though I have not tried to hurt you, the God of our ancestors will know it and punish you."

18God's spirit took control of one of them, Amasai, who later became the commander of "The Thirty," and he called out,

"David son of Jesse, we are yours!
Success to you and those who help you!
God is on your side."

David welcomed them and made them officers in his army.

Followers from Manasseh

19Some soldiers from the tribe of Manasseh went over to David's side when he was marching out with the Philistines to fight King Saul. Actually he did not help the Philistines, for their kings were afraid that he would betray them to his former master Saul, so they sent him back to Ziklag. 20These are the soldiers from Manasseh who went over to David's side when he was returning: Adnah, Jozabad, Jediael, Michael, Jozabad, Elihu, and Zillethai. In Manasseh they had all commanded units of a thousand men. 21They served David as officers over his troops,[m] because they were all outstanding soldiers. Later they were officers in the Israelite army. 22Almost every day new men joined David's forces, so that his army was soon enormous.

List of David's Forces

23-37When David was at Hebron, many trained soldiers joined his army to help make him king in place of Saul, as the LORD had promised. Their numbers were as follows:

Judah: 6,800 well-equipped men, armed with shields and spears;

Simeon: 7,100 well-trained men;

Levi: 4,600 men;

Followers of Jehoiada, descendant of Aaron: 3,700 men;

Relatives of Zadok, an able young fighter: 22 leading men;

Benjamin (Saul's own tribe): 3,000 men (most of the people of Benjamin had remained loyal to Saul);

Ephraim: 20,800 men famous in their own clans;

West Manasseh: 18,000 men chosen to go and make David king;

Issachar: 200 leaders, together with the

[m] **12:21** They served David . . . troops; *or* They helped David fight against the bands of raiders.

men under their command (these leaders knew what Israel should do and the best time to do it);

Zebulun: 50,000 loyal and reliable men ready to fight, trained to use all kinds of weapons;

Naphtali: 1,000 leaders, together with 37,000 men armed with shields and spears;

Dan: 28,600 trained men;

Asher: 40,000 men ready for battle;

Tribes east of the Jordan—Reuben, Gad, and East Manasseh: 120,000 men trained to use all kinds of weapons.

38All these soldiers, ready for battle, went to Hebron, determined to make David king over all Israel. All the rest of the people of Israel were united in the same purpose. 39They spent three days there with David, feasting on the food and drink which their relatives had prepared for them. 40From as far away as the northern tribes of Issachar, Zebulun, and Naphtali, people came bringing donkeys, camels, mules, and oxen loaded with food—flour, figs, raisins, wine, and olive oil. They also brought cattle and sheep to kill and eat. All this was an expression of the joy that was felt throughout the whole country.

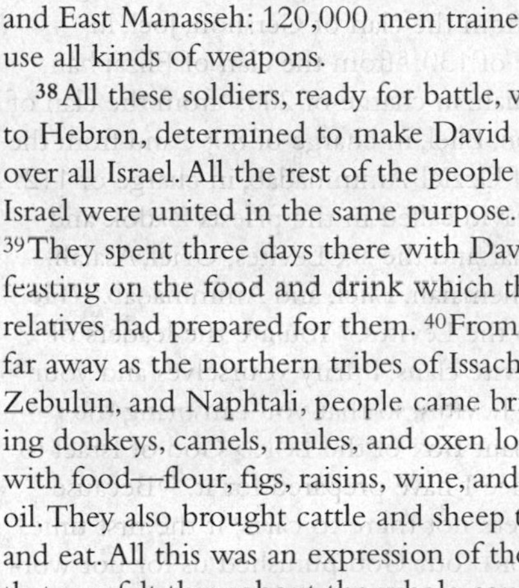

People came bringing donkeys. (12:40)

The Covenant Box Is Moved from Kiriath Jearim
(2 Samuel 6:1–11)

13 King David consulted with all the officers in command of units of a thousand men and units of a hundred men. 2Then he announced to all the people of Israel, "If you give your approval and if it is the will of the LORD our God, let us send messengers to the rest of our people and to the priests and Levites in their towns, and tell them to assemble here with us. 3Then we will go and get God's Covenant Box, which was ignored while Saul was king." 4The people were pleased with the suggestion and agreed to it.

5So David assembled the people of Israel from all over the country, from the Egyptian border in the south to Hamath Pass in the north, in order to bring the Covenant Box from Kiriath Jearim to Jerusalem. 6David and the people went to the city of Baalah, that is, to Kiriath Jearim, in the territory of Judah, to get the Covenant Box of God, which bears the name of the LORD enthroned above the winged creatures. 7At Abinadab's house they brought out the Covenant Box and put it on a new cart. Uzzah and Ahio guided the cart, 8while David and all the people danced with all their might to honor God. They sang and played musical instruments—harps, drums, cymbals, and trumpets.

9As they came to the threshing place of Chidon, the oxen stumbled, and Uzzah reached out and took hold of the Covenant Box. 10At once the LORD became angry with Uzzah and killed him for touching the Box. He died there in God's presence, 11and so that place has been called Perez Uzzah[n] ever since. David was furious because the LORD had punished Uzzah in anger.

12Then David was afraid of God and said, "How can I take the Covenant Box with me now?" 13So David did not take it with him to Jerusalem. Instead, he left it at the house of a man named Obed Edom, a native of the city of Gath. 14It stayed there three months, and the LORD blessed Obed Edom's family and everything that belonged to him.

David's Activities in Jerusalem
(2 Samuel 5:11–16)

14 King Hiram of Tyre sent a trade mission to David; he provided him with cedar logs and with stonemasons and carpenters to build a palace. 2And so David realized that the LORD had established him as king of Israel and was making his kingdom prosperous for the sake of his people.

[n] **13:11** PEREZ UZZAH: *This name in Hebrew means "Punishment of Uzzah."*

13:5 1 Sam 7:1, 2 **13:6** Ex 25:22 **13:12** 2 Macc 7:19 **13:14** 1 Chr 26:4, 5

[3]There in Jerusalem, David married more wives and had more sons and daughters. [4]The following children were born to him in Jerusalem: Shammua, Shobab, Nathan, Solomon, [5]Ibhar, Elishua, Elpelet, [6]Nogah, Nepheg, Japhia, [7]Elishama, Beeliada,[o] and Eliphelet.

Victory over the Philistines
(2 Samuel 5:17–25)

[8]When the Philistines heard that David had now been made king over the whole country of Israel, their army went out to capture him. So David marched out to meet them. [9]The Philistines arrived at Rephaim Valley and began plundering. [10]David asked God, "Shall I attack the Philistines? Will you give me the victory?"

The LORD answered, "Yes, attack! I will give you the victory!"

[11]So David attacked them at Baal Perazim and defeated them. He said, "God has used me to break through the enemy army like a flood." So that place is called Baal Perazim.[p] [12]When the Philistines fled, they left their idols behind, and David gave orders for them to be burned.

[13]Soon the Philistines returned to the valley and started plundering it again. [14]Once more David consulted God, who answered, "Don't attack them from here, but go around and get ready to attack them from the other side, near the balsam trees. [15]When you hear the sound of marching in the treetops, then attack, because I will be marching ahead of you to defeat the Philistine army." [16]David did what God had commanded, and so he drove the Philistines back from Gibeon all the way to Gezer. [17]David's fame spread everywhere, and the LORD made every nation afraid of him.

Getting Ready to Move the Covenant Box

15 For his own use, David built houses in David's City.[q] He also prepared a place for God's Covenant Box and put up a tent for it. [2]Then he said, "Only Levites should carry the Covenant Box, because they are the ones the LORD chose to carry it and to serve him forever." [3]So David summoned all the people of Israel to Jerusalem in order to bring the Covenant Box to the place he had prepared for it. [4]Next he sent for the descendants of Aaron and for the Levites. [5]From the Levite clan of Kohath came Uriel, in charge of 120 members of his clan; [6]from the clan of Merari came Asaiah, in charge of 220; [7]from the clan of Gershon, Joel, in charge of 130; [8]from the clan of Elizaphan, Shemaiah, in charge of 200; [9]from the clan of Hebron, Eliel, in charge of 80; [10]and from the clan of Uzziel, Amminadab, in charge of 112.

[11]David called in the priests Zadok and Abiathar and the six Levites, Uriel, Asaiah, Joel, Shemaiah, Eliel, and Amminadab. [12]He said to the Levites, "You are the leaders of the Levite clans. Purify yourselves and your fellow Levites, so that you can bring the Covenant Box of the LORD God of Israel to the place I have prepared for it. [13]Because you were not there to carry it the first time, the LORD our God punished us for not worshiping him as we should have done."

[14]Then the priests and the Levites purified themselves in order to move the Covenant Box of the LORD God of Israel. [15]The Levites carried it on poles on their shoulders, as the LORD had commanded through Moses.

The Levites carried it on poles. (15:15)

[o] **14:7** BEELIADA: *Called Eliada in 3:8.* [p] **14:11** BAAL PERAZIM: *This name in Hebrew means "Lord of the Breakthrough."* [q] **15:1** DAVID'S CITY: *That part of Jerusalem which David had captured from the original inhabitants, the Jebusites (see 2 Sam 5:6–10).*

15:2 Deut 10:8 **15:15** Ex 25:14

[16]David commanded the leaders of the
Levites to assign various Levites to sing and
to play joyful music on harps and cymbals.
[17-21]From the clans of singers they chose the
following men to play the brass cymbals:
Heman son of Joel, his relative Asaph son of
Berechiah, and Ethan son of Kushaiah, of the
clan of Merari. To assist them they chose the
following Levites to play the high-pitched
harps: Zechariah, Jaaziel, Shemiramoth,
Jehiel, Unni, Eliab, Maaseiah, and Benaiah.
To play the low-pitched harps they chose
the following Levites: Mattithiah, Eliphe-
lehu, Mikneiah, Azaziah, and the Temple
guards, Obed Edom and Jeiel.
[22]Because of his skill in music Chenaniah
was chosen to be in charge of the levitical
musicians. [23-24]Berechiah and Elkanah, along
with Obed Edom and Jehiah, were chosen as
guards for the Covenant Box. The priests
Shebaniah, Joshaphat, Nethanel, Amasai,
Zechariah, Benaiah, and Eliezer were chosen
to blow trumpets in front of the Covenant
Box.

Moving the Covenant Box to Jerusalem

(2 Samuel 6:12–22)

[25]So King David, the leaders of Israel,
and the military commanders went to the
house of Obed Edom to get the Covenant
Box, and they had a great celebration.
[26]They sacrificed seven bulls and seven
sheep, to make sure that God would help the
Levites who were carrying the Covenant
Box. [27]David was wearing a robe made of
the finest linen, and so were the musicians,
Chenaniah their leader, and the Levites who
carried the Box. David also wore a linen
ephod. [28]So all the Israelites accompanied
the Covenant Box up to Jerusalem with
shouts of joy, the sound of trumpets, horns,
and cymbals, and the music of harps.
[29]As the Box was being brought into the
city, Michal, Saul's daughter, looked out of
the window and saw King David dancing
and leaping for joy, and she was disgusted
with him.

16 They took the Covenant Box to the
tent which David had prepared for it
and put it inside. Then they offered sacrifices
and fellowship offerings to God. [2]After David
had finished offering the sacrifices, he blessed
the people in the name of the LORD [3]and
distributed food to them all. He gave each
man and woman in Israel a loaf of bread, a
piece of roasted meat,[r] and some raisins.
[4]David appointed some of the Levites to
lead the worship of the LORD, the God of
Israel, in front of the Covenant Box, by
singing and praising him. [5]Asaph was
appointed leader, with Zechariah as his assis-
tant. Jeiel, Shemiramoth, Jehiel, Mattithiah,

[r] **16:3** a piece of roasted meat; *or* a cake of dates.

With shouts of joy (15:28)

Eliab, Benaiah, Obed Edom, and Jeiel were to
play harps. Asaph was to sound the cymbals,
6 and two priests, Benaiah and Jahaziel, were
to blow trumpets regularly in front of the
Covenant Box. 7 It was then that David first
gave Asaph and the other Levites the responsibility for singing praises to the LORD.

A Song of Praise

(Psalms 105:1–15; 96:1–13; 106:1, 47, 48)

8 Give thanks to the LORD, proclaim his
greatness;
tell the nations what he has done.
9 Sing praise to the LORD;
tell the wonderful things he has done.
10 Be glad that we belong to him;
let all who worship him rejoice!
11 Go to the LORD for help,
and worship him continually.
12-13 You descendants of Jacob, God's servant,
descendants of Israel, whom God
chose,
remember the miracles that God
performed
and the judgments that he gave.
14 The LORD is our God;
his commands are for all the world.
15 Never forget God's covenant,
which he made to last forever,
16 the covenant he made with Abraham,
the promise he made to Isaac.
17 The LORD made a covenant with Jacob,
one that will last forever.
18 "I will give you the land of Canaan," he
said.
"It will be your own possession."

19 God's people were few in number,
strangers in the land of Canaan.
20 They wandered from country to country,
from one kingdom to another.
21 But God let no one oppress them;
to protect them, he warned the kings:
22 "Don't harm my chosen servants;
do not touch my prophets."

23 Sing to the LORD, all the world!
Proclaim every day the good news that
he has saved us.
24 Proclaim his glory to the nations,
his mighty deeds to all peoples.
25 The LORD is great and is to be highly
praised;
he is to be honored more than all the
gods.
26 The gods of all other nations are only
idols,
but the LORD created the heavens.
27 Glory and majesty surround him,
power and joy fill his Temple.
28 Praise the LORD, all people on earth,
praise his glory and might.
29 Praise the LORD's glorious name;
bring an offering and come into his
Temple.
Bow down before the Holy One when
he appears;[s]
30 tremble before him, all the earth!
The earth is set firmly in place and
cannot be moved.
31 Be glad, earth and sky!
Tell the nations that the LORD is king.
32 Roar, sea, and every creature in you;
be glad, fields, and everything in you!
33 The trees in the woods will shout for joy
when the LORD comes to rule the
earth.

34 Give thanks to the LORD, because he is
good;
his love is eternal.
35 Say to him, "Save us, O God our Savior;
gather us together; rescue us from the
nations,
so that we may be thankful
and praise your holy name."
36 Praise the LORD, the God of Israel!
Praise him now and forever!

Then all the people said, "Amen," and
praised the LORD.

Worship at Jerusalem and Gibeon

37 King David put Asaph and the other
Levites in permanent charge of the worship
that was held at the place where the
Covenant Box was kept. They were to per-

[s] **16:29** when he appears; *or* in garments of worship.

16:16 a Gen 12:7; **b** Gen 26:3 **16:17, 18** Gen 28:13 **16:21, 22** Gen 20:3–7 **16:34** 2 Chr 5:13; 7:3; Ezra 3:11; Ps 100:5; 106:1; 107:1; 118:1; 136:1; Jer 33:11

form their duties there day by day. 38Obed
Edom son of Jeduthun and sixty-eight men
of his clan were to assist them. Hosah and
Obed Edom were in charge of guarding the
gates.
39Zadok the priest and his fellow priests,
however, were in charge of the worship of
the LORD at the place of worship in Gibeon.
40Every morning and evening they were to
burn sacrifices whole on the altar in accor-
dance with what was written in the Law
which the LORD gave to Israel. 41There with
them were Heman and Jeduthun and the
others who were specifically chosen to sing
praises to the LORD for his eternal love.
42Heman and Jeduthun also had charge of
the trumpets and cymbals and the other
instruments which were played when the
songs of praise were sung. The members of
Jeduthun's clan were in charge of guarding
the gates.
43Then everyone went home, and David
went home to spend some time with his
family.

Nathan's Message to David

(2 Samuel 7:1–17)

17 King David was now living in his
palace. One day he sent for the
prophet Nathan and said to him, "Here I am
living in a house built of cedar, but the
LORD's Covenant Box is kept in a tent!"
2Nathan answered, "Do whatever you
have in mind, because God is with you."
3But that night God said to Nathan, 4"Go
and tell my servant David that I say to him,
'You are not the one to build a temple for
me to live in. 5From the time I rescued the
people of Israel from Egypt until now I have
never lived in a temple; I have always lived in
tents and moved from place to place. 6In all
my traveling with the people of Israel I
never asked any of the leaders that I appoint-
ed why they had not built me a temple
made of cedar.'
7"So tell my servant David that I, the
LORD Almighty, say to him, 'I took you from
looking after sheep in the fields and made
you the ruler of my people Israel. 8I have
been with you wherever you have gone, and
I have defeated all your enemies as you
advanced. I will make you as famous as the
greatest leaders in the world. 9-10I have cho-
sen a place for my people Israel and have
settled them there, where they will live
without being oppressed any more. Ever
since they entered this land they have been
attacked by violent people, but this will not
happen again. I promise to defeat all your
enemies and to give you descendants.
11When you die and are buried with your
ancestors, I will make one of your sons king
and will keep his kingdom strong. 12He will
be the one to build a temple for me, and I
will make sure that his dynasty continues
forever. 13I will be his father, and he will be
my son. I will not withdraw my support
from him as I did from Saul, whom I
removed so that you could be king. 14I will
put him in charge of my people and my
kingdom forever. His dynasty will never
end.' "
15Nathan told David everything that God
had revealed to him.

David's Prayer of Thanksgiving

(2 Samuel 7:18–29)

16Then King David went into the Tent of
the LORD's presence, sat down, and prayed,
"I am not worthy of what you have already
done for me, LORD God, nor is my family.
17Yet now you are doing even more; you
have made promises about my descendants
in the years to come, and you, LORD God,
are already treating me like someone great.[t]
18What more can I say to you! You know me
well, and yet you honor me, your servant.
19It was your will and purpose to do this for
me and to show me my future greatness.
20LORD, there is none like you; we have
always known that you alone are God.
21There is no other nation on earth like
Israel, whom you rescued from slavery to
make them your own people. The great and
wonderful things you did for them spread
your fame throughout the world. You

[t] **17:17** *Probable text* and you, LORD God . . . great; *Hebrew unclear.*
16:43 2 Sam 6:19, 20 **17:13** 2 Cor 6:18; Heb 1:5

Pray it!

Grandparents' Prayer

Here's a story in which King David takes time out to thank God for God's promises to him. David prays that God will bless his descendants—that is, his children, grandchildren, great-grandchildren, and so on.

One day you may be a grandparent. Is that hard to imagine? Just picture it: you're old (okay, not really, really old, but older than your parents are now), and your own kids are adults and one of them has their own child. Here is a prayer for you to pray for your future grandchildren. (Even if you don't plan on getting married and having kids, you can pray for future generations in this same way.)

Creator God, you made me a child, and a grandchild.
One day I too may be a grandparent.
I pray now for my possible grandchildren and for all the children of the future.
I pray that they know your love and the love of their family.
I pray that they know of your peace.
I pray that they know of your wisdom.
And I pray that they know they were loved even before they were born.
I don't know what will happen, God, but I do know that if I do have kids,
and they have kids, you will be with them. Thank you, God.
Amen.

— 1 Chronicles 17:16–27

rescued your people from Egypt and drove
out other nations as your people advanced.
22 You have made Israel your own people
forever, and you, LORD, have become their
God.
23 "And now, O LORD, fulfill for all time
the promise you made about me and my
descendants, and do what you said you
would. 24 Your fame will be great, and peo-
ple will forever say, 'The LORD Almighty is
God over Israel.' And you will preserve my
dynasty for all time. 25 I have the courage to
pray this prayer to you, my God, because
you have revealed all this to me, your ser-
vant, and have told me that you will make
my descendants kings. 26 You, LORD, are
God, and you have made this wonderful
promise to me. 27 I ask you to bless my
descendants so that they will continue to
enjoy your favor. You, LORD, have blessed
them, and your blessing will rest on them
forever."

David's Military Victories
(2 Samuel 8:1–18)

18 Some time later King David
attacked the Philistines again and
defeated them. He took out of their control
the city of Gath and its surrounding villages.
2 He also defeated the Moabites, who
became his subjects and paid taxes to him.
3 Next, David attacked King Hadadezer of
the Syrian state of Zobah, near the territory
of Hamath, because Hadadezer was trying to
gain control of the territory by the upper
Euphrates River. 4 David captured a thousand
of his chariots, seven thousand cavalry
troops, and twenty thousand foot soldiers.
He kept enough horses for a hundred chari-
ots and crippled all the rest.
5 When the Syrians of Damascus sent
an army to help King Hadadezer, David
attacked it and killed twenty-two thousand
men. 6 Then he set up military camps in
their territory, and they became his subjects

and paid taxes to him. The LORD made David victorious everywhere. [7]David captured the gold shields carried by Hadadezer's officials and took them to Jerusalem. [8]He also took a great quantity of bronze from Tibhath and Kun, cities ruled by Hadadezer. (Solomon later used this bronze to make the tank, the columns, and the bronze utensils for the Temple.)

[9]King Toi of Hamath heard that David had defeated Hadadezer's entire army. [10]So he sent his son Joram to greet King David and congratulate him for his victory over Hadadezer, against whom Toi had fought many times. Joram brought David presents made of gold, silver, and bronze. [11]King David dedicated them for use in worship, along with the silver and gold he took from the nations he conquered—Edom, Moab, Ammon, Philistia, and Amalek.

[12]Abishai, whose mother was Zeruiah, defeated the Edomites in Salt Valley and killed eighteen thousand of them. [13]He set up military camps throughout Edom, and the people there became King David's subjects. The LORD made David victorious everywhere.

[14]David ruled over all Israel and made sure that his people were always treated fairly and justly. [15]Abishai's brother Joab was commander of the army; Jehoshaphat son of Ahilud was in charge of the records; [16]Zadok son of Ahitub and Ahimelech son of Abiathar were priests; Seraiah[u] was court secretary; [17]Benaiah son of Jehoiada was in charge of David's bodyguards; and King David's sons held high positions in his service.

David Defeats the Ammonites and the Syrians

(2 Samuel 10:1–19)

19 Some time later King Nahash of Ammon died, and his son Hanun became king. [2]King David said, "I must show loyal friendship to Hanun, as his father Nahash did to me." So David sent messengers to express his sympathy.

When they arrived in Ammon and called on King Hanun, [3]the Ammonite leaders said to the king, "Do you think that it is in your father's honor that David has sent these men to express sympathy to you? Of course not! He has sent them here as spies to explore the land, so that he can conquer it!"

[4]Hanun seized David's messengers, shaved off their beards, cut off their clothes at the hips, and sent them away. [5]They were too ashamed to return home. When David heard what had happened, he sent word for them to stay in Jericho and not return until their beards had grown again.

[6]King Hanun and the Ammonites realized that they had made David their enemy, so they paid nearly forty tons of silver to hire chariots and charioteers from Upper Mesopotamia and from the Syrian states of Maacah and Zobah. [7]The thirty-two thousand chariots they hired and the army of the king of Maacah came and camped near Medeba. The Ammonites too came out from all their cities and got ready to fight.

[8]When David heard what was happening, he sent out Joab and the whole army. [9]The Ammonites marched out and took up their position at the entrance to Rabbah, their capital city, and the kings who had come to help took up their position in the open countryside.

[10]Joab saw that the enemy troops would attack him in front and from the rear, so he chose the best of Israel's soldiers and put them in position facing the Syrians. [11]He placed the rest of his troops under the command of his brother Abishai, who put them in position facing the Ammonites. [12]Joab said to him, "If you see that the Syrians are defeating me, come and help me, and if the Ammonites are defeating you, I will go and help you. [13]Be strong and courageous! Let's fight hard for our people and for the cities of our God. And may the LORD's will be done."

[14]Joab and his men advanced to attack, and the Syrians fled. [15]When the Ammonites saw the Syrians running away, they fled from Abishai and retreated into the city. Then Joab went back to Jerusalem.

[u] **18:16** *Probable text (see 2 Sam 8:17)* Seraiah; *Hebrew* Shavsha.

18:8 1 Kings 7:40–47; 2 Chr 4:11–18 **18:12** Ps 60 Title

16 The Syrians realized that they had been defeated by the Israelites, so they brought troops from the Syrian states on the east side of the Euphrates River and placed them under the command of Shobach, commander of the army of King Hadadezer of Zobah. 17 When David heard of it, he gathered the Israelite troops, crossed the Jordan River, and put them in position facing the Syrians. The fighting began, 18 and the Israelites drove the Syrian army back. David and his men killed seven thousand Syrian chariot drivers and forty thousand foot soldiers. They also killed the Syrian commander, Shobach. 19 When the kings who were subject to Hadadezer realized that they had been defeated by Israel, they made peace with David and became his subjects. 20 The Syrians were never again willing to help the Ammonites.

David Captures Rabbah
(2 Samuel 12:26–31)

20 The following spring, at the time of the year when kings usually go to war, Joab led out the army and invaded the land of Ammon; King David, however, stayed in Jerusalem. They besieged the city of Rabbah, attacked it, and destroyed it. 2 The Ammonite idol Molech[v] had a gold crown which weighed about seventy-five pounds. In it there was a jewel, which David took and put in his own crown. He also took a large amount of loot from the city. 3 He took the people of the city and put them to work with saws, iron hoes, and axes. He did the same to the people of all the other towns of Ammon. Then he and his men returned to Jerusalem.

Battles against Philistine Giants
(2 Samuel 21:15–22)

4 Later on, war broke out again with the Philistines at Gezer. This was when Sibbecai from Hushah killed a giant named Sippai, and the Philistines were defeated.

5 There was another battle with the Philistines, and Elhanan son of Jair killed Lahmi, the brother of Goliath from Gath, whose spear had a shaft as thick as the bar on a weaver's loom.

6 Another battle took place at Gath, where there was a giant with six fingers on each hand and six toes on each foot. He was a descendant of the ancient giants. 7 He defied the Israelites, and Jonathan, the son of David's brother Shammah, killed him.

8 These three, who were killed by David and his men, were descendants of the giants at Gath.

David Takes a Census
(2 Samuel 24:1–25)

21 Satan wanted to bring trouble on the people of Israel, so he made David decide to take a census. 2 David gave orders to Joab and the other officers, "Go through Israel, from one end of the country to the other, and count the people. I want to know how many there are."

3 Joab answered, "May the LORD make the people of Israel a hundred times more numerous than they are now! Your Majesty, they are all your servants. Why do you want to do this and make the whole nation guilty?" 4 But the king made Joab obey the order. Joab went out, traveled through the whole country of Israel, and then returned to Jerusalem. 5 He reported to King David the total number of men capable of military service: 1,100,000 in Israel and 470,000 in Judah. 6 Because Joab disapproved of the king's command, he did not take any census of the tribes of Levi and Benjamin.

7 God was displeased with what had been done, so he punished Israel. 8 David said to God, "I have committed a terrible sin in doing this! Please forgive me. I have acted foolishly."

9 Then the LORD said to Gad, David's prophet, 10 "Go and tell David that I am giving him three choices. I will do whichever he chooses."

11 Gad went to David, told him what the LORD had said, and asked, "Which is it to be? 12 Three years of famine? Or three months of running away from the armies of

[v] **20:2** Ammonite idol Molech; *or* Ammonite king.
20:1 2 Sam 11:1 **20:5** 1 Sam 17:4–7

your enemies? Or three days during which
the LORD attacks you with his sword and
sends an epidemic on your land, using his
angel to bring death throughout Israel? What
answer shall I give the LORD?"
13 David replied to Gad, "I am in a desper-
ate situation! But I don't want to be pun-
ished by people. Let the LORD himself be the
one to punish me, because he is merciful."
14 So the LORD sent an epidemic on the
people of Israel, and seventy thousand of
them died. 15 Then he sent an angel to
destroy Jerusalem, but he changed his mind
and said to the angel, "Stop! That's enough!"
The angel was standing by the threshing
place of Araunah, a Jebusite.
16 David saw the angel standing in midair,
holding his sword in his hand, ready to
destroy Jerusalem. Then David and the lead-
ers of the people—all of whom were wear-
ing sackcloth—bowed low, with their faces
touching the ground. 17 David prayed, "O
God, I am the one who did wrong. I am the
one who ordered the census. What have these
poor people done? LORD, my God, punish
me and my family, and spare your people."
18 The angel of the LORD told Gad to
command David to go and build an altar to
the LORD at Araunah's threshing place.
19 David obeyed the LORD's command and
went, as Gad had told him to. 20 There at the
threshing place Araunah and his four sons
were threshing wheat, and when they saw
the angel, the sons ran and hid. 21 As soon as
Araunah saw King David approaching, he
left the threshing place and bowed low, with
his face touching the ground. 22 David said to
him, "Sell me your threshing place, so that I
can build an altar to the LORD, to stop the
epidemic. I'll give you the full price."
23 "Take it, Your Majesty," Araunah said,
"and do whatever you wish. Here are these
oxen to burn as an offering on the altar, and
here are the threshing boards to use as fuel,
and wheat to give as an offering. I give it all
to you."
24 But the king answered, "No, I will pay
you the full price. I will not give as an offer-
ing to the LORD something that belongs to
you, something that costs me nothing."
25 And he paid Araunah six hundred gold
coins for the threshing place. 26 He built an
altar to the LORD there and offered burnt
offerings and fellowship offerings. He
prayed, and the LORD answered him by
sending fire from heaven to burn the sacri-
fices on the altar.
27 The LORD told the angel to put his
sword away, and the angel obeyed. 28 David
saw by this that the LORD had answered his
prayer, so he offered sacrifices on the altar at
Araunah's threshing place. 29 The Tent of the
LORD's presence which Moses had made in
the wilderness, and the altar on which sacri-
fices were burned were still at the place of
worship at Gibeon at this time; 30 but David
was not able to go there to worship God,
because he was afraid of the sword of the
LORD's angel.

22 So David said, "This is where the
Temple of the LORD God will be.
Here is the altar where the people of Israel
are to offer burnt offerings."

Preparations for Building the Temple

2 King David gave orders for all the for-
eigners living in the land of Israel to assem-
ble, and he put them to work. Some of them
prepared stone blocks for building the Tem-
ple. 3 He supplied a large amount of iron for
making nails and clamps for the wooden
gates, and so much bronze that no one could
weigh it. 4 He had the people of Tyre and
Sidon bring him a large number of cedar
logs. 5 David thought, "The Temple that my
son Solomon is to build must be splendid
and world-famous. But he is young and
inexperienced, so I must make preparations
for it." So David got large amounts of the
materials ready before he died.
6 He sent for his son Solomon and com-
manded him to build a temple for the
LORD, the God of Israel. 7 David said to him,
"Son, I wanted to build a temple to honor
the LORD my God. 8 But the LORD told me
that I had killed too many people and
fought too many wars. And so, because of all
the bloodshed I have caused, he would not
let me build a temple for him. 9 He did,

22:7–10 2 Sam 7:1–16; 1 Chr 17:1–14

however, make me a promise. He said, 'You
will have a son who will rule in peace,
because I will give him peace from all his
enemies. His name will be Solomon,[w]
because during his reign I will give Israel
peace and security. 10He will build a temple
for me. He will be my son, and I will be his
father. His dynasty will rule Israel forever.' "
11David continued, "Now, son, may the
LORD your God be with you, and may he
keep his promise to make you successful in
building a temple for him. 12And may the
LORD your God give you insight and wis-
dom so that you may govern Israel according
to his Law. 13If you obey all the laws which
the LORD gave to Moses for Israel, you will
be successful. Be determined and confident,
and don't let anything make you afraid. 14As
for the Temple, by my efforts I have accumu-
lated almost four thousand tons of gold and
nearly forty thousand tons of silver to be
used in building it. Besides that, there is an
unlimited supply of bronze and iron. I also
have wood and stone ready, but you must get
more. 15You have many workers. There are
stonecutters to work in the quarries, and
there are masons and carpenters, as well as a
large number of skilled workers of every sort
who can work 16with gold, silver, bronze,
and iron. Now begin the work, and may the
LORD be with you."
17David commanded all the leaders of
Israel to help Solomon. 18He said, "The
LORD your God has been with you and

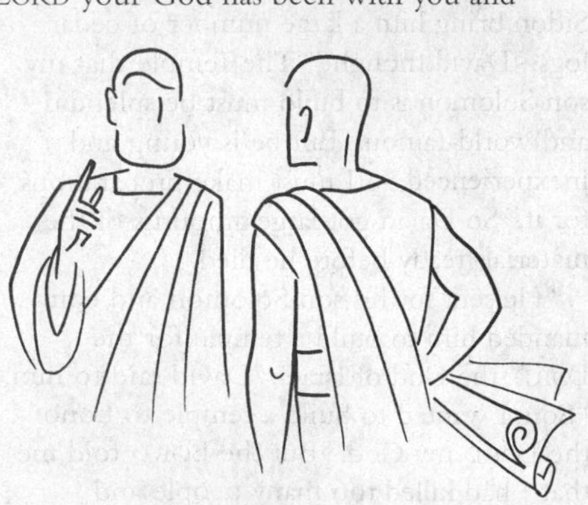

"Now begin the work." (22:16)

given you peace on all sides. He let me con-
quer all the people who used to live in this
land, and they are now subject to you and to
the LORD. 19Now serve the LORD your God
with all your heart and soul. Start building
the Temple, so that you can place in it the
Covenant Box of the LORD and all the other
sacred objects used in worshiping him."

23 When David was very old, he made
his son Solomon king of Israel.

The Work of the Levites

2King David brought together all the
Israelite leaders and all the priests and
Levites. 3He took a census of all the male
Levites aged thirty or older. The total was
thirty-eight thousand. 4The king assigned
twenty-four thousand to administer the
work of the Temple, six thousand to keep
records and decide disputes, 5four thousand
to do guard duty, and four thousand to praise
the LORD, using the musical instruments
provided by the king for this purpose.
6David divided the Levites into three
groups, according to their clans: Gershon,
Kohath, and Merari.
7Gershon had two sons: Ladan and
Shimei. 8Ladan had three sons: Jehiel,
Zetham, and Joel, 9who were the heads of
the clans descended from Ladan. (Shimei had
three sons: Shelomoth, Haziel, and Haran.)[x]
10-11Shimei had four sons: Jahath, Zina,
Jeush, and Beriah, in order of age. Jeush and
Beriah did not have many descendants, so
they were counted as one clan.
12Kohath had four sons: Amram, Izhar,
Hebron, and Uzziel. 13His oldest son,
Amram, was the father of Aaron and Moses.
(Aaron and his descendants were set apart to
be in charge of the sacred objects forever, to
burn incense in the worship of the LORD, to
serve him, and to bless the people in his
name. 14But the sons of Moses, the man of
God, were included among the Levites.)
15Moses had two sons, Gershom and Eliezer.
16The leader among Gershom's sons was
Shebuel. 17Eliezer had only one son, Rehabi-
ah, but Rehabiah had many descendants.

[w] **22:9** SOLOMON: *This name is formed from the Hebrew word "shalom," which means "peace and security."*
[x] **23:9** SHIMEI . . . HARAN: *The relation of this list to the list of Shimei's sons in verse 10 is not clear.*

22:13 Josh 1:6–9 **23:1** 1 Kings 1:1–40 **23:13** Ex 28:1

18Kohath's second son, Izhar, had a son,
Shelomith, the head of the clan. 19Kohath's
third son, Hebron, had four sons: Jeriah,
Amariah, Jahaziel, and Jekameam. 20Kohath's
fourth son, Uzziel, had two sons, Micah and
Isshiah.

21Merari had two sons, Mahli and Mushi.
Mahli also had two sons, Eleazar and Kish,
22but Eleazar died without having any sons,
only daughters. His daughters married their
cousins, the sons of Kish. 23Merari's second
son, Mushi, had three sons: Mahli, Eder, and
Jeremoth.

24These were the descendants of Levi, by
clans and families, every one of them registered by name. Each of his descendants,
twenty years of age or older, had a share in
the work of the LORD's Temple.

25David said, "The LORD God of Israel has
given peace to his people, and he himself will
live in Jerusalem forever. 26So there is no
longer any need for the Levites to carry the
Tent of the LORD's presence and all the
equipment used in worship." 27On the basis
of David's final instructions all Levites were
registered for service when they reached the
age of twenty, 28and were assigned the following duties: to help the priests descended from
Aaron with the Temple worship, to take care
of its courtyards and its rooms, and to keep
undefiled everything that is sacred; 29to be
responsible for the bread offered to God, the
flour used in offerings, the wafers made without yeast, the baked offerings, and the flour
mixed with olive oil; to weigh and measure
the Temple offerings; 30and to praise and glorify the LORD every morning and every
evening 31and whenever offerings to the
LORD are burned on the Sabbath, the New
Moon Festival, and other festivals. Rules were
made specifying the number of Levites
assigned to do this work each time. The
Levites were assigned the duty of worshiping
the LORD for all time. 32They were given the
responsibility of taking care of the Tent of the
LORD's presence and the Temple, and of assisting their relatives, the priests descended from
Aaron, in the Temple worship.

The Work Assigned to the Priests

24 These are the groups to which the
descendants of Aaron belong. Aaron
had four sons: Nadab, Abihu, Eleazar, and
Ithamar. 2Nadab and Abihu died before their
father did, and left no descendants, so their
brothers Eleazar and Ithamar became priests.
3King David organized the descendants of
Aaron into groups according to their duties.
He was assisted in this by Zadok, a descendant
of Eleazar, and by Ahimelech, a descendant of
Ithamar. 4The descendants of Eleazar were
organized into sixteen groups, while the
descendants of Ithamar were organized into
eight; this was done because there were more
male heads of families among the descendants
of Eleazar. 5Since there were Temple officials
and spiritual leaders among the descendants of
both Eleazar and Ithamar, assignments were
made by drawing lots. 6The descendants of
Eleazar and of Ithamar took turns drawing
lots. Then they were registered by Shemaiah
son of Nethanel, a Levite secretary. The king,
his officials, the priest Zadok, Ahimelech son of
Abiathar, and the heads of the priestly families
and of the Levite families, were all witnesses.

7-18This is the order in which the twenty-four family groups were given their assignments: 1) Jehoiarib; 2) Jedaiah; 3) Harim; 4) Seorim; 5) Malchijah; 6) Mijamin; 7) Hakkoz; 8) Abijah; 9) Jeshua; 10) Shecaniah; 11) Eliashib; 12) Jakim; 13) Huppah; 14) Jesheb-eab; 15) Bilgah; 16) Immer; 17) Hezir; 18) Happizzez; 19) Pethahiah; 20) Jehezkel; 21) Jachin; 22) Gamul; 23) Delaiah; 24) Maaziah.

19These men were registered according to
their assignments for going to the Temple
and performing the duties established by
their ancestor Aaron in obedience to the
commands of the LORD God of Israel.

The List of the Levites

20These are other heads of families
descended from Levi:

Jehdeiah, a descendant of Amram through
Shebuel;

21Isshiah, a descendant of Rehabiah;

22Jahath, a descendant of Izhar through
Shelomith;

23:26 Deut 10:8 **23:28–32** Num 3:5–9 **24:2** Lev 10:1, 2

23 Jeriah, Amariah, Jehaziel, and Jekameam,
sons of Hebron, in order of age;
24 Shamir, a descendant of Uzziel through
Micah;
25 Zechariah, a descendant of Uzziel
through Isshiah, Micah's brother;
26 Mahli, Mushi, and Jaaziah, descendants
of Merari. 27 Jaaziah had three sons: Shoham,
Zaccur, and Ibri. 28-29 Mahli had two sons,
Eleazar and Kish. Eleazar had no sons, but
Kish had one son, Jerahmeel. 30 Mushi had
three sons: Mahli, Eder, and Jeremoth.
These are the families of the Levites.
31 The head of each family and one of his
younger brothers drew lots for their assign-
ments, just as their relatives, the priests
descended from Aaron, had done. King
David, Zadok, Ahimelech, and the heads of
families of the priests and of the Levites
were witnesses.

The Temple Musicians

25 King David and the leaders of the
Levites chose the following Levite
clans to lead the worship services: Asaph,
Heman, and Jeduthun. They were to pro-
claim God's messages, accompanied by the
music of harps and cymbals. This is the list of
persons chosen to lead the worship, with the
type of service that each group performed:
2 The four sons of Asaph: Zaccur, Joseph,
Nethaniah, and Asharelah. They were under
the direction of Asaph, who proclaimed God's
messages whenever the king commanded.
3 The six sons of Jeduthun: Gedaliah, Zeri,
Jeshaiah, Shimei, Hashabiah, and Mattithiah.
Under the direction of their father they pro-
claimed God's message, accompanied by the
music of harps, and sang praise and thanks to
the LORD.
4 The fourteen sons of Heman: Bukkiah,
Mattaniah, Uzziel, Shebuel, Jerimoth, Hana-
niah, Hanani, Eliathah, Giddalti, Romamti
Ezer, Joshbekashah, Mallothi, Hothir, and
Mahazioth. 5 God gave to Heman, the king's
prophet, these fourteen sons and also three
daughters, as he had promised, in order to
give power to Heman. 6 All of his sons played
cymbals and harps under their father's direc-
tion, to accompany the Temple worship. And
Asaph, Jeduthun, and Heman were under
orders from the king.
7 All these twenty-four men were experts;
and their fellow Levites were trained musi-
cians. There were 288 men in all.
8 To determine the assignment of duties
they all drew lots, whether they were young
or old, experts or beginners.
9-31 These 288 men were divided accord-
ing to families into twenty-four groups of
twelve, with a leader in charge of each group.
This is the order in which they were on
duty: 1) Joseph of the family of Asaph; 2)
Gedaliah; 3) Zaccur; 4) Zeri; 5) Nethaniah; 6)
Bukkiah; 7) Asharelah; 8) Jeshaiah; 9) Matta-
niah; 10) Shimei; 11) Uzziel; 12) Hashabiah;
13) Shebuel; 14) Mattithiah; 15) Jerimoth;
16) Hananiah; 17) Joshbekashah; 18) Hanani;
19) Mallothi; 20) Eliathah; 21) Hothir; 22)
Giddalti; 23) Mahazioth; 24) Romamti Ezer.

The Temple Guards

26 These are the assignments of work
for the Levites who served as Temple
guards. From the clan of Korah there was
Meshelemiah son of Kore, of the family of
Asaph. 2 He had seven sons, listed in order of
age: Zechariah, Jediael, Zebadiah, Jathniel,
3 Elam, Jehohanan, and Eliehoenai.
4 There was also Obed Edom, whom God
blessed by giving him eight sons, listed in order
of age: Shemaiah, Jehozabad, Joah, Sachar,
Nethanel, 5 Ammiel, Issachar, and Peullethai.
6-7 Obed Edom's oldest son, Shemaiah, had
six sons: Othni, Rephael, Obed, Elzabad,
Elihu, and Semachiah. They were important
men in their clan because of their great abil-
ity; the last two were especially talented.
8 Obed Edom's family furnished a total of
sixty-two highly qualified men for this work.
9 Meshelemiah's family furnished eighteen
qualified men.
10 From the clan of Merari there was
Hosah, who had four sons: Shimri (his father
made him the leader, even though he was not
the oldest son), 11 Hilkiah, Tebaliah, and Zech-
ariah. In all there were thirteen members of
Hosah's family who were Temple guards.

26:4, 5 2 Sam 6:11; 1 Chr 13:14

12 The Temple guards were divided into
groups, according to families, and they were
assigned duties in the Temple, just as the
other Levites were. 13 Each family, regardless
of size, drew lots to see which gate it would
be responsible for. 14 Shelemiah drew the east
gate, and his son Zechariah, a man who
always gave good advice, drew the north
gate. 15 Obed Edom was allotted the south
gate, and his sons were allotted to guard the
storerooms. 16 Shuppim and Hosah were
allotted the west gate and the Shallecheth
Gate on the upper road. Guard duty was
divided into assigned periods, one after
another. 17 On the east, six guards were on
duty each day, on the north, four, and on the
south, four. Four guards were stationed at the
storerooms daily, two at each storeroom.
18 Near the western pavilion there were four
guards by the road and two at the pavilion
itself. 19 This is the assignment of guard duty
to the clan of Korah and the clan of Merari.

Other Temple Duties

20 Others of their fellow Levites[y] were in
charge of the Temple treasury and the store-
rooms for gifts dedicated to God. 21 Ladan,
one of the sons of Gershon, was the ancestor
of several family groups, including the family
of his son Jehiel. 22 Ladan's two other sons,
Zetham and Joel, had charge of the Temple
treasury and storerooms.

23 Duties were also assigned to the descen-
dants of Amram, Izhar, Hebron, and Uzziel.

24 Shebuel, of the clan of Moses' son Ger-
shom, was the chief official responsible for the
Temple treasury. 25 Through Gershom's broth-
er Eliezer he was related to Shelomith. Eliezer
was the father of Rehabiah, who was the
father of Jeshaiah, the father of Joram, the
father of Zichri, the father of Shelomith.
26 Shelomith and the members of his family
were in charge of all the gifts dedicated to
God by King David, the heads of families,
leaders of clan groups, and army officers.
27 They took some of the loot they captured
in battle and dedicated it for use in the Tem-
ple. 28 Shelomith and his family were in charge
of everything that had been dedicated for use
in the Temple, including the gifts brought by
the prophet Samuel, by King Saul, by Abner
son of Ner, and by Joab son of Zeruiah.

Duties of Other Levites

29 Among the descendants of Izhar,
Chenaniah and his sons were assigned
administrative duties: keeping records and
settling disputes for the people of Israel.

30 Among the descendants of Hebron,
Hashabiah and seventeen hundred of his rela-
tives, all outstanding men, were put in charge
of the administration of all religious and civil
matters in Israel west of the Jordan River.
31 Jeriah was the leader of the descendants of
Hebron. In the fortieth year that David was
king, an investigation was made of the family
line of Hebron's descendants, and outstanding
soldiers belonging to this family were found
living at Jazer in the territory of Gilead.
32 King David chose twenty-seven hundred
outstanding heads of families from Jeriah's
relatives and put them in charge of adminis-
tering all religious and civil matters in Israel
east of the Jordan River—the territories of
Reuben, Gad, and East Manasseh.

Military and Civil Organization

27 This is the list of the Israelite heads
of families and clan leaders and their
officials who administered the work of the
kingdom. Each month of the year a different
group of twenty-four thousand men was on
duty under the commander for that month.

2-15 The following were the commanders
for each month:

First month: Jashobeam son of Zabdiel
(he was a member of the clan of
Perez, a part of the tribe of Judah)
Second month: Dodai, a descendant of
Ahohi (Mikloth was his second in
command)[z]
Third month: Benaiah son of Jehoiada
the priest; he was the leader of "The
Thirty" (his son Ammizabad
succeeded him as commander of this
group)

[y] **26:20** *One ancient translation* fellow Levites; *Hebrew* Levites, Ahijah. [z] **27:2-15** *Probable text* Mikloth . . . command; *Hebrew unclear.*

Fourth month: Asahel, brother of Joab (his son Zebadiah succeeded him)
Fifth month: Shamhuth, a descendant of Izhar
Sixth month: Ira son of Ikkesh from Tekoa
Seventh month: Helez, an Ephraimite from Pelon
Eighth month: Sibbecai from Hushah (he was a member of the clan of Zerah, a part of the tribe of Judah)
Ninth month: Abiezer from Anathoth in the territory of the tribe of Benjamin
Tenth month: Maharai from Netophah (he was a member of the clan of Zerah)
Eleventh month: Benaiah from Pirathon in the territory of the tribe of Ephraim
Twelfth month: Heldai from Netophah (he was a descendant of Othniel)

Administration of the Tribes of Israel

16-22 This is the list of the administrators of the tribes of Israel:

Tribe	*Administrator*
Reuben	Eliezer son of Zichri
Simeon	Shephatiah son of Maacah
Levi	Hashabiah son of Kemuel
Aaron	Zadok
Judah	Elihu, one of King David's brothers
Issachar	Omri son of Michael
Zebulun	Ishmaiah son of Obadiah
Naphtali	Jeremoth son of Azriel
Ephraim	Hoshea son of Azaziah
West Manasseh	Joel son of Pedaiah
East Manasseh	Iddo son of Zechariah
Benjamin	Jaasiel son of Abner
Dan	Azarel son of Jeroham

23 King David did not take a census of the people who were under the age of twenty, because of the LORD's promise to make the people of Israel as numerous as the stars in the sky. 24 Joab, whose mother was Zeruiah, began to take a census, but he did not complete it. God punished Israel because of this census, so the final figures were never recorded in King David's official records.

Administrators of the Royal Property

25-31 This is the list of those who administered the royal property:

Royal storerooms: Azmaveth son of Adiel
Local storerooms: Jonathan son of Uzziah
Farm labor: Ezri son of Chelub
Vineyards: Shimei from Ramah
Wine cellars: Zabdi from Shepham
Olive and sycamore trees (in the western foothills): Baal Hanan from Geder
Olive oil storage: Joash
Cattle in the Plain of Sharon: Shitrai from Sharon
Cattle in the valleys: Shaphat son of Adlai
Camels: Obil, an Ishmaelite
Donkeys: Jehdeiah from Meronoth
Sheep and goats: Jaziz, a Hagrite

David's Personal Advisers

32 Jonathan, King David's uncle, was a skillful adviser and a scholar. He and Jehiel son of Hachmoni were in charge of the education of the king's sons. 33 Ahithophel was adviser to the king, and Hushai the Archite was the king's friend and counselor. 34 After Ahithophel died, Abiathar and Jehoiada son of Benaiah became advisers. Joab was commander of the royal army.

David's Instructions for the Temple

28 King David commanded all the officials of Israel to assemble in Jerusalem. So all the officials of the tribes, the officials who administered the work of the kingdom, the leaders of the clans, the supervisors of the property and livestock that belonged to the king and his sons—indeed all the palace officials, leading soldiers, and important men—gathered in Jerusalem.

2 David stood before them and addressed them: "My friends, listen to me. I wanted to build a permanent home for the Covenant

27:23 Gen 15:5; 22:17; 26:4 **27:24** 2 Sam 24:15; 1 Chr 21:1–14 **28:2–7** 2 Sam 7:1–16; 1 Chr 17:1–14

Box, the footstool of the LORD our God. I
have made preparations for building a temple
to honor him, 3but he has forbidden me to
do it, because I am a soldier and have shed
too much blood. 4The LORD, the God of
Israel, chose me and my descendants to rule
Israel forever. He chose the tribe of Judah to
provide leadership, and out of Judah he
chose my father's family. From all that family
it was his pleasure to take me and make me
king over all Israel. 5He gave me many sons,
and out of them all he chose Solomon to
rule over Israel, the LORD's kingdom.

6"The LORD said to me, 'Your son
Solomon is the one who will build my Tem-
ple. I have chosen him to be my son, and I
will be his father. 7I will make his kingdom
last forever if he continues to obey carefully
all my laws and commands as he does now.'

8"So now, my people, in the presence of
our God and of this assembly of all Israel, the
LORD's people, I charge you to obey carefully
everything that the LORD our God has com-
manded us, so that you may continue to pos-
sess this good land and so that you may hand
it on to succeeding generations forever."

9And to Solomon he said, "My son, I
charge you to acknowledge your father's
God and to serve him with an undivided
heart and a willing mind. He knows all our
thoughts and desires. If you go to him, he
will accept you; but if you turn away from
him, he will abandon you forever. 10You
must realize that the LORD has chosen you
to build his holy Temple. Now do it—and
do it with determination."

11David gave Solomon the plans for all
the Temple buildings, for the storerooms and
all the other rooms, and for the Most Holy
Place, where sins are forgiven. 12He also gave
him the plans for all he had in mind for the
courtyards and the rooms around them, and
for the storerooms for the Temple equipment
and the gifts dedicated to the LORD. 13David
also gave him the plans for organizing the
priests and Levites to perform their duties, to
do the work of the Temple, and to take care
of all the Temple utensils. 14He gave instruc-
tions as to how much silver and gold was to
be used for making the utensils, 15for each
lamp and lampstand, 16for the silver tables,
and for each gold table on which were
placed the loaves of bread offered to God.
17He also gave instructions as to how much
pure gold was to be used in making forks,
bowls, and jars, how much silver and gold in
making dishes, 18and how much pure gold
in making the altar on which incense was
burned and in making the chariot for the
winged creatures that spread their wings
over the LORD's Covenant Box. 19King
David said, "All this is contained in the plan
written according to the instructions which
the LORD himself gave me to carry out."

20King David said to his son Solomon,
"Be confident and determined. Start the
work and don't let anything stop you. The
LORD God, whom I serve, will be with you.
He will not abandon you, but he will stay
with you until you finish the work to be
done on his Temple. 21The priests and the
Levites have been assigned duties to perform
in the Temple. Workers with every kind of
skill are eager to help you, and all the people
and their leaders are at your command."

Gifts for Building the Temple

29 King David announced to the whole
assembly: "My son Solomon is the
one whom God has chosen, but he is still
young and lacks experience. The work to be
done is tremendous, because this is not a
palace for people but a temple for the LORD
God. 2I have made every effort to prepare
materials for the Temple—gold, silver,
bronze, iron, timber, precious stones and
gems, stones for mosaics, and quantities of
marble. 3Over and above all this that I have
provided, I have given silver and gold from
my personal property because of my love for
God's Temple. 4I have given 115 tons of the
finest gold and 265 tons of pure silver for
decorating the walls of the Temple 5and for
all the objects which the skilled workers are
to make. Now who else is willing to give a
generous offering to the LORD?"

6Then the heads of the clans, the officials
of the tribes, the commanders of the army,
and the administrators of the royal property

29:1, 2 1 Chr 22:5

"My son Solomon is the one." (29:1)

volunteered to give 7 the following for the
work on the Temple: 190 tons of gold, 380
tons of silver, 675 tons of bronze, and 3,750
tons of iron. 8 Those who had precious
stones gave them to the Temple treasury,
which was administered by Jehiel of the
Levite clan of Gershon. 9 The people had
given willingly to the LORD, and they were
happy that so much had been given. King
David also was extremely happy.

David Praises God

10 There in front of the whole assembly
King David praised the LORD. He said,
"LORD God of our ancestor Jacob, may you
be praised forever and ever! 11 You are great
and powerful, glorious, splendid, and majes-
tic. Everything in heaven and earth is yours,
and you are king, supreme ruler over all.
12 All riches and wealth come from you; you
rule everything by your strength and power;
and you are able to make anyone great and
strong. 13 Now, our God, we give you thanks,
and we praise your glorious name.
14 "Yet my people and I cannot really give
you anything, because everything is a gift
from you, and we have only given back what
is yours already. 15 You know, O LORD, that
we pass through life like exiles and strangers,
as our ancestors did. Our days are like a pass-
ing shadow, and we cannot escape death. 16 O
LORD, our God, we have brought together all
this wealth to build a temple to honor your
holy name, but it all came from you and all
belongs to you. 17 I know that you test every-
one's heart and are pleased with people of
integrity. In honesty and sincerity I have
willingly given all this to you, and I have seen
how your people who are gathered here have
been happy to bring offerings to you.
18 LORD God of our ancestors Abraham, Isaac,
and Jacob, keep such devotion forever strong
in your people's hearts and keep them always
faithful to you. 19 Give my son Solomon a
wholehearted desire to obey everything that
you command and to build the Temple for
which I have made these preparations."
20 Then David commanded the people,
"Praise the LORD your God!" And the whole
assembly praised the LORD, the God of their
ancestors, and they bowed low and gave
honor to the LORD and also to the king.
21 The following day they killed animals as
sacrifices, dedicating them to the LORD, and
then gave them to the people to eat. In addi-
tion, they sacrificed a thousand bulls, a thou-
sand rams, and a thousand lambs, which
they burned whole on the altar. They also
brought the offerings of wine. 22 So that day
they were very happy as they ate and drank
in the presence of the LORD.
For a second time they proclaimed
Solomon king. In the name of the LORD they
anointed him as their ruler and Zadok as
priest. 23 So Solomon succeeded his father
David on the throne which the LORD had
established. He was a successful king, and the
whole nation of Israel obeyed him. 24 All the
officials and soldiers, and even all of David's
other sons, promised to be loyal to Solomon
as king. 25 The LORD made the whole nation
stand in awe of Solomon, and he made him
more glorious than any other king that had
ruled Israel.

Summary of David's Reign

26 David son of Jesse ruled over all Israel
27 for forty years. He ruled in Hebron for seven
years and in Jerusalem for thirty-three. 28 He
died at a ripe old age, wealthy and respected,
and his son Solomon succeeded him as king.
29 The history of King David from beginning
to end is recorded in the records of the three
prophets, Samuel, Nathan, and Gad. 30 The
records tell how he ruled, how powerful he
was, and all the things that happened to him, to
Israel, and to the surrounding kingdoms.

29:11 Mt 6:13 **29:23** 1 Kings 2:12 **29:27** 2 Sam 5:4, 5; 1 Chr 3:4

THE SECOND BOOK OF Chronicles

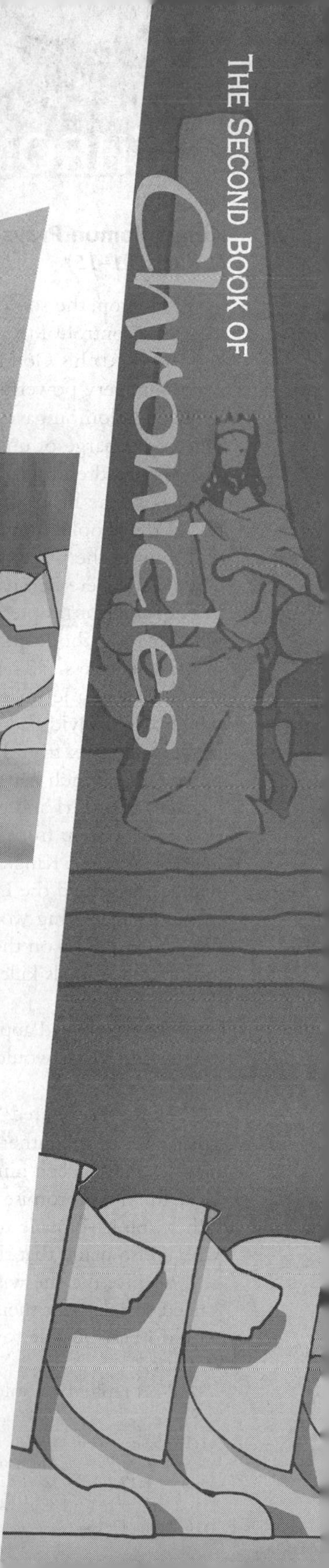

"That was a great movie, but I want to know what happens to the hero. I can't wait for part two! When do you think it'll come out?" When a movie ends and gives a hint that there is another part of the story, most likely a sequel is in the making. It's a good way for moviemakers to get people to come back again. If you just read First Chronicles, you don't have to wait another year to read the sequel. It is right here.

It was natural for the first book to end when David dies and Solomon takes over as king. Second Chronicles continues the history of the Israelite kings and how the kingdom is divided after Solomon's death. But, unlike Second Kings, Second Chronicles focuses on the history and kings of Judah, paying little attention to the northern kingdom of Israel.

Chap. 9:17–19

Headlines

- Work Starts on Temple Building (2:17—3:14)
- Dedication Marked by Fire from Sky (7:1–6)
- African Queen Visits Solomon (9:1–12)
- King Jehoshaphat Begins Reforms (17:1–9)
- King Hezekiah Rededicates Temple (29:18–36)
- Josiah Promises to Keep Covenant (34:29–33)
- Decree Calls for Jews to Return (36:22–23)

FACTOIDS

How does this book fit into the Bible? This book is a continuation of First Chronicles and records the history of Judah from King Solomon to the end of the Babylonian captivity.

Why was it written? It was written to remind the Israelites that God is always with them, even in exile, and to give them hope for the future.

Who are the young people in this book? Joash was seven, Uzziah was sixteen, Manasseh was twelve, Josiah was eight, and Jehoiachin was eighteen when they were named as kings of Judah.

Important themes

- The kings of Judah are measured by their faithfulness to God.
- Israelites must maintain proper worship in the Temple.
- God's faithful people will see Jerusalem and the Temple rebuilt.

2 CHRONICLES

King Solomon Prays for Wisdom
(1 Kings 3:1–15)

1 Solomon, the son of King David, took firm control of the kingdom of Israel, and the LORD his God blessed him and made him very powerful.

2 King Solomon gave an order to all the officers in charge of units of a thousand men and of a hundred men, all the government officials, all the heads of families, and all the rest of the people, 3 commanding them to go with him to the place of worship at Gibeon. They went there because that was where the Tent of the LORD's presence was located, which Moses, the LORD's servant, had made in the wilderness. (4 The Covenant Box, however, was in Jerusalem, kept in a tent which King David had set up when he brought the Box from Kiriath Jearim.) 5 The bronze altar which had been made by Bezalel, the son of Uri and grandson of Hur, was also in Gibeon in front of the Tent of the LORD's presence. King Solomon and all the people worshiped the LORD there. 6 In front of the Tent the king worshiped the LORD by offering sacrifices on the bronze altar; he had a thousand animals killed and burned whole on it.

7 That night God appeared to Solomon and asked, "What would you like me to give you?"

8 Solomon answered, "You always showed great love for my father David, and now you have let me succeed him as king. 9 O LORD God, fulfill the promise you made to my father. You have made me king over a people who are so many that they cannot be counted, 10 so give me the wisdom and knowledge I need to rule over them. Otherwise, how would I ever be able to rule this great people of yours?"

11 God replied to Solomon, "You have made the right choice. Instead of asking for wealth or treasure or fame or the death of your enemies or even for long life for yourself, you have asked for wisdom and knowledge so that you can rule my people, over whom I have made you king. 12 I will give you wisdom and knowledge. And in addition, I will give you more wealth, treasure, and fame than any king has ever had before or will ever have again."

King Solomon's Power and Wealth
(1 Kings 10:26–29)

13 So Solomon left[a] the place of worship at Gibeon, where the Tent of the LORD's presence was, and returned to Jerusalem. There he ruled over Israel. 14 He built up a force of fourteen hundred chariots and twelve thousand cavalry horses. Some of them he kept in Jerusalem, and the rest he stationed in various other cities. 15 During his reign silver and gold became as common in Jerusalem as stone, and cedar was as plentiful as ordinary sycamore in the foothills of Judah. 16 The king's agents controlled the export of horses from Musri[b] and Cilicia,[c] 17 and the export of chariots from Egypt. They supplied the Hittite and Syrian kings with horses and chariots, selling chariots for 600 pieces of silver each and horses for 150 each.[d]

Preparations for Building the Temple
(1 Kings 5:1–18)

2 King Solomon decided to build a temple where the LORD would be worshiped, and also to build a palace for himself. 2 He put 70,000 men to work transporting materials, and 80,000 to work cutting stone in the hill country. There were 3,600 others responsible for supervising the work.

3 Solomon sent a message to King Hiram

[a] **1:13** *Some ancient translations* left; *Hebrew* came to. [b] **1:16** *Probable text* Musri; *Hebrew* Egypt. [c] **1:16** MUSRI AND CILICIA: *Two ancient countries in what is now southeast Turkey which were centers of horse breeding in Solomon's time.* [d] **1:17** *Verses 16–17 in Hebrew are unclear.*

1:4 2 Sam 6:1–17; 1 Chr 13:5–14; 15:25—16:1 **1:5** Ex 38:1–7 **1:9** Gen 13:16; 28:14 **1:14** 1 Kings 4:26 **1:16** Deut 17:16

of Tyre: "Do business with me as you did
with my father, King David, when you sold
him cedar logs for building his palace. [4]I am
building a temple to honor the LORD my
God. It will be a holy place where my peo-
ple and I will worship him by burning
incense of fragrant spices, where we will
present offerings of sacred bread to him con-
tinuously, and where we will offer burnt
offerings every morning and evening, as well
as on Sabbaths, New Moon Festivals, and
other holy days honoring the LORD our
God. He has commanded Israel to do this
forever. [5]I intend to build a great temple,
because our God is greater than any other
god. [6]Yet no one can really build a temple
for God, because even all the vastness of
heaven cannot contain him. How then can I
build a temple that would be anything more
than a place to burn incense to God? [7]Now
send me a man with skill in engraving, in
working gold, silver, bronze, and iron, and in
making blue, purple, and red cloth. He will
work with the craftsmen of Judah and
Jerusalem whom my father David selected.
[8]I know how skillful your lumbermen are, so
send me cedar, cypress, and juniper logs from
Lebanon. I am ready to send my men to
assist yours [9]in preparing large quantities of
timber, because this temple I intend to build
will be large and magnificent. [10]As provi-
sions for your lumbermen, I will send you
100,000 bushels of wheat, 100,000 bushels
of barley, 110,000 gallons of wine, and
110,000 gallons of olive oil."

[11]King Hiram sent Solomon a letter in
reply. He wrote, "Because the LORD loves his
people, he has made you their king. [12]Praise
the LORD God of Israel, Creator of heaven
and earth! He has given King David a wise
son, full of understanding and skill, who now
plans to build a temple for the LORD and a
palace for himself. [13]I am sending you a wise
and skillful master metalworker named
Huram. [14]His mother was a member of the
tribe of Dan and his father was a native of
Tyre. He knows how to make things out of
gold, silver, bronze, iron, stone, and wood.
He can work with blue, purple, and red
cloth, and with linen. He can do all sorts of
engraving and can follow any design sug-
gested to him. Let him work with your
skilled workers and with those who worked
for your father, King David. [15]So now send
us the wheat, barley, wine, and olive oil that
you promised. [16]In the mountains of Leb-
anon we will cut down all the cedars you
need, tie them together in rafts, and float
them by sea as far as Joppa. From there you
can take them to Jerusalem."

Construction of the Temple Begins
(1 Kings 6:1–38)

[17]King Solomon took a census of all the
foreigners living in the land of Israel, similar
to the census his father David had taken.
There were 153,600 resident foreigners.
[18]He assigned 70,000 of them to transport
materials and 80,000 to cut stones in the
mountains, and appointed 3,600 supervisors
to make sure the work was done.

3 King David, Solomon's father, had
already prepared a place for the Temple.
It was in Jerusalem, on Mount Moriah,
where the LORD appeared to David, at the
place which Araunah the Jebusite had used
as a threshing place. King Solomon began
the construction [2]in the second month of
the fourth year that he was king. [3]The Tem-
ple which King Solomon built was 90 feet
long and 30 feet wide. [4]The entrance room
was the full width of the Temple, 30 feet, and
was 180 feet high. The inside of the room
was overlaid with pure gold. [5]The main
room was paneled with cedar and overlaid
with fine gold, in which were worked
designs of palm trees and chain patterns.
[6]The king decorated the Temple with beau-
tiful precious stones and with gold imported
from the land of Parvaim. [7]He used the gold
to overlay the Temple walls, the rafters, the
entryways, and the doors. On the walls the
workers carved designs of winged creatures.[e]
[8]The inner room, called the Most Holy
Place, was 30 feet long and 30 feet wide,
which was the full width of the Temple.
Twenty-five tons of gold were used to cover

[e] **3:7** WINGED CREATURES: *See Word List.*

2:6 1 Kings 8:27; 2 Chr 6:18 **3:1** Gen 22:22 **3:8** Ex 26:33, 34 the walls of the Most Holy Place; 9 twenty ounces of gold were used for making nails, and the walls of the upper rooms were also covered with gold.

10 The king also had his workers make two winged creatures out of metal, cover them with gold, and place them in the Most Holy Place, 11-13 where they stood side by side facing the entrance. Each had two wings, each wing 7½ feet long, which were spread out so that they touched each other in the center of the room and reached to the wall on either side of the room, stretching across the full width of 30 feet. 14 A curtain for the Most Holy Place was made of linen and of other material, which was dyed blue, purple, and red, with designs of the winged creatures worked into it.

The Two Bronze Columns
(1 Kings 7:15–22)

15 The king had two columns made, each one 52 feet tall, and placed them in front of the Temple. Each one had a capital 7½ feet tall. 16 The tops of the columns were decorated with a design of interwoven chains and one hundred bronze pomegranates.[f] 17 The columns were set at the sides of the Temple entrance: the one on the south side was named Jachin[g] and the one on the north side was named Boaz.[h]

Equipment for the Temple
(1 Kings 7:23–51)

4 King Solomon had a bronze altar made, which was 30 feet square and 15 feet high. 2 He also made a round tank of bronze, 7½ feet deep, 15 feet in diameter, and 45 feet in circumference. 3 All around the outer edge of the rim of the tank[i] were two rows of decorations, one above the other. The decorations were in the shape of bulls, which had been cast all in one piece with the rest of the tank. 4 The tank rested on the backs of twelve bronze bulls that faced outward, three facing in each direction. 5 The sides of the tank were 3 inches thick. Its rim was like the rim of a cup, curving outward like the petals of a flower. The tank held about 15,000 gallons. 6 They also made ten basins, five to be placed on the south side of the Temple and five on the north side. They were to be used to rinse the parts of the animals that were burned as sacrifices. The water in the large tank was for the priests to use for washing.

7-8 They made ten gold lampstands according to the usual pattern, and ten tables, and placed them in the main room of the Temple, five lampstands and five tables on each side. They also made a hundred gold bowls.

9 They made an inner courtyard for the priests, and also an outer courtyard. The doors in the gates between the courtyards were covered with bronze. 10 The tank was placed near the southeast corner of the Temple.

11-16 Huram also made pots, shovels, and bowls. He completed all the objects that he had promised King Solomon he would make for the Temple:

- The two columns
- The two bowl-shaped capitals on top of the columns
- The design of interwoven chains on each capital
- The 400 bronze pomegranates arranged in two rows around the design of each capital
- The ten[j] carts
- The ten basins
- The tank
- The twelve bulls supporting the tank
- The pots, shovels, and forks

Huram the master metalworker made all these objects[k] out of polished bronze, as King Solomon had commanded, for use in the Temple of the LORD.

17 The king had them all made in the foundry between Sukkoth and Zeredah[l] in the Jordan Valley. 18 So many objects were

[f] **3:16** *Verse 16 in Hebrew is unclear.* [g] **3:17** JACHIN: *This name sounds like the Hebrew for "he (God) establishes."* [h] **3:17** BOAZ: *This name sounds like the Hebrew for "by his (God's) strength."* [i] **4:3** *Probable text* All around . . . tank; *Hebrew unclear.* [j] **4:11–16** *Probable text (see 1 Kings 7:40–45)* ten; *Hebrew* he made. [k] **4:11–16** *One ancient translation* all these objects; *Hebrew* all their objects. [l] **4:17** ZEREDAH: *(see Zarethan 1 Kings 7:46).*

3:10–13 Ex 25:18–20 **3:14** Ex 26:31 **4:1** Ex 27:1, 2 **4:6** Ex 30:17–21 **4:7** Ex 25:31–40 **4:8** Ex 25:23–30

made that no one determined the total
weight of the bronze used.
19King Solomon also had gold furnishings
made for the Temple: the altar and the tables
for the bread offered to God; 20the lamp-
stands and the lamps of fine gold that were
to burn in front of the Most Holy Place,
according to plan; 21the flower decorations,
the lamps, and the tongs; 22the lamp snuffers,
the bowls, the dishes for incense, and the
pans used for carrying live coals. All these
objects were made of pure gold. The outer
doors of the Temple and the doors to the
Most Holy Place were overlaid with gold.

5 When King Solomon finished all the
work on the Temple, he placed in the
Temple storerooms all the things that his
father David had dedicated to the LORD—
the silver, gold, and other articles.

The Covenant Box Is Brought to the Temple

(1 Kings 8:1–9)

2Then King Solomon summoned all the
leaders of the tribes and clans of Israel to
assemble in Jerusalem, in order to take the
LORD's Covenant Box from Zion, David's
City,[m] to the Temple. 3They all assembled at
the time of the Festival of Shelters. 4When
all the leaders had gathered, then the Levites
lifted the Covenant Box 5and carried it to
the Temple. The priests and the Levites also
moved the Tent of the LORD's presence and
all its equipment to the Temple. 6King
Solomon and all the people of Israel assem-
bled in front of the Covenant Box and sacri-
ficed a large number of sheep and cattle—
too many to count. 7Then the priests carried
the Covenant Box of the LORD into the
Temple and put it in the Most Holy Place,
beneath the winged creatures. 8Their out-
stretched wings covered the Box and the
poles it was carried by. 9The ends of the
poles could be seen by anyone standing
directly in front of the Most Holy Place, but
from nowhere else. (The poles are still there
today.) 10There was nothing inside the
Covenant Box except the two stone tablets
which Moses had placed there at Mount
Sinai, when the LORD made a covenant with
the people of Israel as they were coming
from Egypt.

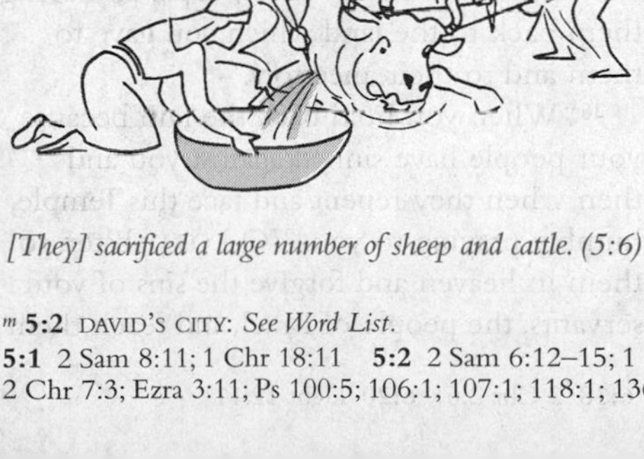

[They] sacrificed a large number of sheep and cattle. (5:6)

The Glory of the LORD

11-14All the priests present, regardless of
the group to which they belonged, had con-
secrated themselves. And all the Levite
musicians—Asaph, Heman, and Jeduthun,
and the members of their clans—were
wearing linen clothing. The Levites stood
near the east side of the altar with cymbals
and harps, and with them were 120 priests
playing trumpets. The singers were accom-
panied in perfect harmony by trumpets,
cymbals, and other instruments, as they
praised the LORD singing:

"Praise the LORD, because he is good,
And his love is eternal."

As the priests were leaving the Temple, it
was suddenly filled with a cloud shining
with the dazzling light of the LORD's pres-
ence, and they could not continue the ser-
vice of worship.

Solomon's Address to the People

(1 Kings 8:12–21)

6 Then King Solomon prayed,
"LORD, you have chosen to live in
clouds and darkness.
2Now I have built a majestic temple for
you,
a place for you to live in forever."
3All the people of Israel were standing
there. The king turned to face them and

[m] **5:2** DAVID'S CITY: *See Word List.*

5:1 2 Sam 8:11; 1 Chr 18:11 **5:2** 2 Sam 6:12–15; 1 Chr 15:25–28 **5:10** Deut 10:5 **5:13** 1 Chr 16:34; 2 Chr 7:3; Ezra 3:11; Ps 100:5; 106:1; 107:1; 118:1; 136:1; Jer 33:11 **5:13, 14** Ex 40:34, 35

asked God's blessing on them. 4He said,
"Praise the LORD God of Israel! He has kept
the promise he made to my father David
when he said to him, 5'From the time I
brought my people out of Egypt until now, I
did not choose any city in the land of Israel
as the place to build a temple where I would
be worshiped, and I did not choose anyone
to lead my people Israel. 6But now I have
chosen Jerusalem as the place where I will
be worshiped, and you, David, to rule my
people.' "

7And Solomon continued, "My father
David planned to build a temple for the
worship of the LORD God of Israel, 8but the
LORD said to him, 'You were right in want-
ing to build a temple for me, 9but you will
never build it. It is your son, your own son,
who will build my temple.'

10"Now the LORD has kept his promise: I
have succeeded my father as king of Israel,
and I have built a temple for the worship of
the LORD God of Israel. 11I have placed in
the Temple the Covenant Box, which con-
tains the stone tablets of the covenant which
the LORD made with the people of Israel."

Solomon's Prayer
(1 Kings 8:22–53)

12Then in the presence of the people
Solomon went and stood in front of the altar
and raised his arms in prayer. (13Solomon
had made a bronze platform and put it in
the middle of the courtyard. It was eight feet
square and five feet high. He mounted this

Solomon . . . raised his arms in prayer. (6:12)

platform, knelt down where everyone could
see him, and raised his hands toward heav-
en.) 14He prayed, "LORD God of Israel, in all
heaven and earth there is no god like you.
You keep your covenant with your people
and show them your love when they live in
wholehearted obedience to you. 15You have
kept the promise you made to my father
David; today every word has been fulfilled.
16Now, LORD God of Israel, keep the other
promise you made to my father when you
told him that there would always be one of
his descendants ruling as king of Israel, pro-
vided that they carefully obeyed your Law
just as he did. 17So now, LORD God of Israel,
let everything come true that you promised
to your servant David.

18"But can you, O God, really live on
earth among men and women? Not even all
of heaven is large enough to hold you, so
how can this Temple that I have built be large
enough? 19LORD my God, I am your servant.
Listen to my prayer and grant the requests I
make to you. 20Watch over this Temple day
and night. You have promised that this is
where you will be worshiped, so hear me
when I face this Temple and pray. 21Hear my
prayers and the prayers of your people Israel
when they face this place and pray. In your
home in heaven hear us and forgive us.

22"When people are accused of wronging
others and are brought to your altar in this
Temple to take an oath that they are inno-
cent, 23O LORD, listen in heaven and judge
your servants. Punish the guilty ones as they
deserve and acquit the innocent.

24"When your people Israel are defeated
by their enemies because they have sinned
against you and then when they turn to you
and come to this Temple, humbly praying to
you for forgiveness, 25listen to them in heav-
en. Forgive the sins of your people and bring
them back to the land which you gave to
them and to their ancestors.

26"When you hold back the rain because
your people have sinned against you and
then when they repent and face this Temple,
humbly praying to you, 27O LORD, listen to
them in heaven and forgive the sins of your
servants, the people of Israel, and teach them

6:4–9 2 Sam 7:1–13; 1 Chr 17:1–12 **6:16** 1 Kings 2:4 **6:18** 2 Chr 2:6 **6:20** Deut 12:11

to do what is right. Then, O LORD, send rain
on this land of yours, which you gave to
your people as a permanent possession.
28 "When there is famine in the land or an
epidemic or the crops are destroyed by
scorching winds or swarms of locusts, or
when your people are attacked by their ene-
mies, or when there is disease or sickness
among them, 29 listen to their prayers. If any
of your people Israel, out of heartfelt sorrow,
stretch out their hands in prayer toward this
Temple, 30 hear their prayer. Listen to them
in your home in heaven and forgive them.
You alone know the thoughts of the human
heart. Deal with each of us as we deserve,
31 so that your people may honor you and
obey you all the time they live in the land
which you gave to our ancestors.
32 "When foreigners who live in a distant
land hear how great and powerful you are
and how you are always ready to act, and
then they come to pray at this Temple, 33 lis-
ten to their prayers. In heaven, where you
live, hear them and do what they ask you to
do, so that all the peoples of the world may
know you and obey you, as your people
Israel do. Then they will know that this Tem-
ple I have built is where you are to be wor-
shiped.
34 "When you command your people to
go into battle against their enemies and they
pray to you, wherever they are, facing this
city which you have chosen and this Temple
which I have built for you, 35 listen to their
prayers. Hear them in heaven and give them
victory.
36 "When your people sin against you—and
there is no one who does not sin—and in
your anger you let their enemies defeat them
and take them as prisoners to some other
land, even if that land is far away, 37 listen to
your people's prayers. If there in that land
they repent and pray to you, confessing how
sinful and wicked they have been, hear their
prayers, O LORD. 38 If in that land they truly
and sincerely repent and pray to you as they
face toward this land which you gave to our
ancestors, this city which you have chosen,
and this Temple which I have built for you,
39 then listen to their prayers. In your home in
heaven hear them and be merciful to them
and forgive all the sins of your people.
40 "Now, O my God, look on us and listen
to the prayers offered in this place. 41 Rise up
now, LORD God, and with the Covenant
Box, the symbol of your power, enter the
Temple and stay here forever. Bless your
priests in all they do, and may all your peo-
ple be happy because of your goodness to
them. 42 LORD God, do not reject the king
you have chosen. Remember the love you
had for your servant David."[n]

The Dedication of the Temple
(1 Kings 8:62–66)

7 When King Solomon finished his prayer,
fire came down from heaven and burned
up the sacrifices that had been offered, and
the dazzling light of the LORD's presence
filled the Temple. 2 Because the Temple was
full of the dazzling light, the priests could not
enter it. 3 When the people of Israel saw the
fire fall from heaven and the light fill the
Temple, they fell face downward on the
pavement, worshiping God and praising him
for his goodness and his eternal love. 4 Then
Solomon and all the people offered sacrifices
to the LORD. 5 He sacrificed 22,000 head of
cattle and 120,000 sheep as fellowship offer-
ings. And so he and all the people dedicated
the Temple. 6 The priests stood in the places
that were assigned to them, and facing them
stood the Levites, praising the LORD with the
musical instruments that King David had
provided and singing the hymn, "His Love Is
Eternal!" as they had been commissioned by
David. The priests blew trumpets while all
the people stood.
7 Solomon consecrated the central part of
the courtyard, the area in front of the Tem-
ple, and then offered there the sacrifices
burned whole, the grain offerings, and the
fat from the fellowship offerings. He did this
because the bronze altar which he had made
was too small for all these offerings.
8 Solomon and all the people of Israel cele-
brated the Festival of Shelters for seven days.

[n] **6:42** the love you . . . David; *or* your servant David's loyal service.

6:41–42 Ps 132:8–10 **7:1** Lev 9:23–24 **7:3** 1 Chr 16:34; 2 Chr 5:11–14; Ezra 3:11; Ps 100:5; 106:1; 107:1; 118:1; 136:1; Jer 33:11

There was a huge crowd of people from as far
away as Hamath Pass in the north and the
Egyptian border in the south. 9They had
spent seven days for the dedication of the altar
and then seven more days for the festival. On
the last day they had a closing celebration,
10and on the following day, the twenty-third
day of the seventh month, Solomon sent the
people home. They were happy about all the
blessings that the LORD had given to his peo-
ple Israel, to David, and to Solomon.

God Appears to Solomon Again
(1 Kings 9:1–9)

11After King Solomon had finished the
Temple and the palace, successfully complet-
ing all his plans for them, 12the LORD
appeared to him at night. He said to him,
"I have heard your prayer, and I accept this
Temple as the place where sacrifices are to be
offered to me. 13Whenever I hold back the
rain or send locusts to eat up the crops or
send an epidemic on my people, 14if they
pray to me and repent and turn away from
the evil they have been doing, then I will
hear them in heaven, forgive their sins, and
make their land prosperous again. 15I will
watch over this Temple and be ready to hear
all the prayers that are offered here, 16because
I have chosen it and consecrated it as the
place where I will be worshiped forever. I
will watch over it and protect it for all time.
17If you serve me faithfully as your father
David did, obeying my laws and doing every-
thing I have commanded you, 18I will keep
the promise I made to your father David
when I told him that Israel would always be
ruled by his descendants. 19But if you and
your people ever disobey the laws and com-
mands I have given you and worship other
gods, 20then I will remove you from the land
that I gave you, and I will abandon this Tem-
ple that I have consecrated as the place where
I am to be worshiped. People everywhere
will ridicule it and treat it with contempt.

21"The Temple is now greatly honored, but
then everyone who passes by it will be amazed
and will ask, 'Why did the LORD do this to
this land and this Temple?' 22People will
answer, 'It is because they abandoned the
LORD their God, who brought their ancestors
out of Egypt. They gave their allegiance to
other gods and worshiped them. That is why
the LORD has brought this disaster on them.' "

Solomon's Achievements
(1 Kings 9:10–28)

8 It took Solomon twenty years to build
the Temple and his palace. 2He also
rebuilt the cities that King Hiram had given
him, and sent Israelites to settle in them. 3He
captured the territory of Hamath and Zobah
4and fortified the city of Palmyra in the
desert. He rebuilt all the cities in Hamath that
were centers for storing supplies. 5Solomon
also rebuilt the following cities: Upper Beth
Horon and Lower Beth Horon (fortified
cities with gates that could be barred), 6the
city of Baalath, all the cities where he stored
supplies, and the cities where his horses and
chariots were stationed. He carried out all his
plans for building in Jerusalem, in Lebanon,
and throughout the territory that he ruled
over. 7-8Solomon employed at forced labor all
the descendants of the people of Canaan
whom the Israelites had not killed when they
took possession of the land. These included
Hittites, Amorites, Perizzites, Hivites, and
Jebusites, whose descendants continue to be
slaves down to the present time. 9Israelites
were not used at forced labor, but served as
soldiers, officers, chariot commanders, and
cavalry troops. 10There were 250 officials in
charge of the forced labor working on the
various building projects.

11Solomon moved his wife, the daughter
of the king of Egypt, from David's City to a
house he built for her. He said, "She must
not live in the palace of King David of
Israel, because any place where the Covenant
Box has been is holy."

12Solomon offered sacrifices to the LORD
on the altar which he had built in front of the
Temple. 13He offered burnt offerings accord-
ing to the requirements of the Law of Moses
for each holy day: Sabbaths, New Moon Fes-
tivals, and the three annual festivals—the Fes-
tival of Unleavened Bread, the Harvest Festi-

7:18 1 Kings 2:4 **8:13** **a** Num 28:9, 10; **b** Num 28:11–15; **c** Ex 23:14–17; 34:22, 23; Num 28:16—29:39; Deut 16:16

val, and the Festival of Shelters. 14Following
the rules laid down by his father David, he
organized the daily work of the priests and of
the Levites who assisted the priests in singing
hymns and in doing their work. He also
organized the Temple guards in sections for
performing their daily duties at each gate, in
accordance with the commands of David, the
man of God. 15The instructions which David
had given the priests and the Levites con-
cerning the storehouses and other matters
were carried out in detail.

16By this time all of Solomon's projects
had been completed. From the laying of the
foundation of the LORD's Temple to its com-
pletion, all the work had been successful.

17Then Solomon went to Eziongeber and
Elath, ports on the shore of the Gulf of
Aqaba, in the land of Edom. 18King Hiram
sent him ships under the command of his
own officers and with experienced sailors.
They sailed with Solomon's officers to the
land of Ophir and brought back to Solomon
about sixteen tons of gold.

The Visit of the Queen of Sheba
(1 Kings 10:1–13)

9 The queen of Sheba heard of King
Solomon's fame, and she traveled to
Jerusalem to test him with difficult ques-
tions. She brought with her a large group of
attendants, as well as camels loaded with
spices, jewels, and a large amount of gold.
When she and Solomon met, she asked him
all the questions that she could think of. 2He
answered them all; there was nothing too
difficult for him to explain. 3The queen of
Sheba heard Solomon's wisdom and saw the
palace he had built. 4She saw the food that
was served at his table, the living quarters for
his officials, the organization of his palace
staff and the uniforms they wore, the cloth-
ing of the servants who waited on him at
feasts, and the sacrifices he offered[o] in the
Temple. It left her breathless and amazed.

5She said to the king, "What I heard in
my own country about you[p] and your wis-
dom is true! 6I did not believe what they
told me until I came and saw for myself. I
had not heard of even half your wisdom. You
are even wiser than people say. 7How fortu-
nate are those who serve you, who are
always in your presence and are privileged to
hear your wise sayings! 8Praise the LORD
your God! He has shown how pleased he is
with you by making you king, to rule in his
name. Because he loves his people Israel and
wants to preserve them forever, he has made
you their king so that you can maintain law
and justice."

9She presented to King Solomon the gifts
she had brought: almost five tons of gold and
a very large amount of spices and jewels.
There have never been any other spices as
fine as those that the queen of Sheba gave to
King Solomon.

(10The sailors of King Hiram and of King
Solomon who brought gold from Ophir also
brought juniper wood and jewels. 11Solo-
mon used the wood to make stairs for the
Temple and for his palace, and to make harps
and lyres for the musicians. Nothing like that
had ever been seen before in the land of
Judah.)

12King Solomon gave the queen of Sheba
everything she asked for. This was in addition
to what he gave her in exchange for the

"I had not heard of even half your wisdom." (9:6)

[o] **9:4** *Probable text (see 1 Kings 10:5)* sacrifices he offered; *Hebrew* his upper rooms. [p] **9:5** you; *or* your deeds.
9:1–9 Mt 12:42; Lk 11:31

gifts[q] she brought to him. Then she and her
attendants returned to the land of Sheba.

King Solomon's Wealth
(1 Kings 10:14–25)

13 Every year King Solomon received over
twenty-five tons of gold, 14 in addition to the
taxes paid by the traders and merchants. The
kings of Arabia and the governors of the
Israelite districts also brought him silver and
gold. 15 Solomon made two hundred large
shields, each of which was covered with
about fifteen pounds of beaten gold, 16 and
three hundred smaller shields, each covered
with about eight pounds of beaten gold. He
had them all placed in the Hall of the Forest
of Lebanon.[r]
17 The king also had a large throne made.
Part of it was covered with ivory and the
rest of it was covered with pure gold. 18 Six
steps led up to the throne, and there was a
footstool attached to it, covered with gold.
There were arms on each side of the throne,
and the figure of a lion stood at each side.
19 Twelve figures of lions were on the steps,
one at either end of each step. No throne
like this had ever existed in any other king-
dom.
20 All of King Solomon's drinking cups
were made of gold, and all the utensils in the
Hall of the Forest of Lebanon were of pure
gold. Silver was not considered valuable in
Solomon's day. 21 He had a fleet of ocean-
going ships sailing with King Hiram's fleet.
Every three years his fleet would return,
bringing gold, silver, ivory, apes, and monkeys.
22 King Solomon was richer and wiser
than any other king in the world. 23 They all
consulted him, to hear the wisdom that God
had given him. 24 Each of them brought
Solomon gifts—articles of silver and gold,
robes, weapons, spices, horses, and mules.
This continued year after year.
25 King Solomon also had four thousand
stalls for his chariots and horses, and had
twelve thousand cavalry horses. Some of
them he kept in Jerusalem and the rest he
stationed in various other cities. 26 He was
supreme ruler of all the kings in the territo-
ry from the Euphrates River to Philistia and
the Egyptian border. 27 During his reign sil-
ver was as common in Jerusalem as stone,
and cedar was as plentiful as ordinary syca-
more in the foothills of Judah. 28 Solomon
imported horses from Musri[s] and from every
other country.

Summary of Solomon's Reign
(1 Kings 11:41–43)

29 The rest of the history of Solomon from
beginning to end is recorded in *The History
of Nathan the Prophet,* in *The Prophecy of Ahi-
jah of Shiloh,* and in *The Visions of Iddo the
Prophet,* which also deal with the reign of
King Jeroboam of Israel. 30 Solomon ruled in
Jerusalem over all Israel for forty years. 31 He
died and was buried in David's City, and his
son Rehoboam succeeded him as king.

The Northern Tribes Revolt
(1 Kings 12:1–20)

10 Rehoboam went to Shechem, where
all the people of northern Israel had
gathered to make him king. 2 When Jeroboam
son of Nebat, who had gone to Egypt to
escape from King Solomon, heard this news,
he returned home. 3 The people of the north-
ern tribes sent for him, and they all went
together to Rehoboam and said to him,
4 "Your father placed heavy burdens on us. If
you make these burdens lighter and make life
easier for us, we will be your loyal subjects."
5 Rehoboam replied, "Give me three days
to consider the matter. Then come back." So
the people left.
6 King Rehoboam consulted the older
men who had served as his father Solomon's
advisers. "What answer do you advise me to
give these people?" he asked.
7 They replied, "If you are kind to these
people and try to please them by giving a
considerate answer, they will always serve
you loyally."

[q] **9:12** *Probable text* he gave her in exchange for the gifts; *Hebrew unclear.* [r] **9:16** HALL OF THE FOREST OF LEBANON: *A large ceremonial hall in the palace, probably so called because it was paneled in cedar.* [s] **9:28** *Probable text (see 1:16)* Musri; *Hebrew* Egypt.

9:25 1 Kings 4:26 **9:26** Gen 15:18; 1 Kings 4:21 **9:28** Deut 17:16

[8]But he ignored the advice of the older men and went instead to the young men who had grown up with him and who were now his advisers. [9]"What do you advise me to do?" he asked. "What shall I say to the people who are asking me to make their burdens lighter?"

[10]They replied, "This is what you should tell them: 'My little finger is thicker than my father's waist.' [11]Tell them, 'My father placed heavy burdens on you; I will make them even heavier. He beat you with whips; I'll flog you with bullwhips!' "

[12]Three days later Jeroboam and all the people returned to King Rehoboam, as he had instructed them. [13]The king ignored the advice of the older men and spoke harshly to the people, [14]as the younger men had advised. He said, "My father placed heavy burdens on you; I will make them even heavier. He beat you with whips; I'll flog you with bullwhips!" [15]It was the will of the LORD God to bring about what he had spoken to Jeroboam son of Nebat through the prophet Ahijah from Shiloh. This is why the king did not pay any attention to the people.

[16]When the people saw that the king would not listen to them, they shouted, "Down with David and his family! What have they ever done for us? People of Israel, let's go home! Let Rehoboam look out for himself!"

So the people of Israel rebelled, [17]leaving Rehoboam as king only of the people who lived in the territory of Judah.

[18]Then King Rehoboam sent Adoniram, who was in charge of the forced labor, to go to the Israelites, but they stoned him to death. At this, Rehoboam hurriedly got in his chariot and escaped to Jerusalem. [19]Ever since that time the people of the northern kingdom of Israel have been in rebellion against the dynasty of David.

Shemaiah's Prophecy

(1 Kings 12:21–24)

11 When King Rehoboam arrived in Jerusalem, he called together 180,000 of the best soldiers from the tribes of Benjamin and Judah. He intended to go to war and restore his control over the northern tribes of Israel. [2]But the LORD told the prophet Shemaiah [3]to give this message to King Rehoboam and to all the people of the tribes of Judah and Benjamin: [4]"Do not attack your own relatives. Go home, all of you. What has happened is my will." They obeyed the LORD's command and did not go to fight Jeroboam.

Rehoboam Fortifies the Cities

[5]Rehoboam remained in Jerusalem and had fortifications built for the following cities of Judah and Benjamin: [6]Bethlehem, Etam, Tekoa, [7]Bethzur, Soco, Adullam, [8]Gath, Mareshah, Ziph, [9]Adoraim, Lachish, Azekah, [10]Zorah, Aijalon, and Hebron. [11]He had them strongly fortified and appointed a commander for each of them, and in each one he placed supplies of food, olive oil, and wine, [12]and also shields and spears. In this way he kept Judah and Benjamin under his control.

Priests and Levites Come to Judah

[13]From all the territory of Israel priests and Levites came south to Judah. [14]The Levites abandoned their pastures and other land and moved to Judah and Jerusalem, because King Jeroboam of Israel and his successors would not let them serve as priests of the LORD. [15]Jeroboam appointed priests of his own to serve at the pagan places of worship and to worship demons and the idols he made in the form of bull-calves. [16]From all the tribes of Israel people who sincerely wanted to worship the LORD, the God of Israel, followed the Levites to Jerusalem, so that they could offer sacrifices to the LORD, the God of their ancestors. [17]This strengthened the kingdom of Judah, and for three years they supported Rehoboam son of Solomon and lived as they had under the rule of King David and King Solomon.

10:16 2 Sam 20:1 **11:15** 1 Kings 12:31

Rehoboam's Family

[18]Rehoboam married Mahalath, whose father was Jerimoth son of David and whose mother was Abihail, the daughter of Eliab and granddaughter of Jesse. [19]They had three sons, Jeush, Shemariah, and Zaham. [20]Later he married Maacah, the daughter of Absalom, and they had four sons: Abijah, Attai, Ziza, and Shelomith. [21]In all, Rehoboam had eighteen wives and sixty concubines, and he fathered twenty-eight sons and sixty daughters. Of all his wives and concubines he loved Maacah best, [22]and he favored her son Abijah over all his other children, choosing him as the one to succeed him as king. [23]Rehoboam wisely assigned responsibilities to his sons and stationed them throughout Judah and Benjamin in the fortified cities. He provided generously for them and also secured many wives for them.

An Egyptian Invasion of Judah
(1 Kings 14:25–28)

12 As soon as Rehoboam had established his authority as king, he and all his people abandoned the Law of the LORD. [2]In the fifth year of Rehoboam's reign their disloyalty to the LORD was punished. King Shishak of Egypt attacked Jerusalem [3]with an army of twelve hundred chariots, sixty thousand cavalry, and more soldiers than could be counted, including Libyan, Sukkite, and Ethiopian[t] troops. [4]He captured the fortified cities of Judah and advanced as far as Jerusalem.

[5]Shemaiah the prophet went to King Rehoboam and the Judean leaders who had gathered in Jerusalem to escape Shishak. He said to them, "This is the LORD's message to you: 'You have abandoned me, so now I have abandoned you to Shishak.' "

[6]The king and the leaders admitted that they had sinned, and they said, "What the LORD is doing is just."

[7]When the LORD saw this, he spoke again to Shemaiah and said to him, "Because they admit their sin, I will not destroy them. But when Shishak attacks, they will barely survive. Jerusalem will not feel the full force of my anger, [8]but Shishak will conquer them, and they will learn the difference between serving me and serving earthly rulers."

[9]King Shishak came to Jerusalem and took the treasures from the Temple and from the palace. He took everything, including the gold shields that King Solomon had made. [10]To replace them, Rehoboam made bronze shields and entrusted them to the officers responsible for guarding the palace gates. [11]Every time the king went to the Temple, the guards carried the shields and then returned them to the guardroom. [12]Because he submitted to the LORD, the LORD's anger did not completely destroy him, and things went well for Judah.

Summary of Rehoboam's Reign

[13]Rehoboam ruled in Jerusalem and increased his power as king. He was forty-one years old when he became king, and he ruled for seventeen years in Jerusalem, the city which the LORD had chosen from all the territory of Israel as the place where he was to be worshiped. Rehoboam's mother was Naamah, from the land of Ammon. [14]He did what was evil, because he did not try to find the LORD's will.

[15]Rehoboam's acts from beginning to end and his family records are found in *The History of Shemaiah the Prophet* and *The History of Iddo the Prophet*. Rehoboam and Jeroboam were constantly at war with each other. [16]Rehoboam died and was buried in the royal tombs in David's City and his son Abijah succeeded him as king.

Abijah's War with Jeroboam
(1 Kings 15:1–8)

13 In the eighteenth year of the reign of King Jeroboam of Israel, Abijah became king of Judah, [2]and he ruled three

[t] **12:3** *Hebrew* Cushite(s): *Cush is the ancient name of the extensive territory south of the First Cataract of the Nile River. This region was called Ethiopia in Graeco-Roman times, and included within its borders most of modern Sudan and some of present-day Ethiopia (Abyssinia).*

12:9 1 Kings 10:16, 17; 2 Chr 9:15, 16

years in Jerusalem. His mother was Micaiah
daughter of Uriel, from the city of Gibeah.
War broke out between Abijah and Jer-
oboam. 3Abijah raised an army of 400,000
soldiers, and Jeroboam opposed him with an
army of 800,000.
4The armies met in the hill country of
Ephraim. King Abijah went up Mount
Zemaraim and called out to Jeroboam and
the Israelites: "Listen to me!" he said.
5"Don't you know that the LORD, the God
of Israel, made an unbreakable covenant
with David, giving him and his descendants
kingship over Israel forever? 6Jeroboam son
of Nebat rebelled against Solomon, his
king. 7Later he gathered together a group
of worthless scoundrels, and they forced
their will on Rehoboam son of Solomon,
who was too young and inexperienced to
resist them. 8Now you propose to fight
against the royal authority that the LORD
gave to David's descendants. You have a
huge army and have with you the gold
bull-calves that Jeroboam made to be your
gods. 9You drove out the LORD's priests,
the descendants of Aaron, and you drove
out the Levites. In their place you appoint-
ed priests in the same way that other
nations do. Anybody who comes along
with a bull or seven sheep can get himself
consecrated as a priest of those so-called
gods of yours.
10"But we still serve the LORD our God
and have not abandoned him. Priests
descended from Aaron perform their duties,
and Levites assist them. 11Every morning and
every evening they offer him incense and
animal sacrifices burned whole. They present
the offerings of bread on a table that is ritu-
ally clean, and every evening they light the
lamps on the gold lampstand. We do what
the LORD has commanded, but you have
abandoned him. 12God himself is our leader
and his priests are here with trumpets, ready
to blow them and call us to battle against
you. People of Israel, don't fight against the
LORD, the God of your ancestors! You can't
win!"
13Meanwhile Jeroboam had sent some of
his troops to ambush the Judean army from
the rear, while the rest faced them from the
front. 14The Judeans looked around and saw
that they were surrounded. They cried to the
LORD for help, and the priests blew the
trumpets. 15The Judeans gave a loud shout,
and led by Abijah, they attacked; God defeat-
ed Jeroboam and the Israelite army. 16The
Israelites fled from the Judeans, and God let
the Judeans overpower them. 17Abijah and
his army dealt the Israelites a crushing
defeat—half a million of Israel's best soldiers
were killed. 18And so the people of Judah
were victorious over Israel, because they
relied on the LORD, the God of their ances-
tors.
19Abijah pursued Jeroboam's army and
occupied some of his cities: Bethel, Jeshanah,
and Ephron, and the villages near each of
these cities. 20Jeroboam never regained his
power during Abijah's reign. Finally the
LORD struck him down, and he died.
21Abijah, however, grew more powerful.
He had fourteen wives and fathered twenty-
two sons and sixteen daughters. 22The rest of
the history of Abijah, what he said and what
he did, is written in *The History of Iddo the
Prophet*.

King Asa Defeats the Ethiopians

14 King Abijah died and was buried in
the royal tombs in David's City. His
son Asa succeeded him as king, and under
Asa the land enjoyed peace for ten years.
2Asa pleased the LORD, his God, by doing
what was right and good. 3He removed the
foreign altars and the pagan places of wor-
ship, broke down the sacred stone columns,
and cut down the symbols of the goddess
Asherah. 4He commanded the people of
Judah to do the will of the LORD, the God
of their ancestors, and to obey his teachings
and commands. 5Because he abolished the
pagan places of worship and the incense
altars from all the cities of Judah, the king-
dom was at peace under his rule. 6He built
fortifications for the cities of Judah during
this time, and for several years there was no
war, because the LORD gave him peace. 7He
told the people of Judah, "Let us fortify the
cities by building walls and towers, and gates
that can be shut and barred. We have control
of the land because we have done the will
of the LORD our God. He has protected us

and given us security on every side." And so
they built and prospered. 8King Asa had an
army of 300,000 men from Judah, armed
with shields and spears, and 280,000 men
from Benjamin, armed with shields and
bows. All of them were brave, well-trained
men.
9An Ethiopian[t] named Zerah invaded
Judah with an army of a million men and
three hundred chariots and advanced as far
as Mareshah. 10Asa went out to fight him,
and both sides took up their positions at
Zephathah Valley near Mareshah. 11Asa
prayed to the LORD his God, "O LORD,
you can help a weak army as easily as a pow-
erful one. Help us now, O LORD our God,
because we are relying on you, and in your
name we have come out to fight against this
huge army. LORD, you are our God; no one
can hope to defeat you."
12The LORD defeated the Ethiopian[t] army
when Asa and the Judean army attacked
them. They fled, 13and Asa and his troops
pursued them as far as Gerar. So many of the
Ethiopians[t] were killed that the army was
unable to rally and fight.[u] They were over-
powered by the LORD and his army, and the
army took large amounts of loot. 14Then
they were able to destroy the cities in the
area around Gerar, because the people there
were terrified of the LORD. The army plun-
dered all those cities and captured large
amounts of loot. 15They also attacked the
camps of some shepherds, capturing large
numbers of sheep and camels. Then they
returned to Jerusalem.

Asa's Reforms

15 The spirit of God came upon Azari-
ah son of Oded, 2and he went to
meet King Asa. He called out, "Listen to me,
King Asa, and all you people of Judah and
Benjamin! The LORD is with you as long as
you are with him. If you look for him, he
will let you find him, but if you turn away,
he will abandon you. 3For a long time Israel
lived without the true God, without priests
to teach them, and without a law. 4But
when trouble came, they turned to the
LORD, the God of Israel. They searched for
him and found him. 5In those days no one
could come and go in safety, because there
was trouble and disorder in every land.
6One nation oppressed another nation, and
one city oppressed another city, because
God was bringing trouble and distress on
them. 7But you must be strong and not be
discouraged. The work that you do will be
rewarded."
8When Asa heard the prophecy that
Azariah son of[v] Oded had spoken, he was
encouraged. He did away with all the idols
in the land of Judah and Benjamin and all
the idols in the cities he had captured in the
hill country of Ephraim. He also repaired the
altar of the LORD that stood in the Temple
courtyard.
9Many people had come over to Asa's
side from Ephraim, Manasseh, and Simeon,
and were living in his kingdom, because
they had seen that the LORD was with him.
Asa summoned all of them and the people
of Judah and Benjamin. 10They assembled in
Jerusalem in the third month of the fif-
teenth year that Asa was king. 11On that day
they offered sacrifices to the LORD from the
loot they had brought back: seven hundred
head of cattle and seven thousand sheep.
12They made a covenant in which they
agreed to worship the LORD, the God of
their ancestors, with all their heart and soul.
13Anyone, young or old, male or female,
who did not worship him was to be put to
death. 14In a loud voice they took an oath
in the LORD's name that they would keep
the covenant, and then they shouted and
blew trumpets. 15All the people of Judah
were happy because they had made this
covenant with all their heart. They took
delight in worshiping the LORD, and he
accepted them and gave them peace on
every side.
16King Asa removed his grandmother

[t] **14:9,12,13** *Hebrew* Cushite(s): *Cush is the ancient name of the extensive territory south of the First Cataract of the Nile River. This region was called Ethiopia in Graeco-Roman times, and included within its borders most of modern Sudan and some of present-day Ethiopia (Abyssinia).* [u] **14:13** So many of the Ethiopians . . . fight; *or* The Ethiopians were completely defeated; not one of them was left alive. [v] **15:8** *Some ancient translations* Azariah son of; *Hebrew does not have these words.*

Maacah from her position as queen mother,
because she had made an obscene idol of the
fertility goddess Asherah. Asa cut down the
idol, chopped it up, and burned the pieces in
Kidron Valley. 17Even though Asa did not
destroy all the pagan places of worship in the
land, he remained faithful to the LORD all
his life. 18He placed in the Temple all the
objects his father Abijah had dedicated to
God, as well as the gold and silver objects
that he himself dedicated. 19There was no
more war until the thirty-fifth year of his
reign.

Asa cut down the idol. (15:16)

Troubles with Israel
(1 Kings 15:17–22)

16 In the thirty-sixth year of the reign
of King Asa of Judah, King Baasha of
Israel invaded Judah and started to fortify
Ramah in order to cut off all traffic in and
out of Judah. 2So Asa took silver and gold
from the treasuries of the Temple and the
palace and sent it to Damascus, to King Ben-
hadad of Syria, with this message: 3"Let us be
allies, as our fathers were. This silver and gold
is a present for you. Now break your alliance
with King Baasha of Israel so that he will
have to pull his troops out of my territory."
4Benhadad agreed to Asa's proposal and
sent his commanding officers and their
armies to attack the cities of Israel. They
captured Ijon, Dan, Abel Beth Maacah, and
all the cities of Naphtali where supplies were
stored. 5When King Baasha heard what was
happening, he stopped fortifying Ramah and
abandoned the work. 6Then King Asa gath-
ered men from throughout Judah and had
them carry off the stones and timbers that
Baasha had been using at Ramah, and they
used them to fortify the cities of Geba and
Mizpah.

The Prophet Hanani

7At that time the prophet Hanani went to
King Asa and said, "Because you relied on the
king of Syria instead of relying on the LORD
your God, the army of the king of Israel[w] has
escaped from you. 8Didn't the Ethiopians[x]
and the Libyans have large armies with many
chariots and cavalry troops? But because you
relied on the LORD, he gave you victory over
them. 9The LORD keeps close watch over the
whole world, to give strength to those whose
hearts are loyal to him. You have acted fool-
ishly, and so from now on you will always be
at war." 10This made Asa so angry with the
prophet that he had him put in chains. It was
at this same time that Asa began treating
some of the people cruelly.

The End of Asa's Reign
(1 Kings 15:23, 24)

11All the events of Asa's reign from begin-
ning to end are recorded in *The History of the
Kings of Judah and Israel.* 12In the thirty-ninth
year that Asa was king, he was crippled by a
severe foot disease; but even then he did not
turn to the LORD for help, but to doctors.
13Two years later he died 14and was buried
in the rock tomb which he had carved out
for himself in David's City. They used spices
and perfumed oils to prepare his body for
burial, and they built a huge bonfire to
mourn his death.

Jehoshaphat Becomes King

17 Jehoshaphat succeeded his father Asa
as king and strengthened his position
against Israel. 2He stationed troops in the

[w] **16:7** *One ancient translation* Israel; *Hebrew* Syria. [x] **16:8** *Hebrew* Cushites: *Cush is the ancient name of the extensive territory south of the First Cataract of the Nile River. This region was called Ethiopia in Graeco-Roman times, and included within its borders most of modern Sudan and some of present-day Ethiopia (Abyssinia).*

fortified cities of Judah, in the Judean countryside, and in the cities which Asa had captured in the territory of Ephraim. 3The LORD blessed Jehoshaphat because he followed the example of his father's early life and did not worship Baal. 4He served his father's God, obeyed God's commands, and did not act the way the kings of Israel did. 5The LORD gave Jehoshaphat firm control over the kingdom of Judah, and all the people brought him gifts, so that he became wealthy and highly honored. 6He took pride in serving the LORD and destroyed all the pagan places of worship and the symbols of the goddess Asherah in Judah.

7In the third year of his reign he sent out the following officials to teach in the cities of Judah: Benhail, Obadiah, Zechariah, Nethanel, and Micaiah. 8They were accompanied by nine Levites and two priests. The Levites were Shemaiah, Nethaniah, Zebadiah, Asahel, Shemiramoth, Jehonathan, Adonijah, Tobijah, and Tobadonijah; and the priests were Elishama and Jehoram. 9They took the book of the Law of the LORD and went through all the towns of Judah, teaching it to the people.

Jehoshaphat's Greatness

10The LORD made all the surrounding kingdoms afraid to go to war against King Jehoshaphat. 11Some of the Philistines brought Jehoshaphat a large amount of silver and other gifts, and some Arabs brought him 7,700 sheep and 7,700 goats. 12So Jehoshaphat continued to grow more and more powerful. Throughout Judah he built fortifications and cities, 13where supplies were stored in huge amounts.

In Jerusalem he stationed outstanding officers, 14according to their clans. Adnah was the commander of the troops from the clans of Judah, and he had 300,000 soldiers under him. 15Second in rank was Jehohanan, with 280,000 soldiers, 16and third was Amasiah son of Zichri, with 200,000. (Amasiah had volunteered to serve the LORD.) 17The commander of the troops from the clans of Benjamin was Eliada, an outstanding soldier, in command of 200,000 men armed with shields and bows. 18His second in command was Jehozabad with 180,000 men, well-equipped for battle. 19These soldiers served the king in Jerusalem, and in addition he stationed others in the other fortified cities of Judah.

The Prophet Micaiah Warns Ahab
(1 Kings 22:1–28)

18 When King Jehoshaphat of Judah became rich and famous, he arranged a marriage between a member of his family and the family of King Ahab of Israel. 2A number of years later Jehoshaphat went to the city of Samaria to visit Ahab. To honor Jehoshaphat and those with him, Ahab had a large number of sheep and cattle slaughtered for a feast. He tried to persuade Jehoshaphat to join him in attacking the city of Ramoth in Gilead. 3He asked, "Will you go with me to attack Ramoth?"

Jehoshaphat replied, "I am ready when you are, and so is my army. We will join you." 4Then he added, "But first let's consult the LORD."

5So Ahab called in the prophets, about four hundred of them, and asked them, "Should I go and attack Ramoth, or not?"

"Attack it," they answered. "God will give you victory."

6But Jehoshaphat asked, "Isn't there another prophet through whom we can consult the LORD?"

7Ahab answered, "There is one more, Micaiah son of Imlah. But I hate him because he never prophesies anything good for me; it's always something bad."

"You shouldn't say that!" Jehoshaphat replied.

8So King Ahab called in a court official and told him to go and get Micaiah at once.

9The two kings, dressed in their royal robes, were sitting on their thrones at the threshing place just outside the gate of Samaria, and all the prophets were prophesying in front of them. 10One of them, Zedekiah son of Chenaanah, made iron horns and said to Ahab, "This is what the LORD says, 'With these you will fight the Syrians and totally defeat them.' " 11All the other prophets said the same thing. "March

All the prophets were prophesying in front of them. (18:9)

against Ramoth and you will win," they said.
"The LORD will give you victory."
12Meanwhile, the official who had gone
to get Micaiah said to him, "All the other
prophets have prophesied success for the
king, and you had better do the same."
13But Micaiah answered, "By the living
LORD I will say what my God tells me to!"
14When he appeared before King Ahab,
the king asked him, "Micaiah, should King
Jehoshaphat and I go and attack Ramoth, or
not?"
"Attack!" Micaiah answered. "Of course
you'll win. The LORD will give you victory."
15But Ahab replied, "When you speak to
me in the name of the LORD, tell the truth!
How many times do I have to tell you that?"
16Micaiah answered, "I can see the army
of Israel scattered over the hills like sheep
without a shepherd. And the LORD said,
'These men have no leader; let them go
home in peace.' "
17Ahab said to Jehoshaphat, "I told you
that he never prophesies anything good for
me; it's always something bad!"
18Micaiah went on: "Now listen to what
the LORD says! I saw the LORD sitting on his
throne in heaven, with all his angels standing
beside him. 19The LORD asked, 'Who will
deceive Ahab so that he will go and get
killed at Ramoth?' Some of the angels said
one thing, and others said something else,
20until a spirit stepped forward, approached
the LORD, and said, 'I will deceive him.'
'How?' the LORD asked. 21The spirit replied,
'I will go and make all of Ahab's prophets
tell lies.' The LORD said, 'Go and deceive
him. You will succeed.' "
22And Micaiah concluded: "This is what
has happened. The LORD has made these
prophets of yours lie to you. But he himself
has decreed that you will meet with disaster!"
23Then the prophet Zedekiah went up to
Micaiah, slapped his face, and asked, "Since
when did the LORD's spirit leave me and
speak to you?"
24"You will find out when you go into
some back room to hide," Micaiah replied.
25Then King Ahab ordered one of his
officers, "Arrest Micaiah and take him to
Amon, the governor of the city, and to
Prince Joash. 26Tell them to throw him in
prison and to put him on bread and water
until I return safely."
27"If you return safely," Micaiah
exclaimed, "then the LORD has not spoken
through me!" And he added, "Listen, everyone, to what I have said!"

The Death of Ahab
(1 Kings 22:29–35)

28Then King Ahab of Israel and King
Jehoshaphat of Judah went to attack the city
of Ramoth in Gilead. 29Ahab said to
Jehoshaphat, "As we go into battle, I will disguise myself, but you wear your royal garments." So the king of Israel went into battle
in disguise.
30The king of Syria had ordered his chariot commanders to attack no one else except
the king of Israel. 31So when they saw King
Jehoshaphat, they all thought that he was the
king of Israel, and they turned to attack him.
But Jehoshaphat gave a shout, and the LORD
God rescued him and turned the attack away
from him. 32The chariot commanders saw
that he was not the king of Israel, so they
stopped pursuing him. 33By chance, however, a Syrian soldier shot an arrow which
struck King Ahab between the joints of his
armor. "I'm wounded!" he cried out to his
chariot driver. "Turn around and pull out of
the battle!" 34While the battle raged on,

18:16 Num 27:17; Ezek 34:5; Mt 9:36; Mk 6:34

King Ahab remained propped up in his char-
iot, facing the Syrians. At sunset he died.

A Prophet Reprimands Jehoshaphat

19 King Jehoshaphat of Judah returned
safely to his palace in Jerusalem. [2]A
prophet, Jehu son of Hanani, went to meet
the king and said to him, "Do you think it is
right to help those who are wicked and to
take the side of those who hate the LORD?
What you have done has brought the LORD's
anger on you. [3]But even so, there is some
good in you. You have removed all the sym-
bols of the goddess Asherah which people
worshiped, and you have tried to follow
God's will."

Jehoshaphat's Reforms

[4]Even though King Jehoshaphat lived in
Jerusalem, he traveled regularly among the
people, from Beersheba in the south to the
edge of the hill country of Ephraim in the
north, in order to call the people back to the
LORD, the God of their ancestors. [5]He
appointed judges in each of the fortified
cities of Judah [6]and instructed them: "Be
careful in pronouncing judgment; you are
not acting on human authority, but on the
authority of the LORD, and he is with you
when you pass sentence. [7]Honor the LORD
and act carefully, because the LORD our God
does not tolerate fraud or partiality or the
taking of bribes."
[8]In Jerusalem Jehoshaphat appointed
Levites, priests, and some of the leading citi-
zens as judges in cases involving a violation
of the Law of the LORD or legal disputes
between inhabitants of the city.[y] [9]He gave
them the following instructions: "You must
perform your duties in reverence for the
LORD, faithfully obeying him in everything
you do. [10]Whenever your fellow citizens
from any of the cities bring before you a
case of homicide or any other violation of a
law or commandment, you must instruct
them carefully how to conduct themselves
during the trial, so that they do not become
guilty of sinning against the LORD. Unless
you do, you and your fellow citizens will feel
the force of the LORD's anger. But if you do
your duty, you will not be guilty. [11]Amariah
the High Priest will have final authority in
all religious cases, and Zebadiah son of Ish-
mael, governor of Judah, will have final
authority in all civil cases. The Levites have
the responsibility of seeing that the decisions
of the courts are carried out. Be courageous
and carry out these instructions, and may the
LORD be on the side of the right!"

War against Edom

20 Some time later the armies of Moab
and Ammon, together with their
allies, the Meunites,[z] invaded Judah. [2]Some
messengers came and announced to King
Jehoshaphat: "A large army from Edom has
come from the other side of the Dead Sea to
attack you. They have already captured Haza-
zon Tamar." (This is another name for En-
gedi.) [3]Jehoshaphat was frightened and prayed
to the LORD for guidance. Then he gave
orders for a fast to be observed throughout
the country. [4]From every city of Judah people
hurried to Jerusalem to ask the LORD for
guidance, [5]and they and the people of Jeru-
salem gathered in the new courtyard of the
Temple. King Jehoshaphat went and stood
before them [6]and prayed aloud, "O LORD
God of our ancestors, you rule in heaven over
all the nations of the world. You are powerful
and mighty, and no one can oppose you. [7]You
are our God. When your people Israel moved
into this land, you drove out the people who
were living here and gave the land to the
descendants of Abraham, your friend, to be
theirs forever. [8]They have lived here and have
built a temple to honor you, knowing [9]that if
any disaster struck them to punish them—a
war,[a] an epidemic, or a famine—then they
could come and stand in front of this Temple
where you are worshiped. They could pray to
you in their trouble, and you would hear
them and rescue them.
[10]"Now the people of Ammon, Moab,
and Edom have attacked us. When our

[y] **19:8** *Some ancient translations* between . . . city; *Hebrew unclear.* [z] **20:1** *One ancient translation* Meunites; *Hebrew* Ammonites. [a] **20:9** struck . . . war; *or* struck them—a devastating war.

20:7 Isa 41:8; Jas 2:23 **20:10** Deut 2:4–19

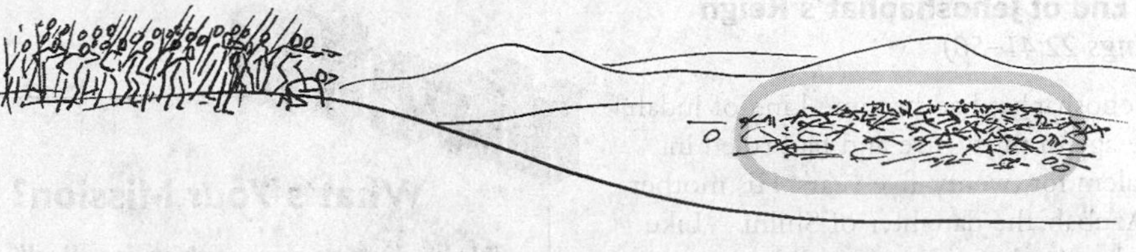

The Judean army . . . saw that the enemy were all lying on the ground dead. (20:24)

ancestors came out of Egypt, you did not
allow them to enter those lands, so our
ancestors went around them and did not
destroy them. 11 This is how they repay us—
they come to drive us out of the land that
you gave us. 12 You are our God! Punish
them, for we are helpless in the face of this
large army that is attacking us. We do not
know what to do, but we look to you for
help."

13 All the men of Judah, with their wives
and children, were standing there at the
Temple. 14 The spirit of the LORD came
upon a Levite who was present in the
crowd. His name was Jahaziel son of
Zechariah; he was a member of the clan
of Asaph and was descended from Asaph
through Mattaniah, Jeiel, and Benaiah.
15 Jahaziel said, "Your Majesty and all you
people of Judah and Jerusalem, the LORD
says that you must not be discouraged or be
afraid to face this large army. The battle
depends on God, not on you. 16 Attack them
tomorrow as they come up the pass at Ziz.
You will meet them at the end of the valley
that leads to the wild country near Jeruel.
17 You will not have to fight this battle. Just
take up your positions and wait; you will see
the LORD give you victory. People of Judah
and Jerusalem, do not hesitate or be afraid.
Go out to battle, and the LORD will be with
you!"

18 Then King Jehoshaphat bowed low,
with his face touching the ground, and all
the people bowed with him and worshiped
the LORD. 19 The members of the Levite
clans of Kohath and Korah stood up and
with a loud shout praised the LORD, the
God of Israel.

20 Early the next morning the people went
out to the wild country near Tekoa. As they
were starting out, Jehoshaphat addressed
them with these words: "People of Judah and
Jerusalem! Put your trust in the LORD your
God, and you will stand your ground.
Believe what his prophets tell you, and you
will succeed." 21 After consulting with the
people, the king ordered some musicians to
put on the robes they wore on sacred occa-
sions and to march ahead of the army,
singing: "Praise the LORD! His love is eter-
nal!"

22 When they began to sing, the LORD
threw the invading armies into a panic.
23 The Ammonites and the Moabites attacked
the Edomite army and completely destroyed
it, and then they turned on each other in
savage fighting. 24 When the Judean army
reached a tower that was in the desert, they
looked toward the enemy and saw that they
were all lying on the ground dead. Not one
had escaped.

25 Jehoshaphat and his troops moved in to
take the loot, and they found many cattle,[b]
supplies, clothing, and other valuable
objects. They spent three days gathering the
loot, but there was so much that they could
not take everything. 26 On the fourth day
they assembled in Beracah Valley and praised
the LORD for all he had done. That is why
the valley is called "Beracah."[c] 27 Jehoshaphat
led his troops back to Jerusalem in triumph,
because the LORD had defeated their ene-
mies. 28 When they reached the city, they
marched to the Temple to the music of
harps and trumpets. 29 Every nation that
heard how the LORD had defeated Israel's
enemies was terrified, 30 so Jehoshaphat
ruled in peace, and God gave him security
on every side.

[b] **20:25** *One ancient translation* cattle; *Hebrew* among them. [c] **20:26** BERACAH: *This name in Hebrew means "praise."*

20:15–17 Deut 20:1–4 **20:17** Ex 14:13, 14

The End of Jehoshaphat's Reign
(1 Kings 22:41–50)

31 Jehoshaphat had become king of Judah
at the age of thirty-five and had ruled in
Jerusalem for twenty-five years. His mother
was Azubah, the daughter of Shilhi. 32 Like
his father Asa before him, he did what was
right in the sight of the LORD; 33 but the
pagan places of worship were not destroyed.
The people still did not turn wholeheartedly
to the worship of the God of their ancestors.
34 Everything else that Jehoshaphat did,
from the beginning of his reign to its end,
is recorded in *The History of Jehu Son of
Hanani,* which is a part of *The History of the
Kings of Israel*.
35 At one time King Jehoshaphat of Judah
made an alliance with King Ahaziah of
Israel, who did many wicked things. 36 At the
port of Eziongeber they built ocean-going
ships. 37 But Eliezer son of Dodavahu, from
the town of Mareshah, warned Jehoshaphat,
"Because you have made an alliance with
Ahaziah, the LORD will destroy what you
have built." And the ships were wrecked and
never sailed.

21 Jehoshaphat died and was buried in
the royal tombs in David's City and
his son Jehoram succeeded him as king.

King Jehoram of Judah
(2 Kings 8:17–24)

2 Jehoram son of King Jehoshaphat of
Judah had six brothers: Azariah, Jehiel,
Zechariah, Azariahu, Michael, and Shephati-
ah. 3 Their father gave them large amounts of
gold, silver, and other valuable possessions,
and placed each one in charge of one of the
fortified cities of Judah. But because Jehoram
was the oldest, Jehoshaphat made him his
successor. 4 When Jehoram was in firm con-
trol of the kingdom, he had all his brothers
killed, and also some Israelite officials.
5 Jehoram became king at the age of thir-
ty-two, and he ruled in Jerusalem for eight
years. 6 He followed the wicked example of
King Ahab and the other kings of Israel,
because he had married one of Ahab's
daughters. He sinned against the LORD, 7 but
the LORD was not willing to destroy the
dynasty of David, because he had made a
covenant with David and promised that his
descendants would always continue to rule.

Live it!

What's Your Mission?

"Nobody was sorry when he died" (2 Chronicles 21:20). That is what they said about Jehoram the king. His only mission seemed to be protecting his power at all costs. He even killed his brothers so they couldn't compete with him for power.

Maybe you've seen a paragraph describing a company's goals on the wall of a fast-food restaurant, at your church, or in a magazine ad. These are called mission statements. A mission statement helps an organization focus on what is important for it to do. And it lets other people know what is important to that organization.

Consider writing your own mission statement. Think about what people will say about you at your funeral. Do you want people to say you were a good family member, student, employee, and friend? Do you want people to say you made lots of money? Do you want people to say you contributed to society, solved problems, or discovered cures? Work whatever you want people to say about you into your mission statement. Write it out and keep it where you can see it every day. Then live out your mission, and people won't say the same thing about you as they did about Jehoram!

— 2 Chronicles 21:2–20

21:7 1 Kings 11:36

8 During Jehoram's reign Edom revolted against Judah and became an independent kingdom. 9 So Jehoram and his officers set out with chariots and invaded Edom. There the Edomite army surrounded them, but during the night they managed to break out and escape. 10 Edom has been independent of[d] Judah ever since. During this same period the city of Libnah also revolted, because Jehoram had abandoned the LORD, the God of his ancestors. 11 He even built pagan places of worship in the Judean highlands and led the people of Judah and Jerusalem to sin against the LORD.

12 The prophet Elijah sent Jehoram a letter, which read as follows: "The LORD, the God of your ancestor David, condemns you, because you did not follow the example of your father, King Jehoshaphat, or that of your grandfather, King Asa. 13 Instead, you have followed the example of the kings of Israel and have led the people of Judah and Jerusalem into being unfaithful to God, just as Ahab and his successors led Israel into unfaithfulness. You even murdered your brothers, who were better men than you are. 14 As a result, the LORD will severely punish your people, your children, and your wives, and will destroy your possessions. 15 You yourself will suffer a painful intestinal disease that will grow worse day by day."

16 Some Philistines and Arabs lived near where some Ethiopians[e] had settled along the coast. The LORD caused them to go to war against Jehoram. 17 They invaded Judah, looted the royal palace, and carried off as prisoners all the king's wives and sons except Ahaziah, his youngest son.

18 Then after all this, the LORD brought on the king a painful disease of the intestines. 19 For almost two years it grew steadily worse until finally the king died in agony. His subjects did not light a bonfire in mourning for him as had been done for his ancestors.

20 Jehoram had become king at the age of thirty-two and had ruled in Jerusalem for eight years. Nobody was sorry when he died. They buried him in David's City, but not in the royal tombs.

King Ahaziah of Judah
(2 Kings 8:25–29; 9:21–28)

22 Some Arabs had led a raid and killed all of King Jehoram's sons except Ahaziah, the youngest. So now the people of Jerusalem made Ahaziah king as his father's successor. 2-3 Ahaziah became king at the age of twenty-two,[f] and he ruled in Jerusalem for one year. Ahaziah also followed the example of King Ahab's family, since his mother Athaliah—the daughter of King Ahab and granddaughter of King Omri of Israel—gave him advice that led him into evil. 4 He sinned against the LORD, because after his father's death other members of King Ahab's family became his advisers, and they led to his downfall. 5 Following their advice, he joined King Joram of Israel in a war against King Hazael of Syria. The armies clashed at Ramoth in Gilead, and Joram was wounded in battle. 6 He returned to the city of Jezreel to recover from his wounds, and Ahaziah went there to visit him.

7 God used this visit to Joram to bring about Ahaziah's downfall. While Ahaziah was there, he and Joram were confronted by a man named Jehu son of Nimshi, whom the LORD had chosen to destroy the dynasty of Ahab. 8 As Jehu was carrying out God's sentence on the dynasty, he came across a group made up of Judean leaders and of Ahaziah's nephews that had accompanied Ahaziah on his visit. Jehu killed them all. 9 A search was made for Ahaziah, and he was found hiding in Samaria. They took him to Jehu and put him to death. But they did bury his body out of respect for his grandfather King Jehoshaphat, who had done all he could to serve the LORD.

No member of Ahaziah's family was left who could rule the kingdom.

[d] **21:10** independent of; *or* in revolt against. [e] **21:16** *Hebrew* Cushites: *Cush is the ancient name of the extensive territory south of the First Cataract of the Nile River. This region was called Ethiopia in Graeco-Roman times, and included within its borders most of modern Sudan and some of present-day Ethiopia (Abyssinia).* [f] **22:2–3** *Some ancient translations (and see 2 Kings 8:26)* twenty-two; *Hebrew* forty-two.

21:8 Gen 27:40

Queen Athaliah of Judah
(2 Kings 11:1–3)

10 As soon as King Ahaziah's mother Athaliah learned of her son's murder, she gave orders for all the members of the royal family of Judah to be killed. 11 Ahaziah had a half sister, Jehosheba, who was married to a priest named Jehoiada. She secretly rescued one of Ahaziah's sons, Joash, took him away from the other princes who were about to be murdered and hid him and a nurse in a bedroom at the Temple. By keeping him hidden, she saved him from death at the hands of Athaliah. 12 For six years he remained there in hiding, while Athaliah ruled as queen.

The Revolt against Athaliah
(2 Kings 11:4–16)

23 After waiting six years Jehoiada the priest decided that it was time to take action. He made a pact with five army officers: Azariah son of Jeroham, Ishmael son of Jehohanan, Azariah son of Obed, Maaseiah son of Adaiah, and Elishaphat son of Zichri. 2 They traveled to all the cities of Judah and brought back with them to Jerusalem the Levites and all the heads of the clans.

3 They all gathered in the Temple, and there they made a covenant with Joash, the king's son. Jehoiada said to them, "Here is the son of the late king. He is now to be king, as the LORD promised that King David's descendants would be. 4 This is what we will do. When the priests and Levites come on duty on the Sabbath, one third of them will guard the Temple gates, 5 another third will guard the royal palace, and the rest will be stationed at the Foundation Gate. All the people will assemble in the Temple courtyard. 6 No one is to enter the Temple buildings except the priests and the Levites who are on duty. They may enter, because they are consecrated, but the rest of the people must obey the LORD's instructions and stay outside. 7 The Levites are to stand guard around the king, with their swords drawn, and are to stay with the king wherever he goes. Anyone who tries to enter the Temple is to be killed."

8 The Levites and the people of Judah carried out Jehoiada's instructions. The men were not dismissed when they went off duty on the Sabbath, so the commanders had available both those coming on duty and those going off. 9 Jehoiada gave the officers the spears and shields that had belonged to King David and had been kept in the Temple. 10 He stationed the men with drawn swords all around the front of the Temple, to protect the king. 11 Then Jehoiada led Joash out, placed the crown on his head, and gave him a copy of the laws governing kingship. And so he was made king. Jehoiada the priest and his sons anointed Joash, and everyone shouted, "Long live the king!"

And so he was made king. (23:11)

12 Athaliah heard the people cheering for the king, so she hurried to the Temple, where the crowd had gathered. 13 There she saw the new king at the Temple entrance, standing by the column reserved for kings and surrounded by the army officers and the trumpeters. All the people were shouting joyfully and blowing trumpets, and the Temple musicians with their instruments were leading the celebration. She tore her clothes in distress and shouted, "Treason! Treason!"

14 Jehoiada did not want Athaliah killed in the Temple area, so he called out the army officers and said, "Take her out between the rows of guards, and kill anyone who tries to rescue her."

15 They seized her, took her to the palace, and there at the Horse Gate they killed her.

23:3 2 Sam 7:12

Jehoiada's Reforms
(2 Kings 11:17–20)

16The priest Jehoiada had King Joash and
the people join him in making a covenant
that they would be the LORD's people.
17Then they all went to the temple of Baal
and tore it down. They smashed the altars
and idols there and killed Mattan, the priest
of Baal, in front of the altars. 18Jehoiada put
the priests and Levites in charge of the work
of the Temple. They were to carry out the
duties assigned to them by King David and
to burn the sacrifices offered to the LORD in
accordance with the Law of Moses. They
were also in charge of the music and the cel-
ebrations. 19Jehoiada also put guards on duty
at the Temple gates to keep out anyone who
was ritually unclean.

20The army officers, the leading citizens,
the officials, and all the rest of the people
joined Jehoiada in a procession that brought
the king from the Temple to the palace. They
entered by the main gate, and the king took
his place on the throne. 21All the people
were filled with happiness, and the city was
quiet, now that Athaliah had been killed.

King Joash of Judah
(2 Kings 12:1–16)

24 Joash became king of Judah at the
age of seven, and he ruled in
Jerusalem for forty years. His mother was
Zibiah from the city of Beersheba. 2He did
what was pleasing to the LORD as long as
Jehoiada the priest was alive. 3Jehoiada chose
two wives for King Joash, and they bore him
sons and daughters.

4After he had been king for a while,
Joash decided to have the Temple repaired.
5He ordered the priests and the Levites to
go to the cities of Judah and collect from all
the people enough money to make the
annual repairs on the Temple. He told them
to act promptly, but the Levites delayed,
6so he called in Jehoiada, their leader, and
demanded, "Why haven't you seen to it
that the Levites collect from Judah and
Jerusalem the tax which Moses, the servant
of the LORD, required the people[g] to pay
for support of the Tent of the LORD's pres-
ence?"

(7The followers of Athaliah, that corrupt
woman,[h] had damaged the Temple and had
used many of the sacred objects in the wor-
ship of Baal.)

8The king ordered the Levites to make a
box for contributions and to place it at the
Temple gate. 9They sent word throughout
Jerusalem and Judah for everyone to bring to
the LORD the tax which Moses, God's ser-
vant, had first collected in the wilderness.
10This pleased the people and their leaders,
and they brought their tax money and filled
the box with it. 11Every day the Levites
would take the box to the royal official who
was in charge of it. Whenever it was full, the
royal secretary and the High Priest's repre-
sentative would take the money out and
return the box to its place. And so they col-
lected a large sum of money.

They brought their tax money. (24:10)

12The king and Jehoiada would give the
money to those who were in charge of
repairing the Temple, and they hired stone-
masons, carpenters, and metalworkers to
make the repairs. 13All of them worked hard,
and they restored the Temple to its original
condition, as solid as ever. 14When the
repairs were finished, the remaining gold and
silver was given to the king and Jehoiada,
who used it to have bowls and other utensils
made for the Temple.

[g] **24:6** *Probable text* required the people; *Hebrew unclear.*
24:6 Ex 30:11–16

[h] **24:7** that corrupt woman; *or* whom she corrupted.

Jehoiada's Policies Are Reversed

As long as Jehoiada was alive, sacrifices
were offered regularly at the Temple. 15 After
reaching the very old age of a hundred and
thirty, he died. 16 They buried him in the
royal tombs in David's City in recognition of
the service he had done for the people of
Israel, for God, and for the Temple.

17 But once Jehoiada was dead, the leaders
of Judah persuaded King Joash to listen to
them instead. 18 And so the people stopped
worshiping in the Temple of the LORD, the
God of their ancestors, and began to worship
idols and the images of the goddess Asherah.
Their guilt for these sins brought the LORD's
anger on Judah and Jerusalem. 19 The LORD
sent prophets to warn them to return to him,
but the people refused to listen. 20 Then the
spirit of God took control of Zechariah son of
Jehoiada the priest. He stood where the peo-
ple could see him and called out, "The LORD
God asks why you have disobeyed his com-
mands and are bringing disaster on yourselves!
You abandoned him, so he has abandoned
you!" 21 King Joash joined in a conspiracy
against Zechariah, and on the king's orders the
people stoned Zechariah in the Temple court-
yard. 22 The king forgot about the loyal service
that Zechariah's father Jehoiada had given
him, and he had Zechariah killed. As Zechari-
ah was dying, he called out, "May the LORD
see what you are doing and punish you!"

The End of Joash's Reign

23 When autumn came that year, the Syrian
army attacked Judah and Jerusalem, killed all
the leaders, and took large amounts of loot
back to Damascus. 24 The Syrian army was
small, but the LORD let them defeat a much
larger Judean army because the people had
abandoned him, the LORD God of their
ancestors. In this way King Joash was pun-
ished. 25 He was severely wounded, and when
the enemy withdrew, two of his officials plot-
ted against him and killed him in his bed to
avenge the murder of the son[i] of Jehoiada the
priest. He was buried in David's City, but not
in the royal tombs. (26 Those who plotted
against him were Zabad, the son of an
Ammonite woman named Shimeath, and
Jehozabad, the son of a Moabite woman
named Shimrith.) 27 The *Commentary on the
Book of Kings* contains the stories of the sons
of Joash, the prophecies spoken against him,
and the record of how he rebuilt the Temple.
His son Amaziah succeeded him as king.

King Amaziah of Judah
(2 Kings 14:2–6)

25 Amaziah became king at the age
of twenty-five, and he ruled in
Jerusalem for twenty-nine years. His mother
was Jehoaddin from Jerusalem. 2 He did what
was pleasing to the LORD, but did it reluc-
tantly. 3 As soon as he was firmly in power,
he executed the officials who had murdered
his father. 4 He did not, however, execute
their children, but followed what the LORD
had commanded in the Law of Moses: "Par-
ents are not to be put to death for crimes
committed by their children, and children
are not to be put to death for crimes com-
mitted by their parents; people are to be put
to death only for crimes they themselves
have committed."

War against Edom
(2 Kings 14:7)

5 King Amaziah organized all the men of
the tribes of Judah and Benjamin into army
units, according to the clans they belonged
to, and placed officers in command of units
of a thousand and units of a hundred. This
included all men twenty years of age or
older, 300,000 in all. They were picked
troops, ready for battle, skilled in using spears
and shields. 6 In addition, he hired 100,000
soldiers from Israel at a cost of about four
tons of silver. 7 But a prophet went to the
king and said to him, "Don't take these
Israelite soldiers with you. The LORD is not
with these people from the Northern King-
dom. 8 You may think that they will make
you stronger[j] in battle, but it is God who has

[i] **24:25** *Some ancient translations* son; *Hebrew* sons. [j] **25:8** *Some ancient translations* You may . . . stronger; *Hebrew unclear.*

24:20, 21 Mt 23:35; Lk 11:51 **25:4** Deut 24:16

the power to give victory or defeat, and he will let your enemies defeat you."

[9]Amaziah asked the prophet, "But what about all that silver I have already paid for them?"

The prophet replied, "The LORD can give you back more than that!" [10]So Amaziah sent the hired troops away and told them to go home. At this they went home, bitterly angry with the people of Judah.

[11]Amaziah summoned up his courage and led his army to Salt Valley. There they fought and killed ten thousand Edomite soldiers [12]and captured another ten thousand. They took the prisoners to the top of the cliff at the city of Sela and threw them off, so that they were killed on the rocks below.

[13]Meanwhile the Israelite soldiers that Amaziah had not allowed to go into battle with him attacked the Judean cities between Samaria and Beth Horon, killed three thousand men, and captured quantities of loot.

[14]When Amaziah returned from defeating the Edomites, he brought their idols back with him, set them up, worshiped them, and burned incense to them. [15]This made the LORD angry, so he sent a prophet to Amaziah. The prophet demanded, "Why have you worshiped foreign gods that could not even save their own people from your power?"

[16]"Since when," Amaziah interrupted, "have we made you adviser to the king? Stop talking, or I'll have you killed!"

The prophet stopped, but not before saying, "Now I know that God has decided to destroy you because you have done all this and have ignored my advice."

War against Israel

(2 Kings 14:8–20)

[17]King Amaziah of Judah and his advisers plotted against Israel. He then sent a message to King Jehoash of Israel, who was the son of Jehoahaz and grandson of Jehu, challenging him to fight.[k] [18]Jehoash sent this answer to Amaziah: "Once a thorn bush in the Lebanon Mountains sent a message to a cedar: 'Give your daughter in marriage to my son.' A wild animal passed by and trampled the bush down. [19]Now Amaziah, you boast that you have defeated the Edomites, but I advise you to stay at home. Why stir up trouble that will only bring disaster on you and your people?"

[20]But Amaziah refused to listen. It was God's will for Amaziah to be defeated, because he had worshiped the Edomite idols. [21]So King Jehoash of Israel went into battle against King Amaziah of Judah. They met at Beth Shemesh in Judah, [22]the Judean army was defeated, and the soldiers fled to their homes. [23]Jehoash captured Amaziah and took him to Jerusalem. There he tore down the city wall from Ephraim Gate to the Corner Gate, a distance of two hundred yards. [24]He took back to Samaria as loot all the gold and silver in the Temple, the Temple equipment guarded by the descendants of Obed Edom, and the palace treasures. He also took hostages with him.

[25]King Amaziah of Judah outlived King Jehoash of Israel by fifteen years. [26]All the other things that Amaziah did from the beginning to the end of his reign are recorded in *The History of the Kings of Judah and Israel.* [27]Ever since the time when he rebelled against the LORD, there had been a plot against him in Jerusalem. Finally he fled to the city of Lachish, but his enemies followed him there and killed him. [28]His body was carried to Jerusalem on a horse, and he was buried in the royal tombs in David's City.

King Uzziah of Judah

(2 Kings 14:21, 22; 15:1–7)

26 All the people of Judah chose Amaziah's sixteen-year-old son Uzziah to succeed his father as king. ([2]It was after the death of Amaziah that Uzziah recaptured Elath and rebuilt the city.)

[3]Uzziah became king at the age of sixteen, and he ruled in Jerusalem for fifty-two years. His mother was Jecoliah from Jerusalem. [4]Following the example of his father, he did what was pleasing to the LORD. [5]As long as Zechariah, his religious

[k] **25:17** challenging him to fight; *or* inviting him to a conference.

He had large herds of livestock. (26:10)

adviser, was living, he served the LORD faith-
fully, and God blessed him.
6Uzziah went to war against the Philis-
tines. He tore down the walls of the cities of
Gath, Jamnia, and Ashdod, and built fortified
cities near Ashdod and in the rest of Philistia.
7God helped him defeat the Philistines, the
Arabs living at Gurbaal, and the Meunites.
8The Ammonites paid tribute to Uzziah, and
he became so powerful that his fame spread
even to Egypt.
9Uzziah strengthened the fortifications of
Jerusalem by building towers at the Corner
Gate, at the Valley Gate, and where the wall
turned. 10He also built fortified towers in
the open country and dug many cisterns,
because he had large herds of livestock in
the western foothills and plains. Because he
loved farming, he encouraged the people to
plant vineyards in the hill country and to
farm the fertile land.
11He had a large army ready for battle. Its
records were kept by his secretaries Jeiel and
Maaseiah under the supervision of Hananiah,
a member of the king's staff. 12The army was
commanded by 2,600 officers. 13Under them
were 307,500 soldiers able to fight effectively
for the king against his enemies. 14Uzziah
supplied the army with shields, spears, hel-
mets, coats of armor, bows and arrows, and
stones for slinging. 15In Jerusalem his inven-
tors made equipment for shooting arrows
and for throwing large stones from the tow-
ers and corners of the city wall. His fame
spread everywhere, and he became very
powerful because of the help he received
from God.

Uzziah Is Punished for His Pride

16But when King Uzziah became strong,
he grew arrogant, and that led to his down-
fall. He defied the LORD his God by going
into the Temple to burn incense on the altar
of incense. 17Azariah the priest, accompanied
by eighty strong and courageous priests, fol-
lowed the king 18to resist him. They said,
"Uzziah! You have no right to burn incense
to the LORD. Only the priests who are
descended from Aaron have been consecrat-
ed to do this. Leave this holy place. You have
offended the LORD God, and you no longer
have his blessing."
19Uzziah was standing there in the Temple
beside the incense altar and was holding an
incense burner. He became angry with the
priests, and immediately a dreaded skin dis-
ease broke out on his forehead. 20Azariah

Immediately a dreaded skin disease broke out. (26:19)

26:18 Ex 30:7, 8; Num 3:10

and the other priests stared at the king's forehead in horror and then forced him to leave the Temple. He hurried to get out, because the LORD had punished him.

21 For the rest of his life King Uzziah was ritually unclean because of his disease. Unable to enter the Temple again, he lived in his own house, relieved of all duties, while his son Jotham governed the country.

22 The prophet Isaiah son of Amoz recorded all the other things that King Uzziah did during his reign. 23 Uzziah died and was buried in the royal burial ground, but because of his disease he was not buried in the royal tombs. His son Jotham succeeded him as king.

King Jotham of Judah
(2 Kings 15:32–38)

27 Jotham became king at the age of twenty-five, and he ruled in Jerusalem for sixteen years. His mother was Jerushah, the daughter of Zadok. 2 He did what was pleasing to the LORD, just as his father had done; but unlike his father he did not sin by burning incense[l] in the Temple. The people, however, went on sinning.

3 It was Jotham who built the North Gate of the Temple and did extensive work on the city wall in the area of Jerusalem called Ophel. 4 In the mountains of Judah he built cities, and in the forests he built forts and towers. 5 He fought against the king of Ammon and his army and defeated them. Then he forced the Ammonites to pay him the following tribute each year for three years: four tons of silver, fifty thousand bushels of wheat, and fifty thousand bushels of barley. 6 Jotham grew powerful because he faithfully obeyed the LORD his God. 7 The other events of Jotham's reign, his wars, and his policies, are all recorded in *The History of the Kings of Israel and Judah.* 8 Jotham was twenty-five years old when he became king, and he ruled in Jerusalem for sixteen years. 9 He died and was buried in David's City and his son Ahaz succeeded him as king.

King Ahaz of Judah
(2 Kings 16:1–4)

28 Ahaz became king at the age of twenty, and he ruled in Jerusalem for sixteen years. He did not follow the good example of his ancestor King David; instead, he did what was not pleasing to the LORD 2 and followed the example of the kings of Israel. He had metal images of Baal made, 3 burned incense in Hinnom Valley, and even sacrificed his own sons as burnt offerings to idols, imitating the disgusting practice of the people whom the LORD had driven out of the land as the Israelites advanced. 4 At the pagan places of worship, on the hills, and under every shady tree Ahaz offered sacrifices and burned incense.

War with Syria and Israel
(2 Kings 16:5)

5-6 Because King Ahaz sinned, the LORD his God let the king of Syria defeat him and take a large number of Judeans back to Damascus as prisoners. The LORD also let the king of Israel, Pekah son of Remaliah, defeat Ahaz and kill 120,000 of the bravest Judean soldiers in one day. The LORD, the God of their ancestors, permitted this to happen, because the people of Judah had abandoned him. 7 An Israelite soldier named Zichri killed King Ahaz' son Maaseiah, the palace administrator Azrikam, and Elkanah, who was second in command to the king. 8 Even though the Judeans were their own relatives, the Israelite army captured 200,000 women and children as prisoners and took them back to Samaria, along with large amounts of loot.

The Prophet Oded

9 A man named Oded, a prophet of the LORD, lived in the city of Samaria. He met the returning Israelite army with its Judean prisoners as it was about to enter the city, and he said, "The LORD God of your ancestors was angry with Judah and let you defeat them, but now he has heard of the vicious

[l] **27:2** he did not sin by burning incense; *or* he did not take part in the worship.

26:23 Isa 6:1 **28:5, 6** 2 Kings 16:5; Isa 7:1

way you slaughtered them. 10And now you
intend to make the men and women of
Jerusalem and Judah your slaves. Don't you
know that you also have committed sins
against the LORD your God? 11Listen to me!
These prisoners are your brothers and sisters.
Let them go, or the LORD will punish you in
his anger."
12Four of the leading men of the North-
ern Kingdom, Azariah son of Jehohanan,
Berechiah son of Meshillemoth, Jehizkiah
son of Shallum, and Amasa son of Hadlai
also opposed the actions of the army. 13They
said, "Don't bring those prisoners here! We
have already sinned against the LORD and
made him angry enough to punish us. Now
you want to do something that will increase
our guilt." 14So then the army handed the
prisoners and the loot over to the people
and their leaders, 15and the four men were
appointed to provide the prisoners with
clothing from the captured loot. They gave
them clothes and sandals to wear, gave them
enough to eat and drink, and put olive oil
on their wounds. Those who were too weak
to walk were put on donkeys, and all the
prisoners were taken back to Judean territo-
ry at Jericho, the city of palm trees. Then the
Israelites returned home to Samaria.

Those who were too weak to walk . . . (28:15)

Ahaz Asks Assyria for Help
(2 Kings 16:7–9)

16-17The Edomites began to raid Judah
again and captured many prisoners, so King
Ahaz asked Tiglath Pileser, the emperor of
Assyria, to send help. 18At this same time the
Philistines were raiding the towns in the
western foothills and in southern Judah.
They captured the cities of Beth Shemesh,
Aijalon, and Gederoth, and the cities of
Soco, Timnah, and Gimzo with their
villages, and settled there permanently.
19Because King Ahaz of Judah had violated
the rights of his people and had defied the
LORD, the LORD brought troubles on Judah.
20The Assyrian emperor, instead of helping
Ahaz, opposed him and caused him trouble.
21So Ahaz took the gold from the Temple,
the palace, and the homes of the leaders of
the people, and gave it to the emperor, but
even this did not help.

The Sins of Ahaz

22When his troubles were at their worst,
that man Ahaz sinned against the LORD
more than ever. 23He offered sacrifices to the
gods of the Syrians, who had defeated him.
He said, "The Syrian gods helped the kings
of Syria, so if I sacrifice to them, they may
help me too." This brought disaster on him
and on his nation. 24In addition, he took all
the Temple equipment and broke it in
pieces. He closed the Temple and set up
altars in every part of Jerusalem. 25In every
city and town in Judah he built pagan places
of worship, where incense was to be burned
to foreign gods. In this way he brought on
himself the anger of the LORD, the God of
his ancestors.
26All the other events of his reign, from
beginning to end, are recorded in *The Histo-
ry of the Kings of Judah and Israel*. 27King
Ahaz died and was buried in Jerusalem, but
not in the royal tombs. His son Hezekiah
succeeded him as king.

28:27 Isa 14:28

King Hezekiah of Judah
(2 Kings 18:1–3)

29 Hezekiah became king of Judah at
the age of twenty-five, and he ruled
in Jerusalem for twenty-nine years. His
mother was Abijah, the daughter of Zechari-
ah. [2]Following the example of his ancestor
King David, he did what was pleasing to the
LORD.

The Purification of the Temple

[3]In the first month of the year after
Hezekiah became king, he reopened the
gates of the Temple and had them repaired.
[4]He assembled a group of priests and Levites
in the east courtyard of the Temple [5]and
spoke to them there. He said, "You Levites
are to consecrate yourselves and purify the
Temple of the LORD, the God of your
ancestors. Remove from the Temple every-
thing that defiles it. [6]Our ancestors were
unfaithful to the LORD our God and did
what was displeasing to him. They aban-
doned him and turned their backs on the
place where he dwells. [7]They closed the
doors of the Temple, let the lamps go out,
and failed to burn incense or offer burnt
offerings in the Temple of the God of Israel.
[8]Because of this the LORD has been angry
with Judah and Jerusalem, and what he has
done to them has shocked and frightened
everyone. You know this very well. [9]Our
fathers were killed in battle, and our wives
and children have been taken away as pris-
oners.

[10]"I have now decided to make a
covenant with the LORD, the God of Israel,
so that he will no longer be angry with us.
[11]My sons, do not lose any time. You are the
ones that the LORD has chosen to burn
incense to him and to lead the people in
worshiping him."

[12-14]The following Levites were there:

From the clan of Kohath, Mahath son of Amasai and Joel son of Azariah
From the clan of Merari, Kish son of Abdi and Azariah son of Jehallelel
From the clan of Gershon, Joah son of Zimmah and Eden son of Joah
From the clan of Elizaphan, Shimri and Jeuel
From the clan of Asaph, Zechariah and Mattaniah
From the clan of Heman, Jehuel and Shimei
From the clan of Jeduthun, Shemaiah and Uzziel

[15]These men assembled their fellow
Levites, and they all made themselves ritually
clean. Then, as the king had commanded
them to do, they began to make the Temple
ritually clean, according to the Law of the
LORD.[m] [16]The priests went inside the Tem-
ple to purify it, and they carried out into the
Temple courtyard everything that was ritual-
ly unclean. From there the Levites took it all
outside the city to Kidron Valley.

[17]The work was begun on the first day of
the first month, and by the eighth day they
had finished it all, including the entrance
room to the Temple. Then they worked for
the next eight days, until the sixteenth of the
month, preparing the Temple for worship.

The Temple Is Rededicated

[18]The Levites made the following report
to King Hezekiah: "We have completed the
ritual purification of the whole Temple,
including the altar for burnt offerings, the
table for the sacred bread, and all their
equipment. [19]We have also brought back all
the equipment which King Ahaz took away
during those years he was unfaithful to God,
and we have rededicated it. It is all in front
of the LORD's altar."

[20]Without delay King Hezekiah assem-
bled the leading men of the city, and togeth-
er they went to the Temple. [21]As an offering
to take away the sins of the royal family and
of the people of Judah and to purify the
Temple, they took seven bulls, seven sheep,
seven lambs, and seven goats. The king told
the priests, who were descendants of Aaron,
to offer the animals as sacrifices on the altar.
[22]The priests killed the bulls first, then the

[m] **29:15** Then, as the king . . . LORD; *or* Then they began to make the Temple ritually clean, as the king, who was acting at the LORD's command, had ordered them to do.

sheep, and then the lambs, and sprinkled the
blood of each sacrifice on the altar. [23]Finally
they took the goats to the king and to the
other worshipers, who laid their hands on
them. [24]Then the priests killed the goats and
poured their blood on the altar as a sacrifice
to take away the sin of all the people, for the
king had commanded that burnt offerings
and sin offerings be made for all Israel.
[25]The king followed the instructions that
the LORD had given to King David through
Gad, the king's prophet, and through the
prophet Nathan; he stationed Levites in the
Temple, with harps and cymbals, [26]instru-
ments like those that King David had used.
The priests also stood there with trumpets.
[27]Hezekiah gave the order for the burnt
offering to be presented; and as the offering
began, the people sang praise to the LORD,
and the musicians began to play the trum-
pets and all the other instruments. [28]Every-
one who was there joined in worship, and
the singing and the rest of the music contin-
ued until all the sacrifices had been burned.
[29]Then King Hezekiah and all the people
knelt down and worshiped God. [30]The king
and the leaders of the nation told the Levites
to sing to the LORD the songs of praise that
were written by David and by Asaph the
prophet. So everyone sang with great joy as
they knelt and worshiped God.
[31]Hezekiah said to the people, "Now that
you are ritually clean, bring sacrifices as
offerings of thanksgiving to the LORD." They
obeyed, and some of them also voluntarily
brought animals to be sacrificed as burnt
offerings. [32]They brought 70 bulls, 100
sheep, and 200 lambs as burnt offerings for
the LORD; [33]they also brought 600 bulls and
3,000 sheep as sacrifices for the people to
eat. [34]Since there were not enough priests to
kill all these animals, the Levites helped them
until the work was finished. By then more
priests had made themselves ritually clean.
(The Levites were more faithful in keeping
ritually clean than the priests were.) [35]In
addition to offering the sacrifices that were
burned whole, the priests were responsible
for burning the fat that was offered from the
sacrifices which the people ate, and for
pouring out the wine that was presented
with the burnt offerings.
And so worship in the Temple was begun
again. [36]King Hezekiah and the people were
happy, because God had helped them to do
all this so quickly.

Preparations for Passover

30 [1-3]The people had not been able to
celebrate the Passover Festival at the
proper time in the first month, because not
enough priests were ritually clean and not
many people had assembled in Jerusalem. So
King Hezekiah, his officials, and the people
of Jerusalem agreed to celebrate it in the sec-
ond month, and the king sent word to all the
people of Israel and Judah. He took special
care to send letters to the tribes of Ephraim
and Manasseh, inviting them to come to the
Temple in Jerusalem to celebrate the Passover
in honor of the LORD, the God of Israel.
[4]The king and the people were pleased with
their plan, [5]so they invited all the Israelites,
from Dan in the north to Beersheba in the
south, to come together in Jerusalem and cel-
ebrate the Passover according to the Law, in
larger numbers than ever before. [6]Messengers
went out at the command of the king and his
officials through all Judah and Israel with the
following invitation:

Messengers went out. (30:6)

"People of Israel, you have survived the
Assyrian conquest of the land. Now return
to the LORD, the God of Abraham, Isaac, and
Jacob, and he will return to you. [7]Do not be
like your ancestors and your Israelite relatives
who were unfaithful to the LORD their God.
As you can see, he punished them severely.

30:2, 3 Num 9:9–11

Aaron & Miriam

Breakthrough!: You two come from a pretty famous family.

Aaron: You could say that; our brother, Moses, is really the famous one.

B: But it would be fair to say that the three of you really worked as a team, wouldn't it?

Miriam: Well, yes. The three of us are very close. Aaron was actually Moses' spokesman. Moses has a bit of a speech problem, you see, and so God said that Aaron could be the one to speak to the people. Later, Aaron became the first high priest of the Israelites.

Aaron: And Miriam acted as the leader of the Hebrew women in the group that escaped from slavery.

B: And if it weren't for you, Miriam, Moses might never have survived to lead the Hebrew slaves out of Egypt, right?

Miriam: Yes, I helped hide him as a baby. Pharaoh had commanded that all the baby boys be thrown into the river and drowned. The Egyptians were afraid that soon there would be so many Hebrew slaves that we would rise up and revolt. My mother made a basket that floated, and I followed the basket and made sure that Moses was safe.

B: Is it true that you two were angry with Moses about the woman he married?

Aaron: Yes, that is true. We thought he should have married a Hebrew woman, but instead he chose an outsider. God let us know that we should trust him and Moses, though. Miriam was struck with leprosy. I pleaded with Moses and Moses pleaded with God for her to be healed.

B: What advice would you like to give our readers?

Miriam: Well, brothers and sisters don't always get along, but with God's help you can be a great support to each other.

Joshua

Breakthrough!: Joshua, you were a great leader, but you had a great teacher, too. Can you tell us who that was?

Joshua: I followed Moses. He was the best! He led the people out of slavery and through the desert. Moses was a really great guy, and so faithful to God.

B: Were you nervous, following in the footsteps of such a fantastic leader?

Joshua: Of course, especially when Moses died just before we were to enter the Promised Land. I didn't know if the people would really follow me. God told me not to be afraid and that he would be with me wherever I went.

B: And was he?

Joshua: Yes. God never left me. We crossed the Jordan River, and God parted the waters for us, just like he did for Moses. Then I led the battle against Jericho, and we won. We kept winning all the battles that God sent us into.

B: The battle of Jericho was pretty amazing, wasn't it?

Joshua: I'll say. The walls of that city were about twenty feet thick. There was no way we were going to get into that city. But God had us march around the city for seven days. The priests led the way carrying the Covenant Box. On the seventh day, the priests blew their horns, our people shouted, and the walls of Jericho caved in!

B: What do you think was the most important thing you did for the people of Israel?

Joshua: Well, I'd have to say that it was keeping them faithful to God. God led us out of slavery and through the desert. I felt like I was always reminding them of that. But it was God's power that led us into the Promised Land.

Deborah

Breakthrough!: Deborah, you were a judge of Israel, is that right?

Deborah: That's right, but in my time that meant something different than it does now.

B: You mean you didn't wear black robes and sit in a courtroom?

Deborah: No, no, no. Actually I sat under a palm tree. I think it's a much better place to make decisions, don't you?

B: I guess so. But what were you responsible for? What was your job?

Deborah: People came to me for advice, and I helped settle disagreements. But I was also a prophet, which meant that I had to deliver God's message to the people. The people had disobeyed the Lord and were suffering under the rule of a cruel king. They cried out to God, and God sent me to lead them.

B: About that, we heard that you told the warrior Barak to go to battle, but that he said he'd go only if you went with him. Is that true?

Deborah: Absolutely! I was not a warrior with an army, so I called Barak to do God's will. I guess Barak felt that if I believed enough in God's will to be at the battle, then he could trust God, too. I teased him a little about it, but I didn't mind going to battle—not much intimidates me. You can read Barak's and my victory song in Judges, chapter 5.

B: Was it unusual for a woman to be a judge in your time?

Deborah: There had been some other women in leadership, but one possible meaning of my name is "spirited woman." God helped other people see my gifts at a time when a woman's leadership was not appreciated.

Gideon

Breakthrough!: Gideon, how did you know that God was calling you to lead the people?

Gideon: Well I was threshing some wheat one day when an angel appeared. He called me brave and mighty, which was kind of cool. It was a little scary, too, though.

B: Scary? In what way?

Gideon: God wanted me to rescue Israel from the Midianites. There were a lot of Midianites, and they were very powerful. I told the angel that I was from a weak tribe and was the least important person in my family. I was definitely thinking that God could have chosen someone more . . . well, prepared than me.

B: But you went on to be a great leader, a judge of Israel, right? You defeated the Midianites and the people loved you!

Gideon: That was really nice, but what was important to me was trusting God. And God sure didn't make it easy for me.

B: What do you mean?

Gideon: Well, there was the time when he told me to send home any of the soldiers who were afraid! I lost two-thirds of my army! And then there was the time he told me to tear down my father's altar to Baal, the foreign god.

B: Was your father mad?

Gideon: Fortunately my father defended me.

B: Defended you? From whom?

Gideon: Basically the whole town wanted to kill me.

B: But you kept following God anyway?

Gideon: I don't think I could have done it if God had not been so patient with me. All along, God would give me signs and show me what he wanted me to do. I learned to trust in God, and our people were blessed with peace for forty years.

Samson

Breakthrough!: Rumor has it that you were a "miracle baby," that your parents thought they couldn't have any children.

Samson: That's right. An angel of the Lord appeared to my mother and told her she would have a baby. The angel was talking about me. He told her that I'd be a nazirite and that I'd fight our enemies, the Philistines.

B: Can you tell us a little bit about what being a nazirite means?

Samson: A nazirite is someone who is dedicated to God. We are not supposed to cut our hair or drink beer or wine.

B: Interesting. The whole haircut thing got to be a problem for you later on, didn't it?

Samson: That's true. My girlfriend Delilah found out that my long hair was the secret to my incredible strength. She was really cute, but she tricked me into telling her and then she told my enemies, the Philistines. It was awful.

B: That's terrible. But before that happened, you got out of a few other tough situations because of your amazing strength, right?

Samson: Seriously! You should have seen it! The people in the city of Gaza, they wanted to kill me. But I tricked them and tore the city gate right out of the ground and carried the whole thing to the top of a hill. It was pretty funny! Then there was the time I killed a lion with my bare hands and another time I killed a thousand men with a donkey's jawbone.

B: Your story has a tragic ending, doesn't it?

Samson: Yes, but it was my fault. I was captured and tortured after Delilah cut my hair. God did answer my prayer one last time, and I was able to destroy the Philistine leaders. If I can tell your readers one thing, it is to never take God's gifts for granted.

Ruth

Breakthrough!: Your story is kind of a sad one, isn't it, Ruth?

Ruth: Oh, I wouldn't say so. I mean, it started out sad; my husband, my father-in-law, and my brother-in-law had all died. My mother-in-law, Naomi, my sister-in-law, Orpah, and I were all widows. In my time widows didn't have any way to support themselves; that's why Naomi decided to go back to her own home. She had come to my country, Moab, when there was a famine in Bethlehem.

B: Didn't Naomi tell you and Orpah to go back to your own families?

Ruth: She did, but when it came time to say good-bye, I just couldn't leave her. We had become so close. I love her. She taught me about life and about God. She is my family now.

B: People say that you were pretty clever. You and Naomi returned to her hometown, and all of sudden you were married to one of the wealthiest men in town!

Ruth: I guess you could say I'm clever. Naomi gave me good advice, though, and Boaz was so kind; he really looked out for me. Boaz was my dead husband's relative, and that made it easier to approach him. But he really didn't have to marry me—because I was a foreign woman and all.

B: So would you say you're a "glass half full" kind of person?

Ruth: Well I've always tried to see the good in any situation. It really helped to learn that the God of the Israelites cared for me, too—a foreign woman. Can you believe that King David, the greatest king of the Israelites, was one of my descendants!

Samuel

Breakthrough!: Tell us, Samuel, did you always know that you'd be a prophet?

Samuel: Well, my mother, Hannah, seemed to think I'd be special. She prayed and prayed that God would send her a son. When I was finally born, she dedicated me to God.

B: You anointed the first king of Israel—that's pretty impressive. How did you feel about that?

Samuel: I actually tried to convince the people that they didn't need a king and that having a king would only bring them trouble. They wanted to be like other nations though. The Lord told me that Saul was the one to anoint.

B: And was he a good king?

Samuel: Hmph! Well, yes and no. Sometimes he was great; he defeated the Ammonites. But there were times when I had to remind Saul that he was supposed to do things God's way, not just do whatever he felt like.

B: Is it true that the first time God spoke to you, you didn't realize it was God?

Samuel: That's actually a pretty funny story. God was calling me in the middle of the night, and I thought it was my master, Eli. I kept waking Eli up thinking he needed something. Eli helped me understand that it was really the Lord who was calling me.

B: Didn't you anoint another king after Saul had disobeyed the Lord?

Samuel: I was pretty depressed after Saul was disobedient to God. God sent me out to Bethlehem to anoint a new king. I almost overlooked David; his older brothers were so much bigger and stronger. But David was handsome, heroic, and he really loved the Lord. Through David, God was able to unite the Twelve Tribes of Israel into one nation.

Saul

Breakthrough!: King Saul, you were the first king of Israel. How were you chosen?

Saul: I was a soldier and a military leader, and one day the prophet Samuel came to me and anointed me to be king. He told me that I had been chosen by God.

B: How did the people respond?

Saul: They seemed pleased to have me for their king, and I tried my best. But somewhere along the line, things started to go bad.

B: What happened?

Saul: I made some decisions that showed my lack of faith in God. Samuel told me that because I disobeyed God, God had turned away from me.

B: So what happened?

Saul: Our enemies, the Philistines, were getting the best of us until David came along and killed Goliath. From then on, everything seemed to go his way. When I found out that he had been anointed to be the next king, it bothered me.

B: What did you do?

Saul: I became very jealous of David and how popular he was getting. He had won over my son Jonathan and my daughter Michal, who became his wife. I know it was wrong, but I was determined to get rid of David.

B: Did you succeed?

Saul: No, and now it doesn't matter. My sons and I lost our lives in a battle on Mount Gilboa, fighting against the Philistines. I pray that David forgives me for my insane jealousy and for persecuting him.

B: Any words for our readers?

Saul: Have faith in God and do not disobey him, especially when God chooses you to be a leader.

8Do not be stubborn as they were, but obey the LORD. Come to the Temple in Jerusalem, which the LORD your God has made holy forever, and worship him so that he will no longer be angry with you. 9If you return to the LORD, then those who have taken your relatives away as prisoners will take pity on them and let them come back home. The LORD your God is kind and merciful, and if you return to him, he will accept you."

10The messengers went to every city in the territory of the tribes of Ephraim and Manasseh, and as far north as the tribe of Zebulun, but people laughed at them and made fun of them. 11Still, there were some from the tribes of Asher, Manasseh, and Zebulun who were willing to come to Jerusalem. 12God was also at work in Judah and united the people in their determination to obey his will by following the commands of the king and his officials.

Passover Is Celebrated

13A great number of people gathered in Jerusalem in the second month to celebrate the Festival of Unleavened Bread. 14They took all the altars that had been used in Jerusalem for offering sacrifices and burning incense and threw them into Kidron Valley. 15And on the fourteenth day of the month they killed the lambs for the Passover sacrifice. The priests and Levites who were not ritually clean became so ashamed that they dedicated themselves to the LORD, and now they could sacrifice burnt offerings in the Temple. 16They took their places in the Temple according to the instructions in the Law of Moses, the man of God. The Levites gave the blood of the sacrifices to the priests, who sprinkled it on the altar. 17Because many of the people were not ritually clean, they could not kill the Passover lambs, so the Levites did it for them and dedicated the lambs to the LORD. 18In addition, many of those who had come from the tribes of Ephraim, Manasseh, Issachar, and Zebulun had not performed the ritual of purification, and so they were observing Passover improperly. King Hezekiah offered this prayer for them: 19"O LORD, the God of our ancestors, in your goodness forgive those who are worshiping you with all their heart, even though they are not ritually clean." 20The LORD answered Hezekiah's prayer; he forgave the people and did not harm them. 21For seven days the people who had gathered in Jerusalem celebrated the Festival of Unleavened Bread with great joy, and day after day the Levites and the priests praised the LORD with all their strength.[n] 22Hezekiah praised the Levites for their skill in conducting the worship of the LORD.

A Second Celebration

After the seven days during which they offered sacrifices in praise of the LORD, the God of their ancestors, 23they all decided to celebrate for another seven days. So they celebrated with joy. 24King Hezekiah contributed 1,000 bulls and 7,000 sheep for the people to kill and eat, and the officials gave them another 1,000 bulls and 10,000 sheep. A large number of priests went through the ritual of purification. 25So everyone was happy—the people of Judah, the priests, the Levites, the people who had come from the north, and the foreigners who had settled permanently in Israel and Judah. 26The city of Jerusalem was filled with joy, because nothing like this had happened since the days of King Solomon, the son of David. 27The priests and the Levites asked the LORD's blessing on the people. In his home in heaven God heard their prayers and accepted them.

Hezekiah Reforms Religious Life

31 After the festival ended, all the people of Israel went to every city in Judah and broke the stone pillars, cut down the symbols of the goddess Asherah, and destroyed the altars and the pagan places of worship. They did the same thing throughout the rest of Judah, and the territories of Benjamin, Ephraim, and Manasseh; then they all returned home.

[n] **30:21** *Probable text* with all their strength; *Hebrew* with mighty instruments.

Receiving the gifts offered to the LORD *and . . . distributing them (31:14)*

2 King Hezekiah reestablished the organization of the priests and Levites, under which they each had specific duties. These included offering the burnt offerings and the fellowship offerings, taking part in the Temple worship, and giving praise and thanks in the various parts of the Temple. 3 From his own flocks and herds he provided animals for the burnt offerings each morning and evening, and for those offered on the Sabbath, at the New Moon Festival, and at the other festivals which are required by the Law of the LORD.

4 In addition, the king told the people of Jerusalem to bring the offerings to which the priests and the Levites were entitled, so that they could give all their time to the requirements of the Law of the LORD. 5 As soon as the order was given, the people of Israel brought gifts of their finest grain, wine, olive oil, honey, and other farm produce, and they also brought the tithes[o] of everything they had. 6 All the people who lived in the cities of Judah brought tithes of their cattle and sheep, and they also brought large quantities of gifts which they dedicated to the LORD their God. 7 The gifts started arriving in the third month and continued to pile up for the next four months. 8 When King Hezekiah and his officials saw how much had been given, they praised the LORD and praised his people Israel. 9 The king spoke to the priests and the Levites about these gifts, 10 and Azariah the High Priest, a descendant of Zadok, said to him, "Since the people started bringing their gifts to the Temple, there has been enough to eat and a large surplus besides. We have all this because the LORD has blessed his people."

11 On the king's orders they prepared storerooms in the Temple area 12 and put all the gifts and tithes in them for safekeeping. They placed a Levite named Conaniah in charge and made his brother Shimei his assistant. 13 Ten Levites were assigned to work under them: Jehiel, Azaziah, Nahath, Asahel, Jerimoth, Jozabad, Eliel, Ismachiah, Mahath, and Benaiah. All this was done under the authority of King Hezekiah and Azariah the High Priest. 14 Kore son of Imnah, a Levite who was chief guard at the East Gate of the Temple, was in charge of receiving the gifts offered to the LORD and of distributing them. 15 In the other cities where priests lived, he was faithfully assisted in this by other Levites: Eden, Miniamin, Jeshua, Shemaiah, Amariah, and Shecaniah. They distributed the food equally to their fellow Levites according to what their duties were, 16 and not by clans. They gave a share to all males thirty[p] years of age or older who had daily responsibilities in the Temple in accordance with their positions. 17 The priests were assigned their duties by clans, and the Levites

[o] **31:5** GIFTS . . . TITHES: *The gifts were for the priests, and the tithes for the Levites (see Num 18).* [p] **31:16** *Probable text* thirty; *Hebrew* three.

31:3 Num 28:1—29:39 **31:4, 5** Num 18:12, 13, 21

twenty years of age or older were assigned
theirs by work groups. 18They were all reg-
istered together with their wives, children,
and other dependents, because they were
required to be ready to perform their sacred
duties at any time. 19Among the priests who
lived in the cities assigned to Aaron's descen-
dants or in the pasture lands belonging to
these cities, there were responsible men who
distributed the food to all the males in the
priestly families and to everyone who was
on the rolls of the Levite clans.

20Throughout all Judah, King Hezekiah
did what was right and what was pleasing to
the LORD his God. 21He was successful,
because everything he did for the Temple or
in observance of the Law, he did in a spirit
of complete loyalty and devotion to his God.

The Assyrians Threaten Jerusalem

(2 Kings 18:13–37; 19:14–19, 35–37;
Isaiah 36:1–22; 37:8–38)

32 After these events, in which King
Hezekiah served the LORD faithfully,
Sennacherib, the emperor of Assyria, invaded
Judah. He besieged the fortified cities and
gave orders for his army to break their way
through the walls. 2When Hezekiah saw that
Sennacherib intended to attack Jerusalem
also, 3-4he and his officials decided to cut off
the supply of water outside the city in order
to keep the Assyrians from having any water
when they got near Jerusalem. The officials
led a large number of people out and
stopped up all the springs, so that no more
water flowed out of them. 5The king
strengthened the city's defenses by repairing
the wall, building towers on it,[q] and building
an outer wall. In addition, he repaired the
defenses built on the land that was filled in
on the east side of the old part of Jerusalem.
He also had a large number of spears and
shields made. 6He placed all the men in the
city under the command of army officers
and had them assemble in the open square at
the city gate. He said to them, 7"Be deter-
mined and confident, and don't be afraid of
the Assyrian emperor or of the army he is
leading. We have more power on our side
than he has on his. 8He has human power,
but we have the LORD our God to help us
and to fight our battles." The people were
encouraged by these words of their king.

9Some time later, while Sennacherib and
his army were still at Lachish, he sent the
following message to Hezekiah and the
people of Judah who were with him in
Jerusalem: 10"I, Sennacherib, Emperor of
Assyria, ask what gives you people the con-
fidence to remain in Jerusalem under siege.
11Hezekiah tells you that the LORD your
God will save you from our power, but
Hezekiah is deceiving you and will let you
die of hunger and thirst. 12He is the one
who destroyed the LORD's shrines and altars
and then told the people of Judah and
Jerusalem to worship and burn incense at
one altar only. 13Don't you know what my
ancestors and I have done to the people of
other nations? Did the gods of any other
nation save their people from the emperor
of Assyria? 14When did any of the gods of
all those countries ever save their country
from us? Then what makes you think that
your god can save you? 15Now don't let
Hezekiah deceive you or mislead you like
that. Don't believe him! No god of any
nation has ever been able to save his people
from any Assyrian emperor. So certainly this
god of yours can't save you!"

16The Assyrian officials said even worse
things about the LORD God and Hezekiah,
the LORD's servant. 17The letter that the
emperor wrote defied the LORD, the God of
Israel. It said, "The gods of the nations have
not saved their people from my power, and
neither will Hezekiah's god save his people
from me." 18The officials shouted this in
Hebrew in order to frighten and discourage
the people of Jerusalem who were on the
city wall, so that it would be easier to cap-
ture the city. 19They talked about the God of
Jerusalem in the same way that they talked
about the gods of the other peoples, idols
made by human hands.

20Then King Hezekiah and the prophet
Isaiah son of Amoz prayed to God and cried
out to him for help. 21The LORD sent an
angel that killed the soldiers and officers of

[q] **32:5** *Some ancient translations* building towers on it; *Hebrew* building on the towers.

Assyrian army. So the emperor went
back to Assyria disgraced. One day when he
was in the temple of his god, some of his
sons killed him with their swords.
22 In this way the LORD rescued King
Hezekiah and the people of Jerusalem from
the power of Sennacherib, the emperor of
Assyria, and also from their other enemies.
He let the people live in peace[r] with all the
neighboring countries. 23 Many people came
to Jerusalem, bringing offerings to the LORD
and gifts to Hezekiah, so that from then on
all the nations held Hezekiah in honor.

Hezekiah's Illness and Pride

(2 Kings 20:1–3, 12–19; Isaiah 38:1–3; 39:1–8)

24 About this time King Hezekiah became
sick and almost died. He prayed, and the
LORD gave him a sign that he would recov-
er. 25 But Hezekiah was too proud to show
gratitude for what the LORD had done for
him, and Judah and Jerusalem suffered for it.
26 Finally, however, Hezekiah and the people
of Jerusalem humbled themselves, and so the
LORD did not punish the people until after
Hezekiah's death.

Hezekiah's Wealth and Splendor

27 King Hezekiah became very wealthy,
and everyone held him in honor. He had
storerooms built for his gold, silver, precious
stones, spices, shields, and other valuable
objects. 28 In addition, he had storehouses
built for his grain, wine, and olive oil; barns
for his cattle; and pens for his sheep.
29 Besides all this, God gave him sheep and
cattle and so much other wealth that he built
many cities. 30 It was King Hezekiah who
blocked the outlet for Gihon Spring and
channeled the water to flow through a tun-
nel to a point inside the walls of Jerusalem.
Hezekiah succeeded in everything he did,
31 and even when the Babylonian ambassa-
dors came to inquire about the unusual
event that had happened in the land, God let
Hezekiah go his own way only in order to
test his character.

The End of Hezekiah's Reign

(2 Kings 20:20, 21)

32 Everything else that King Hezekiah did
and his devotion to the LORD are recorded
in *The Vision of the Prophet Isaiah Son of Amoz*
and in *The History of the Kings of Judah and
Israel.* 33 Hezekiah died and was buried in the
upper section of the royal tombs. All the
people of Judah and Jerusalem paid him
great honor at his death. His son Manasseh
succeeded him as king.

King Manasseh of Judah

(2 Kings 21:1–9)

33 Manasseh was twelve years old when
he became king of Judah, and he
ruled in Jerusalem for fifty-five years. 2 Fol-
lowing the disgusting practices of the nations
whom the LORD had driven out of the land
as his people advanced, Manasseh sinned
against the LORD. 3 He rebuilt the pagan
places of worship that his father Hezekiah
had destroyed. He built altars for the worship
of Baal, made images of the goddess Asherah,
and worshiped the stars. 4 He built pagan
altars in the Temple, the place that the LORD
had said was where he should be worshiped
forever. 5 In the two courtyards of the Temple
he built altars for the worship of the stars.
6 He sacrificed his sons in Hinnom Valley as
burnt offerings. He practiced divination and
magic and consulted fortunetellers and
mediums. He sinned greatly against the
LORD and stirred up his anger. 7 He placed
an image in the Temple, the place about
which God had said to David and his son
Solomon: "Here in Jerusalem, in this Temple,
is the place that I have chosen out of all the
territory of the twelve tribes of Israel as the
place where I am to be worshiped. 8 And if
the people of Israel will obey all my com-
mands and keep the whole Law that my ser-
vant Moses gave them, then I will not allow
them to be driven out of the land that I gave
to their ancestors." 9 Manasseh led the people
of Judah to commit even greater sins than
those committed by the nations whom the

[r] **32:22** *Some ancient translations* He let the people live in peace; *Hebrew* He led the people.

33:2 Jer 15:4 **33:4** 2 Chr 6:6 **33:7, 8** 1 Kings 9:3–5; 2 Chr 7:12–18

He sinned greatly against the LORD. (33:6)

LORD had driven out of the land as his peo-
ple advanced.

Manasseh Repents

[10]Although the LORD warned Manasseh
and his people, they refused to listen. [11]So
the LORD let the commanders of the Assyri-
an army invade Judah. They captured Manas-
seh, stuck hooks in him, put him in chains,
and took him to Babylon. [12]In his suffering
he became humble, turned to the LORD his
God, and begged him for help. [13]God
accepted Manasseh's prayer and answered it
by letting him go back to Jerusalem and rule
again. This convinced Manasseh that the
LORD was God.
[14]After this, Manasseh increased the
height of the outer wall on the east side of
David's City, from a point in the valley near
Gihon Spring north to the Fish Gate and
the area of the city called Ophel. He also
stationed an army officer in command of a
unit of troops in each of the fortified cities
of Judah. [15]He removed from the Temple the
foreign gods and the image that he had
placed there, and the pagan altars that were
on the hill where the Temple stood and in
other places in Jerusalem; he took all these
things outside the city and threw them away.
[16]He also repaired the altar where the LORD
was worshiped, and he sacrificed fellowship
offerings and thanksgiving offerings on it.
He commanded all the people of Judah to
worship the LORD, the God of Israel.
[17]Although the people continued to offer
sacrifices at other places of worship, they
offered them only to the LORD.

The End of Manasseh's Reign

(2 Kings 21:17, 18)

[18]Everything else that Manasseh did, the
prayer he made to his God, and the messages
of the prophets who spoke to him in the
name of the LORD, the God of Israel, are all
recorded in *The History of the Kings of Israel.*
[19]The king's prayer and God's answer to it,
and an account of the sins he committed
before he repented—the evil he did, the
pagan places of worship and the symbols of
the goddess Asherah that he made and the
idols that he worshiped—are all recorded in
The History of the Prophets. [20]Manasseh died
and was buried at the palace, and his son
Amon succeeded him as king.

King Amon of Judah

(2 Kings 21:19–26)

[21]Amon was twenty-two years old when
he became king of Judah, and he ruled in
Jerusalem for two years. [22]Like his father
Manasseh, he sinned against the LORD, and
he worshiped the idols that his father had
worshiped. [23]But unlike his father, he did
not become humble and turn to the LORD;
he was even more sinful than his father had
been.
[24]Amon's officials plotted against him and
assassinated him in the palace. [25]The people
of Judah killed Amon's assassins and made his
son Josiah king.

King Josiah of Judah

(2 Kings 22:1, 2)

34 Josiah was eight years old when he
became king of Judah, and he ruled
in Jerusalem for thirty-one years. [2]He did
what was pleasing to the LORD; he followed
the example of his ancestor King David,
strictly obeying all the laws of God.

34:1 Jer 3:6

Josiah Attacks Pagan Worship

3 In the eighth year that Josiah was king,
while he was still very young, he began to
worship the God of his ancestor King David.
Four years later he began to destroy the
pagan places of worship, the symbols of the
goddess Asherah, and all the other idols.
4 Under his direction the altars where Baal
was worshiped were smashed, and the
incense altars near them were torn down.
They ground to dust the images of Asherah
and all the other idols and then scattered the
dust on the graves of the people who had
sacrificed to them. 5 He burned the bones of
the pagan priests on the altars where they
had worshiped. By doing all this, he made
Judah and Jerusalem ritually clean again. 6 He
did the same thing in the cities and the dev-
astated areas of Manasseh, Ephraim, and
Simeon, and as far north as Naphtali.
7 Throughout the territory of the Northern
Kingdom he smashed the altars and the sym-
bols of Asherah, ground the idols to dust,
and broke into bits all the incense altars.
Then he returned to Jerusalem.

The Book of the Law Is Discovered
(2 Kings 22:3–20)

8 In the eighteenth year of his reign, after
he had purified the land and the Temple by
ending pagan worship, King Josiah sent three
men to repair the Temple of the LORD God:
Shaphan son of Azaliah, Maaseiah, the gover-
nor of Jerusalem, and Joah son of Joahaz, a
high official. 9 The money that the Levite
guards had collected in the Temple was
turned over to Hilkiah the High Priest. (It
had been collected from the people of
Ephraim and Manasseh and the rest of the
Northern Kingdom, and from the people of
Judah, Benjamin, and Jerusalem.) 10 This
money was then handed over to the three
men in charge of the Temple repairs, and
they gave it to 11 the carpenters and the
builders to buy the stones and the timber
used to repair the buildings that the kings of
Judah had allowed to decay. 12 The men who
did the work were thoroughly honest. They
were supervised by four Levites: Jahath and
Obadiah of the clan of Merari, and Zechari-
ah and Meshullam of the clan of Kohath.
(The Levites were all skillful musicians.)
13 Other Levites were in charge of transport-
ing materials and supervising the workers on
various jobs, and others kept records or
served as guards.

14 While the money was being taken out
of the storeroom, Hilkiah found the book of
the Law of the LORD, the Law that God had
given to Moses. 15 He said to Shaphan, "I
have found the book of the Law here in the
Temple." He gave Shaphan the book, 16 and
Shaphan took it to the king. He reported,
"We have done everything that you com-
manded. 17 We have taken the money that
was kept in the Temple and handed it over
to the workers and their supervisors."
18 Then he added, "I have here a book that
Hilkiah gave me." And he read it aloud to
the king.

19 When the king heard the book being
read, he tore his clothes in dismay 20 and gave
the following order to Hilkiah, to Ahikam
son of Shaphan, to Abdon[s] son of Micaiah,
to Shaphan, the court secretary, and to Asa-
iah, the king's attendant: 21 "Go and consult
the LORD for me and for the people who
still remain in Israel and Judah. Find out
about the teachings of this book. The LORD
is angry with us because our ancestors have
not obeyed the word of the LORD and have
not done what this book says must be done."

22 At the king's command, Hilkiah and the
others went to consult a woman named
Huldah, a prophet who lived in the newer
part of Jerusalem. (Her husband Shallum,
the son of Tikvah and grandson of Harhas,
was in charge of the Temple robes.) They
described to her what had happened, 23 and
she told them to go back to the king and
give him 24 the following message from the
LORD: "I am going to punish Jerusalem and
all its people with the curses written in the
book that was read to the king. 25 They have
rejected me and have offered sacrifices to
other gods, and so have stirred up my anger
by all they have done. My anger is aroused

[s] **34:20** ABDON: *Achbor in 2 Kings 22:12.*
34:4 2 Kings 21:3; 2 Chr 33:3 **34:5** 1 Kings 13:2

against Jerusalem, and it will not die down.
26 As for the king himself, this is what I, the
LORD God of Israel, say: You listened to
what is written in the book, 27 and you
repented and humbled yourself before me,
tearing your clothes and weeping, when you
heard how I threatened to punish Jerusalem
and its people. I have heard your prayer,
28 and the punishment which I am going to
bring on Jerusalem will not come until after
your death. I will let you die in peace."

The men returned to King Josiah with
this message.

Josiah Makes a Covenant to Obey the LORD

(2 Kings 23:1–20)

29 King Josiah summoned all the leaders of
Judah and Jerusalem, 30 and together they
went to the Temple, accompanied by the
priests and the Levites and all the rest of the
people, rich and poor alike. Before them all
the king read aloud the whole book of the
covenant, which had been found in the
Temple. 31 He stood by the royal column[t]
and made a covenant with the LORD to
obey him, to keep his laws and commands
with all his heart and soul, and to put into
practice the demands attached to the
covenant, as written in the book. 32 He made
the people of Benjamin and everyone else
present in Jerusalem promise to keep the
covenant. And so the people of Jerusalem
obeyed the requirements of the covenant
they had made with the God of their ances-
tors. 33 King Josiah destroyed all the disgust-
ing idols that were in the territory belong-
ing to the people of Israel, and as long as he
lived, he required the people to serve the
LORD, the God of their ancestors.

Josiah Celebrates the Passover

(2 Kings 23:21–23)

35 King Josiah celebrated the Passover at
Jerusalem in honor of the LORD; on
the fourteenth day of the first month they
killed the animals for the festival. 2 He
assigned to the priests the duties they were to
perform in the Temple and encouraged them
to do them well. 3 He also gave these instruc-
tions to the Levites, the teachers of Israel,
who were dedicated to the LORD: "Put the
sacred Covenant Box in the Temple that
King Solomon, the son of David, built. You
are no longer to carry it from place to place,
but you are to serve the LORD your God and
his people Israel. 4 Take your places in the
Temple by clans, according to the responsi-
bilities assigned to you by King David and
his son King Solomon, 5 and arrange your-
selves so that some of you will be available to
help each family of the people of Israel. 6 You
are to kill the Passover lambs and goats. Now
make yourselves ritually clean and prepare
the sacrifices in order that your fellow
Israelites may follow the instructions which
the LORD gave through Moses."

7 For the use of the people at the Passover,
King Josiah contributed from his own herds
and flocks 30,000 sheep, lambs, and young
goats, and 3,000 bulls. 8 His officials also
made contributions for the people, the
priests, and the Levites to use. And the offi-
cials in charge of the Temple—Hilkiah, the
High Priest, Zechariah, and Jehiel—gave the
priests 2,600 lambs and young goats and 300
bulls for sacrifices during the festival. 9 The
leaders of the Levites—Conaniah, Shemaiah
and his brother Nethanel, Hashabiah, Jeiel,
and Jozabad—contributed 5,000 lambs and
young goats and 500 bulls for the Levites to
offer as sacrifices.

10 When everything was arranged for the
Passover, the priests and the Levites took
their posts, as commanded by the king.
11 After the lambs and goats had been killed,
the Levites skinned them, and the priests
sprinkled the blood on the altar. 12 Then they
divided among the people, by family groups,
the animals for burnt offerings, so that they
could offer them according to the instruc-
tions in the Law of Moses. 13 The Levites
roasted the Passover sacrifices over the fire,
according to the regulations, and boiled the
sacred offerings in pots, kettles, and pans, and
quickly distributed the meat to the people.

[t] **34:31** *Probable text (see 2 Kings 23:3)* by the royal column; *Hebrew* in his place.
35:4 2 Chr 8:14 **35:13** Ex 12:8, 9

14 After this was done, the Levites provided
meat for themselves and for the priests
descended from Aaron, for the priests were
kept busy until night, burning the animals
that were burned whole and the fat of the
sacrifices. 15 The following musicians of the
Levite clan of Asaph were in the places
assigned to them by King David's instruc-
tions: Asaph, Heman, and Jeduthun, the
king's prophet. The guards at the Temple
gates did not need to leave their posts,
because the other Levites prepared the
Passover for them. 16 So, as King Josiah had
commanded, everything was done that day
for the worship of the LORD, the keeping of
the Passover Festival, and the offering of
burnt offerings on the altar. 17 For seven days
all the people of Israel who were present
celebrated the Passover and the Festival of
Unleavened Bread. 18 Since the days of the
prophet Samuel, the Passover had never been
celebrated like this. None of the former
kings had ever celebrated a Passover like this
one celebrated by King Josiah, the priests,
the Levites, and the people of Judah, Israel,
and Jerusalem 19 in the eighteenth year of
Josiah's reign.

The End of Josiah's Reign
(2 Kings 23:28–30)

20 After King Josiah had done all this for
the Temple, King Neco of Egypt led an army
to fight at Carchemish on the Euphrates
River. Josiah tried to stop him, 21 but Neco
sent Josiah this message: "This war I am
fighting does not concern you, King of
Judah. I have not come to fight you, but to
fight my enemies, and God has told me to
hurry. God is on my side, so don't oppose
me, or he will destroy you." 22 But Josiah was
determined to fight. He refused to listen to
what God was saying through King Neco, so
he disguised himself and went into battle on
the plain of Megiddo.
23 During the battle King Josiah was struck
by Egyptian arrows. He ordered his servants,
"Take me away; I'm badly hurt!" 24 They lift-
ed him out of his chariot, placed him in a
second chariot which he had there, and took
him to Jerusalem. There he died and was
buried in the royal tombs. All the people of
Judah and Jerusalem mourned his death.
25 The prophet Jeremiah composed a
lament for King Josiah. It has become a cus-
tom in Israel for the singers, both men and
women, to use this song when they mourn
for him. The song is found in the collection
of laments.
26 Everything that Josiah did—his devotion
to the LORD, his obedience to the Law,
27 and his history from beginning to end—is
all recorded in *The History of the Kings of
Israel and Judah.*

King Joahaz of Judah
(2 Kings 23:30–35)

36 The people of Judah chose Josiah's
son Joahaz and anointed him king in
Jerusalem. 2 Joahaz was twenty-three years
old when he became king of Judah, and he
ruled in Jerusalem for three months. 3 King
Neco of Egypt took him prisoner and made
Judah pay 7,500 pounds of silver and 75
pounds of gold as tribute. 4 Neco made Joa-
haz' brother Eliakim king of Judah and
changed his name to Jehoiakim. Joahaz was
taken to Egypt by Neco.

King Jehoiakim of Judah
(2 Kings 23:36 —24:7)

5 Jehoiakim was twenty-five years old
when he became king of Judah, and he
ruled in Jerusalem for eleven years. He
sinned against the LORD his God. 6 King
Nebuchadnezzar of Babylonia invaded
Judah, captured Jehoiakim, and took him to
Babylonia in chains. 7 Nebuchadnezzar car-
ried off some of the treasures of the Temple
and put them in his palace in Babylon.
8 Everything that Jehoiakim did, including
his disgusting practices and the evil he com-
mitted, is recorded in *The History of the
Kings of Israel and Judah.* His son Jehoiachin
succeeded him as king.

35:15 1 Chr 25:1 **35:17** Ex 12:1–20 **36:4** Jer 22:11, 12 **36:5** Jer 22:18, 19; 26:1–6; 35:1–19 **36:6** Jer 25:1–38; 36:1–32; 45:1–5; Dan 1:1, 2

King Jehoiachin of Judah
(2 Kings 24:8–17)

9 Jehoiachin was eighteen[u] years old when
he became king of Judah, and he ruled in
Jerusalem for three months and ten days. He
too sinned against the LORD. 10 When spring
came, King Nebuchadnezzar took Jehoiachin
to Babylonia as a prisoner and carried off
the treasures of the Temple. Then Nebuchad-
nezzar made Jehoiachin's uncle[v] Zedekiah
king of Judah and Jerusalem.

King Zedekiah of Judah
(2 Kings 24:18–20; Jeremiah 52:1–3a)

11 Zedekiah was twenty-one years old
when he became king of Judah, and he ruled
in Jerusalem for eleven years. 12 He sinned
against the LORD and did not listen humbly
to the prophet Jeremiah, who spoke the
word of the LORD.

The Fall of Jerusalem
(2 Kings 25:1–21; Jeremiah 52:3b–11)

13 Zedekiah rebelled against King Neb-
uchadnezzar, who had forced him to swear
in God's name that he would be loyal. He
stubbornly refused to repent and return to
the LORD, the God of Israel. 14 In addition,
the leaders of Judah, the priests, and the peo-
ple followed the sinful example of the
nations around them in worshiping idols,
and so they defiled the Temple, which the
LORD himself had made holy. 15 The LORD,
the God of their ancestors, had continued to
send prophets to warn his people, because he
wanted to spare them and the Temple. 16 But
they made fun of God's messengers, ignoring
his words and laughing at his prophets, until
at last the LORD's anger against his people
was so great that there was no escape.
17 So the LORD brought the king of Bab-
ylonia to attack them. The king killed the
young men of Judah even in the Temple. He
had no mercy on anyone, young or old, man
or woman, sick or healthy. God handed
them all over to him. 18 The king of Babylo-
nia looted the Temple, the Temple treasury,
and the wealth of the king and his officials,
and took everything back to Babylon. 19 He
burned down the Temple and the city, with
all its palaces and its wealth, and broke
down the city wall. 20 He took all the sur-
vivors to Babylonia, where they served him
and his descendants as slaves until the rise
of the Persian Empire. 21 And so what the
LORD had foretold through the prophet
Jeremiah was fulfilled: "The land will lie
desolate for seventy years, to make up
for the Sabbath rest[w] that has not been
observed."

Cyrus Commands the Jews to Return
(Ezra 1:1–4)

22 In the first year that Cyrus of Persia was
emperor,[x] the LORD made what he had said
through the prophet Jeremiah come true. He
prompted Cyrus to issue the following com-
mand and send it out in writing to be read
aloud everywhere in his empire:
23 "This is the command of Cyrus,
Emperor of Persia. The LORD, the God of
Heaven, has made me ruler over the whole
world and has given me the responsibility of
building a temple for him in Jerusalem in
Judah. Now, all of you who are God's peo-
ple, go there, and may the LORD your God
be with you."

[u] **36:9** *Some ancient translations (and see 2 Kings 24:8)* eighteen; *Hebrew* eight. [v] **36:10** *Some ancient translations (and see 2 Kings 24:17)* uncle; *Hebrew* brother. [w] **36:21** SABBATH REST: *A reference to the requirement of the Law that every seventh year the land was not to be farmed (see Lev 25:1–7).* [x] **36:22** EMPEROR: *King Cyrus of Persia occupied the city of Babylon in 539 B.C. and began to reign as the emperor of Babylonia.*

36:10 **a** Jer 22:24–30; 24:1–10; 29:1, 2; Ezek 17:12; **b** Jer 37:1; Ezek 17:13 **36:11** Jer 27:1–22; 28:1–17 **36:13** Ezek 17:15 **36:17** Jer 21:1–10; 34:1–5 **36:19** 1 Kings 9:8 **36:21** Jer 25:11; 29:10 **36:23** Isa 44:28

THE BOOKS OF *Ezra and Nehemiah*

When the Galliano family left for vacation, they never imagined what would happen. First, they couldn't get home because their car died. When they got the car fixed, they still couldn't go home because of a hurricane. When they finally got back to their home in Florida, they found out the hurricane had ruined part of their house. It seemed so hopeless.

That is probably how the Israelites felt when they returned to Jerusalem—only a whole lot worse. After being in exile for 50 years, they came home to a city that needed a lot of repair. The Temple needed to be rebuilt so they could worship God again, and the city walls needed to be rebuilt for their protection. It was a big job that took a lot of work and cooperation. The books of Ezra and Nehemiah tell part of the rebuilding story.

Headlines

- Jewish Exiles Free After Fifty Years (Ezra 1:1–10)
- Dispute Over Rebuilding the Temple (Ezra 4:1–5)
- Returned Exiles Celebrate Passover (Ezra 6:19–22)
- Ezra Delivers Gifts from King Cyrus (Ezra 8:24–30)
- Nehemiah Asks to Help Rebuild (Nehemiah 2:1–8)
- Wealthy Leaders Take Advantage of Poor People (Nehemiah 5:1–13)
- Nehemiah Dedicates Rebuilt City Wall (Nehemiah 12:27–40)

FACTOIDS

Who wrote these books? The author is unknown, but these books were probably written by a scribe who used personal accounts, or memoirs, from Ezra and Nehemiah to compose them.

What time period do they cover? These books cover the return of the exiles to Jerusalem from the Babylonian captivity to Nehemiah's rule as governor.

Why were they written? These books were written to give an account of the rebuilding of Jerusalem and the Temple after the Exile.

Jesus connection: In the Gospels, Jesus referred to his Resurrection as the rebuilding of the Temple (John 2:19).

Important themes

- The Israelites return from captivity and rebuild Jerusalem and the Temple.
- Prayer, worship, cooperation, strong leadership, and a renewed commitment to God were necessary for the Israelites to rebuild.

Cyrus Commands the Jews to Return

1 In the first year that Cyrus of Persia was
emperor,[a] the LORD made what he had
said through the prophet Jeremiah come
true. He prompted Cyrus to issue the fol-
lowing command and send it out in writing
to be read aloud everywhere in his empire:
2"This is the command of Cyrus, Emper-
or of Persia. The LORD, the God of Heav-
en, has made me ruler over the whole
world and has given me the responsibility
of building a temple for him in Jerusalem
in Judah. 3May God be with all of you
who are his people. You are to go to
Jerusalem and rebuild the Temple of the
LORD, the God of Israel, the God who is
worshiped in Jerusalem. 4If any of his
people in exile need help to return, their
neighbors are to give them this help. They
are to provide them with silver and gold,
supplies and pack animals, as well as offer-
ings to present in the Temple of God in
Jerusalem."
5Then the heads of the clans of the tribes
of Judah and Benjamin, the priests and
Levites, and everyone else whose heart God
had moved got ready to go and rebuild the
LORD's Temple in Jerusalem. 6All their
neighbors helped them by giving them
many things: silver utensils, gold, supplies,
pack animals, other valuables, and offerings
for the Temple.
7Emperor Cyrus gave them back the
bowls and cups that King Nebuchadnezzar
had taken from the Temple in Jerusalem and
had put in the temple of his gods. 8He hand-
ed them over to Mithredath, chief of the
royal treasury, who made an inventory of
them for Sheshbazzar, the governor of Judah,
9-10as follows:

gold bowls for offerings	30
silver bowls for offerings	1,000
other bowls	29
small gold bowls	30
small silver bowls	410
other utensils	1,000

11In all there were 5,400 gold and silver

Study it!

Persian Connection

Persia is an ancient region that is now called Iran. It is in the Middle East, near Iraq, Afghanistan, and Turkey. Three large bodies of water are near it: the Persian Gulf, the Caspian Sea, and the Gulf of Oman. Persia was an important place for the Jewish people who were exiled in Babylon. From Persia came their deliverer, Cyrus the Great.

Cyrus was the emperor in Persia in the sixth century BC. He was called Cyrus the Great because he was a strong warrior, and he also ruled fairly. It is possible that he is the author of the first declaration of human rights. The Jews were finally allowed to return from exile under Cyrus. He also did other good things for the people who lived in his kingdom. The name Cyrus means "like the sun." Even today men are named Cyrus.

Do you know who you are named after and what your name means? If it was someone from the Bible or a saint, find out what he or she did. If not, look up your name in a name book and find out what it means.

— Ezra, chapter 1

[a] **1:1** EMPEROR: *King Cyrus of Persia occupied the city of Babylon in 539 B.C. and began to reign as the emperor of Babylonia.*

1:1 Jer 25:11; 29:10 **1:2** Isa 44:28

bowls and other articles which Sheshbazzar took with him when he and the other exiles went from Babylon to Jerusalem.

The List of Those Who Returned from Exile

(Nehemiah 7:4–73)

2 Many of the exiles left the province of Babylon and returned to Jerusalem and Judah, all to their own hometowns. Their families had been living in exile in Babylonia ever since King Nebuchadnezzar had taken them there as prisoners. 2 Their leaders were Zerubbabel, Joshua, Nehemiah, Seraiah, Reelaiah, Mordecai, Bilshan, Mispar, Bigvai, Rehum, and Baanah.

Many of the exiles left. (2:1)

This is the list of the clans of Israel, with the number of those from each clan who returned from exile:

3-20 Parosh - 2,172
Shephatiah - 372
Arah - 775
Pahath Moab (descendants of Jeshua and Joab) - 2,812
Elam - 1,254
Zattu - 945
Zaccai - 760
Bani - 642
Bebai - 623
Azgad - 1,222
Adonikam - 666
Bigvai - 2,056
Adin - 454
Ater (also called Hezekiah) - 98
Bezai - 323
Jorah - 112
Hashum - 223
Gibbar - 95

21-35 People whose ancestors had lived in the following towns also returned:

Bethlehem - 123
Netophah - 56
Anathoth - 128
Azmaveth - 42
Kiriath Jearim, Chephirah, and Beeroth - 743
Ramah and Geba - 621
Michmash - 122
Bethel and Ai - 223
Nebo - 52
Magbish - 156
The other Elam - 1,254
Harim - 320
Lod, Hadid, and Ono - 725
Jericho - 345
Senaah - 3,630

36-39 This is the list of the priestly clans that returned from exile:

Jedaiah (descendants of Jeshua) - 973
Immer - 1,052
Pashhur - 1,247
Harim - 1,017

40-42 Clans of Levites who returned from exile:

Jeshua and Kadmiel (descendants of Hodaviah) - 74
Temple musicians (descendants of Asaph) - 128
Temple guards (descendants of Shallum, Ater, Talmon, Akkub, Hatita, and Shobai) - 139

43-54 Clans of Temple workers who returned from exile:

Ziha, Hasupha, Tabbaoth,
Keros, Siaha, Padon,
Lebanah, Hagabah, Akkub,
Hagab, Shamlai, Hanan,
Giddel, Gahar, Reaiah,
Rezin, Nekoda, Gazzam,
Uzza, Paseah, Besai,
Asnah, Meunim, Nephisim,
Bakbuk, Hakupha, Harhur,
Bazluth, Mehida, Harsha,
Barkos, Sisera, Temah,
Neziah, and Hatipha

Why would the priests, the Levites, the musicians, the Temple guards, and the Temple workers settle in Jerusalem or nearby towns?

55-57 Clans of Solomon's servants who
returned from exile:
Sotai, Hassophereth, Peruda,
Jaalah, Darkon, Giddel,
Shephatiah, Hattil, Pochereth Hazzebaim,
and Ami
58 The total number of descendants of the
Temple workers and of Solomon's servants
who returned from exile was 392.
59-60 There were 652 belonging to the
clans of Delaiah, Tobiah, and Nekoda who
returned from the towns of Tel Melah, Tel
Harsha, Cherub, Addan, and Immer; but they
could not prove that they were descendants
of Israelites.
61-62 The following priestly clans could
find no record to prove their ancestry: Habaiah, Hakkoz, and Barzillai. (The ancestor of
the priestly clan of Barzillai had married a
woman from the clan of Barzillai of Gilead
and had taken the name of his father-in-law's clan.) Since they were unable to prove
who their ancestors were, they were not
accepted as priests.
63 The Jewish governor
told them that they could not eat the food
offered to God until there was a priest who
could use the Urim and Thummim.[b]
64-67 Total number of exiles who
returned - 42,360
Their male and female servants - 7,337
Male and female musicians - 200
Horses - 736
Mules - 245
Camels - 435
Donkeys - 6,720
68 When the exiles arrived at the LORD's
Temple in Jerusalem, some of the leaders of
the clans gave freewill offerings to help
rebuild the Temple on its old site.
69 They gave
as much as they could for this work, and the
total came to 1,030 pounds of gold, 5,740
pounds of silver, and 100 robes for priests.
70 The priests, the Levites, and some of the
people settled in or near Jerusalem;[c] the
musicians, the Temple guards, and the Temple
workers settled in nearby towns; and the rest
of the Israelites settled in the towns where
their ancestors had lived.

Study it!

Mules, Horses, Camels, and Donkeys

It may seem funny to list the animals that returned from exile. However, the animals were very important for these ancient people. Listing them would be like listing how many cars, trucks, and airplanes a country has today. There is significance to the different types of animals. Mules were associated with royalty. Horses were important for warfare. Camels were important for long-distance travel but were expensive. Only the wealthier people could afford them. And donkeys were the common person's pack animal (like today's compact car!).

If you are good at math, try to figure out how many returning exiles there were for each camel. How many returning exiles for each donkey?

— Ezra 2:64–67

Worship Begins Again

3 By the seventh month the people of
Israel were all settled in their towns.
Then they all assembled in Jerusalem,
2 and
Joshua son of Jehozadak, his fellow priests,
and Zerubbabel son of Shealtiel, together
with his relatives, rebuilt the altar of the God
of Israel, so that they could burn sacrifices on
it according to the instructions written in the
Law of Moses, the man of God.
3 Even
though[d] the returning exiles were afraid of
the people who were living in the land, they
rebuilt the altar where it had stood before.

[b] **2:63** URIM AND THUMMIM: *Two objects used by the priest to determine God's will; it is not known precisely how they were used.* [c] **2:70** *One ancient translation* in or near Jerusalem; *Hebrew does not have these words.* [d] **3:3** Even though; *or* Because.

2:63 Num 27:21 **2:70** 1 Chr 9:2; Neh 11:3 **3:2** Ex 27:1 **3:3** Num 28:1–8

Then they began once again to burn on it
the regular morning and evening sacrifices.
4They celebrated the Festival of Shelters
according to the regulations; each day they
offered the sacrifices required for that day;
5and in addition they offered the regular sac-
rifices to be burned whole and those to be
offered at the New Moon Festival and at all
the other regular assemblies at which the
LORD is worshiped, as well as all the offerings
that were given to the LORD voluntarily.
6Although the people had not yet started to
rebuild the Temple, they began on the first
day of the seventh month to burn sacrifices to
the LORD.

The Rebuilding of the Temple Begins

7The people gave money to pay the
stonemasons and the carpenters and gave
food, drink, and olive oil to be sent to the
cities of Tyre and Sidon in exchange for
cedar trees from Lebanon, which were to be
brought by sea to Joppa. All this was done
with the permission of Emperor Cyrus of
Persia. 8So in the second month of the year
after they came back to the site of the Tem-
ple in Jerusalem, they began work. Zerubba-
bel, Joshua, and the rest of their people, the
priests, and the Levites, in fact all the exiles
who had come back to Jerusalem, joined in
the work. All the Levites twenty years of age
or older were put in charge of the work of
rebuilding the Temple. 9The Levite Jeshua
and his sons and relatives, and Kadmiel and
his sons (the clan of Hodaviah[e]) joined
together in taking charge of the rebuilding
of the Temple. (They were helped by the
Levites of the clan of Henadad.)

10When the builders started to lay the
foundation of the Temple, the priests in their
robes took their places with trumpets in
their hands, and the Levites of the clan of
Asaph stood there with cymbals. They
praised the LORD according to the instruc-
tions handed down from the time of King
David. 11They sang the LORD's praises,
repeating the refrain:

The foundation of the Temple had been started. (3:11)

"The LORD is good, and his love for
Israel is eternal."

Everyone shouted with all their might, prais-
ing the LORD, because the work on the
foundation of the Temple had been started.
12Many of the older priests, Levites, and
heads of clans had seen the first Temple, and
as they watched the foundation of this Tem-
ple being laid, they cried and wailed. But the
others who were there shouted for joy. 13No
one could distinguish between the joyful
shouts and the crying, because the noise they
made was so loud that it could be heard for
miles.

Opposition to the Rebuilding of the Temple

4 The enemies of the people of Judah and
Benjamin heard that those who had
returned from exile were rebuilding the
Temple of the LORD, the God of Israel. 2So
they went to see Zerubbabel and the heads
of the clans and said, "Let us join you in
building the Temple. We worship the same
God you worship, and we have been offering
sacrifices to him ever since Emperor
Esarhaddon of Assyria sent us here to live."

3Zerubbabel, Joshua, and the heads of the
clans told them, "We don't need your help
to build a temple for the LORD our God. We
will build it ourselves, just as Emperor Cyrus
of Persia commanded us."

4Then the people who had been living in
the land tried to discourage and frighten the
Jews and keep them from building. 5They
also bribed Persian government officials to
work against them. They kept on doing this

[e] **3:9** *Probable text (see 2:40)* Hodaviah; *Hebrew* Judah.

3:4 Num 29:12–38 **3:5** Num 28:11—29:39 **3:10** 1 Chr 25:1 **3:11** 1 Chr 16:34; 2 Chr 5:13; 7:3; Ps 100:5; 106:1; 107:1; 118:1; 136:1; Jer 33:11 **3:12** Tob 14:5 **4:2** 2 Kings 17:24–41

throughout the reign of Emperor Cyrus and
into the reign of Emperor Darius.[f]

Opposition to the Rebuilding of Jerusalem

6 At the beginning of the reign of Emper-
or Xerxes, the enemies of the people living
in Judah and Jerusalem brought written
charges against them.
7 Again in the reign of Emperor Artaxerxes
of Persia, Bishlam, Mithredath, Tabeel, and
their associates wrote a letter to the emperor.
The letter was written in Aramaic[g] and was
to be translated when read.[h]
8 Also Rehum, the governor, and
Shimshai, the secretary of the province,
wrote the following letter to Emperor
Artaxerxes about Jerusalem:
9 "From Rehum, the governor, from
Shimshai, secretary of the province, from
their associates, the judges, and from all
the other officials, who are originally from
Erech, Babylon, and Susa in the land of
Elam, 10 together with the other peoples
whom the great and powerful Ashurbani-
pal moved from their homes and settled in
the city of Samaria and elsewhere in West-
of-Euphrates Province."[i]
11 This is the text of the letter:
"To Emperor Artaxerxes from his ser-
vants who live in West-of-Euphrates.
12 "We want Your Majesty to know that
the Jews who came here from your other
territories have settled in Jerusalem and are
rebuilding that evil and rebellious city.
They have begun to rebuild the walls and
will soon finish them. 13 Your Majesty, if
this city is rebuilt and its walls are com-
pleted, the people will stop paying taxes,
and your royal revenues will decrease.
14 Now, because we are under obligation to
Your Majesty, we do not want to see this
happen, and so we suggest 15 that you order
a search to be made in the records your
ancestors kept. If you do, you will discover

Live it!

Keep Trying!

Ezra and the Jewish people returning to rebuild Jerusalem had many obstacles to overcome. They had to find the materials they needed, and they put in lots of long hours in hard, physical labor. They also had people trying to stop them. These people were afraid that they would lose their power once Jerusalem and the Temple were rebuilt. You read the letters they wrote to the new king in chapters 4 and 5. Without the encouragement of Ezra and other leaders, the people might never have finished the rebuilding. It took a long time, and a lot of work, but the result was worth it.

What difficult thing do you have to do? Maybe working on a big school project or completing a scouting award or preparing for a big athletic competition. Find someone to be your "Ezra," someone who can encourage you in completing your task. Choose someone who not only will encourage you but is also wise and can guide you in what you are trying to do. You will find out that having such a person will make your job easier.

— Ezra, chapters 4–5

[f] **4:5** EMPEROR DARIUS: *The account of these events is continued at verse 24. The material in verses 6–23 describes events which took place almost a century later.* [g] **4:7** ARAMAIC: *From 4:8 to 6:18 this book is not in Hebrew, but Aramaic, the official language of the Persian Empire.* [h] **4:7** The letter . . . read; *or* It was in Aramaic and was written in the Aramaic script. [i] **4:10** WEST-OF-EUPHRATES PROVINCE: *Under Persian rule the land of Judah was part of this large Persian province west of the Euphrates River.*

4:6 Esth 1:1

Aramaic *(Ezra 4:7)* **is a language that is still spoken in Syria, Iraq, Turkey, and Iran.**

that this city has always been rebellious
and that from ancient times it has given
trouble to kings and to rulers of provinces.
Its people have always been hard to gov-
ern. This is why the city was destroyed.
16 We therefore are convinced that if this
city is rebuilt and its walls are completed,
Your Majesty will no longer be able to
control West-of-Euphrates Province."
17 The emperor sent this answer:

"To Rehum, the governor, to Shimshai,
secretary of the province, and to their
associates who live in Samaria and in the
rest of West-of-Euphrates, greetings.

18 "The letter which you sent has been
translated and read to me. 19 I gave orders
for an investigation to be made, and it has
indeed been found that from ancient
times Jerusalem has revolted against royal
authority and that it has been full of rebels
and troublemakers. 20 Powerful kings have
reigned there and have ruled over the
entire province of West-of-Euphrates, col-
lecting taxes and revenue. 21 Therefore you
are to issue orders that those men are to
stop rebuilding the city until I give further
commands. 22 Do this at once, so that no
more harm may be done to my interests."
23 As soon as this letter from Emperor
Artaxerxes was read to Rehum, Shimshai,
and their associates, they hurried to
Jerusalem and forced the Jews to stop
rebuilding the city.

Work on the Temple Begins Again

24 Work on the Temple had been stopped
and had remained at a standstill until the
second year of the reign of Emperor Darius
5 of Persia. 1 At that time two prophets,
Haggai and Zechariah son of Iddo, began
to speak in the name of the God of Israel to
the Jews who lived in Judah and Jerusalem.
2 When Zerubbabel son of Shealtiel and
Joshua son of Jehozadak heard their messages,
they began to rebuild the Temple in
Jerusalem, and the two prophets helped them.
3 Almost at once Governor Tattenai of West-
of-Euphrates, Shethar Bozenai, and their fel-
low officials came to Jerusalem and demand-
ed: "Who gave you orders to build this Temple
and equip it?" 4 They[j] also asked for the names
of all the men who were helping build the
Temple. 5 But God was watching over the Jew-
ish leaders, and the Persian officials decided to
take no action until they could write to
Emperor Darius and receive a reply. 6 This is
the report that they sent to the emperor:

7 "To Emperor Darius, may you rule in
peace.

8 "Your Majesty should know that we
went to the province of Judah and found
that the Temple of the great God is being
rebuilt with large stone blocks and with
wooden beams set in the wall. The work
is being done with great care and is mov-
ing ahead steadily.

9 "We then asked the leaders of the peo-
ple to tell us who had given them authori-
ty to rebuild the Temple and to equip it.
10 We also asked them their names so that
we could inform you who the leaders of
this work are.

11 "They answered, 'We are servants of
the God of heaven and earth, and we are
rebuilding the Temple which was originally
built and equipped many years ago by a
powerful king of Israel. 12 But because our
ancestors made the God of Heaven angry,
he let them be conquered by King Neb-
uchadnezzar of Babylonia, a king of the
Chaldean dynasty. The Temple was
destroyed, and the people were taken into
exile in Babylonia. 13 Then in the first year
of the reign of King Cyrus as emperor of
Babylonia, Cyrus issued orders for the Tem-
ple to be rebuilt. 14 He restored the gold and
silver Temple utensils which Nebuchadnez-
zar had taken from the Temple in Jerusalem
and had placed in the temple in Babylon.

[j] **5:4** *Some ancient translations* They; *Aramaic* We.

4:24 Hag 1:1; Zech 1:1 **5:1** Hag 1:1; Zech 1:1 **5:2** Hag 1:12; Zech 4:6–9 **5:12** 2 Kings 25:8–12; 2 Chr 36:17–20; Jer 52:12–15 **5:13** Ezra 1:2–11

At the beginning of Ezra, chapter 5, two prophets are named, Haggai and Zechariah. Can you find their books in the Bible?

Pray it!

Yippee!

The Israelites were very happy when Emperor Darius "found" the original scroll from Emperor Cyrus ordering the rebuilding of the Temple in Jerusalem. They certainly prayed in thanksgiving (most likely after shouting "Yippee!"). If you ask God to help you out, it is good to thank God when your prayers are answered. The next time God answers a prayer, you can use this YIPPEE prayer in thanksgiving.

You, my wonderful God have come to my defense.
I needed you and there you were.
Praise be to you! You came to my defense!
Praise be to you! You answered my prayers!
Every part of me gives thanks.
Every part of me cries "Yippee!"

— Ezra 6:1–12

Emperor Cyrus turned these utensils over to a man named Sheshbazzar, whom he appointed governor of Judah. 15The emperor told him to take them and return them to the Temple in Jerusalem, and to rebuild the Temple where it had stood before. 16So Sheshbazzar came and laid its foundation; construction has continued from then until the present, but it is still not finished.'

17"Now, if it please Your Majesty, have a search made in the royal records in Babylon to find whether or not Emperor Cyrus gave orders for this Temple in Jerusalem to be rebuilt, and then inform us what your will is in this matter."

Emperor Cyrus' Order Is Rediscovered

6 So Emperor Darius issued orders for a search to be made in the royal records that were kept in Babylon. 2But it was in the city of Ecbatana in the province of Media that a scroll was found, containing the following record:

3"In the first year of his reign Emperor Cyrus commanded that the Temple in Jerusalem be rebuilt as a place where sacrifices are made and offerings are burned. The Temple is to be ninety feet high and ninety feet wide. 4The walls are to be built with one layer of wood on top of each three layers of stone. All expenses are to be paid by the royal treasury. 5Also the gold and silver utensils which King Nebuchadnezzar brought to Babylon from the Temple in Jerusalem are to be returned to their proper place in the Jerusalem Temple."

Emperor Darius Orders the Work to Continue

6Then Emperor Darius sent the following reply:

"To Tattenai, governor of West-of-Euphrates, Shethar Bozenai, and your fellow officials in West-of-Euphrates.

"Stay away from the Temple 7and do not interfere with its construction. Let the governor of Judah and the Jewish leaders rebuild the Temple of God where it stood before. 8I hereby command you to help them rebuild it. Their expenses are to be paid promptly out of the royal funds received from taxes in West-of-Euphrates, so that the work is not interrupted. 9Day by day, without fail, you are to give the priests in Jerusalem whatever they tell you they need: young bulls, sheep, or lambs to be burned as offerings to the God of Heaven, or wheat, salt, wine, or olive oil. 10This is to be done so that they can offer sacrifices that are acceptable to the God of Heaven and pray for his blessing on me and my sons. 11I further command that if any disobey this order, a wooden beam is to be torn out of their houses, sharpened on one end, and then driven through their bodies. And their houses are to be made a rubbish heap. 12 May the God who chose Jerusalem as the place where he is to be worshiped overthrow any king or nation that defies this command and tries to destroy the Temple there. I, Darius, have commanded. My command is to be fully obeyed."

The Temple Is Dedicated

13 Then Governor Tattenai, Shethar Bozenai, and their fellow officials did exactly as the emperor had commanded. 14 The Jewish leaders made good progress with the building of the Temple, encouraged by the prophets Haggai and Zechariah. They completed the Temple as they had been commanded by the God of Israel and by Cyrus, Darius, and Artaxerxes, emperors of Persia. 15 They finished the Temple on the third day of the month Adar in the sixth year of the reign of Emperor Darius. 16 Then the people of Israel—the priests, the Levites, and all the others who had returned from exile—joyfully dedicated the Temple. 17 For the dedication they offered 100 bulls, 200 sheep, and 400 lambs as sacrifices, and 12 goats as offerings for sin, one for each tribe of Israel. 18 They also organized the priests and the Levites for the Temple services in Jerusalem, according to the instructions contained in the book of Moses.

The Passover

19 The people who had returned from exile celebrated Passover on the fourteenth day of the first month of the following year. 20 All the priests and the Levites had purified themselves and were ritually clean. The Levites killed the animals for the Passover sacrifices for all the people who had returned, for the priests, and for themselves. 21 The sacrifices were eaten by all the Israelites who had returned from exile and by all those who had given up the pagan ways of the other people who were living in the land and who had come to worship the LORD God of Israel. 22 For seven days they joyfully celebrated the Festival of Unleavened Bread. They were full of joy because the LORD had made the emperor of Assyria[k] favorable to them, so that he supported them in their work of rebuilding the Temple of the God of Israel.

[They] joyfully dedicated the Temple. (6:16)

Ezra Arrives in Jerusalem

7 Many years later, when Artaxerxes was emperor of Persia, there was a man named Ezra. He traced his ancestors back to Aaron, the High Priest, as follows: Ezra was the son of Seraiah, son of Azariah, son of Hilkiah, 2 son of Shallum, son of Zadok, son of Ahitub, 3 son of Amariah, son of Azariah, son of Meraioth, 4 son of Zerahiah, son of Uzzi, son of Bukki, 5 son of Abishua, son of Phinehas, son of Eleazar, son of Aaron.

6-7 Ezra was a scholar with a thorough knowledge of the Law which the LORD, the God of Israel, had given to Moses. Because Ezra had the blessing of the LORD his God, the emperor gave him everything he asked for. In the seventh year of the reign of Artaxerxes, Ezra set out from Babylonia for Jerusalem with a group of Israelites which included priests, Levites, Temple musicians, Temple guards, and workers. 8-9 They left Babylonia on the first day of the first month, and with God's help they arrived in Jerusalem on the first day of the fifth month. 10 Ezra had devoted his life to studying the Law of the LORD, to practicing it, and to teaching all its laws and regulations to the people of Israel.

[k] **6:22** EMPEROR OF ASSYRIA: *Apparently a reference to the Persian emperor who then also ruled the territory once occupied by Assyria, Israel's ancient enemy.*

6:14 a Hag 1:1; **b** Zech 1:1 **6:19** Ex 12:1–20

The Document Which Emperor Artaxerxes Gave to Ezra

11 Emperor Artaxerxes gave the following
document to Ezra, the priest and scholar,
who had a thorough knowledge of the laws
and commands which the LORD had given
to Israel:

12 "From Emperor Artaxerxes[l] to the
priest Ezra, scholar in the Law of the God
of Heaven.[m]

13 "I command that throughout my
empire all the Israelite people, priests, and
Levites that so desire be permitted to go
with you to Jerusalem. 14 I, together with
my seven counselors, send you to investi-
gate the conditions in Jerusalem and Judah
in order to see how well the Law of your
God, which has been entrusted to you, is
being obeyed. 15 You are to take with you
the gold and silver offerings which I and
my counselors desire to give to the God of
Israel, whose Temple is in Jerusalem. 16 You
are also to take all the silver and gold
which you collect throughout the province
of Babylon and the offerings which the
Israelite people and their priests give for
the Temple of their God in Jerusalem.

17 "You are to spend this money care-
fully and buy bulls, rams, lambs, grain, and
wine and offer them on the altar of the
Temple in Jerusalem. 18 You may use the
silver and gold that is left over for whatev-
er you and your people desire, in accor-
dance with the will of your God. 19 You
are to present to God in Jerusalem all the
utensils that have been given to you for
use in the Temple services. 20 And anything
else which you need for the Temple, you
may get from the royal treasury.

21 "I command all the treasury officials in
West of Euphrates Province to provide
promptly for Ezra, the priest and scholar in
the Law of the God of Heaven, everything
he asks you for, 22 up to a limit of 7,500
pounds of silver, 500 bushels of wheat, 550
gallons of wine, 550 gallons of olive oil, and
as much salt as needed. 23 You must be care-
ful to provide everything which the God of
Heaven requires for his Temple, and so
make sure that he is never angry with me
or with those who reign after me. 24 You are
forbidden to collect any taxes from the
priests, Levites, musicians, guards, workers,
or anyone else connected with this Temple.

25 "You, Ezra, using the wisdom which
your God has given you, are to appoint
administrators and judges to govern all the
people in West-of-Euphrates who live by
the Law of your God. You must teach that
Law to anyone who does not know it. 26 If
any disobey the laws of your God or the
laws of the empire, they are to be pun-
ished promptly: by death or by exile or by
confiscation of their property or by
imprisonment."

Ezra Praises God

27 Ezra said, "Praise the LORD, the God of
our ancestors! He has made the emperor
willing to honor in this way the Temple of
the LORD in Jerusalem. 28 By God's grace I
have won the favor of the emperor, of his
counselors, and of all his powerful officials;
the LORD my God has given me courage,
and I have been able to persuade many of
the heads of the clans of Israel to return with
me."

I have been able to persuade many . . . to return with me. (7:28)

[l] **7:12** *Verses 12–26 are in Aramaic (see also 4:7).* [m] **7:12** *Aramaic has an additional word, the meaning of which is unclear.*

Ezra could trace his family tree back sixteen generations. How far back can you trace your family tree?

Pray it!

Answers to Prayer

Do you ever wonder if God really answers prayers? Ezra must have wondered, too. And he learned that God does indeed hear us. In Ezra's prayer (Ezra 7:27–28) he thanks God for answering his plea for courage. Ezra not only won the favor of the emperor but was also given courage.

It can be a good idea to keep a prayer journal of the things you are praying for. In the journal write down when, how, and what you are praying for. A prayer journal is also a good way to see if you are a well-rounded person of prayer. A well-rounded person of prayer remembers to adore God, to pray for others, to pray for him- or herself, and to thank God. Maybe your journal could have sections for each of those areas. Review your journal on a regular basis, and you'll see just how well prayer works. Remember to thank God when you see that your prayer has been answered.

— Ezra 7:27–28

The People Who Returned from Exile

8 This is the list of the heads of the clans who had been in exile in Babylonia and who returned with Ezra to Jerusalem when Artaxerxes was emperor:

2-14 Gershom, of the clan of Phinehas
Daniel, of the clan of Ithamar
Hattush son of Shecaniah, of the clan of David
Zechariah, of the clan of Parosh, with 150 men of his clan (there were records of their family lines)
Eliehoenai son of Zerahiah, of the clan of Pahath Moab, with 200 men
Shecaniah son of Jahaziel, of the clan of Zattu,[n] with 300 men
Ebed son of Jonathan, of the clan of Adin, with 50 men
Jeshaiah son of Athaliah, of the clan of Elam, with 70 men
Zebadiah son of Michael, of the clan of Shephatiah, with 80 men
Obadiah son of Jehiel, of the clan of Joab, with 218 men
Shelomith son of Josiphiah, of the clan of Bani,[o] with 160 men
Zechariah son of Bebai, of the clan of Bebai, with 28 men
Johanan son of Hakkatan, of the clan of Azgad, with 110 men
Eliphelet, Jeuel, and Shemaiah, of the clan of Adonikam, with 60 men (they returned at a later date)
Uthai and Zaccur, of the clan of Bigvai, with 70 men

Ezra Finds Levites for the Temple

15 I assembled the entire group by the canal that runs to the town of Ahava, and we camped there three days. I found that there were priests in the group, but no Levites. 16 I sent for nine of the leaders: Eliezer, Ariel, Shemaiah, Elnathan, Jarib, Elnathan, Nathan, Zechariah, and Meshullam, and for two teachers, Joiarib and Elnathan. 17 I sent them

[n] **8:2–14** *One ancient translation (see also 2:8)* Zattu; *Hebrew does not have this name.* [o] **8:2–14** *One ancient translation (see also 2:10)* Bani; *Hebrew does not have this name.*

How many clans returned with Ezra?

to Iddo, head of the community at Casiphia,
to ask him and his associates, the Temple
workers, to send us people to serve God in
the Temple. 18Through God's grace they sent
us Sherebiah, an able man, a Levite from the
clan of Mahli; and eighteen of his sons and
brothers came with him. 19They also sent
Hashabiah and Jeshaiah of the clan of Me-
rari, with twenty of their relatives. 20In addi-
tion there were 220 Temple workers whose
ancestors had been designated by King
David and his officials to assist the Levites.
They were all listed by name.

Ezra Leads the People in Fasting and Prayer

21There by the Ahava Canal I gave orders
for us all to fast and humble ourselves before
our God and to ask him to lead us on our
journey and protect us and our children and
all our possessions. 22I would have been
ashamed to ask the emperor for a troop of
cavalry to guard us from any enemies during
our journey, because I had told him that our
God blesses everyone who trusts him, but
that he is displeased with and punishes any-
one who turns away from him. 23So we fast-
ed and prayed for God to protect us, and he
answered our prayers.

The Gifts for the Temple

24From among the leading priests I chose
Sherebiah, Hashabiah, and ten others.
25Then I weighed out the silver, the gold,
and the utensils which the emperor, his
advisers and officials, and the people of Israel
had given to be used in the Temple, and I
gave it to the priests. 26-27This is what I gave
them:

silver - 25 tons
100 silver utensils - 150 pounds
gold - 7,500 pounds
20 gold bowls - 270 ounces
2 fine bronze bowls, equal in value to gold bowls

28I said to them, "You are sacred to the
LORD, the God of your ancestors, and so are
all the silver and gold utensils brought to
him as freewill offerings. 29Guard them care-
fully until you reach the Temple. There in
the priests' rooms weigh them and turn
them over to the leaders of the priests and of
the Levites, and to the leaders of the people
of Israel in Jerusalem." 30So the priests and
the Levites took charge of the silver, the
gold, and the utensils, to take them to the
Temple in Jerusalem.

The Return to Jerusalem

31It was on the twelfth day of the first
month that we left the Ahava Canal to go to
Jerusalem. Our God was with us and pro-
tected us from enemy attacks and from
ambush as we traveled. 32When we reached
Jerusalem, we rested three days. 33Then on
the fourth day we went to the Temple,
weighed the silver, the gold, and the utensils,
and turned them over to Meremoth the
priest, son of Uriah. With him were Eleazar
son of Phinehas and two Levites, Jozabad
son of Jeshua and Noadiah son of Binnui.
34Everything was counted and weighed, and
a complete record was made at the same
time.

35All those who had returned from exile
then brought offerings to be burned as sacri-
fices to the God of Israel. They offered 12
bulls for all Israel, 96 rams, and 77 lambs;
they also offered 12 goats to purify them-
selves from sin. All these animals were
burned as sacrifices to the LORD. 36They also
took the document the emperor had given
them and gave it to the governors and offi-
cials of West-of-Euphrates Province, who
then gave their support to the people and
the Temple worship.

Ezra Learns of Intermarriages with Non-Jews

9 After all this had been done, some of
the leaders of the people of Israel came
and told me that the people, the priests, and
the Levites had not kept themselves separate
from the people in the neighboring coun-
tries of Ammon, Moab, and Egypt or from
the Canaanites, Hittites, Perizzites, Jebusites,
and Amorites. They were doing the same
disgusting things which these people did.
2Jewish men were marrying foreign women,
and so God's holy people had become

contaminated. The leaders and officials were
the chief offenders. 3When I heard this, I
tore my clothes in despair, tore my hair and
my beard, and sat down crushed with grief.
4I sat there grieving until the time for the
evening sacrifice to be offered, and people
began to gather around me—all those who
were frightened because of what the God of
Israel had said about the sins of those who
had returned from exile.

5When the time came for the evening
sacrifice, I got up from where I had been
grieving, and still wearing my torn clothes, I
knelt in prayer and stretched out my hands
to the LORD my God. 6I said, "O God, I am
too ashamed to raise my head in your pres-
ence. Our sins pile up higher than our heads;
they reach as high as the heavens. 7From the
days of our ancestors until now, we, your
people, have sinned greatly. Because of our
sins we, our kings, and our priests have fallen
into the hands of foreign kings, and we have
been slaughtered, robbed, and carried away
as prisoners. We have been totally disgraced,
as we still are today. 8Now for a short time,
O LORD our God, you have been gracious
to us and have let some of us escape from
slavery and live in safety in this holy place.
You have let us escape from slavery and have
given us new life. 9We were slaves, but you
did not leave us in slavery. You made the
emperors of Persia favor us and permit us to
go on living and to rebuild your Temple,
which was in ruins, and to find safety here in
Judah and Jerusalem.

10"But now, O God, what can we say after
all that has happened? We have again dis-
obeyed the commands 11that you gave us
through your servants, the prophets. They
told us that the land we were going to occu-
py was an impure land because the people
who lived in it filled it from one end to the
other with disgusting, filthy actions. 12They
told us that we were never to intermarry
with those people and never to help them
prosper or succeed if we wanted to enjoy the
land and pass it on to our descendants forev-
er. 13Even after everything that has happened
to us in punishment for our sins and wrongs,
we know that you, our God, have punished

9:12 Ex 34:11–16; Deut 7:1–5

Study it!

Mixed Marriages

In our time, people often marry someone with a different ethnic or religious background. There are Catholic-Jewish marriages, Protestant-Muslim marriages, American-Chinese marriages and every other combination you can think of. Maybe your own parents are of two different religious or ethnic backgrounds. For our time and culture, this is acceptable. The time of Ezra, however, was much different.

The people returning from the Exile were still learning what their Jewish faith was all about. Leaders like Ezra and Nehemiah were concerned that mixed marriages between Jews and non-Jews would make the Jewish person's faith weaker. They were afraid that the Jewish men in the marriage would be tempted to worship the foreign gods of their wives. They may also have been concerned that non-Jewish children would inherit the father's land. For all these reasons, they forbade Jewish men to marry foreign women.

Even today, mixed marriages have their challenges. When both the husband and wife feel strongly about their different religions or ethnic traditions, a successful marriage requires a great deal of understanding and compromise. Couples considering a mixed marriage must carefully think about how—or even if—they can keep their own beliefs and traditions and still live in harmony with each other.

— Ezra, chapters 9–10

us less than we deserve and have allowed us
to survive. [14]Then how can we ignore your
commandments again and intermarry with
these wicked people? If we do, you will be
so angry that you will destroy us completely
and let no one survive. [15]LORD God of
Israel, you are just, but you have let us sur-
vive. We confess our guilt to you; we have no
right to come into your presence."

The Plan for Ending Mixed Marriages

10 While Ezra was bowing in prayer in
front of the Temple, weeping and
confessing these sins, a large group of
Israelites—men, women, and children—
gathered around him, weeping bitterly.
[2]Then Shecaniah son of Jehiel, of the clan of
Elam, said to Ezra, "We have broken faith
with God by marrying foreign women, but
even so there is still hope for Israel. [3]Now
we must make a solemn promise to our God
that we will send these women and their
children away. We will do what you and the
others who honor God's commands advise
us to do. We will do what God's Law
demands. [4]It is your responsibility to act. We
are behind you, so go ahead and get it
done."

[5]So Ezra began by making the leaders of
the priests, of the Levites, and of the rest of
the people take an oath that they would do
what Shecaniah had proposed. [6]Then he
went from in front of the Temple into the
living quarters of Jehohanan son of Eliashib,
and spent the night[p] there grieving over the
unfaithfulness of the exiles. He did not eat
or drink anything.

[7]A message was sent throughout Jerusalem
and Judah that all those who had returned
from exile were to meet in Jerusalem [8]by
order of the leaders of the people. If any
failed to come within three days, all their
property would be confiscated, and they
would lose their right to be members of the
community. [9]Within the three days, on the
twentieth day of the ninth month, all the
men living in the territory of Judah and
Benjamin came to Jerusalem and assembled
in the Temple square. It was raining hard, and
because of the weather and the importance
of the meeting everyone was trembling.

[10]Ezra the priest stood up and spoke to
them. He said, "You have been faithless and
have brought guilt on Israel by marrying
foreign women. [11]Now then, confess your
sins to the LORD, the God of your ancestors,
and do what pleases him. Separate yourselves
from the foreigners living in our land and
get rid of your foreign wives."

[12]The people shouted in answer, "We will
do whatever you say." [13]But they added,
"The crowd is too big, and it's raining hard.
We can't stand here in the open like this.
This isn't something that can be done in one
or two days, because so many of us are
involved in this sin. [14]Let our officials stay in
Jerusalem and take charge of the matter.
Then let anyone who has a foreign wife
come at a set time, together with the leaders
and the judges of his city. In this way God's
anger over this situation will be turned
away." [15]No one was opposed to the plan
except Jonathan son of Asahel and Jahzeiah
son of Tikvah, who had the support of
Meshullam and of Shabbethai, a Levite.

[16]The returned exiles accepted the plan, so
Ezra the priest appointed[q] men from among
the heads of the clans and recorded their
names. On the first day of the tenth month

"The crowd is too big, and it's raining hard." (10:13)

[p] **10:6** *One ancient translation* spent the night; *Hebrew* went. [q] **10:16** *Some ancient translations* appointed; *Hebrew unclear.*

What are some of the challenges when two people of different religions marry each other? What are some of the positives?

they began their investigation, 17 and within
the next three months they investigated all
the cases of men with foreign wives.

The Men Who Had Foreign Wives

18 This is the list of the men who had for-
eign wives:

Priests, listed by clans:

Clan of Joshua and his brothers, sons of
Jehozadak: Maaseiah, Eliezer, Jarib, and
Gedaliah. 19 They promised to divorce their
wives, and they offered a ram as a sacrifice
for their sins.

20 Clan of Immer: Hanani and Zebadiah

21 Clan of Harim: Maaseiah, Elijah, She-
maiah, Jehiel, and Uzziah

22 Clan of Pashhur: Elioenai, Maaseiah,
Ishmael, Nethanel, Jozabad, and Elasah

23 *Levites:*

Jozabad, Shimei, Kelaiah (also called Keli-
ta), Pethahiah, Judah, and Eliezer

24 *Musicians:*

Eliashib

Temple guards:

Shallum, Telem, and Uri

25 *Others:*

Clan of Parosh: Ramiah, Izziah, Malchijah,
Mijamin, Eleazar, Malchijah, and Benaiah

26 Clan of Elam: Mattaniah, Zechariah,
Jehiel, Abdi, Jeremoth, and Elijah

27 Clan of Zattu: Elioenai, Eliashib, Matta-
niah, Jeremoth, Zabad, and Aziza

28 Clan of Bebai: Jehohanan, Hananiah,
Zabbai, and Athlai

29 Clan of Bani: Meshullam, Malluch, Ada-
iah, Jashub, Sheal, and Jeremoth

30 Clan of Pahath Moab: Adna, Chelal,
Benaiah, Maaseiah, Mattaniah, Bezalel, Bin-
nui, and Manasseh

31-32 Clan of Harim: Eliezer, Isshijah,
Malchijah, Shemaiah, Shimeon, Benjamin,
Malluch, and Shemariah

33 Clan of Hashum: Mattenai, Mattattah,
Zabad, Eliphelet, Jeremai, Manasseh, and
Shimei

34-37 Clan of Bani: Maadai, Amram, Uel,
Benaiah, Bedeiah, Cheluhi, Vaniah, Mere-
moth, Eliashib, Mattaniah, Mattenai, and
Jaasu

38-42 Clan of Binnui: Shimei, Shelemiah,
Nathan, Adaiah, Machnadebai, Shashai,
Sharai, Azarel, Shelemiah, Shemariah, Shal-
lum, Amariah, and Joseph

43 Clan of Nebo: Jeiel, Mattithiah, Zabad,
Zebina, Jaddai, Joel, and Benaiah

44 All these men had foreign wives. They
divorced them and sent them and their chil-
dren away.[r]

[r] **10:44** *Verse 44 in Hebrew is unclear.*

Your Next Step

Congratulations on finishing the Book of Ezra! Use this space to write your thoughts and questions about this book. If you are following the suggested reading plan, the next page begins the Book of Nehemiah. Like Ezra, Nehemiah returns from the Exile to help lead the rebuilding of Jerusalem.

NEHEMIAH

1 This is the account of what Nehemiah son of Hacaliah accomplished.

Nehemiah's Concern for Jerusalem

In the month of Kislev in the twentieth year that Artaxerxes was emperor of Persia, I, Nehemiah, was in Susa, the capital city.
2Hanani, one of my brothers, arrived from Judah with another group, and I asked them about Jerusalem and about the other Jews who had returned from exile in[a] Babylonia.
3They told me that those who had survived and were back in the homeland[b] were in great difficulty and that the foreigners who lived nearby looked down on them. They also told me that the walls of Jerusalem were still broken down and that the gates had not been restored since the time they were
burned. 4When I heard all this, I sat down and wept.

For several days I mourned and did not
eat. I prayed to God, 5"LORD God of Heaven! You are great, and we stand in fear of you. You faithfully keep your covenant with those who love you and do what you command.
6Look at me, LORD, and hear my prayer, as I pray day and night for your servants, the people of Israel. I confess that we, the people of Israel, have sinned. My ancestors and I have sinned.
7We have acted wickedly against you and have not done what you commanded. We have not kept the laws which you gave us through Moses, your
servant. 8Remember now what you told Moses: 'If you people of Israel are unfaithful to me, I will scatter you among the other

[a] **1:2** had returned from exile in; *or* had not been exiled to. [b] **1:3** had survived and . . . homeland; *or* had remained in the homeland and had not gone into exile.
1:8 Lev 26:33

Catholic Connections

Fear of the Lord

In Nehemiah we hear the plea, "LORD God of Heaven! You are great, and we stand in fear of you." Although God is not to be feared like spiders or heights, in the Bible we sometimes hear the phrase "fear of the Lord." You may also hear this phrase when preparing for Confirmation because fear of the Lord is one of the gifts of the Holy Spirit. (Sometimes the gift is called wonder and awe.)

So what does this phrase mean? Aren't we supposed to think of God as a loving parent, not someone to be feared? Well think of fear of the Lord not so much as being afraid of God but as being filled with amazement at God's power and love. It's the feeling that many people get when standing at the edge of the ocean or in a grove of beautiful trees, or when gazing at a starlit sky and realizing how big God is. Today we call the gift of fear of the Lord the gift of awe and wonder. It is the gift of understanding that God is great and wonderful and that God is the perfection of all we desire: perfect knowledge, perfect goodness, perfect power, and perfect love.

— Nehemiah 1:5

nations. 9But then if you turn back to me
and do what I have commanded you, I will
bring you back to the place where I have
chosen to be worshiped, even though you
are scattered to the ends of the earth.'
10"Lord, these are your servants, your own
people. You rescued them by your great power
and strength. 11Listen now to my prayer and
to the prayers of all your other servants who
want to honor you. Give me success today and
make the emperor merciful to me."
In those days I was the emperor's wine
steward.

Nehemiah Goes to Jerusalem

2 One day four months later, when
Emperor Artaxerxes was dining, I took
the wine to him. He had never seen me look
sad before, 2so he asked, "Why are you look-
ing so sad? You aren't sick, so it must be that
you're unhappy."

"Why are you looking so sad?" (2:2)

I was startled 3and answered, "May Your
Majesty live forever! How can I keep from
looking sad when the city where my ances-
tors are buried is in ruins and its gates have
been destroyed by fire?"
4The emperor asked, "What is it that you
want?"
I prayed to the God of Heaven, 5and then
I said to the emperor, "If Your Majesty is
pleased with me and is willing to grant my
request, let me go to the land of Judah, to
the city where my ancestors are buried, so
that I can rebuild the city."
6The emperor, with the empress sitting at
his side, approved my request. He asked me
how long I would be gone and when I
would return, and I told him.
7Then I asked him to grant me the favor
of giving me letters to the governors of
West-of-Euphrates Province,[c] instructing
them to let me travel to Judah. 8I asked also
for a letter to Asaph, keeper of the royal
forests, instructing him to supply me with
timber for the gates of the fort that guards
the Temple, for the city walls, and for the
house I was to live in. The emperor gave me
all I asked for, because God was with me.
9The emperor sent some army officers
and a troop of cavalry with me, and I made
the journey to West-of-Euphrates. There I
gave the emperor's letters to the governors.
10But Sanballat, from the town of Beth
Horon, and Tobiah, an official in the
province of Ammon, heard that someone
had come to work for the good of the peo-
ple of Israel, and they were highly indignant.
11I went on to Jerusalem, and for three
days 12I did not tell anyone what God had
inspired me to do for Jerusalem. Then in the
middle of the night I got up and went out,
taking a few of my companions with me. The
only animal we took was the donkey that I
rode on. 13It was still night as I left the city
through the Valley Gate on the west and went
south past Dragon's Fountain to the Rubbish
Gate. As I went, I inspected the broken walls

I inspected the broken walls. (2:13)

[c] **2:7** WEST-OF-EUPHRATES PROVINCE: *Under Persian rule the land of Israel was part of this large Persian province west of the Euphrates River.*

1:9 Deut 30:1–5 **2:3** 2 Kings 25:8–10; 2 Chr 36:19; Jer 52:12–14

"Listen now to my prayer and to the prayers of all your other servants who want to honor you. Give me success today" *(Nehemiah 1:11)*.

Study it!

Big Deal, a Wall

A wall! Big deal.

Actually, it is a big deal. The walls around ancient cities were important for their defense. They were so important that the building and maintaining of them was considered one of the ruler's most important jobs. In Nehemiah, chapter 2, Nehemiah finds that the walls and gates are in bad shape. So he takes on the task of rebuilding them in order to make the city safer.

In chapter 3, we see how wise Nehemiah is when he assigns different groups different parts of the wall to work on. It gives the people a sense of pride and also some friendly competition. Nehemiah knows that by repairing the gates and the wall, the city will be better protected and more respected.

— Nehemiah, chapters 2–3

of the city and the gates that had been
destroyed by fire. 14 Then on the east side of
the city I went north to the Fountain Gate
and the King's Pool. The donkey I was riding
could not find any path through the rubble,
15 so I went down into Kidron Valley and rode
along, looking at the wall. Then I returned
the way I had come and went back into the
city through the Valley Gate.

16 None of the local officials knew where I
had gone or what I had been doing. So far I
had not said anything to any of the other
Jews—the priests, the leaders, the officials, or
anyone else who would be taking part in the
work. 17 But now I said to them, "See what
trouble we are in because Jerusalem is in
ruins and its gates are destroyed! Let's rebuild
the city walls and put an end to our disgrace."
18 And I told them how God had
been with me and helped me, and what the
emperor had said to me.

They responded, "Let's start rebuilding!"
And they got ready to start the work.

19 When Sanballat, Tobiah, and an Arab
named Geshem heard what we were planning
to do, they laughed at us and said,
"What do you think you're doing? Are you
going to rebel against the emperor?"

20 I answered, "The God of Heaven will
give us success. We are his servants, and we
are going to start building. But you have no
right to any property in Jerusalem, and you
have no share in its traditions."

Rebuilding the Wall of Jerusalem

3 This is how the city wall was rebuilt.[d]
1 The High Priest Eliashib and his fellow
priests rebuilt the Sheep Gate, dedicated it,
and put the gates in place. They dedicated
the wall as far as the Tower of the Hundred
and the Tower of Hananel.

2 The men of Jericho built the next section.
Zaccur son of Imri built the next section.

3 The clan of Hassenaah built the Fish
Gate. They put the beams and the gates in
place, and put in the bolts and bars for locking
the gate.

4 Meremoth, the son of Uriah and grandson
of Hakkoz, built the next section.

Meshullam, the son of Berechiah and
grandson of Meshezabel, built the next section.

Zadok son of Baana built the next section.

5 The men of Tekoa built the next section,
but the leading men of the town refused to
do the manual labor assigned them by the
supervisors.

6 Joiada son of Paseah and Meshullam son
of Besodeiah rebuilt Jeshanah Gate.[e] They
put the beams and the gates in place, and put
in the bolts and bars for locking the gate.

7 Melatiah from Gibeon, Jadon from
Meronoth, and the men of Gibeon and

[d] **3:1** CITY WALL WAS REBUILT: *According to the following report, the rebuilding of the wall started at the middle of the north side and proceeded counterclockwise around the city. Many of the places mentioned cannot be identified.*

[e] **3:6** Jeshanah Gate; *or* the Old Gate.

This is how the city wall was rebuilt. (3:1)

Mizpah built the next section, as far as the res-
idence of the governor of West-of-Euphrates.
8 Uzziel son of Harhaiah, a goldsmith, built
the next section.
Hananiah, a maker of perfumes, built the
next section, as far as Broad Wall.
9 Rephaiah son of Hur, ruler of half of the
Jerusalem District, built the next section.
10 Jedaiah son of Harumaph built the next
section, which was near his own house.
Hattush son of Hashabneiah built the next
section.
11 Malchijah son of Harim and Hasshub
son of Pahath Moab built both the next sec-
tion and the Tower of the Ovens.
12 Shallum son of Hallohesh, ruler of the
other half of the Jerusalem District, built the
next section. (His daughters helped with the
work.)
13 Hanun and the inhabitants of the city of
Zanoah rebuilt the Valley Gate. They put the
gates in place, put in the bolts and the bars
for locking the gate, and repaired the wall
for fifteen hundred feet, as far as the Rub-
bish Gate.
14 Malchijah son of Rechab, ruler of the
Beth Haccherem District, rebuilt the Rub-
bish Gate. He put the gates in place, and put
in the bolts and the bars for locking the gate.
15 Shallum son of Colhozeh, ruler of the
Mizpah District, rebuilt the Fountain Gate.
He covered the gateway, put the gates in
place, and put in the bolts and the bars. At
the Pool of Shelah he built the wall next to
the royal garden, as far as the stairs leading
down from David's City.
16 Nehemiah son of Azbuk, ruler of half of
the Bethzur District, built the next section,
as far as David's tomb, the pool, and the bar-
racks.

Levites Who Worked on the Wall

17 The following Levites rebuilt the next
several sections of the wall:
Rehum son of Bani built the next section;
Hashabiah, ruler of half of the Keilah Dis-
trict, built the next section on behalf of his
district;
18 Bavvai son of Henadad, ruler of the
other half of the Keilah District, built the
next section;
19 Ezer son of Jeshua, ruler of Mizpah,
built the next section in front of the armory,
as far as the place where the wall turns;
20 Baruch son of Zabbai built the next sec-
tion, as far as the entrance to the house of
the High Priest Eliashib;
21 Meremoth, the son of Uriah and grand-
son of Hakkoz, built the next section, up to
the far end of Eliashib's house.

Priests Who Worked on the Wall

22 The following priests rebuilt the next
several sections of the wall:
Priests from the area around Jerusalem
built the next section;

23 Benjamin and Hasshub built the next
section, which was in front of their houses;
Azariah, the son of Maaseiah and grand-
son of Ananiah, built the next section, which
was in front of his house;
24 Binnui son of Henadad built the next
section, from Azariah's house to the corner
of the wall;
25-26 Palal son of Uzai built the next sec-
tion, beginning at the corner of the wall and
the tower of the upper palace near the court
of the guard;
Pedaiah son of Parosh built the next sec-
tion, to a point on the east near the Water
Gate and the tower guarding the Temple.
(This was near that part of the city called
Ophel, where the Temple workers lived.)

Other Builders

27 The men of Tekoa built the next sec-
tion, their second one, from a point opposite
the large tower guarding the Temple as far as
the wall near Ophel.
28 A group of priests built the next sec-
tion, going north from the Horse Gate, each
one building in front of his own house.
29 Zadok son of Immer built the next sec-
tion, which was in front of his house.
Shemaiah son of Shecaniah, keeper of the
East Gate, built the next section.
30 Hananiah son of Shelemiah and Hanun,
the sixth son of Zalaph, built the next sec-
tion, their second one.
Meshullam son of Berechiah built the
next section, which was in front of his
house.
31 Malchijah, a goldsmith, built the next
section, as far as the building used by the
Temple workers and the merchants, which
was by the Miphkad[f] Gate to the Temple,
near the room on top of the northeast cor-
ner of the wall.
32 The goldsmiths and the merchants built
the last section, from the room at the corner
as far as the Sheep Gate.

Nehemiah Overcomes Opposition to His Work

4 When Sanballat heard that we Jews had
begun rebuilding the wall, he became
furious and began to ridicule us. 2 In front of
his companions and the Samaritan troops he
said, "What do these miserable Jews think
they're doing? Do they intend to rebuild the
city? Do they think that by offering sacri-
fices they can finish the work in one day?
Can they make building stones out of heaps
of burnt rubble?"
3 Tobiah was standing there beside him,
and he added, "What kind of wall could they
ever build? Even a fox could knock it
down!"
4 I prayed, "Hear how they make fun of us,
O God! Let their ridicule fall on their own
heads. Let them be robbed of everything
they have, and let them be taken as prisoners
to a foreign land. 5 Don't forgive the evil
they do and don't forget their sins, for they
have insulted us who are building."
6 So we went on rebuilding the wall, and
soon it was half its full height, because the
people were eager to work.
7 Sanballat, Tobiah, and the people of Ara-
bia, Ammon, and Ashdod heard that we were
making progress in rebuilding the wall of
Jerusalem and that the gaps in the wall were
being closed, and they became very angry.
8 So they all plotted together to come and
attack Jerusalem and create confusion, 9 but
we prayed to our God and kept men on
guard against them day and night.
10 The people of Judah had a song they
sang:

"We grow weak carrying burdens;
There's so much rubble to take away.
How can we build the wall today?"

11 Our enemies thought we would not see
them or know what was happening until
they were already upon us, killing us and
putting an end to our work. 12 But time
after time Jews who were living among our
enemies came to warn us of the plans our

[f] **3:31** Miphkad; *or* Mustering, *or* Watch.

People left their regular jobs to help rebuild the walls of Jerusalem. How many different professions are mentioned in the lists of builders?

Pray it!

Stupid!

Let's face it, being made fun of hurts. Nehemiah must have been sad to hear the people making fun of him and his friends who were trying to do something good. The next time someone makes fun of you for something, follow Nehemiah's example and pray.

God my friend,
When others laugh and point fingers at me, it really hurts.
Help me hear your voice instead of their laughter
and to look to you, not at their mocking fingers.
Because it is your opinion that really counts to me,
Not theirs.
It is your voice that calls me,
Not theirs.
I pray for them,
for those who have made fun of me,
so that they may know you as a friend, too.
Amen

— Nehemiah 4:1–5

enemies were making against us.[g] 13So I
armed the people with swords, spears, and bows, and stationed them by clans behind the wall, wherever it was still unfinished.

14I saw that the people were worried, so I
said to them and to their leaders and officials, "Don't be afraid of our enemies. Remember how great and terrifying the Lord is, and fight for your relatives, your children, your wives, and your homes."
15Our enemies heard that we had found out
what they were plotting, and they realized that God had defeated their plans. Then all of us went back to rebuilding the wall.

16From then on half of my men worked
and half stood guard, wearing coats of armor and armed with spears, shields, and bows. And our leaders gave their full support to
the people 17who were rebuilding the wall.
Even those who carried building materials worked with one hand and kept a weapon in the other,
18and everyone who was building kept a sword strapped to their waist. The man who was to sound the alarm on the bugle stayed with me.
19I told the people
and their officials and leaders, "The work is spread out over such a distance that we are

[They] worked with one hand and kept a weapon in another. (4:17)

[g] **4:12** *Probable text* the plans our enemies were making against us; *Hebrew unclear.*

Consider all of Nehemiah's actions. What did he do that shows he is a strong leader?

widely separated from one another on the
wall. 20If you hear the bugle, gather around
me. Our God will fight for us." 21So every
day, from dawn until the stars came out at
night, half of us worked on the wall, while
the other half stood guard with spears.
22During this time I told the men in
charge that they and all their helpers had to
stay in Jerusalem at night, so that we could
guard the city at night as well as work in the
daytime. 23I didn't take off my clothes even
at night, neither did any of my companions
nor my servants nor my bodyguards. And we
all kept our weapons at hand.[h]

Oppression of the Poor

5 Some time later many of the people,
both men and women, began to com-
plain against the other Jews. 2Some said, "We
have large families, we need grain to keep us
alive."
3Others said, "We have had to mortgage
our fields and vineyards and houses to get
enough grain to keep us from starving."
4Still others said, "We had to borrow
money to pay the royal tax on our fields and
vineyards. 5We are of the same race as the
other Jews. Aren't our children just as good
as theirs? But we have to make slaves of our
children. Some of our daughters have already
been sold as slaves. We are helpless because
our fields and vineyards have been taken
away from us."
6When I heard their complaints, I grew
angry 7and decided to act. I denounced the
leaders and officials of the people and told
them, "You are oppressing your own rela-
tives!"
I called a public assembly to deal with the
problem 8and said, "As far as we have been
able, we have been buying back our Jewish
relatives who had to sell themselves to for-
eigners. Now you are forcing your own rela-
tives to sell themselves to you, their own
people!" The leaders were silent and could
find nothing to say.
9Then I said, "What you are doing is
wrong! You ought to obey God and do
what's right. Then you would not give our

Live it!

Nehemiah Works for Justice

In Nehemiah's time, just like in ours, there are people who do not have enough to eat, a place to live, proper clothing or health care. Soup kitchens, food drives, Rice Bowl, clothing, collections, coins for causes, Food Fast, and special collections are all ways to help people in need. These are works of service or charity. This means those in need get immediate help to survive their present situation.

What Nehemiah did was called a work of justice. He talked the rich people into forgiving poor people's debts and giving them land so that they could make their own living. Making a change in society so people no longer need charity is the work of justice. People work for justice by contacting their political leaders about needed changes in laws, protesting unfair business practices, and educating other people about the reasons for injustice.

These two types of works—works of service or charity and works of justice—are called the two feet of service and justice. By using both feet—works of service and works of justice—we can more successfully work to end things like hunger and homelessness.

— Nehemiah 5:1–13

[h] **4:23** *Probable text* weapons at hand; *Hebrew unclear.*
5:7 Ex 22:25; Lev 25. 35–37; Deut 23:19, 20

enemies, the Gentiles, any reason to ridicule
us. 10I have let the people borrow money
and grain from me, and so have my compan-
ions and those who work for me. Now let's
give up all our claims to repayment. 11Can-
cel all the debts[i] they owe you—money or
grain or wine or olive oil. And give them
back their fields, vineyards, olive groves, and
houses right now!"

12The leaders replied, "We'll do as you say.
We'll give the property back and not try to
collect the debts."

I called in the priests and made the leaders
swear in front of them to keep the promise
they had just made. 13Then I took off the
sash[j] I was wearing around my waist and
shook it out. "This is how God will shake
any of you who don't keep your promise," I
said. "God will take away your houses and
everything you own, and will leave you with
nothing."

Everyone who was present said, "Amen!"
and praised the LORD. And the leaders kept
their promise.

Nehemiah's Unselfishness

14During all the twelve years that I was
governor of the land of Judah, from the
twentieth year that Artaxerxes was emperor
until his thirty-second year, neither my rela-
tives nor I ate the food I was entitled to have
as governor. 15Every governor who had been
in office before me had been a burden to the
people and had demanded forty silver coins
a day[k] for food and wine. Even their servants
had oppressed the people. But I acted differ-
ently, because I honored God. 16I put all my
energy into rebuilding the wall and did not
acquire any property. Everyone who worked
for me joined in the rebuilding. 17I regularly
fed at my table a hundred and fifty of the
Jewish people and their leaders, besides all
the people who came to me from the sur-
rounding nations. 18Every day I served one
beef, six of the best sheep, and many chick-
ens, and every ten days I provided a fresh
supply of wine. But I knew what heavy bur-
dens the people had to bear, and so I did not
claim the allowance that the governor is
entitled to.

19I pray you, O God, remember to my
credit everything that I have done for this
people.

Plots against Nehemiah

6 Sanballat, Tobiah, Geshem, and the rest
of our enemies heard that we had fin-
ished building the wall and that there were
no gaps left in it, although we still had not
set up the gates in the gateways. 2So Sanbal-
lat and Geshem sent me a message, suggest-
ing that I meet with them in one of the vil-
lages in the Plain of Ono. This was a trick of
theirs to try to harm me. 3I sent messengers
to say to them, "I am doing important work
and can't go down there. I am not going to
let the work stop just to go and see you."

4They sent me the same message four
times, and each time I sent them the same
reply.

5Then Sanballat sent one of his servants to
me with a fifth message, this one in the form
of an unsealed letter.[l] 6It read:

> "Geshem tells me that a rumor is going
> around among the neighboring peoples
> that you and the Jewish people intend to
> revolt and that this is why you are rebuild-
> ing the wall. He also says you plan to
> make yourself king 7and that you have
> arranged for some prophets to proclaim in
> Jerusalem that you are the king of Judah.
> His Majesty is certain to hear about this,
> so I suggest that you and I meet to talk
> the situation over."

8I sent a reply to him: "Nothing of what
you are saying is true. You have made it all
up yourself."

9They were trying to frighten us into
stopping work. I prayed, "But now, God,
make me strong!"

10About this time I went to visit Shema-
iah, the son of Delaiah and grandson of
Mehetabel, who was unable to leave his
house. He said to me, "You and I must go

[i] **5:11** *One ancient translation* debts; *Hebrew unclear.* [j] **5:13** SASH: *Clothing in those days had no pockets, so small items were tucked into the sash that was worn like a belt around the waist. Shaking it out was a symbol of losing everything.*
[k] **5:15** *One ancient translation* a day; *Hebrew unclear.* [l] **6:5** UNSEALED LETTER: *Leaving a letter unsealed was a deliberate way of making certain that its contents would become widely known.*

and hide together in the Holy Place of the Temple and lock the doors, because they are coming to kill you. Any night now they will come to kill you."

11 I answered, "I'm not the kind of person that runs and hides. Do you think I would try to save my life by hiding in the Temple? I won't do it."

12 When I thought it over, I realized that God had not spoken to Shemaiah, but that Tobiah and Sanballat had bribed him to give
me this warning. 13 They hired him to frighten me into sinning, so that they could ruin my reputation and humiliate me.

14 I prayed, "God, remember what Tobiah and Sanballat have done and punish them. Remember that woman Noadiah and all the other prophets who tried to frighten me."

The Conclusion of the Work

15 After fifty-two days of work the entire wall was finished on the twenty-fifth day of
the month of Elul. 16 When our enemies in the surrounding nations heard this, they realized that they had lost face, since everyone knew that the work had been done with God's help.

17 During all this time the Jewish leaders had been in correspondence with Tobiah.
18 Many people in Judah were on his side because of his Jewish father-in-law, Shecaniah son of Arah. In addition, his son Jehohanan had married the daughter of Meshullam son of Berechiah.
19 People would talk in front of me about all the good deeds Tobiah had done and would tell him everything I said. And he kept sending me letters to try to frighten me.

7 And now the wall had been rebuilt, the gates had all been put in place, and the Temple guards, the members of the sacred choir, and the other Levites had been assigned their work.
2 I put two men in charge of governing the city of Jerusalem: my brother Hanani and Hananiah, commanding officer of the fortress. Hananiah was a reliable and God-fearing man without equal.
3 I told them not to have the gates of Jerusalem opened in the morning until well after sunrise and to have them closed and barred before the guards went off duty at sunset. I also told them to appoint guards from among the people who lived in Jerusalem and to assign some of them to specific posts and others to patrol the area around their own houses.

The List of Those Who Returned from Exile

(Ezra 2:1–70)

4 Jerusalem was a large city, but not many people were living in it, and not many houses had been built yet.
5 God inspired me to assemble the people and their leaders and officials and to check their family records. I located the records of those who had first returned from captivity, and this is the information I found:

6 Many of the exiles left the province of Babylon and returned to Jerusalem and Judah, each to his own hometown. Their families had been living in exile in Babylonia ever since King Nebuchadnezzar had taken them there as prisoners.
7 Their leaders were Zerubbabel, Joshua, Nehemiah, Azariah, Raamiah, Nahamani, Mordecai, Bilshan, Mispereth, Bigvai, Nehum, and Baanah.

8-25 This is the list of the clans of Israel, with the number of those from each clan who returned from exile:

Parosh - 2,172
Shephatiah - 372
Arah - 652
Pahath Moab (descendants of Jeshua and Joab) - 2,818
Elam - 1,254
Zattu - 845
Zaccai - 760
Binnui - 648
Bebai - 628
Azgad - 2,322
Adonikam - 667
Bigvai - 2,067
Adin - 655

"But now, God, make me strong" *(Nehemiah 6:9)*.

Ater (also called Hezekiah) - 98
Hashum - 328
Bezai - 324
Hariph - 112
Gibeon - 95

26-38 People whose ancestors had lived in the following towns also returned:
Bethlehem and Netophah - 188
Anathoth - 128
Beth Azmaveth - 42
Kiriath Jearim, Chephirah, and Beeroth - 743
Ramah and Geba - 621
Michmash - 122
Bethel and Ai - 123
The other Nebo - 52
The other Elam - 1,254
Harim - 320
Jericho - 345
Lod, Hadid, and Ono - 721
Senaah - 3,930

39-42 This is the list of the priestly clans that returned from exile:
Jedaiah (descendants of Jeshua) - 973
Immer - 1,052
Pashhur - 1,247
Harim - 1,017

43-45 Clans of Levites who returned from exile:
Jeshua and Kadmiel (descendants of Hodaviah) - 74
Temple musicians (descendants of Asaph) - 148
Temple guards (descendants of Shallum, Ater, Talmon, Akkub, Hatita, and Shobai) - 138

46-56 Clans of Temple workers who returned from exile:
Ziha, Hasupha, Tabbaoth,
Keros, Sia, Padon,
Lebana, Hagaba, Shalmai,
Hanan, Giddel, Gahar,
Reaiah, Rezin, Nekoda,
Gazzam, Uzza, Paseah,
Besai, Meunim, Nephushesim,
Bakbuk, Hakupha, Harhur,
Bazlith, Mehida, Harsha,
Barkos, Sisera, Temah,
Neziah, and Hatipha.

57-59 Clans of Solomon's servants who returned from exile:
Sotai, Sophereth, Perida,
Jaalah, Darkon, Giddel,
Shephatiah, Hattil, Pochereth Hazzebaim, and Amon.

60 The total number of descendants of the Temple workers and of Solomon's servants who returned from exile was 392.

61-62 There were 642 belonging to the clans of Delaiah, Tobiah, and Nekoda who returned from the towns of Tel Melah, Tel Harsha, Cherub, Addon, and Immer; but they could not prove that they were descendants of Israelites.

63-64 The following priestly clans could find no record to prove their ancestry: Hobaiah, Hakkoz, and Barzillai. (The ancestor of the priestly clan of Barzillai had married a woman from the clan of Barzillai of Gilead and taken the name of his father-in-law's clan.) Since they were unable to prove who their ancestors were, they were not accepted as priests.
65 The Jewish governor told them that they could not eat the food offered to God until there was a priest who could use the Urim and Thummim.[m]

66-69 Total number of exiles who returned - 42,360.
Their male and female servants - 7,337
Male and female musicians - 245
Horses - 736
Mules - 245
Camels - 435
Donkeys - 6,720

70-72 Many of the people contributed to help pay the cost of restoring the Temple:

The governor	270	ounces of gold
	50	ceremonial bowls
	530	robes for priests
Heads of clans	337	pounds of gold
	3,215	pounds of silver

[m] **7:65** URIM AND THUMMIM: *Two objects used by the priest to determine God's will; it is not known precisely how they were used.*

7:65 Ex 28:30; Deut 33:8

When Ezra called the people to praise God, they raised their arms *(Nehemiah 8:6)*. **When have you seen people raise their arms in prayer?**

The rest of the people	337	pounds of gold
	2,923	pounds of silver
	67	robes for priests

73The priests, the Levites, the Temple
guards, the musicians, many of the ordinary
people, the Temple workers—all the people
of Israel—settled in the towns and cities of
Judah.

Ezra Reads the Law to the People

8 By the seventh month the people of
Israel were all settled in their towns. On
the first day of that month they all assembled
in Jerusalem, in the square just inside the
Water Gate. They asked Ezra, the priest and
scholar of the Law which the LORD had given
Israel through Moses, to get the book of the
Law. 2So Ezra brought it to the place where
the people had gathered—men, women, and
the children who were old enough to under-
stand. 3There in the square by the gate he read
the Law to them from dawn until noon, and
they all listened attentively.
4Ezra was standing on a wooden platform
that had been built for the occasion. The fol-
lowing men stood at his right: Mattithiah,
Shema, Anaiah, Uriah, Hilkiah, and Maa-
seiah; and the following stood at his left:
Pedaiah, Mishael, Malchijah, Hashum, Hash-
baddanah, Zechariah, and Meshullam.
5As Ezra stood there on the platform high
above the people, they all kept their eyes
fixed on him. As soon as he opened the
book, they all stood up. 6Ezra said, "Praise
the LORD, the great God!"
All the people raised their arms in the air
and answered, "Amen! Amen!" They knelt in
worship, with their faces to the ground.
7Then they rose and stood in their places,
and the following Levites explained the Law
to them: Jeshua, Bani, Sherebiah, Jamin,
Akkub, Shabbethai, Hodiah, Maaseiah, Keli-
ta, Azariah, Jozabad, Hanan, and Pelaiah.
8They gave an oral translation[n] of God's Law
and explained[o] it so that the people could
understand it.

Live it!

A Big Party

Pete's family planned the party. Everyone would be there—all of his family, including the sixteen cousins, what seemed like half the school, and of course, his scout troop. He didn't know that even his older sister, who was away at college, had flown in. Actually, Pete felt embarrassed to be the center of attention. His mom saw him and asked, "Are you excited?" He shrugged unenthusiastically. "C'mon Pete," his mother said, "It's important to celebrate these things. Earning your Eagle Scout award took a lot of work, and a long time. You deserve it."

Pete thought about it. "You know what, Mom, you're right. I worked really hard. I'm going to change my clothes and have the best party ever." As he walked toward the stairs and saw his sister come in the front door, he grinned with joy. And he remembered to say a quick prayer of thanks to God.

The people in Nehemiah's time took time to celebrate their success at rebuilding the city walls. It is important to celebrate after working hard to achieve a goal. It reminds us of the gifts that God has given us and how we have put those gifts to good use. After you have completed a large task, be sure to take time out to celebrate it—and remember to thank God as part of your celebration.

— Nehemiah, chapter 8

[n] **8:8** TRANSLATION: *The Law was written in Hebrew, but in Babylonia the Jews had adopted Aramaic as the language for daily life. Because of this a translation was necessary.* [o] **8:8** They gave . . . explained; *or* They read God's Law and then translated it, explaining.

7:73 1 Chr 9:2; Neh 11:3

9 When the people heard what the Law required, they were so moved that they began to cry. So Nehemiah, who was the governor, Ezra, the priest and scholar of the Law, and the Levites who were explaining the Law told all the people, "This day is holy to the LORD your God, so you are not to mourn or cry. 10 Now go home and have a feast. Share your food and wine with those who don't have enough. Today is holy to our Lord, so don't be sad. The joy that the LORD gives you will make you strong."

11 The Levites went around calming the people and telling them not to be sad on such a holy day. 12 So all the people went home and ate and drank joyfully and shared what they had with others, because they understood what had been read to them.

The Festival of Shelters

13 The next day the heads of the clans, together with the priests and the Levites, went to Ezra to study the teachings of the Law. 14 They discovered that the Law, which the LORD gave through Moses, ordered the people of Israel to live in temporary shelters during the Festival of Shelters. 15 So they gave the following instructions and sent them[p] all through Jerusalem and the other cities and towns: "Go out to the hills and get branches from pines, olives, myrtles, palms, and other trees to make shelters according to the instructions written in the Law."

16 So the people got branches and built shelters on the flat roofs of their houses, in their yards, in the Temple courtyard, and in the public squares by the Water Gate and by the Ephraim Gate. 17 All the people who had come back from captivity built shelters and lived in them. This was the first time it had been done since the days of Joshua son of Nun, and everybody was excited and happy. 18 From the first day of the festival to the last they read a part of God's Law every day. They celebrated for seven days, and on the eighth day there was a closing ceremony, as required in the Law.

The People Confess Their Sins

9 1-2 On the twenty-fourth day of the same month the people of Israel gathered to fast in order to show sorrow for their sins. They had already separated themselves from all foreigners. They wore sackcloth and put dust on their heads as signs of grief. Then they stood and began to confess the sins that they and their ancestors had committed. 3 For about three hours the Law of the LORD their God was read to them, and for the next three hours they confessed their sins and worshiped the LORD their God.

4 There was a platform for the Levites, and on it stood Jeshua, Bani, Kadmiel, Shebaniah, Bunni, Sherebiah, Bani, and Chenani. They prayed aloud to the LORD their God.

5 The following Levites gave a call to worship: Jeshua, Kadmiel, Bani, Hashabneiah, Sherebiah, Hodiah, Shebaniah, and Pethahiah. They said:

"Stand up and praise the LORD your
    God;
  praise him forever and ever!
Let everyone praise his glorious name,
  although no human praise is great
    enough."

The Prayer of Confession

6 And then the people of Israel prayed this prayer:

"You, LORD, you alone are LORD;
  you made the heavens and the stars of
    the sky.
You made land and sea and everything in
    them;
  you gave life to all.
The heavenly powers bow down and
    worship you.
7 You, LORD God, chose Abram
  and led him out of Ur in Babylonia;
  you changed his name to Abraham.
8 You found that he was faithful to
    you,
  and you made a covenant with him.

p **8:15** *Probable text* So they . . . sent them; *Hebrew* It also ordered that the following instructions be sent.

8:14, 15 Lev 23:33–36, 39–43; Deut 16:13–15 **9:7** **a** Gen 11:31; 12:1; **b** Gen 17:5 **9:8** Gen 15:18–21

Pray it!

Creator God

In the prayer of confession in Nehemiah, chapter 9, there are many references to creator God. After the Exile, this was a popular way to address God. Try writing your own prayer using the themes found in the prayer in chapter 9.

As you write this prayer, here are the things you would want to include:

- **A title for God that describes what he is like for you.**
- **Something about how God helped the people who are part of your family history.**
- **Describe the things that you are sorry for. These can be things you have done wrong or that your family, community, or nation have done wrong.**
- **Ask God for forgiveness.**
- **Give God thanks for his gifts, especially his forgiveness.**

— Nehemiah 9:6–37

You promised to give him the land of the
Canaanites,
the land of the Hittites and the
Amorites,
the land of the Perizzites, the Jebusites,
the Girgashites,
to be a land where his descendants
would live.
You kept your promise, because you are
faithful.

9 "You saw how our ancestors suffered in
Egypt;
you heard their call for help at the Red
Sea.
10 You worked amazing miracles against the
king,
against his officials and the people of
his land,
because you knew how they oppressed
your people.
You won then the fame you still have today.
11 Through the sea you made a path for
your people
and led them through on dry ground.
Those who pursued them drowned in
deep water,
as a stone sinks in the raging sea.
12 With a cloud you led them in daytime,
and at night you lighted their way with
fire.
13 At Mount Sinai you came down from
heaven;
you spoke to your people
and gave them good laws and sound
teachings.
14 You taught them to keep your Sabbaths
holy,
and through your servant Moses you
gave them your laws.

15 "When they were hungry, you gave them
bread from heaven,
and water from a rock when they were
thirsty.
You told them to take control of the land
which you had promised to give them.
16 But our ancestors grew proud and
stubborn
and refused to obey your commands.

9:9 a Ex 3:7; **b** Ex 14:10–12 **9:10** Ex 7:8—12:32 **9:11 a** Ex 14:21–29; **b** Ex 15:4, 5 **9:12** Ex 13:21, 22 **9:13, 14** Ex 19:18—23:33 **9:15 a** Ex 16:4–15; **b** Ex 17:1–7; **c** Deut 1:21 **9:16, 17** Num 14:1–4; Deut 1:26–33

The prayer in Nehemiah, chapter 9, is kind of an overview of the Old Testament. How many of the people and events described do you recognize?

17 They refused to obey; they forgot all you did;
they forgot the miracles you had performed.
In their pride they chose a leader
to take them back to slavery in Egypt.
But you are a God who forgives;
you are gracious and loving, slow to be angry.
Your mercy is great; you did not forsake them.
18 They made an idol in the shape of a bull-calf
and said it was the god who led them from Egypt!
How much they insulted you, LORD!
19 But you did not abandon them there in the desert,
for your mercy is great.
You did not take away the cloud or the fire
that showed them the path by day and night.
20 In your goodness you told them what they should do;
you fed them manna and gave them water to drink.
21 Through forty years in the desert
you provided all that they needed;
their clothing never wore out,
and their feet were not swollen with pain.

22 "You let them conquer nations and kingdoms,
lands that bordered their own.
They conquered the land of Heshbon, where Sihon ruled,
and the land of Bashan, where Og was king.
23 You gave them as many children as there are stars in the sky,
and let them conquer and live in the land
that you had promised their ancestors to give them.
24 They conquered the land of Canaan;
you overcame the people living there.
You gave your people the power to do as they pleased
with the people and kings of Canaan.
25 Your people captured fortified cities,
fertile land, houses full of wealth,
cisterns already dug,
olive trees, fruit trees, and vineyards.
They ate all they wanted and grew fat;
they enjoyed all the good things you gave them.

26 "But your people rebelled and disobeyed you;
they turned their backs on your Law.
They killed the prophets who warned them,
who told them to turn back to you.
They insulted you time after time,
27 so you let their enemies conquer and rule them.
In their trouble they called to you for help,
and you answered them from heaven.
In your great mercy you sent them leaders
who rescued them from their foes.
28 When peace returned, they sinned again,
and again you let their enemies conquer them.
Yet when they repented and asked you to save them,
in heaven you heard, and time after time
you rescued them in your great mercy.
29 You warned them to obey your teachings,
but in pride they rejected your laws,
although keeping your Law is the way to life.
Hard-headed and stubborn, they refused to obey.
30 Year after year you patiently warned them.
You inspired your prophets to speak,
but your people were deaf,
so you let them be conquered by other nations.

9:17 Ex 34:6; Num 14:18 **9:18** Ex 32:1–4 **9:19–21** Deut 8:2–4 **9:22** Num 21:21–35 **9:23** **a** Gen 15:5; 22:17; **b** Josh 3:14–17 **9:24** Josh 11:23 **9:25** Deut 6:10, 11 **9:26–28** Judg 2:11–16 **9:26** Wis 2:10–20 **9:29** Lev 18:5 **9:30** 2 Kings 17:13–18; 2 Chr 36:15, 16

Why, do you think, are the lists of names so important?

31 And yet, because your mercy is great,
you did not forsake or destroy them.
You are a gracious and merciful God!
32 "O God, our God, how great you are!
How terrifying, how powerful!
You faithfully keep your covenant promises.
From the time when Assyrian kings oppressed us,
even till now, how much we have suffered!
Our kings, our leaders, our priests and prophets,
our ancestors, and all our people have suffered.
Remember how much we have suffered!
33 You have done right to punish us;
you have been faithful, even though we have sinned.
34 Our ancestors, our kings, leaders, and priests have not kept your Law.
They did not listen to your commands and warnings.
35 With your blessing, kings ruled your people
when they lived in the broad, fertile land you gave them;
but they failed to turn from sin and serve you.
36 And now we are slaves in the land that you gave us,
this fertile land which gives us food.
37 What the land produces goes to the kings
that you put over us because we sinned.
They do as they please with us and our livestock,
and we are in deep distress!"

The People Sign an Agreement

38 Because of all that has happened, we, the people of Israel, hereby make a solemn written agreement, and our leaders, our Levites, and our priests put their seals to it.

10 The first to sign was the governor, Nehemiah son of Hacaliah, and then Zedekiah signed. The following also signed:

2-8 *Priests:*
Seraiah, Azariah, Jeremiah,
Pashhur, Amariah, Malchijah,
Hattush, Shebaniah, Malluch,
Harim, Meremoth, Obadiah,
Daniel, Ginnethon, Baruch,
Meshullam, Abijah, Mijamin,
Maaziah, Bilgai, and Shemaiah.

9-13 *Levites:*
Jeshua son of Azaniah,
Binnui of the clan of Henadad,
Kadmiel, Shebaniah, Hodiah,
Kelita, Pelaiah, Hanan,
Mica, Rehob, Hashabiah,
Zaccur, Sherebiah, Shebaniah,
Hodiah, Bani, and Beninu.

14-27 *Leaders of the people:*
Parosh, Pahath Moab,
Elam, Zattu, Bani,
Bunni, Azgad, Bebai,
Adonijah, Bigvai, Adin,
Ater, Hezekiah, Azzur,
Hodiah, Hashum, Bezai,
Hariph, Anathoth, Nebai,
Magpiash, Meshullam, Hezir,
Meshezabel, Zadok, Jaddua,
Pelatiah, Hanan, Anaiah,
Hoshea, Hananiah, Hasshub,
Hallohesh, Pilha, Shobek,
Rehum, Hashabnah, Maaseiah,
Ahiah, Hanan, Anan,
Malluch, Harim, and Baanah.

The Agreement

28 We, the people of Israel, the priests, the Levites, the Temple guards, the Temple musicians, the Temple workers, and all others who in obedience to God's Law have separated themselves from the foreigners living in our land, we, together with our wives and all our children old enough to understand,
29 do hereby join with our leaders in an oath, under penalty of a curse if we break it, that we will live according to God's Law, which God gave through his servant Moses; that we will obey all that the LORD, our Lord, commands us; and that we will keep all his laws and requirements.

30 We will not intermarry with the foreigners living in our land.

31 If foreigners bring grain or anything else to sell to us on the Sabbath or on any other holy day, we will not buy from them.

Every seventh year we will not farm the
land, and we will cancel all debts.
32 Every year we will each contribute one-
eighth of an ounce of silver to help pay the
expenses of the Temple.
33 We will provide for the Temple worship
the following: the sacred bread, the daily
grain offering, the animals to be burned each
day as sacrifices, the sacred offerings for Sab-
baths, New Moon Festivals, and other festi-
vals, the other sacred offerings, the offerings
to take away the sins of Israel, and anything
else needed for the Temple.
34 We, the people, priests, and Levites, will
draw lots each year to determine which
clans are to provide wood to burn the sacri-
fices offered to the LORD our God, accord-
ing to the requirements of the Law.
35 We will take to the Temple each year an
offering of the first grain we harvest and of
the first fruit that ripens on our trees.
36 The first son born to each of us we will
take to the priests in the Temple and there, as
required by the Law, dedicate him to God.
We will also dedicate the first calf born to
each of our cows, and the first lamb or kid
born to each of our sheep or goats.
37 We will take to the priests in the Temple
the dough made from the first grain harvest-
ed each year and our other offerings of
wine, olive oil, and all kinds of fruit.

We will take to the Levites, who collect
tithes in our farming villages, the tithes
from the crops that grow on our land.
38 Priests who are descended from Aaron
are to be with the Levites when tithes are
collected, and for use in the Temple the
Levites are to take to the Temple store-
rooms one-tenth of all the tithes they col-
lect. 39 The people of Israel and the Levites
are to take the contributions of grain, wine,
and olive oil to the storerooms where the
utensils for the Temple are kept and where
the priests who are on duty, the Temple
guards, and the members of the Temple
choir have their quarters.

We will not neglect the house of our
God.

The People Who Lived in Jerusalem

11 The leaders settled in Jerusalem, and
the rest of the people drew lots to
choose one family out of every ten to go
and live in the holy city of Jerusalem, while
the rest were to live in the other cities and
towns. 2 The people praised anyone else who
volunteered to live in Jerusalem. 3 In the
other towns and cities the people of Israel,
the priests, the Levites, the Temple workers,
and the descendants of Solomon's servants
lived on their own property in their own
towns.

The following is the list of the leading cit-
izens of the province of Judah who lived in
Jerusalem:

4 *Members of the tribe of Judah:*

Athaiah, the son of Uzziah and grandson
of Zechariah. His other ancestors included
Amariah, Shephatiah, and Mahalalel, descen-
dants of Judah's son Perez.
5 Maaseiah, the son of Baruch and grand-
son of Colhozeh. His other ancestors includ-
ed Hazaiah, Adaiah, Joiarib, and Zechariah,
descendants of Judah's son Shelah.
6 Of the descendants of Perez, 468 out-
standing soldiers lived in Jerusalem.

7 *Members of the tribe of Benjamin:*

Sallu, the son of Meshullam and grandson
of Joed. His other ancestors included Peda-
iah, Kolaiah, Maaseiah, Ithiel, and Jeshaiah.
8 Gabbai and Sallai, close relatives[q] of Sallu.
In all, 928 Benjaminites lived in Jerusalem.
9 Joel son of Zichri was their leader, and Judah
son of Hassenuah was the second ranking
official in the city.

10 *Priests:*

Jedaiah son of Joiarib, and Jachin.
11 Seraiah, the son of Hilkiah and grandson
of Meshullam. His ancestors included
Zadok, Meraioth, and Ahitub, who was the
High Priest. 12 In all, 822 members of this
clan served in the Temple.

Adaiah, the son of Jeroham and grandson
of Pelaliah. His ancestors included Amzi,
Zechariah, Pashhur, and Malchijah. 13 In all,

[q] **11:8** *One ancient translation* close relatives; *Hebrew* after him.

9:32 2 Kings 15:19, 29; 17:3–6; Ezra 4:2, 10 **10:30** Ex 34:16; Deut 7:3 **10:31** **a** Ex 23:10, 11; Lev 25:1–7; **b** Deut 15:1, 2 **10:32** Ex 30:11–16 **10:35** Ex 23:19; 34:26; Deut 26:2 **10:36** Ex 13:2 **10:37** Num 18:21 **10:38** Num 18:26 **11:3, 4** Neh 7:73

242 members of this clan were heads of families.

Amashsai, the son of Azarel and grandson of Ahzai. His ancestors included Meshillemoth and Immer. 14 There were 128 members of this clan who were outstanding soldiers. Their leader was Zabdiel, a member of a leading family.[r]

15 *Levites:*

Shemaiah, the son of Hasshub and grandson of Azrikam. His ancestors included Hashabiah and Bunni.

16 Shabbethai and Jozabad, prominent Levites in charge of the work outside the Temple.

17 Mattaniah, the son of Mica and grandson of Zabdi, a descendant of Asaph. He led the Temple choir in singing the prayer of thanksgiving.

Bakbukiah, who was Mattaniah's assistant.

Abda, the son of Shammua and grandson of Galal, a descendant of Jeduthun.

18 In all, 284 Levites lived in the holy city of Jerusalem.

19 *Temple guards:*

Akkub, Talmon, and their relatives, 172 in all.

20 The rest of the people of Israel and the remaining priests and Levites lived on their own property in the other cities and towns of Judah. 21 The Temple workers lived in the part of Jerusalem called Ophel and worked under the supervision of Ziha and Gishpa.

22 The supervisor of the Levites who lived in Jerusalem was Uzzi, the son of Bani and grandson of Hashabiah. His ancestors included Mattaniah and Mica, and he belonged to the clan of Asaph, the clan that was responsible for the music in the Temple services.
23 There were royal regulations stating how the clans should take turns in leading the Temple music each day.

24 Pethahiah son of Meshezabel, of the clan of Zerah and the tribe of Judah, represented the people of Israel at the Persian court.

The People in Other Towns and Cities

25 Many of the people lived in towns near their farms. Those who were of the tribe of Judah lived in Kiriath Arba, Dibon, and Jekabzeel, and in the villages near these cities.
26 They also lived in the cities of Jeshua, Moladah, Bethpelet, 27 and Hazarshual, and in Beersheba and the villages around it.
28 They lived in the city of Ziklag, in Meconah and its villages, 29 in Enrimmon, in Zorah, in Jarmuth, 30 in Zanoah, in Adullam, and in the villages near these towns. They lived in Lachish and on the farms nearby, and in Azekah and its villages. That is to say, the people of Judah lived in the territory between Beersheba in the south and Hinnom Valley in the north.

31 The people of the tribe of Benjamin lived in Geba, Michmash, Ai, Bethel and the nearby villages, 32 Anathoth, Nob, Ananiah,
33 Hazor, Ramah, Gittaim, 34 Hadid, Zeboim, Neballat, 35 Lod, and Ono, and in Craftsmen's Valley. 36 Some groups of Levites that had lived in the territory of Judah were assigned to live with the people of Benjamin.

List of Priests and Levites

12 The following is a list of the priests and Levites who returned from exile with Zerubbabel son of Shealtiel and with the High Priest Joshua:

2-7 *Priests:*

Seraiah, Jeremiah, Ezra, Amariah, Malluch, Hattush, Shecaniah, Rehum, Meremoth, Iddo, Ginnethoi, Abijah, Mijamin, Maadiah, Bilgah, Shemaiah, Joiarib, Jedaiah, Sallu, Amok, Hilkiah, and Jedaiah.

These men were leaders among all their fellow priests in the days of Joshua.

8 *Levites:*

The following were in charge of the singing of hymns of thanksgiving: Jeshua,

[r] **11:14** a member of a leading family; *or* son of Haggedolim.

The people praised those who volunteered to live in Jerusalem because those people would have to fight if Jerusalem was attacked.

Binnui, Kadmiel, Sherebiah, Judah, and Mat-
taniah.
9 The following formed the choir that
sang the responses: Bakbukiah, Unno, and
their fellow Levites.

Descendants of the High Priest Joshua

10 Joshua was the father of Joiakim;
Joiakim was the father of Eliashib; Eliashib
was the father of Joiada; 11 Joiada was the
father of Jonathan; and Jonathan was the
father of Jaddua.

Heads of the Priestly Clans

12-21 When Joiakim was High Priest, the
following priests were the heads of the
priestly clans:

Priest	*Clan*
Meraiah	Seraiah
Hananiah	Jeremiah
Meshullam	Ezra
Jehohanan	Amariah
Jonathan	Malluchi
Joseph	Shebaniah
Adna	Harim
Helkai	Meraioth
Zechariah	Iddo
Meshullam	Ginnethon
Zichri	Abijah
. . . [s]	Miniamin
Piltai	Moadiah
Shammua	Bilgah
Jehonathan	Shemaiah
Mattenai	Joiarib
Uzzi	Jedaiah
Kallai	Sallai
Eber	Amok
Hashabiah	Hilkiah
Nethanel	Jedaiah

Record of the Priestly and Levite Families

22 A record was kept of the heads of the
Levite families and of the priestly families
during the lifetimes of the following High
Priests: Eliashib, Joiada, Jonathan, and Jaddua.
This record was finished when Darius was
emperor of Persia.
23 The heads of the Levite families, how-
ever, were recorded in the official records
only until the time of Jonathan, the grand-
son of Eliashib.

Assignment of Duties in the Temple

24 Under the direction of Hashabiah,
Sherebiah, Jeshua, Binnui,[t] and Kadmiel, the
Levites were organized into groups. Two
groups at a time praised God responsively
and gave thanks to him, in accordance with
the instructions given by King David, the
man of God.
25 The following Temple guards were in
charge of guarding the storerooms by the
gates to the Temple: Mattaniah, Bakbukiah,
Obadiah, Meshullam, Talmon, and Akkub.
26 These people lived during the time of
Joiakim, the son of Joshua and grandson of
Jehozadak, and the time of Nehemiah the
governor, and the time of Ezra, the priest
who was a scholar of the Law.

Nehemiah Dedicates the City Wall

27 When the city wall of Jerusalem was
dedicated, the Levites were brought in from
wherever they were living, so that they could
join in celebrating the dedication with songs
of thanksgiving and with the music of cym-
bals and harps. 28 The Levite families of
singers gathered from the area where they
had settled around Jerusalem and from the
towns around Netophah, 29 and from
Bethgilgal, Geba, and Azmaveth. 30 The
priests and the Levites performed ritual

[s] **12:12–21** *In Hebrew a name is missing from the list.* [t] **12:24** *Probable text (see 10:9 and 12:8)* Binnui; *Hebrew* son of.

"Remember me, O God, for this also, and spare me because of your great love" *(Nehemiah 13:22)*.

Study it!

The Dedication

When a religious structure, like a church, is finished, it is dedicated. Being dedicated means that a ceremony is held to officially recognize it as a place for gathering God's holy people for prayer and worship.

The wall around Jerusalem, when finished, was dedicated in a similar way. There was a procession, complete with musicians, songs, prayers of thanksgiving, rituals, priests, singers, and sacrifices. There was so much celebration it could be heard for miles. What is the biggest celebration that you have been part of?

— Nehemiah 12:27–43

purification for themselves, the people, the gates, and the city wall.

31 I assembled the leaders of Judah on top of the wall and put them in charge of two large groups to march around the city, giving thanks to God.

The first group went to the right on top of the wall toward the Rubbish Gate.[u] 32 Hoshaiah marched behind the singers, followed by half the leaders of Judah. 33-35 The following priests, blowing trumpets, marched next: Azariah, Ezra, Meshullam, Judah, Benjamin, Shemaiah, and Jeremiah. Next came Zechariah, the son of Jonathan and grandson of Shemaiah. (His ancestors also included Mattaniah, Micaiah, and Zaccur, of the clan of Asaph.) 36 He was followed by other members of his clan—Shemaiah, Azarel, Milalai, Gilalai, Maai, Nethanel, Judah, and Hanani—all of whom carried musical instruments of the kind played by King David, the man of God. Ezra the scholar led this group in the procession. 37 At the Fountain Gate they went up the steps that led to David's City, past David's palace, and back to the wall at the Water Gate, on the east side of the city.

38 The other group of those who gave thanks went to the left along the top of the wall, and I followed with half of the people. We marched past the Tower of the Ovens to the Broad Wall, 39 and from there we went past Ephraim Gate, Jeshanah Gate,[v] the Fish Gate, the Tower of Hananel, and the Tower of the Hundred, to the Sheep Gate. We ended our march near the gate to the Temple.

The other group . . . went to the left. (12:38)

40 So both the groups that were giving thanks to God reached the Temple area.

In addition to the leaders who were with me, 41 my group included the following priests, blowing trumpets: Eliakim, Maaseiah, Miniamin, Micaiah, Elioenai, Zechariah, and Hananiah; 42 and they were followed by Maaseiah, Shemaiah, Eleazar, Uzzi, Jehohanan, Malchijah, Elam, and Ezer. The singers, led by Jezrahiah, sang at the top of their voices.

43 That day many sacrifices were offered, and the people were full of joy because God had made them very happy. The women and the children joined in the celebration, and the noise they all made could be heard for miles.

Providing for Worship in the Temple

44 At that time men were put in charge of the storerooms where contributions for the

[u] **12:31** RUBBISH GATE: *The two groups started somewhere on the southwestern part of the city wall and went in opposite directions until they met in front of the Temple in the northeastern part of the city.* [v] **12:39** Ephraim Gate, Jeshanah Gate; *or* Ephraim Gate (also called the Old Gate).

Temple were kept, including the tithes and the first grain and fruit that ripened each year. These men were responsible for collecting from the farms near the various cities the contributions for the priests and the Levites which the Law required. All the people of Judah were pleased with the priests and the Levites, 45because they performed the ceremonies of purification and the other rituals that God had commanded. The Temple musicians and the Temple guards also performed their duties in accordance with the regulations made by King David and his son Solomon. 46From the time of King David and the musician Asaph long ago, the musicians have led songs of praise and thanksgiving to God. 47In the time of Zerubbabel and also in the time of Nehemiah, all the people of Israel gave daily gifts for the support of the Temple musicians and the Temple guards. The people gave a sacred offering to the Levites, and the Levites gave the required portion to the priests.

Separation from Foreigners

13 When the Law of Moses was being read aloud to the people, they came to the passage that said that no Ammonite or Moabite was ever to be permitted to join God's people. 2This was because the people of Ammon and Moab did not give food and water to the Israelites on their way out of Egypt. Instead, they paid money to Balaam to curse Israel, but our God turned the curse into a blessing. 3When the people of Israel heard this law read, they excluded all foreigners from the community.

Nehemiah's Reforms

4The priest Eliashib, who was in charge of the Temple storerooms, had for a long time been on good terms with Tobiah. 5He allowed Tobiah to use a large room that was intended only for storing offerings of grain and incense, the equipment used in the Temple, the offerings for the priests, and the tithes of grain, wine, and olive oil given to the Levites, to the Temple musicians, and to the Temple guards. 6While this was going on, I was not in Jerusalem, because in the thirty-second year that Artaxerxes[w] was king of Babylon I had gone back to report to him. After some time I received his permission 7and returned to Jerusalem. There I was shocked to find that Eliashib had allowed Tobiah to use a room in the Temple. 8I was furious and threw out all of Tobiah's belongings. 9I gave orders for the rooms to be ritually purified and for the Temple equipment, grain offerings, and incense to be put back.

10I also learned that the Temple musicians and other Levites had left Jerusalem and gone back to their farms, because the people had not been giving them enough to live on. 11I reprimanded the officials for letting the Temple be neglected. And I brought the Levites and musicians back to the Temple and put them to work again. 12Then all the people of Israel again started bringing to the Temple storerooms their tithes of grain, wine, and olive oil. 13I put the following men in charge of the storerooms: Shelemiah, a priest; Zadok, a scholar of the Law; and Pedaiah, a Levite. Hanan, the son of Zaccur and grandson of Mattaniah, was to be their assistant. I knew I could trust these men to be honest in distributing the supplies to the other workers.

14Remember, my God, all these things that I have done for your Temple and its worship.

15At that time I saw people in Judah pressing juice from grapes on the Sabbath. Others were loading grain, wine, grapes, figs, and other things on their donkeys and taking them into Jerusalem; I warned them not to sell anything on the Sabbath. 16Some people from the city of Tyre were living in Jerusalem, and they brought fish and all kinds of goods into the city to sell to our people on the Sabbath. 17I reprimanded the Jewish leaders and told them, "Look at the evil you're doing! You're making the Sabbath unholy. 18This is exactly why God punished your ancestors when he brought destruction on this city. And yet you insist on bringing

[w] **13:6** ARTAXERXES: *As emperor of Persia, Artaxerxes also had the title "King of Babylon."*

12:45 **a** 1 Chr 25:1–8; **b** 1 Chr 26:12 **13:1, 2** Deut 23:3–5 **13:2** Num 22:1–6 **13:10** Deut 12:19 **13:12** Mal 3:10 **13:15** Ex 20:8–10; Deut 5:12–14; Jer 17:21, 22

You're making the Sabbath unholy. (13:17)

more of God's anger down on Israel by profaning the Sabbath."

19 So I gave orders for the city gates to be shut at the beginning of every Sabbath, as soon as evening[x] began to fall, and not to be opened again until the Sabbath was over. I stationed some of my men at the gates to make sure that nothing was brought into the city on the Sabbath. 20 Once or twice merchants who sold all kinds of goods spent Friday night outside the city walls. 21 I warned them, "It's no use waiting out there for morning to come. If you try this again, I'll use force on you." From then on they did not come back on the Sabbath. 22 I ordered the Levites to purify themselves and to go and guard the gates to make sure that the Sabbath was kept holy.

Remember me, O God, for this also, and spare me because of your great love.

23 At that time I also discovered that many of the Jewish men had married women from Ashdod, Ammon, and Moab. 24 Half of their children spoke the language of Ashdod or some other language and didn't know how to speak our language. 25 I reprimanded the men, called down curses on them, beat them, and pulled out their hair. Then I made them take an oath in God's name that never again would they or their children intermarry with foreigners. 26 I told them, "It was foreign women that made King Solomon sin. Here was a man who was greater than any of the kings of other nations. God loved him and made him king over all of Israel, and yet he fell into this sin. 27 Are we then to follow your example and disobey our God by marrying foreign women?"

28 Joiada was the son of Eliashib the High Priest, but one of Joiada's sons married the daughter of Sanballat, from the town of Beth Horon, so I made Joiada leave Jerusalem.

29 Remember, God, how those people defiled both the office of priest and the covenant you made with the priests and the Levites.

30 I purified the people from everything foreign; I prepared regulations for the priests and the Levites so that all of them would know their duties; 31 I arranged for the wood used for burning the offerings to be brought at the proper times, and for the people to bring their offerings of the first grain and the first fruits that ripened.

Remember all this, O God, and give me credit for it.

[x] **13:19** EVENING: *The Jewish day begins at sunset.*

13:23–25 Ex 34:11–16; Deut 7:1–5 **13:26** **a** 2 Sam 12:24, 25; **b** 1 Kings 11:1–8 **13:28** Neh 4:1

Your Next Step

Congratulations on finishing the Book of Nehemiah! Use this space to write your thoughts and questions about this book. If you are following the suggested reading plan, move ahead to the Letter to the Hebrews in the New Testament. The Letter to the Hebrews shows how Jesus is the fulfillment of God's plan, which began in the Old Testament.

The Book of Tobit

Boy meets girl. Boy and girl fall in love. Do they marry and live happily ever after? And what about the angel, the demon, the money, and the blind father?

The Book of Tobit is a novel about Tobit, a faithful Jew, his teenage son, Tobias, and Sarah, the woman Tobias wants to marry. It describes what happens as they try to find love in the world. Tobit was written to encourage the Jewish people to trust in God's protection.

The story includes the archangel Raphael, one of three archangels mentioned in the Bible. Raphael pretends to be a distant relative of Tobit, keeping his true identity a secret until the end, in order to befriend both Tobias' and Sarah's families. *Raphael* means "God heals." And Raphael certainly brings God's healing in this story.

Chap. 8

Headlines

- Tobit Risks Life to Bury the Dead (1:16–20)
- Bird Droppings Cause Blindness! (2:9–10)
- Father Gives Good Advice to Son (4:5–11)
- Undercover Angel Travels with Tobias (5:4–9)
- Young Lovers Marry (7:13–17)
- Blind Tobit Is Healed! (11:10–15)

FACTOIDS

Who wrote this book? An unknown author wrote this book sometime in the second century BC.

What is the literary style? This book is a novel that teaches a truth—when you trust in God, you can get through the bad times and celebrate the good times.

Why was it written? To encourage the Jews who needed hope after Jerusalem was destroyed and they were scattered in foreign lands.

Who are the young people in this book? Tobias and Sarah

Important themes

- God sends us messengers to help and guide us.
- Despite suffering, God does reward the faithful.
- It's best to have faith, even when we feel hopeless.

1 I am Tobit and this is the story of my life. My father was Tobiel, my grandfather was Ananiel, and my great-grandfather was Aduel. Aduel's father was Gabael; his grandfather was Raphael; and his great-grandfather was Raguel, who belonged to the clan of Asiel, a part of the tribe of Naphtali. 2During the time that Shalmaneser was emperor of Assyria, I was taken captive in my hometown of Thisbe, located in northern Galilee, south of Kadesh in Naphtali, northwest of Hazor, and north of Phogor.

Tobit's Early Life

3All my life I have been honest and have tried to do what was right. I often gave money to help needy relatives and other Jews who had been deported with me to Nineveh, the capital of Assyria.

4When I was young, I lived in northern Israel. All the tribes in Israel were supposed to offer sacrifices in Jerusalem. It was the one city that God had chosen from among all the Israelite cities as the place where his Temple was to be built for his holy and eternal home. But my entire tribe of Naphtali rejected the city of Jerusalem and the kings descended from David. 5Like everyone else in this tribe, my own family used to go to the city of Dan in the mountains of northern Galilee to offer sacrifices to the gold bull-calf which King Jeroboam of Israel had set up there.

Tobit's Faithfulness to His Religion

6I was the only one in my family who regularly went to Jerusalem to celebrate the religious festivals, as the Law of Moses commands everyone to do. I would hurry off to Jerusalem with the first part of my harvest, the first-born of my animals, a tenth of my cattle, and the freshly clipped wool from my sheep. Then I would stand before the altar in the Temple, and give these offerings to the priests, the descendants of Aaron. 7I would give a tenth of my grain, wine, olive oil, pomegranates, figs, and other fruits to the Levites who served God in Jerusalem. Every year, except the seventh year when the land was at rest,[a] I would sell a second tenth of my possessions and spend the money in Jerusalem on the festival meal.

8But every third year, I would give a third tithe[b] to widows and orphans and to foreigners living among my people, and we would eat the festival meal together. I did this in keeping with the Law of Moses, which Deborah, the mother of my grandfather Ananiel, had taught me to obey. (I had been left an orphan when my father died.)

Tobit's Faithfulness in Exile

9When I grew up, I married Anna, a member of my own tribe. We had a son and named him Tobias. 10Later, I was taken

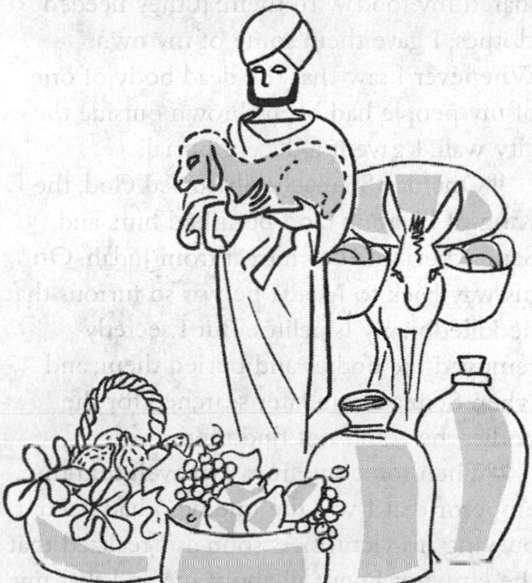

I would hurry off to Jerusalem with the first part of my harvest. (1:6)

[a] **1:7** THE LAND WAS AT REST: *See Lev 25:1–7.* [b] **1:8** a third tithe; *some manuscripts have* the money.

1:2 2 Kings 17:3; 18:9 **1:5** 1 Kings 12:28, 29 **1:6** Deut 16:16

captive and deported to Assyria, and that is how I came to live in Nineveh.

While we lived in Nineveh, all my relatives and the other Jews used to eat the same kind of food as the other people who lived there, [11]but I refused to do so. [12]Since I took seriously the commands of the Most High God, [13]he made Emperor Shalmaneser respect me, and I was placed in charge of purchasing all the emperor's supplies.

[14]Before the emperor died, I made regular trips to the land of Media to buy things for him there. Once, when I was in the city of Rages in Media, I left some bags of money there with Gabael, Gabrias' brother, and asked him to keep them for me. There were more than 600 pounds of silver coins in those bags. [15]When Shalmaneser died, his son Sennacherib succeeded him as emperor. It soon became so dangerous to travel on the roads in Media that I could no longer go there.

Tobit Buries the Dead

[16]While Shalmaneser was still emperor, I took good care of my own people whenever they were in need. [17]If they were hungry, I shared my food with them; if they needed clothes, I gave them some of my own. Whenever I saw that the dead body of one of my people had been thrown outside the city wall, I gave it a decent burial.

[18]One day Sennacherib cursed God, the King of Heaven; God punished him, and Sennacherib had to retreat from Judah. On his way back to Media he was so furious that he killed many Israelites. But I secretly removed the bodies and buried them; and when Sennacherib later searched for the bodies, he could not find them.

[19]Then someone from Nineveh told the emperor that I was the one who had been burying his victims. As soon as I realized that the emperor knew all about me and that my life was in danger, I became frightened. So I ran away and hid. [20]Everything I owned was seized and put in the royal treasury. My wife Anna and my son Tobias were all I had left.

Tobit's Nephew Rescues Him

[21]About six weeks later, two of Sennacherib's sons assassinated him and then escaped to the mountains of Ararat. Another son, Esarhaddon, became emperor and put Ahikar, my brother Anael's son, in charge of all the financial affairs of the empire. [22]This was actually the second time Ahikar was appointed to this position, for when Sennacherib was emperor of Assyria, Ahikar had been wine steward, treasurer, and accountant, and had been in charge of the official seal. Since Ahikar was my nephew, he put in a good word for me with the emperor, and I was allowed to return to Nineveh.

A Family Celebration

2 When I returned home I was reunited with my wife Anna and my son Tobias. At the Harvest Festival, which is also called the Festival of Weeks, I sat down to a delicious meal. [2]When I saw how much food there was on the table, I said to Tobias, "Son, go out and find one of our people who is living in poverty here in exile, someone who takes God's commands seriously. Bring him back with you, so that he can share this festival meal with us. I won't start eating until you come back."

A Murder in Nineveh

[3]So Tobias went out to look for such a person. But he quickly returned, shouting, "Father! Father!"

"Yes, what is it?" I asked.

"One of our people has just been murdered! Someone strangled him and threw his body into the marketplace."

[4]I jumped up and left the table without even touching my food. I removed the body from the street and carried it to a little shed, where I left it until sunset, when I could bury it. [5]Then I returned home and washed, so as to purify myself. In deep sorrow I ate my dinner. [6]I was reminded of what the prophet Amos had said to the people of Bethel,

1:17 Job 31:16–20 **2:1** Ex 23:16 **2:5** Num 19:11–13 **2:6** Am 8:10

"Your festivals will be turned into funerals,
and your glad songs will become cries
of grief."
I began to weep.
[7]After sunset I went out, dug a grave, and
buried the man. [8]My neighbors thought I
was crazy. "Haven't you learned anything?"
they asked. "You have already been hunted
down once for burying the dead, and you
would have been killed if you had not run
away. But here you are doing the same thing
all over again."

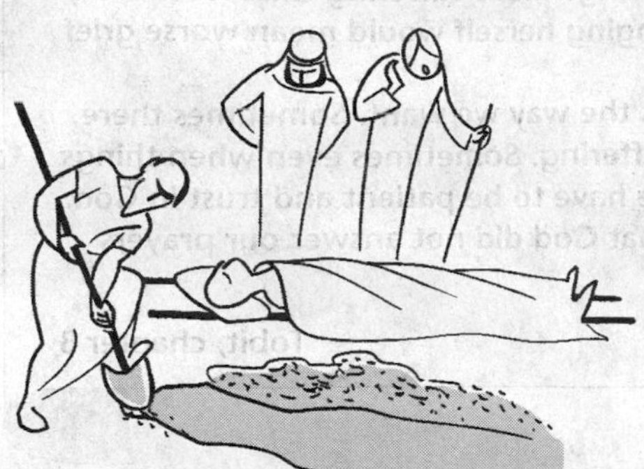

You have already been hunted down once for burying the dead. (2:8)

Tobit Is Blinded

[9]That night I washed, so as to purify
myself, and went out into my courtyard to
sleep by the wall. It was a hot night, and I
did not pull the cover up over my head.
[10]Sparrows were on the wall right above me,
but I did not know it. Their warm droppings
fell into my eyes, causing a white film to
form on them. I went to one doctor after
another, but the more they treated me with
their medicines, the worse my eyes became,
until finally I was completely blind.

For four years I could see nothing. My relatives were deeply concerned about my condition, and Ahikar supported me for two years before he went to the land of Elam.

A Family Quarrel

[11]After Ahikar left, my wife Anna had to
go to work, so she took up weaving, like
many other women. [12]The people she
worked for would pay her when she delivered
the cloth. One spring day, she cut a finished
piece of cloth from the loom and took it to
the people who had ordered it. They paid her
the full price and also gave her a goat.
[13]When Anna came home with the goat,
it began to bleat. I called out, "Where did
that goat come from? You stole it, didn't
you? Take it straight back to its owners. It's
not right to eat stolen food!"
[14]"No!" she replied. "It was given to me
as a gift in addition to what I got for the
cloth." But I didn't believe her, and I blushed
for shame for what she had done. I ordered
her to return the goat to its owners, but she
had the last word. "Now I see what you are
really like!" she shouted. "Where is all that
concern of yours for others? What about all
those good deeds you used to do?"

"Take it straight back to its owners." (2:13)

Tobit's Prayer

3 I was so embarrassed and ashamed that I sighed and began to cry. Then, as I choked back my tears, I prayed:

[2]"You are righteous, O Lord!
You are merciful[c] in all you do,
faithful in all your ways.
You are the judge of this world.[d]
[3-4] I beg you, treat me with kindness.
Do not punish me for my sins,
not even for sins of which I am
unaware.

[c] **3:2** merciful; *some manuscripts add* and just. [d] **3:2** You are the judge of this world; *some manuscripts have* You are always fair and just when you judge.

Pray it!

Praying for Death?

Sarah and Tobit both wanted to die. They each had a horrible problem that seemed hopeless. The only solution they could think of was death. So they prayed to God to end their lives. God heard their prayers, and actually solved their problems, but with a better solution!

For some people, death seems like the only answer to their problems. Tobit and Sarah thought so, too. Sometimes, people don't only pray for death, but they actually attempt suicide. But suicide brings more suffering than it relieves. Sarah understood that—she knew that hanging herself would mean worse grief for her family (Tobit 3:10).

God doesn't always answer our prayers the way we want. Sometimes there is important learning to be gained from suffering. Sometimes even when things seem hopeless and we'd like to just die, we have to be patient and trust in God. Like Sarah and Tobit, we will be relieved that God did not answer our prayers the way we originally asked!

— Tobit, chapter 3

My ancestors rebelled and disobeyed[e]
your commands,
but do not punish me for their sins.
You let our people be plundered,
taken captive and killed.
You made an example of our people,
an object of contempt and disgrace
in all the nations where you scattered
us.
5 You have often judged my ancestors for
their sins
and punished me for mine.
We were disloyal and rejected your
commands,
so our punishment has always been just.

6 "Now treat me as you please.
Take my life away and free me from this
world;
let my body return to the earth.
I would be better off dead.
I am tormented by insults I don't deserve,
and weighed down with despair.
Lord, give the command—
bring all my troubles to an end,
take me to my eternal rest.
Don't reject my prayer.
I would rather die than live in misery
and face such cruel insults."

Sarah's Troubles

7 That same day in the city of Ecbatana in
Media, it happened that Sarah, the daughter
of a man named Raguel, was insulted by one
of her father's servant women. 8 Sarah had
been married seven times, but the evil
demon, Asmodeus, killed each husband
before the marriage could be consummated.
The servant woman said to Sarah, "You hus-
band killer! Look at you! You've already had
seven husbands, but not one of them lived
long enough to give you a son.[f] 9 Why
should you take it out on us? Why don't you
go and join your dead husbands? I hope we
never see a child of yours!"

10 Sarah was so depressed that she burst
into tears and went upstairs determined to
hang herself. But when she thought it over,
she said to herself, "No, I won't do it! People
would insult my father and say, 'You had
only one child, a daughter whom you loved

[e] **3:3–4** My ancestors . . . disobeyed; *some manuscripts have* I disobeyed. [f] **3:8** but . . . son; *some manuscripts have* but it hasn't done you a bit of good.

dearly, but she hanged herself because she felt so miserable.' Such grief would bring my gray-haired father to his grave, and I would be responsible. I won't kill myself; I'll just beg the Lord to let me die. Then I won't have to listen to those insults any longer!"

Sarah's Prayer

11 Then Sarah stood by the window, raised her arms in prayer, and said,

"God of mercy, worthy of our praise,
may your name always be honored,
may all your creation praise you
forever.

Sarah's prayer (3:11)

12 "Lord, I look to you for help.
13 Speak the word and set me free from this
life;
then I will no longer have to hear these
insults.
14 You know, O Lord, that I'm still a virgin;
I have never been defiled by a man.
15 Never have I disgraced myself or my
father's name,
as long as we have lived in this land of
exile.
My father has no other child to be his heir,
and there is no relative[g] whom I can
marry.
I have already lost seven husbands,
so why should I live any longer?
But if it is not your will to take my life,
at least show mercy to me.
Don't let me hear those insults again!"[h]

God Hears the Prayers of Tobit and Sarah

16 As Tobit and Sarah were praying, God in heaven heard their prayers 17 and sent his angel Raphael to help them. He was sent to remove the white film from Tobit's eyes, so that he could see again, and to arrange a marriage between Sarah and Tobit's son Tobias, who, as her cousin, had the right to marry her. Raphael was also ordered to expel the demon Asmodeus from Sarah. At the very moment that Tobit went back into his house from the courtyard, Sarah, in her house in Ecbatana, was coming downstairs.

Tobit's Advice to Tobias

4 That same day, Tobit remembered the money that he had left with Gabael at Rages in Media. 2 He thought to himself, "Now that I have asked God to let me die, I should call my son Tobias and tell him about the money."

3-4 So Tobit called Tobias and said to him, "Son, when I die, give me a proper burial. And after I'm gone, show respect to your mother. Take care of her for the rest of her life, and when she dies, bury her beside me. Remember, she risked her life to bring you into this world, so try to make her happy and never do anything that would worry her.

5 "Every day of your life, keep the Lord our God in mind. Never sin deliberately or disobey any of his commands. Always do what is right and never get involved in anything evil. 6 Be honest, and you will succeed in whatever you do.

7 "Give generously to anyone who faithfully obeys God.[i] If you are stingy in giving to the poor, God will be stingy in giving to you. 8 Give according to what you have. The more you have, the more you should give.

[g] **3:15** RELATIVE: *In Israel it was customary to marry within one's own tribe.* [h] **3:15** at least . . . again; *some manuscripts have* at least listen to my complaint. [i] **4:7** *The translation of verses 7b–19b, accidentally omitted in the Greek manuscript that this translation normally follows, is based on other Greek manuscripts.*

3:17 Num 36:6–9; Tob 6:10–12 **4:7** Deut 15:7, 8; Prov 19:17; Sir 3:30—4:6; 1 Jn 3:17

Even if you have only a little, be sure to give something. 9 This is as good as money saved. You will have your reward in a time of trouble. 10-11 Taking care of the poor is the kind of offering that pleases God in heaven. Do this, and you will be kept safe from the dark world of the dead.

12 "Son, be on your guard against prostitutes. Above all, marry a woman of our tribe, because we are descendants of the prophets. Do not marry anyone who is not related to us. Remember that Noah, Abraham, Isaac and Jacob, our earliest ancestors, all married relatives. God blessed them with children, and so their descendants will inherit the land of Israel. 13 Son, be loyal to your own relatives. Don't be too proud to marry one of them. Such pride leads to terrible frustration and ruin, just as laziness brings on severe poverty and causes starvation.

14 "Pay your workers each day; never keep back their wages overnight. Honor God in this way, and he will reward you. Behave properly at all times. 15 Never do to anyone else anything that you would not want someone to do to you.

"Do not drink so much wine that you get drunk, and do not let drinking become a habit.

16 "Give food to the hungry and clothes to people in need. If you are prosperous, give generously, and do it gladly!

17 "When one of God's faithful people has died, prepare food for the family,[j] but never do this when someone evil dies.

18 "Take the advice of sensible people, and never treat any useful advice lightly.

19 "Take advantage of every opportunity to praise the Lord your God. Ask him to make you prosper in whatever you set out to do. He does not give his wisdom to the people of any other nation. He is the source of all good things, but he can also destroy you and bring you to certain death, if he wishes.

"Remember all my instructions. Don't forget them for one minute.

20 "Tobias, I want you to know that I once left a large sum of money with Gabrias' son, Gabael, at Rages in Media. 21 We're poor now, but don't worry. If you obey God and avoid sin, he will be pleased with you and make you prosperous."

Travel Preparations

5 Then Tobias answered his father, "I'll do everything you told me. 2 But how can I get the money back from Gabael? We have never even met each other. How can I prove to him who I am, so that he will trust me and give me the money? Besides that, I don't know how to get to Media."

3 Tobit replied, "Gabael and I both signed a document. I then tore it in two, and we each took a half. I put his half with the money. That was twenty years ago! Now, go and find a reliable person to travel with you to Media and back, and we will pay him when you return. But you must get the money that I left with Gabael."

Tobias Meets Raphael

4 Tobias then went out to look for someone who knew the way to Media and would travel with him. Almost as soon as he left the house, he found himself face to face with Raphael. Tobias did not know that Raphael was an angel of God, 5 so he asked him where he was from.

"I am an Israelite," Raphael answered, "one of your distant relatives, and I have come here to Nineveh to find work."

"Do you know the way to Media?" Tobias asked.

6 "Yes, I do," Raphael replied. "I have been there many times, and I know all the roads well. I used to stay with our relative Gabael, who lives there in the town of Rages.[k] It takes at least two days to travel there from Ecbatana, the capital city, because Rages is up in the mountains."

7 Then Tobias said to Raphael, "Wait here for me, my friend, while I go in and tell my father. I would like for you to travel with me, and I will pay you for the journey."

8 "All right," Raphael said, "I'll wait, but don't take too long."

[j] **4:17** prepare . . . family; *or* put food on his grave. [k] **5:6** Rages; *Greek* Ecbatana.

4:15 Mt 7:12; Lk 6:31 **4:17** Deut 26:14 **4:21** 1 Tim 6:6–8 **5:4** Heb 13:2

9 Tobias went in and told his father, "I have found an Israelite to travel with me."

"Call the man in," Tobit replied. "I would like to know what family and tribe he belongs to, and whether he is a reliable traveling companion for you."

Tobit Meets Raphael

So Tobias went out and called to Raphael, "My father would like to meet you." When Raphael came in, Tobit greeted him first.

Then Raphael returned the greeting, "I hope all is well with you."

But Tobit replied, "How can all be well with me? I'm blind and can't see a thing. It's like being dead and no longer able to see the light. I might as well be dead! I can hear people talking, but I can't see them."

"Cheer up!" Raphael said to him. "God is going to cure you soon, so don't worry!"

Tobit then said, "My son Tobias wants to go to Media. Can you go with him and show him the way? I will pay you, of course."

Raphael replied, "Certainly I can go with him. I have traveled there many times and I know all the roads in the mountains and on the plains."

10 Tobit questioned him further, "Tell me, my friend, what family and tribe do you belong to?"

11 But Raphael asked, "Why do you need to know that?"

"Tell me the truth," said Tobit. "What is your name, and who are you?"

12 Raphael replied, "My name is Azarias, and I am the son of the older Ananias, one of your relatives."

13 Then Tobit said to him, "Welcome to our home! God bless you, my son. Please don't be offended because I wanted to know the truth about you and your family. As it turns out, you are from a good family and a relative at that! I knew Ananias and Nathan, the two sons of the older Shemaiah. They were always loyal to their religion. We used to travel together to Jerusalem and worship there. Your relatives are fine people, and you come from good stock. Have a safe journey."

14 Tobit continued, "I will pay the normal daily wage plus expenses for both of you. 15 Be a good companion to Tobias, and I will add a bonus to your wages."

16 "I will go with him," Raphael said. "And don't worry; we will get there and back safely. The roads are not dangerous."

"God be with you!" Tobit replied. Then he called Tobias and said to him, "Son, get everything ready that you need for the journey, so that the two of you can be on your way. May God and his angel watch over you both and bring you back to me safe and sound."

Before leaving for Media, Tobias kissed his father and mother good-bye. Tobit said again, "Have a safe journey!"

17 Then his mother began to cry. "How could you send my son away like this?" she complained. "He's our only means of support. Who will take care of us now? 18 Is that money so important to you that you are willing to risk your own son's life to get it back? 19 Why can't we be content to live on what the Lord has given us?"

20 "Calm down," Tobit said to her. "He will get there and back safely, and with your own eyes you will see him return home safe and sound. 21 Now stop worrying about them, dear. A good angel will go with Tobias. He will have a successful journey and will come back in good health." At that, Anna calmed down and stopped crying.

Tobias Catches a Fish

6 So Tobias and the angel started out toward Media, taking Tobias' dog along with them. They walked on until sunset, then camped by the Tigris River. 2 Tobias had gone down to wash his feet in the river, when suddenly a huge fish jumped up out of the water and tried to swallow one of his feet. Tobias let out a yell, 3 and the angel called to him, "Grab that fish! Don't let it get away."

Then Tobias grabbed the fish and dragged it up on the bank.

4 "Cut the fish open," the angel instructed, "and take out its gall bladder, heart, and liver. Keep these with you; they can be used for medicine, but throw away the guts."

5:16 Gen 24:7, 40

Grab that fish! (6:3)

5Tobias did as the angel had told him. Then he cooked the fish, ate part of it, and salted the rest to take along with him.

The two continued on together until they were near Media. 6Then Tobias asked, "Azarias, my friend, what diseases can be cured by this gall bladder, heart, and liver?"

7The angel answered, "The heart and liver can be burned and used to chase away a demon or an evil spirit that is tormenting someone. The attacks will stop immediately, and the person will never be troubled again. 8You can use the gall bladder to treat someone whose eyes are covered with a white film. Just rub it on his eyes and blow on the film, and he will be able to see again."

On the Way to Ecbatana

9When they had reached Media and were approaching the city of Ecbatana, 10Raphael said, "Tobias, my friend."

"Yes, what is it?" Tobias asked.

Raphael continued, "Tonight we will stay at the home of your relative Raguel. He has only one child, a daughter named Sarah, 11and since you are her closest relative, you have the right to marry her. You also have the right to inherit all her father's property. 12She is sensible, brave, and very beautiful; and her father is a good man. Tonight I'll discuss the marriage proposal with her father, and he will consent to give her to you as your bride. Then, when we return home from the town of Rages, we will celebrate the marriage. Raguel cannot refuse to let you marry her, and he cannot let any other man have her. If he did, then according to the Law of Moses he would deserve the death penalty. He knows that you are the only man who has the right to marry his daughter and receive the inheritance, so follow my advice. Raguel and I will discuss the matter tonight and arrange your engagement to Sarah. When we get back from the city of Rages, we will take her home with us."

13Tobias then said to Raphael, "Azarias, my friend, I have already heard about Sarah's seven former husbands, and how each one dropped dead on his wedding night, even before he could get to bed. 14According to the story I heard, a demon killed them. He doesn't harm Sarah, but he kills every man who tries to get near her. I am afraid of this demon. I am an only child, and if I were to die, the sorrow would send my parents to their graves. They don't even have another son to bury them."

15The angel replied, "Have you already forgotten your father's instructions? He told you to marry a woman from your own tribe. So, listen carefully to what I say. Don't worry about the demon. Marry Sarah! I know that tonight Raguel will let Sarah marry you. 16When you go into the bedroom, take the fish's heart and liver with you and place them on the burning incense, 17so that the odor will spread throughout the room. When the demon smells it, he will leave and never come near Sarah again. But before you consummate the marriage, both of you must get up and pray for the Lord in heaven to be merciful to you and to protect you. Don't be afraid. Sarah was meant to be yours from the beginning of creation. You will rescue her from the demon, and she will go with you to your home. You and Sarah will have many children, whom you will love very much. So don't worry!"

Tobias listened very carefully to what Raphael had to say. He knew that Sarah was a relative on his father's side of the family. He began to fall in love with her and looked forward to marrying her.

At Raguel's House

7 When Tobias and the angel Raphael
had entered the city of Ecbatana, Tobias
said, "Azarias, my friend, take me to see
Raguel as quickly as you can." The angel
brought him to Raguel's house, where they
found him sitting at the entrance to his
courtyard. Raphael and Tobias greeted him
first; then he replied, "Come in, my friends.
You are welcome in my home."
Raguel brought them into his house [2]and
said to his wife Edna, "Doesn't this young
man look just like my cousin Tobit?"
[3]Edna asked them, "Where do you come
from?"
"We are Israelites of the tribe of Naph-
tali," Tobias and Raphael answered, "but we
are now living in exile in the city of Nin-
eveh in Assyria."
[4]Edna said, "Do you know our cousin
Tobit?"
"We certainly do know him," they
answered.
"How is he?" she asked.
[5]"He is alive and well," they replied.
Then Tobias added, "Tobit is my father."
[6]At that Raguel got up, and with tears of joy
in his eyes he kissed Tobias. [7]Then he said,
"God bless you, my child. Your father is a
good and noble man. What a terrible tragedy
that such an honest and generous man
should have lost his sight!" He threw his
arms around Tobias' neck and wept on his
shoulder. [8]His wife Edna and his daughter
Sarah also wept for Tobit.
Raguel gave Tobias and Raphael a warm
welcome and had one of his rams slaugh-
tered. After the guests had bathed and were
about to sit down to eat, Tobias said to
Raphael, "Azarias, my friend, when are you
going to ask Raguel to let me marry Sarah?"
[9]But Raguel overheard the question and
said to Tobias, [10]"Eat and drink something
first and enjoy yourself this evening. You
have the right to marry Sarah, and I cannot
let anyone else marry her, because you are
my closest relative. But I must tell you the
truth, my son. [11]I have already given her to
seven men, all of them relatives. Each one
died on his wedding night, as soon as he
entered the bedroom. But now, my son, have
something to eat and drink. The Lord will
take care of you both."
Tobias replied, "I won't eat or drink until
you give me your word."
[12]Raguel agreed. "Certainly I will," he
said. "I will give her to you just as the Law
of Moses commands. God in heaven has
arranged this marriage, so take her as your
wife. From now on, you belong to each
other. Sarah is yours today and forever. May
the Lord of heaven keep both of you safe
tonight. May he be merciful and kind to
you."

The Marriage Ceremony

[13]Then Raguel called his daughter. When
she came in, he took her by the hand and
gave her to Tobias with his blessing, "Take her
to be your wife according to the teachings in
the Law of Moses. Take her safely with you to
your father's house. May the God of heaven
give you a happy life together."
[14]Raguel asked his wife to bring him a
blank scroll so that he could write out the
marriage contract. Edna brought him the
scroll, and Raguel wrote out the agreement,
saying that Sarah was given to Tobias accord-
ing to the teachings in the Law of Moses.
[15]After the ceremony they began the meal.
[16]Raguel called his wife and said, "Get the
spare room ready, my dear, and take Sarah
there."
[17]Edna made up the bed as Raguel had
told her. Then she took Sarah into the room
with her, and Sarah began to cry.[l] But Edna
wiped away her tears and said, [18]"Don't
worry, Sarah. I'm sure the Lord of heaven
will make you happy this time and not sad.
So cheer up, my dear." Then Edna left the
room.

The Demon Is Expelled

8 When they had finished the meal, and it
was time to go to bed, Sarah's parents
led young Tobias to the bedroom. [2]He
remembered Raphael's instructions, so he

[l] **7:17** and Sarah began to cry; *some manuscripts have* and she began to cry.
7:6 Gen 33:4; 45:14; Lk 15:20

took the fish's liver and heart out of the bag where he had been keeping them. Then he placed them on the burning incense. 3The smell drove the demon away from them, and he fled to Egypt.[m] Raphael chased after him and caught him there. At once he bound him hand and foot.

The Prayer of Tobias

4When Tobias and Sarah were alone behind closed doors, Tobias got up from the bed and said to his wife, "Get up, dear. Let's pray for the Lord to be merciful and to protect us." 5Sarah got up so that they could pray together and ask God for his protection. Then Tobias prayed:

"God of our ancestors, you are worthy of praise.
May your name be honored forever and ever
by all your creatures in heaven and on earth.
6You created Adam and gave him his wife Eve
to be his helper and support.
They became the parents of the whole human race.
You said, 'It is not good for man to live alone.
I will make a suitable helper for him.'
7Lord, I have chosen Sarah because it is right,
not because I lusted for her.
Please be merciful to us
and grant that we may grow old together."

8Then they both said "Amen" 9and went to bed for the night.

Anxious Parents

Later that night, Raguel called his servants, and together they went out to dig a grave, 10because Raguel thought, "Tobias will probably die too, and people will laugh and make fun of us." 11When they finished digging the grave, Raguel went back into the house and said to his wife, 12"Send one

They went out to dig a grave. (8:9)

of the servant women to find out if Tobias is still alive. If he isn't, then we will bury him before anyone finds out." 13They then sent a servant woman to take a lamp and see if he was still alive. As she opened the door, she could see that both of them were sound asleep. 14So she went back and told Raguel and Edna that Tobias was alive and unharmed. 15Then Raguel[n] praised the God of heaven:

Raguel's Prayer

"You are worthy of our praise, O God.
May your people praise you forever,
may they praise you with pure hearts.
16I praise you because you have made me glad;
you have been merciful to us,
and my worst fears did not come true.
17You deserve our praise, O Lord;
you were merciful to this young couple,
the only children of their parents.
Now, grant them your mercy and protection.
Let them live out their lives in happiness and love."

18Then Raguel ordered his servants to fill in the grave before dawn.

The Wedding Feast

19Raguel told his wife to bake enough bread for a big feast. Then he went out to the herd and brought back two oxen and four rams, which he ordered his servants to slaughter in preparation for the wedding

[m] **8:3** EGYPT: *Egypt was thought of as the most remote part of the world and the home of demons and evil spirits.*
[n] **8:15** Raguel; *some manuscripts have* they.

8:3 Mt 12:43 **8:5** Dan A:28 **8:6** Gen 2:18

feast. [20]He called for Tobias and vowed[o] that
he would not let him leave for two weeks.
"Stay, and we will eat and drink together,"
he said. "It will do my daughter good after
her terrible suffering. [21]Then you may take
half of what I own and go back to your par-
ents safe and sound. You will inherit the
other half when Edna and I die. Have no
doubts about our love for you; from now on
you are as much our son as Sarah is our
daughter. You can be sure of that, my son."

The Journey to Rages

9 Then Tobias called Raphael and said to
him, [2]"Azarias, take four of the servants
with you, and two camels, and go to Gabael's
house in the town of Rages. Give him the
signed document, so that he will give you
the money. Then bring him back with you
for the wedding feast. [3-4]You know that my
father is counting the days until I come
home, and he will be very upset if I am even
one day late. You know, too, how Raguel
insists that I must stay, and I cannot disap-
point him."
[5]So Raphael and the four servants went
to Rages in Media, where they stayed at
Gabael's house. Raphael gave him the signed
document and told him that Tobit's son
Tobias had recently married, and that
Gabael was invited to the wedding feast. At
once Gabael counted out the bags of
money, which were still sealed, and they
loaded them on the camels.[p] [6]Very early the
next morning, they set out for the wedding
feast. When Raphael and Gabael came to
Raguel's house, they found Tobias at dinner.
Tobias immediately got up and greeted
Gabael. With tears in his eyes Gabael
returned the greeting and added, "You are
just like your honest and generous father.
May the Lord in heaven bless you and your
wife, your mother-in-law, and your father.
Praise God! He has let me live to see my
cousin Tobias, who looks so much like his
father."

Tobit and Anna Are Worried

10 Meanwhile, every day Tobit was
keeping count of the time needed to
travel to Rages and back. When the time was
up and his son had not returned, Tobit said
to his wife, [2]"What can be keeping him? Do
you suppose Gabael has died? Maybe there is
no one to give him the money." [3]Tobit was
very worried.
[4]Then Anna said, "My son is dead. I'm
sure of it." She began to weep and to mourn
for Tobias, [5]"Oh, my son, the joy of my life,
why did I ever let you leave home?"
[6]Tobit tried to comfort her. "Calm down,
my dear," he said. "Don't worry. He will be
all right. Something unexpected is probably
keeping them there longer than we counted
on. Besides, his companion is a reliable man
and a relative at that. Don't let yourself get
so upset over him, dear. I'm sure he is
already on his way home."
[7]But she replied, "Be quiet and leave me
alone! Don't try to fool me. My son is dead."
Each day she would rush out of the house to
the road which Tobias had taken and would
watch for him until sunset. She would let no
one comfort her,[q] and when she returned
home she would weep and mourn for her
son all night long, without sleeping.

Each day she . . . would watch for him until sunset. (10:7)

Departure from Ecbatana

The two-week wedding feast which
Raguel had promised to hold for his daugh-
ter Sarah came to an end. So Tobias went to
him and asked, "Please let me go home now.
I'm certain my parents have given up all
hope of ever seeing me again. Please,

[o] **8:20** vowed; *some manuscripts have* said. [p] **9:5** loaded them on the camels; *some manuscripts have* stacked them up. [q] **10:7** She would let no one comfort her; *some manuscripts have* She would not eat a bite.

8:20 Gen 24:55

Raguel, let me go home to my father. I have
already told you the condition he was in
when I left."

8But Raguel answered, "Stay, my son. Stay
here with me. I will send messengers to your
father to tell him that you are all right."

9But Tobias insisted, "No, I can't! Please
let me go back to my father."

10So Raguel gave Tobias his bride Sarah
without further delay. He also gave Tobias
half of everything he owned: slaves, cattle,
sheep, donkeys, camels, clothes, money, and
furniture. 11Raguel embraced Tobias and sent
them on their way with his blessing, "Good-
bye, my son. Have a safe journey. May the
Lord of heaven protect you and Sarah. And
may I live to see your children." 12Raguel
then said to Sarah, "Go with your husband
and live in his parents' house. From now on
they are as much your parents as your own
mother and I are. Let me hear only good
things about you as long as I live." After say-
ing good-bye he sent them on their way.

Then Edna said to Tobias, "Tobias my dear
child, may the Lord bring you safely home.
And may he let me live to see your children.
The Lord is my witness; I am placing my
daughter in your care. Never, at any time in
your life, do anything that would break her
heart. Have a safe journey, Tobias. From now
on, Sarah is your wife and I am your moth-
er. May we all prosper as long as we live."
Then Edna kissed them both and sent them
safely on their way.

11 When Tobias left, he was as happy as
could be. He praised the Lord of
heaven and earth, the King of all the world,
because his journey had been so successful,
and he promised to honor Raguel and his
wife as long as they lived.[r]

The Homecoming

As they came near the city of Kaserin, just
outside Nineveh, 2Raphael said, "Tobias, you
know the condition your father was in when
we left him. 3We should go on ahead of
your wife and get the house ready before
everyone else arrives. 4Be sure to bring the
fish's gall bladder with you." So they went on
ahead, and Tobias' dog ran along with[s] them.

5Meanwhile, Anna sat looking down the
road for her son. 6Suddenly she saw him
coming and she shouted out to Tobit, "Look!
Our son is coming, and his friend is with
him!"

7Before they reached Tobit, Raphael said to
Tobias, "Your father will be able to see again.
8Just put the fish's gall bladder on his eyes like
a plaster. The medicine will make the white
film shrivel up so that you can peel it off, and
your father will then regain his eyesight."

9Anna ran to her son, threw her arms
around him, and exclaimed, "Now that I
have seen you alive, my child, I can die in
peace!" And she wept for joy.

Tobit's Cure

10Tobit got up and stumbled out through
the entrance of the courtyard. 11Tobias went
up to him, holding the fish's gall bladder in
his hand. He blew on his father's eyes and
steadied him. "Don't worry now, father," he
said. 12-13Tobias then applied the gall, and
beginning from the corners of Tobit's eyes,
he peeled away the white film. 14Tobit threw
his arms around Tobias' neck and wept for
joy. Then he exclaimed, "I can see you! My
son, the light of my eyes!

"Praise God. Praise him for his greatness.
  Praise all his holy angels.
May he continue to bless us.
  Praise all his angels forever.
15He brought this illness upon me,
  but now I can see my son Tobias!"

Then Tobias went happily into the house,
praising God at the top of his voice. He told
his father how successful he had been, that
he had not only brought back the money,
but had married Raguel's daughter Sarah,
who was on her way and would soon arrive.

Sarah's Arrival

16Tobit was excited and praised God as he
went out to meet his son's bride at the city
gate. When the people of Nineveh saw him,

[r] **11:1** successful, and . . . lived; *or* successful. And Raguel made Tobias promise to honor him and Edna as long as they lived. [s] **11:4** Tobias' dog . . . with; *some manuscripts have* the Lord accompanied.
11:12, 13 Acts 9:18

they were amazed, because he was walking on his own, with no one leading him by the hand. 17 Tobit praised God and told everyone how God in his mercy had restored his sight.

Tobit praised God and told everyone . . . (11:17)

When Tobit met Sarah, he greeted her, "Welcome, daughter! Praise God for bringing you to us, my daughter. May God bless your father, as well as you and my son Tobias. Welcome to your new home. May you always be blessed with good health and happiness. Come in, daughter!"

It was a day of great joy for all the Jews of Nineveh. 18 Tobit's nephews Ahikar and Nadab came by to share Tobit's happiness with him.

The Angel Raphael

12 When the wedding feast was over, Tobit called his son Tobias and said to him, "Son, be sure to pay your traveling companion, and don't forget to give him a bonus."

2 Tobias asked him, "Father, how much do you think I should pay him? I wouldn't mind giving him half of everything we brought back with us. 3 He brought me back home safe and sound; he went to get the money for me from Gabael; he rid my wife of a demon; and he cured your blindness. How much of a bonus should I give him?"

4 Tobit answered, "Give him half of what he helped you bring back. He well deserves that."

5 Tobias then called Raphael and said to him, "Here is half of what you helped me bring back. You have earned it; have a safe journey home.

6 Then Raphael called the two men aside and said to them, "Praise God and tell everyone about the good things he has done for you, so that they too will honor him and sing his praises. Let everyone know what God has done. Never stop praising him.

7 "It's a good idea to keep a king's secret, but what God does should be told everywhere, so that he may be praised and honored.

"If you do good, no harm will come to you.

8 "It is better to pray sincerely and to please God by helping the poor than to be rich and dishonest. It is better to give to the poor than to store up gold. 9 Such generosity will save you from death and will wash away all your sins. Those who give to the poor will live full lives, 10 but those who live a life of sin and wickedness are their own worst enemies.

11 "I have already told you that a king's secret ought to be kept, but the things God does should be told to everyone. Now I will reveal to you the full truth and keep nothing back. 12 Tobit, when you and Sarah prayed to the Lord, I was the one who brought your prayers into his glorious presence. I did the same thing each time you buried the dead. 13 On the day you got up from the table without eating your meal in order to bury that corpse, God sent me to test you. 14 But he also sent me to cure you and to rescue your daughter-in-law, Sarah, from her troubles. 15 I am Raphael, one of the seven angels who stand in the glorious presence of the Lord, ready to serve him."

16 Tobit and Tobias were terrified and fell to the ground, trembling with fear. 17 But Raphael said to them, "Don't be afraid; everything is all right. Always remember to praise God. 18 He wanted me to come and help you; I did not come on my own. So sing God's praises as long as you live. 19 When you thought you saw me eating, I did not really

12:8 Sir 29:8–13 **12:9** Prov 11:4; Dan 4:27; Sir 3:30 **12:12** Job 33:23, 24; Acts 10:4; Rev 8:3, 4
12:15 Zech 4:10; Lk 1:19; Rev 8:2

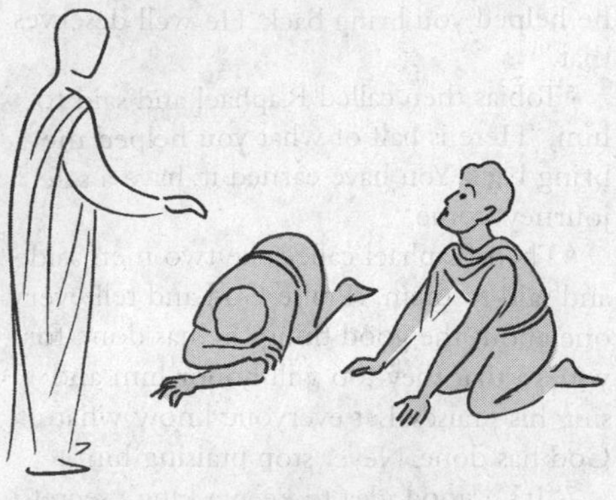

Tobit and Tobias were terrified. (12:16)

eat anything; it only seemed so. 20 While you
are on this earth, you must praise the Lord
God and give him thanks. Now I must go
back to him who sent me. Write down
everything that has happened to you."
21 Then Raphael disappeared into the sky.
Tobit and Tobias stood up, but they could no
longer see him. 22 They began to sing hymns
of praise, giving thanks for all the mighty
deeds God had done while his angel
Raphael had been with them.

Tobit's Song of Praise

13 Then Tobit prayed:

"Praise the eternal God,
praise the one who rules.
2 He punishes us; then he shows us mercy.
He sends us down to the world of the dead,
then he brings us up from the grave.
No one can escape his power.

3 "People of Israel, give thanks among the nations,
where he sent you into exile;
4 even there he showed his great power.
Let all who live hear your praise.
The Lord is our God and father forever.

5 "Though he punished you for your wickedness,
he will be merciful and bring you home
from among the nations where he scattered you.

6 "Turn to him with all your heart and soul,
live in loyal obedience to him.
Then he will turn to you to help you
and will no longer hide himself.
Remember what God has done for you,
and give thanks with all your heart.
Praise the righteous Lord;
honor the eternal King.

"Although I live in exile in a foreign land,
I will give thanks to the Lord
and will speak of his great strength to a nation of sinners.
'Turn away from your sins, and do what pleases God!
Perhaps he will be gracious
and show you his mercy.'

7 "I praise my God and rejoice in his greatness;
my whole being honors the King of heaven.
8 "Let everyone tell of his greatness
and sing his praises in Jerusalem.

9 "Jerusalem, Holy City of our God,
he will punish you for the sins of your people,
but he will be merciful to all who do right.
10 So give thanks to the Lord, for he is good.
Praise the eternal King.[t]
Your Temple will be rebuilt,
and your people will be happy again.

"May the Lord make all your exiles glad,
may he take care of your suffering people
for as long as time shall last.

11 "Jerusalem, your light will shine brightly for all the world,
and from far away many nations will come to you.
Their people will come to honor the Lord your God,
they will bring gifts for the King of heaven.

[t] **13:10** *Some manuscripts do not have verses 6b–10a* Although I live . . . Praise the eternal King.
13:4 Isa 63:16; Jer 3:4; Wis 14:3; Sir 23:1, 4; Mt 6:9 **13:9–18** Isa 60:1–22; Rev 21:9—22:5

In your streets many generations will sing
joyful praise,
your name will endure forever as God's
chosen city.
12 A curse will be on all who make threats
against you,
on all who destroy you and tear down
your walls,
on all who demolish your towers and
burn your homes.
But all who honor you will be blessed
forever.

13 "Rejoice, Jerusalem, because of your
righteous people;
they will be gathered together from
exile
to praise the Lord of the ages.

14 "Happy are all who love you
and are pleased to see you prosper.
Those who mourn over your suffering
now
will one day be happy;
your happiness will bring them joy
forever.

15 "I praise the Lord, the great King;
16 Jerusalem will be rebuilt
and will be his home forever.

"Jerusalem, how happy I will be
when my descendants can see your
splendor
and give thanks to the King of heaven.

"Your gates will be built with sapphires
and emeralds,
and all your walls with precious stones.
Your towers will be made of gold,
and their fortifications of pure gold.
17 Your streets will be paved with rubies and
precious jewels.
18 Joyful songs will ring out from your gates,
and from all your houses people will
shout,
'Praise the Lord! Praise the God of
Israel!'

"Jerusalem, God will bless your people,
and they will praise his holy name
forever."

With these words Tobit ended his song of
praise.

Tobit's Final Advice

14 1-2 Tobit was 62 years old when he
became blind, but after his sight had
been restored, he lived a very full life. Once
again he gave generously to the poor, and he
continued to praise God and tell of his
greatness. Tobit died a peaceful death at the
age of 112, and was given an honorable bur-
ial in Nineveh.
3 But just before Tobit died, he sent for
his son Tobias and told him, 4 "My son, take
your children and go at once to Media.
I believe that God's judgment which his
prophet Nahum announced against Nineveh
is about to take place. Everything that God's
prophets told Israel about Nineveh and
Assyria will happen. It will all come true,
every word of it, when the right time
comes. I am absolutely convinced that
everything God has said is sure to come
true. God does not break his promises. It will
be safer for you in Media than in Assyria or
Babylon.

"Those Jews who live in Israel will all be
scattered and taken from that good land into
exile. All Israel will become a wasteland;
Samaria and Jerusalem will be abandoned
cities. God's Temple will be burned to the
ground and will lie in complete ruin for a
while. 5 But God will have mercy on his
people again, and he will bring them back to
the land of Israel. They will rebuild the Tem-
ple, but it will not be as splendid as the first
Temple, not until the proper time has come.
But when that time does come, all the peo-
ple of Israel will return from exile, and they
will rebuild the city of Jerusalem in all its
former splendor. They will rebuild God's
Temple in Jerusalem, just as Israel's prophets
have foretold.
6 "Then all the nations in the world will
come back to God. They will worship him
as the only true God and give up the idols
that led them into false worship. 7 The
nations of the world will praise the everlast-
ing God by doing what he demands.

14:4 Nah 1:2—3:19

"At that time God will save all the people
of Israel who have been faithful to him. He
will bring them together to Jerusalem, and
let them take possession of the land of Abra-
ham, and there they will live securely forev-
er. All who love God with their heart and
soul will rejoice, but all sinners and evil peo-
ple will be wiped off the face of the earth.

8 "Now, my children, follow my instruc-
tions. Worship God sincerely and do what is
pleasing to him. 9 Bring up your children to
do what is right. Teach them that they must
give to the poor and must always remember
to praise God with all sincerity.

10 "Tobias, my son, leave Nineveh now. Do
not stay here. As soon as you bury your
mother beside me, leave; do not stay another
night within the city limits. It is a wicked
city and full of immorality; the people here
have no sense of shame. Remember what
Nadab did to Ahikar his own uncle who had
brought him up. He tried to kill Ahikar and
forced him to go into hiding in a tomb.
Ahikar came back into the light of day, but
God sent Nadab down into everlasting dark-
ness for what he had done. Ahikar escaped
the deadly trap which Nadab had set for
him, because Ahikar[u] had given generously
to the poor. But Nadab fell into that fatal
trap and it destroyed him. 11 So now, my chil-
dren, you see what happens to those who
show their concern for others, and how
death awaits those who treat others unjustly.
But now I am very weak."

Then they laid Tobit on his bed. He died
and was given an honorable burial. 12 Later
on, Tobit's wife died and was buried beside
her husband. Then Tobias and his wife
moved to Ecbatana in Media, where they
lived with Raguel, Tobias' father-in-law.
13 Tobias took care of Edna and Raguel in
their old age and showed them great respect.
When at last they died, he buried them at
Ecbatana. Tobias inherited Raguel's estate, as
he had inherited the estate of his father
Tobit.

14 At the ripe old age of 117 Tobias died,
15 having lived long enough to hear about
the destruction of Nineveh and to see King
Cyaxares[v] of Media take the people away as
captives. Tobias praised God for the way that
he had punished the people of Nineveh and
Assyria. As long as he lived he gave thanks
for what God had done to Nineveh.

[u] **14:10** Ahikar; *or* I. [v] **14:15** *Probable text* Cyaxares; *Greek unclear.*

THE BOOK OF Judith

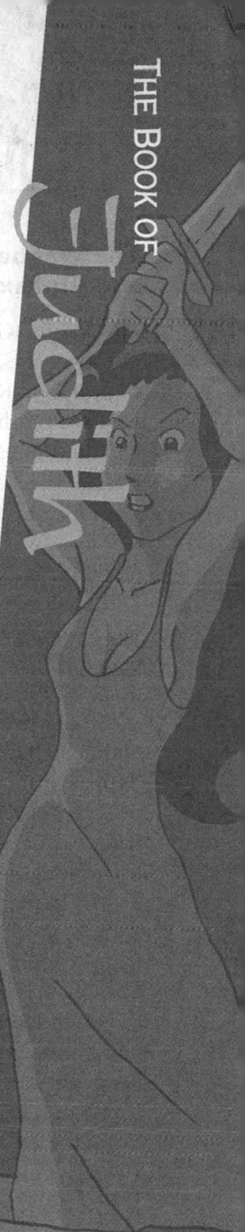

Did you know that women didn't have the right to vote in the United States until 1920? Even today many people think that women are in some ways inferior to men. Those people should read the Book of Judith!

The Book of Judith is a novel about a strong and courageous Jewish woman. She is the underdog of underdogs. The story is remarkable, first, because in the time of this story, women had no rights and were considered property. Second, Judith is a widow without a husband or children—the only way for a woman to have power and influence. And third, Judith lived in Bethulia—an unimportant city. Judith was a brave woman who, because of her faith and devotion to God, saved her people from destruction! How? You'll have to read the book to find out!

Headlines

- King Orders Attack of Israelite Cities (2:4–13)
- Israelites Want to Surrender (7:19–28)
- Widow Advises Town Leaders (8:9–20)
- Judith Carries Out Undercover Plan (10:8—11:4)
- Judith Assassinates General, People Saved (13:1–11)
- Israel Celebrates Victory, Honors Heroine (15:8–13)
- Judith Thanks God for Victory (16:1–17)

FACTOIDS

Who are the central characters? Judith, whose name literally means "Jewish woman," and Holofernes, a general of the Assyrian army.

Who wrote this book? An unknown author probably wrote this at the end of the second century or the beginning of the first century BC.

Why was it written? This book was written to encourage the Jews during the Maccabean persecution. (See 1 and 2 Maccabees.) It teaches that God can bring victory to those who are faithful—even in impossible situations.

What is the literary style? This book is a religious novel. Many of the historical facts in the book are errors.

Important themes

- God's power, not human power, defeats evil and brings victory.
- God loves an underdog and helps those whom others overlook.

JUDITH

The War between Nebuchadnezzar and Arphaxad

1 While King Nebuchadnezzar was ruling
over the Assyrians from his capital city
of Nineveh, King Arphaxad ruled over the
Medes from his capital city of Ecbatana.
2 Around Ecbatana King Arphaxad built a
wall 105 feet high and 75 feet thick of cut
stones; each stone was 4 1/2 feet thick and 9
feet long. 3 At each gate he built a tower 150
feet high, with a foundation 90 feet thick.
4 Each gateway was 105 feet high and 60 feet
wide—wide enough for his whole army to
march through, with the infantry in forma-
tion.

5 In the twelfth year of his reign King
Nebuchadnezzar went to war against King
Arphaxad in the large plain around the city
of Rages. 6 Many nations joined forces with
King Arphaxad—all the people who lived in
the mountains, those who lived along the
Tigris, Euphrates, and Hydaspes rivers, as
well as those who lived in the plain ruled by
King Arioch of Elam. Many nations joined
this Chelodite alliance.

7 Then King Nebuchadnezzar of Assyria
sent a message to the Persians and to the
people to the west, in the regions of Cilicia,
Damascus, Lebanon, Antilebanon, to those
along the coast, 8 and in the regions of
Carmel, Gilead, northern Galilee, and Jezreel
Valley. 9-10 The message also went to the peo-
ple living in Samaria and the nearby towns,
to those in the area west of the Jordan River
as far as the cities of Jerusalem, Bethany,
Chelous, and Kadesh, and to the district of
Goshen. The message was also taken to the
Egyptian cities of Tahpanhes, Rameses, Tanis,
and Memphis, and the district up the Nile
River to the Ethiopian[a] border. 11 But every-
one in this whole region ignored King Neb-
uchadnezzar's appeal and refused to take part
in the war. They thought that he had no
chance of winning the war, so they were not
afraid of him and sent his messengers back
disgraced and empty-handed.

12 This made Nebuchadnezzar so furious
that he vowed he would risk his entire king-
dom to take revenge on all those people. He
vowed that he would put to death the entire
population of Cilicia, Damascus, Syria, Moab,
Ammon, Judah, and Egypt—everyone from
the Mediterranean Sea to the Persian Gulf.

This made Nebuchadnezzar so furious . . . (1:12)

13 In the seventeenth year of his reign
King Nebuchadnezzar led his army into bat-
tle against King Arphaxad. He defeated all of
Arphaxad's forces, including his entire caval-
ry, and all his charioteers. 14 Then Nebuchad-
nezzar occupied all the towns in the land of
Media and advanced against the city of
Ecbatana. He captured the city's towers,
looted its markets, and made that beautiful
city a ruin. 15 He captured King Arphaxad in
the mountains around Rages and killed him.

[a] **1:9–10** *Greek* Ethiopian: *Ethiopia is the name given in Graeco-Roman times to the extensive territory south of the First Cataract of the Nile River. Cush was the ancient (Hebrew) name of this region which included within its borders most of modern Sudan and some of present-day Ethiopia (Abyssinia).*

After Arphaxad's death, 16 Nebuchadnezzar and his entire army returned to Nineveh with all the loot taken in battle. There they relaxed and feasted for four months.

The War against the Nations in the West

2 In the eighteenth year of Nebuchadnezzar's reign, on the twenty-second day of the first month of that year, he and his advisers decided to carry out his threat to take revenge on all those countries that had refused to help him. 2-3 The king called his general staff and senior officers together and reported in detail how those countries had betrayed him. He and his officers agreed that everyone who had refused to help him in the war should be put to death. Then he described to them his plan of attack.

4 At the close of the meeting, Nebuchadnezzar gave the following command to Holofernes, who was the general in command of his armies and second in command to the king: 5 "I, Nebuchadnezzar, the great king and ruler of all the earth, command you to choose some experienced soldiers: 120,000 infantry and 12,000 cavalry. 6 Then attack the lands to the west because they refused to respond to my appeal for help. 7 Warn them that they must prepare their offerings of earth and water to show that they have surrendered unconditionally. I will make them feel the full force of my anger and completely destroy them. My armies will march over every foot of their land and plunder it as they go. 8 I will fill the valleys with their dead bodies and will choke up every stream and river with so many corpses that they will all overflow. 9 I will take captive all those who are left alive and carry them off to the ends of the earth.

10 "But you, Holofernes, are ordered to go ahead of me and occupy all their territories in advance. If they surrender to you, hold them for me until I come to punish them. 11 But if they resist, do not spare them. Kill them and loot the entire region under your control. 12 I have taken a solemn vow, and at the risk of my life and my royal power I am determined to do what I have vowed to do. 13 Do not disobey me in any way. I am your king; remember that, and carry out without delay every order that I have given you."

Holofernes . . . the general in command of the armies (2:4)

The Campaign of Holofernes

14 So Holofernes left the king and called together all the commanders, generals, and officers of the Assyrian army. 15 Just as the king had ordered, he chose 120,000 of the best infantrymen and 12,000 of the best mounted archers 16 and arranged them in battle formation. 17 He also took along a very large number of camels, donkeys, and mules to carry the equipment, as well as many sheep, cattle, and goats for food. 18 Every soldier received plenty of rations and a large payment of gold and silver from the royal treasury.

19 Then Holofernes and his entire army set out, advancing ahead of King Nebuchadnezzar. The chariots, the cavalry, and the infantry marched out to overrun the entire western region. 20 Other troops went with them. There were so many that it was impossible to count them—they were like a swarm of locusts or like grains of sand in the desert.

21 Three days after they had left the city of Nineveh, they reached the plains around Bectileth near the mountains north of Cilicia, where they set up camp. 22 From there Holofernes advanced into the hill country with his entire army, his infantry, cavalry, and chariots. 23 He totally destroyed the countries of Libya and Lydia, then plundered all the people of Rassis and the Ishmaelites who

2:20 Judg 7:12; Joel 2:2–11

lived on the edge of the desert, south of the land of the Chelleans.

24Then Holofernes crossed the Euphrates River and marched through the land of Mesopotamia, completely destroying all the walled towns along the Abron River as far as the sea. 25He seized the territory of Cilicia, killing everyone who resisted him, and went as far as the southern borders of the land of Japheth, near Arabia. 26He surrounded the Midianites, burned down their tents, and slaughtered their sheep.

27Holofernes went down into the plains around Damascus during the wheat harvest, burned all the fields, slaughtered the flocks and herds, looted the towns, devastated the entire countryside, and killed all the young men. 28Panic seized all the people who lived along the Mediterranean Sea, and they shook with fear. Everyone in the towns of Tyre, Sidon, Sur, Ocina, Jamnia, Ashdod, and Ashkelon was terrified.

The Peace Delegation to King Nebuchadnezzar

3 All these nations sent a peace delegation to King Nebuchadnezzar with this message: 2"We remain loyal to you, great King Nebuchadnezzar; we are ready to serve you and obey any command that you may wish to give us. 3Our buildings, all our land, our wheat fields, our livestock, and our tents are at your disposal; use them in any way you wish. 4Our people will be your slaves, and you may use our towns as you please."

5After the peace delegation had brought this message, 6Holofernes led Nebuchadnezzar's army down to the Mediterranean coast. He stationed guards in all the walled towns and selected certain local men in each of the towns as reserve troops. 7The people in the towns and in the surrounding countryside welcomed Holofernes by wearing wreaths of flowers and dancing to the beat of drums. 8But Holofernes destroyed all their places of worship[b] and cut down their sacred trees. He had been ordered to destroy all the gods of the land so that all the nations and tribes would worship only Nebuchadnezzar and pray to him as a god.

9Then Holofernes passed through Jezreel Valley near Dothan, which faces the main ridge of the mountains of Judah, 10and set up camp between Geba and Scythopolis. He stayed there for a month in order to get supplies for his army.

The Israelite Plan for Defense

4 The people of Judah heard what Holofernes, the commander of King Nebuchadnezzar's armies, had done to the other nations. They heard how he had looted and destroyed all their temples, 2and they were terrified of him and afraid of what he might do to Jerusalem and to the Temple of the Lord their God. 3They had only recently returned home to Judah from exile and had just rededicated the Temple and its utensils and its altar after they had been defiled. 4So they sent a warning to the whole region of Samaria and to the towns of Kona, Beth Horon, Belmain, Jericho, Choba, and Aesora, and to Salem Valley. 5They immediately occupied the mountaintops, fortified the villages on the mountains, and stored up food in preparation for war. It was fortunate that they had recently harvested their fields.

6The High Priest Joakim, who was in Jerusalem at that time, wrote to the people in the towns of Bethulia and Betomesthaim, which face Jezreel Valley near Dothan. 7He ordered them to occupy the mountain passes which led into the land of Judah, where it would be easy to withstand an attack, since the approach was only wide enough for two people at a time to pass. 8The Israelites carried out the orders given to them by the High Priest Joakim and the Council which met in Jerusalem.

Prayer before the War

9The leaders of Israel prayed earnestly to God and fasted. 10They put on sackcloth—they and their wives, their children, their livestock, and every resident foreigner, every slave and hired laborer. 11-12They also cov-

[b] **3:8** *One ancient translation* places of worship; *Greek* territory.

3:8 Ex 34:13; 2 Chr 17:6 **4:10–12** Jon 3:7, 8; Esth 4:1–3

They lay there in the Lord's presence. (4:11)

ered the altar with sackcloth. Then all the
men, women, and children in Jerusalem lay
face down on the ground in front of the
Temple; they lay there in the Lord's pres-
ence, all in sackcloth, their heads covered
with ashes. They joined together in earnest
prayer to the God of Israel, begging him not
to let their children be captured, their wives
carried off, or their home towns destroyed.
They pleaded with him not to give the
Gentiles the satisfaction of destroying the
Temple and dishonoring it. 13The Lord
heard their prayers and saw their distress.
For many days the people of Judah and
Jerusalem continued their fast in front of the
Temple of the Lord Almighty. 14The High
Priest Joakim, the priests, and all the others
who served in the Lord's Temple, wore sack-
cloth when they offered the daily burnt
offering, the freewill offerings of the people,
and the offerings made to fulfill a vow.
15They put ashes on their turbans and cried
out in prayer to the Lord, begging him to
have mercy on the whole nation.

The War Council in the Camp of Holofernes

5 When Holofernes, the Assyrian general,
heard that the Israelites had prepared for
war, blocked the mountain passes, fortified
the mountaintops, and set up roadblocks in
the plains, 2he boiled over with anger. He
called together all the Moabite rulers, all the
Ammonite generals, and all the governors of
the region along the Mediterranean coast
3and said to them, "You live in Canaan, so
tell me about the people who live in these
mountains. Which cities do they occupy?
How large is their army? What is the source
of their power and strength? Who is the king
who leads their army? 4Why have they
alone, of all the people in the west, refused
to come out and surrender to me?"

The Speech of Achior

5Then Achior, the leader of all the
Ammonites, answered Holofernes, "Sir, if
you will please be so kind as to listen to me,
I will tell you the truth about these people
who live in the mountains near your camp.
I will not lie to you. 6These people are the
descendants of some Babylonians 7-8who
abandoned the ways of their ancestors in
order to worship the God of heaven. Finally,
they were driven out of their land because
they refused to worship their ancestors' gods.
Then they fled to Mesopotamia, where they
settled and lived for a long time.

9"Afterward, their god told them to leave
Mesopotamia and go to the land of Canaan,
where they settled and became very rich in
gold, silver, and livestock. 10Later, when a
famine struck all the land of Canaan, these
Israelites, as they were later called, went
down to Egypt and stayed there as long as
there was enough food. While they were
there, they became a large nation with so
many people that they could not be count-
ed. 11So the king of Egypt turned against
them. He took advantage of them and put
them to work making bricks. He oppressed
them and made them slaves. 12But they
prayed to their god, and he sent disasters that
left the Egyptians helpless. When the Egyp-
tians drove them out of the country, 13their
god dried up the Red Sea in front of them,
14and then led them along the way to Sinai
and Kadesh Barnea.

"The Israelites drove out all the people
who lived in the southern part of Canaan,
15occupied the land of the Amorites, wiped
out the people of Heshbon, crossed the Jor-
dan River, and took possession of the entire
mountain region. 16They drove out the

4:13 Esth 4:16 **4:14** Joel 2:17 **5:9** Gen 11:31—12:5 **5:10** Gen 42:1–5; Ex 1:7 **5:11** Ex 1:8–14
5:12 Ex 7:1—12:46 **5:13** Ex 14:21, 22

Canaanites, the Perizzites, the Jebusites, the Shechemites, and all the Girgashites. The Israelites have now lived in these mountains for a long time.

17 "Their god hates wickedness, and as long as they did not sin against him, they prospered. 18 But when they disobeyed him, they suffered heavy losses in many wars and were finally taken away as captives to a foreign country. The temple of their god was leveled and their cities were occupied by their enemies. 19 But now that they have returned to their god, they have come back home from the countries where they had been scattered. They have again taken possession of the city of Jerusalem, where their temple is, and have resettled in the mountains that had remained uninhabited.

20 "Sir, if these people are now sinning against their god, even unknowingly, and if we can be sure that they are guilty of some offense, we can successfully attack them. 21 But if they have not disobeyed the law of their god, then you should leave them alone, or he will defend them, and we will be disgraced before the whole world."

The Reaction of the Crowd

22 When Achior had finished his speech, all the people standing around the tent began to protest. Holofernes' own senior officers, as well as the Moabites and those from the Mediterranean coast, demanded that Achior be put to death.

23 "Why should we be afraid of these Israelites?" they asked. "They are weak; they can't put up a strong defense. 24 Let's go ahead! General Holofernes, your great army will slaughter them easily."

The Speech of Holofernes

6 When the noise of the crowd around the council had subsided, Holofernes spoke to Achior in front of the entire group, those from the Mediterranean coast, the Moabites, and the Ammonite mercenaries.[c]

2 "Achior,[d] who do you think you are, acting like a prophet? Who are you to tell us not to go to war against the Israelites because some god will defend them? Nebuchadnezzar is our god, and that's all that matters. He will send his army and wipe these Israelites off the face of the earth. Their god can't help them. 3 But we serve Nebuchadnezzar, and we will beat them as easily as if their whole army were one man. They will not be able to hold their ground against our cavalry; 4 it will overwhelm them. The mountains will be soaked with their blood, and the valleys will be filled with their corpses. After our attack, they will be completely wiped out; not a trace of them will be left. This is the command of Nebuchadnezzar, the lord of the whole earth, and he doesn't speak idle words. 5 Achior, you are nothing but an Ammonite mercenary, and you talk like a traitor. You will not see me again until I come and punish this race of runaway slaves. 6 And when I do, my soldiers will put you to death. You will be just another name on the casualty list.

7 "Now my men will take you into the mountains and leave you in one of the Israelite towns, 8 and you will die with the people there. 9 Why look so worried, Achior? Don't you think the town can stand against me? I will carry out all my threats; you can be sure of that!"

Achior Is Brought to Bethulia

10 Then Holofernes ordered his men, who were waiting in his tent, to seize Achior, take him to Bethulia, and hand him over to the Israelites. 11 So the men seized Achior and took him out of the camp into the valley. From there they led him into the mountains, as far as the spring which was below Bethulia.

12 When the men of that town saw them approaching, they picked up their weapons and ran to the top of the hill. Every man who used a sling as a weapon rained stones down on Holofernes' soldiers, and this stopped them from coming any farther up the mountain. 13 The Assyrians were forced to take cover along the mountainside, where they tied Achior up and left him lying at the

[c] **6:1** the Ammonite mercenaries; *some manuscripts do not have these words.* [d] **6:2** Achior; *some manuscripts add* you and your hired soldiers from Ephraim; *others add* you and your mercenaries from Ammon.

5:17 Deut 28:1–68

foot of the mountain. Then they returned to
Holofernes.

14 Later, when the Israelites came down
from Bethulia, they untied Achior, brought
him into the town, and took him before the
town officials, 15 who at that time were Uzzi-
ah son of Micah, of the tribe of Simeon,
Chabris son of Gothoniel, and Charmis son
of Melchiel. 16 The officials called together
the town elders, and all the women and the
young men also ran to the assembly. Achior
was brought before the people, and Uzziah
began questioning him. 17 Achior told them
what had been said at Holofernes' war coun-
cil, what he himself had said to the Assyrian
officers, and how Holofernes had boasted
about what he would do to the Israelites.
18 When the people heard this, they fell on
their knees and worshiped God. They
prayed: 19 "O Lord God of heaven, look how
our boastful enemies have humiliated your
people! Have pity on us and help us."
20 Then they reassured Achior and praised
him for what he had done. 21 After the
assembly was over, Uzziah took Achior
home with him, and gave a banquet there
for the elders. All that night they prayed to
the God of Israel for help.

The Siege of Bethulia

7 1-2 The next day Holofernes gathered
his whole army together, as well as his
allied forces. It was an immense army, con-
sisting of 170,000 infantry and 12,000 caval-
ry, not counting the support troops who
took care of the equipment. He ordered
them to march on Bethulia, seize the moun-
tain passes, and attack the Israelites. So they
moved out 3 and set up camp beside the
spring in the valley near Bethulia. The camp
was so wide that it spread out toward the
town of Dothan as far as Balbaim, and so
long that it stretched from Bethulia to Cya-
mon, which faces Jezreel Valley.

4 When the Israelites saw the size of the
army, they were terrified and said to one
another, "Those soldiers are going to eat up
everything in sight. There's not enough food
in the mountains, valleys, and hills put
together to feed an army like that." 5 But in
spite of their fear, all the Israelites took up
their weapons, lighted signal fires on the
towers, and remained on guard duty all night.
6 The next day Holofernes led out his entire
cavalry so that the Israelites in Bethulia could
see them. 7 He inspected the approaches to
the town and the springs that supplied its
water. He seized the springs and stationed
guards there, before returning to camp.

8 All the leaders of the Edomite and
Moabite forces, along with the commanders
of the troops from the Mediterranean coast,
came to Holofernes and said, 9 "Sir, if you
listen to our advice, your troops will not suf-
fer heavy losses. 10 These Israelites do not rely
on their weapons for defense but rather on
the height of the mountains where they live,
since the mountains are not easy to climb.
11 So then, General Holofernes, if you do not
make a direct attack on them, your whole
army will suffer no casualties. 12 Stay in your
camp and keep your soldiers in their quar-
ters. Just command your men to blockade
the springs at the foot of the mountains,
13 because that's where the people of Bethu-
lia come to draw their water. Then, when
they are dying of thirst, they will surrender
their town to you. Meanwhile, we and our
men will go up to the tops of the surround-
ing mountains, where we will set up camp
and keep anyone from leaving the town.
14 Everyone will starve to death—men,
women, and children. Even before we attack,
the streets will be littered with their corpses.
15 In this way you can make them pay for
their rebellion and for refusing to surrender
peacefully to you."

16 Holofernes and his entire staff were
pleased with this suggestion, so he gave
orders to put the plan into action. 17 The
Moabites and 5,000 Assyrians moved their
camp into the valley to control the source of
the town's water. 18 The Edomites and the
Ammonites went up into the mountains and
set up their camp opposite the town of
Dothan. They sent some of their men to the
southeast in the direction of Acraba, near
Chusi, which is beside the Mochmur River.
The rest of the Assyrian army set up camp in

7:5 1 Macc 12:28, 29

the valley. Their camp was spread out over
the whole countryside, because the number
of tents and the amount of equipment need-
ed for such a large army were immense.
19 Then the Israelites cried out to the Lord
their God for help. They had lost their
courage, for with the enemy all around them
there was no way to escape. 20 The entire
Assyrian army—infantry, chariots, and caval-
ry—blockaded Bethulia for thirty-four days
until the town ran out of water. 21 All the
reservoirs and cisterns went dry, so that the
drinking water had to be rationed, and not a
day passed when there was enough water to
go around. 22 Children were becoming weak;
everywhere throughout the town women
and young people were collapsing. No one
had any strength left.

No one had any strength left. (7:22)

23 All the people of the town—men,
women, and children alike—gathered around
Uzziah and the town officials and shouted in
protest, 24 "God will punish you for what
you have done to us! You are to blame for
what is happening, because you did not
make peace with the Assyrians. 25 There is no
one to help us now! God has put us in their
power. We are exhausted and dying of thirst.
26 Call the Assyrians now and surrender to
them, and let Holofernes and his army take
the town and loot it. 27 We are better off as
prisoners of war. They will make us slaves,
but at least we will be alive, and we won't
have to watch our wives and children dying
before our eyes. 28 Heaven and earth are wit-
nesses against you, and so is our God, the
Lord of our ancestors, who is punishing us
for their sins as well as ours. We can only
hope and pray that he will not let these ter-
rible things happen to us today."[e]

29 Everyone there began to weep loudly
and to pray to the Lord their God. 30 Then
Uzziah said to them, "Don't give up, my
friends! Let's wait five more days to see if the
Lord our God will be merciful to us. Surely
he will not abandon us completely. 31 But if
no help comes after five days, then I will do
as you say." 32 So Uzziah dismissed the peo-
ple. All the men returned to their guard posts
on the walls and towers, while the women
and children went back to their homes. The
morale of the entire town was very low.

Judith, the Israelite Widow

8 At that time, Judith heard about Uzzi-
ah's decision. She was the daughter of
Merari, the granddaughter of Ox and the
great-granddaughter of Joseph. Joseph's
ancestors were Oziel, Elkiah, Ananias,
Gideon, Raphaim, Ahitub, Elijah, Hilkiah,
Eliab, Nathanael, Salamiel, Sarasadai, and
Israel. 2 Judith's husband Manasseh, who
belonged to the same tribe and clan, had
died during the barley harvest. 3 He had suf-
fered a sunstroke while in the fields supervis-
ing the farm workers and later died in bed at
home in Bethulia. He was buried in the
family tomb in the field between Dothan
and Balamon.
4 For three years and four months, Judith
had lived as a widow. 5 In her grief she built
a little shelter on the roof of her house and
lived there, wearing sackcloth. 6 She fasted
during that entire period except when fast-
ing was forbidden: the day before the Sab-
bath and the Sabbath itself, the eve of the
New Moon Festival and the Festival itself,

[e] **7:28** We can . . . today; *some Greek manuscripts and ancient translations have* We demand that you surrender, as we have asked you to do today.

8:5 Judg 3:20; 2 Kings 4:10

and all the festivals and holidays observed by the people of Israel. [7]Judith was a very beautiful woman. Her husband had left her gold and silver, servants and slaves, livestock and fields. She continued to supervise the estate, [8]and no one ever said anything bad about Judith. She was a very religious woman.

Judith was a very beautiful woman. (8:7)

Judith Meets with the Town Officials

[9]Judith heard how the people were complaining bitterly against Uzziah, now that the water shortage had broken their morale. She learned that in answer to their complaints he had promised to surrender the town to the Assyrians after five days. [10]Judith sent a slave, the woman who managed her business affairs, to invite Uzziah,[f] Chabris, and Charmis, the town officials, to her home.

[11]When the officials arrived, Judith said to them, "Please listen to me. You are the leaders of the people of Bethulia, but you were wrong to speak to the people as you did today. You should not have made a solemn promise before God that you would surrender the town to our enemies if the Lord did not come to our aid within a few days. [12]What right do you have to put God to the test as you have done today? Who are you to put yourselves in God's place in dealing with human affairs? [13]It is the Lord Almighty that you are putting to the test! Will you never learn? [14]There is no way that you can understand what is in the depths of a human heart or find out what a person is thinking. Yet you dare to read God's mind and interpret his thoughts! How can you claim to understand God, the Creator? No, my friends, you must stop arousing the anger of the Lord our God! [15]If he decides not to come to our aid within five days, he still may rescue us at any time he chooses. Or he may let our enemies destroy us. [16]But you must not lay down conditions for the Lord our God! Do you think that he is like one of us? Do you think you can bargain with him or force him to make a decision? [17]No! Instead, we should ask God for his help and wait patiently for him to rescue us. If he wants to, he will answer our cry for help. [18]We do not worship gods made with human hands. Not one of our clans, tribes, towns, or cities has ever done that, even though our ancestors used to do so. [19]That is why God let their enemies kill them and take everything they had. It was a great defeat! [20]But since we worship no other God but the Lord, we can hope that he will not reject us or any of our people.

[21]"If our town is taken by the enemy, the entire region of Judah will then fall, and our Temple in Jerusalem will be looted. And God will make us pay with our lives for allowing the Temple to be defiled. [22]He will hold us responsible for the slaughter and captivity of our people and for the destruction of the land we have inherited. We will be despised and mocked by the people in those nations to which we will be taken as slaves. [23]We are not going to win the favor of our enemies by surrendering to them now.[g] If we do surrender, the Lord our God will see that we are put to shame.

[24]"No, my friends, we should set an example for our own people. Not only their lives, but the fate of the Temple and the altar depend on us. [25]The Lord our God is putting us to the test, just as he tested our ancestors, and we should be thankful for that. [26]Remember how he put Abraham and Isaac to the test, and what happened to Jacob while he was working as a shepherd for his uncle Laban in Mesopotamia. [27]God is not

[f] **8:10** Uzziah; *some Greek manuscripts do not have this word.* [g] **8:23** We are not . . . now; *or* No good will ever come out of our slavery.

8:12 Deut 6:16; Job 38:2 **8:14** Rom 11:33, 34; 1 Cor 2:11 **8:26** Gen 22:1–18; 29:1—31:55

testing our loyalty as severely as he did
theirs. God is not sending this punishment
on us as revenge, but as a warning to us who
worship him."
28 Then Uzziah answered Judith, "Every-
thing you have said makes good sense, and
no one can argue with it. 29 This is not the
first time you have shown wisdom. Ever
since you were a child, all of us have recog-
nized the soundness and maturity of your
judgment. 30 But our people are dying of
thirst. They forced us to say what we did and
to make a solemn promise, which we cannot
break. 31 So now, since you are a deeply reli-
gious woman, pray for our people; ask the
Lord to send rain to fill our cisterns, so that
we can get our strength back."
32 "All right," Judith replied, "I am going
to do something which our Jewish people
will never forget. 33 Tonight, the three of you
must stand guard at the gate so that my slave
woman and I can leave the town. And before
the day comes on which you have promised
to surrender, the Lord will use me to rescue
the people of Israel. 34 But you must not ask
me what I am going to do; I will explain it
to you when it is all over."
35 Uzziah and the other officials said to
her, "You have our blessing. May the Lord
our God guide you as you take revenge on
our enemies." Then they left Judith's rooftop
shelter and returned to their posts.

Judith's Prayer

9 Then Judith put ashes on her head,
opened her robe to reveal the sackcloth
she was wearing under her clothes, and
bowed down with her face to the floor. It
was the time that the evening incense was
being offered in the Temple in Jerusalem,
and Judith prayed in a loud voice: 2 "O Lord,
the God of my ancestor Simeon, remember
how you armed Simeon with a sword to
take revenge on those foreigners who seized
Dinah, who was a virgin, tore off her
clothes,[h] and defiled her; they stripped her
naked and shamed her; they raped her and
disgraced her, even though you had forbid-
den this. 3 That is why you let their leaders
be killed—put to death on the same bed
where they had raped the woman.[i] You
destroyed them all, slaves, princes, and rulers
on their thrones. 4 You let their wives be car-
ried off, their daughters taken captive, and
their possessions plundered by the Israelites,
your chosen people, who were eager to do
your will. Dinah's brothers were furious
because of this disgrace to their family, so
they called on you for help.
"O my God, listen to my prayer, the
prayer of a widow. 5 Your hand guided all
that happened then, and all that happened
before and after. You have planned it all—
what is happening now, and what is yet to
be. Your plans have always been carried out.
6 Whatever you want to be done is as good
as done. You know in advance all that you
will do and what decisions you will make.
7 Now the Assyrians are stronger than ever;
they take pride in their cavalry and their
infantry. They rely on their weapons, but
they do not know that you, O Lord, are a
warrior who ends war. The Lord is your
name. 8 In your anger, use your power to
shatter their mighty army. They plan to defile
your Temple, where you are worshiped, and
to hack off the corners of your altar with
their swords. 9 Look how proud and boastful
they are! Pour out your fury upon them! I
am only a widow, but give me the strength
to carry out my plan. 10 Use my deceitful
words to strike them all dead, master and
slave alike. Let a woman's strength break
their pride. 11 Your power does not depend
on the size and strength of an army. You are
a God who cares for the humble and helps
the oppressed. You give support and protec-
tion to people who are weak and helpless;
you save those who have lost hope. 12 Now
hear my prayer, O God of my ancestor
Simeon, the God in whom Israel trusts, ruler
of heaven and earth, creator of the rivers and
the seas, king of all creation. Hear my prayer
and 13 let my deceitful words wound and kill
those who have planned such cruelty against
your covenant and your holy Temple, against
Mount Zion and the land you have given

[h] **9:2** *Probable text* clothes; *Greek unclear.* [i] **9:3** *Probable text* put to death . . . woman; *Greek unclear.*
9:2 Gen 34:1–31 **9:13** Esth C:24, 25

your people. 14Make your whole nation and
every tribe recognize that you are God,
almighty and all-powerful, and that you
alone protect the people of Israel!"

Judith Goes to the Camp of Holofernes

10 When Judith had finished her prayer
to the God of Israel, 2she stood up,
called her slave woman, and went down into
the house as she always did on Sabbaths and
festival days. 3She took off the sackcloth and
her widow's clothes, took a bath, and put on
rich perfumes. She brushed her hair, tied a
ribbon around it, and dressed herself in the
fine clothes she used to wear on joyful occa-
sions when her husband Manasseh was still
alive. 4She put on sandals and all her finest
jewelry: rings and earrings, and bracelets on
her wrists and ankles. She made herself so
beautiful that she was sure to attract the
attention of any man who saw her. 5Judith
gave her slave woman a leather bag of wine
and a jar of oil to carry. She filled a bag with
roasted barley, cakes of dried figs, and several
loaves of bread baked according to Jewish
food laws. She carefully wrapped all the food
and dishes and gave them to her slave. 6Then
the two women left the house and went to
the gates of Bethulia, where they found
Uzziah and the town officials, Chabris and
Charmis, standing guard. 7When the men
saw Judith after she had changed clothes and
put on make-up, they were struck by her
beauty and said to her, 8"May the God of
our ancestors bless you and make your plan
successful, so that you may bring glory to
Jerusalem and victory to Israel."

Judith prayed 9and then said, "Order the
gates to be opened for me. I am on my way
to do what we were talking about." Then
they ordered the young men to open the
gates for her, 10and Judith and her slave left
the city. The men watched her as she went
down the mountain into the valley, until she
was out of sight.

11As the two women were walking
through the valley, an Assyrian patrol met
them. 12They arrested Judith and questioned
her, "What is your nationality? Where did
you come from, and where are you going?"

"I am a Hebrew," she answered, "but I am
running away from the Israelites because God
is going to let you destroy them. 13I am on
my way to see Holofernes, the general in
command of your army, to give him some
reliable information. I can show him how to
advance into the mountains and take control
of the entire region without a single casualty."

14The men stared at her because she was
so beautiful. They listened to her story and
said, 15"You have saved your life by coming
down here to see our general. Some of us
will take you to his headquarters and present
you to him. 16Do not be afraid of him. Just
tell him what you have told us, and he will
treat you well." 17They assigned a hundred
men to escort Judith and her slave to the
headquarters of Holofernes.

18There was great commotion in the
Assyrian camp as news of Judith's arrival
spread from tent to tent. While she stood
outside the tent of Holofernes waiting to be
presented to him, many Assyrian soldiers
came and stood around her. 19They were
greatly impressed by her beauty and won-
dered what kind of people the Israelites
were. "Who can have contempt for people
whose women are so beautiful?" they asked
one another. "We had better kill all the men,
or else these Jews will be able to charm the
whole world."

They were greatly impressed by her beauty. (10:19)

20Then Holofernes' bodyguard and his
personal servants came out and led Judith
into the tent. 21Holofernes was resting on his
bed under a mosquito net woven of purple

and gold thread and decorated with emeralds
and other precious stones. 22When the men
told him that Judith had arrived, he came to
the outer part of the tent. Silver lamps were
carried ahead of him. 23When Judith came
near him and his servants, they were all
astonished at her beauty. She bowed down to
the ground before Holofernes, but his ser-
vants helped her to her feet.

11 Holofernes said to Judith, "Don't
worry; there's no need for you to be
afraid. I have never hurt anyone who was
willing to serve Nebuchadnezzar, king of the
whole world. 2Even now, if your people up
in the mountains had not insulted me, I
would not have declared war on them. They
have brought all this trouble on themselves.
3But tell me, why have you left them and
come to us? You will be safe here. No need
to be afraid! We have spared your life
tonight, and you are in no danger for the
future. 4No one here will harm you; every-
one will treat you well, like all other servants
of my master, Nebuchadnezzar."

5Then Judith said to Holofernes, "Allow
me to speak to you, my lord, and please lis-
ten to what I have to say. I will tell you the
truth. 6If you follow my advice, God will do
something great with you, and my lord will
not fail in his plan. 7For I swear to you by
the life and strength of Nebuchadnezzar,
king of the whole world, who sent you to
bring order to all the subjects of his king-
dom, that not only have you made people
serve him, but because of you even the wild
animals, the livestock, and the birds obey
him. Because of you, Nebuchadnezzar and
his entire kingdom will prosper.[j] 8We have
heard how wise and clever you are. The
whole world knows that you are the most
competent, skilled, and accomplished general
in the whole Assyrian Empire. 9Achior was
rescued by the men of Bethulia, and has told
us what he said at your war council. 10Please,
sir, do not dismiss lightly what Achior told
you, but take it seriously, because it is true.
No one can harm or conquer our people
unless they sin against their God.

11"But you will not suffer any setbacks,
nor will you fail to achieve your goal. When
the Israelites sin and make their God angry,
they will die. 12Their food supply has
already run out, and the water shortage has
become serious, so they have decided to kill
their livestock and eat foods that God's Law
clearly forbids them to eat. 13They have
decided to eat the wheat set aside from the
early harvest and the tithes of wine and oil,
which are holy and are reserved for the
priests who serve God in Jerusalem. The rest
of us are forbidden even to touch this sacred
food, 14but since the people in Jerusalem
have already broken this law, the people of
our town have sent messengers to the
Council there requesting permission to do
the same. 15On the day that they receive
permission and actually eat the food, you
will be able to destroy them. 16As soon as I
learned about this, I ran away from my peo-
ple. God has sent me to do something with
you that will amaze everyone in the entire
world who hears about it. 17Sir, I am a reli-
gious woman; I worship the God of heaven
day and night. I will stay here in your camp,
and each night I will go out into the valley
to pray to God, and he will tell me when
the Israelites have sinned. 18As soon as I find
out, I will come and tell you, and you can
march out with your whole army. The
Israelites will not be able to defend them-
selves against you. 19I will guide you
through the central part of the land of Judah
until we come to Jerusalem, where I will
crown you king in the center of the city.
You will scatter the people of Jerusalem like
sheep without a shepherd. Not even a dog
will dare to growl at you. God has revealed
these things to me in advance and has sent
me to report them to you."

20Holofernes and his personal servants
were pleased with what Judith had said, and
they admired her wisdom. 21"She must be
the wisest and most beautiful woman in the
world," they commented one to another.

22Then Holofernes said to her, "It's a
good thing that God has sent you here to
bring us victory and to destroy those who
have insulted King Nebuchadnezzar. 23Not

[j] **11:7** not only . . . prosper; *Greek unclear.*

11:7 Jer 27:6; Dan 2:38 **11:13** Ex 23:19; Lev 27:30

only are you beautiful, but you know how to make a speech. If you do as you have promised, your God will be my God. You will live in King Nebuchadnezzar's palace and will be famous throughout the world."

Judith Remains Faithful to Her Religion

12 Holofernes commanded his men to take Judith to the table which was set with his silverware and to serve her some of his own special food and wine. 2But Judith refused. "I cannot eat your food," she said, "for I would be breaking the laws of my God. I will eat only what I have brought with me."

3"But what will you do when your food and wine are gone?" Holofernes asked. "Where will we get more food for you? There are no Israelites here in our camp."

4"Sir," Judith answered, "as surely as you live, I have more than enough food to last until the Lord has used me to carry out his plan."

5Then Holofernes' personal servants led Judith to a tent. She slept there until the time of the morning watch just before dawn, when she got up 6and sent a message to Holofernes requesting permission to go out into the valley to pray. 7Holofernes ordered his guards to let Judith leave the camp. So for three days Judith lived in the camp, and each night she would go out to the valley near Bethulia and bathe at the spring. 8After she had bathed, she would pray to the Lord God to guide her in her plan to bring victory to Israel. 9Then she would return to the camp ritually pure and remain in her tent until after the evening meal.

Holofernes' Banquet

10On the fourth day of Judith's stay in the camp, Holofernes gave a banquet for his highest ranking officers, but he did not invite any of the officers who were on duty. 11He said to Bagoas, the eunuch who was in charge of his personal affairs, "Go and persuade the Hebrew woman, who is in your care, to come to my tent to eat and drink with us. 12It would be a shame to pass up an opportunity to make love to a woman like that. If I don't try to seduce her, she will laugh at me."

13So Bagoas left Holofernes and went to Judith. "Lovely lady," he said, "the general invites you to his tent for some drinks. Come and enjoy yourself like the Assyrian women who serve in Nebuchadnezzar's palace. This is a great honor."

14"I shall be glad to accept," Judith answered. "How could I refuse? I'll remember this happy night as long as I live."

15So Judith got up and put on her prettiest clothes. Her slave woman went ahead of her and placed on the ground in front of Holofernes the lamb skins that Bagoas had given Judith to sit on when she ate. 16Judith came into the tent and sat down there. Holofernes was aroused when he saw her and had an uncontrollable desire to make love to her. From the first day he had seen her, he had been waiting for a chance to seduce her. 17"Join us for a drink and enjoy yourself," he said to her.

18"I'll be glad to, sir," Judith replied; "this is the happiest day of my life." 19But even then Judith ate and drank only what her slave had prepared. 20Holofernes was so charmed by her that he drank more wine than he had ever drunk at one time in his whole life.

13 Finally, when it got late, the guests excused themselves and left. Bagoas then closed up the tent from the outside and prevented Holofernes' servants from going in. So they all went to bed; everyone was very tired because the banquet had lasted so long. 2Judith was left alone in the tent with Holofernes who was lying drunk on his bed. 3Judith's slave woman was waiting outside the tent for Judith to go and pray, as she had done each night. Judith had also told Bagoas that she would be going out to pray as usual.

4All the guests and servants were now gone, and Judith and Holofernes were alone in the tent. Judith stood by Holofernes' bed and prayed silently, "O Lord, God Almighty, help me with what I am about to do for the

12:2 Dan 1:8; Esth C:28

"O Lord . . . help me with what I am about to do." *(13:4)*

glory of Jerusalem. 5Now is the time to res-
cue your chosen people and to help me
carry out my plan to destroy the enemies
who are threatening us." 6Judith went to the
bedpost by Holofernes' head and took down
his sword. 7She came closer, seized
Holofernes by the hair of his head, and said,
"O Lord, God of Israel, give me strength
now." 8Then Judith raised the sword and
struck him twice in the neck as hard as she
could, chopping off his head. 9She rolled his
body off the bed and took down the mos-
quito net from the bedposts. Then she came
out and gave Holofernes' head to her slave,
10who put it in the food bag.

Judith and Her Slave Return to Bethulia

Then the two women left together, as
they always did when they went to pray.
After they had walked through the Assyrian
camp, they crossed the valley and went up
the mountainside until they came to the
gates of Bethulia. 11When they were a short
distance away, Judith called out to the guards
at the gate, "Open the gate! Open the gate!
Our God is still with us. Today he has once
again shown his strength in Israel and used
his power against our enemies."

12When the men heard her voice, they
hurried down to the gates and called for the
town officials. 13Everyone, young and old,
ran together to the gate. No one could
believe that Judith had come back. They
opened the gate for her and her slave and
welcomed them. Then, when they had lit a
fire to give some light and had gathered
around the two women, 14Judith shouted,
"Praise God, give him praise! Praise God,

Study it!

Peace, Not Violence

What Judith did was very violent. What the Israelites did once they had control of the situation was also very violent. It might make you think that violence is okay with God. But that is not really what the Bible teaches. In the Old Testament, many of the victories attributed to God are violent because the Israelites saw military victories as symbolic victories over the gods of other nations. Gradually they came to realize that there aren't any other gods; Yahweh is the only God, and he is God of all people. Jesus reinforced this by teaching that we must love all people, even our enemies, because God loves all people, too.

It's often tempting to use violence because it seems like a quick solution. But it's never a final solution. It always creates more violence, or at least the desire for more violence, once strength is regained. There can never be "a war to end all wars." It's important to put the violence of the Bible in proper perspective. The real message in the Bible is that God is calling us to be peacemakers.

Isaiah (2:4) and Micah (4:3) both speak of a time when people will "hammer their swords into plows," when "nations will never again go to war." That's the vision we need to work toward. Jesus also warned us, "All who take the sword will die by the sword" (Matthew 26:52).

— Judith 13:1–10

When the men heard her voice . . . (13:12)

who has not held back his mercy from the
people of Israel. Tonight he has used me to
destroy our enemies." 15She then took the
head out of the food bag and showed it to
the people. "Here," she said, "is the head of
Holofernes, the general of the Assyrian army,
and here is the mosquito net from his bed,
where he lay in a drunken stupor. The Lord
used a woman to kill him. 16As the Lord
lives, I swear that Holofernes never touched
me, although my beauty deceived him and
brought him to his ruin. I was not defiled or
disgraced; the Lord took care of me through
it all."

17Everyone in the city was utterly
amazed. They bowed down and worshiped
God, praying together, "Our God, you are
worthy of great praise. Today you have tri-
umphed over the enemies of your people."

18Then Uzziah said, "Judith, my dear, the
Most High God has blessed you more than
any other woman on earth. How worthy of
praise is the Lord God who created heaven
and earth! He guided you as you cut off the
head of our deadliest enemy. 19Your trust in
God will never be forgotten by those who
tell of God's power. 20May God give you
everlasting honor for what you have done.
May he reward you with blessings, because
you remained faithful to him and did not
hesitate to risk your own life to relieve the
oppression of your people."

All the people replied, "Amen, amen!"

Judith's Plan

14 Then Judith said to them, "My
friends, please follow my advice. In
the morning, take this head and hang it on
the town wall. 2Appoint a leader for your-
selves, and at sunrise have all your able-bod-
ied men take their weapons and march out
of the town with him, as if they were going
down into the valley to attack the Assyrian
outpost. 3The Assyrian guards will grab their
weapons and rush back to camp to wake up
their officers. The officers will run to
Holofernes' tent but will not find him, and
the whole army will be terrified and retreat
as you advance against them. 4Then you and
all the other Israelites will be able to follow
them and kill them as they retreat. 5But
before you do any of this, send Achior the
Ammonite to me. I want to see if he recog-
nizes Holofernes, the man who spoke of
Israel with contempt and sent Achior to us,
thinking he would be killed along with the
rest of us."

Achior's Conversion

6So they called Achior from Uzziah's
house. But when he came and saw the head
of Holofernes in the hands of one of the
men, Achior fainted and fell to the floor.
7When they had helped him up, Achior
bowed at Judith's feet in respect. "May every
family in the land of Judah praise you," he
said, "and may every nation tremble with
terror when they hear your name. 8Please
tell me how you managed to do this."

While all the people were gathered
around, Judith told him everything that she
had done from the day she left the town
until that moment. 9When she had finished
her story, the people cheered so loudly that
the whole town echoed with sounds of joy.
10When Achior heard all that the God of
Israel had done, he became a firm believer.
He was circumcised and made a member of
the Israelite community, as his descendants
are to the present day.

13:18 Judg 5:24; Lk 1:28, 42

Panic in Holofernes' Camp

11The next morning the Israelites hung
the head of Holofernes on the wall of the
town. All of them took up their weapons
and went out in companies to the slopes in
front of the town. 12When the Assyrians saw
what was happening, they sent word to their
officers, and these reported the matter to
their superiors. 13These men then went to
Holofernes' tent and said to Bagoas, "Wake
up the general! Those worthless Israelites
have dared to come down from the mountain to attack us; they are just asking to be
destroyed."

14Bagoas went in and clapped his hands in
front of the sleeping quarters of the tent,
thinking that Holofernes was in bed with
Judith. 15When there was no answer, he
drew the curtain aside and went in, and
there he found the headless body sprawled
over a footstool. 16Bagoas let out a yell. He
screamed, tore his clothes, and started groaning and weeping. 17He went into the tent
where Judith had stayed, but of course he
did not find her. He rushed out and shouted
to the officers, 18"They have tricked us! One
Israelite woman has disgraced Nebuchadnezzar's whole kingdom. Look in there! Holofernes is lying dead on the ground and his
head is gone!" 19When the officers heard
this, they tore their clothes in grief; and as
the panic spread, wild cries and shouts were
heard throughout the camp.

Israel's Victory

15 When the soldiers heard what had
happened, they were horrified 2and
began to tremble with fear. They all scattered
in different directions from the camp, making no effort to stay together as they tried to
escape along the paths in the mountains and
valleys. 3The soldiers who had camped in
the mountains around Bethulia also began to
retreat. Then all the Israelite soldiers came
charging down on them.

4Uzziah sent messengers to the towns of
Betomesthaim, Bebai, Choba, and Kola, and
throughout the land of Israel to tell everyone
what had happened and to urge them to
join in pursuing and destroying the enemy.
5When they received the message, they all
attacked the Assyrians and chased them as far
as Choba, slaughtering them as they went.
Even the people of Jerusalem and others living in the mountains joined the attack when
the messengers told them what had happened in the Assyrian camp. The people of
the regions of Gilead and Galilee blocked
the path of the retreating Assyrians and
inflicted heavy losses on them. They pursued
them as far as the region around Damascus.

6The rest of the people in Bethulia went
down to the Assyrian camp, plundered it and
carried away enough loot to make themselves very rich. 7When the Israelite soldiers
returned from the slaughter, they helped
themselves to what was left. There was so
much of it that the people of the towns and
villages in the hill country also shared in the
loot.

Israel Celebrates the Victory

8The High Priest Joakim and the Council
of Israel came from Jerusalem to see for
themselves what great things the Lord had
done for his people and to meet Judith and
congratulate her. 9When they arrived, they
all praised her, "You are Jerusalem's crowning
glory, the heroine of Israel, the pride and joy
of our people! 10You have won this great
victory for Israel by yourself. God, the
Almighty, is pleased with what you have
done. May he bless you as long as you live."
All the people responded, "Amen."

11It took the people thirty days to finish

"You are . . . the heroine of Israel!" (15:9)

looting the camp of the Assyrians. Judith was given Holofernes' tent, all his silver, his bowls, his couches, and all his furniture. She took them and loaded as much as she could on her mule; then she brought her wagons and loaded them too.
12 All the Israelite women came to see her; they sang her praises and danced in her honor. On this joyful occasion Judith and the other women waved ivy-covered branches
13 and wore wreaths of olive leaves on their heads. Judith took her place at the head of the procession to lead the women as they danced. All the men of Israel followed, wearing wreaths of flowers on their heads, carrying their weapons, and singing songs of praise.

Judith's Song of Praise

16 Then Judith sang a song of thanksgiving there with all Israel present, and the people joined in this song of praise.
2 She sang,

"Praise my God and sing to him;
praise the Lord with drums and cymbals;
play a new song for him.
Praise him and call on him for help.
3 The Lord is a warrior who ends war.
He rescued me from my pursuers
and brought me back to his people's camp.
4 Down from the mountains of the north
came the Assyrians,
with their tens of thousands of soldiers.
Their troops blocked the rivers in the valleys;
their cavalry covered the mountains.
5 They threatened to set fire to our country,
slaughter our young men,
dash our babies to the ground,
take our children away as captives,
and carry off all our young women.
6 But the Lord Almighty tricked them;
he used a woman to stop them.
7 Their hero was not slain by young soldiers
or attacked and killed by mighty giants.
It was Judith, the daughter of Merari,
who brought him down with her beauty.
8 She gave victory to the oppressed people of Israel,
when she took off her widow's clothes,
and put on a linen dress to entice him.
She put on her rich perfumes
and tied a ribbon around her hair.
9 Her dainty sandal caught his eye;
her beauty captured his heart.
Then the sword slashed through his neck.
10 The Persians trembled at her daring;
the Medes were amazed at her bravery.
11 Then our people shouted in victory.
They had been weak and oppressed,
but they forced the enemy to retreat in panic and fear.
12 We are the descendants of slaves,
but our enemies turned and ran;
we killed them like runaway slaves.
They were destroyed by the army of the Lord.

13 "I will sing a new song to my God.
O Lord, you are strong and glorious!
You have never been defeated.
14 Let all your creatures serve you.
You gave the command,
and all of them came into being;
you breathed on them,
and all of them were created.
No one can oppose your command.
15 The mountains and the seas tremble,
and rocks melt like wax when you come near.
But there is mercy for all who obey you.
16 The Lord is more pleased with those who obey him
than with all the choice meat on the altar,
or with all the most fragrant sacrifices.
17 The nations who rise up against my people are doomed.
The Lord Almighty will punish them on Judgment Day.
He will send fire and worms to devour their bodies,
and they will weep in pain forever."

Judith's Fame

18 When the people arrived in Jerusalem, they purified themselves and worshiped

16:13 Ps 144:9 **16:16** 1 Sam 15:22; Ps 51:16, 17; Hos 6:6

God. They presented their burnt offerings,
freewill offerings, and gifts. 19 Judith dedicat-
ed to God all of Holofernes' property, which
the people had given to her. And as a special
offering in fulfillment of a vow, she present-
ed to the Lord the mosquito net which she
had taken from Holofernes' bed. 20 For three
months the people continued to celebrate in
front of the Temple in Jerusalem, and Judith
stayed there with them.

21 When the celebrations had ended,
everyone returned home, and Judith went
back to Bethulia to live on her own estate.
For the rest of her life she was famous
throughout the land of Israel. 22 Many men
wanted to marry her, but she never remar-
ried after the death of her husband Manas-
seh. 23-24 Her fame continued to spread, and
she lived in the house her husband had left
her. Before she died, Judith divided her
property among her husband's and her own
close relatives and set her slave woman free.
When she died in Bethulia at the age of
105, she was buried beside her husband, and
the people of Israel mourned her death for
seven days. 25 As long as Judith lived, and for
many years after her death, no one dared to
threaten the people of Israel.

THE BOOK OF Esther

Have you ever made an enemy? A grudge can lead to hate, opening the door to power struggles, plots, counterplots . . . and before you know it, more people are involved—and are getting hurt.

This is the unfolding drama in the story of Queen Esther. Her cousin Mordecai, a Jew like her, refuses to honor the court official, Haman's ancestors were enemies of the Jews. He uses his influence with the king in an attempt to destroy not only Mordecai but the entire Jewish population of the empire. Esther courageously seeks the king's help and, with Mordecai, manages to save the Jews. This victory gives birth to the Jewish festival Purim, which is still celebrated today.

Chap. C:12–16

Headlines

- Dream Predicts Future Drama (chapters A and F)
- Queen Defies King, Loses Crown (1:10–20)
- Mordecai Saves King's Life (2:21–23)
- Haman Plots to Kill All Jews (3:1–13)
- Esther Is Called to Save Her People (chapter 4)
- Haman's Evil Plan Is Revealed (chapter 7)

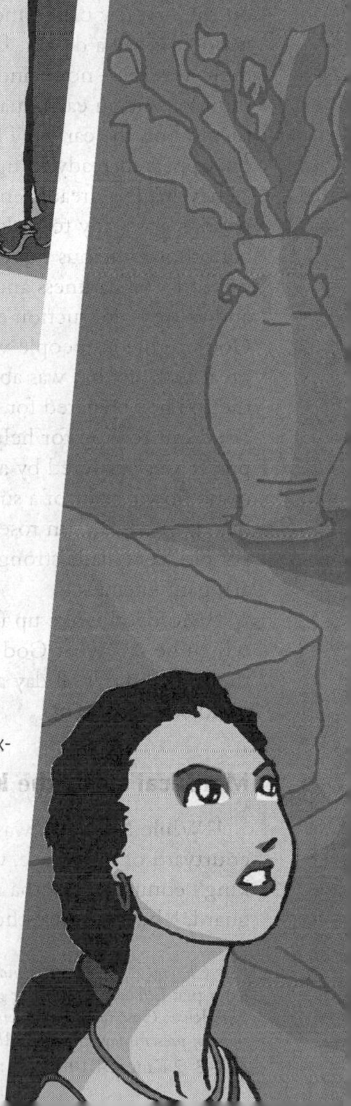

FACTOIDS

Who are the central characters? Queen Esther, her cousin Mordecai, King Xerxes, and his top official Haman

Who wrote this book? Written by unknown author(s), this book has both a Hebrew and Greek version. The parts of both versions are identified by numbers, chapters 1–10. The parts that are only in the Greek version are labeled by letters, chapters A–F. The parts labeled by letters are not part of the Protestant Bible.

What is the literary style? This is a short novel, written to explain the origins of the Jewish festival Purim.

Important themes

- Hatred and jealousy lead to destruction.
- Those in positions of power and esteem have a responsibility to help the powerless.
- God saves the innocent through the courageous acts of people he calls.

ESTHER

Mordecai's Strange Dream

A [a] 1-3 Mordecai, a Jew who belonged to the tribe of Benjamin, was taken into exile, along with King Jehoiachin of Judah, when King Nebuchadnezzar of Babylonia captured Jerusalem. Mordecai was the son of Jair, a descendant of Kish and Shimei. He now lived in the Persian city of Susa, where he was an important official in the royal court of Xerxes the great king.

During the second year of Xerxes' reign, on the first day of the month of Nisan, Mordecai had a dream. 4 He dreamed that there was great noise and confusion, loud thunder, and an earthquake, with terrible turmoil on the earth. 5 Then two huge dragons appeared, ready to fight each other. 6 They made a dreadful noise, and all the nations got ready to make war against God's nation of righteous people. 7 For the world it was a day of darkness and gloom, trouble and distress, destruction and ruin. 8 All of God's righteous people were troubled, in great fear of what was about to happen to them. They prepared for death, 9 but they cried out to God for help. In the dream their prayer was answered by a great river which came flowing out of a small spring. 10 The day dawned, the sun rose, and the humble people were made strong and destroyed their arrogant enemies.

11 Mordecai woke up from this dream in which he saw what God planned to do. He thought about it all day and tried to understand what it meant.

Mordecai Saves the King's Life

12 While Mordecai was resting in the courtyard of the palace, where two of the king's eunuchs, Gabatha and Tharra, were on guard, 13 he overheard them plotting together. He listened carefully to what they were saying and learned that they were making plans to kill the king. So Mordecai went to King Xerxes and told him about the plot of the two eunuchs. 14 The king had them questioned, and when they confessed, they were led away and executed.

He overheard them plotting together. (A:13)

15 The king had an account of this written in the official records, and Mordecai also wrote an account of it. 16 Then the king appointed Mordecai to a position at court and gave him many gifts as a reward for what he had done.

17 But Haman son of Hammedatha, a Bougaean who was respected by the king, tried to cause trouble for Mordecai and his people the Jews, because Mordecai had been responsible for the death of the two eunuchs.

Queen Vashti Defies King Xerxes

1 1-2 These things happened in the time of King Xerxes, who ruled 127 provinces, all the way from India to Ethiopia, [b] from his royal throne in Susa, Persia's capital city. 3 In the third year of his reign, the king gave a banquet for all his advisers, the representatives

[a] **A** *Chapter A:1–17 corresponds to chapters 11:2—12:6 in a number of English translations.* [b] **1:1–2** *Greek* Ethiopia: *Ethiopia is the name given in Graeco-Roman times to the extensive territory south of the First Cataract of the Nile River. Cush was the ancient (Hebrew) name of this region which included within its borders most of modern Sudan and some of present-day Ethiopia (Abyssinia).*

A:1–3 2 Kings 24:10–16 **1:1, 2** Ezra 4:6

of the other countries, the noblemen from Persia and Media, and the governors of the provinces. 4For six whole months he made a show of the riches of the imperial court with magnificent and expensive celebrations.

5After the feast[c] the king gave a banquet for the people of other nations who were in the city. It lasted a week and was held in the palace courtyard, 6which was decorated with linen and cotton curtains, held by cords of purple linen attached to silver and gold blocks on marble and stone columns. Couches made of gold and silver had been placed in the courtyard, which was paved with green and white marble and mother-of-pearl. The couches were spread with a fine, thin fabric of many colors, with roses around the edges. 7There were gold and silver cups, and one of them, decorated with jewels worth more than a thousand tons of silver, had been set out for display. There was plenty of good wine from the king's own supply. 8There were no limits on the drinks. The king had given orders to the palace servants that they should provide him and his guests with as much as they wanted.

9Meanwhile, inside the royal palace Queen Vashti was giving a banquet for the women.

10On the seventh day of his banquet the king was feeling happy, so he called in the seven eunuchs who were his personal servants, Haman, Bazan, Tharra, Boraze, Zatholta, Abataza, and Tharaba.[d] 11He ordered them to bring in the queen, so that he could place the royal crown on her head and show her off to the officials and all his guests, for she was a beautiful woman. 12But Queen Vashti refused to obey and would not come with the servants. This embarrassed the king and made him furious.

13He told his advisers about Vashti's reply and asked them to give a legal opinion about what he should do. 14-15Three of them, who were closest to the king and held the highest offices, came and told him what the law required and what should be done to Queen Vashti for disobeying the command he had given her through his servants. They were Arkesaeus, Sarsathaeus, and Malesear, officials of Persia and Media.[e]

Live it!

R-e-s-p-e-c-t!

Queen Vashti is not about to let herself be used as an object of pleasure for her drunk husband and his friends. Women were not permitted to feast at the king's banquet, but they could be commanded to show up as entertainment! Vashti will not stand for such humiliation, so she refuses to go. Her decision costs her a hefty price—her queenship.

Then, King Xerxes has the nerve to send out a decree to all households in his empire that women should respect their husbands, the masters of their homes! Please! Who needs to respect whom?

Respect is an essential ingredient for strong, healthy, and loving relationships. More importantly, as the courageous Queen Vashti shows us, respect between people must begin with *self*-respect.

— Esther 1:10–22

[c] **1:5** feast; *some manuscripts have* wedding feast. [d] **1:10** *Greek* Haman . . . Tharaba; *Hebrew* Mehuman, Biztha, Harbona, Bigtha, Abagtha, Zethar, and Carkas. [e] **1:14–15** *Greek* Three of them . . . Arkesaeus, Sarsathaeus, and Malesear, officials of Persia and Media; *Hebrew* 14 Those he most often turned to for advice were Carshena, Shethar, Admatha, Tarshish, Meres, Marsena, and Memucan—seven officials of Persia and Media who held the highest offices in the kingdom. 15 He said to these men, "I, King Xerxes, sent my servant to Queen Vashti with a command, and she refused to obey it! What does the law say we should do with her?"

Tribe of Benjamin: One of the twelve tribes of Israel; Benjamin was one of Jacob's twelve sons.

16Then the king told his officials and the
governors of Media and Persia how the
queen had defied him. So Muchaeus[f] said to
the king and everyone present: "Queen
Vashti has insulted not only you but all of us
as well. 17-18As soon as our wives hear what
the queen has done, they will be bold
enough to defy their husbands and treat
them with disrespect in the same way that
Vashti has treated you. 19If, then, it please
Your Majesty, issue a royal proclamation that
Vashti may never again appear before the
king. Have it written into the laws of Media
and Persia. Then give her place as queen to
some better woman. There is no other way.
20When your proclamation is made known
all over this empire, then every woman will
treat her husband with proper respect,
whether he is rich or poor."

21The king and his officials liked this idea,
and the king did as Muchaeus suggested.
22To each of the royal provinces he sent a
message in the language of that province,
saying that every husband must be respected
in his own home.

Esther Becomes Queen

2 Later the king's anger cooled down.
Although he no longer mentioned
Vashti, he kept thinking about how he had
condemned her. 2So some of the king's
advisers suggested, "Why don't you make a
search to find some beautiful young women
of good character? 3You can appoint officials
in every province of the empire and have
them bring all these beautiful young virgins
to your harem here in Susa. Put them in the
care of Hegai, the eunuch who is in charge
of your women, and let them be given cos-
metics and whatever else they may need.
4Then take the young woman you like best
and make her queen in Vashti's place."

The king thought this was good advice, so
he followed it.

5There in Susa lived a Jew named Morde-
cai son of Jair; he was from the tribe of Ben-
jamin and was a descendant of Kish and
Shimei. 6He was among the captives whom
King Nebuchadnezzar of Babylonia had
taken into exile from Jerusalem. 7Mordecai
was the guardian of Esther, the daughter of
his uncle Aminadab.[g] She was a beautiful
young woman, and after the death of her
parents, Mordecai brought her up until she
was grown.[h]

8When the king had issued his new
proclamation, many young women were
being brought to Susa, and Esther was
among them. She too was put in the royal
palace in the care of Hegai, who had charge
of the harem. 9Hegai liked Esther, and she
won his favor. He lost no time in beginning
her beauty treatment of massage and special
diet. He assigned seven young women spe-
cially chosen from the royal palace to serve
her, and he treated her and her servants well.

10Now, on the advice of Mordecai, Esther
had kept secret the fact that she was Jewish.
11Every day Mordecai would walk back and
forth in front of the courtyard of the harem,
watching to see what was going to happen
to her.

12The regular beauty treatment for the
young women lasted a year: massages with
oil of myrrh for six months and with beauty

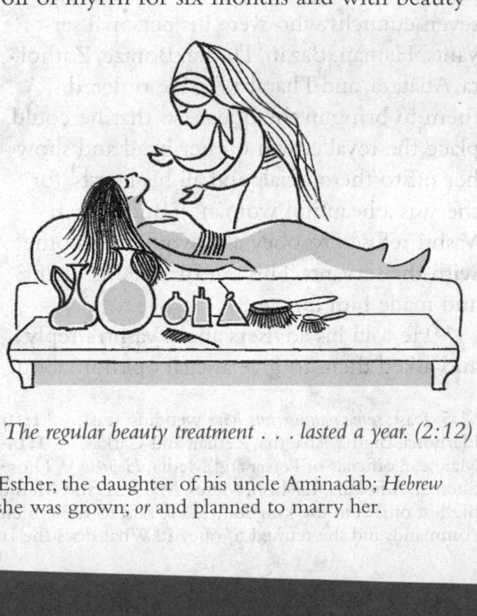

The regular beauty treatment . . . lasted a year. (2:12)

[f] **1:16** *Greek* Muchaeus; *Hebrew* Memucan. [g] **2:7** *Greek* Esther, the daughter of his uncle Aminadab; *Hebrew* Esther, whose Hebrew name was Hadassah. [h] **2:7** until she was grown; *or* and planned to marry her.
2:6 2 Kings 24:10–16; 2 Chr 36:10

What were the qualities King Xerxes was looking for in his new queen?

Supporting Immigrants

Catholic Connections

Mordecai and Esther were part of the Jewish Diaspora—the group of Jews who were forced to move to other places when Jerusalem was destroyed by the Babylonians in 587 BC. In their new homes, they learned new languages and customs, but they also held on to their Jewish traditions. When Esther is chosen as the new queen of Persia, her cousin Mordecai advises her not to reveal her Jewish heritage—to avoid trouble. Only later, when the Jews in her empire are about to be destroyed, does she tell her secret in order to save them.

Immigrants in our country today experience similar challenges. For many reasons, they are forced to leave their homes and move to this country. As they try to fit in, they also try to maintain their religious and cultural identities from their homelands. But often they face hostility from others.

The Catholic bishops in the United States encourage Americans to welcome and support immigrants to this land. Whatever their religious background or customs, immigrants are children of God, and we are called to help them feel safe and at home. How can you help do this in your school or community?

— Esther 2:10–11

creams and cosmetics for six more. [13]After that, each young woman was handed over to the person appointed to conduct her from the harem to the palace, and she was taken to the king. [14]She would go there in the evening, and the next morning she would be taken to another harem and put in the care of Hegai,[i] the eunuch in charge. She would not go to the king again unless he asked for her by name.

[15]The time came for Esther, the daughter of Aminadab[j] the uncle of Mordecai, to go to the king. She had done everything that Hegai had advised, and she was admired by everyone who saw her. [16]So in Xerxes' seventh year as king, in the twelfth month, the month of Adar,[k] she was brought to the king. [17]He fell in love with Esther, who pleased him more than any of the others, and he placed the queen's crown on her head. [18]Then the king gave a week-long banquet for all his advisers and administrators to celebrate his marriage to Esther. He also granted a reduction of taxes for the whole empire.

Mordecai Saves the King's Life

[19]Meanwhile Mordecai had been appointed to a high administrative position. [20]As for Esther, she had still not let it be known that she was Jewish. Mordecai had told her not to tell anyone, and she obeyed him in this, just as she had obeyed him when she was a little girl under his care. She continued to worship God and carry out God's commands, without abandoning her Jewish ways.[l]

[21]When the king promoted Mordecai to a higher position, the two palace eunuchs[m] who were officers of the king's bodyguard became angry and plotted to assassinate the king. [22]Mordecai learned about it and told Queen Esther, who then told the king the

[i] **2:14** *Greek* Hegai; *Hebrew* Shaashgaz. [j] **2:15** *Greek* Aminadab; *Hebrew* Abihail. [k] **2:16** *Greek* twelfth month, the month of Adar; *Hebrew* tenth month, the month of Tebeth. [l] **2:20b** *Greek* She continued to worship God and carry out God's commands, without abandoning her Jewish ways: *These words are not in the Hebrew text.* [m] **2:21** *Greek* the two palace eunuchs; *Hebrew* Bigthana and Teresh, two of the palace eunuchs.

details of the plot. 23 The king had the two men questioned, and both men were hanged. To honor Mordecai, the king ordered an account of this to be written down in the royal records, so that his valuable service would be remembered.

Haman Plots to Destroy the Jews

3 Some time later King Xerxes honored a man named Haman son of Hammedatha, a Bougaean,[n] by promoting him to the position of prime minister. 2 The king ordered all the officials in his service to show their respect for Haman by bowing to him. They all did so, except Mordecai, who refused to bow to Haman. 3 The other officials in the royal service asked him why he was disobeying the king's command. 4 Day after day they urged him to give in, but he would not listen to them. "I am a Jew," he explained, "and I cannot bow to Haman." So they told Haman how Mordecai was defying the king's orders. 5 Haman was furious when he realized that Mordecai was not going to bow to him, 6 and so he made plans to kill every Jew in the whole Persian Empire.

7 In the twelfth year of King Xerxes' reign,[o] Haman ordered the lots to be cast[p] to find out the right day and month to destroy the Jews, all in a single day. The fourteenth day of the month of Adar was the date chosen.

8 So Haman told the king, "There is a certain race of people scattered among the nations all over your empire. They observe customs that are not like those of any other people. Moreover, they do not obey the laws of the empire, so it is not in your best interests to tolerate them. 9 If it please Your Majesty, issue a decree that they are to be put to death. If you do this, I promise to put 375 tons of silver into the royal treasury."[q]

10 The king took off his ring, which was used to stamp official proclamations, and gave it to Haman[r] to seal the decree that was to be written against the Jews. 11 The king told him, "Keep the money, and do whatever you want with that race of people."

12 So on the thirteenth day of the first month, Haman called the king's secretaries and dictated a proclamation to be translated into every language in the empire and to be sent to all the rulers and governors. It was issued in the name of King Xerxes and sent to all the 127 provinces, which stretched from India to Ethiopia.[s] 13 Runners took this

Study it!

The Final Solution

It is amazing how far the evil of one person can reach. Haman is furious with Mordecai, so Haman convinces the king to sign an order to kill every Jewish person in the empire. Wow! But not too long ago one man, Adolf Hitler, actually tried to kill every Jewish person in Europe. He called it the final solution. He was well on his way to doing it, too, before being defeated.

What is even more amazing is that seemingly good people go along with this evil. "Good" soldiers and people in Esther's time would have carried out the king's orders. Soldiers who were otherwise good people carried out Hitler's orders. This is why it is so important that people don't simply follow orders that they know are wrong. We do what God has revealed as good and true—even if it might put us in danger. That is what Queen Esther will do.

— Esther, chapter 3

[n] **3:1** *Greek* a Bougaean; *Hebrew* a descendant of Agag. [o] **3:7** *Greek* twelfth year of King Xerxes' reign; *Hebrew* twelfth year of King Xerxes' rule, in the first month, the month of Nisan. [p] **3:7** *Greek* lots to be cast; *Hebrew* lots to be cast ("purim," they were called). [q] **3:9** *Greek* royal treasury; *Hebrew* royal treasury for the administration of the empire. [r] **3:10** *Greek* Haman; *Hebrew* the enemy of the Jewish people, Haman, son of Hammedatha, the descendant of Agag. [s] **3:12** *Greek* Ethiopia: *Ethiopia is the name given in Graeco-Roman times to the extensive territory south of the First Cataract of the Nile River. Cush was the ancient (Hebrew) name of this region which included within its borders most of modern Sudan and some of present-day Ethiopia (Abyssinia).*

proclamation to every province of the empire. It contained the instructions that on a single day in the twelfth month, the month of Adar, all Jews were to be killed and their belongings confiscated.[t u]

Xerxes' Proclamation against the Jews

B[v] This is a copy of the decree:

"King Xerxes the Great sends the following decree to the governors of his 127 provinces, from India to Ethiopia,[w] and to their subordinate officials:

2"After I became ruler of many nations and master of the whole world, I resolved that my subjects should always live at peace. I wanted this, not because of pride in my power but because I was always reasonable and governed my subjects with kindness. I determined to renew the peace that everyone longs for and to do what was necessary to create a civilized kingdom, safe for travel from one border to another.

3"I asked my advisers how to accomplish this goal, and Haman made a suggestion. He is distinguished among us as a man of great wisdom, and at all times he has demonstrated his concern for the welfare of the kingdom. Because of his unfailing loyalty, he has been raised to the second highest position in the empire. 4Recently Haman told us about a certain unruly people scattered among all the other peoples of the empire. He explained to us that these people have their own laws, are opposed to every other nation, and constantly ignore royal commands. As a result of their attitude, we are not able to establish the kind of unified government which we earnestly intend for the empire.

5"These people are hostile to our government and commit terrible crimes which threaten the security of the empire. They follow strange customs, obey their own laws, and stand alone in their constant opposition to all people. 6In the light of these facts, we recommend the slaughter of the people referred to by Haman, our prime minister. All of them, including women and children, must be put to death; no one is to be spared. They are our enemies; we will show them no pity. This order is to be carried out this year on the fourteenth day of the twelfth month, the month of Adar. 7These people, who have caused so much trouble for so long, will all die a violent death in a single day. From then on, our government will be secure and stable."

3 14The contents of the proclamation were made public in every province, and everyone was ordered to be prepared for that day.

15The decree was also rapidly made public in the capital city of Susa. And while the king and Haman got drunk,[x] the city of Susa was thrown into confusion.

Mordecai Asks for Esther's Help

4 When Mordecai learned of all that had been done, he tore his clothes in anguish. Then he dressed in sackcloth, covered his head with ashes, and ran through the city crying loudly, "An innocent nation is being destroyed!"[y] 2When he came to the entrance of the palace, he stopped. He did not go in because no one in sackcloth and ashes was allowed inside. 3Throughout all the provinces, wherever the king's proclamation was made known, there was loud mourning among the Jews. They wept, wailed, and put on sackcloth and ashes.[z]

4When Esther's servant women and eunuchs told her what Mordecai was doing, she was deeply disturbed. She sent Mordecai

[t] **3:13b** *Greek* on a single day . . . confiscated; *Hebrew* on a single day, the thirteenth day of Adar, all Jews—young and old, women and children—were to be killed. They were to be slaughtered without mercy and their belongings were to be taken. [u] **3:13** *Chapter 3 continues after chapter B.* [v] **B:1** *Chapter B:1–7 corresponds to chapter 13:1–7 in a number of English translations.* [w] **B:1** *Greek* Ethiopia: *Ethiopia is the name given in Graeco-Roman times to the extensive territory south of the First Cataract of the Nile River. Cush was the ancient (Hebrew) name of this region which included within its borders most of modern Sudan and some of present-day Ethiopia (Abyssinia).* [x] **3:15** *Greek* got drunk; *Hebrew* sat down and had a drink. [y] **4:1** *Greek* "An innocent nation is being destroyed!": *These words are not in the Hebrew text.* [z] **4:3** *Greek* They wept . . . ashes; *Hebrew* They fasted, wept, wailed, and most of them put on sackcloth and lay in ashes.

Mordecai refused to bow to Haman because that would have been treating Haman like a god.

some clothes to put on instead of the sack-
cloth, but he would not accept them. 5Then
she called Hathach, one of the palace
eunuchs appointed as her servant, and told
him to go to Mordecai and get the details of
what was happening.[a] 7Mordecai told him
everything that had happened and how
Haman had promised to put 375 tons of sil-
ver into the royal treasury if all the Jews
were killed. 8He gave Hathach a copy of the
proclamation that had been issued in Susa,
ordering the destruction of the Jews. Morde-
cai asked him to take it to Esther so that she
might go and plead with the king and beg
him to have mercy on her people. "Tell her,"
he said, "to remember the days when she
was just an ordinary person being brought
up under my care. Now, since Haman, the
king's prime minister, has spoken against us
and demands our death, she must pray to the
Lord and then speak to the king about us.
She must save us from death."[b]
9So Hathach did this, 10and Esther gave
him this message to take back to Mordecai:
11"If anyone, man or woman, goes to the
inner courtyard and sees the king without
being summoned, that person will be sen-
tenced to death. Everyone in the empire
knows that. Only if the king holds out his
gold scepter to him can his life be spared.
But it has been a month now since the king
has sent for me."
12When Mordecai received Esther's mes-
sage, 13he sent her this warning: "Esther,
don't imagine that you are safer than any of
the other Jews in the empire. 14If you keep
quiet at a time like this, help will come to
the Jews in some other way[c] and they will be
saved, but you will die and your father's fam-
ily will come to an end. Yet, who knows?
Maybe it was for a time like this that you
were made queen!"
15Esther sent Mordecai this reply: 16"Go
and gather all the Jews in Susa together; hold
a fast and pray for me. Don't eat or drink
anything for three days and nights. My ser-
vant women and I will be doing the same.
After that, I will go to the king, even though
it is against the law. If I must die for doing it,
I will die."
17Mordecai then left and did everything
that Esther had told him to do.

Mordecai's Prayer

C[d] Mordecai prayed to the Lord, calling
to mind what the Lord had done in
the past: 2"O Lord, you are the Lord and
King of all creation, and everything obeys
your commands. If you wish to save Israel,
no one can stop you. 3You made heaven and
earth and all the wonderful things on earth.
4You are the Lord of all, and there is no one
who can stand against you. 5You know all
things. You know, Lord, that when I refused
to bow to that arrogant Haman, it was not
because I was arrogant or trying to impress
people. 6-7I simply did not want to honor
any human being more than I honor God. I
refuse to bow to anyone but you, my Lord;
and this is not because of pride. If it would
help to save Israel, I would be willing even
to kiss the soles of his feet.
8-9"And now, O Lord, God and King, God
of Abraham, spare your people; save us from
our enemies. They are determined to destroy
us; they are looking for a chance. Long ago
you chose us to be your people and rescued
us from the land of Egypt. Do not abandon
us now. 10We are your chosen people, so lis-
ten to my prayer and be gracious to us. Turn
our misfortune into joy so that we may live
to sing your praises. Save us from death so
that we can keep on praising you."
11And all the people of Israel prayed loud-
ly and earnestly because they were sure that
they were going to die.

[a] **4:5** *Some manuscripts add verse 6:* Hathach went to Mordecai in the city square at the entrance to the palace.
[b] **4:8b** *Greek* "Tell her," he said . . . "She must save us from death.": *These words are not in the Hebrew text.*
[c] **4:14** *Greek* in some other way; *Hebrew* from heaven. [d] **C:1** *Chapter C:1–30 corresponds to chapters 13:8—14:19 in a number of English translations.*
C:8, 9 Ex 3:6

"Come to our rescue, O Lord. Help me; I am all alone, and I have no one to turn to but you" *(Esther C:25)*.

Pray it!

Let Nothing Disturb You

This prayer is from the great saint Teresa of Ávila, who lived from AD 1515 to 1582. She had great courage and lived a life filled with sacrifice. This prayer could also have been said by Esther.

Let nothing disturb you,
Nothing dismay you.
All things pass.
But God never changes.

Whoever has God lacks nothing.
If you have only God,
You have more than enough.

— Esther C:23–25

Esther's Prayer

12 Queen Esther, in deep agony, turned to
the Lord. 13 She took off her splendid robes
and put on garments of mourning and grief.
Instead of her rich perfumes, she put ashes
and dung on her head. She did all she could
to destroy any dignity in her appearance. She
let her tangled and uncombed hair hang
down over her body that she had always
taken such care to beautify. 14 She prayed to
the Lord God of Israel, "My Lord and King,
only you are God. I am all alone, and I have
no one to turn to but you. Help me! 15 I am

Esther's prayer (C:12)

about to risk my life. 16 O Lord, as long as I
can remember, my family has told me how
you chose Israel from all the nations and
how in ancient times you singled out our
ancestors to be your people forever. You have
kept all your promises to them.
17 "But we sinned against you. You handed
us over to our enemies because we worshiped
their gods. 18 We deserved your punishment,
O Lord. 19 But our enemies are no longer sat-
isfied just to see us in slavery. They have made
a solemn promise to their idols 20 not only to
destroy the people who praise you, but to do
away with your Law and to remove forever
the glory of your house and altar. 21 They
want the whole world to praise worthless
idols and stand in awe of mortal kings forever.
22 "Lord, these gods are nothing; do not
surrender your power to them or give our
enemies the chance to laugh at our down-
fall. Instead, turn their evil plans against
them, and make an example of that man
who first planned our destruction.
23 "Remember us, O Lord. Come to us in
this time of trouble. Give me courage, King of
all gods and Ruler over all earthly powers.
24 Give me the right words to say when I go
in to face Xerxes, that savage lion. Change his
heart so that he will turn against Haman, our

C:24, 25 Jdt 9:13

Live it!

The Courage of a Queen

Like Vashti, who stood up to her husband, the king, Esther must gather all her courage to do the right thing. The royal court had a rule that only those who were summoned by the king could speak with him. If someone dared to approach him without being invited, they were put to death. Esther desperately needs to speak with the king about Haman's plan to destroy Mordecai and all the Jews in the empire. But she knows she could lose her life if she just appears before the king without being invited.

She does it anyway, even though "in her heart she was terror-stricken" (Esther D:5). Esther makes a critical decision to risk her life for the sake of the many Jews who are innocent and do not deserve to be slaughtered. Her courage and her passion to do what is right are truly inspiring!

What are you facing in your life right now that requires courage? What risk do you face if you do the right thing? Who can be there to support and help you?

— Esther 4:9–17; D:1–16

enemy, and destroy him and his gang. [25]Come
to our rescue, O Lord. Help me; I am all
alone, and I have no one to turn to but you.
[26]"You know everything, Lord. You know
that I hate the honor I receive from these
Gentiles. I detest the thought of having sex
with any of these uncircumcised heathen.
[27]But you know that I have no choice. I hate
the crown I have to wear as queen on offi-
cial occasions. I never wear it unless I have
to; it's as disgusting as last month's rag. [28]I
refuse to eat at Haman's table or honor the
king by attending his parties, and I have
never drunk any of the wine dedicated to
his gods. [29]Since I came here, the only thing
that has brought me joy is my worship of
you, Lord God of Abraham.
[30]"Almighty God, listen to the prayer of
your people. Rescue us from these evildoers,
and take away my fear."

Esther Goes to the King

D[e] Queen Esther prayed for three days.
Then she took off the clothes she had
been wearing and put on her splendid robes
again. [2-3]In all her royal splendor, she prayed
again to her God and savior, who sees every-
thing. Walking like a queen, she left her
room accompanied by two servant women,
one of them escorting her by the arm and
[4]the other holding up the train of her robe.
[5]Queen Esther's face was radiantly beautiful.
She looked as cheerful as she was lovely, but
in her heart she was terror-stricken. [6]She
passed through all the doors and entered the
throne room, where she stood before the
king. He was seated on his royal throne,
dressed in his glorious robes, which were
covered with gold and precious jewels. It was
an awe-inspiring sight. [7]His face glowed
with splendor, but when he saw Esther, he
stared at her with fierce anger. She grew
weak and turned pale; she almost fainted and

In all her royal splendor (D:2)

[e] **D:1** *Chapter D:1–15 corresponds to chapter 15:1–16 in a number of English translations.*
C:28 Dan 1:8; Jdt 12:2

had to lean her head on her attendant's shoulder.

[8]But God changed the king's anger into tender concern. He quickly rose from his throne and took her in his arms until she was able to stand. He calmed her with comforting words. [9]"What is it, Esther?" he said to her. "I am your husband. There's no need to be afraid. [10]Our law applies only to ordinary people; you will not die. [11]Come here to me." [12]He lifted his gold scepter and touched her on the neck with it. Then he kissed her and said, "Tell me what you want."

[13]"When I looked at you, my lord, I thought I was seeing an angel of God," the queen answered, "and I was overcome by your awesome majesty. [14]You are so marvelous and your face is so full of kindness."

[15]But while she was speaking, she fainted again. [16]The king was concerned about her, and all his attendants tried to revive her.

Esther Invites the King and Haman to a Banquet

5 [f] [3]"What is it, Esther?" the king asked. "Tell me what you want, and you shall have it—even if it is half of my empire."

[4]Esther replied, "Today is a special day for me. If it please my lord, I would like you and Haman to be my guests tonight at a banquet I am preparing for you."

[5]The king then ordered Haman to come quickly, so that they could be Esther's guests. So the king and Haman went to Esther's banquet. [6]Over the wine the king again said to her, "Tell me what you want, Queen Esther."

[7]Esther replied, [8]"If my lord is kind enough to grant my request, I would like you and Haman to be my guests tomorrow at another banquet that I will prepare for you. It will be just like this one."[g]

Haman Plots to Kill Mordecai

[9]When Haman left the king he was happy and in a good mood, until he saw Mordecai the Jew in the courtyard of the palace. That made him furious, [10]but he went on home.[h] Then he invited his friends to his house and asked his wife Zeresh to join them. [11]He boasted to them about how rich he was[i] and about the honor the king had paid him when he promoted him to high office and made him prime minister. [12]"What is more," Haman said, "Queen Esther gave a banquet for no one but the king and me, and we are invited back tomorrow. [13]But none of this means a thing to me as long as I see that Jew Mordecai sitting in the courtyard of the palace."

[14]Then his wife and all his friends suggested, "Why don't you have a gallows put up, seventy-five feet high? Tomorrow morning you can ask the king to have Mordecai hanged on it, and then you can go with the king to the banquet and enjoy yourself." Haman thought it was a good idea, so he had the gallows built.

The King Honors Mordecai

6 That night the Lord kept the king from sleeping, so the king ordered his private secretary to bring the official records of the empire and read them to him. [2]He read the account of how Mordecai had uncovered a plot to assassinate the king—the plot made by the two eunuchs who served as palace

[f] **5:1** *In Greek, chapter D replaces verses 1 and 2 in Hebrew:* [1] On the third day of her fast Esther put on her royal robes and went and stood in the inner courtyard of the palace, facing the throne room. The king was inside, seated on the royal throne, facing the entrance. [2] When the king saw Queen Esther standing outside, she won his favor, and he held out to her the gold scepter. She then came up and touched the tip of it. [g] **5:8b** *Greek* It will be just like this one; *Hebrew* At that time I will tell you what I want. [h] **5:10** *Greek* but he went on home; *Hebrew* but he controlled himself and went on home. [i] **5:11** *Greek* how rich he was; *Hebrew* how rich he was, how many sons he had.

5:3 Mk 6:23

Esther was terrified to face the king without being summoned. How many times did she faint or almost faint while talking to him?

Pray it!

Forgiving Our Enemies

Mordecai and Haman become enemies whose deep hatred leads to a violent death. Haman wants to hang Mordecai on a gallows seventy-five feet high! Our battles are usually much less intense, but they start with something minor, like this: Jen snickered when she saw Sara's new haircut. It was a quiet little snort, almost unnoticeable, but Sara didn't miss it. This was just like Jen to act that way.

How would you handle this if you were Sara? Find a way to hurt Jen back? Shrug it off and tell yourself she's just insecure? Be extra kind to Jen because you would rather have a friend than an enemy?

Our grudges and battles suck up a lot of energy and time, don't they? Jesus told us to forgive (and love!) our enemies (see Matthew 5:43–48), not just because God desires peace among his children, but because we're healthier and happier when we're not carrying all that hate around. Hate weighs a lot!

Do you have any enemies? Any battles stirring? Talk to God about these and ask for help. Forgiveness is one of the hardest things for humans—we need God's strength to let go of hurts and learn to live peacefully with one another. In the end, we will feel better and stronger.

— Esther 5:9–14

guards.[j] 3The king asked, "How have we
honored and rewarded Mordecai for this?"
His servants answered, "You have done
nothing for him."
4Now just as the king was inquiring about
Mordecai's good deed, Haman entered the
courtyard. He had come to ask the king to
have Mordecai hanged on the gallows that
was now ready.
"Who is that in the courtyard?" the king
asked.
5The servants answered, "It is Haman; he
is waiting to see you."[k]
"Show him in," said the king.
6So Haman came in, and the king said to
him, "There is someone I wish very much to
honor. What should I do for this man?"
Haman thought to himself, "Now who
could the king want to honor so much? Me,
of course."
7-8So he answered the king, "Let the royal
servants bring a fine linen robe for this
man—one that you yourself wear. And let
them bring a horse that you yourself ride.
9Then put that robe on the man you like so
much and then have the nobleman lead him,
mounted on the horse, through the city
square. Have the nobleman announce as they
go: 'See how the king rewards a man whom
he wishes to honor!' "
10Then the king said to Haman, "Fine!
Do all that for Mordecai the Jew, who holds
a high position in the palace;[l] don't leave out
a thing."

[j] **6:2** *Greek* the plot . . . palace guards; *Hebrew* the plot made by Bigthana and Teresh, the two palace eunuchs who had guarded the king's rooms. [k] **6:4–5a** *Greek* Now just as the king . . . he is waiting to see you; *Hebrew* [4] "Are any of my officials in the palace?" the king asked. / Now Haman had just entered the courtyard; he had come to ask the king to have Mordecai hanged on the gallows that was now ready. [5] So the servants answered, "Haman is here, waiting to see you." [l] **6:10b** *Greek* who holds a high position in the palace: *These words are not in the Hebrew text.*

Why did the king first decide to honor Mordecai? What did the king have Haman do for Mordecai that was so humiliating for Haman?

Study it!

Esther and Joseph

Have you seen the musical *Joseph and the Amazing Technicolor Dreamcoat*? It is based on a wonderful story from Genesis about Joseph, the young son of Jacob. If you are not familiar with the story, read Genesis, chapters 37–50. It is entertaining and teaches an important lesson about forgiveness.

Joseph, like Esther and Mordecai, was a Jew who rose to power in a foreign government and ended up having a great deal of influence. None of these Jews sought out their powerful positions, but by strange circumstances wound up there anyway. Joseph, Esther, and Mordecai were able to use their influence to save their people, the Jews.

Joseph's brothers sold him as a slave, hoping to get rid of him for good, and next thing you know, he has saved their lives during a famine. Vashti stood up to the king, and next thing, she is replaced by a new queen, Esther. Esther does what Vashti could not do—save the Jews. God's plans are interesting and complex! At any moment, something could happen to us that is meant to have greater meaning in time. At any moment, someone could enter our life who will change the way we live.

— Esther 6:1–10

. . . and Haman led him through the city. (6:11)

11So Haman got the robe and the horse,
and he put the robe on Mordecai. Mordecai
got on the horse, and Haman led him
through the city square, announcing to the
people as they went: "See how the king
rewards a man whom he wishes to honor!"
12Mordecai then went back to the court-
yard while Haman hurried home, covering
his face in embarrassment. 13He told his
wife and all his friends everything that had
happened to him. Then they all said to
him, "You are beginning to lose power to
Mordecai. He is a Jew, and you cannot over-
come him. He will certainly defeat you, for
the living God is with him!"[m]

Haman Is Put to Death

14While they were still talking, the palace
eunuchs arrived to take Haman to Esther's
banquet.

7 And so the king and Haman went to
eat with Esther 2for a second time.
Over the wine the king asked her again,
"Now, Queen Esther, what do you want?
Tell me and you shall have it. I'll even give
you half the empire."
3Queen Esther answered, "If it please Your
Majesty to grant my humble request, my wish
is that I may live and that my people may live.
4My people and I have been sold into slavery;
our possessions have been plundered, and
now we are to be destroyed—all of us, includ-
ing our children, will be slaves—and so far I
have kept quiet. It isn't right that our enemy
should be a member of the royal court."[n]

[m] **6:13b** *Greek* for the living God is with him!: *These words are not in the Hebrew text.* [n] **7:4** *Greek* My people . . . the royal court; *Hebrew* My people and I have been sold for slaughter. If it were nothing more serious than being sold into slavery, I would have kept quiet [and not bother you about it]; but we are about to be destroyed—exterminated!"; *Probable text* and not . . . it; *Hebrew unclear.*

5Then King Xerxes asked Esther, "Who
dares to do such a thing?"
6Esther answered, "Our enemy is this evil
man Haman!"

"Our enemy is this evil man Haman!" (7:6)

In terror Haman faced the king and
queen. 7The king got up from the table and
went outside to the palace gardens. Haman
could see that he was in a dangerous situa-
tion, so he stayed behind to beg Queen
Esther for his life. 8He had just thrown him-
self down on Esther's couch to beg for
mercy, when the king came back into the
room from the gardens. Seeing this, the king
cried out, "Are you going to rape my wife[o]
here in my own palace?"
When Haman heard this, he turned away
in despair. 9Then one of the eunuchs, whose
name was Bougathan,[p] said, "Haman has
even gone so far as to build a gallows at his
house so that he can hang Mordecai, who
warned Your Majesty about the plot. And it's
seventy-five feet high!"
"Hang Haman on it!" the king command-
ed.
10So Haman was hanged on the gallows
that he had built for Mordecai. Then the
king's anger cooled down.

The Jews Are Told to Fight Back

8 That same day King Xerxes gave Queen
Esther all the property of Haman, the
enemy of the Jews. Esther told the king that
Mordecai was related to her, and Mordecai
was invited to enter the king's presence.
2The king took off his ring with his seal on
it (which he had taken back from Haman)
and gave it to Mordecai. Esther put Morde-
cai in charge of Haman's property.
3Then Esther spoke to the king again,
throwing herself at his feet. She begged him
to do something to stop the evil plot that
Haman[q] had made against the Jews. 4The
king held out the gold scepter to her, so she
stood up 5and said, "If it please Your Majesty
and if you care about me, please issue a
proclamation to keep Haman's orders from
being carried out—those orders he[r] gave for
the destruction of all the Jews in the empire.
6How can I endure it if this disaster comes
on my people? How can I go on living if my
whole nation is destroyed?"
7Then the king said to Esther,[s] "I have
hanged Haman for his plot against the Jews,
and I have given you his property. If that is not
enough, 8you may write to the Jews whatever
you like; and you may write[t] it in my name
and stamp it with the royal seal, for a procla-
mation issued in the king's name and stamped
with the royal seal cannot be revoked."
9On the twenty-third day of the first
month, the month of Nisan,[u] the king's sec-
retaries were called[v] and letters were written
to the Jews and to the governors and admin-
istrators of all 127 provinces from India to
Ethiopia.[w] The letters were written to each
province in its own language. 10They were
written in the name of the king and stamped
with the royal seal and they were delivered
by runners.[x]

[o] **7:8a** *Greek* my wife; *Hebrew* the queen. [p] **7:8, 9** *Greek* When Haman heard this . . . whose name was Bougathan; *Hebrew* The king had no sooner said this than the eunuchs covered Haman's head. Then one of them, who was named Harbonah. [q] **8:3** *Greek* Haman; *Hebrew* Haman, the descendant of Agag.
[r] **8:5b** *Greek* he; *Hebrew* that the son of Hammedatha the descendant of Agag. [s] **8:7** *Greek* to Esther; *Hebrew* to Queen Esther and Mordecai, the Jew. [t] **8:7, 8** *Greek* If that is not enough . . . you may write; *Hebrew* But a proclamation issued in the king's name and stamped with the royal seal cannot be revoked. You may, however, write. [u] **8:9** *Greek* first month, the month of Nisan; *Hebrew* third month, the month of Sivan. [v] **8:9** *Greek* the king's secretaries were called; *Hebrew* Mordecai called the king's secretaries. [w] **8:9** *Greek* Ethiopia: *Ethiopia is the name given in Graeco-Roman times to the extensive territory south of the First Cataract of the Nile River. Cush was the ancient (Hebrew) name of this region which included within its borders most of modern Sudan and some of present-day Ethiopia (Abyssinia).* [x] **8:10** *Greek* by runners; *Hebrew* by riders mounted on fast horses from the royal stables.
8:8 Dan 6:8

Study it!

Saving the Jews

Once King Xerxes learns of Haman's evil plot to kill Mordecai and all the Jews in his kingdom, he takes action. First, he punishes Haman by having him hanged. Unfortunately, he cannot undo the order to kill all the Jews, but he does help Mordecai and Esther to send out another order. This order permits the Jews to form armies and defend themselves against their attackers.

On the day of the planned attack, the Jews are prepared—and so they are saved from destruction. It was a great victory for the Jews, who believed that God was once again on their side, protecting the Chosen People who remained faithful to God.

— Esther 8:1–12

11 These letters explained that the king
would allow the Jews in every city of the
empire to live by their own laws and orga-
nize for self-defense. They were permitted
to treat their opponents and enemies in any
way they liked.[y] 12 This decree was to take
effect throughout the Persian Empire on
the thirteenth day of Adar, the twelfth
month.[z a]

The King's Decree in Favor of the Jews

E[b] This is a copy of the decree:
“Greetings from King Xerxes the
Great to the governors of the 127 provinces,
which extend from India to Ethiopia,[c] and
to all those who are loyal to us.
2 “Many people become increasingly arro-
gant when honors are given to them and
favors are done for them. 3 They do not
know what to do with so much good for-
tune, so they not only try to harm our sub-
jects, but they even scheme against those
who grant them favors. 4 They are never
grateful for what people do for them, and
they even think they can escape the judg-
ment of God, who hates evil and sees every-
thing. In their arrogance they listen to the
flattery of ignorant, sinful people.
5 “It often happens also that friends who
have been entrusted with administrative
responsibilities exert pressure on those in
authority. They make their leaders their part-
ners in killing people and bring about mis-
fortunes that can never be remedied. 6 These
friends, by their lies and deceitful ways, take
advantage of the good will of their rulers.
7 “You can see examples of this misuse of
power not only in the stories that have been
handed down to us from the past, but in the
more recent outrageous things which have
happened among you.
8 “I intend to make sure that in the future
my kingdom will remain untroubled and
peaceful for all people. 9 This can be done by
changing certain policies and by judging fair-
ly each situation that comes to my attention.
10 “Consider, for example, the case of
Haman son of Hammedatha, a Macedonian.
He is a foreigner with no Persian blood and

[y] **8:11** *Greek* These letters . . . in any way they liked; *Hebrew* These letters explained that the king would allow the Jews in every city to organize for self-defense. If armed men of any nationality in any province attacked the Jewish men, their children, or their women, the Jews could fight back and destroy the attackers; they could slaughter them to the last man and take their possessions. [z] **8:12** *Greek* the thirteenth day of Adar, the twelfth month; *Hebrew* the day set for the slaughter of the Jews, the thirteenth of Adar, the twelfth month.
[a] **8:12** *Chapter 8 continues after chapter E.* [b] **E:1** *Chapter E:1–24 corresponds to chapter 16:1–24 in a number of English translations.* [c] **E:1** *Greek* Ethiopia: *Ethiopia is the name given in Graeco-Roman times to the extensive territory south of the First Cataract of the Nile River. Cush was the ancient (Hebrew) name of this region which included within its borders most of modern Sudan and some of present-day Ethiopia (Abyssinia).*

Why do you think Esther invites the king to *two* banquets before she makes her request?

with no trace of my generosity; but I wel-
comed him, 11 and he received the benefit of
my concern and love for all people. He was,
in fact, proclaimed 'Father' of the empire and
received more honor than anyone else,
except the king.
12 "But his arrogance knew no limits, and
he tried to murder me and take over the
empire. 13 In his crafty and deceitful way, he
asked that Mordecai be put to death—
Mordecai, who once saved my life and who
has always supported me. He even asked for
the death of Esther, our blameless queen, and
in fact, the death of all the Jewish people.
14 His purpose was to leave us helpless and to
allow the Macedonians to take over the Per-
sian Empire. 15 Even though this wicked
criminal plotted to wipe out the Jews, I find
that they are not traitors at all but are gov-
erned by very just laws. 16 They worship the
living God, the highest and greatest God,
who has kept our empire in its excellent
condition from the time of our ancestors
until our own day.
17 "Therefore I advise you not to carry
out the instructions issued in the letters sent
out by Haman. 18 He is the person responsi-
ble for all of this, and he has been hanged,
along with his entire family, at the gates of
Susa. God, who governs all things, has given
him the speedy punishment that he
deserved.
19 "I order you to post copies of this
decree in every public place. Permit the Jews
to live by their own customs, 20 and give
them support when they defend themselves
against those who attack them on the day set
for their destruction, the thirteenth day of
Adar, the twelfth month. 21 God, who gov-
erns all things, has turned that day of
destruction into a day of celebration for his
chosen people.
22 "Include this day among your national
holidays and celebrate it as a festival. 23 Now
and in the future it will remind us and all
our allies of the way God watches over our
nation, and those who plot against us will be
reminded of God's threat of destruction.
24 "Every province, every city, without
exception, which does not obey these
orders will feel my anger. It will be destroyed
in battle and burned to the ground. No
human being will ever go there again, and
even the birds and wild animals will avoid it
forever.

8 [d] 13 "Post copies of this decree in plain
view in every province, so that all the
Jews can be ready to fight their enemies
when that day comes."
14 Messengers on horses rode off at top
speed to carry out the orders of the king,
and the decree was also made public in Susa.
15 Mordecai left the palace, wearing royal
robes, a turban of fine purple linen, and a
gold crown. When the people of Susa saw
him, they cheered, 16 and the Jews were
happy and joyful. 17 They held a joyful holi-
day with feasting and happiness in every city
and province, wherever the king's proclama-

Post copies of this decree in plain view in every province . . . Messengers on horses rode off at top speed. (8:13, 14)

[d] **8:13** *Verses 1–12 precede chapter E.*

Read the king's decree in Esther, chapter E. Do you think he is a good king? Why or why not?

tion was posted. In fact, many Gentiles were
circumcised and became Jews, because they
were now afraid of them.

The Jews Destroy Their Enemies

9 On the thirteenth day of Adar, the day
on which the royal proclamation was to
take effect, 2 it was the enemies of the Jews
who were wiped out.[e] People everywhere
were afraid of the Jews, and no one could
stand against them. 3 In fact, the provincial
governors, the administrators, and the royal
scribes showed respect for the Jews, because
they were all afraid of Mordecai. 4-5 The
royal decree had made his name known
throughout the empire.[f]

6 In Susa, the capital city itself, the Jews
killed five hundred people 7-10 and looted
their property.[g] Among them were the ten
sons of Haman son of Hammedatha, a
Bougaean, the enemy of the Jews: Pharsan-
nestain, Delphon, Phasga, Pharadatha, Barea,
Sarbacha, Marmasima, Arouphaeus, Arsaeus,
and Zabouthaeus.[h]

11 That same day the number of people
killed in Susa was reported to the king. 12 He
then said to Esther,[i] "In Susa alone the Jews
have killed five hundred people.[j] What must
they have done out in the provinces! Tell me[k]
what else you want, and you shall have it."

13 Esther answered, "Let the Jews in Susa
do again tomorrow what they were allowed
to do today. And have the bodies of Haman's
ten sons hung up." 14 The king agreed and
permitted the Jews to put the bodies of
Haman's ten sons on public display. 15 On the
fourteenth day of Adar the Jews of Susa got
together again and killed three hundred more
people in the city. But they did no looting.

16 The Jews in the provinces also organized
and defended themselves. They rid themselves
of their enemies by killing 15,000 people[l] on
the thirteenth day of Adar, but they did no
looting. 17 On the next day, the fourteenth,
there was no more killing, and the Jews made
it a joyful holiday of rest and feasting.[m] 18 The
Jews of Susa, however, made the fifteenth a
holiday, since they had slaughtered their ene-
mies on the thirteenth and fourteenth and did
not stop until the fifteenth. 19 This is why Jews
who live in small towns observe the four-
teenth day of the month of Adar as a holiday, a
time of giving gifts of food to one another,
while the Jews in the large cities celebrate the
holiday in the same way on the fifteenth.[n]

The Festival of Purim

20 Mordecai had these events written down
in a book and sent it to all the Jews, near and
far, throughout the Persian Empire, 21 telling
them to observe the fourteenth and fifteenth
days of Adar as holidays.[o] 22 These were the
days on which the Jews had rid themselves of
their enemies. The Jews were to observe the
whole month as a holiday,[p] for this was a
month that had been turned from a time of
grief and despair into a time of joy and hap-
piness. They were told to observe these days
with feasts and parties, giving gifts of food to
friends and to the poor. 23 So the Jews accept-
ed all that Mordecai had written.[q]

24 Mordecai had recorded how Haman son

[e] **9:2** *Greek* it was the enemies . . . wiped out; *Hebrew* 9:1b the day when the enemies of the Jews were hoping to get them in their power. But instead, the Jews triumphed over them. 2 In the Jewish quarter of every city [*or* In every Jewish city] in the empire the Jews organized to attack anyone who tried to harm them. [f] **9:4–5** *Greek* The royal decree . . . empire; *Hebrew* It was well-known throughout the empire that Mordecai was now a powerful man in the palace and was growing more powerful. So the Jews could do what they wanted with their enemies. They attacked them with swords and slaughtered them. [g] **9:7–10** *Greek* and looted their property: *These words are not in the Hebrew text.* [h] **9:7–10** *Greek* Haman son of Hammedatha, a Bougaean . . . Zabouthaeus; *Hebrew* Haman son of Hammedatha, the enemy of the Jews: Parshandatha, Dalphon, Aspatha, Poratha, Adalia, Aridatha, Parmashta, Arisai, Aridai, and Vaizatha. However, there was no looting. [i] **9:12** *Greek* Esther; *Hebrew* Queen Esther. [j] **9:12** *Greek* five hundred people; *Hebrew* five hundred people, including Haman's sons. [k] **9:12** *Greek* provinces! Tell me; *Hebrew* provinces! What do you want now? You shall have it. Tell me. [l] **9:16** *Greek* 15,000 people; *Hebrew* seventy-five thousand people who hated them. [m] **9:17** *Greek* joyful holiday of rest and feasting; *Hebrew* joyful day of feasting. [n] **9:19** *Greek* while the Jews in the larger cities celebrate the holiday in the same way on the fifteenth: *These words are not in the Hebrew text.* [o] **9:21** *Greek* as holidays; *Hebrew* as holidays every year. [p] **9:22** *Greek* The Jews were to observe the whole month as a holiday: *These words are not in the Hebrew text.* [q] **9:23** *Greek* So the Jews accepted all that Mordecai had written; *Hebrew* So the Jews followed Mordecai's instructions, and the celebration became an annual custom.
9:1 1 Macc 7:49; 2 Macc 15:36 **9:24–28** Esth 3:7

Study it!

The Festival of Purim

***Purim* is a Hebrew word that means "lots." The Jewish festival of Purim that celebrates the victory of the Jews was named after the method that decided when the attack would be held. Haman chose lots (similar to picking a date out of a hat) to choose a date. It was on that day, and the next (upon the request of Esther), that the Jews defended themselves against their enemies and were saved. On the days after battle, the Jews celebrated by feasting, giving thanks, and sharing their food with poor people.**

Today, the Jewish people celebrate the courage and determination of Esther and Mordecai on the Festival of Purim. On those days they give thanks to God for his faithfulness, and share gifts and meals with one another, especially with poor people.

— Esther 9:20–31

of Hammedatha, a Macedonian,[r] had fought against the Jewish people, how he had made a decree and cast lots[s] to determine the day he would destroy them, 25 and how he had gone to the king to request that Mordecai be hanged.[t] But Haman suffered the same fate he had planned for the Jews—he and his sons were hanged from the gallows. 26-28 Because of Mordecai's letter,[u] because of all they had suffered, and because of all that had happened to them, the Jews accepted Mordecai's suggestion and made it a rule for themselves, their descendants, and anyone that might become a Jew, that these days should be properly observed as a memorial, generation after generation, in every city, province, and country. The Jews were to remember and observe these days of Purim for all time to come and never neglect them. (The holidays are called Purim because "purim" in their language is the word for "lots.")[v]

29-30 Then Queen Esther, the daughter of Aminadab,[w] along with Mordecai the Jew, wrote down what they had done, putting the queen's full authority behind the letter about Purim. 31 They both took responsibility for establishing the festival and made up their minds to observe it at all costs.[x][y] 32 Esther established the festival forever, and a written record was made of her official decree.

The Greatness of Xerxes and Mordecai

10 King Xerxes imposed taxes[z] on the people of the coastal regions of his empire as well as on those of the interior. 2 His power and virtue, as well as the wealth and splendor of his empire,[a] are recorded in the official records of the kings of Persia and Media. 3 Mordecai[b] was second in rank only to King Xerxes himself. He was a great man in the empire and was honored by his fellow

[r] **9:24** *Greek* a Macedonian; *Hebrew* the descendant of Agog. [s] **9:24** *Greek* cast lots; *Hebrew* cast lots ("purim," they were called). [t] **9:24, 25** *Greek* day he would destroy them . . . that Mordecai would be hanged. But; *Hebrew* for destroying the Jews; he had planned to wipe them out. But Esther went to the king, and the king issued written orders with the result that. [u] **9:26–28** *Greek* Because of Mordecai's letter; *Hebrew* That is why the holidays are called Purim. Because of Mordecai's letter. [v] **9:26–28** *Greek* and never neglect them. (The holidays are called Purim because "purim" in their language is the word for "lots."): *These words are not in the Hebrew text.* [w] **9:29–30** *Greek* Aminadab; *Hebrew* Abihail. [x] **9:31** *Greek* They both . . . at all costs; *Hebrew* 30 The letter was addressed to all the Jews, and copies were sent to all the 127 provinces of the Persian Empire. It wished the Jews peace and security 31 and directed them and their descendants to observe the days of Purim at the proper time, just as they had adopted rules for the observance of fasts and times of mourning. This was commanded by both Mordecai and Queen Esther. [y] **9:31** at all costs; *Greek unclear.* [z] **10:1** *Greek* taxes; *Hebrew* forced labor. [a] **10:2** *Greek* His power and virtue . . . his empire; *Hebrew* All the great and wonderful things he did, as well as the whole story of how he promoted Mordecai to high office. [b] **10:3** *Greek* Mordecai; *Hebrew* Mordecai the Jew.

Jews. He was greatly loved, for he sought the welfare of his people.

Mordecai Remembers His Dream

F[c] Then Mordecai said, "God has caused all these things to happen! 2And I am reminded of the dream I had about all of this. Every detail of the dream has come true: 3the small spring that became a river, the dawn that turned into sunlight, and the abundance of water. The river is Esther, whom the king married and made his queen. 4The two dragons represent Haman and me. 5The nations are all those who have gathered together to destroy the Jews. 6My nation is Israel, which cried out to God for help and was saved. The Lord saved his people! He rescued us from all these evils and performed great miracles and wonders that have never happened among other nations. 7That is because God prepared one destiny for his own people and another for all other nations. 8Then came the day and the hour when these two destinies were to be decided; the time had come for God to make a decision about the nations. 9God remembered his chosen people and gave the verdict in their favor. 10So each year for all time to come God's people will gather together in his presence on the fourteenth and fifteenth of the month of Adar, and celebrate with joy and happiness."

Study it!

Dreams

In ancient times, dreams were believed to be messages from God. Here are some other interesting dreams to check out:

- **Genesis 28:10–22 (Jacob)**
- **Genesis 37:1–11; 40:1—41:36 (Joseph)**
- **1 Samuel 3:1–10 (Samuel)**
- **1 Kings 3:5–15 (Solomon)**
- **Daniel 7:1–14 (Daniel)**
- **Matthew 1:18–25; 2:13–15 (Joseph)**

Does God speak to us in our dreams? It's possible. We believe God dwells inside us, in our hearts and minds. So when our brains are resting (sleeping), what a great time for God to get through to us!

— Esther F:1–10

Postscript

During the fourth year of the reign of Ptolemy and Cleopatra, a man named Dositheus, who claimed to be a levitical priest, brought the preceding letter about the Purim festival. He was accompanied by his son Ptolemy, and they declared that the letter was genuine and that it had been translated by Lysimachus, son of Ptolemy, a member of a Jerusalem family.

[c] **F:1** *Chapter F:1–10 corresponds to chapters 10:4—11:1 in a number of English translations.*

Your Next Step

Congratulations on finishing the Book of Esther! Use this space to write your thoughts and questions about this book. If you are following the suggested reading plan, move ahead to the Book of Daniel in the Old Testament. It is another book with stories about Jewish people living in foreign countries.

The First Book of the Maccabees

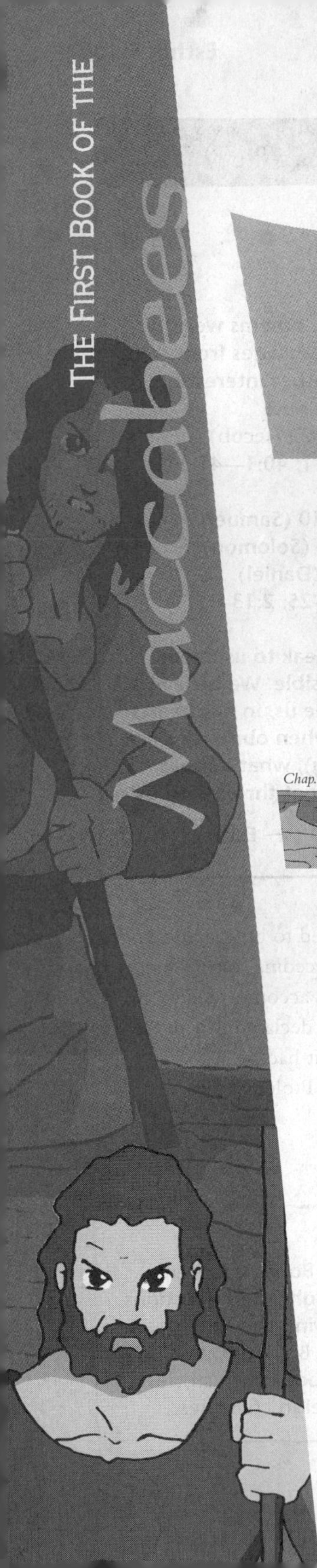

First they came in and took over our country. Then they threw out all the holy objects from our sacred Temple and brought in statues of their pagan gods. Then they wanted us to perform sacrifices to those pagan gods. *Enough!*

This is how the Jews felt when the Greek (Seleucid) rulers took over Palestine (Israel) 150 years before Jesus was born. The First Book of Maccabees has stories of evil rulers, rebellion, courage, and war as it tells the story of the Jewish resistance to the Greek rulers. It focuses on the family of Mattathias and is named for his sons—the Maccabees. Judas Maccabeus is the most famous Maccabee and the one who led much of the revolt against the Greeks.

Chap. 5:40–44

Headlines

- Judas Leads Victories for Israel (3:1–9)
- The Temple Is Purified (4:36–59)
- Judas Dead, Brother Takes Over (9:1–31)
- Traitors' Plans Fail (11:20–27)
- Jonathan Captured and Assumed Dead (12:39–53)
- Simon's Reign Brings Peace to Judea (14:4–15)
- Murderous Plot to Kill Simon Succeeds (16:11–17)

FACTOIDS

Who wrote this book? An unknown author wrote this book sometime after 100 BC.

Who are the central characters? Judas Maccabeus and his brothers, John, Simon, Eleazar, and Jonathan.

What time period does it cover? This book covers from 175 to 134 BC.

Why was it written? It was written to emphasize the kingly and priestly authority of the Maccabees and to help the Israelites see that God used the Maccabees to bring freedom to Israel.

Important themes

- God is absolutely reliable through all generations.
- God, not bloodlines, chooses who will serve and save his people.

1 MACCABEES

Alexander the Great

1 This history begins when Alexander the Great, son of Philip of Macedonia, marched from Macedonia and attacked Darius, king of Persia and Media. Alexander enlarged the Greek Empire by defeating Darius and seizing his throne. 2 He fought many battles, captured fortified cities, and put the kings of the region to death. 3 As he advanced to the ends of the earth, he plundered many nations; and when he had conquered the world, he became proud and arrogant. 4 By building up a strong army, he dominated whole nations and their rulers, and forced everyone to pay him taxes.

5-7 When Alexander had been emperor for twelve years, he fell ill and realized that he was about to die. He called together his generals, noblemen who had been brought up with him since his early childhood, and he divided his empire, giving a part to each of them. 8 After his death, the generals took control, 9 and each had himself crowned king of his own territory. The descendants of these kings ruled for many generations and brought a great deal of misery on the world.

Antiochus Epiphanes and the Renegade Jews
(2 Maccabees 4:7–17)

10 The wicked ruler Antiochus Epiphanes, son of King Antiochus the Third of Syria, was a descendant of one of Alexander's generals. Antiochus Epiphanes had been a hostage in Rome before he became king of Syria in the year 137.[a]

11 At that time there appeared in the land of Israel a group of traitorous Jews who had no regard for the Law and who had a bad influence on many of our people. They said, "Let's come to terms with the Gentiles, for our refusal to associate with them has brought us nothing but trouble." 12 This proposal appealed to many people, 13 and some of them became so enthusiastic about it that they went to the king and received from him permission to follow Gentile customs. 14 They built in Jerusalem a stadium like those in the Greek cities. 15 They had surgery performed to hide their circumcision, abandoned the holy covenant, started associating with[b] Gentiles, and did all sorts of other evil things.

Antiochus Attacks Egypt

16 When Antiochus had firmly established himself as king, he decided to conquer Egypt and rule that country as well as Syria. 17 He invaded Egypt with a large fleet of ships and a powerful army, including chariots, elephants, and cavalry. 18 When the attack came, King Ptolemy of Egypt turned and fled, and many of his soldiers were killed. 19 Antiochus was able to capture the fortified cities of Egypt and plunder the whole land.

Antiochus Persecutes the Jews

20 In the year 143,[c] after the conquest of Egypt, Antiochus marched with a great army against the land of Israel and the city of Jerusalem. 21 In his arrogance, he entered the Temple and took away the gold altar, the lampstand with all its equipment, 22 the table for the bread offered to the Lord, the cups and bowls, the gold fire pans, the curtain, and the crowns. He also stripped all the gold from the front of the Temple 23 and carried off the silver and gold and everything else of value, including all the treasures that he could find stored there. 24 Then he took it all to his own country. He had also murdered many people and boasted arrogantly about it. 25 There was great mourning everywhere in the land of Israel.

[a] **1:10** THE YEAR 137: *The dates in this book are counted from the beginning of the Syrian Kingdom in 312 B.C. The year 137 corresponds to 175 B.C.* [b] **1:15** started associating with; *or* married. [c] **1:20** THE YEAR 143: *This corresponds to 169 B.C.*

1:10 2 Macc 4:7 **1:15** 1 Cor 7:18

Then he took it all to his own country. (1:24)

26 Rulers and leaders groaned in sorrow.
Young men and young women grew weak.
The beauty of our women faded.
27 Every bridegroom sang a funeral song,
and every bride sat mourning in her room.
28 All our people were clothed with shame,
and our land trembled for them.

29 Two years later Antiochus sent a large
army from Mysia[d] against the towns of
Judea. When the soldiers entered Jerusalem,
30 their commander spoke to the people,
offering them terms of peace and completely
deceiving them. Then he suddenly launched
a fierce attack on the city, dealing it a major
blow and killing many of the people. 31 He
plundered the city, set it on fire, and tore
down its buildings and walls. 32 He and his
army took the women and children as pris-
oners and seized the cattle.

33 Then Antiochus and his forces built high
walls and strong towers in the area north of
the Temple, turning it into a fort. 34 They
brought in a group of traitorous Jews and
installed them there. 35 They also brought in
arms and supplies and stored in the fort all
the loot that they had taken in Jerusalem.
This fort became a great threat to the city.

36 The fort was a threat to the Temple,
a constant, evil menace for Israel.
37 Innocent people were murdered around
the altar;
the Holy Place was defiled by murderers.
38 The people of Jerusalem fled in fear,
and the city became a colony of foreigners.
Jerusalem was foreign to its own people,
who had been forced to abandon the city.
39 Her Temple was as empty as a wilderness;
her festivals were turned into days of
mourning,
her Sabbath joy into shame.
Her honor became an object of ridicule.
40 Her shame was as great as her former
glory,
and her pride was turned into deepest
mourning.

41-43 Antiochus now issued a decree that
all nations in his empire should abandon
their own customs and become one people.
All the Gentiles and even many of the
Israelites submitted to this decree. They
adopted the official pagan religion, offered
sacrifices to idols, and no longer observed
the Sabbath.

44 The king also sent messengers with a
decree to Jerusalem and all the towns of
Judea, ordering the people to follow customs
that were foreign to the country. 45 He
ordered them not to offer burnt offerings,
grain offerings, or wine offerings in the
Temple, and commanded them to treat Sab-
baths and festivals as ordinary work days.
46 They were even ordered to defile the Tem-
ple and the holy things in it.[e] 47 They were
commanded to build pagan altars, temples,
and shrines, and to sacrifice pigs and other
unclean animals there. 48 They were forbid-
den to circumcise their sons and were
required to make themselves ritually unclean
in every way they could, 49 so that they
would forget the Law which the Lord had
given through Moses and would disobey all
its commands. 50 The penalty for disobeying
the king's decree was death.

51 The king not only issued the same
decree throughout his whole empire, but he
also appointed officials to supervise the peo-
ple and commanded each town in Judea to
offer pagan sacrifices. 52 Many of the Jews
were ready to forsake the Law and to obey
these officials. They defiled the land with
their evil, 53 and their conduct forced all true
Israelites to hide wherever they could.

54 On the fifteenth day of the month of

[d] **1:29** *Probable text* a large army from Mysia; *Greek* a tax collector with a large army. [e] **1:46** the holy things in it; *or* the priests.

1:54 Dan 9:27; 11:31; 12:11; 1 Macc 6:7; Mt 24:15; Mk 13:14

Study it!

Where Are the Maccabees?

"Wow, I read this great story—actually it was two whole books—in my Bible last night. There were tons of battles and other military stuff. It was so good I stayed up late." Mike was enthusiastic as he talked to his friend, Pat. "Pat, have you read 1 Maccabees yet?"

"Where are the Maccabees?" Pat answered.

"In the Bible, the Maccabees, you know," Mike said.

"I've never heard of them, but I'll look tonight."

The next day they had a big discussion about the Book of Maccabees. Pat couldn't find it in his Bible, and his mom said their Bibles don't include it. Mike couldn't believe it because all the Bibles at his house had it.

They decided to ask around. Pat asked his youth pastor, and Mike asked his youth minister. Both explained to the boys how this happened and why each faith preferred to include or not include these books. Some Protestant Bibles don't have 1 and 2 Maccabees (or Tobit, Judith, Wisdom, Sirach, Baruch, and parts of Esther and Daniel). These Old Testament books were not originally written in Hebrew and have been rejected by some Christians. Other Christians, including Catholics, believe that these books—originally written in Greek—are also inspired books and include them in their Bibles.

Pat and Mike decided that they wouldn't argue over whose Bible was right. There are too many other things they agree on.

Kislev in the year 145,[f] King Antiochus set
up "The Awful Horror" on the altar of the
Temple, and pagan altars were built in the
towns throughout Judea. 55 Pagan sacrifices
were offered in front of houses and in the
streets. 56 Any books of the Law which were
found were torn up and burned, 57 and any-
one who was caught with a copy of the
sacred books or who obeyed the Law was
put to death by order of the king. 58 Month
after month these wicked people used their
power against the Israelites caught in the
towns.
59 On the twenty-fifth of the month, these
same evil people offered sacrifices on the pagan
altar erected on top of the altar in the Temple.
60 Mothers who had allowed their babies to be
circumcised were put to death in accordance
with the king's decree. 61 Their babies were
hung around their necks, and their families and
those who had circumcised them were put to
death. 62 But many people in Israel firmly re-
sisted the king's decree and refused to eat food
that was ritually unclean. 63 They preferred to
die rather than break the holy covenant and eat
unclean food—and many did die. 64 In his
anger God made Israel suffer terribly.

The Faithfulness of Mattathias

2 During that time, a priest of the Jehoiarib
family named Mattathias, who was the
son of John and the grandson of Simeon,
moved from Jerusalem and settled in Modein.
2 Mattathias had five sons: John (also called
Gaddi), 3 Simon (also called Thassi), 4 Judas (also
called Maccabeus), 5 Eleazar (also called
Avaran), and Jonathan (also called Apphus).
6 When Mattathias saw all the sins that
were being committed in Judea and
Jerusalem, 7 he said:

"Why was I born to see these terrible
things,
the ruin of my people and of the holy
city?
Must I sit here helpless
while the city is surrendered to enemies
and the Temple falls into the hands of
foreigners?

[f] **1:54** THE YEAR 145: *This corresponds to 167 B.C.*
1:60 2 Macc 6:10

8 The Temple is like someone without
honor.
9 Its splendid furnishings
have been carried away as loot.
Our children have been killed in the
streets,
and our young men by the sword of
the enemy.
10 Every nation in the world has occupied
the city
and robbed her of her possessions.
11 All her ornaments have been stripped
away;
she is now a slave, no longer free.
12 Look at our Temple, profaned by the
Gentiles,
emptied of all its splendor.
13 Why should we go on living?"

14 In their grief, Mattathias and his sons
tore their clothes, put on sackcloth, and con-
tinued in deep mourning.

15 Then the king's officials, who were forc-
ing the people to turn from God, came to
the town of Modein to force the people
there to offer pagan sacrifices. 16 Many of the
Israelites came to meet them, including Mat-
tathias and his sons. 17 The king's officials said
to Mattathias, "You are a respected leader in
this town, and you have the support of your
sons and relatives. 18 Why not be the first one
here to do what the king has commanded?
All the Gentiles, the people of Judea, and all
the people left in Jerusalem have already
done so. If you do, you and your sons will be
honored with the title of 'Friends of the
King,' and you will be rewarded with silver
and gold and many gifts."

19 Mattathias answered in a loud voice, "I
don't care if every Gentile in this empire has
obeyed the king and yielded to the com-
mand to abandon the religion of his ances-
tors. 20 My children, my relatives, and I will
continue to keep the covenant that God
made with our ancestors. 21 With God's help
we will never abandon his Law or disobey
his commands. 22 We will not obey the king's
decree, and we will not change our way of
worship in the least."

23 Just as he finished speaking, one of the
men from Modein decided to obey the king's

"We will not obey the king's decree." (2:22)

decree and stepped out in front of everyone
to offer a pagan sacrifice on the altar that
stood there. 24 When Mattathias saw him, he
became angry enough to do what had to be
done. Shaking with rage, he ran forward and
killed the man right there on the altar. 25 He
also killed the royal official who was forcing
the people to sacrifice, and then he tore down
the altar. 26 In this way Mattathias showed his
deep devotion for the Law, just as Phinehas
had done when he killed Zimri son of Salu.

The Guerrilla Warfare of Mattathias

27 Then Mattathias went through the town
shouting, "Everyone who is faithful to God's
covenant and obeys his Law, follow me!"
28 With this, he and his sons fled to the
mountains, leaving behind all they owned.

29-30 At that time also many of the
Israelites who were seeking to be right with
God through obedience to the Law went
out to live in the wilderness, taking their
children, their wives, and their livestock with
them, because of the terrible oppression they
were suffering. 31 The report soon reached
the king's officials and the soldiers in the fort
at Jerusalem that some men who had defied
the king's command had gone into hiding in
the wilderness. 32 A large force of soldiers
pursued them, caught up with them, set up
camp opposite them, and prepared to attack
them on the Sabbath. 33 "There is still time,"
they shouted out to the Jews. "Come out
and obey the king's command, and we will
spare your lives."

2:26 Num 25:6–15 **2:32** 2 Macc 6:11

34“We will not come out,” they answered.
“We will not obey the king’s command, and
we will not profane the Sabbath.”
35The soldiers attacked them immediately,
36but the Jews did nothing to resist; they did
not even throw stones or block the entrances
to the caves where they were hiding. 37They
said, “We will all die with a clear conscience.
Let heaven and earth bear witness that you
are slaughtering us unjustly.” 38So the enemy
attacked them on the Sabbath and killed the
men, their wives, their children, and their
livestock. A thousand people died.
39When Mattathias and his friends heard
the news about this, they were greatly sad-
dened 40and said to one another, “If all of us
do as these other Jews have done and refuse
to fight the Gentiles to defend our lives and
our religion, we will soon be wiped off the
face of the earth.” 41On that day they decid-
ed that if anyone attacked them on the Sab-
bath, they would defend themselves, so that
they would not all die as other Jews had died
in the caves.
42Then Mattathias and his friends were
joined by a group of devout and patriotic
Jews, the strongest and bravest men in Israel,
who had all volunteered to defend the Law.
43In addition, everyone who was fleeing
from the persecution joined them and
strengthened their forces. 44Now that they
had an army, they gave vent to their anger by
attacking the renegade Jews. Those who
escaped were forced to flee to the Gentiles
for safety. 45Mattathias and his friends went
everywhere tearing down pagan altars 46and
circumcising by force every uncircumcised
boy they found within the borders of Israel.
47They were also successful in hunting down
the arrogant Gentile officials. 48They rescued
the Law of Moses from the Gentiles and
their kings and broke the power of the
wicked King Antiochus.

The Death of Mattathias

49When the time came for Mattathias to
die, he said to his sons, “These are times of
violence and distress. Arrogant people are in
control and have made us an object of
ridicule. 50But you, my sons, must be devoted
to the Law and ready to die to defend God’s
covenant with our ancestors. 51Remember
what our ancestors did and how much they
accomplished in their day. Follow their exam-
ple, and you will be rewarded with great glory
and undying fame. 52Remember how Abra-
ham put his trust in the Lord when he was
tested and how the Lord was pleased with him
and accepted him. 53Joseph, in his time of
trouble, obeyed God’s commands and became
ruler over the land of Egypt. 54Phinehas, our
ancestor, because of his burning devotion, was
given the promise that his descendants would
always be priests. 55Joshua was made a judge in
Israel because he obeyed the command of
Moses. 56Caleb brought back a good report to
the community and was given a part of the
land as a reward. 57David was made king and
was given the promise that his descendants
would always be kings because of his steadfast
loyalty to God. 58Elijah, because of his great
devotion to the Law, was taken up into heav-
en. 59Hananiah, Azariah, and Mishael were
saved from the flames because they had faith.
60Daniel was a man of integrity, and the Lord
rescued him from the mouth of the lions.
61Take each of these ancestors of ours as an
example, and you will realize that no one who
puts his trust in the Lord will ever lack
strength. 62Don’t be afraid of the threats of a
wicked man. Remember that he will die and
all his splendor will end with worms feeding
on his decaying body. 63Today he may be
highly honored, but tomorrow he will disap-
pear; his body will return to the earth and his
scheming will come to an end. 64But you, my
sons, be strong and courageous in defending
the Law, because it is through the Law that
you will earn great glory.
65“Your brother Simon is wise, so always
listen to him as you would to me. 66Judas
Maccabeus has been strong all his life; he
will be your commander and will lead you
in battle against the enemy. 67Call everyone
who obeys God’s Law to rally around you;
then avenge the wrongs done to your peo-
ple. 68Pay back the Gentiles for what they
have done, and always obey the Law and its
commands.”

2:52 Gen 15:6; 22:15–18 **2:53** Gen 39:1—45:28 **2:55, 56** Num 13:1—14:12 **2:57** 2 Sam 7:16
2:58 2 Kings 2:9–12 **2:59** Dan 3:8–30 **2:60** Dan 6:1–24; Dan C:31–42

69 Then Mattathias gave them his blessing
and died. 70 He was buried in the family
tomb at Modein, and all the people of Israel
went into deep mourning for him. This hap-
pened in the year 146.[g]

The Early Victories of Judas

(2 Maccabees 8:1–7)

3 Judas Maccabeus took the place of his
father Mattathias. 2 All his brothers and
all the loyal followers of his father gave him
their support, and they were happy to carry
on Israel's war.

3 Judas brought greater glory to his people.
In his armor, he was like a giant.
He took up his weapons and went to
war;
with his own sword he defended his
camp.
4 He was like a ferocious lion roaring as it
attacks.
5 Judas hunted down those who broke the
Law
and set fire to all who oppressed his
people.
6 In fear of him, lawless men huddled
together in terror,
not knowing which way to turn.
He advanced the cause of freedom by
what he did.
7 He made life miserable for many kings,
but brought joy to the people of Israel.
We will praise him forever for what he
did.
8 He went through the towns of Judea
and destroyed all the godless men.
He relieved Israel of its terrible suffering.[h]
9 His fame spread to the ends of the earth,
as he gathered together those who
were threatened with death.

10 Then Apollonius assembled a Gentile
army, including a large force from Samaria,
to attack the people of Israel. 11 When Judas
learned of this, he marched out to battle,
defeated the army, and killed Apollonius.
Many Gentiles lost their lives, and the rest
fled. 12 When the spoils of war were collect-
ed, Judas took the sword of Apollonius and
used it in battle until the day he died.

13 Seron, the general of the Syrian forces,
learned that Judas had gathered together an
army, consisting of a band of loyal men who
were ready to fight under his command.
14 Seron said to himself, "I will make a repu-
tation for myself throughout the empire by
defeating Judas and his men, who have no
respect for the king's command." 15 Then he
began a new campaign against Judas and was
joined by a strong force of godless men who
were eager to help him take vengeance on
Israel. 16 When he approached the pass at
Beth Horon, Judas went out to meet him
with a small group of men. 17 When Judas'
men saw the army coming against them,
they asked, "How can our little group of
men fight an army as big as that? Besides, we
have not eaten all day, and we are tired!"

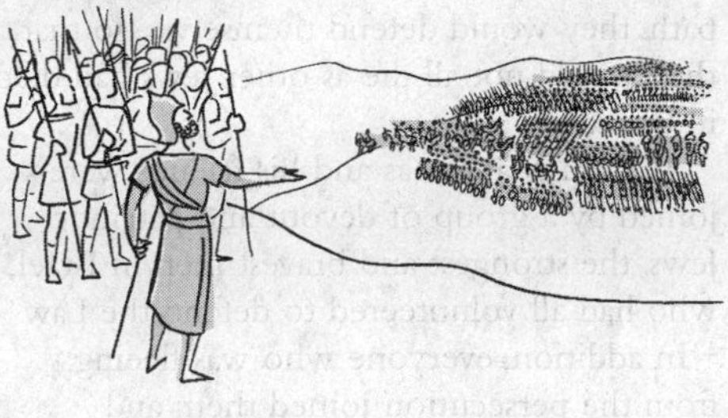

"It is the Lord's power that determines the outcome."
(3:19)

18 "It is not difficult," Judas answered, "for
a small group to overpower a large one. It
makes no difference to the Lord whether we
are rescued by many people or by just a few.
19 Victory in battle does not depend on who
has the largest army; it is the Lord's power
that determines the outcome. 20 Our enemies
are coming against us with great violence,
intending to plunder our possessions and kill
our wives and children. 21 But we are fight-
ing for our lives and for our religion.
22 When we attack, the Lord will crush our
enemies, so don't be afraid of them."

23 As soon as Judas had finished speaking,
he and his men made a sudden attack against
Seron and his army and crushed them.
24 They pursued them down the pass at Beth

[g] **2:70** THE YEAR 146: *This corresponds to 166 B.C.* [h] **3:8** relieved Israel of its terrible suffering; *or* saved Israel from God's anger.

Horon to the plain and killed about 800
men. Those who escaped fled to Philistia.
25After that, Gentiles everywhere began to
be afraid of Judas and his brothers. 26His
fame reached the ears of King Antiochus,
and people in every nation talked about
Judas and his victories.

The King Appoints Lysias as Governor

27When Antiochus heard what had hap-
pened, he was furious. He ordered all the
armies of his empire to assemble in one huge
force. 28From his treasury he paid a full year's
wages to his soldiers and ordered them to be
prepared for any emergency. 29But then he
found that the funds in his treasury were
exhausted. Income from taxes had decreased
because of the disorder and the troubles he
had brought on the world by doing away
with the laws which had been in force from
the earliest times. 30Antiochus had always
given presents more lavishly than earlier
kings, but now he was worried that he might
not be able to continue this, or even to meet
expenses—this had happened once or twice
before. 31He was very disturbed; but finally
he decided to go to Persia, collect the taxes
from the provinces there, and bring together
a large sum of ready cash.

32He appointed Lysias, an important man
who had been granted the title "Relative of
the King," as governor to take care of the
king's affairs in the whole territory between
the Euphrates River and the Egyptian bor-
der. 33The king also made Lysias the
guardian of his son Antiochus the Fifth until
his own return. 34He put Lysias in charge of
all the elephants and of half his army, and
then gave him detailed instructions about
what he wanted done, and in particular,
what he wanted done with the inhabitants
of Judea and Jerusalem. 35Lysias was ordered
to send an army against the Jews, especially
the Jews in Jerusalem, to break their power
and destroy them, so that no trace of them
would remain. 36He was ordered to take
their land and give it to foreigners, who
would settle the whole area. 37Taking the
other half of his army, the king set out from
Antioch, his capital city, in the year 147.[i] He
crossed the Euphrates River and marched
through Mesopotamia.

The Victories of Judas

(2 Maccabees 8:8–29, 34–36)

38Lysias chose Nicanor, Gorgias, and Ptole-
my son of Dorymenes as army commanders;
all three were able men who bore the title
"Friend of the King." 39He put them in
charge of 40,000 infantry and 7,000 cavalry
and ordered them to invade the land of Judea
and destroy it as the king had commanded.
40These commanders set out with their entire
force, and when they came to the plains near
Emmaus, they made camp. 41A force from
Idumea[j] and Philistia joined them. The mer-
chants of the region heard about the strength
of the army, and they came to the camp with
chains and a large amount of money, hoping
to buy some Jewish slaves.

42Judas and his brothers saw that their sit-
uation was getting more and more difficult,
with foreign armies camped within their
own borders. They also learned that the king
had commanded the complete destruction of
the people. 43So they determined to rebuild
their ruined nation and fight for their coun
try and the Temple. 44Then the whole com-
munity came together to prepare for war
and to pray for God's mercy.

45Jerusalem was as empty as a wilderness;
no citizens left or entered the city.
The holy Temple was profaned by
foreigners,
and Gentiles camped in the city's fort;
so joy departed from the people of Israel,
and the sound of music was heard no
more.

46Then Judas and his men assembled and
marched to Mizpah, opposite Jerusalem,
because the people of Israel had previously
had a place of worship there. 47In deep
mourning, they fasted all that day, put on
sackcloth, threw ashes on their heads, and
tore their clothes. 48The Gentiles would
have consulted their idols in such a situation,
but the Israelites unrolled the book of the
Law to search for God's guidance. 49They

[i] **3:37** THE YEAR 147: *This corresponds to 165 B.C.* [j] **3:41** *Probable text* Idumea; *Greek* Syria.

brought the priests' robes, the offerings of
the first grain, and the tithes, and then they
brought in some Nazirites who had com-
pleted their vows. 50 The whole community
prayed, "Lord, what shall we do with these
things? Where shall we take them, 51 now
that your holy Temple has been trampled
and profaned by Gentiles, and your priests
mourn in disgrace? 52 The Gentiles have
come to attack and destroy us. You know
what they plan to do! 53 If you don't help us,
how can we stand up against them?" 54 Then
they blew trumpets and shouted loudly.
55 After that, Judas divided his men into
groups of ten, fifty, a hundred, and a thou-
sand, placing officers in charge of each
group. 56 Then, in obedience to the Law, he
sent home everyone who had recently been
married, built a house, or planted a vineyard,
as well as anyone who was afraid. 57 Finally,
the army marched out and took up positions
south of Emmaus, 58 where Judas said to
them: "Prepare yourselves for battle and be
courageous! Be ready early tomorrow morn-
ing to fight these Gentiles who have joined
forces to attack us and destroy us and our
Temple. 59 It is better for us to die fighting
than to stand idly by and watch the destruc-
tion of our nation and our Temple. 60 But the
Lord will do what he pleases."

4 Gorgias took 5,000 infantry and 1,000
of his most experienced cavalry and left
camp by night, 2 with men from the fort in
Jerusalem as his guides. He had planned to
make a surprise attack on the Jewish army,
3 but Judas learned of the plan and moved
out with his men to attack the king's army at
Emmaus 4 while Gorgias and his troops were
still away from the camp. 5 When Gorgias
and his army reached Judas' camp that night,
they found no one there. They thought Judas
and his men were trying to escape, so they
started looking for them in the mountains.
6 At dawn Judas appeared in the plain with
3,000 men, not all of them as well armed as
they would have liked. 7 They saw the huge
Gentile army of experienced troops wearing
armor and protected by cavalry. 8 But Judas
said to his men, "Don't worry about the size
of their army, and don't be frightened when
they attack. 9 Remember how our ancestors
were saved at the Red Sea when the king of
Egypt was pursuing them with his army!
10 Now let us ask the Lord to have mercy on
us. Let us pray that he will honor his
covenant with our ancestors and crush this
army when we attack today. 11 Then all the
Gentiles will know that Israel has a God
who rescues and saves them."
12 When the Gentiles saw Judas and his
men preparing for battle, 13 they moved out
of their camp to fight. Then Judas and his
men sounded their trumpets 14 and attacked.
The Gentiles broke ranks and fled to the
plain, 15 but all the stragglers were killed. The
Israelites pursued the enemy as far as Gezer,
the plains of Idumea, and the towns of Azo-
tus and Jamnia. Altogether they killed about
3,000 of the enemy.
16 When Judas and his army came back
from the pursuit, 17-18 he said to his men,
"Don't be greedy for loot. Gorgias and his
army are nearby in the mountains, so there is
still heavy fighting ahead of us. We must
stand firm and fight. After that, you can safe-
ly take all the loot you want." 19 Judas was
just finishing his speech when an enemy
patrol on a scouting mission looked down
from the mountains 20 and saw that their
army had been put to flight; they could tell
from the smoke that their camp was burn-
ing. 21 When they saw all this, they were ter-
rified, and when they also saw that Judas'
army was in the plain ready for battle, 22 they
all fled to Philistia. 23 Then Judas returned to
loot the enemy camp; he took large amounts
of gold and silver, blue and purple cloth, and
other rich plunder. 24 When the Jews came
back to their own camp, they sang a hymn:
"The Lord is worthy of praise; his mercy
endures forever." 25 That day brought a great
victory to the people of Israel.

Victory over Lysias
(2 Maccabees 11:1–12)

26 The Gentile troops that escaped went to
Lysias and reported all that had happened.
27 When Lysias heard that his troops had lost
the battle, he was shocked and disappointed

3:56 Deut 20:5–8; Judg 7:3

that Israel had not been defeated as the king
had commanded.
28 In the following year Lysias gathered an
army of 60,000 well-trained infantry and
5,000 cavalry, intending to conquer the Jews.
29 They marched into Idumea and camped at
Bethzur. Judas came to meet them with
10,000 men. 30 When Judas saw how strong
the enemy's army was, he prayed, "We will
praise you, Savior of Israel. You broke the
attack of the giant by the hand of your ser-
vant David and you let Saul's son Jonathan
and the young man who carried his
weapons defeat the entire Philistine army.
31 Now in the same way let your people
Israel defeat our enemy. Put them to shame,
in spite of all their confidence in their
infantry and cavalry. 32 Make them afraid; let
their bold strength melt away; let them trem-
ble at the prospect of defeat. 33 We love and
worship you; so let us kill our enemies, that
we may then sing your praises."
34 The battle began, and in the hand-to-
hand fighting about 5,000 of Lysias' men
were killed. 35 When Lysias saw that his army
was being defeated and when he saw the
reckless courage of Judas and his men, who
showed that they were ready to live or die
with honor, he returned to Antioch. There he
recruited some mercenaries and planned to
return to Judea later with a much larger army.

The Purification of the Temple
(2 Maccabees 10:1–8)

36 Judas and his brothers said, "Now that
our enemies have been defeated, let's go to
Jerusalem to purify the Temple and rededi-
cate it." 37 So the whole army was assembled
and went up to Mount Zion. 38 There they
found the Temple abandoned, the altar pro-
faned, the gates burned down, the courtyards
grown up in a forest of weeds, and the
priests' rooms torn down. 39 In their sorrow,
they tore their clothes, cried loudly, threw
ashes on their heads, 40 and fell face down on
the ground. When the signal was given on
the trumpets, everyone cried out to the
Lord.
41 Then Judas ordered some of his soldiers
to attack the men in the fort, while he puri-
fied the Temple. 42 He chose some priests
who were qualified and who were devoted
to the Law. 43 They purified the Temple and
took the stones that had been defiled and
put them in an unclean place. 44 They dis-
cussed what should be done with the altar of
burnt offerings, which had been desecrated
45 by the Gentiles, and decided to tear it
down, so that it would not stand there as a
monument to their shame. So they tore
down the altar 46 and put the stones in a suit-
able place on the Temple hill, where they
were to be kept until a prophet should
appear and decide what to do with them.
47 Then they took uncut stones, as the Law
of Moses required, and built a new altar like
the old one. 48 They repaired the Temple,
inside and out, and dedicated its courtyards.
49 They made new utensils for worship and
brought the lampstand, the altar of incense,
and the table for the bread into the Temple.
50 They burned incense on the altar and lit
the lamps on the lampstand, and there was
light in the Temple! 51 They placed the loaves
of bread on the table, hung the curtains, and
completed all the work.
52-54 The twenty-fifth day of the ninth
month, the month of Kislev, in the year 148[k]
was the anniversary of the day the Gentiles
had desecrated the altar. On that day a sacri-
fice was offered on the new altar in accor-
dance with the Law of Moses. The new altar
was dedicated and hymns were sung to the
accompaniment of harps, lutes, and cymbals.
55 All the people bowed down with their
faces to the ground and worshiped and
praised the Lord for giving them victory.
56 For eight days they celebrated the
rededication of the altar. With great joy they
brought burnt offerings and offered fellow-
ship offerings and thank offerings. 57 They
decorated the front of the Temple with gold
crowns and shields, rebuilt the gates and the
priests' rooms and put doors on them.
58 Now that the Jews had removed the shame
which the Gentiles had brought, they held a
great celebration. 59 Then Judas, his brothers,

[k] **4:52–54** THE YEAR 148: *This corresponds to 164 B.C.*

4:30 1 Sam 17:41–54; 14:1–23 **4:47** Ex 20:25; Deut 27:5, 6 **4:52–54** 1 Macc 1:54

and the entire community of Israel decreed
that the rededication of the altar should be
celebrated with a festival of joy and gladness
at the same time each year, beginning on the
twenty-fifth of the month of Kislev and last-
ing for eight days.
60 Then they built high walls and strong
towers around Mount Zion, so that the
Gentiles could not come in and trample and
defile it again. 61 Judas placed a detachment
of soldiers there to guard the Temple. He
also fortified the town of Bethzur, so that the
people of Israel would have a fortress facing
Idumea.

Wars with Neighboring Nations
(2 Maccabees 10:14–33; 12:10–45)

5 When the neighboring nations heard
that the Jews had built the altar and
restored the Temple as it had been before,
they were so furious 2 that they made up
their minds to destroy all the Jews who were
living among them. So they began to murder
and kill our people.
3 The Idumeans were blockading the
Israelites, so Judas went to war against them
at Akrabattene, crushed them, and looted
them. 4 He also dealt with the people of
Baean, who were a constant threat to the
people of Israel, because they would lie in
ambush waiting to trap Israelite travelers.
5 He shut the Baeanites up in their forts,
took a solemn oath that he would destroy
them, and burned their forts with everyone
in them. 6 Then he marched against the land
of Ammon, where he met a large and pow-
erful army under the command of a man
named Timothy. 7 Judas won many battles
against them and finally defeated them. 8 He
captured Jazer and its surrounding villages
and then returned to Judea.
9 The Gentiles in Gilead assembled to
attack and destroy the Israelites living in
their territory. But the Israelites fled to the
fortress of Dathema 10-11 and sent the follow-
ing letter to Judas and his brothers: "The
Gentiles around us are joining forces under
Timothy. We have fled to this fortress for
protection, and now they are getting ready
to capture it and destroy us. 12 Many of us
have already been killed. Come rescue us!
13 All the Jewish men in the region of Tob[l]
have been killed, their wives and their chil-
dren have been taken captive, and their pos-
sessions have been carried off. A force of
about 1,000 men has been destroyed there."
14 This letter was still being read when
other messengers, who had torn their clothes
in sorrow, arrived with a report from Galilee.
15 They said, "An army from Ptolemais, Tyre,
Sidon, and all of Galilee has come together
to destroy us."
16 When Judas and the people heard all
this, a great assembly was held to decide
what should be done to help these country-
men, who were in such difficulty under
enemy attack. 17 Judas said to his brother
Simon, "Choose some men and go rescue
our fellow Jews in Galilee; our brother
Jonathan and I will go to Gilead." 18 Judas left
the rest of his army to defend Judea and put
the two leaders, Azariah and Joseph son of
Zechariah, in charge of the people. 19 He
told them: "I am leaving you in command
here, but don't go out and fight the Gentiles
until we get back." 20 Then 3,000 men
joined Simon for the march into Galilee, and
8,000 remained with Judas for the march
into Gilead.
21 Simon went into Galilee and fought
many battles with the Gentiles. He defeated
them 22 and pursued them all the way to the
city of Ptolemais, killing about 3,000 of
them, and taking the loot. 23 Then he took
the Jews who were in Galilee and Arbatta,
with their wives, their children, and all they
owned, and brought them back to Judea
with him. There was great rejoicing.
24 During this time, Judas Maccabeus and
his brother Jonathan had crossed the Jordan
River and had marched for three days
through the desert. 25 They met some friend-
ly Nabateans who told them all that had
happened to the Jews in Gilead. 26 They
reported that many Jews were imprisoned in
the fortified cities of Bozrah, Bosor, Alema,
Chaspho, Maked, and Karnaim, 27 while oth-
ers were imprisoned in the smaller towns of
Gilead. They also reported that the enemy

[l] **5:13** in the region of Tob; *or* who were fighting with Tobias.

was drawn up to make an attack the next day on the Jewish fortresses, hoping to destroy all the Jews in a single day.

28 So Judas and his army suddenly turned and attacked Bozrah by the desert road, captured the town, and killed every man in it. They looted the town and set it on fire. 29 They left there and marched all night to the fortress at Dathema. 30 At dawn Judas and his men saw a vast army attacking the fortress; they were bringing up ladders, siege platforms, and battering rams in an effort to capture it. 31 When Judas heard the noise, the shouts, and the sound of trumpets coming from the city, he realized that the battle had begun, 32 so he said to his men, "Fight today for our fellow Jews!"

Judas and his men saw a vast army attacking the fortress. (5:30)

33 He ordered his men to march in three columns and attack the enemy from the rear. As they moved forward, they blew trumpets and shouted prayers. 34 When the army under Timothy's command saw that it was Judas Maccabeus, the soldiers turned and fled. Judas crushed them and killed about 8,000 men that day.

35 Then Judas turned aside to attack the town of Alema;[m] he captured it and killed all the men in it. He looted the town and set fire to it. 36 From there he went on and captured Chaspho, Maked, Bosor, and the other towns of Gilead.

37 After this, Timothy gathered another army and camped opposite Raphon, on the other side of a river. 38 Judas sent some men to spy on the camp, and they reported back to him that all the Gentiles in the region had joined Timothy and had formed a large army. 39 Timothy had also hired Arab mercenaries to help him, and these were camped on the other side of the river ready to attack Judas. So Judas went out to meet them in battle.

40 As Judas and his army came closer to the water, Timothy said to his officers, "If he keeps on coming and crosses the river, we won't be able to turn back his attack, and he will defeat us. 41 But if he is afraid and stops on the other side of the river, we will cross over to attack and defeat him." 42 When Judas reached the bank of the river, he gave orders to his officers to let no one stop but to push everyone forward into battle. 43 Judas was the first to cross the river against the enemy, and all his men followed him. The Gentiles broke ranks before them, threw away their arms, and fled to the pagan temple at Karnaim. 44 But Judas and his men took the city and burned down the temple with all who were in it. With Karnaim overthrown, the Gentiles could no longer offer any resistance to Judas.

45 Then Judas gathered together all the Jews in Gilead to take them back to Judea with him. It was a large group of all kinds of people, together with their wives and children and all that they owned. 46 They went as far as Ephron, a large, well-fortified town. It was impossible to go around it on either side, and the road passed directly through the town. 47 But the people there would not let them pass and blocked the town gates with stones. 48 Then Judas sent a friendly message to them: "Let us pass through your territory to return home. No one will harm you; we will just pass through." But they still refused to open the gates.

49 So Judas told everyone in the group, except the fighting men, to camp where they were. 50 The fighting men were ordered to take up their positions and attack the town. They fought all day and all night, until they had taken it. 51 Judas had all the men of Ephron put to death, plundered the town, and leveled it. Then he and his army marched through the town over the dead bodies. 52 They crossed the Jordan into the wide plain opposite Beth Shan. 53 Throughout the whole march Judas kept gathering up the stragglers and encouraging the people until they reached the land of Judea. 54 With

[m] **5:35** ALEMA: *The name of the town is not certain.*

thanksgiving and rejoicing, they went up to
Mount Zion and sacrificed burnt offerings
because they had returned safely without a
single loss.
55 While Judas and Jonathan were in
Gilead and their brother Simon was attack-
ing Ptolemais in Galilee, 56 Joseph and Azari-
ah, the commanders of the army in Judea,
heard about their brave deeds and victories.
57 They said to one another, "Let's go to war
with the Gentiles around us and win some
fame for ourselves." 58 So they and their men
attacked Jamnia. 59 Gorgias and his men went
out of the town to meet them in battle.
60 They defeated Joseph and Azariah and
pursued them as far as the borders of Judea.
At least 2,000 Israelite men were killed that
day. 61 This great defeat came about because
the Jewish commanders wanted to be heroes
and refused to obey Judas and his brothers.
62 Besides, they did not belong to the family
of the Maccabees, whom God had chosen to
bring freedom to the people of Israel.
63 But Judas Maccabeus and his brothers
won great respect among all the Israelites
and all the Gentiles. When people heard of
their fame, 64 large crowds gathered to praise
them.
65 Then Judas and his brothers went to war
against the Edomites to the south. He
attacked Hebron and its surrounding towns,
destroyed its fortifications, and burned down
the towers around it. 66 Then he marched
into the land of the Philistines and passed
through Marisa.[n] 67 That day a number of
priests were killed in battle because they
wanted to be heroes and foolishly went out
to fight. 68 Judas turned aside to Azotus in
Philistia. He pulled down the altars, burned
the images of their gods, plundered their
towns, and then returned to Judea.

The Death of Antiochus the Fourth
(2 Maccabees 1:11–17; 9:1–29; 10:9–11)

6 As King Antiochus the Fourth was pass-
ing through Mesopotamia, he heard of a
city in Persia, named Elymais, which was
famous for its riches in silver and gold. 2 The
temple was very rich, containing gold
shields, armor, and weapons left there by
Alexander, son of King Philip of Macedonia,
who was the first to rule the Greek Empire.
3 Antiochus came and tried to take the city
and loot it, but he didn't succeed, because
the citizens had learned what he was plan-
ning to do, 4 and they drew up their troops
to resist him. In great frustration he with-
drew to return to Babylonia.
5 In Persia a messenger reached him with
the news that the armies he had sent into
Judea had been defeated. 6 Lysias and his
strong army had been forced to flee from the
Jews, who were now reinforced by the addi-
tional weapons, supplies, and loot they had
taken from the defeated armies. 7 The Jews
had pulled down the thing they called "The
Awful Horror" that Antiochus had built on
the altar in Jerusalem. They had also sur-
rounded the Temple with high walls, as it
had been before, and had taken and fortified
the town of Bethzur, one of the king's own
towns.
8 When the king heard this report, he was
so dumbfounded and terribly shaken that he
went to bed in a fit of deep depression
because things had not turned out as he had
hoped. 9 He remained ill for a long time, as
waves of despair swept over him, until he
finally realized that he was going to die.
10 He called together all those to whom he
had given the title "Friends of the King" and
said to them, "I cannot sleep, and my heart is
broken with grief and worry. 11 At first I
asked myself why these great waves of trou-
ble were sweeping over me, since I have
been kind and well-liked during my reign.

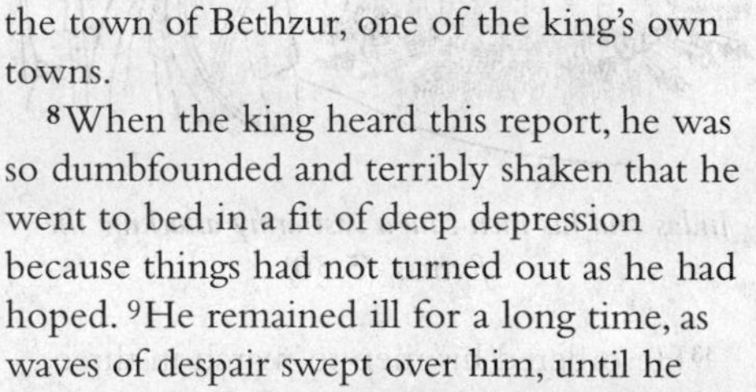

The king . . . went to bed in a fit of deep depression. (6:8)

[n] **5:66** *Some ancient translations* Marisa; *Greek* Samaria.
6:7 1 Macc 1:54

[12]But then I remembered the wrongs I did in Jerusalem when I took all the silver and gold objects from the Temple and tried without any good reason to destroy the inhabitants of Judea. [13]I know this is why all these terrible things have happened to me and I am about to die in deep despair here in this foreign land."

[14]Then he called Philip, one of his most trusted advisers, and put him in charge of his whole empire. [15]He gave him his crown, robe, and official ring, and authorized him to educate his son Antiochus the Fifth and bring him up to be king. [16]King Antiochus died there in the year 149.[o]

[17]When Lysias learned that the king had died, he made the young Antiochus king in place of his father. He had brought up Antiochus from childhood and now gave him the name Eupator.

The Campaign of Antiochus the Fifth and Lysias

(2 Maccabees 13:1–26; 11:22–26)

[18]Meanwhile, the enemies in the fort at Jerusalem had been blockading the people of Israel in the area around the Temple, constantly causing them trouble and giving support to the Gentiles. [19]So Judas decided to get rid of them and called all the people together to besiege the fort. [20]The people assembled and laid siege to the fort in the year 150.[p] They built siege platforms and battering rams.

[21]But some of the men under siege escaped, and together with some of the renegade Jews, they went to the king and said, [22]"How long are you going to wait before you take revenge for what was done to our countrymen? [23]We were willing to serve your father, follow his orders, and obey his decrees. [24]But what good did it do us? Now our own countrymen have become our enemies.[q] In fact, they have killed as many of us as they could find and have stolen our possessions. [25]But we are not the only ones they have harmed; they have attacked all their neighbors. [26]And now they have laid siege to the fort in Jerusalem and are planning to take it. They have also fortified the Temple and Bethzur. [27]Unless you act immediately, they will do even more, and you will not be able to stop them."

[28]When the king heard this, he was furious. He brought together all the army commanders, the cavalry officers, and his most trusted advisers. [29]He also hired mercenary soldiers from other countries and from the Greek islands. [30]His forces numbered 100,000 infantry, 20,000 cavalry, and 32 elephants trained for war. [31]The king and his army passed through Idumea and laid siege to Bethzur, where they fought for a long time. They built battering rams and siege platforms, but the defenders fought bravely and came out of the town and burned down the platforms.

[32]Then Judas withdrew his troops from the fort in Jerusalem and set up his camp at Beth Zechariah, blocking the advance of the king's army. [33]Early the next morning, the king rapidly moved his army along the road to Beth Zechariah, where his troops took up battle positions and blew trumpets. [34]They got the elephants ready for battle by showing them grape juice and mulberry juice. [35]The huge animals were distributed among the infantry units. A thousand men, protected by chain armor and bronze helmets, were stationed with each elephant. Each animal was also accompanied by a special force of 500 cavalry, [36]which always remained with the elephant. [37]A strong, protected wooden platform was securely fastened by a special harness to the back of each elephant. Three[r] soldiers rode on each animal, in addition to the elephant driver. [38]Lysias placed the rest of the cavalry on the two flanks of the army where they could be protected by the infantry while harassing the enemy. [39]The sunlight, reflected off the bronze and gold shields, shone on the mountains and flashed like burning torches. [40]Part of the king's army was spread out over the higher ground of the mountain slopes and part over the lower land, but they all moved forward steadily and in good order. [41]All the people were terrified when they heard the noise

[o] **6:16** THE YEAR 149: *This corresponds to 163 B.C.* [p] **6:20** THE YEAR 150: *This corresponds to 162 B.C.*
[q] **6:21** enemies; *some manuscripts add* and besieged the fort. [r] **6:37** *Probable text* Three; *Greek* Thirty *or* Thirty-two.

made by the clashing of weapons and the
marching of that great and powerful army.
42 Judas and his army advanced into battle,
and immediately killed 600 of the king's
army. 43 When Eleazar Avaran saw that one of
the elephants was larger than the others and
that it was covered with royal armor, he
thought that the king was riding on it.
44 Eleazar sacrificed his life to save his people
and to gain eternal fame. 45 He ran boldly
toward the elephant, which was in the middle
of a battalion of infantry. He rushed forward
killing men to the right and left, so that the
enemy soldiers fell back before him on both
sides. 46 He slipped in under the elephant and
stabbed it to death, and it fell on him and
killed him. 47 But when the Jews realized how
strong the royal army was and how deter-
mined it was to fight, they retreated.

48 The king and his army advanced to
fight the Jews at Jerusalem and laid siege to
the whole of Judea and Jerusalem. 49 He
made peace with the Jews of Bethzur, who
then left the town. There had not been
enough food in the town for them to with-
stand the siege because it was the sabbatical
year, when no crops were planted. 50 The
king occupied Bethzur and stationed a body
of troops there to guard it. 51 Then he sur-
rounded the Temple and besieged it for a
long time. He set up siege platforms, batter-
ing rams, catapults for throwing fire and
stones, and other weapons to throw spears
and rocks. 52 The defenders also made war
machines to oppose those of the enemy, and
so the battle went on for a long time. 53 But
there was no food left in the Temple storage
bins because it was the sabbatical year, and
the people who had fled from the Gentiles
and taken refuge in Judea had eaten all the
food that had been stored there. 54 The
shortage of food had been so severe that
many people had scattered to their homes,
and only a few men were left in the Temple.

55 Meanwhile, Philip, who had been
appointed by King Antiochus before his
death to educate his son to be king,
56 returned from Persia and Media. He had
come back with the royal army and planned
to take control of the government. When
Lysias heard this news, 57 he made rapid
preparations to depart. He said to the young
king, to his officers, and to his men, "We are
growing weaker each day; we are short of
provisions, and this place we are besieging is
strong. Besides, there are pressing govern-
ment affairs which need our attention. 58 So
now let's arrange a truce and make a peace
treaty with the Jews and their whole nation.
59 We will allow them to follow their own
laws and customs as they did before. All this
trouble started when we provoked them by
abolishing their laws and customs."

60 This recommendation was well received
by the king and the officers, so Lysias pro-
posed peace terms to the Jews, and they
accepted them. 61 When the king and his
officers solemnly agreed to abide by these
terms, the Jews came out of their fortress.
62 But when the king entered the Temple
area on Mount Zion and saw the strong for-
tifications, he broke his word and ordered
the walls surrounding the Temple to be torn
down. 63 Then he hurriedly left and returned
to Antioch, where he found Philip in control
of the city. The king attacked the city and
took it by force.

The High Priest Alcimus and the Campaign of Nicanor

(2 Maccabees 14:1–36; 15:1–36)

7 In the year 151,[s] Demetrius son of
Seleucus left Rome and with a few
men landed at a town on the Mediterranean
coast, where he proclaimed himself king. 2 As
he was making his way to the royal palace of
his ancestors, the soldiers arrested Antiochus
the Fifth and Lysias, planning to take them
to Demetrius. 3 When Demetrius heard
about it, he said, "I don't want to see them."
4 So the soldiers killed them, and Demetrius
took the throne.

5 Then all the godless traitorous Jews led
by Alcimus, who wanted to be High Priest,
went to Demetrius. 6 They brought accusa-
tions against the other Jews and said, "Judas
and his brothers have killed everybody who
supported you, and they have driven us out
of our country. 7 We advise you to send

[s] **7:1** THE YEAR 151: *This corresponds to 161 B.C.*

someone whom you can trust to go and inspect all the damage done to our property and the king's territory and to punish Judas, his brothers, and all who support them."

8 King Demetrius chose one of his advisers, a man by the name of Bacchides, who was the governor of Greater Syria. He was an important man in the empire and loyal to the king. 9 He was sent along with the godless Alcimus, whom the king had appointed High Priest; Alcimus had orders to take revenge on the Jews. 10 They left Antioch and arrived in Judea with a large army. Bacchides tried to trick Judas and his brothers by sending to them messengers with offers of peace. 11 But when Judas and his brothers saw what a large army they had brought, they did not believe what the messengers said.

12 A group of teachers of the Law came to Alcimus and Bacchides, asking for justice. 13 These devout and patriotic men were the first of the Jews to try to make peace with Alcimus and Bacchides. 14 They trusted Alcimus, who was a priest descended from Aaron, and they thought he would not cause them any harm. 15 Alcimus assured them of his peaceful intentions and solemnly promised that no harm would come to them or their friends. 16 But as soon as they began to trust him, he arrested 60 of them and put them all to death on the same day. As the scripture says,

17 "The blood of your faithful people was
poured out,
their bodies were scattered around
Jerusalem,
and there was no one left to bury the
dead."

18 When this happened, all the people were afraid of Alcimus and Bacchides, and they said, "They don't know what truth or justice means. They gave their solemn word and then broke it!" 19 Bacchides left Jerusalem and set up his headquarters at Beth Zaith. He ordered the arrest of some of the faithful Jews and even many of the renegades who had willingly joined him; he had them killed and thrown into a deep pit. 20 Bacchides put the country under the control of Alcimus, left troops there to help him, and returned to the king.

21 Alcimus then began his struggle to establish himself as High Priest. 22 Every troublemaker in the country joined him. They gained control of the land of Judea and caused great difficulties for the Jews. 23 Judas saw that the trouble Alcimus and his men had caused was even worse than the damage done by the Gentiles. 24 So he went around the whole country of Judea taking revenge on all the men who had willingly joined Alcimus and preventing them from leaving the towns and going into the country. 25 When Alcimus saw that Judas and his men were growing more powerful and when he realized that he would not be able to stand against them, he returned to the king and accused them of great crimes.

26 Then the king sent Nicanor, one of his most honored officers, who hated the Jews, with orders to exterminate them. 27 Nicanor came to Jerusalem with a big army. He tried to trick Judas and his brothers by sending peace offers. He said, 28 "There need not be any quarrel between you and me. I will come to you with a small escort for a friendly private conversation." 29 When he came to Judas, they exchanged polite greetings, but Judas' enemies were ready to kidnap him. 30 When Judas learned that Nicanor's visit was part of a plot against him, he was afraid and decided not to meet him again. 31 Nicanor realized that his plan had been discovered, so he left Jerusalem to meet Judas in battle near Capharsalama. 32 About 500 of Nicanor's men were killed, and the rest of the army escaped to the fort in Jerusalem.

33 Some time later Nicanor went to Mount Zion. Some of the priests left the Temple and, along with some of the leaders of the people, went to welcome him with words of peace and to show him the burnt offering that was being sacrificed on behalf of the king. 34 But he ridiculed them and made them ceremonially unclean by spitting on them. He spoke proudly 35 and angrily threatened them with an oath, "Unless Judas and his army are surrendered to me immediately, I will burn this Temple down as soon as I return after my victory." And he left in a rage.

7:17 Ps 79:2, 3

36The priests went into the courtyard and
stood facing the altar and the Temple. They
started weeping and prayed, 37"Lord, you
chose this Temple to bear your name and to
be a place of prayer and intercession for your
people. 38Now, take vengeance on this man
and his army; let them die in battle.
Remember how they spoke evil of you, and
let none of them survive."

39Nicanor left Jerusalem and set up his
headquarters at Beth Horon, where the
Syrian army joined him. 40Meanwhile,
Judas set up camp at Adasa with 3,000
men. There Judas prayed, 41"Lord, the
Scriptures tell us that when a king sent
messengers to insult you, your angel went
out and killed 185,000 of his soldiers.
42Now, in the same way, crush this army
before us today and let everyone know that
Nicanor is being punished because he
insulted your holy Temple. Punish him as
his wickedness deserves."

43The armies met in battle on the thir-
teenth day of the month of Adar, and
Nicanor's army was defeated. Nicanor him-
self was the first to be killed in the battle,
44and when his soldiers saw that he was
dead, they threw down their weapons and
fled. 45The Jews pursued them all day long
from Adasa to Gezer. As they followed, they
kept sounding the call to battle on the
trumpets, 46and from all the surrounding
villages of Judea people came out and
attacked the fleeing enemy from the sides.
This forced them back toward the Jews who
were chasing them, and all of the enemy
were killed in the fight. Not one of them
survived.

47The Jews took the loot and then cut off
Nicanor's head and his right arm, which he
had extended so arrogantly. They brought his
head and his arm to be put on display out-
side Jerusalem. 48There was great rejoicing
among the Jews. They set that day aside as a
special day of celebration, 49and decreed that
the thirteenth day of Adar should be
observed as an annual day of celebration.
50There was peace in the land of Judea for a
little while.

The Treaty with the Romans

8 Judas had heard about the Romans and
their reputation as a military power. He
knew that they welcomed all those who
joined them as allies and that those who
came to them could be sure of the friend-
ship of Rome. 2People had told him about
the wars the Romans had fought and their
heroic acts among the Gauls, whom they
had conquered and forced to pay taxes. 3He
had been told what they had done in Spain
when they captured the silver mines and the
gold mines there. 4By careful planning and
persistence, they had conquered the whole
country, even though it was far from Rome.
They had overcome the kings from distant
lands who had fought against them; they had
defeated them so badly that the survivors
had to pay annual taxes. 5They had fought
and conquered Philip and Perseus, kings of
Macedonia, and all who had joined them
against Rome. 6They had even defeated
Antiochus the Great, king of Syria, who had
attacked them with 120 elephants, cavalry,
chariots, and a powerful army. 7They took
him alive and forced him and his successors
to pay heavy taxes, to give hostages, and to
surrender 8India, Media, Lydia, and some of
their best lands. They took these and gave
them to King Eumenes.[t]

9When the Greeks made plans to attack
and destroy them, 10the Romans learned of
the plans and sent a general to fight against
them. The Romans killed many of the
Greeks, took their wives and children cap-
tive, plundered their possessions, occupied
their land, tore down their fortresses, and
made them slaves, as they are today. 11They
also destroyed or made slaves of other king-
doms, the islands, and everyone who had
ever fought against them. 12But they main-
tained their friendship with their allies and
those who relied on them for protection.
They conquered kings near and far, and
everyone who heard of their reputation was
afraid of them. 13They helped some men to
become kings, while they deposed others;
they had become a world power. 14In spite
of all this, no Roman ever tried to advance

[t] **8:8** KING EUMENES: *This is King Eumenes II, king of Pergamum from 197—158 B.C.*
7:41 2 Kings 19:35

his own position by wearing a crown or putting on royal robes. 15They created a senate, and each day 320 senators came together to deliberate about the affairs of the people and their well-being. 16Each year they entrusted to one man the responsibility of governing them and controlling their whole territory. Everyone obeyed this one man, and there was no envy or jealousy among them.

17Judas chose Eupolemus, the son of John and grandson of Accos, and Jason son of Eleazar and sent them to Rome to make a treaty of friendship and alliance with the Romans. 18He did this to eliminate Syrian oppression, since the Jews clearly saw that they were being reduced to slavery. 19After a long and difficult journey, Eupolemus and Jason reached Rome and entered the Senate. They addressed the assembly in these terms: 20"Judas Maccabeus, his brothers, and the Jewish people have sent us here to make a mutual defense treaty with you, so that we may be officially recorded as your friends and allies."

21The Romans accepted the proposal, 22and what follows is a copy of the letter which was engraved on bronze tablets and sent to Jerusalem to remain there as a record of the treaty:

23"May things go well forever for the Romans and for the Jewish nation on land and sea! May they never have enemies, and may they never go to war! 24But if war is declared first against Rome or any of her allies anywhere, 25the Jewish nation will come to her aid with wholehearted support, as the situation may require. 26And to those at war with her, the Jews shall not give or supply food, arms, money, or ships, as was agreed in Rome. The Jews must carry out their obligations without receiving anything in return.

27"In the same way, if war is declared first against the Jewish nation, the Romans will come to their aid with hearty support, as the situation may require. 28And to their enemies there shall not be given or supplied food, arms, money, or ships, as was agreed in Rome. The Romans must carry out their obligations without deception.

29"These are the terms of the treaty that the Romans have made with the Jewish people. 30But if, in the future, both parties shall agree to add or remove anything, they shall act on their decision, and whatever they add or remove shall be valid.

31"Furthermore, concerning the wrongs which King Demetrius is doing against the Jews, we have written him as follows, 'Why have you treated our friends and allies, the Jews, so harshly? 32If they complain to us about you one more time, we will support their cause and go to war against you on land and sea.' "

The Death of Judas

9 When Demetrius heard that Nicanor and his army had been annihilated, he again sent Bacchides and Alcimus to the land of Judea, this time with the Syrian wing of the army. 2They moved along Gilgal Road, laid siege to Mesaloth in Arbela, captured it, and killed many people. 3In the first month of the year 152,[u] they set up camp opposite Jerusalem. 4From there they marched to Berea with 20,000 infantry and 2,000 cavalry.

5Judas had camped at Elasa, with 3,000 experienced soldiers. 6But when they saw the enormous size of the enemy army, they were terrified. So many men deserted that only 800 Jewish soldiers were left. 7When Judas saw that his army was dwindling away and that the battle was about to begin, he was worried because there was not enough time to bring his army together. 8He was discouraged, but he said to those who were still with him, "Let's prepare for the attack; maybe we can still defeat them."

9His men tried to talk him out of it. "We are not strong enough," they said. "Let's retreat now and save our lives. Then we can return with reinforcements and fight the enemy. We don't have enough men now."

10Judas replied, "Never let it be said that I ran from a battle. If our time has come, let's die bravely for our fellow Jews and not leave any stain on our honor."

11The Syrian army came out of the camp

[u] **9:3** THE YEAR 152: *This corresponds to 160 B.C.*

8:17 2 Macc 4:11 **8:22** 1 Macc 14:18

and took up battle positions against the Jews. The cavalry was divided into two parts. The shock troops were in the front lines, but the archers and those who used slings went ahead of the main formation. 12Bacchides took his position on the right. The infantry advanced, protected on both sides by the cavalry, and the war trumpets were blown. The soldiers of Judas also sounded their trumpets. 13The ground shook from the noise when the two armies met, and they fought from morning until evening.

14When Judas saw that Bacchides and the main force of the Syrian army was on the right, all his bravest men joined him, 15and they crushed the Syrians' right wing. They pursued them as far as the foothills.[v] 16But when the Syrians on the left wing saw that their right wing had been crushed, they turned to attack Judas and his men from the rear. 17The fighting became very fierce, and many on both sides were killed. 18Finally Judas himself was killed. Then all his men fled. 19Jonathan and Simon took their brother's body and buried it in the family tomb at Modein, 20and there at the tomb they wept for him. All Israel mourned for him in great sorrow for many days. They said, 21"It can't be! The mighty hero and savior of Israel has been killed!"

22The other deeds of Judas, his battles, his courageous deeds, and his great accomplishments, were too many to write down.

Jonathan Succeeds Judas

23After the death of Judas, the lawless traitors began to reappear everywhere in Judea, and all the wicked people returned. 24Also at that time there was a severe famine, and the whole country went over to the side of the renegades. 25Bacchides deliberately appointed some renegade Jews as rulers over the country. 26These men hunted down the friends of Judas and brought them all before Bacchides, and he subjected them to torture and humiliation. 27It was a time of great trouble for Israel, worse than anything that had happened to them since the time prophets ceased to appear among them.

28Then all the friends of Judas came together and said to Jonathan, 29"Since your brother Judas died, there has been no one like him to lead us against our enemies, against Bacchides and those of our own nation who oppose us. 30So today we choose you to succeed him as our ruler and commander to carry on our war." 31Jonathan accepted the leadership that day and took the place of his brother Judas.

The Campaigns of Jonathan

32When Bacchides learned of this, he made up his mind to kill Jonathan. 33But when this news reached Jonathan, he fled, with his brother Simon and their men, to the wilderness of Tekoa and set up camp at the pool of Asphar. (34Bacchides learned about this on the Sabbath and crossed the Jordan with his whole army.[w]) 35Jonathan sent his brother John, who was responsible for the soldiers' families, to ask the Nabateans, with whom he was on friendly terms, for permission to store with them the large amount of baggage they had. 36But the Jambrites of Medeba attacked John, took him captive, and carried off all the baggage. 37Some time later Jonathan and his brother Simon learned that the Jambrites were about to celebrate an important wedding and that there would be a bridal procession from the town of Nadabath. The bride was the daughter of one of the great princes of Canaan. 38Jonathan and Simon had wanted revenge for the death of their brother John, so they and their men went up on one of the mountains and hid. 39They kept watch and saw a noisy crowd loaded down with baggage. The bridegroom, his friends, and his relatives were on their way to meet the bride's party. They were heavily armed and were playing musical instruments and drums. 40The Jews attacked from their ambush and killed many of them; the rest escaped into the mountains, while the Jews carried off all their possessions. 41So the wedding was turned into a time of mourning and their joyful music into funeral songs. 42Jonathan and Simon had taken full revenge for the death of their brother, and they returned to the marshes along the Jordan.

[v] **9:15** *Probable text* the foothills; *Greek* Mount Azotus.

[w] **9:34** *Verse 34 is probably misplaced and belongs with verse 43.*

They kept watch and saw a noisy crowd loaded down with baggage. (9:39)

43Bacchides heard about this and arrived
on the Sabbath at the banks of the Jordan
with a large army. 44Jonathan said to his
men, "Now we must fight for our lives. We
are in a worse situation than we have ever
been in before. 45The enemy is in front of
us, the river is behind us, and marshes and
thickets are on both sides of us; there is no
way out. 46So pray now for the Lord to save
us from our enemies."

47The battle began and Jonathan and his
men were just about to kill Bacchides, when
he escaped to the rear of the army. 48So
Jonathan and his men jumped into the Jor-
dan and swam to the other side to escape,
and the Syrian army did not cross the river
to follow them. 49That day Bacchides lost
about 1,000 men.

50After Bacchides returned to Jerusalem,
the Syrians built fortifications with high
walls and barred gates for a number of towns
in Judea: Emmaus, Beth Horon, Bethel, Tim-
nath, Pirathon, Tephon, and the fortress in
Jericho. 51In all of these he placed troops to
harass the Jews. 52He also strengthened the
fortifications of the towns of Bethzur and
Gezer and of the fort in Jerusalem. He
placed army units in them and stored up
supplies there. 53Then he took the sons of
the leading men of the country as hostages
and imprisoned them in the fort.

54In the second month of the year 153,[x]
the High Priest Alcimus ordered that the
wall of the inner court of the Temple be
torn down. This would have destroyed what
the prophets had accomplished; but just as
the work began, 55he had a stroke, and work
was stopped. Paralyzed and unable to open
his mouth, he could not speak or even make
a will for his family. 56He died in great tor-
ment. 57When Bacchides learned that
Alcimus was dead, he returned to King
Demetrius, and the land of Judea had peace
for two years.

58Then all the renegades got together and
said, "Look, Jonathan and his men are living
in peace and security. If we bring Bacchides
here now, he can capture them all in a single
night." 59They went to discuss the matter
with Bacchides, 60and he set out with a large
army. He sent secret letters to all his allies in
Judea, asking them to seize Jonathan and his
men. But they were not able to do so
because the plot was discovered. 61Jonathan
and his men captured 50 of the traitorous
leaders who had been involved in the plot
and put them to death. 62Then Jonathan,
Simon, and their forces withdrew to Beth-
basi in the wilderness. They rebuilt the fallen
fortifications and strengthened the town's
defenses. 63When Bacchides learned about
all this, he got his whole army together and
alerted his supporters in Judea. 64He attacked
Bethbasi from all sides and built siege plat-
forms. After the battle had gone on for a
long time, 65Jonathan slipped out into the
country with a small body of men and left
his brother Simon in charge of the town.
66Jonathan defeated Odomera and his peo-
ple, and then attacked and destroyed the
Phasirite camp. Once defeated, they joined
Jonathan and advanced with him in his
attack against Bacchides. 67At the same time,
Simon and his men rushed from the town
and burned the siege platforms. 68In the bat-
tle Bacchides was pressed so hard that all his
plans came to nothing, and he was defeated.
69He was so furious with the traitorous Jews
who had urged him to come to Judea that
he put many of them to death.

Then Bacchides decided to return to his
own country, 70but when Jonathan learned
of this, he sent ambassadors to Bacchides to
arrange for peace terms and the return of
Jewish prisoners. 71Bacchides agreed to do
as Jonathan asked and gave him his solemn
promise that he would let him live in peace
the rest of his life. 72Bacchides handed over
the prisoners and returned to his own

[x] **9:54** THE YEAR 153: *This corresponds to 159 B.C.*

country. Never again did he come into Jew-
ish territory. 73 War came to an end in Israel.
Jonathan settled in Michmash and began to
govern the people and to eliminate the rene-
gade Jews from Israel.

Alexander Epiphanes Makes Jonathan High Priest

10 In the year 160,[y] Alexander
Epiphanes,[z] son of Antiochus the
Fourth, landed at Ptolemais and captured it.
The people welcomed him as their king.
2 When King Demetrius heard of it, he gath-
ered a large army and went out to meet him
in battle. 3 At that time Demetrius sent
Jonathan a friendly letter full of flattery, 4 in
the hope of winning Jonathan over to his
side and making peace with the Jews before
Alexander made a treaty with them against
him. 5 Demetrius thought that Jonathan
would certainly remember all the wrongs he
had done to him, his brothers, and the entire
Jewish nation. 6 And so Demetrius made
Jonathan his ally and gave him authority to
raise an army and equip it. He also ordered
that the hostages held in the fort at
Jerusalem should be handed over to
Jonathan. 7 So Jonathan went to Jerusalem
and read the letter to all the people and to
the men in the fort. 8 These men were terri-
fied when they learned that the king had
given Jonathan authority to raise an army.
9 They handed the hostages over to him, and
he returned them to their parents.

10 Jonathan set up headquarters in
Jerusalem and began to rebuild and restore
the city. 11 He ordered the builders to use
squared stones for the city walls and for the
protecting wall around Mount Zion. This
was done. 12 The foreigners deserted the
fortresses that Bacchides had built; 13 each
man left his post and returned to his own
country. 14 But some of the Jews who had
abandoned the Law of Moses and its com-
mands were still left in Bethzur, which
served as their last place of refuge.

15 King Alexander learned of the promises
Demetrius had made to Jonathan and he also
learned about Jonathan himself, about the
battles he had fought, his courageous deeds,
and the troubles he and his brothers had
endured. 16 He was certain that he would
never find another man like Jonathan and so
decided to make him his friend and ally.
17 He wrote Jonathan a letter:

18 "King Alexander to his friend
Jonathan, greetings.

19 "I have heard that you are a brave man
who has earned the right to be a friend of
the king. 20 I have this day appointed you as
High Priest of your nation and conferred
upon you the title of 'Friend of the King.'
You are to be our ally and give us your
support."

He also sent him a royal robe and a gold
crown. 21 Jonathan put on the robes of the
High Priest in the seventh month of the year
160[a] at the Festival of Shelters. He raised an
army and stored up a large supply of weapons.

Jonathan Supports Alexander Epiphanes

22 When Demetrius heard this, he was dis-
tressed and said, 23 "How did we manage to
let Alexander get ahead of us? He has
strengthened his position by making an
alliance with the Jews. 24 I also will write
them a friendly letter offering high positions
and gifts, so that they will support me."
25 He wrote:

"King Demetrius to the nation of the
Jews, greetings. 26 We are delighted to
learn that you have kept your obligations
under our treaty, remained loyal to us, and
have not gone over to the side of our ene-
mies. 27 Now if you continue to remain
loyal to us, we will reward you well. 28 We
will grant you exemptions from many
taxes and allow you other privileges. 29 I
hereby grant all the Jewish people release
and exemption from payment of regular
taxes, salt taxes, and other special taxes.
30 Furthermore, from this day I release you
from your obligation to pay me one third
of the grain harvest and one half of the
fruit harvest. From now on I will not

[y] **10:1** THE YEAR 160: *This corresponds to 152 B.C.* [z] **10:1** ALEXANDER EPIPHANES: *Alexander Epiphanes is more widely known as Alexander Balas.* [a] **10:21** THE YEAR 160: *This corresponds to 152 B.C.*
10:30 1 Macc 11:34

demand these payments from Judea or
from the three districts that have been
added to Judea from Samaria and Galilee.
31 Jerusalem and its surrounding territory
is to be recognized as a holy city and to
be exempt from the payment of all taxes.
32 I also give up my authority over the fort
in Jerusalem and place it under the High
Priest, who may station there anyone he
wishes to guard it. 33 I freely grant release
to all Jews who are prisoners of war any-
where in my kingdom. All of them will be
exempt from taxes, even on their cattle.[b]
34 No taxes shall be collected from any Jew
anywhere in my kingdom on Sabbaths,
New Moon Festivals, and other holy days.
Furthermore, no taxes shall be collected
three days before or after the major holy
days. 35 No one has the right on any of
these days to demand payment or to trou-
ble you in any way.

36 "Jews may be enlisted in the royal
army up to a total of 30,000 men, and
they will receive the same pay as other
royal troops. 37 Some of them may be sta-
tioned in the great royal fortresses, and
others assigned to responsible positions in
the government. They shall have Jews as
their leaders and officers, and they shall be
allowed to follow their own laws and cus-
toms, just as the king has permitted for
the people of Judea.

38 "The three districts added to Judea
from the territory of Samaria will be
completely incorporated into Judea and
placed under the authority of the High
Priest alone. 39 I give to the Temple in
Jerusalem for its operating expenses the
revenues from the city of Ptolemais and
the lands belonging to it. 40 I also promise
to make an annual gift of 15,000 silver
coins from appropriate accounts within
the royal treasury. 41 The total accumulated
state subsidy, which we have failed to pay
in recent years, shall be paid, and the pay-
ments continued from now on for the
work of the Temple. 42 In addition to this,
we will no longer require the 5,000 silver
coins annually from the Temple income.
This money belongs to the priests serving
in the Temple. 43 Whoever owes a debt to
the king or any other debt and takes
refuge in the Temple in Jerusalem or in
any area that belongs to it may not be
arrested nor may his property anywhere
in my kingdom be confiscated. 44 The
expenses for rebuilding and renovating the
Temple shall be provided from the royal
treasury. 45 Likewise, the expenses for
rebuilding the walls of Jerusalem and its
surrounding fortifications, as well as the
walls of designated towns in Judea, shall be
provided from the royal treasury."

46 When Jonathan and the people heard
the proposals made by King Demetrius, they
refused to believe them or accept them,
because they remembered how harshly he
had treated them and what terrible troubles
he had caused them. 47 They preferred to give
their allegiance to Alexander because he had
been the first to open peace negotiations, and
they remained his allies as long as he lived.

48 King Alexander raised a large army and
took up battle positions facing Demetrius.
49 But when the armies of the two kings met
in battle, the army of Alexander[c] turned and
ran. Demetrius[d] pursued them and won the
battle. 50 Alexander[e] fought bitterly until sun-
down, but Demetrius was killed that day.

51 Then Alexander sent ambassadors to
King Ptolemy the Sixth of Egypt with this
message:

52 "I have returned to my kingdom and
taken my seat on the throne of my ances-
tors. I have taken over the government,
and I am now in control of the country.
53 I made war on Demetrius, defeated him
and his army, and I have taken over his
kingdom. 54 Now I am ready to make an
alliance. Give me your daughter in mar-
riage, and I will give both of you such
gifts as you deserve."

55 King Ptolemy replied, "It was a great
day when you returned to your country and
took the throne of your ancestors. 56 I agree
to your proposals, but first meet me at Ptole-
mais. We can get acquainted there, and I will
give you my daughter in marriage."

[b] **10:33** *This sentence in Greek is unclear.* [c] **10:49** Alexander; *some manuscripts have* Demetrius.
[d] **10:49** Demetrius; *some manuscripts have* Alexander. [e] **10:50** Alexander; *some manuscripts have* Demetrius.

Ptolemy and his daughter Cleopatra left Egypt. (10:57)

[57]So in the year 162[f] Ptolemy and his daughter Cleopatra[g] left Egypt and arrived at Ptolemais. [58]King Alexander met them, and Ptolemy gave him his daughter in marriage. The wedding was celebrated there in Ptolemais with royal splendor.

[59]King Alexander wrote asking Jonathan to come to meet him. [60]So Jonathan, in a show of splendor, went to Ptolemais and met the two kings. He presented them with gifts of silver and gold, and he also gave many gifts to the high officials who had accompanied them. Everyone was favorably impressed with him. [61]At the same time some traitorous Jews who wanted to make trouble for Jonathan made accusations against him, but King Alexander paid no attention to them. [62]He gave orders that Jonathan should be given royal robes to wear, [63]and he honored him by letting him sit at his side. Alexander told his officers to take Jonathan into the center of the city and to announce that no one was to bring charges against him for any reason and no one was to cause him any kind of trouble. [64]When his accusers saw the honors given to him, heard the announcement, and saw him clothed in royal robes, they all fled. [65]The king further honored Jonathan by enrolling him in the First Order of the "Friends of the King" and by making him general and governor of his province. [66]Jonathan returned to Jerusalem pleased and successful.

Jonathan's Victory over Apollonius

[67]In the year 165[h] Demetrius the Second, the son of Demetrius the First, left Crete and arrived in Syria, the land of his ancestors. [68]When King Alexander heard about this, he was worried and returned to Antioch, the capital of Syria. [69]Demetrius reappointed Apollonius governor of Greater Syria. Apollonius raised a large army, set up camp near Jamnia, and sent the following message to Jonathan the High Priest:

[70]"Because of you I am being ridiculed, but why do you, there in your mountains, continue this rebellion when no one supports you? [71]If you really have any confidence in your army, come down here on the plain and fight, where we can test each other's strength. Study the situation, and you will find that I have the support of the forces from the cities. [72]You will learn who I am and who our allies are, and you will discover that you have no chance of standing against us. Your predecessors have already been beaten twice on their own ground; [73]so how do you expect to defeat my cavalry and the kind of army I have here on the plain? Down here there is not so much as a pebble to hide behind and no way to escape."

[74]When Jonathan received this message from Apollonius, he became angry. He took 10,000 elite troops from Jerusalem; his brother Simon also brought troops, and their two forces [75]set up camp outside of Joppa. The men of the city refused to let them in because there was a detachment of Apollonius' troops there, but Jonathan attacked, [76]and the men in the city became so frightened that they opened the gates, allowing Jonathan to capture Joppa. [77]When Apollonius heard what had happened, he took 3,000 cavalry and a large army of infantry and pretended to retreat south toward Azotus. However, relying upon the strength of his cavalry, he marched into the plain with his main force, [78-79]positioning 1,000 cavalry where they could attack Jonathan's forces from the rear. Jonathan continued his pursuit

[f] **10:57** THE YEAR 162: *This corresponds to 150 B.C.* [g] **10:57** CLEOPATRA: *This was Cleopatra Thea, also known as Cleopatra the Third, and not to be confused with Cleopatra the Seventh (69—30 B.C.), who was involved in the history of Caesar and Mark Antony.* [h] **10:67** THE YEAR 165: *This corresponds to 147 B.C.*

as far as Azotus, where the two armies met
in battle. 80 Not until then did Jonathan real-
ize that he was caught in an ambush. His
army was surrounded, and enemy arrows
rained down on them from morning until
evening. 81 But Jonathan's men stood firm, as
he had ordered, and the attacking cavalry
grew tired. 82 Then, when the cavalry was
exhausted, Simon appeared on the scene
with his forces and attacked and over-
whelmed the enemy infantry, who broke
ranks and fled. 83 The cavalry, which by now
was scattered all over the battlefield, fled to
Azotus, where they took refuge in the tem-
ple of Dagon, their god. 84 But Jonathan set
fire to the city and to the temple of Dagon,
burning to death all those who had taken
refuge there. Then he set fire to the sur-
rounding towns and looted them. 85 That day
about 8,000 were either killed in the battle
or burned to death. 86 Jonathan left and set
up camp at Ascalon, where the people of the
city came out to welcome him with great
honors. 87 Jonathan and his men returned to
Jerusalem with large quantities of loot.

88 When King Alexander heard what
Jonathan had done, he gave him even greater
honors. 89 He sent him a gold shoulder buck-
le, which is given only to those honored
with the title "Relative of the King." He also
gave him the city of Ekron and its surround-
ing territory.

The Fall of Alexander Epiphanes

11 King Ptolemy the Sixth of Egypt
assembled an army of soldiers more
numerous than the grains of sand along the
seashore, and he also gathered a great fleet of
ships. He intended to trap Alexander, take his
kingdom, and add it to his own, 2 so he went
to Syria with promises of peace, and the citi-
zens opened their gates to him and wel-
comed him. King Alexander had ordered
them to do this because Ptolemy was his
father-in-law. 3 But as Ptolemy moved north,
he stationed a detachment of troops in each
town. 4 When he reached Azotus, the people
there showed him the burned ruins of the
temple of Dagon and all the destruction in
the city and the surrounding towns. There
were corpses everywhere. The bodies of the
men Jonathan had burned to death during
the battle were now stacked up along Ptole-
my's route. 5 The people told him what
Jonathan had done, hoping that he would
hold him responsible, but Ptolemy said noth-
ing. 6 Jonathan, with all the proper ceremony,
went to Joppa to meet him. They exchanged
greetings and spent the night there. 7 Jonathan
accompanied him as far as the Eleutherus
River before returning to Jerusalem. 8 In this
way King Ptolemy, in his plot against Alexan-
der, took control of the towns along the coast
as far north as Seleucia-by-the-sea.

9 From there King Ptolemy sent this mes-
sage to King Demetrius: "Let's make a treaty.
My daughter is now Alexander's wife, but I
will take her back and give her to you and
let you rule over your father's kingdom. 10 I
regret that I ever gave her to Alexander,
because he has tried to kill me." 11 Ptolemy
made this accusation against Alexander
because he wanted to take over his kingdom.
12 So he took his daughter away from
Alexander and gave her to Demetrius; he
broke off all relations with Alexander, and
they became open enemies. 13 Then Ptolemy
entered Antioch and assumed the crown of
Syria; so he wore both the crown of Egypt
and the crown of Syria.

14 King Alexander was in Cilicia at the time
because the people of that region were in a
state of rebellion. 15 But when he heard what
Ptolemy had done, he moved to attack him.
Ptolemy met him with a large force and won
a decisive victory. 16 While Ptolemy reached
the peak of his power, Alexander fled to Arabia
to find protection, 17 but an Arab named Zab-
diel cut off his head and sent it to Ptolemy.
18 Two days later Ptolemy himself died, and the
troops he had left in the fortresses were then
killed by the local citizens. 19 So in the year
167[i] Demetrius the Second became king.

Jonathan Wins the Favor of Demetrius the Second

20 About that time Jonathan gathered the
men of Judea to attack the fort in Jerusalem.

[i] **11:19** THE YEAR 167: *This corresponds to 145 B.C.*

They built many siege platforms to use in the attack. 21But some traitorous Jews who hated their own nation went to King Demetrius the Second and told him that Jonathan was laying siege to the fort in Jerusalem. 22When Demetrius heard this, he was furious and immediately moved his headquarters to Ptolemais. He wrote to Jonathan and ordered him to lift the siege and to meet him for a conference in Ptolemais without a moment's delay.

23When Jonathan got the message, he gave orders for the siege to continue, and then chose some Jewish leaders and some priests to go with him. At the risk of his life, 24he went to the king in Ptolemais, taking along robes, silver and gold, and many other gifts. He made a good impression on the king. 25Although some lawless traitors of his own nation had made accusations against Jonathan, 26the king still treated him just as his predecessors had done. He honored him in the presence of all his advisers, 27and confirmed him as High Priest, restoring all his former honors and appointing him to the highest rank among the "Friends of the King."

28Jonathan asked the king to release the territory of Judea and the three regions of Samaria[j] from the payment of taxes, promising that if Demetrius would do that, he would pay him a lump sum of 22,000 pounds of silver. 29The king agreed and wrote a letter to Jonathan to confirm all this:

30"King Demetrius to King Jonathan and to the Jewish nation, greetings.

31"For your information I am sending a copy of the letter I have written to the Honorable Lasthenes about you:

32" 'King Demetrius to the Honorable Lasthenes, greetings. 33I have decided to grant the Jewish nation certain benefits because they are our loyal allies and keep their treaty obligations. 34I confirm their rights to the land of Judea and the three regions of Ephraim, Lydda, and Arimathea, which are hereby annexed to Judea from Samaria with all the lands belonging to them. This will be of benefit to everyone who goes to Jerusalem to offer sacrifice, since payments of the annual tax on produce and fruit from these lands will no longer be made to the king, but to the Temple. 35And I also grant them relief from the payment of revenues now due me from tithes, tolls, salt taxes, and special taxes. 36None of the provisions mentioned in this letter shall ever be canceled in the future.

37" 'You are required to see that a complete copy of this decree is made and given to Jonathan, to be posted in a prominent place on the Temple hill.' "

Jonathan Helps Demetrius the Second

38When King Demetrius saw that the land was peaceful under his rule and there was no further resistance, he disbanded his whole army and sent everyone home, except the soldiers he had hired from the Greek islands. This made all the soldiers who had served under his predecessors hate him because they had lost their source of income. 39One of Alexander's former supporters, Trypho, saw that all the soldiers were complaining about Demetrius, so he went to Imalkue, the Arab who was responsible for bringing up Alexander's young son Antiochus. 40Trypho stayed there for a long time and kept urging Imalkue to hand the boy over to him, so that he could make him king in place of his father. He also told Imalkue about the decrees of Demetrius and how the soldiers hated him.

41Jonathan sent a message to King Demetrius asking him to remove his troops from the fort in Jerusalem and from the fortresses in Judea, since they kept harassing the Jews. 42Demetrius replied: "I will do what you request, and when the opportunity presents itself, I will bestow upon you and your nation the highest honors. 43But now you can help me by sending soldiers to fight for me, because all of my troops have revolted."

44So Jonathan sent 3,000 trained soldiers to Antioch. The king was delighted when they arrived, 45because a mob of 120,000 had gathered in the city determined to kill him. 46But he escaped to the palace while the mob took control of the streets and began to riot. 47Then the king called on the

j **11:28** *Probable text* three regions of Samaria; *Greek* three regions and Samaria.
11:34 1 Macc 10:30

Jewish soldiers for help, and they all rushed
to his aid. They went through the whole
city and killed at least 100,000 people.
48 They saved the king's life, but they plun-
dered and burned the city. 49 When the
people saw that the Jews had complete
control of the city, they lost courage and
appealed to the king, requesting 50 him to
arrange a truce and stop the Jewish attack.
51 The rebels threw down their arms and
surrendered. The king and everyone in his
kingdom now had great respect for the Jews,
who returned to Jerusalem with a great deal
of loot. 52 Demetrius was firmly established as
king, and the country was at peace under his
rule, 53 but he broke all his promises and
turned against Jonathan. He did not reward
him for his loyal service, but instead contin-
ued to harass him.

Jonathan Supports Antiochus the Sixth

54 Some time later, Trypho returned with
the young boy Antiochus and crowned him
king. 55 All the soldiers that Demetrius had
dismissed then came to the support of the
young king. They defeated Demetrius, and
he fled. 56 Trypho captured the elephants and
took control of Antioch. 57 The young King
Antiochus wrote to Jonathan and confirmed
him as High Priest and as ruler over the four
regions and gave him the title "Friend of the
King." 58 He sent him a set of gold tableware
and authorized him to drink from gold cups,
to wear a royal robe, and to wear the gold
shoulder buckle awarded to "Relatives of the
King." 59 He also appointed Jonathan's broth-
er Simon as governor of the territory from
the Phoenician coast to the Egyptian border.

60 Jonathan then marched with his army
through the towns of Greater Syria, and all
the Syrian forces joined him as allies. He
went to Ascalon, where the people wel-
comed him with great honors. 61 Then he
went to Gaza, but the people there barred
their gates against him. So he laid siege to
the city and burned and looted the sur-
rounding area. 62 The people of Gaza then
asked for peace, and Jonathan arranged a
truce. He took the sons of the leaders and
sent them to Jerusalem as hostages. After that
he marched on as far as Damascus.

63 Jonathan learned that the officers of
Demetrius had come to Kedesh in Galilee
with a large army, intending to keep him
from carrying out his plan. 64 So he left his
brother Simon in Judea and set out to meet
them in battle. 65 Then Simon laid siege to
Bethzur and fought against it for a long
time. 66 The people asked for peace terms,
and Simon agreed. He then took over the
town, drove the people out, and stationed a
detachment of troops there.

67 Jonathan and his army set up camp by
Lake Galilee. Early the next morning he
marched his troops to the plain of Hazor,
68 where the main force of the foreign army
was advancing to meet him. Unknown to
Jonathan, they had left a detachment of
troops in ambush in the mountains, 69 and
when the men in ambush came out and
attacked, 70 Jonathan's entire army turned and
ran. No one was left, except two officers,
Mattathias son of Absalom and Judas son of
Chalphi. 71 Jonathan was humiliated, so he
tore his clothes, threw dust on his head, and
prayed. 72 Then he turned back to the battle,
crushed the enemy, and put them to flight.
73 When his own fleeing soldiers saw this,
they turned back and joined him in pursuit.
They chased the enemy all the way back to
their camp at Kedesh and then took over the
camp. 74 At least 3,000 enemy soldiers were
killed that day. Jonathan then returned to
Jerusalem.

Alliances with Rome and Sparta

12 When Jonathan saw that things were
working out to his advantage, he
chose ambassadors and sent them to Rome
to confirm and renew friendship with the
Romans. 2 He also sent letters with a similar
message to Sparta and other places. 3 The
ambassadors went to Rome, where they
were admitted to the Senate chamber, and
reported that the High Priest Jonathan and
the Jewish nation had sent them to renew
the earlier ties of friendship and alliance
with Rome. 4 The Romans provided them
with letters to the authorities in each
country through which they would pass,

guaranteeing them safe conduct in their return to the land of Judea.

5 Here is a copy of the letter Jonathan wrote to the Spartans:

6 "Jonathan the High Priest, the national council of leaders, the priests, and the rest of the people of Judea, to our brothers in Sparta, greetings. 7 At an earlier time, your King Arius sent a letter to our High Priest Onias, stating that our two nations are related, as the attached copy shows. 8 Onias received your ambassador with full honors and acknowledged receipt of your letter, which declared our alliance and friendship. 9 And now, although we are not in need of such alliances, since we find our source of strength in the holy books we possess, 10 we have written to renew our ties of brotherhood and friendship with you. We do not wish to become total strangers, and it has now been many years since your last communication. 11 Throughout the years we have taken every opportunity, on our festival days and other suitable days, to remember you when we have offered our sacrifices and made our prayers, as it is fitting and proper for brothers to do. 12 We also are pleased that fame has come to you. 13 But we have had one series of troubles after another and have had to fight many wars, because we have been under constant attack by surrounding nations. 14 During this time of war, we did not wish to trouble you or our other allies and friends, 15 since we do have the help of the Lord, who has defeated our enemies and rescued us from them. 16 So we have chosen Numenius son of Antiochus together with Antipater son of Jason and sent them as ambassadors to Rome to renew our ties of friendship and alliance with the Romans. 17 We have also ordered them to go to you with our greetings and deliver this letter about the renewal of our ties of brotherhood. 18 And now we request an answer to this letter.

19 "The following is a copy of the earlier letter:

20 " 'King Arius of Sparta to Onias the High Priest, greetings. 21 We have found a document about the Spartans and the Jews indicating that we are related and that both of our nations are descended from Abraham. 22 Now that we have discovered this, please send us a report about your situation. 23 In reply, we will send you a letter indicating that we are willing to share our possessions, including cattle and property, if you will do the same. We have given orders to our ambassadors to give you a full report about these matters.' "

Campaigns of Jonathan and Simon

24 Jonathan learned that the officers of Demetrius had returned to attack him with an even larger army than before. 25 Jonathan did not want to give them an opportunity to penetrate his own territory, so he left Jerusalem and went to meet them in the region of Hamath. 26 Jonathan sent spies into the enemy camp, who reported to him that the enemy forces were making plans to attack the Jews by night. 27 At sunset Jonathan ordered all his soldiers to be on the alert and to have their weapons ready for a surprise attack any time during the night. He also stationed guards all around the camp. 28 When the enemy soldiers learned that Jonathan and his men were ready for battle, they were panic-stricken and fled, leaving their campfires burning. 29 Jonathan and his men saw the campfires but did not realize what had happened until the next morning. 30 Jonathan then set out after them, but he could not overtake them because they had already crossed the Eleutherus River. 31 Then Jonathan turned aside and

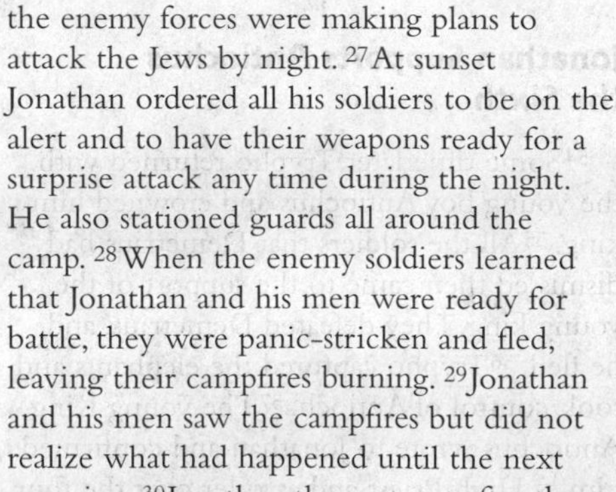

They were panic-stricken and fled, leaving their campfires burning. (12:28)

attacked a tribe of Arabs called Zabadeans. He defeated them and plundered their possessions. 32Then he broke camp and went to Damascus, inspecting the entire area along the way.

33Meanwhile, Simon had also set out on a campaign and had advanced as far as Ascalon and the neighboring fortresses. Then he turned aside to Joppa 34and stationed a detachment of soldiers there because he had heard that the people were planning to hand over the fortress of Joppa to the soldiers of Demetrius.

35When Jonathan returned, he called the council of the leaders together and made plans with them to build fortresses in Judea, 36to increase the height of the walls of Jerusalem, and to build a high wall to separate the fort from the city. This would isolate the fort, making it impossible for the enemy to buy or sell anything. 37The people worked together to strengthen the city's defenses because a part of the east wall along the Kidron Valley had collapsed and the Chaphenatha section was in need of repair. 38Simon also rebuilt the town of Adida in the foothills. He fortified it and constructed barred gates for it.

Trypho Captures Jonathan

39Then Trypho plotted a rebellion against King Antiochus so that he could make himself king of Syria. 40He was afraid, however, that Jonathan would not agree to this and would go to war against him to prevent it. So Trypho got his army ready and went to Beth Shan in the hope of capturing Jonathan and putting him to death. 41But Jonathan also came to Beth Shan with 40,000 well-trained soldiers. 42When Trypho saw how large an army Jonathan had brought with him, he was afraid to take action. 43So he received Jonathan with all honors, presented him to all his advisers, gave him gifts, and ordered his advisers and soldiers to obey Jonathan as they would him. 44He asked Jonathan, "Why have you put these soldiers to so much trouble when we are not at war? 45Why don't you send them home? Choose a few men to stay with you, and then accompany me to Ptolemais. I will hand the city over to you, as well as the rest of the fortresses, the troops, and all the officials. Then I will turn around and leave. In fact, that's why I am here." 46Jonathan believed him, and following his advice, sent his soldiers back to Judea. 47He took 3,000 men with him, but left 2,000 of them in Galilee, while only 1,000 accompanied him the rest of the way. 48But when Jonathan entered Ptolemais, the people of the city locked the gates, arrested him, and killed everyone who had come with him.

49Trypho sent infantry and cavalry units to Galilee and Jezreel Valley to kill the rest of Jonathan's soldiers. 50The Jewish troops thought that Jonathan had been captured and killed, along with all those who had accompanied him, so they encouraged one another and marched out in battle formation. 51When the approaching enemy forces saw that the Jews were ready to fight for their lives, they turned back. 52Then the Jewish soldiers returned to Judea safely, but terribly afraid. The whole nation was in deep mourning, assuming that Jonathan and all his men had been killed. 53All the surrounding nations now tried to destroy them. They thought that the Jews had no leaders or allies and that the time was ripe to annihilate them and put an end to their history.

Simon Leads the Jews

13 Simon learned that Trypho had assembled a large army and that he had plans to invade Judea and devastate it. 2He realized that this news had brought panic and fear to the people, so he went to Jerusalem, called the people together, 3and tried to encourage them by saying, "You know how much my father's family, my brothers, and I have done for the sake of the Law of Moses and the Temple. You also know about the wars we have fought and the troubles we have had. 4All my brothers have been killed fighting for our Law, our Temple, and our nation, and I am the only one left. 5But never let it be said that I tried to save my own life in a time of danger; I do not consider myself better than my brothers. 6Not in the least! It is true that in their hatred all the Gentile nations have gathered together to

destroy us, but I will fight to defend my nation, the Temple, and your loved ones."

7 These words immediately revived the morale of the people, 8 and they answered with a loud shout, "You are now our leader in place of your brothers Judas and Jonathan. 9 Fight our wars, and we will do whatever you ask." 10 So Simon gathered together all the soldiers and hurried to complete the walls of Jerusalem and to strengthen all its defenses. 11 He sent Jonathan son of Absalom to Joppa with a large army. This Jonathan drove out the people who were there and occupied the town.

12 Trypho left Ptolemais with a large army to invade Judea, taking Simon's brother Jonathan along with him as a prisoner. 13 Simon set up camp at Adida at the edge of the plain. 14 When Trypho learned that Simon had succeeded his brother Jonathan and that he was ready to meet him in battle, he sent this message to him: 15 "I am holding your brother Jonathan under arrest because while he was in office he did not pay his debts to the royal treasury. 16 However, I will release him if you will pay me 6,000 pounds of silver and send two of his sons as hostages to guarantee that he will not revolt against us when he is released."

17 Although Simon knew that they were deceiving him, he sent for the money and the two sons because he did not want to arouse the hostility of the Jews. 18 He was afraid that they might later say that Jonathan was put to death because Simon would not send the money and the boys. 19 So he did as Trypho had demanded, but Trypho broke his promise and did not release Jonathan.

20 Then Trypho made his move to invade the land and destroy it, circling around by the road to Adora. But Simon and his army moved along facing him wherever he went. 21 The enemy soldiers in the fort in Jerusalem kept sending messengers to Trypho urging him to come to them quickly by way of the desert and to send them supplies. 22 Trypho got all his cavalry ready for the invasion, but that night there was a heavy snowstorm, and he was not able to move up into the hills. So he withdrew and went into Gilead. 23 When he was near Baskama, he had Jonathan put to death and his body buried there. 24 Then Trypho turned and went back to his own country.

25 Simon had the body of his brother Jonathan brought to Modein, to be buried in the town of their ancestors. 26 Everyone in Israel was in deep sorrow at the loss of Jonathan, and they mourned for him a long time. 27 Over the tomb of his father and his brothers Simon built a high monument that could be seen from a great distance. It was covered front and back with polished stone. 28 He constructed seven pyramids side by side for his father, his mother, and his four brothers. 29 For the pyramids he created a setting of tall columns on which there were carvings. Some of these carvings were of suits of armor and some were of ships. It was a monument to their victories, which travelers from overseas could visit.[k] 30 The tomb which he built in Modein is still there today.

31 Meanwhile, Trypho assassinated the young king, Antiochus the Sixth, 32 and took over his kingdom in Syria. He brought that country great troubles.

33 Simon rebuilt the fortresses of Judea with high towers, strong walls, and barred gates; then he placed stores of supplies there. 34 He sent ambassadors to King Demetrius the Second to ask for tax relief for the land, since Trypho was doing nothing but robbing them. 35 King Demetrius sent the following letter in reply:

> 36 "King Demetrius to the High Priest Simon, the friend of kings, to the Jewish nation, and to their leaders, greetings. 37 I have received the gold crown and the gold palm branch which you sent, and I am prepared to make a peace treaty with you and to instruct our tax officials to grant you exemptions. 38 Our previous agreements with you are confirmed, and the fortresses which you have built are to remain yours. 39 I grant you pardon for treaty violations committed up to the present date, and I release you from payment of the special tax still due and any other taxes that have been collected up to this time in Jerusalem. 40 All Jews who are qualified may enroll in the royal service. Let us have peace."

[k] **13:29** *Verses 28–29 in Greek are unclear.*

41So in the year 170[l] the yoke of the
Gentile oppressors was removed from the
Jews. 42People began to date their docu-
ments and contracts with these words: "In
the first year of Simon, the great High
Priest, commander and leader of the Jews."
43At that time Simon laid siege to Gezer
and surrounded it with his army. He built a
movable siege platform, brought it up to the
town wall, attacked one of the towers, and
captured it. 44The men who had been on
the siege platform then moved rapidly into
the town, and this created great confusion.
45The men of the town, their wives, and
their children tore their clothes in distress
and climbed up on the top of the town wall.
They pleaded loudly with Simon for a truce.
46"Have mercy on us," they begged. "Don't
punish us as we deserve!"
47So Simon came to terms with them and
ended the fighting. He made the people
leave the town; then he purified the houses
in which there had been idols. When that
was done, he and his men entered the town
singing hymns and songs of praise. 48He
eliminated everything that would make the
town ritually unclean and settled it with
people who would obey every command
contained in the Law of Moses. He strength-
ened the defenses of the town and built
himself a palace there.
49Those in the fort in Jerusalem were
now prevented from leaving to buy or sell
anything. They were suffering from severe
hunger and many of them had died of star-
vation. 50Finally they appealed to Simon for
a truce. He agreed, removed them from the
fort, and purified it. 51On the twenty-third
day of the second month, in the year 171,[m]
there was a great celebration in the city
because this terrible threat to the security of
Israel had come to an end. Simon and his
men entered the fort singing hymns of praise
and thanksgiving, while carrying palm
branches and playing harps, cymbals, and
lyres. 52Simon issued a decree that the day
should be joyfully celebrated every year. He
strengthened the defenses of the Temple hill
on the side facing the fort, and he and his
men made their headquarters there.
53Simon's son John was now a grown man,
so Simon made him commander of the
whole army, and John set up headquarters at
Gezer.

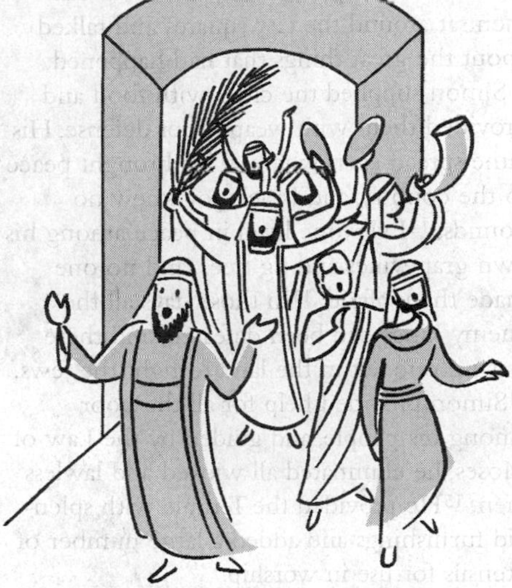

Simon and his men entered the fort. (13:51)

In Praise of Simon

14 In the year 172[n] King Demetrius
the Second gathered his army and
went to Media to seek additional help for
his war against Trypho. 2When King Arsaces
the Sixth of Persia and Media heard that
Demetrius had entered his territory, he sent
one of his commanders with some troops to
capture Demetrius alive. 3They attacked and
defeated the army of Demetrius, took him
captive, and brought him back to King
Arsaces, who threw him in prison.
4The land of Judea was at peace as long as
Simon lived. During his entire reign, he used
his position of power and influence to do
what was good for his people, and they were
always pleased with him as their ruler. 5He
added to his reputation when he captured the
port of Joppa and opened up the route to the
Greek islands. 6He not only enlarged the ter-
ritory of his nation and gained control of the
whole country, 7but he brought back many

[l] **13:41** THE YEAR 170: *This corresponds to 142 B.C.* [m] **13:51** THE YEAR 171: *This corresponds to 141 B.C.*
[n] **14:1** THE YEAR 172: *This corresponds to 140 B.C.*
13:43 2 Macc 10:32–38

prisoners of war and captured Gezer, Bethzur, and the fort in Jerusalem. He purified the fort, and there was no one to oppose him.

[8]The Jews farmed their land in peace; the land produced its crops and the trees bore fruit. [9]The young men showed off their splendid military uniforms, while the old men sat around the city squares and talked about the great things that had happened. [10]Simon supplied the cities with food and provided them with weapons of defense. His fame spread everywhere. [11]He brought peace to the country, and Israel's joy knew no bounds. [12]Everyone lived in peace among his own grapevines and fig trees, and no one made them afraid. [13]In those days all the enemy kings had been defeated, and there was no one left in the land to fight the Jews. [14]Simon provided help for all the poor among his people, and guided by the Law of Moses, he eliminated all wicked and lawless men. [15]He provided the Temple with splendid furnishings and added a large number of utensils for use in worship.

[16]When the news that Jonathan had died reached Rome and Sparta, it brought great sorrow. [17]But when the Spartans heard that Simon had succeeded his brother as High Priest and that he was in control of the country and its towns, [18]they engraved on bronze tablets a renewal of the treaty of friendship which they had made with his brothers Judas and Jonathan and sent the tablets to him. [19]These were read to the assembly in Jerusalem. [20]What follows is a copy of the letter sent by the Spartans:

"The people of Sparta and their rulers to Simon the High Priest, to the leaders and the priests of the Jews, and to all our Jewish brothers, greetings. [21]The delegation that you sent to our people has told us how respected and renowned you are. Their visit has been a source of joy for us, [22]and a report of their visit has been written down in our public records, as follows: 'Numenius son of Antiochus and Antipater son of Jason, honored representatives of the Jews, appeared before us to renew their treaty of friendship. [23]The assembly of the people was pleased to receive these men with all honors and to place a copy of their report in the public archives, so that the people of Sparta may have it on record. A copy of this document has been made for the High Priest Simon.' "

[24]Later, Simon sent Numenius to Rome with the gift of a large gold shield weighing half a ton, to confirm the Jews' alliance with the Romans.

[25]When the people of Israel heard about all this, they asked themselves, "How can we express our thanks to Simon and his sons? [26]He, his brothers, and his father's whole family have been towers of strength for our nation. They have fought off our enemies and set the nation free."

So they recorded this on bronze tablets and set them up on columns on Mount Zion. [27]The inscription read as follows:

"On the eighteenth day of the month of Elul in the year 172,[n] that is, in the third year of Simon, the High Priest,[o] [28]at a great assembly of priests, people, officials, and national leaders the following facts were made known to us: [29]Often when wars broke out in the country, Simon son of Mattathias, a priest of the Jehoiarib family, and his brothers risked their lives in protecting our nation, our Temple, and our Law against our enemies. They have brought great glory to our nation. [30]Jonathan united our people and became the High Priest before he died. [31]The enemies of the Jews plotted to invade the land and defile the Temple. [32]Then Simon assumed command and fought for his country. He spent a large amount of his own money to provide weapons and wages for his nation's armed forces. [33]He fortified the towns of Judea, and especially Bethzur on the border, where enemy weapons had previously been stored. He stationed a detachment of soldiers there. [34]He fortified the seaport of Joppa and the city of Gezer on the border of Azotus, which was previously occupied by enemy soldiers. He settled Jews there and provided the towns with everything that the people needed.[p]

[n] **14:27** THE YEAR 172: *This corresponds to 140 B.C.* [o] **14:27** *Greek has an additional word, the meaning of which is unclear.* [p] **14:34** that the people needed; *or* that was needed to keep them in repair.

14:18 1 Macc 8:22

35 When the people saw Simon's patriotism
and how he wanted to bring glory to his
nation, they made him their leader and
High Priest. They did this because of all
that he had accomplished through his loy-
alty and because he had brought about jus-
tice and had tried in every way to bring
glory to his nation.
36 "Under his leadership the Gentiles
were driven out of the land. Enemy sol-
diers were forced out of the area north of
the Temple, where they had built the fort,
from which the soldiers used to go out
and defile the holy Temple. 37 Simon set-
tled Jews in the fort, strengthened it for
the security of the country and the city of
Jerusalem, and increased the height of the
city walls. 38 As a result, King Demetrius
confirmed him as High Priest, 39 gave him
the title of "Friend of the King," and
treated him with great honor. 40 Deme-
trius did this because he had heard that
the Romans were calling the Jews their
friends, allies, and brothers and that they
had received Simon's delegation with full
honors.
41 "Therefore,[q] the Jews and their
priests are happy to have Simon and his
descendants as their leaders and High
Priests, until a true prophet appears.
42 Simon shall govern their country, have
charge of the Temple, and shall be their
military commander. He shall be in
charge of military supplies, fortifications,
and public works. 43 The people must
obey him in everything. All government
contracts shall be drawn up in his name.
He shall have the right to wear royal robes
with the gold shoulder buckle.
44 "No one, priest or people, shall have
the legal right to annul any of these deci-
sions, to alter or change any of Simon's
orders, to convene any assembly in the
country without his permission, or to
wear royal robes with the gold shoulder
buckle. 45 Anyone who disobeys or disre-
gards these regulations shall be subject to
punishment.
46 "The people gave their unanimous
approval to grant Simon the right to act
in accordance with these regulations.
47 Simon consented and agreed to be
supreme leader: High Priest, commander
of the armies, and governor of the Jews
and the priests."
48 It was decided that this declaration
should be engraved on bronze tablets and set
up in a prominent place within the Temple
area 49 and that copies should be placed in
the Temple treasury, where Simon and his
sons would have access to them.

Antiochus the Seventh Asks for Simon's Support

15 From the Greek islands Antiochus son
of King Demetrius wrote the follow-
ing letter to Simon the High Priest and gover-
nor of the Jews and to the whole nation:
2 "King Antiochus to Simon, the High
Priest and governor, and to the Jewish
nation, greetings. 3 As you know, the king-
dom of my ancestors has been seized by
traitors. I have decided to reclaim it and
restore its former greatness. I have raised a
large army of mercenary troops and have
fitted out warships. 4 I plan to invade the
land and to attack those who have
destroyed many of the towns and ruined
the country.
5 "Now therefore, I confirm all exemp-
tions from taxes and payments granted
you by former kings. 6 I authorize you to
mint your own coins as legal currency in
your own country. 7 Jerusalem and the
Temple shall be free of taxation. All the
weapons that you have manufactured and
the defenses you have built and now
occupy shall remain yours. 8 In addition, all
debts now owed to the royal treasury, or
which may in the future fall due, are per-
manently canceled. 9 As soon as I have
regained control of my kingdom, I will
confer upon you, your nation, and the
Temple such great honors that the glory
of your country will be evident to the
whole world."
10 In the year 174[r] Antiochus invaded the
land of his ancestors. Most of the soldiers
came over to his side, so that there were very

[q] **14:41** Therefore; *some manuscripts have* and that. [r] **15:10** THE YEAR 174: *This corresponds to 138 B.C.*

few left with Trypho. 11 Trypho, pursued by Antiochus, fled to the coastal city of Dor, 12 realizing that he was in a desperate situation, now that all his troops had deserted him. 13 Then Antiochus laid siege to Dor with 120,000 well-trained soldiers and 8,000 cavalry. 14 With his ships joining the attack, he completely surrounded the town and brought such pressure on it that no one was able to enter or leave.

Rome Supports the Jews

15 Meanwhile, Numenius and those with him arrived in Jerusalem from Rome with the following letter addressed to various kings and countries:

> 16 "From Lucius, consul of the Romans, to King Ptolemy, greetings. 17 A delegation from our friends and allies the Jews has come to us to renew the earlier treaty of friendship and alliance. They were sent by the High Priest Simon and the Jewish people, 18 and they have brought as a gift a gold shield weighing half a ton. 19 So we have decided to write to various kings and countries urging them not to harm the Jews, their towns, or their country in any way. They must not make war against the Jews or give support to those who attack them. 20 We have decided to accept the shield and grant them protection. 21 Therefore if any traitors escape from Judea and seek refuge in your land, hand them over to Simon the High Priest, so that he may punish them according to Jewish law."

22 Lucius wrote the same letter to King Demetrius, to Attalus, Ariarathes, and Arsaces, 23 and to all the following countries: Sampsames, Sparta, Delos, Myndos, Sicyon, Caria, Samos, Pamphylia, Lycia, Halicarnassus, Rhodes, Phaselis, Cos, Side, Aradus, Gortyna, Cnidus, Cyprus, and Cyrene. 24 A copy of the letter was also sent to Simon the High Priest.

Antiochus the Seventh Breaks with Simon

25 King Antiochus laid siege to Dor for a second time, keeping it under constant attack. He built siege platforms, and his blockade kept Trypho and his men from going in or out. 26 Simon sent 2,000 well-trained soldiers to help Antiochus, as well as silver and gold and a great deal of equipment. 27 But Antiochus refused to accept them, canceled all the previous agreements that he had made with Simon, and became his enemy. 28 Then Antiochus sent his trusted official Athenobius to negotiate with Simon. He told Simon, "You are occupying Joppa, Gezer, and the fort in Jerusalem, cities that belong to my kingdom. 29 You have devastated those regions and brought great trouble to the country. You have seized control of many places in my kingdom. 30 Now you must hand back these cities that you have captured, and you must give me the tax money that you have taken from places that you occupied outside the territory of Judea. 31 If you are unwilling to do this, then you must pay me 30,000 pounds of silver, and 30,000 additional pounds of silver to compensate me for damages and for lost taxes. If you refuse to do either of these, we will go to war against you."

32 When Athenobius came to Jerusalem and saw the splendor of Simon's court, the gold and silver tableware in his banquet hall, and the rest of the display of great wealth, he was amazed. He delivered the king's message to Simon, 33 and Simon answered, "We have never taken land away from other nations or confiscated anything that belonged to other people. On the contrary, we have simply taken back property that we inherited from our ancestors, land that had been unjustly taken away from us by our enemies at one time or another. 34 We are now only making use of this opportunity to recover our ancestral heritage. 35 As for Joppa and Gezer, which you claim, we will give you 6,000 pounds of silver, in spite of the fact that the people of those cities have done great harm to our nation."

Athenobius made no reply, 36 but he returned to the king in a rage. When he told the king what Simon had said, and reported on the splendor of Simon's court and all that he had seen, the king became violently angry.

John's Victory over Cendebeus

37 In the meantime, Trypho had boarded a ship and escaped to the town of Orthosia.

15:15 1 Macc 12:16

38 King Antiochus appointed Cendebeus as commander of the coastal area, provided him with infantry and cavalry, 39 and gave him orders to move against Judea. He also ordered him to rebuild the town of Kedron and fortify its gates, so that he could fight against the Jewish people. The king himself continued to pursue Trypho.

40 Cendebeus then came to Jamnia and began to harass the Jews by invading Judea, capturing people, and murdering them. 41 He rebuilt Kedron and stationed some cavalry and infantry units there, so that they could make attacks and patrol the roads of Judea, as the king had ordered.

16 Simon's son John left Gezer and went to report to his father what Cendebeus had done. 2 Simon said to John and Judas, his two oldest sons, "All my father's family, my brothers, and I have fought Israel's battles all our lives, and many times we have been successful in saving Israel. 3 I am old now, but you, thanks to God, are in the prime of life. You must take my place and that of my brother in fighting for our nation. And may God himself be with you."

4 Then John raised an Israelite army of 20,000 trained soldiers and cavalry and marched out against Cendebeus. They spent the night in Modein, 5 and then early the next morning they moved into the plain. There a large army of infantry and cavalry moved to meet them, but there was a river between the two armies. 6 John and his army took up battle positions facing the enemy, but when John saw that his soldiers were afraid to cross the river, he crossed ahead of them, and his men saw him and followed. 7 John divided his army and placed his cavalry in the middle of the infantry, because there was a large number of enemy cavalry. 8 The trumpets sounded the attack, and Cendebeus and his army were defeated, and many of them were killed. The rest ran back to their fortress at Kedron. 9 Judas was wounded in the battle, but his brother John continued to pursue the enemy as far as Kedron, which Cendebeus had rebuilt. 10 The escaping soldiers fled to the towers in the fields at Azotus, and John set fire to the city. On that day, 2,000 enemy soldiers were killed, and John returned safely to Judea.

The Murder of Simon and Two of His Sons

11 Simon the High Priest had appointed Ptolemy son of Abubus commander for the Plain of Jericho. Ptolemy was very rich, 12 because he was Simon's son-in-law. 13 But he became too ambitious and wanted to take over the country. So he devised a plan to assassinate Simon and his sons. 14 Simon, together with his sons Mattathias and Judas, was visiting the towns in the area, in order to take care of their needs. They arrived in Jericho in the month of Shebat, the eleventh month, in the year 177.[s] 15 Ptolemy, still plotting to murder Simon and his two sons, received them in a small fortress called Dok, which he had built. He gave a great banquet for them, but he had men hidden within the fortress. 16 When Simon and his sons were drunk, Ptolemy and his men came out of hiding and with swords in hand rushed into the banquet hall, where they killed Simon, his two sons, and some of the servants. 17 With this horrible act of treachery, Ptolemy returned evil for good.

18 Then Ptolemy wrote a report of what he had done and sent it to the king. In the letter he requested that troops be sent to help him and that the country and the cities be turned over to him. 19 He wrote a letter to the army officers inviting them to join him and promising them silver, gold, and gifts. Then he sent some of his men to Gezer to kill John, 20 and others to take control of Jerusalem and the Temple hill. 21 But someone ran to Gezer ahead of Ptolemy's men and reported to John that his father and his brothers had been killed and that Ptolemy was sending his soldiers to kill him. 22 John was horrified at this news, but, because he had been warned in advance, he was able to capture and put to death the men who had been sent to kill him.

23 Now the rest of what John did from the time he succeeded his father: his wars, his deeds of courage, his rebuilding of walls, and his other accomplishments, 24 are all written in the chronicles of his reign as High Priest.

[s] **16:14** THE YEAR 177: *This corresponds to 134 B.C.*

The Second Book of the Maccabees

"What goes around, comes around!" This expresses a simple truth presented in 2 Maccabees. Living a good, just, faithful life—keeping God in front—will bring you great blessings. If not in this life, then your blessings will come in eternal life—heaven. If you are evil and power hungry and thrive on hurting others, you will suffer—either in this life or the next.

The Second Book of Maccabees reveals stories of the best and worst kinds of people. It tells why and how they love God faithfully or reject God completely. As you read this book, you will be inspired, angered, horrified, and challenged by their stories. You will also understand the ups and downs the Jewish people faced during a time of persecution.

Headlines

- Heavenly Warriors Defend Temple (3:1–28)
- Corrupt High Priest Tries to Be Greek (4:7–22)
- Eleazar Remains Faithful, Sets Example for Youth (6:18–31)
- Martyrs Tortured and Die for Faith (chapter 7)
- First Hanukkah Celebrated (10:1–8)
- Judas' Vision Inspires Victory (15:6–37)

FACTOIDS

Who are the central characters? Judas Maccabeus and other faithful Jews who fight to save their faith; Onias, the just and faithful High Priest; corrupt leaders who work to destroy the Jews.

Who wrote this book? An unknown author who was concerned with the meaning of history rather than the facts. Second Maccabees is a summary of a lost five-volume story of the Maccabees written by Jason of Cyrene.

Why was it written? It was written to show how the Jewish faith grew even during difficult years, and to offer the Jews hope in their suffering.

What time period does it cover? From 180 to 160 BC, approximately the same period as 1 Maccabees.

Important themes

- Pray for your enemies. There are many paths to peace—besides war.
- God's faithful may suffer, but justice will eventually be served—if not in this life, then in the resurrection of the dead.
- Pray for those who have died, and know that they pray for you too.

2 MACCABEES

A Letter to the Jews in Egypt

1 "From the Jews of Jerusalem and Judea to those in Egypt, warm greetings.

2"May God be good to you and keep the covenant he made with Abraham, Isaac, and Jacob, his faithful servants. 3May he fill each of you with the desire to worship him and to do his will eagerly with all your heart and soul. 4May he enable you to understand his Law and his commands. May he give you peace, 5answer your prayers, forgive your sins, and never abandon you in times of trouble. 6Here in Judah we are now praying for you.

7"In the year 169,[a] when Demetrius the Second was king of Syria, we wrote to tell you about the persecution and the hard times that came upon us in the years after Jason revolted against authority in the Holy Land. 8Jason and his men set fire to the Temple gates and slaughtered innocent people. Then we prayed to the Lord and he answered our prayers. So we sacrificed animals, gave offerings of grain, lit the lamps in the Temple, and set out the sacred loaves. 9This is why we urge you to celebrate in the month of Kislev a festival similar to the Festival of Shelters. Written in the year 188."[b]

A LETTER TO ARISTOBULUS

The Death of King Antiochus

10"From the Jews of Jerusalem and Judea, the Jewish Senate, and Judas, to Aristobulus, a descendant of priests and the teacher of King Ptolemy, and to the Jews in Egypt, greetings and good health.

11"We thank God because he saved us from great danger. We were like men ready to fight against a king, 12but God drove the enemy from our holy city. 13When King Antiochus arrived in Persia, his army seemed impossible to defeat, but they were cut to pieces in the temple of the goddess Nanea by an act of treachery on the part of her priests. 14King Antiochus had gone to the temple with some of his most trusted advisers, so that he might marry the goddess and then take away most of the temple treasures as a wedding gift. 15After the priests had laid out the treasure, he and a few of his men went into the temple to collect it. But the priests closed the doors behind him 16and stoned him and his men from trap doors hidden in the ceiling. Then they cut up the bodies and threw the heads to the people outside. 17Praise God for punishing those evil men! Praise him for everything!

Fire Consumes Nehemiah's Sacrifice

18"On the twenty-fifth day of the month of Kislev we will celebrate the Festival of Rededication just as we celebrate the Festival of Shelters. We thought it important to remind you of this, so that you too may celebrate this festival. In this way you will remember how fire appeared when Nehemiah offered sacrifices after he had rebuilt the Temple and the altar. 19At the time when our ancestors were being taken to exile in Persia, a few devout priests took some fire from the altar and secretly hid it in the bottom of a dry cistern. They hid the fire so well that no one ever discovered it. 20Years later, when it pleased God, the Persian emperor sent Nehemiah back to Jerusalem, and Nehemiah told the descendants of those priests to find the fire. They reported to us that they had found no fire but only some oily liquid. Nehemiah then told them to scoop some up and bring it to him. 21When everything for the sacrifice had been placed on the altar, he told the priests to pour the liquid over both the wood and the sacrifice. 22After this was done and some time had passed, the sun appeared from behind the clouds, and suddenly everything on the altar burst into flames. Everyone looked on in amazement. 23Then, while the fire was

[a] **1:7** THE YEAR 169: *This corresponds to 143 B.C.* [b] **1:9** THE YEAR 188: *This corresponds to 124 B.C.*
1:13–16 1 Macc 6:1–4; 2 Macc 9:1–10

Everyone looked on in amazement. (1:22)

consuming the sacrifice, Jonathan the High
Priest led the people in prayer, and Nehemi-
ah and all the people responded.

Nehemiah's Prayer

24 "Nehemiah's prayer went something like
this: 'Lord God, Creator of all things, you are
awesome and strong, yet merciful and just.
You alone are king. No one but you is kind;
25 no one but you is gracious and just. You are
almighty and eternal, forever ready to rescue
Israel from trouble. You chose our ancestors to
be your own special people. 26 Accept this sac-
rifice which we offer on behalf of all Israel;
protect your chosen people and make us holy.
27 Free those who are slaves in foreign lands
and gather together our scattered people.
Have mercy on our people, who are mistreat-
ed and despised, so that all other nations will
know that you are our God. 28 Punish the
brutal and arrogant people who have
oppressed us, 29 and then establish your people
in your holy land, as Moses said you would.'

The Persian Emperor Hears about the Fire

30 "Then the priests sang hymns. 31 After
the sacrifices had been consumed, Nehemiah
gave orders for the rest of the liquid to be
poured over some large stones. 32 Immediate-
ly a fire blazed up, but it was extinguished by
a flame from the fire on the altar.
33 "News of what had happened spread
everywhere. The Persian emperor heard that
a liquid had been found in the place where
the priests had hidden the altar fire, just
before they were taken into exile. He also
heard that Nehemiah and his friends had
used this liquid to burn the sacrifice on the
altar. 34 When the emperor investigated the
matter and found out that this was true, he
had the area fenced off and made into a
shrine. 35 It became a substantial source of
income for him, and he used the money for
gifts to anyone who was in his good favor.
36 Nehemiah and his friends called the liquid
nephthar which means 'purification,' but most
people call it 'naphtha.'

Jeremiah Hides the Tent of the Lord's Presence

2 "We know from the records that Jere-
miah the prophet instructed the people
who were being taken into exile to hide
some of the fire from the altar, as we have
just mentioned. 2 We also know that he
taught them God's Law and warned them
not to be deceived by the ornamented gold
and silver idols which they would see in the
land of their exile. 3 And then he urged them
never to abandon the Law.
4 "These same records also tell us that
Jeremiah, acting under divine guidance,
commanded the Tent of the Lord's Presence
and the Covenant Box to follow him to the
mountain where Moses had looked down
on the land which God had promised our
people. 5 When Jeremiah got to the moun-
tain, he found a huge cave and there he hid
the Tent of the Lord's Presence, the
Covenant Box, and the altar of incense. Then
he sealed up the entrance.
6 "Some of Jeremiah's friends tried to fol-
low him and mark the way, but they could
not find the cave. 7 When Jeremiah learned
what they had done, he reprimanded them,
saying, 'No one must know about this place

Read 2 Maccabees 1:2–5 as if it were a blessing being prayed for you.

Pray it!

Please and Thanks, God!

There are lots of ways to pray, including asking God for help. We call prayers asking God for help prayers of petition. God welcomes our requests. But our prayer can't just be about what we need—that's kind of selfish, right? We need to also recognize how much God loves us and cares for us (which is why we know we can come to God for help). Nehemiah gives us a great example of praying this way (2 Maccabees 1:24–29) and so does this young person.

Dear God,

Sometimes I can't believe how lucky I've been to have so many friends in my life. Thank you for each and every one of them! And thanks for teaching me what it means to be a good (not perfect!) friend.

God, my best friend, Molly, and I are in the middle of a terrible fight. I mean, it's bad. It might be the end for us. I won't go into all the details, and you already know what happened. Anyway, we're really stuck.

God, you know all the ins and outs of friendship—being the best friend anyone could have. So please, help Molly and me! Give us the courage to fix this, forgive each other, and start over fresh.

Thanks! Amen.
Love, Amanda

— 2 Maccabees 1:24–29

until God gathers his people together again and shows them mercy. 8At that time he will reveal where these things are hidden, and the dazzling light of his presence will be seen in the cloud, as it was in the time of Moses and on the occasion when Solomon prayed that the Temple might be dedicated in holy splendor.'

. . . but they could not find the cave. (2:6)

How Solomon Celebrated the Festival

9"We are also told how the wise King Solomon offered a sacrifice of dedication at the completion of the Temple, 10and that when he prayed, fire came down from heaven and consumed the sacrifices, just as it had done earlier when Moses prayed. 11Moses had explained that the sin offering was consumed by fire because it was not eaten. 12Solomon celebrated the festival for eight days.

Nehemiah's Library

13"These same facts are found in the royal records and in the memoirs of Nehemiah, who established a library and collected the writings of David, letters of the kings concerning offerings, and books about the kings and prophets. 14Judas also collected the books that had been scattered because of the war, and we still have them. 15If you ever need any of these books, let us know, and we will send them.

2:8 Ex 16:10; 24:16; 1 Kings 8:10, 11

An Invitation to Celebrate the Festival

16"Since we are about to celebrate the
Festival of Rededication, we are writing to
you, advising you to celebrate it as well.
17God has saved all his people and has
restored to all of us our holy land, the king-
ship, the priesthood, and the Temple servic-
es, 18just as he promised in his Law. He has
rescued us from terrible evils and has puri-
fied the Temple, and we are confident that
in his mercy he will soon gather us to his
holy Temple from every nation under the
sun."

Author's Preface

19Jason of Cyrene has recorded in five
volumes the story of Judas Maccabeus and
his brothers, the purification of the great
Temple, and the dedication of its altar. 20He
has described the battles with Antiochus
Epiphanes and with his son Eupator, 21and
he has told of the heavenly visions that
appeared to those who fought bravely and
enthusiastically to defend Judaism. Our
forces were few in number, but they plun-
dered the entire country and routed the hea-
then forces. 22They recaptured the Temple
famous throughout the world, liberated
Jerusalem, and restored the laws that were in
danger of being abolished. They were able to
do all these things because the Lord was
merciful and kind to them.
23I will now try to summarize in a single
book the five volumes written by Jason.
24The number of details and the bulk of
material can be overwhelming for anyone
who wants to read an account of the events.
25But I have attempted to simplify it for all
readers; those who read for sheer pleasure
will find enjoyment and those who want to
memorize the facts will not find it difficult.
26Writing such a summary is a difficult task,
demanding hard work and sleepless nights.
27It is as difficult as preparing a banquet that
people of different tastes will enjoy. But I
am happy to undergo this hardship in order
to please my readers. 28I will leave the mat-
ter of details to the original author and
attempt to give only a summary of the
events. 29I am not the builder of a new
house who is concerned with every detail
of the structure, but simply a painter whose
only concern is to make the house look
attractive. 30The historian must master his
subject, examine every detail, and then
explain it carefully, 31but whoever is merely
writing a summary should be permitted to
give a brief account without going into a
detailed discussion. 32So then, without any
further comment, I will begin my story. It
would be foolish to write such a long intro-
duction that the story itself would have to
be cut short.

Study it!

Hanukkah

Second Maccabees actually starts with two letters written to the Jews in Egypt. In this second letter, the Jews in Egypt are being invited to celebrate the festival of Rededication of the Temple in Jerusalem, also known as Hanukkah. Possibly the Jewish community in Jerusalem wanted to keep the Jews in Egypt connected to their roots. The actual event that Hanukkah is based on is covered later in the book.

Hanukkah is celebrated for eight days during December, to remember how the Maccabees rededicated the Temple after it was robbed and damaged by Antiochus IV Epiphanes (see 1 Maccabees 4:52–56 and 2 Maccabees 10:1–8). Each day a candle is lit as the Jews rejoice and give God thanks that their faith has survived through time. Hanukkah is still celebrated by Jewish people today.

— 2 Maccabees 2:16–18

2:16 1 Macc 4:59

The Argument between Onias and Simon

3 When Onias[c] was High Priest in Jerusalem, the holy city enjoyed peace and prosperity, and its laws were strictly obeyed, because he was devout and hated evil. 2The kings of Syria and Egypt honored the Temple and presented it with expensive gifts, 3and King Seleucus,[d] ruler of all Asia, even used to pay the costs of the Temple sacrifices from the revenues he collected.

4But a man by the name of Simon, of the tribe of Bilgah,[e] the chief administrative official of the Temple, lost an argument he had with Onias over the regulations governing the city market. 5At this time Apollonius son of Thraseus was the governor of Greater Syria. Simon went to him 6and said that there was so much money in the Temple treasury that it could not be counted, and since the money was not needed for sacrifices, it might as well be placed under the king's control.

Heliodorus Is Sent to Jerusalem

7When Apollonius met with the king, he told him about the money, and the king ordered Heliodorus, his chief minister, to get it for him. 8Heliodorus set out at once on his mission, but he claimed that he was only making a tour of inspection of the cities of Greater Syria. 9After he had arrived in Jerusalem and had been warmly received by the High Priest, he explained the real reason for his visit and asked if what he had been told was true. 10-11The High Priest then stated that Simon, that devil of a man, had not been telling the truth. There was indeed some money in the Temple treasury, but part of it was set aside for widows and orphans and part of it belonged to Hyrcanus son of Tobias, a very important man. He also pointed out that the total amount was only 30,000 pounds of silver and 15,000 pounds of gold. 12He added that it was absolutely impossible that anyone should be permitted to take the money of those people who had placed their trust in the sanctity and safety of this world-famous Temple.

Heliodorus Plans to Enter the Temple

13But Heliodorus insisted that the money should be taken for the royal treasury, as the king had ordered. 14So he set a day and went into the Temple to supervise the counting of the money. This caused an uproar throughout the entire city. 15Priests, wearing their priestly robes, threw themselves face downward before the altar and begged God to keep the money safe, since he had given the laws designed to protect the money that people deposited in the Temple. 16It was heartbreaking to see the High Priest. His face turned pale, revealing the agony of his soul, 17and his body was trembling with fear, reflecting the pain in his heart. 18People ran

It was heartbreaking to see the High Priest. (3:16)

[c] **3:1** ONIAS: *This is Onias the Third, son of Simon the Second (see 4:4–6; Sir 50:1–21).* [d] **3:3** SELEUCUS: *This is Seleucus the Fourth, known as Philopator, son of Antiochus the Third, 187—175 B.C.* [e] **3:4** *Some ancient translations* Bilgah *(see Neh 12:5,18); Greek* Benjamin.

Where else in this book, besides 2 Maccabees 2:23–32, does the author of 2 Maccabees write a personal note to his readers, about his writing?

Pray it!

Praying for Enemies

Jesus taught us that when someone hurts us, we should not hurt them back—which is normally just the thing we want to do. Not only should we not hurt them, but, we are supposed to *love* our enemies (see Matthew 5:38–48)! How many examples can you think of when loving an enemy seems impossible?

The High Priest, Onias, shows us one way to do this. The Greek king's representative, Heliodorus, was going to take all the gold from the Jewish treasury in the Temple. But when Heliodorus arrived at the Temple, he was attacked by angels. As Heliodorus lay on the Temple floor, near death, Onias had the perfect chance to destroy him. But what did he do? Onias prayed for Heliodorus! God heard the prayer of Onias and spared the life of Heliodorus. Heliodorus praised God and left the Temple treasury alone.

Loving, forgiving, or praying for an enemy may be one of the hardest things to face in life, but we can ask God for the courage and strength to do it. And we can be sure that God will bless us for loving instead of hating.

— 2 Maccabees 3:29–40

from their houses to join together in prayer
that the Temple might not be defiled.
19 Women, wearing nothing but skirts of
sackcloth, crowded the streets. Young girls
whose parents had never allowed them to be
seen in public ran to the gates or to the walls
of the city, or just stared out of their win-
dows. 20 But wherever they went, they lifted
their hands to God in prayer. 21 What a piti-
ful sight it was to see the High Priest in such
great agony and frustration and to see every-
one in the city confused and lying face
down on the ground.

The Lord Protects His Temple

22 While everyone was begging the Lord
Almighty to protect the money that had
been entrusted to his care, 23 Heliodorus
went on with his plan. 24 But at the very
moment that he and his bodyguards arrived
at the treasury, the Lord of all supernatural
powers caused such a vision to appear that
everyone who had dared to enter with
Heliodorus was panic-stricken and weak
with fear at this display of the Lord's power.
25 In the vision they saw a horse and a rider.
The horse had a richly decorated bridle, and
its rider, dressed in gold armor, was fright-
ening. Suddenly the horse rushed at
Heliodorus, then reared up and struck at
him with its hoofs. 26 Heliodorus also saw
two unusually strong and handsome young
men, wearing very fine clothes. They stood
on either side of him and beat him unmer-
cifully. 27 He immediately fell to the ground
unconscious, and his men put him on a
stretcher 28 and carried him out. Only a
moment earlier this man had entered the
treasury with a large group of men, includ-
ing all his bodyguards, but now he was
being carried away helpless. So they all[f]
openly acknowledged the mighty power of
God.

f **3:28** they all; *some manuscripts have* he.

The Temple also functioned like a bank. It had a special room, the treasury, where gold, silver, and other valuables were kept.

Onias Prays for Heliodorus' Recovery

29 Heliodorus lay there unable to speak and without hope of recovery from this demonstration of God's power. 30 But the Jews praised Almighty God because he had miraculously protected his Temple and had brought great happiness where only minutes before there had been fear and confusion. 31 Some of Heliodorus' friends quickly asked Onias the High Priest to pray that the Most High would spare the life of this man who was at the point of death. 32 So the High Priest offered a sacrifice in the hope that God would save Heliodorus, for he did not want the king to think that the Jews had done this to the man he had sent. 33 While Onias was offering the sacrifice, the two young men, wearing the same clothes as before, again appeared to Heliodorus and said, "Be grateful to the High Priest; the Lord has spared your life because of him. 34 Remember that it was the Lord of heaven who punished you. Now go and tell everyone of his great power." When they had said this, they disappeared.

Heliodorus Praises God

35 So Heliodorus offered a sacrifice to the Lord and made many promises, because the Lord had spared his life. Then he said goodbye to Onias and returned with his army to the king. 36 There he told everyone what the Lord, the most powerful of all gods, had done.

37 When the king asked Heliodorus who would be the best man to send on the next mission to Jerusalem, Heliodorus replied, 38 "If you have an enemy or know of someone plotting against your government, send him. He will come back badly beaten, if he comes back at all, for some strange power from God is at work there. 39 The God of heaven watches over the Temple; he strikes down and destroys anyone who comes to harm it." 40 That is the story of how the Temple treasury was protected from Heliodorus.

Simon Accuses Onias

4 But Simon (mentioned earlier as the one who informed Apollonius about the money and brought trouble on the nation) also lied about Onias, claiming that he was responsible for the attack on Heliodorus and for the difficulties that followed. 2 He dared to accuse Onias of plotting against the government—Onias who not only had made donations to Jerusalem and had protected the Temple, but who was eager to see that all our laws were obeyed. 3-4 Apollonius son of Menestheus, the governor of Greater Syria, encouraged Simon in every evil thing he did, and Simon's opposition finally grew so strong that one of his trusted followers committed several murders. Onias realized how dangerous the situation had become, 5 so he went to the king, not for the purpose of making accusations against his own people, but for the common good of all Jews, both in their private and public lives. 6 He realized that without the king's cooperation there was no hope for peace, and Simon would keep on with his foolishness.

Jason Introduces Greek Customs

7 Later, when King Seleucus died and Antiochus (known as Epiphanes) became king, Jason the brother of Onias became High Priest by corrupt means. 8 He went to see[g] the king and offered him 27,000 pounds of silver with 6,000 more pounds to be paid later. 9 Jason also offered him an additional 11,250 pounds of silver for the authority to establish a stadium where young men could train and to enroll the people of Jerusalem as citizens of Antioch.[h]

10 The king gave his approval, and just as soon as Jason took over the office of High Priest, he made the people of Jerusalem change to the Greek way of life. 11 He began by abolishing the favors that John had secured for the Jews from previous Syrian kings. (John was the father of the Eupolemus who later went to Rome to make an alliance

[g] **4:8** went to see; *or* wrote to. [h] **4:9** the people . . . Antioch; *or* the men of Jerusalem as supporters of King Antiochus.

4:7 1 Macc 1:10 **4:11** 1 Macc 8:17

Study it!

The Price of Evil

Good and faithful Onias has his office of High Priest snatched away by Jason, who later loses his place to Menelaus. Both Jason and Menelaus are selfish, greedy, controlling men whose evil acts bring God's punishment upon the Jews.

Instead of honoring his faith, Jason forced the Greek way of life on the Jewish population. The Temple, the Law, and Jewish values are tossed out the window in favor of Greek customs and ideals (2 Maccabees 4:10–17). Menelaus steals and cheats and even has Onias killed.

Evil does not go unpunished. Unfortunately, innocent people can suffer the consequences of evil, as well as the wicked people who caused the trouble. From this point on in 2 Maccabees, faithful Jews are caught in battle after battle, and many are tortured and killed by their enemies.

What are some of the differences you see in Onias, Jason, and Menelaus—both as religious leaders and as men? What lessons can you learn from them?

— 2 Maccabees, chapter 4

and to establish ties of friendship.) Jason also
did away with our Jewish customs and intro-
duced new customs that were contrary to
our Law. 12 With great enthusiasm he built a
stadium near the Temple hill and led our
finest young men to adopt the Greek custom
of participating in athletic events. 13 Because
of the unrivaled wickedness of Jason, that
ungodly and illegitimate High Priest, the
craze for the Greek way of life and for for-
eign customs reached such a point 14 that
even the priests lost all interest in their sacred
duties. They lost interest in the Temple ser-
vices and neglected the sacrifices. Just as soon
as the signal was given, they would rush off
to take part in the games that were forbidden
by our Law. 15 They did not care about any-
thing their ancestors had valued; they prized
only Greek honors. 16 And this turned out to
be the source of all their troubles, for the
very people whose ways they admired and
whose customs they tried to imitate became
their enemies and oppressed them. 17 It is a
serious thing to disregard God's Law, as you
will see from the following events.

Jerusalem under Syrian Influence

18 Once when the king was present for the
athletic games that were held every five[i]
years in the city of Tyre, 19 that worthless
Jason sent some men there from Jerusalem,
who were also enrolled as citizens of Anti-
och, to take 22,500 pounds of silver to pay
for a sacrifice to the god Hercules. But even
these men did not think it was fitting to use
such a large sum of money for a sacrifice,
and 20 so the money originally intended as a
sacrifice to Hercules was used for the con-
struction of warships.

21 When Apollonius son of Menestheus
was sent to Egypt to attend the crowning of
Philometor as king, Antiochus learned that
Philometor was opposed to his policies.
Antiochus became concerned about the
security of his own kingdom, so he went to
Joppa and then on to Jerusalem. 22 There he
was welcomed with great splendor by Jason
and the people of the city who went out to
greet him, shouting and carrying torches.
From Jerusalem Antiochus led his army to
Phoenicia.

Menelaus Becomes High Priest

23 Three years later, Jason sent Menelaus
(brother of the Simon[j] mentioned earlier) to
take some money to the king and to get his
decision on several important matters. 24 But

[i] **4:18** five; *or* four. [j] **4:23** SIMON: *See 3:4.*

when he stood before the king, Menelaus impressed him with his show of authority and offered 22,500 pounds of silver more than Jason had offered for his appointment to the office of High Priest. [25]As a result Menelaus returned to Jerusalem with papers from the king, confirming him as High Priest. But he possessed no other qualifications; he had the temper of a cruel tyrant and could be as fierce as a wild animal. [26]So Jason, who had cheated his own brother out of the office of High Priest, was now forced to flee to the land of Ammon. [27]Menelaus continued to be High Priest, but he never paid any of the money he had promised the king. [28]However, Sostratus, the captain of the fort in Jerusalem, kept demanding the money, since it was his responsibility to collect it. So finally, the two men were summoned to appear before the king concerning the matter. [29]Menelaus left his brother Lysimachus as acting High Priest, while Sostratus left the fort under the command of Crates, the commander of the mercenary troops from Cyprus.

The Murder of Onias

[30]Meanwhile, there was a revolt in the Cilician cities of Tarsus and Mallus, because the king had given those cities to Antiochis, his mistress. [31]So the king left Andronicus, one of his high officials, in command, while he hurried off to Cilicia to restore order. [32]Menelaus took advantage of this opportunity and presented Andronicus with some of the gold objects he had removed from the Temple in Jerusalem. He had already sold some of them to the city of Tyre and to other nearby cities. [33]When Onias heard about this, he fled for safety to a temple at Daphne near the city of Antioch and openly accused Menelaus. [34]Then Menelaus secretly persuaded Andronicus to kill Onias. So Andronicus went to Onias and deceived him with a friendly greeting and with promises of safety. Although Onias was suspicious, Andronicus finally lured him away from the safety of the temple and immediately murdered him in cold blood.

Andronicus Is Punished

[35]The Jews and Gentiles were very angry because Onias had been murdered. [36]So when the king returned from the territory of Cilicia, the Jews of Antioch went to him and protested against this senseless killing. Many Gentiles felt the same way about the crime. [37]King Antiochus was deeply grieved and was so filled with sorrow that he was moved to tears when he recalled the wisdom and self-control that Onias had shown throughout his life. [38]Antiochus became so angry that he tore off Andronicus' royal robe, stripped him naked, and marched him around the city to the very spot where Onias had been murdered. Then Antiochus had this bloodthirsty murderer put to death. This was how the Lord gave him the punishment he deserved.

Lysimachus Is Killed

[39]Meanwhile, with the support of his brother Menelaus, Lysimachus had on numerous occasions robbed the Jerusalem Temple and had taken many of its gold objects. When word of this spread around, crowds began to gather in protest against Lysimachus. [40]Finally, the crowds were becoming dangerous and were beginning to get out of control, so Lysimachus sent 3,000 armed men to attack them. They were led by Auranus, a man as stupid as he was old. [41]When the Jews in the Temple courtyard realized what was happening, they picked up rocks, pieces of wood, or simply handfuls of ashes from the altar and threw them at Lysimachus and his men in the confusion. [42]They killed a few of Lysimachus' men, wounded many of them, and all the rest ran for their lives. Lysimachus himself, that temple robber, was killed near the Temple treasury.

4:34 Dan 9:26

"It is a serious thing to disregard God's Law" *(2 Maccabees 4:17)*.

Menelaus Is Brought to Trial

43 Because of this incident Menelaus was
brought to trial. 44 When the king came to
the city of Tyre, the Jewish authorities in
Jerusalem sent three men to bring charges
against Menelaus. 45 When Menelaus saw
that he was losing the case, he offered Ptole-
my son of Dorymenes a large bribe to per-
suade the king to decide in his favor.
46 Ptolemy then asked the king to go outside
the courtroom with him, as though to get
some fresh air, and there he persuaded him
to change his mind 47 and declare Menelaus
innocent of the charges against him. So
Menelaus was set free, although he had
caused the trouble; but the three men, whom
even the cruel Scythians would have
declared innocent, were sentenced to death.
48 The three men had spoken in defense of
Jerusalem, its people,[k] and the sacred objects
stolen from the Temple, but they were
quickly and unjustly executed. 49 Some of
the people of Tyre, however, showed their
disgust with this crime and their respect for
these men by giving them a splendid funeral.
50 Menelaus stayed on in his position because
of the greed of those in power. He grew
more evil every day and became the worst
enemy of his own people.

Visions of a Battle

5 About this time Antiochus the Fourth
made a second attack against Egypt.
2 For nearly forty days people all over
Jerusalem saw visions of cavalry troops in
gold armor charging across the sky. The rid-
ers were armed with spears and their swords
were drawn. 3 They were lined up in battle
against one another, attacking and counter-
attacking. Shields were clashing, there was a
rain of spears, and arrows flew through the
air. All the different kinds of armor and the
gold bridles on the horses flashed in the sun-
light. 4 Everyone in the city prayed that these
visions might be a good sign.

Attacking and counterattacking (5:3)

Jason Attacks Jerusalem

5 When a false report began to spread
that Antiochus had died, Jason took more
than a thousand men and suddenly attacked
Jerusalem. They drove back those stationed
on the city walls and finally captured the
city. Menelaus fled for safety to the fort,
near the Temple hill, 6 while Jason and his
men went on slaughtering their fellow Jews
without mercy. Jason did not realize that
success against one's own people is the
worst kind of failure. He even considered
his success a victory over enemies, rather
than a defeat of his own people. 7 But Jason
did not take over the government. Instead
he was forced to flee once again to the ter-
ritory of the Ammonites, and in the end his
evil plot brought him nothing but shame
and disgrace, 8 and he died in misery. Aretas,
the ruler of the Arabs, imprisoned him; he
was looked upon as a criminal and despised
because he had betrayed his own people;
everyone was hunting for him, and he had
to run from town to town. He fled to
Egypt for safety, 9 then to Greece, hoping to
find refuge among the Spartans, who were
related to the Jews. Finally, this man, who
had forced so many others to flee from
their own country, died as a fugitive in a
foreign land. 10 Jason had killed many peo-
ple and left their bodies unburied, but now
his own death was unmourned. He was not
given a funeral or even buried with his
ancestors.

[k] **4:48** its people; *some manuscripts also have* the surrounding villages.

It was bad enough when Jason, the former High Priest, attacked Jerusalem. Then King Antiochus attacked. How many people did he kill?

Antiochus Attacks Jerusalem
(1 Maccabees 1:20–63)

11 When the news of what had happened in Jerusalem reached Antiochus, he thought the whole country of Judea was in revolt, and he became as furious as a wild animal. So he left Egypt and took Jerusalem by storm, 12 giving his men orders to cut down without mercy everyone they met and to slaughter anyone they found hiding in the houses. 13 They murdered everyone—men and women, boys and girls; even babies were butchered. 14 Three days later Jerusalem had lost 80,000 people: 40,000 killed in the attack and at least that many taken away to be sold as slaves.

15 But Antiochus was still not satisfied. He even dared to enter the holiest Temple in all the world, guided by Menelaus, who had become a traitor both to his religion and to his people. 16 With his filthy and unholy hands, Antiochus swept away the sacred objects of worship and the gifts which other kings had given to increase the glory and honor of the Temple. 17 He was so thrilled with his conquest that he did not realize that the Lord had let his holy Temple be defiled because the sin of the people of Jerusalem had made him angry for a while. 18 If the people of Jerusalem had not been involved in so many sins, Antiochus would have been punished immediately and prevented from taking such a foolish action. He would have suffered the same fate as Heliodorus, who was sent by King Seleucus to inspect the treasury. 19 But the Lord did not choose his people for the sake of his Temple; he established his Temple for the sake of his people. 20 So the Temple shared in the people's suffering but also later shared in their prosperity. The Lord abandoned it when he became angry, but restored it when his anger had cooled down.

Another Attack against Jerusalem

21 Antiochus took 135,000 pounds of silver from the Temple and hurried off to Antioch. Such was his arrogance that he felt he could make ships sail across dry land or troops march across the sea. 22 He appointed governors to cause trouble for the people. In Jerusalem he placed Philip, a man from Phrygia who was more evil than Antiochus himself. 23 At Mount Gerizim he placed Andronicus. In addition to these, there was Menelaus, who mistreated his fellow Jews far worse than the governors did. Antiochus hated the Jews so much 24 that he sent an army of 22,000 mercenary troops from Mysia to Jerusalem under the command of a man named Apollonius, with orders to kill every man in the city and to sell the women and boys as slaves. 25 Apollonius arrived in Jerusalem, pretending to be on a peace mission. Then on a Sabbath, when all the Jews were observing the day of rest, he led his troops, who were fully armed, in a parade outside the city. 26 Suddenly he commanded his men to kill everyone who had come out to see them. They rushed into the city and murdered a great many people.

27 But Judas Maccabeus and about nine others escaped into the barren mountains, where they lived like wild animals. In order not to defile themselves, they ate only plants which they found growing there.

The Jews Are Persecuted Because of Their Faith

6 Not long after that, the king sent an elderly Athenian[l] to force the Jews to abandon their religion and the customs of their ancestors. 2 He was also to defile their Temple by dedicating it to the Olympian god Zeus.[m] The temple on Mount Gerizim was to be officially named "Temple of Zeus the God of Hospitality," as the people who lived there had requested.

3 The oppression was harsh and almost intolerable. 4 Gentiles filled the Temple with drinking parties and all sorts of immorality. They even had intercourse with prostitutes there. Forbidden objects were brought into the Temple, 5 and the altar was covered with detestable sacrifices prohibited by our Law. 6 It

[l] **6:1** elderly Athenian; *or* an elder of Athens, *or* Athenaios the elder, *or* Geron an Athenian; *some manuscripts have* an elderly Antiochean; *or* an elder of Antioch. [m] **6:2** ZEUS: *The supreme god of the Greeks; Mount Olympus was thought to be his home.*

was impossible to observe the Sabbath, to cel-
ebrate any of the traditional festivals, or even
so much as to admit to being a Jew. 7Each
month when the king's birthday was celebrat-
ed, the Jews were compelled by brute force to
eat the intestines of sacrificial animals. Then,
during the festival in honor of the wine god
Dionysus, they were required to wear ivy
wreaths on their heads and march in proces-
sion. 8On the advice of Ptolemy,[n] the neigh-
boring Greek cities were also instructed to
require Jews to eat the sacrifices; 9they were
told to put to death every Jew who refused to
adopt the Greek way of life. It was easy to see
that hard times were ahead. 10For example,
two women were arrested for having their
babies circumcised. They were paraded around
the city with their babies hung from their
breasts; then they were thrown down from the
city wall. 11On another occasion, Philip was
told that some Jews had gathered in a nearby
cave to observe the Sabbath in secret. Philip
attacked and burned them all alive. They had
such respect for the Sabbath that they would
not fight to defend themselves.

The Lord Punishes and Shows Mercy

12I beg you not to become discouraged as
you read about the terrible things that hap-
pened. Consider that this was the Lord's way
of punishing his people, not of destroying
them. 13In fact, it is a sign of kindness to pun-
ish a person immediately for his sins, rather
than to wait a long time. 14The Lord does not
treat us as he does other nations: he waits
patiently until they have become deeply
involved in sin before he punishes them, 15but
he punishes us before we have sinned too
much. 16So the Lord is always merciful to us,
his own people. Although he punishes us with
disasters, he never abandons us. 17I have made
these few observations by way of reminder.
We will now get on with the story.

Eleazar Dies for His Faith

18There was an elderly and highly respect-
ed teacher of the Law by the name of
Eleazar, whose mouth was being forced open
to make him eat pork. 19-20But he preferred
an honorable death rather than a life of dis-
grace. So he spit out the meat and went
willingly to the place of torture, showing
how people should have courage to refuse
unclean food, even if it costs them their
lives. 21-22Those in charge of the sacrifice

> **Live it!**
>
> ### Integrity
>
> **Eleazar had the chance to trick the Greeks and save his life. But he wouldn't do it. He was concerned that the young Jews would think he had compromised his faith and believe it was okay for them to do the same.**
>
> **Doing the right thing, no matter the consequences, is what *integrity* is all about. Some people are tempted to think that lying, cheating, or stealing a little isn't so bad if no one seems to get hurt because of it. But when we do these things, they slowly destroy our character. We become untrustworthy, selfish, and greedy. We lose track of what is right and wrong and care less and less about how our actions affect other people.**
>
> **Integrity is important for ourselves, for those around us, and ultimately to the world. We must trust that God sees our actions and blesses us for choosing what is right. A person of integrity is strong, good, and courageous. This is truly a prize for any human—more precious than gold.**
>
> **Who do you know who is like this?**
>
> **— 2 Maccabees 6:18–31**

[n] **6:8** Ptolemy *(see 4:45); some manuscripts have* the people of Ptolemais.

6:10 1 Macc 1:60, 61 **6:11** 1 Macc 2:32–38 **6:18** Lev 11:7, 8; Heb 11:35

had been friends of Eleazar for a long time,
and because of this friendship they told him
privately to bring meat that was lawful for
him to eat. He need only pretend to eat the
pork, they said, and in this way he would not
be put to death.
23 But Eleazar made a decision worthy of
his gray hair and advanced age. All his life he
had lived in perfect obedience to God's holy
laws, so he replied, "Kill me, here and now.
24 Such deception is not worthy of a man of
my years. Many young people would think
that I had denied my faith after I was ninety
years old. 25 If I pretended to eat this meat,
just to live a little while longer, it would
bring shame and disgrace on me and lead
many young people astray. 26 For the present
I might be able to escape what you could do
to me, but whether I live or die, I cannot
escape Almighty God. 27 If I die bravely now,
it will show that I deserved my long life. 28 It
will also set a good example of the way
young people should be willing and glad to
die for our sacred and respected laws."
As soon as he said these things, he went[o]
off to be tortured, 29 and the very people who
had treated him kindly a few minutes before,
now turned against him, because they
thought he had spoken like a madman.
30 When they had beaten him almost to the
point of death, he groaned and said, "The
Lord possesses all holy knowledge. He knows
I could have escaped these terrible sufferings
and death, yet he also knows that I gladly suf-
fer these things, because I fear him."
31 So Eleazar died. But his courageous
death was remembered as a glorious exam-
ple, not only by young people, but by the
entire nation as well.

A Mother and Her Sons Die for Their Faith

7 On another occasion a Jewish mother
and her seven sons were arrested. The
king was having them beaten to force them

His courageous death was remembered as a glorious example. (6:31)

to eat pork. 2 Then one of the young men
said, "What do you hope to gain by doing
this? We would rather die than abandon the
traditions of our ancestors."
3 This made the king so furious that he
gave orders for huge pans and kettles to be
heated red hot, 4 and it was done immediate-
ly. Then he told his men to cut off the
tongue of the one who had spoken and to
scalp him and chop off his hands and feet,
while his mother and six brothers looked
on. 5 After the young man had been reduced
to a helpless mass of breathing flesh, the king
gave orders for him to be carried over and
thrown into one of the pans. As a cloud of
smoke streamed up from the pan, the broth-
ers and their mother encouraged one anoth-
er to die bravely, saying, 6 "The Lord God is
looking on and understands our suffering.
Moses made this clear when he wrote a song
condemning those who had abandoned the
Lord. He said, 'The Lord will have mercy on
those who serve him.' "
7 After the first brother had died in this
way, the soldiers started amusing themselves
with the second one by tearing the hair and
skin from his head. Then they asked him,
"Now will you eat this pork, or do you want
us to chop off your hands and feet one by
one?"
8 He replied in his native language, "I will

[o] **6:28** went; *some manuscripts have* was dragged.
7:1–42 Heb 11:35, 36 **7:6** Deut 32:36

Would people who know you say you are a person of integrity?

Catholic Connections

Eternal Life

This is one of the most painful and gruesome stories in the Bible! Imagine being that mother, watching the slow torture and death of each of her seven sons, then suffering the same fate herself. Why is this story here?

Not only does this family provide us with another example of courage and integrity in the face of religious persecution, but it also teaches us about the reality of eternal life. This family knew that those who live with justice and love, even if they suffer for it, will be raised from the dead and live with God forever. And those who reject God and live a wicked life will be punished for all eternity. This is one of the first places in the Bible that eternal life is spoken about.

— 2 Maccabees, chapter 7

never eat it!" So the soldiers tortured him,
just as they had the first one, 9but with his
dying breath he cried out to the king, "You
butcher! You may kill us, but the King of the
universe will raise us from the dead and give
us eternal life, because we have obeyed his
laws."
10The soldiers began entertaining them-
selves with the third brother. When he was
ordered to stick out his tongue, he quickly
did so. Then he bravely held out his hands
11and courageously said, "God gave these to
me. But his laws mean more to me than my
hands, and I know God will give them back
to me again." 12The king and those with
him were amazed at his courage and at his
willingness to suffer.
13After he had died, the soldiers tortured
the fourth one in the same cruel way, 14but
his final words were, "I am glad to die at
your hands, because we have the assurance
that God will raise us from death. But there
will be no resurrection to life for you, Anti-
ochus!"
15When the soldiers took the fifth boy
and began torturing him, 16he looked the
king squarely in the eye and said, "You have
the power to do whatever you want with us,
even though you also are mortal. But do not
think that God has abandoned our people.
17Just wait. God will use his great power to
torture you and your descendants."
18Then the soldiers took the sixth boy,
and just before he died he said, "Make no
mistake. We are suffering what we deserve,
because we have sinned against our God.
That's why all these terrible things are hap-
pening to us. 19But don't think for a minute
that you will avoid being punished for fight-
ing against God."
20The mother was the most amazing one
of them all, and she deserves a special place
in our memory. Although she saw her seven
sons die in a single day, she endured it with
great courage because she trusted in the
Lord. 21She combined womanly emotion
with manly courage and spoke words of
encouragement to each of her sons in their
native language. 22"I do not know how
your life began in my womb," she would
say, "I was not the one who gave you life
and breath and put together each part of

See Daniel 12:23 for an inspiring description of those who are resurrected from the dead.

Study it!

Nonviolent Resistance

Eleazar and the woman and her seven sons give us wonderful examples of nonviolent resistance to injustice. These Jews did not cooperate with their persecutors. They did not fight them (matching violence with violence), but neither did they just give in to them. They held on firmly to their beliefs and confronted the evil facing them.

In recent times people like Rosa Parks, Martin Luther King, and Mahatma Gandhi powerfully stood up against injustice in a nonviolent way. They fought against racism and neglect of poor people. And each one suffered for it. But they accepted this because they knew God brings good out of the suffering of the just. Many laws protecting human rights have been established because of their nonviolent resistance to injustice.

— 2 Maccabees, chapters 6–7

your body. 23 It was God who did it, God
who created the universe, the human race,
and all that exists. He is merciful and he
will give you back life and breath again,
because you love his laws more than you
love yourself."
24 Antiochus was sure that the mother was
making fun of him, so he did his best to
convince her youngest son to abandon the
traditions of his ancestors. He promised not
only to make the boy rich and famous, but
to place him in a position of authority and
to give him the title "Friend of the King."
25 But the boy paid no attention to him, so
Antiochus tried to persuade the boy's moth-
er to talk him into saving his life, 26 and after
much persuasion she agreed to do so.
27 Leaning over her son, she fooled the cruel
tyrant by saying in her native language, "My
son, have pity on me. Remember that I car-
ried you in my womb for nine months and
nursed you for three years. I have taken care
of you and looked after all your needs up to
the present day. 28 So I urge you, my child, to
look at the sky and the earth. Consider
everything you see there, and realize that
God made it all from nothing, just as he
made the human race. 29 Don't be afraid of
this butcher. Give up your life willingly and
prove yourself worthy of your brothers, so
that by God's mercy I may receive you back
with them at the resurrection."
30 Before she could finish speaking, the
boy said, "King Antiochus, what are you
waiting for? I refuse to obey your orders. I
only obey the commands in the Law which
Moses gave to our ancestors. 31 You have
thought up all kinds of cruel things to do to
our people, but you won't escape the pun-
ishment that God has in store for you. 32-33 It
is true that our living Lord is angry with us
and is making us suffer because of our sins,
in order to correct and discipline us. But this
will last only a short while, for we are still
his servants, and he will forgive us. 34 But you
are the cruelest and most disgusting thing
that ever lived. So don't fool yourself with
illusions of greatness while you punish God's
people. 35 There is no way for you to escape
punishment at the hands of the almighty and
all-seeing God. 36 My brothers suffered
briefly because of our faithfulness to God's
covenant, but now they have entered eternal

"King Antiochus . . . I refuse to obey your orders." (7:30)

life.[p] But you will fall under God's judgment
and be punished as you deserve for your
arrogance. [37]I now give up my body and my
life for the laws of our ancestors, just as my
brothers did. But I also beg God to show
mercy to his people quickly and to torture
you until you are forced to acknowledge
that he alone is God. [38]May my brothers and
I be the last to suffer the anger of Almighty
God, which he has justly brought upon our
entire nation."

[39]These words of ridicule made Antiochus
so furious that he had the boy tortured even
more cruelly than his brothers. [40]And so the
boy died, with absolute trust in the Lord,
never unfaithful for a minute.

[41]Last of all, the mother was put to death.

[42]But I have said enough about the Jews
being tortured and being forced to eat the
intestines of sacrificial animals.

Judas Maccabeus Revolts

(1 Maccabees 3:1–26)

8 Judas Maccabeus and his friends went
secretly from village to village until
they had gathered a force of about 6,000
Jewish men who had remained faithful to
their religion. [2]They begged the Lord to
help his people, now trampled under foot
by all nations, to take pity on the Temple,
now defiled by pagans, [3]and to have mercy
on Jerusalem, now destroyed and almost lev-
eled to the ground. [4]They also asked the
Lord to show his hatred of evil by taking
revenge on those who were murdering his
people, mercilessly slaughtering innocent
children, and saying evil things against the
Lord.

[5]When Judas had finally organized his
forces, the Gentiles were unable to stand
against him, because the Lord's anger against
Israel had now turned to mercy. [6-7]Judas
would make sudden attacks on towns and
villages and burn them. He captured strate-
gic positions and routed many enemy
troops, finding that he was most successful at
night. People everywhere spoke of his brav-
ery.

Study it!

God's Mercy Returns

Judas Maccabeus and his friends have been hiding out, praying for God's help, protection, and strength to fight their enemies. Now Judas has gathered a small army of Jews, and they begin winning battles. They believe God's anger has turned to mercy and that they will be unbeatable.

In 2 Maccabees we once again see the pattern of salvation history that is repeated again and again throughout the Bible:

- **We are blessed and are faithful to God.**
- **We fall into sin.**
- **We suffer because of our sin.**
- **We beg God for help, and we promise to be more faithful.**
- **God is merciful and saves us.**
- **God blesses us again, and we are faithful to God.**

— 2 Maccabees 8:1–7

Ptolemy Sends Nicanor to Attack Judas

(1 Maccabees 3:38–41)

[8]When Philip, governor of Jerusalem, real-
ized that Judas was gaining ground little by
little and that his victories were becoming
more and more frequent, he wrote a letter to
Ptolemy, governor of Greater Syria, request-
ing his help in defending the royal interests.
[9]Ptolemy immediately appointed Nicanor
son of Patroclus, who was also in the closest
circle of the King's Friends, and sent him
with more than 20,000 troops of various
nationalities to wipe out the entire Jewish
race. Ptolemy also appointed Gorgias, a gen-
eral of wide military experience, to go with
him. [10]King Antiochus owed the Romans

[p] **7:36** briefly . . . life; *or* briefly, but now they have entered eternal life because of our covenant with God.

150,000 pounds of silver; Nicanor planned
to pay off the debt by selling Jewish prison-
ers of war as slaves.
11 So he at once sent word to the towns
along the coast, informing them that he
would be selling Jews for less than a pound of
silver each. But he did not know of the judg-
ment that Almighty God had in store for him.

Judas Learns of Nicanor's Plans

(1 Maccabees 3:42–54)

12 Judas learned that Nicanor was advancing
with his army toward Judea, so he informed
his men. 13 Some were cowardly and did not
believe in the justice of God, and they ran
away as fast as they could. 14 But others sold all
their remaining possessions so that the Lord
would consider them worthy to be saved
from the godless Nicanor, who had sold them
as slaves even before the battle had taken
place. 15 They prayed that if God was not will-
ing to do this for their sake alone, he might
be willing to rescue them because of the
covenants he had made with their ancestors,
and because he, the great and wonderful God,
had called them to be his people. 16 Judas
brought together all 6,000 of his men and
encouraged them not to be frightened or to
flee in panic at the sight of the large number
of Gentile troops who were marching against
them without cause. Instead they should fight
bravely, 17 never forgetting the crimes the
Gentiles had committed against the Temple
and how they had made Jerusalem suffer ter-
ribly and had done away with Jewish tradi-
tions. 18 "They rely on their weapons and
their daring," Judas said, "but we trust in
Almighty God, who is able to destroy not
only these troops, but, if necessary, the entire
world, with a mere nod of his head."
19 Then Judas went on to remind them of
the ways God had helped their ancestors:
during the time of Sennacherib 185,000 of
the enemy had been destroyed; 20 and once
in Babylonia 8,000 Jews came to the aid of
4,000 Macedonians, defeating 120,000 Gala-
tians and taking a great deal of loot, all
because of God's help.

Judas Defeats Nicanor

(1 Maccabees 3:55—4:27)

21 Judas' words encouraged his men and
made them willing to die for their religion
and their country. He then divided his army
into four divisions 22 of about 1,500 men
each, with himself and his brothers Simon,
Joseph, and Jonathan each in charge of a
division. 23 After ordering Eleazar to read
aloud[q] from the holy book, he gave his men
the battle cry: "God will help us," and per-
sonally led the attack against Nicanor.
24 Almighty God fought on their side, and
they killed more than 9,000 of the enemy.
They wounded many others and put the
entire enemy army to flight. 25 They seized
the money from the people who had come
to buy them as slaves. Then they pursued the
enemy a long way, until they had to return,
26 because it was almost time for the Sabbath
to begin. 27 When they had collected the
enemy's weapons and looted the dead, they
celebrated the Sabbath, praising the Lord and
giving thanks to him, because he had
brought them safely to that day and had
given them the first sign of his mercy.
28 When the Sabbath was over, they gave
some of the loot to the victims of persecu-
tion and to the widows and orphans; then
they divided the rest among their own fami-
lies. 29 Afterward they joined together in
prayer to the merciful Lord, asking him to
look favorably upon his servants.

Judas Defeats Timothy and Bacchides

30 The Jews later fought against the forces
of Timothy and Bacchides and killed more
than 20,000 of them. They captured some
very high fortresses and took a lot of loot,
which they divided equally among

[q] **8:23** *Probable text* After . . . aloud; *Greek unclear.*
8:23 1 Macc 3:48

Do you think God takes sides in our wars?

themselves and the widows, orphans, old men, and the victims of persecution. 31They carefully collected all the enemy's weapons and stored them in strategic places, but the rest of the loot was taken to Jerusalem. 32They executed the commanding officer of Timothy's forces, a godless man who had caused the Jews much suffering. 33While celebrating their victory in the city of their ancestors, they burned alive those men who had set fire to the Temple gates. The dead included Callisthenes, who had hidden in a small house; and so he received the punishment he deserved for his evil deeds.

34In this way, the evil Nicanor, who had brought a thousand merchants to buy the Jews, 35was defeated with the help of the Lord by the very people he despised so much. He threw off his splendid uniform and fled all alone like a runaway slave, until he reached Antioch. He had succeeded only in destroying his entire army. 36This man, who had tried to pay a debt to Rome by selling the people of Jerusalem, showed that the Jews could not be defeated. God was their mighty Defender, because they obeyed the laws he had given them.

The Lord Punishes Antiochus
(1 Maccabees 6:1–7; 2 Maccabees 1:11–17)

9 About this time Antiochus was retreating in disorder from Persia, 2where he had entered the city of Persepolis and had attempted to rob a temple and take control of the city. The people took up arms and attacked Antiochus, forcing his army to retreat in disgrace. 3When he reached Ecbatana, he was told what had happened to the forces of Nicanor and Timothy. 4He became furious and decided to make the Jews pay for the defeat he had suffered. So he ordered his chariot driver not to stop until they reached Jerusalem. With great arrogance he said, "I will turn Jerusalem into a graveyard full of Jews."

But he did not know that he was heading straight for God's judgment. 5In fact, as soon as he had said these words, the all-seeing Lord, the God of Israel, struck him down with an invisible but fatal blow. He was seized with sharp intestinal pains for which there was no relief— 6a fitting punishment for the man who had tortured others in so many terrible ways! 7But this in no way caused him to give up his pride. Instead he became more arrogant than ever, and breathing out fiery threats against the Jews, he gave orders to drive even faster. As a result he fell out of his chariot with such a thud that it made every bone in his body ache. 8His arrogant pride made him think he had the superhuman strength to make ocean waves obey him and to weigh high mountains on a pair of scales. But suddenly he fell flat on the ground and had to be carried off on a stretcher, a clear sign to everyone of God's power. 9Even the eyes of this godless man were crawling with worms and he lived in terrible pain and agony. The stink was so bad that his entire army was sickened, 10and no one was able to come close enough to carry him around. Yet only a short while before, he thought he could take hold of the stars.

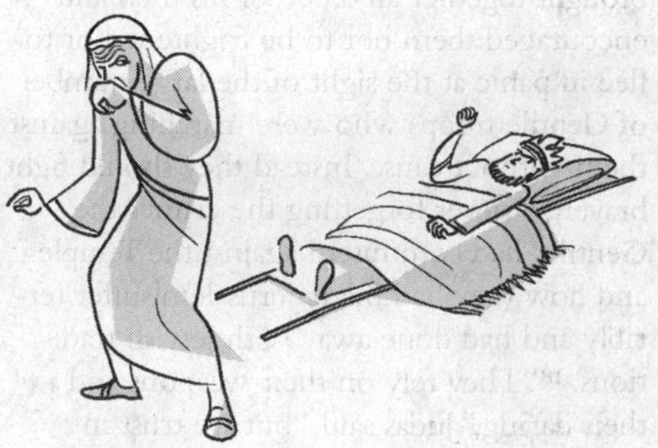

No one was able to come close enough. (9:10)

Antiochus Makes a Promise to God
(1 Maccabees 6:8–17)

11Antiochus was deeply depressed and suffered constant pain because of the punishment that God had brought on him, so he finally came to his senses and gave up his arrogant pride. 12Then, when he could no longer endure his own stink, he said, "It is

What caused Antiochus' change of heart toward the Jews?

right that all mortals should be subject to
God and not think that they are his equal."
13The time of the Lord's mercy had come to
an end for Antiochus, but this worthless man
made the Lord a promise: 14"I once intended
to level Jerusalem to the ground and make
that holy city a graveyard full of Jews," he
said, "but now I declare it a free city. 15I had
planned to throw out the dead bodies of the
Jews and their children for the wild animals
and the birds to eat, for I did not consider
them worth burying. But now I intend to
grant them the same privileges as the citizens
of Athens enjoy. 16I once looted the Temple
and took its sacred utensils, but I will fill it
with splendid gifts and with better utensils
than before, and I will pay the cost of the sac-
rifices from my own resources. 17Besides all
this, I will become a Jew myself and go wher-
ever people live, telling them of God's power."

Antiochus' Letter to the Jews

18Antiochus was in despair and could find
no relief from his pain, because God was
punishing him as he deserved, so he wrote
the following letter to the Jews:

19"King Antiochus to the Jews, my
most distinguished subjects. Warm greet-
ings and best wishes for your health and
prosperity.

20"I hope that you and your families are
in good health and that all goes well with
you. My hope is in God, 21and I remem-
ber with a deep sense of joy the respect
and kindness that you have shown me.

"On my way home from Persia I fell
violently ill, and so I thought it best to
begin making plans for the general wel-
fare of the people. 22I have not given up
hopes of getting well; in fact I am fully
confident that I will recover. 23But I recall
that my father used to appoint a successor
whenever he went on a military campaign
east of the Euphrates. 24He did this so that
if something unexpected happened, or if
some bad news came back, then his sub-
jects would not be afraid, for they knew
who had been left in command. 25Also, I
know how the rulers along the frontiers
of my kingdom are constantly on the
lookout for any opportunity that may
come along. That is why I have appointed
my son Antiochus to succeed me as king.
I have frequently entrusted him to your

Study it!

Is God Violent?

The Maccabees believed God punished evil, therefore God caused their military victories. This thinking can lead us to believe that God is in favor of war and will assist in any violence necessary to defeat evil people. But doesn't this sound odd, when we've been taught to believe that God is all-loving, compassionate, merciful, and more? Does God have a split personality?

No. Jesus made it very clear to us: God is love and calls us to love one another, even our enemies.

So why is God painted to be a great warrior in the Old Testament? The Jews were special to God—God's Chosen People. The survival of the Jews, their faith and customs, and the Temple—all were part of God's will for them. War was what they knew, and they drew upon war as the only way they knew to survive. So it made sense to them that God wanted them to fight violence with violence and that God was behind their victories.

But Jesus corrected this way of thinking and told us that *love,* not violence, was the way to live. We need to trust that God is still close to us, protecting us—even in our suffering. War might sometimes be justifiable in self-defense, but violence and war are not the ultimate answers to injustice. Love, forgiveness, and mercy are.

— 2 Maccabees, chapter 9

care and recommended him to you when I went on my regular visits to the provinces east of the Euphrates. (He is receiving a copy of the letter which follows.) 26 Now I strongly urge each of you to keep in mind the good things that I have done for you, both individually and as a nation, and to continue in your good will toward me and my son. 27 I am confident that he will treat you with fairness and kindness, just as I have always done."

28 And so, this murderer, who had cursed God, suffered the same terrible agonies he had brought on others, and then died a miserable death in the mountains of a foreign land. 29 One of his close friends, Philip, took his body home; but, because he was afraid of Antiochus' son, he went on to King Ptolemy Philometor of Egypt.

The Rededication of the Temple
(1 Maccabees 4:36–61)

10 Judas Maccabeus and his followers, under the leadership of the Lord, recaptured the Temple and the city of Jerusalem. 2 They tore down the altars which foreigners had set up in the marketplace and destroyed the other places of worship that had been built. 3 They purified the Temple and built a new altar. Then, with new fire started by striking flint, they offered sacrifice for the first time in two years, burned incense, lighted the lamps, and set out the sacred loaves. 4 After they had done all this, they lay face down on the ground and prayed that the Lord would never again let such disasters strike them. They begged him to be merciful when he punished them for future sins and not hand them over any more to barbaric, pagan Gentiles. 5 They rededicated the Temple on the twenty-fifth day of the month of Kislev, the same day of the same month on which the Temple had been desecrated by the Gentiles. 6 The happy celebration lasted eight days, like the Festival of Shelters, and the people remembered how only a short time before, they had spent the Festival of Shelters wandering like wild animals in the mountains and living in caves. 7 But now, carrying green palm branches and sticks decorated with ivy, they paraded around, singing grateful praises to him who had brought about the purification of his own Temple. 8 Everyone agreed that the entire Jewish nation should celebrate this festival each year.

Ptolemy Macron Commits Suicide

9 The days of Antiochus Epiphanes had come to an end. 10 Now we will tell about Antiochus Eupator, the son of this godless man, and give a summary of the evil effects of his wars. 11 When he became king he appointed a man by the name of Lysias to be in charge of the affairs of state and to be chief governor of Greater Syria, 12 replacing Ptolemy Macron, who had been the first governor to treat the Jews fairly. Macron had established peaceful relations with them in an attempt to make up for the wrongs they had suffered. 13 As a result the King's Friends went to Eupator and accused Macron of treachery, because he had abandoned the island of Cyprus, which King Philometor of Egypt had placed under his command, and had gone over to Antiochus Epiphanes. In fact, everyone called Macron a traitor. No longer able to maintain the respect that his office demanded, he committed suicide by taking poison.

Judas Maccabeus Defeats the Idumeans
(1 Maccabees 5:1–8)

14 When Gorgias became governor of Idumea, he kept a force of mercenaries and attacked the Jews at every opportunity. 15 Not only this, but the Idumeans themselves controlled certain strategic fortresses and were constantly harassing the Jews. They welcomed those who fled from Jerusalem and did everything they could to keep the country in a perpetual state of war. 16 So Judas Maccabeus and his men, after offering prayers for God's help, rushed out and made a vigorous attack against the Idumean fortresses. 17 They beat back those who were defending the walls and captured the fortresses, killing everyone they found, a total of about 20,000 people.

10:10 1 Macc 6:17

18 About 9,000 of the enemy, however, managed to take refuge in two easily defended forts, with everything they needed to withstand a siege. 19 Judas had to go on to some other places in the country, where he was more urgently needed, but he left behind Simon and Joseph, together with Zacchaeus and his men. This force was large enough to continue the siege, 20 but some of Simon's men were greedy, and when they were offered 140 pounds of silver, they let some of the enemy escape from the forts. 21 When Judas heard what had happened, he called together the leaders of his troops and accused those men of selling their brothers by setting their enemies free to fight against them. 22 Then he executed the traitors and immediately captured the two forts. 23 Judas was always successful in battle, and in his assault on those two forts he killed more than 20,000 men.

> *Pray it!*
>
> **Prayer for Protection**
>
> **Read Psalm 140. Judas and the other Jews who were crying out to God for help may have said a prayer similar to this one. Page through the Book of Psalms and see how many other prayers you can find that have a similar theme. Notice that there are two ideas woven through these prayers: asking God for help and protection and praising God for his love and mercy.**
>
> **Try writing your own prayer to God for protection.**
>
> **— 2 Maccabees 10:25–26**

Judas Defeats Timothy

24 Timothy, who had been defeated by the Jews once before, had gathered a large number of cavalry from Asia and a tremendous force of mercenary troops and was now advancing to take Judea by armed attack. 25 But as the enemy forces were approaching, Judas and his men prayed to God. They put on sackcloth, threw dirt on their heads, 26 and lay face downward on the steps of the altar, begging God to help them by fighting against their enemies, as he had promised in his Law.

27 When they had finished praying, they took up their weapons, went out a good distance from Jerusalem, and stopped for the night not far from the enemy. 28 At daybreak the two armies joined in battle. The Jewish forces depended upon both their bravery and their trust in the Lord for victory, while the enemy relied only on their ability to fight fiercely. 29 When the fighting was at its worst, the enemy saw five handsome men riding on horses with gold bridles and leading the Jewish forces. 30 These five men surrounded Judas, protecting him with their own armor and showering the enemy with arrows and thunderbolts. The enemy forces then became so confused and bewildered that they broke ranks, and the Jews cut them to pieces, 31 slaughtering 20,500 infantry and 600 cavalry.

32 Timothy himself escaped to the strongly defended fort of Gezer, where his brother Chaereas was in command. 33 Judas and his men besieged the fort for four days with great enthusiasm, 34 but those inside trusted to the security of their positions and shouted all sorts of terrible insults against the Jews and their God. 35 At dawn on the fifth day, twenty of Judas' men, burning with anger at these insults, bravely climbed the wall and with savage fury chopped down everyone they met. 36 At the same time, others climbed the walls on the other side of the fort and set the towers on fire. Many of the enemy were burned to death as the flames spread. A third force broke down the gates and let in the rest of Judas' men to capture the city. 37 Timothy had hidden in a cistern, but they killed

When the Maccabees won control of the Temple, they immediately cleaned and purified it. Who is responsible for keeping your church clean and beautiful?

Twenty of Judas' men . . . bravely climbed the wall.
(10:35)

him, as well as his brother Chaereas and
Apollophanes.
38When it was over, the Jews celebrated
by singing hymns and songs of thanksgiving
to the Lord, who had shown them great
kindness and had given them victory.

Judas Maccabeus Defeats Lysias
(1 Maccabees 4:26–35)

11 Not long after Timothy was defeat-
ed, Lysias, the King's guardian and
relative, and head of the government, heard
what had happened. He became angry 2and
led 80,000 infantry and all his cavalry against
the Jews with the intention of turning
Jerusalem into a Greek city. 3The Temple
would be taxed, as were all Gentile places of
worship, and the office of High Priest would
be up for sale each year. 4Lysias was so
pleased with his tens of thousands of
infantry, his thousands of cavalry, and his
eighty elephants that he failed to take into
account the power of God. 5He invaded
Judea and attacked the fort of Bethzur, about
twenty miles south of Jerusalem.
6When Judas and his men heard that
Lysias was laying siege to their forts, they
and all the people cried and wept, begging
the Lord to send a good angel to save them.
7Judas was the first to take up his weapons,
and he urged the others to join him in risk-
ing their lives to help the other Jews. So
with great eagerness they all set out togeth-
er. 8But they had not gone far from
Jerusalem, when suddenly they noticed they
were being led by a horseman dressed in
white and carrying gold weapons. 9Immedi-
ately all of them together thanked God for
his mercy; he had made them brave enough
to attack not only men, but even the most
savage animals or even walls of iron. 10So
they marched in battle formation, and with
them went the one whom the Lord in his
mercy had sent to fight on their side. 11Then
they charged into the enemy like lions,
killing 11,000 infantry and 1,600 cavalry, and
forcing the rest to run for their lives. 12Most
of those who ran were wounded and had
lost their weapons, and Lysias himself man-
aged to escape only because he ran away like
a coward.

Lysias Makes Peace with the Jews
(1 Maccabees 6:56–61)

13Lysias was no fool. As he thought about
the defeat he had suffered, he realized it was
because the mighty God had fought for the
Jews, making it impossible for them to be
defeated. So he sent a message to the Jews,
14trying to persuade them to agree to a just
settlement and promising to do all he could
to make the king friendly toward them.[r]
15Judas Maccabeus considered what would
be best for the people, and so he agreed to
all the proposals Lysias had made, since the
king had granted every written request that
Judas had presented to Lysias.[s]

[r] **11:14** to do . . . them; *Greek unclear.* [s] **11:15** since . . . Lysias; *or* and the king granted every written request that Judas presented to Lysias.

"Immediately all of them together thanked God for his mercy" *(2 Maccabees 11:9)*.

The Letter of Lysias to the Jews

16Here is a copy of the letter which Lysias
wrote to the Jews:
"Lysias to the Jewish people, greetings.
17Your representatives John and Absalom
have delivered to me the official docu-
ment you sent with them, and they have
asked me to agree to what is contained in
it. 18I have informed the king of the mat-
ters that needed to be brought to his
attention, and he has agreed to do what-
ever is possible. 19If you continue to be
loyal to the government, I will do every-
thing I can in the future to benefit your
nation. 20I have instructed your represen-
tatives and mine to meet with you to dis-
cuss the details of these matters. 21May all
go well with you. Dated the twenty-
fourth day of the month of
Dioscorinthius in the year 148."[t]

The King's Letter to Lysias

22Here is a copy of the King's letter:
"King Antiochus to the honorable
Lysias, greetings. 23Now that my father has
gone to be with the gods, I want the sub-
jects of my kingdom to conduct their
own affairs without interference. 24I
understand that the Jews do not wish to
adopt the Greek way of life, as my father
had intended, but prefer their own way of
life and have requested that they be
allowed to live according to their own
customs. 25Since I desire that they live
undisturbed like the other nations in my
empire, I hereby decree that their Temple
be restored to them and that they be
allowed to live according to the customs
of their ancestors. 26Please inform them of
this decision and assure them of my
friendship, so that they may conduct their
own affairs in peace, without anything to
worry about."
27Here is a copy of the king's letter to the
Jewish people:
"King Antiochus to the Jewish leaders
and all the Jews, greetings. 28I hope that
all is going well for you. I am in good
health. 29Menelaus has informed me of
your desire to return home and attend to
your own affairs. 30So then, those of you
who return home by the thirtieth of the
month of Xanthicus may rest assured that
you have nothing to fear. 31You may con-
tinue to observe your food laws and other
laws, as you used to do, and no Jew will
be punished for any crime done in igno-
rance. 32I am sending Menelaus to set
your minds at ease. 33May all go well with
you. Dated the fifteenth day of the month
of Xanthicus in the year 148."[t]

The Letter of the Romans to the Jews

34The Romans also sent the Jews the fol-
lowing letter:
"Quintus Memmius and Titus Manius,
representatives of the Romans, to the Jews,
greetings. 35We are in complete agreement
with all that has been granted to you by
the honorable Lysias. 36We are now on our
way to Antioch, so please examine careful-
ly those matters that Lysias referred to the
king. Then send a reply to us immediately
so that we can represent your best interests
before him. Do this as soon as you can,
37without delay, so that we may know
what you have decided. 38May all go well
with you. Dated the fifteenth day of the
month of Xanthicus in the year 148."

The Jews of Joppa Are Murdered

12 When the peace agreement between
the Jews and the Syrians was com-
pleted, Lysias returned to the king, and the
Jews went back to their farming. 2But some
of the local governors, Timothy and Apollo-
nius son of Gennaeus, as well as Hieronymus
and Demophon, would not let them live in
peace; and neither would Nicanor, the com-
mander of the mercenaries from Cyprus.
3About this time, the people of Joppa did
a cruel thing to the Jews of their city. They
pretended to be friendly to the Jews and
invited them and their families to go sailing
with them on ships they had provided.
4Since all the people of the town had decid-
ed to do this, the Jews suspected nothing and

[t] **11:21, 33** THE YEAR 148: *This corresponds to 164 B.C.*

accepted the invitation out of a feeling of
good will. But when they were out at sea,
the people of Joppa drowned all two hun-
dred of them.

The people of Joppa drowned all two hundred of them. (12:4)

5As soon as Judas heard of this inhuman
thing that had been done to those Jews, he
informed his men. 6After they had prayed to
God, the just judge, they attacked the mur-
derers. Under cover of darkness they set fire
to the harbor, burning all the ships, and
killing everyone they found hiding there.
7The gates of the city were locked, so Judas
withdrew; but he was determined to return
at some other time and wipe out everyone
living there.
8Judas heard that the people of Jamnia had
plans to kill the Jews of their city also. 9So
he attacked Jamnia at night, setting fire to its
harbor and the ships there. The flames could
be seen as far as Jerusalem, thirty miles away.

Judas' Victories in the Region of Gilead
(1 Maccabees 5:9–54)

10When Judas and his men were about a
mile away from Jamnia on their way to meet
Timothy in battle, they were attacked by
more than 5,000 Arabs, supported by 500
cavalry. 11It was a hard fight, but with the
help of God they defeated these desert
tribesmen, who then asked to be on friendly
terms with the Jews, promising to give them
some livestock and offering to help them in
other ways as well. 12Judas thought their
friendship might prove useful in many ways,
so he agreed to make peace with them; after
that the Arabs returned to their tents.
13Judas also attacked the heavily fortified
walled city of Caspin. The people who lived
there were a mixed population of Gentiles
14who relied on the strength of their walls
and felt confident that they had enough food
stored up to last through a siege. So they
made fun of Judas and his men, shouting out
insults against them and profanities against
their God. 15But the Jews prayed to the
Almighty Lord of the universe, who had
torn down the walls of Jericho in the days of
Joshua without using battering rams or siege
weapons. Then they made a fierce attack
against the wall 16and because it was God's
will, they captured the city. The Jews slaugh-
tered so many people that a nearby lake,
which was about a quarter of a mile wide,
seemed to be overflowing with blood.

Judas Defeats Timothy's Army
(1 Maccabees 5:37–44)

17From the city of Caspin, Judas and his
men marched about 95 miles, until they
came to the Jewish settlement of Charax,
near the city of Tob. 18But they did not find
Timothy there, because he had already left
the region. He had been able to do nothing
there except leave behind a strong garrison
in one place. 19Two of Judas' generals,
Dositheus and Sosipater, attacked the garri-
son and killed all 10,000 men stationed
there. 20Then Judas divided his army into
several divisions, placing Dositheus and So-
sipater each in command of a division, and
hurried after Timothy, who had a force of
120,000 infantry and 2,500 cavalry. 21When
Timothy found out that Judas was coming
after him, he sent the women and the chil-
dren on ahead with the baggage to the city
of Karnaim, which was almost impossible to
besiege or even to reach, because of the nar-
row passes that led up to it. 22But at the
moment that Judas' first division came into
sight, the enemy forces were thrown into
panic by a vision sent by God, who sees
everything. In terror they began to run wild-
ly about and many of them were wounded
by the swords of their own men. 23So Judas
and his men pursued them as hard as they

He sent the women and the children on ahead with the baggage. (12:21)

could, killing at least 30,000 of the enemy. 24Timothy himself was captured by the troops of Dositheus and Sosipater. But he was very shrewd and managed to convince them that many of their relatives were his prisoners and would be put to death if anything happened to him. 25Finally, after he had promised to send their relatives home safely, they let him go free.

Judas Wins Other Victories

(1 Maccabees 5:45–54)

26Next, Judas attacked the city of Karnaim and the temple of the goddess Atargatis there, killing 25,000 people 27and completely destroying both the city and the temple. Then he attacked the fortified city of Ephron where Lysias and[u] people of all nationalities were living. Strong young men took up their positions in front of the walls and fought bravely, while inside the city were stored large quantities of military supplies and weapons. 28But the Jews prayed for help to the Lord, who crushes the power of his enemies. So they captured the city and killed about 25,000 people. 29From there they hurried on to the city of Beth Shan, seventy-five miles north of Jerusalem. 30The Jews there told Judas how kindly the people of the city had treated them, especially during hard times. 31So Judas and his men thanked the people and urged them to show the same good will toward the Jews in the future. Then they left for Jerusalem, where they arrived shortly before the Harvest Festival.

Judas Defeats Gorgias

32After Pentecost (as the Harvest Festival is called in Greek) Judas and his men quickly marched out against Gorgias, the governor of Idumea, 33who met them with 3,000 infantry and 400 cavalry. 34In the battle that followed, a few Jews were killed. 35Then a Jew from the city of Tob,[v] a powerful cavalry soldier by the name of Dositheus, grabbed Gorgias by his cloak and started dragging him away by brute force, intending to take the worthless man alive. But suddenly one from the Thracian cavalry rushed at Dositheus and chopped off his arm, allowing Gorgias to escape to the city of Marisa.

36By now the Jewish men under the command of Esdrias had been fighting for a long time and were exhausted. So Judas prayed that the Lord would show that he was on their side and in command of their troops. 37Then, while Judas sang a hymn in his native language as a battle cry, the Jews made a surprise attack against Gorgias and his men and put them to flight.

Prayers for Those Killed in Battle

38After the battle Judas led his men to the town of Adullam. It was the day before the Sabbath, so they purified themselves according to Jewish custom and then observed the holy day. 39By the following day it was urgent that they gather up the bodies of the men who had been killed in battle and bury them in their family tombs. 40But on each of the dead, hidden under their clothes, they found small images of the gods worshiped in Jamnia, which the Law forbids Jews to wear.

[u] **12:27** Lysias and; *some manuscripts do not have these words.* [v] **12:35** a Jew from the city of Tob; *some manuscripts have* one of Bacenor's men.

12:32 Ex 23:16 **12:40** Deut 7:25

Hundreds of thousands of Christians around the world have been killed for defending their faith. Say a prayer today for their souls.

Catholic Connections

Praying for the Dead

The Jewish fighters killed in battle were found wearing small idols of a foreign god. This was a serious sin. Judas Maccabeus made an offering of silver and prayed for the sins of his dead warriors. He believed in the resurrection of the dead and that the dead must be made clean from their sins before they could enjoy God's reward of eternal life in heaven.

This passage supports the Catholic teaching about purgatory. Purgatory is a state where the souls of the dead who died in God's friendship are purified of any remaining sin and of any of the effects of sin which have yet to be healed. Then they will be ready to fully experience the joy of God's immense love in heaven. The Church teaches us to pray for the dead so that God will have mercy on them, forgive their sins, and bring them quickly to heaven.

This is a Catholic prayer (sometimes said with the rosary) that makes this plea to God:

O my Jesus, forgive us our sins, and save us from the fires of hell. Lead all the souls to heaven, especially those in most need of your mercy. Amen.

— 2 Maccabees 12:39–45

Everyone then knew why these men had
been killed. [41]So they praised the ways of the
Lord, the just judge, who reveals what is hid-
den, [42]and they begged him that this sin
might be completely blotted out. Then, Judas,
that great man, urged the people to keep
away from sin, because they had seen for
themselves what had happened to those men
who had sinned. [43]He also took up a collec-
tion from all his men, totaling about four
pounds of silver, and sent it to Jerusalem to
provide for a sin offering. Judas did this noble
thing because he believed in the resurrection
of the dead. [44]If he had not believed that the
dead would be raised, it would have been
foolish and useless to pray for them. [45]In his
firm and devout conviction that all of God's
faithful people would receive a wonderful
reward, Judas made provision for a sin offering
to set free from their sin those who had died.

Menelaus Is Put to Death

13 In the year 149[w] Judas Maccabeus
and his followers found out that
Antiochus Eupator was marching against
Judea with a large army [2]and that Lysias, the
young king's guardian and the head of his
government, was with him. They[x] had a
force of Greek troops consisting of 110,000
infantry, 5,300 cavalry, 22 elephants, and 300
chariots with sharp blades attached to their
wheels.
[3]Menelaus, trying to take advantage of the
situation, went over to their side and urged
them on, not because he was concerned for
the country, but because he hoped to be
confirmed as High Priest. [4]But God, the
King of kings, made Antiochus furious with
Menelaus. Lysias proved to Antiochus that
this criminal had been the source of all his
troubles, so Antiochus ordered him to be

[w] **13:1** THE YEAR 149: *This corresponds to 163 B.C.* [x] **13:2** They; *Greek unclear.*

Check out what Jesus has to say about violence in Matthew 26:51–52.

taken to the city of Berea and put to death
in the way that it was done there. [5]In that
city there is a tower about 75 feet high. It is
filled with ashes, and all around the inside of
the tower is a platform sloping down into
the ashes. [6]People accused of crimes against
the gods or of any other serious crime are
taken there and thrown down to their death.
[7]Menelaus was put to death in that way,
without even having the privilege of a bur-
ial, [8]and that was just what he deserved. He
had often profaned the sacred ashes of the
altar fire in the Temple, and now he met his
death in ashes.

A Battle Near the City of Modein

[9]King Antiochus arrogantly continued his
barbaric invasion of Judah, intending to deal
with the Jews more harshly than his father
had ever done. [10]When Judas learned of this,
he told the people to pray to the Lord day
and night, because they were in danger of
losing their Law, their country, and their
holy Temple. As never before, they needed
his help and protection [11]to keep their
newly restored country from falling into the
hands of godless Gentiles. [12]For three days
the people did nothing but lie face down on
the ground, fasting and crying, begging the
merciful Lord for his help. Then Judas spoke
words of encouragement to the people, urg-
ing them to get ready for action.
[13]Afterward, Judas met privately with the
Jewish leaders and decided to march out
with God's help to battle against the king,
rather than to wait for Antiochus to invade
Judea and besiege Jerusalem. [14]Then, leaving
the outcome of the battle to the Creator of
the world, Judas encouraged his men to
fight bravely and to be willing to die for
their laws, the Temple, Jerusalem, their
country, and their whole way of life. They
set up camp near the city of Modein.
[15]Judas gave his men the battle cry, "Victory
comes from God," and that night, with a
picked force of his bravest young men, he
attacked the area near the king's tent and
killed as many as 2,000 men. They also
stabbed to death[y] the lead elephant and its
keeper. [16]Everyone in camp was terrified
and in panic when Judas and his men finally
left victoriously [17]just before dawn. The
help and protection of the Lord had made
all this possible.

Antiochus the Fifth Makes a Treaty with the Jews

(1 Maccabees 6:48–63)

[18]This taste of Jewish daring was enough
to convince King Antiochus that he had to
find some better way of capturing the Jewish
positions. [19]He attacked the strong Jewish fort
of Bethzur, but was repeatedly beaten back
and finally defeated. [20]Judas sent supplies to
the men who were defending the fort, [21]but a
Jewish soldier by the name of Rhodocus gave
some secret information to the enemy. He
was found out, however, caught, and put to
death. [22]The king made a second attempt to
come to terms with the people of Bethzur,
and when he had reached an agreement with
them, he withdrew his forces. Then he went
to attack Judas, but again he was defeated.
[23]Meanwhile, Philip had been left at Antioch
in charge of the government, but King Anti-
ochus learned that he had revolted. The king
did not know what to do, so he initiated
peace talks with the Jews, agreed to their
terms, and promised to be just in his treat-
ment of them. To put the treaty into effect, he
offered a sacrifice, gave a generous gift to
show his respect for the Temple, [24]and gra-
ciously received Judas Maccabeus. After that,
the king appointed Hegemonides to be gov-
ernor of the territory between the cities of
Ptolemais and Gerar, [25]and then he himself
went on to Ptolemais. The people there were
angry because of the treaty he had made with
the Jews—so angry, in fact, that they wanted
the treaty canceled. [26]But Lysias made a pub-
lic speech, defending the treaty as well as he
could. After he had calmed the people down
and convinced them that he was right, he
returned to Antioch.

In this way King Antiochus' invasion was turned into a retreat.

[y] **13:15** *Probable text* stabbed to death; *Greek unclear.*

Live it!

Peace Talks

King Antiochus saw that war was getting him nowhere, fast! So he sat down with the Jews and tried to talk out a peaceful solution. This isn't an easy way out. In fact, the challenge to make peace through talking and compromise can sometimes be more challenging than a bloody battle.

How do you deal with the battles in your life? Do you enlist friends to turn on the person who hurt you? Do you turn to violence? Or do you try to talk things out? Will you admit where you're wrong and try to understand the other person's actions and feelings?

Next time you find yourself fighting with someone, try a peace talk. Maybe ask for help from a teacher, parent, counselor, or friend who has strong relationship-building skills. Pray to God for wisdom and courage. And peace.

— 2 Maccabees 13:23–26

Alcimus Speaks against Judas
(1 Maccabees 7:1–21)

14 Three years later, Judas and his men
learned that Demetrius son of
Seleucus had sailed into the port of Tripolis
with a powerful army and a fleet. 2It was
reported that he had killed King Antiochus
and his guardian Lysias and had taken over
the country.
3There was a man by the name of
Alcimus, who had formerly been High
Priest but who had gladly adopted the
Greek way of life during the revolt. Realiz-
ing that he could never again be High Priest
and fearful of what the Jews might do to
him, 4he went to see King Demetrius in the
year 151.[z] On this occasion he presented the
king with a gold crown and a palm branch,
together with some olive branches tradition-
ally presented to the Temple, but he said
nothing about his plans. 5Later, however, he
got the chance to put his foolish plans into
effect when Demetrius summoned him to a
meeting of his advisers and asked him what
the Jews were intending to do.
Alcimus said, 6"The followers of Judas
Maccabeus think of themselves as devout
and patriotic; they love war and are con-
stantly inciting the people to rebellion and
will never leave the nation in peace. 7It is
their fault that I no longer hold the glorious
position of High Priest, to which I am enti-
tled by birth. And so I have come here, 8pri-
marily out of a genuine concern for your
interests as king, but also out of considera-
tion for my own people, for the foolish poli-
cies of Judas and his followers have brought
terrible suffering on our entire nation.
9When Your Majesty has examined all the
details of these matters, please act in your

He went to see King Demetrius. (14:4)

[z] **14:4** THE YEAR 151: *This corresponds to 161 B.C.*

usual kind and generous manner to relieve
the oppression of our nation and its people.
10 As long as Judas is alive, it will be impossi-
ble for our nation to enjoy peace."

Demetrius Sends Nicanor to Attack Judas

11 As soon as Alcimus had finished his
speech, the other advisers quickly seized this
opportunity to arouse Demetrius' anger
against Judas, because they also hated him.
12 So King Demetrius immediately appointed
Nicanor, who was the commander of his
elephant forces, to be governor of Judea, and
sent him there 13 with orders to kill Judas,
scatter his followers, and make Alcimus High
Priest of the greatest Temple in all the world.
14 All the foreigners in Judea, who had fled
from Judas' attacks, now rushed to join forces
with Nicanor, because they thought that any
defeat or trouble that came to the Jews
would be to their own advantage.
15 The Jews heard that Nicanor was
attacking and that the foreigners in their
country were giving him their support. So
they threw dirt on themselves and prayed to
their God, who had chosen their nation as
his possession forever and had never failed to
help them in time of need. 16 Then Judas,
their leader, gave the orders, and they imme-
diately marched out to engage the enemy in
battle near the village of Adasa.[a] 17 Judas'
brother Simon was fighting Nicanor but was
gradually losing the battle because of an
unexpected move on the part of the enemy.
18 However, when Nicanor heard how brave-
ly and courageously Judas and his men were
fighting for their country, he decided not to
settle the matter in battle. 19 Instead, he sent
Posidonius, Theodotus, and Mattathias to
make a treaty with the Jews.
20 After the terms of the treaty had been
worked out in detail, Nicanor informed his
troops, and they unanimously agreed. 21 Then a
day was set on which the leaders would meet
in private. Ceremonial chairs were brought out
from each camp and set up. 22 Judas had taken
the precaution of placing battle-ready troops in
strategic places, in case of sudden treachery on
the part of the enemy. But the two leaders had
a friendly meeting. 23 Nicanor stayed on in
Jerusalem for some time after that. He did not
mistreat the Jews in any way, and even sent
away the people who had come over to his
side. 24 The two men became the best of
friends, and Judas was Nicanor's constant com-
panion. 25 Nicanor urged him to marry and
start a family. So Judas did this and settled
down to a peaceful life.

Nicanor Turns against Judas

26 When Alcimus noticed how well Nicanor
and Judas were getting along, he obtained a
copy of the treaty and went to see King
Demetrius. He told the king that Nicanor was
disloyal to the government, because he had
appointed the traitor Judas to be his successor.
27 These false accusations infuriated the king,
and in his anger he wrote to Nicanor, inform-
ing him that he was dissatisfied with the treaty
and ordering him to arrest Judas Maccabeus
and send him to Antioch at once.
28 When this message reached Nicanor, he
was hurt and didn't know what to do, because
he did not like having to break an agreement
with a man who had kept his part of the bar-
gain. 29 Yet it was impossible for him to ignore
the king's command, so he began looking for
a way to trap Judas. 30 Judas, however, noticed
that Nicanor was becoming hostile and rude
toward him, and he knew that this was a bad
sign. So he gathered a large number of his fol-
lowers and went into hiding.
31 When Nicanor realized that Judas had
outsmarted him, he went to the great and
holy Temple at the time when the priests were
offering sacrifice and ordered them to surren-
der Judas to him. 32 But the priests declared
under oath that they had no idea where Judas
was hiding. 33 Then Nicanor raised his right

[a] **14:16** *Probable text* Adasa; *Greek* Dessau.
14:15–25 1 Macc 7:27, 28 **14:31** 1 Macc 7:29, 30

The Greek governor, Nicanor, betrayed his best friend, Judas Maccabeus. Nicanor felt forced to do this by the king. Do you agree with Nicanor?

arm in the direction of the Temple and made a solemn threat: "If you do not hand Judas over to me as a prisoner, I will level God's Temple to the ground, demolish this altar, and on this spot build a glorious temple to Dionysus." 34Then he left, and immediately the priests lifted their arms toward heaven and prayed to God, the faithful Defender of our nation: 35"Lord, you are in need of nothing, yet it has pleased you to place your Temple here and to live among us. 36You alone are holy, and your Temple has only recently been purified, so now protect its holiness forever."

Razis Dies for His Country

37One of the leaders in Jerusalem, a man by the name of Razis, was denounced to Nicanor. It was said that he had helped his people in many ways and was so highly respected by them that he was known as "the Father of the Jews." 38During the early days of the revolution he had risked his life for Judaism and had been brought to trial because of his loyalty. 39Wanting to show clearly how much he disliked the Jews, Nicanor sent more than 500 soldiers to arrest Razis, 40because he thought his arrest would be a crippling blow to the Jews. 41The soldiers were about to capture the tower where Razis had gone. They were forcing open the gates to the courtyard, and the order had been given to set the door on fire. Razis realized there was no escape, so he tried to commit suicide with his sword, 42preferring to die with honor rather than suffer humiliation at the hands of evil men.

43Under the pressure of the moment, Razis misjudged the thrust of the sword, and it did not kill him. So, while the soldiers were swarming into the room, he rushed to the wall and jumped off like a brave hero into the crowd below. 44The crowd quickly moved back, and he fell in the space they left. 45Still alive, and burning with courage, he got up, and with blood gushing from his wounds, he ran through the crowd and finally climbed a steep rock. 46Now completely drained of blood, he tore out his intestines with both hands and threw them at the crowd, and as he did so, he prayed for the Lord of life and breath to give them back to him. That was how he died.

Nicanor's Cruel Plan

15 Nicanor learned that Judas and his men were in the region of Samaria, and so he decided to attack them on a Sabbath, when he could do so without any danger to himself. 2The Jews who were forced to accompany his army begged him not to do such a cruel and savage thing, but to respect the day that the all-seeing God had honored and made the most holy of all days. 3Then Nicanor, the lowest creature on earth, asked if there was some sovereign ruler in heaven who had commanded them to honor the Sabbath. 4And the Jews replied, "Yes; the living Lord, who rules in heaven, commanded us to honor the Sabbath."

5But Nicanor answered, "I am the ruler on earth, and I order you to take up your weapons and to do what the king commands." However, he did not succeed in carrying out his cruel plan.

Judas Prepares His Troops for Battle

6In his arrogance Nicanor had boasted that he would set up a monument in honor of his victory over Judas. 7But Judas was fully confident that the Lord would help him, 8so he urged his men not to be afraid of the enemy. He encouraged them to remember how the Almighty had helped them in times past and to rest assured that he would give them victory this time also. 9He renewed their hope by reading to them from the Law and the Prophets and by reminding them of the battles they had already won. 10When his men were ready for battle, he gave them their orders and at the same time pointed out how the Gentiles could not be trusted, because they never kept their treaties. 11He armed all his men, not by encouraging them to trust in shields and spears, but by inspiring them with

"Lord, you are in need of nothing, yet it has pleased you to place your Temple here and to live among us" *(2 Maccabees 14:35)*.

Intercession of the Saints

Judas is a powerful leader—he prepares his army through prayer and inspires them to be courageous. Before their battle with Nicanor, Judas has a vision about two highly respected Jews who have already died: Onias, the just and faithful High Priest of the Temple, and Jeremiah, the great prophet. In the vision, Onias says that Jeremiah "loves the Jewish people and offers many prayers for us" (2 Maccabees 15:14).

We believe that the faithful saints who have gone to heaven pray for us, as well. We believe in the communion of saints, which means that all believers, living and dead, are connected as one family. The saints in heaven intercede (go to God on our behalf) in prayer for us. The greatest saint of all is Mary, the mother of Jesus. That's why we tell her about our needs; we know her prayers to God for us are very powerful.

— 2 Maccabees 15:11–14

courageous words. He also lifted their morale
by telling them about his dream, a kind of
vision that they could trust in.
12He told them that he had seen a vision
of Onias, the former High Priest, that great
and wonderful man of humble and gentle
disposition, who was an outstanding orator
and who had been taught from childhood
how to live a virtuous life. With outstretched
arms Onias was praying for the entire Jewish
nation. 13Judas then saw an impressive
white-haired man of great dignity and
authority. 14Onias said: "This is God's
prophet Jeremiah, who loves the Jewish people and offers many prayers for us and for
Jerusalem, the holy city."
15Then Jeremiah stretched out his right
hand and gave Judas a gold sword, saying as
he did so, 16"This holy sword is a gift from
God. Take it and destroy your enemies."
17The eloquent words that Judas spoke
encouraged everyone to be brave, and
inspired boys to fight like men. Their city,
their religion, and their Temple were in danger. So the Jews made up their minds not to
waste any time, but to make a daring attack
against the enemy and bravely decide their
fate in hand-to-hand combat. 18They were
not so concerned about their own families
and relatives as they were about their sacred
Temple. 19And the people who had to stay in
Jerusalem were deeply concerned about how
a battle on open ground would turn out.

The Defeat and Death of Nicanor

20Everyone was waiting to see who would
win the battle. The enemy troops were already
moving forward, with their cavalry on each

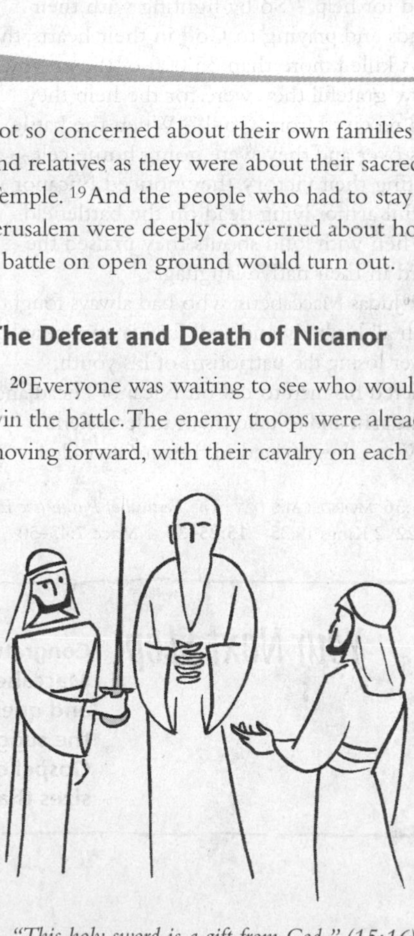

"This holy sword is a gift from God." (15:16)

side of them, and their elephants placed in
strategic positions. [21]Judas Maccabeus looked
at the huge enemy force, the variety of their
weapons, and their fierce elephants. Then he
raised his hands toward heaven and prayed to
the Lord, who works miracles, because he
knew that the Lord gives victory to those
who deserve it, not to those who have a
strong army. [22]Judas said: "Lord, when Hezeki-
ah was king of Judah, you sent your angel,
who killed 185,000 of King Sennacherib's
men. [23]Now once again, Lord of heaven, send
your good angel to make our enemies shake
and tremble with fear. [24]With your great
power, destroy these people who have slan-
dered you and have come out to attack your
chosen people." So Judas ended his prayer.

[25]Nicanor and his army moved forward to
the sound of trumpets and battle songs, [26]but
Judas and his men went into battle calling on
God for help. [27]So by fighting with their
hands and praying to God in their hearts, the
Jews killed more than 35,000 of the enemy.
How grateful they were for the help they
had received from God! [28]When the battle
was over and they were going home cele-
brating their victory, they noticed Nicanor
in full armor lying dead on the battlefield.
[29]Then with loud shouts they praised the
Lord in their native language.

[30]Judas Maccabeus, who had always fought
with all his body and soul for his own people,
never losing the patriotism of his youth,
ordered his men to cut off Nicanor's head and
right arm and to take them to Jerusalem.
[31]When they arrived in the city, he called
together all the people, stationed the priests
before the altar, and sent for the men in the
fort. [32]He showed them the head of the evil
Nicanor and the arm which that wicked man
had arrogantly stretched out against the sacred
Temple of the Almighty God. [33]Then he cut
out the tongue of that godless man, promising
to feed it bit by bit to the birds and to hang
up his head opposite the Temple, as evidence
of what his foolishness did for him. [34]Every-
one there looked up to heaven and praised the
Lord, who had revealed his power and had
kept his Temple from being defiled. [35]Judas
hung Nicanor's head from the wall of the fort,
as a clear proof to everyone of the Lord's help.
[36]By unanimous vote it was decided that this
day would never be forgotten, but would be
celebrated each year on the eve of Mordecai's
Day,[b] which is the thirteenth day of the
twelfth month, called Adar in Aramaic.

Concluding Words

[37]That is how things turned out for
Nicanor. The city of Jerusalem remained in
the possession of the Jewish people from that
time on, so I will end my story here. [38]If it is
well written and to the point, I am pleased;
if it is poorly written and uninteresting, I
have still done my best. [39]We know it is
unhealthy to drink wine or water alone,
whereas wine mixed with water makes a
delightfully tasty drink. So also a good story
skillfully written gives pleasure to those who
read it. With this I conclude.

[b] **15:36** MORDECAI'S DAY: *The Festival of Purim (see Esth 9:17–22).*
15:22 2 Kings 19:35 **15:25–35** 1 Macc 7:43–50 **15:36** 1 Macc 7:49

Your Next Step

Congratulations on finishing the Second Book of the Maccabees! Use this space to write your thoughts and questions about this book. If you are following the suggested reading plan, move ahead to the Gospel of John in the New Testament. John emphasizes that Jesus is the key to the resurrection.

THE BOOK OF Job

Like a volcano that violently and surprisingly erupts, heaping steaming lava upon a city that was minding its own business . . . probably that's what it felt like when Job's good and faithful life shattered to pieces. That's often what tragedy and suffering feel like to us, too. We don't see it coming, we didn't do anything to deserve it, and it shakes our peaceful life to its very core.

Why? Why does God let innocent people suffer? That is the big question in the Book of Job. It is one of the greatest mysteries we ponder in our world. As Job's dramatic story unfolds and you enter into the intense discussions about God's justice, you will learn more about God's deep and awesome wisdom.

Chap. 1:13–22

Headlines

- Tragedy: Job Loses Everything! (1:13–22)
- Curse the Day I Was Born! (3:1–26)
- Friends Blame Job for His Troubles (11:1–20)
- Job Argues His Case (31:5–40)
- Young Bystander Speaks Out (32:1–22)
- God Speaks, Ends Debate! (38:1–41)
- Job Repents, Receives Blessing (chapter 42)

FACTOIDS

Who are the central characters? Job; his three friends, Bildad, Zophar, and Eliphaz; Elihu, a young bystander; and God.

Who wrote this book? An unknown author or authors wrote this book to address questions about suffering, integrity, and the mysterious ways of God, and to teach us about trust.

What literary style is used? Folktale, with poetic speeches.

Who are the young people in this book? Elihu, a young man who had his own ideas to add to the debate between Job and his friends.

Important themes

- Tragedy and suffering happen to everyone and are not punishments sent by God.
- No matter what emotions we feel or thoughts we have, we can share them openly with God.
- God's ways are far beyond our ability to understand, and trusting in God is the only way to have peace of mind and heart.

JOB

Satan tests Job

1 There was a man named Job, living in
the land of Uz,[a] who worshiped God
and was faithful to him. He was a good
man, careful not to do anything evil. 2He
had seven sons and three daughters, 3and
owned seven thousand sheep, three thou-
sand camels, one thousand head of cattle,
and five hundred donkeys. He also had a
large number of servants and was the richest
man in the East.
4Job's sons used to take turns giving a
feast, to which all the others would come,
and they always invited their three sisters to
join them. 5The morning after each feast,
Job would get up early and offer sacrifices
for each of his children in order to purify
them. He always did this because he thought
that one of them might have sinned by
insulting God unintentionally.
6When the day came for the heavenly
beings[b] to appear before the LORD, Satan[c]
was there among them. 7The LORD asked
him, "What have you been doing?"
Satan answered, "I have been walking here
and there, roaming around the earth."
8"Did you notice my servant Job?" the
LORD asked. "There is no one on earth as
faithful and good as he is. He worships me
and is careful not to do anything evil."
9Satan replied, "Would Job worship you if
he got nothing out of it? 10You have always
protected him and his family and everything
he owns. You bless everything he does, and
you have given him enough cattle to fill the
whole country. 11But now suppose you take
away everything he has—he will curse you
to your face!"
12"All right," the LORD said to Satan,
"everything he has is in your power, but
you must not hurt Job himself." So Satan
left.

Live it!

The Fall from a Good Life

What happens to Job is very sad. In the space of a few minutes, he gets the news that all his animals, servants, and even his children have been stolen or killed. It is also possible for us to experience sudden loss. A terrible accident, sickness, a violent fight, death, divorce, natural disaster—life can change for us in an instant! Our good and solid life falls apart, and chaos and sadness take over.

That's why it's so important to be thankful for all you have been given, and to appreciate all of it—*today.* Say thanks when someone is kind to you. Notice the ways your parents show their love for you, and find ways to show it back. Take some time to just hang out with brothers and sisters—what if they weren't there tomorrow? Cherish the good times you have with your friends.

Most of all, *thank God* for all the blessings in your life: family, friends, talents, health, your home, and everything you enjoy doing. Being thankful when times are good helps us remember that God is also with us during times of tragedy and loss.

—Job, chapter 1

[a] **1:1** UZ: *An area whose exact location is unknown.* [b] **1:6** HEAVENLY BEINGS: *Supernatural beings who serve God in heaven.* [c] **1:6** SATAN: *A supernatural being whose name indicates he was regarded as the opponent of human beings.*
1:6 Gen 6:2; Job 38:7; Ps 29:1 **1:9–11** Rev 12:10

Job's Children and Wealth Are Destroyed

13 One day when Job's children were hav-
ing a feast at the home of their oldest broth-
er, 14 a messenger came running to Job. "We
were plowing the fields with the oxen," he
said, "and the donkeys were in a nearby pas-
ture. 15 Suddenly the Sabeans[d] attacked and
stole them all. They killed every one of your
servants except me. I am the only one who
escaped to tell you."

16 Before he had finished speaking, another
servant came and said, "Lightning struck the
sheep and the shepherds and killed them all.
I am the only one who escaped to tell you."

17 Before he had finished speaking, another
servant came and said, "Three bands of
Chaldean[e] raiders attacked us, took away the
camels, and killed all your servants except me.
I am the only one who escaped to tell you."

18 Before he had finished speaking, another
servant came and said, "Your children were
having a feast at the home of your oldest
son, 19 when a storm swept in from the
desert. It blew the house down and killed
them all. I am the only one who escaped to
tell you."

20 Then Job got up and tore his clothes in
grief. He shaved his head and threw himself
face downward on the ground. 21 He said, "I
was born with nothing, and I will die with
nothing. The LORD gave, and now he has
taken away. May his name be praised!"

22 In spite of everything that had hap-
pened, Job did not sin by blaming God.

Satan Tests Job Again

2 When the day came for the heavenly
beings to appear before the LORD again,
Satan was there among them. 2 The LORD
asked him, "Where have you been?"

Satan answered, "I have been walking here
and there, roaming around the earth."

"The LORD gave, and now he has taken away."
(1:21)

3 "Did you notice my servant Job?" the
LORD asked. "There is no one on earth as
faithful and good as he is. He worships me
and is careful not to do anything evil. You
persuaded me to let you attack him for no
reason at all, but Job is still as faithful as
ever."

4 Satan replied, "A person will give up
everything in order to stay alive. 5 But now
suppose you hurt his body—he will curse
you to your face!"

6 So the LORD said to Satan, "All right, he
is in your power, but you are not to kill
him."

7 Then Satan left the LORD's presence and
made sores break out all over Job's body. 8 Job
went and sat by the garbage dump and took
a piece of broken pottery to scrape his sores.
9 His wife said to him, "You are still as faith-
ful as ever, aren't you? Why don't you curse
God and die?"

10 Job answered, "You are talking nonsense!
When God sends us something good, we
welcome it. How can we complain when he
sends us trouble?" Even in all this suffering
Job said nothing against God.

[d] **1:15** SABEANS: *A tribe of wandering raiders from the south.* [e] **1:17** CHALDEANS: *A tribe of wandering raiders from the north.*

1:21 Sir 40:1; 11:14

What do you think of Job's reaction in Job 1:21–22?

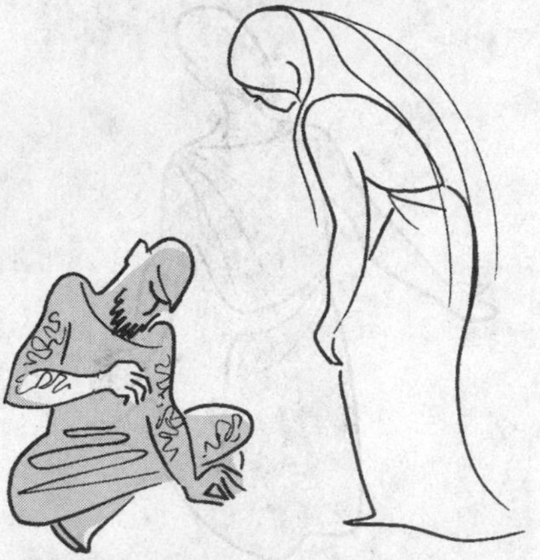

"Why don't you curse God and die?" (2:9)

Job's Friends Come

[11]Three of Job's friends were Eliphaz, from the city of Teman, Bildad, from the land of Shuah, and Zophar, from the land of Naamah. When they heard how much Job had been suffering, they decided to go and comfort him. [12]While they were still a long way off they saw Job, but did not recognize him. When they did, they began to weep and wail, tearing their clothes in grief and throwing dust into the air and on their heads. [13]Then they sat there on the ground with him for seven days and nights without saying a word, because they saw how much he was suffering.

Job's Complaint to God

3 Finally Job broke the silence and cursed the day on which he had been born.

Job

2-3 O God, put a curse on the day I was born;
put a curse on the night when I was conceived!
4 Turn that day into darkness, God.
Never again remember that day;
never again let light shine on it.
5 Make it a day of gloom and thick darkness;
cover it with clouds, and blot out the sun.
6 Blot that night out of the year,
and never let it be counted again;
7 make it a barren, joyless night.
8 Tell the sorcerers to curse that day,
those who know how to control Leviathan.[f]

Live it!

Being There Is Enough

Jenni was getting ready to attend a wake—her first one—for her best friend's dad. She felt sick to her stomach with nervousness because she didn't know what she would say or do. Have you ever been in a situation like this? A friend is suffering, and you don't know how to respond?

Job's friends rushed to his side as soon as they heard about his tragedies. They stayed with him seven days and nights! And they simply sat with him, quietly. No words were necessary.

Sometimes, this is all our friends need from us. Just to be there for them. Having the right words to say isn't important. Simply tell them you're sorry, and let them know you're there if they need you. Then just stay close.

Our presence is the best gift we can offer when someone is suffering.

— Job 2:11–13

[f] **3:8** LEVIATHAN: *Some take this to be the crocodile, others a legendary monster. Magicians were thought to be able to make him cause eclipses of the sun.*

3:1–19 Jer 20:14–18 **3:3** Sir 23:14

Are any of your friends going through a difficult time? How can you show them you are there for them?

Pray it!

Let Me Feel Peace

Job finally lets his grief out in chapter 3. He doesn't hold back. He tells God exactly what he's feeling. Here is a prayer of a young person pouring her heart out to God. Would you feel okay praying like this?

Dear Lord,
Today it feels like everyone hates me. My parents are mad at me, and I'm grounded. My friend Keesha is acting weird and pretty much ignoring me. I don't know what her problem is. I played a horrible game, and my coach and the team really came down hard on me. Geez, everybody has a bad day sometimes. My teachers don't even notice I'm there. And worst of all, Jayden, who I thought was interested in me, started going out with Angelana.

I hate my life! I don't even know why I'm here. Nobody cares, anyway.

God, I need to feel some peace. Show me it won't always be like today. I know you love me, at least. I need your peace and love to fill me up so I can keep going. Help me, Lord!

— Job, chapter 3

9 Keep the morning star from shining;
give that night no hope of dawn.
10 Curse that night for letting me be born,
for exposing me to trouble and grief.

11 I wish I had died in my mother's womb
or died the moment I was born.
12 Why did my mother hold me on her knees?
Why did she feed me at her breast?
13 If I had died then, I would be at rest now,
14 sleeping like the kings and rulers
who rebuilt ancient palaces.
15 Then I would be sleeping like princes
who filled their houses with gold and silver,
16 or sleeping like a stillborn child.
17 In the grave wicked people stop their evil,
and tired workers find rest at last.
18 Even prisoners enjoy peace,
free from shouts and harsh commands.
19 Everyone is there, the famous and the unknown,
and slaves at last are free.
20 Why let people go on living in misery?
Why give light to those in grief
21 They wait for death, but it never comes;
they prefer a grave to any treasure.
22 They are not happy till they are dead and buried;
23 God keeps their future hidden
and hems them in on every side.
24 Instead of eating, I mourn,
and I can never stop groaning.
25 Everything I fear and dread comes true.
26 I have no peace, no rest,
and my troubles never end.

The First Dialogue
(4:1—14:22)

4

Eliphaz

1-2 Job, will you be annoyed if I speak?
I can't keep quiet any longer.
3 You have taught many people
and given strength to feeble hands.
4 When someone stumbled, weak and tired,
your words encouraged him to stand.

3:21 Rev 9:6

Study it!

The (Really, Really) Long Debate

After a week of being quietly present to Job in his grief, his friends try to make some sense out of things. From chapter 4 through chapter 32, Job and his friends get into a huge debate about why Job has suffered so much. Job's friends are certain his tragedies happened because Job or someone in his family sinned against God. They believe God punishes people who are unjust or wicked (this is what the Israelites believed about disaster, disease, and other problems). Job insists he has done nothing wrong to bring on his troubles. He feels like God has abandoned him and treated him unjustly.

What do you think? Are Job's friends correct when they say that God punishes us for our sins? Read on for the answer.

— Job, chapter 4

5 Now it's your turn to be in trouble,
and you are too stunned to face it.
6 You worshiped God, and your life was blameless;
and so you should have confidence and hope.
7 Think back now. Name a single case
where someone righteous met with disaster.
8 I have seen people plow fields of evil
and plant wickedness like seed;
now they harvest wickedness and evil.
9 Like a storm, God destroys them in his anger.
10 The wicked roar and growl like lions,
but God silences them and breaks their teeth.
11 Like lions with nothing to kill and eat,
they die, and all their children are scattered.

12 Once a message came quietly,
so quietly I could hardly hear it.
13 Like a nightmare it disturbed my sleep.
14 I trembled and shuddered;
my whole body shook with fear.
15 A light breeze touched my face,
and my skin crawled with fright.
16 I could see something standing there;
I stared, but couldn't tell what it was.
Then I heard a voice out of the silence:
17 "Can anyone be righteous in the sight of[g] God
or be pure before[h] his Creator?
18 God does not trust his heavenly servants;
he finds fault even with his angels.
19 Do you think he will trust a creature of clay,
a thing of dust that can be crushed like a moth?
20 We may be alive in the morning,
but die unnoticed before evening comes.
21 All that we have is taken away;
we die, still lacking wisdom."

5 Call out, Job. See if anyone answers.
Is there any angel to whom you can turn?
2 To worry yourself to death with resentment
would be a foolish, senseless thing to do.
3 I have seen fools who looked secure,
but I called down a sudden curse on their homes.
4 Their children can never find safety;
no one stands up to defend them in court.
5 Hungry people will eat the fool's crops—
even the grain growing among thorns[i]—
and thirsty people will envy his wealth.

[g] **4:17** righteous in the sight of; *or* more righteous than. [h] **4:17** be pure before; *or* be more pure than.
[i] **5:5** *Probable text* even . . . thorns; *Hebrew unclear.*
4:13 Job 33:15

[6]Evil does not grow in the soil,
nor does trouble grow out of the ground.
[7]No indeed! We bring trouble on ourselves,
as surely as sparks fly up from a fire.[j]

[8]If I were you, I would turn to God
and present my case to him.
[9]We cannot understand the great things he does,
and to his miracles there is no end.
[10]He sends rain on the land
and he waters the fields.
[11]Yes, it is God who raises the humble
and gives joy to all who mourn.
[12-13]He upsets the plans of cunning people,
and traps the wise in their own schemes,
so that nothing they do succeeds;
[14] even at noon they grope in darkness.
[15]But God saves the poor[k] from death;
he saves the needy from oppression.
[16]He gives hope to the poor and silences the wicked.
[17]Happy is the person whom God corrects!
Do not resent it when he rebukes you.
[18]God bandages the wounds he makes;
his hand hurts you, and his hand heals.
[19]Time after time he will save you from harm;
[20] when famine comes, he will keep you alive,
and in war protect you from death.
[21]God will rescue you from slander;
he will save you when destruction comes.
[22]You will laugh at violence and hunger
and not be afraid of wild animals.
[23]The fields you plow will be free of rocks;
wild animals will never attack you.
[24]Then you will live at peace in your tent;
when you look at your sheep, you will find them safe.
[25]You will have as many children
as there are blades of grass in a pasture.
[26]Like wheat that ripens till harvest time,
you will live to a ripe old age.
[27]Job, we have learned this by long study.
It is true, so now accept it.

6

Job

[1-2]If my troubles and griefs were weighed on scales,
[3] they would weigh more than the sands of the sea,
so my wild words should not surprise you.
[4]Almighty God has shot me with arrows,
and their poison spreads through my body.
God has lined up his terrors against me.

[5]A donkey is content when eating grass,
and a cow is quiet when eating hay.
[6]But who can eat flat, unsalted food?
What taste is there in the white of an egg?
[7]I have no appetite for food like that,
and everything I eat makes me sick.[l]

[8]Why won't God give me what I ask?
Why won't he answer my prayer?
[9]If only he would go ahead and kill me!
[10]If I knew he would, I would leap for joy,
no matter how great my pain.
I know that God is holy;
I have never opposed what he commands.
[11]What strength do I have to keep on living?
Why go on living when I have no hope?
[12]Am I made of stone? Is my body bronze?
[13]I have no strength left to save myself;
there is nowhere I can turn for help.

[14]In trouble[m] like this I need loyal friends—
whether I've forsaken God or not.

[j] **5:7** sparks fly up from a fire; *or* birds fly up to the sky. [k] **5:15** *Probable text* poor; *Hebrew unclear.*
[l] **6:7** *Probable text* sick; *Hebrew unclear.* [m] **6:14** *Probable text* trouble; *Hebrew unclear.*
5:9 Sir 43:32 **5:13** 1 Cor 3:19 **5:17** Prov 3:11, 12; Heb 12:5, 6 **5:18** Hos 6:1

Eliphaz encourages Job to talk to God about his problems. Do you need to talk with God about anything in your life?

15 But you, my friends, you deceive me like
streams
that go dry when no rain comes.
16 The streams are choked with snow and
ice,
17 but in the heat they disappear,
and the stream beds lie bare and dry.
18 Caravans get lost looking for water;
they wander and die in the desert.
19 Caravans from Sheba and Tema search,
20 but their hope dies beside dry streams.
21 You are like[n] those streams to me,[o]
you see my fate and draw back in fear.
22 Have I asked you to give me a gift
or to bribe someone on my behalf
23 or to save me from some enemy or
tyrant?
24 All right, teach me; tell me my faults.
I will be quiet and listen to you.
25 Honest words are convincing,
but you are talking nonsense.
26 You think I am talking nothing but wind;
then why do you answer my words of
despair?
27 You would even roll dice for orphan
slaves
and make yourselves rich off your
closest friends!
28 Look me in the face. I won't lie.
29 You have gone far enough. Stop being
unjust.
Don't condemn me. I'm in the right.
30 But you think I am lying—
you think I can't tell right from wrong.

7 Human life is like forced army service,
like a life of hard manual labor,
2 like a slave longing for cool
shade;
like a worker waiting to be paid.

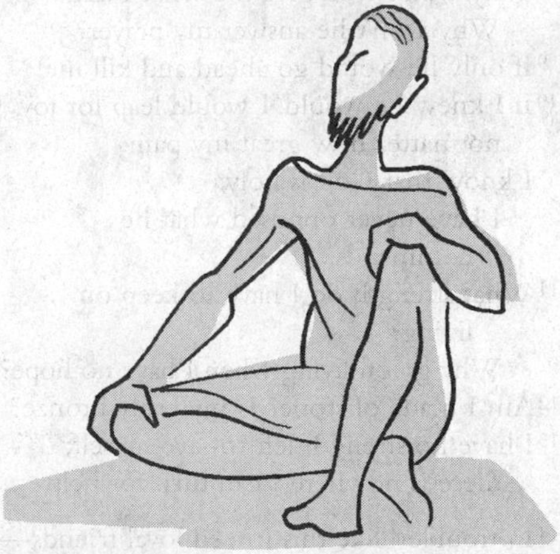

"You think I am talking nothing but wind." (6:26)

Live it!

Open to Criticism?

Sometimes it feels so good to point out someone's faults to them, doesn't it? But what about when someone points out your faults to you? Do you react in anger? Do you brush it off as ridiculous? Do you automatically believe it and add it to your list of reasons you're no good?

Job is struggling to listen to his friends. It's usually a good idea to listen when people point out our faults. Look at yourself honestly: Is there some truth to what they say? Is that fault showing up in the things you say and do? Sometimes they are wrong, but sometimes they are right—especially if it's a person who knows you well. Instead of resenting someone for criticizing you, think of it as an opportunity to check and see if there is some room for personal growth and improvement.

— Job 6:24–25

[n] **6:21** *Probable text* like; *Hebrew* indeed. [o] **6:21** *probable text* to me; *Hebrew unclear*

"Why won't God give me what I ask? / Why won't he answer my prayer?" *(Job 6:8)*.

Pray it!

Honestly, God!

See how honest Job is in talking to God. He's upset with God and lets God know it. Of all the ways there are to pray, God loves it best when we just talk to him. Honestly. We can tell God everything that's on our mind—even what we think of him! God doesn't want us to just say what we think he wants to hear. He already knows our real thoughts, anyway, so why try to hide them?

Sit down and have a conversation with God, or write a letter to God in your journal. Tell God exactly what's going on in your life, how you feel about it, what disappointments you're experiencing, what makes you mad, what your questions and hopes and dreams are, and so on. Tell God everything.

We can be this honest with God. Anytime, anywhere—God welcomes it!

— Job 7:7–21

3 Month after month I have nothing to live
for;
night after night brings me grief.
4 When I lie down to sleep, the hours drag;
I toss all night and long for dawn.
5 My body is full of worms;
it is covered with scabs;
pus runs out of my sores.
6 My days pass by without hope,
pass faster than a weaver's shuttle.[p]
7 Remember, O God, my life is only a
breath;
my happiness has already ended.
8 You see me now, but never again.
If you look for me, I'll be gone.
9-10 Like a cloud that fades and is gone,
we humans die and never return;
we are forgotten by all who knew us.
11 No! I can't be quiet!
I am angry and bitter.
I have to speak.
12 Why do you keep me under guard?
Do you think I am a sea monster?[q]
13 I lie down and try to rest;
I look for relief from my pain.
14 But you—you terrify me with dreams;
you send me visions and nightmares
15 until I would rather be strangled
than live in this miserable body.
16 I give up; I am tired of living.
Leave me alone. My life makes no sense.
17 Why are people so important to you?
Why pay attention to what they do?
18 You inspect them every morning
and test them every minute.
19 Won't you look away long enough
for me to swallow my spit?

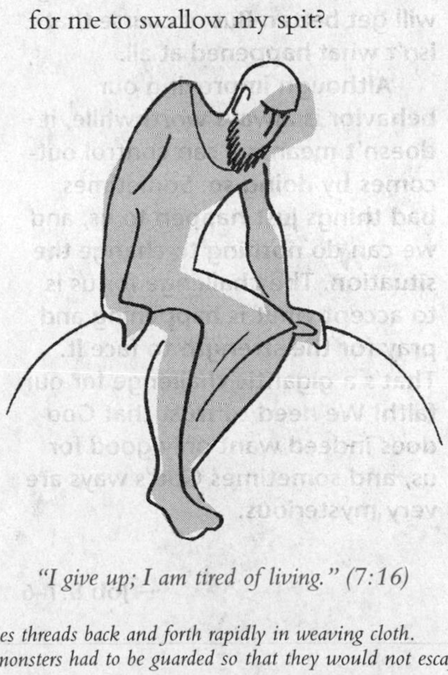

"I give up; I am tired of living." (7:16)

[p] **7:6** WEAVER'S SHUTTLE: *A small device in the loom which carries threads back and forth rapidly in weaving cloth.*
[q] **7:12** SEA MONSTER: *A reference to ancient stories in which sea monsters had to be guarded so that they would not escape and do damage.*

7:9, 10 Wis 2:1–4 **7:17** Ps 8:4; 144:3

20 Are you harmed by my sin, you jailer?
Why use me for your target practice?
Am I so great a burden to you?
21 Can't you ever forgive my sin?
Can't you pardon the wrong I do?
Soon I will be in my grave,
and I'll be gone when you look for me.

8

Bildad

1-2 Are you finally through with your windy
speech?
3 God never twists justice;
he never fails to do what is right.
4 Your children must have sinned against
God,
and so he punished them as they
deserved.
5 But turn now and plead with Almighty
God;
6 if you are so honest and pure,
then God will come and help you
and restore your household as your
reward.
7 All the wealth you lost will be nothing
compared with what God will give you
then.

8 Look for a moment at ancient wisdom;
consider the truths our ancestors
learned.
9 Our life is short, we know nothing at all;
we pass like shadows across the earth.
10 But let the ancient wise people teach you;
listen to what they had to say:
11 "Reeds can't grow where there is no
water;
they are never found outside a swamp.
12 If the water dries up, they are the first to
wither,
while still too small to be cut and used.
13 Godless people are like those reeds;
their hope is gone, once God is
forgotten.
14 They trust a thread—a spider's web.
15 If they lean on a web, will it hold them
up?
If they grab for a thread, will it help
them stand?"

Live it!

Pleading Our Case with God

Last night, Mario's parents told him and his sister that they were getting a divorce. Today, his dad moved out of their house. Mario's head is spinning—he didn't see it coming. Was there something he could have done to stop it? Could he stop it, still? Maybe if he didn't complain so much about helping around the house, or if he wasn't so moody. All that could cause a lot of stress, right? So, if he was more pleasant and helpful, his parents might try again? Maybe if he pleased God *and* his parents, God would bring his family back together again.

Don't we think this way sometimes? Job's friend Bildad thought that way. He said if Job didn't sin, then Job's misfortunes must have been his children's fault. All Job has to do is plead with God and things will get better. But of course that isn't what happened at all.

Although improving our behavior is always worthwhile, it doesn't mean we can control outcomes by doing so. Sometimes bad things just happen to us, and we can do nothing to change the situation. The challenge for us is to accept what is happening and pray for the strength to face it. That's a gigantic challenge for our faith! We need to trust that God does indeed want only good for us, and sometimes God's ways are very mysterious.

— Job 8:1–6

8:8 Sir 8:9

Praying for Help

Catholic Connections

A long tradition of prayer in our Church is intercessory prayer, or prayer of petition. In intercessory prayer, we bring our needs to God and ask for his help and blessing.

Job wonders if it's worth it to ask God for help. He doubts if God is really listening or even if he cares. God truly does care and is always listening to our prayers! But here's the tricky part: we might not get exactly what we ask for. That doesn't mean God doesn't answer our prayers. It just means that God answers our prayers in the ways he knows are best for us.

For instance, Susan's grandmother died of cancer, even though Susan prayed and prayed with all her heart for her grandmother to be healed and to live a long life. Was God busy when Susan was praying? Didn't he get the message? Or did he ignore Susan's prayers?

God did answer Susan's prayers, but not the way she hoped. In time, she realized God showed his love for her in other ways: through the care of friends and family, by showing her how to be kind to someone who is very sick, and by giving her the desire to start hanging out at the nursing home (Susan thought her grandma would really like that).

Trust God—he hears you and is working on your prayer. Keep your eyes and heart open to how your prayer is being answered!

— Job 9:1–16

16 Evil people sprout like weeds in the sun,
like weeds that spread all through the garden.
17 Their roots wrap around the stones
and hold fast to[r] every rock.
18 But then pull them up—
no one will ever know they were there.
19 Yes, that's all the joy evil people have;
others now come and take their places.

20 But God will never abandon the faithful
or ever give help to evil people.
21 He will let you laugh and shout again,
22 but he will bring disgrace on those who hate you,
and the homes of the wicked will vanish.

9

Job

1-2 Yes, I've heard all that before.
But how can a human being win a case against God?
3 How can anyone argue with him?
He can ask a thousand questions
that no one could ever answer.[s]
4 God is so wise and powerful;
no one can stand up against him.
5 Without warning he moves mountains
and in anger he destroys them.
6 God sends earthquakes and shakes the ground;
he rocks the pillars that support the earth.

[r] **8:17** *Probable text* hold fast to; *Hebrew* see. [s] **9:3** He can ask . . . answer; *or* Someone could ask him a thousand questions, and he would not answer.
9:2 Job 4:17

"Are you finally through with your windy speech?" *(Job 8:1–2)*. **Job and his friends sure are honest with one another!**

7 He can keep the sun from rising,
and the stars from shining at night.
8 No one helped God spread out the heavens
or trample the sea monster's back.[t]
9 God hung the stars in the sky—the Dipper,
Orion, the Pleiades, and the stars of the south.
10 We cannot understand the great things he does,
and to his miracles there is no end.

11 God passes by, but I cannot see him.
12 He takes what he wants, and no one can stop him;
no one dares ask him, "What are you doing?"
13 God's anger is constant. He crushed his enemies
who helped Rahab,[u] the sea monster, oppose him.
14 So how can I find words to answer God?
15 Though I am innocent, all I can do
is beg for mercy from God my judge.
16 Yet even then, if he lets me speak,
I can't believe he would listen to me.
17 He sends storms to batter and bruise me
without any reason at all.
18 He won't let me catch my breath;
he has filled my life with bitterness.
19 Should I try force? Try force on God?
Should I take him to court? Could anyone make him go?[v]
20 I am innocent and faithful, but my words sound guilty,
and everything I say seems to condemn me.
21-22 I am innocent, but I no longer care.
I am sick of living. Nothing matters;
innocent or guilty, God will destroy us.
23 When an innocent person suddenly dies,
God laughs.
24 God gave the world to the wicked.
He made all the judges blind.
And if God didn't do it, who did?
25 My days race by, not one of them good.
26 My life passes like the swiftest boat,
as fast as an eagle swooping down on a rabbit.
27-28 If I smile and try to forget my pain,
all my suffering comes back to haunt me;
I know that God does hold me guilty.
29 Since I am held guilty, why should I bother?
30 No soap can wash away my sins.
31 God throws me into a pit with filth,
and even my clothes are ashamed of me.
32 If God were human, I could answer him;
we could go to court to decide our quarrel.
33 But there is no one to step between us—
no one to judge both God and me.
34 Stop punishing me, God!
Keep your terrors away!
35 I am not afraid. I am going to talk
because I know my own heart.

10 I am tired of living.
Listen to my bitter complaint.
2 Don't condemn me, God.
Tell me! What is the charge against me?
3 Is it right for you to be so cruel?
To despise what you yourself have made?
And then to smile on the schemes of wicked people?
4 Do you see things as we do?
5 Is your life as short as ours?
6 Then why do you track down all my sins
and hunt down every fault I have?
7 You know that I am not guilty,
that no one can save me from you.
8 Your hands formed and shaped me,
and now[w] those same hands destroy me.

[t] **9:8** TRAMPLE THE SEA MONSTER'S BACK: *A reference to ancient stories in which a sea monster was killed and then trampled (see also 26:13).* [u] **9:13** RAHAB: *A legendary sea monster which represented the forces of chaos and evil.*
[v] **9:19** *Probable text* make him go; *Hebrew* make me go. [w] **10:8** *Some ancient translations* and now; *Hebrew* together.
9:7, 8 Bar 3:34, 35 **9:9** Job 38:31; Am 5:8 **10:7** Wis 16:15

"We cannot understand the great things he does, / and to his miracles there is no end" *(Job 9:10)*.

9 Remember that you made me from clay;[x]
are you going to crush me back to
dust?
10 You gave my father strength to beget me;
you made me grow in my mother's
womb.
11 You formed my body with bones and
sinews
and covered the bones with muscles
and skin.
12 You have given me life and constant love,
and your care has kept me alive.
13 But now I know that all that time
you were secretly planning to harm
me.
14 You were watching to see if I would sin,
so that you could refuse to forgive me.
15 As soon as I sin, I'm in trouble with you,
but when I do right, I get no credit.
I am miserable and covered with shame.[y]
16 If I have any success at all,
you hunt me down like a lion;
to hurt me you even work miracles.
17 You always have some witness against me;
your anger toward me grows and
grows;
you always plan some new attack.

18 Why, God, did you let me be born?
I should have died before anyone saw
me.
19 To go from the womb straight to the grave
would have been as good as never
existing.
20 Isn't my life almost over? Leave me alone!
Let me enjoy the time I have left.
21 I am going soon and will never come
back—
going to a land that is dark and gloomy,
22 a land of darkness, shadows, and
confusion,
where the light itself is darkness.

11

Zophar

1-2 Will no one answer all this nonsense?
Does talking so much put you in the
right?
3 Job, do you think we can't answer you?
That your mocking words will leave us
speechless?
4 You claim that what you say is true;
you claim you are pure in the sight of
God.
5 How I wish God would answer you!
6 He would tell you there are many sides to
wisdom;
there are things too deep for human
knowledge.
God is punishing you less than you
deserve.

7 Can you discover the limits and bounds
of the greatness and power of God?
8 The sky is no limit for God,
but it lies beyond your reach.
God knows the world of the dead,
but you do not know it.
9 God's greatness is broader than the earth,
wider than the sea.
10 If God arrests you and brings you to trial,
who is there to stop him?
11 God knows which people are worthless;
he sees all their evil deeds.
12 Stupid people will start being wise
when wild donkeys are born tame.

13 Put your heart right, Job. Reach out to
God.
14 Put away evil and wrong from your home.
15 Then face the world again, firm and
courageous.
16 Then all your troubles will fade from
your memory,
like floods that are past and
remembered no more.
17 Your life will be brighter than sunshine at
noon,
and life's darkest hours will shine like
the dawn.
18 You will live secure and full of hope;
God will protect you and give you rest.
19 You won't be afraid of your enemies;
many people will ask you for help.
20 But the wicked will look around in
despair
and find that there is no way to escape.
Their one hope is that death will come.

[x] **10:9** *One ancient translation* from clay; *Hebrew* like clay. [y] **10:15** *Probable text* covered with shame; *Hebrew* see my shame.

10:10 Wis 7:1, 2

Catholic Connections

The Sacrament of Penance and Reconciliation

Job's friend Zophar tells him: "Put your heart right, Job. Reach out to God" (Job 11:13). This is what the sacrament of Penance and Reconciliation is all about for us. We want to put our hearts right and our lives back on track. We know we'll feel better when we admit our sin to God and let him purify us and set us back on the path of goodness. The sacrament lets us reach out to God and ask for forgiveness and healing.

Like the father of the prodigal son (see the parable in Luke 15:11–32), God is waiting for us with open arms, before we even say we're sorry! God will never let us down when we reach out to him. God happily forgives and helps us when we want to change our hearts. Then everything seems lighter and brighter in our lives.

— Job 11:13–18

12

Job

1-2 Yes, you are the voice of the people.
When you die, wisdom will die with you.
3 But I have as much sense as you have;
I am in no way inferior to you;
everyone knows all that you have said.
4 Even my friends laugh at me now;
they laugh, although I am righteous and blameless;
but there was a time when God answered my prayers.
5 You have no troubles, and yet you make fun of me;
you hit someone who is about to fall.
6 But thieves and godless people live in peace,
though their only god is their own strength.
7 Even birds and animals have much they could teach you;
8 ask the creatures of earth and sea for their wisdom.
9 All of them know that the LORD's hand made them.
10 It is God who directs the lives of his creatures;
everyone's life is in his power.
11 But just as your tongue enjoys tasting food,
your ears enjoy hearing words.
12-13 Old people have wisdom,
but God has wisdom and power.
Old people have insight;
God has insight and power to act.
14 When God tears down, who can rebuild,
and who can free those God imprisons?
15 Drought comes when God withholds rain;
floods come when he turns water loose.
16 God is strong and always victorious;
both deceived and deceiver are in his power.
17 He takes away the wisdom of rulers
and makes leaders act like fools.
18 He dethrones kings and makes them prisoners;
19 he humbles priests and men of power.
20 He silences those who are trusted,
and takes the wisdom of old people away.

Study it!

Is God a Director?

Some people believe God controls everything and everybody. They think that he knows exactly what will happen and when, and that he makes it all happen. On the other hand, we are told God gives us free will to make our own choices. So which is it? Is God like a movie director? Does he control us? Or does he give us freedom?

The Bible tells us that we are made in God's image. Which means that God gave us the ability to choose love and goodness. But the flip side of that is we can also choose hate and evil. We are free to choose how to respond to life even if we do not choose everything that happens to us. The mystery is that God sees the whole picture of how our lives are going to unfold, but that doesn't mean he forces it to happen that way.

— Job 12:10

21 He disgraces those in power
and puts an end to the strength of rulers.
22 He sends light to places dark as death.
23 He makes nations strong and great,
but then he defeats and destroys them.
24 He makes their leaders foolish
and lets them wander confused and lost;
25 they grope in the dark and stagger like drunkards.

13 1-2 Everything you say, I have heard before.
I understand it all; I know as much as you do.
I'm not your inferior.
3 But my dispute is with God, not you;
I want to argue my case with him.
4 You cover up your ignorance with lies;
you are like doctors who can't heal anyone.
5 Say nothing, and someone may think you are wise!
6 Listen while I state my case.
7 Why are you lying?
Do you think your lies will benefit God?
8 Are you trying to defend him?
Are you going to argue his case in court?
9 If God looks at you closely, will he find anything good?
Do you think you can fool God the way you fool others?
10 Even though your prejudice is hidden,
he will reprimand you,
11 and his power will fill you with terror.
12 Your proverbs are as useless as ashes;
your arguments are as weak as clay.
13 Be quiet and give me a chance to speak,
and let the results be what they will.

"Be quiet and give me a chance to speak." (13:13)

What choice is facing you today? How can you make it a choice for love and goodness?

14 I am[z] ready to risk my life.
15 I've lost all hope, so what if God kills me?
I am going to state my case to him.
16 It may even be that my boldness will save me,
since no wicked person would dare to face God.
17 Now listen to my words of explanation.
18 I am ready to state my case,
because I know I am in the right.

19 Are you coming to accuse me, God?
If you do, I am ready to be silent and die.
20 Let me ask for two things; agree to them,
and I will not try to hide from you:
21 stop punishing me, and don't crush me with terror.

22 Speak first, O God, and I will answer.
Or let me speak, and you answer me.
23 What are my sins? What wrongs have I done?
What crimes am I charged with?
24 Why do you avoid me?
Why do you treat me like an enemy?
25 Are you trying to frighten me? I'm nothing but a leaf;
you are attacking a piece of dry straw.

26 You bring bitter charges against me,
even for what I did when I was young.
27 You bind chains on my feet;
you watch every step I take,
and even examine my footprints.
28 As a result, I crumble like rotten wood,
like a moth-eaten coat.

14 We are all born weak and helpless.
All lead the same short, troubled life.
2 We grow and wither as quickly as flowers;
we disappear like shadows.
3 Will you even look at me, God,
or put me on trial and judge me?
4 Nothing clean can ever come
from anything as unclean as human beings.
5 The length of our lives is decided beforehand—
the number of months we will live.
You have settled it, and it can't be changed.
6 Look away from us and leave us alone;[a]
let us enjoy our hard life—if we can.[b]

7 There is hope for a tree that has been cut down;
it can come back to life and sprout.

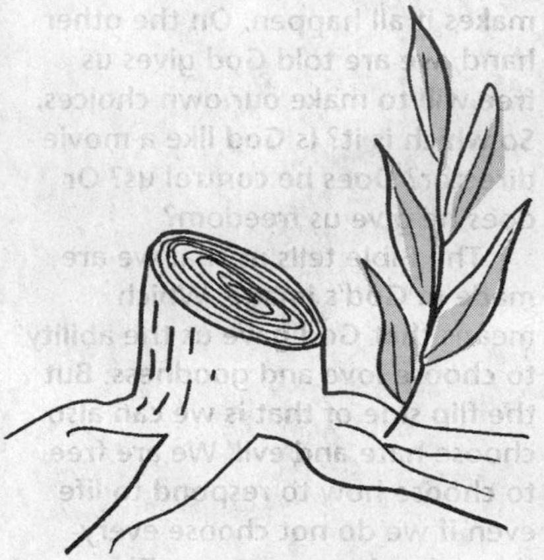

There is hope for a tree that has been cut down. (14:7)

8 Even though its roots grow old,
and its stump dies in the ground,
9 with water it will sprout like a young plant.
10 But we die, and that is the end of us;
we die, and where are we then?

11 Like rivers that stop running,
and lakes that go dry,
12 people die, never to rise.
They will never wake up while the sky endures;
they will never stir from their sleep.
13 I wish you would hide me in the world of the dead;
let me be hidden until your anger is over,
and then set a time to remember me.

[z] **13:14** *One ancient translation* I am; *Hebrew* Why am I. [a] **14:6** *One Hebrew manuscript* and leave us alone; *most Hebrew manuscripts* so that we may rest. [b] **14:6** let us . . . can; *or* until we finish our day of hard work.
13:27 Job 33:11 **14:1, 2** Wis 2:1; Sir 40:1–11; 41:1–4

Think of someone you know who has died. Now imagine him or her living in heaven with God, happier than ever.

Catholic Connections

Eternal Life

Atheists are people who do not believe in the existence of God. They would share the belief of Job: when we die, that's the end of us. Or, as others say, we're just food for the worms. Catholics and all Christians believe something very different! Death is hardly the end, but a new beginning—the beginning of an amazingly wonderful life with God for all of eternity. Forever and ever—more happiness and peace than we can even imagine!

How do we know this? Because when Jesus died, it wasn't over. He rose from the dead! Furthermore, Jesus tells us that those who love God will also share in his Resurrection. We will live forever with God and know complete joy.

When someone we love dies, believing in the Resurrection can bring us great comfort. The Resurrection is God's promise that those people who die in Gods grace shall be raised—body and soul—into a new and incredible life. And when we are facing death one day, we will also have this hope to hold onto. Death isn't the end!

— Job 14:10–12

14 If a man dies, can he come back to life?
But I will wait for better times,
wait till this time of trouble is ended.
15 Then you will call, and I will answer,
and you will be pleased with me, your creature.
16 Then you will watch every step I take,
but you will not keep track of my sins.
17 You will forgive them and put them away;
you will wipe out all the wrongs I have done.

18 There comes a time when mountains fall
and solid cliffs are moved away.
19 Water will wear down rocks,
and heavy rain will wash away the soil;
so you destroy our hope for life.
20 You overpower us and send us away forever;
our faces are twisted in death.
21 Our children win honor, but we never know it,
nor are we told when they are disgraced.
22 We feel only the pain of our own bodies
and the grief of our own minds.

The Second Dialogue
(15:1—21:34)

15
Eliphaz

1-2 Empty words, Job! Empty words!
3 No one who is wise would talk the way you do
or defend himself with such meaningless words.
4 If you had your way, no one would fear God;
no one would pray to him.
5 Your wickedness is evident by what you say;
you are trying to hide behind clever words.
6 There is no need for me to condemn you;
you are condemned by every word you speak.

7 Do you think you were the first person born?
Were you there when God made the mountains?

8 Did you overhear the plans God made?
Does human wisdom belong to you alone?
9 There is nothing you know that we don't know.
10 We learned our wisdom from gray-haired people—
those born before your father.

11 God offers you comfort; why still reject it?
We have spoken for him with calm, even words.
12 But you are excited and glare at us in anger.
13 You are angry with God and denounce him.

14 Can any human being be really pure?
Can anyone be right with God?
15 Why, God does not trust even his angels;
even they are not pure in his sight.
16 And we drink evil as if it were water;
yes, we are corrupt; we are worthless.

17 Now listen, Job, to what I know.
18 Those who are wise have taught me truths
which they learned from their ancestors,
and they kept no secrets hidden.
19 Their land was free from foreigners;
there was no one to lead them away from God.

20 The wicked who oppress others
will be in torment as long as they live.
21 Voices of terror will scream in their ears,
and robbers attack when they think they are safe.
22 They have no hope of escaping from darkness,
for somewhere a sword is waiting to kill them,
23 and vultures[c] are waiting[d] to eat their corpses.
They know their future is dark;
24 disaster, like a powerful king,
is waiting to attack them.

Pray it!

Choosing the Right Path

Eliphaz is trying to prove to Job that our sins cause the hurt and pain we experience. That is often true. What is also true is that sometimes evil or trouble comes our way even when we have tried to make good choices and live moral lives. That's a mystery beyond our understanding. But although we can't control everything that happens to us, we can do our best to bring goodness into our world, by being our best and most faithful selves. Read Psalm 16 and spend some time praying about this.

— Job 15:20–35

25 That is the fate of those
who shake their fists at God
and defy the Almighty.
26-27 They are proud and rebellious;
they stubbornly hold up their shields
and rush to fight against God.

28 They are the ones who captured cities
and seized houses whose owners had fled,
but war will destroy those cities and houses.
29 They will not remain rich for long;
nothing they own will last.
Even their shadows[e] will vanish,
30 and they will not escape from darkness.
They will be like trees
whose branches are burned by fire,
whose blossoms[f] are blown away by the wind.
31 If they are foolish enough to trust in evil,
then evil will be their reward.

[c] **15:23** *One ancient translation* vultures; *Hebrew* where is he? [d] **15:23** *One ancient translation* are waiting; *Hebrew* he wanders. [e] **15:29** *One ancient translation* shadows; *Hebrew unclear.* [f] **15:30** *One ancient translation* blossoms; *Hebrew* mouth.

15:14–16 Job 25:4–6

32 Before their time is up they will wither,[g]
wither like a branch and never be
green again.
33 They will be like vines that lose their
unripe grapes;
like olive trees that drop their blossoms.
34 There will be no descendants for godless
people,
and fire will destroy the homes built by
bribery.
35 These are the ones who plan trouble and
do evil;
their hearts are always full of deceit.

16

Job

1-2 I have heard words like that before;
the comfort you give is only torment.

"The comfort you give is only torment." (16:1)

3 Are you going to keep on talking forever?
Do you always have to have the last
word?
4 If you were in my place and I in yours,
I could say everything you are saying.
I could shake my head wisely
and drown you with a flood of words.
5 I could strengthen you with advice
and keep talking to comfort you.
6 But nothing I say helps,
and being silent does not calm my pain.

Live it!

Shut Up and Just Listen!

At the beginning of Job, chapter 16, Job is tired of hearing his friends giving him advice. It isn't really what he needs right now. When friends have troubles, we often want to help by offering advice or telling a story of a similar experience we had, so they'll know we understand what they're going through. Our intentions are good, but that's not really the best way to help.

When you want to be there for a friend, just listen. Be quiet! Let your friend talk it out. Don't try to fix your friend or their problem. By letting your friend talk, you're allowing them to tap into their own wisdom and find an answer. *Then,* you can talk: Tell your friend that you believe in them and ask how you can help.

— Job 16:1–5

7 You have worn me out, God;
you have let my family be killed.
8 You have seized me; you are my enemy.
I am skin and bones,
and people take that as proof of my
guilt.[h]
9 In anger God tears me limb from limb;
he glares at me with hate.
10 People sneer at me;
they crowd around me and slap my
face.
11 God has handed me over to evil
people.

[g] **15:32** *Some ancient translations* wither; *Hebrew* be filled. [h] **16:8** *Verses 7-8 in Hebrew are unclear.*

Fearing God is another way of saying that we are in awe of God's power and wisdom.

12 I was living in peace,
but God took me by the throat
and battered me and crushed me.
God uses me for target practice
13 and shoots arrows at me from every side—
arrows that pierce and wound me;
and even then he shows no pity.
14 He wounds me again and again;
he attacks like a soldier gone mad with hate.
15 I mourn and wear clothes made of sackcloth,
and I sit here in the dust defeated.
16 I have cried until my face is red,
and my eyes are swollen and circled with shadows,
17 but I am not guilty of any violence,
and my prayer to God is sincere.
18 O Earth, don't hide the wrongs done to me!
Don't let my call for justice be silenced!
19 There is someone in heaven
to stand up for me and take my side.
20 My friends scorn me;
my eyes pour out tears to God.
21 I want someone to plead with God for me,
as one pleads for a friend.
22 My years are passing now,
and I walk the road of no return.

17 1 The end of my life is near. I can hardly breathe;
there is nothing left for me but the grave.
2 I watch how bitterly everyone mocks me.
3 I am being honest, God. Accept my word.
There is no one else to support what I say.
4 You have closed their minds to reason;
don't let them triumph over me now.
5 In the old proverb someone betrays his friends for money,
and his children suffer for it.[i]

Pray it!

The Turning of Friends

alone in my room
no peace joy hope, only tears
bring back just one friend
—Alisha, 13 years old

Like Alisha—and Job—our hearts break when friends turn away from us. When you are sad, confused, lonely, or anxious, it can help to express your feelings creatively. You could try writing a haiku verse, like Alisha's. Haiku is a Japanese form of poetry with three lines of seventeen syllables—five syllables in the first line, seven in the second, and five in the third line. Pour your thoughts and emotions into the words of the haiku. Make a work of art out of it! Writing and creating can bring healing to your heart.

— Job 17:1–6

6 And now people use this proverb against me;
they come and spit in my face.
7 My grief has almost made me blind;
my arms and legs are as thin as shadows.
8 Those who claim to be honest are shocked,
and they all condemn me as godless.
9 Those who claim to be respectable
are more and more convinced they are right.
10 But if all of them came and stood before me,
I would not find even one of them wise.

[i] **17:5** someone . . . suffer for it; *or* someone entertains his friends while his children go hungry.
16:19 Job 19:25

"I want someone to plead with God for me, / as one pleads for a friend" *(Job 16:21)*.

11 My days have passed; my plans have failed;
my hope is gone.
12 But my friends say night is daylight;
they say that light is near,
but I know I remain in darkness.
13 My only hope is the world of the dead,
where I will lie down to sleep in the dark.
14 I will call the grave my father,
and the worms that eat me
I will call my mother and my sisters.
15 Where is there any hope for me?
Who sees any?
16 Hope will not go with me[j]
when I go down to the world of the dead.

18

Bildad

1-2 Job, can't people like you ever be quiet?
If you stopped to listen, we could talk to you.
3 What makes you think we are as stupid as cattle?
4 You are only hurting yourself with your anger.
Will the earth be deserted because you are angry?
Will God move mountains to satisfy you?

5 The light of the wicked will still be put out;
its flame will never burn again.
6 The lamp in their tents will be darkened.
7 Their steps were firm, but now they stumble;
they fall—victims of their own advice.
8 They walk into a net, and their feet are caught;
9 a trap catches their heels and holds them.
10 On the ground a snare is hidden;
a trap has been set in their path.

11 All around them terror is waiting;
it follows them at every step.
12 They used to be rich, but now they go hungry;
disaster stands and waits at their side.

Live it!

The Power of Anger

Anger can be a powerful force in our lives—often a destructive force. When we hold on to our anger, it eats away at us like a disease. We begin concentrating on ways to get revenge, our mood gets darker, we snap at people, and we get ugly lines in our forehead from frowning all the time! At its worst, unhealed anger can result in violence or contribute to serious illness. This is why Job's friend warns Job that he may be hurting himself with his anger. Curiously, our anger hurts us more than it hurts anyone else.

We need to bring our anger to God and ask for healing—for our own good. We experience healing when we choose forgiveness instead of revenge. We are also healed of anger when we focus on the positive things in our lives and see the good in others instead of focusing only on the negative things.

Can anger ever be good? It's never healthy to hold in our feelings, so if we can express anger in a way that is respectful and not violent to others, that's helpful. But then, we need to *let it go* so it doesn't grow deeper in us. Pray for peace in your heart, your words, and your actions!

—Job 18:4

13 A deadly disease spreads over their bodies
and causes their arms and legs to rot.
14 They are torn from the tents where they lived secure,
and are dragged off to face King Death.

[j] **17:16** *One ancient translation* with me; *Hebrew unclear.*
18:5, 6 Job 21:17

15 Now anyone may live in their tents—[k]
after sulfur is sprinkled to disinfect them![l]
16 Their roots and branches are withered
and dry.
17 Their fame is ended at home and abroad;
no one remembers them any more.
18 They will be driven out of the land of the
living,
driven from light into darkness.
19 They have no descendants, no survivors.
20 From east to west, all who hear of their
fate
shudder and tremble with fear.
21 That is the fate of evil people,
the fate of those who care nothing for
God.

19

Job

1-2 Why do you keep tormenting me with
words?
3 Time after time you insult me
and show no shame for the way you
abuse me.
4 Even if I have done wrong,
how does that hurt you?
5 You think you are better than I am,
and regard my troubles as proof of my
guilt.
6 Can't you see it is God who has done this?
He has set a trap to catch me.
7 I protest his violence,
but no one is listening;
no one hears my cry for justice.
8 God has blocked the way, and I can't get
through;
he has hidden my path in darkness.
9 He has taken away all my wealth
and destroyed my reputation.
10 He batters me from every side.
He uproots my hope
and leaves me to wither and die.
11 God is angry and rages against me;
he treats me like his worst enemy.
12 He sends his army to attack me;
they dig trenches and lay siege to my
tent.
13 God has made my own family forsake
me;
I am a stranger to those who knew
me;
14 my relatives and friends are gone.
15 Those who were guests in my house have
forgotten me;
my servant women treat me like a
stranger and a foreigner.
16 When I call a servant, he doesn't
answer—
even when I beg him to help me.
17 My wife can't stand the smell of my
breath,
and my own brothers won't come near
me.
18 Children despise me and laugh when they
see me.
19 My closest friends look at me with
disgust;
those I loved most have turned against
me.
20 My skin hangs loose on my bones;
I have barely escaped with my life.[m]
21 You are my friends! Take pity on me!
The hand of God has struck me down.

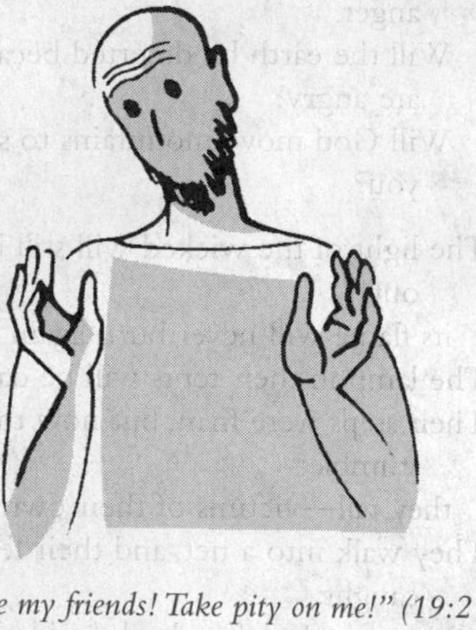

"You are my friends! Take pity on me!" (19:21)

22 Why must you persecute me the way
God does?
Haven't you tormented me enough?

23 How I wish that someone would
remember my words
and record them in a book!

[k] **18:15** Now anyone may live in their tents; *Hebrew unclear.* [l] **18:15** TO DISINFECT THEM: *Sulfur was used in the ancient world as a disinfectant and to clean rooms that had contained corpses.* [m] **19:20** *Verse 20 in Hebrew is unclear.*
19:19 Sir 6:8

Live it!

True Blue Friendship

Marcia was truly at a low point in her life. Some of her problems were her own fault, and others weren't. But she was at her lowest low and felt like everyone was tired of her troubles—and her. This is exactly how Job felt about his family and friends.

What kind of a friend are you during the tough times? Do you get frustrated and walk away? Do you start pointing out faults and try to change your friends? Or do you believe in them and stick by them through thick and thin? Can you wait it out with them, until life gets easier?

This is the kind of friend God is to us. Job doesn't get that—yet!

— Job 19:13–22

24 Or with a chisel carve my words in stone
and write them so that they would last forever.[n]
25 But I know there is someone in heaven
who will come at last to my defense.
26 Even after my skin is eaten by disease,
while still in this body[o] I will see God.[p]
27 I will see him with my own eyes,
and he will not be a stranger.

My courage failed because you said,
28 "How can we torment him?"
You looked for some excuse to attack me.
29 But now, be afraid of the sword—
the sword that brings God's wrath on sin,
so that you will know there is one who judges.[q]

20

Zophar

1-2 Job, you upset me. Now I'm impatient to answer.
3 What you have said is an insult,
but I know how to reply to you.
4 Surely you know that from ancient times,
when we humans were first placed on earth,
5 no wicked people have been happy for long.
6 They may grow great, towering to the sky,
so great that their heads reach the clouds,
7 but they will be blown away like dust.
Those who used to know them
will wonder where they have gone.
8 They will vanish like a dream, like a vision at night,
and never be seen again.
9 The wicked will disappear from the place where they used to live;
10 and their children will make good what they stole from the poor.
11 Their bodies used to be young and vigorous,
but soon they will turn to dust.
12-13 Evil tastes so good to them
that they keep some in their mouths to enjoy its flavor.
14 But in their stomachs the food turns bitter,
as bitter as any poison could be.
15 The wicked vomit up the wealth they stole;
God takes it back, even out of their stomachs.

[n] **19:24** last forever; *or* be on record. [o] **19:26** while still in this body; *or* although not in this body.
[p] **19:26** *Verse 26 in Hebrew is unclear.* [q] **19:29** one who judges; *or* a judgment.
20:8 Wis 5:14

Who has been a true friend to you, even in difficult times?

Live it!

Greed

Is it wrong to be wealthy? Sinful, even? The wicked ones Zophar is talking about are not just wealthy and successful—they are *greedy.* Greed is evil because it leads people to neglect poor people and steal what is not theirs (Job 20:19), so they will have even more wealth. Their money, property, and material things are never enough—like a spoiled child, they want more, more, more, and they're not going to share any of it!

Where do you see greed at work in our world? in our nation? Do you experience greed at school, or in your family? Is greed lurking inside you?

Wealth itself is not evil—but those who are wealthy have a responsibility to be generous with those who have less. And wealthy people need to be careful that money and material things don't start to become the center of their lives. That is the slippery slope toward greed! Our deepest happiness comes when God is at the center of our lives. Everyone, rich and poor, needs to trust that God will take care of all their needs (see Luke 12:22–34).

— Job 20:15–28

16 What the evil people swallow is like poison;
it kills them like the bite of a deadly snake.

17 They will not live to see rivers of olive oil[r]
or streams that flow with milk and honey.
18 They will have to give up all they have worked for;
they will have no chance to enjoy their wealth,
19 because they oppressed and neglected the poor
and seized houses someone else had built.
20 Their greed is never satisfied.
21 When they eat, there is nothing left over,
but now their prosperity comes to an end.
22 At the height of their success
all the weight of misery will crush them.
23 Let them eat all they want!
God will punish them in fury and anger.
24 When they try to escape from an iron sword,
a bronze bow will shoot them down.
25 Arrows stick through their bodies;
the shiny points drip with their blood,
and terror grips their hearts.
26 Everything they have saved is destroyed;
a fire not lit by human hands
burns them and all their family.
27 Heaven reveals their sin,
and the earth gives testimony against them.
28 All their wealth will be destroyed
in the flood of God's anger.
29 This is the fate of wicked people,
the fate that God assigns to them.

21

Job

1-2 Listen to what I am saying;
that is all the comfort I ask from you.
3 Give me a chance to speak and then,
when I am through, sneer if you like.

[r] **20:17** *Probable text* They will . . . oil; *Hebrew unclear.*
20:24 Wis 5:17–23

While reading Job, chapter 20, make a list of all the bad things that Zophar says will happen to wicked or evil people.

4 My quarrel is not with mortals;
I have good reason to be impatient.
5 Look at me. Isn't that enough
to make you stare in shocked silence?
6 When I think of what has happened to me,
I am stunned, and I tremble and shake.

7 Why does God let evil people live,
let them grow old and prosper?
8 They have children and grandchildren,
and live to watch them all grow up.
9 God does not bring disaster on their homes;
they never have to live in terror.
10 Yes, all their cattle breed
and give birth without trouble.
11 Their children run and play like lambs
12 and dance to the music of harps and flutes.
13 They live out their lives in peace
and quietly die without suffering.

14 The wicked tell God to leave them alone;
they don't want to know his will for their lives.
15 They think there is no need to serve God
nor any advantage in praying to him.
16 They claim they succeed by their own strength,
but their way of thinking I can't accept.

17 Was a wicked person's light ever put out?
Did one of them ever meet with disaster?
Did God ever punish the wicked in anger
18 and blow them away like straw in the wind,
or like dust carried away in a storm?

19 You claim God punishes a child for the sins of his father.
No! Let God punish the sinners themselves;
let him show that he does it because of *their* sins.
20 Let sinners bear their own punishment;
let them feel the wrath of Almighty God.
21 When our lives are over,
do we really care whether our children are happy?
22 Can anyone teach God,
who judges even those in high places?

Study it!

Reward and Punishment

The debate seems to be going in endless circles! Job's friends will not give up the idea that Job is being punished for his sins. That was the belief of the Israelites: grief and failure were punishment for unfaithfulness, and happiness and success were rewards for being faithful to God. Job is familiar with that reasoning and doesn't disagree with his friends. And he isn't upset with God because he is suffering. What he's upset about is that he *has* been faithful, and yet he suffers. It doesn't make any sense! This is what he is desperate to have his friends understand.

We know that some people who suffer or struggle with failure are faithful and others are not. And some happy or successful people are faithful, while others are not. Jesus set us straight about how God works: God does not reward and punish in the way the Israelites believed. All people are equally deserving of God's love and generosity. And suffering is a possibility for anyone, not just sinners—Jesus is the best example of this.

So why do innocent people suffer? This is the urgent question in the Book of Job. Keep reading!

— Job, chapter 21

23-24 Some people stay healthy till the day they die;
they die happy and at ease,
their bodies well-nourished.
25 Others have no happiness at all;
they live and die with bitter hearts.
26 But all alike die and are buried;
they all are covered with worms.

27 I know what spiteful thoughts you have.
28 You ask, "Where are the homes of great people now,
those who practiced evil?"

29 Haven't you talked with people who travel?
Don't you know the reports they bring back?
30 On the day God is angry and punishes,
it is the wicked who are always spared.
31 There is no one to accuse the wicked
or pay them back for all they have done.
32 When they are carried to the graveyard,
to their well-guarded tombs,
33 thousands join the funeral procession,
and even the earth lies gently on their bodies.

34 And you! You try to comfort me with nonsense!
Every answer you give is a lie!

The Third Dialogue
(22:1—27:23)

22
Eliphaz

1-2 Is there anyone, even the wisest,
who could ever be of use to God?
3 Does your doing right benefit God,
or does your being good help him at all?
4 It is not because you stand in awe of God
that he reprimands you and brings you to trial.
5 No, it's because you have sinned so much;
it's because of all the evil you do.
6 To make a brother repay you the money he owed,
you took away his clothes and left him nothing to wear.
7 You refused water to those who were tired,
and refused to feed those who were hungry.
8 You used your power and your position
to take over the whole land.
9 You not only refused to help widows,
but you also robbed and mistreated orphans.
10 So now there are pitfalls all around you,
and suddenly you are full of fear.
11 It has grown so dark that you cannot see,
and a flood overwhelms you.

12 Doesn't God live in the highest heavens
and look down on the stars, even though they are high?
13 And yet you ask, "What does God know?
He is hidden by clouds—how can he judge us?"
14 You think the thick clouds keep him from seeing,
as he walks on the dome of the sky.

15 Are you determined to walk in the paths
that evil people have always followed?
16 Even before their time had come,
they were washed away by a flood.
17 These are the ones who rejected God
and believed that he could do nothing to them.
18 And yet it was God who made them prosperous—
I can't understand the thoughts of the wicked.
19 Good people are glad and the innocent laugh
when they see the wicked punished.
20 All that the wicked own is destroyed,
and fire burns up anything that is left.

21 Now, Job, make peace with God
and stop treating him like an enemy;
if you do, then he will bless you.
22 Accept the teaching he gives;
keep his words in your heart.
23 Yes, you must humbly[s] return to God
and put an end to all the evil
that is done in your house.
24 Throw away your gold;
dump your finest gold in the dry stream bed.
25 Let Almighty God be your gold,
and let him be silver, piled high for you.
26 Then you will always trust in God
and find that he is the source of your joy.

[s] **22:23** *One ancient translation* humbly; *Hebrew* be built up.
22:2, 3 Job 35:6–8

27 When you pray, he will answer you,
and you will keep the vows you made.
28 You will succeed in all you do,
and light will shine on your path.
29 God brings down the proud[t]
and saves the humble.
30 He will rescue you if you are innocent,[u]
if what you do is right.[v]

23
Job

1-2 I still rebel and complain against God;
I cannot keep from groaning.
3 How I wish I knew where to find him,
and knew how to go where he is.
4 I would state my case before him
and present all the arguments in my favor.
5 I want to know what he would say
and how he would answer me.
6 Would God use all his strength against me?
No, he would listen as I spoke.
7 I am honest; I could reason with God;
he would declare me innocent[w] once and for all.

8 I have searched in the East, but God is not there;
I have not found him when I searched in the West.
9 God has been at work in the North and the South,
but still I have not seen him.
10 Yet God knows every step I take;
if he tests me, he will find me pure.
11 I follow faithfully the road he chooses,
and never wander to either side.
12 I always do what God commands;
I follow his will, not my own desires.

13 He never changes. No one can oppose him
or stop him from doing what he wants to do.
14 He will fulfill what he has planned for me;
that plan is just one of the many he has;

Pray it!

Where Is God Found?

Job wants a face-to-face meeting with God, and he has looked everywhere, but he can't find him. Where do you find God? Where do you look?

Some people believe Church is where God lives, and in our celebration of the sacraments. Others believe God is found in nature. Still others believe we meet God in other people and in the good works we do. Some find God is as close to them as their heartbeat. Which is correct? All of the above! God is in us and around us and everywhere! God is always waiting for us to seek and find him.

— Job 23:3–9

"I tremble with fear before him." (23:15)

15 I tremble with fear before him.
16-17 Almighty God has destroyed my courage.

[t] **22:29** *Probable text* proud; *Hebrew unclear.* [u] **22:30** *Some ancient translations* innocent; *Hebrew* not innocent.
[v] **22:30** *Verse 30 in Hebrew is unclear.* [w] **23:7** he would declare me innocent; *or* then my rights would be safe.

"Let Almighty God be your gold. . . . / Then you will always trust in God / and find that he is the source of your joy" (*Job 22:25–26*).

It is God, not the dark, that makes me afraid—
even though the darkness has made me blind.

24 Why doesn't God set a time for judging,
a day of justice for those who serve him?
2 People move property lines to get more land;
they steal sheep and put them with their own flocks.
3 They take donkeys that belong to orphans,
and keep a widow's ox till she pays her debts.
4 They prevent the poor from getting their rights
and force the needy to run and hide.

5 So the poor, like wild donkeys,
search for food in the dry wilderness;
nowhere else can they find food for their children.
6 They have to harvest fields they don't own,[x]
and gather grapes in vineyards of the wicked.
7 At night they sleep with nothing to cover them,
nothing to keep them from the cold.
8 They are drenched by the rain that falls on the mountains,
and they huddle beside the rocks for shelter.

9 Evil people make slaves of fatherless infants
and take the children of the poor in payment for debts.
10 But the poor must go out with no clothes to protect them;
they must go hungry while harvesting wheat.
11 They press olives for oil, and grapes for wine,
but they themselves are thirsty.
12 In the cities the wounded and dying cry out,
but God ignores their prayers.

13 There are those who reject the light;
they don't understand it or go where it leads.
14 At dawn the murderer gets up
and goes out to kill the poor,
and at night he steals.
15 The adulterer waits for twilight to come;
he covers his face so that no one can see him.
16 At night thieves break into houses,
but by day they hide and avoid the light.
17 They fear the light of day,
but darkness holds no terror for them.

[Zophar][y]

18 The wicked are swept away by floods,
and the land they own is under God's curse;
they no longer go to work in their vineyards.
19 As snow vanishes in heat and drought,
so sinners vanish from the land of the living.
20 Not even their mothers remember them now;
they are eaten by worms and destroyed like fallen trees.
21 That happens because they mistreated widows
and showed no kindness to childless women.
22 God, in his strength, destroys the mighty;
God acts—and the wicked die.
23 God may let them live secure,
but keeps an eye on them all the time.
24 For a while the wicked prosper,
but then they wither like weeds,
like stalks of grain that have been cut down.
25 Can anyone deny that this is so?
Can anyone prove that my words are not true?

[x] **24:6** FIELDS THEY DON'T OWN: *Having been cheated out of their own land, the poor are forced to work for others for very small pay.* [y] **24:18** Zophar *is not named in the text, but this speech is usually assigned to him.*

Job asks why God doesn't "set a time for judging" ***(Job 24:1)*****. We know that God does! Read Revelation, chapters 20–22, about God's judgment day.**

Pray it!

Whispers of God's Power

Bildad is poetic in his telling of God's power in nature—yet admits we have only hints of God's greatness.

Thank you, God—
for the unconditional love of dogs,
for the amazing way our bodies work,
for the variety of trees and plants and flowers in the world,
for the strength of my dad's arms when he holds me tight,
for the sparkle of fireflies,
for the ability of our hearts to forgive,
for music and sunsets and pizza and electricity!
You are truly an awesome God!

— Job 26:5–14

25

Bildad

1-2 God is powerful; all must stand in awe of him;
he keeps his heavenly kingdom in peace.
3 Can anyone count the angels who serve him?
Is there any place where God's light does not shine?
4 Can anyone be righteous or pure in God's sight?
5 In his eyes even the moon is not bright,
or the stars pure.
6 Then what about a human being, that worm, that insect?
What is a human life worth in God's eyes?

26

Job

1-2 What a big help you are to me—
poor, weak man that I am!
3 You give such good advice
and share your knowledge with a fool like me!
4 Who do you think will hear all your words?
Who inspired you to speak like this?

[Bildad][z]

5 The spirits of the dead tremble
in the waters under the earth.
6 The world of the dead lies open to God;
no covering shields it from his sight.
7 God stretched out the northern sky
and hung the earth in empty space.
8 It is God who fills the clouds with water
and keeps them from bursting with the weight.
9 He hides the full moon behind a cloud.
10 He divided light from darkness
by a circle drawn on the face of the sea.
11 When he threatens the pillars that hold up the sky,
they shake and tremble with fear.
12 It is his strength that conquered the sea;[a]
by his skill he destroyed the monster Rahab.[b]

[z] **26:5** Bildad *is not named in the text, but this speech is usually assigned to him.* [a] **26:12** CONQUERED THE SEA: *A reference to an ancient story in which the sea fought against God.* [b] **26:12** RAHAB: *See 9:13.*

13 It is his breath that made the sky clear,
and his hand that killed the escaping monster.[c]
14 But these are only hints of his power,
only the whispers that we have heard.
Who can know how truly great God is?

27

Job

1-2 I swear by the living Almighty God,
who refuses me justice and makes my life bitter—
3 as long as God gives me breath,
4 my lips will never say anything evil,
my tongue will never tell a lie.
5 I will never say that you men are right;
I will insist on my innocence to my dying day.
6 I will never give up my claim to be right;
my conscience is clear.

7 May all who oppose me and fight against me
be punished like the wicked and the unrighteous.
8 What hope is there for the godless
in the hour when God demands their life?
9 When trouble comes, will God hear their cries?
10 They should have desired the joy he gives;
they should have constantly prayed to him.

11 Let me teach you how great is God's power,
and explain what Almighty God has planned.
12 But no, after all, you have seen for yourselves;
so why do you talk such nonsense?

[Zophar][d]

13 This is how Almighty God
punishes wicked, violent people.
14 They may have many sons,
but all will be killed in war;
their children never have enough to eat.

Live it!

Integrity

This much can be said about Job: he is a person of *integrity.* Integrity means that you know the truth, and you stand by it. You don't give in to pressure from other people's opinions. You do the right thing, no matter what the cost.

Job knows with all his heart that he is innocent. He will not budge on that truth, and, further, he knows God would not want him to back down from the truth either.

Some people keep a list of the things that they know are true. Whenever they learn a new truth about life, they add it to that list. Maybe you want to start such a list. Then make a commitment to live by the truths God has revealed to you. Growing up to be a person of integrity is a gift you can give to the world.

— Job 27:1–6

15 Those who survive will die from disease,
and even their widows will not mourn their death.
16 The wicked may have too much silver to count
and more clothes than anyone needs;
17 but some good person will wear the clothes,
and someone honest will get the silver.
18 The wicked build houses like a spider's web[e]
or like the hut of a slave guarding the fields.
19 One last time[f] they will lie down rich,
and when they wake up, they will find their wealth gone.

[c] **26:13** ESCAPING MONSTER: *See 9:8.* [d] **27:13** Zophar *is not named in the text, but this speech is usually assigned to him.* [e] **27:18** *Some ancient translations* spider's web; *Hebrew* moth *or* bird's nest. [f] **27:19** *Some ancient translations* One last time; *Hebrew* They will not be gathered.

20 Terror will strike like a sudden flood;
a wind in the night will blow them away;
21 the east wind will sweep them from their homes;
22 it will blow down on them without pity
while they try their best to escape.
23 The wind howls at them as they run,
frightening them with destructive power.

In Praise of Wisdom[g]

28 There are mines where silver is dug;
There are places where gold is refined.
2 We dig iron out of the ground
And melt copper out of the stones.
3 Miners explore the deepest darkness.
They search the depths of the earth
And dig for rocks in the darkness.
4 Far from where anyone lives
Or human feet ever travel,
They dig the shafts of mines.
There they work in loneliness,
Clinging to ropes in the pits.
5 Food grows out of the earth,
But underneath the same earth
All is torn up and crushed.
6 The stones of the earth contain sapphires,
And its dust contains gold.
7 No hawk sees the roads to the mines,
And no vulture ever flies over them.
8 No lion or other fierce beast
Ever travels those lonely roads.

9 Miners dig the hardest rocks,
Dig mountains away at their base.
10 As they tunnel through the rocks,
They discover precious stones.
11 They dig to the sources of[h] rivers
And bring to light what is hidden.
12 But where can wisdom be found?
Where can we learn to understand?
13 Wisdom is not to be found among mortals;
No one knows its true value.
14 The depths of the oceans and seas
Say that wisdom is not found there.
15 It cannot be bought with silver or gold.
16 The finest gold and jewels
Cannot equal its value.
17 It is worth more than gold,
Than a gold vase or finest glass.
18 The value of wisdom is more
Than coral or crystal or rubies.
19 The finest topaz and the purest gold
Cannot compare with the value of wisdom.

20 Where, then, is the source of wisdom?
Where can we learn to understand?
21 No living creature can see it,
Not even a bird in flight.
22 Even death and destruction
Admit they have heard only rumors.

23 God alone knows the way,
Knows the place where wisdom is found,
24 Because he sees the ends of the earth,
Sees everything under the sky.
25 When God gave the wind its power
And determined the size of the sea;
26 When God decided where the rain would fall,
And the path that the thunderclouds travel;
27 It was then he saw wisdom and tested its worth—
He gave it his approval.
28 God said to us humans,
"To be wise, you must have reverence for the Lord.
To understand, you must turn from evil."

[g] **28** *The Hebrew text does not indicate who is speaking in this chapter.* [h] **28:11** *Some ancient translations* dig to the sources of; *Hebrew* bind from trickling.

28:12 Sir 1:6; Bar 3:15 **28:13** Bar 3:29–31 **28:23** Bar 3:35–37 **28:27** Sir 1:9, 19 **28:28** Ps 111:10; Prov 1:7; 9:10

"As long as God gives me breath, / my lips will never say anything evil, / my tongue will never tell a lie" *(Job 27:3–4)*.

Pray it!

Keepin' an Eye Out

Job feels that his life crumbled because God stopped watching over him. God abandoned him, he believes, and so began his many troubles. We can certainly understand how someone who experienced Job's losses could feel like this.

This couldn't be further from the truth about how God acts, though. We believe that God is *omnipresent,* meaning, he is watching over everyone (all the billions of us!), all the time, all at once! Don't even try to understand how that can be—it's a great mystery of our faith. Just believe it, and know that problems or not, God never leaves our side for a minute.

— Job 29:2–5

Job's Final Statement of His Case

(29:1—31:40)

29 Job began speaking again.

Job

2 If only my life could once again
be as it was when God watched over
me.
3 God was always with me then
and gave me light as I walked through
the darkness.
4 Those were the days when I was
prosperous,
and the friendship of God protected
my home.
5 Almighty God was with me then,
and I was surrounded by all my
children.
6 My cows and goats gave plenty of milk,
and my olive trees grew in the rockiest
soil.
7 Whenever the city elders met
and I took my place among them,
8 young men stepped aside as soon as
they saw me,
and old men stood up to show me
respect.
9 The leaders of the people would stop
talking;
10 even the most important men kept
silent.
11 Everyone who saw me or heard of me
had good things to say about what I
had done.
12 When the poor cried out, I helped them;
I gave help to orphans who had
nowhere to turn.
13 People who were in deepest misery
praised me,
and I helped widows find security.
14 I have always acted justly and fairly.
15 I was eyes for the blind,
and feet for the lame.
16 I was like a father to the poor
and took the side of strangers in
trouble.
17 I destroyed the power of cruel men
and rescued their victims.
18 I always expected to live a long life
and to die at home in comfort.
19 I was like a tree whose roots always have
water
and whose branches are wet with dew.
20 Everyone was always praising me,
and my strength never failed me.
21 When I gave advice, people were silent
and listened carefully to what I said;

"I smiled on them when they had lost confidence; / my cheerful face encouraged them" *(Job 29:24)*. **Who needs your encouragement today?**

22 they had nothing to add when I had
finished.
My words sank in like drops of rain;
23 everyone welcomed them
just as farmers welcome rain in spring.
24 I smiled on them when they had lost
confidence;
my cheerful face encouraged them.
25 I took charge and made the decisions;
I led them as a king leads his troops,
and gave them comfort in their despair.

30 But men younger than I am make
fun of me now!
Their fathers have always been so
worthless
that I wouldn't let them help my dogs
guard sheep.
2 They were a bunch of worn-out men,
too weak to do any work for me.
3 They were so poor and hungry
that they would gnaw dry roots—
at night, in wild, desolate places.
4 They pulled up the plants of the desert
and ate them,
even the tasteless roots of the broom
tree!
5 Everyone drove them away with shouts,
as if they were shouting at thieves.
6 They had to live in caves,
in holes dug in the sides of cliffs.
7 Out in the wilds they howled like animals
and huddled together under the bushes.
8 A worthless bunch of nameless nobodies!
They were driven out of the land.

9 Now they come and laugh at me;
I am nothing but a joke to them.
10 They treat me with disgust;
they think they are too good for me,
and even come and spit in my face.
11 Because God has made me weak and
helpless,
they turn against me with all their fury.
12 This mob attacks me head-on;
they send me running; they prepare
their final assault.
13 They cut off my escape and try to destroy
me;
and there is no one to stop[i] them.

Study it!

Poetry

The speeches in the Book of Job are written as poems. These are not poems that rhyme or have a certain rhythm (they may have, in the original Hebrew language), but they include a feature of poetry called *parallelism*.

Parallelism can be two lines in which the same thought is repeated: "Now they come and laugh at me; / I am nothing but a joke to them" (Job 30:9).

Or it can be two lines with opposite thoughts: "Where once I heard joyful music, / now I hear only mourning and weeping" (Job 30:31).

Or, the second line can add to or build upon the thought of the first line: "Out in the wilds they howled like animals / and huddled together under the bushes" (Job 30:7).

In your journal, try writing a prayer to God using parallel lines as your pattern.

— Job, chapter 30

14 They pour through the holes in my
defenses
and come crashing down on top of me;
15 I am overcome with terror;
my dignity is gone like a puff of
wind,
and my prosperity like a cloud.

16 Now I am about to die;
there is no relief for my suffering.
17 At night my bones all ache;
the pain that gnaws me never stops.
18 God seizes me by my collar
and twists my clothes out of shape.

[i] **30:13** *Probable text* stop; *Hebrew* help.

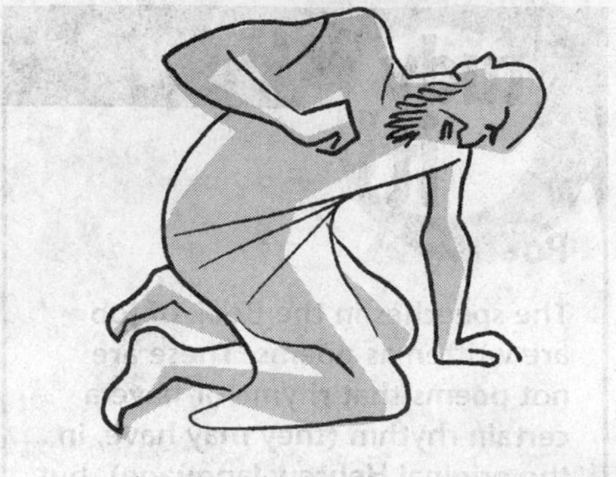

"He throws me down in the mud." (30:19)

19 He throws me down in the mud;
I am no better than dirt.

20 I call to you, O God, but you never answer;
and when I pray, you pay no attention.
21 You are treating me cruelly;
you persecute me with all your power.
22 You let the wind blow me away;
you toss me about in a raging storm.
23 I know you are taking me off to my death,
to the fate in store for everyone.
24 Why do you attack a ruined man,
one who can do nothing but beg for pity?[j]
25 Didn't I weep with people in trouble
and feel sorry for those in need?
26 I hoped for happiness and light,
but trouble and darkness came instead.
27 I am torn apart by worry and pain;
I have had day after day of suffering.
28 I go about in gloom, without any sunshine;
I stand up in public and plead for help.
29 My voice is as sad and lonely
as the cries of a jackal or an ostrich.
30 My skin has turned dark; I am burning with fever.
31 Where once I heard joyful music,
now I hear only mourning and weeping.

31 I have made a solemn promise
never to look with lust at a woman.

2 What does Almighty God do to us?
How does he repay human deeds?
3 He sends disaster and ruin
to those who do wrong.
4 God knows everything I do;
he sees every step I take.

5 I swear I have never acted wickedly
and never tried to deceive others.
6 Let God weigh me on honest scales,
and he will see how innocent I am.
7 If I have turned from the right path
or let myself be attracted to evil,
if my hands are stained with sin,
8 then let my crops be destroyed,
or let others eat the food I grow.

9 If I have been attracted to my neighbor's wife,
and waited, hidden, outside her door,
10 then let my wife cook another man's food
and sleep in another man's bed.
11 Such wickedness should be punished by death.
12 It would be like a destructive, hellish fire,
consuming everything I have.

13 When any of my servants complained against me,
I would listen and treat them fairly.
14 If I did not, how could I then face God?
What could I say when God came to judge me?
15 The same God who created me
created my servants also.

16 I have never refused to help the poor;
never have I let widows live in despair
17 or let orphans go hungry while I ate.
18 All my life I have taken care of them.[k]

19 When I found someone in need,
too poor to buy clothes,
20 I would give him clothing made of wool
that had come from my own flock of sheep.
Then he would praise me with all his heart.

21 If I have ever cheated an orphan,
knowing I could win in court,
22 then may my arms be broken;
may they be torn from my shoulders.
23 Because I fear God's punishment,
I could never do such a thing.

[j] **30:24** *Verse 24 in Hebrew is unclear.* [k] **31:18** All my life . . . them; *Hebrew unclear.*

31:16–18 Tob 4:7–11, 16

Catholic Connections

Examination of Conscience

In his mind, Job was thinking about all his behaviors to see if he had done anything wrong. He thought about his faithfulness to his wife, how he treated the people who work for him, how he cared for poor people, the importance of riches in his life, how he acted toward his enemies, and so on.

We practice this exercise as part of the sacrament of Penance and Reconciliation. Before we confess our sins to the priest, we honestly examine our conscience to determine if and how we are guilty of sin. Many written guides are available to help you think about the different areas of your life. Look for patterns of behavior and attitudes that keep showing up. This helps you prepare what you will confess to God in the sacrament.

Look at Job's list, and see which concerns of his conscience match yours.

How would your examination of conscience differ from Job's?

— Job 31:5–40

24 I have never trusted in riches
25 or taken pride in my wealth.
26 I have never worshiped the sun in its brightness
or the moon in all its beauty.
27 I have not been led astray to honor them
by kissing my hand in reverence to them.
28 Such a sin should be punished by death;
it denies Almighty God.

29 I have never been glad when my enemies suffered,
or pleased when they met with disaster;
30 I never sinned by praying for their death.
31 All those who work for me know
that I have always welcomed strangers.
32 I invited travelers into my home
and never let them sleep in the streets.

33 Others try to hide their sins,
but I have never concealed mine.
34 I have never feared what people would say;
I have never kept quiet or stayed indoors
because I feared their scorn.

35 Will no one listen to what I am saying?
I swear that every word is true.
Let Almighty God answer me.

If the charges my opponent brings against me
were written down so that I could see them,
36 I would wear them proudly on my shoulder
and place them on my head like a crown.
37 I would tell God everything I have done,
and hold my head high in his presence.

38 If I have stolen the land I farm
and taken it from its rightful owners—
39 if I have eaten the food that grew there
but let the farmers that grew it starve—
40 then instead of wheat and barley,
may weeds and thistles grow.

The words of Job are ended.

31:24 Sir 31:5–10

Study it!

The Gifts of Youth

Elihu hesitates to speak up because he is young, but when he gathers up the courage to speak, he has a lot to say! His thoughts reflect the wisdom of a young soul. God calls young people, as well as mature adults, to share their gifts and their wisdom. Here are some stories of young people in the Bible—stories of how they were called by God, the wisdom they possessed, missions they accomplished with courage, and gifts they shared with others:

- **Joseph, son of Jacob (Genesis, chapters 37–50)**
- **Samuel (1 Samuel, chapter 3)**
- **David (1 Samuel, chapters 16–18)**
- **Jeremiah (Jeremiah 1:4–10)**
- **Mary (Luke 1:26–56)**
- **Jesus (Luke 2:41–52)**

Check out these stories, and let them inspire you!

— Job, chapters 32–37

The Speeches of Elihu
(32:1—37:24)

32 Because Job was convinced of his
own innocence, the three men gave
up trying to answer him. 2But a bystander
named Elihu could not control his anger any
longer, because Job was justifying himself and
blaming God. (Elihu was the son of Barakel,
a descendant of Buz, and belonged to the
clan of Ram.) 3He was also angry with Job's
three friends. They could not find any way to
answer Job, and this made it appear that God
was in the wrong. 4Because Elihu was the
youngest one there, he had waited until
everyone finished speaking. 5When he saw
that the three men could not answer Job, he
was angry 6and began to speak.

Elihu

I am young, and you are old,
so I was afraid to tell you what I think.
7I told myself that you ought to speak,
that you older men should share your wisdom.
8But it is the spirit of Almighty God
that comes to us and gives us wisdom.
9It is not growing old that makes us wise
or helps us to know what is right.
10So now I want you to listen to me;
let me tell you what I think.

11I listened patiently while you were speaking
and waited while you searched for wise phrases.
12I paid close attention and heard you fail;
you have not disproved what Job has said.
13How can you claim you have discovered wisdom?
God must answer Job, for you have failed.
14Job was speaking to you, not to me,
but I would never answer the way you did.
15Words have failed them, Job;
they have no answer for you.
16Shall I go on waiting when they are silent?
They stand there with nothing more to say.
17No, I will give my own answer now
and tell you what I think.
18I can hardly wait to speak.
I can't hold back the words.
19If I don't get a chance to speak,
I will burst like a wineskin full of new wine.
20I can't stand it; I have to speak.
21I will not take sides in this debate;
I am not going to flatter anyone.

Wine was made in goatskins that stretched as the fermenting grape juice produced gases—if the skins didn't stretch enough, they would burst.

22 I don't know how to flatter,
and God would quickly punish me if I did.

33

And now, Job, listen carefully
to all that I have to say.
2 I am ready to say what's on my mind.
3 All my words are sincere,
and I am speaking the truth.
4 God's spirit made me and gave me life.
5 Answer me if you can. Prepare your arguments.
6 You and I are the same in God's sight,
both of us were formed from clay.
7 So you have no reason to fear me;
I will not overpower you.
8 Now this is what I heard you say:
9 "I am not guilty; I have done nothing wrong.
I am innocent and free from sin.
10 But God finds excuses for attacking me
and treats me like an enemy.
11 He binds chains on my feet;
he watches every move I make."

12 But I tell you, Job, you are wrong.
God is greater than any human being.
13 Why do you accuse God
of never answering our complaints?
14 Although God speaks again and again,
no one pays attention to what he says.
15 At night when people are asleep,
God speaks in dreams and visions.
16 He makes them listen to what he says,
and they are frightened at his warnings.
17 God speaks to make them stop their sinning
and to save them from becoming proud.
18 He will not let them be destroyed;
he saves them from death itself.
19 God corrects us by sending sickness
and filling our bodies with pain.
20 Those who are sick lose their appetites,
and even the finest food looks revolting.
21 Their bodies waste away to nothing;
you can see all their bones;
22 they are about to go to the world of the dead.

Live it!

God's Messengers

Have you heard the story about the woman who slipped off a cliff, was hanging from a tree limb, and cried out to God: "Help, God! Please save me!" Soon, a helicopter flew near her and a ladder was let down so she could climb up to safety. "No, thanks," she told them, "God's going to save me." Next, a fire truck arrived and a crash pad was placed below her so that she could jump without getting injured. "Thanks, but I'm waiting for God—he'll be saving me any minute now!" Finally, she called out again: "God? Are you there? I don't know how much longer I can hang on! Please save me!" God responded to her, "I sent you a helicopter and a fire truck. What more do you want?"

Elihu tells Job he is wrong about God not answering his prayers. God speaks to us and offers us help all the time, but most of the time we miss it! Some of the ways God can speak to us:

- **through the guidance of parents and other caring adults**
- **through the support and example of friends**
- **when a situation, such as an illness or loss, causes us to look at what is truly important in life**
- **through the dreams and desires that God plants in our hearts**

Ask God to keep your eyes and ears and heart open to his presence in your life.

— Job 33:12–19

33:11 Job 13:27 **33:15** Job 4:13

23 Perhaps an angel may come to their aid—
one of God's thousands of angels,
who remind us of our duty.
24 In mercy the angel will say, "Release them!
They are not to go down to the world of the dead.
Here is the ransom to set them free."
25 Their bodies will grow young and strong again;
26 when they pray, God will answer;
they will worship God with joy;
God will set things right for them again.
27 Each one will say in public, "I have sinned.
I have not done right, but God spared me.
28 He kept me from going to the world of the dead,
and I am still alive."

29 God does all this again and again;
30 each one saves a person's life,
and gives him the joy of living.

31 Now, Job, listen to what I am saying;
be quiet and let me speak.
32 But if you have something to say, let me hear it;
I would gladly admit you are in the right.
33 But if not, be quiet and listen to me,
and I will teach you how to be wise.

34 1-2 You men are so wise, so clever;
listen now to what I am saying.
3 You know good food when you taste it,
but not wise words when you hear them.
4 It is up to us to decide the case.
5 Job claims that he is innocent,
that God refuses to give him justice.
6 He asks, "How could I lie and say I am wrong?
I am fatally wounded, but I am sinless."
7 Have you ever seen anyone like this man Job?
He never shows respect for God.
8 He likes the company of evil people
and goes around with sinners.
9 He says that it never does any good
to try to follow God's will.

10 Listen to me, you men who understand!
Will Almighty God do what is wrong?
11 He rewards people for what they do
and treats them as they deserve.
12 Almighty God does not do evil;
he is never unjust to anyone.
13 Did God get his power from someone else?
Did someone put him in charge of the world?
14 If God took back the breath of life,
15 then everyone living would die
and turn into dust again.

16 Now listen to me, if you are wise.
17 Are you condemning the righteous God?
Do you think that *he* hates justice?
18 God condemns kings and rulers
when they are worthless or wicked.
19 He does not take the side of rulers
nor favor the rich over the poor,
for he created everyone.
20 We may suddenly die at night.
God strikes us down and we perish;
he kills the mighty with no effort at all.
21 He watches every step we take.
22 There is no darkness dark enough
to hide a sinner from God.
23 God does not need to set a time[l]
for us to go and be judged by him.
24 He does not need an investigation
to remove leaders and replace them with others.
25 Because he knows what they do;
he overthrows them and crushes them by night.
26 He punishes sinners where all can see it,
27 because they have stopped following him
and ignored all his commands.
28 They forced the poor to cry out to God,
and he heard their calls for help.

29 If God decided to do nothing at all,
no one could criticize him.
If he hid his face, we would be helpless.
30 There would be nothing that nations could do
to keep godless oppressors from ruling them.

[l] **34:23** *Probable text* a time; *Hebrew* yet.
34:11 Ps 62:12

31 Job, have you confessed your sins to God
and promised not to sin again?
32 Have you asked God to show you your
faults,
and have you agreed to stop doing evil?
33 Since you object to what God does,
can you expect him to do what you
want?
The decision is yours, not mine;
tell us now what you think.

34 Any sensible person will surely agree;
and the wise who hear me will say
35 that Job is speaking from ignorance
and that nothing he says makes sense.
36 Think through everything that Job says;
you will see that he talks like an evil
man.
37 To his sins he adds rebellion;
in front of us all he mocks God.

35 1-2 It is not right, Job, for you to say
that you are innocent in God's sight,
3 or to ask God, "How does my sin affect
you?
What have I gained by not sinning?"
4 I am going to answer you and your
friends too.
5 Look at the sky! See how high the clouds
are!
6 If you sin, that does no harm to God.
If you do wrong many times, does that
affect him?
7 Do you help God by being so righteous?
There is nothing God needs from you.
8 Others suffer from your sins,
and the good you do helps them.

9 When people are oppressed, they groan;
they cry for someone to save them.
10 But they don't turn to God, their Creator,
who gives them hope in their darkest
hours.
11 They don't turn to God, who makes us
wise,
wiser than any animal or bird.

Live it!

Making a Difference

Jackson climbed into bed, and before he fell asleep he thought about his day. He was really sorry that he had borrowed Al's homework to finish his own. He didn't mean to copy quite as much as he did. But they both got caught anyway, and both received big fat zeros for the assignment—a zero he didn't need. Al was pretty mad, and Jackson couldn't blame him. He hoped their friendship wasn't ruined.

Then he remembered the lunchroom incident. Maggie dropped her tray right behind him! Everyone cheered and clapped, of course—that's just what you do during a tray dropping. But something made Jackson turn around in his seat and help her pick up the dishes and food that crashed to the ground. He wasn't sure if he saw tears of embarrassment pooling up in her eyes, but he did recognize gratitude in the smile she gave him.

Our actions do make a difference for other people, as Elihu says in Job 35:8. We choose what *kind* of difference.

— Job 35:8

12 They cry for help, but God doesn't
answer,
for they are proud and evil.
13 It is useless for them to cry out;
Almighty God does not see or hear
them.

35:6–8 Job 22:2, 3

"If God took back the breath of life, / then everyone living would die / and turn into dust again" *(Job 34:14–15)*. **See Genesis 2:7.**

14 Job, you say you can't see God;
but wait patiently—your case is before him.
15 You think that God does not punish,
that he pays little attention to sin.
16 It is useless for you to go on talking;
it is clear you don't know what you are saying.

36 1-2 Be patient and listen a little longer
to what I am saying on God's behalf.
3 My knowledge is wide; I will use what I know
to show that God, my Creator, is just.
4 Nothing I say to you is false;
you see before you a truly wise man.

5 How strong God is! He despises no one;
there is nothing he doesn't understand.
6 He does not let sinners live on,
and he always treats the poor with justice.
7 He protects those who are righteous;
he allows them to rule like kings
and lets them be honored forever.
8 But if people are bound in chains,
suffering for what they have done,
9 God shows them their sins and their pride.
10 He makes them listen to his warning
to turn away from evil.
11 If they obey God and serve him,
they live out their lives in peace and prosperity.
12 But if not, they will die in ignorance
and cross the stream into the world of the dead.

13 Those who are godless keep on being angry,
and even when punished, they don't pray for help.
14 They die while they are still young,
worn out by a life of disgrace.
15 But God teaches people through suffering
and uses distress to open their eyes.

16 God brought you out of trouble,
and let you enjoy security;
your table was piled high with food.
17 But now you are being punished as you deserve.
18 Be careful not to let bribes deceive you,
or riches lead you astray.
19 It will do you no good to cry out for help;
all your strength can't help you now.
20 Don't wish for night to come,
the time when nations will perish.
21 Be careful not to turn to evil;
your suffering was sent to keep you from it.

22 Remember how great is God's power;
he is the greatest teacher of all.
23 No one can tell God what to do
or accuse him of doing evil.
24 He has always been praised for what he does;
you also must praise him.
25 Everyone has seen what he has done;
but we can only watch from a distance.[m]
26 We cannot fully know his greatness
or count the number of his years.

27 It is God who takes water from the earth
and turns it into drops of rain.
28 He lets the rain pour from the clouds
in showers for all human beings.

Everyone has seen what he has done. (36:25)

[m] **36:25** but we can only watch from a distance; *or* no one understands it all.

Have you experienced the death of a close relative or friend? If so, what did you learn or gain from the painful loss you suffered?

Catholic Connections

Euthanasia

"But God teaches people through suffering / and uses distress to open their eyes" (Job 36:15). No one welcomes suffering, no matter whether it is our own or the suffering of someone we love. We pray to God to take suffering away. But we also believe that suffering has a purpose, no matter how bad the pain might be. That is why euthanasia, which is sometimes called mercy killing, is wrong. People who approve of euthanasia feel that it is okay for someone to ask to be killed to end intense suffering. But killing someone before their natural death—even if it is to end the person's suffering—is morally wrong.

What good can come from suffering? Suffering can teach us patience, trust, willingness to let others help us, compassion, humility, faithfulness, and hope, among other lessons. Jesus gave us the best example of facing suffering with courage, forgiveness, and love. Without his violent death, we could not experience his victorious Resurrection, which is the main event of Christianity.

We can't escape suffering—at some point in our lives most of us will experience it. But we can look to God to be near us, to strengthen us, and to teach us important lessons about life, death, and love.

— Job 36:15

29 No one knows how the clouds move
or how the thunder roars
through the sky, where God dwells.
30 He sends lightning through all the sky,
but the depths of the sea remain dark.
31 This is how he feeds[n] the people
and provides an abundance of food.
32 He seizes the lightning with his hands
and commands it to hit the mark.
33 Thunder announces the approaching storm,
and the cattle know it is coming.

37 1 The storm makes my heart beat wildly.
2 Listen, all of you, to the voice of God,
to the thunder that comes from his mouth.
3 He sends the lightning across the sky,
from one end of the earth to the other.
4 Then the roar of his voice is heard,
the majestic sound of thunder,
and all the while the lightning flashes.
5 At God's command amazing things happen,
wonderful things that we can't understand.
6 He commands snow to fall on the earth,
and sends torrents of drenching rain.
7 He brings our work to a stop;
he shows us what he can do.[o]
8 The wild animals go to their dens.
9 The storm winds come from the south,
and the biting cold from the north.
10 The breath of God freezes the waters,
and turns them to solid ice.
11 Lightning flashes from the clouds,[p]
12 as they move at God's will.
They do all that God commands,
everywhere throughout the world.

[n] **36:31** *Probable text* feeds; *Hebrew* judges. [o] **37:7** *One ancient translation* us what he can do; *Hebrew* this to those whom he has made. [p] **37:11** *Verse 11 in Hebrew is unclear.*

13 God sends rain to water the earth;
he may send it to punish us,
or to show us his favor.

14 Pause a moment, Job, and listen;
consider the wonderful things God does.

15 Do you know how God gives the command
and makes lightning flash from the clouds?

16 Do you know how clouds float in the sky,
the work of God's amazing skill?

17 No, you can only suffer in the heat
when the south wind oppresses the land.

18 Can you help God stretch out the sky
and make it as hard as polished metal?

19 Teach us what to say to God;
our minds are blank; we have nothing to say.

20 I won't ask to speak with God;
why should I give him a chance to destroy me?

21 And now the light in the sky is dazzling,
too bright for us to look at it;
and the sky has been swept clean by the wind.

22 A golden glow is seen in the north,
and the glory of God fills us with awe.

23 God's power is so great that we cannot come near him;
he is righteous and just in his dealings with us.

24 No wonder, then, that everyone is awed by him,
and that he ignores those who claim to be wise.

Pray it!

God's View of Creation

God finally speaks up! In chapters 38–39, God asks Job a series of questions, all concerning the creation of the world. Job has no answers to these questions. Awesome, complex, curious, marvelous, amazing—those words can't even begin to describe the miracle of Creation or its architect and maker, God. Spend some time reading those chapters; try reading them out loud as the beautiful poems they are. Let your reading be a prayer, praising God, our Creator.

— Job, chapters 38–39

The LORD Answers Job

38 Then out of the storm the LORD spoke to Job.

The LORD

2 Who are you to question my wisdom
with your ignorant, empty words?

3 Now stand up straight
and answer the questions I ask you.

4 Were you there when I made the world?
If you know so much, tell me about it.

5 Who decided how large it would be?
Who stretched the measuring line over it?
Do you know all the answers?

6 What holds up the pillars that support the earth?
Who laid the cornerstone of the world?

7 In the dawn of that day the stars sang together,
and the heavenly beings[q] shouted for joy.

8 Who closed the gates to hold back the sea[r]
when it burst from the womb of the earth?

9 It was I who covered the sea with clouds
and wrapped it in darkness.

10 I marked a boundary for the sea
and kept it behind bolted gates.

11 I told it, "So far and no farther!
Here your powerful waves must stop."

[q] **38:7** HEAVENLY BEINGS: *See 1:6.* [r] **38:8** TO HOLD BACK THE SEA: *See 26:12.*
38:7 Bar 3:34 **38:8–11** Jer 5:22

12 Job, have you ever in all your life
commanded a day to dawn?
13 Have you ordered the dawn to seize the earth
and shake the wicked from their hiding places?
14 Daylight makes the hills and valleys stand out
like the folds of a garment,
clear as the imprint of a seal on clay.
15 The light of day is too bright for the wicked
and restrains them from doing violence.

16 Have you been to the springs in the depths of the sea?
Have you walked on the floor of the ocean?
17 Has anyone ever shown you the gates
that guard the dark world of the dead?
18 Have you any idea how big the world is?
Answer me if you know.
19 Do you know where the light comes from
or what the source of darkness is?
20 Can you show them how far to go,
or send them back again?
21 I am sure you can, because you're so old
and were there when the world was made!

22 Have you ever visited the storerooms,
where I keep the snow and the hail?
23 I keep them ready for times of trouble,
for days of battle and war.
24 Have you been to the place where the sun comes up,
or the place from which the east wind blows?
25 Who dug a channel for the pouring rain
and cleared the way for the thunderstorm?
26 Who makes rain fall where no one lives?
27 Who waters the dry and thirsty land,
so that grass springs up?
28 Does either the rain or the dew have a father?
29 Who is the mother of the ice and the frost,
30 which turn the waters to stone
and freeze the face of the sea?

31 Can you tie the Pleiades together
or loosen the bonds that hold Orion?
32 Can you guide the stars season by season
and direct the Big and the Little Dipper?
33 Do you know the laws that govern the skies,
and can you make them apply to the earth?

34 Can you shout orders to the clouds
and make them drench you with rain?
35 And if you command the lightning to flash,
will it come to you and say, "At your service"?
36 Who tells the ibis[s] when the Nile will flood,
or who tells the rooster that rain will fall?[t]
37 Who is wise enough to count the clouds
and tilt them over to pour out the rain,
38 rain that hardens the dust into lumps?

39 Do you find food for lions to eat,
and satisfy hungry young lions
40 when they hide in their caves,
or lie in wait in their dens?
41 Who is it that feeds the ravens
when they wander about hungry,
when their young cry to me for food?

39 1 Do you know when mountain goats are born?
Have you watched wild deer give birth?
2 Do you know how long they carry their young?
Do you know the time for their birth?

[s] **38:36** IBIS: *A bird in ancient Egypt that was believed to announce the flooding of the Nile River.* [t] **38:36** *Verse 36 in Hebrew is unclear.*

38:31 Job 9:9; Am 5:8

"Have you ever visited the storerooms, / where I keep the snow and the hail?" *(Job 38:22)*.

Pray it!

Earth Prayer

The beauty of the trees,
the softness of the air,
the fragrance of the grass,
speaks to me.
The summit of the mountain,
the thunder of the sky,
the rhythm of the sea,
speaks to me.
The faintness of the stars,
the freshness of the morning,
the dewdrop on the flower,
speaks to me.
The strength of fire,
the taste of salmon,
the trail of the sun,
and the life that never goes away,
they speak to me.
And my heart soars.
—Chief Dan George

— Job, chapter 39

3 Do you know when they will crouch down
and bring their young into the world?
4 In the wilds their young grow strong;
they go away and don't come back.

5 Who gave the wild donkeys their freedom?
Who turned them loose and let them roam?
6 I gave them the desert to be their home,
and let them live on the salt plains.
7 They keep far away from the noisy cities,
and no one can tame them and make them work.
8 The mountains are the pastures where they feed,
where they search for anything green to eat.

9 Will a wild ox work for you?
Is he willing to spend the night in your stable?
10 Can you hold one with a rope and make him plow?
Or make him pull a harrow in your fields?
11 Can you rely on his great strength
and expect him to do your heavy work?
12 Do you expect him to bring in your harvest
and gather the grain from your threshing place?

13 How fast the wings of an ostrich beat!
But no ostrich can fly like a stork.[u]
14 The ostrich leaves her eggs on the ground
for the heat in the soil to warm them.
15 She is unaware that a foot may crush them
or a wild animal break them.
16 She acts as if the eggs were not hers,
and is unconcerned that her efforts were wasted.
17 It was I who made her foolish
and did not give her wisdom.
18 But when she begins to run,[v]
she can laugh at any horse and rider.

19 Was it you, Job, who made horses so strong
and gave them their flowing manes?
20 Did you make them leap like locusts
and frighten people with their snorting?
21 They eagerly paw the ground in the valley;
they rush into battle with all their strength.
22 They do not know the meaning of fear,
and no sword can turn them back.
23 The weapons which their riders carry
rattle and flash in the sun.
24 Trembling with excitement, the horses race ahead;
when the trumpet blows, they can't stand still.

[u] **39:13** *Verse 13 in Hebrew is unclear.* [v] **39:18** *Probable text* run; *Hebrew unclear.*

Do ostriches make good mothers? Check out Job 39:13–18.

The ostrich . . . the horses . . . an eagle . . . the monster . . . (39:14, 24, 27; 40:15)

25 At each blast of the trumpet they snort;
they can smell a battle before they get near,
and they hear the officers shouting commands.
26 Does a hawk learn from you how to fly
when it spreads its wings toward the south?
27 Does an eagle wait for your command
to build its nest high in the mountains?
28 It makes its home on the highest rocks
and makes the sharp peaks its fortress.
29 From there it watches near and far
for something to kill and eat.
30 Around dead bodies the eagles gather,
and the young eagles drink the blood.

40 1-2 Job, you challenged Almighty God;
will you give up now, or will you answer?

Job

3-4 I spoke foolishly, LORD. What can I answer?
I will not try to say anything else.
5 I have already said more than I should.

6 Then out of the storm the LORD spoke to Job once again.

The LORD

7 Now stand up straight
and answer my questions.
8 Are you trying to prove that I am unjust—
to put me in the wrong and yourself in the right?
9 Are you as strong as I am?
Can your voice thunder as loud as mine?

Study it!

God's Wisdom

So, what is the point of God's speech? Job gets it right away. We cannot even get close to understanding the mind of God. Our brains simply aren't equipped to take in a mystery like that. God is teaching us that, like Creation, human nature is extremely complicated—often beyond our understanding. Why would God allow an innocent person to suffer? Even if God revealed the answer to us, we would not be able to grasp the meaning. God's wisdom is so wide and so deep that it's way beyond the limits of our imagination and control.

Is this supposed to be comforting? We still don't have an answer to the question about why people suffer. Like Job, we each may have times in our lives when all we can do is trust in the wisdom of God's plans—even if we don't like them. For now, we do our best to cope with the mystery of suffering, and to believe that it can teach us, bless us, and deepen our faith and love.

— Job 40:1–5

10 If so, stand up in your honor and pride;
clothe yourself with majesty and glory.
11 Look at those who are proud;
pour out your anger and humble them.
12 Yes, look at them and bring them down;
crush the wicked where they stand.
13 Bury them all in the ground;
bind them in the world of the dead.
14 Then I will be the first to praise you
and admit that you won the victory yourself.

39:30 Mt 24:28; Lk 17:37

15 Look at the monster Behemoth;[w]
I created him and I created you.
He eats grass like a cow,
16 but what strength there is in his body,
and what power there is in his muscles!
17 His tail stands up like a cedar,
and the muscles in his legs are strong.
18 His bones are as strong as bronze,
and his legs are like iron bars.

19 The most amazing of all my creatures!
Only his Creator can defeat him.
20 Grass to feed him grows
on the hills where wild beasts play.[x]
21 He lies down under the thorn bushes,
and hides among the reeds in the swamp.
22 The thorn bushes and the willows by the stream
give him shelter in their shade.
23 He is not afraid of a rushing river;
he is calm when the Jordan dashes in his face.
24 Who can blind his eyes and capture him?
Or who can catch his snout in a trap?

41 Can you catch Leviathan[y] with a fishhook
or tie his tongue down with a rope?
2 Can you put a rope through his snout
or put a hook through his jaws?
3 Will he beg you to let him go?
Will he plead with you for mercy?
4 Will he make an agreement with you
and promise to serve you forever?
5 Will you tie him like a pet bird,
like something to amuse your servant women?
6 Will fishermen bargain over him?
Will merchants cut him up to sell?
7 Can you fill his hide with fishing spears
or pierce his head with a harpoon?
8 Touch him once and you'll never try it again;
you'll never forget the fight!

9 Anyone who sees Leviathan
loses courage and falls to the ground.
10 When he is aroused, he is fierce;
no one would dare to stand before him.
11 Who can attack him and still be safe?
No one in all the world can do it.[z]

12 Let me tell you about Leviathan's legs
and describe how great and strong he is.
13 No one can tear off his outer coat
or pierce the armor[a] he wears.
14 Who can make him open his jaws,
ringed with those terrifying teeth?
15 His back[b] is made of rows of shields,
fastened together and hard as stone.
16 Each one is joined so tight to the next,
not even a breath can come between.
17 They all are fastened so firmly together
that nothing can ever pull them apart.
18 Light flashes when he sneezes,
and his eyes glow like the rising sun.
19 Flames blaze from his mouth,
and streams of sparks fly out.
20 Smoke comes pouring out of his nose,
like smoke from weeds burning under a pot.
21 His breath starts fires burning;
flames leap out of his mouth.
22 His neck is so powerful
that all who meet him are terrified.
23 There is not a weak spot in his skin;
it is as hard and unyielding as iron.
24 His stony heart is without fear,
as unyielding and hard as a millstone.
25 When he rises up, even the strongest[c] are frightened;
they are helpless with fear.
26 There is no sword that can wound him;
no spear or arrow or lance that can harm him.
27 For him iron is as flimsy as straw,
and bronze as soft as rotten wood.
28 There is no arrow that can make him run;
rocks thrown at him are like bits of straw.
29 To him a club is a piece of straw,
and he laughs when men throw spears.

[w] **40:15** BEHEMOTH: *Some identify this with the hippopotamus, others with a legendary creature.* [x] **40:20** *Verse 20 in Hebrew is unclear.* [y] **41:1** LEVIATHAN: *See 3:8.* [z] **41:11** *Verse 11 in Hebrew is unclear.* [a] **41:13** *One ancient translation* armor; *Hebrew* bridle. [b] **41:15** *Some ancient translations* back; *Hebrew* pride. [c] **41:25** strongest; *or* gods.

41:1 Ps 74:14; 104:26; Isa 27:1

30 The scales on his belly are like jagged
pieces of pottery;
they tear up the muddy ground like a
threshing sledge.[d]
31 He churns up the sea like boiling water
and makes it bubble like a pot of oil.
32 He leaves a shining path behind him
and turns the sea to white foam.
33 There is nothing on earth to compare
with him;
he is a creature that has no fear.
34 He looks down on even the proudest
animals;
he is king of all wild beasts.

42 Then Job answered the LORD.

Job

2 I know, LORD, that you are all-powerful;
that you can do everything you want.
3 You ask how I dare question your
wisdom
when I am so very ignorant.
I talked about things I did not
understand,
about marvels too great for me to
know.
4 You told me to listen while you spoke
and to try to answer your questions.
5 In the past I knew only what others had
told me,
but now I have seen you with my own
eyes.
6 So I am ashamed of all I have said
and repent in dust and ashes.

Conclusion

7 After the LORD had finished speaking to Job, he said to Eliphaz, "I am angry with you and your two friends, because you did not speak the truth about me, the way my servant Job did. 8 Now take seven bulls and seven rams to Job and offer them as a sacrifice for yourselves. Job will pray for you, and I will answer his prayer and not disgrace you the way you deserve. You did not speak the truth about me as he did."

Study it!

God's Blessing for Job

Shockingly—to us—God admits that Job was correct. God did indeed allow suffering to trample the life of an innocent person. Job's friends claimed that God would never do such a thing, and God angrily informs them that they spoke untruthfully about him.

The Israelites' view of God's justice—rewarding the good and punishing the wicked—is proven to be too simple. While God does not *cause* or *will* Job's suffering, we are led to understand that God *allows* it. This is not at all comforting to us! But, remember, God's plans are a deep mystery—we cannot grasp all the ways God works in our lives and our world. We are asked to do what seems impossible at times: *trust.*

Because Job spoke the truth about God, God blessed him—twice as much as before! The author's claim that Job lived to the age of 140 is another way of saying that Job's life was good and long (twice as many years as the average life span, to match the twice-as-many blessings), so that he had plenty of time to enjoy all of God's blessings poured upon him.

— Job, chapter 42

[d] **41:30** THRESHING SLEDGES: *These had sharp pieces of iron or stone fastened beneath them.*
42:3 Job 38:2 **42:4** Job 38:3

What do you think is the mightiest object, person, animal, or force in the world? God's might is much greater than that!

The LORD made him prosperous again. (42:10)

9Eliphaz, Bildad, and Zophar did what the
LORD had told them to do, and the LORD
answered Job's prayer.
10Then, after Job had prayed for his three
friends, the LORD made him prosperous
again and gave him twice as much as he had
had before. 11All Job's brothers and sisters
and former friends came to visit him and
feasted with him in his house. They
expressed their sympathy and comforted him
for all the troubles the LORD had brought on
him. Each of them gave him some money
and a gold ring.
12The LORD blessed the last part of Job's
life even more than he had blessed the first.
Job owned fourteen thousand sheep, six
thousand camels, two thousand head of cat-
tle, and one thousand donkeys. 13He was the
father of seven sons and three daughters.
14He called the oldest daughter Jemimah, the
second Keziah, and the youngest Keren
Happuch.[e] 15There were no other women in
the whole world as beautiful as Job's daugh-
ters. Their father gave them a share of the
inheritance along with their brothers.
16Job lived a hundred and forty years after
this, long enough to see his grandchildren
and great-grandchildren. 17And then he died
at a very great age.

[e] **42:14** *In Hebrew the names of Job's daughters suggest beauty both by their sound and by their meaning.* JEMIMAH *means "dove";* KEZIAH *means "cassia," a variety of cinnamon used as a perfume; and* KEREN HAPPUCH *means a small box used for eye make-up.*

42:10 Job 1:1–3

Your Next Step

Congratulations on finishing the Book of Job! Use this space to write your thoughts and questions about this book. If you are following the suggested reading plan, move ahead to the First Letter of Peter in the New Testament. This letter also discusses suffering, connecting our suffering to the suffering of Christ.

THE BOOK OF Psalms

Each Sunday, as the cantor leads the assembly in the responsorial psalm, Debbie sings her heart out. Sometimes, when her youth group plans their special Masses, she leads them in the responsorial psalm. She knows it is good practice, and she likes it a lot. She imagines that one day she will lead the whole church.

Debbie, like many people, loves the Psalms. She especially likes the words and themes of the Psalms. The Psalms are poetic, dramatic, comforting, and inspirational. They sing gratitude for God's blessings, cry for help in times of need, seek wisdom and direction, praise God during worship, and express wonder and awe at the greatness of God. All of these things make the Psalms one of the most beloved books of the Bible.

Psalm 150

Headlines

- The Key to True Happiness! (Psalm 1)
- Fools Say There Is No God (Psalm 14)
- Desperate Cry for Help Is Answered (Psalm 22)
- Hope Found in Time of Despair (Psalm 23)
- Plea for Forgiveness and God's Mercy (Psalm 51)
- Youth Prays for Help (Psalm 102)
- Everyone and Everything Praise God! (Psalms 148–150)

FACTOIDS

Who wrote this book? There are many authors, called psalmists, who contributed to the collection of Psalms.

Why was it written? Psalms was written as a hymnbook and prayer book for God's people. They are still used and sung in Catholic liturgy and devotions, often as a response to another Bible reading.

How is it organized? Psalms is divided into five books: Book 1 (1–41), Book 2 (42–72), Book 3 (73–89), Book 4 (90–106), and Book 5 (107–150).

Jesus connection: Jesus quoted Psalms; some of his last words are from the Psalms (Psalm 22).

Important themes

- There are many kinds of psalms: songs of praise and thanksgiving, songs of lament and petition, songs of wisdom, liturgical or worship psalms, and historical psalms.
- No matter what emotions we are feeling, we can bring them to God in prayer.

PSALMS

BOOK ONE

(Psalms 1–41)

True Happiness

1 Happy are those
who reject the advice of evil people,
who do not follow the example of sinners
or join those who have no use for God.
2 Instead, they find joy in obeying the Law of the LORD,
and they study it day and night.
3 They are like trees that grow beside a stream,
that bear fruit at the right time,
and whose leaves do not dry up.
They succeed in everything they do.

4 But evil people are not like this at all;
they are like straw that the wind blows away.
5 Sinners will be condemned by God
and kept apart from God's own people.
6 The righteous are guided and protected by the LORD,
but the evil are on the way to their doom.

God's Chosen King

2 Why do the nations plan rebellion?
Why do people make their useless plots?
2 Their kings revolt,
their rulers plot together against the LORD
and against the king he chose.
3 "Let us free ourselves from their rule,"
they say;
"let us throw off their control."

4 From his throne in heaven the Lord laughs
and mocks their feeble plans.
5 Then he warns them in anger
and terrifies them with his fury.

Study it!

Sing a Psalm!

Some people like to play a special song or type of music when they are feeling a certain way. They may put on country music when they are feeling low. They might put on rock when they are feeling happy. Maybe they listen to classical music when they need to calm down. This is like the Psalms. There are songs that celebrate as well as ones that express grief. There are songs that are joyful and others that are sad. Almost every emotion can be found in the Psalms.

The Psalms, written in a poetic style, were put to music. They still are! Both Jewish and Christian musicians continue to write music for the Psalms. They are so popular that in many New Testament Bibles (Bibles that only contain the New Testament books), the Psalms are also included. Psalms are included in many Catholic prayer services and liturgies. In a Catholic Mass, a psalm is sung or read after the first reading.

— Psalm 1

6 "On Zion,[a] my sacred hill," he says,
"I have installed my king."

7 "I will announce," says the king, "what the LORD has declared.
He said to me: 'You are my son;
today I have become your father.

[a] **2:6** ZION: *The term "Zion" (originally a designation for "David's City," the Jebusite stronghold captured by King David's forces) was later extended in meaning to refer to the hill on which the Temple stood.*

1:3 Jer 17:8 **2:1, 2** Acts 4:25, 26 **2:7** Acts 13:33; Heb 1:5; 5:5

8 Ask, and I will give you all the nations;
the whole earth will be yours.
9 You will break them with an iron rod;
you will shatter them in pieces like a clay pot.' "

10 Now listen to this warning, you kings;
learn this lesson, you rulers of the world:
11 Serve the LORD with fear;
tremble 12 and bow down to him;[b]
or else his anger will be quickly aroused,
and you will suddenly die.
Happy are all who go to him for protection.

Morning Prayer for Help[c]

3 I have so many enemies, LORD,
so many who turn against me!
2 They talk about me and say,
"God will not help him."

3 But you, O LORD, are always my shield from danger;
you give me victory
and restore my courage.
4 I call to the LORD for help,
and from his sacred hill[d] he answers me.

5 I lie down and sleep,
and all night long the LORD protects me.
6 I am not afraid of the thousands of enemies
who surround me on every side.

7 Come, LORD! Save me, my God!
You punish all my enemies
and leave them powerless to harm me.
8 Victory comes from the LORD —
may he bless his people.

Evening Prayer for Help[e]

4 Answer me when I pray,
O God, my defender!
When I was in trouble, you helped me.
Be kind to me now and hear my prayer.

Pray it!

Sleep Soundly

One way to get a good night's sleep is to do a few things before going to bed. Your parents would probably tell you that before going to bed you should be brushing your teeth and putting your dirty clothes in the laundry. But after the work is done, there is one last thing: prayer. That's right. A good prayer at the end of the day can help you rest well. Psalm 4 can be used as an evening psalm. It probably doesn't describe your average day, but it does remind you that God protects, loves, and blesses you. Those are great thoughts for sweet dreams!

You might even want to write your own closing prayer to end your day. Say a prayer just before going to bed and see how well you sleep.

— Psalm 4

2 How long will you people insult me?
How long will you love what is worthless
and go after what is false?

3 Remember that the LORD has chosen the righteous for his own,
and he hears me when I call to him.

4 Tremble with fear and stop sinning;
think deeply about this,
when you lie in silence on your beds.

[b] **2:12** *Probable text* tremble . . . him; *some other possible texts* with trembling kiss his feet *and* with trembling kiss the Son *and* tremble and kiss the mighty one; *Hebrew unclear.* [c] **3** HEBREW TITLE: *A psalm by David, after he ran away from his son Absalom.* [d] **3:4** SACRED HILL: *See 2:6.* [e] **4** HEBREW TITLE: *A psalm by David.*
2:9 Rev 2:26, 27; 12:5; 19:15 **3 Title** 2 Sam 15:13—17:22 **4:4** Eph 4:26

What do people in our society think makes someone happy? What does Psalm 1 say that really makes a person happy?

5 Offer the right sacrifices to the LORD,
and put your trust in him.

6 There are many who pray:
"Give us more blessings, O LORD.
Look on us with kindness!"
7 But the joy that you have given me
is more than they will ever have
with all their grain and wine.

8 When I lie down, I go to sleep in peace;
you alone, O LORD, keep me perfectly safe.

A Prayer for Protection[e]

5 Listen to my words, O LORD,
and hear my sighs.
2 Listen to my cry for help,
my God and king!

I pray to you, O LORD;
3 you hear my voice in the morning;
at sunrise I offer my prayer[f]
and wait for your answer.

4 You are not a God who is pleased with wrongdoing;
you allow no evil in your presence.
5 You cannot stand the sight of the proud;
you hate all wicked people.
6 You destroy all liars
and despise violent, deceitful people.

7 But because of your great love
I can come into your house;
I can worship in your holy Temple
and bow down to you in reverence.
8 LORD, I have so many enemies!
Lead me to do your will;
make your way plain for me to follow.

9 What my enemies say can never be trusted;
they only want to destroy.
Their words are flattering and smooth,
but full of deadly deceit.
10 Condemn and punish them, O God;
may their own plots cause their ruin.
Drive them out of your presence
because of their many sins
and their rebellion against you.

11 But all who find safety in you will rejoice;
they can always sing for joy.
Protect those who love you;
because of you they are truly happy.
12 You bless those who obey you, LORD;
your love protects them like a shield.

A Prayer for Help in Time of Trouble[g]

6 LORD, don't be angry and rebuke me!
Don't punish me in your anger!
2 I am worn out, O LORD; have pity on me!
Give me strength; I am completely exhausted
3 and my whole being is deeply troubled.
How long, O LORD, will you wait to help me?

4 Come and save me, LORD;
in your mercy rescue me from death.
5 In the world of the dead you are not remembered;
no one can praise you there.

6 I am worn out with grief;
every night my bed is damp from my weeping;
my pillow is soaked with tears.
7 I can hardly see;
my eyes are so swollen
from the weeping caused by my enemies.

8 Keep away from me, you evil people!
The LORD hears my weeping;
9 he listens to my cry for help
and will answer my prayer.
10 My enemies will know the bitter shame of defeat;
in sudden confusion they will be driven away.

[e] **5** HEBREW TITLE: *A psalm by David.* [f] **5:3** prayer; *or* sacrifice. [g] **6** HEBREW TITLE: *A psalm by David.*
5:9 Rom 3:13 **6:1** Ps 38:1 **6:8** Mt 7:23; Lk 13:27

What makes you feel safe? What type of protection do you ask God for?

Live it!

Big Kids Don't Cry?

Maybe you have heard that big kids don't cry. But this can be misleading. It is true that as we age, we learn to control our emotions. But emotions are healthy, and it isn't wrong to show them appropriately. Even tears—for both women and men—have their place. The psalmist isn't afraid to cry. "I am worn out with grief; / every night my bed is damp from my weeping; / my pillow is soaked with tears" (Psalm 6:6).

So, don't worry if every once in a while you feel like crying. It's only human. Life is sad and hard sometimes, and tears can help us express the feelings of frustration and grief. Sometimes people even shed tears when they are feeling great joy. But if you feel like *all* you do is cry (or if you are always angry or sad), talk to an adult you can trust about what you are feeling.

— Psalm 6

A Prayer for Justice[h]

7 O LORD, my God, I come to you for
protection;
rescue me and save me from all who
pursue me,
2 or else like a lion they will carry me off
where no one can save me,
and there they will tear me to pieces.
3-4 O LORD, my God, if I have wronged
anyone,
if I have betrayed a friend
or without cause done violence to my
enemy[i] —
if I have done any of these things—
5 then let my enemies pursue me and catch
me,
let them cut me down and kill me
and leave me lifeless on the ground!
6 Rise in your anger, O LORD!
Stand up against the fury of my enemies;
rouse yourself and help me!
Justice is what you demand,
7 so bring together all the peoples
around you,
and rule over them from above.[j]
8 You are the judge of all people.
Judge in my favor, O LORD;
you know that I am innocent.
9 You are a righteous God
and judge our thoughts and desires.
Stop the wickedness of evildoers
and reward those who are good.

10 God is my protector;
he saves those who obey him.
11 God is a righteous judge
and always condemns the wicked.
12 If they do not change their ways,
God will sharpen his sword.
He bends his bow and makes it ready;
13 he takes up his deadly weapons
and aims his burning arrows.

14 See how wicked people think up evil;
they plan trouble and practice
deception.
15 But in the traps they set for others,
they themselves get caught.
16 So they are punished by their own evil
and are hurt by their own violence.

17 I thank the LORD for his justice;
I sing praises to the LORD, the Most
High.

God's Glory and Human Dignity[k]

8 O LORD, our Lord,
your greatness is seen in all the world!
Your praise reaches up to the heavens;

[h] **7** HEBREW TITLE: *A song which David sang to the LORD because of Cush the Benjaminite.* [i] **7:3–4** without cause done violence to my enemy; *or* shown mercy to someone who wronged me unjustly. [j] **7:7** *Probable text* rule over them from above; *Hebrew* return above over them. [k] **8** HEBREW TITLE: *A psalm by David.*

7:9 Rev 2:23

2 it is sung by children and babies.
You are safe and secure from all your enemies;
you stop anyone who opposes you.

3 When I look at the sky, which you have made,
at the moon and the stars, which you set in their places—
4 what are human beings, that you think of them;
mere mortals, that you care for them?

5 Yet you made them inferior only to yourself;[l]
you crowned them with glory and honor.
6 You appointed them rulers over everything you made;
you placed them over all creation:
7 sheep and cattle, and the wild animals too;
8 the birds and the fish
and the creatures in the seas.

9 O LORD, our Lord,
your greatness is seen in all the world!

Thanksgiving to God for His Justice[m]

9 I will praise you, LORD, with all my heart;
I will tell of all the wonderful things you have done.
2 I will sing with joy because of you.
I will sing praise to you, Almighty God.

I will praise you, LORD. (9:1)

3 My enemies turn back when you appear;
they fall down and die.
4 You are fair and honest in your judgments,
and you have judged in my favor.
5 You have condemned the heathen
and destroyed the wicked;
they will be remembered no more.
6 Our enemies are finished forever;
you have destroyed their cities,
and they are completely forgotten.

7 But the LORD is king forever;
he has set up his throne for judgment.
8 He rules the world with righteousness;
he judges the nations with justice.

9 The LORD is a refuge for the oppressed,
a place of safety in times of trouble.
10 Those who know you, LORD, will trust you;
you do not abandon anyone who comes to you.

11 Sing praise to the LORD, who rules in Zion!
Tell every nation what he has done!
12 God remembers those who suffer;
he does not forget their cry,
and he punishes those who wrong them.

13 Be merciful to me, O LORD!
See the sufferings my enemies cause me!
Rescue me from death, O LORD,
14 that I may stand before the people of Jerusalem
and tell them all the things for which I praise you.
I will rejoice because you saved me.

15 The heathen have dug a pit and fallen in;
they have been caught in their own trap.
16 The LORD has revealed himself by his righteous judgments,
and the wicked are trapped by their own deeds.

[l] **8:5** yourself; *or* the gods, *or* the angels. [m] **9** HEBREW TITLE: *A psalm by David.*

8:2 Mt 21:16 **8:4** Job 7:17, 18; Ps 144:3; Heb 2:6–8 **8:5** Wis 2:23; Sir 17:1–4 **8:6** 1 Cor 15:27; Eph 1:22; Heb 2:8 **9:13** Wis 16:13

17 Death is the destiny of all the wicked,
of all those who reject God.
18 The needy will not always be neglected;
the hope of the poor will not be crushed forever.

19 Come, LORD! Do not let anyone defy you!
Bring the heathen before you
and pronounce judgment on them.
20 Make them afraid, O LORD;
make them know that they are only mortal beings.

A Prayer for Justice

10 Why are you so far away, O LORD?
Why do you hide yourself when we are in trouble?
2 The wicked are proud and persecute the poor;
catch them in the traps they have made.

3 The wicked are proud of their evil desires;
the greedy curse and reject the LORD.
4 The wicked do not care about the LORD;
in their pride they think that God doesn't matter.

"They think that God doesn't matter." (10:4)

5 The wicked succeed in everything.
They cannot understand God's judgments;
they sneer at their enemies.
6 They say to themselves, "We will never fail;
we will never be in trouble."
7 Their speech is filled with curses, lies, and threats;
they are quick to speak hateful, evil words.

8 They hide themselves in the villages,
waiting to murder innocent people.
They spy on their helpless victims;
9 they wait in their hiding place like lions.
They lie in wait for the poor;
they catch them in their traps and drag them away.

10 The helpless victims lie crushed;
brute strength has defeated them.
11 The wicked say to themselves, "God doesn't care!
He has closed his eyes and will never see me!"

12 O LORD, punish those wicked people!
Remember those who are suffering!
13 How can the wicked despise God
and say to themselves, "He will not punish me"?

14 But you do see; you take notice of trouble and suffering
and are always ready to help.
The helpless commit themselves to you;
you have always helped the needy.

15 Break the power of wicked and evil people;
punish them for the wrong they have done
until they do it no more.

16 The LORD is king forever and ever.
Those who worship other gods
will vanish from his land.

17 You will listen, O LORD, to the prayers of the lowly;
you will give them courage.
18 You will hear the cries of the oppressed and the orphans;
you will judge in their favor,
so that mortal men may cause terror no more.

10:7 Rom 3:14

When does it seem like God is hiding? When does it seem that God takes "notice of trouble and suffering" *(Psalm 10:14)***?**

Confidence in the LORD[n]

11 I trust in the LORD for safety.
How foolish of you to say to me,
"Fly away like a bird to the mountains,[o]
2 because the wicked have drawn their
bows and aimed their arrows
to shoot from the shadows at good
people.
3 There is nothing a good person can do
when everything falls apart."

4 The LORD is in his holy temple;
he has his throne in heaven.
He watches people everywhere
and knows what they are doing.
5 He examines the good and the wicked
alike;
the lawless he hates with all his heart.

6 He sends down flaming coals[p] and
burning sulfur on the wicked;
he punishes them with scorching
winds.
7 The LORD is righteous and loves good
deeds;
those who do them will live in his
presence.

Those who do them will live in his presence. (11:7)

A Prayer for Help[q]

12 Help us, LORD!
There is not a good person left;
honest people can no longer be found.
2 All of them lie to one another;
they deceive each other with flattery.
3 Silence those flattering tongues, O LORD!
Close those boastful mouths that say,
4 "With our words we get what we want.
We will say what we wish,
and no one can stop us."

5 "But now I will come," says the LORD,
"because the needy are oppressed
and the persecuted groan in pain.
I will give them the security they long
for."

6 The promises of the LORD can be trusted;
they are as genuine as silver
refined seven times in the furnace.

7-8 The wicked are everywhere,
and everyone praises what is evil.
Keep us always safe, O LORD,
and preserve us from such people.

A Prayer for Help[q]

13 How much longer will you forget
me, LORD? Forever?
How much longer will you hide
yourself from me?
2 How long must I endure trouble?
How long will sorrow fill my heart day
and night?
How long will my enemies triumph
over me?

3 Look at me, O LORD my God, and
answer me.
Restore my strength; don't let me die.
4 Don't let my enemies say, "We have
defeated him."
Don't let them gloat over my downfall.
5 I rely on your constant love;
I will be glad, because you will rescue
me.
6 I will sing to you, O LORD,
because you have been good to me.

[n] **11** HEBREW TITLE: *By David.* [o] **11:1** *Some ancient translations* like a bird to the mountains; *Hebrew* bird, to your *(plural)* mountain. [p] **11:6** *One ancient translation* coals; *Hebrew* traps. [q] **12; 13** HEBREW TITLE: *A psalm by David.*

Who are the needy in your community, and how can you help them?

Study it!

A Psalm for Everything!

Do you know how many psalms there are? If you said 150, you are correct. And do you know how many different types of psalms there are? Thirteen! Psalm 13 is a lament. A lament expresses deep sorrow or grief. There are two types of lament psalms—those of an individual and those of a community. The Israelites experienced many wars and hardships, so they had lots of sorrows and grief.

Other psalm types include thanksgiving by an individual, hymns, songs of Zion, enthronement psalms, royal psalms, wisdom psalms, Torah psalms, entrance psalms, pilgrimage psalms, history psalms, and acrostics. Some people divide the psalms into even more categories. As you read through the psalms, look at the titles—they'll give you a hint as to what type each is. You don't have to know what all these categories mean, though, to appreciate the psalms. When you finish reading all 150, look over them again and decide which type you like best. You may even discover that you have a favorite psalm.

— Psalm 13

Human Wickedness[r]

(Psalm 53)

14 Fools say to themselves,
"There is no God!"
They are all corrupt,
and they have done terrible things;
there is no one who does what is right.
2 The LORD looks down from heaven at us humans
to see if there are any who are wise,
any who worship him.
3 But they have all gone wrong;
they are all equally bad.
Not one of them does what is right,
not a single one.

4 "Don't they know?" asks the LORD.
"Are all these evildoers ignorant?
They live by robbing my people,
and they never pray to me."

5 But then they will be terrified,
for God is with those who obey him.
6 Evildoers frustrate the plans of the humble,
but the LORD is their protection.

7 How I pray that victory
will come to Israel from Zion.
How happy the people of Israel will be
when the LORD makes them prosperous again!

What God Requires[s]

15 LORD, who may enter your Temple?
Who may worship on Zion, your sacred hill?[t]

2 Those who obey God in everything
and always do what is right,
whose words are true and sincere,
3 and who do not slander others.
They do no wrong to their friends
nor spread rumors about their neighbors.
4 They despise those whom God rejects,
but honor those who obey the LORD.
They always do what they promise,
no matter how much it may cost.
5 They make loans without charging interest
and cannot be bribed to testify against the innocent.

Whoever does these things will always be secure.

[r] **14** HEBREW TITLE: *By David.* [s] **15** HEBREW TITLE: *A psalm by David.* [t] **15:1** SACRED HILL: *See 2:6.*

14:1–3 Rom 3:10–12

Live it!

I Don't Need Anyone

"When I grow up, I'm going to depend on myself and not on anyone else," Javier told his mom after school one day. "I won't need parents because I'll have a job. I'll be able to buy my own food and clothes and video games."

His mom sighed, "Javi, it isn't about having all the money and stuff."

"Well, I hate having to ask for stuff all the time. It'll be great when I can get it all myself."

"Javi, your papa and I have good jobs, and we have a house, and you have food and clothes, right?"

"Yes, mama but . . ." he interrupted. She wouldn't let him finish, "Wait a minute, let me finish. We have all that and more, and yet your papa and I still depend on something."

"Yeah, each other, right?" he said.

"That's right, but it isn't the whole story. We also depend on God. Every day we ask God for help."

"Every day?" Javi asked.

"Yes, we depend on God every day. We pray Psalm 16, which says, 'You will show me the path that leads to life; your presence fills me with joy and brings me pleasure forever.' So, even when you're old, and responsible, and buying Papa and me food, remember that! Maybe then you'll understand that you need to depend on God, just like Papa and I do, okay Javi?"

— Psalm 16

A Prayer of Confidence[u]

16 Protect me, O God; I trust in you
for safety.
2 I say to the LORD, "You are my Lord;
all the good things I have come from
you."

3 How excellent are the LORD's faithful
people!
My greatest pleasure is to be with
them.

4 Those who rush to other gods
bring many troubles on themselves.[v]
I will not take part in their sacrifices;
I will not worship their gods.

5 You, LORD, are all I have,
and you give me all I need;
my future is in your hands.
6 How wonderful are your gifts to me;
how good they are!

7 I praise the LORD, because he guides me,
and in the night my conscience warns
me.
8 I am always aware of the LORD's presence;
he is near, and nothing can shake me.

9 And so I am thankful and glad,
and I feel completely secure,
10 because you protect me from the power
of death.
I have served you faithfully,
and you will not abandon me to the
world of the dead.

11 You will show me the path that leads to
life;
your presence fills me with joy
and brings me pleasure forever.

The Prayer of an Innocent Person[w]

17 Listen, O LORD, to my plea for
justice;
pay attention to my cry for help!
Listen to my honest prayer.
2 You will judge in my favor,
because you know what is right.

[u] **16** HEBREW TITLE: *A psalm by David.*
[v] **16:4** *Probable text* Those . . . themselves; *Hebrew unclear.* [w] **17** HEBREW TITLE: *A prayer by David.*
16:10 Acts 13:35 **16:8–11** Acts 2:25–28

3 You know my heart.
You have come to me at night;
you have examined me completely
and found no evil desire in me.
I speak no evil, 4 as others do;
I have obeyed your command
and have not followed paths of violence.
5 I have always walked in your way
and have never strayed from it.

6 I pray to you, O God, because you answer me;
so turn to me and listen to my words.
7 Reveal your wonderful love and save me;
at your side I am safe from my enemies.
8 Protect me as you would your very eyes;
hide me in the shadow of your wings
9 from the attacks of the wicked.

Deadly enemies surround me;
10 they have no pity and speak proudly.
11 They are around me now, wherever I turn,
watching for a chance to pull me down.
12 They are like lions, waiting for me,
wanting to tear me to pieces.
13 Come, LORD! Oppose my enemies and defeat them!
Save me from the wicked by your sword;
14 save me from those who in this life have all they want.
Punish them with the sufferings you have stored up for them;
may there be enough for their children
and some left over for their children's children!

15 But I will see you, because I have done no wrong;
and when I awake, your presence will fill me with joy.

David's Song of Victory[x]
(2 Samuel 22:1–51)

18 How I love you, LORD!
You are my defender.

2 The LORD is my protector;
he is my strong fortress.
My God is my protection,
and with him I am safe.
He protects me like a shield;
he defends me and keeps me safe.
3 I call to the LORD,
and he saves me from my enemies.
Praise the LORD!

4 The danger of death was all around me;
the waves of destruction rolled over me.
5 The danger of death was around me,
and the grave set its trap for me.
6 In my trouble I called to the LORD;
I called to my God for help.
In his temple he heard my voice;
he listened to my cry for help.

7 Then the earth trembled and shook;
the foundations of the mountains rocked and quivered,
because God was angry.
8 Smoke poured out of his nostrils,
a consuming flame and burning coals from his mouth.
9 He tore the sky open and came down
with a dark cloud under his feet.
10 He flew swiftly on his winged creature;[y]
he traveled on the wings of the wind.
11 He covered himself with darkness;
thick clouds, full of water, surrounded him.
12 Hailstones and flashes of fire
came from the lightning before him
and broke through the dark clouds.

13 Then the LORD thundered from the sky;
and the voice of the Most High was heard.[z]

[x] **18** HEBREW TITLE: *The words that David, the LORD's servant, sang to the LORD on the day the LORD saved him from Saul and all his other enemies.* [y] **18:10** WINGED CREATURE: *See Word List.* [z] **18:13** *One ancient translation (and see 2 Sam 22:14)* was heard; *Hebrew* was heard hailstones and flashes of fire.

"Reveal your wonderful love and save me; / at your side I am safe from my enemies" *(Psalm 17:7)*.

14 He shot his arrows and scattered his
enemies;
with flashes of lightning he sent them
running.
15 The floor of the ocean was laid bare,
and the foundations of the earth were
uncovered,
when you rebuked your enemies, LORD,
and roared at them in anger.

16 The LORD reached down from above and
took hold of me;
he pulled me out of the deep waters.
17 He rescued me from my powerful
enemies
and from all those who hate me—
they were too strong for me.
18 When I was in trouble, they attacked me,
but the LORD protected me.
19 He helped me out of danger;
he saved me because he was pleased
with me.

20 The LORD rewards me because I do what
is right;
he blesses me because I am innocent.
21 I have obeyed the law of the LORD;
I have not turned away from my God.
22 I have observed all his laws;
I have not disobeyed his commands.
23 He knows that I am faultless,
that I have kept myself from doing
wrong.
24 And so he rewards me because I do what
is right,
because he knows that I am innocent.

25 O LORD, you are faithful to those who
are faithful to you;
completely good to those who are
perfect.
26 You are pure to those who are pure,
but hostile to those who are wicked.
27 You save those who are humble,
but you humble those who are
proud.

28 O LORD, you give me light;
you dispel my darkness.
29 You give me strength to attack my enemies
and power to overcome their defenses.

30 This God—how perfect are his deeds!
How dependable his words!
He is like a shield
for all who seek his protection.
31 The LORD alone is God;
God alone is our defense.
32 He is the God who makes me strong,
who makes my pathway safe.
33 He makes me sure-footed as a deer;
he keeps me safe on the mountains.
34 He trains me for battle,
so that I can use the strongest bow.

35 O LORD, you protect me and save me;
your care has made me great,
and your power has kept me safe.
36 You have kept me from being captured,
and I have never fallen.
37 I pursue my enemies and catch them;
I do not stop until I destroy them.
38 I strike them down, and they cannot rise;
they lie defeated before me.
39 You give me strength for the battle
and victory over my enemies.
40 You make my enemies run from me;
I destroy those who hate me.
41 They cry for help, but no one saves them;
they call to the LORD, but he does not
answer.
42 I crush them, so that they become like dust
which the wind blows away.
I trample on them like mud in the streets.

43 You saved me from a rebellious people
and made me ruler over the nations;
people I did not know have now
become my subjects.
44 Foreigners bow before me;
when they hear me, they obey.
45 They lose their courage
and come trembling from their
fortresses.

46 The LORD lives! Praise my defender!
Proclaim the greatness of the God who
saves me.

18:33 Hab 3:19

What do you know about King David? Read 2 Samuel 22:1–51 and then read Psalm 18.

[47] He gives me victory over my enemies;
he subdues the nations under me
[48] and saves me from my foes.
O LORD, you give me victory over my
enemies
and protect me from violent people.
[49] And so I praise you among the nations;
I sing praises to you.
[50] God gives great victories to his king;
he shows constant love to the one he
has chosen,
to David and his descendants forever.

God's Glory in Creation[a]

19 How clearly the sky reveals God's
glory!
How plainly it shows what he has
done!
[2] Each day announces it to the following
day;
each night repeats it to the next.
[3] No speech or words are used,
no sound is heard;
[4] yet their message[b] goes out to all the world
and is heard to the ends of the earth.
God made a home in the sky for the sun;
[5] it comes out in the morning like a
happy bridegroom,
like an athlete eager to run a race.
[6] It starts at one end of the sky
and goes across to the other.
Nothing can hide from its heat.

The Law of the LORD

[7] The law of the LORD is perfect;
it gives new strength.
The commands of the LORD are
trustworthy,
giving wisdom to those who lack it.
[8] The laws of the LORD are right,
and those who obey them are happy.
The commands of the LORD are just
and give understanding to the mind.
[9] Reverence for the LORD is good;
it will continue forever.
The judgments of the LORD are just;
they are always fair.

Study it!

Celebrating Saints

Catholics honor saints in many ways. Churches are named after them, statues are built in their honor, and we often take on a saint's name when we are confirmed. Most saints also have feast days, that is, a particular day on which they are remembered each year. On a saint's feast day, special Bible readings can be used at Masses celebrated in honor of the saint. Psalm 19 is the responsorial psalm chosen for saints Andrew, Simon, Jude, Matthew, Philip, and James, on each of their feast days.

What does Psalm 19 have to do with these saints? These saints were all Apostles who preached the gospel message to people who had not heard it. With this in mind, read Psalm 19. Do you see the connection?

If you are interested in a particular saint, you might want to read the Scripture readings chosen for his or her feast day. You can find the readings in a special book called the lectionary. Ask a priest, deacon, or other leader in your church to help you.

— Psalm 19

[10] They are more desirable than the finest
gold;
they are sweeter than the purest
honey.
[11] They give knowledge to me, your servant;
I am rewarded for obeying them.

[a] **19** HEBREW TITLE: *A psalm by David.* [b] **19:4** *Some ancient translations* message; *Hebrew* line.
18:49 Rom 15:9 **19:4** Rom 10:18

12 None of us can see our own errors;
deliver me, LORD, from hidden faults!
13 Keep me safe, also, from willful sins;
don't let them rule over me.
Then I shall be perfect
and free from the evil of sin.

14 May my words and my thoughts be
acceptable to you,
O LORD, my refuge and my redeemer!

A Prayer for Victory[c]

20 May the LORD answer you when
you are in trouble!
May the God of Jacob protect you!
2 May he send you help from his Temple
and give you aid from Mount
Zion.
3 May he accept all your offerings
and be pleased with all your sacrifices.
4 May he give you what you desire
and make all your plans succeed.
5 Then we will shout for joy over your
victory
and celebrate your triumph by praising
our God.
May the LORD answer all your requests.

6 Now I know that the LORD gives victory
to his chosen king;
he answers him from his holy heaven
and by his power gives him great
victories.
7 Some trust in their war chariots
and others in their horses,
but we trust in the power of the LORD
our God.
8 Such people will stumble and fall,
but we will rise and stand firm.

9 Give victory to the king, O LORD;
answer[d] us when we call.

Praise for Victory[e]

21 The king is glad, O LORD, because
you gave him strength;
he rejoices because you made him
victorious.
2 You have given him his heart's desire;
you have answered his request.

3 You came to him with great blessings
and set a crown of gold on his head.
4 He asked for life, and you gave it,
a long and lasting life.

5 His glory is great because of your help;
you have given him fame and majesty.
6 Your blessings are with him forever,
and your presence fills him with joy.

7 The king trusts in the LORD Almighty;
and because of the LORD's constant
love
he will always be secure.
8 The king will capture all his enemies;
he will capture everyone who hates him.
9 He will destroy them like a blazing fire
when he appears.

The LORD will devour them in his anger,
and fire will consume them.
10 None of their descendants will survive;
the king will kill them all.

11 They make their plans, and plot against
him,
but they will not succeed.
12 He will shoot his arrows at them
and make them turn and run.

13 We praise you, LORD, for your great
strength!
We will sing and praise your power.

A Cry of Anguish and a Song of Praise[e]

22 My God, my God, why have you
abandoned me?
I have cried desperately for help,
but still it does not come.
2 During the day I call to you, my God,
but you do not answer;
I call at night,
but get no rest.
3 But you are enthroned as the Holy One,
the one whom Israel praises.
4 Our ancestors put their trust in you;
they trusted you, and you saved them.

[c] **20** HEBREW TITLE: *A psalm by David.* [d] **20:9** *Some ancient translations* answer; *Hebrew* he will answer.
[e] **21; 22** HEBREW TITLE: *A psalm by David.*
22:1 Mt 27:46; Mk 15:34

5 They called to you and escaped from
danger;
they trusted you and were not
disappointed.

6 But I am no longer a human being; I am
a worm,
despised and scorned by everyone!
7 All who see me make fun of me;
they stick out their tongues and shake
their heads.
8 "You relied on the LORD," they say.
"Why doesn't he save you?
If the LORD likes you,
why doesn't he help you?"

9 It was you who brought me safely
through birth,
and when I was a baby, you kept me
safe.
10 I have relied on you since the day I was
born,
and you have always been my God.
11 Do not stay away from me!
Trouble is near,
and there is no one to help.

12 Many enemies surround me like bulls;
they are all around me,
like fierce bulls from the land of
Bashan.
13 They open their mouths like lions,
roaring and tearing at me.

14 My strength is gone,
gone like water spilled on the ground.
All my bones are out of joint;
my heart is like melted wax.
15 My throat[f] is as dry as dust,
and my tongue sticks to the roof of my
mouth.
You have left me for dead in the dust.

16 An evil gang is around me;
like a pack of dogs they close in on
me;
they tear at[g] my hands and feet.

Study it!

Jesus and the Psalms

"My God, my God, why have you abandoned me?"

These are words from Psalm 22 that Jesus cried out from the cross. It is not surprising that the Psalms were part of Jesus' last prayer. He prayed the Psalms his whole life. When he was baptized, a voice from heaven proclaimed words that sound a lot like Psalm 2, "This is my own dear Son, with whom I am pleased" (Matthew 3:17). Jesus knew a lot of Scripture by heart. His parents and rabbis prayed with him and taught him the Psalms. We can imagine him turning to the Psalms, both in times of joy and sorrow. Maybe you will find some psalms that you want to memorize and pray.

— Psalm 22

17 All my bones can be seen.
My enemies look at me and stare.
18 They gamble for my clothes
and divide them among themselves.

19 O LORD, don't stay away from me!
Come quickly to my rescue!
20 Save me from the sword;
save my life from these dogs.
21 Rescue me from these lions;
I am helpless[h] before these wild bulls.

22 I will tell my people what you have done;
I will praise you in their assembly:

[f] **22:15** *Probable text* throat; *Hebrew* strength. [g] **22:16** *Some ancient translations* they tear at; *others* they tie; *Hebrew* like a lion. [h] **22:21** *Some ancient translations* I am helpless; *Hebrew* you answered me.
22:7 Mt 27:39; Mk 15:29; Lk 23:35 **22:8** Mt 27:43 **22:18** Mt 27:35; Mk 15:24; Lk 23:34; Jn 19:24
22:22 Heb 2:12

Read Psalm 22 and see how it moves from hopelessness to praising God.

23 "Praise him, you servants of the LORD!
Honor him, you descendants of Jacob!
Worship him, you people of Israel!
24 He does not neglect the poor or ignore their suffering;
he does not turn away from them,
but answers when they call for help."

25 In the full assembly I will praise you for what you have done;
in the presence of those who worship you
I will offer the sacrifices I promised.
26 The poor will eat as much as they want;
those who come to the LORD will praise him.
May they prosper forever!
27 All nations will remember the LORD.
From every part of the world they will turn to him;
all races will worship him.
28 The LORD is king,
and he rules the nations.
29 All proud people will bow down to him;[i]
all mortals will bow down before him.
30 Future generations will serve him;
they will speak of the Lord to the coming generation.
31 People not yet born will be told:
"The Lord saved his people."

The LORD Our Shepherd[j]

23 The LORD is my shepherd;
I have everything I need.
2 He lets me rest in fields of green grass
and leads me to quiet pools of fresh water.
3 He gives me new strength.
He guides me in the right paths,
as he has promised.
4 Even if I go through the deepest darkness,
I will not be afraid, LORD,
for you are with me.
Your shepherd's rod and staff protect me.

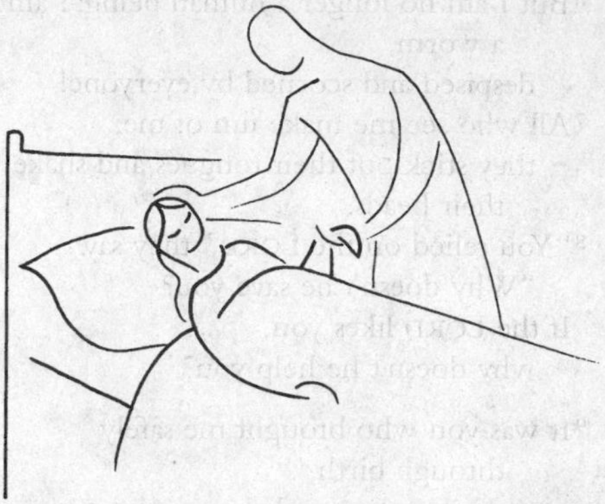

Even if I go through the deepest darkness . . . (23:4)

5 You prepare a banquet for me,
where all my enemies can see me;
you welcome me as an honored guest
and fill my cup to the brim.
6 I know that your goodness and love will be with me all my life;
and your house will be my home as long as I live.

The Great King[j]

24 The world and all that is in it belong to the LORD;
the earth and all who live on it are his.
2 He built it on the deep waters beneath the earth
and laid its foundations in the ocean depths.

3 Who has the right to go up the LORD's hill?[k]
Who may enter his holy Temple?
4 Those who are pure in act and in thought,
who do not worship idols
or make false promises.

[i] **22:29** *Probable text* will bow down to him; *Hebrew* will eat and bow down. [j] **23; 24** HEBREW TITLE: *A psalm by David.* [k] **24:3** THE LORD'S HILL: *The hill in Jerusalem on which the Temple was built.*
23:2 Rev 7:17 **24:1** 1 Cor 10:26 **24:4** Mt 5:8

"The world and all that is in it belong to the LORD; / the earth and all who live on it are his" *(Psalm 24:1)*.

Pray it!

I Trust in You

Psalm 25 is a prayer of trust in God, like this one.

This prayer is for you, God.
You teach me, and I trust in you.
Sometimes I mess up.
I did when I was little, and still do.
You loved me through it all.
Because you are awesome,
you show me what to do, and
I try to do what is good.
I turn to you for help, and
you help me not worry.
I trust in you.
You protect me and keep me safe.
I trust in you.

— Psalm 25

5 The LORD will bless them and save them;
God will declare them innocent.
6 Such are the people who come to God,
who come into the presence of the God of Jacob.

7 Fling wide the gates,
open the ancient doors,
and the great king will come in.
8 Who is this great king?
He is the LORD, strong and mighty,
the LORD, victorious in battle.

9 Fling wide the gates,
open the ancient doors,
and the great king will come in.
10 Who is this great king?
The LORD Almighty—he is the great king!

A Prayer for Guidance and Protection[l]

25 To you, O LORD, I offer my prayer;
2 in you, my God, I trust.
Save me from the shame of defeat;
don't let my enemies gloat over me!
3 Defeat does not come to those who trust in you,
but to those who are quick to rebel against you.

4 Teach me your ways, O LORD;
make them known to me.
5 Teach me to live according to your truth,
for you are my God, who saves me.
I always trust in you.

6 Remember, O LORD, your kindness and constant love
which you have shown from long ago.
7 Forgive the sins and errors of my youth.
In your constant love and goodness,
remember me, LORD!

8 Because the LORD is righteous and good,
he teaches sinners the path they should follow.
9 He leads the humble in the right way
and teaches them his will.
10 With faithfulness and love he leads
all who keep his covenant and obey his commands.

[l] 25 HEBREW TITLE: *By David.*

11 Keep your promise, LORD, and forgive my
sins,
for they are many.
12 Those who have reverence for the LORD
will learn from him the path they
should follow.
13 They will always be prosperous,
and their children will possess the land.
14 The LORD is the friend of those who
obey him
and he affirms his covenant with them.

15 I look to the LORD for help at all times,
and he rescues me from danger.
16 Turn to me, LORD, and be merciful to
me,
because I am lonely and weak.
17 Relieve me of my worries
and save me from all my troubles.
18 Consider my distress and suffering
and forgive all my sins.
19 See how many enemies I have;
see how much they hate me.
20 Protect me and save me;
keep me from defeat.
I come to you for safety.
21 May my goodness and honesty preserve
me,
because I trust in you.

22 From all their troubles, O God,
save your people Israel!

The Prayer of a Good Person[l]

26 Declare me innocent, O LORD,
because I do what is right
and trust you completely.
2 Examine me and test me, LORD;
judge my desires and thoughts.
3 Your constant love is my guide;
your faithfulness always leads me.[m]

4 I do not keep company with worthless
people;
I have nothing to do with hypocrites.
5 I hate the company of the evil
and avoid the wicked.

6 LORD, I wash my hands to show that I am
innocent
and march in worship around your
altar.
7 I sing a hymn of thanksgiving
and tell of all your wonderful deeds.

8 I love the house where you live, O LORD,
the place where your glory dwells.
9 Do not destroy me with the sinners;
spare me from the fate of murderers—
10 those who do evil all the time
and are always ready to take bribes.

11 As for me, I do what is right;
be merciful to me and save me!

12 I am safe from all dangers;
in the assembly of his people I praise
the LORD.

A Prayer of Praise[n]

27 The LORD is my light and my
salvation;
I will fear no one.
The LORD protects me from all danger;
I will never be afraid.

2 When evil people attack me and try to
kill me,
they stumble and fall.
3 Even if a whole army surrounds me,
I will not be afraid;
even if enemies attack me,
I will still trust God.[o]

4 I have asked the LORD for one thing;
one thing only do I want:
to live in the LORD's house all my
life,
to marvel there at his goodness,
and to ask for his guidance.
5 In times of trouble he will shelter me;
he will keep me safe in his Temple
and make me secure on a high rock.
6 So I will triumph over my enemies
around me.
With shouts of joy I will offer sacrifices
in his Temple;
I will sing, I will praise the LORD.

7 Hear me, LORD, when I call to you!
Be merciful and answer me!
8 When you said, "Come worship me,"

[l] **26** HEBREW TITLE: *By David.* [m] **26:3** your faithfulness always leads me; *or* I live in loyalty to you.
[n] **27** HEBREW TITLE: *By David.* [o] **27:3** still trust God; *or* not lose courage.

I answered, "I will come, LORD."
9 Don't hide yourself from me!

Don't be angry with me;
don't turn your servant away.
You have been my help;
don't leave me, don't abandon me,
O God, my savior.
10 My father and mother may abandon me,
but the LORD will take care of me.

11 Teach me, LORD, what you want me to do,
and lead me along a safe path,
because I have many enemies.
12 Don't abandon me to my enemies,
who attack me with lies and threats.

13 I know that I will live to see
the LORD's goodness in this present life.
14 Trust in the LORD.
Have faith, do not despair.
Trust in the LORD.

A Prayer for Help[p]

28 O LORD, my defender, I call to you.
Listen to my cry!
If you do not answer me,
I will be among those who go down to the world of the dead.
2 Hear me when I cry to you for help,
when I lift my hands toward your holy Temple.
3 Do not condemn me with the wicked,
with those who do evil—
those whose words are friendly,
but who have hatred in their hearts.
4 Punish them for what they have done,
for the evil they have committed.
Punish them for all their deeds;
give them what they deserve!
5 They take no notice of what the LORD has done
or of what he has made;
so he will punish them
and destroy them forever.

6 Give praise to the LORD;
he has heard my cry for help.
7 The LORD protects and defends me;
I trust in him.
He gives me help and makes me glad;
I praise him with joyful songs.

8 The LORD protects his people;
he defends and saves his chosen king.
9 Save your people, LORD,
and bless those who are yours.
Be their shepherd,
and take care of them forever.

The Voice of the LORD in the Storm[q]

29 Praise the LORD, you heavenly beings;
praise his glory and power.
2 Praise the LORD's glorious name;
bow down before the Holy One when he appears.[r]

3 The voice of the LORD is heard on the seas;
the glorious God thunders,
and his voice echoes over the ocean.
4 The voice of the LORD is heard
in all its might and majesty.
5 The voice of the LORD breaks the cedars,
even the cedars of Lebanon.
6 He makes the mountains of Lebanon jump like calves
and makes Mount Hermon leap like a young bull.

7 The voice of the LORD makes the lightning flash.
8 His voice makes the desert shake;
he shakes the desert of Kadesh.
9 The LORD's voice shakes the oaks[s]
and strips the leaves from the trees
while everyone in his Temple shouts,
"Glory to God!"

[p] **28** HEBREW TITLE: *By David.* [q] **29** HEBREW TITLE: *A psalm by David.* [r] **29:2** when he appears; *or* in garments of worship; *or* in his beautiful Temple. [s] **29:9** *Probable text* shakes the oaks; *Hebrew* makes the deer give birth.

28:4 Rev 22:12 **29:1, 2** Ps 96:7–9

How many of the qualities in Psalm 26 do you have?

10 The LORD rules over the deep waters;
he rules as king forever.
11 The LORD gives strength to his people
and blesses them with peace.

A Prayer of Thanksgiving[t]

30 I praise you, LORD, because you
have saved me
and kept my enemies from gloating
over me.
2 I cried to you for help, O LORD my God,
and you healed me;
3 you kept me from the grave.
I was on my way to the depths below,[u]
but you restored my life.

4 Sing praise to the LORD,
all his faithful people!
Remember what the Holy One has done,
and give him thanks!
5 His anger lasts only a moment,
his goodness for a lifetime.
Tears may flow in the night,
but joy comes in the morning.

6 I felt secure and said to myself,
"I will never be defeated."
7 You were good to me, LORD;
you protected me like a mountain
fortress.
But then you hid yourself from me,
and I was afraid.
8 I called to you, LORD;
I begged for your help:
9 "What will you gain from my death?
What profit from my going to the grave?
Are dead people able to praise you?
Can they proclaim your unfailing
goodness?
10 Hear me, LORD, and be merciful!
Help me, LORD!"

11 You have changed my sadness into a
joyful dance;
you have taken away my sorrow
and surrounded me with joy.

Live it!

Turning Sadness to Joy

It was Jill's first swim meet, and she was really nervous. She dove in right after the gun went off and swam as fast as she could. She missed her turn, but when she finished, she looked around and no one else was at the edge. "I won!" she thought, then looked to see the rest swimming in. No one was behind her; they had all finished and gotten out of the pool. Embarrassed, she got out of the pool and wanted to disappear.

The next week she almost didn't go to practice, but something told her to go. She went back that week and the next and the next. She practiced her turns each time she went to practice, even if it wasn't a drill.

It was time for her second meet. This time, she didn't finish last and even got out of the pool at the same time as the rest of the heat. By the end of the season, she had won two ribbons—a third place and a second place. The next season she started winning blue ribbons and even a medal in championships. She was so happy, she could barely remember that first meet. The end of Psalm 30 was her motto: "You have changed my sadness into a joyful dance; / you have taken away my sorrow / and surrounded me with joy" (verse 11).

— Psalm 30

[t] **30** HEBREW TITLE: *A song for the dedication of the Temple; a psalm by David.* [u] **30:3** THE DEPTHS BELOW: *The world of the dead (see 6:5).*

Who do you turn to when you need protection? Check out the beginning of Psalm 31 to see who the psalmist turns to.

12 So I will not be silent;
I will sing praise to you.
LORD, you are my God;
I will give you thanks forever.

A Prayer of Trust in God[v]

31 I come to you, LORD, for protection;
never let me be defeated.
You are a righteous God;
save me, I pray!
2 Hear me! Save me now!
Be my refuge to protect me;
my defense to save me.

3 You are my refuge and defense;
guide me and lead me as you have promised.
4 Keep me safe from the trap that has been set for me;
shelter me from danger.
5 I place myself in your care.
You will save me, LORD;
you are a faithful God.

6 You hate those who worship false gods,
but I trust in you.
7 I will be glad and rejoice
because of your constant love.
You see my suffering;
you know my trouble.
8 You have not let my enemies capture me;
you have given me freedom to go where I wish.

9 Be merciful to me, LORD,
for I am in trouble;
my eyes are tired from so much crying;
I am completely worn out.
10 I am exhausted by sorrow,
and weeping has shortened my life.
I am weak from all my troubles;[w]
even my bones are wasting away.

11 All my enemies, and especially my neighbors,
treat me with contempt.
Those who know me are afraid of me;
when they see me in the street, they run away.
12 Everyone has forgotten me, as though I were dead;
I am like something thrown away.
13 I hear many enemies whispering;
terror is all around me.
They are making plans against me,
plotting to kill me.

14 But my trust is in you, O LORD;
you are my God.
15 I am always in your care;
save me from my enemies,
from those who persecute me.
16 Look on your servant with kindness;
save me in your constant love.
17 I call to you, LORD;
don't let me be disgraced.
May the wicked be disgraced;
may they go silently down to the world of the dead.
18 Silence those liars—
all the proud and arrogant
who speak with contempt about the righteous.

19 How wonderful are the good things
you keep for those who honor you!
Everyone knows how good you are,
how securely you protect those who trust you.
20 You hide them in the safety of your presence
from the plots of others;
in a safe shelter you hide them
from the insults of their enemies.

21 Praise the LORD!
How wonderfully he showed his love for me
when I was surrounded and attacked!
22 I was afraid and thought
that he had driven me out of his presence.
But he heard my cry,
when I called to him for help.

23 Love the LORD, all his faithful people.
The LORD protects the faithful,
but punishes the proud as they deserve.
24 Be strong, be courageous,
all you that hope in the LORD.

[v] **31** HEBREW TITLE: *A psalm by David.* [w] **31:10** *Some ancient translations* troubles; *Hebrew* iniquity.

31:5 Lk 23:46

Trinity Sunday

On the Sunday after Pentecost, the Catholic Church celebrates Trinity Sunday. As part of the Mass that Sunday, sometimes the responsorial psalm is from Psalm 33: "Blessed the people the Lord has chosen to be his own." All three persons of the Holy Trinity—Father, Son, and Holy Spirit—make God's love known. They are the one, true God, the God who chooses all people to be his own. If we take Psalm 33 to heart, we will respond by praising, worshiping, and thanking God.

— Psalm 33

Catholic Connections

Confession and Forgiveness[x]

32 Happy are those whose sins are
forgiven,
whose wrongs are pardoned.
2 Happy is the one whom the LORD does
not accuse of doing wrong
and who is free from all deceit.
3 When I did not confess my sins,
I was worn out from crying all day
long.
4 Day and night you punished me, LORD;
my strength was completely drained,
as moisture is dried up by the summer
heat.
5 Then I confessed my sins to you;
I did not conceal my wrongdoings.
I decided to confess them to you,
and you forgave all my sins.
6 So all your loyal people should pray to
you in times of need;[y]
when a great flood of trouble comes
rushing in,
it will not reach them.
7 You are my hiding place;
you will save me from trouble.
I sing aloud of your salvation,
because you protect me.
8 The LORD says, "I will teach you the way
you should go;
I will instruct you and advise you.
9 Don't be stupid like a horse or a mule,
which must be controlled with a bit
and bridle
to make it submit."
10 The wicked will have to suffer,
but those who trust in the LORD
are protected by his constant love.
11 You that are righteous, be glad and rejoice
because of what the LORD has done.
You that obey him, shout for joy!

A Song of Praise

33 All you that are righteous,
shout for joy for what the LORD
has done;
praise him, all you that obey him.
2 Give thanks to the LORD with harps,
sing to him with stringed instruments.
3 Sing a new song to him,
play the harp with skill, and shout for
joy!
4 The words of the LORD are true,
and all his works are dependable.
5 The LORD loves what is righteous and
just;
his constant love fills the earth.
6 The LORD created the heavens by his
command,
the sun, moon, and stars by his spoken
word.

[x] **32** HEBREW TITLE: *A poem by David.* [y] **32:6** *Some ancient translations* need; *Hebrew* finding only.

32:1, 2 Rom 4:7, 8

7 He gathered all the seas into one place;
he shut up the ocean depths in storerooms.

8 Worship the LORD, all the earth!
Honor him, all peoples of the world!
9 When he spoke, the world was created;
at his command everything appeared.

10 The LORD frustrates the purposes of the nations;
he keeps them from carrying out their plans.
11 But his plans endure forever;
his purposes last eternally.
12 Happy is the nation whose God is the LORD;
happy are the people he has chosen for his own!

13 The LORD looks down from heaven
and sees all of us humans.
14 From where he rules, he looks down
on all who live on earth.
15 He forms all their thoughts
and knows everything they do.

16 A king does not win because of his powerful army;
a soldier does not triumph because of his strength.
17 War horses are useless for victory;
their great strength cannot save.

18 The LORD watches over those who obey him,
those who trust in his constant love.
19 He saves them from death;
he keeps them alive in times of famine.

20 We put our hope in the LORD;
he is our protector and our help.
21 We are glad because of him;
we trust in his holy name.

22 May your constant love be with us, LORD,
as we put our hope in you.

In Praise of God's Goodness[z]

34 I will always thank the LORD;
I will never stop praising him.
2 I will praise him for what he has done;
may all who are oppressed listen and be glad!
3 Proclaim with me the LORD's greatness;
let us praise his name together!

4 I prayed to the LORD, and he answered me;
he freed me from all my fears.
5 The oppressed look to him and are glad;
they will never be disappointed.
6 The helpless call to him, and he answers;
he saves them from all their troubles.
7 His angel guards those who honor the LORD
and rescues them from danger.

8 Find out for yourself how good the LORD is.
Happy are those who find safety with him.
9 Honor the LORD, all his people;
those who obey him have all they need.
10 Even lions go hungry for lack of food,
but those who obey the LORD lack nothing good.

11 Come, my young friends, and listen to me,
and I will teach you to honor the LORD.
12 Would you like to enjoy life?
Do you want long life and happiness?
13 Then keep from speaking evil
and from telling lies.
14 Turn away from evil and do good;
strive for peace with all your heart.

15 The LORD watches over the righteous
and listens to their cries;
16 but he opposes those who do evil,
so that when they die, they are soon forgotten.

[z] **34** HEBREW TITLE: *By David, who left the presence of Abimelech after pretending to be crazy and being sent away by him.*

33:16 Jdt 9:7; 1 Macc 3:19 **34 Title** 1 Sam 21:13–15 **34:8** 1 Pet 2:3 **34:12–16** 1 Pet 3:10–12

Which is greater, the time you spend asking God for things, or the time you spend praising God? According to Psalm 34, which should be greater?

17 The righteous call to the LORD, and he
listens;
he rescues them from all their troubles.
18 The LORD is near to those who are
discouraged;
he saves those who have lost all hope.

19 Good people suffer many troubles,
but the LORD saves them from them
all;
20 the LORD preserves them completely;
not one of their bones is broken.
21 Evil will kill the wicked;
those who hate the righteous will be
punished.
22 The LORD will save his people;
those who go to him for protection
will be spared.

A Prayer for Help[a]

35 Oppose those who oppose me,
LORD,
and fight those who fight against me!
2 Take your shield and armor
and come to my rescue.
3 Lift up your spear and war ax
against those who pursue me.
Promise that you will save me.

4 May those who try to kill me
be defeated and disgraced!
May those who plot against me
be turned back and confused!
5 May they be like straw blown by the
wind
as the angel of the LORD pursues them!
6 May their path be dark and slippery
while the angel of the LORD strikes
them down!

7 Without any reason they laid a trap for me
and dug a deep hole to catch me.
8 But destruction will catch them before
they know it;
they will be caught in their own trap
and fall to their destruction!

9 Then I will be glad because of the LORD;
I will be happy because he saved me.
10 With all my heart I will say to the LORD,
"There is no one like you.
You protect the weak from the strong,
the poor from the oppressor."

11 Evil people testify against me
and accuse me of crimes I know
nothing about.
12 They pay me back evil for good,
and I sink in despair.
13 But when they were sick, I dressed in
mourning;
I deprived myself of food;
I prayed with my head bowed low,
14 as I would pray for a friend or a
brother.
I went around bent over in mourning,
as one who mourns for his mother.

15 But when I was in trouble, they were all
glad
and gathered around to make fun of me;
strangers beat me
and kept striking me.
16 Like those who would mock a cripple,[b]
they glared at me with hate.

17 How much longer, Lord, will you just
look on?
Rescue me from their attacks;
save my life from these lions!
18 Then I will thank you in the assembly of
your people;
I will praise you before them all.

19 Don't let my enemies, those liars,
gloat over my defeat.
Don't let those who hate me for no
reason
smirk with delight over my sorrow.
20 They do not speak in a friendly way;
instead they invent all kinds of lies
about peace-loving people.
21 They accuse me, shouting,
"We saw what you did!"

[a] **35** HEBREW TITLE: *By David.* [b] **35:16** *Probable text* Like those . . . cripple; *Hebrew unclear.*

34:20 Jn 19:36 **35:19** Ps 69:4; Jn 15:25

Read Psalm 36:6. Isn't it nice to know that animals are under God's care?

22 But you, O LORD, have seen this.
So don't be silent, Lord;
don't keep yourself far away!
23 Rouse yourself, O Lord, and defend me;
rise up, my God, and plead my cause.
24 You are righteous, O LORD, so declare me innocent;
don't let my enemies gloat over me.
25 Don't let them say to themselves,
"We are rid of him!
That's just what we wanted!"
26 May those who gloat over my suffering
be completely defeated and confused;
may those who claim to be better than I am
be covered with shame and disgrace.
27 May those who want to see me acquitted
shout for joy and say again and again,
"How great is the LORD!
He is pleased with the success of his servant."
28 Then I will proclaim your righteousness,
and I will praise you all day long.

Human Wickedness[c]

36 Sin speaks to the wicked deep in their hearts;
they reject God and do not have reverence for him.
2 Because they think so highly of themselves,
they think that God will not discover their sin and condemn it.
3 Their speech is wicked and full of lies;
they no longer do what is wise and good.
4 They make evil plans as they lie in bed;
nothing they do is good,
and they never reject anything evil.

The Goodness of God

5 LORD, your constant love reaches the heavens;
your faithfulness extends to the skies.
6 Your righteousness is towering like the mountains;
your justice is like the depths of the sea.
People and animals are in your care.

7 How precious, O God, is your constant love!
We find[d] protection under the shadow of your wings.
8 We feast on the abundant food you provide;
you let us drink from the river of your goodness.
9 You are the source of all life,
and because of your light we see the light.

10 Continue to love those who know you
and to do good to those who are righteous.
11 Do not let proud people attack me
or the wicked make me run away.
12 See where evil people have fallen.
There they lie, unable to rise.

The Destiny of the Wicked and of the Good[e]

37 Don't be worried on account of the wicked;
don't be jealous of those who do wrong.
2 They will soon disappear like grass that dries up;
they will die like plants that wither.

3 Trust in the LORD and do good;
live in the land and be safe.
4 Seek your happiness in the LORD,
and he will give you your heart's desire.

5 Give yourself to the LORD;
trust in him, and he will help you;
6 he will make your righteousness shine like the noonday sun.

7 Be patient and wait for the LORD to act;
don't be worried about those who prosper
or those who succeed in their evil plans.

[c] **36** HEBREW TITLE: *By David, the LORD's servant.* [d] **36:7** precious, O God, is . . . find; *or* precious is your constant love! Gods and people find. [e] **37** HEBREW TITLE: *By David.*

36:1 Rom 3:18

Live it!

Cheaters!

"I can't stand it when they cheat; they mess the curve up and make the rest of us look bad," Noah complained to his friends. When tests came back in history, it was obvious that a group of kids had cheated.

"It almost makes me want to cheat too, just to get the grades," Greg answered.

"Yeah, they're getting a movie day, and we have to study on Friday. No fair," Elliot added.

"It's not worth it," Noah tried to calm them a little. "Besides, haven't you ever heard, 'Cheaters never prosper'? I wish I could tell Mr. Shimkis, but I don't have proof!"

"Yeah, I guess there is a chance they'll get caught," Greg said.

"You know, I read a psalm today that said, 'The Lord loves what is right / and does not abandon his faithful people' (Psalm 37:28). We just have to study and do our best. That's what's important," Elliot said.

"Yeah, and let's get a giant order of fries, to help us study!" Noah added.

— Psalm 37

8 Don't give in to worry or anger;
it only leads to trouble.
9 Those who trust in the LORD will possess the land,
but the wicked will be driven out.
10 Soon the wicked will disappear;
you may look for them, but you won't find them;
11 but the humble will possess the land
and enjoy prosperity and peace.
12 The wicked plot against good people
and glare at them with hate.
13 But the Lord laughs at wicked people,
because he knows they will soon be destroyed.
14 The wicked draw their swords and bend their bows
to kill the poor and needy,
to slaughter those who do what is right;
15 but they will be killed by their own swords,
and their bows will be smashed.
16 The little that a good person owns
is worth more than the wealth of all the wicked,
17 because the LORD will take away the strength of the wicked,
but protect those who are good.
18 The LORD takes care of those who obey him,
and the land will be theirs forever.
19 They will not suffer when times are bad;
they will have enough in time of famine.
20 But the wicked will die;
the enemies of the LORD will vanish like wild flowers;
they will disappear like smoke.
21 The wicked borrow and never pay back,
but good people are generous with their gifts.
22 Those who are blessed by the LORD will possess the land,
but those who are cursed by him will be driven out.
23 The LORD guides us in the way we should go
and protects those who please him.
24 If they fall, they will not stay down,
because the LORD will help them up.
25 I am old now; I have lived a long time,
but I have never seen good people abandoned by the LORD
or their children begging for food.

37:11 Mt 5:5

26 At all times they give freely and lend to
others,
and their children are a blessing.

27 Turn away from evil and do good,
and your descendants will always live in
the land;
28 for the LORD loves what is right
and does not abandon his faithful
people.
He protects them forever,
but the descendants of the wicked will
be driven out.
29 The righteous will possess the land
and live in it forever.

30 The words of good people are wise,
and they are always fair.
31 They keep the law of their God in their
hearts
and never depart from it.

32 Wicked people watch good people
and try to kill them;
33 but the LORD will not abandon them to
their enemy's power
or let them be condemned when they
are on trial.

34 Put your hope in the LORD and obey his
commands;
he will honor you by giving you the
land,
and you will see the wicked driven
out.

35 I once knew someone wicked who was a
tyrant;
he towered over everyone like a cedar
of Lebanon;[f]
36 but later I[g] passed by, and he wasn't there;
I looked for him, but couldn't find
him.

37 Notice good people, observe the
righteous;
peaceful people have descendants,
38 but sinners are completely destroyed,
and their descendants are wiped out.

39 The LORD saves the righteous
and protects them in times of trouble.
40 He helps them and rescues them;
he saves them from the wicked,
because they go to him for protection.

The Prayer of a Sufferer[h]

38 O LORD, don't punish me in your
anger!
2 You have wounded me with your arrows;
you have struck me down.

3 Because of your anger, I am in great pain;
my whole body is diseased because of
my sins.
4 I am drowning in the flood of my sins;
they are a burden too heavy to bear.

5 Because I have been foolish,
my sores stink and rot.
6 I am bent over, I am crushed;
I mourn all day long.
7 I am burning with fever
and I am near death.
8 I am worn out and utterly crushed;
my heart is troubled, and I groan with
pain.

9 O Lord, you know what I long for;
you hear all my groans.
10 My heart is pounding, my strength is
gone,
and my eyes have lost their brightness.
11 My friends and neighbors will not come
near me,
because of my sores;
even my family keeps away from me.
12 Those who want to kill me lay traps for
me,
and those who want to hurt me
threaten to ruin me;
they never stop plotting against me.

13 I am like the deaf and cannot hear,
like the dumb and cannot speak.
14 I am like those who do not answer,
because they cannot hear.

[f] **37:35** *One ancient translation* like a cedar of Lebanon; *Hebrew unclear.* [g] **37:36** *Some ancient translations* I; *Hebrew* he. [h] **38** HEBREW TITLE: *A psalm by David; a lament.*

Think of someone you know who is good. What does he or she do that makes you know that? How does it feel to be with that person?

Pray it!

Live Through This

Young people around the world have suffered like the writer of Psalm 38. Here is a poem from a 13-year-old Rwandan-born girl who lost many of her relatives when one tribe of people tried to kill everyone who belonged to a different tribe.

A once peaceful land
With loving neighbors and friends
Torn apart by war.
A saddening event
Too horrible to accept
Yet, it's not the first.
The world shuts them out
A country with such beauty
Now filled with anger
So much bitterness
My heart is soaked with sadness
For I lost so much.
My roots forgotten
The cousins I never met
All ripped apart by hatred.
My blood, family, roots
All lost over ignorance
The Tutsis tortured.
Betrayed by their friends
In their homes, churches and towns
Hiding in horror.
What is our next step?
To regain humanity
Compassion . . . and love?
Is it possible?
Or is it lost forever?
My pride is not lost.

— Psalm 38

(Valerie N. Piraino, Catholic Relief Services)

15 But I trust in you, O LORD;
and you, O Lord my God, will answer me.
16 Don't let my enemies gloat over my distress;
don't let them boast about my downfall!
17 I am about to fall
and am in constant pain.
18 I confess my sins;
they fill me with anxiety.
19 My enemies are healthy and strong;
there are many who hate me for no reason.
20 Those who pay back evil for good
are against me because I try to do right.
21 Do not abandon me, O LORD;
do not stay away, my God!
22 Help me now, O Lord my savior!

The Confession of a Sufferer[i]

39 I said, "I will be careful about what I do
and will not let my tongue make me sin;
I will not say anything
while evil people are near."
2 I kept quiet, not saying a word,
not even about anything good!
But my suffering only grew worse,
3 and I was overcome with anxiety.
The more I thought, the more troubled I became;
I could not keep from asking:
4 "LORD, how long will I live?
When will I die?
Tell me how soon my life will end."
5 How short you have made my life!
In your sight my lifetime seems nothing.
Indeed every living being is no more than a puff of wind,

[i] **39** HEBREW TITLE: *A psalm by David.*

Read Psalm 40:4–11. What does the psalmist suggest that God asks of us?

6 no more than a shadow.
All we do is for nothing;
we gather wealth, but don't know who will get it.

7 What, then, can I hope for, Lord?
I put my hope in you.
8 Save me from all my sins,
and don't let fools make fun of me.
9 I will keep quiet, I will not say a word,
for you are the one who made me suffer like this.
10 Don't punish me any more!
I am about to die from your blows.
11 You punish our sins by your rebukes,
and like a moth you destroy what we love.
Indeed we are no more than a puff of wind!

12 Hear my prayer, LORD,
and listen to my cry;
come to my aid when I weep.
Like all my ancestors
I am only your guest for a little while.
13 Leave me alone so that I may have some happiness
before I go away and am no more.

A Song of Praise[i]

40 I waited patiently for the LORD's help;
then he listened to me and heard my cry.
2 He pulled me out of a dangerous pit,
out of the deadly quicksand.
He set me safely on a rock
and made me secure.
3 He taught me to sing a new song,
a song of praise to our God.
Many who see this will take warning
and will put their trust in the LORD.

4 Happy are those who trust the LORD,
who do not turn to idols
or join those who worship false gods.
5 You have done many things for us,
O LORD our God;
there is no one like you!
You have made many wonderful plans for us.
I could never speak of them all—
their number is so great!

6 You do not want sacrifices and offerings;
you do not ask for animals burned whole on the altar
or for sacrifices to take away sins.
Instead, you have given me ears to hear you,
7 and so I answered, "Here I am;
your instructions for me are in the book of the Law.[j]
8 How I love to do your will, my God!
I keep your teaching in my heart."

9 In the assembly of all your people, LORD,
I told the good news that you save us.
You know that I will never stop telling it.

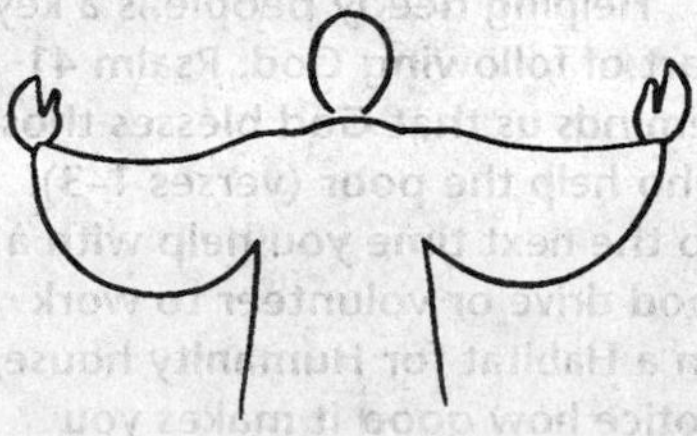

I told the good news. (40:9)

10 I have not kept the news of salvation to myself;
I have always spoken of your faithfulness and help.
In the assembly of all your people I have not been silent
about your loyalty and constant love.

11 LORD, I know you will never stop being merciful to me.
Your love and loyalty will always keep me safe.

A Prayer for Help
(Psalm 70)

12 I am surrounded by many troubles—
too many to count!

[i] **40** HEBREW TITLE: *A psalm by David.* [j] **40:7** your instructions . . . Law; *or* my devotion to you is recorded in your book.

40:6–8 Heb 10:5–7

Live it!

You Want Me to Do What?

If you have poor or homeless people in your community, you may think they look dirty or are weird. Maybe they haven't had a shower for a while. It is hard to shower when you don't have a place to live. (Some homeless people try to use public restroom sinks to get clean.) Some homeless people have mental illnesses that make it hard for them to keep a job and own a home. But they are children of God, just like you and your parents and your friends.

Helping needy people is a key part of following God. Psalm 41 reminds us that God blesses those who help the poor (verses 1–3). So the next time you help with a food drive or volunteer to work on a Habitat for Humanity house, notice how good it makes you feel.

— Psalm 41:1–3

My sins have caught up with me,
and I can no longer see;
they are more than the hairs of my head,
and I have lost my courage.
13 Save me, LORD! Help me now!
14 May those who try to kill me
be completely defeated and confused.
May those who are happy because of my troubles
be turned back and disgraced.
15 May those who make fun of me
be dismayed by their defeat.

16 May all who come to you
be glad and joyful.
May all who are thankful for your salvation
always say, "How great is the LORD!"

17 I am weak and poor, O Lord,
but you have not forgotten me.
You are my savior and my God—
hurry to my aid!

A Prayer in Sickness[k]

41 Happy are those who are concerned for the poor;
the LORD will help them when they are in trouble.
2 The LORD will protect them and preserve their lives;
he will make them happy in the land;
he will not abandon them to the power of their enemies.
3 The LORD will help them when they are sick
and will restore them to health.

4 I said, "I have sinned against you, LORD;
be merciful to me and heal me."
5 My enemies say cruel things about me.
They want me to die and be forgotten.
6 Those who come to see me are not sincere;
they gather bad news about me
and then go out and tell it everywhere.
7 All who hate me whisper to each other about me,
they imagine the worst about[l] me.
8 They say, "He is fatally ill;
he will never leave his bed again."
9 Even my best friend, the one I trusted most,
the one who shared my food,
has turned against me.

10 Be merciful to me, LORD, and restore my health,
and I will pay my enemies back.
11 They will not triumph over me,
and I will know that you are pleased with me.

[k] **41** HEBREW TITLE: *A psalm by David.* [l] **41:7** imagine the worst about; *or* make evil plans to harm.
41:9 Mt 26:23; Mk 14:18; Lk 22:21; Jn 13:18

12 You will help me, because I do what is
right;
you will keep me in your presence
forever.

13 Praise the LORD, the God of Israel!
Praise him now and forever!

Amen! Amen!

BOOK TWO
(Psalms 42–72)

The Prayer of Someone in Exile[m]

42 As a deer longs for a stream of cool
water,
so I long for you, O God.
2 I thirst for you, the living God.
When can I go and worship in your
presence?
3 Day and night I cry,
and tears are my only food;
all the time my enemies ask me,
"Where is your God?"

4 My heart breaks when I remember the
past,
when I went with the crowds to the
house of God
and led them as they walked along,
a happy crowd, singing and shouting
praise to God.
5 Why am I so sad?
Why am I so troubled?
I will put my hope in God,
and once again I will praise him,
my savior and my God.

6-7 Here in exile my heart is breaking,
and so I turn my thoughts to him.
He has sent waves of sorrow over my soul;
chaos roars at me like a flood,
like waterfalls thundering down to the
Jordan
from Mount Hermon and Mount
Mizar.
8 May the LORD show his constant love
during the day,
so that I may have a song at night,
a prayer to the God of my life.

9 To God, my defender, I say,
"Why have you forgotten me?
Why must I go on suffering
from the cruelty of my enemies?"
10 I am crushed by their insults,
as they keep on asking me,
"Where is your God?"

11 Why am I so sad?
Why am I so troubled?
I will put my hope in God,
and once again I will praise him,
my savior and my God.

The Prayer of Someone in Exile
(Continuation of Psalm 42)

43 O God, declare me innocent,
and defend my cause against the
ungodly;
deliver me from lying and evil people!
2 You are my protector;
why have you abandoned me?
Why must I go on suffering
from the cruelty of my enemies?

3 Send your light and your truth;
may they lead me
and bring me back to Zion, your sacred
hill,[n]
and to your Temple, where you live.
4 Then I will go to your altar, O God;
you are the source of my happiness.
I will play my harp and sing praise to you,
O God, my God.

5 Why am I so sad?
Why am I so troubled?
I will put my hope in God,
and once again I will praise him,
my savior and my God.

[m] **42** HEBREW TITLE: *A poem by the clan of Korah.* [n] **43:3** SACRED HILL: *See 2:6.*
41:13 Ps 106:48

"May the LORD show his constant love during the day, / so that I may have a song at night, / a prayer to the God of my life" *(Psalm 42:8)*.

Masses for the Dead

Have you ever been to a Catholic funeral? Do you remember some of the symbols that were used? You may see a white cloth, called a pall, that represents the baptismal cloth. You may also see holy water, a cross, incense, the Book of the Gospels, a Paschal candle, and of course, the bread and wine. These are all symbols that recall God's saving love.

When people plan funerals, they have some choices for the readings that are read at the funeral. Parts of Psalms 42 and 43 are combined as a choice for the responsorial psalm. They express sadness, abandonment, and also hope. Read them over. Can you see how someone who has lost a loved one could relate to these psalms?

— Psalm 43

Catholic Connections

A Prayer for Protection[o]

44 With our own ears we have heard it,
O God—
our ancestors have told us about it,
about the great things you did in their time,
in the days of long ago:
2 how you yourself drove out the heathen
and established your people in their land;
how you punished the other nations
and caused your own to prosper.
3 Your people did not conquer the land
with their swords;
they did not win it by their own power;
it was by your power and your strength,
by the assurance of your presence,
which showed that you loved them.

4 You are my king and my God;
you give[p] victory to your people,
5 and by your power we defeat our enemies.
6 I do not trust in my bow
or in my sword to save me;
7 but you have saved us from our enemies
and defeated those who hate us.
8 We will always praise you
and give thanks to you forever.

9 But now you have rejected us and let us be defeated;
you no longer march out with our armies.
10 You made us run from our enemies,
and they took for themselves what was ours.
11 You allowed us to be slaughtered like sheep;
you scattered us in foreign countries.
12 You sold your own people for a small price
as though they had little value.[q]

13 Our neighbors see what you did to us,
and they mock us and laugh at us.
14 You have made us a joke among the nations;
they shake their heads at us in scorn.
15 I am always in disgrace;
I am covered with shame
16 from hearing the sneers and insults
of my enemies and those who hate me.

[o] **44** HEBREW TITLE: *A poem by the clan of Korah.* [p] **44:4** *Some ancient translations* and my God; you give; *Hebrew* O God; give. [q] **44:12** as . . . value; *or* and made no profit from the sale.

Verse 22 of Psalm 44 is quoted in Romans 8:34–39. Read that passage to see an example of how the New Testament writers referred to the Psalms.

17 All this has happened to us,
even though we have not forgotten you
or broken the covenant you made with
us.
18 We have not been disloyal to you;
we have not disobeyed your
commands.
19 Yet you left us helpless among wild
animals;
you abandoned us in deepest darkness.
20 If we had stopped worshiping our God
and prayed to a foreign god,
21 you would surely have discovered it,
because you know our secret thoughts.
22 But it is on your account that we are
being killed all the time,
that we are treated like sheep to be
slaughtered.
23 Wake up, Lord! Why are you asleep?
Rouse yourself! Don't reject us forever!
24 Why are you hiding from us?
Don't forget our suffering and trouble!
25 We fall crushed to the ground;
we lie defeated in the dust.
26 Come to our aid!
Because of your constant love save us!

A Royal Wedding Song[r]

45 Beautiful words fill my mind,
as I compose this song for the king.
Like the pen of a good writer
my tongue is ready with a poem.
2 You are the most handsome of men;
you are an eloquent speaker.
God has always blessed you.
3 Buckle on your sword, mighty king;
you are glorious and majestic.
4 Ride on in majesty to victory
for the defense of truth and justice![s]
Your strength will win you great
victories!
5 Your arrows are sharp,
they pierce the hearts of your enemies;
nations fall down at your feet.

Study it!

Royal Psalms

Want to be like a king or a queen? Recite Psalm 45! It is called a royal psalm and was probably part of royal weddings. Royal psalms are found throughout the whole Book of Psalms. There may be more than ten royal psalms in it. The king is usually the central figure in a royal psalm. Because in ancient Israel the king was seen as God's representative, by praising the king you are also praising God.

As you read Psalm 45, count the number of times you find words that represent royalty—words such as king, queen, majestic, palace, court, and throne.

— Psalm 45

6 The kingdom that God has given you[t]
will last forever and ever.
You rule over your people with justice;
7 you love what is right and hate what is
evil.
That is why God, your God, has chosen
you
and has poured out more happiness on
you
than on any other king.
8 The perfume of myrrh and aloes is on
your clothes;
musicians entertain you in palaces
decorated with ivory.
9 Among the women of your court are
daughters of kings,
and at the right of your throne stands
the queen,
wearing ornaments of finest gold.

[r] **45** HEBREW TITLE: *A poem by the clan of Korah; a love song.* [s] **45:4** *Probable text* and justice; *Hebrew* and meekness of justice. [t] **45:6** The kingdom that God has given you; *or* Your kingdom, O God; *or* Your divine kingdom.

44:22 Rom 8:36 **45:6, 7** Heb 1:8,9

10 Bride of the king, listen to what I say—
forget your people and your relatives.
11 Your beauty will make the king desire
you;
he is your master, so you must obey
him.
12 The people of Tyre will bring you gifts;
rich people will try to win your favor.
13 The princess is in the palace—how
beautiful she is!
Her gown is made of gold thread.
14 In her colorful gown she is led to the king,
followed by her bridesmaids,
and they also are brought to him.
15 With joy and gladness they come
and enter the king's palace.
16 You, my king, will have many sons
to succeed your ancestors as kings,
and you will make them rulers over the
whole earth.
17 My song will keep your fame alive
forever,
and everyone will praise you for all
time to come.

God Is with Us[u]

46 God is our shelter and strength,
always ready to help in times of
trouble.
2 So we will not be afraid, even if the earth
is shaken
and mountains fall into the ocean
depths;
3 even if the seas roar and rage,
and the hills are shaken by the
violence.

We will not be afraid. (46:2)

4 There is a river that brings joy to the city
of God,
to the sacred house of the Most High.
5 God is in that city, and it will never be
destroyed;
at early dawn he will come to its aid.
6 Nations are terrified, kingdoms are
shaken;
God thunders, and the earth dissolves.
7 The LORD Almighty is with us;
the God of Jacob is our refuge.
8 Come and see what the LORD has
done.
See what amazing things he has done
on earth.
9 He stops wars all over the world;
he breaks bows, destroys spears,
and sets shields on fire.
10 "Stop fighting," he says, "and know that I
am God,
supreme among the nations,
supreme over the world."
11 The LORD Almighty is with us;
the God of Jacob is our refuge.

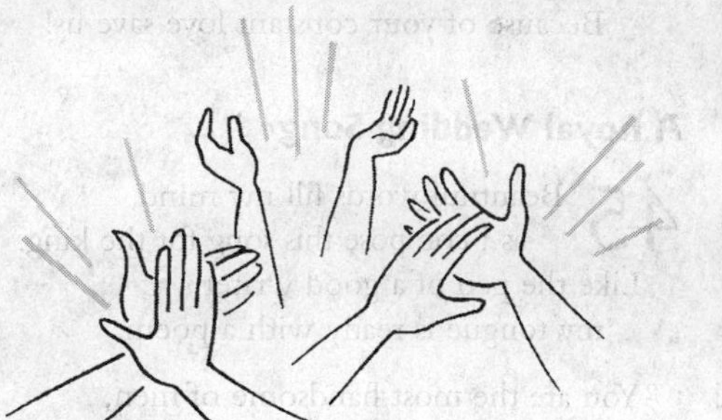

Clap your hands for joy. (47:1)

The Supreme Ruler[v]

47 Clap your hands for joy, all peoples!
Praise God with loud songs!
2 The LORD, the Most High, is to be
feared;
he is a great king, ruling over all the
world.
3 He gave us victory over the peoples;
he made us rule over the nations.

[u] 46 HEBREW TITLE: *A song by the clan of Korah.* [v] 47 HEBREW TITLE: *A psalm by the clan of Korah.*

Ascension Sunday

Catholic Connections

"Let's get going. You don't want to miss this Sunday or be late, do you?" Julio's mom was hurrying him more than usual this morning.

"Uh, it's just like any other Sunday, isn't it?" Julio yawned as he answered.

"No, it's Ascension Sunday! It's like Christmas!" she replied.

This conversation is probably not one that kids and their parents have. It is very unlikely that people invite family over, have big meals, and do all the usual holiday activities on Ascension Sunday. But maybe they should. Ascension is one of the ten days listed in the *Catechism of the Catholic Church* as holy days of obligation. It is celebrated either forty days after Easter or on the following Sunday. Why is the Ascension so special for Catholics? Here are a few reasons:

- **At the Ascension Jesus left this world to return to his Father and be with him forever.**
- **Because of this, we too can spend eternity with God.**
- **Through the Holy Spirit, Jesus is now able to be everywhere, with everyone, for all time!**

— Psalm 47

"Sing praise to God." (47:6)

4 He chose for us the land where we live,
the proud possession of his people,
whom he loves.

5 God goes up to his throne.
There are shouts of joy and the blast of
trumpets,
as the LORD goes up.

6 Sing praise to God;
sing praise to our king!
7 God is king over all the world;
praise him with songs!

8 God sits on his sacred throne;
he rules over the nations.
9 The rulers of the nations assemble
with the people[w] of the God of Abraham.
More powerful than all armies is he;
he rules supreme.

Zion, the City of God[x]

48 The LORD is great and is to be
highly praised
in the city of our God, on his sacred hill.[y]
2 Zion, the mountain of God, is high and
beautiful;
the city of the great king brings joy to
all the world.

[w] **47:9** *Probable text* with the people; *Hebrew* the people. [x] **48** HEBREW TITLE: *A psalm by the clan of Korah; a song.* [y] **48:1** SACRED HILL: *See 2:6.*
48:2 Mt 5:35

Read Psalm 46. How does it feel to know that God is there, even when you are the most scared?

3 God has shown that there is safety with him
inside the fortresses of the city.

4 The kings gathered together
and came to attack Mount Zion.
5 But when they saw it, they were amazed;
they were afraid and ran away.
6 There they were seized with fear and anguish,
like a woman about to bear a child,
7 like ships tossing in a furious storm.

8 We have heard what God has done,
and now we have seen it
in the city of our God, the LORD Almighty;
he will keep the city safe forever.

9 Inside your Temple, O God,
we think of your constant love.
10 You are praised by people everywhere,
and your fame extends over all the earth.
You rule with justice;
11 let the people of Zion be glad!
You give right judgments;
let there be joy in the cities of Judah!

12 People of God, walk around Zion and count the towers;
13 take notice of the walls and examine the fortresses,
so that you may tell the next generation:
14 "This God is our God forever and ever;
he will lead us for all time to come."

The Foolishness of Trusting in Riches[z]

49 Hear this, everyone!
Listen, all people everywhere,
2 great and small alike,
rich and poor together.
3 My thoughts will be clear;
I will speak words of wisdom.
4 I will turn my attention to proverbs
and explain their meaning as I play the harp.

5 I am not afraid in times of danger
when I am surrounded by enemies,
6 by evil people who trust in their riches
and boast of their great wealth.
7 We can never redeem ourselves;
we cannot pay God the price for our lives,
8 because the payment for a human life is too great.
What we could pay would never be enough
9 to keep us from the grave,
to let us live forever.

10 Anyone can see that even the wise die,
as well as the foolish and stupid.
They all leave their riches to their descendants.
11 Their graves[a] are their homes forever;
there they stay for all time,
though they once had lands of their own.
12 Our greatness cannot keep us from death;
we will still die like the animals.

13 See what happens to those who trust in themselves,
the fate of those[b] who are satisfied with their wealth—
14 they are doomed to die like sheep,
and Death will be their shepherd.
The righteous will triumph over them,
as their bodies quickly decay
in the world of the dead far from their homes.[c]
15 But God will rescue me;
he will save me from the power of death.

16 Don't be upset when someone becomes rich,
when his wealth grows even greater;

[z] **49** HEBREW TITLE: *A psalm by the clan of Korah.* [a] **49:11** *Some ancient translations* graves; *Hebrew* inner thoughts. [b] **49:13** *One ancient translation* the fate of those; *Hebrew* after them. [c] **49:14** in . . . homes.; *Hebrew unclear.*
49:10 Sir 11:19

Zion: The hill in Jerusalem the Temple was built on. So the city of Zion was Jerusalem.

17 he cannot take it with him when he dies;
his wealth will not go with him to the grave.

He cannot take it with him when he dies. (49:17)

18 Even if someone is satisfied with this life
and is praised because he is successful,
19 he will join all his ancestors in death,
where the darkness lasts forever.
20 Our greatness cannot keep us from death;
we will still die like the animals.

True Worship[d]

50 The Almighty God, the LORD, speaks;
he calls to the whole earth from east to west.
2 God shines from Zion,
the city perfect in its beauty.

3 Our God is coming, but not in silence;
a raging fire is in front of him,
a furious storm around him.
4 He calls heaven and earth as witnesses
to see him judge his people.
5 He says, "Gather my faithful people to me,
those who made a covenant with me
by offering a sacrifice."
6 The heavens proclaim that God is righteous,
that he himself is judge.

7 "Listen, my people, and I will speak;
I will testify against you, Israel.
I am God, your God.
8 I do not reprimand you because of your sacrifices
and the burnt offerings you always bring me.
9 And yet I do not need bulls from your farms
or goats from your flocks;
10 all the animals in the forest are mine
and the cattle on thousands of hills.
11 All the wild birds are mine
and all living things in the fields.

12 "If I were hungry, I would not ask you for food,
for the world and everything in it is mine.
13 Do I eat the flesh of bulls
or drink the blood of goats?
14 Let the giving of thanks be your sacrifice to God,[e]
and give the Almighty all that you promised.
15 Call to me when trouble comes;
I will save you,
and you will praise me."
16 But God says to the wicked,
"Why should you recite my commandments?
Why should you talk about my covenant?
17 You refuse to let me correct you;
you reject my commands.
18 You become the friend of every thief you see,
and you associate with adulterers.

19 "You are always ready to speak evil;
you never hesitate to tell lies.

All the animals in the forest are mine. (50:10)

[d] **50** HEBREW TITLE: *A psalm by Asaph.* [e] **50:14** Let the giving . . . to God; *or* Offer your thanksgiving sacrifice to God.

Catholic Connections

Examination of Conscience

Psalm 51 is a prayer for forgiveness and reminds Catholics of the sacrament of Penance and Reconciliation. Before celebrating the sacrament, it is a great idea to have an examination of conscience. And no, that is not like going to the doctor for a physical examination, or like taking a final exam. It is something you can do by yourself or with others.

Most group reconciliation services include an examination of conscience. Sometimes that means a person will read some questions based on the Ten Commandments or the Beatitudes or general Christian values. The questions are only for you to answer in your heart. They help you think about your words, actions, and even your failure to act. If the service includes the opportunity to celebrate the actual sacrament of Penance and Reconciliation, the examination of conscience is followed by an opportunity to go to confession.

It is a good idea to examine your conscience on your own each night, while things are still fresh in your mind. Start by asking yourself these simple questions:

- **What did I do today that showed others God's love?**
- **Did any of my actions or words keep me from experiencing God's love?**

— Psalm 51

20 You are ready to accuse your own
relatives
and to find fault with them.
21 You have done all this, and I have said
nothing,
so you thought that I am like you.
But now I reprimand you
and make the matter plain to you.

22 "Listen to this, you that ignore me,
or I will destroy you,
and there will be no one to save you.
23 Giving thanks is the sacrifice that honors
me,
and I will surely save all who obey me."

A Prayer for Forgiveness[f]

51 Be merciful to me, O God,
because of your constant love.
Because of your great mercy
wipe away my sins!
2 Wash away all my evil
and make me clean from my sin!
3 I recognize my faults;
I am always conscious of my sins.
4 I have sinned against you—only against
you—
and done what you consider evil.
So you are right in judging me;
you are justified in condemning me.
5 I have been evil from the day I was born;
from the time I was conceived, I have
been sinful.

6 Sincerity and truth are what you require;
fill my mind with your wisdom.
7 Remove my sin, and I will be clean;
wash me, and I will be whiter than snow.
8 Let me hear the sounds of joy and gladness;
and though you have crushed me and
broken me,
I will be happy once again.

[f] **51** HEBREW TITLE: *A psalm by David, after the prophet Nathan had spoken to him about his adultery with Bathsheba.*
51 Title 2 Sam 12:1–15 **51:4** Rom 3:4

9 Close your eyes to my sins
and wipe out all my evil.
10 Create a pure heart in me, O God,
and put a new and loyal spirit in me.

"Create a pure heart in me, O God." (51:10)

11 Do not banish me from your presence;
do not take your holy spirit away from me.
12 Give me again the joy that comes from your salvation,
and make me willing to obey you.
13 Then I will teach sinners your commands,
and they will turn back to you.
14 Spare my life, O God, and save me,[g]
and I will gladly proclaim your righteousness.
15 Help me to speak, Lord,
and I will praise you.
16 You do not want sacrifices,
or I would offer them;
you are not pleased with burnt offerings.
17 My sacrifice is a humble spirit, O God;
you will not reject a humble and repentant heart.

18 O God, be kind to Zion and help her;
rebuild the walls of Jerusalem.
19 Then you will be pleased with proper sacrifices
and with our burnt offerings;
and bulls will be sacrificed on your altar.

God's Judgment and Grace[h]

52 Why do you boast, great one, of your evil?
God's faithfulness is eternal.
2 You make plans to ruin others;
your tongue is like a sharp razor.
You are always inventing lies.
3 You love evil more than good
and falsehood more than truth.
4 You love to hurt people with your words,
you liar!

5 So God will ruin you forever;
he will take hold of you and snatch you from your home;
he will remove you from the world of the living.
6 Righteous people will see this and be afraid;
then they will laugh at you and say,
7 "Look, here is someone who did not depend on God for safety,
but trusted instead in great wealth
and looked for security in being wicked."

8 But I am like an olive tree growing in the house of God;
I trust in his constant love forever and ever.

[g] **51:14** Spare my life . . . me; *or* O God my savior, keep me from the crime of murder. [h] **52** HEBREW TITLE: *A poem by David, after Doeg the Edomite went to Saul and told him that David had gone to the house of Ahimelech.*
52 Title 1 Sam 22:9, 10

How does Psalm 52 compare those who depend on God and those who do not depend on God?

9 I will always thank you, God, for what
you have done;
in the presence of your people
I will proclaim that you are good.

Human Wickedness[i]

(Psalm 14)

53 Fools say to themselves,
"There is no God."
They are all corrupt,
and they have done terrible things;
there is no one who does what is
right.

2 God looks down from heaven at people
to see if there are any who are wise,
any who worship him.
3 But they have all turned away;
they are all equally bad.
Not one of them does what is right,
not a single one.

4 "Don't they know?" God asks.
"Are these evildoers ignorant?
They live by robbing my people,
and they never pray to me."

5 But then they will become terrified,
as they have never been before,
for God will scatter the bones of the
enemies of his people.
God has rejected them,
and so Israel will totally defeat them.

6 How I pray that victory
will come to Israel from Zion.
How happy the people of Israel will be
when God makes them prosperous
again!

A Prayer for Protection from Enemies[j]

54 Save me by your power, O God;
set me free by your might!
2 Hear my prayer, O God;
listen to my words!
3 Proud people are coming to attack me;
cruel people are trying to kill me—
those who do not care about God.

4 But God is my helper.
The Lord is my defender.
5 May God use their own evil to punish my
enemies.
He will destroy them because he is
faithful.

6 I will gladly offer you a sacrifice,
O LORD;
I will give you thanks
because you are good.
7 You have rescued me from all my
troubles,
and I have seen my enemies defeated.

The Prayer of Someone Betrayed by a Friend[k]

55 Hear my prayer, O God;
don't turn away from my plea!
2 Listen to me and answer me;
I am worn out by my worries.
3 I am terrified by the threats of my
enemies,
crushed by the oppression of the
wicked.
They bring trouble on me;
they are angry with me and hate me.

4 I am terrified,
and the terrors of death crush me.
5 I am gripped by fear and trembling;
I am overcome with horror.
6 I wish I had wings like a dove.
I would fly away and find rest.
7 I would fly far away
and make my home in the desert.
8 I would hurry and find myself a shelter
from the raging wind and the storm.
9 Confuse the speech of my enemies,
O Lord!

I see violence and riots in the city,

[i] **53** HEBREW TITLE: *A poem by David.* [j] **54** HEBREW TITLE: *A poem by David, after the men from Ziph went to Saul and told him that David was hiding in their territory.* [k] **55** HEBREW TITLE: *A poem by David.*

53:1–3 Rom 3:10–12 **54 Title** 1 Sam 23:19; 26:1

"Save me by your power, O God; / set me free by your might!" *(Psalm 54:1)*.

10 surrounding it day and night,
filling it with crime and trouble.
11 There is destruction everywhere;
the streets are full of oppression and fraud.
12 If it were an enemy making fun of me,
I could endure it;
if it were an opponent boasting over me,
I could hide myself from him.
13 But it is you, my companion,
my colleague and close friend.
14 We had intimate talks with each other
and worshiped together in the Temple.
15 May my enemies die before their time;
may they go down alive into the world of the dead!
Evil is in their homes and in their hearts.
16 But I call to the LORD God for help,
and he will save me.
17 Morning, noon, and night
my complaints and groans go up to him,
and he will hear my voice.
18 He will bring me safely back
from the battles that I fight
against so many enemies.
19 God, who has ruled from eternity,
will hear me and defeat them;
for they refuse to change,
and they do not fear him.
20 My former companion attacked his friends;
he broke his promises.
21 His words were smoother than cream,
but there was hatred in his heart;
his words were as soothing as oil,
but they cut like sharp swords.
22 Leave your troubles with the LORD,
and he will defend you;
he never lets honest people be defeated.
23 But you, O God, will bring those
murderers and liars to their graves
before half their life is over.
As for me, I will trust in you.

Live it!

Why Did They Do That?

"I have no friends!"

Have you ever said that? Maybe you said it when a friend or friends did or said something that really hurt you or betrayed you. Most people have had a time in their life when it felt like this. The person who wrote Psalm 55 must have had that same experience. What he wrote in verse 12 is so true: "If it were an enemy making fun of me, I could endure it." When strangers or enemies make fun of us or hurt us, it feels like less of a betrayal than when our friends do it.

This is a great psalm to read when feeling bad about your own friends, but it also is a good reminder of how to live. Think about a friend you may have hurt in the past. Maybe you could take some time to write to him or her, name what happened, and apologize if you haven't already done so. If there isn't someone for you to apologize to, good for you! And keep Psalm 55 in mind whenever you feel like telling a friend's secret or gossiping about something she or he did.

— Psalm 55

A Prayer of Trust in God[l]

56 Be merciful to me, O God,
because I am under attack;
my enemies persecute me all the time.
2 All day long my opponents attack me.
There are so many who fight against me.

[l] **56** HEBREW TITLE: *A psalm by David, after the Philistines captured him in Gath.*
56 Title 1 Sam 21:13–15

3 When I am afraid, O LORD Almighty,
I put my trust in you.
4 I trust in God and am not afraid;
I praise him for what he has promised.
What can a mere human being do to me?

5 My enemies make trouble for me all day long;
they are always thinking up some way to hurt me!
6 They gather in hiding places
and watch everything I do,
hoping to kill me.
7 Punish[m] them, O God, for their evil;
defeat those people in your anger!

8 You know how troubled I am;
you have kept a record of my tears.
Aren't they listed in your book?
9 The day I call to you,
my enemies will be turned back.
I know this: God[n] is on my side—
10 the LORD, whose promises I praise.
11 In him I trust, and I will not be afraid.
What can a mere human being do to me?

12 O God, I will offer you what I have promised;
I will give you my offering of thanksgiving,
13 because you have rescued me from death
and kept me from defeat.
And so I walk in the presence of God,
in the light that shines on the living.

A Prayer for Help[o]

57 Be merciful to me, O God, be merciful,
because I come to you for safety.
In the shadow of your wings I find protection
until the raging storms are over.

2 I call to God, the Most High,
to God, who supplies my every need.
3 He will answer from heaven and save me;
he will defeat my oppressors.
God will show me his constant love
and faithfulness.

4 I am surrounded by enemies,
who are like lions hungry for human flesh.
Their teeth are like spears and arrows;
their tongues are like sharp swords.

5 Show your greatness in the sky, O God,
and your glory over all the earth.

6 My enemies have spread a net to catch me;
I am overcome with distress.
They dug a pit in my path,
but fell into it themselves.
7 I have complete confidence, O God;
I will sing and praise you!
8 Wake up, my soul!
Wake up, my harp and lyre!
I will wake up the sun.
9 I will thank you, O Lord, among the nations.
I will praise you among the peoples.
10 Your constant love reaches the heavens;
your faithfulness touches the skies.
11 Show your greatness in the sky, O God,
and your glory over all the earth.

A Prayer for God to Punish the Wicked[p]

58 Do you rulers[q] ever give a just decision?
Do you judge everyone fairly?
2 No! You think only of the evil you can do,
and commit crimes of violence in the land.

3 Evildoers go wrong all their lives;
they tell lies from the day they are born.
4 They are full of poison like snakes;
they stop up their ears like a deaf cobra,

[m] **56:7** *Probable text* Punish; *Hebrew* Save. [n] **56:9** I know this: God; *or* Because I know that God.
[o] **57** HEBREW TITLE: *A psalm by David, after he fled from Saul in the cave.* [p] **58** HEBREW TITLE: *A psalm by David.*
[q] **58:1** rulers; *or* gods.
57 Title 1 Sam 22:1; 24:3

David

Breakthrough!: King David, how long did you rule over Israel?

David: A total of forty years.

B: Wow, that's a long time. You became king in a rather unusual way. Please describe what happened.

David: Well, I was tending my family's sheep one day, when one of my brothers told me to come to the house. A prophet named Samuel saw me and anointed me with oil! The only problem was that there already was an anointed king, Saul. Plus I had seven older brothers, so I couldn't figure out why I was chosen.

B: What was your relationship with King Saul?

David: At first I was his musician and armor-bearer, and then I got to know two of his children well. Saul's son Jonathan became my best friend, and Saul's daughter Michal became my wife. But Saul became very jealous of me and wanted me dead. I was never sure why. That was hard, because I respected Saul. After all, he had also been anointed king.

B: You accomplished a lot in your life. What are you most proud of?

David: I would say making Jerusalem the capital. It gave my people a city to call their own and a resting place for the Covenant Box.

B: Any regrets?

David: Oh, yes. I very much regret my adultery with Bathsheba and the way I arranged for Uriah to be killed. I was blinded by my desire for Bathsheba, and that led me to break God's laws.

B: Any words for our readers?

David: Yes. I tried to be a person after God's own heart and God worked through me to make the people of Israel a mighty nation. I recommend that your readers try to please God in everything they do.

Solomon

Breakthrough!: King Solomon, you had pretty famous parents, right?

Solomon: Well, my father was King David and my mother was Bathsheba. I grew up in the palace and received a very good education there.

B: You had several older brothers. How is it that you became the third king of Israel?

Solomon: Good question. Some people might say that my mother had a lot to do with it and talked my father into naming me the next king. I believe it was all part of God's plan.

B: Out of all the things you have done, what are you most proud of?

Solomon: That's easy, building the Temple. It took seven long years and lots and lots of workers, but I was finally able to fulfill my father's dream and build a magnificent temple for God.

B: You are also well known for your wisdom. Tell us more about that.

Solomon: Early on, God asked me what I most wanted, and I told him that I wanted an understanding heart. So, he gave me the gift of wisdom. I used that gift to settle disputes among people fairly and justly.

B: Any regrets?

Solomon: Yes, one. I have been criticized for building temples for all my foreign wives and then worshiping their gods. I wanted to keep my wives happy but in doing so I allowed the worship of foreign gods into the kingdom. My heart was turned away from the one, true God.

B: Any words of advice for our Bible readers?

Solomon: I wrote down lots of words of wisdom during my lifetime. Check out the Book of Proverbs to see a sample of the kind of wisdom I taught. It's pretty clever, if I say so myself!

Hezekiah

Breakthrough!: King Hezekiah, the prophet Isaiah spoke highly of you. He says that you were truly faithful to God.

Hezekiah: I really appreciate that. Isaiah gave me messages from God, and those messages were very helpful as we dealt with the Assyrians, who were a constant threat.

B: We heard that the emperor Sennacherib captured forty-six cities of Judah!

Hezekiah: Yes, that's true, but we kept him from capturing our beloved capital city of Jerusalem.

B: How did you do that?

Hezekiah: With God's help. That was part of Isaiah's message to me, that Sennacherib would not enter Jerusalem, and that God would defend and protect his holy city. And so he did.

B: You were also well regarded by the people for your faithfulness to God.

Hezekiah: I tried to obey the Lord's commands. I destroyed several pagan places of worship, broke the stone pillars, and removed the images of the pagan goddess Asherah.

B: You also defeated the Philistines.

Hezekiah: Yes, that's correct. That was before the Assyrians invaded. They had already conquered Samaria. In the end, I just wanted to make sure Jerusalem was not destroyed. And, of course, I tried to remain faithful to God, no matter what.

B: It is easy to see why your people respected you and God favors you.

Hezekiah: It is simply a matter of following God's law, especially the first commandment. Our nation often strayed from the path. But God kept sending prophets to bring us back.

Josiah

Breakthrough!: King Josiah, you became king at a very young age, correct?

Josiah: Yes, I was eight years old when I was made king of Judah.

B: How did that happen?

Josiah: Well, unfortunately, my father, Amon, was assassinated in the palace by some of his own officials. The people had his assassins killed, and they made me king.

B: What would you say were your major accomplishments?

Josiah: I expanded the territory of Judah, but I am most proud of the religious reforms I set in place.

B: Could you explain those reforms?

Josiah: They started with the discovery of a book of the Law of Moses found in the Temple by the priest Hilkiah. I had the book read to me, and I knew what I had to do. I called together all the leaders and all the people of Judah and Jerusalem, and I read the book aloud. Then I made a covenant to obey the Lord and to keep his commands with all my heart and soul.

B: And that meant the end of pagan worship, right?

Josiah: Exactly. I set about destroying every pagan temple in Judah and having the pagan priests killed. The worship of false gods and goddesses had gotten way out of hand and polluted our nation.

B: And you reinstituted the celebration of Passover.

Josiah: Yes, in the eighteenth year of my reign, we celebrated Passover the way it should be celebrated. I donated 30,000 sheep, lambs, and young goats, along with 3,000 bulls.

B: Your people hailed you as the greatest king since David.

Josiah: I don't know about that, but I was determined to bring my people back to the one true God.

Elijah & Elisha

Breakthrough!: So, are you two related? Your names are so similar.

Elijah: Actually, no. Our names are similar, but they mean different things. My name means, "Yahweh is my God," and *Elisha* means, "God is salvation." Remember that "El" in Hebrew means "God."

B: Both of you are prophets. How have you shown to the people that you are God's messengers?

Elisha: One of the signs of a prophet is that he or she can do wonderful things in the name of God and as a sign of God's power.

B: We would call those miracles, right?

Elisha: Yes, and some of the miracles that Elijah did were multiplying food for a starving widow and bringing her dead son back to life.

B: That's very impressive. Any others?

Elisha: Elijah took on the 450 prophets of the false god Baal, and showed them who was boss!

Elijah: Elisha also did great things in God's name. He cured a Syrian commander of leprosy. Plus, he multiplied food for a widow and brought a dead child back to life.

B: So, where can we read about you two? There aren't any books in the Bible named for you, are there?

Elisha: That's right, the words and deeds of some prophets were written down in books named after them. But that is not true for us.

Elijah: You can read about my adventures in the last five chapters of 1 Kings. The beginning of 2 Kings tells how I was taken away and Elisha was left to carry on the work I had started. Let me just say it involved a chariot of fire!

B: Any final words for our readers?

Elijah: Our God is all-powerful. Stay faithful to him, and God will give you everything you need.

Elisha: Amen!

Amos

Breakthrough!: Amos, you come from a small town near Bethlehem, correct?

Amos: That's right. I am from Tekoa in Judah, and I was working as a shepherd and tree trimmer when I got my call from God.

B: You were very critical of the kingdom of Israel, and that got a lot of people upset.

Amos: Yes, that's right. I was ordered to leave the shrine at Bethel because the priest Amaziah didn't like what I was saying.

B: So, then you toned down your message?

Amos: Absolutely not! I would not water down God's message for anyone!

B: And what was God's message?

Amos: Israel and its rulers and its people had gotten fat and lazy. They abused the poor and completely forgot their obligation to serve the less fortunate. They would be destroyed for this.

B: So, you prophesied that Israel was doomed?

Amos: That is exactly what I said. Israel had sinned and turned its back on the poor. They had violated the covenant with God. As a consequence, their kingdom would come to an end.

B: Was there any hope?

Amos: Yes, God would never totally abandon his promises to us. A few people would survive the coming destruction. I knew one day God would restore the kingdom of David.

B: What is your message for our readers?

Amos: To be a follower of God, you must be a person who acts with justice. Then justice will flow like a stream, and righteousness like a river that never goes dry.

Hosea

Breakthrough!: Hosea, I have to get right to the point. You were married to Gomer, correct?

Hosea: Yes, that's right.

B: I'm sure you realize that she had quite a reputation around town. She was a . . . well, she was a prostitute who was unfaithful to you.

Hosea: Yes, I know. It made me very sad.

B: So, why did you stay with her when she clearly did not respect you?

Hosea: That is a very important question, and it gets to the heart of my message to my people. Yes, Gomer was unfaithful. Everyone knew it. But God commanded me to marry her. So I loved her and I stayed with her, despite everything.

B: What is the message you spoke of?

Hosea: My marriage was a public symbol of the relationship between God and his people. God committed himself to us. We were his people. However, we were not faithful to God. We turned away from him time and time again.

B: So you are saying that Gomer was like the people of Israel?

Hosea: That's exactly right. My wife's behavior was very much like Israel's, and yet, God remained faithful through it all. Just as God remained faithful to us, his chosen people, so I remained faithful to Gomer, despite the heartache it caused me.

B: I think I understand now. You are truly an amazing man, Hosea, with a huge heart. Any words for our readers?

Hosea: Yes, they are words I have said before: Return to the Lord. Your sin makes you stumble and fall. Come back to the Lord with all your heart and seek his forgiveness.

Isaiah

Breakthrough!: Hello, Isaiah, it looks like you brought some guests.

Isaiah 1: Actually we are all Isaiahs. There are more than one of us.

B: Say that again?

Isaiah 2: The prophecies in the Book of Isaiah were the work of more than one person. The prophecies at the beginning of the book were from the original Isaiah, but then I came along and prophesied in his name.

Isaiah 3: Then I came along and kept it up.

B: So there were just three of you, right?

Isaiah 1: Well, no one really knows for sure. Maybe there were only two. Or maybe there was a whole group that kept prophesying and writing in my name.

B: And what did you do?

Isaiah 2: We were prophets, meaning we spoke God's truth. Our message had to change with the times. The first Isaiah had to tell the people they were being unfaithful to God and would be punished after that. But then Jerusalem was destroyed and the people taken into slavery. So then I had to speak God's words of hope and promise.

B: What challenges did you three face?

Isaiah 3: I think the hardest thing was being faithful to preaching God's message, even when it seemed like no one was listening. It breaks your heart to see your people ignoring God.

B: What period of time do all your prophecies cover?

Isaiah 1: Our prophecies cover a period of time going from about 740 BC to 500 BC or later. You can see that it would be pretty hard for one person to do.

B: Anything else for our Bible readers?

Isaiah 2: Some of our prophecies were about a leader who would be a suffering servant for his people. I bet you can guess who that turned out to be!

5 which does not hear the voice of the
snake charmer,
or the chant of the clever magician.

6 Break the teeth of these fierce lions,
O God.

7 May they disappear like water draining
away;
may they be crushed like weeds on a
path.[r]

8 May they be like snails that dissolve into
slime;
may they be like a baby born dead that
never sees the light.

9 Before they know it, they are cut down
like weeds;
in his fierce anger God will blow them
away
while they are still living.[s]

10 The righteous will be glad when they see
sinners punished;
they will wade through the blood of
the wicked.

11 People will say, "The righteous are indeed
rewarded;
there is indeed a God who judges the
world."

A Prayer for Safety[t]

59 Save me from my enemies, my God;
protect me from those who attack
me!

2 Save me from those evil people;
rescue me from those murderers!

3 Look! They are waiting to kill me;
cruel people are gathering against
me.
It is not because of any sin or wrong I
have done,
4 nor because of any fault of mine,
O LORD,
that they hurry to their places.

5 Rise, LORD God Almighty, and come to
my aid;
see for yourself, God of Israel!
Wake up and punish the heathen;
show no mercy to evil traitors!

6 They come back in the evening,
snarling like dogs as they go about the
city.

7 Listen to their insults and threats.
Their tongues are like swords in their
mouths,
yet they think that no one hears them.

8 But you laugh at them, LORD;
you mock all the heathen.

9 I have confidence in your strength;
you are my refuge, O God.

10 My God loves me and will come to me;
he will let me see my enemies
defeated.

11 Do not kill them, O God, or my people
may forget.
Scatter them by your strength and
defeat them,
O Lord, our protector.

12 Sin is on their lips; all their words are
sinful;
may they be caught in their pride!
Because they curse and lie,
13 destroy them in your anger;
destroy them completely.
Then everyone will know that God rules
in Israel,
that his rule extends over all the earth.

14 My enemies come back in the evening,
snarling like dogs as they go about the
city,
15 like dogs roaming about for food
and growling if they do not find
enough.

16 But I will sing about your strength;
every morning I will sing aloud of your
constant love.

[r] **58:7** *Probable text may . . .* path; *Hebrew unclear.* [s] **58:9** *Verse 9 in Hebrew is unclear.* [t] **59** HEBREW TITLE: *A psalm by David, after Saul sent men to watch his house in order to kill him.*
59 Title 1 Sam 19:11

How would you describe your enemies? How does the psalmist describe the enemies in Psalm 59?

You have been a refuge for me,
a shelter in my time of trouble.
17 I will praise you, my defender.
My refuge is God,
the God who loves me.

A Prayer for Deliverance[u]

60 You have rejected us, God, and defeated us;
you have been angry with us—but now turn back to us.[v]
2 You have made the land tremble, and you have cut it open;
now heal its wounds, because it is falling apart.
3 You have made your people suffer greatly;
we stagger around as though we were drunk.
4 You have warned those who have reverence for you,
so that they might escape destruction.
5 Save us by your might; answer our prayer,
so that the people you love may be rescued.

6 From his sanctuary[w] God has said,
"In triumph I will divide Shechem
and distribute Sukkoth Valley to my people.
7 Gilead is mine, and Manasseh too;
Ephraim is my helmet
and Judah my royal scepter.
8 But I will use Moab as my washbowl,
and I will throw my sandals on Edom,
as a sign that I own it.
Did the Philistines think they would shout in triumph over me?"

9 Who, O God, will take me into the fortified city?
Who will lead me to Edom?
10 Have you really rejected us?
Aren't you going to march out with our armies?
11 Help us against the enemy;
human help is worthless.
12 With God on our side we will win;
he will defeat our enemies.

A Prayer for Protection[x]

61 Hear my cry, O God;
listen to my prayer!
2 In despair and far from home
I call to you!

Take me to a safe refuge,
3 for you are my protector,
my strong defense against my enemies.

"Take me to a safe refuge." (61:2)

4 Let me live in your sanctuary all my life;
let me find safety under your wings.
5 You have heard my promises, O God,
and you have given me what belongs to those who honor you.

6 Add many years to the king's life;
let him live on and on!
7 May he rule forever in your presence, O God;
protect him with your constant love and faithfulness.

8 So I will always sing praises to you,
as I offer you daily what I have promised.

[u] **60** HEBREW TITLE: *A psalm by David, for teaching, when he fought against the Arameans from Naharaim and from Zobah, and Joab turned back and killed 12,000 Edomites in Salt Valley.* [v] **60:1** angry with us . . . us; *or* angry with us and turned your back on us. [w] **60:6** From his sanctuary; *or* In his holiness. [x] **61** HEBREW TITLE: *By David.*
60 Title 2 Sam 8:13; 1 Chr 18:12

Is God on your side even when you lose at something? How is that similar to or different from what is said in Psalm 60:12?

Pray it!

Every Day?

Did you know that if you do something twenty-one days in a row, it becomes a habit? And that some habits are bad for you (like smoking or eating junk food), but that others are good (like brushing your teeth or exercise)? That's right, if you want to create a good habit, make yourself do something *every day* for twenty-one days in a row. Why not start with prayer? The author of Psalm 61 says he promised to sing to God daily. If you read a psalm or say a memorized prayer or pray spontaneously every day for twenty-one days, you will have a good habit of prayer started.

— Psalm 61:8

Confidence in God's Protection[y]

62 I wait patiently for God to save me;
I depend on him alone.
2 He alone protects and saves me;
he is my defender,
and I shall never be defeated.

3 How much longer will all of you attack
someone
who is no stronger than a broken-down fence?
4 You only want to bring him down from
his place of honor;
you take pleasure in lies.
You speak words of blessing,
but in your heart you curse him.

5 I depend on God alone;
I put my hope in him.
6 He alone protects and saves me;
he is my defender,
and I shall never be defeated.
7 My salvation and honor depend on God;
he is my strong protector;
he is my shelter.

8 Trust in God at all times, my people.
Tell him all your troubles,
for he is our refuge.

9 Human beings are all like a puff of breath;
great and small alike are worthless.
Put them on the scales, and they weigh
nothing;
they are lighter than a mere breath.
10 Don't put your trust in violence;
don't hope to gain anything by robbery;
even if your riches increase,
don't depend on them.

11 More than once I have heard God say
that power belongs to him
12 and that his love is constant.
You yourself, O Lord, reward everyone
according to their deeds.

Longing for God[z]

63 O God, you are my God,
and I long for you.
My whole being desires you;
like a dry, worn-out, and waterless land,
my soul is thirsty for you.
2 Let me see you in the sanctuary;
let me see how mighty and glorious
you are.
3 Your constant love is better than life itself,
and so I will praise you.
4 I will give you thanks as long as I live;
I will raise my hands to you in prayer.
5 My soul will feast and be satisfied,
and I will sing glad songs of praise to
you.

6 As I lie in bed, I remember you;
all night long I think of you,
7 because you have always been my help.
In the shadow of your wings I sing for joy.
8 I cling to you,
and your hand keeps me safe.
9 Those who are trying to kill me
will go down into the world of the
dead.

[y] **62** HEBREW TITLE: *A psalm by David.* [z] **63** HEBREW TITLE: *A psalm by David, when he was in the desert of Judea.*
62:12 Job 34:11; Jer 17:10; Mt 16:27; Rom 2:6; Rev 2:23 **63 Title** 1 Sam 23:14

10 They will be killed in battle,
and their bodies eaten by wolves.
11 Because God gives him victory,
the king will rejoice.
Those who make promises in God's name
will praise him,
but the mouths of liars will be shut.

A Prayer for Protection[a]

64 I am in trouble, God—listen to my
prayer!
I am afraid of my enemies—save my
life!
2 Protect me from the plots of the wicked,
from mobs of evil people.
3 They sharpen their tongues like swords
and aim cruel words like arrows.
4 They are quick to spread their shameless
lies;
they destroy good people with
cowardly slander.
5 They encourage each other in their evil
plots;
they talk about where they will place
their traps.
"No one can see them," they say.
6 They make evil plans and say,
"We have planned a perfect crime."
The human heart and mind are a mystery.
7 But God shoots his arrows at them,
and suddenly they are wounded.
8 He will destroy them because of those
words;[b]
all who see them will shake their
heads.
9 They will all be afraid;
they will think about what God has
done
and tell about his deeds.
10 All righteous people will rejoice
because of what the LORD has done.
They will find safety in him;
all good people will praise him.

Praise and Thanksgiving[c]

65 O God, it is right for us to praise
you in Zion
and keep our promises to you,
2 because you answer prayers.
People everywhere will come to you
3 on account of their sins.
Our faults defeat us,[d]
but you forgive them.
4 Happy are those whom you choose,
whom you bring to live in your
sanctuary.
We shall be satisfied with the good things
of your house,
the blessings of your sacred Temple.
5 You answer us by giving us victory,
and you do wonderful things to save
us.
People all over the world
and across the distant seas trust in
you.
6 You set the mountains in place by your
strength,
showing your mighty power.
7 You calm the roar of the seas
and the noise of the waves;
you calm the uproar of the peoples.
8 The whole world stands in awe
of the great things that you have done.
Your deeds bring shouts of joy
from one end of the earth to the other.
9 You show your care for the land by
sending rain;
you make it rich and fertile.
You fill the streams with water;
you provide the earth with crops.
This is how you do it:
10 you send abundant rain on the plowed
fields
and soak them with water;
you soften the soil with showers
and cause the young plants to grow.
11 What a rich harvest your goodness
provides!
Wherever you go there is plenty.
12 The pastures are filled with flocks;
the hillsides are full of joy.

[a] **64** HEBREW TITLE: *A psalm by David.* [b] **64:8** *Probable text* He will destroy them because of those words; *Hebrew* They will destroy him, those words are against them. [c] **65** HEBREW TITLE: *A psalm by David; a song.* [d] **65:3** *One ancient translation* us; *Hebrew* me.

Thanksgiving

Catholic Connections

The word *thanksgiving* usually brings to mind images of pilgrims and turkeys. For Catholics, thanksgiving isn't something that just happens on a Thursday in November. We are called to be thankful daily, or even more often. The name of our central sacrament, the Eucharist, is a Greek word meaning "thanksgiving." This tells us that the Mass is a form of prayerful thanksgiving.

One of the types of prayer found in the Psalms is thanksgiving. The people writing the Psalms knew how important it is to give thanks to God. How do you give thanks to God? Have you said "thank God" (and made it a prayer) when you got a good grade or won an award? At the end of the day, do you make a list of things to be grateful for and give thanks in your evening prayer? Do you keep a prayer journal that lists your prayers and your thanks when they are answered? If you haven't done anything like these suggestions, try one or more of them. You'll be doing what the writer of Psalm 65 did (and check out what Saint Paul says in 1 Thessalonians 5:18).

— Psalm 65

13 The fields are covered with sheep;
the valleys are full of wheat.
Everything shouts and sings for joy.

A Song of Praise and Thanksgiving[e]

66 Praise God with shouts of joy, all people!
2 Sing to the glory of his name;
offer him glorious praise!
3 Say to God, "How wonderful are the things you do!
Your power is so great
that your enemies bow down in fear before you.
4 Everyone on earth worships you;
they sing praises to you,
they sing praises to your name."

Sing to the glory of his name! (66:2)

5 Come and see what God has done,
his wonderful acts among people.
6 He changed the sea into dry land;
our ancestors crossed the river on foot.
There we rejoiced because of what he did.
7 He rules forever by his might
and keeps his eyes on the nations.
Let no rebels rise against him.
8 Praise our God, all nations;
let your praise be heard.

[e] **66** HEBREW TITLE: *A song.*
66:6 a Ex 14:21; **b** Josh 3:14–17

Psalm 64 complains about cruel words (verse 3). What cruel words have you heard people use to hurt someone else?

Celebrating Mary, Mother of God

Catholic Connections

In the Catholic Church, January 1, the first day of the calendar year, is dedicated to Mary. During the Mass that day, we pray part of Psalm 67, which talks about the mercy of God. Mary knew God's mercy and blessing firsthand and praised God for it just as this psalm does.

This feast day for Mary is celebrated one week after we celebrate Jesus' birth. Why don't you celebrate your mom, or another woman who is significant to you, one week after your birthday? Celebrate it with a psalm you pick just for her by creating a symbol for her and decorating it with the words from the psalm. Surprise her with breakfast in bed or another special meal. Make one week after your birthday *her* day.

— Psalm 67

9 He has kept us alive
and has not allowed us to fall.

10 You have put us to the test, God;
as silver is purified by fire,
so you have tested us.
11 You let us fall into a trap
and placed heavy burdens on our backs.
12 You let our enemies trample us;
we went through fire and flood,
but now you have brought us to a place of safety.[f]

13 I will bring burnt offerings to your house;
I will offer you what I promised.
14 I will give you what I said I would
when I was in trouble.
15 I will offer sheep to be burned on the altar;
I will sacrifice bulls and goats,
and the smoke will go up to the sky.

16 Come and listen, all who honor God,
and I will tell you what he has done for me.
17 I cried to him for help;
I praised him with songs.
18 If I had ignored my sins,
the Lord would not have listened to me.
19 But God has indeed heard me;
he has listened to my prayer.

20 I praise God,
because he did not reject my prayer
or keep back his constant love from me.

A Song of Thanksgiving[g]

67 God, be merciful to us and bless us;
look on us with kindness,
2 so that the whole world may know your will;
so that all nations may know your salvation.

3 May the peoples praise you, O God;
may all the peoples praise you!

4 May the nations be glad and sing for joy,
because you judge the peoples with justice
and guide every nation on earth.

5 May the peoples praise you, O God;
may all the peoples praise you!

[f] **66:12** *Some ancient translations* safety; *Hebrew* overflowing. [g] **67** HEBREW TITLE: *A psalm; a song.*

"God, be merciful to us and bless us; look on us with kindness" (Psalm 67:1).

6 The land has produced its harvest;
God, our God, has blessed us.
7 God has blessed us;
may all people everywhere honor him.

A National Song of Triumph[h]

68 God rises up and scatters his
enemies.
Those who hate him run away in
defeat.
2 As smoke is blown away, so he drives
them off;
as wax melts in front of the fire,
so do the wicked perish in God's
presence.
3 But the righteous are glad and rejoice in
his presence;
they are happy and shout for joy.

4 Sing to God, sing praises to his name;
prepare a way for him who rides on
the clouds.[i]
His name is the LORD—be glad in his
presence!
5 God, who lives in his sacred Temple,
cares for orphans and protects widows.
6 He gives the lonely a home to live in
and leads prisoners out into happy
freedom,
but rebels will have to live in a desolate
land.

7 O God, when you led your people,
when you marched across the
desert,
8 the earth shook, and the sky poured
down rain,
because of the coming of the God of
Sinai,[j]
the coming of the God of Israel.
9 You caused abundant rain to fall
and restored your worn-out land;
10 your people made their home there;
in your goodness you provided for the
poor.

11 The Lord gave the command,
and many women carried the news:
12 "Kings and their armies are running away!"
The women at home divided what was
captured:
13 figures of doves covered with silver,
whose wings glittered with fine gold.
(Why did some of you stay among the
sheep pens on the day of battle?)
14 When Almighty God scattered the kings
on Mount Zalmon,
he caused snow to fall there.

15 What a mighty mountain is Bashan,
a mountain of many peaks!
16 Why from your mighty peaks do you
look with scorn
on the mountain[k] on which God chose
to live?
The LORD will live there forever!

17 With his many thousands of mighty
chariots
the Lord comes from Sinai[l] into the
holy place.
18 He goes up to the heights,
taking many captives with him;
he receives gifts from rebellious people.
The LORD God will live there.

19 Praise the Lord,
who carries our burdens day after day;
he is the God who saves us.
20 Our God is a God who saves;
he is the LORD, our Lord,
who rescues us from death.
21 God will surely break the heads of his
enemies,
of those who persist in their sinful ways.
22 The Lord has said, "I will bring your
enemies back from Bashan;
I will bring them back from the depths
of the ocean,
23 so that you may wade in their blood,
and your dogs may lap up as much as
they want."

24 O God, your march of triumph is seen by
all,
the procession of God, my king, into
his sanctuary.

[h] **68** HEBREW TITLE: *A psalm by David; a song.* [i] **68:4** on the clouds; *or* across the desert. [j] **68:8** GOD OF SINAI: *As the people of Israel went from Egypt to Canaan, God revealed himself to them at Mount Sinai (see Ex 19:16–25).* [k] **68:16** MOUNTAIN: *See 2:6.* [l] **68:17** *Probable text* comes from Sinai; *Hebrew* in them, Sinai.

68:8 Ex 19:18 **68:18** Eph 4:8

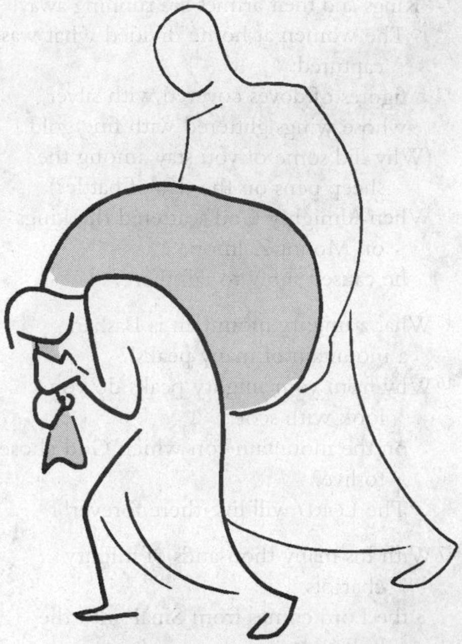

Praise the Lord, who carries our burdens day after day. (68:19)

25 The singers are in front, the musicians are behind,
in between are the young women beating the tambourines.
26 "Praise God in the meeting of his people;
praise the LORD, all you descendants of Jacob!"
27 First comes Benjamin, the smallest tribe,
then the leaders of Judah with their group,
followed by the leaders of Zebulun and Naphtali.
28 Show your power, O God,
the power you have used on our behalf
29 from your Temple in Jerusalem,
where kings bring gifts to you.
30 Rebuke Egypt, that wild animal in the reeds;
rebuke the nations, that herd of bulls with their calves,
until they all bow down and offer you their silver.
Scatter those people who love to make war![m]
31 Ambassadors[n] will come from Egypt;
the Ethiopians[o] will raise their hands in prayer to God.

32 Sing to God, kingdoms of the world,
sing praise to the Lord,
33 to him who rides in the sky,
the ancient sky.
Listen to him shout with a mighty roar.
34 Proclaim God's power;
his majesty is over Israel,
his might is in the skies.
35 How awesome is God as he comes from his sanctuary—
the God of Israel!
He gives strength and power to his people.

Praise God!

A Cry for Help[p]

69 Save me, O God!
The water is up to my neck;
2 I am sinking in deep mud,
and there is no solid ground;
I am out in deep water,
and the waves are about to drown me.
3 I am worn out from calling for help,
and my throat is aching.
I have strained my eyes,
looking for your help.

4 Those who hate me for no reason
are more numerous than the hairs of my head.
My enemies tell lies against me;
they are strong and want to kill me.
They made me give back things I did not steal.
5 My sins, O God, are not hidden from you;
you know how foolish I have been.
6 Don't let me bring shame on those who trust in you,
Sovereign LORD Almighty!

[m] **68:30** *Verse 30 in Hebrew is unclear.* [n] **68:31** *Some ancient translations* Ambassadors; *Hebrew unclear.*
[o] **68:31** *Hebrew* Cushites: *Cush is the ancient name of the extensive territory south of the First Cataract of the Nile River. This region was called Ethiopia in Graeco-Roman time, and included within its borders most of modern Sudan and some of present-day Ethiopia (Abyssinia).* [p] **69** HEBREW TITLE: *By David.*
69:4 Ps 35:19; Jn 15:25

Don't let me bring disgrace to those who
worship you,
O God of Israel!
7 It is for your sake that I have been
insulted
and that I am covered with shame.
8 I am like a stranger to my relatives,
like a foreigner to my family.

9 My devotion to your Temple burns in me
like a fire;
the insults which are hurled at you fall
on me.
10 I humble myself[q] by fasting,
and people insult me;
11 I dress myself in clothes of mourning,
and they laugh at me.
12 They talk about me in the streets,
and drunkards make up songs about me.

13 But as for me, I will pray to you, LORD;
answer me, God, at a time you choose.
Answer me because of your great love,
because you keep your promise to save.
14 Save me from sinking in the mud;
keep me safe from my enemies,
safe from the deep water.
15 Don't let the flood come over me;
don't let me drown in the depths
or sink into the grave.

16 Answer me, LORD, in the goodness of
your constant love;
in your great compassion turn to me!
17 Don't hide yourself from your servant;
I am in great trouble—answer me now!
18 Come to me and save me;
rescue me from my enemies.

19 You know how I am insulted,
how I am disgraced and dishonored;
you see all my enemies.
20 Insults have broken my heart,
and I am in despair.
I had hoped for sympathy, but there was
none;
for comfort, but I found none.
21 When I was hungry, they gave me poison;
when I was thirsty, they offered me
vinegar.

22 May their banquets cause their ruin;
may their sacred feasts cause their
downfall.
23 Strike them with blindness!
Make their backs always weak!
24 Pour out your anger on them;
let your indignation overtake them.
25 May their camps be left deserted;
may no one be left alive in their tents.
26 They persecute those whom you have
punished;
they talk about the sufferings of those
you have wounded.
27 Keep a record of all their sins;
don't let them have any part in your
salvation.
28 May their names be erased from the book
of the living;
may they not be included in the list of
your people.

29 But I am in pain and despair;
lift me up, O God, and save me!

30 I will praise God with a song;
I will proclaim his greatness by giving
him thanks.
31 This will please the LORD more than
offering him cattle,
more than sacrificing a full-grown bull.
32 When the oppressed see this, they will be
glad;
those who worship God will be
encouraged.
33 The LORD listens to those in need
and does not forget his people in
prison.

34 Praise God, O heaven and earth,
seas and all creatures in them.
35 He will save Jerusalem
and rebuild the towns of Judah.

q **69:10** *Some ancient translations* humble myself; *Hebrew* cry.

69:9 **a** Jn 2:17; **b** Rom 15:3 **69:21** Mt 27:48; Mk 15:36; Lk 23:26; Jn 19:28, 29 **69:22, 23** Rom 11:9, 10 **69:25** Acts 1:20 **69:28** Ex 32:32; Rev 3:5; 13:8; 17:8

When do you feel like saying, "The water is up to my neck . . ." *(Psalm 69:1)***? What do you do when you feel that way?**

His people will live there and possess the land;
36 the descendants of his servants will inherit it,
and those who love him will live there.

A Prayer for Help[r]
(Psalm 40:13–17)

70 Save me, O God!
LORD, help me now!
2 May those who try to kill me
be defeated and confused.
May those who are happy because of my troubles
be turned back and disgraced.
3 May those who make fun of me
be dismayed by their defeat.

4 May all who come to you
be glad and joyful.
May all who are thankful for your salvation
always say, "How great is God!"

5 I am weak and poor;
come to me quickly, O God.
You are my savior and my LORD —
hurry to my aid!

The Prayer of an Elderly Person

71 LORD, I have come to you for protection;
never let me be defeated!
2 Because you are righteous, help me and rescue me.
Listen to me and save me!
3 Be my secure shelter
and a strong fortress[s] to protect me;
you are my refuge and defense.

4 My God, rescue me from wicked people,
from the power of cruel and evil people.
5 Sovereign LORD, I put my hope in you;
I have trusted in you since I was young.
6 I have relied on you all my life;
you have protected[t] me since the day I was born.
I will always praise you.

7 My life has been an example to many,
because you have been my strong defender.
8 All day long I praise you
and proclaim your glory.
9 Do not reject me now that I am old;
do not abandon me now that I am feeble.
10 My enemies want to kill me;
they talk and plot against me.
11 They say, "God has abandoned him;
let's go after him and catch him;
there is no one to rescue him."

12 Don't stay so far away, O God;
my God, hurry to my aid!
13 May those who attack me
be defeated and destroyed.
May those who try to hurt me
be shamed and disgraced.
14 I will always put my hope in you;
I will praise you more and more.
15 I will tell of your goodness;
all day long I will speak of your salvation,
though it is more than I can understand.
16 I will go in the strength of the LORD God;
I will proclaim your goodness, yours alone.

17 You have taught me ever since I was young,
and I still tell of your wonderful acts.
18 Now that I am old and my hair is gray,
do not abandon me, O God!
Be with me while I proclaim your power and might
to all generations to come.
19 Your righteousness, God, reaches the skies.
You have done great things;
there is no one like you.

[r] **70** HEBREW TITLE: *A psalm by David; a lament.* [s] **71:3** *One ancient translation* a strong fortress; *Hebrew* to go always you commanded. [t] **71:6** *Some ancient translations* protected; *Hebrew unclear.*

Why, do you think, was the psalmist going to play hymns on a harp *(see Psalm 71:22)*? **What instrument would you use?**

Now that I am old . . . (71:18)

20 You have sent troubles and suffering on me,
but you will restore my strength;
you will keep me from the grave.
21 You will make me greater than ever;
you will comfort me again.
22 I will indeed praise you with the harp;
I will praise your faithfulness, my God.
On my harp I will play hymns to you,
the Holy One of Israel.
23 I will shout for joy as I play for you;
with my whole being I will sing
because you have saved me.
24 I will speak of your righteousness all day long,
because those who tried to harm me
have been defeated and disgraced.

A Prayer for the King[u]

72 Teach the king to judge with your righteousness, O God;
share with him your own justice,
2 so that he will rule over your people with justice
and govern the oppressed with righteousness.
3 May the land enjoy prosperity;
may it experience righteousness.
4 May the king judge the poor fairly;
may he help the needy
and defeat their oppressors.
5 May your people worship you as long as the sun shines,
as long as the moon gives light, for ages to come.

6 May the king be like rain on the fields,
like showers falling on the land.
7 May righteousness flourish in his lifetime,
and may prosperity last as long as the moon gives light.

8 His kingdom will reach from sea to sea,
from the Euphrates to the ends of the earth.
9 The peoples of the desert will bow down before him;
his enemies will throw themselves to the ground.
10 The kings of Spain and of the islands will offer him gifts;
the kings of Sheba and Seba[v] will bring him offerings.
11 All kings will bow down before him;
all nations will serve him.

12 He rescues the poor who call to him,
and those who are needy and neglected.
13 He has pity on the weak and poor;
he saves the lives of those in need.
14 He rescues them from oppression and violence;
their lives are precious to him.

15 Long live the king!
May he be given gold from Sheba;[w]
may prayers be said for him at all times;
may God's blessings be on him always!
16 May there be plenty of grain in the land;
may the hills be covered with crops,
as fruitful as those of Lebanon.
May the cities be filled with people,
like fields full of grass.
17 May the king's name never be forgotten;
may his fame last as long as the sun.
May all nations ask God to bless them
as he has blessed the king.[x]

[u] **72** HEBREW TITLE: *By Solomon.* [v] **72:10** SHEBA AND SEBA: *Sheba was toward the south in Arabia and Seba was on the opposite side of the Red Sea.* [w] **72:15** SHEBA: *See 72:10.* [x] **72:17** as he has blessed the king; *or* and may they wish happiness for the king.

72:8 Zech 9:10; Sir 44:21

Study it!

Dividing the Psalms

You may have noticed that before Psalm 73, there is a heading that says "Book Three (Psalms 73–89)." Psalms is divided into five parts, called books. Book 1 contains Psalms 1–41, Book 2 has Psalms 42–72, Book 3 runs from 73–89, Book 4 includes 90–106, and Book 5 contains Psalms 107–150.

Experts really aren't sure how or why the Psalms were divided into these different books. There is evidence that shows smaller collections of the Psalms were made before the whole group was done. Because psalms were written and sung over a long period of time, scholars say it isn't surprising that we know so little about how they were organized. We do know, however, that they are loved by many people and that they express many different emotions and situations.

— Psalm 73

18 Praise the LORD, the God of Israel!
He alone does these wonderful things.
19 Praise his glorious name forever!
May his glory fill the whole world.

Amen! Amen!

20 This is the end of the prayers of David son of Jesse.

BOOK THREE
(Psalms 73–89)

The Justice of God[y]

73 God is indeed good to Israel,
to those who have pure hearts.
2 But I had nearly lost confidence;
my faith was almost gone
3 because I was jealous of the proud
when I saw that things go well for the wicked.

4 They do not suffer pain;
they are strong and healthy.
5 They do not suffer as other people do;
they do not have the troubles that others have.
6 And so they wear pride like a necklace
and violence like a robe;
7 their hearts pour out evil,[z]
and their minds are busy with wicked schemes.
8 They laugh at other people and speak of evil things;
they are proud and make plans to oppress others.
9 They speak evil of God in heaven
and give arrogant orders to everyone on earth,
10 so that even God's people turn to them
and eagerly believe whatever they say.[a]
11 They say, "God will not know;
the Most High will not find out."
12 That is what the wicked are like.
They have plenty and are always getting more.

13 Is it for nothing, then, that I have kept myself pure
and have not committed sin?
14 O God, you have made me suffer all day long;
every morning you have punished me.

15 If I had said such things,
I would not be acting as one of your people.
16 I tried to think this problem through,
but it was too difficult for me
17 until I went into your Temple.
Then I understood what will happen to the wicked.

18 You will put them in slippery places
and make them fall to destruction!
19 They are instantly destroyed;
they go down to a horrible end.

[y] **73** HEBREW TITLE: *By Asaph.* [z] **73:7** *Some ancient translations* their hearts pour out evil; *Hebrew unclear.*
[a] **73:10** *Verse 10 in Hebrew is unclear.*

20 They are like a dream that goes away in
the morning;
when you rouse yourself, O Lord, they
disappear.
21 When my thoughts were bitter
and my feelings were hurt,
22 I was as stupid as an animal;
I did not understand you.
23 Yet I always stay close to you,
and you hold me by the hand.
24 You guide me with your instruction
and at the end you will receive me
with honor.
25 What else do I have in heaven but you?
Since I have you, what else could I
want on earth?
26 My mind and my body may grow
weak,
but God is my strength;
he is all I ever need.
27 Those who abandon you will certainly
perish;
you will destroy those who are
unfaithful to you.
28 But as for me, how wonderful to be near
God,
to find protection with the Sovereign
LORD
and to proclaim all that he has done!

A Prayer for National Deliverance[b]

74 Why have you abandoned us like
this, O God?
Will you be angry with your own
people forever?
2 Remember your people, whom you
chose for yourself long ago,
whom you brought out of slavery to be
your own tribe.
Remember Mount Zion, where once
you lived.
3 Walk over these total ruins;
our enemies have destroyed everything
in the Temple.
4 Your enemies have shouted in triumph in
your Temple;
they have placed their flags there as
signs of victory.
5 They looked like woodsmen
cutting down trees with their axes.[c]
6 They smashed all the wooden panels
with their axes and sledge hammers.
7 They wrecked your Temple and set it on
fire;
they desecrated the place where you
are worshiped.
8 They wanted to crush us completely;
they burned down every holy place in
the land.
9 All our sacred symbols are gone;
there are no prophets left,
and no one knows how long this will
last.
10 How long, O God, will our enemies
laugh at you?
Will they insult your name forever?
11 Why have you refused to help us?
Why do you keep your hands behind
you?[d]
12 But you have been our king from the
beginning, O God;
you have saved us many times.
13 With your mighty strength you divided
the sea
and smashed the heads of the sea
monsters;
14 you crushed the heads of the monster
Leviathan[e]
and fed his body to desert animals.[f]
15 You made springs and fountains
flow;
you dried up large rivers.
16 You created the day and the night;
you set the sun and the moon in their
places;

[b] **74** HEBREW TITLE: *A poem by Asaph.* [c] **74:5** *Verse 5 in Hebrew is unclear.* [d] **74:11** *Probable text* Why do you keep your hands behind you; *Hebrew unclear.* [e] **74:14** LEVIATHAN: *A legendary monster which was a symbol of the forces of chaos and evil.* [f] **74:14** animals; *or* people.
74:13 Ex 14:21 **74:14** Job 41:1; Ps 104:26; Isa 27:1

"But as for me, how wonderful to be near God, / to find protection with the Sovereign LORD / and to proclaim all that he has done!" *(Psalm 73:28)*.

17 you set the limits of the earth;
you made summer and winter.

18 But remember, O LORD, that your enemies laugh at you,
that they are godless and despise you.
19 Don't abandon your helpless people to their cruel enemies;
don't forget your persecuted people!
20 Remember the covenant you made with us.
There is violence in every dark corner of the land.
21 Don't let the oppressed be put to shame;
let those poor and needy people praise you.

22 Rouse yourself, God, and defend your cause!
Remember that godless people laugh at you all day long.
23 Don't forget the angry shouts of your enemies,
the continuous noise made by your foes.

God the Judge[g]

75 We give thanks to you, O God, we give thanks to you!
We proclaim how great you are
and tell of[h] the wonderful things you have done.

2 "I have set a time for judgment," says God,
"and I will judge with fairness.
3 Though every living creature tremble
and the earth itself be shaken,
I will keep its foundations firm.
4 I tell the wicked not to be arrogant;
5 I tell them to stop their boasting."
6 Judgment does not come from the east or from the west,
from the north or from the south;[i]
7 it is God who is the judge,
condemning some and acquitting others.
8 The LORD holds a cup in his hand,
filled with the strong wine of his anger.
He pours it out, and all the wicked drink it;
they drink it down to the last drop.
9 But I will never stop speaking of the God of Jacob
or singing praises to him.
10 He will break the power of the wicked,
but the power of the righteous will be increased.

God the Victor[j]

76 God is known in Judah;
his name is honored in Israel.
2 He has his home in Jerusalem;
he lives on Mount Zion.
3 There he broke the arrows of the enemy,
their shields and swords, yes, all their weapons.

4 How glorious you are, O God!
How majestic, as you return from the mountains
where you defeated your foes.
5 Their brave soldiers have been stripped of all they had
and now are sleeping the sleep of death;
all their strength and skill was useless.
6 When you threatened them, O God of Jacob,
the horses and their riders fell dead.

7 But you, LORD, are feared by all.
No one can stand in your presence
when you are angry.
8 You made your judgment known from heaven;
the world was afraid and kept silent,
9 when you rose up to pronounce judgment,
to save all the oppressed on earth.

[g] **75** HEBREW TITLE: *A psalm by Asaph; a song.* [h] **75:1** *Some ancient translations* We proclaim how great you are and tell of; *Hebrew* Your name is near and they tell of. [i] **75:6** *Probable text* from the north or from the south; *Hebrew* from the wilderness of the mountains. [j] **76** HEBREW TITLE: *A psalm by Asaph; a song.*

What do you think it means to say that God judges "with fairness"? *(Psalm 75:2)*.

10 Human anger only results in more praise
for you;
those who survive the wars will keep
your festivals.[k]

11 Give the LORD your God what you
promised him;
bring gifts to him, all you nearby
nations.
God makes everyone fear him;
12 he humbles proud princes
and terrifies great kings.

Comfort in Time of Distress[l]

77 I cry aloud to God;
I cry aloud, and he hears me.
2 In times of trouble I pray to the Lord;
all night long I lift my hands in prayer,
but I cannot find comfort.
3 When I think of God, I sigh;
when I meditate, I feel discouraged.

4 He keeps me awake all night;
I am so worried that I cannot speak.
5 I think of days gone by and remember
years of long ago.

6 I spend the night in deep thought;[m]
I meditate, and this is what I ask myself:
7 "Will the Lord always reject us?
Will he never again be pleased with us?
8 Has he stopped loving us?
Does his promise no longer stand?
9 Has God forgotten to be merciful?
Has anger taken the place of his
compassion?"
10 Then I said, "What hurts me most is this—
that God is no longer powerful."[n]

11 I will remember your great deeds, LORD;
I will recall the wonders you did in the
past.
12 I will think about all that you have done;
I will meditate on all your mighty acts.

13 Everything you do, O God, is holy.
No god is as great as you.
14 You are the God who works miracles;
you showed your might among the
nations.
15 By your power you saved your people,
the descendants of Jacob and of Joseph.

16 When the waters saw you, O God, they
were afraid,
and the depths of the sea trembled.
17 The clouds poured down rain;
thunder crashed from the sky,
and lightning flashed in all directions.
18 The crash of your thunder rolled out,
and flashes of lightning lit up the world;
the earth trembled and shook.
19 You walked through the waves;
you crossed the deep sea,
but your footprints could not be seen.
20 You led your people like a shepherd,
with Moses and Aaron in charge.

God and His People[o]

78 Listen, my people, to my teaching,
and pay attention to what I say.
2 I am going to use wise sayings
and explain mysteries from the past,
3 things we have heard and known,
things that our ancestors told us.
4 We will not keep them from our children;
we will tell the next generation
about the LORD's power and his great
deeds
and the wonderful things he has done.

5 He gave laws to the people of Israel
and commandments to the descendants
of Jacob.
He instructed our ancestors
to teach his laws to their children,
6 so that the next generation might learn
them
and in turn should tell their children.
7 In this way they also will put their trust in
God
and not forget what he has done,
but always obey his commandments.
8 They will not be like their ancestors,
a rebellious and disobedient people,
whose trust in God was never firm
and who did not remain faithful to
him.

[k] **76:10** *One ancient translation* will keep your festivals; *verse 10 in Hebrew is unclear.* [l] **77** HEBREW TITLE: *A psalm by Asaph.* [m] **77:6** *Some ancient translations* deep thought; *Hebrew* song. [n] **77:10** *Verse 10 in Hebrew is unclear.*
[o] **78** HEBREW TITLE: *A poem by Asaph.*

78:2 Mt 13:35

Pray it!

Manna from Heaven

Psalm 78 is kind of an overview of the important people and events in the Old Testament. You may recognize the names of some of the people and events mentioned. One of the events was when God provided manna, or food, for the Israelites during a time when they were starving in the desert (verses 23–25).

Many of us often exaggerate our hunger by saying something like, "I'm so hungry I could eat a horse." But for many people around the world, even in the United States, these are real words. Millions of people in the world do not have enough to eat. To help the cause of ending world hunger, join in this prayer:

Giver of life, you helped the Israelites when they were hungry. I know you will continue to help the hungry in our time, too. Help me be more aware of the needs of others, and make me eager to join in works of service to help those who are hungry every day. Amen.

— Psalm 78:23–25

9 The Ephraimites, armed with bows and arrows,
ran away on the day of battle.
10 They did not keep their covenant with God;
they refused to obey his law.
11 They forgot what he had done,
the miracles they had seen him perform.
12 While their ancestors watched, God performed miracles
in the plain of Zoan in the land of Egypt.
13 He divided the sea and took them through it;
he made the waters stand like walls.
14 By day he led them with a cloud
and all night long with the light of a fire.
15 He split rocks open in the desert
and gave them water from the depths.
16 He caused a stream to come out of the rock
and made water flow like a river.

17 But they continued to sin against God,
and in the desert they rebelled against the Most High.
18 They deliberately put God to the test
by demanding the food they wanted.
19 They spoke against God and said,
"Can God supply food in the desert?
20 It is true that he struck the rock,
and water flowed out in a torrent;
but can he also provide us with bread
and give his people meat?"

21 And so the LORD was angry when he heard them;
he attacked his people with fire,
and his anger against them grew,
22 because they had no faith in him
and did not believe that he would save them.
23 But he spoke to the sky above
and commanded its doors to open;
24 he gave them grain from heaven,
by sending down manna for them to eat.
25 So they ate the food of angels,
and God gave them all they wanted.
26 He also caused the east wind to blow,
and by his power he stirred up the south wind;
27 and to his people he sent down birds,
as many as the grains of sand on the shore;
28 they fell in the middle of the camp
all around the tents.
29 So the people ate and were satisfied;
God gave them what they wanted.

78:12 Ex 7:8—12:32 **78:13** Ex 14:21, 22 **78:14** Ex 13:21, 22 **78:12–16** Wis 16:1—19:22 **78:15, 16** Ex 17:1–7; Num 20:2–13 **78:18–31** Ex 16:2–15; Num 11:4–23, 31–35 **78:24** Wis 16:20–29; Jn 6:31

30 But they had not yet satisfied their craving
and were still eating,
31 when God became angry with them
and killed their strongest men,
the best young men of Israel.

32 In spite of all this the people kept sinning;
in spite of his miracles they did not
trust him.
33 So he ended their days like a breath
and their lives with sudden disaster.
34 Whenever he killed some of them,
the rest would turn to him;
they would repent and pray earnestly
to him.
35 They remembered that God was their
protector,
that the Almighty came to their aid.
36 But their words were all lies;
nothing they said was sincere.
37 They were not loyal to him;
they were not faithful to their covenant
with him.

38 But God was merciful to his people.
He forgave their sin
and did not destroy them.
Many times he held back his anger
and restrained his fury.
39 He remembered that they were only
mortal beings,
like a wind that blows by and is gone.

40 How often they rebelled against him in
the desert;
how many times they made him sad!
41 Again and again they put God to the test
and brought pain to the Holy God of
Israel.
42 They forgot his great power
and the day when he saved them from
their enemies
43 and performed his mighty acts and
miracles
in the plain of Zoan in the land of
Egypt.

44 He turned the rivers into blood,
and the Egyptians had no water to
drink.
45 He sent flies among them, that tormented
them,
and frogs that ruined their land.
46 He sent locusts to eat their crops
and to destroy their fields.
47 He killed their grapevines with hail
and their fig trees with frost.
48 He killed their cattle with hail
and their flocks with lightning.[p]
49 He caused them great distress
by pouring out his anger and fierce
rage,
which came as messengers of death.
50 He did not restrain his anger
or spare their lives,
but killed them with a plague.
51 He killed the first-born sons
of all the families of Egypt.

52 Then he led his people out like a
shepherd
and guided them through the desert.
53 He led them safely, and they were not
afraid;
but the sea came rolling over their
enemies.
54 He brought them to his holy land,
to the mountains which he himself
conquered.
55 He drove out the inhabitants as his people
advanced;
he divided their land among the tribes
of Israel
and gave their homes to his people.

56 But they rebelled against Almighty God
and put him to the test.
They did not obey his commandments,
57 but were rebellious and disloyal like
their ancestors,
unreliable as a crooked arrow.

[p] **78:48** hail . . . lightning; *or* terrible disease . . . deadly plague.

78:37 Acts 8:21 **78:44** Ex 7:17–21 **78:45 a** Ex 8:20–24; **b** Ex 8:1–6 **78:46** Ex 10:12–15 **78:47, 48** Ex 9:22–25 **78:51** Ex 12:29 **78:52** Ex 13:17–22 **78:53** Ex 14:26–28 **78:54** Ex 15:17; Josh 3:14–17 **78:55** Josh 11:16–23 **78:56** Judg 2:11–15

Can you find the ten plagues from Exodus in Psalm 78?

58 They angered him with their heathen
places of worship,
and with their idols they made him
furious.
59 God was angry when he saw it,
so he rejected his people completely.
60 He abandoned his tent in Shiloh,[q]
the home where he had lived among
us.
61 He allowed our enemies to capture the
Covenant Box,
the symbol of his power and glory.
62 He was angry with his own people
and let them be killed by their
enemies.
63 Young men were killed in war,
and young women had no one to
marry.
64 Priests died by violence,
and their widows were not allowed to
mourn.

65 At last the Lord woke up as though from
sleep;
he was like a strong man excited by
wine.
66 He drove his enemies back
in lasting and shameful defeat.
67 But he rejected the descendants of Joseph;
he did not select the tribe of Ephraim.
68 Instead he chose the tribe of Judah
and Mount Zion, which he dearly loves.
69 There he built his Temple
like his home in heaven;
he made it firm like the earth itself,
secure for all time.

70 He chose his servant David;
he took him from the pastures,
71 where he looked after his flocks,
and he made him king of Israel,
the shepherd of the people of God.
72 David took care of them with unselfish
devotion
and led them with skill.

A Prayer for the Nation's Deliverance[r]

79 O God, the heathen have invaded
your land.
They have desecrated your holy Temple
and left Jerusalem in ruins.
2 They left the bodies of your people for
the vultures,
the bodies of your servants for wild
animals to eat.
3 They shed your people's blood like water;
blood flowed like water all through
Jerusalem,
and no one was left to bury the dead.
4 The surrounding nations insult us;
they laugh at us and mock us.

5 LORD, will you be angry with us forever?
Will your anger continue to burn like
fire?
6 Turn your anger on the nations that do
not worship you,
on the people who do not pray to you.
7 For they have killed your people;
they have ruined your country.

8 Do not punish us for the sins of our
ancestors.
Have mercy on us now;
we have lost all hope.
9 Help us, O God, and save us;
rescue us and forgive our sins
for the sake of your own honor.
10 Why should the nations ask us,
"Where is your God?"
Let us see you punish the nations
for shedding the blood of your
servants.

11 Listen to the groans of the prisoners,
and by your great power free those
who are condemned to die.
12 Lord, pay the other nations back seven
times
for all the insults they have hurled at
you.

[q] **78:60** SHILOH: *The central place of worship for the people of Israel before the time of King David.* [r] **79** HEBREW TITLE: *A psalm by Asaph.*

78:60 Josh 18:1; Jer 7:12–14; 26:6 **78:61** 1 Sam 4:4–22 **78:70, 71** 1 Sam 16:11, 12; 2 Sam 7:8; 1 Chr 17:7
79:1 2 Kings 25:8–10; 2 Chr 36:17–19; Jer 52:12–14

"Bring us back, O God! / Show us your mercy, and we will be saved!" *(Psalm 80:3)*.

13 Then we, your people, the sheep of your
flock,
will thank you forever
and praise you for all time to come.

A Prayer for the Nation's Restoration[s]

80 Listen to us, O Shepherd of Israel;
hear us, leader of your flock.
Seated on your throne above the winged
creatures,
2 reveal yourself to the tribes of Ephraim,
Benjamin, and Manasseh.
Show us your strength;
come and save us!

3 Bring us back, O God!
Show us your mercy, and we will be
saved!

4 How much longer, LORD God Almighty,
will you be angry with your people's
prayers?
5 You have given us sorrow to eat,
a large cup of tears to drink.
6 You let the surrounding nations fight over
our land;
our enemies insult us.

7 Bring us back, Almighty God!
Show us your mercy, and we will be
saved!

8 You brought a grapevine out of Egypt;
you drove out other nations and
planted it in their land.
9 You cleared a place for it to grow;
its roots went deep, and it spread out
over the whole land.
10 It covered the hills with its shade;
its branches overshadowed the giant
cedars.
11 It extended its branches to the
Mediterranean Sea
and as far as the Euphrates River.
12 Why did you break down the fences
around it?
Now anyone passing by can steal its
grapes;
13 wild hogs trample it down,
and wild animals feed on it.

14 Turn to us, Almighty God!
Look down from heaven at us;
come and save your people!
15 Come and save this grapevine that you
planted,
this young vine you made grow so
strong!

16 Our enemies have set it on fire and cut it
down;
look at them in anger and destroy
them!
17 Preserve and protect the people you have
chosen,
the nation you made so strong.
18 We will never turn away from you again;
keep us alive, and we will praise you.

19 Bring us back, LORD God Almighty.
Show us your mercy, and we will be
saved.

A Song for a Festival[t]

81 Shout for joy to God our defender;
sing praise to the God of Jacob!
2 Start the music and beat the tambourines;
play pleasant music on the harps and
the lyres.
3 Blow the trumpet for the festival,
when the moon is new and when the
moon is full.
4 This is the law in Israel,
an order from the God of Jacob.
5 He gave it to the people of Israel
when he attacked the land of
Egypt.

I hear an unknown voice saying,
6 "I took the burdens off your backs;
I let you put down your loads of
bricks.
7 When you were in trouble, you called to
me, and I saved you.
From my hiding place in the storm, I
answered you.
I put you to the test at the springs of
Meribah.
8 Listen, my people, to my warning;
Israel, how I wish you would listen to
me!

[s] **80** HEBREW TITLE: *A psalm by Asaph; a testimony.* [t] **81** HEBREW TITLE: *By Asaph.*

80:1 Ex 25:22 **81:3** Num 10:10 **81:7** Ex 17:7; Num 20:13

9 You must never worship another god.
10 I am the LORD your God,
who brought you out of Egypt.
Open your mouth, and I will feed you.

11 "But my people would not listen to me;
Israel would not obey me.
12 So I let them go their stubborn ways
and do whatever they wanted.
13 How I wish my people would listen to me;
how I wish they would obey me!
14 I would quickly defeat their enemies
and conquer all their foes.
15 Those who hate me would bow in fear before me;
their punishment would last forever.
16 But I would feed you with the finest wheat
and satisfy you with wild honey."

God the Supreme Ruler[u]

82 God presides in the heavenly council;
in the assembly of the gods he gives his decision:
2 "You must stop judging unjustly;
you must no longer be partial to the wicked!
3 Defend the rights of the poor and the orphans;
be fair to the needy and the helpless.
4 Rescue them from the power of evil people.

5 "How ignorant you are! How stupid!
You are completely corrupt,
and justice has disappeared from the world.
6 'You are gods,' I said;
'all of you are children of the Most High.'
7 But you will die like mortals;
your life will end like that of any prince."

8 Come, O God, and rule the world;
all the nations are yours.

A Prayer for the Defeat of Israel's Enemies[v]

83 O God, do not keep silent;
do not be still, do not be quiet!
2 Look! Your enemies are in revolt,
and those who hate you are rebelling.
3 They are making secret plans against your people;
they are plotting against those you protect.
4 "Come," they say, "let us destroy their nation,
so that Israel will be forgotten forever."

5 They agree on their plan
and form an alliance against you:
6 the people of Edom and the Ishmaelites;
the people of Moab and the Hagrites;
7 the people of Gebal, Ammon, and Amalek,
and of Philistia and Tyre.
8 Assyria has also joined them
as a strong ally of the Ammonites and Moabites, the descendants of Lot.

9 Do to them what you did to the Midianites,
and to Sisera and Jabin at the Kishon River.
10 You defeated them at Endor,
and their bodies rotted on the ground.
11 Do to their leaders what you did to Oreb and Zeeb;
defeat all their rulers as you did Zebah and Zalmunna,
12 who said, "We will take for our own
the land that belongs to God."

13 Scatter them like dust, O God,
like straw blown away by the wind.
14 As fire burns the forest,
as flames set the hills on fire,
15 chase them away with your storm
and terrify them with your fierce winds.
16 Cover their faces with shame, O LORD,
and make them acknowledge your power.
17 May they be defeated and terrified forever;
may they die in complete disgrace.

[u] **82** HEBREW TITLE: *A psalm by Asaph.* [v] **83** HEBREW TITLE: *A psalm by Asaph; a song.*

81:9 Ex 20:2, 3; Deut 5:6, 7 **82:6** Jn 10:34 **83:9 a** Judg 7:1–23; **b** Judg 4:6–22 **83:11 a** Judg 7:25; **b** Judg 8:12

18 May they know that you alone are the
LORD,
supreme ruler over all the earth.

Longing for God's House[w]

84 How I love your Temple, LORD
Almighty!
2 How I want to be there!
I long to be in the LORD's Temple.
With my whole being I sing for joy
to the living God.
3 Even the sparrows have built a nest,
and the swallows have their own home;
they keep their young near your altars,
LORD Almighty, my king and my God.

Even the sparrows have built a nest. (84:3)

4 How happy are those who live in your
Temple,
always singing praise to you.
5 How happy are those whose strength
comes from you,
who are eager to make the pilgrimage
to Mount Zion.
6 As they pass through the dry valley of
Baca,
it becomes a place of springs;
the autumn rain fills it with pools.
7 They grow stronger as they go;
they will see the God of gods on
Zion.

8 Hear my prayer, LORD God Almighty.
Listen, O God of Jacob!
9 Bless our king, O God,
the king you have chosen.

10 One day spent in your Temple
is better than a thousand anywhere
else;
I would rather stand at the gate of the
house of my God
than live in the homes of the wicked.
11 The LORD is our protector and glorious
king,
blessing us with kindness and honor.
He does not refuse any good thing
to those who do what is right.
12 LORD Almighty, how happy are those
who trust in you!

A Prayer for the Nation's Welfare[w]

85 LORD, you have been merciful to
your land;
you have made Israel prosperous again.
2 You have forgiven your people's sins
and pardoned all their wrongs.
3 You stopped being angry with them
and held back your furious rage.
4 Bring us back, O God our savior,
and stop being displeased with us!
5 Will you be angry with us forever?
Will your anger never cease?
6 Make us strong again,
and we, your people, will praise you.
7 Show us your constant love, O LORD,
and give us your saving help.

8 I am listening to what the LORD God is
saying;
he promises peace to us, his own
people,
if we do not go back to our foolish
ways.
9 Surely he is ready to save those who
honor him,
and his saving presence will remain in
our land.

[w] **84; 85** HEBREW TITLE: *A psalm by the clan of Korah.*

"One day spent in your Temple / is better than a thousand anywhere else" *(Psalm 84:10)*.

Live it!

Let God Help

Doing things alone can be difficult! Imagine trying to play tug of war against a whole team—by yourself. Some people think they can live without God's help. But that is like playing tug-of-war by yourself against a whole team. Psalm 85 reminds us that we especially need God's help. If we really listen to the message of verses 10–11, we will hear how good life is when we work with God: "Love and faithfulness will meet; / righteousness and peace will embrace. / Human loyalty will reach up from the earth, / and God's righteousness will look down from heaven."

Can't you just picture your hand reaching up from the earth and God's hand reaching down toward you? If you're trying to go it without God, life will most likely be harder, and the path will be rougher. If there is an area of your life where you can use some strength, remember Psalm 85 and reach your hand out to God. That area might be like a tug-of-war in your heart. Imagine how well you will play with God pulling with you!

— Psalm 85

10 Love and faithfulness will meet;
righteousness and peace will embrace.
11 Human loyalty will reach up from the earth,
and God's righteousness will look down from heaven.
12 The LORD will make us prosperous,
and our land will produce rich harvests.
13 Righteousness will go before the LORD
and prepare the path for him.

A Prayer for Help[x]

86 Listen to me, LORD, and answer me,
for I am helpless and weak.
2 Save me from death, because I am loyal to you;
save me, for I am your servant and I trust in you.
3 You are my God, so be merciful to me;
I pray to you all day long.
4 Make your servant glad, O Lord,
because my prayers go up to you.
5 You are good to us and forgiving,
full of constant love for all who pray to you.

6 Listen, LORD, to my prayer;
hear my cries for help.
7 I call to you in times of trouble,
because you answer my prayers.

8 There is no god like you, O Lord,
not one has done what you have done.
9 All the nations that you have created
will come and bow down to you;
they will praise your greatness.
10 You are mighty and do wonderful things;
you alone are God.

11 Teach me, LORD, what you want me to do,
and I will obey you faithfully;
teach me to serve you with complete devotion.
12 I will praise you with all my heart,
O Lord my God;
I will proclaim your greatness forever.
13 How great is your constant love for me!
You have saved me from the grave itself.

[x] **86** HEBREW TITLE: *A prayer by David.*
86:9 Rev 15:4

"Teach me, LORD, what you want me to do, / and I will obey you faithfully; / teach me to serve you with complete devotion" *(Psalm 86:11)*.

14 Proud people are coming against me,
O God;
a cruel gang is trying to kill me—
people who pay no attention to you.
15 But you, O Lord, are a merciful and
loving God,
always patient, always kind and faithful.
16 Turn to me and have mercy on me;
strengthen me and save me,
because I serve you just as my mother
did.
17 Show me proof of your goodness, LORD;
those who hate me will be ashamed
when they see that you have given me
comfort and help.

In Praise of Jerusalem[y]

87 The LORD built his city on the
sacred hill;[z]
2 more than any other place in Israel
he loves the city of Jerusalem.
3 Listen, city of God,
to the wonderful things he says about
you:
4 "I will include Egypt and Babylonia
when I list the nations that obey me;
the people of Philistia, Tyre, and Ethiopia[a]
I will number among the inhabitants of
Jerusalem."
5 Of Zion it will be said
that all nations belong there
and that the Almighty will make her
strong.
6 The LORD will write a list of the peoples
and include them all as citizens of
Jerusalem.
7 They dance and sing,
"In Zion is the source of all our
blessings."

A Cry for Help[b]

88 LORD God, my savior, I cry out all
day,
and at night I come before you.

Pray it!

Lowest of the Low

Feeling really low, bluer than blue, and just rotten? Check out Psalm 88. It is called the most miserable of all the individual laments (a type of psalm expressing sadness). So you can read it when you're really blue and know that even the psalmist felt that way.

Or maybe you want to write your own individual lament. First, start with a cry to God, then list your troubles, and end with a description of how you are feeling right now. Psalms are very poetic and use symbolic words, so be creative in describing your feelings. Just writing out how you feel can sometimes help you feel better.

— Psalm 88

2 Hear my prayer;
listen to my cry for help!
3 So many troubles have fallen on me
that I am close to death.
4 I am like all others who are about to
die;
all my strength is gone.[c]
5 I am abandoned among the dead;
I am like the slain lying in their
graves,
those you have forgotten completely,
who are beyond your help.
6 You have thrown me into the depths of
the tomb,
into the darkest and deepest pit.
7 Your anger lies heavy on me,
and I am crushed beneath its waves.

[y] **87** HEBREW TITLE: *A psalm by the clan of Korah; a song.* [z] **87:1** SACRED HILL: *See 2:6.* [a] **87:4** *Hebrew* Cush: *Cush is the ancient name of the extensive territory south of the First Cataract of the Nile River. This region was called Ethiopia in Graeco-Roman time, and included within its borders most of modern Sudan and some of present-day Ethiopia (Abyssinia).* [b] **88** HEBREW TITLE: *A psalm by the clan of Korah; a song. A poem by Heman the Ezrahite.* [c] **88:4** all my strength is gone; *or* there is no help for me.

8 You have caused my friends to abandon me;
you have made me repulsive to them.
I am closed in and cannot escape;
9 my eyes are weak from suffering.
LORD, every day I call to you
and lift my hands to you in prayer.
10 Do you perform miracles for the dead?
Do they rise up and praise you?
11 Is your constant love spoken of in the grave
or your faithfulness in the place of destruction?
12 Are your miracles seen in that place of darkness
or your goodness in the land of the forgotten?
13 LORD, I call to you for help;
every morning I pray to you.
14 Why do you reject me, LORD?
Why do you turn away from me?
15 Ever since I was young, I have suffered and been near death;
I am worn out[d] from the burden of your punishments.
16 Your furious anger crushes me;
your terrible attacks destroy me.
17 All day long they surround me like a flood;
they close in on me from every side.
18 You have made even my closest friends abandon me,
and darkness is my only companion.

A Hymn in Time of National Trouble[e]

89 O LORD, I will always sing of your constant love;
I will proclaim your faithfulness forever.
2 I know that your love will last for all time,
that your faithfulness is as permanent as the sky.
3 You said, "I have made a covenant with the man I chose;
I have promised my servant David,
4 'A descendant of yours will always be king;
I will preserve your dynasty forever.' "
5 The heavens sing of the wonderful things you do;
the holy ones sing of your faithfulness, LORD.
6 No one in heaven is like you, LORD;
none of the heavenly beings is your equal.
7 You are feared in the council of the holy ones;
they all stand in awe of you.
8 LORD God Almighty, none is as mighty as you;
in all things you are faithful, O LORD.
9 You rule over the powerful sea;
you calm its angry waves.
10 You crushed the monster Rahab[f] and killed it;
with your mighty strength you defeated your enemies.
11 Heaven is yours, the earth also;
you made the world and everything in it.
12 You created the north and the south;
Mount Tabor and Mount Hermon sing to you for joy.
13 How powerful you are!
How great is your strength!
14 Your kingdom is founded on righteousness and justice;
love and faithfulness are shown in all you do.
15 How happy are the people who worship you with songs,
who live in the light of your kindness!
16 Because of you they rejoice all day long,
and they praise you for your goodness.
17 You give us great victories;
in your love you make us triumphant.
18 You, O LORD, chose our protector;
you, the Holy God of Israel, gave us our king.

[d] **88:15** *Probable text* I am worn out; *Hebrew unclear.* [e] **89** HEBREW TITLE: *A poem by Ethan the Ezrahite.*
[f] **89:10** RAHAB: *A legendary sea monster which represented the forces of chaos and evil.*
89 Title 1 Kings 4:31 **89:4** 2 Sam 7:12–16; 1 Chr 17:11–14; Ps 132:11; Acts 2:30

Catholic Connections

Electing a Pope

"Who will it be?"
"Will he be like the last one?"
"Will it be someone we have heard of?"
"Will it be an Italian?"
"Will it be an African?"

These are some of the many questions that people ask when a pope dies and a new one is soon to be elected. The cardinals elect the pope in a process that includes prayer and conversation. The most important thing in their decision is the Holy Spirit. It is the Holy Spirit that guides the cardinals as they elect their (and our) leader. Masses are held around the world as the new pope is being chosen. The psalm response in these Masses is from Psalm 89, which reminds us that God is faithful in his promises to us.

— Psalm 89

God's Promise to David

19 In a vision long ago you said to your faithful servants,
"I have given help to a famous soldier;
I have given the throne to one I chose from the people.
20 I have made my servant David king
by anointing him with holy oil.
21 My strength will always be with him,
my power will make him strong.
22 His enemies will never succeed against him;
the wicked will not defeat him.
23 I will crush his foes
and kill everyone who hates him.
24 I will love him and be loyal to him;
I will make him always victorious.
25 I will extend his kingdom
from the Mediterranean to the Euphrates River.
26 He will say to me,
'You are my father and my God;
you are my protector and savior.'
27 I will make him my first-born son,
the greatest of all kings.
28 I will always keep my promise to him,
and my covenant with him will last forever.
29 His dynasty will be as permanent as the sky;
a descendant of his will always be king.
30 "But if his descendants disobey my law
and do not live according to my commands,
31 if they disregard my instructions
and do not keep my commandments,
32 then I will punish them for their sins;
I will make them suffer for their wrongs.
33 But I will not stop loving David
or fail to keep my promise to him.
34 I will not break my covenant with him
or take back even one promise I made him.
35 "Once and for all I have promised by my holy name:
I will never lie to David.
36 He will always have descendants,

89:20 **a** 1 Sam 13:14; Acts 13:22; **b** 1 Sam 16:12 **89:27** Rev 1:5

Find the questions the psalmist asks God in Psalm 88. How do you think God would answer them?

and I will watch over his kingdom as
long as the sun shines.
37 It will be as permanent as the moon,
that faithful witness in the sky."

Lament over the Defeat of the King

38 But you are angry with your chosen king;
you have deserted and rejected him.
39 You have broken your covenant with
your servant
and thrown his crown in the dirt.
40 You have torn down the walls of his city
and left his forts in ruins.
41 All who pass by steal his belongings;
all his neighbors laugh at him.
42 You have given the victory to his
enemies;
you have made them all happy.
43 You have made his weapons useless
and let him be defeated in battle.
44 You have taken away his royal scepter[g]
and knocked his throne to the ground.
45 You have made him old before his time
and covered him with disgrace.

A Prayer for Deliverance

46 LORD, will you hide yourself forever?
How long will your anger burn like fire?
47 Remember how short my life is;
remember that you created all of us
mortal!
48 Who can live and never die?
How can we humans keep ourselves
from the grave?

49 Lord, where are the former proofs of your
love?
Where are the promises you made to
David?
50 Don't forget how I, your servant, am
insulted,
how I endure all the curses[h] of the
heathen.
51 Your enemies insult your chosen king,
O LORD!
They insult him wherever he goes.

52 Praise the LORD forever!

Amen! Amen!

BOOK FOUR
(Psalms 90–106)

Of God and Human Beings[i]

90 O Lord, you have always been our
home.
2 Before you created the hills
or brought the world into being,
you were eternally God,
and will be God forever.

3 You tell us to return to what we were;
you change us back to dust.
4 A thousand years to you are like one day;
they are like yesterday, already gone,
like a short hour in the night.
5 You carry us away like a flood;
we last no longer than a dream.
We are like weeds that sprout in the
morning,
6 that grow and burst into bloom,
then dry up and die in the evening.
7 We are destroyed by your anger;
we are terrified by your fury.
8 You place our sins before you,
our secret sins where you can see them.

9 Our life is cut short by your anger;
it fades away like a whisper.
10 Seventy years is all we have—
eighty years, if we are strong;
yet all they bring us is trouble and sorrow;
life is soon over, and we are gone.

11 Who has felt the full power of your
anger?
Who knows what fear your fury can
bring?

[g] **89:44** *Probable text* royal scepter; *Hebrew* purity. [h] **89:50** *Probable text* curses; *Hebrew* crowds. [i] **90** HEBREW TITLE: *A prayer by Moses, the man of God.*
90:4 2 Pet 3:8 **90:10** Sir 18:8, 9

How many minutes "old" would you be if a thousand years were like a day?
(See Psalm 90:4.)

12 Teach us how short our life is,
so that we may become wise.

13 How much longer will your anger last?
Have pity, O LORD, on your servants!
14 Fill us each morning with your constant love,
so that we may sing and be glad all our life.
15 Give us now as much happiness as the sadness you gave us
during all our years of misery.
16 Let us, your servants, see your mighty deeds;
let our descendants see your glorious might.
17 Lord our God, may your blessings be with us.
Give us success in all we do!

God Our Protector

91 Whoever goes to the LORD for safety,
whoever remains under the protection of the Almighty,
2 can say to him,
"You are my defender and protector.
You are my God; in you I trust."
3 He will keep you safe from all hidden dangers
and from all deadly diseases.
4 He will cover you with his wings;
you will be safe in his care;
his faithfulness will protect and defend you.
5 You need not fear any dangers at night
or sudden attacks during the day
6 or the plagues that strike in the dark
or the evils that kill in daylight.

7 A thousand may fall dead beside you,
ten thousand all around you,
but you will not be harmed.
8 You will look and see
how the wicked are punished.

9 You have made the LORD your[j] defender,
the Most High your protector,
10 and so no disaster will strike you,
no violence will come near your home.
11 God will put his angels in charge of you
to protect you wherever you go.
12 They will hold you up with their hands
to keep you from hurting your feet on the stones.
13 You will trample down lions and snakes,
fierce lions and poisonous snakes.

14 God says, "I will save those who love me
and will protect those who acknowledge me as LORD.
15 When they call to me, I will answer them;
when they are in trouble, I will be with them.
I will rescue them and honor them.
16 I will reward them with long life;
I will save them."

A Song of Praise[k]

92 How good it is to give thanks to you, O LORD,
to sing in your honor, O Most High God,
2 to proclaim your constant love every morning
and your faithfulness every night,
3 with the music of stringed instruments
and with melody on the harp.
4 Your mighty deeds, O LORD, make me glad;
because of what you have done, I sing for joy.

5 How great are your actions, LORD!
How deep are your thoughts!
6 This is something a fool cannot know;
someone who is stupid cannot understand:
7 the wicked may grow like weeds,
those who do wrong may prosper;
yet they will be totally destroyed,
8 because you, LORD, are supreme forever.

9 We know that your enemies will die,
and all the wicked will be defeated.
10 You have made me as strong as a wild ox;
you have blessed me with happiness.
11 I have seen the defeat of my enemies
and heard the cries of the wicked.

[j] **91:9** *Probable text* your; *Hebrew* my. [k] **92** HEBREW TITLE: *A psalm; a song for the Sabbath.*

91:11 Mt 4:6; Lk 4:10 **91:12** Mt 4:6; Lk 4:11 **91:13** Lk 10:19 **92:6** Wis 13:1

12 The righteous will flourish like palm trees;
they will grow like the cedars of Lebanon.
13 They are like trees planted in the house of the LORD,
that flourish in the Temple of our God,
14 that still bear fruit in old age
and are always green and strong.
15 This shows that the LORD is just,
that there is no wrong in my protector.

God the King

93 The LORD is king.
He is clothed with majesty and strength.
The earth is set firmly in place
and cannot be moved.
2 Your throne, O LORD, has been firm from the beginning,
and you existed before time began.
3 The ocean depths raise their voice, O LORD;
they raise their voice and roar.
4 The LORD rules supreme in heaven,
greater than the roar of the ocean,
more powerful than the waves of the sea.
5 Your laws are eternal, LORD,
and your Temple is holy indeed,
forever and ever.

God the Judge of All

94 LORD, you are a God who punishes;
reveal your anger!
2 You are the judge of us all;
rise and give the proud what they deserve!
3 How much longer will the wicked be glad?
How much longer, LORD?
4 How much longer will criminals be proud
and boast about their crimes?
5 They crush your people, LORD;
they oppress those who belong to you.
6 They kill widows and orphans,
and murder the strangers who live in our land.
7 They say, "The LORD does not see us;
the God of Israel does not notice."
8 My people, how can you be such stupid fools?
When will you ever learn?
9 God made our ears—can't he hear?
He made our eyes—can't he see?
10 He scolds the nations—won't he punish them?[l]
He is the teacher of us all—hasn't he any knowledge?
11 The LORD knows what we think;
he knows how senseless our reasoning is.
12 LORD, how happy are those you instruct,
the ones to whom you teach your law!
13 You give them rest from days of trouble
until a pit is dug to trap the wicked.
14 The LORD will not abandon his people;
he will not desert those who belong to him.
15 Justice will again be found in the courts,
and all righteous people will support it.
16 Who stood up for me against the wicked?
Who took my side against the evildoers?
17 If the LORD had not helped me,
I would have gone quickly to the land of silence.[m]
18 I said, "I am falling";
but your constant love, O LORD, held me up.
19 Whenever I am anxious and worried,
you comfort me and make me glad.
20 You have nothing to do with corrupt judges,
who make injustice legal,
21 who plot against good people
and sentence the innocent to death.
22 But the LORD defends me;
my God protects me.
23 He will punish them for their wickedness
and destroy them for their sins;
the LORD our God will destroy them.

[l] **94:10** them?; *or* our wicked leaders? [m] **94:17** LAND OF SILENCE: *The world of the dead (see 6:5).*
94:11 1 Cor 3:20

Catholic Connections

Praise and Adoration

Alleluia means "Praise the Lord." And praise is what Psalm 95 is all about. Praise is a type of prayer. The Church teaches that praise is very important because it unites all our other prayers and carries them to God. When we praise God, we recognize his uniqueness, his power, and his love for us. If we didn't recognize those things, we would not be praying to God about anything else!

So praise is different from thanking God for what was done, or for asking God for something, and is certainly different from lamenting to God. It is about the joy of God's love. Praise can be heard in some great music, in many of the psalms, and is described in Paul's letter to the Ephesians (see Ephesians 5:19). Praise is also found in you—it's that feeling you get when you are happy and love God just because God *is*.

— Psalm 95:1–7

A Song of Praise

95 Come, let us praise the LORD!
Let us sing for joy to God, who protects us!
2 Let us come before him with thanksgiving
and sing joyful songs of praise.
3 For the LORD is a mighty God,
a mighty king over all the gods.
4 He rules over the whole earth,
from the deepest caves to the highest hills.
5 He rules over the sea, which he made;
the land also, which he himself formed.

6 Come, let us bow down and worship him;
let us kneel before the LORD, our Maker!
7 He is our God;
we are the people he cares for,
the flock for which he provides.

Listen today to what he says:

"Let us . . . worship him." (95:6)

8 "Don't be stubborn, as your ancestors were at Meribah,
as they were that day in the desert at Massah.
9 There they put me to the test and tried me,
although they had seen what I did for them.

95:7–11 Heb 3:7–11 **95:7, 8** Heb 3:15; 4:7 **95:8, 9** Ex 17:1–7; Num 20:2–13

"He is our God; / we are the people he cares for, / the flock for which he provides" *(Psalm 95:7)*.

10 For forty years I was disgusted with those
people.
I said, 'How disloyal they are!
They refuse to obey my commands.'
11 I was angry and made a solemn promise:
'You will never enter the land
where I would have given you rest.' "

God the Supreme King
(1 Chronicles 16:23–33)

96 Sing a new song to the LORD!
Sing to the LORD, all the world!
2 Sing to the LORD, and praise him!
Proclaim every day the good news that
he has saved us.
3 Proclaim his glory to the nations,
his mighty deeds to all peoples.

4 The LORD is great and is to be highly
praised;
he is to be honored more than all the
gods.
5 The gods of all other nations are only
idols,
but the LORD created the heavens.
6 Glory and majesty surround him;
power and beauty fill his Temple.

7 Praise the LORD, all people on earth;
praise his glory and might.
8 Praise the LORD's glorious name;
bring an offering and come into his
Temple.
9 Bow down before the Holy One when
he appears;[n]
tremble before him, all the earth!

10 Say to all the nations, "The LORD is king!
The earth is set firmly in place and
cannot be moved;
he will judge the peoples with justice."
11 Be glad, earth and sky!
Roar, sea, and every creature in you;
12 be glad, fields, and everything in you!
The trees in the woods will shout for joy

The trees in the woods will shout for joy. (96:12)

13 when the LORD comes to rule the
earth.
He will rule the peoples of the world
with justice and fairness.

God the Supreme Ruler

97 The LORD is king! Earth, be glad!
Rejoice, you islands of the seas!
2 Clouds and darkness surround him;
he rules with righteousness and justice.
3 Fire goes in front of him
and burns up his enemies around him.
4 His lightning lights up the world;
the earth sees it and trembles.
5 The hills melt like wax before the
LORD,
before the Lord of all the earth.
6 The heavens proclaim his righteousness,
and all the nations see his glory.

7 Everyone who worships idols is put to
shame;
all the gods bow down[o] before the
LORD.

[n] **96:9** when he appears; *or* in garments of worship. [o] **97:7** all the gods bow down; *or* bow down, all gods.
95:11 **a** Num 14:20–23; Deut 1:34–36; Heb 4:3, 5; **b** Deut 12:9, 10 **96:7–9** Ps 29:1, 2

Psalm 97 describes God as being a little bit like a superhero. If you were to name God as a superhero, what name would you give God?

8 The people of Zion are glad,
and the cities of Judah rejoice
because of your judgments, O LORD.
9 LORD Almighty, you are ruler of all the earth;
you are much greater than all the gods.

10 The LORD loves those who hate evil;[p]
he protects the lives of his people;
he rescues them from the power of the wicked.
11 Light shines on the righteous,
and gladness on the good.
12 All you that are righteous be glad
because of what the LORD has done!
Remember what the holy God has done,
and give thanks to him.

God the Ruler of the World[q]

98 Sing a new song to the LORD;
he has done wonderful things!
By his own power and holy strength
he has won the victory.
2 The LORD announced his victory;
he made his saving power known to the nations.
3 He kept his promise to the people of Israel
with loyalty and constant love for them.
All people everywhere have seen the victory of our God.

4 Sing for joy to the LORD, all the earth;
praise him with songs and shouts of joy!
5 Sing praises to the LORD!
Play music on the harps!
6 Blow trumpets and horns,
and shout for joy to the LORD, our king.

7 Roar, sea, and every creature in you;
sing, earth, and all who live on you!
8 Clap your hands, you rivers;
you hills, sing together with joy before the LORD,
9 because he comes to rule the earth.
He will rule the peoples of the world
with justice and fairness.

Pray it!

Highest of the High

So did you do the psalm writing as part of the "lowest of the low" (see Psalm 88)? Well, now is a chance to write the "highest of the high." Psalm 98 does that. It shouts out how great God is, and how well God takes care of his people. It ends by inviting everything in the world to clap and sing and praise God.

When you are feeling great, when life is good and it seems like all is well in the world, take time to write a praise psalm of your own. First, decide how you want to address God—for example, as king or with whatever other title you want to use. Then list the great things God has done. Lastly, end by inviting others to rejoice and remember the good things God has done. Remember to use poetic language and to name some specific things God has done for you and for others.

— Psalm 98

God the Supreme King

99 The LORD is king,
and the people tremble.
He sits on his throne above the winged creatures,
and the earth shakes.
2 The LORD is mighty in Zion;
he is supreme over all the nations.
3 Everyone will praise his great and majestic name.
Holy is he!

p 97:10 *Probable text* The LORD loves those who hate evil; *Hebrew* Hate evil, you who love the LORD.
q 98 HEBREW TITLE: *A psalm.*
99:1 Ex 25:22

Catholic Connections

Priestly Promises

"You mean you have to do everything he says?" Ty asked his uncle.

"Well, yes," his uncle replied.

"So, Uncle T, if he asked you to hurt someone, you have to?" Ty was trying to figure out how far his uncle would go. The had just read Psalm 99, and it bothered him that it was about commands. It sounded like the military.

"No, Little Ty, it doesn't mean that. What do you really want to know?" His uncle, also named Ty, knew that Little Ty was up to something.

"I want to know why you are doing it. Why become a priest? Why follow someone's commands?"

"It's about following God. And following what God calls me to do. I know I am supposed to be a priest. It is how I follow God's command."

"Maybe Little Ty will become the second Father Ty *if* his uncle stops calling him Little Ty." The younger Ty smiled up at his uncle, secretly liking to be called Little Ty by him and hoping his uncle would still use that name.

"Sorry, you'll always be my Little Ty. And, if God wants you to be a priest, I'll be there to help you figure it out. And if not, I'll be there to help you figure out what it is you're supposed to do with your life."

— Psalm 99

4 Mighty king,[r] you love what is right;
you have established justice in Israel;
you have brought righteousness and fairness.
5 Praise the LORD our God;
worship before his throne!
Holy is he!

6 Moses and Aaron were his priests,
and Samuel was one who prayed to him;
they called to the LORD, and he answered them.
7 He spoke to them from the pillar of cloud;
they obeyed the laws and commands that he gave them.

8 O LORD, our God, you answered your people;
you showed them that you are a God who forgives,
even though you punished them for their sins.

9 Praise the LORD our God,
and worship at his sacred hill![s]
The LORD our God is holy.

A Hymn of Praise[t]

100 Sing to the LORD, all the world!
2 Worship the LORD with joy;
come before him with happy songs!

3 Acknowledge that the LORD is God.
He made us, and we belong to him;
we are his people, we are his flock.

4 Enter the Temple gates with thanksgiving;
go into its courts with praise.
Give thanks to him and praise him.

5 The LORD is good;
his love is eternal
and his faithfulness lasts forever.

[r] **99:4** *Probable text* Mighty king; *Hebrew* The might of the king. [s] **99:9** SACRED HILL: *See 2:6.* [t] **100** HEBREW TITLE: *A psalm of thanksgiving.*

99:7 Ex 33:9 **100:5** 1 Chr 16:34; 2 Chr 5:13; 7:3; Ezra 3:11; Ps 106:1; 107:1; 118:1; 136:1; Jer 33:11

A King's Promise[u]

101 My song is about loyalty and
justice,
and I sing it to you, O LORD.
2 My conduct will be faultless.
When will you come to me?

I will live a pure life in my house
3 and will never tolerate evil.
I hate the actions of those who turn away
from God;
I will have nothing to do with them.
4 I will not be dishonest[v]
and will have no dealings with evil.[w]
5 I will get rid of anyone
who whispers evil things about
someone else;
I will not tolerate anyone
who is proud and arrogant.

"Enter the Temple gates with thanksgiving." (100:4)

6 I will approve of those who are faithful to
God
and will let them live in my palace.
Those who are completely honest
will be allowed to serve me.

7 No liar will live in my palace;
no hypocrite will remain in my
presence.
8 Day after day I will destroy
the wicked in our land;
I will expel all who are evil
from the city of the LORD.

The Prayer of a Troubled Youth[x]

102 Listen to my prayer, O LORD,
and hear my cry for help!
2 When I am in trouble,
don't turn away from me!
Listen to me,
and answer me quickly when I call!

3 My life is disappearing like smoke;
my body is burning like fire.
4 I am beaten down like dry grass;
I have lost my desire for food.
5 I groan aloud;
I am nothing but skin and bones.
6 I am like a wild bird in the desert,
like an owl in abandoned ruins.
7 I lie awake;
I am like a lonely bird on a housetop.
8 All day long my enemies insult me;
those who mock me use my name in
cursing.

9-10 Because of your anger and fury,
ashes are my food,
and my tears are mixed with my
drink.
You picked me up and threw me away.
11 My life is like the evening shadows;
I am like dry grass.

12 But you, O LORD, are king forever;
all generations will remember you.

[u] **101** HEBREW TITLE: *A psalm by David.* [v] **101:4** not be dishonest; *or* stay away from dishonest people.
[w] **101:4** evil; *or* evil people. [x] **102** HEBREW TITLE: *A prayer by a weary sufferer who pours out his complaints to the LORD.*

The psalmist says to "enter the Temple gates with thanksgiving" *(Psalm 100:4)*. **When you enter your church, do you do so with thanks and praise?**

Pray it!

Prayer for a Troubled Youth

If you're having a rough day, Psalm 102 is a great place for inspiration in prayer. And if you're really having a hard time, try this prayer, inspired by Psalm 103.

Praise the Lord!
How do I praise the Lord when everything is so horrible?
How can I remember how kind God is when everyone else is being unkind?
My life doesn't feel like it is filled with good things.
Wait, though, maybe I can praise the Lord:
I am young
God has forgiven me before.
God does love me.
Even if my parents don't seem kind right now,
they are good people, trying to do their best.
And, if I really do believe,
then God really is here,
even when life is crummy,
when things don't go my way,
and when I'm feeling troubled.
So, yeah, I will praise the Lord!
Praise the Lord!
With God, I will get through this!
Amen.

— Psalm 102

13 You will rise and take pity on Zion;
the time has come to have mercy on her;
this is the right time.
14 Your servants love her,
even though she is destroyed;
they have pity on her,
even though she is in ruins.
15 The nations will fear the LORD;
all the kings of the earth will fear his power.
16 When the LORD rebuilds Zion,
he will reveal his greatness.
17 He will hear his forsaken people
and listen to their prayer.
18 Write down for the coming generation
what the LORD has done,
so that people not yet born will praise him.
19 The LORD looked down from his holy place on high,
he looked down from heaven to earth.
20 He heard the groans of prisoners
and set free those who were condemned to die.
21 And so his name will be proclaimed in Zion,
and he will be praised in Jerusalem
22 when nations and kingdoms come together
and worship the LORD.

"When I am in trouble, / don't turn away from me! / Listen to me, / and answer me quickly when I call!" *(Psalm 102:2).*

23 The LORD has made me weak while I am
still young;
he has shortened my life.
24 O God, do not take me away now
before I grow old.

O LORD, you live forever;
25 long ago you created the earth,
and with your own hands you made
the heavens.
26 They will disappear, but you will
remain;
they will all wear out like clothes.
You will discard them like clothes,
and they will vanish.
27 But you are always the same,
and your life never ends.
28 Our children will live in safety,
and under your protection
their descendants will be secure.

The Love of God[y]

103 Praise the LORD, my soul!
All my being, praise his holy
name!
2 Praise the LORD, my soul,
and do not forget how kind he is.
3 He forgives all my sins
and heals all my diseases.
4 He keeps me from the grave
and blesses me with love and mercy.
5 He fills my life[z] with good things,
so that I stay young and strong like an
eagle.
6 The LORD judges in favor of the
oppressed
and gives them their rights.
7 He revealed his plans to Moses
and let the people of Israel see his
mighty deeds.
8 The LORD is merciful and loving,
slow to become angry and full of
constant love.
9 He does not keep on rebuking;
he is not angry forever.
10 He does not punish us as we deserve
or repay us according to our sins and
wrongs.
11 As high as the sky is above the earth,
so great is his love for those who honor
him.
12 As far as the east is from the west,
so far does he remove our sins from us.
13 As a father is kind to his children,
so the LORD is kind to those who
honor him.
14 He knows what we are made of;
he remembers that we are dust.

15 As for us, our life is like grass.
We grow and flourish like a wild flower;
16 then the wind blows on it, and it is
gone—
no one sees it again.

Then the wind blows on it, and it is gone. (103:16)

17 But for those who honor the LORD, his
love lasts forever,
and his goodness endures for all
generations
18 of those who are true to his covenant
and who faithfully obey his commands.

19 The LORD placed his throne in heaven;
he is king over all.
20 Praise the LORD, you strong and mighty
angels,
who obey his commands,
who listen to what he says.
21 Praise the LORD, all you heavenly
powers,
you servants of his, who do his will!
22 Praise the LORD, all his creatures
in all the places he rules.
Praise the LORD, my soul!

[y] **103** HEBREW TITLE: *By David.* [z] **103:5** *Probable text* my life; *Hebrew unclear.*

102:25–27 Heb 1:10 12 **103:8** Jas 5:11

In Praise of the Creator

104 Praise the LORD, my soul!
O LORD, my God, how great you are!
You are clothed with majesty and glory;
2 you cover yourself with light.
You have spread out the heavens like a tent
3 and built your home on the waters above.[a]
You use the clouds as your chariot
and ride on the wings of the wind.
4 You use the winds as your messengers
and flashes of lightning as your servants.

5 You have set the earth firmly on its foundations,
and it will never be moved.
6 You placed the ocean over it like a robe,
and the water covered the mountains.
7 When you rebuked the waters, they fled;
they rushed away when they heard your shout of command.
8 They flowed over the mountains and into the valleys,
to the place you had made for them.
9 You set a boundary they can never pass,
to keep them from covering the earth again.

10 You make springs flow in the valleys,
and rivers run between the hills.
11 They provide water for the wild animals;
there the wild donkeys quench their thirst.
12 In the trees near by,
the birds make their nests and sing.
13 From the sky you send rain on the hills,
and the earth is filled with your blessings.
14 You make grass grow for the cattle
and plants for us to use,
so that we can grow our crops
15 and produce wine to make us happy,
olive oil to make us cheerful,
and bread to give us strength.
16 The cedars of Lebanon get plenty of rain—
the LORD's own trees, which he planted.
17 There the birds build their nests;
the storks nest in the fir trees.
18 The wild goats live in the high mountains,
and the rock badgers hide in the cliffs.

19 You created the moon to mark the months;
the sun knows the time to set.
20 You made the night, and in the darkness
all the wild animals come out.
21 The young lions roar while they hunt,
looking for the food that God provides.
22 When the sun rises, they go back
and lie down in their dens.
23 Then people go out to do their work
and keep working until evening.

24 LORD, you have made so many things!
How wisely you made them all!
The earth is filled with your creatures.
25 There is the ocean, large and wide,
where countless creatures live,
large and small alike.
26 The ships sail on it, and in it plays Leviathan,
that sea monster which you made.[b]

27 All of them depend on you
to give them food when they need it.
28 You give it to them, and they eat it;
you provide food, and they are satisfied.
29 When you turn away, they are afraid;
when you take away your breath, they die
and go back to the dust from which they came.
30 But when you give them breath,[c] they are created;
you give new life to the earth.

31 May the glory of the LORD last forever!
May the LORD be happy with what he has made!
32 He looks at the earth, and it trembles;
he touches the mountains, and they pour out smoke.

[a] **104:3** THE WATERS ABOVE: *A reference to the waters above the celestial dome (Gen 1:6, 7).* [b] **104:26** in it plays . . . made; *or* Leviathan is there, that sea monster you made to amuse you. [c] **104:30** give them breath; *or* send out your spirit.

104:4 Heb 1:7 **104:26** Job 41:1; Ps 74:14; Isa 27:1

33 I will sing to the LORD all my life;
as long as I live I will sing praises to my God.
34 May he be pleased with my song,
for my gladness comes from him.
35 May sinners be destroyed from the earth;
may the wicked be no more.

Praise the LORD, my soul!
Praise the LORD!

God and His People
(1 Chronicles 16:8–22)

105 Give thanks to the LORD,
proclaim his greatness;
tell the nations what he has done.
2 Sing praise to the LORD;
tell the wonderful things he has done.
3 Be glad that we belong to him;
let all who worship him rejoice.
4 Go to the LORD for help;
and worship him continually.
5-6 You descendants of Abraham, his servant;
you descendants of Jacob, the man he chose:
remember the miracles that God performed
and the judgments that he gave.

7 The LORD is our God;
his commands are for all the world.
8 He will keep his covenant forever,
his promises for a thousand generations.
9 He will keep the agreement he made with Abraham
and his promise to Isaac.
10 The LORD made a covenant with Jacob,
one that will last forever.
11 "I will give you the land of Canaan," he said.
"It will be your own possession."

12 God's people were few in number,
strangers in the land of Canaan.
13 They wandered from country to country,
from one kingdom to another.

Study it!

What About the Women?

Where are the women? Why does Psalm 105 just talk about men: Abraham, Jacob, Joseph, Moses, Aaron? What about their wives, their daughters and sisters—why aren't they mentioned? What about the great women of the Bible—why aren't they mentioned? Keep in mind that in the time the Psalms were written, the roles of women were much different than they are now. Women were not typically leaders, were not usually considered strong, and had little say in what went on in society.

That doesn't mean that the time of the Psalms was better or worse than our time; it was just different. When we read the Bible, it helps to know what was going on in society at the time. Today is different for women; they are recognized for their accomplishments, have more of a voice, and are rulers, presidents, and other political leaders throughout the world.

— Psalm 105

14 But God let no one oppress them;
to protect them, he warned the kings:
15 "Don't harm my chosen servants;
do not touch my prophets."

16 The LORD sent famine to their country
and took away all their food.
17 But he sent a man ahead of them,
Joseph, who had been sold as a slave.

105:9 **a** Gen 12:7; 17:8; **b** Gen 26:3 **105:10, 11** Gen 28:13 **105:14, 15** Gen 20:3–7

Reread the Creation stories in Genesis, chapters 1–3, after reading Psalm 104.

18 His feet were kept in chains,
and an iron collar was around his neck,
19 until what he had predicted came true.
The word of the LORD proved him right.
20 Then the king of Egypt had him released;
the ruler of nations set him free.
21 He put him in charge of his government
and made him ruler over all the land,
22 with power over the king's officials
and authority to instruct his advisers.

23 Then Jacob went to Egypt
and settled in that country.
24 The LORD gave many children to his
people
and made them stronger than their
enemies.
25 He made the Egyptians hate his people
and treat his servants with deceit.

26 Then he sent his servant Moses,
and Aaron, whom he had chosen.
27 They did God's mighty acts
and performed miracles in Egypt.
28 God sent darkness on the country,
but the Egyptians did not obey[d] his
command.
29 He turned their rivers into blood
and killed all their fish.
30 Their country was overrun with frogs;
even the palace was filled with them.
31 God commanded, and flies and gnats
swarmed throughout the whole
country.
32 He sent hail and lightning on their land
instead of rain;
33 he destroyed their grapevines and fig trees
and broke down all the trees.
34 He commanded, and the locusts came,
countless millions of them;
35 they ate all the plants in the land;
they ate all the crops.
36 He killed the first-born sons
of all the families of Egypt.

37 Then he led the Israelites out;
they carried silver and gold,
and all of them were healthy and
strong.
38 The Egyptians were afraid of them
and were glad when they left.
39 God put a cloud over his people
and a fire at night to give them light.
40 They[e] asked, and he sent quails;
he gave them food from heaven to
satisfy them.
41 He opened a rock, and water gushed out,
flowing through the desert like a river.
42 He remembered his sacred promise
to Abraham his servant.

43 So he led his chosen people out,
and they sang and shouted for joy.
44 He gave them the lands of other peoples
and let them take over their fields,
45 so that his people would obey his laws
and keep all his commands.

Praise the LORD!

The LORD's Goodness to His People

106 Praise the LORD!

Give thanks to the LORD, because he is
good;
his love is eternal.
2 Who can tell all the great things he has
done?
Who can praise him enough?
3 Happy are those who obey his
commands,
who always do what is right.

[d] **105:28** *Some ancient translations* did not obey; *Hebrew* obeyed. [e] **105:40** *Some ancient translations* They; *Hebrew* he.

105:16 Gen 41:53–57 **105:17** Gen 37:28; 45:5 **105:18, 19** Gen 39:20—40:23 **105:20** Gen 41:14 **105:21** Gen 41:39–41 **105:23** **a** Gen 46:6; **b** Gen 47:11 **105:24, 25** Ex 1:7–14 **105:26** Ex 3:1—4:17 **105:28** Ex 10:21–23 **105:29** Ex 7:17–21 **105:30** Ex 8:1–6 **105:31** **a** Ex 8:20–24; **b** Ex 8:16, 17 **105:32, 33** Ex 9:22–25 **105:34, 35** Ex 10:12–15 **105:36** Ex 12:29 **105:37, 38** Ex 12:33–36 **105:39** Ex 13:21, 22 **105:40** Ex 16:2–15 **105:41** Ex 17:1–7; Num 20:2–13 **105:44** Josh 11:16–23 **106:1** 1 Chr 16:34; 2 Chr 5:13; 7:3; Ezra 3:11; Ps 100:5; 107:1; 118:1; 136:1; Jer 33:11

Do you remember the story of the gold bull-calf mentioned in Psalm 106? If not, you may want to read Exodus 32:1–21.

4 Remember me, LORD, when you help
your people;
include me when you save them.
5 Let me see the prosperity of your people
and share in the happiness of your
nation,
in the glad pride of those who belong
to you.

6 We have sinned as our ancestors did;
we have been wicked and evil.
7 Our ancestors in Egypt did not
understand God's wonderful acts;
they forgot the many times he showed
them his love,
and they rebelled against the Almighty[f]
at the Red Sea.
8 But he saved them, as he had promised,
in order to show his great power.
9 He gave a command to the Red Sea,
and it dried up;
he led his people across on dry land.
10 He saved them from those who hated
them;
he rescued them from their enemies.
11 But the water drowned their enemies;
not one of them was left.
12 Then his people believed his promises
and sang praises to him.

13 But they quickly forgot what he had
done
and acted without waiting for his
advice.
14 They were filled with craving in the
desert
and put God to the test;
15 so he gave them what they asked for,
but also sent a terrible disease among
them.

16 There in the desert they were jealous of
Moses
and of Aaron, the LORD's holy servant.
17 Then the earth opened up and swallowed
Dathan
and buried Abiram and his family;
18 fire came down on their followers
and burned up those wicked people.
19 They made a gold bull-calf at Sinai
and worshiped that idol;
20 they exchanged the glory of God
for the image of an animal that eats
grass.
21 They forgot the God who had saved
them
by his mighty acts in Egypt.
22 What wonderful things he did there!
What amazing things at the Red Sea!
23 When God said that he would destroy his
people,
his chosen servant, Moses, stood up
against God
and kept his anger from destroying
them.

24 Then they rejected the pleasant land,
because they did not believe God's
promise.
25 They stayed in their tents and
grumbled
and would not listen to the LORD.
26 So he have them a solomn warning
that he would make them die in the
desert
27 and scatter their descendants among
the heathen,
letting them die in foreign countries.

28 Then at Peor, God's people joined in the
worship of Baal
and ate sacrifices offered to dead
gods.
29 They stirred up the LORD's anger by their
actions,
and a terrible disease broke out among
them.
30 But Phinehas stood up and punished the
guilty,
and the plague was stopped.
31 This has been remembered in his favor
ever since
and will be for all time to come.

32 At the springs of Meribah the people
made the LORD angry,
and Moses was in trouble on their
account.

f **106:7** *Probable text* the Almighty; *Hebrew* the sea.

106:7 Ex 14:10–12 **106:9–12** Ex 14:21–31 **106:12** Ex 15:1–21 **106:14, 15** Num 11:4–34 **106:16–18** Num 16:1–35 **106:19–23** Ex 32:1–14 **106:24–26** Num 14:1–35 **106:27** Lev 26:33 **106:28–31** Num 25:1–13 **106:32, 33** Num 20:2–13

33 They made him so bitter
that he spoke without stopping to think.

34 They did not kill the heathen,
as the LORD had commanded them
to do,
35 but they intermarried with them
and adopted their pagan ways.
36 God's people worshiped idols,
and this caused their destruction.
37 They offered their own sons and daughters
as sacrifices to the idols of Canaan.
38 They killed those innocent children,
and the land was defiled by those
murders.
39 They made themselves impure by their
actions
and were unfaithful to God.

40 So the LORD was angry with his people;
he was disgusted with them.
41 He abandoned them to the power of the
heathen,
and their enemies ruled over them.
42 They were oppressed by their enemies
and were in complete subjection to
them.
43 Many times the LORD rescued his people,
but they chose to rebel against him
and sank deeper into sin.
44 Yet the LORD heard them when they
cried out,
and he took notice of their distress.
45 For their sake he remembered his covenant,
and because of his great love he
relented.
46 He made all their oppressors
feel sorry for them.

47 Save us, O LORD our God,
and bring us back from among the
nations,
so that we may be thankful
and praise your holy name.

48 Praise the LORD, the God of Israel;
praise him now and forever!
Let everyone say, "Amen!"

Praise the LORD!

BOOK FIVE
(Psalms 107–150)

In Praise of God's Goodness

107 "Give thanks to the LORD,
because he is good;
his love is eternal!"
2 Repeat these words in praise to the
LORD,
all you whom he has saved.
He has rescued you from your enemies
3 and has brought you back from foreign
countries,
from east and west, from north and
south.[g]

4 Some wandered in the trackless desert
and could not find their way to a city
to live in.
5 They were hungry and thirsty
and had given up all hope.
6 Then in their trouble they called to the
LORD,
and he saved them from their distress.
7 He led them by a straight road
to a city where they could live.
8 They must thank the LORD for his
constant love,
for the wonderful things he did for
them.
9 He satisfies those who are thirsty
and fills the hungry with good things.

10 Some were living in gloom and darkness,
prisoners suffering in chains,
11 because they had rebelled against the
commands of Almighty God
and had rejected his instructions.
12 They were worn out from hard work;
they would fall down, and no one
would help.
13 Then in their trouble they called to the
LORD,
and he saved them from their distress.
14 He brought them out of their gloom and
darkness
and broke their chains in pieces.

[g] **107:3** *Probable text* south; *Hebrew* the Mediterranean Sea (meaning "west").

106:34–36 Judg 2:1–3; 3:5, 6 **106:37** 2 Kings 17:17 **106:38** Num 35:33 **106:40–46** Judg 2:14–18 **106:47, 48** 1 Chr 16:35, 36 **107:1** 1 Chr 16:34; 2 Chr 5:13; 7:3; Ezra 3:11; Ps 100:5; 106:1; 118:1; 136:1; Jer 33:11

15 They must thank the LORD for his
constant love,
for the wonderful things he did for
them.
16 He breaks down doors of bronze
and smashes iron bars.

17 Some were fools, suffering because of
their sins
and because of their evil;
18 they couldn't stand the sight of food
and were close to death.
19 Then in their trouble they called to the
LORD,
and he saved them from their distress.
20 He healed them with his command
and saved them from the grave.
21 They must thank the LORD for his
constant love,
for the wonderful things he did for
them.
22 They must thank him with sacrifices,
and with songs of joy must tell all that
he has done.

23 Some sailed over the ocean in ships,
earning their living on the seas.
24 They saw what the LORD can do,
his wonderful acts on the seas.
25 He commanded, and a mighty wind
began to blow
and stirred up the waves.
26 The ships were lifted high in the air
and plunged down into the depths.
In such danger the sailors lost their
courage;
27 they stumbled and staggered like
drunks—
all their skill was useless.
28 Then in their trouble they called to the
LORD,
and he saved them from their distress.
29 He calmed the raging storm,
and the waves became quiet.
30 They were glad because of the calm,
and he brought them safe to the port
they wanted.
31 They must thank the LORD for his
constant love,
for the wonderful things he did for
them.
32 They must proclaim his greatness in the
assembly of the people
and praise him before the council of
the leaders.

33 The LORD made rivers dry up completely
and stopped springs from flowing.
34 He made rich soil become a salty
wasteland
because of the wickedness of those
who lived there.
35 He changed deserts into pools of water
and dry land into flowing springs.
36 He let hungry people settle there,
and they built a city to live in.
37 They sowed the fields and planted
grapevines
and reaped an abundant harvest.
38 He blessed his people, and they had many
children;
he kept their herds of cattle from
decreasing.

39 When God's people were defeated and
humiliated
by cruel oppression and suffering,
40 he showed contempt for their oppressors
and made them wander in trackless
deserts.
41 But he rescued the needy from their misery
and made their families increase like
flocks.
42 The righteous see this and are glad,
but all the wicked are put to silence.

He brought them safe to the port. (107:30)

107:34 Sir 39:23

How many different great things does God do in Psalm 107?

43 May those who are wise think about
these things;
may they consider the LORD's constant
love.

A Prayer for Help against Enemies[h]
(Psalm 57:7–11; 60:5–12)

108 I have complete confidence,
O God!
I will sing and praise you!
Wake up, my soul!
2 Wake up, my harp and lyre!
I will wake up the sun.
3 I will thank you, O LORD, among the
nations.
I will praise you among the peoples.
4 Your constant love reaches above the
heavens;
your faithfulness touches the skies.

5 Show your greatness in the sky, O God,
and your glory over all the earth.
6 Save us by your might; answer my prayer,
so that the people you love may be
rescued.

7 From his sanctuary[i] God has said,
"In triumph I will divide Shechem
and distribute Sukkoth Valley to my
people.
8 Gilead is mine, and Manasseh too;
Ephraim is my helmet
and Judah my royal scepter.
9 But I will use Moab as my washbowl,
and I will throw my sandals on Edom,
as a sign that I own it.
I will shout in triumph over the
Philistines."

10 Who, O God, will take me into the
fortified city?
Who will lead me to Edom?
11 Have you really rejected us?
Aren't you going to march out with
our armies?
12 Help us against the enemy;
human help is worthless.
13 With God on our side we will win;
he will defeat our enemies.

The Complaint of Someone in Trouble[j]

109 I praise you, God; don't remain
silent!
2 Wicked people and liars have attacked
me.
They tell lies about me,
3 and they say evil things about me,
attacking me for no reason.
4 They oppose me, even though I love
them
and have prayed for them.[k]
5 They pay me back evil for good
and hatred for love.

6 Choose some corrupt judge to try my
enemy,
and let one of his own enemies accuse
him.
7 May he be tried and found guilty;
may even his prayer be considered a
crime!
8 May his life soon be ended;
may someone else take his job!
9 May his children become orphans,
and his wife a widow!
10 May his children be homeless beggars;
may they be driven from[l] the ruins
they live in!
11 May his creditors take away all his
property,
and may strangers get everything he
worked for.
12 May no one ever be kind to him
or care for the orphans he leaves
behind.
13 May all his descendants die,
and may his name be forgotten in the
next generation.

[h] **108** HEBREW TITLE: *A psalm by David; a song.* [i] **108:7** From his sanctuary; *or* In his holiness. [j] **109** HEBREW TITLE: *A psalm by David.* [k] **109:4** *Probable text* have prayed for them; *Hebrew unclear.* [l] **109:10** *One ancient translation* be driven from; *Hebrew* seek.
109:8 Acts 1:20

"Wicked people and liars have attacked me. / . . . They pay me back evil for good / and hatred for love" *(Psalm 109:2–5)* **.**

14 May the LORD remember the evil of his
ancestors
and never forgive his mother's sins.
15 May the LORD always remember their
sins,
but may they themselves be completely
forgotten!
16 That man never thought of being kind;
he persecuted and killed
the poor, the needy, and the helpless.
17 He loved to curse—may he be cursed!
He hated to give blessings—may no
one bless him!
18 He cursed as naturally as he dressed
himself;
may his own curses soak into his body
like water
and into his bones like oil!
19 May they cover him like clothes
and always be around him like a belt!

20 LORD, punish my enemies in that way—
those who say such evil things against
me!
21 But my Sovereign LORD, help me as you
have promised,
and rescue me because of the goodness
of your love.
22 I am poor and needy;
I am hurt to the depths of my heart.
23 Like an evening shadow I am about to
vanish;
I am blown away like an insect.
24 My knees are weak from lack of food;
I am nothing but skin and bones.
25 When people see me, they laugh at me;
they shake their heads in scorn.

26 Help me, O LORD my God;
because of your constant love, save me!
27 Make my enemies know
that you are the one who saves me.
28 They may curse me, but you will bless
me.
May my persecutors be defeated,[m]
and may I, your servant, be glad.
29 May my enemies be covered with disgrace;
may they wear their shame like a robe.

[m] **109:28** *One ancient translation* May my persecutors be defeated; *Hebrew* They persecuted me and were defeated.

109:25 Mt 27:39; Mk 15:29

Study it!

But God!

"Alleluia, alleluia!" The song sounded so joyful, and the people at church were all smiling and singing and seemed to be so happy with God. Not Dena. After Mass, she stayed in the church and looked at Jesus up on the cross. "I am so mad at you!" she said. "I know you did all these great things for humanity, but it doesn't seem like any of it matters for me. I can't believe it!"

"What can't you believe?" Dena almost jumped out of her skin when she heard the voice behind her. It was her second-grade religion teacher, of all people. Dena was embarrassed now.

"Na . . . nothing," she sputtered.

"Well, you sounded pretty mad there," Ms. Jo said.

"I'm not supposed to get mad at God, am I, Ms. Jo?"

"Why not?" Ms. Jo answered.

"Well, you taught us all about God's love, but I'm really mad," Dena said. Dena and Ms. Jo sat on one of the pews.

"Dena, it's okay to get mad at God," Ms. Jo replied. "Don't you remember that we talked about getting close to God? And that one way is by developing a relationship with God? Growing a relationship means being honest, even if we are feeling angry. That doesn't mean we stop loving our friends, or family, or God."

"I think I get it." Dena was thankful for Ms. Jo, just like when she was eight, when Ms. Jo was her teacher. They walked out of church together. Dena was still mad at God, but knew she had someone to talk to about it.

— Psalm 109

30 I will give loud thanks to the LORD;
I will praise him in the assembly of the people,
31 because he defends the poor
and saves them from those who condemn them to death.

The LORD and His Chosen King[n]

110 The LORD said to my lord,
"Sit here at my right side
until I put your enemies under your feet."
2 From Zion the LORD will extend your royal power.
"Rule over your enemies," he says.
3 On the day you fight your enemies,
your people will volunteer.
Like the dew of early morning
your young men will come to you on the sacred hills.[o]
4 The LORD made a solemn promise and will not take it back:
"You will be a priest forever
in the priestly order of Melchizedek."[p]
5 The Lord is at your right side;
when he becomes angry, he will defeat kings.
6 He will pass judgment on the nations
and fill the battlefield with corpses;
he will defeat kings all over the earth.
7 The king will drink from the stream by the road,
and strengthened, he will stand victorious.

In Praise of the LORD

111 Praise the LORD!
With all my heart I will thank the LORD
in the assembly of his people.
2 How wonderful are the things the LORD does!
All who are delighted with them want to understand them.

Pray it!

Acrostic Psalms

An acrostic is a type of poem where the first letter of each line in the poem spells out a word or the entire alphabet. So if you knew Hebrew and saw Psalm 111 written in Hebrew (the language it was first written in), you would see that each line starts with a different letter of the Hebrew alphabet.

Try writing your own acrostic prayer. The first word of each line would start with a different letter of the alphabet. Or for a shorter prayer, write an acrostic based on a word such as *praise.* The first word of the first line would start with *p.* The first word of each of the next five lines would start with one of the following letters, in order: *r, a, i, s, e.* Have fun and be creative!

— Psalm 111

3 All he does is full of honor and majesty;
his righteousness is eternal.
4 The LORD does not let us forget his wonderful actions;
he is kind and merciful.
5 He provides food for those who honor him;
he never forgets his covenant.
6 He has shown his power to his people
by giving them the lands of foreigners.
7 In all he does he is faithful and just;
all his commands are dependable.

[n] **110** HEBREW TITLE: *A psalm by David.* [o] **110:3** *Verse 3 in Hebrew is unclear.* [p] **110:4** in the priestly order of Melchizedek; *or* like Melchizedek; *or* in the line of succession to Melchizedek

110:1 Mt 22:44; Mk 12:36; Lk 20:42, 43; Acts 2:34, 35; 1 Cor 15:25; Eph 1:20–22; Col 3:1; Heb 1:13; 8:1; 10:12, 13 **110:4** Heb 5:6; 6:20; 7:17, 21

8 They last for all time;
they were given in truth and righteousness.
9 He set his people free
and made an eternal covenant with them.
Holy and mighty is he!
10 The way to become wise is to honor the LORD;[q]
he gives sound judgment to all who obey his commands.
He is to be praised forever.

The Happiness of a Good Person

112 Praise the LORD!

Happy is the person who honors the LORD,
who takes pleasure in obeying his commands.
2 The good man's children will be powerful in the land;
his descendants will be blessed.
3 His family will be wealthy and rich,
and he will be prosperous forever.
4 Light shines in the darkness for good people,
for those who are merciful, kind, and just.
5 Happy is the person who is generous with his loans,
who runs his business honestly.
6 A good person will never fail;
he will always be remembered.
7 He is not afraid of receiving bad news;
his faith is strong, and he trusts in the LORD.
8 He is not worried or afraid;
he is certain to see his enemies defeated.
9 He gives generously to the needy,
and his kindness never fails;
he will be powerful and respected.
10 The wicked see this and are angry;
they glare in hate and disappear;
their hopes are gone forever.

Study it!

Words of Wisdom

Is one of your grandparents or an older person you know always giving you little bits of advice? Does it seem like he or she always knows just what to say, better sometimes than your teachers or parents? Listening to these bits of wisdom can help you in your day-to-day life, even if it seems like the same old sayings over and over.

Psalm 112 is one of the wisdom psalms, a group of nearly ten psalms. Becoming wise takes time, and reading about it is one way to help gain wisdom. In the case of Psalm 112, the writer speaks like a wise old person telling the youth the benefits of being a good person. The psalm tells us that the way to become wise is to honor the Lord. If this sounds like the advice you get from older people in your life, then you are receiving true wisdom, indeed!

— Psalm 112

In Praise of the LORD's Goodness

113 Praise the LORD!

You servants of the LORD,
praise his name!
2 May his name be praised,
now and forever.
3 From the east to the west
praise the name of the LORD!

[q] **111:10** The way . . . the LORD; *or* The most important part of wisdom is honoring the LORD.
111:10 Job 28:28; Prov 1:7; 9:10 **112:9** 2 Cor 9:9

"The way to become wise is to honor the LORD" *(Psalm 111:10)*.

4 The LORD rules over all nations;
his glory is above the heavens.

5 There is no one like the LORD our God.
He lives in the heights above,
6 but he bends down
to see the heavens and the earth.
7 He raises the poor from the dust;
he lifts the needy from their misery
8 and makes them companions of princes,
the princes of his people.
9 He honors the childless wife in her home;
he makes her happy by giving her children.

Praise the LORD!

A Passover Song

114 When the people of Israel left Egypt,
when Jacob's descendants left that foreign land,
2 Judah became the Lord's holy people,
Israel became his own possession.

3 The Red Sea looked and ran away;
the Jordan River stopped flowing.
4 The mountains skipped like goats;
the hills jumped around like lambs.

5 What happened, Sea, to make you run away?
And you, O Jordan, why did you stop flowing?
6 You mountains, why did you skip like goats?
You hills, why did you jump around like lambs?

7 Tremble, earth, at the Lord's coming,
at the presence of the God of Jacob,
8 who changes rocks into pools of water
and solid cliffs into flowing springs.

The One True God

115 To you alone, O LORD, to you alone,
and not to us, must glory be given
because of your constant love and faithfulness.

2 Why should the nations ask us,
"Where is your God?"
3 Our God is in heaven;
he does whatever he wishes.
4 Their gods are made of silver and gold,
formed by human hands.
5 They have mouths, but cannot speak,
and eyes, but cannot see.
6 They have ears, but cannot hear,
and noses, but cannot smell.
7 They have hands, but cannot feel,
and feet, but cannot walk;
they cannot make a sound.
8 May all who made them and who trust in them
become[r] like the idols they have made.

9 Trust in the LORD, you people of Israel.
He helps you and protects you.
10 Trust in the LORD, you priests of God.
He helps you and protects you.
11 Trust in the LORD, all you that worship him.
He helps you and protects you.

12 The LORD remembers us and will bless us;
he will bless the people of Israel
and all the priests of God.
13 He will bless everyone who honors him,
the great and the small alike.

14 May the LORD give you children—
you and your descendants!
15 May you be blessed by the LORD,
who made heaven and earth!

16 Heaven belongs to the LORD alone,
but he gave the earth to us humans.

[r] **115:8** May all . . . become; *or* All who made them and who trust in them will become.

114:1 Ex 12:51 **114:3 a** Ex 14:21; **b** Josh 3:16 **114:8** Ex 17:1–7; Num 20:2–13 **115:4–8** Ps 135:15–18; Bar 6:4–73; Rev 9:20 **115:13** Rev 11:18; 19:5

Psalm 114 is a Passover psalm. Remember the Passover story? It can be found in Exodus, chapter 12.

17 The LORD is not praised by the dead,
by any who go down to the land of silence.[s]
18 But we, the living, will give thanks to him
now and forever.

Praise the LORD!

Someone Saved from Death Praises God

116 I love the LORD, because he hears me;
he listens to my prayers.
2 He listens to me
every time I call to him.
3 The danger of death was all around me;
the horrors of the grave closed in on me;
I was filled with fear and anxiety.
4 Then I called to the LORD,
"I beg you, LORD, save me!"

5 The LORD is merciful and good;
our God is compassionate.
6 The LORD protects the helpless;
when I was in danger, he saved me.
7 Be confident, my heart,
because the LORD has been good to me.
8 The LORD saved me from death;
he stopped my tears
and kept me from defeat.
9 And so I walk in the presence of the LORD
in the world of the living.

10 I kept on believing, even when I said,
"I am completely crushed,"
11 even when I was afraid and said,
"No one can be trusted."

12 What can I offer the LORD
for all his goodness to me?
13 I will bring a wine offering to the LORD,
to thank him for saving me.
14 In the assembly of all his people
I will give him what I have promised.

15 How painful it is to the LORD
when one of his people dies!
16 I am your servant, LORD;
I serve you just as my mother did.
You have saved me from death.
17 I will give you a sacrifice of thanksgiving
and offer my prayer to you.
18-19 In the assembly of all your people,
in the sanctuary of your Temple in Jerusalem,
I will give you what I have promised.

Praise the LORD!

In Praise of the LORD

117 Praise the LORD, all nations!
Praise him, all peoples!
2 His love for us is strong,
and his faithfulness is eternal.

Praise the LORD!

Prasie the LORD, all nations! (117:1)

A Prayer of Thanks for Victory

118 Give thanks to the LORD,
because he is good,
and his love is eternal.
2 Let the people of Israel say,
"His love is eternal."
3 Let the priests of God say,
"His love is eternal."

[s] **115:17** LAND OF SILENCE: *The world of the dead (see 6:5).*

116:10 2 Cor 4:13 **117:1** Rom 15:11 **118:1** 1 Chr 16:34; 2 Chr 5:13; 7:3; Ezra 3:11; Ps 100:5; 106:1; 107:1; 136:1; Jer 33:11

Live it!

A Psalm for Confirmation

You will be my witnesses to all the world.
Praise the Lord, all you nations;
glorify him, all you peoples!
You will be witnesses to all the world.
For steadfast is his kindness toward us,
and the fidelity of the Lord endures forever.

Using the words of Acts 1:8 and Psalm 117:1–2, the cantor leads the responsorial psalm during a Rite of Confirmation. Later, the bishop begins his homily by asking the youth being confirmed this question, "How will you be witnesses to all the world?"

One of the girls raises her hand very slowly. Heart pounding, she answers, "I will . . . Oh, never mind, it's stupid." She turns bright red as the bishop walks toward her. He says, "It's okay. Tell us, how will you be a witness?"

As she sees the bishop up close, she sees the kindness in his eyes. He gives her a small smile that gives her a little courage. She answers: "I will ______________."

What did the girl say that answered the bishop's question? How would you answer it?

— Psalm 117

(*The Lectionary for Mass*, p. 605)

4 Let all who worship him say,
"His love is eternal."
5 In my distress I called to the LORD;
he answered me and set me free.
6 The LORD is with me, I will not be afraid;
what can anyone do to me?
7 It is the LORD who helps me,
and I will see my enemies defeated.
8 It is better to trust in the LORD
than to depend on people.
9 It is better to trust in the LORD
than to depend on human leaders.

10 Many enemies were around me;
but I destroyed them by the power of the LORD!
11 They were around me on every side;
but I destroyed them by the power of the LORD!
12 They swarmed around me like bees,
but they burned out as quickly as a brush fire;
by the power of the LORD I destroyed them.
13 I was fiercely attacked and was being defeated,
but the LORD helped me.
14 The LORD makes me powerful and strong;
he has saved me.

15 Listen to the glad shouts of victory in the tents of God's people:
"The LORD's mighty power has done it!
16 His power has brought us victory—
his mighty power in battle!"

17 I will not die; instead, I will live
and proclaim what the LORD has done.
18 He has punished me severely,
but he has not let me die.

19 Open to me the gates of the Temple;
I will go in and give thanks to the LORD!
20 This is the gate of the LORD;
only the righteous can come in.

21 I praise you, LORD, because you heard me,
because you have given me victory.

22 The stone which the builders rejected as worthless
turned out to be the most important of all.

118:6 Heb 13:6 **118:14** Ex 15:2; Isa 12:2 **118:22** Lk 20:17; Acts 4:11; 1 Pet 2:7 **118:22, 23** Mt 21:42; Mk 12:10, 11

23 This was done by the LORD;
what a wonderful sight it is!
24 This is the day of the LORD's victory;
let us be happy, let us celebrate!
25 Save us, LORD, save us!
Give us success, O LORD!
26 May God bless the one who comes in the name of the LORD!
From the Temple of the LORD we bless you.
27 The LORD is God; he has been good to us.
With branches in your hands, start the festival
and march around the altar.

28 You are my God, and I give you thanks;
I will proclaim your greatness.
29 Give thanks to the LORD, because he is good,
and his love is eternal.

The Law of the LORD

119 Happy are those whose lives are faultless,
who live according to the law of the LORD.
2 Happy are those who follow his commands,
who obey him with all their heart.
3 They never do wrong;
they walk in the LORD's ways.
4 LORD, you have given us your laws
and told us to obey them faithfully.
5 How I hope that I shall be faithful
in keeping your instructions!
6 If I pay attention to all your commands,
then I will not be put to shame.
7 As I learn your righteous judgments,
I will praise you with a pure heart.
8 I will obey your laws;
never abandon me!

Live it!

Keeping Commandments

If you break rules, you get punished, right? But is that why rules are there? Think about it. Cheating is against the rules, right? Is it against the rules so your teachers can catch you and punish you, or is it against the rules because cheating is lying, and lying leads to more lying, which leads to being unhappy?

It is the same thing with God's commandments. God did not give us commandments so he would have fun catching us breaking them and punishing us for that. God gives us commandments so that we may be happy, holy, and healthy. The benefit of following God's laws is what Psalm 119 is all about. Look at what it says we get by following the commandments:

- **more understanding and wisdom**
- **happiness and joy**
- **new life and hope**
- **the ability to answer those who insult you**

It may take time and patience to benefit (see verses 81–88, 121–128, and 169–176), but it will be worth it!

— Psalm 119

Obedience to the Law of the LORD

9 How can young people keep their lives pure?
By obeying your commands.

118:25 Mt 21:9; Mk 11:9; Jn 12:13 **118:26** Mt 21:9; 23:39; Mk 11:9; Lk 13:35; 19:38; Jn 12:13

Where have you heard the verse in Psalm 118:22 before? Check the footnotes for places it is quoted in the New Testament.

10 With all my heart I try to serve you;
keep me from disobeying your commandments.
11 I keep your law in my heart,
so that I will not sin against you.
12 I praise you, O LORD;
teach me your ways.
13 I will repeat aloud
all the laws you have given.
14 I delight in following your commands
more than in having great wealth.
15 I study your instructions;
I examine your teachings.
16 I take pleasure in your laws;
your commands I will not forget.

Happiness in the Law of the LORD

17 Be good to me, your servant,
so that I may live and obey your teachings.
18 Open my eyes, so that I may see
the wonderful truths in your law.
19 I am here on earth for just a little while;
do not hide your commands from me.
20 My heart aches with longing;
I want to know your judgments at all times.
21 You reprimand the proud;
cursed are those who disobey your commands.
22 Free me from their insults and scorn,
because I have kept your laws.
23 The rulers meet and plot against me,
but I will study your teachings.
24 Your instructions give me pleasure;
they are my advisers.

Determination to Obey the Law of the LORD

25 I lie defeated in the dust;
revive me, as you have promised.
26 I confessed all I have done, and you answered me;
teach me your ways.
27 Help me to understand your laws,
and I will meditate on your wonderful teachings.[t]
28 I am overcome by sorrow;
strengthen me, as you have promised.
29 Keep me from going the wrong way,
and in your goodness teach me your law.
30 I have chosen to be obedient;
I have paid attention to your judgments.
31 I have followed your instructions, LORD;
don't let me be put to shame.
32 I will eagerly obey your commands,
because you will give me more understanding.

A Prayer for Understanding

33 Teach me, LORD, the meaning of your laws,
and I will obey them at all times.
34 Explain your law to me, and I will obey it;
I will keep it with all my heart.
35 Keep me obedient to your commandments,
because in them I find happiness.
36 Give me the desire to obey your laws
rather than to get rich.
37 Keep me from paying attention to what is worthless;
be good to me, as you have promised.
38 Keep your promise to me, your servant—
the promise you make to those who obey you.
39 Save me from the insults I fear;
how wonderful are your judgments!
40 I want to obey your commands;
give me new life, for you are righteous.

Trusting the Law of the LORD

41 Show me how much you love me, LORD,
and save me according to your promise.
42 Then I can answer those who insult me
because I trust in your word.

[t] **119:27** teachings; *or* deeds.

Is Psalm 119 the longest psalm? Can you find a psalm that is longer?

43 Enable me to speak the truth at all times,
because my hope is in your judgments.
44 I will always obey your law,
forever and ever.
45 I will live in perfect freedom,
because I try to obey your teachings.
46 I will announce your commands to kings
and I will not be ashamed.
47 I find pleasure in obeying your
commands,
because I love them.
48 I respect and love your commandments;
I will meditate on your instructions.

Confidence in the Law of the LORD

49 Remember your promise to me, your
servant;
it has given me hope.
50 Even in my suffering I was comforted
because your promise gave me life.
51 The proud are always scornful of me,
but I have not departed from your
law.
52 I remember your judgments of long
ago,
and they bring me comfort, O LORD.
53 When I see the wicked breaking your
law,
I am filled with anger.
54 During my brief earthly life
I compose songs about your
commands.
55 In the night I remember you, LORD,
and I think about your law.
56 I find my happiness
in obeying your commands.

Devotion to the Law of the LORD

57 You are all I want, O LORD;
I promise to obey your laws.
58 I ask you with all my heart
to have mercy on me, as you have
promised!
59 I have considered my conduct,
and I promise to follow your
instructions.
60 Without delay I hurry
to obey your commands.
61 The wicked have laid a trap for me,
but I do not forget your law.
62 In the middle of the night I wake up
to praise you for your righteous
judgments.
63 I am a friend of all who serve you,
of all who obey your laws.
64 LORD, the earth is full of your constant
love;
teach me your commandments.

The Value of the Law of the LORD

65 You have kept your promise, LORD,
and you are good to me, your servant.
66 Give me wisdom and knowledge,
because I trust in your commands.
67 Before you punished me, I used to go
wrong,
but now I obey your word.
68 How good you are—how kind!
Teach me your commands.
69 The proud have told lies about me,
but with all my heart I obey your
instructions.
70 They have no understanding,
but I find pleasure in your law.
71 My punishment was good for me,
because it made me learn your
commands.
72 The law that you gave means more to
me
than all the money in the world.

The Justice of the Law of the LORD

73 You created me, and you keep me safe;
give me understanding, so that I may
learn your laws.
74 Those who honor you will be glad when
they see me,
because I trust in your promise.
75 I know that your judgments are
righteous, LORD,
and that you punished me because you
are faithful.
76 Let your constant love comfort me,
as you have promised me, your servant.
77 Have mercy on me, and I will live
because I take pleasure in your law.
78 May the proud be ashamed for falsely
accusing me;
as for me, I will meditate on your
instructions.

79 May those who honor you come to me—
all those who know your commands.
80 May I perfectly obey your
commandments
and be spared the shame of defeat.

A Prayer for Deliverance

81 I am worn out, LORD, waiting for you to
save me;
I place my trust in your word.
82 My eyes are tired from watching for what
you promised,
while I ask, "When will you help me?"
83 I am as useless as a discarded wineskin;
yet I have not forgotten your
commands.
84 How much longer must I wait?
When will you punish those who
persecute me?
85 The proud, who do not obey your law,
have dug pits to trap me.
86 Your commandments are all trustworthy;
people persecute me with lies—help
me!
87 They have almost succeeded in killing
me,
but I have not neglected your
commands.
88 Because of your constant love be good to
me,
so that I may obey your laws.

Faith in the Law of the LORD

89 Your word, O LORD, will last forever;
it is eternal in heaven.
90 Your faithfulness endures through all the
ages;
you have set the earth in place, and it
remains.
91 All things remain to this day because of
your command,
because they are all your servants.
92 If your law had not been the source of
my joy,
I would have died from my sufferings.
93 I will never neglect your instructions,
because by them you have kept me
alive.
94 I am yours—save me!
I have tried to obey your commands.
95 The wicked are waiting to kill me,
but I will meditate on your laws.
96 I have learned that everything has limits;
but your commandment is perfect.

Love for the Law of the LORD

97 How I love your law!
I think about it all day long.
98 Your commandment is with me all the
time
and makes me wiser than my enemies.
99 I understand more than all my teachers,
because I meditate on your
instructions.
100 I have greater wisdom than those who are
old,
because I obey your commands.
101 I have avoided all evil conduct,
because I want to obey your word.
102 I have not neglected your instructions,
because you yourself are my teacher.
103 How sweet is the taste of your
instructions—
sweeter even than honey!
104 I gain wisdom from your laws,
and so I hate all bad conduct.

Light from the Law of the LORD

105 Your word is a lamp to guide me
and a light for my path.
106 I will keep my solemn promise
to obey your just instructions.
107 My sufferings, LORD, are terrible indeed;
keep me alive, as you have promised.
108 Accept my prayer of thanks, O LORD,
and teach me your commands.
109 I am always ready to risk my life;
I[u] have not forgotten your law.
110 The wicked lay a trap for me,
but I have not disobeyed your
commands.
111 Your commandments are my eternal
possession;
they are the joy of my heart.
112 I have decided to obey your laws
until the day I die.

[u] **119:109** I am always ready to risk my life; I; *or* My life is in constant danger, but I.

Safety in the Law of the LORD

113 I hate those who are not completely loyal to you,
but I love your law.
114 You are my defender and protector;
I put my hope in your promise.
115 Go away from me, you sinful people.
I will obey the commands of my God.
116 Give me strength, as you promised, and I shall live;
don't let me be disappointed in my hope!
117 Hold me, and I will be safe,
and I will always pay attention to your commands.
118 You reject everyone who disobeys your laws;
their deceitful schemes are useless.
119 You treat all the wicked like rubbish,
and so I love your instructions.
120 Because of you I am afraid;
I am filled with fear because of your judgments.

Obedience to the Law of the LORD

121 I have done what is right and good;
don't abandon me to my enemies!
122 Promise that you will help your servant;
don't let the arrogant oppress me!
123 My eyes are tired from watching for your saving help,
for the deliverance you promised.
124 Treat me according to your constant love,
and teach me your commands.
125 I am your servant; give me understanding,
so that I may know your teachings.
126 LORD, it is time for you to act,
because people are disobeying your law.
127 I love your commands more than gold,
more than the finest gold.
128 And so I follow all your instructions;[v]
I hate all wrong ways.

Desire to Obey the Law of the LORD

129 Your teachings are wonderful;
I obey them with all my heart.
130 The explanation of your teachings gives light
and brings wisdom to the ignorant.
131 In my desire for your commands
I pant with open mouth.
132 Turn to me and have mercy on me
as you do on all those who love you.
133 As you have promised, keep me from falling;
don't let me be overcome by evil.
134 Save me from those who oppress me,
so that I may obey your commands.
135 Bless me with your presence
and teach me your laws.
136 My tears pour down like a river,
because people do not obey your law.

The Justice of the Law of the LORD

137 You are righteous, LORD,
and your laws are just.
138 The rules that you have given
are completely fair and right.
139 My anger burns in me like a fire,
because my enemies disregard your commands.
140 How certain your promise is!
How I love it!
141 I am unimportant and despised,
but I do not neglect your teachings.
142 Your righteousness will last forever,
and your law is always true.
143 I am filled with trouble and anxiety,
but your commandments bring me joy.
144 Your instructions are always just;
give me understanding, and I shall live.

A Prayer for Deliverance

145 With all my heart I call to you;
answer me, LORD, and I will obey your commands!

[v] **119:128** *Some ancient translations* all your instructions; *Hebrew unclear.*

"Your word is a lamp to guide me . . . (*Psalm 119:105*). How does God's word, the Bible, guide your life?

146 I call to you;
save me, and I will keep your laws.
147 Before sunrise I call to you for help;
I place my hope in your promise.
148 All night long I lie awake,
to meditate on your instructions.
149 Because your love is constant, hear me,
O LORD;
show your mercy, and preserve my life!
150 My cruel persecutors are coming
closer,
people who never keep your law.
151 But you are near to me, LORD,
and all your commands are permanent.
152 Long ago I learned about your
instructions;
you made them to last forever.

A Plea for Help

153 Look at my suffering, and save me,
because I have not neglected your law.
154 Defend my cause, and set me free;
save me, as you have promised.
155 The wicked will not be saved,
for they do not obey your laws.
156 But your compassion, LORD, is great;
show your mercy and save me!
157 I have many enemies and oppressors,
but I do not fail to obey your laws.
158 When I look at those traitors, I am filled
with disgust,
because they do not keep your
commands.
159 See how I love your instructions, LORD.
Your love never changes, so save me!
160 The heart of your law is truth,
and all your righteous judgments are
eternal.

Dedication to the Law of the LORD

161 Powerful people attack me unjustly,
but I respect your law.
162 How happy I am because of your
promises—
as happy as someone who finds rich
treasure.
163 I hate and detest all lies,
but I love your law.
164 Seven times each day I thank you
for your righteous judgments.
165 Those who love your law have perfect
security,
and there is nothing that can make
them fall.
166 I wait for you to save me, LORD,
and I do what you command.
167 I obey your teachings;
I love them with all my heart.
168 I obey your commands and your
instructions;
you see everything I do.

A Prayer for Help

169 Let my cry for help reach you,
LORD!
Give me understanding, as you have
promised.
170 Listen to my prayer,
and save me according to your promise!
171 I will always praise you,
because you teach me your laws.
172 I will sing about your law,
because your commands are just.
173 Always be ready to help me,
because I follow your commands.
174 How I long for your saving help,
O LORD!
I find happiness in your law.
175 Give me life, so that I may praise you;
may your instructions help me.
176 I wander about like a lost sheep;
so come and look for me, your servant,
because I have not neglected your laws.

A Prayer for Help

120 When I was in trouble, I called
to the LORD,
and he answered me.
2 Save me, LORD,
from liars and deceivers.
3 You liars, what will God do to you?
How will he punish you?

"My help will come from the LORD, / who made heaven and earth"
(Psalm 121:2).

Live it!

Day and Night

"Is too," Kai said. "Is not," Moe answered. "Is too," Kai repeated. "Is not," Moe said louder.

Sometimes arguments go on like that for a long time. It almost seems as if some people hate peace, like the psalmist says at the end of Psalm 120. Some people argue just for the sake of arguing. Other times they don't stop to see the other person's point of view. Imagine what would happen if everyone, everywhere, instead of arguing, stopped and tried to see what the other person was feeling. A Native American Sioux saying advises that before we judge people, we should walk three miles in their moccasins. That doesn't mean we literally put on their shoes. It just means that we should make every effort to see what they see and experience what they experience. This is one way to start making peace.

So the next time you find yourself in a situation that sounds like the argument between Kai and Moe, take a few minutes to see the other's point of view. Maybe you can be the one who starts the chain of peace.

— Psalm 120:7

4 With a soldier's sharp arrows,
with red-hot coals!

5 Living among you is as bad as living in Meshech
or among the people of Kedar.[w]

6 I have lived too long
with people who hate peace!

7 When I speak of peace,
they are for war.

The LORD Our Protector

121 I look to the mountains;
where will my help come from?
2 My help will come from the LORD,
who made heaven and earth.

3 He will not let you fall;
your protector is always awake.

4 The protector of Israel
never dozes or sleeps.
5 The LORD will guard you;
he is by your side to protect you.
6 The sun will not hurt you during the day,
nor the moon during the night.

7 The LORD will protect you from all danger;
he will keep you safe.
8 He will protect you as you come and go
now and forever.

In Praise of Jerusalem[x]

122 I was glad when they said to me,
"Let us go to the LORD's house."

2 And now we are here,
standing inside the gates of Jerusalem!

3 Jerusalem is a city restored
in beautiful order and harmony.

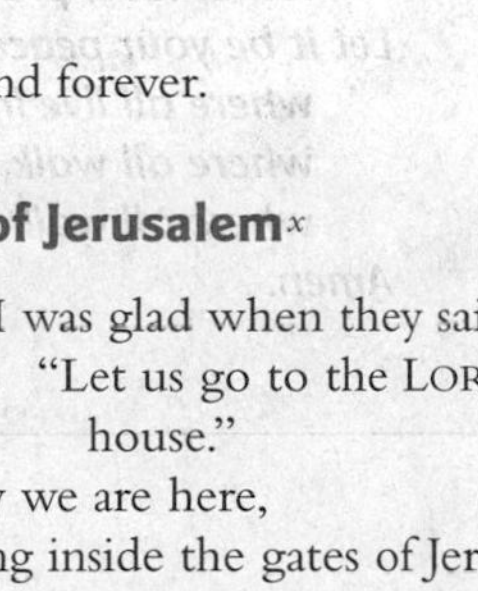

Let us go to the LORD's house. (122:1)

[w] **120:5** MESHECH . . . KEDAR: *Two distant regions, whose people were regarded as savages.* [x] **122** HEBREW TITLE: *By David.*

Pray it!

Peace in Jerusalem

Psalm 122 has a verse about praying for peace in Jerusalem. Even in our time there is much violence in the holy city of Jerusalem. Let's keep praying for peace there and all over the world.

On holy ground they walk.
The people of Jerusalem
going to school
shopping at the markets
talking with friends
running to the bus,
on holy ground they walk.
God, let that holy ground be peaceful.
Let it be your peaceful city.
The place where pilgrims go
to be closer to you,
the place where your people live
in buildings and out in the open.
Let it be your peaceful city,
full of love, prayers, laughter, and freedom.
Let it be your peaceful city,
where all live in unity,
where all walk on holy ground,
where all walk in unity.
Amen.

— Psalm 122

4 This is where the tribes come,
the tribes of Israel,
to give thanks to the LORD
according to his command.
5 Here the kings of Israel
sat to judge their people.

6 Pray for the peace of Jerusalem:
"May those who love you prosper.
7 May there be peace inside your walls
and safety in your palaces."
8 For the sake of my relatives and friends
I say to Jerusalem, "Peace be with
you!"
9 For the sake of the house of the LORD
our God
I pray for your prosperity.

A Prayer for Mercy

123 LORD, I look up to you,
up to heaven, where you
rule.
2 As a servant depends on his master,
as a maid depends on her mistress,
so we will keep looking to you, O LORD
our God,
until you have mercy on us.
3 Be merciful to us, LORD, be
merciful;
we have been treated with so much
contempt.
4 We have been mocked too long by the
rich
and scorned by proud oppressors.

God the Protector of His People[x]

124 What if the LORD had not been on our side?
Answer, O Israel!

2 "If the LORD had not been on our side
when our enemies attacked us,
3 then they would have swallowed us alive
in their furious anger against us;
4 then the flood would have carried us away,
the water would have covered us,
5 the raging torrent would have drowned us."

6 Let us thank the LORD,
who has not let our enemies destroy us.
7 We have escaped like a bird from a hunter's trap;
the trap is broken, and we are free!
8 Our help comes from the LORD,
who made heaven and earth.

The Security of God's People

125 Those who trust in the LORD are like Mount Zion,
which can never be shaken, never be moved.
2 As the mountains surround Jerusalem,
so the LORD surrounds his people,
now and forever.
3 The wicked will not always rule over the land of the righteous;
if they did, the righteous themselves might do evil.
4 LORD, do good to those who are good,
to those who obey your commands.
5 But when you punish the wicked,
punish also those who abandon your ways.

Peace be with Israel!

A Prayer for Deliverance

126 When the LORD brought us back to Jerusalem,[y]
it was like a dream!
2 How we laughed, how we sang for joy!
Then the other nations said about us,
"The LORD did great things for them."
3 Indeed he did great things for us;
how happy we were!

4 LORD, make us prosperous again,[z]
just as the rain brings water back to dry riverbeds.
5 Let those who wept as they planted their crops,
gather the harvest with joy!
6 Those who wept as they went out carrying the seed
will come back singing for joy,
as they bring in the harvest.

Gather the harvest with joy. (126:5)

In Praise of God's Goodness[a]

127 If the LORD does not build the house,
the work of the builders is useless;
if the LORD does not protect the city,
it does no good for the sentries to stand guard.

[x] **124** HEBREW TITLE: *By David.* [y] **126:1** brought us back to Jerusalem; *or* made Jerusalem prosperous again. [z] **126:4** make us prosperous again; *or* take us back to our land. [a] **127** HEBREW TITLE: *By Solomon.*

How would you answer the question, "What if the LORD had not been on our side?" *(Psalm 124:1)*.

Live it!

Holy Families

During the Christmas season, we celebrate the Holy Family: Jesus, Mary, and Joseph. Psalm 128 is the responsorial psalm during Mass that day because it describes a family blessed by God. If we look at the Holy Family, we see an excellent example of a family that followed God. Joseph is an example of doing what God asks even if it results in shame or embarrassment. Remember, Mary, his fiancée, was pregnant, and Joseph wasn't the father.

Mary also risked shame, embarrassment, and more by saying yes to God. In Mary's time, being pregnant without being married meant that Mary would be shunned by nearly everyone. Sometimes it may seem as if following God would be embarrassing, like when your friends want you to do something but you can't because you have to do something with your family. When those times happen, and they will, try to remember the Holy Family.

— Psalm 128

2 It is useless to work so hard for a living,
getting up early and going to bed late.
For the LORD provides for those he loves,
while they are asleep.

3 Children are a gift from the LORD;
they are a real blessing.
4 The sons a man has when he is young
are like arrows in a soldier's hand.
5 Happy is the man who has many such arrows.
He will never be defeated
when he meets his enemies in the place of judgment.

The Reward of Obedience to the LORD

128 Happy are those who obey the LORD,
who live by his commands.

2 Your work will provide for your needs;
you will be happy and prosperous.
3 Your wife will be like a fruitful vine in your home,
and your children will be like young olive trees around your table.
4 A man who obeys the LORD
will surely be blessed like this.

5 May the LORD bless you from Zion!
May you see Jerusalem prosper
all the days of your life!
6 May you live to see your grandchildren!

Peace be with Israel!

A Prayer against Israel's Enemies

129 Israel, tell us how your enemies have persecuted you
ever since you were young.

2 "Ever since I was young,
my enemies have persecuted me cruelly,
but they have not overcome me.
3 They cut deep wounds in my back
and made it like a plowed field.
4 But the LORD, the righteous one,
has freed me from slavery."

5 May everyone who hates Zion
be defeated and driven back.
6 May they all be like grass growing on the housetops,
which dries up before it can grow;

Why, do you think, the psalmist says, "Children are a gift from the LORD; / they are a real blessing" *(Psalm 127:3)***?**

Catholic Connections

What Is Prayer?

Now that you have read most of the Psalms (there are only twenty left), you have experienced quite a few different types of prayer.

So, what is prayer? Is it a complaint to God or praise? Is it a long list of what God has (or hasn't) done? Is it asking God for something, or is it giving thanks? Prayer is all these things, and it is more, too.

Some people might say that prayer is talking to God. But prayer is not just the words we say to God; it is what is in our minds and hearts. Like a good friendship, it includes learning about and loving the other person. In this case, the other is God. So it means that you realize that you are friends with God. God whispers in your heart, "I love you." That is when the power of prayer hits you. But you must be willing to be open and listen with your heart. The great thing is, when you are aware of God's love for you, the more you can share it with others.

— Psalm 130

7 no one gathers it up
or carries it away in bundles.
8 No one who passes by will say,
"May the LORD bless you!
We bless you in the name of the
LORD."

A Prayer for Help

130 From the depths of my despair I
call to you, LORD.
2 Hear my cry, O Lord;
listen to my call for help!
3 If you kept a record of our sins,
who could escape being
condemned?
4 But you forgive us,
so that we should stand in awe of you.

5 I wait eagerly for the LORD's help,
and in his word I trust.
6 I wait for the Lord
more eagerly than sentries wait for the
dawn—
than sentries wait for the dawn.
7 Israel, trust in the LORD,
because his love is constant
and he is always willing to save.
8 He will save his people Israel
from all their sins.

A Prayer of Humble Trust[b]

131 LORD, I have given up my pride
and turned away from my
arrogance.
I am not concerned with great matters
or with subjects too difficult for
me.

. . . more eagerly than sentries wait for the dawn. (130:6)

[b] **131** HEBREW TITLE: *By David.*
130:8 Mt 1:21; Titus 2:14

2 Instead, I am content and at peace.
As a child lies quietly in its mother's arms,
so my heart is quiet within me.
3 Israel, trust in the LORD
now and forever!

In Praise of the Temple

132 LORD, do not forget David
and all the hardships he endured.
2 Remember, LORD, what he promised,
the vow he made to you, the Mighty God of Jacob:
3 "I will not go home or go to bed;
4 I will not rest or sleep,
5 until I provide a place for the LORD,
a home for the Mighty God of Jacob."

6 In Bethlehem we heard about the Covenant Box,
and we found it in the fields of Jearim.
7 We said, "Let us go to the LORD's house;
let us worship before his throne."
8 Come to the Temple, LORD, with the Covenant Box,
the symbol of your power,
and stay here forever.
9 May your priests do always what is right;
may your people shout for joy!

10 You made a promise to your servant David;
do not reject your chosen king, LORD.
11 You made a solemn promise to David—
a promise you will not take back:
"I will make one of your sons king,
and he will rule after you.
12 If your sons are true to my covenant
and to the commands I give them,
their sons, also, will succeed you for all time as kings."

13 The LORD has chosen Zion;
he wants to make it his home:
14 "This is where I will live forever;
this is where I want to rule.
15 I will richly provide Zion with all she needs;
I will satisfy her poor with food.
16 I will bless her priests in all they do,
and her people will sing and shout for joy.
17 Here I will make one of David's descendants a great king;
here I will preserve the rule of my chosen king.
18 I will cover his enemies with shame,
but his kingdom will prosper and flourish."

In Praise of Living in Peace[b]

133 How wonderful it is, how pleasant,
for God's people to live together in harmony!

"How wonderful . . . for God's people to live together in harmony!" (133:1)

2 It is like the precious anointing oil
running down from Aaron's head and beard,
down to the collar of his robes.
3 It is like the dew on Mount Hermon,
falling on the hills of Zion.
That is where the LORD has promised his blessing—
life that never ends.

A Call to Praise God

134 Come, praise the LORD,
all his servants,
all who serve in his Temple at night.
2 Raise your hands in prayer in the Temple,
and praise the LORD!

3 May the LORD, who made heaven and earth,
bless you from Zion!

[b] **133** HEBREW TITLE: *By David.*

132:6–10 2 Chr 6:41, 42 **132:11** 2 Sam 7:12–16; 1 Chr 17:11–14; Ps 89:3, 4; Acts 2:30 **132:17** 1 Kings 11:36

A Hymn of Praise

135 Praise the LORD!
Praise his name, you servants of the LORD,
2 who stand in the LORD's house,
in the Temple of our God.
3 Praise the LORD, because he is good;
sing praises to his name, because he is kind.[c]
4 He chose Jacob for himself,
the people of Israel for his own.

5 I know that our LORD is great,
greater than all the gods.
6 He does whatever he wishes
in heaven and on earth,
in the seas and in the depths below.
7 He brings storm clouds from the ends of the earth;
he makes lightning for the storms,
and he brings out the wind from his storeroom.

8 In Egypt he killed all the first-born
of people and animals alike.
9 There he performed miracles and wonders
to punish the king and all his officials.
10 He destroyed many nations
and killed powerful kings:
11 Sihon, king of the Amorites,
Og, king of Bashan,
and all the kings in Canaan.
12 He gave their lands to his people;
he gave them to Israel.

13 LORD, you will always be proclaimed as God;
all generations will remember you.
14 The LORD will defend his people;
he will take pity on his servants.

15 The gods of the nations are made of silver and gold;
they are formed by human hands.
16 They have mouths, but cannot speak,
and eyes, but cannot see.
17 They have ears, but cannot hear;
they are not even able to breathe.
18 May all who made them and who trust in them
become[d] like the idols they have made!

19 Praise the LORD, people of Israel;
praise him, you priests of God!
20 Praise the LORD, you Levites;
praise him, all you that worship him!
21 Praise the LORD in Zion,
in Jerusalem, his home.

Praise the LORD!

A Hymn of Thanksgiving

136 Give thanks to the LORD,
because he is good;
his love is eternal.
2 Give thanks to the greatest of all gods;
his love is eternal.
3 Give thanks to the mightiest of all lords;
his love is eternal.

4 He alone performs great miracles;
his love is eternal.
5 By his wisdom he made the heavens;
his love is eternal;
6 he built the earth on the deep waters;
his love is eternal.
7 He made the sun and the moon;
his love is eternal;
8 the sun to rule over the day;
his love is eternal;
9 the moon and the stars to rule over the night;
his love is eternal.

10 He killed the first-born sons of the Egyptians;
his love is eternal.
11 He led the people of Israel out of Egypt;
his love is eternal;

[c] **135:3** he is kind; *or* it is pleasant to do so. [d] **135:18** May all . . . become; *or* All who made them and who trust in them will become.

135:15–18 Ps 115:4–8; Rev 9:20 **136:1** 1 Chr 16:34; 2 Chr 5:13; 7:3; Ezra 3:11; Ps 100:5; 106:1; 107:1; 118:1; Jer 33:11 **136:5** Gen 1:1 **136:6** Gen 1:2 **136:7–9** Gen 1:16 **136:10** Ex 12:29

How would your community be different if you were truly living in harmony as suggested by Psalm 133?

Pray it!

His Love Is Eternal

"His love is eternal," is repeated throughout Psalm 136. Maybe you have read lines in other psalms that are repeated. It is one tool the writers use to emphasize a statement about God. Here is another chance to write your own prayer. Choose a statement you would like to make about God (such as, "God Rocks!"). Then write verses about God that can go in between the statement. It is that simple. Have fun!

— Psalm 136

12 with his strong hand, his powerful arm;
his love is eternal.
13 He divided the Red Sea;
his love is eternal;
14 he led his people through it;
his love is eternal;
15 but he drowned the king of Egypt and his army;
his love is eternal.

16 He led his people through the desert;
his love is eternal.
17 He killed powerful kings;
his love is eternal;
18 he killed famous kings;
his love is eternal;
19 Sihon, king of the Amorites;
his love is eternal;
20 and Og, king of Bashan;
his love is eternal.
21 He gave their lands to his people;
his love is eternal;
22 he gave them to Israel, his servant;
his love is eternal.

23 He did not forget us when we were defeated;
his love is eternal;
24 he freed us from our enemies;
his love is eternal.
25 He gives food to every living creature;
his love is eternal.

26 Give thanks to the God of heaven;
his love is eternal.

A Lament of Israelites in Exile

137 By the rivers of Babylon we sat down;
there we wept when we remembered Zion.
2 On the willows near by
we hung up our harps.
3 Those who captured us told us to sing;
they told us to entertain them:
"Sing us a song about Zion."

4 How can we sing a song to the LORD
in a foreign land?
5 May I never be able to play the harp again
if I forget you, Jerusalem!
6 May I never be able to sing again
if I do not remember you,
if I do not think of you as my greatest joy!

7 Remember, LORD, what the Edomites did
the day Jerusalem was captured.
Remember how they kept saying,
"Tear it down to the ground!"

8 Babylon, you will be destroyed.
Happy are those who pay you back
for what you have done to us—
9 who take your babies
and smash them against a rock.

136:11 Ex 12:51 **136:13–15** Ex 14:21–29 **136:19** Num 21:21–30 **136:20** Num 21:31–35 **137:8** Rev 18:6

How many times is the phrase "his love is eternal" repeated in Psalm 136?

Pray it!

Life!

Life—from its very beginning to its natural end—is sacred. It is important to pray for the tiny babies in their mothers' wombs *and* for the aged who are nearing the end of their lives *and* for the person who is on death row. One way to keep life sacred is by praying for all life.

Giver of Life, let us remember that all of life is special. Help us remember the beauty of
life, newly formed, unborn babies, wrinkled and bald,
life, old men and women, wrinkled and bald,
life, sick people, undergoing treatment, wrinkled and bald,
all of life, the old and young, the sick and the healthy, the prisoner and free.
Help me, Giver of Life, to remember that all of them are special.
Amen.

— Psalm 139

A Prayer of Thanksgiving[e]

138 I thank you, LORD, with all my heart;
I sing praise to you before the gods.
2 I face your holy Temple,
bow down, and praise your name
because of your constant love and faithfulness,
because you have shown that your name and your commands are supreme.[f]
3 You answered me when I called to you;
with your strength you strengthened me.

4 All the kings in the world will praise you, LORD,
because they have heard your promises.
5 They will sing about what you have done
and about your great glory.
6 Even though you are so high above,
you care for the lowly,
and the proud cannot hide from you.

7 When I am surrounded by troubles,
you keep me safe.
You oppose my angry enemies
and save me by your power.
8 You will do everything you have promised;
LORD, your love is eternal.
Complete the work that you have begun.

God's Complete Knowledge and Care[g]

139 LORD, you have examined me
and you know me.
2 You know everything I do;
from far away you understand all my thoughts.
3 You see me, whether I am working or resting;
you know all my actions.
4 Even before I speak,
you already know what I will say.
5 You are all around me on every side;
you protect me with your power.
6 Your knowledge of me is too deep;
it is beyond my understanding.
7 Where could I go to escape from you?
Where could I get away from your presence?

[e] **138** HEBREW TITLE: *By David.* [f] **138:2** *Probable text* your name and your commands are supreme; *Hebrew* your command is greater than all your name. [g] **139** HEBREW TITLE: *A psalm by David.*

8 If I went up to heaven, you would be
there;
if I lay down in the world of the dead,
you would be there.
9 If I flew away beyond the east
or lived in the farthest place in the
west,
10 you would be there to lead me,
you would be there to help me.
11 I could ask the darkness to hide me
or the light around me to turn into
night,
12 but even darkness is not dark for you,
and the night is as bright as the day.
Darkness and light are the same to you.

13 You created every part of me;
you put me together in my mother's
womb.
14 I praise you because you are to be feared;
all you do is strange and wonderful.
I know it with all my heart.
15 When my bones were being formed,
carefully put together in my mother's
womb,
when I was growing there in secret,
you knew that I was there—
16 you saw me before I was born.
The days allotted to me
had all been recorded in your book,
before any of them ever began.
17 O God, how difficult I find your
thoughts;[h]
how many of them there are!
18 If I counted them, they would be more
than the grains of sand.
When I awake, I am still with you.

19 O God, how I wish you would kill the
wicked!
How I wish violent people would leave
me alone!
20 They say wicked things about you;
they speak evil things against your
name.[i]
21 O LORD, how I hate those who hate you!
How I despise those who rebel against
you!
22 I hate them with a total hatred;
I regard them as my enemies.

23 Examine me, O God, and know my
mind;
test me, and discover my thoughts.
24 Find out if there is any evil in me
and guide me in the everlasting way.[j]

A Prayer for Protection[k]

140 Save me, LORD, from evildoers;
keep me safe from violent
people.
2 They are always plotting evil,
always stirring up quarrels.
3 Their tongues are like deadly snakes;
their words are like a cobra's poison.

4 Protect me, LORD, from the power of the
wicked;
keep me safe from violent people
who plot my downfall.
5 The proud have set a trap for me;
they have laid their snares,
and along the path they have set traps
to catch me.

6 I say to the LORD, "You are my God."
Hear my cry for help, LORD!
7 My Sovereign LORD, my strong defender,
you have protected me in battle.
8 LORD, don't give the wicked what they
want;
don't let their plots succeed.

9 Don't let my enemies be victorious;[l]
make their threats against me fall back
on them.

10 May red-hot coals fall on them;
may they be thrown into a pit and
never get out.
11 May those who accuse others falsely not
succeed;
may evil overtake violent people and
destroy them.

12 LORD, I know that you defend the cause
of the poor
and the rights of the needy.

[h] **139:17** how difficult I find your thoughts; *or* how precious are your thoughts to me. [i] **139:20** *Probable text* they speak . . . name; *Hebrew unclear.* [j] **139:24** the everlasting way; *or* the ways of my ancestors.
[k] **140** HEBREW TITLE: *A psalm by David.* [l] **140:9** *Probable text* Don't let my enemies be victorious; *Hebrew unclear.*

139:17 Sir 18:5–7 **140:3** Rom 3:13

13 The righteous will praise you indeed;
they will live in your presence.

An Evening Prayer[m]

141 I call to you, LORD; help me now!
Listen to me when I call to you.
2 Receive my prayer as incense,
my uplifted hands as an evening sacrifice.

3 LORD, place a guard at my mouth,
a sentry at the door of my lips.
4 Keep me from wanting to do wrong
and from joining evil people in their wickedness.
May I never take part in their feasts.

5 Good people may punish me and rebuke me in kindness,
but I will never accept honor from evil people,
because I am always praying against their evil deeds.
6 When their rulers are thrown down from rocky cliffs,
the people will admit that my words were true.
7 Like wood that is split and chopped into bits,
so their bones are scattered at the edge of the grave.[n]

8 But I keep trusting in you, my Sovereign LORD.
I seek your protection;
don't let me die!
9 Protect me from the traps they have set for me,
from the snares of those evildoers.
10 May the wicked fall into their own traps
while I go by unharmed.

Study it!

Incense

Using incense is an ancient practice that goes back thousands of years, maybe even as far back as when people lived in caves. There is evidence of the use of incense in many parts of the world. Incense had a very practical purpose; it covered up bad smells when people didn't bathe as frequently as we do. But people also saw the smoke rising from incense as symbolizing their prayers rising to God. The Old Testament has references to incense in the books of Exodus, Leviticus, and Psalms.

Incense is actually a blend of resins from special trees. The Catholic Church uses incense in many of its liturgies—that is, Masses and prayer services. Although it is not usually used every Sunday, incense is frequently used at special times, such as funerals, dedications, and special holy days. It may smell funny at first, but it grows on you; as you get older, it will likely bring back memories of special times of prayer and worship.

— Psalm 141:2

A Prayer for Help[o]

142 I call to the LORD for help;
I plead with him.
2 I bring him all my complaints;
I tell him all my troubles.

[m] **141** HEBREW TITLE: *A psalm by David.* [n] **141:7** *Verses 5–7 in Hebrew are unclear.* [o] **142** HEBREW TITLE: *A poem by David, when he was in the cave; a prayer.*

141:2 Rev 5:8 **142 Title** 1 Sam 22:1; 24:3

What do you do when you are "ready to give up" *(Psalm 142:3)***?**

3 When I am ready to give up,
he knows what I should do.
In the path where I walk,
my enemies have hidden a trap for me.
4 When I look beside me,
I see that there is no one to help me,
no one to protect me.
No one cares for me.
5 LORD, I cry to you for help;
you, LORD, are my protector;
you are all I want in this life.
6 Listen to my cry for help,
for I am sunk in despair.
Save me from my enemies;
they are too strong for me.
7 Set me free from my distress;[p]
then in the assembly of your people I
will praise you
because of your goodness to me.

A Prayer for Help[q]

143 LORD, hear my prayer!
In your righteousness listen to
my plea;
answer me in your faithfulness!
2 Don't put me, your servant, on trial;
no one is innocent in your sight.
3 My enemies have hunted me down
and completely defeated me.
They have put me in a dark prison,
and I am like those who died long
ago.
4 So I am ready to give up;
I am in deep despair.
5 I remember the days gone by;
I think about all that you have
done,
I bring to mind all your deeds.
6 I lift up my hands to you in prayer;
like dry ground my soul is thirsty for
you.
7 Answer me now, LORD!
I have lost all hope.
Don't hide yourself from me,
or I will be among those who go
down to the world of the dead.
8 Remind me each morning of your
constant love,
for I put my trust in you.
My prayers go up to you;
show me the way I should go.
9 I go to you for protection, LORD;
rescue me from my enemies.
10 You are my God;
teach me to do your will.
Be good to me, and guide me on a safe
path.
11 Rescue me, LORD, as you have
promised;
in your goodness save me from my
troubles!
12 Because of your love for me, kill my
enemies
and destroy all my oppressors,
for I am your servant.

A King Thanks God for Victory[r]

144 Praise the LORD, my protector!
He trains me for battle
and prepares me for war.
2 He is my protector and defender,
my shelter and savior,
in whom I trust for safety.
He subdues the nations under me.
3 LORD, what are mortals, that you notice
them;
mere mortals, that you pay attention
to us?
4 We are like a puff of wind;
our days are like a passing shadow.
5 O LORD, tear the sky open and come
down;
touch the mountains, and they will
pour out smoke.

[p] **142:7** distress; *or* prison. [q] **143** HEBREW TITLE: *A psalm by David.* [r] **144** HEBREW TITLE: *By David.*
143:2 Rom 3:20; Gal 2:16 **144:3** Job 7:17, 18; Ps 8:4

Psalm 144 describes good sons and daughters as plants and columns! How do you think your parents would describe you?

Pray it!

Yeah God!

Praise God with instant messages and e-mails!
Praise God with newsflashes and radio announcements!
Praise God with skywriting and billboards!
Praise God with rockets and satellites!
Praise God with electric guitars and synthesizers!

How will you praise God?

As you read Psalms 145–150, notice that the writers were very joyful. Praising God in as many ways as possible, they announce the greatness of God. Music, the stars, princes, kings, all creatures, angels, and all of God's people are invited in the praise.

So, how should we praise God today? Take some time and write your own psalm praising God.

— Psalm 145

6 Send flashes of lightning and scatter your enemies;
shoot your arrows and send them running.
7 Reach down from above,
pull me out of the deep water, and rescue me;
save me from the power of foreigners,
8 who never tell the truth
and lie even under oath.

9 I will sing you a new song, O God;
I will play the harp and sing to you.
10 You give victory to kings
and rescue your servant David.
11 Save me from my cruel enemies;
rescue me from the power of foreigners,
who never tell the truth
and lie even under oath.

12 May our sons in their youth
be like plants that grow up strong.
May our daughters be like stately columns
which adorn the corners of a palace.
13 May our barns be filled
with crops of every kind.
May the sheep in our fields
bear young by the tens of thousands.
14 May our cattle reproduce plentifully
without miscarriage or loss.
May there be no cries of distress in our streets.
15 Happy is the nation of whom this is true;
happy are the people whose God is the LORD!

A Hymn of Praise[s]

145 I will proclaim your greatness,
my God and king;
I will thank you forever and ever.
2 Every day I will thank you;
I will praise you forever and ever.
3 The LORD is great and is to be highly praised;
his greatness is beyond understanding.

4 What you have done will be praised from one generation to the next;
they will proclaim your mighty acts.
5 They will speak of your glory and majesty,
and I will meditate on your wonderful deeds.
6 People will speak of your mighty deeds,
and I will proclaim your greatness.

[s] **145** HEBREW TITLE: *A song of praise by David.*

7 They will tell about all your goodness
and sing about your kindness.
8 The LORD is loving and merciful,
slow to become angry and full of
constant love.
9 He is good to everyone
and has compassion on all he made.

10 All your creatures, LORD, will praise you,
and all your people will give you
thanks.
11 They will speak of the glory of your royal
power
and tell of your might,
12 so that everyone will know your mighty
deeds
and the glorious majesty of your
kingdom.
13 Your rule is eternal,
and you are king forever.

The LORD is faithful to his promises;
he is merciful in all his acts.
14 He helps those who are in trouble;
he lifts those who have fallen.

15 All living things look hopefully to you,
and you give them food when they
need it.
16 You give them enough
and satisfy the needs of all.

17 The LORD is righteous in all he does,
merciful in all his acts.
18 He is near to those who call to him,
who call to him with sincerity.
19 He supplies the needs of those who
honor him;
he hears their cries and saves them.
20 He protects everyone who loves him,
but he will destroy the wicked.

21 I will always praise the LORD;
let all his creatures praise his holy name
forever.

In Praise of God the Savior

146 Praise the LORD!
Praise the LORD, my soul!
2 I will praise him as long as I live;
I will sing to my God all my life.

3 Don't put your trust in human leaders;
no human being can save you.
4 When they die, they return to the
dust;
on that day all their plans come to an
end.

5 Happy are those who have the God of
Jacob to help them
and who depend on the LORD their
God,
6 the Creator of heaven, earth, and sea,
and all that is in them.
He always keeps his promises;
7 he judges in favor of the oppressed
and gives food to the hungry.

The LORD sets prisoners free
8 and gives sight to the blind.
He lifts those who have fallen;
he loves his righteous people.
9 He protects the strangers who live in our
land;
he helps widows and orphans,
but takes the wicked to their ruin.

10 The LORD is king forever.
Your God, O Zion, will reign for all
time.

Praise the LORD!

In Praise of God the Almighty

147 Praise the LORD!

It is good to sing praise to our God;
it is pleasant and right to praise him.
2 The LORD is restoring Jerusalem;
he is bringing back the exiles.
3 He heals the broken-hearted
and bandages their wounds.

4 He has decided the number of the
stars
and calls each one by name.
5 Great and mighty is our Lord;
his wisdom cannot be measured.
6 He raises the humble,
but crushes the wicked to the ground.

7 Sing hymns of praise to the LORD;
play music on the harp to our God.

146:6 Acts 4:24; 14:15

8 He spreads clouds over the sky;
he provides rain for the earth
and makes grass grow on the hills.
9 He gives animals their food
and feeds the young ravens when they call.
10 His pleasure is not in strong horses,
nor his delight in brave soldiers;
11 but he takes pleasure in those who honor him,
in those who trust in his constant love.

12 Praise the LORD, O Jerusalem!
Praise your God, O Zion!
13 He keeps your gates strong;
he blesses your people.
14 He keeps your borders safe
and satisfies you with the finest wheat.

15 He gives a command to the earth,
and what he says is quickly done.
16 He spreads snow like a blanket
and scatters frost like dust.
17 He sends hail like gravel;
no one can endure the cold he sends!
18 Then he gives a command, and the ice melts;
he sends the wind, and the water flows.

19 He gives his message to his people,
his instructions and laws to Israel.
20 He has not done this for other nations;
they do not know his laws.

Praise the LORD!

A Call for the Universe to Praise God

148 Praise the LORD!

Praise the LORD from heaven,
you that live in the heights above.
2 Praise him, all his angels,
all his heavenly armies.

3 Praise him, sun and moon;
praise him, shining stars.
4 Praise him, highest heavens,
and the waters above the sky.[t]

5 Let them all praise the name of the LORD!
He commanded, and they were created;
6 by his command they were fixed in their places forever,
and they cannot disobey.[u]

7 Praise the LORD from the earth,
sea monsters and all ocean depths;
8 lightning and hail, snow and clouds,
strong winds that obey his command.

9 Praise him, hills and mountains,
fruit trees and forests;
10 all animals, tame and wild,
reptiles and birds.

11 Praise him, kings and all peoples,
princes and all other rulers;
12 young women and young men,
old people and children too.

13 Let them all praise the name of the LORD!
His name is greater than all others;
his glory is above earth and heaven.
14 He made his nation strong,
so that all his people praise him—
the people of Israel, so dear to him.

Praise the LORD!

A Hymn of Praise

149 Praise the LORD!

Sing a new song to the LORD;
praise him in the assembly of his faithful people!
2 Be glad, Israel, because of your Creator;
rejoice, people of Zion, because of your king!
3 Praise his name with dancing;
play drums and harps in praise of him.

[t] **148:4** WATERS ABOVE THE SKY: *See Gen 1:6, 7.* [u] **148:6** by his command . . . disobey; *or* he has fixed them in their places for all time, by a command that lasts forever.

"The LORD sets prisoners free / and gives sight to the blind. / He lifts those who have fallen; / he loves his righteous people" *(Psalm 146:7-8)*.

4 The LORD takes pleasure in his
people;
he honors the humble with victory.
5 Let God's people rejoice in their
triumph
and sing joyfully all night long.
6 Let them shout aloud as they praise
God,
with their sharp swords in their hands
7 to defeat the nations
and to punish the peoples;
8 to bind their kings in chains,
their leaders in chains of iron;
9 to punish the nations as God has
commanded.
This is the victory of God's people.

Praise the LORD!

149:6 2 Macc 15:27

Praise the LORD!

150 Praise the LORD!

Praise God in his Temple!
Praise his strength in heaven!
2 Praise him for the mighty things he has
done.
Praise his supreme greatness.
3 Praise him with trumpets.
Praise him with harps and lyres.
4 Praise him with drums and dancing.
Praise him with harps and flutes.
5 Praise him with cymbals.
Praise him with loud cymbals.
6 Praise the LORD, all living creatures!

Praise the LORD!

"Praise the LORD!" (150:1)

Your Next Step

Congratulations on finishing the Book of Psalms! Use this space to write your thoughts and questions about this book. If you are following the suggested reading plan, move ahead to the Letter to the Philippians in the New Testament. Philippians contains a song from the early Church that is like a psalm.

The Book of Proverbs

"Dear Zelda, I have this problem, and I'm not sure what to do about it. . . ." You've probably read letters that begin this way in a magazine or online. People have always looked for help with life's challenges. The Book of Proverbs gives advice on how to be a good person, how to build relationships, how to deal with tough times, and all kinds of other topics that are as important to you today as they were to young people hundreds of years ago.

Proverbs are short, often clever, and easy-to-memorize statements of wisdom and practical truth. The Book of Proverbs is a collection of advice written by different people over a long period of time. All of these people had one goal in mind: to pass along the wisdom that comes from God so that we can understand life better and live it well.

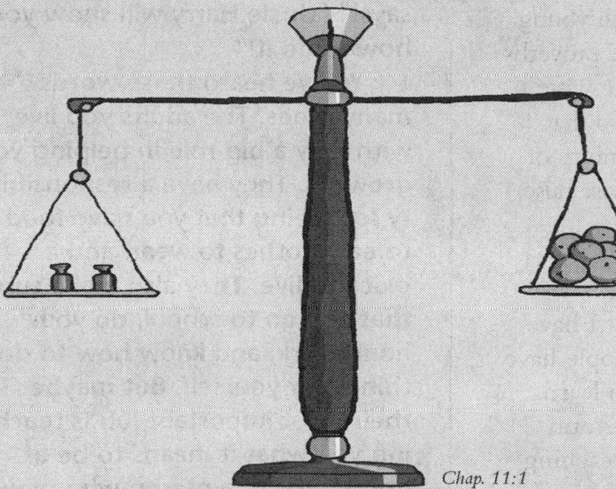

Chap. 11:1

Headlines

- Purpose and Value of Wisdom (1:1–7)
- A Father's Advice (chapter 4)
- Seek Wisdom, Find Happiness (chapter 8)
- Watch Your Temper and Your Tongue! (10:18–21)
- Pick Your Friends Carefully (24:1–2)
- The Sweet Taste of Gossip (26:20–28)
- Honesty Is the Best Policy (28:1–20)

FACTOIDS

Who wrote this book? King Solomon usually gets the credit, but several people wrote different parts of it over a span of about four hundred years, long before Jesus was born.

Why was it written? To give down-to-earth, practical advice on everyday matters, such as family, society, and relationships.

Who was it written for? Even though the advice applies to everyone, much of this book was written specifically for young people.

How is it organized? The book has two main parts. Chapters 1–9 include speeches about how to be wise and live a good life. Chapters 10–31 are collections of short sayings.

Important themes

- Being a wise person means knowing right from wrong and always doing the right thing, no matter how hard it might be.
- Treat people as you want to be treated.
- God is always with us, no matter what.

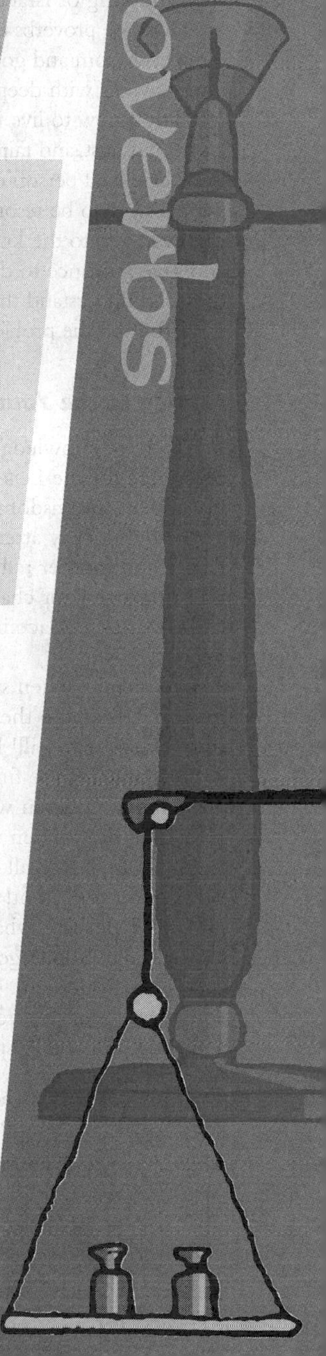

PROVERBS

The Value of Proverbs

1 The proverbs of Solomon, son of David
and king of Israel.
2Here are proverbs that will help you rec-
ognize wisdom and good advice, and under-
stand sayings with deep meaning. 3They can
teach you how to live intelligently and how to
be honest, just, and fair. 4They can make an
inexperienced person clever and teach young
people how to be resourceful. 5These proverbs
can even add to the knowledge of the wise
and give guidance to the educated, 6so that
they can understand the hidden meanings of
proverbs and the problems that the wise raise.

Advice to the Young

7To have knowledge, you must first have
reverence for the LORD.[a] Stupid people have
no respect for wisdom and refuse to learn.
8My child, pay attention to what your
father and mother tell you. 9Their teaching
will improve your character as a handsome
turban or a necklace improves your appear-
ance.
10My child, when sinners tempt you, don't
give in. 11Suppose they say, "Come on; let's
find someone to kill! Let's attack some inno-
cent people for the fun of it! 12They may be
alive and well when we find them, but
they'll be dead when we're through with
them! 13We'll find all kinds of riches and fill
our houses with loot! 14Come and join us,
and we'll all share what we steal."
15My child, don't go with people like that.
Stay away from them. 16They can't wait to do
something bad. They're always ready to kill.
17It does no good to spread a net when the

Live it!

Parental Wisdom

"Go ask your mother!" "Listen to your father!" "See what Grandma says!" "Uncle Harry will show you how to do it!"

You've heard those words many times. The adults you live with play a big role in helping you grow up. They have a responsibility for seeing that you have food to eat, clothes to wear, and a place to live. They also make sure that you go to school, do your homework, and know how to do things for yourself. But maybe their most important job is teaching you what it means to be a good person, a person who makes a positive difference in the world.

The Book of Proverbs starts by telling young people to have reverence for God and to pay attention to their parents. Your parents and other family members have learned a lot in all their years of life. They've had some successes and made mistakes, too. Even though they were teenagers in a very different world, pay close attention to the wisdom they share.

— Proverbs 1:8–9

[a] **1:7** To . . . LORD; *or* The most important part of knowledge is having reverence for the LORD.

1:1 1 Kings 4:32 **1:7** Job 28:28; Ps 111:10; Prov 9:10; Sir 1:14

1:9 *1:11–15* *1:28* *1:33* *2:2*

Pray it!

With Ears and Heart

You listen with your ears, but to really hear and understand someone, you must also listen with your heart. The next time someone needs to talk with you about something important, say this short prayer based on Proverbs 2:1–2.

Dear God,
Open my ears that I may hear the words that are spoken.
Open my heart that I might understand their true meaning.
Open my mind that I may always act out of love and respect.

— Proverbs 2:1–2

bird you want to catch is watching, 18but peo-
ple like that are setting a trap for themselves, a
trap in which they will die. 19Robbery always
claims the life of the robber—this is what hap-
pens to[b] anyone who lives by violence.

Wisdom Calls

20Listen! Wisdom is calling out in the
streets and marketplaces, 21calling loudly at
the city gates and wherever people come
together:
22"Foolish people! How long do you want
to be foolish? How long will you enjoy mak-
ing fun of knowledge? Will you never learn?
23Listen when I reprimand you; I will give
you good advice and share my knowledge
with you. 24I have been calling you, inviting
you to come, but you would not listen. You
paid no attention to me. 25You have ignored
all my advice and have not been willing to
let me correct you. 26So when you get into
trouble, I will laugh at you. I will make fun
of you when terror strikes— 27when it
comes on you like a storm, bringing fierce
winds of trouble, and you are in pain and
misery. 28Then you will call for wisdom, but
I will not answer. You may look for me
everywhere, but you will not find me. 29You
have never had any use for knowledge and
have always refused to obey the LORD. 30You
have never wanted my advice or paid any
attention when I corrected you. 31So then,
you will get what you deserve, and your own
actions will make you sick. 32Inexperienced
people die because they reject wisdom. Stu-
pid people are destroyed by their own lack of
concern. 33But whoever listens to me will
have security. He will be safe, with no reason
to be afraid."

The Rewards of Wisdom

2 My child, learn what I teach you and
never forget what I tell you to do. 2Lis-
ten to what is wise and try to understand it.
3Yes, beg for knowledge; plead for insight.
4Look for it as hard as you would for silver
or some hidden treasure. 5If you do, you will
know what it means to fear the LORD and
you will succeed in learning about God. 6It
is the LORD who gives wisdom; from him
come knowledge and understanding. 7He
provides help and protection for those who

[b] **1:19** *One ancient translation* what happens to; *Hebrew* the path of.
1:20, 21 Prov 8:1–3 **2:6** Wis 9:10; Sir 1:1

"It is the LORD who gives wisdom; from him come knowledge and understanding" *(Proverbs 2:6)*.

Live it!

Wisdom: Guard and Guide

Isabel didn't need to see the hurt in Natalie's eyes to know that what she said was wrong. But the hurt was there. And so were the tears. More than anything, Isabel wanted to eat lunch with Lucy and the other popular girls. As they passed Natalie's table, Lucy made a nasty comment about Natalie's need for special help in reading. When Isabel added her own mean remark, the others giggled. Natalie shot Isabel a glance that said, "Not you, too!" and then her eyes filled with tears. Isabel felt terrible. She was quiet all through lunch at the popular table.

Did you ever do something you knew was wrong, just because someone else did it? God's gift of wisdom does two things: it guards us from evil, and it guides us to make right choices. The gift is yours if you want it. Just ask God.

— Proverbs 2:1–22

are righteous and honest. 8He protects those
who treat others fairly, and guards those who
are devoted to him.
9If you listen to me, you will know what
is right, just, and fair. You will know what
you should do. 10You will become wise, and
your knowledge will give you pleasure.
11Your insight and understanding will pro-
tect you 12and prevent you from doing the
wrong thing. They will keep you away from
people who stir up trouble by what they
say— 13those who have abandoned a righ-
teous life to live in the darkness of sin,
14those who find pleasure in doing wrong
and who enjoy senseless evil, 15unreliable
people who cannot be trusted.
16You will be able to resist any immoral
woman who tries to seduce you with her
smooth talk, 17who is faithless to her own
husband and forgets her sacred vows. 18If
you go to her house, you are traveling the
road to death. To go there is to approach the
world of the dead. 19No one who visits her
ever comes back. He never returns to the
road to life. 20So you must follow the exam-
ple of good people and live a righteous life.
21Righteous people—people of integrity—
will live in this land of ours. 22But God will
snatch the wicked from the land and pull
sinners out of it like plants from the ground.

Advice to the Young

3 My child, don't forget what I teach you.
Always remember what I tell you to do.
2My teaching will give you a long and pros-
perous life. 3Never let go of loyalty and faith-
fulness. Tie them around your neck; write
them on your heart. 4If you do this, both
God and people will be pleased with you.
5Trust in the LORD with all your heart.
Never rely on what you think you know.
6Remember the LORD in everything you
do, and he will show you the right way.
7Never let yourself think that you are wiser
than you are; simply obey the LORD and
refuse to do wrong. 8If you do, it will be like
good medicine, healing your wounds and
easing your pains. 9Honor the LORD by
making him an offering from the best of all
that your land produces. 10If you do, your
barns will be filled with grain, and you will
have too much wine to store it all.
11My child, when the LORD corrects you,
pay close attention and take it as a warning.
12The LORD corrects those he loves, as par-
ents correct a child of whom they are proud.
13Happy is anyone who becomes wise—

3:4 Lk 2:52 **3:7** Rom 12:16 **3:11** Job 5:17 **3:11, 12** Heb 12:5, 6 **3:12** Rev 3:19

Read Proverbs 3:27. How would you apply this teaching in your school? your community? your family?

Pray it!

Trust in the Lord

Dear God, sometimes I wonder,
am I doing what you want me to be doing?
Is everything going to turn out okay?
Why do bad things happen?
When the road ahead looks uncertain or fearful
and I don't know where I'm going,
help me see the path you want me to follow.
I believe you will be with me every step of the way,
when everything is going great,
and in times of trouble, danger, and sorrow.
I trust that you will lead me where you want me to go.
And knowing that brings me joy. **(Koch, Garden of a Thousand Gates, p. 61)**

— Proverbs 3:5–6

who comes to have understanding. 14 There
is more profit in it than there is in silver; it is
worth more to you than gold. 15 Wisdom is
more valuable than jewels; nothing you
could want can compare with it. 16 Wisdom
offers you long life, as well as wealth and
honor. 17 Wisdom can make your life pleas-
ant and lead you safely through it. 18 Those
who become wise are happy; wisdom will
give them life.

19 The LORD created the earth by his
wisdom;
by his knowledge he set the sky in
place.
20 His wisdom caused the rivers to flow
and the clouds to give rain to the earth.

21 My child, hold on to your wisdom and
insight. Never let them get away from you.
22 They will provide you with life—a pleas-
ant and happy life. 23 You can go safely on
your way and never even stumble. 24 You will
not be afraid when you go to bed, and you
will sleep soundly through the night. 25 You
will not have to worry about sudden disas-
ters, such as come on the wicked like a
storm. 26 The LORD will keep you safe. He
will not let you fall into a trap.

27 Whenever you possibly can, do good to
those who need it. 28 Never tell your neigh-
bors to wait until tomorrow if you can help
them now. 29 Don't plan anything that will
hurt your neighbors; they live beside you,
trusting you. 30 Don't argue with others for
no reason when they have never done you
any harm. 31 Don't be jealous of violent peo-
ple or decide to act as they do, 32 because the
LORD hates people who do evil, but he takes
righteous people into his confidence. 33 The
LORD puts a curse on the homes of the
wicked, but blesses the homes of the righ-
teous. 34 He has no use for conceited people,
but shows favor to those who are humble.

3:27, 28 Sir 4:3 **3:34** Jas 4:6; 1 Pet 5:5

2:16 *3:12* *3:20* *3:23* *3:29*

Live it!

Two Ways

Jorge knew that his coach wouldn't let him play this week if he didn't pass his social studies test. The night before the test, he wrote a few facts on his arms; the next day he wore a long-sleeved shirt to cover them. In class he sat near his teammate Derek. He knew Derek would let him copy his answers. After all, last week, he let Derek copy his math homework.

Derek and Jorge heard enough about cheating to know it was wrong. But they told each other that in their case it was the right thing to do. The team needed them more than they needed to know about math or social studies. Neither of them got caught, and they both played in the game.

Every decision we make goes in one of two directions: toward good or toward evil. The end of Proverbs, chapter 4, tells us to have nothing to do with lies and not to take one step off the right way. Which way did Jorge and Derek choose? Which way do you most often choose?

— Proverbs 4:24–27

35 Wise people will gain an honorable repu-
tation, but stupid people will only add to
their own disgrace.

The Benefits of Wisdom

4 My children, listen to what your father
teaches you. Pay attention, and you will
have understanding. 2 What I am teaching
you is good, so remember it all. 3 When I
was only a little boy, my parents' only son,
4 my father would teach me. He would say,
"Remember what I say and never forget it.
Do as I tell you, and you will live. 5 Get wis-
dom and insight! Do not forget or ignore
what I say. 6 Do not abandon wisdom, and
she will protect you; love her, and she will
keep you safe. 7 Getting wisdom is the most
important thing you can do. Whatever else
you get, get insight. 8 Love wisdom, and she
will make you great. Embrace her,[c] and she
will bring you honor. 9 She will be your
crowning glory."

10 Listen to me, my child. Take seriously
what I am telling you, and you will live a
long life. 11 I have taught you wisdom and the
right way to live. 12 Nothing will stand
in your way if you walk wisely, and you
will not stumble when you run. 13 Always
remember what you have learned. Your edu-
cation is your life—guard it well. 14 Do not go
where evil people go. Do not follow the
example of the wicked. 15 Don't do it! Keep
away from evil! Refuse it and go on your
way. 16 Wicked people cannot sleep unless
they have done something wrong. They lie
awake unless they have hurt someone.
17 Wickedness and violence are like food and
drink to them.

18 The road the righteous travel is like the
sunrise, getting brighter and brighter until
daylight has come. 19 The road of the wicked,
however, is dark as night. They fall, but can-
not see what they have stumbled over.

20 My child, pay attention to what I say.
Listen to my words. 21 Never let them get
away from you. Remember them and keep
them in your heart. 22 They will give life and

[c] **4:8** Embrace her; *or* Prize her highly.

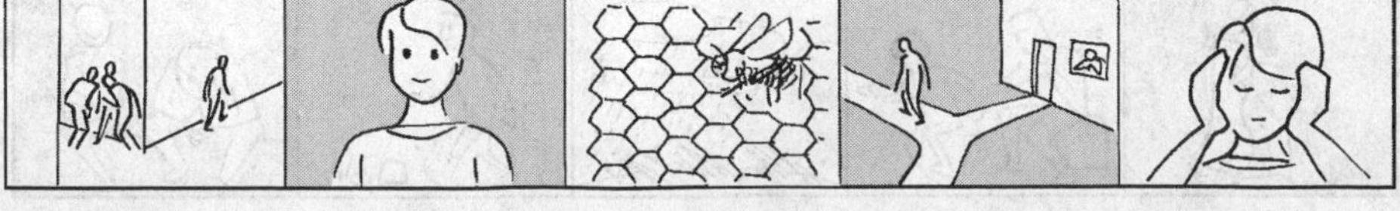

4:15 *4:25* *5:3* *5:8* *5:13*

Catholic Connections

"I Do" Before "Let's Do It"

If you watch television, see movies, listen to music, or read certain magazines, it almost seems like it doesn't matter. It can happen with anyone, anywhere, any age, anytime. What's the "it"? Having sex.

But it most certainly does matter. Sexual feelings are a perfectly normal part of growing up and part of the gift of life God gave to us. But sexual desires, pressure from another person, and curiosity are *never* good reasons for young people to have sex. Chapter 5 of Proverbs warns against adultery but any sex before or outside of marriage is wrong. That's why the Catholic Church teaches that sex is good and holy only when it is between a man and a woman who are married to each other.

— Proverbs, chapter 5

health to anyone who understands them.
23 Be careful how you think; your life is
shaped by your thoughts. 24 Never say any-
thing that isn't true. Have nothing to do
with lies and misleading words. 25 Look
straight ahead with honest confidence; don't
hang your head in shame. 26 Plan carefully
what you do, and whatever you do will turn
out right. 27 Avoid evil and walk straight
ahead. Don't go one step off the right way.

Warning against Adultery

5 My child, pay attention and listen to my
wisdom and insight. 2 Then you will
know how to behave properly, and your
words will show that you have knowledge.
3 The lips of another man's wife may be as
sweet as honey and her kisses as smooth as
olive oil, 4 but when it is all over, she leaves
you nothing but bitterness and pain. 5 She
will take you down to the world of the dead;
the road she walks is the road to death. 6 She
does not stay on the road to life; but wanders
off, and does not realize what is happening.
7 Now listen to me, sons, and never forget
what I am saying. 8 Keep away from such a
woman! Don't even go near her door! 9 If
you do, others will gain the respect that you
once had, and you will die young at the
hands of merciless people. 10 Yes, strangers
will take all your wealth, and what you have
worked for will belong to someone else.
11 You will lie groaning on your deathbed,
your flesh and muscles being eaten away,
12 and you will say, "Why would I never
learn? Why would I never let anyone correct
me? 13 I wouldn't listen to my teachers. I paid
no attention to them. 14 And suddenly I
found myself[d] publicly disgraced."
15 Be faithful to your own wife and give
your love to her alone. 16 Children that you
have by other women will do you no good.
17 Your children should grow up to help you,
not strangers. 18 So be happy with your wife
and find your joy with the woman you mar-
ried— 19 pretty and graceful as a deer. Let
her charms keep you happy; let her surround
you with her love. 20 Son, why should you
give your love to another woman? Why

[d] **5:14** And suddenly . . . myself; *or* I was about to be.
4:26 Heb 12:13

Read Proverbs 4:5–7. The message couldn't be much clearer: Get wisdom, at all costs. Where do you find wisdom?

should you prefer the charms of another
man's wife? 21The LORD sees everything you
do. Wherever you go, he is watching. 22The
sins of the wicked are a trap. They get caught
in the net of their own sin. 23They die
because they have no self-control. Their utter
stupidity will send them to their graves.

More Warnings

6 My child, have you promised to be
responsible for someone else's debts?
2Have you been caught by your own words,
trapped by your own promises? 3Well then, my
child, you are in that person's power, but this is
how to get out of it: hurry to him, and beg
him to release you. 4Don't let yourself go to
sleep or even stop to rest. 5Get out of the trap
like a bird or a deer escaping from a hunter.
6Lazy people should learn a lesson from
the way ants live. 7They have no leader, chief,
or ruler, 8but they store up their food during
the summer, getting ready for winter. 9How
long is the lazy man going to lie around?
When is he ever going to get up? 10"I'll just
take a short nap," he says; "I'll fold my hands
and rest a while." 11But while he sleeps,
poverty will attack him like an armed robber.
12Worthless, wicked people go around
telling lies. 13They wink and make gestures
to deceive you, 14all the while planning evil
in their perverted minds, stirring up trouble
everywhere. 15Because of this, disaster will
strike them without warning, and they will
be fatally wounded.
16-19There are seven things that the LORD
hates and cannot tolerate:
A proud look,
a lying tongue,
hands that kill innocent people,
a mind that thinks up wicked plans,
feet that hurry off to do evil,
a witness who tells one lie after another,
and someone who stirs up trouble
among friends.

Live it!

Bodily Blunders

You wear clothes that make you look nice. You eat foods that keep your body healthy. You visit doctors, dentists, and hair stylists to make sure you stay well and look good. You go to school to build your mind. All those things are important as you grow. Your body does everything for you. It's what you use to take your place in the world.

It's important to give your body a spiritual checkup, too. Chapter 6 contains a list of five bodily blunders that make God angry.

- **eyes that look down on others**
- **a tongue that tells lies**
- **hands that are used for violence**
- **a brain used to think of ways to get away with something wrong**
- **feet that walk toward evil**

How does your body measure up? Check out Romans 12:1–8 and 1 Corinthians 12:12–31 for more spiritual body talk!

— Proverbs 6:16–19

Warning against Adultery

20Son, do what your father tells you and
never forget what your mother taught you.
21Keep their words with you always, locked
in your heart. 22Their teaching will lead you
when you travel, protect you at night, and
advise you during the day. 23Their instruc-
tions are a shining light; their correction can
teach you how to live. 24It can keep you
away from bad women, from the seductive
words of other men's wives. 25Don't be

6:1–5 Sir 29:14–20 **6:10, 11** Prov 24:33, 34 **6:13, 14** Sir 27:22

Scientists say that the earth would thrive without human beings, but it could not survive without ants! Check out Proverbs 6:6–8.

5:15

6:5

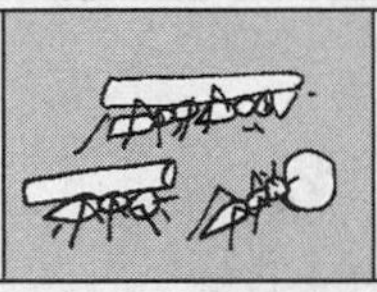
6:6

6:13

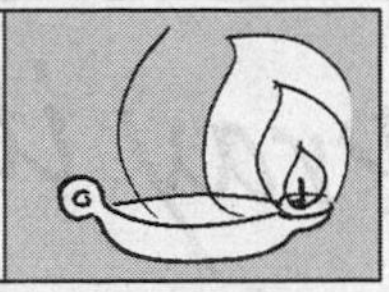
6:23

tempted by their beauty; don't be trapped by
their flirting eyes. 26A man can hire a prosti-
tute for the price of a loaf of bread, but
adultery will cost him all he has.
27Can you carry fire against your chest
without burning your clothes? 28Can you
walk on hot coals without burning your
feet? 29It is just as dangerous to sleep with
another man's wife. Whoever does it will
suffer. 30People don't despise a thief if he
steals food when he is hungry;[e] 31yet if he
is caught, he must pay back seven times
more—he must give up everything he has.
32But a man who commits adultery doesn't
have any sense. He is just destroying himself.
33He will be dishonored and beaten up; he
will be permanently disgraced. 34A husband
is never angrier than when he is jealous; his
revenge knows no limits. 35He will not
accept any payment; no amount of gifts will
satisfy his anger.

7 My child, remember what I say and
never forget what I tell you to do. 2Do
what I say, and you will live. Be as careful to
follow my teaching as you are to protect your
eyes. 3Keep my teaching with you all the
time; write it on your heart. 4Treat wisdom as
your sister, and insight as your closest friend.
5They will keep you away from other men's
wives, from women with seductive words.

The Immoral Woman

6Once I was looking out the window of
my house, 7and I saw many inexperienced
young men, but noticed one foolish fellow in
particular. 8He was walking along the street
near the corner where a certain woman lived.
He was passing near her house 9in the evening
after it was dark. 10And then she met him; she
was dressed like a prostitute and was making
plans. 11She was a bold and shameless woman
who always walked the streets 12or stood wait-
ing at a corner, sometimes in the streets, some-
times in the marketplace. 13She threw her arms
around the young man, kissed him, looked
him straight in the eye, and said, 14"I made my
offerings today and have the meat from the
sacrifices. 15So I came out looking for you. I
wanted to find you, and here you are! 16I've
covered my bed with sheets of colored linen
from Egypt. 17I've perfumed it with myrrh,
aloes, and cinnamon. 18Come on! Let's make
love all night long. We'll be happy in each
other's arms. 19My husband isn't at home. He's
on a long trip. 20He took plenty of money
with him and won't be back for two weeks."
21So she tempted him with her charms, and
he gave in to her smooth talk. 22Suddenly he
was going with her like an ox on the way to
be slaughtered, like a deer prancing into a trap[f]
23where an arrow would pierce its heart. He
was like a bird going into a net—he did not
know that his life was in danger.
24Now then, sons, listen to me. Pay atten-
tion to what I say. 25Do not let such a
woman win your heart; don't go wandering
after her. 26She has been the ruin of many
men and caused the death of too many to
count. 27If you go to her house, you are on
the way to the world of the dead. It is a
shortcut to death.

[e] **6:30** People don't despise . . . hungry; *or* Don't people despise . . . hungry? [f] **7:22** *Probable text* like a deer prancing into a trap; *Hebrew unclear.*

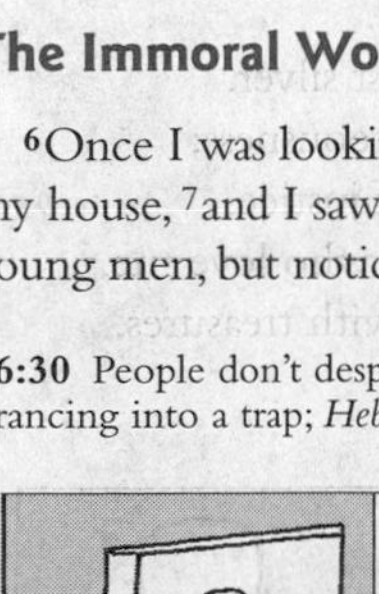
7:6

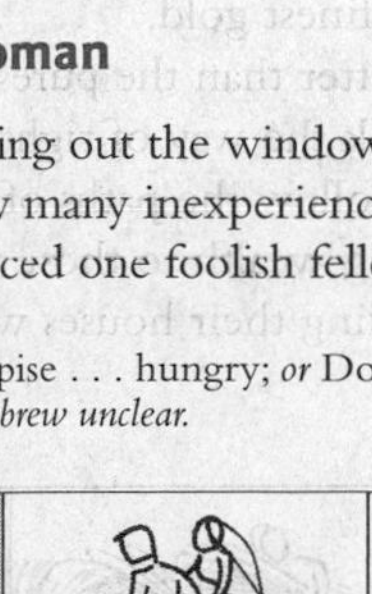
7:10

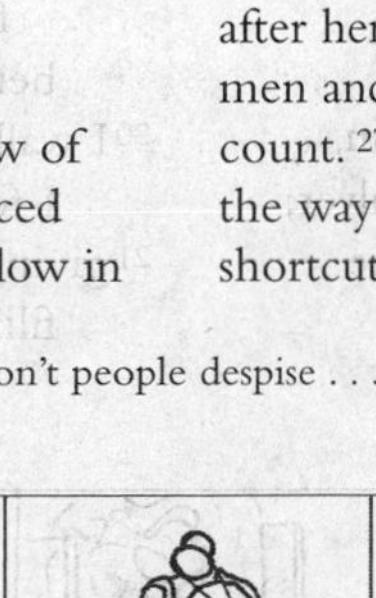
7:13

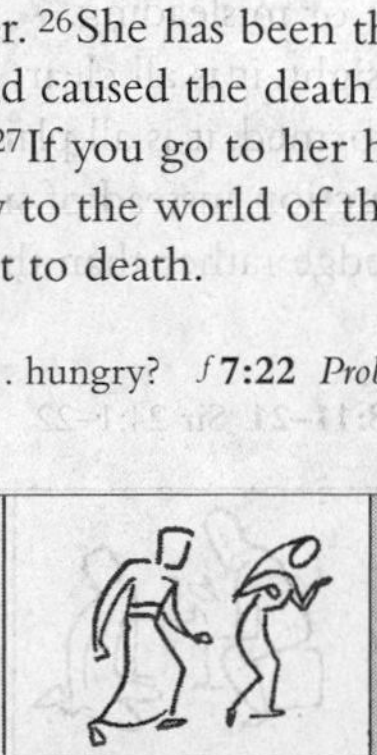
7:22

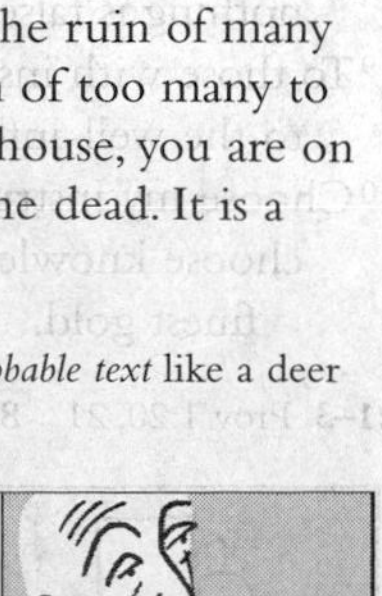
8:13

Pray it!

I Need You, God

They are there, just waiting for you. People who make doing something wrong sound too good to pass up. Just like the woman who lures the young man into having sex in Proverbs, chapter 7. Whether it is a man or a woman who tempts us, we need God's help to escape them!

Dear God,

Sometimes my so-called friends want me to do things that I know are wrong. I want to say no, but I know they would make fun of me. Help me to stand up for what I believe is right. It's not easy to do that, and I really need to know that you are standing right beside me. I can't do it alone. Please, God, I need you. And so do my friends.

— Proverbs 7:24–27

In Praise of Wisdom

8 Listen! Wisdom is calling out.
Reason is making herself heard.
2 On the hilltops near the road
and at the crossroads she stands.
3 At the entrance to the city,
beside the gates, she calls:
4 "I appeal to all of you;
I call to everyone on earth.
5 Are you immature? Learn to be mature.
Are you foolish? Learn to have sense.
6 Listen to my excellent words;
all I tell you is right.
7 What I say is the truth;
lies are hateful to me.
8 Everything I say is true;
nothing is false or misleading.
9 To those with insight, it is all clear;
to the well-informed, it is all plain.
10 Choose my instruction instead of silver;
choose knowledge rather than the finest gold.
11 "I am Wisdom, I am better than jewels;
nothing you want can compare with me.
12 I am Wisdom, and I have insight;
I have knowledge and sound judgment.
13 To honor the LORD is to hate evil;
I hate pride and arrogance,
evil ways and false words.
14 I make plans and carry them out.
I have understanding, and I am strong.
15 I help kings to govern
and rulers to make good laws.
16 Every ruler on earth governs with my help,
officials and nobles alike.
17 I love those who love me;
whoever looks for me can find me.
18 I have riches and honor to give,
prosperity and success.
19 What you get from me is better than the finest gold,
better than the purest silver.
20 I walk the way of righteousness;
I follow the paths of justice,
21 giving wealth to those who love me,
filling their houses with treasures.

8:1–3 Prov 1:20, 21 **8:11–21** Sir 24:1–22

8:34 *9:9* *9:13–14* *10:5* *10:26*

Live it!

Wisdom in the World

"I help kings to govern / and rulers to make good laws. / Every ruler on earth governs with my help, / officials and nobles alike" (Proverbs 8:15–16).

The most important quality a leader can have is wisdom. It is the source of many gifts, such as truth, fairness, respect, understanding, justice, and reverence for all of life. But sometimes it seems as if leaders and lawmakers make decisions out of selfishness, greed, and the need for power and control over other human beings.

- **What do you see happening around you that shows a lack of wisdom?**
- **What would Lady Wisdom have to say about these decisions?**
- **What do you see happening that demonstrates the wisdom of those who made the decision?**

Say a prayer for those who lead our schools, our communities, our country, and our world. They do not have easy jobs.

— Proverbs 8:15–16

22 "The LORD created me first of all,
the first of his works, long ago.
23 I was made in the very beginning,
at the first, before the world began.
24 I was born before the oceans,
when there were no springs of water.
25 I was born before the mountains,
before the hills were set in place,
26 before God made the earth and its fields
or even the first handful of soil.
27 I was there when he set the sky in place,
when he stretched the horizon across
the ocean,
28 when he placed the clouds in the
sky,
when he opened the springs of the
ocean
29 and ordered the waters of the sea
to rise no further than he said.
I was there when he laid the earth's
foundations.
30 I was beside him like an architect,[g]
I was his daily source of joy,
always happy in his presence—
31 happy with the world
and pleased with the human race.

32 "Now, young people, listen to me.
Do as I say, and you will be happy.
33 Listen to what you are taught.
Be wise; do not neglect it.
34 Those who listen to me will be happy—
those who stay at my door every day,
waiting at the entrance to my home.
35 Those who find me find life,
and the LORD will be pleased with
them.
36 Those who do not find me hurt
themselves;
anyone who hates me loves death."

Wisdom and Stupidity

9 Wisdom has built her house and made
seven columns for it. 2 She has had an
animal killed for a feast, mixed spices in the
wine, and set the table. 3 She has sent her ser-
vant women to call out from the highest
place in town: 4 "Come in, ignorant people!"
And to the foolish she says, 5 "Come, eat my
food and drink the wine that I have mixed.
6 Leave the company of ignorant people, and
live. Follow the way of knowledge."
7 If you correct conceited people, you will

[g] **8:30** an architect; *or* a little child.

8:22 Sir 1:4, 9; Rev 3:14 **8:27–31** Wis 9:9; Sir 24:3–6 **8:32** Sir 14:20–27

The poem praising wisdom in Proverbs, chapter 8, makes wisdom sound like an actual person. This is called personification.

Study it!

Who Me? Royalty?

The short sayings in Proverbs, chapters 10–31, were probably written long before the longer speeches of the first nine chapters. The style of the second part of the book is similar to collections of sayings from other parts of the world at that time. In fact, some of the sayings in Proverbs were probably borrowed from other cultures. For example, in Egypt such books of sayings were used to educate princes so that they would become strong, kind, and just rulers.

Make your own wisdom book. Copy into a blank notebook the proverbs from chapters 10–31 that you think will help you and other people your age become strong, kind, and just human beings.

— Proverbs, chapter 10

only be insulted. If you reprimand evil people, you will only get hurt. 8 Never correct conceited people; they will hate you for it. But if you correct the wise, they will respect you. 9 Anything you say to the wise will make them wiser. Whatever you tell the righteous will add to their knowledge.

10 To be wise you must first have reverence for the LORD. If you know the Holy One, you have understanding. 11 Wisdom will add years to your life. 12 You are the one who will profit if you have wisdom, and if you reject it, you are the one who will suffer.

13 Stupidity is like a loud, ignorant, shameless woman.[h] 14 She sits at the door of her house or on a seat in the highest part of town, 15 and calls out to people passing by, who are minding their own business: 16 "Come in, ignorant people!" To the foolish she says, 17 "Stolen water is sweeter. Stolen bread tastes better." 18 Her victims do not know that the people die who go to her house, that those who have already entered are now deep in the world of the dead.

Solomon's Proverbs

10 These are Solomon's proverbs:

Wise children make their fathers proud of them; foolish ones bring their mothers grief.

2 Wealth you get by dishonesty will do you no good, but honesty can save your life.

3 The LORD will not let good people go hungry, but he will keep the wicked from getting what they want.

4 Being lazy will make you poor, but hard work will make you rich.

5 A sensible person gathers the crops when they are ready; it is a disgrace to sleep through the time of harvest.

6 Good people will receive blessings. The words of the wicked hide a violent nature.

7 Good people will be remembered as a blessing, but the wicked will soon be forgotten.

8 Sensible people accept good advice. People who talk foolishly will come to ruin.

9 Honest people are safe and secure, but the dishonest will be caught.

10 Someone who holds back the truth causes trouble, but one who openly criticizes works for peace.[i]

11 A good person's words are a fountain of life, but a wicked person's words hide a violent nature.

12 Hate stirs up trouble, but love forgives all offenses.

[h] **9:13** *Verse 13 in Hebrew is unclear.* [i] **10:10** *One ancient translation* but one . . . peace; *Hebrew repeats verse 8b.*
9:10 Job 28:28; Ps 111:10; Prov 1:7 **10:12** Jas 5:20; 1 Pet 4:8

Proverbs 10:1—22:16 is the first section of short sayings. Can you count how many proverbs are in this section? Hint: The number = (13 x 30) - 15.

Study it!

Who Was Solomon?

You've probably seen the name Solomon a few times so far in the Book of Proverbs. Solomon was the third king of Israel, the son of David and Bathsheba. He was known all over the world for his wisdom. Long after he died he was credited with writing the Proverbs and other wisdom books. Bible scholars tell us this is too simple. Solomon was the source of many wise words, but so were many other people who helped create these writings.

Solomon did many good things, but he also put a high priority on riches and power. He sinned against God by building altars to the gods of foreign nations for the wives he married from other lands. You can read his story in the First Book of Kings, chapters 1–11.

— Proverbs, chapter 10

13 Intelligent people talk sense, but stupid
people need to be punished.
14 The wise get all the knowledge they can,
but when fools speak, trouble is not far off.
15 Wealth protects the rich; poverty
destroys the poor.
16 The reward for doing good is life, but
sin leads only to more sin.
17 People who listen when they are cor-
rected will live, but those who will not
admit that they are wrong are in danger.
18 Anyone who hides hatred is a liar. Any-
one who spreads gossip is a fool.
19 The more you talk, the more likely you
are to sin. If you are wise, you will keep
quiet.
20 A good person's words are like pure sil-
ver; a wicked person's ideas are worthless.
21 A good person's words will benefit
many people, but you can kill yourself with
stupidity.
22 It is the LORD's blessing that makes you
wealthy. Hard work can make you no richer.[j]
23 It is foolish to enjoy doing wrong. Intel-
ligent people take pleasure in wisdom.
24 The righteous get what they want, but
the wicked will get what they fear most.
25 Storms come, and the wicked are blown
away, but honest people are always safe.
26 Never get a lazy person to do some-
thing for you; he will be as irritating as vin-
egar on your teeth or smoke in your eyes.
27 Obey the LORD, and you will live
longer. The wicked die before their time.
28 The hopes of good people lead to joy,
but wicked people can look forward to
nothing.
29 The LORD protects honest people, but
destroys those who do wrong.
30 Righteous people will always have securi-
ty, but the wicked will not survive in the land.
31 Righteous people speak wisdom, but
the tongue that speaks evil will be stopped.
32 Righteous people know the kind thing
to say, but the wicked are always saying
things that hurt.

11 The LORD hates people who use
dishonest scales. He is happy with
honest weights.
2 People who are proud will soon be dis-
graced. It is wiser to be modest.
3 If you are good, you are guided by hon-
esty. People who can't be trusted are
destroyed by their own dishonesty.
4 Riches will do you no good on the day
you face death, but honesty can save your
life.
5 Honesty makes a good person's life easi-
er, but the wicked will cause their own
downfall.
6 Righteousness rescues those who are
honest, but those who can't be trusted are
trapped by their own greed.
7 When the wicked die, their hope dies
with them. Confidence placed in riches
comes to nothing.

[j] **10:22** Hard work . . . richer; *or* And the LORD does not add sorrow to your wealth.

11:1

11:12

11:22

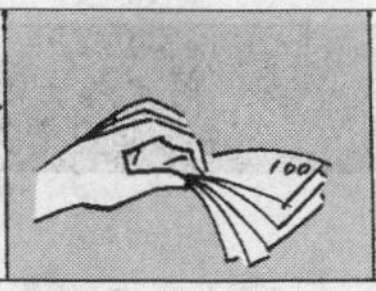
11:25

11:28

8 The righteous are protected from trouble; it comes to the wicked instead.

9 You can be ruined by the talk of godless people, but the wisdom of the righteous can save you.

10 A city is happy when honest people have good fortune, and there are joyful shouts when the wicked die.

11 A city becomes great when the righteous give it their blessing; but a city is brought to ruin by the words of the wicked.

12 It is foolish to speak scornfully of others. If you are smart, you will keep quiet.

13 No one who gossips can be trusted with a secret, but you can put confidence in someone who is trustworthy.

14 A nation will fall if it has no guidance. Many advisers mean security.

15 If you promise to pay a stranger's debt, you will regret it. You are better off if you don't get involved.

16 A gracious woman is respected, but a woman without virtue is a disgrace.

Lazy people will never have money,[k] but aggressive people will get rich.

17 You do yourself a favor when you are kind. If you are cruel, you only hurt yourself.

18 Wicked people do not really gain anything, but if you do what is right, you are certain to be rewarded.

19 Anyone who is determined to do right will live, but anyone who insists on doing wrong will die.

20 The LORD hates evil-minded people, but loves those who do right.

21 You can be sure that evil people will be punished, but the righteous will escape.

22 Beauty in a woman without good judgment is like a gold ring in a pig's snout.

23 What good people want always results in good; when the wicked get what they want, everyone is angry.[l]

24 Some people spend their money freely and still grow richer. Others are cautious, and yet grow poorer.

25 Be generous, and you will be prosperous. Help others, and you will be helped.

26 People curse someone who hoards grain, waiting for a higher price, but they praise the one who puts it up for sale.

27 If your goals are good, you will be respected, but if you are looking for trouble, that is what you will get.

28 Those who depend on their wealth will fall like the leaves of autumn, but the righteous will prosper like the leaves of summer.

29 Those who bring trouble on their families will have nothing at the end.

Foolish people will always be servants to the wise.

30 Righteousness[m] gives life, but violence[n] takes it away.

31 Those who are good are rewarded here on earth, so you can be sure that wicked and sinful people will be punished.

12 Any who love knowledge want to be told when they are wrong. It is stupid to hate being corrected.

2 The LORD is pleased with good people, but condemns those who plan evil.

3 Wickedness does not give security, but righteous people stand firm.

4 A good wife is her husband's pride and joy; but a wife who brings shame on her husband is like a cancer in his bones.

5 Honest people will treat you fairly; the wicked only want to deceive you.

6 The words of the wicked are murderous, but the words of the righteous rescue those who are threatened.

7 The wicked meet their downfall and

[k] **11:16** *One ancient translation* but a woman . . . money; *Hebrew does not have these words.* [l] **11:23** everyone is angry; *or* God punishes them. [m] **11:30** *One ancient translation* Righteousness; *Hebrew* A righteous person. [n] **11:30** *Probable text* violence; *Hebrew* a wise person.

11:14 Wis 6:24 **11:31** 1 Pet 4:18 **12:1** Sir 21:6

Live it!

Keys to Relating

Many of the proverbs give advice about how to treat other people. Check out these verses for some tips on maintaining your relationships.

- **Proverbs 11:1**
- **Proverbs 11:13**
- **Proverbs 11:25**
- **Proverbs 12:10**
- **Proverbs 12:22**
- **Proverbs 12:25**

Can you find any other proverbs in chapters 11–12 that talk about relationships? Add them to the list above.

— Proverbs, chapter 11

leave no descendants, but the families of the righteous live on.

8 If you are intelligent, you will be praised; if you are stupid, people will look down on you.

9 It is better to be an ordinary person working for a living than to play the part of someone great but go hungry.

10 Good people take care of their animals, but wicked people are cruel to theirs.

11 A hard-working farmer has plenty to eat, but it is stupid to waste time on useless projects.

12 All that wicked people want is to find evil things to do, but the righteous stand firm.[o]

13 The wicked are trapped by their own words, but honest people get themselves out of trouble.

14 Your reward depends on what you say and what you do; you will get what you deserve.

15 Stupid people always think they are right. Wise people listen to advice.

16 When a fool is annoyed, he quickly lets it be known. Smart people will ignore an insult.

17 When you tell the truth, justice is done, but lies lead to injustice.

18 Thoughtless words can wound as deeply as any sword, but wisely spoken words can heal.

19 A lie has a short life, but truth lives on forever.

20 Those who plan evil are in for a rude surprise, but those who work for good will find happiness.

21 Nothing bad happens to righteous people, but the wicked have nothing but trouble.

22 The LORD hates liars, but is pleased with those who keep their word.

23 Smart people keep quiet about what they know, but stupid people advertise their ignorance.

24 Hard work will give you power; being lazy will make you a slave.

25 Worry can rob you of happiness, but kind words will cheer you up.

26 The righteous person is a guide to his friend, but the path of the wicked leads them astray.

27 If you are lazy, you will never get what you are after, but if you work hard, you will get a fortune.[p]

28 Righteousness is the road to life; wickedness[q] is the road to death.

13 Wise children pay attention when their parents correct them, but arrogant people never admit they are wrong.

2 Good people will be rewarded for what they say, but those who are deceitful are hungry for violence.

3 Be careful what you say and protect your life. A careless talker destroys himself.

[o] **12:12** *Verse 12 in Hebrew is unclear.* [p] **12:27** *Verse 27 in Hebrew is unclear.* [q] **12:28** *One ancient translation* wickedness; *Hebrew* path.
13:3 Sir 28:25, 26

Find all the proverbs in chapters 12–14 that have to do with lying, cheating, or spreading rumors.

Pray it!

A Prayer for Honesty

Hear me, God.
Only you can help me with this.
Never let me lie or cheat again,
Even when I know the truth will get me in trouble.
Speak to my mind, heart, and soul.
Telling the truth at all times is the way that pleases you.
You, my God, know every truth there is to know.

— Proverbs 13:5

4No matter how much a lazy person may
want something, he will never get it. A hard
worker will get everything he wants.
5Honest people hate lies, but the words of
wicked people are shameful and disgraceful.
6Righteousness protects the innocent;
wickedness is the downfall of sinners.
7Some people pretend to be rich, but have
nothing. Others pretend to be poor, but own
a fortune.
8The rich have to use their money to save
their lives, but no one threatens the poor.
9The righteous are like a light shining
brightly; the wicked are like a lamp flicker-
ing out.
10Arrogance causes nothing but trouble. It
is wiser to ask for advice.
11The more easily you get your wealth,
the sooner you will lose it. The harder it is
to earn, the more you will have.
12When hope is crushed, the heart is
crushed, but a wish come true fills you with
joy.
13If you refuse good advice, you are asking
for trouble; follow it and you are safe.
14The teachings of the wise are a fountain
of life; they will help you escape when your
life is in danger.
15Intelligence wins respect, but those who
can't be trusted are on the road to ruin.[r]
16Sensible people always think before they
act, but stupid people advertise their igno-
rance.
17Unreliable messengers cause trouble, but
those who can be trusted bring peace.
18Someone who will not learn will be
poor and disgraced. Anyone who listens to
correction is respected.
19How good it is to get what you want!
Stupid people refuse to turn away from evil.
20Keep company with the wise and you
will become wise. If you make friends with
stupid people, you will be ruined.
21Trouble follows sinners everywhere, but
righteous people will be rewarded with
good things.
22Good people will have wealth to leave
to their grandchildren, but the wealth of sin-
ners will go to the righteous.
23Unused fields could yield plenty of food
for the poor, but unjust people keep them
from being farmed.[s]
24If you don't punish your children, you
don't love them. If you do love them, you
will correct them.
25The righteous have enough to eat, but
the wicked are always hungry.

[r] **13:15** *One ancient translation* road to ruin; *Hebrew* permanent road. [s] **13:23** *Verse 23 in Hebrew is unclear.*
13:20 Sir 6:33, 34

Virtue: A habit that leads you to do good things and make choices that are morally right.

12:10 12:18 12:27 13:1 13:9

14 Homes are made by the wisdom of
women, but are destroyed by fool-
ishness.
2 Be honest and you show that you have
reverence for the LORD; be dishonest and
you show that you do not.
3 Proud fools talk too much; the words of
the wise protect them.
4 Without any oxen to pull the plow your
barn will be empty, but with them it will be
full of grain.[t]
5 A reliable witness always tells the truth,
but an unreliable one tells nothing but lies.
6 Conceited people can never become
wise, but intelligent people learn easily.
7 Stay away from foolish people; they have
nothing to teach you.
8 Why is a clever person wise? Because he
knows what to do. Why is a stupid person
foolish? Because he only thinks he knows.
9 Foolish people don't care if they sin, but
good people want to be forgiven.[u]
10 Your joy is your own; your bitterness is
your own. No one can share them with you.
11 A good person's house will still be
standing after an evildoer's house has been
destroyed.
12 What you think is the right road may
lead to death.
13 Laughter may hide sadness. When hap-
piness is gone, sorrow is always there.
14 Bad people will get what they deserve.
Good people will be rewarded for their deeds.[v]
15 A fool will believe anything; smart peo-
ple watch their step.
16 Sensible people are careful to stay out of
trouble, but stupid people are careless and act
too quickly.
17 People with a hot temper do foolish
things; wiser people remain calm.[w]
18 Ignorant people get what their foolish-
ness deserves, but the clever are rewarded
with knowledge.
19 Evil people will have to bow down to
the righteous and humbly beg their favor.
20 No one likes the poor, not even their
neighbors, but the rich have many friends.
21 If you want to be happy, be kind to the
poor; it is a sin to despise anyone.
22 You will earn the trust and respect of
others if you work for good; if you work for
evil, you are making a mistake.
23 Work and you will earn a living; if you
sit around talking you will be poor.
24 Wise people are rewarded with wealth,
but fools are known by[x] their foolishness.
25 A witness saves lives when he tells the
truth; when he tells lies, he betrays people.
26 Reverence for the LORD gives confi-
dence and security to a man and his family.
27 Do you want to avoid death? Reverence
for the LORD is a fountain of life.
28 A king's greatness depends on how
many people he rules; without them he is
nothing.

[t] **14:4** your barn will be . . . grain; *or* you may grow a little grain, but with them you can grow much more.
[u] **14:9** *Verse 9 in Hebrew is unclear.* [v] **14:14** *Probable text* for their deeds; *Hebrew* from upon them.
[w] **14:17** *One ancient translation* remain calm; *Hebrew* are hated. [x] **14:24** *Probable text* are known by; *Hebrew unclear.*
14:12 Prov 16:25

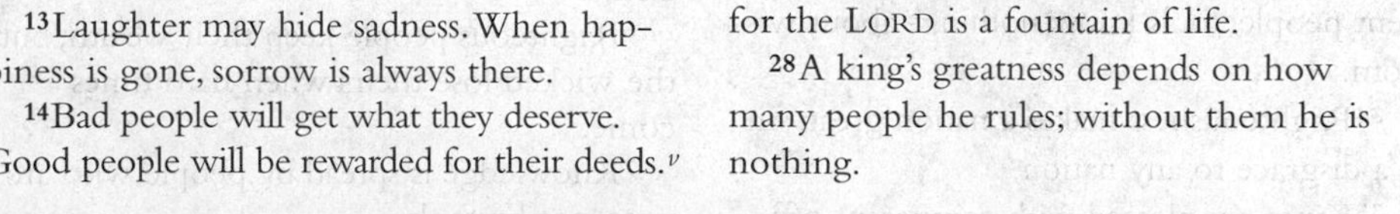

13:24 14:1 14:4 14:20 14:31

Prudence

"Sensible people are careful to stay out of trouble, but stupid people are careless and act too quickly."

"People with a hot temper do foolish things; wiser people remain calm" (Proverbs 14:16–17).

This proverb is describing the virtue of prudence. Prudence means taking the time to make good, thoughtful decisions. When you are feeling strong emotions, it is not the best time to make important decisions. It is better to wait until your emotions calm down and you can think more clearly. That's what prudence is. It helps us avoid evil, follow our conscience, and choose the right path.

Prudence is one of the four cardinal virtues. That means that it is one of the key virtues to have. Pray for prudence the next time you have a tough decision to make about what's right and what's wrong.

— Proverbs 14:15–17

29 If you stay calm, you are wise, but if you
have a hot temper, you only show how stu-
pid you are.
30 Peace of mind makes the body healthy,
but jealousy is like a cancer.
31 If you oppress poor people, you insult
the God who made them; but kindness
shown to the poor is an act of worship.
32 Wicked people bring about their own
downfall by their evil deeds, but good peo-
ple are protected by their integrity.[y]
33 Wisdom is in every thought of intelli-
gent people; fools know nothing[z] about wis-
dom.
34 Righteousness makes a nation great; sin
is a disgrace to any nation.
35 Kings are pleased with competent offi-
cials, but they punish those who fail them.

15 A gentle answer quiets anger, but a
harsh one stirs it up.
2 When wise people speak, they make
knowledge attractive, but stupid people
spout nonsense.
3 The LORD sees what happens every-
where; he is watching us, whether we do
good or evil.
4 Kind words bring life, but cruel words
crush your spirit.
5 It is foolish to ignore what your parents
taught you; it is wise to accept their correc-
tion.
6 Righteous people keep their wealth, but
the wicked lose theirs when hard times
come.
7 Knowledge is spread by people who are
wise, not by fools.
8 The LORD is pleased when good people

[y] **14:32** *Some ancient translations* integrity; *Hebrew* death. [z] **14:33** *One ancient translation* nothing; *Hebrew does not have this word.*

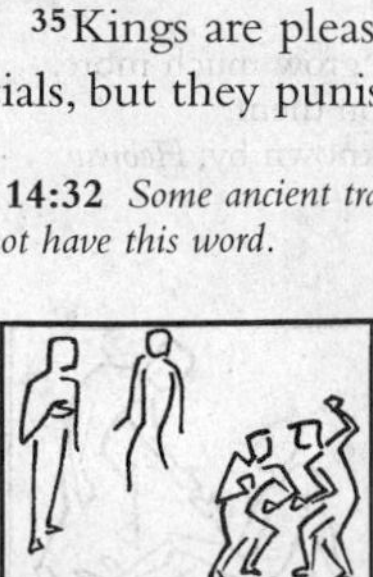
15:1

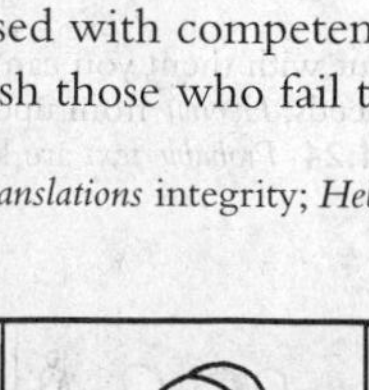
15:13

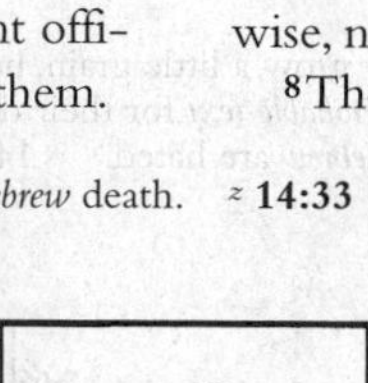
15:17 (1)

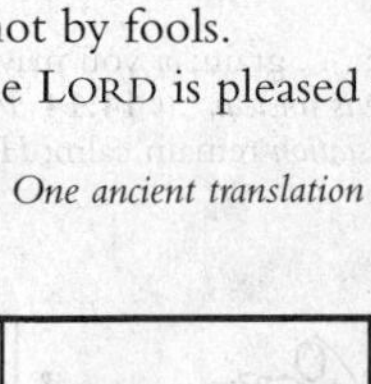
15:17 (2)

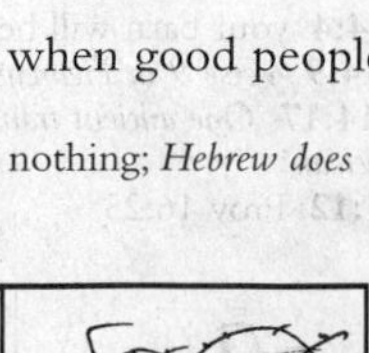
15:19

pray, but hates the sacrifices that the wicked bring him.

9 The LORD hates the ways of evil people, but loves those who do what is right.

10 If you do what is wrong, you will be severely punished; you will die if you do not let yourself be corrected.

11 Not even the world of the dead can keep the LORD from knowing what is there; how then can we hide our thoughts from God?

12 Conceited people do not like to be corrected; they never ask for advice from those who are wiser.

13 When people are happy, they smile, but when they are sad, they look depressed.

14 Intelligent people want to learn, but stupid people are satisfied with ignorance.

15 The life of the poor is a constant struggle, but happy people always enjoy life.

16 Better to be poor and fear the LORD than to be rich and in trouble.

17 Better to eat vegetables with people you love than to eat the finest meat where there is hate.

18 Hot tempers cause arguments, but patience brings peace.

19 If you are lazy, you will meet difficulty everywhere, but if you are honest, you will have no trouble.

20 Wise children make their fathers happy. Only fools despise their mothers.

21 Stupid people are happy with their foolishness, but the wise will do what is right.

22 Get all the advice you can, and you will succeed; without it you will fail.

23 What a joy it is to find just the right word for the right occasion!

24 Wise people walk the road that leads upward to life, not the road that leads downward to death.

25 The LORD will destroy the homes of arrogant men, but he will protect a widow's property.

26 The LORD hates evil thoughts, but he is pleased with friendly words.

27 Try to make a profit dishonestly, and you get your family in trouble. Don't take bribes and you will live longer.

28 Good people think before they answer. Evil people have a quick reply, but it causes trouble.

29 When good people pray, the LORD listens, but he ignores those who are evil.

30 Smiling faces make you happy, and good news makes you feel better.

31 If you pay attention when you are corrected, you are wise.

32 If you refuse to learn, you are hurting yourself. If you accept correction, you will become wiser.

Live it!

JOY Will Get You Through

Have you ever had a bad day? Did you ever feel as though nothing was going right? Have you ever felt sad and depressed? If you answered yes, you are not alone. Everyone has tough times, bad days, and losing streaks. It's part of life. The trick is to learn how to handle them. The next time you feel like nothing is going right, remember these things:

- **Know that tough times do not last forever.**
- **Find positive ways to deal with your stress.**
- **Always have hope.**
- **Remember that JOY will get you through:**
  - **Jesus loves you, no matter what. Trust God.**
  - **Other people are there for you. Talk to them.**
  - **You are wonderful in God's eyes. Believe in yourself.**

— Proverbs 15:13,15

"Kind words bring life, but cruel words crush your spirit" *(Proverbs 15:4)*.

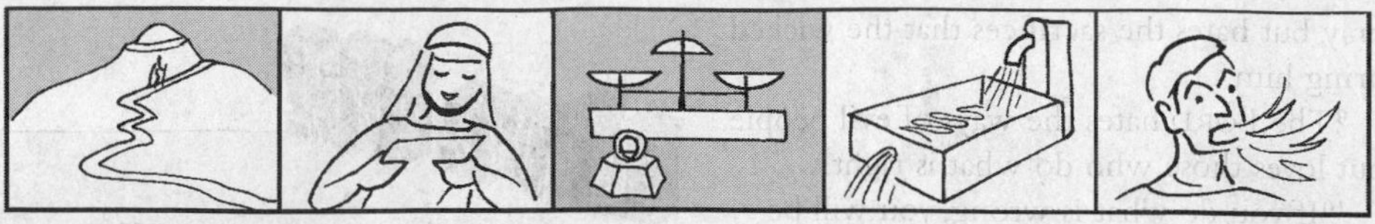

15:24 15:30 16:11 16:22 16:27

33 Reverence for the LORD is an education in itself. You must be humble before you can ever receive honors.

16 We may make our plans, but God has the last word.[a]

2 You may think everything you do is right, but the LORD judges your motives.

3 Ask the LORD to bless your plans, and you will be successful in carrying them out.

4 Everything the LORD has made has its destiny; and the destiny of the wicked is destruction.

5 The LORD hates everyone who is arrogant; he will never let them escape punishment.

6 Be loyal and faithful, and God will forgive your sin. Obey the LORD and nothing evil will happen to you.

7 When you please the LORD, you can make[b] your enemies into friends.

8 It is better to have a little, honestly earned, than to have a large income, dishonestly gained.

9 You may make your plans, but God directs your actions.

10 The king speaks with divine authority; his decisions are always right.

11 The LORD wants weights and measures to be honest and every sale to be fair.

12 Kings cannot tolerate evil,[c] because justice is what makes a government strong.

13 A king wants to hear the truth and will favor those who speak it.

14 A wise person will try to keep the king happy; if the king becomes angry, someone may die.

15 The king's favor is like the clouds that bring rain in the springtime—life is there.

16 It is better—much better—to have wisdom and knowledge than gold and silver.

17 Those who are good travel a road that avoids evil; so watch where you are going—it may save your life.

18 Pride leads to destruction, and arrogance to downfall.

19 It is better to be humble and stay poor than to be one of the arrogant and get a share of their loot.

20 Pay attention to what you are taught, and you will be successful; trust in the LORD and you will be happy.

21 A wise, mature person is known for his understanding. The more pleasant his words, the more persuasive he is.

22 Wisdom is a fountain of life to the wise, but trying to educate stupid people is a waste of time.

23 Intelligent people think before they speak; what they say is then more persuasive.

24 Kind words are like honey—sweet to the taste and good for your health.

25 What you think is the right road may lead to death.

26 A laborer's appetite makes him work harder, because he wants to satisfy his hunger.

27 Evil people look for ways to harm others; even their words burn with evil.

28 Gossip is spread by wicked people; they stir up trouble and break up friendships.

29 Violent people deceive their friends and lead them to disaster.

30 Watch out for people who grin and wink at you; they have thought of something evil.

31 Long life is the reward of the righteous; gray hair is a glorious crown.

[a] **16:1** God . . . word; *or* God inspires our words. [b] **16:7** you can make; *or* he will make. [c] **16:12** Kings . . . evil; *or* It is intolerable for kings to do evil.

16:6 Tob 12:9 **16:8** Tob 12:8 **16:25** Prov 14:12 **16:28** Sir 28:13–26

Read Proverbs 16:1–4. What do these sayings say to you about the plans you make for your life?

Live it!

Gossip

Kristen and Jasmine were great friends. They were together most of the time. They were part of each other's family. Then Katie moved to the area. She was in a class with Jasmine and wanted to be friends with her. She thought she overheard Jasmine telling someone that Kristen was a two-faced liar. She wasn't sure, but she told Kristen anyway. She started rumors and did whatever she could to break up the friendship.

Kristen and Jasmine had a huge fight. They eventually made up, but things were never quite the same.

And Katie? Jasmine's mom helped the girls realize what Katie was doing. She said it was probably because Katie didn't have many friends and was lonely. We can hope she learned that day that gossiping and spreading rumors are *never* good ways to make and keep friends.

— Proverbs 16:27–28

32 It is better to be patient than powerful.
It is better to win control over yourself than
over whole cities.
33 People cast lots to learn God's will, but
God himself determines the answer.
17 Better to eat a dry crust of bread
with peace of mind than have a ban-
quet in a house full of trouble.
2 A shrewd servant will gain authority over
a master's worthless son and receive a part of
the inheritance.
3 Gold and silver are tested by fire, and a
person's heart is tested by the LORD.
4 Evil people listen to evil ideas, and liars
listen to lies.
5 If you make fun of poor people, you
insult the God who made them. You will be
punished if you take pleasure in someone's
misfortune.
6 Grandparents are proud of their grand-
children, just as children are proud of their
parents.
7 Respected people do not tell lies, and
fools have nothing worthwhile to say.
8 Some people think a bribe works like
magic; they believe it can do anything.
9 If you want people to like you, forgive
them when they wrong you. Remembering
wrongs can break up a friendship.
10 An intelligent person learns more from
one rebuke than a fool learns from being
beaten a hundred times.
11 Death will come like a cruel messenger
to wicked people who are always stirring up
trouble.
12 It is better to meet a mother bear
robbed of her cubs than to meet some fool
busy with a stupid project.
13 If you repay good with evil, you will
never get evil out of your house.
14 The start of an argument is like the first
break in a dam; stop it before it goes any
further.
15 Condemning the innocent or letting
the wicked go—both are hateful to the
LORD.
16 It does a fool no good to spend money
on an education, because he has no com-
mon sense.
17 Friends always show their love. What are
relatives for if not to share trouble?
18 Only someone with no sense would

17:17 Sir 6:7–10

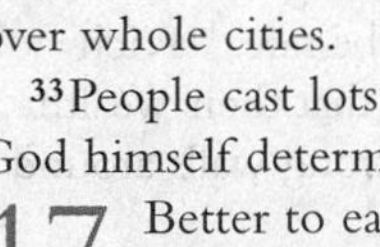

16:30

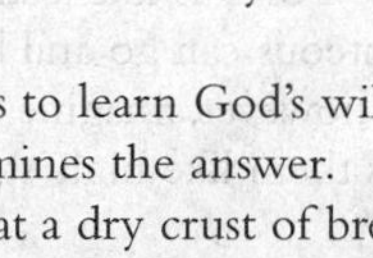

16:31

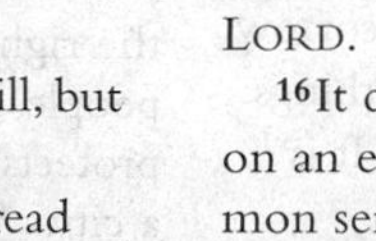

17:6

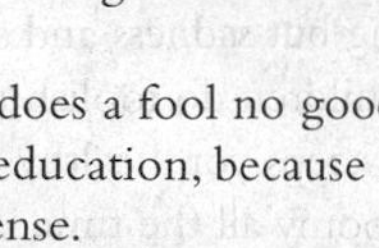

17:14

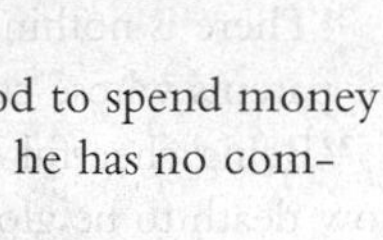

17:17

Pray it!

Prayer of Silence

"Those who are sure of themselves do not talk all the time" (Proverbs 17:27).

Prayer doesn't always mean talking to God, nor does it always involve words. Sometimes it means just being quiet and listening to God speaking to your heart. Sometimes it means just being in God's presence, letting God love you.

Try going to a quiet place in your house or outdoors. Close your eyes and take a few deep breaths. Be aware of all the things around you that show the work of God. For a few minutes just feel God's love all around you. Close your prayer time with a deep breath and a simple amen.

— Proverbs 17:27

promise to be responsible for someone else's
debts.
19 To like sin is to like making trouble. If you
brag all the time,[d] you are asking for trouble.
20 Anyone who thinks and speaks evil can
expect to find nothing good—only disaster.
21 There is nothing but sadness and sorrow
for parents whose children do foolish things.
22 Being cheerful keeps you healthy. It is
slow death to be gloomy all the time.
23 Corrupt judges accept secret bribes, and
then justice is not done.
24 An intelligent person aims at wise
action, but a fool starts off in many directions.
25 Foolish children bring grief to their
fathers and bitter regrets to their mothers.
26 It is not right to make an innocent person pay a fine; justice is perverted when
good people are punished.
27 Those who are sure of themselves do
not talk all the time. People who stay calm
have real insight. 28 After all, even fools may
be thought wise and intelligent if they stay
quiet and keep their mouths shut.

18 People who do not get along with
others are interested only in themselves; they will disagree with what everyone
else knows is right.
2 A fool does not care whether he understands a thing or not; all he wants to do is
show how smart he is.
3 Sin and shame go together. Lose your
honor, and you will get scorn in its place.
4 A person's words can be a source of wisdom, deep as the ocean, fresh as a flowing
stream.
5 It is not right to favor the guilty and
keep the innocent from receiving justice.
6 When some fool starts an argument, he is
asking for a beating.
7 When a fool speaks, he is ruining himself; he gets caught in the trap of his own
words.
8 Gossip is so tasty—how we love to swallow it!
9 A lazy person is as bad as someone who
is destructive.
10 The LORD is like a strong tower, where
the righteous can go and be safe. 11 Rich
people, however, imagine that their wealth
protects them like high, strong walls around
a city.
12 No one is respected unless he is humble; arrogant people are on the way to ruin.

[d] **17:19** brag . . . time; *or* make a show of your wealth.
17:28 Sir 20:5

17:20 *18:4* *18:6* *18:8* *18:10*

18:14 18:22 18:23 19:3 19:6

13 Listen before you answer. If you don't, you are being stupid and insulting.

14 Your will to live can sustain you when you are sick, but if you lose it, your last hope is gone.

15 Intelligent people are always eager and ready to learn.

16 Do you want to meet an important person? Take a gift and it will be easy.

17 The first person to speak in court always seems right until his opponent begins to question him.

18 If two powerful people are opposing each other in court, casting lots can settle the issue.

19 Help your relatives and they will protect you like a strong city wall,[e] but if you quarrel with them, they will close their doors to you.

20 You will have to live with the consequences of everything you say. 21 What you say can preserve life or destroy it; so you must accept the consequences of your words.

22 Find a wife and you find a good thing; it shows that the LORD is good to you.

23 When the poor speak, they have to be polite, but when the rich answer, they are rude.

24 Some friendships do[f] not last, but some friends are more loyal than brothers.

19

It is better to be poor but honest than to be a lying fool.

2 Enthusiasm without knowledge is not good; impatience will get you into trouble.

3 Some people ruin themselves by their own stupid actions and then blame the LORD.

4 Rich people are always finding new friends, but the poor cannot keep the few they have.

5 If you tell lies in court, you will be punished—there will be no escape.

6 Everyone tries to gain the favor of important people; everyone claims the friendship of those who give out favors.

7 Even the relatives of a poor person have no use for him; no wonder he has no friends. No matter how hard he tries, he cannot win any.[g]

8 Do yourself a favor and learn all you can; then remember what you learn and you will prosper.

9 No one who tells lies in court can escape punishment; he is doomed.

10 Fools should not live in luxury, and slaves should not rule over noblemen.

11 If you are sensible, you will control your temper. When someone wrongs you, it is a great virtue to ignore it.

12 The king's anger is like the roar of a lion, but his favor is like welcome rain.

13 Stupid children can bring their parents to ruin. A nagging wife is like water going drip-drip-drip.

14 A man can inherit a house and money from his parents, but only the LORD can give him a sensible wife.

15 Go ahead and be lazy; sleep on, but you will go hungry.

16 Keep God's laws and you will live longer; if you ignore them, you will die.

17 When you give to the poor, it is like lending to the LORD, and the LORD will pay you back.

18 Discipline your children while they are young enough to learn. If you don't, you are helping them destroy themselves.[h]

[e] **18:19** *Some ancient translations* Help . . . wall; *Hebrew unclear.* [f] **18:24** *Some ancient translations* Some friendships do; *Hebrew* Someone with friends does. [g] **19:7** *Probable text* No matter . . . any; *Hebrew unclear.* [h] **19:18** If you . . . themselves; *or* But don't punish them so hard that you kill them.

18:13 Sir 11:8 **18:22** Sir 26:1–4

"Some friendships do not last, but some friends are more loyal than brothers" *(Proverbs 18:24)*.

Live it!

The Real Zeal

The high school football team won the state championship by a score of 49–6. Some of the players said it was because God was on their side and helped them crush their opponents. Two of the opposing players were injured during the game, which the players on the winning team said was a sign that God wanted them to win.

These athletes had *zeal*—enthusiasm for God. However, they were wrong in thinking that God would harm people on the opposing team so that they could win. That's not who God is. God is a fair God who cares for and protects everyone. God does not belong to a person, a team, a country, or any particular religion. God is God of all.

The proverb says, "Enthusiasm without knowledge is not good" (Proverbs 19:2). Religious enthusiasm is a good quality, but only if it is based on the truth about God, not a mistaken belief. Keep on learning all you can about God. Make sure your zeal is real.

— Proverbs 19:2

19 If someone has a hot temper, let him take the consequences. If you get him out of trouble once, you will have to do it again.[i]

20 If you listen to advice and are willing to learn, one day you will be wise.

21 People may plan all kinds of things, but the LORD's will is going to be done.

22 It is a disgrace to be greedy;[j] poor people are better off than liars.

23 Obey the LORD and you will live a long life, content and safe from harm.

24 Some people are too lazy to put food in their own mouths.

25 Arrogance should be punished, so that people who don't know any better can learn a lesson. If you are wise, you will learn when you are corrected.

26 Only a shameful, disgraceful person would mistreat his father or turn his mother away from his home.

27 My child, when you stop learning, you will soon neglect what you already know.

28 There is no justice where a witness is determined to hurt someone. Wicked people love the taste of evil.

29 A conceited fool is sure to get a beating.

20 Drinking too much makes you loud and foolish. It's stupid to get drunk.

2 Fear an angry king as you would a growling lion; making him angry is suicide.

3 Any fool can start arguments; the honorable thing is to stay out of them.

4 A farmer too lazy to plow his fields at the right time will have nothing to harvest.

5 A person's thoughts are like water in a deep well, but someone with insight can draw them out.

6 Everyone talks about how loyal and faithful he is, but just try to find someone who really is!

7 Children are fortunate if they have a father who is honest and does what is right.

8 The king sits in judgment and knows evil when he sees it.

9 Can anyone really say that his conscience is clear, that he has gotten rid of his sin?

10 The LORD hates people who use dishonest weights and measures.

11 Even children show what they are by what they do; you can tell if they are honest and good.

12 The LORD has given us eyes to see with and ears to listen with.

[i] **19:19** get him out . . . again; *or* try to get him out of trouble, you only make things worse. [j] **19:22** It . . . greedy; *or* Loyalty is what is desired in a person.

Read Proverbs 20:18. To whom do you go for advice? Do you consider this person to be truly wise?

13 If you spend your time sleeping, you will be poor. Keep busy and you will have plenty to eat.

14 The customer always complains that the price is too high, but then he goes off and brags about the bargain he got.

15 If you know what you are talking about, you have something more valuable than gold or jewels.

16 Anyone stupid enough to promise to be responsible for a stranger's debts ought to have their own property held to guarantee payment.

17 What you get by dishonesty you may enjoy like the finest food, but sooner or later it will be like a mouthful of sand.

18 Get good advice and you will succeed; don't go charging into battle without a plan.

19 A gossip can never keep a secret. Stay away from people who talk too much.

20 If you curse your parents, your life will end like a lamp that goes out in the dark.

21 The more easily you get your wealth, the less good it will do you.

22 Don't take it on yourself to repay a wrong. Trust the LORD and he will make it right.

23 The LORD hates people who use dishonest scales and weights.

24 The LORD has determined our path; how then can anyone understand the direction his own life is taking?

25 Think carefully before you promise an offering to God. You might regret it later.

26 A wise king will find out who is doing wrong, and will punish him without pity.

27 The LORD gave us mind and conscience; we cannot hide from ourselves.

28 A king will remain in power as long as his rule is honest, just, and fair.

29 We admire the strength of youth and respect the gray hair of age.

30 Sometimes it takes a painful experience to make us change our ways.

Live it!

Parental Privilege

Several proverbs tell us how to treat parents and other people in our lives who care for us. So does the fourth commandment (check out Exodus 20:12). God calls us to love our parents, respect them, listen to them, and honor them. You may not always understand them or agree with them, and they occasionally make mistakes, but they always have your best interest in mind.

- **How do you show love, respect, and honor for your parents or whomever you live with?**
- **What is one thing you can do *today* to show your appreciation for all they do?**

— Proverbs 19:26; 20:20

21

The LORD controls the mind of a king as easily as he directs the course of a stream.

2 You may think that everything you do is right, but remember that the LORD judges your motives.

3 Do what is right and fair; that pleases the LORD more than bringing him sacrifices.

4 Wicked people are controlled by their conceit and arrogance, and this is sinful.

5 Plan carefully and you will have plenty; if you act too quickly, you will never have enough.

6 The riches you get by dishonesty soon disappear, but not before they lead you into the jaws of death.

20:1 *20:12* *20:20* *20:29* *21:8*

21:9

21:13

21:14

21:23

21:25

7 The wicked are doomed by their own
violence; they refuse to do what is right.
8 Guilty people walk a crooked path; the
innocent do what is right.
9 Better to live on the roof than share the
house with a nagging wife.
10 Wicked people are always hungry for
evil; they have no mercy on anyone.
11 When someone who is conceited gets
his punishment, even an unthinking person
learns a lesson. One who is wise will learn
from what he is taught.
12 God, the righteous one, knows what
goes on in the homes of the wicked, and he
will bring the wicked down to ruin.
13 If you refuse to listen to the cry of the
poor, your own cry for help will not be heard.
14 If someone is angry with you, a gift
given secretly will calm him down.
15 When justice is done, good people are
happy, but evil people are brought to despair.
16 Death is waiting for anyone who wan-
ders away from good sense.
17 Indulging in luxuries, wine, and rich
food will never make you wealthy.
18 The wicked bring on themselves the
suffering they try to cause good people.
19 Better to live out in the desert than
with a nagging, complaining wife.
20 Wise people live in wealth and luxury,
but stupid people spend their money as fast
as they get it.
21 Be kind and honest and you will live a
long life; others will respect you and treat
you fairly.
22 A shrewd general can take a city
defended by strong men, and destroy the
walls they relied on.
23 If you want to stay out of trouble, be
careful what you say.
24 Show me a conceited person and I will
show you someone who is arrogant, proud,
and inconsiderate.
25 Lazy people who refuse to work are only
killing themselves; 26 all they do is think about
what they would like to have. The righteous,
however, can give, and give generously.
27 The LORD hates it when wicked people
offer him sacrifices, especially if they do it
from evil motives.
28 The testimony of a liar is not believed,
but the word of someone who thinks mat-
ters through is accepted.
29 Righteous people are sure of them-
selves; the wicked have to pretend as best
they can.
30 Human wisdom, brilliance, insight—
they are of no help if the LORD is against
you.
31 You can get horses ready for battle, but
it is the LORD who gives victory.

22 If you have to choose between a
good reputation and great wealth,
choose a good reputation.
2 The rich and the poor have this in com-
mon: the LORD made them both.
3 Sensible people will see trouble coming
and avoid it, but an unthinking person will
walk right into it and regret it later.
4 Obey the LORD, be humble, and you will
get riches, honor, and a long life.
5 If you love your life, stay away from the
traps that catch the wicked along the way.

21:9 Sir 25:16 **21:27** Sir 7:9

21:31

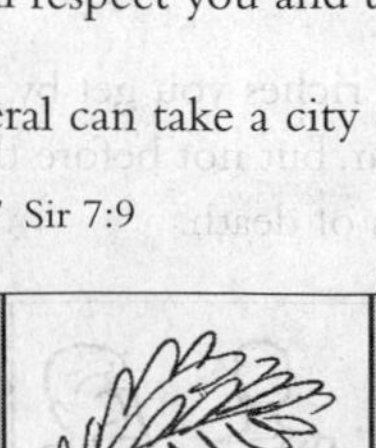
22:5

22:9

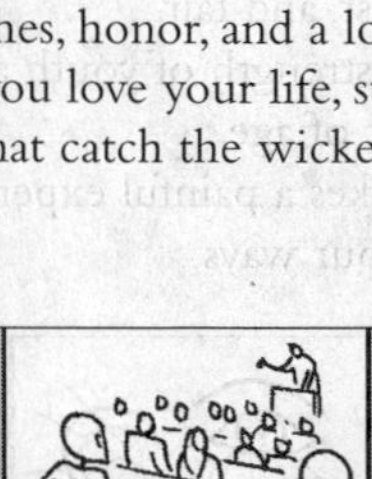
22:17

23:1

Pray it!

The Cry of the Poor

As a young boy learning about his Jewish faith, Jesus studied the proverbs. He may have heard this one many times: "If you refuse to listen to the cry of the poor, your own cry for help will not be heard" (Proverbs 21:13). Jesus showed a special love for poor and powerless people—people who were otherwise ignored by society.

Dear Jesus,
Help me to hear the cry of poor people.
Help me to see the many ways that people can be poor:
By having no friends,
By having special needs,
By being new to our school and community.
Jesus, even though I am young,
inspire me to give of my time and even my money
and to make a difference to someone in need.

— Proverbs 21:13; 22:2, 9, 16, 22

6 Teach children how they should live, and
they will remember it all their life.
7 Poor people are slaves of the rich. Bor-
row money and you are the lender's slave.
8 If you plant the seeds of injustice, disaster
will spring up, and your oppression of others
will end.
9 Be generous and share your food with
the poor. You will be blessed for it.
10 Get rid of a conceited person, and then
there will be no more arguments, quarreling,
or name-calling.
11 If you love purity of heart and gracious-
ness of speech, the king will be your friend.
12 The LORD sees to it that truth is kept
safe by disproving the words of liars.
13 Lazy people stay at home; they say a lion
might get them if they go outside.
14 Adultery is a trap—it catches those with
whom the LORD is angry.
15 Children just naturally do silly, careless
things, but a good spanking will teach them
how to behave.
16 If you make gifts to rich people or
oppress the poor to get rich, you will
become poor yourself.

The Thirty Wise Sayings

17 Listen, and I will teach you what the wise
have said. Study their teachings, 18 and you will
be glad if you remember them and can quote
them. 19 I want you to put your trust in the
LORD; that is why I am going to tell them to
you now. 20 I have written down thirty sayings
for you. They contain knowledge and good
advice, 21 and will teach you what the truth
really is. Then when you are sent to find it
out, you will bring back the right answer.

-1-

22 Don't take advantage of the poor just
because you can; don't take advantage of those

22:6 Sir 6:18

"The rich and the poor have this in common: the LORD made them both" *(Proverbs 22:2)*.

Live it!

Peas in a Pod

"Don't make friends with people who have hot, violent tempers. You might learn their habits and not be able to change" (Proverbs 22:24–25).

The message of this proverb is clear: choose your friends wisely. If you hang around with people who are angry all the time, you will learn to be angry. If your closest friends drink or smoke, chances are so will you. If you are part of a clique that excludes others, you are guilty.

Friends can also be a positive influence on each other. Together you can reach out to people who are excluded. You can support each other in your decisions not to smoke, drink, or do drugs. You can spread joy so that people can't help but smile when they're with you.

You and your friends are like peas in a pod—separate but together. Be sure the pod you're in is one that will lead to a healthy friendship.

— Proverbs 22:24–25

who stand helpless in court. 23The LORD will
argue their case for them and threaten the life
of anyone who threatens theirs.

-2-

24Don't make friends with people who
have hot, violent tempers. 25You might learn
their habits and not be able to change.

-3-

26Don't promise to be responsible for
someone else's debts. 27If you should be
unable to pay, they will take away even your
bed.

-4-

28Never move an old property line that
your ancestors established.

-5-

29Show me someone who does a good
job, and I will show you someone who is
better than most and worthy of the company
of kings.

-6-

23 When you sit down to eat with
someone important, keep in mind
who he is.[k] 2If you have a big appetite,
restrain yourself. 3Don't be greedy for the
fine food he serves; he may be trying to
trick you.

-7-

4Be wise enough not to wear yourself out
trying to get rich. 5Your money can be gone
in a flash, as if it had grown wings and flown
away like an eagle.

-8-

6Don't eat at the table of a stingy person
or be greedy for the fine food he serves.
7"Come on and have some more," he says,
but he doesn't mean it. What he thinks is
what he really is. 8You will vomit up what
you have eaten, and all your flattery will be
wasted.

-9-

9Don't try to talk sense to a fool; he can't
appreciate it.

[k] **23:1** keep . . . is; *or* notice carefully what is before you.

Good advice for school days: Proverbs 23:12.

23:6 23:21 23:22 23:31 23:32

-10-

10 Never move an old property line or take
over land owned by orphans. 11 The LORD is
their powerful defender, and he will argue
their case against you.

-11-

12 Pay attention to your teacher and learn
all you can.

-12-

13 Don't hesitate to discipline children. A
good spanking won't kill them. 14 As a matter
of fact, it may save their lives.

-13-

15 My child, if you become wise, I will be
very happy. 16 I will be proud when I hear
you speaking words of wisdom.

-14-

17 Don't be envious of sinful people; let
reverence for the LORD be the concern of
your life. 18 If it is, you have a bright future.

-15-

19 Listen, my child, be wise and give seri-
ous thought to the way you live. 20 Don't
associate with people who drink too much
wine or stuff themselves with food.
21 Drunkards and gluttons will be reduced to
poverty. If all you do is eat and sleep, you
will soon be wearing rags.

-16-

22 Listen to your father; without him you
would not exist. When your mother is old,
show her your appreciation.
23 Truth, wisdom, learning, and good
sense—these are worth paying for, but too
valuable for you to sell.
24 A righteous person's parents have good
reason to be happy. You can take pride in a
wise child.
25 Let your father and mother be proud of
you; give your mother that happiness.

-17-

26 Pay close attention, son, and let my life
be your example. 27 Prostitutes and immoral
women are a deadly trap. 28 They wait for
you like robbers and cause many men to be
unfaithful.

-18-

29-30 Show me people who drink too
much, who have to try out fancy drinks,
and I will show you people who are miser-
able and sorry for themselves, always causing
trouble and always complaining. Their eyes
are bloodshot, and they have bruises that
could have been avoided. 31 Don't let wine
tempt you, even though it is rich red, and it
sparkles in the cup, and it goes down
smoothly. 32 The next morning you will feel
as if you had been bitten by a poisonous
snake. 33 Weird sights will appear before your
eyes, and you will not be able to think or
speak clearly. 34 You will feel as if you were
out on the ocean, seasick, swinging high up
in the rigging of a tossing ship. 35 "I must
have been hit," you will say; "I must have
been beaten up, but I don't remember it.
Why can't I wake up? I need another
drink."

-19-

24 Don't be envious of evil people, and
don't try to make friends with them.
2 Causing trouble is all they ever think about;
every time they open their mouth someone
is going to be hurt.

Live it!

Winners and Losers

When Mario scored the winning goal in last week's soccer game, he pointed his finger at the goalie and laughed. He scored partly because of his skill and partly because he tripped the defender upfield when the ref wasn't looking.

James was the goalie in that game. Mario's shot took a sharp turn and whizzed right past his outstretched hand. James was angry with himself because it meant losing the league championship. But he went across the field after the game to congratulate Mario on his great shot.

Who was the better player? What can you do to be a good sport on the field, in the classroom, and at home?

— Proverbs 24:17–18

-20-

3 Homes are built on the foundation of
wisdom and understanding.[l] 4 Where there is
knowledge, the rooms are furnished with
valuable, beautiful things.

-21-

5 Being wise is better than being strong;[m]
yes, knowledge is more important than
strength. 6 After all, you must make careful
plans before you fight a battle, and the more
good advice you get, the more likely you are
to win.

-22-

7 Wise sayings are too deep for stupid peo-
ple to understand. They have nothing to say
when important matters are being discussed.

-23-

8 If you are always planning evil, you will
earn a reputation as a troublemaker. 9 Any
scheme a fool thinks up is sinful. People hate
a person who has nothing but scorn for
others.

-24-

10 If you are weak in a crisis, you are weak
indeed.

-25-

11 Don't hesitate to rescue someone who is
about to be executed unjustly. 12 You may say
that it is none of your business, but God
knows and judges your motives. He keeps
watch on you; he knows. And he will reward
you according to what you do.

-26-

13 My child, eat honey; it is good. And just
as honey from the comb is sweet on your
tongue, 14 you may be sure that wisdom is
good for the soul. Get wisdom and you have
a bright future.

-27-

15 Don't be like the wicked who scheme
to rob honest people or to take away their
homes. 16 No matter how often honest peo-
ple fall, they always get up again; but disaster
destroys the wicked.

-28-

17 Don't be glad when your enemies meet
disaster, and don't rejoice when they stum-
ble. 18 The LORD will know if you are gloat-
ing, and he will not like it; and then maybe
he won't punish them.

-29-

19 Don't let evil people worry you; don't
be envious of them. 20 A wicked person has
no future—nothing to look forward to.

[l] **24:3** Homes . . . understanding; *or* It takes care to lay the foundations of a house, and skill to build it.
[m] **24:5** *Some ancient translations* Being wise is better than being strong; *Hebrew* A person is wise in strength.

23:24 24:11 25:9 25:13 25:14

-30-

21 Have reverence for the LORD, my child,
and honor the king. Have nothing to do
with people who rebel against them; 22 such
people could be ruined in a moment. Do
you realize the disaster that God or the king
can cause?

More Wise Sayings

23 The wise have also said these things:
It is wrong for judges to be prejudiced.
24 If they pronounce a guilty person inno-
cent, they will be cursed and hated by every-
one. 25 Judges who punish the guilty, howev-
er, will be prosperous and enjoy a good
reputation.
26 An honest answer is a sign of true
friendship.
27 Don't build your house and establish a
home until your fields are ready, and you are
sure that you can earn a living.
28 Don't give evidence against others with-
out good reason, or say misleading things
about them. 29 Don't say, "I'll do to them just
what they did to me! I'll get even with
them!"
30 I walked through the fields and vine-
yards of a lazy, stupid person. 31 They were
full of thorn bushes and overgrown with
weeds. The stone wall around them had fall-
en down. 32 I looked at this, thought about it,
and learned a lesson from it: 33 Go ahead and
take your nap; go ahead and sleep. Fold your
hands and rest awhile, 34 but while you are
asleep, poverty will attack you like an armed
robber.

More of Solomon's Proverbs

25 Here are more of Solomon's
proverbs, copied by scribes at the
court of King Hezekiah of Judah.
2 We honor God for what he conceals; we
honor kings for what they explain.
3 You never know what a king is thinking;
his thoughts are beyond us, like the heights
of the sky or the depths of the ocean.
4 Take the impurities out of silver and the
artist can produce a thing of beauty. 5 Keep
evil advisers away from the king and his gov-
ernment will be known for its justice.
6 When you stand before the king, don't
try to impress him and pretend to be impor-
tant. 7 It is better to be asked to take a higher
position than to be told to give your place to
someone more important.
8 Don't be too quick to go to court about
something you have seen. If another witness
later proves you wrong, what will you do
then?
9 If you and your neighbor have a difference
of opinion, settle it between yourselves and do
not reveal any secrets. 10 Otherwise everyone
will learn that you can't keep a secret, and you
will never live down the shame.
11 An idea well-expressed is like a design
of gold, set in silver.
12 A warning given by an experienced
person to someone willing to listen is more
valuable than gold rings or jewelry made of
the finest gold.
13 A reliable messenger is refreshing to the
one who sends him, like cold water in the
heat of harvest time.
14 People who promise things that they
never give are like clouds and wind that
bring no rain.

24:33, 34 Prov 6:10, 11 **25:6, 7** Lk 14:8–10

Be fair. Be just. Be honest. Be kind. That's the message of Proverbs 24:23–29.

Do Justice

Like the people who wrote the proverbs, Jesus had a lot to say about how people should treat each other. He often taught the importance of treating all people with love and respect.

We can follow the example of Jesus by keeping this rule in mind: All of human life is holy. This rule is the basis of Catholic teaching about justice. This means that each person must be treated with dignity and respect. No person is better than another. No country is entitled to prosper at the expense of poorer nations. No one has the right to hurt another person in any way, whether it's with weapons or with words.

How do you and your friends do justice? For some hints on living a just life, read the following passages of Proverbs: 24:15–18; 25:21–22; 28:3–8.

— Proverbs 25:21–22

Catholic Connections

15 Patient persuasion can break down the strongest resistance and can even convince rulers.
16 Never eat more honey than you need;
too much may make you vomit. 17 Don't
visit your neighbors too often; they may get tired of you and come to hate you.
18 A false accusation is as deadly as a sword, a club, or a sharp arrow.
19 Depending on an unreliable person in a crisis is like trying to chew with a loose tooth or walk with a crippled foot.
20 Singing to a person who is depressed is like taking off a person's clothes on a cold day or like rubbing salt in a wound.
21 If your enemies are hungry, feed them;
if they are thirsty, give them a drink. 22 You
will make them burn with shame, and the LORD will reward you.
23 Gossip brings anger just as surely as the north wind brings rain.
24 Better to live on the roof than share the house with a nagging wife.
25 Finally hearing good news from a distant land is like a drink of cold water when you are dry and thirsty.
26 A good person who gives in to someone who is evil reminds you of a polluted spring or a poisoned well.
27 Too much honey is bad for you, and so is trying to win too much praise.[n]
28 If you cannot control your anger, you are as helpless as a city without walls, open to attack.

26 Praise for a fool is out of place, like snow in summer or rain at harvest time.
2 Curses cannot hurt you unless you deserve them. They are like birds that fly by and never light.
3 You have to whip a horse, you have to bridle a donkey, and you have to beat a fool.
4 If you answer a silly question, you are just as silly as the person who asked it.
5 Give a silly answer to a silly question, and

[n] **25:27** *Probable text* and so . . . praise; *Hebrew unclear.*
25:21, 22 Rom 12:20

Which of the capital sins *(see Catholic Connections on page 913)* **is a problem for you? Say a prayer asking for God's help to conquer it.**

Catholic Connections

Capital Sins

Read Proverbs 26:13–16. They really come down hard on laziness. Did you know that spiritual laziness (also called sloth) is one of the seven capital sins? Pride, avarice (greed), envy (jealousy), wrath (intense anger), sexual lust, gluttony (eating or drinking too much) are the other six capital sins. They are called capital sins because they can easily lead to other sins. For example, if you are greedy you are probably not paying attention to the needs of poor people. If you are lazy you are not using the gifts God gave you to your best ability.

Try this: List the seven capital sins in a notebook, then make note of the verses in Proverbs, chapters 25–30 that address each one. You may be surprised at how many proverbs address these slippery seven.

— Proverbs 26:13–17

the one who asked it will realize that he's
not as smart as he thinks.
6 If you let a fool deliver a message, you
might as well cut off your own feet; you are
asking for trouble.
7 A fool can use a proverb about as well as
crippled people can use their legs.
8 Praising someone who is stupid makes as
much sense as tying a stone in a sling.
9 A fool quoting a wise saying reminds you
of a drunk trying to pick a thorn out of his
hand.
10 An employer who hires any fool that
comes along is only hurting everybody con-
cerned.[o]
11 A fool doing some stupid thing a sec-
ond time is like a dog going back to its
vomit.
12 The most stupid fool is better off than
those who think they are wise when they
are not.
13 Why don't lazy people ever get out of
the house? What are they afraid of Lions?
14 Lazy people turn over in bed. They get
no farther than a door swinging on its hinges.
15 Some people are too lazy to put food in
their own mouths.
16 A lazy person will think he is smarter
than seven men who can give good reasons
for their opinions.
17 Getting involved in an argument that is
none of your business is like going down the
street and grabbing a dog by the ears.
18-19 Someone who tricks someone else and
then claims that he was only joking is like a
crazy person playing with a deadly weapon.
20 Without wood, a fire goes out; without
gossip, quarreling stops.
21 Charcoal keeps the embers glowing,
wood keeps the fire burning, and trouble-
makers keep arguments alive.
22 Gossip is so tasty! How we love to swal-
low it!
23 Insincere[p] talk that hides what you are
really thinking is like a fine glaze[q] on a
cheap clay pot.

[o] **26:10** *Verse 10 in Hebrew is unclear.* [p] **26:23** *One ancient translation* Insincere; *Hebrew* Burning.
[q] **26:23** *Probable text* fine glaze; *Hebrew* unrefined silver.
26:11 2 Pet 2:22

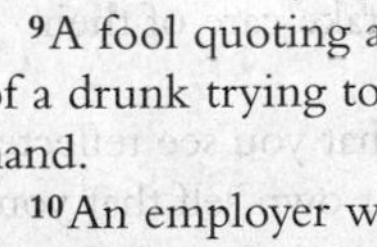
25:18

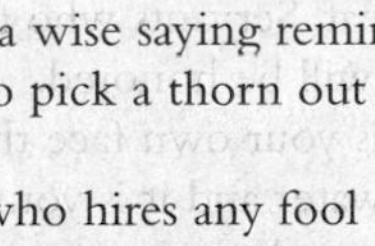
25:25

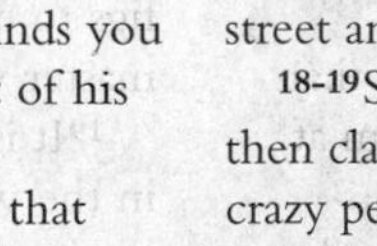
26:3

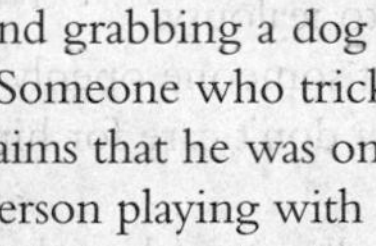
26:11

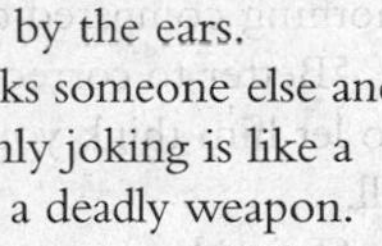
26:17

26:20 26:27 27:9 27:18 27:23

24 A hypocrite hides hate behind flattering
words. 25 They may sound fine, but don't
believe him, because his heart is filled to the
brim with hate. 26 He may disguise his
hatred, but everyone will see the evil things
he does.
27 People who set traps for others get
caught themselves. People who start land-
slides get crushed.
28 You have to hate someone to want to
hurt him with lies. Insincere talk brings
nothing but ruin.

27 Never boast about tomorrow. You
don't know what will happen
between now and then.
2 Let other people praise you—even
strangers; never do it yourself.
3 The weight of stone and sand is nothing
compared to the trouble that stupidity can
cause.
4 Anger is cruel and destructive, but it is
nothing compared to jealousy.
5 Better to correct someone openly than
to let him think you don't care for him at
all.
6 Friends mean well, even when they hurt
you. But when an enemy puts his arm
around your shoulder—watch out!
7 When you are full, you will refuse honey,
but when you are hungry, even bitter food
tastes sweet.
8 Anyone away from home is like a bird
away from its nest.
9 Perfume and fragrant oils make you feel
happier, but trouble shatters your peace of
mind.[r]
10 Do not forget your friends or your
father's friends. If you are in trouble, don't
ask a relative for help; a nearby neighbor can
help you more than relatives who are far
away.
11 Be wise, my child, and I will be happy; I
will have an answer for anyone who criti-
cizes me.
12 Sensible people will see trouble coming
and avoid it, but an unthinking person will
walk right into it and regret it later.
13 Any people stupid enough to promise
to be responsible for a stranger's debts[s]
deserve to have their own property held to
guarantee payment.
14 You might as well curse your friends as
wake them up early in the morning with a
loud greeting.
15 A nagging wife is like water going drip-
drip-drip on a rainy day. 16 How can you
keep her quiet? Have you ever tried to stop
the wind or ever tried to hold a handful of
oil?[t]
17 People learn from one another, just as
iron sharpens iron.
18 Take care of a fig tree and you will have
figs to eat. Servants who take care of their
master will be honored.
19 It is your own face that you see reflected
in the water and it is your own self that you
see in your heart.
20 Human desires are like the world of the
dead—there is always room for more.
21 Fire tests gold and silver; a person's rep-
utation can also be tested.
22 Even if you beat fools half to death, you
still can't beat their foolishness out of them.
23 Look after your sheep and cattle as care-
fully as you can, 24 because wealth is not per-
manent. Not even nations last forever. 25 You
cut the hay and then cut the grass on the
hillsides while the next crop of hay is grow-
ing. 26 You can make clothes from the wool
of your sheep and buy land with the money
you get from selling some of your goats.
27 The rest of the goats will provide milk for

[r] **27:9** *One ancient translation* but trouble . . . mind; *Hebrew unclear.* [s] **27:13** *One ancient translation* stranger's debts; *Hebrew* stranger's debts or those of an immoral woman. [t] **27:16** *Probable text* or ever . . . oil; *Hebrew unclear.*

26:27 Sir 27:25–27 **27:1** Jas 4:13–16

Live it!

Attacking Miss Perfect Life

The way Cameron saw it, Yolanda had a perfect life. She had good grades and a close-knit family. She was on a softball team and played the cello. Everyone liked her, and she always seemed to have a smile.

Cameron's life was pretty awful by comparison. Her family fought a lot, her grades were just okay, she didn't play sports, and she had no interest in music. She was jealous. So she started the rumor that Yolanda was a shoplifter and cheated on tests. Cameron enjoyed seeing Miss Perfect Life upset as she tried to prove that she was neither a thief nor a cheat.

Feeling jealous from time to time is not necessarily a sin. We usally don't choose the feelings we experience. But when you have jealous feelings and keep thinking about them over and over, it becomes a sickness that can drive you to hurt others. Yet Cameron's life was no happier because of what she did to Yolanda. Her energy would have been better spent developing her own interests. That would have been pleasing to God.

— Proverbs 27:4

you and your family, and for your servant
women as well.

28 The wicked run when no one is
chasing them, but an honest person
is as brave as a lion.

2 When a nation sins, it will have one ruler
after another. But a nation will be strong
and endure when it has intelligent, sensible
leaders.
3 Someone in authority who oppresses
poor people is like a driving rain that
destroys the crops.
4 If you have no regard for the law, you are
on the side of the wicked; but if you obey it,
you are against them.
5 Evil people do not know what justice is,
but those who worship the LORD under-
stand it well.
6 Better to be poor and honest than rich
and dishonest.
7 Young people who obey the law are
intelligent. Those who make friends with
good-for-nothings are a disgrace to their
parents.
8 If you get rich by charging interest and
taking advantage of people, your wealth will
go to someone who is kind to the poor.
9 If you do not obey the law, God will find
your prayers too hateful to hear.
10 If you trick an honest person into doing
evil, you will fall into your own trap.
The innocent will be well rewarded.
11 Rich people always think they are wise,
but a poor person who has insight into char-
acter knows better.
12 When good people come to power,
everybody celebrates, but when bad people
rule, people stay in hiding.
13 You will never succeed in life if you try
to hide your sins. Confess them and give
them up; then God will show mercy to you.
14 Always obey the LORD and you will be
happy. If you are stubborn, you will be
ruined.
15 Poor people are helpless against a
wicked ruler; he is as dangerous as a growl-
ing lion or a prowling bear.
16 A ruler without good sense will be a
cruel tyrant. One who hates dishonesty will
rule a long time.
17 Someone guilty of murder is digging his
own grave as fast as he can. Don't try to stop
him.

Many proverbs point out the problems that come with being rich. Is having things important to you? Think about uncluttering your life—and your heart.

Study it!

I Want It All!

As soon as the new video game came out, Victor headed to the store to get it. He had over a hundred games, most of which he didn't play anymore. He wouldn't wear shoes that were not endorsed by major athletes. He spent every penny he got for his birthday on a new bike, even though the two he had were perfectly good. And when his friend Jonas put money in the box at school to help buy gifts for poor children, Victor made fun of him.

Victor is greedy and materialistic, which means that having stuff is more important to him than helping others. He wants everything, and he doesn't care that some people go hungry some days.

Many proverbs address the sin of greed. Look for proverbs in Proverbs, chapter 28, that have to do with being rich and being selfish. Jesus taught about greed, too. Check out what he had to say about it in Matthew 6:19–21, Luke 12:13–21, and John 2:13–17.

— Proverbs 28:8,22,25

18Be honest and you will be safe. If you
are dishonest, you will suddenly fall.
19A hard-working farmer has plenty to eat.
People who waste time will always be poor.
20Honest people will lead a full, happy
life. But if you are in a hurry to get rich, you
are going to be punished.
21Prejudice is wrong. But some judges
will do wrong to get even the smallest bribe.
22Selfish people are in such a hurry to get
rich that they do not know when poverty is
about to strike.
23Correct someone, and afterward he will
appreciate it more than flattery.
24Anyone who thinks it isn't wrong to
steal from his parents is no better than a
common thief.
25Selfishness only causes trouble. You are
much better off to trust the LORD.
26It is foolish to follow your own opinions. Be safe, and follow the teachings of
wiser people.
27Give to the poor and you will never be
in need. If you close your eyes to the poor,
many people will curse you.
28People stay in hiding when the wicked
come to power. But when they fall from
power, the righteous will rule again.

29 If you get more stubborn every time
you are corrected, one day you will
be crushed and never recover.
2Show me a righteous ruler and I will
show you a happy people. Show me a wicked
ruler and I will show you a miserable people.
3If you appreciate wisdom, your parents
will be proud of you.
It is a foolish waste to spend money on
prostitutes.
4When the king is concerned with justice, the nation will be strong, but when he
is only concerned with money, he will ruin
his country.
5If you flatter your friends, you set a trap
for yourself.[u]
6Evil people are trapped in their own sins,
while honest people are happy and free.
7A good person knows the rights of the
poor, but wicked people cannot understand
such things.
8People with no regard for others can
throw whole cities into turmoil. Those who
are wise keep things calm.
9When an intelligent person brings a law-

[u] **29:5** yourself; *or* them.

"If you get more stubborn every time you are corrected, one day you will be crushed and never recover" *(Proverbs 29:1)*.

Pray it!

God Be in Me

"It is dangerous to be concerned with what others think of you, but if you trust the LORD, you are safe" (Proverbs 29:25).

This proverb might have been on the mind of the person who wrote the following prayer almost five hundred years ago. It stresses the importance of trusting in God and asking God to work through you.

God be in my head and in my understanding.
God be in my eyes and in my looking.
God be in my mouth and in my speaking.
God be in my heart and in my thinking.
God be at my end and my departing.
(Sarum Primer, 1527)

— Proverbs 29:25

suit against a fool, the fool only laughs and
becomes loud and abusive.
10Bloodthirsty people hate anyone who's
honest, but righteous people will protect[v]
the life of such a person.
11Stupid people express their anger open-
ly, but sensible people are patient and hold it
back.
12If a ruler pays attention to false informa-
tion, all his officials will be liars.
13A poor person and his oppressor have
this in common—the LORD gave eyes to
both of them.
14If a king defends the rights of the poor,
he will rule for a long time.
15Correction and discipline are good for
children. If they have their own way, they
will make their mothers ashamed of them.
16When evil people are in power, crime
increases. But the righteous will live to see
the downfall of such people.
17Discipline your children and you can
always be proud of them. They will never
give you reason to be ashamed.
18A nation without God's guidance is a
nation without order. Happy are those who
keep God's law!
19You cannot correct servants just by talk-
ing to them. They may understand you, but
they will pay no attention.
20There is more hope for a stupid fool
than for someone who speaks without
thinking.
21If you give your servants everything
they want from childhood on, some day they
will take over everything you own.[w]
22People with quick tempers cause a lot
of quarreling and trouble.
23Arrogance will bring your downfall, but
if you are humble, you will be respected.
24A thief's partner is his own worst enemy.
He will be punished if he tells the truth in
court, and God will curse him if he doesn't.
25It is dangerous to be concerned with

[v] **29:10** *Probable text* protect; *Hebrew* seek. [w] **29:21** they . . . own; *or* you will not be able to control them.
29:19 Sir 33:25–30

28:1 *28:15* *28:27* *29:1* *29:17*

what others think of you, but if you trust the
LORD, you are safe.
26 Everybody wants the good will of the
ruler, but only from the LORD can you get
justice.
27 The righteous hate the wicked, and the
wicked hate the righteous.

The Words of Agur

30 These are the solemn words of Agur
son of Jakeh:
"God is not with me, God is not with
me,
and I am helpless.[x]
2 I am more like an animal than a human
being;
I do not have the sense we humans
should have.
3 I have never learned any wisdom,
and I know nothing at all about God.
4 Have any ever mastered heavenly
knowledge?
Have any ever caught the wind in their
hands?
Or wrapped up water in a piece of cloth?
Or fixed the boundaries of the earth?
Who are they, if you know? Who are their
children?
5 "God keeps every promise he makes. He
is like a shield for all who seek his protec-
tion. 6 If you claim that he said something
that he never said, he will reprimand you
and show that you are a liar."

More Proverbs

7 I ask you, God, to let me have two things
before I die: 8 keep me from lying, and let
me be neither rich nor poor. So give me
only as much food as I need. 9 If I have
more, I might say that I do not need you.
But if I am poor, I might steal and bring dis-
grace on my God.
10 Never criticize servants to their master.
You will be cursed and suffer for it.
11 There are people who curse their
fathers and do not show their appreciation
for their mothers.
12 There are people who think they are
pure when they are as filthy as they can be.
13 There are people who think they are so
good—oh, how good they think they are!
14 There are people who take cruel advan-
tage of the poor and needy; that is the way
they make their living.
15 A leech has two daughters, and both are
named "Give me!"
There are four things that are never satis-
fied:
16 the world of the dead,
a woman without children,
dry ground that needs rain,
and a fire burning out of control.
17 If you make fun of your father or
despise your mother in her old age,[y] you
ought to be eaten by vultures or have your
eyes picked out by wild ravens.
18 There are four things that are too mys-
terious for me to understand:
19 an eagle flying in the sky,
a snake moving on a rock,
a ship finding its way over the sea,
and a man and a woman falling in love.
20 This is how an unfaithful wife acts: she
commits adultery, takes a bath, and says, "But
I haven't done anything wrong!"
21 There are four things that the earth
itself cannot tolerate:
22 a slave who becomes a king,
a fool who has all he wants to eat,
23 a hateful woman who gets married,
and a servant woman who takes the place
of her mistress.

[x] **30:1** *Probable text* "God . . . helpless; *Hebrew unclear. Hebrew* mother's obedience.
[y] **30:17** *One ancient translation* mother in her old age;
30:19 Wis 5:10–12

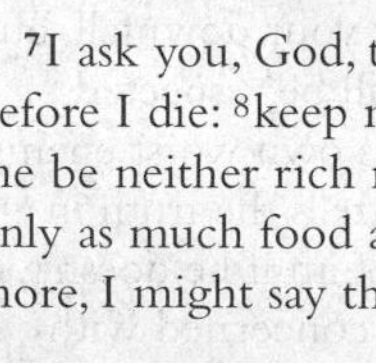
30:13

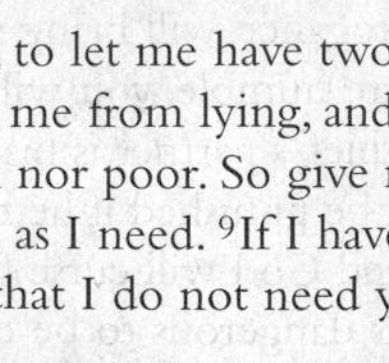
30:19

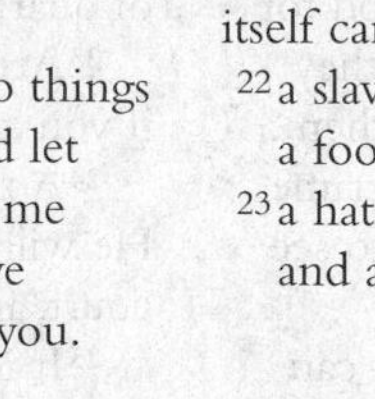
30:32

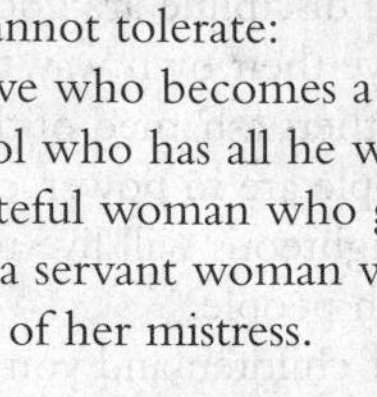
31:8

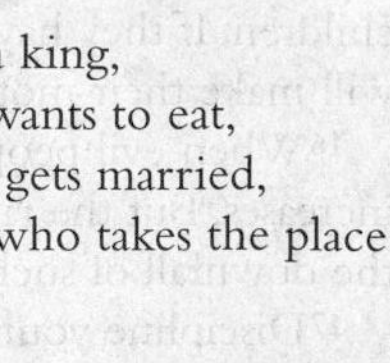
31:28

Pray it!

A Wild Ride

Proverbs, chapter 30, begins with the words of someone who may seem confused about life. Sometimes as we are growing up, we have those feelings, too.

There's so much I don't know, God. I used to think I was pretty smart, but now I'm not so sure. It seems like life is changing too fast for me. I'm different than I was last year. My body is different, I think about different things, and my friends are different, too. It's not a bad kind of different, just different. I don't know what's happening. I suppose it's part of growing up. But I have to tell you, God, it's kind of scary. It's like being on a wild ride at an amusement park.

Now that I'm older I want to get to know you better. I realize that I cannot be the person I want to be without your help. I have a feeling there are more twists and turns up ahead on this wild ride that is my life, and I need you sitting right beside me.

— Proverbs 30:1–4

24 There are four animals in the world that
are small, but very, very clever:
25 Ants: they are weak, but they store up
their food in the summer.
26 Rock badgers: they are not strong either,
but they make their homes among
the rocks.
27 Locusts: they have no king, but they move
in formation.
28 Lizards: you can hold one in your hand,
but you can find them in palaces.
29 There are four things that are impressive
to watch as they walk:
30 lions, strongest of all animals and afraid of
none;
31 goats, strutting roosters,
and kings in front of their people.[z]
32 If you have been foolish enough to be
arrogant and plan evil, stop and think! 33 If
you churn milk, you get butter. If you hit
someone's nose, it bleeds. If you stir up
anger, you get into trouble.

[z] **30:31** *Verse 31 in Hebrew is unclear.*

Advice to a King

31 These are the solemn words which
King Lemuel's mother said to him:
2 "You are my own dear son, the answer to
my prayers. What shall I tell you? 3 Don't
spend all your energy on sex and all your
money on women; they have destroyed
kings. 4 Listen, Lemuel. Kings should not
drink wine or have a craving for alcohol.
5 When they drink, they forget the laws and
ignore the rights of people in need. 6 Alcohol
is for people who are dying, for those who
are in misery. 7 Let them drink and forget
their poverty and unhappiness.
8 "Speak up for people who cannot speak
for themselves. Protect the rights of all who
are helpless. 9 Speak for them and be a righteous judge. Protect the rights of the poor
and needy."

Read Proverbs 30:24-31. Which wonders of God's Creation amaze and delight you?

The Capable Wife

10 How hard it is to find a capable wife!
She is worth far more than jewels!
11 Her husband puts his confidence in her,
and he will never be poor.
12 As long as she lives, she does him good
and never harm.
13 She keeps herself busy making wool and
linen cloth.
14 She brings home food from out-of-the-
way places, as merchant ships do.
15 She gets up before daylight to prepare
food for her family and to tell her servant
women what to do.
16 She looks at land and buys it, and with
money she has earned she plants a vineyard.
17 She is a hard worker, strong and indus-
trious.
18 She knows the value of everything she
makes, and works late into the night.
19 She spins her own thread and weaves
her own cloth.
20 She is generous to the poor and needy.
21 She doesn't worry when it snows,
because her family has warm clothing.
22 She makes bedspreads and wears clothes
of fine purple linen.
23 Her husband is well known, one of the
leading citizens.
24 She makes clothes and belts, and sells
them to merchants.
25 She is strong and respected and not
afraid of the future.
26 She speaks with a gentle wisdom.
27 She is always busy and looks after her
family's needs.
28 Her children show their appreciation,
and her husband praises her.
29 He says, "Many women are good wives,
but you are the best of them all."
30 Charm is deceptive and beauty disap-
pears, but a woman who honors the LORD
should be praised.
31 Give her credit for all she does. She
deserves the respect of everyone.

Live it!

A Maturity Checklist

The last part of the Book of Proverbs describes an ideal women in biblical times. But if you read the passage carefully, it is talking about what it means to be a mature adult—woman or man. Here are a few qualities to strive for:

- **Work hard and use the talents God gave you.**
- **Be responsible; care for others and for the earth.**
- **Be wise, honest, and kind.**
- **Be able to laugh.**
- **Praise God with your actions and words.**

How do the adults in your life measure up? What can you do to grow in these areas?

— Proverbs 31:10–31

Your Next Step

Congratulations on finishing the Book of Proverbs! Use this space to write your thoughts and questions about this book. If you are following the suggested reading plan, move ahead to another wisdom book, the Song of Songs. The Song of Songs is a book of love poetry. Did you know that was in the Bible?

THE BOOK OF Ecclesiastes

Ecclesiastes begins, "Life is useless, all useless." Twelve chapters of down-in-the-dumps, singing-the-blues, depressing kind of stuff! When this book was written, many people believed certain things about God. If you were rich, healthy, and lucky—God loved you more. If you were sick, poor, or unlucky—it must be because you had done something bad. Ecclesiastes disagrees and wants God's people to see that God doesn't work that way.

Most of us know wonderful people who have terrible luck and not-so-wonderful people who get all the breaks. God understands when we are sad and when we complain that life seems unfair. God is the biggest mystery of all. And in some ways, that's the only thing we can be sure of.

Chap. 5:18–20

Headlines

- Nothing New Under the Sun! (1:2–11)
- There Is a Time for Everything (3:1–8)
- Good People Suffer, Evil Rewarded! (8:10–14)
- Enjoy Life! God's Favor Is Now (9:7–10)
- "Young People, Follow Your Heart" (11:9—12:1)

FACTOIDS

Who wrote this book? In this translation "the Philosopher" is named as the author from a Hebrew word that means "teacher" or "preacher." Nothing else is known.

When was it written? Probably the fourth or third century before Christ.

Why was it written? To challenge the belief that God favors certain people. To admit that life is not fair and, yet, there are no easy answers to that mystery.

What literary style is used? It is a collection of short pieces about the unfairness of life.

Important themes

- There are some things we can never understand—love, death, friendship, and why good people suffer and evil people prosper.
- There is a time and a season for everything in life.
- The enthusiasm, hope, and optimism of young people and the wisdom, experience, and knowledge of older people bring balance to how we view life.

ECCLESIASTES

Life Is Useless

1 These are the words of the Philosopher,
David's son, who was king in Jerusalem.
2It is useless, useless, said the Philosopher.
Life is useless, all useless. 3You spend your life
working, laboring, and what do you have to
show for it? 4Generations come and genera-
tions go, but the world stays just the same.
5The sun still rises, and it still goes down,
going wearily back to where it must start all
over again. 6The wind blows south, the wind
blows north—round and round and back
again. 7Every river flows into the sea, but the
sea is not yet full. The water returns to where
the rivers began, and starts all over again.
8Everything leads to weariness—a weariness
too great for words. Our eyes can never see
enough to be satisfied; our ears can never hear
enough. 9What has happened before will
happen again. What has been done before will
be done again. There is nothing new in the
whole world. 10"Look," they say, "here is
something new!" But no, it has all happened
before, long before we were born. 11No one
remembers what has happened in the past,
and no one in days to come will remember
what happens between now and then.

"The world stays just the same." (1:4)

The Philosopher's Experience

12I, the Philosopher, have been king over
Israel in Jerusalem. 13I determined that I
would examine and study all the things that
are done in this world.
God has laid a miserable fate upon us. 14I
have seen everything done in this world, and
I tell you, it is all useless. It is like chasing the
wind. 15You can't straighten out what is
crooked; you can't count things that aren't
there.

"I tell you, it is all useless." (1:14)

16I told myself, "I have become a great
man, far wiser than anyone who ruled
Jerusalem before me. I know what wisdom
and knowledge really are." 17I was deter-
mined to learn the difference between
knowledge and foolishness, wisdom and
madness. But I found out that I might as
well be chasing the wind. 18The wiser you
are, the more worries you have; the more
you know, the more it hurts.

2 I decided to enjoy myself and find out
what happiness is. But I found that this
is useless, too. 2I discovered that laughter is
foolish, that pleasure does you no good.
3Driven on by my desire for wisdom, I
decided to cheer myself up with wine and
have a good time. I thought that this might
be the best way people can spend their short
lives on earth.
4I accomplished great things. I built myself
houses and planted vineyards. 5I planted gar-
dens and orchards, with all kinds of fruit

1:4 Sir 14:18 **1:16** 1 Kings 4:29–31; Sir 47:14–18 **2:4–8** 1 Kings 10:23–27; 2 Chr 9:22–27 trees in them; 6 I dug ponds to irrigate them. 7 I bought many slaves, and there were slaves born in my household. I owned more livestock than anyone else who had ever lived in Jerusalem. 8 I also piled up silver and gold from the royal treasuries of the lands I ruled. Men and women sang to entertain me, and I had all the women a man could want.

9 Yes, I was great, greater than anyone else who had ever lived in Jerusalem, and my wisdom never failed me. 10 Anything I wanted, I got. I did not deny myself any pleasure. I was proud of everything I had worked for, and all this was my reward. 11 Then I thought about all that I had done and how hard I had worked doing it, and I realized that it didn't mean a thing. It was like chasing the wind—of no use at all. 12 After all, a king can only do what previous kings have done.

Anything I wanted, I got. (2:10)

So I started thinking about what it meant to be wise or reckless or foolish. 13 Oh, I know, "Wisdom is better than foolishness, just as light is better than darkness. 14 The wise can see where they are going, and fools cannot." But I also know that the same fate is waiting for us all. 15 I thought to myself, "What happens to fools is going to happen to me, too. So what have I gained from being so wise?" "Nothing," I answered, "not a thing." 16 No one remembers the wise, and no one remembers fools. In days to come, we will all be forgotten. We must all die—wise and foolish alike. 17 So life came to mean nothing to me, because everything in it had brought me nothing but trouble. It had all been useless; I had been chasing the wind.

18 Nothing that I had worked for and earned meant a thing to me, because I knew that I would have to leave it to my successor, 19 and he might be wise, or he might be foolish—who knows? Yet he will own everything I have worked for, everything my wisdom has earned for me in this world. It is all useless. 20 So I came to regret that I had worked so hard. 21 You work for something with all your wisdom, knowledge, and skill, and then you have to leave it all to someone who hasn't had to work for it. It is useless, and it isn't right! 22 You work and worry your way through life, and what do you have to show for it? 23 As long as you live, everything you do brings nothing but worry and heartache. Even at night your mind can't rest. It is all useless.

24 The best thing we can do is eat and drink and enjoy what we have earned. And yet, I realized that even this comes from God. 25 How else could you have anything to eat or enjoy yourself at all? 26 God gives wisdom, knowledge, and happiness to those who please him, but he makes sinners work, earning and saving, so that what they get can be given to those who please him. It is all useless. It is like chasing the wind.

It is like chasing the wind. (2:26)

A Time for Everything

3 Everything that happens in this world
happens at the time God chooses.
2 He sets the time for birth and the time
for death,
the time for planting and the time for
pulling up,

2:7 1 Kings 4:23 **2:8** 1 Kings 10:10, 14–22 **2:9** 1 Chr 29:25 **2:23** Job 5:7; 14:1 **2:24** Eccl 3:13; 5:18; 9:7; Isa 56:12; Lk 12:19; 1 Cor 15:32 **2:26** Job 32:8; Prov 2:6

Pray it!

Things Will Change

The beginning of Ecclesiastes, chapter 3, makes one thing clear: things change. There will be times when you are lucky, and times when you are unlucky, times when you are sad, and times when you are happy. When things go well, enjoy it! When things don't go well, be patient and pray that your situation will change soon.

God of all seasons,
Help me to remember the sun when it's raining.
Help me to remember the rain when the sun is shining.
Teach me to respect the unpopular students when I am popular.
Teach me to respect the popular students when I am unpopular.
When I win a game, help me remember the times I lost.
When I lose a game, help me remember the times I won.
When I am with my friends, remind me of times alone.
When I am alone, remind me of times with friends.
Help me to understand that there is a balance to life.
Amen.

— Ecclesiastes 3:1–8

3 the time for killing and the time for
healing,
the time for tearing down and the time
for building.
4 He sets the time for sorrow and the time
for joy,
the time for mourning and the time for
dancing,
5 the time for making love and the time for
not making love,
the time for kissing and the time for not
kissing.
6 He sets the time for finding and the time
for losing,
the time for saving and the time for
throwing away,
7 the time for tearing and the time for
mending,
the time for silence and the time for talk.
8 He sets the time for love and the time for
hate,
the time for war and the time for peace.
9 What do we gain from all our work? 10 I
know the heavy burdens that God has laid
on us. 11 He has set the right time for
everything. He has given us a desire to
know the future, but never gives us the sat-
isfaction of fully understanding what he
does. 12 So I realized that all we can do is be
happy and do the best we can while we are
still alive. 13 All of us should eat and drink
and enjoy what we have worked for. It is
God's gift.
14 I know that everything God does will
last forever. You can't add anything to it or
take anything away from it. And one thing
God does is to make us stand in awe of him.
15 Whatever happens or can happen has
already happened before. God makes the
same thing happen again and again.

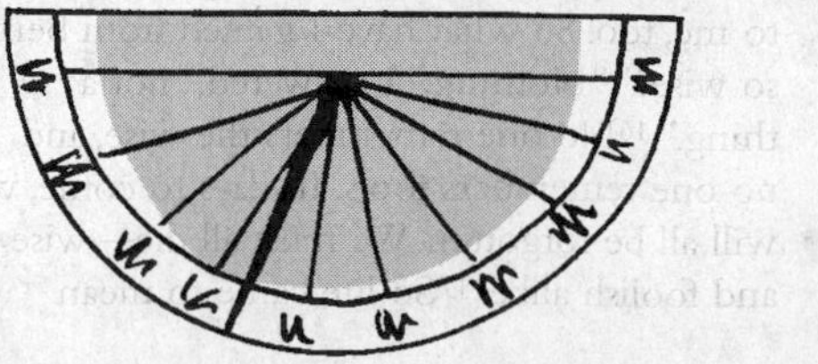

"He has set the right time for everything." (3:11)

Injustice in the World

16 In addition, I have also noticed that in this world you find wickedness where justice and right ought to be. 17 I told myself, "God is going to judge the righteous and the evil alike, because every thing, every action, will happen at its own set time."[a] 18 I decided that God is testing us, to show us that we are no better than animals. 19 After all, the same fate awaits human beings and animals alike. One dies just like the other. They are the same kind of creature. A human being is no better off than an animal, because life has no meaning for either. 20 They are both going to the same place—the dust. They both came from it; they will both go back to it. 21 How can anyone be sure that the human spirit goes upward while an animal's spirit goes down into the ground? 22 So I realized then that the best thing we can do is enjoy what we have worked for. There is nothing else we can do.[b] There is no way for us to know what will happen after we die.

4 Then I looked again at all the injustice that goes on in this world. The oppressed were crying, and no one would help them. No one would help them, because their oppressors had power on their side. 2 I envy those who are dead and gone; they are better off than those who are still alive. 3 But better off than either are those who have never been born, who have never seen the injustice that goes on in this world.

4 I have also learned why people work so hard to succeed: it is because they envy the things their neighbors have. But it is useless. It is like chasing the wind. 5 They say that we would be fools to fold our hands and let ourselves starve to death. 6 Maybe so, but it is better to have only a little, with peace of mind, than be busy all the time with both hands, trying to catch the wind.

"People work so hard to succeed." (4:4)

7 I have noticed something else in life that is useless. 8 Here is someone who lives alone. He has no son, no brother, yet he is always working, never satisfied with the wealth he has. For whom is he working so hard and denying himself any pleasure? This is useless, too—and a miserable way to live.

9 Two are better off than one, because together they can work more effectively. 10 If one of them falls down, the other can help him up. But if someone is alone and falls, it's just too bad, because there is no one to help him. 11 If it is cold, two can sleep together and stay warm, but how can you keep warm by yourself 12 Two people can resist an attack that would defeat one person alone. A rope made of three cords is hard to break.

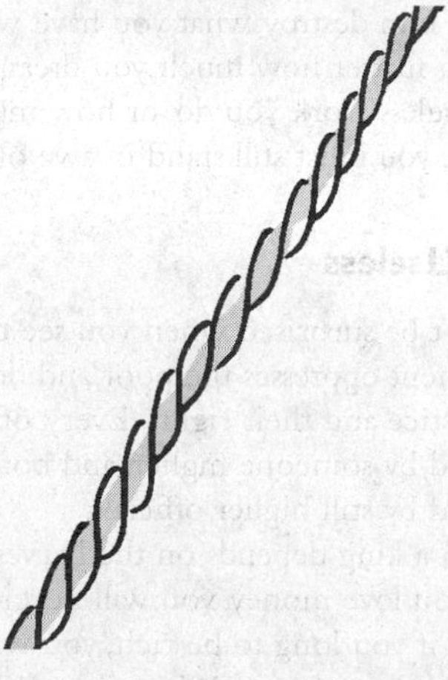

"A rope made of three cords is hard to break." (4:12)

13-14 Someone may rise from poverty to become king of his country, or go from prison to the throne, but if in his old age he is too foolish to take advice, he is not as well off as a young man who is poor but intelligent. 15 I thought about all the people who live in this world, and I realized that somewhere among them there is a young man who will take the king's place. 16 There may be no limit to the number of people a king rules; when he is gone, no one will be grateful for what he has done. It is useless. It is like chasing the wind.

[a] **3:17** *Probable text* its own set time; *Hebrew* its own set time there. [b] **3:22** what we have . . . do; *or* our work, because we are going to have to do it anyway.

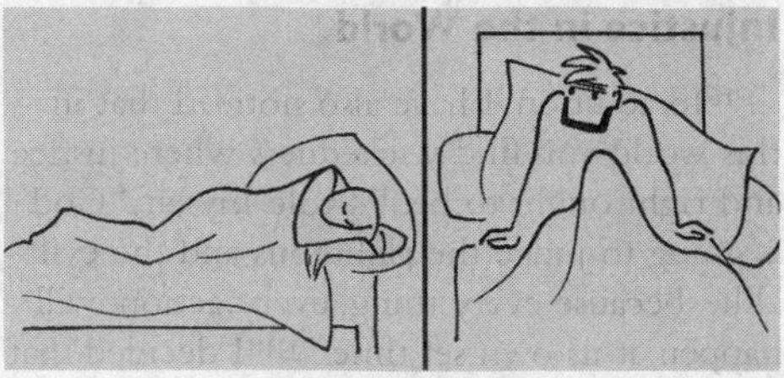

Workers . . . at least they can get a good night's sleep. The rich . . . stay awake worrying. (5:12)

Don't Make Rash Promises

5 Be careful about going to the Temple. It is better to go there to learn than to offer sacrifices like foolish people who don't know right from wrong. 2Think before you speak, and don't make any rash promises to God. He is in heaven and you are on earth, so don't say any more than you have to. 3The more you worry, the more likely you are to have bad dreams, and the more you talk, the more likely you are to say something foolish. 4So when you make a promise to God, keep it as quickly as possible. He has no use for a fool. Do what you promise to do. 5Better not to promise at all than to make a promise and not keep it. 6Don't let your own words lead you into sin, so that you have to tell God's priest that you didn't mean it. Why make God angry with you? Why let him destroy what you have worked for? 7No matter how much you dream, how much useless work you do, or how much you talk, you must still stand in awe of God.

Life Is Useless

8Don't be surprised when you see that the government oppresses the poor and denies them justice and their rights. Every official is protected by someone higher, and both are protected by still higher officials.

9Even a king depends on the harvest.[c]

10If you love money, you will never be satisfied; if you long to be rich, you will never get all you want. It is useless. 11The richer you are, the more mouths you have to feed. All you gain is the knowledge that you are rich. 12Workers may or may not have enough to eat, but at least they can get a good night's sleep. The rich, however, have so much that they stay awake worrying.

13Here is a terrible thing that I have seen in this world: people save up their money for a time when they may need it,[d] 14and then lose it all in some bad deal and end up with nothing left to pass on to their children. 15We leave this world just as we entered it—with nothing. In spite of all our work there is nothing we can take with us. 16It isn't right! We go just as we came. We labor, trying to catch the wind, and what do we get? 17We get to live our lives in darkness and grief,[e] worried, angry, and sick.

18Here is what I have found out: the best thing we can do is eat and drink and enjoy what we have worked for during the short life that God has given us; this is our fate. 19If God gives us wealth and property and lets us enjoy them, we should be grateful and enjoy what we have worked for. It is a gift from God. 20Since God has allowed us to be happy, we will not worry too much about how short life is.

6 I have noticed that in this world a serious injustice is done. 2God will give us wealth, honor, and property, yes, everything we want, but then will not let us enjoy it. Some stranger will enjoy it instead. It is useless, and it just isn't right. 3We may have a hundred children and live a long time, but no matter how long we live, if we do not get our share of happiness and do not receive a decent burial, then I say that a baby born dead is better off. 4It does that baby no good to be born; it disappears into darkness, where it is forgotten. 5It never sees the light of day or knows what life is like, but at least it has found rest— 6more so than the man who never enjoys life, though he may live two thousand years. After all, both of them are going to the same place.

7We do all our work just to get something to eat, but we never have enough. 8How are the wise better off than fools? What good does it do the poor to know how to face life? 9It is useless; it is like chasing the wind.

[c] **5:9** *Verse 9 in Hebrew is unclear.* [d] **5:13** for . . . it; *or* to their own hurt. [e] **5:17** *Some ancient translations* in darkness and grief; *Hebrew* eating in darkness.

5:4 Ps 66:13, 14 **5:15** Job 1:21; Ps 49:17; 1 Tim 6:7

It is better to be satisfied with what you have than to be always wanting something else.

10 Everything that happens was already determined long ago, and we all know that you[f] cannot argue with someone who is stronger than you. 11 The longer you argue, the more useless it is, and you are no better off. 12 How can anyone know what is best for us in this short, useless life of ours—a life that passes like a shadow? How can we know what will happen in the world after we die?

Thoughts about Life

7 A good reputation is better than expensive perfume; and the day you die is better than the day you are born.

2 It is better to go to a home where there is mourning than to one where there is a party, because the living should always remind themselves that death is waiting for us all.

3 Sorrow is better than laughter; it may sadden your face, but it sharpens your understanding.

4 Someone who is always thinking about happiness is a fool. A wise person thinks about death.

5 It is better to have wise people reprimand you than to have stupid people sing your praises.

. . . to have stupid people sing your praises. (7:5)

6 When a fool laughs, it is like thorns crackling in a fire. It doesn't mean a thing.

7 You may be wise, but if you cheat someone, you are acting like a fool. If you take a bribe, you ruin your character.

8 The end of something is better than its beginning.

Patience is better than pride.

9 Keep your temper under control; it is foolish to harbor a grudge.

10 Never ask, "Oh, why were things so much better in the old days?" It's not an intelligent question.

11 Everyone who lives ought to be wise; it is as good as receiving an inheritance 12 and will give you as much security as money can. Wisdom keeps you safe—this is the advantage of knowledge.

13 Think about what God has done. How can anyone straighten out what God has made crooked? 14 When things are going well for you, be glad, and when trouble comes, just remember: God sends both happiness and trouble; you never know what is going to happen next.[g]

15 My life has been useless, but in it I have seen everything. Some good people may die while others live on, even though they are evil. 16 So don't be too good or too wise—why kill yourself 17 But don't be too wicked or too foolish, either—why die before you have to? 18 Avoid both extremes. If you have reverence for God, you will be successful anyway.

. . . take a bribe. (7:7)

19 Wisdom does more for a person than ten rulers can do for a city.

20 There is no one on earth who does

[f] **6:10** and we . . . you; *or* and our nature is already known; you. [g] **7:14** you . . . next; *or* you cannot find fault with him.

7:1 Prov 22:1 **7:9** Jas 1:19

what is right all the time and never makes a mistake.

21 Don't pay attention to everything people say—you may hear your servant insulting you, 22 and you know yourself that you have insulted other people many times.

23 I used my wisdom to test all of this. I was determined to be wise, but it was beyond me. 24 How can anyone discover what life means? It is too deep for us, too hard to understand. 25 But I devoted myself to knowledge and study; I was determined to find wisdom and the answers to my questions, and to learn how wicked and foolish stupidity is.

26 I found something more bitter than death—the woman who is like a trap. The love she offers you will catch you like a net, and her arms around you will hold you like a chain. A man who pleases God can get away, but she will catch the sinner. 27 Yes, said the Philosopher, I found this out little by little while I was looking for answers. 28 I have looked for other answers but have found none. I found one man in a thousand that I could respect, but not one woman. 29 This is all that I have learned: God made us plain and simple, but we have made ourselves very complicated.

8 Only the wise know what things really mean. Wisdom makes them smile and makes their frowns disappear.

"The love she offers you will catch you like a net." (7:26)

Obey the King

2 Do what the king says,[h] and don't make any rash promises to God. 3 The king can do anything he likes, so depart from his presence; don't stay in such a dangerous place. 4 The king acts with authority, and no one can challenge what he does. 5 As long as you obey his commands, you are safe, and a wise person knows how and when to do it. 6 There is a right time and a right way to do everything, but we know so little! 7 None of us knows what is going to happen, and there is no one to tell us. 8 No one can keep from dying or put off the day of death. That is a battle we cannot escape; we cannot cheat our way out.

None of us knows. (8:7)

The Wicked and the Righteous

9 I saw all this when I thought about the things that are done in this world, a world where some people have power and others have to suffer under them. 10 Yes, I have seen the wicked buried and in their graves, but on the way back from the cemetery people praise them in the very city where they did their evil.[i] It is useless.

11 Why do people commit crimes so readily? Because crime is not punished quickly enough. 12 A sinner may commit a hundred crimes and still live. Oh yes, I know what they say: "If you obey God, everything will be all right, 13 but it will not go well for the wicked. Their life is like a shadow and they

[h] **8:2** *Some ancient translations* Do what the king says; *Hebrew unclear.* [i] **8:10** *Verse 10 in Hebrew is unclear.*

will die young, because they do not obey God." 14But this is nonsense. Look at what happens in the world: sometimes the righteous get the punishment of the wicked, and the wicked get the reward of the righteous. I say it is useless.

15So I am convinced that we should enjoy ourselves, because the only pleasure we have in this life is eating and drinking and enjoying ourselves. We can at least do this as we labor during the life that God has given us in this world.

16Whenever I tried to become wise and learn what goes on in the world, I realized that you could stay awake night and day 17and never be able to understand what God is doing. However hard you try, you will never find out. The wise may claim to know, but they don't.

The wise may claim to know . . . (8:17)

9 I thought long and hard about all this and saw that God controls the actions of wise and righteous people, even their love and their hate. No one knows anything about what lies ahead. 2It makes no difference.[j] The same fate comes to the righteous and the wicked, to the good and the bad,[k] to those who are religious and those who are not, to those who offer sacrifices and those who do not. A good person is no better off than a sinner; one who takes an oath is no better off than one who does not. 3One fate comes to all alike, and this is as wrong as anything that happens in this world. As long as people live, their minds are full of evil and madness, and suddenly they die. 4But anyone who is alive in the world of the living has

"A live dog is better off than a dead lion." (9:4)

some hope; a live dog is better off than a dead lion. 5Yes, the living know they are going to die, but the dead know nothing. They have no further reward; they are completely forgotten. 6Their loves, their hates, their passions, all died with them. They will never again take part in anything that happens in this world.

7Go ahead—eat your food and be happy; drink your wine and be cheerful. It's all right with God. 8Always look happy and cheerful. 9Enjoy life with the one you love, as long as you live the useless life that God has given you in this world. Enjoy every useless day of it, because that is all you will get for all your trouble. 10Work hard at whatever you do, because there will be no action, no thought, no knowledge, no wisdom in the world of the dead—and that is where you are going.

11I realized another thing, that in this world fast runners do not always win the races, and the brave do not always win the battles. The wise do not always earn a living, intelligent people do not always get rich, and capable people do not always rise to high positions. Bad luck happens to everyone. 12You never know when your time is coming. Like birds suddenly caught in a trap, like fish caught in a net, we are trapped at some evil moment when we least expect it.

Thoughts on Wisdom and Foolishness

13There is something else I saw, a good example of how wisdom is regarded in this

[j] **9:2** hate. No one . . . difference; *or* hate, but no one knows whether it is out of love or hate.[2] It makes no difference what lies ahead of us. [k] **9:2** *Some ancient translations* and the bad; *Hebrew does not have these words.*

world. 14There was a little town without
many people in it. A powerful king attacked
it. He surrounded it and prepared to break
through the walls. 15Someone lived there
who was poor, but so clever that he could
have saved the town. But no one thought
about him.[l] 16I have always said that wisdom
is better than strength, but no one thinks of
the poor as wise or pays any attention to
what they say. 17It is better to listen to the
quiet words of someone wise than to the
shouts of a ruler at a council of fools. 18Wis-
dom does more good than weapons, but one
sinner can undo a lot of good.

It is better to listen to the quiet words of someone wise . . . (9:17)

10 Dead flies can make a whole bottle
of perfume stink, and a little stupidi-
ty can cancel out the greatest wisdom.
2It is natural for the wise to do the right
thing and for fools to do the wrong thing.
3Their stupidity will be evident even to
strangers they meet along the way; they let
everyone know that they are fools.
4If your ruler becomes angry with you, do
not hand in your resignation; serious wrongs
may be pardoned if you keep calm.[m]
5Here is an injustice I have seen in the
world—an injustice caused by rulers. 6Stupid
people are given positions of authority while
the rich are ignored. 7I have seen slaves on
horseback while noblemen go on foot like
slaves.
8If you dig a pit, you fall in it; if you break
through a wall, a snake bites you. 9If you
work in a stone quarry, you get hurt by
stones. If you split wood, you get hurt doing

I have seen slaves on horseback. (10:7)

it. 10If your ax is dull and you don't sharpen
it, you have to work harder to use it. It is
smarter to plan ahead. 11Knowing how to
charm a snake is of no use if you let the
snake bite first. 12What the wise say brings
them honor, but fools are destroyed by their
own words. 13They start out with silly talk
and end up with pure madness. 14A fool
talks on and on.
No one knows what is going to happen
next, and no one can tell us what will hap-
pen after we die.
15Only someone too stupid to find his way
home would wear himself out with work.
16A country is in trouble when its king is
a youth and its leaders feast all night long.
17But a country is fortunate to have a king
who makes his own decisions and leaders
who eat at the proper time, who control
themselves and don't get drunk.
18When you are too lazy to repair your
roof, it will leak, and the house will fall in.

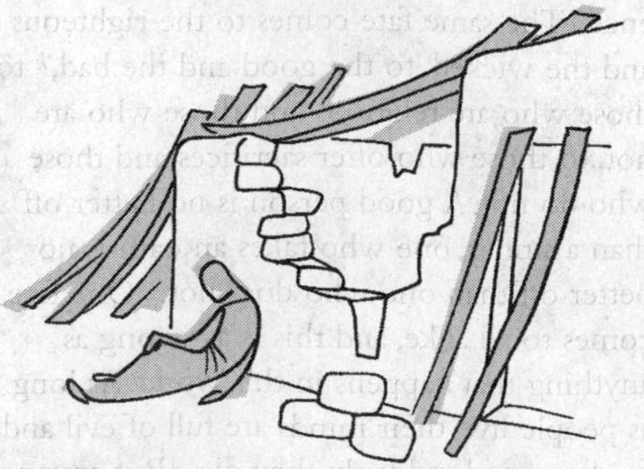

When you are too lazy to repair your roof . . . (10:18)

[l] **9:15** he could have . . . him; *or* he saved the town. But later on no one remembered him. [m] **10:4** keep calm; *or* submit to him.

10:8 Ps 7:15; Prov 26:27; Sir 27:26, 27

19 Feasting makes you happy and wine cheers you up, but you can't have either without money.

20 Don't criticize the king, even silently, and don't criticize the rich, even in the privacy of your bedroom. A bird might carry the message and tell them what you said.

What a Wise Person Does

11 Invest your money in foreign trade, and one of these days you will make a profit. 2 Put your investments in several places—many places even—because you never know what kind of bad luck you are going to have in this world.

3 No matter which direction a tree falls, it will lie where it fell. When the clouds are full, it rains. 4 If you wait until the wind and the weather are just right, you will never plant anything and never harvest anything. 5 God made everything, and you can no more understand what he does than you understand how new life begins in the womb of a pregnant woman. 6 Do your planting in the morning and in the evening, too. You never know whether it will all grow well or whether one planting will do better than the other.

7 It is good to be able to enjoy the pleasant light of day. 8 Be grateful for every year you live. No matter how long you live, remember that you will be dead much longer. There is nothing at all to look forward to.

Advice to Young People

9 Young people, enjoy your youth. Be happy while you are still young. Do what you want to do, and follow your heart's desire. But remember that God is going to judge you for whatever you do.

10 Don't let anything worry you or cause you pain. You aren't going to be young very long.

12 So remember your Creator[n] while you are still young, before those dismal days and years come when you will say, "I don't enjoy life." 2 That is when the light of the sun, the moon, and the stars will grow dim for you, and the rain clouds will never pass away. 3 Then your arms, that have protected you, will tremble, and your legs, now strong, will grow weak. Your teeth will be too few to chew your food, and your eyes too dim to see clearly. 4 Your ears will be deaf to the noise of the street. You will barely be able to hear the mill as it grinds or music as it plays, but even the song of a bird will wake you from sleep. 5 You will be afraid of high places, and walking will be dangerous. Your hair will turn white; you will hardly be able to drag yourself along, and all desire will be gone.

We are going to our final resting place, and then there will be mourning in the streets. 6 The silver chain will snap, and the golden lamp will fall and break; the rope at the well will break, and the water jar will be shattered. 7 Our bodies will return to the dust of the earth, and the breath of life will go back to God, who gave it to us.

8 Useless, useless, said the Philosopher. It is all useless.

The Summing Up

9 But because the Philosopher was wise, he kept on teaching the people what he knew. He studied proverbs and honestly tested their truth. 10 The Philosopher tried to find comforting words, but the words he wrote were honest. 11 The sayings of the wise are like the sharp sticks that shepherds use to

"Remember your Creator while you are still young." (12:1)

[n] **12:1** *The Hebrew expression for* your Creator *sounds like the Hebrew for* your grave.

guide sheep, and collected proverbs are as
lasting as firmly driven nails. They have been
given by God, the one Shepherd of us all.

12 My child, there is something else to watch
out for. There is no end to the writing of
books, and too much study will wear you out.

13 After all this, there is only one thing to
say: Have reverence for God, and obey his
commands, because this is all that we were
created for. 14 God is going to judge every-
thing we do, whether good or bad, even
things done in secret.

THE Song of Songs

In many families if mom and dad start kissing in front of the kids, they'll hear a chorus of "Eeeewwww! That's so gross!" We don't like to think of our parents as anything but mom and dad. But it is because of their love and God's gift of sexuality that you are alive.

The Song of Songs is the opposite of "Eeeewwww!" It is eight whole chapters that celebrate physical attraction and sexual love. Although some versions of the Bible label the two people the bride and bridegroom, this version uses *The Woman* and *The Man*. Throughout the Bible, God's relationship with his chosen people has been compared to two people in love. Some people view the Song of Songs as another example of this. Human love is a reflection of God's love and can teach us about how much God loves us.

Headlines

- Spring Has Arrived, Love Is Blooming! (2:8–15)
- How Beautiful You Are, My Love (4:1–7)
- Nightmare Reveals Lover's Fears (5:2–8)
- Caution: Love Holds Danger (8:6–7)

FACTOIDS

Who wrote this book? The Song of Songs is sometimes credited to Solomon, but the true author is not known.

When was it written? It was probably written sometime after the Babylonian Exile in 583 BC.

Why was it written? It is a collection of love songs and poems that were written to express the goodness of human love and sexuality.

Jesus connection: The Song of Songs is seen as a metaphor for how Christ loves the Church.

Important themes

- Love and sexuality are holy because they are gifts from God.
- The goodness and passion of human love is a reflection of God's love for us.
- Because love is a powerful gift from God, it should be treated with respect.

SONG OF SONGS

1 The most beautiful of songs, by
Solomon.[a]

The First Song

The Woman

2 Your lips cover me with kisses;
your love is better than wine.
3 There is a fragrance about you;
the sound of your name recalls it.
No woman could keep from loving
you.
4 Take me with you, and we'll run away;
be my king and take me to your room.
We will be happy together,
drink deep, and lose ourselves in love.
No wonder all women love you!
5 Women of Jerusalem, I am dark but[b]
beautiful,
dark as the desert tents of Kedar,
but beautiful as the draperies in
Solomon's palace.
6 Don't look down on me because of my
color,
because the sun has tanned me.
My brothers were angry with me
and made me work in the vineyard.
I had no time to care for myself.
7 Tell me, my love,
Where will you lead your flock to
graze?
Where will they rest from the noonday
sun?
Why should I need to look for you
among the flocks of the other
shepherds?[c]

The Man

8 Don't you know the place, loveliest of
women?
Go and follow the flock;
find pasture for your goats
near the tents of the shepherds.

Live it!

Dark and Beautiful

Beauty comes in all shapes, sizes, and colors! Society in every age has had ideas about the right kind of beauty—light skin, dark skin, thin, round, tall, short—but we are all made in the image of God no matter what color we are. Human beings are beautiful, amazing creatures, each one of us! The woman sings of her own dark beauty with confidence. Each of us should follow her example and look in the mirror and say, "I am beautiful!"

— Song of Songs 1:5

9 You, my love, excite men
as a mare excites the stallions of
Pharaoh's chariots.
10 Your hair is beautiful upon your cheeks
and falls along your neck like jewels.
11 But we will make for you a chain of gold
with ornaments of silver.

Loveliest of women (1:8)

[a] **1:1** by Solomon; *or* dedicated to Solomon, *or* about Solomon. [b] **1:5** but; *or* and. [c] **1:7** *Probable text* Why should I . . . shepherds; *Hebrew unclear.*

1:1 1 Kings 4:32

The Woman

12 My king was lying on his couch,
and my perfume filled the air with fragrance.
13 My lover has the scent of myrrh
as he lies upon my breasts.
14 My lover is like the wild flowers
that bloom in the vineyards at Engedi.

The Man

15 How beautiful you are, my love;
how your eyes shine with love!

"How beautiful you are!" (1:15)

The Woman

16 How handsome you are, my dearest;
how you delight me!
The green grass will be our bed;
17 the cedars will be the beams of our house,
and the cypress trees the ceiling.

2 I am only a wild flower in Sharon,
a lily in a mountain valley.

The Man

2 Like a lily among thorns
is my darling among women.

Study it!

The "Best" Song

The Song of Songs is a funny title isn't it? It's actually a way of saying this is the best song or the ultimate song. Other names for this book are the Song of Solomon and the Canticle of Canticles. This book is unlike most of the other books of the Bible. Other Bible books are books of stories, history, laws, and many other things.

But the Song of Songs is a book of love poems, probably even song lyrics, meant to be performed. It's actually not just one song, but a collection of songs. In chapter 2 you probably have the feeling that you're jumping from one topic to the next. That is because it has parts of more than one song, and the song goes back and forth between the woman's part and the man's part. The headings that were added by the translators help you to keep the different songs straight, and they tell you who is singing them.

— Song of Songs, chapter 2

The Woman

3 Like an apple tree among the trees of the forest,
so is my dearest compared to other men.
I love to sit in its shadow,
and its fruit is sweet to my taste.
4 He brought me to his banquet hall
and raised the banner of love over me.
5 Restore my strength with raisins
and refresh me with apples!
I am weak from passion.

Who is the best looking? We waste a lot of time trying to figure that out. Why do you think God made so many kinds and colors of people?

6 His left hand is under my head,
and his right hand caresses me.
7 Promise me, women of Jerusalem;
swear by the swift deer and the gazelles
that you will not interrupt our love.

The Second Song

The Woman

8 I hear my lover's voice.
He comes running over the mountains,
racing across the hills to me.
9 My lover is like a gazelle,
like a young stag.
There he stands beside the wall.
He looks in through the window
and glances through the lattice.
10 My lover speaks to me.

The Man

Come then, my love;
my darling, come with me.
11 The winter is over; the rains have stopped;
12 in the countryside the flowers are in bloom.
This is the time for singing;
the song of doves is heard in the fields.
13 Figs are beginning to ripen;
the air is fragrant with blossoming vines.
Come then, my love;
my darling, come with me.
14 You are like a dove that hides
in the crevice of a rock.
Let me see your lovely face
and hear your enchanting voice.
15 Catch the foxes, the little foxes,
before they ruin our vineyard in bloom.

The Woman

16 My lover is mine, and I am his.
He feeds his flock among the lilies
17 until the morning breezes blow
and the darkness disappears.
Return, my darling, like a gazelle,
like a stag on the mountains of Bether.[d]

3 Asleep on my bed, night after night
I dreamed of the one I love;
I was looking for him, but couldn't find him.
2 I went wandering through the city,
through its streets and alleys.
I looked for the one I love.
I looked, but couldn't find him.
3 The sentries patrolling the city saw me.
I asked them, "Have you found my lover?"
4 As soon as I left them, I found him.
I held him and wouldn't let him go
until I took him to my mother's house,
to the room where I was born.

5 Promise me, women of Jerusalem;
swear by the swift deer and the gazelles
that you will not interrupt our love.

The Third Song

The Woman

6 What is this coming from the desert like a column of smoke,
fragrant with incense and myrrh,
the incense sold by the traders?
7 Solomon is coming, carried on his throne;
sixty soldiers form the bodyguard,
the finest soldiers in Israel.
8 All of them are skillful with the sword;
they are battle-hardened veterans.
Each of them is armed with a sword,
on guard against a night attack.
9 King Solomon is carried on a throne
made of the finest wood.
10 Its posts are covered with silver;
over it is cloth embroidered with gold.
Its cushions are covered with purple cloth,
lovingly woven by the women of Jerusalem.

[d] **2:17** mountains of Bether; *or* rugged mountains.

King Solomon is mentioned in Song of Songs, chapter 3. Is he the male lover in the songs? This is one reason the book is also called the Song of Solomon.

Pray it!

Five Senses

The Song of Songs is full of descriptions of the five senses: sight, hearing, smell, taste, and touch. It celebrates being human and having bodies. Let's use our senses! Try these mini-meditations:

- **The next time you take a bite of your favorite food, eat it slowly, and really taste it!**
- **When you climb in bed, enjoy the feeling of snuggling down into your sheets. If it's a hot summer day, enjoy the coolness of the sheets against your skin. On a cold winter night, notice how quickly the blankets warm up from the heat of your body.**
- **Watch the patterns the shadows of the leaves make when the sun shines through the trees on a breezy day.**
- **When you listen to your favorite music, pay attention to the harmonies and how they fit together, and the sounds of the different instruments.**
- **Do you like the smell of freshly cut grass, blooming flowers, or cookies in the oven? Go through your day noticing all the scents you encounter. Make a list of these and see how many you have at the end of the day.**

Make your own list of meditations based on the five senses and thank God for being human!

— Song of Songs, chapter 3

11 Women of Zion, come and see King
Solomon.
He is wearing the crown that his mother
placed on his head
on his wedding day,
on the day of his gladness and joy.

The Man

4 How beautiful you are, my love!
How your eyes shine with love behind
your veil.
Your hair dances like a flock of goats
bounding down the hills of Gilead.
2 Your teeth are as white as sheep
that have just been shorn and
washed.
Not one of them is missing;
they are all perfectly matched.
3 Your lips are like a scarlet ribbon;
how lovely they are when you speak.
Your cheeks glow behind your veil.
4 Your neck is like the tower of David,
round and smooth,[e]
with a necklace like a thousand shields
hung around it.
5 Your breasts are like gazelles,
twin deer feeding among lilies.
6 I will stay on the hill of myrrh,
the hill of incense,
until the morning breezes blow
and the darkness disappears.
7 How beautiful you are, my love;
how perfect you are!

8 Come with me from the Lebanon
Mountains, my bride;
come with me from Lebanon.
Come down from the top of Mount
Amana,
from Mount Senir and Mount
Hermon,
where the lions and leopards live.

[e] **4:4** round and smooth; *Hebrew unclear.*

Study it!

Fruit and Flowers, Incense and Animals

The author uses many different images from nature to describe love and physical beauty. They give us a picture of what was valued and admired at the time the Song of Songs was written. Can you find these things mentioned in chapters 4–5?

- **For beauty and sweetness: lilies, honey, milk, wine, spices, brooks, incense, a dove, a tower**
- **For strength and good looks: sheep, gazelles, a tree, a king, ivory, alabaster, gold, jewels**

— Song of Songs, chapter 4

9 The look in your eyes, my sweetheart and
bride,
and the necklace you are wearing
have stolen my heart.
10 Your love delights me,
my sweetheart and bride.
Your love is better than wine;
your perfume more fragrant than any
spice.
11 The taste of honey is on your lips, my
darling;
your tongue is milk and honey for me.
Your clothing has all the fragrance of
Lebanon.

12 My sweetheart, my bride, is a secret
garden,
a walled garden, a private spring;
13 there the plants flourish.
They grow like an orchard of
pomegranate trees
and bear the finest fruits.
There is no lack of henna and nard,
14 of saffron, calamus, and cinnamon,
or incense of every kind.
Myrrh and aloes grow there
with all the most fragrant perfumes.
15 Fountains water the garden,
streams of flowing water,
brooks gushing down from the
Lebanon Mountains.

The Woman

16 Wake up, North Wind.
South Wind, blow on my garden;
fill the air with fragrance.
Let my lover come to his garden
and eat the best of its fruits.

The Man

5 I have entered my garden,
my sweetheart, my bride.
I am gathering my spices and myrrh;
I am eating my honey and honeycomb;
I am drinking my wine and milk.

The Women

Eat, lovers, and drink
until you are drunk with love!

The Fourth Song

The Woman

2 While I slept, my heart was awake.
I dreamed my lover knocked at the door.

The Man

Let me come in, my darling,
my sweetheart, my dove.
My head is wet with dew,
and my hair is damp from the mist.

The Woman

3 I have already undressed;
why should I get dressed again?
I have washed my feet;
why should I get them dirty again?

4 My lover put his hand to the door,
and I was thrilled that he was near.
5 I was ready to let him come in.
My hands were covered with myrrh,
my fingers with liquid myrrh,
as I grasped the handle of the door.
6 I opened the door for my lover,
but he had already gone.

How I wanted to hear his voice!
I looked for him, but couldn't find him;
I called to him, but heard no answer.
7 The sentries patrolling the city found me;
they struck me and bruised me;
the guards at the city wall tore off my cape.
8 Promise me, women of Jerusalem,
that if you find my lover,
you will tell him I am weak from passion.

The Women

9 Most beautiful of women,
is your lover different from everyone else?
What is there so wonderful about him
that we should give you our promise?

The Woman

10 My lover is handsome and strong;
he is one in ten thousand.
11 His face is bronzed and smooth;
his hair is wavy,
black as a raven.
12 His eyes are as beautiful as doves by a flowing brook,
doves washed in milk and standing by the stream.[f]
13 His cheeks are as lovely as a garden
that is full of herbs and spices.
His lips are like lilies,
wet with liquid myrrh.
14 His hands are well-formed,
and he wears rings set with gems.
His body is like smooth ivory,[g]
with sapphires set in it.
15 His thighs are columns of alabaster
set in sockets of gold.
He is majestic, like the Lebanon Mountains
with their towering cedars.
16 His mouth is sweet to kiss;
everything about him enchants me.
This is what my lover is like,
women of Jerusalem.

Study it!

Sexuality Versus Sex

Sexuality and sex are not the same thing, but they are very closely related. Sexuality relates to all the things that make us either male or female. Every person has sexuality even if they are not having sex. Sexuality affects every part of our lives—how we see the world, whom we are attracted to, and how we relate to other people, both female and male. Sex often refers to any close physical contact with another person's sexual organs. God did not intend having sex for everybody, only for husbands and wives in marriage.

The Song of Songs celebrates the goodness of both sexuality and sex. The man and woman's attraction for each other is part of sexuality. But the symbolic language of the song indicates that they also desire to be completely united physically. Because this is love poetry, it doesn't talk explicitly about marriage. But we can presume that the couple would be married before they actually have sex. The ultimate commitment of sex is only morally right within marriage.

— Song of Songs, chapter 5

The Women

6 Most beautiful of women,
where has your lover gone?
Tell us which way your lover went,
so that we can help you find him.

[f] **5:12** and standing by the stream; *Hebrew unclear.* [g] **5:14** like smooth ivory; *Hebrew unclear.*

The group of women question, "What's so great about this guy?" What things would make you fall in love with someone else?

Catholic Connections

A Great Gift!

The fact that the Song of Songs is in the Bible makes it clear that our sexuality is beautiful and good. It is a great gift from God and should be treated with the utmost care and respect. Maybe if more people believed in sex as a gift, we wouldn't be so easily misled by advertisers and pornographers who cheapen this wonderful gift. They treat sex as something that is casual, selfish, and without any deeper meaning. No wonder so many people end up seeing sexuality as something dirty or wrong.

Our faith tells us that when sexuality is expressed the way God intended, our relations with other people are good and life-giving. When sex is saved for marriage, it is an amazing reflection of God's love. When sexuality is misused and people have sex outside of marriage, it often results in shame, broken hearts, jealousy, and disease. Both the man and the woman in the Song of Songs declare their love for each other and only each other. "My lover is mine, and I am his. / . . . But I love only one" (Song of Songs 6:3–9).

— Song of Songs 6:1–9

The Woman

2 My lover has gone to his garden,
where the balsam trees grow.
He is feeding his flock in the garden
and gathering lilies.
3 My lover is mine, and I am his;
he feeds his flock among the lilies.

The Fifth Song

The Man

4 My love, you are as beautiful as Jerusalem,
as lovely as the city of Tirzah,
as breathtaking as these great cities.[h]
5 Turn your eyes away from me;
they are holding me captive.
Your hair dances like a flock of goats
bounding down the hills of Gilead.
6 Your teeth are as white as a flock of sheep
that have just been washed.
Not one of them is missing;
they are all perfectly matched.
7 Your cheeks glow behind your veil.
8 Let the king have sixty queens, eighty
concubines,
young women without number!
9 But I love only one,
and she is as lovely as a dove.
She is her mother's only daughter,
her mother's favorite child.
All women look at her and praise her;
queens and concubines sing her praises.

10 Who is this whose glance is like the dawn?
She is beautiful and bright,
as dazzling as the sun or the moon.[i]
11 I have come down among the almond trees
to see the young plants in the valley,
to see the new leaves on the vines
and the blossoms on the pomegranate
trees.
12 I am trembling; you have made me as
eager for love
as a chariot driver is for battle.[j]

[h] **6:4** as breathtaking as . . . cities; *Hebrew unclear.* [i] **6:10** as dazzling as . . . moon; *Hebrew unclear.* [j] **6:12** *Verse 12 in Hebrew is unclear.*

"I love only one, / and she is as lovely as a dove" *(Song of Songs 6:9)*.

The Women

13 Dance, dance,[k] girl of Shulam.
Let us watch you as you dance.

The Woman

Why do you want to watch me
as I dance between the rows of onlookers?

Let us watch you as you dance. (6:13)

The Man

7 What a magnificent young woman you are!
How beautiful are your feet in sandals.
The curve of your thighs
is like the work of an artist.
2 A bowl is there,
that never runs out of spiced wine.
A sheaf of wheat is there,
surrounded by lilies.
3 Your breasts are like twin deer,
like two gazelles.
4 Your neck is like a tower of ivory.
Your eyes are like the pools in the city of Heshbon,
near the gate of that great city.
Your nose is as lovely as the tower of Lebanon
that stands guard at Damascus.
5 Your head is held high like Mount Carmel.
Your braided hair shines like the finest satin;
its beauty[l] could hold a king captive.

6 How pretty you are, how beautiful;
how complete the delights of your love.
7 You are as graceful as a palm tree,
and your breasts are clusters of dates.
8 I will climb the palm tree
and pick its fruit.
To me your breasts are like bunches of grapes,
your breath like the fragrance of apples,
9 and your mouth like the finest wine.

The Woman

Then let the wine flow straight to my lover,
flowing over his lips and teeth.[m]
10 I belong to my lover, and he desires me.
11 Come, darling, let's go out to the countryside
and spend the night in the villages.[n]
12 We will get up early and look at the vines
to see whether they've started to grow,
whether the blossoms are opening
and the pomegranate trees are in bloom.
There I will give you my love.
13 You can smell the scent of mandrakes,
and all the pleasant fruits are near our door.
Darling, I have kept for you
the old delights and the new.

8 I wish that you were my brother,
that my mother had nursed you at her breast.
Then, if I met you in the street,
I could kiss you and no one would mind.
2 I would take you to my mother's house,
where you could teach me love.
I would give you spiced wine,
my pomegranate wine to drink.
3 Your left hand is under my head,
and your right hand caresses me.

4 Promise me, women of Jerusalem,
that you will not interrupt our love.

The Sixth Song

The Women

5 Who is this coming from the desert,
arm in arm with her lover?

[k] **6:13** Dance, dance; *or* Come back, come back. [l] **7:5** beauty; *Hebrew unclear.* [m] **7:9** *Some ancient translations* lips and teeth; *Hebrew* lips of those who sleep. [n] **7:11** villages; *or* fields.

The Woman

Under the apple tree I woke you,
in the place where you were born.
6 Close your heart to every love but mine;
hold no one in your arms but me.
Love is as powerful as death;
passion is as strong as death itself.
It bursts into flame
and burns like a raging fire.
7 Water cannot put it out;
no flood can drown it.
But if any tried to buy love with their wealth,
contempt is all they would get.

The Woman's Brothers

8 We have a young sister,
and her breasts are still small.
What will we do for her
when a young man comes courting?
9 If she is a wall,
we will build her a silver tower.
But if she is a gate,
we will protect her with panels of cedar.

The Woman

10 I am a wall,
and my breasts are its towers.
My lover knows that with him
I find contentment and peace.

The Man

11 Solomon has a vineyard
in a place called Baal Hamon.
There are farmers who rent it from him;
each one pays a thousand silver coins.
12 Solomon is welcome to his thousand coins,
and the farmers to two hundred as their share;
I have a vineyard of my own!

Live it!

The Power of Love

There are other characters in these love poems than the man and woman. In Song of Songs, chapter 8, there are lines by other women and by the brothers of the woman in love. These characters also love the woman and want to protect her. Even when you fall in love with that special person, you are still connected to the other people whom you love and who love you!

Love takes many forms: love between family members, the love friends have for one another, romantic love. All these forms of love are a reflection of the love God has for us. Love can change everything! It can bring peace, healing, and hope. Be a person of love and be a reflection of God's powerful love!

— Song of Songs 8:5–9

13 Let me hear your voice from the garden,
my love;
my companions are waiting to hear you speak.

The Woman

14 Come to me, my lover, like a gazelle,
like a young stag on the mountains
where spices grow.

Your Next Step

Congratulations on finishing the Song of Songs! If you are following the suggested reading plan, go back to the Second Book of Maccabees. Second Maccabees is a book about war, quite a switch from the book you just finished.

THE BOOK OF Wisdom

Have you ever heard stories about life long ago from your parents or grandparents? These stories probably shared some of your family history and traditions. Older people tell these stories so that you know why your family believes certain things and does certain things.

The Wisdom of Solomon is kind of like that. It called the Jews back to their roots and reminded them of the wisdom of their faith. It also spoke about good and evil in a new way—that God rewards good and punishes evil after we have died. It was one of the first Old Testament books that shows a belief in life after death.

The wisdom in this book also calls us back to our Christian roots and helps us remember the wisdom of our faith. It reminds us that sooner or later our actions do have consequences.

Chap. 8–9

Headlines

- World Leaders Called to Love Justice! (1:1–4)
- Why Not Eat, Drink, and Be Merry? (2:6–24)
- Faithful Receive Reward After Death (3:1–9)
- The Awesome Power of Wisdom! (7:22—8:1)
- God's Love and Mercy Is for Everyone (11:21—12:2)
- God's People Protected, Wicked Punished! (19:6–17)

FACTOIDS

Who wrote this book? An unknown author.

When was it written? Around 50 BC. It was probably the last Old Testament book to be written.

Why was it written? Jewish people living in Alexandria, Egypt, were forgetting their Jewish way of life. They needed to remember their family stories and religious traditions.

Jesus connection: Good people can expect to suffer just as Jesus suffered and died unjustly. (See Wisdom 2:12–22.)

Important themes

- Death is not the end of our life. God rewards a holy life, but sometimes not until after death.
- God created each person with care and loves us very much.
- Our actions have consequences. Small sins now can lead to bigger sins later.

WISDOM

The Search for Justice

1 Love justice, you rulers of the world. Set your minds sincerely on the Lord, and look for him with all honesty. 2Those who do not try to test him will find him; he will show himself to those who trust him. 3Dishonest thoughts separate people from God, and if we are foolish enough to test him, his power will put us to shame. 4Wisdom will never be at home with anyone who is deceitful or a slave of sin. 5Everyone who is holy has learned to stay away from deceitful people. He will not stay around when foolish thoughts are being expressed; he will not feel comfortable when injustice is done.

God Is Aware of What We Say

6Wisdom is a spirit that is friendly to people, but she will not forgive anyone who speaks against God, for God knows our feelings and thoughts, and hears our every word. 7Since the Lord's spirit fills the entire world, and holds everything in it together, she knows every word that people say. 8No one who speaks wickedly will escape notice; sooner or later he will receive just punishment. 9The intentions of ungodly people will be closely examined; their words will be reported to the Lord, and then they will get the punishment that their wickedness deserves. 10God will tolerate no challenge, and since he hears everything, you cannot hide your complaining from him. 11So be sure that you do not go around complaining—it does no good—and don't engage in bitter talk. The most secret things you say will have their consequences, and lying will destroy your soul.

God Did Not Create Death

12Do not bring on your own death by sinful actions. 13God did not invent death, and when living creatures die, it gives him no pleasure. 14He created everything so that it might continue to exist, and everything he created is wholesome and good. There is no deadly poison in them. No, death does not rule this world, 15for God's justice does not die.

16Ungodly people have brought death on themselves by the things they have said and done. They yearn for death as if it were a lover. They have gone into partnership with death, and it is just what they deserve.

Wicked Thinking

2 Wicked people are wrong when they say to themselves, "Our life is short and full of sorrow, and when its end comes, there is no escape. No one has ever been known to come back from the world of the dead. 2We were born by chance, and after life is over, we will be as if we had never been born at all. Our breath is no more than a puff of smoke; our mind is nothing more than a spark thrown off by the beating of our heart. 3When that spark dies, our body will crumble into ashes, and our breath will become part of the empty air. 4In time, no one will remember anything we ever did, and even our names will be forgotten. Our lives will pass away like the traces of clouds and vanish like fog in the heat of the sun. 5Our time on earth is like a passing shadow. There is no escape from the day of our death; it is fixed, and no one can postpone it."

6The wicked say, "Come on, then, let's enjoy the good things of life, and live in this world the way we did when we were young and free of care! 7Let's drink the most expensive wines and use the finest perfumes. Let's not miss a single flower in the springtime! 8Before the roses wither, let's pick them and wear them in our hair! 9Let's all join in and leave signs everywhere of our carefree revelry! Life owes us that much!

10"We'll oppress the poor, even if they are righteous. We'll show no respect for widows

1:1 Wis 6:1–11 **1:13** Ezek 18:32; 33:11; 2 Pet 3:9 **1:16** Prov 8:36; Isa 28:15; Sir 14:12 **2:6** Isa 22:13; 1 Cor 15:32

Our lives will pass away like . . . clouds. (2:4)

or old people. 11 We'll call ourselves right if we
are strong enough to get what we want. No
one ever got anywhere by being weak!
12 Righteous people are nothing but a nui-
sance, so let's look for chances to get rid of
them. They are against what we do; they
accuse us of breaking the Law of Moses and
violating the traditions of our ancestors.
13 They claim to know God, and they call
themselves the Lord's children. 14 We can't
stand the sight of people like that; what they
are contradicts our whole way of thinking.
15 They are not like other people; they have
strange ways. 16 They think that our moral
standards are so corrupt that everything we do
should be avoided. They boast of having God
for their Father, and believe that when all is
said and done, only the righteous will be
happy. 17 But we'll see if that's true! Let's see
what will happen when it's time for them to
die! 18 If the righteous really are God's chil-
dren, God will save them from their enemies.
19 So let's put them to the test. We'll be cruel
to them, and torment them; then we'll find
out how calm and reasonable they are! We'll
find out just how much they can stand!
20 We'll condemn them to a shameful death.
After all, they say that God will protect them."

21 That is how evil people think, but they
are wrong. They are blinded by their own
wickedness. 22 They have never known God's
secrets, never hoped for the rewards of a
holy and blameless life. 23 When God created
us, he did not intend for us to die; he made
us like himself. 24 It was the Devil's jealousy
that brought death into the world, and those
who belong to the Devil are the ones who
will die.

The Destiny of the Righteous

3 But righteous people are protected by
God and will never suffer torment. 2 It is
a foolish mistake to think that righteous peo-
ple die and that their death is a terrible evil.
3 They leave us, but it is not a disaster. In fact,
the righteous are at peace. 4 It might appear
that they have suffered punishment, but they
have the confident hope of immortality.
5-6 Their sufferings were minor compared
with the blessings they will receive. God has
tested them, like gold in a furnace, and found
them worthy to be with him. He has accept-
ed them, just as he accepts the sacrifices
which his worshipers burn on the altar.

7 When God comes to reward the righ-
teous, they will blaze out against the wicked
like fire in dry straw. 8 They will rule over
nations and peoples, and the Lord will be
their king forever. 9 Those who have put
their trust in God will come to understand
the truth of his ways. Those who have been
faithful will live with him in his love, for he
is kind and merciful to the ones whom he
has chosen.[a]

The Destiny of the Wicked

10 The ungodly, however, will get the pun-
ishment their wicked thoughts deserve,
because they rebelled against the Lord and
ignored what was right.[b] 11 A man who has
no use for wisdom or education has a miser-
able life in store for him. He has nothing to
hope for. His labors are useless, and he will
never accomplish anything worthwhile.
12 The woman he marries will turn out to be
irresponsible, and his children will go wrong.
13 All his descendants will be under a curse.

[a] **3:9** *Some manuscripts add* and he protects his own people *(see 4:15).* [b] **3:10** what was right; *or* righteous people.

2:23 Gen 1:26, 27 **3:2** Wis 4:17 **3:5, 6** Rom 8:18; 2 Cor 4:17

The Importance of Virtue

On Judgment Day God will reward the
woman who has never been able to have a
child, provided she has not been guilty of
adultery. Then she will be happy. 14On that
day, even the man who has been castrated
will be rewarded with happiness, if he has
kept the Law and has not stored up resent-
ment against the Lord. Because he has been
faithful, he will receive a special reward more
precious than having children: a place in the
Lord's heavenly Temple. 15Honest deeds are
like a tree that bears marvelous fruit. Wis-
dom is like a root that is alive and can always
send up new shoots.

Wisdom is like a root that is alive and can always send up new shoots. (3:15)

16But children born of adultery or of a
forbidden union will die an early death.
17Yet even if they do live a long time, they
will never amount to anything. They will
not be respected in their old age, 18and if
they die young, they will have no hope or
comfort on Judgment Day. 19Children born
of a forbidden union suffer a miserable fate.

4 It is better to have virtue, even if it
means having no children. Your virtue
will be recognized by other people and by
God, and you will be remembered for it for-
ever. 2Virtue provides an example for people
to follow; when it is not there, they miss it. It
has always been the finest prize a person can
win, and it always will be so. It is the noblest
of all the good qualities a person can have.

3No matter how many children are born
of a forbidden union, none of them will ever
amount to anything. They are illegitimate;
they can never lay a firm foundation for
themselves, never take deep root. 4Like trees
with shallow roots, they put out leaves for a
while, but they sway in the wind, and storms
uproot them. 5Their branches snap off
before they mature; their fruit never ripens,
and it is good for nothing. 6On Judgment
Day children born of a forbidden union will
testify to the sin of their parents and act as
witnesses against them.

7Righteous people, however, will find rest,
even if they die young. 8We honor old age,
but not just because a person has lived a
long time. 9Wisdom and righteousness are
signs of the maturity that should come with
old age.

The Example of Enoch

10Once there was a man named Enoch
who pleased God, and God loved him.
While Enoch was still living among sinners,
God took him away, 11so that evil and false-
hood could not corrupt his mind and soul.
(12We all know that people can be so fasci-
nated by evil that they cannot recognize
what is good even when they are looking
right at it. Innocent people can be so cor-
rupted with desire that they can think of
nothing but what they want.) 13This man
Enoch achieved in a few years' time a per-
fection that other people could never attain
in a complete lifetime. 14The Lord was
pleased with Enoch's life and quickly took
him out of this wicked world. People were
aware of his departure but didn't understand.
They never seemed to learn the lesson 15that
God is kind and merciful to his own people;
he protects those whom he has chosen.

The Fate of the Wicked

16Even when righteous people are dead
and gone, they put to shame the wicked
people who live on after them. In their old
age the wicked will be disgraced by young
people who have already achieved perfec-
tion. 17The wise may die young, but the
wicked will never understand that this is the
Lord's way of taking them off to safety.

4:1 Sir 16:3 **4:10–14** Gen 5:21–24; Sir 44:16; Heb 11:5

18 They make light of a wise person's death, but the Lord will soon be laughing at them. When they die, they will not be given an honorable burial. Even the dead will hold them in scorn and disgust forever. 19 God will throw them to the ground and make them speechless. Like buildings shaken from their foundations, they will be reduced to piles of ruins. They will be in torment. People will soon forget all about them. 20 They will come in fear to the Judgment, where their sins will be counted; they will stand condemned by their own lawless actions.

The Regrets of the Wicked

5 On that day someone righteous, full of confidence, will stand before those who oppressed him and made light of his labors. 2 They will be amazed to see him safe and will tremble with terrible fear. 3 Then they will regret what they did, and groaning in anguish they will say to each other: 4 "This is the one we made fun of. We thought he was a joke. What fools we were! We thought he was crazy to live the way he did, and when he died, we didn't honor him. 5 And now here he is, one of God's own children, with a place of his own among God's people. 6 We were the ones who wandered off the right road. We never lived in the light of righteousness; we never caught the first glimmer of its light. 7 All our lives we wandered across unmarked deserts, instead of following the road which the Lord wanted us to travel. And this lawlessness led us to ruin. 8 We were so proud of ourselves—we bragged about how rich we were—and now, what good has it done us? 9 All those things are gone now; they have disappeared like a shadow, like something you hear and then forget.

This is the one we made fun of! (5:4)

10 "A ship sails across the waves of the ocean, but when it is gone, it leaves no trace. You cannot tell it was ever there. 11 A bird flies through the air, but leaves no sign that it has been there. It speeds along, riding through the thin air by the force of its wings, leaving behind no trace of its passing. 12 An arrow splits the air when it is shot at a target, but at once the air closes up behind it, and no one can tell where it passed. 13 It is the same with us—we were born, and then we ceased to be. We left no sign of virtue behind us; we were destroyed by our wickedness."

14 What hope do wicked people have? Only the hope of straw blown about in the wind, the hope of ocean foam[c] that disappears in the storm, the hope of smoke in the breeze. Their hope lasts no longer than our memory of a guest who stays one day and leaves the next.

15 But the righteous live on forever. The Lord will reward them; the Most High will protect them. 16 He will give them royal splendor and a magnificent crown. He will shield them with his powerful arm. 17 He will go out into battle determined to defeat his enemies, and use the creation itself as a weapon. 18 Righteousness will be his armor, genuine justice will be his helmet, 19 holiness will be his invincible shield. 20 He will sharpen his stern anger into a sword, and the forces of nature will join him in battle against those who are foolish enough to oppose him. 21 Bolts of lightning will strike right on target, as if the Lord had made a bow out of the clouds and was shooting arrows. 22 Hailstones will beat down on his enemies with terrible force. The oceans and rivers will come rushing over them in a devastating flood. 23 Great windstorms will blow

[c] **5:14** ocean foam; *some manuscripts have* frost.
5:17–23 Eph 6:11–17

them away like straw. Lawlessness will be the ruin of the whole world. Evil actions will cause governments to fall.

The Responsibility of Rulers

6 So then, you kings, you rulers the world over, listen to what I say, and learn from it. [2]You govern many lands and are proud that so many people are under your rule, [3]but this authority has been given to you by the Lord Most High. He will examine what you have done and what you plan to do. [4]You rule on behalf of God and his kingdom, and if you do not govern justly, if you do not uphold the law, if you do not live according to God's will, [5]you will suffer sudden and terrible punishment. Judgment is especially severe on those in power. [6]Common people may be mercifully forgiven for their wrongs, but those in power will face a severe judgment. [7]The Lord of all is not afraid of anyone, no matter how great they are. He himself made everyone, great and common alike, and he provides for all equally, [8]but he will judge the conduct of rulers more strictly. [9]It is for you, mighty kings, that I write these words, so that you may know how to act wisely and avoid mistakes. [10]These are holy matters, and if you treat them in a holy manner, you yourselves will be considered holy. If you have learned this lesson, you will be able to defend yourselves at the Judgment. [11]So then, make my teaching your treasure and joy, and you will be well instructed.

The Value of Wisdom

[12]Wisdom shines bright and never grows dim; those who love her and look for her can easily find her. [13]She is quick to make herself known to anyone who desires her. [14]Get up early in the morning to find her, and you will have no problem; you will find her sitting at your door. [15]To fasten your attention on Wisdom is to gain perfect understanding. If you look for her, you will soon find peace of mind, [16]because she will be looking for those who are worthy of her, and she will find you wherever you are. She is kind and will be with you in your every thought.

[17]Wisdom begins when you sincerely want to learn. To desire Wisdom is to love her; [18]to love her is to keep her laws; to keep her laws is to be certain of immortality; [19]immortality will bring you close to God. [20]This desire for Wisdom can prepare you to rule a kingdom. [21]So then, you that rule the nations, if you value your thrones and symbols of authority, honor Wisdom so that you may rule forever.

Solomon Wishes to Share His Wisdom

[22]I will tell you what Wisdom is, and how she came to be. I will not keep anything secret. I will trace her history from the beginning and make knowledge of her open to all. I will not ignore any part of the truth. [23]No jealous desire to guard my own knowledge will make me hold back anything. Wisdom has nothing in common with such an attitude. [24]No indeed—the more wise people there are, the safer the world will be. A sensible king can be depended on to give his people this kind of security. [25]So then, learn what I am about to teach you, and you will profit from it.

A King Is Like Everyone Else

7 [1-2]Like every human being, I am mortal. I am a descendant of that first man, who was made from the soil. I was conceived from the sperm of a man, in the pleasure of intercourse. For nine months my flesh took shape in the blood of my mother's womb. [3]When I was born, I came into the world like anyone else. I began to breathe the same air we all breathe; and like everyone else, the first sound I made was a cry. [4]I was wrapped in cloths and cared for. [5]No king ever began life differently. [6]For all of us, there is one way into life, and there is one way out.

Solomon Declares His Love for Wisdom

[7]Realizing that I was only human, I prayed and was given understanding. The

6:3 Rom 13:1 **7:7** 1 Kings 3:6–9; Wis 9:1–18

Catholic Connections

The Gift of Wisdom

"Wisdom is more beautiful than the sun and all the constellations. She is better than light itself" (Wisdom 7:29).

The Wisdom of Solomon speaks of wisdom as if it were an actual person, a woman. Wisdom is something that men should seek and fall in love with, like they would fall in love with the ideal woman.

As Christians we expand on this theme. Wisdom is one of the gifts of the Holy Spirit (see Isaiah 11:2–3 and 1 Corinthians 12:8). We sometimes use Wisdom as a name for the Holy Spirit. The voice from inside our soul, which speaks to us and encourages us to follow God's wisdom, is the Holy Spirit's voice.

So wisdom is a godlike characteristic. When you use the gift of holy wisdom, you are acting in a godlike way. Developing the gifts of the Holy Spirit, such as the gift of wisdom, will help you be a better follower of Jesus and become more like God!

— Wisdom 7:22—8:1

spirit of Wisdom came to me. [8]I regarded
her more highly than any throne or crown.
Wealth was nothing compared to her. [9]Pre-
cious jewels could not equal her worth;
beside Wisdom all the gold in the world is a
handful of sand, and silver is nothing more
than clay. [10]I valued her more than health
and good looks. Hers is a brightness that
never grows dim, and I preferred it to any
other light.
[11]When Wisdom came to me, all good
things came with her. She brought me
untold riches. [12]I was happy with them all,
because Wisdom had brought them to me. I
had not realized before that she was the
source of all these things. [13]I was sincere in
learning from her, and now I am glad to
share what I learned. [14]No one can ever
exhaust the treasures of Wisdom. Use those
treasures and you are God's friends; he
approves of what you learn from her.
[15]I pray to God that my thoughts may be
worthy of what I have learned, and that I
may speak according to his will. He is Wis-
dom's guide; he gives correction to those
who are wise. [16]We are under his power and
authority—we ourselves, our words, all our
understanding and skills. [17]It is he who gave
me true knowledge of the forces of nature:
what the world is made of; how the ele-
ments behave; [18]how the calendar is deter-
mined by the movements of the sun, the
changing seasons, [19]the constellations, and
the cycles of years. [20]He has taught me
about the nature of living creatures, the
behavior of wild animals, the force of the
winds, the reasoning powers of human
beings, the different kinds of plants, and the
use of their roots as medicine. [21]I learned
things that were well known and things that
had never been known before, [22]because
Wisdom, who gave shape to everything that
exists, was my teacher.

The Nature of Wisdom

The spirit of Wisdom is intelligent and
holy. It is of one nature but reveals itself in
many ways. It is not made of any material
substance, and it moves about freely. It is

clear, clean, and confident; it cannot be
harmed.[d] It loves what is good. It is sharp
and unconquerable, [23]kind, and a friend of
humanity. It is dependable and sure, and has
no worries. It has power over everything,
and sees everything. It penetrates every spirit
that is intelligent and pure, no matter how
delicate its substance may be.

[24]Wisdom moves more easily than motion
itself; she is so pure that she penetrates
everything. [25]She is a breath of God's
power—a pure and radiant stream of glory
from the Almighty. Nothing that is defiled
can ever steal its way into Wisdom. [26]She is a
reflection of eternal light, a perfect mirror of
God's activity and goodness. [27]Even though
Wisdom acts alone, she can do anything. She
makes everything new, although she herself
never changes. From generation to genera-
tion she enters the souls of holy people, and
makes them God's friends and prophets.
[28]There is nothing that God loves more than
people who are at home with Wisdom.
[29]Wisdom is more beautiful than the sun
and all the constellations. She is better than
light itself, [30]because night always follows
day, but evil never overcomes Wisdom.

8 [1]Her great power reaches into every
part of the world, and she sets every-
thing in useful order.

Solomon's Love for Wisdom

[2]Wisdom has been my love. I courted her
when I was young and wanted to make her
my bride. I fell in love with her beauty. [3]She
glorifies her noble origin by living with
God, the Lord of all, who loves her. [4]She is
familiar with God's mysteries and helps
determine his course of action.

[5]Is it good to have riches in this life?
Nothing can make you richer than Wisdom,
who makes everything function. [6]Is knowl-
edge a useful thing to have? Nothing is bet-
ter than Wisdom, who has given shape to
everything that exists. [7]Do you love justice?
All the virtues are the result of Wisdom's
work: justice and courage, self-control and
understanding. Life can offer us nothing
more valuable than these. [8]Do you want to
have wide experience? Wisdom knows the
lessons of history and can anticipate the
future. She knows how to interpret what
people say and how to solve problems. She
knows the miracles that God will perform,
and how the movements of history will
develop.

[9]So I decided to take Wisdom home to
live with me, because I knew that she would
give me good advice and encourage me in
times of trouble and grief. [10]I thought to
myself, "Because of her I will be honored
wherever people come together. The old
men will respect me, even though I am
young. [11]They will find that my opinions
show deep insight, and those in power will
admire me. [12]When I am silent, they will
wait for me to speak, and when I speak,
they will pay attention. Even when I speak
at length, they will listen with concentra-
tion. [13]Because of Wisdom I will gain
immortality; I will live forever in the mem-
ory of those who come after me. [14]I will
hold power over nations and peoples;
[15]dreaded tyrants will be seized with fear at
the mention of my name. I will be famous,
as a good king and as a brave soldier.
[16]When I come home to Wisdom, I will
find contentment because there is no con-
flict or pain in living with her, only happi-
ness and joy."

[17]And so I thought it over: to be wedded
to Wisdom is to live forever, [18]to love her is
to be perfectly happy, to do her work is to
be rich beyond measure, to share her com-
pany is to have sound judgment, to converse
with her is to be honored. Then I was deter-
mined to take Wisdom as my bride. [19]I had a
pleasant personality even as a child. I had
been fortunate enough to receive a good
soul, or rather, I was given a sound body to
live in because I was already good. [20]Still, I
realized that I would never receive Wisdom
unless God gave her to me—and knowing
that only God could give her to me was
itself a sign of understanding. So I prayed,
begging the Lord with all my heart:

[d] **7:22** cannot be harmed; *or* does no harm.
8:2 Sir 15:2 **8:4** Prov 8:27–30

Solomon Prays for Wisdom

9 "God of my ancestors, merciful Lord, by your word you created everything. 2By your Wisdom you made us humans to rule all creation, 3to govern the world with holiness and righteousness, to administer justice with integrity. 4Give me the Wisdom that sits beside your throne; give me a place among your children. 5I am your slave, as was my mother before me. I am only human. I am not strong, and my life will be short. I have little understanding of the Law or of how to apply it. 6Even if someone is perfect, he will be thought of as nothing without the Wisdom that comes from you. 7You chose me over everyone else to be the king of your own people, to judge your sons and daughters. 8You told me to build a temple on your sacred mountain, an altar in Jerusalem, the city you chose as your home. It is a copy of that temple in heaven, which you prepared at the beginning. 9Wisdom is with you and knows your actions; she was present when you made the world. She knows what pleases you, what is right and in accordance with your commands. 10Send her from the holy heavens, down from your glorious throne, so that she may work at my side, and I may learn what pleases you. 11She knows and understands everything, and will guide me intelligently in what I do. Her glory will protect me. 12Then I will judge your people fairly, and be worthy of my father's throne. My actions will be acceptable.

13"Who can ever learn the will of God? 14Human reason is not adequate for the task, and our philosophies tend to mislead us, 15because our mortal bodies weigh our souls down. The body is a temporary structure made of earth, a burden to the active mind. 16All we can do is make guesses about things on earth; we must struggle to learn about things that are close to us. Who, then, can ever hope to understand heavenly things? 17No one has ever learned your will, unless you first gave him Wisdom, and sent your holy spirit down to him. 18In this way people on earth have been set on the right path, have learned what pleases you, and have been kept safe by Wisdom."

Wisdom Protected Adam

10 Wisdom protected the father of the world, the first man that was ever formed, when he alone had been created. She saved him from his own sinful act 2and gave him the strength to master everything on earth.

Cain Abandoned Wisdom

3But there was an unrighteous man who abandoned Wisdom; he destroyed himself by killing his brother in a fit of anger.

Wisdom Protected Noah

4Because of that sin, the earth was flooded, but Wisdom saved it again. She guided a righteous man in his flimsy wooden boat.

Wisdom Helped Abraham

5Once when the nations were frustrated in their wicked plans, Wisdom recognized a righteous man and kept him innocent in God's sight. She gave him strength to obey God's command in spite of his love for his son.

Wisdom Rescued Lot

6Wisdom rescued a righteous man while ungodly people were dying. He escaped the flames that destroyed the Five Cities. 7You can still see the evidence of their wickedness. The land there is barren and smoking. The plants bear fruit that never ripens, and a pillar of salt stands as a monument to one who did not believe. 8The people of those cities ignored Wisdom and could not tell right from wrong. Not only that, but the remains of their cities still remind us of the foolish way they lived, so that their failure can never be forgotten. 9But Wisdom rescued her servants from the danger.

9:1–18 1 Kings 3:6–9; Wis 7:7 **10:1, 2** Gen 1:26–28 **10:3** Gen 4:8–13 **10:4** Gen 7:1—8:22 **10:5** Gen 11:1–9; 12:1–3; 22:1–19 **10:6–9** Gen 19:1–29

Wisdom protects. (Numbers refer to verses of chapter 10)

Wisdom Protected Jacob

10A righteous man once had to escape
from his brother's anger, and Wisdom guided
him in the right way. She showed him God's
kingdom and allowed him to know about
holy things.[e] She made him prosperous and
successful in his work. 11When others were
greedy for what he had, and wanted to take
it away from him, Wisdom stood by him and

[e] **10:10** holy things; *or* angels.
10:10–12 Gen 27:43; 28:10–22; 32:24–30

made him rich. 12She protected him from
his enemies who were waiting for a chance
to attack him. She gave him victory in a
hard fight, so that he might realize that
nothing can make a person stronger than
serving God.

Wisdom Rescued Joseph

13Once a righteous man was sold into
slavery, but Wisdom did not abandon him.
She kept him safe from sin. She went to
prison with him 14and never left him until
she had given him power over an empire
and made him the ruler of people who had
once oppressed him. She let it be known
that a false accusation had been made against
him, and she gave him eternal honor.

Wisdom Led the Israelites Out of Egypt

15Wisdom once rescued an innocent and
holy people from a nation of oppressors.
16She entered the soul of one of God's ser-
vants and[f] stood up to dreaded kings by per-
forming miracles. 17She rewarded God's peo-
ple for their hardships. She guided them
along a miraculous journey. She gave them
shade during the day and brilliant starlight at
night. 18She led them through the deep
waters of the Red Sea, 19but she drowned
their enemies and washed their bodies up on
the shore. 20And so the righteous looted the
ungodly. They sang hymns to your holy
name, O Lord; together they praised you for
defending them. 21Wisdom gave speech to
those who could not speak; she even caused
babies to speak clearly.

Wisdom Led the Israelites through the Desert

11 Wisdom brought success to the peo-
ple of Israel through a holy prophet.
2They traveled across a desert where no one
lived and camped in places where no human
being had ever been. 3They stood up to
their enemies and fought them off. 4When
your people grew thirsty, they called to you,
Lord, and you gave them water flowing out
of solid rock. 5The disasters that punished
the Egyptians saved your people when they
were in trouble.

The Punishment of the Egyptians

6-8Because those enemies decreed that the
babies of your people should be killed, you
stirred up the sources of their everflowing
river and made it foul with blood.

In the desert you let your people go
thirsty, to give them a taste of how you had
punished their enemies. And then, when they
least expected it, you gave them plenty of
water. 9When they were being tested, even
though it was a merciful discipline, they
learned how wicked people were tortured
when you judged them in anger. 10You test-
ed your people, as parents test their children,
to warn them. But you judged their enemies
like a stern king and condemned them.
11They suffered, whether they were near
your people or far from them. 12Their sor-
row was doubled; they groaned as they
looked back on what had happened. 13When
they learned that their punishment had been
of benefit to your people, they realized that it
was your work, Lord. 14The Egyptians had
refused to have anything to do with that man
who, long before as a baby, had been thrown
out and exposed; but as things worked out,
they came to be amazed at him. The righ-
teous never suffered a thirst like theirs.

15Their wickedness misled them into silly
ideas, so that they worshiped snakes and
other disgusting animals, creatures without
any powers of reason. Because of this, you
punished them with millions of such ani-
mals, 16and taught them that punishment for
sin takes the same form as the sin itself.
17Your almighty power, Lord, created the
world out of material that had no form at
all. You could easily have punished those
people by sending an invasion of bears or
savage lions. 18You could have created new
and terrible animals, that could breathe fire
or roar and send out clouds of smoke, or

[f] **10:16** and; *or* who.

10:13, 14 Gen 37:12–36; 39:1–23; 41:37–44 **10:15–21** Ex 1:1—15:21 **11:1–5** Ex 15:22—17:16
11:15, 16 Ex 8:1–24; 10:12–15

You could have created new and terrible animals.
(11:18)

shoot out fearful sparks from their eyes.
19 You could have made animals like these
that would not have to attack those people
to kill them, but could scare them to death
just by looking at them. 20 But this was not
necessary. You could have pursued them with
your justice or struck them dead at the
slightest hint of your power. But you have
chosen to measure, count, and weigh every-
thing you do.

God Is Powerful and Merciful

21 You can show your great power any
time you wish, and no one can stand up
against it. 22 In your sight the whole world is
a grain of sand, barely heavy enough to tip a
pair of scales, a drop of dew on the ground
in the morning. 23 You are powerful enough
to do anything, but you are merciful to
everyone; you overlook our sins and give us
time to repent. 24 You love everything that
exists; you do not despise anything that you
have made. If you had not liked it, you
would not have made it in the first place.
25 How could anything last, if you did not
want it to? How could it endure, if you had
not created it? 26 You have allowed it all to
exist, O Lord, because it is yours, and you
love every living thing.

12 Your immortal spirit is in every one
of them, 2 and so you gently correct
those who sin against you. You remind them
of what they are doing, and warn them
about it, so that they may abandon their evil
ways and put their trust in you, Lord.

The Sins of the Canaanites

3-4 You hated the people who lived in
your holy land long ago, because they did
horrible things: they practiced magic and
conducted unholy worship; 5 they killed chil-
dren without mercy and ate the flesh and
blood of human beings. They were initiated
into secret rituals[g] 6 in which parents mur-
dered their own defenseless children. It was
your will for our ancestors to destroy these
people, 7 so that the land which you consider
the most precious of all lands would be a
suitable home for your people. 8 But even in
this you showed mercy toward their ene-
mies, since they were only human beings.
You sent hornets ahead of your army, to
destroy the enemy gradually. 9 You could
have allowed the righteous to destroy those
ungodly people in battle; you could have
wiped them out immediately with wild ani-
mals or with one harsh command. 10 But
instead, you carried out your sentence grad-
ually, to give them a chance to repent, even
though you knew that they came from evil
stock, that they had been wicked since birth,
and that they would never change their way
of thinking. 11 Their whole nation was
cursed from the start, and though you had
not punished them for their sins, it was not
because you were afraid of anyone.

God Is Sovereign

12 You created those wicked people, and
no one can speak in their defense or con-
demn you for destroying them. No one can
question what you have done or challenge
your judgment. 13 All things are under your
care, and there is no other god to whom you
must justify your decisions. 14 No king or
ruler on earth can accuse you of punishing
those people unfairly. 15 You are righteous,

[g] **12:5** They were . . . rituals; *Greek unclear.*
12:3–7 Deut 12:31; 18:9–13 **12:8** Ex 23:28

and you rule everything righteously. You have never used your power to condemn a person who does not deserve to be punished. 16 Your strength is the source of justice. You can show mercy to everyone, because you are the Lord of all. 17 You show your strength when people doubt that your power is perfect, and you punish anyone who knows your power but dares to ignore it. 18 Even though you have absolute power, you are a merciful judge. You could take action against us whenever you like, but instead, you rule us with great patience.

19 By the things you have done you have taught your people that a person who is righteous must also be kind. You have given your people abundant hope by allowing them to repent of their sins. 20 You were very careful and patient in punishing your people's enemies; even when they deserved to die, you gave them every opportunity to give up their sinful ways. 21 But you judged your own people very strictly, even though you had made covenants with their ancestors and had solemnly promised to give them good things.

22 Yes, you punish us, but you punish our enemies ten thousand times more, so that when we judge others, we may remember your goodness, and when we are being judged, we may look for mercy.

The Punishment of the Egyptians

23 And so you tormented those who were foolish enough to live wickedly—you tormented them with the horrible things they worshiped. 24 They had wandered far away from the truth and worshiped the most disgusting and horrible animals. They were deceived as easily as little children. 25 And so you punished them for their stupidity, and your judgment made them look like fools. 26 It was a light punishment, but those who pay no attention to such warnings deserve to feel the full weight of God's judgment. 27 When they were punished with those creatures they considered gods, they became bitterly disillusioned and recognized that the true God was the one they had always refused to acknowledge. That is why they suffered the final punishment.

The Foolishness of Nature Worship

13 Anyone who does not know God is simply foolish. Such people look at the good things around them and still fail to see the living God. They have studied the things he made, but they have not recognized the one who made them. 2 Instead, they suppose that the gods who rule the world are fire or wind or storm or the circling stars or rushing water or the heavenly bodies. 3 People were so delighted with the beauty of these things that they thought they must be gods, but they should have realized that these things have a master and that he is much greater than all of them, for he is the creator of beauty, and he created them. 4 Since people are amazed at the power of these things, and how they behave, they ought to learn from them that their maker is far more powerful. 5 When we realize how vast and beautiful the creation is, we are learning about the Creator at the same time.

6 But maybe we are too harsh with these people. After all, they may have really wanted to find God, but couldn't. 7 Surrounded by God's works, they keep on looking at them, until they are finally convinced that because the things they see are so beautiful, they must be gods. 8 But still, these people really have no excuse. 9 If they had enough intelligence to speculate about the nature of the universe, why did they never find the Lord of all things?

The Foolishness of Idolatry

10 But the most miserable people of all are those who rest their hopes on lifeless things, who worship things that have been made by human hands—images of animals artistically made from gold and silver, or some useless stone carved by someone years ago. 11 A skilled woodworker may saw down some suitable tree, carefully strip off the bark, and then, with skillful craftsmanship, make from it an object that will serve some useful purpose. 12 He will take the leftover pieces and use them as firewood to cook a meal that he can sit down to and enjoy. 13 But among that scrap wood he may take one piece that isn't

13:10—14:31 Isa 44:9–20; Jer 10:1–16; Bar 6:8–73

good for anything—maybe it's crooked and full of knots—and carefully carve it in his leisure time, using spare moments to shape it into the crude image of a person, [14]or maybe of some worthless animal. He paints it all over with red, covering up every flaw in the work. [15]Then he prepares a suitable place in the wall for it and fastens it in place with iron nails. [16]He is careful to keep it from falling, because he knows it is only an idol and needs help; it cannot help itself. [17]But he is not ashamed to pray to this lifeless thing about his marriage, his children, and his possessions. [18]It is weak, but he prays to it for health. It is dead, but he prays to it for life. It has no experience, but he prays to it for help. It cannot walk, but he prays to it for a successful journey. [19]Its hands have no power, but he asks it to help him—in business, in making money, and in his work.

. . . It is dead, but he prays to it for life. (13:18)

Wooden Idols Compared with Noah's Wooden Boat

14 In the same way, a man getting ready to sail on the raging sea will call for help from a piece of wood that is not as strong as the ship he is about to board. [2]Someone designed the ship out of a desire for profit, and a craftsman built it with skill. [3]But it is your care, O Father, that steers it; you give it a safe path through the waves of the sea. [4]People may go to sea even if they have no skill, because you can save them from any danger. [5]It is your will that the things you have made by your wisdom should be put to use. And so people can cross the sea in a boat and come safely to land, because they trust their lives to that small piece of wood.

[6]This was how it was in ancient times, when a proud race of giants was dying away. The hope of the world escaped on such a boat under your guidance and left the world a new generation to carry on the human race. [7]A blessing was on Noah's wooden boat that allowed righteousness to survive, [8]but a curse is on an idol made by human hands. A curse is also on the one who makes it, because he works on this perishable thing and then calls it a god. [9]Ungodly people and these ungodly things they make are equally hated by God, [10]who will punish both the things made and the people who made them. [11]And so God's judgment will fall on pagan idols, because, even though they are made from something God created, they became horrible things that trap the souls of foolish people.

The Origins of Idolatry

[12]Sexual immorality began when idols were invented. They have corrupted human life ever since they were first made. [13]Idols have not always existed, nor will they exist forever. [14]It was human pride that brought them into the world, and that is why a quick end has been planned for them.

[15]Once there was a father who was overwhelmed with grief at the untimely death of his child, so he made an image of that child who had been suddenly taken from him. He then honored a dead human being as a god, and handed on secret rituals and ceremonies to those who were under his authority. [16]As time went on, this ungodly custom became stronger. Finally it became law, and idols were being worshiped at the command of powerful rulers. [17]When people lived too far away to honor a ruler in his presence but were eager to pay honor to this absent king, they would imagine what he must look like, and would then make a likeness of him. [18]The ambitious artists who made these likenesses caused this worship to spread, even among people who did not know the king. [19]An artist might want to please some ruler, and so he would use his skill to make the likeness better looking than the actual person. [20]Then people would be so attracted by the work of art, that the one whom they had

earlier honored now became the object of their worship. [21]So all this became a deadly trap, because people who were grieving, or under royal authority, would take objects of stone or wood, and give them the honor reserved for the One God.

The Results of Idolatry

[22]One thing led to another. It was not enough to be wrong about the knowledge of God. They lived in a state of evil warfare, but they were so ignorant that they called it peace. [23]They murdered children in their initiation rituals, celebrated secret mysteries, and held wild ceremonial orgies with unnatural practices. [24]They no longer kept their lives or their marriages pure. A man might kill another by an act of treachery or cause him grief by committing adultery with his wife. [25]Everything was a complete riot of bloody murder, robbery, deceit, corruption, faithlessness, disorder, falsehood, [26]harassment of innocent people, ingratitude, moral decay, sexual perversion, broken marriages, adultery, and immorality. [27]The worship of idols, whose names should never be spoken, is the beginning and the end, the cause and the result of every evil. [28]People who worship them lose control of themselves in ecstasy, or pass off lies as prophecies, or live wickedly, or break their word without hesitation. [29]They tell lies under oath and expect no punishment, because the idols they put their trust in are lifeless. [30]But punishment will finally catch up with them, for two reasons: first, they were in error about God when they worshiped idols, and second, they had so little regard for holiness that they made false statements to deceive people. [31]When unrighteous people commit sin, they will be hunted down, not by the power of whatever thing they swear by, but by the punishment that sinners deserve.

The True God Gives Immortality

15 But you, our God, are kind and true and patient. You rule the universe with mercy. [2]Even if we sin, we know your power and are still yours. But because we know that we belong to you, we will not sin. [3]Knowing you is perfect righteousness. Recognizing your power is where immortality begins. [4]We have not been misled by any evil product of human skill, by any useless object painted by some artist, or by any idol smeared with different colors. [5]The sight of such things arouses the passions of foolish people and makes them desire a dead, lifeless image. [6]Anyone who makes such a thing or desires it or worships it is in love with something evil, and gets what he deserves when he places his hopes in it.

The Foolishness of Worshiping Clay Idols

[7]A potter works the soft clay and carefully shapes each object for our use. Some things he makes are put to good use, and some are not, but he makes them all from the same clay, and shapes them in the same manner. The potter himself decides which objects shall be used for what purposes. [8]He is a human being who was himself formed from earth only a short while earlier, and after a little while, when he must return the soul

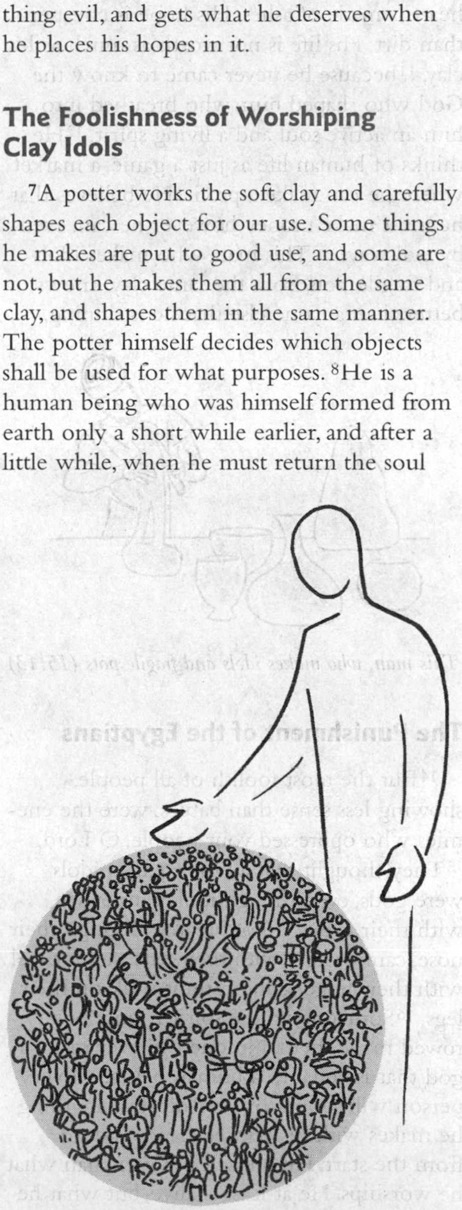

You rule the universe with mercy. (15:1)

that was lent to him, he will go back to the
same earth. He is a human being, but he
wastes his labor shaping a useless god out of
the same clay that he uses to make pots. 9His
life will be short, and he will soon have to
die, but he is not concerned about that. He
wants to compete with those who work in
gold, silver, and bronze, and make things like
they do. He takes great pride in the things
he makes, but they are counterfeit. 10His
heart is made of ashes. His hope is cheaper
than dirt. His life is not worth as much as his
clay, 11because he never came to know the
God who shaped him, who breathed into
him an active soul and a living spirit. 12He
thinks of human life as just a game, a market
where he can make a profit. He believes that
he must make money however he can, even
by evil ways. 13This man, who makes idols
and fragile pots from the same clay, knows
better than anyone else that he is sinning.

This man, who makes idols and fragile pots (15:13)

The Punishment of the Egyptians

14But the most foolish of all people,
showing less sense than babies, were the enemies who oppressed your people, O Lord.
15They thought that all their pagan idols
were gods, even though idols cannot see
with their eyes, cannot breathe through their
nose, cannot hear with their ears, cannot feel
with their fingers, and cannot walk on their
legs. 16Someone whose spirit is only borrowed made them. No one can ever make a
god that is equal to a human being. 17Every
person will sooner or later die, but anything
he makes with his wicked hands is dead
from the start. He himself is better than what
he worships. He at least is alive, but what he
worships is not, and never has been. 18Such
people worship the most disgusting animals,
including even the least intelligent ones.
19Even as animals they are not attractive
enough to make anyone want them. God
himself passed them by when he put his
approval and blessing on the rest of creation.

16 1And so it was appropriate that these
people were punished by such creatures—tormented by swarms of them.

2But you, O Lord, did not punish your
people in this way; instead, you showed them
kindness. You sent them quails to eat, a rare,
delicious food to satisfy their hunger. 3You
did all this so that the idolaters, when they
were hungry, would be unable to eat because
of the disgusting creatures sent to them. Your
people, however, suffered hunger only a
short while, and then they ate the finest
food. 4It was necessary for the oppressors to
suffer relentless need, while your people saw
how their enemies were being tormented.

5When terrible, fierce snakes attacked
your people and were killing them with
their poison, you did not remain angry long
enough to destroy your people. 6This trouble
lasted for only a little while, as a warning.
Then you gave them a healing symbol, the
bronze snake, to remind them of what your
Law requires. 7If a person looked at that
symbol, he was cured of the snakebite—not
by what he saw, but by you, the savior of all
mankind. 8By doing this, you also convinced
our enemies that you are the one who rescues people from every evil. 9Our enemies
died from the bites of locusts and flies; no
way was found to cure them, because they
deserved to be punished by such creatures.
10But even poisonous snakes could not overcome your people, because you had mercy,
helped them, and cured them. 11They were
bitten so that they would remember your
commands, but they were quickly rescued, in
order to keep them from forgetting you
completely and depriving themselves of your
kindness. 12No medicine or ointment cured
them. They were restored to health by your
word, O Lord, the word which heals all
humanity. 13You have power over life and
death; you can bring a person to the brink

16:2 Ex 16:11–13; Num 11:31, 32 **16:5–7** Num 21:6–9

of death and back again. 14 A wicked person
may kill someone, but cannot bring the dead
person back to life or rescue a soul impris-
oned in the world of the dead.

Disastrous Storms Hit Egypt

15 No one can possibly escape from you.
16 Look at those ungodly people: they refused
to recognize you as God, so you punished
them with your great power. They were
overtaken by terrible storms of rain and hail
and were completely destroyed by fire. 17 The
most amazing thing was that the fire burned
all the more fiercely in the water, which
usually puts fire out. All the forces of nature
fight to defend those who are righteous.
18 At one point the flames died down, so that
they wouldn't destroy the creatures sent to
punish the ungodly. Those people had to
learn that they were being overtaken by your
judgment. 19 But at another point, when sur-
rounded by water, the flames burned more
fiercely than fire had ever burned before, and
so destroyed the crops on the land where
those unrighteous people lived.

The Israelites Receive Manna to Eat

20 But this disaster did not strike your peo-
ple. Instead, you gave them the food of
angels. From heaven you sent down bread
that was ready to eat, and they did not have
to prepare it. The food you gave delighted
everyone, no matter what his taste. 21 All this
showed how lovingly you care for your chil-
dren. That food satisfied the desire of every-
one who ate it; it was changed to suit each
person's taste. 22 It was food that under nor-
mal circumstances would vanish away like
snow or ice, but now it did not melt even in
the fire. This was meant to teach your people
that the same fire that was destroying their
enemies' crops during the heavy downpour
of rain and hail 23 held back its power, so that
your own righteous people might have food.

24 You created the universe; it is at your
command. All creation uses its power to
punish unrighteous people, but it becomes
mild and kind to those who put their trust
in you. 25 Creation assumed all kinds of
forms to show how you provide generously
for all who pray to you.[h] 26 This happened so
that the people whom you loved, O Lord,
might learn that they are not fed by what
they can grow. It is your word that maintains
those who put their trust in you. 27 The food
that was not destroyed by the fire melted
when the first ray of sunlight warmed it.
28 This was to teach us that we must get up
before daybreak to give you thanks, and pray
as the sun comes up. 29 But an ungrateful
person's hope will melt away like frost, and
drain away like water that is not being used.

Terror Strikes the Egyptians at Night

17 O Lord, your acts of judgment are
marvelous and hard to explain; that
is why people who had not been taught
about them went astray. 2 When lawless peo-
ple imagined that they had your holy nation
in their power, they were themselves impris-
oned in a long night of darkness. They lay in
their own houses, shut off from your eternal
care. 3 They thought that their sins had been
secret and unnoticed, shielded from view by
a dark curtain of forgetfulness, but now they
were horribly afraid, confused, and terrified
by ghostly forms. 4 Not even the dark cor-
ners where they lay could protect them from
fear. They were surrounded by horrible nois-
es; grim ghosts with gloomy faces appeared
before their eyes. 5 No fire had power to give
them light, and the brilliant stars could do
nothing to relieve that deathly darkness.
6 There was only a dreadful fire, lit by no
human hand, that shone on them, and in
their terror they believed that the real world
was even worse than the things they imag-
ined. 7 The illusions produced by their magic
tricks were put to shame, and all the wisdom
they had boasted of came to nothing. 8 They
had claimed they could drive away all the
fears and illnesses of sick minds, but now
they themselves were sick with silly, ground-
less fears. 9 Even though nothing dangerous
had actually happened, they were terrified by
hissing snakes and animals advancing on
them. 10 And so they died, shaking with fear,

[h] **16:25** pray to you; *or* are in need.
16:20–29 Ex 16:1–36

afraid even to open their eyes, yet unable to
keep them shut.
11 Wickedness is cowardly in itself and
stands self-condemned.[i] Someone with a
guilty conscience will always imagine things
to be worse than they really are. 12 Fear is
nothing but the failure to use the help that
reason gives. 13 When you lack the confi-
dence to rely on reason, you give in to the
fears caused by ignorance.
14 All night long those people slept the
same restless sleep, even though the night
held no power over them, since it came from
the powerless depths of the world of the
dead. 15 They were chased by hideous forms
and lay paralyzed as they surrendered them-
selves to the sudden, unexpected fear that
came over them. 16 People would suddenly
collapse and lie locked in the chains of their
own fear. 17 Farmers, shepherds, and laborers
out in the countryside were captured by the
same inevitable fate and bound in the dark-
ness by the same invisible chain. 18-19 They
were panic-stricken by the sighing of the
wind or by the singing of birds in the trees
or by the roar of rushing water or by the
rumble of falling rock or by the sound of
unseen creatures running about or by the
savage roaring of wild animals or by the
echoes from the mountains. 20 In the full
light of day, the rest of the world went about
its business undisturbed. 21 Only those people
were covered by this heavy night, a foretaste
of the darkness of death that was waiting for
them. They were a burden to themselves that
was even heavier than the darkness.

Light Shines on the Israelites

18 Yet all the while a brilliant light was
shining for your holy people. Their
enemies heard their voices, but couldn't see
them. They envied the good fortune of your
people, who were not suffering. 2 Those ene-
mies could at least be thankful that the peo-
ple they had wronged were not taking
vengeance on them now, and so they begged
them to leave.[j]
3 Then you guided your people as they
traveled through a country they did not
know. You guided them with a pillar of fire.
It was like a sun that would not harm them
on that glorious journey. 4 But their enemies,
who were not allowed to see the light,
deserved to be prisoners in darkness, because
they had made prisoners of your people. And
it was through your people that the eternal
light of the Law was going to be given to
the world.

The Death of the Egyptian First-Born

5 When your enemies were carrying out
their resolve to kill the babies of your holy
people, there was one child who was aban-
doned but later rescued. Then you punished
your enemies by killing a great number of
their own children. You drowned their
whole army at one time in the rushing
waters. 6 But our ancestors had been told in
advance of what would happen that night, so
that they would be cheered and encouraged
by confident trust in your promises to them.
7 Your people knew that you would rescue
the righteous nation and destroy their ene-
mies. 8 With the same act you punished our
enemies and did us the glorious honor of
calling us to yourself.
9 During all this time devout people from
this righteous nation were secretly offering
sacrifices, giving their word to each other
that they would keep God's law and share
each other's blessings and dangers. Already
they were chanting those ancient hymns of
praise. 10 But their enemies' pitiful cries of
grief echoed everywhere, as they mourned
for their dead children. 11 Masters suffered
the same punishment as their slaves; the king
endured the same loss as the common peo-
ple. 12 There were too many dead bodies to
count. There were not enough people left to
bury them all. In a single moment their
dearest children died; all of them met death
in the same way. 13 These people had paid no
attention to any warning, but relied instead
on their magical powers. But when their
first-born sons were killed, then they recog-
nized that Israel was God's son.

[i] **17:11** Wickedness . . . self-condemned; *Greek unclear.* [j] **18:2** begged them to leave; *or* begged their forgiveness for their past hostility.

18:1–4 Ex 13:17–22

14 The short night was half over, and all was quiet and peaceful, 15 when suddenly your threats were carried out! An invincible word of judgment sped from your royal throne in heaven, straight down to that doomed land. It came like a soldier in fierce attack, 16 carrying out your firm command with a fearful weapon, standing with feet on the ground and head touching the sky, filling the land with death. 17 At that moment the people who were about to die had terrible nightmares and were seized by sudden fear. 18 All over the land they lay half-dead and let it be known why they were dying. 19 They knew why they were dying, because their horrible dreams had told them.

Aaron's Prayer Saves the Israelites from Death

20 Death also came to the righteous nation, for an epidemic struck many of them while they were in the desert, but your anger did not last long. 21 There was a certain blameless man who quickly took action to defend them. Acting as their priest, Aaron offered prayers and burned the incense used in asking forgiveness of sins. With prayers and incense as his weapons, he withstood your anger and ended the disaster. By doing this he proved that he was your servant. 22 He overcame the bitter difficulty,[k] but not by his own strength or by military force. Instead, he used prayer to stop the punishment, appealing to the promises you solemnly gave to our ancestors. 23 Dead bodies were already lying in piles, but he stepped in to hold your anger back and to keep it from harming those who were left alive. 24 He wore a long robe decorated with symbols of the universe. In honor of our ancestors he wore four rows of engraved stones on his chest, and your own majesty was represented by the ornament on his turban. 25 The Angel of Death was afraid of these things, and gave up. It was only a slight experience of your wrath, but it was enough.

[k] **18:22** *Probable text* bitter difficulty; *Greek* crowd.
18:20–25 Num 16:41–50

The Suicidal Stupidity of the Egyptians

19 But the godless continued to feel your pitiless anger until the very end. You knew what they would do before they did it. 2 You knew that even though they let your people go and made them leave quickly, they would change their minds and pursue them. 3-4 While the Egyptians were still mourning at the graves of their dead, they forgot why all this had happened, and they foolishly decided that the people they had begged to leave were runaways. So they chased after them. They were led into this as part of the punishment they deserved, so that they would suffer the rest of the torments they were due to receive. 5 They were to meet a strange death, while your people continued on their miraculous journey.

God Guides and Protects His People

6 The whole nature of the universe was changed at your command so that your people would not be harmed. 7 They saw the cloud over their camp and dry land where water had been. There was a grass-covered plain between the stormy waves of the Red Sea, making it easy for them to cross over. 8 All your people, under your protection, saw this miracle and went across. 9 They pranced about like horses let out to pasture; they skipped about like lambs and praised you, Lord, for saving them. 10 They still remembered what life had been like when they were slaves—how the earth bred gnats instead of cattle, how the river produced huge numbers of frogs instead of fish. 11-12 Later, when they desperately wanted better food, quails came up from the sea to satisfy their hunger. The quail was a bird they had never seen before.

The Punishment of the Egyptians

13 But violent thunder gave warning of the punishment that was coming on those

sinners. They suffered a well-deserved pun-
ishment for their great wickedness. No
nation had ever hated strangers so bitterly.
14Other people had been known to refuse
welcome to strangers who came to them,
but these people made slaves of those who
were their guests and who had shown them
kindness. 15Every nation will be punished if
it does not welcome foreigners, 16but these
people, who had earlier welcomed the for-
eigners with happy celebrations and treated
them as equals, later made them suffer cru-
elly. 17These people were also struck with
blindness, like the men of Sodom who
came to the door of that righteous man
Lot. They found themselves in total dark-
ness, as each one groped around to find his
own door.

God's Miraculous Power

18On a harp each string keeps its own
pitch, but each sound can be combined with
others to make different melodies. That is
how it was in those days, when the very ele-
ments entered into new combinations. Look
at what happened! 19Land animals took to
the water, and swimming creatures came up
on the land. 20Fire burned even in water,
which could not put it out. 21And yet the
flames could not burn the flesh of the per-
ishable creatures walking in them and did
not melt that heavenly food that would ordi-
narily have melted like frost.

22Lord, you have made your people
great—glorious in all respects. You have
never neglected them. You have given them
help, always, everywhere.

THE BOOK OF Sirach (ECCLESIASTICUS)

Some of the advice in this book might sound out-of-date. Like something your grandfather would say. Actually, somebody's grandfather did say it years before the birth of Jesus. But it is still good advice today!

The author of this book, Jesus son of Sirach, was a wise Jewish teacher who lived in Jerusalem during a time of great change. He saw many Jews forget the ways of their faith and instead accept the Greek customs and beliefs. The author wrote down all kinds of Jewish wisdom. He wrote for the older generation, who were forgetting, and for the younger generation, who had never learned traditional Jewish beliefs. Then his grandson translated it into Greek, so everyone could appreciate the wisdom of the Jewish faith.

Chap. 3

Headlines

- Youth: Prepare for Difficult Times (2:1–18)
- Advice on Friendship (6:5–17)
- Honor Your Parents (7:27–28)
- Self-Respect Wins Respect (10:28–29)
- Appearances Can Be Deceiving (11:2–6)
- Only Fools Curse (23:13–15)
- The Works of God Are Beautiful! (43:13–33)

FACTOIDS

Who wrote this book? It was written by Jesus son of Sirach, who lived in the second century BC. It was later translated into Greek by his grandson.

Why was it written? To remind the Jews that traditional Jewish wisdom was better than modern Greek ideas.

What literary style is used? It is a collection of prayers, sayings, hymns, lists, and general advice.

Jesus connection: Jesus' parable about the rich fool (Luke 12:16–21) is very similar to Sirach 11:18–19.

Important themes

- God rewards those who do good and punishes the sinful.
- Small sins can lead to bigger sins.
- We should follow the example of our elders and the great heroes of our faith.

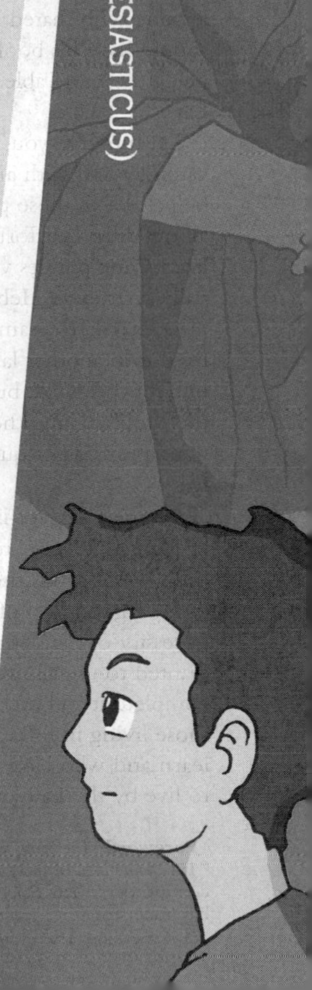

SIRACH

Foreword

The Law, the Prophets, and the later writers have left us a wealth of valuable teachings, and we should praise Israel for the instruction and wisdom they provide. But it is not enough that those who read them should gain understanding for themselves. Anyone who values learning should be able to help others by what he himself says and writes. That is why my grandfather Jesus devoted himself to reading the Law, the Prophets, and the other books of our ancestors. After he had mastered them, he was led to write a book of his own in order to share his wisdom and learning with others, so that anyone who shared his love for learning should have his book available as well, and be all the more able to live according to the Law.

Let me urge you, then, to read this book carefully and with an open mind. And please be patient in those places where, in spite of all my diligent efforts, I may not have translated some phrases vry well. What was originally written in Hebrew does not always have exactly the same sense when it is translated into another language.[a] That is true not only of this book, but even of the Law itself, the Prophets, and the other books. The translations differ quite a bit from the original.

I came to Egypt in the thirty-eighth year of King Euergetes' reign and stayed for some time. While I was there, I had the opportunity for a good deal of study and felt the necessity of translating the following book. I wanted to use all my diligence and skill to complete it and make it available for all those living in foreign lands who wish to learn and who have the strength of character to live by the Law of Moses.

In Praise of Wisdom

1 All wisdom comes from the Lord,
and Wisdom is with him forever.
2 Who can count raindrops or the sand along the shore?
Who can count the days of eternity?
3 How high is the sky? How wide is the earth?
How deep is the ocean? How profound is Wisdom?
Can anyone find answers to these questions?

Who can count raindrops? (1:2)

4 Wisdom was created before anything else;
understanding has always existed.[b]
6 Has anyone ever been shown where Wisdom originates?
Does anyone understand her subtle cleverness?[c]
8 There is only one who is wise,
and we must stand in awe before his throne.
9 The Lord himself created Wisdom;
he saw her and recognized her value,
and so he filled everything he made with Wisdom.

[a] **Foreword** *The book of Sirach was written in Hebrew, but the writer of this foreword translated it into Greek.*
[b] **1:4** *Some manuscripts add verse 5:* The source of Wisdom is the word of God on high; her ways are eternal commands. [c] **1:6** *Some manuscripts add verse 7:* To whom has the knowledge of Wisdom been revealed? Who has understood her great experience?
1:1 Prov 2:6 **1:9** Prov 8:22–31; Sir 24:9

10 He gave some measure of Wisdom to
everyone,
but poured her out on those who love
him.
11 If you fear the Lord, honor and pride will
be yours;
you will be crowned with happiness
and joy.
12 To honor the Lord is a heartfelt delight;
it will give you a long and happy life,
13 and at the end of your days all will go
well for you.
God will bless you on the day of your
death.
14 To fear the Lord is the first step to
Wisdom.
Wisdom is given to the faithful in their
mothers' wombs.
15 She has lived with us from ancient times,
and generations to come will rely on
her.
16 To fear the Lord is Wisdom at her fullest;
she satisfies us completely with her gifts
17 and fills our homes and our barns
with all that our hearts can desire.
18 To fear the Lord is the flower of Wisdom
that blossoms with peace and good
health.[d]
19 She sends knowledge and understanding
like the rain,
and increases the honor of those who
receive her.
20 To fear the Lord is the root of Wisdom;
her branches are long life.[e]

Self-control

22 There is no excuse for unjustified anger;
it can bring about your downfall. 23 Wait and
be patient, and later you will be glad you did.
24 Keep quiet until the right time to speak,
and you will gain a reputation for good sense.

Wisdom and Reverence for God

25 Wisdom has a treasury of wise sayings,
but sinners have nothing but contempt for
godliness. 26 If you want to be wise, keep the
Lord's commands, and he will give you Wis-
dom in abundance. 27 Fearing the Lord is
Wisdom and an education in itself. He is
pleased by loyalty and humility. 28 Be faithful
in the practice of your religion; when you
worship the Lord, do it with all your heart.
29 Be careful about what you say, and don't
be a hypocrite. 30 Don't be arrogant; you may
suffer a fall and be disgraced. The Lord will
reveal your secrets and humble you in front
of everyone in the synagogue, because you
did not come there with reverence for the
Lord, but with a heart full of hypocrisy.

Faithfulness to God

2 My child, if you are going to serve the
Lord, be prepared for times when you
will be put to the test. 2 Be sincere and
determined. Keep calm when trouble comes.
3 Stay with the Lord; never abandon him, and
you will be prosperous at the end of your
days. 4 Accept whatever happens to you.
Even if you suffer humiliation, be patient.
5 Gold is tested by fire, and human character
is tested in the furnace of humiliation. 6 Trust
the Lord, and he will help you. Walk straight
in his ways, and put your hope in him.
7 All you that fear the Lord, wait for him
to show you his mercy. Do not turn away
from him, or you will fall. 8 All you that fear
the Lord, trust him, and you will certainly be
rewarded. 9 All you that fear the Lord, look
forward to his blessings of mercy and eternal
happiness.
10 Think back to the ancient generations
and consider this: has the Lord ever disap-
pointed anyone who put his hope in him?
Has the Lord ever abandoned anyone who
held him in constant reverence? Has the
Lord ever ignored anyone who prayed to
him? 11 The Lord is kind and merciful; he
forgives our sins and keeps us safe in time of
trouble. 12 But those who lose their nerve are
doomed—all those sinners who try to have
it both ways! 13 Doom is sure to come for
those who lose their courage; they have no
faith, and so they will have no protection.
14 Doom is sure to come for those who lose

[d] **1:18** *Some manuscripts add:* He saw her and recognized her value *(see 1:9).* [e] **1:20** *Some manuscripts add verse 21:* Honoring the Lord takes sin away; where the fear of the Lord is found, it turns away anger.

1:17 Wis 7:11 **1:20** Prov 3:16; 4:10 **2:5** Wis 3:5, 6; 1 Pet 1:7

their hope. What will they do when the
Lord comes to judge them?
15 Those who fear the Lord do not dis-
obey his commands; those who love him
will live as he wants them to live. 16 Those
who fear and love the Lord will try to please
him and devote themselves to the Law.
17 Those who fear the Lord are always ready
to serve him. They humble themselves
before him, and say, 18 "We place our destiny
in the hands of the Lord, not in human
hands, because his mercy is as great as his
majesty."

Duties to Parents

3 Children, listen to me; I am your father.
Do what I tell you and you will be safe,
2 for the Lord has given fathers authority
over their children and given children the
obligation to obey their mothers. 3 If you
respect your father, you can make up for
your sins, 4 and if you honor your mother,
you are earning great wealth. 5 If you respect
your father, one day your own children will
make you happy; the Lord will hear your
prayers. 6 If you obey the Lord by honoring
your father and making your mother happy,
you will live a long life. 7 Obey your parents
as if you were their slave. 8 Honor your father

Obey the Lord by . . . making your mother happy. *(3:6)*

in everything you do and say, so that you
may receive his blessing. 9 When parents give
their blessing, they give strength to their
children's homes, but when they curse their
children, they destroy the very foundations.
10 Never seek honor for yourself at your
father's expense; it is not to your credit if he
is dishonored. 11 Your own honor comes
from the respect that you show to your
father. If children do not honor their moth-
ers, it is their own disgrace. 12 My child, take
care of your father when he grows old; give
him no cause for worry as long as he lives.
13 Be sympathetic even if his mind fails him;
don't look down on him just because you
are strong and healthy. 14 The Lord will not
forget the kindness you show to your father;
it will help you make up for your sins.
15 When you are in trouble, the Lord will
remember your kindness and will help you;
your sins will melt away like frost in warm
sunshine. 16 Those who abandon their par-
ents or give them cause for anger may as
well be cursing the Lord; they are already
under the Lord's curse.

Humility

17 My child, be humble in everything you
do, and people will appreciate it more than
gifts.[f] 18 The greater you become, the more
humble you should be; then the Lord will be
pleased with you.[g] 20 The Lord's power is
great, and he is honored by those who are
humble. 21 Don't try to understand things
that are too hard for you, or investigate mat-
ters that are beyond your power to know.
22 Concentrate on the Law, which has been
given to you. You do not need to know
about things which the Lord has not
revealed, 23 so don't concern yourself with
them. After all, what has been shown to you
is beyond human power to understand.
24 Many people have been misled by their
own opinions; their wrong ideas have
warped their judgment.[h]

[f] **3:17** *Hebrew* people . . . gifts; *Greek* those whom the Lord approves will love you. [g] **3:18** *Some Greek manuscripts add verse 19:* Many are exalted and esteemed, but God's secrets are revealed to the humble; *Hebrew:* God's mercy is great, and he reveals his secrets to those who are humble. [h] **3:24** *Some Greek manuscripts add verse 25:* If you have no eyes, you cannot see; don't claim to have knowledge if you don't have it; *Hebrew has, after verse 27:* If you have no eyes, you cannot see; if you have no knowledge, you cannot have Wisdom.

2:15, 16 Wis 6:18; Jn 14:15, 21, 23 **3:8** Ex 20:12 **3:18** Phil 2:3 **3:22** Deut 29:29

The greater you become, the more humble you should be. (3:18)

26 Stubbornness will get you into trouble at the end. If you live dangerously, it will kill you. 27 A stubborn person will be burdened down with troubles. Sinners go on adding one sin to another. 28 There is no cure for the troubles that arrogant people have; wickedness has taken deep root in them. 29 Intelligent people will learn from proverbs and parables. They listen well because they want to learn.

Giving to the Poor

30 Giving to the poor can make up for sin, just as water can put out a blazing fire. 31 Anyone who responds to others with acts of kindness is thinking of the future, because he will find help if he ever falls on hard times.

4 1 My child, don't prevent the poor from making a living, or keep them waiting in their need. 2 Never give a hungry person any cause for resentment or anger. 3 Don't add to the troubles of someone who is already desperate. If he is in need, don't put off giving to him. 4-5 Don't refuse to help a beggar who is in distress. Don't turn your back on a poor person or give him any reason to curse you. 6 If he becomes so bitter that he does curse you, his Creator will hear his prayer.

7 Make yourself popular in the synagogue. Bow your head to men of authority. 8 Listen to what the poor have to say, and answer them politely. 9 Protect people from those who want to wrong them, and be firm in your judgments. 10 Be like a father to orphans, and provide widows with the help their husbands can no longer give them. Then you will be like a child of the Most High, and he will love you more than your own mother does.

Wisdom as a Teacher

11 Wisdom takes care of those who look for her; she raises them to greatness. 12 Loving her is loving life itself; rising early to look for her is pure joy. 13 Anyone who obtains Wisdom will be greatly honored. Wherever he goes, the Lord will bless him. 14 Wisdom's servants are the servants of the Holy One, and the Lord loves everyone who loves her. 15 Those who obey her will give sound judgments;[i] those who pay attention to her have true security. 16 Put your trust in Wisdom, and you will possess her and pass her on to your descendants. 17 At first, Wisdom will lead you along difficult paths. She will make you so afraid that you will think you cannot go on. The discipline she demands will be tormenting, and she will put you to the test with her requirements until she trusts you[j] completely. 18 Then she will come to you with no delay, reveal her secrets to you, and make you happy. 19 But if you go astray, she will abandon you and let you go to your own ruin.

Self-confidence

20 Take advantage of opportunities, but guard yourself against evil. Don't underrate yourself. 21 Humility deserves honor and respect, but a low opinion of yourself leads to sin. 22 Do not let others have their way at your expense; do not bring on your own ruin by giving up your rights. 23 Never hesitate to speak out when the occasion[k] calls for it. Don't hide your wisdom.[l] 24 Your

[i] **4:15** *Hebrew* give sound judgments; *Greek* judge nations. [j] **4:17** she trusts you; *or* you trust her.
[k] **4:23** *Probable text* the occasion; *Greek* safety. [l] **4:23** *Hebrew* Don't hide your wisdom; *most Greek manuscripts do not have these words; other Greek manuscripts* Don't hide your wisdom for the sake of appearances.

wisdom and education can be known only by what you say. 25Do not, however, go against the truth, and remember that you do not know everything. 26Don't be ashamed to confess your sins; there's no point in trying to stop a river from flowing. 27Don't allow yourself to be dominated by someone who is stupid or show partiality to influential people. 28Stand up for what is right, even if it costs you your life; the Lord God will be fighting on your side.

29Don't be quick to speak or lazy and negligent in your work. 30Don't act like a lion at home or be suspicious of your servants. 31Don't stick out your hand to get something if you're going to be tightfisted when the time comes to pay it back.

Don't Be Presumptuous

5 Don't rely on money to make you independent. 2Don't think you have to have everything you want, and then spend your energy trying to get it. 3Don't think that no one can exercise authority over you; if you do, the Lord is certain to punish you. 4Don't think that you can sin and get away with it; the Lord does not mind waiting to punish you. 5Don't be so certain of the Lord's forgiveness that you go on committing one sin after another. 6Don't think that his mercy is so great that he will forgive your sins no matter how many they are. He does show mercy, but he also shows his furious anger with sinners. 7Come back to the Lord quickly. Don't think that you can keep putting it off. His anger can come upon you suddenly, and you will die under his punishment. 8Don't rely on dishonest wealth; it will do you no good on that day of disaster.

Sincerity and Self-control

9-10Be certain about what you believe and consistent in what you say. Don't try to please everyone or agree with everything people say.[m] 11Always be ready to listen, but take your time in answering. 12Answer only if you know what to say, and if you don't know what to say, keep quiet. 13Speaking can bring you either honor or disgrace; what you say can ruin you.

Answer only if you know what to say, and if you don't . . . keep quiet. (5:12)

14Don't get a reputation for being a gossip, and don't tell tales that will hurt people. Just as robbers will suffer disgrace, so liars will suffer severe condemnation. 15Do nothing destructive,[n] whether it seems insignificant or not,

6 1and do not be an enemy when you should be a friend. A bad reputation brings you the disgrace that lying sinners deserve. 2Do not let your passions carry you away; this can tear your soul to pieces like a bull.[o] 3You will be left like a dead tree without any leaves or fruit. 4Evil desire will destroy you and make you a joke to your enemies.

Friendship

5If you are polite and courteous, you will enjoy the friendship of many people. 6Exchange greetings with many, but take advice from only one person out of a thousand. 7When you make friends, don't be too quick to trust them; make sure that they have proved themselves. 8Some people will be your friends only when it is convenient

[m] **5:9–10** *Hebrew* everything people say; *Greek adds* That is what double-tongued sinners do. [n] **5:15** *Hebrew* Do nothing destructive; *Greek* Do not be ignorant in anything. [o] **6:2** *Verse 2 in both Greek and Hebrew is unclear.*

4:31 Acts 20:35 **5:4** Eccl 8:11

for them, but they won't stand by you in trouble. 9 Others will fall out with you over some argument, and then embarrass you by letting everyone know about it. 10-11 Others will sit at your table as long as things are going well; they will stick to you like your shadow and give orders to your servants, but they will not stand by you in trouble. 12 If your situation takes a turn for the worse, they will turn against you, and you won't be able to find them anywhere.

13 Stay away from your enemies and be on guard against your friends. 14 A loyal friend is like a safe shelter; find one, and you have found a treasure. 15 Nothing else is as valuable; there is no way of putting a price on it. 16 A loyal friend is like a medicine that keeps you in good health. Only those who fear the Lord can find such a friend. 17 A person who fears the Lord can make real friendships, because he will treat his friends as he does himself.[p]

Learn from Wisdom

18 My child, learn to value Wisdom while you are young, and you will still be able to find her when you grow old. 19 Work as hard to find Wisdom as a farmer works to plow and plant his fields; then you can expect a good harvest. You will have to work at it for a while, but you will soon be enjoying what you have earned. 20 Undisciplined people find Wisdom's demands too hard and don't have enough determination to meet them. 21 Her requirements are a burden heavier than they are willing to bear, and they quickly lay them aside. 22 "Discipline" means just that—discipline,[q] and not many people are able to discipline themselves.

23 My child, listen to me and take my advice. 24 Put Wisdom's chains around your feet and her yoke around your neck. 25 Carry her on your shoulder and don't be resentful of her bonds. 26 Follow Wisdom, and keep to her ways with all your heart. 27 Go looking for her, and she will reveal herself to you. Take hold of her and don't let go. 28 Then you will discover the peace of mind she offers, and she will become your joy. 29-30 The signs of slavery you wear will become signs of royal majesty. Her chains will be your protection, and you will wear her yoke like a magnificent robe. 31 You will wear Wisdom like a splendid crown.

32 My child, you can learn if you want to. You can be clever if you are determined to be. 33 If you are willing to listen, you will learn and become wise. 34 Go where the old people are; find someone who is wise, and stay with him. 35 Be ready to listen when religious people speak, and don't miss anything that shows insight. 36 If you find someone with understanding, get up early to call on him; wear out his doorstep with your visits.

37 Devote all your time to studying the Lord's commands and thinking about them. He will give you the insight and wisdom you are looking for.

Miscellaneous Advice

7 **1-2** If you do no wrong, no wrong will ever come to you. 3 Do not plow the ground to plant seeds of injustice; you may reap a bigger harvest than you expect.

4 Don't ask the Lord for a place of honor or ask the king for an important position. 5 Don't try to convince the Lord that you are righteous or make a show of your wisdom before the king. 6 Don't set your heart on being a judge, unless you have the strength of character it takes to put an end to injustice. If you let yourself be influenced by someone in a position of power, your integrity will be damaged. 7 Don't commit any crime against the general public, and don't disgrace yourself among your townspeople.

8 Don't commit the same sin twice. The punishment you get the first time ought to be enough.

9 Don't think that God Most High is going to take into account how very generous you are and so accept any offering you decide to make.

10 Never get tired of praying, and never miss a chance to give to the poor.

[p] **6:17** because . . . himself; *or* because his friends will also fear the Lord. [q] **6:22** *Hebrew* "Discipline" . . . discipline; *Greek* "Wisdom" . . . wisdom.

6:19 Jas 5:7, 8 **6:37** Josh 1:8; Ps 1:2

11 Don't laugh at someone who has been
humiliated. It is the Lord who humbles a
person, but the Lord also raises him up
again.
12 Don't think up lies to tell about your
friends. 13 Don't tell lies at all. It never does
any good.
14 In an official assembly, don't get up and
talk a lot of nonsense. And don't repeat
yourself when you pray.
15 Don't try to avoid farm work or other
hard labor; the Most High has given us these
jobs to do.
16 Don't join up with a crowd of sinners;
remember that the Lord's punishment is sure
to come.
17 Be very humble, because the decay of
death awaits us all.[r]

Relations with Others

18 Don't betray a friend for money. Don't
betray a real friend for all the gold in the
world.
19 Don't miss your chance to marry a wise
and good woman. A gracious wife is worth
more than gold.
20 Don't mistreat servants who do their
work well, or employees who do their best
for you.
21 Show the same love to wise servants
that you would show to yourself,[s] and let
them have their freedom.
22 Take good care of any animals you own.
If they make money for you, keep them.
23 If you have sons, educate them. Teach
them self-discipline while they are young.
24 If you have daughters, keep them virtu-
ous, and don't be too indulgent with them.
25 When you give your daughter in marriage,
you have finished a great task, but give her
to a sensible man.
26 If you have a good wife, do not divorce
her, but do not trust yourself to someone
you don't love.
27 Honor your father with all your heart,
and never forget how your mother suffered
when you were born. 28 Remember that you
owe your life to them. How can you ever
repay them for all they have done for you?
29 Fear the Lord with all your heart, and
have respect for his priests. 30 Love your Cre-
ator with all your strength, and give his min-
isters your support. 31 Honor the Lord and
respect the priests. Supply them with what
you have been commanded to give: the first
produce, the offering for sin, the shoulder of
the sacrificial animal—all the required sacri-
fices and offerings.
32 Give your help to the poor, and the
Lord will give you his perfect blessing. 33 Be
generous to every living soul, and be gra-
cious to the memory of the dead. 34 Show
sympathy to those who have lost a loved
one, and mourn with them. 35 Do not hesi-
tate to visit the sick. You will be loved for
things like these. 36 Whatever you do,
remember that some day you must die. As
long as you keep this in mind, you will never
sin.

Teach them self-discipline while they are young. (7:23)

Using Common Sense

8 Do not challenge a person who has
influence; you may fall into his power.
2 Do not quarrel with someone rich; he may
bribe people to turn against you. Gold has
destroyed many people and corrupted kings.
3 Don't argue with someone who talks too
much; you will just be adding fuel to his fire.
4 Don't make fun of someone who has bad
manners; he may insult your ancestors.

[r] **7:17** *Hebrew* the decay . . . all; *Greek* the punishment of the ungodly is fire and worms. [s] **7:21** *Hebrew* Show the same love . . . yourself; *Greek* Show love to a wise servant.
7:21 Ex 21:2; Deut 15:12–15 **7:27, 28** Ex 20:12

5 Don't criticize someone if he is already turning away from sin. Remember that we are all guilty. 6 Never think less of someone because he is old; some of us are growing old, too. 7 Don't be happy over the death of anyone; remember that all of us must die.

8 Do not disregard what the wise have said. Study their proverbs; from them you can learn to be cultured and to serve great people. 9 Pay attention to what old people say, for they learned from those who came before them. You can learn from them, and they can teach you how to have an answer ready when you need one.

10 You should not provide a sinner with more opportunity to sin. You might get hurt yourself; it's as easy as getting burned while adding logs to a fire. 11 You should not get up and walk out on someone who is insolent. He might twist your words and use them against you. 12 You should not lend anything to someone more powerful than you. If you do, you might as well consider it lost. 13 You should not guarantee anyone else's loan to an extent that you cannot afford. You must be prepared to pay any such guarantee. 14 You should not bring a lawsuit against a judge. He will win because of his position. 15 You should not travel with anyone who is reckless. It will cause you nothing but trouble. He will do any foolish thing he pleases, and you will die with him.

16 You should not get into an argument with anyone who has a hot temper or go to some place where the two of you will be alone. Violence means nothing to such a person, and he will attack you when there is no one to help you. 17 You should not ask a stupid person for advice. He will not be able to keep secret what you tell him. 18 You should not do anything in front of a stranger that should be kept secret. There is no way of knowing what will happen if you do. 19 You should not reveal your most private thoughts to anyone. If you do, you may as well throw away any chance of happiness.[t]

Advice about Women

9 Don't be jealous of the wife you love. You will only be teaching her how to do you harm. 2 Do not surrender your dignity to any woman. 3 Keep away from other men's wives[u] or they will trap you. 4 Don't keep company with female musicians; they will trick you. 5 Don't look too intently at a virgin, or you may find yourself forced to pay a bride price. 6 Don't give yourself to prostitutes, or you may lose everything you own. 7 So don't go looking about in the streets or wandering around in the run-down parts of town. 8 When you see a good-looking woman, look the other way; don't let your mind dwell on the beauty of any woman who is not your wife. Many men have been led astray by a woman's beauty. It kindles passion as if it were fire. 9 Don't sit down to eat with another man's wife or join her for a drink. You may give in to the temptation of her charms and be destroyed by your passion.

When you see a good-looking woman, look the other way. (9:8)

Friendships with Others

10 Never abandon old friends; you will never find a new one who can take their place. Friendship is like wine; it gets better as it grows older. 11 Don't be jealous of a sinner's success; you don't know what kind of disaster is in store for him. 12 Don't take

[t] **8:19** *Hebrew* If . . . happiness; *Greek* And don't let anyone do you a favor. [u] **9:3** *Hebrew* other men's wives; *Greek* immoral women.

9:1 Num 5:12–15

pleasure in the things that make ungodly people happy; remember that they will be held guilty as long as they live. 13If you keep away from someone who has the power to put you to death, you will not have to fear for your life; but if you must go near him, be very careful, or he may kill you. Be conscious that you are walking among hidden traps, that you are an easy target.

14Get to know the people around you as well as you can, and take advice only from those who are qualified to give it. 15Engage in conversation with intelligent people, and let the Law of the Most High be the topic of your discussions. 16Choose righteous people for your dinner companions. Your chief pride should be your fear of the Lord.

Rulers

17A skilled worker is admired for the things he makes, and a leader's wisdom is proved by his words. 18Someone who speaks rashly and recklessly is feared and hated by

10 everyone in town. 1A wise ruler will educate his people, and his government will be orderly. 2All the officials and all the citizens will be like their ruler. 3An uneducated king will ruin his people, but a government will grow strong if its rulers are wise. 4The Lord sees to the government of the world and brings the right person to power at the right time. 5The success of that person is in the Lord's hands. The Lord is the source of the honor given to any official.

Pride

6Don't be angry with someone for every little thing he does wrong. Don't do anything out of injured pride. 7Arrogance and injustice are hated by both the Lord and people. 8Injustice, arrogance, and wealth cause nations to fall from power, and others then rise to take their place. 9We are only dust and ashes; what have we got to be proud of? Our body decays even while we are alive.[v] 10A long illness puzzles the doctor.[w] Even a king may be alive today and dead tomorrow. 11When a person dies, all he then possesses is worms, flies, and maggots.

12Pride has its beginning when a person abandons the Lord, his maker. 13Pride is like a fountain pouring out sin, and whoever persists in it will be full of wickedness. That is why the Lord brought terrible punishments on some people and completely destroyed them. 14The Lord has overthrown kings and put humbler people in their place. 15The Lord has pulled up nations by the roots and established humbler ones in their place. 16The Lord has overthrown empires and completely devastated their lands. 17He destroyed some so completely that they are not even remembered any more. 18The Creator never intended for human beings to be arrogant and violent.

People Who Should Be Honored

19Who deserves honor? The human race does, because people fear the Lord. Who does not deserve honor? The human race does not, because people break the Lord's commands. 20A leader should be honored by those who follow him, and the Lord honors those who fear him.[x]

22Rich people, famous people, and poor people all take pride in their fear of the Lord. 23It is not right to refuse honor to a poor person who is intelligent, and it is not right to give honor to a sinner. 24People of influence, rulers, and judges will be honored, but none of them is greater than a person who fears the Lord. 25A slave who is wise will have free citizens serving him; and if they are sensible, they will not resent it.

Humility and Self-respect

26When you do your work, don't make a show of your skill, and don't try to put on a show when you are in trouble. 27It is better to work and have more than you need than to go around boasting but hungry.

28My child, keep your self-respect, but

[v] **10:9** Our body . . . alive; *this sentence in both Greek and Hebrew is unclear.* [w] **10:10** A long . . . doctor; *this sentence in both Greek and Hebrew is unclear.* [x] **10:20** *Some manuscripts add verse 21:* Success begins with fear of the Lord, but failure begins with stubbornness and arrogance.

10:14 1 Sam 2:8; Lk 1:52

remain modest. Value yourself at your true
worth. 29There is no excuse for a person to
run himself down. No one respects a person
who has no respect for himself. 30Poor peo-
ple can be honored for their good sense, and
rich people can be honored for their wealth.
31If someone is honored while he is poor,
think how much he will be honored if he
becomes rich! If someone is despised while
he is rich, think how much more he will be
11 despised if he becomes poor! 1If a
poor person is wise, he has good
reason to be proud, and he will be thought
of as someone great.

Appearances

2Do not compliment a person on his
good looks. On the other hand, do not look
down on someone who is unattractive.
3Compared to most flying things, a bee is
very small, but the honey it makes is the
sweetest of foods. 4Don't make fun of some-
one who has fallen on hard times and is
dressed in rags.[y] The Lord does wonderful
things that human beings never notice.
5Many are the kings who have ended their
careers sitting on the ground, while their
crowns were worn by those no one had
heard of before. 6Many are the rulers who
have suffered disgrace. Many are the famous
people who have fallen into the power of
others.

Be Cautious

7Before you start criticizing, get your facts
straight and think the matter through.
8Don't interrupt while someone is speaking;
hear what he has to say before you answer.
9Don't get into an argument over something
that is none of your business. Don't take part
in decisions that are being made by sinners.
10My child, don't get involved in too
many things. If you try to do too much, you
will suffer for it. You won't be able to finish
your work, and you won't be able to get
away from it either. 11For instance, here is
someone who never stops working like a
slave, but gets further behind all the time.

Live it!

Don't Judge a Book . . .

Have you ever heard an adult say, "Don't judge a book by its cover"? It means don't be fooled by the outside appearance of a person. Do not think that a good-looking person is brave or considerate or smart or trustworthy just because of good looks. And do not think that a plain-looking person is dull or afraid or uncaring or useless just because of plain looks.

Expensive clothes, jewelry, and shoes do not make a person a good friend. What's more important in a friend—money or trust? What's more important—good looks or a caring heart? What's more important—the color of a person's skin or a person's personality? As Sirach says, the bee is very small and ordinary, but it makes honey, something sweeter than anything a larger animal produces!

Money can make you spoiled and demanding. Popularity can make you selfish and inconsiderate. Don't be fooled! Sometimes the most unpopular students in school would make the nicest, most understanding, and appreciative friends. Good relationships are based on values deeper than money, good looks, or popularity. Remember that when you want to invite someone to a movie or a dance!

— Sirach 11:2–6

12On the other hand, someone else may be
very poor and not up to his task. He may be
slow, and he may need help, but the Lord is

[y] **11:4** *Hebrew* Don't . . . rags; *Greek* Don't take pride in fine clothes, and don't let compliments go to your head.

pleased with him and pulls him out of his bad situation. 13When he is back on his feet again, everyone is astounded.

14Everything comes from the Lord: success and failure, poverty and wealth, life and death. 15Wisdom, understanding, knowledge of the Law, love, and the doing of good deeds—all these come from the Lord. 16Error and darkness have been with sinners from the beginning, and those who enjoy evil will have it with them into their old age. 17The Lord's gifts to religious people are gifts that endure. If he approves of you, you will always be successful. 18Someone may grow rich by working hard and denying himself pleasure, but what does he get for it? 19He says to himself, "Now I can finally sit back and enjoy what I have worked for." But he has no idea how long it will be before he must die and leave his wealth to others.

20Stand by your duty and stick to it; grow old at your work. 21Don't be jealous of what sinners achieve; just stick to your own work, and trust the Lord. It is very easy for the Lord to make a poor person suddenly rich. 22Devout people will receive the Lord's blessing as their reward, and that blessing can be given in a moment. 23Don't be concerned about what you need, or what success the future holds for you. 24On the other hand, don't think that you have everything you need or that nothing can go wrong for you in the future. 25When things are going well, people don't think about hard times; and when things are going badly, they forget about prosperity. 26The Lord can easily wait until the day of our death to reward or punish us. 27At that time our deeds are open for all to see; all our happiness can be erased in that one moment of misery. 28So then, don't think of anyone's life as happy until it is over, because all the evidence is not in until the person is dead.[z]

Be Careful in Choosing Friends

29Be careful about the kind of person you invite into your home, because clever people can fool you in many ways. 30A proud person is a decoy to lure you into danger; like a spy, he will look for your weaknesses.[a] 31He will make good appear evil and find fault with the noblest actions. 32A single spark can set a pile of coals ablaze, and a sinner is just waiting for a chance to do violence. 33Watch out for such people and their evil plans; they will ruin you permanently. 34If you bring a stranger home with you, it will only cause trouble, even between you and your own family.

12 When you do a good deed, make sure you know who is benefiting from it; then what you do will not be wasted.[b] 2You will be repaid for any kindness you show to a devout person. If he doesn't repay you, the Most High will. 3No good ever comes to a person who gives comfort to the wicked; it is not a righteous act.[c] 4Give to religious people, but don't help sinners. 5Do good to humble people, but don't give anything to those who are not devout. Don't give them food, or they will use your kindness against you. Every good thing you do for such people will bring you twice as much trouble in return. 6The Most High himself hates sinners, and he will punish them. 7Give to good people, but do not help sinners.

8When things are going well, it is hard to tell who your real friends are, but in hard times you can recognize your enemies; 9even your friends will leave you then. But when you are successful, your enemies will act like friends.[d] 10Never trust an enemy; his

But when you are successful, your enemies will act like friends. (12:9)

[z] **11:28** *Hebrew* all . . . dead; *Greek* a man will be known by his children. [a] **11:30** *Hebrew* look . . . weaknesses; *Greek* wait for your downfall. [b] **12:1** what you do . . . wasted; *or* you will be thanked for what you do. [c] **12:3** *Hebrew* gives . . . act; *Greek* makes evil a habit or refuses to give to the poor. [d] **12:9** *Hebrew* act like friends; *Greek* be sorry.

11:18, 19 Ps 49:10; Lk 12:16–21 **12:1** Mt 7:6

wickedness is as destructive as rust. 11Watch out, and be on guard against him, even if he acts ever so humble. He is like a metal mirror that rusts away if you don't keep it polished. 12Seat an enemy at your right hand, and the next thing you know he'll be trying to get your own place of honor. Put him next to you, and he will overthrow you. Then you will realize the truth of my words, and be stung with regret when you remember them. 13Nobody feels sorry for snake charmers or wild animal tamers who get bitten, 14and nobody will feel sorry for you if you run around with sinners and get involved in their wrongdoing.

15An enemy will stay with you for a while, but not when trouble comes. 16He will speak fine words while he plots how to trap you. He will pretend to share your sorrows, but he will kill you if he gets a chance. 17If trouble comes your way, you will find him waiting, ready to trip you up while he pretends to help you. 18He will be a different person then, rubbing his hands, nodding his head, and spreading rumors about you.

13 If you touch tar, it will stick to you, and if you keep company with arrogant people, you will come to be just like them. 2Don't try to lift something too heavy for you, and don't keep company with people who are richer and more powerful than you. You cannot keep a clay pot next to an iron kettle; the pot will break if it hits the kettle. 3If a rich person wrongs someone, he can afford to add insult to injury; but if a poor person is wronged, he is forced to apologize for himself. 4A rich person will use you as long as he can profit from it, but when you need him, he will leave you helpless. 5He will live with you as long as you have anything and will gladly drain you dry. 6If he needs you, he will trick you with his smiles and cheerful, kindly words. "Do you need anything?" he will ask. 7He will feed you until you are embarrassed. Finally, when he has drained you two or three times over, he will laugh at you. If you see him later, he will pretend he doesn't know you, and will pass you by.

8Be careful not to be misled; you can be enjoying yourself and suddenly find yourself humiliated. 9If you are invited to the home of someone influential, be reserved in your behavior. Then he will invite you more often. 10If you push yourself on him, he will put you in your place. On the other hand, if you keep your distance from him, he will forget about you. 11Don't pretend to be his equal or trust everything he says. In spite of all of his long and polite conversation, he is testing you.

12If a person does not keep confidences, he is cruel; he will not hesitate to hurt you or have you put in jail. 13Keep your secrets to yourself and be very careful, for you are always walking on dangerous ground.[e]

15Every creature prefers its own kind, and people are no different. 16Just as animals of the same species flock together, so people keep company with people like themselves. 17A sinner has no more in common with a devout person than a wolf has with a lamb. 18Rich people have no more in common with poor people than hyenas have with dogs. 19The rich hunt down the poor just as lions hunt down wild donkeys in the open country. 20Arrogant people have nothing but scorn for the humble, and the rich think of the poor in the same way. 21When a rich person stumbles, his friends will steady him, but if a poor person falls, his friends will have nothing to do with him. 22When someone rich makes a mistake, there are many people to cover up for him and

He will feed you until you are embarrassed. (13:7)

[e] **13:13** *Some manuscripts add verses 13b–14:* When you hear this in your sleep, wake up! 14As long as you live, love the Lord and call on him to rescue you.

explain away all the things he never should
have said. But let someone poor make a mis-
take, and he gets nothing but criticism. Even
if what he says makes good sense, nobody
will listen. 23When a rich person speaks,
everyone is silent, and they praise him to the
skies for what he says. But let a poor person
speak, and everybody says, "Who is that?"
They push him down if he so much as
stumbles.

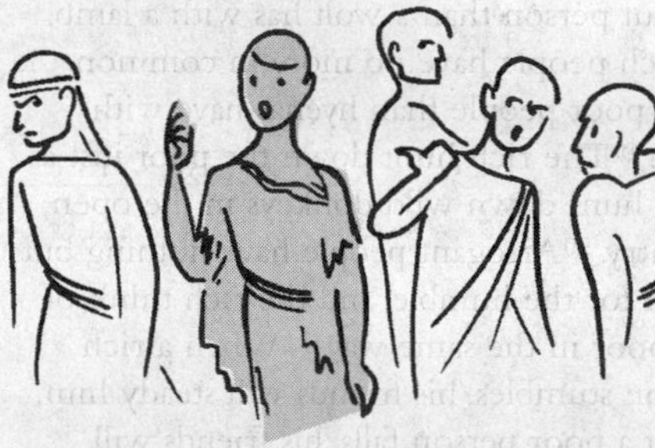

When a rich person speaks, everyone is silent . . .
But let a poor person speak . . . (13:23)

24There is nothing wrong with being
rich if you haven't sinned to get that way.
But there is nothing sinful about being
poor, either. Only the ungodly think so.
25It's what is in your heart that makes the
expression on your face happy or sad. 26If
you feel cheerful, you will look cheerful,
although making up proverbs calls for some
intense thought.

14 If a person never says anything care-
lessly, he is to be congratulated; he
doesn't need to feel guilty. 2If a person has a
clear conscience and never gives up hope, he
is certainly to be congratulated!

Responsible Use of Wealth

3It isn't right for someone who is selfish
to be rich. What use is money to a stingy
person? 4If you deny yourself in order to
accumulate wealth, you are only accumulat-
ing it for someone else. Others will use your
riches to live in luxury. 5How can you be
generous with others if you are stingy with
yourself, if you are not willing to enjoy your
own wealth? 6No one is worse off than
someone who is stingy with himself; it is a
sin that brings its own punishment. 7When
such a person does something good, it is
only by accident; his selfishness will sooner
or later be evident. 8A selfish person is evil;
he turns his back on people's needs 9and is
never satisfied with what he has. Greed[f] will
shrivel up a person's soul. 10Some people are
too stingy to put bread on their own table.
11My child, treat yourself as well as you
can, and bring worthy offerings to the Lord.
12Remember that death is coming for you
some day, and you haven't been told when
that will be. 13Before that day comes, be kind
to your friends; be as generous as you can.
14Don't deny yourself a single day's happiness.
If there is something you want to do and it is
lawful, go ahead! 15Some day all that you have
worked for will be divided up and given to
others. 16So be generous; but also be willing
to receive from others. Enjoy yourself, for you
will not find any pleasures in the world of the
dead. 17The human body wears out like a
piece of clothing. The ancient law decrees
that we must die. 18Human beings are like
leaves on a spreading tree. New growth takes
the place of the fallen leaves; while some of us
die, others are being born. 19Everything made
by human hands will decay and perish, along
with the person who made it.

The Happiness of Having Wisdom

20It is a happy person who is concerned
with Wisdom and who uses good sense.
21Anyone who studies the ways of Wisdom
will also learn her secrets. 22Go after Wisdom
like a hunter looking for game. 23Look into
her windows and listen at her doors. 24Camp

f **14:9** *Probable text* Greed; *Greek* Wicked injustice.
14:20–25 Prov 8:32–35

as close to her house as you can get, 25and
you will have a fine place to live. 26-27Build
your home there, safe beneath her protecting
branches, and shaded from the heat.[g]

15 If you fear the Lord, you will do
this. Master his Law, and you will
find Wisdom. 2She will come to welcome
you, like a mother or a young bride. 3She
will give you wisdom and knowledge like
food and drink. 4Rely on her for support,
and you will never know the disgrace of fail-
ure. 5She will make you more honored than
all your neighbors; when you speak in the
assembly, she will give you the right words.
6You will find happiness and genuine joy;
your name will be remembered forever.

7But people who are foolish or sinful will
never even catch sight of Wisdom. 8She will
have nothing to do with conceited people;
she never enters the mind of liars. 9It is not
appropriate for a sinner to sing hymns of
praise, because his worship is insincere. 10A
hymn should be an expression of wisdom,
inspired by the Lord himself.

Free Will

11Don't blame the Lord for your sin; the
Lord does not cause what he hates.[h] 12Don't
claim that he has misled you; he doesn't
need the help of sinners to accomplish his
purposes. 13The Lord hates evil in all its
forms, and those who fear the Lord find
nothing attractive in evil. 14When, in the
beginning, the Lord created human beings,
he left them free to do as they wished. 15If
you want to, you can keep the Lord's com-
mands. You can decide whether you will be
loyal to him or not. 16He has placed fire and
water before you; reach out and take
whichever you want. 17You have a choice
between life and death; you will get
whichever you choose. 18The Lord's wisdom
and power are great and he sees everything.
19He is aware of everything a person does,
and he takes care of those who fear him.
20He has never commanded anyone to be
wicked or given anyone permission to sin.

God's Punishment of Sinners

16 A large family is nothing to be
desired if the children are worthless.
Godless children are nothing to be proud of.
2No matter how many children you have,
don't look on them with pride unless they
fear the Lord. 3Don't put much hope in
their future or expect them to live a long
time. One child who does the Lord's will is
better than a thousand who do not.[i] It is
better to go to your grave with no children
at all than to have children who are godless.

4A city's population may grow because of
the wisdom of one person, while a whole
tribe of lawless people disappears. 5I have
seen such things many times and have heard
of even more striking examples. 6The Lord's
flaming anger will break out against a small
gathering of sinners or a disobedient nation.
7He did not forgive those ancient giants
who rebelled against him, confident of their
own strength. 8He detested the arrogance of
the people among whom Lot lived, and he
did not spare them. 9He showed no mercy
on that nation which he doomed to destruc-
tion for its sins, 10nor on those 600,000 peo-
ple on the march through the wilderness
who gathered together in stubborn rebel-
lion. 11Even if there had been only one stub-
born person, it would have been a miracle if
he had escaped punishment. The Lord is
merciful, but he can also become angry. He
can be overwhelming in his forgiveness or in
his anger. 12His punishment is as severe as his
mercy is great. He judges people by what
they have done. 13No sinner can escape with
what he has stolen. The Lord will reward the
patience of devout people. 14Every righteous
person will be rewarded;[j] everyone will get
what he deserves.[k]

[g] **14:26–27** *Hebrew* Build . . . heat; *Greek* Let her protect your children. Live safe beneath her branches, shaded from the heat, surrounded by her glory. [h] **15:11** *Hebrew* the Lord does not cause what he hates; *Greek* do not do what the Lord hates. [i] **16:3** *Hebrew* who does . . . do not; *Greek* is better than a thousand.
[j] **16:14** *Hebrew* Every . . . rewarded; *Greek* He makes room for every act of mercy. [k] **16:14** *Some manuscripts add verses 15–16:* The Lord made the king of Egypt so stubborn that he would not acknowledge the Lord, in order that the world might know the Lord's works. 16He shows his mercy to all creation; he has divided his light from darkness with a plumb line.

15:11–20 Sir 17:1–12 **16:7** Gen 6:4; Wis 14:6

17 Never say, "I will hide from the Lord.
Nobody up there is going to give me a
thought. How can I be noticed among so
many people? The creation is so enormous,
what am I worth? 18 When the Lord comes,
everything will tremble: the earth and the
great waters beneath it, the sky and the
heavens above it. 19 The mountains will
shake, and the foundations of the earth will
shudder when he looks at them. 20 The Lord
isn't going to give me a thought. Nobody
cares what I do. 21 If I sin and am secretly
disloyal, nobody will know it.[l] 22 If I do what
is right, nobody will tell the Lord about it.
Who wants to wait for him, anyway? He is
too slow in doing what he has said he
would." 23 Only someone with very little
sense, and foolishly misguided, would think
things like that.

God's Wisdom in Creation

24 My child, listen and pay attention to
me; you will gain knowledge if you do. 25 I
will give you diligent and accurate instruction.

26 In the beginning the Lord did his work of
creation,[m]
and gave everything a place of its own.
27 He arranged everything in an eternal
order
and decreed that it should be that way
forever.
Not one part of creation ever grows
hungry;
no part grows tired or stops its work.
28 The parts do not crowd one another,
and they never disobey his word.
29 When the Lord had made all this,
he looked at the earth and filled it with
good things.
30 He covered it with all kinds of creatures
that must die and return to the dust.

17 Then the Lord formed human
beings from the dust
and sent each of them back to it again.
2 He gave them only a limited time to live,
but he gave them authority over
everything on earth.
3 He made them to be like himself,
and gave them his[n] own strength.
4 He made all other creatures afraid of
them;
he gave them authority over all the
animals and birds.[o]
6 He gave them their tongues, their eyes,
their ears, their minds, and their
consciences.
7 He filled them with knowledge and
understanding
and showed them the difference
between good and evil.
8 He gave them his own insight
to let them see the majesty of his
creation.[p]
10 They will praise his holy name
and proclaim the greatness of all he
does.
11 He made knowledge available to them
and gave them the Law as a source of
life.
12 He made an eternal covenant with them
and revealed his commands to them.
13 They saw the splendor of his majesty
and heard the glory of his voice.
14 He warned them against unrighteousness
and taught each person how to treat
others.

God Is Judge

15 The Lord is always aware of what people
do; there is no way to hide from him.[q] 17 He
gave each nation its own ruler, but Israel is
the Lord's own possession.[r] 19 The Lord is

[l] **16:21** *Hebrew* 20–21 The Lord . . . know it; *Greek* 20 It is altogether too big for the human mind to handle. No one can understand his ways. 21 Most of his works are just as invisible as the storm wind. [m] **16:26** *Hebrew* In . . . creation; *Greek* In the judgment of the Lord his works are from the beginning. [n] **17:3** *Probable text* his; *Greek* their. [o] **17:4** *Some manuscripts add verse 5:* The Lord gave them the five senses, but he also gave them a sixth—intelligence, and a seventh—reason, which enables them to interpret what comes to them through the senses.
[p] **17:8** *Some manuscripts add verse 9:* and he allowed them to take pride forever in his marvelous deeds.
[q] **17:15** *Some manuscripts add verses 16–17a:* From childhood on they tend to be evil; their heart is like stone, and they don't seem to be able to make it more human. 17 He divided the nations of the whole earth.
[r] **17:17** *Some manuscripts add verse 18:* Israel is his first-born, whom he disciplines as he brings him up. He gives him the light of his love and never neglects him.

17:1–3 Gen 1:26–28; 2:7 **17:7** Gen 2:17

always watching what people do; everything
they do is as clear as day to him. 20 None of
their sins are hidden from him; he is aware of
them all.[s] 22 When we give to the poor, the
Lord considers it as precious as a valuable
ring. Human kindness is as precious to him as
life itself. 23 Later he will judge the wicked
and punish them; they will get what they
deserve. 24 But the Lord will allow those who
repent to return to him. He always gives
encouragement to those who are losing hope.

A Call to Repentance

25 Come to the Lord, and leave your sin
behind. Pray sincerely that he will help you
live a better life. 26 Return to the Most High
and turn away from sin. Have an intense
hatred for wickedness. 27 Those who are alive
can give thanks to the Lord, but can anyone
in the world of the dead sing praise to the
Most High? 28 A person who is alive and well
can sing the Lord's praises, but the dead, who
no longer exist, have no way to give him
thanks. 29 How great is the Lord's merciful
forgiveness of those who turn to him! 30 But
this is not the nature of human beings;[t] not
one of us is immortal. 31 Nothing is brighter
than the sun, but even the sun's light fails
during an eclipse. How much easier it is for
human thoughts to be eclipsed by evil! 32 The
Lord can look out over all the stars in the
sky. Human beings? They are dust and ashes.

The Greatness of God

18 The Lord, who lives forever, created
the whole universe, 2 and he alone is
just.[u] 4 He has given no one enough power
to describe what he has done, and no one
can investigate it completely. 5 Who can
measure his majestic power? Who can tell
the whole story of his merciful actions? 6 We
cannot add to them; we cannot subtract
from them. There is no way to comprehend
the marvelous things the Lord has done.
7 When we come to the end of that story, we
have not even begun; we are simply at a loss
for words.

Human Beings Are Nothing

8 What are human beings? Of what use are
we? The good that we do—the evil that we
do—what does it all mean? 9 If we live a hun-
dred years, we have lived an unusually long
time, 10 but compared with all eternity, those
years are like a drop of water in the ocean,
like a single grain of sand. 11 That is why the
Lord is so patient with us, why he is so free
with his mercy. 12 He looks at us and knows
that we are doomed to die; that is why he is
so willing to forgive us. 13 We can show com-
passion to someone we know, but the Lord
shows compassion for all humanity. He cor-
rects us; he disciplines us; he teaches us. Like a
shepherd tending sheep, he brings us back to
himself. 14 He will have compassion on us if
we accept his guidance and are eager for him
to show us where we are wrong.

Kindness and Charity

15 My child, when you help someone,
don't reprimand him at the same time. When
you make a gift, don't say anything that
hurts. 16 Your words count for more than
what you give. Even dew gives some relief
during a spell of hot weather. 17 Yes, kind
words are more effective than the best of
gifts, and if you are really concerned, you
will give both. 18 It is stupid to be unkind
and insulting. No one's eyes are going to
sparkle at a gift that you resent giving.

Self-examination

19 Know what you are talking about before
you speak, and give attention to your health
before you get sick. 20 Examine your con-
science before the Lord judges you; then
when that time comes, he will forgive you.
21 Humble yourself before you are punished
with sickness. When you have sinned, show

[s] **17:20** *Some manuscripts add verse 21:* But the Lord is gracious and knows his creatures; so he has spared them rather than abandon them. [t] **17:30** But . . . human beings; *or* People cannot have everything. [u] **18:2** *Some manuscripts add verses 2b–3:* and there is no other besides him. 3 He guides the world with his hand, and everything obeys him. He is the king of all things, and his power separates what is holy from what is not.

17:25, 26 Jer 3:12 **17:27, 28** Ps 6:5; Isa 38:18; Bar 2:17, 18

. . . a gift you resent giving. (18:18)

repentance. 22If you make a promise to the
Lord, keep it as soon as you can. Don't wait
until you are about to die to set things
straight. 23But before you make such a prom-
ise, be prepared to keep it. Don't try to test
the Lord's patience. 24Think! Do you want
him to be angry with you on the day you
die? When you face his judgment, do you
want him to turn his back on you? 25When
you have all you want, think what it is like to
be hungry, what it is to be poor. 26Things
can change in a single day; the Lord can act
very quickly. 27If you are wise, you will be
careful in everything you do. When sin is all
around you, be especially careful that you do
not become guilty. 28Every intelligent person
can recognize wisdom and will honor any-
one who shows it. 29If you appreciate wis-
dom when you hear it, you will become wise
yourself, and your words will be a source of
wisdom for others.

Self-control

30Don't be controlled by your lust; keep
your passions in check. 31If you allow your-
self to satisfy your every desire, you will be a
joke to your enemies. 32Don't indulge in
luxurious living; the expense of it will ruin
you. 33Don't make yourself a beggar by bor-
rowing for expensive banquets when you
don't have enough money of your own.

19 1If you do, you[v] will never get rich;
if you don't pay attention to small
matters, you will gradually ruin yourself.
2Wine and women make sensible men do
foolish things. A man who goes to prostitutes
gets more and more careless, 3and that care-
lessness will cost him his life. Worms will
feed on his decaying body.

4It is silly to trust people too quickly. If
you sin, you are hurting yourself. 5If wicked-
ness makes you happy, you will be con-
demned.

Loose Talk

6Avoid idle talk, and you will avoid a lot
of trouble. 7Never repeat what you hear, and
you will have no regrets. 8Don't tell it to
your friends or your enemies unless it would
be sinful to keep it to yourself. 9Whoever
hears you will take note of it, and sooner or
later will hate you for it. 10Have you heard a
rumor? Let it die with you. Be brave! It
won't make you explode. 11A foolish person
trying to keep a secret suffers like a woman
in labor. 12Any time he hears a secret, it's like
an arrow stuck in his leg.

13If you hear that a friend has done some-
thing wrong, ask him about it. Maybe it isn't
true. If it is true, he won't do it again. 14If
you hear that a neighbor has said something
he shouldn't, ask him about it. Maybe he
didn't say it. If he did, he won't say it again.
15If you hear something bad about a friend,
ask him about it. It might be a lie. Don't
believe everything you hear. 16A person may
say something carelessly and not really mean
it. Everyone has sinned in this way at one
time or another. 17If you hear something that
makes you angry with your neighbor, ask
him about it before you threaten him. Leave
the matter to the Law of the Most High.[w]

Recognizing Real Wisdom

20Fear the Lord and keep his Law; that is
what Wisdom is all about.[x] 22You may know

[v] **19:1** *Hebrew* If you do, you; *Greek* A worker who drinks too much. [w] **19:17** *Some manuscripts add verses 17c–19:* and don't be angry. 18Fearing the Lord is the first step toward his accepting you; he will love you if you are wise. 19Learn the Lord's commands. It is a discipline that gives life. Those who do what pleases him enjoy the fruit of the tree of immortality. [x] **19:20** *Some manuscripts add verses 20b–21:* and what the knowledge of his omnipotence means. 21If a servant refuses to obey his master, but later does obey, the master is still angry.

everything there is to know about wicked-
ness, but that does not make you wise. It is
not sensible to follow the advice of sinners.
23It is possible to use cleverness for wicked
purposes, but some people act like fools
because they don't know any better. 24A
devout person, even if he is not very intelli-
gent, is better off than the cleverest of sin-
ners. 25It is possible to be marvelously clever
and still be dishonest, or to get what you
want by being absurdly polite.
26Then there are those wicked people
who go about looking very solemn and
mournful, but who are only trying to
deceive you. 27They will turn their faces
away and pretend not to hear you, but they'll
take advantage of you when you least expect
it. 28If for some reason they are unable to sin
now, they'll get around to it at the first
opportunity. 29You can know people by their
appearance. The first time you look at them,
you can tell if they have good sense. 30Their
character shows in the way they dress, the
way they laugh, and the way they walk.

Knowing When to Talk

20 A person can be rebuked in the
wrong way; it may be wiser to keep
quiet than to speak. 2But it is much better
to rebuke the person than to keep your
anger bottled up. 3Admit when you are
wrong, and you will avoid embarrassment.
4Using force to get a point across is like a
castrated man trying to rape a young
woman. 5Some people are thought to be
wise because they don't talk much; others
are disliked because they talk too much.
6Some people keep quiet because they don't
have anything to say; others keep quiet
because they know the right time to speak.
7A wise person will not speak until the
right moment, but a bragging fool doesn't
know when that time is. 8No one can stand
a person who talks too long and will not
give others a chance to speak.

No one can stand a person who talks too long. (20:8)

. . . and pretend not to hear you. (19:27)

Sudden Changes of Fortune

9Bad luck can sometimes lead to success,
and a stroke of good luck can sometimes
lead to loss.
10Generosity will sometimes do you no
good, but at other times it will repay you
double.
11Honor can be followed by disgrace, but
there are people who have risen from obscu-
rity to places of honor.
12Sometimes what seems like a real bar-
gain can turn out to be a very expensive
mistake.
13When a person with good judgment
speaks, he wins friends. A stupid person,
though, can shower compliments on every-
body, and it won't help him a bit. 14If such a
person gives you something, it won't do any
good; it won't be as valuable as he thinks it

is.[y] 15 He isn't generous with anything but criticism, which he will shout for all the world to hear. If he lends you something today, he'll want it back tomorrow. (Don't you hate people like that?) 16 Then that fool will say, "Nobody likes me. Nobody appreciates what I do for them. They'll take what I give them, but then talk about me behind my back." 17 And he's right—he's a constant joke to everyone.

Inappropriate Talk

18 A slip of the tongue is worse than a slip on the pavement; the wicked will go to ruin just as suddenly as a person slips and falls.

19 An impolite person is like one of those off-color stories that ignorant people are always telling.

20 Nobody takes a proverb seriously when some fool quotes it at the wrong time.

21 If a person is too poor to afford sin, he can rest without a guilty conscience.

22 You can lose all your self-respect by being reluctant to speak up in the presence of stupidity.

23 If you promise a friend something because you are too bashful to say no, you're needlessly making an enemy.

24 Lying is an ugly blot on a person's character, but ignorant people do it all the time. 25 A thief is better than a habitual liar, but both are headed for ruin. 26 A liar has no honor. He lives in constant disgrace.

Stewardship of Wisdom

27 Speak wisely, and you will get ahead in the world. Influential people appreciate good sense. 28 They will excuse your errors if they like you, so cultivate the soil and reap the harvest!

29 Gifts and bribes make even the wise blind to the truth, and prevent them from being honest in their criticism.

30 Wisdom that is not expressed is like a treasure that has been hidden—both are useless. 31 But a person who covers up his foolishness is better than one who keeps his wisdom to himself.

Sin

21 My child, have you sinned? Don't do it again, and pray for forgiveness for what you have already done. 2 Avoid sin as if it were a snake. If you get too near, it will sink its teeth into your soul like a lion, and destroy you. 3 Every lawless act leaves an incurable wound, like one left by a double-edged sword.

4 If a person is insolent and arrogant, he may lose everything he has.

5 When poor people pray, God hears them and quickly answers their prayers.

6 If you refuse to accept correction, you are committing a sin; and if you fear the Lord, you will make a sincere change in your ways.

7 Someone may be famous as a good speaker, but when he is wrong, a sensible person will detect it.

8 Anyone who borrows money to build a house is just collecting stones for his own tomb.[z]

9 A group of people who have no respect for the Law is like a pile of kindling; they will meet a fiery end. 10 The road that sinners walk is smooth and paved, but it leads to the world of the dead.

Wisdom and Foolishness

11 Whoever wants to keep the Law must learn what the Law means. If you fear the Lord in every sense of the term, you will have wisdom. 12 You have to be intelligent to learn anything; but there is such a thing as just pretending to be intelligent, which only makes people bitter. 13 A wise person's knowledge is like a river that never runs dry, like an everflowing stream of good advice.

14 A fool, on the other hand, has a mind like a jar with a hole in it; anything he learns is soon lost.

15 When an educated person hears something that shows insight, it stimulates his

[y] **20:14** it won't be . . . it is; *or* he only expects to be repaid. [z] **21:8** his own tomb; *some manuscripts have* the winter.

21:5 Sir 35:17–19

A fool . . . has a mind like a jar with a hole in it. *(21:14)*

mind and leads him on to other ideas. But
when someone who is satisfied with igno-
rance hears it, he won't like it, and will for-
get it as soon as he can. 16Listening to a
foolish person talk is like traveling with a
heavy load on your back, but it is a pleasure
to hear what intelligent people have to say.
17The assembly will be eager to hear from
an intelligent person and will take his opin-
ion seriously.

18To an ignorant person, wisdom is as
useless as a house gone to ruin. He has never
even thought about the things he is so sure
of. 19To a person without any sense, an edu-
cation is like handcuffs, 20-21but to a sensible
person, it is like gold bracelets. An intelligent
person will smile quietly while a fool roars
with laughter. 22-23A stupid person will peep
into someone's house through the door and
then march right in, but someone with
experience and good manners will have
enough respect to wait outside. 24Eavesdrop-
ping at doors is bad manners, and anyone
with a sense of decency would be ashamed
to do it.

25Presumptuous people talk about things
that are none of their business,[a] but the wise
will consider the consequences of what they
say. 26Fools say whatever comes to mind;
wise people think before they speak.

27When a wicked person curses his
enemy[b] he is cursing himself.
28A gossip ruins his own character, and
everyone in the neighborhood hates him.

Laziness and Foolishness

22 1-2Lazy people are no better than
dung; they are repulsive, and no one
wants to get near them.

3It is a disgrace to a father to have an
undisciplined child, especially if it is a
daughter. 4A sensible daughter will get a
husband, but a shameless daughter brings her
father grief. 5A girl with no sense of propri-
ety will disgrace both her husband and her
father; neither will have any respect for her.

6Lecturing your children can sometimes
be as out of place as singing to people in
mourning, but a whipping is a wise choice
of discipline at any time.

7Trying to teach a fool is like gluing a
broken pot back together, like waking some-
one out of a deep sleep. 8Explaining some-
thing to a fool is like explaining it to a
sleepy person; when you have finished, he'll
say, "What was that again?"[c]

11We mourn for the dead because they
have no access to light. We ought to mourn
for fools, because they have no access to
intelligence. In fact, we should go into deep-
er mourning for fools, because the life they
lead is worse than death. The dead are at
least at rest. 12For seven days we mourn the
dead, but a foolish or ungodly person causes
a lifetime of grief.

13Don't visit stupid people or spend a lot
of time talking with them. Avoid them; then
they can't contaminate you, and you can live
in peace without being troubled or worn
down by their foolishness. 14Such people are
a heavier burden to bear than lead; and the
only word that fits them is "fools." 15It is eas-
ier to carry a load of sand, salt, and iron than
to put up with a stupid person.

16A wooden beam can be put into a
building so firmly that an earthquake cannot

[a] **21:25** *Probable text* Presumptuous . . . business; *Greek* The lips of strangers speak of these things. [b] **21:27** his enemy; *or* Satan. [c] **22:8** *Some manuscripts add verses 9–10:* Children who are brought up well do not show the humble origin of their parents. 10Children who are not brought up well, who are arrogant and conceited, are a stain on the noblest family.

22:12 Gen 50:10; Jdt 16:24

shake it loose; a person can be trained to use
reason and good sense so well that he keeps
his head when a crisis comes. 17A mind that
thinks things through intelligently is like a
firm wall, finely decorated. 18Small stones on
top of a wall[d] will not stay put when the
wind blows, and a person whose stupid ideas
have made him timid will not be able to
stand up to frightening situations.

Friendship

19If you stick something in your eye, tears
will flow; and if you hurt a person deeply,
you will discover his true feelings. 20If you
throw rocks at birds, you will scare them
away; and if you insult a friend, you will
break up the friendship. 21-22Even if you
have a violent argument with a friend, and
speak sharply, all is not lost. You can still
make up with him. But any friend will leave
you if you insult him, if you are arrogant, if
you reveal his secrets, or if you turn on him
unexpectedly.

23Gain the confidence of your neighbor if
he is poor; then you can share his happiness
if he becomes successful. Stand by him when
he is in trouble if you want to share with
him when better times come his way.

24Fumes and smoke appear before the
flames do; insults come before violence.

25I will never be afraid to protect a friend,
and I will never turn a friend away if he
needs me. 26If I suffer because of him, every-
one who learns of it will be on guard against
him.

A Prayer for Help against Sin

27I wish that a guard could be placed at
my mouth, that my lips could be wisely
sealed. It would keep me from making mis-
takes and prevent me from destroying myself
with my own tongue!

23 O Lord, my Father and Master of
my life, do not leave me at the
mercy of my own words; don't let them
cause my downfall. 2I wish I could be
whipped for my thoughts, so that Wisdom
could discipline my mind. I would not want
to be spared when I am wrong; I would not
want a single sin to be overlooked! 3Then I
would not keep on sinning, making one
mistake after another. I could not fall to my
enemies and be humiliated by them.

4O Lord, my Father, God of my life, keep
me from being arrogant; 5protect me from
evil desires. 6Keep me from being overcome
by greed or lust; do not leave me at the
mercy of these shameless passions.

Taking Oaths

7My children, listen to what I have to say
about proper speech; do as I teach you and
you will never get trapped. 8Sinners are
caught by their own arrogant, insulting
words.

9Don't fall into the habit of taking oaths,
and don't use God's holy name too freely.
10A slave who is constantly beaten will never
be free of bruises; someone who is always
taking an oath by the Holy Name will never
be free of sin. 11Anyone who takes oaths all
the time is sinful to the core, and punish-
ment is never far away from his household. If
he fails to fulfill his oath, he is guilty. If he
ignores his oath, he is twice as guilty. If his
oath was insincere in the first place, he can-
not be pardoned and will have a house full
of trouble.

Filthy Talk

12There is one way of speaking that is like
death itself—may no Israelite ever be guilty
of it! Devout people do not wallow in such
sin, and they will keep away from such
behavior. 13Don't fall into the habit of
coarse, profane talk; it is sinful. 14You might
forget yourself while in the company of
important people and make a fool of your-
self with some foul word that comes to you
naturally. Think how your parents would
feel! You would curse the day you were born
and wish you were dead! 15If you fall into
the habit of using offensive language, you
will never break yourself of it as long as you
live.

[d] **22:18** Small . . . wall; *some manuscripts have* A fence on top of a hill.

23:9 Mt 5:34; Jas 5:12

Sexual Sins

16 There are any number of ways to sin
and bring down the Lord's anger, but sexual
passion is a hot, blazing fire that cannot be
put out at will; it can only burn itself out. A
man who lives for nothing but sexual enjoy-
ment will keep on until that fire destroys
him. 17 To such a man all women are desir-
able, and he can never get enough as long as
he lives.

18 The man who is unfaithful to his wife
thinks to himself, "No one will ever know.
It's dark in here, and no one sees me. I have
nothing to worry about. As for the Most
High, he won't even notice." 19 This man is
only afraid of other people. He doesn't real-
ize that the eyes of the Lord are 10,000
times brighter than the sun, that he sees
everything we do, even when we try to hide
it. 20 He knew everything before he created
the world, as well as after. 21 That sinful man
will be caught when he least expects it, and
punished publicly.

22 The same is true of a woman who is
unfaithful to her husband and presents him
with a child by another man. 23 In the first
place, she has broken the Law of the Most
High. In the second place, she has wronged
her husband. And in the third place, she has
made a whore of herself by committing
adultery and bearing the child of a man not
her husband. 24-25 The children will suffer for
her sin. They will not be able to find a place
in society or establish families. She herself
will be brought before the assembly 26 and
permanently disgraced. There will be a curse
on her memory. After she is gone, 27 every-
one will realize that nothing is better than
fearing the Lord, nothing is sweeter than
keeping his commands.

In Praise of Wisdom

24 Listen to Wisdom! She proudly sings
her own praises among the Israelites,
her own people, 2 in the assembly of the
Most High, in the presence of his power.[e]

3 "I am the word spoken by the Most
High.
I covered the earth like a mist.
4 I made my home in highest heaven,
my throne on a pillar of cloud.
5 Alone I walked around the circle of the
sky
and walked through the ocean beneath
the earth.
6 I ruled over[f] all the earth and the ocean
waves,
over every nation, over every people.
7 I looked everywhere for a place to settle,
some part of the world to make my
home.
8 Then my Creator, who created the
universe,
told me where I was to live.
'Make your home in Israel,' he said.
'The descendants of Jacob will be your
people.'
9 He created me in eternity, before time
began,
and I will exist for all eternity to come.
10 I served him in the Sacred Tent
and then made my home on Mount
Zion.
11 He settled me in the Beloved City
and gave me authority over Jerusalem.
12 I put down roots among an honored
people
whom the Lord had chosen as his own.
13 I grew tall, like the cedars in Lebanon,
like the cypresses on Mount Hermon,
14 like the palm trees of Engedi,[g]
like the roses of Jericho,
like beautiful olive trees in the fields,
like plane trees growing by the water.
15 My breath was the spicy smell of
cinnamon,
of sweet perfume and finest myrrh,
of stacte, onycha, and galbanum,
the fragrant incense in the Sacred Tent.
16 Like an oak I spread out my branches,
magnificent and graceful.
17 Like a grapevine I put out lovely shoots;
my blossoms gave way to rich and
glorious fruit.[h]

[e] **24:2** power; *or* angels. [f] **24:6** ruled over; *some manuscripts have* gained possession of. [g] **24:14** of Engedi; *some manuscripts have* on the seashore. [h] **24:17** *Some manuscripts add verse 18:* I am the mother of beautiful love, of fear, knowledge, and holy hope. Since I am eternal, I am given to all my children, who are named by him.
24:4 Ex 33:9, 10

[19] Come to me, all you that want me,
and eat your fill of my fruit.
[20] You will remember me as sweeter than honey,
better than honey from the comb.
[21] Eat me, and you will hunger for more;
drink me, and you will thirst for more.
[22] Obey me, and you will never have cause for embarrassment;
do as I say, and you will be safe from sin."

Wisdom and the Law

[23] Wisdom is the Law, the Law which
Moses commanded us to keep, the covenant
of God Most High, the inheritance of the
synagogues of Israel.[i] [25] The Law overflows
with Wisdom like the Pishon River, like the
Tigris at fruit-picking time. [26] The Law
brims over with understanding like the
Euphrates, like the Jordan at harvest time.
[27] It sparkles with teachings like the Nile,[j]
like the Gihon at grape-picking time.
[28] The first human being ever created
never knew Wisdom completely, and the last
person on earth will be no more successful.
[29] The possibilities of Wisdom are vaster
than the ocean; her resources are more pro-
found than the deepest waters beneath the
earth.
[30] As for me, I thought of myself as an
irrigation canal bringing water from a river
into a garden. [31] I only intended to water my
orchard and flower beds, but the canal soon
became a river, and the river became a sea.
[32] And so I present you with my learning; I
hold it high, so that its light can be seen
everywhere, like that of the rising sun.
[33] Like an inspired prophet, I pour out my
teachings, so that future generations can
benefit from them. [34] Please realize that I
have not done all this hard work for myself
alone, but to help anyone who wants to be
wise.

People Who Deserve Praise

25 There are three things in which I
take special delight—things that are
beautiful to the Lord and people alike:[k]
brothers who get along with each other,
neighbors who are friends,
and a married couple who are happy together.
[2] There are three kinds of people I cannot
stand, whose behavior I find highly offen-
sive:
poor people who are arrogant,
rich people who lie,
and foolish old men who commit adultery.
[3] Unless you learn what you can while
you are young, you will never be wise when
you reach old age. [4] Sound judgment, good
advice, and gray hair go together beautifully.

Three things in which I take special delight . . . (25:1)

[i] **24:23** *Some manuscripts add verse 24:* Always be strong in the Lord; stay with him, so that he may make you strong. There is no God but the Lord Almighty, and no savior except him. [j] **24:27** *One ancient translation* It sparkles . . . Nile; *Greek* It makes teachings shine like light. [k] **25:1** *Some ancient translations* There are . . . alike; *Greek* I was made beautiful in three ways and I stood before the Lord and people in beauty.

5 Wisdom, understanding, and sound counsel
are appropriate to the aged and the respect-
ed. 6 Elderly people wear the crown of long
experience, and they can boast of nothing
finer than their fear of the Lord.

7 I will tell you about ten kinds of people
that I feel fortunate to know, especially for-
tunate in the case of the tenth:

someone who takes pride in his children,
someone who lives to see his enemies fall,
8 a man fortunate enough to have an
understanding wife,
a married couple who are well-matched,[l]
a person who never speaks sinfully,
a person who doesn't have to work for
someone less competent than himself,
9 someone fortunate enough to have a real
friend,[m]
a person that people are happy to listen
to,
10 and the really great one: someone who is
wise.
But the greatest one of all is the person
who fears the Lord.

11 Such a person has no equal, because the
fear of the Lord is the most important thing
in the world.[n]

Advice about Women

13 No wound is as serious as wounded
love. No troubles are as serious as the trou-
bles that women cause. 14 No sufferings are
worse than the sufferings caused by people
who hate you. No revenge is worse than
revenge taken by an enemy. 15 No poison is
deadlier than the poison of a snake, and no
anger is deadlier than the anger of a
woman.[o]

16 I would rather live in the same house
with a lion or a dragon than with a bad
wife. 17 When a wife is in a bad mood, her
expression changes until she looks like an
angry bear. 18 Her husband has to go and eat
with the neighbors, where he can't hold
back his bitter sighs.

19 Compared with the troubles caused by a
woman, any other trouble looks small. May
such women suffer the fate of sinners!

20 A quiet man living with a nagging wife
is like an old man climbing up a sandy hill.

21 Never lose your head over a woman's
beauty, and don't try to win a woman
because she is wealthy.[p] 22 When a man is
supported by his wife, there is sure to be
anger, arrogance, and humiliation. 23 A bad
wife will make her husband gloomy and
depressed, and break his heart. Show me a
timid man who can never make up his
mind, and I will show you a wife who
doesn't make her husband happy. 24 Sin
began with a woman, and we must all die
because of her. 25 Don't let a bad wife have
her way, any more than you would allow
water to leak from your cistern. 26 If she
won't do as you tell her, divorce her.

26 The husband of a good wife is a for-
tunate man; he will live twice as
long because of her. 2 A fine wife is a joy to
her husband, and he can live out his years in
peace. 3 A good wife is among the precious
blessings given to those who fear the Lord.
4 Whether such men are rich or poor, they
will be happy and always look cheerful.

5 There are four things that scare me:
vicious rumors spread around town, a gath-
ering mob, false accusations—these are all
worse than death. 6 But a woman jealous of
another woman causes heartache and grief;
her tongue lashes out at everyone.

7 A bad wife is like a yoke that doesn't fit.
Trying to control her is like holding a scor-
pion. 8 A drunken woman is an infuriating
sight; she can't conceal her shameless behav-
ior. 9 You can tell an unfaithful wife by the
bold and flirting look in her eyes.

10 If your daughter is determined to have
her own way, keep a close watch on her. If
you don't, she'll take advantage of any
chance she gets. 11 If she is too self-willed, be
on guard, and don't be surprised if she disap-
points you. 12 She'll spread her legs anywhere
for any man who wants her, just as a thirsty
traveler will drink whatever water is avail-
able.

[l] **25:8** *Hebrew and one ancient translation* a married couple . . . well-matched; *Greek does not have these words.*
[m] **25:9** *Some ancient translations* real friend; *Greek* good sense. [n] **25:11** *Some manuscripts add verse 12:* Fearing the Lord is the first step toward loving him, and faith is the first step toward loyalty to him. [o] **25:15** *Some ancient translations* woman; *Greek* enemy. [p] **25:21** *Hebrew* because she is wealthy; *Greek does not have these words.*

You can tell an unfaithful wife by . . . (26:9)

13 A gracious wife is her husband's delight;
her abilities make him a stronger man.[q] 14 A
wife who doesn't talk too much is a gift
from the Lord. Such restraint is admirable
beyond words. 15 A modest wife has endless
charm; it is a quality too precious to mea-
sure. 16 The beauty of a good wife in her
well-kept home is like the noonday sun
shining in the Lord's sky. 17 Her beautiful face
and attractive figure are[r] as lovely as the light
from the sacred lampstand in the Temple,
18 and like its gold shaft set on its silver base
are her shapely legs and strong ankles.[s,t]

Sad Observations

28 There are two things that make me sad,
and a third that makes me angry:

a soldier who has become poor,
intelligent people who are not respected,
and a righteous person who turns to evil.

The Lord will punish such a person with
death!

29 A merchant can hardly avoid doing
wrong; every salesman is guilty of sin.

27

1 Many people have sinned while
looking for a profit; if you want to
be rich you have to keep blinders on your
eyes. 2 It is hard to remove a peg that is stuck
between two stones of a house, and it is just
as hard to remove dishonesty from buying
and selling. 3 Unless you are determined in
your fear of the Lord, your house is going to
come down on you.

Speech Reflects True Feelings

4 Your talk shows your faults; it is like a
sieve that separates out the rubbish. 5 The
way you think shows your character just as
surely as a kiln shows any flaws in the pot-
tery being fired. 6 You can tell how well a
tree has been cared for by the fruit it bears,
and you can tell a person's feelings by the
way he expresses himself. 7 Never praise any-
one before you hear him talk; that is the real
test.

Honesty

8 If you try to be honest, you can be, and it
will improve your character as handsome
clothing improves your appearance. 9 Birds
come to roost with those of their own kind,
and the habit of honesty comes to those
who try to be honest. 10 Sin waits for those
looking for a chance to sin, just as a lion
waits for prey.

Foolish Talk

11 When devout people talk, what they say
always makes sense, but foolish people are
always contradicting themselves. 12 When

[q] **26:13** her abilities . . . man; *or* she knows how to keep him well-fed. [r] **26:17** and attractive figure are; *or* as she grows older is. [s] **26:18** strong ankles; *some manuscripts have* firm breasts *or* determined heart.
[t] **26:18** *Some manuscripts add verses 19–27:* My child, stay healthy while you are young, and don't give your strength to strangers. 20 Search the whole land for a fertile field, and plant it with your own seed, trusting your own good stock. 21 Then your children will survive and grow up confident of their good family. 22 A prostitute is like spit; a married woman who has affairs brings death to her lovers. 23 A lawless man will get a godless wife, as he deserves, but a man who honors the Lord will have a devout wife. 24 A shameless wife enjoys making a disgrace of herself, but a modest wife will act modestly even alone with her husband. 25 A self-willed woman is a bitch, but a woman with a sense of decency honors the Lord. 26 A wife who honors her husband will seem wise to everyone; but if she dishonors him by her overbearing attitude, everyone will know that she is ungodly. Fortunate is the husband of a good wife, because he will live twice as long. 27 A loud-mouthed, talkative woman is like a trumpet sounding the signal for attack, and any man who has such a wife will spend his life at war.
27:6 Mt 7:17; 12:33; Lk 6:44

you find yourself with stupid people, look
for some excuse to leave, but when you are
with serious-minded people, stay as long as
you can.
13 The stories that foolish people tell are
offensive, and they make jokes about the
worst kinds of sin. 14 When such people
curse, it is enough to make your hair stand
on end, and when they start arguing among
themselves, all you can do is to stop up your
ears. 15 It is painful to listen to them insult
each other, and such blustering can lead to
violence.

All you can do is to stop up your ears. (27:14)

Betraying Secrets

16 If you repeat secrets that have been told
to you, you are destroying the confidence
others have in you, and you will never have
a close friend. 17 Respect your friends, and
keep faith with them. If you do betray a
friend's confidence, you may as well forget
you have a friend. 18 You have killed that
friendship just as surely as if you had taken a
weapon and killed an enemy. 19 Your friend
is gone. You can no more get him back than
you can get a bird to come back to your
hand once you let it go. 20 Don't bother
going after him. It's too late. He is gone, like
a deer escaped from a trap. 21 Wounds can be
bandaged and insults can be forgiven, but if
you betray a confidence, it is hopeless.

Hypocrisy

22 When someone starts winking at you,
he has something bad in mind, and nothing
can stop him from going through with it.
23 When he's with you, his talk is so nice! He
compliments you on every word you say.
But behind your back it's a different story;
he will take what you have said and turn it
against you. 24 There is nothing in the world
that I hate as much as a person like that
and the Lord hates him too.

25 Throw a stone straight up in the air and
it will come down on your head. Strike a
blow, and you yourself will be wounded.
26 People who set traps fall into them them-
selves. 27 People who hurt others will be hurt
by their own actions and will have no idea
why.

28 Arrogant people insult others and make
fun of them,[u] but someone is waiting like a
lion for a chance to take revenge on them.
29 Those who are happy to witness the
downfall of devout people are going to fall
into a trap and die a painful death.

Resentment

30 Anger and a hot temper are horrible
28 things, but sinners have both. 1 The
Lord is taking note of your sins, and
if you take vengeance on someone, the Lord
will take vengeance on you. 2 But if you for-
give someone who has wronged you, your
sins will be forgiven when you pray. 3 You
cannot expect the Lord to pardon you while
you are holding a grudge against someone
else. 4 You yourself are a sinner, and if you
won't forgive another person, you have no
right to pray that the Lord will forgive your
sins. 5 If you cannot get rid of your anger,
you have no hope of forgiveness—you are
only a human being. 6 Think about it! Some
day you will die, and your body will decay.
So give up hate and live by the Lord's com-
mands, 7 the commands in the covenant of
the Most High. Instead of getting upset over
your neighbor's faults, overlook them.

Arguments

8 If you stay out of arguments, you will not
sin so much, because a hot temper gets them
started. 9 It is sinful to break up a friendship

[u] **27:28** insult others . . . them; *or* will be insulted and mocked.

27:16–21 Prov 20:19; 25:9 **28:2** Mt 6:14; Mk 11:25

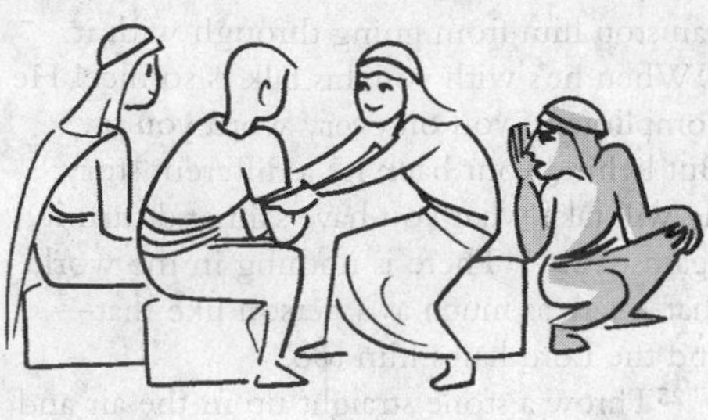

It is sinful to break up a friendship. (28:9)

by creating hostility among people who get
along well together. 10The more fuel, the
hotter the fire. The more stubbornness, the
hotter the argument. And the stronger or
richer people are, the angrier they can afford
to become. 11An argument that blazes out
suddenly can lead to violence. 12You can
blow on a spark to make it glow, or you can
spit on it to put it out. Either way, you do it
with your mouth.

Vicious Talk

13Gossips and liars deserve to be cursed,
because they have been the ruin of many
people who were minding their own busi-
ness. 14Many have had their lives ruined and
have been driven from their homes because
of people who meddled in their business.
Such unwanted interference has resulted in
the destruction of strong cities and the
homes of respected people. 15Meddlers have
caused faithful wives to be divorced, robbed
of everything they had worked for. 16Anyone
who pays attention to slander can never find
peace of mind. 17A whip can raise a welt, but
a vicious tongue can break bones. 18More
people have died as a result of loose talk
than were ever killed by swords. 19-20Count
yourself lucky if you have been spared the
experience of having irresponsible talk
directed against you—if you have never had
that iron yoke around your neck or those
heavy chains on your legs. 21Slander leads to
a miserable death; but in fact, you'd be better
off dead.

22Devout people, however, cannot be
overcome by slander; they cannot be burned
by its flames. 23Its victims are those who
have abandoned the Lord; once the fire of
slander has been lit among them, it cannot
be put out. Slander will pounce on them
like a lion and tear them to pieces like a
leopard.

24Don't you fence in your property?
Don't you lock up your money? 25Well, be
just as careful with what you say. Weigh
every word, and have a lock ready for your
mouth. 26Someone may be waiting for you
to slip, and if you are not careful, you will
stumble over your own words and fall down
in front of him.

Loans and Repayment

29 Be kind enough to lend to your
neighbor when he needs help. You
are keeping the Lord's commands if you help
him. 2If he needs something, lend it to him.
And when you are in debt, pay it back as
soon as you can. 3If you meet your obliga-
tions, you will always be able to borrow
what you need. 4Many people treat a loan as
something they found and can keep, causing
embarrassment to those who helped them.
5Some people will speak politely, bow, and
scrape until they get the loan they want, but
when the time comes to pay it back, they'll
put it off, say that it's inconvenient, and
make a lot of worthless excuses. 6If the
lender insists on being paid, he can count
himself lucky to get back half. If he doesn't
insist, the borrower has robbed him and
made an unnecessary enemy. All the lender
will get from him are curses, insults, and dis-
respect, but never any gratitude.

7Many people refuse to lend at all, not
because they are stingy, but because[v] they
don't want to be cheated if they can avoid it.

Generosity

8Nevertheless, be understanding with
those who are poor. Don't keep them wait-
ing for your generosity. 9The Lord has com-
manded us to help the poor; don't refuse
them the help they need. 10It is better to
lose your money by helping a relative or a
friend than to lose it by letting it rust away

[v] **29:7** not because . . . stingy, but because; *some manuscripts have* therefore, because of this wickedness.

28:13–26 Sir 51:2–6; Jas 3:5–12 **29:1–7** Ex 22:25; Lev 25:35–38

Don't keep them waiting for your generosity. (29:8)

under a rock somewhere. 11 Use your wealth
as the Most High has commanded; this will
do you more good than keeping your
money for yourself. 12 Count among your
treasures the fact that you give to the poor. It
will save you from all kinds of trouble 13 and
will be a better defense against your enemies
than the strongest shield or stoutest spear.

Guaranteeing Debts

14 A good man is willing to guarantee his
neighbor's debts. Only someone who has lost
all sense of decency would refuse to do so.
15 If someone does this favor for you, don't
forget it; he has risked his good name for you.
16 There are some ungrateful sinners who
abandon those who stand behind them, and
they cause them loss of property. 17 Guaran-
teeing loans has ruined many prosperous peo-
ple and caused them unsettling storms of
trouble. 18 Influential people have lost their
homes over it and have had to go wandering
in foreign countries. 19 A sinner who hopes to
make a profit by guaranteeing a loan is going
to find himself involved in lawsuits. 20 So help
your neighbor as much as you can, but pro-
tect yourself against the dangers involved.

Home and Hospitality

21 The necessities of life are water, food,
clothing, and a home where you can have
privacy. 22 It is better to be poor and live
under your own crude roof than to enjoy
lavish banquets in other people's homes.
23 Be happy with what you have, even if it
isn't very much, and don't listen to anyone
who would insult your home and family.[w]
24 Going from house to house is a miserable
way to live. Anywhere you go, you don't
dare speak. 25 You welcome the guests and
pour the drinks, and nobody thanks you.
Instead, people humiliate you by saying
things like: 26 "Stranger! Come here and set
the table! I want to eat what you've got
there! Give it here! 27 Go away, stranger! I've
got an important guest! My brother is com-
ing to visit, and I need the room!"

Going from house to house is a miserable way to live. (29:24)

28 Being denied hospitality or having a
moneylender hound you—these are hard
things for any sensitive person to endure.

Bringing up Children

30 A father who loves his son will whip
him often, so that he can be proud
of him later. 2 If a son is disciplined, he will
be of some use, and his father can boast of
him to his friends. 3 Anyone who gives good
guidance to his son can not only take pride
in him among his friends, but he can make
his enemies jealous. 4-5 While the father is
alive, the sight of his son makes him happy,
and when he dies, he has no regrets. He is
not really dead, because his son is like him.
6 He has left someone to take vengeance on
his enemies and to return the favors he owes
his friends.

[w] **29:23** don't listen . . . family; *or* don't listen to insults from your family; *some manuscripts do not have these words; one ancient translation has* don't get a reputation for living off other people.

. . . so that he can be proud of him later. (30:1)

7But anyone who spoils his son will have
to bandage his wounds.[x] His heart will stop
every time he hears a shout. 8An untamed
horse is going to be stubborn, and an undis-
ciplined son is no different. 9If you pamper
your child and play with him, he will be
a disappointment and a source of grief.
10Laugh with him now, and one day you will
have to cry over him, grinding your teeth in
regret. 11Don't give him freedom while he is
young, and don't overlook what he does
wrong. 12Whip him while he is still a child,
and make him respect your authority. If you
don't, he will be stubborn and disobedient
and cause you nothing but sorrow. 13So dis-
cipline your son and give him work to do, or
else he will be an embarrassment to you.

Health

14It is better to be poor, but strong and
healthy, than to be rich, but in poor health.
15A sound, healthy body and a cheerful atti-
tude[y] are more valuable than gold and jew-
els. 16Nothing can make you richer or give
you greater happiness than those two things.
17It would be better to be dead, asleep forev-
er, than to live in the misery of chronic ill-
ness. 18The finest food means nothing if you
are too sick to eat it; it might as well be
offered to an idol.[z] 19But there is no point
in offering food to an idol; it can't eat it or
smell it. It is just the same with someone
whom the Lord has afflicted. 20He looks at
his food and sighs, like a castrated man hug-
ging a young woman.

The finest food means nothing if you are too sick to eat it. (30:18)

Cheerfulness and Sadness

21Don't deliberately torture yourself by
giving in to depression. 22Happiness makes
for a long life and makes it worth living.
23Enjoy yourself and be happy; don't worry
all the time. Worry never did anybody any
good, and it has destroyed many people. 24It
will make you old before your time. Jealousy
and anger will shorten your life. 25A cheerful
person with a good attitude will have a good
appetite and enjoy his food.

Problems Caused by Money

31 Worrying about money will make
you lose weight and lose sleep. 2Wor-
rying about business[a] will keep you from
sleeping just as surely as a serious illness does.
3Rich people work hard to make a lot of
money; then they can sit back and live in
luxury. 4Poor people work hard and have
nothing to show for it, and when they rest,
they are still poor.

5No one who loves money can be judged
innocent; his efforts to get rich have led him
into sin.[b] 6Many people have been ruined

[x] **30:7** will have . . . wounds; *or* is going to be hurt. [y] **30:15** *Hebrew* a cheerful attitude; *Greek* a strong body.
[z] **30:18** *Hebrew* offered to an idol; *Greek* placed on a grave. [a] **31:2** *Hebrew* Worrying about business; *Greek* Sleepless worry. [b] **31:5** *Hebrew* have . . . sin; *Greek* will destroy him.

30:21–25 Eccl 11:9, 10

because of money, brought face to face with disaster. 7 Money is a trap for those who are fascinated by it, a trap that every fool falls into.

Money is a trap for those who are fascinated by it. *(31:7)*

8 A person who gets rich without sinfully chasing after money is fortunate. 9 Do you know anyone like that? If so, we will congratulate him for performing a miracle that no one else has ever been able to do. 10 If anyone has ever passed this test, he can well be proud. Has anyone ever known that he could get away with cheating someone, and not taken advantage of it? 11 If so, he deserves his wealth, and everyone will praise him for his generosity.

Behavior at Dinner Parties

12 When you sit down at a fancy banquet, don't let your mouth hang open, and don't say, "Look at all that food!" 13 It is impolite to have a greedy eye; remember that. Nothing in creation is greedier than the eye; that is why it sheds tears so often.[c] 14 Don't reach out for everything you see, and don't elbow people out of the way to get at the food. 15 Be considerate of the other people at the table and treat them the way you want to be treated. 16 When you get your food, eat it like a human being. Don't smack and slurp; nobody can stand that. 17 It's good manners to be the first to stop eating; stuffing yourself is offensive. 18 If there are many people present, don't try to be the first to be served. 19 A little bit is plenty for anyone with good manners. Besides, you won't be short of breath when you go to bed. 20 People who eat too much get stomach aches and cannot sleep. If you don't overeat, you can get a good night's sleep and wake up early the next morning feeling fine. 21 But if you do get a stomach ache from eating too much, go off and vomit[d] and you will feel better. 22 My child, if you listen to what I am saying and put it into practice, one of these days you will thank me for it. Be moderate[e] in everything you do, and you will never get sick.

23 People appreciate a generous host, and he deserves their praise. 24 But everybody in town will complain about a host who is stingy with food, and their complaints are justified.

25 Don't try to prove your manhood by how much you can drink. Wine has been the ruin of many. 26 An arrogant person's character shows through when he is in a drunken argument, in the same way that iron is tested when it is heated red-hot and then dipped in water. 27 Wine can put new life into you if you drink it in moderation. What would life be like without it? Wine was created to make us happy. 28 If you drink it in moderation and at the right time, it can lift your spirits and make you cheerful, 29 but if you drink when you are angry and upset, it leads to headaches, embarrassment, and disgrace.[f] 30 A drunken fool can lose his temper and hurt himself. His drinking makes him weak and an easy target for angry blows. 31 Never rebuke a person when you have both been drinking. Don't hurt his feelings while he is having a good time. It's not the time to criticize anyone, or to ask him to pay back a debt.

32 If you are chosen to preside at a banquet, don't put on airs. Just be like everyone else. Look after the guests before you sit down. 2 After you have performed your duties, you can sit down and enjoy yourself with the others. They will respect you for doing a good job.

[c] **31:13** *Hebrew* so often; *Greek* on every face. [d] **31:21** go off and vomit; *some manuscripts have* get up in the middle of the meal. [e] **31:22** *Hebrew* moderate; *Greek* industrious. [f] **31:29** *Hebrew* when you are . . . disgrace; *Greek* too much, it leads to bitterness, offense, and stumbling.

3 If you are older than most of the guests, you may talk; that is your right. But you should know what you are talking about and not interrupt the music. 4 If entertainment is being provided, don't keep up a steady conversation; it's the wrong time to show off your wit. 5 Music at a banquet where wine is served is like a ruby set in gold. 6 Good music and good wine—an emerald set in gold.

7 If you are young, don't speak unless you have to, but never more than twice, and only if someone speaks to you first. 8 Come to the point and say it all in a few words. Show that you are well-informed, but stay quiet. 9 Don't treat important people as if you were their equal and don't make a nuisance of yourself by asking them a lot of questions.[g] 10 The reputation of a modest person goes before him, as lightning before thunder.

11 Leave the party at the right time and never be the last to go. Don't linger at the door; just go straight home. 12 There you can enjoy yourself as you wish, but don't commit the sin of bragging. 13 And don't forget to thank your Creator for letting you enjoy so many good things.

Interpreting the Law

14 If you fear the Lord, you will accept his correction. He will bless those who get up early in the morning to pray. 15 Study his Law, and you will master it, unless you are insincere about it, in which case you will fail. 16 If you fear the Lord, you will know what is right, and you will be famous for your fairness. 17 Sinners have no use for correction, and will interpret the Law to suit themselves.

18 Sensible people will consider every opinion, but arrogant[h] people will let nothing stand in their way. 19 Never do anything without thinking it through, and once you have done something, don't look back and wish you had done something else. 20 Don't take a course of action that is dangerous, and don't make the same mistake twice.[i] 21 Don't be too sure of yourself, even when the way looks easy. 22 Always watch where you are going.[j] 23 Whatever you do be careful;[k] this is keeping the Lord's commands.

24 Believing in the Law means keeping the Lord's commands.

If you trust the Lord, you cannot lose.

33 1 No evil will ever come to a person who fears the Lord; however often danger comes, the Lord will come to the rescue. 2 A person who has no use for the Law doesn't have good sense, and anyone who is insincere about it is going to be tossed about like a boat in a storm. 3 If you are wise, you will believe in the Law; you will find it as reliable as the sacred lots.

4 Prepare what you are going to say and people will listen to you. Use what you have learned before you start talking. 5 A foolish person's mind works like a cartwheel, going round and round in circles. 6 A sarcastic friend is like a wild horse that neighs no matter who tries to ride him.

People Are Not Alike

7 Why are some days holier than others, even though the same sun rises on every day of the year? 8 It is because the Lord made them different by setting them apart as religious holidays and festivals. 9 He made some days holy and important, and made other days ordinary.

10 Every human being was made from the earth, just as Adam was. 11 But the Lord, in his wisdom, made them all different and gave them different tasks. 12 He blessed some, making them honored and holy, keeping them near him. Others he cursed, humbling them and removing them from their positions. 13 Just as clay is in the potter's hands for him to shape as he pleases, so we are in the hands of our Creator for him to do with as he wishes.

14 Good is the opposite of evil, life is the opposite of death, and sin is the opposite of devotion to the Lord. 15 Think about it: the

[g] **32:9** *Hebrew* make . . . questions; *Greek* keep talking when someone else is speaking. [h] **32:18** *Hebrew* arrogant; *Greek* foreign and arrogant. [i] **32:20** *Hebrew* make . . . twice; *Greek* stumble on stones. [j] **32:22** *Hebrew* watch . . . going; *Greek* look out for your children. [k] **32:23** *Hebrew* be careful; *Greek* have confidence in yourself.

33:3 Ex 28:30; Sir 45:10

Most High has made everything in pairs,
each thing the opposite of something else.
16 As for me, I have been the last to come
on duty, as if going through vineyards to
gather whatever the grape-pickers had left
behind. But the Lord blessed me, and I did
well,[l] like a grape-picker who has filled the
wine press. 17 But I want you to know that I
have not done all this work for myself alone,
but for everyone who wants to learn. 18 Lis-
ten to me, all you great leaders! All you lead-
ers of the assemblies, hear what I have to say!

Be Independent

19 Never, as long as you live, give anyone
power over you—whether son, wife, brother,
or friend. Don't give your property to any-
one; you might change your mind and have
to ask for it back. 20 As long as you have
breath in your body, don't let anyone lead
your life for you. 21 It is better that your chil-
dren be dependent on you than the other
way around. 22 Keep control over all that you
do; don't let anything stain your reputation.
23 Wait until the last moment of your life,
when you are breathing your last, and then
divide your property among your heirs.

Treatment of Slaves

24 A donkey should be given its fodder and
its burden, and it should be beaten. A slave
should be given food and work, and should
be disciplined. 25 If you make your slave
work, you can set your mind at ease. If you
don't keep him busy, he will be looking for
freedom. 26 You can use a harness and yoke
to tame an animal, and a slave can be tor-
tured in the stocks. 27 Keep him at work, and
don't let him be idle; idleness can only teach
him how to make trouble. 28 Work is what
he needs. If he won't obey you, put him in
chains.
29 But don't be too severe with anyone,
and never be unfair. 30 If you have a slave,
treat him as you would want to be treated;
you bought him with your hard-earned
money. 31 Treat him as a brother; you need
him as you need yourself. If you mistreat
him and he runs away, where are you going
to look for him?

Dreams Mean Nothing

34 Foolish people are deceived by vain
hopes, and dreams get them all
excited. 2 A person who pays any attention at
all to dreams is like someone who tries to
catch shadows or chase the wind. 3 What you
see in a dream is no more real than the
reflection of your face in a mirror. 4 What is
unreal can no more produce something real
than what is dirty can produce something
clean. 5 Dreams, divination, and omens are all
nonsense. You see in them only what you
want to see.[m] 6 Unless the Most High has
sent you the dream, pay no attention to it.
7 Dreams have misled many people; they put
their faith in them, only to be disappointed.
8 The Law is complete without such false-
hood. Wisdom, as spoken by the righteous, is
also complete without it.

Travel

9 A well-traveled[n] person with wide expe-
rience knows many things and talks sense.
10 You can't know much if you haven't expe-
rienced much, but travel can make you more
clever. 11 In my own travels I have seen many
things and learned more than I can put into
words. 12 I have been in danger of death
many times, but I have always been able to
escape by relying on past experience.

Fear the Lord

13 Those who fear the Lord will live,
because they have put their trust in the one
who can save them. 14 Fear the Lord, and you
will have nothing else to fear. If your trust is
in him, you will never act like a coward.
15 People who fear the Lord are fortunate,
because they know where they can look for
help. 16 The Lord watches over those who
love him; he is their strong protection and
firm support. He shelters them from the

[l] **33:16** did well; *or* overtook the others. [m] **34:5** *Probable text* You see . . . to see; *Greek* The mind has an imagination like a woman in labor. [n] **34:9** A well-traveled; *some manuscripts have* An educated.

34:1–8 Deut 13:1–5; 18:9–14

heat, shades them from the noonday sun, and
keeps them from stumbling and falling. 17He
makes them cheerful and puts a sparkle in
their eyes. He blesses them with life and
health.

Offering Sacrifices

18If you offer as a sacrifice an animal that
you have obtained dishonestly, it is defective
and unacceptable. 19The Most High gets no
pleasure from sacrifices made by ungodly
people; no amount of sacrifices can make
up for their sins. 20Anyone who steals an
animal from the poor to offer as a sacrifice
is like someone who kills a boy before his
father's eyes. 21Food means life itself to
poor people, and taking it away from them
is murder. 22It is murder to deprive some-
one of his living or to cheat an employee of
his wages.

. . . taking it away from them is murder. (34:21)

23When one person builds and somebody
else tears down, has anything been accom-
plished but hard work? 24When one person
blesses and somebody else curses, which one
is the Lord going to listen to? 25If you touch
a dead body and then purify yourself by
washing, but then go and touch it again,
what good did the washing do? 26If you fast
because of your sins, and then go out and
commit the same sins over again, what have
you gained by going without food? Who do
you think is going to listen to your prayers?

35 Keeping the Law is worth many
offerings; it is a fellowship offering
in itself. 2Returning a kindness is like a grain
offering; giving to the poor is like a thanks-
giving offering. 3Keeping away from sin will
please the Lord and make atonement for sin.
4But don't come to the Temple without an
offering; 5the Law requires that you bring
one. 6When someone righteous offers a sac-
rifice and the fat drips down on the altar, a
pleasant smell rises to the Most High. 7The
Lord will accept the offerings made by a
righteous person and will not forget them.
8Praise the Lord by making generous offer-
ings to him; don't be stingy with the first of
your crops. 9Be cheerful with every gift you
make, and when you pay your tithes, do it
gladly. 10Give to the Most High as he has
given to you, just as generously as you can.
11The Lord always repays and will do it
many times over. 12But don't try to bribe
him or rely on offerings that you have
obtained dishonestly. He will not accept
them.

God's Justice

The Lord is fair[o] and does not show par-
tiality. 13He is not prejudiced against the
poor; when someone prays who has been
wronged, the Lord listens. 14When orphans
and widows pour out their prayers, he does
not ignore them. 15The tears running down
a widow's cheek cry out in accusation
against the one who has caused her distress.
16Serve the Lord willingly, and the Lord
will accept you; your prayers will reach the
skies. 17The prayer of a humble person goes
past the clouds and keeps on going until it
reaches the Lord Most High, where it stays
until he answers by seeing that justice is
done and that the guilty are punished.
18And the Lord will act quickly. He will
show no patience with wicked people. He
will take vengeance by crushing the heathen.
He will completely wipe out the merciless
and the arrogant, and will destroy the
authority of the wicked. 19He will give each
of us what our thoughts and actions deserve.
Because of the Lord's mercy, his people will

[o] **35:12** *Hebrew* fair; *Greek* judge.
35:9 2 Cor 9:7

be happy when he has judged their case. 20In
times of trouble his mercy is as welcome as
rain after a long drought.

A Prayer for Israel

36 O Lord God of the universe, look
upon us and have mercy. 2Make
every nation stand in fear of you. 3Take
action against the foreign nations, and let
them witness your power! 4You have used us
to show them how holy you are; now use
them to show us how great you are. 5Let
them learn, as we have learned, that there is
no God, O Lord, but you. 6Give new signs,
perform new miracles; show us your glori-
ous strength! 7-9Bring on that appointed
time when everyone can talk about the great
things you do. Pour out your furious, flam-
ing anger, and let none of our enemies sur-
vive. Destroy those who have oppressed your
people. 10Crush all those enemy rulers who
think they are the only people in the world
who matter! 11Gather the tribes of Israel
together again, and give them back their
land as you gave it to them long ago. 12Lord,
have mercy on Israel, the people who are
known by your name, whom you called
your first-born son. 13Take pity on
Jerusalem, your holy city, where you chose
to stay. 14Fill your Temple[p] on Mount Zion
with your glory and with hymns of praise.
15Testify for your people, whom you created
in the beginning; fulfill the prophecies that
have been spoken in your name. 16Reward
those who have put their faith in you, and
vindicate your prophets. 17You have always
been gracious to your people;[q] listen to your
servants as we pray. Then everyone on earth
will recognize that you are the Lord, the
God of the ages.

Choosing a Wife

18Any kind of food can be eaten, but
some foods are better than others. 19And just
as the tongue can distinguish the flavors of
different kinds of meat, so a sharp mind can
detect lies. 20A person with a warped mind
causes trouble, but an experienced person
knows how to pay it back.

21A woman has to take any man as a hus-
band, but a man must choose his wife care-
fully. 22A woman's beauty makes a man
happy; there is no fairer sight for the human
eye to see. 23If the woman is kind and gentle
in her speech, her husband is the most fortu-
nate of men. 24When a man marries, he gets
the finest thing he will ever have—a wife to
help and encourage him.

25If property is not fenced in, thieves will
wander in and help themselves. And if a man
has no wife, he is a sighing wanderer; 26peo-
ple have no more trust in a homeless person
who sleeps in a different place every night
than they have in a wandering thief who
goes from town to town.

False Friends

37 Anyone can claim to be your friend,
but some people are friends in name
only. 2The grief caused when a close friend-
ship turns sour is as bad as death. 3This evil
impulse we have! Why was it ever formed?
How did it manage to cover the earth with
deceit? 4Some people will be your friend as
long as things are going well, but they will
turn against you when trouble comes. 5A
real[r] friend will help you against your ene-
mies[s] and protect you in the fight. 6Never
forget such companions in battle;[t] share the
results of your victory with them.

When a close friendship turns sour (37:2)

[p] **36:14** *Hebrew* Temple; *Greek* people. [q] **36:17** *Hebrew* You have . . . people; *Greek* According to the blessing of Aaron on your people. [r] **37:5** *Hebrew* real; *Greek does not have this word.* [s] **37:5** *Hebrew* against your enemies; *Greek* hoping to get a meal. [t] **37:6** *Hebrew* in battle; *Greek* in your soul.

Caution in Taking Advice

7Anyone can give advice, but some peo-
ple do so only in their own interest. 8Be
careful when somebody offers you advice.
Find out first what his interest in the matter
is, because you can be sure that he is think-
ing primarily of himself. Why should he
come out on top instead of you?[u] 9He will
assure you that things look good, and then
stand back to watch what happens to you.

10Don't ask advice of anyone who doesn't
trust you, and don't give advice to anyone
who is jealous of you.

11Don't ask a woman for advice about a
rival of hers,

a coward about war,
a merchant about a bargain,
a buyer about selling,
a stingy person about gratitude,
a cruel person about kindness,
a lazy person about work,
a casual worker about finishing a job,
a lazy slave about a difficult task.

Pay no attention to any advice they may
give.

12Instead, rely on someone who is reli-
gious and known to keep the Lord's com-
mands, someone who is sympathetic with
you, who will be sorry to see you fail. 13And
trust your own judgment; no one's advice is
more reliable. 14Sometimes your own intu-
ition can tell you more than seven watch-
men on a high tower. 15Above all, pray to
the Most High that he will show you the
right thing to do.

Wisdom and Confidence

16Planning and thought lie behind every-
thing that is done. 17-18The mind concerns
itself with four things: these are good and
evil, life and death. They all begin in the
mind,[v] but the tongue is their absolute ruler.

19Someone may have the ability to teach,
but still not be of much use to himself. 20He
may be clever with words, but end up starv-
ing because people hate him. 21This may
happen if he doesn't have good sense, if the
Lord has not given him tact. 22Someone may
consider himself wise and let you know that
he is certain about what he knows. 23Any-
one who really is wise will be the teacher of
his people, and they can be certain that what
he teaches is the truth. 24Everyone will
praise such a person and speak of him as for-
tunate. 25A person's life has only a limited
number of days, but the life of Israel cannot
be measured in days at all. 26The wise will
win the confidence of others, and will be
remembered forever.

Controlling the Appetite

27My child, as you go through life, keep
your appetite under control, and don't eat
anything that you know is bad for you. 28All
food doesn't agree with everyone, and every-
one doesn't like the same kinds of food.
29Don't feel that you just have to have all
sorts of fancy food, and don't be a glutton
over any food. 30If you eat too much, you'll
get sick; if you do it all the time, you'll
always have stomach trouble. 31Gluttony has
been the death of many people. Avoid it and
live longer.

Sickness and Medicine

38 Give doctors the honor they
deserve, for the Lord gave them their
work to do.[w] 2Their skill came from the
Most High, and kings reward them for it.
3Their knowledge gives them a position of
importance, and powerful people hold them
in high regard.

4The Lord created medicines from the
earth, and a sensible person will not hesitate
to use them. 5Didn't a tree once make bitter
water fit to drink, so that the Lord's power[x]
might be known? 6He gave medical knowl-
edge to human beings, so that we would
praise him for the miracles he performs.
7-8The druggist mixes these medicines, and
the doctor will use them to cure diseases and

[u] **37:8** *Hebrew* Why . . . you?; *Greek* He may use his influence against you. [v] **37:17–18** *Hebrew* The mind . . . the mind; *Greek* There are four things that show the changes of the heart: good and evil, life and death.
[w] **38:1** *Hebrew* gave them their work to do; *Greek* created them. [x] **38:5** the Lord's power; *or* its healing properties.

38:5 Ex 15:23–25

ease pain. There is no end to the activities of
the Lord, who gives health to the people of
the world.
9My child, when you get sick, don't
ignore it. Pray to the Lord, and he will make
you well. 10Confess all your sins and deter-
mine that in the future you will live a righ-
teous life. 11Offer incense and a grain offer-
ing, as fine as you can afford.[y] 12Then call
the doctor—for the Lord created him—and
keep him at your side; you need him.
13There are times when you have to depend
on his skill. 14The doctor's prayer is that the
Lord will make him able to ease his patients'
pain and make them well again. 15As for the
person who sins against his Creator, he
deserves to be sick.

Mourning for the Dead

16My child, when someone dies, you
should mourn. Weep and wail to show how
deeply you feel the loss. Prepare the body in
the proper way, and be present at the burial.
17Weep bitterly and passionately; observe the
proper period of mourning for the person.
Mourn for a whole day or maybe two, to
keep people from talking, but then pull
yourself together and reconcile yourself to
the loss. 18Grief can undermine your health
and even lead to your own death. 19Grief
lingers on after the death of a loved one, but
it is not wise to let it lead you into poverty.
20Don't lose yourself in sorrow; drive it
away.[z] Remember that we must all die
sometime. 21There is no way to bring the
dead person back. All your sorrow does him
no good, and it hurts you. Don't forget that.
22You will die, just as he did. Today it was his
turn; tomorrow it will be yours. 23When the
dead have been laid to rest, let the memory
of them fade. Once they are gone, take
courage.

Scholarship and Other Occupations

24Scholars must have time to study if they
are going to be wise; they must be relieved
of other responsibilities. 25How can a farm

All your sorrow does him no good. (38:21)

hand gain knowledge, when his only ambi-
tion is to drive the oxen and make them
work, when all he knows to talk about is
livestock? 26He takes great pains to plow a
straight furrow and will work far into the
night to feed the animals.
27It is the same with the artist and the
craftsman, who work night and day engrav-
ing precious stones, carefully working out
new designs. They take great pains to pro-
duce a lifelike image, and will work far into
the night to finish the work.
28It is the same with the blacksmith at his
anvil, planning what he will make from a
piece of iron. The heat from the fire sears his
skin as he sweats away at the forge. The
clanging of the hammer deafens him[a] as he
carefully watches the object he is working
take shape. He takes great pains to complete
his task, and will work far into the night to
bring it to perfection.
29It is the same with the potter, sitting at
his wheel and turning it with his feet, always
concentrating on his work, concerned with
how many objects he can produce. 30He
works the clay with his feet until he can
shape it with his hands; then he takes great
pains to glaze it properly, and will work far
into the night to clean out the kiln.
31All of these people are skilled with their
hands, each of them an expert at his own
craft. 32Without such people there could be
no cities; no one would live or visit where

[y] **38:11** *Hebrew* as fine as you can afford; *Greek unclear.* [z] **38:20** drive it away; *or* put the memory of the person aside. [a] **38:28** *Probable text* deafens him; *Greek* renews his ears.

38:16–23 Sir 22:11, 12

He works the clay with his feet until he can shape it with his hands. (38:30)

these services were not available. 33These people are not sought out to serve on the public councils, and they never attain positions of great importance. They do not serve as judges, and they do not understand legal matters. They have no education and are not known for their wisdom. You never hear them quoting proverbs. 34But the work they do holds this world together. When they do their work, it is the same as offering prayer.[b]

39 But it is different with the person who devotes himself to studying the Law of the Most High. He examines the wisdom of all the ancient writers and concerns himself with the prophecies. 2He memorizes the sayings of famous men and is a skilled interpreter of parables. 3He studies the hidden meaning of proverbs and is able to discuss the obscure points of parables. 4Great people call on him for his services, and he is seen in the company of rulers. He travels to foreign lands in his efforts to learn about human good and evil. 5It is his practice to get up early and pray aloud to the Lord his Creator, asking the Most High to forgive his sins. 6Then, if the great Lord is willing, he will be filled with understanding. He will pour out a stream of wise sayings, and give thanks to the Lord in prayer. 7He will have knowledge to share and good advice to give, as well as insight into the Lord's secrets. 8He will demonstrate his learning in what he teaches,[c] and his pride will be in the Lord's Law and covenant. 9He will be widely praised for his wisdom, and it will never be lost, because people for generations to come will remember him. 10The Gentiles will talk about his wisdom, and he will be praised aloud in the assembly. 11If he lives to old age, he will die famous, but if he is laid to rest before he is famous, he will be content.[d]

A Hymn in Praise of God

12Like the moon, I am full—full of more ideas to be discussed. 13Listen to me, you devout children of mine, and blossom like a rosebush on a stream bank. 14Bloom like a sweet-smelling lily, and send your fragrance into the air like incense. Sing the Lord's praises, and thank him for all that he has done. 15Proclaim his glory in grateful praise! To the music of the harp, sing this song:

16 All that the Lord has done is very good;
  all that he commands is sooner or later done.
17 No one should ask why things are as they are;
  these questions will be answered at the right time.
He commanded, and the water piled up high,
  great walls of water arose when he spoke.
18 Whatever he commands is promptly done;
  there are no limits to his power to save.
19 He sees all that every human being does;
  there is no way to hide from his sight.
20 He sees the whole of time, from beginning to end,
  and nothing takes him by surprise.[e]
21 No one should ask why things are as they are;
  everything in creation has its purpose.
22 His blessings overflow like the Nile,
  enriching the world in a fertile flood.[f]

[b] **38:34** When . . . prayer; *or* When they pray, it is about their work. [c] **39:8** his learning . . . teaches; *or* the wisdom of what he has been taught. [d] **39:11** if he is . . . content; *Greek unclear.* [e] **39:20** takes him by surprise; *or* is too marvelous for him. [f] **39:22** *Hebrew* overflow . . . flood; *Greek* cover the dry land like a river and drench it like a flood.

[23] He turns fresh water into salt water,
and he turns his anger on the nations.
[24] For the devout, his ways are straight;
for the wicked, they are laid with traps.
[25] From the beginning he has made good
things for the good
and terrible things for sinners.
[26] The basic needs of life are these:
water, fire, iron, and salt,
flour, honey, and milk,
wine, clothing, and oil.
[27] All these things are good for those who
are devout,
but they turn into evils for sinners.

[28] There are winds that were created to
bring punishment,
fierce enough to move mountains.[g]
In times of judgment, they unleash their
strength
and calm the anger of their maker.
[29-30] Vicious animals, scorpions, and snakes;
the sword that destroys the wicked;
fire, hail, famine, and disease;
these have all been created as
punishments.
[31] They are all glad to obey the Lord's
command
and are ready to serve him here on
earth.
When their times of duty come,
they never disobey.
([32] I was long convinced of this, so after
thinking it over I put[h] it in writing.)
[33] Everything made by the Lord is good;
he meets every need at the proper
time.
[34] No one can claim that some things are
worse than others,
for everything is good in its proper
place.
[35] Now then, sing praises with all your heart,
and praise the name of the Lord!

The Misery of Human Life

40 Every person has been given a great
deal of work to do. A heavy burden
lies on all of us from the day of our birth
until the day we go back to the earth, the
mother of us all. [2] We are confused and fear-
ful, dreading the day of our death— [3-4] all of
us from the king on his splendid throne
wearing royal robes and a crown, to the
humblest person dressed in burlap and living
in poverty. [5] All through our lives we meet
anger, jealousy, and trouble. Things disturb
us; we live with furious conflicts and with
the fear of death. Even when we go to bed,
we think up new troubles in our sleep. [6] We
get little rest, if any at all. When we sleep, it
is as if we were awake, disturbed by our
imaginations. If we dream that we are run-
ning from an enemy, [7] just as we are about to
be caught,[i] we wake up and are relieved to
find there is nothing to be afraid of.
[8] Here is what all creatures, both human
and animal, must face (but it is seven times
worse for sinners): [9] death, violence, conflict,
murder, disaster, famine, sickness, epidemic.
[10] All these things were created because of
the wicked; they are the ones who have
caused destruction.[j] [11] Everything that comes
from the earth goes back to the earth, just as
all water flows into the sea.

The Results of Evil

[12] Nothing that comes from bribery or
injustice will last, but the effects of loyalty
will remain forever. [13] Wealth that has been
obtained dishonestly is like a stream that
runs full during a thunderstorm, [14] tumbling
rocks along as it flows, but then suddenly
goes dry.[k] [15] The children of ungodly people
will not leave large families; they are like
plants trying to take root on rock, [16] like
reeds along a river bank, withering[l] before
any other plant. [17] Acts of kindness and char-
ity are as lasting as eternity.[m]

The Joys of Human Life

[18] Being independently wealthy or work-
ing for a living—both can make life pleasant,
but it is better to find a treasure.
[19] Your name can be preserved if you have

[g] **39:28** *Hebrew* move mountains; *Greek* lash heavily. [h] **39:32** put; *or* left. [i] **40:7** *Probable text* caught; *Greek* rescued. [j] **40:10** *Hebrew* have caused destruction; *Greek* caused the flood. [k] **40:14** *Verses 13–14 are translated from Hebrew; verse 14 in Greek is unclear.* [l] **40:16** *Hebrew* withering; *Greek* pulled up. [m] **40:17** *Hebrew* Acts . . . eternity; *Greek* Kindness is a blessed garden, and charity lasts forever.

children or if you establish a city, but finding Wisdom is a better way.

Owning livestock and orchards will make you famous,[n] but it is better to have a wife you love.[o]

20 Wine and music can make you happy, but a happy marriage[p] is even better.

21 Flutes and harps make fine music, but a pleasant voice is better than either.

22 Gracefulness and beauty please the eye, but not as much as new growth in the spring.

23 You can't go wrong with a good friend or neighbor, but an intelligent wife is[q] better than either.

24 Relatives and helpers are good to have in times of trouble, but it will be an even greater help if you have made a practice of giving to the poor.

25 Gold and silver provide security, but good advice is better.

26 Wealth and strength give confidence, but the fear of the Lord can give you even greater confidence. When you fear the Lord you need nothing more; it is all the support you need. 27 The fear of the Lord is like a rich garden of blessings; you could not want a more glorious shelter.

Begging

28 My child, don't live the life of a beggar; it is better to die than to beg. 29 If you have to depend on someone else for your food, you are not really living your own life. You pollute yourself by accepting food from another. Begging is torture to the soul of any sensitive person.[r] 30 A shameless person can make begging sound sweet, but something inside him burns.

Death

41 Death! The very thought of it is bitter to someone who is prosperous, living peacefully with his possessions, free of worries, and still able to enjoy his food.

2 Death! Its sentence is welcome to someone living in poverty, with failing health, very old, burdened with worries, blind, and without hope.[s]

3 Do not be afraid of death's decree. Remember that it came to those before you and will come to those after you. 4 The Lord has decreed it for every living creature. Who are you to object to what the Most High wishes? In the world of the dead no one will care whether you lived ten years, a hundred, or a thousand.

The Fate of the Wicked

5 The children of sinners, brought up in ungodly surroundings, turn out to be hateful people. 6 They will lose whatever they inherit, and their own descendants will live in permanent disgrace. 7 The children will put the blame for their disgrace on their ungodly parents.

8 You are doomed, you irreligious people who have abandoned the Law of the Most High God. 9 When you have children, disaster will strike them and you will be left with nothing but sorrow. There will be great joy whenever you stumble,[t] and even after your death you will be cursed. 10 What comes into being from nothing[u] will return to nothing;[u] so it will be with the godless, doomed to extinction.

11 A person's body amounts to nothing,[v] but a good reputation will last forever. 12 Protect your reputation; it will outlive you and last longer than a thousand treasures of gold. 13 A good life lasts only so long, but a good reputation will last forever.

A Sense of Decency

14 My children, do as I teach you and live at peace. Wisdom that is not expressed is like a treasure that has been hidden—both are useless. 15 A person who covers up his fool-

[n] **40:19** *Hebrew* but finding Wisdom . . . famous; *Greek does not have these words.* [o] **40:19** *Hebrew* wife you love; *Greek* blameless wife. [p] **40:20** *Hebrew* a happy marriage; *Greek* the love of Wisdom. [q] **40:23** *Hebrew* an intelligent wife is; *Greek* a wife and a husband are. [r] **40:29** *Hebrew* Begging . . . person; *Greek* An intelligent and understanding person will avoid it. [s] **41:2** *Hebrew* blind, and without hope; *Greek* rebellious and without patience. [t] **41:9** *Hebrew* When you have . . . stumble; *Greek* You are born under a curse. [u] **41:10** *Hebrew* nothing; *Greek* earth. [v] **41:11** *Hebrew* A person's . . . nothing; *Greek* The death of a person's body is mourned.

ishness is better than one who keeps his wisdom to himself.

16 My children, listen and I will teach you the circumstances when it is proper to be ashamed.[w] Sometimes it is entirely out of place.

. . . when it is proper to be ashamed. (41:16)

17 Before your parents, be ashamed of
immoral behavior.
Before a ruler or an important person, be
ashamed of a lie.
18 Before a judge, be ashamed of criminal
behavior.
Before a public assembly, be ashamed of
breaking the law.
Before a friend or partner, be ashamed of
dishonesty.
19 Before your neighbors, be ashamed of
theft.
Be ashamed of breaking a promise,[x]
of leaning on the dinner table with
your elbows,
of stinginess when you are asked for
something,
20 of not returning a greeting,
of staring at a prostitute,
21 of turning down a relative's request,
of depriving someone of what is
rightly his,
of staring at another man's wife,
22 of playing around with his slave
woman (keep away from her bed!)
of insulting your friends,
of following up your gifts with
criticism,
23 of betraying secrets.
These are times when it is proper for you to be ashamed, and people will respect you for it.

A Sense of Pride

42 On the other hand, it is possible to sin by giving in to other people too much. Here are some things you should not be ashamed of:

2 the Law of the Most High and his
covenant,
judging even godless people fairly,
3 sharing expenses with a business partner
or a traveling companion,
sharing an inheritance,
4 using accurate weights and measures,
5 making a profit, whether great or small,
bargaining with a merchant,
disciplining your children often,
beating a disloyal slave until the blood
flows.

6 It is wise to lock things up if you cannot
trust your wife or if too many people are
around. 7 Keep an accurate record of any
deposits you make or of anything you give
or receive. 8 Don't hesitate to correct someone who is acting foolishly or an old man who goes around with prostitutes. All of this is worthwhile advice, and if you follow it, everyone will approve of your behavior.

Fathers and Daughters

9 Although he will not let his daughter know it, a father will lie awake at night worrying about her. If she is young, he worries that she might not get married. If she is already married, he worries about her happiness.
10 If she is a virgin, he worries that she might be seduced and become pregnant while living in his house. If she is married, he worries that she might be unfaithful, or that she might not be able to have children.

11 Keep a close watch over your daughter if she is determined to have her own way. If you don't, she may make a fool of you in front of your enemies. You will be a constant joke to everyone in town, a public disgrace. Make sure that her room has no windows or any place where she can look out to the entrance of the house.[y]
12 Don't let her show

[w] **41:16** *Hebrew* My children . . . ashamed; *Greek* Show respect for what I say. [x] **41:19** *Hebrew* of breaking a promise; *Greek* of yourself before the truth of God. [y] **42:11** *Hebrew* Make sure . . . house; *Greek does not have these words.*

42:9–11 Sir 7:24, 25; 26:10–12

off her beauty in front of men, or spend her time talking with the women.[z] 13 Women hurt other women just as moths damage clothing.

14 A man's wickedness is better than a woman's goodness; women bring shame and disgrace.

The Glory of God in Nature

15 Now I will remind you of the works of the Lord
and describe the things I have seen.
The words of the Lord brought his works into being,
and the whole creation obeys his commands.
16 The light of the sun shines down on everything,
and everything is filled with the Lord's glory.
17 Not even to his holy angels has the Lord given power
to describe all his mighty deeds,
even though he has given them power
to stand unharmed in his glorious presence.[a]
18 He sees into the oceans and into the human heart,
and he knows the secrets of both.
The Most High knows everything that can be known
and understands the signs of the ages.
19 He knows all that has ever been and all that ever will be;
he uncovers the deepest of mysteries.
20 He takes notice of our every thought
and hears our every word.
21 The orderly world shows the greatness of his wisdom;
he is the same forever and ever.[b]
Nothing can be added to him, and nothing taken away;
he needs no one to give him advice.
22 All his works are beautiful,
down to the smallest and faintest spark of light.[c]
23 All these things go on forever,
and all of them have their purpose.
24 All things are in pairs, each the opposite of the other,
but nothing the Lord made is incomplete.
25 Everything completes the goodness of something else.
Could anyone ever see enough of this splendor?

43 How beautiful is the bright, clear sky above us!
What a glorious sight it is!
2 The sun, when it appears, proclaims as it rises
how marvelous a thing it is, made by the Most High.
3 At noon it dries up the land;
no one can stand its blazing heat.
4 The setting sun sets fire to the hilltops,
like a metal furnace glowing from the heat.[d]
It sends out fiery rays,
blinding the eyes with its brightness.
5 The Lord, who made it, is great;
it speeds on its way at his command.

6 There is also the moon, marking the passage of time,[e]
an eternal sign of the changing seasons.
7 The moon determines the holy days.
Its light grows full and then grows dim.
8 The "month" is named after the moon,
marvelous to watch as it grows fuller each night,
a signal light for the heavenly armies,
shining out in the dome of the sky.
9 The shining stars make the night sky lovely,
brilliant ornaments in the Lord's high heavens.
10 They stay in the places assigned to them by the Holy One
and never relax their dutiful watch.

11 Look at the rainbow and praise its Creator!
How magnificent, how radiant, its beauty!

[z] **42:11** *Hebrew* Don't let . . . women; *Greek unclear.* [a] **42:17** *Hebrew* even though . . . presence; *Greek* which the Lord Almighty established so that everything may stand firm in his glory. [b] **42:21** *Hebrew* he is . . . ever; *Greek* he is before eternity and is eternal. [c] **42:22** *Hebrew* down to . . . spark of light; *Greek unclear.*
[d] **43:4** *Hebrew* The setting . . . heat; *Greek* A man at a furnace works with scorching heat, but the sun burns the hills three times as much. [e] **43:6** *Hebrew* marking . . . time; *Greek unclear.*

off her beauty in front of men, or spend her
time talking with the women.[z] 13 Women
hurt other women just as moths damage
clothing.

14 A man's wickedness is better than a
woman's goodness; women bring shame and
disgrace.

The Glory of God in Nature

15 Now I will remind you of the works of
the Lord
and describe the things I have seen.
The words of the Lord brought his works
into being,
and the whole creation obeys his
commands.
16 The light of the sun shines down on
everything,
and everything is filled with the Lord's
glory.
17 Not even to his holy angels has the Lord
given power
to describe all his mighty deeds,
even though he has given them power
to stand unharmed in his glorious
presence.[a]
18 He sees into the oceans and into the
human heart,
and he knows the secrets of both.
The Most High knows everything that
can be known
and understands the signs of the ages.
19 He knows all that has ever been and all
that ever will be;
he uncovers the deepest of mysteries.
20 He takes notice of our every thought
and hears our every word.
21 The orderly world shows the greatness of
his wisdom;
he is the same forever and ever.[b]
Nothing can be added to him, and
nothing taken away;
he needs no one to give him advice.
22 All his works are beautiful,
down to the smallest and faintest spark
of light.[c]
23 All these things go on forever,
and all of them have their purpose.
24 All things are in pairs, each the opposite
of the other,
but nothing the Lord made is
incomplete.
25 Everything completes the goodness of
something else.
Could anyone ever see enough of this
splendor?

43 How beautiful is the bright, clear
sky above us!
What a glorious sight it is!
2 The sun, when it appears, proclaims as it
rises
how marvelous a thing it is, made by
the Most High.
3 At noon it dries up the land;
no one can stand its blazing heat.
4 The setting sun sets fire to the hilltops,
like a metal furnace glowing from the
heat.[d]
It sends out fiery rays,
blinding the eyes with its brightness.
5 The Lord, who made it, is great;
it speeds on its way at his command.

6 There is also the moon, marking the
passage of time,[e]
an eternal sign of the changing seasons.
7 The moon determines the holy days.
Its light grows full and then grows dim.
8 The "month" is named after the moon,
marvelous to watch as it grows fuller
each night,
a signal light for the heavenly armies,
shining out in the dome of the sky.

9 The shining stars make the night sky lovely,
brilliant ornaments in the Lord's high
heavens.
10 They stay in the places assigned to them
by the Holy One
and never relax their dutiful watch.

11 Look at the rainbow and praise its Creator!
How magnificent, how radiant, its
beauty!

[z] **42:11** *Hebrew* Don't let . . . women; *Greek unclear.* [a] **42:17** *Hebrew* even though . . . presence; *Greek* which the Lord Almighty established so that everything may stand firm in his glory. [b] **42:21** *Hebrew* he is . . . ever; *Greek* he is before eternity and is eternal. [c] **42:22** *Hebrew* down to . . . spark of light; *Greek unclear.* [d] **43:4** *Hebrew* The setting . . . heat; *Greek* A man at a furnace works with scorching heat, but the sun burns the hills three times as much. [e] **43:6** *Hebrew* marking . . . time; *Greek unclear.*

ishness is better than one who keeps his wisdom to himself.

16 My children, listen and I will teach you the circumstances when it is proper to be ashamed.[w] Sometimes it is entirely out of place.

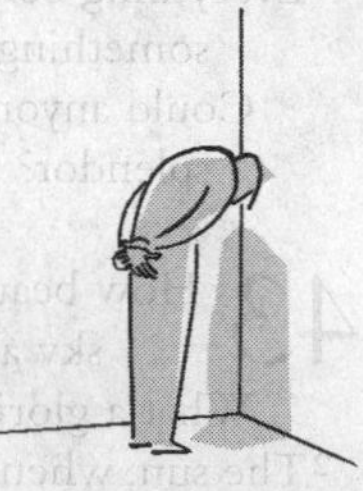

. . . when it is proper to be ashamed. (41:16)

17 Before your parents, be ashamed of
immoral behavior.
Before a ruler or an important person, be
ashamed of a lie.
18 Before a judge, be ashamed of criminal
behavior.
Before a public assembly, be ashamed of
breaking the law.
Before a friend or partner, be ashamed of
dishonesty.
19 Before your neighbors, be ashamed of
theft.
Be ashamed of breaking a promise,[x]
of leaning on the dinner table with
your elbows,
of stinginess when you are asked for
something,
20 of not returning a greeting,
of staring at a prostitute,
21 of turning down a relative's request,
of depriving someone of what is
rightly his,
of staring at another man's wife,
22 of playing around with his slave
woman (keep away from her bed!)
of insulting your friends,
of following up your gifts with
criticism,
23 of betraying secrets.

These are times when it is proper for you to be ashamed, and people will respect you for it.

A Sense of Pride

42 On the other hand, it is possible to sin by giving in to other people too much. Here are some things you should not be ashamed of:

2 the Law of the Most High and his
covenant,
judging even godless people fairly,
3 sharing expenses with a business partner
or a traveling companion,
sharing an inheritance,
4 using accurate weights and measures,
5 making a profit, whether great or small,
bargaining with a merchant,
disciplining your children often,
beating a disloyal slave until the blood
flows.

6 It is wise to lock things up if you cannot trust your wife or if too many people are around. 7 Keep an accurate record of any deposits you make or of anything you give or receive. 8 Don't hesitate to correct someone who is acting foolishly or an old man who goes around with prostitutes. All of this is worthwhile advice, and if you follow it, everyone will approve of your behavior.

Fathers and Daughters

9 Although he will not let his daughter know it, a father will lie awake at night worrying about her. If she is young, he worries that she might not get married. If she is already married, he worries about her happiness. 10 If she is a virgin, he worries that she might be seduced and become pregnant while living in his house. If she is married, he worries that she might be unfaithful, or that she might not be able to have children.

11 Keep a close watch over your daughter if she is determined to have her own way. If you don't, she may make a fool of you in front of your enemies. You will be a constant joke to everyone in town, a public disgrace. Make sure that her room has no windows or any place where she can look out to the entrance of the house.[y] 12 Don't let her show

[w] **41:16** *Hebrew* My children . . . ashamed; *Greek* Show respect for what I say. [x] **41:19** *Hebrew* of breaking a promise; *Greek* of yourself before the truth of God. [y] **42:11** *Hebrew* Make sure . . . house; *Greek does not have these words.*

42:9–11 Sir 7:24, 25; 26:10–12

12 Like a bow bent by the hands of the Most
High,
it spans the horizon in a circle of glory.

It spans the horizon in a circle of glory. (43:12)

13 He commands, and snow begins to fall;
lightning strikes to carry out his
judgments.
14 The storerooms of the sky are thrown
open,
and the clouds roll out like flying birds.
15 With his power he forms great masses of
clouds
and shatters the ice into hailstones.
16-17 He speaks, and thunder twists the earth
in pain;
the mountains are shaken by his
strength.[f]
Whenever he wishes, the south wind
blows,
whirlwinds come, and windstorms
from the north.
He sends the snow fluttering down like
birds,
like locusts lighting on the ground.
18 We marvel at its beautiful whiteness,
and in fascination we watch it fall.
19 He sprinkles frost over the ground like
salt,
and it freezes into thorny flowers of
ice.[g]
20 He sends the cold north wind blowing
and the water hardens into ice;
every lake and pond freezes over,
putting on a coat of icy armor.
21 He scorches the wilderness hills with
drought,
and the grass turns brown from its heat;
22 but a cloudy mist restores it all to life
as the weather cools and dew appears.

23 By his wisdom he calmed the great
oceans
and placed the islands there.
24 Sailors tell about the dangers of the sea,
and we listen to their tales in
amazement.
25 In the sea are strange and marvelous
creatures:
huge monsters and all kinds of living
things.
26 Each of the Lord's messengers succeeds at
its task.
Everything is held together by his
word.

27 We could say much more and never
finish,
but it all means this: the Lord is
everything.
28 How can we find the power to praise
him?
He is greater than all his creation.
29 The Lord is awesome in his greatness;
his power is overwhelming.
30 Though you do your best to praise him,
he is greater than you can ever express.
Though you honor him tirelessly and
with all your strength,
you still cannot praise him enough.
31 No one has seen him, no one can
describe him;
no one can praise him as he deserves.
32 Mysteries greater than these are still
unknown;
we know only a fraction of his works.
33 The Lord made the universe
and then gave wisdom to devout
people.

The Glory of God in History

44 So let us now give praise to godly[h]
men,
our ancestors of generations past,

[f] **43:16–17** *Hebrew* by his strength; *Greek* when he appears.
[g] **43:19** *Hebrew* flowers of ice; *Greek* points.
[h] **44:1** *Hebrew* godly; *Greek* famous.

2 those whom the Lord honored with great
glory,
in whom his greatness has been seen
from the beginning of time.
3 There were some who ruled kingdoms,
and some who were known for their
strength.
Some were wise advisers,
and some spoke prophecies.
4 There were statesmen whose policies
governed the people,
rulers who issued decrees,[i]
scholars who spoke wise words,[j]
and those who used pointed proverbs,[k]
5 poets, and composers of music,
6 rich and powerful men living
peacefully at home.
7 All of these were famous in their own
times,
honored by the people of their day.
8 Some of them left a reputation,
and people still praise them today.
9 There are others who are not
remembered,
as if they had never lived,
who died and were forgotten,
they, and their children after them.

10 But we will praise these godly men,
whose righteous deeds have never been
forgotten.
11 Their reputations will be passed on to
their descendants,
and this will be their inheritance.[l]
12 Their descendants continue to keep the
covenant
and always will, because of what their
ancestors did.
13 Their family line will go on forever,
and their fame will never fade.
14 Their bodies were laid to rest,
but their reputations will live forever.
15 Nations will tell about their wisdom,
and God's people will praise them.

Enoch

16 Enoch pleased the Lord and was taken
up into heaven. He became an inspiration
for repentance for all time to come.

Noah

17 Noah was a perfectly righteous man.
After destruction came, he gave the human
race a new start.[m] Because of him there were
people left on earth when the flood was
over. 18 The Lord made an eternal covenant
with him, promising that life would never
again be destroyed by a flood.

Abraham

19 Abraham was the great ancestor of
many nations; his reputation was faultless.[n]
20 He kept the Law of the Most High and
made a covenant with him, a covenant
marked on his body. When he was put to the
test, he was found faithful. 21 And so the Lord
made him a solemn promise that his descendants would be a blessing to the world; that
their number would be countless, like the
dust of the earth; that they would be honored more than any other people on earth;
and that their land would extend from sea to
sea, from the Euphrates to the ends of the
earth.

Isaac and Jacob

22-23 The Lord renewed that covenant with
Isaac, and then again with Jacob, repeating
the promise that Abraham's descendants
would be a blessing to the whole human
race. The Lord assured Jacob that he would
bless him; he gave him the land that would
be his, dividing it into twelve parts, one for
each of the tribes.

[i] **44:4** *Probable Hebrew text* rulers who issued decrees; *Greek unclear.* [j] **44:4** *Hebrew* scholars . . . words; *Greek unclear.* [k] **44:4** *Hebrew* and those . . . proverbs; *Greek does not have these words.* [l] **44:11** *Verse 11 in Greek is unclear.* [m] **44:17** *Hebrew* gave . . . start; *Greek* was taken in exchange for the human race. [n] **44:19** *Hebrew* his reputation was faultless; *Greek* there was no one like him in reputation.

44:16 Gen 5:24; Heb 11:5; Jude 14 **44:17, 18** Gen 6:9—9:17 **44:19–21** Gen 15:1—17:27; 22:1–18 **44:22, 23** Gen 17:19; 26:3–5; 27:28; 28:14

Moses

45 From Jacob's descendants the Lord raised up a godly man who won the favor of everyone, loved by God and people alike. This man was Moses, whose very memory is a blessing. [2]The Lord made him as glorious as the angels and made his enemies fear him. [3]There in Egypt at his command the disaster struck.[o] The Lord made kings hold him in respect. The Lord gave him his commands for his people and showed him the dazzling light of his presence. [4]The Lord chose Moses out of the whole human race and consecrated him because of his loyalty and humility. [5]He let him hear his voice and led him into the dark cloud, where, face to face, he gave him the commandments, the Law that gives life and knowledge, so that Moses might teach the covenant regulations to the Israelites.

Aaron

[6]The Lord raised up Aaron, a holy man like his brother Moses, of the tribe of Levi. [7]He made an eternal covenant with him, giving him the privilege of serving as priest to the Lord's people. He honored him by clothing him with magnificent robes and fine ornaments, [8]perfect in their splendor. He granted him the symbols of authority: the linen shorts, the shirt, and the robe with the pomegranates around the hem. [9]Gold bells were also around its hem, so that when he walked, their ringing would be heard in the Temple, and the Lord would remember his people. [10]The Lord gave Aaron the sacred robe with the gold, blue, and purple embroidery; the breastpiece with the Urim and Thummim;[p] [11]the red yarn, spun by an expert; the precious stones with names engraved on them, mounted in a gold setting by a jeweler, placed on the breastpiece to remind the Lord of the twelve tribes of Israel. [12]He gave him the turban with the gold ornament engraved with the words "Dedicated to the Lord." It was expertly crafted, a beautiful work of art, and it was a high honor to wear it. [13]Before Aaron's time such beautiful things were never seen. No one but Aaron and his descendants ever wore them, or ever will. [14]The grain offering is to be presented twice a day and burned completely.

[15]Moses ordained Aaron to office by pouring the sacred anointing oil over his head. An eternal covenant was made with him and his descendants, that they would serve the Lord as his priests and bless the people in the Lord's name. [16]The Lord chose Aaron out of the whole human race to offer sacrifices, to burn fragrant incense to remind the Lord of his people, and to take away their sins. [17]He entrusted the commandments to Aaron's keeping and gave him the authority to make legal decisions and to teach Israel the Law.

[18]Once, while the people were in the wilderness, an angry group of jealous outsiders conspired against Moses. These were Dathan, Abiram, and Korah with their supporters. [19]The Lord saw what they were doing and became angry, so furious that he performed a miracle and destroyed them in a blazing fire. [20]Then he rewarded Aaron again, giving him a special honor: the right to the offerings of the first produce, so that the priests should have enough to eat. [21]Their food is the sacrifices offered to the Lord; the Lord gave this to Aaron and his descendants. [22]But Aaron, unlike the rest of the people, was to inherit no land, no special portion of his own. The Lord himself would be all he needed.

Phinehas

[23]Only Moses and Aaron were more famous for their intense devotion to the Lord than Phinehas son of Eleazar. He brought about forgiveness for Israel's sin by standing firm in brave determination when everyone else was in rebellion. [24]And so the Lord made a covenant with him, valid for all time to come, that he should be in charge of

[o] **45:3** *Hebrew* struck; *Greek* stopped. [p] **45:10** URIM AND THUMMIM: *Two objects used by the priest to determine God's will; it is not known precisely how they were used.*

45:1–5 Ex 6:28—11:10; 20:1–21 **45:6** Ex 4:14 **45:7–13** Ex 28:1–43 **45:15** Lev 8:1–36 **45:18, 19** Num 16:1–35 **45:22** Num 18:20; Deut 12:12 **45:23–26** Num 25:7–13

the sanctuary and of his people, that he and
his descendants should hold the office of
High Priest forever. 25 Unlike the covenant
made with David son of Jesse, from the tribe
of Judah, where the kingship passed only
from father to son, the priesthood was to
pass from Aaron to all his descendants.
26 Now praise the Lord, who is good, who

IN PRAISE OF ANCESTORS (Chapters 44-50)

has crowned you with glory![q] May he give
you wisdom to judge his people fairly, so
that their success and your authority[r] may
continue for all time to come.

Joshua

46 Joshua[s] son of Nun was a great sol-
dier and the next of the prophets
after Moses. He lived up to the meaning of
his name as the great deliverer of the Lord's
chosen people. He defeated the enemies that
attacked them, so that Israel could claim its
land. 2How magnificent it was when he
raised his arm and then led the attacks on
the cities! 3No one could stand up to him;[t]
he was fighting a holy war for the Lord.
4Remember how he held back the sun and
made one day as long as two? 5When his
enemies were threatening him from every
side, he prayed to the mighty Lord Most
High, and his prayer was answered with a
hailstorm of devastating force. 6The Lord
hurled the hail down on the enemy[u] and
destroyed them at the pass at Beth Horon, so
that the nations would realize how strong
Joshua was, since he was fighting as a devot-
ed follower of the Lord.

Caleb

7Joshua was loyal as long as Moses lived,
both he and Caleb son of Jephunneh. They
stood up to the whole community, made
them stop their ungrateful complaining, and
kept them from sinning. 8Out of the
600,000 Israelites who marched through the
wilderness, these two were the only ones
spared and allowed to enter the rich and fer-
tile land that was to be theirs. 9The Lord
made Caleb strong, and when he was an old
man, he was still strong enough to go up
into the hill country and capture it for him-
self and his descendants. 10Then all of Israel
could see how good it is to follow the Lord.

The Judges

11Then there were the judges, each of
them famous in their own right, who never
fell into idolatry and never abandoned the
Lord. 12May their memory be honored! May
these whom we honor spring from the grave
to new life in their descendants!

Samuel

13Samuel was loved by the Lord. As the
Lord's prophet he established the kingdom
and appointed rulers for the people. 14He
judged the nation in accordance with the
Law of the Lord, and the Lord protected
Israel. 15Because Samuel was faithful, he was
accepted as a true prophet. People trusted
him as a seer because of his words. 16When
his enemies were threatening him from
every side, he called upon the mighty Lord
and offered him a young lamb as a sacrifice.
17Then the Lord thundered from heaven
with a mighty roar 18and destroyed all the
enemy[v] rulers of Philistia. 19When Samuel
was about to die, he gave assurances before
the Lord and the anointed king that he had
never taken anyone's property, not even so
much as a pair of shoes, and no one contra-
dicted him. 20Even after he died, he prophe-
sied to King Saul how he would die. Out of
the grave he spoke as a prophet, to blot out
his people's wickedness.

Nathan

47 After him came Nathan, who was a
prophet at the time of David.

David

2As the choice fat portion of the fellow-
ship offering is reserved for the Lord, so
David was chosen from among the Israelites.
3He played with lions and bears as if they
were lambs or little goats. 4When he was still

[q] **45:26** *Hebrew* Now praise . . . glory; *Greek does not have these words.* [r] **45:26** *Probable Hebrew text* and your authority; *Greek unclear.* [s] **46:1** JOSHUA: *This name in Hebrew means "the Lord saves."* [t] **46:3** *Hebrew* no one . . . to him; *Greek* No one before had ever been so brave. [u] **46:6** *Probable text* The Lord hurled . . . enemy; *Greek unclear.* [v] **46:18** *Hebrew* enemy; *Greek* rulers of Tyre and.

46:1–6 Josh 1:1—11:23 **46:7–10** Num 14:6–10; 11:21; Josh 14:6–11 **46:11** Judg 1:1—16:31 **46:13–20** 1 Sam 3:19, 20; 7:9–11; 10:1; 12:3; 16:13; 28:18, 19 **47:1** 2 Sam 7:2, 3; 12:1 **47:2–11** 1 Sam 17:34—18:7; 2 Sam 5:7; 8:1; 12:13

a boy, he killed a giant to rescue his people.
He put a stone in his sling, took aim, and
put an end to Goliath's bragging. 5He prayed
to the Lord, the Most High, and was given
the strength to kill that famous soldier, so
that the nations would have respect for the
power of his people. 6The people honored
him for killing his tens of thousands, and
when he was crowned king, they praised
him for being chosen by the Lord. 7He
wiped out all his enemies and permanently
crushed the Philistines, so that they never
again became a threat.
8In everything David did, he gave thanks
and praise to the Holy Lord, the Most High.
He loved his Creator and sang praises to him
with all his heart. 9He put singers at the altar
to provide beautiful music. 10He set the
times of the festivals throughout the year and
made them splendid occasions; the Temple
rang with the Lord's praises all day long.
11The Lord forgave David's sin and estab-
lished his power forever. He made a
covenant with him that he and his descen-
dants would reign in splendor over Israel.

Solomon

12David prepared the way well for his son,
a wise man, to rule after him. 13There was
no war while Solomon was king. God gave
him peace on all his borders, so that he
could build for the Lord a Temple which
would stand forever. 14How wise you were,
Solomon, when you were young! Your
knowledge was like the Nile[w] in flood.
15Your influence reached over all the world;
your proverbs and riddles were known
everywhere. 16You were famous everywhere,
and people loved you for bringing peace.
17Nations around the world held you in
admiration for your songs, proverbs, parables,
and witty sayings. 18You gathered silver and
gold as if it were tin or lead, all in the name
of the Lord God of Israel.
19But your lust for women was your
downfall. 20You stained your reputation and
that of your descendants. They suffered pun-
ishment for that foolishness of yours, which
caused them so much grief. 21It divided the
nation, and a rival kingdom arose in north-
ern Israel. 22But the Lord will always be
merciful and keep all his promises.[x] He will
never destroy the descendants of David,
whom he chose and who loved him. So for
Israel's sake he allowed David's family to sur-
vive.

Rehoboam and Jeroboam

23Solomon followed his ancestors in death
and left one of his sons to rule after him.
This was Rehoboam, a man of little intelli-
gence and great foolishness,[y] whose policies
caused a rebellion.
There was also the unspeakable[z] Jer-
oboam, who led northern Israel in sinful
ways. 24His people became so sinful that
they were exiled from their land. 25They
tried all kinds of wickedness until the Lord
took vengeance on them.

Elijah

48 Then there arose the fiery prophet
Elijah, whose words blazed like a
torch. 2He brought a famine on the people,
and many of them died because of his per-
sistence. 3Speaking in the name of the Lord,
he kept the rain from coming, and on three
occasions he called down fire. 4Elijah, your
miracles were marvelous! No one else can
boast of such deeds! 5In the name of the
Most High, you brought a dead man back to
life. 6You brought a famous king down to
sickness and death. 7At Sinai you heard the
Lord rebuke you and declare his determina-
tion to punish his enemies. 8You anointed a
king to be the instrument of that punish-
ment, and a prophet to take your place. 9You
were taken up to heaven in a fiery whirl-
wind, a chariot drawn by fiery horses. 10The

[w] **47:14** *Hebrew* the Nile; *Greek* a river. [x] **47:22** *Hebrew* keep all his promises; *Greek* will not destroy what he made. [y] **47:23** *Hebrew* great foolishness; *Greek* the people's fool. [z] **47:23** *Hebrew* the unspeakable (one); *Greek* Jeroboam son of Nebat.

47:13–17 1 Kings 4:21–32 **47:18** 1 Kings 10:21, 27 **47:19** 1 Kings 11:1 **47:21** 1 Kings 12:15–20 **47:22** 2 Sam 7:15 **47:23–25** 1 Kings 11:43; 12:10–30; 2 Kings 17:6, 18 **48:1–11** 1 Kings 17:1–24; 18:38; 19:15, 16; 2 Kings 1:10–16; 2:11; Mal 4:5, 6

scripture says that you are ready to appear at
the designated time,[a] to cool God's anger
before it breaks out in fury; that you "will
bring parents and children together again,"
and restore the tribes of Israel. 11Fortunate
are those who live to see you come, as well
as those who have already died in love, for
we too shall live.[b]

Elisha

12When Elijah was hidden by the whirl-
wind, Elisha was filled with his spirit. As long
as he lived, he was not afraid of rulers, and
they could not make him do as they wished.
13Nothing was too hard for him. Even when
he was dead, his body worked a miracle. 14In
life and in death he performed amazing mir-
acles.

15But in spite of all this, the people did
not abandon their sinful ways until they
were taken from their land as prisoners and
scattered all over the world. This left the
nation few in number, but those who
remained were still ruled by the descendants
of David. 16Some of the people did what
was pleasing to the Lord, but others com-
mitted sin after sin.

Hezekiah

17Hezekiah prepared his city to resist a
siege and provided it with a water supply. He
had a tunnel built through solid rock with
iron tools and had cisterns built to hold the
water. 18During his reign Sennacherib
attacked the city and sent his chief official
from Lachish. He challenged Jerusalem and
boasted arrogantly. 19The people lost their
courage and shook with fear; they were in
pain, like a woman in labor. 20But they
prayed to the merciful Lord, the Holy One
in heaven, who quickly answered their
prayers and sent Isaiah to save them. 21The
Lord struck the Assyrian camp; his angel
wiped them out. 22Yes, Hezekiah did what
was pleasing to the Lord and firmly followed
the example of his ancestor David. This was
what was commanded by the great prophet
Isaiah, whose visions were trusted. 23He
made the sun move backward and length-
ened the king's life. 24He comforted the
mourners in Jerusalem. His powerful spirit
looked into the future, 25and he predicted
what was to happen before the end of time,
hidden things that had not yet occurred.

Josiah

49 The memory of Josiah is as sweet as
the fragrance of expertly blended
incense, sweet as honey to the taste,[c] like
music with wine at a banquet. 2He followed
the correct policy of reforming the nation
and removed the horrors of idolatry. 3He
was completely loyal to the Lord and
strengthened true religion in those wicked
times.

Jeremiah

4All the kings, except David, Hezekiah,
and Josiah, were terrible sinners, because
they abandoned the Law of the Most High
to the very end of the kingdom.[d] 5They sur-
rendered their power and honor to foreign-
ers, 6who set fire to the holy city and left its
streets deserted, just as Jeremiah had predict-
ed. 7Jeremiah had been badly treated, even
though he was chosen as a prophet before he
was born, "to uproot and to pull down, to
destroy and to overthrow," but also "to build
and to plant."

Ezekiel

8It was Ezekiel who was shown the vision
of the divine glory over the chariot and the
living creatures. 9He also referred to the
prophet Job, who always did the right thing.[e]

[a] **48:10** *Hebrew* you are . . . time; *Greek unclear.* [b] **48:11** *Verse 11 in Greek is unclear.* [c] **49:1** *Hebrew* to the taste; *Greek* to everyone. [d] **49:4** *Hebrew* to the very end of the kingdom; *Greek* and failed. [e] **49:9** *Probable Hebrew text* He also . . . thing; *Greek unclear.*

48:12 2 Kings 2:9, 13 **48:13** 2 Kings 13:20, 21 **48:15** 2 Kings 18:11, 12 **48:17** 2 Kings 20:20 **48:18** 2 Kings 18:13–17 **48:20, 21** 2 Kings 19:15–20, 35 **48:23** 2 Kings 20:10, 11 **49:1–3** 2 Kings 22:1; 22:11–13; 23:3, 25 **49:6, 7** Jer 1:4–10; 39:8 **49:8, 9** Ezek 1:3–15; 14:14–20

The Twelve Prophets

10May the bones of the twelve prophets
rise to new life, because these men encour-
aged the people of Israel and saved them
with confident hope.

Zerubbabel and Joshua

11How can we praise Zerubbabel? He was
like a signet ring on the Lord's right hand,
12as was Joshua son of Jehozadak. They
rebuilt the Lord's holy Temple, destined for
eternal fame.

Nehemiah

13The memory of Nehemiah is also great.
He rebuilt the ruined walls of Jerusalem,
installing the gates and bars. He rebuilt our
homes.

The Patriarchs

14No one else like Enoch has ever walked
the face of the earth, for he was taken up
from the earth. 15No one else like Joseph has
ever been born;[f] even his bones were hon-
ored.[g] 16Shem, Seth, and Enosh[h] were highly
honored, but Adam's glory was above that of
any other living being.

Simon Son of Onias

50 The greatest of his brothers and the
pride of his people[i] was the High
Priest Simon son of Onias, who repaired the
Temple 2and laid the foundation for the
high double wall and the fortifications of the
Temple.[j] 3The reservoir, as big as the bronze
tank, was dug[k] while he was in office. 4He
made plans to protect his people from attack
and fortified the city so that it could with-
stand a siege.
5How glorious he was when he came out
of the Most Holy Place![l] 6He was like the
morning star shining through the clouds,
like the full moon, 7like the sun shining on
the Temple of the Most High, like the rain-
bow gleaming in glory against the clouds,
8like roses in springtime, like lilies beside a
stream, like the cedars of Lebanon in sum-
mer, 9like burning incense, like a cup made
of hammered gold and decorated with all
kinds of jewels, 10like an olive tree loaded
with fruit, like a cypress tree towering into
the clouds.
11When Simon put on his magnificent
robe and went up to the holy altar dressed
in perfect splendor, he made the Temple
courtyard a majestic sight. 12When the
priests handed him the portions of the sac-
rifice as he stood beside the altar with his
assistants circling him like a wreath, he was
like a young cedar of Lebanon surrounded
by palm trees. 13Those were the descendants
of Aaron in their splendid garments, stand-
ing before the whole assembly of Israel,
holding in their hands the offering made to
the Lord. 14When he had finished the ser-
vice at the altar and had arranged the sacri-
fice to the Most High, the Almighty, 15he
reached for a cup and poured out sweet-
smelling wine at the foot of the altar as an
offering to the Most High, the universal
King. 16Then the priests shouted and blew
their trumpets of hammered silver. They
made a loud noise that the Most High
would hear. 17All the people immediately
bowed down with their faces to the ground
to worship their Lord, the Almighty, the
Most High. 18Then the choir began to sing
his praises, and the beautiful music rang out.
19The people kept praying to the merciful
Lord Most High until the service of wor-
ship had come to a close. 20Then Simon
came down from the altar, raised his hands
over the whole assembly of Israel, and rever-
ently pronounced the blessing from the
Lord, 21while the people bowed a second
time in worship to receive that blessing
from the Most High.

[f] **49:15** *Greek adds* the greatest of his brothers and the pride of his people; *Hebrew and one ancient translation place these words in 50:1.* [g] **49:15** even . . . honored; *or* the Lord watched over his body. [h] **49:16** *Hebrew* Shem, Seth, and Enosh; *Greek* Shem and Seth among people. [i] **50:1** The greatest . . . people; *Hebrew and one ancient translation place the words at this point; Greek places them at 49:15.* [j] **50:2** *Verse 2 in Greek is unclear.* [k] **50:2** *Hebrew* dug; *Greek* reduced. [l] **50:5** *Hebrew* Most Holy Place; *Greek* Most Holy Place among the people.

49:11 Ezra 3:2; Hag 2:23 **49:12** Hag 1:1, 12 **49:13** Neh 6:15 **50:20** Num 6:24–27

A Benediction

22Now then, give praise to the God of the universe, who has done great things everywhere, who brings us up[m] from the time we are born, and deals with us mercifully. 23May he give us happiness and allow us to have peace in Israel forever. 24May he continue his mercy to us and rescue us in our time of need.

Three Hated Nations

25There are two nations that I detest, and a third that does not even deserve to be called a nation. 26These are the Edomites,[n] the inhabitants of the Philistine cities, and the stupid Samaritans.

The Wisdom of Jesus Son of Sirach

27I, Jesus son of Sirach Eleazar[o] of Jerusalem, put all my wisdom into writing this book to provide instruction and knowledge for others. 28May God bless everyone who gives attention to these teachings. Whoever takes them to heart will become wise. 29Whoever lives by them will be strong enough for any occasion, because he will be walking in the light of the Lord.

A Song of Thanksgiving

51 I give you thanks, O Lord and King;
I praise you as my God and Savior.
I give you thanks,
2 for you have helped me and protected me.
You have rescued me from death,
from dangerous lies and slander.
3You helped me when no one else would;
in your great mercy you saved me
from the many troubles I have known:
from the glaring hatred of my enemies,
who wanted to put an end to my life;
4from suffocation in oppressive smoke
rising from fires that I did not light;
5from death itself;
from vicious slander reported to the king.
6I was once brought face to face with death;
7 enemies surrounded me everywhere.
I looked for someone to help me,
but there was no one there.
8But then, O Lord, I remembered how merciful you are
and what you had done in times past.
I remembered that you rescue those who rely on you,
that you save them from their enemies.
9Then from here on earth I prayed to you
to rescue me from death.
10I prayed, "O Lord, you are my father;[p]
do not abandon me to my troubles
when I am helpless against arrogant enemies.
11I will always praise you
and sing hymns of thanksgiving."
You answered my prayer,
12 and saved me from the threat of destruction.
And so I thank you and praise you.
O Lord, I praise you!

The Search for Wisdom

13When I was still young, before I started out on my travels, I boldly prayed for Wisdom. 14I went to the Temple and asked for her, and I will look for her as long as I live. 15From my blossoming youth to my ripe old age she has been my delight. I have followed directly in her path ever since I was young. 16I received Wisdom as soon as I began listening for her, and I have been rewarded with great knowledge. 17I have always been a learner and am grateful to everyone who has been my teacher. 18I was determined to live wisely and was devoted to the cause of goodness. I have no regrets. 19I fought for Wisdom and was strict in my conduct. When I prayed, I sadly confessed how far short of Wisdom I fell. 20But I was determined to have her, and I found her by keeping myself free from sin. I have grown in Wisdom since first I found her, and I will never be without her. 21Because I was driven by the desire to find her, I have been richly rewarded. 22The Lord gave me a gift for words, and I have used it in his praise.

[m] **50:22** brings us up; *or* honors us. [n] **50:26** *Hebrew* Edomites; *Greek* Samaritans. [o] **50:27** Sirach Eleazar; *or* Sirach son of Eleazar. [p] **51:10** *Hebrew* you are my father; *Greek* father of my Lord.

23 Come to me, all you that need instruc-
tion, and learn in my school. 24 Why do you
admit that you are ignorant and do nothing
about it? 25 Here is what I say: It costs nothing
to be wise. 26 Put on the yoke, and be willing
to learn. The opportunity is always near. 27 See
for yourselves! I have really not studied very
hard, but I have found great contentment.
28 No matter how much it costs you to get
Wisdom, it will be well worth it. 29 Be joyfully
grateful for the Lord's mercy, and never be
ashamed to praise him. 30 Do your duty at the
proper time, and the Lord, at the time he
thinks proper, will give you your reward.

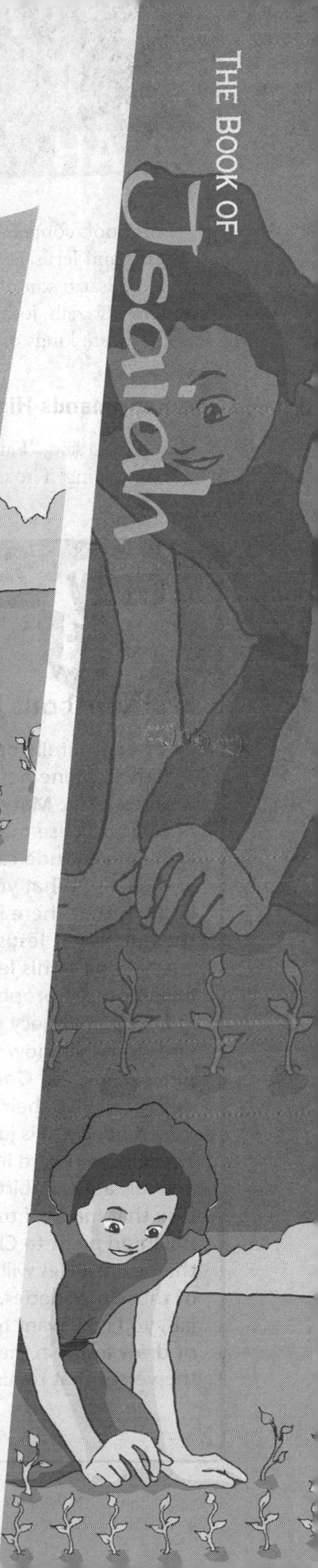

If you take drugs, you can do permanent damage to your brain. If you miss a lot of school and don't do your homework and study, you may not graduate.

These warnings are real, and yet some people don't take them seriously. As a result, many people suffer needless consequences.

The great prophet Isaiah and some of his followers warned the people of God about the dangers of failing to keep God's Covenant. They warned them about the dangers of worshiping foreign gods and treating the poor unfairly. Isaiah called the people to repent of their sins. But they didn't take him seriously. After the people had been taken as slaves into Babylon, Isaiah's disciples offered the people hope that someday they would return from exile and rebuild Israel. They even foretold of a new earth and heaven where God would rule with peace and justice.

Chap. 5

Headlines

- God, Tired of Sacrifices, Wants Justice! (1:10–20)
- Child to Bring Endless Peace (9:2–7)
- New King Will Defend the Helpless (11:1–9)
- Hope Cries Out in the Wilderness! (40:1–5)
- Servant Chosen to Bring Justice (42:1–9)
- Servant Suffers for Sheep (52:13—53:12)
- Good News for God's People (chapter 61)

FACTOIDS

Who wrote this book? Isaiah is divided into three parts. First Isaiah, chapters 1–39, is a collection of poems written by the great prophet Isaiah before the Babylonian Exile. Second Isaiah, chapters 40–55, and Third Isaiah, chapters 56–66, were written by disciples of Isaiah who wrote during and after the Exile.

What time period does it cover? From 745 to 500 BC.

Why was it written? Isaiah was written to warn the leaders about misusing their power. It also offered hope for those living in exile that God would save them and return them to rebuild Israel.

Jesus connection: Jesus is the Messiah and suffering servant prophesied in First and Second Isaiah.

Important themes

- The sacrifice God asks of us is to be faithful and just.
- God is with those who suffer and trust in God's saving power.
- God will send a leader, a descendant of King David, who will be the perfect ruler and will bring justice and peace to God's people.

ISAIAH

1 This book contains the messages about
Judah and Jerusalem which God
revealed to Isaiah son of Amoz during the
time when Uzziah, Jotham, Ahaz, and
Hezekiah were kings of Judah.

God Reprimands His People

2 The LORD said, "Earth and sky, listen to
what I am saying! The children I brought up
have rebelled against me. 3 Cattle know who
owns them, and donkeys know where their
master feeds them. But that is more than my
people Israel know. They don't understand at
all."

4 You are doomed, you sinful nation, you
corrupt and evil people! Your sins drag you
down! You have rejected the LORD, the holy
God of Israel, and have turned your backs on
him. 5 Why do you keep on rebelling? Do
you want to be punished even more? Israel,
your head is already covered with wounds,
and your heart and mind are sick. 6 From
head to foot there is not a healthy spot on
your body. You are covered with bruises and
sores and open wounds. Your wounds have
not been cleaned or bandaged. No medicine
has been put on them.

7 Your country has been devastated, and
your cities have been burned to the ground.
While you look on, foreigners take over
your land and bring everything to ruin.
8 Jerusalem alone is left, a city under siege—
as defenseless as a guard's hut in a vineyard
or a shed in a cucumber field. 9 If the LORD
Almighty had not let some of the people

Study it!

Stories About Jesus?

Does your family or parish put out a nativity scene before Christmas? Besides Jesus, Mary, Joseph, shepherds, and wise men, many nativity scenes include cattle, donkeys, and sheep. What you may not know is that there is a legend that the animals at Jesus' birth knew who he was. This legend was based on the prophecy of Isaiah 1:3. This prophecy says that cattle and donkeys know who their masters are, even if God's people do not recognize their master (God).

That legend is just a legend. There is no record in the Gospels of animals at Jesus' birth. However, it is true that many of the prophecies in Isaiah do point to Christ. Some of the next articles will point out some of those prophecies. As you read Isaiah, you may want to make a list of, or draw a star in the margin next to, the verses that remind you of Jesus.

— Isaiah 1:3

Israel, your head is already covered with wounds. (1:5)

1:1 **a** 2 Kings 15:1–7; 2 Chr 26:1–23; **b** 2 Kings 15:32–38; 2 Chr 27:1–9; **c** 2 Kings 16:1–20; 2 Chr 28:1–27; **d** 2 Kings 18:1—20:21; 2 Chr 29:1—32:33

survive, Jerusalem would have been totally
destroyed, just as Sodom and Gomorrah
were.
10 Jerusalem, your rulers and your people
are like those of Sodom and Gomorrah. Lis-
ten to what the LORD is saying to you. Pay
attention to what our God is teaching you.
11 He says, "Do you think I want all these
sacrifices you keep offering to me? I have
had more than enough of the sheep you
burn as sacrifices and of the fat of your fine
animals. I am tired of the blood of bulls and
sheep and goats. 12 Who asked you to bring
me all this when you come to worship me?
Who asked you to do all this tramping
around in my Temple? 13 It's useless to bring
your offerings. I am disgusted with the smell
of the incense you burn. I cannot stand your
New Moon Festivals, your Sabbaths, and
your religious gatherings; they are all cor-
rupted by your sins. 14 I hate your New
Moon Festivals and holy days; they are a
burden that I am tired of bearing.
15 "When you lift your hands in prayer, I
will not look at you. No matter how much
you pray, I will not listen, for your hands are
covered with blood. 16 Wash yourselves clean.
Stop all this evil that I see you doing. Yes,
stop doing evil 17 and learn to do right. See
that justice is done—help those who are
oppressed, give orphans their rights, and
defend widows."
18 The LORD says, "Now, let's settle the

When you lift your hands in prayer . . . (1:15)

matter. You are stained red with sin, but I
will wash you as clean as snow.[a] Although
your stains are deep red, you will be as white
as wool.[b] 19 If you will only obey me, you
will eat the good things the land produces.
20 But if you defy me, you are doomed to
die. I, the LORD, have spoken."

The Sinful City

21 The city that once was faithful is behav-
ing like a whore! At one time it was filled
with righteous people, but now only mur-
derers remain. 22 Jerusalem, you were once
like silver, but now you are worthless; you
were like good wine, but now you are only
water. 23 Your leaders are rebels and friends
of thieves; they are always accepting gifts and
bribes. They never defend orphans in court
or listen when widows present their case.
24 So now, listen to what the LORD
Almighty, Israel's powerful God, is saying: "I
will take revenge on you, my enemies, and
you will cause me no more trouble. 25 I will
take action against you. I will purify you the
way metal is refined, and will remove all
your impurity. 26 I will give you rulers and
advisers like those you had long ago. Then
Jerusalem will be called the righteous, faith-
ful city."
27 Because the LORD is righteous, he will
save Jerusalem and everyone there who
repents. 28 But he will crush everyone who
sins and rebels against him; he will kill
everyone who forsakes him.
29 You will be sorry that you ever wor-
shiped trees and planted sacred gardens.[c]
30 You will wither like a dying oak, like a
garden that no one waters. 31 Just as straw is
set on fire by a spark, so powerful people
will be destroyed by their own evil deeds,
and no one will be able to stop the destruc-
tion.

[a] **1:18** sin, but . . . snow; *or* sin; do you think I will wash you as clean as snow? [b] **1:18** Although your . . . wool; *or* Your stains are deep red; do you think you will be as white as wool? [c] **1:29** SACRED GARDENS: *People believed that dedicating a garden to a fertility god would cause him to bless their crops.*

1:9 Gen 19:24; Rom 9:29 **1:11–14** Am 5:21, 22

Isaiah spoke to the southern kingdom of Judah around the same time that Hosea was speaking to the northern kingdom of Israel.

Study it!

War or Peace

At the beginning of Isaiah, chapter 2, Isaiah makes a prophecy about a time when God's peace will last forever. This vision of everlasting peace is one that many people have worked for over many centuries. There are even Catholic peace organizations, like Pax Christi, that try to prevent and stop wars and violence. Unfortunately, it seems there are still as many wars as there were at the time of Isaiah. The timelines in history books use wars as markers, and many students (maybe even you) study the dates and places of the various wars.

God doesn't want us to be at war. The Creation stories in Genesis tell us that God created us so that we could all live in peace. Isaiah and other books of the Bible promise us that ultimately God's peace will come and last forever. Until that time it is a good idea to practice peace—right where you are. With God's help if you practice peace and if others practice it too, we will eventually get it right.

— Isaiah 2:2–4

Everlasting Peace
(Micah 4:1–3)

2 Here is the message which God gave to Isaiah son of Amoz about Judah and Jerusalem:

2 In days to come
the mountain where the Temple stands
will be the highest one of all,
towering above all the hills.
Many nations will come streaming to it,
3 and their people will say,
"Let us go up the hill of the LORD,[d]
to the Temple of Israel's God.
He will teach us what he wants us to do;
we will walk in the paths he has chosen.
For the LORD's teaching comes from Jerusalem;
from Zion he speaks to his people."
4 He will settle disputes among great nations.
They will hammer their swords into plows
and their spears into pruning knives.
Nations will never again go to war,
never prepare for battle again.

5 Now, descendants of Jacob, let us walk in the light which the LORD gives us!

Arrogance Will Be Destroyed

6 O God, you have forsaken your people,
the descendants of Jacob! The land is full of
magic practices from the East and from
Philistia.[e] The people follow foreign cus-
toms. 7 Their land is full of silver and gold,
and there is no end to their treasures. Their
land is full of horses, and there is no end to
their chariots. 8 Their land is full of idols, and
they worship objects that they have made
with their own hands.
9 Everyone will be humiliated and dis-
graced. Do not forgive them, LORD!
10 They will hide in caves in the rocky
hills or dig holes in the ground to try to
escape from the LORD's anger and to hide
from his power and glory! 11 A day is coming
when human pride will be ended and
human arrogance destroyed. Then the LORD

[d] 2:3 HILL OF THE LORD: *Mount Zion, the hill in Jerusalem which formed part of the area on which the Temple was built.* [e] 2:6 *Probable text* The land . . . Philistia; *Hebrew unclear.*

2:4 Joel 3:10; Mic 4:3 **2:10** Rev 6:15; 2 Thess 1:9

"They will hammer their swords into plows / and their spears into pruning knives" *(Isaiah 2:4)*.

alone will be exalted. 12On that day the
LORD Almighty will humble everyone who
is powerful, everyone who is proud and con-
ceited. 13He will destroy the tall cedars of
Lebanon and all the oaks in the land of
Bashan. 14He will level the high mountains
and hills, 15every high tower, and the walls of
every fortress. 16He will sink even the largest
and most beautiful ships. 17-18Human pride
will be ended, and human arrogance will be
destroyed. Idols will completely disappear,
and the LORD alone will be exalted on that
day.

19People will hide in caves in the rocky
hills or dig holes in the ground to try to
escape from the LORD's anger and to hide
from his power and glory, when he comes to
shake the earth. 20When that day comes,
they will throw away the gold and silver
idols they have made, and abandon them to
the moles and the bats. 21When the LORD
comes to shake the earth, people will hide in
holes and caves in the rocky hills to try to
escape from his anger and to hide from his
power and glory.

To escape from the LORD's anger (2:19, 21)

22Put no more confidence in mortals.
What are they worth?

Chaos in Jerusalem

3 Now the Lord, the Almighty LORD, is
about to take away from Jerusalem and
Judah everything and everyone that the peo-
ple depend on. He is going to take away
their food and their water, 2their heroes and
their soldiers, their judges and their proph-
ets, their fortunetellers and their statesmen,
3their military and civilian leaders, their
politicians and everyone who uses magic to
control events. 4The LORD will let the peo-
ple be governed by immature boys. 5Every-
one will take advantage of everyone else.
Young people will not respect their elders,
and worthless people will not respect their
superiors.

6A time will come when the members of a
clan will choose one of their number and say
to him, "You at least have something to wear,
so be our leader in this time of trouble."

7But he will answer, "Not me! I can't help
you. I don't have any food or clothes either.
Don't make me your leader!"

8Yes, Jerusalem is doomed! Judah is col-
lapsing! Everything they say and do is against
the LORD; they openly insult God himself.
9Their prejudices will be held against them.
They sin as openly as the people of Sodom
did. They are doomed, and they have
brought it on themselves.

10The righteous will be happy,[f] and things
will go well for them. They will get to enjoy
what they have worked for. 11But evil people
are doomed; what they have done to others
will now be done to them.

12Moneylenders oppress my people, and
their creditors cheat them.

My people, your leaders are misleading
you, so that you do not know which way to
turn.

The LORD Judges His People

13The LORD is ready to state his case; he
is ready to judge his people.[g] 14The LORD is
bringing the elders and leaders of his people
to judgment. He makes this accusation: "You
have plundered vineyards, and your houses
are full of what you have taken from the
poor. 15You have no right to crush my peo-
ple and take advantage of the poor. I, the
Sovereign LORD Almighty, have spoken."

A Warning to the Women of Jerusalem

16The LORD said, "Look how proud the
women of Jerusalem are! They walk along
with their noses in the air. They are always
flirting. They take dainty little steps, and the
bracelets on their ankles jingle. 17But I will

[f] **3:10** *Probable text* The righteous will be happy; *Hebrew* Say to the righteous. [g] **3:13** *Some ancient translations* his people; *Hebrew* the peoples.

punish them—I will shave their heads and
leave them bald."

18 A day is coming when the Lord will
take away from the women of Jerusalem
everything they are so proud of—the orna-
ments they wear on their ankles, on their
heads, on their necks, 19 and on their wrists.
He will take away their veils 20 and their hats;
the magic charms they wear on their arms
and at their waists; 21 the rings they wear on
their fingers and in their noses; 22 all their
fine robes, gowns, cloaks, and purses; 23 their
revealing garments, their linen handkerchiefs,
and the scarves and long veils they wear on
their heads.

24 Instead of using perfumes, they will
stink; instead of fine belts, they will wear
coarse ropes; instead of having beautiful hair,
they will be bald; instead of fine clothes, they
will be dressed in rags; their beauty will be
turned to shame!

With their noses in the air (3:16)
Dressed in rags (3:24)

25 The men of the city, yes, even the
strongest men, will be killed in war. 26 The
city gates will mourn and cry, and the city
itself will be like a woman sitting on the
ground, stripped naked.

4 When that time comes, seven women
will grab hold of one man and say, "We
can feed and clothe ourselves, but please let
us say you are our husband, so that we won't
have to endure the shame of being unmar-
ried."

Jerusalem Will Be Restored

2 The time is coming when the LORD will
make every plant and tree in the land grow
large and beautiful. All the people of Israel
who survive will take delight and pride in
the crops that the land produces. 3 Everyone
who is left in Jerusalem, whom God has
chosen for survival, will be called holy. 4 By
his power the Lord will judge and purify the
nation and wash away the guilt of Jerusalem
and the blood that has been shed there.
5 Then over Mount Zion and over all who
are gathered there, the LORD will send a
cloud in the daytime and smoke and a bright
flame at night. God's glory will cover and
protect the whole city. 6 His glory will shade
the city from the heat of the day and make it
a place of safety, sheltered from the rain and
storm.

The Song of the Vineyard

5 Listen while I sing you this song,
a song of my friend and his vineyard:
My friend had a vineyard
on a very fertile hill.
2 He dug the soil and cleared it of stones;
he planted the finest vines.
He built a tower to guard them,
dug a pit for treading the grapes.
He waited for the grapes to ripen,
but every grape was sour.

3 So now my friend says, "You people who
live in Jerusalem and Judah, judge between
my vineyard and me. 4 Is there anything I
failed to do for it? Then why did it produce
sour grapes and not the good grapes I
expected?

5 "Here is what I am going to do to my
vineyard: I will take away the hedge around it,
break down the wall that protects it, and let
wild animals eat it and trample it down. 6 I
will let it be overgrown with weeds. I will not
trim the vines or hoe the ground; instead, I
will let briers and thorns cover it. I will even
forbid the clouds to let rain fall on it."

7 Israel is the vineyard of the LORD
Almighty;
the people of Judah are the vines he
planted.

4:5 Ex 13:21; 24:16 **5:1, 2** Mt 21:33; Mk 12:1; Lk 20:9

He expected them to do what was
good,
but instead they committed murder.
He expected them to do what was
right,
but their victims cried out for justice.

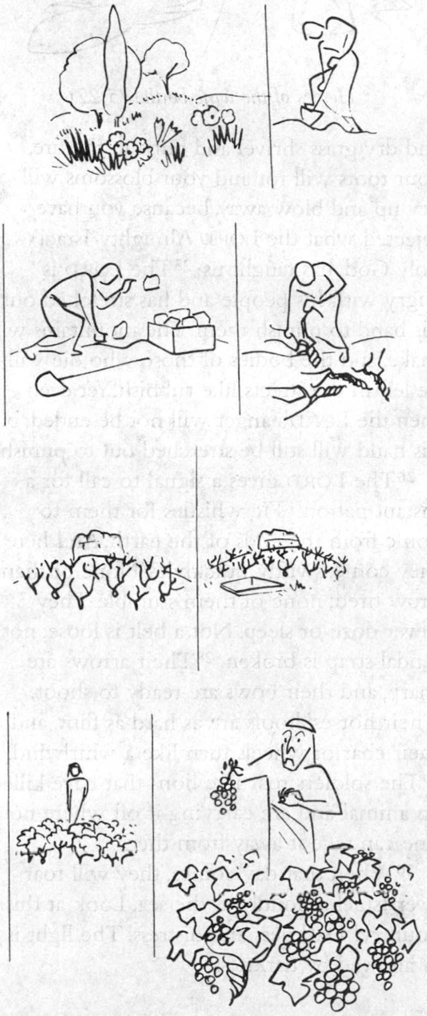

A very fertile hill . . . he dug the soil . . . cleared it of stones . . . he planted the finest vines . . . he built a tower . . . dug a pit . . . he waited for the grapes to ripen, but every grape was sour. (5:1–2)

The Evil That People Do

8You are doomed! You buy more houses
and fields to add to those you already have.
Soon there will be no place for anyone else
to live, and you alone will live in the land. 9I
have heard the LORD Almighty say, "All these
big, fine houses will be empty ruins. 10The
grapevines growing on five acres of land will
yield only five gallons of wine. Ten bushels of
seed will produce only one bushel of grain."
11You are doomed! You get up early in the
morning to start drinking, and you spend
long evenings getting drunk. 12At your feasts
you have harps and tambourines and flutes—
and wine. But you don't understand what the
LORD is doing, 13and so you will be carried
away as prisoners. Your leaders will starve to
death, and the common people will die of
thirst. 14The world of the dead is hungry for
them, and it opens its mouth wide. It gulps
down the nobles of Jerusalem along with the
noisy crowd of common people.
15Everyone will be disgraced, and all who
are proud will be humbled. 16But the LORD
Almighty shows his greatness by doing what
is right, and he reveals his holiness by judg-
ing his people. 17In the ruins of the cities
lambs will eat grass and young goats will
find pasture.[h]
18You are doomed! You are unable to break
free from your sins. 19You say, "Let the LORD
hurry up and do what he says he will, so that
we can see it. Let Israel's holy God carry out
his plans; let's see what he has in mind."
20You are doomed! You call evil good and

In the ruins of the cities. (5:17)

[h] **5:17** *Verse 17 in Hebrew is unclear.*
5:11 Wis 2:7–9

Isaiah, chapter 3, is pretty critical about the way people lived in Isaiah's time. What would a prophet say about the way people live today?

Pray it!

Light and Dark

"You are doomed." Isaiah repeats this phrase several times in Isaiah, chapter 5. Because of the Israelites' wickedness, Isaiah says that God is sending soldiers from a distant nation who will come and punish the Israelites. The light that was supposed to be God's Chosen People will be swallowed by darkness.

Light is a symbol for God's presence throughout the Bible. Darkness is very often used as a symbol for the absence of God. Opposites are used in poems and prayers for drama and as ways of contrasting. Write a prayer using the words *light* and *dark,* and any other sets of opposites (such as happy and sad or wise and foolish) that you want to use. In your prayer, talk about what happens when people follow God and what happens when they do not follow God.

— Isaiah, chapter 5

call good evil. You turn darkness into light
and light into darkness. You make what is bit-
ter sweet, and what is sweet you make bitter.
21You are doomed! You think you are
wise, so very clever.
22You are doomed! Heroes of the wine
bottle! Brave and fearless when it comes to
mixing drinks! 23But for just a bribe you let
the guilty go free, and you keep the innocent
from getting justice. 24So now, just as straw

Heroes of the wine bottle! (5:22)

and dry grass shrivel and burn in the fire,
your roots will rot and your blossoms will
dry up and blow away, because you have
rejected what the LORD Almighty, Israel's
holy God, has taught us. 25The LORD is
angry with his people and has stretched out
his hand to punish them. The mountains will
shake, and the bodies of those who die will
be left in the streets like rubbish. Yet even
then the LORD's anger will not be ended, but
his hand will still be stretched out to punish.
26The LORD gives a signal to call for a
distant nation.[i] He whistles for them to
come from the ends of the earth. And here
they come, swiftly, quickly! 27None of them
grow tired; none of them stumble. They
never doze or sleep. Not a belt is loose; not a
sandal strap is broken. 28Their arrows are
sharp, and their bows are ready to shoot.
Their horses' hoofs are as hard as flint, and
their chariot wheels turn like a whirlwind.
29The soldiers roar like lions that have killed
an animal and are carrying it off where no
one can take it away from them.
30When that day comes, they will roar
over Israel as loudly as the sea. Look at this
country! Darkness and distress! The light is
swallowed by darkness.

God Calls Isaiah to Be a Prophet

6 In the year that King Uzziah died, I saw
the Lord. He was sitting on his throne,
high and exalted, and his robe filled the

[i] **5:26** *Probable text* a distant nation; *Hebrew* distant nations.
6:1 2 Kings 15:7; 2 Chr 26:23

How would you answer if God called you to be a messenger?

whole Temple. 2Around him flaming crea-
tures were standing, each of which had six
wings. Each creature covered its face with
two wings, and its body with two, and used
the other two for flying. 3They were calling
out to each other:
"Holy, holy, holy!
The LORD Almighty is holy!
His glory fills the world."
4The sound of their voices made the
foundation of the Temple shake, and the
Temple itself became filled with smoke.
5I said, "There is no hope for me! I am
doomed because every word that passes my
lips is sinful, and I live among a people
whose every word is sinful. And yet, with my
own eyes I have seen the King, the LORD
Almighty."
6Then one of the creatures flew down to
me, carrying a burning coal that he had
taken from the altar with a pair of tongs.
7He touched my lips with the burning coal
and said, "This has touched your lips, and
now your guilt is gone, and your sins are for-
given."
8Then I heard the Lord say, "Whom shall
I send? Who will be our messenger?"
I answered, "I will go! Send me!"
9So he told me to go and give the people
this message: "No matter how much you lis-
ten, you will not understand. No matter how
much you look, you will not know what is
happening." 10Then he said to me, "Make
the minds of these people dull, their ears
deaf, and their eyes blind, so that they cannot
see or hear or understand. If they did, they
might turn to me and be healed."
11I asked, "How long will it be like this,
Lord?"
He answered, "Until the cities are ruined
and empty—until the houses are uninhabit-
ed—until the land itself is a desolate waste-
land. 12I will send the people far away and
make the whole land desolate. 13Even if one
person out of ten remains in the land, he too
will be destroyed; he will be like the stump
of an oak tree that has been cut down."
(The stump represents a new beginning
for God's people.)

Study it!

Prophets and Prophecy

The Book of Isaiah includes many visions, judgments, predictions, and promises proclaimed by the prophet Isaiah. We call all of these things prophecy. Prophecy isn't magic or fortunetelling, nor is it guessing or hypothesizing. A *prophet* is a person who speaks for another, in this case God. Isaiah and the other prophets were called by God to deliver God's messages to the Israelites. Chapter 6 tells the story of how Isaiah was called by God to be a prophet.

Many times the prophets warned the people about their behavior. And many times the people ignored the warnings. So sometimes the prophets, such as Isaiah, had to tell the people the same warning over and over. The prophets also spoke God's promises of hope and peace when the people needed to hear that message from God. The prophets did not give their own personal message; they always were giving God's message. And sometimes that got the prophets in trouble because people did not always want to hear God's message!

— Isaiah, chapter 6

A Message for King Ahaz

7 When King Ahaz, the son of Jotham and
grandson of Uzziah, ruled Judah, war
broke out. Rezin, king of Syria, and Pekah
son of Remaliah, king of Israel, attacked
Jerusalem, but were unable to capture it.

6:3 Rev 4:8 **6:4** Rev 15:8 **6:9, 10** Mt 13:14, 15; Mk 4:12; Lk 8:10; Jn 12:40; Acts 28:26, 27 **7:1** 2 Kings 16:5; 2 Chr 28:5, 6

Advent

Isaiah 7:10–14 is proclaimed at Mass every three years on the fourth Sunday of Advent, the Sunday just before Christmas. If you are familiar with the Christmas story, you probably know why: "A young woman who is pregnant will have a son and will name him 'Immanuel'" (Isaiah 7:14). These words point toward the birth of Christ. If you read Matthew 1:18–24, which is the Gospel for the fourth Sunday of Advent, you can see how this passage from Isaiah and that Gospel passage go together.

— Isaiah 7:10–14

2 When word reached the king of Judah that the armies of Syria were already in the territory of Israel, he and all his people were so terrified that they trembled like trees shaking in the wind.

3 The LORD said to Isaiah, "Take your son Shear Jashub,[j] and go to meet King Ahaz. You will find him on the road where the cloth makers work, at the end of the ditch that brings water from the upper pool. 4 Tell him to keep alert, to stay calm, and not to be frightened or disturbed. The anger of King Rezin and his Syrians and of King Pekah is no more dangerous than the smoke from two smoldering sticks of wood. 5 Syria, together with Israel and its king, has made a plot. 6 They intend to invade Judah, terrify the people into joining their side, and then put Tabeel's son on the throne.

7 "But I, the LORD, declare that this will never happen. 8 Why? Because Syria is no stronger than Damascus, its capital city, and Damascus is no stronger than King Rezin. As for Israel, within sixty-five years it will be too shattered to survive as a nation. 9 Israel is no stronger than Samaria, its capital city, and Samaria is no stronger than King Pekah.

"If your faith is not enduring, you will not endure."

The Sign of Immanuel

10 The LORD sent another message to Ahaz: 11 "Ask the LORD your God to give you a sign. It can be from deep in the world of the dead or from high up in heaven."

12 Ahaz answered, "I will not ask for a sign. I refuse to put the LORD to the test."

13 To that Isaiah replied, "Listen, now, descendants of King David. It's bad enough for you to wear out the patience of people—do you have to wear out God's patience too? 14 Well then, the Lord himself will give you a sign: a young woman[k] who is pregnant will have a son and will name him 'Immanuel.'[l] 15 By the time he is old enough to make his own decisions, people will be drinking milk and eating honey.[m] 16 Even before that time comes, the lands of those two kings who terrify you will be deserted.

17 "The LORD is going to bring on you, on your people, and on the whole royal family, days of trouble worse than any that have come since the kingdom of Israel separated from Judah—he is going to bring the king of Assyria.

18 "When that time comes, the LORD will whistle as a signal for the Egyptians to come like flies from the farthest branches of the

[j] **7:3** SHEAR JASHUB: *This name in Hebrew means "A few will come back" (see 10:20–22).* [k] **7:14** YOUNG WOMAN: *The Hebrew word here translated "young woman" is not the specific term for "virgin," but refers to any young woman of marriageable age. The use of "virgin" in Mt 1:23 reflects a Greek translation of the Old Testament, made some 500 years after Isaiah.* [l] **7:14** IMMANUEL: *This name in Hebrew means "God is with us."* [m] **7:15** MILK AND HONEY: *These foods were associated with the earlier days of Israel's history.*

7:14 Mt 1:23

Nile, and for the Assyrians to come from
their land like bees. 19They will swarm in
the rugged valleys and in the caves in the
rocks, and they will cover every thorn bush
and every pasture.

20"When that time comes, the Lord will
hire a barber from across the Euphrates—the
emperor of Assyria!—and he will shave off
your beards and the hair on your heads and
your bodies.

21"When that time comes, even if a
farmer has been able to save only one young
cow and two goats, 22they will give so much
milk that he will have all he needs. Yes, the
few survivors left in the land will have milk
and honey to eat.

23"When that time comes, the fine vine-
yards, each with a thousand vines and each
worth a thousand pieces of silver, will be
overgrown with thorn bushes and briers.
24People will go hunting there with bows
and arrows. Yes, the whole country will be
full of briers and thorn bushes. 25All the hills
where crops were once planted will be so
overgrown with thorns that no one will go
there. It will be a place where cattle and
sheep graze."

Isaiah's Son as a Sign to the People

8 The LORD said to me, "Take a large
piece of writing material and write on
it in large letters:[n] 'Quick Loot, Fast Plun-
der.' 2Get two reliable men, the priest Uriah
and Zechariah son of Jeberechiah, to serve as
witnesses."

3Some time later my wife became preg-
nant. When our son was born, the LORD said
to me, "Name him 'Quick-Loot-Fast-Plun-
der.' 4Before the boy is old enough to say
'Mamma' and 'Daddy,' all the wealth of
Damascus and all the loot of Samaria will be
carried off by the king of Assyria."

The Emperor of Assyria Is Coming

5The LORD spoke to me again. 6He said,
"Because these people have rejected the
quiet waters of Shiloah Brook[o] and tremble[p]
before King Rezin and King Pekah, 7I, the
Lord, will bring the emperor of Assyria and
all his forces to attack Judah. They will
advance like the flood waters of the
Euphrates River, overflowing all its banks.
8They will sweep through Judah in a flood,
rising shoulder high and covering every-
thing."

God is with us! His outspread wings pro-
tect the land.[q]

9Gather together in fear, you nations! Lis-
ten, you distant parts of the earth. Get ready
to fight, but be afraid! Yes, get ready, but be
afraid! 10Make your plans! But they will
never succeed. Talk all you want to! But it is
all useless, because God is with us.

The LORD Warns the Prophet

11With his great power the LORD warned
me not to follow the road which the people
were following. He said, 12"Do not join in
the schemes of the people and do not be
afraid of the things that they fear. 13Remem-
ber that I, the LORD Almighty, am holy; I am
the one you must fear. 14Because of my awe-
some holiness I am like a stone that people
stumble over; I am like a trap that will catch
the people of the kingdoms of Judah and
Israel and the people of Jerusalem. 15Many
will stumble; they will fall and be crushed.
They will be caught in a trap."

Warning against Consulting the Dead

16You, my disciples, are to guard and pre-
serve the messages that God has given me.
17The LORD has hidden himself from his
people, but I trust him and place my hope in
him.

[n] **8:1** large letters; *or* letters that everyone can read. [o] **8:6** SHILOAH BROOK: *A stream which flowed from the large spring on the eastern side of Jerusalem.* [p] **8:6** *Probable text* tremble; *Hebrew* rejoice. [q] **8:8** everything." God . . . land; *or* everything. They will spread out over the land. God be with us!"

8:12, 13 1 Pet 3:14, 15 **8:14, 15** 1 Pet 2:8 **8:17** Heb 2:13

The name Immanuel literally means "God is with us."

Live it!

Icky Feelings

Read Isaiah 8:11–15 and then think about this story:

"We have to cheat; it is the only way to pass. If I don't pass, I won't get into the honors program in high school." Sam tried to convince her friends. "Yeah, I *have* to get into that program or my parents will kill me." Claudia agreed.

"And I have the perfect plan," said Karen. "It's just perfect."

"What is it?" Claudia and Sam said at the same time.

"It's . . ." Karen looked at Kenza. "What about you? Are you in or are you out?"

Kenza looked at her friends. It was tempting. Mr. Gratsi's class was so hard, and the test seemed impossible to prepare for. But the thought of cheating gave her such an icky feeling in her stomach. "I don't know."

"Don't know!" cried Sam. "How can you not know? We have to cheat. Let's listen to Karen's plan."

"I don't think so," Kenza said. She knew this meant her friends may get better grades and into the honors program. But she didn't want to be involved in a scheme. "You guys know this is wrong—please don't go through with it."

As she walked away, she heard the girls whispering, but she wasn't afraid or even worried. She was following her conscience, and that good feeling in her stomach was much better than the icky feeling she had earlier.

— Isaiah 8:11–15

18 Here I am with the children the LORD
has given me. The LORD Almighty, whose
throne is on Mount Zion, has sent us as liv-
ing messages to the people of Israel.
19 But people will tell you to ask for mes-
sages from fortunetellers and mediums, who
chirp and mutter. They will say, "After all,
people should ask for messages from the
spirits and consult the dead on behalf of the
living."
20 You are to answer them, "Listen to what
the LORD is teaching you! Don't listen to
mediums—what they tell you cannot keep
trouble away."[r]

A Time of Trouble

21 The people will wander through the
land, discouraged and hungry. In their
hunger and their anger they will curse their
king and their God. They may look up to
the sky 22 or stare at the ground, but they
will see nothing but trouble and darkness,
terrifying darkness into which they are being
9 driven. 1 There will be no way for them
to escape from this time of trouble.

The Future King

The land of the tribes of Zebulun and Naphtali was once disgraced, but the future will bring honor to this region, from the Mediterranean eastward to the land on the other side of the Jordan, and even to Galilee itself, where the foreigners live.

2 The people who walked in darkness
have seen a great light.
They lived in a land of shadows,
but now light is shining on them.
3 You have given them great joy,[s] Lord;
you have made them happy.
They rejoice in what you have done,

[r] **8:20** *Verse 20 in Hebrew is unclear.* [s] **9:3** *Probable text* You have given them great joy; *Hebrew* You have increased the nation.

8:18 Heb 2:13 **9:1** Mt 4:15 **9:2** Mt 4:16; Lk 1:79

Read Isaiah 9:2. How do you feel when you finally get a really sunny day after several cloudy and gloomy days?

Pray it!

Names of God

"Wonderful Counselor," "Mighty God," "Eternal Father," "Prince of Peace" (Isaiah 9:6). All of these are names given to God. Here is a prayer that uses them. You can add to it by using other names that you would give God.

Wonderful

God, you really are wonderful. You do wonderful things and know how to make me feel wonderful. Thank you for being a wonderful friend to me.

Counselor

Jesus you are a counselor. You listen when I call and lead me on the right path. Thank you for being there when I need someone to turn to.

Mighty God

Holy Spirit, you are mighty. You came to Mary and gave courage to the disciples at Pentecost. Thank you for being a mighty force in my life.

Eternal Father

Lord, you are my Eternal Father. You are there for me, like a loving, kind parent, you hold me close. Thank you for being my Eternal Father.

Prince of Peace

Jesus, you are the Prince of Peace. You give me a model for peace and show me that peace is the only way. Thank you for giving me your peace.

— Isaiah 9:6

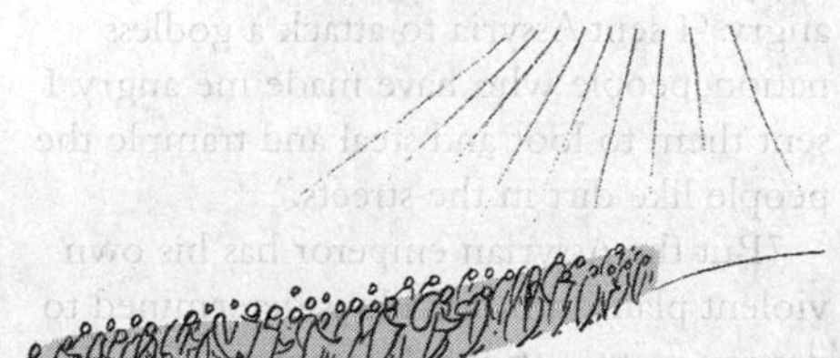

Now light is shining on them. (9:2)

as people rejoice when they harvest
grain
or when they divide captured
wealth.
4 For you have broken the yoke that
burdened them
and the rod that beat their shoulders.
You have defeated the nation
that oppressed and exploited your
people,
just as you defeated the army of Midian
long ago.
5 The boots of the invading army
and all their bloodstained clothing
will be destroyed by fire.
6 A child is born to us!
A son is given to us!
And he will be our ruler.
He will be called, "Wonderful[t]
Counselor,"
"Mighty God," "Eternal Father,"
"Prince of Peace."
7 His royal power will continue to grow;
his kingdom will always be at peace.
He will rule as King David's successor,
basing his power on right and justice,
from now until the end of time.
The LORD Almighty is determined to do
all this.

[t] **9:6** Wonderful; *or* Wise.
9:7 Lk 1:32, 33

The LORD Will Punish Israel

8 The Lord has pronounced judgment on
the kingdom of Israel, on the descendants of
Jacob. 9 All the people of Israel, everyone
who lives in the city of Samaria, will know
that he has done this. Now they are proud
and arrogant. They say, 10 "The brick build-
ings have fallen down, but we will replace
them with stone buildings. The beams of
sycamore wood have been cut down, but we
will replace them with the finest cedar."
11 The LORD has stirred up their enemies[u]
to attack them. 12 Syria on the east and
Philistia on the west have opened their
mouths to devour Israel. Yet even so the
LORD's anger is not ended; his hand is still
stretched out to punish.
13 The people of Israel have not repented;
even though the LORD Almighty has pun-
ished them, they have not returned to him.
14 In a single day the LORD will punish
Israel's leaders and its people; he will cut
them off, head and tail. 15 The old and hon-
orable men are the head—and the tail is the
prophets whose teachings are lies! 16 Those
who lead these people have misled them and
totally confused them. 17 And so the Lord
will not let any of the young men escape,
and he will not show pity on any of the
widows and orphans, because all the people
are godless and wicked and everything they
say is evil. Yet even so the LORD's anger will
not be ended, but his hand will still be
stretched out to punish.
18 The wickedness of the people burns like
a fire that destroys thorn bushes and thistles.
It burns like a forest fire that sends up
columns of smoke. 19 Because the LORD
Almighty is angry, his punishment burns like
a fire throughout the land and destroys the
people, and it is each of us for ourselves.

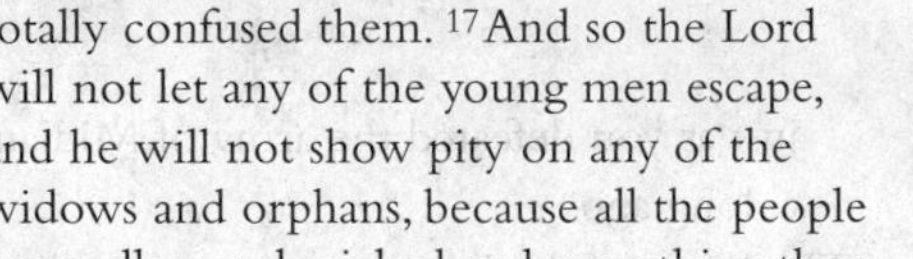

Like a forest fire (9:18)

20 Everywhere in the country people snatch
and eat any bit of food they can find, but
their hunger is never satisfied. They even eat
their own children! 21 The people of Manas-
seh and the people of Ephraim attack each
other, and together they attack Judah. Yet
even so the LORD's anger is not ended; his
hand is still stretched out to punish.

10 You are doomed! You make unjust
laws that oppress my people. 2 That is
how you keep the poor from having their
rights and from getting justice. That is how
you take the property that belongs to wid-
ows and orphans. 3 What will you do when
God punishes you? What will you do when
he brings disaster on you from a distant
country? Where will you run to find help?
Where will you hide your wealth? 4 You will
be killed in battle or dragged off as prison-
ers. Yet even so the LORD's anger will not be
ended; his hand will still be stretched out to
punish.

The Emperor of Assyria as the Instrument of God

5 The LORD said, "Assyria! I use Assyria
like a club to punish those with whom I am
angry. 6 I sent Assyria to attack a godless
nation, people who have made me angry. I
sent them to loot and steal and trample the
people like dirt in the streets."
7 But the Assyrian emperor has his own
violent plans in mind. He is determined to
destroy many nations. 8 He boasts, "Every
one of my commanders is a king! 9 I con-
quered the cities of Calno and Carchemish,
the cities of Hamath and Arpad. I conquered
Samaria and Damascus. 10 I reached out to
punish those kingdoms that worship idols,
idols more numerous than those of
Jerusalem and Samaria. 11 I have destroyed
Samaria and all its idols, and I will do the
same to Jerusalem and the images that are
worshiped there."
12 But the Lord says, "When I finish what I
am doing on Mount Zion and in Jerusalem,
I will punish the emperor of Assyria for all
his boasting and all his pride."

[u] **9:11** *Probable text* their enemies; *Hebrew* the enemies of Rezin.
10:5–34 Isa 14:24–27; Nah 1:1—3:19; Zeph 2:13–15

13 The emperor of Assyria boasts, "I have
done it all myself. I am strong and wise and
clever. I wiped out the boundaries between
nations and took the supplies they had
stored. Like a bull I have trampled the peo-
ple who live there. 14 The nations of the
world were like a bird's nest, and I gathered
their wealth as easily as gathering eggs. Not a
wing fluttered to scare me off; no beak
opened to scream at me!"

15 But the LORD says, "Can an ax claim to
be greater than the one who uses it? Is a saw
more important than the one who saws with
it? A club doesn't lift up a person; a person
lifts up a club."

16 The LORD Almighty is going to send
disease to punish those who are now well-
fed. In their bodies there will be a fire that
burns and burns. 17 God, the light of Israel,
will become a fire. Israel's holy God will
become a flame, which in a single day will
burn up everything, even the thorns and
thistles. 18 The rich forests and farmlands will
be totally destroyed, in the same way that a
fatal sickness destroys someone. 19 There will
be so few trees left that even a child will be
able to count them.

A Few Will Come Back

20 A time is coming when the people of
Israel who have survived will not rely any
more on the nation that almost destroyed
them. They will truly put their trust in the
LORD, Israel's holy God. 21 A few of the peo-
ple of Israel will come back to their mighty
God. 22 Even though now there are as many
people of Israel as there are grains of sand by
the sea, only a few will come back. Destruc-
tion is in store for the people, and it is fully
deserved. 23 Yes, throughout the whole coun-
try the Sovereign LORD Almighty will bring
destruction, as he said he would.

The LORD Will Punish Assyria

24 The Sovereign LORD Almighty says to
his people who live in Zion, "Do not be
afraid of the Assyrians, even though they
oppress you as the Egyptians used to do. 25 In
only a little while I will finish punishing you,
and then I will destroy them. 26 I, the LORD
Almighty, will beat them with my whip as
I did the people of Midian at Oreb Rock.
I will punish Assyria as I punished Egypt.
27 When that time comes, I will free you from
the power of Assyria, and their yoke will no
longer be a burden on your shoulders."[v]

The Invader Attacks

28 The enemy army has captured the city of
Ai![w] They have passed through Migron! They
left their supplies at Michmash! 29 They have
crossed the pass and are spending the night at
Geba! The people in the town of Ramah are
terrified, and the people in King Saul's home-
town of Gibeah have run away. 30 Shout, peo-
ple of Gallim! Listen, people of Laishah!
Answer, people of Anathoth! 31 The people of
Madmenah and Gebim are running for their
lives. 32 Today the enemy are in the town of
Nob, and there they are shaking their fists at
Mount Zion, at the city of Jerusalem.

33 The LORD Almighty will bring them
crashing down like branches cut off a tree.
The proudest and highest of them will be
cut down and humiliated. 34 The LORD will
cut them down as trees in the heart of the
forest are cut down with an ax, as even the
finest trees of Lebanon fall!

The Peaceful Kingdom

11 The royal line of David is like a tree
that has been cut down; but just as
new branches sprout from a stump, so a new
king will arise from among David's descen-
dants.

[v] **10:27** *Hebrew has three additional words, the meaning of which is unclear.* [w] **10:28** AI: *This and the other places mentioned in verses 28–32 were located near Jerusalem, along the way by which an invader would come to attack from the north.*

10:22, 23 Rom 9:27 **11:1** Rev 5:5; 22:16

"Wolves and sheep will live together in peace, / and leopards will lie down with young goats" *(Isaiah 11:6)*.

2 The spirit of the LORD will give him
wisdom
and the knowledge and skill to rule his
people.
He will know the LORD's will and honor
him,
3 and find pleasure in obeying him.
He will not judge by appearance or
hearsay;
4 he will judge the poor fairly
and defend the rights of the helpless.
At his command the people will be
punished,
and evil persons will die.
5 He will rule his people with justice and
integrity.

6 Wolves and sheep will live together in
peace,
and leopards will lie down with young
goats.
Calves and lion cubs will feed[x] together,
and little children will take care of
them.

And little children will take care of them. (11:6)

7 Cows and bears will eat together,
and their calves and cubs will lie down
in peace.
Lions will eat straw as cattle do.
8 Even a baby will not be harmed
if it plays near a poisonous snake.
9 On Zion, God's sacred hill,
there will be nothing harmful or evil.
The land will be as full of knowledge of
the LORD
as the seas are full of water.

The Exiled People Will Return

10 A day is coming when the new king
from the royal line of David will be a symbol
to the nations. They will gather in his royal
city and give him honor. 11 When that day
comes, the Lord will once again use his
power and bring back home those of his peo-
ple who are left in Assyria and Egypt, in the
lands of Pathros, Ethiopia,[y] Elam, Babylonia,
and Hamath, and in the coastlands and on the
islands of the sea. 12 The Lord will raise a sig-
nal flag to show the nations that he is gather-
ing together again the scattered people of
Israel and Judah and bringing them back from
the four corners of the earth. 13 The kingdom
of Israel will not be jealous of Judah any
more, and Judah will not be the enemy of
Israel. 14 Together they will attack the
Philistines on the west and plunder the peo-
ple who live to the east. They will conquer
the people of Edom and Moab, and the peo-
ple of Ammon will obey them. 15 The LORD
will dry up the Gulf of Suez, and he will
bring a hot wind to dry up the Euphrates,
leaving only seven tiny streams, so that anyone
can walk across. 16 There will be a highway
out of Assyria for those of his people Israel
who have survived there, just as there was for
their ancestors when they left Egypt.

Hymn of Thanksgiving

12 A day is coming when people will
sing,
"I praise you, LORD! You were angry with
me,
but now you comfort me and are angry
no longer.

[x] **11:6** *Some ancient translations* will feed; *Hebrew* and well-fed cattle. [y] **11:11** *Hebrew* Cush: *Cush is the ancient name of the extensive territory south of the First Cataract of the Nile River. This region was called Ethiopia in Graeco-Roman times, and included within its borders most of modern Sudan and some of present-day Ethiopia (Abyssinia).*

11:4 2 Thess 2:8 **11:5** Eph 6:14 **11:6–9** Isa 65:25 **11:9** Hab 2:14 **11:10** Rom 15:12 **11:15** Rev 16:12

Zion: **The name for the mountain that the Temple in Jerusalem was built on. Eventually, it became another name for Jerusalem or the whole nation of Israel.**

"Tell them how great he is!" (12:4)

2 God is my savior;
I will trust him and not be afraid.
The LORD gives me power and strength;
he is my savior.
3 As fresh water brings joy to the thirsty,
so God's people rejoice when he saves
them."
4 A day is coming when people will sing,
"Give thanks to the LORD! Call for him
to help you!
Tell all the nations what he has done!
Tell them how great he is!
5 Sing to the LORD because of the great
things he has done.
Let the whole world hear the news.
6 Let everyone who lives in Zion shout and
sing!
Israel's holy God is great,
and he lives among his people."

God Will Punish Babylon

13 This is a message about Babylon,
which Isaiah son of Amoz received
from God.
2 On the top of a barren hill raise the bat-
tle flag! Shout to the soldiers and raise your
arm as the signal for them to attack the gates
of the proud city. 3 The LORD has called out
his proud and confident soldiers to fight a
holy war and punish those he is angry with.
4 Listen to the noise on the mountains—
the sound of a great crowd of people, the
sound of nations and kingdoms gathering.
The LORD of Armies is preparing his troops
for battle. 5 They are coming from far-off
countries at the ends of the earth. In his
anger the LORD is coming to devastate the
whole country.
6 Howl in pain! The day of the LORD is
near, the day when the Almighty brings
destruction. 7 Everyone's hands will hang
limp, and everyone's courage will fail. 8 They
will all be terrified and overcome with pain,
like the pain of a woman in labor. They will
look at each other in fear, and their faces
will burn with shame. 9 The day of the LORD
is coming—that cruel day of his fierce anger

Study it!

Yesua and Yesayahu

Yesua **is the Hebrew word for salvation, and** ***Yesayahu*** **is Isaiah in Hebrew. Does this give you a clue about what Isaiah's message is going to be about? It could be said that Isaiah's words are words of salvation. Salvation has to do with how God is saving us. Maybe you don't think you need to be saved, but the truth is, we all need to be saved. Saved from what? We need to be saved from sin and death.**

The hymn of thanksgiving in Isaiah, chapter 12, is an example of Isaiah's message of salvation. We hear that God is a savior and of the happiness that comes with that. In the whole Book of Isaiah, the words ***salvation, save,*** **and** ***savior*** **are used a total of 78 times.**

— Isaiah, chapter 12

12:2 Ex 15:2; Ps 118:14 **13:1—14:23** Isa 47:1–15; Jer 50:1—51:64 **13:6** Joel 1:15

and fury. The earth will be made a wilder-
ness, and every sinner will be destroyed.
10 Every star and every constellation will stop
shining, the sun will be dark when it rises,
and the moon will give no light.
11 The LORD says, "I will bring disaster on
the earth and punish all wicked people for
their sins. I will humble everyone who is
proud and punish everyone who is arrogant
and cruel. 12 Those who survive will be
scarcer than gold. 13 I will make the heavens
tremble, and the earth will be shaken out of
its place on that day when I, the LORD
Almighty, show my anger.
14 "The foreigners living in Babylon will
run away to their homelands, scattering like
deer escaping from hunters, like sheep with-
out a shepherd. 15 Anyone who is caught will
be stabbed to death. 16 While they look on
helplessly, their babies will be battered to
death, their houses will be looted, and their
wives will be raped."
17 The LORD says, "I am stirring up the
Medes[z] to attack Babylon. They care noth-
ing for silver and are not tempted by gold.
18 With their bows and arrows they will kill
the young men. They will show no mercy to
babies and take no pity on children. 19 Bab-
ylonia is the most beautiful kingdom of all;
it is the pride of its people. But I, the LORD,
will overthrow Babylon as I did Sodom and
Gomorrah! 20 No one will ever live there
again. No wandering Arab will ever pitch a
tent there, and no shepherd will ever pasture
a flock there. 21 It will be a place where
desert animals live and where owls build
their nests. Ostriches will live there, and wild
goats will prance through the ruins. 22 The
towers and palaces will echo with the cries
of hyenas and jackals. Babylon's time has
come! Her days are almost over."

The Return from Exile

14 The LORD will once again be mer-
ciful to his people Israel and choose
them as his own. He will let them live in
their own land again, and foreigners will
come and live there with them. 2 Many
nations will help the people of Israel return
to the land which the LORD gave them, and
there the nations will serve Israel as slaves.
Those who once captured Israel will now be
captured by Israel, and the people of Israel
will rule over those who once oppressed
them.

The King of Babylon in the World of the Dead

3 The LORD will give the people of Israel
relief from their pain and suffering and from
the hard work they were forced to do.
4 When he does this, they are to mock the
king of Babylon and say:
"The cruel king has fallen! He will never
oppress anyone again! 5 The LORD has ended
the power of the evil rulers 6 who angrily
oppressed the peoples and never stopped
persecuting the nations they had conquered.
7 Now at last the whole world enjoys rest
and peace, and everyone sings for joy. 8 The
cypress trees and the cedars of Lebanon
rejoice over the fallen king, because there is
no one to cut them down, now that he is
gone!
9 "The world of the dead is getting ready
to welcome the king of Babylon. The ghosts
of those who were powerful on earth are
stirring about. The ghosts of kings are rising
from their thrones. 10 They all call out to
him, 'Now you are as weak as we are! You
are one of us! 11 You used to be honored
with the music of harps, but now here you
are in the world of the dead. You lie on a
bed of maggots and are covered with a blan-
ket of worms.' "
12 King of Babylon, bright morning star,
you have fallen from heaven! In the past you
conquered nations, but now you have been
thrown to the ground. 13 You were deter-
mined to climb up to heaven and to place
your throne above the highest stars. You
thought you would sit like a king on that
mountain in the north where the gods
assemble. 14 You said you would climb to the
tops of the clouds and be like the Almighty.

[z] **13:17** MEDES: *People of a nation northeast of Babylonia, which became part of the Persian Empire.*

13:10 Ezek 32:7; Mt 24:29; Mk 13:24, 25; Lk 21:25; Rev 6:12, 13; 8:12 **13:19** Gen 19:24 **13:21** Isa 34:14; Zeph 2:14; Rev 18:2 **14:12** Rev 8:10; 9:1 **14:13–15** Mt 11:23; Lk 10:15

15But instead, you have been brought down
to the deepest part of the world of the dead.
16The dead will stare and gape at you.
They will ask, "Is this the man who shook
the earth and made kingdoms tremble? 17Is
this the man who destroyed cities and turned
the world into a desert? Is this the man who
never freed his prisoners or let them go
home?"
18All the kings of the earth lie in their
magnificent tombs, 19but you have no tomb,
and your corpse is thrown out to rot. It is
covered by the bodies of soldiers killed in bat-
tle, thrown with them into a rocky pit, and
trampled down. 20Because you ruined your
country and killed your own people, you will
not be buried like other kings. None of your
evil family will survive. 21Let the slaughter
begin! The sons of this king will die because
of their ancestors' sins. None of them will
ever rule the earth or cover it with cities.

God Will Destroy Babylon

22The LORD Almighty says, "I will attack
Babylon and bring it to ruin. I will leave
nothing—no children, no survivors at all. I,
the LORD, have spoken. 23I will turn Bab-
ylon into a marsh, and owls will live there. I
will sweep Babylon with a broom that will
sweep everything away. I, the LORD
Almighty, have spoken."

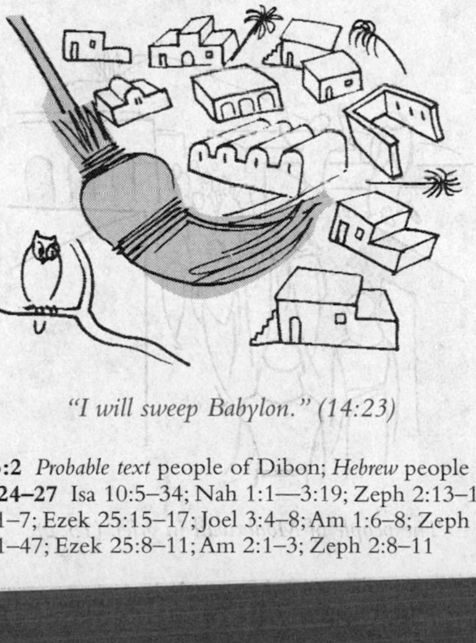

"I will sweep Babylon." (14:23)

God Will Destroy the Assyrians

24The LORD Almighty has sworn an oath:
"What I have planned will happen. What I
have determined to do will be done. 25I will
destroy the Assyrians in my land of Israel and
trample them on my mountains. I will free
my people from the Assyrian yoke and from
the burdens they have had to bear. 26This is
my plan for the world, and my arm is
stretched out to punish the nations." 27The
LORD Almighty is determined to do this; he
has stretched out his arm to punish, and no
one can stop him.

God Will Destroy the Philistines

28This is a message that was proclaimed in
the year that King Ahaz died.
29People of Philistia, the rod that beat you
is broken, but you have no reason to be glad.
When one snake dies, a worse one comes in
its place. A snake's egg hatches a flying drag-
on. 30The LORD will be a shepherd to the
poor of his people and will let them live in
safety. But he will send a terrible famine on
you Philistines, and it will not leave any of
you alive.
31Howl and cry for help, all you Philistine
cities! Be terrified, all of you! A cloud of
dust is coming from the north—it is an army
with no cowards in its ranks.
32How shall we answer the messengers
that come to us from Philistia? We will tell
them that the LORD has established Zion and
that his suffering people will find safety there.

God Will Destroy Moab

15 This is a message about Moab.
The cities of Ar and Kir are
destroyed in a single night, and silence covers
the land of Moab. 2The people of Dibon[a]
climb the hill to weep at the shrine. The
people of Moab wail in grief over the cities

[a] **15:2** *Probable text* people of Dibon; *Hebrew* people and Dibon.
14:24–27 Isa 10:5–34; Nah 1:1—3:19; Zeph 2:13–15 **14:28** 2 Kings 16:20; 2 Chr 28:27 **14:29–31** Jer 47:1–7; Ezek 25:15–17; Joel 3:4–8; Am 1:6–8; Zeph 2:4–7; Zech 9:5–7 **15:1—16:14** Isa 25:10–12; Jer 48:1–47; Ezek 25:8–11; Am 2:1–3; Zeph 2:8–11

The Philistines once lived in Israel and were ancient enemies of the Israelites.°

Pray it!

Our Enemies Destroyed?

The prophecies in these chapters of Isaiah are about God's punishment of nations that are Israel's enemies: Babylon, Assyria, Moab, and Egypt. Isaiah uses strong and violent imagery to describe how these nations and their people will meet their doom. We have to remember to understand the Old Testament in light of what Jesus teaches. Jesus makes it clear that God loves all people and that we should love our enemies and pray for them. Rather than see them destroyed, followers of Jesus try everything possible to show our enemies the goodness of God and how to live in love and peace. Here's a prayer for people who threaten us.

Mighty God,
Sometimes I feel like Isaiah. I want to see people who do evil and hurt others completely destroyed. It is hard to understand how people can be so mean and cruel to other people. But Jesus showed us that you even love mean and evil people. So I pray, Lord, for people who are our enemies. Help them to know your love. Help us to be an example of love and forgiveness so that they might come to believe in you, too. With the help of the Holy Spirit, may we live with understanding, peace, and justice for all people. Amen.

— Isaiah, chapter 15

of Nebo and Medeba; they have shaved their
heads and their beards in grief. 3The people
in the streets are dressed in sackcloth; in the
city squares and on the rooftops people
mourn and cry. 4The people of Heshbon
and Elealeh cry out, and their cry can be
heard as far away as Jahaz. Even the soldiers
tremble; their courage is gone. 5My heart
cries out for Moab! The people have fled to
the town of Zoar, and to Eglath Shelishiyah.
Some climb the road to Luhith, weeping as
they go; some escape to Horonaim, grieving
loudly. 6Nimrim Brook is dry, the grass
beside it has withered, and nothing green is
left. 7The people go across the Valley of Wil-
lows, trying to escape with all their posses-
sions. 8Everywhere at Moab's borders the
sound of crying is heard. It is heard at the
towns of Eglaim and Beerelim. 9At the town
of Dibon the river is red with blood, and
God has something even worse in store for
the people there. Yes, there will be a bloody
slaughter of everyone left in Moab.

The people of Moab wail in grief. (15:2)

"Then one of David's descendants will be king, and he will rule the people with faithfulness and love" *(Isaiah 16:5)*.

Trying to escape with all their possessions (15:7)

Moab's Hopeless Situation

16 From the city of Sela in the desert
the people of Moab send a lamb as a
present to the one who rules in Jerusalem.
2 They wait on the banks of the Arnon River
and move aimlessly back and forth, like birds
driven from their nest.
3 They say to the people of Judah, "Tell us
what to do. Protect us like a tree that casts a
cool shadow in the heat of noon, and let us
rest in your shade. We are refugees; hide us
where no one can find us. 4 Let us stay in
your land. Protect us from those who want
to destroy us."
(Oppression and destruction will end, and
those who are devastating the country will
be gone. 5 Then one of David's descendants
will be king, and he will rule the people
with faithfulness and love. He will be quick
to do what is right, and he will see that jus-
tice is done.)
6 The people of Judah say, "We have heard
how proud the people of Moab are. We
know that they are arrogant and conceited,
but their boasts are empty."
7 The people of Moab will weep because
of the troubles they suffer. They will all weep
when they remember the fine food they
used to eat in the city of Kir Heres. They
will be driven to despair. 8 The farms near
Heshbon and the vineyards of Sibmah are
destroyed—those vineyards whose wine used
to make the rulers of the nations drunk. At
one time the vines spread as far as the city of
Jazer, and eastward into the desert, and west-
ward to the other side of the Dead Sea.
9 Now I weep for Sibmah's vines as I weep
for Jazer. My tears fall for Heshbon and
Elealeh, because there is no harvest to make
the people glad. 10 No one is happy now
in the fertile fields. No one shouts or sings
in the vineyards. No one tramples grapes to
make wine; the shouts of joy are ended.[b] 11 I
groan with sadness for Moab, with grief for
Kir Heres. 12 The people of Moab wear
themselves out going to their mountain
shrines and to their temples to pray, but it
will do them no good.
13 That is the message the LORD gave ear-
lier about Moab. 14 And now the LORD says,
"In exactly three years Moab's great wealth
will disappear. Of its many people, only a
few will survive, and they will be weak."

God Will Punish Syria and Israel

17 The LORD said, "Damascus will not
be a city any longer; it will be only a
pile of ruins. 2 The cities of Syria will be
deserted forever.[c] They will be a pasture for
sheep and cattle, and no one will drive them
away. 3 Israel will be defenseless, and Damas-
cus will lose its independence. Those Syrians
who survive will be in disgrace like the peo-
ple of Israel. I, the LORD Almighty, have spo-
ken."
4 The LORD said, "A day is coming when
Israel's greatness will come to an end, and its
wealth will be replaced by poverty. 5 Israel
will be like a field where the grain has been
cut and harvested, as desolate as a field in
Rephaim Valley when it has been picked
bare. 6 Only a few people will survive, and
Israel will be like an olive tree from which
all the olives have been picked except two or

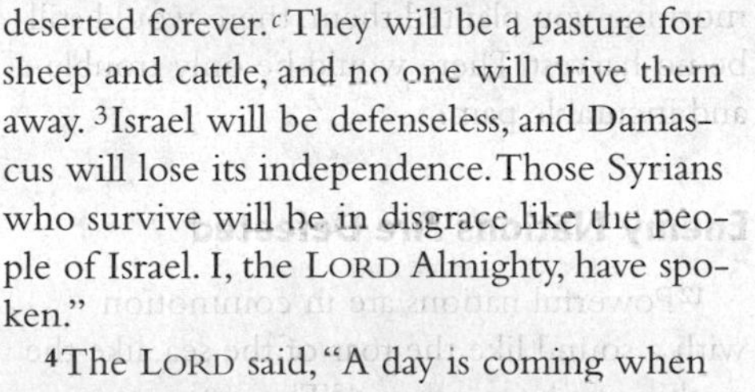

Israel will be like an olive tree. (17:6)

[b] **16:10** *One ancient translation* the shouts of joy are ended; *Hebrew* I have ended the shouts of joy. [c] **17:2** *One ancient translation* The cities . . . forever; *Hebrew* The cities of Aroer are deserted.

17:1–3 Jer 49:23–27; Am 1:3–5; Zech 9:1

three at the very top, or a few that are left on
the lower branches. I, the LORD God of
Israel, have spoken."
[7]When that day comes, people will turn
for help to their Creator, the holy God of
Israel. [8]They will no longer rely on the
altars they made with their own hands, or
trust in their own handiwork—symbols of
the goddess Asherah and altars for burning
incense.
[9]When that day comes, well-defended
cities will be deserted and left in ruins like
the cities that the Hivites and the Amorites[d]
abandoned as they fled from the people of
Israel.
[10]Israel, you have forgotten the God who
rescues you and protects you like a mighty
rock. Instead, you plant sacred gardens[e] in
order to worship a foreign god. [11]But even if
they sprouted and blossomed the very
morning you planted them, there would still
be no harvest. There would be only trouble
and incurable pain.

Enemy Nations Are Defeated

[12]Powerful nations are in commotion
with a sound like the roar of the sea, like the
crashing of huge waves. [13]The nations
advance like rushing waves, but God repri-
mands them and they retreat, driven away
like dust on a mountainside, like straw in a
whirlwind. [14]At evening they cause terror,
but by morning they are gone. That is the
fate of everyone who plunders our land.

God Will Punish Ethiopia

18 Beyond the rivers of Ethiopia[f] there
is a land where the sound of wings is
heard. [2]From that land ambassadors come
down the Nile in boats made of reeds. Go
back home, swift messengers! Take a message
back to your land divided by rivers, to your
strong and powerful nation, to your tall and
smooth-skinned people, who are feared all
over the world.

Study it!

Africans in the Bible

Isaiah, chapters 18–19, are prophecies against the people of Ethiopia and Egypt. What continent do these people come from? Africa, of course! Look on a globe or map and see where Egypt and Ethiopia are located in relation to Israel. You will see that to travel on land from Africa to Europe or Asia you have to cross through Israel. That is why the people of Africa were well known to the Israelites. You can see that Isaiah had a great respect for the Ethiopians, calling them a "strong and powerful nation" (18:2).

— Isaiah, chapter 18

[3]Listen, everyone who lives on earth!
Look for a signal flag to be raised on the
mountaintops! Listen for the blowing of the
bugle! [4]The LORD said to me, "I will look
down from heaven as quietly as the dew
forms in the warm nights of harvest time, as
serenely as the sun shines in the heat of the
day. [5]Before the grapes are gathered, when
the blossoms have all fallen and the grapes
are ripening, the enemy will destroy the
Ethiopians[f] as easily as a knife cuts branches
from a vine. [6]The corpses of their soldiers
will be left exposed to the birds and the wild
animals. In summer the birds will feed on
them, and in winter, the animals."
[7]A time is coming when the LORD
Almighty will receive offerings from this
land divided by rivers, this strong and pow-
erful nation, this tall and smooth-skinned
people, who are feared all over the world.

[d] **17:9** *One ancient translation* the Hivites and the Amorites; *Hebrew* woodland and hill country.
[e] **17:10** SACRED GARDENS: *See 1:29.* [f] **18:1, 5** *Hebrew* Cush(ites): *Cush is the ancient name of the extensive territory south of the First Cataract of the Nile River. This region was called Ethiopia in Graeco-Roman times, and included within its borders most of modern Sudan and some of present-day Ethiopia (Abyssinia).*

18:1–7 Zeph 2:12

They will come to Mount Zion, where the
LORD Almighty is worshiped.

God Will Punish Egypt

19 This is a message about Egypt.
The LORD is coming to Egypt,
riding swiftly on a cloud. The Egyptian idols
tremble before him, and the people of Egypt
lose their courage. 2The LORD says, "I will
stir up civil war in Egypt and turn brother
against brother and neighbor against neigh-
bor. Rival cities will fight each other, and
rival kings will struggle for power. 3I am
going to frustrate the plans of the Egyptians
and destroy their morale. They will ask their
idols to help them, and they will go and
consult mediums and ask the spirits of the
dead for advice. 4I will hand the Egyptians
over to a tyrant, to a cruel king who will
rule them. I, the LORD Almighty, have spo-
ken."
5The water will be low in the Nile, and
the river will gradually dry up. 6The chan-
nels of the river will stink as they slowly go
dry. Reeds and rushes will wither, 7and all
the crops planted along the banks of the
Nile will dry up and be blown away.
8Everyone who earns a living by fishing in
the Nile will groan and cry; their hooks and
their nets will be useless. 9Those who make
linen cloth will be in despair; 10weavers and
skilled workers will be broken and
depressed.
11The leaders of the city of Zoan are
fools! Egypt's wisest people give stupid

Their hooks and their nets will be useless. (19:8)

19:1–25 Jer 46:2–26; Ezek 29:1—32:32

advice! How do they dare to tell the king
that they are successors to the ancient schol-
ars and kings? 12King of Egypt, where are
those clever advisers of yours? Perhaps they
can tell you what plans the LORD Almighty
has for Egypt. 13The leaders of Zoan and
Memphis are fools. They were supposed to
lead the nation, but they have misled it.
14The LORD has made them give confusing
advice. As a result, Egypt does everything
wrong and staggers like a drunk slipping on
his own vomit. 15No one in Egypt, rich or
poor, important or unknown, can offer help.

Egypt Will Worship the LORD

16A time is coming when the people of
Egypt will be as timid as women. They will
tremble in terror when they see that the
LORD Almighty has stretched out his hand
to punish them. 17The people of Egypt will
be terrified of Judah every time they are
reminded of the fate that the LORD
Almighty has prepared for them.
18When that time comes, the Hebrew
language will be spoken in five Egyptian
cities. The people there will take their oaths
in the name of the LORD Almighty. One of
the cities will be called, "City of the Sun."
19When that time comes, there will be an
altar to the LORD in the land of Egypt and a
stone pillar dedicated to him at the Egyptian
border. 20They will be symbols of the LORD
Almighty's presence in Egypt. When the
people there are oppressed and call out to
the LORD for help, he will send someone to
rescue them. 21The LORD will reveal himself
to the Egyptian people, and then they will
acknowledge and worship him, and bring
him sacrifices and offerings. They will make
solemn promises to him and do what they
promise. 22The LORD will punish the Egyp-
tians, but then he will heal them. They will
turn to him, and he will hear their prayers
and heal them.
23When that time comes, there will be a
highway between Egypt and Assyria. The

Many goddesses of foreign nations were worshiped in sacred gardens. This is why Isaiah and the other prophets condemn them *(Isaiah 17:10)*.

Pray it!

Prayer for the Oppressed

In Isaiah, chapter 19, Isaiah makes an interesting prophecy. First, he says that God will punish the Egyptians with a civil war and the Nile will dry up. But they will eventually recognize the Lord and call out to him. Only when they are oppressed do they finally understand their need for God. Like the Egyptians in this prophecy, there are groups of people who have been suffering for a long time. They have been victims of racism, poverty, or hunger. When this happens we say that these people are oppressed.

Find a current newspaper. Look through it for an article on people who are oppressed. Maybe they are people who are losing their land, are not being paid fairly, or are being treated violently by others because of their race or religion. After reading the article, write a prayer for them, asking God to send them the help they need. Pray that prayer often. As part of your prayer, read Isaiah 19:20: "When the people there are oppressed and call out to the LORD for help, he will send someone to rescue them." You may just be the one God is sending to help them!

— Isaiah 19:20

people of these two countries will travel
back and forth between them, and the two
nations will worship together. 24 When that
time comes, Israel will rank with Egypt and
Assyria, and these three nations will be a
blessing to all the world. 25 The LORD
Almighty will bless them and say, "I will
bless you, Egypt, my people; you, Assyria,
whom I created; and you, Israel, my chosen
people."

The Sign of the Naked Prophet

20 Under the orders of Emperor Sar-
gon of Assyria, the commander-in-
chief of the Assyrian army attacked the
Philistine city of Ashdod. 2 Three years ear-
lier the LORD had told Isaiah son of Amoz
to take off his sandals and the sackcloth he
was wearing. He obeyed and went around
naked and barefoot. 3 When Ashdod was
captured, the LORD said, "My servant Isaiah
has been going around naked and barefoot
for three years. This is a sign of what will
happen to Egypt and Ethiopia.[f] 4 The
emperor of Assyria will lead away naked the
prisoners he captures from those two coun-
tries. Young and old, they will walk barefoot
and naked, with their buttocks exposed,
bringing shame on Egypt. 5 Those who
have put their trust in Ethiopia[f] and have
boasted about Egypt will be disillusioned,
their hopes shattered. 6 When that time
comes, the people who live along the coast
of Philistia will say, 'Look at what has hap-
pened to the people we relied on to protect
us from the emperor of Assyria! How will
we ever survive?' "

[f] **20:3, 5** *Hebrew* Cush(ites): *Cush is the ancient name of the extensive territory south of the First Cataract of the Nile River. This region was called Ethiopia in Graeco-Roman times, and included within its borders most of modern Sudan and some of present-day Ethiopia (Abyssinia).*

Isaiah, chapter 20, says that Isaiah went naked and barefoot for three years. He probably wasn't completely naked; he may have just took off his sandals and robe!

A Vision of the Fall of Babylon

21 This is a message about Babylonia.
Like a whirlwind sweeping across
the desert, disaster will come from a terrify-
ing land. 2I have seen a vision of cruel
events, a vision of betrayal and destruction.
Army of Elam, attack! Army of Media, lay
siege to the cities! God will put an end to
the suffering which Babylon has caused.
3What I saw and heard in the vision has
filled me with terror and pain, pain like that
of a woman in labor. 4My head is spinning,
and I am trembling with fear. I had been
longing for evening to come, but it has
brought me nothing but terror.
5In the vision a banquet is ready; rugs are
spread for the guests to sit on. They are eat-
ing and drinking. Suddenly the command
rings out: "Officers! Prepare your shields!"
6Then the Lord said to me, "Go and post
a sentry, and tell him to report what he sees.
7If he sees riders coming on horseback, two
by two, and riders on donkeys and camels,
he is to observe them carefully."
8The sentry calls out, "Sir, I have been
standing guard at my post day and night."
9Suddenly, here they come! Riders on
horseback, two by two. The sentry gives the
news, "Babylon has fallen! All the idols they
worshiped lie shattered on the ground."
10My people Israel, you have been threshed
like wheat, but now I have announced to you
the good news that I have heard from the
LORD Almighty, the God of Israel.

A Message about Edom

11This is a message about Edom.
Someone calls to me from Edom, "Sentry,
how soon will the night be over? Tell me
how soon it will end."
12I answer, "Morning is coming, but night
will come again. If you want to ask again,
come back and ask."

A Message about Arabia

13This is a message about Arabia.
People of Dedan, you whose caravans
camp in the barren country of Arabia, 14give
water to the thirsty people who come to
you. You people of the land of Tema, give
food to the refugees. 15People are fleeing to
escape from swords that are ready to kill
them, from bows that are ready to shoot,
from all the dangers of war.
16Then the Lord said to me, "In exactly
one year the greatness of the tribes of Kedar
will be at an end. 17The archers are the
bravest warriors of Kedar, but few of them
will be left. I, the LORD God of Israel, have
spoken."

A Message about Jerusalem

22 This is a message about the Valley of
Vision.
What is happening? Why are all the peo-
ple of the city celebrating on the roofs of the
houses? 2The whole city is in an uproar,
filled with noise and excitement.
Your people who died in this war did not
die fighting. 3All your leaders ran away and
were captured before they shot a single
arrow. 4Now leave me alone to weep bitterly
over all those of my people who have died.
Don't try to comfort me. 5This is a time of
panic, defeat, and confusion in the Valley of
Vision, and the Sovereign LORD Almighty
has sent it on us. The walls of our city have
been battered down, and cries for help have
echoed among the hills.
6The soldiers from the land of Elam came
riding on horseback, armed with bows and
arrows. Soldiers from the land of Kir had
their shields ready. 7The fertile valleys of
Judah were filled with chariots; soldiers on
horseback stood in front of Jerusalem's gates.
8All of Judah's defenses crumbled.
When that happened, you brought
weapons out of the arsenal. 9-10You found
the places where the walls of Jerusalem
needed repair. You inspected all the houses in
Jerusalem and tore some of them down to
get stones to repair the city walls. In order to
store water, 11you built a reservoir inside the
city to hold the water flowing down from
the old pool. But you paid no attention to
God, who planned all this long ago and who
caused it to happen.

21:9 Rev 14:8; 18:2

Study it!

Huh?

The prophecy in the first half of Isaiah, chapter 22, may leave you scratching your head. It says that God was upset because the people were celebrating and rejoicing. But why would God be upset at that?

It helps to know some background. Isaiah believed that God was sending foreign armies (from Elam) to attack Jerusalem as punishment for their sins. The people of Jerusalem should have recognized this and asked God for forgiveness—by weeping and mourning, shaving their heads, and wearing sackcloth (Isaiah 22:12). Instead they decided to party because they thought they were going to die anyway. God was trying to get their attention so that they could get on the right path—and they totally missed it!

Has God ever tried to get your attention through good or bad events in your life?

— Isaiah 22:1–14

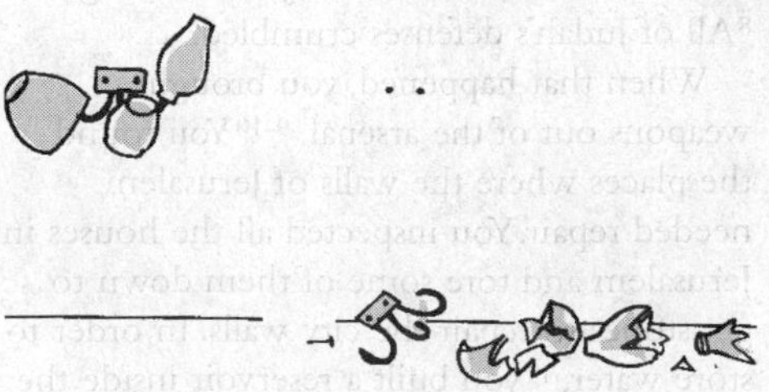

"That will be the end of everything that was hanging on it." (22:25)

12 The Sovereign LORD Almighty was call-
ing you then to weep and mourn, to shave
your heads and wear sackcloth. 13 Instead,
you laughed and celebrated. You killed sheep
and cattle to eat, and you drank wine. You
said, "We might as well eat and drink!
Tomorrow we'll be dead."
14 The Sovereign LORD Almighty himself
spoke to me and said, "This evil will never
be forgiven them as long as they live. I, the
Sovereign LORD Almighty, have spoken."

A Warning to Shebna

15 The Sovereign LORD Almighty told me
to go to Shebna, the manager of the royal
household, and say to him, 16 "Who do you
think you are? What right do you have to
carve a tomb for yourself out of the rocky
hillside? 17 You may be important, but the
LORD will pick you up and throw you away.
18 He will pick you up like a ball and throw
you into a much larger country. You will die
there beside the chariots you were so proud
of. You are a disgrace to your master's house-
hold. 19 The LORD will remove you from
office and bring you down from your high
position."
20 The LORD said to Shebna, "When that
happens, I will send for my servant Eliakim
son of Hilkiah. 21 I will put your official robe
and belt on him and give him all the author-
ity you have had. He will be like a father to
the people of Jerusalem and Judah. 22 I will
give him complete authority under the king,
the descendant of David. He will have the
keys of office; what he opens, no one will
shut, and what he shuts, no one will open.
23 I will fasten him firmly in place like a peg,
and he will be a source of honor to his
whole family.
24 "But all his relatives and dependents will
become a burden to him. They will hang on
him like pots and bowls hanging from a peg!
25 When that happens, the peg that was firm-
ly fastened will pull loose and fall. And that
will be the end of everything that was hang-
ing on it." The LORD has spoken.

22:13 1 Cor 15:32 **22:22** Rev 3:7

A Message about Phoenicia

23 This is a message about Tyre.

Howl with grief, you sailors out on the ocean! Your home port of Tyre has been destroyed; its houses and its harbor are in ruins. As your ships return from Cyprus, you learn the news. 2 Wail, you merchants of Sidon! You sent agents 3 across the sea to buy and sell the grain that grew in Egypt and to do business with all the nations.

4 City of Sidon, you are disgraced! The sea and the great ocean depths disown you and say, "I never had any children. I never raised sons or daughters."

5 Even the Egyptians will be shocked and dismayed when they learn that Tyre has been destroyed.

6 Howl with grief, you people of Phoenicia! Try to escape to Spain! 7 Can this be the joyful city of Tyre, founded so long ago? Is this the city that sent settlers across the sea to establish colonies? 8 Who was it that planned to bring all this on Tyre, that imperial city, whose merchant princes were the most honored men on earth? 9 The LORD Almighty planned it. He planned it in order to put an end to their pride in what they had done and to humiliate their honored ones.

10 Go and farm the land, you people in the colonies in Spain! There is no one to protect you any more.[g] 11 The LORD has stretched out his hand over the sea and overthrown kingdoms. He has commanded that the Phoenician centers of commerce be destroyed. 12 City of Sidon, your happiness has ended, and your people are oppressed. Even if they escape to Cyprus, they will still not be safe.

(13 It was the Babylonians, not the Assyrians, who let the wild animals overrun Tyre. It was the Babylonians who put up siege towers, tore down the fortifications of Tyre, and left the city in ruins.[h])

14 Howl with grief, you sailors out on the ocean! The city you relied on has been destroyed.

15 A time is coming when Tyre will be forgotten for seventy years, the lifetime of a king. When those years are over, Tyre will be like the prostitute in the song:

16 Take your harp, go round the town,
you poor forgotten whore!
Play and sing your songs again
to bring men back once more.

17 When the seventy years are over, the LORD will let Tyre go back to her old trade, and she will hire herself out to all the kingdoms of the world. 18 The money she earns by commerce will be dedicated to the LORD. She will not store it away, but those who worship the LORD will use her money to buy the food and the clothing they need.

The LORD Will Punish the Earth

24 The LORD is going to devastate the earth and leave it desolate. He will twist the earth's surface and scatter its people. 2 Everyone will meet the same fate—the priests and the people, slaves and masters, buyers and sellers, lenders and borrowers, rich and poor. 3 The earth will lie shattered and ruined. The LORD has spoken and it will be done.

4 The earth dries up and withers; the whole world grows weak; both earth and sky decay. 5 The people have defiled the earth by breaking God's laws and by violating the covenant he made to last forever. 6 So God has pronounced a curse on the earth. Its people are paying for what they have done. Fewer and fewer remain alive. 7 The grapevines wither, and wine is becoming scarce. Everyone who was once happy is now sad, 8 and the joyful music of their harps and drums has ceased. 9 There is no more happy singing over wine; no one enjoys its taste any more. 10 In the city everything is in chaos, and people lock themselves in their houses for safety. 11 People shout in the streets because there is no more wine. Happiness is gone forever; it has been banished from the land.

[g] **23:10** *Verse 10 in Hebrew is unclear.* [h] **23:13** *Verse 13 in Hebrew is unclear.*

23:1–18 Ezek 26:1—28:19; Joel 3:4–8; Am 1:9, 10; Zech 9:1–4; Mt 11:21, 22; Lk 10:13, 14

Find Tyre and Sidon on Map 3. Given the location of these cities, what do you think would be the main ways the people of these places made their living?

12 The city is in ruins, and its gates have been
broken down. 13 This is what will happen in
every nation all over the world. It will be like
the end of harvest, when the olives have been
beaten off every tree and the last grapes
picked from the vines.
14 Those who survive will sing for joy.
Those in the West will tell how great the
LORD is, 15 and those in the East will praise
him. The people who live along the sea will
praise the LORD, the God of Israel. 16 From
the most distant parts of the world we will
hear songs in praise of Israel, the righteous
nation.
But there is no hope for me! I am wasting
away! Traitors continue to betray, and their
treachery grows worse and worse. 17 Listen to
me, everyone! There are terrors, pits, and
traps waiting for you. 18 Anyone who tries to
escape from the terror will fall in a pit, and
anyone who escapes from the pit will be
caught in a trap. Torrents of rain will pour
from the sky, and earth's foundations will
shake. 19 The earth will crack and shatter and
split open. 20 The earth itself will stagger like
a drunk, sway like a hut in a storm. The
world is weighed down by its sins; it will
collapse and never rise again.
21 A time is coming when the LORD will
punish the powers above and the rulers of the
earth. 22 God will crowd kings together like
prisoners in a pit. He will shut them in prison
until the time of their punishment comes.
23 The moon will grow dark, and the sun will
no longer shine, for the LORD Almighty will
be king. He will rule in Jerusalem on Mount
Zion, and the leaders of the people will see
his glory.

A Hymn of Praise

25 LORD, you are my God;
I will honor you and praise your
name.
You have done amazing things;
you have faithfully carried out

Kings together like prisoners in a pit (24:22)

the plans you made long ago.
2 You have turned cities into ruins
and destroyed their fortifications.
The palaces which our enemies built
are gone forever.
3 The people of powerful nations will
praise you;
you will be feared in the cities of cruel
nations.
4 The poor and the helpless have fled to
you
and have been safe in times of trouble.
You give them shelter from storms
and shade from the burning heat.
Cruel enemies attack like a winter storm,[i]
5 like drought in a dry land.
But you, LORD, have silenced our enemies;
you silence the shouts of cruel people,
as a cloud cools a hot day.

God Prepares a Banquet

6 Here on Mount Zion the LORD
Almighty will prepare a banquet for all the
nations of the world—a banquet of the rich-
est food and the finest wine. 7 Here he will
suddenly remove the cloud of sorrow that
has been hanging over all the nations. 8 The
Sovereign LORD will destroy death forever!
He will wipe away the tears from everyone's

[i] **25:4** *Probable text* winter storm; *Hebrew* storm against a wall.
25:8 **a** 1 Cor 15:54; **b** Rev 7:17; 21:4

Isaiah 25:8 makes a promise about something God will do. What is that promise, and how did it come true?

Live it!

Habitat for Humanity

In 1976 Millard and Linda Fuller started the organization Habitat for Humanity. They had sold all of their possessions to work for poor people—as a response to Christ's message. Their idea was to provide affordable housing for those who could not afford to buy their own homes. They took Isaiah 25:4 seriously: "The poor and helpless have fled to you / . . . You give them shelter from storms / and shade from the burning heat."

In 1984 former U.S. President Jimmy Carter and his wife Rosalyn became personally involved. Their participation gave Habitat for Humanity the publicity it needed to become nationally known. Today, more than 150,000 houses have been built, giving more than 900,000 people a home of their own. Thousands of volunteers, from many different religions, have helped Habitat for Humanity build the homes.

Many churches work with Habitat for Humanity. Find out if your parish has a connection to Habitat for Humanity. If you are old enough, volunteer to work on a house. It will give you a very good feeling to know you are helping to shelter the homeless—something God is calling us to do.

— Isaiah 25:4

eyes and take away the disgrace his people
have suffered throughout the world. The
LORD himself has spoken.
9 When it happens, everyone will say, "He
is our God! We have put our trust in him,
and he has rescued us. He is the LORD! We
have put our trust in him, and now we are
happy and joyful because he has saved us."

God Will Punish Moab

10 The LORD will protect Mount Zion,
but the people of Moab will be trampled
down the way straw is trampled in manure.
11 They will reach out their hands as if they
were trying to swim, but God will humiliate
them, and their hands will sink helplessly.
12 He will destroy the fortresses of Moab
with their high walls and bring them tum-
bling down into the dust.

God Will Give His People Victory

26 A day is coming when the people will sing this song in the land of Judah:

Our city is strong!
God himself defends its walls!
2 Open the city gates
and let the faithful nation enter,
the nation whose people do what is right.
3 You, LORD, give perfect peace
to those who keep their purpose firm
and put their trust in you.
4 Trust in the LORD forever;
he will always protect us.
5 He has humbled those who were proud;
he destroyed the strong city they lived in,
and sent its walls crashing into the dust.
6 Those who were oppressed walk over it now
and trample it under their feet.

7 LORD, you make the path smooth for good people;
the road they travel is level.
8 We follow your will and put our hope in you;
you are all that we desire.
9 At night I long for you with all my heart;
when you judge the earth and its people,
they will all learn what justice is.
10 Even though you are kind to the wicked,
they never learn to do what is right.

25:10–12 Isa 15:1—16:14; Jer 48:1–47; Ezek 25:8–11; Am 2:1–3; Zeph 2:8–11

Even here in a land of righteous people
they still do wrong;
they refuse to recognize your greatness.
11 Your enemies do not know that you will
punish them.
LORD, put them to shame and let them
suffer;
let them suffer the punishment you
have prepared.
Show them how much you love your
people.

12 You will give us prosperity, LORD;
everything that we achieve
is the result of what you do.[j]
13 LORD our God, we have been ruled by
others,
but you alone are our LORD.
14 Now they are dead and will not live again;
their ghosts will not rise,
for you have punished them and
destroyed them.
No one remembers them any more.
15 LORD, you have made our nation grow,
enlarging its territory on every side;
and this has brought you honor.
16 You punished your people, LORD,
and in anguish they prayed to you.[k]
17 You, LORD, have made us cry out,
as a woman in labor cries out in pain.
18 We were in pain and agony,
but we gave birth to nothing.
We have won no victory for our land;
we have accomplished nothing.[l]
19 Those of our people who have died will
live again!
Their bodies will come back to life.
All those sleeping in their graves
will wake up and sing for joy.
As the sparkling dew refreshes the earth,
so the LORD will revive those who
have long been dead.

Judgment and Restoration

20 Go into your houses, my people, and
shut the door behind you. Hide yourselves
for a little while until God's anger is over.
21 The LORD is coming from his heavenly
dwelling place to punish the people of the
earth for their sins. The murders that were
secretly committed on the earth will be
revealed, and the ground will no longer hide
those who have been killed.

27 On that day the LORD will use his
powerful and deadly sword to punish
Leviathan, that wriggling, twisting dragon,
and to kill the monster[m] that lives in the sea.
2 On that day the LORD will say of his
pleasant vineyard, 3 "I watch over it and
water it continually. I guard it night and day
so that no one will harm it. 4 I am no longer
angry with the vineyard. If there were thorns
and briers to fight against, I would burn
them up completely. 5 But if the enemies of
my people want my protection, let them
make peace with me. Yes, let them make
peace with me."
6 In the days to come the people of Israel,
the descendants of Jacob, will take root like a
tree, and they will blossom and bud. The
earth will be covered with the fruit they
produce.
7 Israel has not been punished by the
LORD as severely as its enemies nor lost as
many people. 8 The LORD punished his peo-
ple by sending them into exile. He took
them away with a cruel wind from the east.[n]
9 But Israel's sins will be forgiven only when
the stones of pagan altars are ground up like
chalk, and no more incense altars or symbols
of the goddess Asherah are left.
10 The fortified city lies in ruins. It is
deserted like an empty wilderness. It has
become a pasture for cattle, where they can
rest and graze. 11 The branches of the trees
are withered and broken, and women gather

The fortified city lies in ruins. (27:10)

[j] **26:12** everything that . . . do; *or* you treat us according to what we do. [k] **26:16** *Verse 16 in Hebrew is unclear.*
[l] **26:18** We have won . . . nothing; *Hebrew unclear.* [m] **27:1** LEVIATHAN . . . MONSTER: *Legendary monsters which were symbols of the nations oppressing Israel.* [n] **27:8** *Verse 8 in Hebrew is unclear.*
26:11 Heb 10:27 **27:1** Job 41:1; Ps 74:14; 104:26

them for firewood. Because the people have
understood nothing, God their Creator will
not pity them or show them any mercy.
12 On that day, from the Euphrates to the
Egyptian border, the LORD will gather his
people one by one, as threshing separates the
wheat from the chaff.
13 When that day comes, a trumpet will be
blown to call back from Assyria and Egypt
all the Israelites who are in exile there. They
will come and worship the LORD in
Jerusalem, on his sacred hill.°

A Warning to the Northern Kingdom

28 The kingdom of Israel is doomed!
Its glory is fading like the crowns of
flowers on the heads of its drunken leaders.
Their proud heads are well perfumed, but
there they lie, dead drunk. 2 The Lord has
someone strong and powerful ready to attack
them, someone who will come like a hail-
storm, like a torrent of rain, like a rushing,
overpowering flood, and will overwhelm the
land. 3 The pride of those drunken leaders
will be trampled underfoot. 4 The fading
glory of those proud leaders will disappear
like the first figs of the season, picked and
eaten as soon as they are ripe.
5 A day is coming when the LORD
Almighty will be like a glorious crown of
flowers for his people who survive. 6 He will
give a sense of justice to those who serve as
judges, and courage to those who defend the
city gates from attack.

Isaiah and the Drunken Prophets of Judah

7 Even the prophets and the priests are so
drunk that they stagger. They have drunk so
much wine and liquor that they stumble in
confusion. The prophets are too drunk to
understand the visions that God sends, and
the priests are too drunk to decide the cases
that are brought to them. 8 The tables where

Live it!

On that Day

There was a lot of bad news in Isaiah's prophecies leading up to Isaiah, chapter 26. Jerusalem, Assyria, Babylon, Philistia, Moab, Syria, Ethiopia, Egypt, Edom, Arabia, Shebna, and Phoenicia all get news of their punishment. It seems like everyone gets bad news. However, throughout those chapters, and especially here in chapters 26–27, Isaiah also has good news. His good news is about a time to come when God's peace and justice will triumph.

Maybe you've been given really bad news sometime in your life. It could be that your parents are splitting up "on that day" or that you have to move to a new city "on that day," or maybe you have to have surgery "on that day." Regardless of the bad news, look for how God is working in a positive way. It could be that you'll meet great new friends in the city you move to, or that by having surgery you'll eventually get better. Sometimes bad news stays bad news, and it is hard to see the good. But most of the time, by looking at all of the angles, we can see that "on that day" God can bring good things out of hard experiences.

— Isaiah, chapter 27

° **27:13** SACRED HILL: *See 2:3.*

In Isaiah 27:5 God says about Israel's enemies, "Let them make peace with me." How do you make peace with God?

So drunk they stagger (28:7)

they sit are all covered with vomit, and not a
clean spot is left.
[9]They complain about me. They say,
"Who does that man think he's teaching?
Who needs his message? It's only good for
babies that have just stopped nursing! [10]He is
trying to teach us letter by letter, line by
line, lesson by lesson."
[11]If you won't listen to me, then God will
use foreigners speaking some strange-sound-
ing language to teach you a lesson. [12]He
offered rest and comfort to all of you, but you
refused to listen to him. [13]That is why the
LORD is going to teach you letter by letter,
line by line, lesson by lesson. Then you will
stumble with every step you take. You will be
wounded, trapped, and taken prisoner.

A Cornerstone for Zion

[14]Now you arrogant leaders who rule
here in Jerusalem over this people, listen to
what the LORD is saying. [15]You boast that
you have made a treaty with death and
reached an agreement with the world of the
dead. You are certain that disaster will spare
you when it comes, because you depend on
lies and deceit to keep you safe. [16]This, now,
is what the Sovereign LORD says: "I am plac-
ing in Zion a foundation that is firm and
strong. In it I am putting a solid cornerstone
on which are written the words, 'Faith that is
firm is also patient.' [17]Justice will be the
measuring line for the foundation, and hon-
esty will be its plumb line."

Hailstorms will sweep away all the lies
you depend on, and floods will destroy your
security. [18]The treaty you have made with
death will be abolished, and your agreement
with the world of the dead will be canceled.
When disaster sweeps down, you will be
overcome. [19]It will strike you again and
again, morning after morning. You will have
to bear it day and night. Each new message
from God will bring new terror! [20]You will
be like the person in the proverb, who tries
to sleep in a bed too short to stretch out on,
with a blanket too narrow to wrap himself
in. [21]The LORD will fight as he did at
Mount Perazim and in the valley of Gibeon,
in order to do what he intends to do—
strange as his actions may seem. He will
complete his work, his mysterious work.

A bed too short, . . . a blanket too narrow (28:20)

[22]Don't laugh at the warning I am giving
you! If you do, it will be even harder for you
to escape. I have heard the LORD Almighty's
decision to destroy the whole country.

God's Wisdom

[23]Listen to what I am saying; pay attention
to what I am telling you. [24]Farmers don't
constantly plow their fields and keep getting
them ready for planting. [25]Once they have
prepared the soil, they plant the seeds of
herbs such as dill and cumin. They plant

28:11, 12 1 Cor 14:21 **28:15** Wis 1:16; Sir 14:12 **28:16** Ps 118:22, 23; Rom 9:33; 10:11; 1 Pet 2:6
28:21 **a** 2 Sam 5:20; 1 Chr 14:11; **b** Josh 10:10–12

"All this wisdom comes from the LORD Almighty! The plans God makes are wise, and they always succeed" *(Isaiah 28:29)*.

Live it!

Keeping God No. 1

Isaiah wanted God's people to listen and to keep God No. 1. He tells them in Isaiah 28:22, "Don't laugh at the warning I am giving you!"

How do you keep God No. 1 in your life? Are there times when you get warnings to change your behavior and ignore them? Are there times when you know you're putting God second or even lower on your list? Most people have times like that. We need to be reminded to keep God No. 1 and look for ways we can do that.

Who do you know who does a good job of keeping God No. 1? Take some time to ask that person how he or she does it. Then spend some time in prayer looking for your own ways of keeping God No. 1. By asking others and praying about it, you can create a plan for keeping God first. Once you have a plan, stick to it. It takes practice and discipline to keep God No. 1.

— Isaiah 28:22–29

rows of wheat and barley,[p] and at the edges
of their fields they plant other grain. [26]They
know how to do their work, because God
has taught them. [27]They never use a heavy
club to beat out dill seeds or cumin seeds;
instead they use light sticks of the proper
size. [28]They do not ruin the wheat by
threshing it endlessly, and they know how to
thresh it by driving a cart over it without
bruising the grains. [29]All this wisdom comes
from the LORD Almighty. The plans God
makes are wise, and they always succeed.

The Fate of Jerusalem

29 God's altar, Jerusalem itself, is
doomed! The city where David
camped is doomed! Let another year or two
come and go, with its feasts and festivals,
[2]and then God will bring disaster on the city
that is called "God's altar." There will be
weeping and wailing, and the whole city will
be like an altar covered with blood. [3]God
will attack the city, surround it, and besiege
it. [4]Jerusalem will be like a ghost struggling
to speak from under the ground, a muffled
voice coming from the dust.

[5]Jerusalem, all the foreigners who attack
you will be blown away like dust, and their
terrifying armies will fly away like straw.
Suddenly and unexpectedly [6]the LORD
Almighty will rescue you with violent thun-
derstorms and earthquakes. He will send
windstorms and raging fire; [7]then all the
armies of the nations attacking the city of
God's altar, all their weapons and equip-
ment—everything—will vanish like a dream,
like something imagined in the night. [8]All
the nations that assemble to attack Jerusalem
will be like a starving person who dreams he
is eating and wakes up hungry, or like some-
one dying of thirst who dreams he is drink-
ing and wakes with a dry throat.

Disregarded Warnings

[9]Go ahead and be stupid! Go ahead and
be blind! Get drunk without any wine! Stag-
ger without drinking a drop! [10]The LORD
has made you drowsy, ready to fall into a
deep sleep. The prophets should be the eyes
of the people, but God has blindfolded them.
[11]The meaning of every prophetic vision will
be hidden from you; it will be like a sealed
scroll. If you take it to someone who knows
how to read and ask him to read it to you, he
will say he can't because it is sealed. [12]If you
give it to someone who can't read and ask
him to read it to you, he will answer that he
doesn't know how.

[13]The Lord said, "These people claim to
worship me, but their words are meaningless,
and their hearts are somewhere else. Their

p **27:25** *Hebrew has an additional word, the meaning of which is unclear.*
29:10 Rom 11:8 **29:13** Mt 15:8, 9; Mk 7:6, 7

Catholic Connections

Just Putting Your Time In

Tina's eyes kept closing, and all she could think of was what she would do when she got out of church. She stood when everyone stood and mumbled the Lord's Prayer, but she wasn't really aware of what she did or said. Afterward her friends were talking about something Father Marco had said. All Tina wanted to do was get to the mall.

While they were shopping, her mom asked what the girls had been talking about after church. When Tina said she didn't know, her mom gave her a hard look. "Tina," she said, "do you listen to anything during church?"

"Mom, don't get on my case. I go. I pray. I stand. I sit. What more do you want?"

"Tina, it isn't about following the rules. It's about putting your heart and soul into it. The prophets made that clear in the Old Testament."

"So, I don't have to sit and stand when you do?"

"Of course it's good to do the gestures, but it's more important to really be part of it. Could you at least try that next week? Maybe what the girls heard was important, and maybe if you really try you'll find something important, too."

"Okay, I'll try," Tina said, "And about these jeans. . ." Tina gave her mom a wink, her signal that she got it.

— Isaiah 29:13–14

religion is nothing but human rules and tra-
ditions, which they have simply memorized.
14So I will startle them with one unexpected
blow after another. Those who are wise will
turn out to be fools, and all their cleverness
will be useless."

Hope for the Future

15Those who try to hide their plans from
the LORD are doomed! They carry out their
schemes in secret and think no one will see
them or know what they are doing. 16They
turn everything upside down. Which is more
important, the potter or the clay? Can some-
thing you have made say, "You didn't make
me"? Or can it say, "You don't know what
you are doing"?
17As the saying goes, before long the
dense forest will become farmland, and the
farmland will go back to forest.
18When that day comes, the deaf will be
able to hear a book being read aloud, and
the blind, who have been living in darkness,
will open their eyes and see. 19Poor and
humble people will once again find the hap-
piness which the LORD, the holy God of
Israel, gives. 20It will be the end of those
who oppress others and show contempt for
God. Every sinner will be destroyed. 21God
will destroy those who slander others, those
who prevent the punishment of criminals,
and those who tell lies to keep honest peo-
ple from getting justice.
22So now the LORD, the God of Israel,
who rescued Abraham from trouble, says,
"My people, you will not be disgraced any
longer, and your faces will no longer be pale
with shame. 23When you see the children
that I will give you, then you will acknowl-
edge that I am the holy God of Israel. You
will honor me and stand in awe of me.

29:14 1 Cor 1:19 **29:16** Isa 45:9; Sir 33:13; Rom 9:20

24 Foolish people will learn to understand,
and those who are always grumbling will be
glad to be taught."

A Useless Treaty with Egypt

30 The LORD has spoken: "Those who
rule Judah are doomed because they
rebel against me. They follow plans that I did
not make, and sign treaties against my will,
piling one sin on another. 2 They go to
Egypt for help without asking for my advice.
They want Egypt to protect them, so they
put their trust in Egypt's king. 3 But the king
will be powerless to help them, and Egypt's
protection will end in disaster. 4 Although
their ambassadors have already arrived at the
Egyptian cities of Zoan and Hanes, 5 the
people of Judah will regret that they ever
trusted that unreliable nation, a nation that
fails them when they expect help."

6 This is God's message about the animals
of the southern desert: "The ambassadors
travel through dangerous country, where
lions live and where there are poisonous
snakes and flying dragons. They load their
donkeys and camels with expensive gifts for a
nation that cannot give them any help. 7 The
help that Egypt gives is useless. So I have
nicknamed Egypt, 'The Harmless Dragon.' "

The Disobedient People

8 God told me to write down in a book
what the people are like, so that there would
be a permanent record of how evil they are.
9 They are always rebelling against God,
always lying, always refusing to listen to the
LORD's teachings. 10 They tell the prophets to
keep quiet. They say, "Don't talk to us about
what's right. Tell us what we want to hear.
Let us keep our illusions. 11 Get out of our
way and stop blocking our path. We don't
want to hear about your holy God of Israel."

12 But this is what the holy God of Israel
says: "You ignore what I tell you and rely on
violence and deceit. 13 You are guilty. You are
like a high wall with a crack running down
it; suddenly you will collapse. 14 You will be
shattered like a clay pot, so badly broken that
there is no piece big enough to pick up hot
coals with or to dip water from a cistern."

15 The Sovereign LORD, the Holy One of
Israel, says to the people, "Come back and
quietly trust in me. Then you will be strong
and secure." But you refuse to do it.
16 Instead, you plan to escape from your ene-
mies by riding fast horses. And you are
right—escape is what you will have to do!
You think your horses are fast enough, but
those who pursue you will be faster! 17 A
thousand of you will run away when you see
one enemy soldier, and five soldiers will be
enough to make you all run away. Nothing
will be left of your army except a lonely
flagpole on the top of a hill. 18 And yet the
LORD is waiting to be merciful to you. He is
ready to take pity on you because he always
does what is right. Happy are those who put
their trust in the LORD.

God Will Bless His People

19 You people who live in Jerusalem will
not weep any more. The LORD is compas-
sionate, and when you cry to him for help,
he will answer you. 20 The Lord will make
you go through hard times, but he himself
will be there to teach you, and you will not
have to search for him any more. 21 If you
wander off the road to the right or the left,
you will hear his voice behind you saying,
"Here is the road. Follow it." 22 You will take
your idols plated with silver and your idols
covered with gold, and will throw them
away like filth, shouting, "Out of my sight!"
23 Whenever you plant your crops, the Lord
will send rain to make them grow and will
give you a rich harvest, and your livestock
will have plenty of pasture. 24 The oxen and
donkeys that plow your fields will eat the
finest and best fodder. 25 On the day when
the forts of your enemies are captured and
their people are killed, streams of water will
flow from every mountain and every hill.
26 The moon will be as bright as the sun, and

Isaiah describes what the people are like in Isaiah 30:8–11. Does that description sound like anyone you know?

Pray it!

Just When

The next time your life seems really bad and you think you can't take it anymore, try this prayer.

Just when I think I can't take it anymore,
there you are,
the God who blesses me.
Just when I have heard so much bad news,
there you are,
the God who brings good news.
Just when I thought I was all wrong,
there you are,
the God who makes me want to do what is right.
Just when I realize that I did wrong,
there you are,
the God who forgives.
Just when I think I can't take it anymore,
there you are,
my wonderful God who never leaves me.
Amen.

— Isaiah 30:19–26

The finest and best fodder (30:24)

the sun will be seven times brighter than usual, like the light of seven days in one. This will all happen when the LORD bandages and heals the wounds he has given his people.

God Will Punish Assyria

27The LORD's power and glory can be
seen in the distance. Fire and smoke show
his anger. He speaks, and his words burn like
fire. 28He sends the wind in front of him like
a flood that carries everything away. It
sweeps nations to destruction and puts an
end to their evil plans. 29But you, God's peo-
ple, will be happy and sing as you do on the
night of a sacred festival. You will be as
happy as those who walk to the music of
flutes on their way to the Temple of the
LORD, the defender of Israel.
30The LORD will let everyone hear his
majestic voice and feel the force of his anger.
There will be flames, cloudbursts, hailstones,
and torrents of rain. 31The Assyrians will be
terrified when they hear the LORD's voice
and feel the force of his punishment. 32As

"Just as a bird hovers over its nest to protect its young, so I, the LORD Almighty, will protect Jerusalem and defend it" *(Isaiah 31:5)*.

the LORD strikes them again and again, his
people will keep time with the music of
drums and harps. God himself will fight
against the Assyrians. 33Long ago a place was
prepared where a huge fire will burn the
emperor of Assyria. It is deep and wide, and
piled high with wood. The LORD will
breathe out a stream of flame to set it on
fire.

God Will Protect Jerusalem

31 Those who go to Egypt for help are
doomed! They are relying on Egypt's
vast military strength—horses, chariots, and
soldiers. But they do not rely on the LORD,
the holy God of Israel, or ask him for help.
2He knows what he is doing! He sends di-
saster. He carries out his threats to punish
evil people and those who protect them.
3The Egyptians are not gods—they are only
human. Their horses are not supernatural.
When the LORD acts, the strong nation will
crumble, and the weak nation it helped will
fall. Both of them will be destroyed.

4The LORD said to me, "No matter how
shepherds yell and shout, they can't scare
away a lion from an animal that it has killed;
in the same way, there is nothing that can
keep me, the LORD Almighty, from pro-
tecting Mount Zion. 5Just as a bird hovers
over its nest to protect its young, so I, the
LORD Almighty, will protect Jerusalem and
defend it."

As a bird hovers over its nest (31:5)

6God said, "People of Israel, you have
sinned against me and opposed me. But now,
come back to me! 7A time is coming when
all of you will throw away the sinful idols
you made out of silver and gold. 8Assyria
will be destroyed in war, but not by human
power. The Assyrians will run from battle,
and their young men will be made slaves.
9Their emperor will run away in terror, and
the officers will be so frightened that they
will abandon their battle flags." The LORD
has spoken—the LORD who is worshiped in
Jerusalem and whose fire burns there for sac-
rifices.

A King with Integrity

32 Some day there will be a king who
rules with integrity, and national
leaders who govern with justice. 2Each of
them will be like a shelter from the wind
and a place to hide from storms. They will
be like streams flowing in a desert, like the
shadow of a giant rock in a barren land.
3Their eyes and ears will be open to the
needs of the people. 4They will not be
impatient any longer, but they will act with
understanding and will say what they mean.
5No one will think that a fool is honorable
or say that a scoundrel is honest. 6A fool
speaks foolishly and thinks up evil things to
do. What he does and what he says are an
insult to the LORD, and he never feeds the
hungry or gives thirsty people anything to
drink. 7A stupid person is evil and does evil
things; he plots to ruin the poor with lies
and to keep them from getting their rights.
8But an honorable person acts honestly and
stands firm for what is right.

Judgment and Restoration

9You women who live an easy life, free
from worries, listen to what I am saying.
10You may be satisfied now, but this time
next year you will be in despair because
there will be no grapes for you to gather.
11You have been living an easy life, free from
worries; but now, tremble with fear! Strip off
your clothes and tie rags around your waist.
12Beat your breasts in grief because the fer-
tile fields and the vineyards have been

destroyed, 13and thorn bushes and briers are
growing on my people's land. Weep for all
the houses where people were happy and for
the city that was full of life. 14Even the
palace will be abandoned and the capital city
totally deserted. Homes and the forts that
guarded them will be in ruins forever. Wild
donkeys will roam there, and sheep will find
pasture there.

15But once more God will send us his
spirit. The wasteland will become fertile, and
fields will produce rich crops. 16Everywhere
in the land righteousness and justice will be
done. 17Because everyone will do what is
right, there will be peace and security forev-
er. 18God's people will be free from worries,
and their homes peaceful and safe. (19But
hail will fall on the forests, and the city will
be torn down.) 20How happy everyone will
be with plenty of water for the crops and
safe pasture everywhere for the donkeys and
cattle.

A Prayer for Help

33 Our enemies are doomed! They
have robbed and betrayed, although
no one has robbed them or betrayed them.
But their time to rob and betray will end,
and they themselves will become victims of
robbery and treachery.

2LORD, have mercy on us. We have put
our hope in you. Protect us day by day and
save us in times of trouble. 3When you fight
for us, nations run away from the noise of
battle. 4Their belongings are pounced upon
and taken as loot.

5How great the LORD is! He rules over
everything. He will fill Jerusalem with justice
and integrity 6and give stability to the
nation. He always protects his people and
gives them wisdom and knowledge. Their
greatest treasure is their reverence for the
LORD.

7The brave are calling for help. The
ambassadors who tried to bring about peace
are crying bitterly. 8The highways are so
dangerous that no one travels on them.
Treaties are broken and agreements are vio-
lated. No one is respected any more. 9The
land lies idle and deserted. The forests of
Lebanon have withered, the fertile valley of

Live it!

The Right Thing

"You can survive if you say and do what is right" (Isaiah 33:15).

"If I become student council president, I will make sure we get extra recess time every day. I will make sure the cafeteria serves McDonald's and pizza. So vote for me!" Eric's opponent ended her speech with that promise.

Eric stepped up to the microphone in the gym. He looked around and then down at his speech. His ideas didn't include extra recess and McDonald's. They did include ideas for making his school safe and ways of helping his classmates to be better students. It seemed unlikely that those ideas would get him elected student body president. But he knew his ideas were realistic and that his classmates felt afraid since the recent violence in a school near theirs. So Eric started his speech. It didn't sound as flashy as his opponent's speech, but what he said must have made sense. There was a lot of applause when he finished.

The next day the principal got on the loudspeaker and announced the winners. Eric was sure everyone had voted for the girl running against him, but it was his name being said over the school PA system, not hers. His classmates were interested in being safe and in succeeding, not just in longer breaks and lunchtimes. A lot of the kids congratulated him in the hallway. Even the popular kids said something to him. Eric realized then that saying and doing what is right is always the best plan.

— Isaiah 33:15

Sharon is like a desert, and in Bashan and on Mount Carmel the leaves are falling from the trees.

The LORD Warns His Enemies

10 The LORD says to the nations, "Now I will act. I will show how powerful I am. 11 You make worthless plans and everything you do is useless. My spirit is like a fire that will destroy you.[q] 12 You will crumble like rocks burned to make lime, like thorns burned to ashes. 13 Let everyone near and far hear what I have done and acknowledge my power."

14 The sinful people of Zion are trembling with fright. They say, "God's judgment is like a fire that burns forever. Can any of us survive a fire like that?" 15 You can survive if you say and do what is right. Don't use your power to cheat the poor and don't accept bribes. Don't join with those who plan to commit murder or to do other evil things. 16 Then you will be safe; you will be as secure as if in a strong fortress. You will have food to eat and water to drink.

The Glorious Future

17 Once again you will see a king ruling in splendor over a land that stretches in all directions. 18 Your old fears of foreign tax collectors and spies will be only a memory. 19 You will no longer see any arrogant foreigners who speak a language that you can't understand. 20 Look at Zion, the city where we celebrate our religious festivals. Look at Jerusalem! What a safe place it will be to live in! It will be like a tent that is never moved, whose pegs are never pulled up and whose ropes never break. 21 The LORD will show us his glory. We will live beside broad rivers and streams, but hostile ships will not sail on them.[r] 22-23 All the rigging on those ships is useless; the sails cannot be spread! We will seize all the wealth of enemy armies, and there will be so much that even the lame can get a share. The LORD himself will be our king; he will rule over us and protect us. 24 No one who lives in our land will ever again complain of being sick, and all sins will be forgiven.

God Will Punish His Enemies

34 Come, people of all nations! Gather around and listen. Let the whole earth and everyone living on it come here and listen. 2 The LORD is angry with all the nations and all their armies. He has condemned them to destruction. 3 Their corpses will not be buried, but will lie there rotting and stinking; and the mountains will be red with blood. 4 The sun, moon, and stars will crumble to dust. The sky will disappear like a scroll being rolled up, and the stars will fall like leaves dropping from a vine or a fig tree.

5 The LORD has prepared his sword in heaven, and now it will strike Edom, those people whom he has condemned to destruction. 6 His sword will be covered with their blood and fat, like the blood and fat of lambs and goats that are sacrificed. The LORD will offer this sacrifice in the city of Bozrah; he will make this a great slaughter in the land of Edom. 7 The people will fall like wild oxen and young bulls, and the earth will be red with blood and covered with fat. 8 This is the time when the LORD will rescue Zion and take vengeance on her enemies.

9 The rivers of Edom will turn into tar, and the soil will turn into sulfur. The whole country will burn like tar. 10 It will burn day and night, and smoke will rise from it forever. The land will lie waste age after age, and no one will ever travel through it again. 11 Owls and ravens will take over the land. The LORD will make it a barren waste again,

[q] **33:11** *One ancient translation* My spirit . . . you; *Hebrew* You are destroying yourselves. [r] **33:21** *Verse 21 in Hebrew is unclear.*

34:4 Mt 24:29; Mk 13:25; Lk 21:26; Rev 6:13, 14 **34:5–17** Isa 63:1–6; Jer 49:7–22; Ezek 25:12–14; 35:1–15; Am 1:11, 12; Ob 1–14; Mal 1:2–5 **34:10** Rev 14:11; 19:3

Isaiah describes a glorious future for the Israelites at the end of Isaiah, chapter 33. How would you describe your glorious future?

Owls and ravens will take over the land. (34:11)

as it was before the creation. 12There will be
no king to rule the country, and the leaders
will all be gone.[s] 13Thorns and thistles will
grow up in all the palaces and walled towns,
and jackals and owls will live in them.
14Wild animals will roam there, and demons
will call to each other. The night monster[t]
will come there looking for a place to rest.
15Owls will build their nests, lay eggs, hatch
their young, and care for them there. Vultures
will gather there, one after another.
16Search in the LORD's book of living
creatures and read what it says. Not one of
these creatures will be missing, and not one
will be without its mate. The LORD has
commanded it to be so; he himself will
bring them together. 17It is the LORD who
will divide the land among them and give
each of them a share. They will live in the
land age after age, and it will belong to them
forever.

The Road of Holiness

35 The desert will rejoice,
and flowers will bloom in the
wastelands.
2The desert will sing and shout for joy;
it will be as beautiful as the Lebanon
Mountains
and as fertile as the fields of Carmel
and Sharon.
Everyone will see the LORD's splendor,
see his greatness and power.

3Give strength to hands that are tired
and to knees that tremble with
weakness.
4Tell everyone who is discouraged,
"Be strong and don't be afraid!
God is coming to your rescue,
coming to punish your enemies."

5The blind will be able to see,
and the deaf will hear.
6The lame will leap and dance,
and those who cannot speak will shout
for joy.
Streams of water will flow through the
desert;
7 the burning sand will become a lake,
and dry land will be filled with springs.
Where jackals used to live,
marsh grass and reeds will grow.

8There will be a highway there,
called "The Road of Holiness."
No sinner will ever travel that road;
no fools will mislead those who follow
it.[u]
9No lions will be there;
no fierce animals will pass that way.
Those whom the LORD has rescued
will travel home by that road.
10They will reach Jerusalem with gladness,
singing and shouting for joy.
They will be happy forever,
forever free from sorrow and grief.

The Assyrians Threaten Jerusalem
(2 Kings 18:13–27; 2 Chronicles 32:1–19)

36 In the fourteenth year that Hezekiah
was king of Judah, Sennacherib, the
emperor of Assyria, attacked the fortified
cities of Judah and captured them. 2Then he
ordered his chief official to go from Lachish
to Jerusalem with a large military force to
demand that King Hezekiah surrender. The
official occupied the road where the cloth
makers work, by the ditch that brings water

[s] **34:12** *Verse 12 in Hebrew begins with a word, the meaning of which is unclear.* [t] **34:14** NIGHT MONSTER: *A female demon, believed to live in desolate places.* [u] **35:8** *Probable text* no fools . . . follow it; *Hebrew unclear.*
35:3 Heb 12:12 **35:5, 6** Mt 11:5; Lk 7:22

The night monster mentioned in Isaiah 34:14 is called Lilith, a female demon, in other Bible translations.

Study it!

Holiness and Healthiness

Isaiah, chapter 35, talks about the Road of Holiness. This is the path that people follow to get to God. It is a marvelous place, where the blind see, and the lame will leap and dance. Did you ever stop and think, though, that the road to holiness is also the road to healthiness?

Some people may think that being a good follower of Christ is just about praying, going to Mass, and avoiding big sins. But God wants more for us. God is interested in all aspects of our life: our bodies, our souls, our hearts, and our minds. This is why the Church teaches that part of the meaning of the fifth commandment, "You shall not kill," is about taking care of our physical health. If we abuse food, alcohol, tobacco, or drugs, we are causing harm to our bodies. We are, in a sense, killing them. This also includes getting enough sleep and eating healthy foods. Equally important is taking care of our mental health. When we have psychological problems and ignore them, we are also not fully obeying the fifth commandment.

God really does want you to be holy and physically healthy. That is the way we are made to be—wonderfully created by our loving God.

— Isaiah, chapter 35

from the upper pool. 3 Three Judeans came
out to meet him: the official in charge of the
palace, Eliakim son of Hilkiah; the court sec-
retary, Shebna; and the official in charge of
the records, Joah son of Asaph. 4 The Assyrian
official told them that the emperor wanted
to know what made King Hezekiah so con-
fident. 5 He demanded, "Do you think that
words can take the place of military skill and
might? Who do you think will help you
rebel against Assyria? 6 You are expecting
Egypt to help you, but that would be like
using a reed as a walking stick—it would
break and would jab your hand. That is what
the king of Egypt is like when anyone relies
on him."

7 The Assyrian official went on, "Or will
you tell me that you are relying on the
LORD your God? It was the LORD's shrines
and altars that Hezekiah destroyed when he
told the people of Judah and Jerusalem to
worship at one altar only. 8 I will make a bar-
gain with you in the name of the emperor. I
will give you two thousand horses if you can
find that many riders. 9 You are no match for
even the lowest ranking Assyrian official, and
yet you expect the Egyptians to send you
chariots and horsemen. 10 Do you think I
have attacked your country and destroyed it
without the LORD's help? The LORD himself
told me to attack it and destroy it."

11 Then Eliakim, Shebna, and Joah told the
official, "Speak Aramaic to us. We understand
it. Don't speak Hebrew; all the people on the
wall are listening."

12 He replied, "Do you think you and the
king are the only ones the emperor sent me
to say all these things to? No, I am also talk-
ing to the people who are sitting on the
wall, who will have to eat their excrement
and drink their urine, just as you will."

13 Then the official stood up and shouted
in Hebrew, "Listen to what the emperor of
Assyria is telling you. 14 He warns you not
to let Hezekiah deceive you. Hezekiah can't
save you. 15 And don't let him persuade you
to rely on the LORD. Don't think that the
LORD will save you and that he will stop
our Assyrian army from capturing your city.
16 Don't listen to Hezekiah! The emperor of
Assyria commands you to come out of the
city and surrender. You will all be allowed
to eat grapes from your own vines and figs
from your own trees, and to drink water

36:6 Ezek 29:6, 7

from your own wells— 17until the emperor resettles you in a country much like your own, where there are vineyards to give wine and there is grain for making bread. 18Don't let Hezekiah fool you into thinking that the LORD will rescue you. Did the gods of any other nations save their countries from the emperor of Assyria? 19Where are they now, the gods of Hamath and Arpad? Where are the gods of Sepharvaim? Did anyone save Samaria? 20When did any of the gods of all these countries ever save their country from our emperor? Then what makes you think the LORD can save Jerusalem?"

21The people kept quiet, just as King Hezekiah had told them to; they did not say a word. 22Then Eliakim, Shebna, and Joah tore their clothes in grief and went and reported to the king what the Assyrian official had said.

The people kept quiet. (36:21)

The King Asks Isaiah's Advice
(2 Kings 19:1–7)

37 As soon as King Hezekiah heard their report, he tore his clothes in grief, put on sackcloth, and went to the Temple of the LORD. 2He sent Eliakim, the official in charge of the palace, Shebna, the court secretary, and the senior priests to the prophet Isaiah son of AmoMz. They also were wearing sackcloth. 3This is the message which he told them to give to Isaiah: "Today is a day of suffering; we are being punished and are in disgrace. We are like a woman who is ready to give birth, but is too weak to do it. 4The Assyrian emperor has sent his chief official to insult the living God. May the LORD your God hear these insults and punish those who spoke them. So pray to God for those of our people who survive."

Study it!

Good King Hezekiah

Chapters 36–39 end the first section of the Book of Isaiah. These chapters tell of King Hezekiah of Judah. These chapters are very similar to the story of Hezekiah in 2 Kings or 2 Chronicles. You will see cross-references to those books under the headings.

Hezekiah was ruling at a difficult time. The Assyrians had just taken over the kingdom of Israel, to the north. Now they were coming for the kingdom of Judah.

Hezekiah could have tried fighting the Assyrians on his own, or he could have surrendered. Instead, he prayed to God and asked Isaiah for help. Isaiah told King Hezekiah to stand firm and have faith and God would take care of things. Sure enough, the Assyrian army left, and the Assyrian emperor was later assassinated by his own sons.

— Isaiah, chapter 36

5When Isaiah received King Hezekiah's message, 6he sent back this answer: "The LORD tells you not to let the Assyrians frighten you by their claims that he cannot save you. 7The LORD will cause the emperor to hear a rumor that will make him go back to his own country, and the LORD will have him killed there."

The Assyrians Send Another Threat
(2 Kings 19:8–19)

8The Assyrian official learned that the emperor had left Lachish and was fighting against the nearby city of Libnah; so he went there to consult him. 9Word reached the Assyrians that the Egyptian army, led by

King Tirhakah of Ethiopia,[v] was coming to
attack them. When the emperor heard this,
he sent a letter to King Hezekiah 10 of Judah
to tell him: "The god you are trusting in has
told you that you will not fall into my
hands, but don't let that deceive you. 11 You
have heard what an Assyrian emperor does
to any country he decides to destroy. Do you
think that you can escape? 12 My ancestors
destroyed the cities of Gozan, Haran, and
Rezeph, and killed the people of Betheden
who lived in Telassar, and none of their gods
could save them. 13 Where are the kings of
the cities of Hamath, Arpad, Sepharvaim,
Hena, and Ivvah?"

14 King Hezekiah took the letter from the
messengers and read it. Then he went to the
Temple, placed the letter there in the pres-
ence of the LORD, 15 and prayed, 16 "Almighty
LORD, God of Israel, seated above the winged
creatures, you alone are God, ruling all the
kingdoms of the world. You created the earth
and the sky. 17 Now, LORD, hear us and look
at what is happening to us. Listen to all the
things that Sennacherib is saying to insult
you, the living God. 18 We all know, LORD,
that the emperors of Assyria have destroyed
many nations, made their lands desolate,
19 and burned up their gods—which were no
gods at all, only images of wood and stone
made by human hands. 20 Now, LORD our
God, rescue us from the Assyrians, so that all
the nations of the world will know that you
alone are God."

Isaiah's Message to the King
(2 Kings 19:20–37)

21 Then Isaiah sent a message telling King
Hezekiah that in answer to the king's prayer
22 the LORD had said, "The city of Jerusalem
laughs at you, Sennacherib, and makes fun of
you. 23 Whom do you think you have been
insulting and ridiculing? You have been dis-
respectful to me, the holy God of Israel.
24 You sent your servants to boast to me that
with all your chariots you had conquered
the highest mountains of Lebanon. You
boasted that there you cut down the tallest
cedars and the finest cypress trees, and that
you reached the deepest parts of the forests.
25 You boasted that you dug wells and drank
water in foreign lands, and that the feet of
your soldiers tramped the Nile River dry.

26 "Have you never heard that I planned
all this long ago? And now I have carried it
out. I gave you the power to turn fortified
cities into piles of rubble. 27 The people who
lived there were powerless; they were fright-
ened and stunned. They were like grass in a
field or weeds growing on a roof when the
hot east wind blasts them.[w]

28 "But I know everything about you,
what you do and where you go. I know how
you rage against me. 29 I have received the
report of that rage and that pride of yours,
and now I will put a hook through your
nose and a bit in your mouth and will take
you back by the same road you came."

30 Then Isaiah said to King Hezekiah,
"Here is a sign of what will happen. This
year and next you will have only wild grain
to eat, but the following year you will be
able to plant grain and harvest it, and plant
vines and eat grapes. 31 Those in Judah who
survive will flourish like plants that send
roots deep into the ground and produce
fruit. 32 There will be people in Jerusalem
and on Mount Zion who will survive,
because the LORD Almighty is determined
to make this happen.

33 "And this is what the LORD has said
about the Assyrian emperor: 'He will not
enter this city or shoot a single arrow against
it. No soldiers with shields will come near
the city, and no siege mounds will be built
around it. 34 He will go back by the same
road he came, without entering this city. I,

[v] **37:9** *Hebrew* Cush: *Cush is the ancient name of the extensive territory south of the First Cataract of the Nile River. This region was called Ethiopia in Graeco-Roman times, and included within its borders most of modern Sudan and some of present-day Ethiopia (Abyssinia).* [w] **37:27** *Probable text* when the hot east wind blasts them; *Hebrew* blasted before they are grown.
37:16 Ex 25:22

How did Isaiah know what to say in reply to King Hezekiah's question *(Isaiah 37:6–7)*?

the LORD, have spoken. 35 I will defend this city and protect it, for the sake of my own honor and because of the promise I made to my servant David.' "

36 An angel of the LORD went to the Assyrian camp and killed 185,000 soldiers. At dawn the next day there they lay, all dead! 37 Then the Assyrian emperor Sennacherib withdrew and returned to Nineveh. 38 One day when he was worshiping in the temple of his god Nisroch, two of his sons, Adrammelech and Sharezer, killed him with their swords and then escaped to the land of Ararat. Another of his sons, Esarhaddon, succeeded him as emperor.

An angel of the LORD went to the Assyrian camp. (37:36)

King Hezekiah's Illness and Recovery

(2 Kings 20:1–11; 2 Chronicles 32:24–26)

38 About this time King Hezekiah became sick and almost died. The prophet Isaiah son of Amoz went to see him and said to him, "The LORD tells you that you are to put everything in order because you will not recover. Get ready to die."

2 Hezekiah turned his face to the wall and prayed: 3 "Remember, LORD, that I have served you faithfully and loyally, and that I have always tried to do what you wanted me to." And he began to cry bitterly.

4 Then the LORD commanded Isaiah 5 to go back to Hezekiah and say to him, "I, the LORD, the God of your ancestor David, have heard your prayer and seen your tears; I will let you live fifteen years longer. 6 I will rescue you and this city of Jerusalem from the emperor of Assyria, and I will continue to protect the city."

21 Isaiah told the king to put a paste made of figs on his boil, and he would get well. 22 Then King Hezekiah asked, "What is the sign to prove that I will be able to go to the Temple?"[x]

7 Isaiah replied, "The LORD will give you a sign to prove that he will keep his promise. 8 On the stairway built by King Ahaz, the LORD will make the shadow go back ten steps." And the shadow moved back ten steps.[y]

9 After Hezekiah recovered from his illness, he wrote this song of praise:

10 I thought that in the prime of life
I was going to the world of the dead,
Never to live out my life.
11 I thought that in this world of the living
I would never again see the LORD
Or any living person.
12 My life was cut off and ended,
Like a tent that is taken down,
Like cloth that is cut from a loom.
I thought that God was ending my life.[z]
13 All night I cried out with pain,
As if a lion were breaking my bones.
I thought that God was ending my life.[a]
14 My voice was thin and weak,
And I moaned like a dove.
My eyes grew tired from looking to heaven.
LORD, rescue me from all this trouble.
15 What can I say? The LORD has done this.
My heart is bitter, and I cannot sleep.[b]
16 Lord, I will live for you, for you alone;
Heal me and let me live.[c]
17 My bitterness will turn into peace.
You save[d] my life from all danger;
You forgive all my sins.

[x] **38:22** *Verses 21–22 are moved here from the end of the chapter (see 2 Kings 20:6–9).* [y] **38:8** stairway . . . ten steps . . . steps; *or* sundial . . . ten degrees . . . degrees *(see 2 Kings 20:9–11).* [z] **38:12** I thought . . . my life; *Hebrew unclear.* [a] **38:13** *Verse 13 in Hebrew is unclear.* [b] **38:15** *One ancient translation suggests* I cannot sleep; *Hebrew unclear.* [c] **38:16** *Verses 15 and 16 in Hebrew are unclear.* [d] **38:17** *Some ancient translations* save; *Hebrew* love.
38:18 Sir 17:27; Bar 2:17

How would you react if you heard great news such as that in Isaiah 39:8?

Live it!

Second Chance

Imagine being really sick and thinking you are going to die. You would probably pray and ask God for help. Imagine then that someone gives you a cure and you get to live. That is what happened to King Hezekiah. He was near death and was even told he would die; then Isaiah told him that he would live. The prayer in chapter 38 is what King Hezekiah wrote after he recovered. Do you think King Hezekiah lived differently after his life was spared?

If you were near death and then you were given a second chance at life, what would you do with it? Would you live your life any differently? Don't wait until you are in King Hezekiah's place. If you need to make changes in your life, make them now. Write a list of how you want to be, what you want to do. As you create your list, keep in mind all you have read here in Isaiah and throughout the Bible.

— Isaiah, chapter 38

18 No one in the world of the dead can
praise you;
The dead cannot trust in your faithfulness.
19 It is the living who praise you,
As I praise you now.
Parents tell their children how faithful
you are.
20 LORD, you have healed me.
We will play harps and sing your praise,
Sing praise in your Temple as long as we
live.[e]

Messengers from Babylonia
(2 Kings 20:12–19)

39 About that same time the king of
Babylonia, Merodach Baladan, son of
Baladan, heard that King Hezekiah had been
sick, so he sent him a letter and a present.
2 Hezekiah welcomed the messengers and
showed them his wealth—his silver and
gold, his spices and perfumes, and all his mil-
itary equipment. There was nothing in his
storerooms or anywhere in his kingdom that
he did not show them. 3 Then the prophet
Isaiah went to King Hezekiah and asked,
"Where did these messengers come from
and what did they say to you?"
Hezekiah answered, "They came from a
very distant country, from Babylonia."
4 "What did they see in the palace?"
"They saw everything. There is nothing in
the storerooms that I didn't show them."
5 Isaiah then told the king, "The LORD
Almighty says that 6 a time is coming when
everything in your palace, everything that
your ancestors have stored up to this day, will
be carried off to Babylonia. Nothing will be
left. 7 Some of your own direct descendants
will be taken away and made eunuchs to
serve in the palace of the king of Babylonia."
8 King Hezekiah understood this to mean
that there would be peace and security dur-
ing his lifetime, so he replied, "The message
you have given me from the LORD is good."

Words of Hope

40 "Comfort my people," says our God.
"Comfort them!
2 Encourage the people of Jerusalem.
Tell them they have suffered long enough
and their sins are now forgiven.[f]
I have punished them in full for all their
sins."

3 A voice cries out,
"Prepare in the wilderness a road for the
LORD!
Clear the way in the desert for our
God!

[e] **38:20** *Verses 21–22 are placed after verse 6.* [f] **40:2** and their sins are now forgiven; *or* they have paid for what they did.

39:7 Dan 1:1–7; 2 Kings 24:10–16; 2 Chr 36:10 **40:3** Sir 48:10; Bar 5:7; Mt 3:3; Mk 1:3; Jn 1:23
40:3–5 Lk 3:4–6

Study it!

A New Section

Chapters 40–66 of Isaiah take a very different turn from the previous chapters. These chapters are sometimes called the Book of Consolation. Consolation means to comfort someone. It is thought that these chapters were written by a follower of the original Isaiah a hundred years or more after the events of chapter 39. They refer to the captivity in Babylon, which was from 587 to 538 B.C. This was the time when the Babylonians had taken over Judah, the southern kingdom, and destroyed Jerusalem and the Temple.

You will notice that these chapters focus on hope and comfort. After the Babylonians destroyed the Temple, many of the people lost all hope. They thought God had abandoned them. The prophet behind these chapters tells the people that God is still with them, and will restore them to their homes once more.

— Isaiah, chapter 40

4 Fill every valley;
level every mountain.
The hills will become a plain,
and the rough country will be made smooth.
5 Then the glory of the LORD will be revealed,
and all people will see it.
The LORD himself has promised this."

6 A voice cries out, "Proclaim a message!"
"What message shall I proclaim?" I ask.
"Proclaim that all human beings are like grass;
they last no longer than wild flowers.
7 Grass withers and flowers fade
when the LORD sends the wind blowing over them.
People are no more enduring than grass.
8 Yes, grass withers and flowers fade,
but the word of our God endures forever."

9 Jerusalem, go up on a high mountain
and proclaim the good news!
Call out with a loud voice, Zion;
announce the good news![g]
Speak out and do not be afraid.
Tell the towns of Judah
that their God is coming!

"Their God is coming!" (40:9)

10 The Sovereign LORD is coming to rule with power,
bringing with him the people he has rescued.[h]
11 He will take care of his flock like a shepherd;
he will gather the lambs together
and carry them in his arms;
he will gently lead their mothers.

[g] **40:9** Jerusalem, go up . . . news!; *or* Go up on a high mountain and proclaim the good news to Jerusalem! Call out with a loud voice and announce the good news to Zion! [h] **40:10** the people he has rescued; *or* the rewards he has for his people.

40:6–8 Jas 1:10, 11; 1 Pet 1:24, 25 **40:10** Isa 62:11; Rev 22:12 **40:11** Ezek 34:15; Jn 10:11

Israel's Incomparable God

12 Can anyone measure the ocean by handfuls
or measure the sky with his hands?
Can anyone hold the soil of the earth in a cup
or weigh the mountains and hills on scales?
13 Can anyone tell the LORD what to do?
Who can teach him or give him advice?
14 With whom does God consult
in order to know and understand
and to learn how things should be done?

15 To the LORD the nations are nothing,
no more than a drop of water;
the distant islands are as light as dust.
16 All the animals in the forests of Lebanon
are not enough for a sacrifice to our God,
and its trees are too few to kindle the fire.
17 The nations are nothing at all to him.

18 To whom can God be compared?
How can you describe what he is like?
19 He is not like an idol that workers make,
that metalworkers cover with gold
and set in a base of silver.
20 Anyone who cannot afford silver or gold[i]
chooses wood that will not rot.
He finds a skillful worker
to make an image that won't fall down.
21 Do you not know?
Were you not told long ago?
Have you not heard how the world began?
22 It was made by the one who sits on his throne
above the earth and beyond the sky;
the people below look as tiny as ants.
He stretched out the sky like a curtain,
like a tent in which to live.
23 He brings down powerful rulers
and reduces them to nothing.
24 They are like young plants,
just set out and barely rooted.
When the LORD sends a wind,
they dry up and blow away like straw.

25 To whom can the holy God be compared?
Is there anyone else like him?
26 Look up at the sky!
Who created the stars you see?
The one who leads them out like an army,
he knows how many there are
and calls each one by name!
His power is so great—
not one of them is ever missing!

27 Israel, why then do you complain
that the LORD doesn't know your troubles
or care if you suffer injustice?
28 Don't you know? Haven't you heard?
The LORD is the everlasting God;
he created all the world.
He never grows tired or weary.
No one understands his thoughts.
29 He strengthens those who are weak and tired.
30 Even those who are young grow weak;
young people can fall exhausted.
31 But those who trust in the LORD for help
will find their strength renewed.
They will rise on wings like eagles;
they will run and not get weary;
they will walk and not grow weak.

God's Assurance to Israel

41 God says,
"Be silent and listen to me, you distant lands!
Get ready to present your case in court;
you will have your chance to speak.
Let us come together to decide who is right.

[i] **40:20** *Verses 19–20a in Hebrew are unclear.*

40:13 Rom 11:34; 1 Cor 2:16 **40:15** Wis 11:22; Sir 10:16, 17 **40:18, 19** Acts 17:29 **40:20** Wis 13:11–19; Bar 6:8–40 **40:26** Bar 3:34, 35

Compare Isaiah, chapter 40, with Isaiah, chapter 6.

Pray it!

FEAR

The dark? spiders? heights? public speaking?

What are you afraid of? A lot of people are afraid of the dark or of spiders or of heights. And being afraid of public speaking is the No. 1 fear. Isaiah knew that the people were afraid and needed courage. He let them know God's message: "Do not be afraid—I am with you! / I am your God—let nothing terrify you!" (Isaiah 41:10). Choose something you are afraid of and include it in this prayer.

I will not be afraid of ______________ because I know that you, my God, are with me. I may get scared, but I will remember you and your message in Isaiah: "Do not be afraid!" Amen.

— Isaiah 41:10

2 "Who was it that brought the conqueror
from the east[j]
and makes him triumphant wherever
he goes?
Who gives him victory over kings and
nations?
His sword strikes them down as if they
were dust.
His arrows scatter them like straw
before the wind.
3 He follows in pursuit and marches safely
on,
so fast that he hardly touches the
ground!
4 Who was it that made this happen?
Who has determined the course of
history?
I, the LORD, was there at the beginning,
and I, the LORD, will be there at the
end.

5 "The people of distant lands have seen
what I have done;
they are frightened and tremble with
fear.
So they all assemble and come.
6 The skilled workers help and encourage
each other.
7 The carpenter says to the goldsmith, 'Well
done!'
The one who beats the idol smooth
encourages the one who nails it
together.
They say, 'The soldering is good'—
and they fasten the idol in place with
nails.

8 "But you, Israel my servant,
you are the people that I have chosen,
the descendants of Abraham, my friend.
9 I brought you from the ends of the earth;
I called you from its farthest corners
and said to you, 'You are my servant.'
I did not reject you, but chose you.
10 Do not be afraid—I am with you!
I am your God—let nothing terrify you!
I will make you strong and help you;
I will protect you and save you.
11 "Those who are angry with you
will know the shame of defeat.
Those who fight against you will die

[j] **41:2** THE CONQUEROR FROM THE EAST: *Cyrus, the emperor of Persia (see 45:1).*
41:8 2 Chr 20:7; Jas 2:23

God is putting the false gods of the nations on trial in chapter 41. Can you find the legal sounding language in verses 1, 21, 22, 28?

12 and will disappear from the earth.
13 I am the LORD your God;
I strengthen you and tell you,
'Do not be afraid; I will help you.'"

14 The LORD says,
"Small and weak as you are, Israel,
don't be afraid; I will help you.
I, the holy God of Israel, am the one who saves you.
15 I will make you like a threshing board,
with spikes that are new and sharp.
You will thresh mountains and destroy them;
hills will crumble into dust.
16 You will toss them in the air;
the wind will carry them off,
and they will be scattered by the storm.
Then you will be happy because I am your God;
you will praise me, the holy God of Israel.

17 "When my people in their need look for water,
when their throats are dry with thirst,
then I, the LORD, will answer their prayer;
I, the God of Israel, will never abandon them.
18 I will make rivers flow among barren hills
and springs of water run in the valleys.
I will turn the desert into pools of water
and the dry land into flowing springs.
19 I will make cedars grow in the desert,
and acacias and myrtles and olive trees.
Forests will grow in barren land,
forests of pine and juniper and cypress.
20 People will see this and know
that I, the LORD, have done it.
They will come to understand
that Israel's holy God has made it happen."

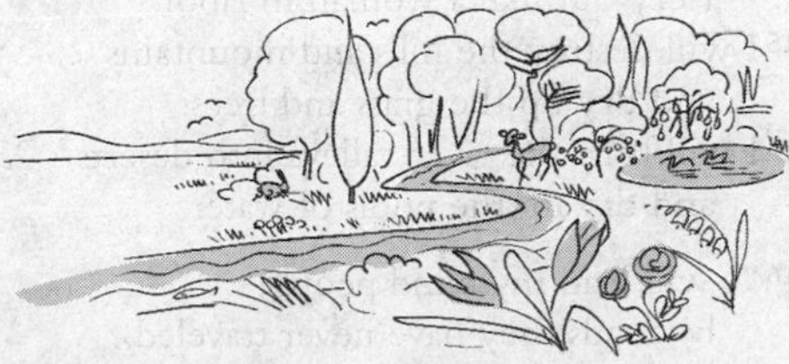

I will turn the desert into pools of water. (41:18)

The LORD's Challenge to False Gods

21 The LORD, the king of Israel, has this to
say:
"You gods of the nations, present your case.
Bring the best arguments you have!
22 Come here and predict what will happen,
so that we will know it when it takes place.
Explain to the court the events of the past,
and tell us what they mean.
23 Tell us what the future holds—
then we will know that you are gods!
Do something good or bring some disaster;
fill us with fear and awe!
24 You and all you do are nothing;
those who worship you are disgusting!

25 "I have chosen a man who lives in the east;[k]
I will bring him to attack from the north.
He tramples on rulers as if they were mud,
like a potter trampling clay.
26 Which of you predicted that this would happen,
so that we could say that you were right?
None of you said a word about it;
no one heard you say a thing!
27 I, the LORD, was the first to tell Zion the news;
I sent a messenger to Jerusalem to say,
'Your people are coming! They are coming home!'[l]
28 When I looked among the gods,
none of them had a thing to say;
not one could answer the questions I asked.
29 All these gods are useless;
they can do nothing at all—
these idols are weak and powerless."

[k] **41:25** A MAN WHO LIVES IN THE EAST: *See 41:2.* [l] **41:27** *Verse 27 in Hebrew is unclear.*

"All these gods are useless." (41:29)

The LORD's Servant

42 The LORD says,
"Here is my servant, whom I strengthen—
the one I have chosen, with whom I am pleased.
I have filled him with my Spirit,
and he will bring justice to every nation.
2 He will not shout or raise his voice
or make loud speeches in the streets.
3 He will not break off a bent reed
nor put out a flickering lamp.
He will bring lasting justice to all.
4 He will not lose hope or courage;
he will establish justice on the earth.
Distant lands eagerly wait for his teaching."

5 God created the heavens and stretched them out;
he fashioned the earth and all that lives there;
he gave life and breath to all its people.
And now the LORD God says to his servant,
6 "I, the LORD, have called you and given you power
to see that justice is done on earth.
Through you I will make a covenant with all peoples;
through you I will bring light to the nations.
7 You will open the eyes of the blind
and set free those who sit in dark prisons.
8 "I alone am the LORD your God.
No other god may share my glory;
I will not let idols share my praise.
9 The things I predicted have now come true.
Now I will tell you of new things
even before they begin to happen."

A Song of Praise

10 Sing a new song to the LORD;
sing his praise, all the world!
Praise him, you that sail the sea;
praise him, all creatures of the sea!
Sing, distant lands and all who live there!
11 Let the desert and its towns praise God;
let the people of Kedar praise him!
Let those who live in the city of Sela
shout for joy from the tops of the mountains!
12 Let those who live in distant lands
give praise and glory to the LORD!
13 The LORD goes out to fight like a warrior;
he is ready and eager for battle.
He gives a war cry, a battle shout;
he shows his power against his enemies.

God Promises to Help His People

14 God says,
"For a long time I kept silent;
I did not answer my people.
But now the time to act has come;
I cry out like a woman in labor.
15 I will destroy the hills and mountains
and dry up the grass and trees.
I will turn the river valleys into deserts[m]
and dry up the pools of water.

16 "I will lead my blind people
by roads they have never traveled.

[m] **42:15** *Probable text* deserts; *Hebrew* coastlands.

42:1 Mt 3:17; 17:5; Mk 1:11; Lk 3:22; 9:35 **42:1–4** Mt 12:18–21 **42:5** Acts 17:24, 25 **42:6** Isa 49:6; Lk 2:32; Acts 13:47; 26:23

I will turn their darkness into light
and make rough country smooth
before them.
These are my promises,
and I will keep them without fail.
17 All who trust in idols,
who call images their gods,
will be humiliated and disgraced."

Israel's Failure to Learn

18 The LORD says,
"Listen, you deaf people!
Look closely, you that are blind!
19 Is anyone more blind than my servant,
more deaf than the messenger I send?
20 Israel, you have seen so much,
but what has it meant to you?
You have ears to hear with,
but what have you really heard?"

21 The LORD is a God who is eager to save,
so he exalted his laws and teachings,
and he wanted his people to honor
them.
22 But now his people have been plundered;
they are locked up in dungeons
and hidden away in prisons.
They were robbed and plundered,
with no one to come to their rescue.

23 Will any of you listen to this?
From now on will you listen with care?
24 Who gave Israel up to the looters?
It was the LORD himself, against whom
we sinned!
We would not live as he wanted us to live
or obey the teachings he gave us.
25 So he made us feel the force of his anger
and suffer the violence of war.
Like fire his anger burned throughout
Israel,
but we never knew what was
happening;
we learned nothing at all from it.

God Promises to Rescue His People

43 Israel, the LORD who created you
says,
"Do not be afraid—I will save you.
I have called you by name—you are
mine.
2 When you pass through deep waters, I
will be with you;
your troubles will not overwhelm you.
When you pass through fire, you will not
be burned;
the hard trials that come will not hurt
you.

When you pass through deep waters . . . (43:2)

3 For I am the LORD your God,
the holy God of Israel, who saves you.
I will give up Egypt to set you free;
I will give up Ethiopia[n] and Seba.
4 I will give up whole nations to save your
life,
because you are precious to me
and because I love you and give you
honor.
5 Do not be afraid—I am with you!
"From the distant east and the farthest
west
I will bring your people home.
6 I will tell the north to let them go
and the south not to hold them back.
Let my people return from distant lands,
from every part of the world.

[n] **43:3** *Hebrew* Cush: *Cush is the ancient name of the extensive territory south of the First Cataract of the Nile River. This region was called Ethiopia in Graeco-Roman times, and included within its borders most of modern Sudan and some of present-day Ethiopia (Abyssinia).*

"Sing a new song to the LORD; / sing his praise, all the world!" (Isaiah 42:10).

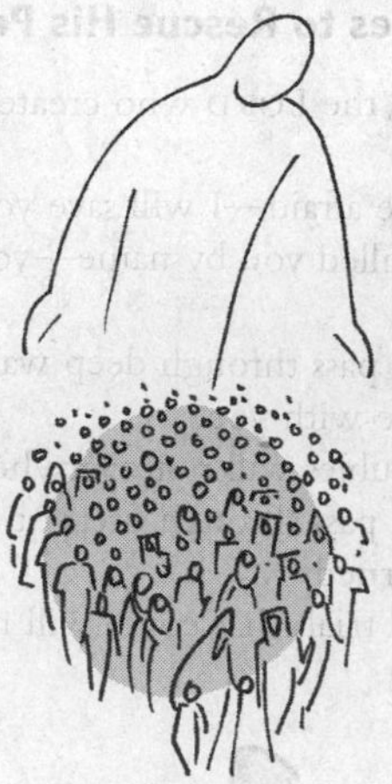

I will bring your people home. (43:5)

7 They are my own people,
and I created them to bring me glory."

Israel Is the LORD's Witness

8 God says,
"Summon my people to court.
They have eyes, but they are blind;
they have ears, but they are deaf!
9 Summon the nations to come to the trial.
Which of their gods can predict the future?
Which of them foretold what is happening now?
Let these gods bring in their witnesses
to prove that they are right,
to testify to the truth of their words.
10 "People of Israel, you are my witnesses;
I chose you to be my servant,
so that you would know me and believe in me
and understand that I am the only God.
Besides me there is no other god;
there never was and never will be.
11 "I alone am the LORD,
the only one who can save you.
12 I predicted what would happen,
and then I came to your aid.
No foreign god has ever done this;
you are my witnesses.
13 I am God and always will be.
No one can escape from my power;
no one can change what I do."

Escape from Babylon

14 Israel's holy God, the LORD who saves you, says,
"To save you, I will send an army against Babylon;
I will break down the city gates,
and the shouts of her people will turn into crying.
15 I am the LORD, your holy God.
I created you, Israel, and I am your king."
16 Long ago the LORD made a road through the sea,
a path through the swirling waters.

The LORD made a road through the sea. (43:16)

17 He led a mighty army to destruction,
an army of chariots and horses.
Down they fell, never to rise,
snuffed out like the flame of a lamp!
18 But the LORD says,
"Do not cling to events of the past
or dwell on what happened long ago.
19 Watch for the new thing I am going to do.
It is happening already—you can see it now!
I will make a road through the wilderness
and give you streams of water there.

In Isaiah, chapter 43, God calls the Israelites to testify that he is the true God. What evidence could they give from their history to prove this?

20 Even the wild animals will honor me;
jackals and ostriches will praise me
when I make rivers flow in the desert
to give water to my chosen people.
21 They are the people I made for myself,
and they will sing my praises!"

Israel's Sin

22 The LORD says,
"But you were tired of me, Israel;
you did not worship me.
23 You did not bring me your burnt
offerings of sheep;
you did not honor me with your
sacrifices.
I did not burden you by demanding
offerings
or wear you out by asking for incense.
24 You didn't buy incense for me
or satisfy me with the fat of your
animals.
Instead you burdened me with your
sins;
you wore me out with the wrongs you
have committed.
25 And yet, I am the God who forgives your
sins,
and I do this because of who I am.
I will not hold your sins against you.

26 "Let us go to court; bring your
accusation!
Present your case to prove you are in
the right!
27 Your earliest ancestor[o] sinned;
your leaders sinned against me,
28 and your rulers profaned[p] my sanctuary.
So I brought destruction on Israel;
I let my own people be insulted."

The LORD Is the Only God

44 The LORD says,
"Listen now, Israel, my servant,
my chosen people, the descendants of
Jacob.
2 I am the LORD who created you;
from the time you were born, I have
helped you.

Live it!

For the Thirsty

You know the person. That one in the lunchroom who sits alone. The one who eats as fast as possible and then disappears. The one who is ignored, or worse, made fun of. Every school has one, probably more.

Did you realize that that kid is thirsty? Even if he or she has something to drink, he or she is thirsty. Thirsty to know a friendly smile or a kind word. Thirsty like the dry ground described in Isaiah 44:3.

Do you know what this person is thirsty for? For you. Yes, for you and your company. It's risky. Your friends might laugh at you or ignore you. They may stop eating with you. But you know it is right. You know it is what you are called to do.

You are called to give water to the thirsty.

— Isaiah 44:3

Do not be afraid; you are my servant,
my chosen people whom I love.

3 "I will give water to the thirsty land
and make streams flow on the dry
ground.
I will pour out my spirit on your children
and my blessing on your descendants.
4 They will thrive like well-watered
grass,
like willows by streams of running
water.

5 "One by one, people will say, 'I am the
LORD's.'
They will come to join the people of
Israel.

[o] **43:27** YOUR EARLIEST ANCESTOR: *A reference to Jacob or to Abraham, or possibly to Adam.* [p] **43:28** *One ancient translation* your rulers profaned; *Hebrew* I profaned the rulers of.

They each will mark the name of the
LORD on their arms
and call themselves one of God's
people."

6 The LORD, who rules and protects Israel,
the LORD Almighty, has this to say:
"I am the first, the last, the only God;
there is no other god but me.
7 Could anyone else have done what I did?
Who could have predicted all that
would happen
from the very beginning to the end of
time?[q]
8 Do not be afraid, my people!
You know that from ancient times until
now
I have predicted all that would happen,
and you are my witnesses.
Is there any other god?
Is there some powerful god I never heard
of?"

Idolatry Is Ridiculed

9 All those who make idols are worthless,
and the gods they prize so highly are useless.
Those who worship these gods are blind and
ignorant—and they will be disgraced. 10 It
does no good to make a metal image to
worship as a god! 11 Everyone who worships
it will be humiliated. The people who make
idols are human beings and nothing more.
Let them come and stand trial—they will be
terrified and will suffer disgrace.
12 The metalworker takes a piece of metal
and works with it over a fire. His strong arm
swings a hammer to pound the metal into
shape. As he works, he gets hungry, thirsty,
and tired.
13 The carpenter measures the wood. He
outlines a figure with chalk, carves it out
with his tools, and makes it in the form of a
man, a handsome human figure, to be placed
in his house. 14 He might cut down cedars to
use, or choose oak or cypress wood from the
forest. Or he might plant a laurel tree and
wait for the rain to make it grow. 15 A person
uses part of a tree for fuel and part of it for
making an idol. With one part he builds a
fire to warm himself and bake bread; with
the other part he makes a god and worships
it. 16 With some of the wood he makes a fire;
he roasts meat, eats it, and is satisfied. He
warms himself and says, "How nice and
warm! What a beautiful fire!" 17 The rest of
the wood he makes into an idol, and then he
bows down and worships it. He prays to it
and says, "You are my god—save me!"
18 Such people are too stupid to know
what they are doing. They close their eyes
and their minds to the truth. 19 The maker of
idols hasn't the wit or the sense to say,
"Some of the wood I burned up. I baked
some bread on the coals, and I roasted meat
and ate it. And the rest of the wood I made
into an idol. Here I am bowing down to a
block of wood!"
20 It makes as much sense[r] as eating ashes.
His foolish ideas have so misled him that he
is beyond help. He won't admit to himself
that the idol he holds in his hand is not a
god at all.

Bowing down to a block of wood (44:19)

The LORD, the Creator and Savior

21 The LORD says,
"Israel, remember this;
remember that you are my servant.
I created you to be my servant,
and I will never forget you.
22 I have swept your sins away like a cloud.
Come back to me; I am the one who
saves you."

[q] **44:7** *Verse 7 in Hebrew is unclear.* [r] **44:20** It makes as much sense; *or* It will do him as much good.
44:6 Isa 48:12; Rev 1:17; 2:8; 22:13 **44:15** Wis 13:11–19

The idol he holds in his hand is not a god at all. (44:20)

[23]Shout for joy, you heavens!
Shout, deep places of the earth!
Shout for joy, mountains, and every tree of the forest!
The LORD has shown his greatness
by saving his people Israel.

[24]"I am the LORD, your savior;
I am the one who created you.
I am the LORD, the Creator of all things.
I alone stretched out the heavens;
when I made the earth, no one helped me.
[25]I make fools of fortunetellers
and frustrate the predictions of astrologers.
The words of the wise I refute
and show that their wisdom is foolishness.
[26]But when my servant makes a prediction,
when I send a messenger to reveal my plans,
I make those plans and predictions come true.
I tell Jerusalem that people will live there again,
and the cities of Judah that they will be rebuilt.
Those cities will rise from the ruins.
[27]With a word of command I dry up the ocean.
[28]I say to Cyrus, 'You are the one who will rule for me;
you will do what I want you to do:
you will order that Jerusalem be rebuilt
and that the foundations of the Temple be laid.' "

The LORD Appoints Cyrus

45 The LORD has chosen Cyrus to be king.
He has appointed him to conquer nations;
he sends him to strip kings of their power;
the LORD will open the gates of cities for him.
To Cyrus the LORD says,
[2]"I myself will prepare your way,
leveling mountains and hills.
I will break down bronze gates
and smash their iron bars.
[3]I will give you treasures from dark, secret places;
then you will know that I am the LORD
and that the God of Israel has called you by name.
[4]I appoint you to help my servant Israel,
the people that I have chosen.
I have given you great honor,
although you do not know me.

[5]"I am the LORD; there is no other god.
I will give you the strength you need,
although you do not know me.
[6]I do this so that everyone
from one end of the world to the other
may know that I am the LORD
and that there is no other god.
[7]I create both light and darkness;
I bring both blessing and disaster.
I, the LORD, do all these things.

44:25 1 Cor 1:20 **44:28** 2 Chr 36:23; Ezra 1:2

Isaiah ridicules people who bow down in worship to idols. Are you bowing down to things like clothes, games, and music?

8 I will send victory from the sky like rain;
the earth will open to receive it
and will blossom with freedom and justice.
I, the LORD, will make this happen."

The LORD of Creation and History

9 Does a clay pot dare argue with its maker,
a pot that is like all the others?
Does the clay ask the potter what he is doing?
Does the pot complain that its maker has no skill?
10 Do we dare say to our parents,
"Why did you make me like this?"
11 The LORD, the holy God of Israel,
the one who shapes the future, says:
"You have no right to question me about my children
or to tell me what I ought to do!
12 I am the one who made the earth
and created human beings to live there.
By my power I stretched out the heavens;
I control the sun, the moon, and the stars.
13 I myself have stirred Cyrus to action
to fulfill my purpose and put things right.
I will straighten out every road that he travels.
He will rebuild my city, Jerusalem,
and set my captive people free.
No one has hired him or bribed him to do this."
The LORD Almighty has spoken.
14 The LORD says to Israel,
"The wealth of Egypt and Ethiopia[s] will be yours,
and the tall men of Seba will be your slaves;
they will follow you in chains.
They will bow down to you and confess,
'God is with you—he alone is God.
15 The God of Israel, who saves his people,
is a God who conceals himself.
16 Those who make idols will all be ashamed;
all of them will be disgraced.
17 But Israel is saved by the LORD,
and her victory lasts forever;
her people will never be disgraced.' "

18 The LORD created the heavens—
he is the one who is God!
He formed and made the earth—
he made it firm and lasting.
He did not make it a desolate waste,
but a place for people to live.
It is he who says, "I am the LORD,
and there is no other god.
19 I have not spoken in secret
or kept my purpose hidden.
I did not require the people of Israel
to look for me in a desolate waste.
I am the LORD, and I speak the truth;
I make known what is right."

The LORD of the World and the Idols of Babylon

20 The LORD says,
"Come together, people of the nations,
all who survive the fall of the empire;
present yourselves for the trial!
The people who parade with their idols of wood
and pray to gods that cannot save them—
those people know nothing at all!
21 Come and present your case in court;
let the defendants consult one another.
Who predicted long ago what would happen?
Was it not I, the LORD, the God who saves his people?
There is no other god.

[s] **45:14** *Hebrew* Cush: *Cush is the ancient name of the extensive territory south of the First Cataract of the Nile River. This region was called Ethiopia in Graeco-Roman times, and included within its borders most of modern Sudan and some of present-day Ethiopia (Abyssinia).*
45:9 Isa 29:16; Rom 9:20

Isaiah, chapter 45, contains the famous image of God as the potter and us as the clay. What would you like to ask God about how you were created?

22 "Turn to me now and be saved,
people all over the world!
I am the only God there is.
23 My promise is true,
and it will not be changed.
I solemnly promise by all that I am:
Everyone will come and kneel before me
and vow to be loyal to me.
24 "They will say that only through me
are victory and strength to be found;
but all who hate me will suffer disgrace.
25 I, the LORD, will rescue all the descendants of Jacob,
and they will give me praise.

46 "This is the end for Babylon's gods!
Bel and Nebo once were worshiped,
but now they are loaded on donkeys,
a burden for the backs of tired animals.
2 The idols cannot save themselves;
they are captured and carried away.
This is the end for Babylon's gods!

The idols cannot save themselves. (46:2)

3 "Listen to me, descendants of Jacob,
all who are left of my people.
I have cared for you from the time you were born.
4 I am your God and will take care of you
until you are old and your hair is gray.
I made you and will care for you;
I will give you help and rescue you.
5 "To whom will you compare me?" says the LORD.
"Is there anyone else like me?
6 People open their purses and pour out gold;
they weigh out silver on the scales.
They hire a goldsmith to make a god;
then they bow down and worship it.
7 They lift it to their shoulders and carry it;
they put it in place, and there it stands,
unable to move from where it is.
If any pray to it, it cannot answer
or save them from disaster.
8 "Remember this, you sinners;
consider what I have done.
9 Remember what happened long ago;
acknowledge that I alone am God
and that there is no one else like me.
10 From the beginning I predicted the outcome;
long ago I foretold what would happen.
I said that my plans would never fail,
that I would do everything I intended to do.
11 I am calling a man to come from the east;[t]
he will swoop down like a hawk
and accomplish what I have planned.
I have spoken, and it will be done.
12 "Listen to me, you stubborn people
who think that victory is far away.
13 I am bringing the day of victory near—
it is not far away at all.
My triumph will not be delayed.
I will save Jerusalem
and bring honor to Israel there."

Judgment on Babylon

47 The LORD says,
"Babylon, come down from your throne,
and sit in the dust on the ground.
You were once like a virgin, a city unconquered,
but you are soft and delicate no longer!
You are now a slave!
2 Turn the millstone! Grind the flour!
Off with your veil! Strip off your fine clothes!
Lift up your skirts to cross the streams![u]
3 People will see you naked;
they will see you humbled and shamed.

[t] **46:11** A MAN TO COME FROM THE EAST: *See 41:2.* [u] **47:2** CROSS THE STREAMS: *This probably refers to going into exile.*

45:23 Rom 14:11; Phil 2:10, 11 **47:1–15** Isa 13:1—14:23; Jer 50:1—51:64

Live it!

Hocus Pocus

Hocus Pocus! Your room is clean. Hocus Pocus! You get an A on a test. Hocus Pocus! Someone gets well.

Wouldn't it be nice to have a magic spell that works that easily? Some books and movies portray worlds where magic is used to make life easier. But, of course, those books are fictional. There is no easy or magical way out of work or life's problems. The Babylonians thought magic spells would work for them. Isaiah's words remind us that magic is really powerless and that the real power lies with God.

Reading novels for fun is fine, even if they contain magical worlds. It can be fun to read about magic and dragons and other fantastic things. Just remember that it is all fiction. *God,* not magic spells, is the only source of life and real freedom.

— Isaiah 47:11–15

I will take vengeance, and no one will
stop me."
4 The holy God of Israel sets us free—
his name is the LORD Almighty.
5 The LORD says to Babylon,
"Sit in silence and darkness;
no more will they call you the queen
of nations!
6 I was angry with my people;
I treated them as no longer mine:
I put them in your power,
and you showed them no mercy;
even the aged you treated harshly.
7 You thought you would always be a
queen,
and did not take these things to heart
or think how it all would end.
8 "Listen to this, you lover of pleasure,
you that think you are safe and secure.
You claim you are as great as God—
that there is no one else like you.
You thought that you would never be a
widow
or suffer the loss of your children.
9 But in a moment, in a single day,
both of these things will happen.
In spite of all the magic you use,
you will lose your husband and
children.
10 "You felt sure of yourself in your evil;
you thought that no one could see you.
Your wisdom and knowledge led you
astray,
and you said to yourself, 'I am God—
there is no one else like me.'
11 Disaster will come upon you,
and none of your magic can stop it.
Ruin will come on you suddenly—
ruin you never dreamed of!
12 Keep all your magic spells and charms;
you have used them since you were
young.
Perhaps they will be of some help to you;
perhaps you can frighten your enemies.
13 You are powerless in spite of the advice
you get.
Let your astrologers come forward and
save you—
those people who study the stars,
who map out the zones of the heavens
and tell you from month to month
what[v] is going to happen to you.
14 "They will be like bits of straw,
and a fire will burn them up!
They will not even be able to save
themselves—
the flames will be too hot for them,
not a cozy fire to warm themselves by.
15 That is all the good they will do you—
those astrologers you've consulted all
your life.

[v] **47:13** *Some ancient translations* what; *Hebrew* from what.

47:8, 9 Rev 18:7, 8

Those people who study the stars (47:13)

They all will leave you and go their own
way,
and none will be left to save you."

God Is LORD of the Future

48 Listen to this, people of Israel,
you that are descended from Judah:
You swear by the name of the LORD
and claim to worship the God of Israel—
but you don't mean a word you say.
2 And yet you are proud to say
that you are citizens of the holy city
and that you depend on Israel's God,
whose name is the LORD Almighty.

3 The LORD says to Israel,
"Long ago I predicted what would take
place;
then suddenly I made it happen.
4 I knew that you would prove to be
stubborn,
as rigid as iron and unyielding as bronze.
5 And so I predicted your future long ago,
announcing events before they took
place,
to keep you from claiming
that your idols and images made them
happen.
6 "All I foretold has now taken place;
you have to admit my predictions were
right.
Now I will tell you of new things to
come,
events that I did not reveal before.
7 Only now am I making them happen;
nothing like this took place in the past.
If it had, you would claim that you knew
all about it.
8 I knew that you couldn't be trusted,
that you have always been known as a
rebel.
That is why you never heard of this at all,
why no word of it ever came to your
ears.

9 "In order that people will praise my
name,
I am holding my anger in check;
I am keeping it back and will not
destroy you.
10 I have tested you in the fire of suffering,
as silver is refined in a furnace.
But I have found that you are worthless.
11 What I do is done for my own sake—
I will not let my name be dishonored
or let anyone else share the glory
that should be mine and mine alone."

Cyrus, the LORD's Chosen Leader

12 The LORD says,
"Listen to me, Israel, the people I have
called!
I am God, the first, the last, the only
God!
13 My hands made the earth's foundations
and spread the heavens out.
When I summon earth and sky,
they come at once and present
themselves.

14 "Assemble and listen, all of you!
None of the gods could predict
that the man I have chosen would
attack Babylon;
he will do what I want him to do.

48:12 Isa 44:6; Rev 1:17; 22:13

King Cyrus of Persia conquered Babylon in 539 BC. He let the Israelites who were in captivity return to rebuild Jerusalem and the Temple.

15 I am the one who spoke and called him;
I led him out and gave him success.

16 "Now come close to me and hear what I say.
From the beginning I have spoken openly
and have always made my words come true."
(Now the Sovereign LORD has given me his power and sent me.)

The LORD's Plan for His People

17 The holy God of Israel,
the LORD who saves you, says:
"I am the LORD your God,
the one who wants to teach you for your own good
and direct you in the way you should go.

18 "If only you had listened to my commands!
Then blessings would have flowed for you
like a stream that never goes dry.
Victory would have come to you
like the waves that roll on the shore.
19 Your descendants would be as numerous
as grains of sand,
and I would have made sure they were never destroyed."

20 Go out from Babylon, go free!
Shout the news gladly; make it known everywhere:
"The LORD has saved his servant Israel!"
21 When the LORD led his people through a hot, dry desert,
they did not suffer from thirst.
He made water come from a rock for them;
he split the rock open, and water flowed out.

22 "There is no safety for sinners," says the LORD.

Israel, A Light to the Nations

49 Listen to me, distant nations,
you people who live far away!
Before I was born, the LORD chose me
and appointed me to be his servant.
2 He made my words as sharp as a sword.
With his own hand he protected me.[w]
He made me like an arrow,
sharp and ready for use.
3 He said to me, "Israel, you are my servant;
because of you, people will praise me."

4 I said, "I have worked, but how hopeless it is!
I have used up my strength, but have accomplished nothing."
Yet I can trust the LORD to defend my cause;
he will reward me for what I do.

5 Before I was born, the LORD appointed me;
he made me his servant to bring back his people,
to bring back the scattered people of Israel.

He made water come from a rock. (48:21)

[w] **49:2** With his own hand . . . me; *or* He kept me hidden in his hand.

48:20 Rev 18:4 **48:22** Isa 57:21 **49:1** Jer 1:5 **49:2** Heb 4:12; Rev 1:16

"Before I was born, the LORD chose me and appointed me to be his servant" *(Isaiah 49:1)*.

The LORD gives me honor;
he is the source of my strength.

6 The LORD said to me,
"I have a greater task for you, my servant.
Not only will you restore to greatness
the people of Israel who have survived,
but I will also make you a light to the
nations—
so that all the world may be saved."

7 Israel's holy God and savior says
to the one who is deeply despised,
who is hated by the nations
and is the servant of rulers:
"Kings will see you released
and will rise to show their respect;
princes also will see it,
and they will bow low to honor you."

This will happen because the LORD has
chosen his servant;
the holy God of Israel keeps his promises.

The Restoration of Jerusalem

8 The LORD says to his people,
"When the time comes to save you, I will
show you favor
and answer your cries for help.
I will guard and protect you
and through you make a covenant with
all peoples.
I will let you settle once again
in your land that is now laid waste.
9 I will say to the prisoners, 'Go free!'
and to those who are in darkness,
'Come out to the light!'
They will be like sheep that graze on the
hills;
10 they will never be hungry or thirsty.
Sun and desert heat will not hurt
them,
for they will be led by one who loves
them.
He will lead them to springs of water.

11 "I will make a highway across the
mountains
and prepare a road for my people to
travel.

Study it!

The Suffering Servant

Have you found many things in Isaiah that remind you of Jesus? (See "Stories About Jesus?" on page 1016.) As part of your search, you definitely want to look at the Servant Songs (they can be read in Isaiah 42:1–4; 49:1–6; 50:4–9 and 52:13—53:12). These are verses in which the prophet tells about an unnamed servant of God. Isaiah prophesies that this servant brings about God's justice, but that he will also suffer. His suffering will not be due to his own sins but those of others. We are told that he will suffer for us, even to death.

Remember that Isaiah was writing hundreds of years before the birth of Jesus. So it is remarkable that in these verses about the suffering servant, we see so much that reminds us of Jesus. When Christians read this passage, we see Jesus as that unnamed servant. The writer tells us that the servant Jesus was appointed by God before he was even born. Knowing that Jesus was born, suffered, and died for us helps us know just how much we are loved.

— Isaiah 49:1–6

12 My people will come from far away,
from the north and the west,
and from Aswan[x] in the south."

13 Sing, heavens! Shout for joy, earth!
Let the mountains burst into song!
The LORD will comfort his people;
he will have pity on his suffering
people.

[x] **49:12** ASWAN: *A city in southern Egypt, where a large Jewish community had settled.*

49:6 a Isa 42:6; Lk 2:32; Acts 26:23; **b** Acts 13:47 **49:8** 2 Cor 6:2 **49:10** Rev 7:16, 17

14 But the people of Jerusalem said,
"The LORD has abandoned us!
He has forgotten us."
15 So the LORD answers,
"Can a woman forget her own baby
and not love the child she bore?
Even if a mother should forget her child,
I will never forget you.
16 Jerusalem, I can never forget you!
I have written your name on the palms
of my hands.
17 "Those who will rebuild you are coming
soon,
and those who destroyed you will
leave.
18 Look around and see what is happening!
Your people are assembling—they are
coming home!
As surely as I am the living God,
you will be proud of your people,
as proud as a bride is of her jewels.

19 "Your country was ruined and desolate—
but now it will be too small
for those who are coming to live there.
And those who left you in ruins
will be far removed from you.
20 Your people who were born in exile
will one day say to you,
'This land is too small—
we need more room to live in!'
21 Then you will say to yourself,
'Who bore all these children for me?
I lost my children and could have no
more.
I was exiled and driven away—
who brought these children up?
I was left all alone—
where did these children come
from?' "

22 The Sovereign LORD says to his people:
"I will signal to the nations,
and they will bring your children
home.
23 Kings will be like fathers to you;
queens will be like mothers.
They will bow low before you and honor
you;
they will humbly show their respect for
you.
Then you will know that I am the LORD;
no one who waits for my help will be
disappointed."

24 Can you take away a soldier's loot?
Can you rescue the prisoners of a
tyrant?
25 The LORD replies,
"That is just what is going to happen.
The soldier's prisoners will be taken away,
and the tyrant's loot will be seized.
I will fight against whoever fights you,
and I will rescue your children.
26 I will make your oppressors kill each
other;
they will be drunk with murder and
rage.
Then all people will know that I am the
LORD,
the one who saves you and sets you free.
They will know that I am Israel's
powerful God."

50 The LORD says,
"Do you think I sent my people
away
like a man who divorces his wife?
Where, then, are the papers of divorce?
Do you think I sold you into captivity
like a man who sells his children as
slaves?
No, you went away captive because of
your sins;
you were sent away because of your
crimes.

2 "Why did my people fail to respond
when I went to them to save them?
Why did they not answer when I called?
Am I too weak to save them?
I can dry up the sea with a command
and turn rivers into a desert,
so that the fish in them die for lack of
water.
3 I can make the sky turn dark,
as if it were in mourning for the dead."

The Obedience of the LORD's Servant

4 The Sovereign LORD has taught me what
to say,

49:22 Bar 5:6 **50:1** Bar 4:6

so that I can strengthen the weary.
Every morning he makes me eager
to hear what he is going to teach me.
5 The LORD has given me understanding,
and I have not rebelled
or turned away from him.
6 I bared my back to those who beat me.
I did not stop them when they insulted
me,
when they pulled out the hairs of my
beard
and spit in my face.
7 But their insults cannot hurt me
because the Sovereign LORD gives me
help.
I brace myself to endure them.
I know that I will not be disgraced,
8 for God is near,
and he will prove me innocent.
Does anyone dare bring charges against
me?
Let us go to court together!
Let him bring his accusation!
9 The Sovereign LORD himself defends
me—
who, then, can prove me guilty?
All my accusers will disappear;
they will vanish like moth-eaten cloth.

10 All of you that honor the LORD
and obey the words of his servant,
the path you walk may be dark indeed,
but trust in the LORD, rely on your
God.
11 All of you that plot to destroy others
will be destroyed by your own plots.
The LORD himself will make this happen;
you will suffer a miserable fate.

Words of Comfort to Jerusalem

51 The LORD says,
"Listen to me, you that want to be
saved,
you that come to me for help.
Think of the rock from which you came,
the quarry from which you were cut.
2 Think of your ancestor, Abraham,
and of Sarah, from whom you are
descended.
When I called Abraham, he was childless,
but I blessed him and gave him children;
I made his descendants numerous.

3 "I will show compassion to Jerusalem,
to all who live in her ruins.
Though her land is a desert, I will make it
a garden,
like the garden I planted in Eden.
Joy and gladness will be there,
and songs of praise and thanks to me.

4 "Listen to me, my people,
listen to what I say:
I give my teaching to the nations;
my laws will bring them light.
5 I will come quickly and save them;
the time of my victory is near.
I myself will rule over the nations.
Distant lands wait for me to come;
they wait with hope for me to save
them.
6 Look up at the heavens; look at the earth!
The heavens will disappear like smoke;
the earth will wear out like old
clothing,
and all its people will die like flies.
But the deliverance I bring will last
forever;
my victory will be final.

7 "Listen to me, you that know what is
right,
who have my teaching fixed in your
hearts.
Do not be afraid when people taunt and
insult you;
8 they will vanish like moth-eaten
clothing!
But the deliverance I bring will last
forever;
my victory will endure for all time."

9 Wake up, LORD, and help us!
Use your power and save us;
use it as you did in ancient times.

50:6 Mt 26:67; Mk 14:65 **50:8, 9** Rom 8:33, 34

Isaiah 50:4–9 is called a suffering servant song. Who does it remind you of?

It was you that cut the sea monster
Rahab[y] to pieces.
10 It was you also who dried up the sea
and made a path through the water,
so that those you were saving could
cross.
11 Those whom you have rescued
will reach Jerusalem with gladness,
singing and shouting for joy.
They will be happy forever,
forever free from sorrow and grief.

12 The LORD says,
"I am the one who strengthens you.
Why should you fear mortals,
who are no more enduring than
grass?
13 Have you forgotten the LORD who made
you,
who stretched out the heavens
and laid the earth's foundations?
Why should you live in constant fear
of the fury of those who oppress
you,
of those who are ready to destroy
you?
Their fury can no longer touch you.
14 Those who are prisoners will soon be set
free;
they will live a long life
and have all the food they need.

15 "I am the LORD your God;
I stir up the sea
and make its waves roar.
My name is the LORD Almighty!
16 I stretched out[z] the heavens
and laid the earth's foundations;
I say to Jerusalem, 'You are my people!
I have given you my teaching,
and I protect you with my hand.' "

The End of Jerusalem's Suffering

17 Jerusalem, wake up!
Rouse yourself and get up!
You have drunk the cup of punishment
that the LORD in his anger gave you to
drink;
you drank it down, and it made you
stagger.
18 There is no one to lead you,
no one among your people
to take you by the hand.

19 A double disaster has fallen on you:
your land has been devastated by war,
and your people have starved.
There is no one to show you sympathy.
20 At the corner of every street
your people collapse from weakness;
they are like deer caught in a hunter's
net.
They have felt the force of God's anger.

21 You suffering people of Jerusalem,
you that stagger as though you were
drunk,
22 the LORD your God defends you and says,
"I am taking away the cup
that I gave you in my anger.
You will no longer have to drink
the wine that makes you stagger.
23 I will give it to those who oppressed you,
to those who made you lie down in
the streets
and trampled on you as if you were
dirt."

God Will Rescue Jerusalem

52 Jerusalem, be strong and great again!
Holy city of God, clothe yourself
with splendor!
The heathen will never enter your gates
again.
2 Shake yourself free, Jerusalem!
Rise from the dust and sit on your
throne!
Undo the chains that bind you,
captive people of Zion!

3 The Sovereign LORD says to his people,

[y] **51:9** RAHAB: *A legendary sea monster, which represented the forces of chaos and evil, was sometimes a symbol of Egypt.*
[z] **51:16** *One ancient translation* stretched out; *Hebrew* planted.
51:17 Rev 14:10; 16:19 **52:1** Rev 21:2, 27

Do you remember what happened to Sarah and Abraham *(see Isaiah 51:2)*? **If not, read Genesis 17:19–22 and 21:1–8.**

"When you became slaves, no money was
paid for you; in the same way nothing will
be paid to set you free. 4When you went to
live in Egypt as foreigners, you did so of
your own free will; Assyria, however, took
you away by force and paid nothing for you.
5And now in Babylonia the same thing has
happened: you are captives, and nothing was
paid for you. Those who rule over you boast
and brag and constantly show contempt for
me. 6In time to come you will acknowledge
that I am God and that I have spoken to
you."

7How wonderful it is to see
a messenger coming across the mountains,
bringing good news, the news of peace!
He announces victory and says to Zion,
"Your God is king!"

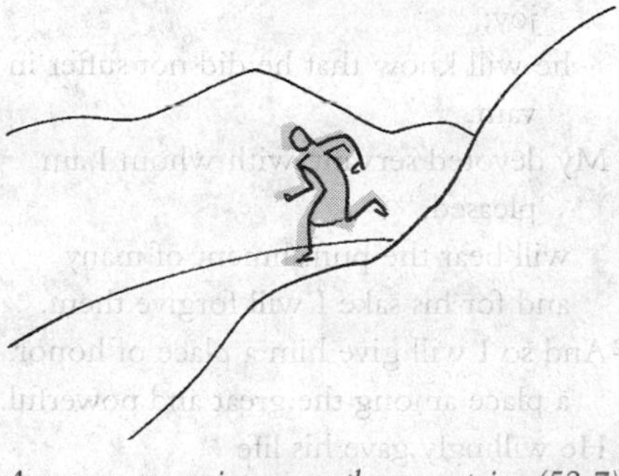

A messenger coming across the mountains (52:7)

8Those who guard the city are shouting,
shouting together for joy.
They can see with their own eyes
the return of the LORD to Zion.

9Break into shouts of joy,
you ruins of Jerusalem!
The LORD will rescue his city
and comfort his people.
10The LORD will use his holy power;
he will save his people,
and all the world will see it.

Pray it!

Beautiful Feet?

The shoes come off
Revealing skin
Tanned a dark brown
With light stripes from sandal straps
Heels cracked and filled with dust
Toenails hiding more brown dirt
These are the beautiful feet of Jesus
The one who came to us
Born simply
Living humbly
Spreading peace
Preaching freedom
Sharing meals
Healing hearts
Loving friends and enemies
Serving all
Arms wide open
Even on the cross
Dying for all
I am thankful for
Those beautiful feet

— Isaiah 52

11Be sure to leave Babylonia,
all you that carry the Temple equipment.
Touch no forbidden thing;[a]
keep yourselves holy and leave.
12This time you will not have to leave in a hurry;
you will not be trying to escape.
The LORD your God will lead you
and protect you on every side.

The Suffering Servant

13The LORD says,
"My servant will succeed in his task;
he will be highly honored.[b]

[a] **52:11** FORBIDDEN THING: *Any object that was considered ritually unclean.* [b] **52:13** he will be highly honored; *or* he will be restored to greatness and honor.

52:5 Rom 2:24 **52:7** Nah 1:15; Rom 10:15; Eph 6:15 **52:11** 2 Cor 6:17

14 Many people were shocked when they
saw him;
he was so disfigured that he hardly
looked human.
15 But now many nations will marvel at him,
and kings will be speechless with
amazement.
They will see and understand
something they had never known."

53 The people reply,
"Who would have believed what we
now report?
Who could have seen the LORD's hand
in this?
2 It was the will of the LORD that his servant
grow like a plant taking root in dry
ground.
He had no dignity or beauty
to make us take notice of him.
There was nothing attractive about him,
nothing that would draw us to him.
3 We despised him and rejected him;
he endured suffering and pain.
No one would even look at him—
we ignored him as if he were nothing.

4 "But he endured the suffering that should
have been ours,
the pain that we should have borne.
All the while we thought that his
suffering
was punishment sent by God.
5 But because of our sins he was wounded,
beaten because of the evil we did.
We are healed by the punishment he
suffered,
made whole by the blows he received.
6 All of us were like sheep that were lost,
each of us going his own way.
But the LORD made the punishment fall
on him,
the punishment all of us deserved.

7 "He was treated harshly, but endured it
humbly;
he never said a word.
Like a lamb about to be slaughtered,
like a sheep about to be sheared,
he never said a word.
8 He was arrested and sentenced and led off
to die,
and no one cared about his fate.
He was put to death for the sins of our
people.
9 He was placed in a grave with those who
are evil,
he was buried with the rich,
even though he had never committed a
crime
or ever told a lie."

10 The LORD says,
"It was my will that he should suffer;
his death was a sacrifice to bring
forgiveness.
And so he will see his descendants;
he will live a long life,
and through him my purpose will
succeed.
11 After a life of suffering, he will again have
joy;
he will know that he did not suffer in
vain.
My devoted servant, with whom I am
pleased,
will bear the punishment of many
and for his sake I will forgive them.
12 And so I will give him a place of honor,
a place among the great and powerful.
He willingly gave his life
and shared the fate of evil men.
He took the place of many sinners
and prayed that they might be
forgiven."[c]

He never said a word. (53:7)

[c] **53:12** prayed that they might be forgiven; *or* suffered the punishment they deserved.

52:15 Rom 15:21 **53:1** Rom 10:16; Jn 12:38 **53:4** Mt 8:17 **53:5** 1 Pet 2:24 **53:6** 1 Pet 2:25
53:7 Rev 5:6 **53:7, 8** Acts 8:32, 33 **53:9** 1 Pet 2:22 **53:12** Mk 15:28; Lk 22:37

The LORD's Love for Israel

54 Jerusalem, you have been like a
childless woman,
but now you can sing and shout for
joy.
Now you will have more children
than a woman whose husband never
left her.
2 Make the tent you live in larger;
lengthen its ropes and strengthen the
pegs!
3 You will extend your boundaries on all
sides;
your people will get back the land
that the other nations now occupy.
Cities now deserted will be filled with
people.

4 Do not be afraid—you will not be
disgraced again;
you will not be humiliated.
You will forget your unfaithfulness as a
young wife,
and your desperate loneliness as a
widow.
5 Your Creator will be like a husband to
you—
the LORD Almighty is his name.
The holy God of Israel will save you—
he is the ruler of all the world.

6 Israel, you are like a young wife,
deserted by her husband and deeply
distressed.
But the LORD calls you back to him and
says:
7 "For one brief moment I left you;
with deep love I will take you back.
8 I turned away angry for only a moment,
but I will show you my love forever."
So says the LORD who saves you.

9 "In the time of Noah I promised
never again to flood the earth.
Now I promise not to be angry with you
again;
I will not reprimand or punish you.

Study it!

Making Connections

If your history teacher talks about a TV show you watch, you will probably listen more carefully to what he or she is talking about. The prophecies of Isaiah also mention popular stories of the Israelite people. Throughout Isaiah there are references to other parts of the Old Testament. In chapter 51 the writer refers to Eden and to Sarah and Abraham. In chapter 54 Isaiah mentions the Covenant God made with Noah after the flood. By using these stories, the prophet encouraged the people to listen closely and make connections with their history.

Is there anyone you know who helps you make the connections between the Bible's stories and our lives today?

— Isaiah 54:9

10 The mountains and hills may crumble,
but my love for you will never end;
I will keep forever my promise of
peace."
So says the LORD who loves you.

The Future Jerusalem

11 The LORD says,
"O Jerusalem, you suffering, helpless
city,
with no one to comfort you,
I will rebuild your foundations with
precious stones.

54:1 Gal 4:27 **54:9** Gen 9:8–17 **54:10** Jdt 16:15 **54:11, 12** Rev 21:18–21 **54:11** Tob 13:16, 17

"We are healed by the punishment he suffered, / made whole by the blows he received" *(Isaiah 53:5)*.

12 I will build your towers with rubies,
your gates with stones that glow like fire,
and the wall around you with jewels.

13 "I myself will teach your people
and give them prosperity and peace.
14 Justice and right will make you strong.
You will be safe from oppression and terror.
15 Whoever attacks you,
does it without my consent;
whoever fights against you will fall.

16 "I create the blacksmith,
who builds a fire and forges weapons.
I also create the soldier,
who uses the weapons to kill.
17 But no weapon will be able to hurt you;
you will have an answer for all who accuse you.
I will defend my servants
and give them victory."

The LORD has spoken.

God's Offer of Mercy

55 The LORD says,
"Come, everyone who is thirsty—
here is water!
Come, you that have no money—
buy grain and eat!
Come! Buy wine and milk—
it will cost you nothing!
2 Why spend money on what does not satisfy?
Why spend your wages and still be hungry?
Listen to me and do what I say,
and you will enjoy the best food of all.

3 "Listen now, my people, and come to me;
come to me, and you will have life!
I will make a lasting covenant with you
and give you the blessings I promised to David.
4 I made him a leader and commander of nations,
and through him I showed them my power.
5 Now you will summon foreign nations;
at one time they did not know you,
but now they will come running to join you!
I, the LORD your God, the holy God of Israel,
will make all this happen;
I will give you honor and glory."

6 Turn to the LORD and pray to him,
now that he is near.
7 Let the wicked leave their way of life
and change their way of thinking.
Let them turn to the LORD, our God;
he is merciful and quick to forgive.
8 "My thoughts," says the LORD, "are not like yours,
and my ways are different from yours.
9 As high as the heavens are above the earth,
so high are my ways and thoughts above yours.

10 "My word is like the snow and the rain
that come down from the sky to water the earth.
They make the crops grow
and provide seed for planting and food to eat.
11 So also will be the word that I speak—
it will not fail to do what I plan for it;
it will do everything I send it to do.

12 "You will leave Babylon with joy;
you will be led out of the city in peace.
The mountains and hills will burst into singing,
and the trees will shout for joy.
13 Cypress trees will grow where now there are briers;
myrtle trees will come up in place of thorns.
This will be a sign that will last forever,
a reminder of what I, the LORD, have done."

54:13 Jn 6:45 **55:1** Rev 21:6; 22:17 **55:2** Sir 24:19–22 **55:3** Acts 13:34 **55:10** 2 Cor 9:10

"My thoughts," says the LORD, "are not like yours. . . . / As high as the heavens are above the earth, / so high are my ways and thoughts above yours" *(Isaiah 55:8–9)*.

God's People Will Include All Nations

56 The LORD says to his people, "Do what is just and right, for soon I will save you. 2I will bless those who always observe the Sabbath and do not misuse it. I will bless those who do nothing evil."

3A foreigner who has joined the LORD's people should not say, "The LORD will not let me worship with his people."

A man who has been castrated should never think that because he cannot have children, he can never be part of God's people. 4The LORD says to such a man, "If you honor me by observing the Sabbath and if you do what pleases me and faithfully keep my covenant, 5then your name will be remembered in my Temple and among my people longer than if you had sons and daughters. You will never be forgotten."

6And the LORD says to those foreigners who become part of his people, who love him and serve him, who observe the Sabbath and faithfully keep his covenant: 7"I will bring you to Zion, my sacred hill,[d] give you joy in my house of prayer, and accept the sacrifices you offer on my altar. My Temple will be called a house of prayer for the people of all nations."

8The Sovereign LORD, who has brought his people Israel home from exile, has promised that he will bring still other people to join them.

Israel's Leaders Are Condemned

9The LORD has told the foreign nations to come like wild animals and devour his people. 10He says, "All the leaders, who are supposed to warn my people, are blind! They know nothing. They are like watch dogs that don't bark—they only lie around and dream. How they love to sleep! 11They are like greedy dogs that never get enough. These leaders have no understanding. They each do as they please and seek their own advantage. 12'Let's get some wine,' these drunkards say, 'and drink all we can hold! Tomorrow will be even better than today!' "

Live it!

All Are Welcome

It really doesn't matter who you are or where you are from. It doesn't matter if you are married or single, if you are rich or poor. It only matters if you love God and keep the Covenant God made with us. God made all of us, equally. God wants all of us—young and old, male and female, foreigner and native—to be included and united.

Read Isaiah 56:1–8. It is pretty clear what God says—all are welcome. If you have been choosing your friends based on where they are from or how they look, think again. Maybe it is time to rethink how you pick your friends and treat outsiders. If you already do a good job of including everyone in your circle of friends, good for you!

— Isaiah 56:1–8

How they love to sleep! (56:10)

Israel's Idolatry Is Condemned

57 Good people die, and no one understands or even cares. But when they die, no calamity can hurt them. 2Those who live good lives find peace and rest in death.

3Come here to be judged, you sinners! You are no better than sorcerers, adulterers, and

[d] **56:7** SACRED HILL: *See 2:3.*

56:4, 5 Wis 3:14, 15 **56:7** Mt 21:13; Mk 11:17; Lk 19:46

prostitutes. 4Who are you making fun of?
Who are you liars jeering at? 5You worship
the fertility gods by having sex under those
sacred trees of yours. You offer your children
as sacrifices in the rocky caves near stream
beds. 6You take smooth stones from there and
worship them as gods. You pour out wine as
offerings to them and bring them grain offer-
ings. Do you think I am pleased with all this?
7You go to the high mountains to offer sacri-
fices and have sex. 8You set up your obscene
idols just inside your front doors. You forsake
me; you take off your clothes and climb in
your large beds with your lovers, whom you
pay to sleep with you. And there you satisfy
your lust. 9You put on your perfumes and
ointments and go to worship the god
Molech. To find gods to worship, you send
messengers far and wide, even to the world of
the dead. 10You wear yourselves out looking
for other gods, but you never give up. You
think your obscene idols give you strength,
and so you never grow weak.

11The LORD says, "Who are these gods
that make you afraid, so that you tell me lies
and forget me completely? Have you stopped
honoring me because I have kept silent for so
long? 12You think that what you do is right,
but I will expose your conduct, and your
idols will not be able to help you. 13When
you cry for help, let those idols of yours save
you! A puff of wind will carry them off But
those who trust in me will live in the land
and will worship me in my Temple."

God's Promise of Help and Healing

14The LORD says, "Let my people return
to me. Remove every obstacle from their
path! Build the road and make it ready!

15"I am the high and holy God, who lives
forever. I live in a high and holy place, but I
also live with people who are humble and
repentant, so that I can restore their confi-
dence and hope. 16I gave my people life, and
I will not continue to accuse them or be
angry with them forever.[e] 17I was angry
with them because of their sin and greed,
and so I punished them and abandoned
them. But they were stubborn and kept on
going their own way.

18"I have seen how they acted, but I will
heal them. I will lead them and help them,
and I will comfort those who mourn. 19I
offer peace to all, both near and far! I will
heal my people. 20But evil people are like
the restless sea, whose waves never stop
rolling in, bringing filth and muck. 21There
is no safety for sinners," says the LORD.

True Fasting

58 The LORD says, "Shout as loud as
you can! Tell my people Israel about
their sins! 2They worship me every day,
claiming that they are eager to know my
ways and obey my laws. They say they want
me to give them just laws and that they take
pleasure in worshiping me."

3The people ask, "Why should we fast if
the LORD never notices? Why should we go
without food if he pays no attention?"

The LORD says to them, "The truth is that
at the same time you fast, you pursue your
own interests and oppress your workers.
4Your fasting makes you violent, and you
quarrel and fight. Do you think this kind of
fasting will make me listen to your prayers?
5When you fast, you make yourselves suffer;
you bow your heads low like a blade of grass
and spread out sackcloth and ashes to lie on.

The kind of fasting I want is this. (58:6-7)

[e] **57:16** I gave my people . . . forever; *or* I will not continue to accuse them or be angry with them forever, for then they would die—the very people to whom I gave life.

57:19 Eph 2:17 **57:21** Isa 48:22

Catholic Connections

It Takes Two Feet

Polluted oceans, children working in sweat shops, homelessness, corrupt governments, hate crimes, and more. These are common headlines. They are also the opposite of what we as Catholics believe God wants for us. The prophets revealed God's desire that we need to work toward the common good. Working toward the common good means we try to live justly and fairly. As Isaiah prophesied, "Remove the chains of oppression and the yoke of injustice, and let the oppressed go free. Share your food with the hungry and open your homes to the homeless poor. Give clothes to those who have nothing to wear, and do not refuse to help your own relatives" (Isaiah 58:6–7).

In addition to doing direct service (such as collecting food, serving meals at shelters, giving away clothes), we also need to work for change. Working for change includes doing things that help remove the causes of hunger, poverty, and prejudice. These types of work include writing letters to challenge unjust laws or publicly protesting things that are wrong. These are the two feet of service and justice. Just like we need two feet to stay balanced and walk forward, working toward the common good takes two feet, too.

By working toward the common good, your steps of service and justice will combine with the steps of millions of other people to create a better world.

— Isaiah 58:6–7

Is that what you call fasting? Do you think I
will be pleased with that?
6"The kind of fasting I want is this:
Remove the chains of oppression and the
yoke of injustice, and let the oppressed go
free. 7Share your food with the hungry and
open your homes to the homeless poor. Give
clothes to those who have nothing to wear,
and do not refuse to help your own relatives.
8"Then my favor will shine on you like
the morning sun, and your wounds will be
quickly healed. I will always be with you to
save you; my presence will protect you on
every side. 9When you pray, I will answer
you. When you call to me, I will respond.

"If you put an end to oppression, to every
gesture of contempt, and to every evil word;
10if you give food to the hungry and satisfy
those who are in need, then the darkness
around you will turn to the brightness of
noon. 11And I will always guide you and
satisfy you with good things. I will keep you
strong and well. You will be like a garden
that has plenty of water, like a spring of
water that never goes dry. 12Your people
will rebuild what has long been in ruins,
building again on the old foundations. You
will be known as the people who rebuilt the
walls, who restored the ruined houses."

The Reward for Keeping the Sabbath

13The LORD says, "If you treat the Sab-
bath as sacred and do not pursue your own

58:7 Mt 25:34

If you want to know the kinds of sinful behaviors people performed in worshiping other gods, read Isaiah 57:3–10.

interests on that day; if you value my holy day and honor it by not traveling, working, or talking idly on that day, 14 then you will find the joy that comes from serving me. I will make you honored all over the world, and you will enjoy the land I gave to your ancestor, Jacob. I, the LORD, have spoken."

The Prophet Condemns the People's Sins

59 Don't think that the LORD is too weak to save you or too deaf to hear your call for help! 2 It is because of your sins that he doesn't hear you. It is your sins that separate you from God when you try to worship him. 3 You are guilty of lying, violence, and murder.

4 You go to court, but you do not have justice on your side. You depend on lies to win your case. You carry out your plans to hurt others. 5-6 The evil plots you make are as deadly as the eggs of a poisonous snake. Crush an egg, out comes a snake! But your plots will do you no good—they are as useless as clothing made of cobwebs! 7 You are always planning something evil, and you can hardly wait to do it. You never hesitate to murder innocent people. You leave ruin and destruction wherever you go, 8 and no one is safe when you are around. Everything you do is unjust. You follow a crooked path, and no one who walks that path will ever be safe.

The People Confess Their Sin

9 The people say, "Now we know why God does not save us from those who oppress us. We hope for light to walk by, but there is only darkness, 10 and we grope about like blind people. We stumble at noon, as if it were night, as if we were in the dark world of the dead. 11 We are frightened and distressed. We long for God to save us from oppression and wrong, but nothing happens.

12 "LORD, our crimes against you are many. Our sins accuse us. We are well aware of them all. 13 We have rebelled against you, rejected you, and refused to follow you. We have oppressed others and turned away from you. Our thoughts are false; our words are lies. 14 Justice is driven away, and right cannot come near. Truth stumbles in the public square, and honesty finds no place there. 15 There is so little honesty that those who stop doing evil find themselves the victims of crime."

The LORD Prepares to Rescue His People

The LORD has seen this, and he is displeased that there is no justice. 16 He is astonished to see that there is no one to help the oppressed. So he will use his own power to rescue them and to win the victory. 17 He will wear justice like a coat of armor and saving power like a helmet. He will clothe himself with the strong desire to set things right and to punish and avenge the wrongs that people suffer. 18 He will punish his enemies according to what they have done, even those who live in distant lands. 19 From east to west everyone will fear him and his great power. He will come like a rushing river, like a strong wind.

20 The LORD says to his people, "I will come to Jerusalem to defend you and to save all of you that turn from your sins. 21 And I make a covenant with you: I have given you my power and my teachings to be yours forever, and from now on you are to obey me and teach your children and your descendants to obey me for all time to come."

The Future Glory of Jerusalem

60 Arise, Jerusalem, and shine like the
sun;
The glory of the LORD is shining on you!
2 Other nations will be covered by
darkness,
But on you the light of the LORD will
shine;

59:7, 8 Rom 3:15–17 **59:16** Isa 63:5 **59:17** Wis 5:17–23; Eph 6:14, 17; 1 Thess 5:8 **59:20** Rom 11:26

"The LORD has seen this, and he is displeased that there is no justice. He is astonished to see that there is no one to help the oppressed" *(Isaiah 59:15–16)*.

Like a strong wind (59:19)

The brightness of his presence will be
with you.
3 Nations will be drawn to your light,
And kings to the dawning of your new
day.

4 Look around you and see what is
happening:
Your people are gathering to come home!
Your sons will come from far away;
Your daughters will be carried like
children.
5 You will see this and be filled with joy;
You will tremble with excitement.
The wealth of the nations will be brought
to you;
From across the sea their riches will
come.
6 Great caravans of camels will come, from
Midian and Ephah.
They will come from Sheba, bringing
gold and incense.
People will tell the good news of what
the LORD has done!
7 All the sheep of Kedar and Nebaioth
Will be brought to you as sacrifices
And offered on the altar to please the
LORD.

Great caravans of camels will come. (60:6)

The LORD will make his Temple more
glorious than ever.

8 What are these ships that skim along like
clouds,
Like doves returning home?
9 They are ships coming from distant lands,
Bringing God's people home.
They bring with them silver and gold
To honor the name of the LORD,
The holy God of Israel,
Who has made all nations honor his
people.

What are these ships? (60:8)

10 The LORD says to Jerusalem,
"Foreigners will rebuild your walls,
And their kings will serve you.
In my anger I punished you,
But now I will show you my favor and
mercy.
11 Day and night your gates will be open,
So that the kings of the nations
May bring you their wealth.
12 But nations that do not serve you
Will be completely destroyed.

13 "The wood of the pine, the juniper, and
the cypress,

60:4 Bar 5:5, 6 **60:11** Rev 21:25, 26

The finest wood from the forests of Lebanon (60:13)

The finest wood from the forests of Lebanon,
Will be brought to rebuild you, Jerusalem,
To make my Temple beautiful,
To make my city glorious.
14 The descendants of those who oppressed you will come
And bow low to show their respect.
All who once despised you will worship at your feet.
They will call you 'The City of the LORD,'
'Zion, the City of Israel's Holy God.'

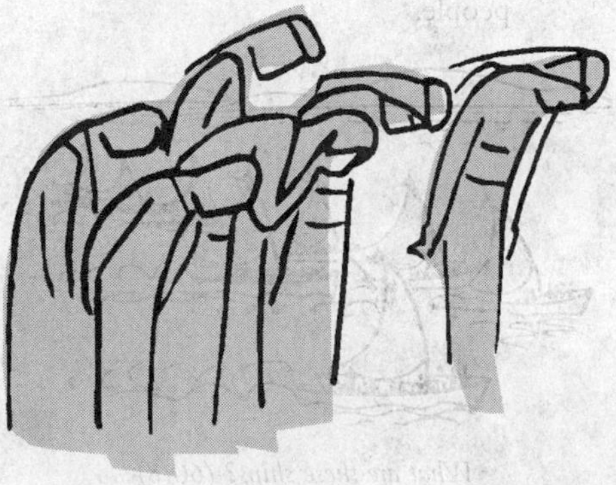

Bow low to show their respect (60:14)

15 "You will no longer be forsaken and hated,
A city deserted and desolate.
I will make you great and beautiful,
A place of joy forever and ever.
16 Nations and kings will care for you
As a mother nurses her child.
You will know that I, the LORD, have saved you,
That the mighty God of Israel sets you free.

17 "I will bring you gold instead of bronze,
Silver and bronze instead of iron and wood,
And iron instead of stone.
Your rulers will no longer oppress you;
I will make them rule with justice and peace.
18 The sounds of violence will be heard no more;
Destruction will not shatter your country again.
I will protect and defend you like a wall;
You will praise me because I have saved you.

19 "No longer will the sun be your light by day
Or the moon be your light by night;
I, the LORD, will be your eternal light;
The light of my glory will shine on you.
20 Your days of grief will come to an end.
I, the LORD, will be your eternal light,
More lasting than the sun and moon.
21 Your people will all do what is right,
And will possess the land forever.

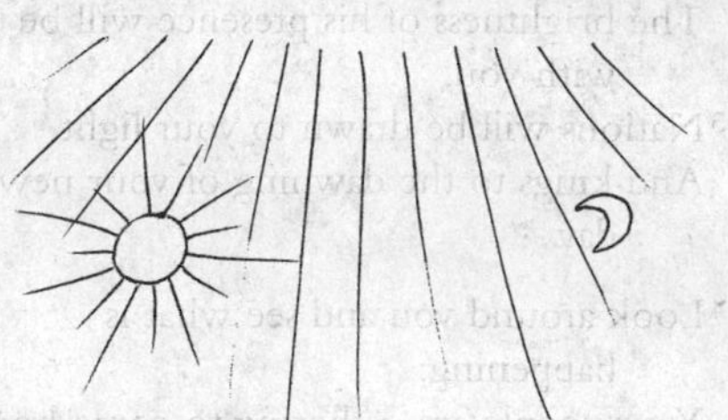

I . . . will be your eternal light. (60:19)

I planted them, I made them,
To reveal my greatness to all.
22 Even your smallest and humblest family
Will become as great as a powerful nation.
When the right time comes,
I will make this happen quickly.
I am the LORD!"

The Good News of Deliverance

61 The Sovereign LORD has filled me with his Spirit.
He has chosen me and sent me
To bring good news to the poor,
To heal the broken-hearted,
To announce release to captives
And freedom to those in prison.

60:14 Rev 3:9 **60:19** Rev 21:23; 22:5 **61:1** Mt 11:5; Lk 7:22 **61:1, 2** Lk 4:18, 19

Study it!

Oh Joy!

The last six chapters of Isaiah are filled with promises of joy. They predict a time when God's love and justice will be brought to all nations. Notice all the nations named in chapter 60 that are sending representatives to honor God. The holy city, Jerusalem, will be rebuilt and become the center of the world's attention. It is a wonderful vision, and we can see some of it repeated in the New Testament, particularly in the Book of Revelation, chapters 21 and 22.

For Christians, the fulfillment of these promises began with Jesus and was confirmed by his death and Resurrection. We live in an in-between time, when Isaiah's promises have begun to be fulfilled but are not yet fully realized. It is an exciting time to be part of. Even though God has triumphed over sin and death, the world is not yet perfect. We are called to be God's messengers, to bring God's good news to the world and help make Isaiah's prophecies more and more real.

— Isaiah, chapter 60

2 He has sent me to proclaim
That the time has come
When the LORD will save his people
And defeat their enemies.
He has sent me to comfort all who
mourn,
3 To give to those who mourn in Zion
Joy and gladness instead of grief,
A song of praise instead of sorrow.
They will be like trees
That the LORD himself has planted.
They will all do what is right,
And God will be praised for what he has
done.
4 They will rebuild cities that have long
been in ruins.

5 My people, foreigners will serve you.
They will take care of your flocks
And farm your land and tend your
vineyards.
6 And you will be known as the priests of
the LORD,
The servants of our God.
You will enjoy the wealth of the nations
And be proud that it is yours.
7 Your shame and disgrace are ended.
You will live in your own land,
And your wealth will be doubled;
Your joy will last forever.
8 The LORD says,
"I love justice and I hate oppression and
crime.
I will faithfully reward my people
And make an eternal covenant with them.
9 They will be famous among the nations;
Everyone who sees them will know
That they are a people whom I have
blessed."

10 Jerusalem rejoices because of what the
LORD has done.
She is like a bride dressed for her wedding.
God has clothed her with salvation and
victory.
11 As surely as seeds sprout and grow,
The Sovereign LORD will save his people,
And all the nations will praise him.

62 I will speak out to encourage
Jerusalem;
I will not be silent until she is saved,
And her victory shines like a torch in the
night.

61:2 Mt 5:4 **61:10** Rev 21:2

Jesus quotes this passage from Isaiah *(61:1–2)* **to announce the start of his ministry** *(see Luke 4:18–19)*.

Live it!

Jesus' Mission Is Yours, Too

good news
healing
freedom
comfort
gladness
rebuilding
joy
blessing
saving
praising

What a great list! Not only did Isaiah promise all these things, Jesus really did them. If you could choose one of the things on the list to be or do for others, which one would you choose? Once you've chosen it, make a list of ways to live it out. Share your ideas with people you trust. These can be your teachers, catechists, youth minister, parents, or priest. See if they can help you live out your idea.

— Isaiah, chapter 61

2 Jerusalem, the nations will see you
victorious!
All their kings will see your glory.
You will be called by a new name,
A name given by the LORD himself.
3 You will be like a beautiful crown for the
LORD.
4 No longer will you be called "Forsaken,"
Or your land be called "The Deserted
Wife."
Your new name will be "God Is Pleased
with Her."
Your land will be called "Happily
Married,"

Like a torch in the night (62:1)

Because the LORD is pleased with you
And will be like a husband to your land.
5 Like a young man taking a virgin as his
bride,
He who formed you will marry you.
As a groom is delighted with his bride,
So your God will delight in you.
6 On your walls, Jerusalem, I have placed
sentries;
They must never be silent day or night.
They must remind the LORD of his
promises
And never let him forget them.
7 They must give him no rest until he
restores Jerusalem
And makes it a city the whole world
praises.
8 The LORD has made a solemn promise,
And by his power he will carry it out:
"Your grain will no longer be food for
your enemies,
And foreigners will no longer drink your
wine.
9 But you that planted and harvested the
grain
Will eat the bread and praise the LORD.
You that tended and gathered the grapes
Will drink the wine in the courts of my
Temple."
10 People of Jerusalem, go out of the city
And build a road for your returning
people!
Prepare a highway; clear it of stones!

"I will tell of the LORD's unfailing love; / I praise him for all he has done for us" *(Isaiah 63:7)*.

Pray it!

Names

In several places Isaiah, chapter 62, talks about old names and new names for places. Jerusalem used to be called Forsaken, but it will be called God Is Pleased with Her or The City That God Loves. These names probably sound really pretty in their original Hebrew language. In the Bible, giving something a new name is a sign that God is at work in a person, a city, or a nation. That is one of the reasons that Catholics have a tradition of taking on a new name at Confirmation.

What is your favorite name for God? What name would you like God to call you? What name would you like for the city or state you live in? Can you write a prayer using all these names?

— Isaiah 62:4,12

Put up a signal so that the nations can
know
11 That the LORD is announcing to all the
earth:
"Tell the people of Jerusalem
That the LORD is coming to save you,
Bringing with him the people he has
rescued."
12 You will be called "God's Holy People,"
"The People the LORD Has Saved."
Jerusalem will be called "The City That
God Loves,"
"The City That God Did Not Forsake."

The LORD's Victory over the Nations

63 "Who is this coming from the city
of Bozrah in Edom? Who is this so
splendidly dressed in red, marching along[f] in
power and strength?"
It is the LORD, powerful to save, coming
to announce his victory.
2 "Why is his clothing so red, like that of
someone who tramples grapes to make
wine?"
3 The LORD answers, "I have trampled the
nations like grapes, and no one came to help
me. I trampled them in my anger, and their
blood has stained all my clothing. 4 I decided
that the time to save my people had come; it
was time to punish their enemies. 5 I was
amazed when I looked and saw that there
was no one to help me. But my anger made
me strong, and I won the victory myself. 6 In
my anger I trampled whole nations and shat-
tered them. I poured out their lifeblood on
the ground."

The LORD's Goodness to Israel

7 I will tell of the LORD's unfailing love;
I praise him for all he has done for us.
He has richly blessed the people of Israel
because of his mercy and constant love.
8 The LORD said, "They are my people;
they will not deceive me." And so he saved
them 9 from all their suffering. It was not an
angel, but the LORD himself who saved
them. In his love and compassion he rescued
them. He had always taken care of them in
the past, 10 but they rebelled against him and
made his holy spirit sad. So the LORD
became their enemy and fought against
them.
11 But then they[g] remembered the past, the
days of Moses, the servant of the LORD, and
they asked, "Where now is the LORD, who
saved the leaders of his people from the sea?

[f] **63:1** *Some ancient translations* marching along; *Hebrew* bowed down. [g] **63:11** *Probable text* they; *Hebrew* he.

62:11 Isa 40:10; Rev 22:12 **63:1–6** Isa 34:5–17; Jer 49:7–22; Ezek 25:12–14; 35:1–15; Am 1:11, 12; Ob 1–14; Mal 1:2–5 **63:3 a** Rev 14:20; 19:15; **b** Rev 19:13 **63:5** Isa 59:16

Where is the LORD, who gave his spirit to Moses? 12-13Where is the LORD, who by his power did great things through Moses, dividing the waters of the sea and leading his people through the deep water, to win everlasting fame for himself"

Led by the LORD, they were as sure-footed as wild horses, and never stumbled. 14As cattle are led into a fertile valley, so the LORD gave his people rest. He led his people and brought honor to his name.

A Prayer for Mercy and Help

15LORD, look upon us from heaven, where you live in your holiness and glory. Where is your great concern for us? Where is your power? Where are your love and compassion? Do not ignore us. 16You are our father. Our ancestors Abraham and Jacob do not acknowledge us, but you, LORD, are our father, the one who has always rescued us. 17Why do you let us stray from your ways? Why do you make us so stubborn that we turn away from you? Come back, for the sake of those who serve you, for the sake of the people who have always been yours.

18We, your holy people, were driven out by our enemies for a little while; they trampled down your sanctuary.[h] 19You treat us as though you had never been our ruler, as though we had never been your people.

64 Why don't you tear the sky open and come down? The mountains would see you and shake with fear. 2They would tremble like water boiling over a hot fire. Come and reveal your power to your enemies, and make the nations tremble at your presence! 3There was a time when you came and did terrifying things that we did not expect; the mountains saw you and shook with fear. 4No one has ever seen or heard of a God like you, who does such deeds for those who put their hope in him. 5You welcome those who find joy in doing what is right, those who remember how you want them to live. You were angry with us, but we went on sinning; in spite of your great anger we have continued to do wrong

Build a road for your returning people! (62:10)

since ancient times.[i] 6All of us have been sinful; even our best actions are filthy through and through. Because of our sins we are like leaves that wither and are blown away by the wind. 7No one turns to you in prayer; no one goes to you for help. You have hidden yourself from us and have abandoned[j] us because of our sins.

8But you are our father, LORD. We are like clay, and you are like the potter. You created us, 9so do not be too angry with us or hold our sins against us forever. We are your people; be merciful to us. 10Your sacred cities are like a desert; Jerusalem is a deserted ruin, 11and our Temple, the sacred and beautiful place where our ancestors praised you, has been destroyed by fire. All the places we loved are in ruins. 12LORD, are you unmoved by all this? Are you going to do nothing and make us suffer more than we can endure?

God's Punishment of the Rebellious

65 The LORD said, "I was ready to answer my people's prayers, but they did not pray. I was ready for them to find me, but they did not even try. The nation did not pray to me, even though I was always ready to answer, 'Here I am; I will help you.' 2I have always been ready to welcome my people, who stubbornly do what is wrong and go their own way. 3They shamelessly keep on making me angry. They offer pagan sacrifices at sacred gardens[k] and burn incense on pagan altars. 4At night they go to caves and tombs to consult the spirits of the dead. They eat pork and drink broth made from meat offered in pagan sacrifices. 5And then they say to others, 'Keep away

[h] **63:18** *Verse 18 in Hebrew is unclear.* [i] **64:5** *Probable text* in spite of . . . ancient times; *Hebrew unclear.*
[j] **64:7** *Some ancient translations* abandoned; *Hebrew* melted. [k] **65:3** SACRED GARDENS: *See 1:29.*

63:12 Ex 14:21 **64:4** 1 Cor 2:9 **65:1** Rom 10:20 **65:2** Rom 10:21

from us; we are too holy for you to touch!' I cannot stand people like that—my anger against them is like a fire that never goes out.

6“I have already decided on their punishment, and their sentence is written down. I will not overlook what they have done, but will repay them 7for their sins and the sins of their ancestors. They have burned incense at pagan hill shrines and spoken evil of me. So I will punish them as their past deeds deserve.”

8The LORD says, “No one destroys good grapes; instead, they make wine with them. Neither will I destroy all my people—I will save those who serve me. 9I will bless the Israelites who belong to the tribe of Judah, and their descendants will possess my land of mountains. My chosen people, who serve me, will live there. 10They will worship me and will lead their sheep and cattle to pasture in the Plain of Sharon in the west and in Trouble Valley in the east.

11“But it will be different for you that forsake me, who ignore Zion, my sacred hill,[l] and worship Gad and Meni, the gods of luck and fate. 12It will be your fate to die a violent death, because you did not answer when I called you or listen when I spoke. You chose to disobey me and do evil. 13And so I tell you that those who worship and obey me will have plenty to eat and drink, but you will be hungry and thirsty. They will be happy, but you will be disgraced. 14They will sing for joy, but you will cry with a broken heart. 15My chosen people will use your name as a curse. I, the Sovereign LORD, will put you to death. But I will give a new name to those who obey me. 16Anyone in the land who asks for a blessing will ask to be blessed by the faithful God. Whoever takes an oath will swear by the name of the faithful God. The troubles of the past will be gone and forgotten.”

The New Creation

17The LORD says, “I am making a new earth and new heavens. The events of the past will be completely forgotten. 18Be glad and rejoice forever in what I create. The new Jerusalem I make will be full of joy, and her people will be happy. 19I myself will be filled with joy because of Jerusalem and her people. There will be no weeping there, no calling for help. 20Babies will no longer die in infancy, and all people will live out their life span. Those who live to be a hundred will be considered young. To die before that would be a sign that I had punished them. 21-22People will build houses and get to live in them—they will not be used by someone else. They will plant vineyards and enjoy the wine—it will not be drunk by others. Like trees, my people will live long lives. They will fully enjoy the things that they have worked for. 23The work they do will be successful, and their children will not meet with disaster. I will bless them and their descendants for all time to come. 24Even before they finish praying to me, I will answer their prayers. 25Wolves and lambs will eat together; lions will eat straw, as cattle do, and snakes will no longer be dangerous. On Zion, my sacred hill,[l] there will be nothing harmful or evil.”

The LORD Judges the Nations

66 The LORD says, “Heaven is my throne, and the earth is my footstool. What kind of house, then, could you build for me, what kind of place for me to live in? 2I myself created the whole universe! I am pleased with those who are humble and repentant, who fear me and obey me.

3“The people do as they please. It's all the same to them whether they kill a bull as a sacrifice or sacrifice a human being; whether they sacrifice a lamb or break a dog's neck;

[l] **65:11, 25** SACRED HILL: *See 2:3.*

65:10 Josh 7:24–26 **65:17** Isa 66:22; 2 Pet 3:13; Rev 21:1 **65:19** Rev 21:4 **65:25** Isa 11:6–9
66:1 a Mt 5:34; 23:22; **b** Mt 5:35 **66:1, 2a** Acts 7:49, 50

“No one has ever seen or heard of a God like you, who does such deeds for those who put their hope in him” *(Isaiah 64:4)*.

Pray it!

Help from the Holy Trinity

At the end of Isaiah are some prophecies about a time in the future when God will judge all people. Some people will be condemned for their sins, but those people who loved God and practiced justice will live in the new Jerusalem. This will be a place of joy and will be free from suffering or injustice.

We don't have to wait to die and go to heaven before experiencing the joy God wants us to have. We just have to look around and be open to the joy that God has in store for us right now. The problem is that some people spend so much time thinking about the past, they can't see what God is doing for them right now. Putting your past behind you can be very freeing. If you find yourself spending too much time thinking about something in the past, maybe this prayer idea can help. It is a prayer that involves all three persons of the Holy Trinity.

- **First, think of the event or problem you keep remembering and ask God the Father to help you put it behind you.**
- **Second, if the event was a sin you committed, ask Jesus to forgive you (and remember to celebrate the sacrament of Penance and Reconciliation).**
- **Third, ask the Holy Spirit for the courage to move into the future.**

— Isaiah 65:17–25

whether they present a grain offering or
offer pigs' blood; whether they offer incense
or pray to an idol. They take pleasure in dis-
gusting ways of worship. 4So I will bring di-
saster upon them—the very things they are
afraid of—because no one answered when I
called or listened when I spoke. They chose
to disobey me and do evil."

5Listen to what the LORD says, you that
fear him and obey him: "Because you are
faithful to me, some of your own people
hate you and will have nothing to do with
you. They mock you and say, 'Let the LORD
show his greatness and save you, so that we
may see you rejoice.' But they themselves
will be disgraced! 6Listen! That loud noise in
the city, that sound in the Temple, is the
sound of the LORD punishing his enemies!

7"My holy city is like a woman who sud-
denly gives birth to a child without ever
going into labor. 8Has anyone ever seen or
heard of such a thing? Has a nation ever
been born in a day? Zion will not have to
suffer long, before the nation is born. 9Do
not think that I will bring my people to the
point of birth and not let them be born."
The LORD has spoken.

10Rejoice with Jerusalem; be glad for her,
all you that love this city!
Rejoice with her now,
all you that have mourned for her!
11You will enjoy her prosperity,
like a child at its mother's breast.

12The LORD says, "I will bring you lasting
prosperity; the wealth of the nations will
flow to you like a river that never goes dry.
You will be like a child that is nursed by its
mother, carried in her arms, and treated with
love. 13I will comfort you in Jerusalem, as a
mother comforts her child. 14When you see

66:7 Rev 12:5

The last chapter of Isaiah is filled with images of negative punishments and positive promises. How many can you find of each?

this happen, you will be glad; it will make
you strong and healthy. Then you will know
that I, the LORD, help those who obey me,
and I show my anger against my enemies."
15 The LORD will come with fire. He will
ride on the wings of a storm to punish those
he is angry with. 16 By fire and sword he will
punish all the people of the world whom he
finds guilty—and many will be put to death.
17 The LORD says, "The end is near for
those who purify themselves for pagan wor-
ship, who go in procession to sacred
gardens,[m] and who eat pork and mice and
other disgusting foods. 18 I know[n] their
thoughts and their deeds. I am coming[o] to
gather the people of all the nations. When
they come together, they will see what my
power can do 19 and will know that I am the
one who punishes them.
"But I will spare some of them and send
them to the nations and the distant lands
that have not heard of my fame or seen my
greatness and power: to Spain, Libya,[p] and
Lydia, with its skilled archers, and to Tubal
and Greece. Among these nations they will
proclaim my greatness. 20 They will bring
back all your people from the nations as a
gift to me. They will bring them to my
sacred hill[q] in Jerusalem on horses, mules,
and camels, and in chariots and wagons, just
as Israelites bring grain offerings to the Tem-
ple in ritually clean containers. 21 I will make
some of them priests and Levites.
22 "Just as the new earth and the new
heavens will endure by my power, so your
descendants and your name will endure.
23 On every New Moon Festival and every
Sabbath people of every nation will come to
worship me here in Jerusalem," says the
LORD. 24 "As they leave, they will see the
dead bodies of those who have rebelled
against me. The worms that eat them will
never die, and the fire that burns them will
never be put out. The sight of them will be
disgusting to all people."

[m] **66:17** SACRED GARDENS: *See 1:29.* [n] **66:18** *Some ancient translations* I know; *Hebrew* I. [o] **66:18** *Some ancient translations* I am coming; *Hebrew* He is coming. [p] **66:19** *One ancient translation* Libya; *Hebrew* Pul. [q] **66:20** SACRED HILL: *See 2:3.*

66:22 Isa 65:17; 2 Pet 3:13; Rev 21:1 **66:24** Jdt 16:17; Mk 9:48

Your Next Step

Congratulations on finishing the Book of Isaiah! Use this space to write your thoughts and questions about this book. If you are following the suggested reading plan, move ahead to the Gospel of Matthew in the New Testament. Look for quotes in Matthew that come from Isaiah.

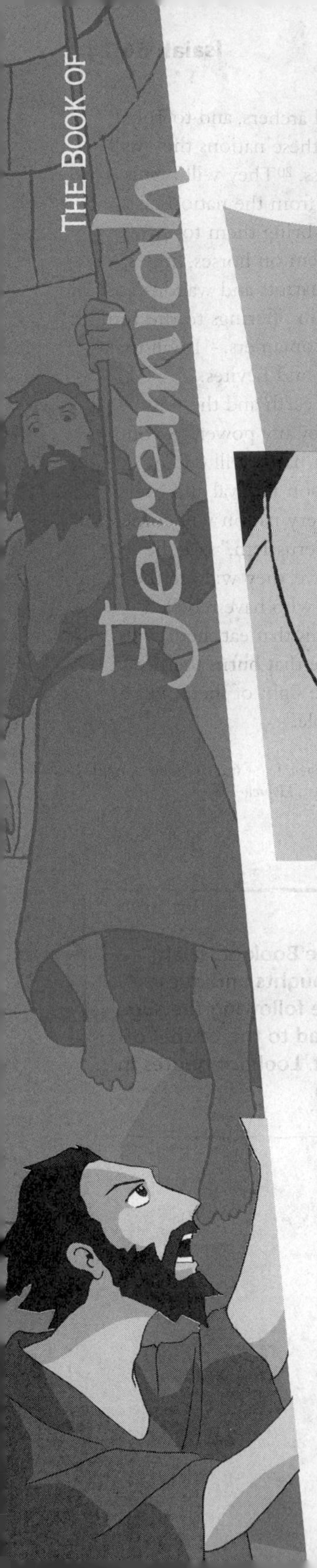

THE BOOK OF Jeremiah

"I just had to tell someone!" Have you ever felt this way? Sometimes we know something that we just can't keep to ourselves, no matter how hard we try.

Jeremiah experienced something similar, except that he knew that what he had to say would get him in trouble. God had chosen him at an early age to be a prophet. He had to proclaim God's words of judgment even though he knew those words would upset people. As a result, Jeremiah was often persecuted because of his message. But he would not back down. Like it or not, he was the one God had chosen to speak the truth—and so he did, no matter what the consequences. And that is the test of a true prophet.

Chap. 38

Headlines

- Youth Chosen As Prophet (1:4–9)
- God's Warning: Keep the Covenant! (11:1–8)
- Jeremiah's Shorts Make a Point (13:1–11)
- Jeremiah Complains to God (20:7–18)
- New Covenant Written on Hearts (31:31–34)
- Prophet Is Rescued from Well (38:1–13)
- God Promises Babylon's Punishment (chapter 51)

FACTOIDS

Who wrote this book? Jeremiah and his disciples, including Baruch.

Why was it written? To tell the story of the prophet Jeremiah and record his messages to God's Chosen People.

What time period does it cover? From 626 to 560 BC.

What literary style is used? This book is part history, part biography, and part prophecy.

Important themes

- God reveals a New Covenant that will be written on the hearts of God's people.
- Sin leads to suffering, but with repentance comes forgiveness and new life.
- Beware of false prophets who tell people what they want to hear.

JEREMIAH

1 This book is the account of what was
said by Jeremiah son of Hilkiah, one of
the priests of the town of Anathoth in the
territory of Benjamin. 2The LORD spoke to
Jeremiah in the thirteenth year that Josiah
son of Amon was king of Judah, 3and he
spoke to him again when Josiah's son
Jehoiakim was king. After that, the LORD
spoke to him many times, until the eleventh
year of the reign of Zedekiah son of Josiah.
In the fifth month of that year the people of
Jerusalem were taken into exile.

The Call of Jeremiah

4The LORD said to me, 5"I chose you
before I gave you life, and before you were
born I selected you to be a prophet to the
nations."
6I answered, "Sovereign LORD, I don't
know how to speak; I am too young."
7But the LORD said to me, "Do not say
that you are too young, but go to the people
I send you to, and tell them everything I
command you to say. 8Do not be afraid of
them, for I will be with you to protect you.
I, the LORD, have spoken!"
9Then the LORD reached out, touched
my lips, and said to me, "Listen, I am giving
you the words you must speak. 10Today I

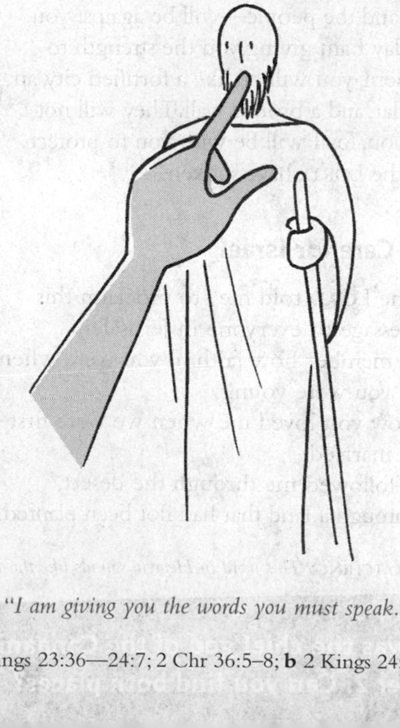

"I am giving you the words you must speak." (1:9)

Live it!

Who, Me?

"Who, me?"

Do those words sound familiar? We have all used them and heard others use them. You can almost picture someone turning around to see who is calling. Or maybe the person saying "Who, me?" isn't excited about being called. This is sort of what Jeremiah is saying at the beginning of his book. It is the story of his call by God. He isn't too excited about being called by God. He knows that prophets are often not treated very well.

So Jeremiah tries to make excuses for why God shouldn't call him. Jeremiah says that he doesn't know how to speak and that he's too young. However, God is not buying it. God has a plan for young Jeremiah, just as he has a plan for each of us. We can make excuses, but God's plan is already in place before we are even born. Jeremiah is called to be a prophet, to speak God's message to people who don't really want to hear it. God also has a plan for each of us, no excuses accepted!

Ask God to help you understand and follow your call.

— Jeremiah 1:4–10

1:2 2 Kings 22:3—23:27; 2 Chr 34:8—35:19 **1:3 a** 2 Kings 23:36—24:7; 2 Chr 36:5–8; **b** 2 Kings 24:18—25:21; 2 Chr 36:11–21 give you authority over nations and kingdoms to uproot and to pull down, to destroy and to overthrow, to build and to plant."

Two Visions

11 The LORD asked me, "Jeremiah, what do you see?"

I answered, "A branch of an almond tree."

12 "You are right," the LORD said, "and I am watching[a] to see that my words come true."

13 Then the LORD spoke to me again. "What else do you see?" he asked.

I answered, "I see a pot boiling in the north, and it is about to tip over this way."

14 He said to me, "Destruction will boil over from the north on all who live in this land,
15 because I am calling all the nations in the north to come. Their kings will set up their thrones at the gates of Jerusalem and around its walls and also around the other cities of
Judah. 16 I will punish my people because they have sinned; they have abandoned me, have offered sacrifices to other gods, and have made
idols and worshiped them. 17 Get ready, Jeremiah; go and tell them everything I command you to say. Do not be afraid of them now, or I will make you even more afraid when you are
with them. 18-19 Listen, Jeremiah! Everyone in this land—the kings of Judah, the officials, the priests, and the people—will be against you. But today I am giving you the strength to resist them; you will be like a fortified city, an iron pillar, and a bronze wall. They will not defeat you, for I will be with you to protect you. I, the LORD, have spoken."

God's Care for Israel

2 The LORD told me 2 to proclaim this message to everyone in Jerusalem.

"I remember how faithful you were when
you were young,
how you loved me when we were first
married;
you followed me through the desert,
through a land that had not been planted.
3 Israel, you belonged to me alone;
you were my sacred possession.
I sent suffering and disaster
on everyone who hurt you.
I, the LORD, have spoken."

The Sin of Israel's Ancestors

4 Listen to the LORD's message, you descendants of Jacob, you tribes of Israel.
5 The LORD says:

"What accusation did your ancestors
bring against me?
What made them turn away from me?
They worshiped worthless idols
and became worthless themselves.
6 They did not care about me,
even though I rescued them from
Egypt
and led them through the wilderness:
a land of deserts and sand pits,
a dry and dangerous land
where no one lives
and no one will even travel.
7 I brought them into a fertile land,
to enjoy its harvests and its other good
things.
But instead they ruined my land;
they defiled the country I had given
them.
8 The priests did not ask, 'Where is the
LORD?'
My own priests did not know me.
The rulers rebelled against me;
the prophets spoke in the name of Baal
and worshiped useless idols.

The LORD's Case against His People

9 "And so I, the LORD, will state my case
against my people again.
I will bring charges against their
descendants.
10 Go west to the island of Cyprus,
and send someone eastward to the land
of Kedar.

[a] **1:12** WATCHING: *This word in Hebrew sounds like the Hebrew for "almond."*

Baal was the chief god of the Canaanites and appears twice in Jeremiah, chapter 2. Can you find both places?

You will see that nothing like this has
ever happened before.
11 No other nation has ever changed its
gods,
even though they were not real.
But my people have exchanged me,
the God who has brought them
honor,
for gods that can do nothing for
them.
12 And so I command the sky to shake with
horror,
to be amazed and astonished,
13 for my people have committed two
sins:
they have turned away from me,
the spring of fresh water,
and they have dug cisterns,
cracked cisterns that can hold no water
at all.

The Results of Israel's Unfaithfulness

14 "Israel is not a slave;
he was not born into slavery.
Why then do his enemies hunt him
down?
15 They have roared at him like lions;
they have made his land a desert,
and his towns lie in ruins, completely
abandoned.
16 Yes, the people of Memphis and
Tahpanhes
have cracked his skull.
17 Israel, you brought this on yourself!
You deserted me, the LORD your
God,
while I was leading you along the
way.
18 What do you think you will gain by
going to Egypt
to drink water from the Nile?
What do you think you will gain by
going to Assyria
to drink water from the Euphrates?
19 Your own evil will punish you,
and your turning from me will
condemn you.
You will learn how bitter and wrong
it is
to abandon me, the LORD your
God,
and no longer to remain faithful to me.
I, the Sovereign LORD Almighty, have
spoken."

Israel Refuses to Worship the LORD

20 The Sovereign LORD says,
"Israel, long ago you rejected my
authority;
you refused to obey me and worship
me.
On every high hill
and under every green tree
you worshiped fertility gods.
21 I planted you like a choice vine
from the very best seed.
But look what you have become!
You are like a rotten, worthless vine.
22 Even if you washed with the strongest
soap,
I would still see the stain of your guilt.
23 How can you say you have not defiled
yourself,
that you have never worshiped Baal?
Look how you sinned in the valley;
see what you have done.
You are like a wild camel in heat,
running around loose,
24 rushing into the desert.[b]
When she is in heat, who can control
her?
No male that wants her has to trouble
himself;
she is always available in mating season.
25 Israel, don't wear your feet out,
or let your throat become dry
from chasing after other gods.
But you say, 'No! I can't turn back.
I have loved foreign gods
and will go after them.' "

Israel Deserves to Be Punished

26 The LORD says, "Just as a thief is dis-
graced when caught, so all you people of
Israel will be disgraced—your kings and

[b] **2:24** *Probable text* rushing into the desert; *Hebrew* a wild donkey used to the desert.

Pray it!

Help! Rescue Me!

"But when you are in trouble, you ask me to come and save you" (Jeremiah 2:27). These words of the Lord can hit home pretty easily. How many times do we pray only when we are in trouble or really need God to help someone we care about? What about when things are going well, when life is good? Take a moment right now and think of five things that happened to you recently that are good things. Think also of five people in your life you would like to pray for. Now, turn to God in prayer, and try this formula:

- **Begin with: "Thank you, God, for these blessings . . ."**
- **Now pray for others in your life: "God, I pray for a blessing upon . . ."**
- **And if you need God's help, end with: "Dear God, please help me to . . ."**

— Jeremiah 2:26–27

officials, your priests and prophets. [27]You will all be disgraced—you that say that a tree is your father and that a rock is your mother. This will happen because you turned away from me instead of turning to me. But when you are in trouble, you ask me to come and save you.

[28]"Where are the gods that you made for yourselves? When you are in trouble, let them save you—if they can! Judah, you have as many gods as you have cities. [29]What is your complaint? Why have you rebelled against me? [30]I punished you, but it did no good; you would not let me correct you. Like a raging lion, you have murdered your prophets. [31]People of Israel, listen to what I am saying. Have I been like a desert to you, like a dark and dangerous land? Why, then, do you say that you will do as you please, that you will never come back to me? [32]Does a young woman forget her jewelry, or a bride her wedding dress? But my people have forgotten me for more days than can be counted. [33]You certainly know how to chase after lovers. Even the worst of women can learn from you. [34]Your clothes are stained with the blood of the poor and innocent, not with the blood of burglars.

"But in spite of all this, [35]you say, 'I am innocent; surely the LORD is no longer angry with me.' But I, the LORD, will punish you because you deny that you have sinned. [36]You have cheapened yourself by turning to the gods of other nations. You will be disappointed by Egypt, just as you were by Assyria. [37]You will turn away from Egypt, hanging your head in shame. I, the LORD, have rejected those you trust; you will not gain anything from them."

Unfaithful Israel

3 The LORD says, "If a man divorces his wife, and she leaves him and becomes another man's wife, he cannot take her back again. This would completely defile the land. But, Israel, you have had many lovers, and now you want to return to me! [2]Look up at the hilltops. Is there any place where you have not acted like a prostitute? You waited for lovers along the roadside, as an Arab waits for victims in the desert. You have defiled the land with your prostitution. [3]That is why the rains were held back, and the spring showers did not come. You even look like a prostitute; you have no shame.

[4]"And now you say to me, 'You are my father, and you have loved me ever since I was a child. [5]You won't always be angry; you won't be mad at me forever.' Israel, that is what you said, but you did all the evil you could."

Worshiping stones and trees (3:9)

Israel and Judah Must Repent

6 When Josiah was king, the LORD said to
me, "Have you seen what Israel, that unfaith-
ful woman, has done? She has turned away
from me, and on every high hill and under
every green tree she has acted like a prosti-
tute. 7 I thought that after she had done all
this, she would surely return to me. But she
did not return, and her unfaithful sister
Judah saw it all. 8 Judah also saw that I
divorced Israel and sent her away because
she had turned from me and had become a
prostitute. But Judah, Israel's unfaithful sister,
was not afraid. She too became a prostitute
9 and was not at all ashamed. She defiled the
land, and she committed adultery by wor-
shiping stones and trees. 10 And after all this,
Judah, Israel's unfaithful sister, only pretend-
ed to return to me; she was not sincere. I,
the LORD, have spoken."
11 Then the LORD told me that, even
though Israel had turned away from him, she
had proved to be better than unfaithful
Judah. 12 He told me to go and say to Israel,
"Unfaithful Israel, come back to me. I am
merciful and will not be angry; I will not be
angry with you forever. 13 Only admit that
you are guilty and that you have rebelled
against the LORD, your God. Confess that
under every green tree you have given your
love to foreign gods and that you have not
obeyed my commands. I, the LORD, have
spoken.

Study it!

The Roots of Racism

In the beginning of Jeremiah, chapter 3, there is the phrase "as an Arab waits for victims in the desert" (verse 2). The word *Arab* here is used to describe bandits who waited for caravans to pass and then attacked and robbed them. Clearly, the word *Arab* here has negative overtones, and we would describe this as a racist comment because not all Arabs are thieves. Perhaps this is why some other English versions of the Bible use the word *nomad* instead of *Arab*.

Today some of us have the tendency to refer to Arabs as terrorists. We have to be very careful when labeling a group of people, especially an ethnic group. Most likely, few Arabs in the time of Jeremiah were thieves, and certainly very few Arabs today are terrorists. Keep your ears open for times when you hear people lumping everyone from an ethnic group or nation together. It is unfair, and it is wrong.

— Jeremiah 3:2

14 "Unfaithful people, come back; you
belong to me. I will take one of you from
each town and two from each clan, and I
will bring you back to Mount Zion. 15 I will
give you rulers who obey me, and they will
rule you with wisdom and understanding.
16 Then when you have become numerous
in that land, people will no longer talk about

3:6 2 Kings 22:1—23:30; 2 Chr 34:1—35:27

Israel is the northern kingdom, and Judah is the southern kingdom. Both are mentioned in Jeremiah, chapter 3. See Map 3 to see their boundaries.

my Covenant Box. They will no longer
think about it or remember it; they will not
even need it, nor will they make another
one. 17 When that time comes, Jerusalem will
be called 'The Throne of the LORD,' and all
nations will gather there to worship me.
They will no longer do what their stubborn
and evil hearts tell them. 18 Israel will join
with Judah, and together they will come
from exile in the country in the north and
will return to the land that I gave your
ancestors as a permanent possession."

The Idolatry of God's People

19 The LORD says,
"Israel, I wanted to accept you as my
child
and give you a delightful land,
the most beautiful land in all the world.
I wanted you to call me father
and never again turn away from me.
20 But like an unfaithful wife,
you have not been faithful to me.
I, the LORD, have spoken."

21 A noise is heard on the hilltops:
it is the people of Israel crying and
pleading
because they have lived sinful lives
and have forgotten the LORD their
God.
22 Return, all of you who have turned away
from the LORD;
he will heal you and make you faithful.

You say, "Yes, we are coming to the LORD
because he is our God. 23 We were not helped
at all by our pagan worship on the hilltops.
Help for Israel comes only from the LORD
our God. 24 But the worship of Baal, the god
of shame, has made us lose flocks and herds,
sons and daughters—everything that our
ancestors have worked for since ancient
times. 25 We should lie down in shame and let
our disgrace cover us. We and our ancestors
have always sinned against the LORD our
God; we have never obeyed his commands."

A Call to Repentance

4 The LORD says, "People of Israel, if you
want to turn, then turn back to me. If
you are faithful to me and remove the idols I
hate, 2 it will be right for you to swear by my
name. Then[c] all the nations will ask me to
bless them, and they will praise me."

Turn back to me. (4:1)

3 The LORD says to the people of Judah
and Jerusalem, "Plow up your unplowed
fields; do not plant your seeds among thorns.
4 Keep your covenant with me, your LORD,
and dedicate yourselves to me, you people of
Judah and Jerusalem. If you don't, my anger
will burn like fire because of the evil things
you have done. It will burn, and there will
be no one to put it out."

Judah Is Threatened with Invasion

5 Blow the trumpet throughout the land!
Shout loud and clear!
Tell the people of Judah and Jerusalem
to run to the fortified cities.
6 Point the way to Zion!
Run for safety! Don't delay!
The LORD is bringing disaster
and great destruction from the north.
7 Like a lion coming from its hiding place,
a destroyer of nations has set out.

[c] **4:2** it will be right . . . name. Then; *or* and if you swear by my name and are truthful, just, and righteous, then.

4:3 Hos 10:12

Sackcloth is a rough material made from goat's hair. It's uncomfortable to wear. Why would people who are mourning wear sackcloth?

The enemy is coming like clouds. (4:13)

He is coming to destroy Judah.
The cities of Judah will be left in ruins,
and no one will live in them.
8 So put on sackcloth, and weep and wail
because the fierce anger of the LORD
has not turned away from Judah.

9 The LORD said, "On that day kings and
officials will lose their courage; priests will
be shocked and prophets will be astonished."
10 Then I said, "Sovereign LORD, you have
completely deceived the people of
Jerusalem! You have said there would be
peace, but a sword is at their throats."
11 The time is coming when the people of
Jerusalem will be told that a scorching wind
is blowing in from the desert toward them. It
will not be a gentle wind that only blows
away the chaff— 12 the wind that comes at
the LORD's command will be much stronger
than that! It is the LORD himself who is pro-
nouncing judgment on his people.

Judah Is Surrounded by Enemies

13 Look, the enemy is coming like clouds.
Their war chariots are like a whirlwind, and
their horses are faster than eagles. We are
lost! We are doomed!
14 Jerusalem, wash the evil from your
heart, so that you may be saved. How long
will you go on thinking sinful thoughts?
15 Messengers from the city of Dan and
from the hills of Ephraim announce the bad
news. 16 They have come to warn the nations
and to tell Jerusalem that enemies are com-
ing from a country far away. These enemies
will shout against the cities of Judah 17 and
will surround Jerusalem like men guarding a
field, because her people have rebelled
against the LORD. The LORD has spoken.
18 Judah, you have brought this on your-
self by the way you have lived and by the
things you have done. Your sin has caused
this suffering; it has stabbed you through the
heart.

Jeremiah's Sorrow for His People

19 The pain! I can't bear the pain!
My heart! My heart is beating wildly!
I can't keep quiet;
I hear the trumpets
and the shouts of battle.
20 One disaster follows another;
the whole country is left in ruins.
Suddenly our tents are destroyed;
their curtains are torn to pieces.
21 How long must I see the battle raging
and hear the blasts of trumpets?
22 The LORD says, "My people are stupid;
they don't know me.
They are like foolish children;
they have no understanding.
They are experts at doing what is evil,
but failures at doing what is good."

Jeremiah's Vision of the Coming Destruction

23 I looked at the earth—it was a barren
waste;
at the sky—there was no light.
24 I looked at the mountains—they were
shaking,
and the hills were rocking back and
forth.
25 I saw that there were no people;
even the birds had flown away.
26 The fertile land had become a desert;
its cities were in ruins
because of the LORD's fierce anger.
(27 The LORD has said that the whole
earth will become a wasteland, but that he
will not completely destroy it.)

Pray it!

Do You Really Mean It?

In one of his prophecies, Jeremiah says, "Even though you claim to worship the LORD, / you do not mean what you say" (Jeremiah 5:2). Do these words apply to us? If we really worship the Lord, then when we go to Mass or participate in a prayer service, do we really pay attention to what we are saying?

It is so easy to mouth the familiar words of prayers we hear every day. But we can do better than that. If we are truly worshiping the Lord, we have to put our heart and soul into it. And we have to live it. Say each of these prayers slowly and try to put meaning into every word:

- **"Lamb of God, you take away the sins of the world, have mercy on us."**
- **"For yours is the kingdom and the power and the glory, now and forever."**
- **"Thanks be to God."**

— Jeremiah 5:2

28 The earth will mourn;
the sky will grow dark.
The LORD has spoken
and will not change his mind.
He has made his decision
and will not turn back.
29 At the noise of the cavalry and archers
everyone will run away.
Some will run to the forest;
others will climb up among the rocks.
Every town will be left empty,
and no one will live in them again.
30 Jerusalem, you are doomed!
Why do you dress in scarlet?
Why do you put on jewelry and paint your eyes?
You are making yourself beautiful for nothing!
Your lovers have rejected you
and want to kill you.
31 I heard a cry, like a woman in labor,
a scream like a woman bearing her first child.
It was the cry of Jerusalem gasping for breath,
stretching out her hand and saying,
"I am doomed!
They are coming to kill me!"

The Sin of Jerusalem

5 People of Jerusalem, run through your streets!
Look around! See for yourselves!
Search the marketplaces!
Can you find one person
who does what is right
and tries to be faithful to God?
If you can, the LORD will forgive Jerusalem.
2 Even though you claim to worship the LORD,
you do not mean what you say.
3 Surely the LORD looks for faithfulness.
He struck you, but you paid no attention;
he crushed you, but you refused to learn.
You were stubborn and would not turn from your sins.
4 Then I thought, "These are only the poor and ignorant.
They behave foolishly;
they don't know what their God requires,
what the LORD wants them to do.
5 I will go to the people in power
and talk with them.
Surely they know what their God requires,
what the LORD wants them to do."

But all of them have rejected the LORD's
authority
and refuse to obey him.
6 That is why lions from the forest will kill
them;
wolves from the desert will tear them
to pieces,
and leopards will prowl through their
towns.
If those people go out, they will be torn
apart
because their sins are numerous
and time after time they have turned
from God.
7 The LORD asked, "Why should I forgive
the sins of my people?
They have abandoned me
and have worshiped gods that are not
real.
I fed my people until they were full,
but they committed adultery
and spent their time with prostitutes.
8 They were like well-fed stallions wild
with desire,
each lusting for his neighbor's wife.
9 Shouldn't I punish them for these
things
and take revenge on a nation such as
this?
10 I will send enemies to cut down my
people's vineyards,
but not to destroy them completely.
I will tell them to strip away the branches,
because those branches are not mine.
11 The people of Israel and Judah
have betrayed me completely.
I, the LORD, have spoken."

The LORD Rejects Israel

12 The LORD's people have denied him
and have said, "He won't really do anything.[d]
We won't have hard times; we won't have
war or famine." 13-14 They have said that the
prophets are nothing but windbags and that
they have no message from the LORD. The
LORD God Almighty said to me, "Jeremiah,
because these people have said such things,
I will make my words like a fire in your
mouth. The people will be like wood, and
the fire will burn them up."
15 People of Israel, the LORD is bringing a
nation from far away to attack you. It is a
strong and ancient nation, a nation whose
language you do not know. 16 Their archers
are mighty soldiers who kill without mercy.
17 They will devour your crops and your
food; they will kill your sons and your
daughters. They will slaughter your flocks
and your herds and destroy your vines and
fig trees. The fortified cities in which you
trust will be destroyed by their army.
18 The LORD says, "Yet even in those days
I will not completely destroy my people.
19 When they ask why I did all these things,
tell them, Jeremiah, that just as they turned
away from me and served foreign gods in
their own land, so they will serve strangers
in a land that is not theirs."

God Warns His People

20 The LORD says, "Tell the descendants
of Jacob, tell the people of Judah: 21 Pay
attention, you foolish and stupid people,
who have eyes, but cannot see, and have
ears, but cannot hear. 22 I am the LORD;
why don't you fear me? Why don't you
tremble before me? I placed the sand as the
boundary of the sea, a permanent boundary
that it cannot cross. The sea may toss, but it
cannot go beyond it; the waves may roar,
but they cannot break through. 23 But you
people! You are stubborn and rebellious;
you have turned aside and left me. 24 You
never thought to honor me, even though I
send the autumn rains and the spring rains
and give you the harvest season each year.
25 Instead, your sins have kept these good
things from you.
26 "Evildoers live among my people; they
lie in wait like those who lay nets to catch

[d] **5:12** He won't . . . anything; *or* We don't want anything to do with him.
5:21 Isa 6:9, 10; Ezek 12:2; Mk 8:18 **5:22** Job 38:8–11

God talks about people "who have eyes, but cannot see, and have ears, but cannot hear" *(Jeremiah 5:20)*. **What do you think God means?**

birds,[e] but they have set their traps to catch
people. 27Just as a hunter fills a cage with
birds, they have filled their houses with loot.
That is why they are powerful and rich,
28why they are fat and well fed. There is no
limit to their evil deeds. They do not give
orphans their rights or show justice to the
oppressed.
29"But I, the LORD, will punish them for
these things; I will take revenge on this
nation. 30A terrible and shocking thing has
happened in the land: 31prophets speak
nothing but lies; priests rule as the prophets
command, and my people offer no objec-
tions. But what will they do when it all
comes to an end?"

Jerusalem Is Surrounded by Enemies

6 People of Benjamin, run for safety!
Escape from Jerusalem! Sound the
trumpet in Tekoa and build a signal fire in
Beth Haccherem. Disaster and destruction
are about to come from the north. 2The city
of Zion is beautiful, but it will be destroyed;
3kings will camp there with their armies.
They will pitch their tents around the city,
and each of them will camp wherever they
want. 4They will say, "Prepare to attack
Jerusalem! Get ready! We'll attack at noon!"
But then they will say, "It's too late, the day
is almost over, and the evening shadows are
growing long. 5We'll attack by night; we'll
destroy the city's fortresses."
6The LORD Almighty has ordered these
kings to cut down trees and build mounds in
order to besiege Jerusalem. He has said, "I
will punish this city because it is full of
oppression. 7As a well keeps its water fresh,
so Jerusalem keeps its evil fresh. I hear vio-
lence and destruction in the city; sickness
and wounds are all I see. 8People of
Jerusalem, let these troubles be a warning to
you, or else I will abandon you; I will turn
your city into a desert, a place where no one
lives."

Rebellious Israel

9The LORD Almighty said to me, "Israel
will be stripped clean like a vineyard from
which every grape has been picked. So you
must rescue everyone you can while there is
still time."
10I answered, "Who would listen to me if
I spoke to them and warned them? They are
stubborn and refuse to listen to your mes-
sage; they laugh at what you tell me to say.
11Your anger against them burns in me too,
LORD, and I can't hold it in any longer."
Then the LORD said to me, "Pour out my
anger on the children in the streets and on
the gatherings of the young people. Hus-
bands and wives will be taken away, and even
the very old will not be spared. 12Their
houses will be given to others, and so will
their fields and their wives. I am going to
punish the people of this land. 13Everyone,
great and small, tries to make money dishon-
estly; even prophets and priests cheat the
people. 14They act as if my people's wounds
were only scratches. 'All is well,' they say,
when all is not well. 15Were they ashamed
because they did these disgusting things? No,
they were not at all ashamed; they don't even
know how to blush. And so they will fall as
others have fallen; when I punish them, that
will be the end of them. I, the LORD, have
spoken."

Israel Rejects God's Way

16The LORD said to his people, "Stand at
the crossroads and look. Ask for the ancient
paths and where the best road is. Walk in it,
and you will live in peace."
But they said, "No, we will not!" 17Then
the LORD appointed sentries to listen for the
trumpet's warning. But they said, "We will
not listen."
18So the LORD said, "Listen, you nations,
and learn what is going to happen to my
people. 19Listen, earth! As punishment for all

[e] **5:26** *Probable text* they . . . birds; *Hebrew unclear.*
6:14 Ezek 13:10 **6:12–15** Jer 8:10–12

Tekoa *(Jeremiah 6:1)* **is the name of a town near Jerusalem. It is the hometown of the prophet Amos. See if you can locate it on Map 3 in the back of this Bible.**

their schemes I am bringing ruin on these people, because they have rejected my teaching and have not obeyed my words. [20]What do I care about the incense they bring me from Sheba, or the spices from a distant land? I will not accept their offerings or be pleased with their sacrifices. [21]And so I will make these people stumble and fall. Parents and children will die, and so will friends and neighbors."

Invasion from the North

[22]The LORD says, "People are coming from a country in the north; a mighty nation far away is preparing for war. [23]They have taken up their bows and swords; they are cruel and merciless. They sound like the roaring sea, as they ride their horses. They are ready for battle against Jerusalem."

[24]"We have heard the news," say the people of Jerusalem, "and our hands hang limp; we are seized by anguish and pain like a woman in labor. [25]We don't dare go to the countryside or walk on the roads, because our enemies are armed and terror is all around us."

"We have heard the news, . . . and our hands hang limp." (6:24)

[26]The LORD says to his people, "Put on sackcloth and roll in ashes. Mourn with bitter tears as you would for an only child, because the one who comes to destroy you will suddenly attack. [27]Jeremiah, test my people, as you would test metal, and find out what they are like. [28]They are all stubborn rebels, hard as bronze and iron. They are all corrupt, going around and spreading gossip. [29]The furnace burns fiercely, but the waste metals do not melt and run off. It is useless to go on refining my people, because those who are evil are not taken away. [30]They will be called worthless dross, because I, the LORD, have rejected them."

Jeremiah Preaches in the Temple

7 [1-3]The LORD sent me to the gate of the Temple where the people of Judah went in to worship. He told me to stand there and announce what the LORD Almighty, the God of Israel, had to say to them: "Change the way you are living and the things you are doing, and I will let you go on living here. [4]Stop believing those deceitful words, 'We are safe! This is the LORD's Temple, this is the LORD's Temple, this is the LORD's Temple!'

[5]"Change the way you are living and stop doing the things you are doing. Be fair in your treatment of one another. [6]Stop taking advantage of aliens, orphans, and widows. Stop killing innocent people in this land. Stop worshiping other gods, for that will destroy you. [7]If you change, I will let you go on living here in the land which I gave your ancestors as a permanent possession.

[8]"Look, you put your trust in deceitful words. [9]You steal, murder, commit adultery, tell lies under oath, offer sacrifices to Baal, and worship gods that you had not known before. [10]You do these things I hate, and then you come and stand in my presence, in my own Temple, and say, 'We are safe!' [11]Do you think that my Temple is a hiding place for robbers? I have seen what you are doing. [12]Go to Shiloh,[f] the first place where I chose to be worshiped, and see what I did to it because of the sins of my people Israel. [13]You have committed all these sins, and even though I spoke to you over and over again, you refused to listen. You would not answer when I called you. [14]And so, what I did to Shiloh I will do to this Temple of

[f] **7:12** SHILOH: *The city where the Covenant Box was kept in the time of Eli (see 1 Sam 1:3). The city was destroyed, probably by the Philistines.*

7:11 Mt 21:13; Mk 11:17; Lk 19:46 **7:12–14** Josh 18:1; Ps 78:60; Jer 26:6

Live it!

This Is the Lord's Temple

The Lord sends Jeremiah to the Temple to deliver a strong message. The people would come to the Temple and say: "We are safe! This is the LORD's Temple" (Jeremiah 7:4). And yet, they would spend the rest of their time breaking almost every commandment possible. They were taking advantage of widows, orphans, and aliens (immigrants)—the most vulnerable (defenseless) groups in Israelite society. They steal, murder, and worship false gods. Yet they still go to God's Temple pretending to be devout followers of God.

It is this hypocritical attitude that God sends Jeremiah to preach against. The people are making a mockery of the Temple by not living holy lives. Sorry, God says through Jeremiah, but it doesn't work that way. Some five hundred years later, Jesus would clear the moneychangers from the Temple because they, too, had made a mockery of God's house. Temples, churches, and mosques are holy places and the people who worship in them are called to live holy lives.

— Jeremiah 7:1–15

mine, in which you trust. Here in this place
that I gave to your ancestors and you, I will
do the same thing that I did to Shiloh. 15I
will drive you out of my sight as I drove out
your relatives, the people of Israel. I, the
LORD, have spoken."

The People's Disobedience

16The LORD said, "Jeremiah, do not pray
for these people. Do not cry or pray on
their behalf; do not plead with me, for I will
not listen to you. 17Don't you see what they
are doing in the cities of Judah and in the
streets of Jerusalem? 18The children gather
firewood, the men build fires, and the
women mix dough to bake cakes for the
goddess they call the Queen of Heaven.
They also pour out offerings of wine to
other gods, in order to hurt me. 19But am I
really the one they are hurting? No, they are
hurting themselves and bringing shame on
themselves. 20And so I, the Sovereign LORD,
will pour out my fierce anger on this Temple. I will pour it out on people and animals
alike, and even on the trees and the crops.
My anger will be like a fire that no one can
put out.

21"My people, some sacrifices you burn
completely on the altar, and some you are
permitted to eat. But what I, the LORD, say
is that you might as well eat them all. 22I
gave your ancestors no commands about
burnt offerings or any other kinds of sacrifices when I brought them out of Egypt.
23But I did command them to obey me, so
that I would be their God and they would
be my people. And I told them to live the
way I had commanded them, so that things
would go well for them. 24But they did not
obey or pay any attention. Instead, they did
whatever their stubborn and evil hearts told
them to do, and they became worse instead
of better. 25From the day that your ancestors
came out of Egypt until this very day I have
kept on sending to you my servants, the
prophets. 26Yet no one listened or paid any
attention. Instead, you became more stubborn and rebellious than your ancestors.

27"So, Jeremiah, you will speak all these
words to my people, but they will not listen
to you; you will call them, but they will not
answer. 28You will tell them that their nation
does not obey me, the LORD their God, or
learn from their punishment. Faithfulness is
dead. No longer is it even talked about.

Sinful Deeds in Hinnom Valley

29"Mourn, people of Jerusalem;
cut off your hair and throw it away.

7:18 Jer 44:17–19

Sing a funeral song on the hilltops,
because I, the LORD, am angry
and have rejected my people.
30 "The people of Judah have done an evil
thing. They have placed their idols, which I
hate, in my Temple and have defiled it. 31 In
Hinnom Valley they have built an altar called
Topheth, so that they can sacrifice their sons
and daughters in the fire. I did not command
them to do this—it did not even enter my
mind. 32 And so, the time will come when it
will no longer be called Topheth or Hinnom
Valley, but Slaughter Valley. They will bury
people there because there will be nowhere
else to bury them. 33 The corpses will be
food for the birds and wild animals, and
there will be no one to scare them off.
34 The land will become a desert. In the
cities of Judah and in the streets of Jerusalem
I will put an end to the sounds of joy and
gladness and to the happy sounds of wed-
ding feasts.

8 "At that time the bones of the kings and
of the officials of Judah, as well as the
bones of the priests, of the prophets, and of
the other people who lived in Jerusalem, will
be taken out of their graves. 2 Instead of being
gathered and buried, their bones will be like
manure lying on the ground. They will be
spread out before the sun, the moon, and the
stars, which these people have loved and
served, and which they have consulted and
worshiped. 3 And the people of this evil
nation who survive, who live in the places
where I have scattered them, will prefer to
die rather than to go on living. I, the LORD
Almighty, have spoken."

Sin and Punishment

4 The LORD told me to say to his people,
"When someone falls down, doesn't he get
back up? If someone misses the road, doesn't
he turn back? 5 Why then, my people, do
you turn away from me without ever turn-
ing back? You cling to your idols and refuse

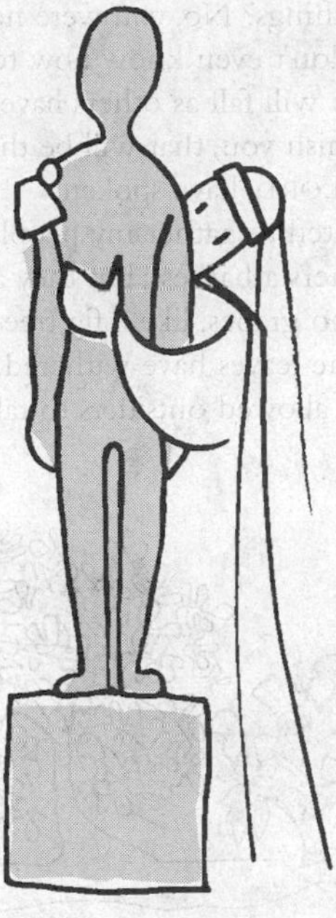

"You cling to your idols." (8:5)

to return to me. 6 I listened carefully, but you
did not speak the truth. Not one of you has
been sorry for your wickedness; not one of
you has asked, 'What have I done wrong?'
Each of you keep on going your own way,
like a horse rushing into battle. 7 Even storks
know when it is time to return; doves, swal-
lows, and thrushes know when it is time to
migrate. But, my people, you do not know
the laws by which I rule you. 8 How can you
say that you are wise and that you know my
laws? Look, the laws have been changed by
dishonest scribes. 9 Your wise men are put to
shame; they are confused and trapped. They
have rejected my words; what wisdom do
they have now? 10 So I will give their fields
to new owners and their wives to other
men. Everyone, great and small, tries to make
money dishonestly. Even prophets and priests
cheat the people. 11 They act as if my peo-
ple's wounds were only scratches. 'All is well,'
they say, when all is not well. 12 My people,
were you ashamed because you did these

7:31 a 2 Kings 23:10; Jer 32:35; **b** Lev 18:21 **7:34** Jer 16:9; 25:10; Bar 2:23; Rev 18:23 **8:11** Ezek 13:10
8:10–12 Jer 6:12–15

Did you know that child sacrifice *(Jeremiah 7:31)* **was still practiced in Old Testament times?**

disgusting things? No, you were not ashamed
at all; you don't even know how to blush!
And so you will fall as others have fallen;
when I punish you, that will be the end of
you. I, the LORD, have spoken.
13 "I wanted to gather my people, as a
farmer gathers a harvest; but they are like a
vine with no grapes, like a fig tree with no
figs; even the leaves have withered. Therefore, I have allowed outsiders to take over
the land."[g]

Like a vine with no grapes (8:13)

14 "Why are we sitting still?" God's people
ask. "Come on, we will run to the fortified
cities and die there. The LORD our God has
condemned us to die; he has given us poison
to drink, because we have sinned against
him. 15 We hoped for peace and a time of
healing, but it was no use; terror came
instead. 16 Our enemies are already in the
city of Dan; we hear the snorting of their
horses. The whole land trembles when their
horses neigh. Our enemies have come to
destroy our land and everything in it, our
city and all its people."
17 "Watch out!" the LORD says, "I am
sending snakes among you, poisonous snakes
that cannot be charmed, and they will bite
you."

Jeremiah's Sorrow for His People

18 My sorrow cannot be healed;[h]
I am sick at heart.

I am sick at heart. (8:18)

19 Listen! Throughout the land
I hear my people crying out,
"Is the LORD no longer in Zion?
Is Zion's king no longer there?"
The LORD, their king, replies,
"Why have you made me angry by
worshiping your idols
and by bowing down to your useless
foreign gods?"
20 The people cry out,
"The summer is gone, the harvest is over,
but we have not been saved."
21 My heart has been crushed
because my people are crushed;
I mourn; I am completely dismayed.
22 Is there no medicine in Gilead?[i]
Are there no doctors there?
Why, then, have my people not been
healed?

9 I wish my head were a well of water,
and my eyes a fountain of tears,
so that I could cry day and night
for my people who have been killed.
2 I wish I had a place to stay in the desert
where I could get away from my
people.
They are all unfaithful,
a mob of traitors.

[g] **8:13** Therefore . . . land; *Hebrew unclear.* [h] **8:18** *Probable text* My sorrow . . . healed; *Hebrew unclear.*
[i] **8:22** GILEAD: *A region east of the Jordan, famous for plants that were used for medicinal purposes.*

Jeremiah expresses his sorrow for his people's suffering, caused because of their sins. What are the sins in our society that cause people to suffer?

3 They are always ready to tell lies;
dishonesty instead of truth rules the land.

The LORD says,
"My people do one evil thing after another
and do not acknowledge me as their God."

4 Everyone must be on guard against their friends,
and no one can trust their relatives;
for all relatives are as deceitful as Jacob,
and everyone slanders their friends.
5-6 They all mislead their friends,
and no one tells the truth;
they have taught their tongues to lie
and will not give up their sinning.
They do one violent thing after another,
and one deceitful act follows another.

The LORD says that his people reject him.
7 Because of this the LORD Almighty says,
"I will refine my people like metal
and put them to the test.
My people have done evil—
what else can I do with them?
8 Their tongues are like deadly arrows;
they always tell lies.
Everyone speaks friendly words to their neighbors,
but they are really setting a trap for them.
9 Will I not punish them for these things?
Will I not take revenge on a nation like this?
I, the LORD, have spoken."

10 I said, "I will mourn for the mountains
and weep for the pastures,
because they have dried up,
and no one travels through them.
The sound of livestock is no longer heard;
birds and wild animals have fled and gone."

11 The LORD says, "I will make Jerusalem a pile of ruins,
a place where jackals live;
the cities of Judah will become a desert,
a place where no one lives."

12 I asked, " LORD, why is the land devastated and dry as a desert, so that no one travels through it? Who is wise enough to understand this? To whom have you explained it so that they can tell others?"

Live it!

The Sharp Tongue

Have you ever seen an arrowhead? In many parts of the United States, particularly near American Indian hunting grounds, arrowheads are fairly common. Chiseled by hand out of small rocks and used as the tips for arrows, they were very effective. Now, imagine someone's tongue being shaped like an arrowhead. All of us know that our tongues can be deadly weapons because we can use them to ruin someone's reputation or to hurt someone by making fun of him or her. Jeremiah says the tongues of people of his time are like deadly arrows (Jeremiah 9:8). Apparently, things haven't changed all that much in 2,500 years! The next time you are tempted to cut someone down, picture your tongue as an arrow that will be shot at someone else. Think about the harm that arrow can do, and stop before you let it loose!

— Jeremiah 9:8

13 The LORD answered, "This has happened because my people have abandoned the teaching that I gave them. They have not obeyed me or done what I told them.
14 Instead, they have been stubborn and have worshiped the idols of Baal as their ancestors
taught them to do. 15 So then, listen to what
I, the LORD Almighty, the God of Israel, will do: I will give my people bitter plants to eat
and poison to drink. 16 I will scatter them
among nations that neither they nor their ancestors have heard about, and I will send

armies against them until I have completely
destroyed them."

The People of Jerusalem Cry Out for Help

17 The LORD Almighty said,
"Think about what is happening!
Call for the mourners to come,
for the women who sing funeral songs."

18 The people said,
"Tell them to hurry and sing a funeral
song for us,
until our eyes fill with tears,
and our eyelids are wet from crying."

19 Listen to the sound of crying in Zion:
"We are ruined!
We are completely disgraced!
We must leave our land;
our homes have been torn down."

20 I said,
"Listen to the LORD, you women,
and pay attention to his words.
Teach your daughters how to mourn,
and your friends how to sing a funeral
song.
21 Death has come in through our windows
and entered our palaces;
it has cut down the children in the streets
and the young men in the
marketplaces.
22 Dead bodies are scattered everywhere,
like piles of manure on the fields,
like grain cut and left behind by the
reapers,
grain that no one gathers.
This is what the LORD has told me to say."

23 The LORD says,
"The wise should not boast of their
wisdom,
nor the strong of their strength,
nor the rich of their wealth.
24 If any want to boast,
they should boast that they know and
understand me,
because my love is constant,
and I do what is just and right.
These are the things that please me.
I, the LORD, have spoken."

25-26 The LORD says, "The time is coming
when I will punish the people of Egypt,
Judah, Edom, Ammon, Moab, and the desert
people, who have their hair cut short.[j] All
these people are circumcised, but have not
kept the covenant it symbolizes. None of
these people and none of the people of
Israel have kept my covenant."

Idolatry and True Worship

10 People of Israel, listen to the message
that the LORD has for you. 2 He says,
"Do not follow the ways of other nations;
do not be disturbed by unusual sights
in the sky,
even though other nations are terrified.
3 The religion of these people is worthless.
A tree is cut down in the forest;
it is carved by the tools of the
woodworker
4 and decorated with silver and gold.
It is fastened down with nails
to keep it from falling over.
5 Such idols are like scarecrows in a field of
melons;
they cannot speak;
they have to be carried
because they cannot walk.
Do not be afraid of them:
they can cause you no harm,
and they can do you no good."

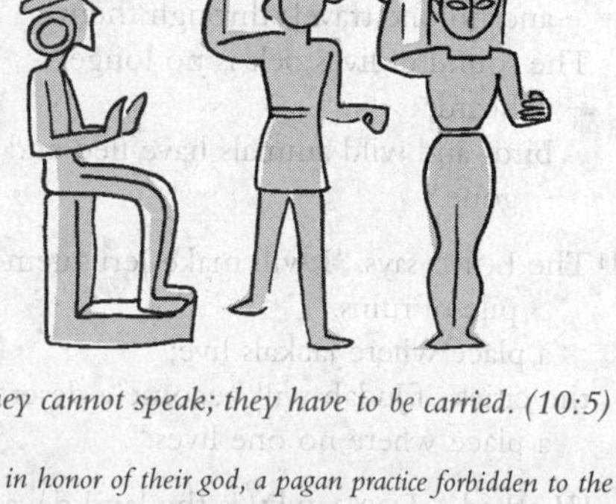

They cannot speak; they have to be carried. (10:5)

[j] 9:25–26 HAIR CUT SHORT: *The desert people cut their hair short in honor of their god, a pagan practice forbidden to the Israelites (see Lev 19:27).*

9:24 1 Cor 1:31; 2 Cor 10:17

6 LORD, there is no one like you;
you are mighty,
and your name is great and powerful.
7 Who would not honor you, the king of all nations?
You deserve to be honored.
There is no one like you
among all the wise men of the nations
or among any of their kings.
8 All of them are stupid and foolish.
What can they learn from wooden idols?[k]
9 Their idols are covered with silver from Spain
and with gold from Uphaz,
all the work of artists;
they are dressed in violet and purple cloth
woven by skilled weavers.
10 But you, LORD, are the true God,
you are the living God
and the eternal king.
When you are angry, the world trembles;
the nations cannot endure your anger.

(11 You people must tell them that the gods who did not make the earth and the sky will be destroyed. They will no longer exist anywhere on earth.)

A Hymn of Praise to God

12 The LORD made the earth by his power;
by his wisdom he created the world
and stretched out the heavens.
13 At his command the waters above the sky[l] roar;
he brings clouds from the ends of the earth.
He makes lightning flash in the rain
and sends the wind from his storeroom.
14 At the sight of this, people feel stupid and senseless;
those who make idols are disillusioned,
because the gods they make are false and lifeless.
15 They are worthless and should be despised;
they will be destroyed when the LORD comes to deal with them.
16 The God of Jacob is not like them;
he is the one who made everything,
and he has chosen Israel to be his very own people.
The LORD Almighty is his name.

The Coming Exile

17 People of Jerusalem, you are under
siege! Gather up your belongings. 18 The
LORD is going to throw you out of this land;
he is going to crush you until not one of
you is left. The LORD has spoken.
19 The people of Jerusalem cried out,
"How badly we are hurt!
Our wounds will not heal.
And we thought this was something we could endure!
20 Our tents are ruined;
the ropes that held them have broken.
Our children have all gone away;
there is no one left to put up our tents again;
there is no one to hang their curtains."

21 I answered, "Our leaders are stupid;
they do not ask the LORD for guidance.
This is why they have failed,
and our people have been scattered.
22 Listen! News has come!
There is a great commotion in a nation to the north;
its army will turn the cities of Judah into a desert,
a place where jackals live."

23 LORD, I know that none of us are in charge of our own destiny;
none of us have control over our own life.

[k] **10:8** What can . . . idols?; *or* What their idols teach is worthless. [l] **10:13** WATERS ABOVE THE SKY: *See Gen 1:6–8.*
10:7 Rev 15:4

Jeremiah says that Jerusalem is "under siege" *(Jeremiah 10:17)*. **This is often how an enemy army would defeat a city. Can you describe the process?**

Study it!

Breaking the Covenant

Why is God so angry with his Chosen People? Why are all these bad things happening? Jeremiah, chapter 11, explains that it is because the Israelites have broken God's Covenant with them. This covenant is the sacred promise or commitment between God and his people. Several covenants are described in the book of Genesis: these include one between God and Noah, one between God and Abraham, and another between God and Jacob.

But the most important covenant was the covenant God made with Moses and the Israelite people at Mount Sinai. You may want to read about that covenant again in Exodus, chapter 24. God's part of the Sinai Covenant was that he would protect the Israelites and give them their own land. Their part of the Sinai Covenant is summarized in the Ten Commandments. Can you see how the Israelites are not keeping their part of the Covenant?

— Jeremiah 11:1–5

24 Correct your people, LORD,
but do not be too hard on us
or punish us when you are angry;
that would be the end of us.
25 Turn your anger on the nations that do
not worship you
and on the people who reject you.
They have killed your people;
they have destroyed us completely
and left our country in ruins.

Jeremiah and the Covenant

11 The LORD said to me, 2“Listen to
the terms of the covenant. Tell the
people of Judah and of Jerusalem 3that I, the
LORD God of Israel, have placed a curse on
everyone who does not obey the terms of
this covenant. 4It is the covenant I made
with their ancestors when I brought them
out of Egypt, the land that was like a blazing
furnace to them. I told them to obey me and
to do everything that I had commanded. I
told them that if they obeyed, they would be
my people and I would be their God. 5Then
I would keep the promise I made to their
ancestors that I would give them the rich
and fertile land which they now have.”
I said, “Yes, LORD.”
6Then the LORD said to me, “Go to the
cities of Judah and to the streets of Jerusalem.
Proclaim my message there and tell the peo-
ple to listen to the terms of the covenant and
to obey them. 7When I brought their ances-
tors out of Egypt, I solemnly warned them to
obey me, and I have kept on warning the
people until this day. 8But they did not listen
or obey. Instead, everyone continued to be as
stubborn and evil as ever. I had commanded
them to keep the covenant, but they refused.
So I brought on them all the punishments
described in it.”
9Then the LORD said to me, “The people
of Judah and of Jerusalem are plotting against
me. 10They have gone back to the sins of
their ancestors, who refused to do what I
said; they have worshiped other gods. Both
Israel and Judah have broken the covenant
that I made with their ancestors. 11So now I,
the LORD, warn them that I am going to
bring destruction on them, and they will not
escape. And when they cry out to me for
help, I will not listen to them. 12Then the
people of Judah and of Jerusalem will go to
the gods to whom they offer sacrifices and
will cry out to them for help. But those gods
will not be able to save them when this
destruction comes. 13The people of Judah
have as many gods as they have cities, and
the inhabitants of Jerusalem have set up as

“When I brought their ancestors out of Egypt, I solemnly warned them to obey me, and I have kept on warning the people until this day” *(Jeremiah 11:7).*

many altars for sacrifices to that disgusting
god Baal as there are streets in the city.
14Jeremiah, don't pray to me or plead with
me on behalf of these people. When they are
in trouble and call to me for help, I will not
listen to them."
15The LORD says, "The people I love are
doing evil things. What right do they have to
be in my Temple? Do they think they can
prevent disaster by making promises[m] and by
offering animal sacrifices? Will they then
rejoice? 16I once called them a leafy olive
tree, full of beautiful fruit; but now, with a
roar like thunder I will set its leaves on fire
and break its branches.

I will set its leaves on fire. (11:16)

17"I, the LORD Almighty, planted Israel
and Judah; but now I threaten them with
disaster. They have brought this on them-
selves because they have done wrong; they
have made me angry by offering sacrifices to
Baal."

A Plot against Jeremiah's Life

18The LORD informed me of the plots
that my enemies were making against me. 19I
was like a trusting lamb taken out to be
killed, and I did not know that it was against
me that they were planning evil things. They
were saying, "Let's chop down the tree while
it is still healthy;[n] let's kill him so that no
one will remember him any more."
20Then I prayed, "Almighty LORD, you
are a just judge; you test people's thoughts

Pray it!

Why?

Read Jeremiah 12:1–4. Jeremiah is asking God several questions. They are hard questions, and we might be tempted to ask the same ones. Why do bad people do well in life? Why do dishonest people succeed? What is striking about Jeremiah is his honesty with God. He does not hesitate to ask God the tough questions, especially when it comes to what seems like injustice. Think of some questions you have for God. Go ahead and ask God about them! Be specific about what is bothering you. God can handle it.

— Jeremiah 12:1–4

and feelings. I have placed my cause in your
hands; so let me watch you take revenge on
these people."
21The people of Anathoth wanted me
killed, and they told me that they would kill
me if I kept on proclaiming the LORD's mes-
sage. 22So the LORD Almighty said, "I will
punish them! Their young men will be killed
in war; their children will die of starvation.
23I have set a time for bringing disaster on
the people of Anathoth, and when that time
comes, none of them will survive."

Jeremiah Questions the LORD

12 "LORD, if I argued my case with you,
you would prove to be right.
Yet I must question you about matters of justice.
Why are the wicked so prosperous?
Why do dishonest people succeed?

[m] **11:15** *One ancient translation* promises; *Hebrew* many. [n] **11:19** *Probable text* while it is still healthy; *Hebrew* with its bread.
11:20 Wis 1:6–9

2 You plant them, and they take root;
they grow and bear fruit.
They always speak well of you,
yet they do not really care about you.
3 But, LORD, you know me;
you see what I do
and how I love you.
Drag these evil people away like sheep to be butchered;
guard them until it is time for them to be slaughtered.
4 How long will our land be dry,
and the grass in every field be withered?
Animals and birds are dying
because of the wickedness of our people,
people who say, 'God doesn't see what we are doing.' "[o]

5 The LORD said,
"Jeremiah, if you get tired racing against people,
how can you race against horses?
If you can't even stand up in open country,
how will you manage in the jungle by the Jordan?
6 Even your relatives, members of your own family, have betrayed you;
they join in the attacks against you.
Do not trust them, even though they speak friendly words."

The LORD's Sorrow because of His People

7 The LORD says,
"I have abandoned Israel;
I have rejected my chosen nation.
I have given the people I love
into the power of their enemies.
8 My chosen people have turned against me;
like a lion in the forest
they have roared at me,
and so I hate them.
9 My chosen people are like a bird
attacked from all sides by hawks.
Call the wild animals
to come and join in the feast!
10 Many foreign rulers have destroyed my vineyard;
they have trampled down my fields;
they have turned my lovely land into a desert.
11 They have made it a wasteland;
it lies desolate before me.
The whole land has become a desert,
and no one cares.
12 Across all the desert highlands
people have come to plunder.
I have sent war to destroy the entire land;
no one can live in peace.
13 My people planted wheat, but gathered weeds;
they have worked hard, but got nothing for it.
Because of my fierce anger
their crops have failed."

The LORD's Promise to Israel's Neighbors

14 The LORD says, "I have something to
say about Israel's neighbors who have ruined
the land I gave to my people Israel. I will
take those wicked people away from their
countries like an uprooted plant, and I will
rescue Judah from them. 15 But after I have
taken them away, I will have mercy on them;
I will bring each nation back to its own land
and to its own country. 16 If with all their
hearts they will accept the religion of my
people and will swear, 'As the LORD lives'—
as they once taught my people to swear by
Baal—then they will also be a part of my
people and will prosper. 17 But if any nation
will not obey, then I will completely uproot
it and destroy it. I, the LORD, have spoken."

The Linen Shorts

13 The LORD told me to go and buy
myself some linen shorts and to put
them on; but he told me not to put them in
water. 2 So I bought them and put them on.
3 Then the LORD spoke to me again and
said, 4 "Go to the Euphrates River and hide
the shorts in a hole in the rocks." 5 So I went
and hid them near the Euphrates.

[o] **12:4** *Some ancient translations* what we are doing; *Hebrew* our latter end.

6 Some time later the LORD told me to go
back to the Euphrates and get the shorts. 7 So
I went back, and when I found the place
where I had hidden them, I saw that they
were ruined and were no longer any good.
8 Then the LORD spoke to me again. He
said, 9 "This is how I will destroy the pride of
Judah and the great pride of Jerusalem.
10 These evil people have refused to obey me.
They have been as stubborn and wicked as
ever, and have worshiped and served other
gods. So then, they will become like these
shorts that are no longer any good. 11 Just as
shorts fit tightly around the waist, so I intend-
ed all the people of Israel and Judah to hold
tightly to me. I did this so that they would be
my people and would bring praise and honor
to my name; but they would not obey me."

The Wine Jar

12 The LORD God said to me, "Jeremiah,
tell the people of Israel that every wine jar
should be filled with wine. They will answer
that they know every wine jar should be
filled with wine. 13 Then tell them that I, the
LORD, am going to fill the people in this
land with wine until they are drunk: the
kings, who are David's descendants, the
priests, the prophets, and all the people of
Jerusalem. 14 Then I will smash them like jars
against one another, old and young alike. No
pity, compassion, or mercy will stop me from
killing them."

Jeremiah Warns against Pride

15 People of Israel, the LORD has spoken!
Be humble and listen to him.
16 Honor the LORD, your God,
before he brings darkness,
and you stumble on the mountains;
before he turns into deep darkness
the light you hoped for.
17 If you will not listen,
I will cry in secret because of your
pride;
I will cry bitterly, and my tears will flow
because the LORD's people have been
taken away as captives.

18 The LORD said to me, "Tell the king
and his mother to come down from their
thrones, because their beautiful crowns have
fallen from their heads.[p] 19 The towns of
southern Judah are under siege; no one can

Live it!

Clinging to God

A pair of linen shorts isn't exactly your typical biblical image, is it? Some translations use the word *loincloth,* which is the type of underwear men would have worn in Old Testament times. Why would God instruct Jeremiah to use such an image? What's the point?

Think about it. As the passage explains, just as shorts fit tightly around the waist, so God wants the people to cling tightly to him. And after the shorts are hidden in a hole in the rocks, they are ruined by the weather and therefore good for nothing. So the people, through their disobedience, have ruined their relationship with God.

So, there it is: a ruined pair of linen shorts is a prop that Jeremiah can use to get his point across. No doubt it got people's attention! Try to think of anything in your room that could be a symbol of your relationship with God.

—Jeremiah 13:1–11

p **13:18** *Some ancient translations* from their heads; *Hebrew unclear.*

In Jeremiah, chapter 12, can you find examples of how the land itself was affected by people's sin? How have we destroyed or hurt the earth in our time?

get through to them. All the people of Judah
have been taken away into exile."
[20]Jerusalem, look! Your enemies are coming
down from the north! Where are the people
entrusted to your care, your people you were
so proud of [21]What will you say when people
you thought were your friends conquer you
and rule over you?[q] You will be in pain like a
woman giving birth. [22]If you ask why all this
has happened to you—why your clothes have
been torn off and you have been raped—it is
because your sin is so terrible. [23]Can people
change the color of their skin, or a leopard
remove its spots? If they could, then you that
do nothing but evil could learn to do what is
right. [24]The LORD will scatter you like straw
that is blown away by the desert wind. [25]He
has said that this will be your fate. This is
what he has decided to do with you, because
you have forgotten him and have trusted in
false gods. [26]The LORD himself will strip off
your clothes and expose you to shame. [27]He
has seen you do the things he hates. He has
seen you go after pagan gods on the hills and
in the fields, like a man lusting after his neigh-
bor's wife or like a stallion after a mare. Peo-
ple of Jerusalem, you are doomed! When will
you ever be pure?

Like straw that is blown away (13:24)

The Terrible Drought

14 The LORD said to me concerning the drought,

[2]"Judah is in mourning;
its cities are dying,
its people lie on the ground in sorrow,
and Jerusalem cries out for help.
[3]The rich people send their servants for water;
they go to the cisterns,
but find no water;
they come back with their jars empty.

They come back with their jars empty. (14:3)

Discouraged and confused,
they hide their faces.
[4]Because there is no rain
and the ground is dried up,
the farmers are sick at heart;
they hide their faces.
[5]In the field the mother deer
abandons her newborn fawn
because there is no grass.
[6]The wild donkeys stand on the hilltops
and pant for breath like jackals;
their eyesight fails them
because they have no food.
[7]My people cry out to me,
'Even though our sins accuse us,
help us, LORD, as you have promised.
We have turned away from you many times;
we have sinned against you.
[8]You are Israel's only hope;
you are the one who saves us from disaster.
Why are you like a stranger in our land,
like a traveler who stays for only one night?
[9]Why are you like someone taken by surprise,
like a soldier powerless to help?
Surely, LORD, you are with us!
We are your people;
do not abandon us.' "

[q] **13:21** *Probable text* What . . . over you; *Hebrew unclear.*

Cistern: **A type of well that holds rainwater. Cisterns are an important source of water for people in dry lands.**

10The LORD says about these people,
"They love to run away from me, and they
will not control themselves. So I am not
pleased with them. I will remember the
wrongs they have done and punish them
because of their sins."
11The LORD said to me, "Do not ask me
to help these people. 12Even if they fast, I
will not listen to their cry for help; and even
if they offer me burnt offerings and grain
offerings, I will not be pleased with them.
Instead, I will kill them in war and by starva-
tion and disease."
13Then I said, "Sovereign LORD, you
know that the prophets are telling the peo-
ple that there will be no war or starvation,
because you have promised, they say, that
there will be only peace in our land."
14But the LORD replied, "The prophets are
telling lies in my name; I did not send them,
nor did I give them any orders or speak one
word to them. The visions they talk about
have not come from me; their predictions are
worthless things that they have imagined. 15I,
the LORD, tell you what I am going to do to
those prophets whom I did not send but
who speak in my name and say war and star-
vation will not strike this land—I will kill
them in war and by starvation. 16The people
to whom they have said these things will be
killed in the same way. Their bodies will be
thrown out into the streets of Jerusalem, and
there will be no one to bury them. This will
happen to all of them—including their
wives, their sons, and their daughters. I will
make them pay for their wickedness."
17The LORD commanded me to tell the
people about my sorrow and to say:

"May my eyes flow with tears day and
night,
may I never stop weeping,
for my people are deeply wounded
and are badly hurt.
18When I go out in the fields,
I see the bodies of men killed in war;
when I go into the towns,
I see people starving to death.
Prophets and priests carry on their work,
but they don't know what they are
doing."[r]

Study it!

False Prophets

One of the reasons Jeremiah was so unpopular is that he preached the truth. He tried to warn the people that bad things would happen to them if they didn't return to the Lord. However, they preferred to listen to other people who called themselves prophets. These prophets told the people what they wanted to hear. But their words did not come from God. So they are called false prophets. As the LORD tells Jeremiah, "The prophets are telling lies in my name" (Jeremiah 14:14).

If the message of a preacher or speaker does not challenge us and only tells us what we want to hear, it is doubtful that these are prophetic words. Check out a more detailed description of false prophets in Jeremiah 23:16–22.

— Jeremiah 14:13–15

The People Plead with the LORD

19LORD, have you completely rejected Judah?
Do you hate the people of Zion?
Why have you hurt us so badly
that we cannot be healed?
We looked for peace, but nothing good
happened;
we hoped for healing, but terror came
instead.
20We have sinned against you, LORD;
we confess our own sins
and the sins of our ancestors.
21Remember your promises and do not
despise us;
do not bring disgrace on Jerusalem,
the place of your glorious throne.

[r] **14:18** Prophets . . . doing; *or* Prophets and priests have been dragged away to a land they know nothing about.

Do not break the covenant you made
with us.
22 None of the idols of the nations can send
rain;
the sky by itself cannot make showers
fall.
We have put our hope in you, O LORD
our God,
because you are the one who does
these things.

Doom for the People of Judah

15 Then the LORD said to me, "Even if
Moses and Samuel were standing
here pleading with me, I would not show
these people any mercy. Make them go
away; make them get out of my sight.
2 When they ask you where they should go,
tell them that I have said:
Some are doomed to die by disease—
that's where they will go!
Others are doomed to die in war—
that's where they will go!
Some are doomed to die of starvation—
that's where they will go!
Others are doomed to be taken away as
prisoners—
that's where they will go!
3 I, the LORD, have decided that four terrible
things will happen to them: they will be
killed in war; their bodies will be dragged off
by dogs; birds will eat them, and wild animals
will devour what is left over. 4 I will make all
the people of the world horrified at them
because of what Hezekiah's son Manasseh
did in Jerusalem when he was king of Judah."
5 The LORD says,
"Who will pity you, people of Jerusalem,
and who will grieve over you?
Who will stop long enough
to ask how you are?
6 You people have rejected me;
you have turned your backs on me.
So I reached out and crushed you
because I was tired of controlling my
anger.[s]
7 In every town in the land
I threw you to the wind like straw.
I destroyed you, my people.
I killed your children
because you did not stop your evil
ways.
8 There are more widows in your land
than grains of sand by the sea.
I killed your young men in their prime
and made their mothers suffer.
I suddenly struck them
with anguish and terror.
9 The mother who lost her seven children
has fainted,
gasping for breath.
Her daylight has turned to darkness;
she is disgraced and sick at heart.
I will let your enemies kill
those of you who are still alive.
I, the LORD, have spoken."

Jeremiah Complains to the LORD

10 What an unhappy man I am! Why did
my mother bring me into the world? I have
to quarrel and argue with everyone in the
land. I have not lent any money or borrowed
any; yet everyone curses me. 11 LORD, may all
their curses come true if I have not served[t]
you well, if I have not pleaded with you on
behalf of my enemies when they were in
trouble and distress. (12 No one can break
iron, especially the iron from the north that
is mixed with bronze.)
13 The LORD said to me, "I will send ene-
mies to carry away the wealth and treasures
of my people, in order to punish them for
the sins they have committed throughout
the land. 14 I will make them serve their ene-
mies in a land they know nothing about,
because my anger is like fire, and it will burn
forever."
15 Then I said, " LORD, you understand.
Remember me and help me. Let me have
revenge on those who persecute me. Do not
be so patient with them that they succeed in
killing me. Remember that it is for your sake
that I am insulted. 16 You spoke to me, and I
listened to every word. I belong to you,
LORD God Almighty, and so your words
filled my heart with joy and happiness. 17 I

[s] **15:6** you because . . . anger; *or* you; I was tired of feeling sorry for you. [t] **15:11** *Probable text* LORD, . . . served; *Hebrew unclear.*

15:1 a Ex 32:11–14; Num 14:13–19; **b** 1 Sam 7:5–9 **15:2** Rev 13:10 **15:4** 2 Kings 21:1–16; 2 Chr 33:1–9

Live it!

Why Me, O Lord?

Check out the conversation between God and Jeremiah in Jeremiah 15:10–21. Jeremiah is unhappy and complains to God. God responds, but Jeremiah has more to say. He has lots of questions for the Lord and doesn't hesitate to ask them. God ends by reassuring Jeremiah that he is not alone. Sometimes that's all we need to know. Think of a time when you sensed God was with you in times of trouble. Are you willing to trust that God is with you even when it seems everyone else is against you?

— Jeremiah 15:10–21

did not spend my time with other people,
laughing and having a good time. In obedi-
ence to your orders I stayed by myself and
was filled with anger. 18Why do I keep on
suffering? Why are my wounds incurable?
Why won't they heal? Do you intend to dis-
appoint me like a stream that goes dry in the
summer?"
19To this the LORD replied, "If you return,
I will take you back, and you will be my ser-
vant again. If instead of talking nonsense you
proclaim a worthwhile message, you will be
my prophet again. The people will come
back to you, and you will not need to go to
them. 20I will make you like a solid bronze
wall as far as they are concerned. They will
fight against you, but they will not defeat
you. I will be with you to protect you and
keep you safe. 21I will rescue you from the
power of wicked and violent people. I, the
LORD, have spoken."

The LORD's Will for Jeremiah's Life

16 Again the LORD spoke to me and
said, 2"Do not marry or have chil-
dren in a place like this. 3I will tell you what
is going to happen to the children who are
born here and to their parents. 4They will
die of terrible diseases, and no one will
mourn for them or bury them. Their bodies
will lie like piles of manure on the ground.
They will be killed in war or die of starva-
tion, and their bodies will be food for the
birds and the wild animals.
5"You must not enter a house where
there is mourning. Do not grieve for any-
one. I will no longer bless my people with
peace or show them love and mercy. 6The
rich and the poor will die in this land, but
no one will bury them or mourn for them.
Not one of you will gash yourself or shave
your head to show your grief. 7No one will
eat or drink with anyone to offer comfort
when a loved one dies. No one will show
sympathy, not even for someone who has
lost a father or mother.
8"Do not enter a house where people are
feasting. Do not sit down with them to eat
and drink. 9Listen to what I, the LORD
Almighty, the God of Israel, have to say. I
will silence the sounds of joy and gladness
and the happy sounds of wedding feasts. The
people here will live to see this happen.
10"When you tell them all this, they will
ask you why I have decided to punish them
so harshly. They will ask what crime they are
guilty of and what sin they have committed
against the LORD their God. 11Then tell
them that the LORD has said, 'Your ancestors
turned away from me and worshiped and
served other gods. They abandoned me and
did not obey my teachings. 12But you have
done even worse than your ancestors. All of
you are stubborn and evil, and you do not
obey me. 13So then, I will throw you out of
this land into a land that neither you nor
your ancestors have ever known. And there

16:9 Jer 7:34; 25:10; Rev 18:23

Moses and Samuel are mentioned at the beginning of Jeremiah, chapter 15. Which of these two men has two books in the Bible named after him?

Catholic Connections

Single for God

God instructs Jeremiah not to marry (Jeremiah 16:2), and so Jeremiah remains single and celibate all his life. He remains single as a sign that the coming destruction is no time to start a family and raise children. Almost all Jewish males married, so staying single would definitely make Jeremiah noticed.

In this way Jeremiah is also like Jesus. Jesus was never married either. Jesus' mission was for all people, and it took all of his energy and time. If he had a wife and children, he could not have been a devoted husband and father and still accomplish his mission.

You are probably aware that in the Catholic Church, priests and women and men in religious communities make vows to remain single for their whole lives. This is also called celibacy. They choose to be single to devote themselves to God's mission and to be a sign that God's love is enough for us.

— Jeremiah 16:1–4

you will serve other gods day and night, and
I will show you no mercy.' "

The Return from Exile

14The LORD says, "The time is coming
when people will no longer swear by me as
the living God who brought the people of
Israel out of the land of Egypt. 15Instead,
they will swear by me as the living God who
brought the people of Israel out of a north-
ern land and out of all the other countries
where I had scattered them. I will bring
them back to their own country, to the land
that I gave their ancestors. I, the LORD, have
spoken."

The Coming Punishment

16The LORD says, "I am sending for
many fishermen to come and catch these
people. Then I will send for many hunters
to hunt them down on every mountain and
hill and in the caves among the rocks. 17I
see everything they do. Nothing is hidden
from me; their sins do not escape my sight.
18I will make them pay double for their sin
and wickedness, because they have defiled
my land with idols that are as lifeless as
corpses, and have filled it with their false
gods."

Jeremiah's Prayer of Confidence in the LORD

19LORD, you are the one who protects me
and gives me strength; you help me in times
of trouble. Nations will come to you from
the ends of the earth and say, "Our ancestors
had nothing but false gods, nothing but use-
less idols. 20Can people make their own
gods? No, if they did, those would not really
be gods."

21"So then," says the LORD, "once and for
all I will make the nations know my power
and my might; they will know that I am the
LORD."

Compare Jeremiah 17:6–8 with Psalm 1.

The Sin and Punishment of Judah

17 The LORD says, "People of Judah,
your sin is written with an iron pen;
it is engraved on your hearts with a diamond
point and carved on the corners of your
altars. 2Your people worship at the altars and
the symbols that have been set up for the
goddess Asherah by every green tree and on
the hilltops 3and on the mountains in the
open country. I will have your enemies take
away your wealth and your treasures because
of all the sins you have committed[u] through-
out your land. 4You will have to give up[v] the
land I gave you, and I will make you serve
your enemies in a land you know nothing
about, because my anger is like a fire, and it
will burn forever."

Various Sayings

5The LORD says,
"I will condemn those
who turn away from me
and put their trust in human beings,
in the strength of mortals.
6He is like a bush in the desert,
which grows in the dry wasteland,
on salty ground where nothing else
grows.
Nothing good ever happens to him.

7"But I will bless the person
who puts his trust in me.
8He is like a tree growing near a stream
and sending out roots to the water.
It is not afraid when hot weather comes,
because its leaves stay green;
it has no worries when there is no rain;
it keeps on bearing fruit.

9"Who can understand the human heart?
There is nothing else so deceitful;
it is too sick to be healed.
10I, the LORD, search the minds
and test the hearts of people.
I treat each of them according to the way
they live,
according to what they do."

He is like a bush in the desert. (17:6)

11The person who gets money dishonestly
is like a bird that hatches eggs it didn't
lay.
In the prime of life he will lose his riches,
and in the end he is nothing but a fool.

12Our Temple is like a glorious throne,
standing on a high mountain from the
beginning.
13LORD, you are Israel's hope;
all who abandon you will be put to
shame.
They will disappear like names written in
the dust,[w]
because they have abandoned you, the
LORD,
the spring of fresh water.

Jeremiah Asks the LORD for Help

14LORD, heal me and I will be completely
well; rescue me and I will be perfectly safe.
You are the one I praise!
15The people say to me, "Where are those
threats the LORD made against us? Let him
carry them out now!"
16But, LORD, I never urged you to bring

[u] **17:3** *Probable text* because of all the sins you have committed; *Hebrew* your high places for sins.
[v] **17:4** *Probable text* You . . . give up; *Hebrew unclear.* [w] **17:13** disappear . . . dust; *or* go to the world of the dead.
17:8 Ps 1:3 **17:10 a** Rev 2:23; **b** Ps 62:12

Pray it!

My Place of Safety

Jeremiah says to God, "You are my place of safety when trouble comes" (Jeremiah 17:17). Where do you go when you are afraid?

Think of a place where you feel safe. Now picture God there with you. Perhaps God is holding you or simply beside you. Stay with this image for a while.

The next time you feel afraid or threatened, try to recapture that image of being in a safe place with God. Let God reassure you and be with you.

— Jeremiah 17:14–18

disaster on them;[x] I did not wish a time of
trouble for them. LORD, you know this; you
know what I have said. 17Do not be a terror
to me; you are my place of safety when
trouble comes. 18Bring disgrace on those
who persecute me, but spare me, LORD. Fill
them with terror, but do not terrify me.
Bring disaster on them and break them to
pieces.

On Observing the Sabbath

19The LORD said to me, "Jeremiah, go and
announce my message at the People's Gate,
through which the kings of Judah enter and
leave the city; then go to all the other gates
of Jerusalem. 20Tell the kings and all the
people of Judah and everyone who lives in
Jerusalem and enters these gates, to listen to
what I say. 21Tell them that if they love their
lives, they must not carry any load on the
Sabbath; they must not carry anything in
through the gates of Jerusalem 22or carry
anything out of their houses on the Sabbath.
They must not work on the Sabbath; they
must observe it as a sacred day, as I com-
manded their ancestors. 23Their ancestors
did not listen to me or pay any attention.
Instead, they became stubborn; they would
not obey me or learn from me.

24"Tell these people that they must obey
all my commands. They must not carry any
load in through the gates of this city on the
Sabbath. They must observe the Sabbath as a
sacred day and must not do any work at all.
25Then their kings and princes will enter the
gates of Jerusalem and have the same royal
power that David had. Together with the
people of Judah and of Jerusalem, they will
ride in chariots and on horses, and the city
of Jerusalem will always be filled with peo-
ple. 26People will come from the towns of
Judah and from the villages around
Jerusalem; they will come from the territory
of Benjamin, from the foothills, from the
mountains, and from southern Judah. They
will bring to my Temple burnt offerings and
sacrifices, grain offerings and incense, as well
as thank offerings. 27But they must obey me
and observe the Sabbath as a sacred day.
They must not carry any load through the
gates of Jerusalem on that day, for if they do,
I will set the gates of Jerusalem on fire. Fire
will burn down the palaces of Jerusalem, and
no one will be able to put it out."

Jeremiah at the Potter's House

18 The LORD said to me, 2"Go down
to the potter's house, where I will
give you my message." 3So I went there and
saw the potter working at his wheel.
4Whenever a piece of pottery turned out
imperfect, he would take the clay and make
it into something else.

5Then the LORD said to me, 6"Don't I
have the right to do with you people of Israel
what the potter did with the clay? You are in
my hands just like clay in the potter's hands.
7If at any time I say that I am going to
uproot, break down, or destroy any nation or
kingdom, 8but then that nation turns from its
evil, I will not do what I said I would. 9On
the other hand, if I say that I am going to

[x] **17:16** *Probable text* bring disaster on them; *Hebrew* from being a shepherd after you.

17:21 Neh 13:15–22 **17:22** Ex 20:8–10; Deut 5:12–14

plant or build up any nation or kingdom,
10but then that nation disobeys me and does
evil, I will not do what I said I would. 11Now
then, tell the people of Judah and of Jerusalem
that I am making plans against them and get-
ting ready to punish them. Tell them to stop
living sinful lives—to change their ways and
the things they are doing. 12They will answer,
'No, why should we? We will all be just as
stubborn and evil as we want to be.' "

The People Reject the LORD

13The LORD says,
"Ask every nation if such a thing
has ever happened before.
The people of Israel have done a
terrible thing!
14Are Lebanon's rocky heights ever without
snow?
Do its cool mountain streams ever run
dry?
15Yet my people have forgotten me;
they burn incense to idols.
They have stumbled in the way they
should go;
they no longer follow the old ways;
they walk on unmarked paths.
16They have made this land a thing of
horror,
to be despised forever.
All who pass by will be shocked at what
they see;
they will shake their heads in
amazement.
17I will scatter my people before their
enemies,
like dust blown by the east wind.
I will turn my back on them;
I will not help them when the disaster
comes."

A Plot against Jeremiah

18Then the people said, "Let's do some-
thing about Jeremiah! There will always be
priests to instruct us, the wise to give us
counsel, and prophets to proclaim God's
message. Let's bring charges against him and
stop listening to what he says."

19So I prayed, " LORD, hear what I am
saying and listen to what my enemies are
saying about me. 20Is evil the payment for
good? Yet they have dug a pit for me to fall
in. Remember how I came to you and spoke
on their behalf, so that you would not deal
with them in anger. 21But now, LORD, let
their children starve to death; let them be
killed in war. Let the women lose their hus-
bands and children; let the men die of dis-
ease and the young men be killed in battle.
22Send a mob to plunder their homes with-
out warning; make them cry out in terror.
They have dug a pit for me to fall in and
have set traps to catch me. 23But, LORD, you
know all their plots to kill me. Do not for-
give their evil or pardon their sin. Throw
them down in defeat and deal with them
while you are angry."

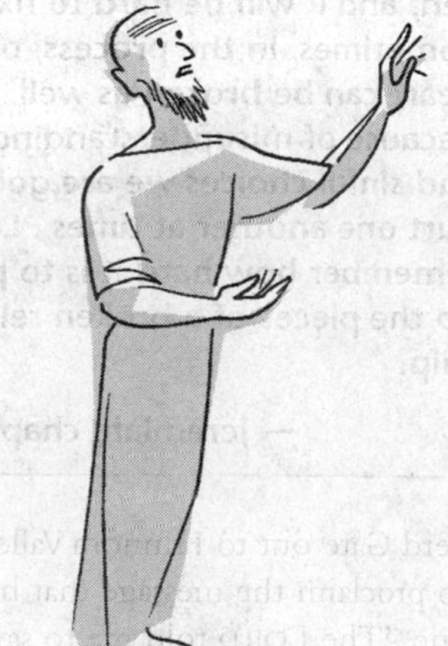

"LORD, hear what I am saying." (18:19)

The Broken Jar

19 The LORD told me to go and buy a
clay jar. He also told me to take
some of the elders of the people and some
of the older priests, 2and to go through

19:2 2 Kings 23:10; Jer 7:30–32; 32:34, 35

How is what the people say against Jeremiah in 18:18 similar to what people said about Jesus in the Gospels?

Live it!

Broken Dreams

God tells Jeremiah to break a clay jar in front of the leaders to let the people know that God is upset with their sins. A shattered clay pot or jar is impossible to fully repair. In fact, it really doesn't make sense to even try to put back together all the broken pieces.

This can happen with relationships as well, especially close friendships. Something happens. A secret told in confidence is shared with others. Or one person gets jealous of another. Angry words become weapons, and then it happens: the friendship is broken, and it will be hard to fix. Sometimes, in the process, our heart can be broken as well. Because of misunderstandings and sinful choices we are going to hurt one another at times . Let's remember how hard it is to pick up the pieces of a broken relationship.

— Jeremiah, chapter 19

Potsherd Gate out to Hinnom Valley. There I
was to proclaim the message that he would
give me. 3The LORD told me to say, "Kings
of Judah and people of Jerusalem, listen to
what I, the LORD Almighty, the God of
Israel, have to say. I am going to bring such a
disaster on this place that everyone who
hears about it will be stunned. 4I am going
to do this because the people have aban-
doned me and defiled this place by offering
sacrifices here to other gods—gods that nei-
ther they nor their ancestors nor the kings of

The LORD told me to break the jar. (19:10)

Judah have known anything about. They
have filled this place with the blood of inno-
cent people, 5and they have built altars for
Baal in order to burn their children in the
fire as sacrifices. I never commanded them to
do this; it never even entered my mind. 6So
then, the time will come when this place
will no longer be called Topheth or Hinnom
Valley. Instead, it will be known as Slaughter
Valley. 7In this place I will frustrate all the
plans of the people of Judah and Jerusalem. I
will let their enemies triumph over them
and kill them in battle. I will give their
corpses to the birds and the wild animals as
food. 8I will bring such terrible destruction
on this city that everyone who passes by will
be shocked and amazed. 9The enemy will
surround the city and try to kill its people.
The siege will be so terrible that the people
inside the city will eat one another and even
their own children."

10Then the LORD told me to break the jar
in front of those who had gone with me
11and to tell them that the LORD Almighty
had said, "I will break this people and this
city, and it will be like this broken clay jar
that cannot be put together again. People
will bury their dead even in Topheth because
there will be nowhere else to bury them. 12I
promise that I will make this city and its
inhabitants like Topheth. 13The houses of
Jerusalem, the houses of the kings of Judah,

19:5 Lev 18:21

"I will break this people and this city, and it will be like this broken clay jar that cannot be put together again" *(Jeremiah 19:11).*

and indeed all the houses on whose roofs
incense has been burned to the stars and
where wine has been poured out as an offer-
ing to other gods—they will all be as
unclean as Topheth."

14 Then I left Topheth, where the LORD
had sent me to proclaim his message. I went
and stood in the court of the Temple and
told all the people 15 that the LORD
Almighty, the God of Israel, had said, "I am
going to bring on this city and on every
nearby town all the punishment that I said I
would, because you are stubborn and will
not listen to what I say."

Jeremiah's Conflict with Pashhur the Priest

20 When the priest Pashhur son of
Immer, who was the chief officer of
the Temple, heard me proclaim these things,
2 he had me beaten and placed in chains near
the upper Benjamin Gate in the Temple.
3 The next morning, after Pashhur had
released me from the chains, I said to him,
"The LORD did not name you Pashhur. The
name he has given you is 'Terror Every-
where.' 4 The LORD himself has said, 'I am
going to make you a terror to yourself and to
your friends, and you will see them all killed
by the swords of their enemies. I am going to
put all the people of Judah under the power
of the king of Babylonia; he will take some
away as prisoners to his country and put oth-
ers to death. 5 I will also let their enemies
plunder all the wealth of this city and seize
all its possessions and property, even the trea-
sures of the kings of Judah, and carry every-
thing off to Babylonia. 6 As for you, Pashhur,
you and all your family will also be captured
and taken off to Babylonia. There you will
die and be buried, along with all your friends
to whom you have told so many lies.' "

Jeremiah Complains to the LORD

7 LORD, you have deceived me,
and I was deceived.
You are stronger than I am,
and you have overpowered me.
Everyone makes fun of me;
they laugh at me all day long.

Live it!

I'm Sick of It!

"Everyone makes fun of me; / they laugh at me all day long" (Jeremiah 20:7).

These words of Jeremiah could easily be our own words, couldn't they? Jeremiah is fed up with his role as a prophet. He is upset and feels that God has tricked him. He is sick and tired of being ridiculed. So Jeremiah complains to God, even cursing the day he was born (Jeremiah 20:14)!

No doubt all of us have been made fun of at one time or another. It can get frustrating, and we want to complain about it. Let God know how you feel. It is dangerous and unwise to keep your feelings bottled up inside of you. If you need to, talk to someone you trust about what is happening. Not so the person can fix it, but so that you can have someone help share your burden. Jeremiah didn't hesitate to share his feelings—maybe that is why he could keep going on.

— Jeremiah 20:7–18

8 Whenever I speak, I have to cry out
and shout, "Violence! Destruction!"
LORD, I am ridiculed and scorned all the time
because I proclaim your message.
9 But when I say, "I will forget the LORD
and no longer speak in his name,"
then your message is like a fire
burning deep within me.
I try my best to hold it in,
but can no longer keep it back.
10 I hear everybody whispering,
"Terror is everywhere!
So let's report him to the authorities!"

Even my close friends wait for my
downfall.
"Perhaps he can be tricked," they say;
"then we can catch him and get
revenge."
11 But you, LORD, are on my side, strong
and mighty,
and those who persecute me will fail.
They will be disgraced forever,
because they cannot succeed.
Their disgrace will never be forgotten.
12 But, Almighty LORD, you test people
justly;
you know what is in their hearts and
minds.
So let me see you take revenge on my
enemies,
for I have placed my cause in your
hands.
13 Sing to the LORD!
Praise the LORD!
He rescues the oppressed from the power
of evil people.

14 Curse the day I was born!
Forget the day my mother gave me birth!
15 Curse the one who made my father glad
by bringing him the news,
"It's a boy! You have a son!"
16 May he be like those cities
that the LORD destroyed without
mercy.
May he hear cries of pain in the morning
and the battle alarm at noon,
17 for not killing me before I was born.
Then my mother's womb would have
been my grave.
18 Why was I born?
Was it only to have trouble and sorrow,
to end my life in disgrace?

Jerusalem's Defeat Is Predicted

21 King Zedekiah of Judah sent to me
Pashhur son of Malchiah and the
priest Zephaniah son of Maaseiah with this
request: 2 "Please speak to the LORD for us,
because King Nebuchadnezzar of Babylonia
and his army are besieging the city. Maybe
the LORD will perform one of his miracles
for us and force Nebuchadnezzar to
retreat."
3 Then the LORD spoke to me, and I told
those who had been sent to me 4 to tell
Zedekiah that the LORD, the God of Israel,
had said, "Zedekiah, I am going to defeat
your army that is fighting against the king of
Babylonia and his army. I will pile up your
soldiers' weapons in the center of the city. 5 I
will fight against you with all my might, my
anger, my wrath, and my fury. 6 I will kill
everyone living in this city; people and ani-
mals alike will die of a terrible disease. 7 But
as for you, your officials, and the people who
survive the war, the famine, and the dis-
ease—I will let all of you be captured by
King Nebuchadnezzar and by your enemies,
who want to kill you. Nebuchadnezzar will
put you to death. He will not spare any of
you or show mercy or pity to any of you. I,
the LORD, have spoken."
8 Then the LORD told me to say to the
people, "Listen! I, the LORD, am giving you
a choice between the way that leads to life
and the way that leads to death. 9 Anyone
who stays in the city will be killed in war or
by starvation or disease. But those who go
out and surrender to the Babylonians, who
are now attacking the city, will not be
killed; they will at least escape with their
life. 10 I have made up my mind not to spare
this city, but to destroy it. It will be given
over to the king of Babylonia, and he will
burn it to the ground. I, the LORD, have
spoken."

Judgment on the Royal House of Judah

11-12 The LORD told me to give this mes-
sage to the royal house of Judah, the
descendants of David: "Listen to what I, the
LORD, am saying. See that justice is done
every day. Protect the person who is being
cheated from the one who is cheating him.
If you don't, the evil you are doing will
make my anger burn like a fire that cannot
be put out. 13 You, Jerusalem, are sitting[y]
high above the valleys, like a rock rising

[y] **21:13** You, Jerusalem, are sitting; *or* You are enthroned.
20:14–18 Job 3:1–19 **21:2** 2 Kings 25:1–11; 2 Chr 36:17–21

above the plain. But I will fight against you.
You say that no one can attack you or
break through your defenses. 14But I will
punish you for what you have done. I will
set your palace on fire, and the fire will
burn down everything around it. I, the
LORD, have spoken."

Jeremiah's Message to the Royal House of Judah

22 1-2The LORD told me to go to the
palace of the king of Judah, the
descendant of David, and there tell the king,
his officials, and the people of Jerusalem to
listen to what the LORD had said: 3"I, the
LORD, command you to do what is just and
right. Protect the person who is being cheat-
ed from the one who is cheating him. Do
not mistreat or oppress aliens, orphans, or
widows; and do not kill innocent people in
this holy place. 4If you really do as I have
commanded, then David's descendants will
continue to be kings. And they, together
with their officials and their people, will
continue to pass through the gates of this
palace in chariots and on horses. 5But if you
do not obey my commands, then I swear to
you that this palace will fall into ruins. I, the
LORD, have spoken.

6"To me, Judah's royal palace is as beauti-
ful as the land of Gilead and as the Lebanon
Mountains; but I will make it a desolate
place where no one lives. 7I am sending men
to destroy it. They will all bring their axes,
cut down its beautiful cedar pillars, and
throw them into the fire.

8"Afterward many foreigners will pass by
and ask one another why I, the LORD, have
done such a thing to this great city. 9Then
they will answer that it is because you have
abandoned your covenant with me, your
God, and have worshiped and served other
gods."

Jeremiah's Message concerning Joahaz

10People of Judah, do not weep for King
Josiah;
do not mourn his death.
But weep bitterly for Joahaz, his son;
they are taking him away, never to
return,
never again to see the land where he
was born.

11The LORD says concerning Josiah's son
Joahaz, who succeeded his father as king of
Judah, "He has gone away from here, never
to return. 12He will die in the country
where they have taken him, and he will
never again see this land."

Jeremiah's Message concerning Jehoiakim

13Doomed is the one who builds his house
by injustice
and enlarges it by dishonesty;
who makes his people work for nothing
and does not pay their wages.
14Doomed is the one who says,
"I will build myself a mansion
with spacious rooms upstairs."
So he puts windows in his house,
panels it with cedar,
and paints it red.
15Does it make you a better king
if you build houses of cedar,
finer than those of others?
Your father enjoyed a full life.
He was always just and fair,
and he prospered in everything he did.
16He gave the poor a fair trial,
and all went well with him.
That is what it means to know the LORD.
17But you can only see your selfish
interests;
you kill the innocent
and violently oppress your people.
The LORD has spoken.

22:5 Mt 23:28; Lk 13:35 **22:11** 2 Kings 23:31–34; 2 Chr 36:1–4

Jeremiah prophesied during the reigns of five kings of Judah: Josiah, Joahaz, Jehoikim, Jehoiachin, and Zedekiah.

Study it!

Fair Is Fair

One of the roles of the prophet is to speak out against injustice, and this is what Jeremiah does in Jeremiah 22:13. His words can easily apply to today's world. In the United States, we have something called minimum wage, which assures that a full-time worker will get at least a certain amount per hour. In many parts of the world, no such laws exist, and often people will take any work they can get, no matter how little it pays. Sometimes, at the end of the day, they are not even paid at all, despite being promised a wage. Jeremiah warns against this injustice to workers and says that those who build their houses on this kind of injustice and dishonesty are doomed.

— Jeremiah 22:13–17

18 So then, the LORD says about Josiah's son Jehoiakim, king of Judah,
"No one will mourn his death or say,
'How terrible, my friend, how terrible!'
No one will weep for him or cry,
'My lord! My king!'
19 With the funeral honors of a donkey,
he will be dragged away
and thrown outside Jerusalem's gates."

Jeremiah's Message about the Fate of Jerusalem

20 People of Jerusalem, go to Lebanon and shout,
go to the land of Bashan and cry;
call out from the mountains of Moab,
because all your allies have been defeated.
21 The LORD spoke to you when you were prosperous,
but you refused to listen.
That is what you've done all your life;
you never would obey the LORD.
22 Your leaders will be blown away by the wind,
your allies taken as prisoners of war,
your city disgraced and put to shame
because of all the evil you have done.
23 You rest secure among the cedars brought from Lebanon;
but how pitiful you'll be when pains strike you,
pains like those of a woman in labor.

God's Judgment on Jehoiachin

24 The LORD said to King Jehoiachin, son of
King Jehoiakim of Judah, "As surely as I am
the living God, even if you were the signet
ring on my right hand, I would pull you off
25 and give you to people you are afraid of,
people who want to kill you. I will give you
to King Nebuchadnezzar of Babylonia and his
soldiers. 26 I am going to force you and your
mother into exile. You will go to a country
where neither of you was born, and both of
you will die there. 27 You will long to see this
country again, but you will never return."
28 I said, "Has King Jehoiachin become
like a broken jar that is thrown away and
that no one wants? Is that why he and his
children have been taken into exile to a land
they know nothing about?"
29 O land, land, land!
Listen to what the LORD has said:
30 "This man is condemned to lose his children,
to be a man who will never succeed.
He will have no descendants
who will rule in Judah
as David's successors.
I, the LORD, have spoken."

22:18 2 Kings 23:36—24:6; 2 Chr 36:5–7 **22:24** 2 Kings 24:8–15; 2 Chr 36:9, 10

King Joahaz ruled only three months before the Egyptian pharaoh took him prisoner and made his brother Jehoiakim king of Judah.

Hope for the Future

23 How terrible will be the LORD's
judgment on those rulers who
destroy and scatter his people! 2 This is what
the LORD, the God of Israel, says about the
rulers who were supposed to take care of his
people: "You have not taken care of my peo-
ple; you have scattered them and driven
them away. Now I am going to punish you
for the evil you have done. 3 I will gather the
rest of my people from the countries where
I have scattered them, and I will bring them
back to their homeland. They will have
many children and increase in number. 4 I
will appoint rulers to take care of them. My
people will no longer be afraid or terrified,
and I will not punish them again.[z] I, the
LORD, have spoken."

5 The LORD says, "The time is coming
when I will choose as king a righteous
descendant of David. That king will rule
wisely and do what is right and just
throughout the land. 6 When he is king, the
people of Judah will be safe, and the people
of Israel will live in peace. He will be called
'The LORD Our Salvation.'

7 "The time is coming," says the LORD,
"when people will no longer swear by me as
the living God who brought the people of
Israel out of the land of Egypt. 8 Instead, they
will swear by me as the living God who
brought the people of Israel out of a north-
ern land and out of all the other countries
where I had scattered them. Then they will
live in their own land."

Jeremiah's Message about the Prophets

9 My heart is crushed,
and I am trembling.
Because of the LORD,
because of his holy words,
I am like a man who is drunk,
someone who has had too much wine.
10 The land is full of people unfaithful to
the LORD;
they live wicked lives and misuse their
power.
Because of the LORD's curse the land
mourns
and the pastures are dry.
11 The LORD says,
"The prophets and the priests are godless;
I have caught them doing evil in the
Temple itself.
12 The paths they follow will be slippery
and dark;
I will make them stumble and fall.
I am going to bring disaster on them;
the time of their punishment is
coming.
I, the LORD, have spoken.
13 I have seen the sin of Samaria's prophets:
they have spoken in the name of Baal
and have led my people astray.
14 But I have seen the prophets in Jerusalem
do even worse:
they commit adultery and tell lies;
they help people to do wrong,
so that no one stops doing what is evil.
To me they are all as bad
as the people of Sodom and
Gomorrah.

15 "So then, this is what I, the LORD
Almighty, say about the prophets of
Jerusalem:
I will give them bitter plants to eat
and poison to drink,
because they have spread ungodliness
throughout the land."

16 The LORD Almighty said to the people
of Jerusalem, "Do not listen to what the
prophets say; they are filling you with false
hopes. They tell you what they have imag-
ined and not what I have said. 17 To the peo-
ple who refuse to listen to what I have said,
they keep saying that all will go well with
them. And they tell everyone who is stub-
born that disaster will never touch them."

18 I said, "None of these prophets has ever
known the LORD's secret thoughts. None of
them has ever heard or understood his mes-
sage, or ever listened or paid attention to
what he said. 19 His anger is a storm, a furi-
ous wind that will rage over the heads of the
wicked, 20 and it will not end until he has

[z] **23:4** I will not punish them again; *or* not one of them will be missing.

23:5, 6 Jer 33:14–16 **23:14** Gen 18:20; Ezek 16:49

done everything he intends to do. In days to
come his people will understand this clearly."
21 The LORD said, "I did not send these
prophets, but even so they went. I did not
give them any message, but still they spoke
in my name. 22 If they had known my secret
thoughts, then they could have proclaimed
my message to my people and could have
made them give up the evil lives they live
and the wicked things they do.
23 "I am a God who is everywhere and
not in one place only. 24 No one can hide
where I cannot see them. Do you not know
that I am everywhere in heaven and on
earth? 25 I know what those prophets have
said who speak lies in my name and claim
that I have given them my messages in their
dreams. 26 How much longer will those
prophets mislead my people with the lies
they have invented? 27 They think that the
dreams they tell will make my people forget
me, just as their ancestors forgot me and
turned to Baal. 28 The prophet who has had a
dream should say it is only a dream, but the
prophet who has heard my message should
proclaim that message faithfully. What good
is straw compared with wheat? 29 My mes-
sage is like a fire and like a hammer that
breaks rocks in pieces. 30 I am against those
prophets who take each other's words and
proclaim them as my message. 31 I am also
against those prophets who speak their own
words and claim they came from me. 32 Lis-
ten to what I, the LORD, say! I am against
the prophets who tell their dreams that are
full of lies. They tell these dreams and lead
my people astray with their lies and their
boasting. I did not send them or order them
to go, and they are of no help at all to the
people. I, the LORD, have spoken."

The LORD's Burden

33 The LORD said to me, "Jeremiah, when
one of my people or a prophet or a priest
asks you, 'What is the LORD's message?' you
are to say, 'You are a burden[a] to the LORD,
and he is going to get rid of you.' 34 If any of
my people or a prophet or a priest even uses
the words 'the LORD's burden,' I will punish
them and their families. 35 Instead, each one
of them should ask their friends and their
relatives, 'What answer has the LORD given?
What has the LORD said?' 36 So they must no
longer use the words 'the LORD's burden,'
because if any of them do, I will make my
message a real burden to them. The people
have perverted the words of their God, the
living God, the LORD Almighty. 37 Jeremiah,
ask the prophets, 'What answer did the
LORD give you? What did the LORD say?'
38 And if they disobey my command and use
the words 'the LORD's burden,' then tell
them that 39 I will certainly pick them up[b]
and throw them far away from me, both
them and the city that I gave to them and
their ancestors. 40 I will bring on them ever-
lasting shame and disgrace that will never be
forgotten."

Two Baskets of Figs

24 The LORD showed me two baskets
of figs placed in front of the Temple.
(This was after King Nebuchadnezzar of
Babylonia had taken away Jehoiakim's son,
King Jehoiachin of Judah, as a prisoner from
Jerusalem to Babylonia, together with the
leaders of Judah, the craftworkers, and the

Two baskets of figs (24:1)

[a] **23:33** *The Hebrew word for* message *and* burden *is the same.* [b] **23:39** *The Hebrew verb for* pick up *comes from the same root as the Hebrew word for* message *and* burden.

23:24 Wis 1:7; Sir 16:17 **24:1** 2 Kings 24:12–16; 2 Chr 36:10

skilled workers.) 2The first basket contained
good figs, those that ripen early; the other
one contained bad figs, too bad to eat.
3Then the LORD said to me, "Jeremiah, what
do you see?"

I answered, "Figs. The good ones are very
good, and the bad ones are very bad, too bad
to eat."

4So the LORD said to me, 5"I, the LORD,
the God of Israel, consider that the people
who were taken away to Babylonia are like
these good figs, and I will treat them with
kindness. 6I will watch over them and bring
them back to this land. I will build them up
and not tear them down; I will plant them
and not pull them up. 7I will give them the
desire to know that I am the LORD. Then
they will be my people, and I will be their
God, because they will return to me with all
their heart.

8"As for King Zedekiah of Judah, the
politicians around him, and the rest of the
people of Jerusalem who have stayed in this
land or moved to Egypt—I, the LORD, will
treat them all like these figs that are too bad
to be eaten. 9I will bring such a disaster on
them that all the nations of the world will be
terrified. People will make fun of them,
make jokes about them, ridicule them, and
use their name as a curse everywhere I scat-
ter them. 10I will bring war, starvation, and
disease on them until there is not one of
them left in the land that I gave to them and
their ancestors."

Live it!

One Bad Apple

Jeremiah, chapter 24, uses the symbol of good figs and bad figs. We are probably more familiar with good apples and bad apples. It's easy to spot a bad or rotten apple. It is bruised, mushy, and has brown spots. No one wants to eat it. Perhaps you have heard the expression, "He is one bad apple." We all know what that means. This individual has been judged to be no good. Perhaps he gets into trouble a lot, or maybe he has been arrested a few times. While it is not fair to judge someone by appearances, we do know that people will judge us by how we act.

Imagine yourself as an apple tree. Are you producing good apples or bad apples? That is, do your actions cause good in the world or evil? What do others see when they look at you—good apples or bad apples? Try to name some of both in your life.

— Jeremiah, chapter 24

The Enemy from the North

25 In the fourth year that Jehoiakim
son of Josiah was king of Judah, I
received a message from the LORD concern-
ing all the people of Judah. (This was the
first year that Nebuchadnezzar was king of
Babylonia.) 2I said to all the people of Judah
and of Jerusalem, 3"For twenty-three years,
from the thirteenth year that Josiah son of
Amon was king of Judah until this very day,
the LORD has spoken to me, and I have
never failed to tell you what he said. But you
have paid no attention. 4You would not lis-
ten or pay attention, even though the LORD
has continued to send you his servants the
prophets. 5They told you to turn from your
wicked way of life and from the evil things
you are doing, so that you could go on liv-
ing in the land that the LORD gave you and
your ancestors as a permanent possession.
6They told you not to worship and serve
other gods and not to make the LORD angry

25:1 2 Kings 24:1; 2 Chr 36:5–7; Dan 1:1, 2

"I am a God who is everywhere and not in one place only. No one can hide where I cannot see them" *(Jeremiah 23:23–24)*.

Live it!

Pay Attention!

Have you ever been daydreaming and suddenly realize that someone is calling your name? That can be pretty embarrassing when it happens in class. Not paying attention can have consequences. Not paying attention while driving can result in an accident and even death. Jeremiah tells the Israelites that they refused to pay attention to the prophets God sent to warn them. Now they have to pay the consequences.

At times all of us have a problem paying attention. Our minds can easily wander. Think about how this can apply to your life. If you aren't paying attention to God, you can easily wander off in a direction different from what God has planned for you. Before long, you find yourself in a situation or problem that makes you wonder, "How did I get into this?" Not paying attention to our soul can also be fatal to our spiritual lives. So Jeremiah's message is pretty clear: pay attention when God is speaking!

— Jeremiah 25:1–7

by worshiping the idols you had made. If
you had obeyed the LORD, then he would
not have punished you. [7]But the LORD him-
self says that you refused to listen to him.
Instead, you made him angry with your idols
and have brought his punishment on your-
selves.
[8]"So then, because you would not listen
to him, the LORD Almighty says, [9]'I am
going to send for all the peoples from the
north and for my servant, King Nebuchad-
nezzar of Babylonia. I am going to bring
them to fight against Judah and its inhabi-
tants and against all the neighboring nations.
I am going to destroy this nation and its
neighbors and leave them in ruins forever, a
terrible and shocking sight. I, the LORD,
have spoken. [10]I will silence their shouts of
joy and gladness and the happy sounds of
wedding feasts. They will have no oil for
their lamps, and there will be no more grain.
[11]This whole land will be left in ruins and
will be a shocking sight, and the neighbor-
ing nations will serve the king of Babylonia
for seventy years. [12]After that I will punish
Babylonia and its king for their sin. I will
destroy that country and leave it in ruins for-
ever. [13]I will punish Babylonia with all the
disasters that I threatened to bring on the
nations when I spoke through Jeremiah—all
the disasters recorded in this book. [14]I will
pay the Babylonians back for what they have
done, and many nations and great kings will
make slaves of them.'"

God's Judgment on the Nations

[15]The LORD, the God of Israel, said to
me, "Here is a wine cup filled with my
anger. Take it to all the nations to whom I
send you, and make them drink from it.
[16]When they drink from it, they will stagger
and go out of their minds because of the war
I am sending against them."
[17]So I took the cup from the LORD's
hand, gave it to all the nations to whom the
LORD had sent me, and made them drink
from it. [18]Jerusalem and all the towns of
Judah, together with its kings and leaders,
were made to drink from it, so that they
would become a desert, a terrible and
shocking sight, and so that people would use
their name as a curse—as they still do.
[19-26]Here is the list of all the others who
had to drink from the cup:

25:10 a Jer 7:34; 16:9; **b** Rev 18:22, 23 **25:11** 2 Chr 36:21; Jer 29:10; Dan 9:2

Locate as many of the lands mentioned in Jeremiah 25:19–26 as you can on Maps 3, 4, and 5 in the back of this Bible.

the king of Egypt, his officials and leaders;
all the Egyptians and all the foreigners in
Egypt;
all the kings of the land of Uz;
all the kings of the Philistine cities of
Ashkelon, Gaza, Ekron, and what
remains of Ashdod;
all the people of Edom, Moab, and
Ammon;
all the kings of Tyre and Sidon;
all the kings of the Mediterranean lands;
the cities of Dedan, Tema, and Buz;
all the people who cut their hair short;
all the kings of Arabia;
all the kings of the desert tribes;
all the kings of Zimri, Elam, and Media;
all the kings of the north, far and near,
one after another.

Every nation on the face of the earth had
to drink from it. Last of all, the king of
Babylonia will drink from it.

27 Then the LORD said to me, "Tell the
people that I, the LORD Almighty, the God
of Israel, am commanding them to drink
until they are drunk and vomit, until they
fall down and cannot get up, because of the
war that I am sending against them. **28** And if
they refuse to take the cup from your hand
and drink from it, then tell them that the
LORD Almighty has said that they will still
have to drink from it. **29** I will begin my
work of destruction in my own city. Do they
think they will go unpunished? No, they will
be punished, for I am going to send war on
all the people on earth. I, the LORD
Almighty, have spoken.

30 "You, Jeremiah, must proclaim every-
thing I have said. You must tell these people,
'The LORD will roar from heaven
and thunder from the heights of
heaven.
He will roar against his people;
he will shout like a man treading
grapes.
Everyone on earth will hear him,
31 and the sound will echo to the ends of
the earth.
The LORD has a case against the
nations.
He will bring all people to trial
and put the wicked to death.
The LORD has spoken.' "

32 The LORD Almighty says that disaster is
coming on one nation after another, and a
great storm is gathering at the far ends of
the earth. **33** On that day the bodies of those
whom the LORD has killed will lie scattered
from one end of the earth to the other. No
one will mourn for them, and they will not
be taken away and buried. They will lie on
the ground like piles of manure.

34 Cry, you leaders, you shepherds of my
people, cry out loud! Mourn and roll in the
dust. The time has come for you to be
slaughtered,[c] and you will be butchered like
rams.[d] **35** There will be no way for you to
escape. **36-37** You moan and cry out in distress
because the LORD in his anger has destroyed
your nation and left your peaceful country
in ruins. **38** The LORD has abandoned his
people[e] like a lion that leaves its cave. The
horrors of war and the LORD's fierce anger
have turned the country into a desert.

Jeremiah Is Brought to Trial

26 Soon after Jehoiakim son of Josiah
became king of Judah, **2** the LORD
said to me, "Stand in the court of the Temple
and proclaim all I have commanded you to
say to the people who come from the towns
of Judah to worship there. Do not leave out
anything. **3** Perhaps the people will listen and
give up their evil ways. If they do, then I will
change my mind about the destruction I
plan to bring on them for all their wicked
deeds."

4 The LORD told me to say to the people,
"I, the LORD, have said that you must obey
me by following the teaching that I gave you,
5 and by paying attention to the words of my
servants, the prophets, whom I have kept on
sending to you. You have never obeyed what
they said. **6** If you continue to disobey, then I
will do to this Temple what I did to Shiloh,[f]
and all the nations of the world will use the
name of this city as a curse."

[c] **25:34** *Hebrew has an additional word, the meaning of which is unclear.* [d] **25:34** *One ancient translation* rams; *Hebrew* vessels. [e] **25:38** The LORD . . . people; *or* The LORD's people run away. [f] **26:6** SHILOH: *See 7:12.*

26:1 2 Kings 23:36—24:6; 2 Chr 36:5–7 **26:6** Josh 18:1; Ps 78:60; Jer 7:12–14

Study it!

Falsely Accused

Even though they lived six hundred years apart, there are some similarities between the life of Jeremiah and the life of Jesus. In Jeremiah, chapter 26, Jeremiah is brought to trial. Read verses 1–16, and then turn to any of these four Gospel accounts of the arrest and trial of Jesus: Matthew 26:47—27:26, Mark 14:43—15:5, Luke 22:47—23:25, and John 18:3—19:16.

What similarities do you notice between Jeremiah's trial and Jesus' trial? What are some differences?

— Jeremiah, chapter 26

7 The priests, the prophets, and all the
people heard me saying these things in the
Temple, 8 and as soon as I had finished all
that the LORD had commanded me to speak,
they grabbed me and shouted, "You ought
to be killed for this! 9 Why have you said in
the LORD's name that this Temple will
become like Shiloh and that this city will be
destroyed and no one will live in it?" Then
the people crowded around me.
10 When the leaders of Judah heard what
had happened, they hurried from the royal
palace to the Temple and took their places at
the New Gate. 11 Then the priests and the
prophets said to the leaders and to the people, "This man deserves to be sentenced to
death because he has spoken against our city.
You heard him with your own ears."
12 Then I said, "The LORD sent me to proclaim everything that you heard me say
against this Temple and against this city.
13 You must change the way you are living
and the things you are doing, and must obey
the LORD your God. If you do, he will
change his mind about the destruction that
he said he would bring on you. 14 As for me,
I am in your power! Do with me whatever
you think is fair and right. 15 But be sure of
this: if you kill me, you and the people of
this city will be guilty of killing an innocent
man, because it is the LORD who sent me to
give you this warning."
16 Then the leaders and the people said to
the priests and the prophets, "This man
spoke to us in the name of the LORD our
God; he should not be put to death."
17 After that, some of the elders stood up
and said to the people who had gathered,
18 "When Hezekiah was king of Judah, the
prophet Micah of Moresheth told all the
people that the LORD Almighty had said,

'Zion will be plowed like a field;
Jerusalem will become a pile of ruins,
and the Temple hill will become a
forest.'

19 King Hezekiah and the people of Judah
did not put Micah to death. Instead, Hezekiah honored the LORD and tried to win his
favor. And the LORD changed his mind
about the disaster that he said he would
bring on them. Now we are about to bring a
terrible disaster on ourselves."
(20 There was another man, Uriah son of
Shemaiah from Kiriath Jearim, who spoke in
the name of the LORD against this city and
nation just as Jeremiah did. 21 When King
Jehoiakim and his soldiers and officials heard
what Uriah had said, the king tried to have
him killed. But Uriah heard about it; so he
fled in terror and escaped to Egypt. 22 King
Jehoiakim, however, sent Elnathan son of
Achbor and some other men to Egypt to get
Uriah. 23 They brought him back to King
Jehoiakim, who had him killed and his body
thrown into the public burial ground.)
24 But because I had the support of
Ahikam son of Shaphan, I was not handed
over to the people and killed.

Jeremiah Wears an Ox Yoke

27 Soon after Josiah's son Zedekiah
became king of Judah, the LORD
told me 2 to make myself a yoke out of
leather straps and wooden crossbars and to

26:18 Mic 3:12 **27:1** 2 Kings 24:18–20; 2 Chr 36:11–13 put it on my neck. 3Then the LORD told me to send a message[g] to the kings of Edom, Moab, Ammon, Tyre, and Sidon through their ambassadors who had come to Jerusalem to see King Zedekiah. 4The LORD Almighty, the God of Israel, told me to command them to tell their kings that the LORD had said: 5"By my great power and strength I created the world, human beings, and all the animals that live on the earth; and I give it to anyone I choose. 6I am the one who has placed all these nations under the power of my servant, King Nebuchadnezzar of Babylonia, and I have made even the wild animals serve him. 7All nations will serve him, and they will serve his son and his grandson until the time comes for his own nation to fall. Then his nation will serve powerful nations and great kings.

8"But if any nation or kingdom will not submit to his rule, then I will punish that nation by war, starvation, and disease until I have let Nebuchadnezzar destroy it completely. 9Do not listen to your prophets or to those who claim they can predict the future, either by dreams or by calling up the spirits of the dead or by magic. They all tell you not to submit to the king of Babylonia. 10They are deceiving you and will cause you to be taken far away from your country. I will drive you out, and you will be destroyed. 11But if any nation submits to the king of Babylonia and serves him, then I will let it stay on in its own land, to farm it and live there. I, the LORD, have spoken."

12I said the same thing to King Zedekiah of Judah, "Submit to the king of Babylonia. Serve him and his people, and you will live. 13Why should you and your people die in war or of starvation or disease? That is what the LORD has said will happen to any nation that does not submit to the king of Babylonia. 14Do not listen to the prophets who tell you not to surrender to him. They are deceiving you. 15The LORD himself has said that he did not send them and that they are lying to you in his name. And so he will drive you out, and you will be killed, you and the prophets who are telling you these lies."

16Then I told the priests and the people that the LORD had said: "Do not listen to the prophets who say that the Temple treasures will soon be brought back from Babylonia. They are lying to you. 17Don't listen to them! Submit to the king of Babylonia and you will live! Why should this city become a pile of ruins? 18If they are really prophets and if they have my message, let them ask me, the LORD Almighty, not to allow the treasures that remain in the Temple and in the royal palace to be taken to Babylonia."

(19-20When King Nebuchadnezzar took away to Babylonia the king of Judah, Jehoiachin son of Jehoiakim, and the leading men of Judah and Jerusalem, he left the columns, the bronze tank, the carts, and some of the other Temple treasures.)

21"Listen to what I, the LORD Almighty, the God of Israel, say about the treasures that are left in the Temple and in the royal palace in Jerusalem: 22They will be taken to Babylonia and will remain there until I turn my attention to them. Then I will bring them back and restore them to this place. I, the LORD, have spoken."

Jeremiah and the Prophet Hananiah

28 That same year,[h] in the fifth month of the fourth year that Zedekiah was king, Hananiah son of Azzur, a prophet from the town of Gibeon, spoke to me in the Temple. In the presence of the priests and of the people he told me 2that the LORD Almighty, the God of Israel, had said: "I have broken the power of the king of Babylonia. 3Within two years I will bring back to this place all the Temple treasures that King Nebuchadnezzar took to Babylonia. 4I will

[g] **27:3** *Probable text* a message; *Hebrew* them. [h] **28:1** *One ancient translation* That same year; *Hebrew* That same year at the beginning of his reign.

27:6 Bar 3:16, 17 **28:1** 2 Kings 24:18–20; 2 Chr 36:11–13

Yoke: **A wood frame put around the neck of an animal, such as an ox. Ropes are attached to the yoke so that the animal can pull a wagon or a plow.**

Study it!

Turning Point

You may notice that Jeremiah's message changes a little in the second half of his book. About this time the Babylonians conquer Jerusalem and take many of the people back to Babylon as captives. The Israelites who survive are hopeless and very upset. They believe that God has abandoned them as a people. So Jeremiah begins to preach a more hopeful message. He prophesies that they will spend years in captivity but that eventually God will have mercy and bring them back to their land. God has not abandoned them!

— Jeremiah 27:21–22

also bring back the king of Judah, Jehoiachin
son of Jehoiakim, along with all of the peo-
ple of Judah who went into exile in Babylo-
nia. Yes, I will break the power of the king of
Babylonia. I, the LORD, have spoken."
5Then in the presence of the priests and
of all the people who were standing in the
Temple, I said to Hananiah, 6"Wonderful! I
hope the LORD will do this! I certainly hope
he will make your prophecy come true and
will bring back from Babylonia all the Tem-
ple treasures and all the people who were
taken away as prisoners. 7But listen to what I
say to you and to the people. 8The prophets
who spoke long ago, before my time and
yours, predicted that war, starvation, and dis-
ease would come to many nations and pow-
erful kingdoms. 9But a prophet who predicts
peace can only be recognized as a prophet
whom the LORD has truly sent when that
prophet's predictions come true."
10Then Hananiah took the yoke off my
neck, broke it in pieces, 11and said in the
presence of all the people, "The LORD has
said that this is how he will break the yoke
that King Nebuchadnezzar has put on the
neck of all the nations; and he will do this
within two years." Then I left.
12Some time after this the LORD told me
13to go and tell Hananiah: "The LORD has
said that you may be able to break a wooden
yoke, but he[i] will replace it with an iron
yoke. 14The LORD Almighty, the God of
Israel, has said that he will put an iron yoke
on all these nations and that they will serve
King Nebuchadnezzar of Babylonia. The
LORD has said that he will make even the
wild animals serve Nebuchadnezzar."
15Then I told Hananiah this, and added,
"Listen, Hananiah! The LORD did not send
you, and you are making these people
believe a lie. 16And so the LORD himself says
that he is going to get rid of you. Before this
year is over you will die because you have
told the people to rebel against the LORD."
17And Hananiah died in the seventh
month of that same year.

Jeremiah's Letter to the Jews in Babylonia

29 I wrote a letter to the priests, the
prophets, the leaders of the people,
and to all the others whom Nebuchadnezzar
had taken away as prisoners from Jerusalem
to Babylonia. 2I wrote it after King
Jehoiachin, his mother, the palace officials,
the leaders of Judah and of Jerusalem, the
engravers, and the skilled workers had been
taken into exile. 3I gave the letter to Elasah
son of Shaphan and to Gemariah son of
Hilkiah, whom King Zedekiah of Judah was

[i] **28:13** *One ancient translation* he; *Hebrew* you.
29:1, 2 2 Kings 24:12–16; 2 Chr 36:10

Hananiah was a false prophet who predicted that Babylonia would only rule for two years. But Babylonia ruled for over fifty years!

Pray it!

Big Plans

Do you spend time wondering where you'll be five or ten years from now? What you'll be doing or who your friends will be? It's all a mystery right now, but one thing is for sure: God knows. Jeremiah, chapter 29, contains a wonderful message from God about our future. The bottom line is God has a plan for us.

For prayer, read through verses 11–13 very slowly. Repeat the words several times. Let them sink in. Imagine God saying them to you.

How do these words make you feel?

Return to this passage whenever you are worried about your future or where your life is headed. Yes, God has big plans for each one of us.

— Jeremiah 29:11–13

sending to King Nebuchadnezzar of Babylo-
nia. It said:
4 “The LORD Almighty, the God of
Israel, says to all those people whom he
allowed Nebuchadnezzar to take away as
prisoners from Jerusalem to Babylonia:
5 ‘Build houses and settle down. Plant gar-
dens and eat what you grow in them.
6 Marry and have children. Then let your
children get married, so that they also may
have children. You must increase in num-
bers and not decrease. 7 Work for the good
of the cities where I have made you go as
prisoners. Pray to me on their behalf,
because if they are prosperous, you will be
prosperous too. 8 I, the LORD, the God of
Israel, warn you not to let yourselves be
deceived by the prophets who live among
you or by any others who claim they can
predict the future. Do not pay any atten-
tion to their[j] dreams. 9 They are telling
you lies in my name. I did not send them.
I, the LORD Almighty, have spoken.’
10 “The LORD says, ‘When Babylonia's
seventy years are over, I will show my
concern for you and keep my promise to
bring you back home. 11 I alone know the
plans I have for you, plans to bring you
prosperity and not disaster, plans to bring
about the future you hope for.[k] 12 Then
you will call to me. You will come and
pray to me, and I will answer you. 13 You
will seek me, and you will find me
because you will seek me with all your
heart. 14 Yes, I say, you will find me, and I
will restore you to your land. I will gather
you from every country and from every
place to which I have scattered you, and
I will bring you back to the land from
which I had sent you away into exile. I,
the LORD, have spoken.’
15 “You say that the LORD has given
you prophets in Babylonia. 16 Listen to
what the LORD says about the king who
rules the kingdom that David ruled and
about the people of this city, that is, your
relatives who were not taken away as pris-
oners with you. 17 The LORD Almighty
says, ‘I am bringing war, starvation, and
disease on them, and I will make them
like figs that are too rotten to be eaten. 18 I
will pursue them with war, starvation, and
disease, and all the nations of the world
will be horrified at what they see. Every-
where I scatter them, people will be
shocked and terrified at what has hap-
pened to them. People will make fun of
them and use their name as a curse. 19 This
will happen to them because they did not
obey the message that I kept on sending

[j] **29:8** *Probable text* their; *Hebrew* your. [k] **29:11** the future you hope for; *or* a future full of hope.

29:10 2 Chr 36:21; Jer 25:11; Dan 9:2 **29:13** Deut 4:29; Wis 6:12, 13

to them through my servants the
prophets. They refused to listen. 20All of
you whom I sent into exile in Babylonia,
listen to what I, the LORD, say.'

21"The LORD Almighty, the God of
Israel, has spoken about Ahab son of Kola-
iah and Zedekiah son of Maaseiah, who
are telling you lies in his name. He has
said that he will hand them over to the
power of King Nebuchadnezzar of Baby-
lonia, who will put them to death before
your eyes. 22When the people who were
taken away as prisoners from Jerusalem to
Babylonia want to bring a curse on some-
one, they will say, 'May the LORD treat
you like Zedekiah and Ahab, whom the
king of Babylonia roasted alive!' 23This
will be their fate because they are guilty
of terrible sins—they have committed
adultery and have told lies in the LORD's
name. This was against the LORD's will; he
knows what they have done, and he is a
witness against them.[l] The LORD has spo-
ken."

The Letter of Shemaiah

24-25The LORD Almighty, the God of
Israel, gave me a message for Shemaiah of
Nehelam, who had sent a letter in his own
name to all the people of Jerusalem and to
the priest Zephaniah son of Maaseiah and to
all the other priests. In this letter Shemaiah
wrote to Zephaniah:

26"The LORD made you a priest in
place of Jehoiada, and you are now the
chief officer[m] in the Temple. It is your
duty to see that every crazy person who
pretends to be a prophet is placed in
chains with an iron collar around the
neck. 27Why haven't you done this to
Jeremiah of Anathoth, who has been
speaking as a prophet to the people? 28He
must be stopped because he told the peo-
ple in Babylonia that they would be pris-
oners there a long time and should build
houses, settle down, plant gardens, and eat
what they grow."

29Zephaniah read the letter to me, 30and
then the LORD told me 31-32to send to all
the prisoners in Babylon this message about
Shemaiah: "I, the LORD, will punish Shema-
iah and all of his descendants. I did not send
him, but he spoke to you as if he were a
prophet, and he made you believe lies. He
will have no descendants among you. He
will not live to see the good things that I am
going to do for my people, because he told
them to rebel against me. I, the LORD, have
spoken."

The LORD's Promises to His People

30 The LORD, the God of Israel, 2said
to me, "Write down in a book
everything that I have told you, 3because the
time is coming when I will restore my peo-
ple, Israel and Judah. I will bring them back
to the land that I gave their ancestors, and
they will take possession of it again. I, the
LORD, have spoken."

4The LORD says to the people of Israel
and Judah,

5"I heard a cry of terror,
a cry of fear and not of peace.
6Now stop and think!
Can a man give birth to a child?
Why then do I see every man with his
hands on his stomach
like a woman in labor?
Why is everyone so pale?
7A terrible day is coming;
no other day can compare with it—
a time of distress for my people,
but they will survive."

8The LORD Almighty says, "When that
day comes, I will break the yoke that is
around their neck and remove their chains,
and they will no longer be the slaves of for-
eigners. 9Instead, they will serve me, the
LORD their God, and a descendant of David,
whom I will enthrone as king.

10"My people, do not be afraid;
people of Israel, do not be terrified.
I will rescue you from that faraway land,
from the land where you are prisoners.

[l] **29:23** done, and he . . . them; *or* done; he saw them do it. [m] **29:26** *Some ancient translations* officer; *Hebrew* officers.

30:10, 11 Jer 46:27, 28

Live it!

It'll Be Okay

What's one of the first things your parent or guardian says when you get hurt or are crying? "It'll be okay." These are reassuring words. We need to hear them from time to time, especially when we're going through rough times. This is the message God is saying to the people in Jeremiah, chapter 30: "It'll be okay." This is the message God wants to say to each of us: "It'll be okay."

"It'll be okay." Think of the last time someone said those words to you. Now try remembering the last time you said them to someone else. Do you know anyone who needs to hear these words right now?

— Jeremiah 30:8–11

You will come back home and live in
peace;
you will be secure, and no one will
make you afraid.
11 I will come to you and save you.
I will destroy all the nations
where I have scattered you,
but I will not destroy you.
I will not let you go unpunished;
but when I punish you, I will be fair.
I, the LORD, have spoken."

12 The LORD says to his people,
"Your wounds are incurable,
your injuries cannot be healed.
13 There is no one to take care of you,
no remedy for your sores,
no hope of healing for you.
14 All your lovers have forgotten you;
they no longer care about you.
I have attacked you like an enemy;
your punishment has been harsh
because your sins are many
and your wickedness is great.
15 Complain no more about your injuries;
there is no cure for you.
I punished you like this
because your sins are many
and your wickedness is great.
16 But now, all who devour you will be
devoured,
and all your enemies will be taken away
as prisoners.
All who oppress you will be oppressed,
and all who plunder you will be
plundered.
17 I will make you well again;
I will heal your wounds,
though your enemies say,
'Zion is an outcast;
no one cares about her.'
I, the LORD, have spoken."

18 The LORD says,
"I will restore my people to their land
and have mercy on every family;
Jerusalem will be rebuilt,
and its palace restored.
19 The people who live there will sing
praise;
they will shout for joy.
By my blessing they will increase in
numbers;
my blessing will bring them honor.
20 I will restore the nation's ancient power
and establish it firmly again;
I will punish all who oppress them.
21-22 Their ruler will come from their own
nation,
their prince from their own people.
He will approach me when I invite him,
for who would dare come uninvited?
They will be my people,
and I will be their God.
I, the LORD, have spoken."

23-24 The LORD's anger is a storm, a furi-
ous wind that will rage over the heads of the
wicked. It will not end until he has done all

"My people, do not be afraid; / people of Israel, do not be terrified. / I will rescue you from that faraway land" *(Jeremiah 30:10).*

that he intends to do. In days to come his people will understand this clearly.

Israel's Return Home

31 The LORD says, "The time is coming
when I will be the God of all the
tribes of Israel, and they will be my people.
2 In the desert I showed mercy to those peo-
ple who had escaped death. When the peo-
ple of Israel longed for rest, 3 I appeared to
them[n] from far away. People of Israel, I have
always loved you, so I continue to show you
my constant love. 4 Once again I will rebuild
you. Once again you will take up your tam-
bourines and dance joyfully. 5 Once again
you will plant vineyards on the hills of
Samaria, and those who plant them will eat
what the vineyards produce. 6 Yes, the time is
coming when sentries will call out on the
hills of Ephraim, 'Let's go up to Zion, to the
LORD our God.' "

7 The LORD says,
"Sing with joy for Israel,
the greatest of the nations.
Sing your song of praise,
'The LORD has saved his[o] people;
he has rescued all who are left.'
8 I will bring them from the north
and gather them from the ends of the earth.

The young women will dance and be happy, and men, young and old, will rejoice. (31:13)

The blind and the lame will come with them,
pregnant women and those about to give birth.
They will come back a great nation.
9 My people will return weeping,
praying as I lead them back.
I will guide them to streams of water,
on a smooth road where they will not stumble.
I am like a father to Israel,
and Ephraim is my oldest son."

10 The LORD says,
"Nations, listen to me
and proclaim my words on the far-off shores.
I scattered my people, but I will gather them
and guard them as a shepherd guards his flock.
11 I have set Israel's people free
and have saved them from a mighty nation.
12 They will come and sing for joy on Mount Zion
and be delighted with my gifts—
gifts of grain and wine and olive oil,
gifts of sheep and cattle.
They will be like a well-watered garden;
they will have everything they need.
13 Then the young women will dance and be happy,
and men, young and old, will rejoice.
I will comfort them and turn their mourning into joy,
their sorrow into gladness.
14 I will fill the priests with the richest food
and satisfy all the needs of my people.
I, the LORD, have spoken."

The LORD's Mercy on Israel

15 The LORD says,
"A sound is heard in Ramah,
the sound of bitter weeping.

[n] **31:3** *One ancient translation* them; *Hebrew* me. [o] **31:7** *Some ancient translations* The LORD has saved his; *Hebrew* LORD save your.

31:15 a Gen 35:16–19; **b** Mt 2:18

Rachel and her children are mentioned in Jeremiah 31:15. Read more about Rachel and her children in Genesis 35:16–19.

Rachel is crying for her children;
they are gone,
and she refuses to be comforted.
16 Stop your crying
and wipe away your tears.
All that you have done for your children
will not go unrewarded;
they will return from the enemy's land.
17 There is hope for your future;
your children will come back home.
I, the LORD, have spoken.

18 "I hear the people of Israel say in grief,
'LORD, we were like an untamed animal,
but you taught us to obey.
Bring us back;
we are ready to return to you,
the LORD our God.
19 We turned away from you,
but soon we wanted to return.
After you had punished us,
we hung our heads in grief.
We were ashamed and disgraced
because we sinned when we were
young.'

20 "Israel, you are my dearest child,
the one I love best.
Whenever I mention your name,
I think[p] of you with love.
My heart goes out to you;
I will be merciful.
21 Set up signs and mark the road;
find again the way by which you left.
Come back, people of Israel,
come home to the towns you left.
22 How long will you hesitate, faithless
people?
I have created something new and
different,
as different as a woman protecting a
man."[q]

Live it!

Wild and Tame

What does it mean to be tame? In the animal kingdom, wild horses and wild dogs run free. They have no master to obey. Tame animals have masters that they follow and who care and provide for them.

In Jeremiah, chapter 31, the people of Israel compare themselves to untamed or wild animals. They did not obey God before they were conquered and led into captivity. Now they tell the Lord, "But you taught us to obey." Aren't we in many ways like that? We enter this world untamed, and our families help to "tame" us by teaching us how to live in peace and harmony. They provide care for us—food, shelter, clothing—and so much more.

Yet it seems there are parts of us that remain untamed. At times, we want to be free and wild. We don't want to have to obey anyone. But we need the people who care for us. We need the love and guidelines they provide to grow and do well in life. We cannot let our "wild" sides get out of control and cut us off from the people we need.

Think about what parts of your life are untamed. Think also about how you can be a more positive member of your family.

— Jeremiah 31:18

The Future Prosperity of God's People

23 The LORD Almighty, the God of Israel, says, "When I restore the people to their land, they will once again say in the land of Judah and in its towns,

'May the LORD bless the sacred hill[r] of
Jerusalem,
the holy place where he lives.'
24 People will live in Judah and in all its
towns, and there will be farmers, and

[p] **31:20** I mention . . . I think; *or* I threaten to punish, I still think. [q] **31:22** as different . . . man; *Hebrew unclear.* [r] **31:23** SACRED HILL: *Mount Zion, the hill in Jerusalem which formed part of the Temple and palace area.*

Live it!

Putting Your Heart in It

You remember that in Exodus, God wrote the original Ten Commandments in stone. Now in Jeremiah, chapter 31, Jeremiah delivers a very important message from God. It is one of the most beautiful prophecies in the whole book. God says he will make a New Covenant, not on stone tablets but on the hearts of the people. In other words, God's New Covenant is with each one of us, and God's law will be within us.

Think of it this way. One of the signs that you are growing up is when you do something just because you know it is the right thing to do. When you are a child, you follow rules so you won't get in trouble. As we mature, we do what is right because the motivation comes from inside of us.

If you avoid doing something wrong because you are afraid of getting caught, that's okay. But if you avoid doing something wrong just because you know it is against God's will, you are following God's law written on your heart!

— Jeremiah 31:31–33

shepherds with their flocks. 25 I will refresh
those who are weary and will satisfy with
food everyone who is weak from hunger.
26 So then, people will say, 'I went to sleep
and woke up refreshed.'
27 "I, the LORD, say that the time is com-
ing when I will fill the land of Israel and
Judah with people and animals. 28 And just as
I took care to uproot, to pull down, to over-
throw, to destroy, and to demolish them, so I
will take care to plant them and to build
them up. 29 When that time comes, people
will no longer say,

'The parents ate the sour grapes,
But the children got the sour taste.'

30 Instead, those who eat sour grapes will
have their own teeth set on edge; and every-
one will die because of their own sin."
31 The LORD says, "The time is coming
when I will make a new covenant with the
people of Israel and with the people of
Judah. 32 It will not be like the old covenant
that I made with their ancestors when I took
them by the hand and led them out of
Egypt. Although I was like a husband to
them, they did not keep that covenant.
33 The new covenant that I will make with
the people of Israel will be this: I will put
my law within them and write it on their
hearts. I will be their God, and they will be
my people. 34 None of them will have to
teach a neighbor to know the LORD,
because all will know me, from the least to
the greatest. I will forgive their sins and I
will no longer remember their wrongs. I, the
LORD, have spoken."

35 The LORD provides the sun for light by day,
the moon and the stars to shine at night.
He stirs up the sea and makes it roar;
his name is the LORD Almighty.
36 He promises that as long as the natural order lasts,
so long will Israel be a nation.
37 If one day the sky could be measured
and the foundations of the earth explored,
only then would he reject the people of Israel
because of all they have done.
The LORD has spoken.

38 "The time is coming," says the LORD,
"when all of Jerusalem will be rebuilt as my
city, from Hananel Tower west to the Corner
Gate. 39 And the boundary line will continue
from there on the west to the hill of Gareb
and then around to Goah. 40 The entire val-
ley, where the dead are buried and garbage is

31:29 Ezek 18:2 **31:31** Mt 26:28; Mk 14:24; Lk 22:20; 1 Cor 11:25; 2 Cor 3:6 **31:31–34** Heb 8:8–12
31:33 Heb 10:16 **31:34** Heb 10:17

dumped, and all the fields above Kidron Brook as far as the Horse Gate to the east, will be sacred to me. The city will never again be torn down or destroyed."

Jeremiah Buys a Field

32 The LORD spoke to me in the tenth year that Zedekiah was king of Judah, which was also the eighteenth year of King Nebuchadnezzar of Babylonia. 2At that time the army of the king of Babylonia was attacking Jerusalem, and I was locked up in the courtyard of the royal palace. 3King Zedekiah had imprisoned me there and had accused me of announcing that the LORD had said, "I am going to let the king of Babylonia capture this city, 4and King Zedekiah will not escape. He will be handed over to the king of Babylonia; he will see him face to face and will speak to him in person. 5Zedekiah will be taken to Babylonia, and he will remain there until I deal with him. Even if he fights the Babylonians, he will not be successful. I, the LORD, have spoken."

6The LORD told me 7that Hanamel, my uncle Shallum's son, would come to me with the request to buy his field at Anathoth in the territory of Benjamin, because I was his nearest relative and had the right to buy it for myself. 8Then, just as the LORD had said, Hanamel came to me there in the courtyard and asked me to buy the field. So I knew that the LORD had really spoken to me. 9I bought the field from Hanamel and weighed out the money to him; the price came to seventeen pieces of silver. 10I signed and sealed the deed, had it witnessed, and weighed out the money on scales. 11Then I took both copies of the deed of purchase— the sealed copy containing the contract and its conditions, and the open copy— 12and gave them to Baruch, the son of Neriah and grandson of Mahseiah. I gave them to him in the presence of Hanamel and of the witnesses who had signed the deed of purchase and of the people who were sitting in the courtyard. 13Before them all I said to Baruch, 14"The LORD Almighty, the God of Israel, has ordered you to take these deeds, both the sealed deed of purchase and the open copy, and to place them in a clay jar, so that they may be preserved for years to come. 15The LORD Almighty, the God of Israel, has said that houses, fields, and vineyards will again be bought in this land."

Jeremiah's Prayer

16After I had given the deed of purchase to Baruch, I prayed, 17"Sovereign LORD, you made the earth and the sky by your great power and might; nothing is too difficult for you. 18You have shown constant love to thousands, but you also punish people for the sins of their parents. You are a great and powerful God; you are the LORD Almighty. 19You make wise plans and do mighty things; you see everything that people do, and you reward them according to their actions. 20Long ago you performed miracles and wonders in Egypt, and you have continued to perform them to this day, both in Israel and among all the other nations, so that you are now known everywhere. 21By means of miracles and wonders that terrified our enemies, you used your power and might to bring your people Israel out of Egypt. 22You gave them this rich and fertile land, as you had promised their ancestors. 23But when they came into this land and took possession of it, they did not obey your commands or live according to your teaching; they did nothing that you had ordered them to do. And so you brought all this destruction on them.

24"The Babylonians have built siege mounds around the city to capture it, and they are attacking. War, starvation, and disease will make the city fall into their hands. You can see that all you have said has come true. 25Yet, Sovereign LORD, you are the one who ordered me to buy the field in the presence of witnesses, even though the city is about to be captured by the Babylonians."

32:1 2 Kings 25:1–7

"The new covenant that I will make with the people of Israel will be this: I will put my law within them and write it on their hearts" *(Jeremiah 31:33).*

26 Then the LORD said to me, 27 "I am the
LORD, the God of all people. Nothing is too
difficult for me. 28 I am going to give this city
over to King Nebuchadnezzar of Babylonia
and his army; they will capture it 29 and set it
on fire. They will burn it down, together
with the houses where people have made me
angry by burning incense to Baal on the
rooftops and by pouring out wine offerings
to other gods. 30 From the very beginning of
their history the people of Israel and the
people of Judah have displeased me and made
me angry by what they have done. 31 The
people of this city have made me angry and
furious from the day it was built. I have
decided to destroy it 32 because of all the evil
that has been done by the people of Judah
and Jerusalem, together with their kings and
leaders, their priests and prophets. 33 They
turned their backs on me; and though I kept
on teaching them, they would not listen and
learn. 34 They even placed their disgusting
idols in the Temple built for my worship, and
they have defiled it. 35 They have built altars
to Baal in Hinnom Valley, to sacrifice their
sons and daughters to the god Molech. I did
not command them to do this, and it did not
even enter my mind that they would do such
a thing and make the people of Judah sin."

A Promise of Hope

36 The LORD, the God of Israel, said to me,
"Jeremiah, the people are saying that war,
starvation, and disease will make this city fall
into the hands of the king of Babylonia.
Now listen to what else I have to say. 37 I am
going to gather the people from all the
countries where I have scattered them in my
anger and fury, and I am going to bring them
back to this place and let them live here in
safety. 38 Then they will be my people, and I
will be their God. 39 I will give them a single
purpose in life: to honor me for all time, for
their own good and the good of their
descendants. 40 I will make an eternal
covenant with them. I will never stop doing
good things for them, and I will make them
fear me with all their heart, so that they will
never turn away from me. 41 I will take plea-
sure in doing good things for them, and I
will establish them permanently in this land.

42 "Just as I have brought this disaster on
these people, so I am going to give them all
the good things that I have promised. 43 The
people are saying that this land will be like a
desert where neither people nor animals live,
and that it will be given over to the Babylo-
nians. But fields will once again be bought
in this land. 44 People will buy them, and the
deeds will be signed, sealed, and witnessed.
This will take place in the territory of Ben-
jamin, in the villages around Jerusalem, in
the towns of Judah, and in the towns in the
hill country, in the foothills, and in southern
Judah. I will restore the people to their land.
I, the LORD, have spoken."

Another Promise of Hope

33 While I was still in prison in the
courtyard, the LORD's message came
to me again. 2 The LORD, who made the
earth, who formed it and set it in place,
spoke to me. He whose name is the LORD
said, 3 "Call to me, and I will answer you; I
will tell you wonderful and marvelous things
that you know nothing about. 4 I, the LORD,
the God of Israel, say that the houses of
Jerusalem and the royal palace of Judah will
be torn down as a result of the siege and the
attack. 5 Some will fight against the Babylo-
nians, who will fill the houses[s] with the
corpses of those whom I am going to strike
down in my anger and fury. I have turned
away from this city because of the evil things
that its people have done. 6 But I will heal
this city and its people and restore them to
health. I will show them abundant peace and
security. 7 I will make Judah and Israel pros-

[s] **33:5** *In verses 4 and 5* as a result . . . houses; *Hebrew unclear.*

32:28 2 Kings 25:1–11; 2 Chr 36:17–21 **32:34** 2 Kings 23:10; Jer 7:30, 31; 19:1–6 **32:35** **a** 2 Kings 23:10; Jer 7:31; **b** Lev 18:21

Nebuchadnezzar was the name of four different kings in ancient Mesopotamia. The most famous is the one who captured Jerusalem in 597 BC.

The LORD's message came to me again. (33:1)

perous, and I will rebuild them as they were
before. 8 I will purify them from the sins that
they have committed against me, and I will
forgive their sins and their rebellion.
9 Jerusalem will be a source of joy, honor, and
pride to me; and every nation in the world
will fear and tremble when they hear about
the good things that I do for the people of
Jerusalem and about the prosperity that I
bring to the city."

10 The LORD said, "People are saying that
this place is like a desert, that it has no peo-
ple or animals living in it. And they are
right; the towns of Judah and the streets of
Jerusalem are empty; no people or animals
live there. But in these places you will hear
again 11 the shouts of gladness and joy and
the happy sounds of wedding feasts. You will
hear people sing as they bring thank offer-
ings to my Temple; they will say,

'Give thanks to the LORD Almighty,
because he is good
and his love is eternal.'

I will make this land as prosperous as it was
before. I, the LORD, have spoken."

12 The LORD Almighty said, "In this land
that is like a desert and where no people or
animals live, there will once again be pastures
where shepherds can take their sheep. 13 In
the towns in the hill country, in the foothills,
and in southern Judah, in the territory of
Benjamin, in the villages around Jerusalem,
and in the towns of Judah, shepherds will
once again count their sheep. I, the LORD,
have spoken."

14 The LORD said, "The time is coming
when I will fulfill the promise that I made to
the people of Israel and Judah. 15 At that time
I will choose as king a righteous descendant
of David. That king will do what is right and
just throughout the land. 16 The people of
Judah and of Jerusalem will be rescued and
will live in safety. The city will be called 'The
LORD Our Salvation.' 17 I, the LORD, promise
that there will always be a descendant of
David to be king of Israel 18 and that there
will always be priests from the tribe of Levi
to serve me and to offer burnt offerings,
grain offerings, and sacrifices."

19 The LORD said to me, 20 "I have made a
covenant with the day and with the night, so
that they always come at their proper times;
and that covenant can never be broken. 21 In
the same way I have made a covenant with
my servant David that he would always have
a descendant to be king, and I have made a
covenant with the priests from the tribe of
Levi that they would always serve me; and
those covenants can never be broken. 22 I will
increase the number of descendants of my
servant David and the number of priests
from the tribe of Levi, so that it will be as
impossible to count them as it is to count
the stars in the sky or the grains of sand on
the seashore."

23 The LORD said to me, 24 "Have you
noticed how people are saying that I have
rejected Israel and Judah, the two families
that I chose? And so they look with con-
tempt on my people and no longer consider
them a nation. 25 But I, the LORD, have a
covenant with day and night, and I have
made the laws that control earth and sky.
26 And just as surely as I have done this, so I
will maintain my covenant with Jacob's
descendants and with my servant David. I
will choose one of David's descendants to
rule over the descendants of Abraham, Isaac,
and Jacob. I will be merciful to my people
and make them prosperous again."

33:11 1 Chr 16:34; 2 Chr 5:13; 7:3; Ezra 3:11; Ps 100:5; 106:1; 107:1; 118:1; 136:1 **33:14–16** Jer 23:5, 6
33:17 2 Sam 7:12–16; 1 Kings 2:4; 1 Chr 17:11–14 **33:18** Num 3:5–10

Pray it!

Night and Day

In our ever-changing world, there are a few things we can count on. One is the twenty-four hour cycle of each day. We know that night will always give way to day, and vice versa. God uses the trustworthiness of night and day as a symbol of the trustworthiness of his covenant with Israel and Judah. You can count on God's promises!

Let God know how grateful you are for those things in your life that you can count on. Begin with the words in Jeremiah 33:20. Think about other parts of God's Creation that we can count on and thank God for. Check out Psalm 104 and Daniel A:29–59 for songs in the Bible that focus on nature and creation.

— Jeremiah 33:19–26

A Message for Zedekiah

34 The LORD spoke to me when King
Nebuchadnezzar of Babylonia and
his army, supported by troops from all the
nations and races that were subject to him,
were attacking Jerusalem and its nearby
towns. [2]The LORD, the God of Israel, told
me to go and say to King Zedekiah of
Judah, "I, the LORD, will hand this city over
to the king of Babylonia, and he will burn it
down. [3]You will not escape; you will be cap-
tured and handed over to him. You will see
him face to face and talk to him in person;
then you will go to Babylonia. [4]Zedekiah,
listen to what I say about you. You will not
be killed in battle. [5]You will die in peace,
and as people burned incense when they
buried your ancestors, who were kings
before you, in the same way they will burn
incense for you. They will mourn over you
and say, 'Our king is dead!' I, the LORD, have
spoken."
[6]Then I gave this message to King
Zedekiah in Jerusalem [7]while the army of
the king of Babylonia was attacking the city.
The army was also attacking Lachish and
Azekah, the only other fortified cities left in
Judah.

Deceitful Treatment of Slaves

[8]King Zedekiah and the people of
Jerusalem had made an agreement to set free
[9]their Hebrew slaves, both male and female,
so that no one would have an Israelite as a
slave. [10]All the people and their leaders
agreed to free their slaves and never to
enslave them again. They did set them free,
[11]but later they changed their minds, took
them back, and forced them to become
slaves again.
[12]Then the LORD, [13]the God of Israel,
told me to say to the people: "I made a
covenant with your ancestors when I res-
cued them from Egypt and set them free
from slavery. I told them that [14]every seven
years they were to set free any Hebrew slave
who had served them for six years. But your
ancestors would not pay any attention to me
or listen to what I said. [15]Just a few days ago
you changed your minds and did what
pleased me. All of you agreed to set all
Israelites free, and you made a covenant in
my presence, in the Temple where I am wor-
shiped. [16]But then you changed your minds
again and dishonored me. All of you took
back the slaves whom you had set free as
they desired, and you forced them into slav-
ery again. [17]So now, I, the LORD, say that
you have disobeyed me; you have not given
all Israelites their freedom. Very well, then, I
will give you freedom: the freedom to die by
war, disease, and starvation. I will make every
nation in the world horrified at what I do
to you. [18-19]The officials of Judah and of
Jerusalem, together with the palace officials,
the priests, and all the leaders, made a
covenant with me by walking between the

34:1 2 Kings 25:1–11; 2 Chr 36:17–21 **34:14** Ex 21:2; Deut 15:12

two halves of a bull that they had cut in two. But they broke the covenant and did not keep its terms. So I will do to these people what they did to the bull. [20]I will hand them over to their enemies, who want to kill them, and their corpses will be eaten by birds and wild animals. [21]I will also hand over King Zedekiah of Judah and his officials to those who want to kill them. I will hand them over to the Babylonian army, which has stopped its attack against you. [22]I will give the order, and they will return to this city. They will attack it, capture it, and burn it down. I will make the towns of Judah like a desert where no one lives. I, the LORD, have spoken."

Jeremiah and the Rechabites

35 When Jehoiakim son of Josiah was king of Judah, the LORD said to me, [2]"Go to the members of the Rechabite clan and talk to them. Then bring them into one of the rooms in the Temple and offer them some wine." [3]So I took the entire Rechabite clan—Jaazaniah (the son of another Jeremiah, who was Habazziniah's son) and all his brothers and sons— [4]and brought them to the Temple. I took them into the room of the disciples of the prophet Hanan son of Igdaliah. This room was above the room of Maaseiah son of Shallum, an important official in the Temple, and near the rooms of the other officials. [5]Then I placed cups and bowls full of wine before the Rechabites, and I said to them, "Have some wine."

[6]But they answered, "We do not drink wine. Our ancestor Jonadab son of Rechab told us that neither we nor our descendants were ever to drink any wine. [7]He also told us not to build houses or farm the land and not to plant vineyards or buy them. He commanded us always to live in tents, so that we might remain in this land where we live like strangers. [8]We have obeyed all the instructions that Jonadab gave us. We ourselves never drink wine, and neither do our wives, our sons, or our daughters. [9-10]We do not build houses for homes—we live in tents—and we own no vineyards, fields, or grain. We have fully obeyed everything that our ancestor Jonadab commanded us. [11]But when King Nebuchadnezzar invaded the country, we decided to come to Jerusalem to get away from the Babylonian and Syrian armies. That is why we are living in Jerusalem."

[12-13]Then the LORD Almighty, the God of Israel, told me to go and say to the people of Judah and Jerusalem, "I, the LORD, ask you why you refuse to listen to me and to obey my instructions. [14]Jonadab's descendants have obeyed his command not to drink wine, and to this very day none of them drink any. But I have kept on speaking to you, and you have not obeyed me. [15]I have continued to send you all my servants the prophets, and they have told you to give up your evil ways and to do what is right. They warned you not to worship and serve other gods, so that you could go on living in the land that I gave you and your ancestors. But you would not listen to me or pay any attention to me. [16]Jonadab's descendants have obeyed the command that their ancestor gave them, but you people have not obeyed me. [17]So now, I, the LORD Almighty, the God of Israel, will bring on you people of Judah and of Jerusalem all the destruction that I promised. I will do this because you would not listen when I spoke to you, and you would not answer when I called you."

[18]Then I told the Rechabite clan that the LORD Almighty, the God of Israel, had said, "You have obeyed the command that your ancestor Jonadab gave you; you have followed all his instructions, and you have done everything he commanded you. [19]So I, the LORD Almighty, the God of Israel, promise that Jonadab son of Rechab will always have a male descendant to serve me."

35:1 2 Kings 23:36—24:6; 2 Chr 36:5–7

Zedekiah was the last king of Judah and was placed on his throne by Nebuchadnezzar in 597 BC.

Baruch wrote it all down on a scroll. Baruch read from the scroll. Then the officials sent Jehudi. (36:4, 10, 14)

Baruch Reads the Scroll in the Temple

36 In the fourth year that Jehoiakim
son of Josiah was king of Judah, the
LORD said to me, 2“Get a scroll and write
on it everything that I have told you about
Israel and Judah and all the nations. Write
everything that I have told you from the
time I first spoke to you, when Josiah was
king, up to the present. 3Perhaps when the
people of Judah hear about all the destruc-
tion that I intend to bring on them, they
will turn from their evil ways. Then I will
forgive their wickedness and their sins.”
4So I called Baruch son of Neriah and
dictated to him everything that the LORD
had said to me. And Baruch wrote it all
down on a scroll. 5Then I gave Baruch the
following instructions: “I am no longer
allowed to go into the Temple. 6But I want
you to go there the next time the people are
fasting. You are to read the scroll aloud, so
that they will hear everything that the LORD
has said to me and that I have dictated to
you. Do this where everyone can hear you,
including the people of Judah who have
come in from their towns. 7Perhaps they will
pray to the LORD and turn from their evil
ways, because the LORD has threatened this
people with his terrible anger and fury.” 8So
Baruch read the LORD's words in the Temple
exactly as I had told him to do.
9In the ninth month of the fifth year that
Jehoiakim was king of Judah, the people fast-
ed to gain the LORD's favor. The fast was kept
by all who lived in Jerusalem and by all who
came there from the towns of Judah. 10Then,
while all the people were listening, Baruch
read from the scroll everything that I had said.
He did this in the Temple, from the room of
Gemariah son of Shaphan, the court secretary.
His room was in the upper court near the
entrance of the New Gate of the Temple.

The Scroll Is Read to the Officials

11Micaiah, the son of Gemariah and
grandson of Shaphan, heard Baruch read
from the scroll what the LORD had said.
12Then he went to the royal palace, to the
room of the court secretary, where all the
officials were in session. Elishama, the court
secretary, Delaiah son of Shemaiah, Elnathan
son of Achbor, Gemariah son of Shaphan,
Zedekiah son of Hananiah, and all the other
officials were there. 13Micaiah told them
everything that he had heard Baruch read to
the people. 14Then the officials sent Jehudi
(the son of Nethaniah, grandson of Shelemi-
ah, and great-grandson of Cushi) to tell
Baruch to bring the scroll that he had read
to the people. Baruch brought them the

36:1 2 Kings 24:1; 2 Chr 36:5–7; Dan 1:1, 2

Baruch was a friend of Jeremiah and served as his secretary, or scribe. He wrote down much of what Jeremiah said.

"We must report this to the king." As soon as Jehudi finished reading three or four columns, the king cut them off . . . Then I took another scroll. (36:16, 23, 32)

scroll. 15"Sit down," they said, "and read the
scroll to us." So Baruch did. 16After he had
read it, they turned to one another in alarm
and said to Baruch, "We must report this to
the king." 17Then they asked him, "Tell us,
now, how did you come to write all this?
Did Jeremiah dictate it to you?"

18Baruch answered, "Jeremiah dictated
every word of it to me, and I wrote it down
in ink on this scroll."

19Then they told him, "You and Jeremiah
must go and hide. Don't let anyone know
where you are."

The King Burns the Scroll

20The officials put the scroll in the room
of Elishama, the court secretary, and went to
the king's court, where they reported every-
thing to the king. 21Then the king sent Jehu-
di to get the scroll. He took it from the room
of Elishama and read it to the king and all
the officials who were standing around him.
22It was winter and the king was sitting in
his winter palace in front of the fire. 23As
soon as Jehudi finished reading three or four
columns, the king cut them off with a small
knife and threw them into the fire. He kept
doing this until the entire scroll was burned
up. 24But neither the king nor any of his offi-
cials who heard all this was afraid or showed
any sign of sorrow. 25Although Elnathan,
Delaiah, and Gemariah begged the king not
to burn the scroll, he paid no attention to
them. 26Then he ordered Prince Jerahmeel,
together with Seraiah son of Azriel and
Shelemiah son of Abdeel, to arrest me and
my secretary Baruch. But the LORD had
hidden us.

Study it!

Scrolls

It's easy to forget that books did not exist in biblical times. Written words were either carved in stone or written on scrolls. Each book of the Bible would actually have been written on one long scroll. That means one continuous sheet of skin or paper. Each end of the scroll would be attached to a rod so that both ends of the scroll could be rolled up toward the middle. They could be unrolled to locate a particular section or passage. Scrolls eventually gave way to books, which were much more convenient to use. It is also good to remember that all copies of books or scrolls were done by hand until the invention of the printing press fourteen hundred years after Christ!

In Jewish worship, scrolls are still used today.

— Jeremiah, chapter 36

Jeremiah Writes Another Scroll

27After King Jehoiakim had burned the
scroll that I had dictated to Baruch, the
LORD told me 28to take another scroll and
write on it everything that had been on the

first one. 29The LORD told me to say to the
king, "You have burned the scroll, and you
have asked Jeremiah why he wrote that the
king of Babylonia would come and destroy
this land and kill its people and its animals.
30So now, I, the LORD, say to you, King
Jehoiakim, that no descendant of yours will
ever rule over David's kingdom. Your corpse
will be thrown out where it will be exposed
to the sun during the day and to the frost at
night. 31I will punish you, your descendants,
and your officials because of the sins all of
you commit. Neither you nor the people of
Jerusalem and of Judah have paid any atten-
tion to my warnings, and so I will bring on
all of you the disaster that I have threat-
ened."

32Then I took another scroll and gave it
to my secretary Baruch, and he wrote down
everything that I dictated. He wrote every-
thing that had been on the first scroll and
similar messages that I dictated to him.

Zedekiah's Request to Jeremiah

37 King Nebuchadnezzar of Babylonia
made Zedekiah son of Josiah king of
Judah in the place of Jehoiachin son of
Jehoiakim. 2But neither Zedekiah nor his
officials nor the people obeyed the message
which the LORD had given me.

3King Zedekiah sent Jehucal son of
Shelemiah and the priest Zephaniah son of
Maaseiah to ask me to pray to the LORD our
God on behalf of our nation. 4I had not yet
been put in prison and was still moving
about freely among the people. 5The Bab-
ylonian army had been besieging Jerusalem,
but when they heard that the Egyptian army
had crossed the Egyptian border, they
retreated.

6Then the LORD, the God of Israel, told
me 7to say to Zedekiah, "The Egyptian army
is on its way to help you, but it will return
home. 8Then the Babylonians will come
back, attack the city, capture it, and burn it
down. 9I, the LORD, warn you not to
deceive yourselves into thinking that the
Babylonians will not come back, because
they will. 10Even if you defeat the whole
Babylonian army, so that only wounded men
are left, lying in their tents, they would still
get up and burn this city to the ground."

Jeremiah Is Arrested and Imprisoned

11The Babylonian army retreated from
Jerusalem because the Egyptian army was
approaching. 12So I started to leave Jerusalem
and go to the territory of Benjamin to take
possession of my share of the family proper-
ty. 13But when I reached the Benjamin Gate,
the officer in charge of the soldiers on duty
there, a man by the name of Irijah, the son
of Shelemiah and grandson of Hananiah,
stopped me and said, "You are deserting to
the Babylonians!"

14I answered, "That's not so! I'm not
deserting." But Irijah would not listen to me.
Instead, he arrested me and took me to the
officials. 15They were furious with me and
had me beaten and locked up in the house
of Jonathan, the court secretary, whose house
had been made into a prison. 16I was put in
an underground cell and kept there a long
time.

17Later on King Zedekiah sent for me,
and there in the palace he asked me private-
ly, "Is there any message from the LORD?"

"There is," I answered, and added, "You
will be handed over to the king of Babylo-
nia." 18Then I asked, "What crime have I
committed against you or your officials or
this people, to make you put me in prison?
19What happened to your prophets who told
you that the king of Babylonia would not
attack you or the country? 20And now, Your
Majesty, I beg you to listen to me and do
what I ask. Please do not send me back to
the prison in Jonathan's house. If you do, I
will surely die there."

21So King Zedekiah ordered me to be
locked up in the palace courtyard. I stayed
there, and each day I was given a loaf of
bread from the bakeries until all the bread in
the city was gone.

37:1 2 Kings 24:17; 2 Chr 36:10

Pray it!

Down and Out

Sometimes you may feel as if you too are at the bottom of a deep pit, as Jeremiah was when he was thrown into the muddy well. Maybe this prayer will help.

Dear God, right now I feel pretty down and out. It seems that no one cares, and I am just sinking deeper. I believe that you are with me in my troubles. And just as Jeremiah was rescued by someone, I pray that you will send someone to help me. Keep my eyes focused on you and fill me with hope. Let me also have the courage to ask for help when I need it. We can't get through life alone. I look forward to brighter days. Thank you, God.

— Jeremiah 38:1–13

Jeremiah in a Dry Well

38 Shephatiah son of Mattan, Gedaliah
son of Pashhur, Jehucal son of
Shelemiah, and Pashhur son of Malchiah
heard that I was telling the people that 2the
LORD had said, "Whoever stays on in the
city will die in war or of starvation or disease. But those who go out and surrender to
the Babylonians will not be killed; they will
at least escape with their life." 3I was also
telling them that the LORD had said, "I am
going to give the city to the Babylonian
army, and they will capture it."
4Then the officials went to the king and
said, "This man must be put to death. By
talking like this he is making the soldiers in
the city lose their courage, and he is doing
the same thing to everyone else left in the
city. He is not trying to help the people; he
only wants to hurt them."
5King Zedekiah answered, "Very well,
then, do what you want to with him; I can't
stop you." 6So they took me and let me
down by ropes into Prince Malchiah's well,
which was in the palace courtyard. There
was no water in the well, only mud, and I
sank down in it.
7However, Ebedmelech the Ethiopian,[t] a
eunuch who worked in the royal palace,
heard that they had put me in the well. At
that time the king was holding court at the
Benjamin Gate. 8So Ebedmelech went there
and said to the king, 9"Your Majesty, what
these men have done is wrong. They have
put Jeremiah in the well, where he is sure to
die of starvation, since there is no more food
in the city." 10Then the king ordered Ebedmelech to take with him three men and to
pull me out of the well before I died. 11So
Ebedmelech went with the men to the
palace storeroom and got some worn-out
clothing which he let down to me by ropes.
12He told me to put the rags under my
arms, so that the ropes wouldn't hurt me. I
did this, 13and they pulled me up out of the
well. After that I was kept in the courtyard.

Zedekiah Asks Jeremiah's Advice

14On another occasion King Zedekiah
had me brought to him at the third entrance
to the Temple, and he said, "I am going to

[t] **38:7** *Hebrew* Cushite: *Cush is the ancient name of the extensive territory south of the First Cataract of the Nile River. This region was called Ethiopia in Graeco-Roman times, and included within its borders most of modern Sudan and some of present-day Ethiopia (Abyssinia).*

Why do you think Jeremiah's message upset people so much that they wanted to throw him in a well and leave him to die?

And they pulled me up out of the well. (38:13)

ask you a question, and I want you to tell
me the whole truth."
15 I answered, "If I tell you the truth, you
will put me to death, and if I give you
advice, you won't pay any attention."
16 So King Zedekiah promised me in
secret, "I swear by the living God, the God
who gave us life, that I will not put you to
death or hand you over to the men who
want to kill you."
17 Then I told Zedekiah that the LORD
Almighty, the God of Israel, had said, "If you
surrender to the king of Babylonia's officers,
your life will be spared, and this city will not
be burned down. Both you and your family
will be spared. 18 But if you do not surrender,
then this city will be handed over to the
Babylonians, who will burn it down, and
you will not escape from them."
19 But the king answered, "I am afraid of
our own people who have deserted to the
Babylonians. I may be handed over to them
and tortured."
20 I said, "You will not be handed over to
them. I beg you to obey the LORD's mes-
sage; then all will go well with you, and your
life will be spared. 21 But the LORD has
shown me in a vision what will happen if
you refuse to surrender. 22 In it I saw all the
women left in Judah's royal palace being led
out to the king of Babylonia's officers. Listen
to what they were saying as they went:

'The king's best friends misled him,
they overruled him.
And now that his feet have sunk in the
mud,
his friends have left him.' "

23 Then I added, "All your women and
children will be taken out to the Babyloni-
ans, and you yourself will not escape from
them. You will be taken prisoner by the king
of Babylonia, and this city will be burned to
the ground."
24 Zedekiah replied, "Don't let anyone
know about this conversation, and your life
will not be in danger. 25 If the officials hear
that I have talked with you, they will come
and ask you what we said. They will promise
not to put you to death if you tell them
everything. 26 Just tell them you were beg-
ging me not to send you back to prison to
die there." 27 Then all the officials came and
questioned me, and I told them exactly what
the king had told me to say. There was noth-
ing else they could do, because no one had
overheard the conversation. 28 And I was kept
in the palace courtyard until the day
Jerusalem was captured.

The Fall of Jerusalem

39 In the tenth month of the ninth year
that Zedekiah was king of Judah,
King Nebuchadnezzar of Babylonia came
with his whole army and attacked Jerusalem.
2 On the ninth day of the fourth month of
Zedekiah's eleventh year as king, the city
walls were broken through.
(3 When Jerusalem was captured,[u] all the
high officials of the king of Babylonia came
and took their places at the Middle Gate,
including Nergal Sharezer, Samgar Nebo,
Sarsechim, and another Nergal Sharezer.[v])

[u] **39:3** When Jerusalem was captured; *these words are moved here from the end of chapter 38.* [v] **39:3** *The names and titles of these men are unclear.*
38:28 Ezek 33:21

Jerusalem was completely taken over by the Babylonians in 587 BC.

The Babylonians burned down the royal palace and the houses. (39:8)

4When King Zedekiah and all his sol-
diers saw what was happening, they tried to
escape from the city during the night. They
left by way of the royal garden, went
through the gateway connecting the two
walls, and escaped in the direction of the
Jordan Valley. 5But the Babylonian army
pursued them and captured Zedekiah in the
plains near Jericho. Then they took him to
King Nebuchadnezzar, who was in the city
of Riblah in the territory of Hamath, and
there Nebuchadnezzar passed sentence on
him. 6At Riblah he put Zedekiah's sons to
death while Zedekiah was looking on, and
he also had the officials of Judah executed.
7After that, he had Zedekiah's eyes put out
and had him placed in chains to be taken to
Babylonia. 8Meanwhile, the Babylonians
burned down the royal palace and the
houses of the people and tore down the
walls of Jerusalem. 9Finally Nebuzaradan,
the commanding officer, took away as pris-
oners to Babylonia the people who were
left in the city, together with those who
had deserted to him. 10He left in the land
of Judah some of the poorest people, who
owned no property, and he gave them vine-
yards and fields.

Jeremiah's Release

11But King Nebuchadnezzar commanded
Nebuzaradan, the commanding officer, to
give the following order: 12"Go and find
Jeremiah and take good care of him. Do not
harm him, but do for him whatever he
wants." 13So Nebuzaradan, together with the
high officials Nebushazban and Nergal
Sharezer and all the other officers of the
king of Babylonia, 14had me brought from
the palace courtyard. They put me under the
care of Gedaliah, the son of Ahikam and
grandson of Shaphan, who was to see that I
got home safely. And so I stayed there among
the people.

Hope for Ebedmelech

15While I was still imprisoned in the
palace courtyard, the LORD told me 16to tell
Ebedmelech the Ethiopian[w] that the LORD
Almighty, the God of Israel, had said, "Just as
I said I would, I am going to bring upon this
city destruction and not prosperity. And
when this happens, you will be there to see
it. 17But I, the LORD, will protect you, and
you will not be handed over to the people
you are afraid of. 18I will keep you safe, and
you will not be put to death. You will escape

[w] **39:16** *Hebrew* Cushite: *Cush is the ancient name of the extensive territory south of the First Cataract of the Nile River. This region was called Ethiopia in Graeco-Roman times, and included within its borders most of modern Sudan and some of present-day Ethiopia (Abyssinia).*

Study it!

Stories After the Fall

Jeremiah, chapters 39–45, read more like history than prophecy. They tell about what happened to Jeremiah and the land of Judah after the Babylonians left. Jeremiah was not forced to go into captivity in Babylon. So he stayed back in Judah, where he had a number of adventures, including being forced to go to Egypt for a while.

The point of it all seems to be that if people just listened to God's message that Jeremiah delivered, everything would have been much better. They could have lived in peace without making the Babylonians angry with them. There would have been no war or destruction of Jerusalem and the Temple. But they continued to refuse to listen to Jeremiah, leading to more killing and hardships.

— Jeremiah, chapter 40

with your life because you have put your
trust in me. I, the LORD, have spoken."

Jeremiah Stays with Gedaliah

40 The LORD spoke to me after Neb-
uzaradan, the commanding officer,
had set me free at Ramah. I had been taken
there in chains, along with all the other peo-
ple from Jerusalem and Judah who were
being taken away as prisoners to Babylonia.
2 The commanding officer took me aside
and said, "The LORD your God threatened
this land with destruction, 3 and now he has
done what he said he would. All this hap-
pened because your people sinned against
the LORD and disobeyed him. 4 Now, I am
taking the chains off your wrists and setting
you free. If you want to go to Babylonia
with me, you may do so, and I will take care
of you. But if you don't want to go, you
don't have to. You have the whole country to
choose from, and you may go wherever you
wish."
5 When I did not answer,[x] Nebuzaradan
said, "Go back to Gedaliah, the son of
Ahikam and grandson of Shaphan, whom
the king of Babylonia has made governor of
the towns of Judah. You may stay with him
and live among the people, or you may go
anywhere you think you should." Then he
gave me a present and some food to take
with me, and let me go on my way. 6 I went
to stay with Gedaliah in Mizpah and lived
among the people who were left in the land.

Gedaliah, Governor of Judah
(2 Kings 25:22–24)

7 Some of the Judean officers and soldiers
had not surrendered. They heard that the
king of Babylonia had made Gedaliah gover-
nor of the land and had placed him in
charge of all those who had not been taken
away to Babylonia—the poorest people in
the land. 8 So Ishmael son of Nethaniah,
Johanan son of Kareah, Seraiah son of Tan-
humeth, the sons of Ephai from Netophah,
and Jezaniah from Maacah went with their
men to Gedaliah at Mizpah. 9 Gedaliah said
to them, "I give you my word that there is
no need for you to be afraid to surrender to
the Babylonians. Settle in this land, serve the
king of Babylonia, and all will go well with
you. 10 I myself will stay in Mizpah and be
your representative when the Babylonians
come here. But you can gather and store up
wine, fruit, and olive oil, and live in the vil-
lages you occupy." 11 Meanwhile, all the
Israelites who were in Moab, Ammon,
Edom, and other countries, heard that the
king of Babylonia had allowed some Isra-
elites to stay on in Judah and that he had
made Gedaliah their governor. 12 So they left
the places where they had been scattered,

[x] **40:5** When I did not answer; *or* Then, before he left.
40:7–9 2 Kings 25:22–24

and returned to Judah. They came to Gedali-
ah at Mizpah, and there they gathered in
large amounts of wine and fruit.

Gedaliah Is Murdered
(2 Kings 25:25, 26)

13 After this, Johanan and the leaders of the
soldiers who had not surrendered came to
Gedaliah at Mizpah 14 and said to him,
"Don't you know that King Baalis of
Ammon has sent Ishmael to murder you?"
But Gedaliah did not believe it. 15 Then
Johanan said privately to him, "Let me go
and kill Ishmael, and no one will know who
did it. Why should he be allowed to murder
you? That would cause all the Jews who
have gathered around you to be scattered,
and it would bring disaster on all the people
who are left in Judah."
16 But Gedaliah answered, "Don't do it!
What you are saying about Ishmael is not
true!"

41 In the seventh month of that year, Ish-
mael, the son of Nethaniah and
grandson of Elishama, a member of the royal
family and one of the king's chief officers,
went to Mizpah with ten men to see Gover-
nor Gedaliah. While they were all eating a
meal together, 2 Ishmael and the ten men with
him pulled out their swords and killed Gedali-
ah. 3 Ishmael also killed all the Israelites who
were with Gedaliah at Mizpah and the Baby-
lonian soldiers who happened to be there.
4 The next day, before anyone knew about
Gedaliah's murder, 5 eighty men arrived from
Shechem, Shiloh, and Samaria. They had
shaved off their beards, torn their clothes, and
gashed themselves. They were taking grain and
incense to offer in the Temple. 6 So Ishmael
went out from Mizpah to meet them, weeping
as he went. When he came to them, he said,
"Please come in to see Gedaliah." 7 As soon as
they were inside the city, Ishmael and his men
killed them and threw their bodies in a well.
8 But there were ten men in the group
who said to Ishmael, "Please don't kill us!
We have wheat, barley, olive oil, and honey
hidden in the fields." So he spared them.
9 The well into which Ishmael threw the
bodies of the men he had killed was the
large one[y] that King Asa had dug when he
was being attacked by King Baasha of Israel.
Ishmael filled the well with the bodies.
10 Then he made prisoners of the king's
daughters and all the rest of the people in
Mizpah, whom Nebuzaradan the command-
ing officer had placed under the care of
Gedaliah. Ishmael took them prisoner and
started off in the direction of the territory
of Ammon.
11 Johanan and all the army leaders with
him heard of the crime that Ishmael had
committed. 12 So they went after him with
their men and overtook him near the large
pool at Gibeon. 13 When Ishmael's prisoners
saw Johanan and the leaders of the forces
with him, they were glad, 14 and turned and
ran to them. 15 But Ishmael and eight of his
men got away from Johanan and escaped to
the land of Ammon.
16 Then Johanan and the leaders of the
forces with him took charge of the people
whom Ishmael had taken away as prisoners
from Mizpah after murdering Gedaliah—
soldiers, women, children, and eunuchs.
17-18 They were afraid of the Babylonians
because Ishmael had murdered Gedaliah,
whom the king of Babylonia had made gov-
ernor of the land. So they set out for Egypt,
in order to get away from the Babylonians.
On the way they stopped at Chimham near
Bethlehem.

The People Ask Jeremiah to Pray for Them

42 Then all the army leaders, including
Johanan son of Kareah and Azariah[z]
son of Hoshaiah, came with people of every

[y] **41:9** *One ancient translation* was the large one; *Hebrew* by means of Gedaliah. [z] **42:1** *One ancient translation (see also 43:2)* Azariah; *Hebrew* Jezaniah.
41:1–3 2 Kings 25:25

King Asa *(Jeremiah 41:9)* **ruled over Judah from 911 to 870 BC. Check out his story in 1 Kings 15:9–24.**

class 2and said to me, "Please do what we ask
you! Pray to the LORD our God for us. Pray
for all of us who have survived. Once there
were many of us; but now only a few of us
are left, as you can see. 3Pray that the LORD
our God will show us the way we should go
and what we should do."

4I answered, "Very well, then. I will pray
to the LORD our God, just as you have
asked, and whatever he says, I will tell you.
I will not keep back anything from you."

5Then they said to me, "May the LORD
be a true and faithful witness against us if
we do not obey all the commands that the
LORD our God gives you for us. 6Whether it
pleases us or not, we will obey the LORD
our God, to whom we are asking you to
pray. All will go well with us if we obey
him."

The LORD's Answer to Jeremiah's Prayer

7Ten days later the LORD spoke to me; 8so
I called together Johanan, all the army lead-
ers who were with him, and all the other
people. 9I said to them, "The LORD, the God
of Israel, to whom you sent me with your
request has said, 10'If you are willing to go
on living in this land, then I will build you
up and not tear you down; I will plant you
and not pull you up. The destruction I
brought on you has caused me great sorrow.
11Stop being afraid of the king of Babylonia.
I am with you, and I will rescue you from
his power. 12Because I am merciful, I will
make him have mercy on you and let you go
back home. I, the LORD, have spoken.'

13-15"But you people who are left in
Judah must not disobey the LORD your God
and refuse to live in this land. You must not
say, 'No, we will go and live in Egypt, where
we won't face war any more or hear the call
to battle or go hungry.' If you say this, then
the LORD Almighty, the God of Israel, says,
'If you are determined to go and live in
Egypt, 16then the war that you fear will
overtake you, and the hunger you dread will
follow you, and you will die there in Egypt.
17All the people who are determined to go
and live in Egypt will die either in war or of
starvation or disease. Not one of them will
survive, not one will escape the disaster that
I am going to bring on them.'

18"The LORD, the God of Israel, says, 'Just
as my anger and fury were poured out on
the people of Jerusalem, so my fury will be
poured out on you if you go to Egypt. You
will be a horrifying sight; people will make
fun of you and use your name as a curse. You
will never see this place again.' "

19Then I continued, "The LORD has told
you people who are left in Judah not to go
to Egypt. And so I warn you now 20that you
are making a fatal mistake. You asked me to
pray to the LORD our God for you, and you
promised that you would do everything that
he commands. 21And now I have told you,
but you are disobeying everything that the
LORD our God sent me to tell you. 22So
then, remember this: you will die in war or
of starvation or disease in the land where
you want to go and live."

Jeremiah Is Taken to Egypt

43 I finished telling the people every-
thing that the LORD their God had
sent me to tell them. 2Then Azariah son of
Hoshaiah and Johanan son of Kareah and
all the other arrogant men said to me, "You
are lying. The LORD our God did not send
you to tell us not to go and live in Egypt.
3Baruch son of Neriah has stirred you up
against us, so that the Babylonians will gain
power over us and can either kill us or take
us away to Babylonia." 4So neither Johanan
nor any of the army officers nor any of the
people would obey the LORD's command to
remain in the land of Judah. 5Then Johanan
and all the army officers took everybody left
in Judah away to Egypt, together with all the
people who had returned from the nations
where they had been scattered: 6the men, the

43:5–7 2 Kings 25:26

"Stop being afraid of the king of Babylonia. I am with you, and I will rescue you from his power" *(Jeremiah 42:11).*

They disobeyed the LORD's command and went into Egypt. (43:7)

women, the children, and the king's daugh-
ters. They took everyone whom Neb-
uzaradan the commanding officer had left
under the care of Gedaliah, including
Baruch and me. 7They disobeyed the LORD's
command and went into Egypt as far as the
city of Tahpanhes.
8There the LORD said to me, 9"Get some
large stones and bury them in the mortar of
the pavement[a] in front of the entrance to the
government building here in the city, and let
some of the Israelites see you do it. 10Then
tell them that I, the LORD Almighty, the God
of Israel, am going to bring my servant King
Nebuchadnezzar of Babylonia to this place,
and he[b] will put his throne over these stones
that you[c] buried, and will spread the royal
tent over them. 11Nebuchadnezzar will
come and defeat Egypt. Those people who
are doomed to die of disease will die of dis-
ease, those doomed to be taken away as pris-
oners will be taken away as prisoners, and
those doomed to be killed in war will be
killed in war. 12I will set fire to the temples
of Egypt's gods, and the king of Babylonia
will either burn their gods or carry them
off. As shepherds pick their clothes clean of
lice, so the king of Babylonia will pick the
land of Egypt clean and then leave victori-
ous. 13He will destroy the sacred stone mon-
uments at Heliopolis in Egypt and will burn
down the temples of the Egyptian gods."

Study it!

Egypt

At the end of his life, Jeremiah was taken off to Egypt, and it is believed that he died there. Egypt plays a very important role in the Bible, and many great figures spent time there.

- **Joseph was sold by his brothers into slavery and spent many years in Egypt, eventually becoming governor and being reunited with his family (Genesis, chapters 37–50).**
- **Moses fled Egypt but was called by God to lead the Israelites out of slavery in Egypt to the Promised Land.**
- **Jesus was taken to Egypt by Mary and Joseph to protect him from death when Herod ordered that all boys under the age of two be murdered (Matthew 2:13–23).**
- **Egypt today is famous for its ancient pyramids. Make sure you can find Egypt on a map.**

— Jeremiah 43:1–6

The LORD's Message to the Israelites in Egypt

44 The LORD spoke to me concerning
all the Israelites living in Egypt, in
the cities of Migdol, Tahpanhes, and Mem-
phis, and in the southern part of the country.
2The LORD Almighty, the God of Israel, said,
"You yourselves have seen the destruction I
brought on Jerusalem and all the other cities
of Judah. Even now they are still in ruins,
and no one lives in them 3because their peo-
ple had done evil and had made me angry.

[a] **43:9** *Probable text* bury them . . . pavement; *Hebrew unclear.* [b] **43:10** *Some ancient translations* he; *Hebrew* I.
[c] **43:10** *Some ancient translations* you; *Hebrew* I.

They offered sacrifices to other gods and
served gods that neither they nor you nor
your ancestors ever worshiped. 4I kept send-
ing you my servants the prophets, who told
you not to do this terrible thing that I hate.
5But you would not listen or pay any atten-
tion. You would not give up your evil prac-
tice of sacrificing to other gods. 6So I
poured out my anger and fury on the towns
of Judah and on the streets of Jerusalem, and
I set them on fire. They were left in ruins
and became a horrifying sight, as they are
today.

7"And so I, the LORD Almighty, the God
of Israel, now ask why you are doing such an
evil thing to yourselves. Do you want to
bring destruction on men and women, chil-
dren and babies, so that none of your people
will be left? 8Why do you make me angry
by worshiping idols and by sacrificing to
other gods here in Egypt, where you have
come to live? Are you doing this just to
destroy yourselves, so that every nation on
earth will make fun of you and use your
name as a curse? 9Have you forgotten all
the wicked things that have been done in
the towns of Judah and in the streets of
Jerusalem by your ancestors, by the kings of
Judah and their wives, and by you and your
wives? 10But to this day you have not hum-
bled yourselves. You have not honored me or
lived according to all the laws that I gave
you and your ancestors.

11"So then, I, the LORD Almighty, the
God of Israel, will turn against you and
destroy all Judah. 12As for the people of
Judah who are left and are determined to go
and live in Egypt, I will see to it that all of
them are destroyed. All of them, great and
small, will die in Egypt, either in war or of
starvation. They will be a horrifying sight;
people will make fun of them and use their
name as a curse. 13I will punish those who
live in Egypt, just as I punished Jerusalem—
with war, starvation, and disease. 14None of
the people of Judah who are left and have
come to Egypt to live will escape or survive.
Not one of them will return to Judah, where
they long to live once again. No one will
return except a few refugees."

15Then all the men who knew that their
wives offered sacrifices to other gods, and all
the women who were standing there,
including the Israelites who lived in south-
ern Egypt—a large crowd in all—said to me,
16"We refuse to listen to what you have told
us in the name of the LORD. 17We will do
everything that we said we would. We will
offer sacrifices to our goddess, the Queen of
Heaven, and we will pour out wine offerings
to her, just as we and our ancestors, our king
and our leaders, used to do in the towns of
Judah and in the streets of Jerusalem. Then
we had plenty of food, we were prosperous,
and had no troubles. 18But ever since we
stopped sacrificing to the Queen of Heaven
and stopped pouring out wine offerings to
her, we have had nothing, and our people
have died in war and of starvation."

19And the women added, "When we
baked cakes shaped like the Queen of Heav-
en, offered sacrifices to her, and poured out
wine offerings to her, our husbands approved
of what we were doing."

20Then I said to all the men and the
women who had answered me in this way,
21"As for the sacrifices which you and your
ancestors, your kings and your leaders, and
the people of the land offered in the towns
of Judah and in the streets of Jerusalem—do
you think that the LORD did not know
about them or that he forgot them? 22This
very day your land lies in ruins and no one
lives in it. It has become a horrifying sight,
and people use its name as a curse because
the LORD could no longer endure your
wicked and evil practices. 23This present di-
saster has come on you because you offered
sacrifices to other gods and sinned against
the LORD by not obeying all his com-
mands."

24-25I told all the people, especially the
women, what the LORD Almighty, the God
of Israel, was saying to the people of Judah
living in Egypt: "Both you and your wives
have made solemn promises to the Queen of
Heaven. You promised that you would offer
sacrifices to her and pour out wine offerings
to her, and you have kept your promises.
Very well, then! Keep your promises! Carry
out your vows! 26But now listen to the vow
that I, the LORD, have made in my mighty
name to all you Israelites in Egypt: Never
again will I let any of you use my name to

make a vow by saying, 'I swear by the living
Sovereign LORD!' 27 I will see to it that you
will not prosper, but will be destroyed. All of
you will die, either in war or of disease, until
not one of you is left. 28 But a few of you
will escape death and return from Egypt to
Judah. Then the survivors will know whose
words have come true, mine or theirs. 29 I,
the LORD, will give you proof that I will
punish you in this place and that my promise
to bring destruction on you will come true.
30 I will hand over King Hophra of Egypt to
his enemies who want to kill him, just as I
handed over King Zedekiah of Judah to
King Nebuchadnezzar of Babylonia, who
was his enemy and wanted to kill him."

God's Promise to Baruch

45 In the fourth year that Jehoiakim
son of Josiah was king of Judah,
Baruch wrote down what I had dictated to
him. Then I told him 2 that the LORD, the
God of Israel, had said, "Baruch, 3 you are
saying, 'I give up! The LORD has added sor-
row to my troubles. I am worn out from
groaning, and I can't find any rest!'
4 "But I, the LORD, am tearing down what
I have built and pulling up what I have
planted. I will do this to the entire earth.
5 Are you looking for special treatment for
yourself? Don't do it. I am bringing disaster
on all people, but you will at least escape
with your life, wherever you go. I, the LORD,
have spoken."

Egypt's Defeat at Carchemish

46 The LORD spoke to me about the
nations, 2 beginning with Egypt. This
is what he said about the army of King
Neco of Egypt, which King Nebuchadnez-
zar of Babylonia defeated at Carchemish
near the Euphrates River in the fourth year
that Jehoiakim was king of Judah:

3 "The Egyptian officers shout,
'Get your shields ready
and march into battle!
4 Harness your horses and mount them!
Fall in line and put on your helmets!
Sharpen your spears!
Put on your armor!'

5 "But what do I see?" asks the LORD.
"They are turning back in terror.
Their soldiers are beaten back;
overcome with fear, they run as fast as
they can
and do not look back.
6 Those who run fast cannot get away;
the soldiers cannot escape.
In the north, by the Euphrates,
they stumble and fall.
7 Who is this that rises like the Nile,
like a river flooding its banks?
8 It is Egypt, rising like the Nile,
like a river flooding its banks.
Egypt said, 'I will rise and cover the world;
I will destroy cities and the people who
live there.
9 Command the horses to go
and the chariots to roll!
Send out the soldiers:
men from Ethiopia[d] and Libya,
carrying shields,
and skilled archers from Lydia.' "

10 This is the day of the Sovereign LORD
Almighty:
today he will take revenge;
today he will punish his enemies.

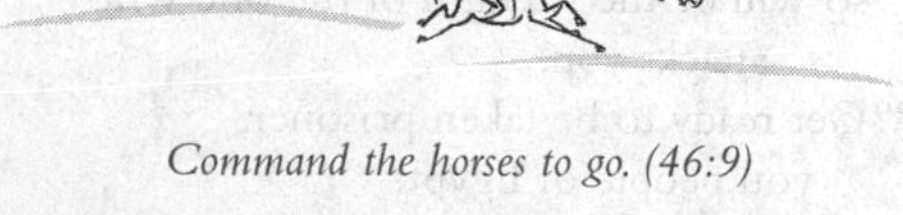

Command the horses to go. (46:9)

[d] **46:9** *Hebrew* Cush: *Cush is the ancient name of the extensive territory south of the First Cataract of the Nile River. This region was called Ethiopia in Graeco-Roman times, and included within its borders most of modern Sudan and some of present-day Ethiopia (Abyssinia).*

44:30 2 Kings 25:1–7 **45:1** 2 Kings 24:1; 2 Chr 36:5–7; Dan 1:1, 2 **46:2–26** Isa 19:1–25; Ezek 29:1—32:32

The Queen of Heaven referred to in Jeremiah 44:17 is not Jesus' mother, Mary, but a false goddess. That title was later given to Mary by the Church.

His sword will eat them until it is full,
and drink their blood until it is satisfied.
Today the Almighty sacrifices his victims
in the north, by the Euphrates.
11 People of Egypt, go to Gilead[e]
and look for medicine!
All your medicine has proved useless;
nothing can heal you.
12 Nations have heard of your shame;
everyone has heard you cry.
One soldier trips over another,
and both of them fall to the ground.

The Coming of Nebuchadnezzar

13 When King Nebuchadnezzar of Babylonia came to attack Egypt, the LORD spoke to me. He said,

14 "Proclaim it in the towns of Egypt,
in Migdol, Memphis, and Tahpanhes:
'Get ready to defend yourselves;
all you have will be destroyed in war!
15 Why has your mighty god Apis fallen?
The LORD has struck him down!'
16 Your soldiers have stumbled and fallen;[f]
each one says to the other,
'Hurry! Let's go home to our people
and escape the enemy's sword!'
17 "Give the king of Egypt a new name—
'Noisy Braggart Who Missed His Chance.'
18 I, the LORD Almighty, am king.
I am the living God.
As Mount Tabor towers above the mountains
and Mount Carmel stands high above the sea,
so will be the strength of the one who attacks you.
19 Get ready to be taken prisoner,
you people of Egypt!
Memphis will be made a desert,
a ruin where no one lives.
20 Egypt is like a splendid cow,
attacked by a stinging fly from the north.
21 Even her hired soldiers
are helpless as calves.
They did not stand and fight;
all of them turned and ran.
The day of their doom had arrived,
the time of their destruction.
22 Egypt runs away, hissing like a snake,
as the enemy's army approaches.
They attack her with axes,
like people cutting down trees
23 and destroying a thick forest.
Their soldiers are too many to count;
they outnumber the locusts.
24 The people of Egypt are put to shame;
they are conquered by the people of the north.
I, the LORD, have spoken."

25 The LORD Almighty, the God of Israel, says, "I am going to punish Amon, the god of Thebes, together with Egypt and its gods and kings. I am going to take the king of Egypt and all who put their trust in him, 26 and hand them over to those who want to kill them, to King Nebuchadnezzar of Babylonia and his army. But later on, people will live in Egypt again, as they did in times past. I, the LORD, have spoken.

The LORD Will Save His People

27 "My people, do not be afraid,
people of Israel, do not be terrified.
I will rescue you from that faraway land,
from the land where you are prisoners.
You will come back home and live in peace;
you will be secure, and no one will make you afraid.
28 I will come to you and save you.
I will destroy all the nations
where I have scattered you,
but I will not destroy you.

[e] **46:11** GILEAD: *See 8:22.* [f] **46:16** *Probable text* Your soldiers . . . fallen; *Hebrew unclear.*
46:13 Jer 43:10–13 **46:27, 28** Jer 30:10, 11

Crete and Gaza still exist today. Crete is an island, and Gaza is part of the Holy Land. See if you can locate them on a map.

Fair Punishment

In Jeremiah 46:28, the Lord says, "I will not let you go unpunished; / but when I punish you, I will be fair."

No one likes to get punished, even when the punishment is deserved. Yet it is easier to accept punishment when you know that it is fair. A fair punishment can help you cool down, be honest and admit that you were wrong, and encourage you to make up for any hurt or damage you have caused. God allowed the Israelites to suffer violence and captivity to help them to be honest about their sinful actions. It was a way of getting their attention. So the next time you are punished for something you did wrong, ask God for the grace to accept punishment without trying to blame someone else. Use it as an opportunity to let God help you be a better person.

— Jeremiah 46:28

I will not let you go unpunished;
but when I punish you, I will be fair.
I, the LORD, have spoken."

The LORD's Message about Philistia

47 Before the king of Egypt attacked Gaza, the LORD spoke to me about Philistia. 2 He said:

"Look! Waters are rising in the north
and will rush like a river in flood.
They will cover the land and everything on it,
cities and the people who live there.
People will call out for help;
everyone on earth will cry bitterly.
3 They will hear the hoofbeats of horses,
the clatter of chariots,
the rumble of wheels.
Parents will not turn back for their children;
their hands will hang limp at their sides.
4 The time has come to destroy Philistia,
to cut off from Tyre and Sidon
all the help that remains.
I, the LORD, will destroy the Philistines,
all who came from the shores of Crete.
5 Great sorrow has come to the people of Gaza,
and Ashkelon's people are silent.
How long will the rest of Philistia mourn?
6 You cry out, 'Sword of the LORD!
How long will you go on slashing?
Go back to your scabbard,
stay there and rest!'
7 But how can it rest,
when I have given it work to do?
I have commanded it to attack Ashkelon
and the people who live on the coast."

The Destruction of Moab

48 This is what the LORD Almighty said about Moab:

"Pity the people of Nebo—
their town is destroyed!
Kiriathaim is captured,
its mighty fortress torn down,
and its people put to shame;
2 the splendor of Moab is gone.
The enemy have captured Heshbon
and plot to destroy the nation of Moab.
The town of Madmen will be silenced;
armies will march against it.
3 The people of Horonaim cry out,
'Violence! Destruction!'

4 "Moab has been destroyed;
listen to the children crying.
5 Hear the sound of their sobs
along the road up to Luhith,
the cries of distress
on the way down to Horonaim.

47:1–7 Isa 14:29–31; Ezek 25:15–17; Joel 3:4–8; Am 1:6–8; Zeph 2:4–7; Zech 9:5–7 **48:1–47** Isa 15:1—16:14; 25:10–12; Ezek 25:8–11; Am 2:1–3; Zeph 2:8–11

6 'Quick, run for your lives!' they say.
'Run like a wild desert donkey!'
7 "Moab, you trusted in your strength and your wealth,
but now even you will be conquered;
your god Chemosh will go into exile,
along with his princes and priests.
8 Not a town will escape the destruction;
both valley and plain will be ruined.
I, the LORD, have spoken.
9 Set up a tombstone for Moab;
it will soon be destroyed.
Its towns will be left in ruins,
and no one will live there again."

(10 Curse those who do not do the LORD's
work with all their heart! Curse those who
do not slash and kill!)

The Cities of Moab Are Destroyed

11 The LORD said, "Moab has always lived
secure and has never been taken into exile.
Moab is like wine left to settle undisturbed
and never poured from jar to jar. Its flavor
has never been ruined, and it tastes as good
as ever.

12 "So now, the time is coming when I will
send people to pour Moab out like wine.
They will empty its wine jars and break
them in pieces. 13 Then the Moabites will be
disillusioned with their god Chemosh, just as
the Israelites were disillusioned with Bethel, a
god in whom they trusted.

14 "Men of Moab, why do you claim to be heroes,
brave soldiers tested in war?
15 Moab and its cities are destroyed;
its finest young men have been slaughtered.
I am the king, the LORD Almighty,
and I have spoken.
16 Moab's doom approaches;
its ruin is coming soon.

17 "Mourn for that nation, you that live nearby,
all of you that know its fame.
Say, 'Its powerful rule has been broken;
its glory and might are no more.'
18 You that live in Dibon,
come down from your place of honor
and sit on the ground in the dust;
Moab's destroyer is here
and has left its forts in ruins.
19 You that live in Aroer,
stand by the road and wait;
ask those who are running away,
find out from them what has happened.
20 'Moab has fallen,' they will answer,
'weep for it; it is disgraced.
Announce along the Arnon River
that Moab is destroyed!'

21 "Judgment has come on the cities of
the plateau: on Holon, Jahzah, Mephaath,
22 Dibon, Nebo, Beth Diblathaim, 23 Kir-
iathaim, Bethgamul, Bethmeon, 24 Kerioth,
and Bozrah. Judgment has come on all the
cities of Moab, far and near. 25 Moab's might
has been crushed; its power has been
destroyed. I, the LORD, have spoken."

Moab Will Be Humbled

26 The LORD said, "Make Moab drunk,
because it has rebelled against me. Moab will
roll in its own vomit, and people will laugh.
27 Moab, remember how you made fun of
the people of Israel? You treated them as
though they had been caught with a gang of
robbers.

28 "You people who live in Moab, leave
your towns! Go and live on the cliffs! Be like
the dove that makes its nest in the sides of a
ravine. 29 Moab is very proud! I have heard
how proud, arrogant, and conceited the peo-
ple are, how much they think of themselves.
30 I, the LORD, know of their arrogance.
Their boasts amount to nothing, and the
things they do will not last. 31 And so I will
weep for everyone in Moab and for the peo-
ple of Kir Heres. 32 I will cry for the people
of Sibmah, even more than for the people of
Jazer. City of Sibmah, you are like a vine
whose branches reach across the Dead Sea
and go as far as Jazer. But now your summer
fruits and your grapes have been destroyed.
33 Happiness and joy have been taken away
from the fertile land of Moab. I have made
the wine stop flowing from the wine presses;
there is no one to make the wine and shout
for joy.

34 "The people of Heshbon and Elealeh

cry out,[g] and their cry can be heard as far as
Jahaz; it can be heard by the people in Zoar,
and it is heard as far as Horonaim and Eglath
Shelishiyah. Even Nimrim Brook has dried
up. 35 I will stop the people of Moab from
making burnt offerings at their places of
worship and from offering sacrifices to their
gods. I, the LORD, have spoken.

36 "So my heart mourns for Moab and for
the people of Kir Heres, like someone play-
ing a funeral song on a flute, because every-
thing they owned is gone. 37 All of them
have shaved their heads and cut off their
beards. They have all made gashes on their
hands, and everyone is wearing sackcloth.
38 On all the housetops of Moab and in all its
public squares there is nothing but mourn-
ing, because I have broken Moab like a jar
that no one wants. 39 Moab has been shat-
tered! Cry out! Moab has been disgraced. It
is in ruins, and all the surrounding nations
make fun of it. I, the LORD, have spoken."

No Escape for Moab

40 The LORD has promised that a nation
will swoop down on Moab like an eagle
with its outspread wings, 41 and the towns
and fortresses will be captured. On that day
Moab's soldiers will be as frightened as a
woman in labor. 42 Moab will be destroyed
and will no longer be a nation, because it
rebelled against me. 43 Terror, pits, and traps
are waiting for the people of Moab. The
LORD has spoken. 44 Whoever tries to escape
the terror will fall into the pits, and whoever
climbs out of the pits will be caught in the
traps, because the LORD has set the time for
Moab's destruction. 45 Helpless refugees try
to find protection in Heshbon, the city that
King Sihon once ruled, but it is in flames.[h]
Fire has burned up the frontiers and the
mountain heights of the war-loving people
of Moab. 46 Pity the people of Moab! The
people who worshiped Chemosh have been
destroyed, and their sons and daughters have
been taken away as prisoners.

47 But in days to come the LORD will
make Moab prosperous again. All of this is
what the LORD has said will happen to
Moab.

The LORD's Judgment on Ammon

49 This is what the LORD said about
Ammon: "Where are the men of
Israel? Is there no one to defend their land?
Why have they let the people who worship
Molech take the territory of the tribe of
Gad and settle there? 2 But the time is com-
ing when I will make the people of the cap-
ital city of Rabbah hear the noise of battle,
and it will be left in ruins and its villages
burned to the ground. Then Israel will take
its land back from those who took it from
them. 3 People of Heshbon, cry out! Ai is
destroyed! Women of Rabbah, go into
mourning! Put on sackcloth and mourn.
Run about in confusion. Your god Molech
will be taken into exile, together with his
priests and princes. 4 Why do you unfaithful
people boast? Your strength is failing. Why
do you trust in your power and say that no
one would dare attack you? 5 I will bring ter-
ror on you from every side. You will all run
away. Each one will run for his life, and there
will be no one to bring your troops together
again.

6 "But later on I will make Ammon pros-
perous again. I, the LORD, have spoken."

The LORD's Judgment on Edom

7 This is what the LORD Almighty said
about Edom: "Have the people of Edom lost
their good judgment? Can their advisers no
longer tell them what to do? Has all their
wisdom disappeared? 8 People of Dedan, turn

[g] **48:34** *Probable text* Heshbon . . . cry out; *Hebrew unclear.* [h] **48:45** Heshbon, the city . . . flames; *or* the city of Heshbon, but it is in flames and the palace of King Sihon is burning.

49:1–6 Ezek 21:28–32; 25:1–7; Am 1:13–15; Zeph 2:8–11 **49:7–22** Isa 34:5–17; 63:1–6; Ezek 25:12–14; 35:1–15; Am 1:11, 12; Ob 1–14; Mal 1:2–5 **49:7** Bar 3:22, 23

Locate Moab and the River Arnon on Map 3 in the back of this Bible. What body of water does the Arnon flow into?

Hide! (49:8)

and run! Hide! I am going to destroy Esau's
descendants because the time has come for
me to punish them. 9When people pick
grapes, they leave a few on the vines, and
when robbers come at night, they take only
what they want. 10But I[i] have stripped Esau's
descendants completely and uncovered their
hiding places, so that they can no longer
hide. All the people of Edom are destroyed.
Not one of them is left. 11Leave your
orphans with me, and I will take care of
them. Your widows can depend on me.

12"If even those who did not deserve to
be punished had to drink from the cup of
punishment, do you think that you will go
unpunished? No, you must drink from the
cup! 13I myself have sworn that the city of
Bozrah will become a horrifying sight and a
desert; people will make fun of it and use its
name as a curse. All the nearby villages will
be in ruins forever. I, the LORD, have spo-
ken."

14I said, "Edom, I have received a message
from the LORD. He has sent a messenger to
tell the nations to assemble their armies and
to get ready to attack you. 15The LORD is
going to make you weak, and no one will
respect you. 16Your pride has deceived you.
No one fears you as much as you think they
do. You live on the rocky cliffs, high on top
of the mountain; but even though you live as
high up as an eagle, the LORD will bring you
down. The LORD has spoken."

17The LORD said, "The destruction that
will come on Edom will be so terrible that
everyone who passes by will be shocked and
terrified. 18The same thing will happen to
Edom that happened to Sodom and
Gomorrah, when they and the nearby towns
were destroyed. No one will ever live there
again. I, the LORD, have spoken. 19Like a
lion coming out of the thick woods along
the Jordan River up to the green pasture
land, I will come and make the Edomites
run away suddenly from their country. Then
the leader I choose will rule the nation.
Who can be compared to me? Who would
dare challenge me? What ruler could oppose
me? 20So listen to the plan that I have made
against the people of Edom, and to what I
intend to do to the people of the city of
Teman. Even their children will be dragged
off, and everyone will be horrified. 21When
Edom falls, there will be such a noise that
the entire earth will shake, and the cries of
alarm will be heard as far away as the Gulf
of Aqaba. 22The enemy will attack Bozrah
like an eagle swooping down with outspread
wings. On that day Edom's soldiers will be
as frightened as a woman in labor."

The LORD's Judgment on Damascus

23This is what the LORD said about Da-
mascus: "The people in the cities of Hamath
and Arpad are worried and troubled because
they have heard bad news. Anxiety rolls over
them like a sea, and they cannot rest. 24The
people of Damascus are weak and have fled
in terror. They are in pain and misery like a
woman in labor. 25The famous city that used
to be happy[j] is completely deserted. 26On
that day her young men will be killed in the
city streets, and all her soldiers destroyed. 27I
will set the walls of Damascus on fire and
will burn down King Benhadad's palaces.
I, the LORD Almighty, have spoken."

[i] **49:10** they leave a few . . . they take only what they want. 10But I; *or* they leave nothing . . . they take everything. 10And so I. [j] **49:25** *Some ancient translations* happy; *Hebrew* my happiness.

49:18 Gen 19:24, 25 **49:19** Wis 12:12 **49:23–27** Isa 17:1–3; Am 1:3–5; Zech 9:1

Read more about Esau's descendants in Genesis, chapter 36. How does this explain why Esau is mentioned in connection with Moab?

Judgment on the Tribe of Kedar and the City of Hazor

28This is what the LORD said about the
tribe of Kedar and the districts controlled by
Hazor, which were conquered by King
Nebuchadnezzar of Babylonia: "Attack the
people of Kedar and destroy that tribe of
eastern people! 29Seize their tents and their
flocks, their tent curtains and everything in
their tents. Take their camels and tell the
people, 'Terror is all around you!'

30"People of Hazor, I, the LORD, warn
you to run far away and hide. King Neb-
uchadnezzar of Babylonia has plotted against
you, and this is what he says, 31'Come on!
We'll attack those people that feel safe and
secure! Their city has no gates or locks and is
completely unprotected.'

32"Take their camels and all their live-
stock! I will scatter in every direction those
people who cut their hair short, and I will
bring disaster on them from every side.
33Hazor will be made a desert forever, a
place where only jackals live. No one will
ever live there again. I, the LORD, have spo-
ken."

The LORD's Judgment on Elam

34Soon after Zedekiah became king of
Judah, the LORD Almighty spoke to me
about the country of Elam. 35He said, "I will
kill all the archers who have made Elam so
powerful. 36I will make winds blow against
Elam from all directions, and I will scatter
her people everywhere, until there is no
country where her refugees have not gone.
37I will make the people of Elam afraid of
their enemies, who want to kill them. In my
great anger I will destroy the people of Elam
and send armies against them until I have
wiped them out. 38I will destroy their kings
and leaders, and set up my throne there.
39But later on I will make the people of
Elam prosperous again. I, the LORD, have
spoken."

50:1—51:64 Isa 13:1—14:23; 47:1–15

Live it!

I, the Lord, Have Spoken

You may notice that the phrase, "I, the LORD, have spoken," appears many times in Jeremiah, chapters 49–52. See if you can count how many times that phrase or something close to it appears. Why, do you think, is it repeated so often?

The words, "I have spoken," have an air of authority about them. You can almost hear God saying after each one, "Period." There is no room for excuses or debate. This is the way it will be. End of discussion.

Sometimes we need to know that something that is said is the final word. "I, the LORD, have spoken," is that kind of statement. The word *amen* works the same way. Whenever we say amen, we are saying, "So be it."

— Jeremiah, chapters 49–52

Babylon's Capture

50 This is the message that the LORD
gave me about the city of Babylon
and its people:

2"Tell the news to the nations! Proclaim it!
Give the signal and announce the
news!
Do not keep it a secret!
Babylon has fallen!
Her god Marduk has been shattered!
Babylon's idols are put to shame;
her disgusting images are crushed!
3"A nation from the north has come to
attack Babylonia and will make it a desert.
People and animals will run away, and no
one will live there."

Israel's Return

4The LORD says, "When that time comes, the people of both Israel and Judah will come weeping, looking for me, their God. 5They will ask the way to Zion and then go in that direction. They will make an eternal covenant with me and never break it.

6"My people are like sheep whose shepherds have let them get lost in the mountains. They have wandered like sheep from one mountain to another, and they have forgotten where their home is. 7They are attacked by all who find them. Their enemies say, 'They sinned against the LORD, and so what we have done is not wrong. Their ancestors trusted in the LORD, and they themselves should have remained faithful to him.'

8"People of Israel, run away from Babylonia! Leave the country! Be the first to leave! 9I am going to stir up a group of strong nations in the north and make them attack Babylonia. They will line up in battle against the country and conquer it. They are skillful hunters, shooting arrows that never miss the mark. 10Babylonia will be looted, and those who loot it will take everything they want. I, the LORD, have spoken."

Babylon's Fall

11The LORD says, "People of Babylonia, you plundered my nation. You are happy and glad, going about like a cow threshing grain or like a neighing horse, 12but your own great city will be humiliated and disgraced. Babylonia will be the least important nation of all; it will become a dry and waterless desert. 13Because of my anger no one will live in Babylon; it will be left in ruins, and all who pass by will be shocked and amazed.

14"Archers, line up for battle against Babylon and surround it. Shoot all your arrows at Babylon, because it has sinned against me, the LORD. 15Raise the war cry all around the city! Now Babylon has surrendered. Its walls have been broken through and torn down.[k] I am taking my revenge on the Babylonians. So take your revenge on them, and treat them as they have treated others. 16Do not let seeds be planted in that country nor let a harvest be gathered. Every foreigner living there will be afraid of the attacking army and will go back home."

Israel's Return

17The LORD says, "The people of Israel are like sheep, chased and scattered by lions. First, they were attacked by the emperor of Assyria, and then King Nebuchadnezzar of Babylonia gnawed on their bones. 18Because of this, I, the LORD Almighty, the God of Israel, will punish King Nebuchadnezzar and his country, just as I punished the emperor of Assyria. 19I will restore the people of Israel to their land. They will eat the food that grows on Mount Carmel and in the region of Bashan, and they will eat all they want of the crops that grow in the territories of Ephraim and Gilead. 20When that time comes, no sin will be found in Israel and no wickedness in Judah, because I will forgive those people whose lives I have spared. I, the LORD, have spoken."

Like sheep . . . scattered by lions (50:17)

God's Judgment on Babylonia

21The LORD says, "Attack the people of Merathaim and of Pekod. Kill and destroy them.[l] Do everything I command you. I, the LORD, have spoken. 22The noise of battle is heard in the land, and there is great destruction. 23Babylonia hammered the whole world to pieces, and now that hammer is shattered! All the nations are shocked at what has happened to that country. 24Babylonia, you fought against me, and you have

[k] **50:15** *Hebrew has an additional word, the meaning of which is unclear.* [l] **50:21** *One ancient translation* them; *Hebrew* after them.

50:8 Rev 18:4

been caught in the trap I set for you, even
though you did not know it. 25 I have
opened the place where my weapons are
stored, and in my anger I have taken them
out, because I, the Sovereign LORD
Almighty, have work to do in Babylonia.
26 Attack it from every side and break open
the places where its grain is stored! Pile up
the loot like piles of grain! Destroy the
country! Leave nothing at all! 27 Kill all their
soldiers! Slaughter them! The people of
Babylonia are doomed! The time has come
for them to be punished!"

(28 Refugees escape from Babylonia and
come to Jerusalem, and they tell how the
LORD our God took revenge for what the
Babylonians had done to his Temple.)

29 "Tell the archers to attack Babylon. Send
out everyone who knows how to use the bow
and arrow. Surround the city and don't let
anyone escape. Pay it back for all it has done,
and treat it as it has treated others, because it
acted with pride against me, the Holy One of
Israel. 30 So its young men will be killed in the
city streets, and all its soldiers will be destroyed
on that day. I, the LORD, have spoken.

31 "Babylonia, you are filled with pride, so
I, the Sovereign LORD Almighty, am against
you! The time has come for me to punish
you. 32 Your proud nation will stumble and
fall, and no one will help you up. I will set
your cities on fire, and everything around
will be destroyed."

33 The LORD Almighty says, "The people
of Israel and of Judah are oppressed. All who
captured them are guarding them closely and
will not let them go. 34 But the one who will
rescue them is strong—his name is the LORD
Almighty. He himself will take up their cause
and will bring peace to the earth, but trouble
to the people of Babylonia."

35 The LORD says,
"Death to Babylonia!
  Death to its people,
  to its rulers, to its people of wisdom.
36 Death to its lying prophets—
  what fools they are!
Death to its soldiers—
  how terrified they are!
37 Destroy its horses and chariots!
Death to its hired soldiers—
  how weak they are!
Destroy its treasures;
  plunder and loot.
38 Bring a drought on its land
  and dry up its rivers.
Babylonia is a land of terrifying idols
  that have made fools of the people.

39 "And so Babylon will be haunted by
demons and evil spirits,[m] and by unclean
birds. Never again will people live there, not
for all time to come. 40 The same thing will
happen to Babylon that happened to Sodom
and Gomorrah, when I destroyed them and
the nearby towns. No one will ever live
there again. I, the LORD, have spoken.

41 "People are coming from a country in the
    north,
  a mighty nation far away;
  many kings are preparing for war.
42 They have taken their bows and swords;
  they are cruel and merciless.
They sound like the roaring sea,
  as they ride their horses.
They are ready for battle against
    Babylonia.
43 The king of Babylonia hears the news,
  and his hands hang limp.
  He is seized by anguish,
  by pain like a woman in labor.

44 "Like a lion coming out of the thick
woods along the Jordan up to the green pas-
ture land, I, the LORD, will come and make
the Babylonians run away suddenly from
their city. Then the leader I choose will rule
the nation. Who can be compared to me?
Who would dare challenge me? What ruler
could oppose me? 45 So listen to the plan
that I have made against the city of Babylon
and to what I intend to do to its people.

[m] **50:39** demons and evil spirits; *or* wildcats and jackals.
50:29 Rev 18:6 **50:39** Rev 18:2 **50:40** Gen 19:24, 25

Jeremiah 50:6 mentions lost sheep, a familiar image in the Bible. Check out Isaiah 53:6 and 1 Peter 2:25.

Even their children will be dragged off, and
everyone will be horrified. 46When Babylon
falls, there will be such a noise that the
entire earth will shake, and the cries of alarm
will be heard by the other nations."

Further Judgment on Babylonia

51 The LORD says, "I am bringing a
destructive wind[n] against Babylonia
and its people. 2I will send foreigners to
destroy Babylonia like a wind that blows
straw away. When that day of destruction
comes, they will attack from every side and
leave the land bare. 3Don't give its soldiers
time to shoot their arrows or to put on their
armor. Do not spare the young men! Destroy
the whole army! 4They will be wounded and
die in the streets of their cities. 5I, the LORD
God Almighty, have not abandoned Israel and
Judah, even though they have sinned against
me, the Holy One of Israel. 6Run away from
Babylonia! Run for your lives! Do not be
killed because of Babylonia's sin. I am now
taking my revenge and punishing it as it
deserves. 7Babylonia was like a gold cup in
my hand, making the whole world drunk.
The nations drank its wine and went out of
their minds. 8Babylonia has suddenly fallen
and is destroyed! Mourn over it! Get medi-
cine for its wounds, and maybe it can be
healed. 9Foreigners living there said, 'We
tried to help Babylonia, but it was too late.
Let's leave now and go back home. God has
punished Babylonia with all his might and
has destroyed it completely.' "

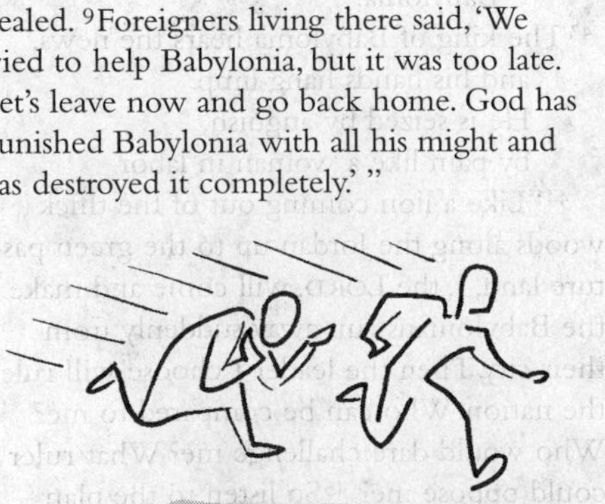

Run for your lives! (51:6)

10The LORD says, "My people shout, 'The
LORD has shown that we are in the right.
Let's go and tell the people in Jerusalem
what the LORD our God has done.' "
11The LORD has stirred up the kings of
Media, because he intends to destroy Bab-
ylonia. That is how he will take revenge for
the destruction of his Temple.

The attacking officers command, "Sharp-
en your arrows! Get your shields ready!
12Give the signal to attack Babylon's walls.
Strengthen the guard! Post the sentries! Place
troops in ambush!"

Give the signal to attack Babylon's walls. (51:12)

The LORD has done what he said he
would do to the people of Babylonia. 13That
country has many rivers and rich treasures,
but its time is up, and its thread of life is cut.
14The LORD Almighty has sworn by his own
life that he will bring many men to attack
Babylonia like a swarm of locusts, and they
will shout with victory.

A Hymn of Praise to God

15The LORD made the earth by his
power;
by his wisdom he created the world
and stretched out the heavens.
16At his command the waters above the
sky[o] roar;
he brings clouds from the ends of the
earth.
He makes lightning flash in the rain
and sends the wind from his storeroom.

[n] **51:1** destructive wind; *or* destroying spirit. [o] **51:16** WATERS ABOVE THE SKY: *See Gen 1:6–8.*
51:7 Rev 17:2–4; 18:3 **51:9** Rev 18:5 **51:13** Rev 17:1

"When Babylon falls, there will be such a noise that the entire earth will shake" *(Jeremiah 50:46)*.

17 At the sight of this, people feel stupid and
senseless;
those who make idols are disillusioned
because the gods they make are false
and lifeless.
18 They are worthless and should be
despised;
they will be destroyed when the LORD
comes to deal with them.
19 The God of Jacob is not like them;
he is the one who made everything,
and he has chosen Israel to be his very
own people.
The LORD Almighty is his name.

The LORD's Hammer

20 The LORD says,
"Babylonia, you are my hammer, my
weapon of war.
I used you to crush nations and
kingdoms,
21 to shatter horses and riders,
to shatter chariots and their drivers,
22 to kill men and women,
to slay old and young,
to kill boys and girls,
23 to slaughter shepherds and their flocks,
to slaughter farmers and their plow
horses,
to crush rulers and high officials."

Babylonia's Punishment

24 The LORD says, "You will see me repay
Babylonia and its people for all the evil they
did to Jerusalem. 25 Babylonia, you are like a
mountain that destroys the whole world, but
I, the LORD, am your enemy. I will take hold
of you, level you to the ground, and leave
you in ashes. 26 None of the stones from your
ruins will ever be used again for building.
You will be like a desert forever. I, the
LORD, have spoken.
27 "Give the signal to attack! Blow the
trumpet so that the nations can hear! Prepare
the nations for war against Babylonia! Tell the
kingdoms of Ararat, Minni, and Ashkenaz to
attack. Appoint an officer to lead the attack.
Bring up the horses like a swarm of locusts.
28 Prepare the nations for war against Babylo-
nia. Send for the kings of Media, their leaders
and officials, and the armies of all the coun-
tries they control. 29 The earth trembles and
shakes because the LORD is carrying out his
plan to make Babylonia a desert, where no
one lives. 30 The Babylonian soldiers have
stopped fighting and remain in their forts.
They have lost their courage and have become
helpless. The city gates are broken down, and
the houses are on fire. 31 Messenger after mes-
senger runs to tell the king of Babylonia that
his city has been broken into from every side.
32 The enemy have captured the river crossing
and have set the fortresses on fire. The Bab-
ylonian soldiers have panicked. 33 Soon the
enemy will cut them down and trample them
like grain on a threshing place. I, the LORD
Almighty, the God of Israel, have spoken."
34 The king of Babylonia cut Jerusalem up
and ate it.
He emptied the city like a jar;
like a monster he swallowed it.

Live it!

The Hammer

A hammer can be either a positive image or a negative one. In Jeremiah 51:21, Babylonia is called God's hammer because it will be used to crush other nations. In this case, it is a weapon of war. But most of the time, a hammer is a positive image. Hammers are used to pound nails and to build things. The international organization Habitat for Humanity, which builds homes for needy people around the world, uses the phrase "Theology of the Hammer." What this means is that a hammer can be a way of witnessing to God. When a hammer is used to build shelter for others, it can be a powerful example of faith in action. Find out if there is a chapter of Habitat for Humanity near you.

— Jeremiah 51:20–23

He took what he wanted
and threw the rest away.
35 Let the people of Zion say,
"May Babylonia be held responsible
for the violence done to us!"
Let the people of Jerusalem say,
"May Babylonia be held responsible
for what we have suffered!"

The LORD Will Help Israel

36 And so the LORD said to the people of
Jerusalem, "I will take up your cause and will
make your enemies pay for what they did to
you. I will dry up the source of Babylonia's
water and make its rivers go dry. 37 That
country will become a pile of ruins where
wild animals live. It will be a horrible sight;
no one will live there, and all who see it will
be terrified. 38 The Babylonians all roar like
lions and growl like lion cubs. 39 Are they
greedy? I will prepare them a feast and make
them drunk and happy. They will go to sleep
and never wake up. 40 I will take them to be
slaughtered, like lambs, goats, and rams. I, the
LORD, have spoken."

That country will become a pile of ruins where wild animals live. (51:37)

Babylon's Fate

41 The LORD says about Babylon: "The
city that the whole world praised has been
captured! What a horrifying sight Babylon
has become to the nations! 42 The sea has
rolled over Babylon and covered it with
roaring waves. 43 The towns have become a
horrifying sight and are like a waterless
desert, where no one lives or even travels. 44 I
will punish Bel, the god of Babylonia, and
make him give up his stolen goods; the
nations will not worship him any more.

"Babylon's walls have fallen. 45 People of
Israel, run away from there! Run for your
life from my fierce anger. 46 Do not lose
courage or be afraid because of the rumors
you hear. Every year a different rumor
spreads—rumors of violence in the land and
of one king fighting another. 47 And so the
time is coming when I will deal with Bab-
ylonia's idols. The whole country will be put
to shame, and all its people will be killed.
48 Everything on earth and in the sky will
shout for joy when Babylonia falls to the
people who come from the north to destroy
it. 49 Babylonia caused the death of people all
over the world, and now Babylonia will fall
because it caused the death of so many
Israelites. I, the LORD, have spoken."

God's Message to the Israelites in Babylonia

50 The LORD says to his people in Babylo-
nia: "You have escaped death! Now go!
Don't wait! Though you are far from home,
think about me, your LORD, and remember
Jerusalem. 51 You say, 'We've been disgraced
and made ashamed; we feel completely help-
less because foreigners have taken over the
holy places in the Temple.' 52 So then, I say
that the time is coming when I will deal
with Babylon's idols, and the wounded will
groan throughout the country. 53 Even if
Babylon could climb to the sky and build a
strong fortress there, I would still send peo-
ple to destroy it. I, the LORD, have spoken."

Further Destruction on Babylon

54 The LORD says,
"Listen to the sound of crying in
Babylon,
of mourning for the destruction in the
land.
55 I am destroying Babylon
and putting it to silence.
The armies rush in like roaring waves
and attack with noisy shouts.
56 They have come to destroy Babylon;
its soldiers are captured,
and their bows are broken.
I am a God who punishes evil,
and I will treat Babylon as it deserves.

51:48 Rev 18:20 **51:49** Rev 18:24

57 I will make its rulers drunk—
men of wisdom, leaders, and soldiers.
They will go to sleep and never wake up.
I, the king, have spoken;
I am the LORD Almighty.
58 The walls of mighty Babylon will be
thrown to the ground,
and its towering gates burned down.
The work of the nations is all for
nothing;
their efforts go up in flames.
I, the LORD Almighty, have spoken."

Jeremiah's Message Is Sent to Babylonia

59 King Zedekiah's personal attendant was
Seraiah, the son of Neriah and grandson of
Mahseiah. In the fourth year that Zedekiah
was king of Judah, Seraiah was going to
Babylonia with him, and I gave him some
instructions. 60 I wrote in a book an account
of all the destruction that would come on
Babylonia, as well as all these other things
about Babylonia. 61 I told Seraiah, "When
you get to Babylon, be sure to read aloud to
the people everything that is written here.
62 Then pray, ' LORD, you have said that you
would destroy this place, so that there would
be no living creatures in it, neither people
nor animals, and it would be like a desert
forever.' 63 Seraiah, when you finish reading
this book to the people, then tie it to a rock
and throw it into the Euphrates River 64 and
say, 'This is what will happen to Babylonia—
it will sink and never rise again because of
the destruction that the LORD is going to
bring on it.' "[p]

The words of Jeremiah end here.

The Fall of Jerusalem
(2 Kings 24:18—25:7)

52 Zedekiah was twenty-one years old
when he became king of Judah, and
he ruled in Jerusalem for eleven years. His

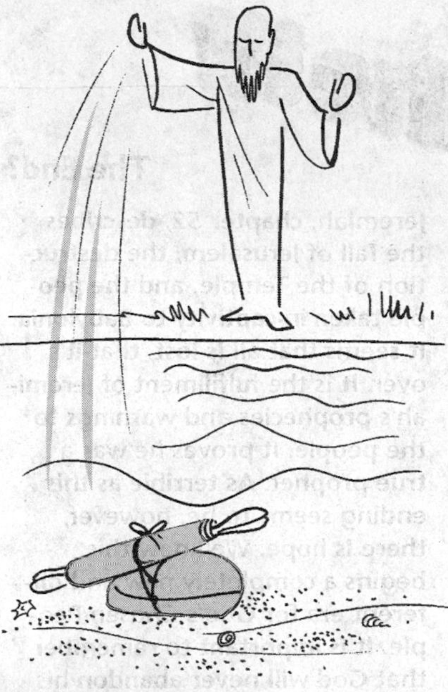

It will sink and never rise again. (51:64)

mother's name was Hamutal, the daughter of
the Jeremiah who lived in the city of Lib-
nah. 2 King Zedekiah sinned against the
LORD, just as King Jehoiakim had done.
3 The LORD became so angry with the peo-
ple of Jerusalem and Judah that he banished
them from his sight.

Zedekiah rebelled against King Neb-
uchadnezzar of Babylonia, 4 and so Neb-
uchadnezzar came with all his army and
attacked Jerusalem on the tenth day of the
tenth month of the ninth year of Zedekiah's
reign. They set up camp outside the city,
built siege walls around it, 5 and kept it under
siege until Zedekiah's eleventh year. 6 On the
ninth day of the fourth month of that same
year, when the famine was so bad that the
people had nothing left to eat, 7 the city walls
were broken through. Although the Babylo-
nians were surrounding the city, all the sol-
diers escaped during the night. They left by
way of the royal garden, went through the
gateway connecting the two walls, and fled

p **51:64** *One ancient translation* on it; *Hebrew* on it and they will become tired out.
51:63, 64 Rev 18:21 **52:4** Ezek 24:2 **52:7** Ezek 33:21

Jeremiah's scroll of prophesies is thrown into the river to sink *(Jeremiah 52:63–64)*. **What is this a sign of?**

> **Live it!**
>
> ### The End?
>
> **Jeremiah, chapter 52, describes the fall of Jerusalem, the destruction of the Temple, and the people taken in captivity to Babylonia. It seems that all is lost, that it's over. It is the fulfillment of Jeremiah's prophecies and warnings to the people. It proves he was a true prophet. As terrible as this ending seems to be, however, there is hope. We know this begins a completely new and different era for God's Chosen People. It is important to remember that God will never abandon his Chosen People. Stay tuned!**
>
> **— Jeremiah, chapter 52**

in the direction of the Jordan Valley. 8 But the
Babylonian army pursued King Zedekiah,
captured him in the plains near Jericho, and
all his soldiers deserted him. 9 Zedekiah was
taken to King Nebuchadnezzar, who was
in the city of Riblah in the territory of
Hamath, and there Nebuchadnezzar passed
sentence on him. 10 At Riblah he put Zed-
ekiah's sons to death while Zedekiah was
looking on and he also had the officials of
Judah executed. 11 After that, he had Zedeki-
ah's eyes put out and had him placed in
chains and taken to Babylon. Zedekiah
remained in prison in Babylon until the day
he died.

The Destruction of the Temple
(2 Kings 25:8–17)

12 On the tenth day of the fifth month of
the nineteenth year of King Nebuchadnezzar
of Babylonia, Nebuzaradan, adviser to the
king and commander of his army, entered
Jerusalem. 13 He burned down the Temple,
the palace, and the houses of all the impor-
tant people in Jerusalem; 14 and his soldiers
tore down the city walls. 15 Then Neb-
uzaradan took away to Babylonia[q] the peo-
ple who were left in the city, the remaining
skilled workers, and those who had deserted
to the Babylonians. 16 But he left in Judah
some of the poorest people, who owned no
property, and he put them to work in the
vineyards and fields.

17 The Babylonians broke in pieces the
bronze columns and the carts that were in
the Temple, together with the large bronze
tank, and they took all the bronze to Bab-
ylon. 18 They also took away the shovels and
the ash containers used in cleaning the altar,
the tools used in tending the lamps, the
bowls used for catching the blood from the
sacrifices, the bowls used for burning
incense, and all the other bronze articles used
in the Temple service. 19 They took away
everything that was made of gold or silver:
the small bowls, the pans used for carrying
live coals, the bowls for holding the blood
from the sacrifices, the ash containers, the
lampstands, the bowls used for incense, and
the bowls used for pouring out wine offer-
ings. 20 The bronze objects that King Sol-
omon had made for the Temple—the two
columns, the carts, the large tank, and the
twelve bulls that supported it—were too
heavy to weigh. 21-22 The two columns were
identical: each one was 27 feet high and 18
feet around. They were hollow, and the metal
was 3 inches thick. On top of each column
was a bronze capital 7½ feet high, and all
around it was a grillwork decorated with
pomegranates, all of which was also made of
bronze. 23 On the grillwork of each column
there were a hundred pomegranates in all,
and ninety-six of these were visible from the
ground.

[q] **52:15** *Probable text* Babylonia; *Hebrew* Babylonia some of the poorest of the people.
52:11 Ezek 12:13 **52:13** 1 Kings 9:8 **52:17–23** 1 Kings 7:15–47

Jeremiah's description of the destruction of the Temple is almost exactly the same as the description in 2 Kings 25:8–17.

So the people of Judah were carried away. (52:27)

The People of Judah Are Taken to Babylonia
(2 Kings 25:18–21, 27–30)

24 In addition, Nebuzaradan, the com-
manding officer, took away as prisoners
Seraiah the High Priest, Zephaniah the
priest next in rank, and the three other
important Temple officials. 25 From the city
he took the officer who had been in com-
mand of the troops, seven of the king's per-
sonal advisers who were still in the city, the
commander's assistant, who was in charge of
military records, and sixty other important
men. 26 Nebuzaradan took them to the king
of Babylonia, who was in the city of Riblah
27 in the territory of Hamath. There the king
had them beaten and put to death.

So the people of Judah were carried away
from their land into exile. 28 This is the
record of the people that Nebuchadnezzar
took away as prisoners: in his seventh year as
king he carried away 3,023; 29 in his eigh-
teenth year, 832 from Jerusalem; 30 and in his
twenty-third year, 745—taken away by Neb-
uzaradan. In all, 4,600 people were taken
away.

31 In the year that Evilmerodach became
king of Babylonia, he showed kindness to
King Jehoiachin of Judah by releasing him
from prison. This happened on the twenty-
fifth day of the twelfth month of the thirty-
seventh year after Jehoiachin had been taken
away as a prisoner. 32 Evilmerodach treated
him kindly and gave him a position of
greater honor than he gave the other kings
who were exiles with him in Babylonia. 33 So
Jehoiachin was permitted to change from his
prison clothes and to dine at the king's table
for the rest of his life. 34 Each day for as long
as he lived, he was given a regular allowance
for his needs.

Your Next Step

Congratulations on finishing the Book of Jeremiah! Use this space to write your thoughts and questions about this book. If you are following the suggested reading plan, move ahead to the Letter from James in the New Testament. The Letter from James also emphasizes the importance of being fair and just in the way you treat others.

THE BOOK OF

Lamentations

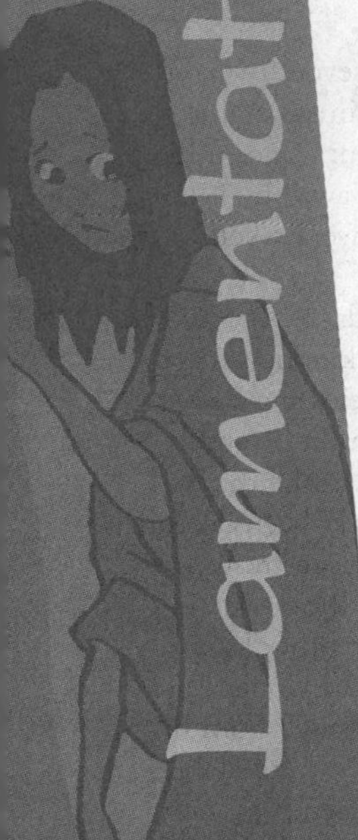

When something bad happens in your life, do you turn to a diary, a sketchpad, or a musical instrument? Many people respond to disasters by writing songs or poetry. The words of country music, rock, blues, and other styles of music are often about people's problems. Countless poems have been written in memory of people who have died or about a traumatic event. The people of Israel were extremely upset over the destruction of their beloved city. They were heartbroken because they were taken as captives to Babylonia. They had lost their homes, their freedom, their capital, and their place of worship—the Temple. As a result of their grief, poems were written. The poems of Lamentations give an idea of how much sorrow the Israelites had.

Headlines

- Jerusalem Is Abandoned! (chapter 1)
- People Worn Out with Weeping (2:10–13)
- A Glimmer of Hope (3:19–42)
- Gotta Get Back to the Lord (5:15–21)

FACTOIDS

Who wrote this book? The author of Lamentations is unknown.

What period is covered? The Babylonian Exile between 587 and 538 BC.

Why was it written? Lamentations was written to give the Israelites living in Babylonia a chance to express their grief. They had lost their country, their freedom, and their worship of God in the Temple. It was also written to help them remember the goodness of God.

How is it organized? Lamentations is a collection of five poems, each of which is a separate chapter, or book. Each of the books has twenty-two verses, except the third, which has sixty-six verses.

Important themes

- Grieving our losses and acknowledging our sins are actions that can lead to healing.
- Recalling God's goodness in the past gives us hope for the future.

The Sorrows of Jerusalem

1 How lonely lies Jerusalem, once so full of people!
Once honored by the world, she is now like a widow;
The noblest of cities has fallen into slavery.

2 All night long she cries; tears run down her cheeks.
Of all her former friends, not one is left to comfort her.
Her allies have betrayed her and are all against her now.

Like a widow . . . all night long she cries. (1:1–2)

3 Judah's people are helpless slaves, forced away from home.[a]
They live in other lands, with no place to call their own—
Surrounded by enemies, with no way to escape.

4 No one comes to the Temple now to worship on the holy days.
The young women who sang there suffer, and the priests can only groan.
The city gates stand empty, and Zion is in agony.

5 Her enemies succeeded; they hold her in their power.
The LORD has made her suffer for all her many sins;
Her children have been captured and taken away.

6 The splendor of Jerusalem is a thing of the past.
Her leaders are like deer that are weak from hunger,
Whose strength is almost gone as they flee from the hunters.

7 A lonely ruin now, Jerusalem recalls her ancient splendor.
When she fell to the enemy, there was no one to help her;
Her conquerors laughed at her downfall.

8 Her honor is gone; she is naked and held in contempt.
She groans and hides her face in shame.
Jerusalem made herself filthy with terrible sin.

9 Her uncleanness was easily seen, but she showed no concern for her fate.
Her downfall was terrible; no one can comfort her.
Her enemies have won, and she cries to the LORD for mercy.

10 The enemies robbed her of all her treasures.
She saw them enter the Temple itself,
Where the LORD had forbidden Gentiles to go.

11 Her people groan as they look for something to eat;
They exchange their treasures for food to keep themselves alive.
"Look at me, LORD," the city cries; "see me in my misery."

12 "Look at me!" she cries to everyone who passes by.[b]

[a] **1:3** are helpless . . . home; *or* fled from home, from the misery of slavery. [b] **1:12** Look . . . by; *or* May this not happen to you that pass by; *or* Does this mean nothing to you that pass by?

1:1 Bar 4:12

"No one has ever had pain like mine,
Pain that the LORD brought on me in
the time of his anger.

13 "He sent fire from above, a fire that
burned inside me.
He set a trap for me and brought me to
the ground.
Then he abandoned me and left me in
constant pain.

14 "He took note of all my sins and tied
them all together;
He hung them around my neck, and I
grew weak beneath the weight.
The Lord gave me to my foes, and I
was helpless against them.

15 "The Lord laughed at all my strongest
soldiers;
He sent an army to destroy my young
men.
He crushed my people like grapes in a
wine press.

16 "That is why my eyes are overflowing
with tears.
No one can comfort me; no one can
give me courage.
The enemy has conquered me; my
people have nothing left.

17 "I stretch out my hands, but no one will
help me.
The LORD has called enemies against
me from every side;
They treat me like some filthy thing.

18 "But the LORD is just, for I have
disobeyed him.
Listen to me, people everywhere; look
at me in my pain.
My young men and women have been
taken away captive.

19 "I called to my allies, but they refused to
help me.
The priests and the leaders died in the
city streets,
Looking for food to keep themselves
alive.

20 "Look, O LORD, at my agony, at the
anguish of my soul!
My heart is broken in sorrow for my
sins.
There is murder in the streets; even
indoors there is death.

21 "Listen[c] to my groans; there is no one to
comfort me.
My enemies are glad that you brought
disaster on me.
Bring[d] the day you promised; make my
enemies suffer as I do.

22 "Condemn them for all their wickedness;
Punish them as you punished me for
my sins.
I groan in misery, and I am sick at
heart."

The Lord's Punishment of Jerusalem

2 The Lord in his anger has covered Zion
with darkness.
Its heavenly splendor he has turned
into ruins.
On the day of his anger he abandoned
even his Temple.

2 The Lord destroyed without mercy every
village in Judah
And tore down the forts that defended
the land.
He brought disgrace on the kingdom
and its rulers.

3 In his fury he shattered the strength of
Israel;
He refused to help us when the enemy
came.
He raged against us like fire, destroying
everything.

4 He aimed his arrows at us like an enemy;
He killed all those who were our joy
and delight.
Here in Jerusalem we felt his burning
anger.

5 Like an enemy, the Lord has destroyed
Israel;
He has left her forts and palaces in ruins.

[c] **1:21** *One ancient translation* Listen; *Hebrew* They listened. [d] **1:21** *One ancient translation* Bring; *Hebrew* You brought.

Catholic Connections

Together We Pray

"I don't need anybody to help me!" Did you ever say this to your parents when you were little and learning to do something new? Even now, you may not want your parents, teachers, or friends to help with some things. You may want to be as independent as possible. But there are times and places when we need other people's help.

One of those times is prayer. Sometimes, praying alone is just what you need. However, there are times when coming together to pray is important to do. At masses, weddings, Baptisms, and Confirmations, people come together to pray. Funerals bring us together in sadness but in trust of eternal life. Whenever there is a tragedy, people find support in sharing their sadness with one another. The Book of Lamentations has poems that helped the Jewish people do that after the horrible events that led to the destruction of Jerusalem and the Temple.

A modern example of this happening is after the tragedy of September 11. In many churches, temples, and synagogues, people came together to pray in sorrow. These services help us remember what has happened, the people affected, and also our own limitations. Not intended to depress us, praying together after a tragedy helps us to care for ourselves and others.

— Lamentations, chapter 2

He has brought on the people of Judah
unending sorrow.

6 He smashed to pieces the Temple where
we worshiped him;
He has put an end to holy days and
Sabbaths.
King and priest alike have felt the force
of his anger.

7 The Lord rejected his altar and deserted
his holy Temple;
He allowed the enemy to tear down its
walls.
They shouted in victory where once
we had worshiped in joy.

8 The LORD was determined that the walls
of Zion should fall;
He measured them off to make sure of
total destruction.
The towers and walls now lie in ruins
together.

9 The gates lie buried in rubble, their bars
smashed to pieces.
The king and the noblemen now are in
exile.
The Law is no longer taught, and the
prophets have no visions from the
LORD.

10 Jerusalem's old men sit on the ground in
silence,
With dust on their heads and sackcloth
on their bodies.
Young women bow their heads to the
ground.

11 My eyes are worn out with weeping; my
soul is in anguish.
I am exhausted with grief at the
destruction of my people.
Children and babies are fainting in the
streets of the city.

12 Hungry and thirsty, they cry to their
mothers;
They fall in the streets as though they
were wounded,
And slowly die in their mothers' arms.

13 O Jerusalem, beloved Jerusalem, what can I say?
How can I comfort you? No one has ever suffered like this.
Your disaster is boundless as the ocean; there is no possible hope.

14 Your prophets had nothing to tell you but lies;
Their preaching deceived you by never exposing your sin.
They made you think you did not need to repent.

15 People passing by the city look at you in scorn.
They shake their heads and laugh at Jerusalem's ruins:
"Is this that lovely city? Is this the pride of the world?"

16 All your enemies mock you and glare at you with hate.
They curl their lips and sneer, "We have destroyed it!
This is the day we have waited for!"

17 The LORD has finally done what he threatened to do:
He has destroyed us without mercy, as he warned us long ago.
He gave our enemies victory, gave them joy at our downfall.

18 O Jerusalem, let your very walls cry out to the Lord![e]
Let your tears flow like rivers night and day;
Wear yourself out with weeping and grief

19 All through the night get up again and again to cry out to the Lord;
Pour out your heart and beg him for mercy on your children—
Children starving to death on every street corner!

20 Look, O LORD! Why are you punishing us like this?
Women are eating the bodies of the children they loved!
Priests and prophets are being killed in the Temple itself

Get up again . . . to cry out to the Lord. (2:19)

21 Young and old alike lie dead in the streets,
Young men and women, killed by enemy swords.
You slaughtered them without mercy on the day of your anger.

22 You invited my enemies to hold a carnival of terror all around me,
And no one could escape on that day of your anger.
They murdered my children, whom I had raised and loved.

Punishment, Repentance, and Hope

3 I am one who knows what it is to be punished by God.
2 He drove me deeper and deeper into darkness
3 And beat me again and again with merciless blows.
4 He has left my flesh open and raw, and has broken my bones.
5 He has shut me in a prison of misery and anguish.
6 He has forced me to live in the stagnant darkness of death.
7 He has bound me in chains; I am a prisoner with no hope of escape.
8 I cry aloud for help, but God refuses to listen;
9 I stagger as I walk; stone walls block me wherever I turn.
10 He waited for me like a bear; he pounced on me like a lion.
11 He chased me off the road, tore me to pieces, and left me.

[e] **2:18** *Probable text* O Jerusalem . . . Lord; *Hebrew* Their hearts cried out to the Lord, O wall of Jerusalem.

God refuses to listen. (3:8)

12 He drew his bow and made me the
target for his arrows.
13 He shot his arrows deep into my body.
14 People laugh at me all day long; I am a
joke to them all.
15 Bitter suffering is all he has given me
for food and drink.
16 He rubbed my face in the ground and
broke my teeth on rocks.
17 I have forgotten what health and peace
and happiness are.
18 I do not have much longer to live; my
hope in the LORD is gone.
19 The thought of my pain, my
homelessness, is bitter poison.
20 I think of it constantly, and my spirit is
depressed.
21 Yet hope returns when I remember this
one thing:
22 The LORD's unfailing love and mercy still
continue,
23 Fresh as the morning, as sure as the
sunrise.
24 The LORD is all I have, and so in him I
put my hope.
25 The LORD is good to everyone who
trusts in him,
26 So it is best for us to wait in patience—
to wait for him to save us—
27 And it is best to learn this patience in
our youth.
28 When we suffer, we should sit alone in
silent patience;
29 We should bow in submission, for there
may still be hope.
30 Though beaten and insulted, we should
accept it all.
31 The Lord is merciful and will not reject
us forever.
32 He may bring us sorrow, but his love
for us is sure and strong.
33 He takes no pleasure in causing us grief
or pain.
34 The Lord knows when our spirits are
crushed in prison;
35 He knows when we are denied the
rights he gave us;
36 When justice is perverted in court, he
knows.
37 The will of the Lord alone is always
carried out.[f]
38 Good and evil alike take place at his
command.
39 Why should we ever complain when
we are punished for our sin?[g]
40 Let us examine our ways and turn back to
the LORD.
41 Let us open our hearts to God in
heaven and pray,
42 "We have sinned and rebelled, and you,
O LORD, have not forgiven us.
43 "You pursued us and killed us; your
mercy was hidden by your anger,
44 By a cloud of fury too thick for our
prayers to get through.
45 You have made us the garbage dump of
the world.
46 "We are insulted and mocked by all our
enemies.
47 We have been through disaster and
ruin; we live in danger and fear.
48 My eyes flow with rivers of tears at the
destruction of my people.

f **3:37** The will . . . out; *or* No one can make anything happen unless the Lord is willing. *g* **3:39** Why should . . . sin?; *or* Why should we complain about being punished for sin, as long as we are still alive?

49 "My tears will pour out in a ceaseless
stream
50 Until the LORD looks down from
heaven and sees us.
51 My heart is grieved when I see what
has happened to the women of the
city.

52 "I was trapped like a bird by enemies
who had no cause to hate me.
53 They threw me alive into a pit and
closed the opening with a stone.
54 Water began to close over me, and I
thought death was near.

55 "From the bottom of the pit, O LORD,
I cried out to you,
56 And when I begged you to listen to
my cry, you heard.
57 You answered me and told me not to
be afraid.

58 "You came to my rescue, Lord, and saved
my life.
59 Judge in my favor; you know the
wrongs done against me.
60 You know how my enemies hate me
and how they plot against me.

61 "You have heard them insult me,
O LORD; you know all their plots.
62 All day long they talk about me and
make their plans.
63 From morning till night they make fun
of me.

64 "Punish them for what they have done,
O LORD;
65 Curse them and fill them with despair!
66 Hunt them down and wipe them off
the earth!"

Jerusalem after Its Fall

4 Our glittering gold has grown dull;
the stones of the Temple lie scattered
in the streets.

2 Zion's young people were as precious to
us as gold,
but now they are treated like common
clay pots.

3 Even a mother wolf will nurse her cubs,
but my people are like ostriches, cruel
to their young.

4 They let their babies die of hunger and
thirst;
children are begging for food that no
one will give them.

5 People who once ate the finest foods die
starving in the streets;
those raised in luxury are pawing
through garbage for food.

6 My people have been punished even
more than the inhabitants of Sodom,
which met a sudden downfall at the
hands of God.

7 Our princes[h] were undefiled and pure as
snow,
vigorous and strong, glowing with
health.

8 Now they lie unknown in the streets,
their faces blackened in death;
their skin, dry as wood, has shriveled
on their bones.

9 Those who died in the war were better
off than those who died later,
who starved slowly to death, with no
food to keep them alive.

10 The disaster that came to my people
brought horror;
loving mothers boiled their own
children for food.

11 The LORD turned loose the full force of
his fury;
he lit a fire in Zion that burned it to
the ground.

12 No one anywhere, not even rulers of
foreign nations,
believed that any invader could enter
Jerusalem's gates.

13 But it happened, because her prophets
sinned and her priests were guilty
of causing the death of innocent
people.

[h] **4:7** princes; *or* Nazirites.

4:6 Gen 19:24 **4:10** Deut 28:57; Ezek 5:10

14 Her leaders wandered through the streets
as though blind,
so stained with blood that no one
would touch them.

15 "Get away!" people shouted. "You're
defiled! Don't touch me!"
So they wandered from nation to
nation, welcomed by no one.

16 The LORD had no more concern for
them; he scattered them himself.
He showed no regard for our priests
and leaders.

17 For help that never came, we looked until
we could look no longer.
We kept waiting for help from a nation
that had none to give.

18 The enemy was watching for us; we could
not even walk in the streets.
Our days were over; the end had come.

19 Swifter than eagles swooping from the
sky, they chased us down.
They tracked us down in the hills; they
took us by surprise in the desert.

20 They captured the source of our life, the
king the LORD had chosen,
the one we had trusted to protect us
from every invader.

21 Laugh on, people of Edom and Uz; be
glad while you can.
Your disaster is coming too; you too
will stagger naked in shame.

22 Zion has paid for her sin; the LORD will
not keep us in exile any longer.
But Edom, the LORD will punish you;
he will expose your guilty acts.

A Prayer for Mercy

5 Remember, O LORD, what has
happened to us.
Look at us, and see our disgrace.

2 Our property is in the hands of strangers;
foreigners are living in our homes.

3 Our fathers have been killed by the enemy,
and now our mothers are widows.

4 We must pay for the water we drink;
we must buy the wood we need for fuel.

5 Driven hard like donkeys or camels,
we are tired, but are allowed no rest.

6 To get food enough to stay alive,
we went begging to Egypt and Assyria.

7 Our ancestors sinned, but now they are
gone,
and we are suffering for their sins.

8 Our rulers are no better than slaves,
and no one can save us from their
power.

9 Murderers roam through the countryside;
we risk our lives when we look for food.

10 Hunger has made us burn with fever
until our skin is as hot as an oven.

11 Our wives have been raped on Mount
Zion itself;
in every Judean village our daughters
have been forced to submit.

12 Our leaders have been taken and hanged;
our elders are shown no respect.

13 Our young men are forced to grind grain
like slaves;
boys go staggering under heavy loads
of wood.

14 The old people no longer sit at the city
gate,
and the young people no longer make
music.

15 Happiness has gone out of our lives;
grief has taken the place of our dances.

16 Nothing is left of all we were proud of.
We sinned, and now we are doomed.

17 We are sick at our very hearts
and can hardly see through our tears,

18 because Mount Zion lies lonely and
deserted,
and wild jackals prowl through its ruins.

19 But you, O LORD, are king forever
and will rule to the end of time.

20 Why have you abandoned us so long?
Will you ever remember us again?

21 Bring us back to you, LORD! Bring us back!
Restore our ancient glory.

22 Or have you rejected us forever?
Is there no limit to your anger?

THE BOOK OF Baruch

Omar, a twelve-year-old boy from Somalia, had been living in refugee camps since he was two. Now he was in a line in an airport in Kenya with what was left of his family, going to a place they had only seen on a map. They were leaving the refugee camp behind, just as they had left their homeland behind years ago. As they boarded the plane, they were full of fear and hope—leaving with only their faith in God, their traditions, and one another. They hoped to return someday.

The Israelites found themselves in a similar situation. Their beloved homeland had been taken over by the Babylonians. Many of the Israelites had been taken into captivity. Now Baruch is telling the Israelites to remember the lessons of the past and pray that God will allow them to return to Jerusalem.

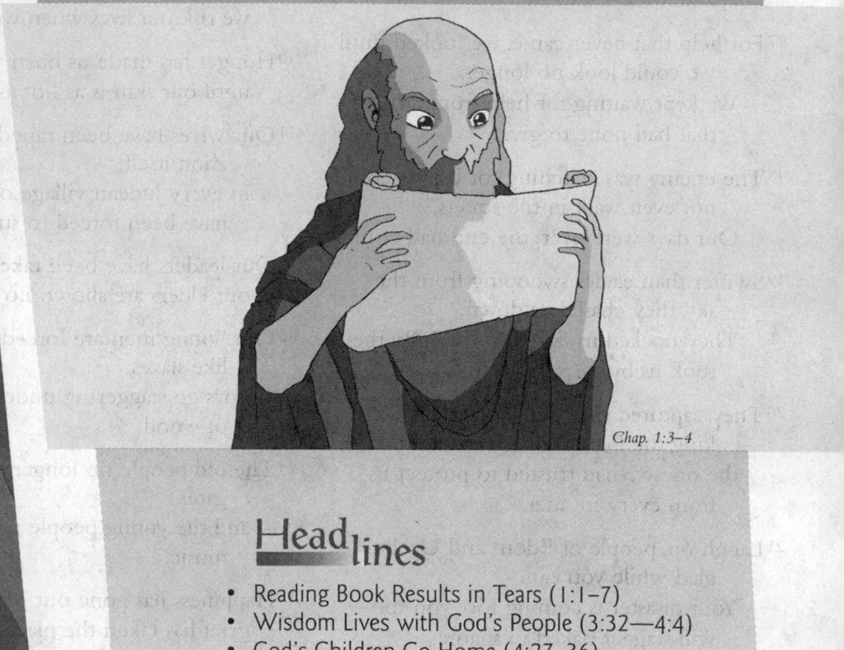

Chap. 1:3–4

Headlines

- Reading Book Results in Tears (1:1–7)
- Wisdom Lives with God's People (3:32—4:4)
- God's Children Go Home (4:27–36)

FACTOIDS

Who wrote this book? The author is unknown, but whoever it was gave credit in the book to Baruch, Jeremiah's secretary.

When was it written? The events took place in the 6th century BC, and the book was written after that. It is estimated that it was written beginning in the second century BC.

Why was it written? It was written to help the Israelite people understand how they could lead a happy and holy life while living in exile.

Important themes

- God's people can find happiness, no matter where they are living, if they are sorry for their sins and try to remain faithful to God's Covenant.
- God's people are able to hold on to their identity in difficult times by remembering and keeping their traditions.

BARUCH

Introduction

1 This book was written by Baruch son of Neraiah, grandson of Mahseiah, and a descendant of Zedekiah, Hasadiah, and Hilkiah. It was written in Babylon 2 on the seventh day of the month[a] in the fifth year after the Babylonians captured Jerusalem and burned it down. 3-4 Baruch read the book aloud to Jehoiachin son of Jehoiakim, king of Judah, and to all the people who lived in Babylon by the Sud River. Everyone came to hear it read—nobles, children of royal families, elders, in fact, all the people, no matter what their status.

5 When the book was read, everyone cried, fasted, and prayed to the Lord. 6 Then they all gave as much money as they could, 7 and the collection was sent to Jerusalem to Jehoiakim the High Priest, son of Hilkiah and grandson of Shallum, and to the other priests and to all the people who were with him in Jerusalem.

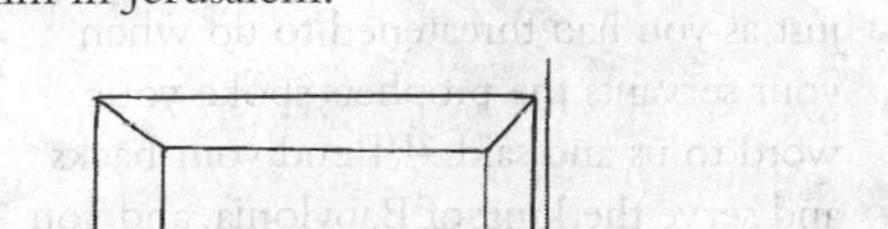

Baruch read the book aloud. (1:3)

8 On the tenth day of the month of Sivan, Baruch took the sacred utensils which had been carried away from the Temple and returned them to Judah. These were the silver utensils which Zedekiah son of King Josiah of Judah had ordered made 9 after King Nebuchadnezzar of Babylonia had deported Jehoiachin, the rulers, the skilled workers,[b] the nobles, and the common people and had taken them from Jerusalem to Babylon.

A Letter to Jerusalem

10 The people wrote:

Please use the money we are sending you to buy animals for the burnt offerings and the sin offerings, to buy incense, and to provide the grain offerings. Offer them on the altar of the Lord our God, 11 and pray for King Nebuchadnezzar of Babylonia and his son Belshazzar, that they may live as long as the heavens last. 12 Then the Lord will strengthen us and be our guide. Nebuchadnezzar and his son Belshazzar will protect us, and we will be loyal to them as long as we live; then they will be pleased with us. 13 We ask you also to pray to the Lord God for us, because we have sinned against him, and he is still angry with us. 14 Please read this book that we are sending you and make your own confession of sin in the Temple on the first day of the Festival of Shelters and on other holy days of assembly.

A Confession of Sin

15 This is the confession you should make: "The Lord our God is righteous, but we are still covered with shame. All of us—the people of Judah, the people of Jerusalem, 16 our kings, our rulers, our priests, our prophets, and our ancestors have been put to shame, 17 because we have sinned against the Lord our God 18 and have disobeyed him. We did not listen to

[a] **1:2** THE MONTH: *The month is probably the fifth month of the Hebrew calendar (see 2 Kings 25:8; Jer 52:12).*
[b] **1:9** skilled workers; *Greek* prisoners.

1:1 Jer 36:4 **1:3, 4** 2 Kings 24:8–17

him or live according to his command-
ments. [19]From the day the Lord brought
our ancestors out of Egypt until the pres-
ent day, we have continued to be unfaith-
ful to him, and we have not hesitated to
disobey him. [20]Long ago, when the Lord
led our ancestors out of Egypt, so that he
could give us a rich and fertile land, he
pronounced curses against us through his
servant Moses. And today we are suffering
because of those curses. [21]We refused to
obey the word of the Lord our God which
he spoke to us through the prophets.
Instead, we all did as we pleased and went
on our own evil way. We turned to other
gods and did things the Lord hates.

2 "So the Lord carried out the threat
he had made against us and against
our judges, our kings, our rulers, and the
people of Israel and Judah. [2]Nowhere else
on earth have such things happened as
happened in Jerusalem when the Lord
carried out the threats written in the Law
of Moses. [3]Things were so bad that we
even ate the flesh of our own sons and
daughters. [4]The Lord scattered our peo-
ple, handing us over to the control of all
the nations around us, and they looked on
us with reproach and horror. [5]We sinned
against the Lord our God and refused to
obey him. Therefore, our nation was con-
quered, instead of being victorious.

6"The Lord our God is always righ-
teous, but we and our ancestors are still
burdened with our guilt. [7]Even though
the Lord punished us as he had threat-
ened, [8]we still did not turn to him and
pray that we would abandon our evil
thoughts. [9-10]We did not obey him or
live by his just commands, so the Lord
brought on us all the punishments he
had kept ready for us.

The Prayer for Deliverance

11"You, O Lord, are the God of Israel
who brought your people out of Egypt
with great power and with signs, miracles,
and wonders. You showed your mighty
strength and gained a glorious reputation,
which is still recognized today. [12]O Lord
our God, we have sinned; we have been
unfaithful; we have disobeyed all your
commands. [13]But do not be angry with us
any longer. Here among the nations where
you have scattered us, only a few of us are
left. [14]Listen to our prayer of petition, Lord,
and rescue us for the sake of your own
honor. Let those who have taken us into
exile be pleased with us. [15]Then the whole
world will know that you are the Lord our
God and that you have chosen the nation
of Israel to be your own people.

16"O Lord, look down from heaven
and see our misery. Listen to our prayer.
[17]Open your eyes and look upon us. Those
in the world of the dead with no breath
left in their bodies cannot offer praises to
you or proclaim how just you are. [18]Only
the living, O Lord, can offer you praise and
acknowledge your justice, even though
they may be suffering greatly, bent and
weak, hungry and with failing eyesight.

19"O Lord our God, we pray to you for
mercy, but not because of any good things
done by our ancestors and our kings. [20]You
turned your anger and wrath against us,
just as you had threatened to do when
your servants the prophets spoke your
word to us and said, [21]'Bend your backs
and serve the king of Babylonia, and you
can remain in the land that I gave to your
ancestors. [22]But if you refuse to obey my
command to serve him, [23]I will bring to an
end every sound of joy and celebration in
the towns of Judah and in Jerusalem. Even
the happy sounds of wedding feasts will no
longer be heard. The whole land will be
desolate and uninhabited.'

24"But we did not obey your command
to serve the king of Babylonia, so you car-
ried out the threat that you had made when
you spoke through your servants the
prophets, when you said that the bones of
our kings and of our ancestors would be
taken from their tombs and scattered. [25]And
now here they lie exposed to the heat of the
day and to the frost of the night. They died
in torment from famine, war, and disease.
[26]And because of the sin of the people of

1:20 Deut 28:15–68 **2:21–23** Jer 7:34; 27:10–12 **2:24** Jer 8:1, 2

Israel and Judah, you have reduced your
own Temple to ruins, even as it is today.
27“But, Lord, you have been patient with
us and have shown us great mercy, 28as you
promised through your servant Moses on
the day you commanded him to write your
Law in the presence of the Israelites. 29‘If
you do not obey me,’ you said, ‘you will be
reduced to a handful among the nations
where I will scatter you. 30I know that you
will not obey me, because you are a stub-
born people. But when you are taken into
exile in another land, you will come to your
senses. 31Then you will realize that I am the
Lord your God, and I will give you a desire
to know and a mind with which to under-
stand. 32There in the land of your exile you
will praise me and remember me. 33You will
stop being so stubborn and wicked, for you
will remember what happened to your
ancestors when they sinned against the
Lord. 34Then I will bring you back to the
land that I solemnly promised to give to
your ancestors, to Abraham, Isaac, and Jacob,
and it will be yours again. I will increase
your population, and you will never again
be reduced to a small number. 35I will make
an everlasting covenant with you; I will be
your God and you will be my people. I will
never again remove you, the people of Israel,
from the land that I gave you.’

3 “O Lord Almighty, God of Israel,
from the depth of our troubled,
weary souls we cry out to you. 2Hear us,
O Lord, and have mercy on us, because
we have sinned against you. 3You reign as
king forever, but we die and are gone for-
ever. 4O Lord Almighty, God of Israel,
hear our prayer. We are no better off than
the dead. Our ancestors sinned against
you, the Lord their God. They refused to
obey you, and we are suffering the conse-
quences of their sin. 5Forget the sinful
things that our ancestors did in the past; at
a time like this, think only of your power
and reputation, 6for you are the Lord our
God, and we will praise you. 7You have
made us fear you, so that we might pray
to you. Here in exile we will praise you
because we have turned away from the
sins of our ancestors. 8You have scattered
us among the nations, and you have made
them despise and curse us. You are punish-
ing us for the sins of our ancestors when
they rebelled against you, the Lord our
God.”

In Praise of Wisdom

9Listen, Israel, to the commands that prom-
ise life; pay attention, and you will become
wise. 10Why is it, Israel, that you find yourself
in an enemy land? Why have you grown old
in a foreign country? You are ritually unclean,
like the dead; 11you are already counted
among the dead. But why? 12It is because you
have left the source of Wisdom! 13If you had
walked in God’s ways, you would have lived
in peace forever. 14Learn where understand-
ing, strength, and insight are to be found.
Then you will know where to find a long
and full life, light to guide you, and peace.
15No one has ever found where Wisdom
lives or has entered her treasure house,
16-17and those who have tried have vanished:
the rulers of the nations, those who hunted
wild animals and birds for sport, those who
accumulated vast fortunes of silver and gold,
which everyone trusts and will do anything to
get, 18and those who worried and schemed to
make money, but who left no trace of their
work behind. 19They have all disappeared and
gone down to the world of the dead. Others
have come along to take their place. 20A later
generation was born and lived in the land, but
they too did not discover the way to knowl-
edge. They did not find the path to Wisdom
or ever reach her. 21Their children also failed.
22Wisdom was not found by the Canaanites.
It has not been discovered by the Edomites
23although they search after knowledge. The
way to Wisdom has not been found by the
merchants of Merran and Tema or by those
who relate fables or by any others who seek
understanding.
24O Israel, how great is the universe in
which God dwells! How vast is all that he
possesses! 25There is no end to it; there is no
way to measure how wide or how high it is.
26Here in early times the famous giants were

2:28, 29 Deut 28:58, 62 **2:35** Jer 32:38–40 **3:9** Prov 4:20–22 **3:15** Job 28:12, 20 **3:26** Gen 6:4; Wis 14:6

Live it!

Where Can You Go?

Consider this type of scavenger hunt—you are told to go to a place where you find the following:

- **insight or wisdom**
- **strength**
- **understanding**

And you are also told to come back with proof that you found those three things.

Where would you look? Who would help you find this place? What would be the proof that you found those three things? If you are having trouble answering this question, don't feel bad. Baruch says, "No one has ever found where Wisdom lives or has entered her treasure house" (3:15). Luckily, Baruch also tells us where to find Wisdom: "Wisdom is the book of God's commandments, the Law that will last forever" (4:1). You can find wisdom, strength, and understanding in this very book you hold! Guess what? You won the scavenger hunt!

— Baruch 3:14–15

born, a mighty race skilled in war. 27 But
God did not choose them to be his people
or show them the way of knowledge. 28 They
died out because they had neither under-
standing nor insight.

29 No one has ever gone up into heaven to
get Wisdom and bring her down out of the
clouds. 30 No one has sailed across the seas to
find Wisdom or bought her with precious
gold. 31 No one knows how to get to her or
how to discover the path that leads to her.

32 The only one who knows Wisdom is
God, and he knows all things. With his
understanding he found her. He established
the earth for all time and filled it with all
kinds of animals. 33 The light trembled and
obeyed when he called. He sent it forth, and
it appeared. 34 He called the stars, and they
promptly answered; they took their places
and gladly shone to please the one who
made them. 35 He is our God, and there is
none like him. 36 He discovered the entire
path leading to understanding and gave Wis-
dom to his servant Israel, whom he loved.
37 From that time on, Wisdom appeared on
earth and lived among us.

4 Wisdom is the book of God's com-
mandments, the Law that will last forev-
er. All who hold onto her will live, but those
who abandon her will die. 2 Turn to Wis-
dom, people of Israel, and take hold of her.
Make your way toward the splendor of her
light. 3 Do not surrender our glorious privi-
leges to any other people. 4 How happy we
are, people of Israel; we have the advantage
of knowing what is pleasing to God!

Comfort for Jerusalem

5 Take courage, my people, you are the
ones who keep Israel's name alive. 6 You were
sold to Gentile nations, but not to be
destroyed. Because you made God angry, he
handed you over to your enemies. 7 When
you offered sacrifices to demons instead of
to God, you angered the one who made
you. 8 You forgot the Eternal God, who had
nourished you as a child, and so you brought
grief to Jerusalem, who had been like a
mother to you. 9 Jerusalem saw that God was
punishing you because he was angry, and she
said to all the neighboring cities, "Look at
the great misery that God has brought on
me. 10 I saw my sons and daughters taken
into captivity, a captivity brought on them
by the Eternal God. 11 I brought up my chil-
dren with great delight, but I cried and
mourned when they were taken from me.
12 Let no one take pleasure in my suffering
now that I am a widow and so many of my
children have been taken from me. They
turned away from God's Law, and their sins
have made me a deserted city. 13 They had
no respect for his commandments and

4:1 Sir 24:23

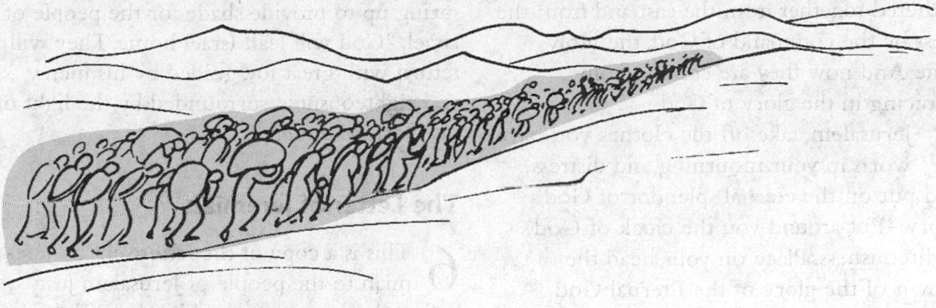

Consider how the Eternal God has sent my people into exile. (4:14)

would not live by them; they refused to let
him guide them in the way of righteousness.
14"All you neighboring cities, come and
consider how the Eternal God has sent my
children into exile. 15He brought against
them a nation from far away, a shameless
nation that speaks a foreign language and has
no respect for the elderly and no pity for
children. 16These people carried off my
beloved sons and took away my daughters,
and I was left a widow, completely alone.
17"My children in exile, I can do nothing
to help you. 18Only the one who brought
this punishment upon you can rescue you
from your enemies. 19Go your own way, my
children; live your own life! I am all alone.
20I have taken off the robes I wore during
days of peace, and I have dressed myself like
a person in mourning. I will cry out to the
Eternal God for help as long as I live.
21"Take courage, my children, and cry out
to God for help. He will rescue you from
oppression, from the power of your enemies.
22I am confident that the Eternal God will
soon set you free. The Holy One, your eter-
nal savior, will make me happy when he
shows you mercy. 23I cried and wailed when
you were taken away, but God will bring you
back and will make me happy forever. 24Just
as the neighboring cities watched as you
were taken captive, so they will soon see the
Eternal God coming in glorious splendor to
rescue you. 25My children, endure God's
punishment with patience. Your enemies have
persecuted you, but you will soon see them
destroyed and at your mercy. 26My children, I
spoiled you with love, but you have had to
follow rugged paths; you were carried off like
sheep caught in an enemy raid.
27"Take courage, my children, and cry out
to God for help. He punished you, but he
will not forget you. 28Just as you were once
determined to turn away from God, now
turn back and serve him with ten times
more determination. 29The one who
brought these calamities upon you will res-
cue you and bring you everlasting joy."

Jerusalem Is Assured of Help

30Take courage, Jerusalem. God, who gave
you your name, will now bring comfort to
you. 31Misery will come to those who mis-
treated you and then rejoiced when you fell.
32Misery will come to those cities that made
your children slaves. Misery will be the fate
of Babylon, that city which swallowed up
your children. 33Just as that city rejoiced
when you fell and took delight in your ruin,
so now she will mourn when she herself is
deserted. 34I will turn her proud boastings
into mourning and take away her large pop-
ulation in which she took pride. 35I, the
Eternal God, will send down fire on her, and
it will burn for many days. Her ruins will be
haunted by demons for a long time to come.
36Look to the east, Jerusalem, and see the
joy that God is bringing to you. 37Look,
your children are coming home, the children
that were taken from you. They have been

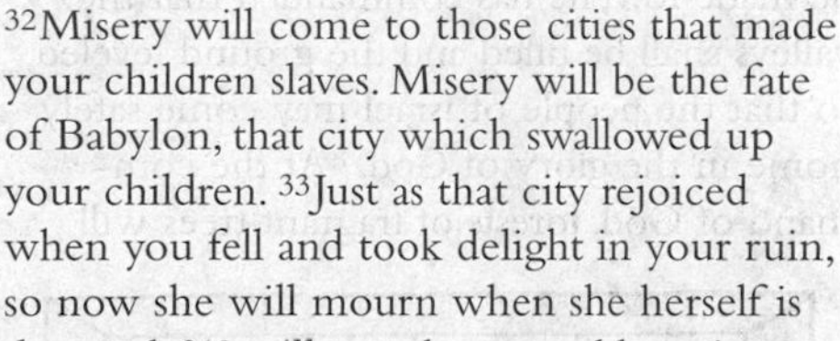

I, the Eternal God, will send down fire on her. (4:35)

gathered together from the east and from the west by the command of God, the Holy One. And now they are coming home, rejoicing in the glory of God.

5 Jerusalem, take off the clothes you have worn in your mourning and distress, and put on the eternal splendor of God's glory. 2 Put around you the cloak of God's righteousness. Place on your head the crown of the glory of the Eternal God. 3 God will show your splendor to every nation on earth. 4 Forever he will say to you: "Your security comes from your righteousness, and your splendor from your devotion to me."[c]

5 Get up, Jerusalem, stand on the mountaintop; see where God, the Holy One, is bringing your children together from the east and from the west. They are rejoicing that God has remembered them. 6 Jerusalem, your children were led away by their enemies; they left you on foot, but God is bringing them back to you, carried in royal splendor. 7 God has commanded that every high mountain and the everlasting hills shall be made low; he has commanded that the valleys shall be filled and the ground leveled, so that the people of Israel may come safely home in the glory of God. 8 At the command of God, forests of fragrant trees will spring up to provide shade for the people of Israel. 9 God will lead Israel home. They will return with great joy, guided by his mercy and righteousness, surrounded by the light of his glorious presence.

God will lead Israel home . . . with great joy. (5:9)

The Letter of Jeremiah

6 This is a copy of the letter sent by Jeremiah to the people of Jerusalem just before they were captured by the Babylonian king and taken to Babylon. It contains the message that God had commanded Jeremiah to give them.

The People Face a Long Captivity

2 You have sinned against God. That is why you are about to be taken away as prisoners to Babylon by King Nebuchadnezzar. 3 You will remain there in exile for many years, as long as seven generations; then God will lead you peacefully home from Babylon.

4 There in Babylon you will see gods made of wood, silver, and gold—gods which people carry on their shoulders and which fill the heathen with fear. 5 You must be careful never to imitate those Gentiles. Don't let their gods fill you with fear when you see them being carried in procession and being worshiped. 6 Instead, say to yourselves, "It is you alone, Lord, that we must worship." 7 God's angel will be there with you; he will take care of you.

The Helplessness of Idols

8 Their idols are plated with silver and gold and have tongues that were carved by woodworkers. But they are not real gods, and they cannot speak. 9 The people make gold crowns and put them on the heads of their gods, as if these idols were girls who love jewelry. 10 Sometimes the priests steal the silver and gold from their gods and spend it on themselves; 11 they even give some of it to the temple prostitutes. People take these gods of wood, silver, and gold, and

[c] **5:4** Forever . . . devotion to me; *or* He will give you this name forever: "Peace from Righteousness and Glory from Godliness."

5:1, 2 Isa 52:1; 61:3, 10; Rev 21:2 **6:1** Jer 29:1

put clothes on them, as if they were human.
12 But even though the gods are dressed in
purple robes like kings, they still cannot keep
themselves from being tarnished or protect
themselves from termites. 13 When dust from
the temple settles on their faces, someone
has to wipe it off for them. 14 Like human
judges they hold scepters in their hands, but
they have no power to punish anyone who
wrongs them. 15 Sometimes they have dag-
gers and axes in their hands, but they cannot
protect themselves from being destroyed in
war or from being carried off by thieves.
16 All of this proves that they are not gods—
do not worship them.

17 Those gods sitting in their temples are
as useless as a broken bowl. Their eyes are
filled with the dust that people kick up
when they come in. 18 The priests fortify the
temples with doors and bars and bolts, so
that thieves cannot break in. The gods are
locked up as securely as a prisoner about to
be executed for a crime against the king.
19 The priests light lamps for the gods, far
more than they need for their own use, but
the idols can't see even one of them. 20 Their
insides are eaten away by termites, just like
the wooden beams of the temple, and their
clothing is destroyed, but they don't even
know it. 21 Their faces are blackened by the
smoke in the temple. 22 Bats, swallows, and
other birds perch on them, and even cats sit
on them. 23 All of this proves that they are
not gods—do not worship them.

24 These idols have been plated with gold
to make them beautiful, but they do not
shine unless someone polishes them. When
they were being poured into molds, they felt
nothing. 25 It makes no difference how high
a price is paid for them; they are still unable
to breathe. 26 See how useless they are! They
can't walk on their own feet, but must be
carried around. 27 Even those who take care
of them are embarrassed when one of their
gods falls to the ground and has to be picked
up again. When someone stands one of them
in a certain place, it cannot move, and if it is
leaning over, it can never straighten itself up.
Offering gifts to them is like giving gifts to a
corpse. 28 Priests sell what is sacrificed to
their gods and use the money on themselves.
And the wives of the priests preserve the
sacrifices with salt for later use, instead of
sharing them with the poor and helpless.
29 Even women who are having their
monthly period or women who have just
given birth are allowed to touch the sacri-
fices. All of this proves that they are not
gods—do not worship them.

30 How can they ever be called gods, when
women are allowed to make offerings to these
things made of wood, silver, and gold? 31 The
priests even sit in the temples when they are
in mourning, with torn clothes and shaved,
uncovered heads. 32 The priests roar and shout
in the presence of their gods as if they were
taking part in a funeral feast. 33 They take the
clothing off their gods and give it to their
wives and children. 34 It doesn't matter
whether a person helps or harms these gods,
since they cannot pay him back. They are not
able to make anyone a king or to dethrone
him, 35 and they cannot make a person
wealthy or give him any money. If someone
makes a vow to them but does not keep it,
they will never make him pay. 36 They can
never rescue a person from death, and they
never help a weak person against one who is
strong. 37 They cannot restore sight to the
blind or save anyone in distress. 38 They can-
not offer any mercy or give help to widows
or orphans. 39 These things made of wood and
covered with silver and gold are as powerless
as stone taken from the mountains; and the
people who worship them will be put to
shame. 40 How can anyone think that they are
gods or call them gods?

They . . . must be carried around. (6:26)

The Foolishness of Worshiping Idols

The Babylonians bring dishonor on their own gods. 41 When someone cannot speak, they take him to the temple and ask Bel to give him the power of speech, as if Bel could understand anything. 42 But even when the people realize that their gods cannot help, they are stupid enough to go on worshiping them. 43 Not only that, but women wrap cords around themselves and sit alongside the road burning incense and offering themselves as prostitutes. When one of them is taken off for sex, she returns to ridicule the woman next to her who was not beautiful enough to be chosen. 44 Everything about these idols is false. How can anyone think that they are gods or call them gods?

45 Woodworkers and goldsmiths make these gods, so they can never be anything other than what these people want them to be. 46 Even their makers do not live long lives, so how are they able to create gods? 47 These people leave nothing but deceit and disgrace as an inheritance for future generations. 48 When wars and disturbances come, the priests plan where they can go into hiding with their gods. 49 These idols are helpless in the face of wars and disturbances. Why can't people realize that these idols are not gods?

50 These idols are nothing more than wood covered with silver and gold; one day it will be clear that they are really not gods at all. 51 All nations and kings will realize that idols are nothing more than the work of human hands. They do not have the power of a god, 52 and anyone should know that they are not really gods.

53 These gods can never make anyone a king or bring rain. 54 They can't make decisions about their own affairs or give justice to someone who has been wronged; they can do absolutely nothing. They are as useless as crows flying around in the air. 55 When a temple catches on fire, the priests run away to save themselves, while the gods made of wood and covered with silver and gold are left to burn like wooden beams. 56 They can't fight kings or go to war against enemies. How can anyone believe that they are gods?

57 These gods of wood, covered with silver and gold, cannot protect themselves from thieves and robbers 58 who take off the silver and gold and the gods' clothing and walk away with all of it. The gods can do nothing to stop them. 59 Anything from a courageous king to a useful piece of pottery is better than a false god. Even a door is better than a false god; a door at least protects the things in the house. Even a wooden pillar in a palace is better than a false god.

60 God provided the sun, the moon, and the stars to give light, and they obey him. 61 The same is true of lightning and wind. The lightning can be seen far and wide, and the wind blows everywhere. 62 When God commands clouds to spread out over the whole world, they obey. 63 When God sends down fire from heaven to burn up mountains and forests, it does what it is told. Idols cannot do these things—they can't even do a good imitation. 64 Why should they be called gods, when they are not able to help us or harm us in any way? 65 You know that they are not gods—do not worship them.

66 These gods have no power over kings; they cannot pronounce curses on them or grant them blessings. 67 They cannot produce for the nations any signs in the sky; they cannot shine like the sun or the moon. 68 Even wild animals are better off than these idols; animals can at least run from danger to protect themselves. 69 So it is absolutely clear that they are not gods—do not worship them.

70 These gods of theirs, made of wood and covered with silver and gold, are about as helpful as a scarecrow in a cucumber patch; they are no protection at all. 71 They do as much good as a thorn bush in a garden; instead of keeping birds away, they provide a perch for them. These gods are like a dead body thrown out into the darkness. 72 The purple linen[d] robes they wear rot away, so we know that they are not gods. Finally they will be eaten by termites, and then no one anywhere will have any use for them.

73 The righteous person has an advantage over others; he does not own any idols, and they can never make a fool of him.

[d] **6:72** linen; *Greek* marble.

6:41 Isa 46:1

The Book of Ezekiel

Are you a science fiction or fantasy fan? Do you like movies with imaginary creatures? Then you'll love the Book of Ezekiel! Ezekiel was one of the greatest prophets of Israel. God sends him wild visions to help the Israelites understand that they sinned against God and that God was very angry with them. Among other things, they worshiped idols and neglected poor people. At first they didn't listen, but terrible things happened—the southern kingdom of Judah was taken over, and the Temple was destroyed. The people who survived were taken to Babylonia as war captives. After that, Ezekiel shares God's message of hope—that God promises to rebuild their homeland and to be with them forever.

Chap. 2:8—3.3

Headlines

- Prophet Has Wild Visions (1:4–28)
- Ezekiel Silenced, Tries Acting (3:22—4:17)
- Children Not Punished for Parents' Sins (18:1–31)
- Ezekiel Does Not Mourn Dead Wife (24:15–27)
- Good Shepherd Rescues His Sheep (34:11–31)
- Dry Bones Come to Life! (37:1–14)
- Plans for New Temple Revealed (40:1–5)

FACTOIDS

Who wrote this book? This book was written by the prophet Ezekiel and people called scribes who recorded his words and actions. Ezekiel did all his prophesying in Babylonia, where he was taken captive before the final fall of Jerusalem.

Why was it written? The book has two major sections. Chapters 1–24 occurred before the destruction of Jerusalem (587 BC.) and warned the Israelites about the coming destruction. Chapters 25–48 occurred after Jerusalem was destroyed. In this section Ezekiel began prophesying about the promise of God's salvation through a new covenant.

What is the literary style? Ezekiel is a combination of historical facts, words of warning and hope to the Israelites, and descriptions of Ezekiel's visions.

Important themes

- The Israelites sinned, and they must repent.
- God is glorious, and the name of God is holy.
- God will restore the Temple and create a new covenant with the Israelites.

EZEKIEL

EZEKIEL'S FIRST VISION OF GOD (1:1—7:27)

God's Throne

1 On the fifth day of the fourth month of the thirtieth year,[a] I, Ezekiel the priest, son of Buzi, was living with the Jewish exiles by the Chebar River in Babylonia. The sky opened, and I saw a vision of God. (2It was the fifth year since King Jehoiachin had been taken into exile.) 3There in Babylonia beside the Chebar River, I heard the LORD speak to me, and I felt his power.

4I looked up and saw a windstorm coming from the north. Lightning was flashing from a huge cloud, and the sky around it was glowing. Where the lightning was flashing, something shone like bronze. 5At the center of the storm I saw what looked like four living creatures in human form, 6but each of them had four faces and four wings. 7Their legs were straight, and they had hoofs like those of a bull. They shone like polished bronze. 8In addition to their four faces and four wings, they each had four human hands, one under each wing. 9Two wings of each creature were spread out so that the creatures formed a square, with their wing tips touching. When they moved, they moved as a group without turning their bodies.

10Each living creature had four different faces: a human face in front, a lion's face at the right, a bull's face at the left, and an eagle's face at the back. 11Two wings[b] of each creature were raised so that they touched the tips of the wings of the creatures next to it, and their other two wings were folded against their bodies. 12Each creature faced all four directions, and so the group could go wherever they wished, without having to turn.

13Among[c] the creatures there was something that looked like a blazing torch, constantly moving. The fire would blaze up and shoot out flashes of lightning. 14The creatures themselves darted back and forth with the speed of lightning.

15As I was looking at the four creatures I saw four wheels touching the ground, one beside each of them.[d] 16All four wheels were

---

Study it!

Seeing Visions

Creatures with four faces, wheels covered with eyes, a crystal dome, windstorms—those are only a few of the images Ezekiel sees in chapter 1. For the Israelites, these images represented familiar characteristics of God. For example, the throne is placed above the dome (Ezekiel 1:26), symbolizing God's location above the sky. Wheels that could move in any direction (1:17) were a sign that God was with them everywhere they went.

Just as Ezekiel did, a prophet trying to get your attention would use familiar images to tell you about God. For example, a picture of the planet earth might mean that God is everywhere. A goldfish surrounded by water could mean that God's love is all around you.

What other symbols and images could a prophet use to tell you and your friends about God?

— Ezekiel 1:4–28

---

[a] **1:1** THIRTIETH YEAR: *It is not known to what year this refers.* [b] **1:11** *Some ancient translations* Two wings; *Hebrew* Their faces, their wings. [c] **1:13** *Some ancient translations* Among; *Hebrew* And the likeness of. [d] **1:15** *Some ancient translations* them; *Hebrew* their faces.

1:1 Rev 19:11 **1:2** 2 Kings 24:10–16; 2 Chr 36:9, 10 **1:5** Rev 4:6 **1:10** Ezek 10:14; Rev 4:7 **1:13** Rev 4:5 **1:15–21** Ezek 10:9–13

alike; each one shone like a precious stone,
and each had another wheel intersecting it
at right angles, 17so that the wheels could
move in any of the four directions. 18The
rims of the wheels were covered with eyes.[e]
19Whenever the creatures moved, the wheels
moved with them, and if the creatures rose
up from the earth, so did the wheels. 20The
creatures went wherever they wished, and
the wheels did exactly what the creatures
did, because the creatures controlled them.
21So every time the creatures moved or
stopped or rose in the air, the wheels did
exactly the same.

22Above the heads of the creatures there
was something that looked like a dome
made of dazzling crystal. 23There under the
dome stood the creatures, each stretching
out two wings toward the ones next to it
and covering its body with the other two
wings. 24I heard the noise their wings made
in flight; it sounded like the roar of the sea,
like the noise of a huge army, like the voice
of Almighty God. When they stopped flying,
they folded their wings, 25but there was still
a sound coming from above the dome over
their heads.

26Above the dome there was something
that looked like a throne made of sapphire,
and sitting on the throne was a figure that
looked like a human being. 27The figure
seemed to be shining like bronze in the
middle of a fire. It shone all over with a
bright light 28that had in it all the colors of
the rainbow. This was the dazzling light
which shows the presence of the LORD.

God Calls Ezekiel to Be a Prophet

2 When I saw this, I fell face downward on
the ground. Then I heard a voice 1saying,
"Mortal man, stand up. I want to talk to
you." 2While the voice was speaking, God's
spirit entered me and raised me to my feet,
and I heard the voice continue, 3"Mortal
man, I am sending you to the people of
Israel. They have rebelled and turned against
me and are still rebels, just as their ancestors
were. 4They are stubborn and do not respect
me, so I am sending you to tell them what I,
the Sovereign LORD, am saying to them.
5Whether those rebels listen to you or not,
they will know that a prophet has been
among them.

6"But you, mortal man, must not be afraid
of them or of anything they say. They will
defy and despise you; it will be like living
among scorpions. Still, don't be afraid of
those rebels or of anything they say. 7You
will tell them whatever I tell you to say,
whether they listen or not. Remember what
rebels they are.

8"Mortal man, listen to what I tell you.
Don't be rebellious like them. Open your
mouth and eat what I am going to give
you." 9I saw a hand reaching out toward me,
and it was holding a scroll. 10The hand
unrolled the scroll, and I saw that there was
writing on both sides—cries of grief were
written there, and wails and groans.

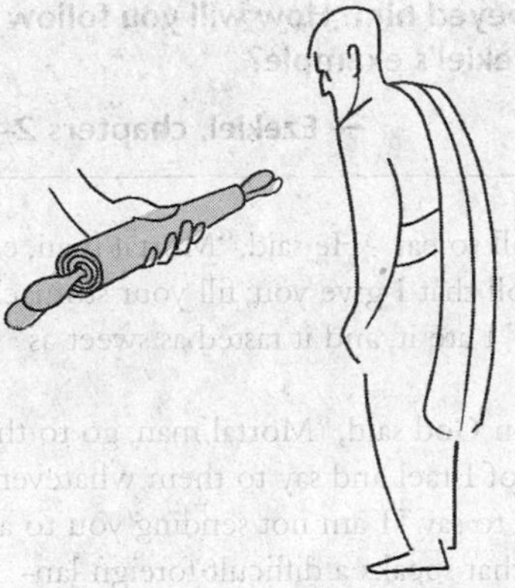

I saw a hand reaching out toward me. (2:9)

3 God said, "Mortal man, eat this scroll;
then go and speak to the people of
Israel."

2So I opened my mouth, and he gave me

[e] 1:18 *Verse 18 in Hebrew is unclear.*

1:18 Rev 4:8 **1:22** Rev 4:6 **1:24** Rev 1:4–15; 19:6 **1:26** Ezek 10:1; Rev 4:2, 3 **1:27** Ezek 8:2
2:9, 10 Rev 5:1

Ezekiel was a priest and led worship in the Temple before he was taken into captivity. As all Jewish priests were, he was a member of the tribe of Levi.

Live it!

Only God Is God

When God talks to Ezekiel, God keeps calling him "mortal man." The use of this phrase emphasizes that God is God and Ezekiel is a human being. God demands honor, respect, and obedience from Ezekiel just because God is God.

God requires the same from us. When we refuse to participate in Sunday Mass or show little reverence in church, we dishonor God. When we use bad language or develop a poor attitude at home, we disrespect God. When we waste precious resources or treat others badly, we disobey God.

Ezekiel listened carefully to God and honored, respected, and obeyed him. How will you follow Ezekiel's example?

— Ezekiel, chapters 2–3

the scroll to eat. [3]He said, "Mortal man, eat
this scroll that I give you; fill your stomach
with it." I ate it, and it tasted as sweet as
honey.
[4]Then God said, "Mortal man, go to the
people of Israel and say to them whatever I
tell you to say. [5]I am not sending you to a
nation that speaks a difficult foreign lan-
guage, but to the Israelites. [6]If I sent you to
great nations that spoke difficult languages
you didn't understand, they would listen to
you. [7]But none of the people of Israel will
be willing to listen; they will not even listen
to me. All of them are stubborn and defiant.
[8]Now I will make you as stubborn and as
tough as they are. [9]I will make you as firm as
a rock, as hard as a diamond; don't be afraid
of those rebels."
[10]God continued, "Mortal man, pay close
attention and remember everything I tell
you. [11]Then go to the people of your nation
who are in exile and tell them what I, the
Sovereign LORD, am saying to them,
whether they pay attention to you or not."
[12]Then God's spirit lifted me up, and I
heard behind me the loud roar of a voice
that said, "Praise the glory of the LORD in
heaven above!" [13]I heard the wings of the
creatures beating together in the air, and the
noise of the wheels, as loud as an earth-
quake. [14]The power of the LORD came on
me with great force, and as his spirit carried
me off, I felt bitter and angry. [15]So I came to
Tel Abib beside the Chebar River, where the
exiles were living, and for seven days I stayed
there, overcome by what I had seen and
heard.

The LORD Appoints Ezekiel as a Lookout

(Ezekiel 33:1–9)

[16]After the seven days had passed, the
LORD spoke to me. [17]"Mortal man," he said,
"I am making you a lookout for the nation
of Israel. You will pass on to them the warn-
ings I give you. [18]If I announce that some-
one evil is going to die but you do not warn
him to change his ways so that he can save
his life, he will die, still a sinner, but I will
hold you responsible for his death. [19]If you
do warn an evil man and he doesn't stop
sinning, he will die, still a sinner, but your
life will be spared.
[20]"If someone truly good starts doing evil
and I put him in a dangerous situation, he
will die if you do not warn him. He will die
because of his sins—I will not remember the
good he did—and I will hold you responsi-
ble for his death. [21]If you do warn a good
man not to sin and he listens to you and
doesn't sin, he will stay alive, and your life
will also be spared."

3:1–3 Rev 10:9, 10

The scroll that God told Ezekiel to eat was covered with cries of grief. So Ezekiel expected it to taste bitter, but instead it tasted sweet.

Ezekiel Will Be Unable to Talk

22 I felt the powerful presence of the LORD
and heard him say to me, "Get up and go
out into the valley. I will talk to you there."
23 So I went out into the valley, and there I
saw the glory of the LORD, just as I had seen
it beside the Chebar River. I fell face down-
ward on the ground, 24 but God's spirit
entered me and raised me to my feet. The
LORD said to me, "Go home and shut your-
self up in the house. 25 You will be tied with
ropes, mortal man, and you will not be able
to go out in public. 26 I will paralyze your
tongue so that you won't be able to warn
these rebellious people. 27 Then, when I
speak to you again and give you back the
power of speech, you will tell them what I,
the Sovereign LORD, am saying. Some of
them will listen, but some will ignore you,
for they are a nation of rebels."

But God's spirit entered me and raised me to my feet. (3:24)

Ezekiel Acts Out the Siege of Jerusalem

4 God said, "Mortal man, get a brick, put
it in front of you, and scratch lines on it
to represent the city of Jerusalem. 2 Then, to
represent a siege, put trenches, earthworks,
camps, and battering rams all around it.
3 Take an iron pan and set it up like a wall
between you and the city. Face the city. It is
under siege, and you are the one besieging
it. This will be a sign to the nation of Israel.
4-5 "Then lie down on your left side, and I[f]
will place on you the guilt of the nation of
Israel. For 390 days you will stay there and
suffer because of their guilt. I have sentenced
you to one day for each year their punish-
ment will last. 6 When you finish that, turn
over on your right side and suffer for the
guilt of Judah for forty days—one day for
each year of their punishment.
7 "Fix your eyes on the siege of Jerusalem.
Shake your fist at the city and prophesy
against it. 8 I will tie you up so that you can-
not turn from one side to the other until the
siege is over.

Shake your fist at the city and prophesy against it. (4:7)

9 "Now take some wheat, barley, beans,
peas, millet, and spelt. Mix them all together
and make bread. That is what you are to eat
during the 390 days you are lying on your
left side. 10 You will be allowed eight ounces
of bread a day, and it will have to last until
the next day. 11 You will also have a limited
amount of water to drink, two cups a day.
12 You are to build a fire out of dried human
excrement, bake bread on the fire, and eat it
where everyone can see you."
13 The LORD said, "This represents the
way the Israelites will have to eat food
which the Law forbids,[g] when I scatter them
to foreign countries."
14 But I replied, "No, Sovereign LORD! I
have never defiled myself. From childhood
on I have never eaten meat from any animal
that died a natural death or was killed by
wild animals. I have never eaten any food
considered unclean."
15 So God said, "Very well. I will let you
use cow dung instead, and you can bake
your bread on that."
16 And he added, "Mortal man, I am going
to cut off the supply of bread for Jerusalem.

[f] **4:4-5** *Probable text* I; *Hebrew* you. [g] **4:13** FOOD WHICH THE LAW FORBIDS: *The Law of Moses prohibited the eating of certain foods as being ritually unclean (see Lev 11).*

Live it!

I.M.s from God?

God had Ezekiel use lots of different ways to deliver his message to the Israelites. It's divine instant messaging. First God tells Ezekiel to make a map of the city and then make it look like it's being destroyed. Then Ezekiel is supposed to lie on his side for 430 days to represent the number of years of punishment. God also tells him to make some bread and bake it over a fire made out of . . . well, check out Ezekiel 4:12. And after that Ezekiel shaves his head.

Many people are trying to get God's message to you. Some of them use unusual means, like Ezekiel did. Some use words. Others share God's message just by living a good life. Keep your eyes and ears open. You never know when an I.M. from God is going to pop up in your life.

— Ezekiel 4:1—5:4

The people there will be distressed and anx-
ious as they measure out the food they eat
and the water they drink. 17They will run
out of bread and water; they will be in
despair, and they will waste away because of
their sins."

Ezekiel Cuts His Hair

5 The LORD said, "Mortal man, take a
sharp sword and use it to shave off your
beard and all your hair. Then weigh the hair
on scales and divide it into three parts.
2Burn up a third of it in the city when the
siege is over. Take another third and chop it
up with your sword as you move around
outside the city. Scatter the remaining third
to the winds, and I will pursue it with my
sword. 3Keep back a few hairs and wrap
them in the hem of your clothes. 4Then take
a few of them out again, throw them in the
fire, and let them burn up. From them fire
will spread to the whole nation of Israel."
5The Sovereign LORD said, "Look at
Jerusalem. I put her at the center of the
world, with other countries all around her.
6But Jerusalem rebelled against my com-
mands and showed that she was more
wicked than the other nations, more disobe-
dient than the countries around her.
Jerusalem rejected my commands and
refused to keep my laws. 7Now listen,
Jerusalem, to what I, the Sovereign LORD,
am saying. By not obeying my laws or keep-
ing my commands, you have caused more
trouble than the nations around you. You
have followed the customs of other nations.
8And so I, the Sovereign LORD, am telling
you that I am your enemy. I will pass judg-
ment on you where all the nations can see
it. 9Because of all the things you do that I
hate, I will punish Jerusalem as I have never
done before and will never do again. 10As a
result, parents in Jerusalem will eat their
children, and children will eat their parents. I
will punish you and scatter in every direc-
tion any who are left alive.
11"Therefore, as I am the living God—this
is the word of the Sovereign LORD—
because you defiled my Temple with all the
evil, disgusting things you did, I will cut you
down without mercy. 12A third of your peo-
ple will die from sickness and hunger in the
city; a third will be cut down by swords out-
side the city; and I will scatter the last third
to the winds and pursue them with a sword.
13"You will feel all the force of my anger
and rage until I am satisfied. When all this
happens, you will be convinced that I, the
LORD, have spoken to you because I am
outraged at your unfaithfulness. 14Everyone
from the nations around you who passes by
will sneer at you and keep their distance.
15"When I am angry and furious with
you and punish you, all the nations around
you will be terrified. They will look at you
with disgust and make fun of you. 16I will
cut off your supply of food and let you

5:10 Lam 4:10

Live it!

Ezekiel's Gift

Ezekiel was not a great poet like some other writers in the Old Testament. He didn't fight bravely in battles. He was not an important leader. But he had an amazing gift for drama. He used this gift to teach others about God.

Do you enjoy acting or playing a musical instrument? Are you good at drawing or painting? Do you like writing stories or poems? Like Ezekiel, you can use these gifts to share God with others. As an artist, a writer, a musician, an actor, or a poet, you reflect God's handiwork and communicate God's message in ways that others cannot.

Look around you. Listen to the sounds of life. Watch people. You will come to know that God is the supreme artist. Keep doing your part to learn about your art and share the gift that God gave you.

— Ezekiel, chapter 5

starve. You[h] will feel the pains of hunger like
sharp arrows sent to destroy you. 17I will
send hunger and wild animals to kill your
children, and will send sickness, violence, and
war to kill you. I, the LORD, have spoken."

The LORD Condemns Idolatry

6 The LORD spoke to me. 2"Mortal
man," he said, "look toward the moun-
tains of Israel and give them my message.
3Tell the mountains of Israel to hear the
Sovereign LORD's word—to hear what I, the
Sovereign LORD, am telling the mountains,
the hills, the gorges, and the valleys: I will
send a sword to destroy the places where
people worship idols. 4The altars will be
torn down and the incense altars broken. All
the people there will be killed in front of
their idols. 5I will scatter the corpses of the
people of Israel; I will scatter their bones all
around the altars. 6All the cities of Israel will
be destroyed, so that all their altars and their
idols will be smashed to pieces, their incense
altars will be shattered, and everything they
made will disappear. 7People will be killed
everywhere, and those who survive will
acknowledge that I am the LORD.
8"I will let some escape the slaughter and
be scattered among the nations, 9where they
will live in exile. There they will remember
me and know that I have punished them and
disgraced them,[i] because their faithless hearts
deserted me and they preferred idols to me.
And they will be disgusted with themselves
because of the evil and degrading things
they have done. 10They will know that I am
the LORD and that my warnings were not
empty threats."
11The Sovereign LORD said, "Wring your
hands! Stamp your feet! Cry in sorrow because
of all the evil, disgusting things the Israelites
have done. They are going to die in war or of
starvation or disease. 12Those far away will get
sick and die; those nearby will be killed in war;
those who survive will starve to death. They
will feel all the force of my anger. 13Corpses
will be scattered among the idols and around

Corpses will be scattered among the idols. (6:13)

[h] **5:16** *Probable text* You; *Hebrew* They. [i] **6:9** *Some ancient translations* disgraced them; *Hebrew* I am disgraced.
5:17 Rev 6:8

People who were captured in war were forced to shave their heads. Ezekiel's shaved head was a symbol of what was to come.

Pray it!

I'm Angry, God

The book of Ezekiel describes God as being angry with the Israelites, and for good reasons. In Ezekiel, chapter 6, he threatens to destroy the mountains and all the places where the people worshiped idols. God sends the message through Ezekiel that they will pay for "all the evil, disgusting things the Israelites have done" (Ezekiel 6:11).

Most people get angry at times. It is not necessarily a sin to feel angry. But anger is such a strong emotion that we must be careful not to be controlled by it. Uncontrolled anger can lead to sinful acts of revenge and violence. The next time you feel angry, say this short prayer asking God to help you control your anger so that you can work out your problems in a mature way.

I'm angry, God,
Help me to understand my feelings.
Help me to see the other person's side of things.
Help me to control my words and my actions.
Help me to look for a solution to the problem
that won't hurt anyone—most of all, me.
Amen.

— Ezekiel, chapter 7

the altars, scattered on every high hill, on the
top of every mountain, under every green tree
and every large oak, in every place where they
burned sacrifices to their idols. Then everyone
will know that I am the LORD. 14 Yes, I will
reach out and destroy their country. I will
make it a wasteland from the southern desert
to the city of Riblah in the north, not sparing
any place where the Israelites live. Then every-
one will know that I am the LORD."

The End Is Near for Israel

7 The LORD spoke to me. 2 "Mortal
man," he said, "this is what I, the Sover-
eign LORD, am saying to the land of Israel:
This is the end for the whole land!
3 "Israel, the end has come. You will feel
my anger, because I am judging you for
what you have done. I will pay you back for
all your disgusting conduct. 4 I will not spare
you or show you any mercy. I am going to
punish you for the disgusting things you
have done, so that you will know that I am
the LORD."
5 This is what the Sovereign LORD is say-
ing: "One disaster after another is coming on
you. 6 It's all over. This is the end. You are fin-
ished. 7 The end is coming for you people
who live in the land. The time is near when
there will be no more celebrations at the
mountain shrines, only confusion.[j]
8 "Very soon now you will feel all the
force of my anger. I am judging you for
what you have done, and I will pay you back
for all your disgusting conduct. 9 I will not
spare you or show you any mercy. I am
going to punish you for the disgusting things
you have done, so that you will know that I

[j] **7:7** *Probable text* celebrations . . . confusion; *Hebrew unclear.*

What are the things that happen in today's world that you think anger God?

am the LORD and that I am the one who
punishes you."
10 The day of disaster is coming. Violence
is flourishing. Pride is at its height.[k] 11 Vio-
lence produces more wickedness. Nothing of
theirs will remain, nothing of their wealth,
their splendor, or their glory.
12 The time is coming. The day is near
when buying and selling will have no more
meaning, because God's punishment will fall
on everyone alike. 13 No merchants will live
long enough to get back what they have
lost, because God's anger is on everyone.
Those who are evil cannot survive.[l] 14 The
trumpet blows, and everyone gets ready. But
no one goes off to war, for God's anger will
fall on everyone alike.

Punishment for Israel's Sins

15 There is fighting in the streets, and sick-
ness and hunger in the houses. Anyone who
is out in the country will die in the fighting,
and anyone in the city will be a victim of
sickness and hunger. 16 Some will escape to
the mountains like doves frightened from
the valleys. All of them will moan over their
sins.[m] 17 Everyone's hands will be weak, and
their knees will shake. 18 They will put on
sackcloth and they will tremble all over.
Their heads will be shaved, and they will all
be disgraced. 19 They will throw their gold
and silver away in the streets like garbage,
because neither silver nor gold can save
them when the LORD pours out his fury.
They cannot use it to satisfy their desires or
fill their stomachs. Gold and silver led them
into sin. 20 Once they were proud of their
beautiful jewels, but they used them to make
disgusting idols. That is why the LORD has
made their wealth repulsive to them.

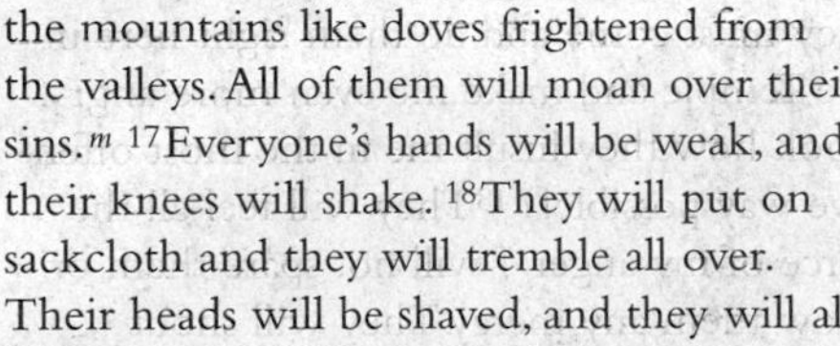

Some will escape to the mountains. (7:16)

21 "I will let foreigners rob them," says the
LORD, "and lawbreakers will take all their
wealth and defile it. 22 I will not interfere
when my treasured Temple is profaned,
when robbers break into it and defile it.

They were proud of their beautiful jewels. (7:20)

23 "Everything is in confusion[n] —the land
is full of murders and the cities are full of
violence. 24 I will bring the most evil nations
here and let them have your homes. Your
strongest men will lose their confidence
when I let the nations profane the places
where you worship. 25 Despair is coming. You
will look for peace and never find it. 26 One
disaster will follow another, and a steady
stream of bad news will pour in. You will
beg the prophets to reveal what they foresee.
The priests will have nothing to teach the
people, and the elders will have no advice to
give. 27 The king will mourn, the prince will
give up hope, and the people will shake with
fear. I will punish you for all you have done,
and will judge you in the same way as you
have judged others. This will show you that I
am the LORD."

[k] **7:10** *Probable text* Pride is at its height; *Hebrew unclear.* [l] **7:13** *Verse 13 in Hebrew is unclear.* [m] **7:16** *Verse 16 in Hebrew is unclear.* [n] **7:23** *One ancient translation* Everything is in confusion; *Hebrew unclear.*

EZEKIEL'S SECOND VISION OF GOD (8:1—10:22)

Idolatry in Jerusalem

8 On the fifth day of the sixth month of the sixth year of our exile, the leaders of the exiles from Judah were sitting in my house with me. Suddenly the power of the Sovereign LORD came on me. 2 I looked up and saw a vision of a fiery human form. From the waist down his body looked like fire, and from the waist up he was shining like polished bronze. 3 He reached out what seemed to be a hand and grabbed me by the hair. Then in this vision God's spirit lifted me high in the air and took me to Jerusalem. He took me to the inner entrance of the north gate of the Temple, where there was an idol that was an outrage to God.

4 There I saw the dazzling light that shows the presence of Israel's God, just as I had seen it when I was by the Chebar River. 5 God said to me, "Mortal man, look toward the north." I looked, and there near the altar by the entrance of the gateway I saw the idol that was an outrage to God.

6 God said to me, "Mortal man, do you see what is happening? Look at the disgusting things the people of Israel are doing here, driving me farther and farther away from my holy place. You will see even more disgraceful things than this."

7 He took me to the entrance of the outer courtyard and showed me a hole in the wall. 8 He said, "Mortal man, break through the wall here." I broke through it and found a door. 9 He told me, "Go in and look at the evil, disgusting things they are doing there." 10 So I went in and looked. The walls were covered with drawings of snakes and other unclean animals,[o] and of the other things which the Israelites were worshiping. 11 Seventy Israelite leaders were there, including Jaazaniah son of Shaphan. Each one was holding an incense burner, and smoke was rising from the incense. 12 God asked me, "Mortal man, do you see what the Israelite leaders are doing in secret? They are all worshiping in a room full of images. Their excuse is: 'The LORD doesn't see us! He has abandoned the country.' "

13 Then the LORD said to me, "You are going to see them do even more disgusting things than that." 14 So he took me to the north gate of the Temple and showed me women weeping over the death of the god Tammuz.[p]

15 He asked, "Mortal man, do you see that? You will see even more disgusting things." 16 So he took me to the inner courtyard of the Temple. There near the entrance of the sanctuary, between the altar and the porch, were about twenty-five men. They had turned their backs to the sanctuary and were bowing low toward the east, worshiping the rising sun.

17 The LORD said to me, "Mortal man, do you see that? These people of Judah are not satisfied with merely doing all the disgusting things you have seen here and with spreading violence throughout the country. No, they must come and do them right here in the Temple and make me even more angry. Look how they insult me in the most offensive way possible![q] 18 They will feel all the force of my anger. I will not spare them or show them any mercy. They will shout prayers to me as loud as they can, but I will not listen to them."

Jerusalem Is Punished

9 Then I heard God shout, "Come here, you men who are going to punish the city. Bring your weapons with you." 2 At once six men came from the outer north gate of the Temple, each one carrying a weapon. With them was a man dressed in linen clothes, carrying something to write with. They all came and stood by the bronze altar.

3 Then the dazzling light of the presence of the God of Israel rose up from the

[o] **8:10** UNCLEAN ANIMALS: *The Law of Moses prohibited the eating of certain animals as being ritually unclean (see 4:13; Lev 11).* [p] **8:14** TAMMUZ: *A god who was thought to die when vegetation died and to come to life the next year. Women would mourn his ritual death.* [q] **8:17** IN THE MOST OFFENSIVE WAY POSSIBLE: *A reference to a pagan rite of putting a branch to the nose.*

8:2 Ezek 1:27 **8:4** Ezek 1:28

winged creatures[r] where it had been, and
moved to the entrance of the Temple. The
LORD called to the man dressed in linen,
4 "Go through the whole city of Jerusalem
and put a mark on the forehead of everyone
who is distressed and troubled because of all
the disgusting things being done in the city."
5 And I heard God say to the other men,
"Follow him through the city and kill. Spare
no one; have mercy on no one. 6 Kill the old
men, young men, young women, mothers,
and children. But don't touch anyone who
has the mark on his forehead. Start here at
my Temple." So they began with the leaders
who were standing there at the Temple.
7 God said to them, "Defile the Temple.
Fill its courtyards with corpses. Get to
work!" So they began to kill the people in
the city.[s]
8 While the killing was going on, I was
there alone. I threw myself face downward
on the ground and shouted, "Sovereign
LORD, are you so angry with Jerusalem that
you are going to kill everyone left in Israel?"
9 God answered, "The people of Israel and
Judah are guilty of terrible sins. They have
committed murder all over the land and
have filled Jerusalem with crime. They say
that I, the LORD, have abandoned their
country and that I don't see them. 10 But I
will not have pity on them; I will do to
them what they have done to others."
11 Then the man wearing linen clothes
returned and reported to the LORD, "I have
carried out your orders."

Live it!

The Mark of Caring

"Go through the whole city of Jerusalem and put a mark on the forehead of everyone who is distressed and troubled because of all the disgusting things being done in the city" (Ezekiel 9:4).

In Ezekiel's vision, the people with a mark on their forehead were the only ones spared when God gave the order to kill the residents of Jerusalem. They were the people who worshiped God as God and treated others fairly. God spared their lives because they cared.

You may not be able to change the attitudes and actions of the people around you, but you can live your life well and care about others. It may be enough to make them think about making some changes. And that's all God asks of you.

— Ezekiel 9:3–6

The Glory of the LORD Leaves the Temple

10 I looked at the dome over the heads
of the living creatures[t] and above
them was something that seemed to be a
throne made of sapphire. 2 God said to the
man wearing linen clothes, "Go between the
wheels under the creatures and fill your
hands with burning coals. Then scatter the
coals over the city."
I watched him go. 3 The creatures were
standing to the south of the Temple when he
went in, and a cloud filled the inner court-
yard. 4 The dazzling light of the LORD's pres-
ence rose up from the creatures and moved
to the entrance of the Temple. Then the
cloud filled the Temple, and the courtyard
was blazing with the light. 5 The noise made
by the creatures' wings was heard even in the

[r] **9:3** WINGED CREATURES: *See 1:5–12.* [s] **9:7** work!" So they . . . city.; *or* work! Go on and start killing the people in the city!" [t] **10:1** LIVING CREATURES: *See 1:5–12.*

9:4 Rev 7:3; 9:4; 14:1 **10:1** Ezek 1:26; Rev 4:2 **10:2** Rev 8:5

"But I will not have pity on them; I will do to them what they have done to others" *(Ezekiel 9:10).*

Study it!

God Is . . .

In Ezekiel's vision, he saw "the dazzling light of the LORD's presence" (Ezekiel 10:4). It is only one of many images that tell us something about God in the Scriptures. Check out these others:

- **an eagle (Deuteronomy 32:10–11)**
- **a shepherd (Psalm 23)**
- **a mother comforting her child (Isaiah 66:13)**
- **a baker woman (Luke 13:20–21)**
- **a vine (John 15:5)**

When you think of God, what images come to mind? Be creative.

— Ezekiel 10:4

outer courtyard. It sounded like the voice of Almighty God.

[6]When the LORD commanded the man wearing linen clothes to take some fire from between the wheels that were under the creatures, the man went in and stood by one of the wheels. [7]One of the creatures reached his hand into the fire that was there among them, picked up some coals, and put them in the hands of the man in linen. The man took the coals and left.

[8]I saw that each creature had what looked like a human hand under each of its wings. [9-10]I also saw that there were four wheels, all alike, one beside each creature. The wheels shone like precious stones, and each one had another wheel which intersected it at right angles. [11]When the creatures moved, they could go in any direction without turning. They all moved together in the direction they wanted to go, without having to turn around. [12]Their bodies, backs, hands, wings, and wheels were covered with eyes. [13]I heard a voice calling out, "Whirling wheels."

[14]Each creature had four faces. The first was the face of a bull, the second a human face, the third the face of a lion, and the fourth the face of an eagle. [15](They were the same creatures that I had seen by the Chebar River.) When the creatures rose in the air [16]and moved, the wheels went with them. Whenever they spread their wings to fly, the wheels still went with them. [17]When the creatures stopped, the wheels stopped; and when the creatures flew, the wheels went with them, because the creatures controlled them.

[18]Then the dazzling light of the LORD's presence left the entrance of the Temple and moved to a place above the creatures. [19]They spread their wings and flew up from the earth while I was watching, and the wheels went with them. They paused at the east gate of the Temple, and the dazzling light was over them. [20]I recognized them as the same creatures which I had seen beneath the God of Israel at the Chebar River.

[21]Each of them had four faces, four wings, and what looked like a human hand under each wing. [22]Their faces looked exactly like the faces[u] I had seen by the Chebar River. Each creature moved straight ahead.

Jerusalem Is Condemned

11 God's spirit lifted me up and took me to the east gate of the Temple. There near the gate I saw twenty-five men, including Jaazaniah son of Azzur and Pelatiah son of Benaiah, two leaders of the nation.

[2]God said to me, "Mortal man, these men make evil plans and give bad advice in this city. [3]They say, 'We will soon be building houses again.[v] The city is like a cooking pot, and we are like the meat in it, but at least it

[u] **10:22** *Probable text* the faces; *Hebrew* the faces and them. [v] **11:3** We will . . . again; *or* We won't be building houses any time soon.

10:9–13 Ezek 1:15–21 **10:12** Rev 4:8 **10:14** Ezek 1:10; Rev 4:7

Ezekiel, chapter 11, introduces a new name for God, Sovereign LORD. ***Soveeign*** **means to have supreme authority and power.**

protects us from the fire.' 4Now then,
denounce them, mortal man."
5The spirit of the LORD took control of
me, and the LORD told me to give the peo-
ple this message: "People of Israel, I know
what you are saying and what you are plan-
ning. 6You have murdered so many people
here in the city that the streets are full of
corpses.
7"So this is what I, the Sovereign LORD,
am saying to you. This city is a cooking pot
all right, but what is the meat? The corpses
of those you have killed! You will not be
here—I will throw you out of the city! 8Are
you afraid of swords? I will bring soldiers
with swords to attack you. 9I will take you
out of the city and hand you over to for-
eigners. I have sentenced you to death, 10and
you will be killed in battle in your own
country. Then everyone will know that I am
the LORD. 11This city will not protect you
the way a pot protects the meat in it. I will
punish you wherever you may be in the land
of Israel. 12You will know that I am the
LORD and that while you were keeping the
laws of the neighboring nations, you were
breaking *my* laws and disobeying *my* com-
mands."
13While I was prophesying, Pelatiah
dropped dead. I threw myself face downward
on the ground and shouted, "No, Sovereign
LORD! Are you going to kill everyone left in
Israel?"

God's Promise to the Exiles

14The LORD spoke to me. 15"Mortal
man," he said, "the people who live in
Jerusalem are talking about you and those of
your nation who are in exile. They say, 'The
exiles are too far away to worship the LORD.
He has given us possession of the land.'
16"Now tell your fellow exiles what I am
saying. I am the one who sent them to live
in far-off nations and scattered them in other
countries. Yet, for the time being I will be
present with them in the lands where they
have gone.
17"So tell them what I, the Sovereign
LORD, am saying. I will gather them out of
the countries where I scattered them, and
will give the land of Israel back to them.
18When they return, they are to get rid of all
the filthy, disgusting idols they find. 19I will
give them a new heart and a new mind. I
will take away their stubborn heart of stone
and will give them an obedient heart.
20Then they will keep my laws and faithfully
obey all my commands. They will be my
people, and I will be their God. 21But I will
punish the people who love to worship
filthy, disgusting idols. I will punish them for
what they have done." The Sovereign LORD
has spoken.

God's Glory Leaves Jerusalem

22The living creatures began to fly, and the
wheels went with them. The dazzling light of
the presence of the God of Israel was over
them. 23Then the dazzling light left the city
and moved to the mountain east of it. 24In
the vision the spirit of God lifted me up and
brought me back to the exiles in Babylonia.
Then the vision faded, 25and I told the exiles
everything that the LORD had shown me.

Pray it!

I Need a New Heart

I need a new heart, God. Not the one that beats inside of me, but the one that makes me understanding and kind to others.

I need a new mind, God. Not the one that gets me through school, but the one that makes me think that I am the center of the universe.

Can you help me, God? Can you take away my stubbornness and replace it with faithfulness? I know that you are my God, and I am yours. I just have to keep remembering.

— Ezekiel 11:19–21

11:19, 20 Ezek 36:26–28 **11:22, 23** Ezek 43:2–5

In the vision . . . (11:24)

The Prophet as a Refugee

12 The LORD spoke to me. 2“Mortal
man,” he said, “you are living among
rebellious people. They have eyes, but they
see nothing; they have ears, but they hear
nothing, because they are rebellious.
3“Now, mortal man, pack a bundle just as
a refugee would and start out before night-
fall. Let everyone see you leaving and going
to another place. Maybe those rebels will
notice you.[w] 4While it is still daylight, pack
your bundle for exile, so that they can see
you, and then let them watch you leave in
the evening as if you were going into exile.
5While they are watching, break a hole
through the wall of your house and take
your pack out through it. 6Let them watch
you putting your pack on your shoulder and
going out into the dark with your eyes cov-
ered, so that you can't see where you are
going. What you do will be a warning to the
Israelites.”
7I did what the LORD told me to do. That
day I packed a bundle as a refugee would,
and that evening as it was getting dark I dug
a hole in the wall with my hands and went
out. While everyone watched, I put the pack
on my shoulder and left.
8The next morning the LORD spoke to
me. 9“Mortal man,” he said, “now that
those Israelite rebels are asking you what
you're doing, 10tell them what I, the Sover-
eign LORD, am saying to them. This mes-
sage is for the prince ruling in Jerusalem
and for all the people who live there. 11Tell
them that what you have done is a sign of
what will happen to them—they will be
refugees and captives. 12The prince who is
ruling them will shoulder his pack in the
dark and escape through a hole that they
dig for him in the wall. He will cover his
eyes and not see where he is going. 13But I
will spread out my net and trap him in it.
Then I will take him to the city of Bab-
ylon, where he will die without having
seen it. 14I will scatter in every direction all
the members of his court and his advisers
and bodyguards, and people will search for
them to kill them.
15“When I scatter them among the other
nations and in foreign countries, they will
know that I am the LORD. 16I will let a few
of them survive the war, the famine, and the
diseases, so that there among the nations
they will realize how disgusting their actions
have been and will acknowledge that I am
the LORD.”

The Sign of the Trembling Prophet

17The LORD spoke to me. 18“Mortal
man,” he said, “tremble when you eat, and
shake with fear when you drink. 19Tell the
whole nation that this is the message of the
Sovereign LORD to the people of Jerusalem
who are still living in their land: They will
tremble when they eat and shake with fear
when they drink. Their land will be stripped
bare, because everyone who lives there is
lawless. 20Cities that are now full of people
will be destroyed, and the country will be
made a wilderness. Then they will know that
I am the LORD.”

[w] **12:3** Maybe those . . . you; *or* Maybe they will then realize that they are rebels.

12:2 Isa 6:9, 10; Jer 5:21; Mk 8:18 **12:13** 2 Kings 25:7; Jer 52:11

A Popular Proverb and an Unpopular Message

21 The LORD spoke to me. 22 "Mortal
man," he said, "why do the people of Israel
repeat this proverb: 'Time goes by, and pre-
dictions come to nothing'? 23 Now tell them
what I, the Sovereign LORD, have to say
about that. I will put an end to that proverb.
It won't be repeated in Israel any more. Tell
them instead: The time has come, and the
predictions are coming true!
24 "Among the people of Israel there will
be no more false visions or misleading
prophecies. 25 I, the LORD, will speak to
them, and what I say will be done. There
will be no more delay. In your own lifetime,
you rebels, I will do what I have warned you
I would do. I have spoken," says the Sover-
eign LORD.
26 The LORD said to me, 27 "Mortal man,
the Israelites think that your visions and
prophecies are about the distant future. 28 So
tell them that I, the Sovereign LORD, am
saying: There will be no more delay. What I
have said will be done. I, the Sovereign
LORD, have spoken!"

Prophecy against False Male Prophets

13 The LORD spoke to me. 2 "Mortal
man," he said, "denounce the prophets
of Israel who make up their own prophecies.
Tell them to listen to the word of the LORD."
3 This is what the Sovereign LORD says:
"These foolish prophets are doomed! They
provide their own inspiration and invent their
own visions. 4 People of Israel, your prophets
are as useless as foxes living among the ruins
of a city. 5 They don't guard the places where
the walls have crumbled, nor do they rebuild
the walls, and so Israel cannot be defended
when war comes on the day of the LORD.
6 Their visions are false, and their predictions
are lies. They claim that they are speaking my
message, but I have not sent them. Yet they
expect their words to come true! 7 I tell them:
Those visions you see are false, and the pre-
dictions you make are lies. You say that they
are my words, but I haven't spoken to you!"
8 So the Sovereign LORD says to them,
"Your words are false, and your visions are
lies. I am against you. 9 I am about to punish
you prophets who have false visions and
make misleading predictions. You will not be
there when my people gather to make deci-
sions; your names will not be included in the
list of the citizens of Israel; you will never
return to your land. Then you will know
that I am the Sovereign LORD.
10 "The prophets mislead my people by

Live it!

The Future is N.O.W.

A cable television show about people living their dreams used the title "N.O.W." The letters stand for "No Opportunity Wasted." That message has a lot to do with God's plan for our lives as well.

The Israelites didn't worry too much about Ezekiel's visions. They thought that his warnings about God's punishment would happen sometime in the future. Their attitude was, "It'll never happen to me." But God had other plans. "There will be no more delay. What I have said will be done" (Ezekiel 12:28).

Every day you learn something new about being the person God wants you to be. What have you learned about yourself and God today or this week? Don't wait to put what you learn into practice. The time is N.O.W.

— Ezekiel 12:26–28

13:10 Jer 6:14; 8:11

God has Ezekiel act out two more signs of coming troubles in Ezekiel, chapter 12, to warn the Israelites. What did Ezekiel do?

saying that all is well. All is certainly not well!
My people have put up a wall of loose
stones, and then the prophets have come and
covered it with whitewash. 11Tell the
prophets that their wall is going to fall down.
I will send a pouring rain. Hailstones will fall
on it, and a strong wind will blow against it.
12The wall will collapse, and everyone will
ask you what good the whitewash did."
13Now this is what the Sovereign LORD
says: "In my anger I will send a strong wind,
pouring rain, and hailstones to destroy the
wall. 14I intend to break down the wall they
whitewashed, to shatter it, and to leave the
foundation stones bare. It will collapse and
kill you all. Then everyone will know that I
am the LORD.

I will send a strong wind, pouring rain, and hailstones to destroy the wall. (13:13)

15"The wall and those who covered it
with whitewash will feel the force of my
anger. Then I will tell you that the wall is
gone and so are those who whitewashed it—
16those prophets who assured Jerusalem that
all was well, when all was not well!" The
Sovereign LORD has spoken.

Prophecy against False Female Prophets

17The LORD said, "Now, mortal man, look
at the women among your people who
make up predictions. Denounce them 18and
tell them what the Sovereign LORD is saying
to them:

"You women are doomed! You sew magic
wristbands for everyone and make magic
scarves for everyone to wear on their heads,
so that they can have power over other peo-
ple's lives. You want to possess the power of
life and death over my people and to use it
for your own benefit. 19You dishonor me in
front of my people in order to get a few
handfuls of barley and a few pieces of bread.
You kill people who don't deserve to die,
and you keep people alive who don't deserve
to live. So you tell lies to my people, and
they believe you."
20Now this is what the Sovereign LORD
says: "I hate the wristbands that you use in
your attempt to control life and death. I will
rip them off your arms and set free the peo-
ple that you were controlling.[x] 21I will rip
off your scarves and let my people escape
from your power once and for all. Then you
will know that I am the LORD.
22"By your lies you discourage good peo-
ple, whom I do not wish to hurt. You pre-
vent evil people from giving up evil and sav-
ing their lives. 23So now your false visions
and misleading predictions are over. I am
rescuing my people from your power, so that
you will know that I am the LORD."

God Condemns Idolatry

14 Some of the leaders of the Israelites
came to consult me about the
LORD's will. 2Then the LORD spoke to me.
3"Mortal man," he said, "these men have
given their hearts to idols and are letting
idols lead them into sin. Do they think I will
give them an answer?
4"Now speak to them and tell them what
I, the Sovereign LORD, am saying to them:
Each of you Israelites who have given your
heart to idols and let them lead you into sin
and who then come to consult a prophet,
will get an answer from me—the answer that
your many idols deserve! 5All those idols
have turned the Israelites away from me, but

[x] **13:20** *In verse 20 in Hebrew a word occurs twice, the meaning of which is unclear.*

Ezekiel 13:17–23 is about fortune-tellers. They sold wristbands and scarves to ward off evil spells.

by my answer I hope to win back their loy-
alty.
6"Now then, tell the Israelites what I, the
Sovereign LORD, am saying: Turn back and
leave your disgusting idols.
7"Whenever one of you Israelites or one
of you foreigners who live in the Israelite
community turn away from me and worship
idols, and then go to consult a prophet, I, the
LORD, will give you your answer! 8I will
oppose you. I will make an example of you.
I will remove you from the community of
my people, so that all of you will know that
I am the LORD.
9"If any prophets are deceived into giving
a false answer, it is because I, the LORD, have
deceived them. I will remove them from the
people of Israel. 10Both prophets and anyone
who consults them will get the same punish-
ment. 11I will do this to keep the Israelites
from deserting me and defiling themselves
by their sins. They are to be my people, and I
will be their God." The Sovereign LORD has
spoken.

Noah, Danel, and Job

12The LORD spoke to me. 13"Mortal
man," he said, "if a country sins and is
unfaithful to me, I will reach out and destroy
its supply of food. I will send a famine and
kill people and animals alike. 14Even if those
three men, Noah, Danel,[y] and Job, were liv-
ing there, their goodness would save only
their own lives." The Sovereign LORD has
spoken.
15"Or I might send wild animals to kill
the people, making the land so dangerous
that no one could travel through it, 16and
even if those three men lived there—as sure-
ly as I, the Sovereign LORD, am the living
God—they would not be able to save even
their own children. They would save only
their own lives, and the land would become
a wilderness.
17"Or I might bring war on that country
and send destructive weapons to wipe out
people and animals alike, 18and even if those
three men lived there—as surely as I, the
Sovereign LORD, am the living God—they
would not be able to save even their chil-
dren, but only their own lives.
19"If I send an epidemic on that country
and in my anger take many lives, killing peo-
ple and animals, 20even if Noah, Danel, and
Job lived there—as surely as I, the Sovereign
LORD, am the living God—they would not
be able to save even their own children. Their
goodness would save only their own lives."
21This is what the Sovereign LORD is say-
ing: "I will send my four worst punishments
on Jerusalem—war, famine, wild animals, and
disease—to destroy people and animals alike.

Study it!

A Few Good Men

Who were Noah, Danel (or Daniel), and Job, and why do their names keep coming up? They are good and holy men from other books of the Bible. Ezekiel brings them into his conversation with God to check if a few good people can save the lives of everyone in a town, even if the others have sinned.

- **Noah and his family were spared from the Flood because he was the only good person in the area (see Genesis, chapters 6–9).**
- **Danel was a king famous for his wisdom and goodness. (There is also the prophet Daniel, but his story is later than Ezekiel's.)**
- **Job was a holy man who was always close to God but endured many trials (see the Book of Job).**

God's message to Ezekiel was simple and direct: each person is responsible for his or her own sinfulness. No one can help you stay close to God but *you*.

— Ezekiel 14:12–23

[y] **14:14** Danel; *or* Daniel *(see 28:3), an ancient hero, known for his righteous life.*
14:21 Rev 6:8

22 If some survive and save their children, look at them when they come to you. See how evil they are, and be convinced that the punishment I am bringing on Jerusalem is justified; 23 then you will know that there was good reason for everything I did." The Sovereign LORD has spoken.

A Parable about a Vine

15 The LORD spoke to me. 2 "Mortal man," he said, "how does a vine compare with a tree? What good is a branch of a grapevine compared with the trees of the forest? 3 Can you use it to make anything? Can you even make a peg out of it to hang things on? 4 It is only good for building a fire. And when the ends are burned up and the middle is charred, can you make anything out of it? 5 It was useless even before it was burned. Now that the fire has burned it and charred it, it is even more useless."

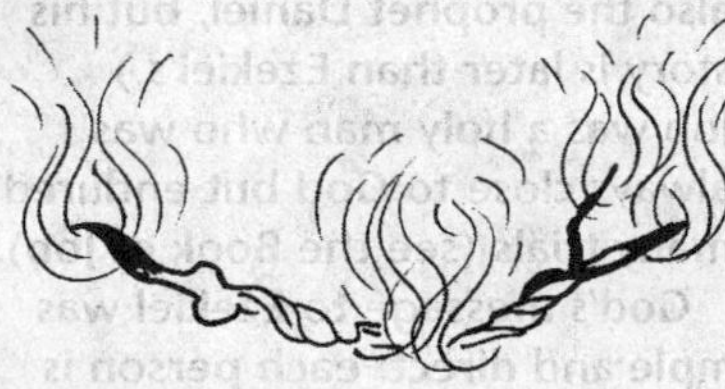

Can you make anything out of it? (15:4)

6 Now this is what the Sovereign LORD is saying: "Just as a vine is taken from the forest and burned, so I will take the people who live in Jerusalem 7 and will punish them. They have escaped one fire, but now fire will burn them up. When I punish them, you will know that I am the LORD. 8 They have been unfaithful to me, and so I will make the country a wilderness." The Sovereign LORD has spoken.

Jerusalem the Unfaithful

16 The LORD spoke to me again. 2 "Mortal man," he said, "point out to Jerusalem what disgusting things she has done. 3 Tell Jerusalem what the Sovereign LORD is saying to her:

"You were born in the land of Canaan. Your father was an Amorite, and your mother was a Hittite.[z] 4 When you were born, no one cut your umbilical cord or washed you[a] or rubbed you with salt or wrapped you in cloths. 5 No one took enough pity on you to do any of these things for you. When you were born, no one loved you. You were thrown out in an open field.

6 "Then I passed by and saw you squirming in your own blood. You were covered with blood, but I wouldn't let you die. 7 I made you grow like a healthy plant. You grew strong and tall and became a young woman.[b] Your breasts were well-formed, and your hair had grown, but you were naked.

8 "As I passed by again, I saw that the time had come for you to fall in love. I covered your naked body with my coat and promised to love you. Yes, I made a marriage covenant with you, and you became mine." This is what the Sovereign LORD says.

9 "Then I took water and washed the blood off you. I rubbed olive oil on your skin. 10 I dressed you in embroidered gowns and gave you shoes of the best leather, a linen headband, and a silk cloak. 11 I put jewels on you—bracelets and necklaces. 12 I gave you a nose ring and earrings and a beautiful crown to wear. 13 You had ornaments of gold and silver, and you always wore clothes of embroidered linen and silk. You ate bread made from the best flour, and had honey and olive oil to eat. Your beauty was dazzling, and you became a queen. 14 You became famous in every nation for your perfect beauty, because I was the one who made you so lovely." This is what the Sovereign LORD says.

15 "But you took advantage of your beauty and fame to sleep with everyone who came along.[c] 16 You used some of your clothes to decorate your places of worship, and just like a prostitute,[d] you gave yourself to everyone. 17 You took the silver and gold jewelry that I had given you, used it to make male images, and committed adultery with them. 18 You

[z] **16:3** AMORITE . . . HITTITE: *The Israelites regarded these people as immoral and idolatrous.* [a] **16:4** *Hebrew has an additional word, the meaning of which is unclear.* [b] **16:7** *Probable text* young woman; *Hebrew unclear.*
[c] **16:15** *Hebrew has two additional words, the meaning of which is unclear.* [d] **16:16** *Hebrew has four additional words, the meaning of which is unclear.*

took the embroidered clothes I gave you and
put them on the images, and you offered to
the images the olive oil and incense I had
given you. 19 I gave you food—the best flour,
olive oil, and honey—but you offered it as a
sacrifice to win the favor of idols." This is
what the Sovereign LORD says.
20 "Then you took the sons and the
daughters you had borne me and offered
them as sacrifices to idols. Wasn't it bad
enough to be unfaithful to me, 21 without
taking my children and sacrificing them to
idols? 22 During your disgusting life as a
prostitute you never once remembered your
childhood—when you were naked, squirming in your own blood."

Jerusalem's Life as a Prostitute

23 The Sovereign LORD said, "You are
doomed! Doomed! You did all that evil, and
then 24 by the side of every road you built
places to worship idols and practice prostitution. 25 You dragged your beauty through the
mud. You offered yourself to everyone who
came by, and you were more of a prostitute
every day. 26 You let your lustful neighbors,
the Egyptians, go to bed with you, and you
used your prostitution to make me angry.
27 "Now I have raised my hand to punish
you and to take away your share of my blessing. I have handed you over to the Philistines, who hate you and are disgusted with
your immoral actions.
28 "Because you were not satisfied by the
others, you went running after the Assyrians.
You were their prostitute, but they didn't satisfy you either. 29 You were also a prostitute
for the Babylonians, that nation of merchants, but they didn't satisfy you either."
30 This[e] is what the Sovereign LORD is
saying: "You have done all this like a shameless prostitute. 31 On every street you built
places to worship idols and practice prostitution. But you are not out for money like a
common prostitute. 32 You are like a woman
who commits adultery with strangers instead
of loving her husband. 33 A prostitute is paid,
but you gave presents to all your lovers and
bribed them to come from everywhere to
sleep with you. 34 You are a special kind of
prostitute. No one forced you to become
one. You didn't get paid; you paid them! Yes,
you are different."

God's Judgment on Jerusalem

35 Now then, Jerusalem, you whore! Hear
what the LORD is saying.
36 This is what the Sovereign LORD says:
"You stripped off your clothes, and like a
prostitute, you gave yourself to your lovers
and to all your disgusting idols, and you
killed your children as sacrifices to idols.
37 Because of this I will bring all your former
lovers together—the ones you liked and the
ones you hated. I will bring them around
you in a circle, and then I will strip off your
clothes and let them see you naked. 38 I will
condemn you for adultery and murder, and
in my anger and fury I will punish you with
death. 39 I will put you in their power, and
they will tear down the places where you
engage in prostitution and worship idols.
They will take away your clothes and jewels
and leave you completely naked.
40 "They will stir up a crowd to stone you,
and they will cut you to pieces with their
swords. 41 They will burn your houses down
and let crowds of women see your punishment. I will make you stop being a prostitute
and make you stop giving gifts to your
lovers. 42 Then my anger will be over, and I
will be calm. I will not be angry or jealous
any more. 43 You have forgotten how I treated you when you were young, and you have
made me angry by all the things you did.
That is why I have made you pay for them
all. Why did you add sexual immorality to all
the other disgusting things you did?" The
Sovereign LORD has spoken.

[e] **16:30** *Verse 30 in Hebrew begins with three words, the meaning of which is unclear.*

Just like the Israelites, we sometimes worship idols. Our idols are money, possessions, power, and physical comforts.

Like Mother, Like Daughter

44The LORD said, "People will use this
proverb about you, Jerusalem: 'Like mother,
like daughter.' 45You really are your mother's
daughter. She detested her husband and her
children. You are like your sisters, who hated
their husbands and their children. You and
your sister cities had a Hittite mother and an
Amorite[f] father.

46"Your older sister, with her villages, is
Samaria, in the north. Your younger sister,
with her villages, is Sodom, in the south.
47Were you satisfied to follow in their foot-
steps and copy their disgusting actions? No,
in only a little while you were acting worse
than they were in everything you did.

48"As surely as I am the living God," the
Sovereign LORD says, "your sister Sodom and
her villages never did the evil that you and
your villages have done. 49She and her
daughters were proud because they had
plenty to eat and lived in peace and quiet,
but they did not take care of the poor and
the underprivileged. 50They were proud and
stubborn and did the things that I hate, so I
destroyed them, as you well know.

51"Samaria did not sin half as much as
you have. You have acted more disgustingly
than she ever did. Your corruption makes
your sisters look innocent by comparison.
52And now you will have to endure your
disgrace. Your sins are so much worse than
those of your sisters that they look innocent
beside you. Now blush and bear your shame,
because you make your sisters look pure."

Sodom and Samaria Will Be Restored

53The LORD said to Jerusalem, "I will
make them prosperous again—Sodom and
her villages and Samaria and her villages. Yes,
I will make you prosperous too. 54You will
be ashamed of yourself, and your disgrace
will show your sisters how well-off they are.
55They will become prosperous again, and
you and your villages will also be restored.
56Didn't you joke about Sodom in those
days when you were proud 57and before the
evil you did had been exposed? Now you
are just like her—a joke to the Edomites, the
Philistines, and your other neighbors who
hate you. 58You must suffer for the obscene,
disgusting things you have done." The LORD
has spoken.

Live it!

Feeling Guilty

Sam was a nice guy. He was funny, smart, and kind. He liked to be in the middle of whatever was going on. He also spent his days in a wheelchair, and his words were hard to understand.

One day Isabel made a rude comment to Sam and made fun of the way he talked. Sam pretended not to hear, but he looked hurt. She thought it was funny, but her best friend got mad and told her that there was nothing funny about it. Isabel felt *really* guilty. She avoided Sam for a while, but it was hard because they were in some of the same classes. She never made fun of Sam again. In fact, she and Sam became good friends. But Isabel never really forgot that day, and never really forgave herself for it.

Sometimes you feel guilty for bad things you've done, even after you've made things right again. But God forgives you and keeps on loving you. And if God can do it, shouldn't you?

— Ezekiel 16:63

[f] **16:45** HITTITE . . . AMORITE: *See 16:3.*

The city of Sodom is often connected to sexual sin. But in Ezekiel God says that Sodom's sin was neglecting poor people *(Ezekiel 16:49).*

A Covenant That Lasts Forever

59 The Sovereign LORD says, "I will treat you the way you deserve, because you ignored your promises and broke the covenant. 60 But I will honor the covenant I made with you when you were young, and I will make a covenant with you that will last forever. 61 You will remember how you have acted, and be ashamed of it when you get your older sister and your younger sister back. I will let them be like daughters to you, even though this was not part of my covenant with you. 62 I will renew my covenant with you, and you will know that I am the LORD. 63 I will forgive all the wrongs you have done, but you will remember them and be too ashamed to open your mouth." The Sovereign LORD has spoken.

The Parable of the Eagles and the Vine

17 The LORD spoke to me. 2 "Mortal man," he said, "tell the Israelites a parable 3 to let them know what I, the Sovereign LORD, am saying to them: There was a giant eagle with beautiful feathers and huge wings, spread wide. He flew to the Lebanon Mountains and broke off the top of a cedar tree, 4 which he carried to a land of commerce and placed in a city of merchants. 5 Then he took a young plant from the land of Israel and planted it in a fertile field,[g] where there was always water to make it grow. 6 The plant sprouted and became a low, wide-spreading grapevine. The branches grew upward toward the eagle, and the roots grew deep. The vine was covered with branches and leaves.

7 "There was another giant eagle with huge wings and thick plumage. And now the vine sent its roots toward him and turned its leaves toward him, in the hope that he would give it more water than there was in the garden where it was growing.[h] 8 But the vine had already been planted in a fertile, well-watered field so that it could grow leaves and bear grapes and be a magnificent vine.

9 "So I, the Sovereign LORD, ask: Will this

He . . . broke off the top of a cedar tree. (17:3)

vine live and grow? Won't the first eagle pull it up by its roots, pull off the grapes, and break off the branches and let them wither? It will not take much strength or a mighty nation to pull it up. 10 Yes, it is planted, but will it live and grow? Won't it wither when the east wind strikes it? Won't it wither there where it is growing?"

It is planted, but will it live and grow? (17:10)

The Parable Is Explained

11 The LORD said to me, 12 "Ask these rebels if they know what the parable means. Tell them that the king of Babylonia came to Jerusalem and took the king and his officials back with him to Babylonia. 13 He took one of the king's family, made a treaty with him, and made him swear to be loyal. He took important men as hostages 14 to keep the nation from rising again and to make sure that the treaty would be kept. 15 But the king of Judah rebelled and sent agents to Egypt to get horses and a large army. Will he succeed? Can he get away with that? He cannot break the treaty and go unpunished!

16 "As surely as I am the living God," says the Sovereign LORD, "this king will die in Babylonia because he broke his oath and the

[g] **17:5** *Hebrew has an additional word, the meaning of which is unclear.* [h] **17:7** And now the vine . . . growing; *or* And now the vine turned away from the garden where it was growing and sent its roots toward him and turned its leaves toward him, in the hope that he would give it water.

17:12–15 2 Kings 24:15–20; 2 Chr 36:10–13

treaty he had made with the king of Babylo-
nia, who put him on the throne. [17]Even the
powerful army of the king of Egypt will not
be able to help him fight when the Babylo-
nians build earthworks and dig trenches in
order to kill many people. [18]He broke his
oath and the treaty he had made. He did all
these things, and now he will not escape."

[19]The Sovereign LORD says, "As surely as
I am the living God, I will punish him for
breaking the treaty which he swore in my
name to keep. [20]I will spread out a hunter's
net and catch him in it. I will take him to
Babylonia and punish him there, because he
was unfaithful to me. [21]His best soldiers will
be killed in battle, and the survivors will be
scattered in every direction. Then you will
know that I, the LORD, have spoken."

I will spread out a hunter's net and catch him in it. (17:20)

God's Promise of Hope

[22]This is what the Sovereign LORD says:
"I will take the top of a tall cedar
and break off a tender sprout;
I will plant it on a high mountain,
23 on Israel's highest mountain.
It will grow branches and bear seed
and become a magnificent cedar.
Birds of every kind will live there
and find shelter in its shade.
[24]All the trees in the land will know
that I am the LORD.
I cut down the tall trees
and make small trees grow tall.
I wither up the green trees
and make the dry trees become green.
I, the LORD, have spoken. I will do what I
have said I would do."

Live it!

You Promised!

Shelby promised her mom that she would clean her room. She went to Laticia's house instead. David promised his teacher that he would finish his assignment. That night he played video games for two hours and never touched it. Grace's dad promised that they would do something together on Saturday. He called her Friday and said he was going to a golf tournament.

Have you ever broken a promise you made to someone? Has anyone ever broken a promise he or she made to you? When you break a promise for no good reason, it's a serious matter. At the end of Ezekiel, chapter 17, God says that King Zedekiah will be punished for breaking his treaties, that is, promises he made to another king. Breaking a promise is a sin against the seventh commandment—just like lying.

Think carefully before you make a promise to someone, and keep the promises you make. You will become known as a person people can trust.

— Ezekiel 17:16–20

Individual Responsibility

18 The LORD spoke to me [2]and said,
"What is this proverb people keep
repeating in the land of Israel?

18:2 Jer 31:29

Birds of every kind will live there. (17:23)

'The parents ate the sour grapes,
But the children got the sour taste.'
3"As surely as I am the living God," says
the Sovereign LORD, "you will not repeat
this proverb in Israel any more. 4The life of
every person belongs to me, the life of the
parent as well as that of the child. The per-
son who sins is the one who will die.
5"Suppose there is a truly good man,
righteous and honest. 6He doesn't worship
the idols of the Israelites or eat the sacrifices
offered at forbidden shrines. He doesn't
seduce another man's wife or have inter-
course with a woman during her period. 7He
doesn't cheat or rob anyone. He returns what
a borrower gives him as security; he feeds the
hungry and gives clothing to the naked. 8He
doesn't lend money for profit. He refuses to
do evil and gives an honest decision in any
dispute. 9Such a man obeys my commands
and carefully keeps my laws. He is righteous,
and he will live," says the Sovereign LORD.
10"Then suppose this man has a son who
robs and kills, who does any[i] of these things
11that the father never did. He eats sacrifices
offered at forbidden shrines and seduces
other men's wives. 12He cheats the poor, he
robs, he keeps what a borrower gives him as
security. He goes to pagan shrines, worships
disgusting idols, 13and lends money for prof-
it. Will he live? No, he will not. He has done
all these disgusting things, and so he will die.
He will be to blame for his own death.
14"Now suppose this second man has a
son. He sees all the sins his father practiced,

Live it!

Be All You Can Be

Alex's family is pretty messed up. His dad left when Alex was a baby. His mom drinks way too much. His older brother is always in trouble with the police. He doesn't really know where his sister is. Thank God for school breakfasts and lunches. Otherwise Alex wouldn't get much to eat.

Alex has a lot of adults watching over him, though. His teachers and his coaches know what's going on. They do their best to guide Alex and to get him the help he needs. He loves his family, and he knows they love him. He also knows that the things they do are wrong. God makes it clear in Ezekiel, chapter 18, that children are not doomed to suffer because their parents do wrong things.

If your family is struggling, talk to someone at school or at church. They will find ways to help you. Rely on the support of people you trust. Above all, know that you are your own person, and you are responsible for yourself. Nothing can stop you from becoming all that you can be. And that's what God wants for you.

— Ezekiel, chapter 18

[i] **18:10** *Some ancient translations* who does any; *Hebrew unclear.*
18:9 Lev 18:5

In Ezekiel's time, many people believed that if a parent sinned, the children would share the punishment for their entire life.

but does not follow his example. 15He
doesn't worship the idols of the Israelites or
eat the sacrifices offered at forbidden shrines.
He doesn't seduce another man's wife 16or
oppress anyone or rob anyone. He returns
what a borrower gives him as security. He
feeds the hungry and gives clothing to the
naked. 17He refuses to do evil[j] and doesn't
lend money for profit. He keeps my laws and
obeys my commands. He will not die
because of his father's sins, but he will cer-
tainly live. 18His father, on the other hand,
cheated and robbed[k] and always did evil to
everyone. And so he died because of the sins
he himself had committed.

19"But you ask, 'Why shouldn't the son
suffer because of his father's sins?' The answer
is that the son did what was right and good.
He kept my laws and followed them careful-
ly, and so he will certainly live. 20It is the one
who sins who will die. A son is not to suffer
because of his father's sins, nor a father
because of the sins of his son. Good people
will be rewarded for doing good, and evil
people will suffer for the evil they do.

21"If someone evil stops sinning and keeps
my laws, if he does what is right and good, he
will not die; he will certainly live. 22All his sins
will be forgiven, and he will live, because he
did what is right. 23Do you think I enjoy see-
ing evil people die?" asks the Sovereign LORD.
"No, I would rather see them repent and live.

24"But if a righteous person stops doing
good and starts doing all the evil, disgusting
things that evil people do, will he go on liv-
ing? No! None of the good he did will be
remembered. He will die because of his
unfaithfulness and his sins.

25"But you say, 'What the Lord does isn't
right.' Listen to me, you Israelites. Do you
think my way of doing things isn't right? It is
your way that isn't right. 26When a righteous
person stops doing good and starts doing evil
and then dies, he dies because of the evil he
has done. 27When someone evil stops sinning
and does what is right and good, he saves his
life. 28He realizes what he is doing and stops
sinning, so he will certainly not die, but go
on living. 29And you Israelites say, 'What the
Lord does isn't right.' You think my way isn't
right, do you? It is your way that isn't right.

He realizes what he is doing and stops sinning. (18:28)

30"Now I, the Sovereign LORD, am telling
you Israelites that I will judge each of you
by what you have done. Turn away from all
the evil you are doing, and don't let your sin
destroy you. 31Give up all the evil you have
been doing, and get yourselves new minds
and hearts. Why do you Israelites want to
die? 32I do not want anyone to die," says the
Sovereign LORD. "Turn away from your sins
and live."

A Song of Sorrow

19 The LORD told me to sing this song
of sorrow for two princes of Israel:

2What a lioness your mother was!
She raised her cubs among the fierce male
lions.
3She raised a cub and taught him to hunt;
he learned to eat people.
4The nations heard about him
and trapped him in a pit.
With hooks they dragged him off to Egypt.
5She waited until she saw all hope was gone.
Then she raised another of her cubs,
and he grew into a fierce lion.

[j] **18:17** *Some ancient translations (see also verse 8)* to do evil; *Hebrew* from the poor. [k] **18:18** *Some ancient translations* robbed; *Hebrew unclear.*

18:20 Deut 24:16 **18:32** Wis 1:13

How do you behave when you do something wrong? Do you take responsibility for your actions?

6 When he was full-grown,
he prowled with the other lions.
He too learned to hunt and eat people.
7 He wrecked forts,[l] he ruined towns.
The people of the land were terrified
every time he roared.
8 The nations gathered to fight him;
people came from everywhere.
They spread their hunting nets
and caught him in their trap.
9 They put him in a cage
and took him to the king of Babylonia.
They kept him under guard,
so that his roar would never be heard
again
on the hills of Israel.

10 Your mother was like a grapevine[m]
planted near a stream.
Because there was plenty of water,
the vine was covered with leaves and
fruit.
11 Its branches were strong
and grew to be royal scepters.
The vine grew tall enough to reach the
clouds;
everyone saw how leafy and tall it was.
12 But angry hands pulled it up by the roots
and threw it to the ground.
The east wind dried up its fruit.
Its branches were broken off;
they dried up and were burned.
13 Now it is planted in the desert,
in a dry and waterless land.
14 The stem of the vine caught fire;
fire burned up its branches and fruit.
The branches will never again be strong,
will never be royal scepters.

This is a song of sorrow; it has been sung again and again.

The LORD's Will and Human Defiance

20 It was the tenth day of the fifth month
of the seventh year of our exile. Some
of the leaders of the Israelite community came
to consult me about the LORD's will, and they
sat down in front of me. 2 Then the LORD
spoke to me. 3 "Mortal man," he said, "speak to
these leaders and tell them that the Sovereign
LORD is saying: You have come to ask my will,
have you? As surely as I am the living God, I
will not let you ask me anything. I, the Sover-
eign LORD, have spoken.

4 "Are you ready to pass sentence on them,
mortal man? Then do so. Remind them of the
disgusting things their ancestors did. 5 Tell
them what I am saying. When I chose Israel,
I made them a promise. I revealed myself to
them in Egypt and told them: I am the LORD
your God. 6 It was then that I promised to take
them out of Egypt and lead them to a land I
had chosen for them, a rich and fertile land,
the finest land of all. 7 I told them to throw
away the disgusting idols they loved and not
to make themselves unclean with the false
gods of Egypt, because I am the LORD their
God. 8 But they defied me and refused to lis-
ten. They did not throw away their disgusting
idols or give up the Egyptian gods. I was ready
to let them feel the full force of my anger
there in Egypt. 9 But I did not, since that
would have brought dishonor to my name, for
in the presence of the people among whom
they were living I had announced to Israel
that I was going to lead them out of Egypt.

10 "And so I led them out of Egypt into
the desert. 11 I gave them my commands and
taught them my laws, which bring life to
anyone who obeys them. 12 I made the keep-
ing of the Sabbath a sign of the agreement
between us, to remind them that I, the
LORD, make them holy. 13 But even in the

I gave them my commands. (20:11)

[l] **19:7** *One ancient translation* wrecked forts; *Hebrew unclear, which is unclear.*

[m] **19:10** *Hebrew has an additional word, the meaning of*

20:5, 6 Ex 6:2–8 **20:11, 13** Lev 18:5 **20:12** Ex 31:13–17 desert they defied me. They broke my laws and rejected my commands, which bring life to anyone who obeys them. They completely profaned the Sabbath. I was ready to let them feel the force of my anger there in the desert and to destroy them. 14But I did not, since that would have brought dishonor to my name among the nations which had seen me lead Israel out of Egypt. 15So I made a vow in the desert that I would not take them to the land I had given them, a rich and fertile land, the finest land of all. 16I made the vow because they had rejected my commands, broken my laws, and profaned the Sabbath—they preferred to worship their idols.

17"But then I took pity on them. I decided not to kill them there in the desert. 18Instead, I warned the young people among them: Do not keep the laws your ancestors made; do not follow their customs or defile yourselves with their idols. 19I am the LORD your God. Obey my laws and my commands. 20Make the Sabbath a holy day, so that it will be a sign of the covenant we made, and will remind you that I am the LORD your God.

21"But that generation also defied me. They broke my laws and did not keep my commands, which bring life to anyone who obeys them. They profaned the Sabbath. I was ready to let them feel the force of my anger there in the desert and to kill them all. 22But I did not, since that would have brought dishonor to my name among the nations which had seen me bring Israel out of Egypt. 23So I made another vow in the desert. I vowed that I would scatter them all over the world. 24I did this because they had rejected my commands, broken my laws, profaned the Sabbath, and worshiped the same idols their ancestors had served.

25"Then I gave them laws that are not good and commands that do not bring life. 26I let them defile themselves with their own offerings, and I let them sacrifice their first-born sons. This was to punish them and show them that I am the LORD.

27"Now then, mortal man, tell the Israelites what I, the Sovereign LORD, am saying to them. This is another way their ancestors insulted me by their unfaithfulness. 28I brought them to the land I had promised to give them. When they saw the high hills and green trees, they offered sacrifices at all of them. They made me angry by the sacrifices they burned and by the wine they brought as offerings. 29I asked them: What are these high places where you go? So they have been called 'High Places'[n] ever since. 30Now tell the Israelites what I am saying: Why must you commit the same sins your ancestors did and go running after their idols? 31Even today you offer the same gifts and defile yourselves with the same idols by sacrificing your children to them in the fire. And then you Israelites still come to ask what my will is! As surely as I, the Sovereign LORD, am the living God, I will not let you ask me anything. 32You have made up your minds that you want to be like the other nations, like the people who live in other countries and worship trees and rocks. But that will never be.

God Punishes and Forgives

33"As surely as I, the Sovereign LORD, am the living God, I warn you that in my anger I will rule over you with a strong hand, with all my power. 34I will show you my power and my anger when I gather you together and bring you back from all the countries where you have been scattered. 35I will bring you into the 'Desert of the Nations,' and there I will condemn you to your face. 36I will now condemn you just as I condemned your ancestors in the Sinai Desert," says the Sovereign LORD.

37"I will take firm control of you and make you obey my covenant. 38I will take away from among you those who are rebellious and sinful. I will take them out of the lands where they are living now, but I will not let them return to the land of Israel. Then you will know that I am the LORD."

39The Sovereign LORD says, "And now, all you Israelites, suit yourselves! Go on and

[n] **20:29** HIGH PLACES: *Pagan places of worship which the Hebrews were forbidden to use. The Hebrew word translated "High Places" sounds like the Hebrew for "where you go."*

20:15 Num 14:26–35 **20:23** Lev 26:33

Live it!

The Dreaded Ms. G

Ms. G was the hardest teacher at school. She gave a lot of homework. She assigned projects that kept people at the library for hours. If you didn't do your very best, she kept after you until she was satisfied. If you messed up, you heard about it.

Ms. G also cared about every person in her class. She made you feel as if you were the most important person in the room. She believed in you and loved you. At the end of the year, people had a hard time saying goodbye to Ms. G. They knew that they had learned a great deal. They had done their very best, and all their hard work paid off.

God is like that, too. So much of Ezekiel's prophecies is about God demanding the very best from the Israelites and warning them when they mess up. God's "classroom" is a tough place to be sometimes. But like Ms. G, God believes in you and loves you. And all your hard work will pay off.

— Ezekiel 20:33–44

serve your idols! But I warn you that after
this you will have to obey me and stop dis-
honoring my holy name by offering gifts to
your idols. 40 There in the land, on my holy
mountain,◦ the high mountain of Israel, all
you people of Israel will worship me. I will
be pleased with you and will expect you to
bring me your sacrifices, your best offerings,
and your holy gifts. 41 After I bring you out
of the countries where you have been scat-
tered and gather you together, I will accept
the sacrifices that you burn, and the nations
will see that I am holy. 42 When I bring you
back to Israel, the land that I promised I
would give to your ancestors, then you will
know that I am the LORD. 43 Then you will
remember all the disgraceful things you did
and how you defiled yourselves. You will be
disgusted with yourselves because of all the
evil things you did. 44 When I act to protect
my honor, you Israelites will know that I am
the LORD, because I do not deal with you as
your wicked, evil actions deserve." The Sov-
ereign LORD has spoken.

Fire in the South

45 The LORD spoke to me. 46 "Mortal
man," he said, "look toward the south. Speak
against the south and prophesy against the
forest of the south. 47 Tell the southern forest
to hear what the Sovereign LORD is saying:
Look! I am starting a fire, and it will burn up
every tree in you, whether green or dry.
Nothing will be able to put it out. It will
spread from south to north, and everyone
will feel the heat of the flames. 48 They will
all see that I, the LORD, set it on fire and that
no one can put it out."

49 But I protested, "Sovereign LORD, don't
make me do it! Everyone is already com-
plaining that I always speak in riddles."

The LORD's Sword

21 The LORD spoke to me. 2 "Mortal
man," he said, "denounce Jerusalem.
Denounce the places where people worship.
Warn the land of Israel 3 that I, the LORD, am
saying: I am your enemy. I will draw my
sword and kill all of you, good and evil alike.
4 I will use my sword against everyone from
south to north. 5 Everyone will know that I,
the LORD, have drawn my sword and that I
will not put it away.

6 "Mortal man, groan as if your heart is

◦ **20:40** HOLY MOUNTAIN: *Mount Zion, the hill in Jerusalem which formed part of the Temple and palace area.*

"I warned the young people among them: Do not keep the laws your ancestors made; do not . . . defile yourselves with their idols" *(Ezekiel 20:18).*

breaking with despair. Groan in sorrow
where everyone can watch you. [7]When they
ask you why you are groaning, tell them it is
because of the news that is coming. When it
comes, their hearts will be filled with fear,
their hands will hang limp, their courage will
fail, and their knees will tremble. The time
has come; it is here." The Sovereign LORD
has spoken.

[8]The LORD said to me, [9]"Mortal man,
prophesy. Tell the people what I, the Lord,
am saying:

A sword, a sword is sharpened and
polished.
[10]It is sharpened to kill,
polished to flash like lightning.
There can be no rejoicing,
for my people have disregarded every
warning and punishment.[p]
[11]The sword is being polished,
to make it ready for use.
It is sharpened and polished,
to be put in the hands of a killer.
[12]Howl in grief, mortal man;
this sword is meant for my people
and for all the leaders of Israel.
They are going to be killed
with all the rest of my people.
Beat your breast in despair!
[13]I am testing my people,
and if they refuse to repent,
all these things will happen to them.[q]

[14]"Now, mortal man, prophesy. Clap your
hands, and the sword will strike again and
again. It is a sword that kills, a sword that
terrifies[r] and slaughters. [15]It makes my peo-
ple lose courage and stumble. I am threaten-
ing their city with a sword[s] that flashes like
lightning and is ready to kill. [16]Cut to the
right and the left, you sharp sword! Cut
wherever you turn.[t] [17]I also will clap my
hands, and my anger will be over. I, the
LORD, have spoken."

The Sword of the King of Babylonia

[18]The LORD spoke to me. [19]"Mortal
man," he said, "mark out two roads by which
the king of Babylonia can come with his
sword. Both of them are to start in the same
country. Put up a signpost where the roads
fork.[u] [20]One will show the king the way to
the Ammonite city of Rabbah, and the other
the way to Judah, to the fortified city,
Jerusalem. [21]The king of Babylonia stands by
the signpost at the fork of the road. To dis-
cover which way to go, he shakes the
arrows;[v] he consults his idols; he examines
the liver of a sacrificed animal. [22]Now! His
right hand holds the arrow marked
'Jerusalem'! It tells him to go and set up bat-
tering rams, to shout the battle cry, to place
battering rams against the gates, to throw up
earthworks, and to dig trenches. [23]The peo-
ple of Jerusalem won't believe this because
of the treaties they have made. But this pre-
diction is to remind them of their sins and
to warn them that they will be captured.
[24]This then is what I, the Sovereign LORD,
am saying: Your sins are exposed. Everyone
knows how guilty you are. You show your
sins in your every action. You stand con-
demned, and I will hand you over to your
enemies.

[25]"You wicked, unholy ruler of Israel,
your day, the day of your final punishment, is
coming. [26]I, the Sovereign LORD, have spo-
ken. Take off your crown and your turban.
Nothing will be the same again. Raise the
poor to power! Bring down those who are
ruling! [27]Ruin, ruin! Yes, I will make the city
a ruin. But this will not happen until the
one comes whom I have chosen to punish
the city. To him I will give it.

[p] **21:10** *Probable text* There . . . punishment; *Hebrew unclear.* [q] **21:13** *Verse 13 in Hebrew is unclear.*
[r] **21:14** *Some ancient translations* terrifies; *Hebrew unclear.* [s] **21:15** *Probable text* threatening . . . sword; *Hebrew unclear.* [t] **21:16** *Verse 16 in Hebrew is unclear.* [u] **21:19** *Probable text* Put . . . fork; *Hebrew unclear.*
[v] **21:21** SHAKES THE ARROWS: *When faced with a decision, people in ancient times would sometimes take a handful of arrows, throw them down, and study the pattern in which they fell, in order to learn what to do.*

In Ezekiel, chapter 21, God has Ezekiel perform several more symbolic actions. Can you find two or three things he must do?

Pray it!

Then and Now

Ezekiel lists the sins of the people of Jerusalem that hurt their relationship with God. Read the list below, which is based on Ezekiel's list. Which of these are we guilty of today?

- **killing and hurting human beings**
- **placing material goods above God**
- **disregarding laws**
- **showing no respect for parents**
- **cheating**
- **not caring for poor people**
- **showing no reverence for churches and other holy places**
- **failing to attend Sunday Mass**
- **lying**
- **needing to have everything we want right now**
- **having sex outside of marriage**
- **stealing**

We need to ask God to help us see where we have sinned. Say a prayer that God will help all people to recognize their sins and ask God's forgiveness for them.

— Ezekiel 22:1–12

A Sword and the Ammonites

28 "Mortal man, prophesy. Announce what
I, the Sovereign LORD, am saying to the
Ammonites, who are insulting Israel. Say to
them:

'A sword is ready to destroy;
It is polished to kill, to flash like lightning.
29 The visions that you see are false, and the
predictions you make are lies. You are wicked
and evil, and your day is coming, the day of
your final punishment. The sword is going to
fall on your necks.

30 " 'Put up the sword! I will judge you in
the place where you were created, in the
land where you were born. 31 You will feel
my anger when I turn it loose on you like a
blazing fire. And I will hand you over to
brutal men, experts at destruction. 32 You will
be destroyed by fire. Your blood will be shed
in your own country, and no one will
remember you any more.' " The LORD has
spoken.

The Crimes of Jerusalem

22 The LORD spoke to me. 2 "Mortal
man," he said, "are you ready to
judge the city that is full of murderers? Make
clear to her all the disgusting things she has
done. 3 Tell the city what I, the Sovereign
LORD, am saying: Because you have mur-
dered so many of your own people and have
defiled yourself by worshiping idols, your
time is coming. 4 You are guilty of those
murders and are defiled by the idols you
made, and so your day is coming, your time
is up! That is why I have let the nations make
fun of you and all the countries sneer at you.
5 Countries nearby and countries far away
sneer at you because of your lawlessness. 6 All
Israel's leaders trust in their own strength and
commit murder. 7 None of you in the city
honor your parents. You cheat foreigners and
take advantage of widows and orphans. 8 You
have no respect for the holy places, and you
don't keep the Sabbath. 9 Some of your

21:28–32 Jer 49:1–6; Ezek 25:1–7; Am 1:3–15; Zeph 2:8–11 **22:7 a** Ex 20:12; Deut 5:16; **b** Ex 22:21, 22; Deut 24:17 **22:8** Lev 19:30; 26:2

people tell lies about others in order to have
them put to death. Some of them eat sacri-
fices offered to idols. Some are always satisfy-
ing their lusts. [10]Some of them sleep with
their father's wife. Some force women to
have intercourse with them during their
period. [11]Some commit adultery, and others
seduce their daughters-in-law or their half
sisters. [12]Some of your people murder for
pay. Some charge interest on the loans they
make to other Israelites and get rich by tak-
ing advantage of them. They have forgotten
me." The Sovereign LORD has spoken.
[13]"I will bring my fist down on your rob-
beries and murders. [14]Do you think you will
have any courage left or have strength
enough to lift your hand when I am finished
with you? I, the LORD, have spoken, and I
keep my word. [15]I will scatter your people
to every country and nation and will put an
end to your evil actions. [16]And so the other
nations will dishonor you, but you will
know that I am the LORD."

God's Refining Furnace

[17]The LORD said to me, [18]"Mortal man,
the Israelites are of no use to me. They are
like waste metal—copper, tin, iron, and
lead—left over after silver has been refined
in a furnace. [19]So now I, the Sovereign
LORD, am telling them that they are just as
useless as that. I will bring them all together
in Jerusalem [20]in the same way that the ore
of silver, copper, iron, lead, and tin is put in a
refining furnace. My anger and rage will
melt them the way fire melts ore. [21]Yes, I
will gather them in Jerusalem, build a fire
under them, and melt them with my anger.
[22]They will be melted in Jerusalem the way
silver is melted in a furnace, and then they
will know that they are feeling the anger of
the LORD."

The Sins of Israel's Leaders

[23]The LORD spoke to me again. [24]"Mor-
tal man," he said, "tell the Israelites that
their land is unholy, and so I am punishing
it in my anger. [25]The leaders[w] are like lions
roaring over the animals they have killed.
They kill the people, take all the money
and property they can get, and by their
murders leave many widows. [26]The priests
break my law and have no respect for what
is holy. They make no distinction between
what is holy and what is not. They do not
teach the difference between clean and
unclean things, and they ignore the Sab-
bath. As a result the people of Israel do not
respect me. [27]The government officials are
like wolves tearing apart the animals they
have killed. They commit murder in order
to get rich. [28]The prophets have hidden
these sins like workers covering a wall with
whitewash. They see false visions and make
false predictions. They claim to speak the
word of the Sovereign LORD, but I, the
LORD, have not spoken to them. [29]The
wealthy cheat and rob. They mistreat the
poor and take advantage of foreigners. [30]I
looked for someone who could build a
wall, who could stand in the places where
the walls have crumbled and defend the
land when my anger is about to destroy it,
but I could find no one. [31]So I will turn my
anger loose on them, and like a fire I will
destroy them for what they have done." The
Sovereign LORD has spoken.

The Sinful Sisters

23 The LORD spoke to me. [2]"Mortal
man," he said, "there were once two
sisters. [3]When they were young, living in
Egypt, they lost their virginity and became
prostitutes. [4]The older one was named Oho-
lah[x] (she represents Samaria), and the
younger one was named Oholibah[y] (she rep-
resents Jerusalem). I married both of them,
and they bore me children. [5]Although she
was mine, Oholah continued to be a prosti-
tute and was full of lust for her lovers from
Assyria. [6]They were soldiers in uniforms of
purple, noblemen and high-ranking officers;
all of them were handsome young cavalry
officers. [7]She was the whore for all the Assyr-
ian officers, and her lust led her to defile her-

[w] **22:25** *One ancient translation* The leaders; *Hebrew* A conspiracy of her prophets. [x] **23:4** OHOLAH: *This name in Hebrew means "her sanctuary."* [y] **23:4** OHOLIBAH: *This name in Hebrew means "my sanctuary is in her."*

22:10, 11 Lev 18:7–20 **22:12** Ex 23:8; Deut 16:19; Ex 22:25; Lev 25:36, 37; Deut 23:19 **22:26** Lev 10:10

self by worshiping Assyrian idols. 8She con-
tinued what she had begun as a prostitute in
Egypt, where she lost her virginity. From the
time she was a young woman, men slept with
her and treated her like a prostitute. 9So I
handed her over to her Assyrian lovers whom
she wanted so much. 10They stripped her
naked, seized her sons and daughters, and
then killed her with a sword. Women every-
where gossiped about her fate.

11"Even though her sister Oholibah saw
this, she was wilder and more of a prostitute
than Oholah had ever been. 12She too was
full of lust for the Assyrian noblemen and
officers—soldiers in bright uniforms—and
for the cavalry officers, all of those handsome
young men. 13I saw that she was completely
immoral, that the second sister was as bad as
the first.

14-15"She sank deeper and deeper in her
immorality. She was attracted by the images of
high Babylonian officials carved into the wall
and painted bright red, with sashes around
their waists and fancy turbans on their heads.
16As soon as she saw them, she was filled with
lust and sent messengers to them in Babylo-
nia. 17The Babylonians came to have sex with
her. They used her and defiled her so much
that finally she became disgusted with them.
18She exposed herself publicly and let every-
one know she was a whore. I was as disgusted
with her as I had been with her sister. 19She
became more of a prostitute than ever, acting
the way she did as a young woman, when she
was a prostitute in Egypt. 20She was filled
with lust for oversexed men who had all
the lustfulness of donkeys or stallions."
(21Oholibah, you wanted to repeat the
immorality you were guilty of as a young
woman in Egypt, where men played with
your breasts and you lost your virginity.)

God's Judgment on the Younger Sister

22"Now then, Oholibah, this is what I, the
Sovereign LORD, am saying to you. You are
tired of those lovers, but I will make them
angry with you and bring them to surround
you. 23I will bring all the Babylonians and
Chaldeans, men from Pekod, Shoa, and Koa,
and all the Assyrians. I will gather all those
handsome young noblemen and officers, all
those important officials and high-ranking
cavalry officers. 24They will attack you from
the north,[z] bringing a large army with char-
iots and supply wagons. Protected by shields
and helmets, they will surround you. I will
hand you over to them, and they will judge
you by their own laws. 25Because I am angry
with you, I will let them deal with you in
their anger. They will cut off your nose and
your ears and kill your children. Yes, they
will take your sons and daughters from you
and burn them alive. 26They will tear off
your clothes and take your jewels. 27I will
put a stop to your lust and to the obscenities
you have committed ever since you were in
Egypt. You won't look at any more idols or
think about Egypt any more."

28This is what the Sovereign LORD says: "I
will hand you over to people you hate and
are disgusted with. 29And because they hate
you, they will take away everything you have
worked for and leave you stripped naked,
exposed like a prostitute. Your lust and your
prostitution 30have brought this on you. You
were a prostitute for the nations and defiled
yourself with their idols. 31You followed in
your sister's footsteps, and so I will give you
the same cup of punishment to drink."

32The Sovereign LORD says,

"You will drink from your sister's cup;
it is large and deep.
Everyone will scorn and mock you;
the cup is full.
33It will make you miserable and drunk,
that cup of fear and ruin,
your sister Samaria's cup.
34You will drink and drain it dry,
and with its broken pieces
tear your breast.
I, the Sovereign LORD, have spoken."

35Now this is what the Sovereign LORD is

[z] **23:24** *One ancient translation* north; *Hebrew unclear.*

Read Ezekiel 22:23–31. Say a prayer that the leaders of the world will listen to God and do what is right.

saying: "Because you forgot me and turned
your back on me, you will suffer for your
lust and your prostitution."

God's Judgment on Both Sisters

36The LORD said to me, "Mortal man, are
you ready to judge Oholah and Oholibah?
Accuse them of the disgusting things they
have done. 37They have committed adultery
and murder—adultery with idols and mur-
der of the children they bore me. They sacri-
ficed my children to their idols. 38And that is
not all they did. They profaned my Temple
and broke the Sabbath, which I had estab-
lished. 39The very day that they killed my
children as sacrifices to idols, they came to
my Temple and profaned it!

40"Again and again they sent messengers
to invite men to come from a great distance,
and the men came. The two sisters would
bathe and put on eye shadow and jewelry.
41They would sit on a beautiful couch, and
in front of them they would have a table
covered with good things, including the
incense and the olive oil that I had given
them. 42The sound of a carefree crowd could
be heard, a group of men brought in from
the desert. They put bracelets on the
women's arms and beautiful crowns on their
heads. 43And I said to myself that they were
using as a prostitute a woman worn out by
adultery.[a] 44They went back to these prosti-
tutes again and again. They went back to
Oholah and Oholibah, those immoral
women. 45Righteous men will condemn
them on the charge of adultery and murder,
because they practice adultery and their
hands are stained with blood."

46This is what the Sovereign LORD says:
"Bring a mob to terrorize them and rob
them. 47Let the mob stone them and attack
them with swords, kill their children, and
burn down their houses. 48Throughout the
land I will put a stop to immorality, as a
warning to every woman not to commit
adultery as they did. 49And you two sisters—
I will punish you for your immorality and
your sin of worshiping idols. Then you will
know that I am the Sovereign LORD."

The Corroded Cooking Pot

24 On the tenth day of the tenth
month of the ninth year of our
exile, the LORD spoke to me. 2"Mortal
man," he said, "write down today's date,
because this is the day that the king of Bab-
ylonia is beginning the siege of Jerusalem.
3Tell my rebellious people this parable that I,
the Sovereign LORD, have for them:

Set the pot on the fire
and fill it up with water.
4Put in the best pieces of meat—

Set the pot on the fire. (24:3)

the shoulders and the legs—
fill it with choice bony pieces too.
5Use the meat of the finest sheep;
pile the wood[b] under the pot.
Let the water boil;
boil the bones and the meat."

6This is what the Sovereign LORD is say-
ing: "The city of murderers is doomed! It is
like a corroded pot that is never cleaned.
Piece after piece of meat is taken out, and
not one is left. 7There was murder in the
city, but the blood was not spilled on the
ground where the dust could hide it; it was

[a] **23:43** *Verses 42–43 in Hebrew are unclear.* [b] **24:5** *Probable text* wood; *Hebrew* bones.
24:2 2 Kings 25:1; Jer 52:4

According to Ezekiel 24:1, the destruction of Jerusalem began on January 15, 588 BC.

Pray it!

Losing Someone Special

Ezekiel's wife died, and God commanded Ezekiel not to show any signs of sorrow or grief. That must have been very hard for Ezekiel. Have you ever lost someone close to you? Losing someone special is one of the hardest things you will go through in life. But death is only one way people leave us. If your parents are divorced, you might feel that you've lost the family you once had. If you and a good friend have a huge fight, you may never be close again. If you move away, you leave part of your heart behind with your old friends and everyone else you were close to.

If you're feeling sad because someone you loved is no longer with you, try this simple prayer: close your eyes and get a picture of the person in your mind. Then say these words over and over, until you feel peaceful: "I will be with you always" (Matthew 28:20). Imagine the person you love is holding God's hand and smiling at you.

— Ezekiel 24:15–27

spilled on a bare rock. 8 I have left the blood
there, where it cannot be hidden, where it
demands angry revenge."
9 This is what the Sovereign LORD is saying: "The city of murderers is doomed! I
myself will pile up the firewood. 10 Bring
more wood! Fan the flames! Cook the meat!
Boil away the broth![c] Burn up the bones!
11 Now set the empty bronze pot on the coals
and let it get red-hot. Then the pot will be
ritually pure again after the corrosion is
burned off, 12 although all that corrosion will
not disappear in the flames.[d] 13 Jerusalem, your
immoral actions have defiled you. Although I
tried to purify you, you remained defiled. You
will not be pure again until you have felt the
full force of my anger. 14 I, the LORD, have
spoken. The time has come for me to act. I
will not ignore your sins or show pity or be
merciful. You will be punished for what you
have done." The Sovereign LORD has spoken.

The Death of the Prophet's Wife

15 The LORD spoke to me. 16 "Mortal
man," he said, "with one blow I am going to
take away the person you love most. You are
not to complain or cry or shed any tears.
17 Don't let your sobbing be heard. Do not
go bareheaded or barefoot as a sign of
mourning. Don't cover your face or eat the
food that mourners eat."
18 Early in the day I was talking with the
people. That evening my wife died, and the
next day I did as I had been told. 19 The peo-
ple asked me, "Why are you acting like this?"
20 So I said to them, "The LORD spoke to
me and told me 21 to give you Israelites this
message: You are proud of the strength of the
Temple. You like to look at it and to visit it,
but the LORD is going to profane it. And the
younger members of your families who are
left in Jerusalem will be killed in war.
22 Then you will do what I have done. You
will not cover your faces or eat the food that
mourners eat. 23 You will not go bareheaded
or barefoot or mourn or cry. You will waste
away because of your sins, and you will
groan to one another. 24 Then I will be a
sign to you; you will do everything I have
done. The LORD says that when this hap-
pens, you will know that he is the Sovereign
LORD."
25 The LORD said, "Now, mortal man, I

[c] **24:10** *Some ancient translations* Boil away the broth!; *Hebrew unclear.* [d] **24:12** *Verse 12 in Hebrew begins with two words, the meaning of which is unclear.*

will take away from them the strong Temple
that was their pride and joy, which they
liked to look at and to visit. And I will take
away their sons and daughters. 26On the day
that I do this, some who escape the destruc-
tion will come and tell you about it. 27That
same day you will get back the power of
speech which you had lost, and you will talk
with them. In this way you will be a sign to
the people, and they will know that I am the
LORD."

Prophecy against Ammon

25 The LORD spoke to me. 2"Mortal
man," he said, "denounce the coun-
try of Ammon. 3Tell them to listen to what
I, the Sovereign LORD, am saying: You were
delighted to see my Temple profaned, to see
the land of Israel devastated, to see the peo-
ple of Judah go into exile. 4Because you
were glad, I will let the tribes from the east-
ern desert conquer you. They will set up
their camps in your country and settle there.
They will eat the fruit and drink the milk
that should have been yours. 5I will turn the
city of Rabbah into a place to keep camels,
and the whole country of Ammon will
become a place to keep sheep, so that you
will know I am the LORD.
6"This is what the Sovereign LORD is say-
ing: You clapped your hands and jumped for
joy. You despised the land of Israel. 7Because
you did, I will hand you over to other
nations who will rob you and plunder you. I
will destroy you so completely that you will
not be a nation any more or have a country
of your own. Then you will know that I am
the LORD."

Prophecy against Moab

8The Sovereign LORD said, "Because
Moab[e] has said that Judah is like all the other
nations, 9I will let the cities that defend the
border of Moab be attacked, including even
the finest cities—Beth Jeshimoth, Baal
Meon, and Kiriathaim. 10I will let the tribes
of the eastern desert conquer Moab, together
with Ammon, so that Moab[f] will no longer
be a nation. 11I will punish Moab, and they
will know that I am the LORD."

Prophecy against Edom

12The Sovereign LORD said, "The people
of Edom took cruel revenge on Judah, and
that revenge has brought lasting guilt on
Edom. 13Now I announce that I will punish

Study it!

God of Mercy

Ammon. Moab. Edom. Philistia. Tyre. Sidon. Egypt. If you're like most people, you only recognize the last name in that list. These are the names of the countries that surrounded Israel and Judah, the land of God's Chosen People. In Ezekiel, chapters 26–32, Ezekiel sends the message that God will punish the nations that were enemies of the Israelites. For example, the Ammonites rejoiced when the Temple fell, and that angered God. The Edomites turned on the Israelites, and God punished them. The Philistines treated the people of Judah horribly.

The first twenty-four chapters show God's anger at the sins of the Israelites. But even though they had sinned against God, God was still willing to protect them and punish those who hurt them. The God of the Israelites—and our God—is a God of justice and mercy.

— Ezekiel, chapter 25

[e] **25:8** *Some ancient translations* Moab; *Hebrew* Moab and Seir. [f] **25:10** *Probable text* Moab; *Hebrew* Ammon.

25:1–7 Jer 49:1–6; Ezek 21:28–32; Am 1:13–15; Zeph 2:8–11 **25:8–11** Isa 15:1—16:14; 25:10–12; Jer 48:1–47; Am 2:1–3; Zeph 2:8–11 **25:12–14** Isa 34:5–17; 63:1–6; Jer 49:7–22; Ezek 35:1–15; Am 1:11, 12; Ob 1–14; Mal 1:2–5

Edom and kill every person and animal
there. I will make it a wasteland, from the
city of Teman to the city of Dedan, and the
people will be killed in battle. 14My people
Israel will take revenge on Edom for me, and
they will make Edom feel my furious anger.
Edom will know what it means to be the
object of my revenge." The Sovereign LORD
has spoken.

Prophecy against Philistia

15The Sovereign LORD said, "The
Philistines have taken cruel revenge on their
agelong enemies and destroyed them in their
hate. 16And so I am announcing that I will
attack the Philistines and wipe them out. I
will destroy everyone left living there on the
Philistine Plain. 17I will punish them severely
and take full revenge on them. They will feel
my anger. Then they will know that I am the
LORD."

Prophecy against Tyre

26 On the first day of the . . . month[g] of
the eleventh year of our exile, the
LORD spoke to me. 2"Mortal man," he said,
"this is what the people in the city of Tyre
are cheering about. They shout, 'Jerusalem is
shattered! Her commercial power is gone!
She won't be our rival any more!'
3"Now then, this is what I, the Sovereign
LORD, am saying: I am your enemy, city of
Tyre. I will bring many nations to attack
you, and they will come like the waves of
the sea. 4They will destroy your city walls
and tear down your towers. Then I will
sweep away all the dust and leave only a bare
rock. 5Fishermen will dry their nets on it,
there where it stands in the sea. I, the Sover-
eign LORD, have spoken. The nations will
plunder Tyre, 6and with their swords they
will kill those who live in her towns on the
mainland. Then Tyre will know that I am the
LORD."
7The Sovereign LORD says, "I am going
to bring the greatest king of all—King
Nebuchadnezzar of Babylonia—to attack
Tyre. He will come from the north with a
huge army, with horses and chariots and
with cavalry. 8Those who live in the towns
on the mainland will be killed in the fight-
ing. The enemy will dig trenches, build
earthworks, and make a solid wall of shields
against you. 9They will pound in your walls
with battering rams and tear down your
towers with iron bars. 10The clouds of dust
raised by their horses will cover you. The
noise of their horses pulling wagons and
chariots will shake your walls as they pass
through the gates of the ruined city. 11Their
cavalry will storm through your streets,
killing your people with their swords. Your
mighty pillars will be thrown to the ground.
12Your enemies will help themselves to your
wealth and merchandise. They will pull
down your walls and shatter your luxurious
houses. They will take the stones and wood
and all the rubble, and dump them into the
sea. 13I will put an end to all your songs, and
I will silence the music of your harps. 14I
will leave only a bare rock where fishermen
can dry their nets. The city will never be
rebuilt. I, the Sovereign LORD, have spo-
ken."
15The Sovereign LORD has this to say to
the city of Tyre: "When you are being con-
quered, the people who live along the coast
will be terrified at the screams of those who
are slaughtered. 16All the kings of the seafar-
ing nations will come down from their
thrones. They will take off their robes and
their embroidered clothes and sit trembling
on the ground. They will be so terrified at
your fate that they will not be able to stop
trembling. 17They will sing this funeral song
for you:

g **26:1** month; *the Hebrew text does not specify the month.*

25:15–17 Isa 14:29–31; Jer 47:1–7; Joel 3:4–8; Am 1:6–8; Zeph 2:4–7; Zech 9:5–7 **26:1—28:19** Isa 23:1–18; Joel 3:4–8; Am 1:9, 10; Zech 9:1–4; Mt 11:21, 22; Lk 10:13, 14 **26:13** Rev 18:22 **26:16–18** Rev 18:9, 10

Ezekiel, chapters 25–32, link the two parts of the Book of Ezekiel: God's judgment in the first half and God's promise in the second half.

That city which stands at the edge of the sea (27:3)

The famous city is destroyed!
Her ships have been swept[h] from the seas.
The people of this city ruled the seas
And terrified all who lived on the coast.
18 Now, on the day it has fallen,
The islands are trembling,
And their people are shocked at such
destruction."

19 The Sovereign LORD says: "I will make
you as desolate as ruined cities where no one
lives. I will cover you with the water of the
ocean depths. 20 I will send you down to the
world of the dead to join the people who
lived in ancient times. I will make you stay
in that underground world among eternal
ruins, keeping company with the dead. As a
result you will never again be inhabited and
take your place[i] in the land of the living. 21 I
will make you a terrifying example, and that
will be the end of you. People may look for
you, but you will never be found." The Sov-
ereign LORD has spoken.

A Funeral Song for Tyre

27 The LORD said to me, 2 "Mortal
man, sing a funeral song for Tyre,
3 that city which stands at the edge of the sea
and does business with the people living on
every seacoast. Tell her what the Sovereign
LORD is saying:

"Tyre, you boasted of your perfect beauty.
4 Your home is the sea.
Your builders made you like a beautiful
ship;
5 They used fir trees from Mount Hermon
for timber
And a cedar from Lebanon for your mast.
6 They took oak trees from Bashan to make
oars;
They made your deck out of pine from
Cyprus
And inlaid it with ivory.
7 Your sails were made of linen,
Embroidered linen from Egypt,
Easily recognized from afar.
Your awnings were made of finest cloth,
Of purple from the island of Cyprus.
8 Your oarsmen were from the cities of
Sidon and Arvad.
Your own skillful men were the sailors.
9 The ship's carpenters
Were well-trained men from Byblos.
Sailors from every seagoing ship
Did business in your shops.
10 "Soldiers from Persia, Lydia, and Libya

[h] **26:17** *Some ancient translations* swept; *Hebrew* inhabited. *Hebrew unclear.*
[i] **26:20** *One ancient translation* and take your place; *Hebrew* I will give beauty.

26:21 Rev 18:21

Check out all the different types of merchandise that were traded in Ezekiel's time *(Ezekiel 27:12–24)*. **How many different things are mentioned?**

served in your army. They hung their shields
and their helmets in your barracks. They are
the men who won glory for you. 11 Soldiers
from Arvad guarded your walls, and troops
from Gamad guarded your towers. They
hung their shields on your walls. They are
the ones who made you beautiful.
12 "You did business in Spain and took sil-
ver, iron, tin, and lead in payment for your
abundant goods. 13 You did business in
Greece, Tubal, and Meshech and traded your
goods for slaves and for articles of bronze.
14 You sold your goods for workhorses, war-
horses, and mules from Beth Togarmah.
15 The people of Rhodes[j] traded with you;
people of many coastal lands gave you ivory
and ebony in exchange for your goods.
16 The people of Syria bought your mer-
chandise and your many products. They gave
emeralds, purple cloth, embroidery, fine
linen, coral, and rubies in payment for your
wares. 17 Judah and Israel paid for your goods
with wheat,[k] honey, olive oil, and spices.
18-19 The people of Damascus bought your
merchandise and your products, paying for
them with wine from Helbon and wool
from Sahar.[l] They traded wrought iron and
spices for your goods. 20 The people of
Dedan traded saddle blankets for your goods.
21 The Arabians and the rulers of the land of
Kedar paid for your merchandise with lambs,
sheep, and goats. 22 For your goods the mer-
chants of Sheba and Raamah traded jewels,
gold, and the finest spices. 23 The cities of
Haran, Canneh, and Eden, the merchants of
Sheba, the cities of Asshur and Chilmad—
they all traded with you. 24 They sold you
luxurious clothing, purple cloth, and
embroidery, brightly colored carpets, and
well-made cords and ropes. 25 Your merchan-
dise was carried in fleets of the largest cargo
ships.

"You were like a ship at sea
Loaded with heavy cargo.
26 When your oarsmen brought you out to
sea,
An east wind wrecked you far from land.
27 All your wealth of merchandise,
All the sailors in your crew,
Your ship's carpenters and your
merchants,
Every soldier on board the ship—
All, all were lost at sea
When your ship was wrecked.
28 The shouts of the drowning sailors
Echoed on the shore.
29 "Every ship is now deserted,
And every sailor has gone ashore.

> **Study it!**
>
> ## Eden, the Sequel
>
> **The people of Tyre had everything. They were rich. The city was perfectly located on the Mediterranean Sea to be the center of trade. Ezekiel 27:12–24 lists some of the products that were traded with other countries in the region.**
>
> **Even though they had little to do with the fall of Jerusalem, the people of Tyre were destroyed by God. Why? Because of their greed and pride. In Ezekiel 26:2, Ezekiel tells us that the people of Tyre were glad to see Jerusalem fall because it meant they would make more money.**
>
> **In the Garden of Eden, Adam and Eve had all that they could ever want or need, but they were not satisfied. So they ate the fruit of the forbidden tree. God punished them for it, just like he punished the people of Tyre.**
>
> **Where do you see greed happening in our world? Do you think people or companies suffer bad things when they get too greedy?**
>
> **— Ezekiel, chapter 27**

[j] **27:15** *One ancient translation* Rhodes; *Hebrew* Dedan. [k] **27:17** *Hebrew has two additional words, the meaning of which is unclear.* [l] **27:18–19** *Hebrew has three additional words, the meaning of which is unclear.*

27:25–36 Rev 18:11–19

30 They all mourn bitterly for you,
Throwing dust on their heads and rolling
in ashes.
31 They shave their heads for you
And dress themselves in sackcloth.
Their hearts are bitter as they weep.
32 They chant a funeral song for you:
'Who can be compared to Tyre,
To Tyre now silent in the sea?
33 When your merchandise went overseas,
You filled the needs of every nation.
Kings were made rich
By the wealth of your goods.
34 Now you are wrecked in the sea;
You have sunk to the ocean depths.
Your goods and all who worked for you
Have vanished with you in the sea.'

35 "Everyone who lives along the coast is
shocked at your fate. Even their kings are
terrified, and fear is written on their faces.
36 You are gone, gone forever, and merchants
all over the world are terrified, afraid that
they will share your fate."

Prophecy against the King of Tyre

28 The LORD spoke to me. 2 "Mortal
man," he said, "tell the ruler of Tyre
what I, the Sovereign LORD, am saying to
him: Puffed up with pride, you claim to be a
god. You say that like a god you sit on a
throne, surrounded by the seas. You may pre-
tend to be a god, but, no, you are mortal, not
divine. 3 You think you are wiser than
Danel,[m] that no secret can be kept from you.
4 Your wisdom and skill made you rich with
treasures of gold and silver. 5 You made clever
business deals and kept on making profits.
How proud you are of your wealth!

6 "Now then, this is what I, the Sovereign
LORD, am saying: Because you think you are
as wise as a god, 7 I will bring ruthless ene-
mies to attack you. They will destroy all the
beautiful things you have acquired by skill
and wisdom. 8 They will kill you and send
you to a watery grave. 9 When they come to
kill you, will you still claim that you are a
god? When you face your murderers, you
will be mortal and not at all divine. 10 You
will die like a dog at the hand of godless for-
eigners. I, the Sovereign LORD, have given
the command."

The Fall of the King of Tyre

11 The LORD spoke to me again. 12 "Mor-
tal man," he said, "grieve for the fate that is
waiting for the king of Tyre. Tell him what I,
the Sovereign LORD, am saying: You were
once an example of perfection. How wise
and handsome you were! 13 You lived in
Eden, the garden of God, and wore gems of
every kind: rubies and diamonds; topaz,
beryl, carnelian, and jasper; sapphires, emer-
alds, and garnets. You had ornaments of gold.
They were made for you[n] on the day you
were created. 14 I put a terrifying angel there
to guard you.[o] You lived on my holy moun-
tain and walked among sparkling gems.
15 Your conduct was perfect from the day
you were created until you began to do evil.
16 You were busy buying and selling, and this
led you to violence and sin. So I forced you
to leave my holy mountain, and the angel
who guarded you drove you away from the
sparkling gems. 17 You were proud of being
handsome, and your fame made you act like
a fool. Because of this I hurled you to the
ground and left you as a warning to other
kings. 18 You did such evil in buying and sell-
ing that your places of worship were cor-
rupted. So I set fire to the city and burned it
to the ground. All who look at you now see
you reduced to ashes. 19 You are gone, gone
forever, and all the nations that had come to
know you are terrified, afraid that they will
share your fate."

Prophecy against Sidon

20 The LORD said to me, 21 "Mortal man,
denounce the city of Sidon. 22 Tell the peo-
ple there what I, the Sovereign LORD, say
about them: I am your enemy, Sidon; people
will praise me because of what I do to you.
They will know that I am the LORD, when I
show how holy I am by punishing those
who live in you. 23 I will send diseases on

[m] **28:3** Danel; *or* Daniel *(see 14:14)*. [n] **28:13** *Probable text* They were made for you; *Hebrew unclear.*
[o] **28:14** *One ancient translation* I put . . . you; *Hebrew unclear.*
28:20–26 Joel 3:4–8; Zech 9:1, 2; Mt 11:21, 22; Lk 10:13, 14

you and make blood flow in your streets. You
will be attacked from every side, and your
people will be killed. Then you will know
that I am the LORD."

Israel Will Be Blessed

24 The LORD said, "None of the surround-
ing nations that treated Israel with scorn will
ever again be like thorns and briers to hurt
Israel. And they will know that I am the
Sovereign LORD."
25 The Sovereign LORD said, "I will bring
back the people of Israel from the nations
where I scattered them, and all the nations
will know that I am holy. The people of
Israel will live in their own land, the land
that I gave to my servant Jacob. 26 They will
live there in safety. They will build houses
and plant vineyards. I will punish all their
neighbors who treated them with scorn, and
Israel will be secure. Then they will know
that I am the LORD their God."

Prophecy against Egypt

29 On the twelfth day of the tenth
month of the tenth year of our exile,
the LORD spoke to me. 2 "Mortal man," he
said, "denounce the king of Egypt. Tell him
how he and all the land of Egypt will be
punished. 3 Say that this is what the Sover-
eign LORD is telling the king of Egypt: I am
your enemy, you monster crocodile, lying in
the river. You say that the Nile is yours and
that you made it.[p] 4 I am going to put a
hook through your jaw and make the fish in
your river stick fast to you. Then I will pull
you up out of the Nile, with all the fish
sticking to you. 5 I will throw you and all
those fish into the desert. Your body will fall
on the ground and be left unburied. I will
give it to the birds and animals for food.

I will pull you up out of the Nile. (29:4)

6 Then all the people of Egypt will know
that I am the LORD."
The LORD says, "The Israelites relied on
you Egyptians for support, but you were no
better than a weak stick. 7 When they leaned
on you, you broke, pierced their armpits, and
made them wrench their backs.[q] 8 Now
then, I, the Sovereign LORD, am telling you
that I will have troops attack you with
swords, and they will kill your people and
your animals. 9 Egypt will become an empty
wasteland. Then you will know that I am the
LORD.
"Because you said that the Nile is yours
and you made it, 10 I am your enemy and the
enemy of your Nile. I will make all of Egypt
an empty wasteland, from the city of Migdol
in the north to the city of Aswan in the
south, all the way to the Ethiopian[r] border.
11 No human being or animal will walk
through it. For forty years nothing will live
there. 12 I will make Egypt the most desolate
country in the world. For forty years the
cities of Egypt will lie in ruins, ruins worse
than those of any other city. I will make the
Egyptians refugees. They will flee to every
country and live among other peoples."
13 The Sovereign LORD says, "After forty
years I will bring the Egyptians back from the
nations where I have scattered them, 14 and I
will let them live in southern Egypt, their
original home. There they will be a weak
kingdom, 15 the weakest kingdom of all, and
they will never again rule other nations. I will
make them so unimportant that they will not

[p] **29:3** *Some ancient translations* you made it; *Hebrew* you made yourself. [q] **29:7** *One ancient translation* wrench their backs; *Hebrew* make their backs stand. [r] **29:10** *Hebrew* Cushite (Cush): *Cush is the ancient name of the extensive territory south of the First Cataract of the Nile River. This region was called Ethiopia in Graeco-Roman times, and included within its borders most of modern Sudan and some of present-day Ethiopia (Abyssinia).*
29:1—32:32 Isa 19:1–25; Jer 46:2–26 **29:6** Isa 36:6

Pride: **Loving yourself or success more than God or others. It is one of the capital sins because it leads to other sins.**

Pray it!

A Prayer for Peace

It seems most of these prophecies against the other nations had to do with war and violence. In Ezekiel, chapter 29, Ezekiel prophesies that there will be war between Egypt and Babylonia. Is there ever an end to war?

God, it seems that war is everywhere. The older I get, the more I hear about it and the more it bothers me. People kill people every day. It happens around the world and right where I live. It seemed like that happened a lot in Ezekiel's time, too. People's lives are shattered because someone they love is hurt or killed, their home is destroyed, or they are wounded beyond repair. I don't know what to do, God, except to pray.

Help me do what I can to change things, God. Please heal the world—one heart at a time. And please start with mine. Amen.

— Ezekiel, chapter 29

be able to bend any other nation to their will.
16 Israel will never again depend on them for
help. Egypt's fate will remind Israel how
wrong it was to rely on them. Then Israel will
know that I am the Sovereign LORD."

King Nebuchadnezzar Will Conquer Egypt

17 On the first day of the first month of
the twenty-seventh year of our exile, the
LORD spoke to me. 18 "Mortal man," he said,
"King Nebuchadnezzar of Babylonia
launched an attack on Tyre. He made his soldiers carry such heavy loads that their heads
were rubbed bald and their shoulders were
worn raw, but neither the king nor his army
got anything for all their trouble. 19 So now
this is what I, the Sovereign LORD, am saying: I am giving the land of Egypt to King
Nebuchadnezzar. He will loot and plunder it
and carry off all the wealth of Egypt as his
army's pay. 20 I am giving him Egypt in payment for his services, because his army was
working for me. I, the Sovereign LORD, have
spoken.

21 "When that happens, I will make the
people of Israel strong and let you, Ezekiel,
speak out where everyone can hear you, so
that they will know that I am the LORD."

The LORD Will Punish Egypt

30 The LORD spoke to me again.
2 "Mortal man," he said, "prophesy
and announce what I, the Sovereign LORD,
am saying. You are to shout these words:

A day of terror is coming!
3 The day is near, the day when the LORD
will act,
A day of clouds and trouble for the
nations.
4 There will be war in Egypt
And great distress in Ethiopia.[r]
Many in Egypt will be killed;
The country will be plundered
And left in ruins.

5 "That war will also kill the soldiers hired
from Ethiopia,[r] Libya, Lydia, Arabia, Kub,
and even from among my own people."

6 The LORD says, "From Migdol in the
north to Aswan in the south, all Egypt's
defenders will be killed in battle. Egypt's
proud army will be destroyed. I, the Sovereign LORD, have spoken. 7 The land will be
the most desolate in the world, and its cities

[r] **30:4, 5** *Hebrew* Cushite (Cush): *Cush is the ancient name of the extensive territory south of the First Cataract of the Nile River. This region was called Ethiopia in Graeco-Roman times, and included within its borders most of modern Sudan and some of present-day Ethiopia (Abyssinia).*

As king of Babylonia, Nebuchadnezzar conquered Israel. Read more about him (and his dreams) in the Book of Daniel.

will be left totally in ruins. 8 When I set fire
to Egypt and all her defenders are killed,
then they will know that I am the LORD.
9 "When that day comes and Egypt is
destroyed, I will send messengers in ships to
arouse the unsuspecting people of Ethiopia,[r]
and they will be terrified. That day is com-
ing!"
10 The Sovereign LORD says, "I will use
King Nebuchadnezzar of Babylonia to put
an end to Egypt's wealth. 11 He and his ruth-
less army will come to devastate the land.
They will attack Egypt with swords, and the
land will be full of corpses. 12 I will dry up
the Nile and put Egypt under the power of
evil people. Foreigners will devastate the
whole country. I, the LORD, have spoken."
13 The Sovereign LORD says, "I will destroy
the idols and the false gods in Memphis.
There will be no one to rule Egypt, and I
will terrify all the people. 14 I will make
southern Egypt desolate and set fire to the
city of Zoan in the north. I will punish the
capital city of Thebes. 15 I will let the city of
Pelusium, Egypt's great fortress, feel my fury. I
will destroy the wealth of Thebes. 16 I will set
fire to Egypt, and Pelusium will be in agony.
The walls of Thebes will be broken down,
and the city will be flooded.[s] 17 The young
men of the cities of Heliopolis and Bubastis
will die in the war, and the other people will
be taken prisoner. 18 Darkness will fall on
Tahpanhes when I break the power of Egypt
and put an end to the strength they were so
proud of. A cloud will cover Egypt, and the
people of all her cities will be taken prisoner.
19 When I punish Egypt in this way, they will
know that I am the LORD."

The Broken Power of the King of Egypt

20 On the seventh day of the first month
of the eleventh year of our exile, the LORD
spoke to me. 21 "Mortal man," he said, "I
have broken the arm of the king of Egypt.
No one has bandaged it or put it in a sling
so that it could heal and be strong enough to
hold a sword again. 22 Now then, this is what
I, the Sovereign LORD, say: I am the enemy
of the king of Egypt. I am going to break
both his arms—the good one and the one
already broken—and the sword will fall from
his hand. 23 I am going to scatter the Egyp-
tians throughout the world. 24 Then I will
make the arms of the king of Babylonia
strong and put my sword in his hands. But I
will break the arms of the king of Egypt, and
he will groan and die in front of his enemy.
25 Yes, I will weaken him and strengthen the
king of Babylonia. When I give him my
sword and he points it toward Egypt, every-
one will know that I am the LORD. 26 I will
scatter the Egyptians throughout the world.
Then they will know that I am the LORD."

Egypt Is Compared to a Cedar Tree

31 On the first day of the third month
of the eleventh year of our exile, the
LORD spoke to me. 2 "Mortal man," he said,
"say to the king of Egypt and all his people:

How powerful you are!
What can I compare you to?
3 You are like[t] a cedar in Lebanon,
With beautiful, shady branches,
A tree so tall it reaches the clouds.[u]
4 There was water to make it grow,
And underground rivers to feed it.
They watered the place where the tree
was growing
And sent streams to all the trees of the
forest.
5 Because it was well-watered,
It grew taller than other trees.
Its branches grew thick and long.
6 Every kind of bird built nests in its
branches;
The wild animals bore their young in its
shelter;
The nations of the world rested in its
shade.
7 How beautiful the tree was—
So tall, with such long branches.
Its roots reached down to the deep-
flowing streams.

[r] **30:9** *Hebrew* Cushite (Cush): *Cush is the ancient name of the extensive territory south of the First Cataract of the Nile River. This region was called Ethiopia in Graeco-Roman times, and included within its borders most of modern Sudan and some of present-day Ethiopia (Abyssinia).* [s] **30:16** *One ancient translation* flooded; *Hebrew unclear.* [t] **31:3** *Probable text* You are like; *Hebrew* Assyria is. [u] **31:3** *One ancient translation* clouds; *Hebrew* thick branches.

Life's Downs and Ups

You've probably heard the saying, "What goes up must come down." That might apply to balls and flying objects, but when it comes to real life, the opposite is true: what goes down often comes up.

In the first part of the Book of Ezekiel, the Israelites are about as down as they can get. They are almost spiritually dead. But God doesn't give up on them. In the second part that is coming up, God promises to lead them home and be with them forever. The Israelites awake from their spiritual death and are making things right with God.

Catholics believe in the *Paschal mystery,* meaning that God saved us through the life, death, and Resurrection of Jesus. Throughout your life, you have dyings and risings, just like the Israelites and Jesus. It's your way of participating in the Paschal mystery of Jesus.

Know that when things are down, it is not the end of our story. God promised new life for those who have faith, and Jesus' Resurrection is the sign and fulfillment of that promise.

— Ezekiel, chapter 31

8 No cedar in God's garden could compare
with it.
No fir tree ever had such branches,
And no plane tree such limbs.
No tree in God's own garden was so
beautiful.
9 I made it beautiful, with spreading
branches.
It was the envy of every tree in Eden, the
garden of God.

10 "Now then, I, the Sovereign LORD, will
tell you what is going to happen to that tree
that grew until it reached the clouds.[u] As it
grew taller it grew proud; 11 so I have rejected
it and will let a foreign ruler have it. He will
give that tree what it deserves for its wicked-
ness. 12 Ruthless foreigners will cut it down
and leave it. Its branches and broken limbs
will fall on every mountain and valley in the
country. All the nations that have been living
in its shade will go away. 13 The birds will
come and perch on the fallen tree, and the
wild animals will walk over its branches.
14 And so from now on, no tree, no matter
how well-watered it is, will grow that tall
again or push its top through the clouds[u] and
reach such a height. All of them are doomed
to die like mortals, doomed to join those
who go down to the world of the dead."

15 This is what the Sovereign LORD says:
"On the day when the tree goes to the world
of the dead, I will make the underground
waters cover it as a sign of mourning. I will
hold back the rivers and not let the many
streams flow out. Because the tree has died, I
will bring darkness over the Lebanon Moun-
tains and make all the trees of the forest
wither. 16 When I send it down to the world
of the dead, the noise of its downfall will
shake the nations. All the trees of Eden and
all the choice, well-watered trees of Lebanon
who have gone to the world below will be
pleased at its downfall. 17 They will go with it
to the world of the dead to join those that
have already fallen. And all who live under its
shadow will be scattered among the nations.[v]

[u] **31:10, 14** *One ancient translation* clouds; *Hebrew* thick branches. [v] **31:17** *Probable text* And all . . . nations; *Hebrew unclear.*
31:8 Gen 2:9

No tree . . . will grow that tall again. (31:14)

18"The tree is the king of Egypt and all
his people. Not even the trees in Eden were
so tall and impressive. But now, like the trees
of Eden, it will go down to the world of the
dead and join the ungodly and those killed
in battle. I have spoken," says the Sovereign
LORD.

The King of Egypt Is Compared to a Crocodile

32 On the first day of the twelfth
month of the twelfth year of our
exile, the LORD spoke to me. 2"Mortal
man," he said, "give a solemn warning to the
king of Egypt. Give him this message from
me: You act like a lion among the nations,
but you are more like a crocodile splashing
through a river. You muddy the water with
your feet and pollute the rivers. 3When
many nations gather, I will catch you in my
net and let them drag the net ashore. 4I will
throw you out on the ground and bring all
the birds and animals of the world to feed
on you. 5I will cover mountains and valleys
with your rotting corpse. 6I will pour out
your blood until it spreads over the moun-
tains and fills the streams. 7When I destroy
you, I will cover the sky and blot out the
stars. The sun will hide behind the clouds,
and the moon will give no light. 8I will put
out all the lights of heaven and plunge your
world into darkness. I, the Sovereign LORD,
have spoken.

9"Many nations will be troubled when I
spread the news of your destruction through
countries you never heard of. 10What I do to
you will shock many nations. When I swing
my sword, kings will shudder with fright.
On the day you fall, all of them will tremble
in fear for their own lives."

11The Sovereign LORD says to the king of
Egypt, "You will face the sword of the king
of Babylonia. 12I will let soldiers from cruel
nations draw their swords and kill all your
people. All your people and everything else
that you are proud of will be destroyed. 13I
will slaughter your cattle at every water hole.
There will be no people or cattle to muddy
the water any more. 14I will let your waters
settle and become clear and let your rivers
run calm. I, the Sovereign LORD, have spo-
ken. 15When I make Egypt a desolate waste-
land and destroy all who live there, they will
know that I am the LORD. 16This solemn
warning will become a funeral song. The
women of the nations will sing it to mourn
for Egypt and all its people. I, the Sovereign
LORD, have spoken."

The World of the Dead

17On the fifteenth day of the first month[w]
of the twelfth year of our exile, the LORD
spoke to me. 18"Mortal man," he said, "mourn
for all the many people of Egypt. Send them
down with the other powerful nations to the
world of the dead. 19Say to them:

[w] **32:17** *One ancient translation* of the first month; *Hebrew does not have these words.*
32:7 Isa 13:10; Mt 24:29; Mk 13:24, 25; Lk 21:25; Rev 6:12, 13; 8:12

Cedar trees were strong, straight, and bug resistant. They were used for ships and large buildings.

Live it!

Hey, Gorgeous!

Are you good-looking? Do you have a nice body? A lot of people your age are concerned with how they look on the outside. Looking your best is important, but it's not the most important part of who you are. Magazines, television shows, movies, and newspapers are full of things that advertisers say will make you look good. They want you to think that you need their product to be attractive. They want you to forget that you are already beautiful. After all, God made you. It doesn't matter what you look like, what clothes you wear, or what shape your body is in—you are gorgeous!

The ancient Egyptians worked hard at looking beautiful. But if you read Ezekiel 32:19, good looks certainly don't matter to God. No one is guaranteed a place in heaven because he or she looks good. What is much more important to God is how you live your life. How beautiful is your life?

— Ezekiel 32:17–19

"Do you think you are more beautiful
than anyone else?
You will go down to the world of the
dead
and lie there among the ungodly.
20"The people of Egypt will fall with
those who are killed in battle. A sword is
ready to kill them all.[x] 21The greatest heroes
and those who fought on the Egyptian side
welcome the Egyptians to the world of the
dead. They shout: 'The ungodly who were
killed in battle have come down here, and
here they lie!'
22"Assyria is there, with the graves of her
soldiers all around. They were all killed in
battle, 23and their graves are in the deepest
parts of the world of the dead. All her sol-
diers fell in battle, and their graves surround
her tomb. Yet once they terrified the land of
the living.
24"Elam is there, with the graves of her
soldiers all around. They were all killed in
battle, and they went down, uncircumcised,
to the world of the dead. In life they spread
terror, but now they lie dead and disgraced.
25Elam lies down among those killed in bat-
tle, and the graves of her soldiers are all
around her. They are all uncircumcised, all
killed in battle. In life they spread terror, but
now they lie dead and disgraced, sharing the
fate of those killed in battle.
26"Meshech and Tubal are there, with the
graves of their soldiers all around. They are
all uncircumcised, all killed in battle. Yet
once they terrified the living. 27They were
not given honorable burial like the heroes of
ancient times,[y] who went fully armed to the
world of the dead, their swords placed under
their heads and their shields[z] over their bod-
ies. These heroes were once powerful
enough to terrify the living.
28"That is how the Egyptians will lie
crushed among the uncircumcised who were
killed in battle.
29"Edom is there with her kings and
rulers. They were powerful soldiers, but now
they lie in the world of the dead with the
uncircumcised who were killed in battle.
30"All the princes of the north are there,
and so are the Sidonians. Their power once
spread terror, but now they go down in dis-
grace with those killed in battle and are laid
to rest, uncircumcised. They share the dis-

[x] **32:20** *Probable text* A sword . . . all; *Hebrew unclear.* [y] **32:27** *Some ancient translations* of ancient times; *Hebrew* of the uncircumcised. [z] **32:27** *Probable text* shields; *Hebrew* iniquities.

Lookouts were usually used for military purposes. But God makes Ezekiel a spiritual lookout.

grace of those who go down to the world of
the dead.
31 "The sight of all these who were killed
in battle will be a comfort to the king of
Egypt and his army," says the Sovereign
LORD.
32 "I caused the king of Egypt to terrorize
the living, but he and all his army will be
killed and laid to rest with all the uncircum-
cised who die in battle." The Sovereign
LORD has spoken.

God Appoints Ezekiel as a Lookout
(Ezekiel 3:16–21)

33 The LORD spoke to me. 2 "Mortal
man," he said, "tell your people what
happens when I bring war to a land. The
people of that country choose one of their
number to be a lookout. 3 When he sees the
enemy approaching, he sounds the alarm to
warn everyone. 4 If someone hears it but pays
no attention and the enemy comes and kills
him, then he is to blame for his own death.
5 His death is his own fault, because he paid
no attention to the warning. If he had paid
attention, he could have escaped. 6 If, howev-
er, the lookout sees the enemy coming and
does not sound the alarm, the enemy will
come and kill those sinners, but I will hold
the lookout responsible for their death.
7 "Now, mortal man, I am making you a
lookout for the nation of Israel. You must
pass on to them the warnings I give you. 8 If
I announce that an evil person is going to
die but you do not warn him to change his
ways so that he can save his life, then he will
die, still a sinner, and I will hold you respon-
sible for his death. 9 If you do warn an evil
person and he doesn't stop sinning, he will
die, still a sinner, but your life will be
spared."

Individual Responsibility

10 The LORD spoke to me. "Mortal man,"
he said, "repeat to the Israelites what they are
saying: 'We are burdened with our sins and
the wrongs we have done. We are wasting
away. How can we live?' 11 Tell them that as
surely as I, the Sovereign LORD, am the liv-
ing God, I do not enjoy seeing sinners die. I
would rather see them stop sinning and live.
Israel, stop the evil you are doing. Why do
you want to die?
12 "Now, mortal man, tell the Israelites that
when someone good sins, the good he has
done will not save him. If an evil person

Live it!

Wrong Secrets

Jonas knew that Max was heading for trouble. He knew that Max got beer from some older guys in exchange for keeping a lookout. He knew that Max was a shoplifter, too, and proud of it. Max knew that he could count on Jonas not to tell adults about these things. "Friends keep secrets." Max told him one day. "You *are* my friend, right?"

God tells Ezekiel, "If I announce that an evil person is going to die but you do not warn him to change his ways so that he can save his life, then he will die" (Ezekiel 33:8). We have a responsibility to challenge other people when they are doing something that is clearly against God's will. Sooner or later their sinful behavior will lead to their being deeply hurt and also maybe hurting others.

Though keeping secrets is an important part of being a friend, sometimes our friends ask us to keep the wrong secrets. If you know that a friend is doing something wrong or is in danger—and they will not listen to you —tell an adult you trust. Your friend may be angry with you, but it's better to lose the friendship than to watch your friend end up deeply hurt or in worse trouble.

— Ezekiel 33:7–9

stops doing evil, he won't be punished, and if a good man starts sinning, his life will not be spared. 13I may promise life to someone good, but if he starts thinking that his past goodness is enough and begins to sin, I will not remember any of the good he did. He will die because of his sins. 14I may warn someone evil that he is going to die, but if he stops sinning and does what is right and good— 15for example, if he returns the security he took for a loan or gives back what he stole—if he stops sinning and follows the laws that give life, he will not die, but live. 16I will forgive the sins he has committed, and he will live because he has done what is right and good.

17"And your people say that what I do isn't right! No, it's their way that isn't right. 18When someone righteous stops doing good and starts doing evil, he will die for it. 19When someone evil quits sinning and does what is right and good, he has saved his life. 20But Israel, you say that what I do isn't right. I am going to judge you by what you do."

The News of Jerusalem's Fall

21On the fifth day of the tenth month of the twelfth year of our exile, someone who had escaped from Jerusalem came and told me that the city had fallen. 22The evening before he came, I had felt the powerful presence of the LORD. When the man arrived the next morning, the LORD gave me back the power of speech.

The Sins of the People

23The LORD spoke to me. 24"Mortal man," he said, "the people who are living in the ruined cities of the land of Israel are saying: 'Abraham was only one man, and he was given the whole land. There are many of us, so now the land is ours.'

25"Tell them what I, the Sovereign LORD, am saying: You eat meat with the blood still in it. You worship idols. You commit murder. What makes you think that the land belongs to you? 26You rely on your swords. Your actions are disgusting. Everyone commits adultery. What makes you think that the land is yours?

27"Tell them that I, the Sovereign LORD, warn them that as surely as I am the living God, the people who live in the ruined cities will be killed. Those living in the country will be eaten by wild animals. Those hiding in the mountains and in caves will die of disease. 28I will make the country a desolate wasteland, and the power they were so proud of will come to an end. The mountains of Israel will be so wild that no one will be able to travel through them. 29When I punish the people for their sins and make the country a wasteland, then they will know that I am the LORD."

The Results of the Prophet's Message

30The LORD said, "Mortal man, your people are talking about you when they meet by the city walls or in the doorways of their houses. They say to one another, 'Let's go and hear what word has come from the LORD now.' 31So my people crowd in to hear what you have to say, but they don't do what you tell them to do. Loving words are on their lips, but they continue their greedy ways. 32To them you are nothing more than an entertainer singing love songs or playing a harp. They listen to all your words and don't obey a single one of them. 33But when all your words come true—and they will come true—then they will know that a prophet has been among them."

They listen to all your words and don't obey a single one of them. (33:32)

33:21 2 Kings 25:3–10; Jer 39:2–8; 52:4–14

Catholic Connections

Do You Know Any Good Shepherds?

You've probably never seen a real, live shepherd. Not many of us have. Shepherds check that the sheep have enough good grass to eat and clear water to drink. They make sure the sheep don't wander off and get lost. They protect them from wild animals and take care of them when they are sick or hurt. It was popular in Bible times to compare leaders to shepherds. Ezekiel talks about the leaders of his time being like poor shepherds, failing to care for their people.

You may have never seen a shepherd, but if you think about it, lots of people in your life are like shepherds to you. They care for you, guide you, provide shelter, and protect you. These people follow God's example when they do these things for you.

Jesus is often called the Good Shepherd because he cares for us like a shepherd cares for sheep. Check out John 10:1–18 for more about how Jesus is the Good Shepherd. In the Catholic Church, bishops are also called shepherds. The bishop's crosier, or staff, is to remind us of the staff used by shepherds.

— Ezekiel, chapter 34

The Shepherds of Israel

34 The LORD spoke to me. 2“Mortal
man,” he said, “denounce the rulers
of Israel. Prophesy to them, and tell them
what I, the Sovereign LORD, say to them:
You are doomed, you shepherds of Israel!
You take care of yourselves, but never tend
the sheep. 3You drink the milk, wear clothes
made from the wool, and kill and eat the
finest sheep. But you never tend the sheep.
4You have not taken care of the weak ones,
healed the ones that are sick, bandaged the
ones that are hurt, brought back the ones
that wandered off, or looked for the ones
that were lost. Instead, you treated them
cruelly. 5Because the sheep had no shep-
herd, they were scattered, and wild animals
killed and ate them. 6So my sheep wandered
over the high hills and the mountains. They
were scattered over the face of the earth,
and no one looked for them or tried to find
them.

7“Now, you shepherds, listen to what I,
the LORD, am telling you. 8As surely as I am
the living God, you had better listen to me.
My sheep have been attacked by wild ani-
mals that killed and ate them because there
was no shepherd. My shepherds did not try
to find the sheep. They were taking care of
themselves and not the sheep. 9So listen to
me, you shepherds. 10I, the Sovereign LORD,
declare that I am your enemy. I will take my
sheep away from you and never again let
you be their shepherds; never again will I let
you take care only of yourselves. I will res-
cue my sheep from you and not let you eat
them.

34:5 Num 27:17; 1 Kings 22:17; Mt 9:36; Mk 6:34

“Loving words are on their lips, but they continue their greedy ways” *(Ezekiel 33:31).*

The Good Shepherd

11 "I, the Sovereign LORD, tell you that I
myself will look for my sheep and take care of
them 12 in the same way as shepherds take
care of their sheep that were scattered and are
brought together again. I will bring them
back from all the places where they were scat-
tered on that dark, disastrous day. 13 I will take
them out of foreign countries, gather them
together, and bring them back to their own
land. I will lead them back to the mountains
and the streams of Israel and will feed them in
pleasant pastures. 14 I will let them graze in
safety in the mountain meadows and the val-
leys and in all the green pastures of the land
of Israel. 15 I myself will be the shepherd of
my sheep, and I will find them a place to rest.
I, the Sovereign LORD, have spoken.

I myself will be the shepherd of my sheep. (34:15)

16 "I will look for those that are lost, bring
back those that wander off, bandage those that
are hurt, and heal those that are sick; but those
that are fat and strong I will destroy, because I
am a shepherd who does what is right.
17 "Now then, my flock, I, the Sovereign
LORD, tell you that I will judge each of you
and separate the good from the bad, the sheep
from the goats. 18 Some of you are not satisfied
with eating the best grass; you even trample
down what you don't eat! You drink the clear
water and muddy what you don't drink! 19 My
other sheep have to eat the grass you trample
down and drink the water you muddy.
20 "So now, I, the Sovereign LORD, tell you
that I will judge between you strong sheep
and the weak sheep. 21 You pushed the sick
ones aside and butted them away from the
flock. 22 But I will rescue my sheep and not
let them be mistreated any more. I will judge
each of my sheep and separate the good
from the bad. 23 I will give them a king like
my servant David to be their one shepherd,
and he will take care of them. 24 I, the LORD,
will be their God, and a king like my servant
David will be their ruler. I have spoken. 25 I
will make a covenant with them that guar-
antees their security. I will get rid of all the
dangerous animals in the land, so that my
sheep can live safely in the fields and sleep in
the forests.
26 "I will bless them and let them live
around my sacred hill.[a] There I will bless
them with showers of rain when they need
it. 27 The trees will bear fruit, the fields will
produce crops, and everyone will live in safe-
ty on his own land. When I break my peo-
ple's chains and set them free from those
who made them slaves, then they will know
that I am the LORD. 28 The heathen nations
will not plunder them any more, and the
wild animals will not kill and eat them. They
will live in safety, and no one will terrify
them. 29 I will give them fertile fields and put
an end to hunger in the land. The other
nations will not sneer at them any more.
30 Everyone will know that I protect Israel
and that they are my people. I, the Sovereign
LORD, have spoken.
31 "You, my sheep, the flock that I feed, are
my people, and I am your God," says the
Sovereign LORD.

God's Punishment of Edom

35 The LORD spoke to me. 2 "Mortal
man," he said, "denounce the coun-
try of Edom. 3 Tell the people what I, the
Sovereign LORD, am saying:

[a] **34:26** SACRED HILL: *See 20:40.*
34:23 Rev 7:17 **34:24** Ezek 37:24 **35:1–15** Isa 34:5–17; 63:1–6; Jer 49:7–22; Ezek 25:12–14; Am 1:11, 12; Ob 1–14; Mal 1:2–5

In New Zealand, there are twenty times as many sheep as there are people.

"I am your enemy, mountains of Edom!
I will make you a desolate wasteland.
4 I will leave your cities in ruins
And your land desolate;
Then you will know that I am the LORD.
5 "You were Israel's constant enemy and
let her people be slaughtered in the time of
her disaster, the time of final punishment for
her sins. 6 So then—as surely as I, the Sover-
eign LORD, am the living God—death is
your fate, and you cannot escape it. You are
guilty of[b] murder, and murder will follow
you. 7 I will make the hill country of Edom a
wasteland and kill everyone who travels
through it. 8 I will cover the mountains with
corpses, and the bodies of those who are
killed in battle will cover the hills and val-
leys. 9 I will make you desolate forever, and
no one will live in your cities again. Then
you will know that I am the LORD.
10 "You said that the two nations, Judah
and Israel, together with their lands,
belonged to you and that you would possess
them, even though I, the LORD, was their
God. 11 So then, as surely as I, the Sovereign
LORD, am the living God, I will pay you
back for your anger, your jealousy, and your
hate toward my people. They will know that
I am punishing you for what you did to
them. 12 Then you will know that I, the
LORD, heard you say with contempt that the
mountains of Israel were desolate and that
they were yours to devour. 13 I have heard
the wild, boastful way you have talked
against me."
14 The Sovereign LORD says, "I will make
you so desolate that the whole world will
rejoice at your downfall, 15 just as you
rejoiced at the devastation of Israel, my own
possession. The mountains of Seir, yes, all the
land of Edom, will be desolate. Then every-
one will know that I am the LORD."

God's Blessing on Israel

36 The LORD said, "Mortal man, speak
to the mountains of Israel and tell
them to listen to the message which I, 2 the
Sovereign LORD, have for them: Israel's ene-
mies gloated and said, 'Now those ancient
hills are ours!'
3 "Prophesy, then, and announce what I,
the Sovereign LORD, am saying. When the
neighboring nations captured and plundered
the mountains of Israel, everyone made fun
of Israel. 4 So now listen to what I, the Sov-
ereign LORD, say to you mountains and hills,
to you brooks and valleys, to you places that
were left in ruins, and to you deserted cities
which were plundered and mocked by all
the surrounding nations.
5 "I, the Sovereign LORD, have spoken out
in the heat of my anger against the surround-
ing nations, and especially against Edom.
With glee and contempt they captured my
land and took possession of its pastures.
6 "So prophesy to the land of Israel; tell the
mountains, hills, brooks, and valleys what I,
the Sovereign LORD, am saying in jealous
anger because of the way the nations have
insulted and humiliated them. 7 I, the

> **Study it!**
>
> ### Punishment and Promises
>
> **In the first part of the Book of Ezekiel, God wants the Israelites to know he is a just God who will punish them for their sins. In the second part, God wants them to know that he is a loving God who forgives them. God also lets them know that he will hear their prayers again and bring them back to the land of their birth. It is God's way of restoring his holy name.**
>
> **Read about all the wonderful promises God makes to the Israelites in Ezekiel, chapter 36. But of all these promises, perhaps the most important is. . . . Well, check out verses 26–27 for the answer.**
>
> **— Ezekiel, chapter 36**

[b] **35:6** *One ancient translation* are guilty of; *Hebrew* hate.

Sovereign LORD, solemnly promise that the
surrounding nations will be humiliated. [8]But
on the mountains of Israel the trees will again
grow leaves and bear fruit for you, my people
Israel. You are going to come home soon. [9]I
am on your side, and I will make sure that
your land is plowed again and crops are plant-
ed on it. [10]I will make your population grow.
You will live in the cities and rebuild every-
thing that was left in ruins. [11]I will make peo-
ple and cattle increase in number. There will
be more of you than ever before, and you will
have many children. I will let you live there as
you used to live, and I will make you more
prosperous than ever. Then you will know
that I am the LORD. [12]I will bring you, my
people Israel, back to live again in the land. It
will be your own land, and it will never again
let your children starve.

[13]"I, the Sovereign LORD, say: It is true
that people say that the land eats people and
that it robs the nation of its children. [14]But
from now on it will no longer eat people and
rob you of your children. I, the Sovereign
LORD, have spoken. [15]The land will no
longer have to listen to the nations making
fun of it or see the peoples sneer at it. The
land will no longer rob the nation of its chil-
dren. I, the Sovereign LORD, have spoken."

Israel's New Life

[16]The LORD spoke to me. [17]"Mortal
man," he said, "when the Israelites were liv-
ing in their land, they defiled it by the way
they lived and acted. I regarded their behav-
ior as being as ritually unclean as a woman is
during her monthly period.[c] [18]I let them
feel the force of my anger because of the
murders they had committed in the land and
because of the idols by which they had
defiled it. [19]I condemned them for the way
they lived and acted, and I scattered them
through foreign countries. [20]Wherever they
went, they brought disgrace on my holy
name, because people would say, 'These are
the people of the LORD, but they had to
leave his land.' [21]That made me concerned
for my holy name, since the Israelites
brought disgrace on it everywhere they
went.

[22]"Now then, give the Israelites the mes-
sage that I, the Sovereign LORD, have for
them: What I am going to do is not for the
sake of you Israelites, but for the sake of my
holy name, which you have disgraced in
every country where you have gone. [23]When
I demonstrate to the nations the holiness of
my great name—the name you disgraced
among them—then they will know that I am
the LORD. I, the Sovereign LORD, have spo-
ken. I will use you to show the nations that I
am holy. [24]I will take you from every nation
and country and bring you back to your own
land. [25]I will sprinkle clean water on you and
make you clean from all your idols and
everything else that has defiled you. [26]I will
give you a new heart and a new mind. I will
take away your stubborn heart of stone and
give you an obedient heart. [27]I will put my
spirit in you and will see to it that you follow
my laws and keep all the commands I have
given you. [28]Then you will live in the land I
gave your ancestors. You will be my people,
and I will be your God. [29]I will save you
from everything that defiles you. I will com-
mand the grain to be plentiful, so that you
will not have any more famines. [30]I will
increase the yield of your fruit trees and your
fields, so that there will be no more famines
to disgrace you among the nations. [31]You
will remember your evil conduct and the
wrongs that you committed, and you will be
disgusted with yourselves because of your
sins and your iniquities. [32]Israel, I want you
to know that I am not doing all this for your
sake. I want you to feel the shame and dis-
grace of what you are doing. I, the Sovereign
LORD, have spoken."

[33]The Sovereign LORD says, "When I
make you clean from all your sins, I will let
you live in your cities again and let you
rebuild the ruins. [34]Everyone who used to
walk by your fields saw how overgrown and
wild they were, but I will let you farm them
again. [35]Everyone will talk about how this
land, which was once a wilderness, has
become like the Garden of Eden, and how

[c] **36:17** RITUALLY UNCLEAN . . . PERIOD: *This is based on the view of ritual uncleanness described in the Law of Moses (see Lev 15:19).*

36:26–28 Ezek 11:19, 20

Pray it!

Praying with New Life

The beginning of Ezekiel's dream sounds like a scene from a horror movie. The ground is covered with dry bones. He has a conversation with God. All of a sudden he hears rattling. He can't quite believe what he's seeing! The bones are forming into bodies! They're being covered with muscles and skin! Then Ezekiel commands the wind (which represents the Holy Spirit) to blow in the name of God. The bodies start to move. They're alive! But it isn't frightening; it is exciting and hopeful.

Our prayer life can sometimes be like dry bones. Have you ever experienced any of the following three situations?

- **You said prayers without thinking about their meaning.**
- **You've gone to Mass but didn't participate.**
- **You talked to God but didn't listen.**

If you said yes, you've experienced a "dry bones" prayer life. Remember what turned a stack of lifeless bones into live bodies: the word of God and the Holy Spirit. When you feel like your prayer life needs new life, listen to God's word and pray to the Holy Spirit to breathe into your heart.

— Ezekiel, chapter 37

the cities which were torn down, looted, and
left in ruins, are now inhabited and fortified.
36 Then the neighboring nations that have
survived will know that I, the LORD, rebuild
ruined cities and replant waste fields. I, the
LORD, have promised that I would do this—
and I will."
37 The Sovereign LORD says, "I will once
again let the Israelites ask me for help, and I
will let them increase in numbers like a flock
of sheep. 38 The cities that are now in ruins
will then be as full of people as Jerusalem
was once full of the sheep which were
offered as sacrifices at a festival. Then they
will know that I am the LORD."

The Valley of Dry Bones

37 I felt the powerful presence of the
LORD, and his spirit took me and set
me down in a valley where the ground was
covered with bones. 2 He led me all around
the valley, and I could see that there were
very many bones and that they were very
dry. 3 He said to me, "Mortal man, can these
bones come back to life?"
I replied, "Sovereign LORD, only you can
answer that!"
4 He said, "Prophesy to the bones. Tell
these dry bones to listen to the word of the
LORD. 5 Tell them that I, the Sovereign
LORD, am saying to them: I am going to put
breath into you and bring you back to life. 6 I
will give you sinews and muscles, and cover
you with skin. I will put breath into you and

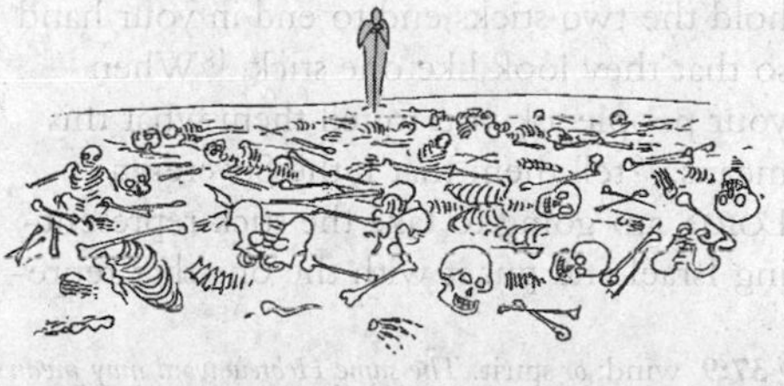

I could see that there were very many bones. (37:2)

"I will take away your stubborn heart of stone and give you an obedient heart" *(Ezekiel 36:26).*

bring you back to life. Then you will know that I am the LORD."

7So I prophesied as I had been told. While I was speaking, I heard a rattling noise, and the bones began to join together. 8While I watched, the bones were covered with sinews and muscles, and then with skin. But there was no breath in the bodies.

9God said to me, "Mortal man, prophesy to the wind.[d] Tell the wind that the Sovereign LORD commands it to come from every direction, to breathe into these dead bodies, and to bring them back to life."

10So I prophesied as I had been told. Breath entered the bodies, and they came to life and stood up. There were enough of them to form an army.

11God said to me, "Mortal man, the people of Israel are like these bones. They say that they are dried up, without any hope and with no future. 12So prophesy to my people Israel and tell them that I, the Sovereign LORD, am going to open their graves. I am going to take them out and bring them back to the land of Israel. 13When I open the graves where my people are buried and bring them out, they will know that I am the LORD. 14I will put my breath in them, bring them back to life, and let them live in their own land. Then they will know that I am the LORD. I have promised that I would do this—and I will. I, the LORD, have spoken."

Judah and Israel in One Kingdom

15The LORD spoke to me again. 16"Mortal man," he said, "take a wooden stick and write on it the words, 'The kingdom of Judah.' Then take another stick and write on it the words, 'The kingdom of Israel.' 17Then hold the two sticks end to end in your hand so that they look like one stick. 18When your people ask you to tell them what this means, 19tell them that I, the Sovereign LORD, am going to take the stick representing Israel and put it with the one that represents Judah. Out of the two I will make one stick and hold it in my hand.

20"Hold in your hand the two sticks and let the people see them. 21Then tell them that I, the Sovereign LORD, am going to take all my people out of the nations where they have gone, gather them together, and bring them back to their own land. 22I will unite them into one nation in the land, on the mountains of Israel. They will have one king to rule over them, and they will no longer be divided into two nations or split into two kingdoms. 23They will not defile themselves with disgusting idols any more or corrupt themselves with sin. I will free them from all the ways in which they sin and betray me. I will purify them; they will be my people, and I will be their God. 24A king like my servant David will be their king. They will all be united under one ruler and will obey my laws faithfully. 25They will live on the land I gave to my servant Jacob, the land where their ancestors lived. They will live there forever, and so will their children and all their descendants. A king like my servant David will rule them forever. 26I will make a covenant with them that guarantees their security forever. I will establish them and increase their population, and will see to it that my Temple stands forever in their land. 27I will live there with them; I will be their God, and they will be my people. 28When I place my Temple there to be among them forever, then the nations will know that I, the LORD, have chosen Israel to be my own people."

Gog as the Instrument of God

38 The LORD spoke to me. 2"Mortal man," he said, "denounce Gog, chief ruler of the nations of Meshech and Tubal in the land of Magog. Denounce him 3and tell him that I, the Sovereign LORD, am his enemy. 4I will turn him around, put hooks in his jaws, and drag him and all his troops

[d] **37:9** wind; *or* spirit. *The same Hebrew word may mean* wind, *or* spirit, *or* breath.

37:10 Rev 11:11 **37:24** Ezek 34:24 **37:27** 2 Cor 6:16; Rev 21:3 **38:2** Rev 20:8

In English, the words *wind, breath,* and *spirit* each have a different meaning. In Hebrew one word, *ruah,* is used to mean all three things.

away. His army, with its horses and uni-
formed riders, is enormous, and every sol-
dier carries a shield and is armed with a
sword. [5]Troops from Persia, Ethiopia,[e] and
Libya are with him, and all have shields and
helmets. [6]All the fighting men of the lands
of Gomer and Beth Togarmah in the north
are with him, and so are men from many
other nations. [7]Tell him to get ready and
have all his troops ready at his command.
[8]After many years I will order him to invade
a country where the people were brought
back together from many nations and have
lived without fear of war. He will invade the
mountains of Israel, which were desolate and
deserted so long, but where all the people
now live in safety. [9]He and his army and the
many nations with him will attack like a
storm and cover the land like a cloud."

10This is what the Sovereign LORD says to
Gog: "When that time comes, you will start
thinking up an evil plan. [11]You will decide
to invade a helpless country where the peo-
ple live in peace and security in unwalled
towns that have no defenses. [12]You will
plunder and loot the people who live in
cities that were once in ruins. They have
been gathered from the nations, and now
they have livestock and property and live at
the crossroads of the world. [13]The people of
Sheba and Dedan and the merchants from
the towns of Spain will ask you, 'Have you
assembled your army and attacked in order
to loot and plunder? Do you intend to get
silver and gold, livestock and property, and
march off with all those spoils?' "

14So the Sovereign LORD sent me to tell
Gog what he was saying to him: "Now
while my people Israel live in security, you
will set out[f] [15]to come from your place in
the far north, leading a large, powerful army
of soldiers from many nations, all of them on
horseback. [16]You will attack my people
Israel like a storm moving across the land.
When the time comes, I will send you to
invade my land in order to show the nations
who I am, to show my holiness by what I do
through you. [17]You are the one I was talking
about long ago, when I announced through
my servants, the prophets of Israel, that in
days to come I would bring someone to
attack Israel." The Sovereign LORD has spo-
ken.

God's Punishment of Gog

18The Sovereign LORD says, "On the day
when Gog invades Israel, I will become furi-
ous. [19]I declare in the heat of my anger that
on that day there will be a severe earthquake
in the land of Israel. [20]Every fish and bird,
every animal large and small, and every
human being on the face of the earth will
tremble for fear of me. Mountains will fall,
cliffs will crumble, and every wall will col-
lapse. [21]I will terrify Gog with all sorts of
calamities.[g] I, the Sovereign LORD, have spo-
ken. His men will turn their swords against
one another. [22]I will punish him with disease
and bloodshed. Torrents of rain and hail,
together with fire and sulfur, will pour down
on him and his army and on the many
nations that are on his side. [23]In this way I
will show all the nations that I am great and
that I am holy. They will know then that I
am the LORD."

The Defeat of Gog

39 The Sovereign LORD said, "Mortal
man, denounce Gog, the chief ruler
of the nations of Meshech and Tubal, and tell
him that I am his enemy. [2]I will turn him in
a new direction and lead him out of the far
north until he comes to the mountains of
Israel. [3]Then I will knock his bow out of his
left hand and his arrows out of his right
hand. [4]Gog and his army and his allies will
fall dead on the mountains of Israel, and I
will let their bodies be food for all the birds
and wild animals. [5]They will fall dead in the
open field. I, the Sovereign LORD, have spo-
ken. [6]I will start a fire in the land of Magog
and along all the seacoasts where people live
undisturbed, and everyone will know that I
am the LORD. [7]I will make sure that my

[e] **38:5** *Hebrew* Cush: *Cush is the ancient name of the extensive territory south of the First Cataract of the Nile River. This region was called Ethiopia in Graeco-Roman times, and included within its borders most of modern Sudan and some of present-day Ethiopia (Abyssinia).* [f] **38:14** *One ancient translation* set out; *Hebrew* know. [g] **38:21** *One ancient translation* terrify . . . calamities; *Hebrew unclear.*

people Israel know my holy name, and I will
not let my name be disgraced any more.
Then the nations will know that I, the
LORD, am the holy God of Israel."
8The Sovereign LORD said, "The day I
spoke about is certain to come. 9The people
who live in the cities of Israel will go out
and collect the abandoned weapons for fire-
wood. They will build fires with the shields,
bows, arrows, spears, and clubs, and have
enough to last for seven years. 10They will
not have to gather firewood in the fields or
cut down trees in the forest, because they
will have the abandoned weapons to burn.
They will loot and plunder those who loot-
ed and plundered them." The Sovereign
LORD has spoken.

The Burial of Gog

11The LORD said, "When all this happens,
I will give Gog a burial ground there in
Israel, in Travelers' Valley, east of the Dead
Sea.[h] Gog and all his army will be buried
there, and the valley will be called 'The
Valley of Gog's Army.' 12It will take the
Israelites seven months to bury all the
corpses and make the land clean again.
13Everyone in the land will help bury them,
and they will be honored for this on the day
of my victory. I, the Sovereign LORD, have
spoken. 14After the seven months are over,
men will be chosen to travel through the
land in order to find and bury those bodies[i]
remaining on the ground, so that they can
make the land clean. 15As they go up and
down the country, every time they find a
human bone, they will put a marker beside
it so that the gravediggers can come and
bury it in the Valley of Gog's Army. 16(There
will be a town nearby named after the
army.) And so the land will be made clean
again."
17The Sovereign LORD said to me, "Mor-
tal man, call all the birds and animals to
come from all around to eat the sacrifice I
am preparing for them. It will be a huge
feast on the mountains of Israel, where they
can eat meat and drink blood. 18They are to
eat the bodies of soldiers and drink the
blood of the rulers of the earth, all of whom
will be killed like rams or lambs or goats or
fat bulls. 19When I kill these people like sac-
rifices, the birds and animals are to eat all the
fat they can hold and to drink blood until
they are drunk. 20At my table they will eat
all they can hold of horses and their riders
and of soldiers and fighting men. I, the Sov-
ereign LORD, have spoken."

The Restoration of Israel

21The LORD said, "I will let the nations
see my glory and show them how I use my
power to carry out my just decisions. 22The
Israelites will know from then on that I am
the LORD their God. 23And the nations will
know that the Israelites went into exile
because of the sins which they committed
against me. I turned away from them and let
their enemies defeat them and kill them in
battle. 24I gave them what they deserved for
their uncleanness and their wickedness, and I
turned away from them."
25The Sovereign LORD said, "But now I
will be merciful to Jacob's descendants, the
people of Israel, and make them prosperous
again. I will protect my holy name. 26When
they are once more living in safety in their
own land, with no one to threaten them,
they will be able to forget how they were
disgraced for having betrayed me. 27In
order to show to the many nations that I
am holy, I will bring my people back from
all the countries where their enemies live.
28Then my people will know that I am the
LORD their God. They will know this,
because I sent them into captivity and now
gather them and bring them back into their
own land, not leaving even one of them
behind. 29I will pour out my spirit on the
people of Israel and never again turn away
from them. I, the Sovereign LORD, have
spoken."

[h] **39:11** *Hebrew has four additional words, the meaning of which is unclear.* [i] **39:14** *Some ancient translations* those bodies; *Hebrew* the travelers.

39:17–20 Rev 19:17, 18

A VISION OF THE FUTURE TEMPLE (40:1—48:35)

Ezekiel Is Taken to Jerusalem

40 It was the tenth day of the new year, which was the twenty-fifth year after we had been taken into exile and the fourteenth year after Jerusalem was captured. On that day I felt the powerful presence of the LORD, and he carried me away. 2In a vision God took me to the land of Israel and put me on a high mountain. I saw in front of me[j] a group of buildings that looked like a city. 3He took me closer, and I saw a man who shone like bronze. He was holding a linen tape measure and a measuring rod and was standing by a gateway.

He was holding a linen tape measure. (40:3)

4He said to me, "Watch, mortal man. Listen carefully and pay close attention to everything I show you, because this is why you were brought here. You are to tell the people of Israel everything you see."

The East Gate

5What I saw was the Temple, and there was a wall around it. The man took his measuring rod, which was 10 feet long, and measured the wall. It was 10 feet high and 10 feet thick. 6Then he went to the gateway that faced east. He went up the steps, and at the top he measured the entrance; it was 10 feet deep.[k] 7Beyond it there was a passageway, which had three guardrooms on each side. Each of the rooms was square, 10 feet on each side, and the walls between them were 8 feet thick. Beyond the guardrooms there was a passageway 10 feet long that led to an entrance room which faced the Temple. 8-9He measured this room and found it was 14 feet deep. It formed that end of the gateway which was nearest the Temple, and at its far end the walls were 4 feet thick. (10These guardrooms on each side of the passageway were all the same size, and the walls between them were all of the same thickness.)

11Next, the man measured the width of the passageway in the gateway. It was 22 feet altogether, and the space between the open gates was 16 feet. 12In front of each of the guardrooms there was a low wall 20 inches high and 20 inches thick. (The rooms were 10 feet square.) 13Then he measured the distance from the back wall[l] of one room to the back wall[l] of the room across the passageway from it, and it was 42 feet. 14The room at the far end led out to a courtyard. He measured that room and found it was 34 feet wide.[m] 15The total length of the gateway from the outside wall of the gate to the far side of the last room was 84 feet. 16There were small openings in the outside walls of all the rooms and also in the inner walls between the rooms. There were palm trees carved on the inner walls that faced the passageway.

The Outer Courtyard

17The man took me through the gateway into the courtyard. There were thirty rooms built against the outer wall, and in front of

[j] **40:2** *One ancient translation* in front of me; *Hebrew* in the south. [k] **40:6** *One ancient translation* deep; *Hebrew* deep, one entrance 10 feet deep. [l] **40:13** *Probable text* back wall; *Hebrew* roof. [m] **40:14** *Verse 14 in Hebrew is unclear.*

40:2 Rev 21:10 **40:3** Rev 11:1; 21:15 **40:5—42:20** 1 Kings 6:1–38; 2 Chr 3:1–9

No one is really sure who or what Gog of Magog is. It may be King Nebuchadnezzar, or it may just refer to evil and chaos.

them there was an area paved with stones,
[18]which extended around the courtyard. This outer courtyard was at a lower level than the inner courtyard.

[19]There was a gateway at a higher level that led to the inner courtyard. The man measured the distance between the two gateways, and it was 168 feet.[n]

The North Gate

[20]Then the man measured the gateway on the north side that led into the outer court-
yard. [21]The three guardrooms on each side of the passageway, the walls between them, and the entrance room all had the same measurements as those in the east gateway. The total length of the gateway was 84 feet
and the width 42 feet. [22]The entrance room, the windows, and the carved palm trees were like those in the east gate. Here seven steps led up to the gate, and the entrance room
was at the end facing the courtyard. [23]Across the courtyard from this north gateway was another gateway leading to the inner courtyard, just as there was on the east side. The man measured the distance between these two gateways, and it was 168 feet.

The South Gate

[24]Next, the man took me to the south side, and there we saw another gateway. He measured its inner walls and its entrance room, and they were the same as the others.
[25]There were windows in the rooms of this gateway just as in the others. The total length of the gateway was 84 feet and the width 42
feet. [26]Seven steps led up to it, and its entrance room was also at the end facing the courtyard. There were palm trees carved on the inner walls that faced the passageway.
[27]Here, too, there was a gateway leading to the inner courtyard. The man measured the distance to this second gateway, and it was 168 feet.

The Inner Courtyard: The South Gate

[28]The man took me through the south gateway into the inner courtyard. He measured the gateway, and it was the same size as the gateways in the outer wall. [29-30]Its guard-
rooms, its entrance room, and its inner walls were the same size as those in the other gateways. There were also windows in the rooms of this gateway. The total length was 84 feet and the width 42 feet. [31]Its entrance
room faced the other courtyard, and palm trees were carved on the walls along the passageway. Eight steps led up to this gate.

The Inner Courtyard: The East Gate

[32]The man took me through the east gateway into the inner courtyard. He measured the gateway, and it was the same size as the others. [33]Its guardrooms, its entrance room, and its inner walls measured the same as those in the other gateways. There were windows all around, and in the entrance room also. The total length was 84 feet and
the width 42 feet. [34]The entrance room faced the outer courtyard. Palm trees were carved on the walls along the passageway. Eight steps led up to this gate.

The Inner Courtyard: The North Gate

[35]Then the man took me to the north gateway. He measured it, and it was the same
size as the others. [36]Like them, it also had guardrooms, decorated inner walls, an entrance room, and windows all around. Its total length
was 84 feet and its width 42 feet. [37]The
entrance room[o] faced the outer courtyard. Palm trees were carved on the walls along the passageway. Eight steps led up to this gate.

Buildings Near the North Gate

[38]In the outer courtyard there was an annex attached to the inner gateway on the

[n] **40:19** *Hebrew has two additional words, the meaning of which is unclear.* [o] **40:37** *Some ancient translations* entrance room; *Hebrew* inner wall.

Check out 1 Corinthians 3:16–17 for Saint Paul's description of the Church as the Temple of the Holy Spirit.

north side. It opened into the entrance room
that faced the courtyard, and there they
washed the carcasses of the animals to be
burned whole as sacrifices. 39 In this entrance
room there were four tables, two on each
side of the room. It was on these tables that
they killed the animals to be offered as sacri-
fices, either to be burned whole or to be
sacrifices for sin or as repayment offerings.
40 Outside the room there were four similar
tables, two on either side of the entrance of
the north gate. 41 Altogether there were eight
tables on which the animals to be sacrificed
were killed: four inside the room and four
out in the courtyard. 42 The four tables in the
annex, used to prepare the offerings to be
burned whole, were of cut stone. They were
20 inches high, and their tops were 30 inch-
es square. All the equipment used in killing
the sacrificial animals was kept on these
tables. 43 Ledges 3 inches wide ran around
the edge of the tables. All the meat to be
offered in sacrifice was placed on the tables.[p]

44 Then he brought me into the inner
court. There were two rooms opening on the
inner court, one facing south beside the north
gateway and the other facing north beside the
south gateway.[q] 45 The man told me that the
room which faced south was for the priests
who served in the Temple, 46 and the room
which faced north was for the priests who
served at the altar. All the priests are descend-
ed from Zadok; they are the only members of
the tribe of Levi who are permitted to go
into the LORD's presence to serve him.

The Inner Courtyard and the Temple Building

47 The man measured the inner courtyard,
and it was 168 feet square. The Temple was on
the west side, and in front of it was an altar.
48 Then he took me into the entrance room
of the Temple. He measured the entranceway:
it was 9 feet deep and 24 feet wide,[r] with
walls 5 feet thick on either side. 49 Steps led
up to the entrance room, which was 34 feet
wide and 20 feet deep.[s] There were two
columns, one on each side of the entrance.

41 Next, the man took me into the
central room, the Holy Place. He
measured the passageway into it: it was 10
feet deep[t] 2 and 18 feet wide, with walls 8
feet thick on either side. He measured the
room itself: it was 68 feet long and 34 feet
wide.

3 Then he went to the innermost room.
He measured the passageway into it: it was 3
feet deep and 10 feet wide, with walls on
either side 12 feet thick.[u] 4 He measured the
room itself, and it was 34 feet square. This
room was beyond the central room. Then he
said to me, "This is the Most Holy Place."

The Rooms Built against the Temple Walls

5 The man measured the thickness of the
inner wall of the Temple building, and it was
10 feet. Against this wall, all around the Tem-
ple, was a series of small rooms 7 feet wide.
6 These rooms were in three stories, with
thirty rooms on each floor. The Temple's
outer wall on each floor was thinner than on
the floor below, so that the rooms could rest
on the wall without being anchored into it.
7 And so the Temple walls, when seen from
the outside, seemed to have the same thick-
ness all the way to the top. Against the Tem-
ple's outer wall, on the outside of the rooms,
two wide stairways were built, so that it was
possible to go from the lower story to the
middle and the upper stories.[v] 8-11 The out-
side wall of these rooms was 8 feet thick;
there was one door into the rooms on the
north side of the Temple, and one into those
on the south side. I saw that there was a ter-
race 8 feet wide around the Temple; it was
10 feet above the ground and it was level
with the foundation of the rooms by the
Temple walls. Between the terrace and the
buildings used by the priests there was an
open space 34 feet across, along the sides of
the Temple.

[p] **40:43** *Verse 43 in Hebrew is unclear.* [q] **40:44** *One ancient translation* Then . . . south gateway; *verse 44 in Hebrew is unclear.* [r] **40:48** *One ancient translation* and 24 feet wide; *Hebrew does not have these words.* [s] **40:49** *One ancient translation* 20 feet deep; *Hebrew* 18 feet deep. [t] **41:1** *Hebrew has two additional words, the meaning of which is unclear.* [u] **41:3** *One ancient translation* with walls on either side 12 feet thick; *Hebrew* and 12 feet thick.
[v] **41:7** *Verse 7 in Hebrew is unclear.*

God, the Builder

Ezekiel's last vision is of a rebuilt Temple in Jerusalem. Chapters 40–42 of Ezekiel are full of measurements, descriptions of areas, and floor plans. Lots of details are included, right down to the palm trees carved on the walls.

The Temple of Jerusalem in Ezekiel's vision was a magnificent place. It was a place where God dwelled again in glory. Ezekiel's vision did come true in the sense that the Temple was rebuilt when King Cyrus allowed the Jews who were in captivity in Babylon to return to Jerusalem.

In the New Testament, Saint Paul calls the Church the Temple of the Holy Spirit. That means that the Holy Spirit lives in all members of the church in a special way. Because of this Catholics do not believe there is only one place where God can be worshiped. Jesus Christ is present with us through the power of the Holy Spirit wherever we gather in God's name.

— Ezekiel 41:15–21

The Building on the West

12 At the far end of the open space on the
west side of the Temple there was a building
150 feet long and 116 feet wide; its walls
were 9 feet thick all around.

The Total Measurements of the Temple Building

13 The man measured the outside of the
Temple, and it was 168 feet long. And from
the back of the Temple, across the open
space to the far side of the building to the
west, the distance was also 168 feet.
14 The
distance across the front of the Temple,
including the open space on either side, was
also 168 feet.
15 He measured the length of
the building to the west, including its gal-
leries on both sides, and it was also 168
feet.

Details of the Temple Building

The entrance room of the Temple, the
Holy Place, and the Most Holy Place
16 were
all paneled with wood from the floor to
the windows. These windows could be
covered.[w]
17 The inside walls of the Temple,
up as high as above the doors, were com-
pletely covered with carvings[x]
18 of palm
trees and winged creatures. Palm trees alter-
nated with creatures, one following the
other, all the way around the room. Each
creature had two faces:
19 a human face that
was turned toward the palm tree on one
side, and a lion's face that was turned toward
the tree on the other side. It was like this all
around the wall,
20 from the floor to above
the doors.
21 The doorposts of the Holy
Place were square.

The Wooden Altar

In front of the entrance of the Most Holy
Place there was something that looked like
22 a wooden altar. It was 5 feet high and 4
feet wide. Its corner posts, its base,[y] and its
sides were all made of wood. The man said
to me, "This is the table which stands in the
presence of the LORD."

[w] **41:16** *Verse 16 in Hebrew is unclear.* [x] **41:17** *Verse 17 in Hebrew is unclear.* [y] **41:22** *Some ancient translations* base; *Hebrew* length.

The Doors

23 There was a door at the end of the pas-
sageway to the Holy Place and one also at
the end of the passageway to the Most Holy
Place. 24 They were double doors that swung
open in the middle. 25 There were palm trees
and winged creatures carved on the doors of
the Holy Place, just as there were on the
walls. And there was a wooden covering over
the outside of the doorway of the entrance
room. 26 At the sides of this room there were
windows, and the walls were decorated with
palm trees.[z]

Two Buildings Near the Temple

42 Then the man took me into the
outer courtyard and led me to a
building on the north side of the Temple, not
far from the building at the west end of the
Temple. 2 This building was 168 feet long and
84 feet wide. 3 On one side it faced the space
34 feet wide which was alongside the Temple,
and on the other side it faced the pavement
of the outer courtyard. It was built on three
levels, each one set further back than the one
below it. 4 Along the north side of this build-
ing was a passageway 16 feet wide and 168
feet long,[a] with entrances on that side. 5 The
rooms at the upper level of the building were
narrower than those at the middle and lower
levels because they were set further back.
6 The rooms at all three levels were on ter-
races and were not supported by columns like
the other buildings in the courtyard. 7-8 At the
lower level the outer wall of the building was
solid for 84 feet, half its length; and there
were rooms in the remaining 84 feet. At the
top level there were rooms in the entire
length of the building. 9-10 Below these rooms
at the east end of the building, where the wall
of the courtyard began,[b] there was an
entrance into the outer courtyard.

At the south[c] side of the Temple there was
an identical building not far from the build-
ing at the west end of the Temple. 11 In front
of the rooms there was a passageway just like
the one on the north side. It had the same
measurements, the same design, and the same
kind of entrances. 12 There was a door under
the rooms on the south side of the building,
at the east end where the wall began.

13 The man said to me, "Both these build-
ings are holy. In them the priests who enter
the LORD's presence eat the holiest offerings.
Because the rooms are holy, the priests will
place the holiest offerings there: the offerings
of grain and the sacrifices offered for sin or
as repayment offerings. 14 When priests have
been in the Temple and want to go to the
outer courtyard, they must leave in these
rooms the holy clothing they wore while
serving the LORD. They must put on other
clothes before going out to the area where
the people gather."

The Measurements of the Temple Area

15 When the man had finished measuring
inside the Temple area, he took me out
through the east gate and then measured the
outside of the area. 16 He took the measuring
rod and measured the east side, and it was
840 feet. 17-19 Then he measured the north
side, the south side, and the west side; each
side had the same length, 840 feet,[d] 20 so that
the wall enclosed a square 840 feet on each
side. The wall served to separate what was
holy from what was not.

The LORD Returns to the Temple

43 The man took me to the gate that
faces east, 2 and there I saw coming
from the east the dazzling light of the pres-
ence of the God of Israel. God's voice

[z] **41:26** *Hebrew has three additional words, the meaning of which is unclear.* [a] **41:4** *Some ancient translations* 168 feet long; *Hebrew* a way of 20 inches. [b] **41:9–10** *One ancient translation* where the wall of the courtyard began; *Hebrew* in the breadth of the wall of the courtyard. [c] **41:9–10** *One ancient translation* south; *Hebrew* east.
[d] **41:17–19** *Verses 16–19 in Hebrew are unclear.*
43:2 Ezek 10:3, 4, 18, 19; 11:22, 23; Rev 1:15

Each wall of the Temple area was 840 feet long. That would make each wall how many football fields long? That is a big area!

sounded like the roar of the sea, and the
earth shone with the dazzling light. 3This
vision was like the one I had seen when
God came to destroy Jerusalem, and the one
I saw by the Chebar River. Then I threw
myself face downward on the ground. 4The
dazzling light passed through the east gate
and went into the Temple.

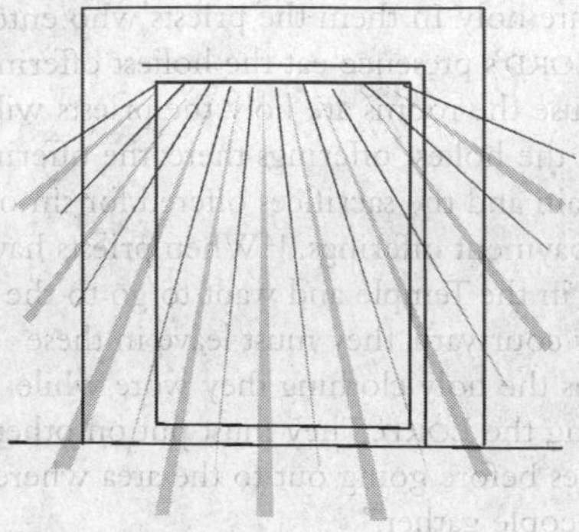

The dazzling light passed through the east gate. (43:4)

5The LORD's spirit lifted me up and took
me into the inner courtyard, where I saw
that the Temple was filled with the glory of
the LORD. 6The man stood beside me there,
and I heard the LORD speak to me out of
the Temple: 7"Mortal man, here is my
throne. I will live here among the people of
Israel and rule them forever. Neither the
people of Israel nor their kings will ever
again disgrace my holy name by worshiping
other gods or by burying the corpses of[e]
their dead kings. 8The kings built the door-
sills and doorposts of their palace right
against the doorsills and doorposts of my
Temple, so that there was only a wall
between us. They disgraced my holy name
by all the disgusting things they did, and so
in my anger I destroyed them. 9Now they
must stop worshiping other gods and remove
the corpses of[f] their kings. If they do, I will
live among them forever."

10And the LORD continued, "Mortal man,
tell the people of Israel about the Temple,
and let them study its plan. Make them
ashamed of their sinful actions. 11Then if
they are ashamed of what they have done,
explain the plan of the Temple to them: its
design, its entrances and exits, its shape, the
arrangement of everything, and all its rules
and regulations. Write all this down for them
so that they can see how everything is
arranged and can carry out all the rules.
12This is the law of the Temple: All the area
surrounding it on the top of the mountain is
sacred and holy."

The Altar

13These are the measurements of the altar,
using the same unit of measure as in measur-
ing the Temple. All around the base of the
altar there was a gutter 20 inches deep and
20 inches wide, with a rim at the outside
edge 10 inches high. 14The lowest section of
the altar, from the top of the base, was 4 feet
high. The next section was set back from the
edge 20 inches all around, and was 7 feet
high. The section after that was also set back
from the edge 20 inches all around. 15This
top section, on which the sacrifices were
burned, was also 7 feet high. The projections
on the four corners were higher than the
rest of the top. 16The top of the altar was a
square, 20 feet on each side. 17The middle
section was also a square, 24 feet on each
side, with a rim at the outside edge 10 inch-
es high. (The gutter was 20 inches wide.)
The steps going up the altar were on the east
side.

The Consecration of the Altar

18The Sovereign LORD said to me, "Mor-
tal man, listen to what I tell you. When the
altar is built, you are to dedicate it by burn-

[e] **43:7** by burying the corpses of; *or* by putting up monuments to. [f] **43:9** remove the corpses of; *or* remove the monuments to.

43:13–17 Ex 27:1, 2; 2 Chr 4:1 **43:18–27** Ex 29:35–37; 1 Macc 4:52–56

The east gate of the Temple was to stay closed, a sign that God would never leave the Israelites again *(Ezekiel 44:1–2).*

ing sacrifices on it and by sprinkling on it the blood of the animals that were sacrificed. 19 Those priests belonging to the tribe of Levi who are descended from Zadok are the only ones who are to come into my presence to serve me. I, the Sovereign LORD, command this. You will give them a young bull to offer as a sacrifice for sin. 20 You are to take some of its blood and put it on the projections on the top corners of the altar, on the corners of the middle section of the altar, and all around its edges. In this way you will purify the altar and consecrate it. 21 You are to take the bull that is offered as a sacrifice for sin and burn it at the specified place outside the Temple area. 22 The next day you are to take a male goat without any defects and offer it as a sacrifice for sin. Purify the altar with its blood the same way you did with the bull. 23 When you have finished doing that, take a young bull and a young ram, both of them without any defects, 24 and bring them to me. The priests will sprinkle salt on them and burn them as an offering to me. 25 Each day for seven days you are to offer a goat, a bull, and a ram as sacrifices for sin. All of them must be without any defects. 26 For seven days the priests are to consecrate the altar and make it ready for use. 27 When the week is over, the priests are to begin offering on the altar the burnt offerings and the fellowship offerings of the people. Then I will be pleased with all of you. I, the Sovereign LORD, have spoken."

The Use of the East Gate

44 The man led me to the outer gate at the east side of the Temple area. The gate was closed, 2 and the LORD said to me, "This gate will stay closed and will never be opened. No human being is allowed to use it, because I, the LORD God of Israel, have entered through it. It is to remain closed. 3 The ruling prince, however, may go there to eat a holy meal in my presence. He is to enter and leave the gateway through the entrance room at the inner end."

Rules for Admission to the Temple

4 Then the man took me through the north gate to the front of the Temple. As I looked, I saw that the Temple of the LORD was filled with the dazzling light of his presence. I threw myself face downward on the ground, 5 and the LORD said to me, "Mortal man, pay attention to everything you see and hear. I am going to tell you the rules and regulations for the Temple. Note carefully which persons are allowed to go in and out of the Temple, and which persons are not allowed.

6 "Tell those rebellious people of Israel that I, the Sovereign LORD, will no longer tolerate the disgusting things that they have been doing. 7 They have profaned my Temple by letting uncircumcised foreigners, people who do not obey me, enter the Temple when the fat and the blood of the sacrifices are being offered to me. So my people have broken my covenant by all the disgusting things they have done. 8 They have not taken charge of the sacred rituals in my Temple, but instead have put foreigners in charge.

9 "I, the Sovereign LORD, declare that no uncircumcised foreigner, no one who disobeys me, will enter my Temple, not even a foreigner who lives among the people of Israel."

The Levites Are Excluded from the Priesthood

10 The LORD said to me, "I am punishing those Levites who, together with the rest of the people of Israel, deserted me and worshiped idols. 11 They may serve me in the Temple by taking charge of the gates and by performing the work of the Temple. They may kill the animals which the people offer for burnt offerings and for sacrifices, and they are to be on duty to serve the people. 12 But because they conducted the worship of idols for the people of Israel and in this way led the people into sin, I, the Sovereign LORD, solemnly swear that they must be punished. 13 They are not to serve me as priests or to go near anything that is holy to me or to enter the Most Holy Place. This is the punishment for the disgusting things they have done. 14 I

am assigning to them the menial work that is
to be done in the Temple."

The Priests

15 The Sovereign LORD said, "Those
priests belonging to the tribe of Levi who
are descended from Zadok, however, contin-
ued to serve me faithfully in the Temple
when the rest of the people of Israel turned
away from me. So now they are the ones
who are to serve me and come into my
presence to offer me the fat and the blood of
the sacrifices. 16 They alone will enter my
Temple, serve at my altar, and conduct the
Temple worship. 17 When they enter the
gateway to the inner courtyard of the Tem-
ple, they are to put on linen clothing. They
must not wear anything made of wool when
they are on duty in the inner courtyard or in
the Temple. 18 So that they won't perspire,
they are to wear linen turbans and linen
trousers, but no belt. 19 Before they go to the
outer courtyard where the people are, they
must first take off the clothes they wore on
duty in the Temple and leave them in the
holy rooms. They are to put on other cloth-
ing in order to keep their sacred clothing
from harming the people.[g]

20 "Priests must neither shave their heads
nor let their hair grow long. They are to
keep it a proper length. 21 Priests must not
drink any wine before going into the inner
courtyard. 22 No priest may marry a divorced
woman; he is to marry only an Israelite vir-
gin or the widow of another priest.

23 "The priests are to teach my people the
difference between what is holy and what is
not, and between what is ritually clean and
what is not. 24 When a legal dispute arises,
the priests are to decide the case according
to my laws. They are to keep the religious
festivals according to my rules and regula-
tions, and they are to keep the Sabbaths holy.

25 "A priest is not to become ritually
unclean by touching a corpse, unless it is one
of his parents, one of his children or a broth-
er or an unmarried sister. 26 After he has
become clean again, he must wait seven days
27 and then go into the inner courtyard of
the Temple and offer a sacrifice for his
purification, so that he can serve in the Tem-
ple again. I, the Sovereign LORD, have spo-
ken.

28 "The priests have the priesthood as their
share of what I have given Israel to be hand-
ed down from one generation to another.
They are not to hold property in Israel; I am
all they need. 29 The grain offerings, the sin
offerings, and the repayment offerings will
be the priests' food, and they are to receive
everything in Israel that is set apart for me.
30 The priests are to have the best of all the
first harvest and of everything else that is
offered to me. Each time the people bake
bread, they are to give the priests the first
loaf as an offering, and my blessing will rest
on their homes. 31 The priests must not eat
any bird or animal that dies a natural death
or is killed by another animal."

The LORD's Portion of the Country

45 When the land is divided to give
each tribe a share, one part is to be
dedicated to the LORD. It is to be 10 miles
long by 8 miles[h] wide. The entire area will
be holy. 2 In this area there is to be a square
plot of land for the Temple, 840 feet on each
side, entirely surrounded by an open space
84 feet wide. 3 Half of this area, a section 10
miles by 4 miles, is to be measured off; it will
contain the Temple, the holiest place of all.
4 It will be a holy part of the country, set
aside for the priests who serve the LORD in
his Temple. It will contain their houses and
the section of land for the Temple. 5 The
other half of the area is to be set aside as the
possession of the Levites, who do the work
in the Temple. There will be towns there for
them to live in.[i]

6 Next to the holy area, another section,

[g] **44:19** HARMING THE PEOPLE: *It was believed that ordinary people would be harmed by touching something holy.*
[h] **45:1** *One ancient translation* 8 miles; *Hebrew* 4 miles. [i] **45:5** *One ancient translation* towns there for them to live in; *Hebrew* twenty rooms.

44:17, 18 Ex 28:39–43; Lev 16:4 **44:19** Lev 16:23 **44:20** Lev 21:5 **44:21** Lev 10:9 **44:22** Lev 21:7, 13, 14 **44:23** Lev 10:10 **44:25** Lev 21:1–4 **44:28** Num 18:20 **44:29, 30** Num 18:8–19 **44:31** Lev 22:8

10 miles long and 2 miles wide, is to be set
aside for a city where any of the people of
Israel may live.

Land for the Prince

7 Land is also to be set aside for the ruling
prince. From the west boundary of the holy
area it will extend west to the Mediter-
ranean Sea; and from the east boundary it
will extend to the eastern border of the
country, so that its length will be the same as
the length of one of the areas allotted to the
tribes of Israel. 8 This area will be the share
the ruling prince will have in the land of
Israel, so that he will no longer oppress the
people, but will let the rest of the country
belong to the tribes of Israel.

Rules for the Prince

9 The Sovereign LORD said, "You have
sinned too long, you rulers of Israel! Stop
your violence and oppression. Do what is
right and just. You must never again drive
my people off their land. I, the Sovereign
LORD, am telling you this.
10 "Everyone must use honest weights and
measures:
11 "The *ephah* for dry measure is to be
equal to the *bath* for liquid measure. The
standard is the *homer.*[j] The resulting measures
are as follows:

1 *homer* = 10 *ephahs* = 10 *baths*

12 "Your weights are to be as follows:

20 *gerahs* = 1 *shekel*[k]

60 *shekels* = 1 *mina*

13-15 "This is the basis on which you are to
make your offerings:

Wheat: 1/60th of your harvest

Barley: 1/60th of your harvest

Olive oil: 1/100th of the yield of your trees
(Measure it by the *bath:* 10 *baths* = 1 *homer* = 1 *kor.*)

Sheep: 1 sheep out of every 200 from the meadows of Israel

"You are to bring grain offerings, animals
to be burned whole, and animals for fellow-
ship offerings, so that your sins will be for-
given. I, the Sovereign LORD, command it.
16 "All the people of the land must take[l]
these offerings to the ruling prince of Israel.
17 It will be his duty to provide the animals
to be burned whole, the grain offerings, and
the wine offerings for the whole nation of
Israel at the New Moon Festivals, the Sab-
baths, and the other festivals. He is to pro-
vide the sin offerings, the grain offerings, the
offerings to be burned whole, and the fel-
lowship offerings, to take away the sins of
the people of Israel."

The Festivals
(Exodus 12:1–20; Leviticus 23:33–43)

18 The Sovereign LORD said, "On the first
day of the first month you are to sacrifice a
bull without any defects and purify the Tem-
ple. 19 The priest will take some of the blood
of this sin offering and put it on the door-
posts of the Temple, on the four corners of
the altar, and on the posts of the gateways to
the inner courtyard. 20 On the seventh day of
the month you are to do the same thing on
behalf of anyone who sins unintentionally or
through ignorance. In this way you will keep
the Temple holy.
21 "On the fourteenth day of the first
month you will begin the celebration of the
Passover Festival. For seven days everyone
will eat bread made without yeast. 22 On the
first day of the festival the ruling prince must
offer a bull as a sacrifice for his sins and for
those of all the people. 23 On each of the
seven days of the festival he is to sacrifice
to the LORD seven bulls and seven rams

[j] **45:11** HOMER: *A unit of dry or liquid measure, about 5 bushels or 175 quarts; so an ephah or a bath would be about 1/2 bushel or 17:5 quarts.* [k] **45:12** SHEKEL: *In Ezekiel's time this unit of weight was about 0:4 ounce or 11:4 grams.*
[l] **45:16** *Probable text* must take; *Hebrew unclear.*
45:10 Lev 19:36 **45:21** Ex 12:1–20; Num 28:16–25

Chapter 23 in the Book of Leviticus also describes many Jewish feasts and festivals.

Catholic Connections

Holy Days

The Jews honored God through special festivals in the Temple. Some of these feasts are described in Ezekiel 45:18–25, including the offering for each event. As Catholics, we also honor God through special feasts of the Church called *holy days of obligation.* We are required to go to Mass on these days just as we do on Sunday. Some holy days, like Easter, always fall on a Sunday. The bishop in your diocese may decide to move a holy day to a Sunday or sometimes excuse people from attending Mass on a particular holy day. Generally, we observe six holy days of obligation during the Church year.

- **December 25: Christmas**
- **January 1: Solemnity of the Blessed Virgin Mary, the Mother of God**
- **Sixth Thursday after Easter: Ascension of the Lord**
- **August 15: Assumption of the Blessed Virgin Mary**
- **November 1: All Saints' Day**
- **December 8: Immaculate Conception of the Blessed Virgin Mary**

— Ezekiel 45:18–26

without any defects and burn them whole.
He is also to sacrifice a male goat each day
as a sin offering. 24For each bull and each
ram that is sacrificed, there is to be an offer-
ing of half a bushel of grain and three quarts
of olive oil.
25"For the Festival of Shelters, which
begins on the fifteenth day of the seventh
month, the prince will offer on each of the
seven days the same sacrifice for sin, the
same offerings to be burned whole, and the
same offerings of grain and olive oil."

The Prince and the Festivals

46 The Sovereign LORD says, "The east
gateway to the inner courtyard must
be kept closed during the six working days,
but it is to be opened on the Sabbath and at
the New Moon Festival. 2The ruling prince
will go from the outer courtyard into the
entrance room of the gateway and stand
beside the posts of the gate while the priests
burn his sacrifices whole and offer his fellow-
ship offerings. There at the gate he must wor-
ship and then go back out. The gate must not
be shut until evening. 3Each Sabbath and
each New Moon Festival all the people are
also to bow down and worship the LORD in
front of the gate. 4On the Sabbath the prince
is to bring to the LORD, as sacrifices to be
burned whole, six lambs and one ram, all
without any defects. 5With each ram he is to
bring an offering of half a bushel of grain,
and with each lamb he is to bring whatever
he wants to give. For each half-bushel of
grain offering he is to bring three quarts of
olive oil. 6At the New Moon Festival he will
offer a young bull, six lambs, and a ram, all
without any defects. 7With each bull and
each ram the offering is to be half a bushel of
grain, and with each lamb the offering is to

45:25 Lev 23:33–36; Num 29:12–38

Notice that Ezekiel refers to the ruler as a prince. Perhaps he wants to emphasize that God alone is king.

be whatever the prince wants to give. Three
quarts of olive oil are to be offered with each
half-bushel of grain. 8 The prince must leave
the entrance room of the gateway and go out
by the same way he went in.

9 "When the people come to worship the
LORD at any festival, those who enter by the
north gate are to leave by the south gate
after they have worshiped, and those who
enter by the south gate are to leave by the
north gate. No one may go out by the same
way he entered, but must leave by the oppo-
site gate. 10 The prince is to come in when
the people come, and leave when they leave.
11 On the feast days and at the festivals the
grain offering will be half a bushel with each
bull or ram, and whatever the worshiper
wants to give with each lamb. Three quarts
of olive oil are to be offered with each half-
bushel of grain.

12 "When the ruling prince wants to make
a voluntary offering to the LORD, either an
offering to be burned whole or a fellowship
offering, the east gate to the inner courtyard
will be opened for him. He is to make the
offering in the same way he does on the
Sabbath, and the gate is to be closed after he
goes back out."

The Daily Offering

13 The LORD says, "Every morning a one-
year-old lamb without any defects is to be
burned whole as an offering to the LORD.
This offering must be made every day. 14 Also
an offering of five pounds of flour is to be
made every morning, along with one quart
of olive oil for mixing with the flour. The
rules for this offering to the LORD are to be
in force forever. 15 The lamb, the flour, and
the olive oil are to be offered to the LORD
every morning forever."

The Prince and the Land

16 The Sovereign LORD commands: "If the
ruling prince gives any of the land he owns
to one of his sons as a present, it will belong
to that son as a part of his family property.
17 But if the ruling prince gives any of his
land to anyone who is in his service, it will
become the prince's property again when
the Year of Restoration[m] comes. It belongs
to him, and only he and his sons can own it
permanently. 18 The ruling prince must not
take any of the people's property away from
them. Any land he gives to his sons must be
from the land that is assigned to him, so that
he will not oppress any of my people by tak-
ing their land."

The Temple Kitchens

19 Then the man took me to the entrance
of the rooms facing north near the gate on
the south side of the inner courtyard. These
are holy rooms for the priests. He pointed
out a place on the west side of the rooms
20 and said, "This is the place where the
priests are to boil the meat offered as sacri-
fices for sin or as repayment offerings, and to
bake the offerings of flour, so that nothing
holy is carried to the outer courtyard, where
it might harm the people."[n]

21-22 Then he led me to the outer court-
yard and showed me that in each of its four
corners there was a smaller[o] courtyard, 68
feet long and 48 feet wide. 23 Each one had a
stone wall around it, with fireplaces built
against the wall. 24 The man told me, "These
are the kitchens where the Temple servants
are to boil the sacrifices the people offer."

The Stream Flowing from the Temple

47 The man led me back to the
entrance of the Temple. Water was
coming out from under the entrance and
flowing east, the direction the Temple faced.
It was flowing down from under the south
part of the Temple past the south side of the
altar. 2 The man then took me out of the
Temple area by way of the north gate and
led me around to the gate that faces east. A

[m] **46:17** YEAR OF RESTORATION: *Every fifty years, all Israelites were required to give freedom to any Israelites who had become slaves because of debts; they were also to give back to the original owner, or his heirs, any ancestral land that had been sold for debt (see Lev 25:8–55).* [n] **46:20** HARM THE PEOPLE: *See 44:19.* [o] **46:21–22** *One ancient translation* smaller; *Hebrew* enclosed.

46:17 Lev 25:10 **47:1** Zech 14:8; Jn 7:38; Rev 22:1

Pray it!

The Water of Life

The Dead Sea in Israel is so filled with dissolved minerals that nothing can live in it. But in Ezekiel's vision, the stream that flowed from the Temple put so much fresh water into the Dead Sea that fish would be able to live in it again. Compare this with the waters of Baptism. When you were baptized, the priest poured holy water over your head. Like the stream in Ezekiel's vision, the waters of Baptism are God's living water for you. They wash away original sin and support you as you grow in faith.

The next time you wash your hands or take a shower, close your eyes and think about God's living water flowing all around you. Imagine that it is washing away the dead parts of your life so that you can start fresh. Think about one thing you will do that day to reflect a new attitude or a new start. Pray that the Holy Spirit will give you the courage to do what you know you need to do.

— Ezekiel 47:1–12

small stream of water was flowing out at the
south side of the gate. 3 With his measuring
rod the man measured 560 yards down-
stream to the east and told me to wade
through the stream there. The water came
only to my ankles. 4 Then he measured
another 560 yards, and the water came up to
my knees. Another 560 yards farther down,
the water was up to my waist. 5 He measured
560 yards more, and there the stream was so
deep I could not wade through it. It was too
deep to cross except by swimming. 6 He said
to me, "Mortal man, note all this carefully."

Then the man took me back to the river-
bank, 7 and when I got there, I saw that there
were very many trees on each bank. 8 He said
to me, "This water flows through the land to
the east and down into the Jordan Valley and
to the Dead Sea. When it flows into the
Dead Sea, it replaces the salt water of that sea
with fresh water. 9 Wherever the stream
flows, there will be all kinds of animals and
fish. The stream will make the water of the
Dead Sea fresh, and wherever it flows, it will
bring life. 10 From the Springs of Engedi all
the way to the Springs of Eneglaim, there
will be fishermen on the shore of the sea,
and they will spread out their nets there to
dry. There will be as many different kinds of
fish there as there are in the Mediterranean
Sea. 11 But the water in the marshes and
ponds along the shore will not be made

The man . . . told me to wade through the stream there. (47:3)

Jeremiah

Breakthrough!: Jeremiah, you are one of the most famous prophets of Israel! God must have chosen you for your great wisdom.

Jeremiah: Actually, I feel like it was just the opposite. I was barely more than a boy when God first called me.

B: Really? Why did you answer God's call?

Jeremiah: Not for the fame; I did it because it was what God wanted of me—to speak for him.

B: What was your life like?

Jeremiah: At first it was easy. Josiah was king when I first started to prophesy. I liked his reforms, and King Josiah respected me. But after Josiah died, King Jehoiakim and King Zedekiah, who followed him, were evil and corrupt men. They were interested in power and money and not in taking care of their people.

B: So things got worse?

Jeremiah: It was then that I had some bad experiences because I spoke out against those kings and their practices. At different times I had to hide from the kings, was in prison, and was beaten. I even was thrown into a well and left to die. But the very worst thing was seeing the great city of Jerusalem totally destroyed by the Babylonians.

B: How did you handle all those bad things?

Jeremiah: (laughing) I was really upset with God, and let him know it. You can see how honest I was with God by reading Jeremiah 20:7–18.

B: What else would you like our readers to know?

Jeremiah: I know the message from God that I gave was very harsh at times. But remember God's message of hope that I also preached. God wants the best for his people!

Ezekiel

Breakthrough!: Ezekiel! We've been looking forward to interviewing you. Tell us about your call from God.

Ezekiel: I was called by God when I was thirty. I was a priest, and God also called me to be a prophet. God had a special name for me, "Mortal man." Oh, yeah, I had to eat a scroll, too. It tasted sweet.

B: How did you feel when you started to have visions of God?

Ezekiel: It was a little scary at first; God's power is so awesome that it tends to be a little overpowering. Some people thought my visions were a little too wild, but I needed to get the message to the people any way I could. I shaved my head once to get the point across.

B: You certainly did some wild things. Did anyone call you crazy? Didn't you once cook your food on . . . ?

Ezekiel: Yes, I cooked my food on dried cow's dung. It was meant to show the people the extreme conditions they would have to face once the kingdom was conquered. I had a good imagination and liked acting, so God used those gifts to make his points.

B: What message did you deliver for God?

Ezekiel: God wanted people to renew their hearts and spirits. I taught that each person is responsible for his or her own sins. I also had hopes that the kingdom of Judah might renew itself and follow God faithfully once again.

B: What was your biggest challenge?

Ezekiel: Getting people to understand and take what I was saying seriously.

B: Anything else you want the Bible readers to know?

Ezekiel: Read the book—you'll get all the wild details.

Ezra & Nehemiah

Breakthrough!: Could you tell us which one of you is which?

Ezra: My name is Ezra.

Nehemiah: And I am Nehemiah.

B: Why are you two put together all the time?

(Both together): Because our stories are very similar. And, originally, our stories were told in one book.

B: Tell us a little about yourselves.

Ezra: I'll go first. I was a priest and scribe, a Jewish religious official who was born in captivity in Babylon.

Nehemiah: And I was an administrator; I actually worked in the emperor's household.

B: So, what was the important part of your story?

Ezra: Well, after years in Babylon, a Persian king conquered Babylon and let us go home and rebuild Jerusalem and the Temple. It was an amazing time.

B: Was it all smooth sailing?

Nehemiah: Ezra had to deal with people who opposed the rebuilding. He also had a big problem with the way Israelite men were marrying foreign women.

Ezra: And Nehemiah first had to convince the emperor to let him go to Jerusalem. Then he really had to deal with rebuilding the city walls. He had a lot of people helping, which took lots of coordination. He had to be sure that all the people had food and a place to live.

B: And what were your joys?

Ezra: I was so happy when God answered our prayers so we could return home. I was also honored to see the gifts the Persian king gave us to help our rebuilding.

Nehemiah: It was a great day when the wall was finished. We had quite a party, dancing and singing so loudly it could be heard from miles away.

Judith

Breakthrough!: Hello, Judith. Can you tell us a little about yourself?

Judith: Yes, and thank you for this opportunity. My story was told to inspire people to be courageous and trust in God. I was very religious and observed all our religious laws.

B: What was your biggest challenge?

Judith: It is really gory.

B: That's okay.

Judith: Well, I beheaded General Holofernes.

B: What!

Judith: I needed to do something that would help the Israelites win a hopeless battle. I made myself very attractive, and Holofernes invited me and my servant into his tent, probably hoping to have sex. Then, when he got very drunk, I chopped off his head with his sword. It created such panic in King Nebuchadnezzar's army that the Israelites had an easy victory.

B: Why do you think people like your story?

Judith: Because it shows the power of people usually thought of as weak. In my society women were thought of as powerless, but my faith in God made me strong.

B: Did you celebrate the victory?

Judith: We sure did. It lasted for three months! I was given rewards (that I offered to God) and I celebrated with the other women. We put olive branches on our heads and danced. The men wore flower wreaths and sang songs of praise as they carried their weapons. I also sang a special song; you can find it in Judith 16:1–17.

B: What else would you like to tell the Bible readers?

Judith: Read the book—it is all in there. And remember how much power you have when you trust in God!

Esther

Breakthrough!: Queen Esther, you certainly look splendid!

Esther: Yes, the king always wants me to look my best for interviews.

B: How is it that you, a Jewish woman, became a queen in Persia?

Esther: Well, the Queen Vashti displeased King Xerxes, and so the king divorced her. The king's advisors looked for a beautiful, young woman to become the next queen, and, amazingly, the king picked me. I never told him about my Jewish faith until later.

B: You were an orphan, too?

Esther: Yes, my relative Mordecai raised me.

B: Didn't Mordecai uncover a plot against your people?

Esther: Actually, Mordecai uncovered a plan to assassinate the king. The king rewarded Mordecai by giving him a high government position. This made another official called Haman jealous. Haman decided to get revenge by telling the king lies about my people. Haman tricked the king into sending out a letter ordering that all Jews be hunted down and killed.

B: How horrible! What happened?

Esther: Mordecai wanted me to go to the king immediately and plead for our people's lives. But no one, not even the queen, could go before the king without being called. I was afraid I would be killed, too. I was not that brave a person. But I found my courage and told the king that I was a Jew and that he had been lied to about my people. The king was so angry he ordered Haman to be hanged. The king let Mordecai send a letter out in the king's name allowing the Jews to defend themselves. Then the king sent out another letter telling the truth about our people.

B: So, do the Jewish people today still remember what you did?

Esther: Yes, they do, in a feast called Purim.

The Maccabees

Breakthrough!: Hi, guys, could you give us your names?

Maccabees: We are Judas, John, Simon, Eleazar, and Jonathan—known as the Maccabees. We lived before Christ was born—about 175 years before. This was when Alexander the Great was dying. We are named after our most famous brother, Judas, who was called Judas Maccabeus, meaning "Judas, the Hammer."

B: Why is Judas most famous?

Maccabees: Our father was Mattathias, and he started a revolt against the Greeks, who were persecuting us. When our father died, Judas was the one who successfully led the revolt and pushed the Greeks out of Jerusalem. He was a brilliant warrior.

B: Was Judas the only leader?

Maccabees: When Judas died, Jonathan took over as leader; he became a High Priest. Unfortunately, he was captured and killed. After him it was Simon who led. He, too, was murdered.

B: Wow, you certainly were a family of leaders willing to give your lives for God's cause. What else are you guys proud of?

Maccabees: Besides the revolt, we also purified the Temple. The Greeks had it filled with statues and images of Greek gods and goddesses, which we threw out.

B: Was that occasion called Hanukkah?

Maccabees: We didn't call it that, but later on the Jewish people named it the feast of Hanukkah, the feast of lights. Jewish people celebrate Hanukkah around the same time Christians celebrate Christmas.

B: What do the Bible readers need to know about your story?

Maccabees: Our story is told in two slightly different versions, 1 Maccabees and 2 Maccabees. We hope you read them.

Job

Breakthrough!: So, Job, tell us a little about yourself.

Job: I had a really hard time for a while. I lost everything, really everything! It was horrible. I was a good man; I followed God and tried not to do anything evil.

B: So what happened?

Job: I lost most of my servants, all of my sheep and camels, and every one of my ten children. Then I got a really bad skin disease. My wife thought I should just curse God and die.

B: Did you?

Job: No, I told her this: "When God sends us something good, we welcome it. How can we complain when he sends us trouble?" (Job 2:10). I never said anything against God, until my friends showed up.

B: Tell us about your friends.

Job: My friends are Eliphaz, Bildad, and Zophar. For seven days they just sat with me in silence. Then we started arguing about why this happened to me.

B: What was your discussion about?

Job: Divine justice, whether my suffering was due to some sin I had committed, that sort of thing. I finally did complain to God. But eventually my friends gave up on me.

B: So, what about God? Didn't you have an encounter with God?

Job: Yes, God did come and help me out. God challenged me about wonderful and awesome things that no human being can explain. He made me realize that some things are beyond human understanding. But God did tell my friends that they weren't right about the cause of my suffering.

B: What happened after that?

Job: God restored my health and all my wealth. And, I had more children and lived to see my grandchildren and great-grandchildren!

Lady Wisdom

Breakthrough!: Lady Wisdom. That is an interesting name.

LW: Lady Wisdom is a name that some ancient Israelites used to describe the wisdom of God. They felt that pursuing wisdom was so important, it was like having a relationship with another person. I'm actually described as a person in Proverbs 1:20–33 and 8:22–31, Sirach 24:1–31, Wisdom 9:9–11 and Job 28:1–28.

B: Tell us some of your major achievements.

LW: First off, I am sort of the inspiration for the Books of Wisdom: Proverbs, Job, Ecclesiastes, Sirach, the Song of Songs, and the Wisdom of Solomon. I also taught people lots of things.

B: Like what things?

LW: Like the need for order in human affairs. There is an order in God's creation that must be respected. I also help them understand that almost all actions have consequences. When you do something, it affects other people and things, for better or worse. For example, if you want to get really good at something you have to practice at it, not just wish for it. That's part of God's order.

B: What was hard to teach people?

LW: Suffering has meaning, living a good life is possible, and humans have the responsibility of caring for God's creation. Some people have a hard time learning these things.

B: Anything else you want to tell the Bible readers?

LW: Yes, I'd like them to know that I do have my limits. Wisdom alone can't tell them everything about God because some things are just beyond our limits. But following the advice in the Books of Wisdom is a good way to live a full and rich life.

fresh. They will remain there as a source of
salt. 12 On each bank of the stream all kinds
of trees will grow to provide food. Their
leaves will never wither, and they will never
stop bearing fruit. They will have fresh fruit
every month, because they are watered by
the stream that flows from the Temple. The
trees will provide food, and their leaves will
be used for healing people."

The Boundaries of the Land

13 The Sovereign LORD said, "These are
the boundaries of the land that is to be
divided among the twelve tribes, with the
tribe of Joseph receiving two sections.[p] 14 I
solemnly promised your ancestors that I
would give them possession of this land; now
divide it equally among you.

15 "The northern boundary runs eastward
from the Mediterranean Sea to the city of
Hethlon, to Hamath Pass, to the city of
Zedad,[q] 16 to the cities of Berothah and
Sibraim (they are located between the terri-
tory of the kingdom of Damascus and that
of the kingdom of Hamath), and to the city
of Ticon (located by the border of the dis-
trict of Hauran). 17 So the northern bound-
ary runs from the Mediterranean eastward to
Enon City, with the border regions of Da-
mascus and Hamath to the north of it.

18 "The eastern boundary runs south from
a point between the territory of Damascus
and that of Hauran, with the Jordan River
forming the boundary between the land of
Israel on the west and Gilead on the east, as
far as Tamar[r] on the Dead Sea.

19 "The southern boundary runs south-
west from Tamar to the oasis of Kadesh
Meribah and then northwest along the
Egyptian border to the Mediterranean Sea.

20 "The western boundary is formed by
the Mediterranean and runs north to a point
west of Hamath Pass.

21 "Divide this land among your tribes; 22 it
is to be your permanent possession. The for-
eigners who are living among you and who
have had children born here are also to
receive their share of the land when you
divide it. They are to be treated like full
Israelite citizens and are to draw lots for
shares of the land along with the tribes of
Israel. 23 All foreign residents will receive
their share with the people of the tribe
among whom they are living. I, the Sover-
eign LORD, have spoken."

The Division of the Land among the Tribes

48 1-7 The northern boundary of the
land runs eastward from the Med-
iterranean Sea to the city of Hethlon, to
Hamath Pass, to Enon City, to the boundary
between the kingdoms of Damascus and
Hamath. Each tribe is to receive one section
of land extending from the eastern boundary
west to the Mediterranean Sea,[s] in the fol-
lowing order from north to south:

Dan
Asher
Naphtali
Manasseh
Ephraim
Reuben
Judah

The Special Section in the Center of the Land

8 The next section of the land is to be set
apart for special use. It is to be 10 miles wide
from north to south, and the same length
from east to west as the sections given to the
tribes. The Temple will be located within
this section.

9 In the center of this section, a special area
10 miles by 8 miles[t] is to be dedicated to the

[p] **47:13** TWO SECTIONS: *The tribes of Manasseh and Ephraim, the sons of Joseph, were each given one section.*
[q] **47:15** *One ancient translation* Hamath Pass, to the city of Zedad; *Hebrew* Zedad Pass to the city of Hamath.
[r] **47:18** *Some ancient translations* Tamar; *Hebrew unclear.*
[s] **48:1–7** *One ancient translation* extending . . . Sea; *Hebrew* having an eastern boundary and a western boundary.
[t] **48:9** *Probable text (see 45:1)* 8 miles; *Hebrew* 4 miles.
47:12 Rev 22:2

The twelve tribes: The twelve family groups of the nation of Israel, each named for a son of Jacob.

LORD. 10 The priests are to have a portion of
this holy area. From east to west their por-
tion is to measure 10 miles, and from north
to south, 4 miles. The Temple of the LORD is
to be located in the middle of this area.
11 This holy area is to be for the priests who
are descendants of Zadok. They served me
faithfully and did not join the rest of the
Israelites in doing wrong, as the other mem-
bers of the tribe of Levi did. 12 So they are to
have a special area next to the area belong-
ing to the Levites, and it will be the holiest
of all. 13 The Levites also are to have a special
area, south of that of the priests. It too is to
be 10 miles from east to west, by 4 miles
from north to south. 14 The area dedicated to
the LORD is the best part of all the land, and
none of it may be sold or exchanged or
transferred to anyone else. It is holy and
belongs to the LORD.
15 The part of the special area that is left,
10 miles by 2 miles, is not holy, but is for the
general use of the people. They may live
there and use the land. The city is to be in
the center of it, 16 and it will be a square,
2,520 yards on each side. 17 All around the
city on each side there will be an open space
140 yards across. 18 The land that is left after
the city has been built in the area immedi-
ately to the south of the holy area—4 miles
by 2 miles on the east and 4 miles by 2 miles
on the west—is to be used as farmland by
the people who live in the city. 19 Anyone
who lives in the city, no matter which tribe
he comes from, may farm that land.
20 And so the total area in the center of
the section which was set apart will be a
square measuring 10 miles on each side, and
it will include the area occupied by the city.
21-22 To the east and to the west of this
area which contains the Temple, the priests'
land, the Levites' land, and the city, the
remaining land belongs to the ruling prince.
It reaches east to the eastern boundary and
west to the Mediterranean Sea, and is
bounded on the north by the section
belonging to Judah and on the south by the
one belonging to Benjamin.

Study it!

A Place Called God

Have you ever felt like God is ignoring you? When you pray, do you wonder if there's really a God out there who is listening? The Israelites probably felt that way, too. In the first half of the Book of Ezekiel, God was so angry with the Israelites that they might have thought that God was ready to give up on them.

In the second part of the book, things change. Jerusalem and the Temple have been destroyed. Many of the people are in exile in Babylon. God shows them that he is forgiving and merciful. He promises to lead them back to their homeland and make it a place where they can live well and worship God only. Ezekiel's visions are a promise that even the Temple will be rebuilt.

God even changes the name of the city of Jerusalem: "The name of the city from now on will be 'The-LORD-Is-Here!'" (Ezekiel 48:35). It will be a rough journey, and it will take a long time to get back, but the Israelites are headed home.

— Ezekiel 48:35

Land for the Other Tribes

23-27 South of this special section, each of
the remaining tribes is to receive one section
of land running from the eastern boundary
west to the Mediterranean Sea, in the fol-
lowing order from north to south:

Zadok *(Ezekiel 48:11)* **was a priest who supported King David and King Solomon. His descendants served as the high priests of the Temple.**

Benjamin
Simeon
Issachar
Zebulun
Gad

28 On the south side of the portion given
to the tribe of Gad, the boundary runs
southwest from Tamar to the oasis of
Kadesh, and then northwest along the
Egyptian border to the Mediterranean Sea.

29 The Sovereign LORD said, "That is the
way the land is to be divided into sections
for the tribes of Israel to possess."

The Gates of Jerusalem

30-34 There are twelve entrances to the city
of Jerusalem. Each of the four walls measures
2,520 yards and has three gates in it, each
named for one of the tribes. The gates in the
north wall are named for Reuben, Judah,
and Levi; those in the east wall, for Joseph,
Benjamin, and Dan; those in the south wall,
for Simeon, Issachar, and Zebulun; and those
in the west wall are named for Gad, Asher,
and Naphtali. 35 The total length of the wall
on all four sides of the city is 10,080 yards.
The name of the city from now on will be
"The-LORD-Is-Here!"

48:30–34 Rev 21:12, 13

Your Next Step

Congratulations on finishing the Book of Ezekiel! Use this space to write your thoughts and questions about this book. If you are following the suggested reading plan, go ahead to the Book of Jonah. Jonah is a story of another prophet, who was even less eager than Ezekiel to speak for God.

THE BOOK OF Daniel

Why are we so fascinated by superheroes? Is it because they are "super," with special gifts that allow them to do great things? Or is it because they are "heroes," willing to put themselves in danger to help other people or even save the planet?

Daniel is a superhero in both senses. In 164 BC, the Jewish people were being treated horribly by an evil king. In their suffering they needed to hear the stories of a Jewish hero from an earlier time. Daniel was that hero. He had a special gift, the ability to interpret dreams, which allowed him to do great things. But he and his friends also put themselves in danger several times in order to remain faithful to God. In the end they always came out ahead—which is the way superhero stories usually end! Daniel's courage gave God's people hope that, in the end, they would be rewarded for their faithfulness.

Headlines

- A King's Disturbing Dream (2:24–45)
- Three Friends Survive Fiery Furnace! (3:19–23; A:23–27)
- Daniel Reads Handwriting on the Wall (5:5–30)
- Daniel Is Thrown to the Lions (6:11–28)
- Susanna Falsely Accused! (chapter B)
- Daniel Slays a Dragon (C:23–32)

FACTOIDS

Who wrote this book? The author is unknown.

Why was it written? These heroic stories and prophetic writings were written to comfort the Jewish people during a time of persecution by Antiochus IV Epiphanes, around 164 BC.

What time period does it cover? A time in the sixth century B.C. during the Babylonian Exile.

Jesus connection: Jesus often calls himself the Son of Man, a term that appears in Daniel (7:13).

Important themes

- It is important to do what is right in the eyes of God.
- God is in control of all events.
- Despite persecution and oppression, God will be victorious, and the Kingdom of God will eventually be realized.

THE STORY OF DANIEL AND HIS FRIENDS (1:1—6:28)

The Young Men at Nebuchadnezzar's Court

1 In the third year that Jehoiakim was king of Judah, King Nebuchadnezzar of Babylonia attacked Jerusalem and surrounded the city. [2]The Lord let him capture King Jehoiakim and seize some of the Temple treasures. He took some prisoners back with him to the temple of his gods in Babylon, and put the captured treasures in the temple storerooms.

[3]The king ordered Ashpenaz, his chief official, to select from among the Israelite exiles some young men of the royal family and of the noble families. [4]They had to be handsome, intelligent, well-trained, quick to learn, and free from physical defects, so that they would be qualified to serve in the royal court. Ashpenaz was to teach them to read and write the Babylonian language. [5]The king also gave orders that every day they were to be given the same food and wine as the members of the royal court. After three years of this training they were to appear before the king. [6]Among those chosen were Daniel, Hananiah, Mishael, and Azariah, all of whom were from the tribe of Judah. [7]The chief official gave them new names: Belteshazzar, Shadrach, Meshach, and Abednego.

[8]Daniel made up his mind not to let himself become ritually unclean by eating the food and drinking the wine of the royal court, so he asked Ashpenaz to help him, [9]and God made Ashpenaz sympathetic to Daniel. [10]Ashpenaz, however, was afraid of the king, so he said to Daniel, "The king has decided what you are to eat and drink, and if you don't look as fit as the other young men, he may kill me."

[11]So Daniel went to the guard whom Ashpenaz had placed in charge of him and his three friends. [12]"Test us for ten days," he said. "Give us vegetables to eat and water to drink. [13]Then compare us with the young men who are eating the food of the royal

Live it!

Eat Your Vegetables!

To avoid eating food that the Law of Moses forbids (such as pork), Daniel and his three friends make a deal with Ashpenaz, the king's chief official. They are granted the right to eat only vegetables and drink water for the next ten days, and they ask to be compared with the other young men of the court who are on a regular diet. When the time is up, Daniel and his friends are actually healthier and stronger than the others are!

The point of this story isn't that a vegetarian diet is better for you, although there might be some truth to that. The point is that our lives are better off when we follow God's commandments. We might think that cheating on a test doesn't hurt us, but it does. We might think that taking time to rest and go to church on Sunday isn't a big deal, but it is.

God doesn't give us commandments to make life difficult. He gives us laws to live by so we can live healthy, happy, and holy lives and be with him forever in heaven. So eat your vegetables and make God's laws the rule of your life.

— Daniel 1:11–16

1:1 2 Kings 24:1; 2 Chr 36:5–7 **1:2–4** 2 Kings 20:17, 18; 24:10–16; 2 Chr 36:10; Isa 39:7, 8

court, and base your decision on how we look."

14 He agreed to let them try it for ten days. 15 When the time was up, they looked healthier and stronger than all those who had been eating the royal food. 16 So from then on the guard let them continue to eat vegetables instead of what the king provided.

17 God gave the four young men knowledge and skill in literature and philosophy. In addition, he gave Daniel skill in interpreting visions and dreams.

18 At the end of the three years set by the king, Ashpenaz took all the young men to Nebuchadnezzar. 19 The king talked with them all, and Daniel, Hananiah, Mishael, and Azariah impressed him more than any of the others. So they became members of the king's court. 20 No matter what question the king asked or what problem he raised, these four knew ten times more than any fortuneteller or magician in his whole kingdom. 21 Daniel remained at the royal court until Cyrus, the emperor of Persia, conquered Babylonia.

Nebuchadnezzar's Dream

2 In the second year that Nebuchadnezzar was king, he had a dream. It worried him so much that he couldn't sleep, 2 so he sent for his fortunetellers, magicians, sorcerers, and wizards to come and explain the dream to him. When they came and stood before the king, 3 he said to them, "I'm worried about a dream I've had. I want to know what it means."

4 They answered the king in Aramaic,[a] "May Your Majesty live forever! Tell us your dream, and we will explain it to you."

5 The king said to them, "I have made up my mind that you must tell me the dream and then tell me what it means. If you can't, I'll have you torn limb from limb and make your houses a pile of ruins. 6 But if you can tell me both the dream and its meaning, I will reward you with gifts and great honor. Now then, tell me what the dream was and what it means."

7 They answered the king again, "If Your Majesty will only tell us what the dream was, we will explain it."

8 At that, the king exclaimed, "Just as I thought! You are trying to gain time, because you see that I have made up my mind 9 to give all of you the same punishment if you don't tell me the dream. You have agreed among yourselves to go on telling me lies because you hope that in time things will change. Tell me what the dream was, and then I will know that you can also tell me what it means."

10 The advisers replied, "There is no one on the face of the earth who can tell Your Majesty what you want to know. No king, not even the greatest and most powerful, has ever made such a demand of his fortunetellers, magicians, and wizards. 11 What Your Majesty is asking for is so difficult that no one can do it for you except the gods, and they do not live among human beings."

12 At that, the king flew into a rage and ordered the execution of all the royal advisers in Babylon. 13 So the order was issued for all of them to be killed, including Daniel and his friends.

God Shows Daniel What the Dream Means

14 Then Daniel went to Arioch, commander of the king's bodyguard, who had been ordered to carry out the execution. Choosing his words carefully, 15 he asked Arioch why the king had issued such a harsh order. So Arioch told Daniel what had happened.

16 Daniel went at once and obtained royal permission for more time, so that he could tell the king what the dream meant. 17 Then Daniel went home and told his friends Hananiah, Mishael, and Azariah what had happened. 18 He told them to pray to the God of heaven for mercy and to ask him to

[a] **2:4** *From here to the end of chapter 7, the language used is Aramaic, not Hebrew. The language of the addition from the ancient Greek translation–The Prayer of Azariah and the Song of the Three Young Men (A.1–68)–between 3.23 and 3.24 is Greek.*

King Jehoiakim ruled over Judah from 609 to 598 BC. Read more about him in 2 Kings 24:1–6.

Pray it!

Daniel's Prayer

Daniel's prayer of praise to God is a beautiful one. Why not adapt it and make it your own? Here's a suggestion.

God, you are wise and powerful! I praise you forever and ever. You control the time and the seasons; you make and unmake presidents and rulers; it is you who give wisdom and understanding. You reveal things that are deep and secret; you know what is hidden in darkness, and you are surrounded by light. I praise you and honor you, God of my parents and grandparents. Please give me wisdom and strength, and let my whole life be a song of praise to you.

— Daniel 2:20–23

explain the mystery to them so that they
would not be killed along with the other
advisers in Babylon. 19 Then that same night
the mystery was revealed to Daniel in a
vision, and he praised the God of heaven:

20 "God is wise and powerful!
Praise him forever and ever.
21 He controls the times and the seasons;
he makes and unmakes kings;
it is he who gives wisdom and
understanding.
22 He reveals things that are deep and secret;
he knows what is hidden in darkness,
and he himself is surrounded by light.
23 I praise you and honor you, God of my
ancestors.
You have given me wisdom and strength;
you have answered my prayer
and shown us what to tell the king."

Daniel Tells the King the Dream and Explains It

24 So Daniel went to Arioch, whom the
king had commanded to execute the royal
advisers. He said to him, "Don't put them to
death. Take me to the king, and I will tell
him what his dream means."
25 At once Arioch took Daniel into King
Nebuchadnezzar's presence and told the
king, "I have found one of the Jewish exiles
who can tell Your Majesty the meaning of
your dream."
26 The king said to Daniel (who was also
called Belteshazzar), "Can you tell me what
I dreamed and what it means?"
27 Daniel replied, "Your Majesty, there is
no wizard, magician, fortuneteller, or
astrologer who can tell you that. 28 But there
is a God in heaven, who reveals mysteries.
He has informed Your Majesty what will
happen in the future. Now I will tell you the
dream, the vision you had while you were
asleep.
29 "While Your Majesty was sleeping, you
dreamed about the future; and God, who
reveals mysteries, showed you what is going
to happen. 30 Now, this mystery was revealed
to me, not because I am wiser than anyone
else, but so that Your Majesty may learn the
meaning of your dream and understand the
thoughts that have come to you.
31 "Your Majesty, in your vision you saw
standing before you a giant statue, bright and
shining, and terrifying to look at. 32 Its head
was made of the finest gold; its chest and
arms were made of silver; its waist and hips
of bronze, 33 its legs of iron, and its feet partly
of iron and partly of clay. 34 While you were
looking at it, a great stone broke loose from
a cliff without anyone touching it, struck the
iron and clay feet of the statue, and shattered
them. 35 At once the iron, clay, bronze, silver,
and gold crumbled and became like the dust
on a threshing place in summer. The wind
carried it all away, leaving not a trace. But
the stone grew to be a mountain that cov-
ered the whole earth.
36 "This was the dream. Now I will tell
Your Majesty what it means. 37 Your
Majesty, you are the greatest of all kings.
The God of heaven has made you emperor

and given you power, might, and honor.
38 He has made you ruler of all the inhabit-
ed earth and ruler over all the animals and
birds. You are the head of gold. 39 After you
there will be another empire, not as great
as yours, and after that a third, an empire of
bronze, which will rule the whole earth.
40 And then there will be a fourth empire,

HIGHLIGHTS FROM NEBUCHADNEZZAR'S DREAM INTERPRETED BY DANIEL

(Numbers refer to chapter and verse in Daniel)

as strong as iron, which shatters and breaks everything. And just as iron shatters everything, it will shatter and crush all the earlier empires. 41 You also saw that the feet and the toes were partly clay and partly iron. This means that it will be a divided empire. It will have something of the strength of iron, because there was iron mixed with the clay. 42 The toes—partly iron and partly clay—mean that part of the empire will be strong and part of it weak. 43 You also saw that the iron was mixed with the clay. This means that the rulers of that empire will try to unite their families by intermarriage, but they will not be able to, any more than iron can mix with clay. 44 At the time of those rulers the God of heaven will establish a kingdom that will never end. It will never be conquered, but will completely destroy all those empires and then last forever. 45 You saw how a stone broke loose from a cliff without anyone touching it and how it struck the statue made of iron, bronze, clay, silver, and gold. The great God is telling Your Majesty what will happen in the future. I have told you exactly what you dreamed, and have given you its true meaning."

The King Rewards Daniel

46 Then King Nebuchadnezzar bowed to the ground and gave orders for sacrifices and offerings to be made to Daniel. 47 The king said, "Your God is the greatest of all gods, the Lord over kings, and the one who reveals mysteries. I know this because you have been able to explain this mystery." 48 Then he gave Daniel a high position, presented him with many splendid gifts, put him in charge of the province of Babylon, and made him the head of all the royal advisers. 49 At Daniel's request the king put Shadrach, Meshach, and Abednego in charge of the affairs of the province of Babylon; Daniel, however, remained at the royal court.

Nebuchadnezzar Commands Everyone to Worship a Gold Statue

3 King Nebuchadnezzar had a gold statue made, ninety feet high and nine feet wide, and he had it set up in the plain of Dura in the province of Babylon. 2 Then the king gave orders for all his officials to come together—the princes, governors, lieutenant governors, commissioners, treasurers, judges, magistrates, and all the other officials of the provinces. They were to attend the dedication of the statue which King Nebuchadnezzar had set up. 3 When all these officials gathered for the dedication and stood in front of the statue, 4 a herald announced in a loud voice, "People of all nations, races, and languages! 5 You will hear the sound of the trumpets, followed by the playing of oboes, lyres, zithers, and harps; and then all the other instruments will join in. As soon as the music starts, you are to bow down and worship the gold statue that King Nebuchadnezzar has set up. 6 Anyone who does not bow down and worship will immediately be thrown into a blazing furnace." 7 And so, as soon as they heard the sound of the instruments, the people of all the nations, races, and languages bowed down and worshiped the gold statue which King Nebuchadnezzar had set up.

Daniel's Three Friends Are Accused of Disobedience

8 It was then that some Babylonians took the opportunity to denounce the Jews. 9 They said to King Nebuchadnezzar, "May Your Majesty live forever! 10 Your Majesty has issued an order that as soon as the music starts, everyone is to bow down and worship the gold statue, 11 and that anyone who does not bow down and worship it is to be thrown into a blazing furnace. 12 There are some Jews whom you put in charge of the province of Babylon—Shadrach, Meshach, and Abednego—who are disobeying Your Majesty's orders. They do not worship your god or bow down to the statue you set up."

Like Daniel, Joseph had the ability to interpret dreams *(see Genesis, chapter 41)*. Both men are given important positions because of their God-given gift.

Live it!

We Believe . . . No Matter What

Daniel's three friends—Shadrach, Meshach, and Abednego—are about to be thrown into a fiery furnace for refusing to worship a gold statue. They tell the king that if God decides to rescue them from the furnace, then they will be saved. But even if he doesn't, It doesn't matter. They will not bow down to the gold statue. No way. Their faith in God is without conditions. They believe, whether they survive or not. Their strong faith makes the king very angry, and he has the furnace heated seven times hotter than usual.

This is a story told to encourage the faith of the Jewish people who were being persecuted several centuries later by the Greeks. After Jesus, the early Christian martyrs were also inspired by the story. It helped them to endure and to know that God would not let them down in the end.

What happens to us when the pressure is on? Do we make excuses about our faith? Do we try to make deals with God? Pray for strong and courageous faith, like that of the three young men in this story.

— Daniel, chapter 3

13 At that, the king flew into a rage and
ordered the three men to be brought before
him. 14 He said to them, "Shadrach,
Meshach, and Abednego, is it true that you
refuse to worship my god and to bow down
to the gold statue I have set up? 15 Now
then, as soon as you hear the sound of the
trumpets, oboes, lyres, zithers, harps, and all
the other instruments, bow down and worship the statue. If you do not, you will
immediately be thrown into a blazing furnace. Do you think there is any god who
can save you?"

16 Shadrach, Meshach, and Abednego
answered, "Your Majesty, we will not try to
defend ourselves. 17 If the God whom we
serve is able to save us from the blazing furnace and from your power, then he will.[b]
18 But even if he doesn't, Your Majesty may
be sure that we will not worship your god,
and we will not bow down to the gold statue that you have set up."

Daniel's Three Friends Are Sentenced to Death

19 Then Nebuchadnezzar lost his temper,
and his face turned red with anger at
Shadrach, Meshach, and Abednego. So he
ordered the furnace to be heated seven times
hotter than usual. 20 And he commanded the
strongest men in his army to tie the three
men up and throw them into the blazing
furnace. 21 So they tied them up, fully
dressed—shirts, robes, caps, and all—and
threw them into the blazing furnace. 22 Now
because the king had given strict orders for
the furnace to be made extremely hot, the
flames burned up the guards who took the
men to the furnace. 23 Then Shadrach,
Meshach, and Abednego, still tied up, fell
into the heart of the blazing fire.

[b] **3:17** If the God . . . will; *or* If it is true that we refuse to worship your god or bow down to the gold statue you set up, the God whom we serve is able to save us from the blazing furnace and from your power—and he will.

3:23 Dan A:1

Not all Bibles include the chapters labeled A, B, and C, which were probably added after the original book was written.

The Prayer of Azariah

A 1 The three young men, Hananiah,
Mishael, and Azariah,[c] started walking
around in the flames, singing hymns to God,
and praising him as Lord. 2 Then Azariah
stood still and there in the fire he prayed
aloud: 3 "O Lord, the God of our ancestors,
we praise and adore you; may your name be
honored forever. 4 You have treated us as we
deserve. In everything you have done to us
you are always honest, and when you bring
us to judgment, you are always fair. 5 You did
what was right when you brought disaster
upon Jerusalem, the holy city of our ances-
tors. We deserved that judgment because of
our sins. 6 We disobeyed you, we turned our
backs on you, and we are guilty of every sin.
7 We did not do the things that you com-
manded us to do. If we had obeyed your
laws, we would have prospered, 8 but now we
deserve the judgment and punishment that
you have brought upon us. 9 You have hand
ed us over to lawless, hateful, and defiant
enemies—to the most wicked king in the
world. 10 And now all of us who worship you
are humiliated; we are too ashamed to open
our mouths.

11 "Yet for the sake of your own honor, do
not break your covenant with us and aban-
don us forever. 12 Do not withhold your
mercy from us. Keep your promises to Abra-
ham, whom you loved, to Isaac, your servant,
and to Jacob, the father of your holy people
Israel. 13 You promised to give them as many
descendants as the stars in the sky or as the
grains of sand along the seashore. 14 But now,
Lord, we are fewer in number than any
other nation; wherever we are, we live in
disgrace because of our sins. 15 We are left
without a king, without any prophets or
leaders. There is no longer a Temple where
we can go to offer you burnt offerings, sacri-
fices, gifts, or incense, no place where we can
make offerings to you and find your mercy.
16 But we come to you with repentant hearts
and humble spirits, begging you to accept us
just as if we had come with burnt offerings
of rams and bulls and thousands of fat lambs.
17 Accept our repentance as our sacrifice to
you today, so that we may obey you with all
our hearts. No one who trusts you will ever
be disappointed. 18-19 Now with all our
hearts we promise to obey you, worship you,
and come to you in prayer. Treat us with
kindness and mercy, and let us never be put
to shame. 20 O Lord, rescue us with one of
your miracles; bring honor to your name.

21 "Bring disgrace and shame on all who
harm us. Take away their might and power
and crush their strength. 22 Let them know
that you alone are Lord and God and that
you rule in majesty over the whole world."

23 The king's servants who had thrown the
three men into the furnace kept the fire hot
by feeding it with oil, tar, flax, and brush-
wood. 24 The flames blazed up to a height of
seventy-five feet 25 and even spread out and
burned up the Babylonians standing near the
furnace. 26 But an angel of the Lord came
down into the fire where the three men
were. He pushed aside the flames 27 so that it
felt as if a cool breeze were blowing, and the
fire did not touch the men at all or hurt
them in any way.

The Song of the Three Young Men

28 There in the furnace the three young
men again started singing together in praise
of God:

29 "We praise you, O Lord, the God of our
ancestors.

The three young men again started singing. (A:28)

[c] **A:1** HANANIAH, MISHAEL, AND AZARIAH: *These are the original names of Shadrach, Meshach, and Abednego (see Dan 1:6, 7).*

A:1 Dan 3:23 **A:26** Tob 5:4

30 May your glorious, holy name
be held in honor and reverence forever.
31 May hymns be sung to your glory forever
and may your holy presence be praised
in that temple,
32 where you sit on your heavenly throne
above the winged creatures
and look down to the world of the
dead.
May you be praised and honored
forever.
33 May you be praised as you sit on your
royal throne.
May hymns be sung to your glory
forever.
34 May you be praised in the dome of the
heavens.
May hymns be sung to your glory
forever.
35 "Praise the Lord, all creation;
sing his praise and honor him forever.
36 Praise the Lord, skies above;
sing his praise and honor him forever.
37 Praise the Lord, all angels of the Lord;
sing his praise and honor him forever.
38 Praise the Lord, all waters above the sky;
sing his praise and honor him forever.
39 Praise the Lord, all heavenly powers;
sing his praise and honor him forever.
40 Praise the Lord, sun and moon;
sing his praise and honor him forever.
41 Praise the Lord, stars of heaven;
sing his praise and honor him forever.
42 Praise the Lord, rain and dew;
sing his praise and honor him forever.
43 Praise the Lord, all winds;
sing his praise and honor him forever.
44 Praise the Lord, fire and heat;
sing his praise and honor him forever.
45 Praise the Lord, bitter cold and scorching
heat;
sing his praise and honor him forever.
46 Praise the Lord, dews and snows;
sing his praise and honor him forever.
47 Praise the Lord, nights and days;
sing his praise and honor him forever.
48 Praise the Lord, daylight and darkness;
sing his praise and honor him forever.
49 Praise the Lord, ice and cold;
sing his praise and honor him forever.
50 Praise the Lord, frost and snow;
sing his praise and honor him forever.

Pray it!

Group Prayer

The long prayer of praise sung by the three men in the furnace seems very repetitive, but try to picture these three young men singing their hearts out and perhaps each taking the first half of each verse, and all three joining in on the refrain, "Sing his praise and honor him forever."

Why not try this in a group—perhaps a class or youth group? Everyone can say together verses 29–34. Then a different person says the first part of each verse, and everyone says the second part together. Better yet, why not get into a rhythm or even set it to music?

Conclude by having everyone say the last three verses together.

— Daniel A:29–68

51 Praise the Lord, lightning and storm
clouds;
sing his praise and honor him forever.
52 "Let the earth praise the Lord;
sing his praise and honor him forever.
53 Praise the Lord, mountains and hills;
sing his praise and honor him forever.
54 Praise the Lord, everything that grows;
sing his praise and honor him forever.
55 Praise the Lord, lakes and rivers;
sing his praise and honor him forever.
56 Praise the Lord, springs of water;
sing his praise and honor him forever.
57 Praise the Lord, whales and sea creatures;
sing his praise and honor him forever.
58 Praise the Lord, all birds;
sing his praise and honor him forever.
59 Praise the Lord, all cattle and wild
animals;
sing his praise and honor him forever.

60 "Praise the Lord, all people on earth;
sing his praise and honor him forever.
61 Praise the Lord, people of Israel;
sing his praise and honor him forever.
62 Praise the Lord, priests of the Lord;
sing his praise and honor him forever.
63 Praise the Lord, servants of the Lord;
sing his praise and honor him forever.
64 Praise the Lord, all faithful people;
sing his praise and honor him forever.
65 Praise the Lord, all who are humble and holy;
sing his praise and honor him forever.
66 Praise the Lord, Hananiah, Azariah, and Mishael;
sing his praise and honor him forever.
He rescued us from the world of the dead
and saved us from the power of death.
He brought us out from the burning furnace
and saved us from the fire.
67 Give thanks to the Lord, for he is good
and his mercy lasts forever.
68 Praise the Lord, all who worship him;
sing praise to the God of gods and give him thanks,
for his mercy lasts forever."

3 24 Suddenly Nebuchadnezzar leaped to his feet in amazement. He asked his officials, "Didn't we tie up three men and throw them into the blazing furnace?"

They answered, "Yes, we did, Your Majesty."

25 "Then why do I see four men walking around in the fire?" he asked. "They are not tied up, and they show no sign of being hurt—and the fourth one looks like an angel." [d]

The Three Men Are Released and Promoted

26 So Nebuchadnezzar went up to the door of the blazing furnace and called out, "Shadrach! Meshach! Abednego! Servants of the Supreme God! Come out!" And they
came out at once. 27 All the princes, gover-
nors, lieutenant governors, and other officials of the king gathered to look at the three men, who had not been harmed by the fire. Their hair was not singed, their clothes were not burned, and there was no smell of smoke on them.

28 The king said, "Praise the God of Shadrach, Meshach, and Abednego! He sent his angel and rescued these men who serve and trust him. They disobeyed my orders and risked their lives rather than bow down and worship any god except their own.

29 "And now I command that if anyone of any nation, race, or language speaks disrespectfully of the God of Shadrach, Meshach, and Abednego, he is to be torn limb from limb, and his house is to be made a pile of ruins. There is no other god who can rescue like this."

30 And the king promoted Shadrach, Meshach, and Abednego to higher positions in the province of Babylon.

The fourth one looks like an angel. (3:25)

Nebuchadnezzar's Second Dream

4 King Nebuchadnezzar sent the following message to the people of all nations, races, and languages in the world:

"Greetings! 2 Listen to my account of the wonders and miracles which the Supreme God has shown me.

[d] **3:25** angel; *or* a son of the gods; *or* a son of God.

"Praise the Lord, all people on earth; / sing his praise and honor him forever" *(Daniel A:60).*

3 "How great are the wonders God shows
us!
How powerful are the miracles he
performs!
God is king forever; he will rule for all
time.
4 "I was living comfortably in my palace,
enjoying great prosperity. 5 But I had a
frightening dream and saw terrifying visions
while I was asleep. 6 I ordered all the royal
advisers in Babylon to be brought to me so
that they could tell me what the dream
meant. 7 Then all the fortunetellers, magi-
cians, wizards, and astrologers were brought
in, and I told them my dream, but they
could not explain it to me. 8 Then Daniel
came in. (He is also called Belteshazzar, after
the name of my god.) The spirit of the holy
gods[e] is in him, so I told him what I had
dreamed. I said to him: 9 Belteshazzar, chief
of the fortunetellers, I know that the spirit of
the holy gods[e] is in you and that you under-
stand all mysteries. This is[f] my dream. Tell me
what it means.
10 "While I was asleep, I had a vision of a
huge tree in the middle of the earth. 11 It
grew bigger and bigger until it reached the
sky and could be seen by everyone in the
world. 12 Its leaves were beautiful, and it was
loaded down with fruit—enough for the
whole world to eat. Wild animals rested in its
shade, birds built nests in its branches, and
every kind of living being ate its fruit.
13 "While I was thinking about the vision,
I saw coming down from heaven an angel,
alert and watchful. 14 He proclaimed in a
loud voice, 'Cut the tree down and chop off
its branches; strip off its leaves and scatter its
fruit. Drive the animals from under it and
the birds out of its branches. 15 But leave the
stump in the ground with a band of iron and
bronze around it. Leave it there in the field
with the grass.
" 'Now let the dew fall on this man, and
let him live with the animals and the plants.
16 For seven years he will not have a human
mind, but the mind of an animal. 17 This is
the decision of the alert and watchful angels.
So then, let all people everywhere know that
the Supreme God has power over human
kingdoms and that he can give them to any-
one he chooses—even to those who are least
important.'
18 "This is the dream I had," said King
Nebuchadnezzar. "Now, Belteshazzar, tell me
what it means. None of my royal advisers
could tell me, but you can, because the spirit
of the holy gods[g] is in you."

Daniel Explains the Dream

19 At this, Daniel, who is also called Belte-
shazzar, was so alarmed that he could not say
anything. The king said to him, "Belteshaz-
zar, don't let the dream and its message alarm
you."
Belteshazzar replied, "Your Majesty, I wish
that the dream and its explanation applied to
your enemies and not to you. 20 The tree, so
tall that it reached the sky, could be seen by
everyone in the world. 21 Its leaves were beau-
tiful, and it had enough fruit on it to feed the

So tall that it reached the sky (4:20)

whole world. Wild animals rested under it,
and birds made their nests in its branches.
22 "Your Majesty, you are the tree, tall and
strong. You have grown so great that you

[e] **4:8, 9** gods; *or* God. [f] **4:9** *Probable text* This is; *Aramaic* Visions of. [g] **4:18** gods; *or* God.

"And now, I, Nebuchadnezzar, praise, honor, and glorify the King of Heaven. Everything he does is right and just" *(Daniel 4:37).*

reach the sky, and your power extends over
the whole world. 23 While Your Majesty was
watching, an angel came down from heaven
and said, 'Cut the tree down and destroy it,
but leave the stump in the ground. Wrap a
band of iron and bronze around it, and leave
it there in the field with the grass. Let the

Leave the stump in the ground. (4:23)

dew fall on this man, and let him live there
with the animals for seven years.'
24 "This, then, is what it means, Your
Majesty, and this is what the Supreme God
has declared will happen to you. 25 You will
be driven away from human society and will
live with wild animals. For seven years you
will eat grass like an ox and sleep in the
open air, where the dew will fall on you.
Then you will admit that the Supreme God
controls all human kingdoms and that he can
give them to anyone he chooses. 26 The
angel ordered the stump to be left in the
ground. This means that you will become
king again when you acknowledge that God
rules all the world. 27 So then, Your Majesty,
follow my advice. Stop sinning, do what is
right, and be merciful to the poor.[h] Then
you will continue to be prosperous."
28 All this did happen to King Nebuchad-
nezzar. 29 Only twelve months later, while he
was walking around on the roof of his royal
palace in Babylon, 30 he said, "Look how
great Babylon is! I built it as my capital city
to display my power and might, my glory
and majesty."
31 Before the words were out of his
mouth, a voice spoke from heaven, "King
Nebuchadnezzar, listen to what I say! Your
royal power is now taken away from you.
32 You will be driven away from human soci-
ety, live with wild animals, and eat grass like
an ox for seven years. Then you will
acknowledge that the Supreme God has
power over human kingdoms and that he
can give them to anyone he chooses."
33 The words came true immediately. Neb-
uchadnezzar was driven out of human socie-
ty and ate grass like an ox. The dew fell on
his body, and his hair grew as long as eagle
feathers and his nails as long as bird claws.

Live it!

Down to Earth

There's a saying that states, The bigger they are, the harder they fall. This certainly seems to be the case with King Nebuchadnezzar. Just as Daniel tells him when he interprets the king's dream, the proud king does indeed spend seven years living as an animal in the wild and eating grass. The word *humility* comes from a word that originally meant "dirt" or "earth." So it seems fitting that the king is suddenly very close to the earth. It is hoped that we don't need to eat grass to be humble, but we do need to remind ourselves—and one another—that we are human beings and need to keep our egos in check.

Think of someone you know who has accomplished much but is still humble. What are some signs of his or her humility?

— Daniel 4:19–33

Nebuchadnezzar Praises God

34 "When the seven years had passed," said
the king, "I looked up at the sky, and my
sanity returned. I praised the Supreme God
and gave honor and glory to the one who
lives forever.

[h] **4:27** Stop sinning . . . to the poor; *or* Make up for your sins by doing what is right and by being merciful to the poor.

4:27 Tob 12:9; Sir 3:30 **4:34** Sir 18:1

"He will rule forever,
and his kingdom will last for all time.
35 He looks on the people of the earth as
nothing;
angels in heaven and people on earth
are under his control.
No one can oppose his will
or question what he does.
36 "When my sanity returned, my honor,
my majesty, and the glory of my kingdom
were given back to me. My officials and my
noblemen welcomed me, and I was given
back my royal power with even greater
honor than before.
37 "And now, I, Nebuchadnezzar, praise,
honor, and glorify the King of Heaven.
Everything he does is right and just, and he
can humble anyone who acts proudly."

Belshazzar's Banquet

5 One night King Belshazzar invited a
thousand noblemen to a great banquet,
and they drank wine together. 2 While they
were drinking, Belshazzar gave orders to
bring in the gold and silver cups and bowls
which his father[i] Nebuchadnezzar had car-
ried off from the Temple in Jerusalem. The
king sent for them so that he, his noblemen,
his wives, and his concubines could drink
out of them. 3 At once the gold cups and
bowls were brought in, and they all drank
wine out of them 4 and praised gods made of
gold, silver, bronze, iron, wood, and stone.
5 Suddenly a human hand appeared and
began writing on the plaster wall of the
palace, where the light from the lamps was
shining most brightly. And the king saw the
hand as it was writing. 6 He turned pale and

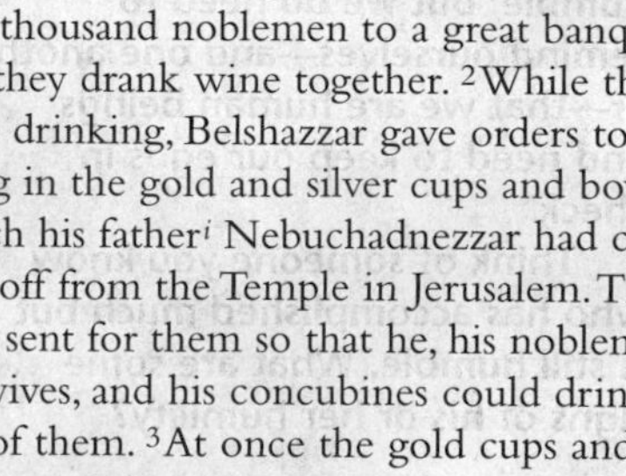

Suddenly a human hand appeared. (5:5)

was so frightened that his knees began to
shake. 7 He shouted for someone to bring in
the magicians, wizards, and astrologers. When
they came in, the king said to them, "Any-
one who can read this writing and tell me
what it means will be dressed in robes of
royal purple, wear a gold chain of honor
around his neck, and be the third in power
in the kingdom." 8 The royal advisers came
forward, but none of them could read the
writing or tell the king what it meant. 9 In
his distress King Belshazzar grew even paler,
and his noblemen had no idea what to do.
10 The queen mother heard the noise
made by the king and his noblemen and
entered the banquet hall. She said, "May
Your Majesty live forever! Please do not be
so disturbed and look so pale. 11 There is a
man in your kingdom who has the spirit of
the holy gods[j] in him. When your father was
king, this man showed good sense, knowl-
edge, and wisdom like the wisdom of the
gods. And King Nebuchadnezzar, your
father,[k] made him chief of the fortunetellers,
magicians, wizards, and astrologers. 12 He has
unusual ability and is wise and skillful in
interpreting dreams, solving riddles, and
explaining mysteries; so send for this man
Daniel, whom the king named Belteshazzar,
and he will tell you what all this means."

Daniel Explains the Writing

13 Daniel was brought at once into the
king's presence, and the king said to him,
"Are you Daniel, that Jewish exile whom my
father the king brought here from Judah? 14 I
have heard that the spirit of the holy gods[l]
is in you and that you are skillful and have
knowledge and wisdom. 15 The advisers and
magicians were brought in to read this writ-
ing and tell me what it means, but they
could not discover the meaning. 16 Now I
have heard that you can find hidden mean-
ings and explain mysteries. If you can read
this writing and tell me what it means, you
will be dressed in robes of royal purple, wear
a gold chain of honor around your neck, and
be the third in power in the kingdom."

[i] **5:2** *There were several kings of Babylonia between Nebuchadnezzar and Belshazzar.* Father *may mean predecessor, or the name* Nebuchadnezzar *may be used for Nabonidus.* [j] **5:11** gods; *or* God. [k] **5:11** your father *(see 5:2).*
[l] **5:14** gods; *or* God.

Live it!

The Writing's on the Wall

Have you ever heard the expression, The writing's on the wall? This is where it comes from: the fifth chapter of the Book of Daniel. It generally means that the end is near. That is certainly true for King Belshazzar. He is told by Daniel that his days are numbered. In fact, Belshazzar is killed that night.

Think about a time when someone might have said this to you. He or she might have been predicting a break-up in a relationship, or perhaps that some goal you had been working toward was about to come true. When someone tells you that the writing is on the wall, he or she is generally telling you that you are about to face the consequences of your actions.

If God were to send you a message written on a wall, what three words do you think would appear? What would they mean?

— Daniel, chapter 5

17 Daniel replied, "Keep your gifts for
yourself or give them to someone else. I will
read for Your Majesty what has been written
and tell you what it means.
18 "The Supreme God made your father
Nebuchadnezzar a great king and gave him
dignity and majesty. 19 He was so great that
people of all nations, races, and languages
were afraid of him and trembled. If he wanted
to kill someone, he did; if he wanted to
keep someone alive, he did. He honored or
disgraced anyone he wanted to. 20 But
because he became proud, stubborn, and
cruel, he was removed from his royal throne
and lost his place of honor. 21 He was driven
away from human society, and his mind
became like that of an animal. He lived with
wild donkeys, ate grass like an ox, and slept
in the open air with nothing to protect him
from the dew. Finally he admitted that the
Supreme God controls all human kingdoms
and can give them to anyone he chooses.
22 "But you, his son, have not humbled
yourself, even though you knew all this.
23 You acted against the Lord of heaven and
brought in the cups and bowls taken from his
Temple. You, your noblemen, your wives, and
your concubines drank wine out of them and
praised gods made of gold, silver, bronze,
iron, wood, and stone—gods that cannot see
or hear and that do not know anything. But
you did not honor the God who determines
whether you live or die and who controls
everything you do. 24 That is why God has
sent the hand to write these words.
25 "This is what was written: 'Number,
number, weight, divisions.' 26 And this is what
it means: *number,* God has numbered the
days of your kingdom and brought it to an
end; 27 *weight,* you have been weighed on the
scales and found to be too light; 28 *divisions,*
your kingdom is divided up and given to the
Medes and Persians."[m]
29 Immediately Belshazzar ordered his servants
to dress Daniel in a robe of royal purple
and to hang a gold chain of honor
around his neck. And he made him the third
in power in the kingdom. 30 That same night
Belshazzar, the king of Babylonia, was killed;
31 and Darius the Mede, who was then sixty-
two years old, seized the royal power.

Daniel in the Pit of Lions

6 Darius decided to appoint a hundred
and twenty governors to hold office
throughout his empire. 2 In addition, he
chose Daniel and two others to supervise the

[m] **5:28** PERSIANS: *In Aramaic the word for "Persians" sounds like the word for "division."*

The gold and silver cups the king is using *(Daniel 5:2)* **were the sacred bowls and cups taken from the Temple in Jerusalem.**

Pray it!

Thrown to the Lions

The incident of Daniel in the lions' pit, or den, is one of the most famous of the Old Testament. Because Daniel was so good at his job, he was promoted. That made his coworkers jealous, and they figured out a way to bring him down. Jealousy and envy can make people do some pretty awful things to others. If you ever feel you are the victim of jealous people, be like Daniel and keep trusting God to protect you.

Heavenly Father,
I didn't mean to make people jealous
or act snobby or proud.
Yet they seem to dislike me anyway.
Dear God, help them to see
that my joy in life comes from you.
Anything good or precious that I have
is the result of your blessing and love.
They can have that, too,
if they only trust in you.

— Daniel, chapter 6

governors and to look after the king's inter-
ests. 3Daniel soon showed that he could do
better work than the other supervisors or
the governors. Because he was so outstand-
ing, the king considered putting him in
charge of the whole empire. 4Then the
other supervisors and the governors tried to
find something wrong with the way Daniel
administered the empire, but they couldn't,
because Daniel was reliable and did not do
anything wrong or dishonest. 5They said to
each other, "We are not going to find any-
thing of which to accuse Daniel unless it is
something in connection with his religion."

6So they went to see the king and said,
"King Darius, may Your Majesty live forever!
7All of us who administer your empire—the
supervisors, the governors, the lieutenant
governors, and the other officials—have
agreed that Your Majesty should issue an
order and enforce it strictly. Give orders that
for thirty days no one be permitted to
request anything from any god or from any
human being except from Your Majesty. Any-
one who violates this order is to be thrown
into a pit filled with lions. 8So let Your
Majesty issue this order and sign it, and it will
be in force, a law of the Medes and Persians,
which cannot be changed." 9And so King
Darius signed the order. 10When Daniel
learned that the order had been signed, he
went home. In an upstairs room of his house
there were windows that faced toward
Jerusalem. There, just as he had always done,
he knelt down at the open windows and
prayed to God three times a day.

11When Daniel's enemies observed him
praying to God, 12all of them went together
to the king to accuse Daniel. They said,
"Your Majesty, you signed an order that for
the next thirty days anyone who requested
anything from any god or from any human
being except you, would be thrown into a
pit filled with lions."

Notice that Daniel faces Jerusalem to pray. Muslims today always face the holy city of Mecca when they pray.

He knelt down at the open windows. (6:10)

The king replied, "Yes, that is a strict
order, a law of the Medes and Persians,
which cannot be changed."
13 Then they said to the king, "Daniel, one
of the exiles from Judah, does not respect
Your Majesty or obey the order you issued.
He prays regularly three times a day."
14 When the king heard this, he was upset
and did his best to find some way to rescue
Daniel. He kept trying until sunset. 15 Then
Daniel's enemies came back to the king and
said to him, "Your Majesty knows that accord-
ing to the laws of the Medes and Persians no
order which the king issues can be changed."
16 So the king gave orders for Daniel to be
taken and thrown into the pit filled with lions.
He said to Daniel, "May your God, whom
you serve so loyally, rescue you." 17 A stone was
put over the mouth of the pit, and the king
placed his own royal seal and the seal of his
noblemen on the stone, so that no one could
rescue Daniel. 18 Then the king returned to
the palace and spent a sleepless night, without
food or any form of entertainment.
19 At dawn the king got up and hurried to
the pit. 20 When he got there, he called out
anxiously, "Daniel, servant of the living God!
Was the God you serve so loyally able to
save you from the lions?"
21 Daniel answered, "May Your Majesty live
forever! 22 God sent his angel to shut the
mouths of the lions so that they would not
hurt me. He did this because he knew that
I was innocent and because I have not
wronged you, Your Majesty."
23 The king was overjoyed and gave orders
for Daniel to be pulled up out of the pit. So
they pulled him up and saw that he had not
been hurt at all, for he trusted God. 24 Then
the king gave orders to arrest all those who
had accused Daniel, and he had them thrown,
together with their wives and children, into
the pit filled with lions. Before they even
reached the bottom of the pit, the lions
pounced on them and broke all their bones.
25 Then King Darius wrote to the people
of all nations, races, and languages on earth:
"Greetings! 26 I command that throughout
my empire everyone should fear and respect
Daniel's God.

"He is a living God,
 and he will rule forever.
His kingdom will never be destroyed,
 and his power will never come to an
 end.
27 He saves and rescues;
 he performs wonders and miracles
 in heaven and on earth.
He saved Daniel from being killed by the
 lions."

28 Daniel prospered during the reign of
Darius and the reign of Cyrus the Persian.

DANIEL DESCRIBES HIS VISIONS (7:1—12:13)

Daniel's Vision of the Four Beasts

7 In the first year that Belshazzar was king
of Babylonia, I had a dream and saw a
vision in the night. I wrote the dream down,
and this is the record 2 of what I saw that
night:

He knew that I was innocent. (6:22)

6:16 Dan C:31–42 **6:22** Tob 4:17; 12:14, 15

Study it!

A Secret Code

The second part of the Book of Daniel is very different from the first. The type of writing in the second part of the book is called apocalyptic writing. *Apocalypse* is a Greek word meaning "to uncover" or "to reveal." Apocalyptic writing often has symbolic images that are revealed in visions. These Images can be confusing to the reader. These symbolic images were like codes meant to reveal God's plans or purposes. Apocalyptic writing sometimes happened during times of persecution, and the code would be understood by the people being persecuted, but not by the persecutors. The last book of the Bible, the Book of Revelation, is almost all apocalyptic writing.

Scholars have identified many of the historical people represented by Daniel's visions. One of them is Alexander the Great (Daniel 11:3–4). The purpose of these visions is to assure the people that God would triumph over all earthly kingdoms and powers.

— Daniel, chapter 7

Winds were blowing from all directions
and lashing the surface of the ocean. 3Four
huge beasts came up out of the ocean, each
one different from the others. 4The first one
looked like a lion, but had wings like an
eagle. While I was watching, the wings were
torn off. The beast was lifted up and made to
stand up straight. And then a human mind
was given to it.
5The second beast looked like a bear
standing on its hind legs. It was holding
three ribs between its teeth, and a voice said
to it, "Go on, eat as much meat as you can!"
6While I was watching, another beast
appeared. It looked like a leopard, but on its
back there were four wings, like the wings of
a bird, and it had four heads. It had a look of
authority about it.
7As I was watching, a fourth beast
appeared. It was powerful, horrible, terrifying. With its huge iron teeth it crushed its
victims, and then it trampled on them.
Unlike the other beasts, it had ten horns.
8While I was staring at the horns, I saw a little horn coming up among the others. It
tore out three of the horns that were already
there. This horn had human eyes and a
mouth that was boasting proudly.

The Vision of the One Who Has Been Living Forever

9While I was looking, thrones were put in
place. One who had been living forever sat
down on one of the thrones. His clothes were
white as snow, and his hair was like pure wool.
His throne, mounted on fiery wheels, was
blazing with fire, 10and a stream of fire was
pouring out from it. There were many thousands of people there to serve him, and millions of people stood before him. The court
began its session, and the books were opened.
11While I was looking, I could still hear
the little horn bragging and boasting. As I
watched, the fourth beast was killed, and
its body was thrown into the flames and
destroyed. 12The other beasts had their
power taken away, but they were permitted
to go on living for a limited time.
13During this vision in the night, I saw
what looked like a human being. He was
approaching me, surrounded by clouds, and
he went to the one who had been living
forever and was presented to him. 14He was
given authority, honor, and royal power, so
that the people of all nations, races, and languages would serve him. His authority
would last forever, and his kingdom would
never end.

7:3 Rev 13:1; 17:8 **7:4–6** Rev 13:2 **7:7** Rev 12:3; 13:1 **7:8** Rev 13:5, 6 **7:9 a** Rev 20:4; **b** Rev 1:14
7:10 a Rev 5:11; **b** Rev 20:12 **7:13** Mt 24:30; 26:64; Mk 13:26; 14:62; Lk 21:27; Rev 1:7, 13; 14:14
7:14 Rev 11:15

The Visions Are Explained

15 The visions I saw alarmed me, and I was
deeply disturbed.[n] 16 I went up to one of
those standing there and asked him to
explain it all. So he told me the meaning.
17 He said, "These four huge beasts are four
empires which will arise on earth. 18 And the
people of the Supreme God will receive
royal power and keep it forever and ever."
19 Then I wanted to know more about the
fourth beast, which was not like any of the
others—the terrifying beast which crushed
its victims with its bronze claws and iron
teeth and then trampled on them. 20 And I
wanted to know about the ten horns on its
head and the horn that had come up after-
ward and had made three of the horns fall. It
had eyes and a mouth and was boasting
proudly. It was more terrifying than any of
the others.
21 While I was looking, that horn made
war on God's people and conquered them.
22 Then the one who had been living forever
came and pronounced judgment in favor of[o]
the people of the Supreme God. The time
had arrived for God's people to receive royal
power.
23 This is the explanation I was given:
"The fourth beast is a fourth empire that
will be on the earth and will be different
from all other empires. It will crush the
whole earth and trample it down. 24 The ten
horns are ten kings who will rule that
empire. Then another king will appear; he
will be very different from the earlier ones
and will overthrow three kings. 25 He will
speak against the Supreme God and oppress
God's people. He will try to change their
religious laws and festivals, and God's people
will be under his power for three and a half
years. 26 Then the heavenly court will sit in
judgment, take away his power, and destroy
him completely. 27 The power and greatness
of all the kingdoms on earth will be given to
the people of the Supreme God. Their royal
power will never end, and all rulers on earth
will serve and obey them."
28 This is the end of the account. I was so
frightened that I turned pale, and I kept
everything to myself.

Daniel's Vision of a Ram and a Goat

8 In the third year that Belshazzar was
king, I saw a second vision.[p] 2 In the
vision I suddenly found myself in the walled
city of Susa in the province of Elam. I was
standing by the Ulai River, 3 and there beside
the river I saw a ram that had two long
horns, one of which was longer and newer
than the other. 4 I watched the ram butting
with his horns to the west, the north, and
the south. No animal could stop him or
escape his power. He did as he pleased and
grew arrogant.
5 While I was wondering what this meant,
a goat came rushing out of the west, moving
so fast that his feet didn't touch the ground.
He had one prominent horn between his
eyes. 6 He came toward the ram, which I had
seen standing beside the river, and rushed at
him with all his force. 7 I watched him attack
the ram. He was so angry that he smashed
into him and broke the two horns. The ram
had no strength to resist. He was thrown to
the ground and trampled on, and there was
no one who could save him.
8 The goat grew more and more arrogant,
but at the height of his power his horn was
broken. In its place four prominent horns
came up, each pointing in a different direc-
tion. 9 Out of one of these four horns grew a
little horn, whose power extended toward
the south and the east and toward the
Promised Land. 10 It grew strong enough to
attack the army of heaven, the stars them-
selves, and it threw some of them to the
ground and trampled on them. 11 It even

[n] **7:15** *Aramaic has two additional words, the meaning of which is unclear.* [o] **7:22** pronounced judgment in favor of; or gave the right to judge to. [p] **8:1** *Beginning at 8:1, the rest of this book is in Hebrew (see 2:4).*

7:18 Rev 22:5 **7:21** Rev 13:7 **7:22** Rev 20:4 **7:24** Rev 17:12 **7:25** Rev 12:14; 13:5, 6 **7:27** **a** Rev 20:4; **b** Rev 22:5 **8:10** Rev 12:4

Other translations of the Bible use the term "son of man" to describe the person in Daniel 7:13–14. This is a title used for Jesus in the New Testament.

defied the Prince of the heavenly army,
stopped the daily sacrifices offered to him,
and ruined the Temple. 12People sinned
there instead of offering the proper daily
sacrifices,[q] and true religion was thrown to
the ground. The horn was successful in
everything it did.
13Then I heard one angel ask another,
"How long will these things that were seen
in the vision continue? How long will an
awful sin replace the daily sacrifices? How
long will the army of heaven and the Temple
be trampled on?"
14I heard the other angel answer, "It will
continue for 2,300 evenings and mornings,
during which sacrifices will not be offered.
Then the Temple will be restored."

The Angel Gabriel Explains the Vision

15I was trying to understand what the
vision meant, when suddenly someone was
standing in front of me. 16I heard a voice call
out over the Ulai River, "Gabriel, explain to
him the meaning of what he saw." 17Gabriel
came and stood beside me, and I was so ter-
rified that I fell to the ground.
He said to me, "Mortal man, understand
the meaning. The vision has to do with the
end of the world." 18While he was talking, I
fell to the ground unconscious. But he took
hold of me, raised me to my feet, 19and said,
"I am showing you what the result of God's
anger will be. The vision refers to the time
of the end.
20"The ram you saw that had two horns
represents the kingdoms of Media and Per-
sia. 21The goat represents the kingdom of
Greece, and the prominent horn between his
eyes is the first king. 22The four horns that
came up when the first horn was broken
represent the four kingdoms into which that
nation will be divided and which will not be
as strong as the first kingdom.
23"When the end of those kingdoms is
near and they have become so wicked that
they must be punished, there will be a stub-
born, vicious, and deceitful king. 24He will
grow strong—but not by his own power. He
will cause terrible destruction and be success-
ful in everything he does. He will bring
destruction on powerful men and on God's
own people. 25Because he is cunning, he will
succeed in his deceitful ways. He will be
proud of himself and destroy many people
without warning. He will even defy the
greatest King of all, but he will be destroyed
without the use of any human power. 26This
vision about the evening and morning sacri-
fices which has been explained to you will

Study it!

The Archangel Gabriel

Most of us know Gabriel as the angel who appeared to Mary to announce to her that she would become the mother of Jesus (see Luke 1:26). But it is here in the Book of Daniel that Gabriel appears for the first time in the Bible as a messenger from God. Gabriel, along with Raphael and Michael, are three archangels, or chief angels. In chapter 8 of Daniel, Gabriel explains to Daniel what his vision means.

Angels are spiritual beings and do not have physical bodies as we do. So why, do you think, are angels usually pictured with wings? It has to do with the role they play in God's plan.

— Daniel 8:15–26

[q] **8:12** People . . . sacrifices; *Hebrew unclear.*
8:16 Lk 1:19, 26

Goats in the Bible are sometimes symbolic of evil or disobedient people.

come true. But keep it secret now, because it
will be a long time before it does come true."
27 I was depressed and ill for several days.
Then I got up and went back to the work
that the king had assigned to me, but I was
puzzled by the vision and could not under-
stand it.

Daniel Prays for His People

9 Darius the Mede, who was the son of
Xerxes, ruled over the kingdom of
Babylonia. 2 In the first year of his reign I
was studying the sacred books and thinking
about the seventy years that Jerusalem would
be in ruins, according to what the LORD had
told the prophet Jeremiah. 3 And I prayed
earnestly to the Lord God, pleading with
him, fasting, wearing sackcloth, and sitting in
ashes. 4 I prayed to the LORD my God and
confessed the sins of my people.
I said, "Lord God, you are great, and we
honor you. You are faithful to your covenant
and show constant love to those who love
you and do what you command.
5 "We have sinned, we have been evil, we
have done wrong. We have rejected what
you commanded us to do and have turned
away from what you showed us was right.
6 We have not listened to your servants the
prophets, who spoke in your name to our
kings, our rulers, our ancestors, and our
whole nation. 7 You, Lord, always do what is
right, but we have always brought disgrace
on ourselves. This is true of all of us who
live in Judea and in Jerusalem and of all the
Israelites whom you scattered in countries
near and far because they were unfaithful to
you. 8 Our kings, our rulers, and our ances-
tors have acted shamefully and sinned
against you, Lord. 9 You are merciful and
forgiving, although we have rebelled against
you. 10 We did not listen to you, O LORD
our God, when you told us to live accord-
ing to the laws which you gave us through
your servants the prophets. 11 All Israel broke
your laws and refused to listen to what you
said. We sinned against you, and so you
brought on us the curses that are written in
the Law of Moses, your servant. 12 You did
what you said you would do to us and our
rulers. You punished Jerusalem more severe-
ly than any other city on earth, 13 giving us
all the punishment described in the Law of
Moses. But even now, O LORD our God, we
have not tried to please you by turning
from our sins or by following your truth.
14 You, O LORD our God, were prepared to
punish us, and you did, because you always
do what is right, and we did not listen to
you.
15 "O Lord our God, you showed your
power by bringing your people out of
Egypt, and your power is still remembered.
We have sinned; we have done wrong. 16 You
have defended us in the past, so do not be
angry with Jerusalem any longer. It is your
city, your sacred hill.[r] All the people in the
neighboring countries look down on
Jerusalem and on your people because of our
sins and the evil our ancestors did. 17 O God,
hear my prayer and pleading. Restore your
Temple, which has been destroyed; restore it
so that everyone will know that you are
God. 18 Listen to us, O God; look at us and
see the trouble we are in and the suffering of
the city that bears your name. We are praying
to you because you are merciful, not because
we have done right. 19 Lord, hear us. Lord,
forgive us. Lord, listen to us, and act! In
order that everyone will know that you are
God, do not delay! This city and these peo-
ple are yours."

"God, do not delay!" (9:19)

[r] **9:16** SACRED HILL: *Mount Zion (see Zion in Word List).*

9:2 Jer 25:11; 29:10 **9:7** Bar 1:15–17 **9:11** Bar 1:19–23 **9:15** Bar 2:11–13 **9:17** Bar 2:14 **9:18** Bar 2:19

Gabriel Explains the Prophecy

[20]I went on praying, confessing my sins
and the sins of my people Israel and pleading
with the LORD my God to restore his holy
Temple. [21]While I was praying, Gabriel,
whom I had seen in the earlier vision, came
flying down to where I was. It was the time
for the evening sacrifice to be offered. [22]He
explained, "Daniel, I have come here to help
you understand the prophecy. [23]When you
began to plead with God, he answered you.
He loves you, and so I have come to tell you
the answer. Now pay attention while I
explain the vision.

[24]"Seven times seventy years is the length
of time God has set for freeing your people
and your holy city from sin and evil. Sin will
be forgiven and eternal justice established, so
that the vision and the prophecy will come
true, and the holy Temple[s] will be rededicat-
ed. [25]Note this and understand it: From the
time the command is given to rebuild
Jerusalem until God's chosen leader comes,
seven times seven years will pass. Jerusalem
will be rebuilt with streets and strong defens-
es, and will stand for seven times sixty-two
years, but this will be a time of troubles.
[26]And at the end of that time God's chosen
leader will be killed unjustly.[t] The city and
the Temple will be destroyed by the invading
army of a powerful ruler. The end will come
like a flood, bringing the war and destruction
which God has prepared. [27]That ruler will
have a firm agreement with many people for
seven years, and when half this time is past,
he will put an end to sacrifices and offerings.
The Awful Horror[u] will be placed on the
highest point of the Temple and will remain
there until the one who put it there meets
the end which God has prepared for him."

Daniel's Vision by the Tigris River

10 In the third year that Cyrus was
emperor of Persia, a message was
revealed to Daniel, who is also called Belte-
shazzar. The message was true but extremely
hard to understand.[v] It was explained to him
in a vision.

[2]At that time I was mourning for three
weeks. [3]I did not eat any rich food or any
meat, drink any wine, or comb my hair until
the three weeks were past.

[4]On the twenty-fourth day of the first
month of the year I was standing on the
bank of the mighty Tigris River. [5]I looked
up and saw someone who was wearing linen
clothes and a belt of fine gold. [6]His body
shone like a jewel. His face was as bright as
a flash of lightning, and his eyes blazed like
fire. His arms and legs shone like polished
bronze, and his voice sounded like the roar
of a great crowd.

[7]I was the only one who saw the vision.
Those who were with me did not see any-
thing, but they were terrified and ran and
hid. [8]I was left there alone, watching this
amazing vision. I had no strength left, and
my face was so changed that no one could
have recognized me. [9]When I heard his
voice, I fell to the ground unconscious and
lay there face downward. [10]Then a hand
took hold of me and raised me to my hands
and knees; I was still trembling.

[11]The angel said to me, "Daniel, God
loves you. Stand up and listen carefully to
what I am going to say. I have been sent to
you." When he had said this, I stood up, still
trembling.

[12]Then he said, "Daniel, don't be afraid.
God has heard your prayers ever since the
first day you decided to humble yourself in
order to gain understanding. I have come in
answer to your prayer. [13]The angel prince
of the kingdom of Persia opposed me for
twenty-one days. Then Michael, one of the
chief angels, came to help me, because I had
been left there alone in Persia. [14]I have come
to make you understand what will happen to
your people in the future. This is a vision
about the future."

[15]When he said this, I stared at the
ground, speechless. [16]Then the angel, who
looked like a human being, reached out and

[s] **9:24** Temple; *or* altar. [t] **9:26** *One ancient translation* unjustly; *Hebrew unclear.* [u] **9:27** THE AWFUL HORROR: *A pagan image set up in the Jerusalem Temple by foreign conquerors (see 1 Macc 1:54–61).* [v] **10:1** but extremely hard to understand; *or* and it was about a great war.

9:21 Lk 1:19, 26 **9:27** Dan 11:31; 12:11; 1 Macc 1:44–50, 54; Mt 24:15; Mk 13:14 **10:5, 6** Rev 1:13–15; 2:18; 19:12 **10:13, 21** Rev 12:7

Catholic Connections

Michael, the Guardian

Michael is the second of the archangels to be introduced in the Book of Daniel. The name Michael means "who is like God?" in Hebrew.

Michael is referred to as Israel's guardian angel in Daniel 10:20–21. He is also famous for leading the good angels in the heavenly battle against the forces of evil in Revelation 12:7. As the guardian angel of Israel, he is responsible for protecting and helping the people of Israel. That is why he is often pictured dressed in armor with a sword.

There are also angels assigned to protect and defend every human being. These angels are also called guardian angels. You can find the story of Raphael, an archangel who helped a man named Tobias, in the Book of Tobit.

The feast of the archangels Michael, Gabriel, and Raphael is celebrated on September 29. The feast of the guardian angels is on October 2.

— Daniel 10:12—11:2

touched my lips. I said to him, "Sir, this
vision makes me so weak that I can't stop
trembling. 17 I am like a slave standing before
his master. How can I talk to you? I have no
strength or breath left in me."

18 Once more he took hold of me, and I
felt stronger. 19 He said, "God loves you, so
don't let anything worry you or frighten
you."

When he had said this, I felt even stronger
and said, "Sir, tell me what you have to say.
You have made me feel better."

20-21 He said, "Do you know why I came
to you? It is to reveal to you what is written
in the book of Truth. Now I have to go back
and fight the guardian angel of Persia. After
that the guardian angel of Greece will appear.
There is no one to help me except Michael,

11 Israel's guardian angel.[w] 1 He is[x]
responsible for helping and defend-
ing me. 2 And what I am now going to tell
you is true."

The Kingdoms of Egypt and Syria

The angel said, "Three more kings will
rule over Persia, followed by a fourth, who
will be richer than all the others. At the
height of his power and wealth he will chal-
lenge the kingdom of Greece.

3 "Then a heroic king will appear. He will
rule over a huge empire and do whatever he
wants. 4 But at the height of his power his
empire will break up and be divided into
four parts. Kings not descended from him
will rule in his place, but they will not have
the power that he had.

5 "The king of Egypt will be strong. One
of his generals, however, will be even
stronger and rule a greater kingdom. 6 After a
number of years the king of Egypt will make
an alliance with the king of Syria and give
him his daughter in marriage. But the
alliance will not last, and she, her husband,
her child,[y] and the servants who went with
her will all be killed. 7 Soon afterward one of
her relatives will become king. He will

[w] **10:20–21** *Probable text* guardian angel; *Hebrew* guardian angel. And I, in the first year of Darius the Mede.
[x] **11:20–21** *One ancient translation* He is; *Hebrew* I am. [y] **11:6** *Some ancient translations* her child; *Hebrew* her father.

The number 7 *(see Daniel 9:24)* **appears often in the Bible and signifies perfection or the right amount of time.**

attack the army of the king of Syria, enter
their fortress, and defeat them. 8 He will
carry back to Egypt the images of their gods
and the articles of gold and silver dedicated
to those gods. After several years of peace
9 the king of Syria will invade Egypt, but he
will be forced to retreat.

10 "The sons of the king of Syria will pre-
pare for war and gather a large army. One of
them will sweep on like a flood and attack
an enemy fortress. 11 In his anger the king of
Egypt will go to war against the king of
Syria and capture his huge army. 12 He will
be proud of his victory and of the many sol-
diers he has killed, but he will not continue
to be victorious.

13 "The king of Syria will go back and
gather a larger army than he had before.
When the proper time comes, he will return
with a large, well-equipped army. 14 Then
many people will rebel against the king of
Egypt. And some violent people from your
nation, Daniel, will rebel because of a vision
they have seen, but they will be defeated.
15 So the king of Syria will lay siege to a for-
tified city and capture it. The soldiers of
Egypt will not continue to fight; even the
best of them will not have enough strength.
16 The Syrian invader will do with them as
he pleases, without opposition. He will stand
in the Promised Land and have it completely
in his power.

17 "The king of Syria will plan an expedi-
tion, using his whole army. Then, in order to
destroy his enemy's kingdom, he will make
an alliance with him and offer him his
daughter[z] in marriage; but his plan will not
succeed. 18 After that he will attack the
nations by the sea and conquer many of
them. But a foreign leader will defeat him
and put an end to his arrogance; indeed he
will turn the arrogance of Syria's king back
on him.[a] 19 The king will return to the
fortresses of his own land, but he will be
defeated, and that will be the end of him.

20 "He will be followed by another king,
who will send an officer to oppress the peo-
ple with taxes in order to increase the wealth
of his kingdom. In a short time that king
will be killed, but not publicly and not in
battle."

The Evil King of Syria

21 The angel went on to explain: "The
next king of Syria will be an evil man who
has no right to be king, but he will come
unexpectedly and seize power by trickery.
22 Anyone who opposes him, even God's
High Priest, will be swept away and wiped
out. 23 By making treaties, he will deceive
other nations, and he will grow stronger and
stronger, even though he rules only a small
nation. 24 He will invade a wealthy province
without warning and will do things that
none of his ancestors ever did. Then he will
divide among his followers the goods and
property he has captured in war. He will
make plans to attack fortresses, but his time
will soon run out.

25 "He will boldly raise a large army to
attack the king of Egypt, who will prepare to
fight back with a huge and powerful army.
But the king of Egypt will be deceived and
will not be successful. 26 His closest advisers
will ruin him. Many of his soldiers will be
killed, and his army will be wiped out.
27 Then the two kings will sit down to eat at
the same table, but their motives will be evil,
and they will lie to each other. They will not
get what they want, because the time for it
has not yet come. 28 The king of Syria will
return home with all the loot he has cap-
tured, determined to destroy the religion of
God's people. He will do as he pleases and
then return to his own land.

29 "Later on he will invade Egypt again,
but this time things will turn out differently.
30 The Romans will come in ships and
oppose him, and he will be frightened.

"Then he will turn back in a rage and try
to destroy the religion of God's people. He

[z] **11:17** his daughter; *or* a young woman. [a] **11:18** *Probable text* his arrogance . . . on him; *Hebrew unclear.*
11:30 2 Macc 5:11

Four nations that still exist today are mentioned in Daniel, chapter 11. Can you identify them and find them on a map?

will follow the advice of those who have abandoned that religion. 31Some of his soldiers will make the Temple ritually unclean. They will stop the daily sacrifices and set up The Awful Horror.[b] 32By deceit the king will win the support of those who have already abandoned their religion, but those who follow God will fight back. 33Wise leaders of the people will share their wisdom with many others. But for a while some of them will be killed in battle or be burned to death, and some will be robbed and made prisoners. 34While the killing is going on, God's people will receive a little help, even though many who join them will do so for selfish reasons. 35Some of those wise leaders will be killed, but as a result of this the people will be purified. This will continue until the end comes, the time that God has set.

36"The king of Syria will do as he pleases. He will boast that he is greater than any god, superior even to the Supreme God. He will be able to do this until the time when God punishes him. God will do exactly what he has planned. 37The king will ignore the god his ancestors served, and also the god that women love. In fact, he will ignore every god, because he will think he is greater than any of them. 38Instead, he will honor the god who protects fortresses. He will offer gold, silver, jewels, and other rich gifts to a god his ancestors never worshiped. 39To defend his fortresses, he will use people who worship a foreign god. He will give great honor to those who accept him as ruler, put them into high offices, and give them land as a reward.

40"When the king of Syria's final hour has almost come, the king of Egypt will attack him, and the king of Syria will fight back with all his power, using chariots, horses, and many ships. He will invade many countries, like the waters of a flood. 41He will even invade the Promised Land and kill tens of thousands, but the countries of Edom, Moab, and what is left of Ammon will escape. 42When he invades all those countries, even Egypt will not be spared. 43He will take away Egypt's hidden treasures of gold and silver and its other prized possessions. He will conquer Libya and Ethiopia.[c] 44Then news that comes from the east and the north will frighten him, and he will fight furiously, killing many people. 45He will even set up his huge royal tents between the sea and the mountain on which the Temple stands. But he will die, with no one there to help him."

The Time of the End

12 The angel wearing linen clothes said, "At that time the great angel Michael, who guards your people, will appear. Then there will be a time of troubles, the worst since nations first came into existence. When that time comes, all the people of your nation whose names are written in God's book will be saved. 2Many of those who have already died will live again: some will enjoy eternal life, and some will suffer eternal disgrace. 3The wise leaders will shine with all the brightness of the sky. And those who have taught many people to do what is right will shine like the stars forever."

4He said to me, "And now, Daniel, close the book and put a seal on it until the end of the world. Meanwhile, many people will

Daniel, close the book. (12:4)

[b] **11:31** THE AWFUL HORROR: *See 9:27.* [c] **11:43** *Hebrew* Cush: *Cush is the ancient name of the extensive territory south of the First Cataract of the Nile River. This region was called Ethiopia in Graeco-Roman times, and included within its borders most of modern Sudan and some of present-day Ethiopia (Abyssinia).*

11:31 Dan 9:27; 12:11; Mt 24:15; Mk 13:14 **11:36** **a** 2 Thess 2:3, 4; **b** Rev 13:5, 6 **12:1** **a** Rev 12:7; **b** Mt 24:21; Mk 13:19; Rev 7:14; 12:7 **12:2** Isa 26:19; 2 Macc 7:9–11, 14; Mt 25:46; Jn 5:29 **12:4** Rev 22:10

waste their efforts trying to understand what
is happening."
5 Then I saw two men standing by a river,
one on each bank. 6 One of them asked the
angel who was standing further upstream,
"How long will it be until these amazing
events come to an end?"
7 The angel raised both hands toward the
sky and made a solemn promise in the name
of the Eternal God. I heard him say, "It will
be three and a half years. When the persecu-
tion of God's people ends, all these things
will have happened."
8 I heard what he said, but I did not
understand it. So I asked, "But, sir, how will
it all end?"
9 He answered, "You must go now, Daniel,
because these words are to be kept secret
and hidden until the end comes. 10 Many
people will be purified. Those who are
wicked will not understand but will go on
being wicked; only those who are wise will
understand.
11 "From the time the daily sacrifices are
stopped, that is, from the time of The Awful
Horror,[d] 1,290 days will pass. 12 Happy are
those who remain faithful until 1,335 days
are over!
13 "And you, Daniel, be faithful to the
end. Then you will die, but you will rise to
receive your reward at the end of time."

Susanna's Beauty Attracts Two Judges

B In Babylon there lived a man named
Joakim, 2 who was married to Susanna,
daughter of Hilkiah. Susanna was a beautiful
woman and deeply religious. 3 Her parents
were devout Jews who had brought up their
daughter to live according to the Law of
Moses. 4 Her husband Joakim was very
wealthy. Lovely gardens surrounded his
house, and the other Jews often gathered
there for meetings, because they all thought
so highly of him. 5-6 Everyone who had a
legal case to present would also go to
Joakim's house, where two judges held
court. These two leaders of the Jewish com-
munity had recently been appointed to
office. They were the ones about whom the
Lord said, "There is wickedness in Babylon;
judges are failing to give guidance to the
people."
7 Every day at noon, when all the people
left for lunch, Susanna used to take a walk in

Live it!

Lust and Self-Control

Do you know what the word *lust* means? A very good example of it is in Daniel, chapter B, the story of Susanna. Lust refers to a strong desire or craving. For example, you can lust after a candy bar, which means you really want a candy bar. Lust usually refers to sexual desire, though. In the story of Susanna, two judges lust after Susanna. They see her only as a sexual object, and they try to force her into having sex. When she refuses, the judges try to condemn her. Daniel saves the day and the life of innocent Susanna.

Lust can lead us to treat others not as human beings but as objects. Pornography is all about lust. What it does is to make sexual objects out of human beings and bring out the worst in us. We need to avoid pornography because it only increases our lust while decreasing our respect for others. Human bodies are wonderful, but not when they are used simply to bring out the worst in us. That is what pornography is about.

Think about why giving in to lust is such a dangerous thing to do.

— Daniel, chapter B

[d] **12:11** THE AWFUL HORROR: *See 9:27.*

12:7 a Rev 10:5; **b** Rev 12:14 **12:10** Rev 22:11 **12:11** Dan 9:27; 11:31; Mt 24:15; Mk 13:14

the gardens. 8The two judges were so attracted to her that they would wait around and watch for her. 9They became so obsessed with their desire for her that they lost interest both in prayer and in their responsibility as judges. 10They each wanted Susanna, but neither told the other how he felt, 11for each was ashamed to admit his lust. 12So day after day they watched eagerly to catch sight of her.

13One day at noon they said to each other, "It's time for lunch; let's go home." 14So they both left and went their separate ways, but soon each one came back for a look at Susanna, and by accident they met each other. At first each tried to explain what he was doing there, but finally they both confessed their desire for Susanna. They decided to watch for a time when they might find her alone. 15-17So they kept waiting for the right opportunity.

Each one came back for a look at Susanna. (B:14)

The Judges Try to Seduce Susanna

One day Susanna went into the garden as usual with her two servant women. No one else was there, except the two judges, who had hidden themselves and were watching Susanna. It was very hot and she decided to take a bath. So she said to her servants, "Bring me some bath oil and some perfume, and lock the gates, so that I won't be disturbed." 18The servants locked the main gates and went out by the side door to get what Susanna had asked for. They did not notice the two men.

19As soon as the servants had left, the two judges jumped out from their hiding place, ran to Susanna, 20and said to her, "The gates are locked and no one will see us. We are burning to have sex with you, so give us what we want. 21If you don't, we will go to court and swear that we saw you send your servants away, so that you could be alone with a young man."

22"There is no way out," Susanna moaned. "If I give in to you, I could be put to death for adultery. If I refuse, you will still have me trapped. 23But I would rather be your innocent victim than sin against the Lord." 24So she started screaming as loud as she could, and the two judges began shouting accusations, 25while one of them ran and unlocked the gates.

26As soon as the servants in the house heard all the noise, they ran into the gardens through the side door to find out what had happened to Susanna. 27The judges told their story, and the servants were shocked and ashamed. Such a thing had never before been said about Susanna.

The Judges Testify against Susanna

28The next day, when the people assembled at Joakim's house, the two judges arrived, fully determined to carry out their wicked plan to have Susanna put to death. 29In front of all the people they said, "Send for Joakim's wife Susanna, the daughter of Hilkiah." When she was called, 30she came in with her parents, her children, and all her other relatives. 31Susanna was so graceful and beautiful 32that the two wicked men ordered her veil to be removed, so that they might

B:22 Lev 20:10; Deut 22:22

In the story of Susanna, Daniel acts like a crime scene detective. What trick does he use to uncover the judges' lies?

enjoy looking at her. 33 Her family and everyone else were in tears.

34 Then the two judges stood up in front of the people, placed their hands on Susanna's head, and began making their accusations against her. 35 She was crying, but she looked up to heaven because she trusted the Lord. 36 The two men gave the following testimony: "We were walking in the gardens when this woman came in with her two servant women. She locked the main gates and asked the servants to leave. 37 Then a young man who had been hiding in the gardens came to her, and they lay down together. 38 We were in a corner of the gardens, and when we saw what was happening, we ran over 39 and caught them in the act. We tried to hold on to the man, but he was too strong for us. He ran and opened the gates and got away, 40 but we were able to hold the woman. We asked her who the man was, but she refused to tell us. We swear that our testimony is true." 41 Because the two men were not only leaders in the community but also judges, the people believed their story and condemned Susanna to death.

Daniel Rescues Susanna

42 Then Susanna cried out in a loud voice, "Eternal God, nothing can be kept secret from you; you know everything before it happens. 43 Here I am about to die, but you know that I am innocent, that these men are lying. Why must I die?"

44 The Lord heard her prayer 45 and led a young man named Daniel to speak out, just as Susanna was being taken away to her death. 46 He shouted, "I refuse to be a party to her death!"

47 Everyone turned around to look at him and asked, "What are you talking about?"

48 Daniel stood up before them and said, "People of Israel, how foolish can you be? Are you going to condemn an Israelite woman to death on this kind of evidence? You haven't even tried to find out the truth. 49 Reopen the case. The testimony these men gave was a lie."

50 So all the people hurried back to where the trial had taken place, and the officials said to Daniel, "God has given you wisdom beyond your years, so come and join us and explain to us what you mean."

51 Daniel said to them, "Separate the two judges, and let me question them one at a time." 52 Then Daniel called the first judge and said, "You wicked old man, now you will have to answer for all the sins you have committed. 53 You have been giving unjust sentences. You have condemned the innocent and released the guilty, even though the Lord has said, 'Do not put an innocent person to death.' 54 Now if you really did see this couple making love, tell me, what tree were they under?"

"Under a small gum tree," he answered.

55 Daniel said, "All right! That lie will cost you your life. God's angel has already been given orders to chop[e] you in two."

56 Then the first judge was led away and the second one was brought before Daniel. "You are more like a Canaanite than a Jew," Daniel said to him. "This woman's beauty has warped your judgment, and lust has corrupted your thinking. 57 You are used to having your way with the women of Israel because they have been afraid of you, but here is a Jewish woman, and she would not give in. 58 Now, tell me what tree you saw them under."

"Under a large oak tree," he answered.

59 Daniel said, "All right! That lie will cost you your life; God's angel is waiting with his sword in his hand, ready to cut[f] you in two. Then we shall be rid of you both."

60 Then all the people shouted and praised God, who saves those who put their trust in him. 61 They turned against the two judges because Daniel had proved that they had lied

[e] **B:55** CHOP: *This word in Greek sounds like the Greek for "a small gum tree."* [f] **B:59** CUT: *This word in Greek sounds like the Greek for "a large oak tree."*

B:53 Ex 23:7

Daniel shows God's power not by force but by cleverness. What clever plan did he use to uncover the secret of the priests of Bel?

under oath. 62 The Law of Moses states that
people who give false testimony shall receive
the same punishment that the accused per-
son would have received. And so the two
judges were put to death, and the life of an
innocent woman was saved. 63 Susanna's par-
ents, her husband, and all her relatives praised
God because she had been proved innocent
of the charges. 64 From that day on, Daniel
was held in high regard.

Daniel and the Priests of Bel

C After the death of King Astyages,
Cyrus of Persia took over his king-
dom. 2 Daniel was one of King Cyrus' closest
companions, and the king thought more
highly of Daniel than of any other of his
advisers.

3 The Babylonians had an idol named Bel.
Each day the people had to provide Bel with
an offering of twelve bushels of fine flour,
forty sheep, and fifty gallons of wine. 4 King
Cyrus believed that Bel was a god, and each
day he used to go and worship it. But Daniel
worshiped his own God.

5 One day the king asked Daniel, "Why
don't you worship Bel?"

Daniel answered, "I do not worship idols
made with human hands. I worship only the
living God, who created heaven and earth
and is the Lord of all human beings."

6 "And don't you believe that our god Bel
is really alive?" asked the king. "Haven't you
seen how much he eats and drinks every
day?"

7 Daniel laughed and said, "Don't be
fooled, Your Majesty. This god you call Bel is
nothing more than clay covered with
bronze; it has never eaten or drunk any-
thing."

8-10 At this the king became angry and
called in all seventy of the priests of Bel. He
said to them, "I warn you that you will be
put to death, unless you can show me that it
is Bel who is eating these offerings. If you
prove to me that it is Bel, then I will have
Daniel put to death for claiming that Bel is
not a god."

Daniel agreed to this proposal.

11 Then they all went with the king into
Bel's temple, where the priests said to the
king, "Your Majesty, we will go out and let
you place the food on the table and prepare
the wine. When you leave, you may lock the
door behind you and seal it with the royal
seal. 12 In the morning when you return, if
you find that Bel has not eaten everything,
you can put us to death. But if he has,
Daniel will die for making false accusations
against us."

13 But the priests were not worried,
because they had made a secret entrance
underneath a table in the temple, so that
they could go in every night and eat the
offerings.

14 When the priests had left, the king set
out the food for Bel. Then Daniel ordered
his servants to bring some ashes and scatter
them all over the floor of the temple. No
one except the king saw them do this. After
that they all went out, locked the door,
sealed it with the royal seal, and left.

The king set out the food for Bel. (C:14)

15 That night, as usual, the priests with
their wives and children came into the tem-
ple by the secret entrance and ate all the
food and drank all the wine.

16 Early the next morning, the king and
Daniel went to the temple. 17 The king
asked, "Have the seals been broken, Daniel?"

"No, Your Majesty, they have not been
broken," he replied.

18 As soon as the door was opened, the
king saw the empty table and shouted, "You
are great, O Bel! You really are a god."

B:62 Deut 19:16–21 **C:3** Isa 46:1; Jer 51:44

19 But Daniel began to laugh and said to the king, "Before you enter the temple, look at the floor and tell me whose footprints you see there."

20 "I see the footprints of men, women, and children," said the king, 21 and he became so angry that he had the priests and their families arrested and brought to him. They showed him the secret doors through which they had come in each night to eat the food placed on the table. 22 So the king had the priests put to death, and he gave Bel to Daniel, who destroyed the idol and tore down its temple.

He gave Bel to Daniel, who destroyed the idol. (C:22)

Daniel Kills the Dragon

23 There was also a huge dragon which the Babylonians worshiped. 24 One day the king said to Daniel, "You can't tell me that this god is not alive. So worship him!"

25 "I worship the Lord," replied Daniel. "He is the only living God. 26 And if Your Majesty will give me permission, I will kill this dragon of yours without using a sword or a club."

"You have my permission," answered the king.

27 So Daniel took some tar, some fat, and some hair and boiled them all together. He made cakes out of the mixture and fed them to the dragon. When the dragon ate them, it swelled up and burst open. "That's the kind of thing you Babylonians worship," said Daniel.

28 When the people of Babylon heard what had happened, they staged an angry demonstration against the king. "The king has become a Jew," they shouted. "First he destroyed Bel and slaughtered the priests, and now he has killed our dragon." 29 They went to the king and demanded that Daniel be handed over to them. "If you refuse," they warned the king, "we will put you and your family to death."

30 When the king saw that they meant what they said, he was forced to hand Daniel over to them. 31 They threw him into a pit of lions, where they left him for six days. 32 There were seven lions in the pit, and normally they were fed two human bodies and two sheep each day. But they were given nothing to eat during these six days, in order to make sure that Daniel would be eaten.

Daniel Is Rescued from the Pit of Lions

33 At that time the prophet Habakkuk was in the land of Judah. He had cooked a stew and crumbled bread into it. He was carrying a bowl of it to the workers who were out in the fields harvesting grain, 34 when an angel of the Lord spoke to him, "Take the food you are carrying and give it to Daniel, who is in Babylon in a pit of lions."

35 Habakkuk answered, "Sir, I have never been to Babylon, and I don't know where the pit of lions is."

36 So the angel grabbed the prophet by the hair and took him to Babylon with the speed of the wind.[g] He set him down near the pit of lions. 37 Habakkuk called out, "Daniel! Daniel! God has sent you some food. Here, take it."

38 When Daniel heard Habakkuk, he prayed, "God, you did remember me; you never abandon those who love you." 39 Then he got up and ate the meal, and God's angel immediately took Habakkuk home.

40 Seven days after Daniel had been thrown to the lions, the king went to the pit to mourn for him. When he got there and looked in, there sat Daniel. 41 The king

[g] **C:36** with the speed of the wind; *or* by the power of his spirit.

C:31, 32 Dan 6:16–24 **C:36** Ezek 8:3

The king shouted, "O Lord, the God of Daniel, how great you are." (C:41)

shouted, "O Lord, the God of Daniel, how great you are. You alone are God." 42So he pulled Daniel out of the pit and had those who had tried to kill Daniel thrown into it. And the lions ate them immediately, while the king watched.

Your Next Step

Congratulations on finishing the Book of Daniel! Use this space to write your thoughts and questions about this book. If you are following the suggested reading plan, go back to the Book of Job in the Old Testament. This book is a reflection on why God allows people to suffer.

THE BOOK OF Hosea

Why would God tell a prophet to marry and have children with a prostitute who would be unfaithful to him? To make a point—to show the people of Israel how they were unfaithful to God.

God told Hosea to marry a prostitute named Gomer. Hosea did what he was told and had three children with her. Their names communicated God's message to his people. Jezreel is named for a place of great bloodshed and tells of God's punishment to come. The second child was named "Unloved," which tells that God no longer shows mercy to Israel. The third, "Not-My-People" tells that God's people were unfaithful. But no matter how often God's people were unfaithful, God is always faithful. Like Hosea's love for Gomer, God's love for us is unfailing.

Chap. 11:3

Headlines

- Prophet Marries Prostitute (1:2–8)
- God's Great Love for His People (2:19–23)
- God Desires Love Not Sacrifice (6:1–6)
- Israelites Sow the Wind, Reap a Storm! (8:1–10)
- God Extends Loving Arms! (11:1–4)

FACTOIDS

Who wrote this book? Hosea, who preached to the northern kingdom of Israel before the Israelites were conquered by the Assyrians.

What period does it cover? Around 786–722 BC.

Why was it written? Hosea used his marriage to the unfaithful prostitute Gomer to illustrate the unfaithfulness of the Israelites and God's faithful and persistent love for them.

Jesus connection: Just as Hosea forgave Gomer every time she left him and was unfaithful, Jesus forgives all of our sins. The reference to Jesus in Matthew 2:15, "I called my Son out of Egypt," is taken from Hosea 11:1.

Important themes

- Those who rely on wealth and power are likely to forget all about God.
- Like a loving parent, God loves us, is waiting for us, and is ready to take us back—even when we are "not worthy."
- Poor choices will have poor results, and evil actions will have evil consequences.

HOSEA

1 This is the message which the LORD
gave Hosea son of Beeri during the
time that Uzziah, Jotham, Ahaz, and Hezeki-
ah were kings of Judah, and Jeroboam son of
Jehoash was king of Israel.

Hosea's Wife and Children

2When the LORD first spoke to Israel
through Hosea, he said to Hosea, "Go and
get married; your wife will be unfaithful, and
your children will be just like her.[a] In the
same way my people have left me and
become unfaithful."

3So Hosea married a woman named
Gomer, the daughter of Diblaim. After the
birth of their first child, a son, 4the LORD said
to Hosea, "Name him 'Jezreel,' because it will
not be long before I punish the king of Israel
for the murders that his ancestor Jehu com-
mitted at Jezreel.[b] I am going to put an end
to Jehu's dynasty.[c] 5And in Jezreel Valley I will
at that time destroy Israel's military power."

6Gomer had a second child—this time it
was a daughter. The LORD said to Hosea,
"Name her 'Unloved,' because I will no
longer show love to the people of Israel or
forgive them. 7But to the people of Judah I
will show love. I, the LORD their God, will
save them, but I will not do it by war—with
swords or bows and arrows or with horses
and horsemen."

8After Gomer had weaned her daughter,
she became pregnant again and had another
son. 9The LORD said to Hosea, "Name him
'Not-My-People,' because the people of Israel
are not my people, and I am not their God."

Israel Is to Be Restored

10The people of Israel will become like
the sand of the sea, more than can be count-
ed or measured. Now God says to them,
"You are not my people," but the day is
coming when he will say to them, "You are
the children of the living God!" 11The peo-
ple of Judah and the people of Israel will be
reunited. They will choose for themselves a
single leader, and once again they will grow
and prosper in their land. Yes, the day of
2 Jezreel[d] will be a great day! 1So call
your fellow Israelites "God's People"
and "Loved-by-the-Lord."

Unfaithful Gomer—Unfaithful Israel

2My children, plead with your mother—
though she is no longer a wife to me, and I
am no longer her husband. Plead with her to
stop her adultery and prostitution. 3If she
does not, I will strip her as naked as she was
on the day she was born. I will make her
like a dry and barren land, and she will die
of thirst. 4-5I will not show mercy to her
children; they are the children of a shameless
prostitute.[e] She herself said, "I will go to my
lovers—they give me food and water, wool
and linen, olive oil and wine."

6So I am going to fence her in with thorn
bushes and build a wall to block her way.
7She will run after her lovers but will not
catch them. She will look for them but will
not find them. Then she will say, "I am going
back to my first husband—I was better off
then than I am now."

8She would never acknowledge that I am
the one who gave her the grain, the wine,
the olive oil, and all the silver and gold that
she used in the worship of Baal. 9So at har-
vest time I will take back my gifts of grain
and wine, and will take away the wool and
the linen I gave her for clothing. 10I will strip
her naked in front of her lovers, and no one
will be able to save her from my power.

[a] **1.2** get married; your wife . . . her; *or* marry a prostitute, and have children by her who will be just as bad as she is. [b] **1.4** JEZREEL: *At this city Jehu assassinated the king of Israel and all the rest of the royal family, and became the first king of a new dynasty (see 2 Kings 9–10).* [c] **1.4** Jehu's dynasty; *or* the kingdom of Israel. [d] **1.11** JEZREEL: *This name in Hebrew means "God sows" and suggests growth and prosperity.* [e] **2.4–5** the children of a shameless prostitute; *or* as shameless as their mother, a prostitute.

1:1 **a** 2 Kings 15:1–7; 2 Chr 26:1–23; **b** 2 Kings 15:32–38; 2 Chr 27:1–8; **c** 2 Kings 16:1–20; 2 Chr 28:1–27; **d** 2 Kings 18:1—20:21; 2 Chr 29:1—32:33; **e** 2 Kings 14:23–29 **1:4** 2 Kings 10:11 **1:10** Rom 9:26

11I will put an end to all her festivities—her
annual and monthly festivals and her Sabbath
celebrations—all her religious meetings. 12I
will destroy her grapevines and her fig trees,
which she said her lovers gave her for serving
them. I will turn her vineyards and orchards
into a wilderness; wild animals will destroy
them. 13I will punish her for the times that
she forgot me, when she burned incense to
Baal and put on her jewelry to go chasing
after her lovers. The LORD has spoken.

The LORD's Love for His People

14So I am going to take her into the
desert again; there I will win her back with
words of love. 15I will give back to her the
vineyards she had and make Trouble Valley a
door of hope. She will respond to me there
as she did when she was young, when she
came from Egypt. 16Then once again she
will call me her husband—she will no
longer call me her Baal.[f] 17I will never let
her speak the name of Baal again.

18At that time I will make a covenant
with all the wild animals and birds, so that
they will not harm my people. I will also
remove all weapons of war from the land, all
swords and bows, and will let my people live
in peace and safety.

Let my people live in peace. (2:18)

19Israel, I will make you my wife;
I will be true and faithful;
I will show you constant love and mercy
and make you mine forever.
20I will keep my promise and make you mine,
and you will acknowledge me as LORD.
21-22At that time I will answer the prayers of my people Israel.[g]
I will make rain fall on the earth,
and the earth will produce grain and grapes and olives.
23I will establish my people in the land and make them prosper.
I will show love to those who were called "Unloved,"
and to those who were called "Not-My-People"
I will say, "You are my people,"
and they will answer, "You are our God."

Hosea and the Unfaithful Woman

3 The LORD said to me, "Go again[h] and
show your love for a woman who is
committing adultery with a lover. You must
love her just as I still love the people of
Israel, even though they turn to other gods
and like to take offerings of raisins to idols."[i]

2So I paid fifteen pieces of silver and
seven bushels of barley to buy her. 3I told
her that for a long time she would have to
wait for me without being a prostitute or
committing adultery; and during this time
I would wait for her. 4In just this way the
people of Israel will have to live for a long
time without kings or leaders, without sacri-
fices or sacred stone pillars, without idols or
images to use for divination. 5But the time
will come when the people of Israel will
once again turn to the LORD their God and
to a descendant of David their king. Then
they will fear the LORD and will receive his
good gifts.

[f] **2.16** BAAL: *This title of the Canaanite god means "Lord"; another meaning of the word is "husband."*
[g] **2.21–22** ISRAEL: *The Hebrew text here refers to Israel as Jezreel (see 1.4, 11).* [h] **3.1** The LORD . . . again; *or* The LORD spoke to me again. He said, "Go . . . " [i] **3.1** OFFERINGS OF RAISINS TO IDOLS: *Dried grapes were used in the worship of fertility gods, who were believed to give abundant harvests to their worshipers.*

2:15 Josh 7:24–26 **2:23** Rom 9:25; 1 Pet 2:10

The LORD's Accusation against Israel

4 The LORD has an accusation to bring
against the people who live in this land.
Listen, Israel, to what he says: "There is no
faithfulness or love in the land, and the peo-
ple do not acknowledge me as God. 2 They
make promises and break them; they lie,
murder, steal, and commit adultery. Crimes
increase, and there is one murder after
another. 3 And so the land will dry up, and
everything that lives on it will die. All the
animals and birds, and even the fish, will
die."

The LORD Accuses the Priests

4 The LORD says, "Let no one accuse the
people or reprimand them—my complaint is
against you priests.[j] 5 Night and day you
blunder on, and the prophets do no better
than you. I am going to destroy Israel, your
mother. 6 My people are doomed because
they do not acknowledge me. You priests
have refused to acknowledge me and have
rejected my teaching, and so I reject you and
will not acknowledge your sons as my
priests.

7 "The more of you priests there are, the
more you sin against me, and so I will turn
your honor into disgrace. 8 You grow rich
from the sins of my people, and so you want
them to sin more and more. 9 You will suffer
the same punishment as the people! I will
punish you and make you pay for the evil
you do. 10 You will eat your share of the sac-
rifices, but still be hungry. You will worship
the fertility gods, but still have no children,
because you have turned away from me to
follow other gods."

The LORD Condemns Pagan Worship

11 The LORD says, "Wine, both old and
new, is robbing my people of their senses!
12 They ask for revelations from a piece of
wood! A stick tells them what they want to

They ask for revelations from a piece of wood! (4:12)

know! They have left me. Like a woman
who becomes a prostitute, they have given
themselves to other gods. 13 At sacred places
on the mountaintops they offer sacrifices,
and on the hills they burn incense under tall,
spreading trees, because the shade is so pleas-
ant!

"As a result, your daughters serve as pros-
titutes, and your daughters-in-law commit
adultery. 14 Yet I will not punish them for
this, because you yourselves go off with tem-
ple prostitutes,[k] and together with them you
offer pagan sacrifices. As the proverb says, 'A
people without sense will be ruined.'

15 "Even though you people of Israel are
unfaithful to me, may Judah not be guilty of
the same thing. Don't worship at Gilgal or
Bethaven,[l] or make promises there in the
name of the living LORD. 16 The people of
Israel are as stubborn as mules. How can I
feed them like lambs in a meadow? 17 The
people of Israel are under the spell of idols.
Let them go their own way. 18 After drinking
much wine, they delight in their prostitution,
preferring disgrace to honor. 19 They will be
carried away as by the wind, and they will be
ashamed of their pagan sacrifices.[m,n]

5 "Listen to this, you priests! Pay atten-
tion, people of Israel! Listen, you that
belong to the royal family! You are supposed

[j] **4.4** *Probable text* my complaint is against you priests; *Hebrew* your people are like those with a complaint against the priests. [k] **4.14** TEMPLE PROSTITUTES: *These women were found in Canaanite temples, where fertility gods were worshiped. It was believed that intercourse with these prostitutes assured fertile fields and herds.* [l] **4.15** BETHAVEN: *This name means "house of evil" or "house of idolatry" and in this passage refers to the city of Bethel, a name which means "house of God." See also 10.8.* [m] **4.19** sacrifices; *some ancient translations* altars. [n] **4.19** *Verses 17–19 in Hebrew are unclear.*

to judge with justice—so judgment will fall
on you! You have become a trap at Mizpah,
a net spread on Mount Tabor, 2a deep pit at
Acacia City,[o] and I will punish all of you. 3I
know what Israel is like—she cannot hide
from me. She has been unfaithful, and her
people are unfit to worship me."

Hosea Warns against Idolatry

4The evil that the people have done keeps
them from returning to their God. Idolatry
has a powerful hold on them, and they do
not acknowledge the LORD. 5The arrogance
of the people of Israel cries out against
them. Their sins make them stumble and fall,
and the people of Judah fall with them.
6They take their sheep and cattle to offer as
sacrifices to the LORD, but it does them no
good. They cannot find him, for he has left
them. 7They have been unfaithful to the
LORD; their children do not belong to him.
So now they and their lands will soon be
destroyed.

War between Judah and Israel

8Blow the war trumpets in Gibeah! Sound
the alarm in Ramah! Raise the war cry at
Bethaven![p] Into battle, men of Benjamin!
9The day of punishment is coming, and
Israel will be ruined. People of Israel, this
will surely happen!

10The LORD says, "I am angry because the
leaders of Judah have invaded Israel and
stolen land from her. So I will pour out pun-
ishment on them like a flood. 11Israel is suf-
fering oppression; she has lost land that was
rightfully hers, because she insisted on going
for help to those who had none to give.[q] 12I
will bring destruction on Israel and ruin on
the people of Judah.

13"When Israel saw how sick she was and
when Judah saw her own wounds, then
Israel went to Assyria to ask the great
emperor for help, but he could not cure
them or heal their wounds. 14I will attack
the people of Israel and Judah like a lion. I
myself will tear them to pieces and then
leave them. When I drag them off, no one
will be able to save them.

15"I will abandon my people until they
have suffered enough for their sins and come
looking for me. Perhaps in their suffering
they will try to find me."

The People's Insincere Repentance

6 The people say, "Let's return to the
LORD! He has hurt us, but he will be
sure to heal us; he has wounded us, but he
will bandage our wounds, won't he? 2In two
or three days he will revive us, and we will
live in his presence. 3Let us try to know the
LORD. He will come to us as surely as the
day dawns, as surely as the spring rains fall
upon the earth."

4But the LORD says, "Israel and Judah,
what am I going to do with you? Your love
for me disappears as quickly as morning
mist; it is like dew, that vanishes early in the
day. 5That is why I have sent my prophets to
you with my message of judgment and
destruction. What I want from you is plain
and clear: 6I want your constant love, not
your animal sacrifices. I would rather have
my people know me than burn offerings
to me.

7"But as soon as they entered the land at
Adam,[r] they broke the covenant I had made
with them. 8Gilead is a city full of evil peo-
ple and murderers. 9The priests are like a
gang of robbers who wait in ambush for
someone. Even on the road to the holy place
at Shechem they commit murder. And they
do all this evil deliberately! 10I have seen a
horrible thing in Israel: my people have
defiled themselves by worshiping idols.

11"And as for you, people of Judah, I have
set a time to punish you also for what you
are doing.

7 "Whenever I want to heal my people
Israel and make them prosperous again,
all I can see is their wickedness and the evil

[o] **5.2** *Probable text* a deep pit at Acacia City; *Hebrew unclear.* [p] **5.8** BETHAVEN: *This name means "house of evil" or "house of idolatry" and in this passage refers to the city of Bethel, a name which means "house of God." See also 10.8.*
[q] **5.11** *Probable text* those who had none to give; *Hebrew* command. [r] **6.7** *Probable text* But . . . at Adam; *Hebrew* But like Adam.

6:6 Mt 9:13; 12:7

they do. They cheat one another; they break
into houses and steal; they rob people in the
streets. 2It never enters their heads that I will
remember all this evil; but their sins sur-
round them, and I cannot avoid seeing
them."

Conspiracy in the Palace

3The LORD says, "People deceive the king
and his officers by their evil plots. 4They are
all treacherous and disloyal. Their hatred
smolders like the fire in an oven, which is
not stirred by the baker until the dough is
ready to bake. 5On the day of the king's cel-
ebration they made the king and his officials
drunk and foolish with wine. 6Yes, they
burned[s] like an oven with their plotting. All
night their anger smoldered, and in the
morning it burst into flames.

7"In the heat of their anger they mur-
dered their rulers. Their kings have been
assassinated one after another, but no one
prays to me for help."

Israel and the Nations

8The LORD says, "The people of Israel are
like a half-baked loaf of bread. They rely on
the nations around them 9and do not realize
that this reliance on foreigners has robbed
them of their strength. Their days are num-
bered, but they don't even know it. 10The
arrogance of the people of Israel cries out
against them. In spite of everything that has
happened, they have not returned to me, the
LORD their God. 11Israel flits around like a
silly pigeon; first her people call on Egypt
for help, and then they run to Assyria! 12But
I will spread out a net and catch them like
birds as they go by. I will punish them for
the evil they have done.[t]

13"They are doomed! They have left me
and rebelled against me. They will be
destroyed. I wanted to save them, but their
worship of me was false. 14They have not
prayed to me sincerely, but instead they
throw themselves down and wail as the hea-
then do. When they pray for grain and wine,
they gash themselves like pagans. What rebels
they are! 15Even though I was the one who
brought them up and made them strong,
they plotted against me. 16They keep on
turning away from me to a god that is pow-
erless.[u] They are as unreliable as a crooked
bow. Because their leaders talk arrogantly,
they will die a violent death, and the Egyp-
tians will laugh."

The LORD Condemns Israel for Idol Worship

8 The LORD says, "Sound the alarm! Ene-
mies are swooping down on my land
like eagles! My people have broken the
covenant I made with them and have
rebelled against my teaching. 2Even though
they call me their God and claim that they
are my people and that they know me, 3they
have rejected what is good. Because of this
their enemies will pursue them.

4"My people chose kings, but they did it
on their own. They appointed leaders, but
without my approval. They took their silver
and gold and made idols—for their own
destruction. 5I hate the gold bull worshiped
by the people of the city of Samaria. I am
furious with them. How long will it be
before they give up their idolatry? 6An
Israelite craftsman made the idol, and it is
not a god at all! The gold bull worshiped in
Samaria will be smashed to pieces! 7When
they sow the wind, they will reap a storm! A
field of grain that doesn't ripen can never
produce any bread. But even if it did, for-
eigners would eat it up. 8Israel has become
like any other nation and is as useless as a
broken pot. 9Stubborn as wild donkeys, the
people of Israel go their own way. They have
gone off to seek help from Assyria and have
paid other nations to protect them. 10But
now I am going to gather them together and
punish them. Soon they will writhe in pain
when the emperor of Assyria oppresses
them.

11"The more altars the people of Israel
build for removing sin, the more places they
have for sinning! 12I write down countless
teachings for the people, but they reject
them as strange and foreign. 13They offer

[s] **7.6** *One ancient translation* burned; *Hebrew* drew near. [t] **7.12** *Probable text* the evil they have done; *Hebrew* the report to their congregation. [u] **7.16** *Probable text* a god that is powerless; *Hebrew unclear.*

sacrifices to me and eat the meat of the sac-
rifices.[v] But I, the LORD, am not pleased
with them, and now I will remember their
sin and punish them for it; I will send them
back to Egypt!
14“The people of Israel have built palaces,
but they have forgotten their own Maker.
The people of Judah have built fortified
cities. But I will send fire that will burn
down their palaces and their cities.”

Hosea Announces Punishment for Israel

9 People of Israel, stop celebrating your
festivals like pagans. You have turned
away from your God and have been unfaith-
ful to him. All over the land you have sold
yourselves like prostitutes to the god Baal and
have loved the grain you thought he paid you
with! 2But soon you will not have enough
grain and olive oil, and there will be no wine.
3The people of Israel will not remain in the
LORD's land, but will have to go back to
Egypt and will have to eat forbidden food[w] in
Assyria. 4In those foreign lands they will not
be able to make wine offerings to the LORD
or bring their sacrifices to him. Their food
will defile everyone who eats it, like food
eaten at funerals. It will be used only to satisfy
their hunger; none of it will be taken as an
offering to the LORD's Temple. 5And when
the time comes for the appointed festivals in
honor of the LORD, what will they do then?
6When the disaster comes and the people are
scattered, the Egyptians will gather them
up—gather them for burial there at Mem-
phis! Their treasures of silver and the places
where their homes once stood will be over-
grown with weeds and thorn bushes.
7The time for punishment has come, the
time when people will get what they
deserve. When that happens, Israel will know
it! “This prophet,” you say, “is a fool. This
inspired man is insane.” You people hate me
so much because your sin is so great. 8God
has sent me as a prophet to warn his people
Israel. Yet wherever I go, you try to trap me
like a bird. Even in God's Temple the people
are the prophet's enemies. 9They are hope-
lessly evil in what they do, just as they were
at Gibeah.[x] God will remember their sin and
punish them for it.

Israel's Sin and Its Consequences

10The LORD says, “When I first found
Israel, it was like finding grapes growing in
the desert. When I first saw your ancestors, it
was like seeing the first ripe figs of the sea-
son. But when they came to Mount Peor,
they began to worship Baal and soon became
as disgusting as the gods they loved. 11Israel's
greatness will fly away like a bird, and there
will be no more children born to them, no
more women pregnant, no more children
conceived. 12But even if they did bring up
children, I would take them away and not
leave one alive. When I abandon these peo-
ple, terrible things will happen to them.”
13LORD, I can see their children being
hunted down[y] and killed. 14What shall I ask
you to do to these people? Make their
women barren! Make them unable to nurse
their babies!

The LORD's Judgment on Israel

15The LORD says, “All their evildoing
began in Gilgal. It was there that I began to
hate them. And because of the evil they have
done, I will drive them out of my land. I will
not love them any more; all their leaders
have rebelled against me. 16The people of
Israel are like a plant whose roots have dried
up and which bears no fruit. They will have
no children, but even if they did, I would kill
the children so dear to them.”

The Prophet Speaks about Israel

17The God I serve will reject his people,
because they have not listened to him. They
will become wanderers among the nations.

[v] **8.13** They offer . . . the sacrifices; *Hebrew unclear.* [w] **9.3** FORBIDDEN FOOD: *The Law of Moses prohibited the eating of certain foods as being ritually unclean (see Lev 11).* [x] **9.9** GIBEAH: *At this city some Israelites of the tribe of Benjamin raped a Levite's concubine; this caused a civil war that almost wiped out the Benjaminites (see Judg 19–21).*
[y] **9.13** *Probable text* being hunted down; *Hebrew unclear.*

9:7 Lk 21:22 **9:9** Judg 19:1–30 **9:10** Num 25:1–5

10 1 The people of Israel were like a
grapevine that was full of grapes.
The more prosperous they were, the more
altars they built. The more productive their
land was, the more beautiful they made the
sacred stone pillars they worship. 2 The peo-
ple whose hearts are deceitful must now suf-
fer for their sins. God will break down their
altars and destroy their sacred pillars.
3 These people will soon be saying, "We
have no king because we did not fear the
LORD. But what could a king do for us any-
way?" 4 They utter empty words and make
false promises and useless treaties. Justice has
become injustice, growing like poisonous
weeds in a plowed field.
5 The people who live in the city of
Samaria will be afraid and will mourn the
loss of the gold bull[z] at Bethaven.[a] They
and the priests who serve the idol will weep
over it. They will wail when it is stripped of
its golden splendor. 6 The idol will be car-
ried off to Assyria as tribute to the great
emperor. The people of Israel will be dis-
graced and put to shame because of the
advice they followed. 7 Their king will be
carried off, like a chip of wood on water.
8 The hilltop shrines of Aven,[a] where the
people of Israel worship idols, will be
destroyed. Thorns and weeds will grow up
over their altars. The people will call out to
the mountains, "Hide us!" and to the hills,
"Cover us!"

Thorns and weeds will grow up over their altars. (10:8)

The LORD Pronounces Judgment on Israel

9 The LORD says, "The people of Israel
have not stopped sinning against me since
the time of their sin at Gibeah.[b] So at
Gibeah war will catch up with them. 10 I
will attack[c] this sinful people and punish
them. Nations will join together against
them, and they will be punished for their
many sins.
11 "Israel was once like a well-trained
young cow, ready and willing to thresh
grain. But I decided to put a yoke[d] on her
beautiful neck and to harness her for harder
work. I made Judah pull the plow and Israel
pull the harrow. 12 I said, 'Plow new ground
for yourselves, plant righteousness, and reap
the blessings that your devotion to me will
produce. It is time for you to turn to me,
your LORD, and I will come and pour out
blessings upon you.' 13 But instead you plant-
ed evil and reaped its harvest. You have eaten
the fruit produced by your lies.
"Because you trusted in your chariots[e]
and in the large number of your soldiers,
14 war will come to your people, and all your
fortresses will be destroyed. It will be like the
day when King Shalman destroyed the city
of Betharbel in battle, and mothers and their
children were crushed to death. 15 That is
what will happen to you, people of Bethel,
because of the terrible evil that you have
done. As soon as the battle begins, the king
of Israel will die."

God's Love for His Rebellious People

11 The LORD says,
"When Israel was a child, I loved
him
and called him out of Egypt as my
son.[f]

[z] **10.5** *Some ancient translations* bull; *Hebrew* cows. [a] **10.5, 8** BETHAVEN: *This name means "house of evil" or "house of idolatry" and in this passage refers to the city of Bethel, a name which means "house of God." In verse 8, Bethaven is called Aven. See also 4.15 and 5.8.* [b] **10.9** GIBEAH: *See 9.9.* [c] **10.10** *One ancient translation* I will attack; *Hebrew* In my desire. [d] **10.11** *Probable text* put a yoke; *Hebrew* spare. [e] **10.13** *One ancient translation* chariots; *Hebrew* way. [f] **11.1** him, and called him . . . son; *or* him; from the time he left Egypt I have called him my son.

10:8 Lk 23:30; Rev 6:16 **10:9** Judg 19:1–30 **10:12** Jer 4:3 **11:1** Ex 4:22; Mt 2:15

[2]But the more I[g] called to him,
the more he turned away from me.[h]
My people sacrificed to Baal;
they burned incense to idols.
[3]Yet I was the one who taught Israel to walk.
I took my people up in my arms,[i]
but they did not acknowledge that I took care of them.
[4]I drew them to me with affection and love.
I picked them up and held them to my cheek;
I bent down to them and fed them.[j]

[5]"They refuse to return to me, and so
they must return to Egypt, and Assyria will
rule them. [6]War will sweep through their
cities and break down the city gates. It will
destroy my people because they do what
they themselves think best. [7]They insist on
turning away from me. They will cry out
because of the yoke that is on them, but no
one will lift it from them.[k]

"They insist on turning away from me." (11:7)

[8]"How can I give you up, Israel?
How can I abandon you?
Could I ever destroy you as I did Admah,
or treat you as I did Zeboiim?
My heart will not let me do it!
My love for you is too strong.
[9]I will not punish you in my anger;
I will not destroy Israel again.
For I am God and not a mere human being.
I, the Holy One, am with you.
I will not come to you in anger.

[10]"My people will follow me when I roar
like a lion at their enemies. They will hurry

Live it!

Parents Sacrifice for Their Children

A section in Hosea, chapter 11, describes God as a loving parent:

Yet I was the one who taught Israel to walk.
I took my people up in my arms,
but they did not acknowledge that I took care of them.
I drew them to me with affection and love.
I picked them up and held them to my cheek;
I bent down to them and fed them. (Verses 3–4)

We often forget about the sacrifices our parents make for us. They did everything for us when we were tiny and completely dependent on them. Sometimes, they have to let us suffer painful consequences in order to learn important lessons. Sometimes in the difficult process of growing up, we rebel against our parents, we insult them, or we even turn away from them. Despite this, most parents continue to love their children.

God also lets us suffer the consequences of our actions. God knows we have to learn the hard way sometimes. But God is always there, like a loving parent, waiting for us to come back. A good thing to think about every day—not just on Mother's Day or Father's Day.

— Hosea 11:1–4

[g] **11.2** *One ancient translation* I; *Hebrew* they. [h] **11.2** *One ancient translation* me; *Hebrew* them. [i] **11.3** *One ancient translation* I . . . my arms; *Hebrew* He . . . his arms. [j] **11.4** *Verse 4 in Hebrew is unclear.* [k] **11.7** *Verse 7 in Hebrew is unclear.*

11:8 Deut 29:23

to me from the west. 11They will come from
Egypt, as swiftly as birds, and from Assyria,
like doves. I will bring them to their homes
again. I, the LORD, have spoken."

Israel and Judah Are Condemned

12The LORD says, "The people of Israel
have surrounded me with lies and deceit,
and the people of Judah are still rebelling
against me, the faithful and holy God.

12 1Everything that the people of Israel
do from morning to night is useless
and destructive. Treachery and acts of violence
increase among them. They make treaties
with Assyria and do business with Egypt."
2The LORD has an accusation to bring
against the people of Judah; he is also going to
punish Israel for the way her people act. He
will pay them back for what they have done.
3Their ancestor Jacob struggled with his twin
brother Esau while the two of them were still
in their mother's womb; when Jacob grew up,
he fought against God— 4he fought against
an angel and won. He wept and asked for a
blessing. And at Bethel God came to our
ancestor Jacob and spoke with him.[l] 5This
was the LORD God Almighty—the LORD is
the name by which he is to be worshiped.
6So now, descendants of Jacob, trust in your
God and return to him. Be loyal and just, and
wait patiently for your God to act.

Further Words of Judgment

7The LORD says, "The people of Israel are
as dishonest as the Canaanites; they love to
cheat their customers with false scales. 8'We
are rich,' they say. 'We've made a fortune.
And no one can accuse us of getting rich
dishonestly.' 9But I, the LORD your God who
led you out of Egypt, I will make you live in
tents again, as you did when I came to you
in the desert.
10"I spoke to the prophets and gave them
many visions, and through the prophets I
gave my people warnings. 11Yet idols are
worshiped in Gilead, and those who worship
them will die. Bulls are sacrificed in Gilgal,
and the altars there will become piles of
stone in the open fields."

The altars there will become piles of stone. (12:11)

12Our ancestor Jacob had to flee to
Mesopotamia, where, in order to get a wife,
he worked for another man and took care of
his sheep. 13The LORD sent a prophet to res-
cue the people of Israel from slavery in
Egypt and to take care of them. 14The peo-
ple of Israel have made the LORD bitterly
angry; they deserve death for their crimes.
Their Lord will punish them for the disgrace
they have brought on him.

Final Judgment on Israel

13 In the past, when the tribe of
Ephraim spoke, the other tribes
of Israel were afraid; they looked up to
Ephraim. But the people sinned by worship-
ing Baal, and for this they will die. 2They
still keep on sinning by making metal images
to worship—idols of silver, designed by
human minds, made by human hands. And
then they say, "Offer sacrifices to them!"
How can anyone kiss those idols—idols in
the shape of bulls![m] 3And so these people
will disappear like morning mist, like the
dew that vanishes early in the day. They will
be like chaff which the wind blows from the
threshing place, like smoke from a chimney.

How can anyone kiss those idols? (13:2)

[l] **12.4** *Some ancient translations* him; *Hebrew* us. [m] **13.2** *Probable text* And then they . . . bulls!; *Hebrew unclear.*

12:3 Gen 25:26 **12:3, 4** Gen 32:24–26 **12:4** Gen 28:10–22 **12:9** Lev 23:42, 43 **12:12** Gen 29:1–20
12:13 Ex 12:50, 51

4The LORD says, "I am the LORD your God, who led you out of Egypt. You have no God but me. I alone am your savior. 5I took care of you in a dry, desert land. 6But when you entered the good land, you became full and satisfied, and then you grew proud and forgot me. 7So I will attack you like a lion. Like a leopard I will lie in wait along your path. 8I will attack you like a bear that has lost her cubs, and I will tear you open. Like a lion I will devour you on the spot, and will tear you to pieces like a wild animal.

9"I will destroy you, people of Israel! Then who can help you?[n] 10You asked for a king and for leaders, but how can they save the nation?[o] 11In my anger I have given you kings, and in my fury I have taken them away.

12"Israel's sin and guilt are on record, and the records are safely stored away. 13Israel has a chance to live, but is too foolish to take it—like a child about to be born, who refuses to come out of the womb. 14I will not save this people from the world of the dead or rescue them from the power of death. Bring on[p] your plagues, death! Bring on[p] your destruction, world of the dead! I will no longer have pity for this people. 15Even though Israel flourishes like weeds,[q] I will send a hot east wind from the desert, and it will dry up their springs and wells. It will take away everything of value. 16Samaria must be punished for rebelling against me. Her people will die in war; babies will be dashed to the ground, and pregnant women will be ripped open."

Hosea's Plea to Israel

14 Return to the LORD your God, people of Israel. Your sin has made you stumble and fall. 2Return to the LORD, and let this prayer be your offering to him: "Forgive all our sins and accept our prayer, and we will praise you as we have promised. 3Assyria can never save us, and war horses cannot protect us. We will never again say to our idols that they are our God. O LORD, you show mercy to those who have no one else to turn to."

Like a leopard I will lie in wait. (13:7)

The LORD Promises New Life for Israel

4The LORD says,

"I will bring my people back to me.
I will love them with all my heart;
no longer am I angry with them.
5I will be to the people of Israel
like rain in a dry land.
They will blossom like flowers;
they will be firmly rooted
like the trees of Lebanon.
6They will be alive with new growth,
and beautiful like olive trees.
They will be fragrant
like the cedars of Lebanon.
7Once again they will live under my
protection.
They will grow crops of grain
and be fruitful like a vineyard.
They will be as famous as the wine of
Lebanon.
8The people of Israel[r] will have nothing
more to do with idols;
I will answer their prayers and take care
of them.
Like an evergreen tree I will shelter them;
I am the source of all their blessings."

Conclusion

9May those who are wise understand what is written here, and may they take it to heart. The LORD's ways are right, and righteous people live by following them, but sinners stumble and fall because they ignore them.

[n] **13.9** *One ancient translation* who can help you?; *Hebrew* in me is your help. [o] **13.10** *Verse 10 in Hebrew is unclear.* [p] **13.14** *Some ancient translations* Bring on; *Hebrew* I will be. [q] **13.15** *Probable text* like weeds; *Hebrew* among brothers. [r] **14.8** *One ancient translation* The people of Israel; *Hebrew* Israel, I.

13:5, 6 Deut 8:11–17 **13:10** 1 Sam 8:5, 6 **13:11 a** 1 Sam 10:17–24; **b** 1 Sam 15:26 **13:14** 1 Cor 15:55

THE BOOK OF Joel

A plague of locusts came and destroyed the land! Locusts swarmed and hopped everywhere! They were destroying everything in their path.

Joel uses the locusts as an opportunity to get people to pay more attention to God. He talks about the "Day of the Lord," which means the end of time, and describes it in two ways—as bad news and good news. The bad news is "The day of the LORD is coming soon. It will be a dark and gloomy day" (2:1–2). The good news is "Be glad . . . rejoice at what the LORD your God has done for you. . . . [God] will give you back what you lost . . . you will have plenty to eat, and be satisfied" (2:23, 25, 26). The bad news is that we sin—that has to stop. But the good news is that God loves us and cares for us—that is a great comfort.

Chap. 1:4

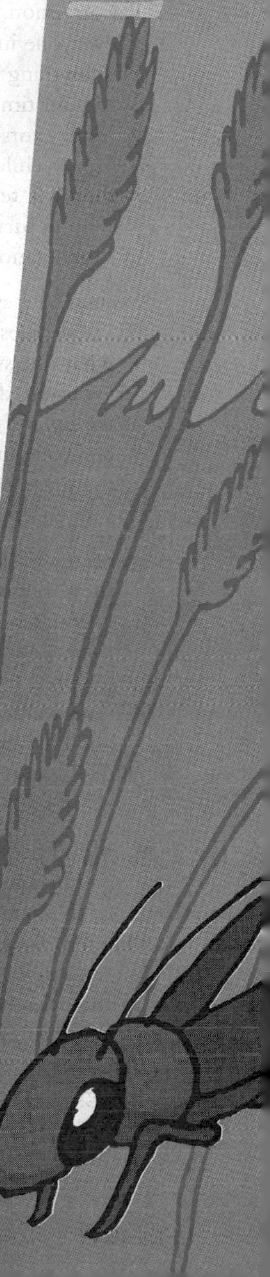

Headlines

- The Day of the Lord Is Near! (1:15—2:1)
- Spirit Poured Out on Women and Men! (2:28–29)
- Stream of Blessings Flow from Temple (3:16–18)

FACTOIDS

Who wrote this book? The prophet Joel, and perhaps other scribes (writers). It was probably written some time after the Babylonian Exile.

Why was it written? To help people cope with the locusts and to understand that despite plagues and natural disasters, there is still hope because God is with them.

Who are the young people in this book? Young people see visions in Joel 2:28–29. This is read each year during Mass on Pentecost Sunday.

Important themes

- God is always with us, in suffering and in celebration.
- Eventually, the wrongs we commit will catch up with us, and we will have to answer to God for our sins.
- All of our blessings come from God. When the time for suffering ends, there will be great joy.

JOEL

1 This is the LORD's message to Joel son of Pethuel.

The People Mourn the Destruction of the Crops

2 Pay attention, you older people;
everyone in Judah, listen.
Has anything like this ever happened
in your time or the time of your ancestors?
3 Tell your children about it;
they will tell their children,
who in turn will tell the next generation.

4 Swarm after swarm of locusts settled on the crops;
what one swarm left, the next swarm devoured.
5 Wake up and weep, you drunkards;
cry, you wine-drinkers;
the grapes for making new wine have been destroyed.

6 An army of locusts has attacked our land;
they are powerful and too many to count;
their teeth are as sharp as those of a lion.
7 They have destroyed our grapevines
and chewed up our fig trees.
They have stripped off the bark,
till the branches are white.

8 Cry, you people, like a young woman
who mourns the death
of the man she was going to marry.
9 There is no grain or wine to offer in the Temple;
the priests mourn because they have no offerings for the LORD.
10 The fields are bare;
the ground mourns
because the grain is destroyed,
the grapes are dried up,
and the olive trees are withered.

The ground mourns. (1:10)

11 Grieve, you farmers;
cry, you that take care of the vineyards,
because the wheat, the barley,
yes all the crops are destroyed.
12 The grapevines and fig trees have withered;
all the fruit trees have wilted and died.
The joy of the people is gone.
13 Put on sackcloth and weep,
you priests who serve at the altar!
Go into the Temple and mourn all night!
There is no grain or wine to offer your God.
14 Give orders for a fast;
call an assembly!
Gather the leaders
and all the people of Judah
into the Temple of the LORD your God
and cry out to him!
15 The day of the LORD is near,
the day when the Almighty brings destruction.
What terror that day will bring!

16 We look on helpless as our crops are destroyed.
There is no joy in the Temple of our God.
17 The seeds die in the dry earth.
There is no grain to be stored,
and so the empty granaries are in ruins.
18 The cattle are bellowing in distress
because there is no pasture for them;
the flocks of sheep also suffer.

1:6 Rev 9:8 **1:15** Isa 13:6

19 I cry out to you, LORD,
because the pastures and trees are dried up,
as though a fire had burned them.
20 Even the wild animals cry out to you
because the streams have become dry.

The Locusts as a Warning of the Day of the LORD

2 Blow the trumpet; sound the alarm
on Zion, God's sacred hill.[a]
Tremble, people of Judah!
The day of the LORD is coming soon.
2 It will be a dark and gloomy day,
a black and cloudy day.
The great army of locusts advances
like darkness spreading over the mountains.
There has never been anything like it,
and there never will be again.
3 Like fire they eat up the plants.
In front of them the land is like the Garden of Eden,
but behind them it is a barren desert.
Nothing escapes them.
4 They look like horses;
they run like war-horses.
5 As they leap on the tops of the mountains,
they rattle like chariots;
they crackle like dry grass on fire.
They are lined up like a great army ready for battle.
6 As they approach, everyone is terrified;
every face turns pale.
7 They attack like warriors;
they climb the walls like soldiers.
They all keep marching straight ahead
and do not change direction
8 or get in each other's way.
They swarm through defenses,
and nothing can stop them.
9 They rush against the city;
they run over the walls;
they climb up the houses
and go in through the windows like thieves.
10 The earth shakes as they advance;
the sky trembles.
The sun and the moon grow dark,
and the stars no longer shine.
11 The LORD thunders commands to his army.
The troops that obey him
are many and mighty.
How terrible is the day of the LORD!
Who will survive it?

A Call to Repentance

12 "But even now," says the LORD,
"repent sincerely and return to me
with fasting and weeping and mourning.
13 Let your broken heart show your sorrow;
tearing your clothes is not enough."
Come back to the LORD your God.
He is kind and full of mercy;
he is patient and keeps his promise;
he is always ready to forgive and not punish.

Let your broken heart show your sorrow. (2:13)

14 Perhaps the LORD your God will change his mind
and bless you with abundant crops.
Then you can offer him grain and wine.
15 Blow the trumpet on Mount Zion;
give orders for a fast and call an assembly!
16 Gather the people together;
prepare them for a sacred meeting;
bring the old people;
gather the children
and the babies too.
Even newly married couples
must leave their homes and come.

[a] **2:1** SACRED HILL: *Mount Zion (see Zion in Word List).*
2:4, 5 Rev 9:7–9 **2:10** Rev 8:12 **2:11** Rev 6:17

Catholic Connections

Ash Wednesday and Lent

Have you heard of prayer, fasting, and almsgiving—the traditional spiritual practices of Lent?

- **By spending more time at prayer, we refocus on God. We remember our sinfulness and God's love.**
- **By fasting, or eating less, we remind ourselves that we depend on God for what we need to live. Fasting also helps make us aware of the needs of people who are poor.**
- **By almsgiving—donating money, food, or clothing to poor and needy people—we put into practice what Jesus taught. Our material things are meant to be shared.**

In the Old Testament reading on Ash Wednesday, we listen to Joel 2:12–18. The prophet reminds us to return to the Lord with all our heart, with fasting and weeping. In the Gospel for Ash Wednesday, Jesus tells us how to be during Lent—humble and quiet. Don't brag about how much money we give to poor people. Don't try to impress people with our perfect prayers. Don't complain about how hungry we are while fasting. Then, by the time Easter comes around, we really will have something to celebrate!

— Joel 2:12–18

17 The priests, serving the LORD
between the altar and the entrance of the Temple,
must weep and pray:
"Have pity on your people, LORD.
Do not let other nations despise us and mock us
by saying, 'Where is your God?' "

God Restores Fertility to the Land

18 Then the LORD showed concern for his land;
he had mercy on his people.
19 He answered them:
"Now I am going to give you
grain and wine and olive oil,
and you will be satisfied.
Other nations will no longer despise you.
20 I will remove the locust army that came from the north
and will drive some of them into the desert.
Their front ranks will be driven into the Dead Sea,
their rear ranks into the Mediterranean.
Their dead bodies will stink.
I will destroy them because of all they have done to you.
21 "Fields, don't be afraid,
but be joyful and glad
because of all the LORD has done for you.
22 Animals, don't be afraid.
The pastures are green;
the trees bear their fruit,
and there are plenty of figs and grapes.
23 "Be glad, people of Zion,
rejoice at what the LORD your God has done for you.

2:17 1 Macc 7:36–38

He has given you the right amount of
autumn rain;[b]
he has poured down the winter rain for
you
and the spring rain as before.
24 The threshing places will be full of grain;
the pits beside the presses will overflow
with wine and olive oil.
25 I will give you back what you lost
in the years when swarms of locusts ate
your crops.
It was I who sent this army against
you.
26 Now you will have plenty to eat, and be
satisfied.
You will praise the LORD your God,
who has done wonderful things for
you.
My people will never be despised
again.
27 Then, Israel, you will know that I am
among you
and that I, the LORD, am your God
and there is no other.
My people will never be despised
again.

The Day of the LORD

28 "Afterward I will pour out my Spirit on
everyone:
your sons and daughters will proclaim
my message;
your old people will have dreams,
and your young people will see visions.
29 At that time I will pour out my Spirit
even on servants, both men and
women.

30 "I will give warnings of that day
in the sky and on the earth;
there will be bloodshed, fire, and clouds
of smoke.
31 The sun will be darkened,
and the moon will turn red as blood
before the great and terrible day of the
LORD comes.
32 But all who ask the LORD for help will be
saved.
As the LORD has said,
'Some in Jerusalem will escape;
those whom I choose will survive.' "

God Will Judge the Nations

3 The LORD says,
"At that time I will restore
the prosperity of Judah and Jerusalem.
2 I will gather all the nations
and bring them to the Valley of
Judgment.
There I will judge them
for all they have done to my people.
They have scattered the Israelites in
foreign countries
and divided Israel, my land.
3 They threw dice to decide
who would get the captives.
They sold boys and girls into slavery
to pay for prostitutes and wine.

4 "What are you trying to do to me, Tyre,
Sidon, and all of Philistia? Are you trying to
pay me back for something? If you are, I will
quickly pay you back! 5 You have taken my
silver and gold and carried my rich treasures
into your temples. 6 You have taken the peo-
ple of Judah and Jerusalem far from their
own country and sold them to the Greeks.
7 Now I am going to bring them out of the
places to which you have sold them. I will
do to you what you have done to them. 8 I
will let your sons and daughters be sold to
the people of Judah; they will sell them to
the far-off Sabeans. I, the LORD, have spo-
ken.

9 "Make this announcement among the
nations:
'Prepare for war;
call your warriors;
gather all your soldiers and march!
10 Hammer the points of your plows into
swords
and your pruning knives into spears.
Even the weak must fight.

[b] **2:23** right amount of autumn rain; *or* autumn rain because he is just.

2:31 Mt 24:29; Mk 13:24, 25; Lk 21:25; Rev 6:12, 13 **2:28–32** Acts 2:17–21 **2:32** Rom 10:13 **3:4–8** Isa 23:1–18; Ezek 26:1—28:26; Am 1:9, 10; Zech 9:1–4; Mt 11:21, 22; Lk 10:13, 14 **3:4–8** Isa 14:29–31; Jer 47:1–7; Ezek 25:15–17; Am 1:6–8; Zeph 2:4–7; Zech 9:5–7 **3:10** Isa 2:4; Mic 4:3

11 Hurry[c] and come,
all you surrounding nations,
and gather in the valley.' "

Send down, O LORD, your army to attack
them!

12 "The nations must get ready
and come to the Valley of Judgment.
There I, the LORD, will sit to judge
all the surrounding nations.
13 They are very wicked;
cut them down like grain
at harvest time;
crush them as grapes are crushed
in a full wine press
until the wine runs over."

14 Thousands and thousands
are in the Valley of Judgment.
It is there that the day of the LORD
will soon come.
15 The sun and the moon grow dark,
and the stars no longer shine.

God Will Bless His People

16 The LORD roars from Mount Zion;
his voice thunders from Jerusalem;
earth and sky tremble.
But he will defend his people.
17 "Then, Israel, you will know that I am
the LORD your God.
I live on Zion, my sacred hill.
Jerusalem will be a sacred city;
foreigners will never conquer it
again.
18 At that time the mountains will be
covered with vineyards,
and cattle will be found on every
hill;
there will be plenty of water for all of
Judah.
A stream will flow from the Temple of the
LORD,
and it will water Acacia Valley.

19 "Egypt will become a desert,
and Edom a ruined waste,
because they attacked the land of Judah
and killed its innocent people.
20-21 I will avenge[d] those who were
killed;
I will not spare the guilty.
But Judah and Jerusalem will be inhabited
forever,
and I, the LORD, will live on Mount
Zion."

[c] **3:11** *Probable text* Hurry; *Hebrew* Help. [d] **3:20–21** *Some ancient translations* avenge; *Hebrew* declare innocent.
3:13 a Rev 14:14–16; **b** Rev 14:19, 20; 19:15 **3:16** Am 1:2

THE BOOK OF AMOS

Isn't it crystal clear? Don't lie, steal, kill, take advantage of poor people, or worship anything other than God. If we live by God's teachings, life is better—for everyone. God gave the Israelites and us laws to live by because he loves us deeply and wants us to know real joy in our day-to-day living. It's so simple. But humanity doesn't seem to be able to pull it off. And people suffer as a result.

That is why Amos is so mad! He is exploding with rage at the people in the northern kingdom of Israel and their neighbors. They disobey God's teachings and take advantage of poor people and worship foreign gods. This time, Amos says, they have gone too far, and God will punish them, Israel most of all because God had done so much for them.

Chap. 2:6–8

Headlines

- Honest People Sold into Slavery! (2:6—3:2)
- Wealthy Women Condemned (4:1–3)
- God Wants Justice, Not Festivals (5:21–27)
- Amos Refuses to Be Silent (7:10–17)
- Merchants Use Crooked Scales! (8:4–6)
- God's Future Plans (9:11–15)

FACTOIDS

Who wrote this book? Amos (or scribes recording his words), the earliest prophet whose words were recorded as a separate book of the Bible.

Why was it written? Amos, a shepherd and farmer, was called by God to prophesy in the northern kingdom of Israel. Amos especially challenged corrupt and greedy people taking advantage of poor people.

What period does it cover? 786–746 BC.

Important themes

- God will punish the sinful, especially those who mistreat poor people.
- Religious acts mean nothing if people will not change their wicked lifestyle.
- God will save those who are faithful, even if there is only a few of them.

AMOS

1 These are the words of Amos, a shepherd from the town of Tekoa. Two years before the earthquake, when Uzziah was king of Judah and Jeroboam son of Jehoash was king of Israel, God revealed to Amos all these things about Israel.

2 Amos said,

"The LORD roars from Mount Zion;
his voice thunders from Jerusalem.
The pastures dry up,
and the grass on Mount Carmel turns brown."

God's Judgment on Israel's Neighbors

Syria

3 The LORD says, "The people of Damascus have sinned again and again, and for this I will certainly punish them. They treated the people of Gilead with savage cruelty. 4 So I will send fire upon the palace built by King Hazael and I will burn down the fortresses of King Benhadad. 5 I will smash the city gates of Damascus and remove the inhabitants of Aven Valley and the ruler of Betheden. The people of Syria will be taken away as prisoners to the land of Kir."

Philistia

6 The LORD says, "The people of Gaza have sinned again and again, and for this I will certainly punish them. They carried off a whole nation and sold them as slaves to the people of Edom. 7 So I will send fire upon the city walls of Gaza and burn down its fortresses. 8 I will remove the rulers of the cities of Ashdod and Ashkelon. I will punish the city of Ekron, and all the Philistines who are left will die."

Tyre

9 The LORD says, "The people of Tyre have sinned again and again, and for this I will certainly punish them. They carried off a whole nation into exile in the land of Edom, and did not keep the treaty of friendship they had made. 10 So I will send fire upon the city walls of Tyre and burn down its fortresses."

"I will send fire." (1:4—2:5)

1:1 a 2 Kings 15:1–7; 2 Chr 26:1–23; **b** 2 Kings 14:23–29 **1:2** Joel 3:16 **1:3–5** Isa 17:1–3; Jer 49:23–27; Zech 9:1 **1:6–8** Isa 14:29–31; Jer 47:1–7; Ezek 25:15–17; Joel 3:4–8; Zeph 2:4–7; Zech 9:5–7 **1:9, 10** Isa 23:1–18; Ezek 26:1—28:19; Joel 3:4–8; Zech 9:1–4; Mt 11:21, 22; Lk 10:13, 14

Study it!

The Sins of the Cities

What's got God in such a rage, according to Amos? What exactly are the sins of Israel and its neighboring cities? Amos accuses them of:

- **treating people with savage cruelty**
- **selling people as slaves**
- **not keeping the promises they had made**
- **showing no mercy, only extreme anger**
- **ripping open pregnant women**
- **dishonoring the king**
- **despising God's teachings and ignoring his Commandments**
- **being led astray by false gods**
- **abusing honest people who had debt, especially poor people**
- **trampling weak, helpless, and poor people**
- **sexual immorality**

If God were addressing your city today, could the people of your city be charged with any of these sins?

— Amos 1:1—2:8

Edom

11 The LORD says, "The people of Edom
have sinned again and again, and for this I
will certainly punish them. They hunted
down their relatives,[a] the Israelites, and
showed them no mercy. Their anger had no
limits, and they never let it die. 12 So I will
send fire upon the city of Teman and burn
down the fortresses of Bozrah."

Ammon

13 The LORD says, "The people of Ammon
have sinned again and again, and for this I
will certainly punish them. In their wars for
more territory they even ripped open preg-
nant women in Gilead. 14 So I will send fire
upon the city walls of Rabbah and burn
down its fortresses. Then there will be shouts
on the day of battle, and the fighting will
rage like a storm. 15 Their king and his offi-
cers will go into exile."

Moab

2 The LORD says, "The people of Moab
have sinned again and again, and for this
I will certainly punish them. They dishon-
ored the bones of the king of Edom by
burning them to ashes. 2 I will send fire upon
the land of Moab and burn down the
fortresses of Kerioth. The people of Moab
will die in the noise of battle while soldiers
are shouting and trumpets are sounding. 3 I
will kill the ruler of Moab and all the leaders
of the land."

Judah

4 The LORD says, "The people of Judah
have sinned again and again, and for this
I will certainly punish them. They have
despised my teachings and have not kept my
commands. They have been led astray by the
same false gods that their ancestors served.
5 So I will send fire upon Judah and burn
down the fortresses of Jerusalem."

God's Judgment on Israel

6 The LORD says, "The people of Israel
have sinned again and again, and for this I

[a] **1:11** THEIR RELATIVES: *The Israelites were descended from Jacob, who was the brother of Esau, the ancestor of the Edomites.*

1:11, 12 Isa 34:5–17; 63:1–6; Jer 49:7–22; Ezek 25:12–14; 35:1–15; Ob 1–14; Mal 1:2–5 **1:13–15** Jer 49:1–6; Ezek 21:28–32; 25:1–7; Zeph 2:8–11 **2:1–3** Isa 15:1—16:14; 25:10–12; Jer 48:1–47; Ezek 25:8–11; Zeph 2:8–11

Find the eight kingdoms or cities named in Amos, chapters 1–2, on Map 3 in the back of this Bible.

will certainly punish them. They sell into
slavery honest people who cannot pay their
debts, the poor who cannot repay even the
price of a pair of sandals. 7They trample[b]
down the weak and helpless and push the
poor out of the way. A man and his father
have intercourse with the same slave woman,
and so profane my holy name. 8At every
place of worship people sleep on clothing
that they have taken from the poor as securi-
ty for debts. In the temple of their God they
drink wine which they have taken from
those who owe them money.

9"And yet, my people, it was for your sake
that I totally destroyed the Amorites, who
were as tall as cedar trees and as strong as
oaks. 10I brought you out of Egypt, led you
through the desert for forty years, and gave
you the land of the Amorites to be your
own. 11I chose some of your sons to be
prophets and some of your young men to be
nazirites.[c] Isn't this true, people of Israel? I,
the LORD, have spoken. 12But you made the
nazirites drink wine, and ordered the
prophets not to speak my message. 13And
now I will crush you to the ground, and you
will groan like a cart loaded with grain.
14Not even fast runners will escape; strong
men will lose their strength, and soldiers will
not be able to save their own lives. 15Archers
will not stand their ground, fast runners will
not get away, and men on horses will not
escape with their lives. 16On that day even
the bravest soldiers will drop their weapons
and run." The LORD has spoken.

3 People of Israel, listen to this message
which the LORD has spoken about you,
the entire nation that he brought out of
Egypt: 2"Of all the nations on earth, you are
the only one I have known and cared for.
That is what makes your sins so terrible, and
that is why I must punish you for them."

Live it!

Test of Holiness

Craig owns a very successful chain of fast-food restaurants that are sweeping the country. In his own town, he and his family are known for their support and generosity in the community and their church.

Not many people know this, but Craig's heart stretches to poor people. There's a guy in town, Samuel, who is homeless and suffers from a variety of problems. He rides a bike everywhere, sleeps outside, depends on the kindness of strangers, and generally causes no trouble. Craig has instructed his employees at his restaurant to take care of Samuel. Samuel comes in twice a day to eat at Craig's restaurant. The workers treat him as respectfully as any other customer, and Samuel always eats for free.

Amos tells us that the real test of holiness is not only what happens in church on Sundays, but how we act outside of church—at work, school, in politics, and community activities. Are we looking out for the needs of poor and powerless people and acting to help them? If not, then our religious practices are empty.

— Amos 2:6–8

The Prophet's Task

3Do two people start traveling together
without arranging to meet?

[b] **2:7** trample; *Hebrew unclear.* [c] **2:11** NAZIRITES: *Israelites who showed their devotion to God by taking vows not to drink wine or beer or cut their hair or touch corpses (see Num 6:1–8).*
2:9 Deut 3:8–11 **2:11** Num 6:1–8

Read Amos 3:10. What kinds of crimes do people commit today to try to gain great wealth?

4Does a lion roar in the forest unless he
has found a victim?
Does a young lion growl in his den unless
he has caught something?
5Does a bird get caught in a trap if the
trap has not been baited?
Does a trap spring unless something sets it
off?
6Does the war trumpet sound in a city
without making the people afraid?
Does disaster strike a city unless the LORD
sends it?
7The Sovereign LORD never does any-
thing without revealing his plan to his ser-
vants, the prophets.
8When a lion roars, who can keep from
being afraid?
When the Sovereign LORD speaks, who
can keep from proclaiming his message?

The Doom of Samaria

9Announce to those who live in the
palaces of Egypt and Ashdod: "Gather
together in the hills around Samaria and see
the great disorder and the crimes being
committed there."
10The LORD says, "These people fill their
mansions with things taken by crime and
violence. They don't even know how to be
honest. 11And so an enemy will surround
their land, destroy their defenses, and plunder
their mansions."
12The LORD says, "As a shepherd recovers
only two legs or an ear of a sheep that a lion
has eaten, so only a few will survive of
Samaria's people, who now recline on luxu-
rious couches.[d] 13Listen now, and warn the
descendants of Jacob," says the Sovereign
LORD Almighty. 14"On the day when I pun-
ish the people of Israel for their sins, I will
destroy the altars of Bethel. The corners of
every altar will be broken off and will fall to
the ground. 15I will destroy winter houses
and summer houses. The houses decorated
with ivory will fall in ruins; every large
house will be destroyed."

4 Listen to this, you women of Samaria,
who grow fat like the well-fed cows of
Bashan, who mistreat the weak, oppress the
poor, and demand that your husbands keep
you supplied with liquor! 2As the Sovereign
LORD is holy, he has promised, "The days
will come when they will drag you away
with hooks; every one of you will be like a

Study it!

Why Is God So Hard on Israel?

Blair is sitting in a jail cell, in shock. She can't believe she got caught stealing. Worse, she can't believe the person who turned her in was her mom! What's the big deal? So she borrowed twenty bucks from the cash register at her mom's store. So what? How horrible can a mother be, to have her own child arrested!

The police officer asked Blair's mom why she turned her daughter in. Blair's mom said: "More than anyone else, she knows better. I've given her everything she could want, and I've taught her right from wrong. She's been warned—this is not the first time I've caught her stealing. I hope it will be her last. She needs to learn that there are consequences when you do something wrong."

This is why God is so angry at Israel. They are his Chosen People. They have been given everything, including the Law of Moses. More than any nation, they should know better than to neglect poor people and allow injustice to grow. Because they know better, God is going to let them experience the full consequences of their sins!

— Amos 3:1–2

[d] **3:12** luxurious couches; *Hebrew unclear.*
3:14 2 Kings 23:15

fish on a hook. 3 You will be dragged to the nearest break in the wall and thrown out."[e]

Israel's Failure to Learn

4 The Sovereign LORD says, "People of Israel, go to the holy place in Bethel and sin, if you must! Go to Gilgal and sin with all your might! Go ahead and bring animals to be sacrificed morning after morning, and bring your tithes every third day. 5 Go on and offer your bread in thanksgiving to God, and brag about the extra offerings you bring! This is the kind of thing you love to do.

6 "I was the one who brought famine to all your cities, yet you did not come back to me. 7 I kept it from raining when your crops needed it most. I sent rain on one city, but not on another. Rain fell on one field, but another field dried up. 8 Weak with thirst, the people of several cities went to a city where they hoped to find water, but there was not enough to drink. Still you did not come back to me.

9 "I sent a scorching wind to dry up your crops. The locusts ate up all your gardens and vineyards, your fig trees and olive trees. Still you did not come back to me.

Still you did not come back to me. (4:9)

10 "I sent a plague on you like the one I sent on Egypt. I killed your young men in battle and took your horses away. I filled your nostrils with the stink of dead bodies in your camps. Still you did not come back to me.

11 "I destroyed some of you as I destroyed Sodom and Gomorrah. Those of you who survived were like a burning stick saved from a fire. Still you did not come back to me," says the LORD. 12 "So then, people of Israel, I am going to punish you. And because I am going to do this, get ready to face my judgment!"

13 God is the one who made the mountains
  and created the winds.
He makes his thoughts known to people;
  he changes day into night.
  He walks on the heights of the earth.
This is his name: the LORD God
  Almighty!

A Call to Repentance

5 Listen, people of Israel, to this funeral song which I sing over you:

2 Virgin Israel has fallen,
Never to rise again!
She lies abandoned on the ground,
And no one helps her up.

3 The Sovereign LORD says, "A city in Israel sends out a thousand soldiers, but only a hundred return; another city sends out a hundred, but only ten come back."

4 The LORD says to the people of Israel, "Come to me, and you will live. 5 Do not go to Beersheba to worship. Do not try to find me at Bethel—Bethel will come to nothing. Do not go to Gilgal—her people are doomed to exile."

6 Go to the LORD, and you will live. If you do not go, he will sweep down like fire on the people of Israel. The fire will burn up the people of Bethel, and no one will be able to put it out. 7 You are doomed, you that twist justice and cheat people out of their rights!

8 The LORD made the stars,
  the Pleiades and Orion.
He turns darkness into daylight
  and day into night.
He calls for the waters of the sea
  and pours them out on the earth.
His name is the LORD.
9 He brings destruction on the mighty and
  their strongholds.

10 You people hate anyone who challenges injustice and speaks the whole truth in

[e] **4:3** *Hebrew has an additional word, the meaning of which is unclear.*
4:6 Wis 12:2, 10 **4:11** Gen 19:24 **5:8** Job 9:9; 38:31

The Working Poor

Olivia's parents work four jobs between them. Still, it seems like they hardly have what they need. Frustrated, she asked: "Why do you work so much? Where is all the money you make?" Her parents helped her understand: They are hard workers, but without college degrees, they cannot get jobs that pay much more than the minimum wage. Plus, none of their employers provide health insurance, which costs around $800 a month—as much as her mom earns. One whole job, just for health insurance! Olivia's parents got angrier as they spoke. It wasn't fair! Business owners who offer only part-time jobs and the lowest possible wages are doing so to save money—but they ignore the needs of the people who work for them. The workers who are struggling to make ends meet just keep struggling and working harder—and never get ahead.

The employers might be acting within the law, but that doesn't mean they are acting justly. Amos pointed this same accusation at Israel: "You are doomed, you that twist justice and cheat people out of their rights!" (Amos 5:7).

How do the businesses in your community treat their workers?

— Amos 5:7–15

court. 11You have oppressed the poor and
robbed them of their grain. And so you will
not live in the fine stone houses you build or
drink wine from the beautiful vineyards you
plant. 12I know how terrible your sins are
and how many crimes you have committed.
You persecute good people, take bribes, and
prevent the poor from getting justice in the
courts. 13And so, keeping quiet in such evil
times is the smart thing to do!
14Make it your aim to do what is right,
not what is evil, so that you may live. Then
the LORD God Almighty really will be with
you, as you claim he is. 15Hate what is evil,
love what is right, and see that justice prevails in the courts. Perhaps the LORD will be
merciful to the people of this nation who
are still left alive.
16And so the Sovereign LORD Almighty
says, "There will be wailing and cries of sorrow in the city streets. Even farmers will be
called to mourn the dead along with those
who are paid to mourn. 17There will be
wailing in all the vineyards. All this will take
place because I am coming to punish you."
The LORD has spoken.

There will be wailing and cries of sorrow. (5:16)

18How terrible it will be for you who
long for the day of the LORD! What good
will that day do you? For you it will be a
day of darkness and not of light. 19It will be
like someone who runs from a lion and
meets a bear! Or like someone who comes
home and puts his hand on the wall—only
to be bitten by a snake! 20The day of the
LORD will bring darkness and not light; it
will be a day of gloom, without any brightness.

No matter what disasters fell upon the Israelites, they would not turn back to God and his Commandments. Why do you think they were so stubborn?

Like someone who runs from a lion (5:19)

21The LORD says, "I hate your religious
festivals; I cannot stand them! 22When you
bring me burnt offerings and grain offerings,
I will not accept them; I will not accept the
animals you have fattened to bring me as
offerings. 23Stop your noisy songs; I do not
want to listen to your harps. 24Instead, let
justice flow like a stream, and righteousness
like a river that never goes dry.

25"People of Israel, I did not demand sac-
rifices and offerings during those forty years
that I led you through the desert. 26But now,
because you have worshiped images of Sak-
kuth, your king god, and of Kaiwan, your
star god, you will have to carry those images
27when I take you into exile in a land
beyond Damascus," says the LORD, whose
name is Almighty God.

The Destruction of Israel

6 How terrible it will be for you that have
such an easy life in Zion and for you
that feel safe in Samaria—you great leaders of
this great nation Israel, you to whom the
people go for help! 2Go and look at the city
of Calneh. Then go on to the great city of
Hamath and on down to the Philistine city
of Gath. Were they any better than the king-
doms of Judah and Israel? Was their territory
larger than yours? 3You refuse to admit that a
day of disaster is coming, but what you do
only brings that day closer. 4How terrible it
will be for you that stretch out on your luxu-
rious couches, feasting on veal and lamb!
5You like to compose songs, as David did,
and play them on harps. 6You drink wine by
the bowlful and use the finest perfumes, but
you do not mourn over the ruin of Israel.
7So you will be the first to go into exile. Your
feasts and banquets will come to an end.

8The Sovereign LORD Almighty has given
this solemn warning: "I hate the pride of the
people of Israel; I despise their luxurious
mansions. I will give their capital city and
everything in it to the enemy."

"I hate the pride of the people of Israel." (6:8)

9If there are ten men left in a family, they
will die. 10The dead man's relative, the one
in charge of the funeral, will take the body
out of the house. The relative will call to
whoever is still left in the house, "Is anyone
else there with you?"

The person will answer, "No!"

Then the relative will say, "Be quiet! We

5:21, 22 Isa 1:11–14 **5:25–27** Acts 7:42, 43

How important are money and material things to you? What do you do to help poor people?

Live it!

Woe to the Wealthy!

Amos is clearly addressing the wealthy people of Israel, not all Israelites. Are we to understand that living a wealthy lifestyle is sinful? Yes, says Amos, if you think only of your own comfort and luxuries. Yes, if your wealth was earned at the expense of poor people, or dishonestly in any way. Yes, if you are not learning about the needs of poor people and how you can help them. But, Amos says, if justice and mercy for poor and weak people are a high priority and you share your wealth generously, then being wealthy is not sinful.

Jesus echoed Amos's warning: "It is much harder for a rich person to enter the Kingdom of God than for a camel to go through the eye of a needle" (Matthew 19:24).

— Amos 6:4–7

must be careful not even to mention the
LORD's name."[f]
11 When the LORD gives the command,
houses large and small will be smashed to
pieces. 12 Do horses gallop on rocks? Does
anyone plow the sea with oxen? Yet you have
turned justice into poison, and right into
wrong.
13 You brag about capturing the town of
Lodebar.[g] You boast, "We were strong
enough to take Karnaim."[h]
14 The LORD God Almighty himself says,
"People of Israel, I am going to send a foreign army to occupy your country. It will
oppress you from Hamath Pass in the north
to the Brook of the Arabah in the south."

A Vision of Locusts

7 I had a vision from the Sovereign
LORD. In it I saw him create a swarm of
locusts just after the king's share of the hay
had been cut and the grass was starting to
grow again. 2 In my vision I saw the locusts
eat up every green thing in the land, and
then I said, "Sovereign LORD, forgive your
people! How can they survive? They are so
small and weak!"
3 The LORD changed his mind and said,
"What you saw will not take place."

A Vision of Fire

4 I had another vision from the Sovereign
LORD. In it I saw him preparing to punish
his people with fire. The fire burned up the
great ocean under the earth and started to
burn up the land. 5 Then I said, "Stop, O
Sovereign LORD! How can your people survive? They are so small and weak!"

"Stop, O Sovereign LORD!" (7:5)

6 The LORD changed his mind again and
said, "This will not take place either."

A Vision of a Plumb Line

7 I had another vision from the LORD. In
it I saw him standing beside a wall that had
been built with the use of a plumb line, and
there was a plumb line in his hand. 8 He
asked me, "Amos, what do you see?"
"A plumb line," I answered.
Then he said, "I am using it to show that
my people are like a wall that is out of line. I
will not change my mind again about punishing them. 9 The places where Isaac's
descendants worship will be destroyed. The

[f] **6:10** *Verse 10 in Hebrew is unclear.* [g] **6:13** LODEBAR: *This name sounds like the Hebrew for "nothing."*
[h] **6:13** KARNAIM: *The name of this small town means "horns," a symbol of strength.*

Pray it!

Called to Be a Prophet

Lord, are you calling me? Like Amos, I get so angry when I see someone acting dishonestly. I want to yell when I am aware of unfairness. In my city, there are homeless people living downtown, and almost everyone pretends they are invisible. God, I know you must be upset about these things. Do you want me to say something?

— Amos, chapter 7

holy places of Israel will be left in ruins. I
will bring the dynasty of King Jeroboam to
an end."

Amos and Amaziah

10 Amaziah, the priest of Bethel, then sent
a report to King Jeroboam of Israel: "Amos is
plotting against you among the people. His
speeches will destroy the country. 11 This is
what he says: 'Jeroboam will die in battle,
and the people of Israel will be taken away
from their land into exile.' "
12 Amaziah then said to Amos, "That's
enough, prophet! Go on back to Judah and
do your preaching there. Let *them* pay you
for it. 13 Don't prophesy here at Bethel any
more. This is the king's place of worship, the
national temple."
14 Amos answered, "I am not the kind of
prophet who prophesies for pay. I am a
herdsman, and I take care of fig trees. 15 But
the LORD took me from my work as a shep-
herd and ordered me to come and prophesy
to his people Israel. 16 So now listen to what
the LORD says. You tell me to stop prophesy-
ing, to stop raving against the people of
Israel. 17 And so, Amaziah, the LORD says to
you, 'Your wife will become a prostitute in
the city, and your children will be killed in
war. Your land will be divided up and given
to others, and you yourself will die in a hea-
then country. And the people of Israel will
certainly be taken away from their own land
into exile.' "

A Vision of a Basket of Fruit

8 I had another vision from the Sovereign
LORD. In it I saw a basket of fruit. 2 The
LORD asked, "Amos, what do you see?"
"A basket of fruit," I answered.
The LORD said to me, "The end[i] has
come for my people Israel. I will not change
my mind again about punishing them. 3 On
that day the songs in the palace will become
cries of mourning. There will be dead bodies
everywhere. They will be cast out in
silence."[j]

Amos, what do you see? "A basket of fruit" (8:2)

Israel's Doom

4 Listen to this, you that trample on the
needy and try to destroy the poor of the
country. 5 You say to yourselves, "We can
hardly wait for the holy days to be over so
that we can sell our grain. When will the
Sabbath end, so that we can start selling
again? Then we can overcharge, use false
measures, and fix the scales to cheat our cus-
tomers. 6 We can sell worthless wheat at a
high price. We'll find someone poor who
can't pay his debts, not even the price of a
pair of sandals, and we'll buy him as a slave."
7 The LORD, the God of Israel, has sworn,
"I will never forget their evil deeds. 8 And so
the earth will quake, and everyone in the
land will be in distress. The whole country

[i] **8:2** END: *The Hebrew words for "end" and "fruit" sound alike.* [j] **8:3** out in silence; *or* out. Silence!

will be shaken; it will rise and fall like the
Nile River. 9The time is coming when I will
make the sun go down at noon and the
earth grow dark in daytime. I, the Sovereign
LORD, have spoken. 10I will turn your festi-
vals into funerals and change your glad songs
into cries of grief. I will make you shave
your heads and wear sackcloth, and you will
be like parents mourning for their only
child. That day will be bitter to the end.
11"The time is coming when I will send
famine on the land. People will be hungry,
but not for bread; they will be thirsty, but
not for water. They will hunger and thirst for
a message from the LORD. I, the Sovereign
LORD, have spoken. 12People will wander
from the Dead Sea to the Mediterranean
and then on around from the north to the
east. They will look everywhere for a mes-
sage from the LORD, but they will not find
it. 13On that day even healthy young men
and women will collapse from thirst.
14Those who swear by the idols of Samaria,
who say, 'By the god of Dan' or 'By the god
of Beersheba'—those people will fall and
not rise again."

The LORD's Judgments

9 I saw the Lord standing by the altar. He
gave the command: "Strike the tops of
the Temple columns so hard that the founda-
tion will shake. Break them off and let them
fall on the heads of the people. I will kill the
rest of the people in war. No one will get
away; not one will escape. 2Even if they dig
their way down to the world of the dead, I
will catch them. Even if they climb up to
heaven, I will bring them down. 3If they
hide on the top of Mount Carmel, I will
search for them and catch them. If they hide
from me at the bottom of the sea, I will
command the sea monster[k] to bite them. 4If
they are taken away into captivity by their
enemies, I will order them to be put to

[k] **9:3** SEA MONSTER: *It was believed that the sea was inhabited by a great monster. This creature, like all others, was regarded as under God's control.*

Live it!

Archbishop Oscar Romero

The 1980s were difficult years for Central American countries. The wealthy families who controlled the military were trying to keep the poor people in their place. Poor families were desperately trying to lift themselves out of poverty. Many religious and human rights workers tried helping the people who lived in poverty, especially through education. And many of them died for their efforts, killed by death squads who worked for the wealthy people in power.

Archbishop Oscar Romero of El Salvador was a good friend of the wealthy citizens of his country. But then he became aware of the severe injustices the poor people in his country suffered. He had a deep change of heart, and became the champion for people living in poverty. He challenged the wealthy leaders to share their wealth and respect the human rights of all people.

Bishop Romero was killed in 1983 while saying Mass. He was one of thousands of martyrs who nonviolently fought against injustice to poor people. Today, faithful followers of Christ are still martyred, or killed, for trying to improve the lives of poor people. Pray for missionaries and others who are tirelessly working on behalf of poor people.

— Amos 8:4–6

"People will be hungry, but not for bread; they will be thirsty, but not for water. They will hunger and thirst for a message from the LORD" *(Amos 8:11).*

Catholic Social Teaching

Catholic Connections

The Catholic Church has been as vocal as Amos about social justice and human dignity. Our concern is rooted in the teachings of the Bible, such as those found in Amos. But the Catholic Church also has a rich collection of documents that explains what is called Catholic social teaching. Some of the key themes of Catholic social teaching are as follows:

- **All people have a unique dignity from God that must be respected.**
- **We must care for the common good of our world community, not just our own individual concerns.**
- **We must have a concern for poor people.**
- **We must protect the rights of workers.**
- **We must care for God's Creation.**
- **We must promote peace and rid ourselves of weapons of mass destruction.**
- **We must work so that the world's wealth is distributed fairly among all people.**

Amos tells the Israelites of the doom that awaits them for their selfish and unjust ways—and how God will one day restore Israel. Catholic social teaching tells us how to live more justly, share more generously, and act with mercy—so that we will not fall into the same kind of sinful behavior as the Israelites.

— Amos, chapters 8–9

death. I am determined to destroy them, not to help them."

5 The Sovereign LORD Almighty touches
the earth,
and it quakes;
all who live there mourn.
The whole world rises and falls like the
Nile River.
6 The LORD builds his home in the heavens,
and over the earth he puts the dome of
the sky.
He calls for the waters of the sea
and pours them out on the earth.
His name is the LORD!

7 The LORD says, "People of Israel, I think
as much of the people of Ethiopia[l] as I do of
you. I brought the Philistines from Crete and
the Syrians from Kir, just as I brought you
from Egypt. 8 I, the Sovereign LORD, am
watching this sinful kingdom of Israel, and I
will destroy it from the face of the earth. But
I will not destroy all the descendants of Jacob.
9 "I will give the command and shake the
people of Israel like grain in a sieve. I will
shake them among the nations to remove all
who are worthless. 10 The sinners among my
people will be killed in war—all those who
say, 'God will not let any harm come near
us.' "

[l] **9:7** *Hebrew* Cush: *Cush is the ancient name of the extensive territory south of the First Cataract of the Nile River. This region was called Ethiopia in Graeco-Roman times, and included within its borders most of modern Sudan and some of present-day Ethiopia (Abyssinia).*

Read Amos' vision of a better world in 9:13–15. How can you tell that he lived in a rural area?

The Future Restoration of Israel

11 The LORD says, "A day is coming when
I will restore the kingdom of David, which
is like a house fallen into ruins. I will repair
its walls and restore it. I will rebuild it and
make it as it was long ago. 12 And so the peo-
ple of Israel will conquer what is left of the
land of Edom and all the nations that were
once mine," says the LORD, who will cause
this to happen.

13 "The days are coming," says the LORD,
"when grain will grow faster than it
can be harvested,
and grapes will grow faster than the
wine can be made.
The mountains will drip with sweet
wine,
and the hills will flow with it.
14 I will bring my people back to their
land.
They will rebuild their ruined cities
and live there;
they will plant vineyards and drink the
wine;
they will plant gardens and eat what
they grow.
15 I will plant my people on the land I gave
them,
and they will not be pulled up
again."
The LORD your God has spoken.

9:11, 12 Acts 15:16–18

Your Next Step

Congratulations on finishing the Book of Amos! Use this space to write your thoughts and questions about this book. If you are following the suggested reading plan, go ahead to the Book of Micah in the Old Testament. Micah is another prophet who spoke out against worshiping foreign gods and treating people unfairly.

THE BOOK OF Obadiah

"Just you wait! You're gonna get it!" You may have heard these words at one time or another, maybe from a brother or sister who was threatening to tell on you. The message is clear—you did something wrong, and you are going to be punished.

Obadiah's message to the Edomites is similar. The Israelites and the Edomites are related through Jacob and his twin brother, Esau. Even though they are related, the Edomites did nothing to help the people of Judah when they were captured by the Babylonians. In fact, the Edomites actually gloated over the ruin of Jerusalem. Obadiah's warning to the Edomites in verse 15 could easily apply to us, too. He says: "What you have done will be done to you. You will get back what you have given."

Headlines

- God to Edom: You Are Warned! (verses 1–9)
- Edom Gets Rich; Judah Suffers (verses 10–14)
- Final Victory Belongs to Judah (verses 15–21)

FACTOIDS

Who wrote this book? Obadiah is the shortest book in the Old Testament. It is thought to have been written by the prophet Obadiah.

Why was it written? Obadiah warns the people of Edom that they will be punished for their abuse of Judah.

What period does it cover? The fifth century, sometime after the Babylonian Exile.

How does it fit into the Bible? Obadiah is one of the minor prophets who wrote after the Babylonian Exile.

Important themes

- What you have done to others will come back to you.
- Even though God's people suffer now, someday they will be reunited and return to the land God promised.

OBADIAH

1 This is the prophecy of Obadiah—what
the Sovereign LORD said about the nation of
Edom.

The LORD Will Punish Edom

The LORD has sent his messenger to the
nations,
and we have heard his message:
"Get ready! Let us go to war against
Edom!"
2 The LORD says to Edom,
"I will make you weak;
everyone will despise you.
3 Your pride has deceived you.
Your capital is a fortress of solid rock;
your home is high in the mountains,
and so you say to yourself,
'Who can ever pull me down?'
4 Even though you make your home
as high as an eagle's nest,
so that it seems to be among the stars,
yet I will pull you down.

Yet I will pull you down. (4)

5 "When thieves come at night,
they take only what they want.
When people gather grapes,
they always leave a few.
But your enemies have wiped you out
completely.
6 Descendants of Esau, your treasures have
been looted.
7 Your allies have deceived you;
they have driven you from your country.
People who were at peace with you have
now conquered you.
Those friends who ate with you have
laid a trap for you;
they say of you, 'Where is all that
cleverness he had?'
8 "On the day I punish Edom,
I will destroy their clever men
and wipe out all their wisdom.
9 The fighting men of Teman will be
terrified,
and every soldier in Edom will be
killed.

Reasons for Edom's Punishment

10 "Because you robbed and killed
your relatives,[a] the descendants of
Jacob,
you will be destroyed and dishonored
forever.
11 You stood aside on that day
when enemies broke down their gates.
You were as bad as those strangers
who carried off Jerusalem's wealth
and divided it among themselves.
12 You should not have gloated
over the misfortune of your relatives in
Judah.
You should not have been glad
on the day of their ruin.
You should not have laughed at them
in their distress.

You should not have gloated. (12)

[a] **10** YOUR RELATIVES: *The Israelites were descended from Jacob, who was the brother of Esau, the ancestor of the Edomites.*

1–14 Isa 34:5–17; 63:1–6; Jer 49:7–22; Ezek 25:12–14; 35:1–15; Am 1:11, 12; Mal 1:2–5

13 You should not have entered the city of
my people
to gloat over their suffering
and to seize their riches
on the day of their disaster.
14 You should not have stood at the
crossroads
to catch those trying to escape.
You should not have handed them over to
the enemy
on the day of their distress.

God Will Judge the Nations

15 "The day is near when I, the LORD,
will judge all nations.
Edom, what you have done
will be done to you.
You will get back what you have given.
16 My people have drunk a bitter cup of
punishment
on my sacred hill.[b]
But all the surrounding nations will drink
a still more bitter cup of punishment;
they will drink it all and vanish away.

The Victory of Israel

17 "But on Mount Zion some will escape,
and it will be a sacred place.
The people of Jacob will possess
the land that is theirs by right.
18 The people of Jacob and of Joseph will be
like fire;
they will destroy the people of
Esau
as fire burns stubble.
No descendant of Esau will survive.
I, the LORD, have spoken.

19 "People from southern Judah will occupy
Edom;
those from the western foothills will
capture Philistia.
Israelites will possess the territory of
Ephraim and Samaria;
the people of Benjamin will take
Gilead.
20 The army of exiles from northern
Israel
will return and conquer Phoenicia as
far north as Zarephath.
The exiles from Jerusalem who are in
Sardis
will capture the towns of southern
Judah.
21 The victorious men of Jerusalem
will attack Edom and rule over it.
And the LORD himself will be king."

[b] **16** SACRED HILL: *Mount Zion (see Zion in Word List).*

Where is Edom? Locate it on Map 3 in the back of this Bible.

THE BOOK OF Jonah

Jonah had an attitude problem. God had a job for him—to go to Nineveh and tell the people to change their ways. Jonah didn't want to go, so he ran away. But God wouldn't let Jonah get away; Jonah ended up in the belly of a large fish. When he finally went to Nineveh, he never expected that the people would listen to him. But amazingly they did! Instead of being happy, Jonah was angry. He didn't want to share God's love with Ninevites. He didn't think they deserved it.

The story of Jonah is full of lessons about respecting others, listening to God, understanding God's love, and believing that God knows best—even when we don't understand God's plans.

Chap. 2

Headlines

- God Calls, Jonah Runs (1:1–16)
- Jonah Becomes Fish Food! (1:17—2:10)
- Jonah Gets a Second Chance (3:1–10)
- God Spares Nineveh, Jonah Throws a Fit! (4:1–10)

FACTOIDS

Who wrote this book? The author is unknown, but the story focuses on the activities of an imaginary prophet named Jonah.

Why was it written? The Israelites believed that God loved only them and that God would destroy their enemies. This book was written to teach them that God cares for everyone, including their enemies.

How does it fit into the Bible? The Book of Jonah is one of eighteen prophetic books and the only one that is a parable, that is, a story that teaches a lesson.

Jesus connection: Just as Jonah spent three days and three nights in the belly of a large fish before being spit up on the shore, Jesus spent three days in the tomb before his Resurrection.

Important themes

- God loves everyone, even those we consider our enemies.
- God forgives those who are sorry for their sins and gives them a second chance.

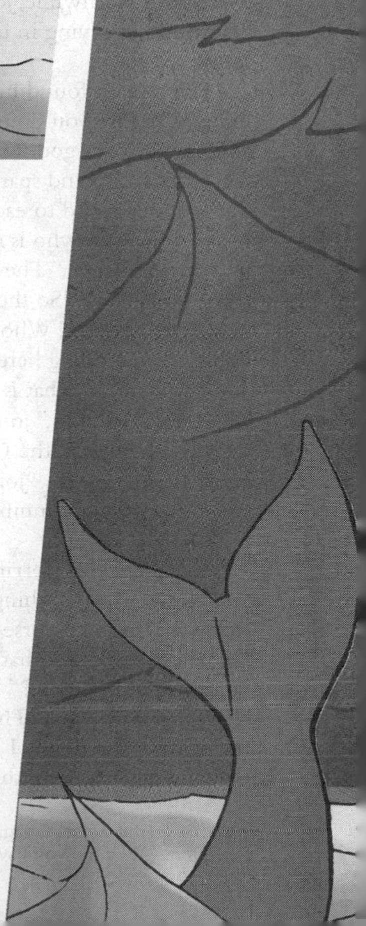

JONAH

Jonah Disobeys the LORD

1 One day the LORD spoke to Jonah son
of Amittai. 2He said, "Go to Nineveh,
that great city, and speak out against it; I am
aware of how wicked its people are." 3Jonah,
however, set out in the opposite direction in
order to get away from the LORD. He went
to Joppa, where he found a ship about to go
to Spain. He paid his fare and went aboard
with the crew to sail to Spain, where he
would be away from the LORD.
4But the LORD sent a strong wind on the
sea, and the storm was so violent that the
ship was in danger of breaking up. 5The
sailors were terrified and cried out for help,
each one to his own god. Then, in order to
lessen the danger,[a] they threw the cargo[b]
overboard. Meanwhile, Jonah had gone
below and was lying in the ship's hold,
sound asleep.
6The captain found him there and said to
him, "What are you doing asleep? Get up
and pray to your god for help. Maybe he will
feel sorry for us and spare our lives."
7The sailors said to each other, "Let's draw
lots and find out who is to blame for getting
us into this danger." They did so, and Jonah's
name was drawn. 8So they said to him,
"Now, then, tell us! Who is to blame for this?
What are you doing here? What country do
you come from? What is your nationality?"
9"I am a Hebrew," Jonah answered. "I
worship the LORD, the God of heaven, who
made land and sea." 10Jonah went on to tell
them that he was running away from the
LORD.

The sailors were terrified, and said to him,
"That was an awful thing to do!"[c] 11The
storm was getting worse all the time, so the
sailors asked him, "What should we do to
you to stop the storm?"
12Jonah answered, "Throw me into the sea,
and it will calm down. I know it is my fault
that you are caught in this violent storm."

Live it!

You Disobey, You Pay

Martin pretended he didn't hear his dad as he rode away on his bike. He was supposed to clean out the garage. Martin knew he would be in trouble, but he and Jon had plans. When he arrived at Jon's house, Martin's dad was waiting for him. He didn't say much, except to tell Martin that he was grounded.

God told Jonah to go to Nineveh, but Jonah boarded a ship instead. God sent a powerful storm, and when the sailors realized that it was Jonah's fault, they threw him overboard and a large fish swallowed him.

Martin and Jonah both realized that wrong actions have unpleasant consequences. Being grounded is no fun. Neither is spending three days in the belly of a fish, only to be vomited up on the shore! It's a hard lesson to learn, but if you disobey, you will pay.

— Jonah, chapter 1

13Instead, the sailors tried to get the ship
to shore, rowing with all their might. But the
storm was becoming worse and worse, and
they got nowhere. 14So they cried out to the
LORD, "O LORD, we pray, don't punish us
with death for taking this man's life! You, O
LORD, are responsible for all this; it is your
doing." 15Then they picked Jonah up and
threw him into the sea, and it calmed down

[a] 1:5 lessen the danger; *or* lighten the ship. [b] 1:5 cargo; *or* equipment. [c] 1:10 and said . . . to do!; *or* and asked him, "Why did you have to run away like that?"

1:1 2 Kings 14:25

Pray it!

Jonah's Prayer, Your Prayer

While he was in the belly of the fish, Jonah had a lot of time to think and pray. He realized that he was running away from God because he didn't want to do what God was asking. In his prayer he did three things:

- **He told God about his fears.**
- **He proclaimed his love for God by praising God.**
- **He promised to do what he had promised to do.**

Jonah's prayer can become your prayer as often as you like. It will change every time, depending on what is going on in your life. Just go to a quiet place and do the same three things that Jonah did.

God answered Jonah's prayer by ordering the fish to spit him out. Don't forget to listen and watch for God's response to you.

— Jonah, chapter 2

at once. 16 This made the sailors so afraid of
the LORD that they offered a sacrifice and
promised to serve him.
17 At the LORD's command a large fish
swallowed Jonah, and he was inside the fish
for three days and three nights.

Jonah's Prayer

2 From deep inside the fish Jonah prayed to the LORD his God:

2 "In my distress, O LORD, I called to you,
and you answered me.
From deep in the world of the dead
I cried for help, and you heard me.
3 You threw me down into the depths,
to the very bottom of the sea,
where the waters were all around me,
and all your mighty waves rolled over me.
4 I thought I had been banished from your presence
and would never see your holy Temple again.
5 The water came over me and choked me;
the sea covered me completely,
and seaweed wrapped around my head.
6 I went down to the very roots of the mountains,
into the land whose gates lock shut forever.[d]
But you, O LORD my God,
brought me back from the depths alive.
7 When I felt my life slipping away,
then, O LORD, I prayed to you,
and in your holy Temple you heard me.
8 Those who worship worthless idols
have abandoned their loyalty to you.
9 But I will sing praises to you;
I will offer you a sacrifice
and do what I have promised.
Salvation comes from the LORD!"
10 Then the LORD ordered the fish to spit
Jonah up on the beach, and it did.

[d] **2:6** THE LAND WHOSE GATES LOCK SHUT FOREVER: *A reference to the world of the dead (see 2:2).*
1:17 Mt 12:40

As a child, you probably heard that Jonah was swallowed by a whale. The Bible just says "a large fish."

Prayer is communicating with God in a relationship of love. What signs do you see of Jonah's love for God in his prayer?

HIGHLIGHTS FROM THE LIFE OF JONAH (1, 2, 3, 4)

Jonah Obeys the LORD

3 Once again the LORD spoke to Jonah.
2He said, "Go to Nineveh, that great
city, and proclaim to the people the message
I have given you." 3So Jonah obeyed the
LORD and went to Nineveh, a city so large
that it took three days to walk through it.
4Jonah started through the city, and after
walking a whole day, he proclaimed, "In
forty days Nineveh will be destroyed!"

5The people of Nineveh believed God's
message. So they decided that everyone
should fast, and all the people, from the
greatest to the least, put on sackcloth to
show that they had repented.

6When the king of Nineveh heard about
it, he got up from his throne, took off his
robe, put on sackcloth, and sat down in
ashes. 7He sent out a proclamation to the
people of Nineveh: "This is an order from
the king and his officials: No one is to eat
anything; all persons, cattle, and sheep are
forbidden to eat or drink. 8All persons and
animals must wear sackcloth. Everyone must
pray earnestly to God and must give up their
wicked behavior and their evil actions. 9Per-
haps God will change his mind; perhaps he
will stop being angry, and we will not die!"

10God saw what they did; he saw that
they had given up their wicked behavior. So
he changed his mind and did not punish
them as he had said he would.

Live it!

One World Under God

Jonah had a strong wish that God would punish the people of Nineveh, whom he considered enemies—mostly because they were not Jews. When he finally agreed to go to the Ninevites with God's message, he was shocked that they listened. He was also angry because it meant that they would not be punished. At the end of the story, God tells Jonah that he has no right to be angry; everyone is entitled to God's love.

The story of Jonah was written to teach the Israelites—and us—a lesson about God: no group of people is any more deserving of God's love than another group. This is true of countries, and it is also true of the groups you belong to. God never chooses sides. He does not care who is popular, athletic, or rich. God's love is big enough for everyone.

— Jonah, chapters 3–4

Jonah's Anger and God's Mercy

4 Jonah was very unhappy about this and
became angry. 2So he prayed, "LORD,
didn't I say before I left home that this is just
what you would do? That's why I did my
best to run away to Spain! I knew that you
are a loving and merciful God, always
patient, always kind, and always ready to
change your mind and not punish. 3Now
then, LORD, let me die. I am better off dead
than alive."

4The LORD answered, "What right do you
have to be angry?"

5Jonah went out east of the city and sat
down. He made a shelter for himself and sat
in its shade, waiting to see what would hap-
pen to Nineveh. 6Then the LORD God
made a plant grow up over Jonah to give
him some shade, so that he would be more
comfortable. Jonah was extremely pleased
with the plant. 7But at dawn the next day, at
God's command, a worm attacked the plant,
and it died. 8After the sun had risen, God
sent a hot east wind, and Jonah was about to
faint from the heat of the sun beating down
on his head. So he wished he were dead.[e] "I
am better off dead than alive," he said.

9But God said to him, "What right do
you have to be angry about the plant?"

[e] **4:8** wished he were dead; *or* prayed that he would die.

3:4, 5 Mt 12:41; Lk 11:32 **4:2** Ex 34:6 **4:3** 1 Kings 19:4

Jonah replied, "I have every right to be
angry—angry enough to die!"
10The LORD said to him, "This plant grew
up in one night and disappeared the next;
you didn't do anything for it and you didn't
make it grow—yet you feel sorry for it!
11How much more, then, should I have pity
on Nineveh, that great city. After all, it has
more than 120,000 innocent children in it,
as well as many animals!"

Your Next Step

Congratulations on finishing the Book of Jonah! Use this space to write your thoughts and questions about this book. If you are following the suggested reading plan, go back to the Book of Ezra. Ezra tells the story of how the people returned to rebuild the city of Jerusalem and the Temple after their captivity in Babylon.

THE BOOK OF Micah

You've probably heard people say: "I've got good news and bad news. Which do you want to hear first?" The Book of Micah is very much like that. The book starts with the bad news. Because the Israelites worship false gods and mistreat one another, their two kingdoms are heading for ruin.

But wait, there is good news. Micah says that after the destruction, God will restore their country. There will also be a new ruler, one who is strong and who will bring peace and justice. And this new ruler will come from a humble place, a small country village called Bethlehem. Any guesses who that might be?

Chap. 2:1–2

Headlines

- Micah Tells of Abuses (2:8–10; 3:1–3)
- Weapons Will Be Farming Tools! (4:1–5)
- Peaceful Ruler Coming from Bethlehem (5:1–5)
- Do You Know What God Requires? (6:6–8)

FACTOIDS

Who wrote this book? Micah (or scribes recording his words), who left his country village and went to the big city of Jerusalem to prophecy when God called.

Why was it written? It was written to record the words of the prophet Micah. He warned God's people that war and violence would be the result of not following God and not treating other people fairly.

Jesus connection: Jesus is the great ruler, born in Bethlehem, who Micah says will bring peace to God's people (5:2–5).

Important themes

- If God's people truly believe in God, then they will care for all people and treat them justly, especially poor people.
- God will not abandon his people; he will send a ruler who will bring a time of peace.

1 During the time that Jotham, Ahaz, and
Hezekiah were kings of Judah, the
LORD gave this message to Micah, who was
from the town of Moresheth. The LORD
revealed to Micah all these things about
Samaria and Jerusalem.

A Lament for Samaria and Jerusalem

2 Hear this, all you nations;
listen to this, all who live on earth!
The Sovereign LORD will testify against
you.
Listen! He speaks from his heavenly
temple.
3 The LORD is coming from his holy place;
he will come down and walk on the
tops of the mountains.
4 Then the mountains will melt under him
like wax in a fire;
they will pour down into the valleys
like water pouring down a hill.

5 All this will happen because the people
of Israel have sinned and rebelled against
God. Who is to blame for Israel's rebellion?
Samaria, the capital city itself! Who is guilty
of idolatry in Judah? Jerusalem itself! 6 So the
LORD says, "I will make Samaria a pile of
ruins in the open country, a place for plant-
ing grapevines. I will pour the rubble of the
city down into the valley, and will lay bare
the city's foundations. 7 All its precious idols
will be smashed to pieces, everything given
to its temple prostitutes will be destroyed by
fire, and all its images will become a desolate
heap. Samaria acquired these things for its
fertility rites, and now her enemies will
carry them off for temple prostitutes else-
where."

8 Then Micah said, "Because of this I will
mourn and lament. To show my sorrow, I
will walk around barefoot and naked. I will
howl like a jackal and wail like an ostrich.

Study it!

Israel and Judah, Samaria and Jerusalem

About 150 years before Micah was born, the Israelite nation split into two separate kingdoms. This happened after the death of King Solomon. The kingdom in the north was called Israel, and the kingdom in the south was called Judah. Samaria was the capital of Israel. Micah first predicts Samaria's destruction (Micah 1:6). Then Micah condemns the sins of Judah and predicts the destruction of Judah's capital, Jerusalem (3:12). Micah realizes that both kingdoms have been unfaithful to God. They will come to a bad end because of this.

— Micah, chapter 1

9 Samaria's wounds cannot be healed, and
Judah is about to suffer in the same way;
destruction has reached the gates of
Jerusalem itself, where my people live."

The Enemy Approaches Jerusalem

10 Don't tell our enemies in Gath about
our defeat; don't let them see you weeping.
People of Beth Leaphrah,[a] show your
despair by rolling in the dust! 11 You peo-
ple of Shaphir, go into exile, naked and
ashamed. Those who live in Zaanan do not
dare to come out of their city. When you
hear the people of Bethezel mourn, you will
know that there is no refuge there. 12 The

[a] **1:10** BETH LEAPHRAH: *The prophet speaks of outlying towns (verses 10–14) which an enemy army approaching Jerusalem would attack.*

1:1 **a** 2 Kings 15:32–38; 2 Chr 27:1–7; **b** 2 Kings 16:1–20; 2 Chr 28:1–27; **c** 2 Kings 18:1—20:21; 2 Chr 29:1—32:33

people of Maroth anxiously wait for relief,
because the LORD has brought disaster close
to Jerusalem. 13 You that live in Lachish,
hitch the horses to the chariots. You imitated
the sins of Israel and so caused Jerusalem to
sin. 14 And now, people of Judah, say good-
bye to the town of Moresheth Gath. The
kings of Israel will get no help from the
town of Achzib.

15 People of Mareshah, the LORD will
hand you over to an enemy, who is going
to capture your town. The leaders of Israel
will go and hide in the cave at Adullam.
16 People of Judah, cut off your hair in
mourning for the children you love. Make
yourselves as bald as vultures, because your
children will be taken away from you into
exile.

The Fate of Those Who Oppress the Poor

2 How terrible it will be for those who
lie awake and plan evil! When morning
comes, as soon as they have the chance, they
do the evil they planned. 2 When they want
fields, they seize them; when they want
houses, they take them. No one's family or
property is safe.

3 And so the LORD says, "I am planning to
bring disaster on you, and you will not be
able to escape it. You are going to find your-
selves in trouble, and then you will not walk
so proudly any more. 4 When that time
comes, people will use the story about you
as an example of disaster, and they will sing
this song of despair about your experience:

> We are completely ruined!
> The LORD has taken our land away
> And given it to those who took us
> captive."[b]

5 So then, when the time comes for the
land to be given back to the LORD's people,
there will be no share for any of you.

6 The people preach at me and say, "Don't
preach at us. Don't preach about all that.
God is not going to disgrace us. 7 Do you
think the people of Israel are under a curse?[c]
Has the LORD lost his patience? Would he
really do such things? Doesn't he[d] speak
kindly to those who do right?"

"Don't preach at us." (2:6)

8 The LORD replies, "You attack my peo-
ple[e] like enemies. Men return from battle,
thinking they are safe at home, but there you
are, waiting to steal the coats off their backs.
9 You drive the women of my people out of
the homes they love, and you have robbed
their children of my blessings forever. 10 Get
up and go; there is no safety here any more.
Your sins have doomed this place to destruc-
tion.

11 "These people want the kind of prophet
who goes around full of lies and deceit and
says, 'I prophesy that wine and liquor will
flow for you.'

12 "But I will gather you together, all you
people of Israel that are left. I will bring you
together like sheep returning to the fold.
Like a pasture full of sheep, your land will
once again be filled with many people."

13 God will open the way for them and
lead them out of exile. They will break out
of the city gates and go free. Their king, the
LORD himself, will lead them out.

[b] **2:4** *Probable text* those who took us captive; *Hebrew* rebels. [c] **2:7** *Probable text* under a curse; *Hebrew unclear.* [d] **2:7** *One ancient translation* Doesn't he; *Hebrew* Don't I. [e] **2:8** *Probable text* You attack my people; *Hebrew* Recently my people have attacked.

Micah may have been a farmer. How many farm images can you find in his book?

Live it!

Peer Pressure

Peer pressure means doing something only because other people tell you to do it. Micah knew about peer pressure. The people kept telling him: "Don't preach at us. Don't preach about all that" (Micah 2:6). But he didn't give in to peer pressure. He preached the message God gave him.

Some of Joe's friends are stealing from a local store. They keep telling Joe that it is exciting and will make him brave. Joe wants to keep his friends, but he knows that stealing is a sin. What do you think Micah would tell Joe? What are some of the peer pressures that you face?

— Micah 2:6–11

Micah Denounces Israel's Leaders

3 Listen, you rulers of Israel! You are sup-
posed to be concerned about justice,
2yet you hate what is good and you love
what is evil. You skin my people alive and
tear the flesh off their bones. 3You eat my
people up. You strip off their skin, break their
bones, and chop them up like meat for the
pot. 4The time is coming when you will cry
out to the LORD, but he will not answer
you. He will not listen to your prayers, for
you have done evil.
5My people are deceived by prophets who
promise peace to those who pay them, but
threaten war for those who don't. To these
prophets the LORD says, 6"Prophets, your
day is almost over; the sun is going down on
you. Because you mislead my people, you
will have no more prophetic visions, and you
will not be able to predict anything." 7Those
who predict the future will be disgraced by
their failure. They will all be humiliated
because God does not answer them.
8But as for me, the LORD fills me with his
spirit and power, and gives me a sense of jus-
tice and the courage to tell the people of
Israel what their sins are. 9Listen to me, you
rulers of Israel, you that hate justice and turn
right into wrong. 10You are building God's
city, Jerusalem, on a foundation of murder
and injustice. 11The city's rulers govern for
bribes, the priests interpret the Law for pay,
the prophets give their revelations for
money—and they all claim that the LORD is
with them. "No harm will come to us," they
say. "The LORD is with us."

The prophets give their revelations for money. (3:11)

12And so, because of you, Zion will be
plowed like a field, Jerusalem will become a
pile of ruins, and the Temple hill will
become a forest.

The LORD's Universal Reign of Peace
(Isaiah 2:2–4)

4 In days to come
the mountain where the Temple stands
will be the highest one of all,
towering above all the hills.
Many nations will come streaming
to it,
2 and their people will say,
"Let us go up the hill of the LORD,[f]
to the Temple of Israel's God.

[f] **4:2** HILL OF THE LORD: *Mount Zion (see Zion in Word List).*

3:12 Jer 26:18

Pray it!

Lord of Peace

Micah says that a time will come when God will bring peace to the whole world. You can pray this prayer for peace, written by Marisa Garfinkel, a high school student. *Adonai Shalom* means "Lord of peace."

Adonai Shalom
Lord, let there be peace in my heart,
so that it may be open to feel love,
kindness, and goodness.

Adonai Shalom
Lord, let there be peace in my life,
so that I can listen to and learn from others
who seem so different from me.

Adonai Shalom
Lord, may I have the opportunity to create
a peaceful environment with lifestyles
that include all my neighbors.

Adonai Shalom
Lord, please grant me peace,
that I may find contentment in your world,
so that "nations will never again go to war, / never prepare for battle again" (Isaiah 2:4).

— Micah 4:1–4

He will teach us what he wants us to do;
we will walk in the paths he has
chosen.
For the LORD's teaching comes from
Jerusalem;
from Zion he speaks to his people."

3 He will settle disputes among the nations,
among the great powers near and far.
They will hammer their swords into plows
and their spears into pruning knives.
Nations will never again go to war,
never prepare for battle again.
4 Everyone will live in peace
among their own vineyards and fig trees,
and no one will make them afraid.
The LORD Almighty has promised this.

5 Each nation worships and obeys its own
god, but we will worship and obey the
LORD our God forever and ever.

Israel Will Return from Exile

6 "The time is coming," says the LORD,
"when I will gather together the people I
punished, those who have suffered in exile.
7 They are crippled and far from home, but I
will make a new beginning with those who
are left, and they will become a great nation.
I will rule over them on Mount Zion from
that time on and forever."
8 And you, Jerusalem, where God, like a
shepherd from his lookout tower, watches
over his people, will once again be the capi-

4:3 Isa 2:4; Joel 3:10 **4:4** Zech 3:10

Catholic Connections

Jesus' Birthplace

Micah predicts that a new ruler will come from Bethlehem, the smallest of towns. That new ruler is Jesus. He was born to poor parents in a little town (see Luke 2:1–7). You might think the Savior of the world should have been born in an important town. But Jesus lived a simple life to show it doesn't matter how wealthy your family is. You do not need to be rich or important to please God—in some ways being rich or famous can make it harder to follow God. What God truly desires is a humble heart—so we recognize that everything we have is a gift from God.

— Micah 5:2–5

tal of the kingdom that was yours. 9 Why do
you cry out so loudly? Why are you suffer-
ing like a woman in labor? Is it because you
have no king, and your counselors are dead?
10 Twist and groan,[g] people of Jerusalem, like
a woman giving birth, for now you will have
to leave the city and live in the open coun-
try. You will have to go to Babylon, but there
the LORD will save you from your enemies.
11 Many nations have gathered to attack you.
They say, "Jerusalem must be destroyed! We
will see this city in ruins!" 12 But these
nations do not know what is in the LORD's
mind. They do not realize that they have
been gathered together to be punished in
the same way that grain is brought in to be
threshed.

13 The LORD says, "People of Jerusalem, go
and punish your enemies! I will make you as
strong as a bull with iron horns and bronze
hoofs. You will crush many nations, and the
wealth they got by violence you will present
to me, the Lord of the whole world."

5 People of Jerusalem, gather your forces![h]
We are besieged! They are attacking the
leader of Israel!

God Promises a Ruler from Bethlehem

2 The LORD says, "Bethlehem Ephrathah,
you are one of the smallest towns in Judah,
but out of you I will bring a ruler for Israel,
whose family line goes back to ancient
times."

3 So the LORD will abandon his people to
their enemies until the woman who is to
give birth has her son. Then those Israelites
who are in exile will be reunited with their
own people. 4 When he comes, he will rule
his people with the strength that comes from
the LORD and with the majesty of the LORD
God himself. His people will live in safety
because people all over the earth will
acknowledge his greatness, 5 and he will
bring peace.

Deliverance and Punishment

When the Assyrians invade our country
and break through our defenses, we will send
our strongest leaders to fight them. 6 By force
of arms they will conquer Assyria, the land
of Nimrod, and they[i] will save us from the
Assyrians when they invade our territory.

[g] **4:10** *Probable text* groan; *Hebrew* bring forth. [h] **5:1** *Probable text* People . . . forces!; *Hebrew unclear.*
[i] **5:6** *Probable text* they; *Hebrew* he.
5:2 Mt 2:6; Jn 7:42 **5:6** Gen 10:8–11

What are some ways you can be a peacemaker in your family? In your school?

7 The people of Israel who survive will be
like refreshing dew sent by the LORD for
many nations, like showers on growing
plants. They will depend on God, not peo-
ple. 8 Those who are left among the nations
will be like a lion hunting for food in a for-
est or a pasture: it gets in among the sheep,
pounces on them, and tears them to
pieces—and there is no hope of rescue.
9 Israel will conquer her enemies and destroy
them all.
10 The LORD says, "At that time I will take
away your horses and destroy your chariots.
11 I will destroy the cities in your land and
tear down all your defenses. 12 I will destroy
the magic charms you use and leave you
without any fortunetellers. 13 I will destroy
your idols and sacred stone pillars; no longer
will you worship the things that you your-
selves have made. 14 I will pull down the
images of the goddess Asherah in your land
and destroy your cities. 15 And in my great
anger I will take revenge on all nations that
have not obeyed me."

The LORD's Case against Israel

6 Listen to the LORD's case against Israel.
Arise, O LORD, and present your
case; let the mountains and the hills hear
what you say.
2 You mountains, you everlasting founda-
tions of the earth, listen to the LORD's case!
The LORD has a case against his people. He
is going to bring an accusation against Israel.
3 The LORD says, "My people, what have I
done to you? How have I been a burden to
you? Answer me. 4 I brought you out of
Egypt; I rescued you from slavery; I sent
Moses, Aaron, and Miriam to lead you. 5 My
people, remember what King Balak of Moab
planned to do to you and how Balaam son
of Beor answered him. Remember the
things that happened on the way from the
camp at Acacia to Gilgal. Remember these
things and you will realize what I did in
order to save you."

What the LORD Requires

6 What shall I bring to the LORD, the God
of heaven, when I come to worship him?
Shall I bring the best calves to burn as offer-
ings to him? 7 Will the LORD be pleased if
I bring him thousands of sheep or endless
streams of olive oil? Shall I offer him my
first-born child to pay for my sins? 8 No, the
LORD has told us what is good. What he
requires of us is this: to do what is just, to
show constant love, and to live in humble
fellowship with our God.
9 It is wise to fear the LORD. He calls to
the city, "Listen, you people who assemble
in the city![j] 10 In the houses of evil people
are treasures which they got dishonestly.
They use false measures, a thing that I
hate.[k] 11 How can I forgive those who use
false scales and weights? 12 Your rich people
exploit the poor, and all of you are liars.
13 So I have already begun[l] your ruin and
destruction because of your sins. 14 You will
eat, but not be satisfied—in fact you will
still be hungry. You will carry things off, but

How can I forgive those who use false scales and weights? (6:11)

[j] **6:9** *Probable text* who assemble in the city; *Hebrew* and who appointed it. Yet. [k] **6:10** *Verse 10 in Hebrew is unclear.* [l] **6:13** *Some ancient translations* begun; *Hebrew* made sick.

6:4 **a** Ex 12:50, 51; **b** Ex 4:10–16; **c** Ex 15:20 **6:5** **a** Num 22:2—24:25; **b** Josh 3:1—4:19

Worship: **To adore God in prayer, particularly as part of a public religious ritual such as the Mass.**

Pray it!

Empty Worship

The Temple at Jerusalem had regular religious rituals to worship God. During the rituals there were animal sacrifices (Micah 6:6). The rituals were attended by all the powerful people of the city. Yet these same people cheated poor people (6:10–12). It upset Micah that these wealthy people pretended to be so religious! Their rituals meant nothing to God if they did not treat others fairly (6:7–8).

Catholics worship God at Mass and other prayer services. But just as in Micah's time, it isn't enough just to attend worship services. We must follow God the rest of the week. To help you remember this, before going to Mass each week, say this prayer:

Dear God, I know I am not perfect. Show me where I need to change. Let Jesus's body and blood in the Eucharist strengthen me to do what is right in the week ahead. Do not let my prayers become empty promises. Amen.

— Micah 6:6–16

you will not be able to save them; anything
you do save I will destroy in war. 15 You
will sow grain, but not harvest the crop.
You will press oil from olives, but never get
to use it. You will make wine, but never
drink it. 16 This will happen because you
have followed the evil practices of King
Omri and of his son, King Ahab. You have
continued their policies, and so I will bring
you to ruin, and everyone will despise you.
People[m] everywhere will treat you with
contempt."[n]

Israel's Moral Corruption

7 It's hopeless! I am like a hungry person
who finds no fruit left on the trees and
no grapes on the vines. All the grapes and all
the tasty figs have been picked. 2 There is not
an honest person left in the land, no one
loyal to God. Everyone is waiting for a
chance to commit murder. Everyone hunts
down their own people. 3 They are all
experts at doing evil. Officials and judges ask
for bribes. The influential people tell them
what they want, and so they scheme togeth-
er.[o] 4 Even the best and most honest of them
are as worthless as weeds.

The day has come when God will punish
the people, as he warned them through their
watchmen, the prophets. Now they are in
confusion. 5 Don't believe your neighbor or
trust your friend. Be careful what you say
even to your husband or wife. 6 In these
times sons treat their fathers like fools,
daughters oppose their mothers, and young
women quarrel with their mothers-in-law;
your enemies are the members of your own
family.

7 But I will watch for the LORD; I will
wait confidently for God, who will save me.
My God will hear me.

The LORD Brings Salvation

8 Our enemies have no reason to gloat over
us. We have fallen, but we will rise again. We
are in darkness now, but the LORD will give
us light. 9 We have sinned against the LORD,
so now we must endure his anger for a
while. But in the end he will defend us and
right the wrongs that have been done to us.

[m] **6:16** *One ancient translation* People; *Hebrew* My people. [n] **6:16** People . . . contempt; *or* As my people you will everywhere be treated with contempt. [o] **7:3** and so they scheme together; *Hebrew unclear.*

6:16 a 1 Kings 16:23–28; **b** 1 Kings 16:29–34; 21:25, 26 **7:6** Mt 10:35, 36; Lk 12:53

Your people will return to you from everywhere. (7:12)

He will bring us out to the light; we will live
to see him save us. 10 Then our enemies will
see this and be disgraced—the same enemies
who taunted us by asking, "Where is the
LORD your God?" We will see them defeat-
ed, trampled[p] down like mud in the streets.
11 People of Jerusalem, the time to rebuild
the city walls is coming. At that time your
territory will be enlarged. 12 Your people will
return to you from everywhere—from
Assyria in the east, from Egypt in the south,
from the region of the Euphrates River,
from distant seas and far-off mountains.
13 But the earth will become a desert because
of the wickedness of those who live on it.

The LORD's Compassion on Israel

14 Be a shepherd to your people, LORD,
the people you have chosen. Although they
live apart in the wilderness, there is fertile
land around them. Let them go and feed in
the rich pastures of Bashan and Gilead, as
they did long ago.
15 Work miracles for us,[q] LORD, as you did
in the days when you brought us out of
Egypt. 16 The nations will see this and be
frustrated in spite of all their strength. In dis-
may they will close their mouths and cover
their ears. 17 They will crawl in the dust like
snakes; they will come from their fortresses,
trembling and afraid. They will turn in fear
to the LORD our God.
18 There is no other god like you, O
LORD; you forgive the sins of your people
who have survived. You do not stay angry
forever, but you take pleasure in showing us
your constant love. 19 You will be merciful to
us once again. You will trample our sins
underfoot and send them to the bottom of
the sea! 20 You will show your faithfulness
and constant love to your people, the
descendants of Abraham and of Jacob, as you
promised our ancestors long ago.

[p] **7:10** We will see . . . trampled; *or* We will gloat over them as they lie trampled. [q] **7:15** *Probable text* Work miracles for us; *Hebrew* I will work miracles for him.

Your Next Step

Congratulations on finishing the Book of Micah! Use this space to write your thoughts and questions about this book. If you are following the suggested reading plan, go back to the Book of Jeremiah in the Old Testament. Jeremiah was a prophet who saw the destruction of Jerusalem and the holy Temple.

THE BOOK OF Nahum

Think about the last time that you were really angry with someone. What made you so angry? How did you deal with your anger? Did you keep it inside? Or did you express your anger? Maybe you talked about it—or "vented"—with a friend.

In this short book, Nahum describes God's anger at the Assyrians. God vows to destroy Nineveh, the glittering capital of the Assyrians, as cruelly as the Assyrians dealt with the Israelites. And that is Nahum's point. God takes care of his Chosen People and punishes the guilty. Nineveh will meet the same fate that it inflicted on others. This may sound like pure revenge, but for the people of Nahum's time, this is simply justice carried out by God.

Chap. 2:4–5

Headlines

- Storm Warning: God's Judgment Coming (chapter 1)
- Nineveh Falls! (2:1—3:19)

FACTOIDS

Who wrote this book? The prophet Nahum.

Why was it written? It was written to the Israelites who had experienced cruel treatment at the hands of the Assyrians. Nahum's prophecies assure God's people that God will avenge them. The book describes the fall of the evil city of Nineveh and celebrates God's victory.

What period does it cover? 663–612 BC.

How does it fit into the Bible? Nahum wrote after the Assyrians had destroyed the northern kingdom of Israel and invaded the southern kingdom of Judah (but before the Babylonian Exile).

Important theme

- God will not allow evil people to go unpunished.
- God protects and comforts those who turn to the Lord in times of trouble.

NAHUM

1 This is a message about Nineveh, the
account of a vision seen by Nahum,
who was from Elkosh.

The LORD's Anger against Nineveh

2 The LORD God tolerates no rivals;
he punishes those who oppose him.
In his anger he pays them back.
3 The LORD does not easily become angry,
but he is powerful
and never lets the guilty go unpunished.

Where the LORD walks, storms arise;
the clouds are the dust raised by his feet!
4 He commands the sea, and it dries up!
He makes the rivers go dry.
The fields of Bashan wither,
Mount Carmel turns brown,
and the flowers of Lebanon fade.
5 Mountains quake in the presence of the LORD;
hills melt before him.
The earth shakes when the LORD appears;
the world and all its people tremble.
6 When he is angry, who can survive?
Who can survive his terrible fury?
He pours out his flaming anger;
rocks crumble to dust before him.

7 The LORD is good;
he protects his people in times of trouble;
he takes care of those who turn to him.
8 Like a great rushing flood he completely destroys his enemies;[a]
he sends to their death those who oppose him.
9 What are you plotting against the LORD?
He will destroy you.
No one opposes him more than once.
10 Like tangled thorns and dry straw
you drunkards will be burned up!

11 From you, Nineveh, there came some-
one full of wicked schemes, who plotted
against the LORD. 12 This is what the LORD

Study it!

Angry God

"He pours out his flaming anger;
rocks crumble to dust before him.

The LORD is good;
he protects his people in times of trouble;
he takes care of those who turn to him." (Nahum 1:6–7)

These two verses follow one another in the Book of Nahum, and seem to describe two different images of God. One is an image of an angry, punishing God. The other is an image of a loving, caring God. The Israelite people had no trouble with these different images of God. They had experienced many wars and conflicts. Throughout this violent time they felt God's support. They had an image of God as a strong warrior, defeating their enemies as long as they remained faithful to their Covenant with God. But they also knew God's love, care, and mercy, and so they also had gentle and tender images of God.

God sent Jesus to fully reveal God's message of love and forgiveness for all people. Because of what Jesus taught us, it has become harder to image God as a warrior, taking one people's side against another people's. Thanks to Jesus, we now see forgiveness—more than victory in battle—as a sign of God's presence.

— Nahum 1:6–7

[a] **1:8** *Some ancient translations* his enemies; *Hebrew* its place.

1:1—3:19 Isa 10:5–34; 14:24–27; Zeph 2:13–15

says to his people Israel: "Even though the Assyrians are strong and numerous, they will be destroyed and disappear. My people, I made you suffer, but I will not do it again.
13 I will now end Assyria's power over you and break the chains that bind you."

14 This is what the LORD has decreed about the Assyrians: "They will have no descendants to carry on their name. I will destroy the idols that are in the temples of their gods. I am preparing a grave for the Assyrians—they don't deserve to live!"

15 Look, a messenger is coming over the mountains with good news! He is on his way to announce the victory! People of Judah, celebrate your festivals and give God what you solemnly promised him. The wicked will never invade your land again. They have been totally destroyed!

The Fall of Nineveh

2 Nineveh, you are under attack!
The power that will shatter you has
come.
Prepare the defenses!
Guard the road!
Prepare for battle!

(2 The LORD is about to restore the glory of Israel, as it was before her enemies plundered her.)

3 The enemy soldiers carry red shields
and wear uniforms of red.
They are preparing to attack!

Look, a messenger is coming! (1:15)

Their chariots flash like fire!
Their horses[b] prance!

4 Chariots dash wildly through the streets,
rushing back and forth in the city
squares.
They flash like torches
and dart about like lightning.

5 The officers are summoned;
they stumble as they press forward.
The attackers rush to the wall
and set up the shield for the battering
ram.

6 The gates by the river burst open;
the palace is filled with terror.

7 The queen is taken captive;
her servants moan like doves
and beat their breasts in sorrow.

8 Like water from a broken dam
the people rush from Nineveh![c]

The fall of Nineveh (2)

[b] **2:3** *Some ancient translations* horses; *Hebrew* cypresses.
[c] **2:8** *Probable text* Like water . . . Nineveh; *Hebrew unclear.*
1:15 Isa 52:7

"Stop! Stop!" the cry rings out—
but no one turns back.

9 Plunder the silver!
Plunder the gold!
The city is full of treasure!

10 Nineveh is destroyed, deserted, desolate!
Hearts melt with fear;
knees tremble, strength is gone;
faces grow pale.

11 Where now is the city
that was like a den of lions,
the place where young lions were fed,
where the lion and the lioness would go
and their cubs would be safe?
12 The lion killed his prey
and tore it to pieces for his mate and
her cubs;
he filled his den with torn flesh.

13 "I am your enemy!" says the LORD
Almighty. "I will burn up your chariots. Your
soldiers will be killed in war, and I will take
away everything that you took from others.
The demands of your envoys will no longer
be heard."

Nineveh's Suffering

3 Doomed is the lying, murderous city,
full of wealth to be looted and
plundered!
2 Listen! The crack of the whip,
the rattle of wheels,
the gallop of horses,
the jolting of chariots!
3 Cavalry troops charge,
swords flash, spears gleam!
Corpses are piled high,
dead bodies without number—
men stumble over them!
4 Nineveh the whore is being punished.
Attractive and full of deadly charms,
she enchanted nations and enslaved[d]
them.

5 The LORD Almighty says,
"I will punish you, Nineveh!
I will strip you naked
and let the nations see you,
see you in all your shame.
6 I will treat you with contempt
and cover you with filth.
People will stare at you in horror.
7 All who see you will shrink back.
They will say, 'Nineveh lies in ruins!
Who has any sympathy for her?
Who will want to comfort her?' "

8 Nineveh, are you any better than Thebes,
the capital of Egypt? She too had a river to
protect her like a wall—the Nile was her
defense. 9 She ruled Ethiopia[e] and Egypt,
there was no limit to her power; Libya was
her ally. 10 Yet the people of Thebes were
carried off into exile. At every street corner
their children were beaten to death. Their
leading men were carried off in chains and
divided among their captors.

11 Nineveh, you too will fall into a drunken
stupor! You too will try to escape from your
enemies. 12 All your fortresses will be like fig
trees with ripe figs: shake the trees, and the
fruit falls right into your mouth! 13 Your sol-
diers are helpless, and your country stands
defenseless before your enemies. Fire will
destroy the bars across your gates. 14 Draw
water to prepare for a siege, and strengthen
your fortresses! Trample the clay to make
bricks, and get the brick molds ready! 15 No
matter what you do, you will still be burned
to death or killed in battle. You will be wiped
out like crops eaten up by locusts.

You multiplied like locusts! 16 You pro-
duced more merchants than there are stars in
the sky! But now they are gone, like locusts
that spread their wings and fly away. 17 Your
officials are like a swarm of locusts that stay
in the walls on a cold day. But when the sun
comes out, they fly away, and no one knows
where they have gone!

18 Emperor of Assyria, your governors are
dead, and your noblemen are asleep forever!
Your people are scattered on the mountains,
and there is no one to bring them home
again. 19 There is no remedy for your
injuries, and your wounds cannot be healed.
All those who hear the news of your
destruction clap their hands for joy. Did any-
one escape your endless cruelty?

[d] **3:4** enslaved; *or* seduced. [e] **3:9** *Hebrew* Cush: *Cush is the ancient name of the extensive territory south of the First Cataract of the Nile River. This region was called Ethiopia in Graeco-Roman times, and included within its borders most of modern Sudan and some of present-day Ethiopia (Abyssinia).*

THE BOOK OF Habakkuk

"O God! All this waiting! What's up with that? What are you waiting for? Why do you let them get away with that, God? If I were in charge of the world, I would do things differently and make things right!"

Habakkuk was right in God's face, telling God what he thought, and offering his own suggestions. Do you ever do that? Sometimes, when we complain to God, we feel guilty. But Habakkuk shows us that it is okay to yell at God. God can take it. God doesn't hold it against us when we get frustrated. Part of growing in faith is learning how to cope with our frustrations. Habakkuk struggled to understand how a loving God could allow evil and suffering. In the end, he placed his trust in God's saving power.

Chap. 1:2

Headlines

- Habbakuk Complains, Debates with God! (1:2–11)
- Habbakuk Rejoices in God's Saving Power (3:1–19)

FACTOIDS

Who wrote this book? Habakkuk, a prophet in the southern kingdom of Judah.

Why was it written? Habakkuk expresses frustration at God's silence when bad things were happening to God's people. He also expresses the importance of having faith in God's eventual justice.

What literary style is used? The reflections in this book are similar to those in the wisdom literature. The dialog sections between Habakkuk and God resemble the Book of Job.

Jesus connection: Habakkuk's cry, "How long, O Lord?" is similar to Jesus' cry to God in the garden at Gethsemane when he asks God to remove the cup of suffering from him. (See Matthew 26:39.)

Important themes

- It is okay for God's people to ask the hard questions, such as, "Why do bad things happen to good people?"
- We may never understand the ways of God while on this earth. Things happen in God's time, not in our own time.

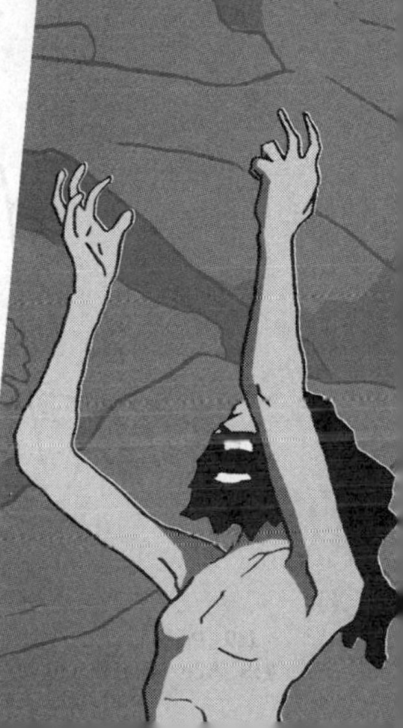

HABAKKUK

1 This is the message that the LORD
revealed to the prophet Habakkuk.

Habakkuk Complains of Injustice

[2]O LORD, how long must I call for help
before you listen, before you save us from
violence? [3]Why do you make me see such
trouble? How can you stand to look on such
wrongdoing? Destruction and violence are
all around me, and there is fighting and
quarreling everywhere. [4]The law is weak and
useless, and justice is never done. Evil people
get the better of the righteous, and so justice
is perverted.

The LORD's Reply

[5]Then the LORD said to his people, "Keep
watching the nations around you, and you
will be astonished at what you see. I am
going to do something that you will not
believe when you hear about it. [6]I am bring-
ing the Babylonians to power, those fierce,
restless people. They are marching out across
the world to conquer other lands. [7]They
spread fear and terror, and in their pride they
are a law to themselves.
[8]"Their horses are faster than leopards,
fiercer than hungry wolves. Their cavalry
troops come riding from distant lands; their
horses paw the ground. They come swoop-
ing down like eagles attacking their prey.
[9]"Their armies advance in violent con-
quest, and everyone is terrified as they
approach.[a] Their captives are as numerous as
grains of sand. [10]They treat kings with con-
tempt and laugh at high officials. No fortress
can stop them—they pile up earth against it
and capture it. [11]Then they sweep on like
the wind and are gone, these men whose
power is their god."

Habakkuk Complains to the LORD Again

[12]LORD, from the very beginning you are
God. You are my God, holy and eternal.
LORD, my God and protector, you have cho-
sen the Babylonians and made them strong
so that they can punish us. [13]But how can
you stand these treacherous, evil men? Your
eyes are too holy to look at evil, and you
cannot stand the sight of people doing
wrong. So why are you silent while they
destroy people who are more righteous than
they are?
[14]How can you treat people like fish or

"LORD . . . how can you stand these treacherous, evil men?" (1:12–13)

[a] **1:9** *Probable text* and everyone . . . approach; *Hebrew unclear.*

1:5 Acts 13:41 **1:6** 2 Kings 24:2

like a swarm of insects that have no ruler to direct them? 15 The Babylonians catch people with hooks, as though they were fish. They drag them off in nets and shout for joy over their catch! 16 They even worship their nets and offer sacrifices to them, because their nets provide them with the best of everything.

17 Are they going to use their swords forever and keep on destroying nations without mercy?

The LORD's Answer to Habakkuk

2 I will climb my watchtower and wait to see what the LORD will tell me to say and what answer he[b] will give to my complaint.

2 The LORD gave me this answer: "Write down clearly on tablets what I reveal to you, so that it can be read at a glance. 3 Put it in writing, because it is not yet time for it to come true. But the time is coming quickly, and what I show you will come true. It may seem slow in coming, but wait for it; it will certainly take place, and it will not be delayed. 4 And this is the message: 'Those who are evil will not survive,[c] but those who are righteous will live because they are faithful to God.' "

Doom on the Unrighteous

5 Wealth is deceitful. Greedy people are proud and restless—like death itself they are never satisfied. That is why they conquer nation after nation for themselves. 6 The conquered people will taunt their conquerors and show their scorn for them. They will say, "You take what isn't yours, but you are doomed! How long will you go on getting rich by forcing your debtors to pay up?"

7 But before you know it, you that have conquered others will be in debt yourselves and be forced to pay interest. Enemies will come and make you tremble. They will plunder you! 8 You have plundered the people of many nations, but now those who have survived will plunder you because of the murders you have committed and because of your violence against the people of the world and its cities.[d]

9 You are doomed! You have made your family rich with what you took by violence, and have tried to make your own home safe from harm and danger! 10 But your schemes have brought shame on your family; by destroying many nations you have only brought ruin on yourself. 11 Even the stones of the walls cry out against you, and the rafters echo the cry.

12 You are doomed! You founded a city on crime and built it up by murder. 13 The nations you conquered wore themselves out in useless labor, and all they have built goes up in flames. The LORD Almighty has done this. 14 But the earth will be as full of the knowledge of the LORD's glory as the seas are full of water.

15 You are doomed! In your fury you humiliated and disgraced your neighbors; you made them stagger as though they were drunk. 16 You in turn will be covered with shame instead of honor. You yourself will drink and stagger. The LORD will make you drink your own cup of punishment, and your honor will be turned to disgrace. 17 You have cut down the forests of Lebanon; now you will be cut down. You killed its animals; now animals will terrify you. This will happen because of the murders you have committed and because of your violence against the people of the world and its cities.[d]

18 What's the use of an idol? It is only something that a human being has made, and it tells you nothing but lies. What good does it do for its maker to trust it—a god that can't even talk! 19 You are doomed! You say to a piece of wood, "Wake up!" or to a block of stone, "Get up!" Can an idol reveal anything to you? It may be covered with silver and gold, but there is no life in it.

20 The LORD is in his holy Temple; let everyone on earth be silent in his presence.

[b] **2:1** *One ancient translation* he; *Hebrew* I. [c] **2:4** *Probable text* will not survive; *Hebrew unclear.* [d] **2:8, 17** the people . . . cities; *or* the land, the city, and those who live in it.

2:3 Heb 10:37 **2:4** Rom 1:17; Gal 3:11; Heb 10:38 **2:13** Sir 14:19 **2:14** Isa 11:9

Pray it!

After Winter, Comes the Spring

Read Habakkuk 3:17–19. How can the prophet say that even if all the crops fail and the animals die, he will still be joyful and glad? The answer is simple: Faith. He is confident that God cares for him and sooner or later things will get better. Can you think of examples like that? When good times follow hard times? How about:

- **After months of painful exercise, I can run faster.**
- **After nine months of preparation and many hours of pain, a new baby is born.**
- **After years of playing boring scales and studying music theory, I become a musician.**
- **After thunder, lightning, and pounding rain, the clouds lighten, and a rainbow forms.**
- **After the suffering death of Good Friday, the glorious life of Easter Sunday comes.**

So Habakkuk's prayer doesn't seem so strange after all. It doesn't mean that praying with the confidence of Habakkuk will be easy. But we need to keep trying to have that kind of faith.

— Habakkuk 3:17–18

A Prayer of Habakkuk

3 This is a prayer of the prophet Habakkuk:[e]

2 O LORD, I have heard of what you have done,
and I am filled with awe.
Now do again in our times
the great deeds you used to do.
Be merciful, even when you are angry.

3 God is coming again from Edom;
the holy God is coming from the hills of Paran.
His splendor covers the heavens,
and the earth is full of his praise.
4 He comes with the brightness of lightning;
light flashes from his hand,
there where his power is hidden.
5 He sends disease before him
and commands death to follow him.
6 When he stops, the earth shakes;
at his glance the nations tremble.
The eternal mountains are shattered;
the everlasting hills sink down,
the hills where he walked in ancient times.

7 I saw the people of Cushan afraid
and the people of Midian tremble.
8 Was it the rivers that made you angry, LORD?
Was it the sea that made you furious?
You rode upon the clouds;
the storm cloud was your chariot,
as you brought victory to your people.
9 You got ready to use your bow,
ready to shoot your arrows.[f]
Your lightning split open the earth.
10 When the mountains saw you, they trembled;
water poured down from the skies.
The waters under the earth roared,
and their waves rose high.

[e] **3:1** *Hebrew has an additional phrase, the meaning of which is unclear.* [f] **3:9** *Probable text* ready to shoot your arrows; *Hebrew unclear.*

[11] At the flash of your speeding arrows
and the gleam of your shining spear,
the sun and the moon stood still.
[12] You marched across the earth in anger;
in fury you trampled the nations.
[13] You went out to save your people,
to save your chosen king.
You struck down the leader of the wicked
and completely destroyed his followers.[g]
[14] Your arrows pierced the commander of his army
when it came like a storm to scatter us,
gloating like those who secretly oppress the poor.[h]
[15] You trampled the sea with your horses,
and the mighty waters foamed.

[16] I hear all this, and I tremble;
my lips quiver with fear.
My body goes limp,
and my feet stumble[i] beneath me.

I will quietly wait for the time to come
when God will punish those who attack us.

[17] Even though the fig trees have no fruit
and no grapes grow on the vines,
even though the olive crop fails
and the fields produce no grain,
even though the sheep all die
and the cattle stalls are empty,
[18] I will still be joyful and glad,
because the LORD God is my savior.
[19] The Sovereign LORD gives me strength.
He makes me sure-footed as a deer
and keeps me safe on the mountains.

[g] **3:13** *Probable text* completely . . . followers; *Hebrew unclear.* [h] **3:14** *Verse 14 in Hebrew is unclear.*
[i] **3:16** *Probable text* my feet stumble; *Hebrew* I am excited, because.
3:19 2 Sam 22:34; Ps 18:33

THE BOOK OF Zephaniah

Gloom and doom. This really could be the title of this book because there are a lot of both. It is a book about sin and the need to repent—to turn back to the Lord. Zephaniah warns his people that gloom and doom lie ahead because they have forgotten who they are. They are worshiping pagan gods such as Baal and Milcom. It is time to shape up and face the consequences—because there are some to face. Whenever we stray from what is good and right, we need to be ready to accept the consequences of our sin.

Yet even though most of this book seems pretty negative, it concludes on a joyful and promising note: "Sing and shout for joy, people of Israel!" (Zephaniah 3:14). There is a happy ending, after all!

Chap. 2:8–15

Headlines

- You Will Hear Wailing! (chapter 1)
- Sing and Shout for Joy! (3:14–20)

FACTOIDS

Who wrote this book? The prophet Zephaniah, who preached to the southern kingdom of Judah around 630 BC, and probably a later editor.

Why was it written? Zephaniah urged the people of Judah to turn from sin and idolatry and to repent.

How does it fit into the Bible? Zephaniah is one of the prophets who wrote during the reign of Josiah (640–609 BC), about the same time as Jeremiah.

Important theme

- God's punishment for sinful actions is meant to teach us, not destroy us. We should never despair, but place our trust in God's loving care.

ZEPHANIAH

1 This is the message that the LORD gave
to Zephaniah during the time that Josi-
ah son of Amon was king of Judah. (Zepha-
niah was descended from King Hezekiah
through Amariah, Gedaliah, and Cushi.)

The Day of the LORD's Judgment

2The LORD said, "I am going to destroy
everything on earth, 3all human beings and
animals, birds and fish. I will bring about the
downfall of[a] the wicked. I will destroy
everyone, and no survivors will be left. I, the
LORD, have spoken.
4"I will punish the people of Jerusalem
and of all Judah. I will destroy the last trace of
the worship of Baal there, and no one will
even remember the pagan priests who serve
him. 5I will destroy anyone who goes up on
the roof and worships the sun, the moon, and
the stars. I will also destroy those who wor-
ship me and swear loyalty to me, but then
take oaths in the name of the god Milcom.
6I will destroy those who have turned back
and no longer follow me, those who do not
come to me or ask me to guide them."
7The day is near when the LORD will sit
in judgment; so be silent in his presence. The
LORD is preparing to sacrifice his people and
has invited enemies to plunder Judah. 8"On
that day of slaughter," says the LORD, "I will
punish the officials, the king's sons, and all
who practice foreign customs. 9I will punish
all who worship like pagans and who steal
and kill in order to fill their master's house[b]
with loot.
10"On that day," says the LORD, "you will
hear the sound of crying at the Fish Gate in
Jerusalem. You will hear wailing in the
newer part of the city and a great crashing
sound in the hills. 11Wail and cry when you
hear this, you that live in the lower part of
the city, because all the merchants will be
dead!
12"At that time I will take a lamp and
search Jerusalem. I will punish the people
who are self-satisfied and confident, who say
to themselves, 'The LORD never does any-
thing, one way or the other.' 13Their wealth
will be looted and their houses destroyed.
They will never live in the houses they are
building or drink wine from the vineyards
they are planting."

The LORD never does anything, one way or the other. (1:12)

14The great day of the LORD is near—very
near and coming fast! That day will be bitter,
for even[c] the bravest soldiers will cry out in
despair! 15It will be a day of fury, a day of
trouble and distress, a day of ruin and destruc-
tion, a day of darkness and gloom, a black and
cloudy day, 16a day filled with the sound of
war trumpets and the battle cry of soldiers
attacking fortified cities and high towers.
17The LORD says, "I will bring such disas-
ters on the human race that everyone will
grope about like someone blind. They have
sinned against me, and now their blood will
be poured out like water, and their dead
bodies will lie rotting on the ground."

[a] **1:3** *Probable text* I will bring about the downfall of; *Hebrew* the stumbling blocks. [b] **1:9** their master's house; *or* the temple of their god. [c] **1:14** That day . . . even; *or* Listen! That terrible day is coming when even.

1:1 2 Kings 22:1—23:30; 2 Chr 34:1—35:27

18 On the day when the LORD shows his fury, not even all their silver and gold will save them. The whole earth will be destroyed by the fire of his anger. He will put an end—a sudden end—to everyone who lives on earth.

A Plea for Repentance

2 Shameless nation, come to your senses 2 before you are driven away like chaff blown by the wind, before the burning anger of the LORD comes upon you, before the day when he shows his fury. 3 Turn to the LORD, all you humble people of the land, who obey his commands. Do what is right, and humble yourselves before the LORD. Perhaps you will escape punishment on the day when the LORD shows his anger.

The Doom of the Nations around Judah

4 No one will be left in the city of Gaza. Ashkelon will be deserted. The people of Ashdod will be driven out in half a day,[d] and the people of Ekron will be driven from their city. 5 You Philistines are doomed, you people who live along the coast. The LORD has passed sentence on you. He will destroy you, and not one of you will be left. 6 Your land by the sea will become open fields with shepherd's huts and sheep pens. 7 The people of Judah who survive will occupy your land. They will pasture their flocks there and sleep in the houses of Ashkelon. The LORD their God will be with them and make them prosper again.

8 The LORD Almighty says, "I have heard the people of Moab and Ammon insulting and taunting my people, and boasting that they would seize their land. 9 As surely as I am the living LORD, the God of Israel, I swear that Moab and Ammon are going to be destroyed like Sodom and Gomorrah. They will become a place of salt pits and everlasting ruin, overgrown with weeds. Those of my people who survive will plunder them and take their land."

10 That is how the people of Moab and Ammon will be punished for their pride and arrogance and for insulting the people of the LORD Almighty. 11 The LORD will terrify them. He will reduce the gods of the earth to nothing, and then every nation will worship him, each in its own land.

12 The LORD will also put the people of Ethiopia[e] to death.

13 The LORD will use his power to destroy Assyria. He will make the city of Nineveh a deserted ruin, a waterless desert. 14 It will be a place where flocks, herds, and animals of every kind will lie down. Owls will live among its ruins and hoot from the windows. Crows[f] will caw on the doorsteps. The cedar wood of her buildings will be stripped away. 15 That is what will happen to the city that is so proud of its own power and thinks it is safe. Its people think that their city is the greatest in the world. What a desolate place it will become, a place where wild animals will rest! Everyone who passes by will shrink back in horror.

Owls will live among its ruins. (2:14)

Jerusalem's Sin and Redemption

3 Jerusalem is doomed, that corrupt, rebellious city that oppresses its own people. 2 It has not listened to the LORD or accepted his discipline. It has not put its trust in the LORD or asked for his help. 3 Its officials are like roaring lions; its judges are

[d] **2:4** in half a day; *or* by a surprise attack at noontime. [e] **2:12** *Hebrew* Cush: *Cush is the ancient name of the extensive territory south of the First Cataract of the Nile River. This region was called Ethiopia in Graeco-Roman times, and included within its borders most of modern Sudan and some of present-day Ethiopia (Abyssinia).* [f] **2:14** *Some ancient translations* Crows; *Hebrew* Desolation.

2:4–7 Isa 14:29–31; Jer 47:1–7; Ezek 25:15–17; Joel 3:4–8; Am 1:6–8; Zech 9:5–7 **2:8–11 a** Isa 15:1—16:14; 25:10–12; Jer 48:1–47; Ezek 25:8–11; Am 1:13–15; **b** Jer 49:1–6; Ezek 21:28–32; 25:1–7; Am 1:13–15 **2:9** Gen 19:24 **2:12** Isa 18:1–7 **2:13–15** Isa 10:5–34; 14:24–27; Nah 1:1—3:19

Pray it!

A Festival of Delight!

Delight is a word some people don't put together with God. Yet that word appears many times in the Bible, especially in the Old Testament. Pray these beautiful lines from Zephaniah, chapter 3.

The LORD will take delight in you,
and in his love he will give you new life.
He will sing and be joyful over you,
as joyful as people at a festival. **(Verses 17–18)**

Now read them a second time, slowly and prayerfully. Imagine God smiling at the thought of you, at the sound of your name. Ask God to help you take delight in others as well. And don't forget to sing, for God sings a song of joy for you!

— Zephaniah 3:17–18

like hungry wolves, too greedy to leave a
bone until morning. 4 The prophets are irre-
sponsible and treacherous; the priests defile
what is sacred, and twist the law of God to
their own advantage. 5 But the LORD is still
in the city; he does what is right and never
what is wrong. Every morning without fail,
he brings justice to his people. And yet the
unrighteous people there keep on doing
wrong and are not ashamed.
6 The LORD says, "I have wiped out whole
nations; I have destroyed their cities and left
their walls and towers in ruins. The cities are
deserted; the streets are empty—no one is
left. 7 I thought that then my people would
have reverence for me and accept my disci-
pline, that they would never forget[g] the les-
son I taught them. But soon they were
behaving as badly as ever.
8 "Just wait," the LORD says. "Wait for the
day when I rise to accuse the nations. I have
made up my mind to gather nations and
kingdoms in order to let them feel the force
of my anger. The whole earth will be
destroyed by the fire of my fury.
9 "Then I will change the people of the
nations, and they will pray to me alone and
not to other gods. They will all obey me.
10 Even from distant Ethiopia[h] my scattered
people will bring offerings to me. 11 At that
time you, my people, will no longer need
to be ashamed that you rebelled against me.
I will remove everyone who is proud and
arrogant, and you will never again rebel
against me on my sacred hill.[i] 12 I will leave
there a humble and lowly people, who will
come to me for help. 13 The people of Israel
who survive will do no wrong to anyone,
tell no lies, nor try to deceive. They will be
prosperous and secure, afraid of no one."

A Song of Joy

14 Sing and shout for joy, people of Israel!
Rejoice with all your heart, Jerusalem!
15 The LORD has stopped your punishment;
he has removed all your enemies.
The LORD, the king of Israel, is with you;
there is no reason now to be afraid.
16 The time is coming when they will say to
Jerusalem,
"Do not be afraid, city of Zion!

[g] **3:7** *Some ancient translations* they would never forget; *Hebrew* their dwelling would not be cut off.
[h] **3:10** *Hebrew* Cush: *Cush is the ancient name of the extensive territory south of the First Cataract of the Nile River. This region was called Ethiopia in Graeco-Roman times, and included within its borders most of modern Sudan and some of present-day Ethiopia (Abyssinia).* [i] **3:11** SACRED HILL: *Mount Zion (see Zion in Word List).*
3:13 Rev 14:5

Do not let your hands hang limp!
17 The LORD your God is with you;
his power gives you victory.
The LORD will take delight in you,
and in his love he will give you new life.[j]
He will sing and be joyful over you,
18 as joyful as people at a festival."
The LORD says,
"I have ended the threat of doom
and taken away your disgrace.[k]
19 The time is coming!
I will punish your oppressors;
I will rescue all the lame
and bring the exiles home.
I will turn their shame to honor,
and all the world will praise them.
20 The time is coming!
I will bring your scattered people home;
I will make you famous throughout the world
and make you prosperous once again."
The LORD has spoken.

[j] **3:17** *Some ancient translations* give you new life; *Hebrew* be silent. [k] **3:18** *Verse 18 in Hebrew is unclear.*

The Book of Haggai

Imagine that your town or neighborhood was hit by a tornado or hurricane. Almost every house and building were destroyed, including the church. What should be rebuilt first? Well, people's homes, of course. Everyone needs a safe place to live. Besides, no one has money to rebuild the church, right?

The prophet Haggai would tell us that it is just as important to rebuild God's house as our own. It's a matter of priorities. Why is the church—or in Haggai's time, the Temple—so important? Having a community place to worship God says that God is very important to a community's life. It's not so important that the new church or temple is the biggest or the best, but rather that God is at the center of our lives together.

Headlines

- Command Issued to Rebuild Temple (chapter 1)
- Future Temple Filled with God's Glory (2:1–9)

FACTOIDS

Who wrote this book? This collection of brief prophetic messages is attributed to the prophet Haggai.

Why was it written? Haggai urged those who have returned to Judah after the Babylonian Exile to rebuild the Temple.

How does it fit into the Bible? Haggai is the first prophet to write after the return from Exile, around 520 BC.

Important theme

- Rebuilding God's Temple will bring blessings and peace to the people.

HAGGAI

The LORD's Command to Rebuild the Temple

1 During the second year that Darius was
emperor of Persia, on the first day of
the sixth month, the LORD spoke through
the prophet Haggai. The message was for the
governor of Judah, Zerubbabel son of She-
altiel, and for the High Priest, Joshua son of
Jehozadak.
2The LORD Almighty said to Haggai,
"These people say that this is not the right
time to rebuild the Temple." 3The LORD
then gave this message to the people through
the prophet Haggai: 4"My people, why
should you be living in well-built houses
while my Temple lies in ruins? 5Don't you
see what is happening to you? 6You have
planted much grain, but have harvested very
little. You have food to eat, but not enough
to make you full. You have wine to drink,
but not enough to get drunk on! You have
clothing, but not enough to keep you warm.
And workers cannot earn enough to live on.
7Can't you see why this has happened?
8Now go up into the hills, get lumber, and
rebuild the Temple; then I will be pleased
and will be worshiped as I should be.
9"You hoped for large harvests, but they
turned out to be small. And when you
brought the harvest home, I blew it away.[a]
Why did I do that? Because my Temple lies
in ruins while every one of you is busy
working on your own house. 10That is why
there is no rain and nothing can grow. 11I
have brought drought on the land—on
its hills, grainfields, vineyards, and olive
orchards—on every crop the ground pro-
duces, on people and animals, on everything
you try to grow."

The People Obey the LORD's Command

12Then Zerubbabel and Joshua and all
the people who had returned from the
exile[b] in Babylonia, did what the LORD
their God told them to do. They were afraid
and obeyed the prophet Haggai, the LORD's

Why should you be living in well-built houses while my Temple lies in ruins? (1:4)

[a] **1:9** I blew it away; *or* I spoiled it. [b] **1:12** who had returned from the exile; *or* who had not gone into exile.
1:1 Ezra 4:24—5:2; 6:14

Pray it!

Working Together

Have you ever been part of a service project where you helped build something? You may have heard of Habitat for Humanity. This organization brings volunteers together to build homes for people who cannot afford to buy a house. The family that will be buying the house (at a very reasonable price) must help build the house, together with lots of volunteers. Habitat is well known and respected because it brings a lot of people together to do a very good thing. This is what happened at the time of Haggai, when the people worked together to rebuild the Temple in Jerusalem.

Is there some local project that you and your friends or classmates can get involved in? See if there is a Habitat for Humanity chapter in your area. And don't forget that Jesus was a carpenter. Try to picture Jesus working right alongside you.

— Haggai 1:12—2:5

messenger. 13 Then Haggai gave the LORD's
message to the people: "I will be with
you—that is my promise." 14 The LORD
inspired everyone to work on the Temple:
Zerubbabel, the governor of Judah; Joshua,
the High Priest, and all the people who had
returned from the exile.[b] They began work-
ing on the Temple of the LORD Almighty,
their God, 15 on the twenty-fourth day of
the sixth month of the second year that
Darius was emperor.

The Splendor of the New Temple

2 On the twenty-first day of the seventh
month of that same year, the LORD
spoke again through the prophet Haggai.
2 He told Haggai to speak to Zerubbabel, the
governor of Judah, to Joshua, the High
Priest, and to the people, and to say to them,
3 "Is there anyone among you who can still
remember how splendid the Temple used to
be? How does it look to you now? It must
seem like nothing at all. 4 But now don't be
discouraged, any of you. Do the work, for I
am with you. 5 When you came out of
Egypt, I promised that I would always be
with you. I am still with you, so do not be
afraid.
6 "Before long I will shake heaven and
earth, land and sea. 7 I will overthrow all the
nations, and their treasures will be brought
here, and the Temple will be filled with
wealth. 8 All the silver and gold of the world
is mine. 9 The new Temple will be more
splendid than the old one, and there I will
give my people prosperity and peace." The
LORD Almighty has spoken.

The Prophet Consults the Priests

10 On the twenty-fourth day of the ninth
month of the second year that Darius was
emperor, the LORD Almighty spoke again to
the prophet Haggai. 11 He said, "Ask the
priests for a ruling on this question: 12 Sup-
pose someone takes a piece of consecrated
meat from a sacrifice and carries it in a fold
of his robe. If he then lets his robe touch any
bread, cooked food, wine, olive oil, or any
kind of food at all, will it make that food
consecrated also?"

[b] **1:14** who had returned from the exile; *or* who had not gone into exile.
2:3 Ezra 3:12 **2:5** Ex 29:45, 46 **2:6** Heb 12:26

When the question was asked, the priests
answered, "No."
13 Then Haggai asked, "Suppose someone
is defiled because he has touched a dead
body. If he then touches any of these foods,
will that make them defiled too?"
The priests answered, "Yes."
14 Then Haggai said, "The LORD says that
the same thing applies to the people of this
nation and to everything they produce; and
so everything they offer on the altar is
defiled."

The LORD Promises His Blessing

15 The LORD says, "Can't you see what has
happened to you? Before you started to
rebuild the Temple, 16 you would go to a pile
of grain expecting to find twenty bushels,
but there would be only ten. You would go
to draw fifty gallons of wine from a vat, but
find only twenty. 17 I sent scorching winds
and hail to ruin everything you tried to
grow, but still you did not repent. 18 Today is
the twenty-fourth day of the ninth month,
the day that the foundation of the Temple
has been completed. See what is going to
happen from now on. 19 Although there is no
grain left, and the grapevines, fig trees,
pomegranates, and olive trees have not yet
produced, yet from now on I will bless you."

The LORD's Promise to Zerubbabel

20 On that same day, the twenty-fourth of
the month, the LORD gave Haggai a second
message 21 for Zerubbabel, the governor of
Judah: "I am about to shake heaven and
earth 22 and overthrow kingdoms and end
their power. I will overturn chariots and
their drivers; the horses will die, and their
riders will kill one another. 23 On that day I
will take you, Zerubbabel my servant, and I
will appoint you to rule in my name. You are
the one I have chosen." The LORD Almighty
has spoken.

2:13 Num 19:11–22

THE BOOK OF Zechariah

Cheer up! Things will get better.

This is the main message of the Book of Zechariah. But you have to read through lots of strange visions to see it. The book has two parts, probably written by two different prophets, just as the Book of Isaiah was. The first part calls the people to rebuild the Temple. Through a series of visions, it also promises a future when God will make everything right. Then the second part tells of a future great battle between good and evil in which God will triumph.

The combined message is meant to give hope to God's people, promising them better days ahead. It's a lot like when we try to comfort people who are going through hard times or suffering from an illness. We try to encourage them and offer them hope that things will eventually get better. That is the main message of this next-to-the-last book of the Old Testament.

Chap. 4:1–14

Headlines

- Vision Foretells Rebuilding of Temple! (1:7–17)
- Vision of a New Jerusalem (2:6–13)
- Woman in a Basket! (5:5–11)
- Future King Rides Donkey (9:9–17)
- God Saves Jerusalem! (12:1–9)

FACTOIDS

Who wrote this book? The prophet Zechariah is thought to have written chapters 1–8 around 520 to 518 BC. But an unknown prophet, (or prophets), is thought to have written chapters 9–14 much later, sometime after 333 BC.

How does it fit into the Bible? Zechariah is one of the prophets who wrote during the same time as Haggai (520 BC).

Jesus connection: Zachariah's prophecies are quoted in the New Testament as proof that Jesus is the promised Messiah. (See Matthew 26:31 and Zechariah 13:7.)

Important theme

- The Temple, Jerusalem, and God's Covenant with the people will be restored.
- The final victory over evil belongs to God.

ZECHARIAH

The LORD Calls His People to Return to Him

1 In the eighth month of the second year
that Darius was emperor of Persia, the
LORD gave this message to the prophet
Zechariah, the son of Berechiah and grand-
son of Iddo. [2]The LORD Almighty told
Zechariah to say to the people, "I, the LORD,
was very angry with your ancestors, [3]but
now I say to you, 'Return to me, and I will
return to you. [4]Do not be like your ances-
tors. Long ago the prophets gave them my
message, telling them not to live evil, sinful
lives any longer. But they would not listen to
me or obey me. [5]Your ancestors and those
prophets are no longer alive. [6]Through my
servants the prophets I gave your ancestors
commands and warnings, but they disregard-
ed them and suffered the consequences. Then
they repented and acknowledged that I, the
LORD Almighty, had punished them as they
deserved and as I had determined to do.' "

The Prophet's Vision of the Horses

[7]In the second year that Darius was
emperor, on the twenty-fourth day of the
eleventh month (the month of Shebat), the
LORD gave me a message in a vision at
night. [8]I saw someone riding a red horse. He
had stopped among some myrtle trees in a
valley, and behind him were other horses—
red, dappled, and white. [9]I asked him, "Sir,
what do these horses mean?"

He answered, "I will show you what they
mean. [10]The LORD sent them to go and
inspect the earth."

[11]They reported to the angel: "We have
been all over the world and have found that
the whole world lies helpless and subdued."

[12]Then the angel said, "Almighty LORD,
you have been angry with Jerusalem and the
cities of Judah for seventy years now. How
much longer will it be before you show
them mercy?"

[13]The LORD answered the angel with
comforting words, [14]and the angel told me
to proclaim what the LORD Almighty had
said: "I have a deep love and concern for
Jerusalem, my holy city, [15]and I am very
angry with the nations that enjoy quiet and
peace. For while I was holding back my
anger against my people, those nations made
the sufferings of my people worse. [16]So I
have come back to Jerusalem to show mercy
to the city. My Temple will be restored, and
the city will be rebuilt."

[17]The angel also told me to proclaim:
"The LORD Almighty says that his cities will
be prosperous again and that he will once
again help Jerusalem and claim the city as his
own."

The Vision of the Horns

[18]In another vision I saw four ox horns.
[19]I asked the angel that had been speaking to
me, "What do these horns mean?"

He answered, "They stand for the world
powers that have scattered the people of
Judah, Israel, and Jerusalem."

[20]Then the LORD showed me four work-
ers with hammers. [21]I asked, "What have
they come to do?"

He answered, "They have come to terrify
and overthrow the nations that completely
crushed the land of Judah and scattered its
people."

The Vision of the Measuring Line

2 In another vision I saw a man with a
measuring line in his hand. [2]"Where are
you going?" I asked.

"To measure Jerusalem," he answered, "to
see how long and how wide it is."

[3]Then I saw the angel who had been
speaking to me step forward, and another
angel came to meet him. [4]The first one said
to the other, "Run and tell that young man
with the measuring line that there are going

1:1 Ezra 4:24—5:1; 6:14 **1:8** a Rev 6:4; **b** Rev 6:2

to be so many people and so much livestock in Jerusalem that it will be too big to have walls. 5 The LORD has promised that he himself will be a wall of fire around the city to protect it and that he will live there in all his glory."

The Exiles Are Called to Come Home

6-7 The LORD said to his people, "I scattered you in all directions. But now, you exiles, escape from Babylonia and return to Jerusalem. 8 Anyone who strikes you strikes what is most precious to me."

So the LORD Almighty[a] sent me with this message for the nations that had plundered his people: 9 "The LORD himself will fight against you, and you will be plundered by the people who were once your servants."

When this happens, everyone will know that the LORD Almighty sent me.

10 The LORD said, "Sing for joy, people of Jerusalem! I am coming to live among you!"

11 At that time many nations will come to the LORD and become his people. He will live among you, and you will know that he has sent me to you. 12 Once again Judah will be the special possession of the LORD in his sacred land, and Jerusalem will be the city he loves most of all.

13 Be silent, everyone, in the presence of the LORD, for he is coming from his holy dwelling place.

The Prophet's Vision of the High Priest

3 In another vision the LORD showed me the High Priest Joshua standing before the angel of the LORD. And there beside Joshua stood Satan,[b] ready to bring an accusation against him. 2 The angel of the LORD[c] said to Satan, "May the LORD condemn you, Satan! May the LORD, who loves Jerusalem, condemn you. This man is like a stick snatched from the fire."

3 Joshua was standing there, wearing filthy clothes. 4 The angel said to his heavenly attendants, "Take away the filthy clothes this man is wearing." Then he said to Joshua, "I have taken away your sin and will give you new clothes to wear."

5 He commanded the attendants to put[d] a clean turban on Joshua's head. They did so, and then they put the new clothes on him while the angel of the LORD stood there.

6 Then the angel told Joshua that 7 the LORD Almighty had said: "If you obey my laws and perform the duties I have assigned you, then you will continue to be in charge of my Temple and its courts, and I will hear your prayers, just as I hear the prayers of the angels who are in my presence. 8 Listen then, Joshua, you who are the High Priest; and listen, you fellow priests of his, you that are the sign of a good future: I will reveal my servant, who is called The Branch! 9 I am placing in front of Joshua a single stone with seven facets. I will engrave an inscription on it, and in a single day I will take away the sin of this land. 10 When that day comes, each of you will invite your neighbor to come and enjoy peace and security, surrounded by your vineyards and fig trees."

A single stone with seven facets (3:9)

The Vision of the Lampstand

4 The angel who had been speaking to me came again and roused me as if I had been sleeping. 2 "What do you see?" he asked.

[a] **2:8** *Hebrew has two additional words, the meaning of which is unclear.* [b] **3:1** SATAN: *A supernatural being whose name indicates he was regarded as the opponent of human beings.* [c] **3:2** *One ancient translation* The angel of the LORD; *Hebrew* The LORD. [d] **3:5** *Some ancient translations* He commanded the attendants to put; *Hebrew* I said, "Let them put.

3:1 a Ezra 5:2; **b** Rev 12:10 **3:2** Jude 9 **3:8** Jer 23:5; 33:15; Zech 6:12 **3:10** Mic 4:4

"A lampstand made of gold," I answered.
"At the top is a bowl for the oil. On the
lampstand are seven lamps, each one with
places for seven wicks. 3 There are two olive
trees beside the lampstand, one on each side
of it." 4 Then I asked the angel, "What do
these things stand for, sir?"
5 "Don't you know?" he asked me.
"No, I don't, sir," I replied.
10b The angel said to me, "The seven
lamps are the seven eyes of the LORD, which
see all over the earth."[e]
11 Then I asked him, "What do the two
olive trees on either side of the lampstand
mean? 12 And what is the meaning of the
two olive branches beside the two gold pipes
from which the olive oil pours?"
13 He asked me, "Don't you know?"
"No, I don't, sir," I answered.
14 Then he said, "These are the two men
whom God has chosen and anointed to
serve him, the Lord of the whole earth."

God's Promise to Zerubbabel

6 The angel told me to give Zerubbabel
this message from the LORD: "You will suc-
ceed, not by military might or by your own
strength, but by my spirit. 7 Obstacles as great
as mountains will disappear before you. You
will rebuild the Temple, and as you put the
last stone in place, the people will shout,
'Beautiful, beautiful!'"
8 Another message came to me from the
LORD. 9 He said, "Zerubbabel has laid the
foundation of the Temple, and he will finish
the building. When this happens, my people
will know that it is I who sent you to them.
10a They are disappointed because so little
progress is being made. But they will see
Zerubbabel continuing to build the Temple,
and they will be glad."

The Vision of the Flying Scroll

5 I looked again, and this time I saw a
scroll flying through the air. 2 The angel
asked me what I saw. I answered, "A scroll
flying through the air; it is thirty feet long
and fifteen feet wide."
3 Then he said to me, "On it is written the
curse that is to go out over the whole land.
On one side of the scroll it says that every
thief will be removed from the land; and on
the other side it says that everyone who tells
lies under oath will also be taken away. 4 The
LORD Almighty says that he will send this
curse out, and it will enter the house of
every thief and the house of everyone who
tells lies under oath. It will remain in their
houses and leave them in ruins."

The Vision of the Woman in the Basket

5 The angel appeared again and said,
"Look! Something else is coming!"
6 "What is it?" I asked.
He replied, "It is a basket, and it stands for
the sin[f] of the whole land."
7 The basket had a lid made of lead. As I
watched, the lid was raised, and there in the
basket sat a woman!

There in the basket sat a woman! (5:7)

8 The angel said, "This represents wicked-
ness." Then he pushed her down into the bas-
ket and put the lid back down. 9 I looked up
and saw two women flying toward me with

[e] **4:10b** *Verses 10b–14 are moved here from the end of the chapter in order to retain the natural sequence of the narrative.*
[f] **5:6** *Some ancient translations* sin; *Hebrew* eye.
4:3 Rev 11:4 **4:6** Ezra 5:2 **4:10** Rev 5:6 **4:11** Rev 11:4

Pray it!

Horses, Flying Scrolls, and Women in Baskets!

Spend some time reading through the eight visions that Zechariah has. Everything from colored horses, to lamps, to a woman in a basket! Notice how many of them are ordinary objects. This is a reminder that almost anything can remind you of God. Look around the room you are in right now. There's probably a light or a window. You are probably sitting on a chair. Are there any pictures on the wall? Focus on one thing and make up a prayer based on how that thing reminds you of God. Here's an example, using the floor:
Dear God, you are the floor of my life. You provide me with support even though I don't realize it. You keep me level. Thank you!

How about an electrical outlet?
Dear God, like an outlet, you are a source of energy. Remind me often to plug myself in to your energy. Let the current of your grace flow through me and keep me going. Amen.

What else can you use around you for prayer?

— Zechariah, chapter 5

powerful wings like those of a stork. They
picked up the basket and flew off with it.
10 I asked the angel, "Where are they taking it?"
11 He answered, "To Babylonia, where they
will build a temple for it. When the temple
is finished, the basket will be placed there to
be worshiped."

The Vision of the Four Chariots

6 I had another vision. This time I saw
four chariots coming out from between
two bronze mountains. 2 The first chariot
was pulled by red horses, the second by
black horses, 3 the third by white horses, and
the fourth by dappled horses. 4 Then I asked
the angel, "Sir, what do these chariots
mean?"
5 He answered, "These are the four winds;
they have just come from the presence of
the Lord of all the earth."
6 The chariot pulled by the black horses
was going north to Babylonia, the white
horses were going to the west, and the dappled horses were going to the country in the
south. 7 As the dappled horses came out, they
were impatient to go and inspect the earth.
The angel said, "Go and inspect the
earth!"—and they did. 8 Then the angel
cried out to me, "The horses that went
north to Babylonia have quieted the LORD's
anger."

The Command to Crown Joshua

9 The LORD gave me this message. 10 He
said, "Take the gifts given by the exiles Heldai, Tobijah, and Jedaiah, and go at once to
the home of Josiah son of Zephaniah. All of
them have returned from exile in Babylonia.
11 Make a crown out of the silver and gold
they have given, and put it on the head of
the High Priest, Joshua son of Jehozadak.
12 Tell him that the LORD Almighty says,
'The man who is called The Branch will
flourish where he is and rebuild the LORD's
Temple. 13 He is the one who will build it
and receive the honor due a king, and he
will rule his people. A priest will stand by
his throne, and they will work together in
peace and harmony.' 14 The crown will be a

6:2 a Rev 6:4; **b** Rev 6:5 **6:3** Rev 6:2 **6:5** Rev 7:1 **6:12** Jer 23:5; 33:15; Zech 3:8

memorial in the LORD's Temple in honor of
Heldai,[g] Tobijah, Jedaiah, and Josiah."[h]
15 Men who live far away will come and
help to rebuild the Temple of the LORD. And
when it is rebuilt, you will know that the
LORD Almighty sent me to you. This will all
happen if you fully obey the commands of
the LORD your God.

The LORD Condemns Insincere Fasting

7 In the fourth year that Darius was
emperor, on the fourth day of the ninth
month (the month of Kislev), the LORD gave
me a message.
2 The people of Bethel had sent Sharezer
and Regemmelech and their men to the
Temple of the LORD Almighty to pray for
the LORD's blessing 3 and to ask the priests
and the prophets this question: "Should we
continue to mourn because of the destruc-
tion of the Temple, by fasting in the fifth
month as we have done for so many years
now?"
4 This is the message of the LORD that
came to me. 5 He said, "Tell the people of the
land and the priests that when they fasted
and mourned in the fifth and seventh
months during these seventy years, it was not
in honor of me. 6 And when they ate and
drank, it was for their own satisfaction."
7 This is what the LORD said through the
earlier prophets at the time when Jerusalem
was prosperous and filled with people and
when there were many people living not
only in the towns around the city but also in
the southern region and in the western
foothills.

Disobedience, the Cause of Exile

8 The LORD gave this message to Zechari-
ah: 9 "Long ago I gave these commands to
my people: 'You must see that justice is
done, and must show kindness and mercy
to one another. 10 Do not oppress widows,
orphans, foreigners who live among you, or
anyone else in need. And do not plan ways
of harming one another.'
11 "But my people stubbornly refused to
listen. They closed their minds 12 and made
their hearts as hard as rock. Because they
would not listen to the teaching which I
sent through the prophets who lived long
ago, I became very angry. 13 Because they did
not listen when I spoke, I did not answer
when they prayed. 14 Like a storm I swept
them away to live in foreign countries. This
good land was left a desolate place, with no
one living in it."

The LORD Promises to Restore Jerusalem

8 The LORD Almighty gave this message
to Zechariah: 2 "I have longed to help
Jerusalem because of my deep love for her
people, a love which has made me angry
with her enemies. 3 I will return to Jeru-
salem, my holy city, and live there. It will be
known as the faithful city, and the hill of the
LORD Almighty[i] will be called the sacred
hill. 4 Once again old men and women, so
old that they use canes when they walk, will
be sitting in the city squares. 5 And the streets
will again be full of boys and girls playing.
6 "This may seem impossible to those of
the nation who are now left, but it's not
impossible for me. 7 I will rescue my people
from the lands where they have been taken,
8 and will bring them back from east and
west to live in Jerusalem. They will be my
people, and I will be their God, ruling over
them faithfully and justly.
9 "Have courage! You are now hearing the
same words the prophets spoke at the time
the foundation was being laid for rebuilding
my Temple. 10 Before that time no one could
afford to hire either men or animals, and no
one was safe from enemies. I turned people
against one another. 11 But now I am treating
the survivors of this nation differently.
12 They will plant their crops in peace. Their
vines will bear grapes, the earth will produce
crops, and there will be plenty of rain. I will
give all these blessings to the people of my
nation who survive. 13 People of Judah and
Israel! In the past foreigners have cursed one
another by saying, 'May the same disasters

[g] **6:14** *One ancient translation* Heldai; *Hebrew* Helem. [h] **6:14** *One ancient translation* Josiah; *Hebrew* Hen.
[i] **8:3** HILL OF THE LORD ALMIGHTY: *Mount Zion (see Zion in Word List).*

fall on you that fell on Judah and Israel!' But I will save you, and then those foreigners will say to one another, 'May you receive the same blessings that came to Judah and Israel!' So have courage and don't be afraid."

May you receive the same blessings that came to Judah and Israel! (8:13)

14 The LORD Almighty says, "When your ancestors made me angry, I planned disaster for them and did not change my mind, but carried out my plans. 15 But now I am planning to bless the people of Jerusalem and Judah. So don't be afraid. 16 These are the things you should do: Speak the truth to one another. In the courts give real justice—the kind that brings peace. 17 Do not plan ways of harming one another. Do not give false testimony under oath. I hate lying, injustice, and violence."

18 The LORD Almighty gave this message to Zechariah: 19 "The fasts held in the fourth, fifth, seventh, and tenth months will become festivals of joy and gladness for the people of Judah. You must love truth and peace."

20 The LORD Almighty says, "The time is coming when people from many[j] cities will come to Jerusalem. 21 Those from one city will say to those from another, 'We are going to worship the LORD Almighty and pray for his blessing. Come with us!' 22 Many[j] peoples and powerful nations will come to Jerusalem to worship the LORD Almighty and to pray for his blessing. 23 In those days ten foreigners will come to one Jew and say, 'We want to share in your destiny, because we have heard that God is with you.' "

Judgment on Neighboring Nations

9 This is the LORD's message:
He has decreed punishment for the land of Hadrach and for the city of Damascus. Not only the tribes of Israel but also the capital of Syria belong to the LORD. 2 Hamath, which borders on Hadrach, also belongs to him, and so do the cities of Tyre and Sidon, with all their skill. 3 Tyre has built fortifications for herself and has piled up so much silver and gold that it is as common as dirt! 4 But the Lord will take away everything she has. He will throw her wealth into the sea, and the city will be burned to the ground.

5 The city of Ashkelon will see this and be afraid. The city of Gaza will see it and suffer great pain. So will Ekron, and her hopes will be shattered. Gaza will lose her king, and Ashkelon will be left deserted. 6 People of mixed race will live in Ashdod. The LORD says, "I will humble all these proud Philistines. 7 They will no longer eat meat with blood in it, or other forbidden food. All the survivors will become part of my people and be like a clan in the tribe of Judah. Ekron will become part of my people, as the Jebusites[k] did. 8 I will guard my land and keep armies from passing through it. I will not allow tyrants to oppress my people any more. I have seen how my people have suffered."

The Future King

9 Rejoice, rejoice, people of Zion!
Shout for joy, you people of Jerusalem!
Look, your king is coming to you!

Look, your king is coming to you! (9:9)

[j] **8:20, 22** many; *or* great. [k] **9:7** JEBUSITES: *The original inhabitants of Jerusalem, who became David's subjects after he captured the city.*

8:16 Eph 4:25 **9:1** Isa 17:1–3; Jer 49:23–27; Am 1:3–5 **9:1–4** Isa 23:1–18; Ezek 26:1—28:26; Joel 3:4–8; Am 1:9, 10; Mt 11:21, 22; Lk 10:13, 14 **9:5–7** Isa 14:29–31; Jer 47:1–7; Ezek 25:15–17; Joel 3:4–8; Am 1:6–8; Zeph 2:4–7 **9:9** Mt 21:5; Jn 12:15

He comes triumphant and victorious,
but humble and riding on a donkey—
on a colt, the foal of a donkey.
10 The LORD says,
"I will remove the war chariots from Israel
and take the horses from Jerusalem;
the bows used in battle will be destroyed.
Your king will make peace among the
nations;
he will rule from sea to sea,
from the Euphrates River to the ends
of the earth."

The Restoration of God's People

11 The LORD says,
"Because of my covenant with you
that was sealed by the blood of
sacrifices,
I will set your people free—
free from the waterless pit of exile.
12 Return, you exiles who now have hope;
return to your place of safety.
Now I tell you that I will repay you twice
over
with blessing for all you have suffered.
13 I will use Judah like a soldier's bow
and Israel like the arrows.
I will use the men of Zion like a sword,
to fight the men of Greece."

14 The LORD will appear above his people;
he will shoot his arrows like lightning.
The Sovereign LORD will sound the
trumpet;
he will march in the storms from the
south.
15 The LORD Almighty will protect his
people,
and they will destroy their enemies.
They will shout in battle like drunk men
and will shed the blood of their
enemies;
it will flow like the blood of a sacrifice
poured on the altar from a bowl.[l]

16 When that day comes, the LORD will save
his people,
as a shepherd saves his flock from
danger.
They will shine in his land
like the jewels of a crown.
17 How good and beautiful the land will be!
The young people will grow strong on
its grain and wine.

The LORD Promises Deliverance

10 Ask the LORD for rain in the spring
of the year. It is the LORD who
sends rain clouds and showers, making the
fields green for everyone. 2 People consult
idols and fortunetellers, but the answers they
get are lies and nonsense. Some interpret
dreams, but only mislead you; the comfort
they give is useless. So the people wander
about like lost sheep. They are in trouble
because they have no leader.
3 The LORD says, "I am angry with those
foreigners who rule my people, and I am
going to punish them. The people of Judah
are mine, and I, the LORD Almighty, will take
care of them. They will be my powerful war-
horses. 4 From among them will come rulers,
leaders, and commanders to govern my peo-
ple.[m] 5 The people of Judah will be victori-
ous like soldiers who trample their enemies
in the mud of the streets. They will fight
because the LORD is with them, and they
will defeat even the enemy cavalry.

6 "I will make the people of Judah strong;
I will rescue the people of Israel.
I will have compassion on them
and bring them all back home.
They will be as though I had never
rejected them.
I am the LORD their God; I will answer
their prayers.
7 The people of Israel will be strong like
soldiers,
happy like those who have been
drinking wine.
Their descendants will remember this
victory
and be glad because of what the LORD
has done.

8 "I will call my people
and gather them together.

[l] **9:15** *Verse 15 in Hebrew is unclear.* [m] **10:4** From among . . . people; *or* All oppressors—rulers, leaders, and commanders—will depart together from Judah.

9:10 Ps 72:8 **9:11** Ex 24:8 **10:2** Mt 9:36; Mk 6:34

I will rescue them
and make them as numerous as they used to be.
9 Though I have scattered them among the nations,
yet in far-off places they will remember me.
They and their children will survive
and return home together.
10 From Egypt and Assyria I will bring them home
and settle them in their own country.
I will settle them in Gilead and Lebanon also;
the whole land will be filled with people.
11 When they pass through their sea of trouble,
I, the LORD, will strike the waves,
and the depths of the Nile will go dry.
Proud Assyria will be humbled,
and mighty Egypt will lose her power.
12 I will make my people strong;
they will worship and obey me."
The LORD has spoken.

The Fall of the Tyrants

11 Open your doors, Lebanon,
so that fire can burn down your cedar trees![n]
2 Weep and wail, cypress trees—
the cedars have fallen;
those glorious trees have been destroyed!
Weep and wail, oaks of Bashan—
the dense forest has been cut down!
3 The rulers cry out in grief;
their glory is gone!
Listen to the roaring of the lions;
their forest home along the Jordan is destroyed!

The Two Shepherds

4 The LORD my God said to me, "Act the
part of the shepherd[o] of a flock of sheep that
are going to be butchered. 5 Their owners
kill them and go unpunished. They sell the
meat and say, 'Praise the LORD! We are rich!'
Even their own shepherds have no pity on
them."

(6 The LORD said, "I will no longer pity
anyone on earth. I myself will put all the
people in the power of their rulers. These
rulers will devastate the earth, and I will not
save it from their power.")

7 Those who bought and sold the sheep
hired me, and I became the shepherd of the
sheep that were going to be butchered. I
took two sticks: one I called "Favor" and the
other "Unity." And I took care of the flock.
8 I lost patience with three other shepherds,
who hated me, and I got rid of them all in a
single month. 9 Then I said to the flock, "I
will not be your shepherd any longer. Let
those die who are to die. Let those be
destroyed who are to be destroyed. Those
who are left will destroy one another."
10 Then I took the stick called "Favor" and
broke it, to cancel the covenant which the
LORD had made with all the nations. 11 So
the covenant was canceled on that day. Those
who bought and sold the sheep were watching me, and they knew that the LORD was
speaking through what I did. 12 I said to
them, "If you are willing, give me my wages.
But if not, keep them." So they paid me
thirty pieces of silver as my wages.

13 The LORD said to me, "Put them in the
Temple treasury."[p] So I took the thirty
pieces of silver—the magnificent sum they
thought I was worth—and put them in the
Temple treasury. 14 Then I broke the second
stick, the one called "Unity," and the unity of
Judah and Israel was shattered.

15 Then the LORD said to me, "Once again
act the part of a shepherd, this time a worthless one. 16 I have put a shepherd in charge of
my flock, but he does not help the sheep
that are threatened by destruction; nor does
he look for the lost, or heal those that are
hurt, or feed the healthy. Instead, he eats the
meat of the fattest sheep and tears off their
hoofs. 17 That worthless shepherd is doomed!

[n] **11:1** CEDAR TREES: *Trees are used here as symbols of powerful nations or their kings.* [o] **11:4** SHEPHERD: *Shepherd is used here as a symbol of a king or leader, and sheep as symbols of his people or followers.* [p] **11:13** *Some ancient translations* Put them in the Temple treasury; *Hebrew* Give them to the potter.

10:9, 10 Bar 2:20–32 **11:12, 13** Mt 27:9, 10 **11:12** Mt 26:15

He has abandoned his flock. (11:17)

He has abandoned his flock. War will totally destroy his power. His arm will wither, and his right eye will go blind."

The Future Deliverance of Jerusalem

12 This is a message about Israel from the LORD, the LORD who spread out the skies, created the earth, and gave life to man. He says, 2"I will make Jerusalem like a cup of wine; the nations around her will drink and stagger like drunks. And when they besiege Jerusalem, the cities of the rest of Judah will also be besieged. 3But when that time comes, I will make Jerusalem like a heavy stone—any nation that tries to lift it will be hurt. All the nations of the world will join forces to attack her. 4At that time I will terrify all their horses and make all their riders go crazy. I will watch over the people of Judah, but I will make the horses of their enemies blind. 5Then the clans of Judah will say to themselves, 'The LORD God Almighty gives strength to his people who live in Jerusalem.'

6"At that time I will make the clans of Judah like a fire in a forest or in a field of ripe grain—they will destroy all the surrounding nations. The people of Jerusalem will remain safe in the city.

7"I, the LORD, will give victory to the armies of Judah first, so that the honor which the descendants of David and the people of Jerusalem will receive will be no greater than that of the rest of Judah. 8At that time the LORD will protect those who live in Jerusalem, and even the weakest among them will become as strong as David was. The descendants of David will lead them like the angel of the LORD, like God himself. 9At that time I will destroy every nation that tries to attack Jerusalem.

10"I will fill the descendants of David and the other people of Jerusalem with the spirit of mercy and the spirit of prayer. They will look at the one whom they stabbed to death, and they will mourn for him like those who mourn for an only child. They will mourn bitterly, like those who have lost their first-born son. 11At that time the mourning in Jerusalem will be as great as the mourning for Hadad Rimmon[q] in the plain of Megiddo. 12-14Each family in the land will mourn by itself: the family descended from David, the family descended from Nathan, the family descended from Levi, the family descended from Shimei, and all the other families. Each family will mourn by itself, and the men of each family will mourn separately from the women.

13 "When that time comes," says the LORD Almighty, "a fountain will be opened to purify the descendants of David and the people of Jerusalem from their sin and idolatry. 2At that time I will remove the names of the idols from the land, and no one will remember them any more. I will get rid of anyone who claims to be a prophet and will take away the desire to worship idols. 3Then if anyone still insists on prophesying, his own father and mother will tell him that he must be put to death, because he claimed to speak the LORD's word, but spoke lies instead. When he prophesies, his own father and mother will stab him to death. 4When that time comes, no prophet will be proud of his visions or act like a prophet or wear a prophet's coarse garment in order to deceive people. 5Instead, he will say, 'I am not a prophet. I am a farmer—I have farmed the land all my life.' 6Then if someone asks him, 'What are those wounds on your chest?' he will answer, 'I got them at a friend's house.' "

The Command to Kill God's Shepherd

7The LORD Almighty says, "Wake up, sword, and attack the shepherd[r] who works for me! Kill him, and the sheep will be scat-

[q] **12:11** HADAD RIMMON: *Probably a name for Baal, the god of vegetation in Canaan and Syria. When the vegetation died each year, the worshipers thought that the god had died, and they mourned his death.* [r] **13:7** SHEPHERD: *See 11:4.*

12:10 Jn 19:37; Rev 1:7 **12:10–14** Mt 24:20; Rev 1:7 **13:7** Mt 26:31; Mk 14:27

tered. I will attack my people 8and through-
out the land two-thirds of the people will
die. 9And I will test the third that survives
and will purify them as silver is purified by
fire. I will test them as gold is tested. Then
they will pray to me, and I will answer them.
I will tell them that they are my people, and
they will confess that I am their God."

Jerusalem and the Nations

14 The day when the LORD will sit in
judgment is near. Then Jerusalem
will be looted, and the loot will be divided
up before your eyes. 2The LORD will bring
all the nations together to make war on
Jerusalem. The city will be taken, the houses
looted, and the women raped. Half of the
people will go into exile, but the rest of
them will not be taken away from the city.
3Then the LORD will go out and fight
against those nations, as he has fought in
times past. 4At that time he will stand on the
Mount of Olives, to the east of Jerusalem.
Then the Mount of Olives will be split in
two from east to west by a large valley. Half
of the mountain will move northward, and
half of it southward. 5You will escape
through this valley that divides the mountain
in two.[s] You will flee as your ancestors did
when the earthquake struck in the time of
King Uzziah of Judah. The LORD my God
will come, bringing all the angels with him.

6When that time comes, there will no
longer be cold or frost,[t] 7nor any darkness.
There will always be daylight, even at night-
time. When this will happen is known only
to the LORD.

8When that day comes, fresh water will
flow from Jerusalem, half of it to the Dead
Sea and the other half to the Mediterranean.
It will flow all year long, in the dry season as
well as the wet. 9Then the LORD will be
king over all the earth; everyone will wor-
ship him as God and know him by the same
name.

10The whole region, from Geba in the
north to Rimmon in the south, will be
made level. Jerusalem will tower above the
land around it; the city will reach from the
Benjamin Gate to the Corner Gate, where
there had been an earlier gate, and from the
Tower of Hananel to the royal wine presses.
11The people will live there in safety, no
longer threatened by destruction.

12The LORD will bring a terrible disease
on all the nations that make war on
Jerusalem. Their flesh will rot away while
they are still alive; their eyes and their
tongues will rot away.

13At that time the LORD will make them
so confused and afraid that everyone will
seize the man next to him and attack him.
14The men of Judah will fight to defend
Jerusalem. They will take as loot the wealth
of all the nations—gold, silver, and clothing
in great abundance.

15A terrible disease will also fall on the
horses, the mules, the camels, and the don-
keys—on all the animals in the camps of the
enemy.

16Then all of the survivors from the
nations that have attacked Jerusalem will go
there each year to worship the LORD
Almighty as king and to celebrate the Festi-
val of Shelters. 17If any nation refuses to go
and worship the LORD Almighty as king,
then rain will not fall on their land. 18If the
Egyptians refuse to celebrate the Festival of
Shelters, then they will be struck by the
same disease that the LORD will send on
every nation that refuses to go. 19This will
be the punishment that will fall on Egypt
and on all the other nations if they do not
celebrate the Festival of Shelters.

20At that time even the harness bells of
the horses will be inscribed with the words
"Dedicated to the LORD." The cooking pots
in the Temple will be as sacred as the bowls
before the altar. 21Every cooking pot in
Jerusalem and in all Judah will be set apart
for use in the worship of the LORD
Almighty. The people who offer sacrifices
will use them for boiling the meat of the
sacrifices. When that time comes, there will
no longer be any merchant in the Temple of
the LORD Almighty.

[s] **14:5** *Probable text* You will escape . . . in two; *Hebrew unclear.* [t] **14:6** *Probable text* cold or frost; *Hebrew unclear.*

14:8 Ezek 47:1; Jn 7:38; Rev 22:1 **14:11** Rev 22:3 **14:16** Lev 23:39–43

THE BOOK OF

Malachi

We expect that when promises are made to us, they will be kept. A broken promise leads to mistrust and hurt.

Malachi calls for faithfulness to promises made to God. This book addresses two areas where men of power broke their promises and were unfaithful—priesthood and marriage. Malachi challenged Israel's priests, who were being dishonest and corrupt, to be faithful in providing good leadership and honoring God. The prophet also challenged husbands, who were divorcing and leaving their Jewish wives for foreign (non-Jewish) wives, to remain faithful to their Jewish wives. Malachi's final prophecy serves as a bridge between the promises God made in the Old Testament and Jesus' fulfillment of those promises in the New Testament.

Chap. 3:1–3

Headlines

- God Sends Warning to Priests! (2:1–9)
- God Hates Broken Promises (2:10–16)
- Messenger Coming to Prepare the People (3:1–5)

FACTOIDS

Who wrote this book? We do not know for sure. Because Malachi means "my messenger," we are not sure if it is the name of an actual prophet. It may be a title describing the book.

Who is this book addressed to? Men of power—priests who were not faithful to the Law and husbands who were not faithful to their wives.

Jesus connection: The messenger who prepares the way for the Lord's coming (Malachi 3:1) is fulfilled in the person of John the Baptist, who prepares the way for Jesus.

Important themes

- God's people are called to keep their promises and to be faithful to God. God will reward those who are just and faithful—all wrongs will be made right.
- The Day of the Lord is coming, and it will be terrible for those who have abused power.

MALACHI

1 This is the message that the LORD gave
Malachi to tell the people of Israel.

The LORD's Love for Israel

[2]The LORD says to his people, "I have
always loved you."

But they reply, "How have you shown
your love for us?"

The LORD answers, "Esau and Jacob were
brothers, but I have loved Jacob and his
descendants, [3]and have hated Esau and his
descendants. I have devastated Esau's hill
country and abandoned the land to jackals."
[4]If Esau's descendants, the Edomites, say,
"Our towns have been destroyed, but we
will rebuild them," then the LORD will reply,
"Let them rebuild—I will tear them down
again. People will call them 'The evil coun-
try' and 'The nation with whom the LORD is
angry forever.' "
[5]The people of Israel are going to see this
with their own eyes, and they will say, "The
LORD is mighty even outside the land of
Israel!"

The LORD Reprimands the Priests

[6]The LORD Almighty says to the priests,
"Children honor their parents, and servants
honor their masters. I am your father—why
don't you honor me? I am your master—
why don't you respect me? You despise me,
and yet you ask, 'How have we despised
you?' [7]This is how—by offering worthless
food on my altar. Then you ask, 'How have
we failed to respect you?' I will tell you—by
showing contempt for my altar. [8]When you
bring a blind or sick or lame animal to sacri-
fice to me, do you think there's nothing
wrong with that? Try giving an animal like
that to the governor! Would he be pleased
with you or grant you any favors?"
[9]Now, you priests, try asking God to be
good to us. He will not answer your prayer,
and it will be your fault. [10]The LORD
Almighty says, "I wish one of you would
close the Temple doors so as to prevent you
from lighting useless fires on my altar. I am
not pleased with you; I will not accept the
offerings you bring me. [11]People from one
end of the world to the other honor me.
Everywhere they burn incense to me and
offer acceptable sacrifices. All of them honor
me! [12]But you dishonor me when you say
that my altar is worthless and when you
offer on it food that you despise. [13]You say,
'How tired we are of all this!' and you turn
up your nose at me. As your offering to me
you bring a stolen animal or one that is lame
or sick. Do you think I will accept that from
you? [14]A curse on the cheater who sacrifices
a worthless animal to me, when he has in his
flock a good animal that he promised to give
me! For I am a great king, and people of all
nations fear me."

One that is lame or sick (1:13)

2 The LORD Almighty says to the priests,
"This command is for you: [2]You must
honor me by what you do. If you will not
listen to what I say, then I will bring a curse
on you. I will put a curse on the things you
receive for your support. In fact, I have
already put a curse on them, because you do
not take my command seriously. [3]I will pun-
ish your children and rub your faces in the
dung of the animals you sacrifice—and you

1:2, 3 Rom 9:13 **1:2–5** Isa 34:5–17; 63:1–6; Jer 49:7–22; Ezek 25:12–14; 35:1–15; Am 1:11, 12; Ob 1–14
1:8 Deut 15:21

will be taken out to the dung heap. 4Then
you will know that I have given you this
command, so that my covenant with the
priests, the descendants of Levi, will not be
broken.

5"In my covenant I promised them life
and well-being, and this is what I gave them,
so that they might respect me. In those days
they did respect and fear me. 6They taught
what was right, not what was wrong. They
lived in harmony with me; they not only did
what was right themselves, but they also
helped many others to stop doing evil. 7It is
the duty of priests to teach the true knowl-
edge of God. People should go to them to
learn my will, because they are the messen-
gers of the LORD Almighty.

8"But now you priests have turned away
from the right path. Your teaching has led
many to do wrong. You have broken the
covenant I made with you. 9So I, in turn,
will make the people of Israel despise you
because you do not obey my will, and when
you teach my people, you do not treat
everyone alike."

The People's Unfaithfulness to God

10Don't we all have the same father?
Didn't the same God create us all? Then
why do we break our promises to one
another, and why do we despise the
covenant that God made with our ances-
tors? 11The people of Judah have broken
their promise to God and done a horrible
thing in Jerusalem and all over the country.
They have defiled the Temple which the
LORD loves. Men have married women who
worship foreign gods. 12May the LORD
remove from the community of Israel those
who did this, and never again let them par-
ticipate in the offerings our nation brings to
the LORD Almighty.[a]

13This is another thing you do. You drown
the LORD's altar with tears, weeping and
wailing because he no longer accepts the
offerings you bring him. 14You ask why he
no longer accepts them. It is because he
knows you have broken your promise to the
wife you married when you were young.
She was your partner, and you have broken
your promise to her, although you promised
before God that you would be faithful to
her. 15Didn't God make you one body and
spirit with her?[b] What was his purpose in
this? It was that you should have children
who are truly God's people. So make sure
that none of you breaks his promise to his
wife. 16"I hate divorce," says the LORD God
of Israel. "I hate it when one of you does
such a cruel thing to his wife. Make sure that
you do not break your promise to be faithful
to your wife."

The Day of Judgment Is Near

17You have tired the LORD out with your
talk. But you ask, "How have we tired him?"
By saying, "The LORD Almighty thinks all
evildoers are good; in fact he likes them." Or
by asking, "Where is the God who is sup-
posed to be just?"

3 The LORD Almighty answers, "I will
send my messenger to prepare the way
for me. Then the Lord you are looking for
will suddenly come to his Temple. The mes-
senger you long to see will come and pro-
claim my covenant."

2But who will be able to endure the day
when he comes? Who will be able to sur-
vive when he appears? He will be like
strong soap, like a fire that refines metal.
3He will come to judge like one who
refines and purifies silver. As a metalworker
refines silver and gold, so the LORD's mes-
senger will purify the priests, so that they
will bring to the LORD the right kind of
offerings. 4Then the offerings which the
people of Judah and Jerusalem bring to the
LORD will be pleasing to him, as they used
to be in the past.

5The LORD Almighty says, "I will appear
among you to judge, and I will testify at
once against those who practice magic,
against adulterers, against those who give
false testimony, those who cheat employees
out of their wages, and those who take

[a] **2:12** *One ancient translation* May . . . Almighty; *Hebrew unclear.* [b] **2:15** *Probable text* Didn't God . . . her; *Hebrew unclear.*

2:4 Num 3:11–13 **2:5** Num 25:12 **3:1** Mt 11:10; Mk 1:2; Lk 1:76; 7:27 **3:2** Joel 2:11; Rev 6:17

advantage of widows, orphans, and foreigners—against all who do not respect me.

The Payment of Tithes

6 "I am the LORD, and I do not change. And so you, the descendants of Jacob, are not yet completely lost. 7 You, like your ancestors

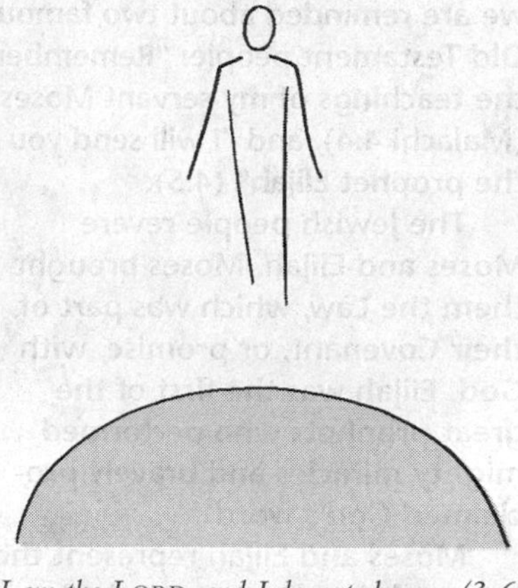

I am the LORD, and I do not change. (3:6)

before you, have turned away from my laws and have not kept them. Turn back to me, and I will turn to you. But you ask, 'What must we do to turn back to you?'
8 I ask you, is it right for a person to cheat God? Of course not, yet you are cheating me. 'How?' you ask. In the matter of tithes and offerings.
9 A curse is on all of you because the whole nation is cheating me.
10 Bring the full amount of your tithes to the Temple, so that there will be plenty of food there. Put me to the test and you will see that I will open the windows of heaven and pour out on you in abundance all kinds of good things.
11 I will not let insects destroy your crops, and your grapevines will be loaded with grapes.
12 Then the people of all nations will call you happy, because your land will be a good place to live.

God's Promise of Mercy

13 "You have said terrible things about me," says the LORD. "But you ask, 'What have we said about you?'
14 You have said, 'It's useless to serve God. What's the use of doing what he says or of trying to show the LORD Almighty that we are sorry for what we have done?
15 As we see it, proud people are the ones who are happy. Evil people not only prosper, but they test God's patience with their evil deeds and get away with it.' "

16 Then the people who feared the LORD spoke to one another, and the LORD listened and heard what they said. In his presence, there was written down in a book a record of those who feared the LORD and respected him.
17 "They will be my people," says the LORD Almighty. "On the day when I act, they will be my very own. I will be merciful to them as parents are merciful to the children who serve them.
18 Once again my people will see the difference between what happens to the righteous and to the wicked, to the person who serves me and the one who does not."

The Day of the LORD Is Coming

4 The LORD Almighty says, "The day is coming when all proud and evil people will burn like straw. On that day they will burn up, and there will be nothing left of them.
2 But for you who obey me, my saving power will rise on you like the sun and bring healing like the sun's rays. You will be as free and happy as calves let out of a stall.

My saving power will rise on you like the sun. (4:2)

3:6 Sir 48:10 **3:10** Lev 27:30; Num 18:21–24; Deut 12:6; 14:22–29; Neh 13:12

3On the day when I act, you will overcome
the wicked, and they will be like dust under
your feet.
4"Remember the teachings of my servant
Moses, the laws and commands which I gave
him at Mount Sinai for all the people of
Israel to obey.
5"But before the great and terrible day of
the LORD comes, I will send you the
prophet Elijah. 6He will bring fathers and
children together again; otherwise I would
have to come and destroy your country."

4:5 Mt 11:14; 17:10–13; Mk 9:11–13; Lk 1:17; Jn 1:21

Study it!

Moses, Elijah, and Jesus

At the end of the Book of Malachi, we are reminded about two famous Old Testament people: "Remember the teachings of my servant Moses" (Malachi 4:4), and "I will send you the prophet Elijah" (4:5).

The Jewish people revere Moses and Elijah. Moses brought them the Law, which was part of their Covenant, or promise, with God. Elijah was the first of the great prophets who performed mighty miracles and bravely proclaimed God's word.

Moses and Elijah represent the Law and the prophets to the Jewish people. No wonder these two men appeared at Jesus' Transfiguration, when Jesus' glory as the Son of God was revealed (Matthew 17:1–9, Mark 9:2–13, Luke 9:28–36). No wonder the three Apostles who saw the sight were amazed. This was one of the most dazzling signs that Jesus was indeed the Messiah, the one they had been waiting for.

Why do you think the last chapter of the last book of the Old Testament has this connection with the life of Jesus to be revealed in the New Testament?

— Malachi, chapter 4

NEW TESTAMENT

The Bible is divided into two major sections, the Old Testament and the New Testament. The New Testament contains twenty-seven books. These books contain several kinds of writings. You will find Gospels, religious history, letters to individuals, letters to communities, homilies, and visions. All these books are in some way about God's biggest breakthrough in history: the coming of Jesus Christ. The New Testament stories tell how Jesus' mission starts with God's Chosen People, who today we call the Jews. They also tell how Jesus' first disciples quickly expanded the mission to include non-Jews, who were called Gentiles.

Testament is another word for *covenant,* and a covenant is a holy promise made between God and human beings. The Old Testament is about the original Covenant that God made with his Chosen People. The New Testament writings show how the promises of the Covenant in the Old Testament were fulfilled by Jesus Christ. Through Jesus, God extended the Covenant to the whole human race. We call this the New Covenant, the promise that every person—Jew or Gentile—can have eternal life with God. This New Testament tells how this was made possible by Jesus' life, death, and Resurrection.

Breakthrough! The Bible for Young Catholics divides the New Testament into two sections. The table of contents shows the books that are in each section. Here's some information on each section:

The Gospels and the Acts of the Apostles. *Gospel* literally means "good news." We call Matthew, Mark, Luke, and John Gospels because they tell the Good News of Jesus Christ. These four books each have their unique picture of Jesus Christ. It is believed that Mark was written first. The writers of Matthew and Luke probably used Mark as a starting point in creating their Gospels. That is why these three Gospels have some very similar stories.

The Gospel of John is quite different from the other three. There are fewer miracles and fewer parables, and John more clearly presents Jesus as God's Son. Having four Gospels gives us a more complete understanding of Jesus than just having one.

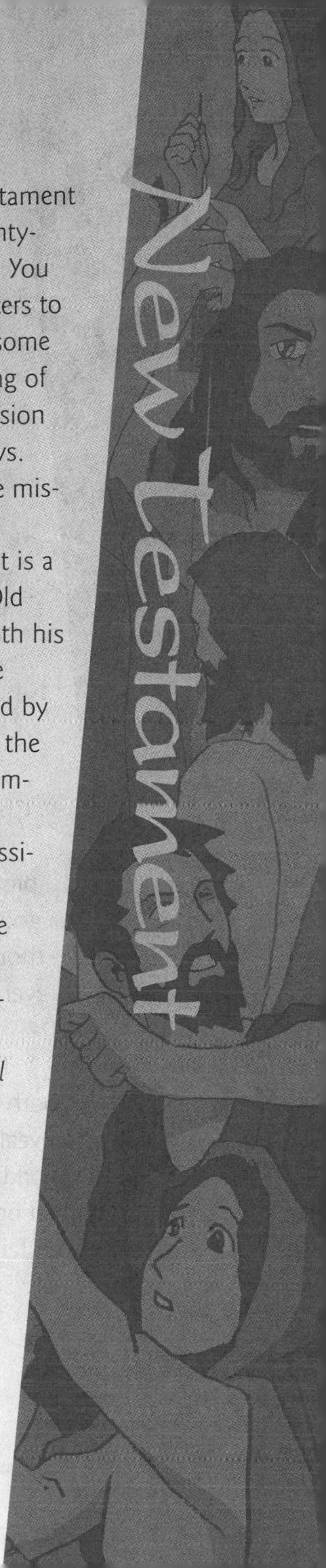

The Acts of the Apostles picks up where the Gospels leave off. It was written by the same person who wrote the Gospel of Luke. Acts tells the exciting story of the first Christians. By traveling and preaching, they spread the Good News of Jesus Christ throughout the known world.

The Letters and Revelation. Back at the time of Jesus, there was no telephone, television, radio, or Internet. So when the early leaders of the Church wanted to communicate, they did so by writing letters. These letters were written to groups and to individuals. They helped the first Christians—and they help us—understand what it means to be a follower of Jesus.

The majority of the letters were written by Saint Paul or by people writing in his name. It was not uncommon at that time to honor a great person by writing letters or books in his or her name. So some letters that say they were written by Saint Paul or Saint Peter may have been written by other early Christians.

The Revelation to John is not a letter but a collection of prophecies and visions. It is about the struggle between the good and evil forces of creation. Revelation promises that even though believers will suffer and be persecuted, God will make everything right in the end.

To fully understand God's plan for the human race, we need both the Old and the New Testaments. The New Testament reveals the great love God has for us by sending his Son into the world. Through the Gospels and letters, God shows us that we can be saved from fear, anxiety, sin, and even death by putting our faith in Jesus Christ. Then, as disciples empowered by the Holy Spirit, we can bring God's love to other people.

The Gospel According to Matthew

If the Gospel of Matthew were a blockbuster movie, it might be titled God Saves. Then the Old Testament books of the Bible might be called *God Saves: The Beginning*. In the Old Testament we hear the story of a God who loves his people and wants to save them from sin and the effects of sin. In the Gospel of Matthew—really in all the books of the New Testament—we hear how God's plans are fulfilled in the life, death, and Resurrection of Jesus Christ.

The Gospel of Matthew shows how Jesus takes the ancient teachings and makes them new. He challenges his followers, including us today, to love as completely as he does. And keep watching! Matthew gives a preview of *God Saves: The Conclusion*, when Jesus will conquer evil and death once and for all at his second coming.

Chap. 28:1–3

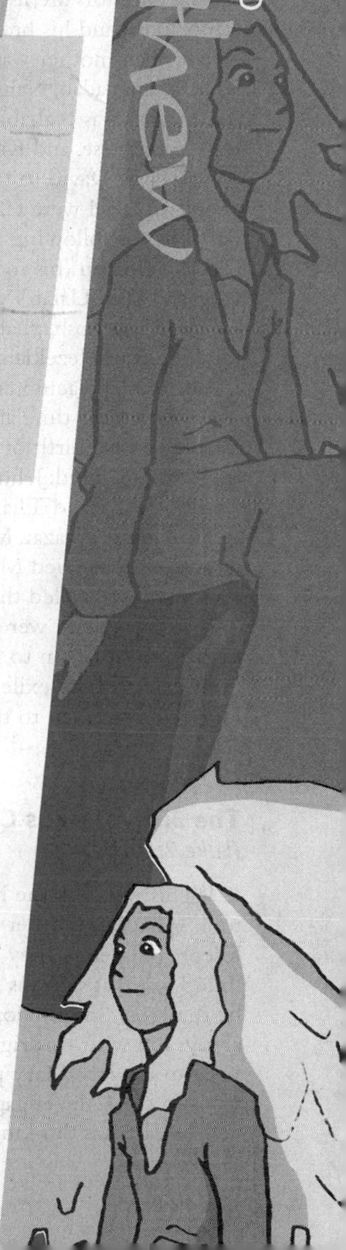

Headlines

- Future King Born In a Stable! (1:1—2:23)
- Jesus' Extreme Message: Love Your Enemies (5:43–48)
- Dead Girl Brought Back to Life! (9:23–26)
- Jesus Responds to Criticisms (12:1–42)
- Jesus Seen Talking to Dead Prophets (17:1–13)
- Women Claim to See Resurrected Jesus! (28:1–9)
- Jesus' Followers Sent to the Whole World (28:16–20)

FACTOIDS

Who wrote this book? An old tradition says it was the Apostle Matthew but no one knows for sure. We do know that the author was a Jew who had become a Christian.

When was it written? Probably between AD 75 and 90, or about fifty years after Jesus' Resurrection.

Whom was it written for? It was originally written for Jews who had become followers of Christ. These Jewish Christians were becoming outcasts in the Jewish community.

Why was it written? Matthew was written to reassure the early Jewish Christians that Jesus was the Messiah promised in the Hebrew Scriptures.

Important themes

- Jesus proclaims the Kingdom of heaven.
- Jesus is in conflict with religious leaders who are not open to his message.
- Jesus has miraculous power over sickness, storms, evil, and even death.

MATTHEW

The Ancestors of Jesus Christ
(Luke 3:23–38)

1 This is the list of the ancestors of Jesus
Christ, a descendant of David, who was
a descendant of Abraham.
2-6a From Abraham to King David, the following ancestors are listed: Abraham, Isaac, Jacob, Judah and his brothers; then Perez and Zerah (their mother was Tamar), Hezron, Ram, Amminadab, Nahshon, Salmon, Boaz (his mother was Rahab), Obed (his mother was Ruth), Jesse, and King David.
6b-11 From David to the time when the people of Israel were taken into exile in Babylon, the following ancestors are listed: David, Solomon (his mother was the woman who had been Uriah's wife), Rehoboam, Abijah, Asa, Jehoshaphat, Jehoram, Uzziah, Jotham, Ahaz, Hezekiah, Manasseh, Amon, Josiah, and Jehoiachin and his brothers.
12-16 From the time after the exile in Babylon to the birth of Jesus, the following ancestors are listed: Jehoiachin, Shealtiel, Zerubbabel, Abiud, Eliakim, Azor, Zadok, Achim, Eliud, Eleazar, Matthan, Jacob, and Joseph, who married Mary, the mother of Jesus, who was called the Messiah.
17 So then, there were fourteen generations from Abraham to David, and fourteen from David to the exile in Babylon, and fourteen from then to the birth of the Messiah.

Study it!

King of Kings

The Gospel of Matthew begins with a genealogy, or listing of Jesus' ancestors. The genealogy shows that God is doing what he promised to do. Look at some of the names in the list. Many of them are names that you will recognize from the Old Testament. God promised Abraham that he would be the father of a great nation (Genesis 12:2). God promised David that the Messiah, the one who would save the people, would be a descendant of David's (2 Samuel 7:12–16).

— Matthew 1:1–17

The Birth of Jesus Christ
(Luke 2:1–7)

18 This was how the birth of Jesus Christ took place. His mother Mary was engaged to Joseph, but before they were married, she found out that she was going to have a baby
by the Holy Spirit. 19 Joseph was a man who always did what was right, but he did not want to disgrace Mary publicly; so he made plans to break the engagement privately.
20 While he was thinking about this, an angel of the Lord appeared to him in a dream and said, "Joseph, descendant of David, do not be afraid to take Mary to be your wife. For it is by the Holy Spirit that she has conceived.
21 She will have a son, and you will name him Jesus—because he will save his people from their sins."
22 Now all this happened in order to make come true what the Lord had said through
the prophet, 23 "A virgin will become pregnant and have a son, and he will be called Immanuel" (which means, "God is with us").
24 So when Joseph woke up, he married Mary, as the angel of the Lord had told him
to. 25 But he had no sexual relations with her before she gave birth to her son. And Joseph named him Jesus.

1:11 2 Kings 24:14, 15; 2 Chr 36:10; Jer 27:20 **1:18** Lk 1:27 **1:21** Sir 46:1; Lk 1:31 **1:23** Isa 7:14 (LXX) **1:25** Lk 2:21

Catholic Connections

The Liturgical Year

After the genealogy Matthew continues with the stories about Jesus' birth and the visit of the wise men, or magi. The Catholic Church celebrates these events during the Christmas season. These are special seasons during the Church year.

The Church has its own calendar called the liturgical calendar. It moves through seasons just like any other calendar does. The seasons are connected to the important moments in Jesus' life. Advent is the season before Christmas. During Advent we remember and celebrate the events leading up to and surrounding the birth of Jesus. The liturgical year reminds us that God's saving action continues today and will be fulfilled when Jesus returns at the end of time.

— Matthew 1:18—2:12

Visitors from the East

2 Jesus was born in the town of Bethle-
hem in Judea, during the time when
Herod was king. Soon afterward, some men
who studied the stars came from the East to
Jerusalem 2and asked, "Where is the baby
born to be the king of the Jews? We saw his
star when it came up in the east, and we
have come to worship him."
3When King Herod heard about this, he
was very upset, and so was everyone else in
Jerusalem. 4He called together all the chief
priests and the teachers of the Law and asked
them, "Where will the Messiah be born?"
5"In the town of Bethlehem in Judea,"
they answered. "For this is what the prophet
wrote:
6'Bethlehem in the land of Judah,
you are by no means the least of the
leading cities of Judah;
for from you will come a leader
who will guide my people Israel.' "
7So Herod called the visitors from the East
to a secret meeting and found out from them
the exact time the star had appeared. 8Then
he sent them to Bethlehem with these
instructions: "Go and make a careful search
for the child; and when you find him, let me
know, so that I too may go and worship him."
9-10And so they left, and on their way they
saw the same star they had seen in the East.
When they saw it, how happy they were,
what joy was theirs! It went ahead of them
until it stopped over the place where the
child was. 11They went into the house, and
when they saw the child with his mother

The star . . . went ahead of them (2:9–10)

2:6 Mic 5:2

Do you think Joseph was scared? How would you feel if an angel asked you to do something for God?

Study it!

Remember Moses?

Jesus was hidden as a baby so that he would not be killed. The same thing happened to Moses (see Exodus 1:22—2:10). The story of Moses was important to the people for whom Matthew's Gospel was written. They were Jews. They would have recognized this comparison to Moses, one of their greatest leaders. Matthew's Gospel includes other similarities between Jesus and Moses. For example, by fleeing to Egypt and returning to Israel, Jesus takes the same journey that Moses and his people, the Israelites, took.

— Matthew 2:13–18

Mary, they knelt down and worshiped him.
They brought out their gifts of gold, frankin-
cense, and myrrh, and presented them to him.
12 Then they returned to their country by
another road, since God had warned them in
a dream not to go back to Herod.

The Escape to Egypt

13 After they had left, an angel of the Lord
appeared in a dream to Joseph and said,
"Herod will be looking for the child in
order to kill him. So get up, take the child
and his mother and escape to Egypt, and stay
there until I tell you to leave."
14 Joseph got up, took the child and his
mother, and left during the night for Egypt,
15 where he stayed until Herod died. This was
done to make come true what the Lord had
said through the prophet, "I called my Son
out of Egypt."

The Killing of the Children

16 When Herod realized that the visitors
from the East had tricked him, he was furi-
ous. He gave orders to kill all the boys in
Bethlehem and its neighborhood who were
two years old and younger—this was done
in accordance with what he had learned
from the visitors about the time when the
star had appeared.
17 In this way what the prophet Jeremiah
had said came true:
18 "A sound is heard in Ramah,
the sound of bitter weeping.
Rachel is crying for her children;
she refuses to be comforted,
for they are dead."

The Return from Egypt

19 After Herod died, an angel of the Lord
appeared in a dream to Joseph in Egypt
20 and said, "Get up, take the child and his
mother, and go back to the land of Israel,
because those who tried to kill the child are
dead." 21 So Joseph got up, took the child and
his mother, and went back to Israel.
22 But when Joseph heard that Archelaus
had succeeded his father Herod as king of
Judea, he was afraid to go there. He was
given more instructions in a dream, so he
went to the province of Galilee 23 and made
his home in a town named Nazareth. And so
what the prophets had said came true: "He
will be called a Nazarene."

The Preaching of John the Baptist
(Mark 1:1–8; Luke 3:1–18; John 1:19–28)

3 At that time John the Baptist came to
the desert of Judea and started preach-
ing. 2 "Turn away from your sins," he said,
"because the Kingdom of heaven is near!"
3 John was the man the prophet Isaiah was

2:15 Hos 11:1 **2:18** Jer 31:15 **2:23** Mk 1:24; Lk 2:39; Jn 1:45 **3:2** Mt 4:17; Mk 1:15

The visitors from the East represent all of us who are not descended from the Jewish people. They show that God's salvation is for everyone.

Pray it!

Announcing God's Kingdom!

John the Baptist went ahead of Jesus. He let everybody know that something special was about to happen. The way his clothes are described would have reminded people of the prophet Elijah (2 Kings 1:8). People of Jesus' time believed that Elijah would return from heaven to announce the coming of the Day of the Lord. The author compares John to Elijah to let people know that Jesus is the one they have been waiting for.

Saving God,
Help me to be like John
by my words and actions.
Help me to announce Jesus' coming.
Help me to make a path for Jesus in my heart.

— Matthew 3:1–12

talking about when he said,
"Someone is shouting in the desert,
'Prepare a road for the Lord;
make a straight path for him to travel!' "
4John's clothes were made of camel's hair;
he wore a leather belt around his waist, and
his food was locusts and wild honey. 5People
came to him from Jerusalem, from the whole
province of Judea, and from all over the
country near the Jordan River. 6They con-
fessed their sins, and he baptized them in the
Jordan.
7When John saw many Pharisees and Sad-
ducees coming to him to be baptized, he
said to them, "You snakes—who told you
that you could escape from the punishment
God is about to send? 8Do those things that
will show that you have turned from your
sins. 9And don't think you can escape pun-
ishment by saying that Abraham is your
ancestor. I tell you that God can take these
rocks and make descendants for Abraham!
10The ax is ready to cut down the trees at
the roots; every tree that does not bear good
fruit will be cut down and thrown in the
fire. 11I baptize you with water to show that
you have repented, but the one who will
come after me will baptize you with the
Holy Spirit and fire. He is much greater than
I am; and I am not good enough even to
carry his sandals. 12He has his winnowing
shovel with him to thresh out all the grain.
He will gather his wheat into his barn, but
he will burn the chaff in a fire that never
goes out."

The Baptism of Jesus

(Mark 1:9–11; Luke 3:21, 22)

13At that time Jesus arrived from Galilee
and came to John at the Jordan to be bap-
tized by him. 14But John tried to make him
change his mind. "I ought to be baptized by
you," John said, "and yet you have come to
me!"
15But Jesus answered him, "Let it be so for
now. For in this way we shall do all that God
requires." So John agreed.
16As soon as Jesus was baptized, he came
up out of the water. Then heaven was
opened to him, and he saw the Spirit of God
coming down like a dove and lighting on
him. 17Then a voice said from heaven, "This
is my own dear Son, with whom I am
pleased."

3:3 Isa 40:3 (LXX) **3:4** 2 Kings 1:8 **3:7** Mt 12:34; 23:33 **3:9** Jn 8:33 **3:10** Mt 7:19 **3:12** Wis 5:14, 23 **3:17** Gen 22:2; Ps 2:7; Isa 42:1; Mt 12:18; 17:5; Mk 1:11; Lk 9:35

Pray it!

Facing the Devil

Jesus is hungry, tired, and probably lonely after fasting for forty days and nights in the desert. The Devil chooses this time to come and tempt him. It is often when we are feeling our worst that temptation is the strongest. When things are going badly at school or at home, when we feel lonely or lost, it is easy to listen to the voice of doubt. It is easy to think that God has abandoned us. Where does Jesus find strength? Jesus relies on God.

Dear God,
I don't feel very good right now.
Like Jesus in the desert, I'm tired.
I feel weak.
Be my strength and my courage.
Help me to rely on you
when I'm tempted to do things that I know I shouldn't.
I know that you will get me through.
Amen.

— Matthew 4:1–11

The Temptation of Jesus

(Mark 1:12, 13; Luke 4:1–13)

4 Then the Spirit led Jesus into the desert
to be tempted by the Devil. 2After
spending forty days and nights without food,
Jesus was hungry. 3Then the Devil came to
him and said, "If you are God's Son, order
these stones to turn into bread."
4But Jesus answered, "The scripture says,
'Human beings cannot live on bread alone,
but need every word that God speaks.' "
5Then the Devil took Jesus to Jerusalem,
the Holy City, set him on the highest point
of the Temple, 6and said to him, "If you are
God's Son, throw yourself down, for the
scripture says,
'God will give orders to his angels about
you;
they will hold you up with their hands,
so that not even your feet will be hurt
on the stones.' "
7Jesus answered, "But the scripture also
says, 'Do not put the Lord your God to the
test.' "
8Then the Devil took Jesus to a very high
mountain and showed him all the kingdoms
of the world in all their greatness. 9"All this I
will give you," the Devil said, "if you kneel
down and worship me."
10Then Jesus answered, "Go away, Satan!
The scripture says, 'Worship the Lord your
God and serve only him!' "

"Order these stones to turn into bread!" (4:3)

4:1 Heb 2:18; 4:15 **4:4** Deut 8:3 **4:6** Ps 91:11, 12 **4:7** Deut 6:16 **4:10** Deut 6:13

11 Then the Devil left Jesus; and angels
came and helped him.

> **Study it!**
>
> **Jesus' Most Famous Sermon**
>
> **Many well-known teachings of Jesus are collected in chapters 5–7 of the Gospel of Matthew, including the Beatitudes, the Golden Rule, and the Lord's Prayer. This section of Matthew's Gospel is called the Sermon on the Mount. Some of these teachings echo ideas that were already present in Jesus' time. Some of them are radical. Jesus says all these things, and then in the chapters to come, we see him live out all these teachings. He trusts in God. When he is treated cruelly, he responds with forgiveness and mercy. Read Matthew, chapters 5 7, carefully. It Is a sneak preview of what lies ahead.**

Jesus Begins His Work in Galilee
(Mark 1:14, 15; Luke 4:14, 15)

12 When Jesus heard that John had been
put in prison, he went away to Galilee. 13 He
did not stay in Nazareth, but went to live in
Capernaum, a town by Lake Galilee, in the
territory of Zebulun and Naphtali. 14 This
was done to make come true what the
prophet Isaiah had said,

15 "Land of Zebulun and land of Naphtali,
on the road to the sea, on the other
side of the Jordan,
Galilee, land of the Gentiles!
16 The people who live in darkness
will see a great light.
On those who live in the dark land of death
the light will shine."

17 From that time Jesus began to preach his
message: "Turn away from your sins, because
the Kingdom of heaven is near!"

Jesus Calls Four Fishermen
(Mark 1:16–20; Luke 5:1–11)

18 As Jesus walked along the shore of Lake
Galilee, he saw two brothers who were fish-
ermen, Simon (called Peter) and his brother
Andrew, catching fish in the lake with a net.
19 Jesus said to them, "Come with me, and I
will teach you to catch people." 20 At once
they left their nets and went with him.

21 He went on and saw two other broth-
ers, James and John, the sons of Zebedee.
They were in their boat with their father
Zebedee, getting their nets ready. Jesus called
them, 22 and at once they left the boat and
their father, and went with him.

Jesus Teaches, Preaches, and Heals
(Luke 6:17–19)

23 Jesus went all over Galilee, teaching in
the synagogues, preaching the Good News
about the Kingdom, and healing people who
had all kinds of disease and sickness. 24 The
news about him spread through the whole
country of Syria, so that people brought to
him all those who were sick, suffering from
all kinds of diseases and disorders: people
with demons, and epileptics, and paralyzed
people—and Jesus healed them all. 25 Large
crowds followed him from Galilee and the
Ten Towns, from Jerusalem, Judea, and the
land on the other side of the Jordan.

The Sermon on the Mount

5 Jesus saw the crowds and went up a hill,
where he sat down. His disciples gath-
ered around him, 2 and he began to teach
them:

4:12 Mt 14:3; Mk 6:17; Lk 3:19,20 **4:13** Jn 2:12 **4:15,16** Isa 9:1,2 **4:17** Mt 3:2 **4:23** Mt 9:35; Mk 1:39

Jesus spent forty days in the desert. Moses and the Israelites spent forty years. What's the connection? (See the article "Remember Moses?" in chapter 2.)

Catholic Connections

A New Law

The Old Covenant is what people of Jesus' time were used to. The Old Covenant was a promise. God promised that the Israelites would be his special people, and the people promised that they would worship him alone. As a sign of their commitment, they followed the special law that God gave to Moses. This Old Law was symbolized by the Ten Commandments.

But the Israelites failed to be faithful to God over and over again. So Jesus brought a New Covenant. The New Covenant had a New Law that did not do away with the Old Law (Matthew 5:17–20) but fulfilled and completed it. The New Law focuses not just on our actions but also on what is in our hearts. In chapter 5 watch for the phrase "You have heard that it was said." Each time this phrase appears, Jesus gives a teaching from the Law of Moses and focuses on its true meaning.

The first section of the Sermon on the Mount is called the Beatitudes. The Beatitudes summarize what God's New Law is all about. They focus on the attitudes in our hearts rather than on specific actions. They are the key to human happiness. In the Beatitudes we see the wisdom of the Old Law brought to a new level.

— Matthew 5:1–12

True Happiness
(Luke 6:20–23)

3 "Happy are those who know they are
spiritually poor;
the Kingdom of heaven belongs to
them!
4 "Happy are those who mourn;
God will comfort them!
5 "Happy are those who are humble;
they will receive what God has
promised!
6 "Happy are those whose greatest desire is
to do what God requires;
God will satisfy them fully!
7 "Happy are those who are merciful to
others;
God will be merciful to them!
8 "Happy are the pure in heart;
they will see God!
9 "Happy are those who work for peace;
God will call them his children!
10 "Happy are those who are persecuted
because they do what God requires;
the Kingdom of heaven belongs to
them!

11 "Happy are you when people insult you
and persecute you and tell all kinds of evil
lies against you because you are my follow-
ers. 12 Be happy and glad, for a great reward
is kept for you in heaven. This is how the
prophets who lived before you were perse-
cuted.

5:4 Isa 61:2 **5:5** Ps 37:11 **5:6** Isa 55:1,2; Sir 24:21 **5:8** Ps 24:3,4 **5:10** 1 Pet 3:14 **5:11** 1 Pet 4:14 **5:12** 2 Chr 36:16; Sir 2:8; Acts 7:52

Salt and Light

(Mark 9:50; Luke 14:34, 35)

13“You are like salt for the whole human race. But if salt loses its saltiness, there is no way to make it salty again. It has become worthless, so it is thrown out and people trample on it.

14“You are like light for the whole world. A city built on a hill cannot be hid. 15No one lights a lamp and puts it under a bowl; instead it is put on the lampstand, where it gives light for everyone in the house. 16In the same way your light must shine before people, so that they will see the good things you do and praise your Father in heaven.

> *Pray it!*
>
> **Shine Bright!**
>
> **In this passage we are told “your light must shine before people” (Matthew 5:16). Light a candle in a dark room. Now shield the flame with your hand. Notice how dark the room gets. Now hold the light up over your head. See how it lights up the whole room? God wants us to do the same thing with our lives. God asks us to live so that the good we do shines on others and lights up the whole world.**
>
> **— Matthew 5:13–16**

Teaching about the Law

17“Do not think that I have come to do away with the Law of Moses and the teachings of the prophets. I have not come to do away with them, but to make their teachings come true. 18Remember that as long as heaven and earth last, not the least point nor the smallest detail of the Law will be done away with—not until the end of all things.[a] 19So then, whoever disobeys even the least important of the commandments and teaches others to do the same, will be least in the Kingdom of heaven. On the other hand, whoever obeys the Law and teaches others to do the same, will be great in the Kingdom of heaven. 20I tell you, then, that you will be able to enter the Kingdom of heaven only if you are more faithful than the teachers of the Law and the Pharisees in doing what God requires.

Teaching about Anger

21“You have heard that people were told in the past, ‘Do not commit murder; anyone who does will be brought to trial.’ 22But now I tell you: if you are angry[b] with your brother you will be brought to trial, if you call your brother ‘You good-for-nothing!’ you will be brought before the Council, and if you call your brother a worthless fool you will be in danger of going to the fire of hell. 23So if you are about to offer your gift to God at the altar and there you remember that your brother has something against you, 24leave your gift there in front of the altar, go at once and make peace with your brother, and then come back and offer your gift to God.

25“If someone brings a lawsuit against you and takes you to court, settle the dispute while there is time, before you get to court. Once you are there, you will be turned over to the judge, who will hand you over to the police, and you will be put in jail. 26There you will stay, I tell you, until you pay the last penny of your fine.

Teaching about Adultery

27“You have heard that it was said, ‘Do not commit adultery.’ 28But now I tell you: anyone who looks at a woman and wants to possess her is guilty of committing adultery with her in his heart. 29So if your right eye causes you to sin, take it out and throw it away! It is

[a] **5:18** the end of all things; *or* all its teachings come true. [b] **5:22** if you are angry; *some manuscripts have* if without cause you are angry.

5:13 Mk 9:50; Lk 14:34,35 **5:14** Jn 8:12; 9:5 **5:15** Mk 4:21; Lk 8:16; 11:33 **5:16** 1 Pet 2:12 **5:18** Lk 16:17 **5:21** Ex 20:13; Deut 5:17 **5:27** Ex 20:14; Deut 5:18 **5:29** Mt 18:9; Mk 9:47

much better for you to lose a part of your
body than to have your whole body thrown
into hell. 30 If your right hand causes you to
sin, cut it off and throw it away! It is much
better for you to lose one of your limbs than
to have your whole body go off to hell.

Teaching about Divorce

(Matthew 19:9; Mark 10:11, 12; Luke 16:18)

31 "It was also said, 'Anyone who divorces
his wife must give her a written notice of
divorce.' 32 But now I tell you: if a man
divorces his wife for any cause other than her
unfaithfulness, then he is guilty of making her
commit adultery if she marries again; and the
man who marries her commits adultery also.

Teaching about Vows

33 "You have also heard that people were
told in the past, 'Do not break your promise,
but do what you have vowed to the Lord to
do.' 34 But now I tell you: do not use any
oath when you make a promise. Do not
swear by heaven, for it is God's throne; 35 nor
by earth, for it is the resting place for his
feet; nor by Jerusalem, for it is the city of the
great King. 36 Do not even swear by your
head, because you cannot make a single hair
white or black. 37 Just say 'Yes' or 'No'—any-
thing else you say comes from the Evil One.

Teaching about Revenge

(Luke 6:29, 30)

38 "You have heard that it was said, 'An eye
for an eye, and a tooth for a tooth.' 39 But
now I tell you: do not take revenge on some-
one who wrongs you. If anyone slaps you on
the right cheek, let him slap your left cheek
too. 40 And if someone takes you to court to
sue you for your shirt, let him have your coat
as well. 41 And if one of the occupation
troops forces you to carry his pack one mile,
carry it two miles. 42 When someone asks you
for something, give it to him; when someone
wants to borrow something, lend it to him.

Love for Enemies

(Luke 6:27, 28, 32–36)

43 "You have heard that it was said, 'Love
your friends, hate your enemies.' 44 But now I
tell you: love your enemies and pray for
those who persecute you, 45 so that you may
become the children of your Father in heav-
en. For he makes his sun to shine on bad
and good people alike, and gives rain to
those who do good and to those who do
evil. 46 Why should God reward you if you
love only the people who love you? Even
the tax collectors do that! 47 And if you speak
only to your friends, have you done anything
out of the ordinary? Even the pagans do
that! 48 You must be perfect—just as your
Father in heaven is perfect.

Teaching about Charity

6 "Make certain you do not perform your
religious duties in public so that people
will see what you do. If you do these things
publicly, you will not have any reward from
your Father in heaven.

2 "So when you give something to a
needy person, do not make a big show of it,
as the hypocrites do in the houses of wor-
ship and on the streets. They do it so that

Do not make a big show of it. (6:2)

5:30 Mt 18:8; Mk 9:43 **5:31** Deut 24:1-4; Mt 19:7; Mk 10:4 **5:32** Mt 19:9; Mk 10:11,12; Lk 16:18; 1 Cor 7:10,11 **5:33** **a** Lev 19:12; **b** Num 30:2; Deut 23:21 **5:34** **a** Jas 5:12; **b** Isa 66:1; Mt 23:22 **5:35** **a** Isa 66:1; **b** Ps 48:2 **5:38** Ex 21:24; Lev 24:20; Deut 19:21 **5:43** Sir 12:4-7 **5:45** Sir 4:10 **5:48** Lev 19:2; Deut 18:13 **6:1** Mt 23:5

people will praise them. I assure you, they
have already been paid in full. 3But when
you help a needy person, do it in such a way
that even your closest friend will not know
about it. 4Then it will be a private matter.
And your Father, who sees what you do in
private, will reward you.

Teaching about Prayer
(Luke 11:2–4)

5"When you pray, do not be like the hyp-
ocrites! They love to stand up and pray in
the houses of worship and on the street cor-
ners, so that everyone will see them. I assure
you, they have already been paid in full. 6But
when you pray, go to your room, close the
door, and pray to your Father, who is
unseen. And your Father, who sees what you
do in private, will reward you.
7"When you pray, do not use a lot of
meaningless words, as the pagans do, who
think that their gods will hear them because
their prayers are long. 8Do not be like them.
Your Father already knows what you need
before you ask him. 9This, then, is how you
should pray:

'Our Father in heaven:
May your holy name be honored;
10 may your Kingdom come;
may your will be done on earth as it
is in heaven.
11 Give us today the food we need.[c]
12 Forgive us the wrongs we have done,
as we forgive the wrongs that others
have done to us.
13 Do not bring us to hard testing,
but keep us safe from the Evil One.'[d]

14"If you forgive others the wrongs they
have done to you, your Father in heaven will
also forgive you. 15But if you do not forgive
others, then your Father will not forgive the
wrongs you have done.

Live it!

No Show-Offs

Hypocrites are people whose beliefs and actions don't match. They say one thing and do the opposite. They may do the right thing, but it is just for show and doesn't really mean anything because their hearts aren't in it. In this section Jesus criticizes this kind of behavior. He tells his followers that when they do something good, they should keep it a secret. When you pray don't show off. When you help someone else, don't brag about it. Then you know that you are doing the right thing for the right reason.

— Matthew 6:5–7

Teaching about Fasting

16"And when you fast, do not put on a
sad face as the hypocrites do. They neglect
their appearance so that everyone will see
that they are fasting. I assure you, they have
already been paid in full. 17When you go
without food, wash your face and comb
your hair, 18so that others cannot know that
you are fasting—only your Father, who is
unseen, will know. And your Father, who
sees what you do in private, will reward
you.

Riches in Heaven
(Luke 12:33, 34)

19"Do not store up riches for yourselves
here on earth, where moths and rust destroy,

[c] **6:11** we need; *or* for today, *or* for tomorrow. [d] **6:13** *Some manuscripts add* For yours is the kingdom, and the power, and the glory forever. Amen.

6:5 Lk 18:10-14 **6:7** Sir 7:14 **6:14,15** Mk 11:25,26 **6:14** Sir 28:1-5 **6:17** Jdt 10:3 **6:19** Jas 5:2,3

During Jesus' time a Roman soldier could force a bystander to carry his pack for a mile *(Matthew 5:41)*. **Such packs weighed about seventy pounds!**

Pray it!

Remember God's Goodness

Do you worry a lot? Many people do. In chapter 6 Matthew reminds us that God takes care of us. The next time you find yourself worrying about the future, use this meditation to regain your perspective.

A flower in the field starts as a seed. The sun warms the seed. The soil feeds the tiny plant through its delicate but growing root system. The rain falls, the plant grows, and finally the bud becomes a bright beautiful blossom. God made this whole process. It takes place without any work or worry on the part of the flower. God has a plan for you too. You are so much more valuable to God than a tiny flower, so much more complex. Imagine the process that has brought you to where you are today—from a tiny creature growing inside your mother to the person you are now. And God's not through with you! God has a plan to make something bright and beautiful happen with you too!

— Matthew 6:25–34

and robbers break in and steal. 20Instead,
store up riches for yourselves in heaven,
where moths and rust cannot destroy, and
robbers cannot break in and steal. 21For your
heart will always be where your riches are.

The Light of the Body
(Luke 11:34–36)

22"The eyes are like a lamp for the body.
If your eyes are sound, your whole body will
be full of light; 23but if your eyes are no
good, your body will be in darkness. So if
the light in you is darkness, how terribly
dark it will be!

God and Possessions
(Luke 16:13; 12:22–31)

24"You cannot be a slave of two masters;
you will hate one and love the other; you
will be loyal to one and despise the other.
You cannot serve both God and money.
25"This is why I tell you: do not be worried about the food and drink you need in
order to stay alive, or about clothes for your
body. After all, isn't life worth more than
food? And isn't the body worth more than
clothes? 26Look at the birds: they do not
plant seeds, gather a harvest and put it in
barns; yet your Father in heaven takes care of
them! Aren't you worth much more than
birds? 27Can any of you live a bit longer[e] by
worrying about it?

Aren't you worth much more than birds? (6:26)

28"And why worry about clothes? Look
how the wild flowers grow: they do not
work or make clothes for themselves. 29But I
tell you that not even King Solomon with
all his wealth had clothes as beautiful as one
of these flowers. 30It is God who clothes the

[e] **6:27** live a bit longer; *or* grow a bit taller.
6:20 Sir 29:11 **6:29** 1 Kings 10:4-7; 2 Chr 9:3-6

Jesus wants more than words! You can't just *say* you believe. You've got to act like you do too!

wild grass—grass that is here today and gone
tomorrow, burned up in the oven. Won't he
be all the more sure to clothe you? What lit-
tle faith you have!
31 “So do not start worrying: 'Where will
my food come from? or my drink? or my
clothes?' 32 (These are the things the pagans
are always concerned about.) Your Father in
heaven knows that you need all these things.
33 Instead, be concerned above everything
else with the Kingdom of God and with
what he requires of you, and he will provide
you with all these other things. 34 So do not
worry about tomorrow; it will have enough
worries of its own. There is no need to add
to the troubles each day brings.

Judging Others
(Luke 6:37, 38, 41, 42)

7 “Do not judge others, so that God will
not judge you, 2 for God will judge you
in the same way you judge others, and he
will apply to you the same rules you apply
to others. 3 Why, then, do you look at the
speck in your brother's eye and pay no atten-
tion to the log in your own eye? 4 How dare
you say to your brother, 'Please, let me take
that speck out of your eye,' when you have a
log in your own eye? 5 You hypocrite! First
take the log out of your own eye, and then
you will be able to see clearly to take the
speck out of your brother's eye.
6 “Do not give what is holy to dogs—they
will only turn and attack you. Do not throw
your pearls in front of pigs—they will only
trample them underfoot.

Ask, Seek, Knock
(Luke 11:9–13)

7 “Ask, and you will receive; seek, and
you will find; knock, and the door will be
opened to you. 8 For everyone who asks will
receive, and anyone who seeks will find, and
the door will be opened to those who
knock. 9 Would any of you who are fathers
give your son a stone when he asks for
bread? 10 Or would you give him a snake
when he asks for a fish? 11 As bad as you are,
you know how to give good things to your
children. How much more, then, will your
Father in heaven give good things to those
who ask him!
12 “Do for others what you want them to
do for you: this is the meaning of the Law of
Moses and of the teachings of the prophets.

The Narrow Gate
(Luke 13:24)

13 “Go in through the narrow gate,
because the gate to hell is wide and the road
that leads to it is easy, and there are many
who travel it. 14 But the gate to life is narrow
and the way that leads to it is hard, and there
are few people who find it.

A Tree and Its Fruit
(Luke 6:43, 44)

15 “Be on your guard against false
prophets; they come to you looking like
sheep on the outside, but on the inside they
are really like wild wolves. 16 You will know
them by what they do. Thorn bushes do not
bear grapes, and briers do not bear figs. 17 A
healthy tree bears good fruit, but a poor tree
bears bad fruit. 18 A healthy tree cannot bear
bad fruit, and a poor tree cannot bear good
fruit. 19 And any tree that does not bear good
fruit is cut down and thrown in the fire. 20 So
then, you will know the false prophets by
what they do.

I Never Knew You
(Luke 13:25–27)

21 “Not everyone who calls me 'Lord,
Lord' will enter the Kingdom of heaven, but
only those who do what my Father in heav-
en wants them to do. 22 When the Judgment
Day comes, many will say to me, 'Lord, Lord!
In your name we spoke God's message, by
your name we drove out many demons and
performed many miracles!' 23 Then I will say
to them, 'I never knew you. Get away from
me, you wicked people!'

7:2 Mk 4:24 **7:12** Tob 4:15; Lk 6:31 **7:13, 14** Sir 15:17 **7:16** Sir 27:6 **7:19** Mt 3:10; Lk 3:9 **7:20** Mt 12:33 **7:23** Ps 6:8

Pray it!

Good as Gold

Even though they might have different ways of saying it, Buddhists, Hindus, Taoists, Jews, Muslims, and Christians all share the central teaching of this section of Matthew, "Do for others what you want them to do for you" (Matthew 7:12). We call this teaching the Golden Rule. The message of the Golden Rule seems to be a part of most cultures and religions. Imagine if everyone in the world lived by this teaching! How would the world be different? How about your own life? In what ways do you live out this teaching?

Loving God,
You showed us how to love one another.
It is easy to say, but sometimes it is hard to do.
When I am angry or tired or annoyed,
it is easy to forget the needs of another person.
It is easy to forget that I should treat them the way I want to be treated.
Please help me to remember each person's humanity.
Help me to remember that each person I meet is your son or daughter.
Help the leaders of this world, Lord.
Whenever they have a decision to make that affects others,
help them remember the Golden Rule.

— Matthew 7:12

The Two House Builders
(Luke 6:47–49)

24 "So then, anyone who hears these words
of mine and obeys them is like a wise man
who built his house on rock. 25 The rain
poured down, the rivers flooded over, and
the wind blew hard against that house. But it
did not fall, because it was built on rock.
26 "But anyone who hears these words of
mine and does not obey them is like a fool-
ish man who built his house on sand. 27 The
rain poured down, the rivers flooded over,
the wind blew hard against that house, and it
fell. And what a terrible fall that was!"

The Authority of Jesus

28 When Jesus finished saying these things,
the crowd was amazed at the way he taught.
29 He wasn't like the teachers of the Law;
instead, he taught with authority.

Jesus Heals a Man
(Mark 1:40–45; Luke 5:12–16)

8 When Jesus came down from the hill,
large crowds followed him. 2 Then a man
suffering from a dreaded skin disease came to
him, knelt down before him, and said, "Sir, if
you want to, you can make me clean."[f]
3 Jesus reached out and touched him. "I do
want to," he answered. "Be clean!" At once
the man was healed of his disease. 4 Then
Jesus said to him, "Listen! Don't tell anyone,
but go straight to the priest and let him
examine you; then in order to prove to
everyone that you are cured, offer the sacri-
fice that Moses ordered."

Jesus Heals a Roman Officer's Servant
(Luke 7:1–10)

5 When Jesus entered Capernaum, a
Roman officer met him and begged for help:

[f] **8:2** MAKE ME CLEAN: *This disease was considered to make a person ritually unclean.*

7:28,29 Mk 1:22; Lk 4:32 **8:4** Lev 14:1-32

6"Sir, my servant is sick in bed at home,
unable to move and suffering terribly."
7"I will go and make him well," Jesus said.
8"Oh no, sir," answered the officer. "I do
not deserve to have you come into my house.
Just give the order, and my servant will get
well. 9I, too, am a man under the authority of
superior officers, and I have soldiers under
me. I order this one, 'Go!' and he goes; and I
order that one, 'Come!' and he comes; and I
order my slave, 'Do this!' and he does it."
10When Jesus heard this, he was surprised
and said to the people following him, "I tell
you, I have never found anyone in Israel
with faith like this. 11I assure you that many
will come from the east and the west and sit
down with Abraham, Isaac, and Jacob at the
feast in the Kingdom of heaven. 12But those
who should be in the Kingdom will be
thrown out into the darkness, where they
will cry and gnash their teeth." 13Then Jesus
said to the officer, "Go home, and what you
believe will be done for you."

And the officer's servant was healed that very moment.

Jesus Heals Many People

(Mark 1:29–34; Luke 4:38–41)

14Jesus went to Peter's home, and there he
saw Peter's mother-in-law sick in bed with a
fever. 15He touched her hand; the fever left
her, and she got up and began to wait on
him.
16When evening came, people brought to
Jesus many who had demons in them. Jesus
drove out the evil spirits with a word and
healed all who were sick. 17He did this to
make come true what the prophet Isaiah had
said, "He himself took our sickness and carried away our diseases."

The Would-Be Followers of Jesus

(Luke 9:57–62)

18When Jesus noticed the crowd around
him, he ordered his disciples to go to the
other side of the lake. 19A teacher of the
Law came to him. "Teacher," he said, "I am
ready to go with you wherever you go."
20Jesus answered him, "Foxes have holes,
and birds have nests, but the Son of Man has
no place to lie down and rest."
21Another man, who was a disciple, said,
"Sir, first let me go back and bury my father."
22"Follow me," Jesus answered, "and let
the dead bury their own dead."

Study it!

Miracles

The miracles in Matthew's Gospel are one more sign that the Kingdom of heaven is not some far off place but right here, right now! The miracles show the power of God clearly present and acting in the world. For example, Jesus comes across a man with a skin disease (Matthew 8:1–3). Because of the laws of the time, the man had to live outside the town, away from his friends and family. By the Jewish Law, people with skin diseases and other illnesses were considered unclean. The law was meant to keep the disease from spreading.

When Jesus healed the man with a skin disease, he not only made the man healthy again but changed his whole life! Now he could go back to his family and friends. Miracles like this are an example of Jesus' healing power. The other miracle stories in chapter 8 show that Jesus also has power over nature and power over evil.

— Matthew, chapter 8

8:9 Bar 3:33-35 **8:11** Lk 13:29 **8:12** Mt 22:13; 25:30; Lk 13:28 **8:17** Isa 53:4 **8:21** Tob 4:3, 4

Love your enemies. Jesus says this *(Matthew 5:44)*, then he does it in chapter 8! Who did Jesus heal who was considered an enemy of the Jews?

Jesus Calms a Storm
(Mark 4:35–41; Luke 8:22–25)

23 Jesus got into a boat, and his disciples
went with him. 24 Suddenly a fierce storm hit
the lake, and the boat was in danger of sink-
ing. But Jesus was asleep. 25 The disciples
went to him and woke him up. "Save us,
Lord!" they said. "We are about to die!"
26 "Why are you so frightened?" Jesus
answered. "What little faith you have!" Then
he got up and ordered the winds and the
waves to stop, and there was a great calm.
27 Everyone was amazed. "What kind of
man is this?" they said. "Even the winds and
the waves obey him!"

Jesus Heals Two Men with Demons
(Mark 5:1–20; Luke 8:26–39)

28 When Jesus came to the territory of
Gadara on the other side of the lake, he was
met by two men who came out of the burial
caves there. These men had demons in them
and were so fierce that no one dared travel
on that road. 29 At once they screamed,
"What do you want with us, you Son of
God? Have you come to punish us before
the right time?"
30 Not far away there was a large herd of
pigs feeding. 31 So the demons begged Jesus,
"If you are going to drive us out, send us
into that herd of pigs."
32 "Go," Jesus told them; so they left and
went off into the pigs. The whole herd
rushed down the side of the cliff into the
lake and was drowned.
33 The men who had been taking care of
the pigs ran away and went into the town,
where they told the whole story and what
had happened to the men with the demons.
34 So everyone from the town went out to
meet Jesus; and when they saw him, they
begged him to leave their territory.

Jesus Heals a Paralyzed Man
(Mark 2:1–12; Luke 5:17–26)

9 Jesus got into the boat and went back
across the lake to his own town,[g]
2 where some people brought to him a para-
lyzed man, lying on a bed. When Jesus saw
how much faith they had, he said to the par-
alyzed man, "Courage, my son! Your sins are
forgiven."
3 Then some teachers of the Law said to
themselves, "This man is speaking blasphe-
my!"
4 Jesus perceived what they were thinking,
and so he said, "Why are you thinking such
evil things? 5 Is it easier to say, 'Your sins are
forgiven,' or to say, 'Get up and walk'? 6 I will
prove to you, then, that the Son of Man has
authority on earth to forgive sins." So he
said to the paralyzed man, "Get up, pick up
your bed, and go home!"
7 The man got up and went home. 8 When
the people saw it, they were afraid, and
praised God for giving such authority to
people.

Jesus Calls Matthew
(Mark 2:13–17; Luke 5:27–32)

9 Jesus left that place, and as he walked
along, he saw a tax collector, named
Matthew, sitting in his office. He said to him,
"Follow me."
Matthew got up and followed him.
10 While Jesus was having a meal in
Matthew's house,[h] many tax collectors and
other outcasts came and joined Jesus and his
disciples at the table. 11 Some Pharisees saw
this and asked his disciples, "Why does your
teacher eat with such people?"
12 Jesus heard them and answered, "People
who are well do not need a doctor, but only
those who are sick. 13 Go and find out what is
meant by the scripture that says: 'It is kindness
that I want, not animal sacrifices.' I have not
come to call respectable people, but outcasts."

[g] **9:1** HIS OWN TOWN: *Capernaum (see 4:13).* [h] **9:10** in Matthew's house; *or* in his (*that is,* Jesus') house.
9:10,11 Lk 15:1,2 **9:13** **a** Mt 12:7; **b** Hos 6:6

***Blasphemy* is insulting God or being disrespectful toward God** *(Matthew 9:3)*.
People thought it was blasphemous to claim to forgive sins.

Live it!

Friends to the Rescue

The man who couldn't walk had to be carried by his friends to Jesus. They took a risk. It could not have been easy to take the man from his house and carry him on a stretcher to where Jesus was. Jesus might have turned them away. Then all their hard work, the risk they took, would have been for nothing. But "when Jesus saw how much faith they had" (Matthew 9:2), he responded by forgiving the man's sins. Sometimes people can be so paralyzed by sin or fear that it is hard for them to ask for what they need from God. They need another person to help them overcome that paralysis.

Think of your friends. Do any of them need help approaching God? Are you being called to "carry" someone to Jesus for healing? How can you help? It can be as easy as telling someone that you will pray for him or her. You can tell them about your own belief in God—that God will always forgive anyone who asks. When someone needs healing, they need to hear about God's love and mercy. You could even share this story with them.

— Matthew 9:1–8

The Question about Fasting

(Mark 2:18–22; Luke 5:33–39)

14Then the followers of John the Baptist
came to Jesus, asking, "Why is it that we and
the Pharisees fast often, but your disciples
don't fast at all?"
15Jesus answered, "Do you expect the
guests at a wedding party to be sad as long as
the bridegroom is with them? Of course
not! But the day will come when the bride-
groom will be taken away from them, and
then they will fast.
16"No one patches up an old coat with a
piece of new cloth, for the new patch will
shrink and make an even bigger hole in the
coat. 17Nor does anyone pour new wine
into used wineskins, for the skins will burst,
the wine will pour out, and the skins will be
ruined. Instead, new wine is poured into
fresh wineskins, and both will keep in good
condition."

The Official's Daughter and the Woman Who Touched Jesus' Cloak

(Mark 5:21–43; Luke 8:40–56)

18While Jesus was saying this, a Jewish offi-
cial came to him, knelt down before him, and
said, "My daughter has just died; but come and
place your hands on her, and she will live."
19So Jesus got up and followed him, and
his disciples went along with him.
20A woman who had suffered from severe
bleeding for twelve years came up behind
Jesus and touched the edge of his cloak.
21She said to herself, "If only I touch his
cloak, I will get well."

"If only I touch his cloak . . ." (9:21)

22Jesus turned around and saw her, and
said, "Courage, my daughter! Your faith has
made you well." At that very moment the
woman became well.
23Then Jesus went into the official's
house. When he saw the musicians for the
funeral and the people all stirred up, 24he
said, "Get out, everybody! The little girl is
not dead—she is only sleeping!" Then they
all started making fun of him. 25But as soon
as the people had been put out, Jesus went

into the girl's room and took hold of her
hand, and she got up. 26 The news about this
spread all over that part of the country.

Jesus Heals Two Blind Men

27 Jesus left that place, and as he walked
along, two blind men started following him.
"Have mercy on us, Son of David!" they
shouted.
28 When Jesus had gone indoors, the two
blind men came to him, and he asked them,
"Do you believe that I can heal you?"
"Yes, sir!" they answered.
29 Then Jesus touched their eyes and said,
"Let it happen, then, just as you believe!"—
30 and their sight was restored. Jesus spoke
sternly to them, "Don't tell this to anyone!"
31 But they left and spread the news about
Jesus all over that part of the country.

Jesus Heals a Man Who Could Not Speak

32 As the men were leaving, some people
brought to Jesus a man who could not talk
because he had a demon. 33 But as soon as
the demon was driven out, the man started
talking, and everyone was amazed. "We have
never seen anything like this in Israel!" they
exclaimed.
34 But the Pharisees said, "It is the chief of
the demons who gives Jesus the power to
drive out demons."

Jesus Has Pity for the People

35 Jesus went around visiting all the towns
and villages. He taught in the synagogues,
preached the Good News about the Kingdom,
and healed people with every kind of
disease and sickness. 36 As he saw the crowds,
his heart was filled with pity for them,
because they were worried and helpless, like
sheep without a shepherd. 37 So he said to his
disciples, "The harvest is large, but there are
few workers to gather it in. 38 Pray to the
owner of the harvest that he will send out
workers to gather in his harvest."

The Twelve Apostles
(Mark 3:13–19; Luke 6:12–16)

10 Jesus called his twelve disciples
together and gave them authority to
drive out evil spirits and to heal every disease
and every sickness. 2 These are the
names of the twelve apostles: first, Simon
(called Peter) and his brother Andrew; James
and his brother John, the sons of Zebedee;
3 Philip and Bartholomew; Thomas and
Matthew, the tax collector; James son of
Alphaeus, and Thaddaeus; 4 Simon the Patriot,
and Judas Iscariot, who betrayed Jesus.

The Mission of the Twelve
(Mark 6:7–13; Luke 9:1–6)

5 These twelve men were sent out by Jesus
with the following instructions: "Do not go
to any Gentile territory or any Samaritan
towns. 6 Instead, you are to go to the lost
sheep of the people of Israel. 7 Go and
preach, 'The Kingdom of heaven is near!'
8 Heal the sick, bring the dead back to life,
heal those who suffer from dreaded skin diseases,
and drive out demons. You have
received without paying, so give without
being paid. 9 Do not carry any gold, silver, or
copper money in your pockets; 10 do not
carry a beggar's bag for the trip or an extra
shirt or shoes or a walking stick. Workers
should be given what they need.
11 "When you come to a town or village,
go in and look for someone who is willing
to welcome you, and stay with him until you
leave that place. 12 When you go into a
house, say, 'Peace be with you.' 13 If the people
in that house welcome you, let your
greeting of peace remain; but if they do not
welcome you, then take back your greeting.
14 And if some home or town will not welcome
you or listen to you, then leave that
place and shake the dust off your feet. 15 I
assure you that on the Judgment Day God
will show more mercy to the people of
Sodom and Gomorrah than to the people of
that town!

9:34 Mt 10:25; 12:24; Mk 3:22; Lk 11:15 **9:35** Mt 4:23; Mk 1:39; Lk 4:44 **9:36** Num 27:17; 1 Kings 22:17; 2 Chr 18:16; Ezek 34:5; Mk 6:34 **9:37,38** Lk 10:2 **10:10** 1 Cor 9:14; 1 Tim 5:18 **10:14** Acts 13:51 **10:15 a** Mt 11:24; **b** Gen 19:24-28 **10:7-15** Lk 10:4-12

Catholic Connections

The Twelve

Twelve is an important number. There were twelve tribes of Israel. The number of Apostles was meant to remind people that Jesus came to save the whole Jewish nation and to be a sign of the connection between the Old Covenant and the New Covenant.

If you look over the list of people at the beginning of Matthew, chapter 10, you might wonder what Jesus was thinking. These were not powerful or important people. One was a tax collector, shunned by others. Simon the Patriot may have been committed to the violent overthrow of the Roman occupation. Judas would betray Jesus. But Jesus knew what he was doing. Eleven of these men, changed by watching and listening to Jesus, would do mighty things. They would endure persecution, torture, and death as the first leaders of the Church, just as Jesus predicts in verses 16–25. All future popes and bishops receive their authority from the authority and mission Christ gave to the original Apostles.

You don't have to be rich or powerful to make a difference. Simple and humble people do great things because greed and pride do not get in the way of God working through them.

— Matthew 10:1–4

Coming Persecutions
(Mark 13:9–13; Luke 21:12–17)

16 "Listen! I am sending you out just like
sheep to a pack of wolves. You must be as
cautious as snakes and as gentle as doves.
17 Watch out, for there will be those who
will arrest you and take you to court, and
they will whip you in the synagogues. 18 For
my sake you will be brought to trial before
rulers and kings, to tell the Good News to
them and to the Gentiles. 19 When they
bring you to trial, do not worry about what
you are going to say or how you will say it;
when the time comes, you will be given
what you will say. 20 For the words you will
speak will not be yours; they will come from
the Spirit of your Father speaking through
you.

21 "People will hand over their own broth-
ers to be put to death, and fathers will do
the same to their children; children will turn
against their parents and have them put to
death. 22 Everyone will hate you because of
me. But whoever holds out to the end will
be saved. 23 When they persecute you in one
town, run away to another one. I assure you
that you will not finish your work in all the
towns of Israel before the Son of Man
comes.

24 "No pupil is greater than his teacher; no
slave is greater than his master. 25 So a pupil
should be satisfied to become like his
teacher, and a slave like his master. If the
head of the family is called Beelzebul, the
members of the family will be called even
worse names!

10:16 Lk 10:3 **10:17-20** Mk 13:9-11; Lk 12:11,12; 21:12-15 **10:21** Mk 13:12; Lk 21:16 **10:22** **a** Mt 24:9; Mk 13:13; Lk 21:17; **b** Mt 24:13; Mk 13:13 **10:24** **a** Lk 6:40; **b** Jn 13:16; 15:20 **10:25** Mt 9:34; 12:24; Mk 3:22; Lk 11:15

Apostle **comes from a Greek word meaning "one who is sent."**

Live it!

Hard Times

Have you ever done the right thing and then gotten in trouble for it? Maybe you told the truth about something, and then someone got mad at you. Maybe you stood up for one friend but lost another friend in the process. This part of chapter 10 is challenging and confusing! Up to this point Jesus has spoken words of love and comfort. Now he is telling his followers that he will cause fighting between family members (Matthew 10:35–36).

Actually this is meant to encourage his followers. He's warning them—especially those who are going out as missionaries—that this is not going to be easy! Even your own family may turn against you. You're doing the right thing, but it's going to be hard!

— Matthew 10:34–39

Whom to Fear
(Luke 12:2–7)

26“So do not be afraid of people. Whatever
is now covered up will be uncovered, and
every secret will be made known. 27What I
am telling you in the dark you must repeat in
broad daylight, and what you have heard in
private you must announce from the house-
tops. 28Do not be afraid of those who kill the
body but cannot kill the soul; rather be afraid
of God, who can destroy both body and soul
in hell. 29For only a penny you can buy two
sparrows, yet not one sparrow falls to the
ground without your Father's consent. 30As
for you, even the hairs of your head have all
been counted. 31So do not be afraid; you are
worth much more than many sparrows!

Confessing and Rejecting Christ
(Luke 12:8, 9)

32“Those who declare publicly that they
belong to me, I will do the same for them
before my Father in heaven. 33But those
who reject me publicly, I will reject before
my Father in heaven.

Not Peace, but a Sword
(Luke 12:51–53; 14:26, 27)

34“Do not think that I have come to bring
peace to the world. No, I did not come to
bring peace, but a sword. 35I came to set sons
against their fathers, daughters against their
mothers, daughters-in-law against their
mothers-in-law; 36your worst enemies will be
the members of your own family.

37“Those who love their father or mother
more than me are not fit to be my disciples;
those who love their son or daughter more
than me are not fit to be my disciples.
38Those who do not take up their cross and
follow in my steps are not fit to be my disci-
ples. 39Those who try to gain their own life
will lose it; but those who lose their life for
my sake will gain it.

Rewards
(Mark 9:41)

40“Whoever welcomes you welcomes me;
and whoever welcomes me welcomes the
one who sent me. 41Whoever welcomes
God's messenger because he is God's mes-
senger, will share in his reward. And whoever
welcomes a good man because he is good,
will share in his reward. 42You can be sure
that whoever gives even a drink of cold
water to one of the least of these my follow-

10:26 Mk 4:22; Lk 8:17 **10:33** 2 Tim 2:12 **10:35,36** Mic 7:6 **10:38** Mt 16:24; Mk 8:34; Lk 9:23
10:39 Mt 16:25; Mk 8:35; Lk 9:24; 17:33; Jn 12:25 **10:40** **a** Lk 10:16; Jn 13:20; **b** Mk 9:37; Lk 9:48

“So do not be afraid; you are worth much move than many sparrows!”
(Matthew 10:31)

ers because he is my follower, will certainly
receive a reward."

The Messengers from John the Baptist
(Luke 7:18–35)

11 When Jesus finished giving these
instructions to his twelve disciples,
he left that place and went off to teach and
preach in the towns near there.
2When John the Baptist heard in prison
about the things that Christ was doing, he
sent some of his disciples to him. 3"Tell us,"
they asked Jesus, "are you the one John said
was going to come, or should we expect
someone else?"
4Jesus answered, "Go back and tell John
what you are hearing and seeing: 5the blind
can see, the lame can walk, those who suffer
from dreaded skin diseases are made clean,[i]
the deaf hear, the dead are brought back to
life, and the Good News is preached to the
poor. 6How happy are those who have no
doubts about me!"
7While John's disciples were leaving, Jesus
spoke about him to the crowds: "When you
went out to John in the desert, what did you
expect to see? A blade of grass bending in
the wind? 8What did you go out to see? A
man dressed up in fancy clothes? People
who dress like that live in palaces! 9Tell me,
what did you go out to see? A prophet? Yes
indeed, but you saw much more than a
prophet. 10For John is the one of whom the
scripture says: 'God said, I will send my mes-
senger ahead of you to open the way for
you.' 11I assure you that John the Baptist is
greater than anyone who has ever lived. But
the one who is least in the Kingdom of
heaven is greater than John. 12From the time
John preached his message until this very day
the Kingdom of heaven has suffered violent
attacks,[j] and violent men try to seize it.
13Until the time of John all the prophets and
the Law of Moses spoke about the King-
dom; 14and if you are willing to believe their
message, John is Elijah, whose coming was
predicted. 15Listen, then, if you have ears!
16"Now, to what can I compare the people
of this day? They are like children sitting in
the marketplace. One group shouts to the
other, 17'We played wedding music for you,
but you wouldn't dance! We sang funeral
songs, but you wouldn't cry!' 18When John
came, he fasted and drank no wine, and every-
one said, 'He has a demon in him!' 19When
the Son of Man came, he ate and drank, and
everyone said, 'Look at this man! He is a glut-
ton and wine drinker, a friend of tax collectors
and other outcasts!' God's wisdom, however, is
shown to be true by its results."

Study it!

The Blind Can See

When John's disciples come to ask Jesus, "Are you the one John said was going to come?" (Matthew 11:3), they are really asking Jesus if he is the Messiah. Jesus answers them with the words of the prophet Isaiah, "The blind can see, the lame can walk" (Matthew 11:5). The people of Jesus' time knew that this prophecy from Isaiah described signs of the coming of the Messiah. So without actually saying so, Jesus is telling John's followers that he is indeed the Messiah.

— Matthew 11:1–6

The Unbelieving Towns
(Luke 10:13–15)

20The people in the towns where Jesus
had performed most of his miracles did not
turn from their sins, so he reproached those
towns. 21"How terrible it will be for you,
Chorazin! How terrible for you too, Beth-
saida! If the miracles which were performed
in you had been performed in Tyre and

[i] **11:5** MADE CLEAN: *See 8:2.* [j] **11:12** has suffered violent attacks; *or* has been coming violently.

11:5 a Isa 35:5,6; **b** Isa 61:1 **11:10** Mal 3:1 **11:12,13** Lk 16:16 **11:14** Mal 4:5; Mt 17:10-13; Mk 9:11-13 **11:21** Isa 23:1-18; Ezek 26:1—28:26; Joel 3:4-8; Am 1:9,10; Zech 9:2-4

Pray it!

Come to Me

At the end of this section, we hear these very comforting words from Jesus, "Come to me, all of you who are tired from carrying heavy loads, and I will give you rest" (Matthew 11:28). Jesus wasn't just talking about being physically tired but being spiritually tired. We can be spiritually tired from the burden of worrying about someone we love or the burden of the guilt of sin. So when you are feeling worn out by life, read these words of Jesus and say this prayer to yourself.

Jesus, help me to remember to come to you
when I am feeling overwhelmed.
You promise to take my heavy burdens,
and replace them with things that are much easier to carry.
When I am tired and sad, remind me to come to you,
the One who loves me, and let me rest in you.

— Matthew 11:25–30

Sidon, the people there would have long ago
put on sackcloth and sprinkled ashes on
themselves, to show that they had turned
from their sins! 22I assure you that on the
Judgment Day God will show more mercy
to the people of Tyre and Sidon than to you!
23And as for you, Capernaum! Did you want
to lift yourself up to heaven? You will be
thrown down to hell! If the miracles which
were performed in you had been performed
in Sodom, it would still be in existence
today! 24You can be sure that on the Judgment
Day God will show more mercy to
Sodom than to you!"

Come to Me and Rest
(Luke 10:21, 22)

25At that time Jesus said, "Father, Lord of
heaven and earth! I thank you because you
have shown to the unlearned what you have
hidden from the wise and learned. 26Yes,
Father, this was how you were pleased to
have it happen.
27"My Father has given me all things. No
one knows the Son except the Father, and
no one knows the Father except the Son
and those to whom the Son chooses to
reveal him.
28"Come to me, all of you who are tired
from carrying heavy loads, and I will give
you rest. 29Take my yoke and put it on you,
and learn from me, because I am gentle and
humble in spirit; and you will find rest. 30For
the yoke I will give you is easy, and the load
I will put on you is light."

Come to me, all of you who are tired. (11:28)

The Question about the Sabbath
(Mark 2:23–28; Luke 6:1–5)

12 Not long afterward Jesus was walk-
ing through some wheat fields on a
Sabbath. His disciples were hungry, so they
began to pick heads of wheat and eat the
grain. 2When the Pharisees saw this, they
said to Jesus, "Look, it is against our Law for
your disciples to do this on the Sabbath!"

11:23 a Isa 14:13-15; **b** Gen 19:24-28 **11:24** Mt 10:15; Lk 10:12 **11:27 a** Jn 3:35; **b** Jn 1:18; 10:15
11:28-30 Sir 6:24-30; 24:19; 51:23-26 **11:29** Jer 6:16 **12:1** Deut 23:25

3 Jesus answered, "Have you never read
what David did that time when he and his
men were hungry? 4 He went into the house
of God, and he and his men ate the bread
offered to God, even though it was against
the Law for them to eat it—only the priests
were allowed to eat that bread. 5 Or have you
not read in the Law of Moses that every
Sabbath the priests in the Temple actually
break the Sabbath law, yet they are not
guilty? 6 I tell you that there is something
here greater than the Temple. 7 The scripture
says, 'It is kindness that I want, not animal
sacrifices.' If you really knew what this
means, you would not condemn people who
are not guilty; 8 for the Son of Man is Lord
of the Sabbath."

The Man with a Paralyzed Hand
(Mark 3:1–6; Luke 6:6–11)

9 Jesus left that place and went to a syna-
gogue, 10 where there was a man who had a
paralyzed hand. Some people were there
who wanted to accuse Jesus of doing wrong,
so they asked him, "Is it against our Law to
heal on the Sabbath?"
11 Jesus answered, "What if one of you has
a sheep and it falls into a deep hole on the
Sabbath? Will you not take hold of it and lift
it out? 12 And a human being is worth much
more than a sheep! So then, our Law does
allow us to help someone on the Sabbath."
13 Then he said to the man with the para-
lyzed hand, "Stretch out your hand."

He stretched it out, and it became well
again, just like the other one. 14 Then the
Pharisees left and made plans to kill Jesus.

God's Chosen Servant

15 When Jesus heard about the plot against
him, he went away from that place; and large
crowds followed him. He healed all the sick
16 and gave them orders not to tell others
about him. 17 He did this so as to make come
true what God had said through the prophet
Isaiah:

18 "Here is my servant, whom I have chosen,
the one I love, and with whom I am
pleased.
I will send my Spirit upon him,

Live it!

The Letter of the Law

The Pharisees criticize Jesus first for allowing his disciples to pick grain on the Sabbath and then for healing a man on the Sabbath. Some religious leaders in Jesus' time saw these actions as violations of the Jewish Law. Jesus responds by reminding the Pharisees that mercy is more important than following their narrow understanding of the Law. We can be like that sometimes too can't we? How might we respond more mercifully to the following people?

- **The young mother who struggles to get to church with her baby and then gets dirty looks from the people around her because the baby makes noise**
- **The homeless man who we make fun of because he smells**
- **The people of a different religion who we label weird because they express their faith in God differently than we do**
- **Any person we judge because we think we're better than them.**

Jesus teaches to not let anything get in the way of reaching out to another person.

— Matthew 12:1–8

12:3,4 1 Sam 21:1-6 **12:4** Lev 24:9 **12:5** Num 28:9,10 **12:7 a** Mt 9:13; **b** Hos 6:6 **12:11** Lk 14:5
12:18-21 Isa 42:1-4 (LXX)

"Come to me, all of you who are tired from carrying heavy loads, and I will give you rest" *(Matthew 11:28)*.

Study it!

Harsh Words

In this section the conflict between Jesus and the religious leaders is steadily increasing. They accuse him of using the power of Beelzebul (another name for Satan) to drive out demons (Matthew 12:24). Jesus calls them snakes (12:34)! This isn't just name-calling though. The religious leaders challenge Jesus' authority and question his understanding of the Jewish Law. Jesus challenges them about whether their hearts are in the right place. Jesus says: "How can you say good things when you are evil? For the mouth speaks what the heart is full of" (12:34).

Jesus' harshest criticism is for people who say one thing and do another or for people who do the right actions but with evil things in their hearts. Jesus will continue to be in conflict with these people for the rest of his ministry, and this conflict will eventually lead to his death. We must all pray for God's help to see when our words, our actions, and our hearts are not acting as one.

— Matthew 12:22–37

and he will announce my judgment to
the nations.
19 He will not argue or shout,
or make loud speeches in the streets.
20 He will not break off a bent reed,
nor put out a flickering lamp.
He will persist until he causes justice to
triumph,
21 and on him all peoples will put their
hope."

Jesus and Beelzebul
(Mark 3:20–30; Luke 11:14–23)

22 Then some people brought to Jesus a
man who was blind and could not talk
because he had a demon. Jesus healed the
man, so that he was able to talk and see.
23 The crowds were all amazed at what Jesus
had done. "Could he be the Son of David?"
they asked.
24 When the Pharisees heard this, they
replied, "He drives out demons only because
their ruler Beelzebul gives him power to
do so."
25 Jesus knew what they were thinking, and
so he said to them, "Any country that divides
itself into groups which fight each other will
not last very long. And any town or family
that divides itself into groups which fight
each other will fall apart. 26 So if one group is
fighting another in Satan's kingdom, this
means that it is already divided into groups
and will soon fall apart! 27 You say that I drive
out demons because Beelzebul gives me the
power to do so. Well, then, who gives your
followers the power to drive them out? What
your own followers do proves that you are
wrong! 28 No, it is not Beelzebul, but God's
Spirit, who gives me the power to drive out
demons, which proves that the Kingdom of
God has already come upon you.
29 "No one can break into a strong man's
house and take away his belongings unless
he first ties up the strong man; then he can
plunder his house.
30 "Anyone who is not for me is really
against me; anyone who does not help me
gather is really scattering. 31 For this reason I
tell you: people can be forgiven any sin and
any evil thing they say;[k] but whoever says
evil things against the Holy Spirit will not

[k] **12:31** evil thing they say; *or* evil thing they say against God.
12:24 Mt 9:34; 10:25 **12:29** Tob 8:3 **12:30** Mk 9:40

Jesus talks about the miracle of Jonah *(Matthew 12:39)*. **The book of the prophet Jonah is very short. Have you read it?**

be forgiven. 32 Anyone who says something
against the Son of Man can be forgiven; but
whoever says something against the Holy
Spirit will not be forgiven—now or ever.

A Tree and Its Fruit
(Luke 6:43–45)

33 “To have good fruit you must have a
healthy tree; if you have a poor tree, you will
have bad fruit. A tree is known by the kind
of fruit it bears. 34 You snakes—how can you
say good things when you are evil? For the
mouth speaks what the heart is full of. 35 A
good person brings good things out of a
treasure of good things; a bad person brings
bad things out of a treasure of bad things.
36 “You can be sure that on the Judgment
Day you will have to give account of every
useless word you have ever spoken. 37 Your
words will be used to judge you—to declare
you either innocent or guilty.”

The Demand for a Miracle
(Mark 8:11, 12; Luke 11:29–32)

38 Then some teachers of the Law and
some Pharisees spoke up. “Teacher,” they said,
“we want to see you perform a miracle.”
39 “How evil and godless are the people of
this day!” Jesus exclaimed. “You ask me for a
miracle? No! The only miracle you will be
given is the miracle of the prophet Jonah.
40 In the same way that Jonah spent three
days and nights in the big fish, so will the
Son of Man spend three days and nights in
the depths of the earth. 41 On the Judgment
Day the people of Nineveh will stand up
and accuse you, because they turned from
their sins when they heard Jonah preach; and
I tell you that there is something here
greater than Jonah! 42 On the Judgment Day
the Queen of Sheba will stand up and
accuse you, because she traveled all the way
from her country to listen to King Solo-
mon's wise teaching; and I assure you that
there is something here greater than
Solomon!

The Return of the Evil Spirit
(Luke 11:24–26)

43 “When an evil spirit goes out of a per-
son, it travels over dry country looking for a
place to rest. If it can't find one, 44 it says to
itself, ‘I will go back to my house.’ So it goes
back and finds the house empty, clean, and
all fixed up. 45 Then it goes out and brings
along seven other spirits even worse than
itself, and they come and live there. So when
it is all over, that person is in worse shape
than at the beginning. This is what will hap-
pen to the evil people of this day.”

Jesus' Mother and Brothers
(Mark 3:31–35; Luke 8:19–21)

46 Jesus was still talking to the people
when his mother and brothers arrived. They
stood outside, asking to speak with him. 47 So
one of the people there said to him, “Look,
your mother and brothers are standing out-
side, and they want to speak with you.”[l]
48 Jesus answered, “Who is my mother?
Who are my brothers?” 49 Then he pointed
to his disciples and said, “Look! Here are my
mother and my brothers! 50 Whoever does
what my Father in heaven wants is my
brother, my sister, and my mother.”

The Parable of the Sower
(Mark 4:1–9; Luke 8:4–8)

13 That same day Jesus left the house
and went to the lakeside, where he
sat down to teach. 2 The crowd that gathered
around him was so large that he got into a
boat and sat in it, while the crowd stood on
the shore. 3 He used parables to tell them
many things.
“Once there was a man who went out to
sow grain. 4 As he scattered the seed in the
field, some of it fell along the path, and the
birds came and ate it up. 5 Some of it fell on
rocky ground, where there was little soil. The
seeds soon sprouted, because the soil wasn't
deep. 6 But when the sun came up, it burned

[l] **12:47** *Some manuscripts do not have verse 47.*

12:32 Lk 12:10 **12:33** Sir 27:6; Mt 7:20; Lk 6:44 **12:34** **a** Mt 3:7; 23:33; Lk 3:7; **b** Mt 15:18; Lk 6:45 **12:38** Mt 16:1; Mk 8:11; Lk 11:16 **12:39** Mt 16:4; Mk 8:12 **12:40** Jon 1:17 **12:41** Jon 3:5 **12:42** 1 Kings 10:1-10; 2 Chr 9:1-12 **13:2** Lk 5:1-3

Pray it!

Are You Good Soil?

The parable of the sower that begins Matthew, chapter 13, is about receiving the word of God and letting it take root in our lives. Even if we hear the good news of God's love, there is so much that can distract us from living the way God wants us to. When we experience disappointment or when we focus on material things, these "rocks and weeds" of the world can choke out the word of God in us. Spend some quiet time reflecting on or even journaling about the following questions:

- **Do you feel like you understand the word of God? What can you do to learn more?**
- **What are the worries and distractions that pull you away from living the life God wants for you? Is there anything you can do to get rid of these things?**
- **What do you need so that you can be "good soil"? Do you need to visit with a mentor or to set aside time for Bible study or to share your faith with other people? Maybe you need a ride to church or to be less busy with activities? How can you make those things happen?**

— Matthew 13:1–23

the young plants; and because the roots had
not grown deep enough, the plants soon
dried up. 7Some of the seed fell among thorn
bushes, which grew up and choked the
plants. 8But some seeds fell in good soil, and
the plants bore grain: some had one hundred
grains, others sixty, and others thirty."
9And Jesus concluded, "Listen, then, if you
have ears!"

The Purpose of the Parables
(Mark 4:10–12; Luke 8:9, 10)

10Then the disciples came to Jesus and
asked him, "Why do you use parables when
you talk to the people?"
11Jesus answered, "The knowledge about
the secrets of the Kingdom of heaven has
been given to you, but not to them. 12For
the person who has something will be given
more, so that he will have more than
enough; but the person who has nothing
will have taken away from him even the lit-
tle he has. 13The reason I use parables in
talking to them is that they look, but do not
see, and they listen, but do not hear or
understand. 14So the prophecy of Isaiah
applies to them:

'This people will listen and listen, but not
understand;
they will look and look, but not see,
15because their minds are dull,
and they have stopped up their ears
and have closed their eyes.
Otherwise, their eyes would see,
their ears would hear,
their minds would understand,
and they would turn to me, says God,
and I would heal them.'

16"As for you, how fortunate you are!
Your eyes see and your ears hear. 17I assure
you that many prophets and many of God's
people wanted very much to see what you
see, but they could not, and to hear what
you hear, but they did not.

Jesus Explains the Parable of the Sower
(Mark 4:13–20; Luke 8:11–15)

18"Listen, then, and learn what the parable
of the sower means. 19Those who hear the
message about the Kingdom but do not
understand it are like the seeds that fell along
the path. The Evil One comes and snatches

13:12 Mt 25:29; Mk 4:25; Lk 8:18; 19:26 **13:14,15** Isa 6:9,10 (LXX) **13:16,17** Lk 10:23,24

away what was sown in them. 20 The seeds
that fell on rocky ground stand for those
who receive the message gladly as soon as
they hear it. 21 But it does not sink deep into
them, and they don't last long. So when
trouble or persecution comes because of the
message, they give up at once. 22 The seeds
that fell among thorn bushes stand for those
who hear the message; but the worries about
this life and the love for riches choke the
message, and they don't bear fruit. 23 And the
seeds sown in the good soil stand for those
who hear the message and understand it:
they bear fruit, some as much as one hun-
dred, others sixty, and others thirty."

The Parable of the Weeds

24 Jesus told them another parable: "The
Kingdom of heaven is like this. A man
sowed good seed in his field. 25 One night,
when everyone was asleep, an enemy came
and sowed weeds among the wheat and
went away. 26 When the plants grew and the
heads of grain began to form, then the
weeds showed up. 27 The man's servants
came to him and said, 'Sir, it was good seed
you sowed in your field; where did the
weeds come from?' 28 'It was some enemy
who did this,' he answered. 'Do you want us
to go and pull up the weeds?' they asked
him. 29 'No,' he answered, 'because as you
gather the weeds you might pull up some
of the wheat along with them. 30 Let the
wheat and the weeds both grow together
until harvest. Then I will tell the harvest
workers to pull up the weeds first, tie them
in bundles and burn them, and then to
gather in the wheat and put it in my
barn.' "

The Parable of the Mustard Seed
(Mark 4:30–32; Luke 13:18, 19)

31 Jesus told them another parable: "The
Kingdom of heaven is like this. A man takes
a mustard seed and sows it in his field. 32 It is
the smallest of all seeds, but when it grows
up, it is the biggest of all plants. It becomes a
tree, so that birds come and make their nests
in its branches."

Pray it!

The God Box

On a retreat, the leaders brought a box filled with all sorts of strange things: marbles, rubber bands, a stick of gum, a toy car, a Super Ball, a red crayon, a smiley face sticker. They called it the God Box. Throughout the retreat, people could pick an item from the box and explain to the rest of the retreatants how God is like that object: "God is like this eraser, erasing all your mistakes." "God is like this glue stick, holding things together." "God is like this pair of glasses, helping us see things clearly."

In this chapter Jesus uses parables to explain the Kingdom of heaven (God). Parables are stories that use objects and activities from people's everyday lives. You can create modern parables by making your own God Box. Decorate the outside of a shoebox and fill it with small, simple objects—a coin, a pebble, a birthday candle. Keep it on your dresser or beside your bed. When you wake up in the morning or before you go to sleep at night, take an object out and think about how it is like God. You might even want to write down your ideas and keep a list inside the box!

— Matthew, chapter 13

***Parables* are stories that use objects and experiences that people are familiar with to explain important ideas about God.**

The Parable of the Yeast
(Luke 13:20, 21)

33 Jesus told them still another parable:
"The Kingdom of heaven is like this. A
woman takes some yeast and mixes it with a
bushel of flour until the whole batch of
dough rises."

Jesus' Use of Parables
(Mark 4:33, 34)

34 Jesus used parables to tell all these things
to the crowds; he would not say a thing to
them without using a parable. 35 He did this
to make come true what the prophet had
said,

"I will use parables when I speak to them;
I will tell them things unknown since
the creation of the world."

Jesus Explains the Parable of the Weeds

36 When Jesus had left the crowd and gone
indoors, his disciples came to him and said,
"Tell us what the parable about the weeds in
the field means."

37 Jesus answered, "The man who sowed
the good seed is the Son of Man; 38 the field
is the world; the good seed is the people
who belong to the Kingdom; the weeds are
the people who belong to the Evil One;
39 and the enemy who sowed the weeds is
the Devil. The harvest is the end of the age,
and the harvest workers are angels. 40 Just as
the weeds are gathered up and burned in the
fire, so the same thing will happen at the end
of the age: 41 the Son of Man will send out
his angels to gather up out of his Kingdom
all those who cause people to sin and all
others who do evil things, 42 and they will
throw them into the fiery furnace, where
they will cry and gnash their teeth. 43 Then
God's people will shine like the sun in their
Father's Kingdom. Listen, then, if you have
ears!

The Parable of the Hidden Treasure

44 "The Kingdom of heaven is like this. A
man happens to find a treasure hidden in a
field. He covers it up again, and is so happy
that he goes and sells everything he has, and
then goes back and buys that field.

The Parable of the Pearl

45 "Also, the Kingdom of heaven is like
this. A man is looking for fine pearls, 46 and
when he finds one that is unusually fine, he
goes and sells everything he has, and buys
that pearl.

The Parable of the Net

47 "Also, the Kingdom of heaven is like
this. Some fishermen throw their net out in
the lake and catch all kinds of fish. 48 When
the net is full, they pull it to shore and sit
down to divide the fish: the good ones go
into the buckets, the worthless ones are
thrown away. 49 It will be like this at the end
of the age: the angels will go out and gather
up the evil people from among the good
50 and will throw them into the fiery furnace,
where they will cry and gnash their teeth.

New Truths and Old

51 "Do you understand these things?" Jesus
asked them.

"Yes," they answered.

52 So he replied, "This means, then, that
every teacher of the Law who becomes a
disciple in the Kingdom of heaven is like a
homeowner who takes new and old things
out of his storage room."

Jesus Is Rejected at Nazareth
(Mark 6:1–6; Luke 4:16–30)

53 When Jesus finished telling these para-
bles, he left that place 54 and went back to his
hometown. He taught in the synagogue, and

13:35 Ps 78:2

Are you willing to do whatever it takes to be part of the Kingdom of heaven?

those who heard him were amazed. "Where
did he get such wisdom?" they asked. "And
what about his miracles? 55Isn't he the car-
penter's son? Isn't Mary his mother, and
aren't James, Joseph, Simon, and Judas his
brothers? 56Aren't all his sisters living here?
Where did he get all this?" 57And so they
rejected him.

Jesus said to them, "A prophet is respected
everywhere except in his hometown and by
his own family." 58Because they did not have
faith, he did not perform many miracles
there.

The Death of John the Baptist
(Mark 6:14–29; Luke 9:7–9)

14 At that time Herod, the ruler of
Galilee, heard about Jesus. 2"He is
really John the Baptist, who has come back
to life," he told his officials. "That is why he
has this power to perform miracles."

3For Herod had earlier ordered John's
arrest, and he had him tied up and put in
prison. He had done this because of Hero-
dias, his brother Philip's wife. 4For some
time John the Baptist had told Herod, "It
isn't right for you to be married to Hero-
dias!" 5Herod wanted to kill him, but he was
afraid of the Jewish people, because they
considered John to be a prophet.

6On Herod's birthday the daughter of
Herodias danced in front of the whole
group. Herod was so pleased 7that he prom-
ised her, "I swear that I will give you any-
thing you ask for!"

8At her mother's suggestion she asked
him, "Give me here and now the head of
John the Baptist on a plate!"

9The king was sad, but because of the
promise he had made in front of all his
guests he gave orders that her wish be grant-
ed. 10So he had John beheaded in prison.
11The head was brought in on a plate and
given to the girl, who took it to her mother.
12John's disciples came, carried away his
body, and buried it; then they went and told
Jesus.

Study it!

Foreshadowing

The story of John the Baptist's death in the middle of Matthew's Gospel, gives us a preview of what will happen at the end of the Gospel. Consider the many parallels between the way John dies and what lies ahead for Jesus himself: John is arrested and treated as a criminal even though he has done nothing wrong (Matthew 14:3), just as Jesus will be. Herod gives in to pressure from others demanding John's death, just as Pilate will give in to the pressure from people who want Jesus sentenced to death. The word *foreshadow* is sometimes used to describe prophecies or events in the Bible that remind us of future events that occur in the life of Jesus.

— Matthew 14:1–12

Jesus Feeds Five Thousand
(Mark 6:30–44; Luke 9:10–17; John 6:1–14)

13When Jesus heard the news about John,
he left there in a boat and went to a lonely
place by himself. The people heard about it,
and so they left their towns and followed him
by land. 14Jesus got out of the boat, and when
he saw the large crowd, his heart was filled
with pity for them, and he healed their sick.

15That evening his disciples came to him
and said, "It is already very late, and this is a
lonely place. Send the people away and let
them go to the villages to buy food for
themselves."

16"They don't have to leave," answered
Jesus. "You yourselves give them something
to eat!"

17"All we have here are five loaves and
two fish," they replied.

13:57 Jn 4:44 **14:3,4** Lk 3:19,20 **14:4** Lev 18:16; 20:21

Live it!

Jesus Rules!

In the middle of the night, the wind was rising, and the waves tossed the boat. Jesus, who rules over fear, who rules over wind and waves, and who rules over chaos walks across the lake. When Peter decides to follow Jesus, his faith isn't quite strong enough. This story tells us these important lessons:

- **Jesus shares in the power of God.**
- **Jesus may challenge us, but he will also rescue us.**
- **Jesus rules!**

The next time you experience a storm in your life—like an argument with your parents or a disagreement with your friends—remember that Jesus is there with you!

— Matthew 14:22–33

18"Then bring them here to me," Jesus
said. 19He ordered the people to sit down on
the grass; then he took the five loaves and
the two fish, looked up to heaven, and gave
thanks to God. He broke the loaves and gave
them to the disciples, and the disciples gave
them to the people. 20Everyone ate and had
enough. Then the disciples took up twelve
baskets full of what was left over. 21The
number of men who ate was about five
thousand, not counting the women and children.

Jesus Walks on the Water
(Mark 6:45–52; John 6:15–21)

22Then Jesus made the disciples get into
the boat and go on ahead to the other side
of the lake, while he sent the people away.
23After sending the people away, he went up
a hill by himself to pray. When evening
came, Jesus was there alone; 24and by this
time the boat was far out in the lake, tossed
about by the waves, because the wind was
blowing against it.
25Between three and six o'clock in the
morning Jesus came to the disciples, walking
on the water. 26When they saw him walking
on the water, they were terrified. "It's a
ghost!" they said, and screamed with fear.
27Jesus spoke to them at once. "Courage!"
he said. "It is I. Don't be afraid!"
28Then Peter spoke up. "Lord, if it is really
you, order me to come out on the water to
you."
29"Come!" answered Jesus. So Peter got
out of the boat and started walking on the
water to Jesus. 30But when he noticed the
strong wind, he was afraid and started to sink
down in the water. "Save me, Lord!" he
cried.
31At once Jesus reached out and grabbed
hold of him and said, "What little faith you
have! Why did you doubt?"
32They both got into the boat, and the
wind died down. 33Then the disciples in the
boat worshiped Jesus. "Truly you are the Son
of God!" they exclaimed.

Jesus Heals the Sick in Gennesaret
(Mark 6:53–56)

34They crossed the lake and came to land
at Gennesaret, 35where the people recognized
Jesus. So they sent for the sick people
in all the surrounding country and brought
them to Jesus. 36They begged him to let the
sick at least touch the edge of his cloak; and
all who touched it were made well.

The Teaching of the Ancestors
(Mark 7:1–13)

15 Then some Pharisees and teachers of
the Law came from Jerusalem to
Jesus and asked him, 2"Why is it that your
disciples disobey the teaching handed down
by our ancestors? They don't wash their
hands in the proper way before they eat!"
3Jesus answered, "And why do you disobey
God's command and follow your own

teaching? 4For God said, 'Respect your
father and your mother,' and 'If you curse
your father or your mother, you are to be
put to death.' 5But you teach that if people
have something they could use to help their
father or mother, but say, 'This belongs to
God,' 6they do not need to honor their
father.[m] In this way you disregard God's
command, in order to follow your own
teaching. 7You hypocrites! How right Isaiah
was when he prophesied about you!

8'These people, says God, honor me with
their words,
but their heart is really far away from
me.
9It is no use for them to worship me,
because they teach human rules as
though they were my laws!'"

The Things That Make a Person Unclean

(Mark 7:14–23)

10Then Jesus called the crowd to him and
said to them, "Listen and understand! 11It is
not what goes into your mouth that makes
you ritually unclean; rather, what comes out
of it makes you unclean."
12Then the disciples came to him and
said, "Do you know that the Pharisees had
their feelings hurt by what you said?"

They are blind leaders of the blind. (15:14)

13"Every plant which my Father in heaven
did not plant will be pulled up," answered
Jesus. 14"Don't worry about them! They are
blind leaders of the blind; and when one blind
man leads another, both fall into a ditch."
15Peter spoke up, "Explain this saying
to us."
16Jesus said to them, "You are still no
more intelligent than the others. 17Don't you
understand? Anything that goes into your
mouth goes into your stomach and then on
out of your body. 18But the things that come
out of the mouth come from the heart, and
these are the things that make you ritually
unclean. 19For from your heart come the
evil ideas which lead you to kill, commit
adultery, and do other immoral things; to
rob, lie, and slander others. 20These are the
things that make you unclean. But to eat
without washing your hands as they say you
should—this doesn't make you unclean."

A Woman's Faith

(Mark 7:24–30)

21Jesus left that place and went off to the
territory near the cities of Tyre and Sidon. 22A
Canaanite woman who lived in that region
came to him. "Son of David!" she cried out.
"Have mercy on me, sir! My daughter has a
demon and is in a terrible condition."
23But Jesus did not say a word to her. His
disciples came to him and begged him,
"Send her away! She is following us and
making all this noise!"
24Then Jesus replied, "I have been sent
only to the lost sheep of the people of Israel."
25At this the woman came and fell at his
feet. "Help me, sir!" she said.
26Jesus answered, "It isn't right to take the
children's food and throw it to the dogs."
27"That's true, sir," she answered, "but
even the dogs eat the leftovers that fall from
their masters' table."
28So Jesus answered her, "You are a
woman of great faith! What you want will

[m] **15:6** their father; *some manuscripts have* their father or mother.

15:4 a Ex 20:12; Deut 5:16; **b** Ex 21:17; Lev 20:9 **15:8,9** Isa 29:13 (LXX) **15:14** Lk 6:39 **15:18** Mt 12:34

Water represents chaos. When Jesus walks on the water, it is a sign that he is divine because he rules over the chaos. Read Psalm 65:7.

Study it!

Feeding the Crowds

At the end of chapter 15, we have a second story about Jesus feeding a large crowd (the first story was in chapter 14). These miracle stories link Jesus with the past and the future. The way the story is told would remind the audience of two important people from the Old Testament: Elisha, and Moses. Elisha fed the people with almost nothing (2 Kings 4:42–44), and so does Jesus. Everyone eats, and there is food left.

We can find a similar story in Exodus, chapter 16. After crossing the Red Sea, God feeds the Israelites with manna—which is like bread—in the wilderness. In Matthew, chapter 14, Jesus crosses Lake Galilee and feeds the people with bread in a deserted place. These stories also foreshadow (see earlier article) the story of the Last Supper and hint at the heavenly banquet at the end of time.

— Matthew 15:32–39

be done for you." And at that very moment
her daughter was healed.

Jesus Heals Many People

29Jesus left there and went along by Lake
Galilee. He climbed a hill and sat down.
30Large crowds came to him, bringing with
them the lame, the blind, the crippled, the
dumb, and many other sick people, whom
they placed at Jesus' feet; and he healed
them. 31The people were amazed as they saw
the dumb speaking, the crippled made
whole, the lame walking, and the blind see-
ing; and they praised the God of Israel.

Jesus Feeds Four Thousand

(Mark 8:1–10)

32Jesus called his disciples to him and said,
"I feel sorry for these people, because they
have been with me for three days and now
have nothing to eat. I don't want to send
them away without feeding them, for they
might faint on their way home."
33The disciples asked him, "Where will
we find enough food in this desert to feed
this crowd?"
34"How much bread do you have?" Jesus
asked.
"Seven loaves," they answered, "and a few
small fish."
35So Jesus ordered the crowd to sit down
on the ground. 36Then he took the seven
loaves and the fish, gave thanks to God,
broke them, and gave them to the disciples;
and the disciples gave them to the people.
37They all ate and had enough. Then the
disciples took up seven baskets full of pieces
left over. 38The number of men who ate was
four thousand, not counting the women and
children.
39Then Jesus sent the people away, got
into a boat, and went to the territory of
Magadan.

The Demand for a Miracle

(Mark 8:11–13; Luke 12:54–56)

16 Some Pharisees and Sadducees who
came to Jesus wanted to trap him, so
they asked him to perform a miracle for
them, to show that God approved of him.
2But Jesus answered, "When the sun is set-
ting, you say, 'We are going to have fine
weather, because the sky is red.' 3And early
in the morning you say, 'It is going to rain,

16:1 Mt 12:38; Lk 11:16

"For if you want to save your own life, you will lose it; but if you lose your life for my sake, you will find it" *(Matthew 16:25)*.

Catholic Connections

Peter the Rock

Once again we read how the religious leaders do not believe in Jesus. In contrast, Peter says confidently, "You are the Messiah, the Son of the living God" (Matthew 16:16). Jesus affirms Peter's faith by telling Peter that he will have a special role in history. Peter's leadership will be the foundation of the Church. He will become the first pope.

This Scripture passage explains why Peter and all the popes that followed him are the spiritual leaders and highest authority of the Church.

Jesus gave Peter a special role as leader of the Apostles. That special role did not end with Peter but is passed on to every pope who followed Peter since the start of the Church.

— Matthew 16:13–20

because the sky is red and dark.' You can pre-
dict the weather by looking at the sky, but
you cannot interpret the signs concerning
these times![n] 4How evil and godless are the
people of this day! You ask me for a miracle?
No! The only miracle you will be given is
the miracle of Jonah."

So he left them and went away.

The Yeast of the Pharisees and Sadducees
(Mark 8:14–21)

5When the disciples crossed over to the
other side of the lake, they forgot to take any
bread. 6Jesus said to them, "Take care; be on
your guard against the yeast of the Pharisees
and Sadducees."

7They started discussing among them-
selves, "He says this because we didn't bring
any bread."

8Jesus knew what they were saying, so he
asked them, "Why are you discussing among
yourselves about not having any bread? What
little faith you have! 9Don't you understand
yet? Don't you remember when I broke the
five loaves for the five thousand men? How
many baskets did you fill? 10And what about
the seven loaves for the four thousand men?
How many baskets did you fill? 11How is it
that you don't understand that I was not
talking to you about bread? Guard your-
selves from the yeast of the Pharisees and
Sadducees!"

12Then the disciples understood that he
was not warning them to guard themselves
from the yeast used in bread but from the
teaching of the Pharisees and Sadducees.

Peter's Declaration about Jesus
(Mark 8:27–30; Luke 9:18–21)

13Jesus went to the territory near the town
of Caesarea Philippi, where he asked his disci-
ples, "Who do people say the Son of Man is?"

14"Some say John the Baptist," they
answered. "Others say Elijah, while others
say Jeremiah or some other prophet."

15"What about you?" he asked them.
"Who do you say I am?"

16Simon Peter answered, "You are the
Messiah, the Son of the living God."

17"Good for you, Simon son of John!"
answered Jesus. "For this truth did not come
to you from any human being, but it was
given to you directly by my Father in heav-
en. 18And so I tell you, Peter: you are a rock,
and on this rock foundation I will build my
church, and not even death will ever be able
to overcome it. 19I will give you the keys of

[n] **16:3** *Some manuscripts do not have the words of Jesus in verses 2-3.*

16:4 Mt 12:39; Lk 11:29 **16:6** Lk 12:1 **16:9** Mt 14:17-21 **16:10** Mt 15:34-38 **16:14** Mt 14:1,2; Mk 6:14,15; Lk 9:7,8 **16:16** Jn 6:68,69 **16:19** Mt 18:18; Jn 20:23

Pray it!

A Glimpse of Glory

"Jesus . . . led them up a high mountain where they were alone. As they looked on, a change came over Jesus: his face was shining like the sun, and his clothes were dazzling white" (Matthew 17:1–2).

Lord Jesus,
I need you to lead me up the mountain
because it is so easy for me to get discouraged.
Let me see your shining presence
because it is so easy for me to get distracted.
Help me focus on what your love requires of me
because it is so easy to want to keep things easy.
Lead me back down the mountain to everyday life
with you by my side
and help me do what God asks me to do in the world.

— Matthew 17:1–13

the Kingdom of heaven; what you prohibit
on earth will be prohibited in heaven, and
what you permit on earth will be permitted
in heaven."
20 Then Jesus ordered his disciples not to
tell anyone that he was the Messiah.

Jesus Speaks about His Suffering and Death
(Mark 8:31—9:1; Luke 9:22–27)

21 From that time on Jesus began to say
plainly to his disciples, "I must go to
Jerusalem and suffer much from the elders,
the chief priests, and the teachers of the Law.
I will be put to death, but three days later I
will be raised to life."
22 Peter took him aside and began to
rebuke him. "God forbid it, Lord!" he said.
"That must never happen to you!"
23 Jesus turned around and said to Peter,
"Get away from me, Satan! You are an obsta-
cle in my way, because these thoughts of
yours don't come from God, but from
human nature."
24 Then Jesus said to his disciples, "If any
of you want to come with me, you must for-
get yourself, carry your cross, and follow me.
25 For if you want to save your own life, you
will lose it; but if you lose your life for my
sake, you will find it. 26 Will you gain any-
thing if you win the whole world but lose
your life? Of course not! There is nothing
you can give to regain your life. 27 For the
Son of Man is about to come in the glory of
his Father with his angels, and then he will
reward each one according to his deeds. 28 I
assure you that there are some here who will
not die until they have seen the Son of Man
come as King."

The Transfiguration
(Mark 9:2–13; Luke 9:28–36)

17 Six days later Jesus took with him
Peter and the brothers James and
John and led them up a high mountain
where they were alone. 2 As they looked on,
a change came over Jesus: his face was shin-
ing like the sun, and his clothes were daz-
zling white. 3 Then the three disciples saw
Moses and Elijah talking with Jesus. 4 So

16:24 Mt 10:38; Lk 14:27 **16:25** Mt 10:39; Lk 17:33; Jn 12:25 **16:27** **a** Mt 25:31; **b** Ps 62:12; Rom 2:6

Peter spoke up and said to Jesus, "Lord, how
good it is that we are here! If you wish, I
will make three tents here, one for you, one
for Moses, and one for Elijah."
5 While he was talking, a shining cloud
came over them, and a voice from the cloud
said, "This is my own dear Son, with whom
I am pleased—listen to him!"
6 When the disciples heard the voice, they
were so terrified that they threw themselves
face downward on the ground. 7 Jesus came
to them and touched them. "Get up," he
said. "Don't be afraid!" 8 So they looked up
and saw no one there but Jesus.
9 As they came down the mountain, Jesus
ordered them, "Don't tell anyone about this
vision you have seen until the Son of Man
has been raised from death."
10 Then the disciples asked Jesus, "Why do
the teachers of the Law say that Elijah has to
come first?"
11 "Elijah is indeed coming first," answered
Jesus, "and he will get everything ready.
12 But I tell you that Elijah has already come
and people did not recognize him, but treat-
ed him just as they pleased. In the same way
they will also mistreat the Son of Man."
13 Then the disciples understood that he
was talking to them about John the Baptist.

Jesus Heals a Boy with a Demon
(Mark 9:14–29; Luke 9:37–43a)

14 When they returned to the crowd, a
man came to Jesus, knelt before him, 15 and
said, "Sir, have mercy on my son! He is an
epileptic and has such terrible attacks that he
often falls in the fire or into water. 16 I
brought him to your disciples, but they
could not heal him."
17 Jesus answered, "How unbelieving and
wrong you people are! How long must I stay
with you? How long do I have to put up
with you? Bring the boy here to me!"
18 Jesus gave a command to the demon, and
it went out of the boy, and at that very
moment he was healed.
19 Then the disciples came to Jesus in pri-
vate and asked him, "Why couldn't we drive
the demon out?"
20 "It was because you do not have
enough faith," answered Jesus. "I assure you
that if you have faith as big as a mustard
seed, you can say to this hill, 'Go from here
to there!' and it will go. You could do any-
thing!"[o]

Jesus Speaks Again about His Death
(Mark 9:30–32; Luke 9:43b–45)

22 When the disciples all came together in
Galilee, Jesus said to them, "The Son of Man
is about to be handed over to those 23 who
will kill him; but three days later he will be
raised to life."
The disciples became very sad.

Payment of the Temple Tax

24 When Jesus and his disciples came to
Capernaum, the collectors of the Temple tax
came to Peter and asked, "Does your teacher
pay the Temple tax?"
25 "Of course," Peter answered.
When Peter went into the house, Jesus
spoke up first, "Simon, what is your opinion?
Who pays duties or taxes to the kings of this
world? The citizens of the country or the
foreigners?"
26 "The foreigners," answered Peter.
"Well, then," replied Jesus, "that means
that the citizens don't have to pay. 27 But we
don't want to offend these people. So go to
the lake and drop in a line. Pull up the first
fish you hook, and in its mouth you will find
a coin worth enough for my Temple tax and
yours. Take it and pay them our taxes."

[o] **17:20** *Some manuscripts add verse 21:* But only prayer and fasting can drive this kind out; nothing else can *(see Mk 9:29).*

17:5 a Gen 22:2; Ps 2:7; Isa 42:1; Mt 3:17; 12:18; Mk 1:11; Lk 3:22; **b** Deut 18:15 **17:1–5** 2 Pet 1:17,18 **17:10** Mal 4:5 **17:11** Sir 48:10 **17:12** Mt 11:14 **17:20** Mt 21:21; Mk 11:23; 1 Cor 13:2 **17:24** Ex 30:13; 38:26

What do Moses and Elijah have in common? Unscramble the letters "sperothp" to find a word that completes this sentence: "They are both __________."

Who Is the Greatest?
(Mark 9:33–37; Luke 9:46–48)

18 At that time the disciples came to
Jesus, asking, "Who is the greatest in
the Kingdom of heaven?"
2So Jesus called a child to come and stand
in front of them, 3and said, "I assure you
that unless you change and become like
children, you will never enter the Kingdom
of heaven. 4The greatest in the Kingdom of
heaven is the one who humbles himself and
becomes like this child. 5And whoever wel-
comes in my name one such child as this,
welcomes me.

"Unless you change and become like children . . ." (18:3)

Temptations to Sin
(Mark 9:42–48; Luke 17:1, 2)

6"If anyone should cause one of these little
ones to lose his faith in me, it would be bet-
ter for that person to have a large millstone
tied around his neck and be drowned in the
deep sea. 7How terrible for the world that
there are things that make people lose their
faith! Such things will always happen—but
how terrible for the one who causes them!
8"If your hand or your foot makes you
lose your faith, cut it off and throw it away! It
is better for you to enter life without a hand
or a foot than to keep both hands and both
feet and be thrown into the eternal fire. 9And
if your eye makes you lose your faith, take it
out and throw it away! It is better for you to
enter life with only one eye than to keep
both eyes and be thrown into the fire of hell.

The Parable of the Lost Sheep
(Luke 15:3–7)

10"See that you don't despise any of these
little ones. Their angels in heaven, I tell you,
are always in the presence of my Father in
heaven.p
12"What do you think a man does who has
one hundred sheep and one of them gets lost?
He will leave the other ninety-nine grazing
on the hillside and go and look for the lost
sheep. 13When he finds it, I tell you, he feels
far happier over this one sheep than over the
ninety-nine that did not get lost. 14In just the

Live it!

When You Are Lost

Isn't it great to know that we have a God who will search for us? The parable of the lost sheep (Matthew 18:10–14) reminds us that God seeks us out even when we have wandered off. When we sin, Jesus the good shepherd comes to find us. We just have to open our hearts and let him in.

This story has a second message: Christians have a responsibility to other people. We should live our lives so that we do not lead others astray. And when a friend, family member, or even a stranger has lost his or her way, it is our responsibility to go and bring them back to God if we can.

— Matthew 18:10–14

p **18:10** *Some manuscripts add verse 11:* For the Son of Man came to save the lost *(see Lk 19:10).*

18:1 Lk 22:24 **18:3** Mk 10:15; Lk 18:17 **18:8** Mt 5:30 **18:9** Mt 5:29 **18:10** Tob 12:15 **18:11** Lk 19:10

Matthew 18:15–17 gives great advice for solving a problem. Would it work for you?

He will go . . . and look for the lost sheep. (18:12)

same way your[q] Father in heaven does not
want any of these little ones to be lost.

When Someone Sins

15"If your brother sins against you,[r] go to
him and show him his fault. But do it pri-
vately, just between yourselves. If he listens
to you, you have won your brother back.
16But if he will not listen to you, take one or
two other persons with you, so that 'every
accusation may be upheld by the testimony
of two or more witnesses,' as the scripture
says. 17And if he will not listen to them, then
tell the whole thing to the church. Finally, if
he will not listen to the church, treat him as
though he were a pagan or a tax collector.

Prohibiting and Permitting

18"And so I tell all of you: what you pro-
hibit on earth will be prohibited in heaven,
and what you permit on earth will be per-
mitted in heaven.

19"And I tell you more: whenever two of
you on earth agree about anything you pray
for, it will be done for you by my Father in
heaven. 20For where two or three come
together in my name, I am there with them."

The Parable of the Unforgiving Servant

21Then Peter came to Jesus and asked,
"Lord, if my brother keeps on sinning
against me, how many times do I have to
forgive him? Seven times?"

22"No, not seven times," answered Jesus,
"but seventy times seven,[s] 23because the
Kingdom of heaven is like this. Once there
was a king who decided to check on his ser-
vants' accounts. 24He had just begun to do
so when one of them was brought in who
owed him millions of dollars. 25The servant
did not have enough to pay his debt, so the
king ordered him to be sold as a slave, with
his wife and his children and all that he had,
in order to pay the debt. 26The servant fell
on his knees before the king. 'Be patient
with me,' he begged, 'and I will pay you
everything!' 27The king felt sorry for him, so
he forgave him the debt and let him go.

28"Then the man went out and met one
of his fellow servants who owed him a few
dollars. He grabbed him and started choking

Live it!

Forgive, Forgive, Then Forgive Again!

In response to Peter's question, "How many times do I have to forgive?" (Matthew 18:21), Jesus tells the parable of the unforgiving servant. This story is a way of saying "You're asking the wrong question Peter!" It's not about how many times you have to forgive someone. It's about being a person of forgiveness, having an attitude of mercy. Is it hard to forgive other people? How can you become a more forgiving person? Remember God's love and mercy for you. Then the next time someone needs your forgiveness, it might not be so hard to forgive that person.

— Matthew 18:21–35

[q] **18:14** your; *some manuscripts have* my. [r] **18:15** *Some manuscripts do not have* against you. [s] **18:22** seventy times seven; *or* seventy-seven times.

18:15 Lk 17:3 **18:16** Deut 19:15 **18:18** Mt 16:19; Jn 20:23 **18:21,22** Lk 17:3,4 **18:22** Gen 4:24

Live it!

Truly Free

As you read this chapter, you might find that the way Jesus describes the Kingdom of heaven can seem confusing! Do not marry for the sake of the Kingdom . . . be like a child . . . sell everything you have and follow me . . . the last shall be first. In our culture these ideas can seem crazy! We like power and prestige; a little child does not have these. We like to own things; giving away our money seems so strange! We like being in first place over almost anything else; choosing to be last is just weird.

Jesus' ideas can seem to make no sense at all—unless you are willing to put your full trust in Jesus, unless you are willing to listen to our saints. Their lives show us that if we can let go of our attachments to things, power, money, and position, then we will be truly free, and we will experience the Kingdom of heaven right now!

— Matthew, chapter 19

him. 'Pay back what you owe me!' he said.
29His fellow servant fell down and begged
him, 'Be patient with me, and I will pay you
back!' 30But he refused; instead, he had him
thrown into jail until he should pay the
debt. 31When the other servants saw what
had happened, they were very upset and
went to the king and told him everything.
32So he called the servant in. 'You worthless
slave!' he said. 'I forgave you the whole
amount you owed me, just because you
asked me to. 33You should have had mercy
on your fellow servant, just as I had mercy
on you.' 34The king was very angry, and he
sent the servant to jail to be punished until
he should pay back the whole amount."
35And Jesus concluded, "That is how my
Father in heaven will treat every one of you
unless you forgive your brother from your
heart."

Jesus Teaches about Divorce
(Mark 10:1–12)

19 When Jesus finished saying these
things, he left Galilee and went to
the territory of Judea on the other side of
the Jordan River. 2Large crowds followed
him, and he healed them there.
3Some Pharisees came to him and tried to
trap him by asking, "Does our Law allow a
man to divorce his wife for whatever reason
he wishes?"
4Jesus answered, "Haven't you read the
scripture that says that in the beginning the
Creator made people male and female? 5And
God said, 'For this reason a man will leave
his father and mother and unite with his
wife, and the two will become one.' 6So they
are no longer two, but one. No human being
must separate, then, what God has joined
together."
7The Pharisees asked him, "Why, then, did
Moses give the law for a man to hand his
wife a divorce notice and send her away?"
8Jesus answered, "Moses gave you permis-
sion to divorce your wives because you are
so hard to teach. But it was not like that at
the time of creation. 9I tell you, then, that
any man who divorces his wife for any cause
other than her unfaithfulness, commits adul-
tery if he marries some other woman."
10His disciples said to him, "If this is how
it is between a man and his wife, it is better
not to marry."
11Jesus answered, "This teaching does not
apply to everyone, but only to those to
whom God has given it. 12For there are dif-
ferent reasons why men cannot marry: some,
because they were born that way; others,
because men made them that way; and oth-
ers do not marry for the sake of the King-
dom of heaven. Let him who can accept this
teaching do so."

19:4 Gen 1:27; 5:2 **19:5** Gen 2:24 **19:7** Deut 24:1–4; Mt 5:31 **19:9** Mt 5:32; 1 Cor 7:10,11

Jesus Blesses Little Children
(Mark 10:13–16; Luke 18:15–17)

13 Some people brought children to Jesus
for him to place his hands on them and to
pray for them, but the disciples scolded the
people. 14 Jesus said, "Let the children come to
me and do not stop them, because the King-
dom of heaven belongs to such as these."
15 He placed his hands on them and then
went away.

The Rich Young Man
(Mark 10:17–31; Luke 18:18–30)

16 Once a man came to Jesus. "Teacher," he
asked, "what good thing must I do to receive
eternal life?"
17 "Why do you ask me concerning what
is good?" answered Jesus. "There is only One
who is good. Keep the commandments if
you want to enter life."
18 "What commandments?" he asked.
Jesus answered, "Do not commit murder;
do not commit adultery; do not steal; do not
accuse anyone falsely; 19 respect your father
and your mother; and love your neighbor as
you love yourself."
20 "I have obeyed all these command-
ments," the young man replied. "What else
do I need to do?"
21 Jesus said to him, "If you want to be
perfect, go and sell all you have and give the
money to the poor, and you will have riches
in heaven; then come and follow me."
22 When the young man heard this, he
went away sad, because he was very rich.
23 Jesus then said to his disciples, "I assure
you: it will be very hard for rich people to
enter the Kingdom of heaven. 24 I repeat: it is
much harder for a rich person to enter the
Kingdom of God than for a camel to go
through the eye of a needle."
25 When the disciples heard this, they were
completely amazed. "Who, then, can be
saved?" they asked.
26 Jesus looked straight at them and
answered, "This is impossible for human
beings, but for God everything is possible."
27 Then Peter spoke up. "Look," he said,
"we have left everything and followed you.
What will we have?"
28 Jesus said to them, "You can be sure that
when the Son of Man sits on his glorious
throne in the New Age, then you twelve fol-
lowers of mine will also sit on thrones, to
rule the twelve tribes of Israel. 29 And every-
one who has left houses or brothers or sisters
or father or mother or children or fields for
my sake, will receive a hundred times more
and will be given eternal life. 30 But many
who now are first will be last, and many
who now are last will be first.

The Workers in the Vineyard

20 "The Kingdom of heaven is like
this. Once there was a man who
went out early in the morning to hire some
men to work in his vineyard. 2 He agreed to
pay them the regular wage, a silver coin a
day, and sent them to work in his vineyard.
3 He went out again to the marketplace at
nine o'clock and saw some men standing
there doing nothing, 4 so he told them, 'You
also go and work in the vineyard, and I will
pay you a fair wage.' 5 So they went. Then at
twelve o'clock and again at three o'clock
he did the same thing. 6 It was nearly five
o'clock when he went to the marketplace
and saw some other men still standing there.
'Why are you wasting the whole day here
doing nothing?' he asked them. 7 'No one
hired us,' they answered. 'Well, then, you go
and work in the vineyard,' he told them.
8 "When evening came, the owner told his
foreman, 'Call the workers and pay them
their wages, starting with those who were
hired last and ending with those who were
hired first.' 9 The men who had begun to
work at five o'clock were paid a silver coin

19:18 **a** Ex 20:13; Deut 5:17; **b** Ex 20:14; Deut 5:18; **c** Ex 20:15; Deut 5:19; **d** Ex 20:16; Deut 5:20
19:19 **a** Ex 20:12; Deut 5:16; **b** Lev 19:18 **19:28** **a** Mt 25:31; **b** Lk 22:30 **19:30** Mt 20:16; Lk 13:30
20:8 Lev 19:13; Deut 24:15

In Jesus' time women had almost no rights. Can you find where Jesus tells husbands to fulfill their responsibilities to their wives?

each. 10 So when the men who were the first to be hired came to be paid, they thought they would get more; but they too were given a silver coin each. 11 They took their money and started grumbling against the employer. 12 'These men who were hired last worked only one hour,' they said, 'while we put up with a whole day's work in the hot sun—yet you paid them the same as you paid us!' 13 'Listen, friend,' the owner answered one of them, 'I have not cheated you. After all, you agreed to do a day's work for one silver coin. 14 Now take your pay and go home. I want to give this man who was hired last as much as I gave you. 15 Don't I have the right to do as I wish with my own money? Or are you jealous because I am generous?' "

16 And Jesus concluded, "So those who are last will be first, and those who are first will be last."

Jesus Speaks a Third Time about His Death
(Mark 10:32–34; Luke 18:31–34)

17 As Jesus was going up to Jerusalem, he took the twelve disciples aside and spoke to them privately, as they walked along. 18 "Listen," he told them, "we are going up to Jerusalem, where the Son of Man will be handed over to the chief priests and the teachers of the Law. They will condemn him to death 19 and then hand him over to the Gentiles, who will make fun of him, whip him, and crucify him; but three days later he will be raised to life."

A Mother's Request
(Mark 10:35–45)

20 Then the wife of Zebedee came to Jesus with her two sons, bowed before him, and asked him for a favor.

21 "What do you want?" Jesus asked her.

She answered, "Promise me that these two sons of mine will sit at your right and your left when you are King."

22 "You don't know what you are asking for," Jesus answered the sons. "Can you drink the cup of suffering that I am about to drink?"

"We can," they answered.

23 "You will indeed drink from my cup," Jesus told them, "but I do not have the right to choose who will sit at my right and my left. These places belong to those for whom my Father has prepared them."

24 When the other ten disciples heard about this, they became angry with the two brothers. 25 So Jesus called them all together and said, "You know that the rulers of the heathen have power over them, and the leaders have complete authority. 26 This, however, is not the way it shall be among you. If one of you wants to be great, you must be the servant of the rest; 27 and if one of you wants to be first, you must be the slave of the others— 28 like the Son of Man, who did not come to be served, but to serve and to give his life to redeem many people."

Jesus Heals Two Blind Men
(Mark 10:46–52; Luke 18:35–43)

29 As Jesus and his disciples were leaving Jericho, a large crowd was following. 30 Two blind men who were sitting by the road heard that Jesus was passing by, so they began to shout, "Son of David! Have mercy on us, sir!"

31 The crowd scolded them and told them to be quiet. But they shouted even more loudly, "Son of David! Have mercy on us, sir!"

32 Jesus stopped and called them. "What do you want me to do for you?" he asked them.

33 "Sir," they answered, "we want you to give us our sight!"

34 Jesus had pity on them and touched their eyes; at once they were able to see, and they followed him.

20:16 Mt 19:30; Mk 10:31; Lk 13:30 **20:25,26** Lk 22:25,26 **20:26,27** Mt 23:11; Mk 9:35; Lk 22:26

The roads of Jesus' time were dirty from travelers and animal wastes. This explains why people would cover it up with palm branches!

Pray it!

Defending Poor People

Jesus has been telling his disciples that he needs to go to Jerusalem. Jerusalem is the political and religious center of Jesus' people. People from all over travel to Jerusalem to offer their sacrifices to God at the Temple. Jesus knew he had to share God's message in that great city.

By now Jesus is so famous that people greet him like a triumphant king. So what is the very first thing that Jesus does? He turns over the tables of the people who sell animals and change money in the Temple. He is angry with them because they are making money unfairly off poor people, and they are doing so in a holy place. Jesus spends so much of his ministry caring for those who have been overlooked or mistreated. Sick and poor people come first for Jesus.

Lord, you showed great care for people that others overlooked.
Help me always be aware of those in need.
Give me the courage to speak out for the people to whom no one else listens.

— Matthew 21:1–17

The Triumphant Entry into Jerusalem
(Mark 11:1–11; Luke 19:28–40; John 12:12–19)

21 As Jesus and his disciples approached
Jerusalem, they came to Bethphage
at the Mount of Olives. There Jesus sent two
of the disciples on ahead 2 with these instruc-
tions: "Go to the village there ahead of you,
and at once you will find a donkey tied up
with her colt beside her. Untie them and
bring them to me. 3 And if anyone says any-
thing, tell him, 'The Master[t] needs them';
and then he will let them go at once."
4 This happened in order to make come
true what the prophet had said:

5 "Tell the city of Zion,
Look, your king is coming to you!
He is humble and rides on a donkey
and on a colt, the foal of a donkey."

6 So the disciples went and did what Jesus
had told them to do: 7 they brought the don-
key and the colt, threw their cloaks over
them, and Jesus got on. 8 A large crowd of
people spread their cloaks on the road while
others cut branches from the trees and spread
them on the road. 9 The crowds walking in

"God bless him who comes in the name of the Lord!" (21:9)

front of Jesus and those walking behind
began to shout, "Praise to David's Son! God
bless him who comes in the name of the
Lord! Praise be to God!"

[t] **21:3** The Master; *or* Their owner.
21:5 Zech 9:9 **21:9** Ps 118:25,26

10 When Jesus entered Jerusalem, the
whole city was thrown into an uproar. "Who
is he?" the people asked.
11 "This is the prophet Jesus, from
Nazareth in Galilee," the crowds answered.

Jesus Goes to the Temple
(Mark 11:15–19; Luke 19:45–48;
John 2:13–22)

12 Jesus went into the Temple and drove
out all those who were buying and selling
there. He overturned the tables of the mon-
eychangers and the stools of those who sold
pigeons, 13 and said to them, "It is written in
the Scriptures that God said, 'My Temple
will be called a house of prayer.' But you are
making it a hideout for thieves!"
14 The blind and the crippled came to him
in the Temple, and he healed them. 15 The
chief priests and the teachers of the Law
became angry when they saw the wonderful
things he was doing and the children shout-
ing in the Temple, "Praise to David's Son!"
16 So they asked Jesus, "Do you hear what
they are saying?"
"Indeed I do," answered Jesus. "Haven't you
ever read this scripture? 'You have trained
children and babies to offer perfect praise.' "
17 Jesus left them and went out of the city
to Bethany, where he spent the night.

Jesus Curses the Fig Tree
(Mark 11:12–14, 20–24)

18 On his way back to the city early next
morning, Jesus was hungry. 19 He saw a fig
tree by the side of the road and went to it,
but found nothing on it except leaves. So he
said to the tree, "You will never again bear
fruit!" At once the fig tree dried up.
20 The disciples saw this and were astound-
ed. "How did the fig tree dry up so quickly?"
they asked.
21 Jesus answered, "I assure you that if you
believe and do not doubt, you will be able to
do what I have done to this fig tree. And not
only this, but you will even be able to say to
this hill, 'Get up and throw yourself in the
sea,' and it will. 22 If you believe, you will
receive whatever you ask for in prayer."

The Question about Jesus' Authority
(Mark 11:27–33; Luke 20:1–8)

23 Jesus came back to the Temple; and as he
taught, the chief priests and the elders came
to him and asked, "What right do you have to
do these things? Who gave you such right?"
24 Jesus answered them, "I will ask you just
one question, and if you give me an answer,
I will tell you what right I have to do these
things. 25 Where did John's right to baptize
come from: was it from God or from human
beings?"
They started to argue among themselves,
"What shall we say? If we answer, 'From
God,' he will say to us, 'Why, then, did you
not believe John?' 26 But if we say, 'From
human beings,' we are afraid of what the
people might do, because they are all con-
vinced that John was a prophet." 27 So they
answered Jesus, "We don't know."
And he said to them, "Neither will I tell
you, then, by what right I do these things.

The Parable of the Two Sons

28 "Now, what do you think? There was
once a man who had two sons. He went to
the older one and said, 'Son, go and work in
the vineyard today.' 29 'I don't want to,' he
answered, but later he changed his mind and
went. 30 Then the father went to the other
son and said the same thing. 'Yes, sir,' he
answered, but he did not go. 31 Which one of
the two did what his father wanted?"
"The older one," they answered.
So Jesus said to them, "I tell you: the tax
collectors and the prostitutes are going into
the Kingdom of God ahead of you. 32 For
John the Baptist came to you showing you
the right path to take, and you would not
believe him; but the tax collectors and the
prostitutes believed him. Even when you saw
this, you did not later change your minds
and believe him.

21:13 Isa 56:7; Jer 7:11 **21:16** Ps 8:2 (LXX) **21:21** Mt 17:20; 1 Cor 13:2 **21:32** Lk 3:12; 7:29,30

The Parable of the Tenants in the Vineyard

(Mark 12:1–12; Luke 20:9–19)

33“Listen to another parable,” Jesus said.
“There was once a landowner who planted
a vineyard, put a fence around it, dug a hole
for the wine press, and built a watchtower.
Then he rented the vineyard to tenants and
left home on a trip. 34When the time came
to gather the grapes, he sent his slaves to
the tenants to receive his share of the har-
vest. 35The tenants grabbed his slaves, beat
one, killed another, and stoned another.
36Again the man sent other slaves, more
than the first time, and the tenants treated
them the same way. 37Last of all he sent his
son to them. ‘Surely they will respect my
son,’ he said. 38But when the tenants saw
the son, they said to themselves, ‘This is the
owner's son. Come on, let's kill him, and we
will get his property!’ 39So they grabbed
him, threw him out of the vineyard, and
killed him.

40“Now, when the owner of the vineyard
comes, what will he do to those tenants?”
Jesus asked.

41“He will certainly kill those evil men,”
they answered, “and rent the vineyard out to
other tenants, who will give him his share of
the harvest at the right time.”

42Jesus said to them, “Haven't you ever
read what the Scriptures say?

‘The stone which the builders rejected as worthless
turned out to be the most important of all.
This was done by the Lord;
what a wonderful sight it is!’

43“And so I tell you,” added Jesus, “the
Kingdom of God will be taken away from
you and given to a people who will produce
the proper fruits.”[u]

45The chief priests and the Pharisees
heard Jesus' parables and knew that he was
talking about them, 46so they tried to arrest
him. But they were afraid of the crowds,
who considered Jesus to be a prophet.

The Parable of the Wedding Feast

(Luke 14:15–24)

22 Jesus again used parables in talking
to the people. 2“The Kingdom of
heaven is like this. Once there was a king
who prepared a wedding feast for his son.
3He sent his servants to tell the invited
guests to come to the feast, but they did not
want to come. 4So he sent other servants
with this message for the guests: ‘My feast is
ready now; my steers and prize calves have
been butchered, and everything is ready.
Come to the wedding feast!’ 5But the invit-
ed guests paid no attention and went about
their business: one went to his farm, another
to his store, 6while others grabbed the ser-
vants, beat them, and killed them. 7The king
was very angry; so he sent his soldiers, who
killed those murderers and burned down
their city. 8Then he called his servants and
said to them, ‘My wedding feast is ready, but
the people I invited did not deserve it.
9Now go to the main streets and invite to
the feast as many people as you find.’ 10So
the servants went out into the streets and
gathered all the people they could find, good
and bad alike; and the wedding hall was
filled with people.

11“The king went in to look at the guests
and saw a man who was not wearing wed-
ding clothes. 12‘Friend, how did you get in
here without wedding clothes?’ the king
asked him. But the man said nothing. 13Then
the king told the servants, ‘Tie him up hand
and foot, and throw him outside in the dark.
There he will cry and gnash his teeth.’ ”

14And Jesus concluded, “Many are invited,
but few are chosen.”

[u] **21:43** *Some manuscripts add verse 44:* Whoever falls on this stone will be cut to pieces; and if the stone falls on someone, it will crush him to dust *(see Lk 20:18).*

21:33 Isa 5:1,2 **21:42** Ps 118:22,23 **22:13** Mt 8:12; 25:30; Lk 13:28

Are you more like the older son or the younger son in the parable of the two sons?

The Question about Paying Taxes
(Mark 12:13–17; Luke 20:20–26)

15 The Pharisees went off and made a plan
to trap Jesus with questions. 16 Then they
sent to him some of their disciples and some
members of Herod's party. "Teacher," they
said, "we know that you tell the truth. You
teach the truth about God's will for people,
without worrying about what others think,
because you pay no attention to anyone's
status. 17 Tell us, then, what do you think? Is
it against our Law to pay taxes to the
Roman Emperor, or not?"
18 Jesus, however, was aware of their evil
plan, and so he said, "You hypocrites! Why
are you trying to trap me? 19 Show me the
coin for paying the tax!"
They brought him the coin, 20 and he asked
them, "Whose face and name are these?"
21 "The Emperor's," they answered.
So Jesus said to them, "Well, then, pay to
the Emperor what belongs to the Emperor,
and pay to God what belongs to God."
22 When they heard this, they were
amazed; and they left him and went away.

The Question about Rising from Death
(Mark 12:18–27; Luke 20:27–40)

23 That same day some Sadducees came to
Jesus and claimed that people will not rise
from death. 24 "Teacher," they said, "Moses said
that if a man who has no children dies, his
brother must marry the widow so that they
can have children who will be considered the
dead man's children. 25 Now, there were seven
brothers who used to live here. The oldest got
married and died without having children, so
he left his widow to his brother. 26 The same
thing happened to the second brother, to the
third, and finally to all seven. 27 Last of all, the
woman died. 28 Now, on the day when the
dead rise to life, whose wife will she be? All of
them had married her."
29 Jesus answered them, "How wrong you
are! It is because you don't know the Scrip-

Live it!

Loving God Full Blast

"Love God with everything you've got!"

In Matthew 22:34–40 the religious leaders try to trap Jesus again with a question that they thought had no right answer. For these religious leaders, all the commandments or laws were equally important. But Jesus avoids the trap by talking about love instead of laws.

How would your life be different if you loved God full blast? With the volume turned all the way up? The second part of Jesus' answer is connected to the first part of his answer. If we truly love God, then we show it by loving the people around us—friends *and* enemies!

— Matthew 22:34–40

tures or God's power. 30 For when the dead
rise to life, they will be like the angels in
heaven and will not marry. 31 Now, as for the
dead rising to life: haven't you ever read
what God has told you? He said, 32 'I am the
God of Abraham, the God of Isaac, and the
God of Jacob.' He is the God of the living,
not of the dead."
33 When the crowds heard this, they were
amazed at his teaching.

The Great Commandment
(Mark 12:28–34; Luke 10:25–28)

34 When the Pharisees heard that Jesus had
silenced the Sadducees, they came together,
35 and one of them, a teacher of the Law, tried

22:23 Acts 23:8 **22:24** Deut 25:5 **22:30** Wis 5:5 **22:32** Ex 3:6

"Love the Lord your God with all your heart, with all your soul, and with all your mind" *(Matthew 22:37)*.

to trap him with a question. [36]"Teacher," he
asked, "which is the greatest commandment
in the Law?"

[37]Jesus answered, " 'Love the Lord your
God with all your heart, with all your soul,
and with all your mind.' [38]This is the great-
est and the most important commandment.
[39]The second most important command-
ment is like it: 'Love your neighbor as you
love yourself.' [40]The whole Law of Moses
and the teachings of the prophets depend on
these two commandments."

The Question about the Messiah
(Mark 12:35–37; Luke 20:41–44)

[41]When some Pharisees gathered together,
Jesus asked them, [42]"What do you think
about the Messiah? Whose descendant is he?"

"He is David's descendant," they answered.

[43]"Why, then," Jesus asked, "did the Spirit
inspire David to call him 'Lord'? David said,
[44]'The Lord said to my Lord:
Sit here at my right side
until I put your enemies under your
feet.'
[45]If, then, David called him 'Lord,' how can
the Messiah be David's descendant?"

[46]No one was able to give Jesus any
answer, and from that day on no one dared
to ask him any more questions.

Jesus Warns against the Teachers of the Law and the Pharisees
(Mark 12:38, 39; Luke 11:43, 46; 20:45, 46)

23 Then Jesus spoke to the crowds and
to his disciples. [2]"The teachers of
the Law and the Pharisees are the authorized
interpreters of Moses' Law. [3]So you must
obey and follow everything they tell you to
do; do not, however, imitate their actions,
because they don't practice what they
preach. [4]They tie onto people's backs loads
that are heavy and hard to carry, yet they
aren't willing even to lift a finger to help
them carry those loads. [5]They do everything

They aren't willing even to lift a finger to help them.
(23:4)

so that people will see them. Look at the
straps with scripture verses on them which
they wear on their foreheads and arms, and
notice how large they are! Notice also how
long are the tassels on their cloaks![v] [6]They
love the best places at feasts and the reserved
seats in the synagogues; [7]they love to be
greeted with respect in the marketplaces and
to have people call them 'Teacher.' [8]You
must not be called 'Teacher,' because you are
all equal and have only one Teacher. [9]And
you must not call anyone here on earth
'Father,' because you have only the one
Father in heaven. [10]Nor should you be called
'Leader,' because your one and only leader is
the Messiah. [11]The greatest one among you
must be your servant. [12]Whoever makes
himself great will be humbled, and whoever
humbles himself will be made great.

Jesus Condemns Their Hypocrisy
(Mark 12:40; Luke 11:39–42, 44, 52; 20:47)

[13]"How terrible for you, teachers of the
Law and Pharisees! You hypocrites! You lock
the door to the Kingdom of heaven in peo-
ple's faces, but you yourselves don't go in,
nor do you allow in those who are trying to
enter![w]

[v] **23:5** TASSELS ON THEIR CLOAKS: *These tassels were worn as a sign of devotion to God (see Num 15:37–41).*
[w] **23:13** *Some manuscripts add verse 14:* How terrible for you, teachers of the Law and Pharisees! You hypocrites! You take advantage of widows and rob them of their homes, and then make a show of saying long prayers! Because of this your punishment will be all the worse! *(see Mk 12:40).*

22:37 Deut 6:5 **22:39** Lev 19:18 **22:35-40** Lk 10:25-28 **22:44** Ps 110:1 **23:5** **a** Mt 6:1; **b** Deut 6:8; **c** Num 15:38 **23:11** Mt 20:26,27; Mk 9:35; 10:43,44; Lk 22:26 **23:12** Lk 14:11; 18:14

How terrible for you, teachers of the Law! (23:15)

15“How terrible for you, teachers of the
Law and Pharisees! You hypocrites! You sail
the seas and cross whole countries to win
one convert; and when you succeed, you
make him twice as deserving of going to
hell as you yourselves are!
16“How terrible for you, blind guides! You
teach, ‘If someone swears by the Temple, he
isn’t bound by his vow; but if he swears by the
gold in the Temple, he is bound.’ 17Blind fools!
Which is more important, the gold or the
Temple which makes the gold holy? 18You
also teach, ‘If someone swears by the altar, he
isn’t bound by his vow; but if he swears by the
gift on the altar, he is bound.’ 19How blind
you are! Which is the more important, the gift
or the altar which makes the gift holy? 20So
then, when a person swears by the altar, he is
swearing by it and by all the gifts on it; 21and
when he swears by the Temple, he is swearing
by it and by God, who lives there; 22and when
someone swears by heaven, he is swearing by
God’s throne and by him who sits on it.
23“How terrible for you, teachers of the
Law and Pharisees! You hypocrites! You give
to God one tenth even of the seasoning
herbs, such as mint, dill, and cumin, but you
neglect to obey the really important teach-
ings of the Law, such as justice and mercy
and honesty. These you should practice,
without neglecting the others. 24Blind
guides! You strain a fly out of your drink,
but swallow a camel!
25“How terrible for you, teachers of the
Law and Pharisees! You hypocrites! You clean
the outside of your cup and plate, while the
inside is full of what you have gotten by vio-
lence and selfishness. 26Blind Pharisee! Clean
what is inside the cup first, and then the
outside will be clean too!
27“How terrible for you, teachers of the
Law and Pharisees! You hypocrites! You are
like whitewashed tombs, which look fine on
the outside but are full of bones and decaying
corpses on the inside. 28In the same way, on
the outside you appear good to everybody,
but inside you are full of hypocrisy and sins.

Jesus Predicts Their Punishment
(Luke 11:47–51)

29“How terrible for you, teachers of the
Law and Pharisees! You hypocrites! You
make fine tombs for the prophets and deco-
rate the monuments of those who lived
good lives; 30and you claim that if you had
lived during the time of your ancestors, you
would not have done what they did and
killed the prophets. 31So you actually admit
that you are the descendants of those who
murdered the prophets! 32Go on, then, and
finish up what your ancestors started! 33You
snakes and children of snakes! How do you
expect to escape from being condemned to
hell? 34And so I tell you that I will send you
prophets and wise men and teachers; you
will kill some of them, crucify others, and
whip others in the synagogues and chase
them from town to town. 35As a result, the
punishment for the murder of all innocent
people will fall on you, from the murder of
innocent Abel to the murder of Zechariah
son of Berechiah, whom you murdered
between the Temple and the altar. 36I tell
you indeed: the punishment for all these
murders will fall on the people of this day!

Jesus’ Love for Jerusalem
(Luke 13:34, 35)

37“Jerusalem, Jerusalem! You kill the
prophets and stone the messengers God has
sent you! How many times I wanted to put

23:22 Isa 66:1; Mt 5:34 **23:23** Lev 27:30 **23:27** Acts 23:3 **23:33** Mt 3:7; 12:34; Lk 3:7 **23:35** **a** Gen 4:8; **b** 2 Chr 24:20,21

Pray it!

Let Me Love You

At the end of Matthew chapter 23 Jesus mourns for the people of Jerusalem. His anger at the religious leaders is turned to sorrow and compassion. "How many times I wanted to put my arms around all your people . . . but you would not let me!" (Matthew 23:37). Jesus wants to give his love to everyone, but our hearts must be open to receiving Jesus.

Jesus, help me to be open to the amazing love you have for me.
I don't want to turn my back on you.
I will follow you; I will accept your love.
I will follow you; I will listen to your words.
I will follow you; I will live as you command.

— Matthew 23:37–39

my arms around all your people, just as a hen gathers her chicks under her wings, but you would not let me!
38 And so your Temple will be abandoned and empty.
39 From now on, I tell you, you will never see me again until you say, 'God bless him who comes in the name of the Lord.' "

Jesus Speaks of the Destruction of the Temple
(Mark 13:1, 2; Luke 21:5, 6)

24 Jesus left and was going away from the Temple when his disciples came to him to call his attention to its buildings.
2 "Yes," he said, "you may well look at all these. I tell you this: not a single stone here will be left in its place; every one of them will be thrown down."

Troubles and Persecutions
(Mark 13:3–13; Luke 21:7–19)

3 As Jesus sat on the Mount of Olives, the disciples came to him in private. "Tell us when all this will be," they asked, "and what will happen to show that it is the time for your coming and the end of the age."

4 Jesus answered, "Watch out, and do not let anyone fool you.
5 Many men, claiming to speak for me, will come and say, 'I am the Messiah!' and they will fool many people.
6 You are going to hear the noise of battles close by and the news of battles far away; but do not be troubled. Such things must happen, but they do not mean that the end has come.
7 Countries will fight each other; kingdoms will attack one another. There will be famines and earthquakes everywhere.
8 All these things are like the first pains of childbirth.

9 "Then you will be arrested and handed over to be punished and be put to death. Everyone will hate you because of me.
10 Many will give up their faith at that time; they will betray one another and hate one another.
11 Then many false prophets will appear and fool many people.
12 Such will be the spread of evil that many people's love will grow cold.
13 But whoever holds out to the end will be saved.
14 And this Good News about the Kingdom will be preached

23:38 Jer 22:5 **23:39** Ps 118:26 **24:9** Mt 10:22 **24:13** Mt 10:22

A *hypocrite* is someone whose actions do not match his or her words. Jesus condemned all hypocrisy.

Study it!

Jesus Comes Again

Jesus promised that he would come back again; he even describes his coming "on the clouds of heaven with power and great glory" (Matthew 24:30). The Church has a special name for the Second Coming of Christ: the Parousia. *Parousia* is a Greek word that means "arrival." The early Christians thought that Jesus would be coming back in their life-time. They looked forward to it with excitement.

Some people are afraid of the Parousia. Sometimes when we don't know what to expect, we can get nervous, even scared. The Catholic Church teaches that Christ will return at the end of time and judge all the nations. His Kingdom will be fully established, and his victory over evil will be complete. Like the early Christians, we should look forward with joy to Jesus' coming again!

— Matthew, chapter 24

through all the world for a witness to all
people; and then the end will come.

The Awful Horror
(Mark 13:14–23; Luke 21:20–24)

15"You will see 'The Awful Horror' of
which the prophet Daniel spoke. It will be
standing in the holy place." (Note to the
reader: understand what this means!)
16"Then those who are in Judea must run
away to the hills. 17Someone who is on the
roof of a house must not take the time to go
down and get any belongings from the
house. 18Someone who is in the field must
not go back to get a cloak. 19How terrible it
will be in those days for women who are
pregnant and for mothers with little babies!
20Pray to God that you will not have to run
away during the winter or on a Sabbath!
21For the trouble at that time will be far
more terrible than any there has ever been,
from the beginning of the world to this very
day. Nor will there ever be anything like it
again. 22But God has already reduced the
number of days; had he not done so, nobody
would survive. For the sake of his chosen
people, however, God will reduce the days.

23"Then, if anyone says to you, 'Look,
here is the Messiah!' or 'There he is!'—do
not believe it. 24For false Messiahs and false
prophets will appear; they will perform great
miracles and wonders in order to deceive
even God's chosen people, if possible. 25Lis-
ten! I have told you this ahead of time.

26"Or, if people should tell you, 'Look, he
is out in the desert!'—don't go there; or if
they say, 'Look, he is hiding here!'—don't
believe it. 27For the Son of Man will come
like the lightning which flashes across the
whole sky from the east to the west.

28"Wherever there is a dead body, the vul-
tures will gather.

The Coming of the Son of Man
(Mark 13:24–27; Luke 21:25–28)

29"Soon after the trouble of those days,
the sun will grow dark, the moon will no
longer shine, the stars will fall from heaven,
and the powers in space will be driven from
their courses. 30Then the sign of the Son of
Man will appear in the sky; and all the peo-
ples of earth will weep as they see the Son
of Man coming on the clouds of heaven

24:15 Dan 9:27; 11:31; 12:11; 1 Macc 1:54; 6:7 **24:17,18** Lk 17:31 **24:21** Dan 12:1; Rev 7:14 **24:26,27** Lk 17:23,24 **24:28** Lk 17:37 **24:29 a** Isa 13:10; Joel 2:10,31; 3:15; Rev 6:12; **b** Isa 13:10; Ezek 32:7; Joel 2:10; 3:15; **c** Isa 34:4; Rev 6:13 **24:30** Dan 7:13; Zech 12:10-14; Rev 1:7

What is the "Awful Horror" mentioned in Matthew 24:15? a war? a plague? A pagan image? A terrible beast? Find out by reading Daniel 9:27.

with power and great glory. 31 The great
trumpet will sound, and he will send out his
angels to the four corners of the earth, and
they will gather his chosen people from one
end of the world to the other.

The Lesson of the Fig Tree
(Mark 13:28–31; Luke 21:29–33)

32 "Let the fig tree teach you a lesson.
When its branches become green and tender
and it starts putting out leaves, you know
that summer is near. 33 In the same way,
when you see all these things, you will
know that the time is near, ready to begin.[x]
34 Remember that all these things will hap-
pen before the people now living have all
died. 35 Heaven and earth will pass away, but
my words will never pass away.

No One Knows the Day and Hour
(Mark 13:32–37; Luke 17:26–30, 34–36)

36 "No one knows, however, when that
day and hour will come—neither the angels
in heaven nor the Son;[y] the Father alone
knows. 37 The coming of the Son of Man
will be like what happened in the time of
Noah. 38 In the days before the flood people
ate and drank, men and women married, up
to the very day Noah went into the boat;
39 yet they did not realize what was happen-
ing until the flood came and swept them all
away. That is how it will be when the Son of
Man comes. 40 At that time two men will be
working in a field: one will be taken away,
the other will be left behind. 41 Two women
will be at a mill grinding meal: one will be
taken away, the other will be left behind.
42 Watch out, then, because you do not know
what day your Lord will come. 43 If the
owner of a house knew the time when the
thief would come, you can be sure that he
would stay awake and not let the thief break
into his house. 44 So then, you also must
always be ready, because the Son of Man will
come at an hour when you are not expect-
ing him.

The Faithful or the Unfaithful Servant
(Luke 12:41–48)

45 "Who, then, is a faithful and wise ser-
vant? It is the one that his master has placed
in charge of the other servants to give them
their food at the proper time. 46 How happy
that servant is if his master finds him doing
this when he comes home! 47 Indeed, I tell
you, the master will put that servant in
charge of all his property. 48 But if he is a bad
servant, he will tell himself that his master
will not come back for a long time, 49 and he
will begin to beat his fellow servants and to
eat and drink with drunkards. 50 Then that
servant's master will come back one day
when the servant does not expect him and
at a time he does not know. 51 The master
will cut him in pieces[z] and make him share
the fate of the hypocrites. There he will cry
and gnash his teeth.

The Parable of the Ten Young Women

25 "At that time the Kingdom of heav-
en will be like this. Once there were
ten young women who took their oil lamps
and went out to meet the bridegroom. 2 Five
of them were foolish, and the other five
were wise. 3 The foolish ones took their
lamps but did not take any extra oil with
them, 4 while the wise ones took containers
full of oil for their lamps. 5 The bridegroom
was late in coming, so they began to nod
and fall asleep.

6 "It was already midnight when the cry
rang out, 'Here is the bridegroom! Come
and meet him!' 7 The ten young women
woke up and trimmed their lamps. 8 Then
the foolish ones said to the wise ones, 'Let us
have some of your oil, because our lamps are
going out.' 9 'No, indeed,' the wise ones
answered, 'there is not enough for you and
for us. Go to the store and buy some for
yourselves.' 10 So the foolish ones went off to
buy some oil; and while they were gone, the
bridegroom arrived. The five who were
ready went in with him to the wedding
feast, and the door was closed.

[x] **24:33** the time is near, ready to begin; *or* he is near, ready to come. [y] **24:36** *Some manuscripts do not have* nor the Son. [z] **24:51** cut him in pieces; *or* throw him out.

24:37 Gen 6:5-8 **24:39** Gen 7:6-24 **24:43,44** Lk 12:39,40 **25:1** Lk 12:35

Pray it!

Find Us Ready, Lord

When you return Lord, I want to be ready.
Help me clean out the dusty corners of my life
and keep my heart ready for your return.
Through prayer I will grow closer to you.
By loving others I will prepare myself for your coming.
By knowing that you might come at any moment,
I will remain ready for your return
because I wish to live always in your love.

— Matthew 25:1–13

11 "Later the others arrived. 'Sir, sir! Let us
in!' they cried out. 12 'Certainly not! I don't
know you,' the bridegroom answered."
13 And Jesus concluded, "Watch out, then,
because you do not know the day or the
hour.

The Parable of the Three Servants
(Luke 19:11–27)

14 "At that time the Kingdom of heaven
will be like this. Once there was a man who
was about to leave home on a trip; he called
his servants and put them in charge of his
property. 15 He gave to each one according to
his ability: to one he gave five thousand gold
coins, to another he gave two thousand, and
to another he gave one thousand. Then he
left on his trip. 16 The servant who had
received five thousand coins went at once
and invested his money and earned another
five thousand. 17 In the same way the servant
who had received two thousand coins
earned another two thousand. 18 But the ser-
vant who had received one thousand coins
went off, dug a hole in the ground, and hid
his master's money.
19 "After a long time the master of those
servants came back and settled accounts with
them. 20 The servant who had received five
thousand coins came in and handed over the
other five thousand. 'You gave me five thou-
sand coins, sir,' he said. 'Look! Here are
another five thousand that I have earned.'
21 'Well done, you good and faithful servant!'
said his master. 'You have been faithful in
managing small amounts, so I will put you in
charge of large amounts. Come on in and
share my happiness!' 22 Then the servant who
had been given two thousand coins came in
and said, 'You gave me two thousand coins,
sir. Look! Here are another two thousand
that I have earned.' 23 'Well done, you good
and faithful servant!' said his master. 'You
have been faithful in managing small
amounts, so I will put you in charge of large
amounts. Come on in and share my happi-
ness!' 24 Then the servant who had received
one thousand coins came in and said, 'Sir, I
know you are a hard man; you reap harvests
where you did not plant, and you gather
crops where you did not scatter seed. 25 I was
afraid, so I went off and hid your money in
the ground. Look! Here is what belongs to
you.' 26 'You bad and lazy servant!' his master
said. 'You knew, did you, that I reap harvests
where I did not plant, and gather crops
where I did not scatter seed? 27 Well, then,
you should have deposited my money in the
bank, and I would have received it all back
with interest when I returned. 28 Now, take
the money away from him and give it to the
one who has ten thousand coins. 29 For to
every person who has something, even more

25:11,12 Lk 13:25 **25:14-30** Lk 19:11-27 **25:29** Mt 13:12; Mk 4:25; Lk 8:18

will be given, and he will have more than
enough; but the person who has nothing,
even the little that he has will be taken away
from him. 30 As for this useless servant—
throw him outside in the darkness; there he
will cry and gnash his teeth.'

The Final Judgment

31 "When the Son of Man comes as King
and all the angels with him, he will sit on his
royal throne, 32 and the people of all the
nations will be gathered before him. Then he
will divide them into two groups, just as a
shepherd separates the sheep from the goats.
33 He will put the righteous people at his
right and the others at his left. 34 Then the
King will say to the people on his right,
'Come, you that are blessed by my Father!
Come and possess the kingdom which has
been prepared for you ever since the cre-
ation of the world. 35 I was hungry and you
fed me, thirsty and you gave me a drink; I
was a stranger and you received me in your
homes, 36 naked and you clothed me; I was
sick and you took care of me, in prison and
you visited me.' 37 The righteous will then
answer him, 'When, Lord, did we ever see
you hungry and feed you, or thirsty and give
you a drink? 38 When did we ever see you a
stranger and welcome you in our homes, or
naked and clothe you? 39 When did we ever
see you sick or in prison, and visit you?'
40 The King will reply, 'I tell you, whenever
you did this for one of the least important of
these followers of mine, you did it for me!'

41 "Then he will say to those on his left,
'Away from me, you that are under God's
curse! Away to the eternal fire which has been
prepared for the Devil and his angels! 42 I was
hungry but you would not feed me, thirsty
but you would not give me a drink; 43 I was a
stranger but you would not welcome me in
your homes, naked but you would not clothe
me; I was sick and in prison but you would
not take care of me.' 44 Then they will answer
him, 'When, Lord, did we ever see you hun-
gry or thirsty or a stranger or naked or sick or
in prison, and we would not help you?' 45 The
King will reply, 'I tell you, whenever you
refused to help one of these least important
ones, you refused to help me.' 46 These, then,
will be sent off to eternal punishment, but the
righteous will go to eternal life."

Live it!

Seeing Christ, Being Christ

Jesus tells his followers that if they show an act of kindness to anyone, it is as if they did it to him (Matthew 25:40). As Christians we are called to see Christ in others and to be Christ for others. You can volunteer at a nursing home or a food pantry. Or encourage your church or school to do a food drive or collect blankets and winter coats. One youth group has a "Change the World" jar. The young people collect all the loose change in people's pockets each week at youth group and then a few times a year donate it to a group that helps poor people. It helps remind them of the people in need. You could have your own "Change the World" jar. Encourage your family, maybe even your whole parish or school, to start this tradition.

— Matthew 25:31–46

The Plot against Jesus

(Mark 14:1, 2; Luke 22:1, 2; John 11:45–53)

26 When Jesus had finished teaching all
these things, he said to his disciples,

25:30 Mt 8:12; 22:13; Lk 13:28 **25:31 a** Mt 16:27; **b** Mt 19:28 **25:35, 36** Sir 7:32-36 **25:46** Dan 12:2

Who are the least important *(Matthew 25:40)* **in the world today? Who is in need of food, clothing, visits? What can you do about it?**

What She Has Done

In a dramatic story at the beginning of Matthew, chapter 26, the unnamed woman anoints Jesus' head in the same way that the kings of the Old Testament were anointed. Anointing on the head was a sign that this person was God's choice. The woman may have suspected that Jesus was in danger of being killed, and this kind of anointing was also a way of preparing a body for burial. She wanted to recognize that Jesus was chosen by God. Jesus in turn recognizes the woman's compassion for him and praises her extravagance in using this very expensive oil. She put her resources at the service of someone in need. It is this act of compassion that will be remembered.

— Matthew 26:6–13

2 "In two days, as you know, it will be the
Passover Festival, and the Son of Man will be
handed over to be crucified."
3 Then the chief priests and the elders met
together in the palace of Caiaphas, the High
Priest, 4 and made plans to arrest Jesus secret-
ly and put him to death. 5 "We must not do
it during the festival," they said, "or the peo-
ple will riot."

Jesus Is Anointed at Bethany
(Mark 14:3–9; John 12:1–8)

6 Jesus was in Bethany at the house of
Simon, a man who had suffered from a
dreaded skin disease. 7 While Jesus was eat-
ing, a woman came to him with an alabaster
jar filled with an expensive perfume, which
she poured on his head. 8 The disciples saw
this and became angry. "Why all this waste?"
they asked. 9 "This perfume could have been
sold for a large amount and the money given
to the poor!"
10 Jesus knew what they were saying, and
so he said to them, "Why are you bothering
this woman? It is a fine and beautiful thing
that she has done for me. 11 You will always
have poor people with you, but you will not
always have me. 12 What she did was to pour
this perfume on my body to get me ready
for burial. 13 Now, I assure you that wherever
this gospel is preached all over the world,
what she has done will be told in memory
of her."

Judas Agrees to Betray Jesus
(Mark 14:10, 11; Luke 22:3–6)

14 Then one of the twelve disciples—the
one named Judas Iscariot—went to the
chief priests 15 and asked, "What will you
give me if I betray Jesus to you?" They
counted out thirty silver coins and gave
them to him. 16 From then on Judas was
looking for a good chance to hand Jesus
over to them.

Thirty silver coins (26:15)

26:2 Ex 12:1-27 **26:7** Lk 7:37,38 **26:11** Deut 15:11 **26:15** Zech 11:12

" 'Take and eat it,' he said; 'this is my body' " *(Matthew 26:26)*.

Jesus Eats the Passover Meal with His Disciples
(Mark 14:12–21; Luke 22:7–13, 21–23; John 13:21–30)

17 On the first day of the Festival of
Unleavened Bread the disciples came to
Jesus and asked him, "Where do you want us
to get the Passover meal ready for you?"
18 "Go to a certain man in the city," he
said to them, "and tell him: 'The Teacher
says, My hour has come; my disciples and I
will celebrate the Passover at your house.' "
19 The disciples did as Jesus had told them
and prepared the Passover meal.
20 When it was evening, Jesus and the
twelve disciples sat down to eat. 21 During
the meal Jesus said, "I tell you, one of you
will betray me."
22 The disciples were very upset and began
to ask him, one after the other, "Surely, Lord,
you don't mean me?"
23 Jesus answered, "One who dips his bread
in the dish with me will betray me. 24 The
Son of Man will die as the Scriptures say he
will, but how terrible for that man who will
betray the Son of Man! It would have been
better for that man if he had never been
born!"
25 Judas, the traitor, spoke up. "Surely,
Teacher, you don't mean me?" he asked.
Jesus answered, "So you say."

The Lord's Supper
(Mark 14:22–26; Luke 22:14–20; 1 Corinthians 11:23–25)

26 While they were eating, Jesus took a
piece of bread, gave a prayer of thanks, broke
it, and gave it to his disciples. "Take and eat
it," he said; "this is my body."
27 Then he took a cup, gave thanks to
God, and gave it to them. "Drink it, all of
you," he said; 28 "this is my blood, which seals
God's covenant, my blood poured out for
many for the forgiveness of sins. 29 I tell you,
I will never again drink this wine until the
day I drink the new wine with you in my
Father's Kingdom."
30 Then they sang a hymn and went out to
the Mount of Olives.

Jesus Predicts Peter's Denial
(Mark 14:27–31; Luke 22:31–34; John 13:36–38)

31 Then Jesus said to them, "This very
night all of you will run away and leave me,
for the scripture says, 'God will kill the shep-
herd, and the sheep of the flock will be scat-
tered.' 32 But after I am raised to life, I will go
to Galilee ahead of you."
33 Peter spoke up and said to Jesus, "I will
never leave you, even though all the rest do!"
34 Jesus said to Peter, "I tell you that before
the rooster crows tonight, you will say three
times that you do not know me."
35 Peter answered, "I will never say that,
even if I have to die with you!"
And all the other disciples said the same
thing.

Jesus Prays in Gethsemane
(Mark 14:32–42; Luke 22:39–46)

36 Then Jesus went with his disciples to a
place called Gethsemane, and he said to
them, "Sit here while I go over there and
pray." 37 He took with him Peter and the two
sons of Zebedee. Grief and anguish came
over him, 38 and he said to them, "The sorrow
in my heart is so great that it almost crushes
me. Stay here and keep watch with me."
39 He went a little farther on, threw him-
self face downward on the ground, and
prayed, "My Father, if it is possible, take this
cup of suffering from me! Yet not what I
want, but what you want."

"Take this cup of suffering from me!" (26:39)

26:23 Ps 41:9 **26:28 a** Ex 24:8; **b** Jer 31:31-34 **26:31** Zech 13:7 **26:32** Mt 28:16

Obstacles to Prayer

Jesus asks his closest friends to "stay here and keep watch with me" (Matthew 26:38). But after a full meal, they fall asleep. The disciples love Jesus. But their human limits keep them from praying as they want to.

Prayer can be a very difficult thing at times. You can be distracted by the radio or television. Maybe noisy people in your house make it difficult to find some quiet. Maybe you are so busy with your friends, family, and school activities that it's hard to find time for prayer.

If you find prayer difficult, don't be discouraged. Even the greatest saints found it very difficult to pray at times. These obstacles can be overcome. Turn off the television and radio. Wake up early or find a quiet room. Pray in the car on your way to or from your activities. Make prayer a priority and keep your relationship with Jesus alive!

— Matthew 26:36–46

40 Then he returned to the three disciples
and found them asleep; and he said to Peter,
"How is it that you three were not able to
keep watch with me for even one hour?
41 Keep watch and pray that you will not fall
into temptation. The spirit is willing, but the
flesh is weak."
42 Once more Jesus went away and prayed,
"My Father, if this cup of suffering cannot
be taken away unless I drink it, your will be
done." 43 He returned once more and found
the disciples asleep; they could not keep
their eyes open.

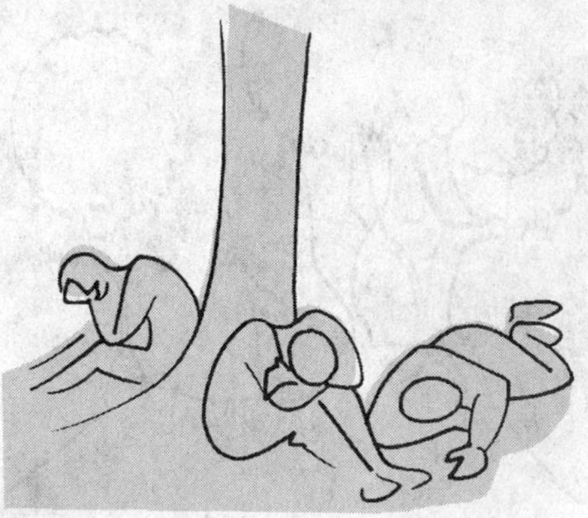

They could not keep their eyes open. (26:43)

44 Again Jesus left them, went away, and
prayed the third time, saying the same words.
45 Then he returned to the disciples and said,
"Are you still sleeping and resting? Look!
The hour has come for the Son of Man to
be handed over to the power of sinners.
46 Get up, let us go. Look, here is the man
who is betraying me!"

The Arrest of Jesus

(Mark 14:43–50; Luke 22:47–53; John 18:3–12)

47 Jesus was still speaking when Judas, one
of the twelve disciples, arrived. With him was
a large crowd armed with swords and clubs
and sent by the chief priests and the elders.
48 The traitor had given the crowd a signal:
"The man I kiss is the one you want. Arrest
him!"
49 Judas went straight to Jesus and said,
"Peace be with you, Teacher," and kissed him.
50 Jesus answered, "Be quick about it,
friend!"[a]
Then they came up, arrested Jesus, and
held him tight. 51 One of those who were
with Jesus drew his sword and struck at the
High Priest's slave, cutting off his ear. 52 "Put

[a] **26:50** Be quick about it, friend!; *or* Why are you here, friend?

your sword back in its place," Jesus said to
him. "All who take the sword will die by the
sword. 53Don't you know that I could call
on my Father for help, and at once he would
send me more than twelve armies of angels?
54But in that case, how could the Scriptures
come true which say that this is what must
happen?"
55Then Jesus spoke to the crowd, "Did
you have to come with swords and clubs to
capture me, as though I were an outlaw?
Every day I sat down and taught in the Tem-
ple, and you did not arrest me. 56But all this
has happened in order to make come true
what the prophets wrote in the Scriptures."
Then all the disciples left him and ran away.

Jesus before the Council
(Mark 14:53–65; Luke 22:54, 55, 63–71; John 18:13, 14, 19–24)

57Those who had arrested Jesus took him
to the house of Caiaphas, the High Priest,
where the teachers of the Law and the elders
had gathered together. 58Peter followed from
a distance, as far as the courtyard of the High
Priest's house. He went into the courtyard
and sat down with the guards to see how it
would all come out. 59The chief priests and
the whole Council tried to find some false
evidence against Jesus to put him to death;
60but they could not find any, even though
many people came forward and told lies
about him. Finally two men stepped up
61and said, "This man said, 'I am able to tear
down God's Temple and three days later
build it back up.' "
62The High Priest stood up and said to
Jesus, "Have you no answer to give to this
accusation against you?" 63But Jesus kept
quiet. Again the High Priest spoke to him,
"In the name of the living God I now put
you under oath: tell us if you are the Messi-
ah, the Son of God."
64Jesus answered him, "So you say. But I
tell all of you: from this time on you will see
the Son of Man sitting at the right side of
the Almighty and coming on the clouds of
heaven!"
65At this the High Priest tore his clothes
and said, "Blasphemy! We don't need any
more witnesses! You have just heard his blas-
phemy! 66What do you think?"
They answered, "He is guilty and must die."
67Then they spat in his face and beat him;
and those who slapped him 68said, "Prophesy
for us, Messiah! Guess who hit you!"

Peter Denies Jesus
(Mark 14:66–72; Luke 22:56–62; John 18:15–18, 25–27)

69Peter was sitting outside in the court-
yard when one of the High Priest's servant
women came to him and said, "You, too,
were with Jesus of Galilee."
70But he denied it in front of them all. "I
don't know what you are talking about," he
answered, 71and went on out to the entrance
of the courtyard. Another servant woman
saw him and said to the men there, "He was
with Jesus of Nazareth."
72Again Peter denied it and answered, "I
swear that I don't know that man!"
73After a little while the men standing
there came to Peter. "Of course you are one
of them," they said. "After all, the way you
speak gives you away!"
74Then Peter said, "I swear that I am
telling the truth! May God punish me if I
am not! I do not know that man!"
Just then a rooster crowed, 75and Peter
remembered what Jesus had told him:
"Before the rooster crows, you will say three
times that you do not know me." He went
out and wept bitterly.

Jesus Is Taken to Pilate
(Mark 15:1; Luke 23:1, 2; John 18:28–32)

27 Early in the morning all the chief
priests and the elders made their
plans against Jesus to put him to death.
2They put him in chains, led him off, and

26:55 Lk 19:47; 21:37 **26:61** Jn 2:19 **26:64** Dan 7:13 **26:65,66** Lev 24:16 **26:67** Isa 50:6

Why did Peter deny Jesus? He was afraid he might be arrested and killed, too.

Catholic Connections

Good Friday

During Holy Week, which begins on Palm Sunday, we remember Jesus' suffering and death on Good Friday. For the Good Friday liturgy, the Church is kept simple, sometimes statues are covered or removed. The Gospel reading is taken from John, chapters 18 and 19, which is another version of what Matthew's Gospel describes here.

The Good Friday liturgy is serious and can even feel sad because we are focusing on Jesus' death. During the liturgy we show special reverence for the cross in appreciation of Christ's sacrifice. This is called the veneration of the cross. This liturgy reminds us of Jesus' sacrifice, but even on Good Friday we are people of hope because we know how the story ends. We leave the Good Friday liturgy knowing that Easter is coming soon!

— Matthew 26:57—27:56

handed him over to Pilate, the Roman governor.

The Death of Judas
(Acts 1:18, 19)

3 When Judas, the traitor, learned that Jesus
had been condemned, he repented and took
back the thirty silver coins to the chief priests
and the elders. 4 "I have sinned by betraying
an innocent man to death!" he said.
"What do we care about that?" they
answered. "That is your business!"
5 Judas threw the coins down in the Temple and left; then he went off and hanged
himself.
6 The chief priests picked up the coins and
said, "This is blood money, and it is against
our Law to put it in the Temple treasury."
7 After reaching an agreement about it, they
used the money to buy Potter's Field, as a
cemetery for foreigners. 8 That is why that
field is called "Field of Blood" to this very day.
9 Then what the prophet Jeremiah had
said came true: "They took the thirty silver
coins, the amount the people of Israel had
agreed to pay for him, 10 and used the money
to buy the potter's field, as the Lord had
commanded me."

Pilate Questions Jesus
(Mark 15:2–5; Luke 23:3–5; John 18:33–38)

11 Jesus stood before the Roman governor,
who questioned him. "Are you the king of
the Jews?" he asked.
"So you say," answered Jesus. 12 But he said
nothing in response to the accusations of the
chief priests and elders.
13 So Pilate said to him, "Don't you hear
all these things they accuse you of?"
14 But Jesus refused to answer a single
word, with the result that the Governor was
greatly surprised.

Jesus Is Sentenced to Death
(Mark 15:6–15; Luke 23:13–25; John 18:39—19:16)

15 At every Passover Festival the Roman
governor was in the habit of setting free any

27:3-8 Acts 1:18,19 **27:9,10** Zech 11:12,13

Matthew 27:25 is also known as the blood curse. It has been wrongly used to justify hatred against the Jewish people.

one prisoner the crowd asked for. 16At that
time there was a well-known prisoner named
Jesus Barabbas. 17So when the crowd gath-
ered, Pilate asked them, "Which one do you
want me to set free for you? Jesus Barabbas
or Jesus called the Messiah?" 18He knew
very well that the Jewish authorities had
handed Jesus over to him because they were
jealous.
19While Pilate was sitting in the judgment
hall, his wife sent him a message: "Have
nothing to do with that innocent man,
because in a dream last night I suffered
much on account of him."
20The chief priests and the elders persuad-
ed the crowd to ask Pilate to set Barabbas
free and have Jesus put to death. 21But Pilate
asked the crowd, "Which one of these two
do you want me to set free for you?"

"Barabbas!" they answered.

22"What, then, shall I do with Jesus called
the Messiah?" Pilate asked them.

"Crucify him!" they all answered.

23But Pilate asked, "What crime has he
committed?"

Then they started shouting at the top of
their voices: "Crucify him!"

24When Pilate saw that it was no use to go
on, but that a riot might break out, he took
some water, washed his hands in front of the
crowd, and said, "I am not responsible for the
death of this man! This is your doing!"
25The whole crowd answered, "Let the
responsibility for his death fall on us and on
our children!"

26Then Pilate set Barabbas free for them;
and after he had Jesus whipped, he handed
him over to be crucified.

The Soldiers Make Fun of Jesus

(Mark 15:16–20; John 19:2, 3)

27Then Pilate's soldiers took Jesus into the
governor's palace, and the whole company
gathered around him. 28They stripped off
his clothes and put a scarlet robe on him.
29Then they made a crown out of thorny
branches and placed it on his head, and put
a stick in his right hand; then they knelt
before him and made fun of him. "Long live
the King of the Jews!" they said. 30They spat
on him, and took the stick and hit him over
the head. 31When they had finished making
fun of him, they took the robe off and put
his own clothes back on him. Then they led
him out to crucify him.

Jesus Is Crucified

(Mark 15:21–32; Luke 23:26–43; John 19:17–27)

32As they were going out, they met a man
from Cyrene named Simon, and the soldiers
forced him to carry Jesus' cross. 33They came
to a place called Golgotha, which means,
"The Place of the Skull." 34There they
offered Jesus wine mixed with a bitter sub-
stance; but after tasting it, he would not
drink it.

35They crucified him and then divided his
clothes among them by throwing dice.
36After that they sat there and watched him.
37Above his head they put the written
notice of the accusation against him: "This is
Jesus, the King of the Jews." 38Then they
crucified two bandits with Jesus, one on his
right and the other on his left.

39People passing by shook their heads and
hurled insults at Jesus: 40"You were going to
tear down the Temple and build it back up
in three days! Save yourself if you are God's
Son! Come on down from the cross!"

41In the same way the chief priests and
the teachers of the Law and the elders made
fun of him: 42"He saved others, but he can-
not save himself! Isn't he the king of Israel?
If he will come down off the cross now, we
will believe in him! 43He trusts in God and
claims to be God's Son. Well, then, let us see
if God wants to save him now!"

44Even the bandits who had been cruci-
fied with him insulted him in the same way.

The Death of Jesus

(Mark 15:33–41; Luke 23:44–49; John 19:28–30)

45At noon the whole country was covered
with darkness, which lasted for three hours.
46At about three o'clock Jesus cried out with

27:24 Deut 21:6-9 **27:34** Ps 69:21 **27:35** Ps 22:18 **27:39** Ps 22:7; 109:25; Sir 12:17,18; 13:7
27:40 Mt 26:61; Jn 2:19 **27:43** Ps 22:8; Wis 2:18-20 **27:46** Ps 22:1

Pray it!

Thank You, Lord

Lord Jesus, when I see you on the cross, it makes me wonder.
Why did you have to suffer? Was this the only way?
I am so amazed that you, the Son of God, were willing to become human, even if that meant enduring the worst treatment that human beings have to offer—mockery, torture, death.
Thank you.
Thank you for following your Father's will.
Thank you for standing in the face of hatred and showing such amazing love.

— Matthew 27:32–50

a loud shout, *"Eli, Eli, lema sabachthani?"*
which means, "My God, my God, why did
you abandon me?"
47Some of the people standing there
heard him and said, "He is calling for
Elijah!" 48One of them ran up at once,
took a sponge, soaked it in cheap wine,
put it on the end of a stick, and tried to
make him drink it.
49But the others said, "Wait, let us see if
Elijah is coming to save him!"
50Jesus again gave a loud cry and breathed
his last.
51Then the curtain hanging in the Temple
was torn in two from top to bottom. The
earth shook, the rocks split apart, 52the
graves broke open, and many of God's peo-
ple who had died were raised to life. 53They
left the graves, and after Jesus rose from
death, they went into the Holy City, where
many people saw them.
54When the army officer and the soldiers
with him who were watching Jesus saw the
earthquake and everything else that hap-
pened, they were terrified and said, "He real-
ly was the Son of God!"
55There were many women there, looking
on from a distance, who had followed Jesus
from Galilee and helped him. 56Among
them were Mary Magdalene, Mary the
mother of James and Joseph, and the wife of
Zebedee.

The Burial of Jesus

(Mark 15:42–47; Luke 23:50–56; John 19:38–42)

57When it was evening, a rich man from
Arimathea arrived; his name was Joseph, and
he also was a disciple of Jesus. 58He went into
the presence of Pilate and asked for the body
of Jesus. Pilate gave orders for the body to be
given to Joseph. 59So Joseph took it, wrapped
it in a new linen sheet, 60and placed it in his
own tomb, which he had just recently dug
out of solid rock. Then he rolled a large stone
across the entrance to the tomb and went
away. 61Mary Magdalene and the other Mary
were sitting there, facing the tomb.

The Guard at the Tomb

62The next day, which was a Sabbath, the
chief priests and the Pharisees met with
Pilate 63and said, "Sir, we remember that
while that liar was still alive he said, 'I will be
raised to life three days later.' 64Give orders,
then, for his tomb to be carefully guarded
until the third day, so that his disciples will
not be able to go and steal the body, and
then tell the people that he was raised from
death. This last lie would be even worse than
the first one."
65"Take a guard," Pilate told them; "go
and make the tomb as secure as you can."

27:48 Ps 69:21 **27:51** Ex 26:31-33 **27:55,56** Lk 8:2,3 **27:63** Mt 16:21; 17:23; 20:19; Mk 8:31; 9:31; 10:33,34; Lk 9:22; 18:31-33

Catholic Connections

Holy Trinity

The Gospel of Matthew ends with two stories of the resurrected Jesus. In the first story he appears to the women leaving the tomb (Matthew 28:9–10). In the second story he appears to the eleven disciples who were also the Apostles. He gives them this command, "Go, then, to all peoples everywhere and make them my disciples: baptize them in the name of the Father, the Son, and the Holy Spirit" (28:19). You probably recognize these words; we say them when we make the sign of the cross.

God the Father, God the Son, and God the Holy Spirit are one God even though they are revealed as three persons. This is why we also call God the Holy Trinity. This belief is a mystery that we do not fully understand. But it does tell us that God is not solitary. The Father, Son, and Holy Spirit are in relationship with one another and form a loving communion. We, too, are not meant to be alone but to live in community. We are all invited to be a part of God's family, as is the whole world!

— Matthew 28:16–20

66So they left and made the tomb secure
by putting a seal on the stone and leaving
the guard on watch.

The Resurrection
(Mark 16:1–10; Luke 24:1–12; John 20:1–10)

28 After the Sabbath, as Sunday morn-
ing was dawning, Mary Magdalene
and the other Mary went to look at the
tomb. 2Suddenly there was a violent earth-
quake; an angel of the Lord came down
from heaven, rolled the stone away, and sat
on it. 3His appearance was like lightning, and
his clothes were white as snow. 4The guards
were so afraid that they trembled and
became like dead men.
5The angel spoke to the women. "You must
not be afraid," he said. "I know you are look-
ing for Jesus, who was crucified. 6He is not
here; he has been raised, just as he said. Come
here and see the place where he was lying.
7Go quickly now, and tell his disciples, 'He has
been raised from death, and now he is going
to Galilee ahead of you; there you will see
him!' Remember what I have told you."
8So they left the tomb in a hurry, afraid
and yet filled with joy, and ran to tell his dis-
ciples.
9Suddenly Jesus met them and said, "Peace
be with you." They came up to him, took
hold of his feet, and worshiped him. 10"Do
not be afraid," Jesus said to them. "Go and
tell my brothers to go to Galilee, and there
they will see me."

The Report of the Guard

11While the women went on their way,
some of the soldiers guarding the tomb went
back to the city and told the chief priests
everything that had happened. 12The chief
priests met with the elders and made their
plan; they gave a large sum of money to the
soldiers 13and said, "You are to say that his
disciples came during the night and stole his
body while you were asleep. 14And if the
Governor should hear of this, we will

"He is not here; he has been raised, just as he said" *(Matthew 28:6)*.

convince him that you are innocent, and you
will have nothing to worry about."
15 The guards took the money and did what
they were told to do. And so that is the report
spread around by the Jews to this very day.

Jesus Appears to His Disciples
(Mark 16:14–18; Luke 24:36–49;
John 20:19–23; Acts 1:6–8)

16 The eleven disciples went to the hill in
Galilee where Jesus had told them to go.
17 When they saw him, they worshiped him,
even though some of them doubted. 18 Jesus
drew near and said to them, "I have been
given all authority in heaven and on earth.
19 Go, then, to all peoples everywhere and
make them my disciples: baptize them in
the name of the Father, the Son, and the
Holy Spirit, 20 and teach them to obey
everything I have commanded you. And I
will be with you always, to the end of the
age."

28:16 Mt 26:32; Mk 14:28 **28:19** Acts 1:8

Your Next Step

Congratulations on finishing the Gospel of Matthew! Use this space to write your thoughts and questions about this book. If you are following the suggested reading plan, go back to the Book of Psalms in the Old Testament. The Psalms were an important part of Jesus and his followers' prayer life.

THE GOSPEL ACCORDING TO Mark

Are you a person who likes to get right to the facts? Then you will definitely enjoy the Gospel according to Mark. It was the first Gospel to be written and is also the shortest of the four Gospels. The Gospel according to Mark was probably intended for new believers in Rome, which was far away from where Jesus walked, taught, and performed miracles.

Mark does not tell about Jesus' teachings as much as the other Gospels do. Instead it focuses on what it really means to be a disciple and how to live what Jesus taught. At the heart of Mark's Gospel is Jesus' suffering. The message to Mark's readers was that someday they would see the risen Jesus because of how they lived and accepted their suffering like Jesus accepted his suffering.

Chap. 15:22–32

Headlines

- Names of Jesus' Apostles Revealed (3:13–19)
- Apostles Struggle to Understand Stories (chapter 4)
- Jesus Asks, "Who Do You Say I Am?" (8:27–30)
- Jesus Predicts Suffering and Death (8:31–38; 9:30–32; 10:32–34)
- Trouble Predicted for Jesus' Disciples (13:3–13)
- Jesus Crucified on Friday! (chapter 15)
- Women Frightened by Empty Tomb (16:1–8)

FACTOIDS

Who wrote this book? An old tradition says the author was a follower of Peter called John Mark, but no one really knows for sure.

When was it written? Probably between AD 60 and 70, about thirty-five years after Jesus' Resurrection.

Who was it written for? Mark was originally written for Christians in Rome who were being persecuted.

How does it fit into the Bible? The Gospels of Matthew, Mark, and Luke are called the *synoptic* Gospels. The authors of Matthew and Luke probably used Mark as the starting point for writing their Gospels.

Important themes

- Jesus suffers and so will his followers.
- Jesus tries to keep his identity secret, but the word still gets out.
- Disciples of Jesus recognize him as their Savior, follow his teachings, and tell other people about Jesus.

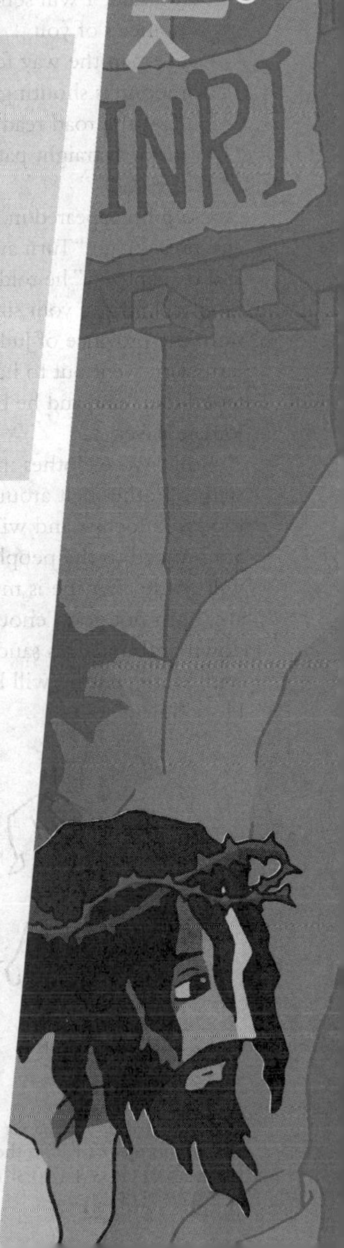

MARK

The Preaching of John the Baptist
(Matthew 3:1–12; Luke 3:1–18; John 1:19–28)

1 This is the Good News about Jesus Christ, the Son of God.[a] 2 It began as the prophet Isaiah had written:

"God said, 'I will send my messenger
ahead of you
to open the way for you.'
3 Someone is shouting in the desert,
'Get the road ready for the Lord;
make a straight path for him to
travel!' "

4 So John appeared in the desert, baptizing and preaching.[b] "Turn away from your sins and be baptized," he told the people, "and God will forgive your sins." 5 Many people from the province of Judea and the city of Jerusalem went out to hear John. They confessed their sins, and he baptized them in the Jordan River.

6 John wore clothes made of camel's hair, with a leather belt around his waist, and his food was locusts and wild honey. 7 He announced to the people, "The man who will come after me is much greater than I am. I am not good enough even to bend down and untie his sandals. 8 I baptize you with water, but he will baptize you with the Holy Spirit."

The Baptism and Temptation of Jesus
(Matthew 3:13—4:11; Luke 3:21, 22; 4:1–13)

9 Not long afterward Jesus came from Nazareth in the province of Galilee, and was baptized by John in the Jordan. 10 As soon as Jesus came up out of the water, he saw heaven opening and the Spirit coming down on him like a dove. 11 And a voice came from heaven, "You are my own dear Son. I am pleased with you."

12 At once the Spirit made him go into the desert, 13 where he stayed forty days, being tempted by Satan. Wild animals were there also, but angels came and helped him.

Jesus Calls Four Fishermen
(Matthew 4:12–22; Luke 4:14, 15; 5:1–11)

14 After John had been put in prison, Jesus went to Galilee and preached the Good News from God. 15 "The right time has come," he said, "and the Kingdom of God is near! Turn away from your sins and believe the Good News!"

16 As Jesus walked along the shore of Lake Galilee, he saw two fishermen, Simon and his brother Andrew, catching fish with a net. 17 Jesus said to them, "Come with me, and I will teach you to catch people." 18 At once they left their nets and went with him.

At once they left their nets. (1:18)

[a] **1:1** *Some manuscripts do not have* the Son of God. [b] **1:4** John appeared in the desert, baptizing and preaching; *some manuscripts have* John the Baptist appeared in the desert, preaching.

1:2 Mal 3:1 **1:3** Isa 40:3 (LXX) **1:6** 2 Kings 1:8 **1:11** Gen 22:2; Ps 2:7; Isa 42:1; Mt 3:17; 12:18; Mk 9:7; Lk 3:22 **1:15** Mt 3:2

Catholic Connections

Lent

Before Jesus began his work of teaching and healing, he went to the desert for forty days to pray and fast (Mark 1:12–13). It was his way of preparing for the road ahead of him, the road that would lead him to his passion, death, and Resurrection.

In memory of Jesus' time in the desert, the Church observes Lent. Lent is a special season of the Church year that is the preparation for the mysteries of Easter. It begins on Ash Wednesday, and lasts forty days, until Easter (the forty days do not include the Sundays during Lent). During that time we focus on our sinfulness and try to change our ways to better follow Christ.

Many people do things to help them focus on God during Lent. They might fast from food, spend extra time in prayer, contribute to causes that help poor people, and reach out to people who are in need of extra help and prayers. How does your family celebrate Lent?

— Mark 1:12–13

19 He went a little farther on and saw two other brothers, James and John, the sons of Zebedee. They were in their boat getting their nets ready. 20 As soon as Jesus saw them, he called them; they left their father Zebedee in the boat with the hired men and went with Jesus.

A Man with an Evil Spirit
(Luke 4:31–37)

21 Jesus and his disciples came to the town of Capernaum, and on the next Sabbath Jesus went to the synagogue and began to teach. 22 The people who heard him were amazed at the way he taught, for he wasn't like the teachers of the Law; instead, he taught with authority.

23 Just then a man with an evil spirit came into the synagogue and screamed, 24 "What do you want with us, Jesus of Nazareth? Are you here to destroy us? I know who you are—you are God's holy messenger!"

25 Jesus ordered the spirit, "Be quiet, and come out of the man!"

26 The evil spirit shook the man hard, gave a loud scream, and came out of him. 27 The people were all so amazed that they started saying to one another, "What is this? Is it some kind of new teaching? This man has authority to give orders to the evil spirits, and they obey him!"

28 And so the news about Jesus spread quickly everywhere in the province of Galilee.

Jesus Heals Many People
(Matthew 8:14–17; Luke 4:38–41)

29 Jesus and his disciples, including James and John, left the synagogue and went straight to the home of Simon and Andrew. 30 Simon's mother-in-law was sick in bed with a fever, and as soon as Jesus arrived, he was told about her. 31 He went to her, took her by the hand, and helped her up. The fever left her, and she began to wait on them.

32 After the sun had set and evening had come, people brought to Jesus all the sick and those who had demons. 33 All the people of the town gathered in front of the house.

1:22 Mt 7:28, 29

How many other events in the Bible can you think of that lasted forty days or forty years?

Took her by the hand, and . . . the fever left her. (1:31)

34Jesus healed many who were sick with
all kinds of diseases and drove out many
demons. He would not let the demons say
anything, because they knew who he was.

Jesus Preaches in Galilee
(Luke 4:42–44)

35Very early the next morning, long
before daylight, Jesus got up and left the
house. He went out of town to a lonely
place, where he prayed. 36But Simon and his
companions went out searching for him,
37and when they found him, they said,
"Everyone is looking for you."

38But Jesus answered, "We must go on to
the other villages around here. I have to preach
in them also, because that is why I came."

39So he traveled all over Galilee, preaching
in the synagogues and driving out demons.

Jesus Heals a Man
(Matthew 8:1–4; Luke 5:12–16)

40A man suffering from a dreaded skin
disease came to Jesus, knelt down, and
begged him for help. "If you want to," he
said, "you can make me clean."[c]

41Jesus was filled with pity,[d] and reached
out and touched him. "I do want to," he
answered. "Be clean!" 42At once the disease
left the man, and he was clean. 43Then Jesus
spoke sternly to him and sent him away at
once, 44after saying to him, "Listen, don't tell
anyone about this. But go straight to the
priest and let him examine you; then in order
to prove to everyone that you are cured, offer
the sacrifice that Moses ordered."

45But the man went away and began to
spread the news everywhere. Indeed, he talked
so much that Jesus could not go into a town
publicly. Instead, he stayed out in lonely places,
and people came to him from everywhere.

Jesus Heals a Paralyzed Man
(Matthew 9:1–8; Luke 5:17–26)

2 A few days later Jesus went back to
Capernaum, and the news spread that he
was at home. 2So many people came together
that there was no room left, not even out in
front of the door. Jesus was preaching the
message to them 3when four men arrived,
carrying a paralyzed man to Jesus. 4Because of
the crowd, however, they could not get the
man to him. So they made a hole in the roof
right above the place where Jesus was. When
they had made an opening, they let the man
down, lying on his mat. 5Seeing how much
faith they had, Jesus said to the paralyzed
man, "My son, your sins are forgiven."

6Some teachers of the Law who were sit-
ting there thought to themselves, 7"How
does he dare talk like this? This is blasphemy!
God is the only one who can forgive sins!"

8At once Jesus knew what they were
thinking, so he said to them, "Why do you
think such things? 9Is it easier to say to this
paralyzed man, 'Your sins are forgiven,' or to
say, 'Get up, pick up your mat, and walk'? 10I
will prove to you, then, that the Son of Man
has authority on earth to forgive sins." So he
said to the paralyzed man, 11"I tell you, get
up, pick up your mat, and go home!"

12While they all watched, the man got up,
picked up his mat, and hurried away. They
were all completely amazed and praised

[c] **1:40** MAKE ME CLEAN: *This disease was considered to make a person ritually unclean.* [d] **1:41** pity; *some manuscripts have* anger.

1:39 Mt 4:23; 9:35 **1:44** Lev 14:1-32

Read Mark 2:13–17. Who are the outcasts in your life? How have you reached out to them? If you haven't, what keeps you from doing it?

God, saying, "We have never seen anything
like this!"

Jesus Calls Levi

(Matthew 9:9–13; Luke 5:27–32)

13Jesus went back again to the shore of
Lake Galilee. A crowd came to him, and he
started teaching them. 14As he walked along,
he saw a tax collector, Levi son of Alphaeus,
sitting in his office. Jesus said to him, "Follow
me." Levi got up and followed him.
15Later on Jesus was having a meal in Levi's
house.[e] A large number of tax collectors and
other outcasts was following Jesus, and many
of them joined him and his disciples at the
table. 16Some teachers of the Law, who were
Pharisees, saw that Jesus was eating with these
outcasts and tax collectors, so they asked his
disciples, "Why does he eat with such people?"
17Jesus heard them and answered, "People
who are well do not need a doctor, but only
those who are sick. I have not come to call
respectable people, but outcasts."

The Question about Fasting

(Matthew 9:14–17; Luke 5:33–39)

18On one occasion the followers of John
the Baptist and the Pharisees were fasting.
Some people came to Jesus and asked him,
"Why is it that the disciples of John the
Baptist and the disciples of the Pharisees fast,
but yours do not?"
19Jesus answered, "Do you expect the
guests at a wedding party to go without
food? Of course not! As long as the bride-
groom is with them, they will not do that.
20But the day will come when the bride-
groom will be taken away from them, and
then they will fast.
21"No one uses a piece of new cloth to
patch up an old coat, because the new patch
will shrink and tear off some of the old
cloth, making an even bigger hole. 22Nor
does anyone pour new wine into used wine-
skins, because the wine will burst the skins,
and both the wine and the skins will be
ruined. Instead, new wine must be poured
into fresh wineskins."

Live it!

Forgiveness

Did you ever ask someone to keep a secret, only to find out that the entire school knows about it? Did you ever get your feelings hurt? Has anyone ever told a lie that got you in trouble? Have you ever done these things to someone else?

When people hurt you, you may be angry and upset. That's a normal human reaction. But eventually you have to get to a point where you can forgive them. Otherwise the negative feelings might begin to affect other relationships. That's why Jesus first forgave the paralyzed man's sins (Mark 2:5). Jesus wanted to show that healing someone from sin is even more important than physical healing.

When you forgive someone, you free yourself to move on to other important concerns. When you are forgiven for your sins—by God and the people you have hurt—you are free to move on and learn from your mistake.

- **God forgives you for all your sins if you are truly sorry. Shouldn't you do the same for others?**
- **Who do you need to forgive?**
- **From whom do you need forgiveness?**

— Mark 2:1–12

The Question about the Sabbath

(Matthew 12:1–8; Luke 6:1–5)

23Jesus was walking through some wheat
fields on a Sabbath. As his disciples walked
along with him, they began to pick the
heads of wheat. 24So the Pharisees said to

[e] **2:15** in Levi's house; *or* in his *(that is,* Jesus') house.
2:23 Deut 23:25

Jesus, "Look, it is against our Law for your
disciples to do that on the Sabbath!"
25 Jesus answered, "Have you never read
what David did that time when he needed
something to eat? He and his men were
hungry, 26 so he went into the house of God
and ate the bread offered to God. This hap-
pened when Abiathar was the High Priest.
According to our Law only the priests may
eat this bread—but David ate it and even
gave it to his men."
27 And Jesus concluded, "The Sabbath was
made for the good of human beings; they
were not made for the Sabbath. 28 So the Son
of Man is Lord even of the Sabbath."

The Man with a Paralyzed Hand

(Matthew 12:9–14; Luke 6:6–11)

3 Then Jesus went back to the synagogue,
where there was a man who had a para-
lyzed hand. 2 Some people were there who
wanted to accuse Jesus of doing wrong; so
they watched him closely to see whether he
would cure the man on the Sabbath. 3 Jesus
said to the man, "Come up here to the
front." 4 Then he asked the people, "What
does our Law allow us to do on the Sab-
bath? To help or to harm? To save someone's
life or to destroy it?"
But they did not say a thing. 5 Jesus was
angry as he looked around at them, but at
the same time he felt sorry for them, because
they were so stubborn and wrong. Then he
said to the man, "Stretch out your hand." He
stretched it out, and it became well again.
6 So the Pharisees left the synagogue and met
at once with some members of Herod's
party, and they made plans to kill Jesus.

A Crowd by the Lake

7 Jesus and his disciples went away to Lake
Galilee, and a large crowd followed him.
They had come from Galilee, from Judea,
8 from Jerusalem, from the territory of
Idumea, from the territory on the east side
of the Jordan, and from the region around
the cities of Tyre and Sidon. All these people
came to Jesus because they had heard of the
things he was doing. 9 The crowd was so
large that Jesus told his disciples to get a boat
ready for him, so that the people would not
crush him. 10 He had healed many people,
and all the sick kept pushing their way to
him in order to touch him. 11 And whenever
the people who had evil spirits in them saw
him, they would fall down before him and
scream, "You are the Son of God!"

The crowd was so large . . . (3:9)

2:26 Lev 24:9 **2:25,26** 1 Sam 21:1-6 **3:9,10** Mk 4:1; Lk 5:1-3

Pray it!

Called and Sent

Jesus chose twelve men to be his closest followers. He called them Apostles, which is from a word that means "one who is sent out." Many other men and women followed Jesus, but the Twelve (as they are often called) were singled out by name. They are listed in Mark 3:16–19.

The number 12 had special meaning to Jesus, who was a devout Jew. It represented the twelve sons of Jacob and the twelve tribes of Israel.

The Apostles were twelve people with different personalities and different jobs. Some were young, some were old. Some were married, some single. The thing they had in common was that they were willing to follow Jesus. After Jesus' Resurrection they continued Jesus' mission in building the Church.

Jesus,
Help me to hear your call.
I want to follow you, wherever you lead me.
I don't need to start a church.
I just need to let the Church guide me and strengthen me
so that I can share your love with others.
Thank you, Jesus, for calling me to be part of your family.
Amen.

— Mark 3:13–19

12 Jesus sternly ordered the evil spirits not
to tell anyone who he was.

Jesus Chooses the Twelve Apostles
(Matthew 10:1–4; Luke 6:12–16)

13 Then Jesus went up a hill and called to
himself the men he wanted. They came to
him, 14 and he chose twelve, whom he
named apostles. "I have chosen you to be
with me," he told them. "I will also send you
out to preach, 15 and you will have authority
to drive out demons."

16 These are the twelve he chose: Simon
(Jesus gave him the name Peter); 17 James and
his brother John, the sons of Zebedee (Jesus
gave them the name Boanerges, which
means "Men of Thunder"); 18 Andrew, Philip,
Bartholomew, Matthew, Thomas, James son
of Alphaeus, Thaddaeus, Simon the Patriot,
19 and Judas Iscariot, who betrayed Jesus.

Jesus and Beelzebul
(Matthew 12:22–32; Luke 11:14–23; 12:10)

20 Then Jesus went home. Again such a large
crowd gathered that Jesus and his disciples had
no time to eat. 21 When his family heard about
it, they set out to take charge of him, because
people were saying, "He's gone mad!"

22 Some teachers of the Law who had come
from Jerusalem were saying, "He has Beelze-
bul in him! It is the chief of the demons who
gives him the power to drive them out."

23 So Jesus called them to him and spoke
to them in parables: "How can Satan drive
out Satan? 24 If a country divides itself into
groups which fight each other, that country

3:22 Mt 9:34; 10:25

The Apostle Judas killed himself after he betrayed Jesus. Do you know who replaced him? Check out Acts 1:15–26.

Catholic Connections

The Church Is the Family of God

In the little story about Jesus' mother and brothers (Mark 3:31–35), it almost seems as if Jesus is putting down his family. But that wasn't his intention. Jesus was trying to make a bigger point. His point is that the family of God is bigger than blood relatives or relationships. The family of God is anyone who believes in Jesus and does what God asks.

Starting with teachings such as this, Jesus put into motion everything that was needed to start the Catholic Church. The Church was in God's plan from the very beginning, from the moment of Creation. God calls everyone together in Jesus and the Holy Spirit and invites everyone to become his children. Jesus started the Church to be God's family on earth—which is why the Church is sometimes called the family of God.

— Mark 3:31–35

will fall apart. 25If a family divides itself into
groups which fight each other, that family
will fall apart. 26So if Satan's kingdom
divides into groups, it cannot last, but will
fall apart and come to an end.
27"No one can break into a strong man's
house and take away his belongings unless
he first ties up the strong man; then he can
plunder his house.
28"I assure you that people can be forgiv-
en all their sins and all the evil things they
may say.[f] 29But whoever says evil things
against the Holy Spirit will never be forgiv-
en, because he has committed an eternal
sin." (30Jesus said this because some people
were saying, "He has an evil spirit in him.")

Jesus' Mother and Brothers

(Matthew 12:46–50; Luke 8:19–21)

31Then Jesus' mother and brothers
arrived. They stood outside the house and
sent in a message, asking for him. 32A crowd
was sitting around Jesus, and they said to
him, "Look, your mother and your brothers
and sisters are outside, and they want you."
33Jesus answered, "Who is my mother?
Who are my brothers?" 34He looked at the
people sitting around him and said, "Look!
Here are my mother and my brothers!
35Whoever does what God wants is my
brother, my sister, my mother."

The Parable of the Sower

(Matthew 13:1–9; Luke 8:4–8)

4 Again Jesus began to teach beside Lake
Galilee. The crowd that gathered around
him was so large that he got into a boat and
sat in it. The boat was out in the water, and
the crowd stood on the shore at the water's
edge. 2He used parables to teach them many
things, saying to them:
3"Listen! Once there was a man who
went out to sow grain. 4As he scattered the
seed in the field, some of it fell along the
path, and the birds came and ate it up.
5Some of it fell on rocky ground, where
there was little soil. The seeds soon sprouted,

[f] **3:28** evil things they may say; *or* evil things they may say against God.
3:29 Lk 12:10 **4:1** Lk 5:1-3

" 'Whoever does what God wants is my brother, my sister, my mother' " *(Mark 3:35)*.

Study it!

Story Time!

When you were a child, you probably heard stories like *The Little Engine That Could, Runaway Bunny,* and *Rainbow Fish.* These are interesting stories that teach a lesson about life.

Jesus also used stories to teach people how to live the way God wants them to. These stories with a spiritual message are called parables. To make his point, Jesus told parables about people, places, and things that were familiar to his audience. But his stories often ended in ways that surprised people and made them think about what God was like.

How many different parables can you find in Mark, chapter 4?

— Mark, chapter 4

because the soil wasn't deep. 6Then, when
the sun came up, it burned the young plants;
and because the roots had not grown deep
enough, the plants soon dried up. 7Some of
the seed fell among thorn bushes, which
grew up and choked the plants, and they
didn't bear grain. 8But some seeds fell in
good soil, and the plants sprouted, grew, and
bore grain: some had thirty grains, others
sixty, and others one hundred."

9And Jesus concluded, "Listen, then, if you
have ears!"

The Purpose of the Parables

(Matthew 13:10–17; Luke 8:9, 10)

10When Jesus was alone, some of those
who had heard him came to him with the
twelve disciples and asked him to explain the
parables. 11"You have been given the secret
of the Kingdom of God," Jesus answered.
"But the others, who are on the outside, hear
all things by means of parables, 12so that,

'They may look and look,
yet not see;
they may listen and listen,
yet not understand.
For if they did, they would turn to God,
and he would forgive them.' "

Jesus Explains the Parable of the Sower

(Matthew 13:18–23; Luke 8:11–15)

13Then Jesus asked them, "Don't you
understand this parable? How, then, will you
ever understand any parable? 14The sower
sows God's message. 15Some people are like
the seeds that fall along the path; as soon as
they hear the message, Satan comes and takes
it away. 16Other people are like the seeds
that fall on rocky ground. As soon as they
hear the message, they receive it gladly. 17But
it does not sink deep into them, and they
don't last long. So when trouble or persecution comes because of the message, they give
up at once. 18Other people are like the seeds
sown among the thorn bushes. These are the
ones who hear the message, 19but the worries about this life, the love for riches, and all
other kinds of desires crowd in and choke
the message, and they don't bear fruit. 20But
other people are like seeds sown in good
soil. They hear the message, accept it, and
bear fruit: some thirty, some sixty, and some
one hundred."

A Lamp under a Bowl

(Luke 8:16–18)

21Jesus continued, "Does anyone ever
bring in a lamp and put it under a bowl or
under the bed? Isn't it put on the lampstand?
22Whatever is hidden away will be brought
out into the open, and whatever is covered
up will be uncovered. 23Listen, then, if you
have ears!"

24He also said to them, "Pay attention to
what you hear! The same rules you use to
judge others will be used by God to judge

4:12 Isa 6:9,10 (LXX) **4:21** Mt 5:15; Lk 11:33 **4:22** Mt 10:26; Lk 12:2 **4:24** Mt 7:2; Lk 6:38

you—but with even greater severity. 25 Those
who have something will be given more, and
those who have nothing will have taken
away from them even the little they have."

The Parable of the Growing Seed

26 Jesus went on to say, "The Kingdom of
God is like this. A man scatters seed in his
field. 27 He sleeps at night, is up and about
during the day, and all the while the seeds
are sprouting and growing. Yet he does not
know how it happens. 28 The soil itself makes
the plants grow and bear fruit; first the ten-
der stalk appears, then the head, and finally
the head full of grain. 29 When the grain is
ripe, the man starts cutting it with his sickle,
because harvest time has come.

The Parable of the Mustard Seed
(Matthew 13:31, 32, 34; Luke 13:18, 19)

30 "What shall we say the Kingdom of God
is like?" asked Jesus. "What parable shall we
use to explain it? 31 It is like this. A man takes
a mustard seed, the smallest seed in the world,
and plants it in the ground. 32 After a while it
grows up and becomes the biggest of all
plants. It puts out such large branches that the
birds come and make their nests in its shade."

33 Jesus preached his message to the people,
using many other parables like these; he told
them as much as they could understand.
34 He would not speak to them without using
parables, but when he was alone with his dis-
ciples, he would explain everything to them.

Jesus Calms a Storm
(Matthew 8:23–27; Luke 8:22–25)

35 On the evening of that same day Jesus
said to his disciples, "Let us go across to the
other side of the lake." 36 So they left the
crowd; the disciples got into the boat in
which Jesus was already sitting, and they
took him with them. Other boats were there
too. 37 Suddenly a strong wind blew up, and
the waves began to spill over into the boat,
so that it was about to fill with water. 38 Jesus
was in the back of the boat, sleeping with his
head on a pillow. The disciples woke him up
and said, "Teacher, don't you care that we are
about to die?"

39 Jesus stood up and commanded the wind,
"Be quiet!" and he said to the waves, "Be still!"
The wind died down, and there was a great
calm. 40 Then Jesus said to his disciples, "Why
are you frightened? Do you still have no faith?"

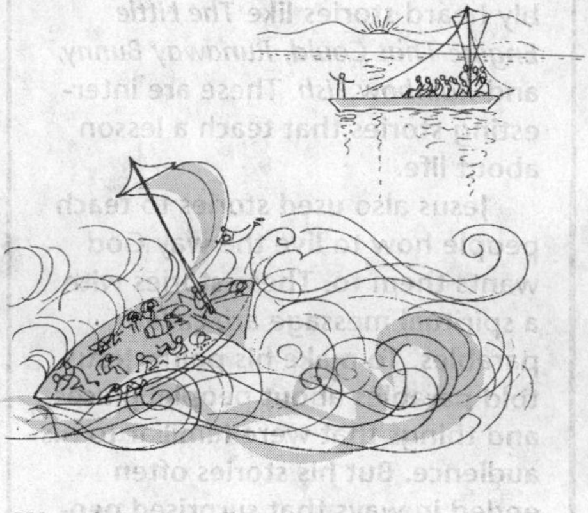

*Waves began to spill over into the boat (4:37) . . .
and there was a great calm. (4:39)*

41 But they were terribly afraid and began
to say to one another, "Who is this man?
Even the wind and the waves obey him!"

Jesus Heals a Man with Evil Spirits
(Matthew 8:28–34; Luke 8:26–39)

5 Jesus and his disciples arrived on the
other side of Lake Galilee, in the terri-
tory of Gerasa. 2 As soon as Jesus got out of
the boat, he was met by a man who came
out of the burial caves there. This man had
an evil spirit in him 3 and lived among the
tombs. Nobody could keep him tied with
chains any more; 4 many times his feet and
his hands had been tied, but every time he
broke the chains and smashed the irons on
his feet. He was too strong for anyone to
control him. 5 Day and night he wandered
among the tombs and through the hills,
screaming and cutting himself with stones.

6 He was some distance away when he saw
Jesus; so he ran, fell on his knees before him,
7 and screamed in a loud voice, "Jesus, Son of
the Most High God! What do you want
with me? For God's sake, I beg you, don't

4:25 Mt 13:12; 25:29; Lk 19:26 **4:29** Joel 3:13

Pray it!

God Is Good!

I know I ask for a lot, God.
Just like the people who saw Jesus at Galilee,
I'm usually asking you for help.
But this prayer is going to be different.
I don't want anything.
I don't need help with a problem.
And I know you're right here with me.
Right now, I just want to say thank you.
Thanks for all you do for me.
Thanks for making me who I am.
Thanks for the people who love me.
Thanks for this wonderful world.
Thanks for being right here with me.
Just one small request: Please give me the courage
to tell my friends how great you are. Amen.

— Mark 5:18–20

punish me!" (8He said this because Jesus was
saying, "Evil spirit, come out of this man!")
9So Jesus asked him, "What is your name?"
The man answered, "My name is 'Mob'—
there are so many of us!" 10And he kept beg-
ging Jesus not to send the evil spirits out of
that region.
11There was a large herd of pigs near by,
feeding on a hillside. 12So the spirits begged
Jesus, "Send us to the pigs, and let us go into
them." 13He let them go, and the evil spirits
went out of the man and entered the pigs.
The whole herd—about two thousand pigs
in all—rushed down the side of the cliff into
the lake and was drowned.
14The men who had been taking care of
the pigs ran away and spread the news in the
town and among the farms. People went out
to see what had happened, 15and when they
came to Jesus, they saw the man who used to
have the mob of demons in him. He was sit-
ting there, clothed and in his right mind; and
they were all afraid. 16Those who had seen it
told the people what had happened to the
man with the demons, and about the pigs.
17So they asked Jesus to leave their territory.
18As Jesus was getting into the boat, the
man who had had the demons begged him,
"Let me go with you!"
19But Jesus would not let him. Instead, he
told him, "Go back home to your family and
tell them how much the Lord has done for
you and how kind he has been to you."
20So the man left and went all through
the Ten Towns, telling what Jesus had done
for him. And all who heard it were amazed.

Jairus' Daughter and the Woman Who Touched Jesus' Cloak

(Matthew 9:18–26; Luke 8:40–56)

21Jesus went back across to the other side
of the lake. There at the lakeside a large
crowd gathered around him. 22Jairus, an offi-
cial of the local synagogue, arrived, and
when he saw Jesus, he threw himself down

Read Mark 4:35–41. What rough and stormy times in your life do you need Jesus' help with?

at his feet 23 and begged him earnestly, "My little daughter is very sick. Please come and place your hands on her, so that she will get well and live!"

24 Then Jesus started off with him. So many people were going along with Jesus that they were crowding him from every side.

25 There was a woman who had suffered terribly from severe bleeding for twelve years, 26 even though she had been treated by many doctors. She had spent all her money, but instead of getting better she got worse all the time. 27 She had heard about Jesus, so she came in the crowd behind him, 28 saying to herself, "If I just touch his clothes, I will get well."

29 She touched his cloak, and her bleeding stopped at once; and she had the feeling inside herself that she was healed of her trouble. 30 At once Jesus knew that power had gone out of him, so he turned around in the crowd and asked, "Who touched my clothes?"

31 His disciples answered, "You see how the people are crowding you; why do you ask who touched you?"

32 But Jesus kept looking around to see who had done it. 33 The woman realized what had happened to her, so she came, trembling with fear, knelt at his feet, and told him the whole truth. 34 Jesus said to her, "My daughter, your faith has made you well. Go in peace, and be healed of your trouble."

35 While Jesus was saying this, some messengers came from Jairus' house and told him, "Your daughter has died. Why bother the Teacher any longer?"

36 Jesus paid no attention to[g] what they said, but told him, "Don't be afraid, only believe." 37 Then he did not let anyone else go on with him except Peter and James and his brother John. 38 They arrived at Jairus' house, where Jesus saw the confusion and heard all the loud crying and wailing. 39 He went in and said to them, "Why all this confusion? Why are you crying? The child is not dead—she is only sleeping!"

40 They started making fun of him, so he put them all out, took the child's father and mother and his three disciples, and went into the room where the child was lying. 41 He took her by the hand and said to her, *"Talitha, koum,"* which means, "Little girl, I tell you to get up!"

42 She got up at once and started walking around. (She was twelve years old.) When this happened, they were completely amazed. 43 But Jesus gave them strict orders not to tell anyone, and he said, "Give her something to eat."

Jesus Is Rejected at Nazareth

(Matthew 13:53–58; Luke 4:16–30)

6 Jesus left that place and went back to his hometown, followed by his disciples. 2 On the Sabbath he began to teach in the synagogue. Many people were there; and when they heard him, they were all amazed. "Where did he get all this?" they asked. "What wisdom is this that has been given him? How does he perform miracles? 3 Isn't he the carpenter, the son of Mary, and the brother of James, Joseph, Judas, and Simon? Aren't his sisters living here?" And so they rejected him.

4 Jesus said to them, "Prophets are respected everywhere except in their own hometown and by their relatives and their family."

5 He was not able to perform any miracles there, except that he placed his hands on a few sick people and healed them. 6 He was greatly surprised, because the people did not have faith.

Jesus Sends Out the Twelve Disciples

(Matthew 10:5–15; Luke 9:1–6)

Then Jesus went to the villages around there, teaching the people. 7 He called the twelve disciples together and sent them out two by two. He gave them authority over the evil spirits 8 and ordered them, "Don't take anything with you on the trip except a walking stick—no bread, no beggar's bag, no

[g] **5:36** paid no attention to; *or* overheard.
5:26 Tob 2:10 **6:4** Jn 4:44

How many miracles did Jesus perform in Mark, chapters 5–6?

money in your pockets. 9 Wear sandals, but
don't carry an extra shirt." 10 He also told
them, "Wherever you are welcomed, stay in
the same house until you leave that place.
11 If you come to a town where people do
not welcome you or will not listen to you,
leave it and shake the dust off your feet. That
will be a warning to them!"

12 So they went out and preached that peo-
ple should turn away from their sins. 13 They
drove out many demons, and rubbed olive oil
on many sick people and healed them.

The Death of John the Baptist
(Matthew 14:1–12; Luke 9:7–9)

14 Now King Herod[h] heard about all this,
because Jesus' reputation had spread every-
where. Some people were saying, "John the
Baptist has come back to life! That is why he
has this power to perform miracles."

15 Others, however, said, "He is Elijah."

Others said, "He is a prophet, like one of
the prophets of long ago."

16 When Herod heard it, he said, "He is
John the Baptist! I had his head cut off, but
he has come back to life!" 17 Herod himself
had ordered John's arrest, and he had him
tied up and put in prison. Herod did this
because of Herodias, whom he had married,
even though she was the wife of his brother
Philip. 18 John the Baptist kept telling Herod,
"It isn't right for you to marry your broth-
er's wife!"

19 So Herodias held a grudge against John
and wanted to kill him, but she could not
because of Herod. 20 Herod was afraid of
John because he knew that John was a good
and holy man, and so he kept him safe. He
liked to listen to him, even though he
became greatly disturbed every time he
heard him.

21 Finally Herodias got her chance. It was
on Herod's birthday, when he gave a feast for
all the top government officials, the military
chiefs, and the leading citizens of Galilee.
22 The daughter of Herodias[i] came in and
danced, and pleased Herod and his guests. So
the king said to the girl, "What would you
like to have? I will give you anything you
want." 23 With many vows he said to her, "I
swear that I will give you anything you ask
for, even as much as half my kingdom!"

24 So the girl went out and asked her
mother, "What shall I ask for?"

"The head of John the Baptist," she
answered.

25 The girl hurried back at once to the
king and demanded, "I want you to give me
here and now the head of John the Baptist
on a plate!"

Live it!

What? No Cell Phone?

Can you imagine going away for a while with nothing but the clothes and shoes you have on? No money, no extra clothes, nothing! That's what Jesus tells the disciples to do when he sends them off to preach (Mark 6:7–9). He tells them to rely on the goodness of the people they meet.

Most of us have too many things. Our lives are cluttered with possessions we think we can't live without. We get so caught up in the things we think we need for day-to-day living that we forget the most important thing: God.

Next time you're packing up for school or to go to a friend's house, remind yourself to pack the knowledge that God is with you, God cares for you, and God wants you to spread the Good News to others. And to do that, you don't need anything but the love in your heart.

— Mark 6:6–13

[h] **6:14** KING HEROD: *Herod Antipas, ruler of Galilee.* [i] **6:22** The daughter of Herodias; *some manuscripts have* His daughter Herodias.

6:11 Acts 13:51 **6:8-11** Lk 10:4-11 **6:13** Jas 5:14 **6:14,15** Mt 16:14; Mk 8:28; Lk 9:19 **6:17,18** Lk 3:19,20

Live it!

Feeding the Hungry

Millions of people in this world—and in this country—don't get enough to eat. Most of us can't understand what such hunger feels like. We can barely make it from lunch to dinner without a snack. But many people get nothing to eat for days.

Jesus took a few loaves of bread and a couple of fish and fed thousands of people who came to see him. You can't perform miracles like that, but you can make a difference in lots of ways:

- **Give up a few treats each week and give the money you save to poor people.**
- **Donate food when your school runs a food drive.**
- **Collect food from your neighbors and friends and donate it.**
- **Pray for people who are starving.**

Jesus is a special friend of poor people, and as members of the Body of Christ, we need to befriend them too. You probably don't know what it's like to go hungry, but you can be a special friend to those who do.

— Mark 6:30–44

26 This made the king very sad, but he could not refuse her because of the vows he had made in front of all his guests. 27 So he sent off a guard at once with orders to bring John's head. The guard left, went to the prison, and cut John's head off; 28 then he brought it on a plate and gave it to the girl, who gave it to her mother. 29 When John's disciples heard about this, they came and got his body, and buried it.

Jesus Feeds Five Thousand

(Matthew 14:13–21; Luke 9:10–17; John 6:1–14)

30 The apostles returned and met with Jesus, and told him all they had done and taught. 31 There were so many people coming and going that Jesus and his disciples didn't even have time to eat. So he said to them, "Let us go off by ourselves to some place where we will be alone and you can rest a while." 32 So they started out in a boat by themselves to a lonely place.

33 Many people, however, saw them leave and knew at once who they were; so they went from all the towns and ran ahead by land and arrived at the place ahead of Jesus and his disciples. 34 When Jesus got out of the boat, he saw this large crowd, and his heart was filled with pity for them, because they were like sheep without a shepherd. So he began to teach them many things. 35 When it was getting late, his disciples came to him and said, "It is already very late, and this is a lonely place. 36 Send the people away, and let them go to the nearby farms and villages in order to buy themselves something to eat."

37 "You yourselves give them something to eat," Jesus answered.

They asked, "Do you want us to go and spend two hundred silver coins[j] on bread in order to feed them?"

38 So Jesus asked them, "How much bread do you have? Go and see."

When they found out, they told him, "Five loaves and also two fish."

39 Jesus then told his disciples to make all the people divide into groups and sit down on the green grass. 40 So the people sat down in rows, in groups of a hundred and groups of fifty. 41 Then Jesus took the five loaves and the two fish, looked up to heaven, and gave thanks to God. He broke the loaves and gave them to his disciples to distribute to the people. He also divided the two fish among them all. 42 Everyone ate and had enough. 43 Then the disciples took up twelve baskets full of what was left of the bread and the fish. 44 The number of men who were fed was five thousand.

[j] **6:37** SILVER COINS: *A silver coin was the daily wage of a rural worker (see Mt 20:2).*
6:34 Num 27:17; 1 Kings 22:17; 2 Chr 18:16; Ezek 34:5; Mt 9:36

"It's a ghost!" (6:49)

Jesus Walks on the Water
(Matthew 14:22–33; John 6:15–21)

45At once Jesus made his disciples get into
the boat and go ahead of him to Bethsaida, on
the other side of the lake, while he sent the
crowd away. 46After saying good-bye to the
people, he went away to a hill to pray. 47When
evening came, the boat was in the middle of
the lake, while Jesus was alone on land. 48He
saw that his disciples were straining at the oars,
because they were rowing against the wind; so
sometime between three and six o'clock in
the morning, he came to them, walking on
the water. He was going to pass them by,[k]
49but they saw him walking on the water. "It's
a ghost!" they thought, and screamed. 50They
were all terrified when they saw him.

Jesus spoke to them at once, "Courage!"
he said. "It is I. Don't be afraid!" 51Then he
got into the boat with them, and the wind
died down. The disciples were completely
amazed, 52because they had not understood
the real meaning of the feeding of the five
thousand; their minds could not grasp it.

Jesus Heals the Sick in Gennesaret
(Matthew 14:34–36)

53They crossed the lake and came to land at
Gennesaret, where they tied up the boat. 54As
they left the boat, people recognized Jesus at
once. 55So they ran throughout the whole
region; and wherever they heard he was, they
brought to him the sick lying on their mats.
56And everywhere Jesus went, to villages,
towns, or farms, people would take their sick
to the marketplaces and beg him to let the
sick at least touch the edge of his cloak. And
all who touched it were made well.

The Teaching of the Ancestors
(Matthew 15:1–9)

7 Some Pharisees and teachers of the Law
who had come from Jerusalem gathered
around Jesus. 2They noticed that some of his
disciples were eating their food with hands
that were ritually unclean—that is, they had
not washed them in the way the Pharisees
said people should.

(3For the Pharisees, as well as the rest of
the Jews, follow the teaching they received
from their ancestors: they do not eat unless
they wash their hands in the proper way;
4nor do they eat anything that comes from
the market unless they wash it first.[l] And
they follow many other rules which they
have received, such as the proper way to
wash cups, pots, copper bowls, and beds.[m])

5So the Pharisees and the teachers of the
Law asked Jesus, "Why is it that your disci-
ples do not follow the teaching handed
down by our ancestors, but instead eat with
ritually unclean hands?"

6Jesus answered them, "How right Isaiah
was when he prophesied about you! You are
hypocrites, just as he wrote:

'These people, says God, honor me with
their words,
but their heart is really far away from
me.
7It is no use for them to worship me,
because they teach human rules
as though they were my laws!'

8"You put aside God's command and
obey human teachings."

9And Jesus continued, "You have a clever
way of rejecting God's law in order to

[k] **6:48** pass them by; *or* join them. [l] **7:4** anything that comes from the market unless they wash it first; *or* anything after they come from the market unless they wash themselves first. [m] **7:4** *Some manuscripts do not have* and beds.
7:6,7 Isa 29:13 (LXX)

Jews followed strict laws for preparing and eating food *(see Mark 7:3–4)*. **Check out Leviticus, chapter 11, for more laws about food.**

uphold your own teaching. 10 For Moses commanded, 'Respect your father and your mother,' and, 'If you curse your father or your mother, you are to be put to death.' 11 But you teach that if people have something they could use to help their father or mother, but say, 'This is Corban' (which means, it belongs to God), 12 they are excused from helping their father or mother. 13 In this way the teaching you pass on to others cancels out the word of God. And there are many other things like this that you do."

The Things That Make a Person Unclean

(Matthew 15:10–20)

14 Then Jesus called the crowd to him once more and said to them, "Listen to me, all of you, and understand. 15 There is nothing that goes into you from the outside which can make you ritually unclean. Rather, it is what comes out of you that makes you unclean."[n]

17 When he left the crowd and went into the house, his disciples asked him to explain this saying. 18 "You are no more intelligent than the others," Jesus said to them. "Don't you understand? Nothing that goes into you from the outside can really make you unclean, 19 because it does not go into your heart but into your stomach and then goes on out of the body." (In saying this, Jesus declared that all foods are fit to be eaten.)

20 And he went on to say, "It is what comes out of you that makes you unclean. 21 For from the inside, from your heart, come the evil ideas which lead you to do immoral things, to rob, kill, 22 commit adultery, be greedy, and do all sorts of evil things; deceit, indecency, jealousy, slander, pride, and folly— 23 all these evil things come from inside you and make you unclean."

A Woman's Faith

(Matthew 15:21–28)

24 Then Jesus left and went away to the territory near the city of Tyre. He went into a house and did not want anyone to know he was there, but he could not stay hidden. 25 A woman, whose daughter had an evil spirit in her, heard about Jesus and came to him at once and fell at his feet. 26 The woman was a Gentile, born in the region of Phoenicia in Syria. She begged Jesus to drive the demon out of her daughter. 27 But Jesus answered, "Let us first feed the children. It isn't right to take the children's food and throw it to the dogs."

28 "Sir," she answered, "even the dogs under the table eat the children's leftovers!"

29 So Jesus said to her, "Because of that answer, go back home, where you will find that the demon has gone out of your daughter!"

30 She went home and found her child lying on the bed; the demon had indeed gone out of her.

Jesus Heals a Deaf-Mute

31 Jesus then left the neighborhood of Tyre and went on through Sidon to Lake Galilee, going by way of the territory of the Ten Towns. 32 Some people brought him a man who was deaf and could hardly speak, and they begged Jesus to place his hands on him. 33 So Jesus took him off alone, away from the crowd, put his fingers in the man's ears, spat, and touched the man's tongue. 34 Then Jesus looked up to heaven, gave a deep groan, and said to the man, *"Ephphatha,"* which means, "Open up!"

35 At once the man was able to hear, his speech impediment was removed, and he began to talk without any trouble. 36 Then Jesus ordered the people not to speak of it to anyone; but the more he ordered them not to, the more they told it. 37 And all who

[n] **7:15** *Some manuscripts add verse 16:* Listen, then, if you have ears! *(see 4:23).*

7:10 **a** Ex 20:12; Deut 5:16; **b** Ex 21:17; Lev 20:9

" 'For from inside, from your heart, come the evil ideas which lead you to do immoral things' " *(Mark 7:21)*.

Live it!

Watch Those "Isms"!

The woman's daughter was sick. She had heard about Jesus and decided to take a chance, even though he was a Jew and she was not. In Jesus' culture Jews were expected to stay away from non-Jews, but out of mercy and love he healed the girl (Mark 7:24–30).

Some people refuse to associate with those who aren't like them. They may believe that people who are different are inferior. These people are *prejudiced,* that is, they "pre-judge" others.

Some common prejudices include *racism* (judging on the basis of skin color or home country), *sexism* (stereotyping or treating someone unfairly because of gender), and *ageism* (discriminating against people because of their age). These attitudes are contrary to Jesus' law of love. They are sinful. What prejudices or "isms" exist in your community? How can you help eliminate them?

— Mark 7:24–30

heard were completely amazed. "How well
he does everything!" they exclaimed. "He
even causes the deaf to hear and the dumb
to speak!"

Jesus Feeds Four Thousand People
(Matthew 15:32–39)

8 Not long afterward another large crowd
came together. When the people had
nothing left to eat, Jesus called the disciples
to him and said, 2"I feel sorry for these peo-
ple, because they have been with me for
three days and now have nothing to eat. 3If I
send them home without feeding them, they
will faint as they go, because some of them
have come a long way."

4His disciples asked him, "Where in this
desert can anyone find enough food to feed
all these people?"

5"How much bread do you have?" Jesus
asked.

"Seven loaves," they answered.

6He ordered the crowd to sit down on
the ground. Then he took the seven loaves,
gave thanks to God, broke them, and gave
them to his disciples to distribute to the
crowd; and the disciples did so. 7They also
had a few small fish. Jesus gave thanks for
these and told the disciples to distribute
them too. 8-9Everybody ate and had
enough—there were about four thousand
people. Then the disciples took up seven bas-
kets full of pieces left over. Jesus sent the
people away 10and at once got into a boat
with his disciples and went to the district of
Dalmanutha.

The Pharisees Ask for a Miracle
(Matthew 16:1–4)

11Some Pharisees came to Jesus and started
to argue with him. They wanted to trap him,
so they asked him to perform a miracle to
show that God approved of him. 12But Jesus
gave a deep groan and said, "Why do the peo-
ple of this day ask for a miracle? No, I tell you!
No such proof will be given to these people!"

13He left them, got back into the boat, and
started across to the other side of the lake.

The Yeast of the Pharisees and of Herod
(Matthew 16:5–12)

14The disciples had forgotten to bring
enough bread and had only one loaf with
them in the boat. 15"Take care," Jesus warned
them, "and be on your guard against the yeast
of the Pharisees and the yeast of Herod."

16They started discussing among them-
selves: "He says this because we don't have
any bread."

17Jesus knew what they were saying, so he
asked them, "Why are you discussing about

8:11 Mt 12:38; Lk 11:16 **8:12** Mt 12:39; Lk 11:29 **8:15** Lk 12:1

Live it!

What's Your Answer?

You've probably noticed that you're changing. Your body is growing, you think deeper thoughts, and your emotions are more complicated. You are on an exciting road to becoming an adult.

Your understanding of God is also changing. When you were a child, your thoughts about God were simple. Now that you're older, you have deeper faith, but you may also have more questions. You may even have doubts.

Your understanding of God must grow with you. Jesus will keep asking the question, "Who do you say I am?" just as he asked his first disciples in the middle of this chapter (Mark 8:29). Keep thinking about your answer and pray for the Holy Spirit to guide your thoughts. Peter must have been thinking for some time about who Jesus was. If you do the same, you can answer Jesus as confidently as he did: "You are the Messiah" (8:29).

— Mark 8:27–30

not having any bread? Don't you know or
understand yet? Are your minds so dull?
18You have eyes—can't you see? You have
ears—can't you hear? Don't you remember
19when I broke the five loaves for the five
thousand people? How many baskets full of
leftover pieces did you take up?"
"Twelve," they answered.
20"And when I broke the seven loaves for
the four thousand people," asked Jesus, "how
many baskets full of leftover pieces did you
take up?"
"Seven," they answered.
21"And you still don't understand?" he
asked them.

Jesus Heals a Blind Man at Bethsaida

22They came to Bethsaida, where some
people brought a blind man to Jesus and
begged him to touch him. 23Jesus took the
blind man by the hand and led him out of
the village. After spitting on the man's eyes,
Jesus placed his hands on him and asked
him, "Can you see anything?"
24The man looked up and said, "Yes, I can
see people, but they look like trees walking
around."
25Jesus again placed his hands on the man's
eyes. This time the man looked intently, his
eyesight returned, and he saw everything
clearly. 26Jesus then sent him home with the
order, "Don't go back into the village."

Peter's Declaration about Jesus
(Matthew 16:13–20; Luke 9:18–21)

27Then Jesus and his disciples went away
to the villages near Caesarea Philippi. On the
way he asked them, "Tell me, who do people
say I am?"
28"Some say that you are John the Bap-
tist," they answered; "others say that you are
Elijah, while others say that you are one of
the prophets."
29"What about you?" he asked them.
"Who do you say I am?"
Peter answered, "You are the Messiah."
30Then Jesus ordered them, "Do not tell
anyone about me."

Jesus Speaks about His Suffering and Death
(Matthew 16:21–28; Luke 9:22–27)

31Then Jesus began to teach his disciples:
"The Son of Man must suffer much and be
rejected by the elders, the chief priests, and
the teachers of the Law. He will be put to
death, but three days later he will rise to
life." 32He made this very clear to them. So
Peter took him aside and began to rebuke
him. 33But Jesus turned around, looked at his
disciples, and rebuked Peter. "Get away from

8:18 Jer 5:21; Ezek 12:2; Mk 4:12 **8:28** Mk 6:14,15; Lk 9:7,8 **8:29** Jn 6:68,69

Catholic Connections

Dazzled by Glory

The scene described at the beginning of Mark, chapter 9, is known as the Transfiguration. It was a moment when Jesus was literally changed so that his glory as the divine Son of God was revealed. The dazzling sight overwhelmed Peter, James, and John, who were with Jesus on the mountaintop that day. It was a sneak peek for the three Apostles of the time when Jesus would be resurrected.

In the Transfiguration the Holy Trinity was present. The Father was the voice, Jesus the Son was there, and the Holy Spirit was represented by the cloud. The Church has many prayers that praise the Holy Trinity. Following is the most common of these prayers. It is usually called the Glory Be. Memorize it and say it the next time you are dazzled by God's brilliance!

Glory be to the Father, and to the Son, and to the Holy Spirit:
As it was in the beginning, is now,
and will be forever. Amen.

— Mark 9:2–8

me, Satan," he said. "Your thoughts don't come from God but from human nature!"

34 Then Jesus called the crowd and his disciples to him. "If any of you want to come with me," he told them, "you must forget yourself, carry your cross, and follow me. 35 For if you want to save your own life, you will lose it; but if you lose your life for me and for the gospel, you will save it. 36 Do you gain anything if you win the whole world but lose your life? Of course not! 37 There is nothing you can give to regain your life. 38 If you are ashamed of me and of my teaching in this godless and wicked day, then the Son of Man will be ashamed of you when he comes in the glory of his Father with the holy angels."

. . . you must forget yourself, carry your cross, and follow me. (8:34)

9 And he went on to say, "I tell you, there are some here who will not die until they have seen the Kingdom of God come with power."

The Transfiguration

(Matthew 17:1–13; Luke 9:28–36)

2 Six days later Jesus took with him Peter, James, and John, and led them up a high mountain, where they were alone. As they looked on, a change came over Jesus, 3 and his clothes became shining white—whiter than anyone in the world could wash them. 4 Then the three disciples saw Elijah and Moses talking with Jesus. 5 Peter spoke up and said to Jesus, "Teacher, how good it is that we are here! We will make three tents,

8:34 Mt 10:38; Lk 14:27 **8:35** Mt 10:39; Lk 17:33; Jn 12:25 **9:2-7** 2 Pet 1:17,18

Jesus probably fed more than five thousand people with the loaves and fishes. Read Mark 6:44 carefully and see if you can explain why.

one for you, one for Moses, and one for Elijah." 6He and the others were so frightened that he did not know what to say.

7Then a cloud appeared and covered them with its shadow, and a voice came from the cloud, "This is my own dear Son—listen to him!" 8They took a quick look around but did not see anyone else; only Jesus was with them.

9As they came down the mountain, Jesus ordered them, "Don't tell anyone what you have seen, until the Son of Man has risen from death."

10They obeyed his order, but among themselves they started discussing the matter, "What does this 'rising from death' mean?" 11And they asked Jesus, "Why do the teachers of the Law say that Elijah has to come first?"

12His answer was, "Elijah is indeed coming first in order to get everything ready. Yet why do the Scriptures say that the Son of Man will suffer much and be rejected? 13I tell you, however, that Elijah has already come and that people treated him just as they pleased, as the Scriptures say about him."

Jesus Heals a Boy with an Evil Spirit
(Matthew 17:14–21; Luke 9:37–43a)

14When they joined the rest of the disciples, they saw a large crowd around them and some teachers of the Law arguing with them. 15When the people saw Jesus, they were greatly surprised, and ran to him and greeted him. 16Jesus asked his disciples, "What are you arguing with them about?"

17A man in the crowd answered, "Teacher, I brought my son to you, because he has an evil spirit in him and cannot talk. 18Whenever the spirit attacks him, it throws him to the ground, and he foams at the mouth, grits his teeth, and becomes stiff all over. I asked your disciples to drive the spirit out, but they could not."

19Jesus said to them, "How unbelieving you people are! How long must I stay with you? How long do I have to put up with you? Bring the boy to me!" 20They brought him to Jesus.

As soon as the spirit saw Jesus, it threw the boy into a fit, so that he fell on the ground and rolled around, foaming at the mouth. 21"How long has he been like this?" Jesus asked the father.

"Ever since he was a child," he replied. 22"Many times the evil spirit has tried to kill him by throwing him in the fire and into water. Have pity on us and help us, if you possibly can!"

23"Yes," said Jesus, "if you yourself can! Everything is possible for the person who has faith."

24The father at once cried out, "I do have faith, but not enough. Help me have more!"

25Jesus noticed that the crowd was closing in on them, so he gave a command to the evil spirit. "Deaf and dumb spirit," he said, "I order you to come out of the boy and never go into him again!"

26The spirit screamed, threw the boy into a bad fit, and came out. The boy looked like a corpse, and everyone said, "He is dead!" 27But Jesus took the boy by the hand and helped him rise, and he stood up.

28After Jesus had gone indoors, his disciples asked him privately, "Why couldn't we drive the spirit out?"

29"Only prayer can drive this kind out," answered Jesus; "nothing else can."

Jesus Speaks Again about His Death
(Matthew 17:22, 23; Luke 9:43b–45)

30Jesus and his disciples left that place and went on through Galilee. Jesus did not want anyone to know where he was, 31because he was teaching his disciples: "The Son of Man will be handed over to those who will kill him. Three days later, however, he will rise to life."

32But they did not understand what this teaching meant, and they were afraid to ask him.

9:7 Mt 3:17; Mk 1:11; Lk 3:22 **9:11** Mal 4:5; Mt 11:14 **9:12** Sir 48:10

"Everything is possible for the person who has faith" *(Mark 9:23)*.

Who Is the Greatest?
(Matthew 18:1–5; Luke 9:46–48)

33They came to Capernaum, and after
going indoors Jesus asked his disciples, "What
were you arguing about on the road?"
34But they would not answer him,
because on the road they had been arguing
among themselves about who was the great-
est. 35Jesus sat down, called the twelve disci-
ples, and said to them, "Whoever wants to be
first must place himself last of all and be the
servant of all." 36Then he took a child and
had him stand in front of them. He put his
arms around him and said to them, 37"Who-
ever welcomes in my name one of these
children, welcomes me; and whoever wel-
comes me, welcomes not only me but also
the one who sent me."

Whoever Is Not against Us Is for Us
(Luke 9:49, 50)

38John said to him, "Teacher, we saw a
man who was driving out demons in your
name, and we told him to stop, because he
doesn't belong to our group."
39"Do not try to stop him," Jesus told
them, "because no one who performs a mir-
acle in my name will be able soon afterward
to say evil things about me. 40For whoever is
not against us is for us. 41I assure you that
anyone who gives you a drink of water
because you belong to me will certainly
receive a reward.

Temptations to Sin
(Matthew 18:6–9; Luke 17:1, 2)

42"If anyone should cause one of these lit-
tle ones to lose faith in me, it would be bet-
ter for that person to have a large millstone
tied around the neck and be thrown into the
sea. 43So if your hand makes you lose your
faith, cut it off! It is better for you to enter
life without a hand than to keep both hands
and go off to hell, to the fire that never goes
out.[o] 45And if your foot makes you lose your
faith, cut it off! It is better for you to enter
life without a foot than to keep both feet
and be thrown into hell.[p] 47And if your eye
makes you lose your faith, take it out! It is
better for you to enter the Kingdom of God
with only one eye than to keep both eyes
and be thrown into hell. 48There 'the worms
that eat them never die, and the fire that
burns them is never put out.'
49"Everyone will be purified by fire as a
sacrifice is purified by salt.
50"Salt is good; but if it loses its saltiness,
how can you make it salty again?
"Have the salt of friendship among your-
selves, and live in peace with one another."

Jesus Teaches about Divorce
(Matthew 19:1–12; Luke 16:18)

10 Then Jesus left that place, went to the
province of Judea, and crossed the
Jordan River. Crowds came flocking to him
again, and he taught them, as he always did.
2Some Pharisees came to him and tried to
trap him. "Tell us," they asked, "does our Law
allow a man to divorce his wife?"
3Jesus answered with a question, "What
law did Moses give you?"
4Their answer was, "Moses gave permis-
sion for a man to write a divorce notice and
send his wife away."
5Jesus said to them, "Moses wrote this law
for you because you are so hard to teach.
6But in the beginning, at the time of cre-
ation, 'God made them male and female,' as
the scripture says. 7'And for this reason a
man will leave his father and mother and
unite with his wife,[q] 8and the two will
become one.' So they are no longer two, but
one. 9No human being must separate, then,
what God has joined together."
10When they went back into the house,
the disciples asked Jesus about this matter.
11He said to them, "A man who divorces his

[o] **9:43** *Some manuscripts add verse 44:* There 'the worms that eat them never die, and the fire that burns them is never put out' *(see verse 48).* [p] **9:45** *Some manuscripts add verse 46:* There 'the worms that eat them never die, and the fire that burns them is never put out' *(see verse 48).* [q] **10:7** *Some manuscripts do not have* and unite with his wife.

9:34 Lk 22:24 **9:35** Mt 20:26,27; 23:11; Mk 10:43,44; Lk 22:26 **9:37** Mt 10:40; Lk 10:16; Jn 13:20 **9:40** Mt 12:30; Lk 11:23 **9:41** Mt 10:42 **9:43** Mt 5:30 **9:47** Mt 5:29 **9:48** Isa 66:24 **9:50** Mt 5:13; Lk 14:34,35 **10:4** Deut 24:1-4; Mt 5:31 **10:6** Gen 1:27; 5:2 **10:7,8** Gen 2:24 **10:11,12** Mt 5:32; 1 Cor 7:10,11

Live it!

The Challenge

It's no wonder the guy was upset. He went to see Jesus, thinking that he was well on his way to heaven. After all, he followed the rules. But Jesus told him that it wasn't enough. He told the man to sell everything, give the money to poor people, and then follow him (Mark 10:17–23).

Jesus made it clear that just following rules is not enough. Just because someone goes to church doesn't mean an automatic ticket to heaven. We have to live the life we hear about in church. That means being honest, being a peacemaker, helping poor people, loving our enemies, praying, and doing all the other things Jesus taught.

The man in the story walked away. We don't know what he did after that. Maybe he did what Jesus told him to do and came back. What would you do?

— Mark 10:17–31

wife and marries another woman commits
adultery against his wife. 12 In the same way, a
woman who divorces her husband and mar-
ries another man commits adultery."

Jesus Blesses Little Children
(Matthew 19:13–15; Luke 18:15–17)

13 Some people brought children to Jesus
for him to place his hands on them, but the
disciples scolded the people. 14 When Jesus
noticed this, he was angry and said to his dis-
ciples, "Let the children come to me, and do
not stop them, because the Kingdom of God
belongs to such as these. 15 I assure you that
whoever does not receive the Kingdom of
God like a child will never enter it." 16 Then
he took the children in his arms, placed his
hands on each of them, and blessed them.

The Rich Man
(Matthew 19:16–30; Luke 18:18–30)

17 As Jesus was starting on his way again, a
man ran up, knelt before him, and asked
him, "Good Teacher, what must I do to
receive eternal life?"

18 "Why do you call me good?" Jesus asked
him. "No one is good except God alone.
19 You know the commandments: 'Do not
commit murder; do not commit adultery; do
not steal; do not accuse anyone falsely; do not
cheat; respect your father and your mother.' "

20 "Teacher," the man said, "ever since I
was young, I have obeyed all these com-
mandments."

21 Jesus looked straight at him with love
and said, "You need only one thing. Go and
sell all you have and give the money to the
poor, and you will have riches in heaven;
then come and follow me." 22 When the man
heard this, gloom spread over his face, and he
went away sad, because he was very rich.

23 Jesus looked around at his disciples and
said to them, "How hard it will be for rich
people to enter the Kingdom of God!"

24 The disciples were shocked at these
words, but Jesus went on to say, "My chil-
dren, how hard it is to enter the Kingdom of
God! 25 It is much harder for a rich person to
enter the Kingdom of God than for a camel
to go through the eye of a needle."

26 At this the disciples were completely
amazed and asked one another, "Who, then,
can be saved?"

27 Jesus looked straight at them and
answered, "This is impossible for human
beings but not for God; everything is possi-
ble for God."

28 Then Peter spoke up, "Look, we have
left everything and followed you."

29 "Yes," Jesus said to them, "and I tell you
that those who leave home or brothers or
sisters or mother or father or children or
fields for me and for the gospel, 30 will

10:15 Mt 18:3 **10:19** **a** Ex 20:13; Deut 5:17; **b** Ex 20:14; Deut 5:18; **c** Ex 20:15; Deut 5:19; **d** Ex 20:16; Deut 5:20; **e** Ex 20:12; Deut 5:16

receive much more in this present age. They
will receive a hundred times more houses,
brothers, sisters, mothers, children, and
fields—and persecutions as well; and in the
age to come they will receive eternal life.
31But many who are now first will be last,
and many who are now last will be first."

Jesus Speaks a Third Time about His Death

(Matthew 20:17–19; Luke 18:31–34)

32Jesus and his disciples were now on the
road going up to Jerusalem. Jesus was going
ahead of the disciples, who were filled with
alarm; the people who followed behind were
afraid. Once again Jesus took the twelve disci-
ples aside and spoke of the things that were
going to happen to him. 33"Listen," he told
them, "we are going up to Jerusalem where
the Son of Man will be handed over to the
chief priests and the teachers of the Law. They
will condemn him to death and then hand
him over to the Gentiles, 34who will make
fun of him, spit on him, whip him, and kill
him; but three days later he will rise to life."

The Request of James and John

(Matthew 20:20–28)

35Then James and John, the sons of
Zebedee, came to Jesus. "Teacher," they said,
"there is something we want you to do for us."
36"What is it?" Jesus asked them.
37They answered, "When you sit on your
throne in your glorious Kingdom, we want
you to let us sit with you, one at your right
and one at your left."
38Jesus said to them, "You don't know
what you are asking for. Can you drink the
cup of suffering that I must drink? Can you
be baptized in the way I must be baptized?"
39"We can," they answered.
Jesus said to them, "You will indeed drink
the cup I must drink and be baptized in the
way I must be baptized. 40But I do not have the
right to choose who will sit at my right and my
left. It is God who will give these places to
those for whom he has prepared them."
41When the other ten disciples heard
about it, they became angry with James and
John. 42So Jesus called them all together to
him and said, "You know that those who are
considered rulers of the heathen have power

Live it!

Me First!

James and John were brothers with big plans—they wanted to be leaders and sit beside Jesus. Jesus gave them a quick lesson in leadership. He said that being a leader is not about being first or most important. "If one of you wants to be great, you must be the servant of the rest" (Mark 10:43).

Are you a leader? People in student government or officers of clubs are leaders. So are people who tutor children, work with young groups of scouts, or help coach sports teams. You are also a leader if you have younger brothers and sisters or babysit children.

Leadership is not about having power over someone. It's not about telling people what to do and what not to do. It's about making hard choices and giving people what they need to be all that God created them to be. It means putting yourself last, not first.

Jesus was the ultimate leader. When you lead someone else, follow his example and be a servant first.

— Mark 10:35–45

10:31 Mt 20:16; Lk 13:30 **10:38** Lk 12:50 **10:42,43** Lk 22:25,26

Chapter 10 of Mark mentions a province and two cities. Name them and find them on the map "Ministry of Jesus" in the back of this Bible.

over them, and the leaders have complete
authority. 43 This, however, is not the way it is
among you. If one of you wants to be great,
you must be the servant of the rest; 44 and if
one of you wants to be first, you must be the
slave of all. 45 For even the Son of Man did
not come to be served; he came to serve and
to give his life to redeem many people."

Jesus Heals Blind Bartimaeus
(Matthew 20:29–34; Luke 18:35–43)

46 They came to Jericho, and as Jesus was
leaving with his disciples and a large crowd,
a blind beggar named Bartimaeus son of
Timaeus was sitting by the road. 47 When he
heard that it was Jesus of Nazareth, he began
to shout, "Jesus! Son of David! Have mercy
on me!"

48 Many of the people scolded him and told
him to be quiet. But he shouted even more
loudly, "Son of David, have mercy on me!"

49 Jesus stopped and said, "Call him."

So they called the blind man. "Cheer up!"
they said. "Get up, he is calling you."

50 So he threw off his cloak, jumped up,
and came to Jesus.

51 "What do you want me to do for you?"
Jesus asked him.

"Teacher," the blind man answered, "I
want to see again."

52 "Go," Jesus told him, "your faith has
made you well."

At once he was able to see and followed
Jesus on the road.

The Triumphant Entry into Jerusalem
(Matthew 21:1–11; Luke 19:28–40;
John 12:12–19)

11 As they approached Jerusalem, near
the towns of Bethphage and
Bethany, they came to the Mount of Olives.
Jesus sent two of his disciples on ahead 2 with
these instructions: "Go to the village there
ahead of you. As soon as you get there, you
will find a colt tied up that has never been
ridden. Untie it and bring it here. 3 And if
someone asks you why you are doing that,
say that the Master[r] needs it and will send it
back at once."

4 So they went and found a colt out in the
street, tied to the door of a house. As they
were untying it, 5 some of the bystanders
asked them, "What are you doing, untying
that colt?"

6 They answered just as Jesus had told
them, and the crowd let them go. 7 They
brought the colt to Jesus, threw their cloaks
over the animal, and Jesus got on. 8 Many
people spread their cloaks on the road, while
others cut branches in the field and spread
them on the road. 9 The people who were in
front and those who followed behind began
to shout, "Praise God! God bless him who
comes in the name of the Lord! 10 God bless
the coming kingdom of King David, our
father! Praise be to God!"

11 Jesus entered Jerusalem, went into the
Temple, and looked around at everything. But
since it was already late in the day, he went
out to Bethany with the twelve disciples.

Jesus Curses the Fig Tree
(Matthew 21:18, 19)

12 The next day, as they were coming back
from Bethany, Jesus was hungry. 13 He saw in
the distance a fig tree covered with leaves, so
he went to see if he could find any figs on
it. But when he came to it, he found only
leaves, because it was not the right time for
figs. 14 Jesus said to the fig tree, "No one shall
ever eat figs from you again!"

And his disciples heard him.

Jesus Goes to the Temple
(Matthew 21:12–17; Luke 19:45–48;
John 2:13–22)

15 When they arrived in Jerusalem, Jesus
went to the Temple and began to drive out all

[r] **11:3** the Master; *or* its owner.

10:43,44 Mt 23:11; Mk 9:35; Lk 22:26 **11:9** Ps 118:25,26

The event described in Mark 11:1–11 is observed in the Church as Palm Sunday, the first day of Holy Week.

Pray it!

Forgive Me, God

Jesus was upset because the religious leaders of his time were more concerned with making money than with true worship of God (Mark 11:15–19). When we sin we also need God's forgiveness.

For being greedy, forgive me, God.
For putting possessions over people, forgive me, God.
For worshiping material things instead of you, forgive me, God.
For being jealous of what others have, forgive me, God.
For not being satisfied with what I have, forgive me, God.
For not being grateful to you for all you have given me, forgive me, God.
Amen.

— Mark 11:15–19

those who were buying and selling. He overturned the tables of the moneychangers and the stools of those who sold pigeons, 16and he would not let anyone carry anything through the Temple courtyards. 17He then taught the people: "It is written in the Scriptures that God said, 'My Temple will be called a house of prayer for the people of all nations.' But you have turned it into a hideout for thieves!"

18The chief priests and the teachers of the Law heard of this, so they began looking for some way to kill Jesus. They were afraid of him, because the whole crowd was amazed at his teaching.

19When evening came, Jesus and his disciples left the city.

The Lesson from the Fig Tree
(Matthew 21:20–22)

20Early next morning, as they walked along the road, they saw the fig tree. It was dead all the way down to its roots. 21Peter remembered what had happened and said to Jesus, "Look, Teacher, the fig tree you cursed has died!"

22Jesus answered them, "Have faith in God. 23I assure you that whoever tells this hill to get up and throw itself in the sea and does not doubt in his heart, but believes that what he says will happen, it will be done for him. 24For this reason I tell you: When you pray and ask for something, believe that you have received it, and you will be given whatever you ask for. 25And when you stand and pray, forgive anything you may have against anyone, so that your Father in heaven will forgive the wrongs you have done."[s]

The Question about Jesus' Authority
(Matthew 21:23–27; Luke 20:1–8)

27They arrived once again in Jerusalem. As Jesus was walking in the Temple, the chief priests, the teachers of the Law, and the elders came to him 28and asked him, "What right do you have to do these things? Who gave you such right?"

29Jesus answered them, "I will ask you just one question, and if you give me an answer, I will tell you what right I have to do these things. 30Tell me, where did John's right to baptize come from: was it from God or from human beings?"

31They started to argue among themselves: "What shall we say? If we answer,

[s] **11:25** *Some manuscripts add verse 26:* If you do not forgive others, your Father in heaven will not forgive the wrongs you have done *(see Mt 6:15).*

11:17 a Isa 56:7; **b** Jer 7:11 **11:23** Mt 17:20; 1 Cor 13:2 **11:25,26** Mt 6:14,15

'From God,' he will say, 'Why, then, did you
not believe John?' 32But if we say, 'From
human beings . . . ' " (They were afraid of
the people, because everyone was convinced
that John had been a prophet.) 33So their
answer to Jesus was, "We don't know."
Jesus said to them, "Neither will I tell you,
then, by what right I do these things."

The Parable of the Tenants in the Vineyard

(Matthew 21:33–46; Luke 20:9–19)

12 Then Jesus spoke to them in parables:
"Once there was a man who planted
a vineyard, put a fence around it, dug a hole
for the wine press, and built a watchtower.
Then he rented the vineyard to tenants and
left home on a trip. 2When the time came to
gather the grapes, he sent a slave to the ten-
ants to receive from them his share of the
harvest. 3The tenants grabbed the slave, beat
him, and sent him back without a thing.
4Then the owner sent another slave; the ten-
ants beat him over the head and treated him
shamefully. 5The owner sent another slave,
and they killed him; and they treated many
others the same way, beating some and killing
others. 6The only one left to send was the
man's own dear son. Last of all, then, he sent
his son to the tenants. 'I am sure they will
respect my son,' he said. 7But those tenants
said to one another, 'This is the owner's son.
Come on, let's kill him, and his property will
be ours!' 8So they grabbed the son and killed
him and threw his body out of the vineyard.
9"What, then, will the owner of the vine-
yard do?" asked Jesus. "He will come and kill
those tenants and turn the vineyard over to
others. 10Surely you have read this scripture?
'The stone which the builders rejected as
worthless
turned out to be the most important of
all.
11This was done by the Lord;
what a wonderful sight it is!' "
12The Jewish leaders tried to arrest Jesus,
because they knew that he had told this
parable against them. But they were afraid of
the crowd, so they left him and went away.

The Question about Paying Taxes

(Matthew 22:15–22; Luke 20:20–26)

13Some Pharisees and some members of
Herod's party were sent to Jesus to trap him
with questions. 14They came to him and
said, "Teacher, we know that you tell the
truth, without worrying about what people
think. You pay no attention to anyone's sta-
tus, but teach the truth about God's will for
people. Tell us, is it against our Law to pay
taxes to the Roman Emperor? Should we
pay them or not?"
15But Jesus saw through their trick and
answered, "Why are you trying to trap me?
Bring a silver coin, and let me see it."
16They brought him one, and he asked,
"Whose face and name are these?"
"The Emperor's," they answered.
17So Jesus said, "Well, then, pay to the
Emperor what belongs to the Emperor, and
pay to God what belongs to God."
And they were amazed at Jesus.

The Question about Rising from Death

(Matthew 22:23–33; Luke 20:27–40)

18Then some Sadducees, who say that
people will not rise from death, came to Jesus
and said, 19"Teacher, Moses wrote this law
for us: 'If a man dies and leaves a wife but no
children, that man's brother must marry the
widow so that they can have children who
will be considered the dead man's children.'
20Once there were seven brothers; the oldest
got married and died without having chil-
dren. 21Then the second one married the
woman, and he also died without having
children. The same thing happened to the
third brother, 22and then to the rest: all seven
brothers married the woman and died with-
out having children. Last of all, the woman
died. 23Now, when all the dead rise to life on
the day of resurrection, whose wife will she
be? All seven of them had married her."
24Jesus answered them, "How wrong you
are! And do you know why? It is because
you don't know the Scriptures or God's
power. 25For when the dead rise to life, they
will be like the angels in heaven and will not

12:1 Isa 5:1,2 **12:10,11** Ps 118:22,23 **12:18** Acts 23:8 **12:19** Deut 25:5

Catholic Connections

Laws of Love

Take a close look at the story in the middle of this chapter with its key question, "Which commandment is the most important of all?" (Mark 12:28). When the man asks the question, everyone looks at Jesus, waiting to see what he will say. To some, it seemed like a trick. After all, how can anyone say one law of God is better than another law? But Jesus is a quick thinker. He quoted the Old Testament, which sums up the first three commandments in one statement: love God (Deuteronomy 6:5). The other seven commandments were also summed up in a second Old Testament statement: love your neighbor as yourself (Leviticus 19:18). These, he says, are the two greatest commandments.

All the moral teachings of the Catholic Church are rooted in these two commandments. If a person does not love God and other people, religion is just meaningless prayers and empty practices.

Write those laws of love in your mind and in your heart. Let them guide everything that you think, do, and say.

— Mark 12:28–34

marry. 26 Now, as for the dead being raised:
haven't you ever read in the Book of Moses
the passage about the burning bush? There it
is written that God said to Moses, 'I am the
God of Abraham, the God of Isaac, and the
God of Jacob.' 27 He is the God of the living,
not of the dead. You are completely wrong!"

The Great Commandment
(Matthew 22:34–40; Luke 10:25–28)

28 A teacher of the Law was there who
heard the discussion. He saw that Jesus had
given the Sadducees a good answer, so he
came to him with a question: "Which commandment is the most important of all?"
29 Jesus replied, "The most important one
is this: 'Listen, Israel! The Lord our God is
the only Lord.[t] 30 Love the Lord your God
with all your heart, with all your soul, with
all your mind, and with all your strength.'
31 The second most important commandment is this: 'Love your neighbor as you love
yourself.' There is no other commandment
more important than these two."
32 The teacher of the Law said to Jesus,
"Well done, Teacher! It is true, as you say,
that only the Lord is God and that there is
no other god but he. 33 And you must love
God with all your heart and with all your
mind and with all your strength; and you
must love your neighbor as you love yourself. It is more important to obey these two
commandments than to offer on the altar
animals and other sacrifices to God."
34 Jesus noticed how wise his answer was,
and so he told him, "You are not far from
the Kingdom of God."

After this nobody dared to ask Jesus any more questions.

[t] **12:29** The Lord our God is the only Lord; *or* The Lord is our God, the Lord alone.

12:26 Ex 3:6 **12:29,30** Deut 6:4,5 **12:31** Lev 19:18 **12:32** Deut 4:35 **12:33** Hos 6:6 **12:28-34** Lk 10:25-28

Jesus said, "Love your neighbor *as you love yourself*" *(Mark 12:31)*. **How are you doing at loving yourself?**

The Question about the Messiah
(Matthew 22:41–46; Luke 20:41–44)

35 As Jesus was teaching in the Temple, he
asked the question, "How can the teachers of
the Law say that the Messiah will be the
descendant of David? 36 The Holy Spirit
inspired David to say:
'The Lord said to my Lord:
Sit here at my right side
until I put your enemies under your
feet.'
37 David himself called him 'Lord'; so how
can the Messiah be David's descendant?"

Jesus Warns against the Teachers of the Law
(Matthew 23:1–36; Luke 20:45–47)

A large crowd was listening to Jesus gladly.
38 As he taught them, he said, "Watch out for
the teachers of the Law, who like to walk
around in their long robes and be greeted
with respect in the marketplace, 39 who
choose the reserved seats in the synagogues
and the best places at feasts. 40 They take
advantage of widows and rob them of their
homes, and then make a show of saying long
prayers. Their punishment will be all the
worse!"

The Widow's Offering
(Luke 21:1–4)

41 As Jesus sat near the Temple treasury, he
watched the people as they dropped in
their money. Many rich people dropped in
a lot of money; 42 then a poor widow came
along and dropped in two little copper
coins, worth about a penny. 43 He called his
disciples together and said to them, "I tell
you that this poor widow put more in the
offering box than all the others. 44 For the
others put in what they had to spare of
their riches; but she, poor as she is, put in
all she had—she gave all she had to live
on."

A poor widow came along. (12:42)

Jesus Speaks of the Destruction of the Temple
(Matthew 24:1, 2; Luke 21:5, 6)

13 As Jesus was leaving the Temple, one
of his disciples said, "Look, Teacher!
What wonderful stones and buildings!"
2 Jesus answered, "You see these great build-
ings? Not a single stone here will be left in its
place; every one of them will be thrown
down."

Troubles and Persecutions
(Matthew 24:3–14; Luke 21:7–19)

3 Jesus was sitting on the Mount of Olives,
across from the Temple, when Peter, James,
John, and Andrew came to him in private.
4 "Tell us when this will be," they said, "and
tell us what will happen to show that the
time has come for all these things to take
place."
5 Jesus said to them, "Watch out, and don't
let anyone fool you. 6 Many men, claiming
to speak for me, will come and say, 'I am
he!' and they will fool many people. 7 And
don't be troubled when you hear the noise
of battles close by and news of battles far
away. Such things must happen, but they do
not mean that the end has come. 8 Countries
will fight each other; kingdoms will attack
one another. There will be earthquakes
everywhere, and there will be famines.

12:36 Ps 110:1

Can you list all the terrible things Jesus talks about in Mark, chapter 13? Of all these things, which do you think is the worst?

Live it!

The End Is Near

Someday the world is going to end. The term commonly used for the end of the world is *apocalypse.* No one knows the time. It may be today, or it may be five billion years away. But it will end. And even if the world doesn't end soon, each of us only has a limited amount of time on earth.

In Mark, chapter 13, Jesus talks about the end of time. It may seem strange to think about the end of life before you even get to high school. But Jesus says that everyone should be prepared because we have no idea when it will happen. Above all, he says, we must remain faithful to God. When the end finally comes—whether it's the end of the world or the end of a life—only those who are watchful and faithful will be united with God for all eternity.

Do you know anyone who died at a young age? If today were the last day of your life on earth, what would you do? Are you ready to meet God face-to-face?

— Mark, chapter 13

These things are like the first pains of child-
birth.
9"You yourselves must watch out. You will
be arrested and taken to court. You will be
beaten in the synagogues; you will stand
before rulers and kings for my sake to tell
them the Good News. 10But before the end
comes, the gospel must be preached to all
peoples. 11And when you are arrested and
taken to court, do not worry ahead of time
about what you are going to say; when the
time comes, say whatever is then given to
you. For the words you speak will not be
yours; they will come from the Holy Spirit.
12Men will hand over their own brothers to
be put to death, and fathers will do the same
to their children. Children will turn against
their parents and have them put to death.
13Everyone will hate you because of me. But
whoever holds out to the end will be saved.

The Awful Horror
(Matthew 24:15–28; Luke 21:20–24)

14"You will see 'The Awful Horror' standing
in the place where he should not be." (Note to
the reader: understand what this means!)
"Then those who are in Judea must run away
to the hills. 15Someone who is on the roof of a
house must not lose time by going down into
the house to get anything to take along.
16Someone who is in the field must not go
back to the house for a cloak. 17How terrible it
will be in those days for women who are preg-
nant and for mothers with little babies! 18Pray
to God that these things will not happen in the
winter! 19For the trouble of those days will be
far worse than any the world has ever known
from the very beginning when God created
the world until the present time. Nor will
there ever be anything like it again. 20But the
Lord has reduced the number of those days; if
he had not, nobody would survive. For the
sake of his chosen people, however, he has
reduced those days.
21"Then, if anyone says to you, 'Look,
here is the Messiah!' or, 'Look, there he is!'—
do not believe it. 22For false Messiahs and
false prophets will appear. They will perform
miracles and wonders in order to deceive
even God's chosen people, if possible. 23Be
on your guard! I have told you everything
ahead of time.

The Coming of the Son of Man
(Matthew 24:29–31; Luke 21:25–28)

24"In the days after that time of trouble
the sun will grow dark, the moon will no
longer shine, 25the stars will fall from heaven,

13:9-11 Mt 10:17-20; Lk 12:11,12 **13:13** Mt 10:22 **13:14** Dan 9:27; 11:31; 12:11; 1 Macc 1:54; 6:7 **13:15,16** Lk 17:31 **13:19** Dan 12:1; Rev 7:14 **13:24** **a** Isa 13:10; Joel 2:10,31; 3:15; Rev 6:12; **b** Isa 13:10; Ezek 32:7 **13:25** **a** Isa 34:4; Rev 6:13; **b** Joel 2:10

and the powers in space will be driven from
their courses. 26 Then the Son of Man will
appear, coming in the clouds with great
power and glory. 27 He will send the angels
out to the four corners of the earth to gather
God's chosen people from one end of the
world to the other.

The Lesson of the Fig Tree
(Matthew 24:32–35; Luke 21:29–33)

28 "Let the fig tree teach you a lesson.
When its branches become green and tender
and it starts putting out leaves, you know
that summer is near. 29 In the same way,
when you see these things happening, you
will know that the time is near, ready to
begin.[u] 30 Remember that all these things
will happen before the people now living
have all died. 31 Heaven and earth will pass
away, but my words will never pass away.

No One Knows the Day or Hour
(Matthew 24:36–44)

32 "No one knows, however, when that
day or hour will come—neither the angels
in heaven, nor the Son; only the Father
knows. 33 Be on watch, be alert, for you do
not know when the time will come. 34 It will
be like a man who goes away from home on
a trip and leaves his servants in charge, after
giving to each one his own work to do and
after telling the doorkeeper to keep watch.
35 Watch, then, because you do not know
when the master of the house is coming—it
might be in the evening or at midnight or
before dawn or at sunrise. 36 If he comes sud-
denly, he must not find you asleep. 37 What I
say to you, then, I say to all: Watch!"

The Plot against Jesus
(Matthew 26:1–5; Luke 22:1, 2; John 11:45–53)

14 It was now two days before the Fes-
tival of Passover and Unleavened
Bread. The chief priests and the teachers of
the Law were looking for a way to arrest
Jesus secretly and put him to death. 2 "We
must not do it during the festival," they said,
"or the people might riot."

Jesus Is Anointed at Bethany
(Matthew 26:6–13; John 12:1–8)

3 Jesus was in Bethany at the house of
Simon, a man who had suffered from a
dreaded skin disease. While Jesus was eating,
a woman came in with an alabaster jar full of
a very expensive perfume made of pure
nard. She broke the jar and poured the per-
fume on Jesus' head. 4 Some of the people
there became angry and said to one another,
"What was the use of wasting the perfume?
5 It could have been sold for more than three
hundred silver coins[v] and the money given
to the poor!" And they criticized her harshly.
6 But Jesus said, "Leave her alone! Why are
you bothering her? She has done a fine and
beautiful thing for me. 7 You will always have
poor people with you, and any time you
want to, you can help them. But you will
not always have me. 8 She did what she
could; she poured perfume on my body to
prepare it ahead of time for burial. 9 Now, I
assure you that wherever the gospel is
preached all over the world, what she has
done will be told in memory of her."

Judas Agrees to Betray Jesus
(Matthew 26:14–16; Luke 22:3–6)

10 Then Judas Iscariot, one of the twelve
disciples, went off to the chief priests in order
to betray Jesus to them. 11 They were pleased
to hear what he had to say, and promised to
give him money. So Judas started looking for
a good chance to hand Jesus over to them.

Jesus Eats the Passover Meal with His Disciples
(Matthew 26:17–25; Luke 22:7–14, 21–23; John 13:21–30)

12 On the first day of the Festival of
Unleavened Bread, the day the lambs for the
Passover meal were killed, Jesus' disciples

[u] **13:29** the time is near, ready to begin; *or* he is near, ready to come. [v] **14:5** SILVER COINS: *See 6:37.*

13:26 Dan 7:13; Rev 1:7 **13:32** Mt 24:36 **13:34** Lk 12:36-38 **14:1** Ex 12:1-27 **14:3** Lk 7:37,38
14:7 Deut 15:11

The Real Deal

"This is my body. . . . This is my blood" (Mark 14:22–24).

Jesus spoke those words at the last Passover meal he had with his Apostles before he died. He didn't say "this bread is *like* my body" or "this wine *represents* my blood." The bread and the wine that you see at Mass is really Jesus Christ, whose body and blood comes to us in that form. We refer to this as the Real Presence.

During the Eucharistic prayer, the priest recites the same words Jesus used at the Last Supper. At that point—which is known as the consecration—the bread and wine are changed into the body and blood of Christ. Later, when you say amen to the person who offers you the host and the cup, you are saying, "Yes, I believe it's really Jesus." Really.

— Mark 14:22–25

asked him, "Where do you want us to go
and get the Passover meal ready for you?"
13 Then Jesus sent two of them with these
instructions: "Go into the city, and a man
carrying a jar of water will meet you. Follow
him 14 to the house he enters, and say to the
owner of the house: 'The Teacher says,
Where is the room where my disciples and I
will eat the Passover meal?' 15 Then he will
show you a large upstairs room, fixed up and
furnished, where you will get everything
ready for us."
16 The disciples left, went to the city, and
found everything just as Jesus had told them;
and they prepared the Passover meal.
17 When it was evening, Jesus came with
the twelve disciples. 18 While they were at
the table eating, Jesus said, "I tell you that
one of you will betray me—one who is eat-
ing with me."
19 The disciples were upset and began to
ask him, one after the other, "Surely you
don't mean me, do you?"
20 Jesus answered, "It will be one of you
twelve, one who dips his bread in the dish
with me. 21 The Son of Man will die as the
Scriptures say he will; but how terrible for
that man who will betray the Son of Man! It
would have been better for that man if he
had never been born!"

The Lord's Supper

(Matthew 26:26–30; Luke 22:14–20; 1 Corinthians 11:23–25)

22 While they were eating, Jesus took a
piece of bread, gave a prayer of thanks, broke

"This is my body." (14:22)

14:18 Ps 41:9

For a description of the event in Jewish history that the feast of Passover recalls, see Exodus 12:1–28.

it, and gave it to his disciples. "Take it," he
said, "this is my body."
23 Then he took a cup, gave thanks to
God, and handed it to them; and they all
drank from it. 24 Jesus said, "This is my blood
which is poured out for many, my blood
which seals God's covenant. 25 I tell you, I
will never again drink this wine until the
day I drink the new wine in the Kingdom
of God."
26 Then they sang a hymn and went out to
the Mount of Olives.

Jesus Predicts Peter's Denial
(Matthew 26:31–35; Luke 22:31–34; John 13:36–38)

27 Jesus said to them, "All of you will run
away and leave me, for the scripture says,
'God will kill the shepherd, and the sheep
will all be scattered.' 28 But after I am raised
to life, I will go to Galilee ahead of you."
29 Peter answered, "I will never leave you,
even though all the rest do!"
30 Jesus said to Peter, "I tell you that before
the rooster crows two times tonight, you will
say three times that you do not know me."
31 Peter answered even more strongly, "I
will never say that, even if I have to die with
you!"
And all the other disciples said the same
thing.

Jesus Prays in Gethsemane
(Matthew 26:36–46; Luke 22:39–46)

32 They came to a place called Gethsem-
ane, and Jesus said to his disciples, "Sit here
while I pray." 33 He took Peter, James, and
John with him. Distress and anguish came
over him, 34 and he said to them, "The sor-
row in my heart is so great that it almost
crushes me. Stay here and keep watch."
35 He went a little farther on, threw him-
self on the ground, and prayed that, if possi-
ble, he might not have to go through that
time of suffering. 36 "Father," he prayed, "my
Father! All things are possible for you. Take
this cup of suffering away from me. Yet not
what I want, but what you want."
37 Then he returned and found the three
disciples asleep. He said to Peter, "Simon, are
you asleep? Weren't you able to stay awake
for even one hour?" 38 And he said to them,
"Keep watch, and pray that you will not fall
into temptation. The spirit is willing, but the
flesh is weak."
39 He went away once more and prayed,

Pray it!

I Messed Up Again, Jesus

I try so hard, Jesus. I try to do everything you said I should do. I love you. I believe in you. I try to be good to others. But sometimes I really make a mess of things. I feel terrible about it. It's like I've got a hole in my soul. I just want things to be right between us again.

Then I remember the Apostles. They messed up too. When you needed them most in the garden at Gethsemane, Peter, James, and John fell asleep (Mark 14:33–41). When the soldiers came to arrest you, the Apostles ran away (Mark 14:50). On top of that, Peter denied that he even knew you (14:66–72). You forgave them all, though.

I know you'll do the same for me, Jesus. I know I keep messing up, but I also keep trying. That is what the Apostles did, and that is what I'll do too.

— Mark 14:32–72

14:24 **a** Ex 24:8; **b** Jer 31:31-34 **14:27** Zech 13:7 **14:28** Mt 28:16

" 'Are you the Messiah, the Son of the Blessed God?' 'I am,' answered Jesus" *(Mark 14:61–62).*

saying the same words. 40 Then he came back
to the disciples and found them asleep; they
could not keep their eyes open. And they did
not know what to say to him.

41 When he came back the third time, he
said to them, "Are you still sleeping and rest-
ing? Enough! The hour has come! Look, the
Son of Man is now being handed over to
the power of sinners. 42 Get up, let us go.
Look, here is the man who is betraying me!"

The Arrest of Jesus

(Matthew 26:47–56; Luke 22:47–53; John 18:3–12)

43 Jesus was still speaking when Judas, one
of the twelve disciples, arrived. With him was
a crowd armed with swords and clubs and
sent by the chief priests, the teachers of the
Law, and the elders. 44 The traitor had given
the crowd a signal: "The man I kiss is the
one you want. Arrest him and take him away
under guard."

So they arrested Jesus and held him tight. (14:46)

45 As soon as Judas arrived, he went up to
Jesus and said, "Teacher!" and kissed him.
46 So they arrested Jesus and held him tight.
47 But one of those standing there drew his
sword and struck at the High Priest's slave,
cutting off his ear. 48 Then Jesus spoke up
and said to them, "Did you have to come
with swords and clubs to capture me, as
though I were an outlaw? 49 Day after day I
was with you teaching in the Temple, and
you did not arrest me. But the Scriptures
must come true."

50 Then all the disciples left him and ran
away.

51 A certain young man, dressed only in a
linen cloth, was following Jesus. They tried
to arrest him, 52 but he ran away naked, leav-
ing the cloth behind.

Jesus before the Council

(Matthew 26:57–68; Luke 22:54, 55, 63–71; John 18:13, 14, 19–24)

53 Then Jesus was taken to the High
Priest's house, where all the chief priests, the
elders, and the teachers of the Law were
gathering. 54 Peter followed from a distance
and went into the courtyard of the High
Priest's house. There he sat down with the
guards, keeping himself warm by the fire.
55 The chief priests and the whole Council
tried to find some evidence against Jesus in
order to put him to death, but they could
not find any. 56 Many witnesses told lies
against Jesus, but their stories did not agree.

57 Then some men stood up and told this
lie against Jesus: 58 "We heard him say, 'I will
tear down this Temple which men have
made, and after three days I will build one
that is not made by men.' " 59 Not even they,
however, could make their stories agree.

60 The High Priest stood up in front of
them all and questioned Jesus, "Have you no
answer to the accusation they bring against
you?"

61 But Jesus kept quiet and would not say a
word. Again the High Priest questioned him,
"Are you the Messiah, the Son of the
Blessed God?"

62 "I am," answered Jesus, "and you will all
see the Son of Man seated at the right side
of the Almighty and coming with the clouds
of heaven!"

63 The High Priest tore his robes and said,
"We don't need any more witnesses! 64 You
heard his blasphemy. What is your decision?"

They all voted against him: he was guilty
and should be put to death.

65 Some of them began to spit on Jesus,
and they blindfolded him and hit him.
"Guess who hit you!" they said. And the
guards took him and slapped him.

14:49 Lk 19:47; 21:37 **14:58** Jn 2:19 **14:62** Dan 7:13 **14:64** Lev 24:16

Peter Denies Jesus
(Matthew 26:69–75; Luke 22:56–62; John 18:15–18, 25–27)

66 Peter was still down in the courtyard when one of the High Priest's servant women came by. 67 When she saw Peter warming himself, she looked straight at him and said, "You, too, were with Jesus of Nazareth."

68 But he denied it. "I don't know . . . I don't understand what you are talking about," he answered, and went out into the passageway. Just then a rooster crowed.[w]

69 The servant woman saw him there and began to repeat to the bystanders, "He is one of them!" 70 But Peter denied it again.

A little while later the bystanders accused Peter again, "You can't deny that you are one of them, because you, too, are from Galilee."

71 Then Peter said, "I swear that I am telling the truth! May God punish me if I am not! I do not know the man you are talking about!"

72 Just then a rooster crowed a second time, and Peter remembered how Jesus had said to him, "Before the rooster crows two times, you will say three times that you do not know me." And he broke down and cried.

He broke down and cried. (14:72)

Jesus before Pilate
(Matthew 27:1, 2, 11–14; Luke 23:1–5; John 18:28–38)

15 Early in the morning the chief priests met hurriedly with the elders, the teachers of the Law, and the whole Council, and made their plans. They put Jesus in chains, led him away, and handed him over to Pilate. 2 Pilate questioned him, "Are you the king of the Jews?"

Jesus answered, "So you say."

3 The chief priests were accusing Jesus of many things, 4 so Pilate questioned him again, "Aren't you going to answer? Listen to all their accusations!"

5 Again Jesus refused to say a word, and Pilate was amazed.

Jesus Is Sentenced to Death
(Matthew 27:15–26; Luke 23:13–25; John 18:39—19:16)

6 At every Passover Festival Pilate was in the habit of setting free any one prisoner the people asked for. 7 At that time a man named Barabbas was in prison with the rebels who had committed murder in the riot. 8 When the crowd gathered and began to ask Pilate for the usual favor, 9 he asked them, "Do you want me to set free for you the king of the Jews?" 10 He knew very well that the chief priests had handed Jesus over to him because they were jealous.

11 But the chief priests stirred up the crowd to ask, instead, that Pilate set Barabbas free for them. 12 Pilate spoke again to the crowd, "What, then, do you want me to do with the one you call the king of the Jews?"

13 They shouted back, "Crucify him!"

14 "But what crime has he committed?" Pilate asked.

They shouted all the louder, "Crucify him!"

15 Pilate wanted to please the crowd, so he set Barabbas free for them. Then he had Jesus whipped and handed him over to be crucified.

The Soldiers Make Fun of Jesus
(Matthew 27:27–31; John 19:2, 3)

16 The soldiers took Jesus inside to the courtyard of the governor's palace and called together the rest of the company. 17 They put a purple robe on Jesus, made a crown out of thorny branches, and put it on his head.

[w] **14:68** *Some manuscripts do not have* Just then a rooster crowed.

18Then they began to salute him: "Long live
the King of the Jews!" 19They beat him over
the head with a stick, spat on him, fell on
their knees, and bowed down to him.
20When they had finished making fun of
him, they took off the purple robe and put
his own clothes back on him. Then they led
him out to crucify him.

Jesus Is Crucified

(Matthew 27:32–44; Luke 23:26–43; John 19:17–27)

21On the way they met a man named
Simon, who was coming into the city from
the country, and the soldiers forced him to
carry Jesus' cross. (Simon was from Cyrene
and was the father of Alexander and Rufus.)
22They took Jesus to a place called Golgo-
tha, which means "The Place of the Skull."
23There they tried to give him wine mixed
with a drug called myrrh, but Jesus would
not drink it. 24Then they crucified him and
divided his clothes among themselves,

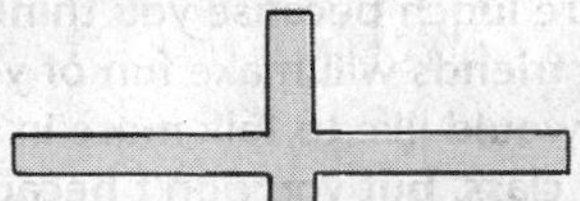

throwing dice to see who would get which
piece of clothing. 25It was nine o'clock in
the morning when they crucified him.

Throwing dice (15:24)

26The notice of the accusation against him
said: "The King of the Jews." 27They also
crucified two bandits with Jesus, one on his
right and the other on his left.[x]
29People passing by shook their heads and
hurled insults at Jesus: "Aha! You were going
to tear down the Temple and build it back
up in three days! 30Now come down from
the cross and save yourself!"
31In the same way the chief priests and
the teachers of the Law made fun of Jesus,
saying to one another, "He saved others, but
he cannot save himself! 32Let us see the
Messiah, the king of Israel, come down from
the cross now, and we will believe in him!"

"Come down from the cross!" (15:30)

And the two who were crucified with
Jesus insulted him also.

The Death of Jesus

(Matthew 27:45–56; Luke 23:44–49; John 19:28–30)

33At noon the whole country was covered
with darkness, which lasted for three hours.
34At three o'clock Jesus cried out with a
loud shout, *"Eloi, Eloi, lema sabachthani?"*
which means, "My God, my God, why did
you abandon me?"
35Some of the people there heard him and

[x] **15:27** *Some manuscripts add verse 28:* In this way the scripture came true which says, "He shared the fate of criminals" *(see Lk 22:37).*

15:21 Rom 16:13 **15:24** Ps 22:18 **15:28** Isa 53:12 **15:29** **a** Ps 22:7; 109:25; **b** Mk 14:58; Jn 2:19 **15:34** Ps 22:1

The words of Jesus in Mark 15:34 are in Aramaic, an ancient language related to Hebrew. Compare the English translation with the opening of Psalm 22.

said, "Listen, he is calling for Elijah!" 36 One
of them ran up with a sponge, soaked it in
cheap wine, and put it on the end of a stick.
Then he held it up to Jesus' lips and said,
"Wait! Let us see if Elijah is coming to bring
him down from the cross!"

37 With a loud cry Jesus died.

38 The curtain hanging in the Temple was
torn in two, from top to bottom. 39 The
army officer who was standing there in front
of the cross saw how Jesus had died.[y] "This
man was really the Son of God!" he said.

40 Some women were there, looking on
from a distance. Among them were Mary
Magdalene, Mary the mother of the younger
James and of Joseph, and Salome. 41 They had
followed Jesus while he was in Galilee and
had helped him. Many other women who
had come to Jerusalem with him were there
also.

The Burial of Jesus

(Matthew 27:57–61; Luke 23:50–56; John 19:38–42)

42-43 It was toward evening when Joseph
of Arimathea arrived. He was a respected
member of the Council, who was waiting
for the coming of the Kingdom of God. It
was Preparation day (that is, the day before
the Sabbath), so Joseph went boldly into the
presence of Pilate and asked him for the
body of Jesus. 44 Pilate was surprised to hear
that Jesus was already dead. He called the
army officer and asked him if Jesus had been
dead a long time. 45 After hearing the offi-
cer's report, Pilate told Joseph he could have
the body. 46 Joseph bought a linen sheet, took
the body down, wrapped it in the sheet, and
placed it in a tomb which had been dug out
of solid rock. Then he rolled a large stone
across the entrance to the tomb. 47 Mary
Magdalene and Mary the mother of Joseph
were watching and saw where the body of
Jesus was placed.

Live it!

An Act of Courage

Joseph of Arimathea was a secret follower of Jesus. He was a leader in the city and was afraid that if he made his beliefs known, he would lose friends and business associates. Still, he was curious about this man who preached a message of hope and freedom. After Jesus died, Joseph took a chance. He found the courage to go to Pilate and asked for Jesus' body so he could bury him. His loyalty to Jesus was no longer a secret.

Sometimes it's hard to talk about God, no matter how deep your faith is. For example, you might be afraid to say a prayer before lunch because you think your friends will make fun of you. You would like to talk more in religion class, but you don't because you're afraid that people will think you're too religious. If you ask for help, the Holy Spirit will give you the right words at the right time in the right place. And like Joseph, your faith won't be a secret anymore.

— Mark 15:42–47

The Resurrection

(Matthew 28:1–8; Luke 24:1–12; John 20:1–10)

16 After the Sabbath was over, Mary
Magdalene, Mary the mother of
James, and Salome bought spices to go and
anoint the body of Jesus. 2 Very early on

[y] **15:39** had died; *some manuscripts have* had cried out and died.
15:36 Ps 69:21 **15:38** Ex 26:31-33 **15:40,41** Lk 8:2,3

The stations of the cross is a Catholic devotion on fourteen scenes from Christ's passion and death.

Live it!

A Model Friend

Mary Magdalene was a close friend of Jesus. She was part of a group of women disciples who followed Jesus and stayed with him during the horrible events of his passion and death. She was the one who discovered the empty tomb and told the Apostles that Jesus had risen.

Mary was a true friend. She supported Jesus when others questioned him. She stuck with him through the roughest time of his life, even though his other friends deserted him. She told the world how wonderful he was. She announced his great moment of glory. But most of all, she was just there for him, walking with him as he made his way through life. She is a model of a great friend.

- **Who are your true friends? What makes them true?**
- **Who would consider you to be a true friend? What do you do to earn that title?**

— Mark 16:1–11

Sunday morning, at sunrise, they went to the
tomb. 3-4On the way they said to one anoth-
er, "Who will roll away the stone for us from
the entrance to the tomb?" (It was a very
large stone.) Then they looked up and saw
that the stone had already been rolled back.
5So they entered the tomb, where they saw a
young man sitting at the right, wearing a
white robe—and they were alarmed.
6"Don't be alarmed," he said. "I know you
are looking for Jesus of Nazareth, who was
crucified. He is not here—he has been
raised! Look, here is the place where he was
placed. 7Now go and give this message to his
disciples, including Peter: 'He is going to
Galilee ahead of you; there you will see him,
just as he told you.' "
8So they went out and ran from the tomb,
distressed and terrified. They said nothing to
anyone, because they were afraid.

So they went out and ran. (16:8)

AN OLD ENDING TO THE GOSPEL[z]

Jesus Appears to Mary Magdalene
(Matthew 28:9, 10; John 20:11–18)

[9After Jesus rose from death early on Sun-
day, he appeared first to Mary Magdalene,
from whom he had driven out seven demons.
10She went and told his companions. They
were mourning and crying; 11and when they
heard her say that Jesus was alive and that she
had seen him, they did not believe her.

Jesus Appears to Two Followers
(Luke 24:13–35)

12After this, Jesus appeared in a different
manner to two of them while they were on
their way to the country. 13They returned and
told the others, but these would not believe it.

Jesus Appears to the Eleven
(Matthew 28:16–20; Luke 24:36–49; John 20:19–23; Acts 1:6–8)

14Last of all, Jesus appeared to the eleven
disciples as they were eating. He scolded
them, because they did not have faith and

[z] **16:8** *Some manuscripts and ancient translations do not have this ending to the Gospel (verses 9–20).*
16:7 Mt 26:32; Mk 14:28

because they were too stubborn to believe
those who had seen him alive. 15He said to
them, "Go throughout the whole world and
preach the gospel to all people. 16Whoever
believes and is baptized will be saved; whoev-
er does not believe will be condemned.
17Believers will be given the power to per-
form miracles: they will drive out demons in
my name; they will speak in strange tongues;
18if they pick up snakes or drink any poison,
they will not be harmed; they will place their
hands on sick people, and these will get well."

Jesus Is Taken Up to Heaven
(Luke 24:50–53; Acts 1:9–11)

19After the Lord Jesus had talked with
them, he was taken up to heaven and sat at
the right side of God. 20The disciples went
and preached everywhere, and the Lord
worked with them and proved that their
preaching was true by the miracles that were
performed.]

The disciples went and preached everywhere. (16:20)

ANOTHER OLD ENDING[a]

[9The women went to Peter and his
friends and gave them a brief account of all
they had been told. 10After this, Jesus himself
sent out through his disciples from the east
to the west the sacred and everliving message
of eternal salvation.]

[a] **16:20** *Some manuscripts and ancient translations have this shorter ending to the Gospel in addition to the longer ending (verses 9–20).*
16:15 Acts 1:8 **16:19** Acts 1:9-11

Your Next Step

Congratulations on finishing the Gospel of Mark! Use this space to write your thoughts and questions about this book. If you are following the suggested reading plan, go back to the Book of Genesis in the Old Testament. This is the first book of the Bible, filled with interesting stories about our ancestors in the faith.

The Gospel According to Luke

"Come on in!"

These are words we are often greeted with as we enter someone's home. They are very welcoming words. In many ways, these words also capture the message of Luke's Gospel. It makes sure to let us know that Jesus welcomes all, not just a certain group of people. Just as the words *come on in* are often said with a smile, Luke also emphasizes the joy that comes with entering into life with Jesus. The Gospel begins and ends with stories of joy and good news. It's almost as if Luke pictures Jesus as standing at the front door with both hands open and saying to us with a welcoming smile: "Come on in—there's room for everyone!"

Chap. 1:26–38

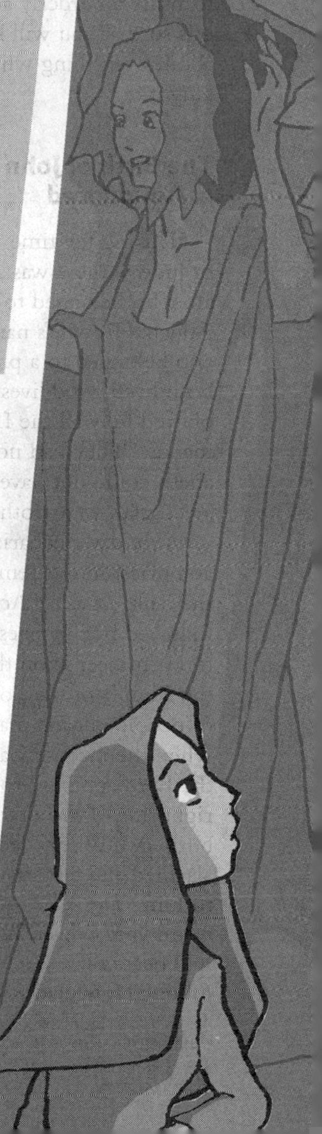

Headlines

- Angel Predicts Miracle Pregnancy (1:26–38)
- Child Jesus Lost for Three Days (2:41–52)
- Jesus Brings Young Man Back to Life (7:11–17)
- Stories Challenge Accepted Beliefs (10:25–37; 15:11–32)
- Rich Challenged to Care for Poor (16:19–31; 18:18–30)
- Jesus Shocks Crowd, Befriends Tax Collector (19:1–10)
- Travelers Surprised by the Risen Jesus (24:13–35)

FACTOIDS

Who wrote this book? Many think the author was a Gentile (non-Jewish) Christian named Luke, who may have traveled with Saint Paul.

When was it written? Probably around AD 80 to 90, about fifty years after the Resurrection of Christ.

Who was it written for? The Gospel is addressed to Theophilus, which means "friend of God" in Greek. So it is for anyone who wishes to be a friend of God.

Why was it written? Luke wanted to share the Good News of Jesus with other Gentile Christians of the early Church.

Important themes

- The action of the Holy Spirit is present and working in our lives.
- Jesus came for everyone: Jew and Gentile, women and men, the poor people and the rich people.
- There is great joy in following Jesus.

Of note: Luke also wrote a sequel to this book called the Acts of the Apostles, which you will find after John's Gospel.

LUKE

Introduction

1 Dear Theophilus:
Many people have done their best to
write a report of the things that have taken
place among us. 2They wrote what we have
been told by those who saw these things
from the beginning and who proclaimed the
message. 3And so, Your Excellency, because I
have carefully studied all these matters from
their beginning, I thought it would be good
to write an orderly account for you. 4I do
this so that you will know the full truth
about everything which you have been
taught.

The Birth of John the Baptist Is Announced

5During the time when Herod was king
of Judea,[a] there was a priest named Zechari-
ah, who belonged to the priestly order of
Abijah. His wife's name was Elizabeth; she
also belonged to a priestly family. 6They
both lived good lives in God's sight and
obeyed fully all the Lord's laws and com-
mands. 7They had no children because Eliz-
abeth could not have any, and she and
Zechariah were both very old.
8One day Zechariah was doing his work
as a priest in the Temple, taking his turn in
the daily service. 9According to the custom
followed by the priests, he was chosen by lot
to burn incense on the altar. So he went into
the Temple of the Lord, 10while the crowd
of people outside prayed during the hour
when the incense was burned. 11An angel of
the Lord appeared to him, standing at the
right side of the altar where the incense was
burned. 12When Zechariah saw him, he was
alarmed and felt afraid. 13But the angel said
to him, "Don't be afraid, Zechariah! God has
heard your prayer, and your wife Elizabeth
will bear you a son. You are to name him
John. 14How glad and happy you will be,
and how happy many others will be when
he is born! 15John will be great in the Lord's
sight. He must not drink any wine or strong
drink. From his very birth he will be filled
with the Holy Spirit, 16and he will bring
back many of the people of Israel to the
Lord their God. 17He will go ahead of the
Lord, strong and mighty like the prophet
Elijah. He will bring fathers and children
together again; he will turn disobedient peo-
ple back to the way of thinking of the righ-
teous; he will get the Lord's people ready for
him."
18Zechariah said to the angel, "How shall
I know if this is so? I am an old man, and
my wife is old also."
19"I am Gabriel," the angel answered. "I
stand in the presence of God, who sent me
to speak to you and tell you this good news.
20But you have not believed my message,
which will come true at the right time.
Because you have not believed, you will be
unable to speak; you will remain silent until
the day my promise to you comes true."
21In the meantime the people were wait-
ing for Zechariah and wondering why he
was spending such a long time in the Tem-
ple. 22When he came out, he could not
speak to them, and so they knew that he had
seen a vision in the Temple. Unable to say a
word, he made signs to them with his hands.
23When his period of service in the Tem-
ple was over, Zechariah went back home.
24Some time later his wife Elizabeth became
pregnant and did not leave the house for five
months. 25"Now at last the Lord has helped
me," she said. "He has taken away my public
disgrace!"

The Birth of Jesus Is Announced

26In the sixth month of Elizabeth's preg-
nancy God sent the angel Gabriel to a town
in Galilee named Nazareth. 27He had a mes-
sage for a young woman promised in mar-

[a] **1:5** JUDEA: *The term here refers to the whole land of Palestine.*

1:5 1 Chr 24:10 **1:15** Num 6:3 **1:17** Mal 4:5, 6; Sir 48:10, 11 **1:19** Dan 8:16; 9:21; Tob 12:15 **1:27** Mt 1:18

Catholic Connections

"Born of the Virgin Mary"

The story of Jesus' conception is one of the greatest and holiest mysteries of the Catholic Church. Catholics believe that Jesus was conceived in the womb of Mary by the power of the Holy Spirit. This means that, unlike normal human births, no human father was involved. Because Jesus was conceived by God and a human parent, we know that Jesus Christ is both fully God and fully human. Mary's virginity is an important sign of that.

When Mary agreed to become the mother of Jesus, she accepted that she would become the mother of the Son of God. The man she was to marry was Joseph, who served as the foster father to Jesus. The moment Mary agreed to become the mother of Jesus, she was helping to set in motion the most important event in human history: the coming of Jesus, the Savior of the World.

— Luke 1:26–38

riage to a man named Joseph, who was a
descendant of King David. Her name was
Mary. 28 The angel came to her and said,
"Peace be with you! The Lord is with you
and has greatly blessed you!"

29 Mary was deeply troubled by the angel's
message, and she wondered what his words
meant. 30 The angel said to her, "Don't be
afraid, Mary; God has been gracious to you.
31 You will become pregnant and give birth to
a son, and you will name him Jesus. 32 He will
be great and will be called the Son of the
Most High God. The Lord God will make
him a king, as his ancestor David was, 33 and
he will be the king of the descendants of
Jacob forever; his kingdom will never end!"

34 Mary said to the angel, "I am a virgin.
How, then, can this be?"

35 The angel answered, "The Holy Spirit
will come on you, and God's power will rest
upon you. For this reason the holy child will
be called the Son of God. 36 Remember your
relative Elizabeth. It is said that she cannot
have children, but she herself is now six
months pregnant, even though she is very
old. 37 For there is nothing that God cannot
do."

38 "I am the Lord's servant," said Mary;
"may it happen to me as you have said." And
the angel left her.

Mary Visits Elizabeth

39 Soon afterward Mary got ready and
hurried off to a town in the hill country of
Judea. 40 She went into Zechariah's house
and greeted Elizabeth. 41 When Elizabeth
heard Mary's greeting, the baby moved with-
in her. Elizabeth was filled with the Holy
Spirit 42 and said in a loud voice, "You are
the most blessed of all women, and blessed is
the child you will bear! 43 Why should this
great thing happen to me, that my Lord's
mother comes to visit me? 44 For as soon as
I heard your greeting, the baby within me
jumped with gladness. 45 How happy you are
to believe that the Lord's message to you will
come true!"

1:31 Mt 1:21 **1:32, 33** 2 Sam 7:12, 13, 16; Isa 9:7 **1:37** Gen 18:14 **1:42** Jdt 13:18

" 'Don't be afraid, Mary; God has been gracious to you' " *(Luke 1:30)*.

Pray it!

Hail Mary!

Elizabeth's greeting to her relative Mary probably sounds familiar to you (Luke 1:42). This greeting forms part of one of the most well-known Catholic prayers, the Hail Mary. The words in this Bible are slightly different from the prayer. See if you can find the part that matches Elizabeth's greeting.

Hail Mary, full of grace,
The Lord is with you!
Blessed are you among women,
and blessed is the fruit of your
womb, Jesus.
Holy Mary, Mother of God,
pray for us sinners,
now and at the hour of our death.
Amen.

By saying yes to God's plan, Mary has become the mother of all of the living. Through the Hail Mary, we can pray with Mary and ask her to pray for us. The Hail Mary also serves as the main prayer of the rosary.

— Luke 1:41–42

Mary's Song of Praise

46 Mary said,
"My heart praises the Lord;
47 my soul is glad because of God my
Savior,
48 for he has remembered me, his lowly
servant!
From now on all people will call me
happy,
49 because of the great things the Mighty
God has done for me.
His name is holy;
50 from one generation to another
he shows mercy to those who honor
him.
51 He has stretched out his mighty arm
and scattered the proud with all their
plans.
52 He has brought down mighty kings from
their thrones,
and lifted up the lowly.
53 He has filled the hungry with good things,
and sent the rich away with empty
hands.
54 He has kept the promise he made to our
ancestors,
and has come to the help of his servant
Israel.
55 He has remembered to show mercy to
Abraham
and to all his descendants forever!"

56 Mary stayed about three months with
Elizabeth and then went back home.

The Birth of John the Baptist

57 The time came for Elizabeth to have
her baby, and she gave birth to a son. 58 Her
neighbors and relatives heard how wonder-
fully good the Lord had been to her, and
they all rejoiced with her.
59 When the baby was a week old, they
came to circumcise him, and they were
going to name him Zechariah, after his
father. 60 But his mother said, "No! His name
is to be John."
61 They said to her, "But you don't have
any relative with that name!" 62 Then they
made signs to his father, asking him what
name he would like the boy to have.
63 Zechariah asked for a writing pad and
wrote, "His name is John." How surprised
they all were! 64 At that moment Zechariah
was able to speak again, and he started praising
God. 65 The neighbors were all filled with fear,
and the news about these things spread

1:48 1 Sam 1:11 **1:52** Job 5:11; 12:19; Sir 10:14 **1:55** Gen 17:7 **1:46–55** 1 Sam 2:1–10 **1:59** Lev 12:3

Mary's song of praise in Luke 1:46–55 is called the *Magnificat* and has become an important prayer in the Catholic Church.

Catholic Connections

Christmas

Santa Claus. Jingle bells. Presents under the Christmas tree. These are all part of the Christmas tradition today, but none of them would exist without the event that the authors of both Luke and Matthew write about at the beginning of their Gospels: the birth of Jesus. Each December 25, just as the days are beginning to get longer, Roman Catholics and most other Christians celebrate the birth of Jesus, the light of the world.

The Christmas story in the Bible is a beautiful and familiar one. As we are busy preparing for this joyful celebration, we need to remember, as the saying goes, that Jesus is the reason for the season. How does your family celebrate the birth of Jesus?

— Luke 2:1–21

through all the hill country of Judea. 66Every-
one who heard of it thought about it and
asked, "What is this child going to be?" For it
was plain that the Lord's power was upon him.

Zechariah's Prophecy

67John's father Zechariah was filled with
the Holy Spirit, and he spoke God's message:

68"Let us praise the Lord, the God of Israel!
He has come to the help of his people
and has set them free.
69He has provided for us a mighty Savior,
a descendant of his servant David.
70He promised through his holy prophets
long ago
71 that he would save us from our enemies,
from the power of all those who hate us.
72He said he would show mercy to our
ancestors
and remember his sacred covenant.
73-74With a solemn oath to our ancestor
Abraham
he promised to rescue us from our
enemies
and allow us to serve him without fear,
75so that we might be holy and righteous
before him
all the days of our life.
76"You, my child, will be called a prophet
of the Most High God.
You will go ahead of the Lord
to prepare his road for him,
77to tell his people that they will be
saved
by having their sins forgiven.
78Our God is merciful and tender.
He will cause the bright dawn of
salvation to rise on us
79 and to shine from heaven on all those
who live in the dark shadow of
death,
to guide our steps into the path of
peace."

80The child grew and developed in body
and spirit. He lived in the desert until the
day when he appeared publicly to the people
of Israel.

The Birth of Jesus

(Matthew 1:18–25)

2 At that time Emperor Augustus ordered
a census to be taken throughout the
Roman Empire. 2When this first census took
place, Quirinius was the governor of Syria.
3Everyone, then, went to register himself,
each to his own hometown.

1:76 Mal 3:1 **1:79** Isa 9:2

4Joseph went from the town of Nazareth
in Galilee to the town of Bethlehem in
Judea, the birthplace of King David. Joseph
went there because he was a descendant of
David. 5He went to register with Mary, who
was promised in marriage to him. She was
pregnant, 6and while they were in Bethle-
hem, the time came for her to have her baby.
7She gave birth to her first son, wrapped him
in cloths and laid him in a manger—there
was no room for them to stay in the inn.

The Shepherds and the Angels

8There were some shepherds in that part of
the country who were spending the night in
the fields, taking care of their flocks. 9An angel
of the Lord appeared to them, and the glory
of the Lord shone over them. They were terri-
bly afraid, 10but the angel said to them, "Don't
be afraid! I am here with good news for you,
which will bring great joy to all the people.
11This very day in David's town your Savior
was born—Christ the Lord! 12And this is
what will prove it to you: you will find a baby
wrapped in cloths and lying in a manger."
13Suddenly a great army of heaven's angels
appeared with the angel, singing praises to
God:

"Glory to God in the highest heaven!" (2:14)

14"Glory to God in the highest heaven,
and peace on earth to those with
whom he is pleased!"

15When the angels went away from them
back into heaven, the shepherds said to one
another, "Let's go to Bethlehem and see this
thing that has happened, which the Lord has
told us."

16So they hurried off and found Mary
and Joseph and saw the baby lying in the
manger. 17When the shepherds saw him,
they told them what the angel had said
about the child. 18All who heard it were
amazed at what the shepherds said. 19Mary
remembered all these things and thought
deeply about them. 20The shepherds went
back, singing praises to God for all they had
heard and seen; it had been just as the angel
had told them.

Mary remembered all these things. (2:19)

Jesus Is Named

21A week later, when the time came for
the baby to be circumcised, he was named
Jesus, the name which the angel had given
him before he had been conceived.

Jesus Is Presented in the Temple

22The time came for Joseph and Mary to
perform the ceremony of purification, as the
Law of Moses commanded. So they took
the child to Jerusalem to present him to the
Lord, 23as it is written in the law of the
Lord: "Every first-born male is to be dedi-
cated to the Lord." 24They also went to offer
a sacrifice of a pair of doves or two young
pigeons, as required by the law of the Lord.

2:9 Tob 5:4 **2:21** **a** Lev 12:3; **b** Lk 1:31 **2:23** Ex 13:2, 12 **2:22–24** Lev 12:6–8

25 At that time there was a man named
Simeon living in Jerusalem. He was a good,
God-fearing man and was waiting for Israel
to be saved. The Holy Spirit was with him
26 and had assured him that he would not die
before he had seen the Lord's promised Mes-
siah. 27 Led by the Spirit, Simeon went into
the Temple. When the parents brought the
child Jesus into the Temple to do for him
what the Law required, 28 Simeon took the
child in his arms and gave thanks to God:

29 "Now, Lord, you have kept your promise,
and you may let your servant go in
peace.
30 With my own eyes I have seen your
salvation,
31 which you have prepared in the
presence of all peoples:
32 A light to reveal your will to the Gentiles
and bring glory to your people Israel."

33 The child's father and mother were
amazed at the things Simeon said about him.
34 Simeon blessed them and said to Mary, his
mother, "This child is chosen by God for the
destruction and the salvation of many in
Israel. He will be a sign from God which
many people will speak against 35 and so
reveal their secret thoughts. And sorrow, like
a sharp sword, will break your own heart."

36-37 There was a very old prophet, a
widow named Anna, daughter of Phanuel of
the tribe of Asher. She had been married for
only seven years and was now eighty-four
years old.[b] She never left the Temple; day
and night she worshiped God, fasting and
praying. 38 That very same hour she arrived
and gave thanks to God and spoke about the
child to all who were waiting for God to set
Jerusalem free.

The Return to Nazareth

39 When Joseph and Mary had finished
doing all that was required by the Law of the
Lord, they returned to their hometown of
Nazareth in Galilee. 40 The child grew and
became strong; he was full of wisdom, and
God's blessings were upon him.

> **Live it!**
>
> **"Where Were You?"**
>
> **Have you ever heard those words? Probably many times, especially if someone was very concerned about you. Jesus faced the same question from his parents when he was twelve years old. They thought he was lost and were very worried about him. On the third day of their frantic search, they found him in the Temple. Jesus seemed surprised at their concern.**
>
> **Like the boy Jesus, you are at an age where you are growing more independent. You will be on your own more, which will be an adjustment for both you and your parents. Try to imagine yourself as the parents of a missing child. Next time you are gone longer than you thought or something comes up, let the adults in your life know where you are. Their concern for your safety is a sign of their love for you, and by staying in touch you show your love for them.**
>
> **— Luke 2:41–51**

The Boy Jesus in the Temple

41 Every year the parents of Jesus went to
Jerusalem for the Passover Festival. 42 When
Jesus was twelve years old, they went to the
festival as usual. 43 When the festival was

[b] **2:36–37** was now eighty-four years old; *or* had been a widow eighty-four years.
2:32 Isa 42:6; 49:6; 52:10 **2:36, 37** Jdt 8:4, 5 **2:39** Mt 2:23 **2:41** Ex 12:1–27; Deut 16:1–8

Augustus was the first emperor of the Roman Empire. Check out the timeline in the front of this Bible to find out when the Romans conquered the Holy Land.

over, they started back home, but the boy
Jesus stayed in Jerusalem. His parents did not
know this; 44 they thought that he was with
the group, so they traveled a whole day and
then started looking for him among their
relatives and friends. 45 They did not find
him, so they went back to Jerusalem looking
for him. 46 On the third day they found him
in the Temple, sitting with the Jewish teach-
ers, listening to them and asking questions.
47 All who heard him were amazed at his
intelligent answers. 48 His parents were aston-
ished when they saw him, and his mother
said to him, "Son, why have you done this to
us? Your father and I have been terribly wor-
ried trying to find you."

. . . sitting with the Jewish teachers (2:46)

49 He answered them, "Why did you have
to look for me? Didn't you know that I had
to be in my Father's house?" 50 But they did
not understand his answer.
51 So Jesus went back with them to
Nazareth, where he was obedient to them.
His mother treasured all these things in her
heart. 52 Jesus grew both in body and in wis-
dom, gaining favor with God and people.

The Preaching of John the Baptist

*(Matthew 3:1–12; Mark 1:1–8;
John 1:19–28)*

3 It was the fifteenth year of the rule of
Emperor Tiberius; Pontius Pilate was
governor of Judea, Herod was ruler of
Galilee, and his brother Philip was ruler of
the territory of Iturea and Trachonitis; Lysa-
nias was ruler of Abilene, 2 and Annas and
Caiaphas were High Priests. At that time the
word of God came to John son of Zechariah
in the desert. 3 So John went throughout the
whole territory of the Jordan River, preach-
ing, "Turn away from your sins and be bap-
tized, and God will forgive your sins." 4 As it
is written in the book of the prophet Isaiah:
"Someone is shouting in the desert:
'Get the road ready for the Lord;
make a straight path for him to travel!
5 Every valley must be filled up,
every hill and mountain leveled off.
The winding roads must be made straight,
and the rough paths made smooth.
6 The whole human race will see God's
salvation!' "
7 Crowds of people came out to John to
be baptized by him. "You snakes!" he said to
them. "Who told you that you could escape
from the punishment God is about to send?
8 Do those things that will show that you
have turned from your sins. And don't start
saying among yourselves that Abraham is
your ancestor. I tell you that God can take
these rocks and make descendants for Abra-
ham! 9 The ax is ready to cut down the trees
at the roots; every tree that does not bear
good fruit will be cut down and thrown in
the fire."
10 The people asked him, "What are we to
do, then?"
11 He answered, "Whoever has two shirts
must give one to the man who has none,
and whoever has food must share it."
12 Some tax collectors came to be bap-
tized, and they asked him, "Teacher, what are
we to do?"
13 "Don't collect more than is legal," he
told them.
14 Some soldiers also asked him, "What
about us? What are we to do?"
He said to them, "Don't take money from
anyone by force or accuse anyone falsely. Be
content with your pay."

2:52 1 Sam 2:26; Prov 3:4 **3:4–6** Isa 40:3–5 (LXX) **3:7** Mt 12:34; 23:33 **3:8** Jn 8:33 **3:9** Mt 7:19
3:12 Lk 7:29

In Luke, chapter 3, we meet Pontius Pilate, Herod, Annas, and Caiaphas. They will play important roles in the arrest and death of Jesus.

Catholic Connections

Advent

"Get the road ready for the Lord." These words of John the Baptist serve as the theme for the season of Advent, which means "coming." John is at the Jordan River, urging people to prepare for the coming of the Messiah. Advent, which begins on the fourth Sunday before Christmas, is a time for us to get a road ready for Jesus in our own lives. The tradition of the Advent wreath with its four candles is a symbol of Advent. Each Sunday another candle is lit as a sign that Jesus is the light that comes into the world. The wreath grows brighter as we get closer to Christmas, and it reminds us to focus on what we need to do to let God enter more fully into our hearts.

— Luke 3:1–18

15 People's hopes began to rise, and they
began to wonder whether John perhaps
might be the Messiah. 16 So John said to all
of them, "I baptize you with water, but
someone is coming who is much greater
than I am. I am not good enough even to
untie his sandals. He will baptize you with
the Holy Spirit and fire. 17 He has his win-
nowing shovel with him, to thresh out all
the grain and gather the wheat into his barn;
but he will burn the chaff in a fire that never
goes out."
18 In many different ways John preached
the Good News to the people and urged
them to change their ways. 19 But John repri-
manded Governor Herod, because he had
married Herodias, his brother's wife, and had
done many other evil things. 20 Then Herod
did an even worse thing by putting John in
prison.

The Baptism of Jesus

(Matthew 3:13–17; Mark 1:9–11)

21 After all the people had been baptized,
Jesus also was baptized. While he was pray-
ing, heaven was opened, 22 and the Holy
Spirit came down upon him in bodily form
like a dove. And a voice came from heaven,
"You are my own dear Son. I am pleased
with you."

The Ancestors of Jesus

(Matthew 1:1–17)

23 When Jesus began his work, he was
about thirty years old. He was the son, so
people thought, of Joseph, who was the son
of Heli, 24 the son of Matthat, the son of
Levi, the son of Melchi, the son of Jannai,
the son of Joseph, 25 the son of Mattathias,
the son of Amos, the son of Nahum, the son
of Esli, the son of Naggai, 26 the son of
Maath, the son of Mattathias, the son of
Semein, the son of Josech, the son of Joda,
27 the son of Joanan, the son of Rhesa, the
son of Zerubbabel, the son of Shealtiel, the
son of Neri, 28 the son of Melchi, the son
of Addi, the son of Cosam, the son of
Elmadam, the son of Er, 29 the son of Joshua,
the son of Eliezer, the son of Jorim, the son
of Matthat, the son of Levi, 30 the son of
Simeon, the son of Judah, the son of Joseph,
the son of Jonam, the son of Eliakim, 31 the
son of Melea, the son of Menna, the son of
Mattatha, the son of Nathan, the son of
David, 32 the son of Jesse, the son of Obed,
the son of Boaz, the son of Salmon, the son
of Nahshon, 33 the son of Amminadab, the

3:19, 20 Mt 14:3, 4; Mk 6:17, 18 **3:22** Gen 22:2; Ps 2:7; Isa 42:1; Mt 3:17; Mk 1:11; Lk 9:35

Live it!

All in the Family

Do you know the names of your great-grandparents? How about *their* great-grandparents? In chapter 3, Luke traces Jesus' ancestors all the way back to Adam, the first human! Family is a very important part of who we are, and we need to take pride in our family and ethnic heritage. Next time you see your grandparents, ask them about their parents and grandparents. Find out what they were like. Each one of us, like Jesus, is part of a long line of people who came before us. And all of us are part of the human family.

— Luke 3:23–38

son of Admin, the son of Arni, the son of
Hezron, the son of Perez, the son of Judah,
34 the son of Jacob, the son of Isaac, the son
of Abraham, the son of Terah, the son of
Nahor, 35 the son of Serug, the son of
Reu, the son of Peleg, the son of Eber, the
son of Shelah, 36 the son of Cainan, the son
of Arphaxad, the son of Shem, the son of
Noah, the son of Lamech, 37 the son of
Methuselah, the son of Enoch, the son of
Jared, the son of Mahalaleel, the son of
Kenan, 38 the son of Enosh, the son of Seth,
the son of Adam, the son of God.

The Temptation of Jesus
(Matthew 4:1–11; Mark 1:12, 13)

4 Jesus returned from the Jordan full of
the Holy Spirit and was led by the Spir-
it into the desert, 2 where he was tempted by
the Devil for forty days. In all that time he
ate nothing, so that he was hungry when it
was over.

3 The Devil said to him, "If you are God's
Son, order this stone to turn into bread."

4 But Jesus answered, "The scripture says,
'Human beings cannot live on bread
alone.' "

5 Then the Devil took him up and showed
him in a second all the kingdoms of the
world. 6 "I will give you all this power and all
this wealth," the Devil told him. "It has all
been handed over to me, and I can give it to
anyone I choose. 7 All this will be yours,
then, if you worship me."

8 Jesus answered, "The scripture says, 'Wor-
ship the Lord your God and serve only
him!' "

9 Then the Devil took him to Jerusalem
and set him on the highest point of the
Temple, and said to him, "If you are God's
Son, throw yourself down from here. 10 For
the scripture says, 'God will order his angels
to take good care of you.' 11 It also says, 'They
will hold you up with their hands so that
not even your feet will be hurt on the
stones.' "

12 But Jesus answered, "The scripture says,
'Do not put the Lord your God to the
test.' "

13 When the Devil finished tempting Jesus
in every way, he left him for a while.

Jesus Begins His Work in Galilee
(Matthew 4:12–17; Mark 1:14, 15)

14 Then Jesus returned to Galilee, and the
power of the Holy Spirit was with him. The
news about him spread throughout all that
territory. 15 He taught in the synagogues and
was praised by everyone.

Jesus Is Rejected at Nazareth
(Matthew 13:53–58; Mark 6:1–6)

16 Then Jesus went to Nazareth, where he
had been brought up, and on the Sabbath he
went as usual to the synagogue. He stood up
to read the Scriptures 17 and was handed the
book of the prophet Isaiah. He unrolled the
scroll and found the place where it is writ-
ten,

18 "The Spirit of the Lord is upon me,
because he has chosen me to bring
good news to the poor.

4:4 Deut 8:3 **4:8** Deut 6:13 **4:10, 11** Ps 91:11, 12 **4:12** Deut 6:16 **4:18, 19** Isa 61:1, 2 (LXX)

He has sent me to proclaim liberty to the
captives
and recovery of sight to the blind,
to set free the oppressed
19 and announce that the time has come
when the Lord will save his people."

20 Jesus rolled up the scroll, gave it back to
the attendant, and sat down. All the people
in the synagogue had their eyes fixed on
him, 21 as he said to them, "This passage of
scripture has come true today, as you heard it
being read."

22 They were all well impressed with him
and marveled at the eloquent words that he
spoke. They said, "Isn't he the son of Joseph?"

23 He said to them, "I am sure that you
will quote this proverb to me, 'Doctor, heal
yourself.' You will also tell me to do here in
my hometown the same things you heard
were done in Capernaum. 24 I tell you this,"
Jesus added, "prophets are never welcomed
in their hometown. 25 Listen to me: it is true
that there were many widows in Israel dur-
ing the time of Elijah, when there was no
rain for three and a half years and a severe
famine spread throughout the whole land.
26 Yet Elijah was not sent to anyone in Israel,
but only to a widow living in Zarephath in
the territory of Sidon. 27 And there were
many people suffering from a dreaded skin
disease who lived in Israel during the time
of the prophet Elisha; yet not one of them
was healed, but only Naaman the Syrian."

28 When the people in the synagogue
heard this, they were filled with anger.
29 They rose up, dragged Jesus out of town,
and took him to the top of the hill on which
their town was built. They meant to throw
him over the cliff, 30 but he walked through
the middle of the crowd and went his way.

A Man with an Evil Spirit
(Mark 1:21–28)

31 Then Jesus went to Capernaum, a town
in Galilee, where he taught the people on
the Sabbath. 32 They were all amazed at the
way he taught, because he spoke with
authority. 33 In the synagogue was a man
who had the spirit of an evil demon in him;
he screamed out in a loud voice, 34 "Ah!
What do you want with us, Jesus of
Nazareth? Are you here to destroy us? I
know who you are: you are God's holy
messenger!"

35 Jesus ordered the spirit, "Be quiet and
come out of the man!" The demon threw
the man down in front of them and went
out of him without doing him any harm.

36 The people were all amazed and said to
one another, "What kind of words are these?
With authority and power this man gives
orders to the evil spirits, and they come
out!" 37 And the report about Jesus spread
everywhere in that region.

Jesus Heals Many People
(Matthew 8:14–17; Mark 1:29–34)

38 Jesus left the synagogue and went to
Simon's home. Simon's mother-in-law was
sick with a high fever, and they spoke to
Jesus about her. 39 He went and stood at her
bedside and ordered the fever to leave her.
The fever left her, and she got up at once
and began to wait on them.

40 After sunset all who had friends who
were sick with various diseases brought them
to Jesus; he placed his hands on every one of
them and healed them all. 41 Demons also
went out from many people, screaming,
"You are the Son of God!"

Jesus gave the demons an order and would
not let them speak, because they knew he
was the Messiah.

Jesus Preaches in the Synagogues
(Mark 1:35–39)

42 At daybreak Jesus left the town and
went off to a lonely place. The people started
looking for him, and when they found him,
they tried to keep him from leaving. 43 But
he said to them, "I must preach the Good

4:24 Jn 4:44 **4:25** 1 Kings 17:1 **4:26** 1 Kings 17:8–16 **4:27** 2 Kings 5:1–14 **4:32** Mt 7:28, 29

Jesus refers to Naaman the Syrian *(Luke 4:27)*. **Check out his story in 2 Kings 5:1–14.**

Pray it!

Turn Down the Noise

Twice Luke mentions that Jesus would go away to a lonely place (Luke 4:42, 5:16). Jesus was almost always surrounded by people, so it makes sense that sometimes he just needed to get away to a quiet spot where he could rest and pray. That's important for us too. We all need to have somewhere to go where we can be alone and spend some time in God's presence. Where is your "lonely", or a quiet place?

Where do you go to be alone with your thoughts? The next time you are there, try this prayer.

God, here I am alone with you.
Life gets so crazy sometimes.
It's good just to hang out with you.
It helps me to know that even Jesus needed to get away once in awhile.
Help me as I sort through what's going on in my life,
especially with my family and friends.
Thank you for being here with me.
Amen.

— Luke 4:42–43

News about the Kingdom of God in other
towns also, because that is what God sent me
to do."
44So he preached in the synagogues
throughout the country.

Jesus Calls the First Disciples
(Matthew 4:18–22; Mark 1:16–20)

5 One day Jesus was standing on the
shore of Lake Gennesaret while the
people pushed their way up to him to listen
to the word of God. 2He saw two boats
pulled up on the beach; the fishermen had
left them and were washing the nets. 3Jesus
got into one of the boats—it belonged to
Simon—and asked him to push off a little
from the shore. Jesus sat in the boat and
taught the crowd.
4When he finished speaking, he said to
Simon, "Push the boat out further to the
deep water, and you and your partners let
down your nets for a catch."
5"Master," Simon answered, "we worked
hard all night long and caught nothing. But if
you say so, I will let down the nets." 6They
let them down and caught such a large num-
ber of fish that the nets were about to break.
7So they motioned to their partners in the
other boat to come and help them. They

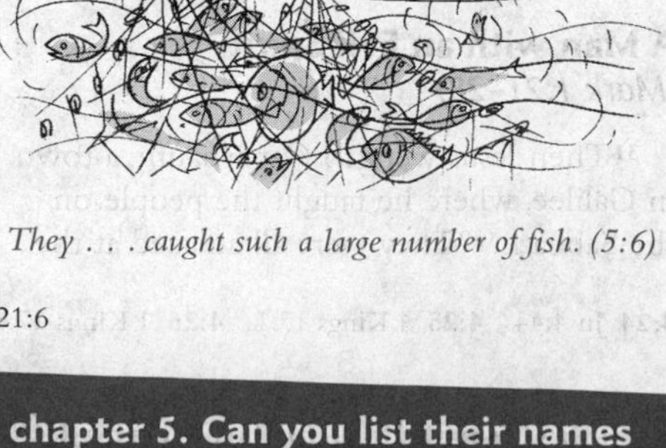

They . . . caught such a large number of fish. (5:6)

5:1–3 Mt 13:1, 2; Mk 3:9, 10; 4:1 **5:5** Jn 21:3 **5:6** Jn 21:6

Jesus calls his first four disciples in Luke, chapter 5. Can you list their names and the jobs they had?

came and filled both boats so full of fish that
the boats were about to sink. 8When Simon
Peter saw what had happened, he fell on his
knees before Jesus and said, "Go away from
me, Lord! I am a sinful man!"
9He and the others with him were all
amazed at the large number of fish they had
caught. 10The same was true of Simon's part-
ners, James and John, the sons of Zebedee.
Jesus said to Simon, "Don't be afraid; from
now on you will be catching people."
11They pulled the boats up on the beach,
left everything, and followed Jesus.

Jesus Heals a Man
(Matthew 8:1–4; Mark 1:40–45)

12Once Jesus was in a town where there
was a man who was suffering from a dreaded
skin disease. When he saw Jesus, he threw
himself down and begged him, "Sir, if you
want to, you can make me clean!"[c]
13Jesus reached out and touched him. "I
do want to," he answered. "Be clean!" At
once the disease left the man. 14Jesus ordered
him, "Don't tell anyone, but go straight to
the priest and let him examine you; then to
prove to everyone that you are cured, offer
the sacrifice as Moses ordered."
15But the news about Jesus spread all the
more widely, and crowds of people came to
hear him and be healed from their diseases.
16But he would go away to lonely places,
where he prayed.

Jesus Heals a Paralyzed Man
(Matthew 9:1–8; Mark 2:1–12)

17One day when Jesus was teaching,
some Pharisees and teachers of the Law
were sitting there who had come from
every town in Galilee and Judea and from
Jerusalem. The power of the Lord was pres-
ent for Jesus to heal the sick. 18Some men
came carrying a paralyzed man on a bed,
and they tried to carry him into the house
and put him in front of Jesus. 19Because of
the crowd, however, they could find no way
to take him in. So they carried him up on
the roof, made an opening in the tiles, and
let him down on his bed into the middle of
the group in front of Jesus. 20When Jesus
saw how much faith they had, he said to
the man, "Your sins are forgiven, my
friend."
21The teachers of the Law and the Phar-
isees began to say to themselves, "Who is this
man who speaks such blasphemy! God is the
only one who can forgive sins!"

They . . . let him down on his bed into the middle of the group. (5:19)

22Jesus knew their thoughts and said to
them, "Why do you think such things? 23Is it
easier to say, 'Your sins are forgiven you,' or
to say, 'Get up and walk'? 24I will prove to
you, then, that the Son of Man has authority
on earth to forgive sins." So he said to the
paralyzed man, "I tell you, get up, pick up
your bed, and go home!"
25At once the man got up in front of
them all, took the bed he had been lying on,
and went home, praising God. 26They were
all completely amazed! Full of fear, they
praised God, saying, "What marvelous things
we have seen today!"

Jesus Calls Levi
(Matthew 9:9–13; Mark 2:13–17)

27After this, Jesus went out and saw a tax
collector named Levi, sitting in his office.
Jesus said to him, "Follow me." 28Levi got
up, left everything, and followed him.
29Then Levi had a big feast in his house

[c] **5:12** MAKE ME CLEAN: *This disease was considered to make a person ritually unclean.*
5:14 Lev 14:1–32

for Jesus, and among the guests was a large
number of tax collectors and other people.
30Some Pharisees and some teachers of the
Law who belonged to their group com-
plained to Jesus' disciples. "Why do you eat
and drink with tax collectors and other out-
casts?" they asked.
31Jesus answered them, "People who are
well do not need a doctor, but only those
who are sick. 32I have not come to call
respectable people to repent, but outcasts."

The Question about Fasting

(Matthew 9:14–17; Mark 2:18–22)

33Some people said to Jesus, "The disci-
ples of John fast frequently and offer prayers,
and the disciples of the Pharisees do the
same; but your disciples eat and drink."
34Jesus answered, "Do you think you can
make the guests at a wedding party go with-
out food as long as the bridegroom is with
them? Of course not! 35But the day will
come when the bridegroom will be taken
away from them, and then they will fast."
36Jesus also told them this parable: "You
don't tear a piece off a new coat to patch up
an old coat. If you do, you will have torn
the new coat, and the piece of new cloth
will not match the old. 37Nor do you pour
new wine into used wineskins, because the
new wine will burst the skins, the wine will
pour out, and the skins will be ruined.
38Instead, new wine must be poured into
fresh wineskins! 39And you don't want new
wine after drinking old wine. 'The old is
better,' you say."

Live it!

Old and New

So what's up with the parable of the patches and the wineskins? When is the last time you had a piece of clothing patched? And what in the world is a wineskin? These are images we have a hard time understanding because they are probably not part of our lives. What Jesus is really talking about here Is the difference between the old and the new. For example, if your family or school has an old computer, and you try to install a brand new program, it probably won't work. The old computer simply can't handle the new software.

Jesus is making a point about the new message he is trying to share with his followers. People were sometimes more concerned with following rules rather than getting closer to God. It's not so much about all the rules, as it is about acting out of love and compassion. That is the good NEWs! That's the new program to install within our hearts and souls.

— Luke 5:36–39

The Question about the Sabbath

(Matthew 12:1–8; Mark 2:23–28)

6 Jesus was walking through some wheat
fields on a Sabbath. His disciples began
to pick the heads of wheat, rub them in
their hands, and eat the grain. 2Some Phar-
isees asked, "Why are you doing what our
Law says you cannot do on the Sabbath?"
3Jesus answered them, "Haven't you read
what David did when he and his men were
hungry? 4He went into the house of God,
took the bread offered to God, ate it, and gave
it also to his men. Yet it is against our Law for
anyone except the priests to eat that bread."
5And Jesus concluded, "The Son of Man
is Lord of the Sabbath."

The Man with a Paralyzed Hand

(Matthew 12:9–14; Mark 3:1–6)

6On another Sabbath Jesus went into a
synagogue and taught. A man was there
whose right hand was paralyzed. 7Some
teachers of the Law and some Pharisees

5:30 Lk 15:1, 2 **6:1** Deut 23:25 **6:4** Lev 24:9 **6:3, 4** 1 Sam 21:1–6

wanted a reason to accuse Jesus of doing
wrong, so they watched him closely to see if
he would heal on the Sabbath. 8But Jesus
knew their thoughts and said to the man,
"Stand up and come here to the front." The
man got up and stood there. 9Then Jesus said
to them, "I ask you: What does our Law
allow us to do on the Sabbath? To help or to
harm? To save someone's life or destroy it?"
10He looked around at them all; then he
said[d] to the man, "Stretch out your hand."
He did so, and his hand became well again.
11They were filled with rage and began to
discuss among themselves what they could
do to Jesus.

Jesus Chooses the Twelve Apostles
(Matthew 10:1–4; Mark 3:13–19)

12At that time Jesus went up a hill to pray
and spent the whole night there praying to
God. 13When day came, he called his disci-
ples to him and chose twelve of them,
whom he named apostles: 14Simon (whom
he named Peter) and his brother Andrew;
James and John, Philip and Bartholomew,
15Matthew and Thomas, James son of
Alphaeus, and Simon (who was called the
Patriot), 16Judas son of James, and Judas
Iscariot, who became the traitor.

Jesus Teaches and Heals
(Matthew 4:23–25)

17When Jesus had come down from the
hill with the apostles, he stood on a level
place with a large number of his disciples.
A large crowd of people was there from all
over Judea and from Jerusalem and from the
coast cities of Tyre and Sidon; 18they had
come to hear him and to be healed of their
diseases. Those who were troubled by evil
spirits also came and were healed. 19All the
people tried to touch him, for power was
going out from him and healing them all.

Happiness and Sorrow
(Matthew 5:1–12)

20Jesus looked at his disciples and said,
"Happy are you poor;
the Kingdom of God is yours!
21"Happy are you who are hungry now;
you will be filled!
"Happy are you who weep now;
you will laugh!
22"Happy are you when people hate you,
reject you, insult you, and say that you are
evil, all because of the Son of Man! 23Be
glad when that happens and dance for joy,
because a great reward is kept for you in
heaven. For their ancestors did the very same
things to the prophets.
24"But how terrible for you who are rich
now;
you have had your easy life!
25"How terrible for you who are full now;
you will go hungry!
"How terrible for you who laugh now;
you will mourn and weep!
26"How terrible when all people speak
well of you; their ancestors said the very
same things about the false prophets.

Love for Enemies
(Matthew 5:38–48; 7:12a)

27"But I tell you who hear me: Love your
enemies, do good to those who hate you,
28bless those who curse you, and pray for
those who mistreat you. 29If anyone hits you
on one cheek, let him hit the other one too;
if someone takes your coat, let him have
your shirt as well. 30Give to everyone who
asks you for something, and when someone
takes what is yours, do not ask for it back.
31Do for others just what you want them to
do for you.
32"If you love only the people who love
you, why should you receive a blessing?
Even sinners love those who love them!
33And if you do good only to those who do

[d] **6:10** said; *some manuscripts have* said angrily.
6:22 1 Pet 4:14 **6:23** 2 Chr 36:16; Acts 7:52 **6:31** Tob 4:15; Mt 7:12

The Beatitudes is the name given to the teachings of Jesus in Luke 6:20–26. See how they compare with the version in Matthew 5:1–12.

Going the Extra Mile

How do we treat people who are mean to us? How do we react to people who we can't stand? Jesus has a pretty clear answer. We are to pray for those who mistreat us and actually bless those people who curse us (to bless someone is to ask God to bring good things to that person)! Jesus goes on to say that it's easy to be nice and kind to the people we like. Anyone can do that. The real challenge—the Christian challenge—is to love the people we don't like and to do good things to and for them.

Who do you have trouble liking? Pray right now that God will bless that person. Think of a specific way that you could follow this tough teaching of Jesus by doing something nice or kind for that person.

— Luke 6:27–36

good to you, why should you receive a bless-
ing? Even sinners do that! 34 And if you lend
only to those from whom you hope to get it
back, why should you receive a blessing?
Even sinners lend to sinners, to get back the
same amount! 35 No! Love your enemies and
do good to them; lend and expect nothing
back. You will then have a great reward, and
you will be children of the Most High God.
For he is good to the ungrateful and the
wicked. 36 Be merciful just as your Father is
merciful.

Judging Others
(Matthew 7:1–5)

37 "Do not judge others, and God will not
judge you; do not condemn others, and God
will not condemn you; forgive others, and
God will forgive you. 38 Give to others, and
God will give to you. Indeed, you will
receive a full measure, a generous helping,
poured into your hands—all that you can
hold. The measure you use for others is the
one that God will use for you."

39 And Jesus told them this parable: "One
blind man cannot lead another one; if he
does, both will fall into a ditch. 40 No pupils
are greater than their teacher; but all pupils,
when they have completed their training,
will be like their teacher.

41 "Why do you look at the speck in your
brother's eye, but pay no attention to the log
in your own eye? 42 How can you say to
your brother, 'Please, brother, let me take that
speck out of your eye,' yet cannot even see
the log in your own eye? You hypocrite!
First take the log out of your own eye, and
then you will be able to see clearly to take
the speck out of your brother's eye.

A Tree and Its Fruit
(Matthew 7:16–20; 12:33–35)

43 "A healthy tree does not bear bad fruit,
nor does a poor tree bear good fruit. 44 Every
tree is known by the fruit it bears; you do
not pick figs from thorn bushes or gather
grapes from bramble bushes. 45 A good per-
son brings good out of the treasure of good
things in his heart; a bad person brings bad
out of his treasure of bad things. For the
mouth speaks what the heart is full of.

The Two House Builders
(Matthew 7:24–27)

46 "Why do you call me, 'Lord, Lord,' and
yet don't do what I tell you? 47 Anyone who
comes to me and listens to my words and

6:35 Sir 4:10, 11 **6:39** Mt 15:14 **6:40** Mt 10:24, 25; Jn 13:16; 15:20 **6:44** Mt 12:33 **6:45** Mt 12:34

" 'Do not judge others, and God will not judge you . . . forgive others, and God will forgive you' " *(Luke 6:37)*.

Live it!

Measure for Measure

Have you ever seen those old-fashioned balances? They are used for weighing and seeing if two things are more-or-less equal. Keep that image in mind as you think about judging another person or about doing a good deed for someone. Jesus tells us that what we do will come back to us (Luke 6:38). If we constantly judge others, the same will happen to us. If we give generously to others, the same will happen to us. Let's try to keep that balance in mind.

— Luke 6:37–42

obeys them—I will show you what he is like.
48He is like a man who, in building his
house, dug deep and laid the foundation on
rock. The river flooded over and hit that
house but could not shake it, because it was
well built. 49But anyone who hears my words
and does not obey them is like a man who
built his house without laying a foundation;
when the flood hit that house it fell at
once—and what a terrible crash that was!"

Jesus Heals a Roman Officer's Servant
(Matthew 8:5–13)

7 When Jesus had finished saying all these
things to the people, he went to Caper-
naum. 2A Roman officer there had a servant
who was very dear to him; the man was sick
and about to die. 3When the officer heard
about Jesus, he sent some Jewish elders to
ask him to come and heal his servant. 4They
came to Jesus and begged him earnestly,
"This man really deserves your help. 5He
loves our people and he himself built a syna-
gogue for us."
6So Jesus went with them. He was not far
from the house when the officer sent friends
to tell him, "Sir, don't trouble yourself. I do
not deserve to have you come into my
house, 7neither do I consider myself worthy
to come to you in person. Just give the
order, and my servant will get well. 8I, too,
am a man placed under the authority of
superior officers, and I have soldiers under
me. I order this one, 'Go!' and he goes; I
order that one, 'Come!' and he comes; and I
order my slave, 'Do this!' and he does it."
9Jesus was surprised when he heard this;
he turned around and said to the crowd fol-
lowing him, "I tell you, I have never found
faith like this, not even in Israel!"
10The messengers went back to the offi-
cer's house and found his servant well.

Jesus Raises a Widow's Son

11Soon afterward[e] Jesus went to a town
named Nain, accompanied by his disciples
and a large crowd. 12Just as he arrived at the
gate of the town, a funeral procession was
coming out. The dead man was the only son
of a woman who was a widow, and a large
crowd from the town was with her. 13When
the Lord saw her, his heart was filled with
pity for her, and he said to her, "Don't cry."
14Then he walked over and touched the cof-
fin, and the men carrying it stopped. Jesus
said, "Young man! Get up, I tell you!" 15The
dead man sat up and began to talk, and Jesus
gave him back to his mother.
16They all were filled with fear and
praised God. "A great prophet has appeared
among us!" they said; "God has come to save
his people!"
17This news about Jesus went out through
all the country and the surrounding territory.

The Messengers from John the Baptist
(Matthew 11:2–19)

18When John's disciples told him about all
these things, he called two of them 19and
sent them to the Lord to ask him, "Are you

[e] **7:11** Soon afterward; *some manuscripts have* The next day.

the one John said was going to come, or
should we expect someone else?"
20 When they came to Jesus, they said,
"John the Baptist sent us to ask if you are
the one he said was going to come, or
should we expect someone else?"
21 At that very time Jesus healed many
people from their sicknesses, diseases, and
evil spirits, and gave sight to many blind
people. 22 He answered John's messengers,
"Go back and tell John what you have seen
and heard: the blind can see, the lame can
walk, those who suffer from dreaded skin
diseases are made clean,[f] the deaf can hear,
the dead are raised to life, and the Good
News is preached to the poor. 23 How happy
are those who have no doubts about me!"
24 After John's messengers had left, Jesus
began to speak about him to the crowds:
"When you went out to John in the desert,
what did you expect to see? A blade of grass
bending in the wind? 25 What did you go
out to see? A man dressed up in fancy
clothes? People who dress like that and live
in luxury are found in palaces! 26 Tell me,
what did you go out to see? A prophet? Yes
indeed, but you saw much more than a
prophet. 27 For John is the one of whom the
scripture says: 'God said, I will send my mes-
senger ahead of you to open the way for
you.' 28 I tell you," Jesus added, "John is
greater than anyone who has ever lived. But
the one who is least in the Kingdom of God
is greater than John."
29 All the people heard him; they and
especially the tax collectors were the ones
who had obeyed God's righteous demands
and had been baptized by John. 30 But the
Pharisees and the teachers of the Law reject-
ed God's purpose for themselves and refused
to be baptized by John.
31 Jesus continued, "Now to what can I
compare the people of this day? What are
they like? 32 They are like children sitting in
the marketplace. One group shouts to the
other, 'We played wedding music for you,
but you wouldn't dance! We sang funeral
songs, but you wouldn't cry!' 33 John the
Baptist came, and he fasted and drank no
wine, and you said, 'He has a demon in him!'

Live it!

It's Always Something

Sometimes you just can't win.

In a certain neighborhood, a small, old building had been empty for a long time, and people complained because it was an eyesore. Then one day the place came alive with construction, and before long, a little grocery opened. It was doing very well, but there wasn't a parking lot, so soon a lot more cars were parking on the streets. People in the neighborhood started complaining because now they couldn't always park right in front of their homes or apartments. They finally complained to the neighborhood council, who put up signs along the streets restricting parking. As the weather got colder, customers of the store started going to other places where parking was easier. Eventually the once-successful grocery went out of business. Once again, the building was empty, and soon the neighbors started complaining about the empty building.

This is the very thing Jesus is talking about in this passage as he compares people's reactions with those of John's followers and his own. Sometimes you just can't win! Think about what you have complained about recently. Can you think of something positive to say as well?

— Luke 7:31–35

34 The Son of Man came, and he ate and
drank, and you said, 'Look at this man! He is
a glutton and wine drinker, a friend of tax

[f] **7:22** MADE CLEAN: *See 5:12.*

7:22 a Isa 35:5,6; **b** Isa 61:1 **7:27** Mal 3:1 **7:29, 30** Mt 21:32; Lk 3:12

collectors and other outcasts!' 35 God's wisdom, however, is shown to be true by all who accept it."

Jesus at the Home of Simon the Pharisee

36 A Pharisee invited Jesus to have dinner with him, and Jesus went to his house and sat down to eat. 37 In that town was a woman who lived a sinful life. She heard that Jesus was eating in the Pharisee's house, so she brought an alabaster jar full of perfume 38 and stood behind Jesus, by his feet, crying and wetting his feet with her tears. Then she dried his feet with her hair, kissed them, and poured the perfume on them. 39 When the Pharisee saw this, he said to himself, "If this man really were a prophet, he would know who this woman is who is touching him; he would know what kind of sinful life she lives!"

40 Jesus spoke up and said to him, "Simon, I have something to tell you."

"Yes, Teacher," he said, "tell me."

41 "There were two men who owed money to a moneylender," Jesus began. "One owed him five hundred silver coins, and the other owed him fifty. 42 Neither of them could pay him back, so he canceled the debts of both. Which one, then, will love him more?"

43 "I suppose," answered Simon, "that it would be the one who was forgiven more."

"You are right," said Jesus. 44 Then he turned to the woman and said to Simon, "Do you see this woman? I came into your home, and you gave me no water for my feet, but she has washed my feet with her tears and dried them with her hair. 45 You did not welcome me with a kiss, but she has not stopped kissing my feet since I came. 46 You provided no olive oil for my head, but she has covered my feet with perfume. 47 I tell you, then, the great love she has shown proves that her many sins have been forgiven. But whoever has been forgiven little shows only a little love."

48 Then Jesus said to the woman, "Your sins are forgiven."

49 The others sitting at the table began to say to themselves, "Who is this, who even forgives sins?"

50 But Jesus said to the woman, "Your faith has saved you; go in peace."

Women Who Accompanied Jesus

8 Some time later Jesus traveled through towns and villages, preaching the Good News about the Kingdom of God. The twelve disciples went with him, 2 and so did some women who had been healed of evil spirits and diseases: Mary (who was called Magdalene), from whom seven demons had been driven out; 3 Joanna, whose husband Chuza was an officer in Herod's court; and Susanna, and many other women who used their own resources to help Jesus and his disciples.

The Parable of the Sower

(Matthew 13:1–9; Mark 4:1–9)

4 People kept coming to Jesus from one town after another; and when a great crowd gathered, Jesus told this parable:

5 "Once there was a man who went out to sow grain. As he scattered the seed in the field, some of it fell along the path, where it was stepped on, and the birds ate it up. 6 Some of it fell on rocky ground, and when the plants sprouted, they dried up because the soil had no moisture. 7 Some of the seed fell among thorn bushes, which grew up with the plants and choked them. 8 And some seeds fell in good soil; the plants grew and bore grain, one hundred grains each."

And Jesus concluded, "Listen, then, if you have ears!"

7:37, 38 Mt 26:7; Mk 14:3; Jn 12:3 **8:2, 3** Mt 27:55, 56; Mk 15:40, 41; Lk 23:49

A glutton *(Luke 7:34)* **is someone who eats or drinks way too much. Gluttony is one of the seven deadly sins.**

Study it!

Jesus: A Friend and Teacher to All

Mary. Joanna. Susanna. Luke provides us with the names of three of the women who followed Jesus along with the twelve disciples. Women are also an important part of the Easter story, as they are the ones who first get the news about Jesus' Resurrection. Luke tells us that many other women used their resources to help Jesus and his disciples.

The status of women in Jesus' time was very different from the status of women today in our culture. Women in Jesus' culture had very few rights and were basically considered the property of their husbands. A woman did not speak to men in public, and a man would not speak to a woman who was not his wife. But Jesus broke through these cultural limitations and reached out to women, who played an important role in his life and mission.

— Luke 8:1–3

The Purpose of the Parables
(Matthew 13:10–17; Mark 4:10–12)

9His disciples asked Jesus what this para-
ble meant, 10and he answered, "The knowl-
edge of the secrets of the Kingdom of God
has been given to you, but to the rest it
comes by means of parables, so that they
may look but not see, and listen but not
understand.

Jesus Explains the Parable of the Sower
(Matthew 13:18–23; Mark 4:13–20)

11"This is what the parable means: the
seed is the word of God. 12The seeds that fell
along the path stand for those who hear; but
the Devil comes and takes the message away
from their hearts in order to keep them from
believing and being saved. 13The seeds that
fell on rocky ground stand for those who
hear the message and receive it gladly. But it
does not sink deep into them; they believe
only for a while but when the time of testing
comes, they fall away. 14The seeds that fell
among thorn bushes stand for those who
hear; but the worries and riches and pleasures
of this life crowd in and choke them, and
their fruit never ripens. 15The seeds that fell
in good soil stand for those who hear the
message and retain it in a good and obedient
heart, and they persist until they bear fruit.

A Lamp under a Bowl
(Mark 4:21–25)

16"No one lights a lamp and covers it
with a bowl or puts it under a bed. Instead,
it is put on the lampstand, so that people will
see the light as they come in.
17"Whatever is hidden away will be
brought out into the open, and whatever is
covered up will be found and brought to light.
18"Be careful, then, how you listen;
because those who have something will be
given more, but whoever has nothing will
have taken away from them even the little
they think they have."

Jesus' Mother and Brothers
(Matthew 12:46–50; Mark 3:31–35)

19Jesus' mother and brothers came to him,
but were unable to join him because of the
crowd. 20Someone said to Jesus, "Your
mother and brothers are standing outside
and want to see you."

8:10 Isa 6:9 (LXX) **8:16** Mt 5:15; Lk 11:33 **8:17** Mt 10:26; Lk 12:2 **8:18** Mt 25:29; Lk 19:26

Jesus casts the demons into a herd of pigs *(Luke 8:32–33)*. **In the Old Law pigs are unclean animals, so Jews did not eat pork.**

21 Jesus said to them all, "My mother and
brothers are those who hear the word of
God and obey it."

Jesus Calms a Storm
(Matthew 8:23–27; Mark 4:35–41)

22 One day Jesus got into a boat with his
disciples and said to them, "Let us go across
to the other side of the lake." So they started
out. 23 As they were sailing, Jesus fell asleep.
Suddenly a strong wind blew down on the
lake, and the boat began to fill with water, so
that they were all in great danger. 24 The dis-
ciples went to Jesus and woke him up, say-
ing, "Master, Master! We are about to die!"

Jesus got up and gave an order to the
wind and to the stormy water; they quieted
down, and there was a great calm. 25 Then he
said to the disciples, "Where is your faith?"

But they were amazed and afraid, and said
to one another, "Who is this man? He gives
orders to the winds and waves, and they
obey him!"

Jesus Heals a Man with Demons
(Matthew 8:28–34; Mark 5:1–20)

26 Jesus and his disciples sailed on over to
the territory of Gerasa,[g] which is across the
lake from Galilee. 27 As Jesus stepped ashore,
he was met by a man from the town who had
demons in him. For a long time this man had
gone without clothes and would not stay at
home, but spent his time in the burial caves.
28 When he saw Jesus, he gave a loud cry,
threw himself down at his feet, and shouted,
"Jesus, Son of the Most High God! What do
you want with me? I beg you, don't punish
me!" 29 He said this because Jesus had ordered
the evil spirit to go out of him. Many times it
had seized him, and even though he was kept
a prisoner, his hands and feet tied with chains,
he would break the chains and be driven by
the demon out into the desert.
30 Jesus asked him, "What is your name?"

"My name is 'Mob,' " he answered—
because many demons had gone into him.
31 The demons begged Jesus not to send
them into the abyss.[h]

32 There was a large herd of pigs near by,
feeding on a hillside. So the demons begged
Jesus to let them go into the pigs, and he let
them. 33 They went out of the man and into
the pigs. The whole herd rushed down the
side of the cliff into the lake and was
drowned.

34 The men who had been taking care of
the pigs saw what happened, so they ran off
and spread the news in the town and among
the farms. 35 People went out to see what had
happened, and when they came to Jesus, they
found the man from whom the demons had
gone out sitting at the feet of Jesus, clothed
and in his right mind; and they were all
afraid. 36 Those who had seen it told the peo-
ple how the man had been cured. 37 Then all
the people from that territory asked Jesus to
go away, because they were terribly afraid. So
Jesus got into the boat and left. 38 The man
from whom the demons had gone out
begged Jesus, "Let me go with you."

But Jesus sent him away, saying, 39 "Go back
home and tell what God has done for you."

The man went through the town, telling
what Jesus had done for him.

Jairus' Daughter and the Woman Who Touched Jesus' Cloak
(Matthew 9:18–26; Mark 5:21–43)

40 When Jesus returned to the other side
of the lake, the people welcomed him,
because they had all been waiting for him.
41 Then a man named Jairus arrived; he was
an official in the local synagogue. He threw
himself down at Jesus' feet and begged him
to go to his home, 42 because his only daugh-
ter, who was twelve years old, was dying.

As Jesus went along, the people were
crowding him from every side. 43 Among
them was a woman who had suffered from
severe bleeding for twelve years; she had
spent all she had on doctors,[i] but no one
had been able to cure her. 44 She came up in
the crowd behind Jesus and touched the

[g] **8:26** Gerasa; *some manuscripts have* Gadara *(see Mt 8:28); others have* Gergesa. [h] **8:31** ABYSS: *It was thought that the demons were to be imprisoned in the depths of the earth until their final punishment.* [i] **8:43** *Some manuscripts do not have* she had spent all she had on doctors.

edge of his cloak, and her bleeding stopped
at once. 45Jesus asked, "Who touched me?"
Everyone denied it, and Peter said, "Mas-
ter, the people are all around you and
crowding in on you."
46But Jesus said, "Someone touched me,
for I knew it when power went out of me."
47The woman saw that she had been found
out, so she came trembling and threw herself
at Jesus' feet. There in front of everybody, she
told him why she had touched him and how
she had been healed at once. 48Jesus said to
her, "My daughter, your faith has made you
well. Go in peace."
49While Jesus was saying this, a messenger
came from the official's house. "Your daugh-
ter has died," he told Jairus; "don't bother the
Teacher any longer."
50But Jesus heard it and said to Jairus,
"Don't be afraid; only believe, and she will be
well."
51When he arrived at the house, he would
not let anyone go in with him except Peter,
John, and James, and the child's father and
mother. 52Everyone there was crying and
mourning for the child. Jesus said, "Don't cry;
the child is not dead—she is only sleeping!"
53They all made fun of him, because they
knew that she was dead. 54But Jesus took her
by the hand and called out, "Get up, child!"
55Her life returned, and she got up at once,
and Jesus ordered them to give her some-
thing to eat. 56Her parents were astounded,
but Jesus commanded them not to tell any-
one what had happened.

Jesus Sends Out the Twelve Disciples

(Matthew 10:5–15; Mark 6:7–13)

9 Jesus called the twelve disciples together
and gave them power and authority to
drive out all demons and to cure diseases.
2Then he sent them out to preach the King-
dom of God and to heal the sick, 3after say-
ing to them, "Take nothing with you for the
trip: no walking stick, no beggar's bag, no
food, no money, not even an extra shirt.
4Wherever you are welcomed, stay in the
same house until you leave that town;
5wherever people don't welcome you, leave
that town and shake the dust off your feet as
a warning to them."
6The disciples left and traveled through all
the villages, preaching the Good News and
healing people everywhere.

Herod's Confusion

(Matthew 14:1–12; Mark 6:14–29)

7When Herod, the ruler of Galilee, heard
about all the things that were happening, he
was very confused, because some people
were saying that John the Baptist had come
back to life. 8Others were saying that Elijah
had appeared, and still others that one of the
prophets of long ago had come back to life.
9Herod said, "I had John's head cut off; but
who is this man I hear these things about?"
And he kept trying to see Jesus.

Jesus Feeds Five Thousand

(Matthew 14:13–21; Mark 6:30–44; John 6:1–14)

10The apostles came back and told Jesus
everything they had done. He took them with
him, and they went off by themselves to a
town named Bethsaida. 11When the crowds
heard about it, they followed him. He wel-
comed them, spoke to them about the King-
dom of God, and healed those who needed it.
12When the sun was beginning to set, the
twelve disciples came to him and said, "Send
the people away so that they can go to the
villages and farms around here and find food
and lodging, because this is a lonely place."
13But Jesus said to them, "You yourselves
give them something to eat."
They answered, "All we have are five
loaves and two fish. Do you want us to go
and buy food for this whole crowd?"
14(There were about five thousand men
there.)

Jesus said to his disciples, "Make the peo-
ple sit down in groups of about fifty each."
15After the disciples had done so, 16Jesus
took the five loaves and two fish, looked up
to heaven, thanked God for them, broke
them, and gave them to the disciples to dis-
tribute to the people. 17They all ate and had

9:5 Acts 13:51 **9:3–5** Lk 10:4–11 **9:7, 8** Mt 16:14; Mk 8:28; Lk 9:19

enough, and the disciples took up twelve
baskets of what was left over.

Peter's Declaration about Jesus

(Matthew 16:13–19; Mark 8:27–29)

18 One day when Jesus was praying alone,
the disciples came to him. "Who do the
crowds say I am?" he asked them.
19 "Some say that you are John the Bap-
tist," they answered. "Others say that you
are Elijah, while others say that one of the
prophets of long ago has come back to life."
20 "What about you?" he asked them.
"Who do you say I am?"
Peter answered, "You are God's Messiah."

They all ate and had enough. (9:17)

Jesus Speaks about His Suffering and Death

(Matthew 16:20–28; Mark 8:30—9:1)

21 Then Jesus gave them strict orders not
to tell this to anyone. 22 He also told them,
"The Son of Man must suffer much and be
rejected by the elders, the chief priests, and
the teachers of the Law. He will be put to
death, but three days later he will be raised
to life."
23 And he said to them all, "If you want to
come with me, you must forget yourself, take
up your cross every day, and follow me. 24 For
if you want to save your own life, you will
lose it, but if you lose your life for my sake,
you will save it. 25 Will you gain anything if
you win the whole world but are yourself
lost or defeated? Of course not! 26 If you are
ashamed of me and of my teaching, then the
Son of Man will be ashamed of you when he
comes in his glory and in the glory of the
Father and of the holy angels. 27 I assure you
that there are some here who will not die
until they have seen the Kingdom of God."

Live it!

Shame on You!

Have you ever been in a situation where you felt embarrassed to be a Catholic? Have you ever felt ashamed about being Christian? Maybe someone was making fun of religion and how stupid it is, and you pretended to agree with them. Or perhaps they made fun of you when you said that you couldn't do something with them because you were going to Church. Whatever was happening, you were in a position where you didn't want to stand out or to stand up for what you believe. Reread Luke 9:26 to hear Jesus' response.

None of us would want Jesus to be ashamed of us. If you need help, remember that one of the gifts of the Holy Spirit is courage. The next time you find yourself embarrassed about being a Catholic, pray to the Holy Spirit—it can make a world of difference!

— Luke 9:23–27

9:19 Mt 14:1, 2; Mk 6:14, 15; Lk 9:7, 8 **9:20** Jn 6:68, 69 **9:23** Mt 10:38; Lk 14:27 **9:24** Mt 10:39; Lk 17:33; Jn 12:25

Learn more about the prophet Elijah in the biography of Elijah and Elisha on page c21.

The Transfiguration
(Matthew 17:1–8; Mark 9:2–8)

28About a week after he had said these
things, Jesus took Peter, John, and James with
him and went up a hill to pray. 29While he
was praying, his face changed its appearance,
and his clothes became dazzling white.
30Suddenly two men were there talking with
him. They were Moses and Elijah, 31who
appeared in heavenly glory and talked with
Jesus about the way in which he would soon
fulfill God's purpose by dying in Jerusalem.
32Peter and his companions were sound
asleep, but they woke up and saw Jesus' glory
and the two men who were standing with
him. 33As the men were leaving Jesus, Peter
said to him, "Master, how good it is that we
are here! We will make three tents, one for
you, one for Moses, and one for Elijah." (He
did not really know what he was saying.)
34While he was still speaking, a cloud
appeared and covered them with its shadow;
and the disciples were afraid as the cloud
came over them. 35A voice said from the
cloud, "This is my Son, whom I have cho-
sen—listen to him!"
36When the voice stopped, there was Jesus
all alone. The disciples kept quiet about all
this and told no one at that time anything
they had seen.

Jesus Heals a Boy with an Evil Spirit
(Matthew 17:14–18; Mark 9:14–27)

37The next day Jesus and the three disciples
went down from the hill, and a large crowd
met Jesus. 38A man shouted from the crowd,
"Teacher! I beg you, look at my son—my
only son! 39A spirit attacks him with a sudden
shout and throws him into a fit, so that he
foams at the mouth; it keeps on hurting him
and will hardly let him go! 40I begged your
disciples to drive it out, but they couldn't."
41Jesus answered, "How unbelieving and
wrong you people are! How long must I stay
with you? How long do I have to put up
with you?" Then he said to the man, "Bring
your son here."
42As the boy was coming, the demon
knocked him to the ground and threw him
into a fit. Jesus gave a command to the evil
spirit, healed the boy, and gave him back to
his father. 43All the people were amazed at
the mighty power of God.

Jesus Speaks Again about His Death
(Matthew 17:22, 23; Mark 9:30–32)

The people were still marveling at every-
thing Jesus was doing, when he said to his
disciples, 44"Don't forget what I am about
to tell you! The Son of Man is going to be
handed over to the power of human beings."
45But the disciples did not know what this
meant. It had been hidden from them so that
they could not understand it, and they were
afraid to ask him about the matter.

Who Is the Greatest?
(Matthew 18:1–5; Mark 9:33–37)

46An argument broke out among the dis-
ciples as to which one of them was the
greatest. 47Jesus knew what they were think-
ing, so he took a child, stood him by his
side, 48and said to them, "Whoever wel-
comes this child in my name, welcomes me;
and whoever welcomes me, also welcomes
the one who sent me. For the one who is
least among you all is the greatest."

Whoever Is Not against You Is for You
(Mark 9:38–40)

49John spoke up, "Master, we saw a man
driving out demons in your name, and we
told him to stop, because he doesn't belong
to our group."
50"Do not try to stop him," Jesus said to
him and to the other disciples, "because
whoever is not against you is for you."

9:35 Isa 42:1; Mt 3:17; 12:18; Mk 1:11; Lk 3:22 **9:28–35** 2 Pet 1:17, 18 **9:46** Lk 22:24 **9:48** Mt 10:40; Lk 10:16; Jn 13:20

Transfiguration: The event where Jesus was revealed in his full glory as the Son of God.

A Samaritan Village Refuses to Receive Jesus

51As the time drew near when Jesus
would be taken up to heaven, he made
up his mind and set out on his way to
Jerusalem. 52He sent messengers ahead of
him, who went into a village in Samaria to
get everything ready for him. 53But the
people there would not receive him,
because it was clear that he was on his way
to Jerusalem. 54When the disciples James
and John saw this, they said, "Lord, do you
want us to call fire down from heaven to
destroy them?"[j]

55Jesus turned and rebuked them.[k] 56Then
Jesus and his disciples went on to another
village.

The Would-Be Followers of Jesus

(Matthew 8:19–22)

57As they went on their way, a man said to
Jesus, "I will follow you wherever you go."
58Jesus said to him, "Foxes have holes, and
birds have nests, but the Son of Man has no
place to lie down and rest."
59He said to another man, "Follow me."
But that man said, "Sir, first let me go
back and bury my father."
60Jesus answered, "Let the dead bury their
own dead. You go and proclaim the King-
dom of God."
61Someone else said, "I will follow you,
sir; but first let me go and say good-bye to
my family."
62Jesus said to him, "Anyone who starts to
plow and then keeps looking back is of no
use for the Kingdom of God."

Jesus Sends Out the Seventy-Two

10 After this the Lord chose another
seventy-two[l] men and sent them out
two by two, to go ahead of him to every
town and place where he himself was about
to go. 2He said to them, "There is a large har-
vest, but few workers to gather it in. Pray to
the owner of the harvest that he will send out
workers to gather in his harvest. 3Go! I am
sending you like lambs among wolves. 4Don't
take a purse or a beggar's bag or shoes; don't
stop to greet anyone on the road. 5Whenever
you go into a house, first say, 'Peace be with
this house.' 6If someone who is peace-loving
lives there, let your greeting of peace remain

Two

When you'r friend and bu y ing, doesn't tin much faster? Jes sit- when he sent his a mission, he made went in pairs (Luke 1). He knew that the miles go much faster when they are sha d. He also knew that two people ravel- ing together could support ne another through the hard tines that would certainly happen. We need each other. That's the way God made us and the way Jesus sends us forth to serve.

When a friend is going through hard times or when a family member is sick and needs extra care, those are times when we are called to be good compan- ions. Sometimes, in a hospital room or at a funeral home, the best thing we can do is just to be there. We don't have to say a lot. We can be a quiet companion. Who are persons you count on as companions on the road of life? How can you be a companion to someone in your life right now?

— Luke 10:1–12

---

[j] **9:54** *Some manuscripts add* as Elijah did. [k] **9:55** *Some manuscripts add* and said, "You don't know what kin
a Spirit you belong to; for the Son of Man did not come to destroy human lives, but to save them."
[l] **10:1** seventy-two; *some manuscripts have* seventy.

9:54 2 Kings 1:9–16 **9:61** 1 Kings 19:20 **10:2** Mt 9:37, 38 **10:3** Mt 10:16

...r greeting
..., eating and
...u, for workers
on that person move around
of peace. 7St... Whenever you
drinking w... re welcome, eat
should be ... all the sick in that
from one ... people there, 'The King-
go into ... to th... hear you.' 10But
what ... has c... a town and are not
town ... you go ... the streets and say,
don... wked, go o... om your town that sticks to
...n the dus... off against you. But remem-
feet we w... gdom of God has come near
...r that the K... you that on the Judgment Day
you!' 12I ass... show more mercy to Sodom than
God will show more mercy to Sodom than
to that town!

The Unbelieving Towns
(Matthew 11:20–24)

13"How terrible it will be for you,
Chorazin! How terrible for you too, Bethsai-
da! If the miracles which were performed in
you had been performed in Tyre and Sidon,
the people there would have long ago sat
down, put on sackcloth, and sprinkled ashes
on themselves, to show that they had turned
from their sins! 14God will show more mercy
on the Judgment Day to Tyre and Sidon than
to you. 15And as for you, Capernaum! Did
you want to lift yourself up to heaven? You
will be thrown down to hell!"
16Jesus said to his disciples, "Whoever lis-
tens to you listens to me; whoever rejects
you rejects me; and whoever rejects me
rejects the one who sent me."

The Return of the Seventy-Two

17The seventy-two[m] men came back in
...d," they said, "even the demons
...e them a command in
...

given you authority, so that you can walk on
snakes and scorpions and overcome all the
power of the Enemy, and nothing will hurt
you. 20But don't be glad because the evil
spirits obey you; rather be glad because your
names are written in heaven."

Jesus Rejoices
(Matthew 11:25–27; 13:16, 17)

21At that time Jesus was filled with joy by
the Holy Spirit[n] and said, "Father, Lord of
heaven and earth! I thank you because you
have shown to the unlearned what you have
hidden from the wise and learned. Yes,
Father, this was how you were pleased to
have it happen.
22"My Father has given me all things. No
one knows who the Son is except the
Father, and no one knows who the Father is
except the Son and those to whom the Son
chooses to reveal him."
23Then Jesus turned to the disciples and
said to them privately, "How fortunate you
are to see the things you see! 24I tell you that
many prophets and kings wanted to see what
you see, but they could not, and to hear
what you hear, but they did not."

The Parable of the Good Samaritan

25A teacher of the Law came up and tried
to trap Jesus. "Teacher," he asked, "what must
I do to receive eternal life?"
26Jesus answered him, "What do the Scrip-
tures say? How do you interpret them?"
27The man answered, " 'Love the Lord
your God with all your heart, with all your
soul, with all your strength, and with all your
mind'; and 'Love your neighbor as you love
yourself.' "
28"You are right," Jesus replied; "do this
and you will live."
29But the teacher of the Law wanted to
justify himself, so he asked Jesus, "Who is my
neighbor?"

...e Holy Spirit; *some manuscripts*
...9:3–5 ... 1:9, 10;

he walked on by on the other side. 32In the
same way a Levite also came there, went
over and looked at the man, and then walked
on by on the other side. 33But a Samaritan
who was traveling that way came upon the
man, and when he saw him, his heart was
filled with pity. 34He went over to him,
poured oil and wine on his wounds and
bandaged them; then he put the man on his
own animal and took him to an inn, where
he took care of him. 35The next day he took
out two silver coins and gave them to the
innkeeper. 'Take care of him,' he told the
innkeeper, 'and when I come back this way, I
will pay you whatever else you spend on
him.' "

Live It

Walk ... ht By

Have you ever walked into a lunchroom and seen someone eating alone? What is your first reaction? Do you think, "Thank God that's not me?" Do you think about joining him or her or maybe inviting him or her to join you at your table? Does it matter whether you know the person or not? Should it matter? Let's not be too quick to judge the priest and the Levite in the good Samaritan story. They had reasons for not stopping. They may have been afraid of being attacked by bandits themselves. Or if they had contact with blood, it would have made them ritually unclean for a week according to the Old Testament Law.

We probably have reasons for walking right by someone we would rather not deal with. But Jesus reminds us that if those reasons mean neglecting a person in need, they probably aren't good reasons. We need to remember that someday we could be the one sitting alone. Let's think about that the next time we see someone sitting alone.

— Luke 10:25–37

His heart was filled with pity. (10:33)

36And Jesus concluded, "In your opinion,
which one of these three acted like a neigh-
bor toward the man attacked by the robbers?"
37The teacher of the Law answered, "The
one who was kind to him."
Jesus replied, "You go, then, and do the
same."

Jesus Visits Martha and Mary

38As Jesus and his disciples went on their
way, he came to a village where a woman
named Martha welcomed him in her home.
39She had a sister named Mary, who sat
down at the feet of the Lord and listened to
his teaching. 40Martha was upset over all the

30Jesus answered, "There was once a man
who was going down from Jerusalem to
Jericho when robbers attacked him, stripped
him, and beat him up, leaving him half dead.
31It so happened that a priest was going
down that road; but when he saw the man,

10:33, 34 2 Chr 28:15 **10:38, 39** Jn 11:1

Many Jews were prejudiced against Samaritans. How does this make the Good Samaritan's actions even more generous?

Catholic Connections

The Our Father: Another Version

As you read through the beginning of Luke, chapter 11, you'll notice a second version of the prayer we often call the Our Father. The version of the prayer in Matthew 6:9–13 i…obably more familiar to you. Study the two versions closely. What si…rities and differences do you notice? What does this tell us about t… Gospel writers?

Because it came directly from J…s, the Our Father is probably the most important prayer that we have. …at is why Christians pray it so often when we gather. If you look carefull… you'll notice that the first part of the prayer praises God and asks that G…d's Kingdom will come. The second part of the prayer is a series of petiti…ns, or requests, for the things that we need. We can follow that pattern …n our own prayer to God.

Here's an idea. Try putting the Our Father in your own words. For example, you might start your prayer by saying, "My Father, Lord of heaven and earth, I praise your holy name." This may help you look at this old prayer in a new way.

— Luke 11:1–4

work she had to do, so she came and said, "Lord, don't you care that my sister has left me to do all the work by myself? Tell her to come and help me!"

41 The Lord answered her, "Martha,
Martha! You are worried and troubled over
so many things, 42 but just one is needed.
Mary has chosen the right thing, and it will
not be taken away from her."

Jesus' Teaching on Prayer
(Matthew 6:9–13; 7:7–11)

11 One day Jesus was praying in a certain place. When he had finished, one of his disciples said to him, "Lord, teach us to pray, just as John taught his disciples."

2 Jesus said to them, "When you pray, say this:

'Father:
May your holy name be honored;
may your Kingdom come.
3 Give us day by day the food we need.°
4 Forgive us our sins,
for we forgive everyone who does us wrong.
And do not bring us to hard testing.' "

5 And Jesus said to his disciples, "Suppose
one of you should go to a friend's house at
midnight and say, 'Friend, let me borrow
three loaves of bread. 6 A friend of mine who
is on a trip has just come to my house, and I
don't have any food for him!' 7 And suppose
your friend should answer from inside, 'Don't
bother me! The door is already locked, and
my children and I are in bed. I can't get up
and give you anything.' 8 Well, what then? I
tell you that even if he will not get up and
give you the bread because you are his
friend, yet he will get up and give you everything you need because you are not ashamed
to keep on asking. 9 And so I say to you: Ask,
and you will receive; seek, and you will find;
knock, and the door will be opened to you.

° **11:3** the food we need; *or* food for the next day.

" 'Ask, and you will receive; seek, and you will find; knock, and the door will …e opened to you' " *(Luke 11:9)*.

Prayers of Petition

"Please help me with this test, God." "Lord, help my sister get better." These are examples of one of the simplest forms of prayer. They are called petitions, meaning that we ask, or petition, God for something. During the Mass we hear the petitions of the whole community after the homily. The petitions at Mass are called the Prayers of the Faithful. The most common response is, "Lord, hear our prayer."

Most of us pray petitions a lot. This isn't wrong; in fact Jesus tells us that we should ask for God's help, and we should expect a response (Luke 11:9–13). Do not hesitate to share with God the needs you have in your heart. Even though it's hard sometimes, it's good to say your prayers out loud. It does two things: it helps to raise awareness of the needs of others, plus it gives others courage to share their own prayers. When you give voice to the needs in your heart and on your mind, others can pray with you. That is the power of community prayer.

—Luke 11:9–13

10 For those who ask will receive, and those
who seek will find, and the door will be
opened to anyone who knocks. 11 Would any
of you who are fathers give your son a snake
when he asks for fish? 12 Or would you give
him a scorpion when he asks for an egg?
13 As bad as you are, you know how to give
good things to your children. How much
more, then, will the Father in heaven give the
Holy Spirit to those who ask him!"

Jesus and Beelzebul

(Matthew 12:22–30; Mark 3:20–27)

14 Jesus was driving out a demon that
could not talk; and when the demon went
out, the man began to talk. The crowds were
amazed, 15 but some of the people said, "It is
Beelzebul, the chief of the demons, who
gives him the power to drive them out."
16 Others wanted to trap Jesus, so they
asked him to perform a miracle to show that
God approved of him. 17 But Jesus knew what
they were thinking, so he said to them, "Any
country that divides itself into groups which
fight each other will not last very long; a
family divided against itself falls apart. 18 So if
Satan's kingdom has groups fighting each
other, how can it last? You say that I drive out
demons because Beelzebul gives me the
power to do so. 19 If this is how I drive them
out, how do your followers drive them out?
Your own followers prove that you are
wrong! 20 No, it is rather by means of God's
power that I drive out demons, and this
proves that the Kingdom of God has already
come to you.
21 "When a strong man, with all his
weapons ready, guards his own house, all his
belongings are safe. 22 But when a stronger
man attacks him and defeats him, he carries
away all the weapons the owner was depending on and divides up what he stole.
23 "Anyone who is not for me is really
against me; anyone who does not help me
gather is really scattering.

The Return of the Evil Spirit

(Matthew 12:43–45)

24 "When an evil spirit goes out of a person, it travels over dry country looking for a

11:15 Mt 9:34; 10:25 **11:16** Mt 12:38; 16:1; Mk 8:11 **11:23** Mk 9:40

place to rest. If it can't find one, it says to
itself, 'I will go back to my house.' 25 So it
goes back and finds the house clean and all
fixed up. 26 Then it goes out and brings seven
other spirits even worse than itself, and they
come and live there. So when it is all over,
that person is in worse shape than at the
beginning."

True Happiness

27 When Jesus had said this, a woman
spoke up from the crowd and said to him,
"How happy is the woman who bore you
and nursed you!"
28 But Jesus answered, "Rather, how happy
are those who hear the word of God and
obey it!"

The Demand for a Miracle
(Matthew 12:38–42)

29 As the people crowded around Jesus, he
went on to say, "How evil are the people of
this day! They ask for a miracle, but none will
be given them except the miracle of Jonah.
30 In the same way that the prophet Jonah
was a sign for the people of Nineveh, so the
Son of Man will be a sign for the people of
this day. 31 On the Judgment Day the Queen
of Sheba will stand up and accuse the people
of today, because she traveled all the way
from her country to listen to King Solomon's
wise teaching; and there is something here,
I tell you, greater than Solomon. 32 On the
Judgment Day the people of Nineveh will
stand up and accuse you, because they turned
from their sins when they heard Jonah
preach; and I assure you that there is some-
thing here greater than Jonah!

The Light of the Body
(Matthew 5:15; 6:22, 23)

33 "No one lights a lamp and then hides it
or puts it under a bowl;[p] instead, it is put on
the lampstand, so that people may see the
light as they come in. 34 Your eyes are like a
lamp for the body. When your eyes are sound,
your whole body is full of light; but when
your eyes are no good, your whole body will
be in darkness. 35 Make certain, then, that the
light in you is not darkness. 36 If your whole
body is full of light, with no part of it in
darkness, it will be bright all over, as when a
lamp shines on you with its brightness."

> **Live it!**
>
> ### The Eyes Have it!
>
> **"Look me in the eyes!" Why is this so important? Jesus says in Luke 11:34 that our eyes are like a lamp for our bodies. An old saying expresses a similar thought: "The eyes are the mirror of the soul." It is very difficult for young children to lie while looking someone in the eye. As we get older, we learn to disguise our emotions better. Imagine what it would be like to gaze into the eyes of Jesus. What would you see in those eyes?**
>
> **— Luke 11:33–36**

Jesus Accuses the Pharisees and the Teachers of the Law
(Matthew 23:1–36; Mark 12:38–40)

37 When Jesus finished speaking, a Pharisee
invited him to eat with him; so he went in
and sat down to eat. 38 The Pharisee was sur-
prised when he noticed that Jesus had not
washed before eating. 39 So the Lord said to
him, "Now then, you Pharisees clean the
outside of your cup and plate, but inside you
are full of violence and evil. 40 Fools! Did not
God, who made the outside, also make the
inside? 41 But give what is in your cups and
plates to the poor, and everything will be
ritually clean for you.
42 "How terrible for you Pharisees! You
give to God one tenth of the seasoning

p **11:33** *Some manuscripts do not have* or puts it under a bowl.

11:29 Mt 16:4; Mk 8:12 **11:30** Jon 3:4 **11:31** 1 Kings 10:1–10; 2 Chr 9:1–12 **11:32** Jon 3:5 **11:33** Mt 5:15; Mk 4:21; Lk 8:16 **11:42** Lev 27:30

herbs, such as mint and rue and all the other
herbs, but you neglect justice and love for
God. These you should practice, without
neglecting the others.
43“How terrible for you Pharisees! You
love the reserved seats in the synagogues and
to be greeted with respect in the market-
places. 44How terrible for you! You are like
unmarked graves which people walk on
without knowing it.”
45One of the teachers of the Law said to
him, “Teacher, when you say this, you insult
us too!”
46Jesus answered, “How terrible also for
you teachers of the Law! You put onto peo-
ple's backs loads which are hard to carry, but
you yourselves will not stretch out a finger to
help them carry those loads. 47How terrible
for you! You make fine tombs for the
prophets—the very prophets your ancestors
murdered. 48You yourselves admit, then, that
you approve of what your ancestors did; they
murdered the prophets, and you build their
tombs. 49For this reason the Wisdom of God
said, ‘I will send them prophets and messen-
gers; they will kill some of them and perse-
cute others.’ 50So the people of this time
will be punished for the murder of all the
prophets killed since the creation of the
world, 51from the murder of Abel to the mur-
der of Zechariah, who was killed between the
altar and the Holy Place. Yes, I tell you, the
people of this time will be punished for them
all!
52“How terrible for you teachers of the
Law! You have kept the key that opens the
door to the house of knowledge; you your-
selves will not go in, and you stop those who
are trying to go in!”
53When Jesus left that place, the teachers
of the Law and the Pharisees began to criti-
cize him bitterly and ask him questions
about many things, 54trying to lay traps for
him and catch him saying something wrong.

A Warning against Hypocrisy
(Matthew 10:26, 27)

12 As thousands of people crowded
together, so that they were stepping
on each other, Jesus said first to his disciples,
“Be on guard against the yeast of the Phar-
isees—I mean their hypocrisy. 2Whatever is
covered up will be uncovered, and every
secret will be made known. 3So then, what-
ever you have said in the dark will be heard
in broad daylight, and whatever you have
whispered in private in a closed room will
be shouted from the housetops.

Whom to Fear
(Matthew 10:28–31)

4“I tell you, my friends, do not be afraid
of those who kill the body but cannot after-
ward do anything worse. 5I will show you
whom to fear: fear God, who, after killing,
has the authority to throw into hell. Believe
me, he is the one you must fear!
6“Aren't five sparrows sold for two pen-
nies? Yet not one sparrow is forgotten by
God. 7Even the hairs of your head have all
been counted. So do not be afraid; you are
worth much more than many sparrows!

Confessing and Rejecting Christ
(Matthew 10:32, 33; 12:32; 10:19, 20)

8“I assure you that those who declare
publicly that they belong to me, the Son of
Man will do the same for them before the
angels of God. 9But those who reject me
publicly, the Son of Man will also reject
them before the angels of God.
10“Whoever says a word against the Son of
Man can be forgiven; but whoever says evil
things against the Holy Spirit will not be for-
given.
11“When they bring you to be tried in
the synagogues or before governors or
rulers, do not be worried about how you

11:51 a Gen 4:8; **b** 2 Chr 24:20, 21 **12:1** Mt 16:6; Mk 8:15 **12:2** Mk 4:22; Lk 8:17 **12:10** Mt 12:32; Mk 3:29 **12:11, 12** Mt 10:19, 20; Mk 13:11; Lk 21:14, 15

The Queen of Sheba appears 1 Kings, chapter 10. Find out who she visits and why.

Live it!

Here Today, Gone Tomorrow

Perhaps you have heard the saying, "You can't take it with you." The parable of the rich fool is about that very idea (Luke 12:13–21). Some rich people are very generous with their money and end up doing a lot of good in the world. But others, like the rich fool in the story, simply hoard what they have and look for ways to get richer.

What does it mean to be rich in God's sight? It certainly doesn't have anything to do with money. There's a young man who invites his friends to his birthday party every year. Instead of bringing gifts for him, he asks his friends to bring specific gifts for a needy school that he knows. What a wonderful way to show that the needs of others should come before our own desires. Now there is a rich young man!

— Luke 12:13–21

will defend yourself or what you will say.
12For the Holy Spirit will teach you at that
time what you should say."

The Parable of the Rich Fool

13A man in the crowd said to Jesus,
"Teacher, tell my brother to divide with me
the property our father left us."
14Jesus answered him, "Friend, who gave
me the right to judge or to divide the property
between you two?" 15And he went on
to say to them all, "Watch out and guard
yourselves from every kind of greed;
because your true life is not made up of the
things you own, no matter how rich you
may be."
16Then Jesus told them this parable:
"There was once a rich man who had land
which bore good crops. 17He began to think
to himself, 'I don't have a place to keep all
my crops. What can I do? 18This is what I
will do,' he told himself; 'I will tear down my
barns and build bigger ones, where I will
store the grain and all my other goods.
19Then I will say to myself, Lucky man! You
have all the good things you need for many
years. Take life easy, eat, drink, and enjoy
yourself!' 20But God said to him, 'You fool!
This very night you will have to give up
your life; then who will get all these things
you have kept for yourself?' "
21And Jesus concluded, "This is how it is
with those who pile up riches for themselves
but are not rich in God's sight."

Trust in God
(Matthew 6:25–34)

22Then Jesus said to the disciples, "And so I
tell you not to worry about the food you
need to stay alive or about the clothes you
need for your body. 23Life is much more
important than food, and the body much
more important than clothes. 24Look at the
crows: they don't plant seeds or gather a harvest;
they don't have storage rooms or barns;
God feeds them! You are worth so much
more than birds! 25Can any of you live a bit

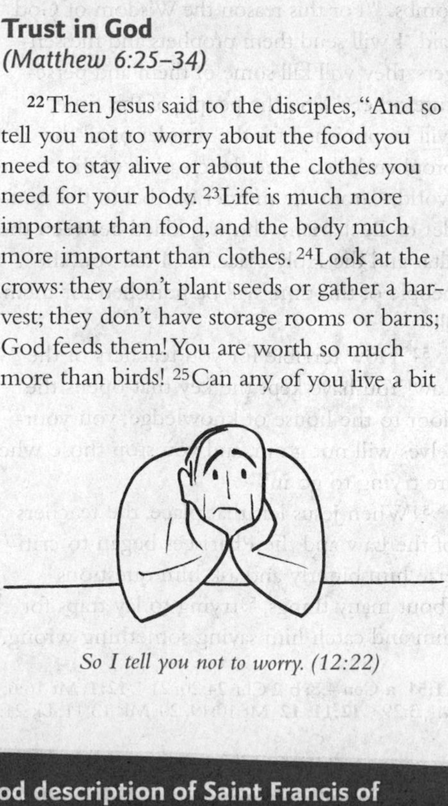

So I tell you not to worry. (12:22)

12:19 Sir 11:19

The words in Luke 12:33–34 serve as a good description of Saint Francis of Assisi, who lived from AD 1182 to 1226. What do you know about Saint Francis?

longer[q] by worrying about it? [26]If you can't
manage even such a small thing, why worry
about the other things? [27]Look how the wild
flowers grow: they don't work or make
clothes for themselves. But I tell you that not
even King Solomon with all his wealth had
clothes as beautiful as one of these flowers.
[28]It is God who clothes the wild grass—grass
that is here today and gone tomorrow, burned
up in the oven. Won't he be all the more sure
to clothe you? What little faith you have!

[29]"So don't be all upset, always concerned
about what you will eat and drink. [30](For
the pagans of this world are always con-
cerned about all these things.) Your Father
knows that you need these things. [31]Instead,
be concerned with his Kingdom, and he will
provide you with these things.

Riches in Heaven
(Matthew 6:19–21)

[32]"Do not be afraid, little flock, for your
Father is pleased to give you the Kingdom.
[33]Sell all your belongings and give the
money to the poor. Provide for yourselves
purses that don't wear out, and save your
riches in heaven, where they will never
decrease, because no thief can get to them,
and no moth can destroy them. [34]For your
heart will always be where your riches are.

Watchful Servants

[35]"Be ready for whatever comes, dressed for
action and with your lamps lit, [36]like servants
who are waiting for their master to come
back from a wedding feast. When he comes
and knocks, they will open the door for him
at once. [37]How happy are those servants
whose master finds them awake and ready
when he returns! I tell you, he will take off his
coat, have them sit down, and will wait on
them. [38]How happy they are if he finds them
ready, even if he should come at midnight or
even later! [39]And you can be sure that if the
owner of a house knew the time when the
thief would come, he would not let the thief
break into his house. [40]And you, too, must be
ready, because the Son of Man will come at
an hour when you are not expecting him."

The Faithful or the Unfaithful Servant
(Matthew 24:45–51)

[41]Peter said, "Lord, does this parable apply
to us, or do you mean it for everyone?"

[42]The Lord answered, "Who, then, is the
faithful and wise servant? He is the one that
his master will put in charge, to run the
household and give the other servants their
share of the food at the proper time. [43]How
happy that servant is if his master finds him
doing this when he comes home! [44]Indeed, I
tell you, the master will put that servant in
charge of all his property. [45]But if that ser-
vant says to himself that his master is taking
a long time to come back and if he begins
to beat the other servants, both the men and
the women, and eats and drinks and gets
drunk, [46]then the master will come back one
day when the servant does not expect him
and at a time he does not know. The master
will cut him in pieces[r] and make him share
the fate of the disobedient.

[47]"The servant who knows what his mas-
ter wants him to do, but does not get himself
ready and do it, will be punished with a
heavy whipping. [48]But the servant who does
not know what his master wants, and yet does
something for which he deserves a whipping,
will be punished with a light whipping.
Much is required from the person to whom
much is given; much more is required from
the person to whom much more is given.

Jesus the Cause of Division
(Matthew 10:34–36)

[49]"I came to set the earth on fire, and
how I wish it were already kindled! [50]I have
a baptism to receive, and how distressed I am
until it is over! [51]Do you suppose that I
came to bring peace to the world? No, not
peace, but division. [52]From now on a family
of five will be divided, three against two and
two against three. [53]Fathers will be against

[q] **12:25** live a bit longer; *or* grow a bit taller. [r] **12:46** cut him in pieces; *or* throw him out.
12:27 1 Kings 10:4–7; 2 Chr 9:3–6 **12:35** Mt 25:1–13 **12:36** Mk 13:34–36 **12:39,40** Mt 24:43, 44
12:50 Mk 10:38 **12:53** Mic 7:6

Live it!

Family Feud

Jesus has some rather startling words in Luke 12:49–53. We are used to words like *peace* and *harmony* as signs of Christ's presence in our lives. But Jesus is telling his followers that some tough times are ahead. By following him, they will get people upset, even within their own families. This happened in the time of Jesus, and it certainly happens today.

When we take our Christianity seriously, our values may be challenging to other family members. We may need to confront a family member who is being abusive to someone or who is lying or who is involved with something illegal. We do this to encourage them to change their lives so that they can know God's love. This can cause a lot of stress and even division in a family. Jesus also uses the image of fire (Luke 12:49) to show that he wants his followers to be on fire with his message. As we all know, fire can bring both warmth and destruction.

— Luke 12:49–53

their sons, and sons against their fathers; mothers will be against their daughters, and daughters against their mothers; mothers-in-law will be against their daughters-in-law, and daughters-in-law against their mothers-in-law."

Understanding the Time
(Matthew 16:2, 3)

54 Jesus said also to the people, "When you
see a cloud coming up in the west, at once
you say that it is going to rain—and it does.
55 And when you feel the south wind blow-
ing, you say that it is going to get hot—and
it does. 56 Hypocrites! You can look at the
earth and the sky and predict the weather; why, then, don't you know the meaning of this present time?

Settle with Your Opponent
(Matthew 5:25, 26)

57 "Why do you not judge for yourselves
the right thing to do? 58 If someone brings a
lawsuit against you and takes you to court, do your best to settle the dispute before you get to court. If you don't, you will be dragged before the judge, who will hand you over to the police, and you will be put in
jail. 59 There you will stay, I tell you, until
you pay the last penny of your fine."

Turn from Your Sins or Die

13 At that time some people were there who told Jesus about the Galileans whom Pilate had killed while they
were offering sacrifices to God. 2 Jesus
answered them, "Because those Galileans were killed in that way, do you think it proves that they were worse sinners than all
other Galileans? 3 No indeed! And I tell you
that if you do not turn from your sins, you
will all die as they did. 4 What about those
eighteen people in Siloam who were killed when the tower fell on them? Do you suppose this proves that they were worse than all the other people living in Jerusalem?
5 No indeed! And I tell you that if you do
not turn from your sins, you will all die as they did."

The Parable of the Unfruitful Fig Tree

6 Then Jesus told them this parable: "There
was once a man who had a fig tree growing in his vineyard. He went looking for figs on
it but found none. 7 So he said to his garden-
er, 'Look, for three years I have been coming here looking for figs on this fig tree, and I haven't found any. Cut it down! Why should
it go on using up the soil?' 8 But the garden-
er answered, 'Leave it alone, sir, just one more year; I will dig around it and put in

Live it!

One More Chance

"Just give me one more chance. I promise I'll do better." No doubt each of us has spoken these words at some time. If the fig tree in the parable (Luke 13:6–9) could talk, this is probably what it would be saying. The gardener seems to sense this and asks the owner to give the fruitless tree one more year. We are not told how the story ends, but we hope that the gardener gets the okay to give the fig tree some more attention. That extra year of care and concern could make all the difference.

Try to think of someone to whom you could give one more chance. Maybe you had a fight with a good friend. Maybe you need to try a little harder to see a parent's point of view. Or maybe there's a teacher who made you upset. Whoever it is, ask God for the patience to make the relationship better again.

— Luke 13:6–9

some fertilizer.
9Then if the tree bears figs
next year, so much the better; if not, then
you can have it cut down.' "

Jesus Heals a Crippled Woman on the Sabbath

10One Sabbath Jesus was teaching in a synagogue.
11A woman there had an evil spirit
that had kept her sick for eighteen years; she
was bent over and could not straighten up at
all.
12When Jesus saw her, he called out to her,
"Woman, you are free from your sickness!"
13He placed his hands on her, and at once she
straightened herself up and praised God.
14The official of the synagogue was angry
that Jesus had healed on the Sabbath, so he
spoke up and said to the people, "There are
six days in which we should work; so come
during those days and be healed, but not on
the Sabbath!"
15The Lord answered him, "You hypocrites! Any one of you would untie your
ox or your donkey from the stall and take
it out to give it water on the Sabbath.
16Now here is this descendant of Abraham
whom Satan has kept in bonds for eighteen
years; should she not be released on the
Sabbath?"
17His answer made his enemies
ashamed of themselves, while the people
rejoiced over all the wonderful things that
he did.

The Parable of the Mustard Seed
(Matthew 13:31, 32; Mark 4:30–32)

18Jesus asked, "What is the Kingdom of
God like? What shall I compare it with?
19It
is like this. A man takes a mustard seed and
plants it in his field. The plant grows and
becomes a tree, and the birds make their
nests in its branches."

The Parable of the Yeast
(Matthew 13:33)

20Again Jesus asked, "What shall I compare the Kingdom of God with?
21It is like
this. A woman takes some yeast and mixes it
with a bushel of flour until the whole batch
of dough rises."

The Narrow Door
(Matthew 7:13, 14, 21–23)

22Jesus went through towns and villages,
teaching the people and making his way

13:14 Ex 20:9, 10; Deut 5:13, 14

Do you know how yeast works? If not, ask someone who bakes. Why is yeast such a good description of the Kingdom of God?

toward Jerusalem. [23]Someone asked him, "Sir, will just a few people be saved?"

Jesus answered them, [24]"Do your best to go in through the narrow door; because many people will surely try to go in but will not be able. [25]The master of the house will get up and close the door; then when you stand outside and begin to knock on the door and say, 'Open the door for us, sir!' he will answer you, 'I don't know where you come from!' [26]Then you will answer, 'We ate and drank with you; you taught in our town!' [27]But he will say again, 'I don't know where you come from. Get away from me, all you wicked people!' [28]How you will cry and gnash your teeth when you see Abraham, Isaac, and Jacob, and all the prophets in the Kingdom of God, while you are thrown out! [29]People will come from the east and the west, from the north and the south, and sit down at the feast in the Kingdom of God. [30]Then those who are now last will be first, and those who are now first will be last."

Jesus' Love for Jerusalem
(Matthew 23:37–39)

[31]At that same time some Pharisees came to Jesus and said to him, "You must get out of here and go somewhere else, because Herod wants to kill you."

[32]Jesus answered them, "Go and tell that fox: 'I am driving out demons and performing cures today and tomorrow, and on the third day I shall finish my work.' [33]Yet I must be on my way today, tomorrow, and the next day; it is not right for a prophet to be killed anywhere except in Jerusalem.

[34]"Jerusalem, Jerusalem! You kill the prophets, you stone the messengers God has sent you! How many times I wanted to put my arms around all your people, just as a hen gathers her chicks under her wings, but you would not let me! [35]And so your Temple will be abandoned. I assure you that you will not see me until the time comes when you say, 'God bless him who comes in the name of the Lord.' "

Jesus Heals a Sick Man

14 One Sabbath Jesus went to eat a meal at the home of one of the leading Pharisees; and people were watching Jesus closely. [2]A man whose legs and arms were swollen came to Jesus, [3]and Jesus spoke up and asked the teachers of the Law and the Pharisees, "Does our Law allow healing on the Sabbath or not?"

[4]But they would not say a thing. Jesus took the man, healed him, and sent him away. [5]Then he said to them, "If any one of you had a child or an ox that happened to fall in a well on a Sabbath, would you not pull it out at once on the Sabbath itself?"

[6]But they were not able to answer him about this.

Humility and Hospitality

[7]Jesus noticed how some of the guests were choosing the best places, so he told this parable to all of them: [8]"When someone invites you to a wedding feast, do not sit down in the best place. It could happen that someone more important than you has been invited, [9]and your host, who invited both of you, would have to come and say to you, 'Let him have this place.' Then you would be embarrassed and have to sit in the lowest place. [10]Instead, when you are invited, go and sit in the lowest place, so that your host will come to you and say, 'Come on up, my friend, to a better place.' This will bring you honor in the presence of all the other guests. [11]For those who make themselves great will be humbled, and those who humble themselves will be made great."

[12]Then Jesus said to his host, "When you give a lunch or a dinner, do not invite your friends or your brothers or your relatives or

13:27 Ps 6:8 **13:28** Mt 22:13; 25:30 **13:28, 29** Mt 8:11, 12 **13:30** Mt 19:30; 20:16; Mk 10:31
13:35 Ps 118:26 **14:5** Mt 12:11 **14:8–10** Prov 25:6, 7 **14:11** Mt 23:12; Lk 18:14

Remember that the Sabbath begins Friday at sunset and ends on Saturday at sunset. For the Jews, this is a time of rest and worship.

Pray it!

Humility and Hospitality

Humility **and** ***hospitality:*** **These two** ***h*** **words are key descriptions of being a true follower of Christ. Humility simply means knowing that we are completely dependent on God and that every one of us is created in God's image. Hospitality is about making people, especially strangers, feel at home and welcome. Take some time to slowly read Luke 14:7–14 and reflect on how important these two virtues are.**

Dear God,
Help me to remember I need the two **h*'s, humility and hospitality.***
Whenever I think that I can handle life all by myself,
remind me that I always need you.
Remind me to look for opportunities to make others feel welcome,
at school, at home, and at church.
Through humility and hospitality, draw me closer to you each day.
Amen.

— Luke 14:7–14

your rich neighbors—for they will invite
you back, and in this way you will be paid
for what you did. 13When you give a feast,
invite the poor, the crippled, the lame, and
the blind; 14and you will be blessed, because
they are not able to pay you back. God will
repay you on the day the good people rise
from death."

The Parable of the Great Feast
(Matthew 22:1–10)

15When one of the guests sitting at the
table heard this, he said to Jesus, "How happy
are those who will sit down at the feast in
the Kingdom of God!"
16Jesus said to him, "There was once a
man who was giving a great feast to which
he invited many people. 17When it was time
for the feast, he sent his servant to tell his
guests, 'Come, everything is ready!' 18But
they all began, one after another, to make
excuses. The first one told the servant, 'I have
bought a field and must go and look at it;
please accept my apologies.' 19Another one
said, 'I have bought five pairs of oxen and am
on my way to try them out; please accept
my apologies.' 20Another one said, 'I have
just gotten married, and for that reason I
cannot come.' 21The servant went back and
told all this to his master. The master was
furious and said to his servant, 'Hurry out to
the streets and alleys of the town, and bring
back the poor, the crippled, the blind, and
the lame.' 22Soon the servant said, 'Your
order has been carried out, sir, but there is
room for more.' 23So the master said to the
servant, 'Go out to the country roads and
lanes and make people come in, so that my
house will be full. 24I tell you all that none
of those who were invited will taste my dinner!'"

The Cost of Being a Disciple
(Matthew 10:37, 38)

25Once when large crowds of people were
going along with Jesus, he turned and said to
them, 26"Those who come to me cannot be
my disciples unless they love me more than
they love father and mother, wife and children, brothers and sisters, and themselves as

14:26 Mt 10:37

well. 27Those who do not carry their own cross and come after me cannot be my disciples. 28If one of you is planning to build a tower, you sit down first and figure out what it will cost, to see if you have enough money to finish the job. 29If you don't, you will not be able to finish the tower after laying the foundation; and all who see what happened will make fun of you. 30'You began to build but can't finish the job!' they will say. 31If a king goes out with ten thousand men to fight another king who comes against him with twenty thousand men, he will sit down first and decide if he is strong enough to face that other king. 32If he isn't, he will send messengers to meet the other king to ask for terms of peace while he is still a long way off. 33In the same way," concluded Jesus, "none of you can be my disciple unless you give up everything you have.

Worthless Salt

(Matthew 5:13; Mark 9:50)

34"Salt is good, but if it loses its saltiness, there is no way to make it salty again. 35It is no good for the soil or for the manure pile; it is thrown away. Listen, then, if you have ears!"

The Lost Sheep

(Matthew 18:12–14)

15 One day when many tax collectors and other outcasts came to listen to Jesus, 2the Pharisees and the teachers of the Law started grumbling, "This man welcomes outcasts and even eats with them!" 3So Jesus told them this parable:

4"Suppose one of you has a hundred sheep and loses one of them—what do you do? You leave the other ninety-nine sheep in the pasture and go looking for the one that got lost until you find it. 5When you find it, you are so happy that you put it on your shoulders 6and carry it back home. Then you call your friends and neighbors together and say to them, 'I am so happy I found my lost sheep. Let us celebrate!' 7In the same way, I tell you, there will be more joy in heaven over one sinner who repents than over ninety-nine respectable people who do not need to repent.

The Lost Coin

8"Or suppose a woman who has ten silver coins loses one of them—what does she do? She lights a lamp, sweeps her house, and looks carefully everywhere until she finds it. 9When she finds it, she calls her friends and neighbors together, and says to them, 'I am so happy I found the coin I lost. Let us celebrate!' 10In the same way, I tell you, the angels of God rejoice over one sinner who repents."

The Lost Son

11Jesus went on to say, "There was once a man who had two sons. 12The younger one said to him, 'Father, give me my share of the property now.' So the man divided his property between his two sons. 13After a few days the younger son sold his part of the property and left home with the money. He went to a country far away, where he wasted his money in reckless living. 14He spent everything he had. Then a severe famine spread over that country, and he was left without a thing. 15So he went to work for one of the citizens of that country, who sent him out to his farm to take care of the pigs. 16He wished he could fill himself with the bean pods the pigs ate, but no one gave him anything to eat. 17At last he came to his senses and said, 'All my father's hired workers have more than they can eat, and here I am about to starve! 18I will get up and go to my father

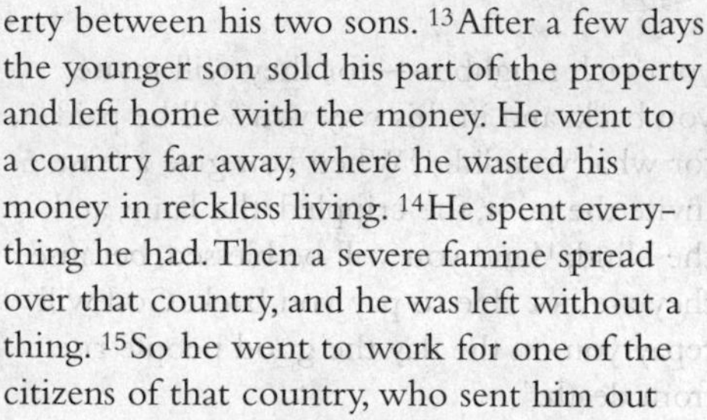

"Here I am about to starve!" (15:17)

14:27 Mt 10:38; 16:24; Mk 8:34; Lk 9:23 **15:1, 2** Lk 5:29, 30

Live it!

Oh, Brother!

If you are the oldest in the family, you might be able to identify with the older brother in the famous parable of the lost son, sometimes called the parable of the prodigal son. Can you blame the older brother for being upset? His spoiled younger brother trashes his life and comes crawling back home. And what happens? Dad throws him a huge party. Thanks a lot, Dad!

The older son most likely feels hurt and angry. What he doesn't realize is that he is as special as his younger brother, and his father loves both brothers with all his heart. But because he has been the good son for so long, he feels ignored and left out when his lost brother returns home.

The father in this parable stands for God, who always welcomes us back, no matter what. How do you think this story ends? What does the older brother do next? What would you do?

—Luke 15:11–32

and say, "Father, I have sinned against God
and against you. 19I am no longer fit to be
called your son; treat me as one of your
hired workers." ' 20So he got up and started
back to his father.

"He was still a long way from home when
his father saw him; his heart was filled with
pity, and he ran, threw his arms around his
son, and kissed him. 21'Father,' the son said, 'I
have sinned against God and against you. I
am no longer fit to be called your son.' 22But
the father called to his servants. 'Hurry!' he
said. 'Bring the best robe and put it on him.
Put a ring on his finger and shoes on his
feet. 23Then go and get the prize calf and
kill it, and let us celebrate with a feast! 24For
this son of mine was dead, but now he is
alive; he was lost, but now he has been
found.' And so the feasting began.

25"In the meantime the older son was out
in the field. On his way back, when he came
close to the house, he heard the music and
dancing. 26So he called one of the servants
and asked him, 'What's going on?' 27'Your

"Now he is alive." (15:24)

brother has come back home,' the servant
answered, 'and your father has killed the prize
calf, because he got him back safe and sound.'
28The older brother was so angry that he
would not go into the house; so his father
came out and begged him to come in. 29But
he spoke back to his father, 'Look, all these
years I have worked for you like a slave, and I
have never disobeyed your orders. What have
you given me? Not even a goat for me to
have a feast with my friends! 30But this son
of yours wasted all your property on prosti-
tutes, and when he comes back home, you
kill the prize calf for him!' 31'My son,' the

The parable of the lost son is also called the parable of the prodigal son.

father answered, 'you are always here with
me, and everything I have is yours. 32But we
had to celebrate and be happy, because your
brother was dead, but now he is alive; he was
lost, but now he has been found.'"

The Shrewd Manager

16 Jesus said to his disciples, "There was
once a rich man who had a servant
who managed his property. The rich man was
told that the manager was wasting his mas-
ter's money, 2so he called him in and said,
'What is this I hear about you? Turn in a
complete account of your handling of my
property, because you cannot be my manager
any longer.' 3The servant said to himself, 'My
master is going to dismiss me from my job.
What shall I do? I am not strong enough to
dig ditches, and I am ashamed to beg. 4Now
I know what I will do! Then when my job is
gone, I shall have friends who will welcome
me in their homes.' 5So he called in all the
people who were in debt to his master. He
asked the first one, 'How much do you owe
my master?' 6'One hundred barrels of olive
oil,' he answered. 'Here is your account,' the
manager told him; 'sit down and write fifty.'
7Then he asked another one, 'And you—how
much do you owe?' 'A thousand bushels of
wheat,' he answered. 'Here is your account,'
the manager told him; 'write eight hundred.'
8As a result the master of this dishonest man-
ager praised him for doing such a shrewd
thing; because the people of this world are
much more shrewd in handling their affairs
than the people who belong to the light."
9And Jesus went on to say, "And so I tell
you: make friends for yourselves with world-
ly wealth, so that when it gives out, you will
be welcomed in the eternal home. 10Who-
ever is faithful in small matters will be faith-
ful in large ones; whoever is dishonest in
small matters will be dishonest in large ones.
11If, then, you have not been faithful in han-
dling worldly wealth, how can you be trust-
ed with true wealth? 12And if you have not
been faithful with what belongs to someone
else, who will give you what belongs to you?
13"No servant can be the slave of two
masters; such a slave will hate one and love
the other or will be loyal to one and despise
the other. You cannot serve both God and
money."

Live it!

Dollars and Sense

Jesus tells his disciples, "You cannot serve both God and money" (Luke 16:13). Why not? The key is in the meaning of the word *serve.* We know that we are called to serve God because God is so much greater than we are and because God has given us so many blessings. It makes sense to serve God. Money, however, is not God. Not even close. But the way some people live, you would think that money is their master. Make God number one in your life, and the other things, including money, will fall into place.

— Luke 16:9–13

Some Sayings of Jesus
(Matthew 11:12, 13; 5:31, 32; Mark 10:11, 12)

14When the Pharisees heard all this, they
made fun of Jesus, because they loved money.
15Jesus said to them, "You are the ones who
make yourselves look right in other people's
sight, but God knows your hearts. For the
things that are considered of great value by
people are worth nothing in God's sight.
16"The Law of Moses and the writings of
the prophets were in effect up to the time of

16:9 Tob 4:9–11 **16:13** Mt 6:24 **16:16** Mt 11:12, 13

Shrewd: to be clever and smart in dealing with people, so that you come out ahead.

Pray it!

It's Too Late!

You almost feel sorry for the rich man in the parable of the rich man and Lazarus. Almost. Then you think of poor Lazarus, covered with sores, hoping for just a crumb of food. All he got was the dogs who came to lick his sores. Here's a prayer to help us see the Lazaruses in our own lives.

Dear God, it is so easy to ignore people we would rather not have to deal with. Give me the grace to notice the forgotten and the ignored, especially the elderly, the homeless, or the people others call crazy. If I can do anything to brighten their day, let me have the courage to do it. Help me to see the unseen.

Take a moment to pray about the forgotten and ignored people in your neighborhood or town. Ask God to open your eyes and heart to people in need. Who might be a Lazarus in your life?

— Luke 16:19–31

John the Baptist; since then the Good News
about the Kingdom of God is being told, and
everyone forces their way in. 17But it is easier
for heaven and earth to disappear than for the
smallest detail of the Law to be done away
with.
18"Any man who divorces his wife and
marries another woman commits adultery;
and the man who marries a divorced woman
commits adultery.

The Rich Man and Lazarus

19"There was once a rich man who
dressed in the most expensive clothes and
lived in great luxury every day. 20There was
also a poor man named Lazarus, covered
with sores, who used to be brought to the
rich man's door, 21hoping to eat the bits of
food that fell from the rich man's table. Even
the dogs would come and lick his sores.
22The poor man died and was carried by the
angels to sit beside Abraham at the feast in
heaven. The rich man died and was buried,
23and in Hades,[s] where he was in great pain,
he looked up and saw Abraham, far away,
with Lazarus at his side. 24So he called out,
'Father Abraham! Take pity on me, and send
Lazarus to dip his finger in some water and
cool off my tongue, because I am in great
pain in this fire!' 25But Abraham said,
'Remember, my son, that in your lifetime
you were given all the good things, while
Lazarus got all the bad things. But now he is
enjoying himself here, while you are in pain.
26Besides all that, there is a deep pit lying
between us, so that those who want to cross
over from here to you cannot do so, nor can
anyone cross over to us from where you are.'
27The rich man said, 'Then I beg you, father
Abraham, send Lazarus to my father's house,
28where I have five brothers. Let him go and
warn them so that they, at least, will not
come to this place of pain.' 29Abraham said,
'Your brothers have Moses and the prophets
to warn them; your brothers should listen to
what they say.' 30The rich man answered,
'That is not enough, father Abraham! But if
someone were to rise from death and go to
them, then they would turn from their sins.'
31But Abraham said, 'If they will not listen to
Moses and the prophets, they will not be
convinced even if someone were to rise
from death.' "

[s] **16:23** HADES: *The world of the dead.*
16:17 Mt 5:18 **16:18** Mt 5:32; 1 Cor 7:10, 11

Sin
(Matthew 18:6, 7, 21, 22; Mark 9:42)

17 Jesus said to his disciples, "Things
that make people fall into sin are
bound to happen, but how terrible for the
one who makes them happen! 2It would be
better for him if a large millstone were tied
around his neck and he were thrown into
the sea than for him to cause one of these
little ones to sin. 3So watch what you do!
"If your brother sins, rebuke him, and if he
repents, forgive him. 4If he sins against you
seven times in one day, and each time he
comes to you saying, 'I repent,' you must for-
give him."

Faith

5The apostles said to the Lord, "Make our
faith greater."
6The Lord answered, "If you had faith as
big as a mustard seed, you could say to this
mulberry tree, 'Pull yourself up by the roots
and plant yourself in the sea!' and it would
obey you.

A Servant's Duty

7"Suppose one of you has a servant who is
plowing or looking after the sheep. When he
comes in from the field, do you tell him to
hurry along and eat his meal? 8Of course not!
Instead, you say to him, 'Get my supper ready,
then put on your apron and wait on me
while I eat and drink; after that you may have
your meal.' 9The servant does not deserve
thanks for obeying orders, does he? 10It is the
same with you; when you have done all you
have been told to do, say, 'We are ordinary
servants; we have only done our duty.' "

Jesus Heals Ten Men

11As Jesus made his way to Jerusalem, he
went along the border between Samaria and
Galilee. 12He was going into a village when he
was met by ten men suffering from a dreaded
skin disease. They stood at a distance 13and
shouted, "Jesus! Master! Have pity on us!"

Live it!

Thanks a Lot

Two of the loveliest words in the English language are *thank you.* So simple, but so easy to forget to say. Think about all the nice things that various people do for you each day. How often do you thank them? Sometimes a grown-up will remind you by asking, "Now, what do you say?"

We shouldn't have to be reminded to express our gratitude. It feels so good to be thanked. How do you think Jesus felt when one of the ten people who were healed came back to thank him (Luke 17:15)? What happened to the other nine? Maybe they were just so excited they forgot. Let's try to make thanking someone the first thing we do rather than an afterthought.

— Luke 17:11–19

14Jesus saw them and said to them, "Go
and let the priests examine you."
On the way they were made clean.[t]
15When one of them saw that he was
healed, he came back, praising God in a loud
voice. 16He threw himself to the ground at
Jesus' feet and thanked him. The man was a
Samaritan. 17Jesus spoke up, "There were ten
who were healed; where are the other nine?
18Why is this foreigner the only one who
came back to give thanks to God?" 19And
Jesus said to him, "Get up and go; your faith
has made you well."

The Coming of the Kingdom
(Matthew 24:23–28, 37–41)

20Some Pharisees asked Jesus when the
Kingdom of God would come. His answer

[t] **17:14** MADE CLEAN: *See 5:12.*
17:3 Mt 18:15 **17:14** Lev 14:1–32

"Where are the other nine?" (17:17)

was, "The Kingdom of God does not come
in such a way as to be seen. [21]No one will
say, 'Look, here it is!' or, 'There it is!'; because
the Kingdom of God is within you."[u]
[22]Then he said to the disciples, "The time
will come when you will wish you could see
one of the days of the Son of Man, but you
will not see it. [23]There will be those who
will say to you, 'Look, over there!' or, 'Look,
over here!' But don't go out looking for it.
[24]As the lightning flashes across the sky and
lights it up from one side to the other, so will
the Son of Man be in his day. [25]But first he
must suffer much and be rejected by the
people of this day. [26]As it was in the time of
Noah so shall it be in the days of the Son of
Man. [27]Everybody kept on eating and drink-
ing, and men and women married, up to the
very day Noah went into the boat and the
flood came and killed them all. [28]It will be as
it was in the time of Lot. Everybody kept on
eating and drinking, buying and selling,
planting and building. [29]On the day Lot left
Sodom, fire and sulfur rained down from
heaven and killed them all. [30]That is how it
will be on the day the Son of Man is
revealed.
[31]"On that day someone who is on the
roof of a house must not go down into the
house to get any belongings; in the same
way anyone who is out in the field must not
go back to the house. [32]Remember Lot's
wife! [33]Those who try to save their own life
will lose it; those who lose their life will save
it. [34]On that night, I tell you, there will be
two people sleeping in the same bed: one
will be taken away, the other will be left
behind. [35]Two women will be grinding meal
together: one will be taken away, the other
will be left behind."[v]
[37]The disciples asked him, "Where, Lord?"
Jesus answered, "Wherever there is a dead
body, the vultures will gather."

The Parable of the Widow and the Judge

18 Then Jesus told his disciples a para-
ble to teach them that they should
always pray and never become discouraged.
[2]"In a certain town there was a judge who
neither feared God nor respected people.
[3]And there was a widow in that same town
who kept coming to him and pleading for
her rights, saying, 'Help me against my
opponent!' [4]For a long time the judge
refused to act, but at last he said to himself,
'Even though I don't fear God or respect
people, [5]yet because of all the trouble this
widow is giving me, I will see to it that she
gets her rights. If I don't, she will keep on
coming and finally wear me out!' "
[6]And the Lord continued, "Listen to what
that corrupt judge said. [7]Now, will God not

[u] **17:21** within you; *or* among you, *or* will suddenly appear among you. [v] **17:35** *Some manuscripts add verse 36:* Two men will be working in a field: one will be taken away, the other will be left behind *(see Mt 24:40)*.

17:26 Gen 6:5–8 **17:27** Gen 7:6–24 **17:28, 29** Gen 18:20—19:25 **17:31** Mt 24:17, 18; Mk 13:15, 16 **17:32** Gen 19:26 **17:33** Mt 10:39; 16:25; Mk 8:35; Lk 9:24; Jn 12:25 **18:7** Sir 35:19

A millstone is a very heavy stone used in a mill to grind wheat. This type of stone was very common in the time of Jesus.

judge in favor of his own people who cry to
him day and night for help? Will he be slow
to help them? 8I tell you, he will judge in
their favor and do it quickly. But will the
Son of Man find faith on earth when he
comes?"

The Parable of the Pharisee and the Tax Collector

9Jesus also told this parable to people who
were sure of their own goodness and
despised everybody else. 10"Once there were
two men who went up to the Temple to
pray: one was a Pharisee, the other a tax col-
lector. 11The Pharisee stood apart by himself
and prayed,[w] 'I thank you, God, that I am
not greedy, dishonest, or an adulterer, like
everybody else. I thank you that I am not
like that tax collector over there. 12I fast two
days a week, and I give you one tenth of all
my income.' 13But the tax collector stood at
a distance and would not even raise his face
to heaven, but beat on his breast and said,
'God, have pity on me, a sinner!' 14I tell
you," said Jesus, "the tax collector, and not
the Pharisee, was in the right with God
when he went home. For those who make
themselves great will be humbled, and those
who humble themselves will be made great."

Jesus Blesses Little Children
(Matthew 19:13–15; Mark 10:13–16)

15Some people brought their babies to
Jesus for him to place his hands on them.
The disciples saw them and scolded them for
doing so, 16but Jesus called the children to
him and said, "Let the children come to me
and do not stop them, because the Kingdom
of God belongs to such as these. 17Remem-
ber this! Whoever does not receive the
Kingdom of God like a child will never
enter it."

Pray it!

Holier Than Thou

Look closely at the two prayers in the parable of the Pharisee and the tax collector. Say each prayer slowly. Describe the attitude revealed in each one. Why does Jesus tell us that the second prayer is better? Why was the tax collector "in the right with God" (Luke 18:14) when he went home? Next time you pray, admit your sinfulness and ask for God's mercy. It's that simple.

— Luke 18:9–14

The Rich Man
(Matthew 19:16–30; Mark 10:17–31)

18A Jewish leader asked Jesus, "Good
Teacher, what must I do to receive eternal
life?"
19"Why do you call me good?" Jesus
asked him. "No one is good except God
alone. 20You know the commandments: 'Do
not commit adultery; do not commit mur-
der; do not steal; do not accuse anyone false-
ly; respect your father and your mother.' "
21The man replied, "Ever since I was
young, I have obeyed all these command-
ments."
22When Jesus heard this, he said to him,
"There is still one more thing you need to
do. Sell all you have and give the money to
the poor, and you will have riches in heaven;
then come and follow me." 23But when the
man heard this, he became very sad, because
he was very rich.
24Jesus saw that he was sad and said, "How

[w] **18:11** stood apart by himself and prayed; *some manuscripts have* stood up and prayed to himself.

18:14 Mt 23:12; Lk 14:11 **18:20** **a** Ex 20:14; Deut 5:18; **b** Ex 20:13; Deut 5:17; **c** Ex 20:15; Deut 5:19; **d** Ex 20:16; Deut 5:20; **e** Ex 20:12; Deut 5:16

In the time of Jesus, tax collectors were hated because they worked for the Romans and often charged much more than they needed to.

hard it is for rich people to enter the King-
dom of God! 25 It is much harder for a rich
person to enter the Kingdom of God than for
a camel to go through the eye of a needle."
26 The people who heard him asked,
"Who, then, can be saved?"
27 Jesus answered, "What is humanly
impossible is possible for God."
28 Then Peter said, "Look! We have left our
homes to follow you."
29 "Yes," Jesus said to them, "and I assure
you that anyone who leaves home or wife or
brothers or parents or children for the sake
of the Kingdom of God 30 will receive much
more in this present age and eternal life in
the age to come."

Jesus Speaks a Third Time about His Death

(Matthew 20:17–19; Mark 10:32–34)

31 Jesus took the twelve disciples aside
and said to them, "Listen! We are going to
Jerusalem where everything the prophets
wrote about the Son of Man will come true.
32 He will be handed over to the Gentiles,
who will make fun of him, insult him, and
spit on him. 33 They will whip him and kill
him, but three days later he will rise to life."
34 But the disciples did not understand any
of these things; the meaning of the words
was hidden from them, and they did not
know what Jesus was talking about.

Jesus Heals a Blind Beggar

(Matthew 20:29–34; Mark 10:46–52)

35 As Jesus was coming near Jericho, there
was a blind man sitting by the road, begging.
36 When he heard the crowd passing by, he
asked, "What is this?"
37 "Jesus of Nazareth is passing by," they
told him.
38 He cried out, "Jesus! Son of David!
Have mercy on me!"
39 The people in front scolded him and
told him to be quiet. But he shouted even
more loudly, "Son of David! Have mercy on
me!"
40 So Jesus stopped and ordered the blind
man to be brought to him. When he came
near, Jesus asked him, 41 "What do you want
me to do for you?"
"Sir," he answered, "I want to see again."
42 Jesus said to him, "Then see! Your faith
has made you well."
43 At once he was able to see, and he fol-
lowed Jesus, giving thanks to God. When the
crowd saw it, they all praised God.

Jesus and Zacchaeus

19 Jesus went on into Jericho and was
passing through. 2 There was a chief
tax collector there named Zacchaeus, who
was rich. 3 He was trying to see who Jesus
was, but he was a little man and could not
see Jesus because of the crowd. 4 So he ran
ahead of the crowd and climbed a sycamore
tree to see Jesus, who was going to pass that
way. 5 When Jesus came to that place, he
looked up and said to Zacchaeus, "Hurry
down, Zacchaeus, because I must stay in
your house today."

He was a little man. (19:3)

6 Zacchaeus hurried down and welcomed
him with great joy. 7 All the people who saw
it started grumbling, "This man has gone as a
guest to the home of a sinner!"
8 Zacchaeus stood up and said to the Lord,
"Listen, sir! I will give half my belongings to
the poor, and if I have cheated anyone, I will
pay back four times as much."
9 Jesus said to him, "Salvation has come to

Live it!

The Long and Short of It

Poor Zacchaeus. He was not only a tax collector but he was also short. The day Jesus came to town, Zacchaeus, like everyone else, wanted to see him. But he came late, and no one was going to make room for him. That didn't stop Zacchaeus. He was determined to see this man whom everyone was talking about. He climbed a tree, and when Jesus saw him, he invited himself over to Zacchaeus's house for dinner.

That encounter changed Zacchaeus's life. One of the morals of the story? Don't let your size or status stop you from following Jesus. Here's another moral. Don't let what others think stop you from being Jesus' friend. Think of little Zacchaeus. Jesus saw inside to his big heart. That's what counts!

— Luke 19:1–10

this house today, for this man, also, is a
descendant of Abraham. 10 The Son of Man
came to seek and to save the lost."

The Parable of the Gold Coins
(Matthew 25:14–30)

11 While the people were listening to this,
Jesus continued and told them a parable. He
was now almost at Jerusalem, and they sup-
posed that the Kingdom of God was just
about to appear. 12 So he said, "There was
once a man of high rank who was going to a
country far away to be made king, after
which he planned to come back home.
13 Before he left, he called his ten servants
and gave them each a gold coin and told
them, 'See what you can earn with this
while I am gone.' 14 Now, his own people
hated him, and so they sent messengers after
him to say, 'We don't want this man to be
our king.'

15 "The man was made king and came
back. At once he ordered his servants to
appear before him, in order to find out how
much they had earned. 16 The first one came
and said, 'Sir, I have earned ten gold coins
with the one you gave me.' 17 'Well done,' he
said; 'you are a good servant! Since you were
faithful in small matters, I will put you in
charge of ten cities.' 18 The second servant
came and said, 'Sir, I have earned five gold
coins with the one you gave me.' 19 To this
one he said, 'You will be in charge of five
cities.' 20 Another servant came and said, 'Sir,
here is your gold coin; I kept it hidden in a
handkerchief. 21 I was afraid of you, because
you are a hard man. You take what is not
yours and reap what you did not plant.' 22 He
said to him, 'You bad servant! I will use your
own words to condemn you! You know that
I am a hard man, taking what is not mine
and reaping what I have not planted. 23 Well,
then, why didn't you put my money in the
bank? Then I would have received it back
with interest when I returned.' 24 Then he
said to those who were standing there, 'Take
the gold coin away from him and give it to
the servant who has ten coins.' 25 But they
said to him, 'Sir, he already has ten coins!'
26 'I tell you,' he replied, 'that to those who
have something, even more will be given;
but those who have nothing, even the little
that they have will be taken away from
them. 27 Now, as for those enemies of mine
who did not want me to be their king, bring
them here and kill them in my presence!' "

The Triumphant Approach to Jerusalem
(Matthew 21:1–11; Mark 11:1–11; John 12:12–19)

28 After Jesus said this, he went on in front
of them toward Jerusalem. 29 As he came
near Bethphage and Bethany at the Mount
of Olives, he sent two disciples ahead 30 with

19:10 Mt 18:11 **19:26** Mt 13:12; Mk 4:25; Lk 8:18 **19:11–27** Mt 25:14–30

these instructions: "Go to the village there
ahead of you; as you go in, you will find a
colt tied up that has never been ridden.
Untie it and bring it here. 31 If someone asks
you why you are untying it, tell him that the
Master[x] needs it."

32 They went on their way and found
everything just as Jesus had told them. 33 As
they were untying the colt, its owners said to
them, "Why are you untying it?"

34 "The Master needs it," they answered,
35 and they took the colt to Jesus. Then they
threw their cloaks over the animal and
helped Jesus get on. 36 As he rode on, people
spread their cloaks on the road.

37 When he came near Jerusalem, at the
place where the road went down the Mount
of Olives, the large crowd of his disciples
began to thank God and praise him in loud
voices for all the great things that they had
seen: 38 "God bless the king who comes in
the name of the Lord! Peace in heaven and
glory to God!"

39 Then some of the Pharisees in the
crowd spoke to Jesus. "Teacher," they said,
"command your disciples to be quiet!"

40 Jesus answered, "I tell you that if they
keep quiet, the stones themselves will start
shouting."

Jesus Weeps over Jerusalem

41 He came closer to the city, and when
he saw it, he wept over it, 42 saying, "If you
only knew today what is needed for peace!
But now you cannot see it! 43 The time will
come when your enemies will surround
you with barricades, blockade you, and
close in on you from every side. 44 They
will completely destroy you and the people
within your walls; not a single stone will
they leave in its place, because you did not
recognize the time when God came to save
you!"

Jesus Goes to the Temple

(Matthew 21:12–17; Mark 11:15–19; John 2:13–22)

45 Then Jesus went into the Temple and
began to drive out the merchants, 46 saying to
them, "It is written in the Scriptures that
God said, 'My Temple will be a house of
prayer.' But you have turned it into a hide-
out for thieves!"

47 Every day Jesus taught in the Temple.
The chief priests, the teachers of the Law,
and the leaders of the people wanted to kill
him, 48 but they could not find a way to do
it, because all the people kept listening to
him, not wanting to miss a single word.

The Question about Jesus' Authority

(Matthew 21:23–27; Mark 11:27–33)

20 One day when Jesus was in the
Temple teaching the people and
preaching the Good News, the chief priests
and the teachers of the Law, together with
the elders, came 2 and said to him, "Tell us,
what right do you have to do these things?
Who gave you such right?"

3 Jesus answered them, "Now let me ask
you a question. Tell me, 4 did John's right to
baptize come from God or from human
beings?"

5 They started to argue among themselves,
"What shall we say? If we say, 'From God,' he
will say, 'Why, then, did you not believe
John?' 6 But if we say, 'From human beings,'
this whole crowd here will stone us, because
they are convinced that John was a prophet."
7 So they answered, "We don't know where it
came from."

8 And Jesus said to them, "Neither will I
tell you, then, by what right I do these
things."

x **19:31** the Master; *or* its owner.
19:38 Ps 118:26 **19:46** Isa 56:7; Jer 7:11 **19:47** Lk 21:37

Did you know that Jesus wept *(Luke 19:41)* **? His heart was so big that when he saw people headed for destruction, he couldn't help but be overcome with grief.**

Live it!

Gotcha!

Twice in Luke, chapter 20, the enemies of Jesus try to trap him with a question, but both times Jesus traps them with his response. They are trying to get Jesus to say something that can be used against him. And they do it in public places where lots of people are gathered so that everyone will hear what he says. It's clear that they are more interested in finding fault with Jesus than in listening to what he has to say.

Jesus is clearly very wise and clever. And the people only grow to admire Jesus even more than before because of how well he handles his questioners. He beats them at their own game.

Sometimes we use words in unkind ways. Examine your heart when you ask a question that may make another person feel mad or sad. Do you really want to know the answer, or are you trying to make yourself look good by making the other person look bad?

— Luke 20:1–8,19–26

The Parable of the Tenants in the Vineyard
(Matthew 21:33–46; Mark 12:1–12)

9Then Jesus told the people this parable:
"There was once a man who planted a vine-
yard, rented it out to tenants, and then left
home for a long time. 10When the time
came to gather the grapes, he sent a slave to
the tenants to receive from them his share of
the harvest. But the tenants beat the slave and
sent him back without a thing. 11So he sent
another slave; but the tenants beat him also,
treated him shamefully, and sent him back
without a thing. 12Then he sent a third slave;
the tenants wounded him, too, and threw
him out. 13Then the owner of the vineyard
said, 'What shall I do? I will send my own
dear son; surely they will respect him!' 14But
when the tenants saw him, they said to one
another, 'This is the owner's son. Let's kill
him, and his property will be ours!' 15So they
threw him out of the vineyard and killed
him.

"What, then, will the owner of the vine-
yard do to the tenants?" Jesus asked. 16"He
will come and kill those men, and turn the
vineyard over to other tenants."

When the people heard this, they said, "Surely not!"

17Jesus looked at them and asked, "What,
then, does this scripture mean?

'The stone which the builders rejected as worthless
turned out to be the most important of all.'

18Everyone who falls on that stone will be
cut to pieces; and if that stone falls on some-
one, that person will be crushed to dust."

The Question about Paying Taxes
(Matthew 22:15–22; Mark 12:13–17)

19The teachers of the Law and the chief
priests tried to arrest Jesus on the spot,
because they knew that he had told this
parable against them; but they were afraid of
the people. 20So they looked for an opportu-
nity. They bribed some men to pretend they
were sincere, and they sent them to trap
Jesus with questions, so that they could hand
him over to the authority and power of the
Roman Governor. 21These spies said to
Jesus, "Teacher, we know that what you say
and teach is right. We know that you pay no
attention to anyone's status, but teach the
truth about God's will for people. 22Tell us, is

20:9 Isa 5:1 **20:17** Ps 118:22

The Hebrew word *Messiah* translates into *Christos* in Greek, which becomes *Christ* in English. All three mean "the anointed one."

Pray it!

Common Cents

In this passage Jesus handles a coin and uses it to make a point. We can use a coin to make a prayer. Take a look at any U. S. coin. Two four-word phrases appear on each. One is, "The United States of America." Can you find the other? That's right. It's "In God We Trust." Check out paper money too.

Interesting that such a religious phrase appears on every piece of U.S. money. So why not let our money—pennies, nickels, dimes, quarters, and dollar bills—be a source for prayer?

Dear God, perhaps the last place I expect to see your name is on a coin or a dollar bill. Yet there you are. Thanks for the reminder that even money calls me to an awareness of your presence in my life and my need to trust in you. Increase my trust in you and decrease my trust in money. And help me be generous with the money I have and spend it wisely. Amen.

— Luke 20:19–26

it against our Law for us to pay taxes to the
Roman Emperor, or not?"
23But Jesus saw through their trick and
said to them, 24"Show me a silver coin.
Whose face and name are these on it?"
"The Emperor's," they answered.
25So Jesus said, "Well, then, pay to the
Emperor what belongs to the Emperor, and
pay to God what belongs to God."
26There before the people they could not
catch him in a thing, so they kept quiet,
amazed at his answer.

The Question about Rising from Death

(Matthew 22:23–33; Mark 12:18–27)

27Then some Sadducees, who say that
people will not rise from death, came to
Jesus and said, 28"Teacher, Moses wrote this
law for us: 'If a man dies and leaves a wife
but no children, that man's brother must
marry the widow so that they can have chil-
dren who will be considered the dead man's
children.' 29Once there were seven brothers;
the oldest got married and died without
having children. 30Then the second one
married the woman, 31and then the third.
The same thing happened to all seven—they
died without having children. 32Last of all,
the woman died. 33Now, on the day when
the dead rise to life, whose wife will she be?
All seven of them had married her."
34Jesus answered them, "The men and
women of this age marry, 35but the men and
women who are worthy to rise from death
and live in the age to come will not then
marry. 36They will be like angels and cannot
die. They are the children of God, because
they have risen from death. 37And Moses
clearly proves that the dead are raised to life.
In the passage about the burning bush he
speaks of the Lord as 'the God of Abraham,
the God of Isaac, and the God of Jacob.'
38He is the God of the living, not of the
dead, for to him all are alive."
39Some of the teachers of the Law spoke
up, "A good answer, Teacher!" 40For they did
not dare ask him any more questions.

The Question about the Messiah

(Matthew 22:41–46; Mark 12:35–37)

41Jesus asked them, "How can it be said
that the Messiah will be the descendant of

20:27 Acts 23:8 **20:28** Deut 25:5 **20:37** Ex 3:6

David? 42For David himself says in the book
of Psalms,
'The Lord said to my Lord:
Sit here at my right side
43 until I put your enemies as a footstool
under your feet.'
44David called him 'Lord'; how, then, can the
Messiah be David's descendant?"

Jesus Warns against the Teachers of the Law

(Matthew 23:1–36; Mark 12:38–40)

45As all the people listened to him, Jesus
said to his disciples, 46"Be on your guard
against the teachers of the Law, who like to
walk around in their long robes and love to
be greeted with respect in the marketplace;
who choose the reserved seats in the syna-
gogues and the best places at feasts; 47who
take advantage of widows and rob them of
their homes, and then make a show of saying
long prayers! Their punishment will be all the
worse!"

The Widow's Offering

(Mark 12:41–44)

21 Jesus looked around and saw rich
people dropping their gifts in the
Temple treasury, 2and he also saw a very
poor widow dropping in two little copper
coins. 3He said, "I tell you that this poor
widow put in more than all the others. 4For
the others offered their gifts from what they
had to spare of their riches; but she, poor as
she is, gave all she had to live on."

Jesus Speaks of the Destruction of the Temple

(Matthew 24:1, 2; Mark 13:1, 2)

5Some of the disciples were talking about
the Temple, how beautiful it looked with its
fine stones and the gifts offered to God. Jesus
said, 6"All this you see—the time will come
when not a single stone here will be left in
its place; every one will be thrown down."

Live it!

You Better Watch Out

Jesus says something very important in this passage. He basically tells his followers that many people will come claiming to speak for him, but Jesus says, "Be careful who you follow."

How do we sort out all the people who claim to speak for Jesus? There are preachers and ministers on television and radio, and all of them claim to be speaking for Jesus. It's easy to be deceived. There are many stories, for instance, where people tell their followers that on a certain date, the world is going to end. Followers make plans and prepare themselves. The date comes and goes, and the world goes on.

The best course to take is to learn all you can about what the Catholic Church teaches. The Catholic Church goes all the way back to Jesus and the Apostles. The Holy Spirit guides the Church into the fullness of truth.

Have you ever been fooled by someone's words or message? Think through what happened and what you will do if it happens again. Ask God to help you stay on the right path and not be misled.

— Luke 21:7–19

Troubles and Persecutions

(Matthew 24:3–14; Mark 13:3–13)

7"Teacher," they asked, "when will this
be? And what will happen in order to show
that the time has come for it to take place?"
8Jesus said, "Watch out; don't be fooled.
Many men, claiming to speak for me, will
come and say, 'I am he!' and, 'The time has

20:42, 43 Ps 110:1

come!' But don't follow them. 9Don't be
afraid when you hear of wars and revolu-
tions; such things must happen first, but they
do not mean that the end is near."
10He went on to say, "Countries will fight
each other; kingdoms will attack one anoth-
er. 11There will be terrible earthquakes,
famines, and plagues everywhere; there will
be strange and terrifying things coming from
the sky. 12Before all these things take place,
however, you will be arrested and persecut-
ed; you will be handed over to be tried in
synagogues and be put in prison; you will be
brought before kings and rulers for my sake.
13This will be your chance to tell the Good
News. 14Make up your minds ahead of time
not to worry about how you will defend
yourselves, 15because I will give you such
words and wisdom that none of your ene-
mies will be able to refute or contradict
what you say. 16You will be handed over by
your parents, your brothers, your relatives,
and your friends; and some of you will be
put to death. 17Everyone will hate you
because of me. 18But not a single hair from
your heads will be lost. 19Stand firm, and
you will save yourselves.

Jesus Speaks of the Destruction of Jerusalem

(Matthew 24:15–21; Mark 13:14–19)

20"When you see Jerusalem surrounded
by armies, then you will know that it will
soon be destroyed. 21Then those who are in
Judea must run away to the hills; those who
are in the city must leave, and those who are
out in the country must not go into the city.
22For those will be 'The Days of Punish-
ment,' to make come true all that the Scrip-
tures say. 23How terrible it will be in those
days for women who are pregnant and for
mothers with little babies! Terrible distress
will come upon this land, and God's punish-
ment will fall on this people. 24Some will be
killed by the sword, and others will be taken
as prisoners to all countries; and the heathen
will trample over Jerusalem until their time
is up.

The Coming of the Son of Man

(Matthew 24:29–31; Mark 13:24–27)

25"There will be strange things happening
to the sun, the moon, and the stars. On earth
whole countries will be in despair, afraid of
the roar of the sea and the raging tides.
26People will faint from fear as they wait for
what is coming over the whole earth, for the
powers in space will be driven from their
courses. 27Then the Son of Man will appear,
coming in a cloud with great power and
glory. 28When these things begin to happen,
stand up and raise your heads, because your
salvation is near."

The Lesson of the Fig Tree

(Matthew 24:32–35; Mark 13:28–31)

29Then Jesus told them this parable:
"Think of the fig tree and all the other trees.
30When you see their leaves beginning to
appear, you know that summer is near. 31In
the same way, when you see these things
happening, you will know that the Kingdom
of God is about to come.
32"Remember that all these things will
take place before the people now living have
all died. 33Heaven and earth will pass away,
but my words will never pass away.

The Need to Watch

34"Be careful not to let yourselves become
occupied with too much feasting and drink-
ing and with the worries of this life, or that
Day may suddenly catch you 35like a trap.
For it will come upon all people everywhere
on earth. 36Be on watch and pray always
that you will have the strength to go safely
through all those things that will happen and
to stand before the Son of Man."

21:14, 15 Lk 12:11, 12 **21:22** Hos 9:7 **21:25** Isa 13:10; Ezek 32:7; Joel 2:31; Rev 6:12, 13 **21:27** Dan 7:13; Rev 1:7

Fig trees are very common in the Holy Land. Have you ever seen or tasted a fig?

37 Jesus spent those days teaching in the
Temple, and when evening came, he would
go out and spend the night on the Mount of
Olives. 38 Early each morning all the people
went to the Temple to listen to him.

The Plot against Jesus
*(Matthew 26:1–5; Mark 14:1, 2;
John 11:45–53)*

22 The time was near for the Festival of
Unleavened Bread, which is called
the Passover. 2 The chief priests and the
teachers of the Law were afraid of the peo-
ple, and so they were trying to find a way of
putting Jesus to death secretly.

Judas Agrees to Betray Jesus
(Matthew 26:14–16; Mark 14:10, 11)

3 Then Satan entered into Judas, called
Iscariot, who was one of the twelve disciples.
4 So Judas went off and spoke with the chief
priests and the officers of the Temple guard
about how he could betray Jesus to them.
5 They were pleased and offered to pay him
money. 6 Judas agreed to it and started look-
ing for a good chance to hand Jesus over to
them without the people knowing about it.

Jesus Prepares to Eat the Passover Meal
*(Matthew 26:17–25; Mark 14:12–21;
John 13:21–30)*

7 The day came during the Festival of
Unleavened Bread when the lambs for the
Passover meal were to be killed. 8 Jesus sent
Peter and John with these instructions: "Go
and get the Passover meal ready for us to
eat."
9 "Where do you want us to get it ready?"
they asked him.
10 He answered, "As you go into the city, a
man carrying a jar of water will meet you.
Follow him into the house that he enters,
11 and say to the owner of the house: 'The
Teacher says to you, Where is the room
where my disciples and I will eat the
Passover meal?' 12 He will show you a large
furnished room upstairs, where you will get
everything ready."
13 They went off and found everything
just as Jesus had told them, and they pre-
pared the Passover meal.

The Lord's Supper
*(Matthew 26:26–30; Mark 14:22–26;
1 Corinthians 11:23–25)*

14 When the hour came, Jesus took his
place at the table with the apostles. 15 He
said to them, "I have wanted so much to eat
this Passover meal with you before I suffer!
16 For I tell you, I will never eat it until it is
given its full meaning in the Kingdom of
God."
17 Then Jesus took a cup, gave thanks to
God, and said, "Take this and share it among
yourselves. 18 I tell you that from now on I
will not drink this wine until the Kingdom
of God comes."
19 Then he took a piece of bread, gave
thanks to God, broke it, and gave it to them,
saying, "This is my body, which is given for
you. Do this in memory of me." 20 In the
same way, he gave them the cup after the
supper, saying, "This cup is God's new
covenant sealed with my blood, which is
poured out for you.[y]
21 "But, look! The one who betrays me is
here at the table with me! 22 The Son of
Man will die as God has decided, but how
terrible for that man who betrays him!"
23 Then they began to ask among them-
selves which one of them it could be who
was going to do this.

The Argument about Greatness

24 An argument broke out among the dis-
ciples as to which one of them should be

y **22:20** *Some manuscripts do not have the words of Jesus after* This is my body *in verse 19, and all of verse 20.*
21:37 Lk 19:47 **22:1** Ex 12:1–27 **22:20** Jer 31:31–34 **22:21** Ps 41:9 **22:24** Mt 18:1; Mk 9:34; Lk 9:46

The Festival of Unleavened Bread is also known as Passover, and it is celebrated each spring by the Jewish people. See Exodus, chapter 12.

Pray it!

Who's Number One?

Try to imagine how Jesus felt at his last meal with his closest followers, when they began to argue about which of them should be thought of as the greatest (Luke 22:24). You can almost hear Jesus saying to himself, "Haven't they been listening to anything I've said?" Following Jesus is about putting others before yourself. It is about serving others and not being served.

Wanting to be number one is definitely *not* what being a Christian is about. Aim to live out the words of Jesus, "I am among you as one who serves." Think of ways that you can be of service to others. Here is a prayer to help you keep your priorities straight.

Dear Jesus, you came to tell us that being number one is* not *what it's all about. Help me to keep you as number one in my life and keep the needs of others close behind. Let me wake up each day and think of how I can serve others, especially at home or in school. Help me to keep my priorities straight, which means they are directed toward you. Amen.

— Luke 22:24–27

thought of as the greatest. 25Jesus said to
them, "The kings of the pagans have power
over their people, and the rulers claim the
title 'Friends of the People.' 26But this is not
the way it is with you; rather, the greatest
one among you must be like the youngest,
and the leader must be like the servant.
27Who is greater, the one who sits down to
eat or the one who serves? The one who sits
down, of course. But I am among you as one
who serves.
28"You have stayed with me all through
my trials; 29and just as my Father has given
me the right to rule, so I will give you the
same right. 30You will eat and drink at my
table in my Kingdom, and you will sit on
thrones to rule over the twelve tribes of
Israel.

Jesus Predicts Peter's Denial
(Matthew 26:31–35; Mark 14:27–31; John 13:36–38)

31"Simon, Simon! Listen! Satan has
received permission to test all of you, to sep-
arate the good from the bad, as a farmer sep-
arates the wheat from the chaff. 32But I have
prayed for you, Simon, that your faith will
not fail. And when you turn back to me, you
must strengthen your brothers."
33Peter answered, "Lord, I am ready to
go to prison with you and to die with
you!"
34"I tell you, Peter," Jesus said, "the rooster
will not crow tonight until you have said
three times that you do not know me."

Purse, Bag, and Sword

35Then Jesus asked his disciples, "When I
sent you out that time without purse, bag, or
shoes, did you lack anything?"
"Not a thing," they answered.
36"But now," Jesus said, "whoever has a
purse or a bag must take it; and whoever
does not have a sword must sell his coat and
buy one. 37For I tell you that the scripture
which says, 'He shared the fate of criminals,'
must come true about me, because what was
written about me is coming true."

22:26 Mt 23:11; Mk 9:35 **22:25, 26** Mt 20:25–27; Mk 10:42–44 **22:27** Jn 13:12–15 **22:30** Mt 19:28
22:35 Mt 10:9, 10; Mk 6:8, 9; Lk 9:3; 10:4 **22:37** Isa 53:12

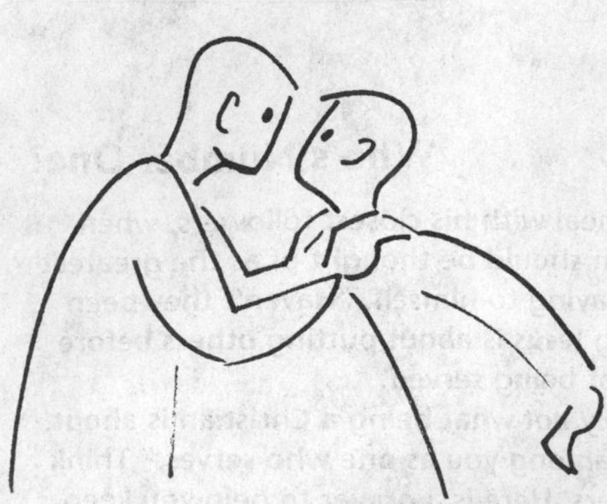

"Simon, Simon! Listen!" (22:31)

38 The disciples said, "Look! Here are two
swords, Lord!"

"That is enough!"[z] he replied.

Jesus Prays on the Mount of Olives

(Matthew 26:36–46; Mark 14:32–42)

39 Jesus left the city and went, as he usually
did, to the Mount of Olives; and the disci-
ples went with him. 40 When he arrived at
the place, he said to them, "Pray that you
will not fall into temptation."

41 Then he went off from them about the
distance of a stone's throw and knelt down
and prayed. 42 "Father," he said, "if you will,
take this cup of suffering away from me. Not
my will, however, but your will be done."
43 An angel from heaven appeared to him
and strengthened him. 44 In great anguish he
prayed even more fervently; his sweat was
like drops of blood falling to the ground.[a]

45 Rising from his prayer, he went back to
the disciples and found them asleep, worn
out by their grief. 46 He said to them, "Why
are you sleeping? Get up and pray that you
will not fall into temptation."

The Arrest of Jesus

(Matthew 26:47–56; Mark 14:43–50; John 18:3–11)

47 Jesus was still speaking when a crowd
arrived, led by Judas, one of the twelve disci-
ples. He came up to Jesus to kiss him. 48 But
Jesus said, "Judas, is it with a kiss that you
betray the Son of Man?"

49 When the disciples who were with Jesus
saw what was going to happen, they asked,
"Shall we use our swords, Lord?" 50 And one
of them struck the High Priest's slave and
cut off his right ear.

51 But Jesus said, "Enough of this!" He
touched the man's ear and healed him.

52 Then Jesus said to the chief priests and
the officers of the Temple guard and the el-
ders who had come there to get him, "Did
you have to come with swords and clubs, as
though I were an outlaw? 53 I was with you
in the Temple every day, and you did not try
to arrest me. But this is your hour to act,
when the power of darkness rules."

Peter Denies Jesus

(Matthew 26:57, 58, 69–75; Mark 14:53, 54, 66–72; John 18:12–18, 25–27)

54 They arrested Jesus and took him away
into the house of the High Priest; and Peter
followed at a distance. 55 A fire had been lit in
the center of the courtyard, and Peter joined
those who were sitting around it. 56 When
one of the servant women saw him sitting
there at the fire, she looked straight at him
and said, "This man too was with Jesus!"

57 But Peter denied it, "Woman, I don't
even know him!"

"Woman, I don't even know him!" (22:57)

58 After a little while a man noticed Peter
and said, "You are one of them, too!"

But Peter answered, "Man, I am not!"

59 And about an hour later another man
insisted strongly, "There isn't any doubt that

[z] **22:38** That is enough; *or* Enough of this. [a] **22:44** *Some manuscripts do not have verses 43–44.*
22:53 Lk 19:47; 21:37

Live it!

It Wasn't Me!

How could Peter do it? Right when Jesus needed him most, three times he denied even knowing him. And Jesus had even warned Peter that he would do it!

We have all been in a situation where we denied doing anything wrong, even though we were guilty. We may have lied about it and maybe even blamed others. Peter was wrong, and once he realized it, he "wept bitterly" (Luke 22:62). Think of the last time you felt regret for not admitting to the truth about something you did. Did you try to blame someone else? Try not to let that happen. It takes courage to face up to the truth, especially when it comes to standing up for a friend. Resist the temptation to deny the truth. You won't regret it.

— Luke 22:54–62

this man was with Jesus, because he also is a
Galilean!"
60But Peter answered, "Man, I don't know
what you are talking about!"
At once, while he was still speaking, a
rooster crowed. 61The Lord turned around
and looked straight at Peter, and Peter
remembered that the Lord had said to him,
"Before the rooster crows tonight, you will
say three times that you do not know me."
62Peter went out and wept bitterly.

Jesus Is Mocked and Beaten
(Matthew 26:67, 68; Mark 14:65)

63The men who were guarding Jesus
made fun of him and beat him. 64They
blindfolded him and asked him, "Who hit
you? Guess!" 65And they said many other
insulting things to him.

Jesus before the Council
(Matthew 26:59–66; Mark 14:55–64; John 18:19–24)

66When day came, the elders, the chief
priests, and the teachers of the Law met
together, and Jesus was brought before the
Council. 67"Tell us," they said, "are you the
Messiah?"
He answered, "If I tell you, you will not
believe me; 68and if I ask you a question, you
will not answer. 69But from now on the Son
of Man will be seated at the right side of
Almighty God."
70They all said, "Are you, then, the Son of
God?"
He answered them, "You say that I am."
71And they said, "We don't need any wit-
nesses! We ourselves have heard what he
said!"

Jesus before Pilate
(Matthew 27:1, 2, 11–14; Mark 15:1–5; John 18:28–38)

23 The whole group rose up and took
Jesus before Pilate, 2where they
began to accuse him: "We caught this man
misleading our people, telling them not to
pay taxes to the Emperor and claiming that
he himself is the Messiah, a king."
3Pilate asked him, "Are you the king of
the Jews?"
"So you say," answered Jesus.
4Then Pilate said to the chief priests and
the crowds, "I find no reason to condemn
this man."
5But they insisted even more strongly,
"With his teaching he is starting a riot
among the people all through Judea. He
began in Galilee and now has come here."

Galilean: someone who lives in Galilee, which is in the north of Judea. Galileans had a distinct accent. Both Jesus and Peter were Galileans.

Jesus before Herod

6When Pilate heard this, he asked, "Is this
man a Galilean?" 7When he learned that
Jesus was from the region ruled by Herod,
he sent him to Herod, who was also in
Jerusalem at that time. 8Herod was very
pleased when he saw Jesus, because he had
heard about him and had been wanting to
see him for a long time. He was hoping to
see Jesus perform some miracle. 9So Herod
asked Jesus many questions, but Jesus made
no answer. 10The chief priests and the teach-
ers of the Law stepped forward and made
strong accusations against Jesus. 11Herod and
his soldiers made fun of Jesus and treated
him with contempt; then they put a fine
robe on him and sent him back to Pilate.
12On that very day Herod and Pilate became
friends; before this they had been enemies.

Jesus Is Sentenced to Death
(Matthew 27:15–26; Mark 15:6–15; John 18:39—19:16)

13Pilate called together the chief priests,
the leaders, and the people, 14and said to
them, "You brought this man to me and said
that he was misleading the people. Now, I
have examined him here in your presence,
and I have not found him guilty of any of
the crimes you accuse him of. 15Nor did
Herod find him guilty, for he sent him back
to us. There is nothing this man has done to
deserve death. 16So I will have him whipped
and let him go."[b]
18The whole crowd cried out, "Kill him!
Set Barabbas free for us!" (19Barabbas had
been put in prison for a riot that had taken
place in the city, and for murder.)
20Pilate wanted to set Jesus free, so he
appealed to the crowd again. 21But they
shouted back, "Crucify him! Crucify him!"
22Pilate said to them the third time, "But
what crime has he committed? I cannot find
anything he has done to deserve death! I will
have him whipped and set him free."
23But they kept on shouting at the top of
their voices that Jesus should be crucified,
and finally their shouting succeeded. 24So
Pilate passed the sentence on Jesus that they
were asking for. 25He set free the man they
wanted, the one who had been put in prison
for riot and murder, and he handed Jesus
over for them to do as they wished.

Jesus Is Crucified
(Matthew 27:32–44; Mark 15:21–32; John 19:17–27)

26The soldiers led Jesus away, and as they
were going, they met a man from Cyrene
named Simon who was coming into the city
from the country. They seized him, put the
cross on him, and made him carry it behind
Jesus.

They . . . put the cross on him, and made him carry it. (23:26)

27A large crowd of people followed him;
among them were some women who were
weeping and wailing for him. 28Jesus turned
to them and said, "Women of Jerusalem!
Don't cry for me, but for yourselves and
your children. 29For the days are coming
when people will say, 'How lucky are the
women who never had children, who never
bore babies, who never nursed them!' 30That
will be the time when people will say to the

[b] **23:16** *Some manuscripts add verse 17:* At every Passover Festival Pilate had to set free one prisoner for them *(see Mk 15:6).*
23:30 Hos 10:8; Rev 6:16

Can you find three wondrous things that happened at Jesus' death? They involved the sun, the Temple, and a Roman officer.

Pray it!

Jesus, Remember Me!

Two criminals were crucified alongside Jesus. One of them insulted Jesus. The other, often referred to as the good thief, respected Jesus and knew he was innocent. He asked to be remembered by Jesus, and Jesus assured him that he would share Paradise with him.

Take a moment to pray for all those accused of crimes, especially the innocent and those given the death penalty.

God, help me always to remember that you love every one of us, no matter what we have done. Your Son was given the death penalty, even though he was innocent. I pray for everyone who has been falsely accused and convicted. I pray also for all those who have been sentenced to death. No matter what they have done, they are still your children. Your love knows no bounds. Remind me of that when my heart is too small and judgmental.

— Luke 23:39–43

mountains, 'Fall on us!' and to the hills, 'Hide
us!' 31 For if such things as these are done
when the wood is green, what will happen
when it is dry?"
32 Two other men, both of them criminals,
were also led out to be put to death with
Jesus. 33 When they came to the place called
"The Skull," they crucified Jesus there, and the
two criminals, one on his right and the other
on his left. 34 Jesus said, "Forgive them, Father!
They don't know what they are doing."[c]
They divided his clothes among themselves by throwing dice. 35 The people stood
there watching while the Jewish leaders
made fun of him: "He saved others; let him
save himself if he is the Messiah whom God
has chosen!"
36 The soldiers also made fun of him: they
came up to him and offered him cheap
wine, 37 and said, "Save yourself if you are the
king of the Jews!"
38 Above him were written these words:
"This is the King of the Jews."
39 One of the criminals hanging there
hurled insults at him: "Aren't you the Messiah? Save yourself and us!"
40 The other one, however, rebuked him,
saying, "Don't you fear God? You received
the same sentence he did. 41 Ours, however,
is only right, because we are getting what we
deserve for what we did; but he has done no
wrong." 42 And he said to Jesus, "Remember
me, Jesus, when you come as King!"
43 Jesus said to him, "I promise you that
today you will be in Paradise with me."

The Death of Jesus
(Matthew 27:45–56; Mark 15:33–41; John 19:28–30)

44-45 It was about twelve o'clock when the
sun stopped shining and darkness covered
the whole country until three o'clock; and
the curtain hanging in the Temple was torn
in two. 46 Jesus cried out in a loud voice,
"Father! In your hands I place my spirit!"
He said this and died.
47 The army officer saw what had happened, and he praised God, saying, "Certainly he was a good man!"
48 When the people who had gathered
there to watch the spectacle saw what happened, they all went back home, beating
their breasts in sorrow. 49 All those who

[c] **23:34** *Some manuscripts do not have* Jesus said, "Forgive them, Father! They don't know what they are doing."
23:34 Ps 22:18 **23:35** Ps 22:7 **23:36** Ps 69:21 **23:45** Ex 26:31–33 **23:46** Ps 31:5 **23:49** Lk 8:2, 3

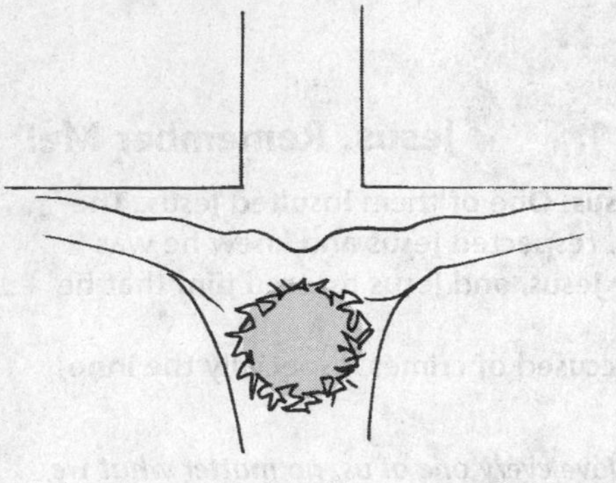

"Father! In your hands I place my spirit!" (23:46)

knew Jesus personally, including the women
who had followed him from Galilee, stood at
a distance to watch.

The Burial of Jesus
(Matthew 27:57–61; Mark 15:42–47; John 19:38–42)

50-51 There was a man named Joseph from
Arimathea, a town in Judea. He was a good
and honorable man, who was waiting for the
coming of the Kingdom of God. Although he
was a member of the Council, he had not
agreed with their decision and action. 52He
went into the presence of Pilate and asked for
the body of Jesus. 53Then he took the body
down, wrapped it in a linen sheet, and placed
it in a tomb which had been dug out of solid
rock and which had never been used. 54It was
Friday, and the Sabbath was about to begin.
55The women who had followed Jesus
from Galilee went with Joseph and saw the
tomb and how Jesus' body was placed in it.
56Then they went back home and prepared
the spices and perfumes for the body.

On the Sabbath they rested, as the Law commanded.

The Resurrection
(Matthew 28:1–10; Mark 16:1–8; John 20:1–10)

24 Very early on Sunday morning the
women went to the tomb, carrying
the spices they had prepared. 2They found
the stone rolled away from the entrance to
the tomb, 3so they went in; but they did not
find the body of the Lord Jesus. 4They stood
there puzzled about this, when suddenly two
men in bright shining clothes stood by
them. 5Full of fear, the women bowed down
to the ground, as the men said to them,
"Why are you looking among the dead for
one who is alive? 6He is not here; he has
been raised. Remember what he said to you
while he was in Galilee: 7'The Son of Man
must be handed over to sinners, be crucified,
and three days later rise to life.' "

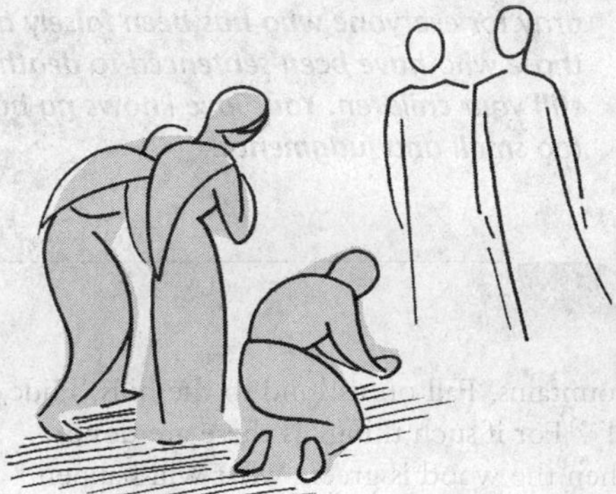

"He is not here; he has been raised." (24:6)

8Then the women remembered his words,
9returned from the tomb, and told all these
things to the eleven disciples and all the rest.
10The women were Mary Magdalene, Joan-
na, and Mary the mother of James; they and
the other women with them told these
things to the apostles. 11But the apostles
thought that what the women said was non-
sense, and they did not believe them. 12But
Peter got up and ran to the tomb; he bent
down and saw the grave cloths but nothing
else. Then he went back home amazed at
what had happened.[d]

The Walk to Emmaus
(Mark 16:12, 13)

13On that same day two of Jesus' followers
were going to a village named Emmaus,
about seven miles from Jerusalem, 14and they

[d] **24:12** *Some manuscripts do not have verse 12.*

23:56 Ex 20:10; Deut 5:14 **24:6, 7** Mt 16:21; 17:22, 23; 20:18, 19; Mk 8:31; 9:31; 10:33, 34; Lk 9:22; 18:31–33

Catholic Connections

Celebrate Easter

Even though the word *Easter* never appears in the Bible, it is the word used in English to describe the most important Christian feast. Easter is the day on which Christians celebrate Jesus' Resurrection from the dead in a special way. It is one of the holiest days of the Church year, and the Easter season lasts fifty days until Pentecost. It truly is a time to celebrate the great joy and wonder of the Resurrection. The Sunday readings focus on the appearances of Jesus that are recorded in the four Gospels and the stories of the start of the Church, from the Acts of the Apostles. The Easter season gives each of us hope and joy because death has been overcome. Throughout the Easter season we sing, "Alleluia!"

— Luke 24:1–12

were talking to each other about all the
things that had happened. 15 As they talked
and discussed, Jesus himself drew near and
walked along with them; 16 they saw him, but
somehow did not recognize him. 17 Jesus said
to them, "What are you talking about to
each other, as you walk along?"

They stood still, with sad faces. 18 One of
them, named Cleopas, asked him, "Are you
the only visitor in Jerusalem who doesn't
know the things that have been happening
there these last few days?"

19 "What things?" he asked.

"The things that happened to Jesus of
Nazareth," they answered. "This man was a
prophet and was considered by God and by
all the people to be powerful in everything
he said and did. 20 Our chief priests and
rulers handed him over to be sentenced to
death, and he was crucified. 21 And we had
hoped that he would be the one who was
going to set Israel free! Besides all that, this is
now the third day since it happened. 22 Some
of the women of our group surprised us;
they went at dawn to the tomb, 23 but could
not find his body. They came back saying
they had seen a vision of angels who told
them that he is alive. 24 Some of our group
went to the tomb and found it exactly as the
women had said, but they did not see him."

25 Then Jesus said to them, "How foolish
you are, how slow you are to believe every-
thing the prophets said! 26 Was it not necessary
for the Messiah to suffer these things and then
to enter his glory?" 27 And Jesus explained to
them what was said about himself in all the
Scriptures, beginning with the books of
Moses and the writings of all the prophets.

28 As they came near the village to which
they were going, Jesus acted as if he were
going farther; 29 but they held him back, say-
ing, "Stay with us; the day is almost over and
it is getting dark." So he went in to stay with
them. 30 He sat down to eat with them, took
the bread, and said the blessing; then he
broke the bread and gave it to them. 31 Then
their eyes were opened and they recognized
him, but he disappeared from their sight.
32 They said to each other, "Wasn't it like a
fire burning in us when he talked to us on
the road and explained the Scriptures to us?"

33 They got up at once and went back to
Jerusalem, where they found the eleven dis-
ciples gathered together with the others
34 and saying, "The Lord is risen indeed! He
has appeared to Simon!"

Mary Magdalene and Joanna are mentioned earlier in this Gospel. Try to find the passage (hint: it's near the parable of the sower).

Pray it!

Walking with Jesus

Doesn't it seem odd that Jesus' followers would not have recognized him after his Resurrection? But Cleopas and his companion were so upset by what had happened to Jesus in Jerusalem, that he was probably the last person they expected to join them on the road. Jesus always seems to be either teaching or healing. In this wonderful Emmaus story, he does both. He helps these two people understand what has happened and then shares a meal with them. Once he breaks the bread—a familiar gesture to Jesus' followers—they know who he is. They can't wait to tell the others the Good News!

You, too, might not always recognize that Jesus is walking with you, but he is there. It is easy to get too distracted by our busy lives or by our worries to notice him. The next time you are feeling alone or upset, find a quiet place and pray. Think about the disciples on the road to Emmaus and remember that Jesus walks with you too. Ask Jesus to let you see his presence. And be sure to remember that when the priest blesses the bread and wine, Jesus is there!

— Luke 24:13–35

35 The two then explained to them what
had happened on the road, and how they
had recognized the Lord when he broke the
bread.

Jesus Appears to His Disciples
(Matthew 28:16–20; Mark 16:14–18; John 20:19–23; Acts 1:6–8)

36 While the two were telling them this,
suddenly the Lord himself stood among
them and said to them, "Peace be with
you."[e]
37 They were terrified, thinking that they
were seeing a ghost. 38 But he said to them,
"Why are you alarmed? Why are these
doubts coming up in your minds? 39 Look at
my hands and my feet, and see that it is I
myself. Feel me, and you will know, for a
ghost doesn't have flesh and bones, as you
can see I have."
40 He said this and showed them his hands
and his feet.[f] 41 They still could not believe,
they were so full of joy and wonder; so he
asked them, "Do you have anything here to
eat?" 42 They gave him a piece of cooked
fish, 43 which he took and ate in their presence.
44 Then he said to them, "These are the
very things I told you about while I was
still with you: everything written about me
in the Law of Moses, the writings of the
prophets, and the Psalms had to come
true."
45 Then he opened their minds to understand the Scriptures,
46 and said to them,
"This is what is written: the Messiah must
suffer and must rise from death three days
later, 47 and in his name the message about
repentance and the forgiveness of sins must
be preached to all nations, beginning in
Jerusalem. 48 You are witnesses of these

[e] **24:36** *Some manuscripts do not have* and said to them, "Peace be with you." [f] **24:40** *Some manuscripts do not have verse 40.*

" 'Everything written about me in the Law of Moses, the writings of the prophets, and the Psalms had to come true' " *(Luke 24:44)*.

things. 49And I myself will send upon you
what my Father has promised. But you
must wait in the city until the power from
above comes down upon you."

Jesus Is Taken Up to Heaven
(Mark 16:19, 20; Acts 1:9–11)

50Then he led them out of the city as far
as Bethany, where he raised his hands and
blessed them. 51As he was blessing them, he
departed from them and was taken up into
heaven.[g] 52They worshiped him and went
back into Jerusalem, filled with great joy,
53and spent all their time in the Temple giv-
ing thanks to God.

As he was blessing them . . . (24:51)

[g] **24:51** *Some manuscripts do not have* and was taken up into heaven.
24:49 Acts 1:4 **24:50, 51** Acts 1:9–11 **24:51** Sir 50:20

Your Next Step

Congratulations on finishing the Gospel of Luke! Use this space to write your thoughts and questions about this book. If you are following the suggested reading plan, move ahead to the Acts of the Apostles. This is the second part of Luke's two-part series and tells the exciting story of the Apostles and the early Church.

The Gospel According to John

Have you ever heard the same family story told by different people? Maybe your grandmother tells it one way, and your dad another, and your serious aunt a very different way. Each of these stories is about the same event and is true, but the story is told from different viewpoints. That is the way it is with John's Gospel. The Gospels of Matthew, Mark, and Luke tell Jesus' story in similar ways, but John is like your serious aunt.

Because of this the Gospel according to John is less action oriented and more teaching oriented. Jesus performs for fewer mircles than he does in the other three Gospels. From the very beginning, John focuses on how Jesus is really the Messiah and the Son of God.

Chap. 11

Headlines

- Wedding Saved! Water Turns to Wine (2:1–12)
- Samaritan Woman's Secrets Revealed (4:4–19)
- A Few Loaves Feed Thousands (6:1–15)
- Dead Man Raised Four Days Later! (11:1–44)
- Jesus Washes Feet, Peter Shocked (chapter 13)
- Jesus Offers Prayer for Friends (chapter 17)
- Mary Magdalene Is First Witness (20:1–18)

FACTOIDS

Who wrote this book? Probably someone who knew John because the Gospel is named after the Apostle John, son of Zebedee.

When was it written? Around AD 90 to 100, about sixty years after Jesus' Resurrection.

Who was it written for? It was originally written for a community of both Jewish and Gentile (non-Jewish) Christians. John shows that Jesus is the Messiah the Jewish people expected and the Savior of all people.

Why was it written? It was written to show that Jesus is the Messiah and the Son of God and that eternal life comes only through faith in him.

What is the literary style? The book is a Gospel, which is a religious explanation of Jesus' life. It uses a lot of symbolic language.

Important themes

- Jesus is the Messiah and the divine Son of God.
- Contrasts between light and darkness, life and death, and truth and lies are made in many places.
- The role of the Holy Spirit is emphasized.

JOHN

Pray it!

In the Beginning

God of all time,
As I learn about you in John's Gospel,
Help me keep my mind on the Word
so that I stay focused on you.
Help me hear the Word
so that I understand it with my heart.
Help me understand the Word
so that I both know and Live It!
And help me live the Word
so that I do more than just think about it.
When I know, and understand, and live,
and do your Word
I will shout Alleluia!
Amen.

— John 1:1–14

The Word of Life

1 In the beginning the Word already exist-
ed; the Word was with God, and the
Word was God. 2From the very beginning
the Word was with God. 3Through him God
made all things; not one thing in all creation
was made without him. 4The Word was the
source of life,[a] and this life brought light to
people. 5The light shines in the darkness, and
the darkness has never put it out.
6God sent his messenger, a man named
John, 7who came to tell people about the
light, so that all should hear the message and
believe. 8He himself was not the light; he
came to tell about the light. 9This was the
real light—the light that comes into the
world and shines on all people.
10The Word was in the world, and though
God made the world through him, yet the
world did not recognize him. 11He came to
his own country, but his own people did not
receive him. 12Some, however, did receive
him and believed in him; so he gave them
the right to become God's children. 13They
did not become God's children by natural
means, that is, by being born as the children
of a human father; God himself was their
Father.
14The Word became a human being and,
full of grace and truth, lived among us. We
saw his glory, the glory which he received as
the Father's only Son.
15John spoke about him. He cried out,
"This is the one I was talking about when I
said, 'He comes after me, but he is greater
than I am, because he existed before I was
born.' "
16Out of the fullness of his grace he has
blessed us all, giving us one blessing after
another. 17God gave the Law through
Moses, but grace and truth came through
Jesus Christ. 18No one has ever seen God.

[a] **1:4** The Word was the source of life; *or* What was made had life in union with the Word.
1:6 Mt 3:1; Mk 1:4; Lk 3:1, 2

The only Son, who is the same as God and
is at the Father's side, he has made him
known.

John the Baptist's Message
(Matthew 3:1–12; Mark 1:1–8;
Luke 3:1–18)

19The Jewish authorities in Jerusalem sent
some priests and Levites to John to ask him,
"Who are you?"
20John did not refuse to answer, but spoke
out openly and clearly, saying: "I am not the
Messiah."
21"Who are you, then?" they asked. "Are
you Elijah?"
"No, I am not," John answered.
"Are you the Prophet?"[b] they asked.
"No," he replied.
22"Then tell us who you are," they said. "We
have to take an answer back to those who sent
us. What do you say about yourself?"
23John answered by quoting the prophet
Isaiah:
"I am 'the voice of someone shouting in
the desert:
Make a straight path for the Lord to
travel!' "
24The messengers, who had been sent by
the Pharisees, 25then[c] asked John, "If you are
not the Messiah nor Elijah nor the Prophet,
why do you baptize?"
26John answered, "I baptize with water,
but among you stands the one you do not
know. 27He is coming after me, but I am not
good enough even to untie his sandals."
28All this happened in Bethany on the
east side of the Jordan River, where John
was baptizing.

The Lamb of God

29The next day John saw Jesus coming to
him, and said, "There is the Lamb of God,
who takes away the sin of the world! 30This
is the one I was talking about when I said,
'A man is coming after me, but he is greater
than I am, because he existed before I was
born.' 31I did not know who he would be,
but I came baptizing with water in order to
make him known to the people of Israel."
32And John gave this testimony: "I saw the
Spirit come down like a dove from heaven
and stay on him. 33I still did not know that
he was the one, but God, who sent me to
baptize with water, had said to me, 'You will
see the Spirit come down and stay on a
man; he is the one who baptizes with the
Holy Spirit.' 34I have seen it," said John, "and
I tell you that he is the Son of God."

I saw the Spirit come down like a dove. (1:32)

The First Disciples of Jesus

35The next day John was standing there
again with two of his disciples, 36when he
saw Jesus walking by. "There is the Lamb of
God!" he said.
37The two disciples heard him say this and

[b] **1:21** THE PROPHET: *The one who was expected to appear and announce the coming of the Messiah.* [c] **1:25** The messengers, who had been sent by the Pharisees, then; *or* Those who had been sent were Pharisees; they.
1:21 **a** Mal 4:5; **b** Deut 18:15, 18; Sir 48:10, 11 **1:23** Isa 40:3 (LXX)

John the Baptist appears in all four Gospels. John's Gospel, though, doesn't have the story of John the Baptist baptizing Jesus.

went with Jesus. 38Jesus turned, saw them following him, and asked, "What are you looking for?"

They answered, "Where do you live, Rabbi?" (This word means "Teacher.")

39"Come and see," he answered. (It was then about four o'clock in the afternoon.) So they went with him and saw where he lived, and spent the rest of that day with him.

40One of them was Andrew, Simon Peter's brother. 41At once he found his brother Simon and told him, "We have found the Messiah." (This word means "Christ.") 42Then he took Simon to Jesus.

Jesus looked at him and said, "Your name is Simon son of John, but you will be called Cephas." (This is the same as Peter and means "a rock.")

Jesus Calls Philip and Nathanael

43The next day Jesus decided to go to Galilee. He found Philip and said to him, "Come with me!" (44Philip was from Bethsaida, the town where Andrew and Peter lived.) 45Philip found Nathanael and told him, "We have found the one whom Moses wrote about in the book of the Law and whom the prophets also wrote about. He is Jesus son of Joseph, from Nazareth."

46"Can anything good come from Nazareth?" Nathanael asked.

"Come and see," answered Philip.

47When Jesus saw Nathanael coming to him, he said about him, "Here is a real Israelite; there is nothing false in him!"

48Nathanael asked him, "How do you know me?"

Jesus answered, "I saw you when you were under the fig tree before Philip called you."

49"Teacher," answered Nathanael, "you are the Son of God! You are the King of Israel!"

50Jesus said, "Do you believe just because I told you I saw you when you were under the fig tree? You will see much greater things than this!" 51And he said to them, "I am telling you the truth: you will see heaven open and God's angels going up and coming down on the Son of Man."

1:51 Gen 28:12

Live it!

What's Your Name?

When Jesus changes Simon's name to Cephas (John 1:42), he's showing the important role Peter would play in the Church. Often people are named for a reason—for example, in honor of a relative or a saint or another significant person. Have your ever found out why you were given the name you have? Do you know what your name means?

Here's an interesting exercise for your imagination. If you were to choose your own secret name, what would it be and why? What does this name say about you and what's important to you? You could even make a symbol of this secret name and keep it on your dresser. It would serve as a reminder of the values you want to live.

— John 1:42

The Wedding in Cana

2 Two days later there was a wedding in the town of Cana in Galilee. Jesus' mother was there, 2and Jesus and his disciples had also been invited to the wedding. 3When the wine had given out, Jesus' mother said to him, "They are out of wine."

4"You must not tell me what to do," Jesus replied. "My time has not yet come."

5Jesus' mother then told the servants, "Do whatever he tells you."

6The Jews have rules about ritual washing, and for this purpose six stone water jars were there, each one large enough to hold between twenty and thirty gallons. 7Jesus said to the servants, "Fill these jars with water." They filled them to the brim, 8and then he told them, "Now draw some water out and take it

Mary as the First Disciple

At the beginning of chapter 2, notice that Jesus was like us—he liked parties! The wedding party was going along great. The bride and groom were happy, and the guests were having a lot of fun. Then Jesus' mother, Mary, noticed that the wine was running out. She believed Jesus could do something about it, and he did!

Mary's belief in Jesus at the wedding feast, her yes to the angel (see Luke 1:26–38), and her place at the foot of the cross (see John 19:25) all show her special place in God's plan. She is so special that she is sometimes called the first disciple. A disciple is a believer. John shows that she was one of the very first people to believe in Jesus' power.

— John 2:1–12

to the man in charge of the feast." They took
him the water, 9which now had turned into
wine, and he tasted it. He did not know
where this wine had come from (but, of
course, the servants who had drawn out the
water knew); so he called the bridegroom
10and said to him, "Everyone else serves the
best wine first, and after the guests have drunk
a lot, he serves the ordinary wine. But you
have kept the best wine until now!"
11Jesus performed this first miracle in
Cana in Galilee; there he revealed his glory,
and his disciples believed in him.

"Fill these jars with water." (2:7)

12After this, Jesus and his mother, broth-
ers, and disciples went to Capernaum and
stayed there a few days.

Jesus Goes to the Temple
(Matthew 21:12, 13; Mark 11:15–17; Luke 19:45, 46)

13It was almost time for the Passover Fes-
tival, so Jesus went to Jerusalem. 14There in
the Temple he found people selling cattle,
sheep, and pigeons, and also the money-
changers sitting at their tables. 15So he made
a whip from cords and drove all the animals
out of the Temple, both the sheep and the
cattle; he overturned the tables of the mon-
eychangers and scattered their coins; 16and
he ordered those who sold the pigeons,
"Take them out of here! Stop making my
Father's house a marketplace!" 17His disciples
remembered that the scripture says, "My
devotion to your house, O God, burns in me
like a fire."
18The Jewish authorities came back at
him with a question, "What miracle can you
perform to show us that you have the right
to do this?"
19Jesus answered, "Tear down this Temple,
and in three days I will build it again."
20"Are you going to build it again in

2:12 Mt 4:13 **2:13** Ex 12:1–27 **2:17** Ps 69:9 **2:19** Mt 26:61; 27:40; Mk 14:58; 15:29

Catholic Connections

Baptism, Born Again!

Have you seen pictures or heard stories about your own Baptism? Most Catholics are baptized as infants and don't remember their Baptism. If you are like many people, you don't remember the water that was poured over your head. You don't remember the holy oil, or chrism, representing the gift of the Holy Spirit that you were crossed with. Maybe your parents kept the candle that was lit for you as a symbol of Christ's light. You might still have your baptismal clothes, which are usually white as a symbol of having our sins washed away. Baptism is the way Christians enter the Church. It is a spiritual rebirth that makes us part of God's family, and it is open to all.

The story of Jesus and Nicodemus is really about Baptism. Nicodemus gets the wrong idea, thinking that Jesus is talking about physical birth. Jesus' answer to Nicodemus tells us how important Baptism is. "'I am telling you the truth,' replied Jesus, 'that no one can enter the Kingdom of God without being born of water and the Spirit'" (John 3:5).

— John 3:1–8

three days?" they asked him. "It has taken
forty-six years to build this Temple!"
21But the temple Jesus was speaking about
was his body. 22So when he was raised from
death, his disciples remembered that he had
said this, and they believed the scripture and
what Jesus had said.

Jesus' Knowledge of Human Nature

23While Jesus was in Jerusalem during the
Passover Festival, many believed in him as
they saw the miracles he performed. 24But
Jesus did not trust himself to them, because
he knew them all. 25There was no need for
anyone to tell him about them, because he
himself knew what was in their hearts.

Jesus and Nicodemus

3 There was a Jewish leader named
Nicodemus, who belonged to the party
of the Pharisees. 2One night he went to
Jesus and said to him, "Rabbi, we know that
you are a teacher sent by God. No one
could perform the miracles you are doing
unless God were with him."
3Jesus answered, "I am telling you the
truth: no one can see the Kingdom of God
without being born again."[d]
4"How can a grown man be born again?"
Nicodemus asked. "He certainly cannot
enter his mother's womb and be born a sec-
ond time!"
5"I am telling you the truth," replied Jesus,
"that no one can enter the Kingdom of God
without being born of water and the Spirit.
6A person is born physically of human par-
ents, but is born spiritually of the Spirit. 7Do
not be surprised because I tell you that you
must all be born again.[d] 8The wind blows
wherever it wishes; you hear the sound it
makes, but you do not know where it comes

[d] **3:3,7** again; *or* from above.

John does not have nearly as many miracles as the other Gospels. Can you count the number of miracle stories in John's Gospel?

from or where it is going. It is like that with
everyone who is born of the Spirit."
9 "How can this be?" asked Nicodemus.
10 Jesus answered, "You are a great teacher
in Israel, and you don't know this? 11 I am
telling you the truth: we speak of what we
know and report what we have seen, yet
none of you is willing to accept our mes-
sage. 12 You do not believe me when I tell
you about the things of this world; how will
you ever believe me, then, when I tell you
about the things of heaven? 13 And no one
has ever gone up to heaven except the Son
of Man, who came down from heaven."[e]
14 As Moses lifted up the bronze snake on
a pole in the desert, in the same way the Son
of Man must be lifted up, 15 so that everyone
who believes in him may have eternal life.
16 For God loved the world so much that he
gave his only Son, so that everyone who
believes in him may not die but have eternal
life. 17 For God did not send his Son into the
world to be its judge, but to be its savior.
18 Those who believe in the Son are not
judged; but those who do not believe have
already been judged, because they have not
believed in God's only Son. 19 This is how the
judgment works: the light has come into the
world, but people love the darkness rather
than the light, because their deeds are evil.
20 Those who do evil things hate the light
and will not come to the light, because they
do not want their evil deeds to be shown up.
21 But those who do what is true come to the
light in order that the light may show that
what they did was in obedience to God.

Live it!

John 3:16

John 3:16 is an important line in the Bible. It is God's plan for saving the human race summed up in a simple statement. The whole Gospel is about God's love but this is the first time it is named. Because it is so important, many people memorize it. Some people even hold up signs at ball games that say "John 3:16" so others will read it.

Some people try to memorize as much of the Bible as they can. Memorizing Bible verses can be fun. Choose one that you would really like to learn. It is a good idea to ask someone (like a teacher, catechist, parent, or priest) to help you understand it first. Once you memorize it, keep it in your heart and live it!

— John 3:16

Jesus and John

22 After this, Jesus and his disciples went to
the province of Judea, where he spent some
time with them and baptized. 23 John also
was baptizing in Aenon, not far from Salim,
because there was plenty of water in that
place. People were going to him, and he was
baptizing them. (24 This was before John had
been put in prison.)
25 Some of John's disciples began arguing
with a Jew[f] about the matter of ritual wash-
ing. 26 So they went to John and told him,
"Teacher, you remember the man who was
with you on the east side of the Jordan, the
one you spoke about? Well, he is baptizing
now, and everyone is going to him!"
27 John answered, "No one can have any-
thing unless God gives it. 28 You yourselves
are my witnesses that I said, 'I am not the
Messiah, but I have been sent ahead of him.'
29 The bridegroom is the one to whom the
bride belongs; but the bridegroom's friend,

[e] **3:13** *The quotation may continue through verse 21.* [f] **3:25** a Jew; *some manuscripts have* some Jews.
3:12 Wis 9:16, 17 **3:13** Bar 3:29 **3:14** Num 21:9; Wis 16:5–7 **3:24** Mt 14:3; Mk 6:17; Lk 3:19, 20
3:28 Jn 1:20

The story about the bronze snake *(John 3:14)* **can be found in Numbers 21:4–9.**

who stands by and listens, is glad when he hears the bridegroom's voice. This is how my own happiness is made complete. 30He must become more important while I become less important."

He Who Comes from Heaven

31He who comes from above is greater than all. He who is from the earth belongs to the earth and speaks about earthly matters, but he who comes from heaven is above all. 32He tells what he has seen and heard, yet no one accepts his message. 33But whoever accepts his message confirms by this that God is truthful. 34The one whom God has sent speaks God's words, because God gives him the fullness of his Spirit. 35The Father loves his Son and has put everything in his power. 36Whoever believes in the Son has eternal life; whoever disobeys the Son will not have life, but will remain under God's punishment.

Jesus and the Samaritan Woman

4 The Pharisees heard that Jesus was winning and baptizing more disciples than John. (2Actually, Jesus himself did not baptize anyone; only his disciples did.) 3So when Jesus heard what was being said, he left Judea and went back to Galilee; 4on his way there he had to go through Samaria.

5In Samaria he came to a town named Sychar, which was not far from the field that Jacob had given to his son Joseph. 6Jacob's well was there, and Jesus, tired out by the trip, sat down by the well. It was about noon.

7A Samaritan woman came to draw some water, and Jesus said to her, "Give me a drink of water." (8His disciples had gone into town to buy food.)

9The woman answered, "You are a Jew, and I am a Samaritan—so how can you ask me for a drink?" (Jews will not use the same cups and bowls that Samaritans use.)[g]

10Jesus answered, "If you only knew what God gives and who it is that is asking you for a drink, you would ask him, and he would give you life-giving water."

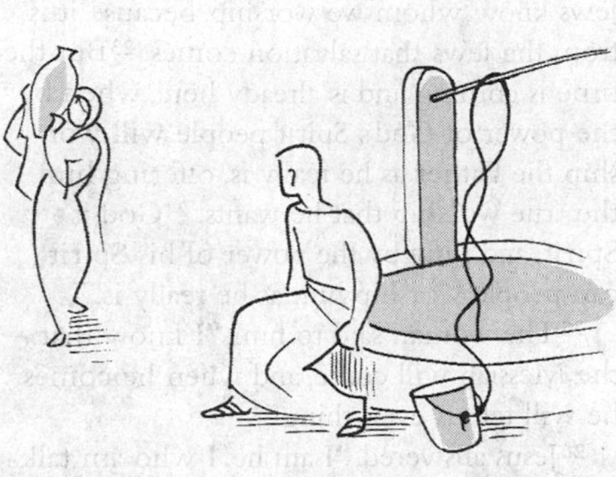

"Give me a drink of water." (4:7)

11"Sir," the woman said, "you don't have a bucket, and the well is deep. Where would you get that life-giving water? 12It was our ancestor Jacob who gave us this well; he and his children and his flocks all drank from it. You don't claim to be greater than Jacob, do you?"

13Jesus answered, "Those who drink this water will get thirsty again, 14but those who drink the water that I will give them will never be thirsty again. The water that I will give them will become in them a spring which will provide them with life-giving water and give them eternal life."

15"Sir," the woman said, "give me that water! Then I will never be thirsty again, nor will I have to come here to draw water."

16"Go and call your husband," Jesus told her, "and come back."

17"I don't have a husband," she answered.

Jesus replied, "You are right when you say you don't have a husband. 18You have been married to five men, and the man you live with now is not really your husband. You have told me the truth."

19"I see you are a prophet, sir," the woman said. 20"My Samaritan ancestors worshiped God on this mountain, but you Jews say that Jerusalem is the place where we should worship God."

21Jesus said to her, "Believe me, woman, the time will come when people will not worship the Father either on this mountain or in Jerusalem. 22You Samaritans do not really know whom you worship; but we

[g] **4:9** Jews will not use the same cups and bowls that Samaritans use; *or* Jews will have nothing to do with Samaritans.

3:35 Mt 11:27; Lk 10:22 **4:5** Gen 33:19; Josh 24:32 **4:9** Ezra 4:1–5; Neh 4:1, 2

Jews know whom we worship, because it is
from the Jews that salvation comes. 23But the
time is coming and is already here, when by
the power of God's Spirit people will wor-
ship the Father as he really is, offering him
the true worship that he wants. 24God is
Spirit, and only by the power of his Spirit
can people worship him as he really is."
25The woman said to him, "I know that
the Messiah will come, and when he comes,
he will tell us everything."
26Jesus answered, "I am he, I who am talk-
ing with you."
27At that moment Jesus' disciples
returned, and they were greatly surprised to
find him talking with a woman. But none of
them said to her, "What do you want?" or
asked him, "Why are you talking with her?"
28Then the woman left her water jar,
went back to the town, and said to the peo-
ple there, 29"Come and see the man who
told me everything I have ever done. Could
he be the Messiah?" 30So they left the town
and went to Jesus.
31In the meantime the disciples were beg-
ging Jesus, "Teacher, have something to eat!"
32But he answered, "I have food to eat
that you know nothing about."
33So the disciples started asking among
themselves, "Could somebody have brought
him food?"
34"My food," Jesus said to them, "is to
obey the will of the one who sent me and to
finish the work he gave me to do. 35You
have a saying, 'Four more months and then
the harvest.' But I tell you, take a good look
at the fields; the crops are now ripe and
ready to be harvested! 36The one who reaps
the harvest is being paid and gathers the
crops for eternal life; so the one who plants
and the one who reaps will be glad together.
37For the saying is true, 'Someone plants,
someone else reaps.' 38I have sent you to reap
a harvest in a field where you did not work;
others worked there, and you profit from
their work."
39Many of the Samaritans in that town
believed in Jesus because the woman had
said, "He told me everything I have ever
done." 40So when the Samaritans came to
him, they begged him to stay with them, and
Jesus stayed there two days.

Live it!

Who Are You Talking To?

"You shouldn't hang out with her at lunch. She is so weird."

"Let's walk this way so we don't have to go near them."

"Why is Tim talking to the new kid? He wears that weird hat and talks so funny."

Maybe you've heard, or even said, things like this. It is common for people to avoid those who are different. What is uncommon is taking a step toward getting to know those who are different. What is great about taking that step is discovering that people who are different from you have a lot to offer. When people of other cultures first came to this country as immigrants, their food and art were considered strange. Now we think of pizza, tacos, and egg rolls as regular food!

Jesus is a great example of someone who is not afraid to reach out to someone who is different from him. Not many Jewish men would talk to a woman in public, especially a Samaritan woman. Men and women were often separated, and Samaritans were disliked by the Jews. But Jesus stepped over those lines and sat with the woman at the well. The next time you come across someone who is different from you, remember how Jesus treated the woman at the well.

— John 4:1–42

41Many more believed because of his mes-
sage, 42and they told the woman, "We believe
now, not because of what you said, but because
we ourselves have heard him, and we know
that he really is the Savior of the world."

Pray it!

Help Me Believe

The father in this story believed in Jesus' power. At first he wanted Jesus to come to his house to heal his son. Jesus did not have to go to the house. He healed the boy because the father believed. Try this prayer when believing is hard for you.

Dear God,
You healed the official's son because he believed in you.
Help me to have that much faith.
Help me believe in you even when it is hard.
Show me how you work in my life.
Teach me to give you my cares,
like the official in the story.
Lead me to where you want me to be.
Amen.

— John 4:46–54

Jesus Heals an Official's Son

43 After spending two days there, Jesus left and went to Galilee. 44 For he himself had said, "Prophets are not respected in their own country." 45 When he arrived in Galilee, the people there welcomed him, because they had gone to the Passover Festival in Jerusalem and had seen everything that he had done during the festival.

46 Then Jesus went back to Cana in Galilee, where he had turned the water into wine. A government official was there whose son was sick in Capernaum. 47 When he heard that Jesus had come from Judea to Galilee, he went to him and asked him to go to Capernaum and heal his son, who was about to die. 48 Jesus said to him, "None of you will ever believe unless you see miracles and wonders."

49 "Sir," replied the official, "come with me before my child dies."

50 Jesus said to him, "Go; your son will live!"

The man believed Jesus' words and went. 51 On his way home his servants met him with the news, "Your boy is going to live!"

52 He asked them what time it was when his son got better, and they answered, "It was one o'clock yesterday afternoon when the fever left him." 53 Then the father remembered that it was at that very hour when Jesus had told him, "Your son will live." So he and all his family believed.

54 This was the second miracle that Jesus performed after coming from Judea to Galilee.

The Healing at the Pool

5 After this, Jesus went to Jerusalem for a religious festival. 2 Near the Sheep Gate in Jerusalem there is a pool[h] with five porches; in Hebrew it is called Bethzatha.[i] 3 A

[h] **5:2** Near the Sheep Gate . . . a pool; *or* Near the Sheep Pool . . . a place. [i] **5:2** Bethzatha; *some manuscripts have* Bethesda.
4:44 Mt 13:57; Mk 6:4; Lk 4:24 **4:45** Jn 2:23 **4:46** Jn 2:1–11

What do you know about water? How much of the human body is made of water? How long can you live without drinking?

Pray it!

Working Together

If at times you feel that your homework or chores are too much, try this prayer:

Jesus, you worked hard healing and caring for others. You were able to do all of this because of the love of your Father. Help me to work and care for others without complaining. Help me be thankful for the ability to work, for my arms and legs—some kids can't use theirs. Help me be thankful for my brain—some kids don't learn well. Help me be thankful for homework—some kids don't have a chance to go to school. Help me be thankful for chores—some kids don't have a kitchen to do dishes in or a rug to vacuum. And most of all, help me remember to be thankful for those who care about me: family, teachers, and, of course, you. Thank you, Jesus, for the example you show me.
Amen.

— John 5:1–18

large crowd of sick people were lying on the
porches—the blind, the lame, and the para-
lyzed.[j] 5 A man was there who had been sick
for thirty-eight years. 6 Jesus saw him lying
there, and he knew that the man had been
sick for such a long time; so he asked him,
"Do you want to get well?"
7 The sick man answered, "Sir, I don't have
anyone here to put me in the pool when the
water is stirred up; while I am trying to get
in, somebody else gets there first."
8 Jesus said to him, "Get up, pick up your
mat, and walk." 9 Immediately the man got
well; he picked up his mat and started walking.
The day this happened was a Sabbath, 10 so
the Jewish authorities told the man who had
been healed, "This is a Sabbath, and it is
against our Law for you to carry your mat."
11 He answered, "The man who made me
well told me to pick up my mat and walk."
12 They asked him, "Who is the man who
told you to do this?"
13 But the man who had been healed did
not know who Jesus was, for there was a
crowd in that place, and Jesus had slipped away.
14 Afterward, Jesus found him in the Tem-
ple and said, "Listen, you are well now; so
stop sinning or something worse may hap-
pen to you."
15 Then the man left and told the Jewish
authorities that it was Jesus who had healed
him. 16 So they began to persecute Jesus,
because he had done this healing on a Sab-
bath. 17 Jesus answered them, "My Father is
always working, and I too must work."
18 This saying made the Jewish authorities
all the more determined to kill him; not
only had he broken the Sabbath law, but he
had said that God was his own Father and in
this way had made himself equal with God.

The Authority of the Son

19 So Jesus answered them, "I tell you the
truth: the Son can do nothing on his own;
he does only what he sees his Father doing.

[j] **5:3** *Some manuscripts add verses 3b–4:* They were waiting for the water to move, 4 because every now and then an angel of the Lord went down into the pool and stirred up the water. The first sick person to go into the pool after the water was stirred up was healed from whatever disease he had.
5:10 Neh 13:19; Jer 17:21 **5:18** Wis 2:16

If you were the sick man, how would you feel after Jesus healed you? How would you feel when the authorities questioned you *(John 5:1–14)***?**

What the Father does, the Son also does. 20 For the Father loves the Son and shows him all that he himself is doing. He will show him even greater things to do than this, and you will all be amazed. 21 Just as the Father raises the dead and gives them life, in the same way the Son gives life to those he wants to. 22 Nor does the Father himself judge anyone. He has given his Son the full right to judge, 23 so that all will honor the Son in the same way as they honor the Father. Whoever does not honor the Son does not honor the Father who sent him.

24 "I am telling you the truth: those who hear my words and believe in him who sent me have eternal life. They will not be judged, but have already passed from death to life. 25 I am telling you the truth: the time is coming—the time has already come—when the dead will hear the voice of the Son of God, and those who hear it will come to life. 26 Just as the Father is himself the source of life, in the same way he has made his Son to be the source of life. 27 And he has given the Son the right to judge, because he is the Son of Man. 28 Do not be surprised at this; the time is coming when all the dead will hear his voice 29 and come out of their graves: those who have done good will rise and live, and those who have done evil will rise and be condemned.

Witnesses to Jesus

30 "I can do nothing on my own authority; I judge only as God tells me, so my judgment is right, because I am not trying to do what I want, but only what he who sent me wants.

31 "If I testify on my own behalf, what I say is not to be accepted as real proof. 32 But there is someone else who testifies on my behalf, and I know that what he says about me is true. 33 John is the one to whom you sent your messengers, and he spoke on behalf of the truth. 34 It is not that I must have a human witness; I say this only in order that you may be saved. 35 John was like a lamp, burning and shining, and you were willing for a while to enjoy his light. 36 But I have a witness on my behalf which is even greater than the witness that John gave: what I do, that is, the deeds my Father gave me to do, these speak on my behalf and show that the Father has sent me. 37 And the Father, who sent me, also testifies on my behalf. You have never heard his voice or seen his face, 38 and you do not keep his message in your hearts, for you do not believe in the one whom he sent. 39 You study the Scriptures, because you think that in them you will find eternal life. And these very Scriptures speak about me! 40 Yet you are not willing to come to me in order to have life.

41 "I am not looking for human praise. 42 But I know what kind of people you are, and I know that you have no love for God in your hearts. 43 I have come with my Father's authority, but you have not received me; when, however, someone comes with his own authority, you will receive him. 44 You like to receive praise from one another, but you do not try to win praise from the one who alone is God; how, then, can you believe me? 45 Do not think, however, that I am the one who will accuse you to my Father. Moses, in whom you have put your hope, is the very one who will accuse you. 46 If you had really believed Moses, you would have believed me, because he wrote about me. 47 But since you do not believe what he wrote, how can you believe what I say?"

Jesus Feeds Five Thousand

(Matthew 14:13–21; Mark 6:30–44; Luke 9:10–17)

6 After this, Jesus went across Lake Galilee (or, Lake Tiberias, as it is also called). 2 A large crowd followed him, because they had seen his miracles of healing the sick. 3 Jesus went up a hill and sat down with his disciples. 4 The time for the Passover Festival was near. 5 Jesus looked around and saw that a large crowd was coming to him, so he asked Philip, "Where can we buy enough food to feed all these people?" (6 He said this to test Philip; actually he already knew what he would do.)

7 Philip answered, "For everyone to have

5:29 Dan 12:2 **5:33** Jn 1:19–27; 3:27–30 **5:35** Sir 48:1 **5:37** Mt 3:17; Mk 1:11; Lk 3:22 **5:39** Bar 4:1

The Eucharist Is Central!

Jesus loved a good meal! He went to weddings and ate, he ate with sinners, and he made sure people didn't go hungry. The story of how a few loaves and fishes fed thousands is in all four Gospels. The Bible references that follow the heading "Jesus Feeds Five Thousand" tell you where this story is in the other Gospels.

In John's Gospel, the story is different from the others. After the miracle, Jesus gives more teaching about the Eucharist (Holy Communion). *Eucharist* means "thanksgiving" in Greek. The Eucharist is central to the Catholic faith. Jesus says, "Those who eat my flesh and drink my blood have eternal life, and I will raise them to life on the last day" (John 6:54). Through the Eucharist we build our relationships with Jesus and with the other members of the Church. As you receive Holy Communion, remind yourself of how it unites you with Christians around the world.

— John, chapter 6

even a little, it would take more than two
hundred silver coins[k] to buy enough bread."
8 Another one of his disciples, Andrew,
who was Simon Peter's brother, said,
9 "There is a boy here who has five loaves of
barley bread and two fish. But they will cer-
tainly not be enough for all these people."
10 "Make the people sit down," Jesus told
them. (There was a lot of grass there.) So all
the people sat down; there were about five
thousand men. 11 Jesus took the bread, gave
thanks to God, and distributed it to the peo-
ple who were sitting there. He did the same
with the fish, and they all had as much as
they wanted. 12 When they were all full, he
said to his disciples, "Gather the pieces left
over; let us not waste a bit." 13 So they gath-
ered them all and filled twelve baskets with
the pieces left over from the five barley
loaves which the people had eaten.
14 Seeing this miracle that Jesus had per-
formed, the people there said, "Surely this is
the Prophet[l] who was to come into the
world!" 15 Jesus knew that they were about to
come and seize him in order to make him
king by force; so he went off again to the
hills by himself.

Jesus Walks on the Water
(Matthew 14:22–33; Mark 6:45–52)

16 When evening came, Jesus' disciples
went down to the lake, 17 got into a boat, and
went back across the lake toward Caper-
naum. Night came on, and Jesus still had not
come to them. 18 By then a strong wind was
blowing and stirring up the water. 19 The
disciples had rowed about three or four miles
when they saw Jesus walking on the water,
coming near the boat, and they were terri-
fied. 20 "Don't be afraid," Jesus told them, "it
is I!" 21 Then they willingly took him into
the boat, and immediately the boat reached
land at the place they were heading for.

The People Seek Jesus

22 Next day the crowd which had stayed
on the other side of the lake realized that
there had been only one boat there. They
knew that Jesus had not gone in it with his

[k] **6:7** SILVER COINS: *A silver coin was the daily wage of a rural worker (see Mt 20:2).* [l] **6:14** THE PROPHET: *See 1:21.*

disciples, but that they had left without him.
23Other boats, which were from Tiberias,
came to shore near the place where the
crowd had eaten the bread after the Lord
had given thanks. 24When the crowd saw
that Jesus was not there, nor his disciples,
they got into those boats and went to
Capernaum, looking for him.

Jesus the Bread of Life

25When the people found Jesus on the
other side of the lake, they said to him,
"Teacher, when did you get here?"
26Jesus answered, "I am telling you the
truth: you are looking for me because you
ate the bread and had all you wanted, not
because you understood my miracles. 27Do
not work for food that spoils; instead, work
for the food that lasts for eternal life. This is
the food which the Son of Man will give
you, because God, the Father, has put his
mark of approval on him."
28So they asked him, "What can we do in
order to do what God wants us to do?"
29Jesus answered, "What God wants you
to do is to believe in the one he sent."
30They replied, "What miracle will you
perform so that we may see it and believe
you? What will you do? 31Our ancestors ate
manna in the desert, just as the scripture says,
'He gave them bread from heaven to eat.' "
32"I am telling you the truth," Jesus said.
"What Moses gave you was not[m] the bread
from heaven; it is my Father who gives you
the real bread from heaven. 33For the bread
that God gives is he who comes down from
heaven and gives life to the world."
34"Sir," they asked him, "give us this bread
always."
35"I am the bread of life," Jesus told them.
"Those who come to me will never be hun-
gry; those who believe in me will never be
thirsty. 36Now, I told you that you have seen
me but will not believe. 37Everyone whom
my Father gives me will come to me. I will
never turn away anyone who comes to me,
38because I have come down from heaven
to do not my own will but the will of him
who sent me. 39And it is the will of him
who sent me that I should not lose any of all
those he has given me, but that I should raise
them all to life on the last day. 40For what
my Father wants is that all who see the Son
and believe in him should have eternal life.
And I will raise them to life on the last day."
41The people started grumbling about
him, because he said, "I am the bread that
came down from heaven." 42So they said,
"This man is Jesus son of Joseph, isn't he? We
know his father and mother. How, then, does
he now say he came down from heaven?"
43Jesus answered, "Stop grumbling among
yourselves. 44People cannot come to me
unless the Father who sent me draws them
to me; and I will raise them to life on the
last day. 45The prophets wrote, 'Everyone
will be taught by God.' Anyone who hears
the Father and learns from him comes to
me. 46This does not mean that anyone has
seen the Father; he who is from God is the
only one who has seen the Father. 47I am
telling you the truth: he who believes has
eternal life. 48I am the bread of life. 49Your
ancestors ate manna in the desert, but they
died. 50But the bread that comes down from
heaven is of such a kind that whoever eats
it will not die. 51I am the living bread that
came down from heaven. If you eat this
bread, you will live forever. The bread that I
will give you is my flesh, which I give so
that the world may live."
52This started an angry argument among
them. "How can this man give us his flesh to
eat?" they asked.
53Jesus said to them, "I am telling you the
truth: if you do not eat the flesh of the Son
of Man and drink his blood, you will not
have life in yourselves. 54Those who eat my
flesh and drink my blood have eternal life,
and I will raise them to life on the last day.
55For my flesh is the real food; my blood is

[m] **6:32** What Moses gave you was not; *or* It was not Moses who gave you.
6:27 Sir 24:19–22 **6:31** Ex 16:4, 15; Ps 78:24; Wis 16:20, 21 **6:45** Isa 54:13

Why would the people want to make Jesus the king *(John 6:15)*? **Why didn't Jesus want to become a king?**

the real drink. 56Those who eat my flesh
and drink my blood live in me, and I live
in them. 57The living Father sent me, and
because of him I live also. In the same way
whoever eats me will live because of me.
58This, then, is the bread that came down
from heaven; it is not like the bread that
your ancestors ate, but then later died.
Those who eat this bread will live forever."
59Jesus said this as he taught in the syna-
gogue in Capernaum.

The Words of Eternal Life

60Many of his followers heard this and
said, "This teaching is too hard. Who can lis-
ten to it?"
61Without being told, Jesus knew that
they were grumbling about this, so he said to
them, "Does this make you want to give up?
62Suppose, then, that you should see the Son
of Man go back up to the place where he
was before? 63What gives life is God's Spirit;
human power is of no use at all. The words I
have spoken to you bring God's life-giving
Spirit. 64Yet some of you do not believe."
(Jesus knew from the very beginning who
were the ones that would not believe and
which one would betray him.) 65And he
added, "This is the very reason I told you
that no people can come to me unless the
Father makes it possible for them to do so."
66Because of this, many of Jesus' followers
turned back and would not go with him any
more. 67So he asked the twelve disciples,
"And you—would you also like to leave?"
68Simon Peter answered him, "Lord, to
whom would we go? You have the words
that give eternal life. 69And now we believe
and know that you are the Holy One who
has come from God."
70Jesus replied, "I chose the twelve of
you, didn't I? Yet one of you is a devil!"
71He was talking about Judas, the son of
Simon Iscariot. For Judas, even though he
was one of the twelve disciples, was going to
betray him.

Live it!

Which Way to Go?

Have you ever thought about not following Jesus? Many of his early followers had a hard time accepting some of the things he said and some left Jesus (John 6:66). His disciples found out it was sometimes hard following Jesus. They also knew that there was no better person to follow. Sometimes we are like the people in this story, and it might seem easier to walk away from what Jesus asks us to do. It might even seem like more fun.

The next time it seems easier not following the things Jesus teaches, ask yourself or someone you trust if it really is. The disciples knew it was better to stick with Jesus. If you give it enough thought, you will realize that doing what Jesus asks is better—not easier, but better.

— John 6:60–71

Jesus and His Brothers

7 After this, Jesus traveled in Galilee; he
did not want to travel in Judea, because
the Jewish authorities there were wanting to
kill him. 2The time for the Festival of Shel-
ters was near, 3so Jesus' brothers said to him,
"Leave this place and go to Judea, so that
your followers will see the things that you
are doing. 4People don't hide what they are
doing if they want to be well known. Since
you are doing these things, let the whole
world know about you!" (5Not even his
brothers believed in him.)

6:63 Wis 9:13–18 **6:68, 69** Mt 16:16; Mk 8:29; Lk 9:20 **7:2** Lev 23:34; Deut 16:13

List all the different things people said about Jesus in chapter 7. Why couldn't they agree on what to think about him?

Pray it!

Loving Either Way

"Stop judging by external standards, and judge by true standards" (John 7:24).

God, you love me whether I am skinny or large, tall or short.
Help me love others who are different from me.
You love me whether I am happy or mad.
Help me love others who are mean or angry.
You love me whether I get straight A's or fail a test.
Help me love others when they seem silly or don't make sense.
You love me whether I win or lose.
Help me love others who compete against me.
You love me no matter what.
Help me to not judge others and to love others the way you do.
Amen.

— John 7:24

6Jesus said to them, "The right time for
me has not yet come. Any time is right for
you. 7The world cannot hate you, but it
hates me, because I keep telling it that its
ways are bad. 8You go on to the festival. I
am not going[n] to this festival, because the
right time has not come for me." 9He said
this and then stayed on in Galilee.

Jesus at the Festival of Shelters

10After his brothers had gone to the festi-
val, Jesus also went; however, he did not go
openly, but secretly. 11The Jewish authorities
were looking for him at the festival. "Where
is he?" they asked.
12There was much whispering about him
in the crowd. "He is a good man," some
people said. "No," others said, "he fools the
people." 13But no one talked about him
openly, because they were afraid of the Jew-
ish authorities.
14The festival was nearly half over when
Jesus went to the Temple and began teaching.
15The Jewish authorities were greatly sur-
prised and said, "How does this man know so
much when he has never been to school?"
16Jesus answered, "What I teach is not
my own teaching, but it comes from God,
who sent me. 17Whoever is willing to do
what God wants will know whether what I
teach comes from God or whether I speak
on my own authority. 18Those who speak
on their own authority are trying to gain
glory for themselves. But he who wants
glory for the one who sent him is honest,
and there is nothing false in him. 19Moses
gave you the Law, didn't he? But not one of
you obeys the Law. Why are you trying to
kill me?"
20"You have a demon in you!" the crowd
answered. "Who is trying to kill you?"
21Jesus answered, "I performed one mira-
cle, and you were all surprised. 22Moses
ordered you to circumcise your sons
(although it was not Moses but your ances-
tors who started it), and so you circumcise a
boy on the Sabbath. 23If a boy is circumcised
on the Sabbath so that Moses' Law is not
broken, why are you angry with me because
I made a man completely well on the Sab-
bath? 24Stop judging by external standards,
and judge by true standards."

[n] **7:8** I am not going; *some manuscripts have* I am not yet going.
7:22 **a** Lev 12:3; **b** Gen 17:10 **7:23** Jn 5:9

Is He the Messiah?

25 Some of the people of Jerusalem said,
"Isn't this the man the authorities are trying
to kill? 26 Look! He is talking in public, and
they say nothing against him! Can it be that
they really know that he is the Messiah?
27 But when the Messiah comes, no one will
know where he is from. And we all know
where this man comes from."
28 As Jesus taught in the Temple, he said in
a loud voice, "Do you really know me and
know where I am from? I have not come on
my own authority. He who sent me, however, is truthful. You do not know him, 29 but I
know him, because I come from him and he
sent me."
30 Then they tried to seize him, but no
one laid a hand on him, because his hour
had not yet come. 31 But many in the crowd
believed in him and said, "When the Messiah comes, will he perform more miracles
than this man has?"

Guards Are Sent to Arrest Jesus

32 The Pharisees heard the crowd whispering these things about Jesus, so they and the
chief priests sent some guards to arrest him.
33 Jesus said, "I shall be with you a little while
longer, and then I shall go away to him who
sent me. 34 You will look for me, but you will
not find me, because you cannot go where I
will be."
35 The Jewish authorities said among
themselves, "Where is he about to go so that
we shall not find him? Will he go to the
Greek cities where our people live, and teach
the Greeks? 36 He says that we will look for
him but will not find him, and that we cannot go where he will be. What does he
mean?"

Streams of Life-Giving Water

37 On the last and most important day of
the festival Jesus stood up and said in a loud
voice, "Whoever is thirsty should come to
me, and 38 whoever believes in me should
drink. As the scripture says, 'Streams of life-giving water will pour out from his side.' "[o]
39 Jesus said this about the Spirit, which those

Live it!

Filling Up

There is a saying, "You are what you eat." Of course it doesn't mean you'll turn into a giant carrot if you eat a lot of vegetables. It means that eating a balanced diet usually results in looking and being healthy. And eating a lot of junk food may result in being overweight and out of shape.

How we feed our minds and souls is a little like that as well. Filling up on violent and sexual images in movies or video games, or on any other negative or destructive ideas in the media, can have a bad influence on our thinking and acting.

Instead of a diet of negative images like these, Jesus said we should come to him for life-giving water (John 7:37). Drinking from Jesus comes in many forms. During Communion we drink from the cup, taking in Jesus in a very special way. Another way to drink is through the word of God. By studying, praying with, and living God's word, you are feeding your mind and soul in a healthy way.

How can you be what you drink? What games, movies, or Internet sites do you avoid or need to avoid? How is the Eucharist and reading the Bible a regular part of your life?

— John 7:37–39

[o] **7:38** *Jesus' words in verses 37–38 may be translated:* "Whoever is thirsty should come to me and drink. 38 As the scripture says, 'Streams of life-giving water will pour out from within anyone who believes in me.' "

7:37 Lev 23:36 **7:38** Ezek 47:1; Zech 14:8

who believed in him were going to receive. At that time the Spirit had not yet been given, because Jesus had not been raised to glory.

Division among the People

40 Some of the people in the crowd heard him say this and said, "This man is really the Prophet!"[p]

41 Others said, "He is the Messiah!"

But others said, "The Messiah will not come from Galilee! 42 The scripture says that the Messiah will be a descendant of King David and will be born in Bethlehem, the town where David lived." 43 So there was a division in the crowd because of Jesus. 44 Some wanted to seize him, but no one laid a hand on him.

The Unbelief of the Jewish Authorities

45 When the guards went back, the chief priests and Pharisees asked them, "Why did you not bring him?"

46 The guards answered, "Nobody has ever talked the way this man does!"

47 "Did he fool you, too?" the Pharisees asked them. 48 "Have you ever known one of the authorities or one Pharisee to believe in him? 49 This crowd does not know the Law of Moses, so they are under God's curse!"

50 One of the Pharisees there was Nicodemus, the man who had gone to see Jesus before. He said to the others, 51 "According to our Law we cannot condemn people before hearing them and finding out what they have done."

52 "Well," they answered, "are you also from Galilee? Study the Scriptures and you will learn that no prophet ever comes[q] from Galilee."

The Woman Caught in Adultery

8 [Then everyone went home, but Jesus went to the Mount of Olives. 2 Early the next morning he went back to the Temple. All the people gathered around him, and he sat down and began to teach them. 3 The teachers of the Law and the Pharisees brought in a woman who had been caught committing adultery, and they made her stand before them all. 4 "Teacher," they said to Jesus, "this woman was caught in the very act of committing adultery. 5 In our Law Moses commanded that such a woman must be stoned to death. Now, what do you say?" 6 They said this to trap Jesus, so that they could accuse him. But he bent over and wrote on the ground with his finger. 7 As they stood there asking him questions, he straightened up and said to them, "Whichever one of you has committed no sin may throw the first stone at her." 8 Then he bent over again and wrote on the ground. 9 When they heard this, they all left, one by one, the older ones first. Jesus was left alone, with the woman still standing there. 10 He straightened up and said to her, "Where are they? Is there no one left to condemn you?"

11 "No one, sir," she answered.

"Well, then," Jesus said, "I do not condemn you either. Go, but do not sin again."][r]

Jesus the Light of the World

12 Jesus spoke to the Pharisees again. "I am the light of the world," he said. "Whoever follows me will have the light of life and will never walk in darkness."

13 The Pharisees said to him, "Now you are testifying on your own behalf; what you say proves nothing."

14 "No," Jesus answered, "even though I do testify on my own behalf, what I say is true, because I know where I came from and

[p] **7:40** THE PROPHET: *See 1:21.* [q] **7:52** no prophet ever comes; *one manuscript has* the Prophet will not come.
[r] **8:11** *Many manuscripts and early translations do not have this passage (8:1–11); others have it after Jn 21:24; others have it after Lk 21:38; one manuscript has it after Jn 7:36.*

7:42 2 Sam 7:12; Mic 5:2 **7:50** Jn 3:1, 2 **8:5** Lev 20:10; Deut 22:22–24 **8:7** Dan B:34 **8:12** Wis 7:26; Mt 5:14; Jn 9:5 **8:13** Jn 5:31

"I am the light of the world. . . . Whoever follows me will have the light of life and will never walk in darkness" *(John 8:12)*.

Study it!

The "I Am" Sayings

In John 8:12 Jesus says, "I am the light of the world." This is one of the "I am" sayings that are found only in the Gospel of John. In these sayings Jesus compares himself to bread (6:35), light (8:12), a gate (10:7), a shepherd (10:11), and a vine (15:5): objects which were common to the people of his time. He also tells us he is "the resurrection and the life" (11:25) and "the way, the truth, and the life" (14:6).

When we read the "I am" sayings, we get a picture of Jesus as one who fills us, lights our way, protects us, provides life, brings us to God, and nurtures us. In these descriptions we come to know and understand that Jesus is the true God.

— John 8:12

where I am going. You do not know where I
came from or where I am going. 15 You
make judgments in a purely human way; I
pass judgment on no one. 16 But if I were to
do so, my judgment would be true, because I
am not alone in this; the Father who sent
me is with me. 17 It is written in your Law
that when two witnesses agree, what they say
is true. 18 I testify on my own behalf, and the
Father who sent me also testifies on my
behalf."
19 "Where is your father?" they asked him.
"You know neither me nor my Father,"
Jesus answered. "If you knew me, you would
know my Father also."
20 Jesus said all this as he taught in the
Temple, in the room where the offering
boxes were placed. And no one arrested him,
because his hour had not come.

You Cannot Go Where I Am Going

21 Again Jesus said to them, "I will go
away; you will look for me, but you will die
in your sins. You cannot go where I am
going."
22 So the Jewish authorities said, "He says
that we cannot go where he is going. Does
this mean that he will kill himself?"
23 Jesus answered, "You belong to this
world here below, but I come from above.
You are from this world, but I am not from
this world. 24 That is why I told you that you
will die in your sins. And you will die in
your sins if you do not believe that 'I Am
Who I Am'."
25 "Who are you?" they asked him.
Jesus answered, "What I have told you
from the very beginning.[s] 26 I have much to
say about you, much to condemn you for.
The one who sent me, however, is truthful,
and I tell the world only what I have heard
from him."
27 They did not understand that Jesus was
talking to them about the Father. 28 So he
said to them, "When you lift up the Son of
Man, you will know that 'I Am Who I Am';
then you will know that I do nothing on my
own authority, but I say only what the
Father has instructed me to say. 29 And he
who sent me is with me; he has not left me
alone, because I always do what pleases him."
30 Many who heard Jesus say these things
believed in him.

The Truth Will Set You Free

31 So Jesus said to those who believed in
him, "If you obey my teaching, you are really
my disciples; 32 you will know the truth, and
the truth will set you free."

[s] **8:25** What I have told you from the very beginning; *or* Why should I speak to you at all?
8:17 Deut 19:15

Chapter eight talks about Jesus' relationship with God the Father. How many times in chapter eight is Father—with a capital F—mentioned?

33“We are the descendants of Abraham,” they answered, “and we have never been anybody’s slaves. What do you mean, then, by saying, ‘You will be free’?”

34Jesus said to them, “I am telling you the truth: everyone who sins is a slave of sin. 35A slave does not belong to a family permanently, but a son belongs there forever. 36If the Son sets you free, then you will be really free. 37I know you are Abraham’s descendants. Yet you are trying to kill me, because you will not accept my teaching. 38I talk about what my Father has shown me, but you do what your father has told you.”

39They answered him, “Our father is Abraham.”

“If you really were Abraham’s children,” Jesus replied, “you would do[t] the same things that he did. 40All I have ever done is to tell you the truth I heard from God, yet you are trying to kill me. Abraham did nothing like this! 41You are doing what your father did.”

“God himself is the only Father we have,” they answered, “and we are his true children.”

42Jesus said to them, “If God really were your Father, you would love me, because I came from God and now I am here. I did not come on my own authority, but he sent me. 43Why do you not understand what I say? It is because you cannot bear to listen to my message. 44You are the children of your father, the Devil, and you want to follow your father’s desires. From the very beginning he was a murderer and has never been on the side of truth, because there is no truth in him. When he tells a lie, he is only doing what is natural to him, because he is a liar and the father of all lies. 45But I tell the truth, and that is why you do not believe me. 46Which one of you can prove that I am guilty of sin? If I tell the truth, then why do you not believe me? 47He who comes from God listens to God’s words. You, however, are not from God, and that is why you will not listen.”

Jesus and Abraham

48They asked Jesus, “Were we not right in saying that you are a Samaritan and have a demon in you?”

49“I have no demon,” Jesus answered. “I honor my Father, but you dishonor me. 50I am not seeking honor for myself. But there is one who is seeking it and who judges in my favor. 51I am telling you the truth: whoever obeys my teaching will never die.”

52They said to him, “Now we know for sure that you have a demon! Abraham died, and the prophets died, yet you say that whoever obeys your teaching will never die. 53Our father Abraham died; you do not claim to be greater than Abraham, do you? And the prophets also died. Who do you think you are?”

54Jesus answered, “If I were to honor myself, that honor would be worth nothing. The one who honors me is my Father—the very one you say is your God. 55You have never known him, but I know him. If I were to say that I do not know him, I would be a liar like you. But I do know him, and I obey his word. 56Your father Abraham rejoiced that he was to see the time of my coming; he saw it and was glad.”

57They said to him, “You are not even fifty years old—and you have seen Abraham?”[u]

58“I am telling you the truth,” Jesus replied. “Before Abraham was born, ‘I Am’.”

59Then they picked up stones to throw at him, but Jesus hid himself and left the Temple.

Jesus Heals a Man Born Blind

9 As Jesus was walking along, he saw a man who had been born blind. 2His disciples asked him, “Teacher, whose sin caused him to be born blind? Was it his own or his parents’ sin?”

3Jesus answered, “His blindness has nothing to do with his sins or his parents’ sins. He is blind so that God’s power might be seen at work in him. 4As long as it is day, we must do the work of him who sent me;

[t] **8:39** If you really were . . . you would do; *some manuscripts have* If you are . . . do. [u] **8:57** you have seen Abraham?; *some manuscripts have* has Abraham seen you?

8:33 Mt 3:9; Lk 3:8 **8:44** Wis 1:13; 2:24

night is coming when no one can work.
5While I am in the world, I am the light for
the world."
6After he said this, Jesus spat on the
ground and made some mud with the spit-
tle; he rubbed the mud on the man's eyes
7and told him, "Go and wash your face in
the Pool of Siloam." (This name means
"Sent.") So the man went, washed his face,
and came back seeing.
8His neighbors, then, and the people who
had seen him begging before this, asked,
"Isn't this the man who used to sit and
beg?"
9Some said, "He is the one," but others
said, "No he isn't; he just looks like him."
So the man himself said, "I am the man."
10"How is it that you can now see?" they
asked him.
11He answered, "The man called Jesus
made some mud, rubbed it on my eyes, and
told me to go to Siloam and wash my face.
So I went, and as soon as I washed, I could
see."
12"Where is he?" they asked.
"I don't know," he answered.

The Pharisees Investigate the Healing

13Then they took to the Pharisees the
man who had been blind. 14The day that
Jesus made the mud and cured him of his
blindness was a Sabbath. 15The Pharisees,
then, asked the man again how he had
received his sight. He told them, "He put
some mud on my eyes; I washed my face,
and now I can see."
16Some of the Pharisees said, "The man
who did this cannot be from God, for he
does not obey the Sabbath law."
Others, however, said, "How could a man
who is a sinner perform such miracles as
these?" And there was a division among them.
17So the Pharisees asked the man once
more, "You say he cured you of your blind-
ness—well, what do you say about him?"
"He is a prophet," the man answered.
18The Jewish authorities, however, were
not willing to believe that he had been blind
and could now see, until they called his par-
ents 19and asked them, "Is this your son? You
say that he was born blind; how is it, then,
that he can now see?"
20His parents answered, "We know that he
is our son, and we know that he was born
blind. 21But we do not know how it is that
he is now able to see, nor do we know who
cured him of his blindness. Ask him; he is
old enough, and he can answer for himself!"
22His parents said this because they were
afraid of the Jewish authorities, who had
already agreed that anyone who said he
believed that Jesus was the Messiah would be
expelled from the synagogue. 23That is why
his parents said, "He is old enough; ask him!"

Live it!

Differently Abled

Keith gets around school using a walker. Kids in the hallway sometimes follow him and imitate his limp. He knows they do it and ignores them because he also knows that he is the best speller in school. Even though he can't join the track team or play football, he always wins the spelling bee.

Jesus didn't care if someone was blind or lame or dirty or different from others. He loved everyone equally. Some people ignored these people; Jesus loved them and helped them. Jesus knew that all people have value and something to share with others.

Today people with disabilities sometimes consider themselves "differently abled." Do you know someone who has a disability that makes them stronger in another area? Take the opportunity to get to know someone who is different or has a disability.

— John 9:1–7

9:5 Mt 5:14; Jn 8:12

24 A second time they called back the man
who had been born blind, and said to him,
"Promise before God that you will tell the
truth! We know that this man who cured
you is a sinner."

25 "I do not know if he is a sinner or not,"
the man replied. "One thing I do know: I
was blind, and now I see."

26 "What did he do to you?" they asked.
"How did he cure you of your blindness?"

27 "I have already told you," he answered,
"and you would not listen. Why do you
want to hear it again? Maybe you, too,
would like to be his disciples?"

28 They insulted him and said, "You are
that fellow's disciple; but we are Moses' disci-
ples. 29 We know that God spoke to Moses;
as for that fellow, however, we do not even
know where he comes from!"

30 The man answered, "What a strange
thing that is! You do not know where he
comes from, but he cured me of my blind-
ness! 31 We know that God does not listen to
sinners; he does listen to people who respect
him and do what he wants them to do.
32 Since the beginning of the world nobody
has ever heard of anyone giving sight to a
person born blind. 33 Unless this man came
from God, he would not be able to do a
thing."

34 They answered, "You were born and
brought up in sin—and you are trying to
teach us?" And they expelled him from the
synagogue.

Spiritual Blindness

35 When Jesus heard what had happened,
he found the man and asked him, "Do you
believe in the Son of Man?"

36 The man answered, "Tell me who he is,
sir, so that I can believe in him!"

37 Jesus said to him, "You have already seen
him, and he is the one who is talking with
you now."

38 "I believe, Lord!" the man said, and
knelt down before Jesus.

39 Jesus said, "I came to this world to
judge, so that the blind should see and those
who see should become blind."

40 Some Pharisees who were there with
him heard him say this and asked him, "Sure-
ly you don't mean that we are blind, too?"

41 Jesus answered, "If you were blind, then
you would not be guilty; but since you claim
that you can see, this means that you are still
guilty."

The Parable of the Shepherd

10 Jesus said, "I am telling you the
truth: the man who does not enter
the sheep pen by the gate, but climbs in
some other way, is a thief and a robber. 2 The
man who goes in through the gate is the
shepherd of the sheep. 3 The gatekeeper
opens the gate for him; the sheep hear his
voice as he calls his own sheep by name, and
he leads them out. 4 When he has brought
them out, he goes ahead of them, and the
sheep follow him, because they know his
voice. 5 They will not follow someone else;
instead, they will run away from such a per-
son, because they do not know his voice."

6 Jesus told them this parable, but they did
not understand what he meant.

Jesus the Good Shepherd

7 So Jesus said again, "I am telling you the
truth: I am the gate for the sheep. 8 All others
who came before me are thieves and robbers,
but the sheep did not listen to them. 9 I am
the gate. Those who come in by me will be
saved; they will come in and go out and find
pasture. 10 The thief comes only in order to
steal, kill, and destroy. I have come in order
that you might have life—life in all its full-
ness.

11 "I am the good shepherd, who is willing
to die for the sheep. 12 When the hired man,
who is not a shepherd and does not own the
sheep, sees a wolf coming, he leaves the sheep
and runs away; so the wolf snatches the sheep

10:11 Sir 18:13

Unscramble these letters to form two words that are the materials Jesus used to heal the man born blind: tpislet, udm.

> ## Study it!
>
> ### Jesus the Firefighter?
>
> **Who protects you? Your parents? Your teachers? The police and fire departments? Who else? Would these people do anything to keep you safe? If Jesus were speaking today, maybe he would say, "I am the good firefighter."**
>
> **In Jesus' time and place, shepherds were common. They were protectors of their flocks. The flock Jesus was talking about in John 10:14–18 is not a flock of sheep. It is a group of people—his people. Jesus is saying that he will do anything to protect his people and to bring them together. He loves everyone so much, he tells them he will even die for them. He tells his followers that he will do all of this because God, his Father, wants him to free everyone, to be the Savior of all.**
>
> **— John 10:7–21**

and scatters them. 13The hired man runs
away because he is only a hired man and
does not care about the sheep. 14-15I am the
good shepherd. As the Father knows me and
I know the Father, in the same way I know
my sheep and they know me. And I am will-
ing to die for them. 16There are other sheep
which belong to me that are not in this
sheep pen. I must bring them, too; they will
listen to my voice, and they will become[v]
one flock with one shepherd.
17"The Father loves me because I am
willing to give up my life, in order that I
may receive it back again. 18No one takes
my life away from me. I give it up of my
own free will. I have the right to give it up,
and I have the right to take it back. This is
what my Father has commanded me to do."
19Again there was a division among the
people because of these words. 20Many of
them were saying, "He has a demon! He is
crazy! Why do you listen to him?"
21But others were saying, "A man with a
demon could not talk like this! How could a
demon give sight to blind people?"

Jesus Is Rejected

22It was winter, and the Festival of the
Dedication of the Temple was being celebrat-
ed in Jerusalem. 23Jesus was walking in
Solomon's Porch in the Temple, 24when the
people gathered around him and asked, "How
long are you going to keep us in suspense?
Tell us the plain truth: are you the Messiah?"
25Jesus answered, "I have already told you,
but you would not believe me. The deeds I
do by my Father's authority speak on my
behalf; 26but you will not believe, for you are
not my sheep. 27My sheep listen to my
voice; I know them, and they follow me. 28I
give them eternal life, and they shall never
die. No one can snatch them away from me.
29What my Father has given me is greater[w]
than everything, and no one can snatch
them away from the Father's care. 30The
Father and I are one."
31Then the people again picked up stones
to throw at him. 32Jesus said to them, "I have
done many good deeds in your presence
which the Father gave me to do; for which
one of these do you want to stone me?"
33They answered, "We do not want to
stone you because of any good deeds, but
because of your blasphemy! You are only a
man, but you are trying to make yourself
God!"

[v] **10:16** they will become; *some manuscripts have* there will be. [w] **10:29** What my Father has given me is greater; *some manuscripts have* My Father, who gave them to me, is greater.

10:15 Mt 11:27; Lk 10:22 **10:22** 1 Macc 4:36, 52–59; 2 Macc 1:18; 10:5 **10:29** Wis 3:1 **10:33** Lev 24:16

"'I am the good shepherd . . . I know my sheep and they know me. And I am willing to die for them'" *(John 10:14-15)*.

34Jesus answered, "It is written in your
own Law that God said, 'You are gods.' 35We
know that what the scripture says is true for-
ever; and God called those people gods, the
people to whom his message was given. 36As
for me, the Father chose me and sent me
into the world. How, then, can you say that I
blaspheme because I said that I am the Son
of God? 37Do not believe me, then, if I am
not doing the things my Father wants me to
do. 38But if I do them, even though you do
not believe me, you should at least believe
my deeds, in order that you may know once
and for all that the Father is in me and that I
am in the Father."

39Once more they tried to seize Jesus, but
he slipped out of their hands.

40Jesus then went back again across the
Jordan River to the place where John had
been baptizing, and he stayed there. 41Many
people came to him. "John performed no
miracles," they said, "but everything he said
about this man was true." 42And many peo-
ple there believed in him.

The Death of Lazarus

11 A man named Lazarus, who lived in
Bethany, became sick. Bethany was
the town where Mary and her sister Martha
lived. (2This Mary was the one who poured
the perfume on the Lord's feet and wiped
them with her hair; it was her brother
Lazarus who was sick.) 3The sisters sent Jesus
a message: "Lord, your dear friend is sick."

4When Jesus heard it, he said, "The final
result of this sickness will not be the death
of Lazarus; this has happened in order to
bring glory to God, and it will be the means
by which the Son of God will receive glory."

5Jesus loved Martha and her sister and
Lazarus. 6Yet when he received the news
that Lazarus was sick, he stayed where he
was for two more days. 7Then he said to the
disciples, "Let us go back to Judea."

8"Teacher," the disciples answered, "just a
short time ago the people there wanted to
stone you; and are you planning to go back?"

9Jesus said, "A day has twelve hours,
doesn't it? So those who walk in broad day-
light do not stumble, for they see the light of
this world. 10But if they walk during the
night they stumble, because they have no
light." 11Jesus said this and then added, "Our
friend Lazarus has fallen asleep, but I will go
and wake him up."

12The disciples answered, "If he is asleep,
Lord, he will get well."

13Jesus meant that Lazarus had died, but
they thought he meant natural sleep. 14So Jesus
told them plainly, "Lazarus is dead, 15but for
your sake I am glad that I was not with him, so
that you will believe. Let us go to him."

16Thomas (called the Twin) said to his fel-
low disciples, "Let us all go along with the
Teacher, so that we may die with him!"

Jesus the Resurrection and the Life

17When Jesus arrived, he found that
Lazarus had been buried four days before.
18Bethany was less than two miles from
Jerusalem, 19and many Judeans had come to
see Martha and Mary to comfort them
about their brother's death.

20When Martha heard that Jesus was com-
ing, she went out to meet him, but Mary
stayed in the house. 21Martha said to Jesus, "If
you had been here, Lord, my brother would
not have died! 22But I know that even now
God will give you whatever you ask him for."

23"Your brother will rise to life," Jesus told
her.

24"I know," she replied, "that he will rise
to life on the last day."

25Jesus said to her, "I am the resurrection
and the life. Those who believe in me will
live, even though they die; 26and those who
live and believe in me will never die. Do you
believe this?"

27"Yes, Lord!" she answered. "I do believe
that you are the Messiah, the Son of God,
who was to come into the world."

Jesus Weeps

28After Martha said this, she went back
and called her sister Mary privately. "The
Teacher is here," she told her, "and is asking
for you." 29When Mary heard this, she got

10:34 Ps 82:6 **10:40** Jn 1:28 **11:1** Lk 10:38, 39 **11:2** Jn 12:3 **11:24** 2 Macc 7:22, 23; 12:44

Pray it!

Jesus Felt Just Like I Do!

Life can be frustrating. If your team loses, if you get a bad grade, if your home life is bad, or if your little sister bugs you too much, it can make you want to cry. Go ahead, Jesus cried when his friend died (John 11:35). Jesus also got upset, had fun with his friends, went to weddings and feasts, and did a lot of other things normal people do. It is great to know that Jesus is really human and that he is really God. So the next time you are feeling some big emotion, remember that Jesus probably felt the same way once too. It can help to take some time and write a prayer to share your emotions with God. Here's a formula you can use.

Jesus, today I feel ______________ (write the emotion) because of ______________ (write what made you feel that way). Did you feel that way too? I thank you for being human; it's nice to know that you felt __________ (the emotion) sometimes. Help me be more like you in other ways too. Amen.

— John 11:28–37

up and hurried out to meet him. (30Jesus
had not yet arrived in the village, but was
still in the place where Martha had met
him.) 31The people who were in the house
with Mary comforting her followed her
when they saw her get up and hurry out.
They thought that she was going to the
grave to weep there.
32Mary arrived where Jesus was, and as
soon as she saw him, she fell at his feet.
"Lord," she said, "if you had been here, my
brother would not have died!"
33Jesus saw her weeping, and he saw how
the people with her were weeping also; his
heart was touched, and he was deeply moved.
34"Where have you buried him?" he asked
them.
"Come and see, Lord," they answered.
35Jesus wept. 36"See how much he loved
him!" the people said.
37But some of them said, "He gave sight
to the blind man, didn't he? Could he not
have kept Lazarus from dying?"

Lazarus Is Brought to Life

38Deeply moved once more, Jesus went to
the tomb, which was a cave with a stone
placed at the entrance. 39"Take the stone
away!" Jesus ordered.
Martha, the dead man's sister, answered,
"There will be a bad smell, Lord. He has
been buried four days!"
40Jesus said to her, "Didn't I tell you that
you would see God's glory if you believed?"
41They took the stone away. Jesus looked up
and said, "I thank you, Father, that you listen
to me. 42I know that you always listen to me,
but I say this for the sake of the people here,
so that they will believe that you sent me."
43After he had said this, he called out in a
loud voice, "Lazarus, come out!" 44He came
out, his hands and feet wrapped in grave
cloths, and with a cloth around his face.
"Untie him," Jesus told them, "and let
him go."

The Plot against Jesus
(Matthew 26:1–5; Mark 14:1, 2; Luke 22:1, 2)

45Many of the people who had come to
visit Mary saw what Jesus did, and they
believed in him. 46But some of them
returned to the Pharisees and told them
what Jesus had done. 47So the Pharisees and

the chief priests met with the Council and said, "What shall we do? Look at all the miracles this man is performing! 48 If we let him go on in this way, everyone will believe in him, and the Roman authorities will take action and destroy our Temple and our nation!"

"Lazarus, come out!" (11:43)

49 One of them, named Caiaphas, who was High Priest that year, said, "What fools you are! 50 Don't you realize that it is better for you to have one man die for the people, instead of having the whole nation destroyed?" 51 Actually, he did not say this of his own accord; rather, as he was High Priest that year, he was prophesying that Jesus was going to die for the Jewish people, 52 and not only for them, but also to bring together into one body all the scattered people of God.

53 From that day on the Jewish authorities made plans to kill Jesus. 54 So Jesus did not travel openly in Judea, but left and went to a place near the desert, to a town named Ephraim, where he stayed with the disciples.

55 The time for the Passover Festival was near, and many people went up from the country to Jerusalem to perform the ritual of purification before the festival. 56 They were looking for Jesus, and as they gathered in the Temple, they asked one another, "What do you think? Surely he will not come to the festival, will he?" 57 The chief priests and the Pharisees had given orders that if anyone knew where Jesus was, he must report it, so that they could arrest him.

Jesus Is Anointed at Bethany
(Matthew 26:6–13; Mark 14:3–9)

12 Six days before the Passover, Jesus went to Bethany, the home of Lazarus, the man he had raised from death. 2 They prepared a dinner for him there, which Martha helped serve; Lazarus was one of those who were sitting at the table with Jesus. 3 Then Mary took a whole pint of a very expensive perfume made of pure nard, poured it on Jesus' feet, and wiped them with her hair. The sweet smell of the perfume filled the whole house. 4 One of Jesus' disciples, Judas Iscariot—the one who was going to betray him—said, 5 "Why wasn't this perfume sold for three hundred silver coins[x] and the money given to the poor?" 6 He said this, not because he cared about the poor, but because he was a thief. He carried the money bag and would help himself from it.

7 But Jesus said, "Leave her alone! Let her keep what she has for the day of my burial. 8 You will always have poor people with you, but you will not always have me."

The Plot against Lazarus

9 A large number of people heard that Jesus was in Bethany, so they went there, not only because of Jesus but also to see Lazarus, whom Jesus had raised from death. 10 So the chief priests made plans to kill Lazarus too, 11 because on his account many Jews were rejecting them and believing in Jesus.

The Triumphant Entry into Jerusalem
(Matthew 21:1–11; Mark 11:1–11; Luke 19:28–40)

12 The next day the large crowd that had come to the Passover Festival heard that Jesus was coming to Jerusalem. 13 So they took branches of palm trees and went out to meet

[x] **12:5** SILVER COINS: *See 6:7.*

12:3 Lk 7:37, 38 **12:8** Deut 15:11 **12:13** Ps 118:25, 26; 1 Macc 13:51

Jesus was very close friends with Martha, Mary, and Lazarus. Read Luke 10:38–42 for another story about Martha and Mary.

him, shouting, "Praise God! God bless him
who comes in the name of the Lord! God
bless the King of Israel!"
14 Jesus found a donkey and rode on it, just
as the scripture says,
15 "Do not be afraid, city of Zion!
Here comes your king,
riding on a young donkey."
16 His disciples did not understand this at
the time; but when Jesus had been raised to
glory, they remembered that the scripture said
this about him and that they had done this for
him.
17 The people who had been with Jesus
when he called Lazarus out of the grave and
raised him from death had reported what
had happened. 18 That was why the crowd
met him—because they heard that he had
performed this miracle. 19 The Pharisees then
said to one another, "You see, we are not
succeeding at all! Look, the whole world is
following him!"

Some Greeks Seek Jesus

20 Some Greeks were among those who
had gone to Jerusalem to worship during the
festival. 21 They went to Philip (he was from
Bethsaida in Galilee) and said, "Sir, we want
to see Jesus."
22 Philip went and told Andrew, and the
two of them went and told Jesus. 23 Jesus
answered them, "The hour has now come
for the Son of Man to receive great glory.
24 I am telling you the truth: a grain of
wheat remains no more than a single grain
unless it is dropped into the ground and
dies. If it does die, then it produces many
grains. 25 Those who love their own life will
lose it; those who hate their own life in this
world will keep it for life eternal. 26 Who-
ever wants to serve me must follow me, so
that my servant will be with me where I
am. And my Father will honor anyone who
serves me.

Live it!

Being Good Seeds

Most kindergarten classes grow beans. The teacher gives each child a paper cup with some earth, then a bean seed. The children cover the seed with soil and they water the seed. Maybe you remember doing this. If so, you probably also remember the wait (which seemed like forever) and the joy when the little sprout first came up from the earth.

Jesus talks about growing things from seeds in John 12:22–26. He talks about how a grain of wheat must fall to the ground in order for plants to grow. In this passage he is talking about himself and how his death will be like a seed that will help others live.

What type of seeds are you planting in your life? If you study and try hard in school, you're planting seeds that may grow into a college education. If you eat a good diet and exercise regularly, you are planting seeds for a healthy body and mind. If you learn about God and follow Jesus, you're planting seeds that will grow into a holy life.

The next time you are making a decision about what to do, ask yourself what type of seed it is that you're planting. If it is a good seed, it'll grow into something good.

— John 12:22–26

12:15 Zech 9:9 **12:25** Mt 10:39; 16:25; Mk 8:35; Lk 9:24; 17:33

Which Sunday of the Church year are we given palm branches in honor of Jesus' triumphant entry into Jerusalem?

Jesus Speaks about His Death

27“Now my heart is troubled—and what
shall I say? Shall I say, ‘Father, do not let this
hour come upon me’? But that is why I
came—so that I might go through this hour
of suffering. 28Father, bring glory to your
name!”

Then a voice spoke from heaven, “I have
brought glory to it, and I will do so again.”
29The crowd standing there heard the
voice, and some of them said it was thunder,
while others said, “An angel spoke to him!”
30But Jesus said to them, “It was not for
my sake that this voice spoke, but for yours.
31Now is the time for this world to be
judged; now the ruler of this world will be
overthrown. 32When I am lifted up from the
earth, I will draw everyone to me.” (33In say-
ing this he indicated the kind of death he
was going to suffer.)
34The crowd answered, “Our Law tells us
that the Messiah will live forever. How, then,
can you say that the Son of Man must be
lifted up? Who is this Son of Man?”
35Jesus answered, “The light will be
among you a little longer. Continue on your
way while you have the light, so that the
darkness will not come upon you; for the
one who walks in the dark does not know
where he is going. 36Believe in the light,
then, while you have it, so that you will be
the people of the light.”

The Unbelief of the People

After Jesus said this, he went off and hid
himself from them. 37Even though he had
performed all these miracles in their pres-
ence, they did not believe in him, 38so that
what the prophet Isaiah had said might
come true:

“Lord, who believed the message we told?
To whom did the Lord reveal his
power?”
39And so they were not able to believe,
because Isaiah also said,
40“God has blinded their eyes
and closed their minds,
so that their eyes would not see,
and their minds would not understand,
and they would not turn to me, says
God,
for me to heal them.”
41Isaiah said this because he saw Jesus’
glory and spoke about him.
42Even then, many Jewish authorities
believed in Jesus; but because of the Phar-
isees they did not talk about it openly, so as
not to be expelled from the synagogue.
43They loved human approval rather than
the approval of God.

Judgment by Jesus’ Words

44Jesus said in a loud voice, “Whoever
believes in me believes not only in me but
also in him who sent me. 45Whoever sees
me sees also him who sent me. 46I have
come into the world as light, so that every-
one who believes in me should not remain
in the darkness. 47If people hear my message
and do not obey it, I will not judge them. I
came, not to judge the world, but to save it.
48Those who reject me and do not accept
my message have one who will judge them.
The words I have spoken will be their judge
on the last day! 49This is true, because I have
not spoken on my own authority, but the
Father who sent me has commanded me
what I must say and speak. 50And I know
that his command brings eternal life. What I
say, then, is what the Father has told me to
say.”

Jesus Washes His Disciples’ Feet

13 It was now the day before the
Passover Festival. Jesus knew that the
hour had come for him to leave this world
and go to the Father. He had always loved
those in the world who were his own, and
he loved them to the very end.
2Jesus and his disciples were at supper. The
Devil had already put into the heart of Judas,
the son of Simon Iscariot, the thought of
betraying Jesus.[y] 3Jesus knew that the Father
had given him complete power; he knew

[y] **13:2** The Devil . . . betraying Jesus; *or* The Devil had already decided that Judas, the son of Simon Iscariot, would betray Jesus.

12:34 Ps 110:4; Isa 9:7; Ezek 37:25; Dan 7:14 **12:38** Isa 53:1 (LXX) **12:40** Isa 6:10 (LXX)

The Triduum, Three Special Days

Catholic Connections

Holy Thursday, Good Friday, and Holy Saturday are three very special days in the Catholic calendar. These three days before Easter Sunday are one celebration called the Triduum. On Holy Thursday, John 13:1–15 is the Gospel read in Church. A foot-washing ritual is part of Thursday's services. On Good Friday, chapters 18–19 of John are read, a dramatic reminder of Jesus' Passion and death. The cross is given special treatment; some people kiss it, and others show love and respect for it in other ways.

On Holy Saturday the Triduum's highlight is the Easter Vigil. The Easter Vigil is the greatest celebration of the year. It is a beautiful liturgy in which we celebrate Christ's Resurrection. The liturgy uses fire and water. It is also the time when the catechumens—those older teens and adults who have been preparing to become Catholic—are baptized, confirmed and receive Holy Communion for the first time.

— John 13:1–17

that he had come from God and was going
to God. 4So he rose from the table, took off
his outer garment, and tied a towel around
his waist. 5Then he poured some water into
a washbasin and began to wash the disciples'
feet and dry them with the towel around his
waist. 6He came to Simon Peter, who said to
him, "Are you going to wash my feet, Lord?"
7Jesus answered him, "You do not under-
stand now what I am doing, but you will
understand later."
8Peter declared, "Never at any time will
you wash my feet!"
"If I do not wash your feet," Jesus
answered, "you will no longer be my disciple."
9Simon Peter answered, "Lord, do not
wash only my feet, then! Wash my hands and
head, too!"
10Jesus said, "Those who have taken a bath
are completely clean and do not have to
wash themselves, except for their feet.[z] All of
you are clean—all except one." (11Jesus
already knew who was going to betray him;
that is why he said, "All of you, except one,
are clean.")
12After Jesus had washed their feet, he put
his outer garment back on and returned to
his place at the table. "Do you understand
what I have just done to you?" he asked.
13"You call me Teacher and Lord, and it is
right that you do so, because that is what I
am. 14I, your Lord and Teacher, have just
washed your feet. You, then, should wash one
another's feet. 15I have set an example for
you, so that you will do just what I have
done for you. 16I am telling you the truth: no
slaves are greater than their master, and no
messengers are greater than the one who sent
them. 17Now that you know this truth, how
happy you will be if you put it into practice!
18"I am not talking about all of you; I
know those I have chosen. But the scripture
must come true that says, 'The man who
shared my food turned against me.' 19I tell
you this now before it happens, so that when
it does happen, you will believe that 'I Am
Who I Am.' 20I am telling you the truth:
whoever receives anyone I send receives me
also; and whoever receives me receives him
who sent me."

[z] **13:10** *Some manuscripts do not have* except for their feet.

13:12–15 Lk 22:27 **13:16** Mt 10:24; Lk 6:40; Jn 15:20 **13:18** Ps 41:9 **13:20** Mt 10:40; Mk 9:37; Lk 9:48; 10:16

Jesus Predicts His Betrayal
(Matthew 26:20–25; Mark 14:17–21; Luke 22:21–23)

21After Jesus had said this, he was deeply
troubled and declared openly, "I am telling
you the truth: one of you is going to betray
me."

The disciples looked at one another. (13:22)

22The disciples looked at one another,
completely puzzled about whom he meant.
23One of the disciples, the one whom Jesus
loved, was sitting next to Jesus. 24Simon
Peter motioned to him and said, "Ask him
whom he is talking about."
25So that disciple moved closer to Jesus'
side and asked, "Who is it, Lord?"
26Jesus answered, "I will dip some bread in
the sauce and give it to him; he is the man."
So he took a piece of bread, dipped it, and
gave it to Judas, the son of Simon Iscariot.
27As soon as Judas took the bread, Satan
entered into him. Jesus said to him, "Hurry
and do what you must!" 28None of the oth-
ers at the table understood why Jesus said
this to him. 29Since Judas was in charge
of the money bag, some of the disciples
thought that Jesus had told him to go and
buy what they needed for the festival, or to
give something to the poor.
30Judas accepted the bread and went out
at once. It was night.

The New Commandment

31After Judas had left, Jesus said, "Now the
Son of Man's glory is revealed; now God's
glory is revealed through him. 32And if
God's glory is revealed through him, then
God will reveal the glory of the Son of Man
in himself, and he will do so at once. 33My
children, I shall not be with you very much

13:33 Jn 7:34

Live it!

Waiting for Heaven

Kali had to wait for everything. She couldn't get her ears pierced until she turned 13 (even though all the other girls in the sixth grade already had their ears done). She couldn't go to the same movies her older brother went to. She couldn't even stay up to see the 10 o'clock shows. To Kali it seemed like she couldn't do anything, and she was always waiting.

Peter didn't want to wait either. When Jesus talked about leaving his disciples, Peter wanted to know where he was going (John 13:36). Jesus said, "You cannot follow me now where I am going." Peter had to learn to wait, and he made a few mistakes before he was able to follow Jesus. In this passage Jesus tells us that we all have a place in heaven. Jesus himself will lead us there. Our time on earth is a preparation—the more we get to know Jesus now, the better prepared we will be for heaven later.

So don't waste your time! Prepare for heaven by getting to know Jesus. The Church gives us lots of ways to know Jesus better. Receiving Holy Eucharist, receiving the sacrament of Penance and Reconciliation, going to religious education classes, and attending youth retreats are all ways you can get to know Jesus better. Are you putting your best energy into these things or just going through the motions?

— John 13:36—14:7

" 'I, your Lord and Teacher, have just washed your feet. You, then, should wash one another's feet' " *(John 13:14)*.

longer. You will look for me; but I tell you
now what I told the Jewish authorities, 'You
cannot go where I am going.' 34And now I
give you a new commandment: love one
another. As I have loved you, so you must
love one another. 35If you have love for one
another, then everyone will know that you
are my disciples."

Jesus Predicts Peter's Denial

(Matthew 26:31–35; Mark 14:27–31; Luke 22:31–34)

36"Where are you going, Lord?" Simon
Peter asked him.
"You cannot follow me now where I am
going," answered Jesus; "but later you will fol-
low me."
37"Lord, why can't I follow you now?"
asked Peter. "I am ready to die for you!"
38Jesus answered, "Are you really ready to
die for me? I am telling you the truth: before
the rooster crows you will say three times
that you do not know me.

Jesus the Way to the Father

14 "Do not be worried and upset,"
Jesus told them. "Believe[a] in God
and believe also in me. 2There are many
rooms in my Father's house, and I am going
to prepare a place for you. I would not tell
you this if it were not so.[b] 3And after I go
and prepare a place for you, I will come
back and take you to myself, so that you
will be where I am. 4You know the way
that leads to the place where I am going."
5Thomas said to him, "Lord, we do not
know where you are going; so how can we
know the way to get there?"
6Jesus answered him, "I am the way, the
truth, and the life; no one goes to the Father
except by me. 7Now that you have known
me," he said to them, "you will know[c] my
Father also, and from now on you do know
him and you have seen him."
8Philip said to him, "Lord, show us the
Father; that is all we need."
9Jesus answered, "For a long time I have
been with you all; yet you do not know me,
Philip? Whoever has seen me has seen the
Father. Why, then, do you say, 'Show us the
Father'? 10Do you not believe, Philip, that I
am in the Father and the Father is in me?
The words that I have spoken to you," Jesus
said to his disciples, "do not come from me.
The Father, who remains in me, does his
own work. 11Believe me when I say that I
am in the Father and the Father is in me. If
not, believe because of the things I do. 12I
am telling you the truth: those who believe
in me will do what I do—yes, they will do
even greater things, because I am going to
the Father. 13And I will do whatever you ask
for in my name, so that the Father's glory
will be shown through the Son. 14If you ask
me[d] for anything in my name, I will do it.

The Promise of the Holy Spirit

15"If you love me, you will obey my com-
mandments. 16I will ask the Father, and he
will give you another Helper, who will stay
with you forever. 17He is the Spirit, who
reveals the truth about God. The world can-
not receive him, because it cannot see him
or know him. But you know him, because
he remains with you and is[e] in you.
18"When I go, you will not be left all
alone; I will come back to you. 19In a little
while the world will see me no more, but
you will see me; and because I live, you also
will live. 20When that day comes, you will
know that I am in my Father and that you
are in me, just as I am in you.
21"Those who accept my commandments
and obey them are the ones who love me.

[a] **14:1** Believe; *or* You believe. [b] **14:2** There are . . . were not so; *or* There are many rooms in my Father's house; if it were not so, would I tell you that I am going to prepare a place for you? [c] **14:7** Now that you have known me . . . you will know; *some manuscripts have* If you had known me . . . you would know. [d] **14:14** *Some manuscripts do not have* me. [e] **14:17** is; *some manuscripts have* will be.

13:34 Jn 15:12, 17; 1 Jn 3:23; 2 Jn 5 **14:6** Bar 3:13, 14 **14:15** Wis 6:18 **14:21** Wis 6:12, 18; Sir 4:14

In other Bible translations, the Holy Spirit is called the *advocate*, which is another word for helper.

Led by the Holy Spirit

Catholic Connections

Imagine your best friend or teacher telling you he or she was going away and that you wouldn't see him or her again. Would you be scared, sad, confused? The disciples probably felt all those emotions when they were told by Jesus that he was going back to God, his Father. To give them courage, he also told them about the Holy Spirit.

The Holy Spirit, who Jesus calls the Helper, would come to them and help them. It would be the Holy Spirit's job to help teach and lead the Apostles. But the Holy Spirit's help didn't end there. The Holy Spirit continues to help and guide the Church throughout all time. Wherever God sends Jesus, the Holy Spirit is also sent. The three persons of the Holy Trinity—Father, Son, and Holy Spirit—have different roles but share the same saving work.

After reading John 14:15–26, read John 20:19–23 and Acts 2:1–12 to see how Jesus' promise was fulfilled.

— John 14:15–26

My Father will love those who love me; I too
will love them and reveal myself to them."
22 Judas (not Judas Iscariot) said, "Lord,
how can it be that you will reveal yourself to
us and not to the world?"
23 Jesus answered him, "Those who love
me will obey my teaching. My Father will
love them, and my Father and I will come to
them and live with them. 24 Those who do
not love me do not obey my teaching. And
the teaching you have heard is not mine, but
comes from the Father, who sent me.
25 "I have told you this while I am still
with you. 26 The Helper, the Holy Spirit,
whom the Father will send in my name, will
teach you everything and make you remember all that I have told you.
27 "Peace is what I leave with you; it is my
own peace that I give you. I do not give it as
the world does. Do not be worried and
upset; do not be afraid. 28 You heard me say
to you, 'I am leaving, but I will come back
to you.' If you loved me, you would be glad
that I am going to the Father; for he is
greater than I. 29 I have told you this now
before it all happens, so that when it does
happen, you will believe. 30 I cannot talk with
you much longer, because the ruler of this
world is coming. He has no power over me,
31 but the world must know that I love the
Father; that is why I do everything as he
commands me.
"Come, let us go from this place.

Jesus the Real Vine

15 "I am the real vine, and my Father is
the gardener. 2 He breaks off every
branch in me that does not bear fruit, and he
prunes every branch that does bear fruit, so
that it will be clean and bear more fruit.
3 You have been made clean already by the
teaching I have given you. 4 Remain united to
me, and I will remain united to you. A branch
cannot bear fruit by itself; it can do so only if
it remains in the vine. In the same way you
cannot bear fruit unless you remain in me.
5 "I am the vine, and you are the branches.
Those who remain in me, and I in them, will
bear much fruit; for you can do nothing
without me. 6 Those who do not remain in
me are thrown out like a branch and dry up;
such branches are gathered up and thrown
into the fire, where they are burned. 7 If you
remain in me and my words remain in you,
then you will ask for anything you wish, and
you shall have it. 8 My Father's glory is shown
by your bearing much fruit; and in this way

you become my disciples. 9 I love you just as
the Father loves me; remain in my love. 10 If
you obey my commands, you will remain in
my love, just as I have obeyed my Father's
commands and remain in his love.
11 "I have told you this so that my joy may
be in you and that your joy may be com-
plete. 12 My commandment is this: love one
another, just as I love you. 13 The greatest
love you can have for your friends is to give
your life for them. 14 And you are my friends
if you do what I command you. 15 I do not
call you servants any longer, because servants
do not know what their master is doing.
Instead, I call you friends, because I have told
you everything I heard from my Father.
16 You did not choose me; I chose you and
appointed you to go and bear much fruit,
the kind of fruit that endures. And so the
Father will give you whatever you ask of
him in my name. 17 This, then, is what I
command you: love one another.

The World's Hatred

18 "If the world hates you, just remember
that it has hated me first. 19 If you belonged
to the world, then the world would love you
as its own. But I chose you from this world,
and you do not belong to it; that is why the
world hates you. 20 Remember what I told
you: 'Slaves are not greater than their master.'
If people persecuted me, they will persecute
you too; if they obeyed my teaching, they
will obey yours too. 21 But they will do all
this to you because you are mine; for they do
not know the one who sent me. 22 They
would not have been guilty of sin if I had
not come and spoken to them; as it is, they
no longer have any excuse for their sin.
23 Whoever hates me hates my Father also.
24 They would not have been guilty of sin if I
had not done among them the things that no
one else ever did; as it is, they have seen what
I did, and they hate both me and my Father.
25 This, however, was bound to happen so
that what is written in their Law may come
true: 'They hated me for no reason at all.'
26 "The Helper will come—the Spirit, who
reveals the truth about God and who comes
from the Father. I will send him to you from
the Father, and he will speak about me. 27 And
you, too, will speak about me, because you
have been with me from the very beginning.
16 "I have told you this, so that you will
not give up your faith. 2 You will be
expelled from the synagogues, and the time

Live it!

Love One Another

"I love ice cream and pizza and my dog and the color yellow and you and my best friend and God," Miko said to her mom.

"Really Miko, do you love me the same as ice cream?" her mom asked.

"Of course not! I love you much more than ice cream," she laughed back.

"Good," her mom said, "I hope you remember too what Jesus said about loving others."

"Yes," Miko said, "Jesus wants us to love one another, but does that mean I have to love the munchkin?"

"Yes, Miko, your brother [the munchkin] is included in 'love one another.' And it also means loving your classmates and even your history teacher, Mr. Wilson."

Miko sighed, "I'll try."

Two times in John 15:11–17, Jesus says to us, "Love one another." He not only tells us to love one another, but he also tells us how much he loves us. He calls us friends. He tells us that he loves us so much he would die for us. He loves us more than ice cream and pizza and the color yellow. He wants us to love one another that much too.

— John 15:1–17

15:12 Jn 13:34; 15:17; 1 Jn 3:23; 2 Jn 5 15:20 Mt 10:24; Lk 6:40; Jn 13:16 15:25 Ps 35:19; 69:4

will come when those who kill you will think that by doing this they are serving God. [3]People will do these things to you because they have not known either the Father or me. [4]But I have told you this, so that when the time comes for them to do these things, you will remember what I told you.

The Work of the Holy Spirit

"I did not tell you these things at the beginning, for I was with you. [5]But now I am going to him who sent me, yet none of you asks me where I am going. [6]And now that I have told you, your hearts are full of sadness. [7]But I am telling you the truth: it is better for you that I go away, because if I do not go, the Helper will not come to you. But if I do go away, then I will send him to you. [8]And when he comes, he will prove to the people of the world that they are wrong about sin and about what is right and about God's judgment. [9]They are wrong about sin, because they do not believe in me; [10]they are wrong about what is right, because I am going to the Father and you will not see me any more; [11]and they are wrong about judgment, because the ruler of this world has already been judged.

[12]"I have much more to tell you, but now it would be too much for you to bear. [13]When, however, the Spirit comes, who reveals the truth about God, he will lead you into all the truth. He will not speak on his own authority, but he will speak of what he hears and will tell you of things to come. [14]He will give me glory, because he will take what I say and tell it to you. [15]All that my Father has is mine; that is why I said that the Spirit will take what I give him and tell it to you.

Sadness and Gladness

[16]"In a little while you will not see me any more, and then a little while later you will see me."

[17]Some of his disciples asked among themselves, "What does this mean? He tells us that in a little while we will not see him, and then a little while later we will see him; and he also says, 'It is because I am going to the Father.' [18]What does this 'a little while' mean? We don't know what he is talking about!"

[19]Jesus knew that they wanted to question him, so he said to them, "I said, 'In a little while you will not see me, and then a little while later you will see me.' Is this what you are asking about among yourselves? [20]I am telling you the truth: you will cry and weep, but the world will be glad; you will be sad, but your sadness will turn into gladness. [21]When a woman is about to give birth, she is sad because her hour of suffering has come; but when the baby is born, she forgets her suffering, because she is happy that a baby has been born into the world. [22]That is how it is with you: now you are sad, but I will see you again, and your hearts will be filled with gladness, the kind of gladness that no one can take away from you.

[23]"When that day comes, you will not ask me for anything. I am telling you the truth: the Father will give you whatever you ask of him in my name.[f] [24]Until now you have not asked for anything in my name; ask and you will receive, so that your happiness may be complete.

Victory over the World

[25]"I have used figures of speech to tell you these things. But the time will come when I will not use figures of speech, but will speak to you plainly about the Father. [26]When that day comes, you will ask him in my name; and I do not say that I will ask him on your behalf, [27]for the Father himself loves you. He loves you because you love me and have believed that I came from God. [28]I did come from the Father, and I came into

[f] **16:23** the Father will give you whatever you ask of him in my name; *some manuscripts have* if you ask the Father for anything, he will give it to you in my name.
16:13 Wis 9:11

The disciples were confused by Jesus' words *(John 16:17)*. **Who can you go to for help in understanding the Bible?**

Study it!

It's Just Too Much!

Tsunamis, hatred, earthquakes, famine, homelessness, war. The list could go on and on. There is so much suffering and sin in the world. Since Adam and Eve's original sin, there always has been. The good news is that Jesus guarantees us victory over suffering and death. Jesus guarantees peace. Jesus says, "The world will make you suffer. But be brave! I have defeated the world!" (John 16:33). So although we will suffer or see others suffer, God's Word assures us that if we are united with Jesus, peace is ours. This also means that we have to do our part to create peace. As you go through your day-to-day activities, remember the promises of Jesus, and let Jesus work through you to make his promises come true for others.

— John 16:25–33

the world; and now I am leaving the world
and going to the Father."
29Then his disciples said to him, "Now
you are speaking plainly, without using fig-
ures of speech. 30We know now that you
know everything; you do not need to have
someone ask you questions. This makes us
believe that you came from God."
31Jesus answered them, "Do you believe
now? 32The time is coming, and is already
here, when all of you will be scattered, each
of you to your own home, and I will be left
all alone. But I am not really alone, because
the Father is with me. 33I have told you this
so that you will have peace by being united
to me. The world will make you suffer. But
be brave! I have defeated the world!"

Jesus Prays for His Disciples

17 After Jesus finished saying this, he
looked up to heaven and said, "Father,
the hour has come. Give glory to your Son, so
that the Son may give glory to you. 2For you
gave him authority over all people, so that he
might give eternal life to all those you gave
him. 3And eternal life means to know you, the
only true God, and to know Jesus Christ,
whom you sent. 4I have shown your glory on
earth; I have finished the work you gave me to
do. 5Father! Give me glory in your presence
now, the same glory I had with you before the
world was made.

"Father, the hour has come." (17:1)

6"I have made you known to those you
gave me out of the world. They belonged to
you, and you gave them to me. They have
obeyed your word, 7and now they know that
everything you gave me comes from you. 8I
gave them the message that you gave me,
and they received it; they know that it is true
that I came from you, and they believe that
you sent me.

17:3 Wis 15:3

"I pray not only for them, but also for those who believe in me because of their message" *(John 17:20)*.

Pray it!

From Me to We

Here is a short poem prayer called a diamond. It has five lines.

Me
Cool Smart
Playing Learning Praying
Together Christians
We

The first line of a diamond poem starts with one word. The second line uses two words to describe the thing in the first line. The fifth line has the name of something new. The fourth line has two words that describe it. The third line ties both things together. It has three words ending in *ing* that describe both things. A diamond poem is often used to show how opposites are related.

Try writing your own diamond poem prayer that asks God for unity. Maybe the first word is *one* and the last word is *many.* After you write it, pray it often. By praying for unity, we are doing what Jesus did in John 17:21. He was praying that all people of all time would be one—one with one another and one with God.

— John 17:20–23

[9]"I pray for them. I do not pray for the
world but for those you gave me, for they
belong to you. [10]All I have is yours, and all
you have is mine; and my glory is shown
through them. [11]And now I am coming to
you; I am no longer in the world, but they
are in the world. Holy Father! Keep them
safe by the power of your name, the name
you gave me,[g] so that they may be one just as
you and I are one. [12]While I was with them,
I kept them safe by the power of your name,
the name you gave me.[h] I protected them,
and not one of them was lost, except the
man who was bound to be lost—so that the
scripture might come true. [13]And now I am
coming to you, and I say these things in the
world so that they might have my joy in their
hearts in all its fullness. [14]I gave them your
message, and the world hated them, because
they do not belong to the world, just as I do
not belong to the world. [15]I do not ask you
to take them out of the world, but I do ask
you to keep them safe from the Evil One.
[16]Just as I do not belong to the world, they
do not belong to the world. [17]Dedicate them
to yourself by means of the truth; your word
is truth. [18]I sent them into the world, just as
you sent me into the world. [19]And for their
sake I dedicate myself to you, in order that
they, too, may be truly dedicated to you.

[20]"I pray not only for them, but also for
those who believe in me because of their
message. [21]I pray that they may all be one.
Father! May they be in us, just as you are in
me and I am in you. May they be one, so
that the world will believe that you sent me.
[22]I gave them the same glory you gave me,
so that they may be one, just as you and I are
one: [23]I in them and you in me, so that they
may be completely one, in order that the
world may know that you sent me and that
you love them as you love me.

[g] **17:11** Keep them safe by the power of your name, the name you gave me; *some manuscripts have* By the power of your name keep safe those you have given me. [h] **17:12** I kept them safe by the power of your name, the name you gave me; *some manuscripts have* By the power of your name I kept safe those you have given me.

17:12 Ps 41:9; Jn 13:18

24“Father! You have given them to me, and
I want them to be with me where I am, so
that they may see my glory, the glory you
gave me; for you loved me before the world
was made. 25Righteous Father! The world
does not know you, but I know you, and
these know that you sent me. 26I made you
known to them, and I will continue to do so,
in order that the love you have for me may be
in them, and so that I also may be in them.”

The Arrest of Jesus
(Matthew 26:47–56; Mark 14:43–50; Luke 22:47–53)

18 After Jesus had said this prayer, he
left with his disciples and went
across Kidron Brook. There was a garden in
that place, and Jesus and his disciples went
in. 2Judas, the traitor, knew where it was,
because many times Jesus had met there
with his disciples. 3So Judas went to the gar-
den, taking with him a group of Roman sol-
diers, and some Temple guards sent by the
chief priests and the Pharisees; they were
armed and carried lanterns and torches.
4Jesus knew everything that was going to
happen to him, so he stepped forward and
asked them, “Who is it you are looking for?”
5“Jesus of Nazareth,” they answered.
“I am he,” he said.
Judas, the traitor, was standing there with
them. 6When Jesus said to them, “I am he,”
they moved back and fell to the ground.
7Again Jesus asked them, “Who is it you are
looking for?”
“Jesus of Nazareth,” they said.
8“I have already told you that I am he,”
Jesus said. “If, then, you are looking for me, let
these others go.” (9He said this so that what
he had said might come true: “Father, I have
not lost even one of those you gave me.”)
10Simon Peter, who had a sword, drew it
and struck the High Priest’s slave, cutting off
his right ear. The name of the slave was
Malchus. 11Jesus said to Peter, “Put your
sword back in its place! Do you think that I
will not drink the cup of suffering which my
Father has given me?”

18:11 Mt 26:39; Mk 14:36; Lk 22:42

Live it!

Nonviolence

Jesus said, “Put your sword back in its place!” (John 18:11) to Peter when Peter cut off the ear of the High Priest’s slave. Jesus was willing to accept his suffering and did not want Peter and the others to resort to violence. Jesus reminds us that suffering is indeed difficult but better than retaliation.

Modern examples of the power of nonviolence similarly inspire us. Martin Luther King Jr. practiced nonviolence during the civil rights movement. It was a time when many white Americans were verbally and physically violent against black Americans. But Martin Luther King Jr. insisted that African Americans not respond with violence themselves. Their courage and willingness to love their persecutors brought about a peaceful revolution in this country.

Probably the best-known advocate of nonviolence was a small, quiet man from India, Mohandas K. Gandhi. His life was dedicated to nonviolence. He once said: “The badge of the violent is his weapon, spear, sword or rifle. God is the shield of the nonviolent.”

If you are in a situation where it seems easier to lash out, hit, or verbally hurt someone, try to remember these examples of nonviolence. Jesus wants us to respond to other people’s violence with love. It is one of the signs that we are truly his followers.

— John 18:1–11

Jesus before Annas

12 Then the Roman soldiers with their
commanding officer and the Jewish guards
arrested Jesus, tied him up, 13 and took him
first to Annas. He was the father-in-law of
Caiaphas, who was High Priest that year. 14 It
was Caiaphas who had advised the Jewish
authorities that it was better that one man
should die for all the people.

Peter Denies Jesus
(Matthew 26:69, 70; Mark 14:66–68; Luke 22:55–57)

15 Simon Peter and another disciple fol-
lowed Jesus. That other disciple was well
known to the High Priest, so he went with
Jesus into the courtyard of the High Priest's
house, 16 while Peter stayed outside by the
gate. Then the other disciple went back out,
spoke to the girl at the gate, and brought
Peter inside. 17 The girl at the gate said to
Peter, "Aren't you also one of the disciples of
that man?"

"No, I am not," answered Peter.

18 It was cold, so the servants and guards
had built a charcoal fire and were standing
around it, warming themselves. So Peter went
over and stood with them, warming himself.

The High Priest Questions Jesus
(Matthew 26:59–66; Mark 14:55–64; Luke 22:66–71)

19 The High Priest questioned Jesus about
his disciples and about his teaching. 20 Jesus
answered, "I have always spoken publicly to
everyone; all my teaching was done in the syn-
agogues and in the Temple, where all the peo-
ple come together. I have never said anything
in secret. 21 Why, then, do you question me?
Question the people who heard me. Ask them
what I told them—they know what I said."

22 When Jesus said this, one of the guards
there slapped him and said, "How dare you
talk like that to the High Priest!"

23 Jesus answered him, "If I have said any-
thing wrong, tell everyone here what it was.
But if I am right in what I have said, why do
you hit me?"

24 Then Annas sent him, still tied up, to
Caiaphas the High Priest.

Peter Denies Jesus Again
(Matthew 26:71–75; Mark 14:69–72; Luke 22:58–62)

25 Peter was still standing there keeping
himself warm. So the others said to him,
"Aren't you also one of the disciples of that
man?"

But Peter denied it. "No, I am not," he
said.

26 One of the High Priest's slaves, a relative
of the man whose ear Peter had cut off,
spoke up. "Didn't I see you with him in the
garden?" he asked.

27 Again Peter said "No"—and at once a
rooster crowed.

Jesus before Pilate
(Matthew 27:1, 2, 11–14; Mark 15:1–5; Luke 23:1–5)

28 Early in the morning Jesus was taken
from Caiaphas' house to the governor's
palace. The Jewish authorities did not go
inside the palace, for they wanted to keep
themselves ritually clean, in order to be able
to eat the Passover meal. 29 So Pilate went
outside to them and asked, "What do you
accuse this man of?"

30 Their answer was, "We would not have
brought him to you if he had not committed
a crime."

31 Pilate said to them, "Then you your-
selves take him and try him according to
your own law."

They replied, "We are not allowed to put
anyone to death." (32 This happened in order
to make come true what Jesus had said
when he indicated the kind of death he
would die.)

18:14 Jn 11:49, 50 **18:32** Jn 3:14; 12:32

How many times did Peter deny Christ before the rooster crowed?

33 Pilate went back into the palace and
called Jesus. "Are you the king of the Jews?"
he asked him.
34 Jesus answered, "Does this question
come from you or have others told you
about me?"
35 Pilate replied, "Do you think I am a
Jew? It was your own people and the chief
priests who handed you over to me. What
have you done?"
36 Jesus said, "My kingdom does not
belong to this world; if my kingdom be-
longed to this world, my followers would
fight to keep me from being handed over to
the Jewish authorities. No, my kingdom does
not belong here!"
37 So Pilate asked him, "Are you a king,
then?"
Jesus answered, "You say that I am a king.
I was born and came into the world for this
one purpose, to speak about the truth. Who-
ever belongs to the truth listens to me."
38 "And what is truth?" Pilate asked.

"And what is truth?" (18:38)

Jesus Is Sentenced to Death

(Matthew 27:15–31; Mark 15:6–20; Luke 23:13–25)

Then Pilate went back outside to the peo-
ple and said to them, "I cannot find any reason
to condemn him. 39 But according to the cus-
tom you have, I always set free a prisoner for
you during the Passover. Do you want me to
set free for you the king of the Jews?"

"No, not him! We want Barabbas!" (18:40)

40 They answered him with a shout, "No,
not him! We want Barabbas!" (Barabbas was
a bandit.)

19 Then Pilate took Jesus and had him
whipped. 2 The soldiers made a
crown out of thorny branches and put it on
his head; then they put a purple robe on him
3 and came to him and said, "Long live the
King of the Jews!" And they went up and
slapped him.
4 Pilate went back out once more and said
to the crowd, "Look, I will bring him out
here to you to let you see that I cannot find
any reason to condemn him." 5 So Jesus came
out, wearing the crown of thorns and the
purple robe. Pilate said to them, "Look! Here
is the man!"
6 When the chief priests and the Temple
guards saw him, they shouted, "Crucify him!
Crucify him!"
Pilate said to them, "You take him, then,
and crucify him. I find no reason to con-
demn him."
7 The crowd answered back, "We have a
law that says he ought to die, because he
claimed to be the Son of God."
8 When Pilate heard this, he was even more
afraid. 9 He went back into the palace and
asked Jesus, "Where do you come from?"
But Jesus did not answer. 10 Pilate said to
him, "You will not speak to me? Remember,
I have the authority to set you free and also
to have you crucified."
11 Jesus answered, "You have authority over
me only because it was given to you by

19:11 Wis 6:3

Breaking the legs of crucified people caused them to die faster because they could no longer push themselves up to fill their lungs with air.

God. So the man who handed me over to
you is guilty of a worse sin."
12 When Pilate heard this, he tried to find
a way to set Jesus free. But the crowd shout-
ed back, "If you set him free, that means that
you are not the Emperor's friend! Anyone
who claims to be a king is a rebel against the
Emperor!"
13 When Pilate heard these words, he took
Jesus outside and sat down on the judge's
seat in the place called "The Stone Pave-
ment." (In Hebrew the name is "Gabbatha.")
14 It was then almost noon of the day before
the Passover. Pilate said to the people, "Here
is your king!"
15 They shouted back, "Kill him! Kill him!
Crucify him!"

Pilate asked them, "Do you want me to
crucify your king?"

The chief priests answered, "The only
king we have is the Emperor!"
16 Then Pilate handed Jesus over to them
to be crucified.

Jesus Is Crucified
(Matthew 27:32–44; Mark 15:21–32; Luke 23:26–43)

So they took charge of Jesus. 17 He went
out, carrying his cross, and came to "The
Place of the Skull," as it is called. (In
Hebrew it is called "Golgotha.") 18 There
they crucified him; and they also crucified
two other men, one on each side, with Jesus
between them. 19 Pilate wrote a notice and
had it put on the cross. "Jesus of Nazareth,
the King of the Jews," is what he wrote.
20 Many people read it, because the place
where Jesus was crucified was not far from
the city. The notice was written in Hebrew,
Latin, and Greek. 21 The chief priests said to
Pilate, "Do not write 'The King of the Jews,'
but rather, 'This man said, I am the King of
the Jews.'"
22 Pilate answered, "What I have written
stays written."
23 After the soldiers had crucified Jesus,
they took his clothes and divided them into
four parts, one part for each soldier. They
also took the robe, which was made of one
piece of woven cloth without any seams in
it. 24 The soldiers said to one another, "Let's
not tear it; let's throw dice to see who will
get it." This happened in order to make the
scripture come true:

"They divided my clothes among
themselves
and gambled for my robe."

And this is what the soldiers did.
25 Standing close to Jesus' cross were his
mother, his mother's sister, Mary the wife of
Clopas, and Mary Magdalene. 26 Jesus saw his
mother and the disciple he loved standing
there; so he said to his mother, "He is your
son."
27 Then he said to the disciple, "She is
your mother." From that time the disciple
took her to live in his home.

The Death of Jesus
(Matthew 27:45–56; Mark 15:33–41; Luke 23:44–49)

28 Jesus knew that by now everything had
been completed; and in order to make the
scripture come true, he said, "I am thirsty."
29 A bowl was there, full of cheap wine; so
a sponge was soaked in the wine, put on a
stalk of hyssop, and lifted up to his lips.
30 Jesus drank the wine and said, "It is fin-
ished!"

Then he bowed his head and gave up his
spirit.

He went out, carrying his cross. (19:17)

19:24 Ps 22:18 **19:28, 29** Ps 69:21; 22:15

Study it!

Our Family

"Who is that little old lady? Is she your grandma?" Lisa asked Leslie.

Leslie answered, "No, my mom just helps her out. First her husband died, and then her kids, so now she is all alone."

That night while Leslie was helping her mom with dinner, she asked, "Mom, why do you help Mrs. Collins? Are you hoping you get her stuff when she dies or something?"

"No, Leslie, I help Mrs. Collins because that is what we do for others. Remember the story of Jesus' death on the cross?"

"Mom, what does that have to do with Mrs. Collins?" asked Leslie.

"Leslie, look it up, John 19:26–27," her mother replied.

Leslie went to her Bible and brought it into the kitchen. After reading it she said, "So, Jesus told the disciple to take care of his mother, not you."

"But that's the point, Leslie," her mom replied. "The things Jesus told his followers then are true for us today. Because we are part of the community, we need to take care of one another."

"Hmm. Mom, don't worry, I'll take care of you when you're old like Mrs. Collins," Leslie said.

"Thanks honey, and remember that the Gospel teaches that Mary is also our Mother and cares for us," her mother answered, giving Leslie a big hug.

— John 19:25–27

Jesus' Side Is Pierced

31 Then the Jewish authorities asked Pilate
to allow them to break the legs of the men
who had been crucified, and to take the
bodies down from the crosses. They request-
ed this because it was Friday, and they did
not want the bodies to stay on the crosses on
the Sabbath, since the coming Sabbath was
especially holy. 32 So the soldiers went and
broke the legs of the first man and then of
the other man who had been crucified with
Jesus. 33 But when they came to Jesus, they
saw that he was already dead, so they did not
break his legs. 34 One of the soldiers, howev-
er, plunged his spear into Jesus' side, and at
once blood and water poured out. (35 The
one who saw this happen has spoken of it, so
that you also may believe.[i] What he said is
true, and he knows that he speaks the truth.)
36 This was done to make the scripture come
true: "Not one of his bones will be broken."
37 And there is another scripture that says,
"People will look at him whom they
pierced."

The Burial of Jesus

(Matthew 27:57–61; Mark 15:42–47; Luke 23:50–56)

38 After this, Joseph, who was from the
town of Arimathea, asked Pilate if he could
take Jesus' body. (Joseph was a follower of
Jesus, but in secret, because he was afraid of
the Jewish authorities.) Pilate told him he
could have the body, so Joseph went and
took it away. 39 Nicodemus, who at first had
gone to see Jesus at night, went with Joseph,
taking with him about one hundred pounds
of spices, a mixture of myrrh and aloes.
40 The two men took Jesus' body and
wrapped it in linen cloths with the spices
according to the Jewish custom of preparing
a body for burial. 41 There was a garden in
the place where Jesus had been put to death,
and in it there was a new tomb where no
one had ever been buried. 42 Since it was the
day before the Sabbath and because the
tomb was close by, they placed Jesus' body
there.

[i] **19:35** believe; *some manuscripts have* continue to believe.

19:36 Ex 12:46; Num 9:12; Ps 34:20 **19:37** Zech 12:10; Rev 1:7 **19:39** Jn 3:1, 2

The two men took Jesus' body. (19:40)

The Empty Tomb
*(Matthew 28:1–8; Mark 16:1–8;
Luke 24:1–12)*

20 Early on Sunday morning, while it
was still dark, Mary Magdalene went
to the tomb and saw that the stone had been
taken away from the entrance. 2She went
running to Simon Peter and the other disci-
ple, whom Jesus loved, and told them, "They
have taken the Lord from the tomb, and we
don't know where they have put him!"
3Then Peter and the other disciple went to
the tomb. 4The two of them were running,
but the other disciple ran faster than Peter
and reached the tomb first. 5He bent over and
saw the linen cloths, but he did not go in.
6Behind him came Simon Peter, and he went
straight into the tomb. He saw the linen
cloths lying there 7and the cloth which had
been around Jesus' head. It was not lying with
the linen cloths but was rolled up by itself.
8Then the other disciple, who had reached
the tomb first, also went in; he saw and
believed. (9They still did not understand the
scripture which said that he must rise from
death.) 10Then the disciples went back home.

Jesus Appears to Mary Magdalene
(Matthew 28:9, 10; Mark 16:9–11)

11Mary stood crying outside the tomb.
While she was still crying, she bent over and
looked in the tomb 12and saw two angels
there dressed in white, sitting where the
body of Jesus had been, one at the head and
the other at the feet. 13"Woman, why are
you crying?" they asked her.
She answered, "They have taken my Lord
away, and I do not know where they have
put him!"
14Then she turned around and saw Jesus
standing there; but she did not know that it
was Jesus. 15"Woman, why are you crying?"
Jesus asked her. "Who is it that you are look-
ing for?"
She thought he was the gardener, so she
said to him, "If you took him away, sir, tell
me where you have put him, and I will go
and get him."
16Jesus said to her, "Mary!"
She turned toward him and said in
Hebrew, "Rabboni!" (This means "Teacher.")
17"Do not hold on to me," Jesus told her,
"because I have not yet gone back up to the
Father. But go to my brothers and tell them
that I am returning to him who is my Father
and their Father, my God and their God."
18So Mary Magdalene went and told the
disciples that she had seen the Lord and
related to them what he had told her.

Jesus Appears to His Disciples
*(Matthew 28:16–20; Mark 16:14–18;
Luke 24:36–49)*

19It was late that Sunday evening, and the
disciples were gathered together behind
locked doors, because they were afraid of the
Jewish authorities. Then Jesus came and
stood among them. "Peace be with you," he
said. 20After saying this, he showed them his
hands and his side. The disciples were filled
with joy at seeing the Lord. 21Jesus said to
them again, "Peace be with you. As the
Father sent me, so I send you." 22Then he
breathed on them and said, "Receive the
Holy Spirit. 23If you forgive people's sins,
they are forgiven; if you do not forgive
them, they are not forgiven."

20:23 Mt 16:19; 18:18

Who first saw Jesus risen from the dead? What did she do after that?

Pray it!

Peace

Jesus said, "Peace be with you," two times to his disciples in John 20:19–21. He wants us to be at peace and to share our peace with others. Here is one way to remember how to practice peace:
Practice peace every day.
Enjoy others, especially those who are different.
Always think before you speak and act.
Create peace at home and school.
Echo Jesus' words.

Notice how each line above begins with one of the letters of the word *peace.* What other ways of practicing peace can you think of? Write your own peace reminder:
P
E
A
C
E

— John 20:19–21

Jesus and Thomas

24 One of the twelve disciples, Thomas (called the Twin), was not with them when Jesus came.
25 So the other disciples told him, "We have seen the Lord!"

Thomas said to them, "Unless I see the scars of the nails in his hands and put my finger on those scars and my hand in his side, I will not believe."

26 A week later the disciples were together again indoors, and Thomas was with them. The doors were locked, but Jesus came and stood among them and said, "Peace be with you."
27 Then he said to Thomas, "Put your finger here, and look at my hands; then reach out your hand and put it in my side. Stop your doubting, and believe!"

28 Thomas answered him, "My Lord and my God!"

29 Jesus said to him, "Do you believe because you see me? How happy are those who believe without seeing me!"

The Purpose of This Book

30 In his disciples' presence Jesus performed many other miracles which are not

Jesus came and stood among them. (20:26)

What is the purpose of this book mentioned at the end of chapter twenty?

Catholic Connections

Penance and Reconciliation

One of the powers that Jesus gave to the Apostles after his Resurrection can be found in John 20:21–23. He tells them that they can forgive the sins of others. This is one of the Bible passages that the sacrament of Penance and Reconciliation is based on. The sacrament of Penance and Reconciliation (sometimes called Confession) allows us to experience God's forgiveness for our sins.

During the sacrament we tell or confess our sins to a priest. The priest is Christ's representative. Confessing our sins to a real person who represents Christ helps us understand that sin has real consequences and that God's forgiveness is also very real. The priest shows God's compassion and understanding to the person who is confessing his or her sins.

Idealy Catholics should go to Penance and Reconciliation at least once a year. If you have committed a very serious (mortal) sin, you should go as soon as you can and not receive the Eucharist until you do so. If it has been a while since your last confession, maybe it is time to go. The priest will help you through it, and you can ask a teacher, or a parent for help. Don't miss this chance to feel the amazing forgiveness of God!

— John 20:19–23

"Look at my hands. . . . Stop your doubting, and believe!" (20:27)

written down in this book. 31But these have
been written in order that you may believe[i]
that Jesus is the Messiah, the Son of God,
and that through your faith in him you may
have life.

Jesus Appears to Seven Disciples

21 After this, Jesus appeared once more
to his disciples at Lake Tiberias. This
is how it happened. 2Simon Peter, Thomas
(called the Twin), Nathanael (the one from
Cana in Galilee), the sons of Zebedee, and
two other disciples of Jesus were all together.
3Simon Peter said to the others, "I am going
fishing."

"We will come with you," they told him.
So they went out in a boat, but all that night
they did not catch a thing. 4As the sun was
rising, Jesus stood at the water's edge, but
the disciples did not know that it was Jesus.
5Then he asked them, "Young men, haven't
you caught anything?"

"Not a thing," they answered.

6He said to them, "Throw your net out
on the right side of the boat, and you will
catch some." So they threw the net out and

[i] **20:31** believe; *some manuscripts have* continue to believe.
21:3 Lk 5:5 **21:6** Lk 5:6

Catholic Connections

Apostolic Succession

In John, chapter 21, the resurrected Jesus tells Peter three times to feed his sheep. Jesus' sheep are all the people of the world, but especially the Church. The Bible establishes Peter as the first pope and the other Apostles as the first bishops (see also John 13:20, 17:20, 20:21). Through the centuries their special leadership roles have been passed to new popes and bishops in a process called apostolic succession.

Apostolic succession is a big phrase. It is also an important one. When Jesus gave the Apostles the Holy Spirit, he began the chain (succession) of bishops and popes. Today, that chain is continued with our current pope and bishops. The Pope's special role can be traced back to the charge that Jesus gave to Peter in John 21:15–19. The Catholic Church has been, and still is, led by the Holy Spirit through the special teaching authority of the Pope and bishops. At Mass we pray for the Pope, bishop, and the other Church leaders. This helps them lead and strengthen the chain.

— John 21:15–19

could not pull it back in, because they had
caught so many fish.
7 The disciple whom Jesus loved said to
Peter, "It is the Lord!" When Peter heard
that it was the Lord, he wrapped his outer
garment around him (for he had taken his
clothes off) and jumped into the water.
8 The other disciples came to shore in the
boat, pulling the net full of fish. They were
not very far from land, about a hundred
yards away. 9 When they stepped ashore, they
saw a charcoal fire there with fish on it and
some bread. 10 Then Jesus said to them,
"Bring some of the fish you have just
caught."
11 Simon Peter went aboard and dragged
the net ashore full of big fish, a hundred and
fifty-three in all; even though there were so
many, still the net did not tear. 12 Jesus said to
them, "Come and eat." None of the disciples
dared ask him, "Who are you?" because they
knew it was the Lord. 13 So Jesus went over,
took the bread, and gave it to them; he did
the same with the fish.
14 This, then, was the third time Jesus
appeared to the disciples after he was raised
from death.

Simon Peter . . . dragged the net ashore. (21:11)

Jesus and Peter

15 After they had eaten, Jesus said to Simon
Peter, "Simon son of John, do you love me
more than these others do?"
"Yes, Lord," he answered, "you know that
I love you."
Jesus said to him, "Take care of my lambs."
16 A second time Jesus said to him, "Simon
son of John, do you love me?"
"Yes, Lord," he answered, "you know that
I love you."

Jesus said to him, "Take care of my sheep."
17 A third time Jesus said, "Simon son of
John, do you love me?"
Peter became sad because Jesus asked him
the third time, "Do you love me?" and so he
said to him, "Lord, you know everything;
you know that I love you!"
Jesus said to him, "Take care of my sheep.
18 I am telling you the truth: when you were
young, you used to get ready and go any-
where you wanted to; but when you are old,
you will stretch out your hands and some-
one else will tie you up and take you where
you don't want to go." 19 (In saying this, Jesus
was indicating the way in which Peter
would die and bring glory to God.) Then
Jesus said to him, "Follow me!"

Jesus and the Other Disciple

20 Peter turned around and saw behind
him that other disciple, whom Jesus loved—
the one who had leaned close to Jesus at the
meal and had asked, "Lord, who is going to
betray you?" 21 When Peter saw him, he
asked Jesus, "Lord, what about this man?"
22 Jesus answered him, "If I want him to live
until I come, what is that to you? Follow me!"
23 So a report spread among the followers
of Jesus that this disciple would not die. But
Jesus did not say he would not die; he said,
"If I want him to live until I come, what is
that to you?"
24 He is the disciple who spoke of these
things, the one who also wrote them down;
and we know that what he said is true.

Conclusion

25 Now, there are many other things that
Jesus did. If they were all written down one
by one, I suppose that the whole world could
not hold the books that would be written.

21:20 Jn 13:25

Your Next Step

Congratulations on finishing the Gospel of John! Use this space to write your thoughts and questions about this book. If you are following the suggested reading plan, move ahead to the First Letter of John. This letter continues to emphasize that God is love!

THE *Acts* OF THE APOSTLES

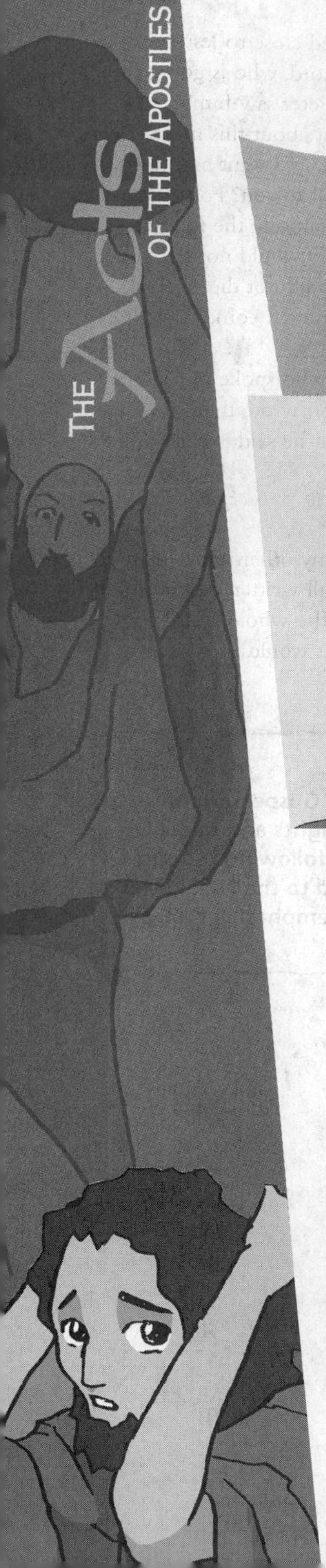

Imagine taking a trip around the world—wouldn't that be a fantastic adventure! In the Acts of the Apostles (Acts) the first followers of Jesus, the Apostles, are on a great journey. But this is no vacation! Instead, they have a huge mission to accomplish: teaching everyone about Jesus and forming new Christian churches.

Acts picks up where the Gospels leave off. The Apostles are on their own, spreading the Good News about Jesus Christ. But they are not really alone, for Jesus has sent them the Holy Spirit to guide them. As they travel about teaching and preaching and healing, they are welcomed by some people and rejected by others. In the midst of it all, a new religion is born: Christianity.

Chap. 7:54–60

Headlines

- Fire! The Spirit's Dramatic Arrival (2:1–13)
- Christians Share Everything (2:43–47)
- Persecutor Becomes Missionary! (9:1–25)
- Jews and Gentiles Form First Church (11:19–26)
- Council Debates Gentile Question (chapter 15)
- Paul Causes Riot in Ephesus! (19:21–41)
- Plot to Assassinate Paul Discovered (23:12–35)

FACTOIDS

Who are the central characters? Peter, Paul, the Apostles, Jewish leaders, Roman leaders, and early Christians.

Who wrote this book? The same person who wrote the Gospel of Luke.

Who was it written for? Just like Luke, Acts is addressed to Theophilus, which means "friend of God" in Greek.

Why was it written? The author wanted to describe how Jesus' mission was carried on by the Apostles after Jesus returned to heaven.

What is the literary style? The style is salvation history. It shows how God's plan for salvation is carried out through special people and events.

Important themes

- Have courage! The Holy Spirit will equip us for the interesting and sometimes perilous journey of living as Christians.
- God wants *all* people on earth to be saved, not only the Jews.
- Living as a Christian means knowing the Gospel, praying together, sharing the Eucharist, and caring for the poor.

1 Dear Theophilus:
In my first book I wrote about all
the things that Jesus did and taught from
the time he began his work 2until the day
he was taken up to heaven. Before he was
taken up, he gave instructions by the power
of the Holy Spirit to the men he had cho-
sen as his apostles. 3For forty days after his
death he appeared to them many times in
ways that proved beyond doubt that he was
alive. They saw him, and he talked with
them about the Kingdom of God. 4And
when they came together,[a] he gave them
this order: "Do not leave Jerusalem, but
wait for the gift I told you about, the gift
my Father promised. 5John baptized with
water, but in a few days you will be bap-
tized with the Holy Spirit."

Jesus Is Taken Up to Heaven

6When the apostles met together with
Jesus, they asked him, "Lord, will you at this
time give the Kingdom back to Israel?"
7Jesus said to them, "The times and occa-
sions are set by my Father's own authority,
and it is not for you to know when they will
be. 8But when the Holy Spirit comes upon
you, you will be filled with power, and you
will be witnesses for me in Jerusalem, in all
of Judea and Samaria, and to the ends of the
earth." 9After saying this, he was taken up to
heaven as they watched him, and a cloud hid
him from their sight.
10They still had their eyes fixed on the sky
as he went away, when two men dressed in
white suddenly stood beside them 11and
said, "Galileans, why are you standing there

[a] **1:4** when they came together; *or* while he was staying with them, *or* while he was eating with them.

1:1 Lk 1:1–4 **1:4** Lk 24:49 **1:5** Mt 3:11; Mk 1:8; Lk 3:16; Jn 1:33 **1:8** Mt 28:19; Mk 16:15; Lk 24:47, 48 **1:9** Mk 16:19; Lk 24:50, 51

Pray it!

Now What?

The Apostles and other disciples of Jesus had given up everything to follow him: homes, families, and jobs. He touched their hearts, and they changed their lives for him. And now in this first chapter of the Acts of the Apostles, Jesus tells them he is leaving. These first followers might have felt hopeless, abandoned, or lost, but Jesus comforts them, telling them to wait (Acts 1:4). He assures them God has promised a gift for them, the Holy Spirit. The Holy Spirit will fill them with power and give them everything they will need to carry on when he is gone.

Lord, I don't always know what's next in my life,
and sometimes the unknown is scary.
But, I will wait for your gifts.
Holy Spirit, help me understand what I need to do
and when I need to do it.
Give me whatever I need to accomplish it.
Amen.

— Acts 1:1–11

looking up at the sky? This Jesus, who was taken from you into heaven, will come back in the same way that you saw him go to heaven."

Judas' Successor

[12]Then the apostles went back to Jerusalem
from the Mount of Olives, which is about
half a mile away from the city. [13]They entered
the city and went up to the room where they
were staying: Peter, John, James and Andrew,
Philip and Thomas, Bartholomew and
Matthew, James son of Alphaeus, Simon the
Patriot, and Judas son of James. [14]They gath-
ered frequently to pray as a group, together
with the women and with Mary the mother
of Jesus and with his brothers.
[15]A few days later there was a meeting of
the believers, about a hundred and twenty
in all, and Peter stood up to speak. [16]"My
friends," he said, "the scripture had to come
true in which the Holy Spirit, speaking
through David, made a prediction about
Judas, who was the guide for those who
arrested Jesus. [17]Judas was a member of our
group, for he had been chosen to have a part
in our work."
([18]With the money that Judas got for his
evil act he bought a field, where he fell to his
death; he burst open and all his insides spilled
out. [19]All the people living in Jerusalem
heard about it, and so in their own language
they call that field Akeldama, which means
"Field of Blood.")
[20]"For it is written in the book of Psalms,

'May his house become empty;
may no one live in it.'

It is also written,

'May someone else take his place of
service.'

[21-22]"So then, someone must join us as a
witness to the resurrection of the Lord Jesus.
He must be one of the men who were in
our group during the whole time that the
Lord Jesus traveled about with us, beginning
from the time John preached his message of
baptism[b] until the day Jesus was taken up
from us to heaven."
[23]So they proposed two men: Joseph, who
was called Barsabbas (also known as Justus),
and Matthias. [24]Then they prayed, "Lord,
you know the thoughts of everyone, so show
us which of these two you have chosen [25]to
serve as an apostle in the place of Judas, who
left to go to the place where he belongs."
[26]Then they drew lots to choose between
the two men, and the one chosen was
Matthias, who was added to the group of
eleven apostles.

The Coming of the Holy Spirit

2 When the day of Pentecost came, all the
believers were gathered together in one
place. [2]Suddenly there was a noise from the
sky which sounded like a strong wind blow-
ing, and it filled the whole house where they
were sitting. [3]Then they saw what looked
like tongues of fire which spread out and
touched each person there. [4]They were all
filled with the Holy Spirit and began to talk
in other languages, as the Spirit enabled
them to speak.
[5]There were Jews living in Jerusalem, reli-
gious people who had come from every
country in the world. [6]When they heard this
noise, a large crowd gathered. They were all
excited, because all of them heard the
believers talking in their own languages. [7]In
amazement and wonder they exclaimed,
"These people who are talking like this are
Galileans! [8]How is it, then, that all of us hear
them speaking in our own native languages?
[9]We are from Parthia, Media, and Elam; from
Mesopotamia, Judea, and Cappadocia; from
Pontus and Asia, [10]from Phrygia and Pam-
phylia, from Egypt and the regions of Libya
near Cyrene. Some of us are from Rome,
[11]both Jews and Gentiles converted to

[b] **1:21–22** John preached his message of baptism; *or* John baptized him.
1:13 Mt 10:2–4; Mk 3:16–19; Lk 6:14–16 **1:18, 19** Mt 27:3–8 **1:20 a** Ps 69:25; **b** Ps 109:8 **1:22 a** Mt 3:16; Mk 1:9; Lk 3:21; **b** Mk 16:19; Lk 24:51 **2:1** Lev 23:15–21; Deut 16:9–11

In the first chapter of Acts, three numbers are mentioned. Can you find them? Do they sound familiar?

Catholic Connections

Confirmation

When the Apostles felt the power of the Holy Spirit inside them, they were changed. Suddenly, they could speak and be understood by people who spoke different languages (Acts 2:4–6)! This miracle proved to the Apostles that God was equipping them with the tools they needed for their mission.

When we are confirmed, God changes us too. Confirmation is a sacrament of initiation, one of the seven sacraments of the Catholic Church. Through Confirmation the gifts of the Holy Spirit—wisdom, understanding, right judgment, courage, knowledge, reverence, wonder and awe in God's presence—grow stronger within us. Just like the Apostles, we become better equipped to live our faith and share it with others.

— Acts 2:1–13

Judaism, and some of us are from Crete and Arabia—yet all of us hear them speaking in our own languages about the great things that God has done!"
12Amazed and confused, they kept asking each other, "What does this mean?"
13But others made fun of the believers, saying, "These people are drunk!"

"Fellow Jews, . . . listen to me!" (2:14)

Peter's Message

14Then Peter stood up with the other eleven apostles and in a loud voice began to speak to the crowd: "Fellow Jews and all of you who live in Jerusalem, listen to me and let me tell you what this means.
15These people are not drunk, as you suppose; it is only nine o'clock in the morning.
16Instead, this is what the prophet Joel spoke about:

17'This is what I will do in the last days, God says:
I will pour out my Spirit on everyone.
Your sons and daughters will proclaim my message;
your young men will see visions,
and your old men will have dreams.
18Yes, even on my servants, both men and women,
I will pour out my Spirit in those days,
and they will proclaim my message.
19I will perform miracles in the sky above
and wonders on the earth below.
There will be blood, fire, and thick smoke;
20 the sun will be darkened,
and the moon will turn red as blood,
before the great and glorious Day of the Lord comes.
21And then, whoever calls out to the Lord for help will be saved.'

2:17–21 Joel 2:28–32 (LXX)

22 "Listen to these words, fellow Israelites!
Jesus of Nazareth was a man whose divine
authority was clearly proven to you by all the
miracles and wonders which God performed
through him. You yourselves know this, for it
happened here among you. 23 In accordance
with his own plan God had already decided
that Jesus would be handed over to you; and
you killed him by letting sinful men crucify
him. 24 But God raised him from death, set-
ting him free from its power, because it was
impossible that death should hold him pris-
oner. 25 For David said about him,
'I saw the Lord before me at all times;
he is near me, and I will not be
troubled.
26 And so I am filled with gladness,
and my words are full of joy.
And I, mortal though I am,
will rest assured in hope,
27 because you will not abandon me in the
world of the dead;
you will not allow your faithful servant
to rot in the grave.
28 You have shown me the paths that lead to
life,
and your presence will fill me with joy.'
29 "My friends, I must speak to you plainly
about our famous ancestor King David. He
died and was buried, and his grave is here
with us to this very day. 30 He was a prophet,
and he knew what God had promised him:
God had made a vow that he would make
one of David's descendants a king, just as
David was. 31 David saw what God was going
to do in the future, and so he spoke about
the resurrection of the Messiah when he said,
'He was not abandoned in the world of
the dead;
his body did not rot in the grave.'
32 God has raised this very Jesus from death,
and we are all witnesses to this fact. 33 He has
been raised to the right side of God, his
Father, and has received from him the Holy
Spirit, as he had promised. What you now
see and hear is his gift that he has poured
out on us. 34 For it was not David who went
up into heaven; rather he said,
'The Lord said to my Lord:
Sit here at my right side
35 until I put your enemies as a footstool
under your feet.'
36 "All the people of Israel, then, are to
know for sure that this Jesus, whom you
crucified, is the one that God has made Lord
and Messiah!"
37 When the people heard this, they were
deeply troubled and said to Peter and the
other apostles, "What shall we do, brothers?"
38 Peter said to them, "Each one of you
must turn away from your sins and be bap-
tized in the name of Jesus Christ, so that
your sins will be forgiven; and you will
receive God's gift, the Holy Spirit. 39 For
God's promise was made to you and your
children, and to all who are far away—all
whom the Lord our God calls to himself."
40 Peter made his appeal to them and with
many other words he urged them, saying,
"Save yourselves from the punishment com-
ing on this wicked people!" 41 Many of them
believed his message and were baptized, and
about three thousand people were added to
the group that day. 42 They spent their time
in learning from the apostles, taking part in
the fellowship, and sharing in the fellowship
meals and the prayers.

Life among the Believers

43 Many miracles and wonders were being
done through the apostles, and everyone was
filled with awe. 44 All the believers continued
together in close fellowship and shared their
belongings with one another. 45 They would
sell their property and possessions, and dis-
tribute the money among all, according to
what each one needed. 46 Day after day they
met as a group in the Temple, and they had
their meals together in their homes, eating
with glad and humble hearts, 47 praising God,
and enjoying the good will of all the people.
And every day the Lord added to their
group those who were being saved.

A Lame Beggar Is Healed

3 One day Peter and John went to the
Temple at three o'clock in the after-
noon, the hour for prayer. 2 There at the

2:23 Mt 27:35; Mk 15:24; Lk 23:33; Jn 19:18 **2:24** Mt 28:5, 6; Mk 16:6; Lk 24:5 **2:25–28** Ps 16:8–11 (LXX) **2:30** Ps 132:11; 2 Sam 7:12, 13 **2:34, 35** Ps 110:1 **2:44** Acts 4:32–35

Beautiful Gate, as it was called, was a man
who had been lame all his life. Every day he
was carried to the gate to beg for money
from the people who were going into the
Temple. [3]When he saw Peter and John going
in, he begged them to give him something.
[4]They looked straight at him, and Peter said,
"Look at us!" [5]So he looked at them,
expecting to get something from them. [6]But
Peter said to him, "I have no money at all,
but I give you what I have: in the name of
Jesus Christ of Nazareth I order you to get
up and walk!" [7]Then he took him by his
right hand and helped him up. At once the
man's feet and ankles became strong; [8]he
jumped up, stood on his feet, and started
walking around. Then he went into the Tem-
ple with them, walking and jumping and
praising God. [9]The people there saw him
walking and praising God, [10]and when they
recognized him as the beggar who had sat at
the Beautiful Gate, they were all surprised
and amazed at what had happened to him.

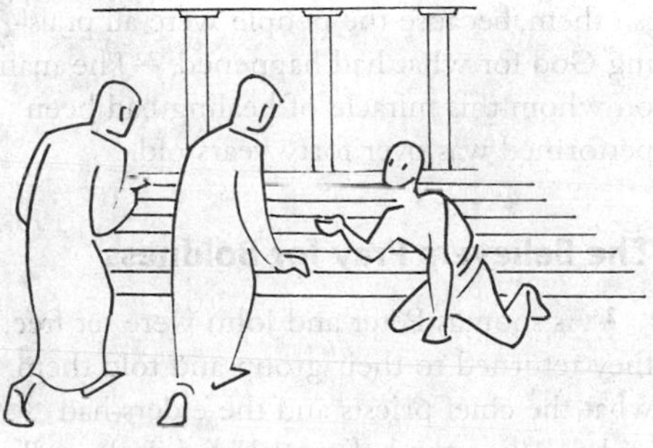

"I . . . give you what I have." (3:6)

Peter's Message in the Temple

[11]As the man held on to Peter and John in
Solomon's Porch, as it was called, the people
were amazed and ran to them. [12]When Peter
saw the people, he said to them, "Fellow
Israelites, why are you surprised at this, and
why do you stare at us? Do you think that it
was by means of our own power or godliness
that we made this man walk? [13]The God of
Abraham, Isaac, and Jacob, the God of our
ancestors, has given divine glory to his Ser-
vant Jesus. But you handed him over to the
authorities, and you rejected him in Pilate's
presence, even after Pilate had decided to set
him free. [14]He was holy and good, but you
rejected him, and instead you asked Pilate to
do you the favor of turning loose a murderer.
[15]You killed the one who leads to life, but
God raised him from death—and we are wit-
nesses to this. [16]It was the power of his name
that gave strength to this lame man. What
you see and know was done by faith in his
name; it was faith in Jesus that has made him
well, as you can all see.

[17]"And now, my friends, I know that what
you and your leaders did to Jesus was due to
your ignorance. [18]God announced long ago
through all the prophets that his Messiah had
to suffer; and he made it come true in this
way. [19]Repent, then, and turn to God, so
that he will forgive your sins. If you do,
[20]times of spiritual strength will come from
the Lord, and he will send Jesus, who is the
Messiah he has already chosen for you. [21]He
must remain in heaven until the time comes
for all things to be made new, as God
announced through his holy prophets of
long ago. [22]For Moses said, 'The Lord your
God will send you a prophet, just as he sent
me,[c] and he will be one of your own people.
You are to obey everything that he tells you
to do. [23]Anyone who does not obey that
prophet shall be separated from God's people
and destroyed.' [24]And all the prophets who
had a message, including Samuel and those
who came after him, also announced what
has been happening these days. [25]The prom-
ises of God through his prophets are for you,
and you share in the covenant which God
made with your ancestors. As he said to
Abraham, 'Through your descendants I will
bless all the people on earth.' [26]And so God
chose his Servant and sent him to you first,

[c] **3:22** just as he sent me; *or* like me.

3:13 Ex 3:15 **3:14** Mt 27:15–23; Mk 15:6–14; Lk 23:13–23; Jn 19:12–15 **3:22** Deut 18:15, 18 (LXX)
3:23 Deut 18:19 **3:25** Gen 22:18

"It was faith in Jesus that has made him well, as you can all see" *(Acts 3:16)*.

to bless you by making every one of you
turn away from your wicked ways."

Peter and John before the Council

4 Peter and John were still speaking to the
people when some priests,[d] the officer
in charge of the Temple guards, and some
Sadducees arrived. 2They were annoyed
because the two apostles were teaching the
people that Jesus had risen from death, which
proved that the dead will rise to life. 3So they
arrested them and put them in jail until the
next day, since it was already late. 4But many
who heard the message believed; and the
number grew to about five thousand.

5The next day the Jewish leaders, the el-
ders, and the teachers of the Law gathered in
Jerusalem. 6They met with the High Priest
Annas and with Caiaphas, John, Alexander,
and the others who belonged to the High
Priest's family. 7They made the apostles stand
before them and asked them, "How did you
do this? What power do you have or whose
name did you use?"

8Peter, full of the Holy Spirit, answered
them, "Leaders of the people and elders: 9if
we are being questioned today about the
good deed done to the lame man and how
he was healed, 10then you should all know,
and all the people of Israel should know, that
this man stands here before you completely
well through the power of the name of Jesus
Christ of Nazareth—whom you crucified
and whom God raised from death. 11Jesus is
the one of whom the scripture says,

'The stone that you the builders despised
turned out to be the most important of
all.'

12Salvation is to be found through him
alone; in all the world there is no one else
whom God has given who can save us."

13The members of the Council were
amazed to see how bold Peter and John
were and to learn that they were ordinary
men of no education. They realized then that
they had been companions of Jesus. 14But
there was nothing that they could say,
because they saw the man who had been
healed standing there with Peter and John.
15So they told them to leave the Council
room, and then they started discussing
among themselves. 16"What shall we do
with these men?" they asked. "Everyone in
Jerusalem knows that this extraordinary mir-
acle has been performed by them, and we
cannot deny it. 17But to keep this matter
from spreading any further among the peo-
ple, let us warn these men never again to
speak to anyone in the name of Jesus."

18So they called them back in and told
them that under no condition were they to
speak or to teach in the name of Jesus. 19But
Peter and John answered them, "You your-
selves judge which is right in God's sight—
to obey you or to obey God. 20For we can-
not stop speaking of what we ourselves have
seen and heard." 21So the Council warned
them even more strongly and then set them
free. They saw that it was impossible to pun-
ish them, because the people were all prais-
ing God for what had happened. 22The man
on whom this miracle of healing had been
performed was over forty years old.

The Believers Pray for Boldness

23As soon as Peter and John were set free,
they returned to their group and told them
what the chief priests and the elders had
said. 24When the believers heard it, they all
joined together in prayer to God: "Master
and Creator of heaven, earth, and sea, and all
that is in them! 25By means of the Holy
Spirit you spoke through our ancestor
David, your servant, when he said,

'Why were the Gentiles furious;
why did people make their useless plots?
26The kings of the earth prepared
themselves,
and the rulers met together
against the Lord and his Messiah.'

[d] **4:1** priests; *some manuscripts have* chief priests.
4:11 Ps 118:22 **4:24** Ex 20:11; Neh 9:6; Ps 146:6 **4:25, 26** Ps 2:1, 2 (LXX)

The Apostles and believers prayed for boldness *(Acts 4:29)*. **What might it look like if you were bold in your faith?**

27For indeed Herod and Pontius Pilate met
together in this city with the Gentiles and
the people of Israel against Jesus, your holy
Servant, whom you made Messiah. 28They
gathered to do everything that you by your
power and will had already decided would
happen. 29And now, Lord, take notice of the
threats they have made, and allow us, your
servants, to speak your message with all bold-
ness. 30Reach out your hand to heal, and
grant that wonders and miracles may be per-
formed through the name of your holy Ser-
vant Jesus."
31When they finished praying, the place
where they were meeting was shaken. They
were all filled with the Holy Spirit and began
to proclaim God's message with boldness.

The Believers Share Their Possessions

32The group of believers was one in mind
and heart. None of them said that any of
their belongings were their own, but they all
shared with one another everything they
had. 33With great power the apostles gave
witness to the resurrection of the Lord Jesus,
and God poured rich blessings on them all.
31There was no one in the group who was
in need. Those who owned fields or houses
would sell them, bring the money received
from the sale, 35and turn it over to the apos-
tles; and the money was distributed accord-
ing to the needs of the people.
36And so it was that Joseph, a Levite born
in Cyprus, whom the apostles called Bar-
nabas (which means "One who Encour-
ages"), 37sold a field he owned, brought the
money, and turned it over to the apostles.

Ananias and Sapphira

5 But there was a man named Ananias,
who with his wife Sapphira sold some
property that belonged to them. 2But with
his wife's agreement he kept part of the
money for himself and turned the rest over
to the apostles. 3Peter said to him, "Ananias,
why did you let Satan take control of you
and make you lie to the Holy Spirit by
keeping part of the money you received for
the property? 4Before you sold the property,
it belonged to you; and after you sold it, the
money was yours. Why, then, did you decide
to do such a thing? You have not lied to
people—you have lied to God!" 5As soon as
Ananias heard this, he fell down dead; and all
who heard about it were terrified. 6The
young men came in, wrapped up his body,
carried him out, and buried him.
7About three hours later his wife, not
knowing what had happened, came in.
8Peter asked her, "Tell me, was this the full
amount you and your husband received for
your property?"
"Yes," she answered, "the full amount."
9So Peter said to her, "Why did you and
your husband decide to put the Lord's Spirit
to the test? The men who buried your hus-
band are at the door right now, and they will
carry you out too!" 10At once she fell down

Live it!

Looking Out for One Another

The early Christian communities were determined that no one would be poor; rather, everyone would have as much as they needed. If a family had more money or possessions than they needed, they gave the extra to the Apostles, who then used it to help those who had less than they needed.

Who are the poor people in your community? How good is your church or your family at noticing who is poor and taking care of them? Find out what groups in your community help poor people, and explore how you and your family might get involved.

— Acts 4:34–35

4:27 **a** Lk 23:7–11; **b** Mt 27:1, 2; Mk 15:1; Lk 23:1; Jn 18:28, 29 **4:32** Acts 2:44, 45 **5:5** Dan B:55

Live it!

Stewardship

Stewardship means sharing generously of our time, our talents, and our money—especially with those in need. God knows what's in our hearts and what we possess. And God knows if we are being generous or selfish; we can fool everyone else, but we can never fool God.

So don't hold back, like Ananias and Sapphira did in the beginning of Acts, chapter 5. Instead, be very generous in sharing your time, talent, and money with others. You may not feel like you have much to offer, but you do. An hour of your time or a couple of dollars of your allowance can make a difference. Then be open to experiencing the abundant blessings God has in store for you for being a good steward!

— Acts 5:1–11

at his feet and died. The young men came in
and saw that she was dead, so they carried
her out and buried her beside her husband.
11 The whole church and all the others who
heard of this were terrified.

Miracles and Wonders

12 Many miracles and wonders were being
performed among the people by the apos-
tles. All the believers met together in
Solomon's Porch. 13 Nobody outside the
group dared join them, even though the
people spoke highly of them. 14 But more
and more people were added to the group—
a crowd of men and women who believed
in the Lord. 15 As a result of what the apos-
tles were doing, sick people were carried out
into the streets and placed on beds and mats
so that at least Peter's shadow might fall on
some of them as he passed by. 16 And crowds
of people came in from the towns around
Jerusalem, bringing those who were sick or
who had evil spirits in them; and they were
all healed.

. . . at least Peter's shadow might fall on some of them. (5:15)

The Apostles Are Persecuted

17 Then the High Priest and all his com-
panions, members of the local party of the
Sadducees, became extremely jealous of the
apostles; so they decided to take action.
18 They arrested the apostles and put them in
the public jail. 19 But that night an angel of
the Lord opened the prison gates, led the
apostles out, and said to them, 20 "Go and
stand in the Temple, and tell the people all
about this new life." 21 The apostles obeyed,
and at dawn they entered the Temple and
started teaching.

The High Priest and his companions
called together all the Jewish elders for a full
meeting of the Council; then they sent
orders to the prison to have the apostles
brought before them. 22 But when the offi-
cials arrived, they did not find the apostles in
prison, so they returned to the Council and
reported, 23 "When we arrived at the jail, we
found it locked up tight and all the guards
on watch at the gates; but when we opened
the gates, we found no one inside!" 24 When
the chief priests and the officer in charge of
the Temple guards heard this, they wondered
what had happened to the apostles. 25 Then a
man came in and said to them, "Listen! The

men you put in prison are in the Temple
teaching the people!" 26So the officer went
off with his men and brought the apostles
back. They did not use force, however,
because they were afraid that the people
might stone them.
27They brought the apostles in, made
them stand before the Council, and the
High Priest questioned them. 28"We gave
you strict orders not to teach in the name of
this man," he said; "but see what you have
done! You have spread your teaching all over
Jerusalem, and you want to make us respon-
sible for his death!"
29Peter and the other apostles answered,
"We must obey God, not men. 30The God
of our ancestors raised Jesus from death, after
you had killed him by nailing him to a cross.
31God raised him to his right side as Leader
and Savior, to give the people of Israel the
opportunity to repent and have their sins
forgiven. 32We are witnesses to these
things—we and the Holy Spirit, who is
God's gift to those who obey him."
33When the members of the Council
heard this, they were so furious that they
wanted to have the apostles put to death.
34But one of them, a Pharisee named
Gamaliel, who was a teacher of the Law and
was highly respected by all the people, stood
up in the Council. He ordered the apostles
to be taken out for a while, 35and then he
said to the Council, "Fellow Israelites, be
careful what you do to these men. 36You
remember that Theudas appeared some time
ago, claiming to be somebody great, and
about four hundred men joined him. But he
was killed, all his followers were scattered,
and his movement died out. 37After that,
Judas the Galilean appeared during the time
of the census; he drew a crowd after him, but
he also was killed, and all his followers were
scattered. 38And so in this case, I tell you, do
not take any action against these men. Leave
them alone! If what they have planned and
done is of human origin, it will disappear,
39but if it comes from God, you cannot pos-
sibly defeat them. You could find yourselves
fighting against God!"
The Council followed Gamaliel's advice.
40They called the apostles in, had them
whipped, and ordered them never again to
speak in the name of Jesus; and then they set
them free. 41As the apostles left the Council,
they were happy, because God had consid-
ered them worthy to suffer disgrace for the
sake of Jesus. 42And every day in the Temple
and in people's homes they continued to
teach and preach the Good News about
Jesus the Messiah.

The Seven Helpers

6 Some time later, as the number of disci-
ples kept growing, there was a quarrel
between the Greek-speaking Jews and the
native Jews. The Greek-speaking Jews
claimed that their widows were being ne-
glected in the daily distribution of funds. 2So
the twelve apostles called the whole group
of believers together and said, "It is not right
for us to neglect the preaching of God's
word in order to handle finances. 3So then,
friends, choose seven men among you who
are known to be full of the Holy Spirit and
wisdom, and we will put them in charge of
this matter. 4We ourselves, then, will give
our full time to prayer and the work of
preaching."
5The whole group was pleased with the
apostles' proposal, so they chose Stephen, a
man full of faith and the Holy Spirit, and
Philip, Prochorus, Nicanor, Timon, Parme-
nas, and Nicolaus, a Gentile from Antioch
who had earlier been converted to Judaism.
6The group presented them to the apostles,
who prayed and placed their hands on them.
7And so the word of God continued to
spread. The number of disciples in Jerusalem
grew larger and larger, and a great number
of priests accepted the faith.

5:28 Mt 27:25 **5:39** 2 Macc 7:19

The Sanhedrin was the great Council of the Jewish leaders, led by the High Priest. They ruled over religious matters.

Catholic Connections

Deacons, Ministers of Service

The job of making sure widows, orphans, and poor people had everything they needed was becoming a huge job! The Apostles needed to concentrate on preaching and healing, so they found helpers who could help keep track of who needed what and pass out donations fairly. Because the Greek word for service to others is *diakonia,* the people doing this work became known as deacons.

Like in the early Church, today we have deacons, who are ordained to serve the community and assist priests in their ministry. Permanent deacons usually do not have a job in the Church but have regular jobs in the community. If your parish has a permanent deacon, talk to him sometime about his special works of service.

— Acts 6:1–7

The Arrest of Stephen

8Stephen, a man richly blessed by God and
full of power, performed great miracles and
wonders among the people. 9But he was
opposed by some men who were members
of the synagogue of the Freedmen[e] (as it was
called), which had Jews from Cyrene and
Alexandria. They and other Jews from the
provinces of Cilicia and Asia started arguing
with Stephen. 10But the Spirit gave Stephen
such wisdom that when he spoke, they could
not refute him. 11So they bribed some men
to say, "We heard him speaking against Moses
and against God!" 12In this way they stirred
up the people, the elders, and the teachers of
the Law. They seized Stephen and took him
before the Council. 13Then they brought in
some men to tell lies about him. "This man,"
they said, "is always talking against our sacred
Temple and the Law of Moses. 14We heard
him say that this Jesus of Nazareth will tear
down the Temple and change all the customs
which have come down to us from Moses!"
15All those sitting in the Council fixed their
eyes on Stephen and saw that his face looked
like the face of an angel.

Stephen's Speech

7 The High Priest asked Stephen, "Is this
true?"
2Stephen answered, "Brothers and fathers,
listen to me! Before our ancestor Abraham
had gone to live in Haran, the God of glory
appeared to him in Mesopotamia 3and said
to him, 'Leave your family and country and
go to the land that I will show you.' 4And so
he left his country and went to live in Haran.
After Abraham's father died, God made him
move to this land where you now live. 5God
did not then give Abraham any part of it as
his own, not even a square foot of ground,
but God promised to give it to him, and that
it would belong to him and to his descen-
dants. At the time God made this promise,
Abraham had no children. 6This is what God
said to him: 'Your descendants will live in a
foreign country, where they will be slaves and
will be badly treated for four hundred years.

[e] **6:9** FREEDMEN: *These were Jews who had been slaves, but had bought or been given their freedom.*

7:2, 3 Gen 12:1 **7:4** **a** Gen 11:31; **b** Gen 12:4 **7:5** Gen 12:7; 13:15; 15:18; 17:8 **7:6, 7** Gen 15:13, 14

Who handles the money at your church? Do you know what the money pays for? To learn more ask your pastor, youth minister, or parents.

7But I will pass judgment on the people that they will serve, and afterward your descendants will come out of that country and will worship me in this place.' 8Then God gave to Abraham the ceremony of circumcision as a sign of the covenant. So Abraham circumcised Isaac a week after he was born; Isaac circumcised his son Jacob, and Jacob circumcised his twelve sons, the famous ancestors of our race.

9"Jacob's sons became jealous of their brother Joseph and sold him to be a slave in Egypt. But God was with him 10and brought him safely through all his troubles. When Joseph appeared before the king of Egypt, God gave him a pleasing manner and wisdom, and the king made Joseph governor over the country and the royal household. 11Then there was a famine all over Egypt and Canaan, which caused much suffering. Our ancestors could not find any food, 12and when Jacob heard that there was grain in Egypt, he sent his sons, our ancestors, on their first visit there. 13On the second visit Joseph made himself known to his brothers, and the king of Egypt came to know about Joseph's family. 14So Joseph sent a message to his father Jacob, telling him and the whole family, seventy-five people in all, to come to Egypt. 15Then Jacob went to Egypt, where he and his sons died. 16Their bodies were taken to Shechem, where they were buried in the grave which Abraham had bought from the clan of Hamor for a sum of money.

17"When the time drew near for God to keep the promise he had made to Abraham, the number of our people in Egypt had grown much larger. 18At last a king who did not know about Joseph began to rule in Egypt. 19He tricked our ancestors and was cruel to them, forcing them to put their babies out of their homes, so that they would die. 20It was at this time that Moses was born, a very beautiful child. He was cared for at home for three months, 21and when he was put out of his home, the king's daughter adopted him and brought him up as her own son. 22He was taught all the wisdom of the Egyptians and became a great man in words and deeds.

23"When Moses was forty years old, he decided to find out how his fellow Israelites were being treated. 24He saw one of them being mistreated by an Egyptian, so he went to his help and took revenge on the Egyptian by killing him. (25He thought that his own people would understand that God was going to use him to set them free, but they did not understand.) 26The next day he saw two Israelites fighting, and he tried to make peace between them. 'Listen, men,' he said, 'you are fellow Israelites; why are you fighting like this?' 27But the one who was mistreating the other pushed Moses aside. 'Who made you ruler and judge over us?' he asked. 28'Do you want to kill me, just as you killed that Egyptian yesterday?' 29When Moses heard this, he fled from Egypt and went to live in the land of Midian. There he had two sons.

30"After forty years had passed, an angel appeared to Moses in the flames of a burning bush in the desert near Mount Sinai. 31Moses was amazed by what he saw, and went near the bush to get a better look. But he heard the Lord's voice: 32'I am the God of your ancestors, the God of Abraham, Isaac, and Jacob.' Moses trembled with fear and dared not look. 33The Lord said to him, 'Take your sandals off, for the place where you are standing is holy ground. 34I have seen the cruel suffering of my people in Egypt. I have heard their groans, and I have come down to set them free. Come now; I will send you to Egypt.'

35"Moses is the one who was rejected by the people of Israel. 'Who made you ruler and judge over us?' they asked. He is the one whom God sent to rule the people and set them free with the help of the angel who appeared to him in the burning bush. 36He led the people out of Egypt, performing miracles and wonders in Egypt and at the Red Sea and for forty years in the desert.

7:7 Ex 3:12 **7:8 a** Gen 17:10–14; **b** Gen 21:2–4; **c** Gen 25:26; **d** Gen 29:31—35:18 **7:9 a** Gen 37:11; **b** Gen 37:28; **c** Gen 39:2, 21 **7:10** Gen 41:39–41 **7:11** Gen 42:1, 2 **7:13 a** Gen 45:1; **b** Gen 45:16 **7:14 a** Gen 45:9, 10, 17, 18; **b** Gen 46:27 (LXX) **7:15 a** Gen 46:1–7; **b** Gen 49:33 **7:16** Gen 23:3–16; 33:19; 50:7–13; Josh 24:32 **7:17, 18** Ex 1:7, 8 **7:19 a** Ex 1:10, 11; **b** Ex 1:22 **7:20** Ex 2:2 **7:21** Ex 2:3–10 **7:23–29** Ex 2:11–15 **7:29** Ex 18:3, 4 **7:30–34** Ex 3:1–10 **7:35** Ex 2:14 **7:36 a** Ex 7:3; **b** Ex 14:21; **c** Num 14:33

Catholic Connections

Martyrdom, the Ultimate Sacrifice

From the beginning of the Church, many Christians have been persecuted for their faith. The enemies of the faith have tried to force these Christians to speak against God or stop their good works, but the Christians refuse to do so. So they are tortured and often killed. The Christians who are killed because of their faith are called *martyrs*.

Acts, chapter 7, tells the story of Stephen, the first martyr of the Christian Church. Right before Stephen died, he said something that sounded very similar to what Jesus said before his death: "Receive my spirit" and "Do not remember this sin against them" (see Luke 23:34,46).

Bishop Oscar Romero from El Salvador is a modern martyr. After noticing the great injustices against poor people of his country, he started speaking out and became a friend and helper of poor people. This was a threat to the military leaders, who were rich and powerful and wanted to keep the poor people in their place. Even though Bishop Romero received death threats, he did not back down from calling for justice in the name of Jesus Christ. So on March 24, 1983, he was shot to death by his enemies while celebrating the Eucharist.

— Acts, chapter 7

37 Moses is the one who said to the people of
Israel, 'God will send you a prophet, just as
he sent me,[f] and he will be one of your own
people.' 38 He is the one who was with the
people of Israel assembled in the desert; he
was there with our ancestors and with the
angel who spoke to him on Mount Sinai,
and he received God's living messages to pass
on to us.
39 "But our ancestors refused to obey him;
they pushed him aside and wished that they
could go back to Egypt. 40 So they said to
Aaron, 'Make us some gods who will lead us.
We do not know what has happened to that
man Moses, who brought us out of Egypt.'
41 It was then that they made an idol in the
shape of a bull, offered sacrifice to it, and had
a feast in honor of what they themselves had
made. 42 So God turned away from them and
gave them over to worship the stars of heav-
en, as it is written in the book of the
prophets:

'People of Israel! It was not to me
that you slaughtered and sacrificed
animals
for forty years in the desert.
43 It was the tent of the god Molech that
you carried,
and the image of Rephan, your star
god;
they were idols that you had made to
worship.
And so I will send you into exile beyond
Babylon.'

44 "Our ancestors had the Tent of God's
presence with them in the desert. It had
been made as God had told Moses to make
it, according to the pattern that Moses had
been shown. 45 Later on, our ancestors who
received the tent from their fathers carried it
with them when they went with Joshua and
took over the land from the nations that
God drove out as they advanced. And it
stayed there until the time of David.

[f] **7:37** just as he sent me; *or* like me.

7:37 Deut 18:15, 18 **7:38** Ex 19:1—20:17; Deut 5:1–33 **7:40** Ex 32:1 **7:41** Ex 32:2–6 **7:42, 43** Am 5:25–27 (LXX) **7:44** Ex 25:9, 40 **7:45** Josh 3:14–17

46He won God's favor and asked God to
allow him to provide a dwelling place for
the God of Jacob.[g] 47But it was Solomon
who built him a house.
48"But the Most High God does not live
in houses built by human hands; as the
prophet says,

49 'Heaven is my throne, says the Lord,
and the earth is my footstool.
What kind of house would you build for
me?
Where is the place for me to live in?
50 Did not I myself make all these things?'

51"How stubborn you are!" Stephen went
on to say. "How heathen your hearts, how
deaf you are to God's message! You are just
like your ancestors: you too have always resis-
ted the Holy Spirit! 52Was there any prophet
that your ancestors did not persecute? They
killed God's messengers, who long ago
announced the coming of his righteous Ser-
vant. And now you have betrayed and mur-
dered him. 53You are the ones who received
God's law, that was handed down by angels—
yet you have not obeyed it!"

The Stoning of Stephen

54As the members of the Council listened
to Stephen, they became furious and ground
their teeth at him in anger. 55But Stephen,
full of the Holy Spirit, looked up to heaven
and saw God's glory and Jesus standing at
the right side of God. 56"Look!" he said. "I
see heaven opened and the Son of Man
standing at the right side of God!"
57With a loud cry the Council members
covered their ears with their hands. Then
they all rushed at him at once, 58threw him
out of the city, and stoned him. The witness-
es left their cloaks in the care of a young
man named Saul. 59They kept on stoning
Stephen as he called out to the Lord, "Lord
Jesus, receive my spirit!" 60He knelt down
and cried out in a loud voice, "Lord! Do not
remember this sin against them!" He said
this and died.

8 And Saul approved of his murder.

Saul Persecutes the Church

That very day the church in Jerusalem
began to suffer cruel persecution. All the
believers, except the apostles, were scattered
throughout the provinces of Judea and
Samaria. 2Some devout men buried Stephen,
mourning for him with loud cries.

Saul approved of his murder. (8:1)

3But Saul tried to destroy the church;
going from house to house, he dragged out
the believers, both men and women, and
threw them into jail.

The Gospel Is Preached in Samaria

4The believers who were scattered went
everywhere, preaching the message. 5Philip
went to the principal city[h] in Samaria and
preached the Messiah to the people there.
6The crowds paid close attention to what
Philip said, as they listened to him and saw
the miracles that he performed. 7Evil spirits
came out from many people with a loud
cry, and many paralyzed and lame people
were healed. 8So there was great joy in that
city.

[g] **7:46** the God of Jacob; *some manuscripts have* the people of Israel. [h] **8:5** the principal city; *some manuscripts have* a city.

7:46 2 Sam 7:1–16; 1 Chr 17:1–14 **7:47** 1 Kings 6:1–38; 2 Chr 3:1–17 **7:49, 50** Isa 66:1, 2 **7:51** Isa 63:10 **8:3** Acts 22:4, 5; 26:9–11

Could you forgive your worst enemies as Stephen forgave his? What is the hardest thing you have ever had to forgive someone for?

Pray it!

You Can't Buy Miracles

Have you ever seen a great magician, or learned magic tricks yourself? Magic involves the work of our minds and hands. Simon the magician saw how people received the Holy Spirit when Peter and John laid their hands on them. It looked like magic to him. And he thought if he paid the Apostles, they would show him that trick (Acts 8:19). Peter set him straight, though: These are not magical powers! And they cannot be bought! True healing that comes from God is the work of the heart and the Holy Spirit. God's power works through us if our hearts are pure or "right in God's sight" (8:21). That means we need to trust and be faithful to God.

Dear Lord, sometimes when I pray, I think I might be looking for miracles that act like magic. I need to trust the mysterious ways your power is at work. I have asked for my grandmother's cancer to disappear and for the ankle I sprained yesterday to be better by the playoffs, tomorrow! I know miracles are possible, but they may not look the way I expect or hope. As I grow up, help me to understand more deeply what it means to trust you and what healing truly means. Amen.

— Acts 8:9–25

9A man named Simon lived there, who
for some time had astounded the Samaritans
with his magic. He claimed that he was
someone great, 10and everyone in the city,
from all classes of society, paid close attention
to him. "He is that power of God known as
'The Great Power,' " they said. 11They paid
this attention to him because for such a long
time he had astonished them with his magic.
12But when they believed Philip's message
about the good news of the Kingdom of
God and about Jesus Christ, they were bap-
tized, both men and women. 13Simon him-
self also believed; and after being baptized,
he stayed close to Philip and was astounded
when he saw the great wonders and miracles
that were being performed.

14The apostles in Jerusalem heard that the
people of Samaria had received the word of
God, so they sent Peter and John to them.
15When they arrived, they prayed for the
believers that they might receive the Holy
Spirit. 16For the Holy Spirit had not yet
come down on any of them; they had only
been baptized in the name of the Lord Jesus.
17Then Peter and John placed their hands on
them, and they received the Holy Spirit.

18Simon saw that the Spirit had been
given to the believers when the apostles
placed their hands on them. So he offered
money to Peter and John, 19and said, "Give
this power to me too, so that anyone I place
my hands on will receive the Holy Spirit."

20But Peter answered him, "May you and
your money go to hell, for thinking that you
can buy God's gift with money! 21You have
no part or share in our work, because your
heart is not right in God's sight. 22Repent,
then, of this evil plan of yours, and pray to
the Lord that he will forgive you for thinking
such a thing as this. 23For I see that you are
full of bitter envy and are a prisoner of sin."

24Simon said to Peter and John, "Please
pray to the Lord for me, so that none of
these things you spoke of will happen to
me."

What did the Ethiopian official feel and do after he was baptized *(Acts 8:39–40)*?

25 After they had given their testimony
and proclaimed the Lord's message, Peter and
John went back to Jerusalem. On their way
they preached the Good News in many vil-
lages of Samaria.

Philip and the Ethiopian Official

26 An angel of the Lord said to Philip, "Get
ready and go south[i] to the road that goes
from Jerusalem to Gaza." (This road is not
used nowadays.)[j] 27-28 So Philip got ready
and went. Now an Ethiopian eunuch, who
was an important official in charge of the
treasury of the queen of Ethiopia, was on his
way home. He had been to Jerusalem to
worship God and was going back home in
his carriage. As he rode along, he was reading
from the book of the prophet Isaiah. 29 The
Holy Spirit said to Philip, "Go over to that
carriage and stay close to it." 30 Philip ran
over and heard him reading from the book
of the prophet Isaiah. He asked him, "Do
you understand what you are reading?"
31 The official replied, "How can I under-
stand unless someone explains it to me?"
And he invited Philip to climb up and sit in
the carriage with him. 32 The passage of
scripture which he was reading was this:

"He was like a sheep that is taken to be
slaughtered,
like a lamb that makes no sound when
its wool is cut off.
He did not say a word.
33 He was humiliated, and justice was denied
him.
No one will be able to tell about his
descendants,
because his life on earth has come to
an end."

34 The official asked Philip, "Tell me, of
whom is the prophet saying this? Of himself
or of someone else?" 35 Then Philip began to
speak; starting from this passage of scripture,
he told him the Good News about Jesus.
36 As they traveled down the road, they came
to a place where there was some water, and
the official said, "Here is some water. What is
to keep me from being baptized?"[k]
38 The official ordered the carriage to stop,
and both Philip and the official went down
into the water, and Philip baptized him.
39 When they came up out of the water, the
Spirit of the Lord took Philip away. The offi-
cial did not see him again, but continued on
his way, full of joy. 40 Philip found himself in
Azotus; he went on to Caesarea, and on the
way he preached the Good News in every
town.

The Conversion of Saul
(Acts 22:6–16; 26:12–18)

9 In the meantime Saul kept up his vio-
lent threats of murder against the fol-
lowers of the Lord. He went to the High
Priest 2 and asked for letters of introduction
to the synagogues in Damascus, so that if he
should find there any followers of the Way of
the Lord, he would be able to arrest them,
both men and women, and bring them back
to Jerusalem.
3 As Saul was coming near the city of
Damascus, suddenly a light from the sky
flashed around him. 4 He fell to the ground
and heard a voice saying to him, "Saul, Saul!
Why do you persecute me?"
5 "Who are you, Lord?" he asked.
"I am Jesus, whom you persecute," the

"Who are you, Lord?" (9:5)

[i] **8:26** south; *or* at midday. [j] **8:26** This road is not used nowadays; *or* This is the desert road. [k] **8:36** *Some manuscripts add verse 37:* Philip said to him, "You may be baptized if you believe with all your heart." "I do," he answered; "I believe that Jesus Christ is the Son of God."
8:32, 33 Isa 53:7, 8 (LXX)

Catholic Connections

Capital Punishment

The Catholic Church teaches that we should not use capital punishment (also known as the death penalty) to punish criminals as long as they can be kept from hurting someone again.

Why? The Church always works to protect and respect life. The lives of all people—living and unborn, healthy and sick, poor and rich, innocent and guilty—must be respected. Even if we commit a terrible sin, God still loves us. Even the worst criminal is able to change his heart and life. So out of respect for God's gift of life, we should not kill someone just to show that killing is wrong.

Also, the death penalty can be so easily misused. Look at Saint Paul: he led a persecution that led to the unjust execution of many Christians. If the Christians had not been forgiving, they might have tried to put Paul to death for this. But then Paul could not have traveled the world to preach the Gospel and bring people to God after his conversion. If God could change Paul's heart, then our worst criminals can become instruments of God as well. Paul is one of our best arguments against the death penalty.

— Acts, chapter 9

voice said. 6 "But get up and go into the city,
where you will be told what you must do."
7 The men who were traveling with Saul
had stopped, not saying a word; they heard
the voice but could not see anyone. 8 Saul
got up from the ground and opened his
eyes, but could not see a thing. So they took
him by the hand and led him into Damas-
cus. 9 For three days he was not able to see,
and during that time he did not eat or drink
anything.
10 There was a believer in Damascus
named Ananias. He had a vision, in which
the Lord said to him, "Ananias!"
"Here I am, Lord," he answered.
11 The Lord said to him, "Get ready and
go to Straight Street, and at the house of
Judas ask for a man from Tarsus named
Saul. He is praying, 12 and in a vision he has
seen a man named Ananias come in and
place his hands on him so that he might see
again."
13 Ananias answered, "Lord, many people
have told me about this man and about all
the terrible things he has done to your peo-
ple in Jerusalem. 14 And he has come to
Damascus with authority from the chief
priests to arrest all who worship you."
15 The Lord said to him, "Go, because I
have chosen him to serve me, to make my
name known to Gentiles and kings and to
the people of Israel. 16 And I myself will
show him all that he must suffer for my
sake."
17 So Ananias went, entered the house
where Saul was, and placed his hands on
him. "Brother Saul," he said, "the Lord has
sent me—Jesus himself, who appeared to
you on the road as you were coming here.
He sent me so that you might see again and
be filled with the Holy Spirit." 18 At once
something like fish scales fell from Saul's
eyes, and he was able to see again. He stood
up and was baptized; 19 and after he had
eaten, his strength came back.

9:18 Tob 11:13–15

Saul Preaches in Damascus

Saul stayed for a few days with the believ-
ers in Damascus. 20He went straight to the
synagogues and began to preach that Jesus
was the Son of God.

21All who heard him were amazed and
asked, "Isn't he the one who in Jerusalem
was killing those who worship that man
Jesus? And didn't he come here for the very
purpose of arresting those people and taking
them back to the chief priests?"

22But Saul's preaching became even more
powerful, and his proofs that Jesus was the
Messiah were so convincing that the Jews
who lived in Damascus could not answer him.

23After many days had gone by, the Jews
met together and made plans to kill Saul,
24but he was told of their plan. Day and night
they watched the city gates in order to kill
him. 25But one night Saul's followers took
him and let him down through an opening in
the wall, lowering him in a basket.

Saul in Jerusalem

26Saul went to Jerusalem and tried to join
the disciples. But they would not believe that
he was a disciple, and they were all afraid of
him. 27Then Barnabas came to his help and
took him to the apostles. He explained to
them how Saul had seen the Lord on the
road and that the Lord had spoken to him.
He also told them how boldly Saul had
preached in the name of Jesus in Damascus.
28And so Saul stayed with them and went all
over Jerusalem, preaching boldly in the name
of the Lord. 29He also talked and disputed
with the Greek-speaking Jews, but they tried
to kill him. 30When the believers found out
about this, they took Saul to Caesarea and
sent him away to Tarsus.

31And so it was that the church through-
out Judea, Galilee, and Samaria had a time of
peace. Through the help of the Holy Spirit it
was strengthened and grew in numbers, as it
lived in reverence for the Lord.

Peter in Lydda and Joppa

32Peter traveled everywhere, and on one
occasion he went to visit God's people who
lived in Lydda. 33There he met a man named
Aeneas, who was paralyzed and had not
been able to get out of bed for eight years.
34"Aeneas," Peter said to him, "Jesus Christ
makes you well. Get up and make your bed."
At once Aeneas got up. 35All the people liv-
ing in Lydda and Sharon saw him, and they
turned to the Lord.

36In Joppa there was a woman named
Tabitha, who was a believer. (Her name in
Greek is Dorcas, meaning "a deer.") She
spent all her time doing good and helping
the poor. 37At that time she got sick and
died. Her body was washed and laid in a
room upstairs. 38Joppa was not very far from
Lydda, and when the believers in Joppa
heard that Peter was in Lydda, they sent two
men to him with the message, "Please hurry
and come to us." 39So Peter got ready and
went with them. When he arrived, he was
taken to the room upstairs, where all the
widows crowded around him, crying and
showing him all the shirts and coats that
Dorcas had made while she was alive. 40Peter
put them all out of the room, and knelt
down and prayed; then he turned to the
body and said, "Tabitha, get up!" She opened
her eyes, and when she saw Peter, she sat up.
41Peter reached over and helped her get up.
Then he called all the believers, including
the widows, and presented her alive to them.
42The news about this spread all over Joppa,
and many people believed in the Lord.
43Peter stayed on in Joppa for many days
with a tanner of leather named Simon.

Peter and Cornelius

10 There was a man in Caesarea named
Cornelius, who was a captain in the
Roman army regiment called "The Italian
Regiment." 2He was a religious man; he and
his whole family worshiped God. He also did

9:23–25 2 Cor 11:32, 33

The early Christians called themselves the Way *(Acts 9:2)*. **Why, do you think, did they call themselves by that name?**

much to help the Jewish poor people and
was constantly praying to God. 3It was about
three o'clock one afternoon when he had a
vision, in which he clearly saw an angel of
God come in and say to him, "Cornelius!"
4He stared at the angel in fear and said,
"What is it, sir?"
The angel answered, "God is pleased with
your prayers and works of charity, and is
ready to answer you. 5And now send some
men to Joppa for a certain man whose full
name is Simon Peter. 6He is a guest in the
home of a tanner of leather named Simon,
who lives by the sea." 7Then the angel went
away, and Cornelius called two of his house
servants and a soldier, a religious man who
was one of his personal attendants. 8He told
them what had happened and sent them off
to Joppa.
9The next day, as they were on their way
and coming near Joppa, Peter went up on the
roof of the house about noon in order to
pray. 10He became hungry and wanted some-
thing to eat; while the food was being pre-
pared, he had a vision. 11He saw heaven
opened and something coming down that
looked like a large sheet being lowered by its
four corners to the earth. 12In it were all
kinds of animals, reptiles, and wild birds. 13A
voice said to him, "Get up, Peter; kill and
eat!"
14But Peter said, "Certainly not, Lord! I
have never eaten anything ritually unclean
or defiled."
15The voice spoke to him again, "Do not
consider anything unclean that God has
declared clean." 16This happened three
times, and then the thing was taken back up
into heaven.
17While Peter was wondering about the
meaning of this vision, the men sent by Cor-
nelius had learned where Simon's house was,
and they were now standing in front of the
gate. 18They called out and asked, "Is there a
guest here by the name of Simon Peter?"
19Peter was still trying to understand what
the vision meant, when the Spirit said, "Lis-

10:9 Jdt 8:5

Live it!

Dreams by God

What's the weirdest dream you've ever had? God sometimes speaks to our hearts through dreams and the symbols they contain. Peter's dream was about God's desire to bring Gentiles (non-Jewish people) into the new Christian community. Jesus was a Jew and preached mostly to Jewish people. So his first followers were Jews. Many of them believed that if you wanted to become a Christian, you first had to become a Jew and follow all the laws of the Jewish religion.

Peter's dream is about Jewish food, or dietary, laws. According to these laws, some animals are unclean, and Jews may not eat them. But Gentiles did not have these kinds of food laws, so they ate those animals. Jewish Christians considered Gentile Christians unclean because of this. In Peter's dream, God was telling Peter that people can follow Christ without following all the Jewish laws about food! Through his dream Peter was being guided to bring Gentiles into the new Church, without them having to first become Jews.

God can still speak to people through dreams. Can you remember any of your dreams? Do you think God is trying to tell you something through the dream?

— Acts 10:9—11:10

***Gentile* is a word used to describe someone who is not Jewish.**

ten! Three[l] men are here looking for you.
20So get ready and go down, and do not
hesitate to go with them, for I have sent
them." 21So Peter went down and said to the
men, "I am the man you are looking for.
Why have you come?"
22"Captain Cornelius sent us," they
answered. "He is a good man who worships
God and is highly respected by all the Jewish
people. An angel of God told him to invite
you to his house, so that he could hear what
you have to say." 23Peter invited the men in
and had them spend the night there.
The next day he got ready and went with
them; and some of the believers from Joppa
went along with him. 24The following day
he arrived in Caesarea, where Cornelius was
waiting for him, together with relatives and
close friends that he had invited. 25As Peter
was about to go in, Cornelius met him, fell
at his feet, and bowed down before him.
26But Peter made him rise. "Stand up," he
said, "I myself am only a man." 27Peter kept
on talking to Cornelius as he went into the
house, where he found many people gath-
ered. 28He said to them, "You yourselves
know very well that a Jew is not allowed by
his religion to visit or associate with Gen-
tiles. But God has shown me that I must not
consider any person ritually unclean or
defiled. 29And so when you sent for me, I
came without any objection. I ask you, then,
why did you send for me?"
30Cornelius said, "It was about this time
three days ago that I was praying[m] in my
house at three o'clock in the afternoon. Sud-
denly a man dressed in shining clothes stood
in front of me 31and said: 'Cornelius! God
has heard your prayer and has taken notice
of your works of charity. 32Send someone to
Joppa for a man whose full name is Simon
Peter. He is a guest in the home of Simon
the tanner of leather, who lives by the sea.'
33And so I sent for you at once, and you
have been good enough to come. Now we
are all here in the presence of God, waiting
to hear anything that the Lord has instructed
you to say."

Peter's Speech

34Peter began to speak: "I now realize that
it is true that God treats everyone on the
same basis. 35Those who fear him and do
what is right are acceptable to him, no matter
what race they belong to. 36You know the
message he sent to the people of Israel, pro-
claiming the Good News of peace through
Jesus Christ, who is Lord of all. 37You know
of the great event that took place throughout
the land of Israel, beginning in Galilee after
John preached his message of baptism. 38You
know about Jesus of Nazareth and how God
poured out on him the Holy Spirit and
power. He went everywhere, doing good and
healing all who were under the power of the
Devil, for God was with him. 39We are wit-
nesses of everything that he did in the land of
Israel and in Jerusalem. Then they put him to
death by nailing him to a cross. 40But God
raised him from death three days later and
caused him to appear, 41not to everyone, but
only to the witnesses that God had already
chosen, that is, to us who ate and drank with
him after he rose from death. 42And he com-
manded us to preach the gospel to the people
and to testify that he is the one whom God
has appointed judge of the living and the
dead. 43All the prophets spoke about him, say-
ing that all who believe in him will have their
sins forgiven through the power of his name."

The Gentiles Receive the Holy Spirit

44While Peter was still speaking, the Holy
Spirit came down on all those who were lis-
tening to his message. 45The Jewish believers
who had come from Joppa with Peter were
amazed that God had poured out his gift of
the Holy Spirit on the Gentiles also. 46For
they heard them speaking in strange tongues
and praising God's greatness. Peter spoke up:
47"These people have received the Holy
Spirit, just as we also did. Can anyone, then,
stop them from being baptized with water?"
48So he ordered them to be baptized in the
name of Jesus Christ. Then they asked him
to stay with them for a few days.

[l] **10:19** Three; *some manuscripts have* Some; *one manuscript has* Two. [m] **10:30** praying; *some manuscripts have* fasting and praying.
10:34 Deut 10:17

Peter's Report to the Church at Jerusalem

11 The apostles and the other believers throughout Judea heard that the Gentiles also had received the word of God. 2When Peter went to Jerusalem, those who were in favor of circumcising Gentiles criticized him, saying, 3"You were a guest in the home of uncircumcised Gentiles, and you even ate with them!" 4So Peter gave them a complete account of what had happened from the very beginning:

5"While I was praying in the city of Joppa, I had a vision. I saw something coming down that looked like a large sheet being lowered by its four corners from heaven, and it stopped next to me. 6I looked closely inside and saw domesticated and wild animals, reptiles, and wild birds. 7Then I heard a voice saying to me, 'Get up, Peter; kill and eat!' 8But I said, 'Certainly not, Lord! No ritually unclean or defiled food has ever entered my mouth.' 9The voice spoke again from heaven, 'Do not consider anything unclean that God has declared clean.' 10This happened three times, and finally the whole thing was drawn back up into heaven. 11At that very moment three men who had been sent to me from Caesarea arrived at the house where I was[n] staying. 12The Spirit told me to go with them without hesitation. These six fellow believers from Joppa accompanied me to Caesarea, and we all went into the house of Cornelius. 13He told us how he had seen an angel standing in his house, who said to him, 'Send someone to Joppa for a man whose full name is Simon Peter. 14He will speak words to you by which you and all your family will be saved.' 15And when I began to speak, the Holy Spirit came down on them just as on us at the beginning. 16Then I remembered what the Lord had said: 'John baptized with water, but you will be baptized with the Holy Spirit.' 17It is clear that God gave those Gentiles the same gift that he gave us when we believed in the Lord Jesus Christ; who was I, then, to try to stop God!"

18When they heard this, they stopped their criticism and praised God, saying, "Then God has given to the Gentiles also the opportunity to repent and live!"

The Church at Antioch

19Some of the believers who were scattered by the persecution which took place when Stephen was killed went as far as Phoenicia, Cyprus, and Antioch, telling the message to Jews only. 20But other believers, who were from Cyprus and Cyrene, went to Antioch and proclaimed the message to Gentiles[o] also, telling them the Good News about the Lord Jesus. 21The Lord's power

Live it!

The More, the Merrier!

God doesn't want us to leave people out just because they are different from us. Variety can make things much more interesting to be a part of. And we can learn more from people who are different from us than from people who are just the same. This is why, as the Church began to form in places such as Antioch, both Jews and Gentiles were included. The variety of histories and gifts made the Church stronger and richer.

Who are the people at your school who get left out because they don't fit in with the popular groups? Try to be the person who looks past their differences and includes them instead of pushing them out. To welcome without judging is a wonderful virtue to possess!

— Acts 11:19–26

[n] **11:11** I was; *some manuscripts have* we were. [o] **11:20** Gentiles; *some manuscripts have* Greek-speaking Jews *or* Greek-speaking people.

11:16 Acts 1:5 **11:19** Acts 8:1–4

Pray it!

The Power of Prayer

After Peter was arrested, everyone in the Church was praying like mad for him! Then, miraculously, Peter escaped from prison.

Do you believe in the power of prayer? Many Catholic parishes have prayer chains. These are groups who make it their business to pray for people. The person on the top of the chain is made aware of a problem, sickness, or other need, then that need gets passed from person to person until everyone in the prayer chain gets the word. Think of something or someone you would want prayers for, then imagine fifty or one hundred or even many hundreds of people praying for your intention. God gets flooded with our prayers!

That's one great thing about being part of a Christian community. We care about what's happening in one another's lives, and when someone is in trouble, we all can pray together for God's help.

Here's an important thing to remember about prayer, however. God always hears and responds to our prayers, but not always in the way we expect or want! Sometimes God's ways are mysterious, but we need to trust in God's constant and deep loving care for us.

— Acts 12:1–19

was with them, and a great number of peo-
ple believed and turned to the Lord.
22 The news about this reached the church
in Jerusalem, so they sent Barnabas to Anti-
och. 23 When he arrived and saw how God
had blessed the people, he was glad and
urged them all to be faithful and true to the
Lord with all their hearts. 24 Barnabas was a
good man, full of the Holy Spirit and faith,
and many people were brought to the Lord.
25 Then Barnabas went to Tarsus to look
for Saul. 26 When he found him, he took him
to Antioch, and for a whole year the two
met with the people of the church and
taught a large group. It was at Antioch that
the believers were first called Christians.
27 About that time some prophets went
from Jerusalem to Antioch. 28 One of them,
named Agabus, stood up and by the power
of the Spirit predicted that a severe famine
was about to come over all the earth. (It
came when Claudius was emperor.) 29 The
disciples decided that they each would send
as much as they could to help their fellow
believers who lived in Judea. 30 They did this,
then, and sent the money to the church el-
ders by Barnabas and Saul.

More Persecution

12 About this time King Herod[p] began
to persecute some members of the
church. 2 He had James, the brother of John,
put to death by the sword. 3 When he saw
that this pleased the Jews, he went ahead and
had Peter arrested. (This happened during
the time of the Festival of Unleavened
Bread.) 4 After his arrest Peter was put in jail,
where he was handed over to be guarded by
four groups of four soldiers each. Herod

[p] **12:1** KING HEROD: *Herod Agrippa I, ruler of all Palestine.*
11:28 Acts 21:10 **12:4** Ex 12:1–27

Antioch is where the believers were first called Christians. Can you find Antioch on Map 7 on page 1906?

planned to put him on trial in public after
Passover. [5]So Peter was kept in jail, but the
people of the church were praying earnestly
to God for him.

Peter Is Set Free from Prison

[6]The night before Herod was going to
bring him out to the people, Peter was
sleeping between two guards. He was tied
with two chains, and there were guards on
duty at the prison gate. [7]Suddenly an angel
of the Lord stood there, and a light shone in
the cell. The angel shook Peter by the shoul-
der, woke him up, and said, "Hurry! Get
up!" At once the chains fell off Peter's hands.
[8]Then the angel said, "Tighten your belt and
put on your sandals." Peter did so, and the
angel said, "Put your cloak around you and
come with me." [9]Peter followed him out of
the prison, not knowing, however, if what
the angel was doing was real; he thought he
was seeing a vision. [10]They passed by the
first guard station and then the second, and
came at last to the iron gate that opens into
the city. The gate opened for them by itself,
and they went out. They walked down a
street, and suddenly the angel left Peter.

[11]Then Peter realized what had happened
to him, and said, "Now I know that it is real-
ly true! The Lord sent his angel to rescue me
from Herod's power and from everything the
Jewish people expected to happen."

[12]Aware of his situation, he went to the
home of Mary, the mother of John Mark,
where many people had gathered and were
praying. [13]Peter knocked at the outside door,
and a servant named Rhoda came to answer
it. [14]She recognized Peter's voice and was so
happy that she ran back in without opening
the door, and announced that Peter was
standing outside. [15]"You are crazy!" they told
her. But she insisted that it was true. So they
answered, "It is his angel."

[16]Meanwhile Peter kept on knocking. At
last they opened the door, and when they
saw him, they were amazed. [17]He motioned
with his hand for them to be quiet, and he
explained to them how the Lord had
brought him out of prison. "Tell this to
James and the rest of the believers," he said;
then he left and went somewhere else.

[18]When morning came, there was a
tremendous confusion among the guards—
what had happened to Peter? [19]Herod gave
orders to search for him, but they could not
find him. So he had the guards questioned
and ordered them put to death.

After this, Herod left Judea and spent
some time in Caesarea.

The Death of Herod

[20]Herod was very angry with the people
of Tyre and Sidon, so they went in a group
to see him. First they convinced Blastus, the
man in charge of the palace, that he should
help them. Then they went to Herod and
asked him for peace, because their country
got its food supplies from the king's country.

[21]On a chosen day Herod put on his royal
robes, sat on his throne, and made a speech
to the people. [22]"It isn't a man speaking, but
a god!" they shouted. [23]At once the angel of
the Lord struck Herod down, because he did
not give honor to God. He was eaten by
worms and died.

[24]Meanwhile the word of God continued
to spread and grow.

[25]Barnabas and Saul finished their mission
and returned from[q] Jerusalem, taking John
Mark with them.

Barnabas and Saul Are Chosen and Sent

13 In the church at Antioch there were
some prophets and teachers: Barna-
bas, Simeon (called the Black), Lucius (from
Cyrene), Manaen (who had been brought up
with Governor Herod[r]), and Saul. [2]While
they were serving the Lord and fasting, the

[q] **12:25** from; *some manuscripts have* to. [r] **13:1** HEROD: *Herod Antipas, ruler of Galilee (see Lk 3:1).*
12:20–23 2 Macc 9:5–28

What needs of others are you aware of that you could pray for? Who else can you ask to pray for those needs?

Holy Spirit said to them, "Set apart for me
Barnabas and Saul, to do the work to which
I have called them."
3They fasted and prayed, placed their
hands on them, and sent them off.

In Cyprus

4Having been sent by the Holy Spirit,
Barnabas and Saul went to Seleucia and
sailed from there to the island of Cyprus.
5When they arrived at Salamis, they
preached the word of God in the syna-
gogues. They had John Mark with them to
help in the work.
6They went all the way across the island
to Paphos, where they met a certain magi-
cian named Bar-Jesus, a Jew who claimed to
be a prophet. 7He was a friend of the gover-
nor of the island, Sergius Paulus, who was an
intelligent man. The governor called Bar-
nabas and Saul before him because he want-
ed to hear the word of God. 8But they were
opposed by the magician Elymas (that is his
name in Greek), who tried to turn the gov-
ernor away from the faith. 9Then Saul—also
known as Paul—was filled with the Holy
Spirit; he looked straight at the magician
10and said, "You son of the Devil! You are
the enemy of everything that is good. You
are full of all kinds of evil tricks, and you
always keep trying to turn the Lord's truths
into lies! 11The Lord's hand will come down
on you now; you will be blind and will not
see the light of day for a time."
At once Elymas felt a dark mist cover his
eyes, and he walked around trying to find
someone to lead him by the hand. 12When
the governor saw what had happened, he
believed; for he was greatly amazed at the
teaching about the Lord.

In Antioch in Pisidia

13Paul and his companions sailed from
Paphos and came to Perga, a city in Pam-
phylia, where John Mark left them and went
back to Jerusalem. 14They went on from
Perga and arrived in Antioch in Pisidia, and
on the Sabbath they went into the syna-
gogue and sat down. 15After the reading
from the Law of Moses and from the

Study it!

Paul's Journeys

In Acts, chapters 13–21, we read about three missionary journeys Paul made over a period of ten years to spread the Gospel message and establish Christian communities, or churches. The first journey (chapters 13–15) begins as a mission to bring Jews to Christ, but soon Paul was converting Gentiles as well. In Acts, the author changes from using Paul's Hebrew name, Saul, to using his Roman name, Paul, symbolizing the importance of his mission. This type of name change happens several other times in the Bible; for example, Abram and Sarai become Abraham and Sarah (Genesis, chapter 17), and Jacob becomes Israel (Genesis, chapter 32).

Paul's second journey (chapters 15 18) takes him into the rest of the Roman Empire, where he begins churches in Thessalonica, Philippi, and Corinth. His letters to these communities (written later) became books in the New Testament: Thessalonians, Philippians, and 1 and 2 Corinthians. Paul also visits the communities he founded on previous journeys.

The third missionary journey (chapters 18–21) is spent primarily in Ephesus and brings Paul back to Jerusalem where he is arrested at the Temple for his preaching about Jesus. Because of his Roman citizenship, he is sent to Rome for a trial and lives the rest of his life there. Check out Map 7 and Map 8 to trace the journeys of Paul.

— Acts, chapters 13–21

Study it!

Jews and Christ

A Jew himself, Paul is trying to convert (change the hearts) of other Jews who did not believe in Jesus. In telling the story of Israel's salvation in the middle of Acts, chapter 13, he is connecting Jewish history to the story of Jesus. This is because he wants the Jews to understand that Jesus is the Messiah that the Jewish prophets spoke of. He is not preaching about some new religion that has nothing to do with Judaism. Rather, Jesus and Christianity have everything to do with Judaism. Paul is trying to bring Jews to the Christian faith by helping them understand that Jesus is the Savior they were waiting for!

— Acts 13:13–43

writings of the prophets, the officials of the
synagogue sent them a message: "Friends, we
want you to speak to the people if you have
a message of encouragement for them."
16Paul stood up, motioned with his hand,
and began to speak:
"Fellow Israelites and all Gentiles here
who worship God: hear me! 17The God of
the people of Israel chose our ancestors and
made the people a great nation during the
time they lived as foreigners in Egypt. God
brought them out of Egypt by his great
power, 18and for forty years he endured[s]
them in the desert. 19He destroyed seven
nations in the land of Canaan and made his
people the owners of the land. 20All of this
took about 450 years.

"After this[t] he gave them judges until the
time of the prophet Samuel. 21And when
they asked for a king, God gave them Saul
son of Kish from the tribe of Benjamin, to
be their king for forty years. 22After remov-
ing him, God made David their king. This is
what God said about him: 'I have found that
David son of Jesse is the kind of man I like, a
man who will do all I want him to do.' 23It
was Jesus, a descendant of David, whom God
made the Savior of the people of Israel, as he
had promised. 24Before Jesus began his work,
John preached to all the people of Israel that
they should turn from their sins and be bap-
tized. 25And as John was about to finish his
mission, he said to the people, 'Who do you
think I am? I am not the one you are wait-
ing for. But listen! He is coming after me,
and I am not good enough to take his san-
dals off his feet.'

26"My fellow Israelites, descendants of
Abraham, and all Gentiles here who worship
God: it is to us that this message of salvation
has been sent! 27For the people who live in
Jerusalem and their leaders did not know that
he is the Savior, nor did they understand the
words of the prophets that are read every
Sabbath. Yet they made the prophets' words
come true by condemning Jesus. 28And even
though they could find no reason to pass the
death sentence on him, they asked Pilate to
have him put to death. 29And after they had
done everything that the Scriptures say about
him, they took him down from the cross and
placed him in a tomb. 30But God raised him
from death, 31and for many days he appeared
to those who had traveled with him from
Galilee to Jerusalem. They are now witnesses
for him to the people of Israel. 32-33And we
are here to bring the Good News to you:
what God promised our ancestors he would
do, he has now done for us, who are their
descendants, by raising Jesus to life. As it is
written in the second Psalm,

'You are my Son;
today I have become your Father.'

[s] **13:18** he endured; *some manuscripts have* he took care of. [t] **13:20** All of this took about 450 years. After this; *or* Some 450 years later.

13:17 a Ex 1:7; **b** Ex 12:51 **13:18** Num 14:34; Deut 1:31 **13:19 a** Deut 7:1; **b** Josh 14:1 **13:20 a** Judg 2:16; **b** 1 Sam 3:20 **13:21 a** 1 Sam 8:5; **b** 1 Sam 10:21 **13:22 a** 1 Sam 13:14; **b** 1 Sam 16:12; Ps 89:20 **13:24** Mk 1:4; Lk 3:3 **13:25 a** Jn 1:20; **b** Mt 3:11; Mk 1:7; Lk 3:16; Jn 1:27 **13:28** Mt 27:22, 23; Mk 15:13, 14; Lk 23:21–23; Jn 19:15 **13:29** Mt 27:57–61; Mk 15:42–47; Lk 23:50–56; Jn 19:38–42 **13:31** Acts 1:3 **13:33** Ps 2:7

34 And this is what God said about raising him from death, never to rot away in the grave:

'I will give you the sacred and sure
blessings
that I promised to David.'

35 As indeed he says in another passage,

'You will not allow your faithful servant
to rot in the grave.'

36 For David served God's purposes in his own time, and then he died, was buried with his ancestors, and his body rotted in the grave. 37 But this did not happen to the one whom God raised from death. 38-39 All of you, my fellow Israelites, are to know for sure that it is through Jesus that the message about forgiveness of sins is preached to you; you are to know that everyone who believes in him is set free from all the sins from which the Law of Moses could not set you free. 40 Take care, then, so that what the prophets said may not happen to you:[u]

41 'Look, you scoffers! Be astonished and
die!
For what I am doing today
is something that you will not believe,
even when someone explains it to
you!' "

42 As Paul and Barnabas were leaving the synagogue, the people invited them to come back the next Sabbath and tell them more about these things. 43 After the people had left the meeting, Paul and Barnabas were followed by many Jews and by many Gentiles who had been converted to Judaism. The apostles spoke to them and encouraged them to keep on living in the grace of God.

44 The next Sabbath nearly everyone in the town came to hear the word of the Lord. 45 When the Jews saw the crowds, they were filled with jealousy; they disputed what Paul was saying and insulted him. 46 But Paul and Barnabas spoke out even more boldly: "It was necessary that the word of God should be spoken first to you. But since you reject it and do not consider yourselves worthy of eternal life, we will leave you and go to the Gentiles. 47 For this is the commandment that the Lord has given us:

'I have made you a light for the Gentiles,
so that all the world may be saved.' "

48 When the Gentiles heard this, they were glad and praised the Lord's message; and those who had been chosen for eternal life became believers.

49 The word of the Lord spread everywhere in that region. 50 But the Jews stirred up the leading men of the city and the Gentile women of high social standing who worshiped God. They started a persecution against Paul and Barnabas and threw them out of their region. 51 The apostles shook the dust off their feet in protest against them and went on to Iconium. 52 The believers in Antioch were full of joy and the Holy Spirit.

In Iconium

14 The same thing happened in Iconium: Paul and Barnabas went to the synagogue and spoke in such a way that a great number of Jews and Gentiles became believers. 2 But the Jews who would not believe stirred up the Gentiles and turned them against the believers. 3 The apostles stayed there for a long time, speaking boldly about the Lord, who proved that their message about his grace was true by giving them the power to perform miracles and wonders. 4 The people of the city were divided: some were for the Jews, others for the apostles.

5 Then some Gentiles and Jews, together with their leaders, decided to mistreat the apostles and stone them. 6 When the apostles learned about it, they fled to the cities of Lystra and Derbe in Lycaonia and to the surrounding territory. 7 There they preached the Good News.

[u] **13:40** *Some manuscripts do not have* to you.

13:34 Isa 55:3 (LXX) **13:35** Ps 16:10 **13:41** Hab 1:5 (LXX) **13:47** Isa 42:6; 49:6 **13:51** Mt 10:14; Mk 6:11; Lk 9:5; 10:11

"The believers in Antioch were full of joy and the Holy Spirit" *(Acts 13:52)*.

In Lystra and Derbe

8 In Lystra there was a crippled man who
had been lame from birth and had never
been able to walk. 9 He sat there and listened
to Paul's words. Paul saw that he believed
and could be healed, so he looked straight at
him 10 and said in a loud voice, "Stand up
straight on your feet!" The man jumped up
and started walking around. 11 When the
crowds saw what Paul had done, they started
shouting in their own Lycaonian language,
"The gods have become like men and have
come down to us!" 12 They gave Barnabas
the name Zeus, and Paul the name Hermes,
because he was the chief speaker. 13 The
priest of the god Zeus, whose temple stood
just outside the town, brought bulls and
flowers to the gate, for he and the crowds
wanted to offer sacrifice to the apostles.
14 When Barnabas and Paul heard what
they were about to do, they tore their
clothes and ran into the middle of the
crowd, shouting, 15 "Why are you doing this?
We ourselves are only human beings like
you! We are here to announce the Good
News, to turn you away from these worth-
less things to the living God, who made
heaven, earth, sea, and all that is in them.
16 In the past he allowed all people to go
their own way. 17 But he has always given
evidence of his existence by the good things
he does: he gives you rain from heaven and
crops at the right times; he gives you food
and fills your hearts with happiness." 18 Even
with these words the apostles could hardly
keep the crowd from offering a sacrifice to
them.
19 Some Jews came from Antioch in Pisidia
and from Iconium; they won the crowds
over to their side, stoned Paul and dragged
him out of the town, thinking that he was
dead. 20 But when the believers gathered
around him, he got up and went back into
the town. The next day he and Barnabas
went to Derbe.

Live it!

Risking Their Necks

In Acts, chapter 14, we learn that Paul and Barnabas were run out of two towns—Iconium and Lystra—and Paul was almost killed. They were just being faithful to the work God sent them to do. The truth is, sometimes being faithful is risky. For example, when we forgive our enemies, we risk having our friends turn on us. When we give our money to poor people instead of spending it on trendy clothes, we risk being judged by what we wear. When we participate in a service project in our free time, we risk being unpopular because we're doing something out of the ordinary.

Don't be afraid of rejection! Jesus warned us we would be persecuted for being faithful. Even though Paul and Barnabas were run out of town, they were successful in helping some people believe in Jesus. Hang in there and believe that what you gain for living faithfully is far greater than anything you have to lose.

— Acts 14:1–20

The Return to Antioch in Syria

21 Paul and Barnabas preached the Good
News in Derbe and won many disciples.
Then they went back to Lystra, to Iconium,
and on to Antioch in Pisidia. 22 They strength-
ened the believers and encouraged them to
remain true to the faith. "We must pass
through many troubles to enter the Kingdom

14:15 Ex 20:11; Ps 146:6

Elders *(Acts 14:23)* **were people appointed by the Apostles to have general responsibility for the work of the Church.**

of God," they taught. 23In each church they
appointed elders, and with prayers and fasting
they commended them to the Lord, in whom
they had put their trust.

24After going through the territory of
Pisidia, they came to Pamphylia. 25There
they preached the message in Perga and then
went to Attalia, 26and from there they sailed
back to Antioch, the place where they had
been commended to the care of God's grace
for the work they had now completed.

27When they arrived in Antioch, they
gathered the people of the church together
and told them about all that God had done
with them and how he had opened the way
for the Gentiles to believe. 28And they stayed
a long time there with the believers.

The Meeting at Jerusalem

15 Some men came from Judea to
Antioch and started teaching the
believers, "You cannot be saved unless you
are circumcised as the Law of Moses
requires." 2Paul and Barnabas got into a
fierce argument with them about this, so it
was decided that Paul and Barnabas and
some of the others in Antioch should go to
Jerusalem and see the apostles and elders
about this matter.

3They were sent on their way by the
church; and as they went through Phoenicia
and Samaria, they reported how the Gentiles
had turned to God; this news brought great
joy to all the believers. 4When they arrived
in Jerusalem, they were welcomed by the
church, the apostles, and the elders, to whom
they told all that God had done through
them. 5But some of the believers who
belonged to the party of the Pharisees stood
up and said, "The Gentiles must be circum-
cised and told to obey the Law of Moses."

6The apostles and the elders met together
to consider this question. 7After a long
debate Peter stood up and said, "My friends,
you know that a long time ago God chose
me from among you to preach the Good
News to the Gentiles, so that they could
hear and believe. 8And God, who knows the
thoughts of everyone, showed his approval of
the Gentiles by giving the Holy Spirit to
them, just as he had to us. 9He made no dif-
ference between us and them; he forgave
their sins because they believed. 10So then,
why do you now want to put God to the
test by laying a load on the backs of the
believers which neither our ancestors nor we
ourselves were able to carry? 11No! We
believe and are saved by the grace of the
Lord Jesus, just as they are."

12The whole group was silent as they
heard Barnabas and Paul report all the mira-
cles and wonders that God had performed
through them among the Gentiles. 13When
they had finished speaking, James spoke up:
"Listen to me, my friends! 14Simon has just
explained how God first showed his care for
the Gentiles by taking from among them a
people to belong to him. 15The words of the
prophets agree completely with this. As the
scripture says,

16'After this I will return, says the Lord,
  and restore the kingdom of David.
I will rebuild its ruins
  and make it strong again.
17And so all the rest of the human race will
    come to me,
  all the Gentiles whom I have called to
    be my own.
18So says the Lord, who made this known
    long ago.'

19"It is my opinion," James went on, "that
we should not trouble the Gentiles who are
turning to God. 20Instead, we should write a
letter telling them not to eat any food that is
ritually unclean because it has been offered
to idols; to keep themselves from sexual
immorality; and not to eat any animal that
has been strangled, or any blood. 21For the
Law of Moses has been read for a very long
time in the synagogues every Sabbath, and
his words are preached in every town."

The Letter to the Gentile Believers

22Then the apostles and the elders,
together with the whole church, decided to
choose some men from the group and send
them to Antioch with Paul and Barnabas.
They chose two men who were highly

15:1 Lev 12:3 **15:7** Acts 10:1–43 **15:8** Acts 10:44; Acts 2:4 **15:16–18** Am 9:11, 12 (LXX) **15:20** **a** Ex 34:15–17; **b** Lev 18:6–23; **c** Lev 17:10–16

respected by the believers, Judas, called
Barsabbas, and Silas, 23 and they sent the fol-
lowing letter by them:
"We, the apostles and the elders, your
brothers, send greetings to all our brothers
of Gentile birth who live in Antioch,
Syria, and Cilicia. 24 We have heard that
some who went from our group have
troubled and upset you by what they said;
they had not, however, received any
instruction from us. 25 And so we have met
together and have all agreed to choose
some messengers and send them to you.
They will go with our dear friends Bar-
nabas and Paul, 26 who have risked their
lives in the service of our Lord Jesus
Christ. 27 We send you, then, Judas and
Silas, who will tell you in person the same
things we are writing. 28 The Holy Spirit
and we have agreed not to put any other
burden on you besides these necessary
rules: 29 eat no food that has been offered
to idols; eat no blood; eat no animal that
has been strangled; and keep yourselves
from sexual immorality. You will do well if
you take care not to do these things. With
our best wishes."
30 The messengers were sent off and went
to Antioch, where they gathered the whole
group of believers and gave them the letter.
31 When the people read it, they were filled
with joy by the message of encouragement.
32 Judas and Silas, who were themselves
prophets, spoke a long time with them, giv-
ing them courage and strength. 33 After
spending some time there, they were sent off
in peace by the believers and went back to
those who had sent them.[v]
35 Paul and Barnabas spent some time in
Antioch, and together with many others
they taught and preached the word of the
Lord.

Paul and Barnabas Separate

36 Some time later Paul said to Barnabas,
"Let us go back and visit the believers in
every town where we preached the word of
the Lord, and let us find out how they are
getting along." 37 Barnabas wanted to take
John Mark with them, 38 but Paul did not
think it was right to take him, because he
had not stayed with them to the end of their
mission, but had turned back and left them
in Pamphylia. 39 There was a sharp argument,
and they separated: Barnabas took Mark and
sailed off for Cyprus, 40 while Paul chose
Silas and left, commended by the believers to
the care of the Lord's grace. 41 He went
through Syria and Cilicia, strengthening the
churches.

Timothy Goes with Paul and Silas

16 Paul traveled on to Derbe and
Lystra, where a Christian named
Timothy lived. His mother, who was also a
Christian, was Jewish, but his father was a
Greek. 2 All the believers in Lystra and Iconi-
um spoke well of Timothy. 3 Paul wanted to
take Timothy along with him, so he circum-
cised him. He did so because all the Jews
who lived in those places knew that Timo-
thy's father was Greek. 4 As they went
through the towns, they delivered to the
believers the rules decided upon by the
apostles and elders in Jerusalem, and they
told them to obey those rules. 5 So the
churches were made stronger in the faith
and grew in numbers every day.

In Troas: Paul's Vision

6 They traveled through the region of
Phrygia and Galatia because the Holy Spirit
did not let them preach the message in the
province of Asia. 7 When they reached the
border of Mysia, they tried to go into the
province of Bithynia, but the Spirit of Jesus
did not allow them. 8 So they traveled right
on through[w] Mysia and went to Troas. 9 That
night Paul had a vision in which he saw a
Macedonian standing and begging him,
"Come over to Macedonia and help us!"
10 As soon as Paul had this vision, we got
ready to leave for Macedonia, because we
decided that God had called us to preach the
Good News to the people there.

[v] **15:33** *Some manuscripts add verse 34:* But Silas decided to stay there. [w] **16:8** traveled right on through; *or* passed by.
15:38 Acts 13:13

In Philippi: the Conversion of Lydia

11 We left by ship from Troas and sailed
straight across to Samothrace, and the next
day to Neapolis. 12 From there we went
inland to Philippi, a city of the first district
of Macedonia;[x] it is also a Roman colony.
We spent several days there. 13 On the Sab-
bath we went out of the city to the river-
side, where we thought there would be a
place where Jews gathered for prayer. We sat
down and talked to the women who gath-
ered there. 14 One of those who heard us was
Lydia from Thyatira, who was a dealer in
purple cloth. She was a woman who wor-
shiped God, and the Lord opened her mind
to pay attention to what Paul was saying.
15 After she and the people of her house had
been baptized, she invited us, "Come and
stay in my house if you have decided that I
am a true believer in the Lord." And she per-
suaded us to go.

In Prison at Philippi

16 One day as we were going to the place
of prayer, we were met by a young servant
woman who had an evil spirit that enabled
her to predict the future. She earned a lot of
money for her owners by telling fortunes.
17 She followed Paul and us, shouting, "These
men are servants of the Most High God!
They announce to you how you can be
saved!" 18 She did this for many days, until
Paul became so upset that he turned around
and said to the spirit, "In the name of Jesus
Christ I order you to come out of her!" The
spirit went out of her that very moment.
19 When her owners realized that their
chance of making money was gone, they
seized Paul and Silas and dragged them to
the authorities in the public square. 20 They
brought them before the Roman officials
and said, "These men are Jews, and they are
causing trouble in our city. 21 They are teach-
ing customs that are against our law; we are
Roman citizens, and we cannot accept these
customs or practice them." 22 And the crowd
joined in the attack against Paul and Silas.
Then the officials tore the clothes off Paul
and Silas and ordered them to be whipped.
23 After a severe beating, they were thrown
into jail, and the jailer was ordered to lock
them up tight. 24 Upon receiving this order,
the jailer threw them into the inner cell and
fastened their feet between heavy blocks of
wood.
25 About midnight Paul and Silas were
praying and singing hymns to God, and the
other prisoners were listening to them.
26 Suddenly there was a violent earthquake,
which shook the prison to its foundations. At
once all the doors opened, and the chains fell
off all the prisoners. 27 The jailer woke up,
and when he saw the prison doors open, he
thought that the prisoners had escaped; so he
pulled out his sword and was about to kill
himself. 28 But Paul shouted at the top of his
voice, "Don't harm yourself! We are all here!"

"Sirs, what must I do to be saved?" (16:30)

29 The jailer called for a light, rushed in,
and fell trembling at the feet of Paul and
Silas. 30 Then he led them out and asked,
"Sirs, what must I do to be saved?"
31 They answered, "Believe in the Lord
Jesus, and you will be saved—you and your
family." 32 Then they preached the word of

[x] **16:12** a city of the first district of Macedonia; *some manuscripts have* a leading city of the district of Macedonia, *or* a leading city of that district in Macedonia.

Lydia was probably a woman of some wealth. Purple dye was expensive, and she was a dealer in purple cloth *(Acts 16:14)*.

Pray it!

Praise God—I'm Miserable!

What would you do if you were put in a prison cell—and you were innocent? Cry? Shout? Curse? Not Paul and Silas! They were praying and singing hymns—loud enough so that all the other prisoners could hear them! The next time you find yourself in trouble or treated unfairly, turn your heart and voice to God:

God, you are amazing!
Over and over you've shown your deep love for me.
I can make it through terrible times because I know you're right here, like always—no matter what happens.
You are as close to me as my heartbeat.
Help me stay strong and hopeful.
Thank you for your blessings in my life!
Amen.

— Acts 16:25

the Lord to him and to all the others in the house. 33 At that very hour of the night the jailer took them and washed their wounds; and he and all his family were baptized at once. 34 Then he took Paul and Silas up into his house and gave them some food to eat. He and his family were filled with joy, because they now believed in God.

35 The next morning the Roman authorities sent police officers with the order, "Let those men go."

36 So the jailer told Paul, "The officials have sent an order for you and Silas to be released. You may leave, then, and go in peace."

37 But Paul said to the police officers, "We were not found guilty of any crime, yet they whipped us in public—and we are Roman citizens! Then they threw us in prison. And now they want to send us away secretly? Not at all! The Roman officials themselves must come here and let us out."

38 The police officers reported these words to the Roman officials; and when they heard that Paul and Silas were Roman citizens, they were afraid. 39 So they went and apologized to them; then they led them out of the prison and asked them to leave the city. 40 Paul and Silas left the prison and went to Lydia's house. There they met the believers, spoke words of encouragement to them, and left.

In Thessalonica

17 Paul and Silas traveled on through Amphipolis and Apollonia and came to Thessalonica, where there was a synagogue. 2 According to his usual habit Paul went to the synagogue. There during three Sabbaths he held discussions with the people, quoting 3 and explaining the Scriptures, and proving from them that the Messiah had to suffer and rise from death. "This Jesus whom I announce to you," Paul said, "is the Messiah." 4 Some of them were convinced and joined Paul and Silas; so did many of the leading women and a large group of Greeks who worshiped God.

5 But some Jews were jealous and gathered worthless loafers from the streets and formed a mob. They set the whole city in an uproar and attacked the home of a man named Jason,

How many different cities did Paul and Silas visit in Acts, chapters 17–18? Match them to the route of Paul's second journey on Map 7 on page 1906.

Live it!

Passing on the Faith

Paul truly had a gift for preaching and teaching! Acts, chapters 17–18, continue the stories of his second missionary journey. Through his speeches and discussions, he spread the news far and wide about Jesus. And many people came to believe in and follow Jesus because of Paul and Silas.

Who taught you about Jesus? Who are the people in your life who continue to show you what living a Christian life means? Take a few minutes to thank God for these people. Better yet, think about sending them a note or small gift that expresses your gratitude.

— Acts, chapters 17–18

in an attempt to find Paul and Silas and bring
them out to the people. 6But when they did
not find them, they dragged Jason and some
other believers before the city authorities and
shouted, "These men have caused trouble
everywhere! Now they have come to our
city, 7and Jason has kept them in his house.
They are all breaking the laws of the Emper-
or, saying that there is another king, whose
name is Jesus." 8With these words they threw
the crowd and the city authorities in an
uproar. 9The authorities made Jason and the
others pay the required amount of money to
be released, and then let them go.

In Berea

10As soon as night came, the believers sent
Paul and Silas to Berea. When they arrived,
they went to the synagogue. 11The people
there were more open-minded than the peo-
ple in Thessalonica. They listened to the mes-
sage with great eagerness, and every day they
studied the Scriptures to see if what Paul said
was really true. 12Many of them believed; and
many Greek women of high social standing
and many Greek men also believed. 13But
when the Jews in Thessalonica heard that
Paul had preached the word of God in Berea
also, they came there and started exciting and
stirring up the mobs. 14At once the believers
sent Paul away to the coast; but both Silas
and Timothy stayed in Berea. 15The men
who were taking Paul went with him as far
as Athens and then returned to Berea with
instructions from Paul that Silas and Timothy
should join him as soon as possible.

In Athens

16While Paul was waiting in Athens for
Silas and Timothy, he was greatly upset when
he noticed how full of idols the city was.
17So he held discussions in the synagogue
with the Jews and with the Gentiles who
worshiped God, and also in the public square
every day with the people who happened to
come by. 18Certain Epicurean and Stoic
teachers also debated with him. Some of
them asked, "What is this ignorant show-off
trying to say?"

Others answered, "He seems to be talking
about foreign gods." They said this because
Paul was preaching about Jesus and the res-
urrection.[y] 19So they took Paul, brought him
before the city council, the Areopagus, and
said, "We would like to know what this new
teaching is that you are talking about.
20Some of the things we hear you say sound
strange to us, and we would like to know
what they mean." (21For all the citizens of
Athens and the foreigners who lived there
liked to spend all their time telling and hear-
ing the latest new thing.)

22Paul stood up in front of the city council
and said, "I see that in every way you Atheni-
ans are very religious. 23For as I walked
through your city and looked at the places
where you worship, I found an altar on
which is written, 'To an Unknown God.'

[y] **17:18** JESUS AND THE RESURRECTION: *In Greek, the feminine noun "resurrection" could be understood to be the name of a goddess.*

17:23 Wis 13:1

Catholic Connections

Welcome the Stranger

In Corinth Paul met Priscilla and Aquila, a married couple who invited him to stay with them. No four-star hotels for Paul! Rather, he stayed in homes of people who welcomed him. Some houses were probably fancier or cleaner or had better food than others. But it didn't matter to Paul. Living with other believers filled him up with the energy he needed to continue his ministry.

Hospitality is a wonderful gift! When you have friends or relatives over to your house, what do you do to make them feel welcome and comfortable? What kinds of preparations are made for their visit? Has your family ever welcomed someone to live with you for several weeks or longer?

"Welcome the stranger" is one of the works of mercy. Dorothy Day is a famous American Catholic who spent her adult life serving poor people in New York. She declared that every Christian home should contain a Christ room (that is, an extra room) or a couch where a homeless person could stay. Talk with your family about ways you can help people who need safe shelter and friendship.

— Acts 18:1–3

That which you worship, then, even though
you do not know it, is what I now proclaim
to you. 24God, who made the world and
everything in it, is Lord of heaven and earth
and does not live in temples made by human
hands. 25Nor does he need anything that we
can supply by working for him, since it is he
himself who gives life and breath and every-
thing else to everyone. 26From one human
being he created all races of people and made
them live throughout the whole earth. He
himself fixed beforehand the exact times and
the limits of the places where they would
live. 27He did this so that they would look
for him, and perhaps find him as they felt
around for him. Yet God is actually not far
from any one of us; 28as someone has said,

'In him we live and move and exist.'

It is as some of your poets have said,

'We too are his children.'

29Since we are God's children, we should not
suppose that his nature is anything like an
image of gold or silver or stone, shaped by
human art and skill. 30God has overlooked the
times when people did not know him, but
now he commands all of them everywhere to
turn away from their evil ways. 31For he has
fixed a day in which he will judge the whole
world with justice by means of a man he has
chosen. He has given proof of this to every-
one by raising that man from death!"
32When they heard Paul speak about a
raising from death, some of them made fun
of him, but others said, "We want to hear
you speak about this again." 33And so Paul
left the meeting. 34Some men joined him
and believed, among whom was Dionysius,
a member of the council; there was also a
woman named Damaris, and some other
people.

In Corinth

18 After this, Paul left Athens and went
on to Corinth. 2There he met a Jew
named Aquila, born in Pontus, who had

17:24, 25 1 Kings 8:27; Isa 42:5; Acts 7:48 **17:25** 2 Macc 14:35 **17:26** 2 Macc 7:23
17:27 Wis 13:6–9

recently come from Italy with his wife Priscilla, for Emperor Claudius had ordered all the Jews to leave Rome. Paul went to see them, 3and stayed and worked with them, because he earned his living by making tents, just as they did. 4He held discussions in the synagogue every Sabbath, trying to convince both Jews and Greeks.

5When Silas and Timothy arrived from Macedonia, Paul gave his whole time to preaching the message, testifying to the Jews that Jesus is the Messiah. 6When they opposed him and said evil things about him, he protested by shaking the dust from his clothes and saying to them, "If you are lost, you yourselves must take the blame for it! I am not responsible. From now on I will go to the Gentiles." 7So he left them and went to live in the house of a Gentile named Titius Justus, who worshiped God; his house was next to the synagogue. 8Crispus, who was the leader of the synagogue, believed in the Lord, together with all his family; and many other people in Corinth heard the message, believed, and were baptized.

9One night Paul had a vision in which the Lord said to him, "Do not be afraid, but keep on speaking and do not give up, 10for I am with you. No one will be able to harm you, for many in this city are my people." 11So Paul stayed there for a year and a half, teaching the people the word of God.

12When Gallio was made the Roman governor of Achaia, Jews there got together, seized Paul, and took him into court. 13"This man," they said, "is trying to persuade people to worship God in a way that is against the law!"

14Paul was about to speak when Gallio said to the Jews, "If this were a matter of some evil crime or wrong that has been committed, it would be reasonable for me to be patient with you Jews. 15But since it is an argument about words and names and your own law, you yourselves must settle it. I will not be the judge of such things!" 16And he drove them out of the court. 17They all grabbed Sosthenes, the leader of the synagogue, and beat him in front of the court. But that did not bother Gallio a bit.

The Return to Antioch

18Paul stayed on with the believers in Corinth for many days, then left them and sailed off with Priscilla and Aquila for Syria. Before sailing from Cenchreae he had his head shaved because of a vow he had taken.[z] 19They arrived in Ephesus, where Paul left Priscilla and Aquila. He went into the synagogue and held discussions with the Jews. 20The people asked him to stay longer, but he would not consent. 21Instead, he told them as he left, "If it is the will of God, I will come back to you." And so he sailed from Ephesus.

22When he arrived at Caesarea, he went to Jerusalem and greeted the church, and then went to Antioch. 23After spending some time there, he left and went through the region of Galatia and Phrygia, strengthening all the believers.

Apollos in Ephesus and Corinth

24At that time a Jew named Apollos, who had been born in Alexandria, came to Ephesus. He was an eloquent speaker and had a thorough knowledge of the Scriptures. 25He had been instructed in the Way of the Lord, and with great enthusiasm he proclaimed and taught correctly the facts about Jesus. However, he knew only the baptism of John. 26He began to speak boldly in the synagogue. When Priscilla and Aquila heard him, they took him home with them and explained to him more correctly the Way of God. 27Apollos then decided to go to Achaia, so the believers in Ephesus helped him by writing to the believers in Achaia, urging them to welcome him. When he arrived, he was a great help to those who through God's

[z] **18:18** A VOW HE HAD TAKEN: *This refers to the Jewish custom of shaving the head as a sign that a vow has been kept.*
18:18 Num 6:18

"Do not be afraid, but keep speaking and do not give up, for I am with you" *(Acts 18:9–10)*.

grace had become believers. 28For with his
strong arguments he defeated the Jews in
public debates by proving from the Scrip-
tures that Jesus is the Messiah.

Paul in Ephesus

19 While Apollos was in Corinth, Paul
traveled through the interior of the
province and arrived in Ephesus. There he
found some disciples 2and asked them, "Did
you receive the Holy Spirit when you
became believers?"

"We have not even heard that there is a
Holy Spirit," they answered.

3"Well, then, what kind of baptism did
you receive?" Paul asked.

"The baptism of John," they answered.

4Paul said, "The baptism of John was for
those who turned from their sins; and he told
the people of Israel to believe in the one
who was coming after him—that is, in Jesus."

5When they heard this, they were baptized
in the name of the Lord Jesus. 6Paul placed
his hands on them, and the Holy Spirit came
upon them; they spoke in strange tongues
and also proclaimed God's message. 7They
were about twelve men in all.

8Paul went into the synagogue and for
three months spoke boldly with the people,
holding discussions with them and trying to
convince them about the Kingdom of God.
9But some of them were stubborn and would
not believe, and before the whole group they
said evil things about the Way of the Lord. So
Paul left them and took the believers with
him, and every day[a] he held discussions in the
lecture hall of Tyrannus. 10This went on for
two years, so that all the people who lived in
the province of Asia, both Jews and Gentiles,
heard the word of the Lord.

The Sons of Sceva

11God was performing unusual miracles
through Paul. 12Even handkerchiefs and
aprons he had used were taken to the sick,
and their diseases were driven away, and the
evil spirits would go out of them. 13Some
Jews who traveled around and drove out evil
spirits also tried to use the name of the Lord
Jesus to do this. They said to the evil spirits,
"I command you in the name of Jesus,

Live it!

Demons and Idols and Riots!

Paul's adventure continues! Chapter 19 describes the beginning of his third missionary journey. In his second journey, Paul was thrown out of cities, beaten, and almost stoned to death. Imagine the courage it took for him to start a new journey of evangelizing and healing. Despite the many dangers he faced, Paul stuck with it. Because he was filled with the Holy Spirit, he possessed the courage needed to wake up each day and preach the Good News to all he met.

We don't have to be faced with a dangerous situation to need courage. It can take courage to be kind to a difficult person whom everyone else makes fun of. It can take courage to accept a tough situation that's beyond our control, like a family death or divorce. What do you need courage for in your life? Ask God to give you plenty of it, then keep moving forward!

— Acts 19:1–10

a **19:9** *Some manuscripts add* from 11:00 a.m. until 4:00 p.m.
19:4 Mt 3:11; Mk 1:4, 7, 8; Lk 3:4, 16; Jn 1:26, 27

Which of the Ten Commandments are the silversmiths breaking in Acts, chapter 19?

whom Paul preaches." 14 Seven brothers, who were the sons of a Jewish High Priest named Sceva, were doing this.

15 But the evil spirit said to them, "I know Jesus, and I know about Paul; but you—who are you?"

16 The man who had the evil spirit in him attacked them with such violence that he overpowered them all. They ran away from his house, wounded and with their clothes torn off. 17 All the Jews and Gentiles who lived in Ephesus heard about this; they were all filled with fear, and the name of the Lord Jesus was given greater honor. 18 Many of the believers came, publicly admitting and revealing what they had done. 19 Many of those who had practiced magic brought their books together and burned them in public. They added up the price of the books, and the total came to fifty thousand silver coins.[b] 20 In this powerful way the word of the Lord[c] kept spreading and growing stronger.

The Riot in Ephesus

21 After these things had happened, Paul made up his mind[d] to travel through Macedonia and Achaia and go on to Jerusalem. "After I go there," he said, "I must also see Rome." 22 So he sent Timothy and Erastus, two of his helpers, to Macedonia, while he spent more time in the province of Asia.

23 It was at this time that there was serious trouble in Ephesus because of the Way of the Lord. 24 A certain silversmith named Demetrius made silver models of the temple of the goddess Artemis, and his business brought a great deal of profit to the workers. 25 So he called them all together with others whose work was like theirs and said to them, "Men, you know that our prosperity comes from this work. 26 Now, you can see and hear for yourselves what this fellow Paul is doing. He says that hand-made gods are not gods at all, and he has succeeded in convincing many people, both here in Ephesus and in nearly the whole province of Asia. 27 There is the danger, then, that this business of ours will get a bad name. Not only that, but there is also the danger that the temple of the great goddess Artemis will come to mean nothing and that her greatness will be destroyed—the goddess worshiped by everyone in Asia and in all the world!"

28 As the crowd heard these words, they became furious and started shouting, "Great is Artemis of Ephesus!" 29 The uproar spread throughout the whole city. The mob grabbed Gaius and Aristarchus, two Macedonians who were traveling with Paul, and rushed with them to the theater. 30 Paul himself wanted to go before the crowd, but the believers would not let him. 31 Some of the provincial authorities, who were his friends, also sent him a message begging him not to show himself in the theater. 32 Meanwhile the whole meeting was in an uproar: some people were shouting one thing, others were shouting something else, because most of them did not even know why they had come together. 33 Some of the people concluded that Alexander was responsible, since the Jews made him go up to the front. Then Alexander motioned with his hand for the people to be silent, and he tried to make a speech of defense. 34 But when they recognized that he was a Jew, they all shouted together the same thing for two hours: "Great is Artemis of Ephesus!"

35 At last the city clerk was able to calm the crowd. "Fellow Ephesians!" he said. "Everyone knows that the city of Ephesus is the keeper of the temple of the great Artemis and of the sacred stone that fell down from heaven. 36 Nobody can deny these things. So then, you must calm down and not do anything reckless. 37 You have brought these men here even though they have not robbed temples or said evil things about our goddess. 38 If Demetrius and his workers have an accusation against anyone, we have the authorities and the regular days for court; charges can be made there. 39 But if there is something more that you want, it will have to be settled in a legal meeting of citizens. 40 For after what has happened today, there is the danger that we will be accused of a riot. There is no excuse for all

[b] **19:19** SILVER COINS: *A silver coin was the daily wage of a rural worker (see Mt 20:2).* [c] **19:19** In this . . . Lord; *or* And so, by the power of the Lord, the message. [d] **19:21** Paul made up his mind; *or* Paul, led by the Spirit, decided.

this uproar, and we would not be able to
give a good reason for it." 41After saying this,
he dismissed the meeting.

To Macedonia and Achaia

20 After the uproar died down, Paul
called together the believers and with
words of encouragement said good-bye to
them. Then he left and went on to Macedo-
nia. 2He went through those regions and
encouraged the people with many messages.
Then he came to Achaia, 3where he stayed
three months. He was getting ready to go to
Syria when he discovered that there were
Jews plotting against him; so he decided to
go back through Macedonia. 4Sopater son of
Pyrrhus, from Berea, went with him; so did
Aristarchus and Secundus, from Thessalonica;
Gaius, from Derbe; Tychicus and Trophimus,
from the province of Asia; and Timothy.
5They went ahead and waited for us in Troas.
6We sailed from Philippi after the Festival of
Unleavened Bread, and five days later we
joined them in Troas, where we spent a
week.

Paul's Last Visit to Troas

7On Saturday[e] evening we gathered
together for the fellowship meal. Paul spoke
to the people and kept on speaking until
midnight, since he was going to leave the
next day. 8Many lamps were burning in the
upstairs room where we were meeting. 9A
young man named Eutychus was sitting in
the window, and as Paul kept on talking,
Eutychus got sleepier and sleepier, until he
finally went sound asleep and fell from the
third story to the ground. When they picked
him up, he was dead. 10But Paul went down
and threw himself on him and hugged him.
"Don't worry," he said, "he is still alive!"
11Then he went back upstairs, broke bread,
and ate. After talking with them for a long
time, even until sunrise, Paul left. 12They
took the young man home alive and were
greatly comforted.

Live it!

You Snooze, You Lose!

Do you ever get bored at Mass? Paul was leading a gathering for a small Christian community at someone's home. It was similar to the Catholic Mass—sharing the word of God and the Eucharist—but more informal. His preaching must have been either boring or too long, because poor Eutychus fell asleep and fell out of the window (Acts 20:9)! The three-story fall killed him, but Paul quickly brought him back to life. Then Paul returned to the group to bless and share the bread and wine. How's that for an interruption in the middle of Mass?

Most people have times when they get bored or tired at Mass. One way to stay alert is by making a mental list before Mass starts of people or situations that need prayers. Then say a prayer to God for each of those after you receive Communion.

— Acts 20:7–12

From Troas to Miletus

13We went on ahead to the ship and sailed
off to Assos, where we were going to take
Paul aboard. He had told us to do this,
because he was going there by land. 14When
he met us in Assos, we took him aboard and
went on to Mitylene. 15We sailed from there
and arrived off Chios the next day. A day
later we came to Samos, and the following
day we reached Miletus. 16Paul had decided
to sail on by Ephesus, so as not to lose any
time in the province of Asia. He was in a
hurry to arrive in Jerusalem by the day of
Pentecost, if at all possible.

[e] **20:7** Saturday; *or* Sunday.

Paul's Farewell Speech to the Elders of Ephesus

17From Miletus Paul sent a message to
Ephesus, asking the elders of the church to
meet him. 18When they arrived, he said to
them, "You know how I spent the whole
time I was with you, from the first day I
arrived in the province of Asia. 19With all
humility and many tears I did my work as
the Lord's servant during the hard times that
came to me because of the plots of some
Jews. 20You know that I did not hold back
anything that would be of help to you as I
preached and taught in public and in your
homes. 21To Jews and Gentiles alike I gave
solemn warning that they should turn from
their sins to God and believe in our Lord
Jesus. 22And now, in obedience to the Holy
Spirit I am going to Jerusalem, not knowing
what will happen to me there. 23I only know
that in every city the Holy Spirit has warned
me that prison and troubles wait for me.
24But I reckon my own life to be worth
nothing to me; I only want to complete my
mission and finish the work that the Lord
Jesus gave me to do, which is to declare the
Good News about the grace of God.
25"I have gone about among all of you,
preaching the Kingdom of God. And now I
know that none of you will ever see me
again. 26So I solemnly declare to you this
very day: if any of you should be lost, I am
not responsible. 27For I have not held back
from announcing to you the whole purpose
of God. 28So keep watch over yourselves and
over all the flock which the Holy Spirit has
placed in your care. Be shepherds of the
church of God,[f] which he made his own
through the blood of his Son.[g] 29I know that
after I leave, fierce wolves will come among
you, and they will not spare the flock. 30The
time will come when some men from your
own group will tell lies to lead the believers
away after them. 31Watch, then, and remem-
ber that with many tears, day and night, I
taught every one of you for three years.
32"And now I commend you to the care
of God and to the message of his grace,
which is able to build you up and give you
the blessings God has for all his people. 33I
have not wanted anyone's silver or gold or
clothing. 34You yourselves know that I have
worked with these hands of mine to provide
everything that my companions and I have
needed. 35I have shown you in all things that
by working hard in this way we must help
the weak, remembering the words that the
Lord Jesus himself said, 'There is more hap-
piness in giving than in receiving.' "
36When Paul finished, he knelt down
with them and prayed. 37They were all cry-
ing as they hugged him and kissed him
good-bye. 38They were especially sad
because he had said that they would never
see him again. And so they went with him to
the ship.

Paul Goes to Jerusalem

21 We said good-bye to them and left.
After sailing straight across, we came
to Cos; the next day we reached Rhodes,
and from there we went on to Patara. 2There
we found a ship that was going to Phoeni-
cia, so we went aboard and sailed away. 3We
came to where we could see Cyprus, and
then sailed south of it on to Syria. We went
ashore at Tyre, where the ship was going to
unload its cargo. 4There we found some
believers and stayed with them a week. By
the power of the Spirit they told Paul not to
go to Jerusalem. 5But when our time with
them was over, we left and went on our way.
All of them, together with their wives and
children, went with us out of the city to the
beach, where we all knelt and prayed. 6Then
we said good-bye to one another, and we
went on board the ship while they went
back home.

f **20:28** God; *some manuscripts have* the Lord. *g* **20:28** through the blood of his Son; *or* through the sacrificial death of his Son; *or* through his own blood.
20:24 2 Tim 4:7

The people of Ephesus were very sad to see Paul leave. What is the saddest good-bye you have had?

Catholic Connections

Blessing Paul

The people at Tyre worried about Paul as he set sail for Jerusalem, even though he was fearless. So they did the best thing a Christian community can do: they got down on their knees and prayed together for his safety and courage (Acts 21:5). When someone leaves on a long journey or begins a new stage of life, it's good to pray a blessing over her or him. A blessing is a special prayer, asking God's special care and grace for someone. Important moments in life are the perfect time to call upon God to help and protect the person.

All cultures have blessing prayers. Here is one from the Apache Native American tradition. It would have been a perfect blessing for Paul.

May the sun bring you new energy by day.
May the moon softly restore you by night.
May the rain wash away your worries
and the breeze blow new strength into your being,
and all of the days of your life may you walk
gently through the world and know its beauty.

— Acts 21:3–6

7 We continued our voyage, sailing from
Tyre to Ptolemais, where we greeted the
believers and stayed with them for a day.
8 On the following day we left and arrived
in Caesarea. There we stayed at the house
of Philip the evangelist, one of the seven
men who had been chosen as helpers in
Jerusalem. 9 He had four unmarried daugh-
ters who proclaimed God's message. 10 We
had been there for several days when a
prophet named Agabus arrived from Judea.
11 He came to us, took Paul's belt, tied up his
own feet and hands with it, and said, "This is
what the Holy Spirit says: The owner of this
belt will be tied up in this way by the Jews
in Jerusalem, and they will hand him over to
the Gentiles."
12 When we heard this, we and the others
there begged Paul not to go to Jerusalem.
13 But he answered, "What are you doing,
crying like this and breaking my heart? I am
ready not only to be tied up in Jerusalem
but even to die there for the sake of the
Lord Jesus."
14 We could not convince him, so we gave
up and said, "May the Lord's will be done."
15 After spending some time there, we got
our things ready and left for Jerusalem.
16 Some of the disciples from Caesarea also
went with us and took us to the house of
the man we were going to stay with[h] —
Mnason, from Cyprus, who had been a
believer since the early days.

Paul Visits James

17 When we arrived in Jerusalem, the
believers welcomed us warmly. 18 The next

[h] **21:16** and took us to the house of the man we were going to stay with; *or* bringing with them the man at whose house we were going to stay.
21:8 Acts 6:5; 8:5 **21:10** Acts 11:28

"May the Lord's will be done" *(Acts 21:14)*.

day Paul went with us to see James; and all the church elders were present. 19 Paul greeted them and gave a complete report of everything that God had done among the Gentiles through his work. 20 After hearing him, they all praised God. Then they said, "Brother Paul, you can see how many thousands of Jews have become believers, and how devoted they all are to the Law. 21 They have been told that you have been teaching all the Jews who live in Gentile countries to abandon the Law of Moses, telling them not to circumcise their children or follow the Jewish customs. 22 They are sure to hear that you have arrived. What should be done, then? 23 This is what we want you to do. There are four men here who have taken a vow. 24 Go along with them and join them in the ceremony of purification and pay their expenses; then they will be able to shave their heads.[i] In this way everyone will know that there is no truth in any of the things that they have been told about you, but that you yourself live in accordance with the Law of Moses. 25 But as for the Gentiles who have become believers, we have sent them a letter telling them we decided that they must not eat any food that has been offered to idols, or any blood, or any animal that has been strangled, and that they must keep themselves from sexual immorality."

26 So Paul took the men and the next day performed the ceremony of purification with them. Then he went into the Temple and gave notice of how many days it would be until the end of the period of purification, when a sacrifice would be offered for each one of them.

Paul Is Arrested in the Temple

27 But just when the seven days were about to come to an end, some Jews from the province of Asia saw Paul in the Temple. They stirred up the whole crowd and grabbed Paul. 28 "People of Israel!" they shouted. "Help! This is the man who goes everywhere teaching everyone against the people of Israel, the Law of Moses, and this Temple. And now he has even brought some Gentiles into the Temple and defiled this holy place!" (29 They said this because they had seen Trophimus from Ephesus with Paul in the city, and they thought that Paul had taken him into the Temple.)

30 Confusion spread through the whole city, and the people all ran together, grabbed Paul, and dragged him out of the Temple. At once the Temple doors were closed. 31 The mob was trying to kill Paul, when a report was sent up to the commander of the Roman troops that all of Jerusalem was rioting. 32 At once the commander took some officers and soldiers and rushed down to the crowd. When the people saw him with the soldiers, they stopped beating Paul. 33 The commander went over to Paul, arrested him, and ordered him to be bound with two chains. Then he asked, "Who is this man, and what has he done?" 34 Some in the crowd shouted one thing, others something else. There was such confusion that the commander could not find out exactly what had happened, so he ordered his men to take Paul up into the fort. 35 They got as far as the steps with him, and then the soldiers had to carry him because the mob was so wild. 36 They were all coming after him and screaming, "Kill him!"

Paul Defends Himself

37 As the soldiers were about to take Paul into the fort, he spoke to the commander: "May I say something to you?"

"You speak Greek, do you?" the commander asked. 38 "Then you are not that Egyptian fellow who some time ago started a revolution and led four thousand armed terrorists out into the desert?"

39 Paul answered, "I am a Jew, born in Tarsus in Cilicia, a citizen of an important city. Please let me speak to the people."

40 The commander gave him permission, so Paul stood on the steps and motioned with his hand for the people to be silent.

[i] **21:24** SHAVE THEIR HEADS: *See 18:18.*

21:23, 24 Num 6:13–21 **21:25** Acts 15:29 **21:29** Acts 20:4

When they were quiet, Paul spoke to them in Hebrew:

22 "My fellow Jews, listen to me as I make my defense before you!" 2When they heard him speaking to them in Hebrew, they became even quieter; and Paul went on:

3"I am a Jew, born in Tarsus in Cilicia, but brought up here in Jerusalem as a student of Gamaliel. I received strict instruction in the Law of our ancestors and was just as dedicated to God as are all of you who are here today. 4I persecuted to the death the people who followed this Way. I arrested men and women and threw them into prison. 5The High Priest and the whole Council can prove that I am telling the truth. I received from them letters written to fellow Jews in Damascus, so I went there to arrest these people and bring them back in chains to Jerusalem to be punished.

Paul Tells of His Conversion

(Acts 9:1–19; 26:12–18)

6"As I was traveling and coming near Damascus, about midday a bright light from the sky flashed suddenly around me. 7I fell to the ground and heard a voice saying to me, 'Saul, Saul! Why do you persecute me?' 8'Who are you, Lord?' I asked. 'I am Jesus of Nazareth, whom you persecute,' he said to me. 9The men with me saw the light, but did not hear the voice of the one who was speaking to me. 10I asked, 'What shall I do, Lord?' and the Lord said to me, 'Get up and go into Damascus, and there you will be told everything that God has determined for you to do.' 11I was blind because of the bright light, and so my companions took me by the hand and led me into Damascus.

12"In that city was a man named Ananias, a religious man who obeyed our Law and was highly respected by all the Jews living there. 13He came to me, stood by me, and said, 'Brother Saul, see again!' At that very moment I saw again and looked at him. 14He said, 'The God of our ancestors has chosen you to know his will, to see his righteous Servant, and to hear him speaking with his own voice. 15For you will be a witness for him to tell everyone what you have seen and heard. 16And now, why wait any longer? Get up and be baptized and have your sins washed away by praying to him.'

Paul's Call to Preach to the Gentiles

17"I went back to Jerusalem, and while I was praying in the Temple, I had a vision, 18in which I saw the Lord, as he said to me, 'Hurry and leave Jerusalem quickly, because the people here will not accept your witness about me.' 19'Lord,' I answered, 'they know very well that I went to the synagogues and arrested and beat those who believe in you. 20And when your witness Stephen was put to death, I myself was there, approving of his murder and taking care of the cloaks of his

Live it!

Turning to God

Conversion simply means turning away from sin and toward God. It means rejecting what is wrong and choosing what is right. At the beginning of Acts, chapter 22, Paul is telling his conversion story to the Jews in Jerusalem, and it's a very dramatic story!

What would you tell people if they asked for your conversion story? Don't panic if you don't have a story like Paul's. Sometimes conversion is connected to a dramatic event in our life. More often, it is about all the little ways we change as we move away from sin and get closer to God. Can you think of one instance when you changed your course—away from sin, toward God? This is part of your conversion story!

— Acts 22:1–21

22:3 Acts 5:34–39 **22:4, 5** Acts 8:3; 26:9–11 **22:20** Acts 7:58

murderers.' 21 'Go,' the Lord said to me, 'for I
will send you far away to the Gentiles.' "
22 The people listened to Paul until he said
this; but then they started shouting at the top
of their voices, "Away with him! Kill him!
He's not fit to live!" 23 They were screaming,
waving their clothes, and throwing dust up
in the air. 24 The Roman commander
ordered his men to take Paul into the fort,
and he told them to whip him in order to
find out why the Jews were screaming like
this against him. 25 But when they had tied
him up to be whipped, Paul said to the offi-
cer standing there, "Is it lawful for you to
whip a Roman citizen who hasn't even been
tried for any crime?"
26 When the officer heard this, he went to
the commander and asked him, "What are
you doing? That man is a Roman citizen!"
27 So the commander went to Paul and
asked him, "Tell me, are you a Roman citi-
zen?"
"Yes," answered Paul.
28 The commander said, "I became one by
paying a large amount of money."
"But I am one by birth," Paul answered.
29 At once the men who were going to
question Paul drew back from him; and the
commander was frightened when he realized
that Paul was a Roman citizen and that he
had put him in chains.

Paul before the Council

30 The commander wanted to find out for
sure what the Jews were accusing Paul of; so
the next day he had Paul's chains taken off
and ordered the chief priests and the whole
Council to meet. Then he took Paul and
made him stand before them.

23 Paul looked straight at the Council
and said, "My fellow Israelites! My
conscience is perfectly clear about the way
in which I have lived before God to this
very day." 2 The High Priest Ananias ordered
those who were standing close to Paul to
strike him on the mouth. 3 Paul said to him,
"God will certainly strike you—you white-
washed wall! You sit there to judge me
according to the Law, yet you break the Law
by ordering them to strike me!"
4 The men close to Paul said to him, "You
are insulting God's High Priest!"
5 Paul answered, "My fellow Israelites, I did
not know that he was the High Priest. The
scripture says, 'You must not speak evil of
the ruler of your people.' "
6 When Paul saw that some of the group
were Sadducees and the others were Phar-
isees, he called out in the Council, "Fellow
Israelites! I am a Pharisee, the son of Phar-
isees. I am on trial here because of the hope
I have that the dead will rise to life!"
7 As soon as he said this, the Pharisees and
Sadducees started to quarrel, and the group
was divided. (8 For the Sadducees say that
people will not rise from death and that
there are no angels or spirits; but the Phar-
isees believe in all three.) 9 The shouting
became louder, and some of the teachers of
the Law who belonged to the party of the
Pharisees stood up and protested strongly:
"We cannot find a thing wrong with this
man! Perhaps a spirit or an angel really did
speak to him!"
10 The argument became so violent that
the commander was afraid that Paul would
be torn to pieces. So he ordered his soldiers
to go down into the group, get Paul away
from them, and take him into the fort.
11 That night the Lord stood by Paul and
said, "Don't be afraid! You have given your
witness for me here in Jerusalem, and you
must also do the same in Rome."

The Plot against Paul's Life

12 The next morning some Jews met
together and made a plan. They took a vow
that they would not eat or drink anything
until they had killed Paul. 13 There were
more than forty who planned this together.
14 Then they went to the chief priests and
elders and said, "We have taken a solemn

23:3 Mt 23:27, 28 **23:5** Ex 22:28 **23:6** Acts 26:5; Phil 3:5 **23:8** Mt 22:23; Mk 12:18; Lk 20:27

What dangers did Paul face in telling his story *(Acts 22:1–25)*? What dangers do you face when you tell how God has worked in your life?

Pray it!

God Works Through Us

While Paul is being held for questioning, his nephew enters the scene, warning the Roman commander of the plot to kill Paul. Lucky for Paul, and thanks to his nephew, the officers and the commander acted swiftly to make sure their prisoner was kept safe.

Paul's nephew, the officers, the commander, and the army of soldiers were acting as instruments of God, keeping Paul safe from danger. This is how God tends to care for us—through people.

God, at the end of each day, help me remember all the people I was with, and how they showed me a little bit of your love and care. A smile, a helping hand, some advice offered sincerely, kind words, fun . . . I don't always think of these as you peeking into my life, but it is! So, God, thank you for all the people who will show me your love today! And help me think of ways I can show your love to all I meet too. Amen.

— Acts 23:12–35

vow together not to eat a thing until we
have killed Paul. 15 Now then, you and the
Council send word to the Roman com-
mander to bring Paul down to you, pretend-
ing that you want to get more accurate
information about him. But we will be ready
to kill him before he ever gets here."
16 But the son of Paul's sister heard about
the plot; so he went to the fort and told Paul.
17 Then Paul called one of the officers and
said to him, "Take this young man to the
commander; he has something to tell him."
18 The officer took him, led him to the com-
mander, and said, "The prisoner Paul called
me and asked me to bring this young man to
you, because he has something to say to you."
19 The commander took him by the hand,
led him off by himself, and asked him,
"What do you have to tell me?"
20 He said, "The Jewish authorities have
agreed to ask you tomorrow to take Paul
down to the Council, pretending that the
Council wants to get more accurate informa-
tion about him. 21 But don't listen to them,
because there are more than forty men who
will be hiding and waiting for him. They
have taken a vow not to eat or drink until
they have killed him. They are now ready to
do it and are waiting for your decision."
22 The commander said, "Don't tell anyone
that you have reported this to me." And he
sent the young man away.

Paul Is Sent to Governor Felix

23 Then the commander called two of his
officers and said, "Get two hundred soldiers
ready to go to Caesarea, together with sev-
enty horsemen and two hundred spearmen,
and be ready to leave by nine o'clock
tonight. 24 Provide some horses for Paul to
ride and get him safely through to Governor
Felix." 25 Then the commander wrote a letter
that went like this:
26 "Claudius Lysias to His Excellency,
Governor Felix: Greetings. 27 The Jews
seized this man and were about to kill
him. I learned that he is a Roman citizen,
so I went with my soldiers and rescued
him. 28 I wanted to know what they were
accusing him of, so I took him down to
their Council. 29 I found out that he had

The Nazarenes *(Acts 24:5)* was another name for Christians because they were followers of Jesus who was from Nazareth.

not done a thing for which he deserved to
die or be put in prison; the accusation
against him had to do with questions
about their own law. 30And when I was
informed that there was a plot against
him, at once I decided to send him to
you. I have told his accusers to make their
charges against him before you."
31The soldiers carried out their orders.
They got Paul and took him that night as far
as Antipatris. 32The next day the foot sol-
diers returned to the fort and left the horse-
men to go on with him. 33They took him to
Caesarea, delivered the letter to the gover-
nor, and turned Paul over to him. 34The
governor read the letter and asked Paul what
province he was from. When he found out
that he was from Cilicia, 35he said, "I will
hear you when your accusers arrive." Then
he gave orders for Paul to be kept under
guard in the governor's headquarters.

The Case against Paul

24 Five days later the High Priest Ana-
nias went to Caesarea with some
elders and a lawyer named Tertullus. They
appeared before Governor Felix and made
their charges against Paul. 2Then Paul was
called in, and Tertullus began to make his
accusation, as follows:
"Your Excellency! Your wise leadership
has brought us a long period of peace, and
many necessary reforms are being made for
the good of our country. 3We welcome this
everywhere and at all times, and we are
deeply grateful to you. 4I do not want to
take up too much of your time, however, so
I beg you to be kind and listen to our brief
account. 5We found this man to be a dan-
gerous nuisance; he starts riots among Jews
all over the world and is a leader of the party
of the Nazarenes. 6He also tried to defile the
Temple, and we arrested him.[j] 8If you ques-
tion this man, you yourself will be able to
learn from him all the things that we are
accusing him of." 9The Jews joined in the
accusation and said that all this was true.

Paul's Defense before Felix

10The governor then motioned to Paul to
speak, and Paul said,
"I know that you have been a judge over
this nation for many years, and so I am
happy to defend myself before you. 11As
you can find out for yourself, it was no
more than twelve days ago that I went to
Jerusalem to worship. 12The Jews did not
find me arguing with anyone in the Temple,
nor did they find me stirring up the people,
either in the synagogues or anywhere else in
the city. 13Nor can they give you proof of
the accusations they now bring against me.
14I do admit this to you: I worship the God
of our ancestors by following that Way
which they say is false. But I also believe in
everything written in the Law of Moses and
the books of the prophets. 15I have the same
hope in God that these themselves have,
namely, that all people, both the good and
the bad, will rise from death. 16And so I do
my best always to have a clear conscience
before God and people.
17"After being away from Jerusalem for
several years, I went there to take some
money to my own people and to offer sacri-
fices. 18It was while I was doing this that
they found me in the Temple after I had
completed the ceremony of purification.
There was no crowd with me and no disor-
der. 19But some Jews from the province of
Asia were there; they themselves ought to
come before you and make their accusations
if they have anything against me. 20Or let
these who are here tell what crime they
found me guilty of when I stood before the
Council— 21except for the one thing I
called out when I stood before them: 'I am
being tried by you today for believing that
the dead will rise to life.' "
22Then Felix, who was well informed
about the Way, brought the hearing to a close.
"When the commander Lysias arrives," he
told them, "I will decide your case." 23He
ordered the officer in charge of Paul to keep
him under guard, but to give him some

j **24:6** *Some manuscripts add verses 6b–8a:* We planned to judge him according to our own law, 7but the commander Lysias came, and with great violence took him from us. 8Then Lysias gave orders that his accusers should come before you.

24:17, 18 Acts 21:17–28 **24:21** Acts 23:6

…m and allow his friends to provide for
…eeds.

…aul before Felix and Drusilla

24 After some days Felix came with his wife
Drusilla, who was Jewish. He sent for Paul
and listened to him as he talked about faith in
Christ Jesus. 25 But as Paul went on discussing
about goodness, self-control, and the coming
Day of Judgment, Felix was afraid and said,
"You may leave now. I will call you again
when I get the chance." 26 At the same time
he was hoping that Paul would give him
some money; and for this reason he would
call for him often and talk with him.
27 After two years had passed, Porcius Fes-
tus succeeded Felix as governor. Felix want-
ed to gain favor with the Jews so he left Paul
in prison.

Paul Appeals to the Emperor

25 Three days after Festus arrived in the
province, he went from Caesarea to
Jerusalem, 2 where the chief priests and the
Jewish leaders brought their charges against
Paul. They begged Festus 3 to do them the
favor of having Paul come to Jerusalem, for
they had made a plot to kill him on the way.
4 Festus answered, "Paul is being kept a pris-
oner in Caesarea, and I myself will be going
back there soon. 5 Let your leaders go to
Caesarea with me and accuse the man if he
has done anything wrong."
6 Festus spent another eight or ten days
with them and then went to Caesarea. On
the next day he sat down in the judgment
court and ordered Paul to be brought in.
7 When Paul arrived, the Jews who had come
from Jerusalem stood around him and started
making many serious charges against him,
which they were not able to prove. 8 But Paul
defended himself: "I have done nothing
wrong against the Law of the Jews or against
the Temple or against the Roman Emperor."
9 But Festus wanted to gain favor with the
Jews, so he asked Paul, "Would you be will-
ing to go to Jerusalem and be tried on these
charges before me there?"
10 Paul said, "I am standing before the
Emperor's own judgment court, where I
should be tried. I have done no wrong to
the Jews, as you yourself well know. 11 If I
have broken the law and done something for
which I deserve the death penalty, I do not
ask to escape it. But if there is no truth in
the charges they bring against me, no one
can hand me over to them. I appeal to the
Emperor."
12 Then Festus, after conferring with his
advisers, answered, "You have appealed to the
Emperor, so to the Emperor you will go."

Study it!

Longest Wait in a Holding Cell

The governor, Felix, doesn't seem to want to deal with Paul's case. He listens respectfully to Paul, and even brings his Jewish wife to listen. Felix knew about the Way (Acts 24:22), which was another name for the early Church. He might even have been secretly interested in this new religion.

Felix tells Paul that he will hold him in custody while deciding his case and orders the officer to give Paul some liberty and to let his friends take care of him. But then Felix simply ignores Paul and leaves him sitting in prison for two years hoping Paul would bribe his way out of jail (24:26). Finally, Felix retired and let Paul be the next governor's problem.

What do you think Felix was afraid of?

— Acts 24:22–27

Paul before Agrippa and Bernice

13 Some time later King Agrippa and Ber-
nice came to Caesarea to pay a visit of wel-
come to Festus. 14 After they had been there
several days, Festus explained Paul's situation to

the king: "There is a man here who was left a
prisoner by Felix; 15and when I went to
Jerusalem, the Jewish chief priests and elders
brought charges against him and asked me to
condemn him. 16But I told them that we
Romans are not in the habit of handing over
any who are accused of a crime before they
have met their accusers face to face and have
had the chance of defending themselves
against the accusation. 17When they came
here, then, I lost no time, but on the very next
day I sat in the judgment court and ordered
the man to be brought in. 18His opponents
stood up, but they did not accuse him of any
of the evil crimes that I thought they would.
19All they had were some arguments with him
about their own religion and about a man
named Jesus, who has died; but Paul claims
that he is alive. 20I was undecided about how I
could get information on these matters, so I
asked Paul if he would be willing to go to
Jerusalem and be tried there on these charges.
21But Paul appealed; he asked to be kept
under guard and to let the Emperor decide his
case. So I gave orders for him to be kept under
guard until I could send him to the Emperor."
22Agrippa said to Festus, "I would like to
hear this man myself."

"You will hear him tomorrow," Festus answered.

23The next day Agrippa and Bernice
came with great pomp and ceremony and
entered the audience hall with the military
chiefs and the leading men of the city. Festus
gave the order, and Paul was brought in.
24Festus said, "King Agrippa and all who are
here with us: You see this man against whom
all the Jewish people, both here and in
Jerusalem, have brought complaints to me.
They scream that he should not live any
longer. 25But I could not find that he had
done anything for which he deserved the
death sentence. And since he himself made
an appeal to the Emperor, I have decided to
send him. 26But I have nothing definite
about him to write to the Emperor. So I
have brought him here before you—and
especially before you, King Agrippa!—so
that, after investigating his case, I may have
something to write. 27For it seems unreason-
able to me to send a prisoner without clearly
indicating the charges against him."

Study it!

Paul Put to the Test

Paul's situation is similar to what Jesus went through at the beginning of his trial. The chief priests and other Jewish leaders accuse Paul of many offenses, none of which are true. Festus, the new Roman governor, doesn't see the problem and would rather not be bothered with this case. Yet he is worried about keeping the peace with the Jews. So when Paul suggests taking the case to the Emperor, Festus eagerly accepts this solution. Festus also drags the local Jewish king into the picture. He asks King Agrippa to listen to Paul to see what crime Paul has committed. But Agrippa also agrees that Paul is not guilty of any crime against the Jewish faith.

But because Paul has asked for his case to go before the Roman Emperor, they have no choice but to send him to Rome to be tried (Acts 26:32). The rest of Acts tells of Paul's travel to Rome and his time there.

— Acts, chapters 25–26

Paul Defends Himself before Agrippa

26 Agrippa said to Paul, "You have per-
mission to speak on your own
behalf." Paul stretched out his hand and
defended himself as follows:

This King Agrippa was actually King Agrippa II. His father, King Agrippa I, was also called King Herod *(see Acts 12:1–5)*.

ng Agrippa! I consider myself fortu-
nat today I am to defend myself before
from all the things these Jews accuse me
3 particularly since you know so well all
e Jewish customs and disputes. I ask you,
hen, to listen to me with patience.
4 "All the Jews know how I have lived ever
since I was young. They know how I have
spent my whole life, at first in my own coun-
try and then in Jerusalem. 5 They have always
known, if they are willing to testify, that from
the very first I have lived as a member of the
strictest party of our religion, the Pharisees.
6 And now I stand here to be tried because of
the hope I have in the promise that God
made to our ancestors— 7 the very thing that
the twelve tribes of our people hope to
receive, as they worship God day and night.
And it is because of this hope, Your Majesty,
that I am being accused by these Jews! 8 Why
do you who are here find it impossible to
believe that God raises the dead?
9 "I myself thought that I should do every-
thing I could against the cause of Jesus of
Nazareth. 10 That is what I did in Jerusalem. I
received authority from the chief priests and
put many of God's people in prison; and
when they were sentenced to death, I also
voted against them. 11 Many times I had
them punished in the synagogues and tried
to make them deny their faith. I was so furi-
ous with them that I even went to foreign
cities to persecute them.

Paul Tells of His Conversion
(Acts 9:1–19; 22:6–16)

12 "It was for this purpose that I went to
Damascus with authority and orders from
the chief priests. 13 It was on the road at mid-
day, Your Majesty, that I saw a light much
brighter than the sun, coming from the sky
and shining around me and the men travel-
ing with me. 14 All of us fell to the ground,
and I heard a voice say to me in Hebrew,
'Saul, Saul! Why are you persecuting me?
You are hurting yourself by hitting back, like
an ox kicking against its owner's stick.'
15 'Who are you, Lord?' I asked. And the
Lord answered, 'I am Jesus, whom you perse-
cute. 16 But get up and stand on your feet. I
have appeared to you to appoint you as my
servant. You are to tell others what you have
seen of me[k] today and what I will show you
in the future. 17 I will rescue you from the
people of Israel and from the Gentiles to
whom I will send you. 18 You are to open
their eyes and turn them from the darkness
to the light and from the power of Satan to
God, so that through their faith in me they
will have their sins forgiven and receive their
place among God's chosen people.'

Paul Tells of His Work

19 "And so, King Agrippa, I did not disobey
the vision I had from heaven. 20 First in Da-
mascus and in Jerusalem and then in the
whole country of Israel and among the Gen-
tiles, I preached that they must repent of their
sins and turn to God and do the things that
would show they had repented. 21 It was for
this reason that these Jews seized me while I
was in the Temple, and they tried to kill me.
22 But to this very day I have been helped by
God, and so I stand here giving my witness to
all, to small and great alike. What I say is the
very same thing which the prophets and
Moses said was going to happen: 23 that the
Messiah must suffer and be the first one to
rise from death, to announce the light of sal-
vation to the Jews and to the Gentiles."
24 As Paul defended himself in this way,
Festus shouted at him, "You are mad, Paul!
Your great learning is driving you mad!"
25 Paul answered, "I am not mad, Your
Excellency! I am speaking the sober truth.
26 King Agrippa! I can speak to you with all
boldness, because you know about these
things. I am sure that you have taken notice

[k] **26:16** *Some manuscripts do not have* of me.

26:5 Acts 23:6; Phil 3:5 **26:8** 2 Macc 7:9 **26:9–11** Acts 8:3; 22:4, 5 **26:20** Acts 9:20, 28, 29
26:23 **a** 1 Cor 15:20; **b** Isa 42:6; 49:6

Unscramble this two-word phrase to see what Paul was doing before his conversion: eeiutpgnsrc sseuj. Find the answer in Acts 26:14.

of every one of them, for this thing has not happened hidden away in a corner. 27 King Agrippa, do you believe the prophets? I know that you do!"

28 Agrippa said to Paul, "In this short time do you think you will make me a Christian?"

29 "Whether a short time or a long time," Paul answered, "my prayer to God is that you and all the rest of you who are listening to me today might become what I am—except, of course, for these chains!"

30 Then the king, the governor, Bernice, and all the others got up, 31 and after leaving they said to each other, "This man has not done anything for which he should die or be put in prison." 32 And Agrippa said to Festus, "This man could have been released if he had not appealed to the Emperor."

Paul Sails for Rome

27 When it was decided that we should sail to Italy, they handed Paul and some other prisoners over to Julius, an officer in the Roman army regiment called "The Emperor's Regiment." 2 We went aboard a ship from Adramyttium, which was ready to leave for the seaports of the province of Asia, and we sailed away. Aristarchus, a Macedonian from Thessalonica, was with us. 3 The next day we arrived at Sidon. Julius was kind to Paul and allowed him to go and see his friends, to be given what he needed. 4 We went on from there, and because the winds were blowing against us, we sailed on the sheltered side of the island of Cyprus. 5 We crossed over the sea off Cilicia and Pamphylia and came to Myra in Lycia. 6 There the officer found a ship from Alexandria that was going to sail for Italy, so he put us aboard.

7 We sailed slowly for several days and with great difficulty finally arrived off the town of Cnidus. The wind would not let us go any farther in that direction, so we sailed down the sheltered side of the island of Crete, passing by Cape Salmone. 8 We kept close to the coast and with great difficulty came to a place called Safe Harbors, not far from the town of Lasea.

9 We spent a long time there, until it became dangerous to continue the voyage, for by now the Day of Atonement[l] was already past. So Paul gave them this advice: 10 "Men, I see that our voyage from here on will be dangerous; there will be great damage to the cargo and to the ship, and loss of life as well." 11 But the army officer was convinced by what the captain and the owner of the ship said, and not by what Paul said. 12 The harbor was not a good one to spend the winter in; so almost everyone was in favor of putting out to sea and trying to reach Phoenix, if possible, in order to spend the winter there. Phoenix is a harbor in Crete that faces southwest and northwest.[m]

The Storm at Sea

13 A soft wind from the south began to blow, and the men thought that they could carry out their plan, so they pulled up the anchor and sailed as close as possible along the coast of Crete. 14 But soon a very strong wind—the one called "Northeaster"—blew down from the island. 15 It hit the ship, and since it was impossible to keep the ship headed into the wind, we gave up trying and let it be carried along by the wind. 16 We got some shelter when we passed to the south of the little island of Cauda. There, with some difficulty we managed to make the ship's boat secure. 17 They pulled it aboard and then fastened some ropes tight around the ship. They were afraid that they might run into the sandbanks off the coast of Libya, so they lowered the sail and let the ship be carried by the wind. 18 The violent storm continued, so on the next day they began to throw some of the ship's cargo overboard, 19 and on the following day they threw part of the ship's equipment overboard. 20 For many days we could not see the sun or the stars, and the wind kept on blowing very hard. We finally gave up all hope of being saved.

21 After everyone had gone a long time without food, Paul stood before them and said, "You should have listened to me and not have sailed from Crete; then we would have avoided all this damage and loss. 22 But

[l] **27:9** DAY OF ATONEMENT: *This was celebrated toward the end of September or beginning of October, at which time bad weather made sailing dangerous.* [m] **27:12** southwest and northwest; *or* northeast and southeast.

ray it!

Holding On for Dear Life

Although this story is made up, it is based on the stories of real people: There were a hundred of us in a boat that should hold only forty people. Then the sea turned into an awful storm, and we were unable to keep everyone safe. When our boat found the shore, weeks later, we had lost twenty-two people. Would we have taken this journey if we had known of the danger? Yes! So terrible is the hatred and violence in Haiti, we could no longer survive there. I believe God heard my cries at sea. It is not easy, but God will help me build a new life here.

Does your life ever seem like you're in the midst of a great storm—things are out of control, you're being tossed about, and it feels like you might never reach safety? That's the perfect time to call out for God!

God, help! This is too big, too scary. I know you are near, but I need to feel your presence—comforting me, protecting me, guiding me to a safe place again. Please calm these waves of trouble, and keep me calm too. And when the storm is over, help me become wiser and stronger and less fearful when the waters of life get choppy again. Thanks, God, for rescuing me—again and again! Amen.

— Acts 27:13–44

now I beg you, take courage! Not one of
you will lose your life; only the ship will be
lost. 23For last night an angel of the God to
whom I belong and whom I worship came
to me 24and said, 'Don't be afraid, Paul! You
must stand before the Emperor. And God in
his goodness to you has spared the lives of all
those who are sailing with you.' 25So take
courage, men! For I trust in God that it will
be just as I was told. 26But we will be driven
ashore on some island."
27It was the fourteenth night, and we
were being driven in the Mediterranean by
the storm. About midnight the sailors sus-
pected that we were getting close to land.
28So they dropped a line with a weight tied
to it and found that the water was one hun-
dred and twenty feet deep; a little later they
did the same and found that it was ninety
feet deep. 29They were afraid that the ship
would go on the rocks, so they lowered four
anchors from the back of the ship and
prayed for daylight. 30Then the sailors tried
to escape from the ship; they lowered the
boat into the water and pretended that they
were going to put out some anchors from
the front of the ship. 31But Paul said to the
army officer and soldiers, "If the sailors don't
stay on board, you have no hope of being
saved." 32So the soldiers cut the ropes that
held the boat and let it go.
33Just before dawn, Paul begged them all
to eat some food: "You have been waiting
for fourteen days now, and all this time you
have not eaten a thing. 34I beg you, then, eat
some food; you need it in order to survive.
Not even a hair of your heads will be lost."
35After saying this, Paul took some bread,
gave thanks to God before them all, broke it,
and began to eat. 36They took courage, and
every one of them also ate some food.
37There was a total of 276[n] of us on board.
38After everyone had eaten enough, they
lightened the ship by throwing all the wheat
into the sea.

The Shipwreck

39When day came, the sailors did not rec-
ognize the coast, but they noticed a bay with

[n] **27:37** 276; *some manuscripts have* 275; *others have* about 76.

a beach and decided that, if possible, they would run the ship aground there. 40So they cut off the anchors and let them sink in the sea, and at the same time they untied the ropes that held the steering oars. Then they raised the sail at the front of the ship so that the wind would blow the ship forward, and we headed for shore. 41But the ship hit a sandbank and went aground; the front part of the ship got stuck and could not move, while the back part was being broken to pieces by the violence of the waves.

The ship hit a sandbank. (27:41)

42The soldiers made a plan to kill all the prisoners, in order to keep them from swimming ashore and escaping. 43But the army officer wanted to save Paul, so he stopped them from doing this. Instead, he ordered everyone who could swim to jump overboard first and swim ashore; 44the rest were to follow, holding on to the planks or to some broken pieces of the ship. And this was how we all got safely ashore.

In Malta

28 When we were safely ashore, we learned that the island was called Malta. 2The natives there were very friendly to us. It had started to rain and was cold, so they built a fire and made us all welcome. 3Paul gathered up a bundle of sticks and was putting them on the fire when a snake came out on account of the heat and fastened itself to his hand. 4The natives saw the snake hanging on Paul's hand and said to one another, "This man must be a murderer, but Fate will not let him live, even though he escaped from the sea." 5But Paul shook the snake off into the fire without being harmed at all. 6They were waiting for him to swell up or suddenly fall down dead. But after waiting for a long time and not seeing anything unusual happening to him, they changed their minds and said, "He is a god!"

7Not far from that place were some fields that belonged to Publius, the chief of the island. He welcomed us kindly and for three days we were his guests. 8Publius' father was in bed, sick with fever and dysentery. Paul went into his room, prayed, placed his hands on him, and healed him. 9When this happened, all the other sick people on the island came and were healed. 10They gave us many gifts, and when we sailed, they put on board what we needed for the voyage.

From Malta to Rome

11After three months we sailed away on a ship from Alexandria, called "The Twin Gods," which had spent the winter in the island. 12We arrived in the city of Syracuse and stayed there for three days. 13From there we sailed on and arrived in the city of Rhegium. The next day a wind began to blow from the south, and in two days we came to the town of Puteoli. 14We found some believers there who asked us to stay with them a week. And so we came to Rome. 15The believers in Rome heard about us and came as far as the towns of Market of Appius and Three Inns to meet us. When Paul saw them, he thanked God and was greatly encouraged.

In Rome

16When we arrived in Rome, Paul was allowed to live by himself with a soldier guarding him.

17After three days Paul called the local Jewish leaders to a meeting. When they had gathered, he said to them, "My fellow Israelites, even though I did nothing against

Where in chapter 27 are we reminded of the Eucharist? How does the Eucharist help us get through the storms of life?

ple or the customs that we received
ur ancestors, I was made a prisoner in
hem and handed over to the Romans.
ter questioning me, the Romans wanted
release me, because they found that I had
one nothing for which I deserved to die.
19 But when the Jews opposed this, I was
forced to appeal to the Emperor, even
though I had no accusation to make against
my own people. 20 That is why I asked to see
you and talk with you. As a matter of fact, I
am bound in chains like this for the sake of
him for whom the people of Israel hope."

21 They said to him, "We have not
received any letters from Judea about you,
nor have any of our people come from there
with any news or anything bad to say about
you. 22 But we would like to hear your ideas,
because we know that everywhere people
speak against this party to which you
belong."

23 So they set a date with Paul, and a large
number of them came that day to the place
where Paul was staying. From morning till
night he explained to them his message
about the Kingdom of God, and he tried to
convince them about Jesus by quoting from
the Law of Moses and the writings of the
prophets. 24 Some of them were convinced
by his words, but others would not believe.
25 So they left, disagreeing among themselves,
after Paul had said this one thing: "How well
the Holy Spirit spoke through the prophet
Isaiah to your ancestors! 26 For he said,

'Go and say to this people:
You will listen and listen, but not
understand;
you will look and look, but not see,
27 because this people's minds are dull,
and they have stopped up their ears
and closed their eyes.
Otherwise, their eyes would see,
their ears would hear,
their minds would understand,
and they would turn to me, says God,
and I would heal them.' "

28 And Paul concluded: "You are to know,

28:19 Acts 25:11 **28:26, 27** Isa 6:9, 10 (LXX)

Live it!

Paul's Last Years

The Book of Acts ends with Paul living alone in Rome as he awaits his trial. For two years we know he lives like this, all the while receiving visitors and preaching about the Kingdom of God "with all boldness and freedom" (Acts 28:31). During that time he also continued writing letters to the Christian communities he helped establish, some of which are included as books in the New Testament. We are not told when or how Paul dies, but ancient tradition claims he was martyred in Rome shortly after that two-year period, around AD 64.

When Paul gathers the Jews to explain his arrest, he quotes the prophet Isaiah (Acts 28:26–27). Paul is pointing out what a tremendous loss their lack of belief is for them. The Jews have waited and waited and waited for the Messiah, yet when he came they could not accept that Jesus was the Messiah.

Through the Holy Spirit, Jesus is present to us. How will we know when we see or hear Jesus? Whenever we experience kindness, comfort, forgiveness, patience, peace, prayerfulness, joy, justice, courage, selflessness, and love—we are meeting Jesus in and through other people.

— Acts 28:17–31

Using Map 8 on page 1906 find the path Paul sailed from Jerusalem to Rome.

then, that God's message of salvation has
been sent to the Gentiles. They will listen!"°
30 For two years Paul lived in a place he
rented for himself, and there he welcomed
all who came to see him. 31 He preached
about the Kingdom of God and taught
about the Lord Jesus Christ, speaking with
all boldness and freedom.

° **28:28** *Some manuscripts add verse 29:* After Paul said this, the Jews left, arguing violently among themselves.

Your Next Step

Congratulations on finishing the Acts of the Apostles! Use this space to write your thoughts and questions about this book. If you are following the suggested reading plan, go back to the Book of Judges in the Old Testament. Like the Apostles, the judges were also leaders who had some pretty exciting adventures.

Have you ever been confused by the directions for playing a new video game? Or have you ever had trouble really understanding a chapter in one of your textbooks?

Reading Paul's letter to the Romans is kind of like that for some people. It's full of messages about being a Christian, but it can be very difficult to understand. Despite this difficulty most people say that it is Saint Paul's most important writing. In the letter he explains how God has a plan to save all people from sin and death. So it may not be easy to read, but it is worth the effort. You will find that Paul's central message is clear enough: We must believe that God sent Jesus to save everyone—and if we believe this, our lives will change.

Chap. 4:1–6;5:14

Headlines

- The Key to Being Right with God (1:16–17)
- Faith Is Answer to Sinner's Plight (3:9–31)
- At War with Yourself! (7:14–25)
- God Works with Those Who Love (8:28–30)
- Need Help? Love God! (10:5–21)
- Paul Reveals Rules for Holy Living (12:1—14:23)

FACTOIDS

Who wrote this book? Saint Paul, in preparation for making a visit to Rome. He wanted to explain his teachings to the Christians who lived there.

When was it written? Around AD 56 to 58, about twenty-five years after Jesus' Resurrection. It was one of Paul's last letters.

Who was it written for? It was written for people who had recently become Christians in Rome.

How does it fit into the Bible? It is one of thirteen letters Paul or his followers wrote to new Christians. It is Paul's longest letter.

Important themes

- Everyone has sinned against God, but instead of punishing us, God sent Jesus to save us.
- The Jewish people have a special place in God's plan. But God's plan also includes salvation for non-Jewish people.
- If we believe in Jesus, we are called to live a life of love and service to others.

ROMANS

1 From Paul, a servant of Christ Jesus and
an apostle chosen and called by God to
preach his Good News.
2 The Good News was promised long ago
by God through his prophets, as written in
the Holy Scriptures. 3 It is about his Son, our
Lord Jesus Christ: as to his humanity, he was
born a descendant of David; 4 as to his divine
holiness, he was shown with great power to
be the Son of God by being raised from
death. 5 Through him God gave me the priv-
ilege of being an apostle for the sake of
Christ, in order to lead people of all nations
to believe and obey. 6 This also includes you
who are in Rome, whom God has called to
belong to Jesus Christ.
7 And so I write to all of you in Rome
whom God loves and has called to be his
own people:
May God our Father and the Lord Jesus
Christ give you grace and peace.

Prayer of Thanksgiving

8 First, I thank my God through Jesus
Christ for all of you, because the whole
world is hearing about your faith. 9 God is
my witness that what I say is true—the God
whom I serve with all my heart by preach-
ing the Good News about his Son. God
knows that I remember you 10 every time I
pray. I ask that God in his good will may at
last make it possible for me to visit you now.
11 For I want very much to see you, in order
to share a spiritual blessing with you to make
you strong. 12 What I mean is that both you
and I will be helped at the same time, you
by my faith and I by yours.
13 You must remember, my friends, that
many times I have planned to visit you, but
something has always kept me from doing
so. I want to win converts among you also, as
I have among other Gentiles. 14 For I have an
obligation to all peoples, to the civilized and
to the savage, to the educated and to the
ignorant. 15 So then, I am eager to preach the
Good News to you also who live in Rome.

The Power of the Gospel

16 I have complete confidence in the
gospel; it is God's power to save all who
believe, first the Jews and also the Gentiles.
17 For the gospel reveals how God puts peo-
ple right with himself: it is through faith
from beginning to end. As the scripture says,
"The person who is put right with God
through faith shall live."[a]

Human Guilt

18 God's anger is revealed from heaven
against all the sin and evil of the people
whose evil ways prevent the truth from
being known. 19 God punishes them, because
what can be known about God is plain to
them, for God himself made it plain. 20 Ever
since God created the world, his invisible
qualities, both his eternal power and his
divine nature, have been clearly seen; they
are perceived in the things that God has
made. So those people have no excuse at all!
21 They know God, but they do not give him
the honor that belongs to him, nor do they
thank him. Instead, their thoughts have
become complete nonsense, and their empty
minds are filled with darkness. 22 They say

Their thoughts have become complete nonsense. (1:21)

[a] **1:17** put right with God through faith shall live; *or* put right with God shall live through faith.

1:13 Acts 19:21 **1:16** Mk 8:38 **1:17** Hab 2:4 **1:20** Wis 13:1–9; Sir 17:8 **1:21** Eph 4:17, 18

...e, but they are fools; 23instead of ...g the immortal God, they worship ...ade to look like mortals or birds or ... or reptiles.

...d so God has given those people over ... the filthy things their hearts desire, and ... do shameful things with each other.

...hey exchange the truth about God for a ...e; they worship and serve what God has created instead of the Creator himself, who is to be praised forever! Amen.

26Because they do this, God has given them over to shameful passions. Even the women pervert the natural use of their sex by unnatural acts. 27In the same way the men give up natural sexual relations with women and burn with passion for each other. Men do shameful things with each other, and as a result they bring upon themselves the punishment they deserve for their wrongdoing.

28Because those people refuse to keep in mind the true knowledge about God, he has given them over to corrupted minds, so that they do the things that they should not do. 29They are filled with all kinds of wickedness, evil, greed, and vice; they are full of jealousy, murder, fighting, deceit, and malice. They gossip 30and speak evil of one another; they are hateful to God, insolent,[b] proud, and boastful; they think of more ways to do evil; they disobey their parents; 31they have no conscience; they do not keep their promises, and they show no kindness or pity for others. 32They know that God's law says that people who live in this way deserve death. Yet, not only do they continue to do these very things, but they even approve of others who do them.

Live it!

Guilty as Charged!

Do you know people who commit the sins Paul describes in Romans 1:28–32? They gossip, fight a lot, and lie. They are greedy and don't care about other people. They say hateful things about their parents and teachers, put down others, and do not keep their promises. They do not respect their own bodies or anyone else's.

Why do they do these things? One simple reason: they don't know God as they should. They refuse to believe that God loves them, has a plan for them, and wants them to be happy forever. If they knew God, they would try to make things right with God by following Jesus.

Remember that through the Bible God speaks to us today too. As you start to read the Letter to the Romans, think about what God might be saying to you. Could Paul have been writing about people at your school? Could he have been writing about you? Are you right with God?

— Romans 1:28–32

God's Judgment

2 Do you, my friend, pass judgment on others? You have no excuse at all, whoever you are. For when you judge others and then do the same things which they do, you condemn yourself. 2We know that God is right when he judges the people who do such things as these. 3But you, my friend, do those very things for which you pass judgment on others! Do you think you will escape God's judgment? 4Or perhaps you despise his great kindness, tolerance, and patience. Surely you know that God is kind, because he is trying to lead you to repent. 5But you have a hard and stubborn heart,

[b] **1:30** are hateful to God, insolent; *or* hate God, and are insolent.

1:23 Deut 4:16–18; Wis 11:15; 12:24; 13:10–19 **2:1** Mt 7:1; Lk 6:37 **2:4** Wis 11:23

How many times does Paul mention the Law (with a capital *L*) in Romans, chapter 2? Why is it so important to the Jews?

and so you are making your own punishment even greater on the Day when God's anger and righteous judgments will be revealed. 6For God will reward each of us according to what we have done. 7Some people keep on doing good, and seek glory, honor, and immortal life; to them God will give eternal life. 8Other people are selfish and reject what is right, in order to follow what is wrong; on them God will pour out his anger and fury. 9There will be suffering and pain for all those who do what is evil, for the Jews first and also for the Gentiles. 10But God will give glory, honor, and peace to all who do what is good, to the Jews first and also to the Gentiles. 11For God judges everyone by the same standard.

12The Gentiles do not have the Law of Moses; they sin and are lost apart from the Law. The Jews have the Law; they sin and are judged by the Law. 13For it is not by hearing the Law that people are put right with God, but by doing what the Law commands. 14The Gentiles do not have the Law; but whenever they do by instinct what the Law commands, they are their own law, even though they do not have the Law. 15Their conduct shows that what the Law commands is written in their hearts. Their consciences also show that this is true, since their thoughts sometimes accuse them and sometimes defend them. 16And so, according to the Good News I preach, this is how it will be on that Day when God through Jesus Christ will judge the secret thoughts of all.

The Jews and the Law

17What about you? You call yourself a Jew; you depend on the Law and boast about God; 18you know what God wants you to do, and you have learned from the Law to choose what is right; 19you are sure that you are a guide for the blind, a light for those who are in darkness, 20an instructor for the foolish, and a teacher for the ignorant. You are certain that in the Law you have the full content of knowledge and of truth. 21You teach others—why don't you teach yourself? You preach, "Do not steal"—but do you yourself steal? 22You say, "Do not commit adultery"—but do you commit adultery? You detest idols—but do you rob temples? 23You boast about having God's law—but do you bring shame on God by breaking his law? 24The scripture says, "Because of you Jews, the Gentiles speak evil of God."

25If you obey the Law, your circumcision is of value; but if you disobey the Law, you might as well never have been circumcised. 26If the Gentile, who is not circumcised, obeys the commands of the Law, will not

Live it!

Know It. Live It.

Carlos can name the Ten Commandments in order. Hannah can recite most parts of the Mass from memory. Loren aced his last religion test, as he usually does. But the three friends declared yesterday "Make Fun of Fat Kids Day." All day they poked fun at people who were overweight and played cruel jokes on them.

Knowing what is right and doing what is right are two different things. Paul makes this point to his Jewish brothers and sisters in the middle of chapter 2 of Romans. Like them, all your life you have been learning the difference between right and wrong. You know the difference. Now it's time to live the difference. Don't put your faith in a notebook and leave it in your locker. Carry it with you in the halls, on the playground, the field, the school bus, the gym, and everyplace else you go. Through your actions give people a good impression about what Christians are like.

— Romans 2:17–29

2:6 Ps 62:12; Prov 24:12 **2:11** Deut 10:17 **2:24** Isa 52:5 (LXX)

…im as though he were circum-
…d so you Jews will be condemned
…ntiles because you break the Law,
…ugh you have it written down and
…umcised; but they obey the Law, even
… they are not physically circumcised.
…er all, who is a real Jew, truly circum-
…d? It is not the man who is a Jew on the
…tside, whose circumcision is a physical
…hing. 29Rather, the real Jew is the person
who is a Jew on the inside, that is, whose
heart has been circumcised, and this is the
work of God's Spirit, not of the written Law.
Such a person receives praise from God, not
from human beings.

3 Do the Jews then have any advantage
over the Gentiles? Or is there any value
in being circumcised? 2Much, indeed, in
every way! In the first place, God trusted his
message to the Jews. 3But what if some of
them were not faithful? Does this mean that
God will not be faithful? 4Certainly not!
God must be true, even though all human
beings are liars. As the scripture says,

"You must be shown to be right when
you speak;
you must win your case when you are
being tried."

5But what if our doing wrong serves to
show up more clearly God's doing right?
Can we say that God does wrong when he
punishes us? (This would be the natural
question to ask.) 6By no means! If God is
not just, how can he judge the world?

7But what if my untruth serves God's
glory by making his truth stand out more
clearly? Why should I still be condemned as
a sinner? 8Why not say, then, "Let us do evil
so that good may come"? Some people,
indeed, have insulted me by accusing me of
saying this very thing! They will be con-
demned, as they should be.

No One Is Righteous

9Well then, are we Jews in any better con-
dition than the Gentiles? Not at all![c] I have
already shown that Jews and Gentiles alike
are all under the power of sin. 10As the
Scriptures say:

"There is no one who is righteous,
11 no one who is wise
or who worships God.
12All have turned away from God;
they have all gone wrong;
no one does what is right, not even one.
13Their words are full of deadly deceit;
wicked lies roll off their tongues,
and dangerous threats, like snake's
poison, from their lips;
14 their speech is filled with bitter curses.
15They are quick to hurt and kill;
16 they leave ruin and destruction
wherever they go.
17They have not known the path of peace,
18 nor have they learned reverence for
God."

19Now we know that everything in the
Law applies to those who live under the Law,
in order to stop all human excuses and bring
the whole world under God's judgment.
20For no one is put right in God's sight by
doing what the Law requires; what the Law
does is to make us know that we have sinned.

How We Are Put Right with God

21But now God's way of putting people
right with himself has been revealed. It has
nothing to do with law, even though the Law
of Moses and the prophets gave their witness
to it. 22God puts people right through their
faith in Jesus Christ. God does this to all who
believe in Christ, because there is no differ-
ence at all: 23everyone has sinned and is far
away from God's saving presence. 24But by
the free gift of God's grace all are put right
with him through Christ Jesus, who sets
them free. 25-26God offered him, so that by
his blood[d] he should become the means by
which people's sins are forgiven through
their faith in him. God did this in order to
demonstrate that he is righteous. In the past
he was patient and overlooked people's sins;

[c] **3:9** any better condition than the Gentiles? Not at all!; *or* any worse condition than the Gentiles? Not altogether. [d] **3:25–26** by his blood; *or* by his sacrificial death.

2:29 Deut 30:6 **3:4** Ps 51:4 (LXX) **3:10–12** Ps 14:1–3 (LXX); Ps 53:1–3 (LXX) **3:13** **a** Ps 5:9 (LXX); **b** Ps 140:3 **3:14** Ps 10:7 (LXX) **3:15–17** Isa 59:7, 8 **3:18** Ps 36:1 **3:20** Ps 143:2; Gal 2:16 **3:22** Gal 2:16

Catholic Connections

Sin Happens

***Sin.* It's a strong word. It's more than a little mistake. Sin is disobeying God on purpose. You can sin by thinking, saying, or doing something that offends God. When you choose to do wrong instead of doing good, you sin. You are not following the example of Jesus. You hurt your relationship with God, with other people, and with yourself.**

Every night before you go to sleep, think about what thoughts, words, and actions hurt your relationships. Say a prayer admitting you were wrong and ask God for forgiveness. This is called an *examination of conscience.*

Along with this daily routine, the sacrament of Penance and Reconciliation gives Catholics a chance to confess their sins. In the sacrament the priest grants you absolution—God's complete forgiveness for your sins.

— Romans 3:9–20

but in the present time he deals with their
sins, in order to demonstrate his righteous-
ness. In this way God shows that he himself is
righteous and that he puts right everyone
who believes in Jesus.
27 What, then, can we boast about? Noth-
ing! And what is the reason for this? Is it that
we obey the Law? No, but that we believe.
28 For we conclude that a person is put right
with God only through faith, and not by
doing what the Law commands. 29 Or is God
the God of the Jews only? Is he not the God
of the Gentiles also? Of course he is. 30 God
is one, and he will put the Jews right with
himself on the basis of their faith, and will
put the Gentiles right through their faith.
31 Does this mean that by this faith we do
away with the Law? No, not at all; instead,
we uphold the Law.

The Example of Abraham

4 What shall we say, then, of Abraham, the
father of our race? What was his experi-
ence? 2 If he was put right with God by the
things he did, he would have something to
boast about—but not in God's sight. 3 The
scripture says, "Abraham believed God, and
because of his faith God accepted him as
righteous." 4 A person who works is paid
wages, but they are not regarded as a gift;
they are something that has been earned.
5 But those who depend on faith, not on
deeds, and who believe in the God who
declares the guilty to be innocent, it is this
faith that God takes into account in order to
put them right with himself. 6 This is what
David meant when he spoke of the happi-
ness of the person whom God accepts as
righteous, apart from anything that person
does:

7 "Happy are those whose wrongs are
forgiven,
whose sins are pardoned!
8 Happy is the person whose sins the Lord
will not keep account of"

9 Does this happiness that David spoke of
belong only to those who are circumcised?
No indeed! It belongs also to those who are
not circumcised. For we have quoted the

3:30 Deut 6:4; Gal 3:20 **4:3** Gen 15:6; Gal 3:6 **4:7, 8** Ps 32:1, 2

An *Act of Contrition* is a prayer telling God you are sorry for your sins.

Study it!

Jew to Jew

Saint Paul was a Jewish Christian. He wrote to both Jews and non-Jews. To get his point across, he used words and names of people that his Jewish readers would understand. In chapter 4 he makes a point about faith by writing about Abraham and Sarah, who had a son even though they were old (see Genesis, chapter 18). He quotes a psalm about forgiveness (see Psalm 32:1–2), because many Jews knew the Psalms by heart. He writes about circumcision, a ritual that was performed on all Jewish males when they were eight days old (see Genesis 17:9–14) to distinguish Jews from non-Jews.

Then Paul says something shocking. He tells them the important thing isn't whether you are circumcised or not but whether you have true faith. Faith in God and faith in Christ. Then he tells them that in God's eyes there is no difference between a circumcised Jew and an uncircumcised non-Jew if they both have faith.

What modern men and women would you name as people who show true faith? What saints, historical figures, and even people you know personally come to mind?

— Romans, chapter 4

scripture, "Abraham believed God, and
because of his faith God accepted him as
righteous." 10 When did this take place? Was it
before or after Abraham was circumcised? It
was before, not after. 11 He was circumcised
later, and his circumcision was a sign to show
that because of his faith God had accepted
him as righteous before he had been circum-
cised. And so Abraham is the spiritual father
of all who believe in God and are accepted as
righteous by him, even though they are not
circumcised. 12 He is also the father of those
who are circumcised, that is, of those who, in
addition to being circumcised, also live the
same life of faith that our father Abraham
lived before he was circumcised.

God's Promise Is Received through Faith

13 When God promised Abraham and his
descendants that the world would belong to
him, he did so, not because Abraham obeyed
the Law, but because he believed and was
accepted as righteous by God. 14 For if what
God promises is to be given to those who
obey the Law, then faith means nothing and
God's promise is worthless. 15 The Law
brings down God's anger; but where there is
no law, there is no disobeying of the law.
16 And so the promise was based on faith,
in order that the promise should be guaran-
teed as God's free gift to all of Abraham's
descendants—not just to those who obey
the Law, but also to those who believe as
Abraham did. For Abraham is the spiritual
father of us all; 17 as the scripture says, "I have
made you father of many nations." So the
promise is good in the sight of God, in
whom Abraham believed—the God who
brings the dead to life and whose command
brings into being what did not exist. 18 Abra-
ham believed and hoped, even when there
was no reason for hoping, and so became
"the father of many nations." Just as the
scripture says, "Your descendants will be as

4:11 Gen 17:10 **4:13** Gen 17:4–6; 22:17, 18; Gal 3:29 **4:14** Gal 3:18 **4:16** Gal 3:7 **4:17** Gen 17:5 **4:18** Gen 15:5

Jews are the spiritual relatives of Christians. We share a special relationship and can learn much from each other.

Pray it!

A Simple Prayer

After reading the section on being right with God (Romans 5:1–11), try praying this prayer. Does it express the relationship you want with God?

More than anything, God, I want to be right with you.
I know that Jesus died for me, just because you love me.
Now it's my turn to show my love.
I want to live the life you want for me.
I want to be the person you made me to be.
I want to feel all the love you have for me.
I want the world to be a better place because I'm in it.
Help me be right with you, God.
Amen.

— Romans 5:1–11

many as the stars." 19He was then almost one
hundred years old; but his faith did not
weaken when he thought of his body, which
was already practically dead, or of the fact
that Sarah could not have children. 20His
faith did not leave him, and he did not
doubt God's promise; his faith filled him
with power, and he gave praise to God. 21He
was absolutely sure that God would be able
to do what he had promised. 22That is why
Abraham, through faith, "was accepted as
righteous by God." 23The words "he was
accepted as righteous" were not written for
him alone. 24They were written also for us
who are to be accepted as righteous, who
believe in him who raised Jesus our Lord
from death. 25Because of our sins he was
given over to die, and he was raised to life in
order to put us right with God.

Right with God

5 Now that we have been put right with
God through faith, we have[e] peace with
God through our Lord Jesus Christ. 2He has
brought us by faith into this experience of
God's grace, in which we now live. And so
we boast[f] of the hope we have of sharing
God's glory! 3We also boast[g] of our troubles,
because we know that trouble produces
endurance, 4endurance brings God's
approval, and his approval creates hope. 5This
hope does not disappoint us, for God has
poured out his love into our hearts by means
of the Holy Spirit, who is God's gift to us.

6For when we were still helpless, Christ
died for the wicked at the time that God
chose. 7It is a difficult thing for someone to
die for a righteous person. It may even be
that someone might dare to die for a good
person. 8But God has shown us how much
he loves us—it was while we were still sin-
ners that Christ died for us! 9By his blood[h]
we are now put right with God; how much
more, then, will we be saved by him from
God's anger! 10We were God's enemies, but
he made us his friends through the death of
his Son. Now that we are God's friends,
how much more will we be saved by
Christ's life! 11But that is not all; we rejoice
because of what God has done through our
Lord Jesus Christ, who has now made us
God's friends.

[e] **5:1** we have; *some manuscripts have* let us have. [f] **5:2** we boast; *or* let us boast. [g] **5:3** We also boast; *or* Let us also boast. [h] **5:9** By his blood; *or* By his sacrificial death.

4:19 Gen 17:17 **4:25** Isa 53:4, 5

Adam and Christ

12 Sin came into the world through one
man, and his sin brought death with it. As a
result, death has spread to the whole human
race because everyone has sinned. 13 There
was sin in the world before the Law was
given; but where there is no law, no account
is kept of sins. 14 But from the time of Adam
to the time of Moses, death ruled over all
human beings, even over those who did not
sin in the same way that Adam did when he
disobeyed God's command.

Adam was a figure of the one who was to
come. 15 But the two are not the same,
because God's free gift is not like Adam's sin.
It is true that many people died because of
the sin of that one man. But God's grace is
much greater, and so is his free gift to so
many people through the grace of the one
man, Jesus Christ. 16 And there is a difference
between God's gift and the sin of one man.
After the one sin, came the judgment of
"Guilty"; but after so many sins, comes the
undeserved gift of "Not guilty!" 17 It is true
that through the sin of one man death began
to rule because of that one man. But how
much greater is the result of what was done
by the one man, Jesus Christ! All who receive
God's abundant grace and are freely put right
with him will rule in life through Christ.

18 So then, as the one sin condemned all
people, in the same way the one righteous act
sets all people free and gives them life. 19 And
just as all people were made sinners as the
result of the disobedience of one man, in the
same way they will all be put right with God
as the result of the obedience of the one man.

20 Law was introduced in order to increase
wrongdoing; but where sin increased, God's
grace increased much more. 21 So then, just as
sin ruled by means of death, so also God's grace
rules by means of righteousness, leading us to
eternal life through Jesus Christ our Lord.

Dead to Sin but Alive in Union with Christ

6 What shall we say, then? Should we
continue to live in sin so that God's
grace will increase? 2 Certainly not! We have
died to sin—how then can we go on living
in it? 3 For surely you know that when we
were baptized into union with Christ Jesus,
we were baptized into union with his death.
4 By our baptism, then, we were buried with
him and shared his death, in order that, just
as Christ was raised from death by the glori-
ous power of the Father, so also we might
live a new life.

5 For since we have become one with him
in dying as he did, in the same way we shall
be one with him by being raised to life as he
was. 6 And we know that our old being has
been put to death with Christ on his cross,
in order that the power of the sinful self
might be destroyed, so that we should no
longer be the slaves of sin. 7 For when we
die, we are set free from the power of sin.
8 Since we have died with Christ, we believe
that we will also live with him. 9 For we
know that Christ has been raised from death
and will never die again—death will no
longer rule over him. 10 And so, because he
died, sin has no power over him; and now he
lives his life in fellowship with God. 11 In the
same way you are to think of yourselves as
dead, so far as sin is concerned, but living in
fellowship with God through Christ Jesus.

So that we should no longer be slaves of sin. (6:6)

12 Sin must no longer rule in your mortal
bodies, so that you obey the desires of your
natural self. 13 Nor must you surrender any
part of yourselves to sin to be used for
wicked purposes. Instead, give yourselves to
God, as those who have been brought from
death to life, and surrender your whole
being to him to be used for righteous pur-

5:12 Gen 3:6; Wis 2:24 **6:4** Col 2:12

Mary of Nazareth

Breakthrough!: Mary, it is an honor to meet you! How old were you when you became the mother of Jesus?

Mary: I was just a teenager—but that was normal for those times.

B: When did you know Jesus was God's son?

Mary: The angel Gabriel told me first, but I'm not sure I really grasped it. My cousin, Elizabeth, knew it immediately when I visited her. But truly, it took all my life for me to fully understand what it meant to be the mother of God's son . . . well, really, the mother of God!

B: What was it like being Jesus' mom?

Mary: He was a good, hard-working boy. Strong-willed, too! But pure joy. Later, when he was a man, I was amazed by his love, and I was crushed when some people returned his love with hate.

B: That must have been hard. What is your favorite memory of Jesus?

Mary: I shared many meals with him, his disciples, and his close friends, Mary, Martha, and Lazarus. I loved seeing him laugh and just relax. And when he brought Lazarus back to life . . . what an amazing day! Of course, Jesus himself was raised later. I don't have words to describe that!

B: You were with him at his death.

Mary: After he died, we brought him down from the cross, and I just held him and kissed him for the longest time. I can still taste his blood on my lips.

B: What would you like your life to teach others?

Mary: From all appearances, I was a poor and insignificant girl, a simple servant of God. But God saw deeper—he saw my faithful, strong, gentle spirit. I would like others to think about those qualities in their lives.

B: What do you think is the most important thing you ever said?

Mary: Saying "yes" to God!

John the Baptist

Breakthrough!: How do you know Jesus?

John: I'm his cousin. When we were grown up, I baptized him and got him started in his ministry.

B: What was it like to baptize Jesus?

John: We both felt very humble about it. When he came out of the water, I saw the Spirit of God rest over Jesus—like a dove, sort of. All of us felt God's presence very powerfully at that moment. I think it was then that Jesus knew it was time to begin his ministry.

B: Tell us a little about your extreme lifestyle.

John: You must be referring to my diet and fashion tastes. It's true; I ate grasshoppers and wild honey, and I wore a camel-hair coat—kind of scratchy, but warm. I lived with a group of believers in the desert. I chose to live very simply so I could keep focused on my mission.

B: What was your mission?

John: I was a baptizer and preacher. I challenged people to change their sinful ways and turn their lives back to God. People said I was a prophet. They also said I was a lot like Jesus, but I knew I wasn't the Messiah; I just pointed people to Jesus, the true Messiah.

B: Your honesty about people's sins got you into trouble, didn't it?

John: Yes, Herod and his illegitimate wife, Herodias, didn't like it when I accused them of adultery. They eventually had me put in prison and killed.

B: Any words you want to leave us with?

John: "Get the road ready for the Lord; / make a straight path for him to travel!" (Mark 1:3). It means, prepare a place in your life for God to live. Clean up your act, people!

Peter

Breakthrough!: Sir, what is your connection to Jesus?

Peter: I was one of his twelve apostles; my brother Andrew and I were the first ones Jesus called to follow him.

B: What did you have to give up to do that?

Peter: Give up? Oh, I gained much more than I gave up. I had a good career as a fisherman, which I took a break from. And my family—I wasn't with them as much. But Jesus filled my life with adventures, miracles, challenges . . . and more love than you can imagine. He taught me things I never dreamed I could understand, do, or say.

B: Like what?

Peter: After Jesus left us, everyone looked to me as their leader. I did my best to carry on Jesus' mission and do the work he did, like healing and preaching. Me—a simple fisherman!

B: People say you were an unlikely candidate for taking over. Did you goof up a lot?

Peter: Hmmm . . . yes, I had my moments! But each time I messed up, I got back up and tried again. I think Jesus appreciated my stick-to-it attitude.

B: What was your greatest failure?

Peter: That's easy. After Jesus was arrested, we were terrified that the Romans would come after us, too. So three times I denied to people that Jesus was my friend. It still makes me feel sick to my stomach to recall this.

B: Did Jesus forgive you for that?

Peter: Yes. And he gave me three opportunities to make it up, to tell him just how much I loved him. That's when Jesus asked me to lead his mission.

B: What words would you like our readers to remember you by?

Peter: I'd rather they remember my favorite saying of Jesus: "Don't be afraid."

Mary Magdalene

Breakthrough!: You're the famous prostitute from the Gospels, right?

Mary: NO! That's a common mistake, a terrible rumor that spread. But it's simply not true. There is a prostitute written about, but it is not me. Nor am I the woman caught in adultery. Geesh, my name gets attached to every sinful woman in the Gospels! And I didn't do anything but be a faithful friend to Jesus!

B: Okay, okay, I'm sorry I hit that nerve! Thanks for setting us all straight. So, tell us more about your friendship with Jesus.

Mary: I was sick—in the head, in the heart—some people say I had demons in me, which is true in a sense. Jesus healed me, and I was so moved by this experience that I became one of his followers. I was with Jesus right up to his death—I stood at the foot of his cross, holding up his mother, Mary. Then, on the morning I went to his tomb with the oils and spices, I discovered his body was gone. Then—sorry, it still moves me to tears—he was alive again and he spoke to me outside the tomb! There is no way to describe how awesome that morning was! I was the first person to announce his Resurrection to his apostles, who were hiding out in fear. My fear didn't stop me from trying to give Jesus a proper burial. I would have died for him.

B: What would you like us to remember about you?

Mary: That I was with Jesus through it all. I heard all his stories, saw the miracles, experienced his healing. I was there on all the good days, and on the bad ones, especially the very worst day, when he was tortured and killed. I would do anything for Jesus. I am saved because of him.

Paul

Breakthrough!: Paul, you are one of the most surprising figures in Christianity.

Paul: I started out as a Pharisee, a devout Jew who lived by the letter of the Law. This new religion, called the Way, was growing rapidly, and some of us felt it had to be stopped before things got out of control. So, I became a defender of the Jewish faith—and ended up persecuting a lot of Christians. I thought I was pleasing God, but I was terribly, terribly misguided.

B: What changed you?

Paul: Jesus appeared to me. To make a long story short, there were flashes from the sky and the voice of Christ saying: "Saul, Saul! Why do you persecute me?" I became a changed man, and learned everything I could about Jesus.

B: Wait, I thought your name was Paul. Why did Christ call you Saul?

Paul: There's an easy explanation. My Jewish name is Saul. But the Roman version of my name is Paul. I became better known as Paul since I spent most of my time preaching in the Roman Empire.

B: You certainly got a lot done after Christ appeared to you.

Paul: I was unstoppable! From the moment of my baptism, I could do nothing but preach the Good News!

B: You must love traveling. You sure got around!

Paul: Honestly, I got terribly seasick! But I had no choice. There were so many people to reach—Jews, Gentiles, the rich, the poor, the educated, the pure of heart. I needed many more years.

B: Under your leadership, the Church expanded from Jerusalem to Rome, the capital of the empire.

Paul: It wasn't just me; there were lots of other Christian missionaries spreading the Good News. It was because of the power of the Holy Spirit. I was just an instrument.

Barnabas

Breakthrough!: How did you first get connected with the apostles?

Barnabas: In the early days of the Way (what Christianity was called early on), all the believers took care of one another; we shared our resources to make sure everyone had what they needed. I sold a field I owned and brought the money to the apostles so they could help the poor among us. Later I introduced the apostles to Paul. He originally was a persecutor of the Christians, you see, and they wanted nothing to do with him. Paul needed me to assure the apostles that God had truly changed Paul's heart.

B: So you believed in Paul when no one else would?

Barnabas: I guess so. Next thing I knew, I was traveling with him and sharing the workload with him.

B: The workload?

Barnabas: Preaching and healing, setting up those first Christian communities, appointing leaders, ironing out conflicts, and so on.

B: But you and Paul had a disagreement and split up, right?

Barnabas: My cousin, John Mark, had to drop out of our first mission before it was over, and Paul really held that against him. I guess he didn't trust John Mark or think he was reliable. Anyway, I felt strongly that we should give John Mark another chance. In the end Paul went one way, John Mark and I went the other.

B: That's too bad.

Barnabas: Eventually we worked it out and got back on the road together. In the end, Jesus and his mission are a lot more important than our petty arguments.

B: Your name means "one who encourages." Seems like it fits you!

Barnabas: I hope so.

Timothy

Breakthrough!: Timothy, how is it that Paul came to choose you as a companion and co-worker in his mission work?

Timothy: I was a convert of Paul's, when I was young. I think he could see that my faith was sincere and that I loved the Scriptures. I guess he saw other gifts in me as well, and felt I had what it takes to be a missionary.

B: Do you give Paul credit for your faith?

Timothy: Partly. My faith was planted in me and nurtured by my mother, Eunice, and my grandmother, Lois. Both women were devout Jews and raised me to love my Jewish faith. When I met Paul and learned about Jesus, God moved my heart to believe in him as the Messiah. I am complete now.

B: Was Paul a good traveling companion?

Timothy: Well, he snores . . . but, yes! I never stopped learning from him and never ceased to be inspired by his courage and determination.

B: Did you travel the entire time with Paul?

Timothy: No, I also spent time in Ephesus as a leader in the Church there. Paul kept in touch with me by letters, encouraging and supporting me in my pastoral work there.

B: Paul called on you to visit him when he was in prison. Why you?

Timothy: Paul looked on me like a son. We had been through a lot together, and we truly loved each other, like father and son. It was natural that he would call me to be by his side during difficult times.

B: And now you are converting and teaching young people, like Paul did for you?

Timothy: That's what the mission is all about—to keep passing the faith from generation to generation.

Priscilla & Aquila

Breakthrough!: You are friends of Paul's, are you not?

Aquila: Yes, Paul lived and worked with my wife and me in Corinth. All three of us were tent-makers. Paul taught us a lot about Jesus.

B: Priscilla, was Paul a good houseguest?

Priscilla: Paul was utterly faithful, and driven to preach the Gospel. It was a privilege to have him in our home. We learned so much from him. Other than his snoring, he was a polite and proper guest!

B: You traveled with Paul a bit, right?

Aquila: It was such an exciting time. We sailed with him to Ephesus. We were partners with Paul in starting the Christian community there.

B: So, you've moved around quite a bit your-selves, it seems.

Aquila: It wasn't easy being a follower of Jesus in those days. Before meeting Paul, Priscilla and I lived in Rome. But the emperor wanted the Jews out, so we came to Corinth where we received our call from God.

B: Your call?

Priscilla: Yes, God called us to spread the message of Jesus and become Church leaders. We started a small home church. The believers met in our home to hear the Scriptures and share the holy meal.

B: And you were also teachers.

Aquila: We did whatever we needed to make sure the Gospel was properly taught. For example, there was Apollos, a powerful preacher.

Priscilla: Apollos' heart was in the right place. But Apollos didn't know about being baptized in Jesus' name. We had to sit him down and make sure he understood the whole story.

B: Do you two know that you are one of the few husband and wife missionary teams in the Bible?

Priscilla: Aquila and I were blessed to be able to share our marriage and our ministry together.

Aquila: Yes, and there are lots of married couples working together in the Church all through history. It is all part of God's plan!

Live it!

Yes, YOU!

"Are you holy?" Megan looked around. "Yes, you, Megan. Are you holy?" She didn't know what to say. The new leader had a habit of asking questions that really made people think—and sometimes squirm a little. Megan thought quickly. She was a good person. She always did her best. When she did something wrong, she was sorry for it. She was kind. Finally, she answered quietly, "I guess so."

The word *holy* comes from the same word as *whole.* The original word meant unbroken, healthy, or complete. Someone who is holy has a solid relationship with God.

Everything God created is holy—including you! Sometimes, though, holiness is hard to recognize. The whole point of chapter 6 is that Christians must always choose holiness. And that means choosing to say no to sin. Are you holy? Yes, YOU!

— Romans, chapter 6

poses. [14]Sin must not be your master; for you
do not live under law but under God's grace.

Slaves of Righteousness

[15]What, then? Shall we sin, because we are
not under law but under God's grace? By no
means! [16]Surely you know that when you
surrender yourselves as slaves to obey some-
one, you are in fact the slaves of the master
you obey—either of sin, which results in
death, or of obedience, which results in
being put right with God. [17]But thanks be
to God! For though at one time you were
slaves to sin, you have obeyed with all your
heart the truths found in the teaching you
received. [18]You were set free from sin and
became the slaves of righteousness. [19](I use
everyday language because of the weakness
of your natural selves.) At one time you sur-
rendered yourselves entirely as slaves to im-
purity and wickedness for wicked purposes.
In the same way you must now surrender
yourselves entirely as slaves of righteousness
for holy purposes.

[20]When you were the slaves of sin, you
were free from righteousness. [21]What did
you gain from doing the things that you are
now ashamed of? The result of those things
is death! [22]But now you have been set free
from sin and are the slaves of God. Your gain
is a life fully dedicated to him, and the result
is eternal life. [23]For sin pays its wage—death;
but God's free gift is eternal life in union
with Christ Jesus our Lord.

An Illustration from Marriage

7 Certainly you will understand what I
am about to say, my friends, because all
of you know about law. The law rules over
people only as long as they live. [2]A married
woman, for example, is bound by the law to
her husband as long as he lives; but if he
dies, then she is free from the law that bound
her to him. [3]So then, if she lives with anoth-
er man while her husband is alive, she will
be called an adulteress; but if her husband
dies, she is legally a free woman and does
not commit adultery if she marries another
man. [4]That is how it is with you, my friends.
As far as the Law is concerned, you also have
died because you are part of the body of
Christ; and now you belong to him who was
raised from death in order that we might be
useful in the service of God. [5]For when we
lived according to our human nature, the
sinful desires stirred up by the Law were at
work in our bodies, and all we did ended in
death. [6]Now, however, we are free from the
Law, because we died to that which once

"For sin pays its wage—death; but God's free gift is eternal life in union with Christ Jesus our Lord" *(Romans 6:23)*.

held us prisoners. No longer do we serve in
the old way of a written law, but in the new
way of the Spirit.

Law and Sin

7Shall we say, then, that the Law itself is
sinful? Of course not! But it was the Law
that made me know what sin is. If the Law
had not said, "Do not desire what belongs to
someone else," I would not have known
such a desire. 8But by means of that com-
mandment sin found its chance to stir up all
kinds of selfish desires in me. Apart from law,
sin is a dead thing. 9I myself was once alive
apart from law; but when the commandment
came, sin sprang to life, 10and I died. And the
commandment which was meant to bring
life, in my case brought death. 11Sin found its
chance, and by means of the commandment
it deceived me and killed me.

12So then, the Law itself is holy, and the
commandment is holy, right, and good.
13But does this mean that what is good
caused my death? By no means! It was sin
that did it; by using what is good, sin
brought death to me, in order that its true
nature as sin might be revealed. And so, by
means of the commandment sin is shown to
be even more terribly sinful.

The Conflict in Us

14We know that the Law is spiritual; but I
am a mortal, sold as a slave to sin. 15I do not
understand what I do; for I don't do what I
would like to do, but instead I do what I
hate. 16Since what I do is what I don't want
to do, this shows that I agree that the Law is
right. 17So I am not really the one who does
this thing; rather it is the sin that lives in me.
18I know that good does not live in me—
that is, in my human nature. For even
though the desire to do good is in me, I am
not able to do it. 19I don't do the good I
want to do; instead, I do the evil that I do
not want to do. 20If I do what I don't want
to do, this means that I am no longer the
one who does it; instead, it is the sin that
lives in me.

21So I find that this law is at work: when I
want to do what is good, what is evil is the
only choice I have. 22My inner being
delights in the law of God. 23But I see a
different law at work in my body—a law
that fights against the law which my mind
approves of. It makes me a prisoner to the
law of sin which is at work in my body.
24What an unhappy man I am! Who will
rescue me from this body that is taking me
to death? 25Thanks be to God, who does
this through our Lord Jesus Christ!

This, then, is my condition: on my own I
can serve God's law only with my mind,
while my human nature serves the law of sin.

Life in the Spirit

8 There is no condemnation now for
those who live in union with Christ
Jesus. 2For the law of the Spirit, which
brings us life in union with Christ Jesus, has
set me[i] free from the law of sin and death.
3What the Law could not do, because
human nature was weak, God did. He con-
demned sin in human nature by sending his
own Son, who came with a nature like our
sinful nature, to do away with sin. 4God did
this so that the righteous demands of the
Law might be fully satisfied in us who live
according to the Spirit, and not according to
human nature. 5Those who live as their
human nature tells them to, have their minds
controlled by what human nature wants.
Those who live as the Spirit tells them to,
have their minds controlled by what the
Spirit wants. 6To be controlled by human
nature results in death; to be controlled by
the Spirit results in life and peace. 7And so
people become enemies of God when they
are controlled by their human nature; for
they do not obey God's law, and in fact they

[i] **8:2** me; *some manuscripts have* you; *others have* us.

7:7 Ex 20:17; Deut 5:21 **7:11** Gen 3:13 **7:15** Gal 5:17

"To be controlled by human nature results in death; to be controlled by the Spirit results in life and peace" *(Romans 8:6)*.

cannot obey it. 8Those who obey their
human nature cannot please God.

9But you do not live as your human
nature tells you to; instead, you live as the
Spirit tells you to—if, in fact, God's Spirit
lives in you. Whoever does not have the
Spirit of Christ does not belong to him.
10But if Christ lives in you, the Spirit is life
for you[j] because you have been put right
with God, even though your bodies are
going to die because of sin. 11If the Spirit of
God, who raised Jesus from death, lives in
you, then he who raised Christ from death
will also give life to your mortal bodies by
the presence of his Spirit in you.

12So then, my friends, we have an obliga-
tion, but it is not to live as our human
nature wants us to. 13For if you live accord-
ing to your human nature, you are going to
die; but if by the Spirit you put to death
your sinful actions, you will live. 14Those
who are led by God's Spirit are God's chil-
dren. 15For the Spirit that God has given
you does not make you slaves and cause you
to be afraid; instead, the Spirit makes you
God's children, and by the Spirit's power we
cry out to God, "Father! my Father!" 16God's
Spirit joins himself to our spirits to declare
that we are God's children. 17Since we are
his children, we will possess the blessings he
keeps for his people, and we will also possess
with Christ what God has kept for him; for
if we share Christ's suffering, we will also
share his glory.

The Future Glory

18I consider that what we suffer at this
present time cannot be compared at all with
the glory that is going to be revealed to us.
19All of creation waits with eager longing
for God to reveal his children. 20For creation
was condemned to lose its purpose, not of its
own will, but because God willed it to be so.
Yet there was the hope 21that creation itself
would one day be set free from its slavery to
decay and would share the glorious freedom
of the children of God. 22For we know that
up to the present time all of creation groans
with pain, like the pain of childbirth. 23But
it is not just creation alone which groans; we
who have the Spirit as the first of God's gifts
also groan within ourselves as we wait for
God to make us his children and[k] set our
whole being free. 24For it was by hope that
we were saved; but if we see what we hope
for, then it is not really hope. For who of us

Live it!

God's Big Job

God created the universe and everything in it. And God promised to take care of everything he created. It's a huge job. Human beings often work against God when it comes to taking care of the planet earth. We pollute the air and water with our cars and factories. We waste natural resources like forests and oil so that we can make life super easy. The earth "groans with pain" because of what people have done to it (see Romans 8:22).

The Native American Iroquois Nations hold to the Great Law, which requires that chiefs think about how their decisions will affect people seven generations later. That means they have to think of how the decision might affect their great-great-great-great-great grandchildren. It's a way of saying that some decisions can affect people and the earth for a long time. The earth would not be groaning as much if everyone followed the Great Law of the Iroquois.

— Romans 8:18–25

[j] **8:10** the Spirit is life for you; *or* your spirit is alive. [k] **8:23** *Some manuscripts do not have* make us his children and.

8:11 1 Cor 3:16 **8:15–17** Gal 4:5–7 **8:15** Mk 14:36; Gal 4:6 **8:18** Wis 3:5, 6 **8:20** Gen 3:17–19
8:23 2 Cor 5:2–4

hopes for something we see? 25 But if we
hope for what we do not see, we wait for it
with patience.

26 In the same way the Spirit also comes to
help us, weak as we are. For we do not know
how we ought to pray; the Spirit himself
pleads with God for us in groans that words
cannot express. 27 And God, who sees into
our hearts, knows what the thought of the
Spirit is; because the Spirit pleads with God
on behalf of his people and in accordance
with his will.

28 We know that in all things God works
for good with those who love him,[l] those
whom he has called according to his pur-
pose. 29 Those whom God had already cho-
sen he also set apart to become like his Son,
so that the Son would be the first among
many believers. 30 And so those whom God
set apart, he called; and those he called, he
put right with himself, and he shared his
glory with them.

God's Love in Christ Jesus

31 In view of all this, what can we say? If
God is for us, who can be against us? 32 Cer-
tainly not God, who did not even keep back
his own Son, but offered him for us all! He
gave us his Son—will he not also freely give
us all things? 33 Who will accuse God's cho-
sen people? God himself declares them not
guilty! 34 Who, then, will condemn them?
Not Christ Jesus, who died, or rather, who
was raised to life and is at the right side of
God, pleading with him for us! 35 Who, then,
can separate us from the love of Christ? Can
trouble do it, or hardship or persecution or
hunger or poverty or danger or death? 36 As
the scripture says,

"For your sake we are in danger of death
at all times;
we are treated like sheep that are going
to be slaughtered."

37 No, in all these things we have complete
victory through him who loved us! 38 For I
am certain that nothing can separate us from
his love: neither death nor life, neither angels
nor other heavenly rulers or powers, neither
the present nor the future, 39 neither the
world above nor the world below—there is
nothing in all creation that will ever be able
to separate us from the love of God which is
ours through Christ Jesus our Lord.

God and His People

9 I am speaking the truth; I belong to
Christ and I do not lie. My conscience,
ruled by the Holy Spirit, also assures me that
I am not lying 2 when I say how great is my
sorrow, how endless the pain in my heart 3 for
my people, my own flesh and blood! For
their sake I could wish that I myself were
under God's curse and separated from Christ.
4 They are God's people; he made them his
children and revealed his glory to them; he
made his covenants[m] with them and gave
them the Law; they have the true worship;
they have received God's promises; 5 they are
descended from the famous Hebrew ances-
tors; and Christ, as a human being, belongs to
their race. May God, who rules over all, be
praised forever![n] Amen.

6 I am not saying that the promise of God
has failed; for not all the people of Israel are
the people of God. 7 Nor are all of Abraham's
descendants the children of God. God said
to Abraham, "It is through Isaac that you will
have the descendants I promised you." 8 This
means that the children born in the usual
way[o] are not the children of God; instead,
the children born as a result of God's prom-
ise are regarded as the true descendants. 9 For
God's promise was made in these words: "At
the right time[p] I will come back, and Sarah
will have a son."

10 And this is not all. For Rebecca's two
sons had the same father, our ancestor Isaac.
11-12 But in order that the choice of one son
might be completely the result of God's own
purpose, God said to her, "The older will

[l] **8:28** in all things God works for good with those who love him; *some manuscripts have* all things work for good for those who love God. [m] **9:4** covenants; *some manuscripts have* covenant. [n] **9:5** May God, who rules over all, be praised forever!; *or* And may he, who is God ruling over all, be praised forever! [o] **9:8** CHILDREN BORN IN THE USUAL WAY: *This refers to the descendants Abraham had through Ishmael, his son by Hagar (see Gal 4:22–23).* [p] **9:9** At the right time; *or* At this time next year.

8:36 Ps 44:22 **9:4** Ex 4:22 **9:7** Gen 21:12 **9:9** Gen 18:10 **9:12** Gen 25:23

Pray it!

A Lump on God's Wheel

In Romans 9:20–21 Paul compares us to a clay pot made by God. Did you ever watch a potter at a wheel? She starts with a cold, wet lump of clay. As the wheel spins, she delicately shapes the clay into a form using her fingers and hands. Sometimes the wheel spins fast, sometimes slowly. The form might be a pot, a cup, a bowl, or anything else the potter wants it to be.

Find a quiet place and sit for a few minutes. Imagine yourself as a lump of clay on God's wheel. Feel yourself spinning around as God's hand forms you into what God wants you to be. Are you spinning fast or slowly? What does it feel like to be shaped by God? What is God shaping you into? Don't resist or try to fight it. God is the potter; you are the clay.

— Romans 9:20–21

serve the younger." He said this before they
were born, before they had done anything
either good or bad; so God's choice was
based on his call, and not on anything they
had done. 13As the scripture says, "I loved
Jacob, but I hated Esau."
14Shall we say, then, that God is unjust?
Not at all. 15For he said to Moses, "I will
have mercy on anyone I wish; I will take
pity on anyone I wish." 16So then, every-
thing depends, not on what we humans
want or do, but only on God's mercy. 17For
the scripture says to the king of Egypt, "I
made you king in order to use you to show
my power and to spread my fame over the
whole world." 18So then, God has mercy on
anyone he wishes, and he makes stubborn
anyone he wishes.

God's Anger and Mercy

19But one of you will say to me, "If this is
so, how can God find fault with anyone?
Who can resist God's will?" 20But who are
you, my friend, to talk back to God? A clay
pot does not ask the man who made it,
"Why did you make me like this?" 21After
all, the man who makes the pots has the right
to use the clay as he wishes, and to make two
pots from the same lump of clay, one for spe-
cial occasions and the other for ordinary use.
22And the same is true of what God has
done. He wanted to show his anger and to
make his power known. But he was very
patient in enduring those who were the
objects of his anger, who were doomed to
destruction. 23And he also wanted to reveal
his abundant glory, which was poured out
on us who are the objects of his mercy, those
of us whom he has prepared to receive his
glory. 24For we are the people he called, not
only from among the Jews but also from
among the Gentiles. 25This is what he says in
the book of Hosea:

"The people who were not mine
I will call 'My People.'
The nation that I did not love
I will call 'My Beloved.'
26And in the very place where they were
told, 'You are not my people,'
there they will be called the children of
the living God."

9:13 Mal 1:2, 3 **9:15** Ex 33:19 **9:17** Ex 9:16 (LXX) **9:20** Isa 29:16; 45:9; Wis 12:12 **9:21** Wis 15:7; Sir 33:13 **9:22** Wis 12:20, 21 **9:25** Hos 2:23 **9:26** Hos 1:10

Check out Isaiah 64:8–12 and Jeremiah 18:1–12 for more images of potter God.

27 And Isaiah exclaims about Israel: "Even if
the people of Israel are as many as the grains
of sand by the sea, yet only a few of them
will be saved; 28 for the Lord will quickly set-
tle his full account with the world." 29 It is as
Isaiah had said before, "If the Lord Almighty
had not left us some descendants, we would
have become like Sodom, we would have
been like Gomorrah."

Israel and the Gospel

30 So we say that the Gentiles, who were
not trying to put themselves right with God,
were put right with him through faith;
31 while God's people, who were seeking a
law that would put them right with God,
did not find it. 32 And why not? Because they
did not depend on faith but on what they
did. And so they stumbled over the "stum-
bling stone" 33 that the scripture speaks of:

"Look, I place in Zion a stone
that will make people stumble,
a rock that will make them fall.
But whoever believes in him will not be
disappointed."

10 My friends, how I wish with all my
heart that my own people might be
saved! How I pray to God for them! 2 I can
assure you that they are deeply devoted to
God; but their devotion is not based on true
knowledge. 3 They have not known the way
in which God puts people right with him-
self, and instead, they have tried to set up
their own way; and so they did not submit
themselves to God's way of putting people
right. 4 For Christ has brought the Law to an
end, so that everyone who believes is put
right with God.

Study it!

Don't Get Too Comfortable!

Paul comes down hard on his people, the Jews. He tells them that even though they are God's special people, they need to follow Jesus. Paul may seem a little harsh with his criticism. As Catholics, we respect other people's faith and honor their beliefs. We know that many of us worship the same God—the God who created us all. But Paul loved his people so much he wanted them to know the fullness of God's love.

Part of the problem was that some Jews were too comfortable or too stubborn. They did things out of habit rather than out of belief. They followed the rules, but didn't take care of people—especially people who were not like them. They thought they were always right and refused to listen to other people's ideas. Paul could have been talking to some of us!

Don't get too comfortable or too stubborn. Think about why you do what you do as a Catholic. Be open to new ideas. Let go of your prejudices. Above all, be *thought-full* and *faith-full*.

— Romans 9:30—10:4

Salvation Is for All

5 Moses wrote this about being put right
with God by obeying the Law: "Whoever
obeys the commands of the Law will live."
6 But what the scripture says about being put
right with God through faith is this: "You
are not to ask yourself, Who will go up into
heaven?" (that is, to bring Christ down).
7 "Nor are you to ask, Who will go down

9:27, 28 Isa 10:22, 23 (LXX) **9:29** Isa 1:9 (LXX) **9:33** Isa 28:16 (LXX) **10:5** Lev 18:5 **10:6–8** Deut 30:12–14

Read Romans 10:14–17. What good news have you heard recently? With whom did you share good news?

Catholic Connections

God's Mighty Messengers

Paul says that the only way people can hear God's Good News is if someone is spreading it. You spread the Good News about Jesus by your words and actions. This is the job of everyone who is baptized. Many Catholics take this job to heart in a special way: they become involved in Church ministries. They read at Mass, sing in the choir, or teach religious education. Some work with young people or the elderly. Others run soup kitchens. Still others help out with the daily tasks of running a parish.

Some men hear a special call from God to be ordained as a priest or a deacon. Still others respond to God's call to join other women or men as a religious sister or brother. They serve the needs of the Church along with those who are married and single. Every young person should listen carefully and be open to whether God is calling him or her in this way.

The Church needs you—now and when you are an adult. As you think about the future, listen carefully to how God is calling you to be a mighty messenger.

— Romans 10:14–17

into the world below?" (that is, to bring
Christ up from death). 8What it says is this:
"God's message is near you, on your lips and
in your heart"—that is, the message of faith
that we preach. 9If you confess that Jesus is
Lord and believe that God raised him from
death, you will be saved. 10For it is by our
faith that we are put right with God; it is by
our confession that we are saved. 11The
scripture says, "Whoever believes in him will
not be disappointed." 12This includes every-
one, because there is no difference between
Jews and Gentiles; God is the same Lord of
all and richly blesses all who call to him.
13As the scripture says, "Everyone who calls
out to the Lord for help will be saved."

14But how can they call to him for help if
they have not believed? And how can they
believe if they have not heard the message?
And how can they hear if the message is not
proclaimed? 15And how can the message be
proclaimed if the messengers are not sent
out? As the scripture says, "How wonderful
is the coming of messengers who bring
good news!" 16But not all have accepted the
Good News. Isaiah himself said, "Lord, who
believed our message?" 17So then, faith
comes from hearing the message, and the
message comes through preaching Christ.

18But I ask: Is it true that they did not
hear the message? Of course they did—for
as the scripture says:

"The sound of their voice went out to all
the world;
their words reached the ends of the
earth."

19Again I ask: Did the people of Israel not
understand? Moses himself is the first one to
answer:

"I will use a so-called nation
to make my people jealous;
and by means of a nation of fools
I will make my people angry."

20And Isaiah is even bolder when he says,

"I was found by those who were not
looking for me;
I appeared to those who were not
asking for me."

10:11 Isa 28:16 (LXX) **10:13** Joel 2:32 **10:15** Isa 52:7 **10:16** Isa 53:1 (LXX) **10:18** Ps 19:4 (LXX) **10:19** Deut 32:21 **10:20** Isa 65:1 (LXX)

21But concerning Israel he says, "All day
long I held out my hands to welcome a dis-
obedient and rebellious people."

God's Mercy on Israel

11 I ask, then: Did God reject his own
people? Certainly not! I myself am
an Israelite, a descendant of Abraham, a
member of the tribe of Benjamin. 2God has
not rejected his people, whom he chose
from the beginning. You know what the
scripture says in the passage where Elijah
pleads with God against Israel: 3"Lord, they
have killed your prophets and torn down
your altars; I am the only one left, and they
are trying to kill me." 4What answer did
God give him? "I have kept for myself seven
thousand men who have not worshiped the
false god Baal." 5It is the same way now:
there is a small number left of those whom
God has chosen because of his grace. 6His
choice is based on his grace, not on what
they have done. For if God's choice were
based on what people do, then his grace
would not be real grace.

7What then? The people of Israel did not
find what they were looking for. It was only
the small group that God chose who found
it; the rest grew deaf to God's call. 8As the
scripture says, "God made their minds and
hearts dull; to this very day they cannot see
or hear." 9And David says,

"May they be caught and trapped at their
feasts;
may they fall, may they be punished!
10May their eyes be blinded so that they
cannot see;
and make them bend under their
troubles at all times."

11I ask, then: When the Jews stumbled, did
they fall to their ruin? By no means! Because
they sinned, salvation has come to the Gen-
tiles, to make the Jews jealous of them.
12The sin of the Jews brought rich blessings
to the world, and their spiritual poverty
brought rich blessings to the Gentiles. Then,
how much greater the blessings will be
when the complete number of Jews is
included!

The Salvation of the Gentiles

13I am speaking now to you Gentiles: As
long as I am an apostle to the Gentiles, I will
take pride in my work. 14Perhaps I can make
the people of my own race jealous, and so be
able to save some of them. 15For when they
were rejected, all other people were changed
from God's enemies into his friends. What
will it be, then, when they are accepted? It
will be life for the dead!

16If the first piece of bread is given to
God, then the whole loaf is his also; and if
the roots of a tree are offered to God, the
branches are his also. 17Some of the branches
of the cultivated olive tree have been broken
off, and a branch of a wild olive tree has
been joined to it. You Gentiles are like that
wild olive tree, and now you share the strong
spiritual life of the Jews. 18So then, you must
not despise those who were broken off like
branches. How can you be proud? You are
just a branch; you don't support the roots—
the roots support you.

19But you will say, "Yes, but the branches
were broken off to make room for me."
20That is true. They were broken off because
they did not believe, while you remain in
place because you do believe. But do not be
proud of it; instead, be afraid. 21God did not
spare the Jews, who are like natural branches;
do you think he will spare you? 22Here we
see how kind and how severe God is. He is
severe toward those who have fallen, but kind
to you—if you continue in his kindness. But
if you do not, you too will be broken off.
23And if the Jews abandon their unbelief,
they will be put back in the place where they
were; for God is able to do that. 24You Gen-
tiles are like the branch of a wild olive tree
that is broken off and then, contrary to
nature, is joined to a cultivated olive tree. The
Jews are like this cultivated tree; and it will be
much easier for God to join these broken-off
branches to their own tree again.

God's Mercy on All

25There is a secret truth, my friends,
which I want you to know, for it will keep

10:21 Isa 65:2 (LXX) **11:1** Phil 3:5 **11:3** 1 Kings 19:10, 14 **11:4** 1 Kings 19:18 **11:8** Deut 29:4; Isa 29:10 **11:9, 10** Ps 69:22, 23 (LXX)

you from thinking how wise you are. It is
that the stubbornness of the people of Israel
is not permanent, but will last only until the
complete number of Gentiles comes to God.
[26]And this is how all Israel will be saved. As
the scripture says,

"The Savior will come from Zion
and remove all wickedness from the
descendants of Jacob.
[27]I will make this covenant with them
when I take away their sins."

[28]Because they reject the Good News, the
Jews are God's enemies for the sake of you
Gentiles. But because of God's choice, they are
his friends because of their ancestors. [29]For
God does not change his mind about whom
he chooses and blesses. [30]As for you Gentiles,
you disobeyed God in the past; but now you
have received God's mercy because the Jews
were disobedient. [31]In the same way, because
of the mercy that you have received, the Jews
now disobey God, in order that they also may
now[q] receive God's mercy. [32]For God has
made all people prisoners of disobedience, so
that he might show mercy to them all.

Praise to God

[33]How great are God's riches! How deep
are his wisdom and knowledge! Who can
explain his decisions? Who can understand
his ways? [34]As the scripture says,

"Who knows the mind of the Lord?
Who is able to give him advice?
[35]Who has ever given him anything,
so that he had to pay it back?"

[36]For all things were created by him, and all
things exist through him and for him. To
God be the glory forever! Amen.

Life in God's Service

12 So then, my friends, because of
God's great mercy to us I appeal to
you: Offer yourselves as a living sacrifice to
God, dedicated to his service and pleasing to
him. This is the true worship that you should
offer. [2]Do not conform yourselves to the
standards of this world, but let God trans-
form you inwardly by a complete change of
your mind. Then you will be able to know
the will of God—what is good and is pleas-
ing to him and is perfect.

[3]And because of God's gracious gift to me
I say to every one of you: Do not think of
yourself more highly than you should.
Instead, be modest in your thinking, and
judge yourself according to the amount of
faith that God has given you. [4]We have
many parts in the one body, and all these
parts have different functions. [5]In the same
way, though we are many, we are one body
in union with Christ, and we are all joined
to each other as different parts of one body.
[6]So we are to use our different gifts in
accordance with the grace that God has

Pray it!

Start Your Day Right

"To God be the glory forever! Amen" (Romans 11:36).

The last line of chapter 11 is a powerful statement of faith in an awesome God. Write the verse on a card and put it where you will see it every morning. At the start of each day, read the statement out loud. Think about it during the day. Let everything you do, every decision you make, every word you say reflect God's power in your life.

— Romans 11:36

[q] **11:31** *Some manuscripts do not have* now.

11:26 Isa 59:20, 21 (LXX) **11:27** Isa 27:9 (LXX) **11:33** Isa 55:8; Wis 17:1 **11:34** Isa 40:13 (LXX) **11:35** Job 41:11 **11:36** 1 Cor 8:6 **12:4, 5** 1 Cor 12:12 **12:6–8** 1 Cor 12:4–11

***Mercy* is having loving kindness for a person who does something wrong, just as God has mercy on us.**

given us. If our gift is to speak God's mes-
sage, we should do it according to the faith
that we have; 7if it is to serve, we should
serve; if it is to teach, we should teach; 8if it
is to encourage others, we should do so.
Whoever shares with others should do it
generously; whoever has authority should
work hard; whoever shows kindness to oth-
ers should do it cheerfully.

9Love must be completely sincere. Hate
what is evil, hold on to what is good. 10Love
one another warmly as Christians, and be
eager to show respect for one another.
11Work hard and do not be lazy. Serve the
Lord with a heart full of devotion. 12Let your
hope keep you joyful, be patient in your
troubles, and pray at all times. 13Share your
belongings with your needy fellow Chris-
tians, and open your homes to strangers.

14Ask God to bless those who persecute
you—yes, ask him to bless, not to curse. 15Be
happy with those who are happy, weep with
those who weep. 16Have the same concern
for everyone. Do not be proud, but accept
humble duties.[r] Do not think of yourselves as
wise.

17If someone has done you wrong, do not
repay him with a wrong. Try to do what
everyone considers to be good. 18Do every-
thing possible on your part to live in peace
with everybody. 19Never take revenge, my
friends, but instead let God's anger do it. For
the scripture says, "I will take revenge, I will
pay back, says the Lord." 20Instead, as the
scripture says: "If your enemies are hungry,
feed them; if they are thirsty, give them a
drink; for by doing this you will make them
burn with shame." 21Do not let evil defeat
you; instead, conquer evil with good.

Live it!

Whose Rules?

- **What do your favorite television shows tell you about what it means to be successful?**
- **What do your favorite magazines tell you about what it means to be a man or a woman?**
- **What do your favorite video games tell you about how to handle conflict?**

You learn a lot from the world around you. The world tells you that you need a certain body shape or you won't be attractive to others. It tells you that violence is the best way to resolve differences. It tells you that you need a lot of money and material things to be happy and successful.

Sometimes certain messages in our world try to teach us things that are not what God wants for us. In chapter 12 Paul gives us a list of rules for living the life that God intended. Notice how different that list is from some of the things you see or hear every day. Make a list of these rules from Paul. Keep it near your bed. Before you go to sleep, look it over and think about your day. Whose rules did you follow that day? the world's? or God's?

— Romans, chapter 12

Duties toward State Authorities

13 Everyone must obey state authori-
ties, because no authority exists
without God's permission, and the existing
authorities have been put there by God.
2Whoever opposes the existing authority
opposes what God has ordered; and anyone

[r] **12:16** accept humble duties; *or* make friends with humble people.

12:14 Mt 5:44; Lk 6:28 **12:15** Sir 7:34 **12:16** Prov 3:7 **12:19** Deut 32:35 **12:20** Prov 25:21, 22 (LXX)
13:1 Wis 6:3

"If you love others, you will never do them wrong" *(Romans 13:10)*.

who does so will bring judgment on him-
self. 3For rulers are not to be feared by those
who do good, but by those who do evil.
Would you like to be unafraid of those in
authority? Then do what is good, and they
will praise you, 4because they are God's ser-
vants working for your own good. But if you
do evil, then be afraid of them, because their
power to punish is real. They are God's ser-
vants and carry out God's punishment on
those who do evil. 5For this reason you must
obey the authorities—not just because of
God's punishment, but also as a matter of
conscience.

6That is also why you pay taxes, because
the authorities are working for God when
they fulfill their duties. 7Pay, then, what you
owe them; pay them your personal and
property taxes, and show respect and honor
for them all.

Duties toward One Another

8Be under obligation to no one—the only
obligation you have is to love one another.
Whoever does this has obeyed the Law. 9The
commandments, "Do not commit adultery;
do not commit murder; do not steal; do not
desire what belongs to someone else"—all
these, and any others besides, are summed up
in the one command, "Love your neighbor
as you love yourself." 10If you love others,
you will never do them wrong; to love, then,
is to obey the whole Law.

11You must do this, because you know
that the time has come for you to wake up
from your sleep. For the moment when we
will be saved is closer now than it was when
we first believed. 12The night is nearly over,
day is almost here. Let us stop doing the
things that belong to the dark, and let us
take up weapons for fighting in the light.
13Let us conduct ourselves properly, as peo-
ple who live in the light of day—no orgies
or drunkenness, no immorality or indecency,
no fighting or jealousy. 14But take up the
weapons of the Lord Jesus Christ, and stop
paying attention to your sinful nature and
satisfying its desires.

Study it!

And the Greatest Is Love

Jesus' most important message while he was on earth can be summed up in one word: *love.* Paul shared that message with new believers often, as he does in 13:8–10. He says that if you look through the eyes of love, you could never hurt another person. Loving others the way Jesus taught us to makes a person complete.

Check out some of these other teachings about love in the Bible. Try to memorize some of the verses so that they remain in your mind and your heart.

- **Leviticus 19:18**
- **Matthew 5:43–48**
- **Mark 12:28–31**
- **John 13:34–35**
- **Romans 13:8–10**

— 1 Corinthians 13:4–13

Do Not Judge Others

14 Welcome those who are weak in
faith, but do not argue with them
about their personal opinions. 2Some peo-
ple's faith allows them to eat anything, but
the person who is weak in the faith eats only
vegetables. 3The person who will eat any-
thing is not to despise the one who doesn't;
while the one who eats only vegetables is
not to pass judgment on the one who will
eat anything; for God has accepted that per-
son. 4Who are you to judge the servants of
someone else? It is their own Master who

13:6, 7 Mt 22:21; Mk 12:17; Lk 20:25 **13:9 a** Ex 20:14; Deut 5:18; **b** Ex 20:13; Deut 5:17; **c** Ex 20:15; Deut 5:19; **d** Ex 20:17; Deut 5:21; **e** Lev 19:18 **14:1–6** Col 2:16

Live it!

A World of Difference

Amelia rides the school bus with students who were born in other countries. Most of them are just learning English. A few wear clothing from their native countries. Some of her classmates poke fun at them. Some just ignore them. No one talks to them. Amelia is not sure what to do.

One day an elderly neighbor asked Amelia about school. Amelia told her about her multicultural bus ride. Mrs. Kowalski shared her own story. Her parents came from Poland. When she went to school, her classmates made fun of her accent, her clothing, and everything else about her. She told Amelia how much it hurt and how she didn't want to go to school. It got better, but she never forgot what it felt like to be made fun of, just because she was different. She knew in her heart she was the same on the inside as everyone else.

After that Amelia made a promise to herself to talk to at least one person from another country each day. She learned it was important not to judge people because of what they eat or the clothes they wear or how they talk.

— Romans 14:1–12

will decide whether they succeed or fail.
And they will succeed, because the Lord is
able to make them succeed.
5Some people think that a certain day is
more important than other days, while others
think that all days are the same. We each
should firmly make up our own minds.
6Those who think highly of a certain day do
so in honor of the Lord; those who will eat
anything do so in honor of the Lord, because
they give thanks to God for the food. Those
who refuse to eat certain things do so in
honor of the Lord, and they give thanks to
God. 7We do not live for ourselves only, and
we do not die for ourselves only. 8If we live,
it is for the Lord that we live, and if we die, it
is for the Lord that we die. So whether we
live or die, we belong to the Lord. 9For
Christ died and rose to life in order to be the
Lord of the living and of the dead. 10You
then, who eat only vegetables—why do you
pass judgment on others? And you who eat
anything—why do you despise other believers? All of us will stand before God to be
judged by him. 11For the scripture says,

"As surely as I am the living God, says the
Lord,
everyone will kneel before me,
and everyone will confess that I am
God."

12Every one of us, then, will have to give an
account to God.

Do Not Make Others Fall

13So then, let us stop judging one another.
Instead, you should decide never to do anything that would make others stumble or fall
into sin. 14My union with the Lord Jesus
makes me certain that no food is of itself ritually unclean; but if you believe that some food
is unclean, then it becomes unclean for you.
15If you hurt others because of something
you eat, then you are no longer acting from
love. Do not let the food that you eat ruin the
person for whom Christ died! 16Do not let
what you regard as good get a bad name.
17For God's Kingdom is not a matter of eating and drinking, but of the righteousness,
peace, and joy which the Holy Spirit gives.
18And when you serve Christ in this way, you
please God and are approved by others.
19So then, we must always aim[s] at those
things that bring peace and that help
strengthen one another. 20Do not, because of
food, destroy what God has done. All foods

[s] **14:19** we must always aim; *some manuscripts have* we always aim.

14:10 2 Cor 5:10 **14:11** Isa 45:23 (LXX)

may be eaten, but it is wrong to eat anything
that will cause someone else to fall into sin.
21The right thing to do is to keep from eat-
ing meat, drinking wine, or doing anything
else that will make other believers fall.
22Keep what you believe about this matter,
then, between yourself and God. Happy are
those who do not feel guilty when they do
something they judge is right! 23But if they
have doubts about what they eat, God con-
demns them when they eat it, because their
action is not based on faith. And anything
that is not based on faith is sin.

Please Others, Not Yourselves

15 We who are strong in the faith
ought to help the weak to carry
their burdens. We should not please our-
selves. 2Instead, we should all please other
believers for their own good, in order to
build them up in the faith. 3For Christ did
not please himself. Instead, as the scripture
says, "The insults which are hurled at you
have fallen on me." 4Everything written in
the Scriptures was written to teach us, in

Help the weak. (15:1)

order that we might have hope through
the patience and encouragement which
the Scriptures give us. 5And may God, the
source of patience and encouragement,
enable you to have the same point of view
among yourselves by following the example
of Christ Jesus, 6so that all of you together
may praise with one voice the God and
Father of our Lord Jesus Christ.

The Gospel to the Gentiles

7Accept one another, then, for the glory
of God, as Christ has accepted you. 8For I
tell you that Christ's life of service was on
behalf of the Jews, to show that God is faith-
ful, to make his promises to their ancestors
come true, 9and to enable even the Gentiles
to praise God for his mercy. As the scripture
says,

"And so I will praise you among the
Gentiles;
I will sing praises to you."

10Again it says,

"Rejoice, Gentiles, with God's people!"

11And again,

"Praise the Lord, all Gentiles;
praise him, all peoples!"

12And again, Isaiah says,

"A descendant of Jesse will appear;
he will come to rule the Gentiles,
and they will put their hope in him."

13May God, the source of hope, fill you
with all joy and peace by means of your faith
in him, so that your hope will continue to
grow by the power of the Holy Spirit.

Paul's Reason for Writing So Boldly

14My friends: I myself feel sure that you
are full of goodness, that you have all knowl-
edge, and that you are able to teach one
another. 15But in this letter I have been quite
bold about certain subjects of which I have
reminded you. I have been bold because of
the privilege God has given me 16of being a

15:3 Ps 69:9 **15:4** 1 Macc 12:9; 2 Macc 15:9 **15:9** 2 Sam 22:50; Ps 18:49 **15:10** Deut 32:43 **15:11** Ps 117:1 **15:12** Isa 11:10 (LXX)

The three *theological virtues* are faith, hope, and love. They are gifts to us from God. Can you find all three in chapter 15?

Catholic Connections

Hopeful People

"I'm hoping for a new bike."

"I hope she cancels that test."

"I hope we win this game."

Many of our hopes are really wishes and wants. We *wish* for something that will make life easier or more fun. We *want* something good to happen. When we truly *hope* for something, we expect it. We don't just want it or wish for it, we *expect* it, and we wait for it to happen.

The Church calls hope a *theological virtue.* We hope for God's blessings and grace, that is, we expect these things from God. We hope that when we die, we will be with God, meaning that we are confident that God will make good on his promise if we lead a good life. A hopeful person trusts God, has faith in Jesus, and relies on the Holy Spirit.

— Romans 15:13

servant of Christ Jesus to work for the Gen-
tiles. I serve like a priest in preaching the
Good News from God, in order that the
Gentiles may be an offering acceptable to
God, dedicated to him by the Holy Spirit.
[17]In union with Christ Jesus, then, I can be
proud of my service for God. [18]I will be
bold and speak only about what Christ has
done through me to lead the Gentiles to
obey God. He has done this by means of
words and deeds, [19]by the power of miracles
and wonders, and by the power of the Spirit
of God. And so, in traveling all the way from
Jerusalem to Illyricum, I have proclaimed
fully the Good News about Christ. [20]My
ambition has always been to proclaim the
Good News in places where Christ has not
been heard of, so as not to build on a foun-
dation laid by someone else. [21]As the scrip-
ture says,

"Those who were not told about him
will see,
and those who have not heard will
understand."

Paul's Plan to Visit Rome

[22]And so I have been prevented many
times from coming to you. [23]But now that I
have finished my work in these regions and
since I have been wanting for so many years
to come to see you, [24]I hope to do so now. I
would like to see you on my way to Spain,
and be helped by you to go there, after I have
enjoyed visiting you for a while. [25]Right
now, however, I am going to Jerusalem in the
service of God's people there. [26]For the
churches in Macedonia and Achaia have
freely decided to give an offering to help the
poor among God's people in Jerusalem.
[27]That decision was their own; but, as a mat-
ter of fact, they have an obligation to help
them. Since the Jews shared their spiritual
blessings with the Gentiles, the Gentiles
ought to use their material blessings to help
the Jews. [28]When I have finished this task
and have turned over to them all the money
that has been raised for them, I shall leave
for Spain and visit you on my way there.
[29]When I come to you, I know that I shall

15:21 Isa 52:15 (LXX) **15:22** Rom 1:13 **15:25, 26** 1 Cor 16:1–4 **15:27** 1 Cor 9:11

"Greet one another with the kiss of peace" *(Romans 16:16)*.

come with a full measure of the blessing of
Christ.
30 I urge you, friends, by our Lord Jesus
Christ and by the love that the Spirit gives:
join me in praying fervently to God for me.
31 Pray that I may be kept safe from the
unbelievers in Judea and that my service in
Jerusalem may be acceptable to God's people
there. 32 And so I will come to you full of
joy, if it is God's will, and enjoy a refreshing
visit with you. 33 May God, our source of
peace, be with all of you. Amen.

Personal Greetings

16 I recommend to you our sister
Phoebe, who serves the church at
Cenchreae. 2 Receive her in the Lord's name,
as God's people should, and give her any
help she may need from you; for she herself
has been a good friend to many people and
also to me.
3 I send greetings to Priscilla and Aquila,
my fellow workers in the service of Christ
Jesus; 4 they risked their lives for me. I am
grateful to them—not only I, but all the
Gentile churches as well. 5 Greetings also to
the church that meets in their house.
Greetings to my dear friend Epaenetus,
who was the first in the province of Asia to
believe in Christ. 6 Greetings to Mary, who
has worked so hard for you. 7 Greetings also
to Andronicus and Junia,[t] fellow Jews who
were in prison with me; they are well
known among the apostles, and they became
Christians before I did.
8 My greetings to Ampliatus, my dear
friend in the fellowship of the Lord. 9 Greet-
ings also to Urbanus, our fellow worker in
Christ's service, and to Stachys, my dear
friend. 10 Greetings to Apelles, whose loyalty
to Christ has been proved. Greetings to
those who belong to the family of Aristobu-
lus. 11 Greetings to Herodion, a fellow Jew,
and to the Christians in the family of Nar-
cissus.
12 My greetings to Tryphaena and
Tryphosa, who work in the Lord's service,
and to my dear friend Persis, who has done
so much work for the Lord. 13 I send greet-
ings to Rufus, that outstanding worker in
the Lord's service, and to his mother, who
has always treated me like a son. 14 My greet-
ings to Asyncritus, Phlegon, Hermes,
Patrobas, Hermas, and all the other Chris-
tians with them. 15 Greetings to Philologus
and Julia, to Nereus and his sister, to Olym-
pas and to all of God's people who are with
them.
16 Greet one another with the kiss of
peace. All the churches of Christ send you
their greetings.

Study it!

Side by Side

In the final chapter of Paul's letter to the Romans, he mentions several people by name, both women and men. The first person he refers to is Phoebe. She was a friend of his, and she served the growing Church. Paul thanks her for her help and support.

Next Paul names Priscilla and Aquila, a married couple who sometimes traveled with Paul and supported his ministry. They opened their house for Christians to gather for the Eucharist.

Even though women were not allowed to be leaders in the government at that time, they played an important role in the early Church. Even though traveling was dangerous, married couples went on missionary journeys. Working side by side, single women, single men, and married couples spread the Good News of Jesus Christ.

— Romans 16:1–16

[t] **16:7** Junia; *or* Junias; *some manuscripts have* Julia.
16:3 Acts 18:2 **16:13** Mk 15:21

Greet one another with the kiss of peace. (16:16)

Final Instructions

17 I urge you, my friends: watch out for
those who cause divisions and upset people's
faith and go against the teaching which you
have received. Keep away from them! 18 For
those who do such things are not serving
Christ our Lord, but their own appetites. By
their fine words and flattering speech they
deceive innocent people. 19 Everyone has
heard of your loyalty to the gospel, and for
this reason I am happy about you. I want
you to be wise about what is good, but
innocent in what is evil. 20 And God, our
source of peace, will soon crush Satan under
your feet.
The grace of our Lord Jesus be with you.[u]
21 Timothy, my fellow worker, sends you
his greetings; and so do Lucius, Jason, and
Sosipater, fellow Jews.
22 I, Tertius, the writer of this letter, send
you Christian greetings.
23 My host Gaius, in whose house the
church meets, sends you his greetings; Eras-
tus, the city treasurer, and our brother Quar-
tus send you their greetings.[v]

Concluding Prayer of Praise

25 Let us give glory to God! He is able to
make you stand firm in your faith, according
to the Good News I preach about Jesus
Christ and according to the revelation of the
secret truth which was hidden for long ages
in the past. 26 Now, however, that truth has
been brought out into the open through the
writings of the prophets; and by the com-
mand of the eternal God it is made known
to all nations, so that all may believe and
obey.
27 To the only God, who alone is all-wise,
be glory through Jesus Christ forever!
Amen.[w]

[u] **16:20** *Some manuscripts omit this sentence.* [v] **16:23** *Some manuscripts add verse 24:* The grace of our Lord Jesus Christ be with you all. Amen; *others add this after verse 27.* [w] **16:27** *Some manuscripts have verses 25–27 here and after 14:23; others have them only after 14:23; one has them after 15:33.*

16:21 Acts 16:1 **16:23** **a** Acts 19:29; 1 Cor 1:14; **b** 2 Tim 4:20

Your Next Step

Congratulations on finishing the Letter to the Romans! Use this space to write your thoughts and questions about this book. If you are following the suggested reading plan, go back to the Book of Proverbs in the Old Testament. Like the Letter to the Romans, it has lots of wise advice for how to live your life.

The First Letter to the Corinthians

Do you ever get tired of your parents correcting you? Even though it might get annoying, you probably know deep down that they do it because they care about you. Your parents want you to learn important lessons while you are young—lessons that will serve you well as a teenager and adult.

The Christian church in the city of Corinth was very young. Paul started the church there. He felt it was his responsibility to correct the people when they were acting badly. He wanted to keep teaching them the important truths about being a Christian. He was acting like a parent—out of love—by correcting his spiritual children.

Chap. 3:5–9

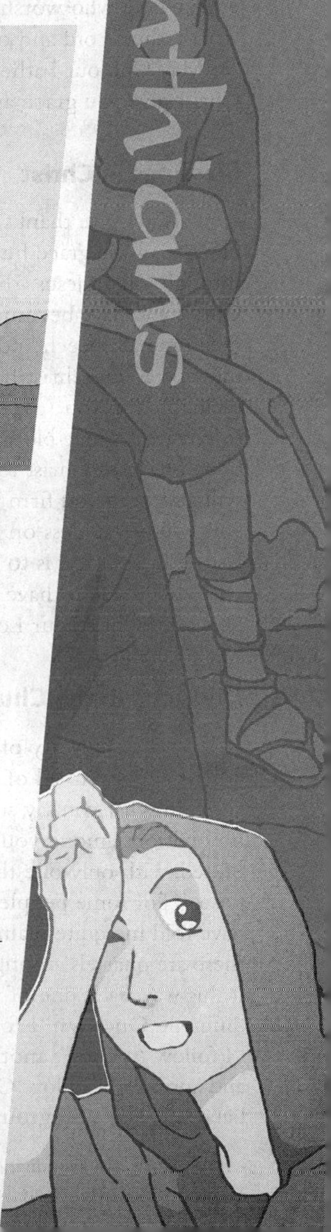

Headlines

- Divisions Threaten New Church (1:10–13)
- Avoid Immoral People! (5:9–13)
- Use Your Body for God's Glory (6:12–20)
- Dangers of Idolatry (10:1–10)
- Paul Says, "Respect the Lord's Supper" (11:17–34)
- Body Parts and the Body of Christ (12:12–31)
- The Primacy of Love (chapter 13)
- Resurrection: Truth or Fiction? (15:12–58)

FACTOIDS

Who are the central characters? Paul, Apollos, and the Christians in Corinth.

Who wrote this book? Saint Paul.

When was it written? A few years after Paul had started the church in Corinth.

Why was it written? Paul wrote to correct mistakes in the new church. He wanted to reinforce some important teachings about the Christian faith.

Jesus connection. In this letter Paul speaks a lot about Jesus' Resurrection. He makes it clear that Christ's Resurrection is the guarantee that we also will be resurrected into new life (15:12–28).

Important themes

- God's wisdom seems like foolishness to some people.
- Christians are not free to do anything they want. We must live moral lives, especially regarding our bodies.
- We are each a part of one body, the Church. The Spirit gives different gifts to each person, all for serving God and the Church.

1 CORINTHIANS

1 From Paul, who was called by the will
of God to be an apostle of Christ Jesus,
and from our brother Sosthenes—
2To the church of God which is in
Corinth, to all who are called to be God's
holy people, who belong to him in union
with Christ Jesus, together with all people
everywhere who worship our Lord Jesus
Christ, their Lord and ours:
3May God our Father and the Lord Jesus
Christ give you grace and peace.

Blessings in Christ

4I always give thanks to my God for you
because of the grace he has given you
through Christ Jesus. 5For in union with
Christ you have become rich in all things,
including all speech and all knowledge. 6The
message about Christ has become so firmly
established in you 7that you have not failed
to receive a single blessing, as you wait for
our Lord Jesus Christ to be revealed. 8He
will also keep you firm to the end, so that
you will be faultless on the Day of our Lord
Jesus Christ. 9God is to be trusted, the God
who called you to have fellowship with his
Son Jesus Christ, our Lord.

Divisions in the Church

10By the authority of our Lord Jesus
Christ I appeal to all of you, my friends, to
agree in what you say, so that there will be
no divisions among you. Be completely
united, with only one thought and one pur-
pose. 11For some people from Chloe's family
have told me quite plainly, my friends, that
there are quarrels among you. 12Let me put
it this way: each one of you says something
different. One says, "I follow Paul"; another,
"I follow Apollos"; another, "I follow Peter";
and another, "I follow Christ." 13Christ has
been divided[a] into groups! Was it Paul who
died on the cross for you? Were you baptized
as Paul's disciples?
14I thank God that I did not baptize any of
you except Crispus and Gaius. 15No one can
say, then, that you were baptized as my disci-
ples. (16Oh yes, I also baptized Stephanas and
his family; but I can't remember whether I
baptized anyone else.) 17Christ did not send
me to baptize. He sent me to tell the Good
News, and to tell it without using the lan-
guage of human wisdom, in order to make
sure that Christ's death on the cross is not
robbed of its power.

> **Study it!**
>
> ### The Scoop on Corinth
>
> **Corinth was a seaport city in Greece with a mixture of cultures and religions, as well as very rich and very poor people. Corinth was well-known for its thriving businesses, sports events, variety of people, and—unfortunately—its lack of morality. The church that Paul began there was made up mostly of non-Jewish Christians but also some Jewish Christians. He lived with them about eighteen months, then left the church in the hands of Apollos while he continued his mission in other places. When Paul began hearing reports of divisions, problems with morality, and lack of attention to poor people, he wrote this letter to the Corinthian church to teach and correct its members.**
>
> **— 1 Corinthians 1:4–9**

[a] **1:13** Christ has been divided; *some manuscripts have* Christ cannot be divided.
1:2 Acts 18:1 **1:12** Acts 18:24 **1:14** **a** Acts 18:8; **b** Acts 19:29; Rom 16:23 **1:16** 1 Cor 16:15

Live it!

Cliques

It's said that variety is good. It makes life interesting. Right? So why, then, are we so quick to label people? He's popular. She's a jock. He's smart. She's religious. And on and on. Cliques are here to stay, it seems. Paul tells the Corinthians that divisions—or cliques—are useless, and worse, they are destructive. Have you ever experienced division in your family, class, team, or even in your group of friends? Loyalties change, people are let in or left out, and emotions rage . . . it can get ugly. And what is accomplished?

Being united, as Paul teaches (1 Corinthians 1:10), means keeping your focus on what is truly important. It's important that nobody gets hurt. It's important to treat other people with kindness. It's important to be respected and appreciated—in spite of differences. It's that simple. Judging, labeling, leaving people out, putting people down . . . that's just the opposite of what's important.

Think about the cliques in your school or neighborhood—both those you're part of and not part of. What causes the divisions? How do you treat people inside and outside of the cliques? Are you willing to help build bridges between groups?

— 1 Corinthians 1:10–13

Christ the Power and the Wisdom of God

18 For the message about Christ's death on
the cross is nonsense to those who are being
lost; but for us who are being saved it is
God's power. 19 The scripture says,

"I will destroy the wisdom of the wise
and set aside the understanding of the
scholars."

20 So then, where does that leave the wise? or
the scholars? or the skillful debaters of this
world? God has shown that this world's wis-
dom is foolishness!

21 For God in his wisdom made it impossi-
ble for people to know him by means of their
own wisdom. Instead, by means of the so-
called "foolish" message we preach, God
decided to save those who believe. 22 Jews
want miracles for proof, and Greeks look for
wisdom. 23 As for us, we proclaim the crucified
Christ, a message that is offensive to the Jews
and nonsense to the Gentiles; 24 but for those
whom God has called, both Jews and Gentiles,
this message is Christ, who is the power of
God and the wisdom of God. 25 For what
seems to be God's foolishness is wiser than
human wisdom, and what seems to be God's
weakness is stronger than human strength.

26 Now remember what you were, my
friends, when God called you. From the
human point of view few of you were wise
or powerful or of high social standing. 27 God
purposely chose what the world considers
nonsense in order to shame the wise, and he
chose what the world considers weak in order
to shame the powerful. 28 He chose what the
world looks down on and despises and thinks
is nothing, in order to destroy what the world
thinks is important. 29 This means that no one
can boast in God's presence. 30 But God has
brought you into union with Christ Jesus, and
God has made Christ to be our wisdom. By
him we are put right with God; we become
God's holy people and are set free. 31 So then,
as the scripture says, "Whoever wants to boast
must boast of what the Lord has done."

1:19 Isa 29:14 (LXX) **1:20** **a** Job 12.17, **b** Isa 44.25 **1:21** Wis 13.1–9 **1:31** Jer 9.24

"God has shown that this world's wisdom is foolishness!" *(1 Corinthians 1:20)*. **What do you think that means?**

The Message about the Crucified Christ

2 When I came to you, my friends, to
preach God's secret truth,[b] I did not use
big words and great learning. 2For while I
was with you, I made up my mind to forget
everything except Jesus Christ and especially
his death on the cross. 3So when I came to
you, I was weak and trembled all over with
fear, 4and my teaching and message were not
delivered with skillful words of human wis-
dom, but with convincing proof of the power
of God's Spirit. 5Your faith, then, does not rest
on human wisdom but on God's power.

God's Wisdom

6Yet I do proclaim a message of wisdom to
those who are spiritually mature. But it is not
the wisdom that belongs to this world or to
the powers that rule this world—powers that
are losing their power. 7The wisdom I pro-
claim is God's secret wisdom, which is hid-
den from human beings, but which he had
already chosen for our glory even before the
world was made. 8None of the rulers of this
world knew this wisdom. If they had known
it, they would not have crucified the Lord of
glory. 9However, as the scripture says,

"What no one ever saw or heard,
what no one ever thought could
happen,
is the very thing God prepared for
those who love him."

10But[c] it was to us that God made known
his secret by means of his Spirit. The Spirit
searches everything, even the hidden depths
of God's purposes. 11It is only our own spirit
within us that knows all about us; in the
same way, only God's Spirit knows all about
God. 12We have not received this world's
spirit; instead, we have received the Spirit
sent by God, so that we may know all that
God has given us.

13So then, we do not speak in words
taught by human wisdom, but in words
taught by the Spirit, as we explain spiritual
truths to those who have the Spirit.[d]
14Whoever does not have the Spirit cannot
receive the gifts that come from God's Spirit.
Such a person really does not understand
them, and they seem to be nonsense, because
their value can be judged only on a spiritual
basis. 15Whoever has the Spirit, however, is
able to judge the value of everything, but no
one is able to judge him. 16As the scripture
says,

"Who knows the mind of the Lord?
Who is able to give him advice?"

We, however, have the mind of Christ.

Servants of God

3 As a matter of fact, my friends, I could
not talk to you as I talk to people who
have the Spirit; I had to talk to you as
though you belonged to this world, as chil-
dren in the Christian faith. 2I had to feed
you milk, not solid food, because you were
not ready for it. And even now you are not
ready for it, 3because you still live as the
people of this world live. When there is jeal-
ousy among you and you quarrel with one
another, doesn't this prove that you belong
to this world, living by its standards? 4When
one of you says, "I follow Paul," and another,
"I follow Apollos"—aren't you acting like
worldly people?

5After all, who is Apollos? And who is
Paul? We are simply God's servants, by
whom you were led to believe. Each one of
us does the work which the Lord gave him
to do: 6I planted the seed, Apollos watered
the plant, but it was God who made the
plant grow. 7The one who plants and the
one who waters really do not matter. It is
God who matters, because he makes the
plant grow. 8There is no difference between

[b] **2:1** God's secret truth; *some manuscripts have* the testimony about God. [c] **2:10** But; *some manuscripts have* For.
[d] **2:13** to those who have the Spirit; *or* with words given by the Spirit.

2:3 Acts 18:9 **2:8** Bar 3:14–17 **2:9** Isa 64:4; Sir 1:9, 10 **2:16** Isa 40:13 (LXX) **3:2** Heb 5:12, 13
3:4 1 Cor 1:12 **3:6** **a** Acts 18:4–11; **b** Acts 18:24–28

The Day of Christ *(1 Corinthians 3:13)* **refers to the Final Judgment, which Jesus describes in Matthew, chapter 25.**

It was God who made the plant grow. (3:6)

the one who plants and the one who waters;
God will reward each one according to the
work each has done. 9For we are partners
working together for God, and you are
God's field.

You are also God's building. 10Using the
gift that God gave me, I did the work of an
expert builder and laid the foundation, and
someone else is building on it. But each of
you must be careful how you build. 11For
God has already placed Jesus Christ as the
one and only foundation, and no other
foundation can be laid. 12Some will use gold
or silver or precious stones in building on
the foundation; others will use wood or grass
or straw. 13And the quality of each person's
work will be seen when the Day of Christ
exposes it. For on that Day fire will reveal
everyone's work; the fire will test it and
show its real quality. 14If what was built on
the foundation survives the fire, the builder
will receive a reward. 15But if your work is
burnt up, then you will lose it; but you your-
self will be saved, as if you had escaped
through the fire.

16Surely you know that you are God's
temple and that God's Spirit lives in you!
17God will destroy anyone who destroys
God's temple. For God's temple is holy, and
you yourselves are his temple.

18You should not fool yourself. If any of
you think that you are wise by this world's
standards, you should become a fool, in
order to be really wise. 19For what this world
considers to be wisdom is nonsense in God's
sight. As the scripture says, "God traps the
wise in their cleverness"; 20and another
scripture says, "The Lord knows that the
thoughts of the wise are worthless." 21No
one, then, should boast about what human
beings can do. Actually everything belongs

Live it!

U-Build It

If you were a building, what would you look like? a skyscraper made of glass and steel? a log cabin? a concrete warehouse? a stone castle? Is it a welcoming place? Could it survive a hurricane or an earthquake?

In chapter 3 Saint Paul uses this image to have us pay attention to how we are building our character and our life. Then it's up to us to design and build the rest. For example, take a look at your personality—are you kind or mean to others? Are your friendships strong or stormy? Do you treat your family members with patience or is there a lot of yelling that you're part of? What about your interests—is your life all about video games or shopping, or do you take time to help out others? What about your values—do you value honesty, or are you okay with doing something wrong as long as you can get away with it? All of your personality qualities, values, interests, and relationships are indicators of what your building will look like. Lastly, ask yourself: Is Jesus at the heart of it all? Is the Spirit living within you?

— 1 Corinthians 3:9–15

3:16 1 Cor 6:19; 2 Cor 6:16 **3:19** Job 5:13 **3:20** Ps 94:11

to you: 22 Paul, Apollos, and Peter; this world,
life and death, the present and the future—
all these are yours, 23 and you belong to
Christ, and Christ belongs to God.

Apostles of Christ

4 You should think of us as Christ's ser-
vants, who have been put in charge of
God's secret truths. 2 The one thing required
of such servants is that they be faithful to
their master. 3 Now, I am not at all con-
cerned about being judged by you or by any
human standard; I don't even pass judgment
on myself. 4 My conscience is clear, but that
does not prove that I am really innocent. The
Lord is the one who passes judgment on me.
5 So you should not pass judgment on any-
one before the right time comes. Final judg-
ment must wait until the Lord comes; he
will bring to light the dark secrets and
expose the hidden purposes of people's
minds. And then all will receive from God
the praise they deserve.

6 For your sake, my friends, I have applied
all this to Apollos and me, using the two of
us as an example, so that you may learn what
the saying means, "Observe the proper rules."
None of you should be proud of one person
and despise another. 7 Who made you superi-
or to others? Didn't God give you everything
you have? Well, then, how can you boast, as if
what you have were not a gift?

8 Do you already have everything you
need? Are you already rich? Have you
become kings, even though we are not?
Well, I wish you really were kings, so that we
could be kings together with you. 9 For it
seems to me that God has given the very last
place to us apostles, like people condemned
to die in public as a spectacle for the whole
world of angels and of human beings. 10 For
Christ's sake we are fools; but you are wise
in union with Christ! We are weak, but you
are strong! We are despised, but you are hon-
ored! 11 To this very moment we go hungry
and thirsty; we are clothed in rags; we are
beaten; we wander from place to place; 12 we
wear ourselves out with hard work. When
we are cursed, we bless; when we are perse-
cuted, we endure; 13 when we are insulted,
we answer back with kind words. We are no
more than this world's garbage; we are the
scum of the earth to this very moment!

14 I write this to you, not because I want to
make you feel ashamed, but to instruct you as
my own dear children. 15 For even if you have
ten thousand guardians in your Christian life,
you have only one father. For in your life in
union with Christ Jesus I have become your
father by bringing the Good News to you.
16 I beg you, then, to follow my example.
17 For this purpose I am sending to you Tim-
othy, who is my own dear and faithful son in
the Christian life. He will remind you of the
principles which I follow in the new life in
union with Christ Jesus and which I teach in
all the churches everywhere.

18 Some of you have become proud
because you have thought that I would not
be coming to visit you. 19 If the Lord is will-
ing, however, I will come to you soon, and

Pray it!

Prayer for Humility

Dear God,
Help me understand what it means to be humble. There are some things I can do really well, and some parts of me that are easy to like. I want to remember that you have given all that to me. Whenever I am complimented by others or I am feeling good about myself, let me stop and whisper a thanks to you. If I start feeling like I'm better than others, stop me in my tracks and remind me where my gifts come from. And, on those days when I don't believe there is anything good about me, show me the best parts of myself that you've helped build inside me. Amen.

— 1 Corinthians 4:7

4:4 Wis 17:11 **4:12** Acts 18:3 **4:16** 1 Cor 11:1; Phil 3:17

then I will find out for myself the power
which these proud people have, and not just
what they say. 20For the Kingdom of God is
not a matter of words but of power. 21Which
do you prefer? Shall I come to you with a
whip, or in a spirit of love and gentleness?

Immorality in the Church

5 Now, it is actually being said that there is
sexual immorality among you so terrible
that not even the heathen would be guilty of
it. I am told that a man is sleeping with his
stepmother! 2How, then, can you be proud?
On the contrary, you should be filled with
sadness, and the man who has done such a
thing should be expelled from your fellow-
ship. 3-4And even though I am far away from
you in body, still I am there with you in spir-
it; and as though I were there with you, I
have in the name of our Lord Jesus already
passed judgment on the man who has done
this terrible thing. As you meet together, and
I meet with you in my spirit, by the power of
our Lord Jesus present with us, 5you are to
hand this man over to Satan for his body to
be destroyed, so that his spirit may be saved
in the Day of the Lord.

6It is not right for you to be proud! You
know the saying, "A little bit of yeast makes
the whole batch of dough rise." 7You must
remove the old yeast of sin so that you will
be entirely pure. Then you will be like a new
batch of dough without any yeast, as indeed
I know you actually are. For our Passover
Festival is ready, now that Christ, our
Passover lamb, has been sacrificed. 8Let us
celebrate our Passover, then, not with bread
having the old yeast of sin and wickedness,
but with the bread that has no yeast, the
bread of purity and truth.

9In the letter that I wrote you I told you
not to associate with immoral people.
10Now I did not mean pagans who are
immoral or greedy or are thieves, or who
worship idols. To avoid them you would
have to get out of the world completely.
11What I meant was that you should not
associate with a person who calls himself a
believer but is immoral or greedy or wor-
ships idols or is a slanderer or a drunkard or
a thief. Don't even sit down to eat with such
a person.

12-13After all, it is none of my business to
judge outsiders. God will judge them. But

Live it!

Help from Your Friends

From the time we are babies, people have been teaching us right from wrong: our parents, grandparents, teachers, coaches, and priests to name a few. We also learn about morality from the Bible and from our Church teachings. It gets exhausting!

Our friends and peers can teach us about living morally too. Sometimes they teach us good things, and sometimes not so good. We make our own choices, but we can be influenced to act one way or another. Paul has this to say, straight and simply: Stay away from immoral people! Their bad morals can rub off on us. Don't be judgmental or rude toward them, but don't hang out with them either. Paul's talking about peer pressure at its worst!

Pray that God will help you resist the bad influences that are all around us. Pray, too, to be surrounded by people who are trying to live good, moral lives—to be influenced by peer pressure at its best!

— 1 Corinthians 5:9–11

5:1 Deut 22:30 **5:6** Gal 5:9 **5:7** Ex 12:5 **5:8** Ex 13:7; Deut 16:3

Occasionally, Saint Paul used sarcasm to make his point *(1 Corinthians 4:8–14)*. **He must have been pretty frustrated!**

should you not judge the members of your own fellowship? As the scripture says, "Remove the evil person from your group."

Lawsuits against Fellow Christians

6 If any of you have a dispute with another Christian, how dare you go before heathen judges instead of letting God's people settle the matter? [2]Don't you know that God's people will judge the world? Well, then, if you are to judge the world, aren't you capable of judging small matters? [3]Do you not know that we shall judge the angels? How much more, then, the things of this life! [4]If such matters come up, are you going to take them to be settled by people who have no standing in the church? [5]Shame on you! Surely there is at least one wise person in your fellowship who can settle a dispute between fellow Christians. [6]Instead, one Christian goes to court against another and lets unbelievers judge the case!

[7]The very fact that you have legal disputes among yourselves shows that you have failed completely. Would it not be better for you to be wronged? Would it not be better for you to be robbed? [8]Instead, you yourselves wrong one another and rob one another, even other believers! [9]Surely you know that the wicked will not possess God's Kingdom. Do not fool yourselves; people who are immoral or who worship idols or are adulterers or homosexual perverts [10]or who steal or are greedy or are drunkards or who slander others or are thieves—none of these will possess God's Kingdom. [11]Some of you were like that. But you have been purified from sin; you have been dedicated to God; you have been put right with God by the Lord Jesus Christ and by the Spirit of our God.

Use Your Bodies for God's Glory

[12]Someone will say, "I am allowed to do anything." Yes; but not everything is good for you. I could say that I am allowed to do anything, but I am not going to let anything make me its slave. [13]Someone else will say, "Food is for the stomach, and the stomach is for food." Yes; but God will put an end to both. The body is not to be used for sexual immorality, but to serve the Lord; and the Lord provides for the body. [14]God raised the Lord from death, and he will also raise us by his power.

[15]You know that your bodies are parts of the body of Christ. Shall I take a part of Christ's body and make it part of the body of a prostitute? Impossible! [16]Or perhaps you don't know that the man who joins his body to a prostitute becomes physically one with her? The scripture says quite plainly, "The two will become one body." [17]But he who joins himself to the Lord becomes spiritually one with him.

[18]Avoid immorality. Any other sin a man commits does not affect his body; but the man who is guilty of sexual immorality sins against his own body. [19]Don't you know that your body is the temple of the Holy Spirit, who lives in you and who was given to you by God? You do not belong to yourselves but to God; [20]he bought you for a price. So use your bodies for God's glory.

Questions about Marriage

7 Now, to deal with the matters you wrote about.

A man does well not to marry.[e] [2]But because there is so much immorality, every man should have his own wife, and every woman should have her own husband. [3]A man should fulfill his duty as a husband, and a woman should fulfill her duty as a wife, and each should satisfy the other's needs. [4]A wife is not the master of her own body, but her husband is; in the same way a husband is not the master of his own body, but his wife is. [5]Do not deny yourselves to each other, unless you first agree to do so for a while in order to spend your time in prayer; but then resume

[e] **7:1** A man does well not to marry; *or* You say that a man does well not to marry.

5:13 Deut 13:5; 17:7 (LXX) **6:12** 1 Cor 10:23 **6:16** Gen 2:24 **6:19** 1 Cor 3:16; 2 Cor 6:16

"The body is not to be used for sexual immorality, but to serve the Lord" *(1 Corinthians 6:13)*.

Vocations

Do you think you'll get married someday? Most people do believe that when they're young, but not everyone is meant to be married. God might want you to be single. These are two examples of vocations that Paul speaks about in 1 Corinthians, chapter 7. Both of these—marriage and single life—offer special gifts, as well as many opportunities to serve God and other people.

Marriage offers the gifts of lifelong companionship, children, and daily lessons in becoming a less self-centered person. At the end of a long life, the greatest gift of marriage is sharing your days and memories with your best friend. Single life offers freedom to do and be many things, to go anywhere, and to be available for whatever might pop up. If you let God steer your life, it's amazing how many people and adventures fill it up!

You might also receive God's call to become a religious sister or brother, or a priest. These are also wonderful vocations and bring you deeply into prayer and doing the work Jesus showed us how to do: helping poor people, comforting sick people, providing the sacraments, teaching, and confronting injustice, for example.

— 1 Corinthians, chapter 7

normal marital relations. In this way you will
be kept from giving in to Satan's temptation
because of your lack of self-control.
6I tell you this not as an order, but simply
as a permission. 7Actually I would prefer that
all of you were as I am; but each one has a
special gift from God, one person this gift,
another one that gift.
8Now, to the unmarried and to the widows
I say that it would be better for you to continue to live alone as I do. 9But if you cannot
restrain your desires, go ahead and marry—it
is better to marry than to burn with passion.
10For married people I have a command
which is not my own but the Lord's: a wife
must not leave her husband; 11but if she
does, she must remain single or else be reconciled to her husband; and a husband must
not divorce his wife.
12To the others I say (I, myself, not the
Lord): if a Christian man has a wife who is
an unbeliever and she agrees to go on living
with him, he must not divorce her. 13And if
a Christian woman is married to a man who
is an unbeliever and he agrees to go on living with her, she must not divorce him.
14For the unbelieving husband is made
acceptable to God by being united to his
wife, and the unbelieving wife is made
acceptable to God by being united to her
Christian husband. If this were not so, their
children would be like pagan children; but as
it is, they are acceptable to God. 15However,
if the one who is not a believer wishes to
leave the Christian partner, let it be so. In
such cases the Christian partner, whether
husband or wife, is free to act. God has
called you to live in peace. 16How can you
be sure, Christian wife, that you will not
save[f] your husband? Or how can you be
sure, Christian husband, that you will not
save[f] your wife?

[f] 7:16 How can you be sure . . . that you will not save; *or* How do you know . . . that you will save.

7:10, 11 Mt 5:32; 19:9; Mk 10:11, 12; Lk 16:18

Live As God Called You

17Each of you should go on living accord-
ing to the Lord's gift to you, and as you were
when God called you. This is the rule I teach
in all the churches. 18If a circumcised man
has accepted God's call, he should not try to
remove the marks of circumcision; if an
uncircumcised man has accepted God's call,
he should not get circumcised. 19For whether
or not a man is circumcised means nothing;
what matters is to obey God's command-
ments. 20Each of you should remain as you
were when you accepted God's call. 21Were
you a slave when God called you? Well, never
mind; but if you have a chance to become
free, use it.[g] 22For a slave who has been called
by the Lord is the Lord's free person; in the
same way a free person who has been called
by Christ is his slave. 23God bought you for a
price; so do not become slaves of people.
24My friends, each of you should remain in
fellowship with God in the same condition
that you were when you were called.

Questions about the Unmarried and the Widows

25Now, concerning what you wrote about
unmarried people: I do not have a command
from the Lord, but I give my opinion as one
who by the Lord's mercy is worthy of trust.

26Considering the present distress, I think
it is better for a man to stay as he is. 27Do
you have a wife? Then don't try to get rid of
her. Are you unmarried? Then don't look for
a wife. 28But if you do marry, you haven't
committed a sin; and if an unmarried
woman marries, she hasn't committed a sin.
But I would rather spare you the everyday
troubles that married people will have.

29What I mean, my friends, is this: there is
not much time left, and from now on mar-
ried people should live as though they were
not married; 30those who weep, as though
they were not sad; those who laugh, as
though they were not happy; those who buy,
as though they did not own what they
bought; 31those who deal in material goods,
as though they were not fully occupied with
them. For this world, as it is now, will not
last much longer.

32I would like you to be free from worry.
An unmarried man concerns himself with
the Lord's work, because he is trying to
please the Lord. 33But a married man con-
cerns himself with worldly matters, because
he wants to please his wife; 34and so he is
pulled in two directions. An unmarried
woman or a virgin concerns herself with the
Lord's work, because she wants to be dedicat-
ed both in body and spirit; but a married
woman concerns herself with worldly mat-
ters, because she wants to please her husband.

35I am saying this because I want to help
you. I am not trying to put restrictions on
you. Instead, I want you to do what is right
and proper, and to give yourselves complete-
ly to the Lord's service without any reserva-
tion.

36In the case of an engaged couple who
have decided not to marry: if the man feels
that he is not acting properly toward the
young woman and if his passions are too
strong and he feels that they ought to marry,
then they should get married, as he wants
to.[h] There is no sin in this. 37But if a man,
without being forced to do so, has firmly
made up his mind not to marry,[i] and if he
has his will under complete control and has
already decided in his own mind what to
do—then he does well not to marry the
young woman.[j] 38So the man who marries[k]
does well, but the one who doesn't marry[l]
does even better.

39A married woman is not free as long as
her husband lives; but if her husband dies,
then she is free to be married to any man
she wishes, but only if he is a Christian.
40She will be happier, however, if she stays as
she is. That is my opinion, and I think that I
too have God's Spirit.

[g] **7:21** but if you have a chance to become free, use it; *or* but even if you have a chance to become free, choose rather to make the best of your condition as a slave. [h] **7:36** an engaged couple . . . as he wants to; *or* a man and his unmarried daughter: if he feels that he is not acting properly toward her, and if she is at the right age to marry, then he should do as he wishes and let her get married. [i] **7:37** not to marry; *or* not to let his daughter get married. [j] **7:37** marry the young woman; *or* let her get married. [k] **7:38** marries; *or* lets his daughter get married. [l] **7:38** doesn't marry; *or* doesn't let her get married.

7:18 1 Macc 1:15

The Question about Food Offered to Idols

8 Now, concerning what you wrote about
food offered to idols.
It is true, of course, that "all of us have
knowledge," as they say. Such knowledge,
however, puffs a person up with pride; but
love builds up. 2Those who think they know
something really don't know as they ought
to know. 3But the person who loves God is
known by him.
4So then, about eating the food offered to
idols: we know that an idol stands for some-
thing that does not really exist; we know
that there is only the one God. 5Even if
there are so-called "gods," whether in heaven
or on earth, and even though there are many
of these "gods" and "lords," 6yet there is for
us only one God, the Father, who is the
Creator of all things and for whom we live;
and there is only one Lord, Jesus Christ,
through whom all things were created and
through whom we live.
7But not everyone knows this truth. Some
people have been so used to idols that to this
day when they eat such food they still think
of it as food that belongs to an idol; their
conscience is weak, and they feel they are
defiled by the food. 8Food, however, will not
improve our relation with God; we shall not
lose anything if we do not eat, nor shall we
gain anything if we do eat.
9Be careful, however, not to let your free-
dom of action make those who are weak in
the faith fall into sin. 10Suppose a person
whose conscience is weak in this matter sees
you, who have so-called "knowledge," eating
in the temple of an idol; will not this
encourage him to eat food offered to idols?
11And so this weak person, your brother for
whom Christ died, will perish because of
your "knowledge"! 12And in this way you
will be sinning against Christ by sinning
against other Christians and wounding their
weak conscience. 13So then, if food makes a
believer sin, I will never eat meat again, so as
not to make a believer fall into sin.

Rights and Duties of an Apostle

9 Am I not a free man? Am I not an
apostle? Haven't I seen Jesus our Lord?
And aren't you the result of my work for the
Lord? 2Even if others do not accept me as
an apostle, surely you do! Because of your
life in union with the Lord you yourselves
are proof of the fact that I am an apostle.
3When people criticize me, this is how I
defend myself: 4Don't I have the right to be
given food and drink for my work? 5Don't I
have the right to follow the example of the
other apostles and the Lord's brothers and
Peter, by taking a Christian wife with me on
my trips? 6Or are Barnabas and I the only
ones who have to work for our living?
7What soldiers ever have to pay their own
expenses in the army? What farmers do not
eat the grapes from their own vineyard?
What shepherds do not use the milk from
their own sheep?
8I don't have to limit myself to these
everyday examples, because the Law says the
same thing. 9We read in the Law of Moses,
"Do not muzzle an ox when you are using it
to thresh grain." Now, is God concerned
about oxen? 10Didn't he really mean us
when he said that? Of course that was writ-
ten for us. Anyone who plows and anyone
who reaps should do their work in the hope
of getting a share of the crop. 11We have
sown spiritual seed among you. Is it too
much if we reap material benefits from you?
12If others have the right to expect this from
you, don't we have an even greater right?
But we haven't made use of this right.
Instead, we have endured everything in
order not to put any obstacle in the way of
the Good News about Christ. 13Surely you
know that the men who work in the Temple
get their food from the Temple and that
those who offer the sacrifices on the altar get
a share of the sacrifices. 14In the same way,

9:9 Deut 25:4; 1 Tim 5:18 **9:11** Rom 15:27 **9:13** Deut 18:1 **9:14** Mt 10:10; Lk 10:7

In Corinth much of the meat sold in markets was from animals slaughtered in pagan temples as sacrifices to a god or a goddess.

Live it!

Focus on the Finish Line

On your mark! Get set! Go!

Corinth was well-known for its sports events, so when Paul spoke of running, he caught people's attention. But the race he talks about is our life here on earth; the finish line is our eternal life with God. Eternal life is the treasured prize that we can look forward to after a well-run race, that is, a faithful life.

To reach the prize, we need to stay focused on God—in the same way a good athlete stays focused on his or her game. When we stay focused, God gives us strength and endurance in our race, and we will win our prize.

— 1 Corinthians 9:23–27

the Lord has ordered that those who preach
the gospel should get their living from it.
[15]But I haven't made use of any of these
rights, nor am I writing this now in order to
claim such rights for myself. I would rather
die first! Nobody is going to turn my right-
ful boast into empty words! [16]I have no right
to boast just because I preach the gospel.
After all, I am under orders to do so. And
how terrible it would be for me if I did not
preach the gospel! [17]If I did my work as a
matter of free choice, then I could expect
to be paid; but I do it as a matter of duty,
because God has entrusted me with this task.
[18]What pay do I get, then? It is the privilege
of preaching the Good News without charg-
ing for it, without claiming my rights in my
work for the gospel.
[19]I am a free man, nobody's slave; but I
make myself everybody's slave in order to
win as many people as possible. [20]While
working with the Jews, I live like a Jew in
order to win them; and even though I myself
am not subject to the Law of Moses, I live as
though I were when working with those
who are, in order to win them. [21]In the same
way, when working with Gentiles, I live like
a Gentile, outside the Jewish Law, in order
to win Gentiles. This does not mean that I
don't obey God's law; I am really under
Christ's law. [22]Among the weak in faith I
become weak like one of them, in order to
win them. So I become all things to all peo-
ple, that I may save some of them by what-
ever means are possible.
[23]All this I do for the gospel's sake, in order
to share in its blessings. [24]Surely you know
that many runners take part in a race, but
only one of them wins the prize. Run, then,
in such a way as to win the prize. [25]Every
athlete in training submits to strict discipline,
in order to be crowned with a wreath that
will not last; but we do it for one that will last
forever. [26]That is why I run straight for the
finish line; that is why I am like a boxer who
does not waste his punches. [27]I harden my
body with blows and bring it under complete
control, to keep myself from being disquali-
fied after having called others to the contest.

Only one of them wins the prize. (9:24)

Warnings against Idols

10 I want you to remember, my friends,
what happened to our ancestors
who followed Moses. They were all under

9:25 Wis 4:2; 5:16 **10:1 a** Ex 13:21, 22; **b** Ex 14:22–29

Read 1 Corinthians 10:16–17. Do you see how the Body of Christ names three things? (1) Jesus himself, (2) the consecrated bread, and (3) the people of God.

the protection of the cloud, and all passed
safely through the Red Sea. 2In the cloud
and in the sea they were all baptized as fol-
lowers of Moses. 3All ate the same spiritual
bread 4and drank the same spiritual drink.
They drank from the spiritual rock that went
with them; and that rock was Christ himself.
5But even then God was not pleased with
most of them, and so their dead bodies were
scattered over the desert.

6Now, all of this is an example for us, to
warn us not to desire evil things, as they did,
7nor to worship idols, as some of them did.
As the scripture says, "The people sat down
to a feast which turned into an orgy of
drinking and sex." 8We must not be guilty of
sexual immorality, as some of them were—
and in one day twenty-three thousand of
them fell dead. 9We must not put the Lord[m]
to the test, as some of them did—and they
were killed by snakes. 10We must not com-
plain, as some of them did—and they were
destroyed by the Angel of Death.

11All these things happened to them as
examples for others, and they were written
down as a warning for us. For we live at a
time when the end is about to come.

12If you think you are standing firm you
had better be careful that you do not fall.
13Every test that you have experienced is the
kind that normally comes to people. But
God keeps his promise, and he will not allow
you to be tested beyond your power to
remain firm; at the time you are put to the
test, he will give you the strength to endure
it, and so provide you with a way out.

14So then, my dear friends, keep away
from the worship of idols. 15I speak to you as
sensible people; judge for yourselves what I
say. 16The cup we use in the Lord's Supper
and for which we give thanks to God: when
we drink from it, we are sharing in the
blood of Christ. And the bread we break:
when we eat it, we are sharing in the body
of Christ. 17Because there is the one loaf of
bread, all of us, though many, are one body,
for we all share the same loaf.

18Consider the people of Israel; those who

Live it!

American Idols

Money. Popularity. Sports. Fashion. Sex. Food. Success. Comfort. Beauty. These are examples of things that we can idolize. One or more of these can become more important to us than anything else, even God.

In the first commandment, we're told God and only God should come first in our life. "I am the LORD your God. . . . Do not bow down to any idol or worship it" (Exodus 20:2–5). And Paul stresses it again. He goes so far as to call idolatry evil (1 Corinthians 10:6).

Do you have idols in your life? Think about how you spend your money or your time. Is God or the Church anywhere in your priorities? Do you often or always brush these aside for something you consider more fun or interesting? If so, some idols might have snuck into your life.

God has made the most amazing promise to us: he will be with us always, through thick and thin—no matter what. But if we've got a bunch of idols crowding our life—there's not much room left to experience God's promised love. It might even seem like life is falling apart sometimes. But if we put God first, our problems seem lighter, and we just feel more peaceful.

— 1 Corinthians 10:1–13

m **10:9** the Lord; *some manuscripts have* Christ.

10:3 Ex 16:35 **10:4** Ex 17:6; Num 20:11 **10:5** Num 14:29, 30 **10:6** Num 11:4 **10:7** Ex 32:6 **10:8** Num 25:1–18 **10:9** Num 21:5, 6 **10:10** Num 16:41–49 **10:13** Jdt 8:25–27; Sir 15:11–20 **10:16** Mt 26:26–28; Mk 14:22–24; Lk 22:19, 20 **10:18** Lev 7:6

We all share the same loaf. (10:17)

eat what is offered in sacrifice share in the
altar's service to God. 19 Do I imply, then, that
an idol or the food offered to it really amounts
to anything? 20 No! What I am saying is that
what is sacrificed on pagan altars is offered to
demons, not to God. And I do not want you
to be partners with demons. 21 You cannot
drink from the Lord's cup and also from the
cup of demons; you cannot eat at the Lord's
table and also at the table of demons. 22 Or do
we want to make the Lord jealous? Do we
think that we are stronger than he?

23 "We are allowed to do anything," so
they say. That is true, but not everything is
good. "We are allowed to do anything"—but
not everything is helpful. 24 None of you
should be looking out for your own inter-
ests, but for the interests of others.

25 You are free to eat anything sold in the
meat market, without asking any questions
because of your conscience. 26 For, as the
scripture says, "The earth and everything in
it belong to the Lord."

27 If an unbeliever invites you to a meal
and you decide to go, eat what is set before
you, without asking any questions because of
your conscience. 28 But if someone tells you,
"This food was offered to idols," then do not
eat that food, for the sake of the one who
told you and for conscience' sake— 29 that is,
not your own conscience, but the other per-
son's conscience.

"Well, then," someone asks, "why should
my freedom to act be limited by another
person's conscience? 30 If I thank God for my
food, why should anyone criticize me about
food for which I give thanks?"

31 Well, whatever you do, whether you eat
or drink, do it all for God's glory. 32 Live in
such a way as to cause no trouble either to
Jews or Gentiles or to the church of God.
33 Just do as I do; I try to please everyone in all
that I do, not thinking of my own good, but
of the good of all, so that they might be saved.

11 Imitate me, then, just as I imitate
Christ.

Covering the Head in Worship

2 I praise you because you always remem-
ber me and follow the teachings that I have
handed on to you. 3 But I want you to
understand that Christ is supreme over every
man, the husband is supreme over his wife,
and God is supreme over Christ. 4 So a man
who prays or proclaims God's message in
public worship with his head covered dis-
graces Christ. 5 And any woman who prays
or proclaims God's message in public wor-
ship with nothing on her head disgraces her
husband; there is no difference between her
and a woman whose head has been shaved.
6 If the woman does not cover her head, she
might as well cut her hair. And since it is a
shameful thing for a woman to shave her
head or cut her hair, she should cover her
head. 7 A man has no need to cover his head,
because he reflects the image and glory of
God. But woman reflects the glory of man;
8 for man was not created from woman, but
woman from man. 9 Nor was man created for
woman's sake, but woman was created for
man's sake. 10 On account of the angels, then,
a woman should have a covering over her
head to show that she is under her husband's
authority. 11 In our life in the Lord, however,
woman is not independent of man, nor is
man independent of woman. 12 For as
woman was made from man, in the same
way man is born of woman; and it is God
who brings everything into existence.

13 Judge for yourselves whether it is proper
for a woman to pray to God in public wor-
ship with nothing on her head. 14 Why,
nature itself teaches you that long hair on a

10:20 Deut 32:17 (LXX) **10:22** Deut 32:21 **10:23** 1 Cor 6:12 **10:26** Ps 24:1 **11:1** 1 Cor 4:16; Phil 3:17 **11:7** Gen 1:26, 27 **11:8, 9** Gen 2:18–23

Catholic Connections

The Eucharistic Meal

Do you ever find yourself during Communion time looking around to see who's walking up the aisle, worrying about tomorrow's big test, remembering the fight you had earlier that morning with your dad, observing the cute three-year-old in front of you, or thinking about the soccer game coming up? A million distractions, right there in church or in our heads!

Saint Paul teaches us that receiving the body and blood of Christ is precious—so take it seriously (1 Corinthians 11:29)! Next time you're at Mass and it's time to receive the Eucharist, really concentrate on what you're doing. Listen to the words, take communion, be quiet and focus on the presence of Jesus within you. For in the same way that bread and wine is changed into Jesus' body and blood, when we eat and drink the Eucharist, we are changed. Jesus becomes part of us, so we become more like Jesus. Pray to feel the power of that change happening inside you. Pray that the love of Jesus will be noticeable in the things you say and do. Pray for peace—in you and around you.

— 1 Corinthians 11:23–33

man is a disgrace, 15but on a woman it is a thing of beauty. Her long hair has been given her to serve as a covering. 16But if anyone wants to argue about it, all I have to say is that neither we nor the churches of God have any other custom in worship.

The Lord's Supper

(Matthew 26:26–29; Mark 14:22–25; Luke 22:14–20)

17In the following instructions, however, I do not praise you, because your meetings for worship actually do more harm than good.
18In the first place, I have been told that there are opposing groups in your meetings; and this I believe is partly true. (19No doubt there must be divisions among you so that the ones who are in the right may be clearly seen.) 20When you meet together as a group, it is not the Lord's Supper that you eat. 21For as you eat, you each go ahead with your own meal, so that some are hungry while others get drunk. 22Don't you have your own homes in which to eat and drink? Or would you rather despise the church of God and put to shame the people who are in need? What do you expect me to say to you about this? Shall I praise you? Of course I don't!

23For I received from the Lord the teaching that I passed on to you: that the Lord Jesus, on the night he was betrayed, took a piece of bread, 24gave thanks to God, broke it, and said, "This is my body, which is for you. Do this in memory of me." 25In the same way, after the supper he took the cup and said, "This cup is God's new covenant, sealed with my blood. Whenever you drink it, do so in memory of me."

26This means that every time you eat this bread and drink from this cup you proclaim the Lord's death until he comes. 27It follows that if one of you eats the Lord's bread or drinks from his cup in a way that dishonors

11:25 **a** Ex 24:8; Jer 31:31–34; **b** Ex 24:6–8

"Every time you eat this bread and drink from this cup you proclaim the Lord's death until he comes" *(1 Corinthians 11:26)*. **Where have you heard this before?**

Pray it!

Come, Holy Spirit!

The beginning of 1 Corinthians, chapter 12, talks about the gifts of the Holy Spirit, gifts that we receive more fully during the sacrament of Confirmation. The bishop prays this blessing over the Confirmation candidates before they are anointed with oil:

> *All powerful God, Father of our Lord Jesus Christ,*
> *by water and the Holy Spirit*
> *you freed your sons and daughters from sin*
> *And gave them new life.*
> *Send your Holy Spirit upon them*
> *to be their helper and guide.*
> *Give them the spirit of wisdom and understanding,*
> *the spirit of right judgment and courage,*
> *the spirit of knowledge and reverence.*
> *Fill them with the spirit of wonder and awe in your presence.*
> *We ask this through Christ our Lord*
> **(The Rites of the Catholic Church)**

— 1 Corinthians 12:1–11

him, you are guilty of sin against the Lord's
body and blood. 28So then, you should each
examine yourself first, and then eat the bread
and drink from the cup. 29For if you do not
recognize the meaning of the Lord's body
when you eat the bread and drink from the
cup, you bring judgment on yourself as you eat
and drink. 30That is why many of you are sick
and weak, and several have died. 31If we would
examine ourselves first, we would not come
under God's judgment. 32But we are judged
and punished by the Lord, so that we shall not
be condemned together with the world.

33So then, my friends, when you gather
together to eat the Lord's Supper, wait for
one another. 34And if any of you are hungry,
you should eat at home, so that you will not
come under God's judgment as you meet
together. As for the other matters, I will set-
tle them when I come.

Gifts from the Holy Spirit

12 Now, concerning what you wrote
about the gifts from the Holy Spirit.
I want you to know the truth about them,
my friends. 2You know that while you were
still heathen, you were led astray in many
ways to the worship of lifeless idols. 3I want
you to know that no one who is led by
God's Spirit can say "A curse on Jesus!" and
no one can confess "Jesus is Lord," without
being guided by the Holy Spirit.

4There are different kinds of spiritual
gifts, but the same Spirit gives them. 5There
are different ways of serving, but the same
Lord is served. 6There are different abilities
to perform service, but the same God gives
ability to all for their particular service. 7The
Spirit's presence is shown in some way in
each person for the good of all. 8The Spirit
gives one person a message full of wisdom,
while to another person the same Spirit

12:4–11 Rom 12:6–8

"Set your hearts, then, on the more important gifts" *(1 Corinthians 12:31)*.

gives a message full of knowledge. 9One and
the same Spirit gives faith to one person,
while to another person he gives the power
to heal. 10The Spirit gives one person the
power to work miracles; to another, the gift
of speaking God's message; and to yet anoth-
er, the ability to tell the difference between
gifts that come from the Spirit and those
that do not. To one person he gives the abili-
ty to speak in strange tongues, and to anoth-
er he gives the ability to explain what is said.
11But it is one and the same Spirit who does
all this; as he wishes, he gives a different gift
to each person.

One Body with Many Parts

12Christ is like a single body, which has
many parts; it is still one body, even though it
is made up of different parts. 13In the same
way, all of us, whether Jews or Gentiles,
whether slaves or free, have been baptized
into the one body by the same Spirit, and we
have all been given the one Spirit to drink.
14For the body itself is not made up of
only one part, but of many parts. 15If the
foot were to say, "Because I am not a hand, I
don't belong to the body," that would not
keep it from being a part of the body. 16And
if the ear were to say, "Because I am not an
eye, I don't belong to the body," that would
not keep it from being a part of the body.
17If the whole body were just an eye, how
could it hear? And if it were only an ear,
how could it smell? 18As it is, however, God
put every different part in the body just as
he wanted it to be. 19There would not be a
body if it were all only one part! 20As it is,
there are many parts but one body.
21So then, the eye cannot say to the hand,
"I don't need you!" Nor can the head say to
the feet, "Well, I don't need you!" 22On the
contrary, we cannot do without the parts of
the body that seem to be weaker; 23and those
parts that we think aren't worth very much
are the ones which we treat with greater
care; while the parts of the body which don't
look very nice are treated with special mod-
esty, 24which the more beautiful parts do not
need. God himself has put the body together
in such a way as to give greater honor to
those parts that need it. 25And so there is no
division in the body, but all its different parts
have the same concern for one another. 26If
one part of the body suffers, all the other
parts suffer with it; if one part is praised, all
the other parts share its happiness.
27All of you are Christ's body, and each
one is a part of it. 28In the church God has
put all in place: in the first place apostles, in
the second place prophets, and in the third
place teachers; then those who perform mira-
cles, followed by those who are given the
power to heal or to help others or to direct
them or to speak in strange tongues. 29They
are not all apostles or prophets or teachers.
Not everyone has the power to work miracles
30or to heal diseases or to speak in strange
tongues or to explain what is said. 31Set your
hearts, then, on the more important gifts.
Best of all, however, is the following way.

Love

13 I may be able to speak the languages
of human beings and even of angels,
but if I have no love, my speech is no more
than a noisy gong or a clanging bell. 2I may
have the gift of inspired preaching; I may
have all knowledge and understand all
secrets; I may have all the faith needed to
move mountains—but if I have no love, I am
nothing. 3I may give away everything I have,
and even give up my body to be burned[n] —
but if I have no love, this does me no good.
4Love is patient and kind; it is not jealous
or conceited or proud; 5love is not ill-man-
nered or selfish or irritable; love does not
keep a record of wrongs; 6love is not happy
with evil, but is happy with the truth. 7Love
never gives up; and its faith, hope, and
patience never fail.
8Love is eternal. There are inspired mes-
sages, but they are temporary; there are gifts
of speaking in strange tongues, but they will
cease; there is knowledge, but it will pass.
9For our gifts of knowledge and of inspired
messages are only partial; 10but when what is

[n] **13:3** to be burned, *some manuscripts have* in order to boast.

12:12 Rom 12:4, 5 **12:28** Eph 4:11 **13:2** Mt 17:20; 21:21; Mk 11:23

Live it!

True Love

Think of five things you said or did today. Five concrete examples. Now, reread 1 Corinthians 13:4–7. How do your words and actions measure up? Do they show that you are patient? kind? unselfish?

It's one thing to say, "I love God" or "I love my parents" or "I love my best friend." It's another thing to really live in a loving way.

Write out the words of these verses, and hang them up where you'll see them every day. This is a good way to keep checking if you are being faithful to the kind of love God is asking us to offer to ourselves and others.

— 1 Corinthians 13:4–7

perfect comes, then what is partial will dis-
appear.
11 When I was a child, my speech, feelings,
and thinking were all those of a child; now
that I am an adult, I have no more use for
childish ways. 12 What we see now is like a
dim image in a mirror; then we shall see face
to face. What I know now is only partial;

What we see now is like a dim image in a mirror. (13:12)

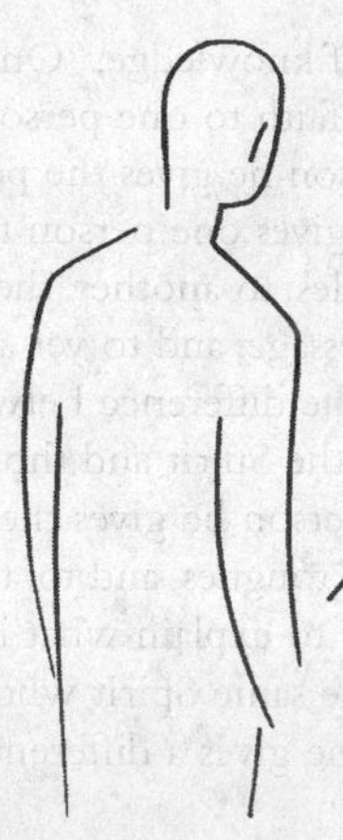

Then we shall see face to face. (13:12)

then it will be complete—as complete as
God's knowledge of me.
13 Meanwhile these three remain: faith,
hope, and love; and the greatest of these is
love.

More about Gifts from the Spirit

14 It is love, then, that you should strive
for. Set your hearts on spiritual gifts,
especially the gift of proclaiming God's mes-
sage. 2 Those who speak in strange tongues
do not speak to others but to God, because
no one understands them. They are speaking
secret truths by the power of the Spirit. 3 But
those who proclaim God's message speak to
people and give them help, encouragement,
and comfort. 4 Those who speak in strange
tongues help only themselves, but those who
proclaim God's message help the whole
church.
5 I would like for all of you to speak in
strange tongues; but I would rather that you
had the gift of proclaiming God's message.
For the person who proclaims God's message
is of greater value than the one who speaks
in strange tongues—unless there is someone
present who can explain what is said, so that
the whole church may be helped. 6 So when
I come to you, my friends, what use will I
be to you if I speak in strange tongues? Not
a bit, unless I bring you some revelation
from God or some knowledge or some
inspired message or some teaching.
7 Take such lifeless musical instruments as
the flute or the harp—how will anyone

Pray it!

Strange Tongues?

What does it mean to speak in strange tongues? It's a way of praying. Some people possess this gift of the Spirit described in 1 Corinthians, chapter 14. When they pray out loud, it sometimes sounds like strange, foreign-sounding words. This is said to be the Holy Spirit speaking through them, even though they have no idea what it means. They are praying with their spirit, not their mind. Paul explains that while some people have the gift of speaking in tongues, others might have the gift of understanding what they are saying.

If you ever hear someone speaking in tongues, it can be shocking or disturbing at first. But trust that it is prayer and is another mysterious way that God can work in us.

Paul is making a more important point, however. What comes out of your mouth? Everything we say is important. Our words can offer "help, encouragement, and comfort" (1 Corinthians 14:3). Or our words can be hurtful and destructive or useless. Screaming and cursing is harmful. Laughter and singing can bring joy.

Think about that the next time you're about to open your mouth to God in prayer!

— 1 Corinthians 14:1–6

know the tune that is being played unless the
notes are sounded distinctly? 8And if the one
who plays the bugle does not sound a clear
call, who will prepare for battle? 9In the same
way, how will anyone understand what you
are talking about if your message given in
strange tongues is not clear? Your words will
vanish in the air! 10There are many different
languages in the world, yet none of them is
without meaning. 11But if I do not know the
language being spoken, those who use it will
be foreigners to me and I will be a foreigner
to them. 12Since you are eager to have the
gifts of the Spirit, you must try above every-
thing else to make greater use of those which
help to build up the church.

13The person who speaks in strange
tongues, then, must pray for the gift to
explain what is said. 14For if I pray in this
way, my spirit prays indeed, but my mind has
no part in it. 15What should I do, then? I will
pray with my spirit, but I will pray also with
my mind; I will sing with my spirit, but I will
sing also with my mind. 16When you give
thanks to God in spirit only, how can ordi-
nary people taking part in the meeting say
"Amen" to your prayer of thanksgiving? They
have no way of knowing what you are saying.
17Even if your prayer of thanks to God is
quite good, other people are not helped at all.

18I thank God that I speak in strange
tongues much more than any of you. 19But
in church worship I would rather speak five
words that can be understood, in order to
teach others, than speak thousands of words
in strange tongues.

20Do not be like children in your think-
ing, my friends; be children so far as evil is
concerned, but be grown up in your think-
ing. 21In the Scriptures it is written,

14:21 Isa 28:11, 12

Speaking in strange tongues *(1 Corinthians 14:2)* **sometimes happens in charismatic prayer groups that are part of some Catholic parishes.**

"By means of people speaking strange
languages
I will speak to my people, says the Lord.
I will speak through lips of foreigners,
but even then my people will not listen
to me."
22So then, the gift of speaking in strange
tongues is proof for unbelievers, not for
believers, while the gift of proclaiming God's
message is proof for believers, not for unbe-
lievers.
23If, then, the whole church meets togeth-
er and everyone starts speaking in strange
tongues—and if some ordinary people or
unbelievers come in, won't they say that you
are all crazy? 24But if everyone is proclaiming
God's message when some unbelievers or
ordinary people come in, they will be con-
vinced of their sin by what they hear. They
will be judged by all they hear, 25their secret
thoughts will be brought into the open, and
they will bow down and worship God, con-
fessing, "Truly God is here among you!"

Order in the Church

26This is what I mean, my friends. When
you meet for worship, one person has a
hymn, another a teaching, another a revela-
tion from God, another a message in strange
tongues, and still another the explanation of
what is said. Everything must be of help to
the church. 27If someone is going to speak in
strange tongues, two or three at the most
should speak, one after the other, and some-
one else must explain what is being said.
28But if no one is there who can explain,
then the one who speaks in strange tongues
must be quiet and speak only to himself and
to God. 29Two or three who are given God's
message should speak, while the others are
to judge what they say. 30But if someone sit-
ting in the meeting receives a message from
God, the one who is speaking should stop.
31All of you may proclaim God's message,
one by one, so that everyone will learn and
be encouraged. 32The gift of proclaiming
God's message should be under the speaker's
control, 33because God does not want us to
be in disorder but in harmony and peace.
As in all the churches of God's people,
34the women should keep quiet in the meet-
ings. They are not allowed to speak; as the
Jewish Law says, they must not be in charge.
35If they want to find out about something,
they should ask their husbands at home. It is
a disgraceful thing for a woman to speak in a
church meeting.
36Or could it be that the word of God
came from you? Or are you the only ones to
whom it came? 37If anyone supposes he is
God's messenger or has a spiritual gift, he
must realize that what I am writing to you is
the Lord's command. 38But if he does not
pay attention to this, pay no attention to him.
39So then, my friends, set your heart on
proclaiming God's message, but do not forbid
the speaking in strange tongues. 40Everything
must be done in a proper and orderly way.

The Resurrection of Christ

15 And now I want to remind you, my
friends, of the Good News which I
preached to you, which you received, and on
which your faith stands firm. 2That is the
gospel, the message that I preached to you.
You are saved by the gospel if you hold
firmly to it—unless it was for nothing that
you believed.
3I passed on to you what I received, which
is of the greatest importance: that Christ died
for our sins, as written in the Scriptures; 4that
he was buried and that he was raised to life
three days later, as written in the Scriptures;
5that he appeared to Peter and then to all
twelve apostles. 6Then he appeared to more
than five hundred of his followers at once,
most of whom are still alive, although some
have died. 7Then he appeared to James, and
afterward to all the apostles.
8Last of all he appeared also to me—even

15:3 Isa 53:5–12 **15:4** Ps 16:8–10; Mt 12:40; Acts 2:24–32 **15:5** **a** Lk 24:34; **b** Mt 28:16, 17; Mk 16:14; Lk 24:36; Jn 20:19 **15:8** Acts 9:3–6

Read 1 Corinthians 15:19. Would you be a Christian if you didn't believe in the Resurrection?

Study it!

An African Creed

In 1 Corinthians 15:3–5, Paul proclaims one of the earliest creeds of the Church. A creed is a statement of beliefs about our faith, especially about the death and Resurrection of Jesus. Here is the beginning of another creed from the Masai tribe of the African tradition:

We believe in the one High God, who out of love created the beautiful world and everything good in it. He created man and wanted man to be happy in the world. God loves the world and every nation and tribe on the earth. We have known this High God in the darkness, and now we know him in the light. God promised in the book of his word, the Bible, that he would save the world and all the nations and tribes.

We believe that God made good his promise by sending his Son, Jesus Christ, a man in the flesh, a Jew by tribe, born poor in a little village, who left his home and was always on safari doing good, curing people by the power of God, teaching about God and man, showing that the meaning of religion is love. He was rejected by his people, tortured and nailed hands and feet to a cross, and died.

—1 Corinthians 15:3–5

though I am like someone whose birth was
abnormal.[o] 9For I am the least of all the apos-
tles—I do not even deserve to be called an
apostle, because I persecuted God's church.
10But by God's grace I am what I am, and the
grace that he gave me was not without effect.
On the contrary, I have worked harder than
any of the other apostles, although it was not
really my own doing, but God's grace work-
ing with me. 11So then, whether it came from
me or from them, this is what we all preach,
and this is what you believe.

Our Resurrection

12Now, since our message is that Christ has
been raised from death, how can some of you
say that the dead will not be raised to life? 13If
that is true, it means that Christ was not
raised; 14and if Christ has not been raised from
death, then we have nothing to preach and
you have nothing to believe. 15More than that,
we are shown to be lying about God, because
we said that he raised Christ from death—but
if it is true that the dead are not raised to life,
then he did not raise Christ. 16For if the dead
are not raised, neither has Christ been raised.
17And if Christ has not been raised, then your
faith is a delusion and you are still lost in your
sins. 18It would also mean that the believers in
Christ who have died are lost. 19If our hope in
Christ is good for this life only and no more,[p]
then we deserve more pity than anyone else in
all the world.

20But the truth is that Christ has been
raised from death, as the guarantee that those
who sleep in death will also be raised. 21For

Those who sleep in death will also be raised. (15:20)

[o] **15:8** whose birth was abnormal; *or* who was born at the wrong time. [p] **15:19** If our hope in Christ is good for this life only and no more; *or* If all we have in this life is our hope in Christ.
15:9 Acts 8:3

just as death came by means of a man, in the
same way the rising from death comes by
means of a man. 22 For just as all people die
because of their union with Adam, in the
same way all will be raised to life because of
their union with Christ. 23 But each one will
be raised in proper order: Christ, first of all;
then, at the time of his coming, those who
belong to him. 24 Then the end will come;
Christ will overcome all spiritual rulers,
authorities, and powers, and will hand over
the Kingdom to God the Father. 25 For
Christ must rule until God defeats all ene-
mies and puts them under his feet. 26 The last
enemy to be defeated will be death. 27 For
the scripture says, "God put *all* things under
his feet." It is clear, of course, that the words
"all things" do not include God himself,
who puts all things under Christ. 28 But
when all things have been placed under
Christ's rule, then he himself, the Son, will
place himself under God, who placed all
things under him; and God will rule com-
pletely over all.

29 Now, what about those people who are
baptized for the dead? What do they hope to
accomplish? If it is true, as some claim, that
the dead are not raised to life, why are those
people being baptized for the dead? 30 And as
for us—why would we run the risk of dan-
ger every hour? 31 My friends, I face death
every day! The pride I have in you, in our
life in union with Christ Jesus our Lord,
makes me declare this. 32 If I have, as it were,
fought "wild beasts" here in Ephesus simply
from human motives, what have I gained?
But if the dead are not raised to life, then, as
the saying goes, "Let us eat and drink, for
tomorrow we will die."

33 Do not be fooled. "Bad companions
ruin good character." 34 Come back to your
right senses and stop your sinful ways. I
declare to your shame that some of you do
not know God.

The Resurrection Body

35 Someone will ask, "How can the dead
be raised to life? What kind of body will
they have?" 36 You fool! When you plant a
seed in the ground, it does not sprout to life
unless it dies. 37 And what you plant is a bare
seed, perhaps a grain of wheat or some other
grain, not the full-bodied plant that will later
grow up. 38 God provides that seed with the
body he wishes; he gives each seed its own
proper body.

39 And the flesh of living beings is not all
the same kind of flesh; human beings have
one kind of flesh, animals another, birds
another, and fish another.

40 And there are heavenly bodies and
earthly bodies; the beauty that belongs to
heavenly bodies is different from the beauty
that belongs to earthly bodies. 41 The sun has
its own beauty, the moon another beauty,
and the stars a different beauty; and even
among stars there are different kinds of
beauty.

42 This is how it will be when the dead are
raised to life. When the body is buried, it is
mortal; when raised, it will be immortal.
43 When buried, it is ugly and weak; when
raised, it will be beautiful and strong.
44 When buried, it is a physical body; when
raised, it will be a spiritual body. There is, of
course, a physical body, so there has to be a
spiritual body. 45 For the scripture says, "The
first man, Adam, was created a living being";
but the last Adam is the life-giving Spirit.
46 It is not the spiritual that comes first, but
the physical, and then the spiritual. 47 The
first Adam, made of earth, came from the
earth; the second Adam came from heaven.
48 Those who belong to the earth are like the
one who was made of earth; those who are
of heaven are like the one who came from
heaven. 49 Just as we wear the likeness of the
man made of earth, so we will wear[q] the
likeness of the Man from heaven.

50 What I mean, friends, is that what is
made of flesh and blood cannot share in
God's Kingdom, and what is mortal cannot
possess immortality.

51-52 Listen to this secret truth: we shall not
all die, but when the last trumpet sounds, we
shall all be changed in an instant, as quickly
as the blinking of an eye. For when the

[q] **15:49** we will wear; *some manuscripts have* let us wear.

15:25 Ps 110:1 **15:27** Ps 8:6 **15:29** 2 Macc 12:44 **15:32** Isa 22:13 **15:45** Gen 2:7
15:51, 52 1 Thess 4:15–17

Study it!

Eternal Life

When someone we love dies, it's the saddest moment of our lives. It feels as though we have lost that person forever—and a big, horrible, painful hole is left inside us. But wait—there's great news! Because of Jesus' Resurrection, we believe death is not the end. Our loved ones will be raised up from the dead and given new, resurrected bodies! And we will be together again one day.

If Jesus had died, and that was that—then you wouldn't be reading this right now because it would all be meaningless. But death wasn't the end! Jesus rose from the dead, and that event is at the heart of all our religious beliefs.

Death isn't the end for us, either. We, too, will rise and be with God forever and ever—we call this eternal life. What do you think that will be like? Paul says we will not look the same, just as a seed planted in the soil looks completely different after it dies and rises up out of the ground as a plant or flower (1 Corinthians 15:35–37). Our new bodies will be "spiritual bodies," and they will be "beautiful and strong" (15:44,43).

This is truly the best news of all the Good News!

— 1 Corinthians, chapter 15

trumpet sounds, the dead will be raised,
never to die again, and we shall all be
changed. 53For what is mortal must be
changed into what is immortal; what will die
must be changed into what cannot die. 54So
when this takes place, and the mortal has
been changed into the immortal, then
the scripture will come true: "Death is
destroyed; victory is complete!"
55 "Where, Death, is your victory?
Where, Death, is your power to hurt?"
56Death gets its power to hurt from sin, and
sin gets its power from the Law. 57But thanks
be to God who gives us the victory through
our Lord Jesus Christ!
58So then, my dear friends, stand firm and
steady. Keep busy always in your work for
the Lord, since you know that nothing you
do in the Lord's service is ever useless.

The Offering for Needy Believers

16 Now, concerning what you wrote
about the money to be raised to
help God's people in Judea. You must do
what I told the churches in Galatia to do.
2Every Sunday each of you must put aside
some money, in proportion to what you
have earned, and save it up, so that there will
be no need to collect money when I come.
3After I come, I shall give letters of introduction to those you have approved, and
send them to take your gift to Jerusalem. 4If
it seems worthwhile for me to go, then they
can go along with me.

Paul's Plans

5I shall come to you after I have gone
through Macedonia—for I have to go
through Macedonia. 6I shall probably spend
some time with you, perhaps the whole
winter, and then you can help me to continue my trip, wherever it is I shall go next. 7I
want to see you more than just briefly in
passing; I hope to spend quite a long time
with you, if the Lord allows.

15:54 Isa 25:8 **15:55** Hos 13:14 (LXX) **16:1** Rom 15:25, 26 **16:5** Acts 19:21

"Where, Death, is your victory? Where, Death, is your power to hurt?"
(1 Corinthians 15:55).

Catholic Connections

Tithing

Saint Paul instructs the Corinthians to put aside an amount of money "in proportion to what you have earned" (1 Corinthians 16:2) for poor people. Our church calls this the practice of tithing (also described in Deuteronomy 26:12). A tithe means 10 percent and is the amount of crops required in Deuteronomy to set aside for poor and needy people.

If you were to practice tithing, it would look like this: If you earn $20 for a job, you save 10 percent ($2) to give to poor people. If you bring home a paycheck of $2,000, then $200 of it goes to charity—before it gets spent on other things!

Today, the Church doesn't require people to give 10 percent, but we are all challenged to give as generously as we can. Some people might be able to give more than 10 percent, and for others 5 percent is a big commitment. Tithing is something to start now. Do you get an allowance? Figure out how much 10 percent of it is, and before you spend a penny of your allowance, put that amount aside and give it to someone or some group that helps poor people.

—1 Corinthians 16:1–2

8I will stay here in Ephesus until the day
of Pentecost. 9There is a real opportunity
here for great and worthwhile work, even
though there are many opponents.

10If Timothy comes your way, be sure
to make him feel welcome among you,
because he is working for the Lord, just
as I am. 11No one should look down on
him, but you must help him continue his
trip in peace, so that he will come back to
me; for I am expecting him back with the
believers.

12Now, about brother Apollos. I have
often encouraged him to visit you with the
other believers, but he is not completely
convinced[r] that he should go at this time.
When he gets the chance, however, he
will go.

Final Words

13Be alert, stand firm in the faith, be
brave, be strong. 14Do all your work in love.

15You know about Stephanas and his family; they are the first Christian converts in
Achaia and have given themselves to the
service of God's people. I beg you, my
friends, 16to follow the leadership of such
people as these, and of anyone else who
works and serves with them.

17I am happy about the coming of
Stephanas, Fortunatus, and Achaicus; they
have made up for your absence 18and have
cheered me up, just as they cheered you up.
Such men as these deserve notice.

19The churches in the province of Asia
send you their greetings; Aquila and Priscilla
and the church that meets in their house

[r] **16:12** he is not completely convinced; *or* it is not at all God's will.

16:8 Lev 23:15–21; Deut 16:9–11 **16:8, 9** Acts 19:8–10 **16:10** 1 Cor 4:17 **16:15** 1 Cor 1:16 **16:19** Acts 18:2

Do the names of Paul's co-workers sound familiar: Timothy, Apollos, Aquila, and Priscilla? We met them in the Acts of the Apostles.

send warm Christian greetings. 20 All the
believers here send greetings.
Greet one another with the kiss of peace.
21 With my own hand I write this: *Greet-
ings from Paul.*

22 Whoever does not love the Lord—a
curse on him!
Maran atha—Our Lord, come!
23 The grace of the Lord Jesus be with you.
24 My love be with you all in Christ Jesus.

Your Next Step

Congratulations on finishing the First Letter to the Corinthians! Use this space to write your thoughts and questions about this book. If you are following the suggested reading plan, move back to the Second Book of Samuel in the Old Testament. This book tells the story of King David.

The Second Letter to the Corinthians

Nobody likes to be put down, especially by people you thought were your friends. When Paul wrote his first letter to the people of Corinth, they had a good relationship. But then some outsiders came to the city and criticized Paul. They said he was a bad person, he was a poor speaker, and he was untrustworthy.

Paul didn't like this conflict. He wrote this second letter to the Christians in Corinth to defend himself and help them get back on the right track. He also wanted to encourage them to be generous to the needs of the poor.

Chap. 8:1–9

Headlines

- Paul Does Everything Out of Love! (1:12—2:4)
- Treasure Contained in Clay Pots (4:1–15)
- Faith, Not Sight, Guides Believers (5:6–7)
- Corinthians Told to Be Generous (8:1–15)
- Paul Describes His Amazing Life (11:16–33)

FACTOIDS

Who wrote this book? It was written by Saint Paul, who started Christian communities in several cities, including Corinth.

When was it written? Around AD 57, about a year after Paul wrote his first letter to the Corinthians.

Why was it written? Paul wanted to defend himself and his ministry against the people who criticized him. He wanted to improve his relationship with the Christian people of Corinth.

Jesus connection. Jesus was without sin. When we unite ourselves to Christ by believing in him, his goodness is reflected in us. This changes us from God's enemies into his friends! (5:16–21)

Important themes

- Paul shows us how to stay faithful to Jesus even when we are personally attacked or put down.
- We are weak and imperfect so that everyone knows that treasure of faith we have comes from God.
- We must be generous in sharing what we have with those in need.

2 CORINTHIANS

1 From Paul, an apostle of Christ Jesus by God's will, and from our brother Timothy—

To the church of God in Corinth, and to all God's people throughout Achaia:

2 May God our Father and the Lord Jesus Christ give you grace and peace.

Paul Gives Thanks to God

3 Let us give thanks to the God and Father of our Lord Jesus Christ, the merciful Father, the God from whom all help comes! 4 He helps us in all our troubles, so that we are able to help others who have all kinds of troubles, using the same help that we ourselves have received from God. 5 Just as we have a share in Christ's many sufferings, so also through Christ we share in God's great help. 6 If we suffer, it is for your help and salvation; if we are helped, then you too are helped and given the strength to endure with patience the same sufferings that we also endure. 7 So our hope in you is never shaken; we know that just as you share in our sufferings, you also share in the help we receive.

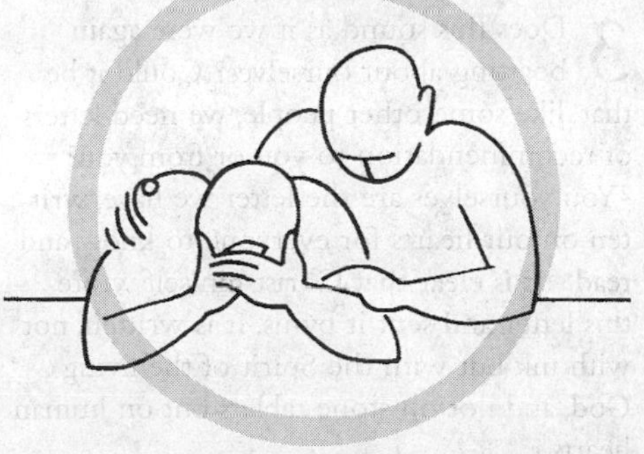

Help others who have all kinds of troubles. (1:4)

8 We want to remind you, friends, of the trouble we had in the province of Asia. The burdens laid upon us were so great and so heavy that we gave up all hope of staying alive. 9 We felt that the death sentence had been passed on us. But this happened so that we should rely, not on ourselves, but only on God, who raises the dead. 10 From such terrible dangers of death[a] he saved us, and will save us; and we have placed our hope in him that he will save us again, 11 as you help us by means of your prayers for us. So it will be that the many prayers for us will be answered, and God will bless us; and many will raise their voices to him in thanksgiving for us.

The Change in Paul's Plans

12 We are proud that our conscience assures us that our lives in this world, and especially our relations with you, have been ruled by God-given frankness[b] and sincerity, by the power of God's grace and not by human wisdom. 13-14 We write to you only what you can read and understand. But even though you now understand us only in part, I hope that you will come to understand us completely, so that in the Day of our Lord Jesus you can be as proud of us as we shall be of you.

15 I was so sure of all this that I made plans at first to visit you, in order that you might be blessed twice. 16 For I planned to visit you on my way to Macedonia and again on my way back, in order to get help from you for my trip to Judea. 17 In planning this, did I appear fickle? When I make my plans, do I make them from selfish motives, ready to say "Yes, yes" and "No, no" at the same time? 18 As surely as God speaks the truth, my promise to you was not a "Yes" and a "No." 19 For Jesus Christ, the Son of God, who was preached among you by Silas, Timothy, and myself, is not one who is "Yes" and "No." On the contrary, he is God's "Yes"; 20 for it is he who is the "Yes" to all of God's promises. This is why through Jesus Christ our "Amen" is said to the glory of God. 21 It is

[a] **1:10** terrible dangers of death; *some manuscripts have* terrible death. [b] **1:12** frankness; *some manuscripts have* holiness.

1:1 Acts 18:1 **1:8** 1 Cor 15:32 **1:16** Acts 19:21 **1:19** Acts 18:5

God himself who makes us, together with
you, sure of our life in union with Christ; it
is God himself who has set us apart, 22who
has placed his mark of ownership upon us,
and who has given us the Holy Spirit in our
hearts as the guarantee of all that he has in
store for us.

23I call God as my witness—he knows my
heart! It was in order to spare you that I
decided not to go to Corinth. 24We are not
trying to dictate to you what you must
believe; we know that you stand firm in the
faith. Instead, we are working with you for
your own happiness.

2 So I made up my mind not to come to
you again to make you sad. 2For if I
were to make you sad, who would be left to
cheer me up? Only the very persons I had
made sad. 3That is why I wrote that letter to
you—I did not want to come to you and be
made sad by the very people who should
make me glad. For I am convinced that
when I am happy, then all of you are happy
too. 4I wrote you with a greatly troubled and
distressed heart and with many tears; my
purpose was not to make you sad, but to
make you realize how much I love you all.

Forgiveness for the Offender

5Now, if anyone has made somebody sad,
he has not done it to me but to all of you—
in part, at least. (I say this because I do not
want to be too hard on him.) 6It is enough
that this person has been punished in this
way by most of you. 7Now, however, you
should forgive him and encourage him, in
order to keep him from becoming so sad as
to give up completely. 8And so I beg you to
let him know that you really do love him. 9I
wrote you that letter because I wanted to
find out how well you had stood the test and
whether you are always ready to obey my
instructions. 10When you forgive people for
what they have done, I forgive them too. For
when I forgive—if, indeed, I need to forgive
anything—I do it in Christ's presence
because of you, 11in order to keep Satan
from getting the upper hand over us; for we
know what his plans are.

Paul's Anxiety in Troas

12When I arrived in Troas to preach the
Good News about Christ, I found that the
Lord had opened the way for the work
there. 13But I was deeply worried, because I
could not find our brother Titus. So I said
good-bye to the people there and went on
to Macedonia.

Victory through Christ

14But thanks be to God! For in union
with Christ we are always led by God as
prisoners in Christ's victory procession. God
uses us to make the knowledge about Christ
spread everywhere like a sweet fragrance.
15For we are like a sweet-smelling incense
offered by Christ to God, which spreads
among those who are being saved and those
who are being lost. 16For those who are
being lost, it is a deadly stench that kills; but
for those who are being saved, it is a fra-
grance that brings life. Who, then, is capable
for such a task? 17We are not like so many
others, who handle God's message as if it
were cheap merchandise; but because God
has sent us, we speak with sincerity in his
presence, as servants of Christ.

Servants of the New Covenant

3 Does this sound as if we were again
boasting about ourselves? Could it be
that, like some other people, we need letters
of recommendation to you or from you?
2You yourselves are the letter we have, writ-
ten on our hearts for everyone to know and
read. 3It is clear that Christ himself wrote
this letter and sent it by us. It is written, not
with ink but with the Spirit of the living
God, and not on stone tablets but on human
hearts.

4We say this because we have confidence
in God through Christ. 5There is nothing in
us that allows us to claim that we are capable
of doing this work. The capacity we have
comes from God; 6it is he who made us
capable of serving the new covenant, which
consists not of a written law but of the Spir-

2:12, 13 Acts 20:1 **3:3** **a** Ex 24:12; **b** Jer 31:33; Ezek 11:19; 36:26 **3:6** Jer 31:31

it. The written law brings death, but the
Spirit gives life.
7The Law was carved in letters on stone
tablets, and God's glory appeared when it
was given. Even though the brightness on
Moses' face was fading, it was so strong that
the people of Israel could not keep their eyes
fixed on him. If the Law, which brings death
when it is in force, came with such glory,
8how much greater is the glory that belongs
to the activity of the Spirit! 9The system
which brings condemnation was glorious;
how much more glorious is the activity
which brings salvation! 10We may say that
because of the far brighter glory now the
glory that was so bright in the past is gone.
11For if there was glory in that which lasted
for a while, how much more glory is there
in that which lasts forever!
12Because we have this hope, we are very
bold. 13We are not like Moses, who had to
put a veil over his face so that the people of
Israel would not see the brightness fade and
disappear. 14Their minds, indeed, were
closed; and to this very day their minds are
covered with the same veil as they read the
books of the old covenant. The veil is
removed only when a person is joined to
Christ. 15Even today, whenever they read the
Law of Moses, the veil still covers their
minds. 16But it can be removed, as the scrip-
ture says about Moses: "His veil was removed
when he turned to the Lord."[c] 17Now, "the
Lord" in this passage is the Spirit; and where
the Spirit of the Lord is present, there is
freedom. 18All of us, then, reflect the glory
of the Lord with uncovered faces; and that
same glory, coming from the Lord, who is
the Spirit, transforms us into his likeness in
an ever greater degree of glory.

Spiritual Treasure in Clay Pots

4 God in his mercy has given us this work
to do, and so we do not become dis-
couraged. 2We put aside all secret and
shameful deeds; we do not act with deceit,
nor do we falsify the word of God. In the
full light of truth we live in God's sight and
try to commend ourselves to everyone's
good conscience. 3For if the gospel we
preach is hidden, it is hidden only from
those who are being lost. 4They do not
believe, because their minds have been kept
in the dark by the evil god of this world. He
keeps them from seeing the light shining on
them, the light that comes from the Good
News about the glory of Christ, who is the
exact likeness of God. 5For it is not ourselves
that we preach; we preach Jesus Christ as
Lord, and ourselves as your servants for Jesus'
sake. 6The God who said, "Out of darkness
the light shall shine!" is the same God who
made his light shine in our hearts, to bring
us the knowledge of God's glory shining in
the face of Christ.
7Yet we who have this spiritual treasure
are like common clay pots, in order to show
that the supreme power belongs to God, not
to us. 8We are often troubled, but not
crushed; sometimes in doubt, but never in
despair; 9there are many enemies, but we are
never without a friend; and though badly
hurt at times, we are not destroyed. 10At all
times we carry in our mortal bodies the
death of Jesus, so that his life also may be
seen in our bodies. 11Throughout our lives
we are always in danger of death for Jesus'
sake, in order that his life may be seen in this
mortal body of ours. 12This means that death
is at work in us, but life is at work in you.
13The scripture says, "I spoke because I
believed." In the same spirit of faith we also
speak because we believe. 14We know that
God, who raised the Lord Jesus to life, will
also raise us up with Jesus and take us,
together with you, into his presence. 15All
this is for your sake; and as God's grace
reaches more and more people, they will
offer to the glory of God more prayers of
thanksgiving.

Living by Faith

16For this reason we never become dis-
couraged. Even though our physical being is
gradually decaying, yet our spiritual being is
renewed day after day. 17And this small and
temporary trouble we suffer will bring us a
tremendous and eternal glory, much greater

[c] **3:16** *Verse 16 may be translated:* But the veil is removed whenever someone turns to the Lord.

3:7 Ex 34:29 **3:13** Ex 34:33 **3:16** Ex 34:34 **4:6** Gen 1:3 **4:13** Ps 116:10 (LXX)

Pray it!

Are You a Clay Pot?

"Yet we who have this spiritual treasure are like common clay pots" (2 Corinthians 4:7). Saint Paul knew the Jewish Scriptures. He knew that the prophet Isaiah describes us as clay in the hands of God, the potter (Isaiah 64:8).

Almighty God, our potter,
I am the work of your hands.
Even though I am like an ordinary clay pot,
you trust me to carry the wonderful treasure of Jesus, your Son.
Help me keep my body, mind, and soul healthy and strong
so that I am worthy of this great honor.
And keep me humble, always pointing others to Jesus
and not to myself.
Because I am just an ordinary clay pot
made beautiful by you living within me.
Amen.

— 2 Corinthians 4:5–7

than the trouble. 18 For we fix our attention,
not on things that are seen, but on things that
are unseen. What can be seen lasts only for a
time, but what cannot be seen lasts forever.

5 For we know that when this tent we
live in—our body here on earth—is
torn down, God will have a house in heaven
for us to live in, a home he himself has
made, which will last forever. 2 And now we
sigh, so great is our desire that our home
which comes from heaven should be put on
over us; 3 by being clothed with it we shall
not be without a body. 4 While we live in
this earthly tent, we groan with a feeling of
oppression; it is not that we want to get rid
of our earthly body, but that we want to
have the heavenly one put on over us, so
that what is mortal will be transformed by
life. 5 God is the one who has prepared us for
this change, and he gave us his Spirit as the
guarantee of all that he has in store for us.

6 So we are always full of courage. We
know that as long as we are at home in the
body we are away from the Lord's home.
7 For our life is a matter of faith, not of sight.
8 We are full of courage and would much
prefer to leave our home in the body and be
at home with the Lord. 9 More than anything
else, however, we want to please him,
whether in our home here or there. 10 For all
of us must appear before Christ, to be
judged by him. We will each receive what
we deserve, according to everything we have
done, good or bad, in our bodily life.

Friendship with God through Christ

11 We know what it means to fear the
Lord, and so we try to persuade others. God
knows us completely, and I hope that in
your hearts you know me as well. 12 We are
not trying again to recommend ourselves to
you; rather, we are trying to give you a good
reason to be proud of us, so that you will be
able to answer those who boast about peo-
ple's appearance and not about their charac-
ter. 13 Are we really insane? It is for God's
sake. Or are we sane? Then it is for your

5:1 Wis 9:15 **5:10** Rom 14:10

sake. 14We are ruled by the love of Christ,
now that we recognize that one man died
for everyone, which means that they all share
in his death. 15He died for all, so that those
who live should no longer live for them-
selves, but only for him who died and was
raised to life for their sake.

16No longer, then, do we judge anyone by
human standards. Even if at one time we
judged Christ according to human standards,
we no longer do so. 17Anyone who is joined
to Christ is a new being; the old is gone, the
new has come. 18All this is done by God,
who through Christ changed us from ene-
mies into his friends and gave us the task of
making others his friends also. 19Our mes-
sage is that God was making all human
beings his friends through Christ.[d] God did
not keep an account of their sins, and he has
given us the message which tells how he
makes them his friends.

20Here we are, then, speaking for Christ,
as though God himself were making his
appeal through us. We plead on Christ's
behalf: let God change you from enemies
into his friends! 21Christ was without sin,
but for our sake God made him share our
sin in order that in union with him we
might share the righteousness of God.

6 In our work together with God, then, we
beg you who have received God's grace
not to let it be wasted. 2Hear what God says:

"When the time came for me to show
 you favor,
 I heard you;
when the day arrived for me to save you,
 I helped you."

Listen! This is the hour to receive God's
favor; today is the day to be saved!

3We do not want anyone to find fault
with our work, so we try not to put obsta-
cles in anyone's way. 4Instead, in everything
we do we show that we are God's servants
by patiently enduring troubles, hardships, and
difficulties. 5We have been beaten, jailed, and
mobbed; we have been overworked and have
gone without sleep or food. 6By our purity,
knowledge, patience, and kindness we have
shown ourselves to be God's servants—by
the Holy Spirit, by our true love, 7by our
message of truth, and by the power of God.
We have righteousness as our weapon, both
to attack and to defend ourselves. 8We are
honored and disgraced; we are insulted and
praised. We are treated as liars, yet we speak
the truth; 9as unknown, yet we are known
by all; as though we were dead, but, as you
see, we live on. Although punished, we are
not killed; 10although saddened, we are
always glad; we seem poor, but we make
many people rich; we seem to have nothing,
yet we really possess everything.

11Dear friends in Corinth! We have spo-
ken frankly to you; we have opened our
hearts wide. 12It is not we who have closed
our hearts to you; it is you who have closed
your hearts to us. 13I speak now as though
you were my children: show us the same
feelings that we have for you. Open your
hearts wide!

Warning against Pagan Influences

14Do not try to work together as equals
with unbelievers, for it cannot be done. How
can right and wrong be partners? How can
light and darkness live together? 15How can
Christ and the Devil agree? What does a
believer have in common with an unbeliev-
er? 16How can God's temple come to terms
with pagan idols? For we are the temple of
the living God! As God himself has said,

"I will make my home with my people
 and live among them;
I will be their God,
 and they shall be my people."

17And so the Lord says,

"You must leave them
 and separate yourselves from them.
Have nothing to do with what is unclean,
 and I will accept you.
18I will be your father,
 and you shall be my sons and
 daughters,
 says the Lord Almighty."

[d] **5:19** God was making all human beings his friends through Christ; *or* God was in Christ making all human beings his friends.

6:2 Isa 49:8 **6:5** Acts 16:23 **6:16 a** 1 Cor 3:16; 6:19; **b** Lev 26:12; Ezek 37:27 **6:17** Isa 52:11
6:18 2 Sam 7:14; 1 Chr 17:13; Isa 43:6; Jer 31:9

7 All these promises are made to us, my
dear friends. So then, let us purify our-
selves from everything that makes body or
soul unclean, and let us be completely holy
by living in awe of God.

Paul's Joy

2Make room for us in your hearts. We
have wronged no one; we have ruined no
one, nor tried to take advantage of anyone.
3I do not say this to condemn you; for, as I
have said before, you are so dear to us that
we are always together, whether we live or
die. 4I am so sure of you; I take such pride in
you! In all our troubles I am still full of
courage; I am running over with joy.

5Even after we arrived in Macedonia, we
did not have any rest. There were troubles
everywhere, quarrels with others, fears in our
hearts. 6But God, who encourages the
downhearted, encouraged us with the com-
ing of Titus. 7It was not only his coming that
cheered us, but also his report of how you
encouraged him. He told us how much you
want to see me, how sorry you are, how
ready you are to defend me; and so I am
even happier now.

8For even if that letter of mine made you
sad, I am not sorry I wrote it. I could have
been sorry when I saw that it made you sad
for a while. 9But now I am happy—not
because I made you sad, but because your
sadness made you change your ways. That
sadness was used by God, and so we caused
you no harm. 10For the sadness that is used
by God brings a change of heart that leads
to salvation—and there is no regret in that!
But sadness that is merely human causes
death. 11See what God did with this sadness
of yours: how earnest it has made you, how
eager to prove your innocence! Such indig-
nation, such alarm, such feelings, such devo-
tion, such readiness to punish wrongdoing!
You have shown yourselves to be without
fault in the whole matter.

12So, even though I wrote that letter, it
was not because of the one who did wrong
or the one who was wronged. Instead, I
wrote it to make plain to you, in God's sight,
how deep your devotion to us really is.
13That is why we were encouraged.

Not only were we encouraged; how
happy Titus made us with his happiness over
the way in which all of you helped to cheer
him up! 14I did boast of you to him, and you
have not disappointed me. We have always
spoken the truth to you, and in the same
way the boast we made to Titus has proved
true. 15And so his love for you grows
stronger, as he remembers how all of you
were ready to obey his instructions, how you
welcomed him with fear and trembling.
16How happy I am that I can depend on you
completely!

Christian Giving

8 Our friends, we want you to know
what God's grace has accomplished in
the churches in Macedonia. 2They have
been severely tested by the troubles they
went through; but their joy was so great that
they were extremely generous in their giv-
ing, even though they are very poor. 3I can
assure you that they gave as much as they
could, and even more than they could. Of
their own free will 4they begged us and
pleaded for the privilege of having a part in
helping God's people in Judea. 5It was more
than we could have hoped for! First they
gave themselves to the Lord; and then, by
God's will they gave themselves to us as well.
6So we urged Titus, who began this work, to
continue it and help you complete this spe-
cial service of love. 7You are so rich in all
you have: in faith, speech, and knowledge, in
your eagerness to help and in your love for
us.[e] And so we want you to be generous also
in this service of love.

8I am not laying down any rules. But by
showing how eager others are to help, I am
trying to find out how real your own love is.
9You know the grace of our Lord Jesus
Christ; rich as he was, he made himself poor
for your sake, in order to make you rich by
means of his poverty.

10My opinion is that it is better for you to
finish now what you began last year. You
were the first, not only to act, but also to be

[e] **8:7** your love for us; *some manuscripts have* our love for you.

7:5 2 Cor 2:13 **8:1–4** Rom 15:26

willing to act. 11 On with it, then, and finish the job! Be as eager to finish it as you were to plan it, and do it with what you now have. 12 If you are eager to give, God will accept your gift on the basis of what you have to give, not on what you don't have.

13-14 I am not trying to relieve others by putting a burden on you; but since you have plenty at this time, it is only fair that you should help those who are in need. Then, when you are in need and they have plenty, they will help you. In this way both are treated equally. 15 As the scripture says, "The one who gathered much did not have too much, and the one who gathered little did not have too little."

Titus and His Companions

16 How we thank God for making Titus as eager as we are to help you! 17 Not only did he welcome our request; he was so eager to help that of his own free will he decided to go to you. 18 With him we are sending the brother who is highly respected in all the churches for his work in preaching the gospel. 19 And besides that, he has been chosen and appointed by the churches to travel with us as we carry out this service of love for the sake of the Lord's glory and in order to show that we want to help.

20 We are being careful not to stir up any complaints about the way we handle this generous gift. 21 Our purpose is to do what is right, not only in the sight of the Lord, but also in the sight of others.

22 So we are sending our brother with them; we have tested him many times and found him always very eager to help. And now that he has so much confidence in you, he is all the more eager to help. 23 As for Titus, he is my partner and works with me to help you; as for the other brothers who are going with him, they represent the churches and bring glory to Christ. 24 Show your love to them, so that all the churches will be sure of it and know that we are right in boasting about you.

Help for Needy Believers

9 There is really no need for me to write you about the help being sent to God's people in Judea. 2 I know that you are willing to help, and I have boasted of you to the people in Macedonia. "The believers in Achaia," I said, "have been ready to help since last year." Your eagerness has stirred up most of them. 3 Now I am sending these believers, so that our boasting about you in this matter may not turn out to be empty words. But, just as I said, you will be ready with your help. 4 However, if the people from Macedonia should come with me and find out that you are not ready, how ashamed we would be—not to speak of your shame—for feeling so sure of you! 5 So I thought it was necessary to urge these believers to go to you ahead of me and get ready in advance the gift you promised to make. Then it will be ready when I arrive, and it will show that you give because you want to, not because you have to.

6 Remember that the person who plants few seeds will have a small crop; the one who plants many seeds will have a large crop. 7 You should each give, then, as you have decided, not with regret or out of a sense of duty; for God loves the one who gives gladly. 8 And God is able to give you more than you need, so that you will always have all you need for yourselves and more than enough for every good cause. 9 As the scripture says,

> "He gives generously to the needy;
> his kindness lasts forever."

10 And God, who supplies seed for the sower and bread to eat, will also supply you with all the seed you need and will make it grow and produce a rich harvest from your generosity. 11 He will always make you rich enough to be generous at all times, so that many will thank God for your gifts which they receive from us. 12 For this service you perform not only meets the needs of God's people, but also produces an outpouring of gratitude to God. 13 And because of the proof which this service of yours brings, many will give glory to God for your loyalty to the gospel of Christ, which you profess, and for your generosity in sharing with them

8:15 Ex 16:18 **8:21** Prov 3:4 (LXX) **9:7** Sir 20:10–15 **9:9** Ps 112:9 **9:10** Isa 55:10

and everyone else. 14And so with deep affec-
tion they will pray for you because of the
extraordinary grace God has shown you.
15Let us thank God for his priceless gift!

Paul Defends His Ministry

10 I, Paul, make a personal appeal to
you—I who am said to be meek and
mild when I am with you, but harsh with
you when I am away. By the gentleness and
kindness of Christ 2I beg you not to force
me to be harsh when I come; for I am sure I
can deal harshly with those who say that we
act from worldly motives. 3It is true that we
live in the world, but we do not fight from
worldly motives. 4The weapons we use in
our fight are not the world's weapons but
God's powerful weapons, which we use to
destroy strongholds. We destroy false argu-
ments; 5we pull down every proud obstacle
that is raised against the knowledge of God;
we take every thought captive and make it
obey Christ. 6And after you have proved
your complete loyalty, we will be ready to
punish any act of disloyalty.

7You are looking at the outward appear-
ance of things. Are there some there who
reckon themselves to belong to Christ? Well,
let them think again about themselves,
because we belong to Christ just as much as
they do. 8For I am not ashamed, even if I
have boasted somewhat too much about the
authority that the Lord has given us—
authority to build you up, not to tear you
down. 9I do not want it to appear that I am
trying to frighten you with my letters.
10Someone will say, "Paul's letters are severe
and strong, but when he is with us in per-
son, he is weak, and his words are nothing!"
11Such a person must understand that there
is no difference between what we write in
our letters when we are away and what we
will do when we are there with you.

12Of course we would not dare classify
ourselves or compare ourselves with those
who rate themselves so highly. How stupid
they are! They make up their own standards
to measure themselves by, and they judge
themselves by their own standards! 13As for

Preach the Good News in other countries beyond you. (10:16)

us, however, our boasting will not go beyond
certain limits; it will stay within the limits of
the work which God has set for us, and this
includes our work among you. 14And since
you are within those limits, we were not
going beyond them when we came to you,
bringing the Good News about Christ. 15So
we do not boast about the work that others
have done beyond the limits God set for us.
Instead, we hope that your faith may grow
and that we may be able to do a much
greater work among you, always within the
limits that God has set. 16Then we can
preach the Good News in other countries
beyond you and shall not have to boast about
work already done in someone else's field.

17But as the scripture says, "Whoever
wants to boast must boast about what the
Lord has done." 18For it is when the Lord
thinks well of us that we are really approved,
and not when we think well of ourselves.

Paul and the False Apostles

11 I wish you would tolerate me, even
when I am a bit foolish. Please do!
2I am jealous for you, just as God is; you are
like a pure virgin whom I have promised in
marriage to one man only, Christ himself. 3I
am afraid that your minds will be corrupted
and that you will abandon your full and pure
devotion to Christ—in the same way that
Eve was deceived by the snake's clever lies.
4For you gladly tolerate anyone who comes
to you and preaches a different Jesus, not the
one we preached; and you accept a spirit and

10:17 Jer 9:24 **11:3** Gen 3:1–5, 13

a gospel completely different from the Spirit and the gospel you received from us!

5I do not think that I am the least bit inferior to those very special so-called "apostles" of yours! 6Perhaps I am an amateur in speaking, but certainly not in knowledge; we have made this clear to you at all times and in all conditions.

7I did not charge you a thing when I preached the Good News of God to you; I humbled myself in order to make you important. Was that wrong of me? 8While I was working among you, I was paid by other churches. I was robbing them, so to speak, in order to help you. 9And during the time I was with you I did not bother you for help when I needed money; the believers who came from Macedonia brought me everything I needed. As in the past, so in the future: I will never be a burden to you! 10By Christ's truth in me, I promise that this boast of mine will not be silenced anywhere in all of Achaia. 11Do I say this because I don't love you? God knows I love you!

12I will go on doing what I am doing now, in order to keep those other "apostles" from having any reason for boasting and saying that they work in the same way that we do. 13Those men are not true apostles—they are false apostles, who lie about their work and disguise themselves to look like real apostles of Christ. 14Well, no wonder! Even Satan can disguise himself to look like an angel of light! 15So it is no great thing if his servants disguise themselves to look like servants of righteousness. In the end they will get exactly what their actions deserve.

Paul's Sufferings as an Apostle

16I repeat: no one should think that I am a fool. But if you do, at least accept me as a fool, just so I will have a little to boast of. 17Of course what I am saying now is not what the Lord would have me say; in this matter of boasting I am really talking like a fool. 18But since there are so many who boast for merely human reasons, I will do the same. 19You yourselves are so wise, and so you gladly tolerate fools! 20You tolerate anyone who

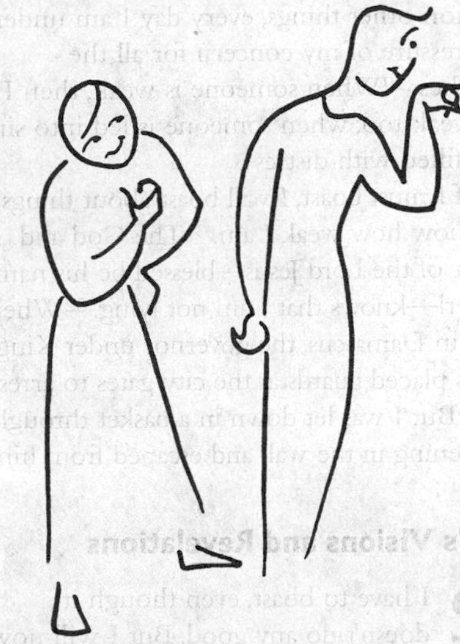

Satan can disguise himself. (11:14)

orders you around or takes advantage of you or traps you or looks down on you or slaps you in the face. 21I am ashamed to admit that we were too timid to do those things!

But if anyone dares to boast about something—I am talking like a fool—I will be just as daring. 22Are they Hebrews? So am I. Are they Israelites? So am I. Are they Abraham's descendants? So am I. 23Are they Christ's servants? I sound like a madman—but I am a better servant than they are! I have worked much harder, I have been in prison more times, I have been whipped much more, and I have been near death more often. 24Five times I was given the thirty-nine lashes by the Jews; 25three times I was whipped by the Romans; and once I was stoned. I have been in three shipwrecks, and once I spent twenty-four hours in the water. 26In my many travels I have been in danger from floods and from robbers, in danger from my own people and from Gentiles; there have been dangers in the cities, dangers in the wilds, dangers on the high seas, and dangers from false friends. 27There has been work and toil; often I have gone without sleep; I have been hungry and thirsty; I have often been without enough food, shelter, or clothing. 28And not to

11:9 Phil 4:15–18 **11:23** Acts 16:23 **11:24** Deut 25:3 **11:25 a** Acts 16:22; **b** Acts 14:19 **11:26 a** Acts 9:23; **b** Acts 14:5

mention other things, every day I am under
the pressure of my concern for all the
churches. 29When someone is weak, then I
feel weak too; when someone is led into sin,
I am filled with distress.
30If I must boast, I will boast about things
that show how weak I am. 31The God and
Father of the Lord Jesus—blessed be his name
forever!—knows that I am not lying. 32When
I was in Damascus, the governor under King
Aretas placed guards at the city gates to arrest
me. 33But I was let down in a basket through
an opening in the wall and escaped from him.

Paul's Visions and Revelations

12 I have to boast, even though it
doesn't do any good. But I will now
talk about visions and revelations given me
by the Lord. 2I know a certain Christian
man who fourteen years ago was snatched
up to the highest heaven (I do not know
whether this actually happened or whether
he had a vision—only God knows). 3-4I
repeat, I know that this man was snatched to
Paradise (again, I do not know whether this
actually happened or whether it was a
vision—only God knows), and there he
heard things which cannot be put into
words, things that human lips may not speak.
5So I will boast about this man—but I will
not boast about myself, except the things
that show how weak I am. 6If I wanted to
boast, I would not be a fool, because I would
be telling the truth. But I will not boast,
because I do not want any of you to have a
higher opinion of me than you have as a
result of what you have seen me do and
heard me say.
7But to keep me from being puffed up
with pride because of the many wonderful
things I saw, I was given a painful physical
ailment, which acts as Satan's messenger to
beat me and keep me from being proud.
8Three times I prayed to the Lord about this
and asked him to take it away. 9But his
answer was: "My grace is all you need, for
my power is greatest when you are weak."
I am most happy, then, to be proud of my
weaknesses, in order to feel the protection of
Christ's power over me. 10I am content with
weaknesses, insults, hardships, persecutions,
and difficulties for Christ's sake. For when I
am weak, then I am strong.

Paul's Concern for the Corinthians

11I am acting like a fool—but you have
made me do it. You are the ones who ought
to show your approval of me. For even if I
am nothing, I am in no way inferior to those
very special "apostles" of yours. 12The many
miracles and wonders that prove that I am an
apostle were performed among you with
much patience. 13How were you treated any
worse than the other churches, except that I
did not bother you for financial help? Please
forgive me for being so unfair!
14This is now the third time that I am
ready to come to visit you—and I will not
make any demands on you. It is you I want,
not your money. After all, children should
not have to provide for their parents, but
parents should provide for their children. 15I
will be glad to spend all I have, and myself as
well, in order to help you. Will you love me
less because I love you so much?
16You will agree, then, that I was not a
burden to you. But someone will say that
I was tricky, and trapped you with lies.
17How? Did I take advantage of you through
any of the messengers I sent? 18I begged
Titus to go, and I sent the other believer
with him. Would you say that Titus took
advantage of you? Do not he and I act from
the very same motives and behave in the
same way?
19Perhaps you think that all along we have
been trying to defend ourselves before you.
No! We speak as Christ would have us speak
in the presence of God, and everything we
do, dear friends, is done to help you. 20I am
afraid that when I get there I will find you
different from what I would like you to be
and you will find me different from what
you would like me to be. I am afraid that I
will find quarreling and jealousy, hot tempers
and selfishness, insults and gossip, pride and
disorder. 21I am afraid that the next time I
come my God will humiliate me in your

11:32, 33 Acts 9:23–25

presence, and I shall weep over many who
sinned in the past and have not repented of
the immoral things they have done—their
lust and their sexual sins.

Final Warnings and Greetings

13 This is now the third time that I am
coming to visit you. "Any accusation
must be upheld by the evidence of two or
more witnesses"—as the scripture says. 2 I
want to tell those of you who have sinned in
the past, and all the others; I said it before
during my second visit to you, but I will say
it again now that I am away: the next time I
come nobody will escape punishment. 3 You
will have all the proof you want that Christ
speaks through me. When he deals with you,
he is not weak; instead, he shows his power
among you. 4 For even though it was in
weakness that he was put to death on the
cross, it is by God's power that he lives. In
union with him we also are weak; but in our
relations with you we shall share God's
power in his life.
5 Put yourselves to the test and judge
yourselves, to find out whether you are liv-
ing in faith. Surely you know that Christ
Jesus is in you?—unless you have completely
failed. 6 I trust you will know that we are not
failures. 7 We pray to God that you will do
no wrong—not in order to show that we are
a success, but so that you may do what is
right, even though we may seem to be fail-
ures. 8 For we cannot do a thing against the
truth, but only for it. 9 We are glad when we
are weak but you are strong. And so we also
pray that you will become perfect. 10 That is
why I write this while I am away from you;
it is so that when I arrive I will not have to
deal harshly with you in using the authority
that the Lord has given me—authority to
build you up, not to tear you down.
11 And now, my friends, good-bye! Strive
for perfection; listen to my appeals; agree
with one another; live in peace. And the
God of love and peace will be with you.
12 Greet one another with the kiss of
peace.

All of God's people send you their greet-
ings.
13 The grace of the Lord Jesus Christ, the
love of God, and the fellowship of the Holy
Spirit be with you all.

13:1 Deut 17:6; 19:15

The Letter to the Galatians

Do you sometimes know what your mom, dad, or teacher is feeling just by their voice? The people of Galatia knew what Paul was feeling just by reading the first few paragraphs of this letter: *angry!*

The Galatians were a group of people Paul had visited. When he visited them, he helped them learn about Jesus and probably set up house-churches. After Paul left, some of those he taught started to change the way they acted and who they believed. When Paul heard about their behavior, he wrote this letter. He wrote it to remind them of the importance of faith and to get them back on track.

Chap. 2:11–14

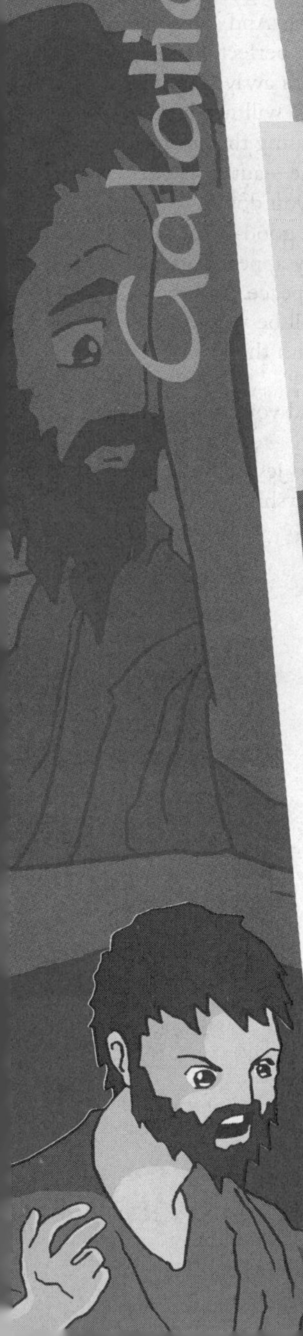

Headlines

- An Angry Message (1:6–10)
- Paul Defends His Role as Apostle (1:11—2:14)
- Galatians Warned That Only Faith Saves (3:1–14)
- Galatians Told to Live Like Christians! (5:16–26)

FACTOIDS

Who wrote this book? Saint Paul, after his missionary trip to Galatia.

When was it written? Around AD 54 to 55, about twenty years after Jesus' Resurrection.

Who was it written for? Paul wrote this letter to the Gentile (non-Jewish) Christians in Galatia who were being influenced by missionaries who were preaching something different from what Paul had taught.

Why was it written? Paul wrote to remind the Galatians that they must live by faith in Christ and that non-Jewish Christians were not required to follow Jewish ceremonial laws.

Jesus connection. Paul reminds the Galatians of Jesus' commandment to love one another (5:1–15).

Important themes

- Salvation comes from faith, not just from following rules.
- All God's children are equal and have the same rights and responsibilities.
- Living as faithful Christians means loving and caring for one another.

GALATIANS

1 From Paul, whose call to be an apostle
did not come from human beings or by
human means, but from Jesus Christ and
God the Father, who raised him from death.
2 All the believers who are here join me in
sending greetings to the churches of Galatia:
3 May God our Father and the Lord Jesus
Christ give you grace and peace.
4 In order to set us free from this present
evil age, Christ gave himself for our sins, in
obedience to the will of our God and
Father. 5 To God be the glory forever and
ever! Amen.

The One Gospel

6 I am surprised at you! In no time at all
you are deserting the one who called you by
the grace of Christ,[a] and are accepting
another gospel. 7 Actually, there is no "other
gospel," but I say this because there are some
people who are upsetting you and trying to
change the gospel of Christ. 8 But even if we
or an angel from heaven should preach to
you a gospel that is different from the one
we preached to you, may he be condemned
to hell! 9 We have said it before, and now I
say it again: if anyone preaches to you a
gospel that is different from the one you
accepted, may he be condemned to hell!
10 Does this sound as if I am trying to win
human approval? No indeed! What I want is
God's approval! Am I trying to be popular
with people? If I were still trying to do so,
I would not be a servant of Christ.

How Paul Became an Apostle

11 Let me tell you, my friends, that the
gospel I preach is not of human origin. 12 I
did not receive it from any human being,
nor did anyone teach it to me. It was Jesus
Christ himself who revealed it to me.
13 You have been told how I used to live
when I was devoted to the Jewish religion,
how I persecuted without mercy the church
of God and did my best to destroy it. 14 I was
ahead of most other Jews of my age in my
practice of the Jewish religion, and was
much more devoted to the traditions of our
ancestors.
15 But God in his grace chose me even
before I was born, and called me to serve
him. And when he decided 16 to reveal his
Son to me, so that I might preach the Good
News about him to the Gentiles, I did not
go to anyone for advice, 17 nor did I go to
Jerusalem to see those who were apostles
before me. Instead, I went at once to Arabia,
and then I returned to Damascus. 18 It was
three years later that I went to Jerusalem to
obtain information from Peter, and I stayed
with him for two weeks. 19 I did not see any
other apostle except James,[b] the Lord's
brother.
20 What I write is true. God knows that I
am not lying!
21 Afterward I went to places in Syria and
Cilicia. 22 At that time the members of the
churches in Judea did not know me person-
ally. 23 They knew only what others were
saying: "The man who used to persecute us
is now preaching the faith that he once tried
to destroy!" 24 And so they praised God
because of me.

Paul and the Other Apostles

2 Fourteen years later I went back to
Jerusalem with Barnabas, taking Titus
along with me. 2 I went because God
revealed to me that I should go. In a private
meeting with the leaders I explained the
gospel message that I preach to the Gentiles.
I did not want my work in the past or in the
present to be a failure. 3 My companion
Titus, even though he is Greek, was not
forced to be circumcised, 4 although some

[a] **1:6** by the grace of Christ; *some manuscripts have* by his grace. [b] **1:19** any other apostle except James; *or* any other apostle; the only other person I saw was James.

1:13 Acts 8:3; 22:4, 5; 26:9–11 **1:14** Acts 22:3 **1:15, 16** Acts 9:3–6; 22:6–10; 26:13–18 **1:18** Acts 9:26–30 **2:1** Acts 11:30; 15:2

Salvation by Faith

Catholic Connections

Do you know someone who does things to look like they have a good and honest life but when you talk to them, it seems like something is missing? They may be missing an important part of a relationship with God: faith. In Galatians Saint Paul insists that having faith in Jesus Christ as our Savior is what saves us from sin and death. The Old Law that emphasized doing the right things is not enough. Because of original sin we can never live perfectly. Our own actions alone will never restore our true relationship with God.

The Catholic Church teaches that actions are important but faith is necessary for salvation. Salvation means our relationship with God is restored to what God intended from the beginning. This means that you can do all sorts of things to look like you have a good life, but it is faith that is the first step toward salvation.

— Galatians 2:15—3:5

wanted it done. Pretending to be believers,
these men slipped into our group as spies, in
order to find out about the freedom we have
through our union with Christ Jesus. They
wanted to make slaves of us, 5but in order to
keep the truth of the gospel safe for you, we
did not give in to them for a minute.
6But those who seemed to be the leaders—
I say this because it makes no difference to me
what they were; God does not judge by outward appearances—those leaders, I say, made
no new suggestions to me. 7On the contrary,
they saw that God had given me the task of
preaching the gospel to the Gentiles, just as
he had given Peter the task of preaching the
gospel to the Jews. 8For by God's power I was
made an apostle to the Gentiles, just as Peter
was made an apostle to the Jews. 9James, Peter,
and John, who seemed to be the leaders, recognized that God had given me this special
task; so they shook hands with Barnabas and
me, as a sign that we were all partners. We
agreed that Barnabas and I would work
among the Gentiles and they among the Jews.
10All they asked was that we should remember the needy in their group, which is the
very thing I have[c] been eager to do.

Paul Rebukes Peter at Antioch

11But when Peter came to Antioch, I
opposed him in public, because he was clearly wrong. 12Before some men who had been
sent by James arrived there, Peter had been
eating with the Gentile believers. But after
these men arrived, he drew back and would
not eat with the Gentiles, because he was
afraid of those who were in favor of circumcising them. 13The other Jewish believers
also started acting like cowards along with
Peter; and even Barnabas was swept along by
their cowardly action. 14When I saw that
they were not walking a straight path in line
with the truth of the gospel, I said to Peter
in front of them all, "You are a Jew, yet you
have been living like a Gentile, not like a

[c] **2:10** have; *or* had.
2:6 Deut 10:17

Saint Paul sure could get upset when people were falling away from the truth. Read Galatians 3:1–4 to find out just how mad he was.

Jew. How, then, can you try to force Gentiles
to live like Jews?"

Jews and Gentiles Are Saved by Faith

15Indeed, we are Jews by birth and not
"Gentile sinners," as they are called. 16Yet we
know that a person is put right with God
only through faith in Jesus Christ, never by
doing what the Law requires. We, too, have
believed in Christ Jesus in order to be put
right with God through our faith in Christ,
and not by doing what the Law requires. For
no one is put right with God by doing what
the Law requires. 17If, then, as we try to be
put right with God by our union with
Christ, we are found to be sinners, as much as
the Gentiles are—does this mean that Christ
is serving the cause of sin? By no means! 18If
I start to rebuild the system of Law that I tore
down, then I show myself to be someone
who breaks the Law. 19So far as the Law is
concerned, however, I am dead—killed by the
Law itself—in order that I might live for
God. I have been put to death with Christ on
his cross, 20so that it is no longer I who live,
but it is Christ who lives in me. This life that I
live now, I live by faith in the Son of God,
who loved me and gave his life for me. 21I
refuse to reject the grace of God. But if a per-
son is put right with God through the Law, it
means that Christ died for nothing!

Law or Faith

3 You foolish Galatians! Who put a spell
on you? Before your very eyes you had
a clear description of the death of Jesus
Christ on the cross! 2Tell me this one thing:
did you receive God's Spirit by doing what
the Law requires or by hearing the gospel
and believing it? 3How can you be so fool-
ish! You began by God's Spirit; do you now
want to finish by your own power? 4Did all
your experience mean nothing at all? Surely
it meant something! 5Does God give you
the Spirit and work miracles among you
because you do what the Law requires or
because you hear the gospel and believe it?

6Consider the experience of Abraham; as
the scripture says, "He believed God, and
because of his faith God accepted him as
righteous." 7You should realize, then, that the
real descendants of Abraham are the people
who have faith. 8The scripture predicted that
God would put the Gentiles right with him-
self through faith. And so the scripture
announced the Good News to Abraham:
"Through you God will bless all people."
9Abraham believed and was blessed; so all
who believe are blessed as he was.

10Those who depend on obeying the Law
live under a curse. For the scripture says,
"Whoever does not always obey everything
that is written in the book of the Law is under
God's curse!" 11Now, it is clear that no one is
put right with God by means of the Law,
because the scripture says, "Only the person
who is put right with God through faith shall
live."[d] 12But the Law has nothing to do with
faith. Instead, as the scripture says, "Whoever
does everything the Law requires will live."

13But by becoming a curse for us Christ
has redeemed us from the curse that the Law
brings; for the scripture says, "Anyone who is
hanged on a tree is under God's curse."
14Christ did this in order that the blessing
which God promised to Abraham might be
given to the Gentiles by means of Christ
Jesus, so that through faith we might receive
the Spirit promised by God.

The Law and the Promise

15My friends, I am going to use an every-
day example: when two people agree on a
matter and sign an agreement, no one can
break it or add anything to it. 16Now, God
made his promises to Abraham and to his
descendant. The scripture does not use the
plural "descendants," meaning many people,
but the singular "descendant," meaning one
person only, namely, Christ. 17What I mean
is that God made a covenant with Abraham
and promised to keep it. The Law, which was
given four hundred and thirty years later,
cannot break that covenant and cancel God's
promise. 18For if God's gift depends on the

[d] **3:11** put right with God through faith shall live; *or* put right with God shall live through faith.

2:16 a Ps 143:2; Rom 3:20; **b** Rom 3:22 **3:6** Gen 15:6; Rom 4:3 **3:7** Rom 4:16 **3:8** Gen 12:3
3:10 Deut 27:26 (LXX) **3:11** Hab 2:4 **3:12** Lev 18:5 **3:13** Deut 21:23 **3:17** Ex 12:40 **3:18** Rom 4:14

Study it!

Who Is Equal?

Sometimes in the Old Testament, some people are treated better than others. Men had more freedom and privileges than women. People who were wealthy enough to own slaves thought God favored them over poor people. Jewish people believed that God favored them over all other peoples.

Jesus' message of equality and his new commandment to love one another changed that thinking. His message that all people are equally loved by God was scary to the Jews who had been living with the Old Law. Paul had to remind the Galatians that his teaching about faith, and not the Old Law his opponents were trying to bring back, was the truth revealed by Jesus. Paul reminded the Galatians that equality was one of the cornerstones of Jesus' message. Paul's list included gender (man and woman), religion (Jews and Gentiles), and status (free or slave). What categories would Paul write about if he looked at our society?

— Galatians 3:26–29

Law, then it no longer depends on his prom-
ise. However, it was because of his promise
that God gave that gift to Abraham.
19 What, then, was the purpose of the Law?
It was added in order to show what wrongdo-
ing is, and it was meant to last until the com-
ing of Abraham's descendant, to whom the
promise was made. The Law was handed down
by angels, with a man acting as a go-between.
20 But a go-between is not needed when only
one person is involved; and God is one.[e]

The Purpose of the Law

21 Does this mean that the Law is against
God's promises? No, not at all! For if human
beings had received a law that could bring
life, then everyone could be put right with
God by obeying it. 22 But the scripture says
that the whole world is under the power of
sin; and so the gift which is promised on the
basis of faith in Jesus Christ is given to those
who believe.
23 But before the time for faith came, the
Law kept us all locked up as prisoners until
this coming faith should be revealed. 24 And
so the Law was in charge of us until Christ
came, in order that we might then be put
right with God through faith. 25 Now that
the time for faith is here, the Law is no
longer in charge of us.
26 It is through faith that all of you are
God's children in union with Christ Jesus.
27 You were baptized into union with Christ,
and now you are clothed, so to speak, with
the life of Christ himself. 28 So there is no
difference between Jews and Gentiles,
between slaves and free people, between men
and women; you are all one in union with
Christ Jesus. 29 If you belong to Christ, then

You are all one in union with Christ Jesus. (3:28)

[e] **3:20** and God is one; *or* and God acts alone.

3:29 Rom 4:13

you are the descendants of Abraham and will receive what God has promised.

4 But now to continue—the son who will receive his father's property is treated just like a slave while he is young, even though he really owns everything. 2While he is young, there are men who take care of him and manage his affairs until the time set by his father. 3In the same way, we too were slaves of the ruling spirits of the universe before we reached spiritual maturity. 4But when the right time finally came, God sent his own Son. He came as the son of a human mother and lived under the Jewish Law, 5to redeem those who were under the Law, so that we might become God's children.

6To show that you are[f] his children, God sent the Spirit of his Son into our hearts, the Spirit who cries out, "Father, my Father." 7So then, you are no longer a slave but a child. And since you are his child, God will give you all that he has for his children.

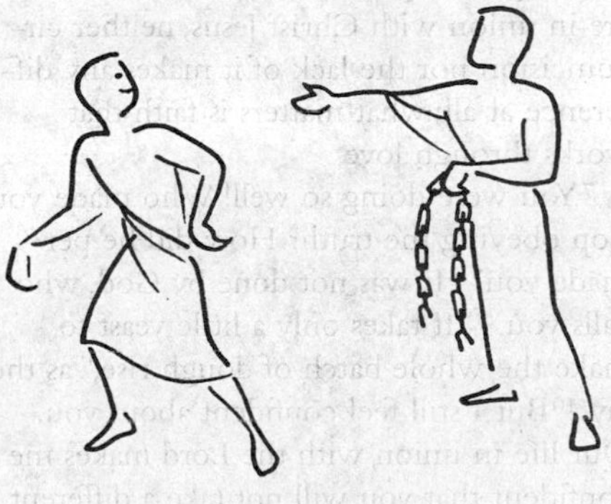

You are not longer a slave. (4:7)

Paul's Concern for the Galatians

8In the past you did not know God, and so you were slaves of beings who are not gods. 9But now that you know God—or, I should say, now that God knows you—how is it that you want to turn back to those weak and pitiful ruling spirits? Why do you want to become their slaves all over again? 10You pay special attention to certain days, months, seasons, and years. 11I am worried about you! Can it be that all my work for you has been for nothing?

12I beg you, my friends, be like me. After all, I am like you. You have not done me any wrong. 13You remember why I preached the gospel to you the first time; it was because I was sick. 14But even though my physical condition was a great trial to you, you did not despise or reject me. Instead, you received me as you would an angel from heaven; you received me as you would Christ Jesus. 15You were so happy! What has happened? I myself can say that you would have taken out your own eyes, if you could, and given them to me. 16Have I now become your enemy by telling you the truth?

17Those other people show a deep interest in you, but their intentions are not good. All they want is to separate you from me, so that

Live it!

Shape Up!

Paul might sound a little conceited in Galatians 4:12. But he's not bragging. It was common in his time to use this method to tell people how to behave. So he tells the Galatians to act better. He reminds them about how happily they first received his message (4:13–15). He reminds them that he cares about them deeply, in fact, so much that he calls them his children (4:19).

If you have friends that need to act better, what is a way for you to be a good example to them, without bragging?

— Galatians 4:8–21

[f] **4:6** To show that you are; *or* Because you are.
4:5–7 Rom 8:15–17

"There is no difference between Jews and Gentiles . . . slaves and free people . . . men and women; you are all one in union with Christ Jesus" *(Galatians 3:28)*.

you will have the same interest in them as
they have in you. 18Now, it is good to have
such a deep interest if the purpose is good—
this is true always, and not merely when I
am with you. 19My dear children! Once
again, just like a mother in childbirth, I feel
the same kind of pain for you until Christ's
nature is formed in you. 20How I wish I
were with you now, so that I could take a
different attitude toward you. I am so wor-
ried about you!

The Example of Hagar and Sarah

21Let me ask those of you who want to be
subject to the Law: do you not hear what
the Law says? 22It says that Abraham had two
sons, one by a slave woman, the other by a
free woman. 23His son by the slave woman
was born in the usual way, but his son by the
free woman was born as a result of God's
promise. 24These things can be understood
as a figure: the two women represent two
covenants. The one whose children are born
in slavery is Hagar, and she represents the
covenant made at Mount Sinai. 25Hagar,
who stands for Mount Sinai in Arabia, is[g] a
figure of the present city of Jerusalem, in
slavery with all its people. 26But the heavenly
Jerusalem is free, and she is our mother.
27For the scripture says,

"Be happy, you childless woman!
Shout and cry with joy, you who never
felt the pains of childbirth!
For the woman who was deserted will
have more children
than the woman whose husband never
left her."

28Now, you, my friends, are God's children
as a result of his promise, just as Isaac was.
29At that time the son who was born in the
usual way persecuted the one who was born
because of God's Spirit; and it is the same
now. 30But what does the scripture say? It
says, "Send the slave woman and her son
away; for the son of the slave woman will
not have a part of the father's property along
with the son of the free woman." 31So then,
my friends, we are not the children of a slave
woman but of a free woman.

Preserve Your Freedom

5 Freedom is what we have—Christ has
set us free! Stand, then, as free people,
and do not allow yourselves to become
slaves again.

2Listen! I, Paul, tell you that if you allow
yourselves to be circumcised, it means that
Christ is of no use to you at all. 3Once more
I warn any man who allows himself to be
circumcised that he is obliged to obey the
whole Law. 4Those of you who try to be put
right with God by obeying the Law have cut
yourselves off from Christ. You are outside
God's grace. 5As for us, our hope is that God
will put us right with him; and this is what
we wait for by the power of God's Spirit
working through our faith. 6For when we
are in union with Christ Jesus, neither cir-
cumcision nor the lack of it makes any dif-
ference at all; what matters is faith that
works through love.

7You were doing so well! Who made you
stop obeying the truth? How did he per-
suade you? 8It was not done by God, who
calls you. 9"It takes only a little yeast to
make the whole batch of dough rise," as they
say. 10But I still feel confident about you.
Our life in union with the Lord makes me
confident that you will not take a different
view and that whoever is upsetting you will
be punished by God.

11But as for me, my friends, if I continue
to preach that circumcision is necessary, why
am I still being persecuted? If that were true,
then my preaching about the cross of Christ
would cause no trouble. 12I wish that the
people who are upsetting you would go all
the way; let them go on and castrate them-
selves!

13As for you, my friends, you were called

g **4:25** Hagar . . . is; *some manuscripts have* Sinai is a mountain in Arabia, and it is.

4:22 a Gen 16:15; **b** Gen 21:2 **4:27** Isa 54:1 **4:29** Gen 21:9 **4:30** Gen 21:10 **5:9** 1 Cor 5:6

The things listed in Galatians 5:22–23 are called the *fruits of the Holy Spirit:* love, joy, peace, patience, kindness, goodness, faithfulness, humility, and self-control.

Live it!

Who Do You Follow?

"C'mon, just do it. One little puff won't kill you." It seemed like every guy in Jack's class had tried smoking. Even Jack's best friend, Carlo, was now urging him to try it. Jack just walked home, ignoring Carlo and the other guys. He heard them laughing as he walked away and felt hurt.

Jack was surprised when Carlo called him that night. He asked Carlo who had convinced him to try smoking. When Carlo didn't answer, Jack said, "It doesn't matter who it is, what matters is that we shouldn't be doing it. I don't want to lose my new curfew over a stupid cigarette." Carlo didn't answer for a little bit then said, "Whatever Jack. I'll talk to you tomorrow, and maybe we can hang out after school, and avoid the other guys together. It's probably better that I follow you."

Saint Paul is concerned that someone has turned the Galatians away from the truth (Galatians 5:7). He hopes his good example and urging can bring them back. How can you help the people you know stay on the right path?

— Galatians 5:7–10

to be free. But do not let this freedom
become an excuse for letting your physical
desires control you. Instead, let love make
you serve one another. 14 For the whole Law
is summed up in one commandment: "Love
your neighbor as you love yourself." 15 But if
you act like wild animals, hurting and harm-
ing each other, then watch out, or you will
completely destroy one another.

The Spirit and Human Nature

16 What I say is this: let the Spirit direct
your lives, and you will not satisfy the desires
of the human nature. 17 For what our human
nature wants is opposed to what the Spirit
wants, and what the Spirit wants is opposed
to what our human nature wants. These two
are enemies, and this means that you cannot
do what you want to do. 18 If the Spirit leads
you, then you are not subject to the Law.

19 What human nature does is quite plain.
It shows itself in immoral, filthy, and inde-
cent actions; 20 in worship of idols and
witchcraft. People become enemies and they
fight; they become jealous, angry, and ambi-
tious. They separate into parties and groups;
21 they are envious, get drunk, have orgies,
and do other things like these. I warn you
now as I have before: those who do these
things will not possess the Kingdom of
God.

22 But the Spirit produces love, joy, peace,
patience, kindness, goodness, faithfulness,
23 humility, and self-control. There is no law
against such things as these. 24 And those
who belong to Christ Jesus have put to
death their human nature with all its pas-
sions and desires. 25 The Spirit has given us
life; he must also control our lives. 26 We
must not be proud or irritate one another
or be jealous of one another.

Bear One Another's Burdens

6 My friends, if someone is caught in any
kind of wrongdoing, those of you who
are spiritual should set him right; but you
must do it in a gentle way. And keep an eye
on yourselves, so that you will not be tempt-
ed, too. 2 Help carry one another's burdens,
and in this way you will obey[h] the law of

Help carry one another's burdens. (6:2)

[h] **6:2** you will obey; *some manuscripts have* obey.
5:14 Lev 19:18 **5:17** Rom 7:15–23

Pray it!

The Real Me

Some people act like they are more than they really are. Maybe you have tried to be something you aren't. The next time you need help in being yourself, say this prayer.

Dear God,
I want to be me.
But my parents tell me to be one thing,
my friends tell me to be my own person,
and television, music, and movies make me think
I should be something else.
It's all very confusing.
Then I remember you.
Who do you want me to be?
You have given me direction in your word.
Help me to hear your call.
Help me be the person you created me to be.
The real me.
Amen.

— Galatians 6:3–4

Christ. 3If you think you are something
when you really are nothing, you are only
deceiving yourself. 4You should each judge
your own conduct. If it is good, then you
can be proud of what you yourself have
done, without having to compare it with
what someone else has done. 5For each of
you have to carry your own load.

6If you are being taught the Christian
message, you should share all the good things
you have with your teacher.

7Do not deceive yourselves; no one
makes a fool of God. You will reap exactly
what you plant. 8If you plant in the field of
your natural desires, from it you will gather
the harvest of death; if you plant in the field
of the Spirit, from the Spirit you will gather
the harvest of eternal life. 9So let us not
become tired of doing good; for if we do
not give up, the time will come when we
will reap the harvest. 10So then, as often as
we have the chance, we should do good to
everyone, and especially to those who
belong to our family in the faith.

Final Warning and Greeting

11See what big letters I make as I write
to you now with my own hand! 12The
people who are trying to force you to be
circumcised are the ones who want to
show off and boast about external matters.
They do it, however, only so that they may
not be persecuted for the cross of Christ.
13Even those who practice circumcision do
not obey the Law; they want you to be cir-
cumcised so that they can boast that you
submitted to this physical ceremony. 14As
for me, however, I will boast only about
the cross of our Lord Jesus Christ; for by
means of his cross the world is dead to me,
and I am dead to the world. 15It does not
matter at all whether or not one is circum-
cised; what does matter is being a new
creature. 16As for those who follow this

rule in their lives, may peace and mercy be
with them—with them and with all of
God's people!
17 To conclude: let no one give me any
more trouble, because the scars I have on my
body show that I am the slave of Jesus.
18 May the grace of our Lord Jesus Christ
be with you all, my friends. Amen.

Your Next Step

Congratulations on finishing the Letter to the Galatians! Use this space to write your thoughts and questions about this book. If you are following the suggested reading plan, go back to the Book of Esther in the Old Testament. It is a fascinating story about people who put their faith in God and who God saved from destruction.

THE LETTER TO THE Ephesians

Have you ever disagreed with someone on what was important to believe as a Christian? Saint Paul's letter to the Ephesians was about overcoming disagreements between the Christians who were circumcised (Jewish Christians) and those who were not circumcised (the Gentile Christians). Think of the conflicts in our time between Jews and Arabs and between Christians, Jews, and Muslims. This lesson of unity is still important for us to learn today.

This letter also uses images of war to speak about peace. Chapter 6 mentions the armor of God, the breastplate of righteousness, the shield of faith, the helmet of salvation, and the sword of the Spirit. The way to find peace is to begin with the struggles and conflicts inside of us. Once we are peaceful people ourselves, then we can start to bring peace to others.

Chap. 5:21–33

Headlines

- Prayer for God's People (1:15–23)
- Unite in Christ! (2:11–22; 4:1–6)
- A Beautiful Prayer (3:14–21)
- Rules for Living as God's Children (5:1–10; 6:1–4)
- Prepare for Spiritual Battle! (6:10–20)

FACTOIDS

Who wrote this book? Probably a follower of Paul who wanted to summarize or introduce Paul's teachings about church.

When was it written? After Paul died, sometime between AD 70 and 95.

Who was it written for? Most likely this letter was not written directly for the people in the city of Ephesus, even though it's called the Letter to the Ephesians. It was a general letter, written for Christian communities in several different places.

Important themes

- There is a need for unity and peace, especially among Jews and Gentiles (non-Jews).
- Jesus' followers require inner strength to resist evil and do God's work.

EPHESIANS

1 From Paul, who by God's will is an
apostle of Christ Jesus—
To God's people in Ephesus,[a] who are
faithful in their life in union with Christ Jesus:
2May God our Father and the Lord Jesus
Christ give you grace and peace.

Spiritual Blessings in Christ

3Let us give thanks to the God and Father
of our Lord Jesus Christ! For in our union
with Christ he has blessed us by giving us
every spiritual blessing in the heavenly
world. 4Even before the world was made,
God had already chosen us to be his through
our union with Christ, so that we would be
holy and without fault before him.
Because of his love 5God[b] had already
decided that through Jesus Christ he would
make us his children—this was his pleasure
and purpose. 6Let us praise God for his glo-
rious grace, for the free gift he gave us in his
dear Son! 7For by the blood of Christ[c] we
are set free, that is, our sins are forgiven.
How great is the grace of God, 8which he
gave to us in such large measure!
In all his wisdom and insight 9God did
what he had purposed, and made known to
us the secret plan he had already decided to
complete by means of Christ. 10This plan,
which God will complete when the time is
right, is to bring all creation together, every-
thing in heaven and on earth, with Christ as
head.
11All things are done according to God's
plan and decision; and God chose us to be
his own people in union with Christ
because of his own purpose, based on what
he had decided from the very beginning.
12Let us, then, who were the first to hope in
Christ, praise God's glory!
13And you also became God's people
when you heard the true message, the Good
News that brought you salvation. You
believed in Christ, and God put his stamp of

Let us . . . praise God's glory. (1:12)

ownership on you by giving you the Holy
Spirit he had promised. 14The Spirit is the
guarantee that we shall receive what God has
promised his people, and this assures us that
God will give complete freedom to those
who are his. Let us praise his glory!

Paul's Prayer

15For this reason, ever since I heard of
your faith in the Lord Jesus and your love
for all of God's people, 16I have not stopped
giving thanks to God for you. I remember
you in my prayers 17and ask the God of our
Lord Jesus Christ, the glorious Father, to
give you the Spirit, who will make you wise
and reveal God to you, so that you will
know him. 18I ask that your minds may be
opened to see his light, so that you will
know what is the hope to which he has
called you, how rich are the wonderful
blessings he promises his people, 19and how
very great is his power at work in us who
believe. This power working in us is the
same as the mighty strength 20which he

[a] **1:1** *Some manuscripts do not have* in Ephesus. [b] **1:5** before him. Because of his love God; *or* before him, and to live in love. God. [c] **1:7** by the blood of Christ; *or* by the sacrificial death of Christ.

1:1 Acts 18:19–21; 19:1 **1:7** Col 1:14 **1:20** Ps 110:1

used when he raised Christ from death and seated him at his right side in the heavenly world. 21 Christ rules there above all heavenly rulers, authorities, powers, and lords; he has a title superior to all titles of authority in this world and in the next. 22 God put all things under Christ's feet and gave him to the church as supreme Lord over all things. 23 The church is Christ's body, the completion of him who himself completes all things everywhere.[d]

From Death to Life

2 In the past you were spiritually dead because of your disobedience and sins. 2 At that time you followed the world's evil way; you obeyed the ruler of the spiritual powers in space, the spirit who now controls the people who disobey God. 3 Actually all of us were like them and lived according to our natural desires, doing whatever suited the wishes of our own bodies and minds. In our natural condition we, like everyone else, were destined to suffer God's anger.

4 But God's mercy is so abundant, and his love for us is so great, 5 that while we were spiritually dead in our disobedience he brought us to life with Christ. It is by God's grace that you have been saved. 6 In our union with Christ Jesus he raised us up with him to rule with him in the heavenly world. 7 He did this to demonstrate for all time to come the extraordinary greatness of his grace in the love he showed us in Christ Jesus. 8-9 For it is by God's grace that you have been saved through faith. It is not the result of your own efforts, but God's gift, so that no one can boast about it. 10 God has made us what we are, and in our union with Christ Jesus he has created us for a life of good deeds, which he has already prepared for us to do.

One in Christ

11 You Gentiles by birth—called "the uncircumcised" by the Jews, who call themselves the circumcised (which refers to what men do to their bodies)—remember what you were in the past. 12 At that time you were apart from Christ. You were foreigners and did not belong to God's chosen people. You had no part in the covenants, which were based on God's promises to his people, and you lived in this world without hope and without God. 13 But now, in union with Christ Jesus you, who used to be far away, have been brought near by the blood of Christ.[e] 14 For Christ himself has brought us peace by making Jews and Gentiles one people. With his own body he broke down the wall that separated them and kept them enemies. 15 He abolished the Jewish Law with its commandments and rules, in order to create out of the two races one new people in union with himself, in this way making peace. 16 By his death on the cross Christ destroyed their enmity; by means of the cross he united both races into one body and brought them back to God. 17 So Christ came and preached the Good News of peace to all—to you Gentiles, who were far away from God, and to the Jews, who were near to him. 18 It is through Christ that all of us, Jews and Gentiles, are able to come in the one Spirit into the presence of the Father.

19 So then, you Gentiles are not foreigners or strangers any longer; you are now citizens together with God's people and members of the family of God. 20 You, too, are built upon the foundation laid by the apostles and prophets,[f] the cornerstone being Christ Jesus himself. 21 He is the one who holds the whole building together and makes it grow into a sacred temple dedicated to the Lord. 22 In union with him you too are being built together with all the others into a place where God lives through his Spirit.

Paul's Work for the Gentiles

3 For this reason I, Paul, the prisoner of Christ Jesus for the sake of you Gentiles, pray to God. 2 Surely you have heard

[d] **1:23** who himself completes all things everywhere; *or* who is himself completely filled with God's fullness.
[e] **2:13** by the blood of Christ; *or* by the sacrificial death of Christ. [f] **2:20** the foundation laid by the apostles and prophets; *or* the foundation, that is, the apostles and prophets.

1:22 Ps 8:6 **1:22, 23** Col 1:18 **2:1–5** Col 2:13 **2:15** Col 2:14 **2:16** Col 1:20 **2:17** Isa 57:19

Pray it!

This Is a Prayer for Us!

The writer of the Letter to the Ephesians is praying an awesome prayer for us in chapter 3. It's not just for people long ago but for anyone who reads it throughout all time. Here's a simple version of the Ephesians' prayer you can say yourself.

I kneel before the Creator of heaven and earth.
I ask to receive the power of the Holy Spirit to strengthen my inner self.
I pray that Jesus Christ lives in my heart.
I pray that my life is built on love.
I pray that I can know how huge God's love is for me and for all the world.
Finally, I pray that God's power will work in me to do more
than I can ever imagine or think to ask for.
Glory to God forever!
Amen.

— Ephesians 3:14–21

that God in his grace has given me this work
to do for your good. 3God revealed his
secret plan and made it known to me. (I
have written briefly about this, 4and if you
will read what I have written, you can learn
about my understanding of the secret of
Christ.) 5In past times human beings were
not told this secret, but God has revealed it
now by the Spirit to his holy apostles and
prophets. 6The secret is that by means of the
gospel the Gentiles have a part with the Jews
in God's blessings; they are members of the
same body and share in the promise that
God made through Christ Jesus.

7I was made a servant of the gospel by
God's special gift, which he gave me through
the working of his power. 8I am less than the
least of all God's people; yet God gave me
this privilege of taking to the Gentiles the
Good News about the infinite riches of
Christ, 9and of making all people see how
God's secret plan is to be put into effect.
God, who is the Creator of all things, kept
his secret hidden through all the past ages,
10in order that at the present time, by means
of the church, the angelic rulers and powers
in the heavenly world might learn of his wis-
dom in all its different forms. 11God did this
according to his eternal purpose, which he
achieved through Christ Jesus our Lord. 12In
union with Christ and through our faith in
him we have the boldness to go into God's
presence with all confidence. 13I beg you,
then, not to be discouraged because I am suf-
fering for you; it is all for your benefit.

The Love of Christ

14For this reason I fall on my knees before
the Father, 15from whom every family in
heaven and on earth receives its true name.
16I ask God from the wealth of his glory to
give you power through his Spirit to be
strong in your inner selves, 17and I pray that
Christ will make his home in your hearts
through faith. I pray that you may have your
roots and foundation in love, 18so that you,
together with all God's people, may have the
power to understand how broad and long,
how high and deep, is Christ's love. 19Yes,
may you come to know his love—although
it can never be fully known—and so be
completely filled with the very nature of
God.

3:4–6 Col 1:26, 27 **3:18** Sir 1:3

20 To him who by means of his power
working in us is able to do so much more
than we can ever ask for, or even think of:
21 to God be the glory in the church and in
Christ Jesus for all time, forever and ever!
Amen.

The Unity of the Body

4 I urge you, then—I who am a prisoner
because I serve the Lord: live a life that
measures up to the standard God set when
he called you. 2 Be always humble, gentle, and
patient. Show your love by being tolerant
with one another. 3 Do your best to preserve
the unity which the Spirit gives by means of
the peace that binds you together. 4 There is
one body and one Spirit, just as there is one
hope to which God has called you. 5 There is
one Lord, one faith, one baptism; 6 there is
one God and Father of all people, who is
Lord of all, works through all, and is in all.

7 Each one of us has received a special gift
in proportion to what Christ has given. 8 As
the scripture says,

"When he went up to the very heights,
he took many captives with him;
he gave gifts to people."

9 Now, what does "he went up" mean? It
means that first he came down to the lowest
depths of the earth.[g] 10 So the one who came
down is the same one who went up, above
and beyond the heavens, to fill the whole
universe with his presence. 11 It was he who
"gave gifts to people"; he appointed some to
be apostles, others to be prophets, others to
be evangelists, others to be pastors and
teachers. 12 He did this to prepare all God's
people for the work of Christian service, in
order to build up the body of Christ. 13 And
so we shall all come together to that oneness
in our faith and in our knowledge of the
Son of God; we shall become mature people,
reaching to the very height of Christ's full
stature. 14 Then we shall no longer be chil-
dren, carried by the waves and blown about
by every shifting wind of the teaching of
deceitful people, who lead others into error
by the tricks they invent. 15 Instead, by speak-
ing the truth in a spirit of love, we must
grow up in every way to Christ, who is the
head. 16 Under his control all the different
parts of the body fit together, and the whole
body is held together by every joint with
which it is provided. So when each separate
part works as it should, the whole body
grows and builds itself up through love.

The New Life in Christ

17 In the Lord's name, then, I warn you: do
not continue to live like the heathen, whose
thoughts are worthless 18 and whose minds
are in the dark. They have no part in the life
that God gives, for they are completely igno-
rant and stubborn. 19 They have lost all feel-
ing of shame; they give themselves over to
vice and do all sorts of indecent things with-
out restraint.

20 That was not what you learned about
Christ! 21 You certainly heard about him, and
as his followers you were taught the truth
that is in Jesus. 22 So get rid of your old self,
which made you live as you used to—the
old self that was being destroyed by its
deceitful desires. 23 Your hearts and minds
must be made completely new, 24 and you
must put on the new self, which is created in
God's likeness and reveals itself in the true
life that is upright and holy.

25 No more lying, then! Each of you must
tell the truth to the other believer, because we
are all members together in the body of
Christ. 26 If you become angry, do not let your
anger lead you into sin, and do not stay angry
all day. 27 Don't give the Devil a chance. 28 If
you used to rob, you must stop robbing and

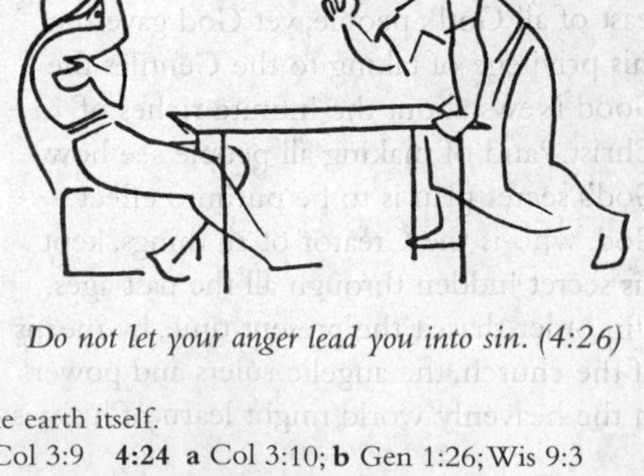

Do not let your anger lead you into sin. (4:26)

[g] **4:9** the lowest depths of the earth; *or* the lower depths, the earth itself.

4:2 Col 3:12, 13 **4:8** Ps 68:18 **4:16** Col 2:19 **4:22** Col 3:9 **4:24 a** Col 3:10; **b** Gen 1:26; Wis 9:3
4:25 Zech 8:16 **4:26** Ps 4:4 (LXX)

start working, in order to earn an honest liv-
ing for yourself and to be able to help the
poor. 29 Do not use harmful words, but only
helpful words, the kind that build up and pro-
vide what is needed, so that what you say will
do good to those who hear you. 30 And do
not make God's Holy Spirit sad; for the Spirit
is God's mark of ownership on you, a guaran-
tee that the Day will come when God will set
you free. 31 Get rid of all bitterness, passion,
and anger. No more shouting or insults, no
more hateful feelings of any sort. 32 Instead, be
kind and tender-hearted to one another, and
forgive one another, as God has forgiven you
through Christ.

Living in the Light

5 Since you are God's dear children, you
must try to be like him. 2 Your life must
be controlled by love, just as Christ loved us
and gave his life for us as a sweet-smelling
offering and sacrifice that pleases God.

3 Since you are God's people, it is not right
that any matters of sexual immorality or
indecency or greed should even be men-
tioned among you. 4 Nor is it fitting for you
to use language which is obscene, profane, or
vulgar. Rather you should give thanks to
God. 5 You may be sure that no one who is
immoral, indecent, or greedy (for greed is a
form of idolatry) will ever receive a share in
the Kingdom of Christ and of God.

6 Do not let anyone deceive you with
foolish words; it is because of these very
things that God's anger will come upon
those who do not obey him. 7 So have noth-
ing at all to do with such people. 8 You your-
selves used to be in the darkness, but since
you have become the Lord's people, you are
in the light. So you must live like people
who belong to the light, 9 for it is the light[h]
that brings a rich harvest of every kind of
goodness, righteousness, and truth. 10 Try to
learn what pleases the Lord. 11 Have nothing
to do with the worthless things that people
do, things that belong to the darkness.
Instead, bring them out to the light. (12 It is
really too shameful even to talk about the
things they do in secret.) 13 And when all
things are brought out to the light, then
their true nature is clearly revealed; 14 for
anything that is clearly revealed becomes
light.[i] That is why it is said,

"Wake up, sleeper,
  and rise from death,
and Christ will shine on you."

15 So be careful how you live. Don't live
like ignorant people, but like wise people.
16 Make good use of every opportunity you
have, because these are evil days. 17 Don't be
fools, then, but try to find out what the Lord
wants you to do.

18 Do not get drunk with wine, which will
only ruin you; instead, be filled with the
Spirit. 19 Speak to one another with the
words of psalms, hymns, and sacred songs;
sing hymns and psalms to the Lord with
praise in your hearts. 20 In the name of our
Lord Jesus Christ, always give thanks for
everything to God the Father.

Wives and Husbands

21 Submit yourselves to one another
because of your reverence for Christ.

22 Wives, submit yourselves to your hus-
bands as to the Lord. 23 For a husband has
authority over his wife just as Christ has
authority over the church; and Christ is
himself the Savior of the church, his body.
24 And so wives must submit themselves
completely to their husbands just as the
church submits itself to Christ.

25 Husbands, love your wives just as Christ
loved the church and gave his life for it. 26 He
did this to dedicate the church to God by his
word, after making it clean by washing it in
water, 27 in order to present the church to
himself in all its beauty—pure and faultless,
without spot or wrinkle or any other imper-
fection. 28 Men ought to love their wives just
as they love their own bodies. A man who
loves his wife loves himself. (29 None of us
ever hate our own bodies. Instead, we feed
them, and take care of them, just as Christ

[h] **5:9** the light; *some manuscripts have* the Spirit. [i] **5:14** anything that is clearly revealed becomes light; *or* it is light that clearly reveals everything.

4:32 Col 3:13 **5:2** Ex 29:18; Ps 40:6 **5:16** Col 4:5 **5:19, 20** Col 3:16, 17 **5:22** Col 3:18; 1 Pet 3:1 **5:25** Col 3:19; 1 Pet 3:7

does the church; 30 for we are members of his
body.) 31 As the scripture says, "For this reason
a man will leave his father and mother and
unite with his wife, and the two will become
one." 32 There is a deep secret truth revealed
in this scripture, which I understand as apply-
ing to Christ and the church. 33 But it also
applies to you: every husband must love his
wife as himself, and every wife must respect
her husband.

Children and Parents

6 Children, it is your Christian duty to[j]
obey your parents, for this is the right
thing to do. 2 "Respect your father and moth-
er" is the first commandment that has a prom-
ise added: 3 "so that all may go well with you,
and you may live a long time in the land."
4 Parents, do not treat your children in
such a way as to make them angry. Instead,
raise them with Christian discipline and
instruction.

Slaves and Masters

5 Slaves, obey your human masters with
fear and trembling; and do it with a sincere
heart, as though you were serving Christ.
6 Do this not only when they are watching
you, because you want to gain their
approval; but with all your heart do what
God wants, as slaves of Christ. 7 Do your
work as slaves cheerfully, as though you
served the Lord, and not merely human
beings. 8 Remember that the Lord will
reward each of us, whether slave or free, for
the good work we do.
9 Masters, behave in the same way toward
your slaves and stop using threats. Remem-
ber that you and your slaves belong to the
same Master in heaven, who judges everyone
by the same standard.

The Whole Armor of God

10 Finally, build up your strength in union
with the Lord and by means of his mighty
power. 11 Put on all the armor that God gives
you, so that you will be able to stand up
against the Devil's evil tricks. 12 For we are
not fighting against human beings but
against the wicked spiritual forces in the
heavenly world, the rulers, authorities, and
cosmic powers of this dark age. 13 So put on
God's armor now! Then when the evil day
comes, you will be able to resist the enemy's
attacks; and after fighting to the end, you
will still hold your ground.
14 So stand ready, with truth as a belt
tight around your waist, with righteousness
as your breastplate, 15 and as your shoes the
readiness to announce the Good News of
peace. 16 At all times carry faith as a shield;
for with it you will be able to put out all
the burning arrows shot by the Evil One.
17 And accept salvation as a helmet, and the
word of God as the sword which the Spirit
gives you. 18 Do all this in prayer, asking for
God's help. Pray on every occasion, as the
Spirit leads. For this reason keep alert and
never give up; pray always for all God's
people. 19 And pray also for me, that God
will give me a message when I am ready to
speak, so that I may speak boldly and make
known the gospel's secret. 20 For the sake of
this gospel I am an ambassador, though
now I am in prison. Pray that I may be
bold in speaking about the gospel as I
should.

Final Greetings

21 Tychicus, our dear brother and faithful
servant in the Lord's work, will give you all
the news about me, so that you may know
how I am getting along. 22 That is why I
am sending him to you—to tell you how
all of us are getting along and to encourage
you.
23 May God the Father and the Lord Jesus
Christ give to all Christians peace and love
with faith. 24 May God's grace be with all
those who love our Lord Jesus Christ with
undying love.

[j] **6:1** *Some manuscripts do not have* it is your Christian duty to.

5:31 Gen 2:24 **6:1** Col 3:20 **6:2, 3** Ex 20:12; Deut 5:16 **6:4** Col 3:21 **6:5–8** Col 3:22–25 **6:9 a** Col 4:1; **b** Deut 10:17; Col 3:25 **6:11** Wis 5:17 **6:14–17** Wis 5:18–23 **6:14 a** Isa 11:5; **b** Isa 59:17 **6:15** Isa 52:7 **6:17** Isa 59:17 **6:21** Acts 20:4; 2 Tim 4:12 **6:21, 22** Col 4:7, 8

THE LETTER TO THE Philippians

Have you heard the song "Joy to the World"? *Joy* seems to be one of those words that we don't hear or see a lot, except in church. Yet for Paul, who is writing from prison, the word *joy* is very important. It captures the attitude that he wants the new Christians in Philippi to live out. It is more than just having a positive attitude; it is about recognizing the many gifts that we have been given by God through Jesus. The best gift is, of course, Jesus himself. Paul feels very close to the Christians in Philippi, and this short letter contains some of his most beautiful messages.

Chap. 3:1–14

Headlines

- Paul Sends Joyful Prayer from Prison (1:3–11)
- Well-Known Song About Jesus (2:5–11)
- The Prize Worth Running For (3:12–14)

FACTOIDS

Who wrote this book? Paul, probably while he was in prison.
When was it written? About AD 55 to 63.
Why was it written? Paul wanted to express his thanks to the Christians in Philippi and to teach and encourage the people in their faith.
Jesus connection. A famous and beautiful hymn about Jesus talks about him as true God and true man (2:6–11).
Important themes

- The letter speaks often about joy and rejoicing. Can you count the number of times these words appear in this book?
- Those who continue to try to follow Christ, no matter how many times they fail, will be rewarded.

PHILIPPIANS

1 From Paul and Timothy, servants of
Christ Jesus—
To all God's people in Philippi who are in
union with Christ Jesus, including the
church leaders and helpers:
2May God our Father and the Lord Jesus
Christ give you grace and peace.

Paul's Prayer for His Readers

3I thank my God for you every time I
think of you; 4and every time I pray for you
all, I pray with joy 5because of the way in
which you have helped me in the work of
the gospel from the very first day until now.
6And so I am sure that God, who began this
good work in you, will carry it on until it is
finished on the Day of Christ Jesus. 7You are
always in my heart! And so it is only right
for me to feel as I do about you. For you
have all shared with me in this privilege that
God has given me, both now that I am in
prison and also while I was free to defend
the gospel and establish it firmly. 8God is my
witness that I tell the truth when I say that
my deep feeling for you all comes from the
heart of Christ Jesus himself.
9I pray that your love will keep on grow-
ing more and more, together with true
knowledge and perfect judgment, 10so that
you will be able to choose what is best. Then
you will be free from all impurity and blame
on the Day of Christ. 11Your lives will be
filled with the truly good qualities which
only Jesus Christ can produce, for the glory
and praise of God.

To Live Is Christ

12I want you to know, my friends, that the
things that have happened to me have really
helped the progress of the gospel. 13As a
result, the whole palace guard and all the
others here know that I am in prison
because I am a servant of Christ. 14And my
being in prison has given most of the believ-
ers more confidence in the Lord, so that
they grow bolder all the time to preach the
message[a] fearlessly.
15Of course some of them preach Christ
because they are jealous and quarrelsome,
but others from genuine good will. 16These
do so from love, because they know that
God has given me the work of defending
the gospel. 17The others do not proclaim
Christ sincerely, but from a spirit of selfish
ambition; they think that they will make
more trouble for me while I am in prison.
18It does not matter! I am happy about
it—just so Christ is preached in every way
possible, whether from wrong or right
motives. And I will continue to be happy,
19because I know that by means of your

Live it!

Heart to Heart

In Paul's greetings to the Philippians, he says, "You are always in my heart!" (1:7). What a beautiful way to express the friendship and closeness we feel to another person or a group of friends. It is clear that Paul feels a strong bond of friendship with the members of the church in Philippi. What are some ways that you express in words your close friendship with others? Why not write a letter to someone you feel close to and let him or her know how much his or her friendship means to you? Or use the words from this passage to make a birthday card or a get-well card for someone you know.

— Philippians 1:3–11

[a] **1:14** the message; *some manuscripts have* God's message.
1:1 Acts 16:12 **1:13** Acts 28:30

Catholic Connections

True God and True Man

You may notice that the words of Philippians 2:6–11 are set apart. It is believed that they were part of an early Christian song. This beautiful hymn provides an excellent description of who Jesus Christ is for us. In Jesus, the human and divine are perfectly united. This mystery is called the Incarnation. As the *Catechism of the Catholic Church* teaches: "[Jesus] is truly the Son of God who, without ceasing to be God and Lord, became a man and our brother" (number 469). This is a core belief for all Christians. Read over these verses slowly and prayerfully. Jesus Christ is Lord!

— Philippians 2:5–11

prayers and the help which comes from the
Spirit of Jesus Christ I shall be set free. 20 My
deep desire and hope is that I shall never fail
in my duty, but that at all times, and especial-
ly right now, I shall be full of courage, so
that with my whole being I shall bring
honor to Christ, whether I live or die. 21 For
what is life? To me, it is Christ. Death, then,
will bring more. 22 But if by continuing to
live I can do more worthwhile work, then I
am not sure which I should choose. 23 I am
pulled in two directions. I want very much
to leave this life and be with Christ, which is
a far better thing; 24 but for your sake it is
much more important that I remain alive. 25 I
am sure of this, and so I know that I will
stay. I will stay on with you all, to add to
your progress and joy in the faith, 26 so that
when I am with you again, you will have
even more reason to be proud of me in your
life in union with Christ Jesus.

27 Now, the important thing is that your
way of life should be as the gospel of Christ
requires, so that, whether or not I am able to
go and see you, I will hear that you are
standing firm with one common purpose
and that with only one desire you are fight-
ing together for the faith of the gospel.
28 Don't be afraid of your enemies; always be
courageous, and this will prove to them that
they will lose and that you will win, because
it is God who gives you the victory. 29 For
you have been given the privilege of serving
Christ, not only by believing in him, but also
by suffering for him. 30 Now you can take
part with me in the battle. It is the same bat-
tle you saw me fighting in the past, and as
you hear, the one I am fighting still.

Christ's Humility and Greatness

2 Your life in Christ makes you strong,
and his love comforts you. You have
fellowship with the Spirit,[b] and you have
kindness and compassion for one another.
2 I urge you, then, to make me completely
happy by having the same thoughts, sharing
the same love, and being one in soul and
mind. 3 Don't do anything from selfish
ambition or from a cheap desire to boast,
but be humble toward one another, always
considering others better than yourselves.
4 And look out for one another's interests,
not just for your own. 5 The attitude you
should have is the one that Christ Jesus
had:

[b] **2:1** You have fellowship with the Spirit; *or* The Spirit has brought you into fellowship with one another.
1:30 Acts 16:19–40

"I am sure that God, who began this good work in you, will carry it on until it is finished on the Day of Christ Jesus" *(Philippians 1:6)*.

6 He always had the nature of God,
but he did not think that by force he
should try to remain[c] equal with God.
7 Instead of this, of his own free will he
gave up all he had,
and took the nature of a servant.
He became like a human being
and appeared in human likeness.
8 He was humble and walked the path of
obedience all the way to death—
his death on the cross.
9 For this reason God raised him to the
highest place above
and gave him the name that is greater
than any other name.
10 And so, in honor of the name of Jesus
all beings in heaven, on earth, and in
the world below[d]
will fall on their knees,
11 and all will openly proclaim that Jesus
Christ is Lord,
to the glory of God the Father.

Shining as Lights in the World

12 So then, dear friends, as you always
obeyed me when I was with you, it is even
more important that you obey me now
while I am away from you. Keep on working
with fear and trembling to complete your
salvation, 13 because God is always at work in
you to make you willing and able to obey
his own purpose.
14 Do everything without complaining or
arguing, 15 so that you may be innocent and
pure as God's perfect children, who live in a
world of corrupt and sinful people. You must
shine among them like stars lighting up the
sky, 16 as you offer them the message of life. If
you do so, I shall have reason to be proud of
you on the Day of Christ, because it will
show that all my effort and work have not
been wasted.
17 Perhaps my life's blood is to be poured
out like an offering on the sacrifice that your
faith offers to God. If that is so, I am glad
and share my joy with you all. 18 In the same
way, you too must be glad and share your joy
with me.

Timothy and Epaphroditus

19 If it is the Lord's will, I hope that I will
be able to send Timothy to you soon, so that
I may be encouraged by news about you.
20 He is the only one who shares my feelings
and who really cares about you. 21 Everyone
else is concerned only with their own affairs,
not with the cause of Jesus Christ. 22 And you
yourselves know how he has proved his
worth, how he and I, like a son and his
father, have worked together for the sake of
the gospel. 23 So I hope to send him to you as

Study it!

Stop Whining!

Paul tells the Christians of Philippi to do everything without complaining or arguing (Philippians 2:14). Does this advice sound familiar? No doubt you have heard the words, "Do what you're told and stop complaining!" Have you ever noticed how quickly an attitude of grumbling and complaining can spread? Soon everyone is whining about something. So why not decide to just be upbeat? Today when you hear someone complaining about something, try to think of something positive to say. You can help spread the Good News!

— Philippians 2:12–18

[c] **2:6** remain; *or* become. [d] **2:10** WORLD BELOW: *It was thought that the dead continued to exist in a dark world under the ground.*

2:10, 11 Isa 45:23 (LXX) **2:15** Deut 32:5

Timothy *(Philippians 2:19)* **is an early Church leader and companion who Paul relied on. Two letters in the New Testament are addressed to Timothy.**

soon as I know how things are going to turn
out for me. [24]And I trust in the Lord that I
myself will be able to come to you soon.
[25]I have thought it necessary to send to
you our brother Epaphroditus, who has
worked and fought by my side and who has
served as your messenger in helping me.
[26]He is anxious to see you all and is very
upset because you had heard that he was
sick. [27]Indeed he was sick and almost died.
But God had pity on him, and not only on
him but on me, too, and spared me an even
greater sorrow. [28]I am all the more eager,
then, to send him to you, so that you will
be glad again when you see him, and my
own sorrow will disappear. [29]Receive him,
then, with joy, as a believer in the Lord.
Show respect to all such people as he,
[30]because he risked his life and nearly died
for the sake of the work of Christ, in order
to give me the help that you yourselves
could not give.

Receive him . . . as a believer. (2:29)

The True Righteousness

3 In conclusion, my friends, be joyful in
your union with the Lord. I don't mind
repeating what I have written before, and
you will be safer if I do so. [2]Watch out for
those who do evil things, those dogs, those
who insist on cutting the body. [3]It is we, not
they, who have received the true circumci-
sion, for we worship God by means of his
Spirit and rejoice in our life in union with
Christ Jesus. We do not put any trust in
external ceremonies. [4]I could, of course, put
my trust in such things. If any of you think
you can trust in external ceremonies, I have
even more reason to feel that way. [5]I was cir-
cumcised when I was a week old. I am an
Israelite by birth, of the tribe of Benjamin, a
pure-blooded Hebrew. As far as keeping the
Jewish Law is concerned, I was a Pharisee,
[6]and I was so zealous that I persecuted the
church. As far as a person can be righteous
by obeying the commands of the Law, I was
without fault. [7]But all those things that I
might count as profit I now reckon as loss
for Christ's sake. [8]Not only those things; I
reckon everything as complete loss for the
sake of what is so much more valuable, the
knowledge of Christ Jesus my Lord. For his
sake I have thrown everything away; I con-
sider it all as mere garbage, so that I may
gain Christ [9]and be completely united with
him. I no longer have a righteousness of my
own, the kind that is gained by obeying the
Law. I now have the righteousness that is
given through faith in Christ, the righteous-
ness that comes from God and is based on
faith. [10]All I want is to know Christ and to
experience the power of his resurrection, to
share in his sufferings and become like him
in his death, [11]in the hope that I myself will
be raised from death to life.

Running toward the Goal

[12]I do not claim that I have already suc-
ceeded or have already become perfect. I
keep striving to win the prize for which
Christ Jesus has already won me to himself.
[13]Of course, my friends, I really do not[e]
think that I have already won it; the one
thing I do, however, is to forget what is
behind me and do my best to reach what is
ahead. [14]So I run straight toward the goal in
order to win the prize, which is God's call
through Christ Jesus to the life above.
[15]All of us who are spiritually mature
should have this same attitude. But if some
of you have a different attitude, God will
make this clear to you. [16]However that may
be, let us go forward according to the same
rules we have followed until now.
[17]Keep on imitating me, my friends. Pay
attention to those who follow the right
example that we have set for you. [18]I have

[e] **3:13** not; *some manuscripts have* not yet.

3:5 a Rom 11:1; **b** Acts 23:6; 26:5 **3:6** Acts 8:3; 22:4; 26:9–11 **3:17** 1 Cor 4:16; 11:1

I run straight toward the goal. (3:14)

told you this many times before, and now I
repeat it with tears: there are many whose
lives make them enemies of Christ's death
on the cross. 19They are going to end up in
hell, because their god is their bodily desires.
They are proud of what they should be
ashamed of, and they think only of things
that belong to this world. 20We, however, are
citizens of heaven, and we eagerly wait for
our Savior, the Lord Jesus Christ, to come
from heaven. 21He will change our weak
mortal bodies and make them like his own
glorious body, using that power by which he
is able to bring all things under his rule.

Their god is their bodily desires. (3:19)

Instructions

4 So then, my friends, how dear you are to
me and how I miss you! How happy
you make me, and how proud I am of
you!—this, dear friends, is how you should
stand firm in your life in the Lord.

2Euodia and Syntyche, please, I beg you,
try to agree as sisters in the Lord. 3And you
too, my faithful partner, I want you to help
these women; for they have worked hard
with me to spread the gospel, together with
Clement and all my other fellow workers,
whose names are in God's book of the living.

4May you always be joyful in your union
with the Lord. I say it again: rejoice!

5Show a gentle attitude toward everyone.
The Lord is coming soon. 6Don't worry

Live it!

Keep at it!

The summer Olympics are held every four years. Athletes from all over the world come together to compete in a variety of events. The winners receive gold, silver, and bronze medals. That is often what we see on television or in photos, but we know that behind those medals are years of practice, often for long hours seven days a week. Paul uses the image of a runner trying to win first prize to help us understand that following God's call takes work and dedication. The prize is not a medal, but rather full life in Jesus—in this life and in heaven.

Star athletes may complain about practice, but they know they have to put in their time to be successful. They make a practice schedule to motivate them. Why not make a practice schedule for your spiritual life? When and how long will you spend reading the Bible? When will you spend time learning about your faith? When will you get together to pray with others?

— Philippians 3:12–14

about anything, but in all your prayers ask
God for what you need, always asking him
with a thankful heart. 7And God's peace,
which is far beyond human understanding,
will keep your hearts and minds safe in
union with Christ Jesus.
8In conclusion, my friends, fill your minds
with those things that are good and that
deserve praise: things that are true, noble,
right, pure, lovely, and honorable. 9Put into
practice what you learned and received from
me, both from my words and from my
actions. And the God who gives us peace
will be with you.

Thanks for the Gift

10In my life in union with the Lord it is a
great joy to me that after so long a time you
once more had the chance of showing that
you care for me. I don't mean that you had
stopped caring for me—you just had no
chance to show it. 11And I am not saying
this because I feel neglected, for I have
learned to be satisfied with what I have. 12I
know what it is to be in need and what it is
to have more than enough. I have learned
this secret, so that anywhere, at any time, I
am content, whether I am full or hungry,
whether I have too much or too little. 13I
have the strength to face all conditions by
the power that Christ gives me.
14But it was very good of you to help
me in my troubles. 15You Philippians know
very well that when I left Macedonia in the
early days of preaching the Good News,
you were the only church to help me; you
were the only ones who shared my profits
and losses. 16More than once when I need-
ed help in Thessalonica, you sent it to me.
17It is not that I just want to receive gifts;
rather, I want to see profit added to your
account. 18Here, then, is my receipt for
everything you have given me—and it has
been more than enough! I have all I need
now that Epaphroditus has brought me all
your gifts. They are like a sweet-smelling
offering to God, a sacrifice which is accept-
able and pleasing to him. 19And with all his
abundant wealth through Christ Jesus, my
God will supply all your needs. 20To our
God and Father be the glory forever and
ever! Amen.

Final Greetings

21Greetings to each one of God's people
who belong to Christ Jesus. The believers
here with me send you their greetings. 22All
God's people here send greetings, especially
those who belong to the Emperor's palace.
23May the grace of the Lord Jesus Christ
be with you all.

4:16 Acts 17:1 **4:15, 16** 2 Cor 11:9 **4:18** Ex 29:18

Your Next Step

Congratulations on finishing the Letter to the Philippians! Use this space to write your thoughts and questions about this book. If you are following the suggested reading plan, go back to the Book of Amos in the Old Testament. This prophet had a real dedication to following God by practicing justice.

The Letter to the Colossians

Did you ever ask anyone for good advice? Even though the Letter to the Colossians was written more than two thousand years ago, it still has good advice for us today. It begins with a rich description of who Christ is. The second chapter warns us about false teachers and incorrect ideas. The third chapter describes how we need to live our lives, and the last chapter closes with final greetings to particular people by name. Those who follow this advice will become happier people, better Christians, and better friends.

Chap. 1:15–18

Headlines

- God Makes Peace Through Son's Death (1:15–20)
- The Secret to a Full Life Revealed! (2:6–10)
- How-To Guide: Living Life in Christ (3:5—4:1)

FACTOIDS

Who wrote this book? Paul or one of Paul's followers using the name of Paul. The author is familiar with Paul's teachings and uses Paul's themes.

When was it written? If Paul wrote it, around AD 61. If one of Paul's followers wrote it, probably after AD 61.

Why was it written? It seems that a group of people were teaching some unusual ideas and practices. This letter reminds the Christian community at Colossae that Jesus needs to be central to their faith.

Jesus connection. Jesus is described as supreme—as the head of the body, the head of the Church. If we know who Christ is, then we know how we must live.

Important themes

- Do not try to be popular by following the latest fads.
- Do not listen to just anyone for advice.
- Know what a Christian needs to do and follow that way of life.

COLOSSIANS

1 From Paul, who by God's will is an apostle of Christ Jesus, and from our brother Timothy—

2 To God's people in Colossae, who are our faithful friends in union with Christ:

May God our Father give you grace and peace.

Prayer of Thanksgiving

3 We always give thanks to God, the Father of our Lord Jesus Christ, when we pray for you. 4 For we have heard of your faith in Christ Jesus and of your love for all God's people. 5 When the true message, the Good News, first came to you, you heard about the hope it offers. So your faith and love are based on what you hope for, which is kept safe for you in heaven. 6 The gospel keeps bringing blessings and is spreading throughout the world, just as it has among you ever since the day you first heard about the grace of God and came to know it as it really is. 7 You learned of God's grace from Epaphras, our dear fellow servant, who is Christ's faithful worker on our[a] behalf. 8 He has told us of the love that the Spirit has given you.

9 For this reason we have always prayed for you, ever since we heard about you. We ask God to fill you with the knowledge of his will, with all the wisdom and understanding that his Spirit gives. 10 Then you will be able to live as the Lord wants and will always do what pleases him. Your lives will produce all kinds of good deeds, and you will grow in your knowledge of God. 11-12 May you be made strong with all the strength which comes from his glorious power, so that you may be able to endure everything with patience. And with joy give thanks to[b] the Father, who has made you fit to have your share of what God has reserved for his people in the kingdom of light. 13 He rescued us from the power of darkness and brought us safe into the kingdom of his dear Son, 14 by whom we are set free, that is, our sins are forgiven.

The Person and Work of Christ

15 Christ is the visible likeness of the invisible God. He is the first-born Son, superior to all created things. 16 For through him God created everything in heaven and on earth, the seen and the unseen things, including spiritual powers, lords, rulers, and authorities. God created the whole universe through him and for him. 17 Christ existed before all things, and in union with him all things have their proper place. 18 He is the head of his body, the church; he is the source of the body's life. He is the first-born Son, who was raised from death, in order that he alone might have the first place in all things. 19 For it was by God's own decision that the Son has in himself the full nature of God. 20 Through the Son, then, God decided to bring the whole universe back to himself. God made peace through his Son's blood[c] on the cross and so brought back to himself all things, both on earth and in heaven.

21 At one time you were far away from God and were his enemies because of the evil things you did and thought. 22 But now, by means of the physical death of his Son, God has made you his friends, in order to bring you, holy, pure, and faultless, into his presence. 23 You must, of course, continue faithful on a firm and sure foundation, and must not allow yourselves to be shaken from the hope you gained when you heard the gospel. It is of this gospel that I, Paul, became a servant—this gospel which has been preached to everybody in the world.

[a] **1:7** our; *some manuscripts have* your. [b] **1:11-12** with patience. And with joy give thanks to; *or* with patience and joy. And give thanks to. [c] **1:20** his Son's blood; *or* his Son's sacrificial death.

1:7 Col 4:12; Philem 23 **1:14** Eph 1:7 **1:15** Wis 7:26 **1:18** Eph 1:22, 23 **1:20** Eph 2:16

Paul's Work as a Servant of the Church

24 And now I am happy about my suffer-
ings for you, for by means of my physical suf-
ferings I am helping to complete what still
remains of Christ's sufferings on behalf of his
body, the church. 25 And I have been made a
servant of the church by God, who gave me
this task to perform for your good. It is the
task of fully proclaiming his message, 26 which
is the secret he hid through all past ages from
all human beings but has now revealed to his
people. 27 God's plan is to make known his
secret to his people, this rich and glorious
secret which he has for all peoples. And the
secret is that Christ is in you, which means
that you will share in the glory of God. 28 So
we preach Christ to everyone. With all possi-
ble wisdom we warn and teach them in
order to bring each one into God's presence
as a mature individual in union with Christ.
29 To get this done I toil and struggle, using
the mighty strength which Christ supplies
and which is at work in me.

2 Let me tell you how hard I have
worked for you and for the people in
Laodicea and for all others who do not
know me personally. 2 I do this in order that
they may be filled with courage and may be
drawn together in love, and so have the full
wealth of assurance which true understand-
ing brings. In this way they will know God's
secret, which is Christ himself.[d] 3 He is the
key that opens all the hidden treasures of
God's wisdom and knowledge.

4 I tell you, then, do not let anyone
deceive you with false arguments, no matter
how good they seem to be. 5 For even
though I am absent in body, yet I am with
you in spirit, and I am glad as I see the res-
olute firmness with which you stand togeth-
er in your faith in Christ.

Fullness of Life in Christ

6 Since you have accepted Christ Jesus as
Lord, live in union with him. 7 Keep your
roots deep in him, build your lives on him,
and become stronger in your faith, as you
were taught. And be filled with thanksgiving.

8 See to it, then, that no one enslaves you
by means of the worthless deceit of human
wisdom, which comes from the teachings
handed down by human beings and from
the ruling spirits of the universe, and not
from Christ. 9 For the full content of divine
nature lives in Christ, in his humanity, 10 and
you have been given full life in union with
him. He is supreme over every spiritual ruler
and authority.

11 In union with Christ you were circum-
cised, not with the circumcision that is made
by human beings, but with the circumcision
made by Christ, which consists of being freed
from the power of this sinful self. 12 For when
you were baptized, you were buried with
Christ, and in baptism you were also raised
with Christ through your faith in the active
power of God, who raised him from death.
13 You were at one time spiritually dead
because of your sins and because you were
Gentiles without the Law. But God has now
brought you to life with Christ. God forgave
us all our sins; 14 he canceled the unfavorable
record of our debts with its binding rules and
did away with it completely by nailing it to
the cross. 15 And on that cross Christ freed
himself from the power of the spiritual rulers
and authorities;[e] he made a public spectacle
of them by leading them as captives in his
victory procession.

16 So let no one make rules about what
you eat or drink or about holy days or the
New Moon Festival or the Sabbath. 17 All
such things are only a shadow of things in
the future; the reality is Christ. 18 Do not
allow yourselves to be condemned by any-
one who claims to be superior because of
special visions and who insists on false
humility and the worship of angels. For no
reason at all, such people are all puffed up by
their human way of thinking 19 and have
stopped holding on to Christ, who is the
head of the body. Under Christ's control the
whole body is nourished and held together

[d] **2:2** God's secret, which is Christ himself; *some manuscripts have* God's secret; *others have* the secret of God the Father of Christ; *others have* the secret of the God and Father, and of Christ. [e] **2:15** Christ freed himself from the power of the spiritual rulers and authorities; *or* Christ stripped the spiritual rulers and authorities of their power.

2:12 Rom 6:4 **2:13** Eph 2:1–5 **2:14** Eph 2:15 **2:16** Rom 14:1–6 **2:19** Eph 4:16

by its joints and ligaments, and it grows as
God wants it to grow.

Dying and Living with Christ

20 You have died with Christ and are set
free from the ruling spirits of the universe.
Why, then, do you live as though you
belonged to this world? Why do you obey
such rules as 21 "Don't handle this," "Don't
taste that," "Don't touch the other"? 22 All
these refer to things which become useless
once they are used; they are only human
rules and teachings. 23 Of course such rules
appear to be based on wisdom in their
forced worship of angels, and false humility,
and severe treatment of the body; but they
have no real value in controlling physical
passions.

3 You have been raised to life with Christ,
so set your hearts on the things that are
in heaven, where Christ sits on his throne at
the right side of God. 2 Keep your minds
fixed on things there, not on things here on
earth. 3 For you have died, and your life is
hidden with Christ in God. 4 Your real life is
Christ and when he appears, then you too
will appear with him and share his glory!

The Old Life and the New

5 You must put to death, then, the earth-
ly desires at work in you, such as sexual
immorality, indecency, lust, evil passions,
and greed (for greed is a form of idolatry).
6 Because of such things God's anger will
come upon those who do not obey him.[f]
7 At one time you yourselves used to live
according to such desires, when your life
was dominated by them.

8 But now you must get rid of all these
things: anger, passion, and hateful feelings.
No insults or obscene talk must ever come
from your lips. 9 Do not lie to one another,
for you have put off the old self with its
habits 10 and have put on the new self. This is
the new being which God, its Creator, is
constantly renewing in his own image, in
order to bring you to a full knowledge of
himself. 11 As a result, there is no longer any
distinction between Gentiles and Jews, cir-
cumcised and uncircumcised, barbarians, sav-
ages, slaves, and free, but Christ is all, Christ
is in all.

12 You are the people of God; he loved
you and chose you for his own. So then, you

Live it!

Fashion Advice and More

The Letter to the Colossians has some interesting fashion advice. It says we need to clothe ourselves with compassion, kindness, humility, gentleness, and patience (3:12). What should we take off? Colossians says we need to get rid of sexual immorality, lust, greed (3:5), anger, hateful feelings, insults, obscene language (3:8) and anything else that Jesus wouldn't be part of.

In the world we live in, there are lots of false messages about what's important in life. Colossians challenges many of these false messages. It says we should be tolerant with one another, forgive one another, and love one another. What kind of friend do you want to be? Someone with cool clothes, but bad attitudes? Or someone with less stuff, but who is caring and concerned about your friends and their feelings?

What kind of person do you want to be when you are all grown? Now is the time to start thinking about that. Now is the time to start developing good habits. The advice in chapter 3 is still good for all of us to follow.

— Colossians 3:1–17

f 3:6 *Some manuscripts do not have* upon those who do not obey him.

3:1 Ps 110:1 **3:9** Eph 4:22 **3:10** **a** Eph 4:24; **b** Gen 1:26 **3:12, 13** Eph 4:2

must clothe yourselves with compassion,
kindness, humility, gentleness, and patience.
13Be tolerant with one another and forgive
one another whenever any of you has a
complaint against someone else. You must
forgive one another just as the Lord has for-
given you. 14And to all these qualities add
love, which binds all things together in per-
fect unity. 15The peace that Christ gives is
to guide you in the decisions you make; for
it is to this peace that God has called you
together in the one body. And be thankful.
16Christ's message in all its richness must live
in your hearts. Teach and instruct one anoth-
er with all wisdom. Sing psalms, hymns, and
sacred songs; sing to God with thanksgiving
in your hearts. 17Everything you do or say,
then, should be done in the name of the
Lord Jesus, as you give thanks through him
to God the Father.

Personal Relations in the New Life

18Wives, submit yourselves to your hus-
bands, for that is what you should do as
Christians.

19Husbands, love your wives and do not
be harsh with them.

20Children, it is your Christian duty to
obey your parents always, for that is what
pleases God.

21Parents, do not irritate your children, or
they will become discouraged.

22Slaves, obey your human masters in all
things, not only when they are watching you
because you want to gain their approval; but
do it with a sincere heart because of your
reverence for the Lord. 23Whatever you do,
work at it with all your heart, as though you
were working for the Lord and not for peo-
ple. 24Remember that the Lord will give you
as a reward what he has kept for his people.
For Christ is the real Master you serve.
25And all wrongdoers will be repaid for the
wrong things they do, because God judges
everyone by the same standard.

4 Masters, be fair and just in the way you
treat your slaves. Remember that you
too have a Master in heaven.

Instructions

2Be persistent in prayer, and keep alert as
you pray, giving thanks to God. 3At the same
time pray also for us, so that God will give
us a good opportunity to preach his message
about the secret of Christ. For that is why I
am now in prison. 4Pray, then, that I may
speak, as I should, in such a way as to make
it clear.

5Be wise in the way you act toward those
who are not believers, making good use of
every opportunity you have. 6Your speech
should always be pleasant and interesting,
and you should know how to give the right
answer to everyone.

Final Greetings

7Our dear friend Tychicus, who is a faith-
ful worker and fellow servant in the Lord's
work, will give you all the news about me.
8That is why I am sending him to you, in
order to cheer you up by telling you how all
of us are getting along. 9With him goes
Onesimus, that dear and faithful friend, who
belongs to your group. They will tell you
everything that is happening here.

10Aristarchus, who is in prison with me,
sends you greetings, and so does Mark, the
cousin of Barnabas. (You have already
received instructions to welcome Mark if he
comes your way.) 11Joshua, also called Justus,
sends greetings too. These three are the only
Jewish believers who work with me for the
Kingdom of God, and they have been a
great help to me.

12Greetings from Epaphras, another mem-
ber of your group and a servant of Christ
Jesus. He always prays fervently for you, ask-
ing God to make you stand firm, as mature
and fully convinced Christians, in complete
obedience to God's will. 13I can personally
testify to his hard work for you and for the

3:13 Eph 4:32 **3:16, 17** Eph 5:19, 20 **3:18** Eph 5:22; 1 Pet 3:1 **3:19** Eph 5:25; 1 Pet 3:7 **3:20** Eph 6:1 **3:21** Eph 6:4 **3:22–25** Eph 6:5–8 **3:25** Deut 10:17; Eph 6:9 **4:1** Eph 6:9 **4:5** Eph 5:16 **4:6** Wis 8:12 **4:7** Acts 20:4; 2 Tim 4:12 **4:7, 8** Eph 6:21, 22 **4:9** Philem 10–12 **4:10** **a** Acts 19:29; 27:2; Philem 24; **b** Acts 12:12, 25; 13:13; 15:37–39 **4:12** Col 1:7; Philem 23

people in Laodicea and Hierapolis. 14 Luke,
our dear doctor, and Demas send you their
greetings.

15 Give our best wishes to the believers in
Laodicea and to Nympha and the church
that meets in her house.[g] 16 After you read
this letter, make sure that it is read also in the
church at Laodicea. At the same time, you
are to read the letter that the believers in
Laodicea will send you. 17 And tell Archip-
pus, "Be sure to finish the task you were
given in the Lord's service."

18 With my own hand I write this: *Greet-
ings from Paul.* Do not forget my chains!

May God's grace be with you.

[g] **4:15** Nympha . . . her house; *some manuscripts have* Nymphas . . . his house.

4:14 **a** 2 Tim 4:11; Philem 24; **b** 2 Tim 4:10; Philem 24 **4:17** Philem 2

The First Letter to the Thessalonians

One of life's most difficult experiences is when someone who is close to you dies. We pray that our loved one is at peace with God. We might wonder if we will be united with our loved one again in heaven. It was partly due to concerns like these that Paul wrote to the Thessalonians.

Like many early Christians, the Thessalonians thought that Jesus would come back while they were still alive. They were concerned about their friends who had already died and wondered if they would rise up again when the Lord returned. In this letter Paul wanted to reassure them and tell them not to worry. Christ's final coming is sometimes called the Second Coming of Christ or the Day of the Lord or the Parousia. When that great day arrives, all the dead who had faith in Christ will be united with Christ and one another.

Chap. 2:9

Headlines

- Missionary Life Is Not Easy (2:8–12)
- Paul Encouraged by Community's Love (3:6–13)
- Death Is Not the End! (4:13–18)
- Followers Told to Stay Awake (5:1–11)

FACTOIDS

Who wrote this book? Paul. He spent time preaching at Thessalonica and started a new Christian community there.

When was it written? This is the oldest book in the New Testament. Most likely it was written around AD 50 to 51. That's only twenty years or so after the death and Resurrection of Jesus. First Thessalonians is even older than the Gospels!

Who was it written for? It was written to the church in Thessalonica, people who were mostly non-Jewish Christians.

Important themes

- Jesus died and rose; so God will raise up all people who have "fallen asleep" (died).
- We do not know when the world will end, but there is no need to be afraid.

1 THESSALONIANS

1 From Paul, Silas, and Timothy—
To the people of the church in Thes-
salonica, who belong to God the Father and
the Lord Jesus Christ:
May grace and peace be yours.

The Life and Faith of the Thessalonians

2We always thank God for you all and
always mention you in our prayers. 3For we
remember before our God and Father how
you put your faith into practice, how your
love made you work so hard, and how your
hope in our Lord Jesus Christ is firm. 4Our
friends, we know that God loves you and has
chosen you to be his own. 5For we brought
the Good News to you, not with words
only, but also with power and the Holy Spir-
it, and with complete conviction of its truth.
You know how we lived when we were
with you; it was for your own good. 6You
imitated us and the Lord; and even though
you suffered much, you received the message
with the joy that comes from the Holy Spir-
it. 7So you became an example to all believ-
ers in Macedonia and Achaia. 8For not only
did the message about the Lord go out from
you throughout Macedonia and Achaia, but
the news about your faith in God has gone
everywhere. There is nothing, then, that we
need to say. 9All those people speak about
how you received us when we visited you,
and how you turned away from idols to
God, to serve the true and living God 10and
to wait for his Son to come from heaven—
his Son Jesus, whom he raised from death
and who rescues us from God's anger that is
coming.

Paul's Work in Thessalonica

2 Our friends, you yourselves know that
our visit to you was not a failure. 2You
know how we had already been mistreated
and insulted in Philippi before we came to
you in Thessalonica. And even though there
was much opposition, our God gave us
courage to tell you the Good News that
comes from him. 3Our appeal to you is not
based on error or impure motives, nor do we
try to trick anyone. 4Instead, we always speak
as God wants us to, because he has judged us
worthy to be entrusted with the Good
News. We do not try to please people, but to
please God, who tests our motives. 5You
know very well that we did not come to
you with flattering talk, nor did we use
words to cover up greed—God is our wit-
ness! 6We did not try to get praise from any-
one, either from you or from others, 7even
though as apostles of Christ we could have
made demands on you. But we were gentle
when we were with you, like a mother[a] tak-
ing care of her children. 8Because of our
love for you we were ready to share with
you not only the Good News from God but
even our own lives. You were so dear to us!
9Surely you remember, our friends, how we
worked and toiled! We worked day and
night so that we would not be any trouble to
you as we preached to you the Good News
from God.

10You are our witnesses, and so is God,
that our conduct toward you who believe
was pure, right, and without fault. 11You
know that we treated each one of you just as
parents treat their own children. 12We
encouraged you, we comforted you, and we
kept urging you to live the kind of life that
pleases God, who calls you to share in his
own Kingdom and glory.

13And there is another reason why we
always give thanks to God. When we
brought you God's message, you heard it and
accepted it, not as a message from human
beings but as God's message, which indeed it
is. For God is at work in you who believe.
14Our friends, the same things happened to

[a] **2:7** we were gentle when we were with you, like a mother; *some manuscripts have* we were like children when we were with you; we were like a mother.

1:1 Acts 17:1 **1:6** Acts 17:5–9 **2:2** **a** Acts 16:19–24; **b** Acts 17:1–9

Live it!

Paul's a Working Man

Saint Paul reminds the Thessalonians that he worked very hard when he was with them. He probably worked hard so that he wouldn't have to beg for his food. But he probably also did it as an example for others to follow. The hard work that Paul and his companions did on their journeys accomplished something huge—it helped establish the Church throughout the Roman Empire.

Work is important. When you do work, it contributes to your community. Maybe you are thinking about what kind of job you might be able to find as a teenager. Maybe you already work—perhaps you have a paper route or you babysit. Some jobs may seem pointless. But almost all honest jobs serve a purpose and help to make the community a better place. So be responsible like Paul, and do your best whenever and wherever you work.

— 1 Thessalonians 2:9–12

you that happened to the churches of God
in Judea, to the people there who belong to
Christ Jesus. You suffered the same persecu-
tions from your own people that they suf-
fered from the Jews, 15who killed the Lord
Jesus and the prophets, and persecuted us.
How displeasing they are to God! How hos-
tile they are to everyone! 16They even tried
to stop us from preaching to the Gentiles the
message that would bring them salvation. In
this way they have brought to completion all
the sins they have always committed. And
now God's anger has at last come down on
them!

Paul's Desire to Visit Them Again

17As for us, friends, when we were sepa-
rated from you for a little while—not in our
thoughts, of course, but only in body—how
we missed you and how hard we tried to see
you again! 18We wanted to return to you. I
myself tried to go back more than once, but
Satan would not let us. 19After all, it is you—
you, no less than others!—who are our
hope, our joy, and our reason for boasting of
our victory in the presence of our Lord Jesus
when he comes. 20Indeed, you are our pride
and our joy!

3 Finally, we could not bear it any longer.
So we decided to stay on alone in
Athens 2while we sent Timothy, our brother
who works with us for God in preaching the
Good News about Christ. We sent him to
strengthen you and help your faith, 3so that
none of you should turn back because of
these persecutions. You yourselves know that
such persecutions are part of God's will for
us. 4For while we were still with you, we
told you ahead of time that we were going
to be persecuted; and as you well know, that
is exactly what happened. 5That is why I had
to send Timothy. I could not bear it any
longer, so I sent him to find out about your
faith. Surely it could not be that the Devil
had tempted you and all our work had been
for nothing!

6Now Timothy has come back, and he has
brought us the welcome news about your
faith and love. He has told us that you always
think well of us and that you want to see us
just as much as we want to see you. 7So, in
all our trouble and suffering we have been
encouraged about you, friends. It was your
faith that encouraged us, 8because now we
really live if you stand firm in your life in
union with the Lord. 9Now we can give
thanks to our God for you. We thank him
for the joy we have in his presence because
of you. 10Day and night we ask him with all
our heart to let us see you personally and
supply what is needed in your faith.

11May our God and Father himself and
our Lord Jesus prepare the way for us to
come to you! 12May the Lord make your
love for one another and for all people grow

2:14 Acts 17:5 **2:15** Acts 9:23, 29; 13:45, 50; 14:2, 5, 19; 17:5, 13; 18:12 **3:1** Acts 17:15 **3:6** Acts 18:5

more and more and become as great as our love for you. 13 In this way he will strengthen you, and you will be perfect and holy in the presence of our God and Father when our Lord Jesus comes with all who belong to him.[b]

A Life That Pleases God

4 Finally, our friends, you learned from us how you should live in order to please God. This is, of course, the way you have been living. And now we beg and urge you in the name of the Lord Jesus to do even more. 2 For you know the instructions we gave you by the authority of the Lord Jesus. 3 God wants you to be holy and completely free from sexual immorality. 4 Each of you should know how to live with your wife[c] in a holy and honorable way, 5 not with a lustful desire, like the heathen who do not know God. 6 In this matter, then, none of you should do wrong to other Christians or take advantage of them. We have told you this before, and we strongly warned you that the Lord will punish those who do that. 7 God did not call us to live in immorality, but in holiness. 8 So then, whoever rejects this teaching is not rejecting a human being, but God, who gives you his Holy Spirit.

9 There is no need to write you about love for each other. You yourselves have been taught by God how you should love one another. 10 And you have, in fact, behaved like this toward all the believers in all of Macedonia. So we beg you, our friends, to do even more. 11 Make it your aim to live a quiet life, to mind your own business, and to earn your own living, just as we told you before. 12 In this way you will win the respect of those who are not believers, and you will not have to depend on anyone for what you need.

The Lord's Coming

13 Our friends, we want you to know the truth about those who have died, so that you will not be sad, as are those who have no hope. 14 We believe that Jesus died and rose again, and so we believe that God will take back with Jesus those who have died believing in him.

15 What we are teaching you now is the Lord's teaching: we who are alive on the day the Lord comes will not go ahead of those who have died. 16 There will be the shout of command, the archangel's voice, the sound of God's trumpet, and the Lord himself will come down from heaven. Those who have died believing in Christ will rise to life first; 17 then we who are living at that time will be gathered up along with them in the clouds to meet the Lord in the air. And so we will always be with the Lord. 18 So then, encourage one another with these words.

Be Ready for the Lord's Coming

5 There is no need to write you, friends, about the times and occasions when these things will happen. 2 For you yourselves know very well that the Day of the Lord will come as a thief comes at night. 3 When people say, "Everything is quiet and safe," then suddenly destruction will hit them! It will come as suddenly as the pains that come upon a woman in labor, and people will not escape. 4 But you, friends, are not in the darkness, and the Day should not take you by surprise like a thief. 5 All of you are people who belong to the light, who belong to the day. We do not belong to the night or to the darkness. 6 So then, we should not be sleeping like the others; we should be awake and sober. 7 It is at night when people sleep; it is at night when they get drunk. 8 But we belong to the day, and we should be sober. We must wear faith and love as a breastplate, and our hope of salvation as a helmet. 9 God did not choose us to suffer his anger, but to possess salvation through our Lord Jesus Christ, 10 who died for us in order that we might live together with him, whether we are alive or dead when he comes. 11 And so encourage one another and help one another, just as you are now doing.

[b] **3:13** all who belong to him; *or* all his angels. [c] **4:4** live with your wife; *or* control your body.

4:15–17 1 Cor 15:51, 52 **4:15** Sir 48:11 **5:2** Mt 24:43; Lk 12:39; 2 Pet 3:10 **5:8** Isa 59:17; Eph 6:13–17

Final Instructions and Greetings

12 We beg you, our friends, to pay proper
respect to those who work among you, who
guide and instruct you in the Christian life.
13 Treat them with the greatest respect and
love because of the work they do. Be at
peace among yourselves.

14 We urge you, our friends, to warn the
idle, encourage the timid, help the weak, be
patient with everyone. 15 See that no one
pays back wrong for wrong, but at all times
make it your aim to do good to one another
and to all people.

16 Be joyful always, 17 pray at all times, 18 be
thankful in all circumstances. This is what
God wants from you in your life in union
with Christ Jesus.

19 Do not restrain the Holy Spirit; 20 do
not despise inspired messages. 21 Put all things
to the test: keep what is good 22 and avoid
every kind of evil.

23 May the God who gives us peace make
you holy in every way and keep your whole
being—spirit, soul, and body—free from
every fault at the coming of our Lord Jesus
Christ. 24 He who calls you will do it,
because he is faithful.

25 Pray also for us, friends.

26 Greet all the believers with the kiss of
peace.

27 I urge you by the authority of the Lord
to read this letter to all the believers.

28 The grace of our Lord Jesus Christ be
with you.

The Second Letter to the Thessalonians

Do you ever think about the end of the world? The Thessalonians did. In his first letter to the Thessalonians, Paul reassures the people who are concerned about the Second Coming of Christ.

This second letter was written much later. But the concerns of the people in Thessalonica are the same—only worse. They are much more worried about when Jesus will return, and some people have even stopped working. They just want to sit around and wait for the end of the world. This letter assures them and tells them to keep working, to keep living their lives normally. No one can predict when Jesus will return. The lesson from this letter is still good advice today. Don't worry. Keep living your life. Have confidence in God.

Chap. 1:6–7

Headlines

- The Final Judgment (chapter 1)
- People Warned About Laziness (3:6–15)

FACTOIDS

When was this book written? If Paul wrote it, around AD 51. If Paul's followers wrote it, which is most likely, sometime between AD 70 and 90.

Who was it written for? Although it was addressed to the church in Thessalonica, it might also have been written for other churches that were having similar troubles.

Why was it written? Paul wanted to reassure the Thessalonians who were confused about the Second Coming of Christ.

Jesus connection. Jesus Christ will come once more at the end of time to bring God's judgment on every person.

Important themes

- Those who do evil and persecute innocent people will receive their just punishment.
- Do not be troubled by news about the end of the world.

2 THESSALONIANS

1 From Paul, Silas, and Timothy—
To the people of the church in Thes-
salonica, who belong to God our Father and
the Lord Jesus Christ:
2 May God our Father and the Lord Jesus
Christ give you grace and peace.

The Judgment at Christ's Coming

3 Our friends, we must thank God at all
times for you. It is right for us to do so,
because your faith is growing so much and
the love each of you has for the others is
becoming greater. 4 That is why we ourselves
boast about you in the churches of God. We
boast about the way you continue to endure
and believe through all the persecutions and
sufferings you are experiencing.
5 All of this proves that God's judgment is
just and as a result you will become worthy
of his Kingdom, for which you are suffering.
6 God will do what is right: he will bring
suffering on those who make you suffer,
7 and he will give relief to you who suffer
and to us as well. He will do this when the
Lord Jesus appears from heaven with his
mighty angels, 8 with a flaming fire, to punish
those who reject God and who do not obey
the Good News about our Lord Jesus. 9 They
will suffer the punishment of eternal
destruction, separated from the presence of
the Lord and from his glorious might,
10 when he comes on that Day to receive
glory from all his people and honor from all
who believe. You too will be among them,
because you have believed the message that
we told you. 11 That is why we always pray
for you. We ask our God to make you wor-
thy of the life he has called you to live. May
he fulfill by his power all your desire for
goodness and complete your work of faith.
12 In this way the name of our Lord Jesus
will receive glory from you, and you from
him, by the grace of our God and of the
Lord[a] Jesus Christ.

The Wicked One

2 Concerning the coming of our Lord
Jesus Christ and our being gathered
together to be with him: I beg you, my
friends, 2 not to be so easily confused in your
thinking or upset by the claim that the Day
of the Lord has come. Perhaps it is thought
that we said this while prophesying or
preaching, or that we wrote it in a letter.
3 Do not let anyone deceive you in any way.
For the Day will not come until the final
Rebellion takes place and the Wicked One
appears, who is destined to hell. 4 He will
oppose every so-called god or object of
worship and will put himself above them all.
He will even go in and sit down in God's
Temple and claim to be God.
5 Don't you remember? I told you all this
while I was with you. 6 Yet there is some-
thing that keeps this from happening now,
and you know what it is. At the proper time,
then, the Wicked One will appear. 7 The
Mysterious Wickedness is already at work,
but what is going to happen will not happen
until the one who holds it back is taken out
of the way. 8 Then the Wicked One will be
revealed, but when the Lord Jesus comes, he
will kill him with the breath from his mouth
and destroy him with his dazzling presence.
9 The Wicked One will come with the
power of Satan and perform all kinds of false
miracles and wonders, 10 and use every kind
of wicked deceit on those who will perish.
They will perish because they did not wel-
come and love the truth so as to be saved.
11 And so God sends the power of error to
work in them so that they believe what is
false. 12 The result is that all who have not
believed the truth, but have taken pleasure in
sin, will be condemned.

You Are Chosen for Salvation

13 We must thank God at all times for you,
friends, you whom the Lord loves. For God

[a] **1:12** our God and of the Lord; *or* our God and Lord.

1:1 Acts 17:1 **1:9** Isa 2:10 **2:1** 1 Thess 4:15–17 **2:4** Dan 11:36; Ezek 28:2 **2:8** Isa 11:4 **2:9** Mt 24:24

Live it!

God Has Chosen You!

There's something very comforting about this idea: God chose me to do something important with my life. God has chosen me. I have a calling.

Our calling in life is our vocation. A vocation is not just a career. A vocation means listening for who God is calling you to be; a career is a call to some particular kind of work. A vocation is connected to your state in life, as a single or married person, or as a priest or a religious sister or brother. Often, the greatest fulfillment comes when your vocation helps to determine your career.

Some adults try to figure out which career will bring them the most money. Then to be successful in their career, they may ignore their vocation to their family, their friends, and their Church. And they end up being very unhappy. Other adults listen for the vocations God is calling them to. When they find it, they make sure that their careers support their vocations. And often, they are very happy. When people keep their commitment to their vocations, they are usually successful in their careers too.

When you think about future jobs and careers, ask God to help you see the vocation he is calling you to. That should help guide all your career choices.

– 2 Thessalonians 2:13–17

chose you as the first[b] to be saved by the
Spirit's power to make you his holy people
and by your faith in the truth. 14God called
you to this through the Good News we
preached to you; he called you to possess
your share of the glory of our Lord Jesus
Christ. 15So then, our friends, stand firm and
hold on to those truths which we taught
you, both in our preaching and in our letter.
16May our Lord Jesus Christ himself and
God our Father, who loved us and in his
grace gave us unfailing courage and a firm
hope, 17encourage you and strengthen you
to always do and say what is good.

Pray for Us

3 Finally, our friends, pray for us that the
Lord's message may continue to spread
rapidly and be received with honor, just as it
was among you. 2Pray also that God will rescue
us from wicked and evil people; for not
everyone believes the message.
3But the Lord is faithful, and he will
strengthen you and keep you safe from the
Evil One. 4And the Lord gives us confidence
in you, and we are sure that you are doing
and will continue to do what we tell you.
5May the Lord lead you into a greater
understanding of God's love and the
endurance that is given by Christ.

The Obligation to Work

6Our friends, we command you in the
name of our Lord Jesus Christ to keep away
from all believers who are living a lazy life
and who do not follow the instructions that
we gave them. 7You yourselves know very
well that you should do just what we did.
We were not lazy when we were with you.
8We did not accept anyone's support without
paying for it. Instead, we worked and
toiled; we kept working day and night so as
not to be an expense to any of you. 9We did
this, not because we do not have the right to
demand our support; we did it to be an
example for you to follow. 10While we were
with you, we used to tell you, "Whoever
refuses to work is not allowed to eat."
11We say this because we hear that there
are some people among you who live lazy
lives and who do nothing except meddle in

[b] **2:13** as the first; *some manuscripts have* from the beginning.

Do not treat them as enemies. (3:15)

other people's business. 12In the name of the
Lord Jesus Christ we command these people
and warn them to lead orderly lives and
work to earn their own living.
13But you, friends, must not become tired
of doing good. 14It may be that some there
will not obey the message we send you in
this letter. If so, take note of them and have
nothing to do with them, so that they will
be ashamed. 15But do not treat them as ene-
mies; instead, warn them as believers.

Final Words

16May the Lord himself, who is our
source of peace, give you peace at all times
and in every way. The Lord be with you
all.
17With my own hand I write this: *Greet-
ings from Paul*. This is the way I sign every
letter; this is how I write.
18May the grace of our Lord Jesus Christ
be with you all.

THE FIRST LETTER TO Timothy

Being young has its advantages and its disadvantages. Most of us are familiar with being told that we're too young for things, or to wait until we're older, or that because of our age we shouldn't try to do or say certain things. Timothy probably felt this way too. This letter encourages Timothy, a young leader in the early Church, and reminds him that he is not too young. This message can be a reminder for anyone who feels too young to serve as a leader. "Do not let anyone look down on you because you are young" (1 Timothy 4:12) are good words to live by. And following Timothy's example is a good practice to live by.

Chap. 2:1–8

Headlines

- Beware of False Teachers (1:3–10)
- Church Roles Defined (3:1–13)
- How to Live a Godly Life (4:6–15)

FACTOIDS

Who wrote this book? The author used Paul's name, but the book was probably written by followers of Paul.

When was it written? If Paul wrote it, around AD 65. If Paul's followers wrote it, between AD 90 and 100.

Why was it written? The author wanted to counteract some people who were teaching false beliefs and pulling new Christians away from the truth.

Who are the young people in this book? Timothy is a young church leader.

Important themes

- Prayer and worship are important in helping others come to know Jesus.
- Church leadership requires preparation, sincerity, good character, and spiritual training
- Leaders in the Church, whether young or old, serve as examples for all believers.

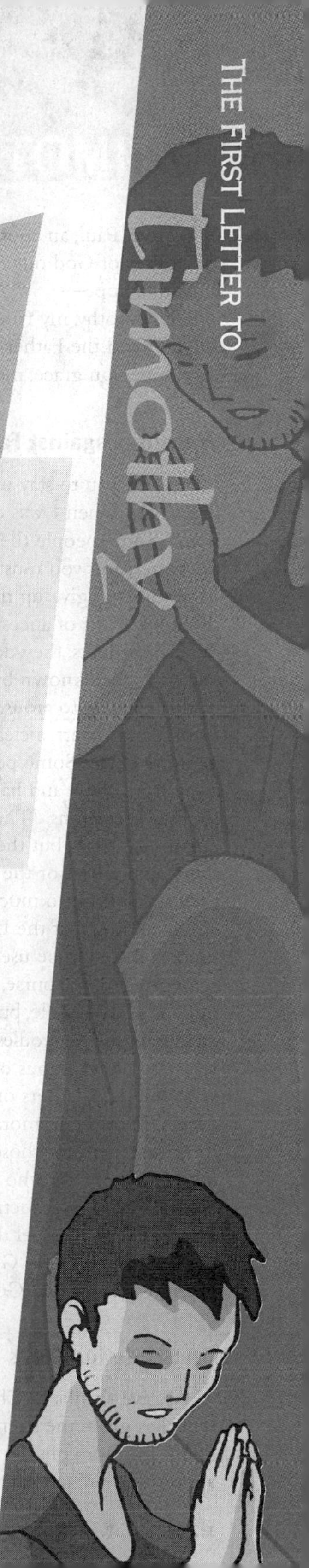

1 TIMOTHY

1 From Paul, an apostle of Christ Jesus by
order of God our Savior and Christ
Jesus our hope—
2 To Timothy, my true son in the faith:
May God the Father and Christ Jesus our
Lord give you grace, mercy, and peace.

Warnings against False Teaching

3 I want you to stay in Ephesus, just as I
urged you when I was on my way to Mace-
donia. Some people there are teaching false
doctrines, and you must order them to stop.
4 Tell them to give up those legends and
those long lists of ancestors, which only pro-
duce arguments; they do not serve God's
plan, which is known by faith. 5 The purpose
of this order is to arouse the love that comes
from a pure heart, a clear conscience, and a
genuine faith. 6 Some people have turned
away from these and have lost their way in
foolish discussions. 7 They want to be teach-
ers of God's law, but they do not understand
their own words or the matters about which
they speak with so much confidence.
8 We know that the Law is good if it is
used as it should be used. 9 It must be
remembered, of course, that laws are made,
not for good people, but for lawbreakers and
criminals, for the godless and sinful, for those
who are not religious or spiritual, for those
who kill their fathers or mothers, for mur-
derers, 10 for the immoral, for sexual perverts,
for kidnappers, for those who lie and give
false testimony or who do anything else
contrary to sound doctrine. 11 That teaching
is found in the gospel that was entrusted to
me to announce, the Good News from the
glorious and blessed God.

Gratitude for God's Mercy

12 I give thanks to Christ Jesus our Lord,
who has given me strength for my work. I
thank him for considering me worthy and
appointing me to serve him, 13 even though
in the past I spoke evil of him and persecut-
ed and insulted him. But God was merciful
to me because I did not yet have faith and so
did not know what I was doing. 14 And our
Lord poured out his abundant grace on me
and gave me the faith and love which are
ours in union with Christ Jesus. 15 This is a
true saying, to be completely accepted and
believed: Christ Jesus came into the world to
save sinners. I am the worst of them, 16 but
God was merciful to me in order that Christ
Jesus might show his full patience in dealing
with me, the worst of sinners, as an example
for all those who would later believe in him
and receive eternal life. 17 To the eternal
King, immortal and invisible, the only
God—to him be honor and glory forever
and ever! Amen.
18 Timothy, my child, I entrust to you this
command, which is in accordance with the
words of prophecy spoken in the past about

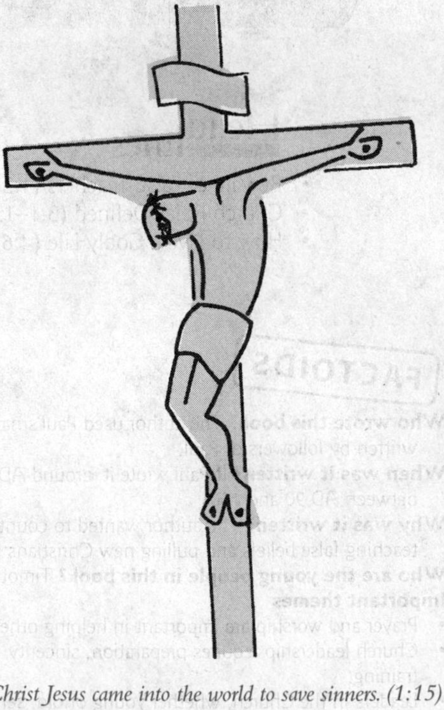

Christ Jesus came into the world to save sinners. (1:15)

1:2 Acts 16:1 **1:13** Acts 8:3; 9:4, 5

Pray it!

It's PPRT-Y Easy to Pray!

Ricardo tried to lead prayer at the junior high gathering and was tongue-tied. The youth minister whispered in his ear, "Pert, Ricardo, remember pert?" Ricardo took a deep breathe and led the prayer. It was easy, once he remembered *PPRT* (which sounds like *pert*).

PPRT are the initials of directions for prayer given in 1 Timothy 2:1. The first *P* is "prayers," which simply means taking time out to pray. The second *P* is "petitions." Petitions are your own needs that you pray for. The *R* is for "requests." Requests are other people's needs that you pray for. The *T* is for "thanksgiving." Thanksgiving is taking time to thank God for the things you are grateful for.

Praying out loud in front of a group can be hard, especially if you haven't had time to practice. So just remember it is pert-y easy to pray if you remember *PPRT*. Give it a try right now.

Prayers: Take a few minutes to pray.
Petitions: Pray for your own personal needs.
Requests: Pray for needs of other people, especially the things people asked you to pray for.
Thanksgiving: Thank God for the things, people, and events you are grateful for.

— 1 Timothy 2:1

you. Use those words as weapons in order to
fight well, 19and keep your faith and a clear
conscience. Some people have not listened
to their conscience and have made a ruin of
their faith. 20Among them are Hymenaeus
and Alexander, whom I have punished by
handing them over to the power of Satan;
this will teach them to stop their blasphemy.

Church Worship

2 First of all, then, I urge that petitions,
prayers, requests, and thanksgivings be
offered to God for all people; 2for kings and
all others who are in authority, that we may
live a quiet and peaceful life with all rever-
ence toward God and with proper conduct.
3This is good and it pleases God our Savior,
4who wants everyone to be saved and to
come to know the truth. 5For there is one
God, and there is one who brings God and
human beings together, the man Christ
Jesus, 6who gave himself to redeem the
whole human race. That was the proof at the
right time that God wants everyone to be
saved, 7and that is why I was sent as an apos-
tle and teacher of the Gentiles, to proclaim
the message of faith and truth. I am not
lying; I am telling the truth!
8In every church service I want the men
to pray, men who are dedicated to God and
can lift up their hands in prayer without
anger or argument. 9I also want the women
to be modest and sensible about their clothes
and to dress properly; not with fancy hair
styles or with gold ornaments or pearls or

2:7 2 Tim 1:11 **2:9** 1 Pet 3:3

***Doctrines* are the official teachings of the Church based on what God revealed through Jesus Christ under the guidance of the Holy Spirit.**

Catholic Connections

Leading the Way

In some other Bibles the Church leaders mentioned in 1 Timothy, chapter 3, are called bishops. The Church helpers mentioned in chapter 3 are called deacons. First Timothy was written when the churches that Paul and other missionaries started were getting bigger. They needed strong spiritual leaders to stay on track. This letter provided spiritual advice to those early bishops and deacons for leading their churches.

Over time the Holy Spirit shaped the roles of bishop, priest, and deacon into the ministries we have today. The leaders of the early Church helped maintain true teaching and guided the Church's service, and so do our bishops, priests, and deacons today. DREs, music ministers, youth ministers, and pastoral ministers serve as leaders in many parishes too. Are you called to serve the Church in a leadership role?

— 1 Timothy 3:1–13

expensive dresses, 10but with good deeds, as
is proper for women who claim to be reli-
gious. 11Women should learn in silence and
all humility. 12I do not allow them to teach
or to have authority over men; they must
keep quiet. 13For Adam was created first,
and then Eve. 14And it was not Adam who
was deceived; it was the woman who was
deceived and broke God's law. 15But a
woman will be saved through having chil-
dren,[a] if she perseveres[b] in faith and love and
holiness, with modesty.

Leaders in the Church

3 This is a true saying: If a man is eager to
be a church leader, he desires an excel-
lent work. 2A church leader must be without
fault; he must have only one wife,[c] be sober,
self-controlled, and orderly; he must wel-
come strangers in his home; he must be able
to teach; 3he must not be a drunkard or a
violent man, but gentle and peaceful; he
must not love money; 4he must be able to
manage his own family well and make his
children obey him with all respect. 5For if a
man does not know how to manage his own
family, how can he take care of the church
of God? 6He must be mature in the faith, so
that he will not swell up with pride and be
condemned, as the Devil was. 7He should be
a man who is respected by the people out-
side the church, so that he will not be dis-
graced and fall into the Devil's trap.

Helpers in the Church

8Church helpers must also have a good
character and be sincere; they must not drink
too much wine or be greedy for money;
9they should hold to the revealed truth of the
faith with a clear conscience. 10They should
be tested first, and then, if they pass the test,
they are to serve. 11Their wives[d] also must be
of good character and must not gossip; they
must be sober and honest in everything. 12A

[a] **2:15** will be saved through having children; *or* will be kept safe through childbirth. [b] **2:15** if she perseveres; *or* if they persevere. [c] **3:2** have only one wife; *or* be married only once. [d] **3:11** Their wives; *or* Women helpers.

2:13 a Gen 2:7; **b** Gen 2:21, 22 **2:14** Gen 3:1–6 **3:2–7** Titus 1:6–9

At the time this letter was written, Church leaders could still be married. The requirement of priests and bishops staying unmarried developed later.

church helper must have only one wife,[e] and
be able to manage his children and family
well. 13 Those helpers who do their work
well win for themselves a good standing and
are able to speak boldly about their faith in
Christ Jesus.

The Great Secret

14 As I write this letter to you, I hope to
come and see you soon. 15 But if I delay, this
letter will let you know how we should con-
duct ourselves in God's household, which is
the church of the living God, the pillar and
support of the truth. 16 No one can deny
how great is the secret of our religion:

He appeared in human form,
was shown to be right by the Spirit,[f]
and was seen by angels.
He was preached among the nations,
was believed in throughout the world,
and was taken up to heaven.

False Teachers

4 The Spirit says clearly that some people
will abandon the faith in later times;
they will obey lying spirits and follow the
teachings of demons. 2 Such teachings are
spread by deceitful liars, whose consciences
are dead, as if burnt with a hot iron. 3 Such
people teach that it is wrong to marry and
to eat certain foods. But God created those
foods to be eaten, after a prayer of thanks, by
those who are believers and have come to
know the truth. 4 Everything that God has
created is good; nothing is to be rejected, but
everything is to be received with a prayer of
thanks, 5 because the word of God and the
prayer make it acceptable to God.

A Good Servant of Christ Jesus

6 If you give these instructions to the
believers, you will be a good servant of
Christ Jesus, as you feed yourself spiritually
on the words of faith and of the true teach-
ing which you have followed. 7 But keep
away from those godless legends, which are
not worth telling. Keep yourself in training
for a godly life. 8 Physical exercise has some
value, but spiritual exercise is valuable in
every way, because it promises life both for
the present and for the future. 9 This is a true
saying, to be completely accepted and
believed. 10 We struggle[g] and work hard,
because we have placed our hope in the liv-
ing God, who is the Savior of all and espe-
cially of those who believe.

11 Give them these instructions and these
teachings. 12 Do not let anyone look down
on you because you are young, but be an
example for the believers in your speech,
your conduct, your love, faith, and purity.
13 Until I come, give your time and effort to
the public reading of the Scriptures and to
preaching and teaching. 14 Do not neglect
the spiritual gift that is in you, which was
given to you when the prophets spoke and
the elders laid their hands on you. 15 Practice
these things and devote yourself to them, in
order that your progress may be seen by all.
16 Watch yourself and watch your teaching.
Keep on doing these things, because if you
do, you will save both yourself and those
who hear you.

Responsibilities toward Believers

5 Do not rebuke an older man, but appeal
to him as if he were your father. Treat
the younger men as your brothers, 2 the older
women as mothers, and the younger women
as sisters, with all purity.

3 Show respect for widows who really are
all alone. 4 But if a widow has children or
grandchildren, they should learn first to
carry out their religious duties toward their
own family and in this way repay their par-
ents and grandparents, because that is what
pleases God. 5 A widow who is all alone,
with no one to take care of her, has placed
her hope in God and continues to pray and
ask him for his help night and day. 6 But a
widow who gives herself to pleasure has
already died, even though she lives. 7 Give
them these instructions, so that no one will
find fault with them. 8 But if any do not take

[e] **3:12** have only one wife; *or* be married only once. [f] **3:16** was shown to be right by the Spirit; *or* and, in spiritual form, was shown to be right. [g] **4:10** struggle; *some manuscripts have* are reviled.

5:5 Jdt 8:4–6

Live it!

Never Too Young

While growing up, Jeff was constantly reminded that his older brother, Brett, was a good role model. Brett won athletic awards, was class president at the middle school, and all his teachers remembered how great he was. Brett was now in high school and was beginning to do things that his parents weren't too happy about. Jeff was worried that Brett was starting to do bad stuff, and one day told him so. Brett replied, "You're only 12, what do you know?" which of course made Jeff feel hurt.

Imagine Jeff's surprise at the dinner table that night when his parents said to Brett, "You know, you should follow the example of your little brother, he is respectful to us and is well-behaved at school. You could learn from him." Jeff almost fell off his chair.

Because Timothy was a young leader in the Church, other people may not have given him the respect he deserved (1 Timothy 4:12). The author of this letter reminds Timothy—and us—that anyone of any age can be an example by their speech and conduct. Even though you are young, you can be an inspiration for others, even people much older than you!

— 1 Timothy 4:11–16

care of their relatives, especially the members
of their own family, they have denied the
faith and are worse than an unbeliever.
9Do not add any widow to the list of
widows unless she is over sixty years of age.
In addition, she must have been married
only once[h] 10and have a reputation for good
deeds: a woman who brought up her children well, received strangers in her home, performed humble duties for other Christians, helped people in trouble, and devoted herself to doing good.
11But do not include younger widows in
the list; because when their desires make
them want to marry, they turn away from
Christ, 12and so become guilty of breaking
their earlier promise to him. 13They also
learn to waste their time in going around from house to house; but even worse, they learn to be gossips and busybodies, talking of
things they should not. 14So I would prefer
that the younger widows get married, have children, and take care of their homes, so as to give our enemies no chance of speaking
evil of us. 15For some widows have already
turned away to follow Satan. 16But if any
Christian woman has widows in her family, she must take care of them and not put the burden on the church, so that it may take care of the widows who are all alone.
17The elders who do good work as leaders should be considered worthy of receiving double pay, especially those who work hard at preaching and teaching. 18For the scrip-
ture says, "Do not muzzle an ox when you are using it to thresh grain" and "Workers should be given their pay." 19Do not listen
to an accusation against an elder unless it is brought by two or more witnesses.
20Rebuke publicly all those who commit
sins, so that the rest may be afraid.
21In the presence of God and of Christ
Jesus and of the holy angels I solemnly call upon you to obey these instructions without showing any prejudice or favor to anyone in anything you do. 22Be in no hurry to lay
hands on people to dedicate them to the Lord's service. Take no part in the sins of others; keep yourself pure.
23Do not drink water only, but take a little
wine to help your digestion, since you are sick so often.
24The sins of some people are plain to see,
and their sins go ahead of them to judgment; but the sins of others are seen only

[h] **5:9** married only once; *or* faithful to her husband.
5:18 **a** Deut 25:4; **b** Mt 10:10; Lk 10:7 **5:19** Deut 17:6; 19:15

later. 25In the same way good deeds are
plainly seen, and even those that are not so
plain cannot be hidden.

6 Those who are slaves must consider their
masters worthy of all respect, so that no
one will speak evil of the name of God and
of our teaching. 2Slaves belonging to Chris-
tian masters must not despise them, for they
are believers too. Instead, they are to serve
them even better, because those who benefit
from their work are believers whom they
love.

False Teaching and True Riches

You must teach and preach these things.
3Whoever teaches a different doctrine and
does not agree with the true words of our
Lord Jesus Christ and with the teaching of
our religion 4is swollen with pride and
knows nothing. He has an unhealthy desire
to argue and quarrel about words, and this
brings on jealousy, disputes, insults, evil sus-
picions, 5and constant arguments from peo-
ple whose minds do not function and who
no longer have the truth. They think that
religion is a way to become rich.
6Well, religion does make us very rich, if
we are satisfied with what we have. 7What
did we bring into the world? Nothing!
What can we take out of the world? Noth-
ing! 8So then, if we have food and clothes,
that should be enough for us. 9But those
who want to get rich fall into temptation
and are caught in the trap of many foolish
and harmful desires, which pull them down
to ruin and destruction. 10For the love of
money is a source of all kinds of evil. Some
have been so eager to have it that they
have wandered away from the faith and
have broken their hearts with many sor-
rows.

What did we bring into the world? Nothing! What can we take out of the world? Nothing! (6:7)

Live it!

Strive

You can strive for the same character qualities Timothy was told to work toward in 1 Timothy 6:11. For each of the qualities, write a phrase that starts with the same letter as the word. The phrase should explain how you will work toward attaining these qualities. For example, the first word, *righteousness,* begins with *R.* So your phrase might be "Resist cheating." Give it a try:

Righteousness:
R____________________

Godliness:
G____________________

Faith:
F____________________

Love:
L____________________

Endurance:
E____________________

Gentleness:
G____________________

Once you write your phrases, copy them onto nice paper, decorate the sheet, and put it somewhere to remind yourself of the qualities you are striving for.

— 1 Timothy 6:11–14

Righteousness **is the quality of doing what is right, fair, and just.**

Personal Instructions

[11]But you, man of God, avoid all these
things. Strive for righteousness, godliness,
faith, love, endurance, and gentleness. [12]Run
your best in the race of faith, and win eter-
nal life for yourself; for it was to this life that
God called you when you firmly professed
your faith before many witnesses. [13]Before
God, who gives life to all things, and before
Christ Jesus, who firmly professed his faith
before Pontius Pilate, I command you [14]to
obey your orders and keep them faithfully
until the Day when our Lord Jesus Christ
will appear. [15]His appearing will be brought
about at the right time by God, the blessed
and only Ruler, the King of kings and the
Lord of lords. [16]He alone is immortal; he
lives in the light that no one can approach.
No one has ever seen him; no one can ever
see him. To him be honor and eternal
power! Amen.
[17]Command those who are rich in the
things of this life not to be proud, but to
place their hope, not in such an uncertain
thing as riches, but in God, who generously
gives us everything for our enjoyment.
[18]Command them to do good, to be rich in
good works, to be generous and ready to
share with others. [19]In this way they will
store up for themselves a treasure which will
be a solid foundation for the future. And
then they will be able to win the life which
is true life.
[20]Timothy, keep safe what has been
entrusted to your care. Avoid the profane
talk and foolish arguments of what some
people wrongly call "Knowledge." [21]For
some have claimed to possess it, and as a
result they have lost the way of faith.

God's grace be with you all.

6:13 Jn 18:33-38

Your Next Step

Congratulations on finishing the First Letter of Timothy! Use this space to write your thoughts and questions about this book. Now move ahead to the Second Letter of Timothy to read even more advice to this young church leader.

The Second Letter to Timothy

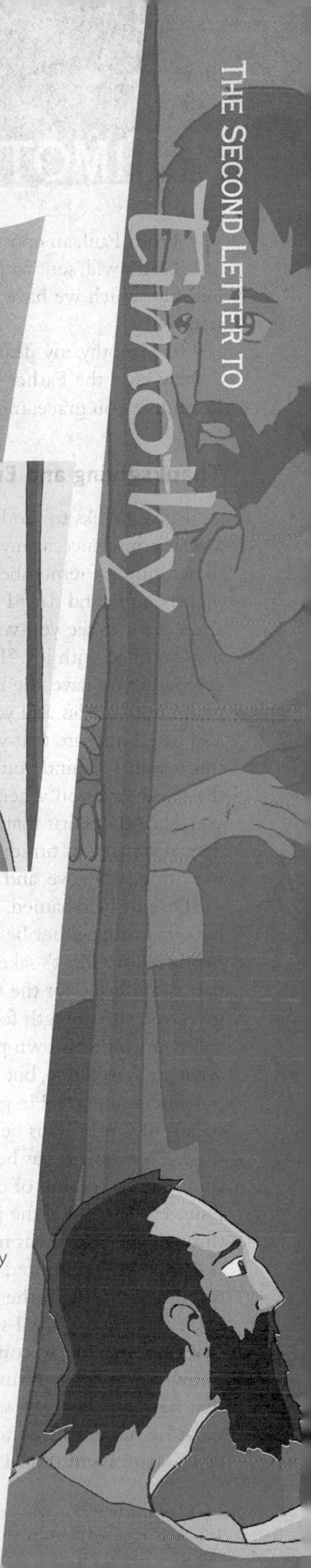

Did you ever get into trouble for something you didn't do? Then you know how this writer feels. Imagine someone who was put in jail—simply for being a Christian!

This letter expresses the sadness of a church leader who has suffered for the faith. Yet the author still has faith, still has persistence, and still wants to encourage others (especially Timothy) to be strong. It is clear that the author knows Timothy's family well and that he loves and cares about Timothy very much. This letter ends with the author recalling details about many personal friends. Imagine how lonely it would feel to sit in jail without any friends. . . . It seems to make this letter even more special.

Chap. 4:9–15

Headlines

- Encouraging Words from an Apostle (1:8–14)
- The Power of the Word of God! (3:14–17)
- God's Prize Waits for Us (4:7–8)

FACTOIDS

Who wrote this book? Possibly Paul, but more likely one of Paul's followers.

When was it written? If Paul wrote it, possibly as early as AD 65, but more likely around AD 90 to 100.

Who was it written for? It was written for Church leaders in the name of Timothy, a young leader in the early Church.

Why Was It Written? The author wanted to encourage and give advice to Church leaders.

Important themes

- Do not be ashamed of your faith.
- It helps to remember that Jesus suffered, died, and rose again.
- Be persistent in your faith and remember what you have been taught.
- Keep teaching others about the Gospel story.

2 TIMOTHY

1 From Paul, an apostle of Christ Jesus by
God's will, sent to proclaim the prom-
ised life which we have in union with Christ
Jesus—
[2]To Timothy, my dear son:
May God the Father and Christ Jesus our
Lord give you grace, mercy, and peace.

Thanksgiving and Encouragement

[3]I give thanks to God, whom I serve with
a clear conscience, as my ancestors did. I
thank him as I remember you always in my
prayers night and day. [4]I remember your tears,
and I want to see you very much, so that I
may be filled with joy. [5]I remember the sin-
cere faith you have, the kind of faith that your
grandmother Lois and your mother Eunice
also had. I am sure that you have it also. [6]For
this reason I remind you to keep alive the gift
that God gave you when I laid my hands on
you. [7]For the Spirit that God has given us
does not make us timid; instead, his Spirit fills
us with power, love, and self-control.
[8]Do not be ashamed, then, of witnessing
for our Lord; neither be ashamed of me, a
prisoner for Christ's sake. Instead, take your
part in suffering for the Good News, as God
gives you the strength for it. [9]He saved us and
called us to be his own people, not because of
what we have done, but because of his own
purpose and grace. He gave us this grace by
means of Christ Jesus before the beginning of
time, [10]but now it has been revealed to us
through the coming of our Savior, Christ
Jesus. He has ended the power of death and
through the gospel has revealed immortal life.
[11]God has appointed me as an apostle and
teacher to proclaim the Good News, [12]and it
is for this reason that I suffer these things.
But I am still full of confidence, because I
know whom I have trusted, and I am sure
that he is able to keep safe until that Day
what he has entrusted to me.[a] [13]Hold firmly
to the true words that I taught you, as the
example for you to follow, and remain in the
faith and love that are ours in union with
Christ Jesus. [14]Through the power of the
Holy Spirit, who lives in us, keep the good
things that have been entrusted to you.
[15]You know that everyone in the province
of Asia, including Phygelus and Hermogenes,
has deserted me. [16]May the Lord show mercy
to the family of Onesiphorus, because he
cheered me up many times. He was not
ashamed that I am in prison, [17]but as soon as
he arrived in Rome, he started looking for me
until he found me. [18]May the Lord grant him
his mercy on that Day! And you know very
well how much he did for me in Ephesus.

A Loyal Soldier of Christ Jesus

2 As for you, my son, be strong through
the grace that is ours in union with
Christ Jesus. [2]Take the teachings that you
heard me proclaim in the presence of many
witnesses, and entrust them to reliable peo-
ple, who will be able to teach others also.
[3]Take your part in suffering, as a loyal sol-
dier of Christ Jesus. [4]A soldier on active duty
wants to please his commanding officer and
so does not get mixed up in the affairs of
civilian life. [5]An athlete who runs in a race
cannot win the prize unless he obeys the
rules. [6]The farmer who has done the hard
work should have the first share of the har-
vest. [7]Think about what I am saying, because
the Lord will enable you to understand it all.
[8]Remember Jesus Christ, who was raised
from death, who was a descendant of David,
as is taught in the Good News I preach.
[9]Because I preach the Good News, I suffer
and I am even chained like a criminal. But
the word of God is not in chains, [10]and so I
endure everything for the sake of God's cho-
sen people, in order that they too may
obtain the salvation that comes through
Christ Jesus and brings eternal glory. [11]This
is a true saying:

[a] **1:12** what he has entrusted to me; *or* what I have entrusted to him.

1:2 Acts 16:1 **1:5** Acts 16:1 **1:11** 1 Tim 2:7

Pray it!

The Passions of Youth

Joan and Jacob had been seeing each other for two months. It was Joan's first relationship with a guy, and she felt deeply in love. One day at school Jacob said, "Joan, it's been great, but I think we should just be friends. I'm not ready to date just one person." Joan felt deeply hurt, and without thinking she burst out, "That's not fair. We love each other. You can't decide that by yourself." They got into a big argument. All of a sudden they looked around, and it felt like the whole school was staring at them.

As a young person, it is natural that you will feel deep emotions. You will love more, be angrier about injustices, and feel hurt more easily. This is what it means to be passionate, and it is a good thing. So what does 2 Timothy mean when it says, "Avoid the passions of youth" (2:22)? The author is talking about not letting your deep emotions take control of you. Don't let your love or your anger or your hurt lead you to say or do something that you will later regret. When you are feeling strong emotions, take a break. Share your feelings with God in prayer. Talk with someone a little older who can help you sort out what you are feeling and what to say or do.

— 2 Timothy 2:22–26

"If we have died with him,
we shall also live with him.
12 If we continue to endure,
we shall also rule with him.
If we deny him,
he also will deny us.
13 If we are not faithful,
he remains faithful,
because he cannot be false to himself."

An Approved Worker

14 Remind your people of this, and give
them a solemn warning in God's presence
not to fight over words. It does no good, but
only ruins the people who listen. 15 Do your
best to win full approval in God's sight, as a
worker who is not ashamed of his work, one
who correctly teaches the message of God's
truth. 16 Keep away from profane and foolish
discussions, which only drive people farther
away from God. 17 Such teaching is like an
open sore that eats away the flesh. Two men
who have taught such things are Hymenaeus
and Philetus. 18 They have left the way of
truth and are upsetting the faith of some
believers by saying that our resurrection has
already taken place. 19 But the solid founda-
tion that God has laid cannot be shaken; and
on it are written these words: "The Lord
knows those who are his" and "Those who
say that they belong to the Lord must turn
away from wrongdoing."
20 In a large house there are dishes and
bowls of all kinds: some are made of silver
and gold, others of wood and clay; some are
for special occasions, others for ordinary use.
21 Those who make themselves clean from all
those evil things, will be used for special
purposes, because they are dedicated and
useful to their Master, ready to be used for
every good deed. 22 Avoid the passions of
youth, and strive for righteousness, faith,
love, and peace, together with those who

2:12 Mt 10:33; Lk 12:9 **2:19** Num 16:5

The saying in 2 Timothy 2:11–13 may have been part of an early Christian hymn. Can you create a song using these words?

Catholic Connections

God's Revealed Truth

Are there certain Bible stories you know really well? Maybe you know them because you've heard them all your life. They are probably the stories your grandparents, parents, catechists, and priests told you as you grew up. This is like Timothy, who from an early age learned Scripture (2 Timothy 3:14–15). The advantage you have is that this edition of the Bible is created just for young people. It is important to have parents and teachers teaching you about the Bible, and this Bible will also help you understand the meaning of the Bible stories.

The truth is that by reading and praying with the Bible, you are getting to know God. God is revealed in the Bible, and the more stories about God and the people of God you become familiar with, the easier it is to know God. God also reveals himself and his truths in sacred Tradition. Sacred Tradition includes the truths revealed by Jesus Christ that were taught and passed on by the Apostles, the popes, and the bishops. Sacred Tradition and the Bible are the ways God's revelation for all people is handed on.

— 2 Timothy 3:14–17

with a pure heart call out to the Lord for
help. 23But keep away from foolish and
ignorant arguments; you know that they end
up in quarrels. 24As the Lord's servant, you
must not quarrel. You must be kind toward
all, a good and patient teacher, 25who is gen-
tle as you correct your opponents, for it may
be that God will give them the opportunity
to repent and come to know the truth.
26And then they will come to their senses
and escape from the trap of the Devil, who
had caught them and made them obey his
will.

The Last Days

3 Remember that there will be difficult
times in the last days. 2People will be
selfish, greedy, boastful, and conceited; they
will be insulting, disobedient to their par-
ents, ungrateful, and irreligious; 3they will
be unkind, merciless, slanderers, violent, and
fierce; they will hate the good; 4they will be
treacherous, reckless, and swollen with
pride; they will love pleasure rather than
God; 5they will hold to the outward form
of our religion, but reject its real power.
Keep away from such people. 6Some of
them go into people's houses and gain con-
trol over weak women who are burdened by
the guilt of their sins and driven by all kinds
of desires, 7women who are always trying to
learn but who can never come to know the
truth. 8As Jannes and Jambres were opposed
to Moses, so also these people are opposed
to the truth—people whose minds do not
function and who are failures in the faith.
9But they will not get very far, because
everyone will see how stupid they are. That
is just what happened to Jannes and Jam-
bres.

3:8 Ex 7:11

Holy Scriptures,* or *Scripture *(2 Timothy 3:15–16)*, **is another name for the Bible. Timothy read the Hebrew Scriptures, or the Old Testament.**

Live it!

Long, Full Life

This letter was probably written in the name of Paul, recalling the time when Paul was in prison. In prison Paul was sad. He missed Timothy and his other friends and begged them to visit him. He was worried about how everyone was holding up, but he had faith in the people of God. He sensed that he might not live much longer, and he said about his life, "I have done my best in the race, I have run the full distance, and I have kept the faith" (2 Timothy 4:7). The writer knew that Paul was ready to accept his death, and was grateful that he had had such a full life.

Is there someone you know who has lived a long, full life? Perhaps an aging relative or a neighbor? Take a moment to be thankful for that person. Pray for that person's needs. Then decide to spend time with that person and enjoy him or her. Maybe you can get some good advice for your life, as Timothy did.

— 2 Timothy 4:6–8

Last Instructions

10But you have followed my teaching, my
conduct, and my purpose in life; you have
observed my faith, my patience, my love, my
endurance, 11my persecutions, and my suffer-
ings. You know all that happened to me in
Antioch, Iconium, and Lystra, the terrible
persecutions I endured! But the Lord res-
cued me from them all. 12Everyone who
wants to live a godly life in union with
Christ Jesus will be persecuted; 13and evil
persons and impostors will keep on going
from bad to worse, deceiving others and
being deceived themselves. 14But as for you,
continue in the truths that you were taught
and firmly believe. You know who your
teachers were, 15and you remember that ever
since you were a child, you have known the
Holy Scriptures, which are able to give you
the wisdom that leads to salvation through
faith in Christ Jesus. 16All Scripture is
inspired by God and is useful[b] for teaching
the truth, rebuking error, correcting faults,
and giving instruction for right living, 17so
that the person who serves God may be fully
qualified and equipped to do every kind of
good deed.

4 In the presence of God and of Christ
Jesus, who will judge the living and the
dead, and because he is coming to rule as
King, I solemnly urge you 2to preach the
message, to insist upon proclaiming it
(whether the time is right or not), to con-
vince, reproach, and encourage, as you teach
with all patience. 3The time will come
when people will not listen to sound doc-
trine, but will follow their own desires and
will collect for themselves more and more
teachers who will tell them what they are
itching to hear. 4They will turn away from
listening to the truth and give their atten-
tion to legends. 5But you must keep control
of yourself in all circumstances; endure suf-
fering, do the work of a preacher of the
Good News, and perform your whole duty
as a servant of God.

6As for me, the hour has come for me to
be sacrificed; the time is here for me to leave
this life. 7I have done my best in the race, I
have run the full distance, and I have kept
the faith.[c] 8And now there is waiting for me
the victory prize of being put right with
God, which the Lord, the righteous Judge,
will give me on that Day—and not only to
me, but to all those who wait with love for
him to appear.

[b] **3:16** All Scripture is inspired by God and is useful; *or* Every scripture inspired by God is also useful.
[c] **4:7** kept the faith; *or* been true to my promise.
3:11 **a** Acts 13:14–52; **b** Acts 14:1–7; **c** Acts 14:8–20

The victory prize . . . (4:8)

Personal Words

9Do your best to come to me soon.
10Demas fell in love with this present world
and has deserted me, going off to Thessalonica.
Crescens went to Galatia, and Titus to
Dalmatia. 11Only Luke is with me. Get Mark
and bring him with you, because he can
help me in the work. 12I sent Tychicus to
Ephesus. 13When you come, bring my coat
that I left in Troas with Carpus; bring the
books too, and especially the ones made of
parchment.
14Alexander the metalworker did me great
harm; the Lord will reward him according to
what he has done. 15Be on your guard
against him yourself, because he was violently
opposed to our message.
16No one stood by me the first time I
defended myself; all deserted me. May God
not count it against them! 17But the Lord
stayed with me and gave me strength, so that
I was able to proclaim the full message for all
the Gentiles to hear; and I was rescued from
being sentenced to death. 18And the Lord
will rescue me from all evil and take me
safely into his heavenly Kingdom. To him be
the glory forever and ever! Amen.

Final Greetings

19I send greetings to Priscilla and Aquila
and to the family of Onesiphorus. 20Erastus
stayed in Corinth, and I left Trophimus in
Miletus, because he was sick. 21Do your best
to come before winter.

Eubulus, Pudens, Linus, and Claudia send their greetings, and so do all the other Christians.

22The Lord be with your spirit.
God's grace be with you all.

4:10 **a** Col 4:14; Philem 24; **b** 2 Cor 8:23; Gal 2:3; Titus 1:4 **4:11** **a** Col 4:14; Philem 24; **b** Acts 12:12, 25; 13:13; 15:37–39; Col 4:10; Philem 24 **4:12** Acts 20:4; Eph 6:21, 22; Col 4:7, 8 **4:13** Acts 20:6 **4:14** **a** 1 Tim 1:20; **b** Ps 62:12; Rom 2:6 **4:19** **a** Acts 18:2; **b** 2 Tim 1:16, 17 **4:20** **a** Acts 19:22; Rom 16:23; **b** Acts 20:4; 21:29

Your Next Step

Congratulations on finishing the Second Letter of Timothy! Use this space to write your thoughts and questions about this book. If you are following the suggested reading plan, move back to the First Letter to the Corinthians. This letter is about some of the issues an early Christian church faced.

THE LETTER TO Titus

Did you ever want to give advice to a bishop or leader of the Church? This short letter does exactly that.

It was written to a Church leader and is filled with advice: Advice for elders and leaders (called presbyters and bishops in some Bible translations) and for rebellious people. Advice for men and women, both young and old. Advice for Church leaders on what to do and not to do. There is even advice for slaves.

After reading it, you might think about your answer to this question, "If I were a Church leader, what advice would I want to follow?"

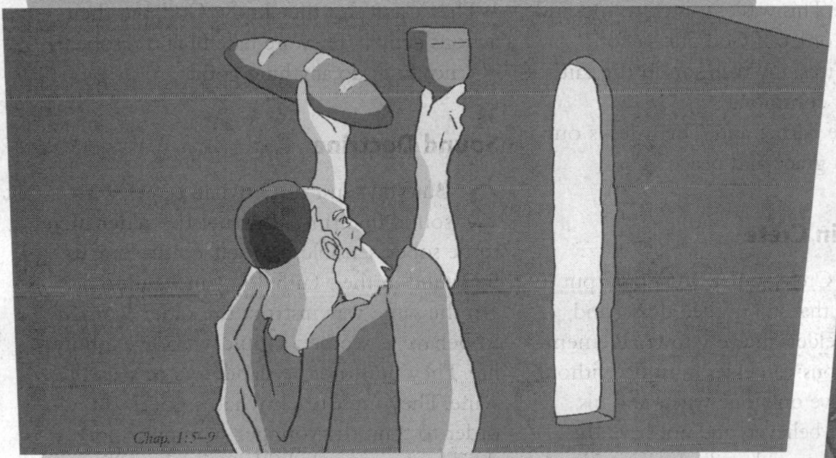

Chap. 1:5–9

Headlines

- What Makes a Worthy Bishop? (1:5–9)
- Tips for Teaching the Christian Life (2:1–8)
- Be Good in Every Way! (3:1–11)

FACTOIDS

Who wrote this book? Possibly Paul, but more likely one of Paul's followers.

When was it written? If Paul wrote it, as early as AD 65, but more likely between AD 90 and 100.

Who was it written for? This letter was written to Titus, a trusted leader in the early Church.

Why was it written? It was written to encourage Titus in his role as pastor and to give him advice.

Important themes

- Pastors are given advice for teaching people how to live as Christians.
- People need encouragement to keep good habits.

TITUS

1 From Paul, a servant of God and an
apostle of Jesus Christ.
I was chosen and sent to help the faith of
God's chosen people and to lead them to the
truth taught by our religion, 2which is based
on the hope for eternal life. God, who does
not lie, promised us this life before the begin-
ning of time, 3and at the right time he revealed
it in his message. This was entrusted to me, and
I proclaim it by order of God our Savior.
4I write to Titus, my true son in the faith
that we have in common.
May God the Father and Christ Jesus our
Savior give you grace and peace.

Titus' Work in Crete

5I left you in Crete, so that you could put in
order the things that still needed doing and
appoint church elders in every town. Remem-
ber my instructions: 6an elder must be without
fault; he must have only one wife,[a] and his
children must be believers and not have the
reputation of being wild or disobedient. 7For
since a church leader is in charge of God's
work, he should be without fault. He must not
be arrogant or quick-tempered, or a drunkard
or violent or greedy for money. 8He must be
hospitable and love what is good. He must be
self-controlled, upright, holy, and disciplined.
9He must hold firmly to the message which
can be trusted and which agrees with the doc-
trine. In this way he will be able to encourage
others with the true teaching and also to show
the error of those who are opposed to it.
10For there are many, especially the converts
from Judaism, who rebel and deceive others
with their nonsense. 11It is necessary to stop
their talk, because they are upsetting whole
families by teaching what they should not, and
all for the shameful purpose of making money.
12-13It was a Cretan himself, one of their own
prophets, who spoke the truth when he said,
"Cretans are always liars, wicked beasts, and
lazy gluttons." For this reason you must rebuke
them sharply, so that they may have a healthy
faith 14and no longer hold on to Jewish leg-
ends and to human commandments which
come from people who have rejected the
truth. 15Everything is pure to those who are
themselves pure; but nothing is pure to those
who are defiled and unbelieving, for their
minds and consciences have been defiled.
16They claim that they know God, but their
actions deny it. They are hateful and disobedi-
ent, not fit to do anything good.

Sound Doctrine

2 But you must teach what agrees with
sound doctrine. 2Instruct the older men
to be sober, sensible, and self-controlled; to
be sound in their faith, love, and endurance.
3In the same way instruct the older women
to behave as women should who live a holy
life. They must not be slanderers or slaves to
wine. They must teach what is good, 4in
order to train the younger women to love
their husbands and children, 5to be self-con-
trolled and pure, and to be good housewives
who submit themselves to their husbands, so
that no one will speak evil of the message
that comes from God.
6In the same way urge the young men to
be self-controlled. 7In all things you yourself
must be an example of good behavior. Be
sincere and serious in your teaching. 8Use
sound words that cannot be criticized, so
that your enemies may be put to shame by
not having anything bad to say about us.
9Slaves are to submit themselves to their
masters and please them in all things. They
must not talk back to them 10or steal from
them. Instead, they must show that they are
always good and faithful, so as to bring credit
to the teaching about God our Savior in all
they do.
11For God has revealed his grace for the sal-
vation of all people. 12That grace instructs us
to give up ungodly living and worldly passions,

[a] **1:6** have only one wife; *or* be married only once.
1:4 2 Cor 8:23; Gal 2:3; 2 Tim 4:10 **1:6–9** 1 Tim 3:2–7

and to live self-controlled, upright, and godly
lives in this world, 13as we wait for the blessed
Day we hope for, when the glory of our great
God and Savior Jesus Christ[b] will appear. 14He
gave himself for us, to rescue us from all
wickedness and to make us a pure people who
belong to him alone and are eager to do good.
15Teach these things and use your full
authority as you encourage and rebuke your
hearers. Let none of them look down on you.

Live it!

Making Big Things from Small Beginnings

The Letter to Titus is very short and was written to a Church leader who did not become very famous. And yet a passage from this letter (2:11–14) is used every year at Christmas midnight Mass. Four little verses that are read at Mass begin with, "Beloved: The grace of God has appeared, saving all and training us to reject godless ways and worldly desires" (*The Lectionary,* p. 106).

The Christmas story itself has other examples of God making big things from small beginnings. Mary is just a young girl—a teenager—and she becomes the mother of God. Bethlehem is a tiny town, not very well known for anything, and it becomes the birthplace of our Messiah.

God is very good at making surprising things happen. So don't ever doubt the importance of whatever you do for God. Even if you think it's small, God can make very big things come from it.

— Titus 2:11–14

Christian Conduct

3 Remind your people to submit to rulers
and authorities, to obey them, and to be
ready to do good in every way. 2Tell them not
to speak evil of anyone, but to be peaceful
and friendly, and always to show a gentle atti-
tude toward everyone. 3For we ourselves were
once foolish, disobedient, and wrong. We
were slaves to passions and pleasures of all
kinds. We spent our lives in malice and envy;
others hated us and we hated them. 4But
when the kindness and love of God our Sav-
ior was revealed, 5he saved us. It was not
because of any good deeds that we ourselves
had done, but because of his own mercy that
he saved us, through the Holy Spirit, who
gives us new birth and new life by washing
us. 6God poured out the Holy Spirit abun-
dantly on us through Jesus Christ our Savior,
7so that by his grace we might be put right
with God and come into possession of the
eternal life we hope for. 8This is a true saying.
I want you to give special emphasis to these
matters, so that those who believe in God may
be concerned with giving their time to doing
good deeds, which are good and useful for
everyone. 9But avoid stupid arguments, long
lists of ancestors, quarrels, and fights about the
Law. They are useless and worthless. 10Give at
least two warnings to those who cause divi-
sions, and then have nothing more to do with
them. 11You know that such people are cor-
rupt, and their sins prove that they are wrong.

Final Instructions

12When I send Artemas or Tychicus to you,
do your best to come to me in Nicopolis,
because I have decided to spend the winter
there. 13Do your best to help Zenas the
lawyer and Apollos to get started on their
travels, and see to it that they have everything
they need. 14Our people must learn to spend
their time doing good, in order to provide for
real needs; they should not live useless lives.
15All who are with me send you greetings.
Give our greetings to our friends in the faith.
God's grace be with you all.

[b] **2:13** our great God and Savior Jesus Christ; *or* the great God and our Savior Jesus Christ.

2:14 **a** Ps 130:8; **b** Ex 19:5; Deut 4:20; 7:6; 14:2; 1 Pet 2:9 **3:12** Acts 20:4; Eph 6:21, 22; Col 4:7, 8; 2 Tim 4:12 **3:13** Acts 18:24; 1 Cor 16:12

The Letter to Philemon

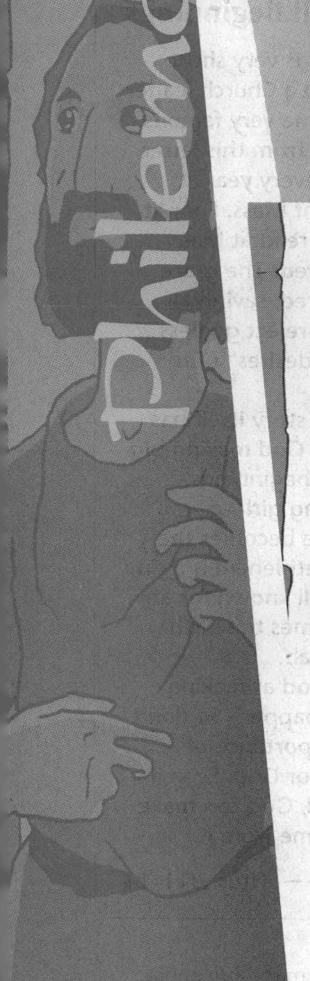

Have you ever seen a movie or a TV show about slavery? Have you ever thought about what it's like to be a slave? Masters don't usually treat their slaves very well. In fact, the treatment is often horrible.

While he was in prison, Paul wrote this letter to a slave owner named Philemon. Onesimus was Philemon's slave. He ran away and somehow ended up in prison with Paul, and became a Christian. Paul is trying to convince Philemon to accept Onesimus back as his brother in Christ. Not only does Paul want Onesimus to escape all punishment, he also wants Philemon to give Onesimus freedom.

Picture one of those slave masters in a movie or TV show you have seen. Can you imagine such a person changing his ways and accepting one of his runaway slaves as a brother? That's exactly what Paul is asking.

Headlines

- Paul Begs, "Accept Slave as Brother" (verses 17–22)
- Paul gives thanks for Philemon's love and faith (verses 4–7)

FACTOIDS

Who wrote this book? Paul, writing from prison.
When was it written? Around AD 61 to 63.
Who was it written for? It was written to Philemon, one of Paul's friends, who once owned Onesimus as a slave.
Why was it written? The author wanted to convince Philemon to welcome back his former slave Onesimus and accept him as a fellow Christian.
Important theme
- Paul encourages Philemon to accept Onesimus back to his home, no longer just a slave, but now a brother in Christ.

PHILEMON

1 From Paul, a prisoner for the sake of
Christ Jesus, and from our brother Timo-
thy—

To our friend and fellow worker Phile-
mon, 2 and the church that meets in your
house, and our sister Apphia, and our fellow
soldier Archippus:

3 May God our Father and the Lord Jesus
Christ give you grace and peace.

Philemon's Love and Faith

4 Brother Philemon, every time I pray, I
mention you and give thanks to my God.
5 For I hear of your love for all of God's peo-
ple and the faith you have in the Lord Jesus.
6 My prayer is that our fellowship with you
as believers will bring about a deeper under-
standing of every blessing which we have in
our life in union with Christ. 7 Your love,
dear brother, has brought me great joy and
much encouragement! You have cheered the
hearts of all of God's people.

A Request for Onesimus

8 For this reason I could be bold enough,
as your brother in Christ, to order you to do
what should be done. 9 But because I love
you, I make a request instead. I do this even
though I am Paul, the ambassador of Christ
Jesus, and at present also a prisoner for his
sake.[a] 10 So I make a request to you on behalf
of Onesimus, who is my own son in Christ;
for while in prison I have become his spiri-
tual father. 11 At one time he was of no use
to you, but now he is useful[b] both to you
and to me.

[a] **9** the ambassador of Christ Jesus, and at present also a prisoner for his sake; *or* an old man, and at present a prisoner for the sake of Christ Jesus. [b] **11** *The Greek name Onesimus means "useful."*

2 Col 4:17 **10** Col 4:9

Pray it!

Slaves Today

Paul probably didn't believe in slavery. In another part of the Bible, he says this: "So there is no difference between Jews and Gentiles, between slaves and free people, between men and women; you are all one in union with Christ Jesus" (Galatians 3:28). In those days, each of these three relationships had one person who was above the other person in some way. Paul is essentially saying, "Not anymore."

In this letter Paul is asking Philemon to welcome Onesimus as a brother in Christ. Paul wants Onesimus to be a free man, not a slave anymore. Even in today's modern world, there are still slaves. People are forced to work in factories or sweatshops. Women and children are kidnapped and forced to work as prostitutes. In some places people are kidnapped and forced to be soldiers.

Think about being chained in a factory and forced to sew clothing or stitch soccer balls. Or worse, forced to sell your body for sex or to kill other people. Think about that cruel existence, day after day, year after year. Say a prayer that some day soon, every country and company in the world will recognize the rights of freedom for all people. Pray that slavery will truly be "not anymore."

Welcome him back. (17)

12 I am sending him back to you now, and
with him goes my heart. 13 I would like to
keep him here with me, while I am in
prison for the gospel's sake, so that he could
help me in your place. 14 However, I do not
want to force you to help me; rather, I
would like for you to do it of your own free
will. So I will not do anything unless you
agree.

15 It may be that Onesimus was away from
you for a short time so that you might have
him back for all time. 16 And now he is not
just a slave, but much more than a slave: he is
a dear brother in Christ. How much he
means to me! And how much more he will
mean to you, both as a slave and as a brother
in the Lord!

17 So, if you think of me as your partner,
welcome him back just as you would wel-
come me. 18 If he has done you any wrong
or owes you anything, charge it to my
account. 19 Here, I will write this with my
own hand: *I, Paul, will pay you back* (I should
not have to remind you, of course, that you
owe your very self to me.) 20 So, my brother,
please do me this favor for the Lord's sake; as
a brother in Christ, cheer me up!

21 I am sure, as I write this, that you will
do what I ask—in fact I know that you will
do even more. 22 At the same time, get a
room ready for me, because I hope that God
will answer the prayers of all of you and give
me back to you.

Final Greetings

23 Epaphras, who is in prison with me for
the sake of Christ Jesus, sends you his greet-
ings, 24 and so do my co-workers Mark,
Aristarchus, Demas, and Luke.

25 May the grace of the Lord Jesus Christ
be with you all.

23 Col 1:7; 4:12 **24** **a** Acts 12:12, 25; 13:13; 15;37–39; Col 4:10; **b** Acts 19:29; 27:2; Col 4:10; **c** Col 4:14; 2 Tim 4:10; **d** Col 4:14; 2 Tim 4:11

The Letter to the Hebrews

Have you ever gone to Mass and the priest said something during the homily that really gave you a good idea of who Jesus is? The Letter to the Hebrews is sort of like that but in writing. It is filled with messages of encouragement and great descriptions of Jesus. The writer lets us know just how wonderful Jesus is and tells us that Jesus is more important than the angels. The letter makes a strong case that Jesus is the divine Son of God and that only he could take away the sins of the world.

The writer also encourages Christians (both then and now) to hold fast to the faith that has been given them and to continue moving toward Christ. We can endure whatever comes our way if we keep our faith in Jesus Christ.

Headlines

- Who Is Greater Than the Angels? (1:4–14)
- God's Son Saves People from Sin! (2:9–10)
- God's Promise Is an Anchor (6:13–17)
- Jesus Is the Perfect High Priest (9:6–15)
- Jewish Heroes Kept the Faith (11:1–35)

FACTOIDS

Who wrote this book? Unknown, but sometimes attributed to Paul.

When was it written? Around AD 80 to 90.

Who was it written for? It was written to a group of Greek-speaking Christians, some of whom were possibly Jewish Christians who were in danger of losing their faith.

Why was it written? It was written to tell the Christians to hold on to their faith and to move toward Christ.

What is its literary style? Although called a letter, it is really more like a sermon filled with explanations and metaphors.

Jesus connection. This letter contains many references to Jesus that are found in the Old Testament. The author does this to prove that Jesus fulfills the Jewish Law and is the sacrifice that ends all sacrifices (Hebrews 10:5–7).

Important themes

- God saves us through Jesus' sacrifice.
- Hold fast to faith and move toward Christ.

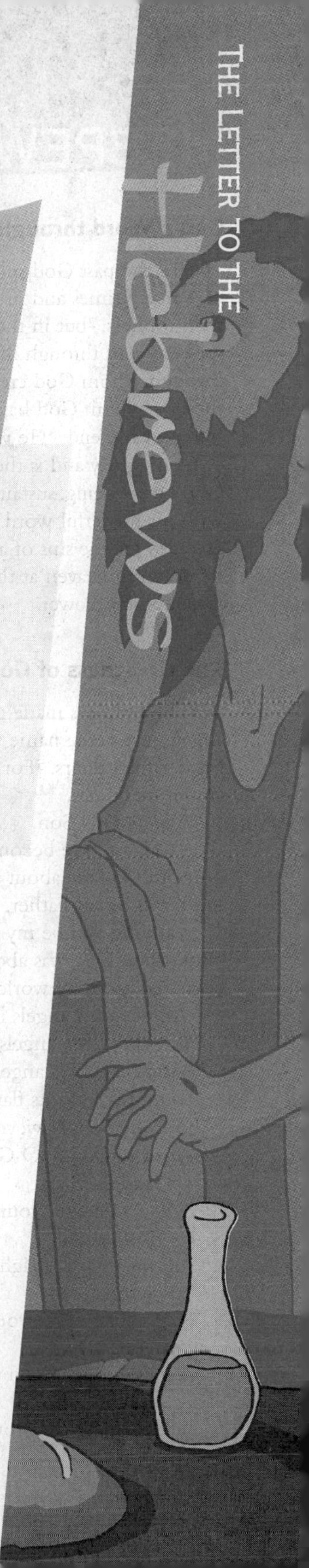

HEBREWS

God's Word through His Son

1 In the past God spoke to our ancestors many times and in many ways through the prophets, 2but in these last days he has spoken to us through his Son. He is the one through whom God created the universe, the one whom God has chosen to possess all things at the end. 3He reflects the brightness of God's glory and is the exact likeness of God's own being, sustaining the universe with his powerful word. After achieving forgiveness for the sins of all human beings, he sat down in heaven at the right side of God, the Supreme Power.

The Greatness of God's Son

4The Son was made greater than the angels, just as the name that God gave him is greater than theirs. 5For God never said to any of his angels,

"You are my Son;
today I have become your Father."

Nor did God say about any angel,

"I will be his Father,
and he will be my Son."

6But when God was about to send his first-born Son into the world, he said,

"All of God's angels must worship him."

7But about the angels God said,

"God makes his angels winds,
and his servants flames of fire."

8About the Son, however, God said:

"Your kingdom, O God, will last[a] forever and ever!
You rule over your[b] people with justice.
9You love what is right and hate what is wrong.
That is why God, your God, has chosen you
and has given you the joy of an honor far greater
than he gave to your companions."

10He also said,

"You, Lord, in the beginning created the earth,
and with your own hands you made the heavens.
11They will disappear, but you will remain;
they will all wear out like clothes.
12You will fold them up like a coat,
and they will be changed like clothes.
But you are always the same,
and your life never ends."

13God never said to any of his angels:

"Sit here at my right side
until I put your enemies
as a footstool under your feet."

14What are the angels, then? They are spirits who serve God and are sent by him to help those who are to receive salvation.

The Great Salvation

2 That is why we must hold on all the more firmly to the truths we have heard, so that we will not be carried away. 2The message given to our ancestors by the angels was shown to be true, and those who did not follow it or obey it received the punishment they deserved. 3How, then, shall we escape if we pay no attention to such a great salvation? The Lord himself first announced this salvation, and those who heard him proved to us that it is true. 4At the same time God added his witness to theirs by performing all kinds of miracles and wonders and by distributing the gifts of the Holy Spirit according to his will.

The One Who Leads Us to Salvation

5God has not placed the angels as rulers over the new world to come—the world of

[a] **1:8** Your kingdom, O God, will last; *or* God is your kingdom. [b] **1:8** your; *some manuscripts have* his.

1:2 Wis 7:22 **1:3** Wis 7:25, 26; 8:1 **1:5** **a** Ps 2:7; **b** 2 Sam 7:14; 1 Chr 17:13 **1:6** Deut 32:43 (LXX) **1:7** Ps 104:4 (LXX) **1:8, 9** Ps 45:6, 7 **1:10–12** Ps 102:25–27 (LXX) **1:13** Ps 110:1 **1:14** Tob 12:14, 15

Angels

Do you believe in angels? Whether you do or not, they are real. In chapters 1 and 2 of Hebrews, the author refers to angels several times. At one point he defines what angels are, "They are spirits who serve God and are sent by him to help those who are to receive salvation" (1:14). The Catholic Church teaches that angels belong to the unseen part of Creation. They cannot be seen, heard, touched, or smelled. They are spiritual beings without physical bodies, and they are immortal; that is, they will live forever. When angels interact with human beings, it is often to deliver messages from God.

But as great and wonderful as angels are, the Letter to the Hebrews makes it clear that Christ Jesus is greater than the angels. Angels are beings created by God, but Jesus is God's Son (1:5) who has existed with God forever (1:2). Jesus, not the angels, will rule the new world to come forever (1:8; 2:5). Angels are wonderful, and it is comforting to know they exist. But Jesus is still greater, and our salvation comes from him.

— Hebrews 1:4—2:8

which we speak. 6Instead, as it is said some-
where in the Scriptures:
"What are human beings, O God, that
you should think of them;
mere human beings, that you should
care for them?
7You made them for a little while lower
than the angels;
you crowned them with glory and
honor,[c]
8 and made them rulers over all things."
It says that God made them "rulers over all
things"; this clearly includes everything. We
do not, however, see human beings ruling
over all things now. 9But we do see Jesus,
who for a little while was made lower than
the angels, so that through God's grace he
should die for everyone. We see him now
crowned with glory and honor because of
the death he suffered. 10It was only right that
God, who creates and preserves all things,
should make Jesus perfect through suffering,
in order to bring many children to share his
glory. For Jesus is the one who leads them to
salvation.

11He purifies people from their sins, and
both he and those who are made pure all
have the same Father. That is why Jesus is
not ashamed to call them his family. 12He
says to God,
"I will tell my people what you have
done;
I will praise you in their meeting."
13He also says, "I will put my trust in God."
And he also says, "Here I am with the chil-
dren that God has given me."

14Since the children, as he calls them, are
people of flesh and blood, Jesus himself
became like them and shared their human
nature. He did this so that through his death
he might destroy the Devil, who has the
power over death, 15and in this way set free

[c] **2:7** *Many manuscripts add:* You made them rulers over everything you made *(see Ps 8:6).*
2:6–8 Ps 8:4–6 **2:12** Ps 22:22 **2:13 a** Isa 8:17 (LXX); **b** Isa 8:18

"In the past God spoke to our ancestors . . . through the prophets, but in these last days he has spoken to us through his Son" *(Hebrews 1:1–2)*.

those who were slaves all their lives because
of their fear of death. 16 For it is clear that it
is not the angels that he helps. Instead, he
helps the descendants of Abraham. 17 This
means that he had to become like his people
in every way, in order to be their faithful and
merciful High Priest in his service to God,
so that the people's sins would be forgiven.
18 And now he can help those who are
tempted, because he himself was tempted
and suffered.

Jesus Is Greater than Moses

3 My Christian friends, who also have
been called by God! Think of Jesus,
whom God sent to be the High Priest of the
faith we profess. 2 He was faithful to God,
who chose him to do this work, just as Moses
was faithful in his work in God's house. 3 A
man who builds a house receives more honor
than the house itself. In the same way Jesus is
worthy of much greater honor than Moses.
4 Every house, of course, is built by some-
one—and God is the one who has built all
things. 5 Moses was faithful in God's house as
a servant, and he spoke of the things that God
would say in the future. 6 But Christ is faithful
as the Son in charge of God's house. We are
his house if we keep up our courage and our
confidence in what we hope for.

A Rest for God's People

7 So then, as the Holy Spirit says,
"If you hear God's voice today,
8 do not be stubborn, as your ancestors
were when they rebelled against God,
as they were that day in the desert
when they put him to the test.
9 There they put me to the test and tried
me, says God,
although they had seen what I did for
forty years.
10 And so I was angry with those people
and said,
'They are always disloyal
and refuse to obey my commands.'
11 I was angry and made a solemn promise:
'They will never enter the land where I
would have given them rest!' "

12 My friends, be careful that none of you
have a heart so evil and unbelieving that you
will turn away from the living God.
13 Instead, in order that none of you be
deceived by sin and become stubborn, you
must help one another every day, as long as
the word "Today" in the scripture applies to
us. 14 For we are all partners with Christ if
we hold firmly to the end the confidence
we had at the beginning.
15 This is what the scripture says:
"If you hear God's voice today,
do not be stubborn, as your ancestors
were
when they rebelled against God."

16 Who were the people who heard God's
voice and rebelled against him? All those
who were led out of Egypt by Moses.
17 With whom was God angry for forty
years? With the people who sinned, who fell
down dead in the desert. 18 When God made
his solemn promise, "They will never enter
the land where I would have given them
rest"—of whom was he speaking? Of those
who rebelled. 19 We see, then, that they were
not able to enter the land, because they did
not believe.

4 Now, God has offered us the promise
that we may receive that rest he spoke
about. Let us take care, then, that none of
you will be found to have failed to receive
that promised rest. 2 For we have heard the
Good News, just as they did. They heard the
message, but it did them no good, because
when they heard it, they did not accept it
with faith. 3 We who believe, then, do receive
that rest which God promised. It is just as he
said,
"I was angry and made a solemn promise:
'They will never enter the land where I
would have given them rest!' "

2:16 Isa 41:8, 9 **3:2** Num 12:7 **3:7–11** Ps 95:7–11 (LXX) **3:15** Ps 95:7, 8 (LXX) **3:16–18** Num 14:1–35 **4:3** Ps 95:11

Hebrews 3:7-11 is based on Psalm 95:7-11. Find that psalm and compare it with this passage in Hebrews.

He said this even though his work had been finished from the time he created the world. 4 For somewhere in the Scriptures this is said about the seventh day: "God rested on the seventh day from all his work." 5 This same matter is spoken of again: "They will never enter that land where I would have given them rest." 6 Those who first heard the Good News did not receive that rest, because they did not believe. There are, then, others who are allowed to receive it. 7 This is shown by the fact that God sets another day, which is called "Today." Many years later he spoke of it through David in the scripture already quoted:

"If you hear God's voice today,
do not be stubborn."

8 If Joshua had given the people the rest that God had promised, God would not have spoken later about another day. 9 As it is, however, there still remains for God's people a rest like God's resting on the seventh day. 10 For those who receive that rest which God promised will rest from their own work, just as God rested from his. 11 Let us, then, do our best to receive that rest, so that no one of us will fail as they did because of their lack of faith.

12 The word of God is alive and active, sharper than any double-edged sword. It cuts all the way through, to where soul and spirit meet, to where joints and marrow come together. It judges the desires and thoughts of the heart. 13 There is nothing that can be hid from God; everything in all creation is exposed and lies open before his eyes. And it is to him that we must all give an account of ourselves.

Jesus the Great High Priest

14 Let us, then, hold firmly to the faith we profess. For we have a great High Priest who has gone into the very presence of God—Jesus, the Son of God. 15 Our High Priest is not one who cannot feel sympathy for our weaknesses. On the contrary, we have a High Priest who was tempted in every way that we are, but did not sin. 16 Let us have confidence, then, and approach God's throne,

Live it!

Power of God's Word

The Bible has many gory parts, and Hebrews 4:12–13 is just one example. The image of the word of God slicing through someone is not supposed to be realistic, though. Rather, it is meant to show the power of God's word. The word of God is so powerful that nothing in our lives can be hidden from it. Even if you are trying to hide something from others, the word of God will make it clear whether your life is about doing good or doing bad.

We cannot hide from God's love and concern for us; and we cannot hide our actions, thoughts, and desires from God. This should help us remember to keep God number one in our lives. List the top 10 things that influence the way you live your life. If God isn't on the top of your list, what can you do to put God there?

— Hebrews 4:12–13

where there is grace. There we will receive mercy and find grace to help us just when we need it.

5 Every high priest is chosen from his fellow-men and appointed to serve God on their behalf, to offer sacrifices and offerings for sins. 2 Since he himself is weak in many ways, he is able to be gentle with those who are ignorant and make mistakes. 3 And because he is himself weak, he must offer sacrifices not only for the sins of the people but also for his own sins. 4 No one chooses for himself the honor of being a high priest. It is only by God's call that a man is made a high priest—just as Aaron was.

4:4 Gen 2:2 **4:5** Ps 95:11 **4:7** Ps 95:7, 8 (LXX) **4:8** Deut 31:7; Josh 22:4 **4:10** Gen 2:2 **4:13** Wis 1:6 **5:3** Lev 9:7 **5:4** Ex 28:1

5In the same way, Christ did not take
upon himself the honor of being a high
priest. Instead, God said to him,

"You are my Son;
today I have become your Father."

6He also said in another place,

"You will be a priest forever,
in the priestly order of Melchizedek."[d]

7In his life on earth Jesus made his prayers
and requests with loud cries and tears to
God, who could save him from death.
Because he was humble and devoted, God
heard him. 8But even though he was God's
Son, he learned through his sufferings to be
obedient. 9When he was made perfect, he
became the source of eternal salvation for all
those who obey him, 10and God declared
him to be high priest, in the priestly order of
Melchizedek.[d]

Warning against Abandoning the Faith

11There is much we have to say about this
matter, but it is hard to explain to you,
because you are so slow to understand.
12There has been enough time for you to be
teachers—yet you still need someone to
teach you the first lessons of God's message.
Instead of eating solid food, you still have to
drink milk. 13Anyone who has to drink milk
is still a child, without any experience in the
matter of right and wrong. 14Solid food, on
the other hand, is for adults, who through
practice are able to distinguish between good
and evil.

6 Let us go forward, then, to mature teach-
ing and leave behind us the first lessons
of the Christian message. We should not lay
again the foundation of turning away from
useless works and believing in God; 2of the
teaching about baptisms[e] and the laying on of
hands; of the resurrection of the dead and the
eternal judgment. 3Let us go forward! And
this is what we will do, if God allows.

4For how can those who abandon their
faith be brought back to repent again? They
were once in God's light; they tasted heaven's
gift and received their share of the Holy
Spirit; 5they knew from experience that
God's word is good, and they had felt the
powers of the coming age. 6And then they
abandoned their faith! It is impossible to
bring them back to repent again, because
they are again crucifying the Son of God
and exposing him to public shame.

7God blesses the soil which drinks in the
rain that often falls on it and which grows
plants that are useful to those for whom it is
cultivated. 8But if it grows thorns and
weeds, it is worth nothing; it is in danger of
being cursed by God and will be destroyed
by fire.

9But even if we speak like this, dear
friends, we feel sure about you. We know
that you have the better blessings that belong

Live it!

God's Sure Promise

"I promise to call you tonight," Josefina said to her friend Beth. Beth had had a really bad day and wanted to talk to Josefina about it. When Josefina called her that night, Beth felt better and was able to turn her day around. By keeping her promise, Josefina showed Beth that Beth could trust her.

Chapter 6 in Hebrews tells us that God keeps his promises. This gives us hope and can be a comfort. It gives us an anchor. Anchors keep boats in place through bad weather, and that is what God does for us. The next time you need some hope, read Hebrews 6:9–19 and remind yourself of how God keeps promises.

— Hebrews 6:9–19

[d] **5:6, 10** in the priestly order of Melchizedek; *or* like Melchizedek; *or* in the line of succession to Melchizedek.
[e] **6:2** baptisms; *or* purification ceremonies.

5:5 Ps 2:7 **5:6** Ps 110:4 **5:7** Mt 26:36–46; Mk 14:32–42; Lk 22:39–46 **5:12, 13** 1 Cor 3:2 **6:8** Gen 3:17, 18

to your salvation. 10God is not unfair. He
will not forget the work you did or the love
you showed for him in the help you gave
and are still giving to other Christians. 11Our
great desire is that each of you keep up your
eagerness to the end, so that the things you
hope for will come true. 12We do not want
you to become lazy, but to be like those
who believe and are patient, and so receive
what God has promised.

God's Sure Promise

13When God made his promise to Abra-
ham, he made a vow to do what he had
promised. Since there was no one greater
than himself, he used his own name when
he made his vow. 14He said, "I promise you
that I will bless you and give you many
descendants." 15Abraham was patient, and so
he received what God had promised.
16When we make a vow, we use the name of
someone greater than ourselves, and the vow
settles all arguments. 17To those who were to
receive what he promised, God wanted to
make it very clear that he would never
change his purpose; so he added his vow to
the promise. 18There are these two things,
then, that cannot change and about which
God cannot lie. So we who have found safe-
ty with him are greatly encouraged to hold
firmly to the hope placed before us. 19We
have this hope as an anchor for our lives. It is
safe and sure, and goes through the curtain
of the heavenly temple into the inner sanc-
tuary. 20On our behalf Jesus has gone in
there before us and has become a high priest
forever, in the priestly order of
Melchizedek.[f]

The Priest Melchizedek

7 This Melchizedek was king of Salem
and a priest of the Most High God. As
Abraham was coming back from the battle
in which he defeated the four kings,
Melchizedek met him and blessed him, 2and
Abraham gave him one tenth of all he had
taken. (The first meaning of Melchizedek's
name is "King of Righteousness"; and
because he was king of Salem, his name also
means "King of Peace.") 3There is no record
of Melchizedek's father or mother or of any
of his ancestors; no record of his birth or of
his death. He is like the Son of God; he
remains a priest forever.

4You see, then, how great he was. Abra-
ham, our famous ancestor, gave him one
tenth of all he got in the battle. 5And those
descendants of Levi who are priests are com-
manded by the Law to collect one tenth
from the people of Israel, that is, from their
own people, even though they are also
descendants of Abraham. 6Melchizedek was
not descended from Levi, but he collected
one tenth from Abraham and blessed him,
the man who received God's promises.
7There is no doubt that the one who blesses
is greater than the one who is blessed. 8In
the case of the priests the tenth is collected
by men who die; but as for Melchizedek the
tenth was collected by one who lives, as the
scripture says. 9And, so to speak, when Abra-
ham paid the tenth, Levi (whose descendants
collect the tenth) also paid it. 10For Levi had
not yet been born, but was, so to speak, in
the body of his ancestor Abraham when
Melchizedek met him.

11It was on the basis of the levitical priest-
hood that the Law was given to the people
of Israel. Now, if the work of the levitical
priests had been perfect, there would have
been no need for a different kind of priest to
appear, one who is in the priestly order of
Melchizedek,[f] not of Aaron. 12For when the
priesthood is changed, there also has to be a
change in the law. 13And our Lord, of whom
these things are said, belonged to a different
tribe, and no member of his tribe ever
served as a priest. 14It is well known that he
was born a member of the tribe of Judah;

f **6:20; 7:11** in the priestly order of Melchizedek *(see 5:6).*
6:14 Gen 22:16, 17 **6:19** Lev 16:2 **6:20** Ps 110:4 **7:1, 2** Gen 14:17–20 **7:5** Num 18:21

"God is not unfair. He will not forget the work you did or the love you showed for him in the help you gave" *(Hebrews 6:10)*.

Study it!

Melchizedek

"Melcheesy who?" Joellen said to Father Raul after Mass.

"Melchizedek, Mel-kiss-a-deck."

Joellen had never heard the Eucharistic prayer that Father Raul prayed at Mass. "So, who is Melchizedek, anyway?" Father Raul explained that Melchizedek was a priest and king who, according to the Book of Genesis, offered a sacrifice of bread and wine to God (14:17–20). Because Melchizedek did this, he became Abraham's priest. Father Raul finished his story of Melchizedek by telling Joellen that some early Christians saw similarities between Jesus and Melchizedek. They both offered bread and wine to God.

Melchizedek was an early (but not complete) example of Jesus' priesthood, which is explained in the Letter to the Hebrews.

— Hebrews, chapter 7

and Moses did not mention this tribe when
he spoke of priests.

Another Priest, like Melchizedek

15 The matter becomes even plainer; a dif-
ferent priest has appeared, who is like
Melchizedek. 16 He was made a priest, not by
human rules and regulations, but through
the power of a life which has no end. 17 For
the scripture says, "You will be a priest for-
ever, in the priestly order of Melchizedek."[f]
18 The old rule, then, is set aside, because it
was weak and useless. 19 For the Law of
Moses could not make anything perfect. And
now a better hope has been provided
through which we come near to God.
20 In addition, there is also God's vow.
There was no such vow when the others
were made priests. 21 But Jesus became a
priest by means of a vow when God said to
him,

"The Lord has made a solemn promise
and will not take it back:
'You will be a priest forever.' "

22 This difference, then, also makes Jesus the
guarantee of a better covenant.
23 There is another difference: there were
many of those other priests, because they
died and could not continue their work.
24 But Jesus lives on forever, and his work as
priest does not pass on to someone else.
25 And so he is able, now and always, to save
those who come to God through him,
because he lives forever to plead with God
for them.
26 Jesus, then, is the High Priest that meets
our needs. He is holy; he has no fault or sin
in him; he has been set apart from sinners
and raised above the heavens. 27 He is not
like other high priests; he does not need to
offer sacrifices every day for his own sins
first and then for the sins of the people. He
offered one sacrifice, once and for all, when
he offered himself. 28 The Law of Moses
appoints men who are imperfect to be high
priests; but God's promise made with the
vow, which came later than the Law,
appoints the Son, who has been made per-
fect forever.

Jesus Our High Priest

8 The whole point of what we are saying
is that we have such a High Priest, who
sits at the right of the throne of the Divine
Majesty in heaven. 2 He serves as high priest
in the Most Holy Place, that is, in the real

[f] **7:17** in the priestly order of Melchizedek *(see 5:6)*.
7:17 Ps 110:4 **7:21** Ps 110:4 **7:27** Lev 9:7 **8:1** Ps 110:1

The *high priest* of the Jewish people was the only one who could enter the most sacred part of the Temple and offer sacrifice to God.

tent which was put up by the Lord, not by
human hands.
3 Every high priest is appointed to present
offerings and animal sacrifices to God, and
so our High Priest must also have something
to offer. 4 If he were on earth, he would not
be a priest at all, since there are priests who
offer the gifts required by the Jewish Law.
5 The work they do as priests is really only a
copy and a shadow of what is in heaven. It is
the same as it was with Moses. When he was
about to build the Sacred Tent, God told
him, "Be sure to make everything according
to the pattern you were shown on the
mountain." 6 But now, Jesus has been given
priestly work which is superior to theirs, just
as the covenant which he arranged between
God and his people is a better one, because
it is based on promises of better things.
7 If there had been nothing wrong with
the first covenant, there would have been no
need for a second one. 8 But God finds fault
with his people when he says,

"The days are coming, says the Lord,
when I will draw up a new covenant
with the people of Israel and with
the people of Judah.
9 It will not be like the covenant that I
made with their ancestors
on the day I took them by the hand
and led them out of Egypt.
They were not faithful to the covenant I
made with them,
and so I paid no attention to them.
10 Now, this is the covenant that I will make
with the people of Israel
in the days to come, says the Lord:
I will put my laws in their minds
and write them on their hearts.
I will be their God,
and they will be my people.
11 None of them will have to teach their
friends
or tell their neighbors,
'Know the Lord.'
For they will all know me,
from the least to the greatest.
12 I will forgive their sins
and will no longer remember their
wrongs."

13 By speaking of a new covenant, God has
made the first one old; and anything that
becomes old and worn out will soon disap-
pear.

Earthly and Heavenly Worship

9 The first covenant had rules for worship
and a place made for worship as well.
2 A tent was put up, the outer one, which
was called the Holy Place. In it were the
lampstand and the table with the bread
offered to God. 3 Behind the second curtain
was the tent called the Most Holy Place. 4 In
it were the gold altar for the burning of
incense and the Covenant Box all covered
with gold and containing the gold jar with
the manna in it, Aaron's stick that had
sprouted leaves, and the two stone tablets
with the commandments written on them.
5 Above the Box were the winged creatures
representing God's presence, with their
wings spread over the place where sins were
forgiven. But now is not the time to explain
everything in detail.
6 This is how those things have been
arranged. The priests go into the outer tent
every day to perform their duties, 7 but only
the high priest goes into the inner tent, and
he does so only once a year. He takes with
him blood which he offers to God on behalf
of himself and for the sins which the people
have committed without knowing they were
sinning. 8 The Holy Spirit clearly teaches
from all these arrangements that the way
into the Most Holy Place has not yet been
opened as long as the outer tent still stands.
9 This is a symbol which points to the pres-
ent time. It means that the offerings and ani-
mal sacrifices presented to God cannot make
the worshiper's heart perfect, 10 since they
have to do only with food, drink, and vari-
ous purification ceremonies. These are all
outward rules, which apply only until the
time when God will establish the new order.
11 But Christ has already come as the High
Priest of the good things that are already

8:5 Ex 25:40 **8:8–12** Jer 31:31–34 (LXX) **9:2** **a** Ex 26:1–30; **b** Ex 25:31–40; **c** Ex 25:23–30 **9:3** Ex 26:31–33 **9:4** **a** Ex 30:1–6; **b** Ex 25:10–16; **c** Ex 16:33; **d** Num 17:8–10; **e** Ex 25:16; Deut 10:3–5 **9:5** Ex 25:18–22 **9:6** Num 18:2–6 **9:7** Lev 16:2–34

here.[g] The tent in which he serves is greater
and more perfect; it is not a tent made by
human hands, that is, it is not a part of this
created world. 12 When Christ went through
the tent and entered once and for all into
the Most Holy Place, he did not take the
blood of goats and bulls to offer as a sacri-
fice; rather, he took his own blood and
obtained eternal salvation for us. 13 The
blood of goats and bulls and the ashes of a
burnt calf are sprinkled on the people who
are ritually unclean, and this purifies them
by taking away their ritual impurity. 14 Since
this is true, how much more is accomplished
by the blood of Christ! Through the eternal
Spirit he offered himself as a perfect sacrifice
to God. His blood will purify our con-
sciences from useless rituals, so that we may
serve the living God.
15 For this reason Christ is the one who
arranges a new covenant, so that those who
have been called by God may receive the
eternal blessings that God has promised.
This can be done because there has been a
death which sets people free from the
wrongs they did while the first covenant
was in effect.
16 In the case of a will it is necessary to
prove that the person who made it has died,
17 for a will means nothing while the person
who made it is alive; it goes into effect only
after his death. 18 That is why even the first
covenant[h] went into effect only with the use
of blood. 19 First, Moses proclaimed to the
people all the commandments as set forth in
the Law. Then he took the blood of bulls
and goats, mixed it with water, and sprinkled
it on the book of the Law and all the peo-
ple, using a sprig of hyssop and some red
wool. 20 He said, "This is the blood which
seals the covenant that God has commanded
you to obey." 21 In the same way Moses also
sprinkled the blood on the Sacred Tent and
over all the things used in worship. 22 Indeed,
according to the Law almost everything is
purified by blood, and sins are forgiven only
if blood is poured out.

Christ's Sacrifice Takes Away Sins

23 Those things, which are copies of the
heavenly originals, had to be purified in that
way. But the heavenly things themselves
require much better sacrifices. 24 For Christ
did not go into a Holy Place made by
human hands, which was a copy of the real
one. He went into heaven itself, where he
now appears on our behalf in the presence
of God. 25 The Jewish high priest goes into
the Most Holy Place every year with the
blood of an animal. But Christ did not go in
to offer himself many times, 26 for then he
would have had to suffer many times ever
since the creation of the world. Instead, now
when all ages of time are nearing the end, he
has appeared once and for all, to remove sin
through the sacrifice of himself. 27 Everyone
must die once, and after that be judged by
God. 28 In the same manner Christ also was
offered in sacrifice once to take away the sins
of many. He will appear a second time, not
to deal with sin, but to save those who are
waiting for him.

10 The Jewish Law is not a full and
faithful model of the real things; it is
only a faint outline of the good things to
come. The same sacrifices are offered forever,
year after year. How can the Law, then, by
means of these sacrifices make perfect the
people who come to God? 2 If the people
worshiping God had really been purified
from their sins, they would not feel guilty of
sin any more, and all sacrifices would stop.
3 As it is, however, the sacrifices serve year
after year to remind people of their sins. 4 For
the blood of bulls and goats can never take
away sins.
5 For this reason, when Christ was about
to come into the world, he said to God:

"You do not want sacrifices and offerings,
 but you have prepared a body for me.
6 You are not pleased with animals burned
 whole on the altar
 or with sacrifices to take away sins.
7 Then I said, 'Here I am,
 to do your will, O God,

[g] **9:11** already here; *some manuscripts have* coming. [h] **9:18** COVENANT: *In Greek the same word means "will" and "covenant."*

9:13 a Lev 16:15, 16; **b** Num 19:9, 17–19 **9:19, 20** Ex 24:6–8 **9:21** Lev 8:15 **9:22** Lev 17:11 **9:28** Isa 53:12 **10:5–7** Ps 40:6–8 (LXX)

just as it is written of me in the book
of the Law.' "
8 First he said, "You neither want nor are you
pleased with sacrifices and offerings or with
animals burned on the altar and the sacrifices
to take away sins." He said this even though
all these sacrifices are offered according to
the Law. 9 Then he said, "Here I am, O God,
to do your will." So God does away with all
the old sacrifices and puts the sacrifice of
Christ in their place. 10 Because Jesus Christ
did what God wanted him to do, we are all
purified from sin by the offering that he
made of his own body once and for all.

11 Every Jewish priest performs his services
every day and offers the same sacrifices many
times; but these sacrifices can never take
away sins. 12 Christ, however, offered one sac-
rifice for sins, an offering that is effective
forever, and then he sat down at the right
side of God. 13 There he now waits until
God puts his enemies as a footstool under
his feet. 14 With one sacrifice, then, he has
made perfect forever those who are purified
from sin.

15 And the Holy Spirit also gives us his
witness. First he says,

16 "This is the covenant that I will make
with them
in the days to come, says the Lord:
I will put my laws in their hearts
and write them on their minds."

17 And then he says, "I will not remember
their sins and evil deeds any longer." 18 So
when these have been forgiven, an offering
to take away sins is no longer needed.

Let Us Come Near to God

19 We have, then, my friends, complete
freedom to go into the Most Holy Place by
means of the death of Jesus. 20 He opened for
us a new way, a living way, through the cur-
tain—that is, through his own body. 21 We
have a great priest in charge of the house of
God. 22 So let us come near to God with a
sincere heart and a sure faith, with hearts
that have been purified from a guilty con-
science and with bodies washed with clean
water. 23 Let us hold on firmly to the hope
we profess, because we can trust God to
keep his promise. 24 Let us be concerned for
one another, to help one another to show
love and to do good. 25 Let us not give up
the habit of meeting together, as some are
doing. Instead, let us encourage one another
all the more, since you see that the Day of
the Lord is coming nearer.

Let us not give up the habit of meeting together.
(10:25)

26 For there is no longer any sacrifice that
will take away sins if we purposely go on
sinning after the truth has been made known
to us. 27 Instead, all that is left is to wait in
fear for the coming Judgment and the fierce
fire which will destroy those who oppose
God! 28 Anyone who disobeys the Law of
Moses is put to death without any mercy
when judged guilty from the evidence of
two or more witnesses. 29 What, then, of
those who despise the Son of God? who
treat as a cheap thing the blood of God's
covenant which purified them from sin?
who insult the Spirit of grace? Just think
how much worse is the punishment they
will deserve! 30 For we know who said, "I
will take revenge, I will repay"; and who also
said, "The Lord will judge his people." 31 It is
a terrifying thing to fall into the hands of
the living God!

10:11 Ex 29:38 **10:12, 13** Ps 110:1 **10:16** Jer 31:33 **10:17** Jer 31:34 **10:22** Lev 8:30; Ezek 36:25
10:27 Isa 26:11 (LXX) **10:28** Deut 17:6; 19:15 **10:29** Ex 24:8 **10:30** **a** Deut 32:35; **b** Deut 32:36

"Christ also was offered in sacrifice once to take away the sins of many"
(Hebrews 9:28).

Pray it!

Find Me, God

Staying on God's path can be hard. But going off that path, or turning away from it, gets us lost. In Hebrews 10:39 we are told that "we have faith and are saved." The next time you are feeling lost, try this prayer:

Find me God, I am feeling lost.
Help me get back on your path.
Find me God, I'm ready to turn back.
Help me stay with you.
Find me God, I'm slowing down.
Help me know my faith.
Find me God, I want to be with you.
Help me remember that you never leave.
Amen.

— Hebrews 10:39

32 Remember how it was with you in the
past. In those days, after God's light had
shone on you, you suffered many things, yet
were not defeated by the struggle. 33 You
were at times publicly insulted and mistreat-
ed, and at other times you were ready to join
those who were being treated in this way.
34 You shared the sufferings of prisoners, and
when all your belongings were seized, you
endured your loss gladly, because you knew
that you still possessed something much bet-
ter, which would last forever. 35 Do not lose
your courage, then, because it brings with it
a great reward. 36 You need to be patient, in
order to do the will of God and receive
what he promises. 37 For, as the scripture says,

"Just a little while longer,
and he who is coming will come;
he will not delay.
38 My righteous people, however, will
believe and live;
but if any of them turns back,
I will not be pleased with them."

39 We are not people who turn back and are
lost. Instead, we have faith and are saved.

Faith

11 To have faith is to be sure of the
things we hope for, to be certain of
the things we cannot see. 2 It was by their
faith that people of ancient times won God's
approval.

3 It is by faith that we understand that the
universe was created by God's word, so that
what can be seen was made out of what
cannot be seen.

4 It was faith that made Abel offer to God
a better sacrifice than Cain's. Through his
faith he won God's approval as a righteous
man, because God himself approved of his
gifts. By means of his faith Abel still speaks,
even though he is dead.

5 It was faith that kept Enoch from dying.
Instead, he was taken up to God, and
nobody could find him, because God had

10:37, 38 Hab 2:3, 4 (LXX) **11:2** Sir 44:10—50:21; 1 Macc 2:51–64 **11:3** Gen 1:1; Ps 33:6, 9; Jn 1:3
11:4 Gen 4:3–10 **11:5** Gen 5:21–24 (LXX); Sir 44:16

Hebrews, chapter 11, gives many examples of people from the Old Testament who had faith in God. How many people are named in chapter 11?

To be certain of the things we cannot see (11:1)

taken him up. The scripture says that before
Enoch was taken up, he had pleased God.
6No one can please God without faith, for
whoever comes to God must have faith that
God exists and rewards those who seek him.
7It was faith that made Noah hear God's
warnings about things in the future that he
could not see. He obeyed God and built a
boat in which he and his family were saved.
As a result, the world was condemned, and
Noah received from God the righteousness
that comes by faith.
8It was faith that made Abraham obey
when God called him to go out to a country
which God had promised to give him. He
left his own country without knowing
where he was going. 9By faith he lived as a
foreigner in the country that God had
promised him. He lived in tents, as did Isaac
and Jacob, who received the same promise
from God. 10For Abraham was waiting for
the city which God has designed and built,
the city with permanent foundations.
11It was faith that made Abraham able to
become a father, even though he was too old
and Sarah herself could not have children.
He[i] trusted God to keep his promise.
12Though Abraham was practically dead,
from this one man came as many descen-
dants as there are stars in the sky, as many as
the numberless grains of sand on the
seashore.

Live it!

It Was Faith

Wow! Faith sure has helped a lot of people in the Bible. Chapter 11 of Hebrews gives many examples of how faith helped people live a godly life. It tells us of these men and women, how they lived, how they obeyed God, and what happened as a result.

Write your own version of Hebrews, chapter 11. Start a paragraph like this: "It was faith that helped me . . . ." In the paragraph list the ways faith has helped you live the way God wants you to live. Write another paragraph of the ways faith can help you in the future. Keep the paragraphs in a place where you look often. If you have a locker, put them there, or put them on your bedside table, in a notebook, or anywhere you'll see them daily. Add to your paragraphs as new faith-filled events happen in your life.

— Hebrews, chapter 11

13It was in faith that all these persons died.
They did not receive the things God had
promised, but from a long way off they saw
them and welcomed them, and admitted
openly that they were foreigners and refugees
on earth. 14Those who say such things make
it clear that they are looking for a country of
their own. 15They did not keep thinking
about the country they had left; if they had,
they would have had the chance to return.
16Instead, it was a better country they longed
for, the heavenly country. And so God is not
ashamed for them to call him their God,
because he has prepared a city for them.

[i] **11:11** It was faith . . . children. He; *some manuscripts have* It was faith that made Sarah herself able to conceive, even though she was too old to have children. She.

11:7 Gen 6:13–22 **11:8** Gen 12:1–5 **11:9** Gen 35:27 **11:11** Gen 18:11–14; 21:2 **11:12** Gen 15:5; 22:17; 32:12 **11:13** Gen 23:4; 1 Chr 29:15; Ps 39:12

17 It was faith that made Abraham offer his
son Isaac as a sacrifice when God put Abra-
ham to the test. Abraham was the one to
whom God had made the promise, yet he
was ready to offer his only son as a sacrifice.
18 God had said to him, "It is through Isaac
that you will have the descendants I prom-
ised." 19 Abraham reckoned that God was able
to raise Isaac from death—and, so to speak,
Abraham did receive Isaac back from death.

20 It was faith that made Isaac promise
blessings for the future to Jacob and Esau.

21 It was faith that made Jacob bless each
of the sons of Joseph just before he died. He
leaned on the top of his walking stick and
worshiped God.

22 It was faith that made Joseph, when he
was about to die, speak of the departure of
the Israelites from Egypt, and leave instruc-
tions about what should be done with his
body.

23 It was faith that made the parents of
Moses hide him for three months after he
was born. They saw that he was a beautiful
child, and they were not afraid to disobey
the king's order.

24 It was faith that made Moses, when he
had grown up, refuse to be called the son of
the king's daughter. 25 He preferred to suffer
with God's people rather than to enjoy sin
for a little while. 26 He reckoned that to suf-
fer scorn for the Messiah was worth far
more than all the treasures of Egypt, for he
kept his eyes on the future reward.

27 It was faith that made Moses leave
Egypt without being afraid of the king's
anger. As though he saw the invisible God,
he refused to turn back. 28 It was faith that
made him establish the Passover and order
the blood to be sprinkled on the doors, so
that the Angel of Death would not kill the
first-born sons of the Israelites.

29 It was faith that made the Israelites able
to cross the Red Sea as if on dry land; when
the Egyptians tried to do it, the water swal-
lowed them up.

30 It was faith that made the walls of Jeri-
cho fall down after the Israelites had
marched around them for seven days. 31 It
was faith that kept the prostitute Rahab
from being killed with those who disobeyed
God, for she gave the Israelite spies a friend-
ly welcome.

32 Should I go on? There isn't enough
time for me to speak of Gideon, Barak, Sam-
son, Jephthah, David, Samuel, and the
prophets. 33 Through faith they fought whole
countries and won. They did what was right
and received what God had promised. They
shut the mouths of lions, 34 put out fierce
fires, escaped being killed by the sword. They
were weak, but became strong; they were
mighty in battle and defeated the armies of
foreigners. 35 Through faith women received
their dead relatives raised back to life.

Others, refusing to accept freedom, died
under torture in order to be raised to a bet-
ter life. 36 Some were mocked and whipped,
and others were put in chains and taken off
to prison. 37 They were stoned, they were
sawed in two, they were killed by the sword.
They went around clothed in skins of sheep
or goats—poor, persecuted, and mistreated.
38 The world was not good enough for them!
They wandered like refugees in the deserts
and hills, living in caves and holes in the
ground.

39 What a record all of these have won by
their faith! Yet they did not receive what
God had promised, 40 because God had
decided on an even better plan for us. His
purpose was that only in company with us
would they be made perfect.

God Our Father

12 As for us, we have this large crowd
of witnesses around us. So then, let
us rid ourselves of everything that gets in the
way, and of the sin which holds on to us so
tightly, and let us run with determination
the race that lies before us. 2 Let us keep our
eyes fixed on Jesus, on whom our faith
depends from beginning to end. He did not

11:17 Gen 22:1–14 **11:18** Gen 21:12 **11:20** Gen 27:27–29, 39, 40 **11:21** **a** Gen 48:1–20; **b** Gen 47:31 (LXX) **11:22** Gen 50:24, 25; Ex 13:19 **11:23** **a** Ex 2:2; **b** Ex 1:22 **11:24** Ex 2:10–12 **11:28** Ex 12:21–30 **11:29** Ex 14:21–31 **11:30** Josh 6:12–21 **11:31** **a** Josh 6:22–25; **b** Josh 2:1–21 **11:32** **a** Judg 6:11—8:32; **b** Judg 4:6—5:31; **c** Judg 13:2—16:31; **d** Judg 11:1—12:7; **e** 1 Sam 16:1—1 Kings 2:11; **11:33** Dan 6:1–27 **11:34** Dan 3:1–30 **11:35** 1 Kings 17:17–24; 2 Kings 4:25–37; 2 Macc 6:18—7:42 **11:36** 1 Kings 22:26, 27; 2 Chr 18:25, 26; Jer 20:2; 37:15; 38:6 **11:37** 2 Chr 24:21

give up because of the cross! On the con-
trary, because of the joy that was waiting for
him, he thought nothing of the disgrace of
dying on the cross, and he is now seated at
the right side of God's throne.
3Think of what he went through; how he
put up with so much hatred from sinners! So
do not let yourselves become discouraged
and give up. 4For in your struggle against sin
you have not yet had to resist to the point of
being killed. 5Have you forgotten the
encouraging words which God speaks to
you as his children?

"My child, pay attention when the Lord
corrects you,
and do not be discouraged when he
rebukes you.
6Because the Lord corrects everyone he
loves,
and punishes everyone he accepts as a
child."

7Endure what you suffer as being a father's
punishment; your suffering shows that God
is treating you as his children. Was there ever
a child who was not punished by his father?
8If you are not punished, as all his children
are, it means you are not real children, but
bastards. 9In the case of our human fathers,
they punished us and we respected them.
How much more, then, should we submit to
our spiritual Father and live! 10Our human
fathers punished us for a short time, as it
seemed right to them; but God does it for
our own good, so that we may share his
holiness. 11When we are punished, it seems
to us at the time something to make us sad,
not glad. Later, however, those who have
been disciplined by such punishment reap
the peaceful reward of a righteous life.

Instructions and Warnings

12Lift up your tired hands, then, and
strengthen your trembling knees! 13Keep
walking on straight paths, so that the lame
foot may not be disabled, but instead be
healed.
14Try to be at peace with everyone, and
try to live a holy life, because no one will see
the Lord without it. 15Guard against turning
back from the grace of God. Let no one
become like a bitter plant that grows up and
causes many troubles with its poison. 16Let
no one become immoral or unspiritual like
Esau, who for a single meal sold his rights as
the older son. 17Afterward, you know, he
wanted to receive his father's blessing; but he
was turned back, because he could not find
any way to change what he had done, even
though in tears he looked for it.[i]
18You have not come, as the people of
Israel came, to what you can feel, to Mount
Sinai with its blazing fire, the darkness and
the gloom, the storm, 19the blast of a trum-
pet, and the sound of a voice. When the
people heard the voice, they begged not to
hear another word, 20because they could not
bear the order which said, "If even an animal
touches the mountain, it must be stoned to
death." 21The sight was so terrifying that
Moses said, "I am trembling and afraid!"
22Instead, you have come to Mount Zion
and to the city of the living God, the heav-
enly Jerusalem, with its thousands of angels.
23You have come to the joyful gathering of
God's first-born, whose names are written in
heaven. You have come to God, who is the
judge of all people, and to the spirits of good
people made perfect. 24You have come to
Jesus, who arranged the new covenant, and
to the sprinkled blood that promises much
better things than does the blood of Abel.
25Be careful, then, and do not refuse to
hear him who speaks. Those who refused to
hear the one who gave the divine message
on earth did not escape. How much less shall
we escape, then, if we turn away from the
one who speaks from heaven! 26His voice

i **12:17** he looked for it; *or* he tried to get the blessing.

12:5, 6 Job 5:17; Prov 3:11, 12 (LXX) **12:12** Isa 35:3 (LXX) **12:13** Prov 4:26 (LXX) **12:15** Deut 29:18 (LXX) **12:16** Gen 25:29–34 **12:17** Gen 27:30–40 **12:18, 19** Ex 19:16–22; 20:18–21; Deut 4:11, 12; 5:22–27 **12:20** Ex 19:12, 13 **12:21** Deut 9:19 **12:24** Gen 4:10 **12:25** Ex 20:22 **12:26** Hag 2:6 (LXX)

"Let us keep our eyes fixed on Jesus, on whom our faith depends from beginning to end" *(Hebrews 12:2)*.

shook the earth at that time, but now he has
promised, "I will once more shake not only
the earth but heaven as well." 27The words
"once more" plainly show that the created
things will be shaken and removed, so that
the things that cannot be shaken will remain.
28Let us be thankful, then, because we
receive a kingdom that cannot be shaken. Let
us be grateful and worship God in a way that
will please him, with reverence and awe;
29because our God is indeed a destroying fire.

How to Please God

13 Keep on loving one another as
Christians. 2Remember to welcome
strangers in your homes. There were some
who did that and welcomed angels without
knowing it. 3Remember those who are in
prison, as though you were in prison with
them. Remember those who are suffering, as
though you were suffering as they are.
4Marriage is to be honored by all, and
husbands and wives must be faithful to each
other. God will judge those who are
immoral and those who commit adultery.
5Keep your lives free from the love of
money, and be satisfied with what you have.
For God has said, "I will never leave you; I
will never abandon you." 6Let us be bold,
then, and say,

"The Lord is my helper,
I will not be afraid.
What can anyone do to me?"

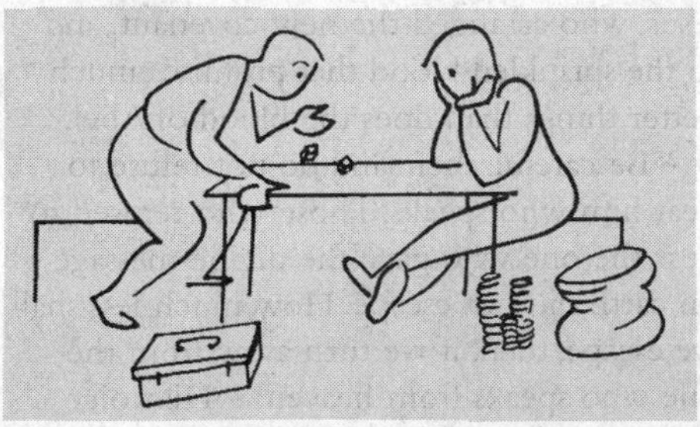

Keep your lives free from the love of money. (13:5)

Live it!

Love of Money

Some Native American tribes have a special ceremony called the *otuhan.* In an *otuhan* a person gives away some or all of his or her belongings to mark a special occasion. It is a way of acknowledging the importance of other people in your life. It is also a recognition that a happy life does not come from owning things.

Hebrews reminds us to "Keep your lives free from the love of money" (13:5). Loving stuff is like loving money. The Church calls loving stuff materialism and teaches that materialism is a spiritual danger. If loving stuff stops you from loving people, it is time for a change. People are always more important. You might want to look at all you have and decide if you really need it. If you give some of your extra things away, you may find yourself with more time for people.

— Hebrews 13:5–6

7Remember your former leaders, who
spoke God's message to you. Think back on
how they lived and died, and imitate their
faith. 8Jesus Christ is the same yesterday,
today, and forever. 9Do not let all kinds of
strange teachings lead you from the right
way. It is good to receive inner strength from
God's grace, and not by obeying rules about
foods; those who obey these rules have not
been helped by them.
10The priests who serve in the Jewish

12:29 Deut 4:24 **13:2** Gen 18:1–8; 19:1–3; Tob 5:4, 5 **13:4** Wis 3:13 **13:5** Deut 31:6, 8; Josh 1:5 **13:6** Ps 118:6 (LXX)

"Jesus Christ is the same yesterday, today, and forever" *(Hebrews 13:8)*.

place of worship have no right to eat any of
the sacrifice on our altar. 11 The Jewish high
priest brings the blood of the animals into
the Most Holy Place to offer it as a sacrifice
for sins; but the bodies of the animals are
burned outside the camp. 12 For this reason
Jesus also died outside the city, in order to
purify the people from sin with his own
blood. 13 Let us, then, go to him outside the
camp and share his shame. 14 For there is no
permanent city for us here on earth; we are
looking for the city which is to come. 15 Let
us, then, always offer praise to God as our
sacrifice through Jesus, which is the offering
presented by lips that confess him as Lord.
16 Do not forget to do good and to help one
another, because these are the sacrifices that
please God.

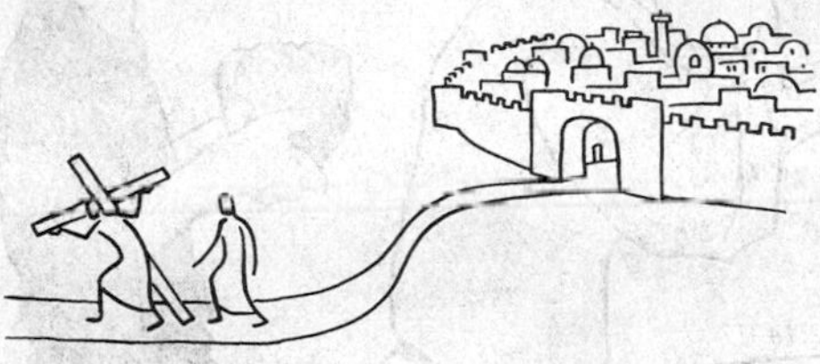

For this reason Jesus also died outside the city. (13:12)

17 Obey your leaders and follow their
orders. They watch over your souls without
resting, since they must give to God an
account of their service. If you obey them,
they will do their work gladly; if not, they
will do it with sadness, and that would be of
no help to you.

18 Keep on praying for us. We are sure we
have a clear conscience, because we want to
do the right thing at all times. 19 And I beg
you even more earnestly to pray that God
will send me back to you soon.

Closing Prayer

20-21 God has raised from death our Lord
Jesus, who is the Great Shepherd of the
sheep as the result of his blood,[k] by which
the eternal covenant is sealed. May the God
of peace provide you with every good thing
you need in order to do his will, and may
he, through Jesus Christ, do in us what
pleases him. And to Christ be the glory for-
ever and ever! Amen.

Final Words

22 I beg you, my friends, to listen patiently
to this message of encouragement; for this
letter I have written you is not very long. 23 I
want you to know that our brother Timothy
has been let out of prison. If he comes soon
enough, I will have him with me when I see
you.

24 Give our greetings to all your leaders
and to all God's people. The believers from
Italy send you their greetings.

25 May God's grace be with you all.

[k] **13:20–21** his blood; *or* his sacrificial death.
13:11 Lev 16:27

Your Next Step

Congratulations on finishing the Letter to the Hebrews! Use this space to write your thoughts and questions about this book. If you are following the suggested reading plan, move back to the Letter to the Romans. Romans is one of the most difficult letters to understand, but it tells us even more about the importance of faith.

The Letter of James

Ahhhh . . . freedom! When is the last time you felt this? When you finished a big project or had no homework on a weekend? When you were getting along great with all your friends?

James describes freedom as the way we will feel when we practice living God's law of love. For example we are most free when we avoid anger, don't judge people, do good deeds for others, be patient, and take care of the poor. God's law isn't meant to be hard on us. Rather, if we were all following it, our lives would be better and easier. People would treat each other with deeper kindness, respect, and care.

Living in God's love brings true freedom, and James offers lots of practical advice for living that way.

Chap. 2:14–17

Headlines

- Pray Confidently for What You Need! (1:2–7)
- Faith Is Useless Without Action (1:19–27; 2:14–26)
- The Power of the Tongue (3:1–12)
- Boasting Is Bad (4:1–10)
- Prayer Produces Wonders! (5:13–20)

FACTOIDS

Who wrote this book? Possibly James, a relative of Jesus and the first leader of the Christian community in Jerusalem.

When was it written? If James wrote it, around AD 57 to 62. If a later admirer of James wrote it, between AD 70 and 150.

Who was it written for? It was written for Christians living in either Palestine, Syria, or Rome.

What is the literary style? It is a letter to Christians, but it is almost like a Christian advice column.

Important themes

- God is generous and gracious to us, even during difficult times.
- Beware of judging others by their appearance, especially the rich and the poor.
- Our actions and words should reflect our faith.
- Be patient with one another and pray for all in need.

1

1 From James, a servant of God and of the
Lord Jesus Christ:
Greetings to all God's people scattered
over the whole world.

Faith and Wisdom

2My friends, consider yourselves fortunate
when all kinds of trials come your way, 3for
you know that when your faith succeeds in
facing such trials, the result is the ability to
endure. 4Make sure that your endurance car-
ries you all the way without failing, so that
you may be perfect and complete, lacking
nothing. 5But if any of you lack wisdom,
you should pray to God, who will give it to
you; because God gives generously and gra-
ciously to all. 6But when you pray, you must
believe and not doubt at all. Whoever doubts
is like a wave in the sea that is driven and
blown about by the wind. 7-8If you are like
that, unable to make up your mind and
undecided in all you do, you must not think
that you will receive anything from the
Lord.

Poverty and Riches

9Those Christians who are poor must be
glad when God lifts them up, 10and the rich
Christians must be glad when God brings
them down. For the rich will pass away like
the flower of a wild plant. 11The sun rises
with its blazing heat and burns the plant; its
flower falls off, and its beauty is destroyed. In
the same way the rich will be destroyed
while they go about their business.

Testing and Tempting

12Happy are those who remain faithful
under trials, because when they succeed in
passing such a test, they will receive as their
reward the life which God has promised to
those who love him. 13If we are tempted by
such trials, we must not say, "This temptation
comes from God." For God cannot be
tempted by evil, and he himself tempts no
one. 14But we are tempted when we are
drawn away and trapped by our own evil
desires. 15Then our evil desires conceive and
give birth to sin; and sin, when it is full-
grown, gives birth to death.

16Do not be deceived, my dear friends!
17Every good gift and every perfect present
comes from heaven; it comes down from
God, the Creator of the heavenly lights, who
does not change or cause darkness by turn-
ing. 18By his own will he brought us into
being through the word of truth, so that we
should have first place among all his crea-
tures.

Hearing and Doing

19Remember this, my dear friends! Every-
one must be quick to listen, but slow to
speak and slow to become angry. 20Human
anger does not achieve God's righteous pur-
pose. 21So get rid of every filthy habit and all
wicked conduct. Submit to God and accept
the word that he plants in your hearts, which
is able to save you.

22Do not deceive yourselves by just listen-
ing to his word; instead, put it into practice.
23If you listen to the word, but do not put it
into practice you are like people who look
in a mirror and see themselves as they are.
24They take a good look at themselves and
then go away and at once forget what they
look like. 25But if you look closely into the
perfect law that sets people free, and keep on
paying attention to it and do not simply lis-
ten and then forget it, but put it into prac-
tice—you will be blessed by God in what
you do.

26Do any of you think you are religious? If
you do not control your tongue, your religion
is worthless and you deceive yourself. 27What
God the Father considers to be pure and

1:1 Mt 13:55; Mk 6:3; Acts 15:13; Gal 1:19 **1:2** Wis 3:5, 6 **1:5** Wis 8:20; Sir 51:13, 14 **1:10, 11** Isa 40:6, 7 (LXX) **1:13** Sir 15:11–20 **1:19** Sir 5:11

Live it!

Empty Faith?

Mom: **Well, that was a nice homily today. Not too long—but lots of pearls of wisdom. I need all the help I can get to become more patient!**
Daughter: **That last song was cool. I love it when they play drums at Church!**
Dad: **What is this jerk doing? Hey buddy, move it! Where did you get your license? Out of a cereal box?**
Daughter: **Geez, Dad.**
Mom: **Honey, did you hear anything at Church today? Did anything at all sink in?**
Dad: **Can't you just be happy that I went to Church? Get off my back!**

The author of James reminds Christians that listening to God's word and saying we have faith isn't worth much if we don't show it in our words and actions. What are some ways you see people slipping up on practicing what we claim to believe?

— James 1:19–25

genuine religion is this: to take care of orphans
and widows in their suffering and to keep
oneself from being corrupted by the world.

Warning against Prejudice

2 My friends, as believers in our Lord
Jesus Christ, the Lord of glory, you must
never treat people in different ways accord-
ing to their outward appearance. 2Suppose a
rich man wearing a gold ring and fine
clothes comes to your meeting, and a poor
man in ragged clothes also comes. 3If you
show more respect to the well-dressed man
and say to him, "Have this best seat here,"
but say to the poor man, "Stand over there,
or sit here on the floor by my feet," 4then
you are guilty of creating distinctions among
yourselves and of making judgments based
on evil motives.

5Listen, my dear friends! God chose the
poor people of this world to be rich in faith
and to possess the kingdom which he prom-
ised to those who love him. 6But you dishon-
or the poor! Who are the ones who oppress
you and drag you before the judges? The rich!
7They are the ones who speak evil of that
good name which has been given to you.

8You will be doing the right thing if you
obey the law of the Kingdom, which is
found in the scripture, "Love your neighbor
as you love yourself." 9But if you treat peo-
ple according to their outward appearance,
you are guilty of sin, and the Law condemns
you as a lawbreaker. 10Whoever breaks one
commandment is guilty of breaking them
all. 11For the same one who said, "Do not
commit adultery," also said, "Do not commit
murder." Even if you do not commit adul-
tery, you have become a lawbreaker if you
commit murder. 12Speak and act as people
who will be judged by the law that sets us
free. 13For God will not show mercy when
he judges the person who has not been mer-
ciful; but mercy triumphs over judgment.

Faith and Actions

14My friends, what good is it for one of
you to say that you have faith if your actions
do not prove it? Can that faith save you?
15Suppose there are brothers or sisters who
need clothes and don't have enough to eat.
16What good is there in your saying to
them, "God bless you! Keep warm and eat
well!"—if you don't give them the necessi-
ties of life? 17So it is with faith: if it is alone
and includes no actions, then it is dead.

2:8 Lev 19:18 **2:11** **a** Ex 20:14; Deut 5:18; **b** Ex 20:13; Deut 5:17

"If you do not control your tongue, your religion is worthless and you deceive yourself" *(James 1:26)*.

Live it!

Guilty!
(of Being a Christian)

Someone once posed this question: If you were on trial for being a Christian, would there be enough proof to find you guilty?

The Letter from James suggests that one proof would be your attitude and behavior toward people who are poor, unpopular, unattractive, or just hard to be around. In his earthly life, Jesus spent much of his time with poor people and the people considered the losers of society. He taught us that the least among us are especially blessed—they are precious to God. By his preaching and example, Jesus was teaching us to love and care for poor and outcast people too.

Quickly think of ten things you did and said the past few days. Which things showed patience, fairness, compassion, forgiveness, or generosity? Which things showed acceptance and care for people who are unpopular or less fortunate?

— James 2:1–7

18 But someone will say, "One person has
faith, another has actions." My answer is,
"Show me how anyone can have faith with-
out actions. I will show you my faith by my
actions." 19 Do you believe that there is only
one God? Good! The demons also believe—
and tremble with fear. 20 You fool! Do you
want to be shown that faith without actions
is useless?[a] 21 How was our ancestor Abraham
put right with God? It was through his
actions, when he offered his son Isaac on the
altar. 22 Can't you see? His faith and his
actions worked together; his faith was made
perfect through his actions. 23 And the scrip-
ture came true that said, "Abraham believed
God, and because of his faith God accepted
him as righteous." And so Abraham was
called God's friend. 24 You see, then, that it is
by our actions that we are put right with
God, and not by our faith alone.

25 It was the same with the prostitute
Rahab. She was put right with God through
her actions, by welcoming the Israelite spies
and helping them to escape by a different
road.

26 So then, as the body without the spirit
is dead, also faith without actions is dead.

The Tongue

3 My friends, not many of you should
become teachers. As you know, we
teachers will be judged with greater strictness
than others. 2 All of us often make mistakes.
But if a person never makes a mistake in
what he says, he is perfect and is also able to
control his whole being. 3 We put a bit into
the mouth of a horse to make it obey us, and
we are able to make it go where we want.
4 Or think of a ship: big as it is and driven by
such strong winds, it can be steered by a very
small rudder, and it goes wherever the pilot
wants it to go. 5 So it is with the tongue: small
as it is, it can boast about great things.

Just think how large a forest can be set on
fire by a tiny flame! 6 And the tongue is like
a fire. It is a world of wrong, occupying its
place in our bodies and spreading evil
through our whole being. It sets on fire the
entire course of our existence with the fire
that comes to it from hell itself. 7 We humans
are able to tame and have tamed all other
creatures—wild animals and birds, reptiles
and fish. 8 But no one has ever been able to
tame the tongue. It is evil and uncontrol-
lable, full of deadly poison. 9 We use it to
give thanks to our Lord and Father and also
to curse other people, who are created in the
likeness of God. 10 Words of thanksgiving
and cursing pour out from the same mouth.

[a] **2:20** useless; *some manuscripts have* dead.

2:21 Gen 22:1–14; Sir 44:19–21; 1 Macc 2:52 **2:23** **a** Gen 15:6, **b** 2 Chr 20:7; Isa 41:8 **2:25** Josh 2:1–21 **3:2** Sir 5:9–15; 14:1; 28:13–26 **3:6** Sir 5:13; 28:22 **3:9** Gen 1:26

Live it!

You Can Prevent Forest Fires!

Shauna just saw something she couldn't believe. She saw William and Denise holding hands in the drama room after school. But Denise was going out with Travis. Shauna had to tell someone, and soon all their friends knew about it. Travis even tried to start a fight with William. Only later did Shauna hear that Denise and William were only practicing their parts for the school play.

James compares our mean or untrue gossip to a spark that starts a huge forest fire. The words that come out of our mouths can be encouraging and kind, or they can be deadly. God is the best one to help us control our tongues. Ask God to help you stop and think before you speak—so you don't set some person's or some group's reputation on fire!

— James 3:5–12

My friends, this should not happen! 11No
spring of water pours out sweet water and
bitter water from the same opening. 12A fig
tree, my friends, cannot bear olives; a
grapevine cannot bear figs, nor can a salty
spring produce sweet water.

The Wisdom from Above

13Are there any of you who are wise and
understanding? You are to prove it by your
good life, by your good deeds performed
with humility and wisdom. 14But if in your
heart you are jealous, bitter, and selfish, don't
sin against the truth by boasting of your wis-
dom. 15Such wisdom does not come down
from heaven; it belongs to the world, it is
unspiritual and demonic. 16Where there is
jealousy and selfishness, there is also disorder
and every kind of evil. 17But the wisdom
from above is pure first of all; it is also peace-
ful, gentle, and friendly; it is full of compas-
sion and produces a harvest of good deeds; it
is free from prejudice and hypocrisy. 18And
goodness is the harvest that is produced from
the seeds the peacemakers plant in peace.

Friendship with the World

4 Where do all the fights and quarrels
among you come from? They come from
your desires for pleasure, which are constantly
fighting within you. 2You want things, but
you cannot have them, so you are ready to
kill; you strongly desire things, but you cannot
get them, so you quarrel and fight. You do not
have what you want because you do not ask
God for it. 3And when you ask, you do not
receive it, because your motives are bad; you
ask for things to use for your own pleasures.
4Unfaithful people! Don't you know that to
be the world's friend means to be God's
enemy? If you want to be the world's friend,
you make yourself God's enemy. 5Don't think
that there is no truth in the scripture that
says, "The spirit that God placed in us is filled
with fierce desires."[b] 6But the grace that God
gives is even stronger. As the scripture says,
"God resists the proud, but gives grace to the
humble."

7So then, submit yourselves to God. Resist
the Devil, and he will run away from you.
8Come near to God, and he will come near
to you. Wash your hands, you sinners! Purify
your hearts, you hypocrites! 9Be sorrowful,
cry, and weep; change your laughter into
crying, your joy into gloom! 10Humble
yourselves before the Lord, and he will lift
you up.

Warning against Judging One Another

11Do not criticize one another, my
friends. If you criticize or judge another

[b] **4:5** The spirit . . . fierce desires; *or* God yearns jealously over the spirit that he placed in us.

3:13 Sir 19:20–30 **4:6** Prov 3:34 (LXX)

Pray it!

Is Nice in Me?

Dear Lord,

Yesterday I was really going at it! Judging people, I mean. I had a clever put-down for quite a few of my classmates—mostly the ones who are "good." Kids who always follow the rules, never get in trouble, are A students . . . the kind of kids you must really love, God!

All that judging felt good at the time because everyone was laughing at the stuff I said. Later, though, I felt kind of sick—a big pit in my stomach. Is that what guilt feels like?

What I'm trying to say, God, is I'm sorry. You know, I can be really snotty. I'm actually getting tired of it, though. And I think other people are getting tired of me. I can't really blame them.

There's this guy in my school, Anthony. He's just nice—plain and simple. I don't think I've ever heard him say a mean thing about anyone. And everybody really likes him. He's popular just because he's nice to everyone. How simple is that? Lord, do you think I can become like that? Can you help me?

— James 4:11–12

Christian, you criticize and judge the Law. If you judge the Law, then you are no longer one who obeys the Law, but one who
judges it. 12God is the only lawgiver and judge. He alone can save and destroy. Who do you think you are, to judge someone else?

Warning against Boasting

13Now listen to me, you that say, "Today or tomorrow we will travel to a certain city, where we will stay a year and go into business and make a lot of money."
14You don't even know what your life tomorrow will be! You are like a puff of smoke, which appears for a moment and then disappears.
15What you should say is this: "If the Lord is willing, we will live and do this or that."
16But now you are proud, and you boast; all such boasting is wrong.
17So then, if we do not do the good we know we should do, we are guilty of sin.

Warning to the Rich

5 And now, you rich people, listen to me! Weep and wail over the miseries that are coming upon you!
2Your riches have rotted away, and your clothes have been eaten by moths.
3Your gold and silver are covered with rust, and this rust will be a witness against you and will eat up your flesh like fire. You have piled up riches in these last days.
4You have not paid any wages to those who work in your fields. Listen to their complaints! The cries of those who gather in your crops have reached the ears of God, the Lord Almighty.
5Your life here on earth has been full of luxury and pleasure. You have made yourselves fat for the day of slaughter.
6You have condemned and

4:13, 14 Prov 27:1 **4:13** Wis 2:4; 5:9–13 **5:2, 3** Mt 6:19 **5:3** Sir 29:10–12 **5:4** Deut 24:14, 15 **5:6** Wis 2:10–20

"Do not criticize one another, my friends" *(James 4:11)*.

Prayers of the Faithful

Catholic Connections

Who do you know who needs God's help? One of the best things we can do for one another is pray.

Each week after we pray the Nicene Creed at Mass, usually we pray for our world, our Church, the dead and the sick, and other needs in our community. These prayers are called the Prayers of the Faithful. They are a type of prayer called a petition. After each prayer of petition is read, we say together, "Lord, hear our prayer," or some similar response.

Depending on the size of your church, there might be 100 people joining in those prayers or 600 people or a thousand—all praying to God for the same thing. When we pray alone, we know God hears us. But hundreds of prayers together—imagine how that must get God's attention! Remember, James tells us that our prayers are very powerful (James 5:16).

— James 5:13–18

murdered innocent people, and they do not resist you.[c]

Patience and Prayer

7Be patient, then, my friends, until the
Lord comes. See how patient farmers are as
they wait for their land to produce precious
crops. They wait patiently for the autumn
and spring rains. 8You also must be patient.
Keep your hopes high, for the day of the
Lord's coming is near.

9Do not complain against one another,
my friends, so that God will not judge you.
The Judge is near, ready to appear. 10My
friends, remember the prophets who spoke
in the name of the Lord. Take them as
examples of patient endurance under suffer-
ing. 11We call them happy because they
endured. You have heard of Job's patience,
and you know how the Lord provided for
him in the end. For the Lord is full of mercy
and compassion.

12Above all, my friends, do not use an
oath when you make a promise. Do not
swear by heaven or by earth or by anything
else. Say only "Yes" when you mean yes, and
"No" when you mean no, and then you will
not come under God's judgment.

13Are any among you in trouble? They
should pray. Are any among you happy?

This prayer made in faith will heal the sick. (5:15)

[c] **5:6** people, and they do not resist you; *or* people. Will God not resist you?

5:11 **a** Job 1:21, 22; 2:10; **b** Ps 103:8 **5:12** Mt 5:34–37

"The prayer of a good person has a powerful effect" *(James 5:16)*. **Who needs your prayers today?**

They should sing praises. 14 Are any among
you sick? They should send for the church
elders, who will pray for them and rub olive
oil on them in the name of the Lord. 15 This
prayer made in faith will heal the sick; the
Lord will restore them to health, and the sins
they have committed will be forgiven. 16 So
then, confess your sins to one another and
pray for one another, so that you will be
healed. The prayer of a good person has a
powerful effect. 17 Elijah was the same kind
of person as we are. He prayed earnestly that
there would be no rain, and no rain fell on
the land for three and a half years. 18 Once
again he prayed, and the sky poured out its
rain and the earth produced its crops.

19 My friends, if any of you wander away
from the truth and another one brings you
back again, 20 remember this: whoever turns
a sinner back from the wrong way will save
that sinner's soul[d] from death and bring
about the forgiveness of many sins.

[d] **5:20** that sinner's soul; *or* his own soul.

5:14 Mk 6:13 **5:16** Sir 4:26 **5:17** 1 Kings 17:1; 18:1; Sir 48:2, 3 **5:18** 1 Kings 18:42–45 **5:20** Prov 10:12; Tob 12:9; 1 Pet 4:8

Your Next Step

Congratulations on finishing the Letter of James! Use this space to write your thoughts and questions about this book. If you are following the suggested reading plan, move back to the Letter to the Galatians. Galatians also talks about faith and salvation and a particular issue that almost divided the early Church.

The First Letter of Peter

Have you ever been picked on or teased? We have all been hurt at some point. It's part of life. It's part of being a human being. The First Letter of Peter was addressed to early Christians who had changed their way of living. For many this new life was very difficult. They were being picked on for being followers of Christ, but it was much more serious than that. They were often mistreated and even persecuted. Suffering for their faith was a way of life.

These Christians lived a long way from Jerusalem and Rome, so you can understand why they needed encouragement. This letter reminded these new Christians of their Baptism and their call to live a good and holy life. It pointed out that their suffering is to be expected because Christ also suffered. In the end, they will be rewarded for their faith. In the meantime, they, like us, need to stay alert and cheer one another on.

Chap. 4:12–16

Headlines

- Rich Blessings Await Us (1:3–5)
- God Will Bless Your Suffering (2:18–25; 3:8–17; 4:12–19)
- Watch Out for the Devil! (5:8–11)

FACTOIDS

Who wrote this book? Possibly Peter, but most likely one of his followers.

When was it written? If it was written by Peter, around AD 60 to 63; if by a follower, AD 70 to 90.

Who was it written for? It was written to Christians living in Asia Minor who were being ridiculed for the way they lived.

Why was it written? The author wanted to encourage the Christian community and help the people make sense of their suffering.

Important themes

- Suffering for following Christ is to be expected.
- Despite suffering, it is important to keep faith in Jesus.
- Older Christians should be good examples. Younger Christians should be open to what their elders have to teach them.

1 PETER

1 From Peter, apostle of Jesus Christ—
To God's chosen people who live as
refugees scattered throughout the provinces
of Pontus, Galatia, Cappadocia, Asia, and
Bithynia. 2You were chosen according to the
purpose of God the Father and were made a
holy people by his Spirit, to obey Jesus
Christ and be purified by his blood.
May grace and peace be yours in full
measure.

A Living Hope

3Let us give thanks to the God and Father
of our Lord Jesus Christ! Because of his
great mercy he gave us new life by raising
Jesus Christ from death. This fills us with a
living hope, 4and so we look forward to pos-
sessing the rich blessings that God keeps for
his people. He keeps them for you in heav-
en, where they cannot decay or spoil or fade
away. 5They are for you, who through faith
are kept safe by God's power for the salva-
tion which is ready to be revealed at the end
of time.
6Be glad about this, even though it may
now be necessary for you to be sad for a
while because of the many kinds of trials
you suffer. 7Their purpose is to prove that
your faith is genuine. Even gold, which can
be destroyed, is tested by fire; and so your
faith, which is much more precious than
gold, must also be tested, so that it may
endure. Then you will receive praise and
glory and honor on the Day when Jesus
Christ is revealed. 8You love him, although
you have not seen him, and you believe in
him, although you do not now see him. So
you rejoice with a great and glorious joy
which words cannot express, 9because you
are receiving the salvation of your souls,
which is the purpose of your faith in him.
10It was concerning this salvation that the
prophets made careful search and investiga-
tion, and they prophesied about this gift
which God would give you. 11They tried to
find out when the time would be and how

Catholic Connections

Prayer of Blessing

"God bless you!" This is a common expression in English, and a beautiful one. It is a simple form of prayer. A blessing prayer is one that calls on God's power to care for a person, place, thing, or undertaking. A blessing prayer often includes praise for God and for his gifts. First Peter 1:3–9 has several elements of a blessing prayer, beginning with giving thanks and praise to God.

Think of times when a blessing prayer could be used: before a trip, on a birthday or anniversary, before a retreat. There are many ways to pray a blessing, including having all those doing the blessing raise their hands over the person or group to be blessed. The blessing might also involve placing a hand on the person's shoulder or head. No matter how we do it or what words we say, what it comes down to is that we are sharing a simple but deep prayer: "God bless you!"

— 1 Peter 1:3–9

it would come.[a] This was the time to which
Christ's Spirit in them was pointing, in pre-
dicting the sufferings that Christ would have
to endure and the glory that would follow.
12 God revealed to these prophets that their
work was not for their own benefit, but for
yours, as they spoke about those things
which you have now heard from the mes-
sengers who announced the Good News by
the power of the Holy Spirit sent from
heaven. These are things which even the
angels would like to understand.

A Call to Holy Living

13 So then, have your minds ready for
action. Keep alert and set your hope com-
pletely on the blessing which will be given
you when Jesus Christ is revealed. 14 Be obe-
dient to God, and do not allow your lives to
be shaped by those desires you had when
you were still ignorant. 15 Instead, be holy in
all that you do, just as God who called you is
holy. 16 The scripture says, "Be holy because I
am holy."

17 You call him Father, when you pray to
God, who judges all people by the same
standard, according to what each one has
done; so then, spend the rest of your lives
here on earth in reverence for him. 18 For
you know what was paid to set you free
from the worthless manner of life handed
down by your ancestors. It was not some-
thing that can be destroyed, such as silver or
gold; 19 it was the costly sacrifice of Christ,
who was like a lamb without defect or flaw.
20 He had been chosen by God before the
creation of the world and was revealed in
these last days for your sake. 21 Through him
you believe in God, who raised him from
death and gave him glory; and so your faith
and hope are fixed on God.

22 Now that by your obedience to the
truth you have purified yourselves and have
come to have a sincere love for other believ-
ers, love one another earnestly with all your
heart.[b] 23 For through the living and eternal
word of God you have been born again as
the children of a parent who is immortal,
not mortal. 24 As the scripture says,

"All human beings are like grass,
and all their glory is like wild flowers.
The grass withers, and the flowers fall,
25 but the word of the Lord remains
forever."

This word is the Good News that was pro-
claimed to you.

The Living Stone and the Holy Nation

2 Rid yourselves, then, of all evil; no more
lying or hypocrisy or jealousy or insult-
ing language. 2 Be like newborn babies, always
thirsty for the pure spiritual milk, so that by
drinking it you may grow up and be saved.
3 As the scripture says, "You have found out
for yourselves how kind the Lord is."

4 Come to the Lord, the living stone
rejected by people as worthless but chosen
by God as valuable. 5 Come as living stones,
and let yourselves be used in building the
spiritual temple, where you will serve as holy
priests to offer spiritual and acceptable sacri-
fices to God through Jesus Christ. 6 For the
scripture says,

"I chose a valuable stone,
which I am placing as the cornerstone
in Zion;
and whoever believes in him will never
be disappointed."

7 This stone is of great value for you that
believe; but for those who do not believe:

"The stone which the builders rejected as
worthless
turned out to be the most important of
all."

8 And another scripture says,

[a] **1:11** when the time would be and how it would come; *or* who the person would be and when he would come. [b] **1:22** with all your heart; *some manuscripts have* with a pure heart.

1:16 Lev 11:44, 45; 19:2 **1:24, 25** Isa 40:6–8 (LXX) **2:3** Ps 34:8 **2:6** Isa 28:16 (LXX) **2:7** Ps 118:22 **2:8** Isa 8:14, 15

The *heathen* (1 Peter 2:12) are those people who do not worship God as revealed in the Bible.

"This is the stone that will make people
stumble,
the rock that will make them fall."
They stumbled because they did not believe
in the word; such was God's will for them.
[9]But you are the chosen race, the King's
priests, the holy nation, God's own people,
chosen to proclaim the wonderful acts of
God, who called you out of darkness into his
own marvelous light. [10]At one time you
were not God's people, but now you are his
people; at one time you did not know God's
mercy, but now you have received his mercy.

Slaves of God

[11]I appeal to you, my friends, as strangers
and refugees in this world! Do not give in to
bodily passions, which are always at war
against the soul. [12]Your conduct among the
heathen should be so good that when they
accuse you of being evildoers, they will have
to recognize your good deeds and so praise
God on the Day of his coming.
[13]For the sake of the Lord submit your-
selves to every human authority: to the
Emperor, who is the supreme authority,
[14]and to the governors, who have been
appointed by him to punish the evildoers
and to praise those who do good. [15]For God
wants you to silence the ignorant talk of
foolish people by the good things you do.
[16]Live as free people; do not, however, use
your freedom to cover up any evil, but live
as God's slaves. [17]Respect everyone, love
other believers, honor God, and respect the
Emperor.

The Example of Christ's Suffering

[18]You servants must submit yourselves to
your masters and show them complete
respect, not only to those who are kind and
considerate, but also to those who are harsh.
[19]God will bless you for this, if you endure
the pain of undeserved suffering because you
are conscious of his will. [20]For what credit is
there if you endure the beatings you deserve
for having done wrong? But if you endure
suffering even when you have done right,
God will bless you for it. [21]It was to this that
God called you, for Christ himself suffered
for you and left you an example, so that you
would follow in his steps. [22]He committed
no sin, and no one ever heard a lie come
from his lips. [23]When he was insulted, he did
not answer back with an insult; when he suf-
fered, he did not threaten, but placed his
hopes in God, the righteous Judge. [24]Christ
himself carried our sins in his body to the
cross, so that we might die to sin and live for
righteousness. It is by his wounds that you
have been healed. [25]You were like sheep that
had lost their way, but now you have been
brought back to follow the Shepherd and
Keeper of your souls.

Wives and Husbands

3 In the same way you wives must submit
yourselves to your husbands, so that if
any of them do not believe God's word, your
conduct will win them over to believe. It
will not be necessary for you to say a word,
[2]because they will see how pure and rever-
ent your conduct is. [3]You should not use
outward aids to make yourselves beautiful,
such as the way you fix your hair, or the
jewelry you put on, or the dresses you wear.
[4]Instead, your beauty should consist of your
true inner self, the ageless beauty of a gentle
and quiet spirit, which is of the greatest
value in God's sight. [5]For the devout women
of the past who placed their hope in God
used to make themselves beautiful by sub-
mitting themselves to their husbands. [6]Sarah
was like that; she obeyed Abraham and called
him her master. You are now her daughters if
you do good and are not afraid of anything.
[7]In the same way you husbands must live
with your wives with the proper under-
standing that they are more delicate than
you. Treat them with respect, because they
also will receive, together with you, God's
gift of life. Do this so that nothing will inter-
fere with your prayers.

2:9 a Ex 19:5, 6; Isa 43:20 (LXX); **b** Ex 19:5; Deut 4:20; 7:6; 14:2; Titus 2:14; **c** Isa 43:21; **d** Isa 9:2 **2:10** Hos 2:23 **2:22** Isa 53:9 **2:23** Isa 53:7 **2:24, 25** Isa 53:5, 6 (LXX) **3:1** Eph 5:22; Col 3:18 **3:3** 1 Tim 2:9 **3:6** Gen 18:12 **3:7** Eph 5:25; Col 3:19

Suffering for Doing Right

8 To conclude: you must all have the same
attitude and the same feelings; love one
another, and be kind and humble with one
another. 9 Do not pay back evil with evil or
cursing with cursing; instead, pay back with
a blessing, because a blessing is what God
promised to give you when he called you.
10 As the scripture says,

"If you want to enjoy life
and wish to see good times,
you must keep from speaking evil
and stop telling lies.
11 You must turn away from evil and do
good;
you must strive for peace with all your
heart.
12 For the Lord watches over the righteous
and listens to their prayers;
but he opposes those who do evil."

13 Who will harm you if you are eager to
do what is good? 14 But even if you should
suffer for doing what is right, how happy
you are! Do not be afraid of anyone, and do
not worry. 15 But have reverence for Christ
in your hearts, and honor him as Lord. Be
ready at all times to answer anyone who asks
you to explain the hope you have in you,
16 but do it with gentleness and respect. Keep
your conscience clear, so that when you are
insulted, those who speak evil of your good
conduct as followers of Christ will become
ashamed of what they say. 17 For it is better
to suffer for doing good, if this should be
God's will, than for doing evil. 18 For Christ
died[c] for sins once and for all, a good man
on behalf of sinners, in order to lead you to
God. He was put to death physically, but
made alive spiritually, 19 and in his spiritual
existence he went and preached to the
imprisoned spirits. 20 These were the spirits
of those who had not obeyed God when he
waited patiently during the days that Noah
was building his boat. The few people in the
boat—eight in all—were saved by the water,
21 which was a symbol pointing to baptism,
which now saves you. It is not the washing
off of bodily dirt, but the promise made to
God from a good conscience. It saves you
through the resurrection of Jesus Christ,
22 who has gone to heaven and is at the right
side of God, ruling over all angels and heav-
enly authorities and powers.

Live it!

You Are Beautiful

What makes a woman beautiful? If you asked advertisers, you would get a variety of answers: the right makeup, the perfect hairstyle, or just the right piece of jewelry, not to mention wearing the latest fashion.

These were pretty much the same things that people in the Roman Empire valued at the time 1 Peter was written (1 Peter 3:3). But the author of this letter suggests that if you asked God the same question, there is little doubt how God would respond: true beauty lies within a person. First Peter 3:4 is a lovely way of describing what real beauty is. And that is true for men as well as women.

Have you ever seen a picture of Mother Teresa? There is more beauty in her wrinkled face than in a hundred fashion models, because we know what lies within her. Nothing is wrong with taking reasonable measures to make ourselves look our best. But when people obsess over makeup and clothes, they are forgetting that what we look like does not define who we are.

How would you define beauty by the world's standards? How would you define beauty by God's standards? Which will you choose to follow?

— 1 Peter 3:3–4

[c] **3:18** died; *many manuscripts have* suffered.

3:10–12 Ps 34:12–16 (LXX) **3:14** Mt 5:10 **3:14, 15** Isa 8:12, 13 **3:20** Gen 6:1—7:24

Changed Lives

4 Since Christ suffered physically, you too
must strengthen yourselves with the
same way of thinking that he had; because
whoever suffers physically is no longer
involved with sin. 2 From now on, then, you
must live the rest of your earthly lives con-
trolled by God's will and not by human
desires. 3 You have spent enough time in the
past doing what the heathen like to do. Your
lives were spent in indecency, lust, drunken-
ness, orgies, drinking parties, and the disgust-
ing worship of idols. 4 And now the heathen
are surprised when you do not join them in
the same wild and reckless living, and so
they insult you. 5 But they will have to give
an account of themselves to God, who is
ready to judge the living and the dead. 6 That
is why the Good News was preached also to
the dead, to those who had been judged in
their physical existence as everyone is
judged; it was preached to them so that in
their spiritual existence they may live as God
lives.

Good Managers of God's Gifts

7 The end of all things is near. You must be
self-controlled and alert, to be able to pray.
8 Above everything, love one another earnest-
ly, because love covers over many sins. 9 Open
your homes to each other without complain-
ing. 10 Each one, as a good manager of God's
different gifts, must use for the good of oth-
ers the special gift he has received from God.
11 Those who preach must preach God's mes-
sages; those who serve must serve with the
strength that God gives them, so that in all
things praise may be given to God through
Jesus Christ, to whom belong glory and
power forever and ever. Amen.

Suffering as a Christian

12 My dear friends, do not be surprised at
the painful test you are suffering, as though
something unusual were happening to you.
13 Rather be glad that you are sharing
Christ's sufferings, so that you may be full of

Live it!

Watch Out!

When someone tells you to watch out, they are usually giving you a warning. That is exactly what the author is doing in this letter; he tells these Christians to be alert (1 Peter 4:7, 5:8). Why? Because they are being challenged and persecuted because of their faith in Jesus Christ.

It is so easy to get sucked into doing the wrong thing, if we don't stay alert. During a time of national crisis, a government will often raise the alert level. It is a reminder to keep our eyes and ears open and to be aware of what is going on around us. In a way, that is what this letter is telling us: if we are a follower of Christ, our alert level needs to be raised. Because we live in a world that does not yet recognize Jesus as the Lord of all creation, we will get tempted to do things that are not good for us and go against our beliefs.

Think of ways we can help one another to be alert. Church involvement will help you to stay on the right track. Check and see how you can be involved at your Church. If you don't find a way that works for you, talk to your youth minister or parish priest about how you would like to be involved.

— 1 Peter 4:7, 5:8

4:8 Prov 10:12; Tob 12:9

"If you suffer because you are a Christian, don't be ashamed of it, but thank God that you bear Christ's name" *(1 Peter 4:16)*.

joy when his glory is revealed. 14Happy are
you if you are insulted because you are
Christ's followers; this means that the glori-
ous Spirit, the Spirit of God, is resting on
you. 15If you suffer, it must not be because
you are a murderer or a thief or a criminal
or a meddler in other people's affairs.
16However, if you suffer because you are a
Christian, don't be ashamed of it, but thank
God that you bear Christ's name.
17The time has come for judgment to
begin, and God's own people are the first to
be judged. If it starts with us, how will it end
with those who do not believe the Good
News from God? 18As the scripture says,

"It is difficult for good people to be
saved;
what, then, will become of godless
sinners?"

19So then, those who suffer because it is
God's will for them, should by their good
actions trust themselves completely to their
Creator, who always keeps his promise.

The Flock of God

5 I, who am an elder myself, appeal to the
church elders among you. I am a wit-
ness of Christ's sufferings, and I will share in
the glory that will be revealed. I appeal to
you 2to be shepherds of the flock that God
gave you and to take care of it willingly, as
God wants you to, and not unwillingly. Do
your work, not for mere pay, but from a real
desire to serve. 3Do not try to rule over
those who have been put in your care, but
be examples to the flock. 4And when the
Chief Shepherd appears, you will receive the
glorious crown which will never lose its
brightness.
5In the same way you younger people
must submit yourselves to your elders. And
all of you must put on the apron of humility,
to serve one another; for the scripture says,
"God resists the proud, but shows favor to

The kiss of Christian love (5:14)

the humble." 6Humble yourselves, then,
under God's mighty hand, so that he will lift
you up in his own good time. 7Leave all
your worries with him, because he cares for
you.
8Be alert, be on watch! Your enemy, the
Devil, roams around like a roaring lion,
looking for someone to devour. 9Be firm in
your faith and resist him, because you know
that other believers in all the world are
going through the same kind of sufferings.
10But after you have suffered for a little
while, the God of all grace, who calls you to
share his eternal glory in union with Christ,
will himself perfect you and give you firm-
ness, strength, and a sure foundation. 11To
him be the power forever! Amen.

Final Greetings

12I write you this brief letter with the
help of Silas, whom I regard as a faithful
Christian. I want to encourage you and give

4:18 Prov 11:31 (LXX) **5:2** Jn 21:15–17 **5:5** Prov 3:34 (LXX) **5:6** Mt 23:12; Lk 14:11; 18:14 **5:7** Sir 2:1–18

Some of the early Christians used *Babylon* as a code word for Rome. They saw the Romans persecuting Christians like the Babylonians persecuted the Jewish people.

my testimony that this is the true grace of
God. Stand firm in it.
13 Your sister church in Babylon,[d] also
chosen by God, sends you greetings, and so
does my son Mark. 14 Greet one another
with the kiss of Christian love.
May peace be with all of you who belong
to Christ.

[d] **5:13** BABYLON: *As in the book of Revelation, this probably refers to Rome.*

5:12 Acts 15:22, 40 **5:13** Acts 12:12, 25; 13:13; 15:37–39; Col 4:10; Philem 24

Your Next Step

Congratulations on finishing the First Letter of Peter! Use this space to write your thoughts and questions about this book. If you are following the suggested reading plan, go back to the Book of Ezekiel in the Old Testament. Like Peter, Ezekiel encourages his people to live their lives as God wants them to.

The Second Letter of Peter

When it seems that many things we see and listen to today try to lead us in the wrong direction, this letter gives us hope. Jesus has given us everything we need to live right. It's all a matter of faith, goodness, knowledge, self-control, endurance, godliness, mutual affection, and love.

What about God's promises? When will Jesus return? What will happen?

These are good questions, but we cannot know the answers. To God, one day is like a thousand years, and a thousand years are like one day. We have to be patient and wait. And while we are waiting, let's keep living right.

Chap. 1:16–18

Headlines

- Eyewitness to Christ's Glory (1:16–18)
- False Prophets Will Be Punished (chapter 2)
- New Heavens and New Earth Promised (3:10–13)

FACTOIDS

Who wrote this book? An unknown person, writing in Peter's name.

When was it written? Around AD 130, about one hundred years after Jesus' death and Resurrection.

Who was it written for? It was written for a community of early Christians, both Jewish and Gentile (non-Jewish), beginning to question their beliefs.

Why was it written? The author wanted to convince early Christians to ignore false teachings and to hold on to their true faith.

Jesus connection. The author mentions the Transfiguration of Jesus, an event that happened on a mountain while Peter, James, and John were present (Matthew 17:1–8, Mark 9:2–13, and Luke 9:28–36).

Important themes

- Ignore the teachings of false prophets.
- Remain faithful to true Christian teachings.
- Wait patiently and have faith that when the time is right God will make all things new.

2 PETER

1 From Simon Peter, a servant and apostle of Jesus Christ—

To those who through the righteousness of our God and Savior Jesus Christ have been given a faith as precious as ours:

2 May grace and peace be yours in full measure through your knowledge of God and of Jesus our Lord.

God's Call and Choice

3 God's divine power has given us everything we need to live a truly religious life through our knowledge of the one who called us to share in his own[a] glory and goodness. 4 In this way he has given us the very great and precious gifts he promised, so that by means of these gifts you may escape from the destructive lust that is in the world, and may come to share the divine nature. 5 For this very reason do your best to add goodness to your faith; to your goodness add knowledge; 6 to your knowledge add self-control; to your self-control add endurance; to your endurance add godliness; 7 to your godliness add Christian affection; and to your Christian affection add love. 8 These are the qualities you need, and if you have them in abundance, they will make you active and effective in your knowledge of our Lord Jesus Christ. 9 But if you do not have them, you are so shortsighted that you cannot see and have forgotten that you have been purified from your past sins.

10 So then, my friends, try even harder to make God's call and his choice of you a permanent experience; if you do so, you will never abandon your faith.[b] 11 In this way you will be given the full right to enter the eternal Kingdom of our Lord and Savior Jesus Christ.

12 And so I will always remind you of these matters, even though you already know them and are firmly grounded in the truth you have received. 13 I think it only

To make God's call . . . a permanent experience (1:10)

right for me to stir up your memory of these matters as long as I am still alive. 14 I know that I shall soon put off this mortal body, as our Lord Jesus Christ plainly told me. 15 I will do my best, then, to provide a way for you to remember these matters at all times after my death.

Eyewitnesses of Christ's Glory

16 We have not depended on made-up stories in making known to you the mighty coming of our Lord Jesus Christ. With our own eyes we saw his greatness. 17 We were there when he was given honor and glory by God the Father, when the voice came to him from the Supreme Glory, saying, "This is my own dear Son, with whom I am pleased!" 18 We ourselves heard this voice coming from heaven, when we were with him on the holy mountain.

19 So we are even more confident of the message proclaimed by the prophets. You will do well to pay attention to it, because it is like a lamp shining in a dark place until the Day dawns and the light of the morning

[a] **1:3** to share in his own; *some manuscripts have* through his. [b] **1:10** abandon your faith; *or* fall into sin.

1:17, 18 Mt 17:1–5; Mk 9:2–7; Lk 9:28–35

star shines in your hearts. [20]Above all else, however, remember that none of us can explain by ourselves a prophecy in the Scriptures. [21]For no prophetic message ever came just from the human will, but people were under the control of the Holy Spirit as they spoke the message that came from God.

False Teachers

2 False prophets appeared in the past among the people, and in the same way false teachers will appear among you. They will bring in destructive, untrue doctrines, and will deny the Master who redeemed them, and so they will bring upon themselves sudden destruction. [2]Even so, many will follow their immoral ways; and because of what they do, others will speak evil of the Way of truth. [3]In their greed these false teachers will make a profit out of telling you made-up stories. For a long time now their Judge has been ready, and their Destroyer has been wide awake!

[4]God did not spare the angels who sinned, but threw them into hell, where they are kept chained in darkness,[c] waiting for the Day of Judgment. [5]God did not spare the ancient world, but brought the flood on the world of godless people; the only ones he saved were Noah, who preached righteousness, and seven other people. [6]God condemned the cities of Sodom and Gomorrah, destroying them with fire, and made them an example of what will happen to the godless. [7]He rescued Lot, a good man, who was distressed by the immoral conduct of lawless people. [8]That good man lived among them, and day after day he suffered agony as he saw and heard their evil actions. [9]And so the Lord knows how to rescue godly people from their trials and how to keep the wicked under punishment for the Day of Judgment, [10]especially those who follow their filthy bodily lusts and despise God's authority.

These false teachers are bold and arrogant, and show no respect for the glorious beings above; instead, they insult them. [11]Even the angels, who are so much stronger and mightier than these false teachers, do not accuse them with insults in the presence of the Lord. [12]But these people act by instinct, like wild animals born to be captured and killed; they attack with insults anything they do not understand. They will be destroyed like wild animals, [13]and they will be paid with suffering for the suffering they have caused. Pleasure for them is to do anything in broad daylight that will satisfy their bodily appetites; they are a shame and a disgrace as they join you in your meals, all the while enjoying their deceitful ways! [14]They want to look for nothing but the chance to commit adultery; their appetite for sin is never satisfied. They lead weak people into a trap. Their hearts are trained to be greedy. They are under God's curse! [15]They have left the straight path and have lost their way; they have followed the path taken by Balaam son of Beor, who loved the money he would get for doing wrong [16]and was rebuked for his sin. His donkey spoke with a human voice and stopped the prophet's insane action.

17These people are like dried-up springs, like clouds blown along by a storm; God has reserved a place for them in the deepest darkness. [18]They make proud and stupid statements, and use immoral bodily lusts to trap those who are just beginning to escape from among people who live in error. [19]They promise them freedom while they themselves are slaves of destructive habits—for we are slaves of anything that has conquered us. [20]If people have escaped from the corrupting forces of the world through their knowledge of our Lord and Savior Jesus Christ, and then are again caught and conquered by them, such people are in worse condition at the end than they were at the beginning. [21]It would have been much better for them never to have known the way of righteousness than to know it and then turn away from the sacred command that was given them. [22]What happened to them shows that the proverbs are true: "A dog goes back to what it has vomited" and "A pig that has been washed goes back to roll in the mud."

[c] **2:4** chained in darkness; *some manuscripts have* in dark pits.

2:5 Gen 6:1—7:24; Wis 10:4 **2:6** Gen 19:24 **2:7** Gen 19:1–16; Wis 10:6–8 **2:15, 16** Num 22:4–35 **2:22** Prov 26:11

The Promise of the Lord's Coming

3 My dear friends, this is now the second
letter I have written you. In both letters
I have tried to arouse pure thoughts in your
minds by reminding you of these things. 2I
want you to remember the words that were
spoken long ago by the holy prophets, and
the command from the Lord and Savior
which was given you by your apostles. 3First
of all, you must understand that in the last
days some people will appear whose lives are
controlled by their own lusts. They will
make fun of you 4and will ask, "He promised
to come, didn't he? Where is he? Our ances-
tors have already died, but everything is still
the same as it was since the creation of the
world!" 5They purposely ignore the fact that
long ago God gave a command, and the
heavens and earth were created. The earth
was formed out of water and by water, 6and
it was also by water, the water of the flood,
that the old world was destroyed. 7But the
heavens and the earth that now exist are
being preserved by the same command of
God, in order to be destroyed by fire. They
are being kept for the day when godless
people will be judged and destroyed.
8But do not forget one thing, my dear
friends! There is no difference in the Lord's
sight between one day and a thousand years;
to him the two are the same. 9The Lord is
not slow to do what he has promised, as
some think. Instead, he is patient with you,
because he does not want anyone to be
destroyed, but wants all to turn away from
their sins.
10But the Day of the Lord will come like
a thief. On that Day the heavens will disap-
pear with a shrill noise, the heavenly bodies
will burn up and be destroyed, and the
earth with everything in it will vanish.[d]
11Since all these things will be destroyed in
this way, what kind of people should you
be? Your lives should be holy and dedicated
to God, 12as you wait for the Day of God
and do your best to make it come soon—
the Day when the heavens will burn up and
be destroyed, and the heavenly bodies will
be melted by the heat. 13But we wait for
what God has promised: new heavens and a
new earth, where righteousness will be at
home.
14And so, my friends, as you wait for that
Day, do your best to be pure and faultless in

Live it!

What Kind of Person?

The end of 2 Peter talks about the Second Coming of Christ. The letter is saying that even though Christ has not yet returned, he will at some point. "There is no difference in the Lord's sight between one day and a thousand years" (3:8). Knowing that Christ will return when we least expect, we need to consider our response to the question, "What kind of people should you be?" (3:11). Why would the letter writer ask this question? Because the writer knows that every individual life has purpose and meaning in God's plan. Not just the lives of famous people, but the lives of all people.

"Your lives should be holy and dedicated to God" (3:11), not just some of the time but all of the time. What you do each day matters. What you do each day affects your family, your neighborhood, the people in your school, and all of your friends.

What kind of person must you be to have a positive effect on all of those people? What kind of person would have a negative effect? The choice is yours. The results are important. God knows this. So do you.

— 2 Peter 3:1–13

[d] **3:10** vanish; *some manuscripts have* be found; *others have* be burned up; *one has* be found destroyed.

3:3 Jude 18 **3:5** Gen 1:6–9 **3:6** Gen 7:11 **3:8** Ps 90:4 **3:10** Mt 24:43; Lk 12:39; 1 Thess 5:2; Rev 16:15 **3:13** Isa 65:17; 66:22; Rev 21:1

God's sight and to be at peace with him.
15Look on our Lord's patience as the oppor-
tunity he is giving you to be saved, just as
our dear friend Paul wrote to you, using the
wisdom that God gave him. 16This is what
he says in all his letters when he writes on
the subject. There are some difficult things in
his letters which ignorant and unstable peo-
ple explain falsely, as they do with other pas-
sages of the Scriptures. So they bring on
their own destruction.

17But you, my friends, already know this.
Be on your guard, then, so that you will not
be led away by the errors of lawless people
and fall from your safe position. 18But con-
tinue to grow in the grace and knowledge of
our Lord and Savior Jesus Christ. To him be
the glory, now and forever! Amen.

THE LETTERS OF John

Has anyone ever asked your advice about something important? Maybe it was a younger brother or sister, or maybe it was a friend. They looked up to you because you were older or because they respected you.

The author of these three letters was considered a respected adviser, or elder, of a Christian community that the Gospel of John had been written for.

In the First Letter of John, the author calls the members of the community little children not because they were actually young people but because the writer cared about them as a spiritual father. In the Second Letter of John, this leader warns the community not to follow those spreading false teachings—to totally avoid them. In the Third Letter of John, the author praises those who show love and care for others and warns against those who cause division in the community.

2 John

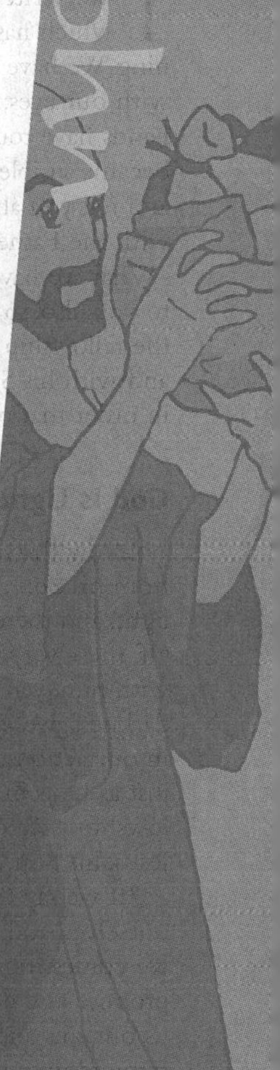

Headlines

- Live in God's Light (1 John 2:7–17)
- Love One Another (1 John 3:11–18)
- Perfect Love Drives Out Fear (1 John 4:16–18)
- Deceivers Teach Christ Wasn't Human (2 John, verses 4–11)
- Church Leader Applauded (3 John, verses 5–8)

FACTOIDS

Who wrote these books? A member of the community that produced the Gospel of John, called the elder.

When were they written? Around AD 100.

Who were they written for? They were written for Christians suffering from a split in their community.

Why were they written? The authors wanted to encourage believers to live the right way and to love one another. They also wanted to warn against people teaching falsely about Jesus Christ.

What is the literary style? First John is a teaching homily, and Second John and Third John are both letters.

Important themes

- We are called to walk in the light that is God, in both our words and actions, and to avoid the darkness of sin.
- When we love others, we are showing our love for God.
- Jesus was a real human being even though he was also God's Son.

1 JOHN

The Word of Life

1 We write to you about the Word of life,
which has existed from the very begin-
ning. We have heard it, and we have seen it
with our eyes; yes, we have seen it, and our
hands have touched it. 2When this life
became visible, we saw it; so we speak of it
and tell you about the eternal life which was
with the Father and was made known to us.
3What we have seen and heard we announce
to you also, so that you will join with us in
the fellowship that we have with the Father
and with his Son Jesus Christ. 4We write this
in order that our[a] joy may be complete.

God Is Light

5Now the message that we have heard
from his Son and announce is this: God is
light, and there is no darkness at all in him.
6If, then, we say that we have fellowship
with him, yet at the same time live in the
darkness, we are lying both in our words and
in our actions. 7But if we live in the light—
just as he is in the light—then we have fel-
lowship with one another, and the blood of
Jesus, his Son, purifies us from every sin.
8If we say that we have no sin, we deceive
ourselves, and there is no truth in us. 9But if
we confess our sins to God, he will keep his
promise and do what is right: he will forgive
us our sins and purify us from all our
wrongdoing. 10If we say that we have not
sinned, we make a liar out of God, and his
word is not in us.

Christ Our Helper

2 I am writing this to you, my children, so
that you will not sin; but if anyone does
sin, we have someone who pleads with the
Father on our behalf—Jesus Christ, the righ-
teous one. 2And Christ himself is the means
by which our sins are forgiven, and not our
sins only, but also the sins of everyone.
3If we obey God's commands, then we are
sure that we know him. 4If we say that we
know him, but do not obey his commands,
we are liars and there is no truth in us. 5But
if we obey his word, we are the ones whose
love for God has really been made perfect.
This is how we can be sure that we are in

Live it!

Live in the Light

It was a dark night. There was a thick blanket of clouds that covered the stars. Kim was camping with her family. She was already in her sleeping bag when she remembered that she had left her backpack on the picnic table. If she got up now and tried to find it in the dark, she knew she'd probably trip and fall. She might even get lost in the woods if she strayed off the path. As she lay in the inky blackness, she saw a pinprick of light through the window of her tent, then another. The sky was beginning to clear. Soon the full moon shone round and bright, and everything outside the tent was clearly outlined in silvery white light. Kim knew she could go safely now and find her backpack.

This letter urges the early Christians—and us—to "live in the light" to follow God (1 John 1:7). In the same way that Kim needed the starlight to find her backpack, we need the light of Christ. Jesus Christ will lead us to true happiness and eternal life!

— 1 John 1:5–7

[a] **1:4** our; *some manuscripts have* your.
1:1 Jn 1:1 **1:2** Jn 1:14

union with God: 6if we say that we remain
in union with God, we should live just as
Jesus Christ did.

The New Command

7My dear friends, this command I am
writing you is not new; it is the old com-
mand, the one you have had from the very
beginning. The old command is the message
you have already heard. 8However, the com-
mand I now write you is new, because its
truth is seen in Christ and also in you. For
the darkness is passing away, and the real
light is already shining.
9If we say that we are in the light, yet hate
others, we are in the darkness to this very
hour. 10If we love others, we live in the light,
and so there is nothing in us that will cause
someone else[b] to sin. 11But if we hate others,
we are in the darkness; we walk in it and do
not know where we are going, because the
darkness has made us blind.

If we love others . . . if we hate others. (2:10, 11)

12I write to you, my children, because
your sins are forgiven for the sake of Christ.
13I write to you, fathers, because you know
him who has existed from the beginning. I
write to you, young people, because you
have defeated the Evil One.
14I write to you, my children, because you
know the Father. I write to you, fathers,
because you know him who has existed
from the beginning. I write to you, young
people, because you are strong; the word of
God lives in you, and you have defeated the
Evil One.
15Do not love the world or anything that
belongs to the world. If you love the world,
you do not love the Father. 16Everything
that belongs to the world—what the sinful
self desires, what people see and want, and
everything in this world that people are so
proud of—none of this comes from the
Father; it all comes from the world. 17The
world and everything in it that people desire
is passing away; but those who do the will of
God live forever.

The Enemy of Christ

18My children, the end is near! You were
told that the Enemy of Christ would come;
and now many enemies of Christ have
already appeared, and so we know that the
end is near. 19These people really did not
belong to our fellowship, and that is why
they left us; if they had belonged to our fel-
lowship, they would have stayed with us. But
they left so that it might be clear that none
of them really belonged to us.
20But you have had the Holy Spirit
poured out on you by Christ, and so all of
you know the truth. 21I write you, then,
not because you do not know the truth;
instead, it is because you do know it, and
you also know that no lie ever comes from
the truth.
22Who, then, is the liar? It is those who
say that Jesus is not the Messiah. Such peo-
ple are the Enemy of Christ—they reject
both the Father and the Son. 23For those
who reject the Son reject also the Father;
those who accept the Son have the Father
also.
24Be sure, then, to keep in your hearts the
message you heard from the beginning. If
you keep that message, then you will always
live in union with the Son and the Father.

[b] **2:10** someone else; *or* us.
2:7 Jn 13:34

The author of I John uses very personal language. In chapter 2 how many different names does he use for the people he is writing to?

Pray it!

Bigger, Better, Faster

What is the opposite of God? What are the things that pull us away from love? The author warns us away from "anything that belongs to the world" (1 John 2:15). How will you know what these things are? They would be anything that causes you to be selfish, lustful, boastful, or greedy. As Christians we must be especially careful not to be tempted by advertisers who want us to buy the latest gadget or the fastest car. These things will not last. They are "passing away" (2:17).

Holy Spirit,
Help me not to love the things of this world.
Give me the wisdom to know that having the latest and greatest does not bring true happiness.
Give me the courage to say no to people who promise me good times but only lead me away from you.
Give me the strength to resist the things that promise instant happiness but in reality bring unhappiness and even death.
Help me to know the difference between the things that are of God and the things that are only passing away.

— 1 John 2:15–17

25 And this is what Christ himself promised
to give us—eternal life.
26 I am writing this to you about those
who are trying to deceive you. 27 But as for
you, Christ has poured out his Spirit on you.
As long as his Spirit remains in you, you do
not need anyone to teach you. For his Spirit
teaches you about everything, and what
he teaches is true, not false. Obey the Spirit's
teaching, then, and remain in union with
Christ.
28 Yes, my children, remain in union with
him, so that when he appears we may be full
of courage and need not hide in shame from
him on the Day he comes. 29 You know that
Christ is righteous; you should know, then,
that everyone who does what is right is
God's child.

Children of God

3 See how much the Father has loved us!
His love is so great that we are called
God's children—and so, in fact, we are. This
is why the world does not know us: it has
not known God. 2 My dear friends, we are
now God's children, but it is not yet clear
what we shall become. But we know that
when Christ appears, we shall be like him,
because we shall see him as he really is.
3 Everyone who has this hope in Christ
keeps himself pure, just as Christ is pure.
4 Whoever sins is guilty of breaking God's
law, because sin is a breaking of the law.
5 You know that Christ appeared in order to
take away sins,[c] and that there is no sin in
him. 6 So everyone who lives in union with
Christ does not continue to sin; but whoever

[c] **3:5** sins; *some manuscripts have* our sins.
3:1 Jn 1:12 **3:5** Jn 1:29

The author of this letter was connected to the author of the Gospel of John. Look for similarities between 1 John 3:11–18 and John 15:17–18.

continues to sin has never seen him or
known him.
7 Let no one deceive you, my children!
Whoever does what is right is righteous, just
as Christ is righteous. 8 Whoever continues
to sin belongs to the Devil, because the
Devil has sinned from the very beginning.
The Son of God appeared for this very rea-
son, to destroy what the Devil had done.
9 Those who are children of God do not
continue to sin, for God's very nature is in
them; and because God is their Father, they
cannot continue to sin. 10 Here is the clear
difference between God's children and the
Devil's children: those who do not do what
is right or do not love others are not God's
children.

Love One Another

11 The message you heard from the very
beginning is this: we must love one another.
12 We must not be like Cain; he belonged to
the Evil One and murdered his own brother
Abel. Why did Cain murder him? Because
the things he himself did were wrong, and
the things his brother did were right.
13 So do not be surprised, my friends, if
the people of the world hate you. 14 We
know that we have left death and come over
into life; we know it because we love others.
Those who do not love are still under the
power of death. 15 Those who hate others are
murderers, and you know that murderers do
not have eternal life in them. 16 This is how
we know what love is: Christ gave his life for
us. We too, then, ought to give our lives for
others! 17 If we are rich and see others in
need, yet close our hearts against them, how
can we claim that we love God? 18 My chil-
dren, our love should not be just words and
talk; it must be true love, which shows itself
in action.

Courage before God

19 This, then, is how we will know that we
belong to the truth; this is how we will be
confident in God's presence. 20 If our con-
science condemns us, we know that God is
greater than our conscience and that he
knows everything. 21 And so, my dear friends,
if our conscience does not condemn us, we
have courage in God's presence. 22 We
receive from him whatever we ask, because
we obey his commands and do what pleases
him. 23 What he commands is that we believe
in his Son Jesus Christ and love one another,
just as Christ commanded us. 24 Those who
obey God's commands live in union with
God and God lives in union with them. And
because of the Spirit that God has given us
we know that God lives in union with us.

Study it!

A Closed Heart

It is not wealth alone, but a closed heart, that is contrary to the will of God (1 John 3:17). God's care for poor people is spoken of again and again in the Bible. The Old Law in the Old Testament specifically required that those who have more must share with those who are going without (Deuteronomy 24:10–22).

But the Old Law was not enough. If people's hearts were closed, they found ways around caring for poor people. So Jesus told stories to warn us against having a closed, hard heart. The story of the rich man and Lazarus (Luke 16:19–31), the warning against the teachers of the Law (Mark 12:38–40), and the story of the final judgment (Matthew 25:31–46) are examples of these stories.

What other stories told by Jesus can you think of or find that challenged people to open their hearts to people in need?

— 1 John 3:17–18

3:11 Jn 13:34 **3:12** Gen 4:8 **3:14** Jn 5:24 **3:23** Jn 13:34; 15:12, 17

Pray it!

God Is Love

Here is a meditation prayer you can try. Read 1 John 4:7–21. Then quiet yourself and imagine you are surrounded by the people you love. Put everyone in the picture: family, friends, other people who have shown love to you, and people whom you have cared about. Now remember what the passage says, "No one has ever seen God, but if we love one another, God lives in union with us, and his love is made perfect in us" (4:12). Imagine all those people's love for you, knowing that through them you are experiencing God's love. Then thank God for all of the love you have been blessed with.

As a follow-up to this meditation, you might want to make a collage with pictures of all the people you imagined. Keep it where you see it regularly to keep in mind God's love for you. Let it serve as a reminder to you to share that love with others.

— 1 John 4:7–21

The True Spirit and the False Spirit

4 My dear friends, do not believe all who
claim to have the Spirit, but test them
to find out if the spirit they have comes
from God. For many false prophets have
gone out everywhere. 2This is how you will
be able to know whether it is God's Spirit:
anyone who acknowledges that Jesus Christ
came as a human being has the Spirit who
comes from God. 3But anyone who denies
this about Jesus does not have the Spirit
from God. The spirit that he has is from the
Enemy of Christ; you heard that it would
come, and now it is here in the world
already.

4But you belong to God, my children, and
have defeated the false prophets, because the
Spirit who is in you is more powerful than
the spirit in those who belong to the world.
5Those false prophets speak about matters of
the world, and the world listens to them
because they belong to the world. 6But we
belong to God. Whoever knows God listens
to us; whoever does not belong to God does
not listen to us. This, then, is how we can tell
the difference between the Spirit of truth
and the spirit of error.

God Is Love

7Dear friends, let us love one another,
because love comes from God. Whoever
loves is a child of God and knows God.
8Whoever does not love does not know
God, for God is love. 9And God showed his
love for us by sending his only Son into the
world, so that we might have life through
him. 10This is what love is: it is not that we
have loved God, but that he loved us and
sent his Son to be the means by which our
sins are forgiven.

11Dear friends, if this is how God loved
us, then we should love one another. 12No
one has ever seen God, but if we love one
another, God lives in union with us, and his
love is made perfect in us.

13We are sure that we live in union with
God and that he lives in union with us,
because he has given us his Spirit. 14And we
have seen and tell others that the Father sent
his Son to be the Savior of the world. 15If
we declare that Jesus is the Son of God, we
live in union with God and God lives in
union with us. 16And we ourselves know
and believe the love which God has for us.

God is love, and those who live in love
live in union with God and God lives in

4:12 Jn 1:18

union with them. [17]Love is made perfect in
us in order that we may have courage on the
Judgment Day; and we will have it because
our life in this world is the same as Christ's.
[18]There is no fear in love; perfect love drives
out all fear. So then, love has not been made
perfect in anyone who is afraid, because fear
has to do with punishment.

Perfect love drives out all fear. (4:18)

19We love because God first loved us. [20]If
we say we love God, but hate others, we are
liars. For we cannot love God, whom we
have not seen, if we do not love others,
whom we have seen. [21]The command that
Christ has given us is this: whoever loves
God must love others also.

Our Victory over the World

5 Whoever believes that Jesus is the Mes-
siah is a child of God; and whoever
loves a father loves his child also. [2]This is

Whoever believes that Jesus is the Messiah is a child of God. (5:1)

how we know that we love God's children: it
is by loving God and obeying his com-
mands. [3]For our love for God means that we
obey his commands. And his commands are
not too hard for us, [4]because every child of
God is able to defeat the world. And we win
the victory over the world by means of our
faith. [5]Who can defeat the world? Only the
person who believes that Jesus is the Son of
God.

The Witness about Jesus Christ

6Jesus Christ is the one who came with
the water of his baptism and the blood of
his death. He came not only with the
water, but with both the water and the
blood. And the Spirit himself testifies that
this is true, because the Spirit is truth.
[7]There are three witnesses: [8]the Spirit, the
water, and the blood; and all three give the
same testimony. [9]We believe human testi-
mony; but God's testimony is much
stronger, and he has given this testimony
about his Son. [10]So those who believe in
the Son of God have this testimony in their
own heart; but those who do not believe
God, have made a liar of him, because they
have not believed what God has said about
his Son. [11]The testimony is this: God has
given us eternal life, and this life has its
source in his Son. [12]Whoever has the Son
has this life; whoever does not have the Son
of God does not have life.

Eternal Life

13I am writing this to you so that you
may know that you have eternal life—you
that believe in the Son of God. [14]We have
courage in God's presence, because we are
sure that he hears us if we ask him for any-
thing that is according to his will. [15]He hears
us whenever we ask him; and since we know
this is true, we know also that he gives us
what we ask from him.
16If you see a believer commit a sin that

5:3 Jn 14:15 **5:12** Jn 3:36

"If we say we love God, but hate others, we are liars" *(1 John 4:20)*.

does not lead to death, you should pray to
God, who will give that person life. This
applies to those whose sins do not lead to
death. But there is sin which leads to death,
and I do not say that you should pray to
God about that. 17 All wrongdoing is sin,
but there is sin which does not lead to
death.
18 We know that no children of God keep
on sinning, for the Son of God keeps them
safe, and the Evil One cannot harm them.
19 We know that we belong to God even
though the whole world is under the rule of
the Evil One.
20 We know that the Son of God has come
and has given us understanding, so that we
know the true God. We live in union with
the true God—in union with his Son Jesus
Christ. This is the true God, and this is eter-
nal life.
21 My children, keep yourselves safe from
false gods!

Your Next Step

Congratulations on finishing the First Letter of John! Use this space to write your thoughts and questions about this book. If you are following the suggested reading plan, move ahead to the Revelation to John. This book is filled with symbolic figures and stories that teach that God's love will triumph over all evil!

The Evil One is another name for Satan or the Devil.

2 JOHN

1 From the Elder—
To the dear Lady and to her children,[a]
whom I truly love. And I am not the only
one, but all who know the truth love you,
2 because the truth remains in us and will be
with us forever.
3 May God the Father and Jesus Christ, the
Father's Son, give us grace, mercy, and peace;
may they be ours in truth and love.

Truth and Love

4 How happy I was to find that some of
your children live in the truth, just as the
Father commanded us. 5 And so I ask you,
dear Lady: let us all love one another. This is
no new command I am writing you; it is the
command which we have had from the
beginning. 6 This love I speak of means that
we must live in obedience to God's com-
mands. The command, as you have all heard
from the beginning, is that you must all live
in love.
7 Many deceivers have gone out over the
world, people who do not acknowledge that
Jesus Christ came as a human being. Such a
person is a deceiver and the Enemy of
Christ. 8 Be on your guard, then, so that you
will not lose what we[b] have worked for, but
will receive your reward in full.
9 Anyone who does not stay with the
teaching of Christ, but goes beyond it, does
not have God. Whoever does stay with the
teaching has both the Father and the Son.
10 So then, if some come to you who do not
bring this teaching, do not welcome them in
your homes; do not even say, "Peace be with
you." 11 For anyone who wishes them peace
becomes their partner in the evil things they
do.

[a] **1** LADY AND . . . HER CHILDREN: *This probably refers to a church and its members (also in verses 4, 5).* [b] **8** we; *some manuscripts have* you.
5 Jn 13:34; 15:12, 17

Catholic Connections

He Came as a Human Being

It seems strange that a Church leader would warn someone *not* to welcome another person. The Second Letter of John reveals a serious conflict within this early Church. The belief that Jesus was a real human being was under attack (verse 7).

This elder writing the letter was worried that believers might be misled. He was very clear that those who taught that Jesus wasn't a human being were deceivers and enemies of Christ (verse 7).

Christians believe that Jesus Christ was both fully God and fully human; or as we sometimes say, "true God and true man." This teaching is called the mystery of the Incarnation. How wonderful to know that Jesus was flesh and blood, just like us! He was hungry, he was tired, he was happy, he was sad, just like us. He was like us in every way except that he never sinned—he never disobeyed God, his Father. Because the Son of God was willing to become a true human being, we know how much we are loved!

— 2 John

Final Words

12I have so much to tell you, but I would
rather not do it with paper and ink; instead,
I hope to visit you and talk with you personally, so that we shall be completely
happy.
13The children of your dear Sister[c] send
you their greetings.

[c] **13** CHILDREN OF YOUR DEAR SISTER: *This probably refers to the members of the church to which the writer belonged.*

3 JOHN

1 From the Elder—
To my dear Gaius, whom I truly love.
2 My dear friend, I pray that everything
may go well with you and that you may be
in good health—as I know you are well in
spirit. 3 I was so happy when some Christians
arrived and told me how faithful you are to
the truth—just as you always live in the
truth. 4 Nothing makes me happier than to
hear that my children live in the truth.

Gaius Is Praised

5 My dear friend, you are so faithful in the
work you do for other Christians, even
when they are strangers. 6 They have spoken
to the church here about your love. Please
help them to continue their trip in a way
that will please God. 7 For they set out on
their trip in the service of Christ without
accepting any help from unbelievers. 8 We
Christians, then, must help these people, so
that we may share in their work for the
truth.

Diotrephes and Demetrius

9 I wrote a short letter to the church; but
Diotrephes, who likes to be their leader, will
not pay any attention to what I say. 10 When
I come, then, I will bring up everything he
has done: the terrible things he says about us
and the lies he tells! But that is not enough
for him; he will not receive the Christians
when they come, and even stops those who
want to receive them and tries to drive them
out of the church!
11 My dear friend, do not imitate what is
bad, but imitate what is good. Whoever does
good belongs to God; whoever does what is
bad has not seen God.
12 Everyone speaks well of Demetrius;
truth itself speaks well of him. And we add
our testimony, and you know that what we
say is true.

Final Greetings

13 I have so much to tell you, but I do not
want to do it with pen and ink. 14 I hope to
see you soon, and then we will talk person-
ally.
15 Peace be with you.
All your friends send greetings. Greet all
our friends personally.

Live it!

What a Guy!

Gaius, the man whom the Third Letter of John is addressed to, was a friend, maybe even a student, of the Elder. Gaius had welcomed missionaries in the past and is now being asked to do so again. He has been a faithful Christian and helped the mission of the Church. Are you like Gaius? Do others recognize you for your faithfulness and love? Even as a young person, you can support the mission of the Church. Get involved in projects sponsored by your parish, school, or community that help other people. Then you will build a reputation as a generous and welcoming person too.

— 3 John

1 Acts 19:29; Rom 16:23; 1 Cor 1:14

The Letter of Jude

If you're lucky, you have never met one of the people that the Letter from Jude talks about—people who lie and twist things to look important and cause division. They only seem happy when other people are unhappy. They pretend to like you, but then cause trouble. They are nice to your face, but they complain behind your back. They create problems wherever they go.

These people can be very smooth talkers. They might make you doubt the things you have always known to be true. When you meet one—and you will—don't be fooled. Do as Jude says and "keep yourselves in the love of God" (verse 21).

Verse 7

Headlines

- Harsh Criticism for False Teachers (verses 5–16)
- How to Respond to Manipulators (verses 20–22)

FACTOIDS

Who wrote this book? Unknown.

When was it written? Possibly around AD 90.

Who was it written for? It is unknown who the audience was.

Why was it written? The author wanted to warn people about false teachers and to encourage people to remain faithful.

Important themes

- False teachers are criticized.
- Believers are reminded to stay faithful and pray in the Holy Spirit.

JUDE

[1]From Jude, servant of Jesus Christ, and
brother of James—
To those who have been called by God,
who live in the love of God the Father and
the protection of Jesus Christ:
[2]May mercy, peace, and love be yours in
full measure.

False Teachers

[3]My dear friends, I was doing my best to
write to you about the salvation we share in
common, when I felt the need of writing at
once to encourage you to fight on for the
faith which once and for all God has given
to his people. [4]For some godless people have
slipped in unnoticed among us, persons who
distort the message about the grace of our
God in order to excuse their immoral ways,
and who reject Jesus Christ, our only Master
and Lord. Long ago the Scriptures predicted
the condemnation they have received.
[5]For even though you know all this, I
want to remind you of how the Lord[a] once
rescued the people of Israel from Egypt, but
afterward destroyed those who did not
believe. [6]Remember the angels who did not
stay within the limits of their proper author-
ity, but abandoned their own dwelling place:
they are bound with eternal chains in the
darkness below, where God is keeping them
for that great Day on which they will be
condemned. [7]Remember Sodom and
Gomorrah, and the nearby towns, whose
people acted as those angels did and
indulged in sexual immorality and perver-
sion: they suffer the punishment of eternal
fire as a plain warning to all.
[8]In the same way also, these people have
visions which make them sin against their
own bodies; they despise God's authority and
insult the glorious beings above. [9]Not even
the chief angel Michael did this. In his quarrel
with the Devil, when they argued about who
would have the body of Moses, Michael did
not dare condemn the Devil with insulting
words, but said, "The Lord rebuke you!"
[10]But these people attack with insults any-
thing they do not understand; and those
things that they know by instinct, like wild
animals, are the very things that destroy them.
[11]How terrible for them! They have followed
the way that Cain took. For the sake of
money they have given themselves over to
the error that Balaam committed. They have
rebelled as Korah rebelled, and like him they
are destroyed. [12]With their shameless carous-
ing they are like dirty spots in your fellowship
meals. They take care only of themselves.
They are like clouds carried along by the
wind, but bringing no rain. They are like trees
that bear no fruit, even in autumn, trees that
have been pulled up by the roots and are
completely dead. [13]They are like wild waves
of the sea, with their shameful deeds showing
up like foam. They are like wandering stars,
for whom God has reserved a place forever in
the deepest darkness.
[14]It was Enoch, the seventh[b] direct descen-
dant from Adam, who long ago prophesied
this about them: "The Lord will come with
many thousands of his holy angels [15]to bring
judgment on all, to condemn them all for the
godless deeds they have performed and for all
the terrible words that godless sinners have
spoken against him!"
[16]These people are always grumbling and
blaming others; they follow their own evil
desires; they brag about themselves and flat-
ter others in order to get their own way.

Warnings and Instructions

[17]But remember, my friends, what you
were told in the past by the apostles of our
Lord Jesus Christ. [18]They said to you,

[a] **5** the Lord; *some manuscripts have* Jesus, *which in Greek is the same as* Joshua. [b] **14** SEVENTH: *This numbering includes both the first and the last in the series of seven names from Adam to Enoch.*

1 Mt 13:55; Mk 6:3 **5 a** Ex 12:51; **b** Num 14:29, 30 **7** Gen 19:1–24 **9 a** Dan 10:13, 21; 12:1; Rev 12:7; **b** Deut 34:6; **c** Zech 3:2 **11 a** Gen 4:3–8; **b** Num 22:1–35; **c** Num 16:1–35 **14** Gen 5:18, 21–24 **18** 2 Pet 3:3

Pray it!

End with Prayer

The Letter from Jude is full of criticism about some troublesome people. These people are distorting the Christian message and practicing immoral behavior (verse 4). They are even making trouble at the fellowship meals, or the celebration of the Eucharist (verse 12). The author even calls them dirty spots, autumn trees without fruit, wild waves, and wandering stars (verses 12–13). Yet despite all of this negativity, the letter has a lovely, prayerful ending (verses 20–25).

This can serve as a reminder to us during hard times. When you are feeling attacked, when things aren't going your way, when you start feeling negative about life, stop and pray. In your prayer, remember God's love for you. Ask God's help with the things that are bothering you. Pray for the people who seem to be against you. When you stop and pray, you might be surprised by how quickly things can change.

— Jude

"When the last days come, people will
appear who will make fun of you, people
who follow their own godless desires."
19 These are the people who cause divisions,
who are controlled by their natural desires,
who do not have the Spirit. 20 But you, my
friends, keep on building yourselves up on
your most sacred faith. Pray in the power of
the Holy Spirit, 21 and keep yourselves in the
love of God, as you wait for our Lord Jesus
Christ in his mercy to give you eternal life.
22 Show mercy toward those who have
doubts; 23 save others by snatching them out
of the fire; and to others show mercy mixed
with fear, but hate their very clothes, stained
by their sinful lusts.

Prayer of Praise

24 To him who is able to keep you from
falling and to bring you faultless and joyful
before his glorious presence— 25 to the only
God our Savior, through Jesus Christ our
Lord, be glory, majesty, might, and authority,
from all ages past, and now, and forever and
ever! Amen.

The Revelation to John

Life can seem like it's falling apart at times, even when you're trying to live right. This is what the early Christians felt as they were being persecuted and killed by the Romans who were threatened by their faith. They needed a big dose of hope!

Revelation is filled with weird symbols, coded language, and images that seem like science fiction. But the meaning of it all is that no matter how scary and difficult life gets, there is a happy, hopeful ending. God's love for us is greater than any suffering or evil we experience. If we trust God and try to be faithful in following Jesus, we will one day know the pure joy of being with God forever.

Chap. 12:7–9

Headlines

- Jesus Appears to John! (1:9–20)
- All Heaven Worships the Lamb (chapters 4–5)
- 144,000 Faithful People Saved (7:1–8)
- War Breaks Out in Heaven (12:7–9)
- The Fall of an Evil Empire (18:1–3)
- Judgment Day Arrives for All (20:11–15)
- No More Sadness: God Lives with Us (21:1–4)

FACTOIDS

Who wrote this book? John, a prophet and disciple of the Apostle John.

When was it written? Probably around AD 92 to 96.

Who was it written for? It was written for Christians of the early Church who were being persecuted and killed by the Roman Empire because of their faith.

Why was it written? To offer hope to the persecuted Christians by reminding them that God ultimately wins over evil, so we must have courage during difficult times and trust in God.

What is the literary style? This book is written in apocalyptic language containing visions, symbols, animals, numbers, coded language, natural disasters, and horrors. It is not meant to be taken literally.

Important themes

- Don't be lukewarm about your faith!
- Jesus is the beginning and end of the entire universe and all history.
- God is victorious over evil; in all things, trust God and have hope!
- A new earth and heaven is waiting for us!

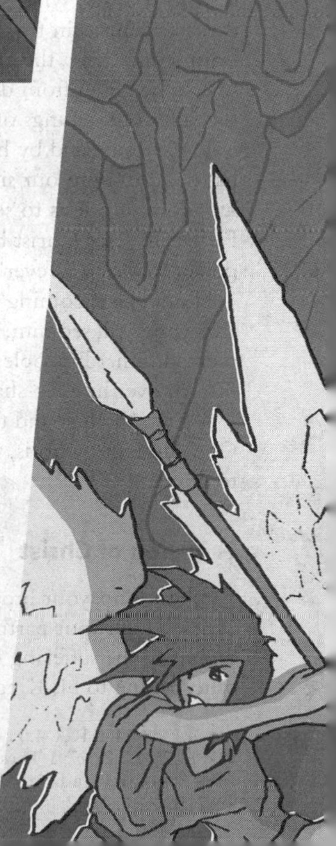

REVELATION

1 This book is the record of the events
that Jesus Christ revealed. God gave him
this revelation in order to show to his ser-
vants what must happen very soon. Christ
made these things known to his servant John
by sending his angel to him, 2 and John has
told all that he has seen. This is his report
concerning the message from God and the
truth revealed by Jesus Christ. 3 Happy is the
one who reads this book, and happy are
those who listen to the words of this
prophetic message and obey what is written
in this book! For the time is near when all
these things will happen.

Greetings to the Seven Churches

4 From John to the seven churches in the
province of Asia:
Grace and peace be yours from God, who
is, who was, and who is to come, and from
the seven spirits in front of his throne, 5 and
from Jesus Christ, the faithful witness, the
first to be raised from death and who is also
the ruler of the kings of the world.
He loves us, and by his sacrificial death he
has freed us from our sins 6 and made us a
kingdom of priests to serve his God and
Father. To Jesus Christ be the glory and
power forever and ever! Amen.
7 Look, he is coming on the clouds!
Everyone will see him, including those who
pierced him. All peoples on earth will
mourn over him. So shall it be!
8 "I am the first and the last," says the Lord
God Almighty, who is, who was, and who is
to come.

A Vision of Christ

9 I am John, your brother, and as a follower
of Jesus I am your partner in patiently
enduring the suffering that comes to those
who belong to his Kingdom. I was put on
the island of Patmos because I had pro-
claimed God's word and the truth that Jesus
revealed. 10 On the Lord's day the Spirit took
control of me, and I heard a loud voice, that
sounded like a trumpet, speaking behind me.
11 It said, "Write down what you see, and
send the book to the churches in these seven
cities: Ephesus, Smyrna, Pergamum, Thyatira,
Sardis, Philadelphia, and Laodicea."
12 I turned around to see who was talking
to me, and I saw seven gold lampstands,
13 and among them there was what looked
like a human being, wearing a robe that
reached to his feet, and a gold band around
his chest. 14 His hair was white as wool, or as
snow, and his eyes blazed like fire; 15 his feet
shone like brass that has been refined and
polished, and his voice sounded like a roar-
ing waterfall. 16 He held seven stars in his
right hand, and a sharp two-edged sword
came out of his mouth. His face was as
bright as the midday sun. 17 When I saw
him, I fell down at his feet like a dead man.
He placed his right hand on me and said,
"Don't be afraid! I am the first and the last.
18 I am the living one! I was dead, but now I
am alive forever and ever. I have authority
over death and the world of the dead.
19 Write, then, the things you see, both the
things that are now and the things that will
happen afterward. 20 Here is the secret mean-
ing of the seven stars that you see in my
right hand, and of the seven gold lampstands:
the seven stars are the angels of the seven
churches, and the seven lampstands are the
seven churches.

The Message to Ephesus

2 "To the angel of the church in Ephesus
write:
"This is the message from the one who
holds the seven stars in his right hand and
who walks among the seven gold lamp-

1:4 a Ex 3:14; **b** Rev 4:5 **1:5 a** Isa 55:4; **b** Ps 89:27 **1:6** Ex 19:6; Rev 5:10 **1:7 a** Dan 7:13; Mt 24:30; Mk 13:26; Lk 21:27; 1 Thess 4:17; **b** Zech 12:10; Jn 19:34, 37; **c** Zech 12:10; Mt 24:30 **1:8 a** Rev 22:13; **b** Ex 3:14 **1:13 a** Dan 7:13; **b** Dan 10:5 **1:14** Dan 7:9 **1:14, 15** Dan 10:6 **1:15** Ezek 1:24; 43:2 **1:17** Isa 44:6; 48:12; Rev 2:8; 22:13

Pray it!

Hair as White as Snow?

Have you ever imagined Jesus with white hair? Not only that, but in John's vision of Jesus, he had a gold band around his chest, eyes blazing, feet shining like polished brass, his face as bright as the sun (Revelation 1:13–16). Jesus' voice sounded like a trumpet and then a rushing waterfall. The Jesus who appeared in John's vision seems nothing like the Jesus we imagine! Jesus lived in the Middle East, and like other men from that region, he probably had dark skin and hair. But remember, after Jesus' Resurrection, when he appeared to his friends, they didn't recognize him. His glorified body looked completely different than when he was alive.

Close your eyes and picture yourself in a quiet, peaceful place. Imagine that Jesus comes along and sits next to you. What does he look like to you? What do you think he would like to say to you in a meeting like that? What would you share about your life with him? (Meeting Jesus in your imagination is one way to pray, and it can be very comforting and peaceful. You can pray like this anytime, anywhere!)

— Revelation 1:10–16

stands. [2]I know what you have done; I know
how hard you have worked and how patient
you have been. I know that you cannot tol-
erate evil people and that you have tested
those who say they are apostles but are not,
and have found out that they are liars. [3]You
are patient, you have suffered for my sake,
and you have not given up. [4]But this is what
I have against you: you do not love me now
as you did at first. [5]Think how far you have
fallen! Turn from your sins and do what you
did at first. If you don't turn from your sins, I
will come to you and take your lampstand
from its place. [6]But this is what you have in
your favor: you hate what the Nicolaitans
do, as much as I do.
[7]"If you have ears, then, listen to what the
Spirit says to the churches!
"To those who win the victory I will give
the right to eat the fruit of the tree of life
that grows in the Garden of God.

The Message to Smyrna

[8]"To the angel of the church in Smyrna
write:
"This is the message from the one who is
the first and the last, who died and lived
again. [9]I know your troubles; I know that
you are poor—but really you are rich! I
know the evil things said against you by
those who claim to be Jews but are not; they
are a group that belongs to Satan! [10]Don't be
afraid of anything you are about to suffer.
Listen! The Devil will put you to the test by
having some of you thrown into prison, and
your troubles will last ten days. Be faithful to
me, even if it means death, and I will give
you life as your prize of victory.
[11]"If you have ears, then, listen to what
the Spirit says to the churches!
"Those who win the victory will not be
hurt by the second death.

2:7 **a** Gen 2:9; Rev 22:2; **b** Ezek 28:13; 31:8 (LXX) **2:8** Isa 44:6; 48:12; Rev 1:17; 22:13 **2:11** Rev 20:14; 21:8

"'I am the first and the last,' says the Lord God Almighty" *(Revelation 1:8)*.

The Message to Pergamum

12“To the angel of the church in Perga-
mum write:
“This is the message from the one who
has the sharp two-edged sword. 13I know
where you live, there where Satan has his
throne. You are true to me, and you did not
abandon your faith in me even during the
time when Antipas, my faithful witness, was
killed there where Satan lives. 14But there are
a few things I have against you: there are
some among you who follow the teaching of
Balaam, who taught Balak how to lead the
people of Israel into sin by persuading them
to eat food that had been offered to idols and
to practice sexual immorality. 15In the same
way you have people among you who follow
the teaching of the Nicolaitans. 16Now turn
from your sins! If you don’t, I will come to
you soon and fight against those people with
the sword that comes out of my mouth.
17“If you have ears, then, listen to what
the Spirit says to the churches!
“To those who win the victory I will give
some of the hidden manna. I will also give
each of them a white stone on which is
written a new name that no one knows
except the one who receives it.

The Message to Thyatira

18“To the angel of the church in Thyatira
write:
“This is the message from the Son of
God, whose eyes blaze like fire, whose feet
shine like polished brass. 19I know what you
do. I know your love, your faithfulness, your
service, and your patience. I know that you
are doing more now than you did at first.
20But this is what I have against you: you
tolerate that woman Jezebel, who calls her-
self a messenger of God. By her teaching she
misleads my servants into practicing sexual
immorality and eating food that has been
offered to idols. 21I have given her time to

Live it!

Report Cards for Seven Churches

Your heart is racing as you wait for your name to be called. Finally, your teacher calls you up to receive your first-quarter report card. You open it and eagerly read her comments about you: “Paolo shows much patience with his fellow students. He is such a friendly and helpful boy, a real pleasure to have in class. But his constant talking is a problem. Because of it, he doesn’t hear directions, and he distracts others who are trying to listen. This behavior must change.”

In John’s vision, Jesus has written a letter to each of the seven churches of Asia Minor. The letters sound a bit like report cards. He offers praise and encouragement to the communities, but he also points out their weaknesses and tells them strongly that they must change and become more faithful.

Remember, these were new churches, still trying to figure out all the ins and outs of living as Christians. They needed guidance and sometimes correction to keep on the right path. If Jesus were writing a letter to your church, what positive things would he have to say? What would he tell you needs to change?

— Revelation, chapters 2–3

2:14 **a** Num 22:5, 7; 31:16; Deut 23:4; **b** Num 25:1–3 **2:17** **a** Ex 16:14, 15; 16:33, 34; Jn 6:48–50; **b** Isa 62:2; 65:15 **2:20** 1 Kings 16:31; 2 Kings 9:22, 30

What does Jesus promise to the seven churches if they are faithful?

repent of her sins, but she does not want to
turn from her immorality. 22 And so I will
throw her on a bed where she and those
who committed adultery with her will suffer
terribly. I will do this now unless they repent
of the wicked things they did with her. 23 I
will also kill her followers, and then all the
churches will know that I am the one who
knows everyone's thoughts and wishes. I will
repay each of you according to what you
have done.
24 "But the rest of you in Thyatira have
not followed this evil teaching; you have not
learned what the others call 'the deep secrets
of Satan.' I say to you that I will not put any
other burden on you. 25 But until I come,
you must hold firmly to what you have.
26-28 To those who win the victory, who
continue to the end to do what I want, I
will give the same authority that I received
from my Father: I will give them authority
over the nations, to rule them with an iron
rod and to break them to pieces like clay
pots. I will also give them the morning star.
29 "If you have ears, then, listen to what
the Spirit says to the churches!

The Message to Sardis

3 "To the angel of the church in Sardis
write:
"This is the message from the one who
has the seven spirits of God and the seven
stars. I know what you are doing; I know
that you have the reputation of being alive,
even though you are dead! 2 So wake up, and
strengthen what you still have before it dies
completely. For I find that what you have
done is not yet perfect in the sight of my
God. 3 Remember, then, what you were
taught and what you heard; obey it and turn
from your sins. If you do not wake up, I will
come upon you like a thief, and you will not
even know the time when I will come. 4 But
a few of you there in Sardis have kept your
clothes clean. You will walk with me, clothed
in white, because you are worthy to do so.
5 Those who win the victory will be clothed
like this in white, and I will not remove their
names from the book of the living. In the
presence of my Father and of his angels I
will declare openly that they belong to me.
6 "If you have ears, then, listen to what the
Spirit says to the churches!

The Message to Philadelphia

7 "To the angel of the church in Philadel-
phia write:
"This is the message from the one who is
holy and true. He has the key that belonged
to David, and when he opens a door, no one
can close it, and when he closes it, no one
can open it. 8 I know what you do; I know
that you have a little power; you have fol-
lowed my teaching and have been faithful to
me. I have opened a door in front of you,
which no one can close. 9 Listen! As for that
group that belongs to Satan, those liars who
claim that they are Jews but are not, I will
make them come and bow down at your
feet. They will all know that I love you.
10 Because you have kept my command to
endure, I will also keep you safe from the
time of trouble which is coming upon the
world to test all the people on earth. 11 I am
coming soon. Keep safe what you have, so
that no one will rob you of your victory
prize. 12 I will make those who are victorious
pillars in the temple of my God, and they
will never leave it. I will write on them the
name of my God and the name of the city
of my God, the new Jerusalem, which will
come down out of heaven from my God. I
will also write on them my new name.
13 "If you have ears, then, listen to what
the Spirit says to the churches!

The Message to Laodicea

14 "To the angel of the church in Laodicea
write:
"This is the message from the Amen, the
faithful and true witness, who is the origin[a]
of all that God has created. 15 I know what
you have done; I know that you are neither

[a] **3:14** origin; *or* ruler.

2:23 **a** Ps 7:9; Jer 17:10; **b** Ps 62:12 **2:26, 27** Ps 2:8, 9 (LXX) **3:3** Mt 24:43, 44; Lk 12:39, 40; Rev 16:15 **3:5** **a** Ex 32:32, 33; Ps 69:28; Rev 20:12; **b** Mt 10:32; Lk 12:8 **3:7** Isa 22:22; Job 12:14 **3:9** **a** Isa 49:23; 60:14; **b** Isa 43:4 **3:12** **a** Rev 21:2; **b** Isa 62:2; 65:15 **3:14** Prov 8:22

cold nor hot. How I wish you were either
one or the other! 16But because you are
lukewarm, neither hot nor cold, I am going
to spit you out of my mouth! 17You say, 'I am
rich and well off; I have all I need.' But you
do not know how miserable and pitiful you
are! You are poor, naked, and blind. 18I advise
you, then, to buy gold from me, pure gold, in
order to be rich. Buy also white clothing to
dress yourself and cover up your shameful
nakedness. Buy also some ointment to put on
your eyes, so that you may see. 19I rebuke and
punish all whom I love. Be in earnest, then,
and turn from your sins. 20Listen! I stand at
the door and knock; if any hear my voice
and open the door, I will come into their
house and eat with them, and they will eat
with me. 21To those who win the victory I
will give the right to sit beside me on my
throne, just as I have been victorious and
now sit by my Father on his throne.

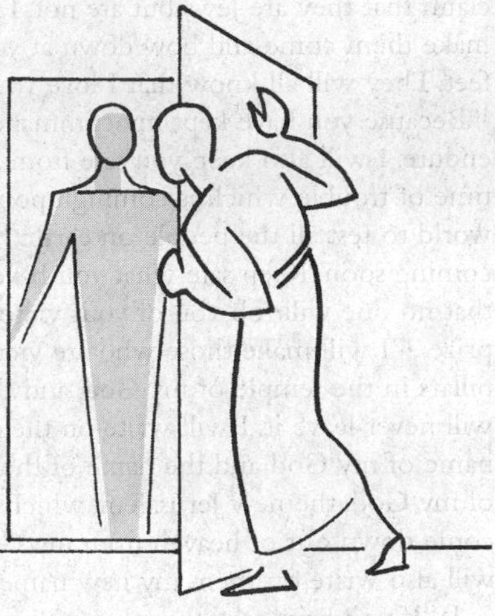

I stand at the door and knock. (3:20)

22"If you have ears, then, listen to what
the Spirit says to the churches!"

Worship in Heaven

4 At this point I had another vision and
saw an open door in heaven.
And the voice that sounded like a trum-
pet, which I had heard speaking to me
before, said, "Come up here, and I will show
you what must happen after this." 2At once
the Spirit took control of me. There in heav-
en was a throne with someone sitting on it.
3His face gleamed like such precious stones
as jasper and carnelian, and all around the
throne there was a rainbow the color of an
emerald. 4In a circle around the throne were
twenty-four other thrones, on which were
seated twenty-four elders dressed in white
and wearing crowns of gold. 5From the

Live it!

Lukewarm Faith

Jesus is upset with the church in Laodicea because it's boring! "I know that you are neither cold nor hot. How I wish you were either one or the other!" (Revelation 3:15). If these Christians were hot, they'd be on fire with their faith, and of course this is what he wants from all of us. But why would Jesus rather see us cold in our faith than lukewarm? If our faith was cold, we would be greatly in need of saving. Jesus said in the Gospels that he came to save lost, sinful, poor, and suffering people, and those who don't believe. Having a cold faith gives him a lot to work with!

But lukewarm faith is a problem. People with faith that is lukewarm aren't necessarily sinners, but their faith is dull, half-hearted. They just don't care. They might not be bad people, but they don't see any reason to become any better either. And Jesus is saying it's harder to move the hearts of those people.

What's the temperature of your faith?

— Revelation 3:14–15

3:19 Prov 3:12; Heb 12:6 **4:2, 3** Ezek 1:26–28; 10:1 **4:5 a** Ex 19:16; Tob 12:15; Rev 8:5; 11:19; 16:18; **b** Ezek 1:13; **c** Rev 1:4; Zech 4:2

throne came flashes of lightning, rumblings,
and peals of thunder. In front of the throne
seven lighted torches were burning, which
are the seven spirits of God. 6 Also in front of
the throne there was what looked like a sea
of glass, clear as crystal.
Surrounding the throne on each of its sides,
were four living creatures covered with eyes in
front and behind. 7 The first one looked like a
lion; the second looked like a bull; the third
had a face like a human face; and the fourth
looked like an eagle in flight. 8 Each one of the
four living creatures had six wings, and they
were covered with eyes, inside and out. Day
and night they never stop singing:
"Holy, holy, holy, is the Lord God Almighty,
who was, who is, and who is to come."
9 The four living creatures sing songs of
glory and honor and thanks to the one who
sits on the throne, who lives forever and
ever. When they do so, 10 the twenty-four
elders fall down before the one who sits on
the throne, and worship him who lives for-
ever and ever. They throw their crowns
down in front of the throne and say,
11 "Our Lord and God! You are worthy
to receive glory, honor, and power.
For you created all things,
and by your will they were given
existence and life."

The Scroll and the Lamb

5 I saw a scroll in the right hand of the
one who sits on the throne; it was cov-
ered with writing on both sides and was
sealed with seven seals. 2 And I saw a mighty
angel, who announced in a loud voice,
"Who is worthy to break the seals and open
the scroll?" 3 But there was no one in heaven
or on earth or in the world below[b] who
could open the scroll and look inside it. 4 I
cried bitterly because no one could be
found who was worthy to open the scroll or
look inside it. 5 Then one of the elders said

> **Study it!**
>
> ### Unlocking the Code
>
> **The language in Revelation was coded so that while the faithful followers of Jesus could understand John's message, their persecutors could not. Here is the meaning of some of the symbols in Revelation:**
>
> - ***Throne in heaven:* God is seated on a throne, meaning that he holds authority over all of history.**
> - ***Twenty-four thrones around God with twenty-four elders seated:* Twelve, like seven, is symbolic of fullness or perfection; double that, and it is even more perfect. The first twelve thrones are the twelve tribes of Israel and the second twelve thrones are the twelve Apostles. Together they symbolize the fullness of the faith—the Old Covenant and the New Covenant.**
> - ***Four living creatures:* Four means universal (as in the four directions). God rules the entire universe, and all creation praises him. The lion, bull, human being, and eagle represent what is noblest, strongest, wisest, and swiftest in creation.**
>
> **This first part of John's vision reminds us that God is at the center of everything: all history, the universe, and our faith. That's a good reason for the creatures to be singing God's praise!**
>
> **— Revelation, chapter 4**

[b] **5:3** WORLD BELOW: *The world of the dead (see 1:18).*

4:6 Ezek 1:22 **4:6, 7** Ezek 1:5–10; 10:14 **4:8 a** Ezek 1:18; 10:12; **b** Isa 6:2, 3 **5:1** Ezek 2:9, 10; Isa 29:11
5:5 a Gen 49:9; **b** Isa 11:1, 10

What prayer do we sing at Mass that is similar to the song in Revelation 4:8?

to me, "Don't cry. Look! The Lion from
Judah's tribe, the great descendant of David,
has won the victory, and he can break the
seven seals and open the scroll."
6 Then I saw a Lamb standing in the cen-
ter of the throne, surrounded by the four liv-
ing creatures and the elders. The Lamb
appeared to have been killed. It had seven
horns and seven eyes, which are the seven
spirits of God that have been sent through
the whole earth. 7 The Lamb went and took
the scroll from the right hand of the one
who sits on the throne. 8 As he did so, the
four living creatures and the twenty-four
elders fell down before the Lamb. Each had
a harp and gold bowls filled with incense,
which are the prayers of God's people.
9 They sang a new song:

"You are worthy to take the scroll
and to break open its seals.
For you were killed, and by your
sacrificial death you bought for God
people from every tribe, language,
nation, and race.
10 You have made them a kingdom of
priests to serve our God,
and they shall rule on earth."

11 Again I looked, and I heard angels,
thousands and millions of them! They stood
around the throne, the four living creatures,
and the elders, 12 and sang in a loud voice:

"The Lamb who was killed is worthy
to receive power, wealth, wisdom, and
strength,
honor, glory, and praise!"

13 And I heard every creature in heaven, on
earth, in the world below, and in the sea—all
living beings in the universe—and they were
singing:

"To him who sits on the throne and to
the Lamb,
be praise and honor, glory and might,
forever and ever!"

14 The four living creatures answered,
"Amen!" And the elders fell down and wor-
shiped.

Study it!

The Lamb of God

As the vision continues, it is helpful to understand the meaning of these symbols in Revelation:

- ***Sealed scroll:* Contains messages to sinners, as well as God's plan for the world.**
- ***Lamb:* Jesus, who had been killed and is now resurrected from the dead. He is in the form of a lamb because he is the Lamb of God. We call Jesus the Lamb of God because he was sacrificed for our sake like the Passover lambs (see Exodus, chapter 12).**

His seven horns symbolize perfect power, and his seven eyes symbolize his perfect knowledge. Only he can read the scroll because he alone can reveal and carry out God's divine plan.

Read on to see what messages the scroll contains.

— Revelation, chapter 5

The Seals

6 Then I saw the Lamb break open the
first of the seven seals, and I heard one
of the four living creatures say in a voice that
sounded like thunder, "Come!" 2 I looked,
and there was a white horse. Its rider held a
bow, and he was given a crown. He rode out
as a conqueror to conquer.
3 Then the Lamb broke open the second
seal; and I heard the second living creature
say, "Come!" 4 Another horse came out, a red
one. Its rider was given the power to bring

5:6 a Isa 53:7; **b** Zech 4:10 **5:8** Ps 141:2 **5:9** Ps 33:3; 98:1; Isa 42:10 **5:10** Ex 19:6; Rev 1:6 **5:11** Dan 7:10 **6:2** Zech 1:8; 6:3, 6 **6:4** Zech 1:8; 6:2

Chapter 5 of Revelation contains one of many songs of praise to God in the Book of Revelation. How many others can you find in this book?

war on the earth, so that people should kill
each other. He was given a large sword.
5 Then the Lamb broke open the third
seal; and I heard the third living creature say,
"Come!" I looked, and there was a black
horse. Its rider held a pair of scales in his
hand. 6 I heard what sounded like a voice
coming from among the four living crea-
tures, which said, "A quart of wheat for a
day's wages, and three quarts of barley for a
day's wages. But do not damage the olive
trees and the vineyards!"
7 Then the Lamb broke open the fourth
seal; and I heard the fourth living creature
say, "Come!" 8 I looked, and there was a pale-
colored horse. Its rider was named Death,
and Hades[c] followed close behind. They
were given authority over one fourth of the
earth, to kill by means of war, famine, dis-
ease, and wild animals.
9 Then the Lamb broke open the fifth seal.
I saw underneath the altar the souls of those
who had been killed because they had pro-
claimed God's word and had been faithful in
their witnessing. 10 They shouted in a loud
voice, "Almighty Lord, holy and true! How
long will it be until you judge the people on
earth and punish them for killing us?"
11 Each of them was given a white robe, and
they were told to rest a little while longer,
until the complete number of other servants
and believers were killed, as they had been.
12 And I saw the Lamb break open the
sixth seal. There was a violent earthquake,
and the sun became black like coarse black
cloth, and the moon turned completely red
like blood. 13 The stars fell down to the
earth, like unripe figs falling from the tree
when a strong wind shakes it. 14 The sky dis-
appeared like a scroll being rolled up, and
every mountain and island was moved from
its place. 15 Then the kings of the earth, the
rulers and the military chiefs, the rich and
the powerful, and all other people, slave and
free, hid themselves in caves and under rocks
on the mountains. 16 They called out to the
mountains and to the rocks, "Fall on us and
hide us from the eyes of the one who sits on
the throne and from the anger of the Lamb!
17 The terrible day of their anger is here, and
who can stand up against it?"

Study it!

Forces of Human Nature Unleashed

Just because we're human, we're bound to have problems! In this vision, seals hold the scroll shut. As the Lamb breaks open the first four seals, horses and riders come out. The riders of the four horses represent power, war, famine, and death—the difficulties and disasters generally brought on by human sin. They are sometimes called the four horsemen of the apocalypse.

Beneath the fifth seal are the martyrs—people who have died for being true to their faith. White is symbolic of joy and victory, and in receiving white robes, they are comforted with knowing their faith will win out over death.

Breaking the sixth seal brings on a violent earthquake, turns the sun black and the moon blood red, and all the stars fall out of the sky. These events symbolize that when God judges us at the end of time, all creation will be affected

What are some of the terrible things going on around the world today—both those caused by natural forces and those brought on by humans? What are people most afraid of? How do you think God might judge our world in these times?

— Revelation, chapter 6

[c] **6:8** HADES *The world of the dead (see 1:18).*

6:5 Zech 6:2, 6 **6:8** Ezek 14:21 **6:12 a** Rev 11:13; 16:18; **b** Isa 13:10; Joel 2:10, 31; 3:15; Mt 24:29; Mk 13:24, 25; Lk 21:25 **6:13, 14** Isa 34:4 **6:14** Rev 16:20 **6:15** Isa 2:19, 21 **6:16** Hos 10:8; Lk 23:30 **6:17** Joel 2:11; Mal 3:2

Pray it!

Comfort for Those Who Suffer

There are many symbolic numbers in Revelation. What does the number 144,000 mean? One thousand is symbolic of a large number of people, more than can be counted. From each of the twelve tribes of Israel, there are twelve (perfection) thousand (too many to count) people. So twelve tribes multiplied by twelve thousand in each tribe equals 144,000 people.

Revelation isn't saying that exactly 144,000 people are saved. It really means that an enormous number have been faithful to God throughout history—even enduring persecution and death. They had already suffered enough, and now God was going to comfort and refresh them and take away all their pain.

Dear God, too many people are suffering in our world today—from disease, hunger, war, hurricanes, earthquakes, hatred, addictions, violence, and other terrible things. Some live far from me, and some are right here in my town and in my school. You depend on us to help bring your comfort to one another, so help me to listen to those who are afraid, or give a hug to those who are sad, or provide assistance to those who have lost homes and belongings. Let me show them there is hope and that they are loved by you. Amen.

— Revelation, chapter 7

The 144,000 People of Israel

7 After this I saw four angels standing at
the four corners of the earth, holding
back the four winds so that no wind should
blow on the earth or the sea or against any
tree. 2And I saw another angel coming up
from the east with the seal of the living
God. He called out in a loud voice to the
four angels to whom God had given the
power to damage the earth and the sea. 3The
angel said, "Do not harm the earth, the sea,
or the trees, until we mark the servants of
our God with a seal on their foreheads."
4And I was told that the number of those
who were marked with God's seal on their
foreheads was 144,000. They were from the
twelve tribes of Israel, 5-8twelve thousand
from each tribe: Judah, Reuben, Gad, Asher,
Naphtali, Manasseh, Simeon, Levi, Issachar,
Zebulun, Joseph, and Benjamin.

The Enormous Crowd

9After this I looked, and there was an
enormous crowd—no one could count all
the people! They were from every race, tribe,
nation, and language, and they stood in front
of the throne and of the Lamb, dressed in
white robes and holding palm branches in
their hands. 10They called out in a loud
voice: "Salvation comes from our God, who
sits on the throne, and from the Lamb!" 11All
the angels stood around the throne, the el-
ders, and the four living creatures. Then they
threw themselves face downward in front of
the throne and worshiped God, 12saying,
"Amen! Praise, glory, wisdom, thanksgiving,
honor, power, and might belong to our God
forever and ever! Amen!"
13One of the elders asked me, "Who are
these people dressed in white robes, and
where do they come from?"
14"I don't know, sir. You do," I answered.
He said to me, "These are the people who

7:1 Jer 49:36; Dan 7:2; Zech 6:5 **7:3** Ezek 9:4, 6 **7:14** Dan 12:1; Mt 24:21; Mk 13:19

have come safely through the terrible perse-
cution. They have washed their robes and
made them white with the blood of the
Lamb. 15 That is why they stand before God's
throne and serve him day and night in his
temple. He who sits on the throne will pro-
tect them with his presence. 16 Never again
will they hunger or thirst; neither sun nor
any scorching heat will burn them, 17 because
the Lamb, who is in the center of the
throne, will be their shepherd, and he will
guide them to springs of life-giving water.
And God will wipe away every tear from
their eyes."

The Seventh Seal

8 When the Lamb broke open the sev-
enth seal, there was silence in heaven for
about half an hour. 2 Then I saw the seven
angels who stand before God, and they were
given seven trumpets.
3 Another angel, who had a gold incense
container, came and stood at the altar. He
was given a lot of incense to add to the
prayers of all God's people and to offer it on
the gold altar that stands before the throne.
4 The smoke of the burning incense went up
with the prayers of God's people from the
hands of the angel standing before God.
5 Then the angel took the incense container,
filled it with fire from the altar, and threw it
on the earth. There were rumblings and
peals of thunder, flashes of lightning, and an
earthquake.

The Trumpets

6 Then the seven angels with the seven
trumpets prepared to blow them.
7 The first angel blew his trumpet. Hail
and fire, mixed with blood, came pouring
down on the earth. A third of the earth was
burned up, a third of the trees, and every
blade of green grass.
8 Then the second angel blew his trumpet.
Something that looked like a huge mountain
on fire was thrown into the sea. A third of
the sea was turned into blood, 9 a third of the

Live it!

Many Problems, One Solution

When the seventh seal is broken, there is great silence—like a calm before a storm. Then terrible things start happening, and it seems the entire world is going to be destroyed. Six trumpets blow, each announcing natural disasters, plagues, violent deaths, and more horror than we can imagine!

But wait! The message of this vision is not that the world is coming to an end. This vision, like all of Revelation, is about *hope.* For all those people who lived faithful lives and were marked by God's seal are kept safe from the destruction (Revelation 9:4). God protects them from harm.

This is a hopeful message for us, as well. We no doubt will face suffering or evil in our lives. But if we remain faithful to God, we will not be destroyed by it. Even if it brings physical pain or death here on earth, in eternity we will know nothing but joy and peace.

What does living a faithful life mean to you? Think of five qualities or behaviors that might describe a faithful person. How do you fit the description? How can you be more faithful to God's call?

— Revelation, chapters 8–9

7:16 Isa 49:10 **7:17 a** Ps 23:1; Ezek 34:23; **b** Ps 23:2; Isa 49:10; **c** Isa 25:8 **8:3 a** Am 9:1; **b** Ex 30:1, 3
8:5 a Lev 16:12; Ezek 10:2; **b** Ex 19:16; Rev 11:19; 16:18 **8:6, 7** Wis 11:5—12:2 **8:7** Ex 9:23–25; Ezek 38:22

"And God will wipe away every tear from their eyes" *(Revelation 7:17)*.

living creatures in the sea died, and a third of
the ships were destroyed.
10 Then the third angel blew his trumpet.
A large star, burning like a torch, dropped
from the sky and fell on a third of the rivers
and on the springs of water. 11 (The name of
the star is "Bitterness.") A third of the water
turned bitter, and many people died from
drinking the water, because it had turned
bitter.
12 Then the fourth angel blew his trumpet.
A third of the sun was struck, and a third of
the moon, and a third of the stars, so that
their light lost a third of its brightness; there
was no light during a third of the day and a
third of the night also.
13 Then I looked, and I heard an eagle that
was flying high in the air say in a loud voice,
"O horror! horror! How horrible it will be
for all who live on earth when the sound
comes from the trumpets that the other
three angels must blow!"

9 Then the fifth angel blew his trumpet. I
saw a star which had fallen down to the
earth, and it was given the key to the abyss.[d]
2 The star opened the abyss, and smoke
poured out of it, like the smoke from a large
furnace; the sunlight and the air were dark-
ened by the smoke from the abyss. 3 Locusts
came down out of the smoke upon the earth,
and they were given the same kind of power
that scorpions have. 4 They were told not to
harm the grass or the trees or any other plant;
they could harm only the people who did
not have the mark of God's seal on their fore-
heads. 5 The locusts were not allowed to kill
these people, but only to torture them for five
months. The pain caused by the torture is like
the pain caused by a scorpion's sting. 6 During
those five months they will seek death, but
will not find it; they will want to die, but
death will flee from them.
7 The locusts looked like horses ready for
battle; on their heads they had what seemed
to be crowns of gold, and their faces were
like human faces. 8 Their hair was like
women's hair, their teeth were like lions'
teeth. 9 Their chests were covered with what
looked like iron breastplates, and the sound
made by their wings was like the noise of
many horse-drawn chariots rushing into bat-
tle. 10 They have tails and stings like those of
a scorpion, and it is with their tails that they
have the power to hurt people for five
months. 11 They have a king ruling over
them, who is the angel in charge of the
abyss. His name in Hebrew is Abaddon; in
Greek the name is Apollyon (meaning "The
Destroyer").
12 The first horror is over; after this there
are still two more horrors to come.
13 Then the sixth angel blew his trumpet. I
heard a voice coming from the four corners
of the gold altar standing before God. 14 The
voice said to the sixth angel, "Release the
four angels who are bound at the great
Euphrates River!" 15 The four angels were
released; for this very hour of this very day
of this very month and year they had been
kept ready to kill a third of all the human
race. 16 I was told the number of the mount-
ed troops: it was two hundred million. 17 And
in my vision I saw the horses and their rid-
ers: they had breastplates red as fire, blue as
sapphire, and yellow as sulfur. The horses'
heads were like lions' heads, and from their
mouths came out fire, smoke, and sulfur. 18 A
third of the human race was killed by those
three plagues: the fire, the smoke, and the
sulfur coming out of the horses' mouths.
19 For the power of the horses is in their
mouths and also in their tails. Their tails are
like snakes with heads, and they use them to
hurt people.
20 The rest of the human race, all those
who had not been killed by these plagues,
did not turn away from what they them-
selves had made. They did not stop worship-

[d] **9:1** ABYSS: *The place in the depths of the earth where the demons were imprisoned until their final punishment.*

8:10 Isa 14:12 **8:11** Jer 9:15 **8:12** Isa 13:10; Ezek 32:7; Joel 2:10, 31; 3:15 **9:2** Gen 19:28 **9:3** Ex 10:12–15; Wis 16:9 **9:4** Ezek 9:4 **9:6** Job 3:21; Jer 8:3 **9:7** Joel 2:4 **9:8** Joel 1:6 **9:9** Joel 2:5 **9:13** Ex 30:1–3 **9:17** Wis 11:17, 18 **9:20** Ps 115:4–7; 135:15–17; Dan 5:23

The angel burns incense in heaven to help the prayers of people on earth *(Revelation 8:3)*. **When and where have you seen incense used with prayers?**

ing demons, nor the idols of gold, silver,
bronze, stone, and wood, which cannot see,
hear, or walk. 21 Nor did they repent of their
murders, their magic, their sexual immorali-
ty, or their stealing.

The Angel and the Little Scroll

10 Then I saw another mighty angel
coming down out of heaven. He was
wrapped in a cloud and had a rainbow
around his head; his face was like the sun,
and his legs were like columns of fire. 2 He
had a small scroll open in his hand. He put
his right foot on the sea and his left foot on
the land, 3 and called out in a loud voice that
sounded like the roar of lions. After he had
called out, the seven thunders answered with
a roar. 4 As soon as they spoke, I was about to
write. But I heard a voice speak from heav-
en, "Keep secret what the seven thunders
have said; do not write it down!"
5 Then the angel that I saw standing on
the sea and on the land raised his right hand
to heaven 6 and took a vow in the name of
God, who lives forever and ever, who created
heaven, earth, and the sea, and everything in
them. The angel said, "There will be no
more delay! 7 But when the seventh angel
blows his trumpet, then God will accomplish
his secret plan, as he announced to his ser-
vants, the prophets."
8 Then the voice that I had heard speaking
from heaven spoke to me again, saying, "Go
and take the open scroll which is in the
hand of the angel standing on the sea and on
the land."
9 I went to the angel and asked him to
give me the little scroll. He said to me, "Take
it and eat it; it will turn sour in your stom-
ach, but in your mouth it will be sweet as
honey."
10 I took the little scroll from his hand and
ate it, and it tasted sweet as honey in my
mouth. But after I swallowed it, it turned
sour in my stomach. 11 Then I was told,
"Once again you must proclaim God's mes-
sage about many nations, races, languages,
and kings."

The Two Witnesses

11 I was then given a stick that looked
like a measuring-rod, and was told,
"Go and measure the temple of God and the
altar, and count those who are worshiping in
the temple. 2 But do not measure the outer
courts, because they have been given to the
heathen, who will trample on the Holy City
for forty-two months. 3 I will send my two
witnesses dressed in sackcloth, and they will
proclaim God's message during those 1, 260
days."
4 The two witnesses are the two olive trees
and the two lamps that stand before the Lord
of the earth. 5 If anyone tries to harm them,
fire comes out of their mouths and destroys
their enemies; and in this way whoever tries
to harm them will be killed. 6 They have
authority to shut up the sky so that there
will be no rain during the time they pro-
claim God's message. They have authority
also over the springs of water, to turn them
into blood; they have authority also to strike
the earth with every kind of plague as often
as they wish.
7 When they finish proclaiming their mes-
sage, the beast that comes up out of the abyss
will fight against them. He will defeat them
and kill them, 8 and their bodies will lie in
the street of the great city, where their Lord
was crucified. The symbolic name of that
city is Sodom, or Egypt. 9 People from all
nations, tribes, languages, and races will look
at their bodies for three and a half days and
will not allow them to be buried. 10 The
people of the earth will be happy because of
the death of these two. They will celebrate
and send presents to each other, because
those two prophets brought much suffering
upon the whole human race. 11 After three
and a half days a life-giving breath came
from God and entered them, and they stood
up; and all who saw them were terrified.
12 Then the two prophets heard a loud voice
say to them from heaven, "Come up here!"
As their enemies watched, they went up into
heaven in a cloud. 13 At that very moment
there was a violent earthquake; a tenth of the

10:5–7 Ex 20:11; Deut 32:40; Dan 12:7; Am 3:7 **10:8–10** Ezek 2:8—3:3 **11:1** Ezek 40:3; Zech 2:1, 2 **11:2** Lk 21:24 **11:4** Zech 4:3, 11–14 **11:6** **a** 1 Kings 17:1; **b** Ex 7:17–19; **c** 1 Sam 4:8 **11:7** **a** Dan 7:7; Rev 13:5–7; 17:8; **b** Dan 7:21 **11:8** Isa 1:9, 10 **11:11** Ezek 37:10 **11:12** 2 Kings 2:11 **11:13** Rev 6:12; 16.18

The Paschal Mystery

How have you experienced suffering in your life? Sickness, depression, death of a loved one, anger, poverty—or something else? Maybe you have suffered for standing up for what is right and moral?

At the heart of the Christian faith is the reality that suffering and death are not the end of life for those with faith in Jesus. God will resurrect us and raise us to a new life, free from the chains of sin and pain and death. Jesus own suffering, death, and Resurrection is called the Paschal mystery. Those of us who have been baptized already have some share in this mystery. The Paschal mystery promises that if we remain faithful to Jesus, after we die we shall also be raised to new life.

We can get a taste of the Paschal mystery here on earth when we go through a time of pain and suffering with faith. Many people find they come through those times with greater faith or as better people.

Sometimes, though, our suffering can last a lifetime. Know that God never abandons you. And at the end of your life, death will not be the end! Like the prophets, we will have new life with Christ—a heaven so wonderful, we can't even imagine it!

— Revelation 11:11–12

city was destroyed, and seven thousand peo-
ple were killed. The rest of the people were
terrified and praised the greatness of the
God of heaven.
14 The second horror is over, but the third
horror will come soon!

The Seventh Trumpet

15 Then the seventh angel blew his trum-
pet, and there were loud voices in heaven,
saying, "The power to rule over the world
belongs now to our Lord and his Messiah,
and he will rule forever and ever!" 16 Then
the twenty-four elders who sit on their
thrones in front of God threw themselves
face downward and worshiped God, 17 say-
ing:

"Lord God Almighty, the one who is and
who was!
We thank you that you have taken your
great power
and have begun to rule!
18 The heathen were filled with rage,
because the time for your anger has
come,
the time for the dead to be judged.
The time has come to reward your
servants, the prophets,
and all your people, all who have
reverence for you,
great and small alike.
The time has come to destroy those who
destroy the earth!"

19 God's temple in heaven was opened, and
the Covenant Box was seen there. Then
there were flashes of lightning, rumblings
and peals of thunder, an earthquake, and
heavy hail.

The Woman and the Dragon

12 Then a great and mysterious sight
appeared in the sky. There was a
woman, whose dress was the sun and who
had the moon under her feet and a crown of

11:15 Ex 15:18; Dan 2:44; 7:14, 27 **11:18** **a** Ps 2:5; 110:5; **b** Ps 115:13 **11:19** 2 Macc 2:4–8; **a** Rev 8:5; 16:18; **b** Rev 16:21

twelve stars on her head. 2She was soon to
give birth, and the pains and suffering of
childbirth made her cry out.
3Another mysterious sight appeared in the
sky. There was a huge red dragon with seven
heads and ten horns and a crown on each of
his heads. 4With his tail he dragged a third
of the stars out of the sky and threw them
down to the earth. He stood in front of the
woman, in order to eat her child as soon as it
was born. 5Then she gave birth to a son,
who will rule over all nations with an iron
rod. But the child was snatched away and
taken to God and his throne. 6The woman
fled to the desert, to a place God had pre-
pared for her, where she will be taken care
of for 1, 260 days.
7Then war broke out in heaven. Michael
and his angels fought against the dragon, who
fought back with his angels; 8but the dragon
was defeated, and he and his angels were not
allowed to stay in heaven any longer. 9The
huge dragon was thrown out—that ancient
serpent, named the Devil, or Satan, that
deceived the whole world. He was thrown
down to earth, and all his angels with him.
10Then I heard a loud voice in heaven say-
ing, "Now God's salvation has come! Now
God has shown his power as King! Now his
Messiah has shown his authority! For the one
who stood before our God and accused
believers day and night has been thrown out
of heaven. 11They won the victory over him
by the blood of the Lamb and by the truth
which they proclaimed; and they were will-
ing to give up their lives and die. 12And so be
glad, you heavens, and all you that live there!
But how terrible for the earth and the sea!
For the Devil has come down to you, and he
is filled with rage, because he knows that he
has only a little time left."
13When the dragon realized that he had
been thrown down to the earth, he began to
pursue the woman who had given birth to
the boy. 14She was given the two wings of a
large eagle in order to fly to her place in the
desert, where she will be taken care of for
three and a half years, safe from the dragon's
attack. 15And then from his mouth the drag-
on poured out a flood of water after the
woman, so that it would carry her away.
16But the earth helped the woman; it

Study it!

Evil Wages War

This vision symbolizes the battle between Jesus and Satan. The woman is Israel, and the child she gives birth to is Jesus. The pains and sufferings of childbirth are all the problems the Israelites suffered through before God sent them Jesus as their Savior.

The huge red dragon is a symbol of Satan or the terrible forces of evil, ready to devour the child when he is born. But the child is protected and taken to heaven. Satan follows into heaven and war breaks out. Satan and his angels lose the war and are thrown out of heaven, where they once again try to find and destroy the woman. Now, the woman symbolizes the new Christian churches and Jesus' mother, Mary, who brings Christ to the world. She escapes on the wings of a great eagle, which represents the power and swiftness of divine help. But the dragon goes off to continue torturing God's people.

In what ways do you think people are tortured by evil?

— Revelation, chapter 12

12:3 Dan 7:7 **12:4** Dan 8:10 **12:5 a** Isa 66:7; **b** Ps 2:9 **12:7** Dan 10:13, 21; 12:1; Jude 9 **12:9 a** Gen 3:1; **b** Lk 10:18 **12:10** Job 1:9–11; Zech 3:1 **12:14** Dan 7:25; 12:7

Michael *(Revelation 12:7)* **is an archangel, one of God's chief angels. His name was the war cry in the battle against Satan and his followers.**

opened its mouth and swallowed the water
that had come from the dragon's mouth.
17 The dragon was furious with the woman
and went off to fight against the rest of her
descendants, all those who obey God's com-
mandments and are faithful to the truth
revealed by Jesus. 18 And the dragon stood[e]
on the seashore.

The Two Beasts

13 Then I saw a beast coming up out
of the sea. It had ten horns and
seven heads; on each of its horns there was a
crown, and on each of its heads there was a
name that was insulting to God. 2 The beast
looked like a leopard, with feet like a bear's
feet and a mouth like a lion's mouth. The
dragon gave the beast his own power, his
throne, and his vast authority. 3 One of the
heads of the beast seemed to have been fatal-
ly wounded, but the wound had healed. The
whole earth was amazed and followed the
beast. 4 Everyone worshiped the dragon
because he had given his authority to the
beast. They worshiped the beast also, saying,
"Who is like the beast? Who can fight
against it?"

5 The beast was allowed to make proud
claims which were insulting to God, and it
was permitted to have authority for forty-
two months. 6 It began to curse God, his
name, the place where he lives, and all those
who live in heaven. 7 It was allowed to fight
against God's people and to defeat them, and
it was given authority over every tribe,
nation, language, and race. 8 All people living
on earth will worship it, except those whose
names were written before the creation of
the world in the book of the living which
belongs to the Lamb that was killed.

9 "Listen, then, if you have ears! 10 Who-
ever is meant to be captured will surely be
captured; whoever is meant to be killed by
the sword will surely be killed by the sword.

Live it!

Evil Today

In Revelation, chapter 13, the vision of the two beasts continues the story about how evil tries to destroy God's people. The power of evil in our world is very real, and it can be terrifying. Just open a newspaper, and stories of murder, war, rape, and other horrible crimes fill the pages.

Evil must be resisted. Like the beasts, it grows in power when good people do not stand against it. It may seem too powerful, too big to do anything about. It happens when a group of good young people gradually get involved deeper and deeper in drinking, drugs, and sexual activity. It starts small, just one drink or some sexual touching. If no one steps in to say this is wrong, the sinful behavior just gets worse and worse.

The way to fight off evil is to keep turning to God. First, pay attention to your sinfulness and do not allow it to get the best of you. Pray for God's strength. Second, speak out when you see sinful behavior happening—even if it isn't the popular thing to do. You may get persecuted. Just remember Revelation. For even though the evil beasts seem powerful, God's love is a million times more powerful.

— Revelation, chapter 13

[e] **12:18** And the dragon stood; *some manuscripts have* And I stood, *connecting this verse with what follows.*

13:1 a Dan 7:3; **b** Rev 17:3, 7-12 **13:2** Dan 7:4–6 **13:5, 6** Dan 7:8, 25; 11:36 **13:7** Dan 7:21 **13:8** Ps 69:28 **13:10** Jer 15:2; 43:11

"This calls for endurance and faith on the part of God's people" *(Revelation 13:10)*.

This calls for endurance and faith on the part of God's people."

11 Then I saw another beast, which came up out of the earth. It had two horns like a lamb's horns, and it spoke like a dragon. 12 It used the vast authority of the first beast in its presence. It forced the earth and all who live on it to worship the first beast, whose wound had healed. 13 This second beast performed great miracles; it made fire come down out of heaven to earth in the sight of everyone. 14 And it deceived all the people living on earth by means of the miracles which it was allowed to perform in the presence of the first beast. The beast told them to build an image in honor of the beast that had been wounded by the sword and yet lived. 15 The second beast was allowed to breathe life into the image of the first beast, so that the image could talk and put to death all those who would not worship it. 16 The beast forced all the people, small and great, rich and poor, slave and free, to have a mark placed on their right hands or on their foreheads. 17 No one could buy or sell without this mark, that is, the beast's name or the number that stands for the name.

18 This calls for wisdom. Whoever is intelligent can figure out the meaning of the number of the beast, because the number stands for the name of someone. Its number is 666.

The Lamb and His People

14 Then I looked, and there was the Lamb standing on Mount Zion; with him were 144,000 people who have his name and his Father's name written on their foreheads. 2 And I heard a voice from heaven that sounded like a roaring waterfall, like a loud peal of thunder. It sounded like the music made by musicians playing their harps. 3 The 144,000 people stood before the throne, the four living creatures, and the elders; they were singing a new song, which only they could learn. Of the whole human race they are the only ones who have been redeemed. 4 They are the men who have kept themselves pure by not having sexual relations with women; they are virgins. They follow the Lamb wherever he goes. They have been redeemed from the rest of the human race and are the first ones to be offered to God and to the Lamb. 5 They have never been known to tell lies; they are faultless.

The Three Angels

6 Then I saw another angel flying high in the air, with an eternal message of Good News to announce to the peoples of the earth, to every race, tribe, language, and nation. 7 He said in a loud voice, "Honor God and praise his greatness! For the time has come for him to judge all people. Worship him who made heaven, earth, sea, and the springs of water!"

8 A second angel followed the first one, saying, "She has fallen! Great Babylon has fallen! She made all peoples drink her wine—the strong wine of her immoral lust!"

9 A third angel followed the first two, saying in a loud voice, "Those who worship the beast and its image and receive the mark on their forehead or on their hand 10 will themselves drink God's wine, the wine of his fury, which he has poured at full strength into the cup of his anger! All who do this will be tormented in fire and sulfur before the holy angels and the Lamb. 11 The smoke of the fire that torments them goes up forever and ever. There is no relief day or night for those who worship the beast and its image, for anyone who has the mark of its name."

12 This calls for endurance on the part of God's people, those who obey God's commandments and are faithful to Jesus.

13 Then I heard a voice from heaven saying, "Write this: Happy are those who from now on die in the service of the Lord!"

"Yes indeed!" answers the Spirit. "They will enjoy rest from their hard work, because the results of their service go with them."

The Harvest of the Earth

14 Then I looked, and there was a white cloud, and sitting on the cloud was what looked like a human being, with a crown of gold on his head and a sharp sickle in his

14:1 Ezek 9:4; Rev 7:3 **14:5** Zeph 3:13 **14:8** Isa 21:9; Jer 51:8; Rev 18:2 **14:10** **a** Isa 51:17; **b** Gen 19:24; Ezek 38:22 **14:11** Isa 34:10 **14:14** Dan 7:13

Pray it!

End of the Day Checkup

It's hard to think about our whole life being judged at the end of time as described in Revelation 14:7! What about just taking one day at a time? How would God judge you at the end of today—for this day only?

Try this self-examination when you go to bed tonight: Think back upon your day, and recall five very specific things you're thankful for. Maybe your coach encouraged you, or you got a new babysitting job. Now, thank God for these five things, events, or people.

Second, think of five things you said or did that you believe were pleasing to God. Ask God to continue to show you how to live faithfully, and to give you the stamina to keep it up every day.

Third, ask yourself—honestly: Were there any times during the day when your actions or words would have disappointed God? Talk to God about those and express your sorrow for those words or actions. Remember how deeply God loves you and wants to help you be forgiving, patient, kind, and caring. If you take care of one day at a time, God's judgment at the end of time doesn't look so scary!

— Revelation 14:6–13

hand. 15 Then another angel came out from
the temple and cried out in a loud voice to
the one who was sitting on the cloud, "Use
your sickle and reap the harvest, because the
time has come; the earth is ripe for the har-
vest!" 16 Then the one who sat on the cloud
swung his sickle on the earth, and the earth's
harvest was reaped.

17 Then I saw another angel come out of
the temple in heaven, and he also had a
sharp sickle.

18 Then another angel, who is in charge of
the fire, came from the altar. He shouted in a
loud voice to the angel who had the sharp
sickle, "Use your sickle, and cut the grapes
from the vineyard of the earth, because the
grapes are ripe!" 19 So the angel swung his
sickle on the earth, cut the grapes from the
vine, and threw them into the wine press of
God's furious anger. 20 The grapes were
squeezed out in the wine press outside the
city, and blood came out of the wine press in
a flood two hundred miles long and about
five feet deep.

The Angels with the Last Plagues

15 Then I saw in the sky another mys-
terious sight, great and amazing.
There were seven angels with seven plagues,
which are the last ones, because they are the
final expression of God's anger.

2 Then I saw what looked like a sea of glass
mixed with fire. I also saw those who had
won the victory over the beast and its image
and over the one whose name is represented
by a number. They were standing by the sea
of glass, holding harps that God had given
them 3 and singing the song of Moses, the
servant of God, and the song of the Lamb:

"Lord God Almighty,
how great and wonderful are your
deeds!
King of the nations,[f]
how right and true are your ways!
4 Who will not stand in awe of you, Lord?
Who will refuse to declare your
greatness?
You alone are holy.

f **15:3** nations; *some manuscripts have* ages.

14:15 Joel 3:13 **14:20** Isa 63:3; Lam 1:15; Rev 19:15 **15:3** Ex 15:1 **15:4 a** Jer 10:7; **b** Ps 86:9

All the nations will come
and worship you,
because your just actions are seen by
all."
5 After this I saw the temple in heaven
open, with the Sacred Tent in it. 6 The seven
angels who had the seven plagues came out
of the temple, dressed in clean shining linen
and with gold bands tied around their chests.
7 Then one of the four living creatures gave
the seven angels seven gold bowls full of the
anger of God, who lives forever and ever.
8 The temple was filled with smoke from the
glory and power of God, and no one could
go into the temple until the seven plagues
brought by the seven angels had come to an
end.

The Bowls of God's Anger

16 Then I heard a loud voice speaking
from the temple to the seven angels:
"Go and pour out the seven bowls of God's
anger on the earth!"
2 The first angel went and poured out his
bowl on the earth. Terrible and painful sores
appeared on those who had the mark of the
beast and on those who had worshiped its
image.
3 Then the second angel poured out his
bowl on the sea. The water became like the
blood of a dead person, and every living
creature in the sea died.
4 Then the third angel poured out his
bowl on the rivers and the springs of water,
and they turned into blood. 5 I heard the
angel in charge of the waters say, "The judg-
ments you have made are just, O Holy One,
you who are and who were! 6 They poured
out the blood of God's people and of the
prophets, and so you have given them blood
to drink. They are getting what they
deserve!" 7 Then I heard a voice from the
altar saying, "Lord God Almighty! True and
just indeed are your judgments!"
8 Then the fourth angel poured out his
bowl on the sun, and it was allowed to burn
people with its fiery heat. 9 They were
burned by the fierce heat, and they cursed
the name of God, who has authority over
these plagues. But they would not turn from
their sins and praise his greatness.
10 Then the fifth angel poure out his
bowl on the throne of the beast Darkness
fell over the beast's kingdom nd people bit
their tongues because of th pain, 11 and
they cursed the God of ven for their
pains and sores. But th d not turn from
their evil ways. el poured out his
12 Then the sixthrates River. The river
bowl on the gr way for the kings who
dried up, to p 13 Then I saw three
come from looked like frogs. They
unclean s of the mouth of the drag-
were co f the beast, and the mouth
on, th phet. 14 They are the spirits of
of t

Study it!

More Disaster Strikes!

The seven bowls described are like the seven seals and seven trumpets. These symbols in Revelation each release a disaster or plague upon the sinful people. Check out the plagues in Exodus, chapters 7 to 12. Each plague came as a warning to the Egyptians to stop tormenting the Israelites and free them from slavery. Again, here in Revelation, disasters and plagues are sent as warnings for people to change their hearts and turn away from evil.

— Revelation, chapter 16

15:5 Ex 38:21 **15:8** Ex 40:34; 1 Kings 8:10, 11; 2 Chr
Ps 78:44 **16:10** Ex 10:21 **16:12** Isa 11:15 **16:2** Ex 9:10 **16:4** Ex 7:17–21;

"Lord God Almighty, / how great a l are your deeds! / King of the nations, / how right and true are yo *(Revelation 15:3)*

demons that perform miracles. These three
spirits go out to all the kings of the world, to
bring them together for the battle on the
great Day of Almighty God.
15 "Listen! I am coming like a thief!
Happy is he who stays awake and guards his
clothes, so that he will not walk around
naked and be ashamed in public!"
16 Then the spirits brought the kings
together in the place that in Hebrew is
called Armageddon.
17 Then the seventh angel poured out his
bowl in the air. A loud voice came from the
throne in the temple, saying, "It is done!"
18 There were flashes of lightning, rumblings
and peals of thunder, and a terrible earth-
quake. There has never been such an earth-
quake since the creation of human beings;
this was the worst earthquake of all! 19 The
great city was split into three parts, and the
cities of all countries were destroyed. God
remembered great Babylon and made her
drink the wine from his cup—the wine of
his furious anger. 20 All the islands disap-
peared, all the mountains vanished. 21 Huge
hailstones, each weighing as much as a hun-
dred pounds, fell from the sky on people,
who cursed God on account of the plague
of hail, because it was such a terrible plague.

The Famou Prostitute

17 Theron of the seven angels who
had th seven bowls came to me and
said, "Come, ar will show you how the
famous prostitu to be punished, that
great city that is near many rivers. 2 The
kings of the earth and thced sexual immorali-
ty with her, and the of the world
became drunk from ng the wine of
her immorality."
3 The Spirit took c
angel carried me to a c me, and the
woman sitting on a red ere I saw a
insulting to God written had names
the beast
had seven heads and ten horns. 4 The woman
was dressed in purple and scarlet, and cov-
ered with gold ornaments, precious stones,
and pearls. In her hand she held a gold cup
full of obscene and filthy things, the result of
her immorality. 5 On her forehead was writ-
ten a name that has a secret meaning: "Great
Babylon, the mother of all prostitutes and
perverts in the world." 6 And I saw that the
woman was drunk with the blood of God's

Live it!

Sins of Nations

The prostitute in Revelation, chapter 17, probably stood for the Roman Empire at the time of John. When John had his visions, the Roman Empire was filled with immoral behavior, greed, and abuse of power. How many nations or empires since then have fallen victim to the same evils? How easy it can be for powerful nations and their leaders to get sucked into the vacuum of sin!

How do you think our country and its leaders measure up in the area of morality? If you could meet with the president, which sins of our nation would you choose to discuss? What concrete suggestions would you make for getting us back on track as a nation that values moral living? If you could deliver a speech to our nation's citizens, what important points would you make?

— Revelation, chapter 17

16:15 Mt 24:43, 44; Lk 12:39, **16:16** 2 Kings 23:29; Zech 12:11 **16:18** Rev 8:5; 11:13, 19 **16:19** Isa 51:17 **16:20** Rev 6: 9:23; Rev 11:19 **17:1** Jer 51:13 **17:2** Isa 23:17; Jer 51:7 **17:3** Rev 13:1 **17:4** Jer 51:7

The author of Revelation troubles caused by another ome to the Old Testament by telling the Babylon *(see 2 Kings 25:1–21)*.

All the nations will come
and worship you,
because your just actions are seen by
all."
5After this I saw the temple in heaven
open, with the Sacred Tent in it. 6The seven
angels who had the seven plagues came out
of the temple, dressed in clean shining linen
and with gold bands tied around their chests.
7Then one of the four living creatures gave
the seven angels seven gold bowls full of the
anger of God, who lives forever and ever.
8The temple was filled with smoke from the
glory and power of God, and no one could
go into the temple until the seven plagues
brought by the seven angels had come to an
end.

The Bowls of God's Anger

16 Then I heard a loud voice speaking
from the temple to the seven angels:
"Go and pour out the seven bowls of God's
anger on the earth!"
2The first angel went and poured out his
bowl on the earth. Terrible and painful sores
appeared on those who had the mark of the
beast and on those who had worshiped its
image.
3Then the second angel poured out his
bowl on the sea. The water became like the
blood of a dead person, and every living
creature in the sea died.
4Then the third angel poured out his
bowl on the rivers and the springs of water,
and they turned into blood. 5I heard the
angel in charge of the waters say, "The judg-
ments you have made are just, O Holy One,
you who are and who were! 6They poured
out the blood of God's people and of the
prophets, and so you have given them blood
to drink. They are getting what they
deserve!" 7Then I heard a voice from the
altar saying, "Lord God Almighty! True and
just indeed are your judgments!"
8Then the fourth angel poured out his

Study it!

More Disaster Strikes!

The seven bowls described are like the seven seals and seven trumpets. These symbols in Revelation each release a disaster or plague upon the sinful people. Check out the plagues in Exodus, chapters 7 to 12. Each plague came as a warning to the Egyptians to stop tormenting the Israelites and free them from slavery. Again, here in Revelation, disasters and plagues are sent as warnings for people to change their hearts and turn away from evil.

— Revelation, chapter 16

bowl on the sun, and it was allowed to burn
people with its fiery heat. 9They were
burned by the fierce heat, and they cursed
the name of God, who has authority over
these plagues. But they would not turn from
their sins and praise his greatness.
10Then the fifth angel poured out his
bowl on the throne of the beast. Darkness
fell over the beast's kingdom, and people bit
their tongues because of their pain, 11and
they cursed the God of heaven for their
pains and sores. But they did not turn from
their evil ways.
12Then the sixth angel poured out his
bowl on the great Euphrates River. The river
dried up, to provide a way for the kings who
come from the east. 13Then I saw three
unclean spirits that looked like frogs. They
were coming out of the mouth of the drag-
on, the mouth of the beast, and the mouth
of the false prophet. 14They are the spirits of

15:5 Ex 38:21 **15:8** Ex 40:34; 1 Kings 8:10, 11; 2 Chr 5:13, 14; Isa 6:4 **16:2** Ex 9:10 **16:4** Ex 7:17–21; Ps 78:44 **16:10** Ex 10:21 **16:12** Isa 11:15

"Lord God Almighty, / how great and wonderful are your deeds! / King of the nations, / how right and true are your ways!" *(Revelation 15:3)*

demons that perform miracles. These three
spirits go out to all the kings of the world, to
bring them together for the battle on the
great Day of Almighty God.
15“Listen! I am coming like a thief!
Happy is he who stays awake and guards his
clothes, so that he will not walk around
naked and be ashamed in public!”
16Then the spirits brought the kings
together in the place that in Hebrew is
called Armageddon.
17Then the seventh angel poured out his
bowl in the air. A loud voice came from the
throne in the temple, saying, “It is done!”
18There were flashes of lightning, rumblings
and peals of thunder, and a terrible earth-
quake. There has never been such an earth-
quake since the creation of human beings;
this was the worst earthquake of all! 19The
great city was split into three parts, and the
cities of all countries were destroyed. God
remembered great Babylon and made her
drink the wine from his cup—the wine of
his furious anger. 20All the islands disap-
peared, all the mountains vanished. 21Huge
hailstones, each weighing as much as a hun-
dred pounds, fell from the sky on people,
who cursed God on account of the plague
of hail, because it was such a terrible plague.

The Famous Prostitute

17 Then one of the seven angels who
had the seven bowls came to me and
said, “Come, and I will show you how the
famous prostitute is to be punished, that
great city that is built near many rivers. 2The
kings of the earth practiced sexual immorali-
ty with her, and the people of the world
became drunk from drinking the wine of
her immorality.”
3The Spirit took control of me, and the
angel carried me to a desert. There I saw a
woman sitting on a red beast that had names
insulting to God written all over it; the beast
had seven heads and ten horns. 4The woman
was dressed in purple and scarlet, and cov-
ered with gold ornaments, precious stones,
and pearls. In her hand she held a gold cup
full of obscene and filthy things, the result of
her immorality. 5On her forehead was writ-
ten a name that has a secret meaning: “Great
Babylon, the mother of all prostitutes and
perverts in the world.” 6And I saw that the
woman was drunk with the blood of God’s

Live it!

Sins of Nations

The prostitute in Revelation, chapter 17, probably stood for the Roman Empire at the time of John. When John had his visions, the Roman Empire was filled with immoral behavior, greed, and abuse of power. How many nations or empires since then have fallen victim to the same evils? How easy it can be for powerful nations and their leaders to get sucked into the vacuum of sin!

How do you think our country and its leaders measure up in the area of morality? If you could meet with the president, which sins of our nation would you choose to discuss? What concrete suggestions would you make for getting us back on track as a nation that values moral living? If you could deliver a speech to our nation’s citizens, what important points would you make?

— Revelation, chapter 17

16:15 Mt 24:43, 44; Lk 12:39, 40; Rev 3:3 **16:16** 2 Kings 23:29; Zech 12:11 **16:18** Rev 8:5; 11:13, 19 **16:19** Isa 51:17 **16:20** Rev 6:14 **16:21** Ex 9:23; Rev 11:19 **17:1** Jer 51:13 **17:2** Isa 23:17; Jer 51:7 **17:3** Rev 13:1 **17:4** Jer 51:7

The author of Revelation connects Rome to the Old Testament by telling the troubles caused by another evil empire, Babylon *(see 2 Kings 25:1–21)*.

people and the blood of those who were killed because they had been loyal to Jesus.

When I saw her, I was completely amazed. 7“Why are you amazed?” the angel asked me. “I will tell you the secret meaning of the woman and of the beast that carries her, the beast with seven heads and ten horns. 8That beast was once alive, but lives no longer; it is about to come up from the abyss and will go off to be destroyed. The people living on earth whose names have not been written before the creation of the world in the book of the living, will all be amazed as they look at the beast. It was once alive; now it no longer lives, but it will reappear.

9“This calls for wisdom and understanding. The seven heads are seven hills, on which the woman sits. They are also seven kings: 10five of them have fallen, one still rules, and the other one has not yet come; when he comes, he must rule only a little while. 11And the beast that was once alive, but lives no longer, is itself an eighth king who is one of the seven and is going off to be destroyed.

12“The ten horns you saw are ten kings who have not yet begun to rule, but who will be given authority to rule as kings for one hour with the beast. 13These ten all have the same purpose, and they give their power and authority to the beast. 14They will fight against the Lamb; but the Lamb, together with his called, chosen, and faithful followers, will defeat them, because he is Lord of lords and King of kings.”

15The angel also said to me, “The waters you saw, on which the prostitute sits, are nations, peoples, races, and languages. 16The ten horns you saw and the beast will hate the prostitute; they will take away everything she has and leave her naked; they will eat her flesh and destroy her with fire. 17For God has placed in their hearts the will to carry out his purpose by acting together and giving to the beast their power to rule until God’s words come true.

18“The woman you saw is the great city that rules over the kings of the earth.”

The Fall of Babylon

18 After this I saw another angel coming down out of heaven. He had great authority, and his splendor brightened the whole earth. 2He cried out in a loud voice: “She has fallen! Great Babylon has fallen! She is now haunted by demons and unclean spirits; all kinds of filthy and hateful birds live in her. 3For all the nations have drunk her wine—the strong wine of her immoral lust. The kings of the earth practiced sexual immorality with her, and the merchants of the world grew rich from her unrestrained lust.”

4Then I heard another voice from heaven, saying,

“Come out, my people! Come out from
her!
You must not take part in her sins;
you must not share in her punishment!
5For her sins are piled up as high as
heaven,
and God remembers her wicked ways.
6Treat her exactly as she has treated you;
pay her back double for all she has
done.
Fill her cup with a drink twice as strong
as the drink she prepared for you.
7Give her as much suffering and grief
as the glory and luxury she gave
herself.
For she keeps telling herself:
‘Here I sit, a queen!
I am no widow,
I will never know grief!’
8Because of this, in one day she will be
struck with plagues—
disease, grief, and famine.
And she will be burned with fire,
because the Lord God, who judges her,
is mighty.”

9The kings of the earth who took part in her immorality and lust will cry and weep over the city when they see the smoke from the flames that consume her. 10They stand a long way off, because they are afraid of sharing in her suffering. They say, “How terrible! How awful! This great and mighty city

17:8 a Dan 7:7; Rev 11:7; **b** Ps 69:28 **17:12** Dan 7:24 **18:2 a** Isa 21:9; Jer 51:8; Rev 14:8; **b** Isa 13:21; Jer 50:39 **18:3** Isa 23:17; Jer 51:7 **18:4** Isa 48:20; Jer 50:8; 51:6, 45 **18:5** Gen 18:20, 21; Jer 51:9 **18:6** Ps 137:8; Jer 50:29 **18:7, 8** Isa 47:7–9 **18:9, 10** Ezek 26:16, 17

This great and mighty city Babylon! (18:10)

Babylon! In just one hour you have been
punished!"
[11]The merchants of the earth also cry and
mourn for her, because no one buys their
goods any longer; [12]no one buys their gold,
silver, precious stones, and pearls; their goods
of linen, purple cloth, silk, and scarlet cloth;
all kinds of rare woods and all kinds of
objects made of ivory and of expensive
wood, of bronze, iron, and marble; [13]and cin-
namon, spice, incense, myrrh, and frankin-
cense; wine and oil, flour and wheat, cattle
and sheep, horses and carriages, slaves, and
even human lives. [14]The merchants say to
her, "All the good things you longed to own
have disappeared, and all your wealth and
glamor are gone, and you will never find
them again!" [15]The merchants, who became
rich from doing business in that city, will
stand a long way off, because they are afraid
of sharing in her suffering. They will cry and
mourn, [16]and say, "How terrible! How awful
for the great city! She used to dress herself in
linen, purple, and scarlet, and cover herself
with gold ornaments, precious stones, and
pearls! [17]And in one hour she has lost all this
wealth!"
All the ships' captains and passengers, the
sailors and all others who earn their living
on the sea, stood a long way off, [18]and cried
out as they saw the smoke from the flames
that consumed her: "There never has been
another city like this great city!" [19]They
threw dust on their heads, they cried and
mourned, saying, "How terrible! How awful
for the great city! She is the city where all
who have ships sailing the seas became rich
on her wealth! And in one hour she has lost
everything!"
[20]Be glad, heaven, because of her destruc-
tion! Be glad, God's people and the apostles
and prophets! For God has condemned her
for what she did to you!
[21]Then a mighty angel picked up a stone
the size of a large millstone and threw it into
the sea, saying, "This is how the great city
Babylon will be violently thrown down and
will never be seen again. [22]The music of
harps and of human voices, of players of the
flute and the trumpet, will never be heard in
you again! No workman in any trade will
ever be found in you again; and the sound of
the millstone will be heard no more!
[23]Never again will the light of a lamp be
seen in you; no more will the voices of
brides and grooms be heard in you. Your
merchants were the most powerful in all the

18:11 Ezek 27:31, 36 **18:12, 13** Ezek 27:12, 13, 22 **18:15** Ezek 27:31, 36 **18:17** Isa 23:14; Ezek 27:26–30 **18:18** Ezek 27:32 **18:19** Ezek 27:30–34 **18:20** Deut 32:43; Jer 51:48 **18:21** **a** Jer 51:63, 64; **b** Ezek 26:21 **18:22** Ezek 26:13; Isa 24:8 **18:22, 23** Jer 7:34; 25:10

world, and with your magic you deceived all
the peoples of the world!"
24 Babylon was punished because the
blood of prophets and of God's people was
found in the city; yes, the blood of all those
who have been killed on earth.

19 After this I heard what sounded like
the roar of a large crowd of people
in heaven, saying, "Praise God! Salvation,
glory, and power belong to our God! 2 True
and just are his judgments! He has con-
demned the prostitute who was corrupting
the earth with her immorality. God has pun-
ished her because she killed his servants."
3 Again they shouted, "Praise God! The
smoke from the flames that consume the
great city goes up forever and ever!" 4 The
twenty-four elders and the four living crea-
tures fell down and worshiped God, who
was seated on the throne. They said, "Amen!
Praise God!"

The Wedding Feast of the Lamb

5 Then there came from the throne the
sound of a voice, saying, "Praise our God, all
his servants and all people, both great and
small, who have reverence for him!" 6 Then I
heard what sounded like a crowd, like the
sound of a roaring waterfall, like loud peals
of thunder. I heard them say, "Praise God!
For the Lord, our Almighty God, is King!
7 Let us rejoice and be glad; let us praise his
greatness! For the time has come for the
wedding of the Lamb, and his bride has pre-
pared herself for it. 8 She has been given
clean shining linen to wear." (The linen is
the good deeds of God's people.)

9 Then the angel said to me, "Write this:
Happy are those who have been invited to
the wedding feast of the Lamb." And the
angel added, "These are the true words of
God."

10 I fell down at his feet to worship him,
but he said to me, "Don't do it! I am a ser-
vant together with you and with other
believers, all those who hold to the truth
that Jesus revealed. Worship God!"

For the truth that Jesus revealed is what
inspires the prophets.

The Rider on the White Horse

11 Then I saw heaven open, and there was
a white horse. Its rider is called Faithful and
True; it is with justice that he judges and
fights his battles. 12 His eyes were like a flame
of fire, and he wore many crowns on his
head. He had a name written on him, but no
one except himself knows what it is. 13 The
robe he wore was covered with blood. His
name is "The Word of God." 14 The armies
of heaven followed him, riding on white
horses and dressed in clean white linen.
15 Out of his mouth came a sharp sword,
with which he will defeat the nations. He
will rule over them with a rod of iron, and
he will trample out the wine in the wine
press of the furious anger of the Almighty
God. 16 On his robe and on his thigh was
written the name: "King of kings and Lord
of lords."

17 Then I saw an angel standing on the
sun. He shouted in a loud voice to all the
birds flying in midair: "Come and gather
together for God's great feast! 18 Come and
eat the flesh of kings, generals, and soldiers,
the flesh of horses and their riders, the flesh
of all people, slave and free, great and small!"

19 Then I saw the beast and the kings of
the earth and their armies gathered to fight
against the one who was riding the horse
and against his army. 20 The beast was taken
prisoner, together with the false prophet
who had performed miracles in his presence.
(It was by those miracles that he had
deceived those who had the mark of the
beast and those who had worshiped the

18:24 Jer 51:49 **19:2** Deut 32:43; 2 Kings 9:7 **19:3** Isa 34:10 **19:5** Ps 115:13 **19:6** **a** Ezek 1:24; **b** Ps 93:1; 97:1; 99:1 **19:9** Mt 22:2, 3 **19:11** **a** Ezek 1:1; **b** Ps 96:13; Isa 11:4 **19:12** Dan 10:6 **19:13** Wis 18:14–18 **19:15** **a** Ps 2:9; **b** Isa 63:3; Joel 3:13; Rev 14:20 **19:17, 18** Ezek 39:17–20 **19:20** Rev 13:1–18

Chapter 19 of Revelation includes a wedding feast. See Matthew 22:1–14 and John 2:1–11 for other stories about wedding feasts.

Pray it!

Delivery from Evil!

Just when everything seems to have been swallowed up by evil and destruction, Revelation takes a dramatic turn. Riding into the scene on a white (symbolizing victory and joy) horse is Jesus, called "Faithful and True" (19:11) and "the Word of God" (19:13). The beast is thrown into the lake of fire and all his kings and armies are killed by Jesus and the heavenly armies (the martyrs and all who have been faithful to God). Justice has come at last! Jesus is victorious over evil!

Every time we pray the Our Father, we pray, "Lead us not into temptation, but deliver us from evil." Jesus gave us that prayer (see Matthew 6:13). He knows that we may come face to face with evil, though we often don't even recognize it. Jesus knows we need God's protection from evil and help with resisting temptations to sin.

Try to pray the Our Father each day and remember who leads the charge against evil—Jesus Christ.

— Revelation 19:11–21

image of the beast.) The beast and the false
prophet were both thrown alive into the lake
of fire that burns with sulfur. 21 Their armies
were killed by the sword that comes out of
the mouth of the one who was riding the
horse; and all the birds ate all they could of
their flesh.

The Thousand Years

20 Then I saw an angel coming down
from heaven, holding in his hand the
key of the abyss and a heavy chain. 2 He
seized the dragon, that ancient serpent—that
is, the Devil, or Satan—and chained him up
for a thousand years. 3 The angel threw him
into the abyss, locked it, and sealed it, so that
he could not deceive the nations any more
until the thousand years were over. After that
he must be set loose for a little while.
4 Then I saw thrones, and those who sat
on them were given the power to judge. I
also saw the souls of those who had been
executed because they had proclaimed the
truth that Jesus revealed and the word of
God. They had not worshiped the beast or
its image, nor had they received the mark of
the beast on their foreheads or their hands.
They came to life and ruled as kings with
Christ for a thousand years. 5 (The rest of the
dead did not come to life until the thousand
years were over.) This is the first raising of
the dead. 6 Happy and greatly blessed are
those who are included in this first raising of
the dead. The second death has no power
over them; they shall be priests of God and
of Christ, and they will rule with him for a
thousand years.

The Defeat of Satan

7 After the thousand years are over, Satan
will be set loose from his prison, 8 and he
will go out to deceive the nations scattered
over the whole world, that is, Gog and
Magog. Satan will bring them all together

20:2 Gen 3:1 **20:4** Dan 7:9, 22 **20:8 a** Ezek 7:2; **b** Ezek 38:2, 9, 15

Gog and Magog represent pagan nations—those that have no religion and are interested only in what brings them pleasure *(see Ezekiel, chapters 38–39)*.

Study it!

The End . . .

In this vision the dragon (Satan) is chained up or imprisoned for a thousand years. The number 1,000 symbolizes *many*—too many to count. The dragon is not dead, yet, but he doesn't have much power because he's chained. After many years he will be set loose on the earth and cause destruction again. There will be another war between him and God's people, and this time the dragon will be thrown into hell for good. Christ will be victorious over evil for all time! Then all the dead will meet God and be "judged according to what they had done" (Revelation 20:13) with their lives.

—Revelation, chapter 20

for battle, as many as the grains of sand on
the seashore. 9 They spread out over the earth
and surrounded the camp of God's people
and the city that he loves. But fire came
down from heaven and destroyed them.
10 Then the Devil, who deceived them, was
thrown into the lake of fire and sulfur, where
the beast and the false prophet had already
been thrown; and they will be tormented
day and night forever and ever.

The Final Judgment

11 Then I saw a great white throne and the
one who sits on it. Earth and heaven fled
from his presence and were seen no more.
12 And I saw the dead, great and small alike,
standing before the throne. Books were
opened, and then another book was opened,
the book of the living. The dead were
judged according to what they had done, as
recorded in the books. 13 Then the sea gave
up its dead. Death and the world of the dead
also gave up the dead they held. And all were
judged according to what they had done.
14 Then death and the world of the dead
were thrown into the lake of fire. (This lake
of fire is the second death.) 15 Those who did
not have their name written in the book of
the living were thrown into the lake of fire.

The New Heaven and the New Earth

21 Then I saw a new heaven and a new
earth. The first heaven and the first
earth disappeared, and the sea vanished.
2 And I saw the Holy City, the new Jeru-
salem, coming down out of heaven from
God, prepared and ready, like a bride dressed
to meet her husband. 3 I heard a loud voice
speaking from the throne: "Now God's
home is with people! He will live with
them, and they shall be his people. God him-
self will be with them, and he will be their
God. 4 He will wipe away all tears from their
eyes. There will be no more death, no more
grief or crying or pain. The old things have
disappeared."

5 Then the one who sits on the throne
said, "And now I make all things new!" He
also said to me, "Write this, because these
words are true and can be trusted." 6 And he
said, "It is done! I am the first and the last,
the beginning and the end. To anyone who
is thirsty I will give the right to drink from
the spring of the water of life without pay-
ing for it. 7 Those who win the victory will
receive this from me: I will be their God,
and they will be my children. 8 But cowards,
traitors, perverts, murderers, the immoral,
those who practice magic, those who wor-
ship idols, and all liars—the place for them is
the lake burning with fire and sulfur, which
is the second death."

The New Jerusalem

9 One of the seven angels who had the
seven bowls full of the seven last plagues

20:11, 12 Dan 7:9, 10 **21:1** Isa 65:17; 66:22; 2 Pet 3:13 **21:2** **a** Isa 52:1; **b** Rev 3:12; **c** Isa 61:10
21:3 Ezek 37:27; Lev 26:11, 12 **21:4** **a** Isa 25:8; **b** Isa 35:10; 65:19 **21:6** Isa 55:1 **21:7** 2 Sam 7:14;
Ps 89:26, 27

Study it!

. . . And a Beginning

Genesis begins with creation, and Revelation ends with a new creation! All of earth and heaven are full of God's goodness that we were always meant to enjoy. In this holy city—the new Jerusalem which is a symbol of heaven—there will be nothing that causes us sadness or pain. We will experience only joy and love. The beauty of this city could take your breath away, because the glory of God shines on it and there is no night. Fresh delicious fruit grows all year, and a sparkling river—the river of life—flows from God's throne, for all to drink whenever they wish.

But this hasn't happened yet! John's visions are meant to bring hope to the early Christians when they are being persecuted. This new creation he dreams of will come to us when all evil and suffering are ended. Until that day comes, there will still be people who try to do good with their lives, as well as those who are wrapped up in sinful living. So we must do our part: try to be faithful; remember that God is stronger than pain and evil; and hold on to the hope that one day we will live in God's holy city forever!

— Revelation, chapter 21

came to me and said, "Come, and I will show
you the Bride, the wife of the Lamb." 10 The
Spirit took control of me, and the angel car-
ried me to the top of a very high mountain.
He showed me Jerusalem, the Holy City,
coming down out of heaven from God 11 and
shining with the glory of God. The city
shone like a precious stone, like a jasper, clear
as crystal. 12 It had a great, high wall with
twelve gates and with twelve angels in charge
of the gates. On the gates were written the
names of the twelve tribes of the people of
Israel. 13 There were three gates on each side:
three on the east, three on the south, three
on the north, and three on the west. 14 The
city's wall was built on twelve foundation
stones, on which were written the names of
the twelve apostles of the Lamb. 15 The angel
who spoke to me had a gold measuring stick
to measure the city, its gates, and its wall.
16 The city was perfectly square, as wide as it
was long. The angel measured the city with
his measuring stick: it was fifteen hundred
miles long and was as wide and as high as it
was long. 17 The angel also measured the wall,
and it was 216 feet high,[g] according to the
standard unit of measure which he was
using.[h] 18 The wall was made of jasper, and
the city itself was made of pure gold, as clear
as glass. 19 The foundation stones of the city
wall were adorned with all kinds of precious
stones. The first foundation stone was jasper,
the second sapphire, the third agate, the
fourth emerald, 20 the fifth onyx, the sixth
carnelian, the seventh yellow quartz, the
eighth beryl, the ninth topaz, the tenth chal-
cedony, the eleventh turquoise, the twelfth
amethyst. 21 The twelve gates were twelve
pearls; each gate was made from a single
pearl. The street of the city was of pure gold,
transparent as glass.

22 I did not see a temple in the city,
because its temple is the Lord God Almighty
and the Lamb. 23 The city has no need of the
sun or the moon to shine on it, because the
glory of God shines on it, and the Lamb is
its lamp. 24 The peoples of the world will
walk by its light, and the kings of the earth
will bring their wealth into it. 25 The gates of
the city will stand open all day; they will
never be closed, because there will be no
night there. 26 The greatness and the wealth

[g] **21:17** high; *or* thick. [h] **21:17** *In verses 16 and 17 the Greek text speaks of "12,000 furlongs" and "144 cubits" which may have symbolic significance.*

21:10 Ezek 40:2 **21:12, 13** Ezek 48:30–35 **21:15** Ezek 40:3 **21:18–21** Isa 54:11, 12
21:18 Tob 13:16, 17 **21:23** Isa 60:19, 20 **21:24** Isa 60:3 **21:25, 26** Isa 60:11

Catholic Connections

Heaven and Hell

Some of our images of heaven and hell come from chapters 20 and 21 of Revelation. Hell is described as "the lake of fire and sulfur" where "they will be tormented day and night forever and ever" (20:10). Heaven is like the Holy City described in chapter 21—everything is perfect and amazing. Heaven and hell are not physical places like the images John presents or in the way we usually think of places. But they are very real. And throughout our lives, the choices we make lead us to where we will spend eternity—with or without God, in pure joy or utter despair.

Being with God in heaven will be perfect and amazing! Heaven means perfect unity and joy with God, for eternity. We get glimpses of this on earth. Think of a really fun vacation you've taken or the thrilling moment of victory you share with teammates after a tough game. Those feelings are just a tiny fraction of the joy you'll feel *forever and ever* in heaven!

We experience hell-like moments as well: the death of a family member or getting caught in a serious lie. The sick, horrifying feeling in the pit of your stomach is nothing compared with the misery that hell brings. In life, the person who rejects God moves deeper into sin and unhappiness. At death the separation from God is complete and the suffering is unbearable.

— Revelation, chapters 20–21

of the nations will be brought into the city.
27But nothing that is impure will enter the
city, nor anyone who does shameful things
or tells lies. Only those whose names are
written in the Lamb's book of the living will
enter the city.

22 The angel also showed me the river
of the water of life, sparkling like
crystal, and coming from the throne of God
and of the Lamb 2and flowing down the
middle of the city's street. On each side of
the river was the tree of life, which bears
fruit twelve times a year, once each month;
and its leaves are for the healing of the
nations. 3Nothing that is under God's curse
will be found in the city.
The throne of God and of the Lamb will
be in the city, and his servants will worship
him. 4They will see his face, and his name
will be written on their foreheads. 5There
shall be no more night, and they will not
need lamps or sunlight, because the Lord
God will be their light, and they will rule as
kings forever and ever.

The Coming of Jesus

6Then the angel said to me, "These words
are true and can be trusted. And the Lord
God, who gives his Spirit to the prophets,
has sent his angel to show his servants what
must happen very soon."

21:27 Isa 52:1; Ezek 44:9 **22:1** Ezek 47:1; Zech 14:8 **22:2** Gen 2:9 **22:3** Zech 14:11 (cp. Gen 3:17) **22:5** **a** Isa 60:19; **b** Dan 7:18

"There will be no more death, no more grief or crying or pain" *(Revelation 21:4)*.

Live it!

Have Hope!

Poor Antonia. She has three tests this week plus a major project due—and the rest of her project teammates aren't pulling their weight, so she's getting stuck with all the work! She got a detention for chewing gum in class, her volleyball team lost in the last seconds of finals because she missed a play, her parents are constantly fighting, her grandpa's cancer seems to be getting worse, and she caught her best friend saying nasty things about her behind her back. On top of that, she's got a big zit on her nose! She feels like she's getting crushed under the pressure of it all.

Isn't that how life is sometimes? Some days feel like everything is falling apart around us, and it will all come crashing down on us and squish us like a bug!

Hang in there, and keep reading the Book of Revelation! John's message for us is the same one the early Christians needed to hear: Have hope! God is keeping us afloat in our sea of troubles. All the pain, embarrassment, unfairness, anxiety—it will not get the best of us!

— Revelation, chapter 22

7 "Listen!" says Jesus. "I am coming soon!
Happy are those who obey the prophetic
words in this book!"

8 I, John, have heard and seen all these
things. And when I finished hearing and see-
ing them, I fell down at the feet of the angel
who had shown me these things, and I was
about to worship him. 9 But he said to me,
"Don't do it! I am a servant together with
you and with your brothers the prophets and
of all those who obey the words in this
book. Worship God!" 10 And he said to me,
"Do not keep the prophetic words of this
book a secret, because the time is near when
all this will happen. 11 Whoever is evil must
go on doing evil, and whoever is filthy must
go on being filthy; whoever is good must go
on doing good, and whoever is holy must go
on being holy."

12 "Listen!" says Jesus. "I am coming soon!
I will bring my rewards with me, to give to
each one according to what he has done. 13 I
am the first and the last, the beginning and
the end."

14 Happy are those who wash their robes
clean and so have the right to eat the fruit
from the tree of life and to go through the
gates into the city. 15 But outside the city are
the perverts and those who practice magic,
the immoral and the murderers, those who
worship idols and those who are liars both
in words and deeds.

16 "I, Jesus, have sent my angel to an-
nounce these things to you in the churches.
I am descended from the family of David; I
am the bright morning star."

17 The Spirit and the Bride say, "Come!"
Everyone who hears this must also say,
"Come!"

Come, whoever is thirsty; accept the water
of life as a gift, whoever wants it.

Conclusion

18 I, John, solemnly warn everyone who
hears the prophetic words of this book: if
any add anything to them, God will add to
their punishment the plagues described in
this book. 19 And if any take anything away

22:11 Dan 12:10 **22:12** **a** Isa 40:10; 62:11; **b** Ps 28:4; Isa 40:10; Jer 17:10 **22:13** **a** Rev 1:8; **b** Isa 44:6; 48:12; Rev 1:17; 2:8 **22:14** Gen 2:9; 3:22 **22:16** Isa 11:1, 10 **22:17** Isa 55:1 **22:18, 19** Deut 4:2; 12:32

The phrase "So be it" ***(Revelation 3:20)*** **is a translation of the word** ***amen.*** **Whenever we pray, "Amen," we are saying, "So be it!"**

from the prophetic words of this book, God will take away from them their share of the fruit of the tree of life and of the Holy City, which are described in this book.

20 He who gives his testimony to all this
says, "Yes indeed! I am coming soon!"
So be it. Come, Lord Jesus!
21 May the grace of the Lord Jesus be with
everyone.[i]

[i] **22:21** everyone; *some manuscripts have* God's people; *others have* all of God's people.

Your Next Step

Congratulations on finishing the Book of Revelation! Use this space to write your thoughts and questions about this book. If you have been reading through the books in order, you have come to the end of this Bible reading plan. But your journey is not over! Here are a few suggestions for continuing your Bible journey:

- **Read some of the books that this reading plan skipped.**
- **Each week read the Gospel that will be read in the upcoming Sunday Mass. You can find Sunday readings listed in "Reading the Bible with the Church," starting on page 1883.**
- **Go back and reread some of the books or sections you found especially interesting or confusing. Ask a leader in your church for some help in understanding them.**

Let reading and studying the Bible become a lifelong practice!

Study Helps

Where To Find It?

Old Testament Stories

These stories are listed in the order in which they first appear in the Bible.

Creation, *Genesis, chapters 1–2*
original sin and its punishment, *Genesis, chapter 3*
Cain and Abel, *Genesis 4:1–16*
Noah and the Great Flood, *Genesis, chapters 6–9*
God's covenant with Abraham, *Genesis 17:1—18:15*
God's command to sacrifice Isaac, *Genesis 22:1–19*
Isaac's blessing of Jacob, *Genesis 27:1–29*
Jacob's dream, *Genesis 28:10–22*
Joseph and his brothers, *Genesis, chapters 37–46*
birth and youth of Moses, *Exodus 2:1–10*
Moses at the burning bush, *Exodus 3:1–12*
plagues on Egypt, *Exodus, chapters 7–12*
Passover and the Exodus, *Exodus, chapters 12–14*
Ten Commandments, *Exodus 20:1–17*
destruction of Jericho, *Joshua 5:13—6:27*
Gideon and the fleece, *Judges 6:36–40*
Samson, *Judges, chapters 13–16*
Samuel's birth and calling, *1 Samuel, chapters 1–3*
David and Goliath, *1 Samuel, chapter 17*
David and Bathsheba, *2 Samuel, chapter 11*
Solomon's wisdom, *1 Kings, chapter 3*
Elijah's triumph over the priests of Baal, *1 Kings 18:21–40*
miracles of Elisha, *2 Kings 4:1—6:23*
return from Exile, *Ezra, chapter 1*
battles of Judas Maccabeus, *1 Maccabees, chapters 3–5*
Ezekiel and the valley of dry bones, *Ezekiel 37:1–14*
Daniel, *Daniel, chapters 1–6*
Jonah and the Ninevites, *Jonah, chapters 1–3*

New Testament Stories

These stories are listed in the order in which they first appear in the Bible.

birth of Jesus, *Matthew 1:18—2:12; Luke, chapters 1–2*
baptism of Jesus, *Matthew 3:13–17; Mark 1:9–11; Luke 3:21–22*
temptation of Jesus, *Matthew 4:1–11; Mark 1:12–13; Luke 4:1–13*
Peter's declaration about Jesus, *Matthew 16:13–20; Mark 8:27–30; Luke 9:18–20*
Transfiguration of Jesus, *Matthew 17:1–13; Mark 9:2–13; Luke 9:28–36*
Jesus' triumphal entry into Jerusalem, *Matthew 21:1–11; Mark 11:1–11; Luke 19:28–40; John 12:12–19*
Jesus in the Temple, *Matthew 21:12–17; Mark 11:15–19; Luke 19:45–48; John 2:13–17*
Judas's betrayal of Jesus, *Matthew 26:14–16,47–56; Mark 14:10–11,43–52; Luke 22:1–53; John 13:21–30; 18:1–5*
Last Supper, *Matthew 26:17–30; Mark 14:12–26; Luke 22:7–38; 1 Corinthians 11:23–26*

Jesus at Gethsemane, *Matthew 26:36–56; Mark 14:32–52; Luke 22:39–53*
Peter's denial of Christ, *Matthew 26:69–75; Mark 14:66–72; Luke 22:54–62; John 18:15–18,25–27*
Crucifixion, *Matthew 27:32–56; Mark 15:21–41; Luke 23:26–49; John 19:16–30*
Resurrection and appearances, *Matthew, chapter 28; Mark, chapter 16; Luke, chapter 24; John, chapters 20–21; Acts 1:1–11*
Jesus washing his disciples' feet, *John 13:1–17*
Holy Spirit at Pentecost, *Acts 2:1–41*
stoning of Stephen, *Acts, chapters 6–7*
conversion of Saul, *Acts 9:1–30*
Peter's escape from prison, *Acts 12:1–19*
Paul and Silas's escape from prison, *Acts 16:16–40*
Paul's journey to Rome for his trial, *Acts, chapters 27–28*

Prayers

These prayers are listed in the order in which they first appear in the Bible.

The LORD bless you and take care of you, *Numbers 6:24–27*
Hannah's prayer, *1 Samuel 2:1–10*
Speak, LORD, for your servant is listening, *1 Samuel 3:9–10*
Blessed be the Lord, *1 Kings 8:56–61*
Tobit's thanksgiving, *Tobit, chapter 13*
Judith's hymn of praise, *Judith 16:1–17*
The LORD is my shepherd, *Psalm 23*
Be merciful to me, O God, *Psalm 51*
LORD, you have examined me and you know me, *Psalm 139*
Holy, holy, holy (Hosanna), *Isaiah 6:3; Matthew 21:9; Mark 11:9–10; Luke 19:38; John 12:13; Revelation 4:8*
Lord's Prayer, *Matthew 6:9–15; Luke 11:2–4*
Lord, I am not worthy, *Matthew 8:8*
Jesus' prayer for deliverance, *Matthew 26:39; Mark 14:36; Luke 22:42*
Mary's song of praise, *Luke 1:46–55*
Zechariah's prophecy, *Luke 1:68–79*
Glory to God in the highest, *Luke 2:14*
Simeon's prayer, *Luke 2:29–32*
God, have pity on me, a sinner!, *Luke 18:13*
Lamb of God, *John 1:29*
Jesus' prayer for his disciples, *John, chapter 17*
Paul's prayer for the Ephesians, *Ephesians 3:14–21*
Amen, *1 Peter 5:11; Jude, verse 25; Revelation 1:6–7; 22:20–21*

Miracles of Jesus

These miracle stories are listed in the order in which they first appear in the Bible.

Healing Individuals

sin disease, *Matthew 8:1–4; Mark 1:40–45; Luke 5:12–16*
centurion's servant, *Matthew 8:5–13; Luke 7:1–10*
many at Peter's house, *Matthew 8:14–17; Mark 1:29–34; Luke 4:38–41*
Gadarene (Gerasene) demoniacs, *Matthew 8:28–34; Mark 5:1–20; Luke 8:26–39*
paralytic, *Matthew 9:1–8; Mark 2:1–12; Luke 5:17–26*
woman with bleeding, *Matthew 9:20–22; Mark 5:25–34; Luke 8:43–48*
two blind men, *Matthew 9:27–31*
mute man, *Matthew 9:32–34*

man with a paralyzed hand,
Matthew 12:9–13; Mark 3:1–5; Luke 6:6–11
blind, mute, and possessed man,
Matthew 12:22
Canaanite woman's daughter,
Matthew 15:21–28; Mark 7:24–30
boy with a demon, *Matthew 17:14–21; Mark 9:14–29; Luke 9:37–43*
blind man (Bartimaeus),
Matthew 20:29–34; Mark 10:46–52; Luke 18:35–43
man with an unclean spirit,
Mark 1:21–28; Luke 4:31–37
deaf man, *Mark 7:31–37*
blind man at Bethsaida, *Mark 8:22–26*
crippled woman, *Luke 13:11–13*
sick man, *Luke 14:1–4*
ten men with skin diseases,
Luke 17:11–19
High Priest's slave, *Luke 22:50–51*
official's son, *John 4:46–54*
man at the pool of Bethzatha,
John 5:1–9

Controlling Nature

stilling the storm, *Matthew 8:23–27; Mark 4:35–41; Luke 8:22–25*
feeding five thousand,
Matthew 14:13–21; Mark 6:30–44; Luke 9:10–17; John 6:1–14
walking on water, *Matthew 14:22–33; Mark 6:45–52; John 6:16–21*
feeding four thousand,
Matthew 15:32–39; Mark 8:1–10
fish with a coin, *Matthew 17:24–27*
fig tree withers, *Matthew 21:18–22; Mark 11:12–14,20–25*
huge catch of fish, *Luke 5:1–11; John 21:1–11*
turning water into wine, *John 2:1–11*

Raising the Dead

Jairus's daughter,
Matthew 9:18–19,23–26; Mark 5:21–24,35–43; Luke 8:40–42,49–56
widow's son at Nain, *Luke 7:11–17*
Lazarus, *John 11:1–44*

Parables of Jesus

These parables are listed in alphabetical order.

unfruitful fig tree, *Luke 13:6–9*
canceled debts, *Luke 7:41–43*
cost of discipleship, *Luke 14:25–33*
dishonest manager, *Luke 16:1–8*
faithful or unfaithful slave,
Matthew 24:45–51; Luke 12:42–48
fig tree, *Matthew 24:32–35; Mark 13:28–31; Luke 21:29–33*
good Samaritan, *Luke 10:30–37*
great feast, *Luke 14:16–24*
growing seed, *Mark 4:26–29*
hidden treasure and pearl,
Matthew 13:44–46
honor at a banquet, *Luke 14:7–14*
workers in the vineyard,
Matthew 20:1–16
light of the world, *Matthew 5:14–16*
lost coin, *Luke 15:8–10*
lost sheep, *Matthew 18:12–14; Luke 15:3–7*
mustard seed, *Matthew 13:31–32; Mark 4:30–32; Luke 13:18–19*
net, *Matthew 13:47–50*
new wine in old wineskins,
Matthew 9:16–17; Mark 2:21–22; Luke 5:36–39
persistent friend, *Luke 11:5–8*
persistent widow, *Luke 18:2–8*
Pharisee and the tax collector,
Luke 18:10–14
lost son, *Luke 15:11–32*
rich fool, *Luke 12:16–21*

Teachings of Jesus

These teachings are listed in alphabetical order.

Catholic Connections article list

The "Catholic Connections" articles show how the teachings of the Catholic Church are rooted in the Bible. If you read them all, the "Catholic Connections" articles provide a simple overview of the Catholic faith. This index will help you find those articles. The articles are arranged to reflect the order in which they are explained in the *Catechism of the Catholic Church*. Keep in mind that there is much more to be learned about the Catholic faith than what is covered in these short articles.

The Creed (Part One of the *Catechism of the Catholic Church*)

Liturgy and the Sacraments (Part Two of the *Catechism of the Catholic Church*)

Christian Morality (Part Three of the *Catechism of the Catholic Church*)

Christian Prayer (Part Four of the *Catechism of the Catholic Church*)

Bible Passages for Special Occasions

God speaks to us though the words of the Bible. Here are some suggestions for passages to read and reflect on at important moments in your life. Approach these passages in confidence that God wants you to feel his love and presence.

When you need a good friend or want to be a good friend:
- ☐ 1 Samuel, chapter 20
- ☐ Sirach 6:5–17
- ☐ John 15:12–17
- ☐ Colossians 3:12–17

When you are feeling hopeless:
- ☐ Psalm 42
- ☐ Matthew 11:28–30
- ☐ Romans 8:18–39
- ☐ 1 Peter 1:3–9

When you are feeling happy:
- ☐ Psalm 40
- ☐ Psalm 150
- ☐ Sirach 25:1–11
- ☐ Philippians 4:4–9

When you are acting as a leader:
- ☐ 1 Kings 3:4–14
- ☐ Mark 10:35–45
- ☐ 1 Timothy 4:4–12

When preparing for a big game or competition:
- ☐ 1 Corinthians 9:23–27
- ☐ 2 Timothy 2:5

When someone you love has died:
- ☐ Psalm 90
- ☐ John 3:16–17
- ☐ 1 Corinthians 15:50–57
- ☐ 1 Thessalonians 4:13–18

When you are facing temptation:
- ☐ Genesis 3:1–21
- ☐ Matthew 4:1–11
- ☐ 1 Timothy 6:6–10
- ☐ James 1:12–18

At the beginning of the school year:
- ☐ Proverbs, chapter 1
- ☐ Proverbs 10:1,4,13–14,23
- ☐ 1 Corinthians 2:6–8

When you want to be a better follower of Jesus:
- ☐ Mark 8:34–38
- ☐ Luke 6:20–49

When you want to be a better follower of Jesus: ***(continued)***
- ☐ Ephesians 5:1–20
- ☐ James 1:19–27

When you are feeling angry or want revenge:
- ☐ Proverbs 25:21–22
- ☐ Matthew 5:21–24,38–42
- ☐ Romans 12:17–21
- ☐ Ephesians 4:25–32

When you want to know that God loves you:
- ☐ Exodus 34:5–6
- ☐ Psalm 36:5–12
- ☐ Psalm 59:16–17
- ☐ Psalm 139
- ☐ John 15:1–17
- ☐ Romans 5:6–8

When you or someone you know is sick:
- ☐ Psalm 23
- ☐ Luke 7:21–23
- ☐ James 5:14–15
- ☐ 1 Peter 3:3–17

When you are having problems controlling your tongue:
- ☐ Proverbs 10:18–21
- ☐ Sirach 28:12–26
- ☐ Matthew 12:33–37
- ☐ James 3:1–12

During times of violence or war:
- ☐ Proverbs 3:31–33
- ☐ Micah 4:1–4
- ☐ Luke 12:4–7
- ☐ John 14:27–31

When you are overcome by sexual feelings:
- ☐ Genesis 1:26–31
- ☐ Matthew 19:3–9
- ☐ 1 Corinthians 6:12–20
- ☐ Ephesians 5:1–5

Word List

This word list identifies many objects or cultural features whose meaning may not be known to all readers.

Abib. The first month of the Hebrew calendar, corresponding to the period from about mid-March to about mid-April. This month is also called Nisan.

Abyss. The place in the depths of the earth where the demons were imprisoned until their final punishment.

Acacia. A flowering tree, a type of mimosa, with hard and durable wood.

Adar. The twelfth month of the Hebrew calendar, corresponding to the period from about mid-February to about mid-March.

Agate. A semiprecious stone of various colors, but usually white and brown.

Alabaster. A soft stone of usually light, creamy color; vases and jars were made from it.

Aloes. A sweet-smelling substance, derived from a plant. It was used medicinally and as a perfume.

Amen. A Hebrew word that means "it is so" or "may it be so." It can also be translated "certainly," "truly," or "surely." In Revelation 3:14 it is used as a title for Christ.

Amethyst. A semiprecious stone, usually purple or violet in color.

Anoint. To pour or rub olive oil on someone in order to honor him or appoint him to some special work. The Israelite kings were anointed as a sign of their taking office, and so the king could be called "the anointed one." In a figurative sense, "The Anointed One" is the title of the one whom God chose and appointed as Savior and Lord.

Apostle. Principally one of the group of twelve men whom Jesus chose to be his special followers and helpers. It is also used in the New Testament to refer to Paul. The word means "one who is sent."

Areopagus. A hill in Athens where the city council used to meet. For this reason the council itself was called Areopagus, even after it no longer met on the hill.

Artemis. The Greek name of an ancient goddess of fertility, worshiped especially in Asia Minor.

Asherah. A goddess of fertility worshiped by the Canaanites; her male counterpart was Baal. After the Hebrews invaded Canaan, many of them began worshiping these two gods.

Astarte. A goddess of fertility and war who was widely worshiped in the ancient Near East.

Atonement, Day of. The most important of Israel's holy days, when the High Priest would offer a sacrifice for the sins of the people of Israel (Leviticus, chapter 16). It was held on the tenth day of the seventh month of the Hebrew calendar (around October 1). The Jewish name for this day is Yom Kippur.

Baal. The god of fertility worshiped by the Canaanites; his female counterpart was Asherah. After the Hebrews invaded Canaan, many of them began worshiping these two gods.

Baal-of-the-Covenant. A name by which the god Baal was known by the people of Shechem.

Babylon. The name of a city and an empire that existed in the ancient Middle East. The Babylonians destroyed Jerusalem and Solomon's Temple in 587 BC. Some early Christians used the name Babylon as a code word for the Roman Empire. They saw the Romans persecuting Christians like the Babylonians persecuted the Israelites.

Balsam. A tree from which sweet-smelling resin was obtained; the resin was used for perfume and medicine.

Barley. A cultivated grain similar to wheat, grown as a food crop.

Beelzebul. A New Testament name given to the Devil as the chief of the evil spirits.

Beryl. A semiprecious stone, usually green or bluish green in color.

Blasphemy. Insulting God or being disrespectful toward God. People thought Jesus was committing blasphemy by claiming to forgive sins.

Breastplate. Part of a soldier's armor, made of leather or metal; it covered the chest and sometimes the back as a protection against arrows and the blows of a sword.

Bul. The eighth month of the Hebrew calendar, corresponding to the period from about mid-October to about mid-November.

Burnt offering. A type of sacrifice in which all the parts of the animal were completely burned on the altar; in other sacrifices only certain parts of the animal were burned.

Calamus. A sweet-smelling reed-like plant.

Capital. The top part of a column supporting a roof.

Carnelian. A semiprecious stone, usually red in color.

Cassia. A spice made from the bark of a tree; it closely resembles cinnamon.

Chalcedony. A semiprecious stone, usually milky or gray in color.

Christ. Originally a title, the Greek equivalent of the Hebrew word *Messiah*. It means "the anointed one." Jesus was called the Christ because he was the one whom God chose and sent as Savior and Lord.

Circumcise. To cut off the foreskin of the penis. As a sign of God's covenant with his people, Israelite boys were circumcised eight days after they were born (Genesis 17:9–14).

Cistern. A type of well that holds rainwater. Cisterns are an important source of water for people in dry lands.

City of refuge. When the people of Israel moved into the land of Canaan, they were told to name certain towns as cities of refuge. If anyone accidentally killed someone, he could escape to one of these cities and be safe from revenge (see Numbers 35:9–34; Deuteronomy 4:41–43, 19:1–13; Joshua 20:1–9).

Concubine. A servant woman who, although not a wife, had sexual relations with her master. She had important legal rights, and her master was referred to as her husband.

Coral. A brightly colored stony substance found in the sea; it was used as jewelry.

Council. The supreme religious court of the Jews, composed of seventy leaders of the Jewish people and presided over by the High Priest.

Covenant. An agreement, either between persons or between God and a person or a people. God made a covenant with Noah (Genesis 9:8–17) and with Abraham (Genesis 17:1–8), but in the Old Testament, the term usually refers to the covenant made between God and the people of Israel at the time of Moses (Exodus 24:4–8).

Covenant Box. The wooden chest covered with gold in which were kept the two stone tablets on which were written the Ten Commandments. It has traditionally been called the Ark of the Covenant.

Cumin. A small plant whose seeds are ground up and used for seasoning foods.

Cush. The term *Cush* in the Old Testament Hebrew text normally designates the territory extending south from the First Cataract of the Nile River at Aswan. It was known in Graeco-Roman times as Ethiopia (Greek, *Aithiopia*), and later as Nubia. In Genesis, chapter 10, the Table of Nations, verses 8–12 are included under the genealogy of Egyptian Cush, yet all the peoples named are in Mesopotamia. Apparently the Hebrew designation for the Babylonian Kassites was "Cush" as well, thus resulting in the mixing of the two regions. Genesis 2:13 may be another reference to Babylonian Cush.

Cymbals. A pair of thin pieces of metal held in the hands and struck together rhythmically in music.

David's City. In the Old Testament, the reference is generally to that part of the city of Jerusalem that was captured from the Jebusites by King David. In the New Testament, the reference is to the town of Bethlehem, David's boyhood home, where Jesus was born.

Dedication, Festival of. The Jewish festival, lasting eight days, that celebrated the restoration and rededication in 165 BC of the Temple altar by the Jewish patriot Judas Maccabeus. The festival began on the twenty-fifth day of the month Kislev (around December 10). The Jewish name for this festival is Hanukkah.

Defile. To make ritually unclean or impure. Certain foods and practices were prohibited by the Law of Moses because they were thought to make a person ritually or ceremonially unclean. Such a person could not take part in the public worship until he had performed certain rituals that would remove the defilement.

Demon. An evil spirit with the power to harm people; it was regarded as a messenger and servant of the Devil.

Dill. A Small garden plant whose stems, leaves, and seeds are used for seasoning food.

Dipper: Big Dipper and Little Dipper. Two groups of stars that in the Northern Hemisphere are visible in the northern sky. The star at the end of the "handle" of the Little Dipper is Polaris, the North Star.

Disciple. A person who follows and learns from someone else. In the New Testament, the word is used of the followers of John the Baptist and especially of the followers of Jesus, particularly the twelve Apostles.

Divination. The attempt to discover a message from God or the gods by examining such things as marked stones or the liver of a sacrificed animal.

Dragon. A legendary beast, thought to be like a huge lizard. It is also called a serpent and appears as a figure of the Devil (Revelation 12:3—13:4; 20:2,3).

Elders. In the Old Testament, this is a name given to certain respected leaders of a tribe, nation, or city. In the New Testament, three different groups are called elders: (1) in the Gospels the elders were influential Jewish religious leaders, some of whom were members of the supreme Council; (2) in Acts, chapters 11–21 and the Letters, the elders are Christian Church officers who had a general responsibility for the work of the Church; (3) in Revelation the twenty-four elders are part of God's court in heaven, perhaps as representatives of God's people.

Elul. The sixth month of the Hebrew calendar, corresponding to the period from about mid-August to about mid-September.

Ephod. The Hebrew term traditionally transliterated as "ephod" is of uncertain meaning in a number of contexts. Generally it refers to some type of priestly garment that was worn over the shoulder by the High Priest and with which the Urim and Thummim were associated. In certain contexts, however, the Hebrew term refers to an object of worship, and in some other passages, it evidently refers to an object used to foretell future events.

Epicureans. Those who followed the teaching of Epicurus (died 270 BC), a Greek philosopher who taught that happiness is the highest good in life.

Epileptic. A person who suffers from a nervous disease causing convulsions and fainting.

Ethanim. The seventh month of the Hebrew calendar, corresponding to the period from about mid-September to about mid-October; it was later called Tishri.

Ethiopia. *See* Cush.

Eunuch. A man who has been made physically incapable of having normal sexual relations. Eunuchs were often important officials in the courts of ancient kings, and the term may have come to be used of such officials in general, regardless of their sexual condition.

Exile, the. About 721 BC the Assyrians conquered northern Israel and the Israelite territory east of the Jordan River and deported the people (see 2 Kings 15:29; 1 Chronicles 5:22). In 587 BC the Babylonians conquered the southern kingdom of Judah, destroyed Jerusalem and the Temple, and deported the people to Babylon (see 2 Kings 25; 2 Chronicles 36:5–21). This is called the Exile.

Exodus. A term that means "departure." The main event in the book with this name is the departure of the Israelites from Egypt.

Fast. To go without food for a while as a religious duty.

Feldspar. A colorful, rather hard rock, often glassy in appearance.

Fellowship offerings. A type of sacrifice offered to ensure a right relationship with God. Only a portion of the animal was burned on the altar; the rest was eaten by the worshipers or the priests.

Flax. A Small cultivated plant; the fibers of its stem are spun into thread used in making linen cloth.

Frankincense. A valuable incense, made from the sap of a certain tree. This incense was probably imported from Arabia.

Fruits of the Holy Spirit. The effects in a person's life that come from the work of the Holy Spirit. See Galatians 5:22–23, where the fruits are listed as love, joy, peace, patience, kindness, goodness, faithfulness, humility, and self-control.

Garnet. A semiprecious stone, usually red in color.

Gazelle. A kind of antelope, known for its beauty and gracefulness.

Genesis. A word that means "source" or "beginning." It means that the Book of Genesis is about the beginning of things: the world, human beings, sin, the Covenant with God.

Gentile. A person who is not a Jew.

Hades. The Greek name used in the New Testament to refer to the world of the dead.

Harrow. A farm implement used to break up the ground and level it after plowing.

Harvest Festival. The Israelite festival celebrating the wheat harvest, held in the latter part of May or early June, fifty days after Passover. The Jewish name for this festival is Shavuoth (the Feast of Weeks). It has also been called Pentecost.

Heathens. People who do not worship God as revealed in the Bible.

Hermes. The name of a Greek god who served as messenger of the gods.

Herod's party. A political party in New Testament times composed of Jews who favored being ruled by one of the descendants of Herod the Great rather than by the Roman governor.

High Priest. The priest who occupied the highest office in the Jewish priestly system and was president of the supreme Council of the Jews. Once a year (on the Day of Atonement) he would enter the Most Holy Place in the Temple and offer sacrifice for himself and for the sins of the people of Israel.

Hyssop. A small, bushy plant used in religious ceremonies to sprinkle liquids.

Idolatry. Worshiping false gods, people, or material things in a way that is fitting for God alone.

Incense. Material that is burned to produce a pleasant smell. The Israelites used it in their worship.

Jackal. A small wild animal resembling a fox.

Jasper. A semiprecious stone of various colors. The jasper mentioned in the Bible was probably green, or else clear.

Javelin. A short, light spear used by soldiers in ancient times.

Justice. Being right and fair in relationships with other people. For the prophets it especially meant the quality of caring for the poor and outcast.

Kislev. The ninth month of the Hebrew calendar, corresponding to the period from about mid-November to about mid-December.

Law. The name the Jews applied to the first five books of the Old Testament, also called the Torah or the Pentateuch. Sometimes, however, the name is applied in a more general way to the entire Old Testament.

Leviathan. A legendary animal associated with water, in some passages identified by some scholars as the crocodile. In a figurative sense, it may represent the chaos that existed before God created the world (Job 3:8; Psalm 74:14; Isaiah 27:1).

Levite. (1) A member of the tribe of Levi; (2) a man who assisted the priest in the performance of religious duties.

Levitical priest. A Hebrew priest descended from the tribe of Levi. All priests were supposed to be members of the tribe of Levi, but in later times not all members of the tribe of Levi were priests.

Living creatures. Also referred to as "winged creatures" and traditionally called "cherubim," they were symbols of God's majesty and associated with his presence. For a description of such creatures, see Exodus 25:18–20; Ezekiel 1:5–13, chapter 10; Revelation 4:6–9.

Lord. Where the Hebrew text has Yahweh, sometimes transliterated as Jehovah, this translation employs Lord with capital letters, following a usage that is widespread in English versions. See, for example, Genesis 2:4 and Exodus 3:14. This corresponds either to the occurrence of the name itself or to a pronoun standing for the name.

Lyre. A kind of harp.

Mandrake. A small plant; it was believed that eating its root or fruit would make a woman more easily able to have children.

Manna. A food eaten by the Israelites during their travels in the wilderness. It was white and flaky and looked like small seeds (Exodus 16:14–21; Numbers 11:7–9).

Medium. A person who believes that he or she can communicate with the dead.

Mercy. Having forgiveness and loving kindness for a person who does something wrong.

Messiah. A Hebrew title (meaning "the anointed one") given to the promised Savior, whose coming was foretold by the Hebrew prophets; the corresponding Greek term "the Christ" has the same meaning.

Michael. An archangel, one of God's chief angels. His name was the war cry of the good angels in the battle against Satan and his followers.

Mildew. A fungus that appears on various objects, especially in damp weather.

Millet. A cultivated grain grown as a food crop.

Molech. One of the gods of the ancient people of Canaan.

Most Holy Place. The innermost room of the Tent of the Lord's presence or the Temple. The Covenant Box was kept there. Only the High Priest could enter the Most Holy Place, and he did so only once a year, on the Day of Atonement.

Mustard. A large plant that grows from a very small seed. The seeds were ground into powder and used as spice on food.

Myrrh. A sweet-smelling resin that was highly prized. It served as a medicine (Mark 15:23) and was used by the Jews in preparing bodies for burial (John 19:39).

Myrtle. A kind of evergreen shrub or tree.

Nard. An expensive perfume made from a plant.

Nazarene. Someone from the town of Nazareth. The name was used as a title for Jesus and also as a name for the early Christians (Acts 24:5).

Nazirite. A person who took a special vow of self-dedication. Such a person was not to drink beer or wine, cut his hair, or touch a dead body (Numbers 6:1–21). The vow could be taken for a certain period of time, but some persons were dedicated to God as Nazirites from their birth.

New Moon Festival. A religious observance held by the Israelites on the day of each new moon.

New Year Festival. The Jewish name for this festival is Rosh Hashanah.

Nisan. The first month of the Hebrew calendar, corresponding to the period from about mid-March to about mid-April. The month is also called Abib.

Onyx. A semiprecious stone of various colors.

Orion. A group of prominent stars visible during winter evenings.

Outcasts. In the Gospels this name, which in many translations appears as "sinners," refers to those Jews who had been excluded from synagogue worship because they violated rules about foods that should not be eaten and about associating with people who were not Jews. Such outcasts were despised by many of their fellow Jews, and Jesus was criticized for associating with them (Mark 2:15–17; Luke 7:34; 15:1–2).

Parable. A story that uses objects and experiences that people are familiar with to teach spiritual truth. It was often used by Jesus.

Paradise. A name for heaven (Luke 23:43; 2 Corinthians 12:3).

Passover. The Israelite festival which begins on the evening after the fourteenth day of the month Nisan (around April 1), that celebrated the deliverance of the ancient Hebrews from their captivity in Egypt. The Angel of Death killed the first-born in the Egyptian homes but passed over the Hebrew homes (Exodus 12:23–27). The Jewish name for this festival is Pesach.

Pentecost, Day of. The Greek name for the Israelite festival of wheat harvest (*see* Harvest Festival). The name Pentecost (meaning "fiftieth") comes from the fact that the feast was held fifty days after Passover.

Pervert. One who commits unnatural sexual acts.

Pharisees. A Jewish religious party during the time of Jesus. They were strict in obeying the Law of Moses and other regulations that had been added to it through the centuries.

Pistachio nut. A small, greenish nut.

Plagues. Disastrous evils or afflictions that cause much destruction and sometimes death.

Pleiades. A small group of stars visible during winter evenings.

Pomegranate. A reddish fruit about the size of a large apple; it has a hard rind and is full of tasty seeds.

Preparation, Day of. The sixth day of the week (Friday), on which the Jews made the required preparation to observe the Sabbath (Saturday).

Pride. Loving yourself or loving success more than God or others. It is one of the capital sins because it leads to other sins.

Prophet. A person who proclaims a message from God. The term usually refers to certain men and women in the Old Testament, but the New Testament speaks of prophets in the early Church. John the Baptist is also called a prophet.

Purim. The Jewish religious holiday held on the fourteenth day of the month Adar (around March 1), celebrating the deliverance of the Jews from Haman by Esther and Mordecai. The story is told in the book of Esther.

Quartz. A semiprecious stone of various colors, but usually clear.

Rabbi. A Hebrew word that means "my teacher."

Rahab. (1) A legendary sea monster that represented the forces of chaos and evil (Psalm 89:10) and was sometimes used as a symbol of Egypt (Isaiah, chapter 51); (2) a Canaanite woman who helped the Israelite spies escape from Jericho (Joshua, chapter 2; Hebrews 11:31).

Red Sea. Evidently referred originally to (1) a series of lakes and marshes between the head of the Gulf of Suez and the Mediterranean, the region generally regarded as the site of the events described in Exodus, chapter 13, and was also used to designate (2) the Gulf of Suez, and (3) the Gulf of Aqaba.

Rephan. The name of an ancient god that was worshiped as the ruler of the planet Saturn.

Resin. A fragrant, gummy substance produced from the sap of certain trees and shrubs.

Restoration, Year of. The year, coming every fifty years, when the ancient Israelites returned to the original owner any property they were holding, freed their Israelite slaves, and did not cultivate their fields.

Sabbath. The seventh day of the Jewish week (from sundown on Friday to sundown on Saturday), a holy day on which no work was permitted.

Sackcloth. A coarse cloth made of goats' hair, which was worn as a sign of mourning or distress.

Sadducees. A small Jewish religious party in New Testament times, composed largely of priests. They based their beliefs primarily on the first five books of the Old Testament and differed in several matters of belief and practice from the larger party of the Pharisees.

Samaritan. A name used to refer to a native of Samaria, the region between Judea and Galilee. Because of differences in politics, race, customs, and religion (including especially the central place of worship), there was much bad feeling between the Jews and the Samaritans.

Sanctuary. A building dedicated to the worship of God. Sometimes the word refers to the central place of worship and not to the whole building.

Sapphire. A very valuable stone, usually blue in color.

Scepter. A short rod held by kings to symbolize their authority.

Scorpion. A small creature that has eight legs and a long tail with a poisonous sting. It can inflict a very painful, and sometimes fatal, wound.

Scribe. A person whose business it was to write documents for others or to copy written material. Some scribes were employed by ancient kings to prepare official documents, and some of them became important officials.

Scriptures. In the New Testament, the word refers to the collected body of Hebrew sacred writings known to Christians as the Old Testament. Various names are used: the Law (or the Law of Moses) and the prophets (Matthew 5:17; 7:12; Luke 2:22; 24:44; Acts 13:15; 28:23), the Holy Scriptures (Romans 1:2; 2 Timothy 3:15), the old covenant (2 Corinthians 3:14). For Christians, the Scriptures is another name for the Bible, containing both the Old and New Testaments.

Serpent. A name given to the dragon that appears in the New Testament as a figure of the Devil (Revelation 12:3–17; 20:2, 3).

Seventh year. The year, coming every seventh year, when the ancient Israelites did not cultivate their fields and when debts were canceled.

Shebat. The eleventh month of the Hebrew calendar, corresponding to the period from about mid-January to about mid-February.

Shelters, Festival of. A joyous festival celebrated by the Israelites in the fall after the completion of the harvest. To help them remember the years when their ancestors wandered through the wilderness, the Israelites constructed rough shelters to live in during the festival. The Jewish name for this festival is Sukkoth. It has been traditionally called the Feast of Tabernacles or the Feast of Booths.

Shiloh. The central place of worship for the people of Israel before the time of King David. It was here that the Covenant Box was kept in the time of the priest Eli (1 Samuel 1:3). The city was most likely destroyed by the Philistines.

Sickle. A tool consisting of a curved metal blade and a wooden handle, used for cutting wheat and other crops.

Sinai. As the people of Israel went from Egypt to Canaan, God revealed himself to Moses and the people at Mount Sinai, a mountain located somewhere on the Sinai Peninsula but whose exact location is uncertain. It was on this mountain that God gave the Law to Moses (Exodus 19:16–25; 31:18).

Sivan. The third month of the Hebrew calendar, corresponding to the period from about mid-May to about mid-June.

Snuffer. The Hebrew word translated "snuffer" apparently identifies an implement used to trim the oil lamps used in the Tent of the LORD's presence or the Temple.

Sorcerer. A person who works magic for evil purposes.

Stoics. Those who followed the teachings of the Greek philosopher Zeno (died 265 BC), who taught that happiness is to be found in being free from pleasure and pain.

Sulfur. In the Bible this refers to a sulfur compound that burns with great heat and produces an unpleasant smell.

Synagogue. A place where Jews met every Sabbath day for their public worship. It probably also served as a center for Jewish social life and a school for Jewish children.

Tambourine. A small drum with pieces of metal in the rim, held in the hand and shaken. In biblical times it was generally used by women.

Tassel. A group of threads or cords fastened together at one end and loose at the other. The Israelites were commanded to wear these on their clothes (Numbers 15:37–41).

Teachers of the Law. Men who in New Testament times taught and interpreted the teachings of the Old Testament, especially the first five books.

Tebeth. The tenth month of the Hebrew calendar, corresponding to the period from about mid-December to about mid-January.

Tenant. A man who grows crops on land owned by someone else, and turns over a part of the harvest to the owner to pay for the use of his land.

Tent of the LORD's presence. The large tent described in detail in Exodus, chapter 26, where the Israelites worshiped God until Solomon built the Temple. It has traditionally been called the Tabernacle or Tent of meeting.

Threshing, threshing floor, and threshing sledge. Threshing is the process by which farmers separate the edible grain from the husks of crops like wheat and rye. First the stalks are placed on a hard surface called a threshing floor. The farmer then beats the stalks or uses animals to trample them in order to separate the grain from the husks. Sometimes farmers would ride a sledge pulled by oxen over the stalks to speed up the process. These sledges often had bits of iron or stone fastened beneath them. The farmer then used a winnowing shovel to complete the process of separating and gathering the grain (*see* Winnowing shovel). See also 1 Chronicles 21:18–30; Isaiah 41:15.

Tithe. A tenth part of a person's produce or income, given for religious purposes. See Numbers 18:25–32; Deuteronomy 14:22–29.

Topaz. A semiprecious stone, usually yellow in color.

Turban. A head covering worn by men, made by cloth wrapped around the head.

Turquoise. A semiprecious stone, blue or bluish green in color.

Twelve tribes. The twelve family groups of the nation of Israel, each named for a son of Jacob.

Unleavened Bread, Festival of. The Israelite festival, lasting seven days after Passover; it also celebrated the deliverance of the ancient Hebrews from Egypt. The name came from the practice of not using leaven (yeast) in making bread during that week (Exodus 12:14–20). It was held from the fifteenth to the twenty-second day of the month Nisan (around the first week of April).

Urim and Thummim. Two small objects used by Israelite priests to determine God's will; it is not known precisely how they were used (Numbers 27:21).

Virtue. A habit that leads you to do good things and make choices that are morally right.

Vow. A strong declaration or promise, usually made while calling upon God to punish the speaker if the statement should prove to be not true or if the promise were not kept.

Winged creatures. Also referred to as "living creatures" and traditionally called "cherubim," they were symbols of God's majesty and associated with his presence. For a description of such creatures, see Exodus 25:18–20; Ezekiel 1:5–13, chapter 10; Revelation 4:6–9.

Winnowing shovel. A tool like a shovel or a large fork, used to separate the wheat from the chaff. See Matthew 3:12.

Worship. To adore God in prayer, particularly as part of a public religious ritual.

Wreath. Flowers or leaves arranged in a circle, to be placed on a person's head. In ancient times a wreath of leaves was the prize given to winners in athletic contests.

Year of Restoration. Every fifty years, all Israelites were required to give freedom to any Israelites who had become slaves because of debts; they were also to give back to the original owner, or his heirs, any ancestral land that had been sold for debt (Leviticus 25:8–55; Ezekiel 46:17).

Yeast. A substance, also called leaven, that is added to dough made from the flour of wheat or barley to make it rise before being baked into bread.

Yoke. A heavy bar of wood fitted over the necks of two oxen to make it possible for them to pull a plow or a cart. The word is used figuratively to describe the moral lessons that a teacher passes on to his pupils.

Zeus. The name of the supreme god of the Greeks.

Zion. Originally a name for "David's City," the Jebusite stronghold captured by King David's forces. The term *Zion* was later extended in meaning to refer to the hill on which the Temple stood.

Ziv. The second month of the Hebrew calendar, corresponding to the period from about mid-April to about mid-May.

Article Subject Index

This subject index is not an index to the Bible itself (sometimes called a concordance). Rather, it is an index to the subjects covered in the various articles in *Breakthrough!*.

A

B

C

G

H

O

P

S

T

U

New Testament Passages Quoted or Paraphrased from the Septuagint

The writers of the New Testament often directly quoted or paraphrased the ancient Greek translation of the Old Testament, commonly known as the Septuagint Version (LXX). The LXX was translated from the original Hebrew version of the Old Testament some two hundred years before the time of Christ. In a number of instances, the LXX differs significantly in meaning from the Masoretic Hebrew text. However, the Old Testament in this Bible was translated from the Hebrew text. Thus, many Old Testament quotations in the New Testament will be different from the way those verses appear in this Bible.

As a special help to the reader, such occurrences of LXX quotations, paraphrases, or evident allusions are listed here. The following translations of the LXX passages reflect in general the wording of Today's English Version of the New Testament (TEV). When, however, an LXX quotation occurs several times in the New Testament, the TEV wording of the translation may vary because of evident differences in meaning or emphasis reflected in the different contexts. Chapter and verse numbers are those of the English Bible.

Matthew 1:23 (Isaiah 7:14)
A virgin will become pregnant and have a son.

Matthew 3:3 (Isaiah 40:3)
Someone is shouting in the desert, "Prepare a road for the Lord; make a straight path for our God to travel!"

Matthew 12:21 (Isaiah 42:4)
And on him all people will put their hope.

Matthew 13:14,15 (Isaiah 6:9,10)
This people will listen and listen, but not understand; they will look and look, but not see, because their minds are dull, and they have stopped up their ears, and have closed their eyes. Otherwise, their eyes would see, their ears would hear, their minds would understand, and they would turn to me, says God, and I would heal them.

Matthew 15:8,9 (Isaiah 29:13)
These people, says God, . . . honor me with their words, but their heart is really far away from me. It is no use for them to worship me, because they teach man-made rules and laws.

Matthew 21:16 (Psalm 8:2)
You have trained children and babies to offer perfect praise.

Mark 1:3 (Isaiah 40:3)
Someone is shouting in the desert, "Get the road ready for the Lord; make a straight path for our God to travel!"

Mark 4:12 (Isaiah 6:9,10)
This people will listen and listen, but not understand; they will look and look, but not see . . .; for if they did . . ., they would turn to me, says God, and I would heal them.

Mark 7:6,7 (Isaiah 29:13)
These people, says God, . . . honor me with their words, but their heart is really far away from me. It is no use for them to worship me, because they teach man-made rules and laws.

Luke 3:4–6 (Isaiah 40:3–5)
Someone is shouting in the desert: "Get the road ready for the Lord, make a straight path for our God to travel! Every valley must be filled up, every hill and mountain leveled off. All the winding roads must be made straight, and the rough paths made smooth. . . . All people will see God's salvation!"

Luke 4:18 (Isaiah 61:1)
The Spirit of the Lord is upon me, because he has chosen me to bring good news to the poor. He has sent me . . . to proclaim liberty to the captives and the recovery of sight to the blind.

Luke 8:10 (Isaiah 6:9)
You will listen and listen, but not understand; you will look and look, but not see.

John 1:23 (Isaiah 40:3)
The voice of someone shouting in the desert: . . . "Make a straight path for our God to travel!"

John 12:38 (Isaiah 53:1)
Lord, who believed the message we told?

John 12:40 (Isaiah 6:10)
This people's minds are dull, and they have stopped up their ears and have closed their eyes. Otherwise, their eyes would see, and their ears would hear, their minds would understand, and they would turn to me, says God, for me to heal them.

Acts 2:19,20 (Joel 2:30,31)
There will be blood, fire, and thick smoke; the sun will be darkened, and the moon will turn red as blood, before the great and glorious Day of the Lord comes.

Acts 2:25–28 (Psalm 16:8–11)
I saw the Lord before me at all times. He is near me, and I will not be troubled. And so I am filled with gladness, and my words are full of joy. And I, mortal though I am, will rest assured in hope, because you will not abandon me in the world of the dead; you will not allow your faithful servant to rot in the grave. You have shown me the paths that lead to life, and your presence will fill me with joy.

Acts 3:22 (Deuteronomy 18:15)
You are to obey him in all things.

Acts 4:25,26 (Psalm 2:1,2)
Why were the Gentiles furious; why did people make their useless plots? The kings of the earth prepared themselves, and the rulers met together.

Acts 7:14 (Genesis 46:27)
Seventy-five people.

Acts 7:42,43 (Amos 5:25–27)
People of Israel! It was not to me that you slaughtered and sacrificed animals for forty years in the desert. It was the tent of the god Molech that you carried, and the image of Rephan, your star god; they were idols that you had made for yourselves. And so I will send you into exile beyond Damascus.

Acts 8:33 (Isaiah 53:8)
He was humiliated, and justice was denied him. No one will be able to tell about his descendants, because his life on earth has come to an end.

Acts 13:34 (Isaiah 55:3)
I will make an everlasting covenant with you, the sacred and sure blessings I promised to David.

Acts 13:41 (Habakkuk 1:5)
Look, you scoffers! Be much astonished and die!

Acts 15:16,17 (Amos 9:11,12)
In that day, says the Lord, I will restore the kingdom of David. I will rebuild its ruins, and make it strong again. . . . And so all the rest of the human race will come to me, all the Gentiles whom I have called to be my own.

Acts 28:26,27 (Isaiah 6:9,10)
Go and say to this people: You will listen and listen, but not understand; you will look and look, but not see, because this people's minds are dull, and they have stopped up their ears and closed their eyes. Otherwise, their eyes would see, their ears would hear, their minds would understand, and they would turn to me, says God, and I would heal them.

Romans 2:24 (Isaiah 52:5)
Because of you Jews, the Gentiles continually speak evil of God.

Romans 3:4 (Psalm 51:4)
You must be shown to be right when you speak; you must win your case when you are being tried.

Romans 3:12 (Psalms 14:3; 53:3)
All have turned away from God; they have all gone wrong.

Romans 3:13 (Psalm 5:9)
Wicked lies roll off their tongues.

Romans 3:14 (Psalm 10:7)
Their speech is filled with bitter curses and guile.

Romans 9:17 (Exodus 9:16)
To use you to show my power.

Romans 9:27,28 (Isaiah 10:22, 23)
Even if the people of Israel are as many as the grains of sand by the sea, yet only a few of them will be saved; for God will quickly and justly settle his full account with all the world.

Romans 9:29 (Isaiah 1:9)
If the Lord Almighty had not left us some descendants.

Romans 9:33 (Isaiah 28:16)
Whoever believes in him will not be disappointed.

Romans 10:11 (Isaiah 28:16)
Whoever believes in him will not be disappointed.

Romans 10:16 (Isaiah 53:1)
Lord, who believed our message?

Romans 10:18 (Psalm 19:4)
The sound of their voice went out to all the world; their words reached the ends of the earth.

Romans 10:20 (Isaiah 65:1)
I appeared to those who were not looking for me, I was found by those who were not asking for me.

Romans 10:21 (Isaiah 65:2)
All day long I held out my hands to welcome a disobedient and rebellious people.

Romans 11:9,10 (Psalm 69:22,23)
May they fall, may they be punished!
. . . Make them bend under their troubles at all times.

Romans 11:26,27 (Isaiah 59:20,21)
The Savior will come for the sake of Zion, and remove all wickedness from the descendants of Jacob. I will make this covenant with them (Isaiah 27:9), when I take away their sins.

Romans 11:34 (Isaiah 40:13)
Who knows the mind of the Lord?

Romans 12:20 (Proverbs 25:21,22)
If your enemies are hungry, feed them; if they are thirsty, give them a drink; for by doing this you will make them burn with shame.

Romans 14:11 (Isaiah 45:23)
Everyone will kneel before me, and everyone will confess that I am God.

Romans 15:12 (Isaiah 11:10)
On that day a descendant of Jesse will appear; he will come to rule the Gentiles, and they will put their hope in him.

Romans 15:21 (Isaiah 52:15)
Those who were not told about him will see, and those who have not heard will understand.

1 Corinthians 1:19 (Isaiah 29:14)
I will destroy the wisdom of the wise, and hide the understanding of the scholars.

1 Corinthians 2:16 (Isaiah 40:13)
Who knows the mind of the Lord?

1 Corinthians 5:13 (Deuteronomy 17:7)
Remove the evil man from your group.

1 Corinthians 10:20 (Deuteronomy 32:17)
What is sacrificed on pagan altars is offered to demons, not to God.

1 Corinthians 15:55 (Hosea 13:14)
Where, Death, is your punishment?
Where, Hades, is your power to hurt?

2 Corinthians 4:13 (Psalm 116:10)
I spoke because I believed.

2 Corinthians 8:21 (Proverbs 3:4)
Make it your purpose to do what is right, not only in the sight of the Lord, but also in the sight of man.

Galatians 3:10 (Deuteronomy 27:26)
Whoever does not always obey everything that is written in this Law is under God's curse.

Ephesians 4:26 (Psalm 4:4)
If you become angry, do not let your anger lead you into sin.

Philippians 2:11 (Isaiah 45:23)
And all will openly proclaim God.

Hebrews 1:6 (Deuteronomy 32:43)
All of God's sons must worship him.

Hebrews 1:7 (Psalm 104:4)
God makes his angels winds, and his servants a flaming fire.

Hebrews 1:10–12 (Psalm 102:25–27)
You, Lord, in the beginning created the earth. . . . You will fold them up like a coat, and they will be changed.

Hebrews 2:7 (Psalm 8:5)
You made him for a little while lower than the angels.

Hebrews 3:7–9 (Psalm 95:7–9)
If you hear God's voice today, do not be stubborn as your ancestors were when they rebelled against God, as they were that day in the desert when they put him to the test. There they put me to the test and tried me, says God, although they saw what I did.

Hebrews 3:15 (Psalm 95:7,8)
If you hear God's voice today, do not be stubborn as your ancestors were when they rebelled against God.

Hebrews 4:7 (Psalm 95:7,8)
If you hear God's voice today, do not be stubborn.

Hebrews 8:9 (Jeremiah 31:32)
They were not faithful to the covenant I made with them, and so I paid no attention to them.

Hebrews 10:5 (Psalm 40:6)
You do not want sacrifices and offerings, but you have prepared a body for me.

Hebrews 10:27 (Isaiah 26:11)
The fierceness . . . and now fire will destroy those who oppose God.

Hebrews 10:38b (Habakkuk 2:4a)
If he turns back, I will not be pleased with him.

Hebrews 11:5 (Genesis 5:24)
Enoch pleased God, and nobody could find him, because God had taken him up.

Hebrews 11:21 (Genesis 47:31)
He leaned on the top of his walking stick and worshiped God.

Hebrews 12:5,6 (Proverbs 3:11,12)
Son, pay attention when the Lord corrects you, and do not be discouraged when he rebukes you. Because the Lord corrects everyone he loves, and punishes everyone he accepts as a son.

Hebrews 12:13 (Proverbs 4:26)
Keep walking on straight paths.

Hebrews 12:15 (Deuteronomy 29:18)
A bitter plant that grows up.

Hebrews 12:26 (Haggai 2:6)
I will once more shake heaven and earth.

Hebrews 13:6 (Psalm 118:6)
The Lord is my helper; I will not fear what anyone may do to me.

James 1:10,11 (Isaiah 40:6,7)
Like the flower of a wild plant. . . . Its flower falls off.

James 4:6 (Proverbs 3:34)
The Lord resists the proud, but gives grace to the humble.

1 Peter 1:24 (Isaiah 40:6,7)
All human beings are like grass, and all their glory is like wild flowers. The grass withers, and the flowers fall.

1 Peter 2:6 (Isaiah 28:16)
I chose a valuable and costly stone, which I am placing as the cornerstone in the foundations of Zion, and whoever believes in him will never be disappointed.

1 Peter 2:9 (Isaiah 43:20)
The chosen race (Exodus 19:5,6), the King's priests, the holy nation (Isaiah 43:21), my own people, chosen to proclaim my wonderful acts.

1 Peter 3:10 (Psalm 34:12)
Whoever wishes life and wants to see good times.

1 Peter 4:18 (Proverbs 11:31)
It is difficult for good people to be saved; what, then, will become of godless sinners?

1 Peter 5:5 (Proverbs 3:34)
The Lord resists the proud, but shows favor to the humble.

Revelation 2:7 (Ezekiel 28:13; 31:8,9)
The Garden of God.

Revelation 2:27 (Psalm 2:9)
You will rule them with an iron rod.

Reading the Bible with the Church Year

The feast days and holy days celebrated by Catholics and other Christians follow a yearly pattern. This pattern is called the liturgical year; it is different from the calendar year. Here is a description of the major seasons in the liturgical year. As you read this, refer to the chart on the next page.

Advent begins the liturgical year four Sundays before Christmas. It is a time of preparation for the coming of Christ. The Advent season can be found on the liturgical year wheel in November and December. It is represented by the small graphic of an Advent wreath.

The **Christmas** season lasts twelve days, beginning with Christmas Day and concluding with the feast of the Baptism of the Lord. This season is found at the top part of the liturgical year wheel. The cross reminds us that the wood of the manger becomes the wood of the cross.

Lent begins with Ash Wednesday and lasts forty days. It is a solemn time of fasting, prayer, and almsgiving in preparation for Easter. The small picture of the palms and cross in the liturgical year wheel symbolizes all of Lent as a journey toward Palm Sunday, when the same crowd that waves palms and yells "Hosanna!" ends up waving angry fists and shouting "Crucify him!"

The **Easter Triduum** is the celebration of Holy Thursday, Good Friday, and the Easter Vigil on Holy Saturday. At this one, continuous, three-day liturgy, Christians remember the Lord's Supper, Christ's Passion and death, and his Resurrection. These feasts are at the heart of the liturgical year. They are represented by the picture of the Easter candle, which makes its appearance in the darkness of the Easter Vigil. The vestments and altar cloths seen are red on Good Friday and white on the other two days.

The **Easter** Season lasts fifty days, beginning with Easter Sunday and ending with the feast of Pentecost. The symbol of the lamb represents Jesus, the innocent sacrificial lamb of God. The symbol of the Holy Spirit reminds us that the Holy Spirit came to the disciples, in the rush of wind and tongues of fire. The altar cloths and vestments are white throughout the Easter season, and then red on Pentecost. Red is the color of the Holy Spirit (as in Confirmation Mass) and of the celebration of feast days associated with martyrs, people killed for their faith (such as the feast of Saints Peter and Paul).

The season of **Ordinary Time** is made up of the days between Christmas and Lent, and the days between Easter and Advent. The bread and wine show us that the main focus of Ordinary Time is the ministry of Jesus, represented by the grapes and bread of communion. There are some special feast days during Ordinary Time that are not celebrated with green vestments and altar cloths, such as Trinity Sunday and the Feast of the Body and Blood of Christ, the first two Sundays after Pentecost, and the Feast of Christ the King, the last Sunday before Advent. You'll see white on all three of those days. The particular dates and days these feasts fall upon vary from year to year.

Christmas is always December 25, so counting backwards four Sundays shows the four Sundays of Advent. Sometimes Advent includes Thanksgiving weekend, and sometimes it doesn't, depending on which day of the week Christmas is.

Easter is always the first Sunday after the first full moon in the spring. Counting backwards six Sundays and then one Wednesday shows when Ash Wednesday and Lent begin. Sometimes Easter is in March, and sometimes it is in April.

On the next page, you will find the Bible readings heard on Sundays throughout the liturgical year. The first reading is usually from the Old Testament. The second reading is usually from a New Testament letter. The third reading is always from one of the four Gospels.

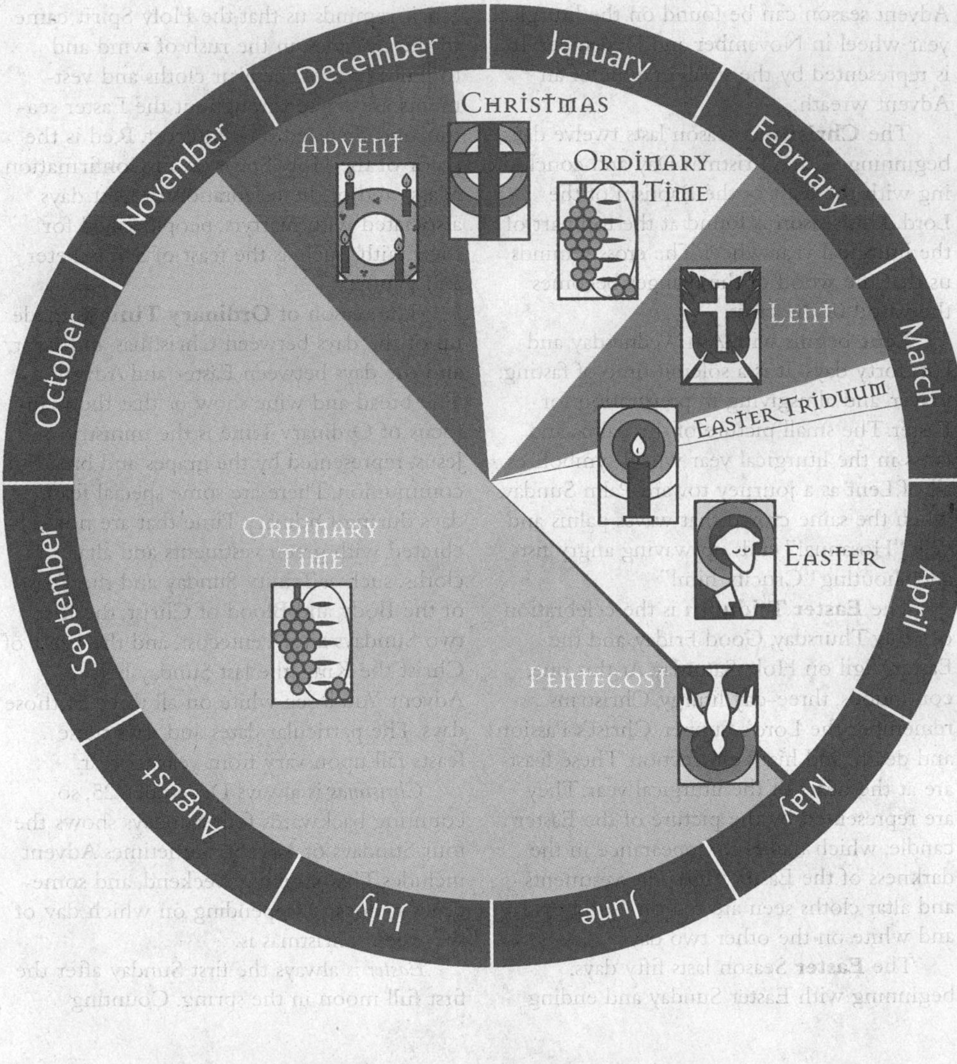

This chart lists the Sunday Bible readings from the liturgical, or Church, year.

ADVENT AND CHRISTMAS

Year A (2007, 2010, 2013)	Year B (2005, 2008, 2011)	Year C (2006, 2009, 2012)
The First Sunday of Advent		
Isa 2:1–5	Isa 63:16–17,19; 64:2–7	Jer 33:14–16
Rom 13:11–14	1 Cor 1:3–9	1 Thess 3:12—4:2
Mt 24:37–44	Mk 13:33–37	Lk 21:25–28,34–36
The Second Sunday of Advent		
Isa 11:1–10	Isa 40:1–5,9–11	Bar 5:1–9
Rom 15:4–9	2 Pet 3:8–14	Phil 1:4–6,8–11
Mt 3:1–12	Mk 1:1–8	Lk 3:1–6
The Third Sunday of Advent		
Isa 35:1–6,10	Isa 61:1–2,10–11	Zeph 3:14–18
Jas 5:7–10	1 Thess 5:16–24	Phil 4:4–7
Mt 11:2–11	Jn 1:6–8,19–28	Lk 3:10–18
The Fourth Sunday of Advent		
Isa 7:10–14	2 Sam 7:1–5,8–11,14,16	Mic 5:1–4
Rom 1:1–7	Rom 16:25–27	Heb 10:5–10
Mt 1:18–24	Lk 1:26–38	Lk 1:39–45
Midnight Mass *(25 December, every year: readings are the same for all cycles)*		
Isa 9:1–6	Isa 9:1–6	Isa 9:1–6
Titus 2:11–14	Titus 2:11–14	Titus 2:11–14
Lk 2:1–14	Lk 2:1–14	Lk 2:1–14
Feast of the Holy Family		
Sir 3:2–7,12–14	Sir 3:2–7,12–14	Sir 3:2–7,12–14
Col 3:12–21	Col 3:12–21	Col 3:12–21
Mt 2:13–15,19–23	Lk 2:22–40 or 2:22,39–40	Lk 2:41–52
Solemnity of Mary, Mother of God *(1 January, every year, readings are the same for all cycles)*		
Num 6:22–27	Num 6:22–27	Num 6:22–27
Gal 4:4–7	Gal 4:4–7	Gal 4:4–7
Lk 2:16–21	Lk 2:16–21	Lk 2:16–21
Epiphany *(readings are the same for all cycles)*		
Isa 60:1–6	Isa 60:1–6	Isa 60:1–6
Eph 3:2–3,5–6	Eph 3:2–3,5–6	Eph 3:2–3,5–6
Mt 2:1–12	Mt 2:1–12	Mt 2:1–12
Baptism of the Lord		
Isa 42:1–4,6–7	Isa 42:1–4,6–7	Isa 42:1–4,6–7
Acts 10:34–38	Acts 10:34–38	Acts 10:34–38
Mt 3:13–17	Mk 1:7–11	Lk 3:15–16,21–22

LENT AND EASTER

Year A (2008, 2011, 2014)	Year B (2006, 2009, 2012)	Year C (2007, 2010, 2013)
Ash Wednesday *(readings are the same for all cycles)*		
Joel 2:12–18	Joel 2:12–18	Joel 2:12–18
2 Cor 5:20—6:2	2 Cor 5:20—6:2	2 Cor 5:20—6:2
Mt 6:1–6,16–18	Mt 6:1–6,16–18	Mt 6:1–6,16–18
The First Sunday of Lent		
Gen 2:7–9; 3:1–7	Gen 9:8–15	Deut 26:4–10
Rom 5:12–19	1 Pet 3:18–22	Rom 10:8–13
Mt 4:1–11	Mk 1:12–15	Lk 4:1–13
The Second Sunday of Lent		
Gen 12:1–4	Gen 22:1–2,9,10–13,15–18	Gen 15:5–12,17–18
2 Tim 1:8–10	Rom 8:31–34	Phil 3:17—4:1
Mt 17:1–9	Mk 9:2–10	Lk 9:28–36

LENT AND EASTER *(continued)*

Year A (2008, 2011, 2014)	Year B (2006, 2009, 2012)	Year C (2007, 2010, 2013)
The Third Sunday of Lent		
Ex 17:3–7	Ex 20:1–17	Ex 3:1–8,13–15
Rom 5:1–2,5–8	1 Cor 1:22–25	1 Cor 10:1–6,10–12
Jn 4:5–42	Jn 2:13–25	Lk 13:1–9
The Fourth Sunday of Lent		
1 Sam 16:1,6–7,10–13	2 Chr 36:14–17,19–23	Josh 5:9,10–12
Eph 5:8–14	Eph 2:4–10	2 Cor 5:17–21
Jn 9:1–41	Jn 3:14–21	Lk 15:1–3,11–32
The Fifth Sunday of Lent		
Ezek 37:12–14	Jer 31:31–34	Isa 43:16–21
Rom 8:8–11	Heb 5:7–9	Phil 3:8–14
Jn 11:1–45	Jn 12:20–33	Jn 8:1–11
Passion Sunday (Palm Sunday)		
Isa 50:4–7	Isa 50:4–7	Isa 50:4–7
Phil 2:6–11	Phil 2:6–11	Phil 2:6–11
Mt 26:14—27:66	Mk 14:1—15:47	Lk 22:14—23:56
Holy Thursday *(readings are the same for all cycles)*		
Ex 12:1–8,11–14	Ex 12:1–8,11–14	Ex 12:1–8,11–14
1 Cor 11:23–26	1 Cor 11:23–26	1 Cor 11:23–26
Jn 13:1–15	Jn 13:1–15	Jn 13:1–15
Good Friday *(readings are the same for all cycles)*		
Isa 52:13—53:12	Isa 52:13—53:12	Isa 52:13—53:12
Heb 4:14–16; 5:7–9	Heb 4:14–16; 5:7–9	Heb 4:14–16; 5:7–9
Jn 18:1—19:42	Jn 18:1—19:42	Jn 18:1—19:42
Easter Sunday *(readings are the same for all cycles)*		
Acts 10:34,37–43	Acts 10:34,37–43	Acts 10:34,37–43
Col 3:1–4 or 1 Cor 5:6–8	Col 3:1–4 or 1 Cor 5:6–8	Col 3:1–4 or 1 Cor 5:6–8
Jn 20:1–9	Jn 20:1–9	Jn 20:1–9
Second Sunday of Easter		
Acts 2:42–47	Acts 4:32–35	Acts 5:12–16
1 Pet 1:3–9	1 Jn 5:1–6	Rev 1:9–11,12–13,17–19
Jn 20:19–31	Jn 20:19–31	Jn 20:19–31
Third Sunday of Easter		
Acts 2:14,22–28	Acts 3:13–15,17–19	Acts 5:27–32,40–41
1 Pet 1:17–21	1 Jn 2:1–5	Rev 5:11–14
Lk 24:13–35	Lk 24:35–48	Jn 21:1–19 or 1–14
Fourth Sunday of Easter		
Acts 2:14,36–41	Acts 4:8–12	Acts 13:14,43–52
1 Pet 2:20–25	1 Jn 3:1–2	Rev 7:9,14–17
Jn 10:1–10	Jn 10:11–18	Jn 10:27–30
Fifth Sunday of Easter		
Acts 6:1–7	Acts 9:26–31	Acts 14:21–27
1 Pet 2:4–9	1 Jn 3:18–24	Rev 21:1–5
Jn 14:1–12	Jn 15:1–8	Jn 13:31–35
Sixth Sunday of Easter		
Acts 8:5–8,14–17	Acts 10:25–26,34–35,44–48	Acts 15:1–2,22–29
1 Pet 3:15–18	1 Jn 4:7–10	Rev 21:10–14,22–23
Jn 14:15–21	Jn 15:9–17	Jn 14:23–29
Seventh Sunday of Easter		
Acts 1:12–14	Acts 1:15–17,20–26	Acts 7:55–60
1 Pet 4:13–16	1 Jn 4:11–16	Rev 22:12–14,16–17,20
Jn 17:1–11	Jn 17:11–19	Jn 17:20–26
Pentecost Sunday *(readings are the same for all cycles)*		
Acts 2:1–11	Acts 2:1–11	Acts 2:1–11
1 Cor 12:3–7,12–13	1 Cor 12:3–7,12–13	1 Cor 12:3–7,12–13
Jn 20:19–23	Jn 20:19–23	Jn 20:19–23

ORDINARY TIME

Year A (2008, 2011, 2014)	Year B (2006, 2009, 2012)	Year C (2007, 2010, 2013)
First Sunday in Ordinary Time *(see the Feast of the Baptism of the Lord under "Advent and Christmas")*		
Second Sunday in Ordinary Time		
Isa 49:3,5–6	1 Sam 3:3b–10,19	Isa 62:1–5
1 Cor 1:1–3	1 Cor 6:13c–15a,17–20	1 Cor 12:4–11
Jn 1:29–34	Jn 1:35–42	Jn 2:1–11
Third Sunday in Ordinary Time		
Isa 8:23–9:3	Jon 3:1–5,10	Neh 8:2–4a,5–6,8–10
1 Cor 1:10–13,17	1 Cor 7:29–31	1 Cor 12:12–30
Mt 4:12 23	Mk 1:14–20	Lk 1:1–4; 4:14–21
Fourth Sunday in Ordinary Time		
Zeph 2:3; 3:12–13	Deut 18:15–20	Jer 1:4–5,17–19
1 Cor 1:26–31	1 Cor 7:32–35	1 Cor 12:31—13:13
Mt 5:1–12a	Mk 1:21–28	Lk 4:21–30
Fifth Sunday in Ordinary Time		
Isa 58:7–10	Job 7:1–4,6–7	Isa 6:1–2a,3–8
1 Cor 2:1–5	1 Cor 9:16–19,22–23	1 Cor 15:1–11
Mt 5:13–16	Mk 1:29–39	Lk 5:1–11
Sixth Sunday in Ordinary Time		
Sir 15:15–20	Lev 13:1–2,44–46	Jer 17:5–8
1 Cor 2:6–10	1 Cor 10:31—11:1	1 Cor 15:12,16–20
Mt 5:17–37	Mk 1:40–45	Lk 6:17,20–26
Seventh Sunday in Ordinary Time		
Lev 19:1–2,17–18	Isa 43:18–19,21–22,24b–25	1 Sam 26:2,7–9,12–13,22–23
1 Cor 3:16–23	2 Cor 1:18–22	1 Cor 15:45–49
Mt 5:38–48	Mk 2:1–12	Lk 6:27–38
Eighth Sunday in Ordinary Time		
Isa 49:14–15	Hos 2:16b,17b,21–22	Sir 27:4–7
1 Cor 4:1–5	2 Cor 3:1b–6	1 Cor 15:54–58
Mt 6:24–34	Mk 2:18–22	Lk 6:39–45
Ninth Sunday in Ordinary Time		
Deut 11:18,26–28,32	Deut 5:12–15	1 Kings 8:41–43
Rom 3:21–25a,28	2 Cor 4:6–11	Gal 1:1–2,6–10
Mt 7:21–27	Mk 2:23—3:6	Lk 7:1–10
Tenth Sunday in Ordinary Time		
Hos 6:3–6	Gen 3:9–15	1 Kings 17:17–24
Rom 4:18–25	2 Cor 4:13—5:1	Gal 1:11–19
Mt 9:9–13	Mk 3:20–35	Lk 7:11–17
Eleventh Sunday in Ordinary Time		
Ex 19:2–6a	Ezek 17:22–24	2 Sam 12:7–10,13
Rom 5:6–11	2 Cor 5:6–10	Gal 2:16,19–21
Mt 9:36—10:8	Mk 4:26–34	Lk 7:36—8:3
Twelfth Sunday in Ordinary Time		
Jer 20:10–13	Job 38:1,8–11	Zech 12:10–11; 13:1
Rom 5:12–15	2 Cor 5:14–17	Gal 3:26–29
Mt 10:26–33	Mk 4:35–41	Lk 9:18–24
Thirteenth Sunday in Ordinary Time		
2 Kings 4:8–11,14–16a	Wis 1:13–15; 2:23–24	1 Kings 19:16b,19–21
Rom 6:3–4,8–11	2 Cor 8:7,9,13–15	Gal 5:1,13–18
Mt 10:37–42	Mk 5:21–43	Lk 9:51–62
Fourteenth Sunday in Ordinary Time		
Zech 9:9–10	Ezek 2:2–5	Isa 66:10–14c
Rom 8:9,11–13	2 Cor 12:7–10	Gal 6:14–18
Mt 11:25–30	Mk 6:1–6	Lk 10:1–12,17–20

ORDINARY TIME *(continued)*

	Year A (2008, 2011, 2014)	Year B (2006, 2009, 2012)	Year C (2007, 2010, 2013)
Fifteenth Sunday in Ordinary Time			
	Isa 55:10–11	Am 7:12–15	Deut 30:10–14
	Rom 8:18–23	Eph 1:3–14	Col 1:15–20
	Mt 13:1–23	Mk 6:7–13	Lk 10:25–37
Sixteenth Sunday in Ordinary Time			
	Wis 12:13,16–19	Jer 23:1–6	Gen 18:1–10a
	Rom 8:26–27	Eph 2:13–18	Col 1:24–28
	Mt 13:24–43	Mk 6:30–34	Lk 10:38–42
Seventeenth Sunday in Ordinary Time			
	1 Kings 3:5,7–12	2 Kings 4:42–44	Gen 18:20–32
	Rom 8:28–30	Eph 4:1–6	Col 2:12–14
	Mt 13:44–52	Jn 6:1–15	Lk 11:1–13
Eighteenth Sunday in Ordinary Time			
	Isa 55:1–3	Ex 16:2–4,12–15	Eccl 1:2; 2:21–23
	Rom 8:35,37–39	Eph 4:17,20–24	Col 3:1–5,9–11
	Mt 14:13–21	Jn 6:24–35	Lk 12:13–21
Nineteenth Sunday in Ordinary Time			
	1 Kings 19:9a,11–13a	1 Kings 19:4–8	Wis 18:6–9
	Rom 9:1–5	Eph 4:30—5:2	Heb 11:1–2,8–19
	Mt 14:22–33	Jn 6:41–51	Lk 12:32–48
Twentieth Sunday in Ordinary Time			
	Isa 56:1,6–7	Prov 9:1–6	Jer 38:4–6,8–10
	Rom 11:13–15,29–32	Eph 5:15–20	Heb 12:1–4
	Mt 15:21–28	Jn 6:51–58	Lk 12:49–53
Twenty-First Sunday in Ordinary Time			
	Isa 22:19–23	Josh 24:1–2a,15–17,18b	Isa 66:18–21
	Rom 11:33–36	Eph 5:21–32	Heb 12:5–7,11–13
	Mt 16:13–20	Jn 6:60–69	Lk 13:22–30
Twenty-Second Sunday in Ordinary Time			
	Jer 20:7–9	Deut 4:1–2,6–8	Sir 3:17–18,20,28–29
	Rom 12:1–2	Jas 1:17–18,21b–22,27	Heb 12:18–19,22–24a
	Mt 16:21–27	Mk 7:1–8,14–15,21–23	Lk 14:1,7–14
Twenty-Third Sunday in Ordinary Time			
	Ezek 33:7–9	Isa 35:4–7a	Wis 9:13–18b
	Rom 13:8–10	Jas 2:1–5	Philem 9–10,12–17
	Mt 18:15–20	Mk 7:31–37	Lk 14:25–33
Twenty-Fourth Sunday in Ordinary Time			
	Sir 27:30—28:9	Isa 50:5–9a	Ex 32:7–11,13–14
	Rom 14:7–9	Jas 2:14–18	1 Tim 1:12–17
	Mt 18:21–35	Mk 8:27–35	Lk 15:1–32
Twenty-Fifth Sunday in Ordinary Time			
	Isa 55:6–9	Wis 2:12,17–20	Am 8:4–7
	Phil 1:20c–24,27a	Jas 3:16—4:3	1 Tim 2:1–8
	Mt 20:1–16a	Mk 9:30–37	Lk 16:1–13
Twenty-Sixth Sunday in Ordinary Time			
	Ezek 18:25–28	Num 11:25–29	Am 6:1a,4–7
	Phil 2:1–11	Jas 5:1–6	1 Tim 6:11–16
	Mt 21:28–32	Mk 9:38–43,45,47–48	Lk 16:19–31
Twenty-Seventh Sunday in Ordinary Time			
	Isa 5:1–7	Gen 2:18–24	Hab 1:2–3; 2:2–4
	Phil 4:6–9	Heb 2:9–11	2 Tim 1:6–8,13–14
	Mt 21:33–43	Mk 10:2–16	Lk 17:5–10
Twenty-Eighth Sunday in Ordinary Time			
	Isa 25:6–10a	Wis 7:7–11	2 Kings 5:14–17
	Phil 4:12–14,19–20	Heb 4:12–13	2 Tim 2:8–13
	Mt 22:1–14	Mk 10:17–30	Lk 17:11–19

ORDINARY TIME (*continued*)

	Year A (2008, 2011, 2014)	Year B (2006, 2009, 2012)	Year C (2007, 2010, 2013)
Twenty-Ninth Sunday in Ordinary Time			
	Isa 45:1,4–6	Isa 53:10–11	Ex 17:8–13
	1 Thess 1:1–5b	Heb 4:14–16	2 Tim 3:14—4:2
	Mt 22:15–21	Mk 10:35–45	Lk 18:1–8
Thirtieth Sunday in Ordinary Time			
	Ex 22:20–26	Jer 31:7–9	Sir 35:12–14,16–18
	1 Thess 1:5c–10	Heb 5:1–6	2 Tim 4:6–8,16–18
	Mt 22:34–40	Mk 10:46–52	Lk 18:9–14
Thirty–First Sunday in Ordinary Time			
	Mal 1:14b—2:2b,8–10	Deut 6:2–6	Wis 11:22—12:2
	1 Thess 2:7b–9,13	Heb 7:23–28	2 Thess 1:11—2:2
	Mt 23:1–12	Mk 12:28b–34	Lk 19:1–10
Thirty–Second Sunday in Ordinary Time			
	Wis 6:12–16	1 Kings 17:10–16	2 Macc 7:1–2,9–14
	1 Thess 4:13–18	Heb 9:24–28	2 Thess 2:16—3:5
	Mt 25:1–13	Mk 12:38–44	Lk 20:27–38
Thirty–Third Sunday in Ordinary Time			
	Prv 31:10–13,19–20,30–31	Dan 12:1–3	Mal 3:19–20a
	1 Thess 5:1–6	Heb 10:11–14,18	2 Thess 3:7–12
	Mt 25:14–30	Mk 13:24–32	Lk 21:5–19
Thirty–Fourth Sunday in Ordinary Time *(The Solemnity of Our Lord Jesus Christ the King)*			
	Ezek 34:11–12,15–17	Dan 7:13–14	2 Sam 5:1–3
	1 Cor 15:20–26,28	Rev 1:5–8	Col 1:12–20
	Mt 25:31–46	Jn 18:33b–37	Lk 23:35–43

About this Translation

In September 1966 the American Bible Society published *The New Testament in Today's English Version*, the first publication of a new Bible translation intended for people everywhere for whom English is either their mother tongue or an acquired language. Shortly thereafter the United Bible Societies (UBS) requested the American Bible Society (ABS) to undertake on its behalf a translation of the Old Testament following the same principles. Accordingly the American Bible Society appointed a group of translators to prepare the translation. In 1971 this group added a British consultant recommended by the British and Foreign Bible Society. The translation of the Old Testament, which was completed in 1976, was joined to the fourth edition New Testament, thus completing the first edition of the translation that came to be known as the *Good News Bible.*

Two Ways to Present the Deuterocanonical Books

The translation of the books of the Deuterocanon and others classed as Apocrypha was completed in 1978, and the first edition of the *Good News Bible* with Deuterocanonicals and Apocrypha was published in 1979, with the Imprimatur of the Most Reverend John F. Whealon, Archbishop of Hartford, Connecticut. The 1979 publication was an interconfessional edition in which these books were grouped in a separate section between the Old and the New Testaments.

In this present edition, the deuterocanonical books are arranged in the order most familiar to Roman Catholics. The books of Tobit, Judith, and 1 and 2 Maccabees follow the historical books Ezra and Nehemiah. The Book of Esther and its six additions follow Judith in this grouping. Most of these books were written or have their settings in the last several centuries BC. The book of Baruch and the Letter of Jeremiah are positioned after Lamentations, as part of the Jeremiah grouping. The books of the Wisdom of Solomon and Sirach, being wisdom books, are located among the other Old Testament Wisdom books, immediately following Song of Songs. The three additions to the book of Daniel, which are presented as separate books in the interconfessional edition of the Good News Bible, are presented here in the way most familiar to Roman Catholics. Susanna and Bel and the Dragon are traditionally treated as chapters 13 and 14 of Daniel. The third addition has its location between verses 23 and 24 of chapter 3 in the Hebrew text because this is the position it holds in the Septuagint. Known as the Prayer of Azariah and the Song of the Three Young Men, this addition to Daniel provides the text of the prayer offered by Azariah and of the song he and his companions sang while in the midst of the flames in the fiery furnace. The result is an Old Testament with forty-six books, several of which contain significant additions. These books formed part of the Septuagint, the Greek translation of the Old Testament that was in circulation at the time of Christ.

Prior to Jerome's great Latin translation, which came to be known as the *Vulgata* (the common language), there were numerous Latin translations in circulation, all of which had been done from the Greek Septuagint. The great significance of Jerome's work, at least for the Old Testament (AD 389–405), is that he broke from that tradition and based his translation on the received consonantal Hebrew text. His knowledge of Hebrew was excellent, and he had recourse to Jewish text scholars wherever he had questions. For the sections of Esther and Daniel not in the Hebrew canon, Jerome worked from the ancient Greek text. For Tobit and Judith, his base texts were (no longer extant) Aramaic editions of these books. Already before taking on the Old Testament books, Jerome had prepared a revised edition of the Gospels (revising the Old Latin text in light of the best Greek manuscripts available to him). The rest of the Vulgate New Testament text is also attributed to Jerome. The influence of the Vulgate in western Christendom remained unsurpassed from his time until the era of the Reformation and the proliferation of vernacular Bible translations, well over one thousand years later.

The Text Used for This Translation

The basic Hebrew (and Aramaic) text for the Old Testament is the Masoretic text, made available through printed editions published by the UBS, and since 1977 under the title of *Biblia Hebraica Stuttgartensia*. In some instances the words of the printed consonantal text have been divided differently or have been read with a different set of vowels; at times a variant reading in the margin of the Hebrew text *(qere)* has been followed instead of the reading in the text *(kethiv);* and in other instances a variant reading supported by one or more Hebrew manuscripts has been adopted. Where no Hebrew source yields a satisfactory meaning in the context, the translation has either followed one or more of the ancient versions (for example, Greek, Syriac, Latin) or has adopted a reconstructed text (technically referred to as a conjectural emendation) based on scholarly consensus; such departures from the Hebrew are indicated in footnotes.

The basic text for the deuterocanonical books is the Greek text printed in the Septuagint (third edition, 1949), edited by Alfred Rahlfs. For some of these books, the more recently published Goettingen edition of the Septuagint was also consulted.

The basic text for the translation of the New Testament is the *Greek New Testament* published by the UBS (third edition, 1975), but in a few instances the translation is based on a variant reading supported by one or more Greek manuscripts.

The Translation Process

Drafts of the translation in its early stages were sent for comments and suggestions to a Review Panel comprising prominent theologians and biblical scholars appointed by the American Bible Society Board of Managers in its capacity as trustee for the translation. In addition, drafts were sent to major English-speaking Bible Societies throughout the world. Final approval of the translation on behalf of the United Bible Societies was given by the American Bible Society's Board of Managers upon recommendation of its Translations Committee.

The primary concern of the translators was to provide a faithful translation of the meaning of the Hebrew, Aramaic, and Greek texts. Their first task was to understand correctly the meaning of the original. At times the original meaning cannot be precisely known, not only because the meaning of some words and phrases cannot be determined with a great degree of assurance, but also because the underlying cultural and historical context is sometimes beyond recovery. All aids available were used in this task, including the ancient versions (for example, the Septuagint Greek text of the Old Testament, the Vulgate of Jerome, and Old Latin texts as available) and the modern translations in English and other languages.

After ascertaining as accurately as possible the meaning of the original, the translators' next task was to express that meaning in a manner and form easily understood by the readers. Because this translation is intended for all who use English as a means of communication, the translators have tried to avoid words and forms not in current or widespread use; but no artificial limit has been set to the range of the vocabulary employed. Every effort has been made to use language that is natural, clear, simple, and unambiguous. Consequently there has been no attempt to reproduce in English the parts of speech, sentence structure, word order, and grammatical devices of the original languages. Faithfulness in translation also includes a faithful representation of the cultural and historical features of the original. Certain features, however, such as the hours of the day and the measures of weight, capacity, distance, and area, are given their modern equivalents, because the information in those terms conveys more meaning to the reader than the biblical form of those terms.

In cases where a person or place is called by two or more different names in the original, this translation has normally used only the more familiar name in all places: for example, King Jehoiachin of Judah (Jeremiah 52:31), also called Jeconiah (Jeremiah 24:1) and Coniah (Jeremiah 37:1). Where a proper name is spelled two or more different ways in the original text, this translation has used only one spelling: for example, Nebuchadnezzar, also spelled Nebuchadrezzar (Jeremiah 29:3 and 29:21); and Priscilla, also spelled Prisca (Acts 18:26 and Romans 16:3).

Following an ancient tradition, begun by the first translation of the Hebrew Scriptures into Greek (the Septuagint) and followed by the vast majority of English translations, the distinctive Hebrew name for God (usually transliterated *Yahweh,* and earlier *Jehovah)* is in this translation represented by "LORD." When *Adonai*, normally translated "Lord," is followed by *Yahweh*, the combination is rendered by the phrase "Sovereign LORD."

The Revision of the Good News Bible

Since the initial appearance of the *Good News Bible* in *Today's English Version* in 1976, some minor editorial changes and corrections of printing errors have been introduced into the text in connection with various printings. The New Testament was already in its fourth edition at the time the full Bible appeared, but for the Old Testament and the Deuterocanonicals/ Apocrypha of the *Good News Bible*, there was no revised edition until 1992. The preparation and publication of the second edition of the full *Good News Bible* in two formats, with and without the Deuterocanonicals and Apocrypha, is the result of a broad international process of careful review and evaluation of the Good News translation by many scholars and experts over a period of several years. This Catholic edition is consequently the beneficiary of all those corrections and revisions.

In December 1986, acting in response to a mounting perception of a need for text revisions, the ABS Board of Managers approved the undertaking of a revision of the Good News translation. The revision was restricted to two main areas of concern that had been raised and discussed over the years since the first appearance of the translation: (1) passages in which the English style had been unnecessarily exclusive and inattentive to gender concerns, and (2) passages in which the translation had been seen as problematic from either a stylistic or an exegetical viewpoint.

The process followed in preparing this revised edition was one of first inviting and collecting proposals for needed revisions from all English-language Bible Societies and English-speaking UBS translations consultants around the world, as well as numerous scholarly consultants in the United States and representatives of various American churches. The proposals received were then assembled for review and evaluation by the same broad array of experts whose specializations included translation, linguistics, English usage, literary and poetic style, biblical studies, and theology. In a series of four stages, consensus was sought on which proposals were necessary and valid, and at each of these review stages, the number of proposals under consideration was reduced until widespread agreement was reached. On the recommendation of the program committee of the ABS Board of Trustees (formerly Board of Managers) and its Translations subcommittee, the ABS Board acted to approve the revisions for the Good News Second Edition.

In the decade and a half since the initial publication of the Good News Bible, many Bible readers had become sensitive to the negative effects of exclusive language; that is, to the ways in which the built-in linguistic biases of the ancient languages and the English language toward the masculine gender has led some Bible readers to feel excluded from being addressed by the scriptural word. This concern has led to the revision of most major English translations during the 1980s, and, increasingly, readers of the Good News translation wrote to request that the Bible Society take this concern into consideration in preparing any revision. In practical terms what this means is that, where references in particular passages are to both men and women, the revision aims at language that is not exclusively masculine-oriented. At the same time, however, great care was taken not to distort the historical reality of the ancient patriarchal culture of Bible times.

Helps for the Reader

To make the text easier to understand, various kinds of readers' helps are supplied. The text itself has been divided into sections, and headings are provided to indicate the contents of the section. Where there are parallel accounts elsewhere in the Bible, as happens frequently in the Gospels, a reference to such a passage appears within parentheses below the heading. There are, in addition, several kinds of notes that appear at the bottom of the page.

(1) *Cultural or historical notes.* These provide information required to enable the modern reader to understand the meaning of the text in terms of its original setting (for example, the explanation of *Rahab* in Psalm 89:10; and the explanation of *Day of Atonement* in Acts 27:9).

(2) *Textual notes.* In the Old Testament, these indicate primarily those passages where the Hebrew word or words may be unclear in meaning, or where one or more of the ancient translations (for example, the Septuagint, Vulgate, or Syriac) appears to preserve the original wording better than the received Hebrew text. In Exodus 8:23, for example, all the above ancient translations have a word meaning "distinction" (cf. Vulgate, *divisionem*) rather than "redemption," which the Hebrew word *pedut* means. The ancient translations point to a Hebrew word *pelut* (division), which is only one letter different from *pedut* (redemption). Where one or more of the ancient versions were followed, the note indicates this by *One ancient translation* (for example, Genesis 1:26) or *Some ancient translations* (for example, Genesis 4:8); where a conjectural emendation was adopted, the note reads *Probable text* (for example, Genesis 10:14). Where the Greek is the primary text, such as in the New Testament or in the Old Testament books based on the Septuagint (also known as the deuterocanonicals), textual notes indicate some of the places where significant differences exist among the ancient manuscripts. These differences may consist of additions to the text (for example, Matthew 21:43), deletions (for example, Matthew 24:36), or substitutions (for example, Mark 1:41).

(3) *Alternative renderings.* In many places the precise meaning of the original text is in dispute, and there are two or more different ways in which the text may be understood. In some of the more important of such instances, an alternative rendering is given (e.g. Genesis 2:9; Matthew 6:11).

(4) *References to other passages.* In addition, many editions of the Good News Bible include references (by book, chapter, and verse) to other places in the Bible where identical or similar matters or ideas are dealt with.

The line drawings that accompany the text were specially prepared for this translation.

The numbering of chapters and verses in this translation follows the traditional system of major English translations of the Bible. In some instances, however, where the order of thought or events in two or more verses is more clearly represented by a rearrangement of the material, two or more verse numbers are joined (for example, Exodus 2:15–16; Acts 1:21–22). In Old Testament books where additions from the Septuagint have been integrated with the Hebrew text, various strategies of versification have been employed. For these, it will be helpful for the reader to consult the book's introductions and footnotes for guidance.

A Bible that Brings Good News

No one knows better than the translators how difficult their task has been. But they have performed it gladly, conscious always of the presence of the Holy Spirit and of the tremendous debt they owe to the dedication and scholarship of those who have preceded them. The Bible is not simply great literature to be admired and revered; it is Good News for all people everywhere—a message both to be understood and to be applied in daily life. It is with prayer and thankfulness that the translator and staff of the United Bible Societies and American Bible Society offer this translation to the Lord; it is with humility that we pray God will make it fruitful. And to Christ be the glory forever and ever!

Acknowledgments

The lyrics of "Open My Eyes" on page 426 are from *Spirit and Song* (Portland, OR: OCP Publications, 1999), number 196. Copyright © 1999 by OCP Publications. Song copyright © 1988 by Jesse Manibusan. Published by spiritandsong.com®, 5536 NE Hassalo, Portland, OR 97213. All rights reserved. Used with permission.

The prayer on page 766 is from *Best of Chief Dan George* by Chief Dan George and Helmut Hirnschall (Blaine, WA: Hancock House Publishers, 1989), page 83. Copyright © 1974, 1989 by Chief Dan George and Helmut Hirnschall. Used with permission.

The prayer on page 798 is by Valerie Piraino, in "Rwanda: Ten Years After Genocide," by Catholic Relief Services at *www.catholicrelief.org,* accessed July 18, 2005. Used with permission.

The prayer on page 887 is adapted from *Garden of a Thousand Gates: Pathways to Prayer,* by Carl Koch (Winona, MN: Saint Mary's Press, 1998), page 61. Copyright © 1998 by Saint Mary's Press. All rights reserved.

The "Joy" article on page 901 is adapted from *Teaching Guide for Dealing with Tough Times,* by Marilyn Kielbasa (Winona, MN: Saint Mary's Press, 1999), pages 30–31. Copyright © 1999 by Saint Mary's Press. All rights reserved.

The prayer by Marisa T. Garfinkel on page 1338 is taken from the Saint Mary's Press Web site, at *www.smp.org/resourcepage.cfm?Article=372&Print=Yes,* accessed August 3, 2005. Copyright © 2005 by Saint Mary's Press.

The quotation on page 1574 is by Mahatma Gandhi, from the Mahatma Gandhi Canadian Foundation for World Peace Web site, at *www.gandhi.ca,* accessed July 18, 2005.

The prayer on page 1676 and the refrains on page 860 are from *The Rites of the Catholic Church,* volume one (Collegeville, MN: Liturgical Press, 1990), pages 500 and 605. Excerpts from the English translation of *Rite of Confirmation,* 2nd edition © 1975, by ICEL, Inc. All rights reserved. Copyright © 1990 by the International Commission on English in the Liturgy. Used with permission.

The article on page 1681 is from *Christianity Rediscovered: An Epistle from the Masai,* by Vincent J. Donovan (Notre Dame, IN: Fides/Claretian, 1978), page 200. Copyright © 1978 by Fides/Claretian. Used with permission.

The excerpt on page 1717 is from the English translation of the *Catechism of the Catholic Church* for use in the United States of America, number 469. Copyright © 1994 by the United States Catholic Conference, Inc.—Libreria Editrice Vaticana. Used with permission.

The Scripture quotation on page 1753 is taken from the *Lectionary for Mass,* volume one, by the National Conference of Catholic Bishops (New York: Catholic Book Publishing Company, 1998), page 106. Copyright © 1998, 1997, 1970 by the Confraternity of Christian Doctrine.

To view copyright terms and conditions for Internet materials cited here, log on to the home pages for the referenced Web sites.

During this book's preparation, all citations, facts, figures, names, addresses, telephone numbers, Internet URLs, and other pieces of information cited within were verified for accuracy. The authors and Saint Mary's Press staff have made every attempt to reference current and valid sources, but we cannot guarantee the content of any source, and we are not responsible for any changes that may have occurred since our verification. If you find an error in, or have a question or concern about, any of the information or sources listed within, please contact Saint Mary's Press.

Illustration Credits

Line drawings by Annie Vallotton.

Cover and inside illustrations by Alex Christ and Erik Lervold of Pernsteiner Creative Group, Inc.

The timeline was created by Maps.com.

Notes

Notes

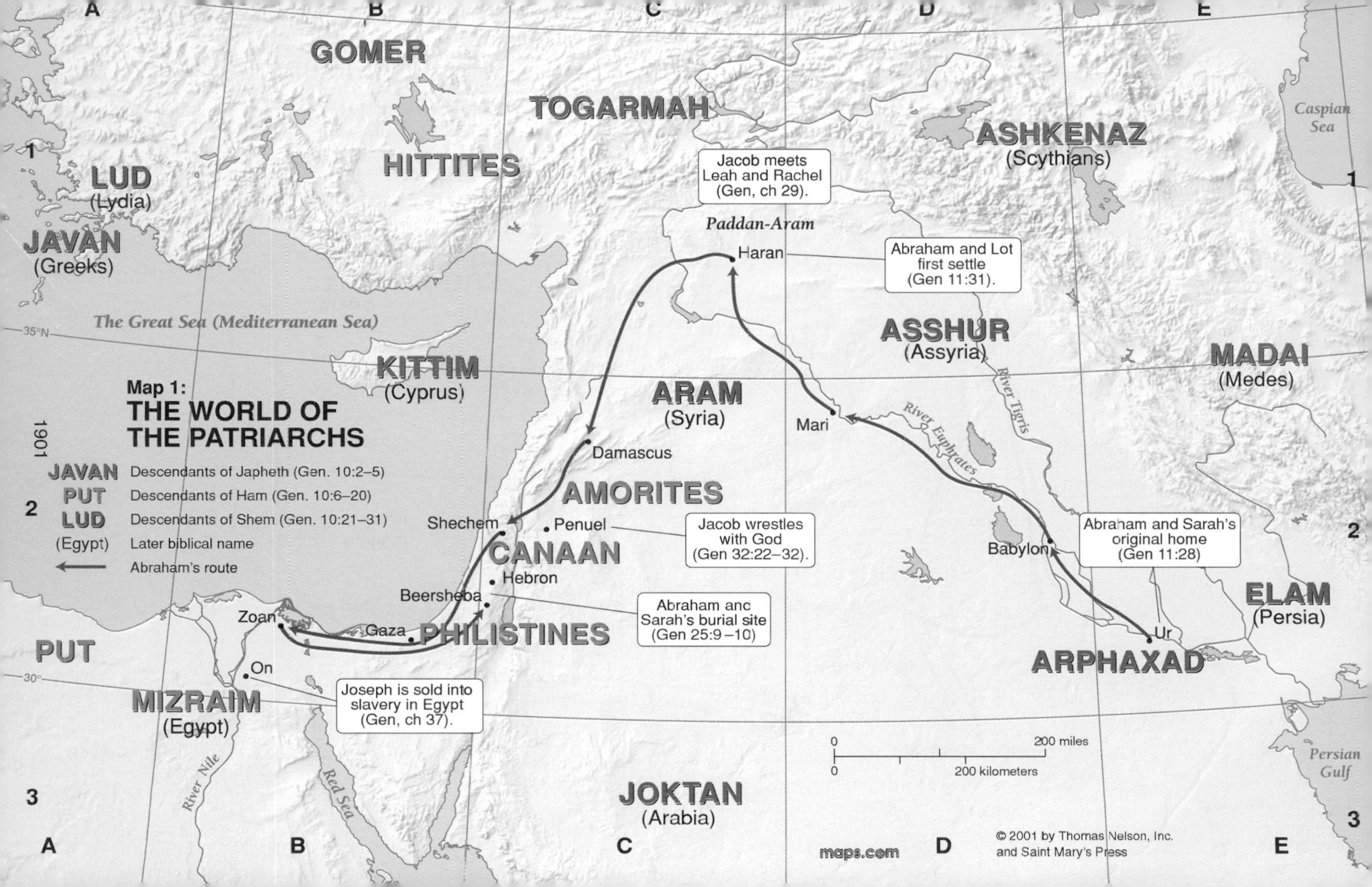

© 2001 by Thomas Nelson, Inc. and Saint Mary's Press

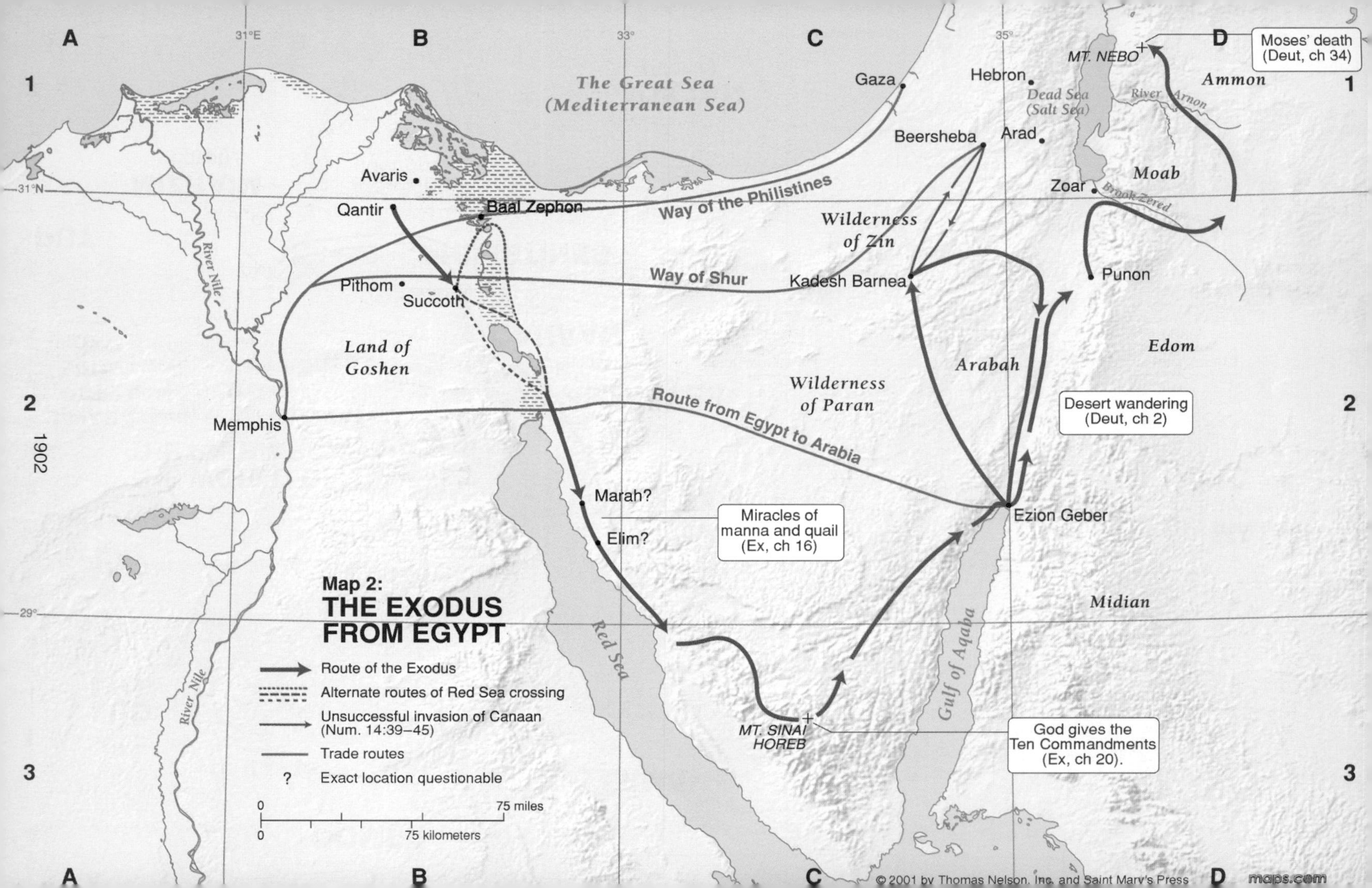
Map 2:
THE EXODUS FROM EGYPT
Route of the Exodus
Alternate routes of Red Sea crossing
Unsuccessful invasion of Canaan (Num. 14:39–45)
Trade routes
? Exact location questionable
0 75 miles
0 75 kilometers
A
B
C
D
1
2
3
31°E
33°
35°
31°N
29°
The Great Sea (Mediterranean Sea)
Gaza
Hebron
Dead Sea (Salt Sea)
Beersheba
Arad
MT. NEBO
Moses' death (Deut, ch 34)
Ammon
River Arnon
Moab
Zoar
Brook Zered
Avaris
Qantir
Baal Zephon
Way of the Philistines
Wilderness of Zin
Way of Shur
Kadesh Barnea
Pithom
Succoth
Punon
Land of Goshen
Arabah
Edom
Wilderness of Paran
Route from Egypt to Arabia
Memphis
Desert wandering (Deut, ch 2)
River Nile
Marah?
Elim?
Miracles of manna and quail (Ex, ch 16)
Ezion Geber
Midian
Red Sea
Gulf of Aqaba
MT. SINAI HOREB
God gives the Ten Commandments (Ex, ch 20).
© 2001 by Thomas Nelson, Inc. and Saint Mary's Press
maps.com

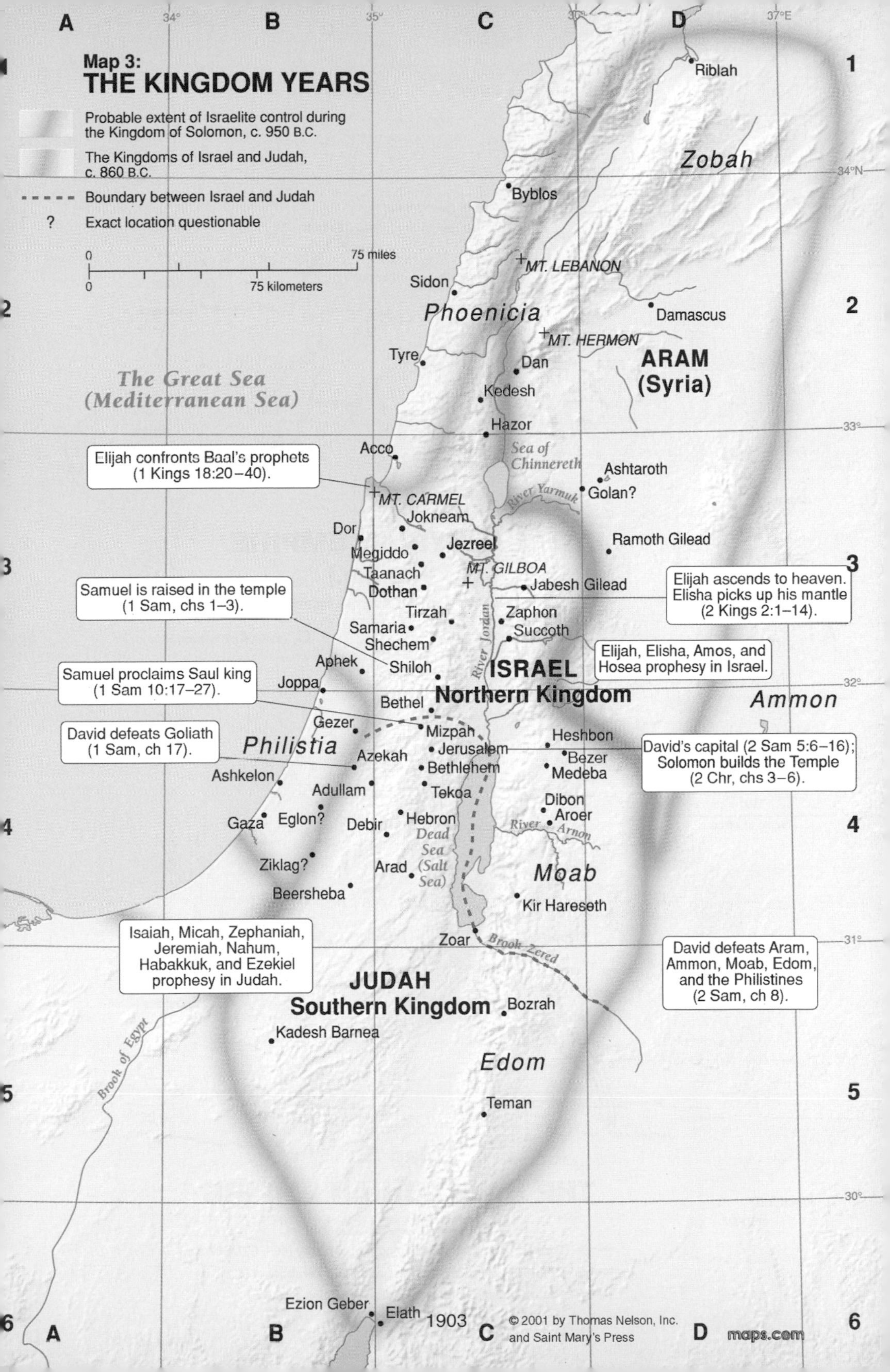

© 2001 by Thomas Nelson, Inc. and Saint Mary's Press
maps.com

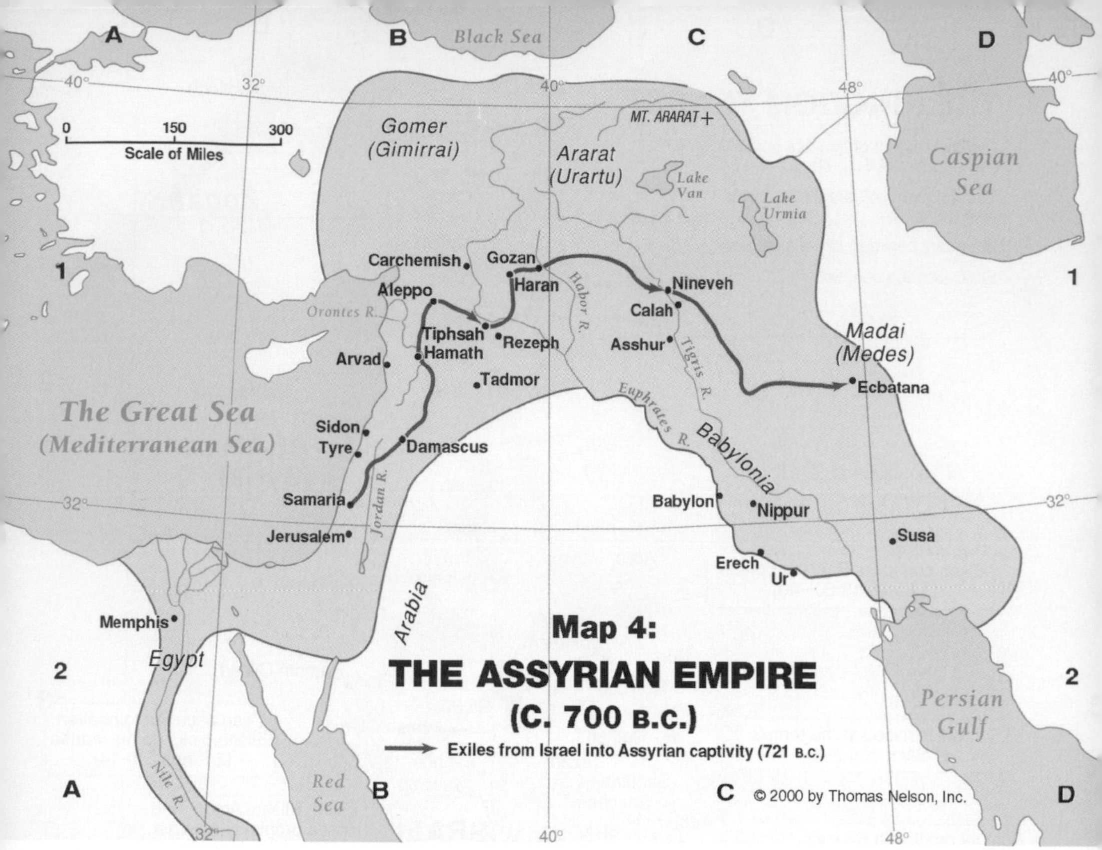
Map 4:
THE ASSYRIAN EMPIRE
(C. 700 B.C.)
Exiles from Israel into Assyrian captivity (721 B.C.)
© 2000 by Thomas Nelson, Inc.
A
B
C
D
1
2
40°
32°
48°
0
150
300
Scale of Miles
Black Sea
Gomer
(Gimirrai)
MT. ARARAT
Ararat
(Urartu)
Lake
Van
Lake
Urmia
Caspian
Sea
Carchemish
Gozan
Haran
Habor R.
Nineveh
Calah
Aleppo
Orontes R.
Tiphsah
Hamath
Rezeph
Asshur
Tigris R.
Madai
(Medes)
Arvad
Tadmor
Ecbatana
The Great Sea
(Mediterranean Sea)
Euphrates R.
Babylonia
Sidon
Tyre
Damascus
Samaria
Jordan R.
Babylon
Nippur
Jerusalem
Susa
Erech
Ur
Arabia
Memphis
Egypt
Persian
Gulf
Nile R.
Red
Sea

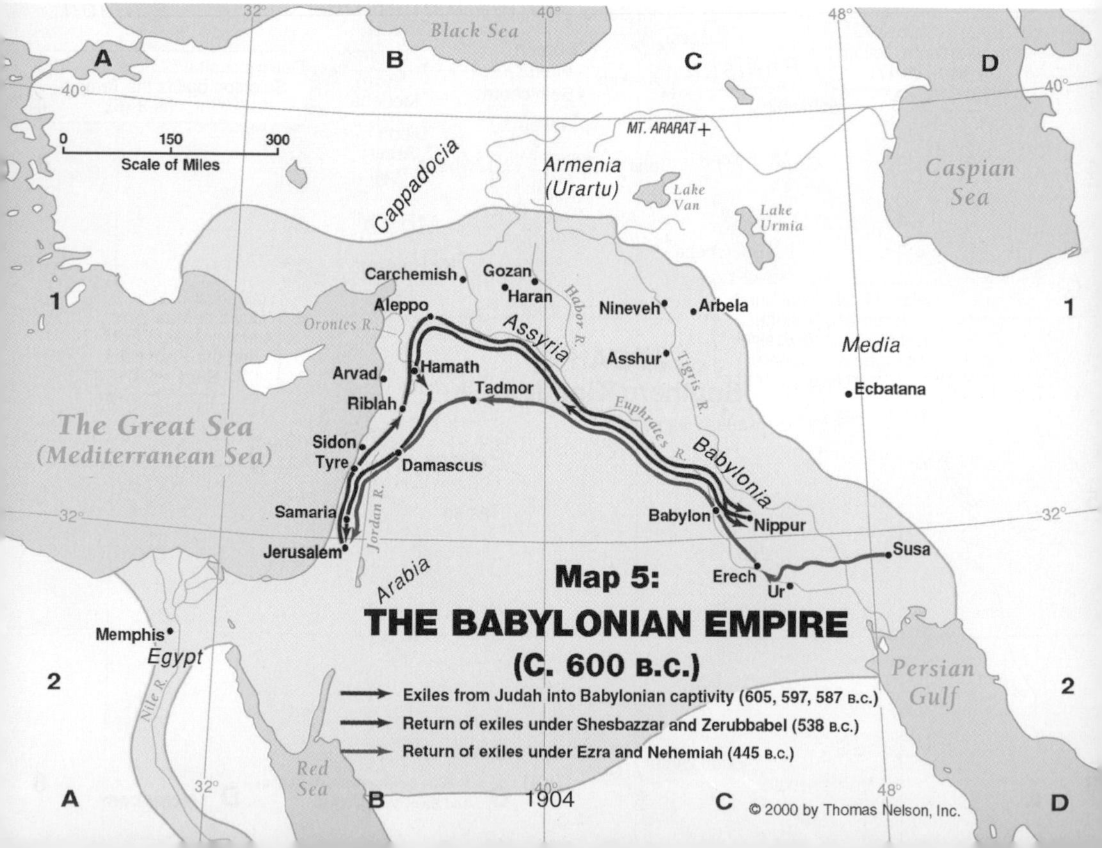
Map 5:
THE BABYLONIAN EMPIRE
(C. 600 B.C.)
Exiles from Judah into Babylonian captivity (605, 597, 587 B.C.)
Return of exiles under Shesbazzar and Zerubbabel (538 B.C.)
Return of exiles under Ezra and Nehemiah (445 B.C.)
© 2000 by Thomas Nelson, Inc.
A
B
C
D
1
2
40°
32°
48°
0
150
300
Scale of Miles
Black Sea
MT. ARARAT
Cappadocia
Armenia
(Urartu)
Lake
Van
Lake
Urmia
Caspian
Sea
Carchemish
Gozan
Haran
Habor R.
Nineveh
Arbela
Aleppo
Orontes R.
Assyria
Media
Hamath
Asshur
Tigris R.
Arvad
Tadmor
Ecbatana
Riblah
Euphrates R.
The Great Sea
(Mediterranean Sea)
Sidon
Tyre
Babylonia
Damascus
Samaria
Jordan R.
Babylon
Nippur
Jerusalem
Susa
Arabia
Erech
Ur
Memphis
Egypt
Nile R.
Persian
Gulf
Red
Sea

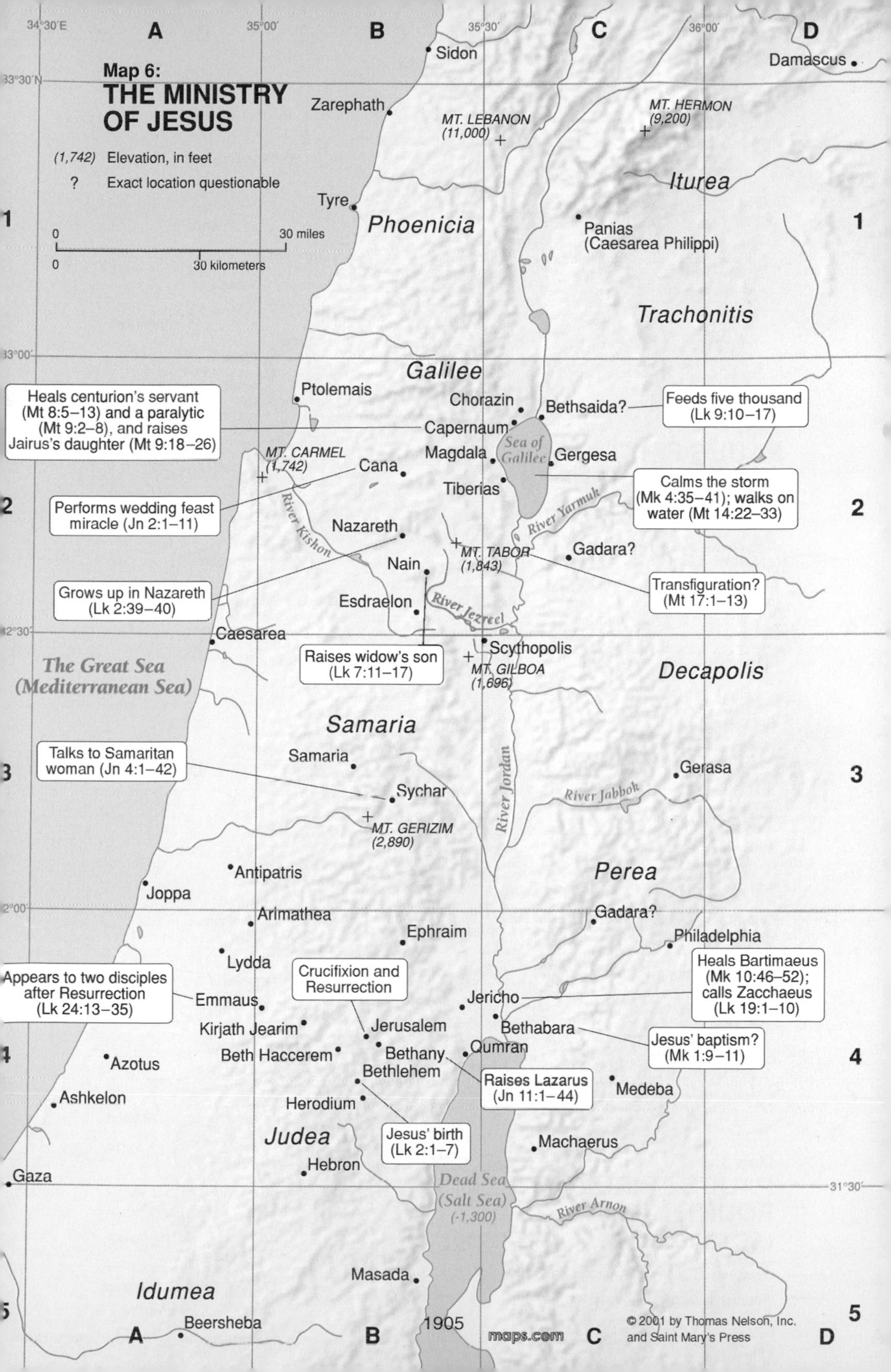

Map 6:
THE MINISTRY OF JESUS
(1,742) Elevation, in feet
? Exact location questionable
0 30 miles
0 30 kilometers
34°30′E
35°00′
35°30′
36°00′
33°30′N
33°00′
32°30′
32°00′
31°30′
A
B
C
D
1
2
3
4
5
Sidon
Damascus
Zarephath
MT. LEBANON (11,000)
MT. HERMON (9,200)
Iturea
Tyre
Phoenicia
Panias (Caesarea Philippi)
Trachonitis
Galilee
Ptolemais
Chorazin
Bethsaida?
Feeds five thousand (Lk 9:10–17)
Heals centurion's servant (Mt 8:5–13) and a paralytic (Mt 9:2–8), and raises Jairus's daughter (Mt 9:18–26)
Capernaum
Sea of Galilee
MT. CARMEL (1,742)
Magdala
Gergesa
Cana
Tiberias
Calms the storm (Mk 4:35–41); walks on water (Mt 14:22–33)
Performs wedding feast miracle (Jn 2:1–11)
River Kishon
River Yarmuk
Nazareth
MT. TABOR (1,843)
Gadara?
Nain
Transfiguration? (Mt 17:1–13)
Grows up in Nazareth (Lk 2:39–40)
Esdraelon
River Jezreel
Caesarea
Scythopolis
Raises widow's son (Lk 7:11–17)
MT. GILBOA (1,696)
The Great Sea (Mediterranean Sea)
Decapolis
Samaria
Talks to Samaritan woman (Jn 4:1–42)
Samaria
Gerasa
Sychar
River Jordan
River Jabbok
MT. GERIZIM (2,890)
Antipatris
Perea
Joppa
Arimathea
Gadara?
Ephraim
Philadelphia
Lydda
Crucifixion and Resurrection
Heals Bartimaeus (Mk 10:46–52); calls Zacchaeus (Lk 19:1–10)
Appears to two disciples after Resurrection (Lk 24:13–35)
Emmaus
Jericho
Kirjath Jearim
Jerusalem
Bethabara
Jesus' baptism? (Mk 1:9–11)
Beth Haccerem
Bethany
Qumran
Azotus
Bethlehem
Raises Lazarus (Jn 11:1–44)
Medeba
Ashkelon
Herodium
Judea
Jesus' birth (Lk 2:1–7)
Machaerus
Hebron
Gaza
Dead Sea (Salt Sea) (-1,300)
River Arnon
Masada
Idumea
Beersheba
maps.com
© 2001 by Thomas Nelson, Inc. and Saint Mary's Press

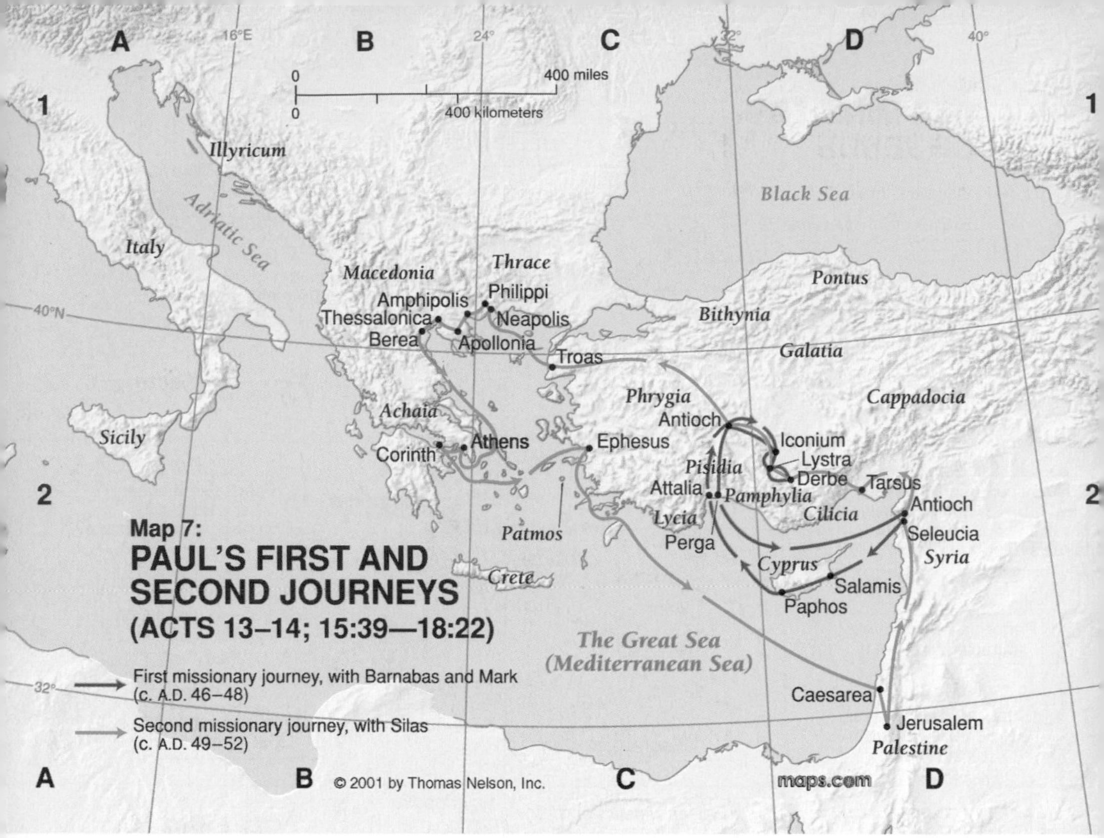

Map 7:
PAUL'S FIRST AND SECOND JOURNEYS
(ACTS 13–14; 15:39—18:22)

First missionary journey, with Barnabas and Mark (c. A.D. 46–48)

Second missionary journey, with Silas (c. A.D. 49–52)

© 2001 by Thomas Nelson, Inc.

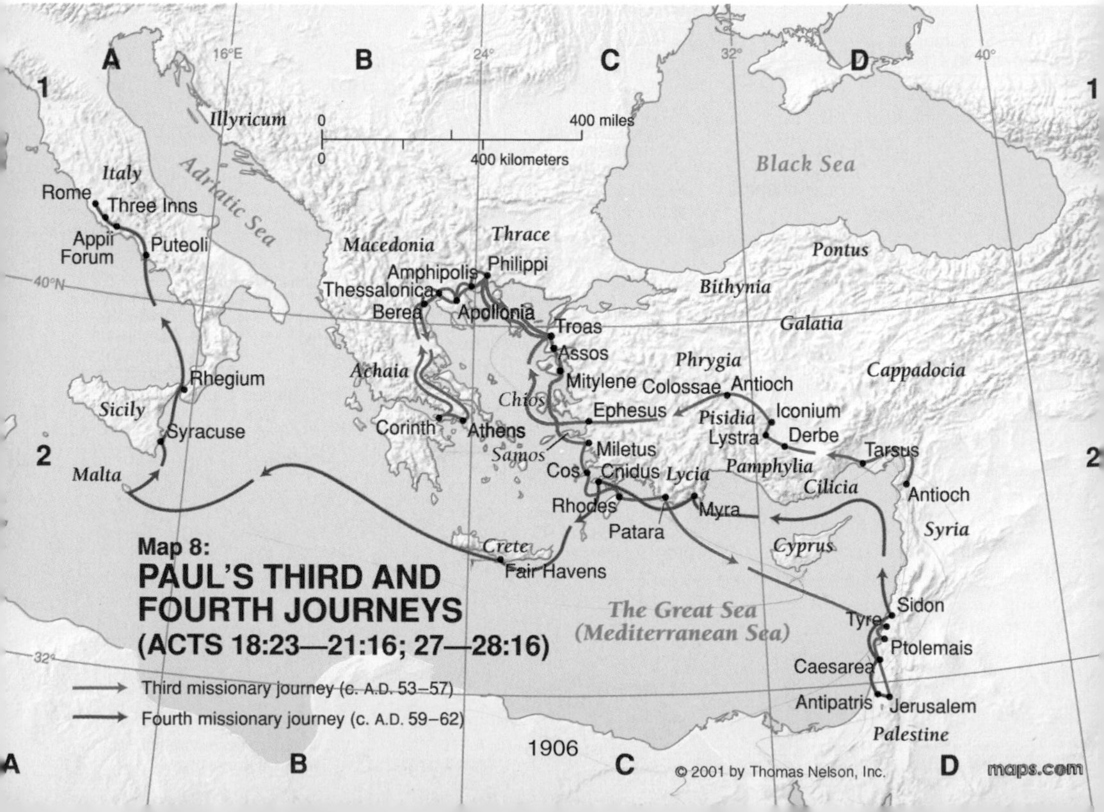

Map 8:
PAUL'S THIRD AND FOURTH JOURNEYS
(ACTS 18:23—21:16; 27—28:16)

Third missionary journey (c. A.D. 53–57)

Fourth missionary journey (c. A.D. 59–62)

© 2001 by Thomas Nelson, Inc.

© 2001 by Thomas Nelson, Inc.

Alphabetical List of Bible Books and Abbreviations

All scripture is inspired by God and is useful for teaching, for reproof, for correction, and for training in righteousness, so that everyone who belongs to God may be proficient, equipped for every good work.
(2 Tim 3:16–17)